Collins
ITALIAN
DICTIONARY

HarperCollins Publishers
Westerhill Road
Bishopbriggs
Glasgow
G64 2QT

Fourth Edition 2018

10 9 8 7 6 5 4 3 2 1

© HarperCollins Publishers 2008, 2010, 2014, 2018

ISBN 978-0-00-824140-7

Collins® is a registered trademark of HarperCollins Publishers Limited

www.collinsdictionary.com
www.collins.co.uk

A catalogue record for this book is available from the British Library

HarperCollins Publishers
195 Broadway
New York
NY10007

Seventh Edition 2018

ISBN 978-0-06-287617-1

Typeset by Palimpsest Book Production Limited and Davidson Publishing Solutions

Printed in Italy by Grafica Veneta S.p.A.

Acknowledgements
We would like to thank those authors and publishers who kindly gave permission for copyright material to be used in the Collins Corpus. We would also like to thank Times Newspapers Ltd for providing valuable data.

EDITOR
Susie Beattie

CONTRIBUTORS
Mirella Alessio
Anne Benson
Cordelia Lilly
Persephone Lock
Donald Watt

FOR THE PUBLISHER
Gerry Breslin
Janice McNeillie
Sheena Shanks

TECHNICAL SUPPORT
Claire Dimeo
Ross Taggart
Agnieszka Urbanowicz

Indice

Contents

Introduzione

Se desiderate imparare l'inglese o approfondire le conoscenze già acquisite, se volete leggere o redigere dei testi in inglese, oppure conversare con interlocutori di madrelingua inglese, se siete studenti, turisti, uomini o donne d'affari avete scelto il compagno di viaggio ideale per esprimervi e comunicare in inglese sia a voce che per iscritto. Strumento pratico e moderno, il vostro dizionario dà largo spazio al linguaggio quotidiano in campi quali l'attualità, gli affari, la gestione d'ufficio, l'informatica e il turismo. Come in tutti i nostri dizionari, grande importanza è stata data alla lingua contemporanea e alle espressioni idiomatiche.

Come usare il dizionario

Troverete qui di seguito alcune spiegazioni sul modo in cui le informazioni sono state presentate nel testo. L'obiettivo del dizionario è quello di darvi il maggior numero possibile di informazioni senza tuttavia sacrificare la chiarezza all'interno delle voci.

Le voci

Qui di seguito verranno descritti i vari elementi di cui si compone una voce tipo del vostro dizionario.

La trascrizione fonetica

Come regola generale è stata data la pronuncia di tutte le parole inglesi e quella delle parole italiane che potevano presentare qualche difficoltà per il parlante inglese. Nella parte inglese–italiano, tuttavia, per la pronuncia di nomi composti formati da due parole non unite dal trattino si dovrà cercare la trascrizione di ciascuna di queste parole alla rispettiva posizione alfabetica. La pronuncia si trova tra parentesi quadre, subito dopo il lemma. Come nella maggior parte dei dizionari moderni è stato adottato il sistema noto come "alfabeto fonetico internazionale". Troverete qui di seguito, a pagina xiii e xiv, un elenco completo dei caratteri utilizzati in questo sistema.

Sillabe accentate in italiano

In italiano, l'accento di solito cade sulla penultima sillaba. Per ogni lemma italiano, in questo dizionario, la sillaba su cui cade l'accento è preceduta dal simbolo '.

Le categorie grammaticali

Tutte le parole appartengono ad una categoria grammaticale, cioè possono essere sostantivi, verbi, aggettivi, avverbi, pronomi, articoli o congiunzioni.

I sostantivi possono essere singolari o plurali, sia in italiano che in inglese, e maschili o femminili in italiano. I verbi possono essere transitivi o intransitivi in entrambe le lingue, ma anche riflessivi o impersonali in italiano; nella sezione italiano–inglese, i verbi più comuni sono seguiti da un numero in grassetto che rimanda alle tavole dei verbi nelle pagine xvi-xix. La categoria grammaticale appare in maiuscoletto subito dopo la pronuncia ed eventuali informazioni di tipo morfologico (plurali irregolari ecc.).

Numerose voci sono state suddivise in varie categorie grammaticali. Per esempio, la parola italiana **bene** può essere sia un avverbio che un aggettivo o un sostantivo, e la parola inglese **sneeze** può essere sia un sostantivo ("starnuto") che un verbo intransitivo ("starnutire"). Analogamente il verbo italiano **correre** può essere usato sia come verbo intransitivo ("correre alla stazione") che come transitivo ("correre un rischio"). Per presentare la voce con maggiore chiarezza e permettervi di trovare rapidamente la traduzione che cercate, è stato introdotto un triangolino nero ▶ per contrassegnare il passaggio da una categoria grammaticale ad un'altra.

Suddivisioni semantiche

La maggior parte delle parole ha più di un significato. Per esempio, la parola **fiocco** può essere sia un'annodatura di un nastro che una falda di neve. Molte parole si traducono in modo diverso a seconda del contesto in cui sono usate: per esempio **scala** si tradurrà in inglese con "staircase" o "stairs" se si tratta di una scala con gradini, con "ladder" se è una scala a pioli. Per permettervi di scegliere la traduzione giusta per ciascuno dei contesti in cui la parola si può trovare, le voci sono state suddivise in categorie di significato. Ciascuna suddivisione è introdotta da un "indicatore d'uso" tra parentesi in *corsivo*. Le voci **fiocco** e **scala** compariranno quindi nel testo nel modo seguente:

> **fi'occo, -chi** SM (*di nastro*) bow; (*di stoffa, lana*)
> flock; (*di neve*) flake; ...

> **'scala** SF (*a gradini ecc*) staircase, stairs *pl*;
> (*a pioli, di corda*) ladder; ...

Per segnalare la traduzione appropriata sono stati introdotti anche degli indicatori d'ambito d'uso in *corsivo* con la prima lettera maiuscola, tra parentesi, spesso in forma abbreviata, come per esempio nel caso della voce **tromba**:

> **'tromba** SF (*Mus*) trumpet; (*Aut*) horn; ...

L'elenco completo delle abbreviazioni adottate nel dizionario è riportato alle pagine xi e xii.

Le traduzioni

Per la maggior parte delle parole inglesi ed italiane ci sono traduzioni precise a seconda del significato o del contesto, come risulta dagli esempi riportati fin qui. A volte, tuttavia, le parole non hanno un preciso equivalente nella lingua d'arrivo: in questi casi è stato fornito un equivalente approssimativo, preceduto dal segno ≈, come ad esempio per l'abbreviazione **RAC**, per cui è stato dato l'equivalente italiano "A.C.I.", dato che le due associazioni svolgono nei due paesi funzioni analoghe:

> **RAC** N ABBR (*BRIT*: = *Royal Automobile Club*)
> ≈ A.C.I. *m* (= *Automobile Club d'Italia*)

A volte è impossibile trovare un equivalente approssimativo. Questo è il caso, per esempio, di piatti tipici di un certo paese, come ad esempio **pandoro**:

pan'doro SM *type of sponge cake eaten at Christmas*

In questi casi, al posto della traduzione, che non esiste, comparirà una spiegazione: per maggiore chiarezza, questa spiegazione o glossa è stata messa in *corsivo*.

Molto spesso la traduzione di una parola può non funzionare all'interno di una data locuzione. Ad esempio alla voce **dare**, verbo spesso tradotto con "to give" in inglese, troviamo varie locuzioni per alcune delle quali la traduzione fornita all'inizio della voce non si può utilizzare: **quanti anni mi dai?** "how old do you think I am?" **danno ancora quel film?** "is that film still showing?", **dare per certo qc** "to consider sth certain", e così via. Ed è proprio in questi casi che potrete verificare l'utilità e la completezza del dizionario, che contiene una ricca gamma di composti, locuzioni e frasi idiomatiche.

Il registro linguistico
In italiano sapete istintivamente scegliere l'espressione corretta da usare a seconda del contesto in cui vi esprimete. Per esempio saprete quando dire **Non me ne importa!** e quando invece potete dire **Chi se ne frega?** Più difficile sarà farlo in inglese, dove avete minore consapevolezza delle sfumature di registro linguistico. Per questo motivo nella parte inglese–italiano le parole ed espressioni inglesi di uso più familiare sono segnalate dall'abbreviazione (*col*), mentre (*col!*) segnala le parole ed espressioni volgari. Nella parte italiano–inglese (!) dopo una traduzione segnala che si tratta di una parola od espressione offensiva o volgare.

Parole chiave
Come vedrete, ad alcune voci è stato riservato un trattamento particolare sia dal punto di vista grafico che da quello linguistico. Si tratta di voci come **essere** o **fare**, o dei loro equivalenti inglesi **be** e **do**, che per la loro importanza e complessità meritano una strutturazione più articolata ed un maggior numero di locuzioni illustrative. Queste voci sono strutturate in diverse categorie di significato contrassegnate da numeri, e le costruzioni sintattiche e locuzioni che illustrano quel particolare significato sono riportate all'interno della relativa categoria.

Informazioni culturali
Le voci che appaiono in un riquadro a sfondo grigio con i bordi arrotondati trattano aspetti della cultura italiana o di quella dei paesi di lingua inglese in argomenti quali la politica, la scuola, i mass media e le festività nazionali.

Note linguistiche
Sono state introdotte numerose note sulla lingua inglese per completare le informazioni contenute in ogni voce. Queste note d'uso consentono di evitare gli errori più comuni in inglese e spiegano in modo più dettagliato alcune delle differenze tra le due lingue.

Introduction

You may be starting to learn Italian, or you may wish to extend your knowledge of the language. Perhaps you want to read and study Italian books, newspapers and magazines, or perhaps simply have a conversation with Italian speakers. Whatever the reason, whether you're a student, a tourist or want to use Italian for business, this is the ideal book to help you understand and communicate. This modern, user-friendly dictionary gives priority to everyday vocabulary and the language of current affairs, business and tourism. As in all Collins dictionaries, the emphasis is firmly placed on contemporary language and expressions.

How to use the dictionary

Below you will find an outline of how information is presented in this dictionary. Our aim is to give you the maximum amount of detail in the clearest and most helpful way.

Entries

A typical entry in this dictionary will be made up of the following elements:

Phonetic transcription

Phonetics appear in square brackets immediately after the headword. They are shown using the International Phonetic Alphabet (IPA), and a complete list of the symbols used in this system can be found on pages xiii and xiv.

Stressed syllables in Italian

In Italian, stress usually falls on the penultimate syllable. In each Italian entry in this dictionary, the stressed syllable is preceded by the symbol '.

Grammatical information

All words belong to one of the following parts of speech: noun, verb, adjective, adverb, pronoun, article, conjunction, preposition.

Nouns can be singular or plural and, in Italian, masculine or feminine. Verbs can be transitive, intransitive, reflexive or impersonal: on the Italian side, the most common verbs are followed by a number in bold, which corresponds to verb tables on pages xvi–xix. Parts of speech appear in SMALL CAPS immediately after the phonetic spelling of the headword.

Often a word can have more than one part of speech. Just as the English word **chemical** can be an adjective or a noun, the Italian word **fondo** can be an adjective ("deep") or a masculine noun ("bottom"). In the same way the verb **to walk** is sometimes transitive, i.e. it takes an object ("to walk the dog") and sometimes intransitive, i.e. it doesn't take an object ("to walk to school"). To help you find the meaning you are looking for quickly and for clarity of presentation, the different part of speech categories are separated by a solid black triangle ▶.

Meaning divisions

Most words have more than one meaning. Take, for example, **punch** which can be, amongst other things, a blow with the fist or an object used for making holes. Other words are translated differently depending on the context in which they are used. The transitive verb **to roll up**, for example, can be translated by "arrotolare" or "rimboccare" depending on what it is you are rolling up. To help you select the most appropriate translation in every context, entries are divided according to meaning. Each different meaning is introduced by an "indicator" in *italics* and in brackets. Thus, the examples given above will be shown as follows:

> **punch** [pʌntʃ] N (*blow*) pugno; (*fig: force*) forza;
> (*tool*) punzone *m*; ...

> ▶ **roll up** VI (*col: arrive*) arrivare ▶ VT (*carpet,
> cloth, map*) arrotolare; (*sleeves*) rimboccare ...

Likewise, some words can have a different meaning when used to talk about a specific subject area or field. For example, **bishop**, which is generally used to mean a high-ranking member of the clergy, is also the name of a chess piece. To show English speakers which translation to use, we have added "subject field labels" in *italics*, starting with a capital letter, and in brackets, in this case (*Chess*):

> **bishop** [ˈbɪʃəp] N vescovo; (*Chess*) alfiere *m*

Field labels are often shortened to save space. You will find a complete list of abbreviations used in the dictionary on pages xi and xii.

Translations

Most English words have a direct translation in Italian and vice versa, as shown in the examples given above. Sometimes, however, no exact equivalent exists in the target language. In such cases we have given an approximate equivalent, indicated by the sign ≈. Such is the case of **National Insurance**, the Italian equivalent of which is "Previdenza Sociale". This is not an exact translation since the systems of the two countries in question are quite different:

> **National Insurance** N (*BRIT*) ≈ Previdenza
> Sociale

On occasion it is impossible to find even an approximate equivalent. This may be the case, for example, with the names of types of food:

> **cottage pie** N *piatto a base di carne macinata in
> sugo e purè di patate*

Here the translation (which doesn't exist) is replaced by an explanation. For increased clarity the explanation, or "gloss", is shown in *italics*.

It is often the case that a word, or a particular meaning of a word, cannot be translated in isolation. The translation of **Dutch**, for example, is "olandese". However, the phrase **to go Dutch** is rendered by "fare alla romana". Even a term as simple as **washing powder** needs a separate translation since it translates as "detersivo (in polvere)", not "polvere per lavare". This is where your dictionary will prove to be particularly informative and useful since it contains an abundance of compounds, phrases and idiomatic expressions.

Levels of formality and familiarity

In English you instinctively know when to say **I'm broke** or **I'm a bit short of cash** and when to say **I don't have any money**. When you are trying to understand someone who is speaking Italian, however, or when you yourself try to speak Italian, it is important to know what is polite and what is less so, and what you can say in a relaxed situation but not in a formal context. To help you with this, on the Italian–English side we have added the label (col) to show that an Italian word or expression is colloquial, while those words or expressions which are vulgar or offensive are given an exclamation mark (!), warning you they can cause serious offence. Note also that on both the Italian–English side and the English–Italian side, translations which are vulgar are followed by an exclamation mark in brackets.

Keywords

Words such as **be** and **do** or their Italian equivalents **essere** and **fare**, have been given special treatment because they form the basic elements of the language. These entries are presented on a grey shaded background with the keyword itself at the top, inside an outlined box. This extra help will ensure that you are able to use these complex words with confidence.

Cultural information

Entries which appear inside a grey shaded box with rounded edges explain aspects of culture in Italy and in English-speaking countries. Subject areas covered include politics, education, media and national festivals.

Language notes

Notes on the Italian language have been added to supplement the information given in the entries themselves. These usage notes help avoid common errors in Italian made by English speakers, and to explain in more detail the difference between the two languages.

Abbreviazioni   Abbreviations

abbreviazione	ABBR	abbreviation
aggettivo	ADJ, AG	adjective
amministrazione	*Admin*	administration
avverbio	ADV	adverb
aeronautica, viaggi aerei	*Aer*	flying, air travel
aggettivo	AG	adjective
agricoltura	*Agr*	agriculture
amministrazione	*Amm*	administration
anatomia	*Anat*	anatomy
architettura	*Archit*	architecture
astronomia, astrologia	*Astr*	astronomy, astrology
l'automobile	*Aut*	the motor car and motoring
verbo ausiliare	AUX VB	auxiliary verb
avverbio	AV	adverb
aeronautica, viaggi aerei	*Aviat*	flying, air travel
biologia	*Biol*	biology
botanica	*Bot*	botany
inglese della Gran Bretagna	BRIT	British English
chimica	*Chim, Chem*	chemistry
familiare (! da evitare)	*col(!)*	colloquial usage (! particularly offensive)
commercio, finanza, banca	*Comm*	commerce, finance, banking
informatica	*Comput*	computing
congiunzione	CONG	conjunction
congiunzione	CONJ	conjunction
edilizia	*Constr*	building, construction industry
sostantivo usato come aggettivo, non può essere usato dopo il sostantivo qualificato	CPD	compound element: noun used as adjective and not able to follow the noun it qualifies
cucina	*Cuc, Culin*	cookery
davanti a	*dav*	before
determinante: articolo, aggettivo dimostrativo o indefinito ecc	DET	determiner: article, demonstrative, etc
diritto	*Dir*	law
economia	*Econ*	economics
edilizia	*Edil*	building, construction industry
elettricità, elettronica	*Elettr, Elec*	electricity, electronics
esclamazione, interiezione	*escl, excl*	exclamation, interjection
specialmente	*esp*	especially
femminile	*f*	feminine
ferrovia	*Ferr*	railways

figurato	*fig*	figurative use
fisiologia	*Fisiol*	physiology
fotografia	*Fot*	photography
nella maggior parte dei sensi; generalmente	*gen*	in most or all senses; generally
geografia, geologia	*Geo*	geography, geology
geometria	*Geom*	geometry
impersonale	*impers*	impersonal
informatica	*Inform*	computing
insegnamento, sistema scolastico e universitario	*Ins*	schooling, schools and universities
invariabile	*inv*	invariable
irregolare	*irreg*	irregular
grammatica, linguistica	*Ling*	grammar, linguistics
maschile	*m*	masculine
matematica	*Mat(h)*	mathematics
termine medico, medicina	*Med*	medical term, medicine
il tempo, meteorologia	*Meteor*	the weather, meteorology
maschile o femminile	*m/f*	either masculine or feminine depending on sex
esercito, linguaggio militare	*Mil*	military matters
musica	*Mus*	music
sostantivo	N	noun
nautica	*Naut*	sailing, navigation
sostantivo che non si usa al plurale	*no pl*	uncountable noun: not used in the plural
numerale (aggettivo, sostantivo)	NUM	numeral (adjective or noun)
	o.s.	oneself
peggiorativo	*peg, pej*	derogatory, pejorative
fotografia	*Phot*	photography
fisiologia	*Physiol*	physiology
plurale	*pl*	plural
politica	*Pol*	politics
participio passato	*pp*	past participle
preposizione	PREP	preposition
pronome	PRON	pronoun
psicologia, psichiatria	*Psic, Psych*	psychology, psychiatry
tempo passato	*pt*	past tense
qualcosa	*qc*	
qualcuno	*qn*	
religione, liturgia	*Rel*	religions, church service
sostantivo	S	noun
	sb	somebody
insegnamento, sistema scolastico e universitario	*Scol*	schooling, schools and universities

singolare	*sg*	singular
soggetto (grammaticale)	*sog*	(grammatical) subject
	sth	something
congiuntivo	*sub*	subjunctive
soggetto (grammaticale)	*subj*	(grammatical) subject
termine tecnico, tecnologia	*Tecn, Tech*	technical term, technology
telecomunicazioni	*Tel*	telecommunications
tipografia	*Tip*	typography, printing
televisione	TV	television
tipografia	*Typ*	typography, printing
inglese degli Stati Uniti	US	American English
vocale	*v*	vowel
verbo (ausiliare)	VB (AUS)	(auxiliary) verb
verbo o gruppo verbale con funzione intransitiva	VI	verb or phrasal verb used intransitively
verbo riflessivo	VR	reflexive verb
verbo o gruppo verbale con funzione transitiva	VT	verb or phrasal verb used transitively
verbo inglese la cui particella è inseparabile dal verbo	VT FUS	phrasal verb where the particle cannot be separated from main verb
zoologia	*Zool*	zoology
marchio registrato	®	registered trademark
da evitare	!	particularly offensive or vulgar
introduce un'equivalenza culturale	≈	introduces a cultural equivalent

Trascrizione fonetica

Consonanti

N.B. **p, b, t, d, k, g** sono seguite da un'aspirazione in inglese.

Consonants

NB **p, b, t, d, k, g** are not aspirated in Italian.

*p*adre	p	*pup*py
*b*am*b*ino	b	*b*a*b*y
tu*tt*o	t	*t*en*t*
*d*a*d*o	d	*d*ad*d*y
cane *ch*e	k	*c*ork *k*iss *ch*ord
*g*ola *gh*iro	g	*g*a*g g*uess
*s*ano	s	*s*o ri*c*e *k*iss
*s*vago e*s*ame	z	cou*s*in buz*z*
*sc*ena	ʃ	*sh*eep *s*ugar
	ʒ	plea*s*ure bei*ge*
pe*c*e lan*c*iare	tʃ	*ch*ur*ch*
*g*iro *g*ioco	dʒ	*j*ud*ge* *g*eneral
a*f*a *f*aro	f	*f*arm ra*ff*le
*v*ero bra*v*o	v	*v*ery re*v*
	θ	*th*in ma*th*s
	ð	*th*at o*th*er
*l*etto a*l*a	l	*l*itt*l*e ba*ll*
*gl*i	ʎ	
*r*ete a*r*co	r	*r*at *br*at
*r*amo *m*adre	m	*m*u*mm*y co*mb*
*n*o fuma*n*te	n	*n*o ra*n*
*gn*omo	ɲ	
	ŋ	si*ng*ing ba*nk*
	h	*h*at re*h*eat
bu*i*o p*i*acere	j	*y*et
*u*omo g*u*aio	w	*w*all be*w*ail
	x	lo*ch*

Varie

per l'inglese: la "r" finale viene pronunciata se seguita da una vocale

precede la sillaba accentata

Miscellaneous

ʳ

ˈ precedes the stressed syllable

Come regola generale, in tutte le voci la trascrizione fonetica in parentesi quadra segue il termine cui si riferisce. Tuttavia, nella parte inglese–italiano del dizionario, per la pronuncia di composti che sono formati da più parole non unite da trattino che appaiono comunque nel dizionario, si veda la trascrizione fonetica di ciascuna di queste parole alla rispettiva posizione alfabetica.

Phonetic transcription

Vocali		Vowels
N.B. L'associazione di certi suoni indica solo una rassomiglianza approssimativa.		NB The pairing of some vowel sounds only indicates approximate equivalence.
vino idea	i iː	heel bead
	ɪ	hit pity
stella edera	e	
epoca eccetto	ɛ	set tent
mamma amore	a æ	apple bat
	ɑː	after car calm
	ʌ	fun cousin
	ə	over above
	əː	urn fern work
rosa occhio	ɔ	wash pot
	ɔː	born cork
ponte ognuno	o	
utile zucca	u	full soot
	uː	boon lewd

Dittonghi		Diphthongs
	ɪə	beer tier
	ɛə	tear fair there
	eɪ	date plaice day
	aɪ	life buy cry
	au	owl foul now
	əu	low no
	ɔɪ	boil boy oily
	uə	poor tour

In general, we give the pronunciation of each entry in square brackets after the word in question. However, on the English–Italian side, where the entry is composed of two or more unhyphenated words, each of which is given elsewhere in this dictionary, you will find the pronunciation of each word in its alphabetical position.

Italian pronunciation

Vowels

Where the vowel **e** or the vowel **o** appears in a stressed syllable it can be either open [ɛ], [ɔ] or closed [e], [o]. As the open or closed pronunciation of these vowels is subject to regional variation, the distinction is of little importance to the user of this dictionary. Phonetic transcription for headwords containing these vowels will therefore only appear where other pronunciation difficulties are present.

Consonants

c before "e" or "i" is pronounced *tch*.
ch is pronounced like the "k" in "kit".
g before "e" or "i" is pronounced like the "j" in "jet".
gh is pronounced like the "g" in "get".
gl before "e" or "i" is normally pronounced like the "lli" in "million", and in a few cases only like the "gl" in "glove".
gn is pronounced like the "ny" in "canyon".
sc before "e" or "i" is pronounced *sh*.
z is pronounced like the "ts" in "stetson", or like the "d's" in "bird's eye".

Headwords containing the above consonants and consonantal groups have been given full phonetic transcription in this dictionary.

NB All double written consonants in Italian are fully sounded: e.g. the *tt* in "tutto" is pronounced as in "hat trick".

Italian verbs

a Gerund **b** Past participle **c** Present **d** Imperfect **e** Past historic **f** Future **g** Conditional **h** Present subjunctive **i** Imperfect subjunctive **j** Imperative

1 abbattere e abbattei, abbattesti *(doesn't have alternative forms* -etti, -ette, -ettero)

2 accendere b acceso **e** accesi, accendesti

3 accludere b accluso **e** acclusi, accludesti

4 accorgersi b accorto **e** mi accorsi, ti accorgesti

5 aggiungere b aggiunto **e** aggiunsi, aggiungesti

6 andare c vado, vai, va, andiamo, andate, vanno **f** andrò *etc* **h** vada **j** va'!, vada!, andate!, vadano!

7 apparire b apparso **c** appaio, appari *or* apparisci, appare *or* apparisce, appaiono *or* appariscono **e** apparvi *or* apparsi, apparisti, apparve *or* apparì *or* apparse, apparvero *or* apparirono *or* apparsero **h** appaia *or* apparisca

8 appendere b appeso **e** appesi, appendesti

9 aprire b aperto **c** apro **e** aprii, apristi **h** apra

10 ardere b arso **e** arsi, ardesti

11 assistere b assistito **e** assistei *or* assistetti, assistesti

12 assumere b assunto **e** assunsi, assumesti

13 AVERE c ho, hai, ha, abbiamo, avete, hanno **e** ebbi, avesti, ebbe, avemmo, aveste, ebbero **f** avrò *etc* **h** abbia *etc* **j** abbi!, abbia!, abbiate!, abbiano!

14 baciare *when the ending begins with* -e, *the* i *is dropped* → bacerò (*not* bacierò)

15 bagnare c bagniamo, bagniate **h** bagniamo, bagniate (*not* bagnamo, bagnate)

16 bere a bevendo **b** bevuto **c** bevo *etc* **d** bevevo *etc* **e** bevvi *or* bevetti, bevesti **f** berrò *etc* **h** beva *etc* **i** bevessi *etc*

17 bollire c bollo *or* bollisco, bolli *or* bollisci *etc*

18 cadere e caddi, cadesti **f** cadrò *etc*

19 cambiare *drops the* i *of the root if the ending starts with* i (cambi, cambino *not* cambii, cambiino (*cf.* inviare)

20 caricare *when* c *in the root is* -i *followed by* -i *or* -e *an* h *should be inserted* (*i.e.* carichi, carichiamo, caricherò)

21 chiedere b chiesto **e** chiesi, chiedesti

22 chiudere b chiuso **e** chiusi, chiudesti

23 cogliere b colto **c** colgo, colgono **e** colsi, cogliesti **h** colga

24 compiere b compiuto **e** compii, compisti

25 confondere b confuso **e** confusi, confondesti

26 conoscere b conosciuto **e** conobbi, conoscesti

27 consigliare *when the ending begins with* -i, *the* i *of the root is dropped* → consigli (*not* consiglii)

28 correre b corso **e** corsi, corresti

29 CREDERE a credendo **b** creduto **c** credo, credi, crede, crediamo, credete, credono **d** credevo, credevi, credeva, credevamo, credevate, credevano **e** credei *or* credetti, credesti, credé *or* credette, credemmo, credeste, crederono *or* credettero **f** crederò, crederai, crederà, crederemo, crederete, crederanno **g** crederei, crederesti, crederebbe, crederemmo, credereste, crederebbero **h** creda, creda, creda, crediamo, crediate, credano **i** credessi, credessi, credesse, credessimo, credeste, credessero **j** credi!, creda!, credete!, credano!

30 crescere b cresciuto **e** crebbi, crescesti

31 cucire *when* c *or* g *in the root is followed by* -o *or* -a, *an* i *should be inserted* (*i.e.* cucio, cucia)

32 cuocere b cotto c cuocio, cuociamo, cuociono e cossi, cocesti

33 dare b do, dai, dà, diamo, date, danno e diedi *or* detti, desti f darò *etc* h dia *etc* i dessi *etc* j da'! *or* dai!, dia!, date!, diano!

34 decidere b deciso e decisi, decidesti

35 deludere b deluso e delusi, deludesti

36 difendere b difeso e difesi, difendesti

37 dipingere b dipinto e dipinsi, dipingesti

38 dire a dicendo b detto c dico, dici, dice, diciamo, dite, dicono d dicevo *etc* e dissi, dicesti f dirò *etc* h dica, diciamo, diciate, dicano i dicessi *etc* j di'!, dica!, dite!, dicano!

39 dirigere b diretto e diressi, dirigesti

40 discutere b discusso e discussi, discutesti

41 disfare *like* fare *but* c disfo, disfi *etc* f disferò, disferai *etc* i disfi, disfi *etc(regular forms)*

42 distinguere b distinto e distinsi, distinguesti

43 dividere b diviso e divisi, dividesti

44 dolere c dolgo, duoli, duole, dolgono e dolsi, dolesti f dorrò *etc* h dolga

45 DORMIRE a dormendo b dormito c dormo, dormi, dorme, dormiamo, dormite, dormono d dormivo, dormivi, dormiva, dormivamo, dormivate, dormivano e dormii, dormisti, dormì, dormimmo, dormiste, dormirono f dormirò, dormirai, dormirà, dormiremo, dormirete, dormiranno g dormirei, dormiresti, dormirebbe, dormiremmo, dormireste, dormirebbero h dorma, dorma, dorma, dormiamo, dormiate, dormano i dormissi, dormissi, dormisse, dormissimo, dormiste, dormissero j dormi!, dorma!, dormite!, dormano!

46 dovere c devo *or* debbo, devi, deve, dobbiamo, dovete, devono *or* debbono f dovrò *etc* h debba, dobbiamo, dobbiate, devano *or* debbano

47 esigere b esatto *(not common)* e esigei *or* esigetti, esigesti

48 espellere b espulso e espulsi, espellesti

49 esplodere b esploso e esplosi, esplodesti

50 esprimere b espresso e espressi, esprimesti

51 ESSERE b stato c sono, sei, è, siamo, siete, sono d ero, eri, era, eravamo, eravate, erano e fui, fosti, fu, fummo, foste, furono f sarò *etc* h sia *etc* i fossi, fossi, fosse, fossimo, foste, fossero j sii!, sia!, siate!, siano!

52 evadere b evaso e evasi, evadesti

53 fare a facendo b fatto c faccio, fai, fa, facciamo, fate, fanno d facevo *etc* e feci, facesti f farò *etc* h faccia *etc* i facessi *etc* j fa'!, faccia!, fate!, facciano!

54 fingere b finto e finsi, fingesti

55 FINIRE a finendo b finito c finisco, finisci, finisce, finiamo, finite, finiscono d finivo, finivi, finiva, finivamo, finivate, finivano e finii, finisti, finì, finimmo, finiste, finirono f finirò, finirai, finirà, finiremo, finirete, finiranno g finirei, finiresti, finirebbe, finiremmo, finireste, finirebbero h finisca, finisca, finisca, finiamo, finiate, finiscano i finissi, finissi, finisse, finissimo, finiste, finissero j finisci!, finisca!, finite!, finiscano!

56 friggere b fritto e frissi, friggesti

57 giacere b giaciuto e giacqui, giacesti

58 godere f godrò, godrai *etc* g godrei, godresti *etc*

59 immergere b immerso e immersi, immergesti

60 inviare c (tu) invii f (essi) inviino

61 leggere b letto e lessi, leggesti

62 mangiare *when the ending begins with -e, the i is dropped* → mangerò (*not* mangierò)

63 mettere b messo e misi, mettesti

64 mordere b morso e morsi, mordesti

65 morire b morto c muoio, muori, muore, moriamo, morite, muoiono f morirò *or* morrò *etc* h muoia

66 muovere b mosso e mossi, muovesti

67 nascere b nato e nacqui, nascesti

68 nascondere b nascosto e nascosi, nascondesti

69 nuocere b nuociuto c nuoccio, nuoci, nuoce, nociamo *or* nuociamo, nuocete, nuocciono d nuocevo *etc* e nocqui, nuocesti f nuocerò *etc* g nuoccia

70 offrire b offerto c offro e offersi *or* offrii, offristi h offra

71 parere b parso c paio, paiamo, paiono e parvi *or* parsi, paresti f parrò *etc* h paia, paiamo, paiate, paiano

72 PARLARE a parlando b parlato c parlo, parli, parla, parliamo, parlate, parlano d parlavo, parlavi, parlava, parlavamo, parlavate, parlavano e parlai, parlasti, parlò, parlammo, parlaste, parlarono f parlerò, parlerai, parlerà, parleremo, parlerete, parleranno g parlerei, parleresti, parlerebbe, parleremmo, parlereste, parlerebbero h parli, parli, parli, parliamo, parliate, parlino i parlassi, parlassi, parlasse, parlassimo, parlaste, parlassero j parla!, parli!, parlate!, parlino!

73 perdere b perso *or* perduto e persi, perdesti

74 piacere b piaciuto c piaccio, -piacciamo, piacciono e piacqui, piacesti h piaccia *etc*

75 piangere b pianto e piansi, piangesti

76 piovere b piovuto e piovve

77 porre a ponendo b posto c pongo, poni, pone, poniamo, ponete, pongono d ponevo *etc* e posi, ponesti f porrò *etc* h ponga, poniamo, poniate, pongano i ponessi *etc*

78 potere c posso, puoi, può, possiamo, potete, possono f potrò *etc* h possa, possiamo, possiate, possano

79 prefiggersi b prefisso e mi prefissi, ti prefiggesti

80 pregare *when g in the root is -followed by -i or -e, an h should be inserted* (i.e. preghi, preghiamo, pregherò)

81 prendere b preso e presi, prendesti

82 prevedere *like* vedere *but* f prevederò, prevederai *etc* g prevederei *etc*

83 proteggere b protetto e protessi, proteggesti

84 pungere b punto e punsi, pungesti

85 radere b raso e rasi, radesti

86 redimere b redento e redensi, redimesti

87 reggere b retto e ressi, reggesti

88 rendere b reso e resi, rendesti

89 ridere b riso e risi, ridesti

90 ridurre a riducendo b ridotto c riduco *etc* d riducevo *etc* e ridussi, riducesti f ridurrò *etc* h riduca *etc* i riducessi *etc*

91 riempire a riempiendo c riempio, riempi, riempie, riempiono

92 riflettere b riflettuto *or* riflesso

93 rimanere b rimasto c rimango, rimangono e rimasi, rimanesti f rimarrò *etc* h rimanga

94 risolvere b risolto e risolsi, risolvesti

95 rispondere b risposto e risposi, rispondesti

96 rivolgere b rivolto e rivolsi, rivolgesti

97 rompere b rotto e ruppi, rompesti

98 salire c salgo, sali, salgono h salga

99 sapere c so, sai, sa, sappiamo, sapete, sanno e seppi, sapesti f saprò *etc* h sappia *etc* j sappi!, sappia!, sappiate!, sappiano!

100 scegliere b scelto c scelgo, scegli, sceglie, scegliamo, scegliete, scelgono e scelsi, scegliesti h scelga, scegliamo, scegliate, scelgano j scegli!, scelga!, scegliamo!, scegliete!, scelgano!

101 scendere b sceso e scesi, scendesti

102 scindere b scisso e scissi, scindesti

103 sciogliere b sciolto c sciolgo, sciogli, scioglie, sciogliamo, sciogliete, sciolgono e sciolsi, sciogliesti h sciolga, sciogliamo, sciogliate, sciolgano j sciogli!, sciolga!, sciogliamo!, sciogliete!, sciolgano!

104 sconfiggere b sconfitto e sconfissi, sconfiggesti

105 scrivere b scritto **e** scrissi, scrivesti
106 scuotere b scosso **e** scossi, scuotesti
107 sedere c siedo, siedi, siede, siedono
  h sieda
108 solere b solito **e** soglio, suoli, suole,
  sogliamo, solete, sogliono **h** soglia
  (*regular imperfect, gerund, past participle; no
  other verb forms*)
109 sorgere b sorto **e** sorse, sorsero
110 spandere b spanto **e** spansi, spandesti
111 spargere b sparso **e** sparse, sparsero
112 sparire e sparii, sparisti
113 spegnere b spento **c** spengo,
  spengono **e** spensi, spegnesti **h** spenga
114 spingere b spinto **e** spinsi, spingesti
115 sporgere b sporto **e** sporsi, sporgesti
116 stare b stato **c** sto, stai, sta, stiamo,
  state, stanno **e** stetti, stesti **f** starò *etc*
  h stia *etc* **i** stessi *etc* **j** sta'!, stia!, state!,
  stiano!
117 stringere b stretto **e** strinsi,
  stringesti
118 succedere b successo **e** successi,
  succedesti
119 tacere b taciuto **c** taccio, tacciono
  e tacqui, tacesti **h** taccia

120 tendere b teso **e** tesi, tendesti
121 tenere c tengo, tieni, tiene,
  tengono **e** tenni, tenesti **f** terrò *etc*
  h tenga
122 togliere b tolto **c** tolgo, togli, toglie,
  togliamo, togliete, tolgono **e** tolsi,
  togliesti **h** tolga **j** togli!, tolga!,
  togliamo!, togliete!, tolgano!
123 trarre a traendo **b** tratto **c** traggo,
  trai, trae, traiamo, traete, traggono
  d traevo *etc* **e** trassi, traesti **f** trarrò *etc*
  h tragga **i** traessi *etc*
124 udire c odo, odi, ode, odono **h** oda
125 uscire c esco, esci, esce, escono **h** esca
126 valere b valso **c** valgo, valgono
  e valsi, valesti **f** varrò *etc* **h** valga
127 vedere b visto *or* veduto **e** vidi, vedesti
  f vedrò *etc*
128 venire b venuto **c** vengo, vieni, viene,
  vengono **e** venni, venisti **f** verrò *etc*
  h venga
129 vincere b vinto **e** vinsi, vincesti
130 vivere b vissuto **e** vissi, vivesti
131 volere c voglio, vuoi, vuole, vogliamo,
  volete, vogliono **e** volli, volesti **f** vorrò
  etc **h** voglia *etc* **j** *not common*

For additional information on Italian verb formation, see pages 6–125 of the
Grammar section.

Verbi inglesi

PRESENT	PT	PP
arise	arose	arisen
awake	awoke	awoken
be (am, is, are; being)	was, were	been
bear	bore	born(e)
beat	beat	beaten
become	became	become
befall	befell	befallen
begin	began	begun
behold	beheld	beheld
bend	bent	bent
beset	beset	beset
bet	bet, betted	bet, betted
bid (at auction, cards)	bid	bid
bid (say)	bade	bidden
bind	bound	bound
bite	bit	bitten
bleed	bled	bled
blow	blew	blown
break	broke	broken
breed	bred	bred
bring	brought	brought
build	built	built
burn	burnt, burned	burnt, burned
burst	burst	burst
buy	bought	bought
can	could	(been able)
cast	cast	cast
catch	caught	caught
choose	chose	chosen
cling	clung	clung
come	came	come
cost	cost	cost
cost (work out price of)	costed	costed
creep	crept	crept
cut	cut	cut
deal	dealt	dealt
dig	dug	dug
do (3rd person: he/she/it does)	did	done
draw	drew	drawn
dream	dreamed, dreamt	dreamed, dreamt

PRESENT	PT	PP
drink	drank	drunk
drive	drove	driven
dwell	dwelt	dwelt
eat	ate	eaten
fall	fell	fallen
feed	fed	fed
feel	felt	felt
fight	fought	fought
find	found	found
flee	fled	fled
fling	flung	flung
fly	flew	flown
forbid	forbad(e)	forbidden
forecast	forecast	forecast
forget	forgot	forgotten
forgive	forgave	forgiven
forsake	forsook	forsaken
freeze	froze	frozen
get	got	got, (US) gotten
give	gave	given
go (goes)	went	gone
grind	ground	ground
grow	grew	grown
hang	hung	hung
hang (execute)	hanged	hanged
have	had	had
hear	heard	heard
hide	hid	hidden
hit	hit	hit
hold	held	held
hurt	hurt	hurt
keep	kept	kept
kneel	knelt, kneeled	knelt, kneeled
know	knew	known
lay	laid	laid
lead	led	led
lean	leant, leaned	leant, leaned
leap	leapt, leaped	leapt, leaped
learn	learnt, learned	learnt, learned
leave	left	left
lend	lent	lent
let	let	let

PRESENT	PT	PP	PRESENT	PT	PP
lie (lying)	lay	lain	sow	sowed	sown, sowed
light	lit, lighted	lit, lighted			
lose	lost	lost	speak	spoke	spoken
make	made	made	speed	sped, speeded	sped, speeded
may	might	—			
mean	meant	meant	spell	spelt, spelled	spelt, spelled
meet	met	met			
mistake	mistook	mistaken	spend	spent	spent
mow	mowed	mown, mowed	spill	spilt, spilled	spilt, spilled
			spin	spun	spun
must	(had to)	(had to)	spit	spat	spat
pay	paid	paid	spoil	spoiled, spoilt	spoiled, spoilt
put	put	put			
quit	quit, quitted	quit, quitted	spread	spread	spread
			spring	sprang	sprung
read	read	read	stand	stood	stood
rid	rid	rid	steal	stole	stolen
ride	rode	ridden	stick	stuck	stuck
ring	rang	rung	sting	stung	stung
rise	rose	risen	stink	stank	stunk
run	ran	run	stride	strode	stridden
saw	sawed	sawed, sawn	strike	struck	struck
			strive	strove	striven
say	said	said	swear	swore	sworn
see	saw	seen	sweep	swept	swept
seek	sought	sought	swell	swelled	swollen, swelled
sell	sold	sold			
send	sent	sent	swim	swam	swum
set	set	set	swing	swung	swung
sew	sewed	sewn	take	took	taken
shake	shook	shaken	teach	taught	taught
shear	sheared	shorn, sheared	tear	tore	torn
			tell	told	told
shed	shed	shed	think	thought	thought
shine	shone	shone	throw	threw	thrown
shoot	shot	shot	thrust	thrust	thrust
show	showed	shown	tread	trod	trodden
shrink	shrank	shrunk	wake	woke, waked	woken, waked
shut	shut	shut			
sing	sang	sung	wear	wore	worn
sink	sank	sunk	weave	wove	woven
sit	sat	sat	weave (wind)	weaved	weaved
slay	slew	slain	wed	wedded, wed	wedded, wed
sleep	slept	slept			
slide	slid	slid	weep	wept	wept
sling	slung	slung	win	won	won
slit	slit	slit	wind	wound	wound
smell	smelt, smelled	smelt, smelled	wring	wrung	wrung
			write	wrote	written

I numeri

Numbers

Italiano		English
uno(a)	1	one
due	2	two
tre	3	three
quattro	4	four
cinque	5	five
sei	6	six
sette	7	seven
otto	8	eight
nove	9	nine
dieci	10	ten
undici	11	eleven
dodici	12	twelve
tredici	13	thirteen
quattordici	14	fourteen
quindici	15	fifteen
sedici	16	sixteen
diciassette	17	seventeen
diciotto	18	eighteen
diciannove	19	nineteen
venti	20	twenty
ventuno	21	twenty-one
ventidue	22	twenty-two
ventitré	23	twenty-three
ventotto	28	twenty-eight
trenta	30	thirty
quaranta	40	forty
cinquanta	50	fifty
sessanta	60	sixty
settanta	70	seventy
ottanta	80	eighty
novanta	90	ninety
cento	100	a hundred, one hundred
centouno	101	a hundred and one
duecento	200	two hundred
mille	1 000	a thousand, one thousand
milleduecentodue	1 202	one thousand two hundred and two
cinquemila	5 000	five thousand
un milione	1 000 000	a million, one million

I numeri

Numbers

primo(a), 1°	first, 1st
secondo(a), 2°	second, 2nd
terzo(a), 3°	third, 3rd
quarto(a)	fourth, 4th
quinto(a)	fifth, 5th
sesto(a)	sixth, 6th
settimo(a)	seventh
ottavo(a)	eighth
nono(a)	ninth
decimo(a)	tenth
undicesimo(a)	eleventh
dodicesimo(a)	twelfth
tredicesimo(a)	thirteenth
quattordicesimo(a)	fourteenth
quindicesimo(a)	fifteenth
sedicesimo(a)	sixteenth
diciassettesimo(a)	seventeenth
diciottesimo(a)	eighteenth
diciannovesimo(a)	nineteenth
ventesimo(a)	twentieth
ventunesimo(a)	twenty-first
ventiduesimo(a)	twenty-second
ventitreesimo(a)	twenty-third
ventottesimo(a)	twenty-eighth
trentesimo(a)	thirtieth
centesimo(a)	hundredth
centunesimo(a)	hundred-and-first
millesimo(a)	thousandth
milionesimo(a)	millionth

L'ora

The time

che ora è ?, che ore sono?	*what time is it?*
è ..., sono ...	*it's ...*
mezzanotte	midnight
l'una (del mattino)	one o'clock (in the morning), one (a.m.)
l'una e cinque	five past one
l'una e dieci	ten past one
l'una e un quarto, l'una e quindici	a quarter past one, one fifteen
l'una e venticinque	twenty-five past one, one twenty-five
l'una e mezzo *o* mezza, l'una e trenta	half past one, one thirty
l'una e trentacinque	twenty-five to two, one thirty-five
le due meno venti, l'una e quaranta	twenty to two, one forty
le due meno un quarto, l'una e quarantacinque	a quarter to two, one forty-five
le due meno dieci, l'una e cinquanta	ten to two, one fifty
mezzogiorno	twelve o'clock, midday, noon
le tre (del pomeriggio), le quindici	three o'clock (in the afternoon), three (p.m.)
le sette (di sera), le diciannove	seven o'clock (in the evening), seven (p.m.)

a che ora?	*at what time?*
a mezzanotte	at midnight
alle sette	at seven o'clock
fra venti minuti	in twenty minutes
venti minuti fa	twenty minutes ago

La data

The date

oggi	today
domani	tomorrow
dopodomani	the day after tomorrow
ieri	yesterday
l'altro ieri	the day before yesterday
il giorno prima	the day before, the previous day
il giorno dopo	the next *or* following day
la mattina	morning
la sera	evening
stamattina	this morning
stasera	this evening
questo pomeriggio	this afternoon

ieri mattina	yesterday morning
ieri sera	yesterday evening
domani mattina	tomorrow morning
domani sera	tomorrow evening
nella notte tra sabato e domenica	during Saturday night, during the night of Saturday to Sunday
viene sabato	he's coming on Saturday
il sabato	on Saturdays
tutti i sabati	every Saturday
sabato scorso, lo scorso sabato	last Saturday
il prossimo sabato	next Saturday
fra due sabati	a week on Saturday
fra tre sabati	a fortnight *or* two weeks on Saturday
da lunedì a sabato	from Monday to Saturday
tutti i lunedì	every Monday
una volta alla settimana	once a week
una volta al mese	once a month
due volte alla settimana	twice a week
una settimana fa	a week ago
quindici giorni fa	a fortnight *or* two weeks ago
l'anno scorso *or* passato	last year
fra due giorni	in two days
fra una settimana	in a week
fra quindici giorni	in a fortnight *or* two weeks
il mese prossimo	next month
l'anno prossimo	next year

che giorno è oggi?
il primo/24 ottobre 2018

what day is it?
the 1st/24th of October 2018, October 1st/24th 2018

nel 2018	in 2018
il millenovecentonovantacinque	nineteen ninety-five
44 a.C.	44 BC
14 d.C.	14 AD
nel diciannovesimo secolo, nel XIX secolo, nell'Ottocento	in the nineteenth century
negli anni Trenta	in the thirties
c'era una volta …	once upon a time …

ITALIANO – INGLESE

ITALIAN – ENGLISH

Aa

A, a [a] SM O F INV (*lettera*) A, a; **A come Ancona** ≈ A for Andrew (BRIT), ≈ A for Able (US); **dalla a alla z** from a to z

A ABBR (= *altezza*) h; (= *area*) A; (= *autostrada*) ≈ M (BRIT)

---

a

(*a + il* = **al**, *a + lo* = **allo**, *a + l'* = **all'**, *a + la* = **alla**, *a + i* = **ai**, *a + gli* = **agli**, *a + le* = **alle**) PREP **1** (*stato in luogo*) at; (: *in*) in; **essere alla stazione** to be at the station; **essere a casa/a scuola/a Roma** to be at home/at school/in Rome; **è a 10 km da qui** it's 10 km from here, it's 10 km away; **restare a cena** to stay for dinner

2 (*moto a luogo*) to; **andare a casa/a scuola/alla stazione** to go home/to school/to the station; **andare a Roma/al mare** to go to Rome/to the seaside

3 (*tempo*) at; (: *epoca, stagione*) in; **alle cinque** at five (o'clock); **a mezzanotte/Natale** at midnight/Christmas; **al mattino** in the morning; **a maggio/primavera** in May/spring; **a cinquant'anni** at fifty (years of age); **a domani!** see you tomorrow!; **a lunedì!** see you on Monday!; **a giorni** within (a few) days

4 (*complemento di termine*) to; **dare qc a qn** to give sb sth, give sth to sb; **l'ho chiesto a lui** I asked him

5 (*mezzo, modo*) with, by; **a piedi/cavallo** on foot/horseback; **viaggiare a 100 km all'ora** to travel at 100 km o per hour; **alla televisione/radio** on television/the radio; **fatto a mano** made by hand, handmade; **una barca a motore** a motorboat; **una stufa a gas** a gas heater; **a uno a uno** one by one; **a fatica** with difficulty; **all'italiana** the Italian way, in the Italian fashion

6 (*rapporto*) a, per; (: *con prezzi*) at; **due volte al giorno/mese** twice a day/month; **prendo 2000 euro al mese** I get 2000 euro a o per month; **pagato a ore** paid by the hour; **vendere qc a 2 euro il chilo** to sell sth at 2 euros a o per kilo; **cinque a zero** (*punteggio*) five nil

---

AA SIGLA = **Alto Adige**

AAST SIGLA F = **Azienda Autonoma di Soggiorno e Turismo**

AA.VV. ABBR = **autori vari**

ab. ABBR = **abitante**

a'bate SM abbot

abbacchi'ato, -a [abbak'kjato] AG downhearted, in low spirits

abbacin'are [abbatʃi'nare] /**72**/ VT to dazzle

abbagli'ante [abbaʎ'ʎante] AG dazzling ■ **abbaglianti** SMPL (*Aut*): **accendere gli abbaglianti** to put one's headlights on full (BRIT) o high (US) beam

abbagli'are [abbaʎ'ʎare] /**27**/ VT to dazzle; (*illudere*) to delude

ab'baglio [ab'baʎʎo] SM blunder; **prendere un ~** to blunder, make a blunder

abbai'are /**19**/ VI to bark

abba'ino SM dormer window; (*soffitta*) attic room

abbando'nare /**72**/ VT to leave, abandon, desert; (*trascurare*) to neglect; (*rinunciare a*) to abandon, give up ■ **abbandonarsi** VPR to let o.s. go; **~ il campo** (*Mil*) to retreat; **~ la presa** to let go; **abbandonarsi a** (*ricordi, vizio*) to give o.s. up to

abbando'nato, -a AG (*casa*) deserted; (*miniera*) disused; (*trascurato: terreno, podere*) neglected; (: *bambino*) abandoned

abban'dono SM abandoning; neglecting; (*stato*) abandonment; neglect; (*Sport*) withdrawal; (*fig*) abandon; **in ~** (*edificio, giardino*) neglected

abbarbi'carsi /**61**/ VPR: **~ (a)** (*anche fig*) to cling (to)

abbassa'mento SM lowering; (*di pressione, livello dell'acqua*) fall; (*di prezzi*) reduction; **~ di temperatura** drop in temperature

abbas'sare /**72**/ VT to lower; (*radio*) to turn down ■ **abbassarsi** VPR (*chinarsi*) to stoop; (*livello, sole*) to go down; (*fig: umiliarsi*) to demean o.s.; **~ i fari** (*Aut*) to dip (BRIT) o dim (US) one's lights; **~ le armi** (*Mil*) to lay down one's arms

ab'basso ESCL: **~ il re!** down with the king!

abbas'tanza [abbas'tantsa] AV (*a sufficienza*) enough; (*alquanto*) quite, rather, fairly; **non è ~ furbo** he's not shrewd enough; **un vino ~ dolce**

quite a sweet wine, a fairly sweet wine; **averne ~ di qn/qc** to have had enough of sb/sth

ab'battere /**1**/ vт (*muro, casa, ostacolo*) to knock down; (*albero*) to fell; (: *vento*) to bring down; (*bestie da macello*) to slaughter; (*cane, cavallo*) to destroy, put down; (*selvaggina, aereo*) to shoot down; (*fig: malattia, disgrazia*) to lay low ∎ **abbattersi** vрr (*avvilirsi*) to lose heart; **abbattersi a terra** *o* **al suolo** to fall to the ground; **abbattersi su** (*maltempo*) to beat down on; (*disgrazia*) to hit, strike

abbatti'mento sм knocking down; felling; (*di casa*) demolition; (*prostrazione: fisica*) exhaustion; (: *morale*) despondency

abbat'tuto, -a ag (*fig*) despondent, depressed

abba'zia [abbat'tsia] sf abbey

abbece'dario [abbetʃe'darjo] sм primer

abbelli'mento sм embellishment

abbel'lire /**55**/ vт to make beautiful; (*ornare*) to embellish

abbeve'rare /**72**/ vт to water ∎ **abbeverarsi** vрr to drink

abbevera'toio sм drinking trough

'abbi vв *vedi* **avere**

'abbia vв *vedi* **avere**

abbi'amo vв *vedi* **avere**

'abbiano vв *vedi* **avere**

abbi'ate vв *vedi* **avere**

abbicci [abbit'tʃi] sм inv alphabet; (*sillabario*) primer; (*fig*) rudiments *pl*

abbi'ente ag well-to-do, well-off ∎ **abbienti** sмpl: **gli abbienti** the well-to-do

abbi'etto, -a ag = **abietto**

abbiezi'one [abbjet'tsjone] sf = **abiezione**

abbiglia'mento [abbiʎʎa'mento] sм dress *no pl*; (*indumenti*) clothes *pl*; (*industria*) clothing industry

abbigli'are [abbiʎ'ʎare] /**27**/ vт to dress up

abbina'mento sм combination; linking; matching

abbi'nare /**72**/ vт: **~ (con** *o* **a)** (*gen*) to combine (with); (*nomi*) to link (with); **~ qc a qc** (*colori ecc*) to match sth with sth

abbindo'lare /**72**/ vт (*fig*) to cheat, trick

abbocca'mento sм (*colloquio*) talks *pl*, meeting; (*Tecn: di tubi*) connection

abboc'care /**20**/ vт (*tubi, canali*) to connect, join up ▶ vι (*pesce*) to bite; (*tubi*) to join; **~ (all'amo)** (*fig*) to swallow the bait

abboc'cato, -a ag (*vino*) sweetish

abbona'mento sм subscription; (*alle ferrovie ecc*) season ticket; **in ~** for subscribers only; for season ticket holders only; **fare l'~ (a)** to take out a subscription (to); to buy a season ticket (for)

abbo'nare /**72**/ vт (*cifra*) to deduct; (*fig: perdonare*) to forgive ∎ **abbonarsi** vрr: **abbonarsi a un**

giornale to take out a subscription to a newspaper; **abbonarsi al teatro/alle ferrovie** to take out a season ticket for the theatre/the train

abbo'nato, -a sм/ғ subscriber; season-ticket holder; **elenco degli abbonati** telephone directory

abbon'dante ag abundant, plentiful; (*giacca*) roomy

abbon'danza [abbon'dantsa] sf abundance; plenty

abbon'dare /**72**/ vι to abound, be plentiful; **~ in** *o* **di** to be full of, abound in

abbor'dabile ag (*persona*) approachable; (*prezzo*) reasonable

abbor'dare /**72**/ vт (*nave*) to board; (*persona*) to approach; (*argomento*) to tackle; **~ una curva** to take a bend

abbotto'nare /**72**/ vт to button up, do up ∎ **abbottonarsi** vрr to button (up)

abbotto'nato, -a ag (*camicia ecc*) buttoned (up); (*fig*) reserved

abbottona'tura sf buttons *pl*; **questo cappotto ha l'~ da uomo/da donna** this coat buttons on the man's/woman's side

abboz'zare [abbot'tsare] /**72**/ vт to sketch, outline; (*Scultura*) to rough-hew; **~ un sorriso** to give a hint of a smile

ab'bozzo [ab'bɔttso] sм sketch, outline; (*Dir*) draft

abbracci'are [abbrat'tʃare] /**14**/ vт to embrace; (*persona*) to hug, embrace; (*professione*) to take up; (*contenere*) to include ∎ **abbracciarsi** vрr to hug *o* embrace (one another)

ab'braccio [ab'brattʃo] sм hug, embrace

abbrevi'are /**19**/ vт to shorten; (*parola*) to abbreviate, shorten

abbreviazi'one [abbrevjat'tsjone] sf abbreviation

abbron'zante [abbron'dzante] ag tanning, sun *cpd*

abbron'zare [abbron'dzare] /**72**/ vт (*pelle*) to tan; (*metalli*) to bronze ∎ **abbronzarsi** vрr to tan, get a tan

abbron'zato, -a [abbron'dzato] ag (sun)tanned

abbronza'tura [abbrondza'tura] sf tan, suntan

abbrusto'lire /**55**/ vт (*pane*) to toast; (*caffè*) to roast ∎ **abbrustolirsi** vрr to toast; (*fig: al sole*) to soak up the sun

abbruti'mento sм exhaustion; degradation

abbru'tire /**55**/ vт (*snervare, stancare*) to exhaust; (*degradare*) to degrade; **essere abbrutito dall'alcool** to be ruined by drink

abbuffarsi /**72**/ vрr (*col*): **~ di qc** to stuff o.s. (with sth)

abbuf'fata sf (*col*) nosh-up; (*fig*) binge; **farsi un'~** to stuff o.s.

abbuo'nare /72/ vt = **abbonare**

abbu'ono sm (*Comm*) allowance, discount; (*Sport*) handicap

abdi'care /20/ vi to abdicate; ~ **a** to give up, renounce

abdicazi'one [abdikat'tsjone] sf abdication

aberrazi'one [aberrat'tsjone] sf aberration

abe'taia sf fir wood

a'bete sm fir (tree); ~ **bianco** silver fir; ~ **rosso** spruce

abi'etto, -a ag despicable, abject

abiezi'one [abjet'tsjone] sf abjection

'**abile** ag (*idoneo*): ~ **(a qc/a fare qc)** fit (for sth/to do sth); (*capace*) able; (*astuto*) clever; (*accorto*) skilful; ~ **al servizio militare** fit for military service

abilità sf inv ability; cleverness; skill

abili'tante ag qualifying; **corsi abilitanti** (*Ins*) = teacher training *sg*

abili'tare /72/ vt: ~ **qn a qc/a fare qc** to qualify sb for sth/to do sth; **è stato abilitato all'insegnamento** he has qualified as a teacher

abili'tato, -a ag qualified; (*Tel*) which has an outside line

abilitazi'one [abilitat'tsjone] sf qualification

abis'sale ag abysmal; (*fig: senza limiti*) profound

abis'sino, -a ag, sm/f Abyssinian

a'bisso sm abyss, gulf

abitabilità sf: **licenza di** ~ *document stating that a property is fit for habitation*

abi'tacolo sm (*Aer*) cockpit; (*Aut*) inside; (*di camion*) (driver's) cab

abi'tante smf inhabitant

abi'tare /72/ vt to live in, dwell in ▶ vi: ~ **in campagna/a Roma** to live in the country/in Rome; **dove abita?** where do you live?

abi'tato, -a ag inhabited; lived in ▶ sm (*anche:* **centro abitato**) built-up area

abitazi'one [abitat'tsjone] sf residence; house

'**abito** sm dress *no pl*; (*da uomo*) suit; (*da donna*) dress; (*abitudine, disposizione, Rel*) habit ■ **abiti** smpl (*vestiti*) clothes; **in ~ da cerimonia** in formal dress; **in ~ da sera** in evening dress; "**è gradito l'~ scuro**" "dress formal"; ~ **mentale** way of thinking

abitu'ale ag usual, habitual; (*cliente*) regular

abitual'mente av usually, normally

abitu'are /72/ vt: ~ **qn a** to get sb used *o* accustomed to; **abituarsi a** to get used to, accustom o.s. to

abitudi'nario, -a ag of fixed habits ▶ sm/f creature of habit

abi'tudine sf habit; **aver l'~ di fare qc** to be in the habit of doing sth; **d'~** usually; **per ~** from *o* out of habit

abiu'rare /72/ vt to renounce

abla'tivo sm ablative

abnegazi'one [abnegat'tsjone] sf (self-)abnegation, self-denial

ab'norme ag (*enorme*) extraordinary; (*anormale*) abnormal

abo'lire /55/ vt to abolish; (*Dir*) to repeal

abolizi'one [abolit'tsjone] sf abolition; repeal

abomi'nevole ag abominable

abo'rigeno, -a [abo'ridʒeno] sm/f aborigine

abor'rire /17/ vt to abhor, detest

abor'tire /55/ vi (*Med: accidentalmente*) to miscarry, have a miscarriage; (: *deliberatamente*) to have an abortion; (*fig*) to miscarry, fail

abor'tista, -i, -e ag pro-choice, pro-abortion ▶ sm/f pro-choicer

a'borto sm miscarriage; abortion; (*fig*) freak; ~ **clandestino** backstreet abortion

abrasi'one sf abrasion

abra'sivo, -a ag, sm abrasive

abro'gare /80/ vt to repeal, abrogate

abrogazi'one [abrogat'tsjone] sf repeal

abruz'zese [abrut'tsese] ag of (*o* from) the Abruzzi

A'bruzzo [a'bruttso] sm: **l'~, gli Abruzzi** the Abruzzi

ABS [abi'esse] sigla m (= *Anti-Blockier System*) ABS (= *anti-lock braking system*)

'**abside** sf apse

'**Abu 'Dhabi** sf Abu Dhabi

a'bulico, -a, -ci, -che ag lacking in willpower

abu'sare /72/ vi: ~ **di** to abuse, misuse; (*approfittare, violare*) to take advantage of; ~ **dell'alcool/dei cibi** to drink/eat to excess

abusi'vismo sm (*anche:* **abusivismo edilizio**) unlawful building, building without planning permission (*Brit*)

abu'sivo, -a ag unauthorized, unlawful; (**occupante**) ~ (*di una casa*) squatter

a'buso sm abuse, misuse; excessive use; **fare ~ di** (*stupefacenti, medicine*) to abuse

a.C. abbr (= *avanti Cristo*) BC

a'cacia, -cie [a'katʃa] sf (*Bot*) acacia

'**acca** sf letter H; **non capire un'~** not to understand a thing

ac'cadde vb *vedi* **accadere**

acca'demia sf (*società*) learned society; (*scuola: d'arte, militare*) academy; **A~ di Belle Arti** art school

acca'demico, -a, -ci, -che ag academic ▶ sm academician

acca'dere /18/ vb impers to happen, occur

acca'duto sm event; **raccontare l'~** to describe what has happened

accalappia'cani sm inv dog-catcher

accalappi'are /19/ vt to catch; (*fig*) to trick, dupe

accal'care /20/ VT, **accal'carsi** VPR to crowd, throng

accal'darsi /61/ VPR to grow hot

accal'dato, -a AG hot

accalo'rarsi /61/ VPR (fig) to get excited

accampa'mento SM camp

accam'pare /72/ VT to encamp; (fig) to put forward, advance ▪ **accamparsi** VPR to camp; ~ **scuse** to make excuses

accani'mento SM fury; (tenacia) tenacity, perseverance

acca'nirsi /55/ VPR (infierire) to rage; (ostinarsi) to persist

accanita'mente AV fiercely; assiduously

acca'nito, -a AG (odio, gelosia) fierce, bitter; (lavoratore) assiduous; (giocatore, fumatore) inveterate; (tifoso, sostenitore) keen; **fumatore** ~ chain smoker

ac'canto AV near, nearby; ~ **a** prep near, beside, close to; **la casa** ~ the house next door

accanto'nare /72/ VT (problema) to shelve; (somma) to set aside

accaparra'mento SM (Comm) cornering, buying up

accapar'rare /72/ VT (Comm) to corner, buy up; (versare una caparra) to pay a deposit on ▪ **accaparrarsi** VPR: **accaparrarsi qc** (fig: simpatia, voti) to secure sth (for o.s.)

accapigli'arsi [akkapiʎˈʎarsi] /27/ VPR to come to blows; (fig) to quarrel

accappa'toio SM bathrobe

accappo'nare /72/ VI: **far** ~ **la pelle a qn** (fig) to bring sb out in goosepimples

accarez'zare [akkaretˈtsare] /72/ VT to caress, stroke, fondle; (fig) to toy with

accartocci'are [akkartotˈtʃare] /14/ VT (carta) to roll up, screw up ▪ **accartocciarsi** VPR (foglie) to curl up

acca'sarsi /27/ VPR to set up house; to get married

accasci'arsi [akkaʃˈʃarsi] /14/ VPR to collapse; (fig) to lose heart

accatas'tare /72/ VT to stack, pile

accatto'naggio [akkattoˈnaddʒo] SM begging

accat'tone, -a SM/F beggar

accaval'lare /72/ VT (gambe) to cross ▪ **accavallarsi** VPR (sovrapporsi) to overlap; (addensarsi) to gather

acce'care [attʃeˈkare] /20/ VT to blind ▶ VI to go blind

ac'cedere [atˈtʃɛdere] /29/ VI: ~ **a** to enter; (richiesta) to grant, accede to; (fonte) to gain access to

accele'rare [attʃeleˈrare] /72/ VT to speed up ▶ VI (Aut) to accelerate; ~ **il passo** to quicken one's pace

accele'rato, -a [attʃeleˈrato] AG quick, rapid ▶ SM (Ferr) local train, stopping train

accelera'tore [attʃeleraˈtore] SM (Aut) accelerator

accelerazi'one [attʃelератˈtsjone] SF acceleration

ac'cendere [atˈtʃɛndere] /2/ VT (fuoco, sigaretta) to light; (luce, televisione) to put o switch o turn on; (Aut: motore) to switch on; (Comm: conto) to open; (: debito) to contract; (: ipoteca) to raise; (fig: suscitare) to inflame, stir up ▪ **accendersi** VPR (luce) to come o go on; (legna) to catch fire, ignite; (fig: lotta, conflitto) to break out

accen'dino [attʃenˈdino], **accendi'sigaro** [attʃendiˈsigaro] SM (cigarette) lighter

accen'nare [attʃenˈnare] /72/ VT to indicate, point out; (Mus) to pick out the notes of; to hum ▶ VI: ~ **a** (fig: alludere a) to hint at; (: far atto di) to make as if; ~ **un saluto** (con la mano) to make as if to wave; (col capo) to half nod; ~ **un sorriso** to half smile; **accenna a piovere** it looks as if it's going to rain

ac'cenno [atˈtʃenno] SM (cenno) sign; nod; (allusione) hint

accensi'one [attʃenˈsjone] SF (vedi accendere) lighting; switching on; opening; (Aut) ignition

accen'tare [attʃenˈtare] /72/ VT (parlando) to stress; (scrivendo) to accent

accentuazi'one [attʃentatˈtsjone] SF accentuation; stressing

ac'cento [atˈtʃento] SM accent; (Fonetica, fig) stress; (inflessione) tone (of voice)

accentra'mento [attʃentraˈmento] SM centralization

accen'trare [attʃenˈtrare] /72/ VT to centralize

accentra'tore, -'trice [attʃentraˈtore] AG (persona) unwilling to delegate; **politica accentratrice** policy of centralization

accentu'are [attʃentuˈare] /72/ VT to stress, emphasize ▪ **accentuarsi** VPR to become more noticeable

accerchi'are [attʃerˈkjare] /19/ VT to surround, encircle

accerta'mento [attʃertaˈmento] SM check; assessment

accer'tare [attʃerˈtare] /72/ VT to ascertain; (verificare) to check; (reddito) to assess ▪ **accertarsi** VPR: **accertarsi (di qc/che)** to make sure (of sth/that)

ac'ceso, -a [atˈtʃeso] PP di **accendere** ▶ AG lit; on; open; (colore) bright; ~ **di** (ira, entusiasmo ecc) burning with

acces'sibile [attʃesˈsibile] AG (luogo) accessible; (persona) approachable; (prezzo) reasonable; (idea): ~ **a qn** within the reach of sb

ac'cesso [atˈtʃesso] SM (anche Inform) access; (Med) attack, fit; (impulso violento) fit, outburst; **programmi dell'**~ (TV) educational programmes; **tempo di** ~ (Inform) access time; ~

casuale/seriale/sequenziale (*Inform*) random/serial/sequential access

accessori'ato, -a [attʃesso'rjato] AG with accessories

acces'sorio, -a [attʃes'sɔrjo] AG secondary, of secondary importance ◾ **accessori** SMPL accessories

ac'cetta [at'tʃetta] SF hatchet

accet'tabile [attʃet'tabile] AG acceptable

accet'tare [attʃet'tare] /**72**/ VT to accept; **~ di fare qc** to agree to do sth

accettazi'one [attʃettat'tsjone] SF acceptance; (*locale di servizio pubblico*) reception; **~ bagagli** (*Aer*) check-in (desk); **~ con riserva** qualified acceptance

ac'cetto, -a [at'tʃetto] AG (*persona*) welcome; **(ben) ~ a tutti** well-liked by everybody

accezi'one [attʃet'tsjone] SF meaning

acchiap'pare [akkjap'pare] /**72**/ VT to catch; (*afferrare*) to seize

ac'chito [ak'kito] SM: **a primo ~** at first sight

acciac'cato, -a [attʃak'kato] AG (*persona*) full of aches and pains; (*abito*) crushed

acci'acco, -chi [at'tʃakko] SM ailment ◾ **acciacchi** SMPL aches and pains

acciaie'ria [attʃaje'ria] SF steelworks *sg*

acci'aio [at'tʃajo] SM steel; **~ inossidabile** stainless steel

acciden'tale [attʃiden'tale] AG accidental

accidental'mente [attʃidental'mente] AV (*per caso*) by chance; (*non deliberatamente*) accidentally, by accident

acciden'tato, -a [attʃiden'tato] AG (*terreno ecc*) uneven

acci'dente [attʃi'dɛnte] SM (*caso imprevisto*) accident; (*disgrazia*) mishap; **accidenti!** (*col: per rabbia*) damn (it)!; (: *per meraviglia*) good heavens!; **accidenti a lui!** damn him!; **non vale un ~** it's not worth a damn; **non capisco un ~** it's as clear as mud to me; **mandare un ~ a qn** to curse sb

ac'cidia [at'tʃidja] SF (*Rel*) sloth

accigli'ato, -a [attʃiʎ'ʎato] AG frowning

ac'cingersi [at'tʃindʒersi] /**54**/ VPR: **~ a fare** to be about to do

acciotto'lato [attʃotto'lato] SM cobbles *pl*

acciuf'fare [attʃuf'fare] /**72**/ VT to seize, catch

acci'uga, -ghe [at'tʃuga] SF anchovy; **magro come un'~** as thin as a rake

accla'mare /**72**/ VT (*applaudire*) to applaud; (*eleggere*) to acclaim

acclamazi'one [akklamat'tsjone] SF applause; acclamation

acclima'tare /**72**/ VT to acclimatize ◾ **acclimatarsi** VPR to become acclimatized

acclimatazi'one [akklimatat'tsjone] SF acclimatization

ac'cludere /**3**/ VT to enclose

ac'cluso, -a PP *di* **accludere** ▶ AG enclosed

accocco'larsi /**72**/ VPR to crouch

acco'darsi /**72**/ VPR to follow, tag on (behind)

accogli'ente [akkoʎ'ʎɛnte] AG welcoming, friendly

accogli'enza [akkoʎ'ʎɛntsa] SF reception; welcome; **fare una buona ~ a qn** to welcome sb

ac'cogliere [ak'kɔʎʎere] /**23**/ VT (*ricevere*) to receive; (*dare il benvenuto*) to welcome; (*approvare*) to agree to, accept; (*contenere*) to hold, accommodate

ac'colgo *ecc* VB *vedi* **accogliere**

accol'lare /**72**/ VT: **~ qc a qn** (*fig*) to force sth on sb ◾ **accollarsi** VPR: **accollarsi qc** to take sth upon o.s., shoulder sth

accol'lato, -a AG (*vestito*) high-necked

ac'colsi *ecc* VB *vedi* **accogliere**

accoltel'lare /**72**/ VT to knife, stab

ac'colto, -a PP *di* **accogliere**

accoman'dita SF (*Dir*) limited partnership

accomia'tare /**72**/ VT to dismiss ◾ **accomiatarsi** VPR: **accomiatarsi (da)** to take one's leave (of)

accomoda'mento SM agreement, settlement

accomo'dante AG accommodating

accomo'dare /**72**/ VT (*aggiustare*) to repair, mend; (*riordinare*) to tidy; (*sistemare: questione, lite*) to settle ◾ **accomodarsi** VPR (*sedersi*) to sit down; (*fig: risolversi: situazione*) to work out; **si accomodi!** (*venga avanti*) come in!; (*si sieda*) take a seat!

accompagna'mento [akkompaɲɲa'mento] SM (*Mus*) accompaniment; (*Comm*): **lettera di ~** accompanying letter

accompa'gnare [akkompaɲ'ɲare] /**15**/ VT to accompany, come *o* go with; (*Mus*) to accompany; (*unire*) to couple ◾ **accompagnarsi** VPR (*armonizzarsi*) to go well together; **~ qn a casa** to see sb home; **~ qn alla porta** to show sb out; **~ un regalo con un biglietto** to put in *o* send a card with a present; **~ qn con lo sguardo** to follow sb with one's eyes; **~ la porta** to close the door gently; **accompagnarsi a** (*frequentare*) to frequent; (*colori*) to go with, match; (*cibi*) to go with

accompagna'tore, -'trice [akkompaɲɲa'tore] SM/F companion, escort; (*Mus*) accompanist; (*Sport*) team manager; **~ turistico** courier; tour guide

accomu'nare /**72**/ VT to pool, share; (*avvicinare*) to unite

acconcia'tura [akkontʃa'tura] SF hairstyle

accondiscen'dente [akkondiʃʃen'dɛnte] AG affable

accondi'scendere [akkondiʃ'ʃendere] /**101**/ VI: **~ a** to agree *o* consent to

accondi'sceso, -a [akkondiʃ'ʃeso] PP *di* **accondiscendere**

acconsen'tire /17/ VI: ~ **(a)** to agree o consent (to); **chi tace acconsente** silence means consent

acconten'tare /72/ VT to satisfy ∎ **accontentarsi** VPR: **accontentarsi di** to be satisfied with, content o.s. with; **chi si accontenta gode** there's no point in complaining

ac'conto SM part payment; **pagare una somma in** ~ to pay a sum of money as a deposit; ~ **di dividendo** interim dividend

accoppia'mento SM pairing off; mating; (Elettr, Inform) coupling

accoppi'are /19/ VT to couple, pair off; (Biol) to mate ∎ **accoppiarsi** VPR to pair off; to mate

accoppia'tore SM (Tecn) coupler; ~ **acustico** (Inform) acoustic coupler

acco'rato, -a AG heartfelt

accorci'are [akkor'tʃare] /14/ VT to shorten ∎ **accorciarsi** VPR to become shorter; (vestiti: nel lavaggio) to shrink

accor'dare /72/ VT to reconcile; (colori) to match; (Mus) to tune; (Ling): ~ **qc con qc** to make sth agree with sth; (Dir) to grant ∎ **accordarsi** VPR to agree, come to an agreement; (colori) to match

ac'cordo SM agreement; (armonia) harmony; (Mus) chord; **essere d'**~ to agree; **andare d'**~ to get on well together; **d'**~**!** all right!, agreed!; **mettersi d'**~ **(con qn)** to agree o come to an agreement (with sb); **prendere accordi con** to reach an agreement with; ~ **commerciale** trade agreement; **A**~ **generale sulle tariffe ed il commercio** General Agreement on Tariffs and Trade, GATT

ac'corgersi [ak'kɔrdʒersi] /4/ VPR: ~ **di** to notice; (fig) to realize

accorgi'mento [akkordʒi'mento] SM shrewdness no pl; (espediente) trick, device

ac'correre /28/ VI to run up

ac'corsi VB vedi **accorgersi; accorrere**

ac'corso, -a PP di **accorrere**

accor'tezza [akkor'tettsa] SF (avvedutezza) good sense; (astuzia) shrewdness

ac'corto, -a PP di **accorgersi** ▶ AG shrewd; **stare** ~ to be on one's guard

accosta'mento SM (di colori ecc) combination

accos'tare /72/ VT (avvicinarsi a) to approach; (socchiudere: imposte) to half-close; (: porta) to leave ajar ▶ VI: ~ **(a)** (Naut) to come alongside; (Aut) to draw up (at) ∎ **accostarsi** VPR: **accostarsi a** to draw near, approach; (somigliare) to be like, resemble; (fede, religione) to turn to; (idee politiche) to come to agree with; ~ **qc a** (avvicinare) to bring sth near to, put sth near to; (colori, stili) to match sth with; (appoggiare: scala ecc) to lean sth against

accovacci'arsi [akkovat'tʃarsi] /14/ VPR to crouch

accoz'zaglia [akkot'tsaʎʎa] SF (peg: di idee, oggetti) jumble, hotchpotch; (: di persone) odd assortment

ac'crebbi ecc VB vedi **accrescere**

accredi'tare /72/ VT (notizia) to confirm the truth of; (Comm) to credit; (diplomatico) to accredit ∎ **accreditarsi** VPR (fig) to gain credit

ac'credito SM (Comm: atto) crediting; (: effetto) credit

ac'crescere [ak'kreʃʃere] /30/ VT to increase ∎ **accrescersi** VPR to increase, grow

accresci'mento [akkreʃʃi'mento] SM increase, growth

accresci'tivo, -a [akkreʃʃi'tivo] AG, SM (Ling) augmentative

accresci'uto, -a [akkreʃ'ʃuto] PP di **accrescere**

accucci'arsi [akkut'tʃarsi] /14/ VPR (cane) to lie down; (persona) to crouch down

accu'dire /55/ VI: ~ **a** to attend to ▶ VT to look after

acculturazi'one [akkulturat'tsjone] SF (Sociologia) integration

accumu'lare /72/ VT to accumulate ∎ **accumularsi** VPR to accumulate; (Finanza) to accrue

accumula'tore SM (Elettr) accumulator

accumulazi'one [akkumulat'tsjone] SF accumulation

ac'cumulo SM accumulation

accurata'mente AV carefully

accura'tezza [akkura'tettsa] SF care; accuracy

accu'rato, -a AG (diligente) careful; (preciso) accurate

ac'cusa SF accusation; (Dir) charge; **l'**~, **la pubblica** ~ (Dir) the prosecution; **mettere qn sotto** ~ to indict sb; **in stato di** ~ committed for trial

accu'sare /72/ VT (sentire: dolore) to feel; ~ **qn di qc** to accuse sb of sth; (Dir) to charge sb with sth; ~ **ricevuta di** (Comm) to acknowledge receipt of; ~ **la fatica** to show signs of exhaustion; **ha accusato il colpo** (anche fig) you could see that he had felt the blow

accusa'tivo SM accusative

accu'sato, -a SM/F accused

accusa'tore, -'trice AG accusing ▶ SM/F accuser ▶ SM (Dir) prosecutor

a'cerbo, -a [a'tʃerbo] AG bitter; (frutta) sour, unripe; (persona) immature

'acero ['atʃero] SM maple

a'cerrimo, -a [a'tʃerrimo] AG very fierce

ace'tato [atʃe'tato] SM acetate

a'ceto [a'tʃeto] SM vinegar; **mettere sotto** ~ to pickle

ace'tone [atʃe'tone] SM nail varnish remover

'A.C.I. ['atʃi] SIGLA M (= Automobile Club d'Italia) ≈ AA (BRIT), ≈ AAA (US)

acidità [atʃidiˈta] SF acidity; sourness; **~ (di stomaco)** heartburn

'acido, -a [ˈatʃido] AG (sapore) acid, sour; (Chim, colore) acid ▸ SM (Chim) acid

a'cidulo, -a [aˈtʃidulo] AG slightly sour, slightly acid

'acino [ˈatʃino] SM berry; **~ d'uva** grape

'ACLI SIGLA FPL (= Associazioni Cristiane dei Lavoratori Italiani) Christian Trade Union Association

'acme SF (fig) acme, peak; (Med) crisis

'acne SF acne

ACNUR SIGLA M (= Alto Commissariato delle Nazioni Unite per i Rifugiati) UNHCR

'acqua SF water; (pioggia) rain ▪ **acque** SFPL (di mare, fiume ecc) waters; **fare ~** (Naut) to leak, take in water; **essere con** o **avere l'~ alla gola** to be in great difficulty; **tirare ~ al proprio mulino** to feather one's own nest; **navigare in cattive acque** (fig) to be in deep water; **~ in bocca!** mum's the word!; **~ corrente** running water; **~ dolce** fresh water; **~ di mare** sea water; **~ minerale** mineral water; **~ ossigenata** hydrogen peroxide; **~ piovana** rain water; **~ potabile** drinking water; **~ salata** o **salmastra** salt water; **~ tonica** tonic water

acqua'bike [akkwaˈbaik] SF aquabiking, aquacycling

acqua'forte (pl **acqueforti**) SF etching

acqua'gym [akkwaˈdʒim] SF aquacise

a'cquaio SM sink

acqua'ragia [akkwaˈradʒa] SF turpentine

a'cquario SM aquarium; **A~** Aquarius; **essere dell'A~** to be Aquarius

acquartie'rare /72/ VT (Mil) to quarter

acqua'santa SF holy water

acquas'cooter [akkwasˈkuter] SM INV Jet Ski®

a'cquatico, -a, -ci, -che AG aquatic; (sport, sci) water cpd

acquat'tarsi /72/ VPR to crouch (down)

acqua'vite SF brandy

acquaz'zone [akkwatˈtsone] SM cloudburst, heavy shower

acque'dotto SM aqueduct; waterworks pl, water system

'acqueo, -a AG: **vapore ~** water vapour (BRIT) o vapor (US); **umore ~** aqueous humour (BRIT) o humor (US)

acque'rello SM watercolour (BRIT), watercolor (US)

acque'rugiola [akkweˈrudʒola] SF drizzle

acquie'tare /72/ VT to appease; (dolore) to ease ▪ **acquietarsi** VPR to calm down

acqui'rente SMF purchaser, buyer

acqui'sire /55/ VT to acquire

acquisizi'one [akkwizitˈtsjone] SF acquisition

acquis'tare /72/ VT to purchase, buy; (fig) to gain ▸ VI to improve; **~ in bellezza** to become more beautiful; **ha acquistato in salute** his health has improved

a'cquisto SM purchase; **fare acquisti** to go shopping; **ufficio acquisti** (Comm) purchasing department; **~ rateale** instalment purchase, hire purchase (BRIT)

acqui'trino SM bog, marsh

acquo'lina SF: **far venire l'~ in bocca a qn** to make sb's mouth water

a'cquoso, -a AG watery

'acre AG acrid, pungent; (fig) harsh, biting

a'credine SF (fig) bitterness

a'crilico, -a, -ci, -che AG, SM acrylic

a'critico, -a, -ci, -che AG uncritical

acro'bata, -i, -e SM/F acrobat

acro'batico, -a, -ci, -che AG (ginnastica) acrobatic; (Aer) aerobatic ▸ SF acrobatics sg

acroba'zia [akrobatˈtsia] SF acrobatic feat; **acrobazie aeree** aerobatics

a'cronimo SM acronym

a'cropoli SF INV: **l'A~** the Acropolis

acu'ire /55/ VT to sharpen ▪ **acuirsi** VPR (gen) to increase; (crisi) to worsen

a'culeo SM (Zool) sting; (Bot) prickle

a'cume SM acumen, perspicacity

acumi'nato, -a AG sharp

a'custico, -a, -ci, -che AG acoustic ▸ SF (scienza) acoustics sg; (di una sala) acoustics pl; **apparecchio ~** hearing aid; **cornetto ~** ear trumpet

acu'tezza [akuˈtettsa] SF sharpness; shrillness; acuteness; high pitch; intensity; keenness

acutiz'zare [akutidˈdzare] /72/ VT (fig) to intensify ▪ **acutizzarsi** VPR (fig: crisi, malattia) to become worse, worsen

a'cuto, -a AG (appuntito) sharp, pointed; (suono, voce) shrill, piercing; (Mat, Ling, Med) acute; (Mus) high-pitched; (fig: dolore, desiderio) intense; (: perspicace) acute, keen ▸ SM (Mus) high note

ad PREP (dav V) = **a**

adagi'are [adaˈdʒare] /62/ VT to lay o set down carefully ▪ **adagiarsi** VPR to lie down, stretch out

a'dagio [aˈdadʒo] AV slowly ▸ SM (Mus) adagio; (proverbio) adage, saying

ada'mitico, -a, -ci, -che AG: **in costume ~** in one's birthday suit

adat'tabile AG adaptable

adattabi'lità SF adaptability

adatta'mento SM adaptation; **avere spirito di ~** to be adaptable

adat'tare /72/ VT to adapt; (sistemare) to fit ▪ **adattarsi** VPR: **adattarsi (a)** (ambiente, tempi) to adapt (to); (essere adatto) to be suitable (for);

adattarsi a qc/a fare qc (*accontentarsi*) to make the best of sth/of doing sth

adatta'tore SM (*Elettr*) adapter, adaptor

a'datto, -a AG: ~ **(a)** suitable (for), right (for)

addebi'tare /72/ VT: ~ **qc a qn** to debit sb with sth; (*fig: incolpare*) to blame sb for sth

ad'debito SM (*Comm*) debit

addensa'mento SM thickening; gathering

adden'sare /72/ VT to thicken ■ **addensarsi** VPR to thicken; (*nuvole*) to gather

adden'tare /72/ VT to bite into

adden'trarsi /72/ VPR: ~ **in** to penetrate, go into

ad'dentro AV (*fig*): **essere molto ~ in qc** to be well-versed in sth

addestra'mento SM training; ~ **aziendale** company training

addes'trare /72/ VT, **addes'trarsi** VPR to train; **addestrarsi in qc** to practise (BRIT) o practice (US) sth

ad'detto, -a AG: ~ **a** (*persona*) assigned to; (*oggetto*) intended for ▶ SM/F employee; (*funzionario*) attaché; ~ **commerciale/stampa** commercial/press attaché; ~ **al telex** telex operator; **gli addetti ai lavori** authorized personnel; (*fig*) those in the know; **"vietato l'ingresso ai non addetti ai lavori"** "authorized personnel only"

addì AV (*Amm*): ~ **3 luglio 2017** on the 3rd of July 2017 (BRIT), on July 3rd 2017 (US)

addi'accio [ad'djattʃo] SM (*Mil*) bivouac; **dormire all'~** to sleep in the open

addi'etro AV (*indietro*) behind; (*nel passato, prima*) before, ago

ad'dio SM, ESCL goodbye, farewell

addirit'tura AV (*veramente*) really, absolutely; (*perfino*) even; (*direttamente*) directly, right away

ad'dirsi /38/ VPR: ~ **a** to suit, be suitable for

'Addis A'beba SF Addis Ababa

addi'tare /72/ VT to point out; (*fig*) to expose

addi'tivo SM additive

addizio'nale [addittsjo'nale] AG additional ▶ SF (*anche:* **imposta addizionale**) surtax

addizio'nare [addittsjo'nare] /72/ VT (*Mat*) to add (up)

addizi'one [addit'tsjone] SF addition

addob'bare /72/ VT to decorate

ad'dobbo SM decoration

addol'cire [addol'tʃire] /55/ VT (*caffè ecc*) to sweeten; (*acqua, fig: carattere*) to soften ■ **addolcirsi** VPR (*fig*) to mellow, soften; ~ **la pillola** (*fig*) to sugar the pill

addolo'rare /72/ VT to pain, grieve ■ **addolorarsi** VPR: **addolorarsi (per)** to be distressed (by)

addolo'rato, -a AG distressed, upset; **l'Addolorata** (*Rel*) Our Lady of Sorrows

ad'dome SM abdomen

addomesti'care /20/ VT to tame

addomi'nale AG abdominal; **(muscoli) addominali** stomach muscles

addormen'tare /72/ VT to put to sleep ■ **addormentarsi** VPR to fall asleep, go to sleep

addormen'tato, -a AG sleeping, asleep; (*fig: tardo*) stupid, dopey

addos'sare /72/ VT (*appoggiare*): ~ **qc a qc** to lean sth against sth; (*fig*): ~ **la colpa a qn** to lay the blame on sb ■ **addossarsi: addossarsi qc** (*responsabilità ecc*) to shoulder sth

ad'dosso AV (*sulla persona*) on; ~ **a** prep (*sopra*) on; (*molto vicino*) right next to; **mettersi ~ il cappotto** to put one's coat on; **andare (o venire) ~ a** (*Aut: altra macchina*) to run into; (: *pedone*) to run over; **non ho soldi ~** I don't have any money on me; **stare ~ a qn** (*fig*) to breathe down sb's neck; **dare ~ a qn** (*fig*) to attack sb; **mettere gli occhi ~ a qn/qc** to take quite a fancy to sb/sth; **mettere le mani ~ a qn** (*picchiare*) to hit sb; (*catturare*) to seize sb; (*molestare: donna*) to touch sb up

ad'dotto, -a PP *di* **addurre**

ad'duco *ecc* VB *vedi* **addurre**

ad'durre /90/ VT (*Dir*) to produce; (*citare*) to cite

ad'dussi *ecc* VB *vedi* **addurre**

adegu'are /72/ VT: ~ **qc a** to adjust sth to ■ **adeguarsi** VPR to adapt

adegua'tezza [adegwa'tettsa] SF adequacy; suitability; fairness

adegu'ato, -a AG adequate; (*conveniente*) suitable; (*equo*) fair

a'dempiere /24/ VT to fulfil (BRIT), fulfill (US), carry out; (*comando*) to carry out

adempi'mento SM fulfilment (BRIT), fulfillment (US); carrying out; **nell'~ del proprio dovere** in the performance of one's duty

adem'pire /17/ VT = **adempiere**

'Aden SM: **il golfo di ~** the Gulf of Aden

ade'noidi SFPL adenoids

a'depto, -a SM/F disciple, follower

ade'rente AG adhesive; (*vestito*) close-fitting ▶ SMF follower

ade'renza [ade'rentsa] SF adhesion ■ **aderenze** SFPL (*fig*) connections, contacts

ade'rire /55/ VI (*stare attaccato*) to adhere, stick; ~ **a** to adhere to, stick to; (*fig: società, partito*) to join; (: *opinione*) to support; (: *richiesta*) to agree to

ades'care /20/ VT (*attirare*) to lure, entice; (*Tecn: pompa*) to prime

adesi'one SF adhesion; (*fig: assenso*) agreement, acceptance; (*appoggio*) support

ade'sivo, -a AG, SM adhesive

a'desso AV (*ora*) now; (*or ora, poco fa*) just now; (*tra poco*) any moment now; **da ~ in poi** from now on; **per ~** for the moment, for now

adia'cente [adja'tʃente] AG adjacent

adi'bire /55/ VT (*usare*): ~ qc a to turn sth into

'Adige ['adidʒe] SM: l'~ the Adige

'adipe SM fat

adi'poso, -a AG (*tessuto, zona*) adipose

adi'rarsi /72/ VPR: ~ **(con** o **contro qn per qc)** to get angry (with sb over sth)

adi'rato, -a AG angry

a'dire /55/ VT (*Dir*): ~ **le vie legali** to take legal proceedings; ~ **un'eredità** to take legal possession of an inheritance

'adito SM: **dare ~ a** (*sospetti*) to give rise to

adocchi'are [adok'kjare] /19/ VT (*scorgere*) to catch sight of; (*occhieggiare*) to eye

adole'scente [adoleʃ'ʃente] AG, SMF adolescent

adole'scenza [adoleʃ'ʃentsa] SF adolescence

adolescenzi'ale [adoleʃʃen'tsjale] AG adolescent

adom'brarsi /72/ VPR (*cavallo*) to shy; (*persona*) to grow suspicious; (: *aversene a male*) to be offended

adope'rare /72/ VT to use ∎ **adoperarsi** VPR to strive; **adoperarsi per qn/qc** to do one's best for sb/sth

ado'rabile AG adorable

ado'rare /72/ VT to adore; (*Rel*) to adore, worship

adorazi'one [adorat'tsjone] SF adoration; worship

ador'nare /72/ VT to adorn

a'dorno, -a AG: ~ **(di)** adorned (with)

adot'tare /72/ VT to adopt; (*decisione, provvedimenti*) to pass

adot'tivo, -a AG (*genitori*) adoptive; (*figlio, patria*) adopted

adozi'one [adot'tsjone] SF adoption; ~ **a distanza** child sponsorship

adrena'linico, -a, -ci, -che AG (*fig: vivace, eccitato*) charged-up

adri'atico, -a, -ci, -che AG Adriatic ▶ SM: l'A~, **il mare A~** the Adriatic, the Adriatic Sea

ADSL SIGLA M ADSL (= *asymmetric digital subscriber line*)

adu'lare /72/ VT to flatter

adula'tore, -'trice SM/F flatterer

adula'torio, -a AG flattering

adulazi'one [adulat'tsjone] SF flattery

adulte'rare /72/ VT to adulterate

adul'terio SM adultery

a'dultero, -a AG adulterous ▶ SM/F adulterer (adulteress)

a'dulto, -a AG adult; (*fig*) mature ▶ SM/F adult, grown-up

adu'nanza [adu'nantsa] SF assembly, meeting

adu'nare /72/ VT, **adu'narsi** VPR to assemble, gather

adu'nata SF (*Mil*) parade, muster

a'dunco, -a, -chi, -che AG hooked

aerazi'one [aerat'tsjone] SF ventilation; (*Tecn*) aeration

a'ereo, -a AG air *cpd*; (*radice*) aerial ▶ SM aerial; (*aeroplano*) plane; ~ **da caccia** fighter (plane); ~ **di linea** airliner; ~ **a reazione** jet (plane)

ae'robica SF aerobics *sg*

aerodi'namico, -a, -ci, -che AG aerodynamic; (*affusolato*) streamlined ▶ SF aerodynamics *sg*

aeromo'dello SM model aircraft

aero'nautica SF (*scienza*) aeronautics *sg*; ~ **militare** air force

aerona'vale AG (*forze, manovre*) air and sea *cpd*

aero'plano SM (aero)plane (*BRIT*), (air)plane (*US*)

aero'porto SM airport

aeroportu'ale AG airport *cpd*

aeros'calo SM airstrip

aero'sol SM INV aerosol

aerospazi'ale [aerospat'tsjale] AG aerospace

aeros'tatico, -a, -ci, -che AG aerostatic; **pallone ~** air balloon

ae'rostato SM aerostat

A.F. ABBR (= *alta frequenza*) HF; (*Amm*) = **assegni familiari**

'afa SF sultriness

af'fabile AG affable

affabilità SF affability

affaccen'darsi [affattʃen'darsi] /72/ VPR: ~ **intorno a qc** to busy o.s. with sth

affaccen'dato, -a [affattʃen'dato] AG (*persona*) busy

affacci'arsi [affat'tʃarsi] /14/ VPR: ~ **(a)** to appear (at); ~ **alla vita** to come into the world

affa'mato, -a AG starving; (*fig*): ~ **(di)** eager (for)

affan'nare /72/ VT to leave breathless; (*fig*) to worry ∎ **affannarsi** VPR: **affannarsi per qn/qc** to worry about sb/sth

af'fanno SM breathlessness; (*fig*) anxiety, worry

affannosa'mente AV with difficulty; anxiously

affan'noso, -a AG (*respiro*) difficult; (*fig*) troubled, anxious

af'fare SM (*faccenda*) matter, affair; (*Comm*) piece of business, (business) deal; (*occasione*) bargain; (*Dir*) case; (*col: cosa*) thing ∎ **affari** SMPL (*Comm*) business *sg*; ~ **fatto!** done!, it's a deal!; **sono affari miei** that's my business; **bada agli affari tuoi!** mind your own business!; **uomo d'affari** businessman; **ministro degli Affari Esteri** Foreign Secretary (*BRIT*), Secretary of State (*US*)

affa'rista, -i, -e SM profiteer, unscrupulous businessman(-woman)

affasci'nante [affaʃʃi'nante] AG fascinating

affasci'nare [affaʃʃi'nare] /72/ VT to bewitch; (*fig*) to charm, fascinate

affatica'mento SM tiredness

affati'care /20/ VT to tire ▪ **affaticarsi** VPR (durar fatica) to tire o.s. out

affati'cato, -a AG tired

af'fatto AV completely; **non ... ~** not ... at all; **niente ~** not at all

affer'mare /72/ VI (dire di sì) to say yes ▶ VT (dichiarare) to maintain, affirm ▪ **affermarsi** VPR to assert o.s., make one's name known

affermativa'mente AV in the affirmative, affirmatively

afferma'tivo, -a AG affirmative

affer'mato, -a AG established, well-known

affermazi'one [affermat'tsjone] SF affirmation, assertion; (successo) achievement

affer'rare /72/ VT to seize, grasp; (fig: idea) to grasp ▪ **afferrarsi** VPR: **afferrarsi a** to cling to

affet'tare /72/ VT (tagliare a fette) to slice; (ostentare) to affect

affet'tato, -a AG sliced; affected ▶ SM sliced cold meat

affetta'trice [affetta'tritʃe] SF meat slicer

affettazi'one [affettat'tsjone] SF affectation

affet'tivo, -a AG emotional, affective

affetto, -a AG: **essere ~ da** to suffer from ▶ SM affection; **gli affetti familiari** one's nearest and dearest

affettuosa'mente AV affectionately; (nelle lettere): **(ti saluto) ~, Maria** love, Maria

affettuosità SF INV affection ▶ SFPL (manifestazioni) demonstrations of affection

affettu'oso, -a AG affectionate

affezio'narsi [affettsjo'narsi] /72/ VPR: **~ a** to grow fond of

affezio'nato, -a [affettsjo'nato] AG: **~ a qn/qc** fond of sb/sth; (attaccato) attached to sb/sth

affezi'one [affet'tsjone] SF (affetto) affection; (Med) ailment, disorder

affian'care /20/ VT to place side by side; (Mil) to flank; (fig) to support; **~ qc a qc** to place sth next to o **affiancarsi** VPR: **affiancarsi a qn** to stand beside sb

affiata'mento SM understanding

affia'tato, -a AG: **essere affiatati** to work well together o get on; **formano una squadra affiatata** they make a good team

affibbi'are /19/ VT to buckle, do up; (fig: dare) to give

affi'dabile AG reliable

affidabilità SF reliability

affida'mento SM (Dir: di bambino) custody; (fiducia): **fare ~ su qn** to rely on sb; **non dà nessun ~** he's not to be trusted

affi'dare /72/ VT: **~ qc o qn a qn** to entrust sth o sb to sb ▪ **affidarsi** VPR: **affidarsi a** to place one's trust in

affievo'lirsi /55/ VPR to grow weak

af'figgere [af'fiddʒere] /104/ VT to stick up, post up

affi'lare /72/ VT to sharpen

affi'lato, -a AG (gen) sharp; (volto, naso) thin

affili'are /19/ VT to affiliate ▪ **affiliarsi** VPR: **affiliarsi a** to become affiliated to

affi'nare /72/ VT to sharpen

affin'ché [affin'ke] CONG in order that, so that

af'fine AG similar

affinità SF INV affinity

affio'rare /72/ VI to emerge

af'fissi ecc VB vedi **affiggere**

affissi'one SF billposting

af'fisso, -a PP di **affiggere** ▶ SM bill, poster; (Ling) affix

affitta'camere SM INV/F INV landlord (landlady)

affit'tare /72/ VT (dare in affitto) to let, rent (out); (prendere in affitto) to rent

af'fitto SM rent; (contratto) lease; **dare in ~** to rent (out), let; **prendere in ~** to rent

affittu'ario SM lessee

af'fliggere [af'fliddʒere] /104/ VT to torment ▪ **affliggersi** VPR to grieve

af'flissi ecc VB vedi **affliggere**

af'flitto, -a PP di **affliggere**

afflizi'one [afflit'tsjone] SF distress, torment

afflosci'arsi [afflɔʃ'ʃarsi] /14/ VPR to go limp; (frutta) to go soft

afflu'ente SM tributary

afflu'enza [afflu'entsa] SF flow; (di persone) crowd

afflu'ire /55/ VI to flow; (fig: merci, persone) to pour in

af'flusso SM influx

affo'gare /80/ VT, VI to drown ▪ **affogarsi** VPR to drown; (deliberatamente) to drown o.s.

affo'gato, -a AG drowned; (Cuc: uova) poached

affolla'mento SM crowding; (folla) crowd

affol'lare /72/ VT, **affol'larsi** VPR to crowd

affol'lato, -a AG crowded

affonda'mento SM (di nave) sinking

affon'dare /72/ VT to sink

affran'care /20/ VT to free, liberate; (Amm) to redeem; (lettera) to stamp; (: meccanicamente) to frank (BRIT), meter (US) ▪ **affrancarsi** VPR to free o.s.

affranca'trice [affranka'tritʃe] SF franking machine (BRIT), postage meter (US)

affranca'tura SF (di francobollo) stamping; franking (BRIT), metering (US); (tassa di spedizione) postage; **~ a carico del destinatario** postage paid

af'franto, -a AG (esausto) worn out; (abbattuto) overcome

af'fresco, -schi SM fresco

affret'tare /72/ VT to quicken, speed up ■ **affrettarsi** VPR to hurry; **affrettarsi a fare qc** to hurry o hasten to do sth

affret'tato, -a AG (*veloce: passo, ritmo*) quick, fast; (*frettoloso: decisione*) hurried, hasty; (: *lavoro*) rushed

affron'tare /72/ VT (*pericolo ecc*) to face; (*assalire: nemico*) to confront ■ **affrontarsi** VPR (*reciproco*) to confront each other

af'fronto SM affront, insult; **fare un ~ a qn** to insult sb

affumi'care /20/ VT to fill with smoke; to blacken with smoke; (*alimenti*) to smoke

affumi'cato, -a AG (*prosciutto, aringa ecc*) smoked

affuso'lato, -a AG tapering

af'gano, -a AG, SM/F Afghan

Af'ghanistan [af'ganistan] SM: **l'~** Afghanistan

af'ghano, -a AG, SM/F = **afgano**

afo'risma, -i SM aphorism

a'foso, -a AG sultry, close

'Africa SF: **l'~** Africa

afri'cano, -a AG, SM/F African

afroasi'atico, -a, -ci, -che AG Afro-Asian

afrodi'siaco, -a, -ci, -che AG, SM aphrodisiac

AG SIGLA = **Agrigento**

a'genda [a'dʒɛnda] SF diary; **~ tascabile/da tavolo** pocket/desk diary

---
Do not translate the Italian word **agenda** by *agenda*.

---

a'gente [a'dʒɛnte] SM (*anche Chim, ecc*) agent; **resistente agli agenti atmosferici** weather-resistant ▶ SM/F: **~ di cambio** stockbroker; **~ di custodia** prison officer; **~ marittimo** shipping agent; **~ di polizia** police officer; **~ segreto(a)** secret agent; **~ provocatore(-trice)** agent provocateur; **~ delle tasse** tax inspector; **~ di vendita** sales agent

agen'zia [adʒen'tsia] SF agency; (*succursale*) branch; **~ di collocamento** employment agency; **~ immobiliare** estate agent's (office) (BRIT), real estate office (US); **A~ Internazionale per l'Energia Atomica** International Atomic Energy Agency; **~ matrimoniale** marriage bureau; **~ pubblicitaria** advertising agency; **~ di stampa** press agency; **~ viaggi** travel agency

agevo'lare [adʒevo'lare] /72/ VT to facilitate, make easy

agevolazi'one [adʒevolat'tsjone] SF (*facilitazione economica*) facility; **~ di pagamento** payment on easy terms; **agevolazioni creditizie** credit facilities; **agevolazioni fiscali** tax concessions

a'gevole [a'dʒevole] AG easy; (*strada*) smooth

agganci'are [aggan'tʃare] /14/ VT to hook up;

(*Ferr*) to couple ■ **agganciarsi** VPR: **agganciarsi a** to hook up to; (*fig: pretesto*) to seize on

ag'gancio [ag'gantʃo] SM (*Tecn*) coupling; (*fig: conoscenza*) contact

ag'geggio [ad'dʒeddʒo] SM gadget, contraption

agget'tivo [addʒet'tivo] SM adjective

agghiac'ciante [aggjat'tʃante] AG (*fig*) chilling

agghiacci'are [aggjat'tʃare] /14/ VT to freeze; (*fig*) to make one's blood run cold ■ **agghiacciarsi** VPR to freeze

agghin'darsi [aggin'darsi] /61/ VPR to deck o.s. out

aggiorna'mento [addʒorna'mento] SM updating; revision; postponement; **corso di ~** refresher course

aggior'nare [addʒor'nare] /72/ VT (*opera, manuale*) to bring up-to-date; (: *rivedere*) to revise; (*listino*) to maintain, up-date; (*seduta ecc*) to postpone ■ **aggiornarsi** VPR to bring (o keep) o.s. up-to-date

aggior'nato, -a [addʒor'nato] AG up-to-date

aggio'taggio [addʒo'taddʒo] SM (*Econ*) rigging the market

aggi'rare [addʒi'rare] /72/ VT to go round; (*fig: ingannare*) to trick ■ **aggirarsi** VPR to wander about; **il prezzo s'aggira sul milione** the price is around the million mark

aggiudi'care [addʒudi'kare] /20/ VT to award; (*all'asta*) to knock down; **aggiudicarsi qc** to win sth

aggi'ungere [ad'dʒundʒere] /5/ VT to add; (*Inform*): **~ alla propria lista di amici** to add to one's friend list; **grazie per avermi aggiunto (come amico)** thanks for the add

aggi'unsi *ecc* [ad'dʒunsi] VB *vedi* **aggiungere**

aggi'unto, -a [ad'dʒunto] PP *di* **aggiungere** ▶ AG assistant *cpd* ▶ SM assistant ▶ SF addition; **sindaco ~** deputy mayor; **in aggiunta ...** what's more ...

aggius'tare [addʒus'tare] /72/ VT (*accomodare*) to mend, repair; (*riassettare*) to adjust; (*fig: lite*) to settle ■ **aggiustarsi** VPR (*arrangiarsi*) to make do; (*con senso reciproco*) to come to an agreement; **ti aggiusto io!** I'll fix you!

agglome'rato SM (*di rocce*) conglomerate; (*di legno*) chipboard; **~ urbano** built-up area

aggrap'parsi /72/ VPR: **~ a** to cling to

aggrava'mento SM worsening

aggra'vante AG (*Dir*) aggravating ▶ SF aggravation

aggra'vare /72/ VT (*aumentare*) to increase; (*appesantire: anche fig*) to weigh down, make heavy; (*fig: pena*) to make worse ■ **aggravarsi** VPR (*fig*) to worsen, become worse

ag'gravio SM: **~ di costi** increase in costs

aggrazi'ato, -a [aggrat'tsjato] AG graceful

aggre'dire /55/ VT to attack, assault

aggre'gare /80/ VT: ~ **qn a qc** to admit sb to sth ■ **aggregarsi** VPR to join; **aggregarersi a** to join, become a member of

aggre'gato, -a AG associated ▶ SM aggregate; ~ **urbano** built-up area

aggrega'tore SM (*Inform*) aggregator

aggressi'one SF aggression; (*atto*) attack, assault; ~ **a mano armata** armed assault

aggressività SF aggressiveness

aggres'sivo, -a AG aggressive

aggres'sore SM aggressor, attacker

aggrot'tare /72/ VT: ~ **le sopracciglia** to frown

aggrovigli'are [aggrovi Λ ' Λ are] /27/ VT to tangle ■ **aggrovigliarsi** VPR (*fig*) to become complicated

agguan'tare /72/ VT to catch, seize

aggu'ato SM trap; (*imboscata*) ambush; **tendere un ~ a qn** to set a trap for sb

agguer'rito, -a AG (*sostenitore, nemico*) fierce

agia'tezza [adʒa'tettsa] SF prosperity

agi'ato, -a [a'dʒato] AG (*vita*) easy; (*persona*) well-off, well-to-do

'agile ['adʒile] AG agile, nimble

agilità [adʒili'ta] SF agility, nimbleness

'agio ['adʒo] SM ease, comfort ■ **agi** SMPL comforts; **mettersi a proprio ~** to make o.s. at home *o* comfortable; **dare ~ a qn di fare qc** to give sb the chance of doing sth

a'gire [a'dʒire] /55/ VI to act; (*esercitare un'azione*) to take effect; (*Tecn*) to work, function; ~ **contro qn** (*Dir*) to take action against sb

agi'tare [adʒi'tare] /72/ VT (*bottiglia*) to shake; (*mano, fazzoletto*) to wave; (*fig: turbare*) to disturb; (: *incitare*) to stir (up); (: *dibattere*) to discuss ■ **agitarsi** VPR (*mare*) to be rough; (*malato, dormitore*) to toss and turn; (*bambino*) to fidget; (*emozionarsi*) to get upset; (*Pol*) to agitate

agi'tato, -a [adʒi'tato] AG rough; restless; fidgety; upset, perturbed

agita'tore, -'trice [adʒita'tore] SM/F (*Pol*) agitator

agitazi'one [adʒitat'tsjone] SF agitation; (*Pol*) unrest, agitation; **mettere in ~ qn** to upset *o* distress sb

'agli ['aʎʎi] PREP + DET *vedi* **a**

'aglio ['aʎʎo] SM garlic

a'gnello [aɲ'ɲɛllo] SM lamb

a'gnostico, -a, -ci, -che [aɲ'ɲɔstiko] AG, SM/F agnostic

'ago (*pl* **aghi**) SM needle; ~ **da calza** knitting needle

ago. ABBR (= *agosto*) Aug.

ago'nia SF agony

ago'nistico, -a, -ci, -che AG athletic; (*fig*) competitive

agoniz'zante [agonid'dzante] AG dying

agoniz'zare [agonid'dzare] /72/ VI to be dying

agopun'tura SF acupuncture

agorafo'bia SF agoraphobia

a'gosto SM August; *vedi anche* **luglio**

a'grario, -a AG agrarian, agricultural; (*riforma*) land *cpd* ▶ SM landowner ▶ SF agriculture

a'gricolo, -a AG agricultural, farm *cpd*

agricol'tore, -trice SM/F farmer

agricol'tura SF agriculture, farming

agri'foglio [agri'fɔʎʎo] SM holly

agrimen'sore SM land surveyor

agritu'rismo SM (*luogo*) farm where you can stay on holiday; (*tipo di vacanza*) farm holidays *pl*; (*Econ*) agritourism

> The term **agriturismo** covers a large number of different services available in the countryside, from simple affordable farm holidays to stays in old houses or farms converted into luxury villas. Various types of accommodation are on offer, with or without meals provided, in bed and breakfasts, cottages, villas, or apartments. Many *agriturismi* also provide a variety of activities or services: working on a farm, sampling and buying regional products, fine dining, swimming, riding, etc.

agritu'ristico, -a, -ci, -che AG farm holiday *cpd*

'agro, -a AG sour, sharp

agrobiotecnolo'gia [agrobioteknolo'dʒia] SF agricultural biotechnology, agrobiotechnology

agro'dolce [agro'doltʃe] AG bittersweet; (*salsa*) sweet and sour

agroecolo'gia [agroekolo'dʒia] SF agroecology

agrono'mia SF agronomy

a'gronomo SM agronomist

a'grume SM (*spesso al pl: pianta*) citrus; (: *frutto*) citrus fruit

agru'meto SM citrus grove

aguz'zare [agut'tsare] /72/ VT to sharpen; ~ **gli orecchi** to prick up one's ears; ~ **l'ingegno** to use one's wits

aguz'zino, -a [agud'dzino] SM/F jailer; (*fig*) tyrant

a'guzzo, -a [a'guttso] AG sharp

'ahi ESCL (*dolore*) ouch!

ahimè ESCL alas!

'ai PREP + DET *vedi* **a**

'Aia SF: **L'~** The Hague

'aia SF threshing floor

AIDDA SIGLA F (= *Associazione Imprenditrici Donne Dirigenti d'Azienda*) association of women entrepreneurs and managers

AIDS ['aids] ABBR M/ABBR F AIDS

AIE SIGLA F (= *Associazione Italiana degli Editori*) *publishers' association*

AIEA SIGLA F = **Agenzia Internazionale per l'Energia Atomica**

AIED SIGLA F (= *Associazione Italiana Educazione Demografica*) ≈ FPA (= *Family Planning Association*)

AIG SIGLA F (= *Associazione Italiana Alberghi per la Gioventù*) ≈ YHA (*BRIT*)

ai'ola SF = **aiuola**

air'bag [er'bag] SM INV air bag

AIRC ABBR F = **Associazione Italiana per la Ricerca sul Cancro**

ai'rone SM heron

ai'tante AG robust

aiu'ola SF flower bed

aiu'tante SMF assistant ▶ SM (*Mil*) adjutant; (*Naut*) master-at-arms; **~ di campo** aide-de-camp

aiu'tare /**72**/ VT to help; **~ qn (a fare)** to help sb (to do) ▪ **aiutarsi** VPR to help each other; **~ qn in qc/a fare qc** to help sb with sth/to do sth; **può aiutarmi?** can you help me?

ai'uto SM help, assistance, aid; (*aiutante*) assistant; **venire in ~ di qn** to come to sb's aid; **~ chirurgo** assistant surgeon

aiz'zare [ait'tsare] /**72**/ VT to incite; **~ i cani contro qn** to set the dogs on sb

al PREP + DET *vedi* **a**

a.l. ABBR = **anno luce**

'ala (*pl* **ali**) SF wing; **fare ~** to fall back, make way; **~ destra/sinistra** (*Sport*) right/left wing

ala'bastro SM alabaster

'alacre AG quick, brisk

alacrità SF promptness, speed

alam'bicco, -chi SM still (*Chim*)

a'lano SM Great Dane

a'lare AG wing *cpd* ▪ **alari** SMPL firedogs

A'laska SF: **l'~** Alaska

a'lato, -a AG winged

'alba SF dawn; **all'~** at dawn

alba'nese AG, SMF Albanian

Alba'nia SF: **l'~** Albania

'albatro SM albatross

albeggi'are [albed'dʒare] /**62**/ VI, VB IMPERS to dawn

albe'rato, -a AG (*viale, piazza*) lined with trees, tree-lined

albera'tura SF (*Naut*) masts *pl*

alber'gare /**80**/ VT (*dare albergo*) to accommodate ▶ VI (*poetico*) to dwell

alberga'tore, -'trice SM/F hotelier, hotel owner

alberghi'ero, -a [alber'gjɛro] AG hotel *cpd*

al'bergo, -ghi SM hotel; **~ diurno** *public toilets with washing and shaving facilities etc*; **~ della gioventù** youth hostel

'albero SM tree; (*Naut*) mast; (*Tecn*) shaft; **~ a camme** camshaft; **~ genealogico** family tree; **~ a gomiti** crankshaft; **~ maestro** mainmast; **~ di Natale** Christmas tree; **~ di trasmissione** transmission shaft

albi'cocca, -che SF apricot

albi'cocco, -chi SM apricot tree

al'bino, -a AG, SM/F albino

'albo SM (*registro*) register, roll; (*Amm*) notice board

'album SM INV album; **~ da disegno** sketch book

al'bume SM albumen; (*bianco d'uovo*) egg white

albu'mina SF albumin

'alce ['altʃe] SM elk

al'chimia [al'kimja] SF alchemy

alchi'mista, -i [alki'mista] SM alchemist

'alcol SM INV = **alcool**

alcolicità [alkolitʃi'ta] SF alcohol(ic) content

al'colico, -a, -ci, -che AG alcoholic ▶ SM alcoholic drink

alco'lismo SM alcoholism

alco'lista, -i, -e SM/F alcoholic

alcoliz'zato, -a [alkolid'dzato] SM/F alcoholic

'alcool SM INV alcohol; **~ denaturato** methylated spirits *pl* (*BRIT*), wood alcohol (*US*); **~ etilico** ethyl alcohol; **~ metilico** methyl alcohol

alco'olico *ecc vedi* **alcolico** *ecc*

'alcopop SM alcopop

alco'test SM INV Breathalyser® (*BRIT*), Breathalyzer® (*US*)

al'cova SF alcove

al'cuno, -a DET (*dav sm:* **alcun** + C, V, **alcuno** + *s impura, gn, pn, ps, x, z; dav sf:* **alcuna** + C, **alcun'** + V: *nessuno*): **non … ~** no, not any ▪ **alcuni, e** DET PL, PRON PL some, a few; **non c'è alcuna fretta** there's no hurry, there isn't any hurry; **senza alcun riguardo** without any consideration

aldilà SM INV: **l'~** the next life, the after-life

alea'torio, -a AG (*incerto*) uncertain

aleggi'are [aled'dʒare] /**62**/ VI (*fig: profumo, sospetto*) to be in the air

Ales'sandria SF (*anche:* **Alessandria d'Egitto**) Alexandria

a'letta SF (*Tecn*) fin; tab

alet'tone SM (*Aer*) aileron

Aleu'tine SFPL: **le isole ~** the Aleutian Islands

alfa'betico, -a, -ci, -che AG alphabetical

alfa'beto SM alphabet

alfanu'merico, -a, -ci, -che AG alphanumeric

alfi'ere SM standard-bearer; (*Scacchi*) bishop

al'fine AV finally, in the end

'alga, -ghe SF seaweed *no pl*, alga

'algebra ['aldʒebra] SF algebra

Al'geri [al'dʒeri] SF Algiers

Alge'ria [aldʒe'ria] SF: **l'~** Algeria

alge'rino, -a [aldʒe'rino] AG, SM/F Algerian

algo'ritmo SM algorithm

ALI SIGLA F (= *Associazione Librai Italiani*) booksellers' association

ali'ante SM (*Aer*) glider

'alibi SM INV alibi

a'lice [a'litʃe] SF anchovy

alie'nare /72/ VT (*Dir*) to transfer; (*rendere ostile*) to alienate; **alienarsi qn** to alienate sb

alie'nato, -a AG alienated; transferred; (*fuor di senno*) insane ▸ SM/F insane person

alienazi'one [aljenat'tsjone] SF alienation; transfer; insanity

ali'eno, -a AG (*avverso*): **~ (da)** opposed (to), averse (to) ▸ SM/F alien

alimen'tare /72/ VT to feed; (*Tecn*) to feed, supply; (*fig*) to sustain ▸ AG food *cpd* ■ **alimentari** SMPL foodstuffs; (*anche*: **negozio di alimentari**) grocer's shop; **regime ~** diet

alimenta'tore SM (*Elettr*) feeder

alimentazi'one [alimentat'tsjone] SF feeding; supplying; sustaining; (*cibi*) diet; **~ di fogli** (*Inform*) sheet feed

ali'mento SM food ■ **alimenti** SMPL food *sg*; (*Dir*) alimony

a'liquota SF share; **~ d'imposta** tax rate; **~ minima** (*Fisco*) basic rate

alis'cafo SM hydrofoil

'alito SM breath

all. ABBR (= *allegato*) enc., encl.

'alla PREP + DET *vedi* a

allaccia'mento [allattʃa'mento] SM (*Tecn*) connection

allacci'are [allat'tʃare] /14/ VT (*scarpe*) to tie, lace (up); (*cintura*) to do up, fasten; (*due località*) to link; (*luce, gas*) to connect; (*amicizia*) to form ■ **allacciarsi** VPR (*vestito*) to fasten; **~ o allacciarsi la cintura** to fasten one's belt

allaccia'tura [allattʃa'tura] SF fastening

allaga'mento SM flooding *no pl*; flood

alla'gare /80/ VT, **alla'garsi** VPR to flood

allampa'nato, -a AG lanky

allar'gare /80/ VT to widen; (*vestito*) to let out; (*aprire*) to open; (*fig: dilatare*) to extend ■ **allargarsi** VPR (*gen*) to widen; (*scarpe, pantaloni*) to stretch; (*fig: problema, fenomeno*) to spread

allar'mare /72/ VT to alarm ■ **allarmarsi** VPR to become alarmed

al'larme SM alarm; **mettere qn in ~** to alarm sb; **~ aereo** air-raid warning

allar'mismo SM scaremongering

allar'mista, -i, -e SM/F scaremonger, alarmist

allat'tare /72/ VT (*donna*) to (breast-)feed; (*ani-*

male) to suckle; **~ artificialmente** to bottle-feed

'alle PREP + DET *vedi* a

alle'anza [alle'antsa] SF alliance; **A~ Democratica** (*Pol*) moderate centre-left party; **A~ Nazionale** (*Pol*) party on the far right

alle'arsi /72/ VPR to form an alliance

alle'ato, -a AG allied ▸ SM/F ally

alleg. ABBR = **all.**

alle'gare /80/ VT (*accludere*) to enclose; (*Dir: citare*) to cite, adduce; (*denti*) to set on edge

alle'gato, -a AG enclosed ▸ SM enclosure; (*di e-mail*) attachment; **in ~** enclosed; **in ~ Vi inviamo ...** please find enclosed ...

allegge'rire [alleddʒe'rire] /55/ VT to lighten, make lighter; (*fig: sofferenza*) to alleviate, lessen; (*: lavoro, tasse*) to reduce

allego'ria SF allegory

alle'gorico, -a, -ci, -che AG allegorical

alle'gria SF gaiety, cheerfulness

al'legro, -a AG cheerful, merry; (*un po' brillo*) merry, tipsy; (*vivace: colore*) bright ▸ SM (*Mus*) allegro

allena'mento SM training

alle'nare /72/ VT, **alle'narsi** VPR to train

allena'tore, -trice SM/F (*Sport*) trainer, coach

allen'tare /72/ VT to slacken; (*disciplina*) to relax ■ **allentarsi** VPR to become slack; (*ingranaggio*) to work loose

aller'gia, -'gie [aller'dʒia] SF allergy

al'lergico, -a, -ci, -che [al'lerdʒiko] AG allergic

allesti'mento SM preparation, setting up; **in ~** in preparation

alles'tire /55/ VT (*cena*) to prepare; (*esercito, nave*) to equip, fit out; (*spettacolo*) to stage

allet'tante AG attractive, alluring

allet'tare /72/ VT to lure, entice

alleva'mento SM breeding, rearing; (*luogo*) stock farm; **pollo d'~** battery hen

alle'vare /72/ VT (*animale*) to breed, rear; (*bambino*) to bring up

alleva'tore, -trice SM/F breeder

allevi'are /19/ VT to alleviate

alli'bire /55/ VI to turn pale; (*essere turbato*) to be disconcerted

alli'bito, -a AG pale; disconcerted; astounded

allibra'tore SM bookmaker

allie'tare /72/ VT to cheer up, gladden

alli'evo, -a SM/F pupil; (*apprendista*) apprentice; **~ ufficiale** cadet

alliga'tore SM alligator

allinea'mento SM alignment

alline'are /72/ VT (*persone, cose*) to line up; (*Tip*) to align; (*fig: economia, salari*) to adjust, align ■ **allinearsi** VPR to line up; (*fig: a idee*) **allinearsi a** to come into line with

alline'ato, -a AG aligned, in line; **paesi non allineati** (*Pol*) non-aligned countries

'allo PREP + DET *vedi* **a**

allo'care /20/ VT to allocate

al'locco, -a, -chi, -che SM/F oaf ▶ SM tawny owl

allocuzi'one [allokut'tsjone] SF address, solemn speech

al'lodola SF (sky)lark

alloggi'are [allod'dʒare] /62/ VT to accommodate ▶ VI to live

al'loggio [al'lɔddʒo] SM lodging, accommodation (BRIT), accommodations (US); (*appartamento*) flat (BRIT), apartment (US)

allontana'mento SM removal; dismissal; estrangement

allonta'nare /72/ VT to send away, send off; (*impiegato*) to dismiss; (*pericolo*) to avert, remove; (*estraniare*) to alienate ■ **allontanarsi** VPR: **allontanarsi (da)** to go away (from); (*estraniarsi*) to become estranged (from)

al'lora AV (*in quel momento*) then ▶ CONG (*in questo caso*) well then; (*dunque*) well then, so; **la gente d'~** people then *o* in those days; **da ~ in poi** from then on; **e ~?** (*che fare?*) what now?; (*e con ciò?*) so what?

allor'ché [allor'ke] CONG (*formale*) when, as soon as

al'loro SM laurel; **riposare** *o* **dormire sugli allori** to rest on one's laurels

'alluce ['allutʃe] SM big toe

alluci'nante [allutʃi'nante] AG (*scena, spettacolo*) awful, terrifying; (*col: incredibile*) amazing

alluci'nato, -a [allutʃi'nato] AG terrified; (*fuori di sé*) bewildered, confused

allucinazi'one [allutʃinat'tsjone] SF hallucination

al'ludere /35/ VI: **~ a** to allude to, hint at

allu'minio SM aluminium (BRIT), aluminum (US)

allu'naggio [allu'naddʒo] SM moon landing

allu'nare /72/ VI to land on the moon

allun'gare /80/ VT to lengthen; (*distendere*) to prolong, extend; (*diluire*) to water down ■ **allungarsi** VPR to lengthen; (*ragazzo*) to stretch, grow taller; (*sdraiarsi*) to lie down, stretch out; **~ le mani** (*rubare*) to pick pockets; **gli allungò uno schiaffo** he took a swipe at him

al'lusi *ecc* VB *vedi* **alludere**

allusi'one SF hint, allusion

al'luso, -a PP *di* **alludere**

alluvi'one SF flood

alma'nacco, -chi SM almanac

al'meno AV at least ▶ CONG: **(se) ~** if only; **(se) ~ piovesse!** if only it would rain!

a'logeno, -a [a'lɔdʒeno] AG: **lampada alogena** halogen lamp

a'lone SM halo

al'pestre AG (*delle alpi*) alpine; (*montuoso*) mountainous

'Alpi SFPL: **le ~** the Alps

alpi'nismo SM mountaineering, climbing

alpi'nista, -i, -e SM/F mountaineer, climber

al'pino, -a AG Alpine; mountain *cpd* ■ **alpini** SMPL (*Mil*) Italian Alpine troops

al'quanto AV rather, a little ▶ DET: **~(-a)** a certain amount of, some ▶ PRON a certain amount, some ■ **alquanti, e** DET PL, PRON PL several, quite a few

Al'sazia [al'sattsja] SF Alsace

alt ESCL halt!, stop! ▶ SM: **dare l'~** to call a halt

alta'lena SF (*a funi*) swing; (*in bilico, anche fig*) seesaw

alta'mente AV extremely, highly

al'tare SM altar

alte'rare /72/ VT to alter, change; (*cibo*) to adulterate; (*registro*) to falsify; (*persona*) to irritate ■ **alterarsi** VPR to alter; (*cibo*) to go bad; (*persona*) to lose one's temper

alterazi'one [alterat'tsjone] SF alteration, change; adulteration; falsification; annoyance

al'terco, -chi SM altercation, wrangle

alter'nanza [alter'nantsa] SF alternation; (*Agr*) rotation

alter'nare /72/ VT, **alter'narsi** VPR to alternate

alterna'tivo, -a AG alternative ▶ SF alternative; **non abbiamo alternative** we have no alternative

alter'nato, -a AG alternate; (*Elettr*) alternating

alterna'tore SM alternator

al'terno, -a AG alternate; **a giorni alterni** on alternate days, every other day; **circolazione a targhe alterne** (*Aut*) system of restricting vehicle use to odd/even registrations on alternate days

al'tero, -a AG proud

al'tezza [al'tettsa] SF (*di edificio, persona*) height; (*di tessuto*) width, breadth; (*di acqua, pozzo*) depth; (*di suono*) pitch; (*Geo*) latitude; (*titolo*) highness; (*fig: nobiltà*) greatness; **essere all'~ di** to be on a level with; (*fig*) to be up to *o* equal to; **all'~ della farmacia** near the chemist's

altez'zoso, -a [altet'tsoso] AG haughty

al'ticcio, -a, -ci, -ce [al'tittʃo] AG tipsy

altipi'ano SM = **altopiano**

altiso'nante AG (*fig*) high-sounding, pompous

alti'tudine SF altitude

'alto, -a AG high; (*persona*) tall; (*tessuto*) wide, broad; (*sonno, acque*) deep; (*suono*) high(-pitched); (*Geo*) upper; (*: settentrionale*) northern ▶ SM top (part) ▶ AV high; (*parlare*) aloud, loudly; **il palazzo è ~ 20 metri** the building is 20 metres high; **il tessuto è ~ 70 cm** the material is 70 cm wide; **ad alta voce** aloud; **a notte alta**

in the dead of night; **in ~** up, upwards; at the top; **mani in ~!** hands up!; **dall'~ in *o* al basso** up and down; **degli alti e bassi** (*fig*) ups and downs; **andare a testa alta** (*fig*) to carry one's head high; **essere in ~ mare** (*fig*) to be far from a solution; **alta fedeltà** high fidelity, hi-fi; **alta finanza/società** high finance/society; **alta moda** haute couture; **l'A~ Medioevo** the Early Middle Ages; **l'~ Po** the upper reaches of the Po; **alta velocità** (*Ferr*) high speed rail system

---

Alto si traduce generalmente con **high**, *ma quando ci si riferisce a una persona si usa* **tall**. *una signora molto alta* **a very tall woman**

---

altoate'sino, -a AG of (*o* from) the Alto Adige

alto'forno SM blast furnace

altolo'cato, -a AG of high rank, highly placed

altopar'lante SM loudspeaker

altopi'ano (*pl* **altipiani**) SM upland plain, plateau

'Alto 'Volta SM: **l'~** Upper Volta

altret'tanto, -a AG, PRON as much; (*pl*) as many ▸ AV equally; **tanti auguri! — grazie, ~** all the best! — thank you, the same to you

'altri PRON INV (*qualcuno*) somebody; (: *in espressioni negative*) anybody; (*un'altra persona*) another (person)

altri'menti AV otherwise

'altro, -a

DET **1** (*diverso*) other, different; **questa è un'altra cosa** that's another *o* a different thing; **passami l'altra penna** give me the other pen **2** (*supplementare*) other; **prendi un altro cioccolatino** have another chocolate; **hai avuto altre notizie?** have you had any more *o* any other news?; **hai altro pane?** have you got any more bread?

3 (*nel tempo*): **l'altro giorno** the other day; **l'altr'anno** last year; **l'altro ieri** the day before yesterday; **domani l'altro** the day after tomorrow; **quest'altro mese** next month **4**: **d'altra parte** on the other hand

▸ PRON **1** (*persona: cosa diversa o supplementare*): **un altro, un'altra** another (one); **lo farà un altro** someone else will do it; **altri, e** others; **gli altri** (*la gente*) others, other people; **l'uno e l'altro** both (of them); **aiutarsi l'un l'altro** to help one another; **prendine un altro** have another (one); **da un giorno all'altro** from day to day; (*nel giro di 24 ore*) from one day to the next; (*da un momento all'altro*) any day now **2** (*sostantivato: solo maschile*) something else; (: *in espressioni interrogative*) anything else; **non ho altro da dire** I have nothing else *o* I don't have anything else to say; **desidera altro?** do you want anything else?; **più che altro** above all; **se non altro** if nothing else, at least; **tra l'altro** among other things; **ci mancherebbe altro!** that's all we need!; **non faccio altro che lavorare** I do nothing but work; **contento? — altro che!** are you pleased? — I certainly am!; *vedi anche* **senza**; **noialtri**; **voialtri**; **tutto**

altroché [altro'ke] ESCL certainly!, and how!

al'tronde AV: **d'~** on the other hand

al'trove AV elsewhere, somewhere else

al'trui AG INV other people's ▸ SM: **l'~** other people's belongings *pl*

altru'ismo SM altruism

altru'ista, -i, -e AG altruistic ▸ SM/F altruist

al'tura SF (*rialto*) height, high ground; (*alto mare*) open sea; **pesca d'~** deep-sea fishing

a'lunno, -a SM/F pupil

alve'are SM hive

'alveo SM riverbed

alzabandi'era [altsaban'djera] SM INV (*Mil*): **l'~** the raising of the flag

al'zare [al'tsare] /72/ VT to raise, lift; (*issare*) to hoist; (*costruire*) to build, erect ■ **alzarsi** VPR to rise; (*dal letto*) to get up; (*crescere*) to grow tall (*o* taller); **~ le spalle** to shrug one's shoulders; **~ le carte** to cut the cards; **~ il gomito** to drink too much; **~ le mani su qn** to raise one's hand to sb; **~ i tacchi** to take to one's heels; **alzarsi in piedi** to stand up, get to one's feet; **alzarsi col piede sbagliato** to get out of bed on the wrong side

al'zata [al'tsata] SF lifting, raising; **un'~ di spalle** a shrug

a'mabile AG lovable; (*vino*) sweet

'AMAC SIGLA F = **Aeronautica Militare-Aviazione Civile**

a'maca, -che SF hammock

amalga'mare /72/ VT, **amalga'marsi** VPR to amalgamate

a'mante AG: **~ di** (*musica ecc*) fond of ▸ SMF lover (mistress)

amara'mente AV bitterly

ama'ranto SM (*Bot*) love-lies-bleeding ▸ AG INV: **color ~** reddish purple

a'mare /72/ VT to love; (*amico, musica, sport*) to like ■ **amarsi** VPR to love each other

amareggi'are [amared'dʒare] /62/ VT to sadden, upset ■ **amareggiarsi** VPR to get upset; **amareggiarsi la vita** to make one's life a misery

amareggi'ato, -a [amared'dʒato] AG upset, saddened

ama'rena SF sour black cherry

ama'retto SM (*dolce*) macaroon; (*liquore*) bitter liqueur made with almonds

ama'rezza [ama'rettsa] SF bitterness

a'maro, -a AG bitter ▸ SM bitterness; (*liquore*) bitters *pl*

ama'rognolo, -a [ama'roɲɲolo] AG slightly bitter

a'mato, -a AG beloved, loved, dear ▶ SM/F loved one

ama'tore, -'trice SM/F (*amante*) lover; (*intenditore: di vini ecc*) connoisseur; (*dilettante*) amateur

a'mazzone [a'maddzone] SF (*Mitologia*) Amazon; (*cavallerizza*) horsewoman; (*abito*) riding habit; **cavalcare all'~** to ride sidesaddle; **il Rio delle Amazzoni** the (river) Amazon

Amaz'zonia [amad'dzɔnja] SF Amazonia

amaz'zonico, -a, -ci, -che [amad'dzɔniko] AG Amazonian; Amazon *cpd*

ambasce'ria [ambaʃʃe'ria] SF embassy

ambasci'ata [ambaʃ'ʃata] SF embassy; (*messaggio*) message

ambascia'tore, -'trice [ambaʃʃa'tore] SM/F ambassador (ambassadress)

ambe'due AG INV: **~ i ragazzi** both boys ▶ PRON INV both

ambi'destro, -a AG ambidextrous

ambien'tale AG (*temperatura*) ambient *cpd*; (*problemi, tutela*) environmental

ambienta'lismo SM environmentalism

ambienta'lista, -i, -e AG environmental ▶ SM/F environmentalist

ambien'tare /72/ VT to acclimatize; (*romanzo, film*) to set ■ **ambientarsi** VPR to get used to one's surroundings

ambientazi'one [ambjentat'tsjone] SF setting

ambi'ente SM environment; (*fig: insieme di persone*) milieu; (*stanza*) room

ambiguità SF INV ambiguity

am'biguo, -a AG ambiguous; (*persona*) shady

am'bire /55/ VT, VI: **~ a** to aspire to; **un premio molto ambito** a much sought-after prize

'ambito SM sphere, field

ambiva'lente AG ambivalent; **questo apparecchio è ~** this is a dual-purpose device

ambizi'one [ambit'tsjone] SF ambition

ambizi'oso, -a [ambit'tsjoso] AG ambitious

'ambo AG INV both ▶ SM (*al gioco*) double

'ambra SF amber; **~ grigia** ambergris

ambu'lante AG travelling, itinerant ▶ SM peddler

ambu'lanza [ambu'lantsa] SF ambulance; **chiamate un'~** call an ambulance

ambulatori'ale AG (*Med*) outpatients *cpd*; **operazione ~** operation as an outpatient; **visita ~** visit to the doctor's surgery (BRIT) *o* office (US)

ambula'torio SM (*studio medico*) surgery (BRIT), doctor's office (US)

a'meba SF amoeba (BRIT), ameba (US)

amenità SF INV pleasantness *no pl*; (*facezia*) pleasantry

a'meno, -a AG pleasant; (*strano*) funny, strange; (*spiritoso*) amusing

A'merica SF: **l'~** America; **l'~ latina** Latin America; **l'~ del sud** South America

america'nata SF (*peg*): **le Olimpiadi sono state una vera ~** the Olympics were a typically vulgar American extravaganza

america'nismo SM Americanism; (*ammirazione*) love of America

ameri'cano, -a AG, SM/F American

ame'tista SF amethyst

AMI ABBR = **Aeronautica Militare Italiana**

ami'anto SM asbestos

a'mica SF *vedi* **amico**

ami'chevole [ami'kevole] AG friendly

ami'cizia [ami'tʃittsja] SF friendship ■ **amicizie** SFPL (*amici*) friends; **fare ~ con qn** to make friends with sb

a'mico, -a, -ci, -che SM/F friend; (*amante*) boyfriend (girlfriend); **~ del cuore** *o* **intimo** bosom friend; **~ d'infanzia** childhood friend; **aggiungere come ~** (*Internet*) to friend

'amido SM starch

ammac'care /20/ VT (*pentola*) to dent; (*persona*) to bruise ■ **ammaccarsi** VPR to bruise

ammacca'tura SF dent; bruise

ammaes'trare /72/ VT (*animale*) to train; (*persona*) to teach

ammai'nare /72/ VT to lower, haul down

amma'larsi /72/ VPR to fall ill

amma'lato, -a AG ill, sick ▶ SM/F sick person; (*paziente*) patient

ammali'are /19/ VT (*fig*) to enchant, charm

ammalia'tore, -'trice SM/F enchanter (enchantress)

am'manco, -chi SM (*Econ*) deficit

ammanet'tare /72/ VT to handcuff

ammani'cato, -a, ammanigli'ato, -a [ammaniʎ'ʎato] AG (*fig*) with friends in high places

amman'sire /55/ VT (*animale*) to tame; (*fig: persona*) to calm down, placate

amman'tarsi /72/ VPR: **~ di** (*persona*) to wrap o.s. in; (*fig: prato ecc*) to be covered in

amma'raggio [amma'raddʒo] SM (*sea*) landing; splashdown

amma'rare /72/ VI (*Aer*) to make a sea landing; (*astronave*) to splash down

ammas'sare /72/ VT (*ammucchiare*) to amass; (*raccogliere*) to gather together ■ **ammassarsi** VPR to pile up; to gather

am'masso SM mass; (*mucchio*) pile, heap; (*Econ*) stockpile

ammat'tire /55/ VI to go mad

ammaz'zare [ammat'tsare] /72/ VT to kill ■ **ammazzarsi** VPR (*uccidersi*) to kill o.s.; (*rima-*

nere ucciso) to be killed; **ammazzarsi di lavoro** to work o.s. to death

am'menda SF amends *pl*; (*Dir, Sport*) fine; **fare ~ di qc** to make amends for sth

am'messo, -a PP *di* **ammettere** ▶ CONG: **~ che** supposing that

am'mettere /63/ VT to admit; (*riconoscere: fatto*) to acknowledge, admit; (*permettere*) to allow, accept; (*supporre*) to suppose; **ammettiamo che** ... let us suppose that ...

ammez'zato [ammed'dzato] SM (*anche:* **piano ammezzato**) entresol, mezzanine

ammic'care /20/ VI: **~ (a)** to wink (at)

amminis'trare /72/ VT to run, manage; (*Rel, Dir*) to administer

amministra'tivo, -a AG administrative

amministra'tore, -trice SM/F administrator; (*di condominio*) apartment block manager; (*Comm*) director; **~ aggiunto(a)** associate director; **~ delegato(a)** managing director; **~ fiduciario(a)** trustee; **~ unico(a)** sole director

amministrazi'one [amministrat'tsjone] SF management; administration; **consiglio d'~** board of directors; **l'~ comunale** local government; **~ fiduciaria** trust

ammi'raglia [ammi'raʎʎa] SF flagship

ammiragli'ato [ammiraʎ'ʎato] SM admiralty

ammi'raglio [ammi'raʎʎo] SM admiral

ammi'rare /72/ VT to admire

ammira'tore, -'trice SM/F admirer

ammirazi'one [ammirat'tsjone] SF admiration

am'misi *ecc* VB *vedi* **ammettere**

ammis'sibile AG admissible, acceptable

ammissi'one SF admission; (*approvazione*) acknowledgment

Amm.ne ABBR = **amministrazione**

ammobili'are /19/ VT to furnish

ammobili'ato, -a AG (*camera, appartamento*) furnished

ammoder'nare /72/ VT to modernize

am'modo, a 'modo AV properly ▶ AG INV respectable, nice

ammogli'are [ammoʎ'ʎare] /27/ VT to find a wife for ■ **ammogliarsi** VPR to marry, take a wife

am'mollo SM: **lasciare in ~** to leave to soak

ammo'niaca SF ammonia

ammoni'mento SM warning; admonishment

ammo'nire /55/ VT (*avvertire*) to warn; (*rimproverare*) to admonish; (*Dir*) to caution

ammonizi'one [ammonit'tsjone] SF (*monito: anche Sport*) warning; (*rimprovero*) reprimand; (*Dir*) caution

ammon'tare /72/ VI: **~ a** to amount to ▶ SM (*total*) amount

ammonticchi'are [ammontik'kjare] /19/ VT to pile up, heap up

ammor'bare /72/ VT (*diffondere malattia*) to infect; (*odore*) to taint, foul

ammorbi'dente SM fabric softener

ammorbi'dire /55/ VT to soften

ammorta'mento SM redemption; amortization; **~ fiscale** capital allowance

ammor'tare /72/ VT (*Finanza: debito*) to pay off, redeem; (*: spese d'impianto*) to write off

ammortiz'zare [ammortid'dzare] /72/ VT (*Finanza*) to pay off, redeem; (*: spese d'impianto*) to write off; (*Aut, Tecn*) to absorb, deaden

ammortizza'tore [ammortiddza'tore] SM (*Aut, Tecn*) shock absorber

ammucchi'are [ammuk'kjare] /19/ VT, **ammucchi'arsi** VPR to pile up, accumulate

ammuf'fire /55/ VI to go mouldy (BRIT) o moldy (US)

ammutina'mento SM mutiny

ammuti'narsi /72/ VPR to mutiny

ammuti'nato, -a AG mutinous ▶ SM mutineer

ammuto'lire /55/ VI to be struck dumb

amne'sia SF amnesia

amnis'tia SF amnesty

'amo SM (*Pesca*) hook; (*fig*) bait

amo'rale AG amoral

a'more SM love ■ **amori** SMPL love affairs; **il tuo bambino è un ~** your baby's a darling; **fare l'~** o **all'~** to make love; **andare d'~ e d'accordo con qn** to get on like a house on fire with sb; **per ~ o per forza** by hook or by crook; **amor proprio** self-esteem, pride

amoreggi'are [amored'dʒare] /62/ VI to flirt

amo'revole AG loving, affectionate

a'morfo, -a AG amorphous; (*fig: persona*) lifeless

amo'rino SM cupid

amo'roso, -a AG (*affettuoso*) loving, affectionate; (*d'amore: sguardo*) amorous; (*: poesia, relazione*) love *cpd*

am'pere [ã'pɛr] SM INV amp(ère)

ampi'ezza [am'pjettsa] SF width, breadth; spaciousness; (*fig: importanza*) scale, size; **~ di vedute** broad-mindedness

'ampio, -a AG wide, broad; (*spazioso*) spacious; (*abbondante: vestito*) loose; (*: gonna*) full; (*: spiegazione*) ample, full

am'plesso SM (*sessuale*) intercourse

amplia'mento SM (*di strada*) widening; (*di aeroporto*) expansion; (*fig*) broadening

ampli'are /19/ VT (*ingrandire*) to enlarge; (*allargare*) to widen; (*fig: discorso*) to enlarge on ■ **ampliarsi** VPR to grow, increase; **~ la propria cultura** to broaden one's mind

amplifi'care /20/ VT to amplify; (*magnificare*) to extol

amplifica'tore SM (*Tecn, Mus*) amplifier

amplificazi'one [amplifikat'tsjone] SF amplification

am'polla SF (*vasetto*) cruet

ampol'loso, -a AG bombastic, pompous

ampu'tare **/72/** VT (*Med*) to amputate

amputazi'one [amputat'tsjone] SF amputation

'Amsterdam SF Amsterdam

amu'leto SM lucky charm

AN SIGLA = **Ancona**

anabbagli'ante [anabbaʎ'ʎante] AG (*Aut*) dipped (BRIT), dimmed (US) ▪ **anabbaglianti** SMPL dipped *or* dimmed headlights

anaboliz'zante [anabolid'dzante] SM anabolic steroid ▸ AG anabolic

anacro'nismo SM anachronism

a'nagrafe SF (*registro*) register of births, marriages and deaths; (*ufficio*) registry office (BRIT), office of vital statistics (US)

ana'grafico, -a, -ci, -che AG (*Amm*): **dati anagrafici** personal data; **comune di residenza anagrafica** district where resident

ana'gramma, -i SM anagram

anal'colico, -a, -ci, -che AG non-alcoholic ▸ SM soft drink; **bevanda analcolica** soft drink

a'nale AG anal

analfa'beta, -i, -e AG, SM/F illiterate

analfabe'tismo SM illiteracy

anal'gesico, -a, -ci, -che [anal'dʒeziko] AG, SM analgesic

a'nalisi SF INV analysis; (*Med: esame*) test; **in ultima ~** in conclusion, in the final analysis; **~ grammaticale** parsing; **~ del sangue** blood test; **~ dei sistemi/costi** systems/cost analysis

ana'lista, -i, -e SM/F analyst; (*Psic*) (psycho)analyst; **~ finanziario** financial analyst; **~ di sistemi** systems analyst

ana'litico, -a, -ci, -che AG analytic(al)

analiz'zare [analid'dzare] **/72/** VT to analyse (BRIT), analyze (US); (*Med*) to test

analo'gia, -'gie [analo'dʒia] SF analogy

ana'logico, -a, -ci, -che [ana'lɔdʒiko] AG analogical; (*calcolatore, orologio*) analog(ue)

a'nalogo, -a, -ghi, -ghe AG analogous

'ananas SM INV pineapple

anar'chia [anar'kia] SF anarchy

a'narchico, -a, -ci, -che [a'narkiko] AG anarchic(al) ▸ SM/F anarchist

anarco-insurreziona'lista [anarko insurrettsjona'lista] AG anarcho-revolutionary

'A.N.A.S. SIGLA F (= *Azienda Nazionale Autonoma delle Strade*) national roads department

ana'tema, -i SM anathema

anato'mia SF anatomy

ana'tomico, -a, -ci, -che AG anatomical; (*sedile*) contoured

'anatra SF duck; **~ selvatica** mallard

ana'troccolo SM duckling

'ANCA SIGLA F = **Associazione Nazionale Cooperative Agroalimentari**

'anca, -che SF (*Anat*) hip; (*Zool*) haunch

ANCC SIGLA F = **Associazione Nazionale Carabinieri**

'anche ['anke] CONG (*inoltre, pure*) also, too; (*perfino*) even; **vengo anch'io!** I'm coming too!; **~ se** even if; **~ volendo, non finiremmo in tempo** even if we wanted to, we wouldn't finish in time

> *Anche,* quando si traduce con **also**, segue il verbo.
> *È stata anche una grande artista.* **She was also a great artist.**
> Quando si usa **too** va alla fine della frase.
> *È una cantante e anche un'attrice.* **She's a singer and an actress too.**
> *Vengo anch'io.* **I'm coming too.**

ancheggi'are [anked'dʒare] **/62/** VI to wiggle (one's hips)

anchilo'sato, -a [ankilo'zato] AG stiff

'ANCI ['antʃi] SIGLA F (= *Associazione Nazionale dei Comuni Italiani*) national confederation of local authorities

ancone'tano, -a AG of (*o* from) Ancona

an'cora¹ AV still; (*di nuovo*) again; (*di più*) some more; (*persino*): **~ più forte** even stronger; **non ~** not yet; **~ una volta** once more, once again; **~ un po'** a little more; (*di tempo*) a little longer

an'cora² SF anchor; **gettare/levare l'~** to cast/weigh anchor; **~ di salvezza** (*fig*) last hope

anco'raggio [anko'raddʒo] SM anchorage

anco'rare **/72/** VT, **anco'rarsi** VPR to anchor

ANCR SIGLA F (= *Associazione Nazionale Combattenti e Reduci*) servicemen's and ex-servicemen's association

Andalu'sia SF: **l'~** Andalusia

anda'luso, -a AG, SM/F Andalusian

anda'mento SM (*di strada, malattia*) course; (*del mercato*) state

an'dante AG (*corrente*) current; (*di poco pregio*) cheap, second-rate ▸ SM (*Mus*) andante

an'dare **/6/** SM: **a lungo ~** in the long run; **con l'andar del tempo** with the passing of time; **racconta storie a tutto ~** she's forever talking rubbish ▸ VI (*gen*) to go; **~ a** (*essere adatto*) to suit; **il suo comportamento non mi va** (*piace*) I don't like the way he behaves; **ti va di ~ al cinema?** do you feel like going to the cinema?; **~ a cavallo** to ride; **~ in macchina/aereo** to go by car/plane; **~ a fare qc** to go and do sth; **~ a pescare/sciare** to go fishing/skiing; **andarsene** to go away; **questa camicia va lavata** this shirt needs a wash *o* should be washed;

vado e vengo I'll be back in a minute; **~ per i 50** (*età*) to be getting on for 50; **~ a male** to go bad; **~ fiero di qc/qn** to be proud of sth/sb; **~ perduto** to be lost; **come va?** (*lavoro, progetto*) how are things?; **come va? — bene, grazie!** how are you? — fine, thanks!; **va fatto entro oggi** it's got to be done today; **ne va della nostra vita** our lives are at stake; **se non vado errato** if I'm not mistaken; **le mele vanno molto** apples are selling well; **va da sé** (*è naturale*) it goes without saying; **per questa volta vada** let's say no more about it this time

an'data SF going; (*viaggio*) outward journey; **biglietto di sola ~** single (*BRIT*) o one-way ticket; **biglietto di ~ e ritorno** return (*BRIT*) o round-trip (*US*) ticket

anda'tura SF (*modo di andare*) walk, gait; (*Sport*) pace; (*Naut*) tack

an'dazzo [an'dattso] SM (*peg*): **prendere un brutto ~** to take a turn for the worse

'Ande SFPL: **le ~** the Andes

'AMDI SIGLA F = **Associazione Nazionale Dentisti Italiani**

an'dino, -a AG Andean

andirivi'eni SM INV coming and going

'andito SM corridor, passage

An'dorra SF Andorra

andrò *ecc* VB *vedi* **andare**

an'drone SM entrance hall

a'neddoto SM anecdote

ane'lare /72/ VI: **~ a** (*fig*) to long for, yearn for

a'nelito SM (*fig*): **~ di** longing o yearning for

a'nello SM ring; (*di catena*) link ■ **anelli** SMPL (*Ginnastica*) rings

ane'mia SF anaemia (*BRIT*), anemia (*US*)

a'nemico, -a, -ci, -che AG anaemic (*BRIT*), anemic (*US*)

a'nemone SM anemone

aneste'sia SF anaesthesia (*BRIT*), anesthesia (*US*)

aneste'sista, -i, -e SM/F anaesthetist (*BRIT*), anesthetist (*US*)

anes'tetico, -a, -ci, -che AG, SM anaesthetic (*BRIT*), anesthetic (*US*)

anestetiz'zare [anestetid'dzare] /72/ VT to anaesthetize (*BRIT*), anesthetize (*US*)

anfeta'mina SF amphetamine

anfeta'minico, -a, -ci, -che AG (*fig*) hyper

an'fibio, -a AG amphibious ▶ SM amphibian; (*Aut*) amphibious vehicle

anfite'atro SM amphitheatre (*BRIT*), amphitheater (*US*)

anfitri'one SM host

'anfora SF amphora

an'fratto SM ravine

an'gelico, -a, -ci, -che [an'dʒɛliko] AG angelic(al)

'angelo ['andʒelo] SM angel; **~ custode** guardian angel; **l'~ del focolare** (*fig*) the perfect housewife

anghe'ria [ange'ria] SF vexation

an'gina [an'dʒina] SF tonsillitis; **~ pectoris** angina

angli'cano, -a AG, SM/F Anglican

angli'cismo [angli'tʃizmo] SM anglicism

an'glofilo, -a AG anglophilic ▶ SM/F anglophile

anglo'sassone AG Anglo-Saxon

An'gola SF: **l'~** Angola

ango'lano, -a AG, SM/F Angolan

ango'lare AG angular

angolazi'one [angolat'tsjone] SF (*di angolo*) angulation; (*Fot, Cine, TV, fig*) angle

'angolo SM corner; (*Mat*) angle; **~ cottura** (*di appartamento ecc*) cooking area; **fare ~ con** (*strada*) to run into; **dietro l'~** (*anche fig*) round the corner

ango'loso, -a AG (*oggetto*) angular; (*volto, corpo*) angular, bony

an'gora SF: **lana d'~** angora

an'goscia, -sce [an'gɔʃʃa] SF deep anxiety, anguish *no pl*

angosci'are [angoʃ'ʃare] /14/ VT to cause anguish to ■ **angosciarsi** VPR: **angosciarsi (per)** (*preoccuparsi*) to become anxious (about); (*provare angoscia*) to get upset (about o over)

angosci'oso, -a [angoʃ'ʃoso] AG (*d'angoscia*) anguished; (*che dà angoscia*) distressing, painful

angu'illa SF eel

an'guria SF watermelon

an'gustia SF (*ansia*) anguish, distress; (*povertà*) poverty, want

angusti'are /19/ VT to distress ■ **angustiarsi** VPR: **angustiarsi (per)** to worry (about)

an'gusto, -a AG (*stretto*) narrow; (*fig*) mean, petty

'anice ['anitʃe] SM (*Cuc*) aniseed; (*Bot*) anise; (*liquore*) anisette

ani'dride SF (*Chim*): **~ carbonica/solforosa** carbon/sulphur dioxide

'anima SF soul; (*abitante*) inhabitant; **~ gemella** soul mate; **un'~ in pena** (*anche fig*) a tormented soul; **non c'era ~ viva** there wasn't a living soul; **volere un bene dell'~ a qn** to be extremely fond of sb; **rompere l'~ a qn** to drive sb mad; **il nonno buon'~ ...** Grandfather, God rest his soul ...

ani'male SM, AG animal; **~ domestico** pet

anima'lesco, -a, -schi, -sche AG (*gesto, atteggiamento*) animal-like

anima'lista, -i, -e AG animal rights *cpd* ▶ SM/F animal rights activist

ani'mare /72/ VT to give life to, liven (up); (*incoraggiare*) to encourage ■ **animarsi** VPR to become animated, come to life

ani'mato, -a AG animate; (*vivace*) lively, animated; (*: strada*) busy

anima'tore, -'trice SM/F guiding spirit; (*Cine*) animator; (*di festa*) life and soul

animazi'one [animat'tsjone] SF liveliness; (*di strada*) bustle; (*Cine*) animation; **~ teatrale** amateur dramatics

'animo SM (*mente*) mind; (*cuore*) heart; (*coraggio*) courage; (*disposizione*) character, disposition; **avere in ~ di fare qc** to intend *o* have a mind to do sth; **farsi ~** to pluck up courage; **fare qc di buon/mal ~** to do sth willingly/unwillingly; **perdersi d'~** to lose heart

animosità SF animosity

A'NITA SIGLA F = **Associazione Naturista Italiana**

'anitra SF = **anatra**

'Ankara SF Ankara

ANM SIGLA F (= *Associazione Nazionale dei Magistrati*) national association of Magistrates

anna'cquare /72/ VT to water down, dilute

annaffi'are /19/ VT to water

annaffia'toio SM watering can

an'nali SMPL annals

annas'pare /72/ VI (*nell'acqua*) to flounder; (*fig: nel buio, nell'incertezza*) to grope

an'nata SF year; (*importo annuo*) annual amount; **vino d'~** vintage wine

annebbi'are /19/ VT (*fig*) to cloud ■ **annebbiarsi** VPR to become foggy; (*vista*) to become dim

annega'mento SM drowning

anne'gare /80/ VT, VI to drown ■ **annegarsi** VPR (*accidentalmente*) to drown; (*deliberatamente*) to drown o.s.

anne'rire /55/ VT to blacken ▶ VI to become black

annessi'one SF (*Pol*) annexation

an'nesso, -a PP *di* **annettere** ▶ AG attached; (*Pol*) annexed; **... e tutti gli annessi e connessi** ... and so on and so forth

an'nettere /63/ VT (*Pol*) to annex; (*accludere*) to attach

annichi'lire [anniki'lire] /55/ VT to annihilate

anni'darsi /72/ VPR to nest

annienta'mento SM annihilation, destruction

annien'tare /72/ VT to annihilate, destroy

anniver'sario SM anniversary; **~ di matrimonio** wedding anniversary

'anno SM year; **quanti anni hai? — ho 40 anni** how old are you? — I'm 40 (years old); **gli anni 20** the 20s; **porta bene gli anni** she doesn't look her age; **porta male gli anni** she looks older than she is; **~ commerciale** business year; **~ giudiziario** legal year; **~ luce** light year; **gli anni di piombo** *the Seventies in Italy, characterized by terrorist attacks and killings*

anno'dare /72/ VT to knot, tie; (*fig: rapporto*) to form

annoi'are /19/ VT to bore; (*seccare*) to annoy ■ **annoiarsi** VPR to be bored; to be annoyed

an'noso, -a AG (*albero*) old; (*fig: problema ecc*) age-old

anno'tare /72/ VT (*registrare*) to note, note down (BRIT); (*commentare*) to annotate

annotazi'one [annotat'tsjone] SF note; annotation

annove'rare /72/ VT to number

annu'ale AG annual

annual'mente AV annually, yearly

annu'ario SM yearbook

annu'ire /55/ VI to nod; (*acconsentire*) to agree

annulla'mento SM annihilation, destruction; cancellation; annulment; quashing

annul'lare /72/ VT to annihilate, destroy; (*contratto, francobollo*) to cancel; (*matrimonio*) to annul; (*sentenza*) to quash; (*risultati*) to declare void

annunci'are [annun'tʃare] /14/ VT to announce; (*dar segni rivelatori*) to herald

annuncia'tore, -'trice [annuntʃa'tore] SM/F (*Radio, TV*) announcer

Annunciazi'one [annuntʃat'tsjone] SF (*Rel*): **l'~** the Annunciation

an'nuncio [an'nuntʃo] SM announcement; (*fig*) sign; **~ pubblicitario** advertisement; **annunci economici** classified advertisements, small ads; **piccoli annunci** small ads, classified ads; **annunci mortuari** (*colonna*) obituary column

'annuo, -a AG annual, yearly

annu'sare /72/ VT to sniff, smell; **~ tabacco** to take snuff

annuvola'mento SM clouding (over)

annuvo'lare /72/ VT to cloud ■ **annuvolarsi** VPR to become cloudy, cloud over

'ano SM anus

'anodo SM anode

anoma'lia SF anomaly

a'nomalo, -a AG anomalous

anoni'mato SM anonymity; **conservare l'~** to remain anonymous

a'nonimo, -a AG anonymous ▶ SM (*autore*) anonymous writer (*o painter etc*); **un tipo ~** (*peg*) a colourless (BRIT) *o* colorless (US) character; **società anonima** (*Comm*) joint stock company

anores'sia SF anorexia; **~ nervosa** anorexia nervosa

ano'ressico, -a, -ci, -che AG anorexic

anor'male AG abnormal ▶ SMF person with learning difficulties

anormalità SF INV abnormality

'ANSA SIGLA F (= *Agenzia Nazionale Stampa Associata*) national press agency

'ansa SF (*manico*) handle; (*di fiume*) bend, loop

an'sante AG out of breath, panting

'ANSEA SIGLA F (= *Associazione delle Nazioni del Sud-Est asiatico*) ASEAN

'ansia SF anxiety; **stare in ~ (per qn/qc)** to be anxious (about sb/sth)

ansietà SF anxiety

ansi'mare /72/ VI to pant

ansi'oso, -a AG anxious

'anta SF (*di finestra*) shutter; (*di armadio*) door

antago'nismo SM antagonism

antago'nista, -i, -e SM/F antagonist

an'tartico, -a, -ci, -che AG Antarctic ▶ SM: **l'A~** the Antarctic

An'tartide SF: **l'~** Antarctica

ante'bellico, -a, -ci, -che AG prewar *cpd*

antece'dente [antetʃe'dɛnte] AG preceding, previous

ante'fatto SM previous events *pl*; previous history

ante'guerra SM pre-war period

ante'nato SM ancestor, forefather

an'tenna SF (*Radio, TV*) aerial; (*Zool*) antenna, feeler; (*Naut*) yard; **rizzare le antenne** (*fig*) to prick up one's ears; **~ parabolica** (*TV*) satellite dish

ante'porre /77/ VT: **~ qc a qc** to place *o* put sth before sth

ante'posto, -a PP *di* **anteporre**

ante'prima SF preview; **~ di stampa** (*Inform*) print preview

anteri'ore AG (*ruota, zampa*) front *cpd*; (*fatti*) previous, preceding

antesi'gnano [antesiɲ'ɲano] SM (*Storia*) standard-bearer; (*fig*) forerunner

antiade'rente AG non-stick

antia'ereo, -a AG anti-aircraft *cpd*

antial'lergico, -a [antial'lɛrdʒiko] AG, SM hypoallergenic

antia'tomico, -a, -ci, -che AG anti-nuclear; **rifugio ~** fallout shelter

antibi'otico, -a, -ci, -che AG, SM antibiotic

anti'caglia [anti'kaʎʎa] SF junk *no pl*

antical'care AG (*prodotto, detersivo*) anti-limescale

anti'camera SF anteroom; **fare ~** to be kept waiting; **non mi passerebbe neanche per l'~ del cervello** it wouldn't even cross my mind

anti'carie AG INV which fights tooth decay

antichità [antiki'ta] SF INV antiquity; (*oggetto*) antique

antici'clone [antitʃi'klone] SM anticyclone

antici'pare [antitʃi'pare] /72/ VT (*consegna, visita*) to bring forward, anticipate; (*somma di denaro*) to pay in advance; (*notizia*) to disclose ▶ VI to be ahead of time

antici'pato, -a [antitʃi'pato] AG (*prima del previsto*) early; **pagamento ~** payment in advance

anticipazi'one [antitʃipat'tsjone] SF anticipation; (*di notizia*) advance information; (*somma di denaro*) advance

an'ticipo [an'titʃipo] SM anticipation; (*di denaro*) advance; **in ~** early, in advance; **con un sensibile ~** well in advance

anti'clan AG INV (*magistrato, processo*) anti-Mafia

an'tico, -a, -chi, -che AG (*quadro, mobili*) antique; (*dell'antichità*) ancient; **all'antica** old-fashioned

anticoncezio'nale [antikontʃettsjo'nale] SM contraceptive

anticonfor'mista, -i, -e AG, SM/F nonconformist

anticonge'lante [antikondʒe'lante] AG, SM antifreeze

anticongiuntu'rale [antikondʒuntu'rale] AG (*Econ*): **misure anticongiunturali** measures to remedy the economic situation

anti'corpo SM antibody

anticostituzio'nale [antikostituttsjo'nale] AG unconstitutional

antidepres'sivo, -a AG, SM antidepressant

antidiluvi'ano, -a AG (*fig*: *antiquato*) ancient

antidolo'rifico, -ci SM painkiller

anti'doping SM INV (*Sport*) dope test ▶ AG INV drug-testing; **test ~** drugs (BRIT) *o* drug (US) test

an'tidoto SM antidote

anti'droga AG INV anti-drugs *cpd*

antie'stetico, -a, -ci, -che AG unsightly

antieurope'ista AG anti-European

an'tifona SF (*Mus, Rel*) antiphon; **capire l'~** (*fig*) to take the hint

anti'forfora AG INV anti-dandruff

anti'furto SM anti-theft device

anti'gelo [anti'dʒelo] AG INV antifreeze *cpd* ▶ SM (*per motore*) antifreeze; (*per cristalli*) de-icer

an'tigene [an'tidʒene] SM antigen

antigi'enico, -a, -ci, -che [anti'dʒɛniko] AG unhygienic

antiglobalizza'zione [antiglobaliddza'tsjone] AG anti-globalization

An'tille SFPL: **le ~** the West Indies

an'tilope SF antelope

anti'mafia AG INV anti-mafia *cpd*

antin'cendio [antin'tʃendjo] AG INV fire *cpd*; **bombola ~** fire extinguisher

anti'nebbia SM INV (*anche*: **faro antinebbia**: *Aut*) fog lamp

antine'vralgico, -a, -ci, -che [antine'vraldʒiko] AG painkilling ▶ SM painkiller

antin'fiammatorio, -a AG, SM anti-inflammatory

antio'rario AG: **in senso ~** in an anticlockwise (BRIT) o counterclockwise (US) direction, anticlockwise (BRIT) o counterclockwise (US)

anti'pasto SM hors d'œuvre

antipa'tia SF antipathy, dislike

anti'patico, -a, -ci, -che AG unpleasant, disagreeable

anti'placca AG INV (*dentifricio*) anti-plaque

an'tipodi SMPL: **essere agli ~** (*fig: di idee opposte*) to be poles apart

antipro'iettile AG INV bulletproof

antiquari'ato SM antique trade; **un pezzo d'~** an antique

anti'quario SM antique dealer

anti'quato, -a AG antiquated, old-fashioned

antirici'claggio [antiritʃi'kladdʒo] AG INV (*attività, operazioni*) anti-laundering

antiri'flesso AG INV (*schermo*) non-glare cpd

anti'ruggine [anti'ruddʒine] AG INV anti-rust cpd ▶ SM INV rust-preventer

anti'rughe [anti'ruge] AG INV (*crema, prodotto*) anti-wrinkle

antise'mita, -i, -e AG anti-semitic

antisemi'tismo SM anti-semitism

anti'settico, -a, -ci, -che AG, SM antiseptic

antista'minico, -a, -ci, -che AG, SM antihistamine

anti'stante AG opposite

anti'tartaro AG INV anti-tartar

antiterro'rismo SM anti-terrorist measures *pl*

an'titesi SF antithesis

antitraspi'rante AG antiperspirant

anti'vipera AG INV: **siero ~** remedy for snake bites

antivi'rale AG antiviral

anti'virus [anti'virus] SM INV antivirus software *no pl* ▶ AG INV antivirus

antolo'gia, -'gie [antolo'dʒia] SF anthology

antono'masia SF antonomasia; **per ~** par excellence

antra'cite [antra'tʃite] SF anthracite

'antro SM cavern

antro'pofago, -a, -gi, -ghe SM/F cannibal

antropolo'gia [antropolo'dʒia] SF anthropology

antropo'logico, -a, -ci, -che [antropo'lɔdʒiko] AG anthropological

antro'pologo, -a, -gi, -ghe SM/F anthropologist

anu'lare AG ring cpd ▶ SM ring finger

An'versa SF Antwerp

'anzi ['antsi] AV (*invece*) on the contrary; (*o meglio*) or rather, or better still

anzianità [antsjani'ta] SF old age; (*Amm*) seniority

anzi'ano, -a [an'tsjano] AG old; (*Amm*) senior ▶ SM/F old person; senior member

anziché [antsi'ke] CONG rather than

anzi'tempo [antsi'tɛmpo] AV (*in anticipo*) early

anzi'tutto [antsi'tutto] AV first of all

AO SIGLA = **Aosta**

a'orta SF aorta

aos'tano, -a AG of (o from) Aosta

AP SIGLA = **Ascoli Piceno**

apar'titico, -a, -ci, -che AG (*Pol*) non-party cpd

apa'tia SF apathy, indifference

a'patico, -a, -ci, -che AG apathetic, indifferent

a.p.c. ABBR = **a pronta cassa**

'ape SF bee

aperi'cena [aperi'tʃena] SF *one drink plus an all-you-can-eat buffet in a bar*

aperi'tivo SM apéritif

aperta'mente AV openly

a'perto, -a PP di **aprire** ▶ AG open ▶ SM: **all'~** in the open (air); **rimanere a bocca aperta** (*fig*) to be taken aback

aper'tura SF opening; (*ampiezza*) width, spread; (*Pol*) approach; (*Fot*) aperture; **~ alare** wing span; **~ mentale** open-mindedness; **~ di credito** (*Comm*) granting of credit

API SIGLA F = **Associazione Piccole e Medie Industrie**

'apice ['apitʃe] SM apex; (*fig*) height

apicol'tore SM beekeeper

apicol'tura SF beekeeping

ap'nea SF: **immergersi in ~** to dive without breathing apparatus

apoca'lisse SF apocalypse

apo'geo [apo'dʒɛo] SM (*Astr*) apogee; (*fig: culmine*) zenith

a'polide AG stateless

apo'litico, -a, -ci, -che AG (*neutrale*) nonpolitical; (*indifferente*) apolitical

apolo'gia, -'gie [apolo'dʒia] SF (*difesa*) apologia; (*esaltazione*) praise; **~ di reato** attempt to defend criminal acts

apoples'sia SF (*Med*) apoplexy

apop'lettico, -a, -ci, -che AG apoplectic; **colpo ~** apoplectic fit

a'postolo SM apostle

apostro'fare /72/ VT (*parola*) to write with an apostrophe; (*persona*) to address

a'postrofo SM apostrophe

app. ABBR (= *appendice*) app.

appaga'mento SM satisfaction; fulfilment

appa'gare /80/ VT to satisfy; (*desiderio*) to fulfil ■ **appagarsi** VPR: **appagarsi di** to be satisfied with

appa'gato, -a AG satisfied

appai'are /19/ VT to couple, pair

ap'paio *ecc* VB *vedi* **apparire**

appallotto'lare /72/ VT (*carta, foglio*) to screw into a ball ■ **appallottolarsi** VPR (*gatto*) to roll up into a ball

appalta'tore, -trice SM/F contractor

ap'palto SM (*Comm*) contract; **dare/prendere in ~ un lavoro** to let out/undertake a job on contract

appan'naggio [appan'nadd3o] SM (*compenso*) annuity; (*fig*) privilege, prerogative

appan'nare /72/ VT (*vetro*) to mist; (*metallo*) to tarnish; (*vista*) to dim ■ **appannarsi** VPR to mist over; to tarnish; to grow dim

appa'rato SM equipment, machinery; (*Anat*) apparatus; **~ scenico** (*Teat*) props *pl*

apparecchi'are [apparek'kjare] /19/ VT to prepare; (*tavola*) to set ► VI to set the table

apparecchia'tura [apparekkja'tura] SF equipment; (*macchina*) machine, device

appa'recchio [appa'rekkjo] SM piece of apparatus, device; (*aeroplano*) aircraft *inv*; **apparecchi sanitari** bathroom *o* sanitary appliances; **~ acustico** hearing aid; **~ televisivo/telefonico** television set/telephone

appa'rente AG apparent

apparente'mente AV apparently

appa'renza [appa'rɛntsa] SF appearance; **in** *o* **all'~** apparently, to all appearances

appa'rire /7/ VI to appear; (*sembrare*) to seem, appear

appari'scente [appariʃ'ʃɛnte] AG (*colore*) garish, gaudy; (*bellezza*) striking

apparizi'one [apparit'tsjone] SF apparition

ap'parso, -a PP *di* **apparire**

apparta'mento SM flat (*Brit*), apartment (*US*)

appar'tarsi /72/ VPR to withdraw

appar'tato, -a AG (*luogo*) secluded

apparte'nenza [apparte'nɛntsa] SF: **~ (a)** (*gen*) belonging (to); (*a un partito, club*) membership (of)

apparte'nere /121/ VI: **~ a** to belong to

ap'parvi *ecc* VB *vedi* **apparire**

appassio'nante AG thrilling, exciting

appassio'nare /72/ VT to thrill; (*commuovere*) to move ■ **appassionarsi** VPR: **appassionarsi a qc** to take a great interest in sth; to be deeply moved by sth

appassio'nato, -a AG passionate; (*entusiasta*): **~ (di)** keen (on)

appas'sire /55/ VI to wither

appas'sito, -a AG dead

appel'larsi /72/ VPR (*ricorrere*): **~ a** to appeal to; (*Dir*) **~ contro** to appeal against

ap'pello SM roll-call; (*implorazione, Dir*) appeal; (*sessione d'esame*) exam session; **fare ~ a** to

appeal to; **fare l'~** (*Ins*) to call the register *o* roll; (*Mil*) to call the roll

ap'pena AV (*a stento*) hardly, scarcely; (*solamente, da poco*) just ► CONG as soon as; **(non) ~ furono arrivati ...** as soon as they had arrived ...; **~ ... che** *o* **quando** no sooner ... than; **basta ~ a sfamarli** it's scarcely enough to feed them; **ho ~ finito** I've just finished

---

Hardly e **scarcely** si usano davanti al verbo principale e dopo un ausiliare o un modale, anche se **hardly** è più comune.
Riusciva appena a parlare. **He could hardly speak.**
La conosco appena. **I hardly** o **scarcely know her.**
Barely si usa di solito davanti a una cifra.
Aveva appena 5 anni! **She was barely 5 years old!**

---

ap'pendere /8/ VT to hang (up)

appendi'abiti SM INV hook, peg; (*mobile*) hall stand (*Brit*), hall tree (*US*)

appen'dice [appen'ditʃe] SF appendix; **romanzo d'~** popular serial

appendi'cite [appendi'tʃite] SF appendicitis

appen'dino SM (coat) hook

Appen'nini SMPL: **gli ~** the Apennines

appesan'tire /55/ VT to make heavy ■ **appesantirsi** VPR to grow stout

ap'peso, -a PP *di* **appendere**

appe'tito SM appetite

appeti'toso, -a AG appetising; (*fig*) attractive, desirable

appezza'mento [appettsa'mento] SM (*anche*: **appezzamento di terreno**) plot, piece of ground

appia'nare /72/ VT to level; (*fig*) to smooth away, iron out ■ **appianarsi** VPR (*divergenze*) to be ironed out

appiat'tire /55/ VT to flatten ■ **appiattirsi** VPR to become flatter; (*farsi piatto*) to flatten o.s.; **appiattirsi al suolo** to lie flat on the ground

appic'care /20/ VT: **~ il fuoco a** to set fire to, set on fire

appicci'care [appittʃi'kare] /20/ VT to stick; (*fig*): **~ qc a qn** to palm sth off on sb ■ **appiccicarsi** VPR to stick; (*fig: persona*) to cling

appiccica'ticcio, -a, -ci, -ce [appittʃika'tittʃo], **appicci'coso, -a** [appittʃi'koso] AG sticky; (*fig: persona*): **essere ~** to cling like a leech

appie'dato, -a AG: **rimanere ~** to be left without means of transport

appi'eno AV fully

appigli'arsi [appiʎ'ʎarsi] /27/ VPR: **~ a** (*afferrarsi*) to take hold of; (*fig*) to cling to

ap'piglio [ap'piʎʎo] SM hold; (*fig*) pretext

appiop'pare /72/ VT: ~ qc a qn (nomignolo) to pin sth on sb; (compito difficile) to saddle sb with sth; **gli ha appioppato un pugno sul muso** he punched him in the face

appiso'larsi /72/ VPR to doze off

applau'dire /45/ VT, VI to applaud

ap'plauso SM applause no pl

appli'cabile AG: ~ **(a)** applicable (to)

appli'care /20/ VT to apply; (regolamento) to enforce ▪ **applicarsi** VPR to apply o.s.

appli'cato, -a AG (arte, scienze) applied ▶ SM (Amm) clerk

applica'tore SM applicator

applicazi'one [applikat'tsjone] SF application; enforcement; ~ **per il cellulare** mobile app; **applicazioni tecniche** (Ins) practical subjects

appoggi'are [appod'dʒare] /62/ VT (fig: sostenere) to support; ~ **qc a qc** (mettere contro) to lean o rest sth against sth ▪ **appoggiarsi** VPR: **appoggiarsi a** to lean against; (fig) to rely upon

ap'poggio [ap'pɔddʒo] SM support

appollai'arsi /72/ VPR (anche fig) to perch

ap'pongo, ap'poni ecc VB vedi **apporre**

ap'porre /77/ VT to affix

appor'tare /72/ VT to bring

ap'porto SM (gen, Finanza) contribution

ap'posi ecc VB vedi **apporre**

apposita'mente AV (apposta) on purpose; (specialmente) specially

ap'posito, -a AG appropriate

ap'posta AV on purpose, deliberately; **neanche a farlo ~,** ... by sheer coincidence, ...

appos'tarsi /72/ VPR to lie in wait

ap'posto, -a PP di **apporre**

ap'prendere /81/ VT (imparare) to learn; (comprendere) to grasp

apprendi'mento SM learning

appren'dista, -i, -e SM/F apprentice

apprendi'stato SM apprenticeship

apprensi'one SF apprehension

appren'sivo, -a AG apprehensive

ap'preso, -a PP di **apprendere**

ap'presso AV (accanto, vicino) close by, near; (dietro) behind; (dopo, più tardi) after, later ▶ AG INV (dopo): **il giorno ~** the next day; ~ **a** prep (vicino a) near, close to

appres'tare /72/ VT to prepare, get ready ▪ **apprestarsi** VPR: **apprestarsi a fare qc** to prepare o get ready to do sth

ap'pretto SM starch

apprez'zabile [appret'tsabile] AG (notevole) noteworthy, significant; (percepibile) appreciable

apprezza'mento [apprettsa'mento] SM appreciation; (giudizio) opinion; (commento) comment

apprez'zare [appret'tsare] /72/ VT to appreciate

ap'proccio [ap'prɔttʃo] SM approach

appro'dare /72/ VI (Naut) to land; (fig): **non ~ a nulla** to come to nothing

ap'prodo SM landing; (luogo) landing place

approfit'tare /72/ VI: ~ **di** (situazione) to make the most of; (persona) to take advantage of; (occasione, opportunità) to make the most of, profit by

approfon'dire /55/ VT to deepen; (fig) to study in depth ▪ **approfondirsi** VPR (gen, fig) to deepen; (peggiorare) to get worse

appron'tare /72/ VT to prepare, get ready

appropri'arsi /19/ VPR: ~ **di qc** to appropriate sth, take possession of sth; ~ **indebitamente di** to embezzle

appropri'ato, -a AG appropriate

appropriazi'one [approprjat'tsjone] SF appropriation; ~ **indebita** (Dir) embezzlement

approssi'mare /72/ VT (cifra): ~ **per eccesso/per difetto** to round up/down ▪ **approssimarsi** VPR: **approssimarsi a** to approach, draw near

approssima'tivo, -a AG approximate, rough; (impreciso) inexact, imprecise

approssimazi'one [approssimat'tsjone] SF approximation; **per ~** approximately, roughly

appro'vare /72/ VT (condotta, azione) to approve of; (candidato) to pass; (progetto di legge) to approve

approvazi'one [approvat'tsjone] SF approval

approvigiona'mento [approvvidʒona'mento] SM supplying; stocking up ▪ **approvvigionamenti** SMPL (Mil) supplies

approvvigio'nare [approvvidʒo'nare] /72/ VT to supply ▪ **approvvigionarsi** VPR to lay in provisions, stock up; ~ **qn di qc** to supply sb with sth

appunta'mento SM appointment; (amoroso) date; **darsi ~** to arrange to meet (one another); **ho un ~ con...** I have an appointment with ...; **vorrei prendere un ~** I'd like to make an appointment

appun'tare /72/ VT (rendere aguzzo) to sharpen; (fissare) to pin, fix; (annotare) to note down

appun'tato SM (Carabinieri) corporal

appun'tino AV perfectly

appun'tire /55/ VT to sharpen

ap'punto SM note; (rimprovero) reproach; (Inform): **Appunti** Clipboard sg ▶ AV (proprio) exactly, just; **per l'~!, ~!** exactly!

appu'rare /72/ VT to check, verify

apr. ABBR (= aprile) Apr.

apribot'tiglie [apribot'tiʎʎe] SM INV bottle opener

a'prile SM April; **pesce d'~!** April Fool!; vedi anche **luglio**

a'prire /9/ VT to open; (via, cadavere) to open up; (gas, luce, acqua) to turn on ▶ VI to open ■ aprirsi VPR to open; ~ le ostilità (Mil) to start up o begin hostilities; ~ una sessione (Inform) to log on; aprirsi a qn to confide in sb, open one's heart to sb; mi si è aperto lo stomaco I feel rather peckish; apriti cielo! heaven forbid!

apris'catole SM INV tin (BRIT) o can opener

APT SIGLA F (= Azienda di Promozione Turistica) = tourist board

AQ SIGLA = L'Aquila

aqua'gym [akwa'dʒim] SF aquarobics

a'quario SM = acquario

'aquila SF (Zool) eagle; (fig) genius

aqui'lino, -a AG aquiline

aqui'lone SM (giocattolo) kite; (vento) North wind

AR SIGLA = Arezzo

A/R ABBR (= andata e ritorno) return (ticket) (BRIT), round-trip ticket (US)

ara'besco, -schi SM (decorazione) arabesque

A'rabia Sau'dita SF: l'~ Saudi Arabia

a'rabico, -a, -ci, -che AG: il Deserto ~ the Arabian Desert

a'rabile AG arable

'arabo, -a AG, SM/F Arab ▶ SM (Ling) Arabic; parlare ~ (fig) to speak double Dutch (BRIT)

a'rachide [a'rakide] SF peanut

ara'gosta SF crayfish; spiny lobster

a'raldica SF heraldry

a'raldo SM herald

aran'ceto [aran'tʃeto] SM orange grove

a'rancia, -ce [a'rantʃa] SF orange

aranci'ata [aran'tʃata] SF orangeade

a'rancio [a'rantʃo] SM (Bot) orange tree; (colore) orange ▶ AG INV (colore) orange; fiori di ~ orange blossom sg

aranci'one [aran'tʃone] AG INV: (color) ~ bright orange

a'rare /72/ VT to plough (BRIT), plow (US)

ara'tore SM ploughman (BRIT), plowman (US)

a'ratro SM plough (BRIT), plow (US)

ara'tura SF ploughing (BRIT), plowing (US)

a'razzo [a'rattso] SM tapestry

arbi'traggio [arbi'traddʒo] SM (Sport) refereeing; umpiring; (Dir) arbitration; (Comm) arbitrage

arbi'trare /72/ VT (Sport) to referee; to umpire; (Dir) to arbitrate

arbi'trario, -a AG arbitrary

arbi'trato SM arbitration

ar'bitrio SM will; (abuso, sopruso) arbitrary act

'arbitro SM arbiter, judge; (Dir) arbitrator; (Sport) referee; (: Tennis, Cricket) umpire

ar'busto SM shrub

'arca, -che SF (sarcofago) sarcophagus; l'~ di Noè Noah's ark

ar'caico, -a, -ci, -che AG archaic

arca'ismo SM (Ling) archaism

ar'cangelo [ar'kandʒelo] SM archangel

ar'cano, -a AG arcane, mysterious ▶ SM mystery

ar'cata SF (Archit, Anat) arch; (ordine di archi) arcade

archeolo'gia [arkeolo'dʒia] SF arch(a)eology

archeo'logico, -a, -ci, -che [arkeo'lɔdʒiko] AG arch(a)eological

arche'ologo, -a, -gi, -ghe [arke'ɔlogo] SM/F arch(a)eologist

ar'chetipo [ar'kɛtipo] SM archetype

ar'chetto [ar'ketto] SM (Mus) bow

architet'tare [arkitet'tare] /72/ VT (fig: ideare) to devise; (: macchinare) to plan, concoct

archi'tetto [arki'tetto] SM architect

architet'tonico, -a, -ci, -che [arkitet'tɔniko] AG architectural

architet'tura [arkitet'tura] SF architecture

archivi'are [arki'vjare] /19/ VT (documenti) to file; (Dir) to dismiss

archiviazi'one [arkivjat'tsjone] SF filing; dismissal

ar'chivio [ar'kivjo] SM archives pl; (Inform) file; ~ principale (Inform) master file

archi'vista, -i, -e [arki'vista] SM/F (Amm) archivist; (in ufficio) filing clerk

'ARCI ['artʃi] SIGLA F (= Associazione Ricreativa Culturale Italiana) cultural society

arci'duca, -chi [artʃi'duka] SM archduke

arci'ere [ar'tʃɛre] SM archer

ar'cigno, -a [ar'tʃiɲɲo] AG grim, severe

arci'pelago, -ghi [artʃi'pɛlago] SM archipelago

arci'vescovo [artʃi'veskovo] SM archbishop

'arco, -chi SM (arma, Mus) bow; (Archit) arch; (Mat) arc; nell'~ di 3 settimane within the space of 3 weeks; ~ costituzionale political parties involved in formulating Italy's post-war constitution

arcoba'leno SM rainbow

arcu'ato, -a AG curved, bent; dalle gambe arcuate bow-legged

ar'dente AG burning; (fig) burning, ardent

'ardere /10/ VT, VI to burn; legna da ~ firewood

ar'desia SF slate

ardi'mento SM daring

ar'dire /55/ VI to dare ▶ SM daring

ar'dito, -a AG brave, daring, bold; (sfacciato) bold

ar'dore SM blazing heat; (fig) ardour, fervour

'arduo, -a AG arduous, difficult

'area SF area; (Edil) land, ground; nell'~ dei partiti di sinistra among the parties of the left; ~ fabbricabile building land; ~ di rigore (Sport) penalty area; **~ di servizio** (*Aut*) service area

a'rena SF arena; (*per corride*) bullring; (*sabbia*) sand

are'naria SF sandstone

are'narsi /72/ VPR to run aground; (*fig: trattative*) to come to a standstill

areo'plano SM = **aeroplano**

are'tino, -a AG of (*o* from) Arezzo

'argano SM winch

argen'tato, -a [ardʒen'tato] AG silver-plated; (*colore*) silver, silvery; (*capelli*) silver(-grey)

ar'genteo, -a [ar'dʒɛnteo] AG silver, silvery

argente'ria [ardʒente'ria] SF silverware, silver

Argen'tina [ardʒen'tina] SF: **l'~** Argentina

argen'tino, -a AG, SM/F (*dell'Argentina*) Argentinian ▸ SF crewneck sweater

ar'gento [ar'dʒento] SM silver; **~ vivo** quicksilver; **avere l'~ (vivo) addosso** (*fig*) to be fidgety

ar'gilla [ar'dʒilla] SF clay

argil'loso, -a [ardʒil'loso] AG (*contenente argilla*) clayey; (*simile ad argilla*) clay-like

argi'nare [ardʒi'nare] /72/ VT (*fiume, acque*) to embank; (*: con diga*) to dyke up; (*fig: inflazione, corruzione*) to check; (*: spese*) to limit

'argine ['ardʒine] SM embankment, bank; (*diga*) dyke, dike; **far ~ a, porre un ~ a** (*fig*) to check, hold back

argomen'tare /72/ VI to argue

argo'mento SM argument; (*motivo*) motive; (*materia, tema*) subject; **tornare sull'~** to bring the matter up again

argu'ire /55/ VT to deduce

ar'guto, -a AG sharp, quick-witted; (*spiritoso*) witty

ar'guzia [ar'guttsja] SF wit; (*battuta*) witty remark

'aria SF air; (*espressione, aspetto*) air, look; (*Mus: melodia*) tune; (*: di opera*) aria; **all'~ aperta** in the open (air); **manca l'~** it's stuffy; **andare all'~** (*piano, progetto*) to come to nothing; **mandare all'~ qc** to ruin *o* upset sth; **darsi delle arie** to put on airs and graces; **ha la testa per ~** his head is in the clouds; **che ~ tira?** (*fig: atmosfera*) what's the atmosphere like?

aridità SF aridity, dryness; (*fig*) lack of feeling

'arido, -a AG arid

arieggi'are [arjed'dʒare] /62/ VT (*cambiare aria*) to air; (*imitare*) to imitate

ari'ete SM ram; (*Mil*) battering ram; **A~** Aries; **essere dell'A~** to be Aries

a'ringa, -ghe SF herring *inv*; **~ affumicata** smoked herring, kipper; **~ marinata** pickled herring

ari'oso, -a AG (*ambiente, stanza*) airy; (*Mus*) ariose

'arista SF (*Cuc*) chine of pork

aristo'cratico, -a, -ci, -che AG aristocratic

aristocra'zia [aristokrat'tsia] SF aristocracy

arit'metica SF arithmetic

arit'metico, -a, -ci, -che AG arithmetical

arlec'chino [arlek'kino] SM harlequin

'arma, -i SF weapon, arm; (*parte dell'esercito*) arm; **alle armi!** to arms!; **chiamare alle armi** to call up (*BRIT*), draft (*US*); **sotto le armi** in the army (*o* forces); **combattere ad armi pari** (*anche fig*) to fight on equal terms; **essere alle prime armi** (*fig*) to be a novice; **passare qn per le armi** to execute sb; **~ a doppio taglio** (*anche fig*) double-edged weapon; **~ atomica/nucleare** atomic/nuclear weapon; **~ da fuoco** firearm; **armi convenzionali/non convenzionali** conventional/unconventional weapons; **armi di distruzione di massa** weapons of mass destruction

arma'dietto SM (*di medicinali*) medicine cabinet; (*in palestra ecc*) locker; (*in cucina*) (kitchen) cupboard

ar'madio SM cupboard; (*per abiti*) wardrobe; **~ a muro** built-in cupboard

armamen'tario SM equipment, instruments *pl*

arma'mento SM (*Mil*) armament; (*: materiale*) arms *pl*, weapons *pl*; (*Naut*) fitting out; manning; **la corsa agli armamenti** the arms race

ar'mare /72/ VT to arm; (*arma da fuoco*) to cock; (*Naut: nave*) to rig, fit out; to man; (*Edil: volta, galleria*) to prop up, shore up ▪ **armarsi** VPR to arm o.s.; (*Mil*) to take up arms

ar'mato, -a AG: **~ (di)** (*anche fig*) armed (with) ▸ SF (*Mil*) army; (*Naut*) fleet; **rapina a mano armata** armed robbery

arma'tore SM shipowner

arma'tura SF (*struttura di sostegno*) framework; (*impalcatura*) scaffolding; (*Storia*) armour *no pl* (*BRIT*), armor *no pl* (*US*), suit of armour

armeggi'are [armed'dʒare] /62/ VI (*affaccendarsi*): **~ (intorno a qc)** to mess about (with sth)

ar'meno, -a AG, SM/F Armenian

arme'ria SF (*deposito*) armoury (*BRIT*), armory (*US*); (*collezione*) collection of arms

armis'tizio [armis'tittsjo] SM armistice

armo'nia SF harmony

ar'monico, -a, -ci, -che AG harmonic; (*fig*) harmonious ▸ SF (*Mus*) harmonica; **armonica a bocca** mouth organ

armoni'oso, -a AG harmonious

armoniz'zare [armonid'dzare] /72/ VT to harmonize; (*colori, abiti*) to match ▸ VI to be in harmony; to match

ar'nese SM tool, implement; (*oggetto indeterminato*) thing, contraption; **male in ~** (*malvestito*) badly dressed; (*di salute malferma*) in poor health; (*di condizioni economiche*) down-at-heel

'arnia SF hive

a'roma, -i SM aroma; fragrance ■ **aromi** SMPL (*Cuc*) herbs and spices; **aromi naturali/artificiali** natural/artificial flavouring *sg* (*BRIT*) *o* flavoring *sg* (*US*)

aromatera'pia SF aromatherapy

aro'matico, -a, -ci, -che AG aromatic; (*cibo*) spicy

aromatiz'zare [aromatid'dzare] /**72**/ VT to season, flavour (*BRIT*), flavor (*US*)

'arpa SF (*Mus*) harp

ar'peggio [ar'peddʒo] SM (*Mus*) arpeggio

ar'pia SF (*anche fig*) harpy

arpi'one SM (*gancio*) hook; (*cardine*) hinge; (*Pesca*) harpoon

arrabat'tarsi /**72**/ VPR to do all one can, strive

arrabbi'are /**19**/ VI (*cane*) to be affected with rabies ■ **arrabbiarsi** VPR (*essere preso dall'ira*) to get angry, fly into a rage

arrabbi'ato, -a AG (*cane*) rabid, with rabies; (*persona*) furious, angry

arrabbia'tura SF: **prenderси un'~ (per qc)** to become furious (over sth)

arraf'fare /**72**/ VT to snatch, seize; (*sottrarre*) to pinch

arrampi'carsi /**20**/ VPR to climb (up); **~ sui vetri** *o* **sugli specchi** (*fig*) to clutch at straws

arrampi'cata SF climb

arrampica'tore, -'trice SM/F (*gen, Sport*) climber; **~ sociale** (*fig*) social climber

arran'care /**20**/ VI to limp, hobble; (*fig*) to struggle along

arrangia'mento [arrandʒa'mento] SM (*Mus*) arrangement

arran'giare [arran'dʒare] /**62**/ VT to arrange ■ **arrangiarsi** VPR to manage, do the best one can

arre'care /**20**/ VT to bring; (*causare*) to cause

arreda'mento SM (*studio*) interior design; (*mobili ecc*) furnishings *pl*

arre'dare /**72**/ VT to furnish

arreda'tore, -'trice SM/F interior designer

ar'redo SM fittings *pl*, furnishings *pl*; **~ per uffici** office furnishings

arrem'baggio [arrem'baddʒo] SM (*Naut*) boarding

ar'rendersi /**88**/ VPR to surrender; **~ all'evidenza (dei fatti)** to face (the) facts

arren'devole AG (*persona*) yielding, compliant

arrendevo'lezza [arrendevo'lettsa] SF compliancy

ar'reso, -a PP *di* **arrendersi**

arres'tare /**72**/ VT (*fermare*) to stop, halt; (*catturare*) to arrest ■ **arrestarsi** VPR (*fermarsi*) to stop

arres'tato, -a SM/F person under arrest

ar'resto SM (*cessazione*) stopping; (*fermata*) stop; (*cattura, Med*) arrest; (*Comm: in produzione*) stoppage; **subire un ~** to come to a stop *o* standstill; **mettere agli arresti** to place under arrest; **arresti domiciliari** (*Dir*) house arrest *sg*

arre'trare /**72**/ VT, VI to withdraw

arre'trato, -a AG (*lavoro*) behind schedule; (*paese, bambino*) backward; (*numero di giornale*) back *cpd* ■ **arretrati** SMPL arrears; **gli arretrati dello stipendio** back pay *sg*

arricchi'mento [arrikki'mento] SM enrichment

arric'chire [arrik'kire] /**55**/ VT to enrich ■ **arricchirsi** VPR to become rich

arric'chito, -a [arrik'kito] SM/F nouveau riche

arricci'are [arrit'tʃare] /**14**/ VT to curl; **~ il naso** to turn up one's nose

ar'ridere /**89**/ VI: **~ a qn** (*fortuna, successo*) to smile on sb

ar'ringa, -ghe SF harangue; (*Dir*) address by counsel

arrischi'are [arris'kjare] /**19**/ VT to risk ■ **arrischiarsi** VPR to venture, dare

arrischi'ato, -a [arris'kjato] AG risky; (*temerario*) reckless, rash

ar'riso, -a PP *di* **arridere**

arri'vare /**72**/ VI to arrive; (*avvicinarsi*) to come; (*accadere*) to happen, occur; **~ a** (*livello, grado ecc*) to reach; **lui arriva a Roma alle 7** he gets to *o* arrives at Rome at 7; **~ a fare qc** to manage to do sth, succeed in doing sth; **non ci arrivo** I can't reach it; (*fig: non capisco*) I can't understand it

arri'vato, -a AG (*persona, di successo*) successful ▶ SM/F: **essere un ~** to have made it; **nuovo ~** newcomer; **ben ~!** welcome!; **non sono l'ultimo ~!** (*fig*) I'm no fool!

arrive'derci [arrive'dertʃi] ESCL goodbye!

arrive'derla ESCL (*forma di cortesia*) goodbye!

arri'vismo SM (*ambizione*) ambitiousness; (*sociale*) social climbing

arri'vista, -i, -e SM/F go-getter

ar'rivo SM arrival; (*Sport*) finish, finishing line

arro'gante AG arrogant

arro'ganza [arro'gantsa] SF arrogance

arro'gare /**80**/ VT: **arrogarsi il diritto di fare qc** to assume the right to do sth; **arrogarsi il merito di qc** to claim credit for sth

arrossa'mento SM reddening

arros'sare /**72**/ VT (*occhi, pelle*) to redden, make red ■ **arrossarsi** VPR to go *o* become red

arros'sire /**55**/ VI (*per vergogna, timidezza*) to blush; (*per gioia*) to flush, blush

arros'tire /**55**/ VT to roast; (*pane*) to toast; (*ai ferri*) to grill

ar'rosto SM, AG INV roast; **~ di manzo** roast beef

arro'tare /**72**/ VT to sharpen; (*investire con un veicolo*) to run over

arro'tino SM knife-grinder

arroto'lare /72/ VT to roll up

arron'dare /72/ VT (*forma, oggetto*) to round; (*stipendio*) to add to; (*somma*) to round off

arrovel'larsi /72/ VPR (*anche:* **arrovellarsi il cervello**) to rack one's brains

arroven'tato, -a AG red-hot

arruf'fare /72/ VT to ruffle; (*fili*) to tangle; (*fig: questione*) to confuse

arruggi'nire [arruddʒi'nire] /55/ VT to rust ▪ **arrugginirsi** VPR to rust; (*fig*) to become rusty

arruggi'nito, -a [arruddʒin'nito] AG rusty

arruola'mento SM (*Mil*) enlistment

arruo'lare /72/ VT (*Mil*) to enlist ▪ **arruolarsi** VPR to enlist, join up

arse'nale SM (*Mil*) arsenal; (*cantiere navale*) dockyard

ar'senico SM arsenic

'arsi VB *vedi* **ardere**

'arso, -a PP *di* **ardere** ▶ AG (*bruciato*) burnt; (*arido*) dry

ar'sura SF (*calore opprimente*) burning heat; (*siccità*) drought

art. ABBR (= *articolo*) art.

'arte SF art; (*abilità*) skill; **a regola d'~** (*fig*) perfectly; **senz'~ né parte** penniless and out of a job; **arti figurative** visual arts

arte'fatto, -a AG (*stile, modi*) affected; (*cibo*) adulterated

ar'tefice [ar'tefitʃe] SMF craftsman(-woman); (*autore*) author

ar'teria SF artery; **~ stradale** main road

arterioscle'rosi SF arteriosclerosis, hardening of the arteries

arteri'oso, -a AG arterial

'artico, -a, -ci, -che AG Arctic ▶ SM: **l'A~** the Arctic; **il Circolo polare ~** the Arctic Circle; **l'O-ceano ~** the Arctic Ocean

artico'lare /72/ AG (*Anat*) of the joints, articular ▶ VT to articulate; (*suddividere*) to divide, split up ▪ **articolarsi** VPR: **articolarsi in** (*discorso, progetto*) to be divided into

artico'lato, -a AG (*linguaggio*) articulate; (*Aut*) articulated

articolazi'one [artikolat'tsjone] SF (*Anat, Tecn*) joint; (*di voce, concetto*) articulation

ar'ticolo SM article; **~ di fondo** (*Stampa*) leader, leading article; **articoli di marca** branded goods; **un bell'~** (*fig*) a real character

'Artide SM: **l'~** the Arctic

artifici'ale [artifi'tʃale] AG artificial

artifici'ere [artifi'tʃɛre] SM (*Mil*) artificer; (: *per disinnescare bombe*) bomb-disposal expert

arti'ficio [arti'fitʃo] SM (*espediente*) trick, artifice; (*ricerca di effetto*) artificiality

artifici'oso, -a [artifi'tʃoso] AG cunning; (*non spontaneo*) affected

artigia'nale [artidʒa'nale] AG craft *cpd*

artigia'nato [artidʒa'nato] SM craftsmanship; craftsmen *pl*

artigi'ano, -a [arti'dʒano] SM/F craftsman(-woman)

artigli'ere [artiʎ'ʎere] SM artilleryman

artiglie'ria [artiʎʎe'ria] SF artillery

ar'tiglio [ar'tiʎʎo] SM claw; (*di rapaci*) talon; **sfoderare gli artigli** (*fig*) to show one's claws

ar'tista, -i, -e SM/F artist; **un lavoro da ~** (*fig*) a professional piece of work

ar'tistico, -a, -ci, -che AG artistic

'arto SM (*Anat*) limb

ar'trite SF (*Med*) arthritis

ar'trosi SF osteoarthritis

arzigogo'lato, -a [ardzigogo'lato] AG tortuous

ar'zillo, -a [ar'dzillo] AG lively, sprightly

a'scella [aʃ'ʃella] SF (*Anat*) armpit

ascen'dente [aʃʃen'dɛnte] SM ancestor; (*fig*) ascendancy; (*Astr*) ascendant

a'scendere [aʃ'ʃendere] /101/ VI: **~ al trono** to ascend the throne

ascensi'one [aʃʃen'sjone] SF (*Alpinismo*) ascent; (*Rel*): **l'A~** the Ascension; **isola dell'A~** Ascension Island

ascen'sore [aʃʃen'sore] SM lift

a'scesa [aʃ'ʃesa] SF ascent; (*al trono*) accession; (*al potere*) rise

a'scesi [aʃ'ʃezi] SF asceticism

a'sceso, -a [aʃ'ʃeso] PP *di* **ascendere**

a'scesso [aʃ'ʃɛsso] SM (*Med*) abscess

a'sceta, -i [aʃ'ʃeta] SM ascetic

'ascia ['aʃʃa] (*pl* **asce**) SF axe

asciugaca'pelli [aʃʃugaka'pelli] SM INV hair dryer

asciuga'mano [aʃʃuga'mano] SM towel

asciu'gare [aʃʃu'gare] /80/ VT to dry ▪ **asciugarsi** VPR to dry o.s.; (*diventare asciutto*) to dry

asciuga'trice [aʃʃuga'tritʃe] SF tumble dryer

asciut'tezza [aʃʃut'tettsa] SF dryness; leanness; curtness

asci'utto, -a [aʃ'ʃutto] AG dry; (*fig: magro*) lean; (: *burbero*) curt ▶ SM: **restare all'~** (*fig*) to be left penniless; **restare a bocca asciutta** (*fig*) to be disappointed

asco'lano, -a AG of (*o* from) Ascoli

ascol'tare /72/ VT to listen to; **~ il consiglio di qn** to listen to *o* heed sb's advice

ascolta'tore, -'trice SM/F listener

as'colto SM: **essere** *o* **stare in ~** to be listening; **dare** *o* **prestare ~ (a)** to pay attention (to); **indice di ~** (*TV, Radio*) audience rating

AS. COM. SIGLA F = **Associazione Commercianti**

as'critto, -a PP *di* **ascrivere**

as'crivere /105/ vt (*attribuire*): **~ qc a qn** to attribute sth to sb; **~ qc a merito di qn** to give sb credit for sth

a'settico, -a, -ci, -che AG aseptic

asfal'tare /72/ vt to asphalt

as'falto SM asphalt

asfis'sia SF asphyxia, asphyxiation

asfissi'ante AG (*gas*) asphyxiating; (*fig: calore, ambiente*) stifling, suffocating; (: *persona*) tiresome

asfissi'are /19/ vt to asphyxiate, suffocate; (*fig: opprimere*) to stifle; (: *infastidire*) to get on sb's nerves ▶ vi to suffocate, asphyxiate

'Asia SF: **l'~** Asia

asi'atico, -a, -ci, -che AG, SM/F Asiatic, Asian

a'silo SM refuge, sanctuary; **~ (d'infanzia)** nursery(-school); **~ nido** day nursery, crèche (*for children aged 0 to 3*); **~ politico** political asylum

asim'metrico, -a, -ci, -che AG asymmetric(al)

'asino SM donkey, ass; **la bellezza dell'~** (*fig: di ragazza*) the beauty of youth; **qui casca l'~!** there's the rub!

ASL [azl] SIGLA F (= *Azienda Sanitaria Locale*) local health centre

'asma SF asthma

as'matico, -a, -ci, -che AG, SM/F asthmatic

asoci'ale [aso't∫ale] AG antisocial

'asola SF buttonhole

as'parago, -gi SM asparagus *no pl*

as'pergere [as'pɛrdʒere] /59/ vt: **~ (di o con)** to sprinkle (with)

asperità SF INV roughness *no pl*; (*fig*) harshness *no pl*

as'persi *ecc* vb *vedi* **aspergere**

as'perso, -a PP *di* **aspergere**

aspet'tare /72/ vt to wait for; (*anche Comm*) to await; (*aspettarsi*) to expect; (*essere in serbo: notizia, evento ecc*) to be in store for, lie ahead of ▶ vi to wait; **aspettarsi qc** to expect sth; **~ un bambino** to be expecting (a baby); **questo non me l'aspettavo** I wasn't expecting this; **me l'aspettavo!** I thought as much!

aspetta'tiva SF expectation; **inferiore all'~** worse than expected; **essere/mettersi in ~** (*Amm*) to be on/take leave of absence

as'petto SM (*apparenza*) aspect, appearance, look; (*punto di vista*) point of view; **di bell'~** good-looking

aspi'rante AG (*attore ecc*) aspiring ▶ SMF candidate, applicant

aspira'polvere SM INV vacuum cleaner

aspi'rare /72/ vt (*respirare*) to breathe in, inhale; (*apparecchi*) to suck (up) ▶ vi: **~ a** to aspire to

aspira'tore SM extractor fan

aspirazi'one [aspirat'tsjone] SF (*Tecn*) suction; (*anelito*) aspiration

aspi'rina SF aspirin

aspor'tare /72/ vt (*anche Med*) to remove, take away

as'prezza [as'prettsa] SF sourness, tartness; pungency; harshness; roughness; rugged nature

'aspro, -a AG (*sapore*) sour, tart; (*odore*) acrid, pungent; (*voce, clima, fig*) harsh; (*superficie*) rough; (*paesaggio*) rugged

Ass. ABBR = **assicurazione**; **assicurato**; **assegno**

assaggi'are [assad'dʒare] /62/ vt to taste

assag'gini [assad'dʒini] SMPL (*Cuc*) selection of first courses

as'saggio [as'saddʒo] SM tasting; (*piccola quantità*) taste; (*campione*) sample

as'sai AV (*molto*) a lot, much; (: *con ag*) very; (*a sufficienza*) enough ▶ AG INV (*quantità*) a lot of, much; (*numero*) a lot of, many; **~ contento** very pleased

as'salgo *ecc* VB *vedi* **assalire**

assa'lire /98/ vt to attack, assail

assali'tore, -'trice SM/F attacker, assailant

assal'tare /72/ vt (*Mil*) to storm; (*banca*) to raid; (*treno, diligenza*) to hold up

as'salto SM attack, assault; **prendere d'~** (*fig: negozio, treno*) to storm; (: *personalità*) to besiege; **d'~** (*editoria, giornalista ecc*) aggressive

assapo'rare /72/ vt to savour (BRIT), savor (US)

assassi'nare /72/ vt to murder; (*Pol*) to assassinate; (*fig*) to ruin

assas'sinio SM murder; assassination

assas'sino, -a AG murderous ▶ SM/F murderer; assassin

'asse SM (*Tecn*) axle; (*Mat*) axis ▶ SF board; **~ da stiro** ironing board

assecon'dare /72/ vt: **~ qn (in qc)** to go along with sb (in sth); **~ i desideri di qn** to go along with sb's wishes; **~ i capricci di qn** to give in to sb's whims

assedi'are /19/ vt to besiege

as'sedio SM siege

asse'gnare [asseɲ'ɲare] /15/ vt to assign, allot; (*premio*) to award

assegna'tario [asseɲɲa'tarjo] SM (*Dir*) assignee; (*Comm*) recipient; **l'~ del premio** the person awarded the prize

assegnazi'one [asseɲɲat'tsjone] SF (*di casa, somma*) allocation; (*di carica*) assignment; (*di premio, borsa di studio*) awarding

as'segno [as'seɲɲo] SM allowance; (*anche:* **assegno bancario**) cheque (BRIT), check (US); **~ contro** ~ cash on delivery; **~ circolare** bank draft; **~ di malattia** *o* **di invalidità** sick pay/disability benefit; **~ post-datato** post-dated cheque; **~ sbarrato** crossed cheque; **~ non**

sbarrato uncrossed cheque; **~ di studio** study grant; **"~ non trasferibile"** "account payee only"; **~ di viaggio** travel(l)er's cheque; **~ a vuoto** dud cheque; **assegni alimentari** alimony *sg*; **assegni familiari** ≈ child benefit *sg*

assem'blaggio [assem'bladdʒo] SM (*Industria*) assembly

assem'blare /72/ VT to assemble

assem'blea SF assembly; (*raduno, adunanza*) meeting

assembra'mento SM public gathering; **divieto di ~** ban on public meetings

assen'nato, -a AG sensible

as'senso SM assent, consent

assen'tarsi /72/ VPR to go out

as'sente AG absent; (*fig*) faraway, vacant ▶ SMF absentee

assente'ismo SM absenteeism

assente'ista, -i, -e SM/F (*dal lavoro*) absentee

assen'tire /45/ VI: **~ (a)** to agree (to), assent (to)

as'senza [as'sɛntsa] SF absence

asse'rire /55/ VT to maintain, assert

asserragli'arsi [asserraʎ'ʎarsi] /27/ VPR: **~ (in)** to barricade o.s. (in)

asser'vire /55/ VT to enslave; (*fig: animo, passioni*) to subdue ■ **asservirsi** VPR: **asservirsi (a)** to submit (to)

asserzi'one [asser'tsjone] SF assertion

assesso'rato SM councillorship

asses'sore SM councillor

assesta'mento SM (*sistemazione*) arrangement; (*Edil, Geo*) settlement

asses'tare /72/ VT (*mettere in ordine*) to put in order, arrange ■ **assestarsi** VPR to settle in; (*Geo*) to settle; **~ un colpo a qn** to deal sb a blow

asse'tato, -a AG thirsty, parched

as'setto SM order, arrangement; (*Naut, Aer*) trim; **in ~ di guerra** on a war footing; **~ territoriale** country planning

assicu'rare /72/ VT (*accertare*) to ensure; (*infondere certezza*) to assure; (*fermare, legare*) to make fast, secure; (*fare un contratto di assicurazione*) to insure ■ **assicurarsi** VPR: **assicurarsi (di)** (*accertarsi*) to make sure (of); **assicurarsi (contro)** (*il furto ecc*) to insure o.s. (against)

assicu'rato, -a AG insured ▶ SF (*anche:* **lettera assicurata**) registered letter

assicura'tore, -'trice AG insurance *cpd* ▶ SM/F insurance agent; **società assicuratrice** insurance company

assicurazi'one [assikurat'tsjone] SF assurance; insurance; **~ multi-rischio** comprehensive insurance

assidera'mento SM exposure

asside'rare /72/ VT to freeze ■ **assiderarsi** VPR to freeze; **morire assiderato** to die of exposure

as'siduo, -a AG (*costante*) assiduous; (*regolare*) regular

assi'eme AV (*insieme*) together ▶ PREP: **~ a** (together) with

assil'lante AG (*dubbio, pensiero*) nagging; (*creditore*) pestering

assil'lare /72/ VT to pester, torment

as'sillo SM (*fig*) worrying thought

assimi'lare /72/ VT to assimilate

assimilazi'one [assimilat'tsjone] SF assimilation

assi'oma, -i SM axiom

assio'matico, -a, -ci, -che AG axiomatic

as'sise SFPL (*Dir*) assizes (BRIT); **corte d'~** court of assizes, ≈ crown court (BRIT)

assis'tente SMF assistant; **~ sociale** social worker; **~ universitario** (assistant) lecturer; **~ di volo** (*Aer*) steward (stewardess)

assis'tenza [assis'tɛntsa] SF assistance; **~ legale** legal aid; **~ ospedaliera** free hospital treatment; **~ sanitaria** health service; **~ sociale** welfare services *pl*

assistenzi'ale [assisten'tsjale] AG (*ente, organizzazione*) welfare *cpd*; (*opera*) charitable

assistenzia'lismo [assistentsja'lizmo] SM (*peg*) excessive state aid

as'sistere /11/ VT (*aiutare*) to assist, help; (*curare*) to treat ▶ VI: **~ (a qc)** (*essere presente*) to be present (at sth), attend (sth)

assis'tito, -a PP *di* **assistere**

'asso SM ace; **piantare qn in ~** to leave sb in the lurch

associ'are [asso't ʃare] /14/ VT to associate; (*rendere partecipe*): **~ qn a** (*affari*) to take sb into partnership in; (*partito*) to make sb a member of ■ **associarsi** VPR to enter into partnership; **associarsi a** to become a member of, join; (*dolori, gioie*) to share in; **~ qn alle carceri** to take sb to prison

associazi'one [assot ʃat'tsjone] SF association; (*Comm*) association, society; **~ di categoria** trade association; **~ a o per delinquere** (*Dir*) criminal association; **A~ Europea di Libero Scambio** European Free Trade Association, EFTA; **~ in partecipazione** (*Comm*) joint venture

asso'dare /72/ VT (*muro, posizione*) to strengthen; (*fatti, verità*) to ascertain

asso'dato, -a AG well-founded

assogget'tare [assoddʒet'tare] /72/ VT to subject, subjugate ■ **assoggettarsi** VPR: **assoggettarsi a** to submit to

asso'lato, -a AG sunny

assol'dare /72/ VT to recruit

as'solsi *ecc* VB *vedi* **assolvere**

as'solto, -a PP *di* **assolvere**

assoluta'mente AV absolutely

asso'luto, -a AG absolute

assoluzi'one [assolut'tsjone] SF (Dir) acquittal; (Rel) absolution

as'solvere /94/ VT (Dir) to acquit; (Rel) to absolve; (adempiere) to carry out, perform

assomigli'are [assomiʎ'ʎare] /27/ VI: ~ **a** to resemble, look like ■ **assomigliarsi** VPR to look alike; (nel carattere) to be alike

asson'nato, -a AG sleepy

asso'pirsi /55/ VPR to doze off

assor'bente AG absorbent ▶ SM: ~ **igienico/esterno** sanitary towel; ~ **interno** tampon

assor'bire /17/ VT to absorb; (fig: far proprio) to assimilate

assor'dante AG (rumore, musica) deafening

assor'dare /72/ VT to deafen

assorti'mento SM assortment

assor'tire /55/ VT (disporre) to arrange

assor'tito, -a AG assorted; (colori) matched, matching

as'sorto, -a AG absorbed, engrossed

assottigli'are [assottiʎ'ʎare] /27/ VT to make thin, thin; (aguzzare) to sharpen; (ridurre) to reduce ■ **assottigliarsi** VPR to grow thin; (fig: ridursi) to be reduced

assue'fare /41/ VT to accustom ■ **assuefarsi** VPR: **assuefarsi a** to get used to, accustom o.s. to

assue'fatto, -a PP di **assuefare**

assuefazi'one [assuefat'tsjone] SF (Med) addiction

as'sumere /12/ VT (impiegato) to take on, engage; (responsabilità) to assume, take upon o.s.; (contegno, espressione) to assume, put on; (droga) to consume

as'sunsi ecc VB vedi **assumere**

as'sunto, -a PP di **assumere** ▶ SM (tesi) proposition

assunzi'one [assun'tsjone] SF (di impiegati) employment, engagement; (Rel): **l'A~** the Assumption

assurdità SF INV absurdity; **dire delle ~** to talk nonsense

as'surdo, -a AG absurd

'asta SF pole; (modo di vendita) auction

as'tante SMF bystander

astante'ria SF casualty department

as'temio, -a AG teetotal ▶ SM/F teetotaller

aste'nersi /121/ VPR: ~ **(da)** to abstain (from), refrain (from); (Pol) to abstain (from)

astensi'one SF abstention

astensio'nista, -i, -e SM/F (Pol) abstentionist

aste'risco, -schi SM asterisk

aste'roide SM asteroid

'astice ['astitʃe] SM lobster

astigi'ano, -a [asti'dʒano] AG of (o from) Asti

astig'matico, -a, -ci, -che AG astigmatic

asti'nenza [asti'nɛntsa] SF abstinence; **essere in crisi di ~** to suffer from withdrawal symptoms

'astio SM rancour, resentment

asti'oso, -a AG resentful

astrat'tismo SM (Arte) abstract art

as'tratto, -a AG abstract

astrin'gente [astrin'dʒɛnte] AG, SM astringent

'astro SM star

'astro PREFISSO astro

astrolo'gia [astrolo'dʒia] SF astrology

astro'logico, -a, -ci, -che [astro'lɔdʒiko] AG astrological

as'trologo, -a, -ghi, -ghe SM/F astrologer

astro'nauta, -i, -e SM/F astronaut

astro'nautica SF astronautics sg

astro'nave SF space ship

astrono'mia SF astronomy

astro'nomico, -a, -ci, -che AG astronomic(al)

as'tronomo SM astronomer

as'truso, -a AG (discorso, ragionamento) abstruse

as'tuccio [as'tuttʃo] SM case, box, holder

as'tuto, -a AG astute, cunning, shrewd

as'tuzia [as'tuttsja] SF astuteness, shrewdness; (azione) trick

AT SIGLA = Asti

ATA SIGLA F = **Associazione Turistica Albergatori**

a'tavico, -a, -ci, -che AG atavistic

ate'ismo SM atheism

ate'lier [atə'lje] SM INV (laboratorio) workshop; (studio) studio; (sartoria) fashion house

A'tene SF Athens

ate'neo SM university

ateni'ese AG, SMF Athenian

'ateo, -a AG, SM/F atheist

a'tipico, -a, -ci, -che AG atypical

at'lante SM atlas; **i Monti dell'A~** the Atlas Mountains

at'lantico, -a, -ci, -che AG Atlantic ▶ SM: **l'A~**, **l'Oceano A~** the Atlantic, the Atlantic Ocean

at'leta, -i, -e SM/F athlete

at'letica SF athletics sg; ~ **leggera** track and field events pl; ~ **pesante** weightlifting and wrestling

atmos'fera SF atmosphere

atmos'ferico, -a, -ci, -che AG atmospheric

a'tollo SM atoll

a'tomico, -a, -ci, -che AG atomic; (nucleare) atomic, atom cpd, nuclear

atomizza'tore [atomiddza'tore] SM (di acqua, lacca) spray; (di profumo) atomizer

'atomo SM atom

'atono, -a AG (*Fonetica*) unstressed

'atrio SM entrance hall, lobby

a'troce [a'trotʃe] AG (*che provoca orrore*) dreadful; (*terribile*) atrocious

atrocità [atrotʃi'ta] SF INV atrocity

atro'fia SF atrophy

attacca'brighe [attakka'brige] SM INV/F INV quarrelsome person

attacca'mento SM (*fig*) attachment, affection

attac'cante SMF (*Sport*) forward

attacca'panni SM hook, peg; (*mobile*) hall stand

attac'care /20/ VT (*unire*) to attach; (*cucire*) to sew on; (*far aderire*) to stick (on); (*appendere*) to hang (up); (*assalire: anche fig*) to attack; (*iniziare*) to begin, start; (*fig: contagiare*) to pass on ▶ VI to stick, adhere ■ **attaccarsi** VPR to stick, adhere; (*trasmettersi per contagio*) to be contagious; (*afferrarsi*) **attaccarsi (a)** to cling (to); (*fig: affezionarsi*) to become attached (to); **~ discorso** to start a conversation; **con me non attacca!** that won't work with me!

attacca'ticcio, -a, -ci, -ce [attakka'tittʃo] AG sticky

attacca'tura SF (*di manica*) join; **~ (dei capelli)** hairline

at'tacco, -chi SM (*azione offensiva: anche fig*) attack; (*Med*) attack, fit; (*Sci*) binding; (*Elettr*) socket; **~ informatico** cyber attack

attanagli'are [attanaʎ'ʎare] /27/ VT (*anche fig*) to grip

attar'darsi /72/ VPR: **~ a fare qc** (*fermarsi*) to stop to do sth; (*stare più a lungo*) to stay behind to do sth

attec'chire [attek'kire] /55/ VI (*pianta*) to take root; (*fig*) to catch on

atteggia'mento [atteddʒa'mento] SM attitude

atteggi'arsi [atted'dʒarsi] /62/ VPR: **~ a** to pose as

attem'pato, -a AG elderly

atten'dente SM (*Mil*) orderly, batman

at'tendere /120/ VT to wait for, await ▶ VI: **~ a** to attend to

atten'dibile AG (*scusa, storia*) credible; (*fonte, testimone, notizia*) reliable; (*persona*) trustworthy

atte'nersi /121/ VPR: **~ a** to keep o stick to

atten'tare /72/ VI: **~ a** to make an attempt on

atten'tato SM attack; **~ alla vita di qn** attempt on sb's life

attenta'tore, -'trice SM/F bomber; **~ suicida** suicide bomber

at'tento, -a AG attentive; (*accurato*) careful, thorough ▶ ESCL be careful!; **stare ~ a qc** to pay attention to sth; **attenti!** (*Mil*) attention!; **attenti al cane** beware of the dog

attenu'ante SF (*Dir*) extenuating circumstance

attenu'are /72/ VT to alleviate, ease; (*diminuire*) to reduce ■ **attenuarsi** VPR to ease, abate

attenuazi'one [attenuat'tsjone] SF alleviation; easing; reduction

attenzi'one [atten'tsjone] SF attention ▶ ESCL watch out!, be careful! ■ **attenzioni** SFPL (*premure*) attentions; **fare ~ a** to watch out for; **coprire qn di attenzioni** to lavish attention on sb

atter'raggio [atter'raddʒo] SM landing; **~ di fortuna** emergency landing

atter'rare /72/ VT to bring down ▶ VI to land

atter'rire /55/ VT to terrify

at'tesa SF waiting; (*tempo trascorso aspettando*) wait; **essere in ~ di qc** to be waiting for sth; **in ~ di una vostra risposta** (*Comm*) awaiting your reply; **restiamo in ~ di Vostre ulteriori notizie** (*Comm*) we look forward to hearing (further) from you

at'tesi *ecc* VB *vedi* **attendere**

at'teso, -a PP *di* **attendere**

attes'tare /72/ VT: **~ qc/che** to testify to sth/(to the fact) that

attes'tato SM certificate

attestazi'one [attestat'tsjone] SF (*certificato*) certificate; (*dichiarazione*) statement

'attico, -ci SM attic

at'tiguo, -a AG adjacent, adjoining

attil'lato, -a AG (*vestito*) close-fitting, tight; (*persona*) dressed up

'attimo SM moment; **in un ~** in a moment

atti'nente AG: **~ a** relating to, concerning

atti'nenza [atti'nɛntsa] SF connection

at'tingere [at'tindʒere] /37/ VT: **~ a o da** (*acqua*) to draw from; (*denaro, notizie*) to obtain from

at'tinto, -a PP *di* **attingere**

atti'rare /72/ VT to attract; **attirarsi delle critiche** to incur criticism

atti'tudine SF (*disposizione*) aptitude; (*atteggiamento*) attitude

atti'vare /72/ VT to activate; (*far funzionare*) to set going, start

atti'vista, -i, -e SM/F activist

attività SF INV activity; (*Comm*) assets *pl*; **~ liquide** (*Comm*) liquid assets

at'tivo, -a AG active; (*Comm*) profit-making, credit *cpd* ▶ SM (*Comm*) assets *pl*; **in ~** in credit; **chiudere in ~** to show a profit; **avere qc al proprio ~** (*fig*) to have sth to one's credit

attiz'zare [attit'tsare] /72/ VT (*fuoco*) to poke; (*fig*) to stir up

attizza'toio [attittsa'tojo] SM poker

'atto, -a AG: **~ a** fit for, capable of ▶ SM act; (*azione, gesto*) action, act, deed; (*Dir: documento*) deed, document ■ **atti** SMPL (*di congressi ecc*) proceedings; **essere in ~** to be under way; **mettere in ~** to put into action; **fare ~ di fare qc** to make as if to do sth; **all'~ pratico** in practice; **dare ~ a qn di qc** to give sb credit for sth; **~ di nascita/morte** birth/death certificate; **~ di proprietà** title deed; **~ pubblico** official document; **~ di vendita** bill of sale; **atti osceni (in luogo pubblico)** (*Dir*) indecent exposure; **atti verbali** transactions

at'tonito, -a AG dumbfounded, astonished

attorcigli'are [attortʃiʎ'ʎare] /27/ VT, **attorcigli'arsi** VPR to twist

at'tore, -'trice SM/F actor (actress)

attorni'are /19/ VT (*circondare*) to surround ▪ **attorniarsi** VPR: **attorniarsi di** to surround o.s. with

at'torno AV round, around, about ▸ PREP: **~ a** round, around, about

attrac'care /20/ VT, VI (*Naut*) to dock, berth

at'tracco, -chi SM (*Naut: manovra*) docking, berthing; (: *luogo*) berth

at'trae *ecc* VB *vedi* **attrarre**

attra'ente AG attractive

at'traggo *ecc* VB *vedi* **attrarre**

at'trarre /123/ VT to attract

at'trassi *ecc* VB *vedi* **attrarre**

attrat'tiva SF attraction, charm

at'tratto, -a PP *di* **attrarre**

attraversa'mento SM crossing; **~ pedonale** pedestrian crossing

attraver'sare /72/ VT to cross; (*città, bosco, fig: periodo*) to go through; (*fiume*) to run through

attra'verso PREP through; (*da una parte all'altra*) across

attrazi'one [attrat'tsjone] SF attraction

attrez'zare [attret'tsare] /72/ VT to equip; (*Naut*) to rig

attrezza'tura [attrettsa'tura] SF equipment *no pl*; rigging; **attrezzature per uffici** office equipment

at'trezzo [at'trettso] SM tool, instrument; (*Sport*) piece of equipment

attribu'ire /55/ VT: **~ qc a qn** (*assegnare*) to give o award sth to sb; (*quadro ecc*) to attribute sth to sb

attri'buto SM attribute

at'trice [at'tritʃe] SF *vedi* **attore**

at'trito SM (*anche fig*) friction

attu'abile AG feasible

attuabilità SF feasibility

attu'ale AG (*presente*) present; (*di attualità*) topical; (*che è in atto*) actual

---
Do not translate the Italian word **attuale** by *actual*.

---

attualità SF INV topicality; (*avvenimento*) current event; **notizie d'~** (*TV*) the news *sg*

attualiz'zare [attualid'dzare] /72/ VT to update, bring up to date

attual'mente AV at the moment, at present

attu'are /72/ VT to carry out ▪ **attuarsi** VPR to be realized

attuazi'one [attuat'tsjone] SF carrying out

attu'tire /55/ VT to deaden, reduce ▪ **attutirsi** VPR to die down

A.U. ABBR = **allievo ufficiale**

au'dace [au'datʃe] AG audacious, daring, bold; (*provocante*) provocative; (*sfacciato*) impudent, bold

au'dacia [au'datʃa] SF audacity, daring; boldness; provocativeness; impudence

'audio SM (*TV, Radio, Cine*) sound

audiocas'setta SF (audio) cassette

audiodescri'zione [audjodeskrit'tsjone] SF audio description

audio'guida SF audioguide

audio'leso, -a SM/F person who is hard of hearing

audiovi'sivo, -a AG audiovisual

audi'torio SM, **audi'torium** SM INV auditorium

audizi'one [audit'tsjone] SF hearing; (*Mus*) audition

'auge ['audʒe] SF (*della gloria, carriera*) height, peak; **essere in ~** to be at the top

augu'rale AG: **messaggio ~** greeting; **biglietto ~** greetings card

augu'rare /72/ VT to wish; **augurarsi qc** to hope for sth

au'gurio SM (*presagio*) omen; (*voto di benessere ecc*) (good) wish; **essere di buon/cattivo ~** to be of good omen/be ominous ▪ **auguri** SMPL best wishes; **fare gli auguri a qn** to give sb one's best wishes; **tanti auguri!** best wishes!; (*per compleanno*) happy birthday!

'aula SF (*scolastica*) classroom; (*universitaria*) lecture theatre; (*di edificio pubblico*) hall; **~ magna** main hall; **~ del tribunale** courtroom

aumen'tare /72/ VT, VI to increase; **~ di peso** (*persona*) to put on weight; **la produzione è aumentata del 50%** production has increased by 50%

au'mento SM increase

'aureo, -a AG (*di oro*) gold *cpd*; (*fig: colore, periodo*) golden

au'reola SF halo

au'rora SF dawn

ausili'are AG, SM/F auxiliary

au'silio SM aid

auspi'cabile AG desirable

auspi'care /20/ VT to call for, express a desire for

aus'picio [aus'pitʃo] SM omen; (*protezione*)

patronage; **sotto gli auspici di** under the auspices of; **è di buon ~** it augurs well

austerità SF INV austerity

aus'tero, -a AG austere

aus'trale AG southern

Aus'tralia SF: **l'~** Australia

australi'ano, -a AG, SM/F Australian

'Austria SF: **l'~** Austria

aus'triaco, -a, -ci, -che AG, SM/F Austrian

au'tarchico, -a, -ci, -che [au'tarkiko] AG (*sistema*) self-sufficient, autarkic; (*prodotto*) home *cpd*, home-produced

'aut 'aut SM INV ultimatum

autenti'care /**20**/ VT to authenticate

autenticità [autentitʃi'ta] SF authenticity

au'tentico, -a, -ci, -che AG (*quadro, firma*) authentic, genuine; (*fatto*) true, genuine

au'tista, -i SM driver; (*personale*) chauffeur

'auto SF INV car; **~ blu** official car

autoabbron'zante AG self-tanning

autoade'sivo, -a AG self-adhesive ▶ SM sticker

autoartico'lato SM articulated lorry (*BRIT*), semi (trailer) (*US*)

autobiogra'fia SF autobiography

autobio'grafico, -a, -ci, -che AG autobiographic(al)

auto'blinda SF armoured (*BRIT*) o armored (*US*) car

auto'bomba SF INV car carrying a bomb; **l'~ si trovava a pochi metri** the car bomb was a few metres away

auto'botte SF tanker

'autobus SM INV bus

autocari'cabile AG: **scheda ~** top-up card

auto'carro SM lorry (*BRIT*), truck

autocertificazi'one [autotʃertifikat'tsjone] SF self-declaration

autocis'terna [autotʃis'tɛrna] SF tanker

autoco'lonna SF convoy

autocon'trollo SM self-control

autocopia'tivo, -a AG: **carta autocopiativa** carbonless paper

autocorri'era SF coach, bus

auto'cratico, -a, -ci, -che AG autocratic

auto'critica, -che SF self-criticism

au'toctono, -a AG, SM/F native

autodemolizi'one [autodemolit'tsjone] SF breaker's yard (*BRIT*), wrecking yard (*US*)

autodi'datta, -i, -e SM/F autodidact, self-taught person

autodi'fesa SF self-defence

autodistrut'tivo, -a AG self-destructive

autoferrotranvi'ario, -a AG public transport *cpd*

autogesti'one [autodʒes'tjone] SF worker management

autoges'tito, -a [autodʒes'tito] AG under worker management

auto'gol SM INV own goal

au'tografo, -a AG, SM autograph

auto'grill® SM INV motorway café (*BRIT*), roadside restaurant (*US*)

autoim'mune AG autoimmune

autolesio'nismo SM (*fig*) self-destruction; (*Med*) self-harm

auto'linea SF bus route

au'toma, -i SM automaton

auto'matico, -a, -ci, -che AG automatic ▶ SM (*bottone*) snap fastener; (*fucile*) automatic; **selezione automatica** (*Tel*) direct dialling

automazi'one [automat'tsjone] SF: **~ delle procedure d'ufficio** office automation

automedicazi'one [automedikat'tsjone] SF (*medicine, farmaci*): **medicinale di ~** self-medication

auto'mezzo [auto'mɛddzo] SM motor vehicle

auto'mobile SF (motor) car; **~ da corsa** racing car (*BRIT*), race car (*US*)

automobi'lismo SM (*gen*) motoring; (*Sport*) motor racing

automobi'lista, -i, -e SM/F motorist

automobi'listico, -a, -ci, -che AG car *cpd* (*BRIT*), automobile *cpd* (*US*); (*sport*) motor *cpd*

autono'leggio [autono'leddʒo] SM car hire (*BRIT*), car rental

autono'mia SF autonomy; (*di volo*) range

au'tonomo, -a AG autonomous; (*sindacato, pensiero*) independent

auto'parco, -chi SM (*parcheggio*) car park (*BRIT*), parking lot (*US*); (*insieme di automezzi*) transport fleet

auto'pompa SF fire engine

autop'sia SF post-mortem (examination), autopsy

auto'radio SF INV (*apparecchio*) car radio; (*autoveicolo*) radio car

au'tore, -'trice SM/F author; **l'~ del furto** the person who committed the robbery; **diritti d'~** copyright *sg*; (*compenso*) royalties

autoreg'gente [autored'dʒente] AG: **calze autoreggenti** hold ups

autoregolamentazi'one [autoregolament-at'tsjone] SF self-regulation

auto'revole AG authoritative; (*persona*) influential

autoricari'cabile AG: **scheda ~** top-up card

autori'messa SF garage

autorità SF INV authority

autori'tratto SM self-portrait

autoriz'zare [autorid'dzare] /**72**/ VT (*permettere*)

to authorize, give permission for; (*giustificare*) to allow, sanction

autorizzazi'one [autoriddzat'tsjone] SF authorization; **~ a procedere** (*Dir*) authorization to proceed

autos'catto SM (*Fot*) timer

autos'contro SM dodgem car (*BRIT*), bumper car (*US*)

autoscu'ola SF driving school

autosno'dato SM articulated vehicle

autos'tima SF self-esteem

autos'top SM hitchhiking

autostop'pista, -i, -e SM/F hitchhiker

autos'trada SF motorway (*BRIT*), highway (*US*); **~ informatica** information superhighway

> You have to pay to use Italian motorways. To avoid queuing at tollbooths, you can buy an automatic payment card (*Telepass*) in advance. They are indicated by an *A* followed by a number on a green sign. The speed limit on Italian motorways is 130 kph.

autosuffici'ente [autosuffi'tʃɛnte] AG self-sufficient

autosuffici'enza [autosuffi'tʃɛntsa] SF self-sufficiency

auto'treno SM articulated lorry (*BRIT*), semi (trailer) (*US*)

autove'icolo SM motor vehicle

auto'velox® SM INV (police) speed camera

autovet'tura SF (motor) car

autun'nale AG (*di autunno*) autumn *cpd*; (*da autunno*) autumnal

au'tunno SM autumn

AV SIGLA = **Avellino**

aval'lare /72/ VT (*Finanza*) to guarantee; (*fig: sostenere*) to back; (: *confermare*) to confirm

a'vallo SM (*Finanza*) guarantee

avam'braccio [avam'brattʃo] (*pl(f)* **avambraccia**) SFPL forearm

avam'posto SM (*Mil*) outpost

A'vana SF: **l'~** Havana

a'vana SM INV (*sigaro*) Havana (cigar); (*colore*) Havana brown

avangu'ardia SF vanguard; (*Arte*) avant-garde

avansco'perta SF (*Mil*) reconnaissance; **andare in ~** to reconnoitre

a'vanti AV (*stato in luogo*) in front; (*moto: andare, venire*) forward; (*tempo: prima*) before ▶ PREP (*luogo*): **~ a** before, in front of; (*tempo*) **~ Cristo** before Christ ▶ ESCL (*entrate*) come (*o* go) in!; (*Mil*) forward!; (*coraggio*) come on! ▶ SM INV (*Sport*) forward; **il giorno ~** the day before; **~ e indietro** backwards and forwards; **andare ~** to go forward; (*continuare*) to go on; (*precedere*) to go (on) ahead; (*orologio*) to be fast; **essere ~ negli**

studi to be well advanced with one's studies; **mandare ~ la famiglia** to provide for one's family; **mandare ~ un'azienda** to run a business; **~ il prossimo!** next please!

avan'treno SM (*Aut*) front chassis

avanza'mento [avantsa'mento] SM (*gen*) advance; (*fig*) progress; promotion

avan'zare [avan'tsare] /72/ VT (*spostare in avanti*) to move forward, advance; (*domanda*) to put forward; (*promuovere*) to promote; (*essere creditore*): **~ qc da qn** to be owed sth by sb ▶ VI (*andare avanti*) to move forward, advance; (*fig: progredire*) to make progress; (*essere d'avanzo*) to be left, remain; **basta e avanza** that's more than enough

avan'zato, -a [avan'tsato] AG (*teoria, tecnica*) advanced ▶ SF (*Mil*) advance; **in età avanzata** advanced in years, up in years

a'vanzo [a'vantso] SM (*residuo*) remains *pl*, leftovers *pl*; (*Mat*) remainder; (*Comm*) surplus; (*eccedenza di bilancio*) profit carried forward; **averne d'~ di qc** to have more than enough of sth; **~ di cassa** cash in hand; **~ di galera** (*fig*) jailbird

ava'ria SF (*guasto*) damage; (: *meccanico*) breakdown

avari'ato, -a AG (*merce*) damaged; (*cibo*) off

ava'rizia [ava'rittsja] SF avarice; **crepi l'~!** to hang with the expense!

a'varo, -a AG avaricious, miserly ▶ SM/F miser

a'vena SF oats *pl*

---

a'vere

/13/ SM (*Comm*) credit; **gli averi** (*ricchezze*) wealth *sg*, possessions

▶ VT **1** (*possedere*) to have; **ha due bambini/una bella casa** she has (got) two children/a lovely house; **ha i capelli lunghi** he has (got) long hair; **non ho da mangiare/bere** I've (got) nothing to eat/drink, I don't have anything to eat/drink

2 (*indossare*) to wear, have on; **aveva una maglietta rossa** he was wearing *o* he had on a red T-shirt; **ha gli occhiali** he wears *o* has glasses

3 (*ricevere*) to get; **hai avuto l'assegno?** did you get *o* have you had the cheque?

4 (*età, dimensione*) to be; **la stanza ha 3 metri di lunghezza** the room is 3 metres in length; **ha 9 anni** he is 9 (years old); *vedi* **fame; paura; sonno** *ecc*

5 (*tempo*): **quanti ne abbiamo oggi?** what's the date today?; **ne hai per molto?** will you be long?

6 (*fraseologia*): **avercela con qn** to be angry with sb; **cos'hai?** what's wrong *o* what's the matter (with you)?; **non ha niente a che vedere** *o* **fare con me** it's got nothing to do with me

▶ VB AUS **1** to have; **aver bevuto/mangiato** to

have drunk/eaten; **l'ho già visto** I have seen it already; **l'ho visto ieri** I saw it yesterday; **ci ha creduto?** did he believe it?

2 (+ *da* + *infinito*): **avere da fare qc** to have to do sth; **non ho niente da dire** I have nothing to say; **non hai che da chiederlo** you only have to ask him

avi'ario, -a AG bird *cpd*; **influenza aviaria** bird flu

avia'tore, -'trice SM/F aviator, pilot

aviazi'one [avjat'tsjone] SF aviation; (*Mil*) air force; **~ civile** civil aviation

avicol'tura SF bird breeding; (*di pollame*) poultry farming

avidità SF eagerness; greed

'avido, -a AG eager; (*peg*) greedy

avi'ere SM (*Mil*) airman

avitami'nosi SF vitamin deficiency

'avo SM (*antenato*) ancestor; **i nostri avi** our ancestors

avo'cado SM avocado

a'vorio SM ivory

a'vulso, -a AG: **parole avulse dal contesto** words out of context; **~ dalla società** (*fig*) cut off from society

Avv. ABBR = **avvocato**

avva'lersi /126/ VPR: **~ di** to avail o.s. of

avvalla'mento SM sinking *no pl*; (*effetto*) depression

avvalo'rare /72/ VT to confirm

avvantaggi'are [avvantad'dʒare] /62/ VT to favour (*BRIT*), favor (*US*) ■ **avvantaggiarsi** VPR (*trarre vantaggio*): **avvantaggiarsi di** to take advantage of; **avvantaggiarsi negli affari/sui concorrenti** (*prevalere*) to get ahead in business/ of one's competitors

avve'dersi /127/ VPR: **~ di qn/qc** to notice sb/sth

avve'duto, -a AG (*accorto*) prudent; (*scaltro*) astute

avvelena'mento SM poisoning

avvele'nare /72/ VT to poison

avve'nente AG attractive, charming

avve'nenza [avve'nentsa] SF good looks *pl*

av'vengo *ecc* VB *vedi* **avvenire**

avveni'mento SM event

avve'nire /128/ VI, VB IMPERS to happen, occur ▶ SM future

av'venni *ecc* VB *vedi* **avvenire**

avven'tarsi /72/ VPR: **~ su** *o* **contro qn/qc** to hurl o.s. *o* rush at sb/sth

avven'tato, -a AG rash, reckless

avven'tizio, -a [avven'tittsjo] AG (*impiegato*) temporary; (*guadagno*) casual

av'vento SM advent, coming; (*Rel*): **l'A~** Advent

avven'tore SM customer

avven'tura SF adventure; (*amorosa*) affair; **avere spirito d'~** to be adventurous

avventu'rarsi /72/ VPR to venture

avventuri'ero, -a SM/F adventurer (adventuress)

avventu'roso, -a AG adventurous

avve'nuto, -a PP *di* **avvenire**

avve'rarsi /72/ VPR to come true

av'verbio SM adverb

avverrò *ecc* VB *vedi* **avvenire**

avver'sare /72/ VT to oppose

avver'sario, -a AG opposing ▶ SM/F opponent, adversary

avversi'one SF aversion

avversità SF INV adversity, misfortune

av'verso, -a AG (*contrario*) contrary; (*sfavorevole*) unfavourable (*BRIT*), unfavorable (*US*)

avver'tenza [avver'tentsa] SF (*ammonimento*) warning; (*cautela*) care; (*premessa*) foreword ■ **avvertenze** SFPL (*istruzioni per l'uso*) instructions

avverti'mento SM warning

avver'tire /45/ VT (*avvisare*) to warn; (*rendere consapevole*) to inform, notify; (*percepire*) to feel

av'vezzo, -a [av'vettso] AG: **~ a** used to

avvia'mento SM (*atto*) starting; (*effetto*) start; (*Aut*) starting; (: *dispositivo*) starter; (*Comm*) goodwill

avvi'are /60/ VT (*mettere sul cammino*) to direct; (*impresa, trattative*) to begin, start; (*motore*) to start ■ **avviarsi** VPR to set off, set out

avvicenda'mento [avvitʃenda'mento] SM alternation; (*Agr*) rotation; **c'è molto ~ di personale** there is a high turnover of staff

avvicen'dare [avvitʃen'dare] /72/ VT, **avvicen'darsi** VPR to alternate

avvicina'mento [avvitʃina'mento] SM approach

avvici'nare [avvitʃi'nare] /72/ VT to bring near; (*trattare con: persona*) to approach ■ **avvicinarsi** VPR: **avvicinarsi (a qn/qc)** to approach (sb/ sth), draw near (to sb/sth); (*somigliare*) to be similar (to sb/sth), be close (to sb/sth)

avvi'lente AG (*umiliante*) humiliating; (*scoraggiante*) discouraging, disheartening

avvili'mento SM humiliation; disgrace; discouragement

avvi'lire /55/ VT (*umiliare*) to humiliate; (*degradare*) to disgrace; (*scoraggiare*) to dishearten, discourage ■ **avvilirsi** VPR (*abbattersi*) to lose heart

avvi'lito, -a AG discouraged

avvilup'pare /72/ VT (*avvolgere*) to wrap up; (*ingarbugliare*) to entangle

avvinaz'zato, -a [avvinat'tsato] AG drunk

avvin'cente [avvin'tʃente] AG (*film, racconto*) enthralling

av'vincere [av'vintʃere] /**129**/ vt to charm, enthral

avvinghi'are [avvin'gjare] /**19**/ vt to clasp ▪ **avvinghiarsi** vpr: **avvinghiarsi a** to cling to

av'vinsi *ecc* vb *vedi* **avvincere**

av'vinto, -a pp *di* **avvincere**

av'vio sm start, beginning; **dare l'~ a qc** to start sth off; **prendere l'~** to get going, get under way

avvi'saglia [avvi'zaʎʎa] sf (*sintomo: di temporale ecc*) sign; (*di malattia*) manifestation, sign, symptom; (*scaramuccia*) skirmish

avvi'sare /**72**/ vt (*far sapere*) to inform; (*mettere in guardia*) to warn

avvisa'tore sm (*apparecchio d'allarme*) alarm; **~ acustico** horn; **~ d'incendio** fire alarm

av'viso sm warning; (*annuncio*) announcement; (*affisso*) notice; (*inserzione pubblicitaria*) advertisement; **a mio ~** in my opinion; **mettere qn sull'~** to put sb on their guard; **fino a nuovo ~** until further notice; **~ di chiamata** (*servizio*) call waiting; (*segnale*) call waiting signal; **~ di consegna/spedizione** (*Comm*) delivery/consignment note; **~ di garanzia** (*Dir*) notification (*of impending investigation and of the right to name a defence laywer*); **~ di pagamento** (*Comm*) payment advice

avvista'mento sm sighting

avvis'tare /**72**/ vt to sight

avvi'tare /**72**/ vt to screw down (*o* in)

avviz'zire [avvit'tsire] /**55**/ vi to wither

avvo'cato, -'essa sm/f (*Dir*) barrister (*BRIT*), lawyer; (*fig*) defender, advocate; **~ del diavolo, fare l'~ del diavolo** to play devil's advocate; **~ difensore** counsel for the defence; **~ di parte civile** counsel for the plaintiff

av'volgere [av'vɔldʒere] /**96**/ vt to roll up; (*bobina*) to wind up; (*avviluppare*) to wrap up ▪ **avvolgersi** vpr (*avvilupparsi*) to wrap o.s. up

avvol'gibile [avvol'dʒibile] sm roller blind (*BRIT*), blind

avvolgi'mento sm winding

av'volsi *ecc* vb *vedi* **avvolgere**

av'volto, -a pp *di* **avvolgere**

avvol'toio sm vulture

aza'lea [addza'lɛa] sf azalea

Azerbaigi'an [addzɛrbai'dʒan] sm Azerbaijan

azerbaig'iano, -a [addzɛrbai'dʒano] ag Azerbaijani ▪ sm/f (*abitante*) Azerbaijani ▪ sm (*Ling*) Azerbaijani

a'zero, -a [ad'dzɛro] sm/f Azeri

azi'enda [ad'dzjɛnda] sf business, firm, concern; **~ agricola** farm; **~ (autonoma) di soggiorno** tourist board; **~ a partecipazione statale** business in which the State has a financial interest; **aziende pubbliche** public corporations

azien'dale [addzjen'dale] ag company *cpd*; **organizzazione ~** business administration

azio'nare [attsjo'nare] /**72**/ vt to activate

azio'nario, -a [attsjo'narjo] ag share *cpd*; **capitale ~** share capital; **mercato ~** stock market

azi'one [at'tsjone] sf action; (*Comm*) share; **~ sindacale** industrial action; **azioni preferenziali** preference shares (*BRIT*), preferred stock *sg* (*US*)

azio'nista, -i, -e [attsjo'nista] sm/f (*Comm*) shareholder

a'zoto [ad'dzɔto] sm nitrogen

az'teco, -a, -ci, -che [as'tɛko] ag, sm/f Aztec

azzan'nare [attsan'nare] /**72**/ vt to sink one's teeth into

azzar'dare [addzar'dare] /**72**/ vt (*soldi, vita*) to risk, hazard; (*domanda, ipotesi*) to hazard, venture ▪ **azzardarsi** vpr: **azzardarsi a fare** to dare (to) do

azzar'dato, -a [addzar'dato] ag (*impresa*) risky; (*risposta*) rash

az'zardo [ad'dzardo] sm risk; **gioco d'~** game of chance

azzec'care [attsek'kare] /**20**/ vt (*bersaglio*) to hit, strike; (*risposta, pronostico*) to get right; (*fig: indovinare*) to guess

azzera'mento [addzera'mento] sm (*Inform*) reset

azze'rare [addze'rare] /**72**/ vt (*Mat, Fisica*) to make equal to zero, reduce to zero; (*Tecn: strumento*) to (re)set to zero

'azzimo, -a ['addzimo] ag unleavened ▪ sm unleavened bread

azzop'pare [attsop'pare] /**72**/ vt to lame, make lame

Az'zorre [ad'dzorre] sfpl: **le ~** the Azores

azzuf'farsi [attsuf'farsi] /**72**/ vpr to come to blows

az'zurro, -a [ad'dzurro] ag blue ▪ sm (*colore*) blue; **gli azzurri** (*Sport*) the Italian national team

azzur'rognolo, -a [addzur'roɲɲolo] ag bluish

Bb

B, b [bi] SM O F INV (*lettera*) B, b; **B come Bologna** ≈ B for Benjamin (*BRIT*), ≈ B for Baker (*US*)

BA SIGLA = **Bari**

ba'bau SM INV ogre, bogey man

bab'beo SM simpleton

'babbo SM (*col*) dad, daddy; **B~ Natale** Father Christmas

bab'buccia, -ce [bab'buttʃa] SF slipper; (*per neonati*) bootee

babbu'ino SM baboon

babilo'nese AG, SMF Babylonian

Babi'lonia SF Babylonia

ba'bordo SM (*Naut*) port side

baby'sitter ['beɪbɪsɪter] SM INV/F INV baby-sitter

ba'cato, -a AG worm-eaten, rotten; (*fig: mente*) diseased; (: *persona*) corrupt

'bacca, -che SF berry

baccalà SM dried salted cod; (*fig: peg*) dummy

bac'cano SM din, clamour (*BRIT*), clamor (*US*)

bac'cello [bat'tʃɛllo] SM pod

bac'chetta [bak'ketta] SF (*verga*) stick, rod; (*di direttore d'orchestra*) baton; (*di tamburo*) drumstick; **comandare a ~** to rule with a rod of iron; **~ magica** magic wand

ba'checa, -che [ba'kɛka] SF (*mobile*) showcase, display case; (*Università, in ufficio*) notice board (*BRIT*), bulletin board (*US*)

bacia'mano [batʃa'mano] SM: **fare il ~ a qn** to kiss sb's hand

baci'are [ba'tʃare] /14/ VT to kiss ■ **baciarsi** VPR to kiss (one another)

ba'cillo [ba'tʃillo] SM bacillus, germ

baci'nella [batʃi'nɛlla] SF basin

ba'cino [ba'tʃino] SM basin; (*Mineralogia*) field, bed; (*Anat*) pelvis; (*Naut*) dock; **~ carbonifero** coalfield; **~ di carenaggio** dry dock; **~ petrolifero** oilfield; **~ d'utenza** catchment area

'bacio ['batʃo] SM kiss

back'up [be'kap] SM INV (*Inform*) backup

'baco, -chi SM worm; **~ da seta** silkworm

'bada SF: **tenere qn a ~** (*tener d'occhio*) to keep an eye on sb; (*tenere a distanza*) to hold sb at bay

ba'dante SMF care worker

ba'dare /72/ VI (*fare attenzione*) to take care, be careful; **~ a** (*occuparsi di*) to look after, take care of; (*dar ascolto*) to pay attention to; **è un tipo che non bada a spese** money is no object to him; **bada ai fatti tuoi!** mind your own business!

ba'dia SF abbey

ba'dile SM shovel

'baffi SMPL moustache *sg*, mustache *sg* (*US*); (*di animale*) whiskers; **leccarsi i ~** to lick one's lips; **ridere sotto i ~** to laugh up one's sleeve

bagagli'aio [bagaʎ'ʎajo] SM luggage van (*BRIT*) o car (*US*); (*Aut*) boot (*BRIT*), trunk (*US*)

ba'gaglio [ba'gaʎʎo] SM luggage *no pl*, baggage *no pl*; **fare/disfare i bagagli** to pack/unpack; **~ a mano** hand luggage

> *Bagagli* si traduce con **luggage**, non prende la **~s** finale e si usa con il verbo al singolare.
> *I suoi bagagli sono troppo pesanti.* **Your luggage is too heavy.**
> Quando si deve tradurre una sola borsa al singolare si usa **piece of luggage**.
> *un solo bagaglio a mano* **only one piece of hand luggage**

bagat'tella SF trifle, trifling matter

Bag'dad SF Baghdad

baggia'nata [baddʒa'nata] SF foolish action; **dire baggianate** to talk nonsense

bagli'ore [baʎ'ʎore] SM flash, dazzling light; **un ~ di speranza** a (sudden) ray of hope

ba'gnante [baɲ'ɲante] SMF bather

ba'gnare [baɲ'ɲare] /15/ VT to wet; (*inzuppare*) to soak; (*innaffiare*) to water; (*fiume*) to flow through; (: *mare*) to wash, bathe; (*brindare*) to drink to, toast ■ **bagnarsi** VPR to get wet; (*al mare*) to go swimming o bathing; (*in vasca*) to have a bath

ba'gnato, -a [baɲ'ɲato] AG wet; **era come un pulcino ~** he looked like a drowned rat

ba'gnino, -a [baɲ'ɲino] SM/F lifeguard

'bagno ['baɲɲo] SM bathroom; (*locale*) (*toilette*) toilet ■ **bagni** SMPL (*stabilimento*) baths; **fare il ~** to have a bath; (*nel mare*) to go swimming *o* bathing; **fare il ~ a qn** to give sb a bath; **mettere a ~** to soak

bagnoma'ria [baɲɲoma'ria] SM: **cuocere a ~** to cook in a double saucepan (*BRIT*) *o* double boiler (*US*)

bagnoschi'uma [baɲɲo'skjuma] SM INV bubble bath

Ba'hama [ba'ama] SFPL: **le ~** the Bahamas

Bah'rein [ba'rein] SM: **il ~** Bahrain *o* Bahrein

'baia SF bay

baio'netta SF bayonet

'baita SF mountain hut

balaus'trata SF balustrade

balbet'tare /72/ VI to stutter, stammer; (*bimbo*) to babble ▶ VT to stammer out

bal'buzie [bal'buttsje] SF stammer

balbuzi'ente [balbut'tsjɛnte] AG stuttering, stammering

Bal'cani SMPL: **i ~** the Balkans

bal'canico, -a, -ci, -che AG Balkan

bal'cone SM balcony

baldac'chino [baldak'kino] SM canopy; **letto a ~** four-poster (bed)

bal'danza [bal'dantsa] SF self-confidence; boldness

'baldo, -a AG bold, daring

bal'doria SF: **fare ~** to have a riotous time

Bale'ari SFPL: **le isole ~** the Balearic Islands

ba'lena SF whale

bale'nare /72/ VB IMPERS: **balena** there's lightning ▶ VI to flash; **mi balenò un'idea** an idea flashed through my mind

baleni'era SF (*per la caccia*) whaler, whaling ship

ba'leno SM flash of lightning; **in un ~** in a flash

ba'lera SF (*locale*) dance hall; (*pista*) dance floor

ba'lestra SF crossbow

'balia¹ SF wet-nurse; **~ asciutta** nanny

ba'lia² SF: **in ~ di** at the mercy of; **essere lasciato in ~ di se stesso** to be left to one's own devices

ba'lilla SM INV (*Storia*) member of Fascist youth group

ba'listico, -a, -ci, -che AG ballistic ▶ SF ballistics *sg*; **perito ~** ballistics expert

'balla SF (*di merci*) bale; (*fandonia*) (tall) story

bal'labile SM dance number, dance tune

bal'lare /72/ VT, VI to dance

bal'lata SF ballad

balla'toio SM (*terrazzina*) gallery

balle'rina SF dancer; ballet dancer; (*scarpa*) pump, ballet shoe; **~ di rivista** chorus girl

balle'rino SM dancer; ballet dancer

bal'letto SM ballet

'ballo SM dance; (*azione*) dancing *no pl*; **~ in maschera** *o* **mascherato** fancy-dress ball; **essere in ~** (*fig: persona*) to be involved; (: *cosa*) to be at stake; **tirare in ~ qc** to bring sth up, raise sth

ballot'taggio [ballot'taddʒo] SM (*Pol*) second ballot

balne'are AG seaside *cpd*; (*stagione*) bathing

ba'locco, -chi SM toy

ba'lordo, -a AG stupid, senseless

bal'samico, -a, -ci, -che AG (*aria, brezza*) balmy; **pomata balsamica** balsam

'balsamo SM (*aroma*) balsam; (*lenimento, fig*) balm; (*per capelli*) conditioner

'baltico, -a, -ci, -che AG Baltic; **il (mar) B~** the Baltic (Sea)

balu'ardo SM bulwark

'balza ['baltsa] SF (*dirupo*) crag; (*di stoffa*) frill

bal'zano, -a [bal'tsano] AG (*persona, idea*) queer, odd

bal'zare [bal'tsare] /72/ VI to bounce; (*lanciarsi*) to jump, leap; **la verità balza agli occhi** the truth of the matter is obvious

'balzo ['baltso] SM bounce; jump, leap; (*del terreno*) crag; **prendere la palla al ~** (*fig*) to seize one's opportunity

bam'bagia [bam'badʒa] SF (*ovatta*) cotton wool (*BRIT*), absorbent cotton (*US*); (*cascame*) cotton waste; **tenere qn nella ~** (*fig*) to mollycoddle sb

bam'bina SF *vedi* bambino

bambi'naia SF nanny, nurse(maid)

bam'bino, -a SM/F child; **fare il ~** to behave childishly

bam'boccio [bam'bɔttʃo] SM plump child; (*pupazzo*) rag doll

'bambola SF doll

bambo'lotto SM male doll

bambù SM bamboo

ba'nale AG banal, commonplace

banalità SF INV banality

ba'nana SF banana

ba'nano SM banana tree

'banca, -che SF bank; **~ d'affari** merchant bank; **~ (di) dati** data bank

Outside big cities, where the major banks are open all day, Italian **banche** are open Monday to Friday, usually from 8.30 to 1.30 and from 2.45 to 4.45.

banca'rella SF stall

ban'cario, -a AG banking, bank *cpd* ▶ SM bank clerk

banca'rotta SF bankruptcy; **fare ~** to go bankrupt

bancarotti'ere SM bankrupt

ban'chetto [ban'ketto] SM banquet

banchi'ere, -a [ban'kjɛre] SM/F banker

ban'china [ban'kina] SF (*di porto*) quay; (*per*

pedoni, ciclisti) path; (*di stazione*) platform; **~ cedevole** (*Aut*) soft verge (*Brit*) o shoulder (*US*); **~ spartitraffico** (*Aut*) central reservation (*Brit*), median (strip) (*US*)

ban'chisa [ban'kiza] SF pack ice

'banco, -chi SM bench; (*di negozio*) counter; (*di mercato*) stall; (*di officina*) (work)bench; (*Geo, banca*) bank; **sotto ~** (*fig*) under the counter; **tenere il ~** (*nei giochi*) to be (the) banker; **tener ~** (*fig*) to monopolize the conversation; **medicinali da ~** over-the-counter medicines; **~ di chiesa** pew; **~ di corallo** coral reef; **~ degli imputati** dock; **~ del Lotto** lottery-ticket office; **~ di prova** (*fig*) testing ground; **~ dei testimoni** witness box (*Brit*) o stand (*US*); **~ dei pegni** pawnshop; **~ di nebbia** bank of fog

banco'giro [banko'dʒiro] SM credit transfer

'Bancomat® SM INV automated banking; (*tessera*) cash card; (*sportello automatico*) cashpoint

banco'nota SF banknote

'banda SF band; (*di stoffa*) band, stripe; (*lato, parte*) side; (*di calcolatore*) tape; **~ larga** broadband; **~ perforata** punch tape

banderu'ola SF (*Meteor*) weathercock, weathervane; **essere una ~** (*fig*) to be fickle

bandi'era SF flag, banner; **battere ~ italiana** (*nave ecc*) to fly the Italian flag; **cambiare ~** (*fig*) to change sides; **~ di comodo** flag of convenience

ban'dire /55/ VT to proclaim; (*esiliare*) to exile; (*fig*) to dispense with

ban'dito SM outlaw, bandit

bandi'tore SM (*di aste*) auctioneer

'bando SM proclamation; (*esilio*) exile, banishment; **mettere al ~ qn** to exile sb; (*fig*) to freeze sb out; **~ alle ciance!** that's enough talk!; **~ di concorso** announcement of a competition

'bandolo SM (*di matassa*) end; **trovare il ~ della matassa** (*fig*) to find the key to the problem

Bang'kok [ban'kɔk] SF Bangkok

Bangla'desh [bangla'dɛʃ] SM: **il ~** Bangladesh

ban'nare VT (*da un forum*) to ban

bar SM INV bar

'bara SF coffin

ba'racca, -che SF shed, hut; (*peg*) hovel; **mandare avanti la ~** to keep things going; **piantare ~ e burattini** to throw everything up

barac'cato, -a SM/F *person living in temporary camp*

barac'chino [barak'kino] SM (*chiosco*) stall; (*apparecchio*) CB radio

barac'cone SM booth, stall ■ **baracconi** SMPL (*luna park*) funfair *sg* (*Brit*), amusement park; **fenomeno da ~** circus freak

barac'copoli SF INV shanty town

bara'onda SF hubbub, bustle

ba'rare /72/ VI to cheat

'baratro SM abyss

barat'tare /72/ VT: **~ qc con** to barter sth for, swap sth for

ba'ratto SM barter

ba'rattolo SM (*di latta*) tin; (*di vetro*) jar; (*di coccio*) pot

'barba SF beard; **farsi la ~** to shave; **farla in ~ a qn** (*fig*) to do sth to sb's face; **servire qn di ~ e capelli** (*fig*) to teach sb a lesson; **che ~!** what a bore!

barbabi'etola SF beetroot (*Brit*), beet (*US*); **~ da zucchero** sugar beet

Bar'bados SF Barbados

bar'barico, -a, -ci, -che AG (*invasione*) barbarian; (*usanze, metodi*) barbaric

bar'barie SF barbarity

'barbaro, -a AG barbarous ▸ SM barbarian; **i Barbari** the Barbarians

'barbecue ['barbikju:] SM INV barbecue

barbi'ere, -a SM/F barber

barbi'turico, -a, -ci, -che AG barbituric ▸ SM barbiturate

bar'bone SM (*cane*) poodle; (*vagabondo*) tramp

bar'buto, -a AG bearded

'barca, -che SF boat; **una ~ di** (*fig*) heaps of, tons of; **mandare avanti la ~** (*fig*) to keep things going; **~ a motore** motorboat; **~ a remi** rowing boat (*Brit*), rowboat (*US*); **~ a vela** sailing boat (*Brit*), sailboat (*US*)

barcai'olo SM boatman

barcame'narsi /72/ VPR (*nel lavoro*) to get by; (*a parole*) to beat about the bush

Barcel'lona [bartʃel'lona] SF Barcelona

barcol'lare /72/ VI to stagger

bar'cone SM (*per ponti di barche*) pontoon

ba'rella SF (*lettiga*) stretcher

'Barents: il mar di ~ *sm* the Barents Sea

ba'rese AG of (o from) Bari

bari'centro [bari'tʃentro] SM centre (*Brit*) o center (*US*) of gravity

ba'rile SM barrel, cask

ba'rista, -i, -e SM/F barman (barmaid); (*proprietario*) bar owner

ba'ritono SM baritone

bar'lume SM glimmer, gleam

'baro SM (*Carte*) cardsharp

ba'rocco, -a, -chi, -che AG, SM baroque

ba'rometro SM barometer

ba'rone SM baron; **i baroni della medicina** (*fig, peg*) the top brass in the medical faculty

baro'nessa SF baroness

'barra SF bar; (*Naut*) helm; (*linea grafica*) line, stroke

bar'rare /72/ VT to bar

barri'care /20/ VT to barricade ■ **barricarsi** VPR to barricade o.s.

barri'cata SF barricade; **essere dall'altra parte della ~** (*fig*) to be on the other side of the fence

barri'era SF barrier; (*Geo*) reef; **la Grande B~ Corallina** the Great Barrier Reef

bar'roccio [bar'rɔttʃo] SM cart

ba'ruffa SF scuffle; **fare ~** to squabble

barzel'letta [bardzel'letta] SF joke, funny story

basa'mento SM (*parte inferiore, piedestallo*) base; (*Tecn*) bed, base plate

ba'sare /72/ VT to base, found ■ **basarsi** VPR: **basarsi su** (*fatti, prove*) to be based *o* founded on; (*persona*) to base one's arguments on

'basco, -a, -schi, -sche AG Basque ▶ SM/F Basque ▶ SM (*lingua*) Basque; (*copricapo*) beret

bas'culla SF weighing machine, weighbridge

'base SF base; (*fig: fondamento*) basis; (*Pol*) rank and file; **di ~** basic; **in ~ a** on the basis of, according to; **in ~ a ciò …** on that basis …; **a ~ di caffè** coffee-based; **essere alla ~ di qc** to be at the root of sth; **gettare le basi per qc** to lay the basis *o* foundations for sth; **avere buone basi** (*Ins*) to have a sound educational background

'baseball ['beisbɔːl] SM baseball

ba'setta SF sideburn

basi'lare AG basic, fundamental

Basi'lea SF Basle

ba'silica, -che SF basilica

ba'silico SM basil

'basket ['basket] SM basketball

bas'sezza [bas'settsa] SF (*d'animo, di sentimenti*) baseness; (*azione*) base action

bas'sista, -i, -e SM/F bass player

'basso, -a AG low; (*di statura*) short; (*meridionale*) southern ▶ SM bottom, lower part; (*Mus*) bass; **a occhi bassi** with eyes lowered; **a ~ prezzo** cheap; **scendere da ~** to go downstairs; **cadere in ~** (*fig*) to come down in the world; **la bassa Italia** southern Italy; **il ~ Medioevo** the late Middle Ages

basso'fondo (*pl* **bassifondi**) SM (*Geo*) shallows *pl*; **i bassifondi (della città)** the seediest parts of the town

bassorili'evo SM bas-relief

bas'sotto, -a AG squat ▶ SM (*cane*) dachshund

'basta ESCL (that's) enough!, that will do!

bas'tardo, -a AG (*animale, pianta*) hybrid, cross-breed; (*persona*) illegitimate, bastard (*peg*) ▶ SM/F illegitimate child, bastard (*peg*); (*cane*) mongrel

bas'tare /72/ VI, VB IMPERS to be enough, be sufficient; **~ a qn** to be enough for sb; **~ a se stesso** to be self-sufficient; **basta chiedere** *o* **che chieda a un vigile** you have only to *o* need only ask a policeman; **basti dire che …** suffice it to say that …; **basta!** that's enough!, that will do!; **basta così?** (*al bar ecc*) will that be all?;

basta così, grazie that's enough, thanks; **punto e basta!** and that's that!

basti'an SM: **~ contrario** awkward customer

basti'mento SM ship, vessel

basti'one SM bastion

basto'nare /72/ VT to beat, thrash; **avere l'aria di un cane bastonato** to look crestfallen

basto'nata SF blow (with a stick); **prendere qn a bastonate** to give sb a good beating

baston'cino [baston'tʃino] SM (*piccolo bastone*) small stick; (*Tecn*) rod; (*Sci*) ski pole; **bastoncini di pesce** (*Cuc*) fish fingers (BRIT), fish sticks (US)

bas'tone SM stick ■ **bastoni** SMPL (*Carte*) suit in Neapolitan pack of cards; **~ da passeggio** walking stick; **mettere i bastoni fra le ruote a qn** to put a spoke in sb's wheel

bat'tage [ba'taʒ] SM INV: **~ promozionale** *o* **pubblicitario** publicity campaign

bat'taglia [bat'taʎʎa] SF battle; fight

bat'taglio [bat'taʎʎo] SM (*di campana*) clapper; (*di porta*) knocker

battagli'one [battaʎ'ʎone] SM battalion

bat'tello SM boat

bat'tente SM (*imposta: di porta*) wing, flap; (*: di finestra*) shutter; (*batacchio: di porta*) knocker; (*: di orologio*) hammer; **chiudere i battenti** (*fig*) to shut up shop

'battere /1/ VT to beat; (*grano*) to thresh; (*percorrere*) to scour; (*rintoccare: le ore*) to strike ▶ VI (*bussare*) to knock; (*pioggia, sole*) to beat down; (*cuore*) to beat; (*Tennis*) to serve; (*urtare*): **~ contro** to hit *o* strike against ■ **battersi** VPR to fight; **~ le mani** to clap; **~ i piedi** to stamp one's feet; **~ su un argomento** to hammer home an argument; **~ a macchina** to type; **~ bandiera italiana** to fly the Italian flag; **~ il marciapiede** (*peg*) to walk the streets, be on the game; **~ un rigore** (*Calcio*) to take a penalty; **~ in testa** (*Aut*) to knock; **in un batter d'occhio** in the twinkling of an eye; **senza ~ ciglio** without batting an eyelid; **battersela** to run off

batte'ria SF battery; (*Mus*) drums *pl*; **~ da cucina** pots and pans *pl*

bat'terio SM bacterium ■ **batteri** SMPL bacteria

batteriolo'gia [batterjolo'dʒia] SF bacteriology

batte'rista, -i, -e SM/F drummer

bat'tesimo SM (*sacramento*) baptism; (*rito*) baptism; christening; **tenere qn a ~** to be godfather (*o* godmother) to sb

battez'zare [batted'dzare] /72/ VT to baptize; to christen

battiba'leno SM: **in un ~** in a flash

batti'becco, -chi SM squabble

batticu'ore SM palpitations *pl*; **avere il ~** to be frightened to death

bat'tigia [bat'tidʒa] SF water's edge

batti'mano SM applause

batti'panni SM INV carpet-beater

battis'tero SM baptistry

battis'trada SM INV (di pneumatico) tread; (di gara) pacemaker

battitap'peto SM INV upright vacuum cleaner

'battito SM beat, throb; **~ cardiaco** heartbeat; **~ della pioggia/dell'orologio** beating of the rain/ticking of the clock

batti'tore SM (Cricket) batsman; (Baseball) batter; (Caccia) beater

batti'tura SF (anche: **battitura a macchina**) typing; (: del grano) threshing

bat'tuta SF blow; (di macchina da scrivere) stroke; (Mus) bar; beat; (Teat) cue; (frase spiritosa) witty remark; (di caccia) beating; (Polizia) combing, scouring; (Tennis) service; **fare una ~** to crack a joke, make a witty remark; **aver la ~ pronta** (fig) to have a ready answer; **è ancora alle prime battute** it's just started

ba'tuffolo SM wad

ba'ule SM trunk; (Aut) boot (BRIT), trunk (US)

bau'xite [bauk'site] SF bauxite

'bava SF (di animale) slaver, slobber; (di lumaca) slime; (di vento) breath

bava'glino [bavaʎ'ʎino] SM bib

ba'vaglio [ba'vaʎʎo] SM gag

bava'rese AG, SM/F Bavarian

'bavero SM collar

Bavi'era SF Bavaria

ba'zar [bad'dzar] SM INV bazaar

baz'zecola [bad'dzekola] SF trifle

bazzi'care [battsi'kare] /20/ VT (persona) to hang about with; (posto) to hang about ▶ VI: **~ in/con** to hang about/hang about with

BCE SIGLA F (= Banca centrale europea) ECB

be'arsi /72/ VPR: **~ di qc/a fare qc** to delight in sth/in doing sth; **~ alla vista di** to enjoy looking at

beati'tudine SF bliss

be'ato, -a AG blessed; (fig) happy; **~ te!** lucky you!

bebè SM INV baby

bec'caccia, -ce [bek'kattʃa] SF woodcock

bec'care /20/ VT to peck; (fig: raffreddore) to catch, pick up ▪ **beccarsi** VPR (fig) to squabble; **beccarsi qc** to catch sth

bec'cata SF peck

beccheggi'are [bekked'dʒare] /62/ VI to pitch

beccherò ecc [bekke'rɔ] VB vedi **beccare**

bec'chime [bek'kime] SM birdseed

bec'chino [bek'kino] SM gravedigger

'becco, -chi SM beak, bill; (di caffettiera ecc) spout; lip; (fig: col) cuckold; **mettere ~** (col) to butt in; **chiudi il ~!** (col) shut your mouth!, shut your trap!; **non ho il ~ di un quattrino** (col) I'm broke

Be'fana SF old woman who, according to legend, brings children their presents at the Epiphany; (Epifania) Epiphany; (donna brutta): **befana** hag, witch

Marking the end of the traditional 12 days of Christmas on 6 January, the **Befana**, or the feast of the Epiphany, is a national holiday in Italy. It is named after the ugly but kindly old woman who, legend has it, rides a broomstick and comes down the chimney the night before, bringing gifts in a stocking (calza della Befana) to children who have been good during the year and leaving lumps of coal for those who have not.

'beffa SF practical joke; **farsi ~ o beffe di qn** to make a fool of sb

bef'fardo, -a AG scornful, mocking

bef'fare /72/ VT (anche: **beffarsi di**) to make a fool of, mock

'bega, -ghe SF quarrel

'begli ['beʎʎi], **'bei** AG vedi **bello**

'beige [bɛʒ] AG INV beige

Bei'rut SF Beirut

bel AG vedi **bello**

be'lare /72/ VI to bleat

be'lato SM bleating

'belga, -gi, -ghe AG, SM/F Belgian

'Belgio ['bɛldʒo] SM: **il ~** Belgium

Bel'grado SF Belgrade

'bella SF (Sport) decider; vedi **bello**

bel'lezza [bel'lettsa] SF beauty; **chiudere o finire qc in ~** to finish sth with a flourish; **che ~!** fantastic!; **ho pagato la ~ di 300 euro** I paid 300 euro, no less

belli'coso, -a AG warlike

bellige'rante [bellidʒe'rante] AG belligerent

bellim'busto SM dandy

'bello, -a

(ag: dav sm **bel** + C, **bell'** + V, **bello** + s impura, gn, pn, ps, x, z, pl **bei** + C, **begli** + s impura ecc o V) AG **1** (oggetto, donna, paesaggio) beautiful, lovely; (uomo) handsome; (tempo) beautiful, fine, lovely; **farsi bello di qc** to show off about sth; **fare la bella vita** to have an easy life; **le belle arti** fine arts

2 (quantità): **una bella cifra** a considerable sum of money; **un bel niente** absolutely nothing

3 (rafforzativo): **è una truffa bella e buona!** it's a real fraud!; **oh bella!, anche questa è bella!** (ironico) that's nice!; **è bell'e finito** it's already finished

▶ SM/F (innamorato) sweetheart

▶ SM **1** (bellezza) beauty; (tempo) fine weather

2: **adesso viene il bello** now comes the best bit; **sul più bello** at the crucial point; **cosa fai**

di bello? are you doing anything interesting?
▶ SF **1** (anche: **bella copia**) fair copy
2 (Sport, Carte) decider
▶ AV: **fa bello** the weather is fine, it's fine;
alla bell'e meglio somehow or other

Bello per descrivere una donna o una ragazza
si traduce con **beautiful**; per un uomo si
usano **handsome** o **good-looking**.

---

bellu'nese AG of (o from) Belluno

'belva SF wild animal

belve'dere SM INV panoramic viewpoint

benché [ben'ke] CONG although

'benda SF bandage; (per gli occhi) blindfold

ben'daggio [ben'daddʒo] SM bandages; **fare un ~ a qc** to bandage sth up; **~ gastrico** gastric band surgery

ben'dare /72/ VT to bandage; to blindfold

bendis'posto, -a AG: **~ a qn/qc** well disposed towards sb/sth

'bene AV well; (completamente, affatto): **è ben difficile** it's very difficult ▶ AG INV: **gente ~** well-to-do people ▶ SM good; (Comm) asset ■ **beni** SMPL (averi) property sg, estate sg; **io sto ~/poco ~** I'm well/not very well; **va ~** all right; **ben più lungo/caro** much longer/more expensive; **lo spero ~** I certainly hope so; **volere un ~ dell'anima a qn** to love sb very much; **un uomo per ~** a respectable man; **fare ~** to do the right thing; **fare ~ a** (salute) to be good for; **fare del ~ a qn** to do sb a good turn; **di ~ in meglio** better and better; **beni ambientali** environmental assets; **beni di consumo** consumer goods; **beni di consumo durevole** consumer durables; **beni culturali** cultural heritage; **beni immateriali** immaterial o intangible assets; **beni patrimoniali** fixed assets; **beni privati** private property sg; **beni pubblici** public property sg; **beni reali** tangible assets

bene'detto, -a PP di **benedire** ▶ AG blessed, holy

bene'dire /38/ VT to bless; to consecrate; **l'ho mandato a farsi ~** (fig) I told him to go to hell

benedizi'one [benedit'tsjone] SF blessing

benedu'cato, -a AG well-mannered

benefat'tore, -'trice SM/F benefactor (benefactress)

benefi'cenza [benefi'tʃɛntsa] SF charity

benefici'are [benefi'tʃare] /14/ VI: **~ di** to benefit by, benefit from

benefici'ario, -a [benefi'tʃarjo] AG, SM/F beneficiary

bene'ficio [bene'fitʃo] SM benefit; **con ~ d'inventario** (fig) with reservations

be'nefico, -a, -ci, -che AG beneficial; charitable

'Benelux SM: **il ~** Benelux, the Benelux countries

beneme'renza [beneme'rɛntsa] SF merit

bene'merito, -a AG meritorious

bene'placito [bene'platʃito] SM (approvazione) approval; (permesso) permission

be'nessere SM well-being

benes'tante AG well-to-do

benes'tare SM consent, approval

benevo'lenza [benevo'lɛntsa] SF benevolence

be'nevolo, -a AG benevolent

ben'godi SM land of plenty

benia'mino, -a SM/F favourite (BRIT), favorite (US)

be'nigno, -a [be'niɲɲo] AG kind, kindly; (critica ecc) favourable (BRIT), favorable (US); (Med) benign

benintenzio'nato, -a [benintentsjo'nato] AG well-meaning

benin'teso AV of course; **~ che** cong provided that

benpen'sante SMF conformist

benser'vito SM: **dare il ~ a qn** (sul lavoro) to give sb the sack, fire sb; (fig) to send sb packing

ben'sì CONG but (rather)

benve'nuto, -a AG, SM welcome; **dare il ~ a qn** to welcome sb

ben'visto, -a AG: **essere ~ (da)** to be well thought of (by)

benvo'lere /131/ VT: **farsi ~ da tutti** to win everybody's affection; **prendere a ~ qn/qc** to take a liking to sb/sth

ben'zina [ben'dzina] SF petrol (BRIT), gas (US); **fare ~** to get petrol o gas; **rimanere senza ~** to run out of petrol o gas; **~ verde** unleaded petrol, lead-free petrol

benzi'naio, -a [bendzi'najo] SM/F petrol (BRIT) o gas (US) pump attendant

be'one SM heavy drinker

'bere /16/ VT to drink; (assorbire) to soak up; **darla a ~ a qn** (fig) to fool sb; **questa volta non me la dai a ~!** I won't be taken in this time!

berga'masco, -a, -schi, -sche AG of (o from) Bergamo

'Bering ['beriŋ]: **il mar di ~** sm the Bering Sea

ber'lina SF (Aut) saloon (car) (BRIT), sedan (US); **mettere alla ~** (fig) to hold up to ridicule

Ber'lino SF Berlin; **~ est/ovest** East/West Berlin

Ber'muda SFPL: **le ~** Bermuda sg

ber'muda SMPL (calzoncini) Bermuda shorts

'Berna SF Bern

ber'noccolo SM bump; (inclinazione) flair

ber'retto SM cap

ber'rò ecc VB vedi **bere**

bersagli'are [bersaʎ'ʎare] /27/ ᴠᴛ to shoot at; (*colpire ripetutamente*, *fig*) to bombard; **bersagliato dalla sfortuna** dogged by ill fortune

bersagli'ere [bersaʎ'ʎɛre] sᴍ *member of rifle regiment in Italian army*

ber'saglio [ber'saʎʎo] sᴍ target

bescia'mella [beʃʃa'mɛlla] sꜰ béchamel sauce

bes'temmia sꜰ curse; (*Rel*) blasphemy

bestemmi'are /19/ ᴠɪ to curse, swear; to blaspheme ▶ ᴠᴛ to curse, swear at; to blaspheme; **~ come un turco** to swear like a trooper

'bestia sꜰ animal; **lavorare come una ~** to work like a dog; **andare in ~** (*fig*) to fly into a rage; **una ~ rara** (*fig: persona*) an oddball; **~ da soma** beast of burden

besti'ale ᴀɢ beastly; animal *cpd*; (*col*): **fa un caldo ~** it's terribly hot; **fa un freddo ~** it's bitterly cold

bestialità sꜰ ɪɴᴠ (*qualità*) bestiality; **dire/fare una ~ dopo l'altra** to say/do one idiotic thing after another

besti'ame sᴍ livestock; (*bovino*) cattle *pl*

Bet'lemme sꜰ Bethlehem

betoni'era sꜰ cement mixer

'bettola sꜰ (*peg*) dive

be'tulla sꜰ birch

be'vanda sꜰ drink, beverage; **~ energetica** energy drink

bevi'tore, -'trice sᴍ/ꜰ drinker

'bevo *ecc* ᴠʙ *vedi* **bere**

be'vuto, -a ᴘᴘ *di* **bere** ▶ sꜰ drink

'bevvi *ecc* ᴠʙ *vedi* **bere**

BG sɪɢʟᴀ = **Bergamo**

BI sɪɢʟᴀ ꜰ = **Banca d'Italia** ▶ sɪɢʟᴀ = **Biella**

bi'ada sꜰ fodder

bianche'ria [bjanke'ria] sꜰ linen; **~ intima** underwear; **~ da donna** ladies' underwear, lingerie; **~ femminile** lingerie

bi'anco, -a, -chi, -che ᴀɢ white; (*non scritto*) blank ▶ sᴍ white; (*intonaco*) whitewash ▶ sᴍ/ꜰ white, white man/woman; **in ~** (*foglio, assegno*) blank; **in ~ e nero** (TV, *Fot*) black and white; **mangiare in ~** to follow a bland diet; **pesce in ~** boiled fish; **andare in ~** (*non riuscire*) to fail; (*in amore*) to be rejected; **notte bianca** *o* **in ~** sleepless night; **voce bianca** (*Mus*) treble (voice); **votare scheda bianca** to return a blank voting slip; **~ dell'uovo** egg-white

bianco'segno [bjanko'seɲɲo] sᴍ signature to a blank document

biancos'pino sᴍ hawthorn

biasci'care [bjaʃʃi'kare] /20/ ᴠᴛ to mumble

biasi'mare /72/ ᴠᴛ to disapprove of, censure

bi'asimo sᴍ disapproval, censure

'bibbia sꜰ (*anche fig*) bible

bibe'ron sᴍ ɪɴᴠ feeding bottle

'bibita sꜰ (soft) drink

bibliogra'fia sꜰ bibliography

biblio'teca, -che sꜰ library; (*mobile*) bookcase

bibliote'cario, -a sᴍ/ꜰ librarian

bicame'rale ᴀɢ (*Pol*) two-chamber *cpd*

bicarbo'nato sᴍ: **~ (di sodio)** bicarbonate (of soda)

bicchi'ere [bik'kjɛre] sᴍ glass; **è (facile) come bere un bicchier d'acqua** it's as easy as pie

bici'cletta [bitʃi'kletta] sꜰ bicycle; **andare in ~** to cycle

bi'cipite [bi'tʃipite] sᴍ bicep

bidè sᴍ ɪɴᴠ bidet

bi'dello, -a sᴍ/ꜰ (*Ins*) janitor

bi'det sᴍ ɪɴᴠ = **bidè**

bidirezio'nale [bidirettsjo'nale] ᴀɢ bidirectional

bido'nare /72/ ᴠᴛ (*col: piantare in asso*) to let down; (*: imbrogliare*) to cheat, swindle

bido'nata sꜰ (*col*) swindle

bi'done sᴍ drum, can; (*anche*: **bidone dell'immondizia**) (dust)bin; (*col: truffa*) swindle; **fare un ~ a qn** (*col*) to let sb down; to cheat sb

bidon'ville [bidɔ'vil] sꜰ ɪɴᴠ shanty town

bi'eco, -a, -chi, -che ᴀɢ sinister

bi'ella sꜰ (*Tecn*) connecting rod

Bielo'russia sꜰ Belarus, Belorussia

bielo'russo, -a ᴀɢ, sᴍ/ꜰ Belarussian, Belorussian

bien'nale ᴀɢ biennial ▶ sꜰ: **la B~ di Venezia** the Venice Arts Festival

---

Dating back to 1895, the **Biennale di Venezia** is an international festival of the contemporary arts. It takes place every two years in the *Giardini Pubblici* and the *Arsenale*. The various countries taking part each put on exhibitions in their own pavilions. There is a section dedicated to the work of young artists, as well as a special exhibition on a specific theme for that year.

---

bi'ennio sᴍ period of two years

bi'erre sᴍꜰ *member of the Red Brigades*

bi'etola sꜰ beet

bifami'liare ᴀɢ (*villa, casetta*) semi-detached

bifo'cale ᴀɢ bifocal

bi'folco, -a, -chi, -che sᴍ/ꜰ (*peg*) bumpkin

'bifora sꜰ (*Archit*) mullioned window

bifor'carsi /20/ ᴠᴘʀ to fork

biforcazi'one [biforkat'tsjone] sꜰ fork

bifor'cuto, -a ᴀɢ (*anche fig*) forked

biga'mia sꜰ bigamy

'bigamo, -a ᴀɢ bigamous ▶ sᴍ/ꜰ bigamist

bighello'nare [bigello'nare] /72/ ᴠɪ to loaf (about)

bighel'lone, -a [bigel'lone] sᴍ/ꜰ loafer

bigiotte'ria [bidʒotte'ria] sꜰ costume jewellery (BRIT) o jewelry (US); (negozio) jeweller's (shop) (BRIT) o jewelry store (US: selling only costume jewellery)

bigli'ardo [biʎ'ʎardo] SM = **biliardo**

bigliet'taio, -a [biʎʎet'tajo] SM/F (nei treni) ticket inspector; (in autobus ecc) conductor (conductress); (Cine, Teat) box-office attendant

bigliette'ria [biʎʎette'ria] SF (di stazione) ticket office; booking office; (di teatro) box office

bigli'etto [biʎ'ʎetto] SM (per viaggi, spettacoli ecc) ticket; (cartoncino) card; **~ di banca** (bank)note; (anche: **biglietto d'auguri/da visita**) greetings/visiting card; **~ di andata e ritorno** return (BRIT) o round-trip (US) ticket; **~ di sola andata** single (ticket); **~ elettronico** e-ticket; **~ omaggio** complimentary ticket

bignè [biɲ'ɲɛ] SM INV cream puff

bigo'dino SM roller, curler

bi'gotto, -a AG over-pious ▶ SM/F church fiend

bi'kini SM INV bikini

bi'lancia, -ce [bi'lantʃa] SF (pesa) scales pl; (: di precisione) balance; **B~** Libra; **essere della B~** to be Libra; **~ commerciale/dei pagamenti** balance of trade/payments

bilanci'are [bilan'tʃare] /**14**/ VT (pesare) to weigh; (: fig) to weigh up; **~ le uscite e le entrate** (Comm) to balance expenditure and revenue

bi'lancio [bi'lantʃo] SM (Comm) balance (sheet); (statale) budget; **far quadrare il ~** to balance the books; **chiudere il ~ in attivo/passivo** to make a profit/loss; **fare il ~ di** (fig) to assess; **~ consolidato** consolidated balance; **~ consuntivo** (final) balance; **~ preventivo** budget; **~ pubblico** national budget; **~ di verifica** trial balance

bilate'rale AG bilateral

'bile SF bile; (fig) rage, anger

biliar'dino SM pinball

bili'ardo SM billiards sg; (tavolo) billiard table

'bilico, -chi SM: **essere in ~** to be balanced; (fig) to be undecided; **tenere qn in ~** to keep sb in suspense

bi'lingue AG bilingual

bili'one SM (mille milioni) thousand million, billion (US); (milione di milioni) billion (BRIT), trillion (US)

bilo'cale SM two-room flat (BRIT) o apartment (US)

'bimbo, -a SM/F little boy (girl)

bimen'sile AG fortnightly

bimes'trale AG two-monthly, bimonthly

bi'mestre SM two-month period; **ogni ~** every two months

bi'nario, -a AG (sistema) binary ▶ SM (railway) track o line; (piattaforma) platform; **~ morto** dead-end track

bi'nocolo SM binoculars pl

bio... PREFISSO bio

biocarbu'rante SM biofuel

bio'chimica [bio'kimika] SF biochemistry

biodegra'dabile AG biodegradable

bio'diesel [bio'dizel] SM INV biodiesel

biodi'namico, -a, -ci, -che AG biodynamic

biodiversità SF biodiversity

bio'etica SF bioethics sg

bio'etico, -a, -ci, -che AG bioethical

bio'fabbrica SF factory producing biological control agents

bio'fisica SF biophysics sg

biogra'fia SF biography

bio'grafico, -a, -ci, -che AG biographical

bi'ografo, -a SM/F biographer

biolo'gia [biolo'dʒia] SF biology

bio'logico, -a, -ci, -che [bio'lɔdʒiko] AG (scienze, fenomeni ecc) biological; (agricoltura, prodotti) organic; **guerra biologica** biological warfare

bi'ologo, -a, -ghi, -ghe SM/F biologist

bi'ondo, -a AG blond, fair

bi'onico, -a, -ci, -che AG bionic

biop'sia SF biopsy

bio'ritmo SM biorhythm

bios'fera SF biosphere

biotecnolo'gia [bioteknolo'dʒia] SF biotechnology

biov'egano, -a AG organic vegan

bipar'tito, -a AG (Pol) two-party cpd ▶ SM (Pol) two-party alliance

bipo'lare AG bipolar

'birba SF rascal, rogue

bir'bante SM rascal, rogue

birbo'nata SF naughty trick

bir'bone, -a AG (bambino) naughty ▶ SM/F little rascal

biri'chino, -a [biri'kino] AG mischievous ▶ SM/F scamp, little rascal

bi'rillo SM skittle (BRIT), pin (US) ■ **birilli** SMPL (gioco) skittles sg (BRIT), bowling no pl (US)

Bir'mania SF: **la ~** Burma

bir'mano, -a AG, SM/F Burmese (inv)

'biro® SF INV biro®

'birra SF beer; **~ chiara/scura** lager/stout; **a tutta ~** (fig) at top speed

birre'ria SF (locale) ≈ bierkeller; (fabbrica) brewery

bis ESCL, SM INV encore ▶ AG INV (treno, autobus) relief cpd (BRIT), additional; (numero): **12 ~** 12a

bi'saccia, -ce [bi'zattʃa] SF knapsack

Bi'sanzio [bi'zantsjo] SF Byzantium

bis'betico, -a, -ci, -che AG ill-tempered, crabby

bisbigli'are [bizbiʎ'ʎare] /**27**/ VT, VI to whisper

bis'biglio¹ [biz'biʎʎo] sm whisper; (*notizia*) rumour (*Brit*), rumor (*US*)

bisbi'glio² [bizbiʎ'ʎio] sm whispering

bis'boccia, -ce [biz'bɔttʃa] sf binge, spree; **fare ~** to have a binge

'bisca, -sche sf gambling house

Bis'caglia [bis'kaʎʎa] sf: **il golfo di ~** the Bay of Biscay

'bischero ['biskero] sm (*Mus*) peg ▶ smf (*col: toscano*) fool, idiot

'biscia, -sce ['biʃʃa] sf snake; **~ d'acqua** water snake

biscot'tato, -a AG crisp; **fette biscottate** rusks

bis'cotto sm biscuit

bisessu'ale AG, smf bisexual

bises'tile AG: **anno ~** leap year

bisezi'one [biset'tsjone] sf dichotomy

bis'lacco, -a, -chi, -che AG odd, weird

bis'lungo, -a, -ghi, -ghe AG oblong

bis'nonno, -a sm/f great grandfather/grandmother

biso'gnare [bizoɲ'ɲare] /15/ VB IMPERS: **bisogna che tu parta/lo faccia** you'll have to go/do it; **bisogna parlargli** we'll (*o* I'll) have to talk to him ▶ vi (*esser utile*) to be necessary

bi'sogno [bi'zoɲɲo] sm need ▪ **bisogni** SMPL (*necessità corporali*): **fare i propri bisogni** to relieve o.s.; **avere ~ di qc/di fare qc** to need sth/to do sth; **ha ~ di qualcosa?** do you need anything?; **al ~**, **in caso di ~** if need be

biso'gnoso, -a [bizoɲ'ɲoso] AG needy, poor; **~ di** in need of, needing

bi'sonte sm (*Zool*) bison

bis'tecca, -che sf steak, beefsteak; **~ al sangue/ai ferri** rare/grilled steak

bisticci'are [bistit'tʃare] /14/ VI to quarrel, bicker ▪ **bisticciarsi** VPR to quarrel, bicker

bis'ticcio [bis'tittʃo] sm quarrel, squabble; (*gioco di parole*) pun

bistrat'tare /72/ VT to maltreat

'bisturi sm INV scalpel

bi'sunto, -a AG very greasy

bi'torzolo [bi'tortsolo] sm (*sulla testa*) bump; (*sul corpo*) lump

'bitter sm INV bitters *pl*

bi'tume sm bitumen

bivac'care /20/ VI (*Mil*) to bivouac; (*fig*) to bed down

bi'vacco, -chi sm bivouac

'bivio sm fork; (*fig*) dilemma

bizan'tino, -a [biddzan'tino] AG Byzantine

'bizza ['biddza] sf tantrum; **fare le bizze** to throw a tantrum

biz'zarro, -a [bid'dzarro] AG bizarre, strange

biz'zeffe [bid'dzɛffe]: **a ~** *av* in plenty, galore

BL SIGLA = **Belluno**

blan'dire /55/ VT to soothe; to flatter

'blando, -a AG mild, gentle

blas'femo, -a AG blasphemous ▶ sm/f blasphemer

bla'sone sm coat of arms

blate'rare /72/ VI to chatter

'blatta sf cockroach

blin'dare /72/ VT to armour (*Brit*), armor (*US*)

blin'data sf (*macchina*) armoured (*Brit*) *o* armored (*US*) car *o* limousine

blin'dato, -a AG armoured (*Brit*), armored (*US*); **camera blindata** strongroom; **mezzo ~** armoured vehicle; **porta blindata** reinforced door; **vita blindata** life amid maximum security; **vetro ~** bulletproof glass

bloc'care /20/ VT to block; (*isolare*) to isolate, cut off; (*porto*) to blockade; (*prezzi, beni*) to freeze; (*meccanismo*) to jam ▪ **bloccarsi** VPR (*motore*) to stall; (*freni, porta*) to jam, stick; (*ascensore*) to get stuck, stop; **ha bloccato la macchina** (*Aut*) he jammed on the brakes

bloccas'terzo [blokkas'tɛrtso] sm (*Aut*) steering lock

bloccherò *ecc* [blokke'rɔ] VB *vedi* **bloccare**

bloc'chetto [blok'ketto] sm notebook; (*di biglietti*) book

'blocco, -chi sm block; (*Mil*) blockade; (*dei fitti*) restriction; (*quadernetto*) pad; (*fig: unione*) coalition; (*il bloccare*) blocking; isolating; cutting-off; blockading; freezing; jamming; **in ~** (*nell'insieme*) as a whole; (*Comm*) in bulk; **~ cardiaco** cardiac arrest; **~ stradale** road block

bloc-'notes [blɔk'nɔt] sm INV notebook, notepad

blog [blog] sm INV blog

'bloggare /80/ VI to blog

blogos'fera [blogos'fɛra] sf blogosphere

blu AG INV, sm INV dark blue

bluff [blɛf] sm INV bluff

bluf'fare /72/ VI (*anche fig*) to bluff

'blusa sf (*camiciotto*) smock; (*camicetta*) blouse

BN SIGLA = **Benevento**

BO SIGLA = **Bologna**

'boa sm INV (*Zool*) boa constrictor; (*sciarpa*) feather boa ▶ sf buoy

bo'ato sm rumble, roar

bob [bɔb] sm INV bobsleigh

bo'bina sf reel, spool; (*di pellicola*) spool; (*di film*) reel; (*Elettr*) coil

'bocca, -che sf mouth; **essere di buona ~** to be a hearty eater; (*fig*) to be easily satisfied; **essere sulla ~ di tutti** (*persona, notizia*) to be the talk of the town; **rimanere a ~ asciutta** to have nothing to eat; (*fig*) to be disappointed; **in ~ al lupo!** good luck!; **~ di leone** (*Bot*) snapdragon

boc'caccia, -ce [bok'kattʃa] SF (*malalingua*) gossip; (*smorfia*): **fare le boccacce** to pull faces

boc'caglio [bok'kaʎʎo] SM (*Tecn*) nozzle; (*di respiratore*) mouthpiece

boc'cale SM jug; **~ da birra** tankard

bocca'scena [bokkaʃ'ʃena] SM INV proscenium

boc'cata SF mouthful; (*di fumo*) puff; **prendere una ~ d'aria** to go out for a breath of (fresh) air

boc'cetta [bot'tʃetta] SF small bottle

boccheggi'are [bokked'dʒare] /62/ VI to gasp

boc'chino [bok'kino] SM (*di sigaretta, sigaro: cannella*) cigarette-holder; cigar-holder; (*di pipa, strumenti musicali*) mouthpiece

'boccia, -ce ['bottʃa] SF bottle; (*da vino*) decanter, carafe; (*palla di legno, metallo*) bowl; **gioco delle bocce** bowls *sg*

bocci'are [bot'tʃare] /14/ VT (*proposta, progetto*) to reject; (*Ins*) to fail; (*Bocce*) to hit

boccia'tura [bottʃa'tura] SF failure

bocci'olo [bot'tʃɔlo] SM bud

'boccolo SM curl

boccon'cino [bokkon'tʃino] SM (*pietanza deliziosa*) delicacy

boc'cone SM mouthful, morsel; **mangiare un ~** to have a bite to eat

boc'coni AV face downwards

Bo'emia SF Bohemia

bo'emo, -a AG, SM/F Bohemian

bofonchi'are [bofon'kjare] /19/ VI to grumble

Bogotá SF Bogotá

'boia SM INV executioner; hangman; **fa un freddo ~** (*col*) it's cold as hell; **mondo ~!**, **~ d'un mondo ladro!** (*col*) damn!, blast!

boi'ata SF botch

boicot'taggio [boikot'taddʒo] SM boycott

boicot'tare /72/ VT to boycott

'bolgia, -ge ['boldʒa] SF (*fig*): **c'era una tale ~ al cinema** the cinema was absolutely mobbed

'bolide SM (*Astr*) meteor; (*macchina: da corsa*) racing car (*BRIT*), race car (*US*); (: *elaborata*) performance car; **come un ~** like a flash, at top speed; **entrare/uscire come un ~** to charge in/out

Bo'livia SF: **la ~** Bolivia

bolivi'ano, -a AG, SM/F Bolivian

'bolla SF bubble; (*Med*) blister; (*Comm*) bill, receipt; **finire in una ~ di sapone** (*fig*) to come to nothing; **~ di accompagnamento** waybill; **~ di consegna** (*Comm*) delivery note; **~ papale** papal bull

bol'lare /72/ VT to stamp; (*fig*) to brand

bol'lente AG boiling; boiling hot; **calmare i bollenti spiriti** to sober up, calm down

bol'letta SF bill; (*ricevuta*) receipt; **essere in ~** to be hard up; **~ di consegna** delivery note; **~ doganale** clearance certificate; **~ di trasporto aereo** air waybill

bollet'tino SM bulletin; (*Comm*) note; **~ meteorologico** weather forecast; **~ di ordinazione** order form; **~ di spedizione** consignment note

bolli'cina [bolli'tʃina] SF bubble; **acqua con le bollicine** fizzy water

bol'lire /17/ VT, VI to boil; **qualcosa bolle in pentola** (*fig*) there's something brewing

bol'lito SM (*Cuc*) boiled meat

bolli'tore SM (*Tecn*) boiler; (*Cuc: per acqua*) kettle; (: *per latte*) milk pan

bolli'tura SF boiling

'bollo SM stamp; **imposta di ~** stamp duty; **~ auto** road tax; **~ per patente** driving licence tax; **~ postale** postmark

bol'lore SM: **dare un ~ a qc** to bring sth to the boil (*BRIT*) o a boil (*US*); **i bollori della gioventù** youthful enthusiasm *sg*

Bo'logna [bo'lɔɲɲa] SF Bologna

bolo'gnese [bolɔɲ'ɲese] AG Bolognese; **spaghetti alla ~** spaghetti bolognese

'bomba SF bomb; **tornare a ~** (*fig*) to get back to the point; **sei stato una ~!** you were tremendous!; **~ atomica** atom bomb; **~ a mano** hand grenade; **~ ad orologeria** time bomb

bombarda'mento SM bombardment; bombing

bombar'dare /72/ VT to bombard; (*da aereo*) to bomb

bombardi'ere SM bomber

bom'betta SF bowler (hat) (*BRIT*), derby (*US*)

'bombola SF cylinder; **~ del gas** gas cylinder

bombo'letta SF spray can

bomboni'era SF box of sweets (*as souvenir at weddings, first communions etc*)

bo'naccia, -ce [bo'nattʃa] SF dead calm

bonacci'one, -a [bonat'tʃone] AG good-natured ▶ SM/F good-natured sort

bo'nario, -a AG good-natured, kind

bo'nifica, -che SF reclamation; reclaimed land

bo'nifico, -ci SM (*riduzione, abbuono*) discount; (*versamento a terzi*) credit transfer

Bonn SF Bonn

bontà SF goodness; (*cortesia*) kindness; **aver la ~ di fare qc** to be good o kind enough to do sth

'bonus-'malus SM INV ≈ no-claims bonus

bor'bonico, -a, -ci, -che AG Bourbon; (*fig*) backward, out of date

borbot'tare /72/ VI to mumble; (*stomaco*) to rumble

borbot'tio, -ii SM mumbling; rumbling

'borchia ['borkja] SF stud

borda'tura SF (*Sartoria*) border, trim

bor'deaux [bor'dɔ] AG INV maroon ▶ SM INV (*colore*) burgundy, maroon; (*vino*) Bordeaux

bor'dello SM brothel

'bordo SM (*Naut*) ship's side; (*orlo*) edge; (*striscia di guarnizione*) border, trim; **a ~ di** (*nave, aereo*) aboard, on board; (*macchina*) in; **sul ~ della strada** at the roadside; **persona d'alto ~** VIP

bor'dura SF border

bor'gata SF hamlet; (*a Roma*) working-class suburb

bor'ghese [bor'geze] AG (*spesso peg*) middle-class; bourgeois; **abito ~** civilian dress; **poliziotto in ~** plainclothes policeman

borghe'sia [borge'zia] SF middle classes *pl*; bourgeoisie

'borgo, -ghi SM (*paesino*) village; (*quartiere*) district; (*sobborgo*) suburb

'boria SF self-conceit, arrogance

bori'oso, -a AG arrogant

bor'lotto SM kidney bean

'Borneo SM: **il ~** Borneo

boro'talco SM talcum powder

bor'raccia, -ce [bor'rattʃa] SF canteen, water-bottle

'borsa SF bag; (*anche:* **borsa da signora**) handbag; (*Econ*) **la B~ (valori)** the Stock Exchange; **~ dell'acqua calda** hot-water bottle; **B~ merci** commodity exchange; **~ nera** black market; **~ della spesa** shopping bag; **~ di studio** grant

borsai'olo SM pickpocket

bor'seggio [bor'seddʒo] SM pickpocketing

borsel'lino SM purse

bor'sello SM gent's handbag

bor'setta SF handbag

bor'sista, -i, -e SM/F (*Econ*) speculator; (*Ins*) grant-holder

bos'caglia [bos'kaʎʎa] SF woodlands *pl*

bosciai'olo, boscaiu'olo SM woodcutter; forester

bos'chetto [bos'ketto] SM copse, grove

'bosco, -schi SM wood

bos'coso, -a AG wooded

bos'niaco, -a, -ci, -che AG, SM/F Bosnian

'Bosnia-Erze'govina ['bɔsnja erdze'govina] SF: **la ~** Bosnia and Herzegovina

'bossolo SM cartridge case

Bot SIGLA M INV (= *Buono ordinario del Tesoro*) short-term Treasury bond

bo'tanico, -a, -ci, -che AG botanical ▶ SM botanist ▶ SF botany

'botola SF trap door

Bots'wana [bots'vana] SM: **il ~** Botswana

'botta SF blow; (*rumore*) bang; **dare (un sacco di) botte a qn** to give sb a good thrashing; **~ e risposta** (*fig*) cut and thrust

'botte SF barrel, cask; **essere in una ~ di ferro** (*fig*) to be as safe as houses; **volere la ~ piena e la moglie ubriaca** to want to have one's cake and eat it

bot'tega, -ghe SF shop; (*officina*) workshop; **stare a ~ da qn** to serve one's apprenticeship (with sb); **le Botteghe Oscure** headquarters of the DS, Italian left-wing party

botte'gaio, -a SM/F shopkeeper

botte'ghino [botte'gino] SM ticket office; (*del lotto*) public lottery office

bot'tiglia [bot'tiʎʎa] SF bottle

bottiglie'ria [bottiʎʎe'ria] SF wine shop

bot'tino SM (*di guerra*) booty; (*di rapina, furto*) loot; **fare ~ di qc** (*anche fig*) to make off with sth

'botto SM bang; crash; **di ~** suddenly; **d'un ~** (*col*) in a flash

bot'tone SM button; (*Bot*) bud; **stanza dei bottoni** control room; (*fig*) nerve centre; **attaccare (un) ~ a qn** to buttonhole sb

bo'vino, -a AG bovine ■ **bovini** SMPL cattle

box [bɔks] SM INV (*per cavalli*) horsebox; (*per macchina*) lock-up; (*per macchina da corsa*) pit; (*per bambini*) playpen

boxe [bɔks] SF boxing

'boxer ['bɔkser] SM INV (*cane*) boxer ▶ SMPL (*mutande*) **un paio di ~** a pair of boxer shorts

'bozza ['bɔttsa] SF draft; (*Tip*) proof; **~ di stampa/impaginata** galley/page proof

boz'zetto [bot'tsetto] SM sketch

'bozzolo ['bɔttsolo] SM cocoon

BR SIGLA FPL = **Brigate Rosse** ▶ SIGLA = **Brindisi**

'braca, -che SF (*gamba di pantalone*) trouser leg ■ **brache** SFPL (*col*) trousers, pants (*US*); (*mutandoni*) drawers; **calare le brache** (*fig: col*) to chicken out

brac'care /20/ VT to hunt

brac'cetto [brat'tʃetto] SM: **a ~** arm in arm

braccherò *ecc* [brakke'rɔ] VB *vedi* **braccare**

bracci'ale [brat'tʃale] SM bracelet; (*per nuotare, anche distintivo*) armband

braccia'letto [brattʃa'letto] SM bracelet, bangle

bracci'ante [brat'tʃante] SMF (*Agr*) day labourer

bracci'ata [brat'tʃata] SF armful; (*nel nuoto*) stroke

'braccio (*pl(f)* **braccia**: *Anat*; *pl(m)* **bracci**: *di gru, fiume*) ['brattʃo] SM arm; (*di edificio*) wing; **camminare sotto ~** to walk arm in arm; **è il suo ~ destro** he's his right-hand man; **~ di ferro** (*anche fig*) trial of strength; **~ di mare** sound

bracci'olo [brat'tʃɔlo] SM (*appoggio*) arm

'bracco, -chi SM hound

bracconi'ere SM poacher

'brace ['bratʃe] SF embers *pl*

braci'ere [bra'tʃɛre] SM brazier

braci'ola [bra'tʃɔla] SF (*Cuc*) chop

'bradipo SM (*Zool*) sloth

'brado, -a AG: **allo stato ~** in the wild *o* natural state

'brama SF: ~ **(di/di fare)** longing (for/to do), yearning (for/to do)

bra'mare /72/ VT: ~ **(qc/di fare qc)** to long (for sth/to do sth), yearn (for sth/to do sth)

bramo'sia SF: ~ **(di)** longing (for), yearning (for)

'branca, -che SF branch

'branchia ['brankja] SF (Zool) gill

'branco, -chi SM (di cani, lupi) pack; (di uccelli, pecore) flock; (peg: di persone) gang, pack

branco'lare /72/ VI to grope, feel one's way

'branda SF camp bed

bran'dello SM scrap, shred; **a brandelli** in tatters, in rags; **fare a brandelli** to tear to shreds

bran'dina SF camp bed (BRIT), cot (US)

bran'dire /55/ VT to brandish

'brano SM piece; (di libro) passage

bra'sare /72/ VT to braise

bra'sato SM braised beef

Bra'sile SM: **il ~** Brazil

Bra'silia SF Brasilia

brasili'ano, -a AG, SM/F Brazilian

bra'vata SF (azione spavalda) act of bravado

'bravo, -a AG (abile) clever, capable, skilful; (buono) good, honest; (: bambino) good; (coraggioso) brave; **~!** well done!; (al teatro) bravo!; **su da ~!** (col) there's a good boy!; **mi sono fatto le mie brave 8 ore di lavoro** I put in a full 8 hours' work

bra'vura SF cleverness, skill

'breccia, -ce ['brettʃa] SF breach; **essere sulla ~** (fig) to be going strong; **fare ~ nell'animo** o **nel cuore di qn** to find the way to sb's heart

'Brema SF Bremen

bre'saola SF kind of dried salted beef

bresci'ano, -a [breʃ'ʃano] AG of (o from) Brescia

Bre'tagna [bre'taɲɲa] SF: **la ~** Brittany

bre'tella SF (Aut) link ▪ **bretelle** SFPL (di calzoni) braces

bret(t)one AG, SMF Breton

'breve AG brief, short; **in ~** in short; **per farla ~** to cut a long story short; **a ~** (Comm) short-term

brevet'tare /72/ VT to patent

bre'vetto SM patent; **~ di pilotaggio** pilot's licence (BRIT) o license (US)

brevità SF brevity

'brezza ['breddza] SF breeze

'bricco, -chi SM jug; **~ del caffè** coffeepot

bricco'nata SF mischievous trick

bric'cone, -a SM/F rogue, rascal

'briciola ['britʃola] SF crumb

'briciolo ['britʃolo] SM (fig) bit

'bridge [bridʒ] SM bridge

'briga, -ghe SF (fastidio) trouble, bother; **attaccar ~** to start a quarrel; **pigliarsi la ~ di fare qc** to take the trouble to do sth

brigadi'ere SM (dei carabinieri ecc) ≈ sergeant

bri'gante SM bandit

bri'gata SF (Mil) brigade; (gruppo) group, party; **le Brigate Rosse** (Pol) the Red Brigades

briga'tismo SM phenomenon of the Red Brigades

briga'tista, -i, -e SM/F (Pol) member of the Red Brigades

'briglia ['briʎʎa] SF rein; **a ~ sciolta** at full gallop; (fig) at full speed

bril'lante AG bright; (anche fig) brilliant; (che luccica) shining ▶ SM diamond

brillan'tina SF brilliantine

bril'lare /72/ VI to shine; (mina) to blow up ▶ VT (mina) to set off

'brillo, -a AG merry, tipsy

'brina SF hoarfrost

brin'dare /72/ VI: ~ **a qn/qc** to drink to o toast sb/sth

'brindisi SM INV toast

'brio SM liveliness, go

bri'oche [bri'ɔʃ] SF INV brioche (bun)

bri'oso, -a AG lively

'briscola SF type of card game; (seme vincente) trump(s); (carta) trump card

bri'tannico, -a, -ci, -che AG British ▶ SM/F Briton; **i Britannici** the British pl

'brivido SM shiver; (di ribrezzo) shudder; (fig) thrill; **racconti del ~** suspense stories

brizzo'lato, -a [brittso'lato] AG (persona) going grey; (barba, capelli) greying

'brocca, -che SF jug

broc'cato SM brocade

'broccoli SMPL broccoli sg

bro'daglia [bro'daʎʎa] SF (peg) dishwater

'brodo SM broth; (per cucinare) stock; **~ ristretto** consommé; **lasciare (cuocere) qn nel suo ~** to let sb stew (in his own juice); **tutto fa ~** every little bit helps

'broglio ['brɔʎʎo] SM: **~ elettorale** gerrymandering ▪ **brogli** SMPL (Dir) malpractices

'bromo SM (Chim) bromine

bron'chite [bron'kite] SF (Med) bronchitis

'broncio ['brontʃo] SM sulky expression; **tenere il ~** to sulk

'bronco, -chi SM bronchial tube

bronto'lare /72/ VI to grumble; (tuono, stomaco) to rumble

bronto'lio SM grumbling, mumbling

bronto'lone, -a AG grumbling ▶ SM/F grumbler

bron'zina [bron'dzina] SF (Tecn) bush

'bronzo ['brondzo] SM bronze; **che faccia di ~!** what a brass neck!

bross. ABBR = **in brossura**

bros'sura SF: **in ~** (libro) limpback

'browser ['brauzer] SM INV (*Inform*) browser

bru'care /**20**/ VT to browse on, nibble at

bruche'rà *ecc* [bruke'ra] VB *vedi* **brucare**

bruciacchi'are [brutʃak'kjare] /**19**/ VT to singe, scorch ▪ **bruciacchiarsi** VPR to become singed *o* scorched

brucia'pelo [brutʃa'pelo]: **a ~** *av* point-blank

bruci'are [bru'tʃare] /**14**/ VT to burn; (*scottare*) to scald ▶ VI to burn ▪ **bruciarsi** VPR to burn o.s.; (*fallire*) to ruin one's chances; **~ gli avversari** (*Sport, fig*) to leave the rest of the field behind; **~ le tappe** *o* **i tempi** (*Sport, fig*) to shoot ahead; **bruciarsi la carriera** to put an end to one's career

brucia'tore [brutʃa'tore] SM burner

brucia'tura [brutʃa'tura] SF (*atto*) burning *no pl*; (*segno*) burn; (*scottatura*) scald

bruci'ore [bru'tʃore] SM burning *o* smarting sensation

'bruco, -chi SM grub; (*di farfalla*) caterpillar

'brufolo SM pimple, spot

brughi'era [bru'gjɛra] SF heath, moor

bruli'care /**20**/ VI to swarm

bruli'chio, -ii [bruli'kio] SM swarming

'brullo, -a AG bare, bleak

'bruma SF mist

'brunch ['brantʃ] SM INV brunch

'bruno, -a AG brown, dark; (*persona*) dark(-haired)

brusca'mente AV (*frenare, fermarsi*) suddenly; (*rispondere, reagire*) sharply

'brusco, -a, -schi, -sche AG (*sapore*) sharp; (*modi, persona*) brusque, abrupt; (*movimento*) abrupt, sudden

bru'sio SM buzz, buzzing

bru'tale AG brutal

brutalità SF INV brutality

'bruto, -a AG (*forza*) brute *cpd* ▶ SM brute

'brutta SF *vedi* **brutto**

brut'tezza [brut'tettsa] SF ugliness

'brutto, -a AG ugly; (*cattivo*) bad; (*malattia, strada, affare*) nasty, bad ▶ SM: **guardare qn di ~** to give sb a nasty look ▶ SF rough copy, first draft; **~ tempo** bad weather; **passare un ~ quarto d'ora** to have a nasty time of it; **vedersela brutta** (*per un attimo*) to have a nasty moment; (*per un periodo*) to have a bad time of it

brut'tura SF (*cosa brutta*) ugly thing; (*sudiciume*) filth; (*azione meschina*) mean action

Bru'xelles [bry'sɛl] SF Brussels

BS SIGLA = **Brescia**

BSE [biessɛ'e] SIGLA F BSE (= *bovine spongiform encephalopathy*)

B.T. ABBR (= *bassa tensione*) LT ▶ SIGLA M INV = **buono del Tesoro**

btg ABBR = **battaglione**

BTP SIGLA M = **Buono del Tesoro poliennale**; *vedi* **buono**

bub'bone SM swelling

'buca, -che SF hole; (*avvallamento*) hollow; **~ delle lettere** letterbox

buca'neve SM INV snowdrop

bu'care /**20**/ VT (*forare*) to make a hole (*o* holes) in; (*pungere*) to pierce; (*biglietto*) to punch ▪ **bucarsi** VPR (*con eroina*) to mainline; **~ una gomma** to have a puncture; **avere le mani bucate** (*fig*) to be a spendthrift

'Bucarest SF Bucharest

bu'cato SM (*operazione*) washing; (*panni*) wash, washing

'buccia, -ce ['buttʃa] SF skin, peel; (*corteccia*) bark

bucherel'lare [bukerel'lare] /**72**/ VT to riddle with holes

bucherò *ecc* [buke'rɔ] VB *vedi* **bucare**

'buco, -chi SM hole; **fare un ~ nell'acqua** to fail, draw a blank; **farsi un ~** (*col: drogarsi*) to have a fix; **~ nero** (*anche fig*) black hole

'Budapest SF Budapest

'Budda SM INV Buddha

bud'dismo SM Buddhism

bu'dello SM intestine; (*fig: tubo*) tube; (*vicolo*) alley ▪ **budella** SFPL bowels, guts

bu'dino SM pudding

'bue (*pl* **buoi**) SM ox; (*anche*: **carne di bue**) beef; **uovo all'occhio di ~** fried egg

Bu'enos 'Aires SF Buenos Aires

'bufalo SM buffalo

bu'fera SF storm

buf'fetto SM flick

'buffo, -a AG funny; (*Teat*) comic

buffo'nata SF (*azione*) prank, jest; (*parola*) jest

buf'fone SM buffoon

bugge'rare [buddʒe'rare] /**72**/ VT to swindle, cheat

bu'gia, -'gie [bu'dʒia] SF lie; (*candeliere*) candle-holder; **dire una ~** to tell a lie

bugi'ardo, -a [bu'dʒardo] AG lying, deceitful ▶ SM/F liar

bugi'gattolo [budʒi'gattolo] SM poky little room

'buio, -a AG dark ▶ SM dark, darkness; **fa ~ pesto** it's pitch-dark

'bulbo SM (*Bot*) bulb; **~ oculare** eyeball

Bulga'ria SF: **la ~** Bulgaria

'bulgaro, -a AG, SM/F Bulgarian

buli'mia SF bulimia

bu'limico, -a, -ci, -che AG bulimic

bul'lismo SM bullying

bulliz'zare [bullid'dzare] VT to bully

'bullo SM (*persona*) tough

bul'lone SM bolt

bu'oi SMPL *di* **bue**

buona'fede SF good faith

buon'anima SF = **buon'anima**; *vedi* **anima**

buona'notte ESCL good night! ▶ SF: **dare la ~ a** to say good night to

buona'sera ESCL good evening!

buoncos'tume SM public morality; **la (squadra del) ~** (*Polizia*) the vice squad

buondì ESCL hello!

buongi'orno [bwon'dʒorno] ESCL good morning (*o* afternoon)!

buon'grado AV: **di ~** willingly

buongus'taio, -a SM/F gourmet

buon'gusto SM good taste

---

bu'ono, -a

(*ag: dav sm* **buon** + C *o* V, **buono** + s *impura*, gn, pn, ps, z; *dav sf* **buon'** + V) AG (*gen*) good; **un buon pranzo/ristorante** a good lunch/restaurant; **(stai) buono!** behave!; **che buono!** (*cibo*) this is nice!

2 (*benevolo*): **buono (con)** good (to), kind (to)

3 (*giusto, valido*) right; **al momento buono** at the right moment

4 (*adatto*): **buono a/da** fit for/to; **essere buono a nulla** to be no good *o* use at anything

5 (*auguri*): **buon anno!** happy New Year!; **buon appetito!** enjoy your meal!; **buon compleanno!** happy birthday!; **buon divertimento!** have a nice time!; **buona fortuna!** good luck!; **buon riposo!** sleep well!; **buon viaggio!** bon voyage!, have a good trip!

6: **ad ogni buon conto** in any case; **tante buone cose!** all the best!; **di buon cuore** (*persona*) goodhearted; **di buon grado** willingly; **le buone maniere** good manners; **di buon mattino** early in the morning; **a buon mercato** cheap; **di buon'ora** early; **mettere una buona parola** to put in a good word; **di buon passo** at a good pace; **buon pro ti faccia!** much good may it do you!; **buon senso** common sense; **la buona società** the upper classes; **una buona volta** once and for all; **fare qc alla buona** to do sth simply *o* in a simple way; **un tipo alla buona** an easy-going sort

▶ SM/F: **essere un buono/una buona** to be a good person; **buono a nulla** good for nothing; **i buoni e i cattivi** (*in storia, film*) the goodies and the baddies; **accetterà con le buone o con le cattive** one way or another he's going to agree to it

▶ SM 1 (*bontà*) goodness, good

2 (*Comm*) voucher, coupon; **buono d'acquisto** credit note; **buono di cassa** cash voucher;

---

buono di consegna delivery note; **buono fruttifero** interest-bearing bond; **buono ordinario del Tesoro** short-term Treasury bond; **buono postale fruttifero** interest-bearing bond (*issued by Italian Post Office*); **buono del Tesoro** Treasury bill

buon'senso SM = **buon senso**

buontem'pone, -a SM/F jovial person

buonu'scita [bwonuʃ'ʃita] SF (*Industria*) golden handshake; (*di affitti*) sum paid for the relinquishing of tenancy rights

buratti'naio, -a SM/F puppeteer

burat'tino SM puppet

'burbero, -a AG surly, gruff

'burla SF prank, trick

bur'lare /72/ VT: **~ qc/qn**, **burlarsi di qc/qn** to make fun of sth/sb

bu'rocrate SM bureaucrat

buro'cratico, -a, -ci, -che AG bureaucratic

burocra'zia [burokrat'tsia] SF bureaucracy

bur'rasca, -sche SF storm

burras'coso, -a AG stormy

'burro SM butter

bur'rone SM ravine

bus'care /20/ VT (*raffreddore*: *anche*: **buscarsi**) to get, catch; **buscarle** (*col*) to get a hiding

buscherò *ecc* [buske'rɔ] VB *vedi* **buscare**

bus'sare /72/ VI to knock; **~ a quattrini** (*fig*) to ask for money

'bussola SF compass; **perdere la ~** (*fig*) to lose one's bearings

'busta SF (*da lettera*) envelope; (*astuccio*) case; **in ~ aperta/chiusa** in an unsealed/sealed envelope; **~ paga** pay packet

busta'rella SF bribe, backhander

bus'tina SF (*piccola busta*) envelope; (*di cibi, farmaci*) sachet; (*Mil*) forage cap; **~ di tè** tea bag

'busto SM bust; (*indumento*) corset, girdle; **a mezzo ~** (*fotografia, ritratto*) half-length

bu'tano SM butane

but'tare /72/ VT to throw; (*anche*: **buttare via**) to throw away ■ **buttarsi** VPR (*saltare*) to jump; **~ giù** (*scritto*) to scribble down, dash off; (*cibo*) to gulp down; (*edificio*) to pull down, demolish; (*pasta, verdura*) to put into boiling water; **ho buttato là una frase** I mentioned it in passing; **buttiamoci!** (*saltiamo*) let's jump!; (*rischiamo*) let's have a go at!; **buttarsi dalla finestra** to jump out of the window

'buzzo ['buddzo] SM (*col: pancia*) belly, paunch; **di ~ buono** (*con impegno*) with a will

byte ['bait] SM INV byte

Cc

C, c [tʃi] SM O F INV (*lettera*) C, c ▶ABBR (*Geo*) = **capo**; (= *Celsius, centigrado*) C; (= *conto*) a/c; **C come Como** ≈ C for Charlie

CA SIGLA = **Cagliari**

c.a. ABBR (*Elettr*) *vedi* **corrente alternata**; (*Comm*) = **corrente anno**

caba'ret [kaba'rε] SM INV cabaret

ca'bina SF (*di nave*) cabin; (*da spiaggia*) beach hut; (*di autocarro, treno*) cab; (*di aereo*) cockpit; (*di ascensore*) cage; **~ di pilotaggio** cockpit; **~ di proiezione** (*Cine*) projection booth; **~ di registrazione** recording booth; **~ telefonica** callbox, (tele) phone box o booth

cabi'nato SM cabin cruiser

ca'blaggio [ka'bladdʒo] SM wiring

cablo'gramma SM cable(gram)

ca'cao SM cocoa

'cacca SF (*col: anche fig*) shit (!)

'caccia ['kattʃa] SF hunting; (*con fucile*) shooting; (*inseguimento*) chase; (*cacciagione*) game ▶ SM INV (*aereo*) fighter; (*nave*) destroyer; **andare a ~** to go hunting; **andare a ~ di guai** to be asking for trouble; **~ grossa** big-game hunting; **~ all'uomo** manhunt

cacciabombardi'ere [kattʃabombar'djεre] SM fighter-bomber

cacciagi'one [kattʃa'dʒone] SF game

cacci'are [kat'tʃare] /**14**/ VT to hunt; (*mandar via*) to chase away; (*ficcare*) to shove, stick ▶ VI to hunt ▪ **cacciarsi** VPR (*col: mettersi*): **cacciarsi tra la folla** to plunge into the crowd; **~ fuori qc** to whip o pull sth out; **~ un urlo** to let out a yell; **dove s'è cacciata la mia borsa?** where has my bag got to?; **cacciarsi nei guai** to get into trouble

caccia'tora [kattʃa'tora] SF (*giacca*) hunting jacket; (*Cuc*): **pollo** *ecc* **alla ~** chicken *ecc* chasseur

caccia'tore [kattʃa'tore] SM hunter; **~ di frodo** poacher; **~ di dote** fortune-hunter

cacciatorpedini'ere [kattʃatorpedi'njεre] SM destroyer

caccia'vite [kattʃa'vite] SM INV screwdriver

cache'mire [kaʃ'mir] SM INV cashmere

ca'chet [ka'ʃε] SM (*Med*) capsule; (: *compressa*) tablet; (*compenso*) fee; (*colorante per capelli*) rinse

'cachi ['kaki] SM INV (*albero, frutto*) persimmon; (*colore*) khaki ▶ AG INV khaki

'cacio ['katʃo] SM cheese; **essere come il ~ sui maccheroni** (*fig*) to turn up at the right moment

'cactus SM INV cactus

ca'davere SM (dead) body, corpse

cada'verico, -a, -ci, -che AG (*fig*) deathly pale

'caddi *ecc* VB *vedi* **cadere**

ca'dente AG falling; (*casa*) tumbledown; (*persona*) decrepit

ca'denza [ka'dεntsa] SF cadence; (*andamento ritmico*) rhythm; (*Mus*) cadenza

ca'dere /**18**/ VI to fall; (*denti, capelli*) to fall out; (*tetto*) to fall in; **questa gonna cade bene** this skirt hangs well; **lasciar ~** (*anche fig*) to drop; **~ dal sonno** to be falling asleep on one's feet; **~ ammalato** to fall ill; **~ dalle nuvole** (*fig*) to be taken aback

ca'detto SM cadet

cadrò *ecc* VB *vedi* **cadere**

ca'duta SF fall; **la ~ dei capelli** hair loss; **~ di temperatura** drop in temperature; **~ del sistema** (*Inform*) system failure

ca'duto, -a AG (*morto*) dead ▶ SM dead soldier; **monumento ai caduti** war memorial

caffè SM INV coffee; (*locale*) café; **~ corretto** coffee with liqueur; **~ in grani** coffee beans; **~ macchiato** coffee with a dash of milk; **~ macinato** ground coffee

caffe'ina SF caffeine

caffel'latte SM INV white coffee

caffette'ria SF coffee shop

caffetti'era SF coffeepot

ca'fone, -a SM/F (*contadino*) peasant; (*peg*) boor

cagio'nare [kadʒo'nare] /**72**/ VT to cause, be the cause of

cagio'nevole [kadʒo'nevole] AG delicate, weak

cagli'are [kaʎ'ʎare] /**27**/ VI to curdle

cagliari'tano, -a [kaʎʎari'tano] AG of (o from) Cagliari

'cagna ['kaɲɲa] SF (*Zool, peg*) bitch (*anche!*)

ca'gnara [kaɲ'nara] SF (*fig*) uproar

ca'gnesco, -a, -schi, -sche [kaɲ'nesko] AG (*fig*): **guardare qn in ~** to scowl at sb

CAI SIGLA M = **Club Alpino Italiano**

'Cairo SM: **il ~** Cairo

cala'brese AG, SMF Calabrian

cala'brone SM hornet

Cala'hari [kala'ari]: **il Deserto di ~** SM the Kalahari Desert

cala'maio SM inkpot; inkwell

cala'maro SM squid

cala'mita SF magnet

calamità SF INV calamity, disaster; **~ naturale** natural disaster

ca'lare /**72**/ VT (*far discendere*) to lower; (*Maglia*) to decrease ▶ VI (*discendere*) to go (*o* come) down; (*tramontare*) to set, go down; **~ di peso** to lose weight

ca'lata SF (*invasione*) invasion

'calca SF throng, press

cal'cagno [kal'kaɲɲo] SM heel

cal'care /**20**/ SM limestone; (*incrostazione*) (lime) scale ▶ VT (*premere coi piedi*) to tread, press down; (*premere con forza*) to press down; (*mettere in rilievo*) to stress; **~ la mano** to overdo it, exaggerate; **~ le scene** (*fig*) to be on the stage; **~ le orme di qn** (*fig*) to follow in sb's footsteps

'calce ['kaltʃe] SM: **in ~** at the foot of the page ▶ SF lime; **~ viva** quicklime

calces'truzzo [kaltʃes'truttso] SM concrete

cal'cetto [kal'tʃetto] SM (*calcio-balilla*) table football; (*calcio a cinque*) five-a-side (football)

calcherò ecc [kalke'rɔ] VB vedi **calcare**

calci'are [kal'tʃare] /**14**/ VT, VI to kick

calcia'tore, -trice [kaltʃa'tore] SM/F footballer (BRIT), (football) player

cal'cina [kal'tʃina] SF (lime) mortar

calci'naccio [kaltʃi'nattʃo] SM flake of plaster

'calcio ['kaltʃo] SM (*pedata*) kick; (*sport*) football, soccer; (*di pistola, fucile*) butt; (*Chim*) calcium; **~ d'angolo** (*Sport*) corner (kick); **~ di punizione** (*Sport*) free kick; **~ di rigore** penalty

'calco, -chi SM (*Arte*) casting, moulding (BRIT), molding (US); cast, mo(u)ld

calco'lare /**72**/ VT to calculate, work out, reckon; (*ponderare*) to weigh (up)

calcola'tore, -'trice AG calculating ▶ SM calculator ▶ SM/F (*fig*) calculating person ▶ SF (*anche:* **macchina calcolatrice**) calculator; **~ digitale** digital computer; **~ elettronico** computer; **~ da tavolo** desktop computer

calcola'trice SF calculator

'calcolo SM (*anche Mat*) calculation; (*infinitesimale ecc*) calculus; (*Med*) stone; **fare il ~ di qc** to work sth out; **fare i propri calcoli** (*fig*) to weigh the pros and cons; **per ~** out of self-interest

cal'daia SF boiler

caldar'rosta SF roast chestnut

caldeggi'are [kalded'dʒare] /**62**/ VT to support

'caldo, -a AG warm; (*molto caldo*) hot; (*fig: appassionato*) keen; hearty ▶ SM heat; **ho ~** I'm warm; I'm hot; **fa ~** it's warm; it's hot; **non mi fa né ~ né freddo** I couldn't care less; **a ~** (*fig*) in the heat of the moment

caleidos'copio SM kaleidoscope

calen'dario SM calendar

ca'lende SFPL calends; **rimandare qc alle ~ greche** to put sth off indefinitely

ca'lesse SM gig

'calibro SM (*di arma*) calibre, bore; (*Tecn*) callipers *pl*; (*fig*) calibre; **di grosso ~** (*fig*) prominent

'calice ['kalitʃe] SM goblet; (*Rel*) chalice

Cali'fornia SF California

californi'ano, -a AG Californian

ca'ligine [ka'lidʒine] SF fog; (*mista con fumo*) smog

call 'center [kol'sɛnter] SM INV call centre (BRIT), call center (US)

calligra'fia SF (*scrittura*) handwriting; (*arte*) calligraphy

'callo SM callus; (*ai piedi*) corn; **fare il ~ a qc** to get used to sth

'calma SF calm; **faccia con ~** take your time

cal'mante SM sedative, tranquillizer

cal'mare /**72**/ VT to calm; (*lenire*) to soothe ■ **calmarsi** VPR to grow calm, calm down; (*vento*) to abate; (*dolori*) to ease

calmi'ere SM controlled price

'calmo, -a AG calm, quiet

'calo SM (*Comm: di prezzi*) fall; (: *di volume*) shrinkage; (: *di peso*) loss

ca'lore SM warmth; (*intenso, Fisica*) heat; **essere in ~** (*Zool*) to be on heat

calo'ria SF calorie

calo'rifero SM radiator

calo'roso, -a AG warm; **essere ~** not to feel the cold

calpes'tare /**72**/ VT to tread on, trample on; **"è vietato ~ l'erba"** "keep off the grass"

ca'lunnia SF slander; (*scritta*) libel

calunni'are /**19**/ VT to slander

cal'vario SM (*fig*) affliction, cross

cal'vizie [kal'vittsje] SF baldness

'calvo, -a AG bald

'calza ['kaltsa] SF (*da donna*) stocking; (*da uomo*) sock; **fare la ~** to knit; **calze di nailon** nylons, (nylon) stockings

calza'maglia [kaltsa'maʎʎa] SF tights *pl*; (*per danza, ginnastica*) leotard

cal'zare [kal'tsare] /**72**/ VT (*scarpe, guanti: mettersi*)

to put on; (: *portare*) to wear ▶ vɪ to fit; **~ a pennello** to fit like a glove

calza'tura [kaltsa'tura] sғ footwear

calzaturi'ficio [kaltsaturi'fitʃo] sᴍ shoe o footwear factory

cal'zetta [kal'tsetta] sϝ ankle sock; **una mezza
~** (*fig*) a nobody

calzet'tone [kaltset'tone] sᴍ heavy knee-
length sock

cal'zino [kal'tsino] sᴍ sock

calzo'laio, -a [kaltso'lajo] sᴍ/ϝ shoemaker;
(*che ripara scarpe*) cobbler

calzole'ria [kaltsole'ria] sϝ (*negozio*) shoe shop;
(*arte*) shoemaking

calzon'cini [kaltson'tʃini] sᴍᴘʟ shorts; **~ da
bagno** (swimming) trunks

cal'zone [kal'tsone] sᴍ trouser leg; (*Cuc*) savoury
turnover made with pizza dough ■ **calzoni** sᴍᴘʟ
(*pantaloni*) trousers (*Bʀɪᴛ*), pants (*US*)

camale'onte sᴍ chameleon

cambi'ale sϝ bill (of exchange); (*pagherò cambiario*) promissory note; **~ di comodo** o **di favore**
accommodation bill

cambia'mento sᴍ change; **cambiamenti climatici** climate change *sg*

cambi'are /19/ ᴠᴛ to change; (*modificare*) to alter,
change; (*barattare*): **~ (qc con qn/qc)** to
exchange (sth with sb/for sth) ▶ vɪ to change,
alter ■ **cambiarsi** ᴠᴘʀ (*variare abito*) to change; **~
casa** to move (house); **~ idea** to change one's
mind; **~ treno** to change trains; **~ le carte in
tavola** (*fig*) to change one's tune; **~ (l')aria in
una stanza** to air a room; **è ora di ~ aria** (*andarsene*) it's time to move on

cambiava'lute sᴍ ɪɴᴠ exchange office

'cambio sᴍ change; (*modifica*) alteration,
change; (*scambio, Comm*) exchange; (*corso dei
cambi*) rate (of exchange); (*Tecn, Aut*) gears pl; **in
~ di** in exchange for; **dare il ~ a qn** to take over
from sb; **fare il** o **un ~** to change (over); **~ a termine** (*Comm*) forward exchange

'Cambital sɪɢʟᴀ ᴍ = **Ufficio Italiano dei Cambi**

Cam'bogia [kam'bɔdʒa] sϝ: **la ~** Cambodia

cambogi'ano, -a [kambo'dʒano] ᴀɢ, sᴍ/ϝ
Cambodian

cam'busa sϝ storeroom

'camera sϝ room; (*anche:* **camera da letto**) bedroom; (*Pol*) chamber, house; **~ ardente** mortuary chapel; **~ d'aria** inner tube; (*di pallone*)
bladder; **~ blindata** strongroom; **C~ di Commercio** Chamber of Commerce; **C~ dei Deputati** Chamber of Deputies, ≈ House of
Commons (*Bʀɪᴛ*), ≈ House of Representatives
(*US*); **~ a gas** gas chamber; **~ del lavoro** trades
union centre (*Bʀɪᴛ*), labor union center (*US*); **~
a un letto/a due letti/matrimoniale** single/
twin-bedded/double room; **~ oscura** (*Fot*) dark
room; **~ da pranzo** dining room

The **Camera dei deputati** is the lower house of
the Italian Parliament and is presided over by
the *Presidente della Camera*, who is chosen by the
deputati. Elections to the Chamber are normally
held every 5 years. Since the electoral reform of
1993 members have been voted in via a system
which combines a first-past-the-post element
with proportional representation. See also **parlamento**

Do not translate the Italian word **camera** by
camera.

came'rata, -i, -e sᴍ/ϝ companion, mate ▶ sϝ
dormitory

camera'tismo sᴍ comradeship

cameri'era sϝ (*domestica*) maid; (*che serve a
tavola*) waitress; (*che fa le camere*) chambermaid

cameri'ere sᴍ (man)servant; (*di ristorante*)
waiter

came'rino sᴍ (*Teat*) dressing room

'Camerun sᴍ: **il ~** Cameroon

'camice ['kamitʃe] sᴍ (*Rel*) alb; (*per medici ecc*)
white coat

cami'cetta [kami'tʃetta] sϝ blouse

ca'micia, -cie [ka'mitʃa] sϝ (*da uomo*) shirt; (*da
donna*) blouse; **nascere con la ~** (*fig*) to be born
lucky; **sudare sette camicie** (*fig*) to have a hell
of a time; **~ di forza** straitjacket; **~ da notte** (*da
donna*) nightdress; (*da uomo*) nightshirt; **C~
nera** (*fascista*) Blackshirt

camici'aio, -a [kami'tʃajo] sᴍ/ϝ (*sarto*) shirt-
maker; (*che vende camicie*) shirtseller

camici'ola [kami'tʃɔla] sϝ vest

camici'otto [kami'tʃɔtto] sᴍ casual shirt; (*per
operai*) smock

cami'netto sᴍ hearth, fireplace

ca'mino sᴍ chimney; (*focolare*) fireplace,
hearth

'camion sᴍ ɪɴᴠ lorry (*Bʀɪᴛ*), truck (*US*)

camion'cino [kamjon'tʃino] sᴍ van

camio'netta sϝ jeep

camio'nista, -i sᴍ lorry driver (*Bʀɪᴛ*), truck
driver (*US*)

'camma sϝ cam; **albero a camme** camshaft

cam'mello sᴍ (*Zool*) camel; (*tessuto*) camel hair

cam'meo sᴍ cameo

cammi'nare /72/ vɪ to walk; (*funzionare*) to work,
go; **~ a carponi** o **a quattro zampe** to go on all
fours

cammi'nata sϝ walk; **fare una ~** to go for a
walk

cam'mino sᴍ walk; (*sentiero*) path; (*itinerario,
direzione, tragitto*) way; **mettersi in ~** to set o start
off; **cammin facendo** on the way; **riprendere il
~** to continue on one's way

camo'milla sϝ camomile; (*infuso*) camomile tea

ca'morra sϝ Camorra; (*fig*) racket

camor'rista, -i, -e SM/F member of the Camorra; (*fig*) racketeer

ca'moscio [ka'mɔʃʃo] SM chamois; **di ~** (*scarpe, borsa*) suede cpd

cam'pagna [kam'paɲɲa] SF country, countryside; (*Pol, Comm, Mil*) campaign; **in ~** in the country; **andare in ~** to go to the country; **fare una ~** to campaign; **~ promozionale vendite** sales campaign; **~ pubblicitaria** advertising campaign

> Anche se **country** e **countryside** sono spesso intercambiabili, quando si parla di paesaggio, specie se si esprime un giudizio estetico, si usa **countryside**.
> *la splendida campagna romana* **the beautiful Roman countryside**
> Si usa **country** in frasi come: *viviamo/ci siamo trasferiti in campagna* **we live in/moved to the country**.

campa'gnolo, -a [kampaɲ'ɲɔlo] AG country cpd ▶ SF (*Aut*) cross-country vehicle

cam'pale AG field cpd; (*fig*): **una giornata ~** a hard day

cam'pana SF bell; (*anche*: **campana di vetro**) bell jar; **sordo come una ~** as deaf as a doorpost; **sentire l'altra ~** (*fig*) to hear the other side of the story; **~ (per la raccolta del vetro)** bottle bank

campa'nella SF small bell; (*di tenda*) curtain ring

campa'nello SM (*all'uscio, da tavola*) bell

campa'nile SM bell tower, belfry

campani'lismo SM parochialism

cam'pano, -a AG of (*o* from) Campania

cam'pare /72/ VI to live; (*tirare avanti*) to get by, manage; **~ alla giornata** to live from day to day

cam'pato, -a AG: **~ in aria** unsound, unfounded

campeggi'are [kamped'dʒare] /62/ VI to camp; (*risaltare*) to stand out

campeggia'tore, -'trice [kampeddʒa'tore] SM/F camper

cam'peggio [kam'peddʒo] SM camping; (*terreno*) camp site; **fare (del) ~** to go camping

'camper ['kamper] SM INV motor caravan (BRIT), motor home (US)

cam'pestre AG country cpd, rural; **corsa ~** cross-country race

Campi'doglio [kampi'dɔʎʎo] SM: **il ~** the Capitol

> The **Campidoglio**, one of the Seven Hills of Rome, has been inhabited since the Bronze Age and was at the centre of political life in the city during the Middle Ages. Its square, designed by Michelangelo, houses the *Palazzo Senatorio* together with the *palazzi* of the *Museo Capitolino* and the *Museo dei Conservatori*. The *Palazzo Senatorio* is the home of the *Comune di Roma*. The *Campidoglio* is often used to mean the mayor of Rome's office.

'camping ['kæmpiŋ] SM INV camp site

campiona'mento SM sampling

campio'nario, -a AG: **fiera campionaria** trade fair ▶ SM collection of samples

campio'nato SM championship

campiona'tura SF (*Comm*) production of samples; (*Statistica*) sampling

campi'one, -'essa SM/F (*Sport*) champion ▶ SM (*Comm*) sample; **~ gratuito** free sample; **prelievi di ~** product samples

'campo SM (*gen*) field; (*Mil*) field; (: *accampamento*) camp; (*spazio delimitato: sportivo ecc*) ground; field; (*di quadro*) background; **i campi** (*campagna*) the countryside; **padrone del ~** (*fig*) victor; **~ da aviazione** airfield; **~ di battaglia** (*Mil, fig*) battlefield; **~ di concentramento** concentration camp; **~ di golf** golf course; **~ profughi** refugee camp; **~ sportivo** sports ground; **~ lungo** (*Cine, TV, Fot*) long shot; **~ nomadi** travellers' camp; **~ da tennis** tennis court; **~ visivo** field of vision

campobas'sano, -a AG of (*o* from) Campobasso

campo'santo (*pl* **campisanti**) SM cemetery

camuf'fare /72/ VT to disguise ■ **camuffarsi** VPR: **camuffarsi (da)** to disguise o.s. (as); (*per ballo in maschera*) to dress up (as)

CAN ABBR (= *Costo, Assicurazione e Nolo*) CIF

Can. ABBR (*Geo*) = **canale**

'Canada SM: **il ~** Canada

cana'dese AG, SMF Canadian ▶ SF (*anche*: **tenda canadese**) ridge tent

ca'naglia [ka'naʎʎa] SF rabble, mob; (*persona*) scoundrel, rogue

ca'nale SM (*anche fig*) channel; (*artificiale*) canal

'canapa SF hemp; **~ indiana** (*droga*) cannabis

Ca'narie SFPL: **le (isole) ~** the Canary Islands, the Canaries

cana'rino SM canary

Can'berra SF Canberra

cancel'lare [kantʃel'lare] /72/ VT (*con la gomma*) to rub out, erase; (*con la penna*) to strike out; (*annullare*) to annul, cancel; (*disdire*) to cancel; (*Inform*) to delete

cancel'lata [kantʃel'lata] SF railing(s) pl

cancelle'ria [kantʃelle'ria] SF chancery; (*quanto necessario per scrivere*) stationery

cancelli'ere [kantʃel'ljɛre] SM chancellor; (*di tribunale*) clerk of the court

can'cello [kan'tʃɛllo] SM gate

cance'rogeno, -a [kantʃe'rɔdʒeno] AG carcinogenic ▶ SM carcinogen

cance'rologo, -a, -gi, -ghe [kantʃe'rɔlogo] SM/F cancer specialist

cance'roso, -a [kantʃe'roso] AG cancerous ▶ SM/F cancer patient

can'crena SF gangrene

'cancro SM (*Med*) cancer; **C~** Cancer; **essere del C~** to be Cancer

candeggi'are [kanded'dʒare] /**62**/ VT to bleach

candeg'gina [kanded'dʒina] SF bleach

can'deggio [kan'deddʒo] SM bleaching

can'dela SF candle; **~ (di accensione)** (*Aut*) spark(ing) plug; **una lampadina da 100 candele** (*Elettr*) a 100 watt bulb; **a lume di ~** by candlelight; **tenere la ~** (*fig*) to play gooseberry (*Brit*), act as chaperone

cande'labro SM candelabra

candeli'ere SM candlestick

cande'lotto SM candle; **~ di dinamite** stick of dynamite; **~ lacrimogeno** tear gas grenade

candi'dare /**72**/ VT to present as candidate ∎ **candidarsi** VPR to present o.s. as candidate

candi'dato, -a SM/F candidate; (*aspirante a una carica*) applicant

candida'tura SF candidature; application

'candido, -a AG white as snow; (*puro*) pure; (*sincero*) sincere, candid

can'dito, -a AG candied

can'dore SM brilliant white; purity, sincerity, candour (*Brit*), candor (*US*)

'cane SM dog; (*di pistola, fucile*) cock; **fa un freddo ~** it's bitterly cold; **non c'era un ~** there wasn't a soul; **quell'attore è un ~** he's a rotten actor; **~ da caccia** hunting dog; **~ da guardia** guard dog; **~ lupo** alsatian; **~ da salotto** lap dog; **~ da slitta** husky; **~ pastore** sheepdog

ca'nestro SM basket; **fare un ~** (*Sport*) to shoot a basket

'canfora SF camphor

cangi'ante [kan'dʒante] AG iridescent; **seta ~** shot silk

can'guro SM kangaroo

ca'nicola SF scorching heat

ca'nile SM kennel; (*di allevamento*) kennels *pl*; **~ municipale** dog pound

ca'nino, -a AG, SM canine

'canna SF (*pianta*) reed; (: *indica, da zucchero*) cane; (*bastone*) stick, cane; (*di fucile*) barrel; (*di organo*) pipe; (*col: Droga*) joint; **~ fumaria** chimney flue; **~ da pesca** (fishing) rod; **~ da zucchero** sugar cane

can'nella SF (*Cuc*) cinnamon; (*di conduttura, botte*) tap

cannel'loni SMPL *pasta tubes stuffed with sauce and baked*

can'neto SM bed of reeds

can'nibale SMF cannibal

cannocchi'ale [kannok'kjale] SM telescope

canno'nata SF: **è una vera ~!** (*fig*) it's (*o* he's *etc*) fantastic!

can'none SM (*Mil*) gun; (: *Storia*) cannon; (*tubo*) pipe, tube; (*piega*) box pleat; (*fig*) ace; **donna ~** fat woman

cannoni'ere SM (*Naut*) gunner; (*Calcio*) goal scorer

can'nuccia, -ce [kan'nuttʃa] SF (drinking) straw

ca'noa SF canoe

'canone SM canon, criterion; (*mensile, annuo*) rent; fee; **legge dell'equo ~** fair rent act

ca'nonica, -che SF presbytery

ca'nonico, -ci SM (*Rel*) canon

canoniz'zare [kanonid'dzare] /**72**/ VT to canonize

ca'noro, -a AG (*uccello*) singing, song *cpd*

ca'notta SF vest

canot'taggio [kanot'taddʒo] SM rowing

canotti'era SF vest (*Brit*), undershirt (*US*)

ca'notto SM small boat, dinghy; canoe

cano'vaccio [kano'vattʃo] SM (*tela*) canvas; (*strofinaccio*) duster; (*trama*) plot

can'tante SMF singer

can'tare /**72**/ VT, VI to sing; **~ vittoria** to crow; **fare ~ qn** (*fig*) to make sb talk

canta'storie SM INV/F INV storyteller

cantau'tore, -'trice SM/F singer-composer

canterel'lare /**72**/ VT, VI to hum, sing to o.s.

canticchi'are [kantik'kjare] /**19**/ VT, VI to hum, sing to o.s.

canti'ere SM (*Edil*) (building) site; (*anche:* **cantiere navale**) shipyard

canti'lena SF (*filastrocca*) lullaby; (*fig*) singsong voice

can'tina SF (*locale*) cellar; (*bottega*) wine shop; **~ sociale** cooperative winegrowers' association

'canto SM song; (*arte*) singing; (*Rel*) chant; chanting; (*Poesia*) poem, lyric; (*parte di una poesia*) canto; (*parte, lato*): **da un ~** on the one hand; **d'altro ~** on the other hand

canto'nata SF (*di edificio*) corner; **prendere una ~** (*fig*) to blunder

can'tone SM (*in Svizzera*) canton

cantoni'era AG: **(casa) ~** road inspector's house

can'tuccio [kan'tuttʃo] SM corner, nook

ca'nuto, -a AG white, whitehaired

canzo'nare [kantso'nare] /**72**/ VT to tease

canzona'tura [kantsona'tura] SF teasing; (*beffa*) joke

can'zone [kan'tsone] SF song; (*Poesia*) canzone

canzoni'ere [kantso'njɛre] SM (*Mus*) songbook; (*Letteratura*) collection of poems

'caos SM INV chaos

ca'otico, -a, -ci, -che AG chaotic

CAP SIGLA M = **codice di avviamento postale**

cap. ABBR (= *capitolo*) ch.

ca'pace [ka'patʃe] AG able, capable; (*ampio, vasto*) large, capacious; **sei ~ di farlo?** can you *o* are you able to do it?; **~ d'intendere e di volere** (*Dir*) in full possession of one's faculties

capacità [kapatʃi'ta] SF INV ability; (*Dir, di recipiente*) capacity; **~ produttiva** production capacity

capaci'tarsi [kapatʃi'tarsi] /72/ VPR: **~ di** to make out, understand

ca'panna SF hut

capan'nello SM knot (of people)

ca'panno SM (*di cacciatori*) hide; (*da spiaggia*) bathing hut

capan'none SM (*Agr*) barn; (*fabbricato industriale*) (factory) shed

caparbietà SF stubbornness

ca'parbio, -a AG stubborn

ca'parra SF deposit, down payment

capa'tina SF: **fare una ~ da qn/in centro** to pop in on sb/into town

capeggi'are [kaped'dʒare] /62/ VT (*rivolta ecc*) to head, lead

ca'pello SM hair ■ **capelli** SMPL (*capigliatura*) hair *sg*; **averne fin sopra i capelli di qc/qn** to be fed up to the (back) teeth with sth/sb; **mi ci hanno tirato per i capelli** (*fig*) they dragged me into it; **tirato per i capelli** (*spiegazione*) far-fetched

> *Capelli*, nel senso di chioma, si traduce **hair** con il verbo al singolare.
> *I capelli di Mirella sono troppo lunghi.* **Mirella's hair is too long.**
> Se invece si intende individuarne una quantità specifica si usa il plurale, quindi con la **–s**, e il verbo va ovviamente al plurale.
> *Ci sono tre lunghi capelli ricci sulla tua giacca.* **There are three long curly hairs on your jacket.**

capel'lone, -a SM/F hippie

capel'luto, -a AG: **cuoio ~** scalp

capez'zale [kapet'tsale] SM bolster; (*fig*) bedside

ca'pezzolo [ka'pettsolo] SM nipple

capi'ente AG capacious

capi'enza [ka'pjentsa] SF capacity

capiglia'tura [kapiλλa'tura] SF hair

capil'lare AG (*fig*) detailed ▶ SM (*Anat: anche:* **vaso capillare**) capillary

ca'pire /55/ VT to understand; **~ al volo** to catch on straight away; **si capisce!** (*certamente!*) of course!, certainly!

capi'tale AG (*mortale*) capital; (*fondamentale*) main *cpd*, chief *cpd* ▶ SF (*città*) capital ▶ SM (*Econ*) capital; **~ azionario** equity capital, share capital; **~ d'esercizio** working capital; **~ fisso** capital assets, fixed capital; **~ immobile** real estate; **~ liquido** cash assets *pl*; **~ mobile** movables *pl*; **~ di rischio** risk capital; **~ sociale** (*di società*) authorized capital; (*di club*) funds *pl*; **~ di ventura** venture capital, risk capital

capita'lismo SM capitalism

capita'lista, -i, -e AG, SM/F capitalist

capitaliz'zare [kapitalid'dzare] /72/ VT to capitalize

capitalizzazi'one [kapitaliddzat'tsjone] SF capitalization

capita'nare /72/ VT to lead; (*Calcio*) to captain

capitane'ria SF: **~ (di porto)** port authorities *pl*

capi'tano SM captain; **~ di lungo corso** master mariner; **~ di ventura** (*Storia*) mercenary leader

capi'tare /72/ VI (*giungere casualmente*) to happen to go, find o.s.; (*accadere*) to happen; (*presentarsi: cosa*) to turn up, present itself ▶ VB IMPERS to happen; **~ a proposito/bene/male** to turn up at the right moment/at a good time/at a bad time; **mi è capitato un guaio** I've had a spot of trouble

capi'tello SM (*Archit*) capital

capito'lare /72/ VI to capitulate

capitolazi'one [kapitolat'tsjone] SF capitulation

ca'pitolo SM chapter ■ **capitoli** SMPL (*Comm*) items; **non ho voce in ~** (*fig*) I have no say in the matter

capi'tombolo SM headlong fall, tumble

'capo SM (*Anat*) head; (*persona*) head, leader; (*: in ufficio*) head, boss; (*: in tribù*) chief; (*estremità: di tavolo, scale*) head, top; (*: di filo*) end; (*Geo*) cape; **andare a ~** to start a new paragraph; **"punto a ~"** "full stop — new paragraph"; **da ~** over again; **in ~ a** (*tempo*) within; **da un ~ all'altro** from one end to the other; **fra ~ e collo** (*all'improvviso*) out of the blue; **un discorso senza né ~ né coda** a senseless o meaningless speech; **~ d'accusa** (*Dir*) charge; **~ di bestiame** head *inv* of cattle; **C~ di Buona Speranza** Cape of Good Hope; **~ di vestiario** item of clothing

capo'banda (*pl* **capibanda**) SM (*Mus*) bandmaster; (*di malviventi, fig*) gang leader

ca'poccia [ka'pottʃa] SM INV (*di lavoranti*) overseer; (*peg: capobanda*) boss

capo'classe (*mpl* **capiclasse**, *fpl* **~**) SM/F (*Ins*) ≈ form captain (BRIT), class president (US)

capocu'oco, -chi SM head cook

Capo'danno SM New Year

capofa'miglia [kapofa'miλλa] (*mpl* **capifamiglia**, *fpl* **~**) SM/F head of the family

capo'fitto: a ~ AV headfirst, headlong

capo'giro [kapo'dʒiro] SM dizziness *no pl*; **da ~** (*fig*) astonishing, staggering

capo'gruppo (*mpl* **capigruppo**, *fpl* **~**) SM/F group leader

capola'voro, -i SM masterpiece

capo'linea (*pl* **capilinea**) SM terminus; (*fig*) end of the line

capo'lino SM: **far ~** to peep out (*o in etc*)

capo'lista (*mpl* **capilista**, *fpl* **~**) SM/F (*Pol*) *top candidate on electoral list*

capolu'ogo (*pl* **capoluoghi** *o* **capiluoghi**) SM chief town, administrative centre (*BRIT*) *o* center (*US*)

capo'mastro (*pl* **capomastri** *o* **capimastri**) SM master builder

capo'rale SM (*Mil*) lance corporal (*BRIT*), private first class (*US*)

capore'parto (*mpl* **capireparto**, *fpl* **~**) SM/F (*di operai*) foreman; (*di ufficio, negozio*) head of department

capo'sala SM *o* F INV (*Med*) head nurse; (: *woman*) ward sister

capo'saldo (*pl* **capisaldi**) SM stronghold; (*fig*: *fondamento*) basis, cornerstone

capo'squadra (*pl* **capisquadra**) SM (*di operai*) foreman, ganger; (*Mil*) squad leader; (*Sport*) team captain

capostazi'one [kapostat'tsjone] (*pl* **capistazione**) SM station master

capos'tipite SM progenitor; (*fig*) earliest example

capo'tavola (*mpl* **capitavola**, *fpl* **~**) SM/F (*persona*) head of the table; **sedere a ~** to sit at the head of the table

ca'pote [ka'pɔt] SF INV (*Aut*) hood (*BRIT*), soft top

capo'treno (*pl* **capitreno** *o* **capotreni**) SM guard

capouf'ficio [kapouf'fitʃo] SM INV/F INV head clerk

'Capo 'Verde SM: **il ~** Cape Verde

capo'verso SM (*di verso, periodo*) first line; (*Tip*) indent; (*paragrafo*) paragraph; (*Dir*: *comma*) section

capo'volgere [kapo'vɔldʒere] /**96**/ VT to overturn; (*fig*) to reverse ◼ **capovolgersi** VPR to overturn; (*barca*) to capsize; (*fig*) to be reversed

capovolgi'mento [kapovoldʒi'mento] SM (*fig*) reversal, complete change

capo'volto, -a PP *di* **capovolgere** ▶ AG upside down; (*barca*) capsized

'cappa SF (*mantello*) cape, cloak; (*del camino*) hood

cap'pella SF (*Rel*) chapel

cappel'lano SM chaplain

cap'pello SM hat; **Tanto di ~!** (*fig*) I take my hat off to you!; **~ a bombetta** bowler (hat), derby (*US*); **~ a cilindro** top hat; **~ di paglia** straw hat

'cappero SM caper

cap'pone SM capon

cappot'tare /**72**/ VI (*Aut*) to overturn

cap'potto SM (over)coat

cappuc'cino [kapput'tʃino] SM (*frate*) Capuchin monk; (*bevanda*) cappuccino

cap'puccio [kap'puttʃo] SM (*copricapo*) hood; (*della biro*) cap

'capra SF (she-)goat

ca'prese AG from (*o* of) Capri

ca'pretto SM kid

ca'priccio [ka'prittʃo] SM caprice, whim; (*bizza*) tantrum; **fare i capricci** to be very naughty; **~ della sorte** quirk of fate

capricci'oso, -a [kaprit'tʃoso] AG capricious, whimsical; naughty

Capri'corno SM Capricorn; **essere del ~** (*dello zodiaco*) to be Capricorn

capri'foglio [kapri'fɔʎʎo] SM honeysuckle

capri'ola SF somersault

capri'olo SM roe deer

'capro SM billy-goat; **~ espiatorio** (*fig*) scapegoat

ca'prone SM billy-goat

'capsula SF capsule; (*di arma, per bottiglie*) cap

cap'tare /**72**/ VT (*Radio, TV*) to pick up; (*cattivarsi*) to gain, win

CAR SIGLA M = **Centro Addestramento Reclute**

cara'bina SF rifle

carabini'ere SM *member of Italian military police force*

Forming part of the armed forces, the **Carabinieri** are police who have civil as well as military duties and are responsible for maintaining public order. They include paratroop units and mounted divisions and report to the Minister of Defence. The emergency telephone number for the *Carabinieri* is 112.

Ca'racas SF Caracas

ca'raffa SF carafe

Ca'raibi SMPL: **il mar dei ~** the Caribbean (Sea)

cara'ibico, -a, -ci, -che AG Caribbean

cara'mella SF sweet

cara'mello SM caramel

ca'rato SM (*di oro, diamante ecc*) carat

ca'rattere SM character; (*caratteristica*) characteristic, trait; **avere un buon ~** to be good-natured; **informazione di ~ tecnico/confidenziale** information of a technical/confidential nature; **essere in ~ con qc** (*intonarsi*) to be in harmony with sth; **~ jolly** wild card

caratte'rino SM difficult nature *o* character

caratte'ristico, -a, -ci, -che AG characteristic ▶ SF characteristic, feature, trait; **segni caratteristici** (*su passaporto ecc*) distinguishing marks

caratteriz'zare [karatterid'dzare] /**72**/ VT to characterize, distinguish

carboi'drato SM carbohydrate

carbo'naio SM (*chi fa carbone*) charcoal-burner; (*commerciante*) coalman, coal merchant

car'bone SM coal; **~ fossile** (pit) coal; **essere** *o* **stare sui carboni ardenti** to be like a cat on hot bricks

car'bonio SM (*Chim*) carbon

carboniz'zare [karbonid'dzare] /**72**/ VT (*legna*) to carbonize; (: *parzialmente*) to char; **morire carbonizzato** to be burned to death

carbu'rante SM (*motor*) fuel

carbura'tore SM carburettor

car'cassa SF carcass; (*fig: peg: macchina ecc*) (old) wreck

carce'rato, -a [kartʃe'rato] SM/F prisoner

'carcere ['kartʃere] SM prison; (*pena*) imprisonment; **~ di massima sicurezza** top-security prison

carceri'ere, -a [kartʃe'rjɛre] SM/F (*anche fig*) jailer

carci'ofo [kar'tʃɔfo] SM artichoke

cardel'lino SM goldfinch

car'diaco, -a, -ci, -che AG cardiac, heart *cpd*

cardi'nale AG, SM cardinal

'cardine SM hinge

cardiolo'gia [kardjolo'dʒia] SF cardiology

cardi'ologo, -gi SM heart specialist, cardiologist

'cardo SM thistle

ca'rente AG: **~ di** lacking in

ca'renza [ka'rɛntsa] SF lack, scarcity; (*vitaminica*) deficiency

cares'tia SF famine; (*penuria*) scarcity, dearth

ca'rezza [ka'rettsa] SF caress; **dare** *o* **fare una ~ a** (*persona*) to caress; (*animale*) to stroke, pat

carez'zare [karet'tsare] /**20**/ VT to caress, stroke, fondle

carez'zevole [karet'tsevole] AG sweet, endearing

'cargo, -ghi SM (*nave*) cargo boat, freighter; (*aereo*) freighter

cari'are /**20**/ VT, **cari'arsi** VPR (*denti*) to decay

'carica SF *vedi* **carico**

caricabatte'ria SM INV (*Elettr*) battery charger

cari'care /**20**/ VT (*merce*) to load; (*aggravare: anche fig*) to weigh down; (*orologio*) to wind up; (*batteria, Mil*) to charge; (*Inform*) to load ∎ **caricarsi** VPR: **caricarsi di** to burden *o* load o.s. with; (*fig: di responsabilità, impegni*) to burden o.s. with

carica'tura SF caricature

'carico, -a, -chi, -che AG (*fucile*) loaded; (*orologio*) wound up; (*batteria*) charged; (*colore*) deep; (*caffè, tè*) strong; **~ di** (*che porta un peso*) loaded *o* laden with ▸ SM (*il caricare*) loading; (*ciò che si carica*) load; (*Comm*) shipment; (*fig: peso*) burden, weight ▸ SF (*mansione ufficiale*) office, position; (*Mil, Tecn, Elettr*) charge; **~ di debiti** up to one's ears in debt; **persona a ~** dependant; **essere a ~ di qn** (*spese ecc*) to be charged to sb; (*accusa, prova*) to be against sb; **testimone a ~** witness for the prosecution; **farsi ~ di** (*problema, responsabilità*) to take on; **a ~ del cliente** at the customer's expense; **~ di lavoro** (*di ditta, reparto*) workload; **~ utile** payload; **capacità di ~** cargo capacity; **entrare/essere in carica** to come into/be in office; **ricoprire** *o* **rivestire una carica** to hold a position; **uscire di carica** to leave office; **dare la carica a** (*orologio*) to wind up; (*fig: persona*) to back up; **tornare alla carica** (*fig*) to insist, persist; **ha una forte carica di simpatia** he's very likeable

'carie SF (*dentaria*) decay

ca'rino, -a AG (*grazioso*) lovely, pretty, nice; (*simpatico*) nice

ca'risma [ka'rizma] SM charisma

caris'matico, -a, -ci, -che AG charismatic

carità SF charity; **per ~!** (*escl di rifiuto*) good heavens, no!

carita'tevole AG charitable

carnagi'one [karna'dʒone] SF complexion

car'nale AG (*amore*) carnal; (*fratello*) blood *cpd*

'carne SF flesh; (*bovina, ovina ecc*) meat; **in ~ e ossa** in the flesh, in person; **essere (bene) in ~** to be well padded, be plump; **non essere né ~ né pesce** (*fig*) to be neither fish nor fowl; **~ di manzo/maiale/pecora** beef/pork/mutton; **~ in scatola** tinned *o* canned meat; **~ tritata** *o* **macinata** mince (BRIT), hamburger meat (US), minced (BRIT) *o* ground (US) meat

car'nefice [kar'nefitʃe] SM executioner; hangman

carnefi'cina [karnefi'tʃina] SF carnage; (*fig*) disaster

carne'vale SM carnival; **C~** *see note*

Carnevale is the name given to the period between Epiphany (6 January) and the beginning of Lent, when people throw parties, buy the traditional fried pasta tubes with sweet fillings, put on processions with spectacular floats, build bonfires in the *piazze* and dress up in fabulous costumes and masks. Building to a peak just before Lent, *Carnevale* culminates in the festivities of *Martedì grasso* (Shrove Tuesday). Two of the most famous are held in Venice and Viareggio.

---

car'nivoro, -a AG carnivorous

car'noso, -a AG fleshy; (*pianta, frutto, radice*) pulpy; (*labbra*) full

'caro, -a AG (*amato*) dear; (*costoso*) dear, expensive; **se ti è cara la vita** if you value your life; **è troppo ~** it's too expensive

ca'rogna [ka'roɲɲa] SF carrion; (*fig: col*) swine

caro'sello SM merry-go-round

ca'rota SF carrot

caro'vana SF caravan

caro'vita SM high cost of living

'carpa SF carp

Car'pazi [kar'patsi] SMPL: **i ~** the Carpathian Mountains

carpente'ria SF carpentry

carpenti'ere SM carpenter

car'pire /55/ VT: ~ **qc a qn** (*segreto ecc*) to get sth out of sb

car'poni AV on all fours

car'rabile AG suitable for vehicles; **"passo ~"** "keep clear"

car'raio, -a AG: **passo ~** vehicle entrance

carré SM (*acconciatura*) bob

carreggi'ata [karred'dʒata] SF carriageway (BRIT), roadway; **rimettersi in ~** (*fig: recuperare*) to catch up; **tenersi in ~** (*fig*) to keep to the right path

carrel'lata SF (*Cine, TV: tecnica*) tracking; (: *scena*) running shot; **~ di successi** medley of hit tunes

car'rello SM trolley; (*Aer*) undercarriage; (*Cine*) dolly; (*di macchina da scrivere*) carriage; (*Internet*) shopping basket (BRIT), shopping cart (US)

car'retta SF: **tirare la ~** (*fig*) to plod along

car'retto SM handcart

carri'era SF career; **fare ~** to get on; **ufficiale di ~** (*Mil*) regular officer; **a gran ~** at full speed

carri'ola SF wheelbarrow

'carro SM cart, wagon; **il Gran/Piccolo C~** (*Astr*) the Great/Little Bear; **mettere il ~ avanti ai buoi** (*fig*) to put the cart before the horse; **~ armato** tank; **~ attrezzi** (*Aut*) breakdown van (BRIT), tow truck (US); **~ funebre** hearse; **~ merci/bestiame** (*Ferr*) goods/animal wagon

car'roccio [kar'rɔtʃo] SM (*Pol*): **il C~** *symbol of Lega Nord*

car'rozza [kar'rɔttsa] SF carriage, coach; **~ letto** (*Ferr*) sleeper; **~ ristorante** (*Ferr*) dining car

carroz'zella [karrot'tsɛlla] SF (*per bambini*) pram (BRIT), baby carriage (US); (*per invalidi*) wheelchair

carrozze'ria [karrottse'ria] SF body, coachwork (BRIT); (*officina*) coachbuilder's workshop (BRIT), body shop

carrozzi'ere [karrot'tsjere] SM (*Aut: progettista*) car designer; (: *meccanico*) coachbuilder

carroz'zina [karrot'tsina] SF pram (BRIT), baby carriage (US)

carroz'zone [karrot'tsone] SM (*da circo, di zingari*) caravan

car'rucola SF pulley

'carta SF paper; (*al ristorante*) menu; (*Geo*) map; plan; (*documento*) card; (*costituzione*) charter ■ **carte** SFPL (*documenti*) papers, documents; **alla ~** (*al ristorante*) à la carte; **cambiare le carte in tavola** (*fig*) to shift one's ground; **fare carte false** (*fig*) to go to great lengths; **~ assegni** bank card; **~ assorbente** blotting paper; **~ bollata** o **da bollo** (*Amm*) official stamped paper; **~ (da gioco)** playing card; **~ di credito** credit card; **~**

di debito cash card; **~ fedeltà** loyalty card; **~ (geografica)** map; **~ d'identità** identity card; **~ igienica** toilet paper; **~ d'imbarco** (*Aer, Naut*) boarding card, boarding pass; **~ da lettere** writing paper; **~ libera** (*Amm*) unstamped paper; **~ stradale** road map; **~ millimetrata** graph paper; **~ oleata** waxed paper; **~ da pacchi**, **~ da imballo** wrapping paper, brown paper; **~ da parati** wallpaper; **~ verde** (*Aut*) green card; **~ vetrata** sandpaper; **~ da visita** visiting card

cartacar'bone (*pl* **cartecarbone**) SF carbon paper

car'taccia, -ce [kar'tattʃa] SF waste paper

cartamo'dello SM (*Cucito*) paper pattern

cartamo'neta SF paper money

carta'pecora SF parchment

carta'pesta SF papier-mâché

cartas'traccia [kartas'trattʃa] SF waste paper

car'teggio [kar'teddʒo] SM correspondence

car'tella SF (*scheda*) card; (*custodia: di cartone, Inform*) folder; (: *di uomo d'affari ecc*) briefcase; (: *di scolaro*) schoolbag, satchel; **~ clinica** (*Med*) case sheet; **~ della posta in arrivo** (*Inform*) inbox; **~ della posta in uscita** (*Inform*) outbox

cartel'lino SM (*etichetta*) label; (*su porta*) notice; (*scheda*) card; **timbrare il ~** (*all'entrata*) to clock in; (*all'uscita*) to clock out; **~ di presenza** clock card, timecard

car'tello SM sign; (*pubblicitario*) poster; (*stradale*) sign, signpost; (*in dimostrazioni*) placard; (*Econ*) cartel; **~ stradale** sign

cartel'lone SM (*della tombola*) scoring frame; (*Teat*) playbill; **tenere il ~** (*spettacolo*) to have a long run; **~ pubblicitario** advertising poster

carti'era SF paper mill

carti'lagine [karti'ladʒine] SF cartilage

car'tina SF (*Aut, Geo*) map

car'toccio [kar'tɔttʃo] SM paper bag; **cuocere al ~** (*Cuc*) to bake in tinfoil

cartogra'fia SF cartography

carto'laio, -a SM/F stationer

cartolarizzazi'one [kartolariddza'tsjone] SF securitization

cartole'ria SF stationer's (shop (BRIT))

carto'lina SF postcard; **~ di auguri** greetings card; **~ precetto** o **rosa** (*Mil*) call-up card; **~ postale** ready-stamped postcard; **~ virtuale** e-card

carto'mante SMF fortune-teller (*using cards*)

carton'cino [karton'tʃino] SM (*materiale*) thin cardboard; (*biglietto*) card; **~ della società** compliments slip

car'tone SM cardboard; (*del latte, dell'aranciata*) carton; (*Arte*) cartoon; **cartoni animati** (*Cine*) cartoons

car'tuccia, -ce [kar'tuttʃa] SF cartridge; **~ a**

salve blank cartridge; **mezza ~** (fig: persona) good-for-nothing

'**casa** SF house; (specialmente la propria casa) home; (Comm) firm, house; **essere a ~** to be at home; **vado a ~ mia/tua** I'm going home/to your house; **~ di correzione** ≈ community home (BRIT), reformatory (US); **vino della ~** house wine; **~ di cura** nursing home; **~ editrice** publishing house; **C~ delle Libertà** House of Liberties, centre-right coalition; **~ di riposo** (old people's) home, care home; **~ dello studente** student hostel; **~ di tolleranza, ~ d'appuntamenti** brothel; **case popolari** ≈ council houses (o flats) (BRIT), ≈ public housing units (US)

ca'**sacca, -che** SF military coat; (di fantino) blouse

ca'**sale** SM (gruppo di case) hamlet; (casa di campagna) farmhouse

casa'**lingo, -a, -ghi, -ghe** AG household, domestic; (fatto a casa) home-made; (semplice) homely; (amante della casa) home-loving ▶ SF housewife ■ **casalinghi** SMPL (oggetti) household articles; **cucina casalinga** plain home cooking

ca'**sata** SF family lineage

ca'**sato** SM family name

casca'**morto** SM woman-chaser; **fare il ~** to chase women

cas'**care** /20/ VI to fall; **~ bene/male** (fig) to land lucky/unlucky; **~ dalle nuvole** (fig) to be taken aback; **~ dal sonno** to be falling asleep on one's feet; **caschi il mondo** no matter what; **non cascherà il mondo se …** it won't be the end of the world if …

cas'**cata** SF fall; (d'acqua) cascade, waterfall

casche'**rò** ecc [kaske'rɔ] VB vedi **cascare**

ca'**scina** [kaʃ'ʃina] SF farmstead

casci'**nale** [kaʃʃi'nale] SM (casolare) farmhouse; (cascina) farmstead

'**casco** (pl **caschi**) SM helmet; (del parrucchiere) hair-dryer; (di banane) bunch; **~ blu** (Mil) blue helmet (UN soldier)

caseggi'**ato** [kased'dʒato] SM (edificio) large block of flats (BRIT) o apartment building (US); (gruppo di case) group of houses

casei'**ficio** [kazei'fitʃo] SM creamery

ca'**sella** SF pigeonhole; **~ email** mailbox; **~ di posta elettronica** mailbox; **~ postale** post office box

casel'**lario** SM (mobile) filing cabinet; (raccolta di pratiche) files pl; **~ giudiziale** court records pl; **~ penale** police files pl

ca'**sello** SM (di autostrada) tollgate

case'**reccio, -a, -ci, -ce** [kase'rettʃo] AG home-made

ca'**serma** SF barracks

caser'**tano, -a** AG of (o from) Caserta

ca'**sino** SM (col: confusione) row, racket; (casa di prostituzione) brothel

casi'**nò** SM INV casino

ca'**sistica** SF (Med) record of cases; **secondo la ~ degli incidenti stradali** according to road accident data

'**caso** SM chance; (fatto, vicenda) event, incident; (possibilità) possibility; (Med, Ling) case; **a ~** at random; **per ~** by chance, by accident; **in ogni ~, in tutti i casi** in any case, at any rate; **in ~ contrario** otherwise; **al ~** should the opportunity arise; **nel ~ che** in case; **~ mai** if by chance; **far ~ a qc/qn** to pay attention to sth/sb; **fare o porre o mettere il ~ che** to suppose that; **fa proprio al ~ nostro** it's just what we need; **guarda ~ …** strangely enough …; **è il ~ che ce ne andiamo** we'd better go; **~ limite** borderline case

caso'**lare** SM cottage

'**Caspio** SM: **il mar ~** the Caspian Sea

'**caspita** ESCL (di sorpresa) good heavens!; (di impazienza) for goodness' sake!

'**cassa** SF case, crate, box; (bara) coffin; (mobile) chest; (involucro: di orologio ecc) case; (macchina) cash register, till; (luogo di pagamento) cash desk, checkout (counter); (fondo) fund; (istituto bancario) bank; **battere ~** (fig) to come looking for money; **~ automatica prelievi** automatic telling machine, cash dispenser; **~ continua** night safe; **mettere in ~ integrazione** ≈ to lay off; **C~ del Mezzogiorno** development fund for the South of Italy; **~ mutua o malattia** health insurance scheme; **~ di risonanza** (Mus) soundbox; (fig) platform; **~ di risparmio** savings bank; **~ rurale e artigiana** credit institution (serving farmers and craftsmen); **~ toracica** (Anat) chest

cassa'**forte** (pl **casseforti**) SF safe

cassa'**panca** (pl **cassapanche** o **cassepanche**) SF settle

casseru'**ola, casse'rola** SF saucepan

cas'**setta** SF box; (per registratore) cassette; (Cine, Teat) box-office takings pl; **pane a o in ~** toasting loaf; **film di ~** (commerciale) box-office draw; **far ~** to be a box-office success; **~ delle lettere** letterbox; **~ di sicurezza** strongbox

cas'**setto** SM drawer

casset'**tone** SM chest of drawers

cassi'**ere, -a** SM/F cashier; (di banca) teller

cassinte'**grato, -a** SM/F person who has been laid off

cas'**sone** SM (cassa) large case, large chest

casso'**netto** SM wheelie-bin

'**casta** SF caste

cas'**tagna** [kas'taɲɲa] SF chestnut; **prendere qn in ~** (fig) to catch sb in the act

cas'**tagno** [kas'taɲɲo] SM chestnut (tree)

cas'**tano, -a** AG chestnut (brown)

cas'**tello** SM castle; (Tecn) scaffolding

casti'gare /80/ vt to punish

casti'gato, -a AG (*casto, modesto*) pure, chaste; (*emendato: prosa, versione*) expurgated, amended

cas'tigo, -ghi SM punishment; **mettere/ essere in ~** to punish/be punished

castità SF chastity

'casto, -a AG chaste, pure

cas'toro SM beaver

cas'trante AG frustrating

cas'trare /72/ vt to castrate; to geld; to doctor (BRIT), fix (US); (*fig: iniziativa*) to frustrate

castrone'ria SF (*col*): **dire castronerie** to talk rubbish

casu'ale AG chance *cpd*; (*Inform*) random *cpd*

ca'supola SF simple little cottage

catac'lisma, -i SM (*fig*) catastrophe

cata'comba SF catacomb

cata'fascio [kata'faʃʃo] SM: **andare a ~** to collapse; **mandare a ~** to wreck

cata'litico, -a, -ci, -che AG: **marmitta catalitica** (*Aut*) catalytic converter

cataliz'zare [katalid'dzare] /72/ vt (*fig*) to act as a catalyst (up)on

cataliz'zato, -a [katalid'dzato] AG (*Aut*) with catalytic converter

catalizza'tore [kataliddza'tore] SM (*anche fig*) catalyst; (*Aut*) catalytic converter

Cata'logna [kata'loɲɲa] SF: **la ~** Catalonia

ca'talogo, -ghi SM catalogue; **~ dei prezzi** price list

cata'nese AG of (*o* from) Catania

catanza'rese [katandza'rese] AG of (*o* from) Catanzaro

cata'pecchia [kata'pekkja] SF hovel

cata'pulta SF catapult

catarifran'gente [katarifran'dʒɛnte] SM (*Aut*) reflector

ca'tarro SM catarrh

ca'tarsi SF INV catharsis

ca'tasta SF stack, pile

ca'tasto SM land register; land registry office

ca'tastrofe SF catastrophe, disaster

catas'trofico, -a, -ci, -che AG (*evento*) catastrophic; (*persona, previsione*) pessimistic

catastro'fista, -i, -e AG, SM/F doom-monger; **non fare il ~** don't be so pessimistic

cate'chismo [kate'kizmo] SM catechism

catego'ria SF category; (*di albergo*) class

cate'gorico, -a, -ci, -che AG categorical

ca'tena SF chain; **reazione a ~** chain reaction; **susseguirsi a ~** to follow in quick succession; **~ alimentare** food chain; **~ di montaggio** assembly line; **~ montuosa** mountain range; **catene da neve** (*Aut*) snow chains

cate'naccio [kate'nattʃo] SM bolt

cate'nella SF (*ornamento*) chain; (*di orologio*) watch chain; (*di porta*) door chain

cate'nina SF (*gioiello*) (thin) chain

cate'ratta SF cataract; (*chiusa*) sluice gate

ca'terva SF (*di cose*) loads *pl*, heaps *pl*; (*di persone*) horde

cate'tere SM (*Med*) catheter

cati'nella SF: **piovere a catinelle** to pour, rain cats and dogs

ca'tino SM basin

ca'todico, -a, -ci, -che AG: **tubo a raggi catodici** cathode-ray tube

ca'torcio [ka'tɔrtʃo] SM (*peg*) old wreck

ca'trame SM tar

'cattedra SF teacher's desk; (*di università*) chair; **salire *o* montare in ~** (*fig*) to pontificate

catte'drale SF cathedral

catte'dratico, -a, -ci, -che AG (*insegnamento*) university *cpd*; (*ironico*) pedantic ▸ SM/F professor

catti'veria SF (*qualità*) wickedness, malice; (*di bambino*) naughtiness; (*azione*) spiteful act; (*parole*) malicious *o* spiteful remark; **fare una ~** to do something wicked; to be naughty

cattività SF captivity

cat'tivo, -a AG bad; (*malvagio*) bad, wicked; (*turbolento: bambino*) bad, naughty; (*: mare*) rough; (*odore, sapore*) nasty, bad ▸ SM/F bad *o* wicked person; **farsi ~ sangue** to worry, get in a state; **farsi un ~ nome** to earn o.s. a bad reputation; **i cattivi** (*nei film*) the baddies (*BRIT*), the bad guys (*US*)

cattocomu'nista, -i, -e AG *combining Catholic and communist ideas*

cattoli'cesimo [kattoli'tʃezimo] SM Catholicism

cat'tolico, -a, -ci, -che AG, SM/F (Roman) Catholic

cat'tura SF capture

cattu'rare /72/ vt to capture

cau'casico, -a, -ci, -che AG, SM/F Caucasian

'Caucaso SM: **il ~** the Caucasus

cauccìù [kaut'tʃu] SM rubber

'causa SF cause; (*Dir*) lawsuit, case, action; **a ~ di, per ~ di** because of; **per ~ sua** because of him; **fare *o* muovere ~ a qn** to take legal action against sb; **parte in ~** litigant

cau'sale AG (*Ling*) causal ▸ SF cause, reason

cau'sare /72/ vt to cause

'caustico, -a, -ci, -che AG caustic

cau'tela SF caution, prudence

caute'lare /72/ vt to protect ▪ **cautelarsi** VPR: **cautelarsi (da *o* contro)** to take precautions (against)

'cauto, -a AG cautious, prudent

cauzio'nare [kauttsjo'nare] /72/ vt to guarantee

cauzi'one [kaut'tsjone] SF security; (*Dir*) bail; **rilasciare dietro ~** to release on bail

cav. ABBR = **cavaliere**

'cava SF quarry

caval'care /20/ VT (*cavallo*) to ride; (*muro*) to sit astride; (*ponte*) to span

caval'cata SF ride; (*gruppo di persone*) riding party

cavalca'via SM INV flyover

cavalci'oni [kaval'tʃoni]: **a ~ di** *prep* astride

cavali'ere SM rider; (*feudale, titolo*) knight; (*soldato*) cavalryman; (*al ballo*) partner

cavalleg'gero [kavalled'dʒɛro] SM (*Mil*) light cavalryman

cavalle'resco, -a, -schi, -sche AG chivalrous

cavalle'ria SF chivalry; (*milizia a cavallo*) cavalry

cavalle'rizzo, -a [kavalle'rittso] SM/F riding instructor; circus rider

caval'letta SF grasshopper; (*dannosa*) locust

caval'letto SM (*Fot*) tripod; (*da pittore*) easel

caval'lina SF (*Ginnastica*) horse; (*gioco*) leap-frog; **correre la ~** (*fig*) to sow one's wild oats

ca'vallo SM horse; (*Scacchi*) knight; (*Aut: anche*: **cavallo vapore**) horsepower; (*dei pantaloni*) crotch; **a ~** on horseback; **a ~ di** astride, straddling; **siamo a ~** (*fig*) we've made it; **da ~** (*fig: dose*) drastic; (: *febbre*) raging; **vivere a ~ tra due periodi** to straddle two periods; **~ di battaglia** (*Teat*) tour de force; (*fig*) hobbyhorse; **~ da corsa** racehorse; **~ a dondolo** rocking horse; **~ da sella** saddle horse; **~ da soma** packhorse

ca'vare /72/ VT (*togliere*) to draw out, extract, take out; (: *giacca, scarpe*) to take off; (: *fame, sete, voglia*) to satisfy ▪ **cavarsi** VPR: **cavarsi da** (*guai, problemi*) to get out of; **cavarsela** to get away with it; to manage, get on all right; **non ci caverà un bel nulla** you'll get nothing out of it (*o him etc*)

cava'tappi SM INV corkscrew

ca'verna SF cave

caver'noso, -a AG (*luogo*) cavernous; (*fig: voce*) deep; (: *tosse*) raucous

ca'vezza [ka'vettsa] SF halter

'cavia SF guinea pig

cavi'ale SM caviar

ca'viglia [ka'viʎʎa] SF ankle

cavil'lare /72/ VI to quibble

ca'villo SM quibble

cavil'loso, -a AG quibbling, hair-splitting

cavità SF INV cavity

'cavo, -a AG hollow ▶ SM (*Anat*) cavity; (*grossa corda*) rope, cable; (*Elettr, Tel*) cable

cavo'lata SF (*col*) stupid thing

cavo'letto SM: **~ di Bruxelles** Brussels sprout

cavolfi'ore SM cauliflower

'cavolo SM cabbage; **non m'importa un ~** (*col*) I don't give a hoot; **che ~ vuoi?** (*col*) what the heck do you want?

caz'zata [kat'tsata] SF (!: *stupidaggine*) stupid thing, something stupid

'cazzo ['kattso] SM (!: *pene*) prick (!); **non gliene importa un ~** (*fig*: !) he doesn't give a damn about it; **fatti i cazzi tuoi** (*fig*: !) mind your own damn business

caz'zotto [kat'tsɔtto] SM punch; **fare a cazzotti** to have a punch-up

cazzu'ola [kat'tswɔla] SF trowel

CB SIGLA = **Campobasso**

CC ABBR = **Carabinieri**

cc ABBR (= *centimetro cubico*) cc

C.C. ABBR = **codice civile**

c.c. ABBR (= *conto corrente*) c/a, a/c; (*Elettr*) *vedi* **corrente continua**

c/c ABBR (= *conto corrente*) c/a, a/c

CCI SIGLA F (= *Camera di Commercio Internazionale*) ICC (= *International Chamber of Commerce*)

CCIAA ABBR = **Camera di Commercio Industria, Agricoltura e Artigianato**

CCT SIGLA M = **certificato di credito del Tesoro**

C.D. ABBR (= *Corpo Diplomatico*) CD ▶ SM INV (= *compact disc*) CD; (*lettore*) CD player

c.d. ABBR = **cosiddetto**

C.d.A. ABBR = **Consiglio di Amministrazione**

c.d.d. ABBR (= *come dovevasi dimostrare*) QED (= *quod erat demonstrandum*)

CD-Rom [tʃidi'rɔm] SIGLA M INV (= *Compact Disc Read Only Memory*) CD-Rom

CE SIGLA = **Caserta**

ce [tʃe] PRON, AV *vedi* **ci**

C.E. SIGLA = **Consiglio d'Europa**

cec'chino [tʃek'kino] SM sniper; (*Pol*) member of parliament who votes against his own party

'cece ['tʃetʃe] SM chickpea, garbanzo (*US*)

Ce'cenia [tʃe'tʃenja] SF Chechnya

ce'ceno, -a [tʃe'tʃeno] AG, SM/F Chechen

cecità [tʃetʃi'ta] SF blindness

'ceco, -a, -chi, -che ['tʃɛko] AG, SM/F, SM Czech; **la Repubblica Ceca** the Czech Republic, Czechia

Cecoslo'vacchia [tʃekozlo'vakkja] SF (*Storia*): **la ~** Czechoslovakia

cecoslo'vacco, -a, -chi, -che [tʃekozlo'vakko] AG, SM/F (*Storia*) Czechoslovakian

CED [tʃɛd] SIGLA M = **centro elaborazione dati**

'cedere ['tʃedere] /29/ VT (*concedere: posto*) to give up; (*Dir*) to transfer, make over ▶ VI (*cadere*) to give way, subside; **~ (a)** to surrender (to), yield (to), give in (to); **~ il passo (a qn)** to let (sb) pass in front; **~ il passo a qc** (*fig*) to give way to sth; **~ la parola (a qn)** to hand over (to sb)

ce'devole [tʃe'devole] AG (*terreno*) soft; (*fig*) yielding '**cedola** ['tʃɛdola] SF (*Comm*) coupon; voucher

ce'drata [tʃe'drata] SF citron juice

'**cedro** ['tʃɛdro] SM cedar; (*albero da frutto, frutto*) citron

'**CEE** ['tʃee] SIGLA F = **Comunità Economica Europea**

'**ceffo** ['tʃɛffo] SM (*peg*) ugly mug

cef'fone [tʃef'fone] SM slap, smack

'**ceko, -a** ['tʃɛko] AG, SM/F = **ceco**

ce'lare [tʃe'lare] /**72**/ VT to conceal ■ **celarsi** VPR to hide

cele'brare [tʃele'brare] /**72**/ VT to celebrate; (*cerimonia*) to hold; **~ le lodi di qc/qn** to sing the praises of sth/sb

celebrazi'one [tʃelebrat'tsjone] SF celebration

'**celebre** ['tʃɛlebre] AG famous, celebrated

celebrità [tʃelebri'ta] SF INV fame; (*persona*) celebrity

'**celere** ['tʃɛlere] AG fast, swift; (*corso*) crash *cpd* ▶ SF (*Polizia*) riot police

ce'leste [tʃe'lɛste] AG celestial; heavenly; (*colore*) sky-blue

'**celia** [tʃɛlja] SF joke; **per ~** for a joke

celi'bato [tʃeli'bato] SM celibacy

'**celibe** ['tʃɛlibe] AG single, unmarried ▶ SM bachelor

'**cella** ['tʃɛlla] SF cell; **~ di rigore** punishment cell; **~ frigorifera** cold store

cello'phane® [sɛlo'fan] SM cellophane®

'**cellula** ['tʃɛllula] SF (*Biol, Elettr, Pol*) cell

cellu'lare [tʃellu'lare] AG cellular ▶ SM (*furgone*) police van; (*telefono*) mobile phone (BRIT), cellphone (US); **segregazione ~** (*Dir*) solitary confinement

cellu'lite [tʃellu'lite] SF cellulite

'**celta** ['tʃɛlta] SMF Celt

'**celtico, -a, -ci, -che** ['tʃɛltiko] AG, SM Celtic

cembalo ['tʃembalo] SM (*Mus*) harpsichord

cemen'tare [tʃemen'tare] /**72**/ VT (*anche fig*) to cement

cementifica'zione [tʃemɛntifikat'tsjone] SF overbuilding

ce'mento [tʃe'mento] SM cement; **~ armato** reinforced concrete

'**cena** ['tʃena] SF dinner; (*leggera*) supper

ce'nacolo [tʃe'nakolo] SM (*circolo*) coterie, circle; (*Rel, dipinto*) Last Supper

ce'nare [tʃe'nare] /**72**/ VI to dine, have dinner

'**cencio** ['tʃentʃo] SM piece of cloth, rag; (*per spolverare*) duster; **essere bianco come un ~** to be as white as a sheet

'**cenere** ['tʃenere] SF ash

Cene'rentola [tʃene'rɛntola] SF (*anche fig*) Cinderella

'**cenno** ['tʃenno] SM (*segno*) sign, signal; (*gesto*)

gesture; (*col capo*) nod; (*con la mano*) wave; (*allusione*) hint, mention; (*breve esposizione*) short account; **far ~ di sì/no** to nod (one's head)/ shake one's head; **~ d'intesa** sign of agreement; **cenni di storia dell'arte** an outline of the history of art

censi'mento [tʃensi'mento] SM census

cen'sire [tʃen'sire] /**55**/ VT to take a census of

'**CENSIS** ['tʃensis] SIGLA M (= *Centro Studi Investimenti Sociali*) *independent institute carrying out research on Italy's social and cultural welfare*

cen'sore [tʃen'sore] SM censor

cen'sura [tʃen'sura] SF censorship; censor's office; (*fig*) censure

censu'rare [tʃensu'rare] /**72**/ VT to censor; to censure

cent. ABBR = **centesimo**

centelli'nare [tʃentelli'nare] /**72**/ VT to sip; (*fig*) to savour (BRIT), savor (US)

cente'nario, -a [tʃente'narjo] AG (*che ha cento anni*) hundred-year-old; (*che ricorre ogni cento anni*) centennial, centenary *cpd* ▶ SM/F centenarian ▶ SM centenary

cen'tesimo, -a [tʃen'tezimo] AG, SM hundredth; (*di euro, dollaro*) cent; **essere senza un ~** to be penniless

cen'tigrado, -a [tʃen'tigrado] AG centigrade; **20 gradi centigradi** 20 degrees centigrade

cen'tilitro [tʃen'tilitro] SM centilitre

cen'timetro [tʃen'timetro] SM centimetre (BRIT), centimeter (US); (*nastro*) measuring tape (*in centimetres*)

centi'naio [tʃenti'najo] (*pl(f)* **centinaia**) SM: **un ~ (di)** a hundred; about a hundred

'**cento** ['tʃento] NUM a hundred, one hundred; **per ~** per cent; **al ~ per ~** a hundred per cent; **~ di questi giorni!** many happy returns (of the day)!

centodi'eci [tʃento'djetʃi] NUM one hundred and ten; **~ e lode** (*Università*) ≈ first-class honours

cento'mila [tʃento'mila] NUM a o one hundred thousand; **te l'ho detto ~ volte** (*fig*) I've told you a thousand times

Cen'trafrica [tʃen'trafrika] SM: **il ~** the Central African Republic

cen'trale [tʃen'trale] AG central ▶ SF: **~ elettrica** electric power station; **~ eolica** wind farm; **~ del latte** dairy; **~ di polizia** police headquarters *pl*; **~ telefonica** (telephone) exchange; **sede ~** head office

centrali'nista [tʃentrali'nista] SMF operator

centra'lino [tʃentra'lino] SM (telephone) exchange; (*di albergo ecc*) switchboard

centraliz'zare [tʃentralid'dzare] /**72**/ VT to centralize

centraliz'zato, -a [tʃentralid'dzato] AG central

cen'trare [tʃenˈtrare] /**72**/ vт to hit the centre (BRIT) o center (US) of; (Tecn) to centre; **~ una risposta** to get the right answer; **ha centrato il problema** you've hit the nail on the head

centra'vanti [tʃentraˈvanti] sм iɴv centre forward

cen'trifuga [tʃenˈtrifuga] sf spin-dryer

centrifu'gare [tʃentrifuˈgare] /**80**/ vт (Tecn) to centrifuge; (biancheria) to spin-dry

'centro [ˈtʃentro] sм centre (BRIT), center (US); **fare ~** to hit the bull's eye; (Calcio) to score; (fig) to hit the nail on the head; **~ balneare** seaside resort; **~ civico** civic centre; **~ commerciale** shopping centre; (città) commercial centre; **~ di costo** cost centre; **~ elaborazione dati** data-processing unit; **~ ospedaliero** hospital complex; **~ di permanenza temporanea** reception centre; **~ sociale** community centre; **centri vitali** (anche fig) vital organs

centro'destra [tʃentroˈdɛstra] sм (Pol) centre right

centromedi'ano [tʃentromeˈdjano] sм (Calcio) centre half

centrosi'nistra [tʃentrosiˈnistra] sм (Pol) centre left

'ceppo [ˈtʃeppo] sм (di albero) stump; (pezzo di legno) log

'cera [ˈtʃera] sf wax; (aspetto) appearance, look; **~ per pavimenti** floor polish

cera'lacca [tʃeraˈlakka] sf sealing wax

ce'ramica [tʃeˈramika] (pl **ceramiche**) sf ceramic; (Arte) ceramics sg

cerbi'atto [tʃerˈbjatto] sм (Zool) fawn

'cerca [ˈtʃerka] sf: **in** o **alla ~ di** in search of

cercaper'sone [tʃerkaperˈsone] sм iɴv bleeper

cer'care [tʃerˈkare] /**20**/ vт to look for, search for ▸ vi: **~ di fare qc** to try to do sth

cercherò ecc [tʃerkeˈrɔ] vв vedi **cercare**

'cerchia [ˈtʃerkja] sf circle

cerchi'ato, -a [tʃerˈkjato] ʌɢ: **occhiali cerchiati d'osso** horn-rimmed spectacles; **avere gli occhi cerchiati** to have dark rings under one's eyes

cer'chietto [tʃerˈkjetto] sм (per capelli) hairband

'cerchio [ˈtʃerkjo] sм circle; (giocattolo, di botte) hoop; **dare un colpo al ~ e uno alla botte** (fig) to keep two things going at the same time

cerchi'one [tʃerˈkjone] sм (wheel)rim

cere'ale [tʃereˈale] sм cereal

cere'brale [tʃereˈbrale] ʌɢ cerebral

ceri'monia [tʃeriˈmɔnja] sf ceremony; **senza tante cerimonie** (senza formalità) informally; (bruscamente) unceremoniously, without so much as a by-your-leave

cerimoni'ale [tʃerimoˈnjale] sм etiquette; ceremonial

cerimoni'ere [tʃerimoˈnjɛre] sм master of ceremonies

cerimoni'oso, -a [tʃerimoˈnjoso] ʌɢ formal, ceremonious

ce'rino [tʃeˈrino] sм wax match

CERN [tʃern] sɪɢʟʌ м (= Comitato Europeo di Ricerche Nucleari) CERN

'cernia [ˈtʃernja] sf (Zool) stone bass

cerni'era [tʃerˈnjɛra] sf hinge; **~ lampo** zip (fastener) (BRIT), zipper (US)

'cernita [ˈtʃernita] sf selection; **fare una ~ di** to select

'cero [ˈtʃero] sм (church) candle

ce'rone [tʃeˈrone] sм (trucco) greasepaint

ce'rotto [tʃeˈrɔtto] sм sticking plaster

certa'mente [tʃertaˈmente] ʌv certainly, surely

cer'tezza [tʃerˈtettsa] sf certainty

certifi'care [tʃertifiˈkare] /**20**/ vт to certify

certifi'cato [tʃertifiˈkato] sм certificate; **~ medico/di nascita/di morte** medical/birth/death certificate; **~ di credito del Tesoro** treasury bill

certificazi'one [tʃertifikatˈtsjone] sf certification; **~ di bilancio** (Comm) external audit

---

'certo, -a [ˈtʃerto]

ʌɢ (sicuro): **certo (di/che)** certain o sure (of/that)

▸ DET **1** (tale) certain; **un certo signor Smith** a (certain) Mr Smith

2 (qualche: con valore intensivo) some; **dopo un certo tempo** after some time; **un fatto di una certa importanza** a matter of some importance; **di una certa età** past one's prime, not so young

▸ PRON: **certi, e** (pl) some

▸ ʌv (certamente) certainly; (senz'altro) of course; **di certo** certainly; **no (di) certo!, certo che no!** certainly not!; **sì certo** yes indeed, certainly

---

certo'sino [tʃertoˈzino] sм Carthusian monk; (liquore) chartreuse; **è un lavoro da ~** it's a pernickety job

cer'tuni [tʃerˈtuni] pʀoɴ pʟ some (people)

ce'rume [tʃeˈrume] sм (ear) wax

'cerva [ˈtʃerva] sf (female) deer, doe

cer'vello [tʃerˈvɛllo] (pl **cervelli**, pl(f) **cervella**) sм (Anat) brain; **~ elettronico** computer; **avere il** o **essere un ~ fino** to be sharp-witted; **è uscito di ~, gli è dato di volta il ~** he's gone off his head

cervi'cale [tʃerviˈkale] ʌɢ cervical

'cervo, -a [ˈtʃervo] sм/ꜰ stag (hind) ▸ sм deer; **~ volante** stag beetle

cesel'lare [tʃezelˈlare] /**72**/ vт to chisel; (incidere) to engrave

ce'sello [tʃeˈzɛllo] sм chisel

ce'soie [tʃe'zoje] sf pl shears

ces'puglio [tʃes'puʎʎo] sm bush

ces'sare [tʃes'sare] /**72**/ vi, vt to stop, cease; **~ di fare qc** to stop doing sth; **"cessato allarme"** "all clear"

ces'sate il fu'oco [tʃes'sate-] sm ceasefire

cessazi'one [tʃessat'tsjone] sf cessation; (*interruzione*) suspension

cessi'one [tʃes'sjone] sf transfer

'cesso ['tʃɛsso] sm (*col: gabinetto*) bog

'cesta ['tʃesta] sf (large) basket

ces'tello [tʃes'tɛllo] sm (*per bottiglie*) crate; (*di lavatrice*) drum

cesti'nare [tʃesti'nare] /**72**/ vt to throw away; (*fig: proposta*) to turn down; (*: romanzo*) to reject

ces'tino [tʃes'tino] sm basket; (*per la carta straccia*) wastepaper basket; (*Inform*) recycle bin; **~ da viaggio** (*Ferr*) packed lunch (*o* dinner)

'cesto ['tʃesto] sm basket

ce'sura [tʃe'zura] sf caesura

ce'taceo [tʃe'tatʃeo] sm sea mammal

'ceto ['tʃɛto] sm (social) class

'cetra ['tʃɛtra] sf zither; (*fig: di poeta*) lyre

cetrio'lino [tʃetrio'lino] sm gherkin

cetri'olo [tʃetri'ɔlo] sm cucumber

Cf., Cfr. abbr (= *confronta*) cf.

CFC [tʃiɛffe'tʃi] abbr mpl (= *clorofluorocarburi*) CFC

Cfr. abbr (= *confronta*) cf

CFS sigla m (= *Corpo Forestale dello Stato*) body responsible for the planting and management of forests

cg abbr (= *centigrammo*) cg

C.G.I.L. [tʃidʒi'ɛlle] sigla f (= *Confederazione Generale Italiana del Lavoro*) trades union organization

CH sigla = **Chieti**

cha'let [ʃa'lɛ] sm inv chalet

cham'pagne [ʃã'paɲ] sm inv champagne

'chance [ʃãs] sf inv chance

'charme [ʃarm] sm charm

'charter ['tʃartər] ag inv (*volo*) charter cpd; (*aereo*) chartered ▶ sm inv chartered plane

chat'line [tʃæt'laen] sf inv chat room

chat'tare [tʃat'tare] /**72**/ vi to chat; (*online*) to chat

chat'tata [tʃat'tata] sf chat

---

che [ke]

pron **1** (*relativo: persona: soggetto*) who; (*: oggetto*) whom, that; (*: cosa, animale*) which, that; **il ragazzo che è venuto** the boy who came; **l'uomo che io vedo** the man (whom) I see; **il libro che è sul tavolo** the book which *o* that is on the table; **il libro che vedi** the book (which *o* that) you see; **la sera che ti ho visto** the evening I saw you

2 (*interrogativo, esclamativo*) what; **che (cosa) fai?** what are you doing?; **a che (cosa) pensi?** what are you thinking about?; **non sa che (cosa) fare** he doesn't know what to do; **sai di che si tratta?** do you know what it's about?; **che (cosa) succede?** what's happening?; **ma che dici!** what are you saying!

3 (*indefinito*): **quell'uomo ha un che di losco** there's something suspicious about that man; **un certo non so che** an indefinable something; **non è un gran che** it's nothing much

▶ det **1** (*interrogativo: tra tanti*) what; (*: tra pochi*) which; **che tipo di film preferisci?** what sort of film do you prefer?; **che vestito ti vuoi mettere?** what (*o* which) dress do you want to put on?

2 (*esclamativo: seguito da aggettivo*) how; (*: seguito da sostantivo*) what; **che buono!** how delicious!; **che bel vestito!** what a lovely dress!; **che macchina!** what a car!

▶ cong **1** (*con proposizioni subordinate*) that; **credo che verrà** I think he'll come; **voglio che tu studi** I want you to study; **so che tu c'eri** I know (that) you were there; **non che sia sbagliato, ma ...** not that it's wrong, but ...

2 (*finale*) so that; **vieni qua, che ti veda** come here, so (that) I can see you; **stai attento che non cada** mind it doesn't fall

3 (*temporale*): **arrivai che eri già partito** you had already left when I arrived; **sono anni che non lo vedo** I haven't seen him for years

4 (*in frasi imperative, concessive*): **che venga pure!** let him come by all means!; **che tu sia benedetto!** may God bless you!; **che tu venga o no partiamo lo stesso** we're going whether you come or not

5 (*comparativo: con più, meno*) than; **è più lungo che largo** it's longer than it's wide; **più bella che mai** more beautiful than ever; *vedi anche* **più**; **meno**

6 *vedi anche* **così** ecc

'checca, -che ['kekka] sf (*col: omosessuale*) fairy

chef [ʃef] sm inv chef

chemiotera'pia [kemjotera'pia] sf chemotherapy

chero'sene [kero'zɛne] sm kerosene

cheru'bino [keru'bino] sm cherub

che'tare [ke'tare] /**72**/ vt to hush, silence ▪ **che-tarsi** vpr to quieten down, fall silent

cheti'chella [keti'kɛlla] av: **alla ~** stealthily, unobtrusively; **andarsene alla ~** to slip away

'cheto, -a ['keto] ag quiet, silent

---

chi [ki]

pron **1** (*interrogativo: soggetto*) who; (*: oggetto*) who, whom; **chi è?** who is it?; **di chi è questo libro?** whose book is this?, whose is this book?; **con chi parli?** who are you talking to?; **a chi pensi?** who are you thinking about?; **chi di voi?** which of you?; **non so a chi rivolgermi** I don't know who to ask

2 (*relativo*) whoever, anyone who; **dillo a chi vuoi** tell whoever you like; **portate chi volete** bring anyone you like; **so io di chi parlo** I know who I'm talking about; **lo riferirò a chi di dovere** I'll pass it on to the relevant person

3 (*indefinito*): **chi … chi …** some … others …; **chi dice una cosa, chi dice un'altra** some say one thing, others say another

chiacchie'rare [kjakkje'rare] /72/ vi to chat; (*discorrere futilmente*) to chatter; (*far pettegolezzi*) to gossip

chiacchie'rata [kjakkje'rata] sf chat; **farsi una ~** to have a chat

chi'acchiere ['kjakkjere] sfpl chatter *no pl*; gossip *no pl*; **fare due** o **quattro ~** to have a chat; **perdersi in ~** to waste time talking

chiacchie'rone, -a [kjakkje'rone] ag talkative, chatty gossipy ▶ sm/f chatterbox; gossip

chia'mare [kja'mare] /72/ vt to call; (*rivolgersi a qn*) to call (in), send for ■ **chiamarsi** vpr (*aver nome*) to be called; **come ti chiami?** what's your name?; **mi chiamo Paolo** my name is Paolo, I'm called Paolo; **mandare a ~ qn** to send for sb, call sb in; **~ alle armi** to call up; **~ in giudizio** to summon; **~ qn da parte** to take sb aside

chia'mata [kja'mata] sf (*Tel*) call; (*Mil*) call-up; **~ interurbana** long-distance call; **~ con preavviso** person-to-person call; **~ alle urne** (*Pol*) election

chi'appa ['kjappa] sf (*col: natica*) cheek ■ **chiappe** sfpl bottom *sg*

chi'ara ['kjara] sf egg white

chia'rezza [kja'rettsa] sf clearness; clarity

chiarifi'care [kjarifi'kare] /20/ vt (*anche fig*) to clarify

chiarificazi'one [kjarifikat'tsjone] sf clarification

chiari'mento [kjari'mento] sm clarification *no pl*, explanation

chia'rire [kja'rire] /55/ vt to make clear; (*fig: spiegare*) to clear up, explain ■ **chiarirsi** vpr to become clear; **si sono chiariti** they've sorted things out

chi'aro, -a ['kjaro] ag clear; (*luminoso*) clear, bright; (*colore*) pale, light ▶ av (*parlare, vedere*) clearly; **si sta facendo ~** the day is dawning; **sia chiara una cosa** let's get one thing straight; **mettere in ~ qc** (*fig*) to clear sth up; **parliamoci ~** let's be frank; **trasmissione in ~** (*TV*) uncoded broadcast

chia'rore [kja'rore] sm (diffuse) light

chiaroveg'gente [kjaroved'dʒɛnte] smf clairvoyant

chi'asso ['kjasso] sm uproar, row; **far ~** to make a din; (*fig*) to make a fuss; (*: notizia*) to cause a stir

chias'soso, -a [kjas'soso] ag noisy, rowdy; (*vistoso*) showy, gaudy

'chiatta ['kjatta] sf barge

chi'ave ['kjave] sf key ▶ ag inv key *cpd*; **chiudere a ~** to lock; **~ d'accensione** (*Aut*) ignition key; **~ a forcella** fork spanner; **~ inglese** monkey wrench; **in ~ politica** in political terms; **~ di volta** (*anche fig*) keystone; **chiavi in mano** (*contratto*) turn-key *cpd*; **prezzo chiavi in mano** (*di macchina*) on-the-road price; **~ hardware** (*Inform*) dongle; **~ USB** (*Inform*) USB key

chia'vetta [kja'vetta] sf (*Inform*) dongle; **~ USB** USB stick

chiavis'tello [kjavis'tɛllo] sm bolt

chi'azza ['kjattsa] sf stain, splash; **~ di petrolio** oil slick

chiaz'zare [kjat'tsare] /72/ vt to stain, splash

chic [ʃik] ag inv chic, elegant

chicches'sia [kikkes'sia] pron anyone, anybody

chicco, -chi ['kikko] sm (*di cereale, riso*) grain; (*di caffè*) bean; **~ di grandine** hailstone; **~ d'uva** grape

chi'edere [kjedere] /21/ vt (*per sapere*) to ask; (*per avere*) to ask for ▶ vi: **~ di qn** to ask after sb; (*al telefono*) to ask for o want sb ■ **chiedersi** vpr: **chiedersi (se)** to wonder (whether); **~ qc a qn** to ask sb sth; to ask sb for sth; **~ scusa a qn** to apologize to sb; **~ l'elemosina** to beg; **non chiedo altro** that's all I want

chieri'chetto [kjeri'ketto] sm altar boy

chi'erico, -ci ['kjeriko] sm cleric; altar boy

chi'esa ['kjeza] sf church

chi'esi ecc ['kjɛzi] vb *vedi* **chiedere**

chi'esto, -a ['kjɛsto] pp *di* **chiedere**

'Chigi ['kidʒi]: **palazzo ~** sm (*Pol*) offices of the Italian Prime Minister

'chiglia ['kiʎʎa] sf keel

'chilo ['kilo] sm kilo

chilo'grammo [kilo'grammo] sm kilogram(me)

chilome'traggio [kilome'traddʒo] sm (*Aut*) ≈ mileage

chilo'metrico, -a, -ci, -che [kilo'mɛtriko] ag kilometric; (*fig*) endless

chi'lometro [ki'lɔmetro] sm kilometre (BRIT), kilometer (US)

'chimico, -a, -ci, -che ['kimiko] ag chemical ▶ sm/f chemist ▶ sf chemistry

chi'mono [ki'mɔno] sm inv kimono

'china ['kina] sf (*pendio*) slope, descent; (*Bot*) cinchona; **(inchiostro di) ~** Indian ink; **risalire la ~** (*fig*) to be on the road to recovery

chi'nare [ki'nare] **/72/** VT to lower, bend ∎ **chinarsi** VPR to stoop, bend

chincaglie'ria [kinka'ʎʎe'ria] SF fancy-goods shop ∎ **chincaglierie** SFPL fancy goods, knick-knacks

chi'nino [ki'nino] SM quinine

'chino, -a ['kino] AG: **a capo ~, a testa china** head bent o bowed

chi'occia, -ce ['kjɔttʃa] SF brooding hen

chi'occio, -a, -ci, -ce ['kjɔttʃo] AG (voce) clucking

chi'occiola ['kjɔttʃola] SF snail; (di indirizzo e-mail) at (symbol); **scala a ~** spiral staircase

chi'odo ['kjɔdo] SM nail; (fig) obsession; **~ scaccia ~** (proverbio) one problem drives away another; **roba da chiodi!** it's unbelievable!; **~ di garofano** (Cuc) clove

chi'oma ['kjɔma] SF (capelli) head of hair; (di albero) foliage

chi'osco, -schi ['kjɔsko] SM kiosk, stall

chi'ostro ['kjɔstro] SM cloister

chiro'mante [kiro'mante] SMF palmist; (indovino) fortune-teller

chirur'gia [kirur'dʒia] SF surgery; **~ estetica** cosmetic surgery

chi'rurgico, -a, -ci, -che [ki'rurdʒiko] AG (anche fig) surgical

chi'rurgo, -ghi, -gi [ki'rurgo] SM surgeon

chissà [kis'sa] AV who knows, I wonder

chi'tarra [ki'tarra] SF guitar

chitar'rista, -i, -e [kitar'rista] SM/F guitarist, guitar player

chi'udere ['kjudere] **/22/** VT to close, shut; (luce, acqua) to put off, turn off; (definitivamente: fabbrica) to close down, shut down; (strada) to close, to enclose; (porre termine a) to end ▸ VI to close, shut; to close down, shut down, to end ∎ **chiudersi** VPR to shut, close; (ritirarsi: anche fig) to shut o.s. away; (ferita) to close up; **~ un occhio su** (fig) to turn a blind eye to; **chiudi la bocca!** o **il becco!** (col) shut up!

chi'unque [ki'unkwe] PRON (relativo) whoever; (indefinito) anyone, anybody; **~ sia** whoever it is

'chiusi ecc ['kjusi] VB vedi **chiudere**

chi'uso, -a ['kjuso] PP di **chiudere** ▸ AG (porta) shut, closed; (: a chiave) locked; (senza uscita: strada ecc) blocked off; (rubinetto) off; (persona) uncommunicative; (ambiente, club) exclusive ▸ SM: **stare al ~** (fig) to be shut up ▸ SF (di corso d'acqua) sluice, lock; (recinto) enclosure; (di discorso ecc) conclusion, ending; **"~"** (negozio ecc) "closed"; **"~ al pubblico"** "no admittance to the public"

chiu'sura [kju'sura] SF closing; shutting; closing o shutting down; ending; (dispositivo) catch; fastening; fastener; **orario di ~** closing time; **~ lampo®** zip (fastener) (BRIT), zipper (US)

---

ci [tʃi]

(dav lo, la, li, le, ne diventa **ce**) PRON **1** (personale: complemento oggetto) us; (: a noi: complemento di termine) (to) us; (: riflessivo) ourselves; (: reciproco) each other, one another; (: impersonale): **ci si veste** we get dressed; **ci ha visti** he's seen us; **non ci ha dato niente** he gave us nothing; **ci vestiamo** we get dressed; **ci amiamo** we love one another o each other; **ci siamo divertiti** we had a good time

2 (dimostrativo: di ciò, su ciò, in ciò ecc) about (o on o of) it; **non ci capisco nulla** I can't make head nor tail of it; **non so cosa farci** I don't know what to do about it; **che ci posso fare?** what can I do about it?; **che c'entro io?** what have I got to do with it?; **ci puoi giurare** you can bet on it; **ci puoi contare** you can depend on it; **ci sei?** (sei pronto?) are you ready?; (hai capito?) are you with me?

▸ AV (qui) here; (lì) there; (moto attraverso luogo): **ci passa sopra un ponte** a bridge passes over it; **non ci passa più nessuno** nobody comes this way any more; **qui ci abito da un anno** I've been living here for a year; **esserci** vedi **essere**

C.I. ABBR = **carta d'identità**

CIA ['tʃia] SIGLA F (= Central Intelligence Agency) CIA

C.ia ABBR (= compagnia) Co

cia'batta [tʃa'batta] SF mule, slipper; (pane) ciabatta

ciabat'tino [tʃabat'tino] SM cobbler

ciac [tʃak] SM (Cine) clapper board; **~, si gira!** action!

Ci'ad [tʃad] SM: **il ~** Chad

ci'alda ['tʃalda] SF (Cuc) wafer

cial'trone, -a [tʃal'trone] SM/F good-for-nothing

ciam'bella [tʃam'bɛlla] SF (Cuc) ring-shaped cake; (salvagente) rubber ring

ci'ancia, -ce ['tʃantʃa] SF gossip no pl, tittle-tattle no pl

cianfru'saglie [tʃanfru'zaʎʎe] SFPL bits and pieces

cia'nuro [tʃa'nuro] SM cyanide

ci'ao ['tʃao] ESCL (all'arrivo) hello!; (alla partenza) cheerio! (BRIT), bye!

ciar'lare [tʃar'lare] **/72/** VI to chatter; (peg) to gossip

ciarla'tano [tʃarla'tano] SM charlatan

cias'cuno, -a [tʃas'kuno] (dav sm: **ciascun** + C, V, **ciascuno** + s impura, gn, pn, ps, x, z; dav sf: **ciascuna** + C, **ciascun'** + V) DET every, each; (ogni) every ▸ PRON each (one); (tutti) everyone, everybody

ci'bare [tʃi'bare] **/72/** VT to feed ∎ **cibarsi** VPR: **cibarsi di** to eat

ci'barie [tʃi'barje] SFPL foodstuffs

ciber'nauta, -i, -e [tʃiber'nauta] SM/F internet surfer

ciber'netica [tʃiber'nɛtika] SF cybernetics *sg*

ciber'spazio [tʃiber'spattsjo] SM cyberspace

'cibo ['tʃibo] SM food

ci'cala [tʃi'kala] SF cicada

cica'trice [tʃika'tritʃe] SF scar

cicatriz'zarsi [tʃikatrid'dzarsi] /72/ VPR to form a scar, heal (up)

'cicca, -che ['tʃikka] SF cigarette end; (*col: sigaretta*) fag; **non vale una ~** (*fig*) it's worthless

'ciccia ['tʃittʃa] SF (*col: carne*) meat; (: *grasso umano*) fat, flesh

cicci'one, -a [tʃit'tʃone] SM/F (*col*) fatty

cice'rone [tʃitʃe'rone] SM guide

cicla'mino [tʃikla'mino] SM cyclamen

ci'clismo [tʃi'klizmo] SM cycling

ci'clista, -i, -e [tʃi'klista] SM/F cyclist

'ciclo ['tʃiklo] SM cycle; (*di malattia*) course

ciclomo'tore [tʃiklomo'tore] SM moped

ci'clone [tʃi'klone] SM cyclone

ciclos'tile [tʃiklos'tile] SM cyclostyle (BRIT)

ci'cogna [tʃi'koɲɲa] SF stork

ci'coria [tʃi'kɔrja] SF chicory

ci'eco, -a, -chi, -che ['tʃɛko] AG blind ▶ SM/F blind man(-woman); **alla cieca** (*anche fig*) blindly

ciel'lino, -a [tʃiel'lino] SM/F (*Pol*) member of CL movement

ci'elo ['tʃɛlo] SM sky; (*Rel*) heaven; **toccare il ~ con un dito** (*fig*) to walk on air; **per amor del ~!** for heavens' sake!

'cifra ['tʃifra] SF (*numero*) figure, numeral; (*somma di denaro*) sum, figure; (*monogramma*) monogram, initials *pl*; (*codice*) code, cipher

ci'frare [tʃi'frare] /72/ VT (*messaggio*) to code; (*lenzuola ecc*) to embroider with a monogram

'ciglio ['tʃiʎʎo] SM (*margine*) edge, verge; (*pl(f) ciglia: delle palpebre*) (eye)lash; (eye)lid; (*sopracciglio*) eyebrow; **non ha battuto ~** (*fig*) he didn't bat an eyelid

'cigno ['tʃiɲɲo] SM swan

cigo'lante [tʃigo'lante] AG squeaking, creaking

cigo'lare [tʃigo'lare] /72/ VI to squeak, creak

'Cile ['tʃile] SM: **il ~** Chile

ci'lecca [tʃi'lekka] SF: **far ~** to fail

ci'leno, -a [tʃi'lɛno] AG, SM/F Chilean

cili'egia, -gie, -ge [tʃi'ljɛdʒa] SF cherry

cilie'gina, -gie, -ge [tʃilje'dʒina] SF glacé cherry; **la ~ sulla torta** (*fig*) the icing *o* cherry on the cake

cili'egio [tʃi'ljɛdʒo] SM cherry tree

cilin'drata [tʃilin'drata] SF (*Aut*) (cubic) capacity; **una macchina di grossa ~** a big-engined car

ci'lindro [tʃi'lindro] SM cylinder; (*cappello*) top hat

CIM [tʃim] SIGLA M = **centro d'igiene mentale**

'cima ['tʃima] SF (*sommità*) top; (*di monte*) top, summit; (*estremità*) end; (*fig: persona*) genius; **in ~ a** at the top of; **da ~ a fondo** from top to bottom; (*fig*) from beginning to end

ci'melio [tʃi'mɛljo] SM relic

cimen'tarsi [tʃimen'tarsi] /72/ VPR: **~ in** (*atleta, concorrente*) to try one's hand at

'cimice ['tʃimitʃe] SF (*Zool*) bug; (*puntina*) drawing pin (BRIT), thumbtack (US)

cimini'era [tʃimi'njɛra] SF chimney; (*di nave*) funnel

cimi'tero [tʃimi'tero] SM cemetery

ci'murro [tʃi'murro] SM (*di cani*) distemper

'Cina ['tʃina] SF: **la ~** China

cin'cin, cin cin [tʃin'tʃin] ESCL cheers!

cincischi'are [tʃintʃis'kjare] /19/ VI to mess about

'cine ['tʃine] SM INV (*col*) cinema

cine'asta, -i, -e [tʃine'asta] SM/F person in the film industry; film-maker

cinegior'nale [tʃinedʒor'nale] SM newsreel

'cinema ['tʃinema] SM INV cinema; **~ muto** silent films; **~ d'essai** (*locale*) avant-garde cinema, experimental cinema

cinemato'grafico, -a, -ci, -che [tʃinemato'grafiko] AG (*attore, critica*) movie *cpd*; film *cpd*; (*festival*) film *cpd*; **sala cinematografica** cinema; **successo ~** box-office success

cinema'tografo [tʃinema'tografo] SM cinema

cinepanet'tone [tʃinepanet'tone] SM *Christmas comedy film*

cine'presa [tʃine'presa] SF cine-camera

ci'nese [tʃi'nese] AG, SMF, SM Chinese *inv*

cine'teca, -che [tʃine'tɛka] SF (*collezione*) film collection; (*locale*) film library

ci'netico, -a, -ci, -che [tʃi'nɛtiko] AG kinetic

cinetur'ismo [tʃinetur'izmo] SM film tourism

'cingere ['tʃindʒere] /54/ VT (*attorniare*) to surround, encircle; **~ la vita con una cintura** to put a belt round one's waist; **~ d'assedio** to besiege, lay siege to

'cinghia ['tʃingja] SF strap; (*cintura, Tecn*) belt; **tirare la ~** (*fig*) to tighten one's belt

cinghi'ale [tʃin'gjale] SM wild boar

cinguet'tare [tʃingwet'tare] /72/ VI to twitter

'cinico, -a, -ci, -che ['tʃiniko] AG cynical ▶ SM/F cynic

ci'nismo [tʃi'nizmo] SM cynicism

cin'quanta [tʃin'kwanta] NUM fifty

cinquante'nario [tʃinkwante'narjo] SM fiftieth anniversary

cinquan'tenne [tʃinkwan'tɛnne] SMF fifty-year-old man/woman

cinquan'tesimo, -a [tʃinkwan'tɛzimo] NUM fiftieth

cinquan'tina [tʃinkwan'tina] sf (serie): **una ~ (di)** about fifty; (età) **essere sulla ~** to be about fifty

'cinque ['tʃinkwe] num five; **avere ~ anni** to be five (years old); **il ~ dicembre 2008** the fifth of December 2008; **alle ~** (ora) at five (o'clock); **siamo in ~** there are five of us

cinquecen'tesco, -a, -schi, -sche [tʃinkwetʃen'tesko] ag sixteenth-century

cinque'cento [tʃinkwe'tʃento] num five hundred ▶ sm: **il C~** the sixteenth century

cinque'mila [tʃinkwe'mila] num five thousand

'cinsi ecc ['tʃinsi] vb vedi **cingere**

'cinta ['tʃinta] sf (anche: **cinta muraria**) city walls pl; **muro di ~** (di giardino ecc) surrounding wall

cin'tare [tʃin'tare] /72/ vt to enclose

'cinto, -a ['tʃinto] pp di **cingere**

'cintola ['tʃintola] sf (cintura) belt; (vita) waist

cin'tura [tʃin'tura] sf belt; **~ di salvataggio** lifebelt (Brit), life preserver (US); **~ di sicurezza** (Aut, Aer) safety o seat belt

cintu'rino [tʃintu'rino] sm strap; **~ dell'orologio** watch strap

CIO sigla m (= Comitato Internazionale Olimpico) IOC (= International Olympic Committee)

ciò [tʃɔ] pron this; that; **~ che** what; **~ nonostante** o **nondimeno** nevertheless, in spite of that; **con tutto ~** for all that, in spite of everything

ci'occa, -che ['tʃɔkka] sf (di capelli) lock

ciocco'lata [tʃokko'lata] sf chocolate; (bevanda) (hot) chocolate; **~ al latte/fondente** milk/plain chocolate

cioccola'tino [tʃokkola'tino] sm chocolate

ciocco'lato [tʃokko'lato] sm chocolate

cio'è [tʃo'ɛ] av that is (to say)

ciondo'lare [tʃondo'lare] /72/ vt (far dondolare) to dangle, swing ▶ vi to dangle; (fig) to loaf (about)

ci'ondolo ['tʃondolo] sm pendant; **~ portafortuna** charm

ciondo'loni [tʃondo'loni] av: **con le braccia/gambe ~** with arms/legs dangling

ciononos'tante [tʃononos'tante] av nonetheless, nevertheless

ci'otola ['tʃɔtola] sf bowl

ci'ottolo ['tʃɔttolo] sm pebble; (di strada) cobble(stone)

CIPE ['tʃipe] sigla m = **Comitato Interministeriale per la Programmazione Economica**; vedi **comitato**

ci'piglio [tʃi'piʎʎo] sm frown

ci'polla [tʃi'polla] sf onion; (di tulipano ecc) bulb

cipol'lina [tʃipol'lina] sf onion; **cipolline sottaceto** pickled onions; **cipolline sottolio** baby onions in oil

ci'presso [tʃi'presso] sm cypress (tree)

'cipria ['tʃiprja] sf (face) powder

cipri'ota, -i, -e [tʃipri'ɔta] ag, sm/f Cypriot

'Cipro ['tʃipro] sm Cyprus

'circa ['tʃirka] av about, roughly ▶ prep about, concerning; **a mezzogiorno ~** about midday

'circo, -chi ['tʃirko] sm circus

circo'lare [tʃirko'lare] /72/ vi to circulate; (Aut) to drive (along), move (along) ▶ ag circular ▶ sf (Amm) circular; (di autobus) circle (line); **circola voce che ...** there is a rumour going about that ...; **assegno ~** banker's draft

circolazi'one [tʃirkolat'tsjone] sf circulation; (Aut): **la ~** (the) traffic; **libretto di ~** log book, registration book; **tassa di ~** road tax; **~ a targhe alterne** see note

> **Circolazione a targhe alterne** is used by some town councils to combat the increase in traffic and pollution in town centres. It stipulates that on days with an even date, only cars whose number plate ends in an even number or a zero may be on the road; on days with an odd date, only cars with odd registration numbers may be used. Public holidays are generally, but not always, exempt.

'circolo ['tʃirkolo] sm circle; **entrare in ~** (Anat) to enter the bloodstream

circoncisi'one [tʃirkontʃi'zjone] sf circumcision

circon'dare [tʃirkon'dare] /72/ vt to surround ■ **circondarsi** vpr: **circondarsi di** to surround o.s. with

circondari'ale [tʃirkonda'rjale] ag: **casa di pena ~** district prison

circon'dario [tʃirkon'darjo] sm (Dir) administrative district; (zona circostante) neighbourhood (Brit), neighborhood (US)

circonfe'renza [tʃirkonfe'rentsa] sf circumference

circonvallazi'one [tʃirkonvallat'tsjone] sf ring road (Brit), beltway (US); (per evitare una città) by-pass

circos'critto, -a [tʃirkos'kritto] pp di **circoscrivere**

circos'crivere [tʃirkos'krivere] /105/ vt to circumscribe; (fig) to limit, restrict

circoscrizi'one [tʃirkoskrit'tsjone] sf (Amm) district, area; **~ elettorale** constituency

circos'petto, -a [tʃirkos'petto] ag circumspect, cautious

circos'tante [tʃirkos'tante] ag surrounding, neighbouring (Brit), neighboring (US)

circos'tanza [tʃirkos'tantsa] sf circumstance; (occasione) occasion; **parole di ~** words suited to the occasion

circu'ire [tʃirku'ire] /55/ vt (fig) to fool, take in

cir'cuito [tʃir'kuito] SM circuit; **andare in** o **fare corto ~** to short-circuit; **~ integrato** integrated circuit

ci'rillico, -a, -ci, -che [tʃi'rilliko] AG Cyrillic

cir'rosi [tʃir'rɔzi] SF: **~ epatica** cirrhosis (of the liver)

'C.I.S.A.L. ['tʃizal] SIGLA F (= Confederazione Italiana Sindacati Autonomi dei Lavoratori) trades union organization

CISL [tʃizl] SIGLA F (= Confederazione Italiana Sindacati Lavoratori) trades union organization

'C.I.S.N.A.L. ['tʃiznal] SIGLA F (= Confederazione Italiana Sindacati Nazionali dei Lavoratori) trades union organization

'ciste ['tʃiste] SF = **cisti**

cis'terna [tʃis'terna] SF tank, cistern

'cisti ['tʃisti] SF INV cyst

cis'tite [tʃis'tite] SF cystitis

cit. ABBR = **citato**; (= citata) cit.

ci'tare [tʃi'tare] /72/ VT (Dir) to summon; (autore) to quote; (a esempio, modello) to cite; **~ qn per danni** to sue sb

citazi'one [tʃitat'tsjone] SF summons sg; quotation; (di persona) mention

ci'tofono [tʃi'tɔfono] SM entry phone; (in uffici) intercom

cito'logico, -a, -ci, -che [tʃito'lɔdʒiko] AG: **esame ~** test for detection of cancerous cells

'citrico, -a, -ci, -che ['tʃitriko] AG citric

città [tʃit'ta] SF INV town; (importante) city; **~ giardino** garden city; **~ mercato** shopping centre, mall; **~ universitaria** university campus; **C~ del Capo** Cape Town

citta'della [tʃitta'della] SF citadel, stronghold

cittadi'nanza [tʃittadi'nantsa] SF citizens pl, inhabitants pl of a town (o city); (Dir) citizenship

citta'dino, -a [tʃitta'dino] AG town cpd; city cpd ▶ SM/F (di uno Stato) citizen; (abitante di città) town dweller, city dweller

ci'uccio ['tʃuttʃo] SM (col) comforter, dummy (BRIT), pacifier (US)

ci'uco, -a, -chi, -che ['tʃuko] SM/F ass

ci'uffo ['tʃuffo] SM tuft

ci'urma ['tʃurma] SF (di nave) crew

ci'vetta [tʃi'vetta] SF (Zool) owl; (fig: donna) coquette, flirt ▶ AG INV: **auto/nave ~** decoy car/ship; **fare la ~ con qn** to flirt with sb

civet'tare [tʃivet'tare] /72/ VT to flirt

civette'ria [tʃivette'ria] SF coquetry, coquettishness

civettu'olo, -a [tʃivet'twɔlo] AG flirtatious

'civico, -a, -ci, -che ['tʃiviko] AG civic; (museo) municipal, town cpd; city cpd; **guardia civica** town policeman; **senso ~** public spirit

ci'vile [tʃi'vile] AG civil; (non militare) civilian; (nazione) civilized ▶ SM civilian; **stato ~** marital status; **abiti civili** civvies

civi'lista, -i, -e [tʃivi'lista] SM/F (avvocato) civil lawyer; (studioso) expert in civil law

civiliz'zare [tʃivilid'dzare] /72/ VT to civilize

civilizzazi'one [tʃiviliddzat'tsjone] SF civilization

civiltà [tʃivil'ta] SF civilization; (cortesia) civility

ci'vismo [tʃi'vizmo] SM public spirit

CL [tʃi'elle] SIGLA F (Pol: = Comunione e Liberazione) Catholic youth movement ▶ SIGLA = **Caltanissetta**

cl ABBR (= centilitro) cl

'clacson SM INV (Aut) horn

cla'more SM (frastuono) din, uproar, clamour (BRIT), clamor (US); (fig) outcry

clamo'roso, -a AG noisy; (fig) sensational

clan SM INV clan

clandestinità SF (di attività) secret nature; **vivere nella ~** to live in hiding; (ricercato politico) to live underground

clandes'tino, -a AG clandestine; (Pol) underground, clandestine; (immigrato) illegal ▶ SM/F stowaway; (anche: **immigrato clandestino**) illegal immigrant

clari'netto SM clarinet

'classe SF class; **di ~** (fig) with class; of excellent quality; **~ operaia** working class; **~ turistica** (Aer) economy class

classi'cismo [klassi'tʃizmo] SM classicism

'classico, -a, -ci, -che AG classical; (tradizionale: moda) classic(al) ▶ SM classic; classical author; (anche: **liceo classico**) secondary school with emphasis on the humanities

clas'sifica, -che SF classification; (Sport) placings pl; (di dischi) charts pl, hit parade

classifi'care /20/ VT to classify; (candidato, compito) to grade ■ **classificarsi** VPR to be placed

classifica'tore SM filing cabinet

classificazi'one [klassifikat'tsjone] SF classification; grading

clas'sista, -i, -e AG class-conscious ▶ SM/F class-conscious person

claudi'cante AG (zoppo) lame; (fig: prosa) halting

'clausola SF (Dir) clause

claustro'fobico, -a, -ci, -che AG claustrophobic

clau'sura SF (Rel): **monaca di ~** nun belonging to an enclosed order; **fare una vita di ~** (fig) to lead a cloistered life

'clava SF club

clavi'cembalo [klavi'tʃembalo] SM harpsichord

cla'vicola SF (Anat) collarbone

cle'mente AG merciful; (clima) mild

cle'menza [kle'mentsa] SF mercy, clemency; mildness

clep'tomane SM F kleptomaniac

cleri'cale AG clerical

'clero SM clergy

cles'sidra SF (a sabbia) hourglass; (ad acqua) water clock

clic'care /20/ VI (Inform): ~ su to click on

cliché [kli'ʃe] SM INV (Tip) plate; (fig) cliché

cli'ente SMF customer, client

> Cliente si traduce con **client** quando è riferito a un libero professionista.
> il cliente di un avvocato **a lawyer's client**
> Chi acquista qualcosa in un negozio o su un sito web è un **customer**.
> una buona cliente **a good customer**

clien'tela SF customers pl, clientèle

cliente'lismo SM: ~ **politico** political nepotism

'clima, -i SM climate

cli'matico, -a, -ci, -che AG climatic; **stazione climatica** health resort

climatizza'tore [klimatiddza'tore] SM air conditioner

climatizzazi'one [klimatiddzat'tsjone] SF air conditioning

'clinico, -a, -ci, -che AG clinical ▶ SM (medico) clinician ▶ SF (scienza) clinical medicine; (casa di cura) clinic, nursing home; (settore d'ospedale) clinic; **quadro ~** anamnesis; **avere l'occhio ~** (fig) to have an expert eye

clis'tere SM (Med) enema; (: apparecchio) device used to give an enema

clo'aca, -che SF sewer

cloche [klɔʃ] SF INV control stick, joystick; **cambio a ~** (Aut) floor-mounted gear lever

clo'nare /72/ VT to clone

clona'zione [klonat'tsjone] SF (Biol, fig) cloning

'cloro SM chlorine

cloro'filla SF chlorophyll

cloro'formio SM chloroform

'cloud com'puting [klaud kom'pjutin] SM INV cloud computing

club SM INV club

cm ABBR (= centimetro) cm

c.m. ABBR (= corrente mese) inst.

CN SIGLA = **Cuneo**

CNEN SIGLA M (= Comitato Nazionale per l'Energia Nucleare) ≈ AEA (BRIT), AEC (US)

CNR SIGLA M (= Consiglio Nazionale delle Ricerche) science research council

CNRN SIGLA M = **Comitato Nazionale Ricerche Nucleari**

CO SIGLA = **Como**

Co. ABBR (= compagnia) Co.

c/o ABBR (= care of) c/o

coabi'tare /72/ VI to live together, live under the same roof

coagu'lare /72/ VT to coagulate ▶ VI (anche: coagularsi) to coagulate; (: latte) to curdle

coalizi'one [koalit'tsjone] SF coalition

co'atto, -a AG (Dir) compulsory, forced; **condannare al domicilio ~** to place under house arrest

'COBAS SIGLA MPL (= Comitati di base) independent trades unions

'cobra SM INV cobra

'coca SF (bibita) Coke®; (droga) cocaine

'coca 'cola® SF coca cola®

coca'ina SF cocaine

coc'carda SF cockade

cocchi'ere [kok'kjɛre] SM coachman

'cocchio ['kɔkkjo] SM (carrozza) coach; (biga) chariot

cocci'nella [kottʃi'nɛlla] SF ladybird (BRIT), ladybug (US)

'coccio ['kɔttʃo] SM earthenware; (vaso) earthenware pot ▪ **cocci** SMPL fragments (of pottery)

cocciu'taggine [kottʃu'taddʒine] SF stubbornness, pig-headedness

cocci'uto, -a [kot'tʃuto] AG stubborn, pig-headed

'cocco, -chi SM (pianta) coconut palm; (frutto): **noce di ~** coconut ▶ SM/F (col) darling; **è il ~ della mamma** he's mummy's darling

cocco'drillo SM crocodile

cocco'lare /72/ VT to cuddle, fondle

co'cente [ko'tʃɛnte] AG (anche fig) burning

cocerò ecc [kotʃe'rɔ] VB vedi **cuocere**

co'comero SM watermelon

co'cuzzolo [ko'kuttsolo] SM top; (di capo, cappello) crown

cod. ABBR = **codice**

'coda SF tail; (fila di persone, auto) queue (BRIT), line (US); (di abiti) train; **con la ~ dell'occhio** out of the corner of one's eye; **mettersi in ~** to queue (up) (BRIT), line up (US); to join the queue o line; **~ di cavallo** (acconciatura) ponytail; **avere la ~ di paglia** (fig) to have a guilty conscience; **~ di rospo** (Cuc) frogfish tail

codar'dia SF cowardice

co'dardo, -a AG cowardly ▶ SM/F coward

co'desto, -a AG, PRON (poetico) this; that

'codice ['kɔditʃe] SM code; (manoscritto antico) codex; **~ di avviamento postale** postcode (BRIT), zip code (US); **~ a barre** bar code; **~ civile** civil code; **~ fiscale** tax code; **~ penale** penal code; **~ segreto** (di tessera magnetica) PIN (number); **~ di sicurezza** security code; **~ della strada** highway code

co'difica SF codification; (Inform: di programma) coding

codifi'care /20/ VT (Dir) to codify; (cifrare) to code

codificazi'one [kodifikat'tsjone] SF coding

coercizi'one [koertʃit'tsjone] SF coercion

coe'rente AG coherent

coe'renza [koe'rɛntsa] SF coherence

coesi'one SF cohesion

coe'sistere /11/ VI to coexist

coe'taneo, -a AG, SM/F contemporary; **essere ~ di qn** to be the same age as sb

cofa'netto SM casket; **~ dei gioielli** jewel case

'cofano SM (Aut) bonnet (BRIT), hood (US); (forziere) chest

'coffa SF (Naut) top

'cogli ['koʎʎi] PREP + DET vedi **con**

'cogliere ['kɔʎʎere] /23/ VT (fiore, frutto) to pick, gather; (sorprendere) to catch, surprise; (bersaglio) to hit; (fig: momento opportuno ecc) to grasp, seize, take; (: capire) to grasp; **~ l'occasione (per fare)** to take the opportunity (to do); **~ sul fatto o in flagrante/alla sprovvista** to catch red-handed/unprepared; **~ nel segno** (fig) to hit the nail on the head

cogli'one, -a [koʎ'ʎone] SM (!: testicolo): **coglioni** balls (!); **rompere i coglioni a qn** to get on sb's tits (!) ▶ SM/F (fig: persona sciocca) jerk

co'gnac [kɔ'ɲak] SM INV cognac

co'gnato, -a [koɲ'ɲato] SM/F brother-in-law(-sister-in-law)

cogni'tivo, -a [koɲɲi'tivo] AG cognitive

cognizi'one [koɲɲit'tsjone] SF knowledge; **con ~ di causa** with full knowledge of the facts

co'gnome [koɲ'ɲome] SM surname

> In Italy, married women officially keep their maiden name. However, in practice, many women often use their husband's surname.

'coi PREP + DET vedi **con**

coi'bente AG insulating

coinci'denza [kointʃi'dɛntsa] SF coincidence; (Ferr, Aer, di autobus) connection

coin'cidere [koin'tʃidere] /34/ VI to coincide

coin'ciso, -a [koin'tʃizo] PP di **coincidere**

coinqui'lino SM fellow tenant

cointeres'senza [kointeres'sɛntsa] SF (Comm): **avere una ~ in qc** to own shares in sth; **~ dei lavoratori** profit-sharing

coin'volgere [koin'vɔldʒere] /96/ VT: **~ in** to involve in

coinvolgi'mento [koinvoldʒi'mento] SM involvement

coin'volto, -a PP di **coinvolgere**

col PREP + DET vedi **con**

Col. ABBR (= colonnello) Col.

colà AV there

cola'brodo SM INV strainer

cola'pasta SM INV colander

co'lare /72/ VT (liquido) to strain; (pasta) to drain; (oro fuso) to pour ▶ VI (sudore) to drip; (botte) to leak; (cera) to melt; **~ a picco** VT (nave) to sink

co'lata SF (di lava) flow; (Industria) casting

colazi'one [kolat'tsjone] SF (anche: **prima colazione**) breakfast; (anche: **seconda colazione**) lunch; **fare ~** to have breakfast (o lunch); **~ di lavoro** working lunch

Coldi'retti ABBR F (= Confederazione nazionale coltivatori diretti) federation of Italian farmers

co'lei PRON vedi **colui**

co'lera SM (Med) cholera

coleste'rolo SM cholesterol

colf ABBR F = **collaboratrice familiare**

'colgo ecc VB vedi **cogliere**

colibrì SM hummingbird

'colica SF (Med) colic

co'lino SM strainer

'colla PREP + DET vedi **con** ▶ SF glue; (di farina) paste

collabo'rare /72/ VI to collaborate; (con la polizia) to co-operate; **~ a** to collaborate on; (giornale) to contribute to

collabora'tore, -'trice SM/F collaborator; (di giornale, rivista) contributor; **~ esterno** freelance; **collaboratrice familiare** home help; **~ di giustizia** = **pentito**

collaborazi'one [kollaborat'tsjone] SF collaboration; contribution

col'lana SF necklace; (collezione) collection, series

col'lant [kɔ'lɑ̃] SM INV tights pl

col'lare SM collar

col'lasso SM (Med) collapse

collate'rale AG collateral; **effetti collaterali** side effects

collau'dare /72/ VT to test, try out

col'laudo SM testing no pl; test

'colle PREP + DET vedi **con** ▶ SM hill

col'lega, -ghi, -ghe SM/F colleague

collega'mento SM connection; (Mil) liaison; (Radio) link(-up); (Inform) link; **ufficiale di ~** liaison officer; **~ ipertestuale** hyperlink

colle'gare /80/ VT to connect, join, link ▪ **collegarsi** VPR (Radio, TV) to link up; **collegarsi con** (Tel) to get through to

collegi'ale [kolle'dʒale] AG (riunione, decisione) collective; (Ins) boarding school cpd ▶ SM/F boarder; (fig: persona timida e inesperta) schoolboy(-girl)

col'legio [kol'lɛdʒo] SM college; (convitto) boarding school; **~ elettorale** (Pol) constituency

'collera SF anger; **andare in ~** to get angry

col'lerico, -a, -ci, -che AG quick-tempered, irascible

col'letta SF collection

collettività SF community

collet'tivo, -a AG collective; (*interesse*) general, everybody's; (*biglietto, visita ecc*) group cpd ▶ SM (*Pol*) (political) group; **società in nome ~** (*Comm*) partnership

col'letto SM collar; **colletti bianchi** (*fig*) white-collar workers

collezio'nare [kollettsjo'nare] /72/ VT to collect

collezi'one [kollet'tsjone] SF collection

collezio'nista [kollettsjo'nista] SMF collector

colli'mare /72/ VI to correspond, coincide

col'lina SF hill

colli'nare AG hill cpd

col'lirio SM eyewash

collisi'one SF collision

'collo PREP + DET vedi **con** ▶ SM neck; (*di abito*) neck, collar; (*pacco*) parcel; **~ del piede** instep

colloca'mento SM (*impiego*) employment; (*disposizione*) placing, arrangement; **ufficio di ~** ≈ Jobcentre (*Brit*), state (*o* federal) employment agency (*US*); **~ a riposo** retirement

collo'care /20/ VT (*libri, mobili*) to place; (*persona: trovare un lavoro per*) to find a job for, place; (*Comm: merce*) to find a market for; **~ qn a riposo** to retire sb

collocazi'one [kollokat'tsjone] SF placing; (*di libro*) classification

colloqui'ale AG (*termine ecc*) colloquial; (*tono*) informal

col'loquio SM conversation, talk; (*ufficiale, per un lavoro*) interview; (*Ins*) preliminary oral exam; **avviare un ~ con qn** (*Pol ecc*) to start talks with sb

col'loso, -a AG sticky

col'lottola SF nape *o* scruff of the neck; **afferrare qn per la ~** to grab sb by the scruff of the neck

collusi'one SF (*Dir*) collusion

colluttazi'one [kolluttat'tsjone] SF scuffle

col'mare /72/ VT: **~ di** (*anche fig*) to fill with; (*dare in abbondanza*) to load *o* overwhelm with; **~ un divario** (*fig*) to bridge a gap

'colmo, -a AG: **~ (di)** full (of) ▶ SM summit, top; (*fig*) height; **al ~ della disperazione** in the depths of despair; **è il ~!** it's the last straw!; **e per ~ di sfortuna ...** and to cap it all ...

co'lomba SF vedi **colombo**

Co'lombia SF: **la ~** Colombia

colombi'ano, -a AG, SM/F Colombian

co'lombo, -a SM/F dove; pigeon; **colombi** (*fig: col*) lovebirds

Co'lonia SF Cologne

co'lonia SF colony; (*per bambini*) holiday camp; **(acqua di) ~** (eau de) cologne

coloni'ale AG colonial ▶ SMF colonist, settler

co'lonico, -a, -ci, -che AG: **casa colonica** farmhouse

coloniz'zare [kolonid'dzare] /72/ VT to colonize

co'lonna SF column; **~ sonora** (*Cine*) sound track; **~ vertebrale** spine, spinal column

colon'nello SM colonel

co'lono SM (*coltivatore*) tenant farmer

colo'rante SM colouring (*Brit*), coloring (*US*)

colo'rare /72/ VT to colour (*Brit*), color (*US*); (*disegno*) to colour in

co'lore SM colour (*Brit*), color (*US*); (*Carte*) suit; **a colori** in colour, colour cpd; **la gente di ~** coloured people; **diventare di tutti i colori** to turn scarlet; **farne di tutti i colori** to get up to all sorts of mischief; **passarne di tutti i colori** to go through all sorts of problems

colo'rito, -a AG coloured (*Brit*), colored (*US*); (*viso*) rosy, pink; (*linguaggio*) colourful (*Brit*), colorful (*US*) ▶ SM (*tinta*) colour (*Brit*), color (*US*); (*carnagione*) complexion

co'loro PRON PL vedi **colui**

colos'sale AG colossal, enormous

co'losso SM colossus

'colpa SF fault; (*biasimo*) blame; (*colpevolezza*) guilt; (*azione colpevole*) offence (*Brit*) *o* offense (*US*); (*peccato*) sin; **di chi è la ~?** whose fault is it?; **è ~ sua** it's his fault; **per ~ di** through, owing to; **senso di ~** sense of guilt; **dare la ~ a qn di qc** to blame sb for sth

col'pevole AG guilty

colpevoliz'zare [kolpevolid'dzare] /72/ VT: **~ qn** to make sb feel guilty

col'pire /55/ VT to hit, strike; (*fig*) to strike; **rimanere colpito da qc** to be amazed *o* struck by sth; **è stato colpito da ordine di cattura** there is a warrant out for his arrest; **~ nel segno** (*fig*) to hit the nail on the head, be spot on (*Brit*)

'colpo SM (*urto*) knock; (*fig: affettivo*) blow, shock; (*: aggressivo*) blow; (*di pistola*) shot; (*Med*) stroke; (*furto*) raid; **di ~, tutto d'un ~** suddenly; **fare ~** to make a strong impression; **il motore perde colpi** the engine is misfiring; **è morto sul ~** he died instantly; **mi hai fatto venire un ~!** what a fright you gave me!; **ti venisse un ~!** (*col*) drop dead!; **~ d'aria** chill; **~ in banca** bank job *o* raid; **~ basso** (*Pugilato, fig*) punch below the belt; **~ di fulmine** love at first sight; **~ di grazia** coup de grâce; (*fig*) finishing blow; **a ~ d'occhio** at a glance; **~ di scena** (*Teat*) coup de théâtre; (*fig*) dramatic turn of events; **~ di sole** sunstroke; **colpi di sole** (*nei capelli*) highlights; **~ di Stato** coup d'état; **~ di telefono** phone call; **~ di testa** (*sudden*) impulse *o* whim; **~ di vento** gust (of wind)

col'poso, -a AG: **omicidio ~** manslaughter

'colsi ecc VB vedi **cogliere**

coltel'lata SF stab

col'tello SM knife; **avere il ~ dalla parte del**

manico (*fig*) to have the whip hand; **~ a serra-manico** clasp knife

colti'vare /**72**/ VT to cultivate; (*verdura*) to grow, cultivate

coltiva'tore, -trice SM/F farmer; **~ diretto(a)** small independent farmer

coltivazi'one [koltivat'tsjone] SF cultivation; growing; **~ intensiva** intensive farming

'colto, -a PP *di* **cogliere** ▶ AG (*istruito*) cultured, educated

'coltre SF blanket

col'tura SF cultivation; **~ alternata** crop rotation

co'lui (*f* **colei**, *pl* **coloro**) PRON the one; **~ che parla** the one *o* the man *o* the person who is speaking; **colei che amo** the one *o* the woman *o* the person (whom) I love

com. ABBR = **comunale**; **commissione**

'coma SM INV coma

comanda'mento SM (*Rel*) commandment

coman'dante SM (*Mil*) commander, commandant; (*di reggimento*) commanding officer; (*Naut*, *Aer*) captain

coman'dare /**72**/ VI to be in command ▶ VT to command; (*imporre*) to order, command; **~ a qn di fare** to order sb to do

co'mando SM (*ingiunzione*) order, command; (*autorità*) command; (*Tecn*) control; **~ generale** general headquarters *pl*; **~ a distanza** remote control

co'mare SF (*madrina*) godmother; (*donna pettegola*) gossip

co'masco, -a, -schi, -sche AG of (*o* from) Como

combaci'are [komba'tʃare] /**14**/ VI to meet; (*fig*: *coincidere*) to coincide, correspond

combat'tente AG fighting ▶ SM combatant; **ex-combattente** ex-serviceman

com'battere /**1**/ VT to fight; (*fig*) to combat, fight against ▶ VI to fight

combatti'mento SM fight; fighting *no pl*; (*di pugilato*) match; **mettere fuori ~** to knock out

combat'tivo, -a AG pugnacious

combat'tuto, -a AG (*incerto*: *persona*) uncertain, undecided; (*gara*, *partita*) hard fought

combi'nare /**72**/ VT to combine; (*organizzare*) to arrange; (*col*: *fare*) to make, cause ▶ VI (*corrispondere*): **~ (con)** to correspond (with)

combinazi'one [kombinat'tsjone] SF combination; (*caso fortuito*) coincidence; **per ~** by chance

com'briccola SF (*gruppo*) party; (*banda*) gang

combus'tibile AG combustible ▶ SM fuel; **~ fossile** fossil fuel

combusti'one SF combustion

com'butta SF (*peg*) gang; **in ~** in league

'come

AV **1** (*alla maniera di*) like; **ti comporti come lui** you behave like him *o* like he does; **bianco come la neve** (as) white as snow; **come se** as if, as though; **com'è vero Dio!** as God is my witness!

2 (*in qualità di*) as a; **lavora come autista** he works as a driver

3 (*interrogativo*) how; **come ti chiami?** what's your name?; **come sta?** how are you?; **com'è il tuo amico?** what is your friend like?; **come?** (*prego?*) pardon?, sorry?; **come mai?** how come?; **come mai non ci hai avvertiti?** how come you didn't warn us?

4 (*esclamativo*): **come sei bravo!** how clever you are!; **come mi dispiace!** I'm terribly sorry!

▶ CONG **1** (*in che modo*) how; **mi ha spiegato come l'ha conosciuto** he told me how he met him; **non so come sia successo** I don't know how it happened; **attento a come parli!** watch your mouth!

2 (*correlativo*) as; (: *con comparativi di maggioranza*) than; **non è bravo come pensavo** he isn't as clever as I thought; **è meglio di come pensassi** it's better than I thought

3 (*quasi se*) as; **è come se fosse ancora qui** it's as if he was still here; **come se niente fosse** as if nothing had happened; **come non detto!** let's forget it!

4 (*appena che*, *quando*) as soon as; **come arrivò, iniziò a lavorare** as soon as he arrived, he set to work

5 *vedi anche* **così**; **oggi**; **ora**; **tanto**

---

come'done SM blackhead

co'meta SF comet

'comico, -a, -ci, -che AG (*Teat*) comic; (*buffo*) comical ▶ SM (*attore*) comedian, comic actor; (*comicità*) comic spirit, comedy

co'mignolo [ko'miɲɲolo] SM chimney top

cominci'are [komin'tʃare] /**14**/ VT, VI to begin, start; **~ a fare/col fare** to begin to do/by doing; **cominciamo bene!** (*ironico*) we're off to a fine start!

comi'tato SM committee; **~ direttivo** steering committee; **~ di gestione** works council; **~ interministeriale prezzi** interdepartmental committee on prices; **~ interministeriale per la programmazione economica** interdepartmental committee for economic planning; **~ interministeriale per lo sviluppo industriale** interdepartmental committee for industrial development

comi'tiva SF party, group

co'mizio [ko'mittsjo] SM (*Pol*) meeting, assembly; **~ elettorale** election rally

'comma, -i SM (*Dir*) subsection

com'mando SM INV commando (squad)

com'media SF comedy; (*opera teatrale*) play; (*: che fa ridere*) comedy; (*fig*) playacting *no pl*

commedi'ante SMF (*peg*) third-rate actor (actress); (*: fig*) sham

commedi'ografo, -a SM/F (*autore*) comedy writer

commemo'rare /**72**/ VT to commemorate

commemorazi'one [kommemorat'tsjone] SF commemoration

commenda'tore SM *official title awarded for services to one's country*

commen'sale SMF table companion

commen'tare /**72**/ VT to comment on; (*testo*) to annotate; (*Radio, TV*) to give a commentary on

commenta'tore, -'trice SM/F commentator

com'mento SM comment; (*a un testo, Radio, TV*) commentary; **~ musicale** (*Cine*) background music

commerci'ale [kommer'tʃale] AG commercial, trading; (*peg*) commercial

commercia'lista, -i, -e [kommertʃa'lista] SM/F (*laureato*) graduate in economics and commerce; (*consulente*) business consultant

commercializ'zare [kommertʃalid'dzare] /**72**/ VT to market

commercializzazi'one [kommertʃaliddzat'tsjone] SF marketing

commerci'ante [kommer'tʃante] SMF trader, dealer; (*negoziante*) shopkeeper; **~ all'ingrosso** wholesaler; **~ in proprio** sole trader

commerci'are [kommer'tʃare] /**14**/ VI: **~ in** to deal o trade in ▶ VT to deal o trade in

com'mercio [kom'mertʃo] SM trade, commerce; **essere in ~** (*prodotto*) to be on the market o on sale; **essere nel ~** (*persona*) to be in business; **~ all'ingrosso/al dettaglio** wholesale/retail trade

com'messo, -a PP *di* **commettere** ▶ SM/F shop assistant (*Brit*), sales clerk (*US*) ▶ SM (*impiegato*) clerk ▶ SF (*Comm*) order; **~ viaggiatore** commercial traveller

commes'tibile AG edible ■ **commestibili** SMPL foodstuffs

com'mettere /**63**/ VT to commit; (*ordinare*) to commission, order

commi'ato SM leave-taking; **prendere ~ da qn** to take one's leave of sb

commi'nare /**72**/ VT (*Dir*) to make provision for

commise'rare /**72**/ VT to sympathize with, commiserate with

commiserazi'one [kommizerat'tsjone] SF commiseration

com'misi *ecc* VB *vedi* **commettere**

commissaria'mento SM temporary receivership

commissari'are /**19**/ VT to put under temporary receivership

commissari'ato SM (*Amm*) commissionership; (*: sede*) commissioner's office; (*: di polizia*) police station

commis'sario SM commissioner; (*di pubblica sicurezza*) ≈ (police) superintendent (*Brit*), ≈ (police) captain (*US*); (*Sport*) steward; (*membro di commissione*) member of a committee o board; **alto ~** high commissioner; **~ di bordo** (*Naut*) purser; **~ d'esame** member of an examining board; **~ di gara** race official; **~ tecnico** (*Sport*) national coach

commissio'nare /**72**/ VT to order, place an order for

commissio'nario SM (*Comm*) agent, broker

commissi'one SF (*incarico*) errand; (*comitato, percentuale*) commission; (*Comm: ordinazione*) order ■ **commissioni** SFPL (*acquisti*) shopping *sg*; **~ d'esame** examining board; **~ d'inchiesta** committee of enquiry; **~ permanente** standing committee; **commissioni bancarie** bank charges

commit'tente SMF (*Comm*) purchaser, customer

com'mosso, -a PP *di* **commuovere**

commo'vente AG moving

commozi'one [kommot'tsjone] SF emotion, deep feeling; **~ cerebrale** (*Med*) concussion

commu'overe /**66**/ VT to move, affect ■ **commuoversi** VPR to be moved

commu'tare /**72**/ VT (*pena*) to commute; (*Elettr*) to change o switch over

commutazi'one [kommutat'tsjone] SF (*Dir, Elettr*) commutation

comò SM INV chest of drawers

como'dino SM bedside table

comodità SF INV comfort; convenience

'comodo, -a AG comfortable; (*facile*) easy; (*conveniente*) convenient; (*utile*) useful, handy ▶ SM comfort; convenience; **con ~** at one's convenience o leisure; **fare il proprio ~** to do as one pleases; **far ~** to be useful o handy; **stia ~!** don't bother to get up!

'compact disc SM INV compact disc

compae'sano, -a SM/F fellow-countryman (-woman); person from the same town

com'pagine [kom'padʒine] SF (*squadra*) team

compa'gnia [kompaɲ'ɲia] SF company; (*gruppo*) gathering; **fare ~ a qn** to keep sb company; **essere di ~** to be sociable

com'pagno, -a [kom'paɲɲo] SM/F (*di classe, gioco*) companion; (*Pol*) comrade; **~ di lavoro** workmate; **~ di scuola** schoolfriend; **~ di viaggio** fellow traveller

com'paio *ecc* VB *vedi* **comparire**

compa'rare /**72**/ VT to compare

compara'tivo, -a AG, SM comparative

comparazi'one [komparat'tsjone] SF comparison

com'pare SM (*padrino*) godfather; (*complice*) accomplice; (*col: amico*) old pal, old mate

compa'rire /7/ VI to appear; ~ **in giudizio** (*Dir*) to appear before the court

comparizi'one [komparit'tsjone] SF (*Dir*) appearance; **mandato di** ~ summons *sg*

com'parso, -a PP *di* **comparire** ▶ SF appearance; (*Teat*) walk-on; (*Cine*) extra

comparteci'pare [kompartetʃi'pare] /72/ VI (*Comm*): ~ **a** to have a share in

compartecipazi'one [kompartetʃipat'tsjone] SF sharing; (*quota*) share; ~ **agli utili** profit-sharing; **in** ~ jointly

comparti'mento SM compartment; (*Amm*) district

com'parvi *ecc* VB *vedi* **comparire**

compas'sato, -a AG (*persona*) composed; **freddo e** ~ cool and collected

compassi'one SF compassion, pity; **avere** ~ **di qn** to feel sorry for sb, pity sb; **fare** ~ to arouse pity

compassio'nevole AG compassionate

com'passo SM (pair of) compasses *pl*; callipers *pl*

compa'tibile AG (*scusabile*) excusable; (*conciliabile, Inform*) compatible

compati'mento SM compassion; indulgence; **con aria di** ~ with a condescending air

compa'tire /55/ VT (*aver compassione di*) to sympathize with, feel sorry for; (*scusare*) to make allowances for

compatri'ota, -i, -e SM/F compatriot

compat'tezza [kompat'tettsa] SF (*solidità*) compactness; (*fig: unità*) solidarity

com'patto, -a AG compact; (*roccia*) solid; (*folla*) dense; (*fig: gruppo, partito*) united, close-knit

com'pendio SM summary; (*libro*) compendium

compen'sare /72/ VT (*equilibrare*) to compensate for, make up for ▪ **compensarsi** VPR (*reciproco*) to balance each other out; ~ **qn di** (*rimunerare*) to pay *o* remunerate sb for; (*risarcire*) to pay compensation to sb for; (*fig: fatiche, dolori*) to reward sb for

compen'sato SM (*anche:* **legno compensato**) plywood

com'penso SM compensation; payment, remuneration; reward; **in** ~ (*d'altra parte*) on the other hand

'**compera** SF purchase; **fare le compere** to do the shopping

compe'rare /72/ VT = **comprare**

'**compere** SFPL: **fare** ~ to do the shopping

compe'tente AG competent; (*mancia*) apt, suitable; (*capace*) qualified; **rivolgersi all'ufficio** ~ to apply to the office concerned

compe'tenza [kompe'tɛntsa] SF competence; (*Dir: autorità*) jurisdiction; (*Tecn, Comm*) expertise ▪ **competenze** SFPL (*onorari*) fees; **definire le competenze** to establish responsibilities

com'petere /45/ VI to compete, vie; (*Dir*): (*spettare*) ~ **a** to lie within the competence of

competitività SF INV competitiveness

competi'tivo, -a AG competitive

competi'tore, -'trice SM/F competitor

competizi'one [kompetit'tsjone] SF competition; **spirito di** ~ competitive spirit

compia'cente [kompja'tʃɛnte] AG courteous, obliging

compia'cenza [kompja'tʃɛntsa] SF courtesy

compia'cere [kompja'tʃere] /74/ VI: ~ **a** to gratify, please ▶ VT to please ▪ **compiacersi** VPR: **compiacersi di** *o* **per qc** (*provare soddisfazione*) to be delighted at sth; **compiacersi con qn** (*rallegrarsi*) to congratulate sb; **compiacersi di fare** (*degnarsi*) to be so good as to do

compiaci'mento [kompjatʃi'mento] SM satisfaction

compiaci'uto, -a [kompja'tʃuto] PP *di* **compiacere**

compi'angere [kom'pjandʒere] /75/ VT to sympathize with, feel sorry for

compi'anto, -a PP *di* **compiangere** ▶ AG: **il** ~ **presidente** the late lamented president ▶ SM mourning, grief

'**compiere** /24/ VT (*concludere*) to finish, complete; (*adempiere*) to carry out, fulfil ▪ **compiersi** VPR (*avverarsi*) to be fulfilled, come true; ~ **gli anni** to have one's birthday

compi'lare /72/ VT to compile; (*modulo*) to complete, fill in (BRIT), fill out (US)

compila'tore, -'trice SM/F compiler

compilazi'one [kompilat'tsjone] SF compilation; completion

compi'mento SM (*termine, conclusione*) completion, fulfilment; **portare a** ~ **qc** to conclude sth, bring sth to a conclusion

com'pire /92/ VB = **compiere**

'**compito**[1] SM (*incarico*) task, duty; (*dovere*) duty; (*Ins*) exercise; (*: a casa*) piece of homework; **fare i compiti** to do one's homework

com'pito[2], **-a** AG well-mannered, polite

compiu'tezza [kompju'tettsa] SF (*completezza*) completeness; (*perfezione*) perfection

compi'uto, -a PP *di* **compiere** ▶ AG: **a 20 anni compiuti** at 20 years of age, at age 20; **un fatto** ~ a fait accompli

comple'anno SM birthday

complemen'tare AG complementary; (*Ins: materia*) subsidiary

comple'mento SM complement; (*Mil*) reserve (troops); ~ **oggetto** (*Ling*) direct object

comples'sato, -a AG, SM/F: **essere (un)** ~ to be full of complexes *o* hang-ups (*col*)

complessità SF complexity

complessiva'mente AV (*nell'insieme*) on the whole; (*in tutto*) altogether

comples'sivo, -a AG (*globale*) comprehensive, overall; (*totale: cifra*) total; **visione complessiva** overview

com'plesso, -a AG complex ▸ SM (*Psic, Edil*) complex; (*Mus: corale*) ensemble; (: *orchestrina*) band; (: *di musica pop*) group; **in** *o* **nel ~** on the whole; **~ alberghiero** hotel complex; **~ edilizio** building complex; **~ vitaminico** vitamin complex

completa'mente AV completely

completa'mento SM completion

comple'tare /72/ VT to complete **com'pleto, -a** AG complete; (*teatro, autobus*) full ▸ SM suit; **al ~** full; **essere al ~** (*teatro*) to be sold out; **~ da sci** ski suit

compli'care /20/ VT to complicate ■ **complicarsi** VPR to become complicated

complicazi'one [komplikat'tsjone] SF complication; **salvo complicazioni** unless any difficulties arise

'complice ['kɔmplitʃe] SMF accomplice

complicità [komplitʃi'ta] SF INV complicity; **un sorriso/uno sguardo di ~** a knowing smile/look

complimen'tarsi /72/ VPR: **~ con** to congratulate

compli'mento SM compliment ■ **complimenti** SMPL (*cortesia eccessiva*) ceremony *sg*; (*ossequi*) regards, compliments; **complimenti!** congratulations!; **senza complimenti!** don't stand on ceremony!; make yourself at home!; help yourself!

complot'tare /72/ VI to plot, conspire

complot'tista SMF conspiracy theorist ▸ AG conspiracy-theorist

com'plotto SM plot, conspiracy

com'pone *ecc* VB *vedi* **comporre**

compo'nente SMF member ▸ SM component

com'pongo *ecc* VB *vedi* **comporre**

compo'nibile AG (*mobili, cucina*) fitted

componi'mento SM (*Dir*) settlement; (*Ins*) composition; (*poetico, teatrale*) work

com'porre /77/ VT (*musica, testo*) to compose; (*mettere in ordine*) to arrange; (*Dir: lite*) to settle; (*Tip*) to set; (*Tel*) to dial ■ **comporsi** VPR: **comporsi di** to consist of, be composed of

comportamen'tale AG behavioural (*BRIT*), behavioral (*US*)

comporta'mento SM behaviour (*BRIT*), behavior (*US*); (*di prodotto*) performance

compor'tare /72/ VT (*implicare*) to involve, entail; (*consentire*) to permit, allow (of) ■ **comportarsi** VPR (*condursi*) to behave

com'posi *ecc* VB *vedi* **comporre**

composi'tore, -'trice SM/F composer; (*Tip*) compositor, typesetter

composizi'one [kompozit'tsjone] SF composition; (*Dir*) settlement

com'posta SF *vedi* **composto**

compos'tezza [kompos'tettsa] SF composure; decorum

com'posto, -a PP *di* **comporre** ▸ AG (*persona*) composed, self-possessed; (: *decoroso*) dignified; (*formato da più elementi*) compound *cpd* ▸ SM compound; (*Cuc ecc*) mixture ▸ SF (*Cuc*) stewed fruit *no pl*; (*Agr*) compost

com'prare /72/ VT to buy; (*corrompere*) to bribe

compra'tore, -'trice SM/F buyer, purchaser

compra'vendita SF (*Comm*) (contract of) sale; **un atto di ~** a deed of sale

com'prendere /81/ VT (*contenere*) to comprise, consist of; (*capire*) to understand

compren'donio SM: **essere duro di ~** to be slow on the uptake

compren'sibile AG understandable

comprensi'one SF understanding

compren'sivo, -a AG (*prezzo*): **~ di** inclusive of; (*indulgente*) understanding

compren'sorio SM area, territory; (*Amm*) district

com'preso, -a PP *di* **comprendere** ▸ AG (*incluso*) included; **tutto ~** all included, all-in (*BRIT*)

com'pressa SF *vedi* **compresso**

compressi'one SF compression

com'presso, -a PP *di* **comprimere** ▸ AG (*vedi comprimere*) pressed; compressed; repressed ▸ SF (*Med: garza*) compress; (: *pastiglia*) tablet

compres'sore SM compressor; (*anche: rullo compressore*) steamroller

compri'mario, -a SM/F (*Teat*) supporting actor(-actress)

com'primere /50/ VT (*premere*) to press; (*Fisica*) to compress; (*fig*) to repress

compro'messo, -a PP *di* **compromettere** ▸ SM compromise

compro'mettere /63/ VT to compromise ■ **compromettersi** VPR to compromise o.s.

comproprietà SF (*Dir*) joint ownership

compro'vare /72/ VT to confirm

com'punto, -a AG contrite; **con fare ~** with a solemn air

compunzi'one [kompun'tsjone] SF contrition; solemnity

compu'tare /72/ VT to calculate; (*addebitare*): **~ qc a qn** to debit sb with sth

com'puter [kəm'pju:tər] SM INV computer; **~ fisso** desktop computer

computeriz'zato, -a [komputerid'dzato] AG computerized

computerizzazi'one [komputeriddzat'tsjone] SF computerization

computiste'ria SF accounting, book-keeping

'computo SM calculation; **fare il ~ di** to count

comu'nale AG municipal, town *cpd*; **consiglio/palazzo ~** town council/hall; **è un impiegato ~** he works for the local council

Co'mune SM (*Amm*) town council; (*sede*) town hall

The **Comune** is the smallest autonomous political and administrative unit. It keeps records of births, marriages and deaths and has the power to levy taxes and vet proposals for public works and town planning. It is run by a *Giunta comunale*, which is elected by the *Consiglio Comunale* (town council). The *Comune* is headed by the *sindaco* (mayor), who since 1993 has been elected directly by the citizens.

co'mune AG common; (*consueto*) common, everyday; (*di livello medio*) average; (*ordinario*) ordinary ▶ SF (*di persone*) commune; **fuori del ~** out of the ordinary; **avere in ~** to have in common, share; **mettere in ~** to share; **un nostro ~ amico** a mutual friend of ours; **fare cassa ~** to pool one's money

comuni'care /20/ VT (*notizia*) to pass on, convey; (*malattia*) to pass on; (*ansia ecc*) to communicate; (*trasmettere: calore ecc*) to transmit, communicate; (*Rel*) to administer communion to ▶ VI to communicate ■ **comunicarsi** VPR (*propagarsi*): **comunicarsi a** to spread to; (*Rel*) to receive communion

comunica'tivo, -a AG (*sentimento*) infectious; (*persona*) communicative ▶ SF communicativeness

comuni'cato SM communiqué; **~ stampa** press release

comunicazi'one [komunikat'tsjone] SF communication; (*annuncio*) announcement; (*Tel*): **~ (telefonica)** (telephone) call; **dare la ~ a qn** to put sb through; **ottenere la ~** to get through; **salvo comunicazioni contrarie da parte Vostra** unless we hear from you to the contrary

comuni'one SF communion; **~ dei beni** (*Dir: tra coniugi*) joint ownership of property

comu'nismo SM communism

comu'nista, -i, -e AG, SM/F communist

comunità SF INV community; **C~ Economica Europea** European Economic Community; **~ terapeutica** *rehabilitation centre run by voluntary organizations for people with drug, alcohol ecc dependency*

comuni'tario, -a AG community *cpd*

co'munque CONG however, no matter how ▶ AV (*in ogni modo*) in any case; (*tuttavia*) however, nevertheless

con PREP (*nei seguenti casi* **con** *può fondersi con l'articolo definito:* **con** + *il* = **col**, **con** + *la* = **colla**, **con** + *gli* = **cogli**, **con** + *i* = **coi**, **con** + *le* = **colle**) with; **partire col treno** to leave by train; **~ mio grande stu-**

pore to my great astonishment; **~ la forza** by force; **~ questo freddo** in this cold weather; **~ il 1° di ottobre** as of October 1st; **~ tutto ciò** in spite of that, for all that; **~ tutto che era arrabbiato** even though he was angry, in spite of the fact that he was angry; **e ~ questo?** so what?

co'nato SM: **~ di vomito** retching

'conca, -che SF (*Geo*) valley

concate'nare /72/ VT to link up, connect ■ **concatenarsi** VPR to be connected

'concavo, -a AG concave

con'cedere [kon'tʃedere] /29/ VT (*accordare*) to grant; (*ammettere*) to admit, concede; **concedersi qc** to treat o.s. to sth, allow o.s. sth

concentra'mento [kontʃentra'mento] SM concentration

concen'trare [kontʃen'trare] /72/ VT, **concen'trarsi** VPR to concentrate

concen'trato [kontʃen'trato] SM concentrate; **~ di pomodoro** tomato purée

concentrazi'one [kontʃentrat'tsjone] SF concentration; **~ orizzontale/verticale** (*Econ*) horizontal/vertical integration

con'centrico, -a, -ci, -che [kon'tʃentriko] AG concentric

conce'pibile [kontʃe'pibile] AG conceivable

concepi'mento [kontʃepi'mento] SM conception

conce'pire [kontʃe'pire] /55/ VT (*bambino*) to conceive; (*progetto, idea*) to conceive (of); (*metodo, piano*) to devise; (*situazione*) to imagine, understand

con'cernere [kon'tʃernere] /45/ VT to concern; **per quanto mi concerne** as far as I'm concerned

concer'tare [kontʃer'tare] /72/ VT (*Mus*) to harmonize; (*ordire*) to devise, plan ■ **concertarsi** VPR to agree

concer'tista, -i, -e [kontʃer'tista] SM/F (*Mus*) concert performer

con'certo [kon'tʃerto] SM (*Mus*) concert; (*: componimento*) concerto

con'cessi *ecc* [kon'tʃessi] VB *vedi* **concedere**

concessio'nario [kontʃessjo'narjo] SM (*Comm*) agent, dealer; **~ esclusivo (di)** sole agent (for)

concessi'one [kontʃes'sjone] SF concession

con'cesso, -a [kon'tʃesso] PP *di* **concedere**

con'cetto [kon'tʃetto] SM (*pensiero, idea*) concept; (*opinione*) opinion; **è un impiegato di ~** ≈ he's a white-collar worker

concezi'one [kontʃet'tsjone] SF conception; (*idea*) view, idea

con'chiglia [kon'kiʎʎa] SF shell

'concia ['kontʃa] SF (*di pelli*) tanning; (*di tabacco*) curing; (*sostanza*) tannin

conci'are [kon'tʃare] /14/ VT (*pelli*) to tan; (*tabacco*) to cure; (*fig: ridurre in cattivo stato*) to beat up ■ **con-**

ciarsi VPR (*sporcarsi*) to get in a mess; (*vestirsi male*) to dress badly; **ti hanno conciato male** *o* **per le feste!** they've really beaten you up!

concili'abile [kontʃi'ljabile] AG compatible

concili'abolo [kontʃi'ljabolo] SM secret meeting

concili'ante [kontʃi'ljante] AG conciliatory

concili'are [kontʃi'ljare] /19/ VT to reconcile; (*contravvenzione*) to pay on the spot; (*favorire: sonno*) to be conducive to, induce; (*procurare: simpatia*) to gain; **conciliarsi qc** to gain *o* win sth (for o.s.); **conciliarsi qn** to win sb over; **conciliarsi con** to be reconciled with

conciliazi'one [kontʃiljat'tsjone] SF reconciliation; (*Dir*) settlement; **la C~** (*Storia*) the Lateran Pact

con'cilio [kon'tʃiljo] SM (*Rel*) council

conci'mare [kontʃi'mare] /72/ VT to fertilize; (*con letame*) to manure

con'cime [kon'tʃime] SM manure; (*chimico*) fertilizer

concisi'one [kontʃi'zjone] SF concision, conciseness

con'ciso, -a [kon'tʃizo] AG concise, succinct

conci'tato, -a [kontʃi'tato] AG excited, emotional

concitta'dino, -a [kontʃitta'dino] SM/F fellow citizen

con'clave SM conclave

con'cludere /3/ VT to conclude; (*portare a compimento*) to conclude, finish, bring to an end; (*operare positivamente*) to achieve ▸ VI (*essere convincente*) to be conclusive ◼ **concludersi** VPR to come to an end, close

conclusi'one SF conclusion; (*risultato*) result

conclu'sivo, -a AG conclusive; (*finale*) final

con'cluso, -a PP di **concludere**

concomi'tanza [konkomi'tantsa] SF (*di circostanze, fatti*) combination

concor'danza [konkor'dantsa] SF (*anche Ling*) agreement

concor'dare /72/ VT (*prezzo*) to agree on; (*Ling*) to make agree ▸ VI to agree; **~ una tregua** to agree to a truce

concor'dato SM agreement; (*Rel*) concordat

con'corde AG (*d'accordo*) in agreement; (*simultaneo*) simultaneous

con'cordia SF harmony, concord

concor'rente AG competing; (*Mat*) concurrent ▸ SMF (*Sport, Comm*) competitor; (*Ins*) candidate; (*a un concorso di bellezza*) contestant

concor'renza [konkor'rɛntsa] SF competition; **~ sleale** unfair competition; **a prezzi di ~** at competitive prices

concorrenzi'ale [konkorren'tsjale] AG competitive

con'correre /28/ VI: **~ (in)** (*Mat*) to converge *o*

meet (in); **~ (a)** (*competere*) to compete (for); (*Ins: a una cattedra*) to apply (for); (*partecipare: a un'impresa*) to take part (in), contribute (to)

con'corso, -a PP di **concorrere** ▸ SM competition; (*esame*) competitive examination; **~ di bellezza** beauty contest; **~ di circostanze** combination of circumstances; **~ di colpa** (*Dir*) contributory negligence; **un ~ ippico** a showjumping event; **~ in reato** (*Dir*) complicity in a crime; **~ per titoli** competitive examination for qualified candidates

con'creto, -a AG concrete ▸ SM: **in ~** in reality

concu'bina SF concubine ▸ SM: **sono concubini** they are living together

concussi'one SF (*Dir*) extortion

con'danna SF condemnation; sentence; conviction; **~ a morte** death sentence

condan'nare /72/ VT (*disapprovare*) to condemn; (*Dir*): **~ a** to sentence to; **~ per** to convict of

condan'nato, -a SM/F convict

con'densa SF condensation

conden'sare /72/ VT, **conden'sarsi** VPR to condense

condensa'tore SM capacitor

condensazi'one [kondensat'tsjone] SF condensation

condi'mento SM seasoning; dressing

con'dire /55/ VT to season; (*insalata*) to dress

condiscen'dente [kondiʃʃen'dɛnte] AG obliging; compliant

condiscen'denza [kondiʃʃen'dɛntsa] SF (*disponibilità*) obligingness; (*arrendevolezza*) compliance

condi'scendere [kondiʃ'ʃendere] /101/ VI: **~ a** to agree to

condi'sceso, -a [kondiʃ'ʃeso] PP di **condiscendere**

condi'videre /43/ VT to share

condi'viso, -a PP di **condividere**

condizio'nale [kondittsjo'nale] AG conditional ▸ SM (*Ling*) conditional ▸ SF (*Dir*) suspended sentence

condiziona'mento [kondittsjona'mento] SM conditioning; **~ d'aria** air conditioning

condizio'nare [kondittsjo'nare] /72/ VT to condition; **ad aria condizionata** air-conditioned

condiziona'tore [kondittsjona'tore] SM air conditioner

condizi'one [kondit'tsjone] SF condition ◼ **condizioni** SFPL (*di pagamento ecc*) terms, conditions; **a ~ che** on condition that, provided that; **a nessuna ~** on no account; **condizioni a convenirsi** terms to be arranged; **condizioni di lavoro** working conditions; **condizioni di vendita** sales terms

condogli'anze [kondoʎ'ʎantse] SFPL condolences

condomini'ale AG: **riunione ~** residents' meeting; **spese condominiali** common charges

condo'minio SM joint ownership; (*edificio*) jointly-owned building

con'domino SM joint owner

condo'nare /72/ VT (*Dir*) to remit

con'dono SM remission; **~ fiscale** *conditional amnesty for people evading tax*

con'dotta SF *vedi* **condotto**

con'dotto, -a PP *di* **condurre** ▶ AG: **medico ~** local authority doctor (*in country district*) ▶ SM (*canale, tubo*) pipe, conduit; (*Anat*) duct ▶ SF (*modo di comportarsi*) conduct, behaviour (*BRIT*), behavior (*US*); (*di un affare ecc*) handling; (*di acqua*) piping; (*incarico sanitario*) *country medical practice controlled by a local authority*

condu'cente [kondu'tʃɛnte] SMF driver

con'duco *ecc* VB *vedi* **condurre**

con'durre /90/ VT to conduct; (*azienda*) to manage; (*accompagnare: bambino*) to take; (: *automobile*) to drive; (*trasportare: acqua, gas*) to convey, conduct; (*fig*) to lead ▶ VI to lead ■ **condursi** VPR to behave, conduct o.s.; **~ a termine** to conclude

con'dussi *ecc* VB *vedi* **condurre**

condut'tore, -'trice AG: **filo ~** (*fig*) thread; **motivo ~** leitmotiv ▶ SM (*di mezzi pubblici*) driver; (*Fisica*) conductor

condut'tura SF (*gen*) pipe; (*di acqua, gas*) main

conduzi'one [kondut'tsjone] SF (*di affari, ditta*) management; (*Dir: locazione*) lease; (*Fisica*) conduction

confabu'lare /72/ VI to confab

confa'cente [konfa'tʃɛnte] AG: **~ a qn/qc** suitable for sb/sth; **clima ~ alla salute** healthy climate

CONFAGRICOL'TURA ABBR F (= *Confederazione generale dell'Agricoltura Italiana*) *confederation of Italian farmers*

CON'FAPI SIGLA F = **Confederazione Nazionale della Piccola Industria**

con'farsi /53/ VPR: **~ a** to suit, agree with

CONFARTIGIA'NATO [konfartidʒa'nato] ABBR F = **Confederazione Generale dell'Artigianato Italiano**

con'fatto, -a PP *di* **confarsi**

CONFCOM'MERCIO [konfkom'mɛrtʃo] ABBR F = **Confederazione Generale del Commercio**

confederazi'one [konfederat'tsjone] SF confederation; **~ imprenditoriale** employers' association

confe'renza [konfe'rɛntsa] SF (*discorso*) lecture; (*riunione*) conference; **~ stampa** press conference

conferenzi'ere, -a [konferen'tsjɛre] SM/F lecturer

conferi'mento SM conferring, awarding

confe'rire /55/ VT: **~ qc a qn** to give sth to sb, confer sth on sb ▶ VI to confer

con'ferma SF confirmation

confer'mare /72/ VT to confirm

confes'sare /72/ VT, **confes'sarsi** VPR to confess; **andare a confessarsi** (*Rel*) to go to confession

confessio'nale AG, SM confessional

confessi'one SF confession; (*setta religiosa*) denomination

con'fesso, -a AG: **essere reo ~** to have pleaded guilty

confes'sore SM confessor

con'fetto SM sugared almond; (*Med*) pill

confet'tura SF (*gen*) jam; (*di arance*) marmalade

confezio'nare [konfettsjo'nare] /72/ VT (*vestito*) to make (up); (*merci, pacchi*) to package

confezi'one [konfet'tsjone] SF (*di abiti: da uomo*) tailoring; (: *da donna*) dressmaking; (*imballaggio*) packaging; **~ regalo** gift pack; **~ risparmio** economy size; **~ da viaggio** travel pack; **confezioni per signora** ladies' wear *no pl*; **confezioni da uomo** menswear *no pl*

confic'care /20/ VT: **~ qc in** to hammer *o* drive sth into ■ **conficcarsi** VPR to stick

confi'dare /72/ VI: **~ in** to confide in, rely on ▶ VT to confide; **confidarsi con qn** to confide in sb

confi'dente SMF (*persona amica*) confidant (confidante); (*informatore*) informer

confi'denza [konfi'dɛntsa] SF (*familiarità*) intimacy, familiarity; (*fiducia*) trust, confidence; (*rivelazione*) confidence; **prendersi (troppe) confidenze** to take liberties; **fare una ~ a qn** to confide something to sb

confidenzi'ale [konfiden'tsjale] AG familiar, friendly; (*segreto*) confidential; **in via ~** confidentially

configu'rare /72/ VT (*Inform*) to set ■ **configurarsi** VPR: **configurarsi a** to assume the shape *o* form of

configurazi'one [konfigurat'tsjone] SF configuration; (*Inform*) setting

confi'nante AG neighbouring (*BRIT*), neighboring (*US*)

confi'nare /72/ VI: **~ con** to border on ▶ VT (*Pol*) to intern; (*fig*) to confine ■ **confinarsi** VPR (*isolarsi*): **confinarsi in** to shut o.s. up in

confi'nato, -a AG interned ▶ SM/F internee

CONFIN'DUSTRIA SIGLA F (= *Confederazione Generale dell'Industria Italiana*) *employers' association*, ≈ CBI (*BRIT*)

con'fine SM boundary; (*di paese*) border, frontier; **territorio di ~** border zone

con'fino SM internment

con'fisca SF confiscation

confis'care /20/ VT to confiscate

conflagrazi'one [konflagrat'tsjone] SF conflagration

con'flitto SM conflict; **essere in ~ con qc** to

clash with sth; **essere in ~ con qn** to be at loggerheads with sb; **~ d'interessi** conflict of interests

conflittu'ale AG: **rapporto ~** relationship based on conflict

conflittualità SF conflicts pl

conflu'enza [konflu'ɛntsa] SF (di fiumi) confluence; (di strade) junction

conflu'ire /55/ VI (fiumi) to flow into each other, meet; (strade) to meet

con'fondere /25/ VT to mix up, confuse; (imbarazzare) to embarrass ■ **confondersi** VPR (mescolarsi) to mingle; (turbarsi) to be confused; (sbagliare) to get mixed up; **~ le idee a qn** to mix sb up, confuse sb

confor'mare /72/ VT (adeguare): **~ a** to adapt o conform to ■ **conformarsi** VPR: **conformarsi (a)** to conform (to)

con'forme AG: **~ a** (simile) similar to; (corrispondente) in keeping with

conforme'mente AV accordingly; **~ a** in accordance with

confor'mismo SM conformity

confor'mista, -i, -e SM/F conformist

conformità SF conformity; **in ~ a** in conformity with

confor'tare /72/ VT to comfort, console

confor'tevole AG (consolante) comforting; (comodo) comfortable

con'forto SM (consolazione, sollievo) comfort, consolation; (conferma) support; **a ~ di qc** in support of sth; **i conforti (religiosi)** the last sacraments

confra'ternita SF brotherhood

confron'tare /72/ VT to compare ■ **confrontarsi** VPR (scontrarsi) to have a confrontation

con'fronto SM comparison; (Dir, Mil, Pol) confrontation; **in** o **a ~** in comparison with, compared to; **nei miei (o tuoi etc) confronti** towards me (o you etc)

con'fusi ecc VB vedi **confondere**

confusi'one SF confusion; (imbarazzo) embarrassment; **far ~** (disordine) to make a mess; (chiasso) to make a racket; (confondere) to confuse things

con'fuso, -a PP di **confondere** ▶ AG (vedi confondere) confused; embarrassed

confu'tare /72/ VT to refute

conge'dare [kondʒe'dare] /72/ VT to dismiss; (Mil) to demobilize ■ **congedarsi** VPR to take one's leave

con'gedo [kon'dʒedo] SM (anche Mil) leave; **prendere ~ da qn** to take one's leave of sb; **~ assoluto** (Mil) discharge

conge'gnare [kondʒeɲ'ɲare] /15/ VT to construct, put together

con'gegno [kon'dʒeɲɲo] SM device, mechanism

congela'mento [kondʒela'mento] SM (gen) freezing; (Med) frostbite; **~ salariale** wage freeze

conge'lare [kondʒe'lare] /72/ VT, **congelarsi** VPR to freeze

congela'tore [kondʒela'tore] SM freezer

con'genito, -a [kon'dʒɛnito] AG congenital

con'gerie [kon'dʒɛrje] SF INV (di oggetti) heap; (di idee) muddle, jumble

congestio'nare [kondʒestjo'nare] /72/ VT to congest; **essere congestionato** (persona, viso) to be flushed; (zona: per traffico) to be congested

congesti'one [kondʒes'tjone] SF congestion

conget'tura [kondʒet'tura] SF conjecture, supposition

con'giungere [kon'dʒundʒere] /5/ VT, **con' giungersi** VPR to join (together)

congiunti'vite [kondʒunti'vite] SF conjunctivitis

congiun'tivo [kondʒun'tivo] SM (Ling) subjunctive

congi'unto, -a [kon'dʒunto] PP di **congiungere** ▶ AG (unito) joined ▶ SM/F (parente) relative

congiun'tura [kondʒun'tura] SF (giuntura) junction, join; (Anat) joint; (circostanza) juncture; (Econ) economic situation

congiuntu'rale [kondʒuntu'rale] AG of the economic situation; **crisi ~** economic crisis

congiunzi'one [kondʒun'tsjone] SF (Ling) conjunction

congi'ura [kon'dʒura] SF conspiracy

congiu'rare [kondʒu'rare] /72/ VI to conspire

conglome'rato SM (Geo) conglomerate; (fig) conglomeration; (Edil) concrete

'Congo SM: **il ~** the Congo

congo'lese AG, SMF Congolese inv

congratu'larsi /72/ VPR: **~ con qn per qc** to congratulate sb on sth

congratulazi'oni [kongratulat'tsjoni] SFPL congratulations

con'grega, -ghe SF band, bunch

congregazi'one [kongregat'tsjone] SF congregation

congres'sista, -i, -e SM/F participant at a congress

con'gresso SM congress

'congruo, -a AG (prezzo, compenso) adequate, fair; (ragionamento) coherent, consistent

conguagli'are [kongwaʎ'ʎare] /27/ VT to balance; (stipendio) to adjust

congu'aglio [kon'gwaʎʎo] SM balancing; adjusting; (somma di denaro) balance; **fare il ~ di** to balance; to adjust

C.O.N.I. SIGLA M (= Comitato Olimpico Nazionale Italiano) Italian Olympic Games Committee

coni'are /19/ VT to mint, coin; (fig) to coin

83

coniazi'one [konjat'tsjone] SF mintage

'**conico, -a, -ci, -che** AG conical

co'nifere SFPL conifers

conigli'era [koniʎ'ʎɛra] SF (gabbia) rabbit hutch; (più grande) rabbit run

conigli'etta [koniʎ'ʎetta] SF bunny girl

conigli'etto [koniʎ'ʎetto] SM bunny

co'niglio [ko'niʎʎo] SM rabbit; **sei un ~!** (fig) you're chicken!

coniu'gale AG (amore, diritti) conjugal; (vita) married, conjugal

coniu'gare /80/ VT to combine; (Ling) to conjugate ◼ **coniugarsi** VPR to get married

coniu'gato, -a AG (Amm) married

coniugazi'one [konjugat'tsjone] SF (Ling) conjugation

'**coniuge** ['kɔnjudʒe] SMF spouse

connatu'rato, -a AG inborn

connazio'nale [konnattsjo'nale] SMF fellow-countryman(-woman)

connessi'one SF connection

con'nesso, -a PP di **connettere**

con'nettere /63/ VT to connect, join ▶ VI (fig) to think straight

connet'tore SM (Elettr) connector

conni'vente AG conniving

conno'tati SMPL distinguishing marks; **rispondere ai ~** to fit the description; **cambiare i ~ a qn** (col) to beat sb up

con'nubio SM (matrimonio) marriage; (fig) union

'**cono** SM cone; **~ gelato** ice-cream cone

co'nobbi ecc VB vedi **conoscere**

cono'scente [konoʃ'ʃɛnte] SMF acquaintance

cono'scenza [konoʃ'ʃɛntsa] SF (il sapere) knowledge no pl; (persona) acquaintance; (facoltà sensoriale) consciousness no pl; **essere a ~ di qc** to know sth; **portare qn a ~ di qc** to inform sb of sth; **per vostra ~** for your information; **fare la ~ di qn** to make sb's acquaintance; **perdere ~** to lose consciousness; **~ tecnica** know-how

co'noscere [ko'noʃʃere] /26/ VT to know; **ci siamo conosciuti a Firenze** we (first) met in Florence ◼ **conoscersi** VPR to know o.s.; (reciproco) to know each other; (incontrarsi) to meet; **~ qn di vista** to know sb by sight; **farsi ~** (fig) to make a name for o.s.

conosci'tore, -'trice [konoʃʃi'tore] SM/F connoisseur

conosci'uto, -a [konoʃ'ʃuto] PP di **conoscere** ▶ AG well-known

con'quista SF conquest

conquis'tare /72/ VT to conquer; (fig) to gain, win

conquista'tore, -'trice SM/F (in guerra) conqueror ▶ SM (seduttore) lady-killer

cons. ABBR = **consiglio**

consa'crare /72/ VT (Rel) to consecrate; (: sacerdote) to ordain; (dedicare) to dedicate; (fig: uso ecc) to sanction; **consacrarsi a** to dedicate o.s. to

consangu'ineo, -a SM/F blood relation

consa'pevole AG: **~ di** aware of

consapevo'lezza [konsapevo'lettsa] SF awareness, consciousness

conscia'mente [konʃa'mente] AV consciously

'**conscio, -a, -sci, -sce** ['kɔnʃo] AG: **~ di** aware o conscious of

consecu'tivo, -a AG consecutive; (successivo: giorno) following, next

con'segna [kon'seɲɲa] SF delivery; (merce consegnata) consignment; (custodia) care, custody; (Mil: ordine) orders pl; (: punizione) confinement to barracks; **alla ~** on delivery; **dare qc in ~ a qn** to entrust sth to sb; **passare le consegne a qn** to hand over to sb; **~ a domicilio** home delivery; **~ in contrassegno, pagamento alla ~** cash on delivery; **~ sollecita** prompt delivery

conse'gnare [konseɲ'ɲare] /15/ VT to deliver; (affidare) to entrust, hand over; (Mil) to confine to barracks

consegna'tario [konseɲɲa'tarjo] SM consignee

consegu'ente AG consequent

conseguente'mente AV consequently

consegu'enza [konse'gwɛntsa] SF consequence; **per o di ~** consequently

consegui'mento SM (di scopo, risultato ecc) achievement, attainment; **al ~ della laurea** on graduation

consegu'ire /17/ VT to achieve ▶ VI to follow, result; **~ la laurea** to graduate, obtain one's degree

con'senso SM approval, consent; **~ informato** informed consent

consensu'ale AG (Dir) by mutual consent

consen'tire /45/ VI: **~ a** to consent o agree to ▶ VT to allow, permit; **mi si consenta di ringraziare ...** I would like to thank ...

consenzi'ente [konsen'tsjɛnte] AG (gen, Dir) consenting

con'serto, -a AG: **a braccia conserte** with one's arms folded

con'serva SF (Cuc) preserve; **~ di frutta** jam; **~ di pomodoro** tomato purée; **conserve alimentari** tinned (o canned o bottled) foods

conser'vante SM (per alimenti) preservative

conser'vare /72/ VT (Cuc) to preserve; (custodire) to keep; (: dalla distruzione ecc) to preserve, conserve ◼ **conservarsi** VPR to keep

conserva'tore, -'trice AG, SM/F (Pol) conservative

conserva'torio SM (di musica) conservatory

conservato'rismo SM (Pol) conservatism

conservazi'one [konservat'tsjone] SF preservation; conservation; **istinto di ~** instinct for self-preservation; **a lunga ~** (*latte, panna*) long-life *cpd*

con'sesso SM (*assemblea*) assembly; (*riunione*) meeting

conside'rabile AG worthy of consideration

conside'rare /72/ VT to consider; (*reputare*) to consider, regard; **~ molto qn** to think highly of sb ▪ **considerarsi** VPR to consider o.s.

conside'rato, -a AG (*prudente*) cautious, careful; (*stimato*) highly thought of, esteemed

considerazi'one [konsiderat'tsjone] SF (*esame, riflessione*) consideration; (*stima*) regard, esteem; (*pensiero, osservazione*) observation; **prendere in ~** to take into consideration

conside'revole AG considerable

consigli'abile [konsiʎ'ʎabile] AG advisable

consigli'are [konsiʎ'ʎare] /27/ VT (*persona*) to advise; (*metodo, azione*) to recommend, advise, suggest ▪ **consigliarsi** VPR: **consigliarsi con qn** to ask sb for advice

consigli'ere, -a [konsiʎ'ʎɛre] SM/F adviser ▶ SM: **~ d'amministrazione** board member; **~ comunale** town councillor; **~ delegato** (*Comm*) managing director

con'siglio [kon'siʎʎo] SM (*suggerimento*) advice *no pl*, piece of advice; (*assemblea*) council; **~ d'amministrazione** board; **C~ d'Europa** Council of Europe; **~ di fabbrica** works council; **il C~ dei Ministri** (*Pol*) ≈ the Cabinet; **C~ di stato** *advisory body to the Italian government on administrative matters and their legal implications*; **C~ superiore della magistratura** *state body responsible for judicial appointments and regulations*

> *Consigli* si traduce **advice**, che non prende la **–s**, con il verbo al singolare.
> *I tuoi consigli mi sono stati preziosi.* **Your advice was invaluable to me.**
> Quando si tratta di un singolo *consiglio* si usa: **a piece of/some advice.**
> *Questo è il miglior consiglio che mi sia mai stato dato.* **This is the best piece of advice I have ever been given.**

con'simile AG similar

consis'tente AG thick; solid; (*fig*) sound, valid

consis'tenza [konsis'tɛntsa] SF (*di impasto*) consistency; (*di stoffa*) texture; **senza ~** (*sospetti, voci*) ill-founded, groundless; **~ di cassa/di magazzino** cash/stock in hand; **~ patrimoniale** financial solidity

con'sistere /11/ VI: **~ in** to consist of

consis'tito, -a PP *di* **consistere**

'CONSOB SIGLA F (= *Commissione nazionale per le società e la borsa*) *regulatory body for the Italian Stock Exchange*

consoci'arsi [konso'tʃarsi] /14/ VPR to go into partnership

consociati'vismo [konsotʃati'vizmo] SM (*Pol*) pact-building

consocia'tivo, -a [konsotʃa'tivo] AG (*Pol: democrazia*) based on pacts

consoci'ato, -a [konso'tʃato] AG associated ▶ SM/F associate

conso'lante AG consoling, comforting

conso'lare /72/ AG consular ▶ VT (*confortare*) to console, comfort; (*rallegrare*) to cheer up ▪ **consolarsi** VPR to be comforted; to cheer up

conso'lato SM consulate

consolazi'one [konsolat'tsjone] SF consolation, comfort

'console¹ ['kɔnsole] SM consul

'console² ['kɔsɔl] SF (*quadro di comando*) console

consolida'mento SM strengthening; consolidation

consoli'dare /72/ VT to strengthen, reinforce; (*Mil, terreno*) to consolidate ▪ **consolidarsi** VPR to consolidate

consolidazi'one [konsolidat'tsjone] SF strengthening; consolidation

consommé [kɔsɔ'me] SM INV consommé

conso'nante SF consonant

conso'nanza [konso'nantsa] SF consonance

'consono, -a AG: **~ a** consistent with, consonant with

con'sorte SMF consort

con'sorzio [kon'sɔrtsjo] SM consortium; **~ agrario** farmers' cooperative; **~ di garanzia** (*Comm*) underwriting syndicate

con'stare /72/ VI: **~ di** to consist of ▶ VB IMPERS: **mi consta che** it has come to my knowledge that, it appears that; **a quanto mi consta** as far as I know

consta'tare /72/ VT to establish, verify; (*notare*) to notice, observe

constatazi'one [konstatat'tsjone] SF observation; **~ amichevole** (*in incidenti*) jointly-agreed statement for insurance purposes

consu'eto, -a AG habitual, usual ▶ SM: **come di ~** as usual

consuetudi'nario, -a AG: **diritto ~** (*Dir*) common law

consue'tudine SF habit; (*usanza*) custom

consu'lente SMF consultant; **~ aziendale/tecnico** management/technical consultant

consu'lenza [konsu'lɛntsa] SF consultancy; **~ medica/legale** medical/legal advice; **ufficio di ~ fiscale** tax consultancy office; **~ tecnica** technical consultancy *o* advice

consul'tare /72/ VT to consult ▪ **consultarsi** VPR: **consultarsi con qn** to seek the advice of sb

consultazi'one [konsultat'tsjone] SF consultation ▪ **consultazioni** SFPL (*Pol*) talks, consultations; **libro di ~** reference book

consul'tivo, -a AG consultative

consul'torio SM: **~ familiare** family planning clinic; **~ matrimoniale** marriage guidance centre; **~ pediatrico** children's clinic

consu'mare /72/ VT (*logorare: abiti, scarpe*) to wear out; (*usare*) to consume, use up; (*mangiare, bere*) to consume; (*Dir*) to consummate ■ **consumarsi** VPR to wear out; to be used up; (*anche fig*) to be consumed; (*combustibile*) to burn out

consu'mato, -a AG (*vestiti, scarpe, tappeto*) worn; (*persona: esperto*) accomplished

consuma'tore SM consumer

consumazi'one [konsumat'tsjone] SF (*bibita*) drink; (*spuntino*) snack; (*Dir*) consummation

consu'mismo SM consumerism

con'sumo SM consumption; wear; use; **generi o beni di ~** consumer goods; **beni di largo ~** basic commodities; **imposta sui consumi** tax on consumer goods

consun'tivo SM (*Econ*) final balance

con'sunto, -a AG worn-out; (*viso*) wasted

'conta SF (*nei giochi*): **fare la ~** to see who is going to be "it"

con'tabile AG accounts *cpd*, accounting ▶ SMF accountant

contabilità SF (*attività, tecnica*) accounting, accountancy; (*insieme dei libri ecc*) books *pl*, accounts *pl*; **(ufficio) ~** accounts department; **~ finanziaria** financial accounting; **~ di gestione** management accounting

contachi'lometri [kontaki'lɔmetri] SM INV ≈ mileometer

conta'dino, -a SM/F countryman(-woman); farm worker; (*peg*) peasant

contagi'are [konta'dʒare] /62/ VT to infect

con'tagio [kon'tadʒo] SM infection; (*per contatto diretto*) contagion; (*epidemia*) epidemic

contagi'oso, -a [konta'dʒoso] AG infectious; contagious

conta'giri [konta'dʒiri] SM INV (*Aut*) rev counter

conta'gocce [konta'gottʃe] SM INV (*Med*) dropper

contami'nare /72/ VT to contaminate

contaminazi'one [kontaminat'tsjone] SF contamination

con'tante SM cash; **pagare in contanti** to pay cash; **non ho contanti** I haven't got any cash

con'tare /72/ VT to count; (*considerare*) to consider ▶ VI to count, be of importance; **~ su qn** to count *o* rely on sb; **~ di fare qc** to intend to do sth; **ha i giorni contati, ha le ore contate** his days are numbered; **la gente che conta** people who matter

contas'catti SM INV telephone meter

conta'tore SM meter

contat'tare /72/ VT to contact

con'tatto SM contact; **essere in ~ con qn** to be in touch with sb; **fare ~** (*Elettr: fili*) to touch

'conte SM count

con'tea SF (*Storia*) earldom; (*Amm*) county

conteggi'are [konted'dʒare] /62/ VT to charge, put on the bill

con'teggio [kon'teddʒo] SM calculation

con'tegno [kon'teɲɲo] SM (*comportamento*) behaviour (BRIT), behavior (US); (*atteggiamento*) attitude; **darsi un ~** (*ostentare disinvoltura*) to act nonchalant; (*ricomporsi*) to pull o.s. together

conte'gnoso, -a [konteɲ'ɲoso] AG reserved, dignified

contem'plare /72/ VT to contemplate, gaze at; (*Dir*) to make provision for

contempla'tivo, -a AG contemplative

contemplazi'one [kontemplat'tsjone] SF contemplation

con'tempo SM: **nel ~** meanwhile, in the meantime

contemporanea'mente AV simultaneously; at the same time

contempo'raneo, -a AG, SM/F contemporary

conten'dente SMF opponent, adversary

con'tendere /120/ VI (*competere*) to compete; (*litigare*) to quarrel ▶ VT: **~ qc a qn** to contend with *o* be in competition with sb for sth

conte'nere /121/ VT to contain ■ **contenersi** VPR to contain o.s.

conteni'tore SM container

conten'tabile AG: **difficilmente ~** difficult to please

conten'tare /72/ VT to please, satisfy ■ **contentarsi** VPR: **contentarsi di** to be satisfied with, content o.s. with; **si contenta di poco** he is easily satisfied

conten'tezza [konten'tettsa] SF contentment

conten'tino SM sop

con'tento, -a AG pleased, glad; **~ di** pleased with

conte'nuto AG (*ira, entusiasmo*) restrained, suppressed; (*forza*) contained ▶ SM contents *pl*; (*argomento*) content

contenzi'oso, -a [konten'tsjɔso] AG (*Dir*) contentious ▶ SM (*Amm: ufficio*) legal department

con'teso, -a PP *di* **contendere** ▶ SF dispute, argument

con'tessa SF countess

contes'tare /72/ VT (*Dir*) to notify; (*fig*) to dispute; **~ il sistema** to protest against the system

contesta'tore, -'trice AG anti-establishment ▶ SM/F protester

contestazi'one [kontestat'tsjone] SF (*Dir: disputa*) dispute; (*: notifica*) notification; (*Pol*) anti-establishment activity; **in caso di ~** if there are any objections

con'testo SM context

con'tiguo, -a AG: **~ (a)** adjacent (to)

continen'tale AG, SMF continental

conti'nente AG continent ▶ SM (Geo) continent; (: *terra ferma*) mainland

conti'nenza [konti'nɛntsa] SF continence

contin'gente [kontin'dʒɛnte] AG contingent ▶ SM (Comm) quota; (Mil) contingent

contin'genza [kontin'dʒɛntsa] SF circumstance; **(indennità di)** ~ cost-of-living allowance

continua'mente AV (*senza interruzione*) continuously, nonstop; (*ripetutamente*) continually

continu'are /72/ VT to continue (with), go on with ▶ VI to continue, go on; ~ **a fare qc** to go on o continue doing sth; **continua a nevicare/a fare freddo** it's still snowing/cold

continua'tivo, -a AG (*occupazione*) permanent; (*periodo*) consecutive

continuazi'one [kontinuat'tsjone] SF continuation

continuità SF continuity

con'tinuo, -a AG (*numerazione*) continuous; (*pioggia*) continual, constant; (*Elettr: corrente*) direct; **di** ~ continually

'conto SM (*calcolo*) calculation; (Comm, Econ) account; (*di ristorante, albergo*) bill; (*fig: stima*) consideration, esteem; **avere un** ~ **in sospeso (con qn)** to have an outstanding account (with sb); (*fig*) to have a score to settle (with sb); **fare i conti con qn** to settle one's account with sb; **fare** ~ **su qn** to count o rely on sb; **fare** ~ **che** (*supporre*) to suppose that; **rendere** ~ **a qn di qc** to be accountable to sb for sth; **rendersi** ~ **di qc/che** to realize sth/that; **tener** ~ **di qn/qc** to take sb/sth into account; **tenere qc da** ~ to take great care of sth; **ad ogni buon** ~ in any case; **di poco/nessun** ~ of little/no importance; **per** ~ **di** on behalf of; **per** ~ **mio** as far as I'm concerned; (*da solo*) on my own; **a conti fatti, in fin dei conti** all things considered; **mi hanno detto strane cose sul suo** ~ I've heard some strange things about him; ~ **capitale** capital account; ~ **cifrato** numbered account; ~ **corrente** current account (BRIT), checking account (US); ~ **corrente postale** Post Office account; ~ **economico** profit and loss account; ~ **in partecipazione** joint account; ~ **passivo** account payable; ~ **profitti e perdite** profit and loss account; ~ **alla rovescia** countdown; ~ **valutario** foreign currency account

con'torcere [kon'tɔrtʃere] /106/ VT to twist; (*panni*) to wring (out) ▪ **contorcersi** VPR to twist, writhe

contor'nare /72/ VT to surround ▪ **contornarsi** VPR: **contornarsi di** to surround o.s. with

con'torno SM (*linea*) outline, contour; (*ornamento*) border; (Cuc) vegetables pl; **fare da** ~ **a** to surround

contorsi'one SF contortion

con'torto, -a PP di **contorcere**

contrabban'dare /72/ VT to smuggle

contrabbandi'ere, -a SM/F smuggler

contrab'bando SM smuggling, contraband; **merce di** ~ contraband, smuggled goods pl

contrab'basso SM (Mus) (double) bass

contraccambi'are /19/ VT (*favore ecc*) to return; **vorrei** ~ I'd like to show my appreciation

contraccet'tivo, -a [kontrattʃet'tivo] AG, SM contraceptive

contrac'colpo SM rebound; (*di arma da fuoco*) recoil; (*fig*) repercussion

con'trada SF street; district; *vedi anche* **palio**

contrad'detto, -a PP di **contraddire**

contrad'dire /38/ VT to contradict ▪ **contraddirsi** VPR to contradict o.s.; (*uso reciproco: persone*) to contradict each other o one another; (: *testimonianze ecc*) to be contradictory

contraddis'tinguere /42/ VT (*merce*) to mark; (*fig: atteggiamento, persona*) to distinguish

contraddis'tinto, -a PP di **contraddistinguere**

contraddit'torio, -a AG contradictory; (*sentimenti*) conflicting ▶ SM (Dir) cross-examination

contraddizi'one [kontraddit'tsjone] SF contradiction; **cadere in** ~ to contradict o.s.; **essere in** ~ (*tesi, affermazioni*) to contradict one another; **spirito di** ~ argumentativeness

con'trae ecc VB vedi **contrarre**

contra'ente SMF contractor

contra'erea SF (Mil) anti-aircraft artillery

contra'ereo, -a AG anti-aircraft

contraf'fare /41/ VT (*persona*) to mimic; (*alterare: voce*) to disguise; (: *firma*) to forge, counterfeit

contraf'fatto, -a PP di **contraffare** ▶ AG counterfeit

contraffazi'one [kontraffat'tsjone] SF mimicking no pl; disguising no pl; forging no pl; (*cosa contraffatta*) forgery

contraf'forte SM (Archit) buttress; (Geo) spur

con'traggo ecc VB vedi **contrarre**

con'tralto SM (Mus) contralto

contrap'pello SM (Mil) second roll call

contrappe'sare /72/ VT to counterbalance; (*fig: decisione*) to weigh up

contrap'peso SM counterbalance, counterweight

contrap'porre /77/ VT: ~ **qc a qc** to counter sth with sth; (*paragonare*) to compare sth with sth ▪ **contrapporsi** VPR: **contrapporsi a qc** to contrast with sth, be opposed to sth

contrap'posto, -a PP di **contrapporre**

contraria'mente AV: ~ **a** contrary to

contrari'are /19/ VT (*contrastare*) to thwart, oppose; (*irritare*) to annoy, bother ▪ **contrariarsi** VPR to get annoyed

contrari'ato, -a AG annoyed

contrarietà SF adversity; (fig) aversion

con'trario, -a AG opposite; (sfavorevole) unfavourable (BRIT), unfavorable (US) ▶ SM opposite; **essere ~ a qc** (persona) to be against sth; **al ~** on the contrary; **in caso ~** otherwise; **avere qualcosa in ~** to have some objection; **non ho niente in ~** I have no objection

con'trarre /123/ VT (malattia, debito) to contract; (muscoli) to tense; (abitudine, vizio) to pick up; (accordo, patto) to enter into ■ **contrarsi** VPR to contract; **~ matrimonio** to marry

contrasse'gnare [kontrassenˈɲare] /15/ VT to mark

contras'segno [kontrasˈseɲɲo] SM (distintivo) distinguishing mark; **spedire in ~** (Comm) to send COD

con'trassi ecc VB vedi **contrarre**

contras'tante AG contrasting

contras'tare /72/ VT (avversare) to oppose; (impedire) to bar; (negare: diritto) to contest, dispute ▶ VI: **~ (con)** (essere in disaccordo) to contrast (with); (lottare) to struggle (with)

con'trasto SM contrast; (conflitto) conflict; (litigio) dispute

contrat'tacco SM counterattack; **passare al ~** (fig) to fight back

contrat'tare /72/ VT, VI to negotiate

contrat'tempo SM hitch

con'tratto, -a PP di **contrarre** ▶ SM contract; **~ di acquisto** purchase agreement; **~ di affitto, ~ di locazione** lease; **~ collettivo di lavoro** collective agreement; **~ di lavoro** contract of employment; **~ a termine** forward contract

contrattu'ale AG contractual; **forza ~** (di sindacato) bargaining power

contrattualizza'zione [kontrattualiddzaˈtsjone] SF employment on contract

contravve'nire /128/ VI: **~ a** (legge) to contravene; (obbligo) to fail to meet

contravven'tore, -'trice SM/F offender

contravve'nuto, -a PP di **contravvenire**

contravvenzi'one [kontravvenˈtsjone] SF contravention; (ammenda) fine

contrazi'one [kontratˈtsjone] SF contraction; (di prezzi ecc) reduction

contribu'ente SMF taxpayer; ratepayer (BRIT), property tax payer (US)

contribu'ire /55/ VI to contribute

contribu'tivo, -a AG contributory

contri'buto SM contribution; (sovvenzione) subsidy, contribution; (tassa) tax; **contributi previdenziali** = national insurance (BRIT) o welfare (US) contributions; **contributi sindacali** trade union dues

con'trito, -a AG contrite, penitent

'contro PREP against; **~ di me/lui** against me/

him; **pastiglie ~ la tosse** throat lozenges; **~ pagamento** (Comm) on payment; **~ ogni mia aspettativa** contrary to my expectations; **per ~** on the other hand

contro'battere /1/ VT (fig: a parole) to answer back; (: confutare) to refute

controbilanci'are [kontrobilanˈtʃare] /14/ VT to counterbalance

controcor'rente AV: **andare ~** (anche fig) to swim against the tide

controcul'tura SF counterculture

contro'esodo SM return from holiday

contro'fax SM INV reply to a fax

controffen'siva SF counteroffensive

controfi'gura SF (Cine) double

controfir'mare /72/ VT to countersign

control'lare /72/ VT (accertare) to check; (sorvegliare) to watch, control; (tenere nel proprio potere, fig: dominare) to control ■ **controllarsi** VPR to control o.s.

control'lato, -a AG (persona) self-possessed; (reazioni) controlled ▶ SF (Comm: società) associated company

con'trollo SM check; watch; control; **base di ~** (Aer) ground control; **telefono sotto ~** tapped telephone; **visita di ~** (Med) checkup; **~ doganale** customs inspection; **~ di gestione** management control; **~ delle nascite** birth control; **~ di qualità** quality control

control'lore SM (Ferr, Aut) (ticket) inspector; **~ di volo** o **del traffico aereo** air traffic controller

contro'luce [kontroˈlutʃe] SF INV (Fot) backlit shot ▶ AV: **(in) ~** against the light; (fotografare) into the light

contro'mano AV: **guidare ~** to drive on the wrong side of the road; (in un senso unico) to drive the wrong way up a one-way street

contropar'tita SF (fig: compenso): **come ~** in return

contropi'ede SM (Sport): **azione di ~** sudden counter-attack; **prendere qn in ~** (fig) to catch sb off his (o her) guard

controprodu'cente [kontroproduˈtʃɛnte] AG counterproductive

con'trordine SM counter-order; **salvo ~** unless I (o you etc) hear to the contrary

contro'senso SM (contraddizione) contradiction in terms; (assurdità) nonsense

controspio'naggio [kontrospioˈnaddʒo] SM counterespionage

controva'lore SM equivalent (value)

contro'vento AV against the wind; **navigare ~** (Naut) to sail to windward

contro'versia SF controversy; (Dir) dispute; **~ sindacale** industrial dispute

contro'verso, -a AG controversial

contro'voglia [kontro'vɔʎʎa] AV unwillingly

contu'mace [kontu'matʃe] AG (*Dir*): **rendersi ~** to default, fail to appear in court ▶ SMF (*Dir*) defaulter

contu'macia [kontu'matʃa] SF (*Dir*) default

contun'dente AG: **corpo ~** blunt instrument

contur'bante AG (*sguardo, bellezza*) disturbing

contur'bare /**72**/ VT to disturb, upset

contusi'one SF (*Med*) bruise

convale'scente [konvaleʃ'ʃente] AG, SMF convalescent

convale'scenza [konvaleʃ'ʃentsa] SF convalescence

con'valida SF (*Dir*) confirmation; (*di biglietto*) stamping

convali'dare /**72**/ VT (*Amm*) to validate; (*fig: sospetto, dubbio*) to confirm

con'vegno [kon'veɲɲo] SM (*incontro*) meeting; (*congresso*) convention, congress; (*luogo*) meeting place

conve'nevoli SMPL civilities

conveni'ente AG suitable; (*vantaggioso*) profitable; (: *prezzo*) cheap

conveni'enza [konve'njentsa] SF suitability; advantage; cheapness ■ **convenienze** SFPL social conventions

conve'nire /**128**/ VT to agree upon ▶ VI (*riunirsi*) to gather, assemble; (*concordare*) to agree; (*tornare utile*) to be worthwhile ▶ VB IMPERS: **conviene fare questo** it is advisable to do this; **conviene andarsene** we should go; **ne convengo** I agree; **come convenuto** as agreed; **in data da ~** on a date to be agreed; **come (si) conviene ad una signorina** as befits a young lady

conven'ticola SF (*cricca*) clique; (*riunione*) secret meeting

con'vento SM (*di frati*) monastery; (*di suore*) convent

conve'nuto, -a PP di **convenire** ▶ SM (*cosa pattuita*) agreement ▶ SM/F (*Dir*) defendant; **i convenuti** (*i presenti*) those present

convenzio'nale [konventsjo'nale] AG conventional

convenzio'nato, -a [konventsjo'nato] AG (*ospedale, clinica*) providing free health care, ≈ National Health Service *cpd* (*BRIT*)

convenzi'one [konven'tsjone] SF (*Dir*) agreement; (*nella società*) convention; **le convenzioni (sociali)** social conventions

conver'gente [konver'dʒente] AG convergent

conver'genza [konver'dʒentsa] SF convergence

con'vergere [kon'verdʒere] /**59**/ VI to converge

con'versa SF (*Rel*) lay sister

conver'sare /**72**/ VI to have a conversation, converse

conversazi'one [konversat'tsjone] SF conversation; **fare ~** (*chiacchierare*) to chat, have a chat

conversi'one SF conversion; **~ ad U** (*Aut*) U-turn

con'verso, -a PP di **convergere**; **per ~** conversely

conver'tire /**45**/ VT (*trasformare*) to change; (*Inform, Pol, Rel*) to convert ■ **convertirsi** VPR: **convertirsi (a)** to be converted (to)

conver'tito, -a SM/F convert

converti'tore SM (*Elettr*) converter

con'vesso, -a AG convex

convin'cente [konvin'tʃente] AG convincing

con'vincere [kon'vintʃere] /**129**/ VT to convince ■ **convincersi** VPR: **convincersi (di qc)** to convince o.s. (of sth); **~ qn di qc** to convince sb of sth; (*Dir*) to prove sb guilty of sth; **~ qn a fare qc** to persuade sb to do sth

con'vinto, -a PP di **convincere** ▶ AG: **reo ~** (*Dir*) convicted criminal

convinzi'one [konvin'tsjone] SF conviction, firm belief

convis'suto, -a PP di **convivere**

convi'tato, -a SM/F guest

con'vitto SM (*Ins*) boarding school

convi'vente SMF common-law husband/wife

convi'venza [konvi'ventsa] SF living together; (*Dir*) cohabitation

con'vivere /**130**/ VI to live together

convivi'ale AG convivial

convo'care /**20**/ VT to call, convene; (*Dir*) to summon

convocazi'one [konvokat'tsjone] SF meeting; summons *sg*; **lettera di ~** (letter of) notification to appear o attend

convogli'are [konvoʎ'ʎare] /**27**/ VT to convey; (*dirigere*) to direct, send

con'voglio [kon'vɔʎʎo] SM (*di veicoli*) convoy; (*Ferr*) train; **~ funebre** funeral procession

convo'lare /**72**/ VI: **~ a (giuste) nozze** (*scherzoso*) to tie the knot

convulsi'one SF convulsion

con'vulso, -a AG (*pianto*) violent, convulsive; (*attività*) feverish

COOP ABBR F = **cooperativa**

coope'rare /**72**/ VI: **~ (a)** to cooperate (in)

coopera'tiva SF cooperative

cooperazi'one [kooperat'tsjone] SF cooperation

coordina'mento SM coordination

coordi'nare /**72**/ VT to coordinate

coordi'nato, -a AG (*movimenti*) coordinated ▶ SF (*Ling, Geo, Mat*) coordinate ▶ SMPL: **coordinati** (*Moda*) coordinates

coordinazi'one [koordinat'tsjone] SF coordination

co'perchio [koˈpɛrkjo] SM cover; (di pentola) lid

co'perta SF cover; (di lana) blanket; (da viaggio) rug; (Naut) deck

coper'tina SF (Stampa) cover, jacket

co'perto, -a PP di **coprire** ▶ AG covered; (cielo) overcast ▶ SM place setting; (posto a tavola) place; (al ristorante) cover charge; **~ di** covered in o with

coper'tone SM (telo impermeabile) tarpaulin; (Aut) rubber tyre

coper'tura SF (anche Econ, Mil) cover; (di edificio) roofing; **fare un gioco di ~** (Sport) to play a defensive game; **~ assicurativa** insurance cover

'copia SF copy; (Fot) print; **brutta/bella ~** rough/final copy; **~ conforme** (Dir) certified copy; **~ omaggio** presentation copy

'copia e in'colla SM INV copy and paste

copi'are /19/ VT to copy

copia'trice [kopjaˈtritʃe] SF copier, copying machine

copincol'lare /72/ VT to copy and paste

copin'collo SM copy and paste

copi'one SM (Cine, Teat) script

'coppa SF (bicchiere) goblet; (per frutta, gelato) dish; (trofeo) cup, trophy ■ **coppe** SFPL (Carte) suit in Neapolitan pack of cards; **~ dell'olio** oil sump (BRIT) o pan (US)

'coppia SF (di persone) couple; (di animali, Sport) pair

cop'rente AG (colore, cosmetico) covering; (calze) opaque

copri'capo SM headgear; (cappello) hat

coprifu'oco, -chi SM curfew

copri'letto SM bedspread

copripiu'mino SM INV duvet cover

co'prire /9/ VT to cover; (occupare: carica, posto) to hold ■ **coprirsi** VPR (cielo) to cloud over; (vestirsi) to wrap up, cover up; (Econ) to cover o.s.; **coprirsi di** (macchie, muffa) to become covered in; **~ qn di baci** to smother sb with kisses; **~ le spese** to break even; **coprirsi le spalle** (fig) to cover o.s.

coque [kɔk] SF: **uovo alla ~** boiled egg

co'raggio [koˈraddʒo] SM courage, bravery; **~!** (forza!) come on!; (animo!) cheer up!; **farsi ~** to pluck up courage; **hai un bel ~!** (sfacciataggine) you've got a nerve o a cheek!

coraggi'oso, -a [koradˈdʒoso] AG courageous, brave

co'rale AG choral; (approvazione) unanimous

co'rallo SM coral; **il mar dei Coralli** the Coral Sea

Co'rano SM (Rel) Koran

co'razza [koˈrattsa] SF armour (BRIT), armor (US); (di animali) carapace, shell; (Mil) armour(-plating)

coraz'zato, -a [koratˈtsato] AG (Mil) armoured (BRIT), armored (US) ▶ SF battleship

corazzi'ere [koratˈtsjɛre] SM (Storia) cuirassier; (guardia presidenziale) carabiniere of the President's guard

corbelle'ria SF stupid remark ■ **corbellerie** SFPL (sciocchezze) nonsense no pl

'corda SF cord; (fune) rope; (spago, Mus) string; **dare ~ a qn** (fig) to let sb have his (o her) way; **tenere sulla ~ qn** (fig) to keep sb on tenterhooks; **tagliare la ~** (fig) to slip away, sneak off; **essere giù di ~** to feel down; **corde vocali** vocal cords

cor'data SF (Alpinismo) roped party; (fig) alliance system in financial and business world

cordi'ale AG cordial, warm ▶ SM (bevanda) cordial

cordialità SF INV warmth, cordiality ▶ SFPL (saluti) best wishes

'cordless [ˈkɔrdlɪs] SM INV cordless phone

cor'doglio [korˈdɔʎʎo] SM grief; (lutto) mourning

cor'done SM cord, string; (linea: di polizia) cordon; **~ ombelicale** umbilical cord; **~ sanitario** quarantine line

Co'rea SF: **la ~** Korea; **la ~ del Nord/Sud** North/South Korea

core'ano, -a AG, SM/F Korean

coreogra'fia SF choreography

core'ografo, -a SM/F choreographer

cori'aceo, -a [koˈrjatʃeo] AG (Bot, Zool) coriaceous; (fig) tough

cori'andolo SM (Bot) coriander ■ **coriandoli** SMPL (per carnevale ecc) confetti no pl

cori'care /20/ VT to put to bed ■ **coricarsi** VPR to go to bed

coricherò ecc [korikeˈrɔ] VB vedi **coricare**

Co'rinto SF Corinth

co'rista, -i, -e SM/F (Rel) choir member, chorister; (Teat) member of the chorus

'corna SFPL vedi **corno**

cor'nacchia [korˈnakkja] SF crow

corna'musa SF bagpipes pl

'cornea SF (Anat) cornea

'corner SM INV (Calcio) corner (kick); **salvarsi in ~** (fig: in gara, esame ecc) to get through by the skin of one's teeth

cor'netta SF (Mus) cornet; (Tel) receiver

cor'netto SM (Cuc) croissant; (gelato) cone; **~ acustico** ear trumpet

cor'nice [korˈnitʃe] SF frame; (fig) background, setting

cornici'one [korniˈtʃone] SM (di edificio) ledge; (Archit) cornice

'corno SM (pl(f) **corna**: Zool) horn; (pl(m) **corni**: Mus) horn; (col) **fare le corna a qn** to be unfaith ful to sb; **dire peste e corna di qn** to call sb every name under the sun; **un ~!** not on your life!

Corno'vaglia [korno'vaλλa] SF: **la ~** Cornwall

cor'nuto, -a AG (con corna) horned; (col: marito) cuckolded ▶ SM (col) cuckold; (: insulto) bastard (!)

'**coro** SM chorus; (Rel) choir

corol'lario SM corollary

co'rona SF crown; (di fiori) wreath

corona'mento SM (di impresa) completion; (di carriera) crowning achievement; **il ~ dei propri sogni** the fulfilment of one's dreams

coro'nare /72/ VT to crown

coro'naria SF coronary artery

'**corpo** SM body; (cadavere) (dead) body; (militare, diplomatico) corps inv; (di opere) corpus; **prendere ~** to take shape; **darsi anima e ~ a** to give o.s. heart and soul to; **a ~ a ~** hand-to-hand; **~ d'armata** army corps; **~ di ballo** corps de ballet; **~ dei carabinieri** ≈ police force; **~ celeste** heavenly body; **~ di guardia** (soldati) guard; (locale) guardroom; **~ insegnante** teaching staff; **~ del reato** material evidence

corpo'rale AG bodily; (punizione) corporal

corpora'tura SF build, physique

corporazi'one [korporat'tsjone] SF corporation

cor'poreo, -a AG bodily, physical

cor'poso, -a AG (vino) full-bodied

corpu'lento, -a AG stout, corpulent

corpu'lenza [korpu'lɛntsa] SF stoutness, corpulence

cor'puscolo SM corpuscle

corre'dare /72/ VT: **~ di** to provide o furnish with; **domanda corredata dai seguenti documenti** application accompanied by the following documents

cor'redo SM equipment; (di sposa) trousseau

cor'reggere [kor'reddʒere] /87/ VT to correct; (compiti) to correct, mark

cor'rente AG (fiume) flowing; (acqua del rubinetto) running; (moneta, prezzo) current; (comune) everyday ▶ SM: **essere al ~ (di)** to be well-informed (about) ▶ SF (movimento di liquido) current, stream; (spiffero) draught; (Elettr, Meteor) current; (fig) trend, tendency; **mettere al ~ (di)** to inform (of); **la vostra lettera del 5 ~ mese** (in lettere commerciali) your letter of the 5th inst.; **articoli di qualità ~** average-quality products; **~ alternata** alternating current; **~ continua** direct current

corrente'mente AV (comunemente) commonly; **parlare una lingua ~** to speak a language fluently

corren'tista, -i, -e SM/F (current (BRIT) o checking (US)) account holder

cor'reo, -a SM/F (Dir) accomplice

'**correre** /28/ VI to run; (precipitarsi) to rush; (partecipare a una gara) to race, run; (fig: diffondersi) to go round ▶ VT (Sport: gara) to compete in; (rischio) to run; (pericolo) to face; **~ dietro a qn** to run after sb; **corre voce che ...** it is rumoured that ...

corresponsabilità SF joint responsibility; (Dir) joint liability

corresponsi'one SF payment

cor'ressi ecc VB vedi **correggere**

corret'tezza [korret'tettsa] SF (di comportamento) correctness; (Sport) fair play

cor'retto, -a PP di **correggere** ▶ AG (comportamento) correct, proper; **caffè ~ al cognac** coffee laced with brandy

corret'tore, -'trice SM/F: **~ di bozze** proofreader ▶ SM: **(liquido) ~** correction fluid; **~ ortografico** (Inform) spellchecker

correzi'one [korret'tsjone] SF correction; marking; **~ di bozze** proofreading

cor'rida SF bullfight

corri'doio SM corridor; (in aereo, al cinema) aisle; **manovre di ~** (Pol) lobbying sg

corri'dore SM (Sport) runner; (: su veicolo) racer

corri'era SF coach (BRIT), bus

corri'ere SM (diplomatico, di guerra, postale) courier; (spedizioniere) carrier

corri'mano SM handrail

corrispet'tivo SM amount due; **versare a qn il ~ di una prestazione** to pay sb the amount due for his (o her) services

corrispon'dente AG corresponding ▶ SMF correspondent

corrispon'denza [korrispon'dɛntsa] SF correspondence; **~ in arrivo/partenza** incoming/outgoing mail

corris'pondere /95/ VI (equivalere): **~ (a)** to correspond (to); (per lettera): **~ con** to correspond with ▶ VT (stipendio) to pay; (fig: amore) to return

corris'posto, -a PP di **corrispondere**

corrobo'rare /72/ VT to strengthen, fortify; (fig) to corroborate, bear out

cor'rodere /49/ VT, **cor'rodersi** VPR to corrode

cor'rompere /97/ VT to corrupt; (comprare) to bribe

corrosi'one SF corrosion

corro'sivo, -a AG corrosive

cor'roso, -a PP di **corrodere**

corrotta'mente AV corruptly

cor'rotto, -a PP di **corrompere** ▶ AG corrupt

corrucci'arsi [korrut'tʃarsi] /14/ VPR to grow angry o vexed

corru'gare /80/ VT to wrinkle; **~ la fronte** to knit one's brows

cor'ruppi *ecc* VB *vedi* **corrompere**

corrut'tela SF corruption, depravity

corruzi'one [korrut'tsjone] SF corruption; bribery; **~ di minorenne** (*Dir*) corruption of a minor

'**corsa** SF running *no pl*; (*gara*) race; (*di autobus, taxi*) journey, trip; **fare una ~** to run, dash; (*Sport*) to run a race; **andare** *o* **essere di ~** to be in a hurry; **~ automobilistica/ciclistica** motor/cycle race; **~ campestre** cross-country race; **~ ad ostacoli** (*Ippica*) steeplechase; (*Atletica*) hurdles race

cor'saro, -a AG: **nave corsara** privateer ▶ SM privateer

'**corsi** *ecc* VB *vedi* **correre**

cor'sia SF (*Aut, Sport*) lane; (*di ospedale*) ward; **~ di emergenza** (*Aut*) hard shoulder; **~ preferenziale** ≈ bus lane; (*fig*) fast track; **~ di sorpasso** (*Aut*) overtaking lane

'**Corsica** SF: **la ~** Corsica

cor'sivo SM cursive (writing); (*Tip*) italics *pl*

'**corso, -a** PP *di* **correre** ▶ AG, SM/F Corsican ▶ SM course; (*strada cittadina*) main street; (*di unità monetaria*) circulation; (*di titoli, valori*) rate, price; **dar libero ~ a** to give free expression to; **in ~** in progress, under way; (*annata*) current; **~ d'acqua** river; stream; (*artificiale*) waterway; **~ d'aggiornamento** refresher course; **~ serale** evening class; **aver ~ legale** to be legal tender

'**corte** SF (*court*)yard; (*Dir, regale*) court; **fare la ~ a qn** to court sb; **~ d'appello** court of appeal; **~ di cassazione** final court of appeal; **C~ dei Conti** State audit court; **C~ Costituzionale** special court dealing with constitutional and ministerial matters; **~ marziale** court-martial

cor'teccia, -ce [kor'tettʃa] SF bark

corteggia'mento [korteddʒa'mento] SM courtship

corteggi'are [korted'dʒare] /62/ VT to court

corteggia'tore [korteddʒa'tore] SM suitor

cor'teo SM procession; **~ funebre** funeral cortège

cor'tese AG courteous

corte'sia SF courtesy; **fare una ~ a qn** to do sb a favour; **per ~, dov'è ...?** excuse me, please, where is ...?

cortigi'ano, -a [korti'dʒano] SM/F courtier ▶ SF courtesan

cor'tile SM (*court*)yard

cor'tina SF curtain; (*anche fig*) screen

corti'sone SM cortisone

'**corto, -a** AG short ▶ AV: **tagliare ~** to come straight to the point; **essere a ~ di** to be short of sth; **essere a ~ di parole** to be at a loss for words; **la settimana corta** the 5-day week; **~ circuito** short-circuit

cortocir'cuito [kortotʃir'kuito] SM = **corto circuito**

cortome'traggio [kortome'traddʒo] SM short (feature film)

cor'vino, -a AG (*capelli*) jet-black

'**corvo** SM raven

'**cosa** SF thing; (*faccenda*) affair, matter, business *no pl*; (**che**) **~?** what?; (**che**) **cos'è?** what is it?; **a ~ pensi?** what are you thinking about?; **tante belle cose!** all the best!; **ormai è ~ fatta!** (*positivo*) it's in the bag!; (*negativo*) it's done now!; **a cose fatte** when it's all over

'**Cosa 'Nostra** SF Cosa Nostra

'**cosca, -sche** SF (*di mafiosi*) clan

'**coscia, -sce** ['kɔʃʃa] SF thigh; **~ di pollo** (*Cuc*) chicken leg

cosci'ente [koʃ'ʃente] AG conscious; **~ di** conscious *o* aware of

cosci'enza [koʃ'ʃentsa] SF conscience; (*consapevolezza*) consciousness; **~ politica** political awareness

coscienzi'oso, -a [koʃʃen'tsjoso] AG conscientious

cosci'otto [koʃ'ʃotto] SM (*Cuc*) leg

cos'critto SM (*Mil*) conscript

coscrizi'one [koskrit'tsjone] SF conscription

---

così

AV **1** (*in questo modo*) like this, (in) this way; (*in tal modo*) so; **le cose stanno così** this is the way things stand; **non ho detto così!** I didn't say that!; **come stai? — (e) così** how are you? — so-so; **e così via** and so on; **per così dire** so to speak; **così sia** amen
2 (*tanto*) so; **così lontano** so far away; **un ragazzo così intelligente** such an intelligent boy
▶ AG INV (*tale*): **non ho mai visto un film così** I've never seen such a film
▶ CONG **1** (*perciò*) so, therefore; **e così ho deciso di lasciarlo** so I decided to leave him
2: **così ... come** as ... as; **non è così bravo come te** he's not as good as you; **così ... che** so ... that

---

cosicché [kosik'ke] CONG so (that)

cosid'detto, -a AG so-called

cos'mesi SF (*scienza*) cosmetics *sg*; (*prodotti*) cosmetics *pl*; (*trattamento*) beauty treatment

cos'metico, -a, -ci, -che AG, SM cosmetic

'**cosmico, -a, -ci, -che** AG cosmic

'**cosmo** SM cosmos

cosmo'nauta, -i, -e SM/F cosmonaut

cosmopo'lita, -i, -e AG cosmopolitan

'**coso** SM (*col: oggetto*) thing, thingumajig; (: *aggeggio*) contraption; (: *persona*) what's his name, thingumajig

cos'pargere [kos'pardʒere] /111/ vt: ~ **di** to sprinkle with

cos'parso, -a pp di **cospargere**

cos'petto sm: **al ~ di** in front of; in the presence of

cospicuità sf vast quantity

cos'picuo, -a ag considerable, large

cospi'rare /72/ vi to conspire

cospira'tore, -'trice sm/f conspirator

cospirazi'one [kospirat'tsjone] sf conspiracy

'cossi ecc vb vedi **cuocere**

Cost. abbr = **costituzione**

'costa sf (tra terra e mare) coast(line); (litorale) shore; (pendio) slope; (Anat) rib; **navigare sotto ~** to hug the coast; **la C~ Azzurra** the French Riviera; **la C~ d'Avorio** the Ivory Coast; **velluto a coste** corduroy

costà av there

cos'tante ag constant; (persona) steadfast ▶ sf constant

cos'tanza [kos'tantsa] sf (gen) constancy; (fermezza) constancy, steadfastness; **il Lago di C~** Lake Constance

cos'tare /72/ vi, vt to cost; **~ caro** to be expensive, cost a lot; **~ un occhio della testa** to cost a fortune; **costi quel che costi** no matter what

'Costa 'Rica sf: **la ~** Costa Rica

cos'tata sf (Cuc: di manzo) large chop

cos'tato sm (Anat) ribs pl

costeggi'are [kosted'dʒare] /62/ vt to be close to; to run alongside

cos'tei pron vedi **costui**

costellazi'one [kostellat'tsjone] sf constellation

coster'nare /72/ vt to dismay

coster'nato, -a ag dismayed

costernazi'one [kosternat'tsjone] sf dismay, consternation

costi'ero, -a ag coastal, coast cpd ▶ sf stretch of coast

costi'pato, -a ag (stitico) constipated

costitu'ire /55/ vt (comitato, gruppo) to set up, form; (collezione) to put together, build up; (elementi, parati: comporre) to make up, constitute; (rappresentare) to constitute; (Dir) to appoint ■ **costituirsi** vpr: **costituirsi (alla polizia)** to give o.s. up (to the police); **costituirsi parte civile** (Dir) to associate in an action with the public prosecutor for damages; **il fatto non costituisce reato** this is not a crime

costitu'tivo, -a ag constituent, component; **atto ~** (Dir: di società) memorandum of association

costituzio'nale [kostituttsjo'nale] ag constitutional

costituzi'one [kostitut'tsjone] sf setting up; building up; constitution

'costo sm cost; **sotto ~** for less than cost price; **a ogni** o **qualunque ~, a tutti i costi** at all costs; **costi di esercizio** running costs; **costi fissi** fixed costs; **costi di gestione** operating costs; **costi di produzione** production costs

'costola sf (Anat) rib; **ha la polizia alle costole** the police are hard on his heels

costo'letta sf (Cuc) cutlet

cos'toro pron vedi **costui**

cos'toso, -a ag expensive, costly

cos'tretto, -a pp di **costringere**

cos'tringere [kos'trindʒere] /117/ vt: **~ qn a fare qc** to force sb to do sth

costrit'tivo, -a ag coercive

costrizi'one [kostrit'tsjone] sf coercion

costru'ire /55/ vt to construct, build

costrut'tivo, -a ag (Edil) building cpd; (fig) constructive

costruzi'one [kostrut'tsjone] sf construction, building; **di ~ inglese** British-made

cos'tui (f **costei**, pl **costoro**) pron (soggetto) he (she); (pl) they; (complemento) him (her); (pl) them; **si può sapere chi è ~?** (peg) just who is that fellow?

cos'tume sm (uso) custom; (foggia di vestire, indumento) costume; **il buon ~** public morality; **donna di facili costumi** woman of easy morals; **~ da bagno** bathing o swimming costume (Brit), swimsuit; (da uomo) bathing o swimming trunks pl

costu'mista, -i, -e sm/f costume maker, costume designer

co'tenna sf bacon rind

co'togna [ko'toɲɲa] sf quince

coto'letta sf (di maiale, montone) chop; (di vitello, agnello) cutlet

coto'nare /72/ vt (capelli) to backcomb

co'tone sm cotton; **~ idrofilo** cotton wool (Brit), absorbent cotton (US)

cotoni'ficio [kotoni'fitʃo] sm cotton mill

'cotta sf (Rel) surplice; (col: innamoramento) crush

'cottimo sm: **lavorare a ~** to do piecework

'cotto, -a pp di **cuocere** ▶ ag cooked; (col: innamorato) head-over-heels in love ▶ sm brickwork; **~ a puntino** cooked to perfection; **dirne di cotte e di crude a qn** to call sb every name under the sun; **farne di cotte e di crude** to get up to all kinds of mischief; **mattone di ~** fired brick; **pavimento in ~** tile floor; **ben ~** (carne) well done

cot'tura sf cooking; (in forno) baking; (in umido) stewing; **~ a fuoco lento** simmering; **angolo (di) ~** cooking area

co'vare /72/ vt to hatch; (fig: malattia) to be sickening for; (: *odio, rancore*) to nurse ▶ VI (*fuoco, fig*) to smoulder (BRIT), smolder (US)

co'vata SF (*anche fig*) brood

'covo SM den; **~ di terroristi** terrorist base

co'vone SM sheaf

'cozza ['kɔttsa] SF mussel

coz'zare [kot'tsare] /72/ VI: **~ contro** to bang into, collide with

'cozzo ['kɔttso] SM collision

C.P. ABBR (= *cartolina postale*) pc; (*Posta*) *vedi* **casella postale**; (*Naut*) = **capitaneria (di porto)**; (*Dir*) = **codice penale**

crac'care /20/ VT (*Inform*) to crack

crack SM INV (*droga*) crack

Cra'covia SF Cracow

'crampo SM cramp; **ho un ~ alla gamba** I've got cramp in my leg

'cranio SM skull

cra'tere SM crater

cra'vatta SF tie; **~ a farfalla** bow tie

cravat'tino SM bow tie

cre'anza [kre'antsa] SF manners *pl*; **per buona ~** out of politeness

cre'are /72/ VT to create

creativit à SF creativity

cre'ato SM creation

crea'tore, -'trice AG creative ▶ SM/F creator; **un ~ di alta moda** fashion designer; **andare al C~** to go to meet one's maker

crea'tura SF creature; (*bimbo*) baby, infant

creazi'one [kreat'tsjone] SF creation; (*fondazione*) foundation, establishment

'crebbi *ecc* VB *vedi* **crescere**

cre'dente SMF (*Rel*) believer

cre'denza [kre'dentsa] SF belief; (*armadio*) sideboard

credenzi'ali [kreden'tsjali] SFPL credentials

'credere /29/ VT to believe ▶ VI: **~ in, ~ a** to believe in; **~ qn onesto** to believe sb (to be) honest; **~ che** to believe *o* think that; **credersi furbo** to think one is clever; **lo credo bene!** I can well believe it!; **fai quello che credi** *o* **come credi** do as you please

cre'dibile AG credible, believable

credibilit à SF credibility

credi'tizio, -a [kredi'tittsjo] AG credit

'credito SM (*anche Comm*) credit; (*reputazione*) esteem, repute; **comprare a ~** to buy on credit; **~ agevolato** easy credit terms; **~ d'imposta** tax credit

credi'tore, -'trice SM/F creditor

'credo SM INV creed

'credulo, -a AG credulous

credu'lone, -a SM/F simpleton, sucker (*col*)

'crema SF cream; (*con uova, zucchero ecc*) custard; **~ idratante** moisturizing cream; **~ pasticciera** confectioner's custard; **~ solare** sun cream

cre'mare /72/ VT to cremate

crema'torio SM crematorium

cremazi'one [kremat'tsjone] SF cremation

'cremisi AG INV, SM INV crimson

Crem'lino SM: **il ~** the Kremlin

cremo'nese AG of (*o* from) Cremona

cre'moso, -a AG creamy

'crepa SF crack

cre'paccio [kre'pattʃo] SM large crack, fissure; (*di ghiacciaio*) crevasse

crepacu'ore SM broken heart

crepa'pelle AV: **ridere a ~** to split one's sides laughing

cre'pare /72/ VI (*col: morire*) to snuff it (BRIT), kick the bucket; **~ dalle risa** to split one's sides laughing; **~ dall'invidia** to be green with envy

crêpe [krɛp] SF INV pancake

crepi'tare /72/ VI (*fuoco*) to crackle; (*pioggia*) to patter

crepi'tio, -ii SM crackling; pattering

cre'puscolo SM twilight, dusk

cre'scendo [kreʃ'ʃendo] SM (*Mus*) crescendo

cre'scente [kreʃ'ʃente] AG (*gen*) growing, increasing; (*luna*) waxing

'crescere ['kreʃʃere] /30/ VI to grow ▶ VT (*figli*) to raise

cre'scione [kreʃ'ʃone] SM watercress

'crescita ['kreʃʃita] SF growth

cresci'uto, -a [kreʃ'ʃuto] PP *di* **crescere**

cresima SF (*Rel*) confirmation

cresi'mare /72/ VT to confirm

'crespo, -a AG (*capelli*) frizzy; (*tessuto*) puckered ▶ SM crêpe

'cresta SF crest; (*di polli, uccelli*) crest, comb; **alzare la ~** (*fig*) to become cocky; **abbassare la ~** (*fig*) to climb down; **essere sulla ~ dell'onda** (*fig*) to be riding high

'Creta SF Crete

'creta SF (*gesso*) chalk; (*argilla*) clay

cre'tese AG, SMF Cretan

creti'nata SF (*col*): **dire/fare una ~** to say/do a stupid thing

cre'tino, -a AG stupid ▶ SM/F idiot, fool

CRI SIGLA F = **Croce Rossa Italiana**

cric SM INV (*Tecn*) jack

'cricca, -che SF clique

'cricco, -chi SM = **cric**

cri'ceto [kri'tʃeto] SM hamster

crimi'nale AG, SMF criminal

criminalit à SF crime; **~ organizzata** organized crime

'Criminalpol ABBR = **polizia criminale**

'crimine SM (*Dir*) crime

criminolo'gia [kriminolo'dʒia] SF criminology

crimi'noso, -a AG criminal

cri'nale SM ridge

'crine SM horsehair

crini'era SF mane

'cripta SF crypt

crip'tare /**72**/ VT (TV: *programma*) to encrypt

crip'tato, -a AG (*programma, messaggio*) encrypted

crisan'temo SM chrysanthemum; *vedi anche* **giorno**

'crisi SF INV crisis; (*Med*) attack, fit; **essere in ~** (*partito, impresa ecc*) to be in a state of crisis; **~ energetica** energy crisis; **~ di nervi** attack o fit of nerves

cristalle'ria SF (*fabbrica*) crystal glassworks *sg*; (*oggetti*) crystalware

cristal'lino, -a AG (*Mineralogia*) crystalline; (*fig: suono, acque*) crystal clear ▶ SM (*Anat*) crystalline lens

cristalliz'zare [kristallid'dzare] /**72**/ VI, **cristalliz'zarsi** VPR to crystallize; (*fig*) to become fossilized

cris'tallo SM crystal; **cristalli liquidi** liquid crystals

cristia'nesimo SM Christianity

cristianità SF Christianity; (*i cristiani*) Christendom

cristi'ano, -a AG, SM/F Christian; **un povero ~** (*fig*) a poor soul o beggar; **comportarsi da ~** (*fig*) to behave in a civilized manner

'cristo SM: **C~** Christ; **(un) povero ~** (a) poor beggar

cri'terio SM criterion; (*buon senso*) (common) sense

'critica, -che SF *vedi* **critico**

criti'care /**20**/ VT to criticize

'critico, -a, -ci, -che AG critical ▶ SM critic ▶ SF criticism; **la critica** (*attività*) criticism; (*persone*) the critics *pl*

criti'cone, -a SM/F faultfinder

crivel'lare /**72**/ VT: **~ (di)** to riddle (with)

cri'vello SM riddle

cro'ato, -a AG, SM/F Croatian, Croat

Cro'azia [kro'attsja] SF: **la ~** Croatia

croc'cante AG crisp, crunchy ▶ SM (*Cuc*) almond crunch

'crocchia ['krɔkkja] SF chignon, bun

'crocchio ['krɔkkjo] SM (*di persone*) small group, cluster

'croce ['krotʃe] SF cross; **in ~** (*di traverso*) crosswise; (*fig*) on tenterhooks; **mettere in ~** (*anche fig: criticare*) to crucify; (: *tormentare*) to nag to death; **la C~ Rossa** the Red Cross; **~ uncinata** swastika

croce'figgere *ecc* [krotʃe'fiddʒere] = **crocifiggere** *ecc*

croceros'sina [krotʃeros'sina] SF Red Cross nurse

croce'via [krotʃe'via] SM INV crossroads *sg*

croci'ato, -a [kro'tʃato] AG cross-shaped ▶ SM (*anche fig*) crusader ▶ SF crusade

cro'cicchio [kro'tʃikkjo] SM crossroads *sg*

croci'era [kro'tʃera] SF (*viaggio*) cruise; (*Archit*) transept; **altezza di ~** (*Aer*) cruising height; **velocità di ~** (*Aer, Naut*) cruising speed

croci'figgere [krotʃi'fiddʒere] /**104**/ VT to crucify

crocifissi'one [krotʃifis'sjone] SF crucifixion

croci'fisso, -a [krotʃi'fisso] PP *di* **crocifiggere** ▶ SM crucifix

crogio'larsi [krodʒo'larsi] /**72**/ VPR: **~ al sole** to bask in the sun

crogi'olo [kro'dʒɔlo], **crogiu'olo** [kro'dʒwɔlo] SM crucible; (*fig*) melting pot

crol'lare /**72**/ VI to collapse

'crollo SM collapse; (*di prezzi*) slump, sudden fall; **~ in Borsa** *slump in prices on the Stock Exchange*

'croma SF (*Mus*) quaver (BRIT), eighth note (US)

cro'mato, -a AG chromium-plated

'cromo SM chrome, chromium

cromo'soma, -i SM chromosome

'cronaca, -che SF chronicle; (*Stampa*) news *sg*; (: *rubrica*) column; (TV, *Radio*) commentary; **fatto** o **episodio di ~** news item; **~ nera** crime news *sg*; crime column

'cronico, -a, -ci, -che AG chronic

cro'nista, -i SMF (*Stampa*) reporter, columnist

cronis'toria SF chronicle; (*fig: ironico*) blow-by-blow account

cro'nografo SM (*strumento*) chronograph

cronolo'gia [kronolo'dʒia] SF chronology

cronome'trare /**72**/ VT to time

cro'nometro SM chronometer; (*a scatto*) stopwatch

'crosta SF crust; (*Med*) scab; (*Zool*) shell; (*di ghiaccio*) layer; (*fig: peg: quadro*) daub

cros'tacei [kros'tatʃei] SMPL shellfish

cros'tata SF (*Cuc*) tart

cros'tino SM (*Cuc*) croûton; (: *da antipasto*) canapé

crowd'sourcing [kraud'sursin(g)] SM crowdsourcing

crucci'are [krut'tʃare] /**14**/ VT to torment, worry ■ **crucciarsi** VPR: **crucciarsi per** to torment o.s. over

'cruccio ['kruttʃo] SM worry, torment

cruci'ale [kru'tʃale] AG crucial

cruci'verba [krutʃi'vɛrba] SM INV crossword (puzzle)

cru'dele AG cruel

crudeltà SF cruelty

'crudo, -a AG (*non cotto*) raw; (*aspro*) harsh, severe

cru'ento, -a AG bloody

cru'miro, -a SM/F (*peg*) blackleg (BRIT), scab

'cruna SF eye (of a needle)

'crusca SF bran

crus'cotto SM (*Aut*) dashboard

CS SIGLA = **Cosenza**

c.s. ABBR = **come sopra**

CSI [tʃi'ɛsse'i] SIGLA F (= *Comunità di Stati Indipendenti*) CIS

CSM [tʃiɛsse'ɛmme] SIGLA M (= *consiglio superiore della magistratura*) Magistrates' Board of Supervisors

CT SIGLA = **Catania**

c.t. ABBR = **commissario tecnico**

'Cuba SF Cuba

cu'bano, -a AG, SM/F Cuban

cu'betto SM (small) cube; **~ di ghiaccio** ice cube

'cubico, -a, -ci, -che AG cubic

cu'bista, -i, -e AG (*Arte*) Cubist ▶ SF podium dancer, *dancer who performs on stage in a club*

'cubo, -a AG cubic ▶ SM cube; **elevare al ~** (*Mat*) to cube

cuc'cagna [kuk'kaɲɲa] SF: **paese della ~** land of plenty; **albero della ~** greasy pole (*fig*)

cuc'cetta [kut'tʃetta] SF (*Ferr*) couchette; (*Naut*) berth

cucchiai'ata [kukkja'jata] SF spoonful; tablespoonful

cucchia'ino [kukkja'ino] SM teaspoon; coffee spoon

cucchi'aio [kuk'kjajo] SM spoon; (*da tavola*) tablespoon; (*cucchiaiata*) spoonful; tablespoonful

'cuccia, -ce ['kuttʃa] SF dog's bed; **a ~!** down!

cuccio'lata [kuttʃo'lata] SF litter

'cucciolo ['kuttʃolo] SM cub; (*di cane*) puppy

cu'cina [ku'tʃina] SF (*locale*) kitchen; (*arte culinaria*) cooking, cookery; (*le vivande*) food, cooking; (*apparecchio*) cooker; **di ~** (*libro, lezione*) cookery *cpd*; **~ componibile** fitted kitchen; **~ economica** kitchen range

cuci'nare [kutʃi'nare] /**72**/ VT to cook

cuci'nino [kutʃi'nino] SM kitchenette

cu'cire [ku'tʃire] /**31**/ VT to sew, stitch; **~ la bocca a qn** (*fig*) to shut sb up

cu'cito, -a [ku'tʃito] SM sewing; (*Ins*) sewing, needlework

cuci'trice [kutʃi'tritʃe] SF (*Tip: per libri*) stitching machine; (*per fogli*) stapler

cuci'tura [kutʃi'tura] SF sewing, stitching; (*costura*) seam

cucù SM INV, **cu'culo** SM cuckoo

'cuffia SF bonnet, cap; (*da infermiera*) cap; (*da bagno*) (bathing) cap; (*per ascoltare*) headphones *pl*, headset

cu'gino, -a [ku'dʒino] SM/F cousin

'cui

PRON **1** (*nei complementi indiretti: persona*) whom; (: *oggetto, animale*) which; **la persona a cui accennavi** the person/people you were referring *o* to whom you were referring; **la penna con cui scrivo** the pen I'm writing with; **il paese da cui viene** the country he comes from; **i libri di cui parlavo** the books I was talking about *o* about which I was talking; **parla varie lingue, fra cui l'inglese** he speaks several languages, including English; **il quartiere in cui abito** the district where I live; **visto il modo in cui ti ha trattato ...** considering how he treated you ...; **la ragione per cui** the reason why; **per cui non so più che fare** that's why I don't know what to do **2** (*inserito tra articolo e sostantivo*) whose; **la donna i cui figli sono scomparsi** the woman whose children have disappeared; **il signore, dal cui figlio ho avuto il libro** the man from whose son I got the book

---

culi'naria SF cookery

culi'nario, -a AG culinary

'culla SF cradle

cul'lare /**72**/ VT to rock; (*fig: idea, speranza*) to cherish ■ **cullarsi** VPR (*gen*) to sway; **cullarsi in vane speranze** (*fig*) to cherish fond hopes; **cullarsi nel dolce far niente** (*fig*) to sit back and relax

culmi'nante AG: **posizione ~** (*Astr*) highest point; **punto** *o* **momento ~** (*fig*) climax

culmi'nare /**72**/ VI: **~ in** *o* **con** to culminate in

'culmine SM top, summit

'culo SM (*col*) arse (BRIT !), ass (US !); (: *fig: fortuna*): **aver ~** to have the luck of the devil; **prendere qn per il ~** to take the piss out of sb (!)

'culto SM (*religione*) religion; (*adorazione*) worship, adoration; (*venerazione: anche fig*) cult

cul'tura SF (*gen*) culture; (*conoscenza*) education, learning; **di ~** (*persona*) cultured; (*istituto*) cultural, of culture; **~ generale** general knowledge; **~ di massa** mass culture

cultu'rale AG cultural

cultu'rismo SM body-building

cumu'lare /**72**/ VT to accumulate, amass

cumula'tivo, -a AG cumulative; (*prezzo*) inclusive; (*biglietto*) group *cpd*

'cumulo SM (*mucchio*) pile, heap; (*Meteor*) cumulus; **~ dei redditi** (*Fisco*) combined incomes; **~ delle pene** (*Dir*) consecutive sentences

'cuneo SM wedge

cu'netta SF (*di strada ecc*) bump; (*scolo: nelle strade di città*) gutter; (: *di campagna*) ditch; (*avvallamento*) dip cu'nicolo SM (*galleria*) tunnel; (*di miniera*) pit, shaft; (*di talpa*) hole

cu'oca SF *vedi* **cuoco**

cu'ocere ['kwɔtʃere] /32/ VT (*alimenti*) to cook; (*mattoni ecc*) to fire ▶ VI to cook; **~ in umido/a vapore/in padella** to stew/steam/fry; **~ al forno** (*pane*) to bake; (*arrosto*) to roast

cu'oco, -a, -chi, -che SM/F cook; (*di ristorante*) chef

cuoi'ame SM leather goods *pl*

cu'oio SM leather; **~ capelluto** scalp; **tirare le cuoia** (*col*) to kick the bucket

cu'ore SM heart ◼ **cuori** SMPL (*Carte*) hearts; **avere buon ~** to be kind-hearted; **stare a ~ a qn** to be important to sb; **un grazie di ~** heartfelt thanks; **ringraziare di ~** to thank sincerely; **nel profondo del ~** in one's heart of hearts; **avere la morte nel ~** to be sick at heart; **club dei cuori solitari** lonely hearts club

cupi'digia [kupi'didʒa] SF greed, covetousness

'cupo, -a AG dark; (*suono*) dull; (*fig*) gloomy, dismal

'cupola SF dome; (*più piccola*) cupola; (*fig*) Mafia high command

'cura SF care; (*Med: trattamento*) (course of) treatment; **aver ~ di** (*occuparsi di*) to look after; **a ~ di** (*libro*) edited by; **fare una ~** to follow a course of treatment; **~ dimagrante** diet

cu'rabile AG curable

cu'rante AG: **medico ~** doctor (in charge of a patient)

cu'rare /72/ VT (*malato, malattia*) to treat; (: *guarire*) to cure; (*aver cura di*) to take care of; (*testo*) to edit ◼ **curarsi** VPR to take care of o.s.; (*Med*) to follow a course of treatment; **curarsi di** to pay attention to; (*occuparsi di*) to look after

cu'rato SM parish priest; (*protestante*) vicar, minister

cura'tore, -'trice SM/F (*Dir*) trustee; (*di antologia ecc*) editor; **~ fallimentare** (official) receiver

'curdo, -a AG Kurdish ▶ SM/F Kurd

'curia SF (*Rel*): **la ~ romana** the Roman curia; **~ notarile** notaries' association *o* guild

curio'saggine [kurjo'saddʒine] SF nosiness

curio'sare /72/ VI to look round, wander round; (*tra libri*) to browse; **~ nei negozi** to look *o* wander round the shops; **~ nelle faccende altrui** to poke one's nose into other people's affairs

curiosità SF INV curiosity; (*cosa rara*) curio, curiosity

curi'oso, -a AG (*che vuol sapere*) curious, inquiring; (*ficcanaso*) curious, inquisitive; (*bizzarro*) strange, curious ▶ SM/F busybody, nosy parker; **essere ~ di** to be curious about; **una folla di curiosi** a crowd of onlookers

cur'riculum SM INV: **~ (vitae)** curriculum vitae

cur'sore SM (*Inform*) cursor

'curva SF curve; (*stradale*) bend, curve

cur'vare /72/ VT to bend ▶ VI (*veicolo*) to take a bend; (*strada*) to bend, curve ◼ **curvarsi** VPR to bend; (*legno*) to warp

'curvo, -a AG curved; (*piegato*) bent

'curvy ['kervi] AG INV curvy, curvaceous

CUS SIGLA M = **Centro Universitario Sportivo**

cusci'netto [kuʃʃi'netto] SM pad; (*Tecn*) bearing ▶ AG INV: **stato ~** buffer state; **~ a sfere** ball bearing

cu'scino [kuʃ'ʃino] SM cushion; (*guanciale*) pillow

'cuspide SF (*Archit*) spire

cus'tode SMF (*di museo*) keeper, custodian; (*di parco*) warden; (*di casa*) concierge; (*di fabbrica, carcere*) guard

cus'todia SF care; (*Dir*) custody; (*astuccio*) case, holder; **avere qc in ~** to look after sth; **dare qc in ~ a qn** to entrust sth to sb's care; **agente di ~** prison warder; **~ delle carceri** prison security; **~ cautelare** (*Dir*) remand

custo'dire /55/ VT (*conservare*) to keep; (*assistere*) to look after, take care of; (*fare la guardia*) to guard

customiz'zare [kustomid'dzare] /72/ VT (*Inform*) to customize

'cute SF (*Anat*) skin

cu'ticola SF cuticle

C.V. ABBR (= *cavallo vapore*) h.p.

c.v.d. ABBR (= *come volevasi dimostrare*) QED (= *quod erat demonstrandum*)

c.vo ABBR = **corsivo**

cyberat'tacco [tʃiberat'takko] SM cyberattack

cyberbul'lismo [tʃiberbu'lizmo] SM cyberbullying

cyberca'ffè [tʃiberka'fe] SM INV cybercafé

cyber'nauta, -i, -e SM/F internet surfer

cybersicu'rezza [tʃibersiku'rettsa] SF cybersecurity

cyber'spazio SM cyberspace

cy'clette® [si'klɛt] SF INV exercise bike

CZ SIGLA = **Catanzaro**

Dd

D¹, d [di] SM O F INV (*lettera*) D, d; **D come Domo-dossola** ≈ D for David (BRIT), D for Dog (US)

D² ABBR (= *destra*) R; (*Ferr*) = **diretto**

---

da

(*da + il* = **dal**, *da + lo* = **dallo**, *da + l'* = **dall'**, *da + la* = **dalla**, *da + i* = **dai**, *da + gli* = **dagli**, *da + le* = **dalle**)
PREP **1** (*agente*) by; **dipinto da un grande artista** painted by a great artist
2 (*causa*) with; **tremare dalla paura** to tremble with fear
3 (*stato in luogo*) at; **abito da lui** I'm living at his house *o* with him; **sono dal giornalaio** I'm at the newsagent's; **era da Francesco** she was at Francesco's (house)
4 (*moto a luogo*) to; (*moto per luogo*) through; **vado da Pietro/dal giornalaio** I'm going to Pietro's (house)/to the newsagent's; **sono passati dalla finestra** they came in through the window
5 (*provenienza, allontanamento*) from; **da ... a** from ... to; **arrivare/partire da Milano** to arrive/depart from Milan; **scendere dal treno/dalla macchina** to get off the train/out of the car; **viene da una famiglia povera** he comes from a poor background; **viene dalla Scozia** he comes from Scotland; **ti chiamo da una cabina** I'm phoning from a call box; **si trova a 5 km da qui** it's 5 km from here
6 (*tempo: durata*) for; (: *a partire da: nel passato*) since; (: *nel futuro*) from; **vivo qui da un anno** I've been living here for a year; **è dalle 3 che ti aspetto** I've been waiting for you since 3 (o'clock); **da mattina a sera** from morning till night; **da oggi in poi** from today onwards; **da bambino** as a child, when I (*o* he *etc*) was a child
7 (*modo, maniera*) like; **comportarsi da uomo** to behave like a man; **l'ho fatto da me** I did it (by) myself; **non è da lui** it's not like him
8 (*descrittivo*): **una macchina da corsa** a racing car; **è una cosa da poco** it's nothing special; **una ragazza dai capelli biondi** a girl with blonde hair; **sordo da un orecchio** deaf in one ear; **abbigliamento da uomo** menswear; **un vestito da 100 euro** a 100 euro dress; **qualcosa da bere/mangiare** something to drink/eat

---

La preposizione **da**, nella domanda relativa alla provenienza, si traduce **from**, che si mette al fondo.
Da dove vieni? **Where do you come from?**
Quando *da* si riferisce a un'azione, iniziata nel passato e che ancora continua, si usa il verbo al passato. Si traduce con **for** se la durata è vaga come in: *Studia italiano da 5 anni.* **She's been learning Italian for five years**.
Se invece il momento in cui l'azione è ben definito, si traduce con **since**.
Sono qua dall'inizio di giugno. **I've been here since the beginning of June.**
Per tradurre *da quanto (tempo)* si usa **how long** e il verbo al passato.
Da quanto sei qui? **How long have you been here?**

---

dà VB *vedi* **dare**

dab'bene AG INV honest, decent

'Dacca SF Dacca

dac'capo, da 'capo AV (*di nuovo*) (once) again; (*dal principio*) all over again, from the beginning

dacché [dak'ke] CONG since

'dado SM (*da gioco*) dice *o* die; (*Cuc*) stock cube (BRIT), bouillon cube (US); (*Tecn*) (screw) nut ■ **dadi** SMPL (game of) dice; **giocare a dadi** to play dice

daf'fare, da 'fare SM work, toil; **avere un gran ~** to be very busy

'dagli ['daʎʎi], **'dai** PREP + DET *vedi* **da**

'daino SM (fallow) deer inv; (*pelle*) buckskin

Da'kar SF Dakar

dal¹ PREP + DET *vedi* **da**

dal² ABBR (= *decalitro*) dal

dall', 'dalla, 'dalle, 'dallo PREP + DET *vedi* **da**

dal'tonico, -a, -ci, -che AG colour-blind (BRIT), colorblind (US)

dam ABBR (= *decametro*) dam

'dama SF lady; (*nei balli*) partner; (*gioco*) draughts sg (BRIT), checkers sg (US); **far ~** (*nel gioco*) to make a crown; **~ di compagnia** lady's companion; **~ di corte** lady-in-waiting

Da'masco SF Damascus

dami'gella [dami'dʒɛlla] SF (*Storia*) damsel;

(: *titolo*) mistress; **~ d'onore** (*di sposa*) bridesmaid

damigi'ana [dami'dʒana] SF demijohn

dam'meno AG INV: **per non essere ~ di qn** so as not to be outdone by sb

DAMS SIGLA M: **Discipline delle Arti, della Musica, dello Spettacolo** *study of the performing arts*

da'naro SM = **denaro**

dana'roso, -a AG wealthy

da'nese AG Danish ▶ SMF Dane ▶ SM (*Ling*) Danish

Dani'marca SF: **la ~** Denmark

dan'nare /72/ VT (*Rel*) to damn ▪ **dannarsi** VPR: **dannarsi per** (*fig: tormentarsi*) to be worried to death (by); **far ~ qn** to drive sb mad; **dannarsi l'anima per qc** (*affannarsi*) to work o.s. to death for sth; (*tormentarsi*) to worry o.s. to death over sth

dan'nato, -a AG damned

dannazi'one [dannat'tsjone] SF damnation

danneggi'are [danned'dʒare] /62/ VT to damage; (*rovinare*) to spoil; (*nuocere*) to harm; **la parte danneggiata** (*Dir*) the injured party

'danno VB *vedi* **dare** ▶ SM damage; (*a persona*) harm, injury ▪ **danni** SMPL (*Dir*) damages; **a ~ di qn** to sb's detriment; **chiedere/risarcire i danni** to sue for/pay damages

dan'noso, -a AG: **~ (a o per)** harmful (to), bad (for)

dan'tesco, -a, -schi, -sche AG Dantesque; **l'opera dantesca** Dante's work

Da'nubio SM: **il ~** the Danube

'danza ['dantsa] SF: **la ~** dancing; **una ~** a dance

dan'zante [dan'tsante] AG dancing; **serata ~** dance

dan'zare [dan'tsare] /72/ VT, VI to dance

danza'tore, -'trice [dantsa'tore] SM/F dancer

dapper'tutto AV everywhere

dap'poco AG INV inept; worthless

dap'prima AV at first

Darda'nelli SMPL: **i ~** the Dardanelles

'dardo SM dart

'dare /33/ SM (*Comm*) debit ▶ VT to give; (*produrre: frutti, suono*) to produce ▶ VI (*guardare*): **~ su** to look (out) onto ▪ **darsi** VPR: **darsi a** to dedicate o.s. to; **quanti anni mi dai?** how old do you think I am?; **danno ancora quel film?** is that film still showing?; **~ da mangiare a qn** to give sb something to eat; **~ per certo qc** to consider sth certain; **~ ad intendere a qn che ...** to lead sb to believe that ...; **~ per morto qn** to give sb up for dead; **~ qc per scontato** to take sth for granted; **darsi ammalato** to report sick; **darsi alla bella vita** to have a good time; **darsi al bere** to take to drink; **darsi al commercio** to go into business; **darsi da fare per fare qc** to go to a lot of bother to do sth; **darsi per vinto** to give

in; **può darsi** maybe, perhaps; **si dà il caso che ...** it so happens that ...; **darsela a gambe** to take to one's heels; **il ~ e l'avere** (*Econ*) debits and credits *pl*

Dar-es-Sa'laam SF Dar-es-Salaam

'darsena SF dock

'data SF date; **in ~ da destinarsi** on a date still to be announced; **in ~ odierna** as of today; **amicizia di lunga o vecchia ~** long-standing friendship; **~ di emissione** date of issue; **~ di nascita** date of birth; **~ di scadenza** expiry date; **~ limite d'utilizzo o di consumo** (*Comm*) best-before date

'data 'base SM INV (*Inform*) database

da'tare /72/ VT to date ▶ VI: **~ da** to date from

da'tato, -a AG dated

da'tivo SM dative

'dato, -a AG (*stabilito*) given ▶ SM datum ▪ **dati** SMPL data *pl*; **~ che** given that; **in dati casi** in certain cases; **è un ~ di fatto** it's a fact; **dati sensibili** sense data

da'tore, -'trice SM/F: **~ di lavoro** employer

'dattero SM date (*Bot*)

dattilogra'fare /72/ VT to type

dattilogra'fia SF typing

datti'lografo, -a SM/F typist

dattilos'critto SM typescript

da'vanti AV in front; (*dirimpetto*) opposite ▶ AG INV front ▶ SM front; **~ a** *prep* in front of; (*dirimpetto a*) facing, opposite; (*in presenza di*) before, in front of

davan'zale [davan'tsale] SM windowsill

da'vanzo, d'a'vanzo [da'vantso] AV more than enough

dav'vero AV really, indeed; **dico ~** I mean it

dazi'ario, -a [dat'tsjarjo] AG excise *cpd*

'dazio ['dattsjo] SM (*somma*) duty; (*luogo*) customs *pl*; **~ d'importazione** import duty

db ABBR (= *decibel*) dB

DC SIGLA F (*former political party*) = **la Democrazia Cristiana**

d.C. ABBR (= *dopo Cristo*) A.D.

D.D.T. ABBR M (= *dicloro-difenil-tricloroetano*) D.D.T.

'dea SF goddess

'debbo *ecc* VB *vedi* **dovere**

debel'lare /72/ VT to overcome, conquer

debili'tare /72/ VT to debilitate

debita'mente AV duly, properly

'debito, -a AG due, proper ▶ SM debt; (*Comm: dare*) debit; **a tempo ~** at the right time; **portare a ~ di qn** to debit sb with; **~ consolidato** consolidated debt; **~ d'imposta** tax liability; **~ pubblico** national debt

debi'tore, -'trice SM/F debtor

'debole AG weak, feeble; (*suono*) faint; (*luce*) dim ▶ SM weakness

debo'lezza [debo'lettsa] SF weakness

debut'tante SMF (gen) beginner, novice; (Teat) actor (actress) (at the beginning of his (or her) career)

debut'tare /72/ VI to make one's début

de'butto SM début

'decade SF period of ten days

deca'dente AG decadent

deca'denza [deka'dɛntsa] SF decline; (Dir) loss, forfeiture

deca'dere /18/ VI to decline

deca'duto, -a AG (persona) impoverished; (norma) lapsed

decaffei'nato, -a AG decaffeinated

de'calogo SM (fig) rulebook

de'cano SM (Rel) dean

decan'tare /72/ VT (virtù, bravura ecc) to praise; (persona) to sing the praises of

decapi'tare /72/ VT to decapitate, behead

decappot'tabile AG, SF convertible

dece'duto, -a [detʃe'duto] AG deceased

decele'rare [detʃele'rare] /72/ VT, VI to decelerate, slow down

decen'nale [detʃen'nale] AG (che dura 10 anni) ten-year cpd; (che ricorre ogni 10 anni) ten-yearly, every ten years ▶ SM (ricorrenza) tenth anniversary

de'cenne [de'tʃɛnne] AG: **un bambino ~** a ten-year-old child, a child of ten

de'cennio [de'tʃɛnnjo] SM decade

de'cente [de'tʃɛnte] AG decent, respectable, proper; (accettabile) satisfactory, decent

decentraliz'zare [detʃentralid'dzare] /72/ VT (Amm) to decentralize

decentra'mento [detʃentra'mento] SM decentralization

decen'trare [detʃen'trare] /72/ VT to decentralize, move out of o away from the centre

de'cenza [de'tʃɛntsa] SF decency, propriety

de'cesso [de'tʃɛsso] SM death; **atto di ~** death certificate

de'cidere [de'tʃidere] /34/ VI to decide, make up one's mind ▶ VT: **~ qc** to decide on sth; (questione, lite) to settle sth ■ **decidersi** VPR: **decidersi (a fare)** to decide (to do), make up one's mind (to do); **~ di fare/che** to decide to do/that; **~ di qc** (cosa) to determine sth

deci'frare [detʃi'frare] /72/ VT to decode; (fig) to decipher, make out

de'cilitro [de'tʃilitro] SM decilitre (BRIT), deciliter (US)

deci'male [detʃi'male] AG decimal

deci'mare [detʃi'mare] /72/ VT to decimate

de'cimetro [de'tʃimetro] SM decimetre

'decimo, -a ['dɛtʃimo] NUM tenth

de'cina [de'tʃina] SF ten; (circa dieci): **una ~ (di)** about ten

de'cisi ecc [de'tʃizi] VB vedi **decidere**

decisio'nale [detʃizjo'nale] AG decision-making cpd

decisi'one [detʃi'zjone] SF decision; **prendere una ~** to make a decision; **con ~** decisively, resolutely

deci'sivo, -a [detʃi'zivo] AG (gen) decisive; (fattore) deciding

de'ciso, -a [de'tʃizo] PP di **decidere** ▶ AG (persona, carattere) determined; (tono) firm, resolute

declas'sare /72/ VT to downgrade; to lower in status; **1ª declassata** (Ferr) first-class carriage which may be used by second-class passengers

decli'nare /72/ VI (pendio) to slope down; (fig: diminuire) to decline; (: tramontare) to set, go down ▶ VT to decline; **~ le proprie generalità** (fig) to give one's particulars; **~ ogni responsabilità** to disclaim all responsibility

declinazi'one [deklinat'tsjone] SF (Ling) declension

de'clino SM decline

de'clivio SM (downward) slope

decodifi'care /20/ VT to decode

decodifica'tore SM (Tel) decoder

decol'lare /72/ VI (Aer) to take off

décolleté [dekol'te] AG INV (abito) low-necked, low-cut ▶ SM (di abito) low neckline; (di donna) cleavage

de'collo SM take-off

decolo'rare /72/ VT to bleach

decom'porre /77/ VT, **decom'porsi** VPR to decompose

decomposizi'one [dekompozit'tsjone] SF decomposition

decom'posto, -a PP di **decomporre**

decompressi'one SF decompression

deconge'lare [dekondʒe'lare] /72/ VT to defrost

decongestio'nare [dekondʒestjo'nare] /72/ VT (Med, traffico) to relieve congestion in

deco'rare /72/ VT to decorate

decora'tivo, -a AG decorative

decora'tore, -'trice SM/F (interior) decorator

decorazi'one [dekorat'tsjone] SF decoration

de'coro SM decorum

deco'roso, -a AG decorous, dignified

decor'renza [dekor'rɛntsa] SF: **con ~ da** (as) from

de'correre /28/ VI to pass, elapse; (avere effetto) to run, have effect

de'corso, -a PP di **decorrere** ▶ SM (evoluzione: anche Med) course

de'crebbi ecc VB vedi **decrescere**

de'crepito, -a AG decrepit

de'crescere [de'kreʃʃere] /30/ VI (diminuire) to decrease, diminish; (acque) to subside, go down; (prezzi) to go down decresci'uto, -a [dekreʃ'ʃuto] PP di decrescere

decre'tare /72/ VT (norma) to decree; (mobilitazione) to order; ~ lo stato d'emergenza to declare a state of emergency; ~ la nomina di qn to decide on the appointment of sb

de'creto SM decree; ~ legge decree with the force of law; ~ di sfratto eviction order

decrip'tare [dekrip'tare] VT to decrypt

decur'tare /72/ VT (debito, somma) to reduce

decurtazi'one [dekurtat'tsjone] SF reduction

'dedalo SM maze, labyrinth

'dedica, -che SF dedication

dedi'care /20/ VT to dedicate ■ dedicarsi VPR: dedicarsi a (votarsi) to devote o.s. to

dediche'rò ecc [dedike'rɔ] VB vedi dedicare

'dedito, -a AG: ~ a (studio ecc) dedicated o devoted to; (vizio) addicted to

de'dotto, -a PP di dedurre

de'duco ecc VB vedi dedurre

de'durre /90/ VT (concludere) to deduce; (defalcare) to deduct

de'dussi ecc VB vedi dedurre

deduzi'one [dedut'tsjone] SF deduction

defal'care /20/ VT to deduct

defenes'trare /72/ VT to throw out of the window; (fig) to remove from office

defe'rente AG respectful, deferential

defe'rire /55/ VT (Dir): ~ a to refer to

defezi'one [defet'tsjone] SF defection, desertion

defici'ente [defi'tʃɛnte] AG (insufficiente) insufficient; ~ di (mancante) deficient in ▶ SMF (peg: cretino) idiot

defici'enza [defi'tʃɛntsa] SF deficiency; (carenza) shortage; (fig: lacuna) weakness

'deficit ['dɛfitʃit] SM INV (Econ) deficit

defi'nire /55/ VT to define; (risolvere) to settle; (questione) to finalize

defini'tivo, -a AG definitive, final ▶ SF: in definitiva (dopotutto) when all is said and done; (dunque) hence

defi'nito, -a AG definite; ben ~ clear, clear cut

definizi'one [definit'tsjone] SF (gen) definition; (di disputa, vertenza) settlement; (di tempi, obiettivi) establishment

deflagrazi'one [deflagrat'tsjone] SF explosion

deflazi'one [deflat'tsjone] SF (Econ) deflation

deflet'tore SM (Aut) quarterlight (BRIT), deflector (US)

deflu'ire /55/ VI: ~ da (liquido) to flow away from; (fig: capitali) to flow out of

de'flusso SM (della marea) ebb

deforesta'zione [deforestat'tsjone] SF deforestation

defor'mare /72/ VT (alterare) to put out of shape; (corpo) to deform; (pensiero, fatto) to distort ■ deformarsi VPR to lose its shape

deformazi'one [deformat'tsjone] SF (Med) deformation; questa è ~ professionale! that's force of habit because of your (o his etc) job!

de'forme AG deformed; disfigured

deformità SF INV deformity

defrau'dare /72/ VT: ~ qn di qc to defraud sb of sth, cheat sb out of sth

de'funto, -a AG late cpd ▶ SM/F deceased

degene'rare [dedʒene'rare] /72/ VI to degenerate

degenerazi'one [dedʒenerat'tsjone] SF degeneration

de'genere [de'dʒɛnere] AG degenerate

de'gente [de'dʒɛnte] SMF bedridden person; (ricoverato in ospedale) in-patient

de'genza [de'dʒɛntsa] SF confinement to bed; ~ ospedaliera period in hospital

'degli ['deʎʎi] PREP + DET vedi di

deglu'tire /55/ VT to swallow

de'gnare [deɲ'ɲare] /15/ VT: ~ qn della propria presenza to honour sb with one's presence ■ degnarsi VPR: degnarsi di fare qc to deign o condescend to do sth; non mi ha degnato di uno sguardo he wouldn't even look at me

'degno, -a ['deɲɲo] AG dignified; ~ di worthy of; ~ di lode praiseworthy

degra'dare /72/ VT (Mil) to demote; (privare della dignità) to degrade ■ degradarsi VPR to demean o.s

de'grado SM: ~ urbano urban decline

degus'tare /72/ VT to sample, taste

degustazi'one [degustat'tsjone] SF sampling, tasting; ~ di vini (locale) specialist wine bar; ~ di caffè (locale) specialist coffee shop

'dei SMPL di dio ▶ PREP + DET vedi di

del PREP + DET vedi di

dela'tore, -'trice SM/F police informer

delazi'one [delat'tsjone] SF informing

'delega, -ghe SF (procura) proxy; per ~ notarile = through a solicitor (BRIT) o lawyer

dele'gare /80/ VT to delegate

dele'gato SM delegate

delegazi'one [delegat'tsjone] SF delegation

deleghe'rò ecc [delege'rɔ] VB vedi delegare

dele'terio, -a AG damaging; (per salute ecc) harmful

del'fino SM (Zool) dolphin; (Storia) dauphin; (fig) probable successor

'Delhi ['dɛli] SF Delhi

de'libera SF decision

delibe'rare /72/ VT to come to a decision on ▶ VI (Dir): ~ (su qc) to rule (on sth)

delica'tezza [delika'tettsa] SF delicacy; frailty; thoughtfulness; tactfulness

deli'cato, -a AG delicate; (*salute*) delicate, frail; (*fig: gentile*) thoughtful, considerate; (: *che dimostra tatto*) tactful

delimi'tare /72/ VT (*anche fig*) to delimit

deline'are /72/ VT to outline ■ **delinearsi** VPR to be outlined; (*fig*) to emerge

delin'quente SMF criminal, delinquent; **~ abituale** regular offender, habitual offender

delin'quenza [delin'kwɛntsa] SF criminality, delinquency; **~ minorile** juvenile delinquency

de'liquio SM (*Med*) swoon; **cadere in ~** to swoon

deli'rante AG (*Med*) delirious; (*fig: folla*) frenzied; (: *discorso, mente*) insane

deli'rare /72/ VI to be delirious, rave; (*fig*) to rave

de'lirio SM delirium; (*ragionamento insensato*) raving; (*fig*): **andare/mandare in ~** to go/send into a frenzy

de'litto SM crime; **~ d'onore** crime committed to avenge one's honour

delittu'oso, -a AG criminal

de'lizia [de'littsja] SF delight

delizi'are [delit'tsjare] /19/ VT to delight ■ **deliziarsi** VPR: **deliziarsi di qc/a fare qc** to take delight in sth/in doing sth

delizi'oso, -a [delit'tsjoso] AG delightful; (*cibi*) delicious

dell', 'della, 'delle, 'dello PREP + DET *vedi* **di**

'delta SM INV delta

delta'plano SM hang-glider; **volo col ~** hang-gliding

delucidazi'one [delutʃidat'tsjone] SF clarification *no pl*

delu'dente AG disappointing

de'ludere /35/ VT to disappoint

delusi'one SF disappointment

de'luso, -a PP *di* **deludere** ▶ AG disappointed

dema'gogico, -a, -ci, -che [dema'gɔdʒiko] AG popularity-seeking, demagogic

dema'gogo, -ghi SM demagogue

de'manio SM state property

de'mente AG (*Med*) demented, mentally deranged; (*fig*) crazy, mad

de'menza [de'mɛntsa] SF dementia; madness; **~ senile** senile dementia

demenzi'ale [demen'tsjale] AG (*fig*) off-the-wall

'demmo VB *vedi* **dare**

demo'cratico, -a, -ci, -che AG democratic

democra'zia [demokrat'tsia] SF democracy; **la D~ Cristiana** the Christian Democrat Party

democristi'ano, -a AG, SM/F Christian Democrat

demogra'fia SF demography

demo'grafico, -a, -ci, -che AG demographic; **incremento ~** increase in population

demo'lire /55/ VT to demolish

demolizi'one [demolit'tsjone] SF demolition

'demone SM demon

de'monio SM demon, devil; **il D~** the Devil

demoniz'zare [demonid'dzare] /72/ VT to make a monster of

demonizzazi'one [demoniddzat'tsjone] SF demonizing, demonization

demoraliz'zare [demoralid'dzare] /72/ VT to demoralize ■ **demoralizzarsi** VPR to become demoralized

de'mordere /64/ VI: **non ~ (da)** to refuse to give up

demoti'vare /72/ VT: **~ qn** to take away sb's motivation

demoti'vato, -a AG unmotivated, lacking motivation

de'naro SM money ■ **denari** SMPL (*Carte*) suit in Neapolitan pack of cards

denatu'rato, -a AG *vedi* **alcool**

deni'grare /72/ VT to denigrate, run down

denomi'nare /72/ VT to name ■ **denominarsi** VPR to be named o called

denomina'tore SM (*Mat*) denominator

denominazi'one [denominat'tsjone] SF name; denomination; **~ di origine controllata** label guaranteeing the quality and origin of a wine

deno'tare /72/ VT to denote, indicate

densità SF INV density; (*di nebbia*) thickness, denseness; **ad alta/bassa ~ di popolazione** densely/sparsely populated

'denso, -a AG thick, dense

den'tale AG dental

den'tario, -a AG dental

denta'tura SF set of teeth, teeth *pl*; (*Tecn: di ruota*) serration

'dente SM tooth; (*di forchetta*) prong; (*Geo: cima*) jagged peak; **al ~** (*Cuc: pasta*) al dente; **mettere i denti** to teethe; **mettere qc sotto i denti** to have a bite to eat; **avere il ~ avvelenato contro** o **con qn** to bear sb a grudge; **~ di leone** (*Bot*) dandelion; **denti del giudizio** wisdom teeth; **denti da latte** milk teeth

'dentice ['dɛntitʃe] SM (*Zool*) sea bream

denti'era SF (set of) false teeth *pl*

denti'fricio [denti'fritʃo] SM toothpaste

den'tista, -i, -e SM/F dentist

'dentro AV inside; (*in casa*) indoors; (*fig: nell'intimo*) inwardly ▶ PREP: **~ (a)** in; **piegato in ~** folded over; **qui/là ~** in here/there; **~ di sé** (*pensare, brontolare*) to oneself; **tenere tutto ~** to keep everything bottled up (inside o.s.); **darci ~** (*fig: col*) to slog away, work hard

denucleariz'zato, -a [denuklearid'dzato] AG denuclearized, nuclear-free

denu'dare /72/ VT (*persona*) to strip; (*parte del corpo*) to bare ■ **denudarsi** VPR to strip

de'nuncia [de'nuntʃa] (pl -ce o -cie), **de'nunzia** [de'nuntsja] SF denunciation; declaration; **fare una ~** o **sporgere ~ contro qn** (Dir) to report sb to the police; **~ del reddito** (income) tax return

denunci'are [denun'tʃare] /14/, **denunzi'are** [denun'tsjare] VT to denounce; (dichiarare) to declare; **~ qn/qc (alla polizia)** to report sb/sth to the police

denu'trito, -a AG undernourished

denutrizi'one [denutrit'tsjone] SF malnutrition

deodo'rante SM deodorant

deontolo'gia [deontolo'dʒia] SF (professionale) professional code of conduct

depenalizzazi'one [depenaliddzat'tsjone] SF decriminalization

dépen'dance [depã'dãs] SF INV outbuilding

depe'ribile AG perishable; **merce ~** perishables pl, perishable goods pl

deperi'mento SM (di persona) wasting away; (di merci) deterioration

depe'rire /55/ VI to waste away

depi'lare /72/ VT to depilate ▪ **depilarsi** VPR: **depilarsi (le gambe)** (con rasoio) to shave (one's legs); (con ceretta) to wax (one's legs)

depila'torio, -a AG hair-removing cpd, depilatory ▸ SM hair remover, depilatory

depilazi'one [depilat'tsjone] SF hair removal, depilation

depis'taggio [depis'taddʒo] SM diversion

depis'tare /72/ VT to set on the wrong track

dépli'ant [depli'ã] SM INV leaflet; (opuscolo) brochure

deplo'rare /72/ VT to deplore; to lament

deplo'revole AG deplorable

de'pone, de'pongo ecc VB vedi **deporre**

de'porre /77/ VT (depositare) to put down; (rimuovere: da una carica) to remove; (: re) to depose; (Dir) to testify; **~ le armi** (Mil) to lay down arms; **~ le uova** to lay eggs

depor'tare /72/ VT to deport

depor'tato, -a SM/F deportee

deportazi'one [deportat'tsjone] SF deportation

de'posi ecc VB vedi **deporre**

deposi'tante SM (Comm) depositor

deposi'tare /72/ VT (gen, Geo, Econ) to deposit; (lasciare) to leave; (merci) to store ▪ **depositarsi** VPR (sabbia, polvere) to settle

deposi'tario SM (Comm) depository

de'posito SM deposit; (luogo) warehouse; depot; (: Mil) depot; **~ bagagli** left-luggage office; **~ di munizioni** ammunition dump

deposizi'one [depozit'tsjone] SF deposition; (da una carica) removal; **rendere una falsa ~** to perjure o.s.

de'posto, -a PP di **deporre**

depra'vare /72/ VT to corrupt, pervert

depra'vato, -a AG depraved ▸ SM/F degenerate

depre'care /20/ VT to deprecate, deplore

depre'dare /72/ VT to rob, plunder

depressi'one SF depression; **area** o **zona di ~** (Meteor) area of low pressure; (Econ) depressed area

de'presso, -a PP di **deprimere** ▸ AG depressed

deprezza'mento [deprettsa'mento] SM depreciation

deprez'zare [depret'tsare] /72/ VT (Econ) to depreciate

depri'mente AG depressing

de'primere /50/ VT to depress

depu'rare /72/ VT to purify

depura'tore SM: **~ d'acqua** water purifier; **~ di gas** scrubber

depu'tato, -a SM/F (Pol) deputy, ≈ Member of Parliament (BRIT), ≈ Congressman(-woman) (US); vedi anche **Camera dei Deputati**

deputazi'one [deputat'tsjone] SF deputation; (Pol) position of deputy, ≈ parliamentary seat (BRIT), ≈ seat in Congress (US)

deraglia'mento [deraʎʎa'mento] SM derailment

deragli'are [deraʎ'ʎare] /27/ VI to be derailed; **far ~** to derail

dera'pare /72/ VI (veicolo) to skid; (Sci) to sideslip

derattizzazi'one [derattiddzat'tsjone] SF rodent control

deregolamen'tare /72/ VT to deregulate

deregolamentazi'one [deregolamentat'tsjone] SF deregulation

dere'litto, -a AG derelict

dere'tano SM (col) bottom, buttocks pl

de'ridere /89/ VT to mock, deride

de'risi ecc VB vedi **deridere**

derisi'one SF derision, mockery

de'riso, -a PP di **deridere**

deri'sorio, -a AG (gesto, tono) mocking

de'riva SF (Naut, Aer) drift; (dispositivo: Aer) fin; (: Naut) centre-board (BRIT), centerboard (US); **andare alla ~** (anche fig) to drift

deri'vare /72/ VI: **~ da** to derive from ▸ VT to derive; (corso d'acqua) to divert

deri'vato, -a AG derived ▸ SM (Chim, Ling) derivative; (prodotto) by-product

derivazi'one [derivat'tsjone] SF derivation; diversion

derma'tite SF dermatitis

dermatolo'gia [dermatolo'dʒia] SF dermatology

derma'tologo, -a, -gi, -ghe SM/F dermatologist

dermoprotet'tivo, -a AG (*crema, azione*) protecting the skin

'deroga, -ghe SF (special) dispensation; **in ~ a** as a (special) dispensation to

dero'gare /80/ VI: **~ a** (*Dir*) to repeal in part

der'rate SFPL commodities; **~ alimentari** foodstuffs

deru'bare /72/ VT to rob

des'critto, -a PP *di* **descrivere**

des'crivere /105/ VT to describe

descrizi'one [deskrit'tsjone] SF description

de'serto, -a AG deserted ▶ SM (*Geo*) desert; **isola deserta** desert island

deside'rabile AG desirable

deside'rare /72/ VT to want, wish for; (*sessualmente*) to desire; **~ fare/che qn faccia** to want *o* wish to do/sb to do; **desidera fare una passeggiata?** would you like to go for a walk?; **farsi ~** (*fare il prezioso*) to play hard to get; (*farsi aspettare*) to take one's time; **lascia molto a ~** it leaves a lot to be desired

desi'derio SM wish; (*più intenso, carnale*) desire

deside'roso, -a AG: **~ di** longing *o* eager for

desi'gnare [desiɲ'ɲare] /15/ VT to designate, appoint; (*data*) to fix; **la vittima designata** the intended victim

designazi'one [desiɲɲat'tsjone] SF designation, appointment

desi'nare /72/ VI to dine, have dinner ▶ SM dinner

desi'nenza [dezi'nɛntsa] SF (*Ling*) ending, inflexion

de'sistere /11/ VI: **~ da** to give up, desist from

desis'tito, -a PP *di* **desistere**

'desktop ['desktop] SM INV (*Inform*) desktop

deso'lante AG distressing

deso'lato, -a AG (*paesaggio*) desolate; (*persona: spiacente*) sorry

desolazi'one [dezolat'tsjone] SF desolation

'despota, -i SM despot

'dessi *ecc* VB *vedi* **dare**

destabiliz'zare [destabilid'dzare] /72/ VT to destabilize

des'tare /72/ VT to wake (up); (*fig*) to awaken, arouse ▪ **destarsi** VPR to wake (up)

'deste *ecc* VB *vedi* **dare**

desti'nare /72/ VT to destine; (*assegnare*) to appoint, assign; (*indirizzare*) to address; **~ qc a qn** to intend to give sth to sb, intend sb to have sth

destina'tario, -a SM/F (*di lettera*) addressee; (*di merce*) consignee; (*di mandato*) payee

destinazi'one [destinat'tsjone] SF destination; (*uso*) purpose

des'tino SM destiny, fate

destitu'ire /55/ VT to dismiss, remove

destituzi'one [destitut'tsjone] SF dismissal, removal

'desto, -a AG (wide) awake

'destra SF *vedi* **destro**

destreggi'arsi [destred'dʒarsi] /62/ VPR to manoeuvre (*Brit*), maneuver (*US*)

des'trezza [des'trettsa] SF skill, dexterity

'destro, -a AG right, right-hand; (*abile*) skilful (*Brit*), skillful (*US*), adroit ▶ SF (*mano*) right hand; (*parte*) right (side); (*Pol*): **la destra** the right ▶ SM (*Pugilato*) right; **a destra** (*essere*) on the right; (*andare*) to the right; **tenere la destra** to keep to the right

de'sumere /12/ VT (*dedurre*) to infer, deduce; (*trarre: informazioni*) to obtain

de'sunto, -a PP *di* **desumere**

detas'sare /72/ VT to remove the duty (*o* tax) from

dete'nere /121/ VT (*incarico, primato*) to hold; (*proprietà*) to have, possess; (*in prigione*) to detain, hold

de'tengo, de'tenni *ecc* VB *vedi* **detenere**

deten'tivo, -a AG: **mandato ~** imprisonment order; **pena detentiva** prison sentence

deten'tore, -'trice SM/F (*di titolo, primato ecc*) holder

dete'nuto, -a SM/F prisoner

detenzi'one [deten'tsjone] SF holding; possession; detention

deter'gente [deter'dʒɛnte] AG (*crema, latte*) cleansing ▶ SM cleanser

de'tergere [de'tɛrdʒere] /111/ VT (*gen*) to clean; (*pelle, viso*) to cleanse; (*sudore*) to wipe (away)

deteriora'mento SM: **~ (di)** deterioration (in)

deterio'rare /72/ VT to damage ▪ **deteriorarsi** VPR to deteriorate

deteri'ore AG (*merce*) second-rate; (*significato*) pejorative; (*tradizione letteraria*) lesser, minor

determi'nante AG decisive, determining

determi'nare /72/ VT to determine

determina'tivo, -a AG determining; **articolo ~** (*Ling*) definite article

determi'nato, -a AG (*gen*) certain; (*particolare*) specific; (*risoluto*) determined, resolute

determinazi'one [determinat'tsjone] SF determination; (*decisione*) decision

deter'rente AG, SM deterrent

deter'rò *ecc* VB *vedi* **detenere**

deter'sivo SM detergent; (*per bucato: in polvere*) washing powder (*Brit*), soap powder

de'terso, -a PP *di* **detergere**

detes'tare /72/ VT to detest, hate

deti'ene *ecc* VB *vedi* **detenere**

deto'nare /72/ VI to detonate

detona'tore SM detonator

detonazi'one [detonat'tsjone] SF (*di esplosivo*)

detonation, explosion; (*di arma*) bang; (*di motore*) pinking (BRIT), knocking

de'trae, de'traggo *ecc* VB *vedi* **detrarre**

de'trarre /123/ VT: ~ (da) to deduct (from), take away (from)

de'trassi *ecc* VB *vedi* **detrarre**

de'tratto, -a PP *di* **detrarre**

detrazi'one [detrat'tsjone] SF deduction; ~ d'imposta tax allowance

detri'mento SM detriment, harm; a ~ di to the detriment of

de'trito SM (*Geo*) detritus

detroniz'zare [detronid'dzare] /72/ VT to dethrone

'detta SF: a ~ di according to

dettagli'ante [dettaʎ'ʎante] SMF (*Comm*) retailer

dettagli'are [dettaʎ'ʎare] /27/ VT to detail, give full details of

dettagliata'mente [dettaʎʎata'mente] AV in detail

det'taglio [det'taʎʎo] SM detail; (*Comm*): il ~ retail; al ~ (*Comm*) retail; separately

det'tame SM dictate, precept

det'tare /72/ VT to dictate; ~ legge (*fig*) to lay down the law

det'tato SM dictation

detta'tura SF dictation

'detto, -a PP *di* dire ▶ AG (*soprannominato*) called, known as; (*già nominato*) above-mentioned ▶ SM saying; ~ fatto no sooner said than done; presto ~! it's easier said than done!

detur'pare /72/ VT to disfigure; (*moralmente*) to sully

devas'tante AG (*anche fig*) devastating

devas'tare /72/ VT to devastate; (*fig*) to ravage

devastazi'one [devastat'tsjone] SF devastation, destruction

devi'are /19/ VI: ~ (da) to turn off (from) ▶ VT to divert

devi'ato, -a AG (*fig: persona, organizzazione*) corrupt, bent (*col*)

deviazi'one [devjat'tsjone] SF (*anche Aut*) diversion; fare una ~ to make a detour

'devo *ecc* VB *vedi* **dovere**

devo'luto, -a PP *di* **devolvere**

devoluzi'one [devolut'tsjone] SF (*Dir*) devolution, transfer

de'volvere /94/ VT (*Dir*) to transfer, devolve; ~ qc in beneficenza to give sth to charity

de'voto, -a AG (*Rel*) devout, pious; (*affezionato*) devoted

devozi'one [devot'tsjone] SF devoutness; (*anche Rel*) devotion

dezip'pare [dedzip'pare] /72/ VT (*Inform*) to unzip

dg ABBR (= *decigrammo*) dg

---

di

(*di + il* = **del**, *di + lo* = **dello**, *di + l'* = **dell'**, *di + la* = **della**, *di + i* = **dei**, *di + gli* = **degli**, *di + le* = **delle**) PREP **1** (*possesso, specificazione*) of; (*composto da, scritto da*) by; la macchina di Paolo/di mio fratello Paolo's/my brother's car; un amico di mio fratello a friend of my brother's, one of my brother's friends; la grandezza della casa the size of the house; le foto delle vacanze the holiday photos; la città di Firenze the city of Florence; il nome di Maria the name Mary; un quadro di Botticelli a painting by Botticelli

2 (*caratterizzazione, misura*) of; una casa di mattoni a brick house, a house made of bricks; un orologio d'oro a gold watch; un bimbo di 3 anni a child of 3, a 3-year-old child; una trota di un chilo a trout weighing a kilo; una strada di 10 km a road 10 km long; un quadro di valore a valuable picture

3 (*causa, mezzo, modo*) with; tremare di paura to tremble with fear; morire di cancro to die of cancer; spalmare di burro to spread with butter

4 (*argomento*) about, of; discutere di sport to talk about sport; parlare di politica/lavoro to talk about politics/work

5 (*luogo: provenienza*) from; out of; essere di Roma to be from Rome; uscire di casa to come out of *o* leave the house

6 (*tempo*) in; d'estate/d'inverno in (the) summer/winter; di notte by night, at night; di mattina/sera in the morning/evening; di lunedì on Mondays; di ora in ora by the hour

7 (*partitivo*) of; alcuni di voi/noi some of you/us; il più bravo di tutti the best of all; il migliore del mondo the best in the world; non c'è niente di peggio there's nothing worse

8 (*paragone*) than; più veloce di me faster than me; guadagna meno di me he earns less than me

▶ DET (*una certa quantità di*) some; (: *negativo*) any; (: *interrogativo*) any; some; del pane (some) bread; delle caramelle (some) sweets; degli amici miei some friends of mine; vuoi del vino? do you want some *o* any wine?

dì SM day; buon dì! hallo!; a dì = addì

DIA SIGLA F = Direzione investigativa antimafia

dia'bete SM diabetes *sg*

dia'betico, -a, -ci, -che AG, SM/F diabetic

dia'bolico, -a, -ci, -che AG diabolical

di'acono SM (*Rel*) deacon

dia'dema, -i SM diadem; (*di donna*) tiara

di'afano, -a AG (*trasparente*) diaphanous; (*pelle*) transparent

dia'framma, -i SM (*divisione*) screen; (*Anat, Fot: contraccettivo*) diaphragm

di'agnosi [di'aɲɲozi] SF diagnosis *sg*

diagnosti'care [diaɲɲosti'kare] /20/ VT to diagnose

dia'gnostico, -a, -ci, -che [diaɲ'nɔstiko] AG diagnostic; **aiuti diagnostici** (*Inform*) debugging aids

diago'nale AG, SF diagonal

dia'gramma, -i SM diagram; ~ **a barre** bar chart; ~ **di flusso** flow chart

dialet'tale AG dialectal; **poesia** ~ poetry in dialect

dia'letto SM dialect

> In Italy the official language is Italian, but there are a large number of important and distinctive **dialetti** which many Italians use in their daily lives.

di'alisi SF dialysis *sg*

dialo'gante AG: **unità** ~ (*Inform*) interactive terminal

dialo'gare /80/ VI: ~ **(con)** to have a dialogue (with); (*conversare*) to converse (with) ▶ VT (*scena*) to write the dialogue for

di'alogo, -ghi SM dialogue

dia'mante SM diamond

di'ametro SM diameter

di'amine ESCL: **che ~ ...?** what on earth ...?

diapo'rama [djapo'rama] SM INV slide show

diaposi'tiva SF transparency, slide

di'aria SF daily (expense) allowance

di'ario SM diary; ~ **di bordo** (*Naut*) log(book); ~ **di classe** (*Ins*) class register; ~ **degli esami** (*Ins*) exam timetable

diar'rea SF diarrhoea

dia'triba SF diatribe

diavole'ria SF (*azione*) act of mischief; (*aggeggio*) weird contraption

di'avolo, -essa SM/F devil; **è un buon** ~ he's a good sort; **avere un** ~ **per capello** to be in a foul temper; **avere una fame/un freddo del** ~ to be ravenously hungry/frozen stiff; **mandare qn al** ~ (*col*) to tell sb to go to hell; **fare il** ~ **a quattro** to kick up a fuss

di'battere /1/ VT to debate, discuss ▪ **dibattersi** VPR to struggle

dibatti'mento SM (*dibattito*) debate, discussion; (*Dir*) hearing

di'battito SM debate, discussion

dic. ABBR (= *dicembre*) Dec

dicas'tero SM ministry

'dice ['ditʃe] VB *vedi* **dire**

di'cembre [di'tʃɛmbre] SM December; *vedi anche* **luglio**

dice'ria [ditʃe'ria] SF rumour (*Brit*), rumor (*US*), piece of gossip

dichia'rare [dikja'rare] /72/ VT to declare ▪ **dichiararsi** VPR to declare o.s.; (*innamorato*) to declare one's love; **si dichiara che ...** it is hereby declared that ...; **dichiararsi vinto** to admit defeat

dichia'rato, -a [dikja'rato] AG (*nemico, ateo*) avowed

dichiarazi'one [dikjarat'tsjone] SF declaration; ~ **dei redditi** statement of income; (*modulo*) tax return

dician'nove [ditʃan'nɔve] NUM nineteen

dicianno'venne [ditʃanno'vɛnne] AG, SMF nineteen-year-old

dicias'sette [ditʃas'sɛtte] NUM seventeen

diciasset'tenne [ditʃasset'tɛnne] AG, SMF seventeen-year-old

diciot'tenne [ditʃot'tɛnne] AG, SMF eighteen-year-old

dici'otto [di'tʃɔtto] NUM eighteen ▶ SM INV (*Ins*) *minimum satisfactory mark awarded in Italian universities*

dici'tura [ditʃi'tura] SF words *pl*, wording

'dico *ecc* VB *vedi* **dire**

didasca'lia SF (*di illustrazione*) caption; (*Cine*) subtitle; (*Teat*) stage directions *pl*

di'dattico, -a, -ci, -che AG didactic; (*metodo, programma*) teaching; (*libro*) educational ▶ SF didactics *sg*; teaching methodology

di'dentro AV inside, indoors

didi'etro AV behind ▶ AG INV (*ruota, giardino*) back, rear *cpd* ▶ SM (*di casa*) rear; (*col: sedere*) backside

di'eci ['djetʃi] NUM ten

dieci'mila [djetʃi'mila] NUM ten thousand

die'cina [dje'tʃina] SF = **decina**

di'edi *ecc* VB *vedi* **dare**

di'eresi SF dieresis *sg*

'diesel ['diːzəl] SM INV diesel engine

dies'sino, -a AG (*Pol*) of o belonging to the Democrats of the Left (*Italian left-wing party*) ▶ SM/F *member of the DS political party*

di'eta SF diet; **essere a** ~ to be on a diet

die'tetica SF dietetics *sg*

die'tologo, -a, -gi, -ghe SM/F dietician

di'etro AV behind; (*in fondo*) at the back ▶ PREP behind; (*tempo: dopo*) after ▶ SM (*di foglio, giacca*) back; (*di casa*) back, rear ▶ AG INV back *cpd*; **le zampe di** ~ the hind legs; ~ **ricevuta** against receipt; ~ **richiesta** on demand; (*scritta*) on application; **andare** ~ **a** (*anche fig*) to follow; **stare** ~ **a qn** (*sorvegliare*) to keep an eye on sb; (*corteggiare*) to hang around sb; **portarsi** ~ **qn/qc** to bring sb/sth with one, bring sb/sth along; **gli hanno riso/parlato** ~ they laughed at/talked about him behind his back

di'etro 'front ESCL about turn! (*Brit*), about face! (*US*) ▶ SM (*Mil*) about-turn, about-face;

d

(fig) volte-face, about-turn, about-face; **fare ~** *(Mil, fig)* to about-turn, about-face; *(tornare indietro)* to turn round

di'fatti CONG in fact, as a matter of fact

di'fendere /36/ VT to defend ■ **difendersi** VPR *(cavarsela)* to get by; **difendersi da/contro** to defend o.s. from/against; **difendersi dal freddo** to protect o.s. from the cold; **sapersi ~** to know how to look after o.s.

difen'sivo, -a AG defensive ▶ SF: **stare sulla difensiva** *(anche fig)* to be on the defensive

difen'sore, -a SM/F defender; **avvocato ~** counsel for the defence *(BRIT)* o defense *(US)*

di'fesa SF *vedi* **difeso**

di'fesi *ecc* VB *vedi* **difendere**

di'feso, -a PP *di* **difendere** ▶ SF defence *(BRIT)*, defense *(US)*; **prendere le difese di qn** to defend sb, take sb's part

difet'tare /72/ VI to be defective; **~ di** to be lacking in, lack

difet'tivo, -a AG defective

di'fetto SM *(mancanza)*: **~ di** lack of; shortage of; *(di fabbricazione)* fault, flaw, defect; *(morale)* fault, failing, defect; *(fisico)* defect; **far ~** to be lacking; **in ~** at fault; in the wrong

difet'toso, -a AG defective, faulty

diffa'mare /72/ VT *(a parole)* to slander; *(per iscritto)* to libel

diffama'torio, -a AG slanderous; libellous

diffamazi'one [diffamat'tsjone] SF slander; libel

diffe'rente AG different

diffe'renza [diffe'rɛntsa] SF difference; **a ~ di** unlike; **non fare ~ (tra)** to make no distinction (between)

differenzi'ale [differen'tsjale] AG, SM differential; **classi differenziali** *(Ins)* special classes *(for backward children)*

differenzi'are [differen'tsjare] /19/ VT to differentiate; **differenziarsi da** to differentiate o.s. from; to differ from

diffe'rire /55/ VT to postpone, defer ▶ VI to be different

diffe'rita SF: **in ~** *(trasmettere)* prerecorded

difficile [dif'fitʃile] AG difficult; *(persona)* hard to please, difficult (to please); *(poco probabile)*: **è ~ che sia libero** it is unlikely that he'll be free ▶ SMF: **fare il(la) ~** to be difficult, be awkward ▶ SM difficult part; difficulty; **essere ~ nel mangiare** to be fussy about one's food

difficil'mente [diffitʃil'mente] AV *(con difficoltà)* with difficulty; **~ verrà** he's unlikely to come

difficoltà SF INV difficulty

difficol'toso, -a AG *(compito)* difficult, hard; *(persona)* difficult, hard to please; **digestione difficoltosa** poor digestion

diffida SF *(Dir)* warning, notice

diffi'dare /72/ VI: **~ di** to be suspicious o distrustful of ▶ VT *(Dir)* to warn; **~ qn dal fare qc** to warn sb not to do sth, caution sb against doing sth

diffi'dente AG suspicious, distrustful

diffi'denza [diffi'dɛntsa] SF suspicion, distrust

diffondere /25/ VT *(luce, calore)* to diffuse; *(notizie)* to spread, circulate ■ **diffondersi** VPR to spread

diffusi *ecc* VB *vedi* **diffondere**

diffusi'one SF diffusion; spread; *(anche di giornale)* circulation; *(Fisica)* scattering

diffuso, -a PP *di* **diffondere** ▶ AG *(Fisica)* diffuse; *(fenomeno, notizia, malattia ecc)* widespread; **è opinione diffusa che ...** it's widely held that ....

difi'lato AV *(direttamente)* straight, directly; *(subito)* straight away

difte'rite SF diphtheria

'diga, -ghe SF dam; *(portuale)* breakwater

dige'rente [didʒe'rɛnte] AG *(apparato)* digestive

dige'rire [didʒe'rire] /55/ VT to digest

digesti'one [didʒes'tjone] SF digestion

diges'tivo, -a [didʒes'tivo] AG digestive ▶ SM *(after-dinner)* liqueur

Digi'one [di'dʒone] SF Dijon

digi'tale [didʒi'tale] AG digital; *(delle dita)* finger *cpd*, digital ▶ SF *(Bot)* foxglove

digi'tare [didʒi'tare] /72/ VT *(dati)* to key (in); *(tasto)* to press

digiu'nare [didʒu'nare] /72/ VI to starve o.s.; *(Rel)* to fast

digi'uno, -a [di'dʒuno] AG: **essere ~** not to have eaten ▶ SM fast; **a ~** on an empty stomach

dignità [diɲɲi'ta] SF INV dignity

digni'tario [diɲɲi'tarjo] SM dignitary

digni'toso, -a [diɲɲi'toso] AG dignified

'DIGOS SIGLA F (= *Divisione Investigazioni Generali e Operazioni Speciali*) police department dealing with political security

digressi'one SF digression

digri'gnare [digriɲ'ɲare] /15/ VT: **~ i denti** to grind one's teeth

dila'gare /80/ VI to flood; *(fig)* to spread

dilani'are /19/ VT to tear to pieces

dilapi'dare /72/ VT to squander, waste

dila'tare /72/ VT to dilate; *(gas)* to cause to expand; *(passaggio, cavità)* to open (up) ■ **dilatarsi** VPR to dilate; *(Fisica)* to expand

dilatazi'one [dilatat'tsjone] SF *(Anat)* dilation; *(di gas, metallo)* expansion

dilazio'nare [dilattsjo'nare] /72/ VT to delay, defer

dilazi'one [dilat'tsjone] SF deferment

dileggi'are [diled'dʒare] /62/ VT to mock, deride

dilegu'are /72/ VI, **dilegu'arsi** VPR to vanish, disappear

di'lemma, -i SM dilemma

dilet'tante SMF dilettante; (*anche Sport*) amateur

dilet'tare /72/ VT to give pleasure to, delight ■ **dilettarsi** VPR: **dilettarsi di** to take pleasure in, enjoy

dilet'tevole AG delightful

di'letto, -a AG dear, beloved ▶ SM/F beloved, dear one ▶ SM pleasure, delight

dili'gente [dili'dʒɛnte] AG (*scrupoloso*) diligent; (*accurato*) careful, accurate

dili'genza [dili'dʒɛntsa] SF diligence; care; (*carrozza*) stagecoach

dilu'ire /55/ VT to dilute

dilun'garsi /80/ VPR (*fig*): ~ **su** to talk at length on o about

diluvi'are /19/ VB IMPERS to pour (down)

di'luvio SM downpour; (*inondazione, fig*) flood; **il ~ universale** the Flood

dima'grante AG slimming *cpd*

dima'grire /55/ VI to get thinner, lose weight

dime'nare /72/ VT to wave, shake ■ **dimenarsi** VPR to toss and turn; (*fig*) to struggle; ~ **la coda** (*cane*) to wag its tail

dimensi'one SF dimension; (*grandezza*) size; **considerare un discorso nella sua ~ politica** to look at a speech in terms of its political significance

dimenti'canza [dimenti'kantsa] SF forgetfulness; (*errore*) oversight, slip; **per ~** inadvertently

dimenti'care /20/ VT to forget ■ **dimenticarsi** VPR: **dimenticarsi di qc** to forget sth

dimentica'toio SM (*scherzoso*): **cadere/mettere nel ~** to sink into/consign to oblivion

di'mentico, -a, -chi, -che AG: ~ **di** (*che non ricorda*) forgetful of; (*incurante*) oblivious of, unmindful of

di'messo, -a PP *di* **dimettere** ▶ AG (*voce*) subdued; (*uomo, abito*) modest, humble

dimesti'chezza [dimesti'kettsa] SF familiarity

di'mettere /63/ VT: ~ **qn da** to dismiss sb from; (*dall'ospedale*) to discharge sb from ■ **dimettersi** VPR: **dimettersi (da)** to resign (from)

dimez'zare [dimed'dzare] /72/ VT to halve

diminu'ire /55/ VT to reduce, diminish; (*prezzi*) to bring down, reduce ▶ VI to decrease, diminish; (*rumore*) to die down, die away; (*prezzi*) to fall, go down

diminu'tivo, -a AG, SM diminutive

diminuzi'one [diminut'tsjone] SF decreasing, diminishing; **in ~** on the decrease; ~ **della produttività** fall in productivity

di'misi *ecc* VB *vedi* **dimettere**

dimissio'nario, -a AG outgoing, resigning

dimissi'oni SFPL resignation *sg*; **dare** o **presentare le ~** to resign, hand in one's resignation

di'mora SF residence; **senza fissa ~** of no fixed address o abode

dimo'rare /72/ VI to reside

dimos'trante SMF (*Pol*) demonstrator

dimos'trare /72/ VT to demonstrate, show; (*provare*) to prove, demonstrate ■ **dimostrarsi** VPR: **dimostrarsi molto abile** to show o.s. o prove to be very clever; **non dimostra la sua età** he doesn't look his age; **dimostra 30 anni** he looks about 30 (years old)

dimostra'tivo, -a AG (*anche Ling*) demonstrative

dimostrazi'one [dimostrat'tsjone] SF demonstration; proof

di'namico, -a, -ci, -che AG dynamic ▶ SF dynamics *sg*

dina'mismo SM dynamism

dinami'tardo, -a AG: **attentato ~** dynamite attack ▶ SM/F dynamiter

dina'mite SF dynamite

'dinamo SF INV dynamo

di'nanzi [di'nantsi]: ~ **a** *prep* in front of

dinas'tia SF dynasty

dini'ego, -ghi SM (*rifiuto*) refusal; (*negazione*) denial

dinocco'lato, -a AG lanky; **camminare ~** to walk with a slouch

dino'sauro SM dinosaur

din'torno AV round, (round) about ■ **dintorni** SMPL outskirts; **nei dintorni di** in the vicinity o neighbourhood of

'dio (*pl* **dei**) SM god; **D~** God; **gli dei** the gods; **si crede un ~** he thinks he's wonderful; **D~ mio!** my God!; **D~ ce la mandi buona** let's hope for the best; **D~ ce ne scampi e liberi!** God forbid!

di'ocesi [di'ɔtʃezi] SF INV diocese

dios'sina SF dioxin

dipa'nare /72/ VT (*lana*) to wind into a ball; (*fig*) to disentangle, sort out

diparti'mento SM department

dipen'dente AG dependent ▶ SMF employee; ~ **statale** state employee

dipen'denza [dipen'dɛntsa] SF dependence; **essere alle dipendenze di qn** to be employed by sb o in sb's employ

di'pendere /8/ VI: ~ **da** to depend on; (*finanziariamente*) to be dependent on; (*derivare*) to come from, be due to

di'pesi *ecc* VB *vedi* **dipendere**

di'peso, -a PP *di* **dipendere**

di'pingere [di'pindʒere] /37/ VT to paint

di'pinsi *ecc* VB *vedi* **dipingere**

di'pinto, -a PP *di* **dipingere** ▶ SM painting

di'ploma, -i SM diploma

diplo'mare /72/ VT to award a diploma to, graduate (*US*) ▶ VI to obtain a diploma, graduate (*US*)

diplo'matico, -a, -ci, -che AG diplomatic ▶ SM diplomat

diplo'mato, -a AG qualified ▶ SM/F qualified person, holder of a diploma

diploma'zia [diplomat'tsia] SF diplomacy

di'porto SM: **imbarcazione da ~** pleasure craft

dira'dare /72/ VT to thin (out); (visite) to reduce, make less frequent ■ **diradarsi** VPR to disperse; (nebbia) to clear (up)

dira'mare /72/ VT to issue ▶ VI (strade: anche: **diramarsi**) to branch

'dire /38/ VT to say; (segreto, fatto) to tell; **~ qc a qn** to tell sb sth; **~ a qn di fare qc** to tell sb to do sth; **~ di si/no** to say yes/no; **si dice che ...** they say that ...; **mi si dice che ...** I am told that ...; **si direbbe che ...** it looks (o sounds) as though ...; **dica, signora?** (in un negozio) yes, Madam, can I help you?; **sa quello che dice** he knows what he's talking about; **lascialo ~** (esprimersi) let him have his say; (ignoralo) just ignore him; **come sarebbe a ~?** what do you mean?; **che ne diresti di andarcene?** how about leaving?; **chi l'avrebbe mai detto!** who would have thought it!; **si dicono esperti** they say they are experts; **per così ~** so to speak; **a dir poco** to say the least; **non c'è che ~** there's no doubt about it; **non dico di no** I can't deny it; **il che è tutto ~** need I say more?

Quando si introduce il discorso diretto *dire* si traduce **say** e non **tell**.
Mi ha detto: 'Sono molto stanca'. **She said 'I am very tired'.**
Per introdurre il discorso indiretto si possono usare indifferentemente **say** o **tell**, facendo attenzione alla costruzione: **say ... to somebody**, ma **tell somebody ...**
Mi ha detto che andava al cinema. **She said to me (that)** o **She told me (that) she was going to the cinema.**

---

di'ressi ecc VB vedi **dirigere**

di'retta SF: **in ~** (trasmettere) live; **un incontro di calcio in ~** a live football match; vedi **diretto**

diretta'mente AV (immediatamente) directly, straight; (personalmente) directly; (senza intermediari) direct, straight

diret'tissima SF (tragitto) most direct route; (Dir): **processo per ~** summary trial

diret'tissimo SM (Ferr) fast (through) train

diret'tivo, -a AG (Pol, Amm) executive; (Comm) managerial, executive ▶ SM leadership, leaders pl ▶ SF directive, instruction

di'retto, -a PP di **dirigere** ▶ AG direct ▶ SM (Ferr) through train ▶ SF: **in (linea) diretta** (Radio, TV) live; **il mio ~ superiore** my immediate superior

diret'tore, -'trice SM/F (di azienda) director, manager (manageress); (di scuola elementare) head (teacher) (BRIT), principal (US); **~ amministrativo** company secretary (BRIT), corporate

executive secretary (US); **~ del carcere** prison governor (BRIT) o warden (US); **~ di filiale** branch manager; **~ d'orchestra** conductor; **~ di produzione** (Cine) producer; **~ sportivo** team manager; **~ tecnico** (Sport) trainer, coach; **~ vendite** sales director o manager

direzi'one [diret'tsjone] SF board of directors; management; (senso: anche fig) direction; (conduzione: gen) running; (: di partito) leadership; (: di società) management; (: di giornale) editorship; (direttori) management; **in ~ di** in the direction of, towards

diri'gente [diri'dʒɛnte] AG managerial ▶ SMF executive; (Pol) leader ▶ AG: **classe ~** ruling class

diri'genza [diri'dʒɛntsa] SF management; (Pol) leadership

dirigenzi'ale [diridʒen'tsjale] AG managerial

di'rigere [di'ridʒere] /39/ VT to direct; (impresa) to run, manage; (Mus) to conduct ■ **dirigersi** VPR: **dirigersi verso** o **a** to make o head for; **~ i propri passi verso** to make one's way towards; **il treno era diretto a Pavia** the train was heading for Pavia

diri'gibile [diri'dʒibile] SM airship

dirim'petto AV opposite; **~ a** prep opposite, facing

di'ritto, -a AG straight; (onesto) straight, upright ▶ AV straight, directly ▶ SM right side; (Tennis) forehand; (Maglia) plain stitch, knit stitch; (prerogativa) right; (leggi, scienza): **il ~** law ■ **diritti** SMPL (tasse) duty sg; **stare ~** to stand up straight; **aver ~ a qc** to be entitled to sth; **punto ~** plain (stitch); **andare ~** to go straight on; **a buon ~** quite rightly; **diritti (d'autore)** royalties; **~ di successione** right of succession

dirit'tura SF (Sport) straight; (fig) rectitude

diroc'cato, -a AG tumbledown, in ruins

dirom'pente AG (anche fig) explosive

dirotta'mento SM: **~ (aereo)** hijack

dirot'tare /72/ VT (nave, aereo) to change the course of; (aereo: sotto minaccia) to hijack; (traffico) to divert ▶ VI (nave, aereo) to change course

dirotta'tore, -'trice SM/F hijacker

di'rotto, -a AG (pioggia) torrential; (pianto) unrestrained; **piovere a ~** to pour, rain cats and dogs; **piangere a ~** to cry one's heart out

di'rupo SM crag, precipice

di'sabile SMF person with a disability ▶ AG with a disability; **i disabili** people with disabilities

disabi'tato, -a AG uninhabited

disabitu'arsi /72/ VPR: **~ a** to get out of the habit of

disac'cordo SM disagreement

disadat'tato, -a AG (Psic) maladjusted

disa'dorno, -a AG plain, unadorned

disaffezi'one [dizaffet'tsjone] SF disaffection

disa'gevole [disa'dʒevole] AG (*scomodo*) uncomfortable; (*difficile*) difficult

disagi'ato, -a [diza'dʒato] AG poor, needy; (*vita*) hard

di'sagio [di'zadʒo] SM discomfort; (*disturbo*) inconvenience; (*fig: imbarazzo*) embarrassment ▪ **disagi** SMPL hardship *sg*, poverty *sg*; **essere a ~** to be ill at ease

di'samina SF close examination

disappro'vare /72/ VT to disapprove of

disapprovazi'one [dizapprovat'tsjone] SF disapproval

disap'punto SM disappointment

disarcio'nare [dizartʃo'nare] /72/ VT to unhorse

disar'mante AG (*fig*) disarming

disar'mare /72/ VT, VI to disarm

di'sarmo SM (*Mil*) disarmament

di'sastro SM disaster

disas'troso, -a AG disastrous

disat'tento, -a AG inattentive

disattenzi'one [dizatten'tsjone] SF carelessness, lack of attention

disatti'vare /72/ VT (*bomba*) to de-activate, defuse

disa'vanzo [diza'vantso] SM (*Econ*) deficit

disavven'tura SF misadventure, mishap

dis'brigo, -ghi SM (*prompt*) clearing up *o* settlement

dis'capito SM: **a ~ di** to the detriment of

dis'carica, -che SF (*di rifiuti*) rubbish tip *o* dump

discen'dente [diʃʃen'dɛnte] AG descending ▶ SMF descendant

di'scendere [diʃ'ʃɛndere] /101/ VT to go (*o come*) down ▶ VI to go (*o come*) down; (*strada*) to go down; (*smontare*) to get off; **~ da** (*famiglia*) to be descended from; **~ dalla macchina/dal treno** to get out of the car/out of *o* off the train; **~ da cavallo** to dismount, get off one's horse

di'scepolo, -a [diʃ'ʃepolo] SM/F disciple

di'scernere [diʃ'ʃɛrnere] /29/ VT to discern

discerni'mento [diʃʃerni'mento] SM discernment

di'scesa [diʃ'ʃesa] SF descent; (*pendio*) slope; **in ~** (*strada*) downhill *cpd*, sloping; **~ libera** (*Sci*) downhill (race)

disce'sista [diʃʃe'sista] SMF downhill skier

di'sceso, -a [diʃ'ʃeso] PP *di* **discendere** ▶ SF descent; (*pendio*) slope; **in discesa** (*strada*) downhill *cpd*, sloping; **discesa libera** (*Sci*) downhill race

dischi'udere [dis'kjudere] /22/ VT (*aprire*) to open; (*fig: rivelare*) to disclose, reveal

dischi'usi *ecc* [dis'kjusi] VB *vedi* **dischiudere**

dischi'uso, -a [dis'kjuso] PP *di* **dischiudere**

di'scinto, -a [diʃ'ʃinto] AG (*anche:* **in abiti discinti**) half-undressed

disci'ogliere [diʃ'ʃɔʎʎere] /103/ VT, **disci'ogliersi** VPR to dissolve; (*fondere*) to melt

disci'plina [diʃʃi'plina] SF discipline

discipli'nare [diʃʃipli'nare] /72/ AG disciplinary ▶ VT to discipline

'disco, -schi SM disc, disk; (*Sport*) discus; (*fonografico*) record; (*Inform*) disk; **~ magnetico** (*Inform*) magnetic disk; **~ orario** (*Aut*) parking disc; **~ rigido** (*Inform*) hard disk; **~ volante** flying saucer

discogra'fia SF (*tecnica*) recording, record-making; (*industria*) record industry

disco'grafico, -a, -ci, -che AG record *cpd*, recording *cpd* ▶ SM/F record producer; **casa discografica** record(ing) company

'discolo, -a AG (*bambino*) undisciplined, unruly ▶ SM/F rascal

discol'pare /72/ VT to clear of blame ▪ **discolparsi** VPR to clear o.s., prove one's innocence; (*giustificarsi*) to excuse o.s.

disco'noscere [disko'noʃʃere] /26/ VT (*figlio*) to disown; (*meriti*) to ignore, disregard

disconosci'uto, -a [diskonoʃ'ʃuto] PP *di* **disconoscere**

discon'tinuo, -a AG (*linea*) broken; (*rendimento, stile*) irregular; (*interesse*) sporadic

dis'corde AG conflicting, clashing

dis'cordia SF discord; (*dissidio*) disagreement, clash

dis'correre /28/ VI: **~ (di)** to talk (about)

dis'corso, -a PP *di* **discorrere** ▶ SM speech; (*conversazione*) conversation, talk

dis'costo, -a AG faraway, distant ▶ AV far away; **~ da** *prep* far from

disco'teca, -che SF (*raccolta*) record library; (*luogo di ballo*) disco(theque)

dis'count [dis'kaunt] SM INV (*supermercato*) cut-price supermarket

discre'panza [diskre'pantsa] SF discrepancy

dis'creto, -a AG discreet; (*abbastanza buono*) reasonable, fair

discrezi'one [diskret'tsjone] SF discretion; (*giudizio*) judgment, discernment; **a ~ di** at the discretion of

discrimi'nante AG (*fattore, elemento*) decisive ▶ SF (*Dir*) extenuating circumstance

discrimi'nare /72/ VT to discriminate

discriminazi'one [diskriminat'tsjone] SF discrimination

dis'cussi *ecc* VB *vedi* **discutere**

discussi'one SF discussion; (*litigio*) argument; **mettere in ~** to bring into question; **fuori ~** out of the question

dis'cusso, -a PP *di* **discutere**

dis'cutere /40/ VT to discuss, debate; (*contestare*) to question, dispute ▶ VI (*litigare*) to argue; (*conversare*): **~ (di)** to discuss

discu'tibile AG questionable

disde'gnare [dizdeɲ'ɲare] /**15**/ vt to scorn

dis'degno [diz'deɲɲo] sm scorn, disdain

disde'gnoso, -a [dizdeɲ'ɲoso] AG disdainful, scornful

dis'detto, -a PP di **disdire** ▶ SF (di prenotazione ecc) cancellation; (sfortuna) bad luck

disdi'cevole [dizdi'tʃevole] AG improper, unseemly

dis'dire /**38**/ vt (prenotazione) to cancel; ~ **un contratto d'affitto** (Dir) to give notice (to quit)

dise'gnare [diseɲ'ɲare] /**15**/ vt to draw; (progettare) to design; (fig) to outline

disegna'tore, -'trice [diseɲɲa'tore] sm/f designer

di'segno [di'zeɲɲo] sm drawing; (su stoffa ecc) design; (fig: schema) outline; ~ **industriale** industrial design; ~ **di legge** (Dir) bill

diser'bante sm weedkiller

disere'dare /**72**/ vt to disinherit

diser'tare /**72**/ vt, vi to desert

diser'tore sm (Mil) deserter

diserzi'one [dizer'tsjone] SF (Mil) desertion

disfaci'mento [disfatʃi'mento] sm (di cadavere) decay; (fig: di istituzione, impero, società) decline, decay; **in ~** in decay

dis'fare /**41**/ vt to undo; (valigie) to unpack; (meccanismo) to take to pieces; (lavoro, paese) to destroy; (neve) to melt ▪ **disfarsi** VPR to come undone; (neve) to melt; ~ **il letto** to strip the bed; **disfarsi di qn** (liberarsi) to get rid of sb

dis'fatta SF vedi **disfatto**

disfat'tista, -i, -e sm/f defeatist

dis'fatto, -a PP di **disfare** ▶ AG (gen) undone, untied; (letto) unmade; (persona: sfinito) exhausted, worn-out; (: addolorato) grief-stricken ▶ SF (sconfitta) rout

disfunzi'one [disfun'tsjone] SF (Med) dysfunction; ~ **cardiaca** heart trouble

disge'lare [dizdʒe'lare] /**72**/ vt, vi, **disge'larsi** VPR to thaw

dis'gelo [diz'dʒelo] sm thaw

dis'grazia [diz'grattsja] SF (sventura) misfortune; (incidente) accident, mishap

disgrazi'ato, -a [dizgrat'tsjato] AG unfortunate ▶ sm/f wretch

disgre'gare /**80**/ vt, **disgre'garsi** VPR to break up

disgu'ido sm hitch; ~ **postale** error in postal delivery

disgus'tare /**72**/ vt to disgust ▪ **disgustarsi** VPR: **disgustarsi di** to be disgusted by

dis'gusto sm disgust

disgus'toso, -a AG disgusting

disidra'tare /**72**/ vt to dehydrate

disidra'tato, -a AG dehydrated

disil'ludere /**35**/ vt to disillusion, disenchant

disillusi'one SF disillusion, disenchantment

disimpa'rare /**72**/ vt to forget

disimpe'gnare [dizimpeɲ'ɲare] /**15**/ vt (oggetto dato in pegno) to redeem, get out of pawn; ~ **da** (persona: da obblighi) to release from ▪ **disimpegnarsi** VPR: **disimpegnarsi da** (obblighi) to release o.s. from, free o.s. from

disincagli'are [dizinkaʎ'ʎare] /**27**/ vt (barca) to refloat ▪ **disincagliarsi** VPR to get afloat again

disincan'tato, -a AG disenchanted, disillusioned

disincenti'vare [dizintʃenti'vare] /**72**/ vt to discourage

disinfes'tare /**72**/ vt to disinfest

disinfestazi'one [dizinfestat'tsjone] SF disinfestation

disinfet'tante AG, sm disinfectant

disinfet'tare /**72**/ vt to disinfect

disinfezi'one [dizinfet'tsjone] SF disinfection

disingan'nare /**72**/ vt to disillusion

disin'ganno sm disillusion

disini'bito, -a AG uninhibited

disinnes'care /**20**/ vt to defuse

disinnes'tare /**72**/ vt (marcia) to disengage

disinqui'nare /**72**/ vt to free from pollution

disinstal'lare /**72**/ vt (software) to uninstall

disinte'grare /**72**/ vt, vi to disintegrate ▪ **disintegrarsi** VPR to disintegrate

disinteres'sarsi /**72**/ VPR: ~ **di** to take no interest in

disinte'resse sm indifference; (generosità) unselfishness

disintossi'care /**20**/ vt (alcolizzato, drogato) to treat for alcoholism (o drug addiction) ▪ **disintossicarsi** VPR to clear out one's system; (alcolizzato, drogato) to be treated for alcoholism (o drug addiction)

disintossicazi'one [dizintossikat'tsjone] SF detox; treatment for alcoholism (o drug addiction)

disin'volto, -a AG casual, free and easy

disinvol'tura SF casualness, ease

disles'sia SF dyslexia

disli'vello SF difference in height; (fig) gap

dislo'care /**20**/ vt to station, position

dismi'sura SF excess; **a ~** to excess, excessively

disobbe'dire ecc = **disubbidire** ecc

disoccu'pato, -a AG unemployed ▶ sm/f unemployed person

disoccupazi'one [dizokkupat'tsjone] SF unemployment

disonestà SF dishonesty

diso'nesto, -a AG dishonest

disono'rare /**45**/ vt to dishonour (Brit), dishonor (US), bring disgrace upon

111

diso'nore SM dishonour (BRIT), dishonor (US), disgrace

di'sopra AV (con contatto) on top; (senza contatto) above; (al piano superiore) upstairs ▶ AG INV (superiore) upper ▶ SM INV top, upper part; **la gente ~** the people upstairs; **il piano ~** the floor above

disordi'nare /72/ VT to mess up, disarrange; (Mil) to throw into disorder

disordi'nato, -a AG untidy; (privo di misura) irregular, wild

di'sordine SM (confusione) disorder, confusion; (sregolatezza) debauchery ▪ **disordini** SMPL (Pol ecc) disorder sg; (tumulti) riots

disor'ganico, -a, -ci, -che AG incoherent, disorganized

disorganiz'zato, -a [dizorganid'dzato] AG disorganized

disorienta'mento SM (fig) confusion, bewilderment

disorien'tare /72/ VT to disorientate ▪ **disorientarsi** VPR (fig) to get confused, lose one's bearings

disorien'tato, -a AG disorientated

disos'sare /72/ VT (Cuc) to bone

di'sotto AV below, underneath; (in fondo) at the bottom; (al piano inferiore) downstairs ▶ AG INV (inferiore) lower; bottom cpd ▶ SM INV (parte inferiore) lower part; bottom; **la gente ~** the people downstairs; **il piano ~** the floor below

dis'paccio [dis'pattʃo] SM dispatch

dispa'rato, -a AG disparate

'dispari AG INV odd, uneven

disparità SF INV disparity

dis'parte AV: **in ~** (da lato) aside, apart; **tenersi** o **starsene in ~** to keep to o.s., hold aloof

dis'pendio SM (di denaro, energie) expenditure; (: spreco) waste

dispendi'oso, -a AG expensive

dis'pensa SF pantry, larder; (mobile) sideboard; (Dir) exemption; (Rel) dispensation; (fascicolo) number, issue

dispen'sare /72/ VT (elemosine, favori) to distribute; (esonerare) to exempt

dispe'rare /72/ VI: **~ (di)** to despair (of) ▪ **disperarsi** VPR to despair

dispe'rato, -a AG (persona) in despair; (caso, tentativo) desperate

disperazi'one [disperat'tsjone] SF despair

dis'perdere /73/ VT (disseminare) to disperse; (Mil) to scatter, rout; (fig: consumare) to waste, squander ▪ **disperdersi** VPR to disperse; to scatter

dispersi'one SF dispersion, dispersal; (Fisica, Chim) dispersion

disper'sivo, -a AG (lavoro ecc) disorganized

dis'perso, -a PP di **disperdere** ▶ SM/F missing person; (Mil) missing soldier

dis'petto SM spite no pl, spitefulness no pl; **fare**

un ~ a qn to play a (nasty) trick on sb; **a ~ di** in spite of; **con suo grande ~** much to his annoyance

dispet'toso, -a AG spiteful

dispia'cere [dispja'tʃere] /74/ SM (rammarico) regret, sorrow; (dolore) grief ▶ VI: **~** to displease ▶ VB IMPERS: **mi dispiace (che)** I am sorry (that); **le dispiace se...?** do you mind if ...? ▪ **dispiaceri** SMPL (preoccupazioni) troubles, worries; **se non le dispiace, me ne vado adesso** if you don't mind, I'll go now

dispiaci'uto, -a [dispja'tʃuto] PP di **dispiacere** ▶ AG sorry

dis'pone, dis'pongo ecc VB vedi **disporre**

dispo'nibile AG available; (persona: solerte, gentile) helpful

disponibilità SF INV availability; (solerzia, gentilezza) helpfulness ▶ SFPL (economiche) resources

dis'porre /77/ VT (sistemare) to arrange; (preparare) to prepare; (Dir) to order; (persuadere): **~ qn a** to incline o dispose sb towards ▶ VI (decidere) to decide; (usufruire): **~ di** to use, have at one's disposal; (essere dotato): **~ di** to have ▪ **disporsi** VPR (ordinarsi) to place o.s., arrange o.s.; **disporsi a fare** to get ready to do; **disporsi all'attacco** to prepare for an attack; **disporsi in cerchio** to form a circle

dis'posi ecc VB vedi **disporre**

disposi'tivo SM (meccanismo) device; (Dir) pronouncement; **~ di controllo** o **di comando** control device; **~ di sicurezza** (gen) safety device; (di arma da fuoco) safety catch

disposizi'one [dispozit'tsjone] SF arrangement, layout; (stato d'animo) mood; (tendenza) bent, inclination; (comando) order; (Dir) provision, regulation; **a ~ di qn** at sb's disposal; **per ~ di legge** by law; **~ testamentaria** provisions of a will

dis'posto, -a PP di **disporre** ▶ AG (incline): **~ a fare** disposed o prepared to do

dis'potico, -a, -ci, -che AG despotic

dispo'tismo SM despotism

disprez'zare [dispret'tsare] /72/ VT to despise

dis'prezzo [dis'prettso] SM contempt; **con ~ del pericolo** with a total disregard for the danger involved

'disputa SF dispute, quarrel

dispu'tare /72/ VT (contendere) to dispute, contest; (Sport: partita) to play; (: gara) to take part in ▶ VI to quarrel; **~ di** to discuss; **disputarsi qc** to fight for sth

disqui'sire /55/ VI to discourse on

disquisizi'one [diskwizit'tsjone] SF detailed analysis

dissa'crare /72/ VT to desecrate

dissangua'mento SM loss of blood

dissangu'are /72/ VT (fig: persona) to bleed white; (: patrimonio) to suck dry ▪ **dissanguarsi**

VPR (*Med*) to lose blood; (*fig*) to ruin o.s.; **morire dissanguato** to bleed to death

dissa'pore SM slight disagreement

'disse VB *vedi* **dire**

disse'care /20/ VT to dissect

dissec'care /20/ VT, **dissec'carsi** VPR to dry up

dissemi'nare /72/ VT to scatter; (*fig: notizie*) to spread

dissenna'tezza [dissenna'tettsa] SF foolishness

dis'senso SM dissent; (*disapprovazione*) disapproval

dissente'ria SF dysentery

dissen'tire /45/ VI: **~ (da)** to disagree (with)

disseppel'lire /55/ VT (*esumare: cadavere*) to disinter, exhume; (*dissotterrare: anche fig*) to dig up, unearth; (*rancori*) to resurrect

dissertazi'one [dissertat'tsjone] SF dissertation

disser'vizio [disser'vittsjo] SM inefficiency

disses'tare /72/ VT (*Econ*) to ruin

disses'tato, -a AG (*fondo stradale*) uneven; (*economia, finanze*) shaky; **"strada dissestata"** (*per lavori in corso*) "road up" (BRIT), "road out" (US)

dis'sesto SM (financial) ruin

disse'tante AG refreshing

disse'tare /72/ VT to quench the thirst of ■ **dissetarsi** VPR to quench one's thirst

dissezi'one [disset'tsjone] SF dissection

'dissi VB *vedi* **dire**

dissi'dente AG, SMF dissident

dis'sidio SM disagreement

dis'simile AG different, dissimilar

dissimu'lare /72/ VT (*fingere*) to dissemble; (*nascondere*) to conceal

dissimula'tore, -'trice SM/F dissembler

dissimulazi'one [dissimulat'tsjone] SF dissembling; concealment

dissi'pare /72/ VT to dissipate; (*scialacquare*) to squander, waste

dissipa'tezza [dissipa'tettsa] SF dissipation

dissi'pato, -a AG dissolute, dissipated

dissipazi'one [dissipat'tsjone] SF squandering

dissoci'are [disso'tʃare] /14/ VT to dissociate

dis'solto, -a PP *di* **dissolvere**

disso'lubile AG soluble

dissolu'tezza [dissolu'tettsa] SF dissoluteness

dissolu'tivo, -a AG (*forza*) divisive; **processo ~** (*anche fig*) process of dissolution

disso'luto, -a PP *di* **dissolvere** ▶ AG dissolute, licentious

dissol'venza [dissol'vɛntsa] SF (*Cine*) fading

dis'solvere /94/ VT to dissolve; (*neve*) to melt; (*fumo*) to disperse ■ **dissolversi** VPR to dissolve; to melt; to disperse

disso'nante AG discordant

disso'nanza [disso'nantsa] SF (*fig: di opinioni*) clash

dissotter'rare /72/ VT (*cadavere*) to disinter, exhume; (*tesori, rovine*) to dig up, unearth; (*fig: sentimenti, odio*) to bring up again, resurrect

dissu'adere /88/ VT: **~ qn da** to dissuade sb from

dissuasi'one SF dissuasion

dissu'aso, -a PP *di* **dissuadere**

dissua'sore SM: **~ di velocità** (*Aut*) speed bump

distacca'mento SM (*Mil*) detachment

distac'care /20/ VT to detach, separate; (*Sport*) to leave behind ■ **distaccarsi** VPR to be detached; (*fig*) to stand out; **distaccarsi da** (*fig: allontanarsi*) to grow away from

dis'tacco, -chi SM (*separazione*) separation; (*fig: indifferenza*) detachment; (*Sport*): **vincere con un ~ di ...** to win by a distance of ...

dis'tante AV far away ▶ AG distant, far away; **essere ~ (da)** to be a long way (from); **è ~ da qui?** is it far from here?; **essere ~ nel tempo** to be in the distant past

dis'tanza [dis'tantsa] SF distance; **comando a ~** remote control; **a ~ di 2 giorni** 2 days later; **tener qn a ~** to keep sb at arm's length; **prendere le distanze da qc/qn** to dissociate o.s. from sth/sb; **tenere** o **mantenere le distanze** to keep one's distance; **~ focale** focal length; **~ di sicurezza** safe distance; (*Aut*) braking distance; **~ di tiro** range; **~ di visibilità** visibility

distanzi'are [distan'tsjare] /19/ VT to space out, place at intervals; (*Sport*) to outdistance; (*fig: superare*) to outstrip, surpass

dis'tare /72/ VI: **distiamo pochi chilometri da Roma** we are only a few kilometres (away) from Rome; **dista molto da qui?** is it far (away) from here?; **non dista molto** it's not far (away); **quanto dista il centro da qui?** how far is the town centre?

dis'tendere /120/ VT (*coperta*) to spread out; (*gambe*) to stretch (out); (*mettere a giacere*) to lay; (*rilassare: muscoli, nervi*) to relax ■ **distendersi** VPR (*rilassarsi*) to relax; (*sdraiarsi*) to lie down

distensi'one SF stretching; relaxation; (*Pol*) détente

disten'sivo, -a AG (*gen*) relaxing, restful; (*farmaco*) tranquillizing; (*Pol*) conciliatory

dis'teso, -a PP *di* **distendere** ▶ AG (*allungato: persona, gamba*) stretched out; (*rilassato: persona, atmosfera*) relaxed ▶ SF expanse, stretch; **avere un volto ~** to look relaxed

distil'lare /72/ VT to distil

distil'lato SM distillate

distillazi'one [distillat'tsjone] SF distillation

distille'ria SF distillery

dis'tinguere /42/ VT to distinguish ■ **distinguersi** VPR (*essere riconoscibile*) to be distinguished; (*emergere*) to stand out, be conspicuous, distinguish o.s.; **un vino che si distingue per il suo aroma** a wine with a distinctive bouquet

dis'tinguo SM INV distinction

dis'tinta SF (*nota*) note; (*elenco*) list; ~ **di pagamento** receipt; ~ **di versamento** pay-in slip

distin'tivo, -a AG distinctive; distinguishing ▶ SM badge

dis'tinto, -a PP *di* **distinguere** ▶ AG (*dignitoso ed elegante*) distinguished; **distinti saluti** (*in lettera*) yours faithfully

distinzi'one [distin'tsjone] SF distinction; **non faccio distinzioni** (*tra persone*) I don't discriminate; (*tra cose*) it's all one to me; **senza ~ di razza/religione ...** no matter what one's race/creed ...

dis'togliere [dis'tɔʎʎere] /122/ VT: ~ **da** to take away from; (*fig*) to dissuade from

dis'tolto, -a PP *di* **distogliere**

dis'torcere [dis'tɔrtʃere] /106/ VT to twist; (*fig*) to twist, distort ■ **distorcersi** VPR (*contorcersi*) to twist

distorsi'one SF (*Med*) sprain; (*Fisica, Ottica*) distortion

dis'torto, -a PP *di* **distorcere**

dis'trarre /123/ VT to distract; (*divertire*) to entertain, amuse ■ **distrarsi** VPR (*non fare attenzione*) to be distracted, let one's mind wander; (*svagarsi*) to amuse o enjoy o.s.; ~ **lo sguardo** to look away; **non distrarti!** pay attention!

distratta'mente AV absent-mindedly, without thinking

dis'tratto, -a PP *di* **distrarre** ▶ AG absent-minded; (*disattento*) inattentive

distrazi'one [distrat'tsjone] SF absent-mindedness; inattention; (*svago*) distraction, entertainment; **errori di ~** careless mistakes

dis'tretto SM district

distribu'ire /55/ VT to distribute; (*Carte*) to deal (out); (*consegnare: posta*) to deliver; (: *lavoro*) to allocate, assign; (*ripartire*) to share out

distribu'tore SM (*di benzina*) petrol (BRIT) o gas (US) pump; (*Aut, Elettr*) distributor; (*automatico*) vending machine

distribuzi'one [distribut'tsjone] SF distribution; delivery; allocation, assignment; sharing out

distri'care /20/ VT to disentangle, unravel ■ **districarsi** VPR (*fig: cavarsela*) to manage, get by; (*tirarsi fuori*): **districarsi da** to get out of, disentangle o.s. from

dis'truggere [dis'truddʒere] /83/ VT to destroy

distrut'tivo, -a AG destructive

dis'trutto, -a PP *di* **distruggere**

distruzi'one [distrut'tsjone] SF destruction

distur'bare /72/ VT to disturb, trouble; (*sonno, lezioni*) to disturb, interrupt ■ **disturbarsi** VPR to put o.s. out; **non si disturbi** please don't bother

dis'turbo SM trouble, bother, inconvenience; (*indisposizione*) (slight) disorder, ailment ■ **disturbi** SMPL (*Radio, TV*) static sg; ~ **della quiete pubblica** (*Dir*) disturbance of the peace; **disturbi di stomaco** stomach trouble sg

disubbidi'ente AG disobedient

disubbidi'enza [dizubbi'djɛntsa] SF disobedience; ~ **civile** civil disobedience

disubbi'dire /55/ VI: ~ **(a qn)** to disobey (sb)

disuguagli'anza [dizugwaʎ'ʎantsa] SF inequality

disugu'ale AG unequal; (*diverso*) different; (*irregolare*) uneven

disumanità SF inhumanity

disu'mano, -a AG inhuman; **un grido ~** a terrible cry

disuni'one SF disunity

disu'nire /55/ VT to divide, disunite

di'suso SM: **andare** o **cadere in ~** to fall into disuse

'dita SFPL *di* **dito**

di'tale SM thimble

di'tata SF (*colpo*) jab (with one's finger); (*segno*) fingermark

'dito (*pl(f)* **dita**) SM finger; (*misura*) finger, finger's breadth; ~ **(del piede)** toe; **mettersi le dita nel naso** to pick one's nose; **mettere il ~ sulla piaga** (*fig*) to touch a sore spot; **non ha mosso un ~ (per aiutarmi)** he didn't lift a finger (to help me); **ormai è segnato a ~** everyone knows about him now

'ditta SF firm, business; **macchina della ~** company car

dit'tafono SM Dictaphone®

ditta'tore SM dictator

ditta'tura SF dictatorship

dit'tongo, -ghi SM diphthong

di'urno, -a AG day *cpd*, daytime *cpd*; **ore diurne** daytime sg; **spettacolo ~** matinee; **turno ~** day shift; *vedi anche* **albergo**

'diva SF *vedi* **divo**

diva'gare /80/ VI to digress

divagazi'one [divagat'tsjone] SF digression; **divagazioni sul tema** variations on a theme

divam'pare /72/ VI to flare up, blaze up

di'vano SM sofa; (*senza schienale*) divan; ~ **letto** bed settee, sofa bed

divari'care /20/ VT to open wide

di'vario SM difference

di'vengo *ecc* VB *vedi* **divenire**

dive'nire /128/ VI = **diventare**

di'venni *ecc* VB *vedi* **divenire**

diven'tare /72/ VI to become; **~ famoso/professore** to become famous/a teacher; **~ vecchio** to grow old; **c'è da ~ matti** it's enough to drive you mad

dive'nuto, -a PP *di* **divenire**

di'verbio SM altercation

diver'gente [diver'dʒɛnte] AG divergent

diver'genza [diver'dʒɛntsa] SF divergence; **~ d'opinioni** difference of opinion

di'vergere [di'vɛrdʒere] /59/ VI to diverge

diverrò *ecc* VB *vedi* **divenire**

diversa'mente AV (*in modo differente*) differently; (*altrimenti*) otherwise; **~ da quanto stabilito** contrary to what had been decided

diversifi'care /20/ VT to diversify, vary; to differentiate ■ **diversificarsi** VPR: **diversificarsi (per)** to differ (in)

diversificazi'one [diversifikat'tsjone] SF diversification; difference

diversi'one SF diversion

diversità SF INV difference, diversity; (*varietà*) variety

diver'sivo, -a AG diversionary ▶ SM diversion, distraction; **fare un'azione diversiva** to create a diversion

di'verso, -a AG (*differente*): **~ (da)** different (from) ▶ SM (*omosessuale*) homosexual ■ **diversi, e** DET PL, PRON PL several, various; (*Comm*) sundry; several people, many (people)

diver'tente AG amusing

diverti'mento SM amusement, pleasure; (*passatempo*) pastime, recreation; **buon ~!** enjoy yourself!, have a nice time!

diver'tire /45/ VT to amuse, entertain ■ **divertirsi** VPR to amuse *o* enjoy o.s.; **divertiti!** enjoy yourself, have a good time!; **divertirsi alle spalle di qn** to have a laugh at sb's expense

diver'tito, -a AG amused

divi'dendo SM dividend

di'videre /43/ VT (*anche Mat*) to divide; (*distribuire, ripartire*) to divide (up), split (up) ■ **dividersi** VPR (*persone*) to separate, part; (*coppia*) to separate; (*ramificarsi*) to fork; **dividere (in)** (*scindersi*) to divide (into), split up (into); **è diviso dalla moglie** he's separated from his wife; **si divide tra casa e lavoro** he divides his time between home and work

divi'eto SM prohibition; **"~ di accesso"** "no entry"; **"~ di caccia"** "no hunting"; **"~ di parcheggio"** "no parking"; **"~ di sosta"** (*Aut*) "no waiting"

divinco'larsi /72/ VPR to wriggle, writhe

divinità SF INV divinity

di'vino, -a AG divine

di'visa SF (*Mil ecc*) uniform; (*Comm*) foreign currency

di'visi *ecc* VB *vedi* **dividere**

divisi'one SF division; **~ in sillabe** syllable division; (*a fine riga*) hyphenation

di'vismo SM (*esibizionismo*) playing to the crowd

di'viso, -a PP *di* **dividere**

divi'sorio, -a AG (*siepe, muro esterno*) dividing; (*muro interno*) dividing, partition *cpd* ▶ SM (*in una stanza*) partition

'divo, -a SM/F star; **come una diva** like a prima donna

divo'rare /72/ VT to devour; **~ qc con gli occhi** to eye sth greedily

divorzi'are [divor'tsjare] /19/ VI: **~ (da qn)** to divorce (sb)

divorzi'ato, -a [divor'tsjato] AG divorced ▶ SM/F divorcee

di'vorzio [di'vɔrtsjo] SM divorce

divul'gare /80/ VT to divulge, disclose; (*rendere comprensibile*) to popularize ■ **divulgarsi** VPR to spread

divulgazi'one [divulgat'tsjone] SF (*vedi vb*) disclosure; popularization; spread

dizio'nario [dittsjo'narjo] SM dictionary

dizi'one [dit'tsjone] SF diction; pronunciation

DJ [di'dʒei] SIGLA M/SIGLA F (= *Disc Jockey*) DJ

Dja'karta [dʒa'karta] SF Djakarta

dl ABBR (= *decilitro*) dl

dm ABBR (= *decimetro*) dm

DNA [di'ennea] SIGLA M (*Biol*: = *acido deossiribonucleico*) DNA ▶ SIGLA F = **direzione nazionale antimafia**

do SM (*Mus*) C; (: *solfeggiando la scala*) do(h)

dobbi'amo VB *vedi* **dovere**

doc. ABBR = **documento**

D.O.C. [dɔk] SIGLA (= *denominazione di origine controllata*) *label guaranteeing the quality of wine*

'doccia, -ce ['dottʃa] SF (*bagno*) shower; (*condotto*) pipe; **fare la ~** to have a shower; **~ fredda** (*fig*) slap in the face

docciaschi'uma [dottʃas'kjuma] SM INV shower gel

do'cente [do'tʃɛnte] AG teaching ▶ SM/F teacher; (*di università*) lecturer; **personale non ~** non-teaching staff

do'cenza [do'tʃɛntsa] SF university teaching *o* lecturing; **ottenere la libera ~** to become a lecturer

D.O.C.G. SIGLA (= *denominazione di origine controllata e garantita*) *label guaranteeing the quality and origin of a wine*

'docile ['dɔtʃile] AG docile

docilità [dotʃili'ta] SF docility

documen'tare /72/ VT to document ■ **documentarsi** VPR: **documentarsi (su)** to gather information *o* material (about)

documen'tario, -a AG, SM documentary

documentazi'one [dokumentat'tsjone] SF documentation

docu'mento SM document ▪ **documenti** SMPL (*d'identità ecc*) papers

Dodecan'neso SM: **le Isole del ~** the Dodecanese Islands

dodi'cenne [dodi'tʃɛnne] AG, SMF twelve-year-old

dodi'cesimo, -a [dodi'tʃɛzimo] NUM twelfth

'dodici ['doditʃi] NUM twelve

do'gana SF (*ufficio*) customs pl; (*tassa*) (customs) duty; **passare la ~** to go through customs

doga'nale AG customs cpd

dogani'ere, -a SM/F customs officer

'doglie ['dɔʎʎe] SFPL (*Med*) labour sg (BRIT), labor sg (US), labour pains

'dogma, -i SM dogma

dog'matico, -a, -ci, -che AG dogmatic

'dolce ['doltʃe] AG sweet; (*colore*) soft; (*carattere, persona*) gentle, mild; (*fig: mite: clima*) mild; (*non ripido: pendio*) gentle ▶ SM (*sapore dolce*) sweetness, sweet taste; (*Cuc: portata*) sweet, dessert; (*: torta*) cake; **il ~ far niente** sweet idleness

dolce'mente [doltʃe'mente] AV (*baciare, trattare*) gently; (*sorridere, cantare*) sweetly; (*parlare*) softly

dol'cezza [dol'tʃettsa] SF sweetness; softness; mildness; gentleness

dolci'ario, -a [dol'tʃarjo] AG confectionery cpd

dolci'astro, -a [dol'tʃastro] AG (*sapore*) sweetish

dolcifi'cante [doltʃifi'kante] AG sweetening ▶ SM sweetener

dolci'umi [dol'tʃumi] SMPL sweets

do'lente AG sorrowful, sad

do'lere /44/ VI to be sore, hurt, ache ▪ **dolersi** VPR to complain; (*essere spiacente*) **dolersi di** to be sorry for; **mi duole la testa** my head aches, I've got a headache

'dolgo ecc VB vedi **dolere**

'dollaro SM dollar

'dolo SM (*Dir*) malice; (*frode*) fraud, deceit

Dolo'miti SFPL: **le ~** the Dolomites

dolo'rante AG aching, sore

do'lore SM (*fisico*) pain; (*morale*) sorrow, grief; **se lo scoprono sono dolori!** if they find out there'll be trouble!

dolo'roso, -a AG painful; sorrowful, sad

dolo'loso, -a AG (*Dir*) malicious; **incendio ~** arson

'dolsi ecc VB vedi **dolere**

dom. ABBR (= *domenica*) Sun

do'manda SF (*interrogazione*) question; (*richiesta*) demand; (*: cortese*) request; (*Dir: richiesta scritta*) application; (*Econ*): **la ~** demand; **fare una ~ a qn** to ask sb a question; **fare ~ (per un lavoro)** to apply (for a job); **far regolare ~ (di qc)** to apply through the proper channels (for sth); **fare ~ all'autorità giudiziaria** to apply to the courts; **~ di divorzio** divorce petition; **~ di matrimonio** proposal

doman'dare /72/ VT (*per avere*) to ask for; (*per sapere*) to ask; (*esigere*) to demand ▪ **domandarsi** VPR to wonder; to ask o.s.; **~ qc a qn** to ask sb for sth; to ask sb sth

do'mani AV tomorrow ▶ SM (*l'indomani*) the next day, the following day; **il ~** (*il futuro*) the future; (*il giorno successivo*) the next day; **un ~** some day; **~ l'altro** the day after tomorrow; **~ (a) otto** tomorrow week, a week tomorrow; **a ~!** see you tomorrow!

do'mare /72/ VT to tame

doma'tore, -'trice SM/F (*gen*) tamer; **~ di cavalli** horsebreaker; **~ di leoni** lion tamer

domat'tina AV tomorrow morning

do'menica, -che SF Sunday; **di** o **la ~** on Sundays; vedi anche **martedì**

domeni'cale AG Sunday cpd

domeni'cano, -a AG, SM/F Dominican

do'mestica, -che SF vedi **domestico**

do'mestico, -a, -ci, -che AG domestic ▶ SM/F servant, domestic; **le pareti domestiche** one's own four walls; **animale ~** pet; **una domestica a ore** a daily (woman)

domicili'are [domitʃi'ljare] AG vedi **arresto**

domicili'arsi [domitʃi'ljarsi] /19/ VPR to take up residence

domi'cilio [domi'tʃiljo] SM (*Dir*) domicile, place of residence; **visita a ~** (*Med*) house call; **"recapito a ~"** "deliveries"; **violazione di ~** (*Dir*) breaking and entering

domi'nante AG (*colore, nota*) dominant; (*opinione*) prevailing; (*idea*) main cpd, chief cpd; (*posizione*) dominating cpd; (*classe, partito*) ruling cpd

domi'nare /72/ VT to dominate; (*fig: sentimenti*) to control, master ▶ VI to be in the dominant position ▪ **dominarsi** VPR (*controllarsi*) to control o.s.; **~ su** (*fig*) to surpass, outclass

domina'tore, -'trice AG ruling cpd ▶ SM/F ruler

dominazi'one [dominat'tsjone] SF domination

domini'cano, -a AG: **la Repubblica Dominicana** the Dominican Republic

do'minio SM dominion; (*fig: campo*) field, domain; **domini coloniali** colonies; **essere di ~ pubblico** (*notizia ecc*) to be common knowledge

do'motica SF home automation, domotics

don SM (*Rel*) Father

do'nare /72/ VT to give, present; (*per beneficenza ecc*) to donate ▶ VI (*fig*): **~ a** to suit, become; **~ sangue** to give blood

dona'tore, -'trice SM/F donor; **~ di sangue/di organi** blood/organ donor

donazi'one [donat'tsjone] SF donation; **atto di ~** (*Dir*) deed of gift

'donde AV (*poetico*) whence

dondo'lare /72/ VT (*cullare*) to rock ▪ **dondolarsi** VPR to swing, sway

'dondolo SM: **sedia/cavallo a ~** rocking chair/ horse

dongio'vanni [dondʒo'vanni] SM Don Juan, ladies' man

'donna SF woman; (*titolo*) Donna; (*Carte*) queen; **figlio di buona ~!** (*col*) son of a bitch!; **~ di casa** housewife; home-loving woman; **~ a ore** daily (help *o* woman); **~ delle pulizie** cleaning lady, cleaner; **~ di servizio** maid; **~ di vita** *o* **di strada** prostitute, streetwalker

donnai'olo SM ladykiller

'donnola SF weasel

'dono SM gift

'doping SM doping

'dopo AV (*tempo*) afterwards; (: *più tardi*) later; (*luogo*) after, next ▶ PREP after ▶ CONG (*temporale*): **~ aver studiato** after having studied ▶ AG INV: **il giorno ~** the following day; **~ mangiato va a dormire** after having eaten *o* after a meal he goes for a sleep; **un anno ~** a year later; **~ di me/ lui** after me/him; **~, a ~!** see you later!; **~ che = dopoché**

dopo'barba SM INV after-shave

dopoché [dopo'ke] CONG after, when

dopodiché [dopodi'ke] AV after which

dopodo'mani AV the day after tomorrow

dopogu'erra SM postwar years *pl*

dopola'voro SM recreational club

dopo'pranzo [dopo'prandzo] AV after lunch (*o* dinner)

doposcì [dopoʃ'ʃi] SM INV après-ski outfit

doposcu'ola SM INV *school club offering extra tuition and recreational facilities*

dopo'sole SM INV, AG INV: **(lozione/crema) ~** aftersun (lotion/cream)

dopo'tutto AV (*tutto considerato*) after all

doppi'aggio [dop'pjaddʒo] SM (*Cine*) dubbing

doppi'are /19/ VT (*Naut*) to round; (*Sport*) to lap; (*Cine*) to dub

doppia'tore, -'trice SM/F dubber

doppi'etta SF (*fucile*) double-barrelled (BRIT) *o* double-barreled (US) shotgun; (*sparo*) shot from both barrels; (*Calcio*) double; (*Pugilato*) one-two; (*Aut*) double-declutch (BRIT), double-clutch (US)

doppi'ezza [dop'pjettsa] SF (*fig: di persona*) duplicity, double-dealing

'doppio, -a AG double; (*fig: falso*) double-dealing, deceitful ▶ SM (*quantità*): **il ~ (di)** twice as much (*o* many), double the amount (*o* number) of; (*Sport*) doubles *pl* ▶ AV double; **fare il ~ gioco** (*fig*) to play a double game; **chiudere a doppia mandata** to double-lock; **~ senso** double entendre; **frase a ~ senso** sentence with a double meaning; **un utensile a ~ uso** a dual-purpose utensil

doppio'fondo SM (*di valigia*) false bottom; (*Naut*) double hull

doppi'one SM duplicate (copy)

doppio'petto SM double-breasted jacket

dop'pista SMF (*Tennis*) doubles player

do'rare /72/ VT to gild; (*Cuc*) to brown; **~ la pillola** (*fig*) to sugar the pill

do'rato, -a AG golden; (*ricoperto d'oro*) gilt, gilded

dora'tura SF gilding

dormicchi'are [dormik'kjare] /19/ VI to doze

dormi'ente AG sleeping ▶ SMF sleeper

dormigli'one, -a [dormiʎ'ʎone] SM/F sleepy-head

dor'mire /45/ VI to sleep; **andare a ~** to go to bed; (*essere addormentato*) to be asleep, be sleeping; **il caffè non mi fa ~** coffee keeps me awake; **~ come un ghiro** to sleep like a log; **~ della grossa** to sleep soundly, be dead to the world; **~ in piedi** (*essere stanco*) to be asleep on one's feet

dor'mita SF: **farsi una ~** to have a good sleep

dormi'torio SM dormitory; **~ pubblico** doss house (BRIT) *o* flophouse (US: *run by local authority*)

dormi'veglia [dormi'veʎʎa] SM drowsiness

dorrò *ecc* VB *vedi* **dolere**

dor'sale AG: **spina ~** backbone, spine

'dorso SM back; (*di montagna*) ridge, crest; (*di libro*) spine; (*Nuoto*) backstroke; **a ~ di cavallo** on horseback

do'saggio [do'zaddʒo] SM (*atto*) measuring out; **sbagliare il ~** to get the proportions wrong

do'sare /72/ VT to measure out; (*Med*) to dose

'dose SF quantity, amount; (*Med*) dose

dossi'er [do'sje] SM INV dossier, file

'dosso SM (*rilievo*) rise; (: *di strada*) bump; (*dorso*): **levarsi di ~ i vestiti** to take one's clothes off; **levarsi un peso di ~** (*fig*) to take a weight off one's mind

do'tare /72/ VT: **~ di** to provide *o* supply with; (*fig*) to endow with

do'tato, -a AG: **~ di** (*attrezzature*) equipped with; (*bellezza, intelligenza*) endowed with; **un uomo ~** a gifted man

dotazi'one [dotat'tsjone] SF (*insieme di beni*) endowment; (*di macchine ecc*) equipment; **dare qc in ~ a qn** to issue sb with sth, issue sth to sb; **i macchinari in ~ alla fabbrica** the machinery in use in the factory

'dote SF (*di sposa*) dowry; (*assegnata a un ente*) endowment; (*fig*) gift, talent

Dott. ABBR (= *dottore*) Dr

'dotto, -a AG (*colto*) learned ▶ SM (*sapiente*) scholar; (*Anat*) duct

dotto'rato SM degree; **~ di ricerca** doctorate, doctor's degree

dot'tore, -'essa SM/F doctor

In Italy, anyone who has a degree in any subject can use the title **dottore**. Thus, a person who is addressed as *dottore* is not necessarily a doctor of medicine.

dot'trina SF doctrine

Dott.ssa ABBR (= *dottoressa*) Dr

double-'face [dubl'fas] AG INV reversible

'**dove** AV (*gen*) where; (*in cui*) where, in which; (*dovunque*) wherever ▶ CONG (*mentre, laddove*) whereas ▶ SM: **per ogni ~** everywhere; **~ sei?/vai?** where are you?/are you going?; **dimmi dov'è** tell me where it is; **di dov'è?** where are you from?; **da ~ abito vedo tutta la città** I can see the whole city from where I live; **per ~ si passa?** which way should we go?; **le dò una mano fin ~ posso** I'll help you as much as I can; **la città ~ abito** the town where *o* in which I live; **siediti ~ vuoi** sit wherever you like

do'vere /**46**/ SM (*obbligo*) duty ▶ VT (*essere debitore*): **~ qc (a qn)** to owe (sb) sth ▶ VI (*seguito dall'infinito: obbligo*) to have to; **devo partire domani** I'm due (to) leave tomorrow; **dev'essere tardi** (*probabilità*) it must be late; **lui deve farlo** he has to do it, he must do it; **quanto le devo?** how much do I owe you?; **è dovuto partire** he had to leave; **ha dovuto pagare** he had to pay; **doveva accadere** it was bound to happen; **avere il senso del ~** to have a sense of duty; **rivolgersi a chi di ~** to apply to the appropriate authority *o* person; **a ~** (*bene*) properly; (*debitamente*) as he (*o* she *etc*) deserves; **come si deve** (*bene*) properly; (*meritatamente*) properly, as he (*o* she *etc*) deserves; **una persona come si deve** a respectable person

dove'roso, -a AG (right and) proper

do'vizia [do'vittsja] SF abundance

dovrò *ecc* VB *vedi* **dovere**

do'vunque AV (*in qualunque luogo*) wherever; (*dappertutto*) everywhere; **~ io vada** wherever I go

dovuta'mente AV (*debitamente: redigere, compilare*) correctly; (*: rimproverare*) as he (*o* she *etc*) deserves

do'vuto, -a AG (*causato*): **~ a** due to ▶ SM due; **nel modo ~** in the proper way; **ho lavorato più del ~** I worked more than was necessary

doz'zina [dod'dzina] SF dozen; **una ~ di uova** a dozen eggs; **di** *o* **da ~** (*scrittore, spettacolo*) second-rate

dozzi'nale [doddzi'nale] AG cheap, second-rate

DP SIGLA F (= *Democrazia Proletaria*) *political party*

'**draga, -ghe** SF dredger

dra'gare /**80**/ VT to dredge

dragherò *ecc* [drage'rɔ] VB *vedi* **dragare**

'**drago, -ghi** SM dragon; (*fig: col*) genius

'**dramma, -i** SM drama; **fare un ~ di qc** to make a drama out of sth

dram'matico, -a, -ci, -che AG dramatic

drammatiz'zare [drammatid'dzare] /**72**/ VT to dramatize

dramma'turgo, -ghi SM playwright

drappeggi'are [drapped'dʒare] /**62**/ VT to drape

drap'peggio [drap'peddʒo] SM (*tessuto*) drapery; (*di abito*) folds

drap'pello SM (*Mil*) squad; (*gruppo*) band, group

'**drappo** SM cloth

'**drastico, -a, -ci, -che** AG drastic

dre'naggio [dre'naddʒo] SM drainage

dre'nare /**72**/ VT to drain

'**Dresda** SF Dresden

drib'blare /**72**/ VI (*Calcio*) to dribble ▶ VT (*avversario*) to dodge, avoid

'**dritto, -a** AG, AV = **diritto** ▶ SM/F (*col: furbo*): **è un ~** he's a crafty *o* sly one ▶ SF (*destra*) right, right hand; (*Naut*) starboard; **a dritta e a manca** (*fig*) on all sides, right, left and centre

driz'zare [drit'tsare] /**72**/ VT (*far tornare diritto*) to straighten; (*volgere: sguardo, occhi*) to turn, direct; (*innalzare: antenna, muro*) to erect ■ **drizzarsi** VPR to stand up; **~ le orecchie** to prick up one's ears; **drizzarsi in piedi** to rise to one's feet; **drizzarsi a sedere** to sit up

'**droga, -ghe** SF (*sostanza aromatica*) spice; (*stupefacente*) drug; **droghe pesanti/leggere** hard/soft drugs

dro'gare /**80**/ VT to drug, dope ■ **drogarsi** VPR to take drugs

dro'gato, -a SM/F drug addict

droghe'ria [droge'ria] SF grocer's (shop) (BRIT), grocery (store) (US)

drogherò *ecc* [droge'rɔ] VB *vedi* **drogare**

droghi'ere, -a [dro'gjɛre] SM/F grocer

drome'dario SM dromedary

'**drone** [dron] SM INV drone

DS [di'ɛsse] SMPL (= *Democratici di Sinistra*) Democrats of the Left (*Italian left-wing party*)

'**dubbio, -a** AG (*incerto*) doubtful, dubious; (*ambiguo*) dubious ▶ SM (*incertezza*) doubt; **avere il ~ che** to be afraid that, suspect that; **essere in ~ fra** to hesitate between; **mettere in ~ qc** to question sth; **nutrire seri dubbi su qc** to have grave doubts about sth; **senza ~** doubtless, no doubt

dubbi'oso, -a AG doubtful, dubious

dubi'tare /**72**/ VI: **~ di** (*onestà*) to doubt; (*risultato*) to be doubtful of; **~ di qn** to mistrust sb; **~ di sé** to be unsure of o.s.

Du'blino SF Dublin

'**duca, -chi** SM duke

'**duce** ['dutʃe] SM (*Storia*) captain; (*: del fascismo*) duce

du'chessa [du'kessa] SF duchess

'due NUM two; **a ~ a ~** two at a time, two by two; **dire ~ parole** to say a few words; **ci metto ~ minuti** I'll have it done in a jiffy

duecen'tesco, -a, -schi, -sche [duetʃen'tesko] AG thirteenth-century

due'cento [due'tʃento] NUM two hundred ▶ SM: **il D~** the thirteenth century

duel'lare /72/ VI to fight a duel

du'ello SM duel

due'mila NUM two thousand ▶ SM INV: **il ~** the year two thousand

due'pezzi [due'pɛttsi] SM (costume da bagno) two-piece swimsuit; (abito femminile) two-piece suit

du'etto SM duet

'dulcis in 'fundo ['dultʃisin'fundo] AV to cap it all

'duna SF dune

'dunque CONG (perciò) so, therefore; (riprendendo il discorso) well (then) ▶ SM INV: **venire al ~** to come to the point

'duo SM INV (Mus) duet; (Teat, Cine, fig) duo

du'ole ecc VB vedi **dolere**

du'omo SM cathedral

'duplex SM INV (Tel) party line

dupli'cato SM duplicate

'duplice ['duplitʃe] AG double, twofold; **in ~ copia** in duplicate

duplicità [duplitʃi'ta] SF (fig) duplicity

du'rante PREP during; **vita natural ~** for life

du'rare /72/ VI to last; **non può ~!** this can't go on any longer!; **~ fatica a** to have difficulty in; **~ in carica** to remain in office

du'rata SF length (of time); duration; **per tutta la ~ di** throughout; **~ media della vita** life expectancy

dura'turo, -a, du'revole AG (ricordo) lasting; (materiale) durable

du'rezza [du'rettsa] SF hardness; stubbornness; harshness; toughness

'duro, -a AG (pietra, lavoro, materasso, problema) hard; (persona: ostinato) stubborn, obstinate; (: severo) harsh, hard; (voce) harsh; (carne) tough ▶ SM/F hardness; (difficoltà) hard part; (persona) tough one ▶ AV: **tener ~** (resistere) to stand firm, hold out; **avere la pelle dura** (fig: persona) to be tough; **fare il ~** to act tough; **~ di comprendonio** slow-witted; **~ d'orecchi** hard of hearing

du'rone SM hard skin

'duttile AG (sostanza) malleable; (fig: carattere) docile, biddable; (: stile) adaptable

DVD [divu'di] SM INV DVD; (lettore) DVD player

d

Ee

E, e [e] SM O F INV (*lettera*) E, e; **E come Empoli** ≈ E for Edward (*BRIT*), E for Easy (*US*)

E ABBR (= *est*) E; (*Aut*) = **itinerario europeo**

e (*dav V spesso* **ed**) CONG and; (*avversativo*) but; (*eppure*) and yet; **e lui?** what about him?; **e compralo!** well buy it then!

è VB *vedi* **essere**

E.A.D. SIGLA F = **elaborazione automatica dei dati**

ebaniste'ria SF cabinet-making; (*negozio*) cabinet-maker's shop

'ebano SM ebony

eb'bene CONG well (then)

'ebbi *ecc* VB *vedi* **avere**

eb'brezza [eb'brettsa] SF intoxication

'ebbro, -a AG drunk; ~ **di** (*gioia ecc*) beside o.s. *o* wild with

'ebete AG stupid, idiotic

ebe'tismo SM stupidity

ebollizi'one [ebollit'tsjone] SF boiling; **punto di** ~ boiling point

e'braico, -a, -ci, -che AG Hebrew, Hebraic ▶ SM (*Ling*) Hebrew

e'breo, -a AG Jewish ▶ SM/F Jewish person, Jew

'Ebridi SFPL: **le (isole)** ~ the Hebrides

e'burneo, -a AG ivory *cpd*

EC ABBR (= *Eurocity*) *fast train connecting Western European cities*

E/C ABBR = **estratto conto**

eca'tombe SF (*strage*) slaughter, massacre

ecc. ABBR (= *eccetera*) etc

ecce'dente [ettʃe'dɛnte] SM surplus

ecce'denza [ettʃe'dɛntsa] SF excess, surplus; (*Inform*) overflow

ec'cedere [et'tʃɛdere] /29/ VT to exceed ▶ VI to go too far; ~ **nel bere/mangiare** to indulge in drink/food to excess

eccel'lente [ettʃel'lɛnte] AG excellent; (*cadavere, arresto*) of a prominent person

eccel'lenza [ettʃe'lɛntsa] SF excellence; (*titolo*): **Sua E**~ His Excellency

ec'cellere [et'tʃɛllere] /45/ VI: ~ **(in)** to excel (at); ~ **su tutti** to surpass everyone

ec'celso, -a [et'tʃɛlso] PP *di* **eccellere** ▶ AG (*cima, montagna*) high; (*fig: ingegno*) great, exceptional

ec'centrico, -a, -ci, -che [et'tʃɛntriko] AG eccentric

ecces'sivo, -a [ettʃes'sivo] AG excessive

ec'cesso [et'tʃɛsso] SM excess; **all'~** (*gentile, generoso*) to excess, excessively; **dare in eccessi** to fly into a rage; ~ **di velocità** (*Aut*) speeding; ~ **di zelo** overzealousness

ec'cetera [et'tʃetera] AV et cetera, and so on

ec'cetto [et'tʃɛtto] PREP except, with the exception of; ~ **che** *cong* except, other than; ~ **che (non)** unless

eccettu'are [ettʃettu'are] /72/ VT to except; **eccettuati i presenti** present company excepted

eccezio'nale [ettʃettsjo'nale] AG exceptional; **in via del tutto** ~ in this instance, exceptionally

eccezi'one [ettʃet'tsjone] SF exception; (*Dir*) objection; **a** ~ **di** with the exception of, except for; **d'**~ exceptional; **fare un'**~ **alla regola** to make an exception to the rule

ec'chimosi [ek'kimozi] SF INV bruise

ec'cidio [et'tʃidjo] SM massacre

ecci'tante [ettʃi'tante] AG (*gen*) exciting; (*sostanza*) stimulating ▶ SM stimulant

ecci'tare [ettʃi'tare] /72/ VT (*curiosità, interesse*) to excite, arouse; (*folla*) to incite ■ **eccitarsi** VPR to get excited; (*sessualmente*) to become aroused

eccitazi'one [ettʃitat'tsjone] SF excitement

ecclesi'astico, -a, -ci, -che AG ecclesiastical, church *cpd*; clerical ▶ SM ecclesiastic

'ecco AV (*per dimostrare*): ~ **il treno!** here's *o* here comes the train!; (*dav pronome*) **eccomi!** here I am!; **eccone uno!** here's one (of them)!; (*dav pp*) ~ **fatto!** there, that's it done!

ec'come AV rather; **ti piace? – ~!** do you like it? — I'll say! o and how! o rather! (BRIT)

ECG SIGLA M = **elettrocardiogramma**

echeggi'are [eked'dʒare] /**62**/ VI to echo

e'clettico, -a, -ci, -che AG, SM/F eclectic

eclet'tismo SM eclecticism

eclis'sare /**72**/ VT to eclipse; (fig) to eclipse, overshadow ▪ **eclissarsi** VPR (persona: scherzoso) to slip away

e'clisse SF eclipse

e'clissi SF eclipse

'eco (pl(m) **echi**) SM O F echo; **suscitò o ebbe una profonda ~** it caused quite a stir

ecogra'fia SF (Med) ultrasound

ecolo'gia [ekolo'dʒia] SF ecology

eco'logico, -a, -ci, -che [eko'lɔdʒiko] AG ecological

ecolo'gista, -i, -e [ekolo'dʒista] AG ecological ▪ SM/F ecologist, environmentalist

e'cologo, -a, -gi, -ghe SM/F ecologist

eco'mafia SF mafia involved in crimes related to the environment, in particular the illegal disposal of waste

econo'mato SM (Ins) bursar's office

econo'mia SF economy; (scienza) economics sg; (risparmio: azione) saving; **fare ~** to economize, make economies; **l'~ sommersa** the black (BRIT) o underground (US) economy; **~ di mercato** market economy; **~ pianificata** planned economy

eco'nomico, -a, -ci, -che AG economic; (poco costoso) economical; **edizione economica** economy edition

econo'mista, -i SMF economist

economiz'zare [ekonomid'dzare] /**72**/ VT, VI to save

e'conomo, -a AG thrifty ▪ SM/F (Ins) bursar

ecorespon'sabile AG eco-friendly, environmentally friendly

ecosis'tema, -i SM ecosystem

ecosoli'dale AG environmentally and socially conscious; **turismo ~** ethical tourism

eco'tassa [eko'tassa] SF green tax

ecotu'rismo SM ecotourism

'ecstasy ['ɛkstasi] SF INV ecstasy

'Ecuador SM: **l'~** Ecuador

ecu'menico, -a, -ci, -che AG ecumenical

ec'zema [ek'dzɛma] SM eczema

ed CONG vedi **e**

Ed. ABBR = **editore**

ed. ABBR = **edizione**

'edera SF ivy

e'dicola SF newspaper kiosk o stand (US)

edico'lante SMF news vendor (in kiosk)

edifi'cante AG edifying

edifi'care /**20**/ VT to build; (fig: teoria, azienda) to establish; (indurre al bene) to edify

edi'ficio [edi'fitʃo] SM building; (fig) structure

e'dile AG building cpd

edi'lizio, -a [edi'littsjo] AG building cpd ▪ SF building, building trade

Edim'burgo SF Edinburgh

'edito, -a AG published

edi'tore, -'trice AG publishing cpd ▪ SM/F publisher

edito'ria SF publishing

editori'ale AG publishing cpd ▪ SM (articolo di fondo) editorial, leader

e'ditto SM edict

edizi'one [edit'tsjone] SF edition; (tiratura) printing; **~ a tiratura limitata** limited edition; **~ straordinaria** special edition

edo'nismo SM hedonism

e'dotto, -a AG informed; **rendere qn ~ su qc** to inform sb about sth

edu'canda SF boarder

edu'care /**20**/ VT to educate; (gusto, mente) to train; **~ qn a fare** to train sb to do

educa'tivo, -a AG educational

edu'cato, -a AG polite, well-mannered

educazi'one [edukat'tsjone] SF education; (familiare) upbringing; (comportamento) (good) manners pl; **per ~** out of politeness; **questa è pura mancanza d'~!** this is sheer bad manners!; **~ fisica** (Ins) physical training o education

educherò ecc [eduke'rɔ] VB vedi **educare**

E.E.D. SIGLA F = **elaborazione elettronica dei dati**

EEG SIGLA M = **elettroencefalogramma**

e'felide SF freckle

effemi'nato, -a AG effeminate

effe'rato, -a AG brutal, savage

efferve'scente [efferveʃ'ʃente] AG effervescent

effettiva'mente AV (in effetti) in fact; (a dire il vero) really, actually

effet'tivo, -a AG (reale) real, actual; (impiegato, professore) permanent; (Mil) regular ▪ SM (Mil) strength; (di patrimonio ecc) sum total

ef'fetto SM effect; (Comm: cambiale) bill; (fig: impressione) impression; **far ~** (medicina) to take effect, (start to) work; **cercare l'~** to seek attention; **in effetti** in fact, actually; **effetti attivi** (Comm) bills receivable; **effetti passivi** (Comm) bills payable; **effetti personali** personal effects, personal belongings; **~ serra** greenhouse effect; **effetti speciali** (Cine) special effects

effettu'are /**72**/ VT to effect, carry out

effi'cace [effi'katʃe] AG effective

effi'cacia [effi'katʃa] SF effectiveness

effici'ente [effi'tʃɛnte] AG efficient

121

efficien'tismo [effitʃen'tizmo] SM maximum efficiency

effici'enza [effi'tʃɛntsa] SF efficiency

effigi'are [effi'dʒare] /**62**/ VT to represent, portray

effigie [ef'fidʒe] SF INV effigy

ef'fimero, -a AG ephemeral

ef'fluvio SM (anche peg, ironico) scent, perfume

effusi'one SF effusion

e.g. ABBR (= exempli gratia) e.g.

egemo'nia [edʒemo'nia] SF hegemony

E'geo [e'dʒɛo] SM: **l'~, il mare ~** the Aegean (Sea)

'egida ['ɛdʒida] SF: **sotto l'~ di** under the aegis of

E'gitto [e'dʒitto] SM: **l'~** Egypt

egizi'ano, -a [edʒit'tsjano] AG, SM/F Egyptian

e'gizio, -a [e'dʒittsjo] AG, SM/F (ancient) Egyptian

'egli ['eʎʎi] PRON he; **~ stesso** he himself

'ego SM INV (Psic) ego

ego'centrico, -a, -ci, -che [ego'tʃɛntriko] AG egocentric(al) ▶ SM/F self-centred (BRIT) o self-centered (US) person

egocen'trismo [egotʃen'trizmo] SM egocentricity

ego'ismo SM selfishness, egoism

ego'ista, -i, -e AG selfish, egoistic ▶ SM/F egoist

ego'istico, -a, -ci, -che AG egoistic, selfish

ego'tismo SM egotism

ego'tista, -i, -e AG egotistic ▶ SM/F egotist

Egr. ABBR = **egregio**

e'gregio, -a, -gi, -gie [e'grɛdʒo] AG distinguished; (nelle lettere): **E~ Signore** Dear Sir

eguagli'anza ecc [egwaʎ'ʎantsa] vedi **uguaglianza** ecc

eguali'tario, -a AG, SM/F egalitarian

E.I. ABBR = **Esercito Italiano**

eiaculazi'one [ejakulat'tsjone] SF ejaculation; **~ precoce** premature ejaculation

elabo'rare /**72**/ VT (progetto) to work out, elaborate; (dati) to process; (digerire) to digest

elabora'tore SM (Inform): **~ elettronico** computer

elaborazi'one [elaborat'tsjone] SF elaboration; processing; digestion; **~ automatica dei dati** (Inform) automatic data processing; **~ elettronica dei dati** (Inform) electronic data processing; **~ testi** (Inform) text processing

elar'gire [elar'dʒire] /**55**/ VT to hand out

elargizi'one [elardʒit'tsjone] SF donation

elasticiz'zato, -a [elastitʃid'dzato] AG (tessuto) stretch cpd

e'lastico, -a, -ci, -che AG elastic; (fig: andatura) springy; (: decisione, vedute) flexible ▶ SM (gommino) rubber band; (per il cucito) elastic no pl

ele'fante, -essa SM/F elephant

ele'gante AG elegant

ele'ganza [ele'gantsa] SF elegance

e'leggere [e'lɛddʒere] /**61**/ VT to elect

elemen'tare AG elementary; **le (scuole) elementari** sfpl primary (BRIT) o grade (US) school; **prima ~** first year of primary school, ≈ reception class (BRIT), ≈ 1st grade (US)

ele'mento SM element; (parte componente) element, component, part ▪ **elementi** SMPL (della scienza ecc) elements, rudiments

ele'mosina SF charity, alms pl; **chiedere l'~** to beg

elemosi'nare /**72**/ VT to beg for, ask for ▶ VI to beg

elen'care /**20**/ VT to list

elencherò ecc [elenke'rɔ] VB vedi **elencare**

e'lenco, -chi SM list; **~ nominativo** list of names; **~ telefonico** telephone directory

e'lessi ecc VB vedi **eleggere**

elet'tivo, -a AG (carica ecc) elected

e'letto, -a PP di **eleggere** ▶ SM/F (nominato) elected member

eletto'rale AG electoral, election cpd

eletto'rato SM electorate

elet'tore, -'trice SM/F voter, elector

elet'trauto SM INV workshop for car electrical repairs; (tecnico) car electrician

elettri'cista, -i [elettri'tʃista] SM electrician

elettricità [elettritʃi'ta] SF electricity

e'lettrico, -a, -ci, -che AG electric(al)

elettrifi'care /**20**/ VT to electrify

elettriz'zante [elettrid'dzante] AG (fig) electrifying, thrilling

elettriz'zare [elettrid'dzare] /**72**/ VT to electrify ▪ **elettrizzarsi** VPR to become charged with electricity; (fig: persona) to be thrilled

e'lettro... PREFISSO electro...

elettrocardio'gramma, -i SM electrocardiogram

e'lettrodo SM electrode

elettrodo'mestico, -a, -ci, -che AG: **apparecchi elettrodomestici** domestic (electrical) appliances

elettroencefalo'gramma, -i [elettroentʃefalo'gramma] SM electroencephalogram

elet'trogeno, -a [elet'trɔdʒeno] AG: **gruppo ~** generator

elet'trolisi SF electrolysis

elettroma'gnetico, -a, -ci, -che [elettromaɲ'ɲetiko] AG electromagnetic

elettromo'trice [elettromo'tritʃe] SF electric train

elet'trone SM electron

elet'tronico, -a, -ci, -che AG electronic ▶ SF electronics sg

elettro'shock [elettroʃ'ʃɔk] SM INV (electro) shock treatment

elettro'tecnico, -a, -ci, -che AG electrotechnical ► SM electrical engineer

ele'vare /72/ VT to raise; (edificio) to erect; (multa) to impose; **~ un numero al quadrato** to square a number

eleva'tezza [eleva'tettsa] SF (altezza) elevation; (di animo, pensiero) loftiness

ele'vato, -a AG (gen) high; (cime) high, lofty; (fig: stile, sentimenti) lofty

elevazi'one [elevat'tsjone] SF elevation; (l'elevare) raising

elezi'one [elet'tsjone] SF election ◼ **elezioni** SFPL (Pol) election(s); **patria d'~** chosen country

'elica, -che SF propeller

eli'cottero SM helicopter

e'lidere /89/ VT (Fonetica) to elide ◼ **elidersi** VPR (forze) to cancel each other out, neutralize each other

elimi'nare /72/ VT to eliminate

elimina'toria SF eliminating round

eliminazi'one [eliminat'tsjone] SF elimination

'elio SM helium

eli'porto SM heliport

elisabetti'ano, -a AG Elizabethan

eli'sir SM INV elixir

e'liso, -a PP di **elidere**

elisoc'corso SM helicopter ambulance

eli'tario, -a AG elitist

é'lite [e'lit] SF INV élite

'ella PRON she; (forma di cortesia) you; **~ stessa** she herself; you yourself

el'lisse SF ellipse

el'littico, -a, -ci, -che AG elliptic(al)

el'metto SM helmet

'elmo SM helmet

elogi'are [elo'dʒare] /62/ VT to praise

elogia'tivo, -a [elodʒa'tivo] AG laudatory

e'logio [e'lɔdʒo] SM (discorso, scritto) eulogy; (lode) praise; **~ funebre** funeral oration

elo'quente AG eloquent; **questi dati sono eloquenti** these facts speak for themselves

elo'quenza [elo'kwɛntsa] SF eloquence

e'loquio SM speech, language

elucu'brare /72/ VT to ponder about o over

elucubrazi'oni [elukubrat'tsjoni] SFPL (anche ironico) cogitations, ponderings

e'ludere /35/ VT to evade

e'lusi ecc VB vedi **eludere**

elusi'one SF: **~ d'imposta** tax evasion

elu'sivo, -a AG evasive

e'luso, -a PP di **eludere**

el'vetico, -a, -ci, -che AG Swiss

emaci'ato, -a [ema'tʃato] AG emaciated

e-'mail, e'mail [e'mɛil] SF INV (messaggio, sistema) email ► AG INV email; **indirizzo ~** email address

ema'nare /72/ VT to send out, give off; (fig: leggi) to promulgate; (: decreti) to issue ► VI: **~ da** to come from

emanazi'one [emanat'tsjone] SF (di raggi, calore) emanation; (di odori) exhalation; (di legge) promulgation; (di ordine, circolare) issuing

emanci'pare [emantʃi'pare] /72/ VT to emancipate ◼ **emanciparsi** VPR (fig) to become liberated o emancipated

emancipazi'one [emantʃipat'tsjone] SF emancipation

emargi'nare [emardʒi'nare] /72/ VT (fig: socialmente) to cast out

emargi'nato, -a [emardʒi'nato] SM/F outcast

emargina'zione [emardʒinat'tsjone] SF marginalization

ematolo'gia [ematolo'dʒia] SF haematology (BRIT), hematology (US)

ema'toma, -i SM haematoma (BRIT), hematoma (US)

embed'dato, -a AG embedded

em'blema, -i SM emblem

emble'matico, -a, -ci, -che AG emblematic; (fig: atteggiamento, parole) symbolic

embo'lia SF embolism

embrio'nale, -i, -e AG embryonic, embryo cpd; **allo stadio ~** at the embryo stage

embri'one SM embryo

emenda'mento SM amendment

emen'dare /72/ VT to amend

emer'gente [emer'dʒɛnte] AG emerging

emer'genza [emer'dʒɛntsa] SF emergency; **in caso di ~** in an emergency

---

Emergency telephone numbers in Italy are as follows: police 113, Carabinieri 112, ambulance 118, fire brigade 115, car breakdown service 116.

---

e'mergere [e'mɛrdʒere] /59/ VI to emerge; (sommergibile) to surface; (fig: distinguersi) to stand out

e'merito, -a AG (insigne) distinguished; **è un ~ cretino!** he's a complete idiot!

e'mersi ecc VB vedi **emergere**

e'merso, -a PP di **emergere** ► AG (Geo): **terre emerse** lands above sea level

e'messo, -a PP di **emettere**

e'mettere /63/ VT (suono, luce) to give out, emit; (onde radio) to send out; (assegno, francobollo, ordine) to issue; (fig: giudizio) to express, voice; **~ la sentenza** (Dir) to pass sentence

emi'crania SF migraine

emi'grante AG, SM/F emigrant

emi'grare /72/ VI to emigrate

emi'grato, -a AG emigrant ▶ SM/F emigrant; (*Storia*) émigré

emigrazi'one [emigrat'tsjone] SF emigration

emili'ano, -a AG of (*o* from) Emilia

emi'nente AG eminent, distinguished

emi'nenza [emi'nɛntsa] SF eminence; **~ grigia** (*fig*) éminence grise

emi'rato SM emirate; **gli Emirati Arabi Uniti** the United Arab Emirates

e'miro SM emir

emis'fero SM hemisphere; **~ boreale/australe** northern/southern hemisphere

e'misi *ecc* VB *vedi* **emettere**

emis'sario SM (*Geo*) outlet, effluent; (*inviato*) emissary

emissi'one SF (*vedi* **emettere**) emission; sending out; issue; (*Radio*) broadcast

emit'tente AG (*banca*) issuing; (*Radio*) broadcasting, transmitting ▶ SF (*Radio*) transmitter

emofi'lia SF haemophilia (BRIT), hemophilia (US)

emofi'liaco, -a, -ci, -che AG, SM/F haemophiliac (BRIT), hemophiliac (US)

emoglo'bina SF haemoglobin (BRIT), hemoglobin (US)

emolli'ente AG soothing

emorra'gia, -'gie [emorra'dʒia] SF haemorrhage (BRIT), hemorrhage (US)

emor'roidi SFPL haemorrhoids *pl* (BRIT), hemorrhoids *pl* (US)

emos'tatico, -a, -ci, -che AG haemostatic (BRIT), hemostatic (US); **laccio ~** tourniquet; **matita emostatica** styptic pencil

emotività SF emotionalism

emo'tivo, -a AG emotional

emozio'nante [emottsjo'nante] AG exciting, thrilling

emozio'nare [emottsjo'nare] /72/ VT (*appassionare*) to excite, thrill; (*commuovere*) to move; (*agitare*) to make nervous; (*innervosire*) to upset ▪ **emozionarsi** VPR to be excited; to be moved; to be nervous; to be upset

emozion'ato, -a [emottsjo'nato] AG (*commosso*) moved; (*agitato*) nervous; (*elettrizzato*) excited

emozi'one [emot'tsjone] SF emotion; (*agitazione*) excitement

'empio, -a AG (*sacrilego*) impious; (*spietato*) cruel, pitiless; (*malvagio*) wicked, evil

em'pirico, -a, -ci, -che AG empirical

em'porio SM general store

emu'lare /72/ VT to emulate

'emulo, -a SM/F imitator

emulsi'one SF emulsion

EN SIGLA = **Enna**

en'ciclica, -che [en'tʃiklika] SF (*Rel*) encyclical

enciclope'dia [entʃiklope'dia] SF encyclop(a)edia

encomi'abile AG commendable, praiseworthy

encomi'are /19/ VT to commend, praise

en'comio SM commendation; **~ solenne** (*Mil*) mention in dispatches

endove'noso, -a AG (*Med*) intravenous ▶ SF intravenous injection

E'NEA SIGLA F = **Comitato nazionale per la ricerca e lo sviluppo dell'Energia Nucleare e delle Energie Alternative**

'E.N.E.L. SIGLA M (= *Ente Nazionale per l'Energia Elettrica*) national electricity company

ener'getico, -a, -ci, -che [ener'dʒɛtiko] AG (*risorse, crisi*) energy *cpd*; (*sostanza, alimento*) energy-giving

ener'gia, -'gie [ener'dʒia] SF (*Fisica*) energy; (*fig*) energy, strength, vigour (BRIT), vigor (US); **~ eolica** wind power; **~ rinnovabile** renewable energy; **~ solare** solar energy, solar power; **~ sostenibile** sustainable energy

e'nergico, -a, -ci, -che [e'nɛrdʒiko] AG energetic, vigorous

'enfasi SF emphasis; (*peg*) bombast, pomposity

en'fatico, -a, -ci, -che AG emphatic; pompous

enfatiz'zare [enfatid'dzare] /72/ VT to emphasize, stress

enfi'sema SM emphysema

'ENI SIGLA M = **Ente Nazionale Idrocarburi**

e'nigma, -i SM enigma

enig'matico, -a, -ci, -che AG enigmatic

'ENIT SIGLA M (= *Ente Nazionale Italiano per il Turismo*) *Italian tourist authority*

en'nesimo, -a AG (*Mat, fig*) nth; **per l'ennesima volta** for the umpteenth time

enolo'gia [enolo'dʒia] SF oenology (BRIT), enology (US)

e'nologo, -gi SM wine expert

e'norme AG enormous, huge

enormità SF INV enormity, huge size; (*assurdità*) absurdity; **non dire ~!** don't talk nonsense!

eno'teca, -che SF (*negozio*) wine bar

'E.N.P.A. SIGLA M (= *Ente Nazionale Protezione Animali*) ≈ RSPCA (BRIT), ≈ SPCA (US)

'ente SM (*istituzione*) body, board, corporation; (*Filosofia*) being; **~ locale** local authority (BRIT), local government (US); **~ pubblico** public body; **~ di ricerca** research organization

ente'rite SF enteritis

entità SF INV (*Filosofia*) entity; (*di perdita, danni, investimenti*) extent; (*di popolazione*) size; **di molta/poca ~** (*avvenimento, incidente*) of great/little importance

en'trambi, -e PRON PL both (of them) ▶ AG PL: **~ i ragazzi** both boys, both of the boys

en'trante AG (*prossimo: mese, anno*) next, coming

en'trare /72/ VI to enter, go (*o* come) in; **~ in** (*luogo*) to enter, go (*o* come) into; (*trovar posto,* *poter stare*) to fit into; (*essere ammesso a: club ecc*) to join, become a member of; **~ in automobile** to get into the car; **far ~ qn** (*visitatore ecc*) to show sb in; **~ in società/in commercio con qn** to go into partnership/business with sb; **questo non c'entra** (*fig*) that's got nothing to do with it

en'trata SF entrance, entry; **dov'è l'~?** where's the entrance? ■ **entrate** SFPL (*Comm*) receipts, takings; (*Econ*) income *sg*; **"~ libera"** "admission free"; **con l'~ in vigore dei nuovi provvedimenti ...** once the new measures come into effect ...; **entrate tributarie** tax revenue *sg*

'entro PREP (*temporale*) within; **~ domani** by tomorrow; **~ e non oltre il 25 aprile** no later than 25th April

entro'terra SM INV hinterland

entusias'mante AG exciting

entusias'mare /72/ VT to excite, fill with enthusiasm ■ **entusiasmarsi** VPR: **entusiasmarsi (per qc/qn)** to become enthusiastic (about sth/sb)

entusi'asmo SM enthusiasm

entusi'asta, -i, -e AG enthusiastic ▶ SM/F enthusiast

entusi'astico, -a, -ci, -che AG enthusiastic

enucle'are /72/ VT (*formale: chiarire*) to explain

enume'rare /72/ VT to enumerate, list

enunci'are [enun'tʃare] /14/ VT (*teoria*) to enunciate, set out

en'zima, -i SM enzyme

e'olico, -a, -chi, -che AG wind; **energia eolica** wind power

e'patico, -a, -ci, -che AG hepatic; **cirrosi epatica** cirrhosis of the liver

epa'tite SF hepatitis

'epico, -a, -ci, -che AG epic

epide'mia SF epidemic

epi'dermico, -a, -ci, -che AG (*Anat*) skin *cpd*; (*fig: interesse, impressioni*) superficial

epi'dermide SF skin, epidermis

Epifa'nia SF Epiphany

e'pigono SM imitator

e'pigrafe SF epigraph; (*su libro*) dedication

epiles'sia SF epilepsy

epi'lettico, -a, -ci, -che AG, SM/F epileptic

e'pilogo, -ghi SM conclusion

epi'sodico, -a, -ci, -che AG (*romanzo, narrazione*) episodic; (*fig: occasionale*) occasional

epi'sodio SM episode; **sceneggiato a episodi** serial

e'pistola SF epistle

episto'lare AG epistolary; **essere in rapporto** *o* **relazione ~ con qn** to correspond *o* be in correspondence with sb

e'piteto SM epithet

'epoca, -che SF (*periodo storico*) age, era; (*tempo*) time; (*Geo*) age; **mobili d'~** period furniture; **fare ~** (*scandalo*) to cause a stir; (*cantante, moda*) to mark a new era

epo'pea SF (*anche fig*) epic

ep'pure CONG and yet, nevertheless

EPT SIGLA M (= *Ente Provinciale per il Turismo*) district tourist bureau

epu'rare /72/ VT (*Pol*) to purge

equ'anime AG (*imparziale*) fair, impartial

equa'tore SM equator

equazi'one [ekwat'tsjone] SF (*Mat*) equation

e'questre AG equestrian

equi'latero, -a AG equilateral

equili'brare /72/ VT to balance

equili'brato, -a AG (*carico, fig: giudizio*) balanced; (*vita*) well-regulated; (*persona*) stable, well-balanced

equi'librio SM balance, equilibrium; **perdere l'~** to lose one's balance; **stare in ~ su** (*persona*) to balance on; (*oggetto*) to be balanced on

equili'brismo SM tightrope walking; (*fig*) juggling

e'quino, -a AG horse *cpd*, equine

equi'nozio [ekwi'nɔttsjo] SM equinox

equipaggia'mento [ekwipaddʒa'mento] SM (*operazione: di nave*) equipping, fitting out; (: *di spedizione, esercito*) equipping, kitting out; (*attrezzatura*) equipment

equipaggi'are [ekwipad'dʒare] /62/ VT (*di persone*) to man; (*di mezzi*) to equip ■ **equipaggiarsi** VPR to equip o.s.

equi'paggio [ekwi'paddʒo] SM crew

equipa'rare /72/ VT to make equal

é'quipe [e'kip] SF (*Sport, gen*) team

equità SF equity, fairness

equitazi'one [ekwitat'tsjone] SF (horse-) riding

equiva'lente AG, SM equivalent

equiva'lenza [ekwiva'lɛntsa] SF equivalence

equiva'lere /126/ VI: **~ a** to be equivalent to ■ **equivalersi** VPR (*forze ecc*) to counterbalance each other; (*soluzioni*) to amount to the same thing; **equivale a dire che ...** that is the same as saying that ...

equi'valso, -a PP *di* equivalere

equivo'care /20/ VI to misunderstand

e'quivoco, -a, -ci, -che AG equivocal, ambiguous; (*sospetto*) dubious ▶ SM misunderstanding; **a scanso di equivoci** to avoid any misunderstanding; **giocare sull'~** to equivocate

'equo, -a AG fair, just; **commercio ~ solidale** fair trade; **prodotto ~ solidale** fair-trade product

'era SF era

'era *ecc* VB *vedi* essere

erari'ale AG: **ufficio ~** = tax office; **imposte era-**

riali revenue taxes; **spese erariali** public expenditure *sg*

e'rario SM: l'~ = the Treasury

'erba SF grass; in ~ (*fig*) budding; fare di ogni ~ un fascio (*fig*) to lump everything (*o* everybody) together; **erbe aromatiche** herbs; ~ **medica** lucerne

er'baccia, -ce [er'battʃa] SF weed

er'bivoro, -a AG herbivorous ▶ SM/F herbivore

erbo'rista, -i, -e SM/F herbalist

erboriste'ria SF (*scienza*) study of medicinal herbs; (*negozio*) herbalist's (shop)

er'boso, -a AG grassy

e'rede SMF heir(-ess); ~ **legittimo** heir-at-law

eredità SF (*Dir*) inheritance; (*Biol*) heredity; **lasciare qc in ~ a qn** to leave *o* bequeath sth to sb

eredi'tare /72/ VT to inherit

eredi'tario, -a AG hereditary

erediti'era SF heiress

ere'mita, -i SM hermit

eremi'taggio [eremi'taddʒo] SM hermitage

'eremo SM hermitage; (*fig*) retreat

ere'sia SF heresy

e'ressi *ecc* VB *vedi* **erigere**

e'retico, -a, -ci, -che AG heretical ▶ SM/F heretic

e'retto, -a PP *di* **erigere** ▶ AG erect, upright

erezi'one [eret'tsjone] SF (*Fisiol*) erection

ergasto'lano, -a SM/F prisoner serving a life sentence, lifer (*col*)

er'gastolo SM (*Dir: pena*) life imprisonment; (: *luogo di pena*) prison (*for those serving life sentences*)

ergono'mia SF ergonomics *sg*

ergo'nomico, -a, -ci, -che AG ergonomic(al)

'erica SF heather

e'rigere [e'ridʒere] /39/ VT to erect, raise; (*fig: fondare*) to found

eri'tema SM (*Med*) inflammation, erythema; ~ solare sunburn

Eri'trea SF Eritrea

ermel'lino SM ermine

er'metico, -a, -ci, -che AG hermetic

'ernia SF (*Med*) hernia; ~ **del disco** slipped disc

'ero VB *vedi* **essere**

e'rodere /49/ VT to erode

e'roe SM hero

ero'gare /80/ VT (*somme*) to distribute; (*gas, servizi*) to supply

erogazi'one [erogat'tsjone] SF distribution; supply

e'roico, -a, -ci, -che AG heroic

ero'ina SF heroine; (*droga*) heroin

ero'ismo SM heroism

'eros SM Eros

erosi'one SF erosion

e'roso, -a PP *di* **erodere**

e'rotico, -a, -ci, -che AG erotic

ero'tismo SM eroticism

'erpete SM herpes *sg*

'erpice ['erpitʃe] SM (*Agr*) harrow

er'rare /72/ VI (*vagare*) to wander, roam; (*sbagliare*) to be mistaken

er'rato, -a AG wrong

er'roneo, -a AG erroneous, wrong

er'rore SM error, mistake; (*morale*) error; per ~ by mistake; **ci dev'essere un ~** there must be some mistake; ~ **giudiziario** miscarriage of justice

'erto, -a AG (very) steep ▶ SF steep slope; stare all'erta to be on the alert

eru'dire /55/ VT to teach, educate

eru'dito, -a AG learned, erudite

erut'tare /72/ VT (*vulcano*) to throw out, belch

eruzi'one [erut'tsjone] SF eruption; (*Med*) rash

es. ABBR (= *esempio*) e.g.

E.S. SIGLA M (= *elettroshock*) ECT

E.S.A. ['eza] SIGLA M (= *European Space Agency*) ESA

esacer'bare [ezatʃer'bare] /72/ VT to exacerbate

esage'rare [ezadʒe'rare] /72/ VT to exaggerate ▶ VI to exaggerate; (*eccedere*) to go too far; **senza ~** without exaggeration

esage'rato, -a [ezadʒe'rato] AG (*notizia, proporzioni*) exaggerated; (*curiosità, pignoleria*) excessive; (*prezzo*) exorbitant ▶ SM/F: **sei il solito ~** you are exaggerating as usual

esagerazi'one [esadʒerat'tsjone] SF exaggeration

esago'nale AG hexagonal

e'sagono SM hexagon

esa'lare /72/ VT (*odori*) to give off ▶ VI: ~ **(da)** to emanate (from); ~ **l'ultimo respiro** (*fig*) to breathe one's last

esalazi'one [ezalat'tsjone] SF (*emissione*) exhalation; (*odore*) fumes *pl*

esal'tante AG exciting

esal'tare /72/ VT to exalt; (*entusiasmare*) to excite, stir ■ **esaltarsi** VPR: **esaltarsi (per qc)** to grow excited (about sth)

esal'tato, -a SM/F fanatic

esaltazi'one [ezaltat'tsjone] SF (*elogio*) extolling, exalting; (*nervosa*) intense excitement; (*mistica*) exaltation

e'same SM examination; (*Ins*) exam, examination; fare *o* dare un ~ to sit *o* take an exam; fare un ~ di coscienza to search one's conscience; ~ **di guida** driving test; ~ **del sangue** blood test

esami'nare /72/ VT to examine

e'sangue AG bloodless; *(fig: pallido)* pale, wan; *(: privo di vigore)* lifeless

e'sanime AG lifeless

esaspe'rare /**72**/ VT to exasperate; *(situazione)* to exacerbate ■ **esasperarsi** VPR to become annoyed *o* exasperated

esasperazi'one [ezasperat'tsjone] SF exasperation

esatta'mente AV exactly; accurately, precisely

esat'tezza [ezat'tettsa] SF exactitude, accuracy, precision; **per l'~** to be precise

e'satto, -a PP di **esigere** ▶ AG *(calcolo, ora)* correct, right, exact; *(preciso)* accurate, precise; *(puntuale)* punctual

esat'tore SM *(di imposte ecc)* collector

esat'to'ria SF: **~ comunale** district rates office (BRIT) *o* assessor's office (US)

esau'dire /**55**/ VT to grant, fulfil (BRIT), fulfill (US)

esauri'ente AG exhaustive

esauri'mento SM exhaustion; **~ nervoso** nervous breakdown; **svendita (fino) ad ~ della merce** clearance sale

esau'rire /**55**/ VT *(stancare)* to exhaust, wear out; *(provviste, miniera)* to exhaust ■ **esaurirsi** VPR to exhaust o.s., wear o.s. out; *(provviste)* to run out

esau'rito, -a AG exhausted; *(merci)* sold out; *(libri)* out of print; **essere ~** *(persona)* to be run down; **registrare il tutto ~** *(Teat)* to have a full house

e'sausto, -a AG exhausted

esauto'rare /**72**/ VT *(dirigente, funzionario)* to deprive of authority

esazi'one [ezat'tsjone] SF collection (of taxes)

'esca *(pl* **esche)** SF bait

escamo'tage [ɛskamɔ'taʒ] SM subterfuge

escande'scenza [eskandeʃ'ʃentsa] SF: **dare in escandescenze** to lose one's temper, fly into a rage

'esce ['eʃʃe] VB *vedi* **uscire**

eschi'mese [eski'mese] AG, SMF, SM Eskimo

'esci ['eʃʃi] VB *vedi* **uscire**

escl. ABBR (= *escluso*) excl

escla'mare /**72**/ VI to exclaim, cry out

esclama'tivo, -a AG: **punto ~** exclamation mark

esclamazi'one [esklamat'tsjone] SF exclamation

es'cludere /**3**/ VT to exclude

es'clusi *ecc* VB *vedi* **escludere**

esclusi'one SF exclusion; **a ~ di, fatta ~ per** except (for), apart from; **senza ~ (alcuna)** without exception; **procedere per ~** to follow a process of elimination; **senza ~ di colpi** *(fig)* with no holds barred; **~ sociale** social exclusion

esclu'siva SF *vedi* **esclusivo**

esclusiva'mente AV exclusively, solely

esclu'sivo, -a AG exclusive ▶ SF *(Dir, Comm)* exclusive *o* sole rights *pl*

es'cluso, -a PP di **escludere** ▶ AG: **nessuno ~** without exception; **IVA esclusa** excluding VAT, exclusive of VAT

'esco VB *vedi* **uscire**

escogi'tare [eskod'ʒi'tare] /**72**/ VT to devise, think up

'escono VB *vedi* **uscire**

escoriazi'one [eskorjat'tsjone] SF abrasion, graze

escre'menti SMPL excrement *sg*, faeces

escursi'one SF *(gita)* excursion, trip; *(: a piedi)* hike, walk; *(Meteor)*: **~ termica** temperature range

escursio'nista, -i, -e SM/F *(gitante)* (day) tripper; *(a piedi)* hiker, walker

ese'crare /**72**/ VT to loathe, abhor

esecu'tivo, -a AG, SM executive

esecu'tore, -'trice SM/F *(Mus)* performer; *(Dir)* executor

esecuzi'one [ezekut'tsjone] SF execution, carrying out; *(Mus)* performance; **~ capitale** execution

ese'geta, -i [eze'dʒɛta] SM commentator

esegu'ire /**45**/ VT to carry out, execute; *(Mus)* to perform, execute

e'sempio SM example; **per ~** for example, for instance; **fare un ~** to give an example

esem'plare AG exemplary ▶ SM example; *(copia)* copy; *(Bot, Zool, Geo)* specimen

esemplifi'care /**20**/ VT to exemplify

esen'tare /**72**/ VT: **~ qn/qc da** to exempt sb/sth from

esen'tasse AG INV tax-free

e'sente AG: **~ da** *(dispensato da)* exempt from; *(privo di)* free from

esenzi'one [ezen'tsjone] SF exemption

e'sequie SFPL funeral rites; funeral service *sg*

eser'cente [ezer'tʃɛnte] SMF trader, dealer; shopkeeper

eserci'tare [ezertʃi'tare] /**72**/ VT *(professione)* to practise (BRIT), practice (US); *(allenare: corpo, mente)* to exercise, train; *(: diritto)* to exercise; *(: influenza, pressione)* to exert ■ **esercitarsi** VPR to practise; **esercitarsi nella guida** to practise one's driving

esercitazi'one [ezertʃitat'tsjone] SF *(scolastica, militare)* exercise; **esercitazioni di tiro** target practice *sg*

e'sercito [e'zertʃito] SM army

eser'cizio [ezer'tʃittsjo] SM practice; *(compito, movimento)* exercise; *(azienda)* business, concern; exercising; *(fisico: di matematica)* exercise; *(Econ)*: **~ finanziario** financial year; **in ~** *(medico ecc)* practising (BRIT), practicing (US); **nell'~ delle**

e

127

proprie funzioni in the execution of one's duties

esfoli'ante SM exfoliator

esi'bire /55/ VT to exhibit, display; (*documenti*) to produce, present ■ **esibirsi** VPR (*attore*) to perform; (*fig*) to show off

esibizi'one [ezibit'tsjone] SF exhibition; (*di documento*) presentation; (*spettacolo*) show, performance

esibizio'nista, -i, -e [ezibittsjo'nista] SM/F exhibitionist

esi'gente [ezi'dʒɛnte] AG demanding

esi'genza [ezi'dʒɛntsa] SF demand, requirement

e'sigere [e'zidʒere] /47/ VT (*pretendere*) to demand; (*richiedere*) to demand, require; (*imposte*) to collect

esi'gibile [ezi'dʒibile] AG payable

e'siguo, -a AG small, slight

esila'rante AG hilarious; **gas ~** laughing gas

'esile AG (*persona*) slender, slim; (*stelo*) thin; (*voce*) faint

esili'are /19/ VT to exile

esili'ato, -a AG exiled ▶ SM/F exile

e'silio SM exile

e'simere /29/ VT: **~ qn/qc da** to exempt sb/sth from ■ **esimersi** VPR: **esimersi da** to get out of

esis'tente AG existing; (*attuale*) present, current

esis'tenza [ezis'tɛntsa] SF existence

esistenzia'lismo [ezistentsja'lizmo] SM existentialism

e'sistere /11/ VI to exist; **esiste più di una versione dell'opera** there is more than one version of the work; **non esiste!** (*col*) no way!

esis'tito, -a PP *di* esistere

esi'tante AG hesitant; (*voce*) faltering

esi'tare /72/ VI to hesitate

esitazi'one [ezitat'tsjone] SF hesitation

'esito SM result, outcome

'eskimo SM (*giaccone*) parka

'esodo SM exodus

e'sofago, -gi SM oesophagus (BRIT), esophagus (US)

esone'rare /72/ VT: **~ qn da** to exempt sb from

esopia'neta SM exoplanet

esorbi'tante AG exorbitant, excessive

esor'cismo [ezor'tʃizmo] SM exorcism

esor'cista, -i [ezor'tʃista] SM exorcist

esorciz'zare [ezortʃid'dzare] /72/ VT to exorcize

esordi'ente SMF beginner

e'sordio SM debut

esor'dire /55/ VI (*nel teatro*) to make one's debut; (*fig*) to start out, begin (one's career); **esordì dicendo che …** he began by saying (that) …

esor'tare /72/ VT: **~ qn a fare** to urge sb to do

esortazi'one [ezortat'tsjone] SF exhortation

e'soso, -a AG (*prezzo*) exorbitant; (*persona: avido*) grasping

eso'terico, -a, -ci, -che AG esoteric

e'sotico, -a, -ci, -che AG exotic

es'pandere /110/ VT to expand; (*confini*) to extend; (*influenza*) to extend, spread ■ **espandersi** VPR to expand

espansi'one SF expansion; **~ di memoria** (*Inform*) memory upgrade

espansività SF expansiveness

espan'sivo, -a AG expansive, communicative

es'panso, -a PP *di* espandere

espatri'are /19/ VI to leave one's country

es'patrio SM expatriation; **permesso di ~** authorization to leave the country

espedi'ente SM expedient; **vivere di espedienti** to live by one's wits

es'pellere /48/ VT to expel

esperi'enza [espe'rjɛntsa] SF experience; (*Sci: prova*) experiment; **parlare per ~** to speak from experience

esperi'mento SM experiment; **fare un ~** to carry out *o* do an experiment

es'perto, -a AG, SM/F expert

espi'anto SM (*Med*) removal

espi'are /60/ VT to atone for

espiazi'one [espiat'tsjone] SF: **~ (di)** expiation (of), atonement (for)

espi'rare /72/ VT, VI to breathe out

esplea'mento SM (*Amm*) carrying out

esple'tare /72/ VT (*Amm*) to carry out

espli'care /20/ VT (*attività*) to carry out, perform

esplica'tivo, -a AG explanatory

es'plicito, -a [es'plitʃito] AG explicit

es'plodere /49/ VI (*anche fig*) to explode ▶ VT to fire

esplo'rare /72/ VT to explore

esplora'tore, -'trice SM/F explorer; (*anche: giovane esploratore*) (boy) scout/(girl) guide (BRIT) *o* scout (US) ▶ SM (*Naut*) scout (ship)

esplorazi'one [esplorat'tsjone] SF exploration; **mandare qn in ~** (*Mil*) to send sb to scout ahead

esplosi'one SF (*anche fig*) explosion

esplo'sivo, -a AG, SM explosive

es'ploso, -a PP *di* esplodere

es'pone *ecc* VB *vedi* **esporre**

espo'nente SMF (*rappresentante*) representative

esponenzi'ale [esponen'tsjale] AG (*Mat*) exponential

es'pongo, es'poni *ecc* VB *vedi* **esporre**

es'porre /77/ VT (*merci*) to display; (*quadro*) to exhibit, show; (*fatti, idee*) to explain, set out; (*porre in pericolo, Fot*) to expose ■ **esporsi** VPR:

esporsi a (*sole, pericolo*) to expose o.s. to; (*critiche*) to lay o.s. open to

espor'tare /72/ vt to export

esporta'tore, -'trice AG exporting ▶ SM/F exporter

esportazi'one [esportat'tsjone] SF (*azione*) exportation, export; (*insieme di prodotti*) exports *pl*

es'pose *ecc* VB *vedi* **esporre**

espo'simetro SM exposure meter

esposizi'one [espozit'tsjone] SF displaying; exhibiting; setting out; (*anche Fot*) exposure; (*mostra*) exhibition; (*narrazione*) explanation, exposition

es'posto, -a PP *di* **esporre** ▶ AG: **~ a nord** facing north, north-facing ▶ SM (*Amm*) statement, account; (: *petizione*) petition

espressi'one SF expression

espres'sivo, -a AG expressive

es'presso, -a PP *di* **esprimere** ▶ AG express ▶ SM (*lettera*) express letter; (*anche:* **treno espresso**) express train; (*anche:* **caffè espresso**) espresso

es'primere /50/ vt to express ▪ **esprimersi** VPR to express o.s.

espropri'are /19/ vt (*terreni, edifici*) to place a compulsory purchase order on; (*persona*) to dispossess

espropriazi'one [esproprjat'tsjone] SF, **es'proprio** SM expropriation; **~ per pubblica utilità** compulsory purchase

espu'gnare [espuɲ'ɲare] /15/ vt to take by force, storm

es'pulsi *ecc* VB *vedi* **espellere**

espulsi'one SF expulsion

es'pulso, -a PP *di* **espellere**

'essa PRON F (*pl* **esse**) *vedi* **esso**

es'senza [es'sɛntsa] SF essence

essenzi'ale [essen'tsjale] AG essential; (*stile, linea*) simple ▶ SM: **l'~** the main o most important thing

---

'essere

/51/ SM being; **essere umano** human being
▶ VB COPULATIVO **1** (*con attributo, sostantivo*) to be; **sei giovane/simpatico** you are o you're young/nice; **è medico** he is o he's a doctor
2 (+ *di: appartenere*) to be; **di chi è la penna?** whose pen is it?; **è di Carla** it is o it's Carla's, it belongs to Carla
3 (+ *di: provenire*) to be; **è di Venezia** he is o he's from Venice
4 (*data, ora*): **è il 15 agosto** it is o it's the 15th of August; **è lunedì** it is o it's Monday; **che ora è?, che ore sono?** what time is it?; **è l'una** it is o it's one o'clock; **sono le due** it is o it's two o'clock
5 (*costare*): **quant'è?** how much is it?; **sono 20**

euro it's 20 euros
▶ VB AUS **1** (*attivo*): **essere arrivato/venuto** to have arrived/come; **è già partita** she has already left
2 (*passivo*) to be; **essere fatto da** to be made by; **è stata uccisa** she has been killed
3 (*riflessivo*): **si sono lavati** they washed, they got washed
4 (+ *da* + *infinito*): **è da farsi subito** it must be done o is to be done immediately
▶ VI **1** (*esistere, trovarsi*) to be; **sono a casa** I'm at home; **essere in piedi/seduto** to be standing/sitting
2 (*succedere*): **sarà quel che sarà** what will be will be; **sia quel che sia, io me ne vado** come what may, I'm going now
3: **esserci**: **c'è** there is; **ci sono** there are; **che c'è?** what's the matter?, what is it?; **non c'è niente da fare** there's nothing we can do; **c'è da sperare che …** one can only hope that …; **ci sono!** (*sono pronto*) I'm ready; (*ho capito*) I get it!
▶ VB IMPERS: **è tardi/Pasqua** it's late/Easter; **è mezzanotte** it's midnight; **è bello/caldo/freddo** it's nice/hot/cold; **è possibile che venga** he may come; **è così** that's the way it is

'essi PRON MPL *vedi* **esso**

essic'care /20/ vt (*gen*) to dry; (*legname*) to season; (*cibi*) to desiccate; (*bacino, palude*) to drain ▪ **essiccarsi** VPR (*fiume, pozzo*) to dry up; (*vernice*) to dry (out)

'esso, -a PRON PRON it; (*riferito a persona: soggetto*) he (she); (: *complemento*) him (her) ▪ **essi, e** PRON PL (*soggetto*) they; (*complemento*) them

est SM east; **i paesi dell'E~** the Eastern bloc *sg*

'estasi SF ecstasy

estasi'are /19/ vt to send into raptures ▪ **estasiarsi** VPR: **estasiarsi (davanti a)** to go into ecstasies (over), go into raptures (over)

es'tate SF summer

es'tatico, -a, -ci, -che AG ecstatic

estempo'raneo, -a AG (*discorso*) extempore, impromptu; (*brano musicale*) impromptu

es'tendere /120/ vt to extend ▪ **estendersi** VPR (*diffondersi*) to spread; (*territorio, confini*) to extend

estensi'one SF extension; (*di superficie*) expanse; (*di voce*) range

estenu'ante AG wearing, tiring

estenu'are /72/ vt (*stancare*) to wear out, tire out

esteri'ore AG outward, external

esteriorità SF INV outward appearance

esterioriz'zare [esterjorid'dzare] /72/ vt (*gioia ecc*) to show

ester'nare /72/ vt to express; **~ un sospetto** to voice a suspicion

es'terno, -a AG (*porta, muro*) outer, outside; (*scala*) outside; (*alunno, impressione*) external ▶ SM outside, exterior ▶ SM/F (*allievo*) day pupil ▪ **esterni** SM PL (*Cine*) location shots; **"per uso ~"** "for external use only"; **all'~** outside; **gli esterni sono stati girati a Glasgow** the location shots were taken in Glasgow

'**estero, -a** AG foreign ▶ SM: **all'~** abroad; **Ministero degli Esteri, gli Esteri** Ministry for Foreign Affairs, ≈ Foreign Office (BRIT), ≈ State Department (US)

esterofi'lia SF *excessive love of foreign things*

esterre'fatto, -a AG (*costernato*) horrified; (*sbalordito*) astounded

es'tesi *ecc* VB *vedi* **estendere**

es'teso, -a PP *di* **estendere** ▶ AG extensive, large; **scrivere per ~** to write in full

estetica'mente AV aesthetically

es'tetico, -a, -ci, -che AG aesthetic ▶ SF (*disciplina*) aesthetics *sg*; (*bellezza*) attractiveness; **chirurgia estetica** cosmetic surgery; **cura estetica** beauty treatment

este'tista, -i, -e SM/F beautician

'**estimo** SM valuation; (*disciplina*) surveying

es'tinguere /42/ VT to extinguish, put out; (*debito*) to pay off; (*conto*) to close ▪ **estinguersi** VPR to go out; (*specie*) to become extinct

es'tinsi *ecc* VB *vedi* **estinguere**

es'tinto, -a PP *di* **estinguere**

estin'tore SM (fire) extinguisher

estinzi'one [estin'tsjone] SF putting out; (*di specie*) extinction; (*di debito*) payment; (*di conto*) closing

estir'pare /72/ VT (*pianta*) to uproot, pull up; (*dente*) to extract; (*tumore*) to remove; (*fig: vizio*) to eradicate

es'tivo, -a AG summer *cpd*

'**estone** AG, SMF, SM Estonian

Es'tonia SF: **l'~** Estonia

es'torcere [es'tɔrtʃere] /106/ VT: **~ qc (a qn)** to extort sth (from sb)

estorsi'one SF extortion

es'torto, -a PP *di* **estorcere**

estra'dare /72/ VT to extradite

estradizi'one [estradit'tsjone] SF extradition

es'trae, es'traggo *ecc* VB *vedi* **estrarre**

es'traneo, -a AG foreign; (*discorso*) extraneous, unrelated ▶ SM/F stranger; **rimanere ~ a qc** to take no part in sth; **sentirsi ~ a** (*famiglia, società*) to feel alienated from; **"ingresso vietato agli estranei"** "no admittance to unauthorized personnel"

estrani'arsi /19/ VPR: **~ (da)** to cut o.s. off (from)

es'trarre /123/ VT to extract; (*minerali*) to mine; (*sorteggiare*) to draw; **~ a sorte** to draw lots

es'trassi *ecc* VB *vedi* **estrarre**

es'tratto, -a PP *di* **estrarre** ▶ SM extract; (*di documento*) abstract; **~ conto** (bank) statement; **~ di nascita** birth certificate

estrazi'one [estrat'tsjone] SF extraction; mining; drawing *no pl*; draw

estrema'mente AV extremely

estre'mismo SM extremism

estre'mista, -i, -e SM/F extremist

estremità SF INV extremity, end ▶ SFPL (*Anat*) extremities

es'tremo, -a AG extreme; (*ultimo: ora, tentativo*) final, last ▶ SM extreme; (*di pazienza, forza*) limit, end ▪ **estremi** SMPL (*Dir*) essential elements; (*Amm: dati essenziali*) details, particulars; **l'E~ Oriente** the Far East

estrinse'care /20/ VT to express, show

'**estro** SM (*capriccio*) whim, fancy; (*ispirazione creativa*) inspiration

estro'messo, -a PP *di* **estromettere**

estro'mettere /63/ VT: **~ (da)** (*partito, club ecc*) to expel (from); (*discussione*) to exclude (from)

estromissi'one SF expulsion

es'troso, -a AG whimsical, capricious; inspired

estro'verso, -a AG, SM extrovert

estu'ario SM estuary

esube'rante AG exuberant; (*Comm*) redundant (BRIT)

esube'ranza [ezube'rantsa] SF (*di persona*) exuberance; **~ di personale** (*Comm*) overmanning (BRIT), over-staffing (US)

e'subero SM: **~ di personale** surplus staff; **in ~** redundant, due to be laid off

esu'lare /72/ VI: **~ da** (*competenza*) to be beyond; (*compiti*) not to be part of

'**esule** SMF exile

esul'tanza [ezul'tantsa] SF exultation

esul'tare /72/ VI to exult

esu'mare /72/ VT (*salma*) to exhume, disinter; (*fig*) to unearth

età SF INV age; **all'~ di 8 anni** at the age of 8, at 8 years of age; **ha la mia ~** he (*o* she) is the same age as me *o* as I am; **di mezza ~** middle-aged; **raggiungere la maggiore ~** to come of age; **essere in ~ minore** to be under age; **in ~ avanzata** advanced in years

eta'nolo SM ethanol

etc. ABBR etc.

'**etere** SM ether; **via ~** on the airwaves

e'tereo, -a AG ethereal

eternità SF eternity

e'terno, -a AG eternal; (*interminabile: lamenti, attesa*) never-ending; **in ~** for ever, eternally

etero'geneo, -a [etero'dʒɛneo] AG heterogeneous

eterosessu'ale AG, SMF heterosexual

'**etica** SF *vedi* **etico**

eti'chetta [eti'ketta] SF label; (*cerimoniale*): **l'~** etiquette

'**etico, -a, -ci, -che** AG ethical ▶ SF ethics *sg*

eti'lometro SM Breathalyzer®

etimolo'gia, -'gie [etimolo'dʒia] SF etymology

etimo'logico, -a, -ci, -che [etimo'lɔdʒiko] AG etymological

e'tiope AG, SMF Ethiopian

Eti'opia SF: l'~ Ethiopia

eti'opico, -a, -ci, -che AG, SM (*Ling*) Ethiopian

'Etna SM: l'~ Etna

'etnico, -a, -ci, -che AG ethnic

e'trusco, -a, -schi, -sche AG, SM/F Etruscan

'ettaro SM hectare (*10,000 m2*)

'etto ABBR M (= *ettogrammo*) 100 grams

etto'grammo SM hectogram(me) (= *100 grams*)

et'tolitro SM hectolitre (*BRIT*), hectoliter (*US*)

et'tometro SM hectometre

EU ABBR = **Europa**

euca'lipto SM eucalyptus

Eucaris'tia SF: l'~ the Eucharist

eufe'mismo SM euphemism

eufe'mistico, -a, -ci, -che AG euphemistic

eufo'ria SF euphoria

eu'forico, -a, -ci, -che AG euphoric

Eu'rasia SF Eurasia

eurasi'atico, -a, -ci, -che AG, SM/F Eurasian

Eura'tom SIGLA F (= *Comunità Europea dell'Energia Atomica*) Euratom

eu'ristico, -a, -ci, -che AG heuristic

'euro SM INV (*divisa*) euro

euro'corpo SM European force

eurodepu'tato SM Euro MP

eurodi'visa SF Eurocurrency

euro'dollaro SM Eurodollar

eur'ofobo, -a AG Europhobic ▶ SM/F Europhobe

Euro'landia SF Euroland

euromer'cato SM Euromarket

euro'missile SM Euro-missile

Eu'ropa SF: l'~ Europe

europarlamen'tare SMF Member of the European Parliament, MEP

euro'peo, -a AG, SM/F European

euro'scettico, -a, -ci, -che [euroʃ'ʃettiko] SM/F Euro-sceptic

eutana'sia SF euthanasia

evacu'are /72/ VT to evacuate

evacuazi'one [evakuat'tsjone] SF evacuation

e'vadere /52/ VI (*fuggire*): ~ **da** to escape from ▶ VT (*sbrigare*) to deal with, dispatch; (*tasse*) to evade

evan'gelico, -a, -ci, -che [evan'dʒɛliko] AG evangelical

evange'lista, -i [evandʒe'lista] SM evangelist

evapo'rare /72/ VI to evaporate

evaporazi'one [evaporat'tsjone] SF evaporation

e'vasi *ecc* VB *vedi* **evadere**

evasi'one SF (*vedi evadere*) escape; dispatch; **dare ~ ad un ordine** to carry out *o* execute an order; **letteratura d'~** escapist literature; **~ fiscale** tax evasion

eva'sivo, -a AG evasive

e'vaso, -a PP *di* **evadere** ▶ SM/F escapee

eva'sore SM: ~ (**fiscale**) tax evader

eveni'enza [eve'njentsa] SF: **nell'~ che ciò succeda** should that happen; **essere pronto ad ogni ~** to be ready for anything *o* any eventuality

e'vento SM event

eventu'ale AG possible

Do not translate the Italian word **eventuale** by *eventual*.

---

eventualità SF INV eventuality, possibility; **nell'~ di** in the event of

eventual'mente AV if need be, if necessary

'Everest SM: l'~, **il Monte ~** (Mount) Everest

eversi'one SF subversion

ever'sivo, -a AG subversive

evi'dente AG evident, obvious

evidente'mente AV evidently; (*palesemente*) obviously, evidently

evi'denza [evi'dɛntsa] SF obviousness; **mettere in ~** to point out, highlight; **tenere in ~ qc** to bear sth in mind

evidenzi'are [eviden'tsjare] /19/ VT (*sottolineare*) to emphasize, highlight; (*con evidenziatore*) to highlight

evidenzia'tore [evidentsja'tore] SM (*penna*) highlighter

evi'rare /72/ VT to castrate

evi'tabile AG avoidable

evi'tare /72/ VT to avoid; ~ **di fare** to avoid doing; ~ **qc a qn** to spare sb sth

'evo SM age, epoch

evo'care /20/ VT to evoke

evoca'tivo, -a AG evocative

evocherò *ecc* [evoke'rɔ] VB *vedi* **evocare**

evolu'tivo, -a AG (*gen, Biol*) evolutionary; (*Med*) progressive

evo'luto, -a PP *di* **evolversi** ▶ AG (*popolo, civiltà*) (highly) developed, advanced; (*persona: emancipato*) independent; (: *senza pregiudizi*) broadminded

evoluzi'one [evolut'tsjone] SF evolution

e'volversi /94/ VPR to evolve; **con l'~ della situazione** as the situation develops

ev'viva ESCL hurrah!; ~ **il re!** long live the king!, hurrah for the king!

ex... PREFISSO ex-, former ▶ SM INV/F INV ex-boy-friend/girlfriend

ex 'aequo [ɛg'zɛkwo] AV: **classificarsi primo ~** to come joint first, come equal first

'extra AG INV first-rate; top-quality ▶ SM INV extra

extracomuni'tario, -a AG non-EU ▶ SM/F non-EU citizen (*often referred to non-European immigrant*)

extraconiu'gale AG extramarital

extraparlamen'tare AG extraparliamentary

extrasensori'ale AG: **percezione ~** extrasensory perception

extrater'restre AG, SMF extraterrestrial

extraur'bano, -a AG suburban

Ff

F, f [ˈɛffe] SM O F INV (*lettera*) F, f; **F come Firenze** ≈ F for Frederick (*BRIT*), F for Fox (*US*)

F ABBR (= *Fahrenheit*) F

F. ABBR (= *fiume*) R

fa VB *vedi* **fare** ▸ SM INV (*Mus*) F; (: *solfeggiando la scala*) fa ▸ AV: **10 anni fa** 10 years ago

fabbi'sogno [fabbiˈzoɲɲo] SM needs *pl*, requirements *pl*; **il ~ nazionale di petrolio** the country's oil requirements; **~ del settore pubblico** public sector borrowing requirement (*BRIT*), government debt borrowing (*US*)

'fabbrica SF factory

fabbri'cante SM manufacturer, maker

fabbri'care /**20**/ VT to build; (*produrre*) to manufacture, make; (*fig*) to fabricate, invent

fabbri'cato SM building

fabbricazi'one [fabbrikatˈtsjone] SF building, fabrication; making, manufacture, manufacturing

'fabbro SM (black)smith

fac'cenda [fatˈtʃɛnda] SF matter, affair; (*cosa da fare*) task, chore; **le faccende domestiche** the housework *sg*

faccendi'ere [fattʃenˈdjɛre] SM wheeler-dealer, (shady) operator

fac'cetta [fatˈtʃetta] SF (*di pietra preziosa*) facet

fac'chino [fakˈkino] SM porter

'faccia, -ce [ˈfattʃa] SF face; (*di moneta, medaglia*) side; **~ a ~** face to face; **di ~** opposite, facing; **avere la ~ (tosta) di dire/fare qc** to have the cheek o nerve to say/do sth; **fare qc alla ~ di qn** to do sth to spite sb; **leggere qc in ~ a qn** to see sth written all over sb's face

facci'ata [fatˈtʃata] SF façade; (*di pagina*) side

fac'cina [fatˈtʃina] SF (*Inform*) emoticon

'faccio *ecc* [ˈfattʃo] VB *vedi* **fare**

'Facebook® [ˈfeisbuk] SM Facebook®

fa'cente [faˈtʃɛnte]: **~ funzione** *sm* (*Amm*) deputy

fa'cessi *ecc* [faˈtʃessi] VB *vedi* **fare**

fa'ceto, -a [faˈtʃeto] AG witty, humorous

fa'cevo *ecc* [faˈtʃevo] VB *vedi* **fare**

fa'cezia [faˈtʃɛttsja] SF witticism, witty remark

fa'chiro [faˈkiro] SM fakir

'facile [ˈfatʃile] AG easy; (*affabile*) easy-going; (*disposto*): **~ a** inclined to, prone to; (*probabile*): **è ~ che piova** it's likely to rain; **donna di facili costumi** woman of easy virtue, loose woman

facilità [fatʃiliˈta] SF easiness; (*disposizione, dono*) aptitude

facili'tare [fatʃiliˈtare] /**72**/ VT to make easier

facilitazi'one [fatʃilitatˈtsjone] SF (*gen*) facilities *pl*; **facilitazioni di pagamento** easy terms, credit facilities

facil'mente [fatʃilˈmente] AV (*gen*) easily; (*probabilmente*) probably

faci'lone, -a [fatʃiˈlone] SM/F (*peg*) happy-go-lucky person

facino'roso, -a [fatʃinoˈroso] AG violent

facoltà SF INV faculty; (*Chim*) property; (*autorità*) power

facolta'tivo, -a AG optional; (*fermata d'autobus*) request *cpd*

facol'toso, -a AG wealthy, rich

fac'simile SM facsimile

'faggio [ˈfaddʒo] SM beech

fagi'ano [faˈdʒano] SM pheasant

fagio'lino [fadʒoˈlino] SM French (*BRIT*) o string bean

fagi'olo [faˈdʒɔlo] SM bean; **capitare a ~** to come at the right time

fagoci'tare [fagotʃiˈtare] /**72**/ VT (*fig: industria ecc*) to absorb, swallow up; (*scherzoso: cibo*) to devour

fa'gotto SM bundle; (*Mus*) bassoon; **far ~** (*fig*) to pack up and go

'Fahrenheit [ˈfaːrənheit] SM Fahrenheit

'fai VB *vedi* **fare**

'faida SF feud

'fai-da-'te SM INV DIY, do-it-yourself

fa'ina SF (*Zool*) stone marten

fa'lange [faˈlandʒe] SF (*Anat*, *Mil*) phalanx

fal'cata SF stride

'falce [ˈfaltʃe] SF scythe; **~ e martello** (*Pol*) hammer and sickle

fal'cetto [falˈtʃetto] SM sickle

falci'are [fal'tʃare] /**14**/ VT to cut; (fig) to mow down

falcia'trice [faltʃa'tritʃe] SF (per fieno) reaping machine; (per erba) mowing machine

'falco, -chi SM (anche fig) hawk

fal'cone SM falcon

'falda SF (Geo) layer, stratum; (di cappello) brim; (di cappotto) tails pl; (di monte) lower slope; (di tetto) pitch; (di neve) flake; **abito a falde** tails pl

fale'gname [falɛɲ'ɲame] SM joiner

fa'lena SF (Zool) moth

'Falkland ['fɔːlklənd] SFPL: **le isole ~** the Falkland Islands

fal'lace [fal'latʃe] AG misleading, deceptive

'fallico, -a, -ci, -che AG phallic

fallimen'tare AG (Comm) bankruptcy cpd; **bilancio ~** negative balance, deficit; **diritto ~** bankruptcy law

falli'mento SM failure; bankruptcy

fal'lire /**55**/ VI (Dir) to go bankrupt; (non riuscire): **~ (in)** to fail (in) ▶ VT (colpo, bersaglio) to miss

fal'lito, -a AG unsuccessful; bankrupt ▶ SM/F bankrupt

'fallo SM error, mistake; (imperfezione) defect, flaw; (Sport) foul; fault; (Anat) phallus; **senza ~** without fail; **cogliere qn in ~** to catch sb out; **mettere il piede in ~** to slip

fal'locrate SM male chauvinist

falò SM INV bonfire

fal'sare /**72**/ VT to distort, misrepresent

falsa'riga, -ghe SF lined page, ruled page; **sulla ~ di ...** (fig) along the lines of ...

fal'sario, -a SM/F forger; counterfeiter

falsifi'care /**20**/ VT to forge; (monete) to forge, counterfeit

falsità SF INV (di persona, notizia) falseness; (bugia) falsehood, lie

'falso, -a AG false; (errato) wrong; (falsificato) forged; fake; (: oro, gioielli) imitation cpd ▶ SM forgery; **essere un ~ magro** to be heavier than one looks; **giurare il ~** to commit perjury; **~ in atto pubblico** forgery (of a legal document)

'fama SF fame; (reputazione) reputation, name

'fame SF hunger; **aver ~** to be hungry; **fare la ~** (fig) to starve, exist at subsistence level

fa'melico, -a, -ci, -che AG ravenous

famige'rato, -a [famidʒe'rato] AG notorious, ill-famed

fa'miglia [fa'miʎʎa] SF family

famili'are AG (della famiglia) family cpd; (ben noto) familiar; (rapporti, atmosfera) friendly; (Ling) informal, colloquial ▶ SMF relative, relation; **una vettura ~** a family car

familiarità SF familiarity; friendliness; informality

familiariz'zare [familjarid'dzare] /**72**/ VI: **~ con**

qn to get to know sb; **abbiamo familiarizzato subito** we got on well together from the start

fa'moso, -a AG famous, well-known

fa'nale SM (Aut) light, lamp (BRIT); (luce stradale, Naut) light; (di faro) beacon

fa'natico, -a, -ci, -che AG fanatical; (del teatro, calcio ecc): **~ di o per** mad o crazy about ▶ SM/F fanatic; (tifoso) fan

fana'tismo SM fanaticism

fanciul'lezza [fantʃul'lettsa] SF childhood

fanci'ullo, -a [fan'tʃullo] SM/F child

fan'donia SF tall story ■ **fandonie** SFPL nonsense sg

fan'fara SF brass band; (musica) fanfare

fanfa'rone SM braggart

fan'ghiglia [fan'giʎʎa] SF mire, mud

'fango, -ghi SM mud; **fare i fanghi** (Med) to take a course of mud baths

fan'goso, -a AG muddy

'fanno VB vedi **fare**

fannul'lone, -a SM/F idler, loafer

fantasci'enza [fantaʃ'ʃentsa] SF science fiction

fanta'sia SF fantasy, imagination; (capriccio) whim, caprice ▶ AG INV: **vestito ~** patterned dress

fantasi'oso, -a AG (dotato di fantasia) imaginative; (bizzarro) fanciful, strange

fan'tasma, -i SM ghost, phantom

fantasti'care /**20**/ VI to daydream

fantastiche'ria [fantastike'ria] SF daydream

fan'tastico, -a, -ci, -che AG fantastic; (potenza, ingegno) imaginative

'fante SM infantryman; (Carte) jack, knave (BRIT)

fante'ria SF infantry

fan'tino SM jockey

fan'toccio [fan'tɔttʃo] SM puppet

fanto'matico, -a, -ci, -che AG (nave, esercito) phantom cpd; (personaggio) mysterious

FAO SIGLA F (= Food and Agriculture Organization) FAO

fara'butto SM crook

fara'ona SF guinea fowl

fara'one SM (Storia) Pharaoh

fara'onico, -a, -ci, -che AG of the Pharaohs; (fig) enormous, huge

far'cire [far'tʃire] /**55**/ VT (carni, peperoni ecc) to stuff; (torte) to fill

fard [far] SM INV blusher

far'dello SM bundle; (fig) burden

'fare

/**53**/ SM 1 (modo di fare): **con fare distratto** absent-mindedly; **ha un fare simpatico** he has a pleasant manner

2: **sul far del giorno/della notte** at daybreak/nightfall

▶ VT **1** (*fabbricare, creare*) to make; (: *casa*) to build; (: *assegno*) to make out; **fare un pasto/una promessa/un film** to make a meal/promise/a film; **fare rumore** to make a noise **2** (*effettuare: lavoro, attività, studi*) to do; (: *sport*) to play; **cosa fa?** (*adesso*) what are you doing?; (*di professione*) what do you do?; **fare psicologia/italiano** (*Ins*) to do psychology/Italian; **fare tennis** to play tennis; **fare un viaggio** to go on a trip o journey; **fare una passeggiata** to go for a walk; **fare la spesa** to do the shopping

3 (*funzione*) to be; (: *Teat*) to play, be; **fare il medico** to be a doctor; **fare il malato** (*fingere*) to act the invalid

4 (*suscitare: sentimenti*): **fare paura a qn** to frighten sb; **mi fa rabbia** it makes me angry; **(non) fa niente** (*non importa*) it doesn't matter **5** (*ammontare*): **3 più 3 fa 6** 3 and 3 are o make 6; **fanno 6 euro** that's 6 euros; **Roma fa oltre 2.000.000 di abitanti** Rome has over 2,000,000 inhabitants; **che ora fai?** what time do you make it?

6 (+ *infinito*): **far fare qc a qn** (*obbligare*) to make sb do sth; (*permettere*) to let sb do sth; **fare piangere/ridere qn** to make sb cry/laugh; **fare venire qn** to send for sb; **fammi vedere** let me see; **far partire il motore** to start (up) the engine; **far riparare la macchina/costruire una casa** to get o have the car repaired/a house built

7: farsi: **farsi una gonna** to make o.s. a skirt; **farsi un nome** to make a name for o.s.; **farsi la permanente** to get a perm; **farsi notare** to get o.s. noticed; **farsi tagliare i capelli** to get one's hair cut; **farsi operare** to have an operation

8 (*fraseologia*): **farcela** to succeed, manage; **non ce la faccio più** I can't go on; **ce la faremo** we'll make it; **me l'hanno fatta!** (*imbrogliare*) I've been done!; **lo facevo più giovane** I thought he was younger; **fare sì/no con la testa** to nod/shake one's head

▶ VI **1** (*agire*) to act, do; **fate come volete** do as you like; **fare presto** to be quick; **fare da** to act as; **non c'è niente da fare** it's no use; **saperci fare con qn/qc** to know how to deal with sb/sth; **ci sa fare** she's very good at it; **faccia pure!** go ahead!

2 (*dire*) to say; **"davvero?" fece** "really?" he said

3: fare per (*essere adatto*) to be suitable for; **fare per fare qc** to be about to do sth; **fece per andarsene** he made as if to leave

4: farsi: **si fa così** you do it like this, this is the way it's done; **non si fa così!** (*rimprovero*) that's no way to behave!; **la festa non si fa** the party is off

5: fare a gara con qn to compete with sb; **fare a pugni** to come to blows; **fare in tempo a fare** to be in time to do

▶ VB IMPERS: **fa bel tempo** the weather is fine;

fa caldo/freddo it's hot/cold; **fa notte** it's getting dark

▶ VPR **1** (*diventare*) to become; **farsi prete** to become a priest; **farsi grande/vecchio** to grow tall/old

2 (*spostarsi*): **farsi avanti/indietro** to move forward/back; **fatti più in là** move along a bit **3** (*col: drogarsi*) to be a junkie

fa'retra SF quiver

far'falla SF butterfly

farfugli'are [farfuʎ'ʎare] /**27**/ VT, VI to mumble, mutter

fa'rina SF flour; **~ gialla** maize (BRIT) o corn (US) flour; **~ integrale** wholemeal (BRIT) o wholewheat (US) flour; **questa non è ~ del tuo sacco** (*fig*) this isn't your own idea (o work)

fari'nacei [fari'natʃei] SMPL starches

fa'ringe [fa'rindʒe] SF (*Anat*) pharynx

farin'gite [farin'dʒite] SF pharyngitis

fari'noso, -a AG (*patate*) floury; (*neve, mela*) powdery

farma'ceutico, -a, -ci, -che [farma'tʃeutiko] AG pharmaceutical

farma'cia, -'cie [farma'tʃia] SF pharmacy; (*negozio*) chemist's (shop) (BRIT), pharmacy

farma'cista, -i, -e [farma'tʃista] SM/F chemist (BRIT), pharmacist

'farmaco, -ci, -chi SM drug, medicine

farneti'care /**20**/ VI to rave, be delirious

'faro SM (*Naut*) lighthouse; (*Aer*) beacon; (*Aut*) headlight, headlamp (BRIT)

farragi'noso, -a [farradʒi'noso] AG (*stile*) muddled, confused

'farsa SF farce

far'sesco, -a, -schi, -sche AG farcical

fasc. ABBR = **fascicolo**

'fascia, -sce ['faʃʃa] SF band, strip; (*Med*) bandage; (*di sindaco, ufficiale*) sash; (*parte di territorio*) strip, belt; (*di contribuenti ecc*) group, band; **essere in fasce** (*anche fig*) to be in one's infancy; **~ oraria** time band

fasci'are [faʃ'ʃare] /**14**/ VT to bind; (*Med*) to bandage; (*bambino*) to put a nappy (BRIT) o diaper (US) on

fascia'tura [faʃʃa'tura] SF (*azione*) bandaging; (*fascia*) bandage

fa'scicolo [faʃ'ʃikolo] SM (*di documenti*) file, dossier; (*di rivista*) issue, number; (*opuscolo*) booklet, pamphlet

'fascino ['faʃʃino] SM charm, fascination

'fascio ['faʃʃo] SM bundle, sheaf; (*di fiori*) bunch; (*di luce*) beam; (*Pol*): **il F~** the Fascist Party

fa'scismo [faʃ'ʃizmo] SM fascism

fa'scista, -i, -e [faʃ'ʃista] AG, SM/F fascist

'fase SF phase; (*Tecn*) stroke; **in ~ di espansione** in a period of expansion; **essere fuori ~** (*motore*) to be rough (*BRIT*), run roughly; (*fig*) to feel rough (*BRIT*) o rotten

fas'tidio SM bother, trouble; **dare ~ a qn** to bother o annoy sb; **sento ~ allo stomaco** my stomach's upset; **avere fastidi con la polizia** to have trouble o bother with the police

fastidi'oso, -a AG annoying, tiresome; (*schifiltoso*) fastidious

'fasto SM pomp, splendour (*BRIT*), splendor (*US*)

fas'toso, -a AG sumptuous, lavish

fa'sullo, -a AG (*gen*) fake; (*dichiarazione, persona*) false; (*pretesto*) bogus

'fata SF fairy

fa'tale AG fatal; (*inevitabile*) inevitable; (*fig*) irresistible

fata'lismo SM fatalism

fatalità SF INV inevitability; (*avversità*) misfortune; (*fato*) fate, destiny

fa'tato, -a AG (*spada, chiave*) magic; (*castello*) enchanted

fa'tica, -che SF hard work, toil; (*sforzo*) effort; (*di metalli*) fatigue; **a ~** with difficulty; **respirare a ~** to have difficulty (in) breathing; **fare ~ a fare qc** to find it difficult to do sth; **animale da ~** beast of burden

fati'caccia, -ce SF: **fu una ~** it was hard work, it was a hell of a job (*col*)

fati'care /20/ VI to toil; **~ a fare qc** to have difficulty doing sth

fati'cata SF hard work

fa'tichi *ecc* [fa'tiki] VB *vedi* **faticare**

fati'coso, -a AG (*viaggio, camminata*) tiring, exhausting; (*lavoro*) laborious

fa'tidico, -a, -ci, -che AG fateful

'fato SM fate, destiny

Fatt. ABBR (= *fattura*) inv

fat'taccio [fat'tattʃo] SM foul deed

fat'tezze [fat'tettse] SFPL features

fat'tibile AG feasible, possible

fattis'pecie [fattis'pɛtʃe] SF: **nella** o **in ~** in this case o instance

'fatto, -a PP *di* **fare** ▶ AG: **un uomo ~** a grown man ▶ SM fact; (*azione*) deed; (*avvenimento*) event, occurrence; (*di romanzo, film*) action, story; **~ a mano/in casa** hand-/home-made; **è ben fatta** she has a nice figure; **cogliere qn sul ~** to catch sb red-handed; **il ~ sta** o **è che** the fact remains o is that; **in ~ di** as for, as far as ... is concerned; **fare i fatti propri** to mind one's own business; **è uno che sa il ~ suo** he knows what he's about; **gli ho detto il ~ suo** I told him what I thought of him; **porre qn di fronte al ~ compiuto** to present sb with a fait accompli; **coppia/unione di ~** long-standing relationship

fat'tore SM (*Agr*) farm manager; (*Mat: elemento costitutivo*) factor; **~ di protezione** (*di lozione solare*) factor

fatto'ria SF farm; (*casa*) farmhouse

Do not translate the Italian word **fattoria** by *factory*.

fatto'rino SM errand boy; (*di ufficio*) office boy; (*d'albergo*) porter

fattucchi'era [fattuk'kjɛra] SF witch

fat'tura SF (*Comm*) invoice; (*di abito*) tailoring; (*malia*) spell; **pagamento contro presentazione ~** payment on invoice

fattu'rare /72/ VT (*Comm*) to invoice; (*prodotto*) to produce; (*vino*) to adulterate

fattu'rato SM (*Comm*) turnover

fatturazi'one [fatturat'tsjone] SF billing, invoicing

'fatuo, -a AG vain, fatuous; **fuoco ~** (*anche fig*) will-o'-the-wisp

'fauci ['fautʃi] SFPL (*di leone ecc*) jaws; (*di vulcano*) mouth *sg*

'fauna SF fauna

'fausto, -a AG (*formale*) happy; **un ~ presagio** a good omen

fau'tore, -'trice SM/F advocate, supporter

'fava SF broad bean

fa'vella SF speech

fa'villa SF spark

'favo SM (*di api*) honeycomb

'favola SF (*fiaba*) fairy tale; (*d'intento morale*) fable; (*fandonia*) yarn; **essere la ~ del paese** (*oggetto di critica*) to be the talk of the town; (*zimbello*) to be a laughing stock

favo'loso, -a AG fabulous; (*incredibile*) incredible

fa'vore SM favour (*BRIT*), favor (*US*); **per ~** please; **prezzo/trattamento di ~** preferential price/treatment; **condizioni di ~** (*Comm*) favo(u)rable terms; **fare un ~ a qn** to do sb a favo(u)r; **col ~ delle tenebre** under cover of darkness

favoreggia'mento [favoreddʒa'mento] SM (*Dir*) aiding and abetting

favo'revole AG favourable (*BRIT*), favorable (*US*)

favo'rire /55/ VT to favour (*BRIT*), favor (*US*); (*il commercio, l'industria, le arti*) to promote, encourage; **vuole ~?** won't you help yourself?; **favorisca in salotto** please come into the sitting room; **mi favorisca i documenti** please may I see your papers?

favori'tismo SM favouritism (*BRIT*), favoritism (*US*)

favo'rito, -a AG, SM/F favourite (*BRIT*), favorite (*US*)

fax SM INV fax; **mandare qc via ~** to fax sth

fa'xare /72/ VT to fax

fazi'one [fat'tsjone] SF faction

faziosità [fattsjosi'ta] SF sectarianism

fazzo'letto [fattso'letto] SM handkerchief; (*per la testa*) (head)scarf; **~ di carta** tissue

F.B.I. SIGLA F (= *Federal Bureau of Investigation*) FBI

F.C. ABBR = **fuoricorso**

f.co ABBR = **franco**

FE SIGLA = **Ferrara**

febb. ABBR (= *febbraio*) Feb

feb'braio SM February; *vedi anche* **luglio**

'febbre SF fever; **aver la ~** to have a high temperature; **~ da fieno** hay fever

feb'brile AG (*anche fig*) feverish

'feccia, -ce ['fettʃa] SF dregs *pl*

'feci ['fetʃi] SFPL faeces, excrement *sg*

'feci *ecc* ['fetʃi] VB *vedi* **fare**

'fecola SF potato flour

fecon'dare /72/ VT to fertilize

fecondazi'one [fekondat'tsjone] SF fertilization; **~ artificiale** artificial insemination

fecondità SF fertility

fe'condo, -a AG fertile

'Fedcom SIGLA M = **Fondo Europeo di Cooperazione Monetaria**

'fede SF (*credenza*) belief, faith; (*Rel*) faith; (*fiducia*) faith, trust; (*fedeltà*) loyalty; (*anello*) wedding ring; (*attestato*) certificate; **aver ~ in qn** to have faith in sb; **tener ~ a** (*ideale*) to remain loyal to; (*giuramento, promessa*) to keep; **in buona/cattiva ~** in good/bad faith; **"in ~"** (*Dir*) "in witness whereof"

fe'dele AG (*leale, veritiero*) true, accurate; **~ (a)** faithful (to) ▶ SMF follower; **i fedeli** (*Rel*) the faithful

fedeltà SF faithfulness; (*coniugale*) fidelity; (*esattezza: di copia, traduzione*) accuracy; **alta ~** (*Radio*) high fidelity

'federa SF pillowslip, pillowcase

fede'rale AG federal

federa'lismo SM (*Pol*) federalism

federa'lista, -i, -e AG, SM/F (*Pol*) federalist

federazi'one [federat'tsjone] SF federation

Feder'caccia [feder'kattʃa] ABBR F (= *Federazione Italiana della Caccia*) *hunting federation*

Feder'calcio [feder'kaltʃo] ABBR M (= *Federazione Italiana Gioco Calcio*) *Italian football association*

Federcon'sorzi [federkon'sɔrtsi] ABBR F (= *Federazione Italiana dei Consorzi Agrari*) *federation of farmers' cooperatives*

fe'difrago, -a, -ghi, -ghe AG faithless, perfidious

fe'dina SF (*Dir*): **~ (penale)** record; **avere la ~ penale sporca** to have a police record

'fegato SM liver; (*fig*) guts *pl*, nerve; **mangiarsi o rodersi il ~** to be consumed with rage

'felce ['feltʃe] SF fern

fe'lice [fe'litʃe] AG happy; (*fortunato*) lucky

felicità [felitʃi'ta] SF happiness

felici'tarsi [felitʃi'tarsi] /72/ VPR (*congratularsi*): **~**
con qn per qc to congratulate sb on sth

felicitazi'oni [felitʃitat'tsjoni] SFPL congratulations

fe'lino, -a AG, SM feline

'felpa SF sweatshirt

fel'pato, -a (*tessuto*) brushed; (*passo*) stealthy; **con passo ~** stealthily

'feltro SM felt

'femmina SF (*Zool, Tecn*) female; (*figlia*) girl, daughter; (*spesso peg*) woman

femmini'cidio [femmini'tʃidjo] SM femicide

femmi'nile AG feminine; (*sesso*) female; (*lavoro, giornale*) woman's, women's; (*moda*) women's ▶ SM (*Ling*) feminine

femminilità SF femininity

femmi'nismo SM feminism

femmi'nista, -i, -e AG, SM/F feminist

'femore SM thighbone, femur

'fendere /36/ VT to cut through

fendi'nebbia SM (*Aut*) fog lamp

fendi'tura SF (*gen*) crack; (*di roccia*) cleft, crack

fe'nomeno SM phenomenon

'feretro SM coffin

feri'ale AG: **giorno ~** weekday, working day

'ferie SFPL holidays (*BRIT*), vacation *sg* (*US*); **andare in ~** to go on holiday o vacation; **25 giorni di ~ pagate** 25 days' holiday o vacation with pay

feri'mento SM wounding

fe'rire /55/ VT to injure; (*deliberatamente: Mil ecc*) to wound; (*colpire*) to hurt ■ **ferirsi** VPR to hurt o.s., injure o.s.

fe'rito, -a SM/F wounded o injured man/woman ▶ SF injury; wound

feri'toia SF slit

'ferma SF (*Mil*) (period of) service; (*Caccia*): **cane da ~** pointer

ferma'carte SM INV paperweight

fermacra'vatta SM INV tiepin (*BRIT*), tie tack (*US*)

fer'maglio [fer'maʎʎo] SM clasp; (*gioiello*) brooch; (*per documenti*) clip

ferma'mente AV firmly

fer'mare /72/ VT to stop, halt; (*Polizia*) to detain, hold; (*bottone ecc*) to fasten, fix ▶ VI to stop ■ **fermarsi** VPR to stop, halt; **fermarsi a fare qc** to stop to do sth

fer'mata SF stop; **~ dell'autobus** bus stop

fermen'tare /72/ VI to ferment; (*fig*) to be in a ferment

fermentazi'one [fermentat'tsjone] SF fermentation

fer'mento SM (*anche fig*) ferment; (*lievito*) yeast; **fermenti lattici** probiotics, probiotic bacteria

fer'mezza [fer'mettsa] SF (*fig*) firmness, steadfastness

'fermo, -a AG still, motionless; (*veicolo*) stationary; (*orologio*) not working; (*saldo: anche fig*) firm; (*voce, mano*) steady ▶ ESCL stop!; keep still! ▶ SM (*chiusura*) catch, lock; (*Dir*): **~ di polizia** police detention; **~ restando che ...** it being understood that ...

'fermo 'posta AV, SM INV poste restante (*BRIT*), general delivery (*US*)

fe'roce [fe'rɔtʃe] AG (*animale*) wild, fierce, ferocious; (*persona*) cruel, fierce; (*fame, dolore*) raging; **le bestie feroci** wild animals

fe'rocia, -cie [fe'rɔtʃa] SF ferocity

Ferr. ABBR = **ferrovia**

fer'raglia [fer'raʎʎa] SF scrap iron

ferra'gosto SM (*festa*) feast of the Assumption; (*periodo*) August holidays pl (*BRIT*) o vacation (*US*)

> **Ferragosto**, 15 August, is a national holiday. Marking the feast of the Assumption, its origins are religious, but in recent years it has simply become the most important public holiday of the summer season. Most people take some extra time off work and head out of town to the holiday resorts. Consequently, most of industry and commerce grinds to a standstill.

ferra'menta SFPL ironmongery *sg* (*BRIT*), hardware *sg*; **negozio di ~** ironmonger's (*BRIT*), hardware shop o store (*US*)

fer'rare /72/ VT (*cavallo*) to shoe

fer'rato, -a AG (*Ferr*): **strada ferrata** railway line (*BRIT*), railroad line (*US*); **essere ~ in** (*fig: materia*) to be well up in

ferra'vecchio [ferra'vɛkkjo] SM scrap merchant

'ferreo, -a AG iron *cpd*

ferri'era SF ironworks *inv*

'ferro SM iron; **una bistecca ai ferri** a grilled steak; **mettere a ~ e fuoco** to put to the sword; **essere ai ferri corti** (*fig*) to be at daggers drawn; **tocca ~!** I touch wood!; **~ battuto** wrought iron; **~ di cavallo** horseshoe; **~ da stiro** iron; **ferri da calza** knitting needles; **i ferri del mestiere** the tools of the trade

ferrotranvi'ario, -a AG public transport *cpd*

Ferrotranvi'eri ABBR F (= *Federazione Nazionale Lavoratori Autoferrotranvieri e Internavigatori*) *transport workers' union*

ferro'vecchio [ferro'vɛkkjo] SM = **ferravecchio**

ferro'via SF railway (*BRIT*), railroad (*US*)

ferrovi'ario, -a AG railway *cpd* (*BRIT*), railroad *cpd* (*US*)

ferrovi'ere SM railwayman (*BRIT*), railroad man (*US*)

'fertile AG fertile

fertilità SF fertility

fertiliz'zante [fertilid'dzante] SM fertilizer

fertiliz'zare [fertilid'dzare] /72/ VT to fertilize

fer'vente AG fervent, ardent

'fervere /29/ VI: **fervono i preparativi per ...** they are making feverish preparations for ...

'fervido, -a AG fervent, ardent

fer'vore SM fervour (*BRIT*), fervor (*US*), ardour (*BRIT*), ardor (*US*); (*punto culminante*) height

'fesa SF (*Cuc*) rump of veal

fesse'ria SF stupidity; **dire fesserie** to talk nonsense

'fesso, -a PP *di* **fendere** ▶ AG (*col: sciocco*) crazy, cracked

fes'sura SF crack, split; (*per gettone, moneta*) slot

'festa SF (*religiosa*) feast; (*pubblica*) holiday; (*compleanno*) birthday; (*onomastico*) name day; (*ricevimento*) celebration, party; **far ~** to have a holiday; (*far baldoria*) to live it up; **far ~ a qn** to give sb a warm welcome; **essere vestito a ~** to be dressed up to the nines; **~ comandata** (*Rel*) holiday of obligation; **la ~ della mamma/del papà** Mother's/Father's Day; **la F~ della Repubblica** *see note*

> The **Festa della Repubblica**, 2 June, celebrates the founding of the Italian Republic after the fall of the monarchy and the subsequent referendum in 1946. In Rome a wreath is laid on the Tomb of the Unknown Soldier, and there is a military parade along the *via dei Fori Imperiali*. In the afternoon the gardens of the *Quirinale* palace, the official residence of the president of the Republic, are opened to the public and military bands give performances.

festeggia'menti [festeddʒa'menti] SMPL celebrations

festeggi'are [fested'dʒare] /62/ VT to celebrate; (*persona*) to have a celebration for

fes'tino SM party; (*con balli*) ball

fes'tivo, -a AG (*atmosfera*) festive; **giorno ~** holiday

fes'toso, -a AG merry, joyful

fe'tente AG (*puzzolente*) fetid; (*comportamento*) disgusting ▶ SMF (*col*) stinker, rotter (*BRIT*)

fe'ticcio [fe'tittʃo] SM fetish

'feto SM foetus (*BRIT*), fetus (*US*)

fe'tore SM stench, stink

'fetta SF slice

fet'tuccia, -ce [fet'tuttʃa] SF tape, ribbon

fettuc'cine [fettut'tʃine] SFPL (*Cuc*) ribbon-shaped pasta

feu'dale AG feudal

'feudo SM (*Storia*) fief; (*fig*) stronghold

ff ABBR (*Amm*) = **facente funzione**; (= *fogli*) pp

FF.AA ABBR = **forze armate**

FF.SS. ABBR = **Ferrovie dello Stato**

FG SIGLA = **Foggia**

FI SIGLA = **Firenze** ▶ ABBR (= *Forza Italia*) *Italian centre-right political party*

fi'aba SF fairy tale

fia'besco, -a, -schi, -sche AG fairy-tale *cpd*

fi'acca SF weariness; (*svogliatezza*) listlessness; **battere la ~** to shirk

fiac'care /20/ VT to weaken

fiaccherò *ecc* [fjakke'rɔ] VB *vedi* **fiaccare**

fi'acco, -a, -chi, -che AG (*stanco*) tired, weary; (*svogliato*) listless; (*debole*) weak; (*mercato*) slack

fi'accola SF torch

fiacco'lata SF torchlight procession

fi'ala SF phial

fi'amma SF flame; (*Naut*) pennant

fiam'mante AG (*colore*) flaming; **nuovo ~** brand new

fiam'mata SF blaze

fiammeggi'are [fjammed'dʒare] /62/ VI to blaze

fiam'mifero SM match

fiam'mingo, -a, -ghi, -ghe AG Flemish ▶ SM/F Fleming ▶ SM (*Ling*) Flemish; (*Zool*) flamingo; **i Fiamminghi** the Flemish

fian'cata SF (*di nave ecc*) side; (*Naut*) broadside

fiancheggi'are [fjanked'dʒare] /62/ VT to border; (*fig*) to support, back (up); (*Mil*) to flank

fi'anco, -chi SM side; (*di persona*) hip; (*Mil*) flank; **di ~** sideways, from the side; **a ~ a ~** side by side; **prestare il proprio ~ alle critiche** to leave o.s. open to criticism; **~ destr/sinistr!** (*Mil*) right/left turn!

Fi'andre SFPL: **le ~** Flanders *sg*

fiaschette'ria [fjaskette'ria] SF wine shop

fi'asco, -schi SM flask; (*fig*) fiasco; **fare ~** to fail

fia'tare /72/ VI (*fig: parlare*): **senza ~** without saying a word

fi'ato SM breath; (*resistenza*) stamina ▪ **fiati** SMPL (*Mus*) wind instruments; **avere il ~ grosso** to be out of breath; **prendere ~** to catch one's breath; **bere qc tutto d'un ~** to drink sth in one go *o* gulp

'fibbia SF buckle

'fibra SF fibre, fiber (*US*); (*fig*) constitution; **~ ottica** optical fibre; **~ di vetro** fibreglass (*BRIT*), fiberglass (*US*)

ficca'naso (*mpl* **ficcanasi**, *fpl* **~**) SM/F busybody, nos(e)y parker

fic'care /20/ VT to push, thrust, drive ▪ **ficcarsi** VPR (*andare a finire*) to get to; **~ il naso negli affari altrui** (*fig*) to poke *o* stick one's nose into other people's business; **ficcarsi nei pasticci** *o* **nei guai** to get into hot water *o* a fix

ficcherò *ecc* [fikke'rɔ] VB *vedi* **ficcare**

'fiche [fiʃ] SF INV (*nei giochi d'azzardo*) chip

'fico, -chi SM (*pianta*) fig tree; (*frutto*) fig; **~ d'India** prickly pear; **~ secco** dried fig

'fiction ['fikʃon] SF INV TV drama

fidanza'mento [fidantsa'mento] SM engagement

fidan'zarsi [fidan'tsarsi] /72/ VPR to get engaged

fidan'zato, -a [fidan'tsato] SM/F fiancé (fiancée)

fi'darsi /72/ VPR: **~ di** to trust; **~ è bene non ~ è meglio** (*proverbio*) better safe than sorry

fi'dato, -a AG reliable, trustworthy

fide'ismo SM unquestioning belief

fide'istico, -a, -ci, -che AG (*atteggiamento, posizione*) totally uncritical

fideius'sore SM (*Dir*) guarantor

fideliz'zare [fidelid'dzare] /72/ VT: **~ la clientela** to build customer loyalty ▪ **fidelizzarsi** VPR to stay loyal

'fido, -a AG faithful, loyal ▶ SM (*Comm*) credit

fi'ducia [fi'dutʃa] SF confidence, trust; **incarico di ~** position of trust, responsible position; **persona di ~** reliable person; **è il mio uomo di ~** he is my right-hand man; **porre la questione di ~** (*Pol*) to ask for a vote of confidence

fiduci'oso, -a [fidu'tʃoso] AG trusting

fi'ele SM (*Med*) bile; (*fig*) bitterness

fie'nile SM barn; hayloft

fi'eno SM hay

fi'era SF fair; (*animale*) wild beast; **~ di beneficenza** charity bazaar; **~ campionaria** trade fair

fie'rezza [fje'rettsa] SF pride

fi'ero, -a AG proud; (*crudele*) fierce, cruel; (*audace*) bold

fi'evole AG (*luce*) dim; (*suono*) weak

'fifa SF (*col*): **aver ~** to have the jitters

F.I.F.A. SIGLA F (= *Fédération Internationale de Football Association*) FIFA

fi'fone, -a SM/F (*col, scherzoso*) coward

fig. ABBR (= *figura*) fig

FIGC SIGLA F (= *Federazione Italiana Gioco Calcio*) Italian football association

'Figi ['fidʒi] SFPL: **le isole ~** Fiji, the Fiji Islands

'figlia ['fiʎʎa] SF daughter; (*Comm*) counterfoil (*BRIT*), stub

figli'are [fiʎ'ʎare] /27/ VI to give birth

figli'astro, -a [fiʎ'ʎastro] SM/F stepson (-daughter)

'figlio ['fiʎʎo] SM son; (*senza distinzione di sesso*) child; **~ d'arte: essere ~ d'arte** to come from a theatrical (*o* musical *etc*) family; **~ di puttana** (!) son of a bitch (!); **~ di papà** spoilt, wealthy young man; **~ unico** only child

figli'occio, -a, -ci, -ce [fiʎ'ʎɔttʃo] SM/F godchild, godson(-daughter)

figli'ola [fiʎ'ʎɔla] SF daughter; (*fig: ragazza*) girl

figli'olo [fiʎ'ʎɔlo] SM (*anche fig: ragazzo*) son

fi'gura SF figure; (*forma, aspetto esterno*) form, shape; (*illustrazione*) picture, illustration; **far ~** to look smart; **fare una brutta ~** to make a bad impression; **che ~!** how embarrassing!

figu'raccia, -ce [figu'rattʃa] SF: **fare una ~** to create a bad impression

figu'rare /72/ VI to appear ▶ VT: **figurarsi qc** to imagine sth ■ **figurarsi** VPR: **figurati!** imagine that!; **ti do noia? — ma figurati!** am I disturbing you? — not at all!

figura'tivo, -a AG figurative

figu'rina SF (*statuetta*) figurine; (*cartoncino*) picture card

figuri'nista, -i, -e SM/F dress designer

figu'rino SM fashion sketch

fi'guro SM: **un losco ~** a suspicious character

figu'rone SM: **fare un ~** (*persona, oggetto*) to look terrific; (*persona: con un discorso ecc*) to make an excellent impression

'fila SF row, line; (*coda*) queue; (*serie*) series, string; **di ~** in succession; **fare la ~** to queue; **in ~ indiana** in single file

fila'mento SM filament

fi'lanca® SF *stretch material*

fi'landa SF spinning mill

fi'lante AG: **stella ~** (*stella cadente*) shooting star; (*striscia di carta*) streamer

filantro'pia SF philanthropy

filan'tropico, -a, -ci, -che AG philanthropic(al)

fi'lantropo SM philanthropist

fi'lare /72/ VT to spin; (*Naut*) to pay out ▶ VI (*baco, ragno*) to spin; (*formaggio fuso*) to go stringy; (*liquido*) to trickle; (*discorso*) to hang together; (*col: amoreggiare*) to go steady; (*muoversi a forte velocità*) to go at full speed; (*andarsene lestamente*) to make o.s. scarce ▶ SM (*di alberi ecc*) row, line; **~ diritto** (*fig*) to toe the line; **~ via** to dash off

filar'monico, -a, -ci, -che AG philharmonic

filas'trocca, -che SF nursery rhyme

filate'lia SF philately, stamp collecting

fi'lato, -a AG spun ▶ SM yarn ▶ AV: **vai dritto ~ a casa** go straight home; **3 giorni filati** 3 days running o on end

fila'tura SF spinning; (*luogo*) spinning mill

'file ['fail] SM INV (*Inform*) file

file' sharing [fail'ʃerin(g)] SM (*Inform*) file sharing

fi'letto SM (*ornamento*) braid, trimming; (*di vite*) thread; (*di carne*) fillet

fili'ale AG filial ▶ SF (*di impresa*) branch

filibusti'ere SM pirate; (*fig*) adventurer

fili'grana SF (*in oreficeria*) filigree; (*su carta*) watermark

fi'lippica SF invective

Filip'pine SFPL: **le ~** the Philippines

filip'pino, -a AG, SM/F Filipino

'film SM INV film

fil'mare /72/ VT to film

fil'mato SM short film

fil'mina SF film strip

'filo SM (*anche fig*) thread; (*filato*) yarn; (*metallico*) wire; (*di lama, rasoio*) edge; **con un ~ di voce** in a whisper; **un ~ d'aria** (*fig*) a breath of air; **dare del ~ da torcere a qn** to create difficulties for sb, make life difficult for sb; **fare il ~ a qn** (*corteggiare*) to be after sb, chase sb; **per ~ e per segno** in detail; **~ d'erba** blade of grass; **~ interdentale** dental floss; **~ di perle** string of pearls; **~ di Scozia** fine cotton yarn; **~ spinato** barbed wire

filoameri'cano, -a AG pro-American

'filobus SM INV trolley bus

filodiffusi'one SF rediffusion

filodram'matico, -a, -ci, -che AG: (**compagnia**) **filodrammatica** amateur dramatic society ▶ SM/F amateur actor (actress)

filon'cino [filon'tʃino] SM ≈ French stick

fi'lone SM (*di minerali*) seam, vein; (*pane*) ≈ Vienna loaf; (*fig*) trend

filoso'fia SF philosophy

filo'sofico, -a, -ci, -che AG philosophical

fi'losofo, -a SM/F philosopher

filosovi'etico, -a, -ci, -che AG pro-Soviet

filo'via SF (*linea*) trolley line; (*bus*) trolley bus

fil'trare /72/ VT, VI to filter

'filtro SM filter; (*pozione*) potion; **~ dell'olio** (*Aut*) oil filter

'filza ['filtsa] SF (*anche fig*) string

FIN SIGLA F = **Federazione Italiana Nuoto**

fin AV, PREP = **fino**

fi'nale AG final ▶ SM (*di libro, film*) end, ending; (*Mus*) finale ▶ SF (*Sport*) final

fina'lista, -i, -e SM/F finalist

finalità SF (*scopo*) aim, purpose

finaliz'zare [finalid'dzare] /72/ VT: **~ a** to direct towards

final'mente AV finally, at last

fi'nanza [fi'nantsa] SF finance ■ **finanze** SFPL (*di individuo, Stato*) finances; (**Guardia di**) **~** (*di frontiera*) ≈ Customs and Excise (*BRIT*), ≈ Customs Service (*US*); (**Intendenza di**) **~** ≈ Inland Revenue (*BRIT*), ≈ Internal Revenue Service (*US*); **Ministro delle finanze** Minister of Finance, ≈ Chancellor of the Exchequer (*BRIT*), ≈ Secretary of the Treasury (*US*)

finanzia'mento [finantsja'mento] SM (*azione*) financing; (*denaro fornito*) funds pl

finanzi'are [finan'tsjare] /19/ VT to finance, fund

finanzi'ario, -a [finan'tsjarjo] AG financial ▶ SF (*anche*: **società finanziaria**) investment company; (*anche*: **legge finanziaria**) finance act, ≈ budget (*BRIT*)

finanzia'tore, -'trice AG: **ente ~** backer ▶ SM/F backer

finanzi'ere [finan'tsjɛre] SM financier; (*guardia*

di finanza: doganale) customs officer; (: *tributaria*) Inland Revenue official (BRIT), Internal Revenue official (US)

finché [fin'ke] CONG (*per tutto il tempo che*) as long as; (*fino al momento in cui*) until; **~ vorrai** as long as you like; **aspetta ~ non esca** wait until he goes (*o* comes) out; **aspetta ~ io (non) sia ritornato** wait until I get back

'**fine** AG (*lamina, carta*) thin; (*capelli, polvere*) fine; (*vista, udito*) keen, sharp; (*persona: raffinata*) refined, distinguished; (*osservazione*) subtle ▶ SF end ▶ SM aim, purpose; (*esito*) result, outcome; **in** *o* **alla ~** in the end, finally; **alla fin ~** at the end of the day, in the end; **che ~ ha fatto?** what became of him?; **buona ~ e buon principio!** (*augurio*) happy New Year!; **a fin di bene** with the best of intentions; **al ~ di fare qc** (in order) to do sth; **condurre qc a buon ~** to bring sth to a successful conclusion; **secondo ~** ulterior motive

'**fine setti'mana** SM *o* F INV weekend

fi'nestra SF window

fines'trino SM (*di treno, auto*) window

fi'nezza [fi'nettsa] SF thinness; fineness; keenness, sharpness; refinement; subtlety

'**fingere** ['findʒere] /**54**/ VT to feign; (*supporre*) to imagine, suppose ■ **fingersi** VPR: **fingersi ubriaco/pazzo** to pretend to be drunk/crazy; **~ di fare** to pretend to do

fini'menti SMPL (*di cavallo ecc*) harness *sg*

fini'mondo SM pandemonium

fi'nire /**55**/ VT to finish ▶ VI to finish, end ▶ SM: **sul ~ della festa** towards the end of the party; **~ di fare** (*compiere*) to finish doing; (*smettere*) to stop doing; **~ in galera** to end up *o* finish up in prison; **farla finita** (*con la vita*) to put an end to one's life; **farla finita con qc** to have done with sth; **com'è andata a ~?** what happened in the end?; **finiscila!** stop it!

fini'tura SF finish

finlan'dese AG Finnish ▶ SMF Finn ▶ SM (*Ling*) Finnish

Fin'landia SF: **la ~** Finland

'**fino, -a** AG (*capelli, seta*) fine; (*oro*) pure; (*fig: acuto*) shrewd ▶ AV (*spesso troncato in fin: pure, anche*) even ▶ PREP (*spesso troncato in fin*): **fin quando?** till when?; **fin qui** as far as here; **~ a** (*tempo*) until, till; (*luogo*) as far as, (up) to; **fin da domani** from tomorrow onwards; **fin da ieri** since yesterday; **fin dalla nascita** from *o* since birth

fi'nocchio [fi'nɔkkjo] SM fennel; (*col, peg: omosessuale*) queer (!)

fi'nora AV up till now

'**finsi** *ecc* VB *vedi* **fingere**

'**finto, -a** PP *di* **fingere** ▶ AG (*capelli, dente*) false; (*fiori*) artificial; (*cuoio, pelle*) imitation *cpd*; (*fig: simulato: pazzia ecc*) feigned, sham ▶ SF pretence

(BRIT), pretense (US), sham; (*Sport*) feint; **far finta (di fare)** to pretend (to do); **l'ho detto per finta** I was only pretending; (*per scherzo*) I was only kidding

finzi'one [fin'tsjone] SF pretence (BRIT), pretense (US), sham

fioc'care /**20**/ VI (*neve*) to fall; (*fig: insulti ecc*) to fall thick and fast

fi'occo, -chi SM (*di nastro*) bow; (*di stoffa, lana*) flock; (*di neve*) flake; (*Naut*) jib; **coi fiocchi** (*fig*) first-rate; **fiocchi di avena** oatflakes; **fiocchi di granoturco** cornflakes

fi'ocina ['fjɔtʃina] SF harpoon

fi'oco, -a, -chi, -che AG faint, dim

fi'onda SF catapult

fio'raio, -a SM/F florist

fiorda'liso SM (*Bot*) cornflower

fi'ordo SM fjord

fi'ore SM flower ■ **fiori** SMPL (*Carte*) clubs; **nel ~ degli anni** in one's prime; **a fior d'acqua** on the surface of the water; **a fior di labbra** in a whisper; **aver i nervi a fior di pelle** to be on edge; **fior di latte** cream; **è costato fior di soldi** it cost a pretty penny; **il fior ~ della società** the cream of society; **~ all'occhiello** feather in the cap; **fiori di campo** wild flowers

fio'rente AG (*industria, paese*) flourishing; (*salute*) blooming; (*petto*) ample

fioren'tino, -a AG, SM/F Florentine ▶ SF (*Cuc*) T-bone steak

fio'retto SM (*Scherma*) foil

fio'rino SM florin

fio'rire /**55**/ VI (*rosa*) to flower; (*albero*) to blossom; (*fig*) to flourish

fio'rista, -i, -e SM/F florist

fiori'tura SF (*di pianta*) flowering, blooming; (*di albero*) blossoming; (*fig: di commercio, arte*) flourishing; (*insieme dei fiori*) flowers *pl*; (*Mus*) fioritura

fi'otto SM (*di lacrime*) flow, flood; (*di sangue*) gush, spurt

'**FIPE** SIGLA F = **Federazione Italiana Pubblici Esercizi**

Fi'renze [fi'rentse] SF Florence

'**firma** SF signature; (*reputazione*) name

> Do not translate the Italian word **firma** by firm.

firma'mento SM firmament

fir'mare /**72**/ VT to sign; **un abito firmato** a designer suit

firma'tario, -a SM/F signatory

fisar'monica, -che SF accordion

fis'cale AG fiscal, tax *cpd*; (*meticoloso*) punctilious; **medico ~** doctor employed by Social Security to verify cases of sick leave

fisca'lista, -i, -e SM/F tax consultant

fiscaliz'zare [fiskalid'dzare] /**72**/ VT to exempt from taxes

fischi'are [fis'kjare] /**19**/ VI to whistle ▶VT to whistle; (*attore*) to boo, hiss; **mi fischiano le orecchie** my ears are ringing; (*fig*) my ears are burning

fischiet'tare [fiskjet'tare] /**72**/ VI, VT to whistle

fischi'etto [fis'kjetto] SM (*strumento*) whistle

'fischio ['fiskjo] SM whistle; **prendere fischi per fiaschi** to get hold of the wrong end of the stick

'fisco SM tax authorities *pl*, ≈ HM Revenue & Customs (BRIT), ≈ Internal Revenue Service (US)

'fisica SF *vedi* **fisico**

fisica'mente AV physically

'fisico, -a, -ci, -che AG physical ▶SM/F physicist ▶SM physique ▶SF physics *sg*

'fisima SF fixation

fisiolo'gia [fizjolo'dʒia] SF physiology

fisiono'mia SF face, physiognomy

fisiotera'pia SF physiotherapy

fisiotera'pista SMF physiotherapist

fis'saggio [fis'saddʒo] SM (*Fot*) fixing

fis'sante AG (*spray, lozione*) holding

fis'sare /**72**/ VT to fix, fasten; (*guardare intensamente*) to stare at; (*data, condizioni*) to fix, establish, set; (*prenotare*) to book ■ **fissarsi** VPR: **fissarsi su** (*sguardo, attenzione*) to focus on; (*fig: idea*) to become obsessed with

fissazi'one [fissat'tsjone] SF (*Psic*) fixation

fissi'one SF fission

'fisso, -a AG fixed; (*stipendio, impiego*) regular ▶AV: **guardare ~ qn/qc** to stare at sb/sth; **avere un ragazzo ~** to have a steady boyfriend; **senza fissa dimora** of no fixed abode; **telefono ~** landline

fitoterma'lismo SM herbal hydrotherapy

'fitta SF *vedi* **fitto**

fit'tavolo SM tenant

fit'tizio, -a [fit'tittsjo] AG fictitious, imaginary

'fitto, -a AG thick, dense; (*pioggia*) heavy ▶SM depths *pl*, middle; (*affitto, pigione*) rent ▶SF sharp pain; **una fitta al cuore** (*fig*) a pang of grief; **nel ~ del bosco** in the heart o depths of the wood

fiu'mana SF torrent; (*fig*) stream, flood

fi'ume SM river ▶AG INV: **processo ~** long-running trial; **scorrere a fiumi** (*acqua, sangue*) to flow in torrents

fiu'tare /**72**/ VT to smell, sniff; (*animale*) to scent; (*fig: inganno*) to get wind of, smell; **~ tabacco** to take snuff; **~ cocaina** to snort cocaine

fi'uto SM (*sense of*) smell; (*fig*) nose

'flaccido, -a ['flattʃido] AG flabby

fla'cone SM bottle

flagel'lare [fladʒel'lare] /**72**/ VT to flog, scourge; (*onde*) to beat against

fla'gello [fla'dʒello] SM scourge

fla'grante AG flagrant; **cogliere qn in ~** to catch sb red-handed

fla'nella SF flannel

flash [flaʃ] SM INV (*Fot*) flash; (*giornalistico*) news-flash

flau'tista, -i SM/F flautist

'flauto SM flute

'flebile AG faint, feeble

fle'bite SF phlebitis

'flemma SF (*calma*) coolness, phlegm; (*Med*) phlegm

flem'matico, -a, -ci, -che AG phlegmatic, cool

fles'sibile AG pliable; (*fig: che si adatta*) flexible

flessibili'tà SF (*anche fig*) flexibility

flessi'one SF (*gen*) bending; (*Ginnastica: a terra*) sit-up; (: *in piedi*) forward bend; (: *sulle gambe*) knee-bend; (*diminuzione*) slight drop, slight fall; (*Ling*) inflection; **fare una ~** to bend; **una ~ economica** a downward trend in the economy

'flesso, -a PP *di* **flettere**

flessu'oso, -a AG supple, lithe; (*andatura*) flowing, graceful

'flettere /**92**/ VT to bend

'flipper ['flipper] SM INV pinball machine

flirt [flərt] SM INV brief romance, flirtation

flir'tare /**72**/ VI to flirt

F.lli ABBR (= *fratelli*) Bros

'flora SF flora

'florido, -a AG flourishing; (*fig*) glowing with health

'floscio, -a, -sci, -sce ['floʃʃo] AG (*cappello*) floppy, soft; (*muscoli*) flabby

'flotta SF fleet

flot'tante SM (*Econ*): **titoli a largo ~** blue chips, stocks on the market

'fluido, -a AG, SM fluid

flu'ire /**55**/ VI to flow

fluore'scente [fluoreʃ'ʃɛnte] AG fluorescent

flu'oro SM fluorine

fluo'ruro SM fluoride

'flusso SM flow; (*Fisica, Med*) flux; **~ e riflusso** ebb and flow; **~ di cassa** (*Comm*) cash flow

'flutti SMPL waves

fluttu'are /**72**/ VI to rise and fall; (*Econ*) to fluctuate

fluvi'ale AG river *cpd*, fluvial

FM ABBR *vedi* **modulazione di frequenza**

FMI SIGLA M (= *Fondo Monetario Internazionale*) IMF

FO SIGLA = Forlì

fo'bia SF phobia

'foca, -che SF (*Zool*) seal

fo'caccia, -ce [fo'kattʃa] SF kind of pizza; (*dolce*) bun; **rendere pan per ~** to get one's own back, give tit for tat

fo'cale AG focal

focaliz'zare [fokalid'dzare] /72/ VT (Fot: immagine) to get into focus; (fig: situazione) to get into perspective; **~ l'attenzione su** to focus one's attention on

'foce ['fotʃe] SF (Geo) mouth

fo'chista, -i [fo'kista] SM (Ferr) stoker, fireman

foco'laio SM (Med) centre (BRIT) o center (US) of infection; (fig) hotbed

foco'lare SM hearth, fireside; (Tecn) furnace

fo'coso, -a AG fiery; (cavallo) mettlesome, fiery

'fodera SF (di vestito) lining; (di libro, poltrona) cover

fode'rare /72/ VT to line; to cover

'fodero SM (di spada) scabbard; (di pugnale) sheath; (di pistola) holster

'foga SF enthusiasm, ardour (BRIT), ardor (US)

'foggia, -ge ['fɔddʒa] SF (maniera) style; (aspetto) form, shape; (moda) fashion, style

foggi'are [fod'dʒare] /62/ VT to shape; to style

'foglia ['fɔʎʎa] SF leaf; **ha mangiato la ~** (fig) he's caught on; **~ d'argento/d'oro** silver/gold leaf

fogli'ame [foʎ'ʎame] SM foliage, leaves pl

fogli'etto [foʎ'ʎetto] SM (piccolo foglio) slip of paper, piece of paper; (manifestino) leaflet, handout

'foglio ['fɔʎʎo] SM (di carta) sheet (of paper); (di metallo) sheet; (documento) document; (banconota) (bank)note; **~ di calcolo** (Inform) spreadsheet; **~ rosa** (Aut) provisional licence; **~ di via** (Dir) expulsion order; **~ volante** pamphlet

'fogna ['foɲɲa] SF drain, sewer

fogna'tura [foɲɲa'tura] SF drainage, sewerage

föhn [fon] SM INV hair-dryer

fo'lata SF gust

fol'clore SM folklore

folclo'ristico, -a, -ci, -che AG folk cpd

folgo'rare /72/ VT (fulmine) to strike down; (: alta tensione) to electrocute

folgorazi'one [folgorat'tsjone] SF electrocution; **ebbe una ~** (fig: idea) he had a brainwave

'folgore SF thunderbolt

folksono'mia SF (Inform) folksonomy

'folla SF crowd, throng

'folle AG mad, insane; (Tecn) idle; **in ~** (Aut) in neutral

folleggi'are [folled'dʒare] /62/ VI (divertirsi) to paint the town red

fol'letto SM elf

fol'lia SF folly, foolishness; foolish act; (pazzia) madness, lunacy; **amare qn alla ~** to love sb to distraction; **costare una ~** to cost the earth

'folto, -a AG thick

fomen'tare /72/ VT to stir up, foment

fon SM INV = **föhn**

fon'dale SM (del mare) bottom; (Teat) backdrop; **il ~ marino** the sea bed

fondamen'tale AG fundamental, basic

fondamenta'lista, -i, -e AG, SM/F (Rel) fundamentalist

fonda'mento SM foundation ▪ **fondamenta** SFPL (Edil) foundations

fon'dare /72/ VT to found; (fig: dar base): **~ qc su** to base sth on ▪ **fondarsi** VPR (teorie): **fondarsi (su)** to be based (on)

fonda'tezza [fonda'tettsa] SF (di ragioni) soundness; (di dubbio, sospetto) basis in fact

fon'dato, -a AG (ragioni) sound; (dubbio, sospetto) well-founded

fondazi'one [fondat'tsjone] SF foundation

fon'dente AG: **cioccolato ~** plain o dark chocolate

'fondere /25/ VT (neve) to melt; (metallo) to fuse, melt; (fig: colori) to merge, blend; (: imprese, gruppi) to merge ▶ VI to melt ▪ **fondersi** VPR to melt; (fig: partiti, correnti) to unite, merge

fonde'ria SF foundry

fondi'ario, -a AG land cpd

fon'dina SF (piatto fondo) soup plate; (portapistola) holster

'fondo, -a AG deep ▶ SM (di recipiente, pozzo) bottom; (di stanza) back; (quantità di liquido che resta, deposito) dregs pl; (sfondo) background; (unità immobiliare) property, estate; (somma di denaro) fund; (Sport) long-distance race ▪ **fondi** SMPL (denaro) funds; **a notte fonda** at dead of night; **in ~ a** at the bottom of; at the back of; (strada) at the end of; **laggiù in ~** (lontano) over there; (in profondità) down there; **in ~** (fig) after all, all things considered; **andare fino in ~ a** (fig) to examine thoroughly; **andare a ~** (nave) to sink; **conoscere a ~** to know inside out; **dar ~ a** (provviste, soldi) to use up; **toccare il ~** (fig) to plumb the depths; **~ perduto** (Comm) without security; **~ comune di investimento** investment trust; **F~ Monetario Internazionale** International Monetary Fund; **~ di previdenza** social insurance fund; **~ di riserva** reserve fund; **~ urbano** town property; **fondi di caffè** coffee grounds; **fondi d'esercizio** working capital sg; **fondi liquidi** ready money sg, liquid assets; **fondi di magazzino** old o unsold stock sg; **fondi neri** slush fund sg

fondo'tinta SM INV (cosmetico) foundation

fo'nema SM phoneme

fo'netica SF phonetics sg

fo'netico, -a, -ci, -che AG phonetic

fon'tana SF fountain

fonta'nella SF drinking fountain

'fonte SF spring, source; (fig) source ▶ SM: **~ battesimale** (Rel) font; **~ energetica** source of energy

fon'tina SM full fat hard, sweet cheese

'footing ['futiŋ] SM jogging

forag'giare [forad'dʒare] /**62**/ vт (*cavalli*) to fodder; (*fig: partito ecc*) to bankroll

fo'raggio [fo'raddʒo] sм fodder, forage

fo'rare /**72**/ vт to pierce, make a hole in; (*pallone*) to burst; (*pneumatico*) to puncture; (*biglietto*) to punch ■ **forarsi** vPR (*gen*) to develop a hole; (*Aut, pallone, timpano*) to burst; **~ una gomma** to burst a tyre (BRIT) o tire (US)

fora'tura sғ piercing; bursting; puncturing; punching

'forbici ['fɔrbitʃi] sғPL scissors

forbi'cina [forbi'tʃina] sғ earwig

for'bito, -a AG (*stile, modi*) polished

'forca, -che sғ (*Agr*) fork, pitchfork; (*patibolo*) gallows sg

for'cella [for'tʃɛlla] sғ (*Tecn*) fork; (*di monte*) pass

for'chetta [for'ketta] sғ fork; **essere una buona ~** to enjoy one's food

for'cina [for'tʃina] sғ hairpin

'forcipe ['fɔrtʃipe] sм forceps pl

for'cone sм pitchfork

fo'rense AG (*linguaggio*) legal; **avvocato ~** barrister (BRIT), lawyer

fo'resta sғ forest; **la F~ Nera** the Black Forest; **~ pluviale** rainforest

fores'tale AG forest cpd; **guardia ~** forester

foreste'ria sғ (*di convento, palazzo ecc*) guest rooms pl, guest quarters pl

foresti'ero, -a AG foreign ▶ sм/ғ foreigner

for'fait [fɔr'fe] sм INV: **(prezzo a) ~** fixed price, set price; **dichiarare ~** (*Sport*) to withdraw; (*fig*) to give up

forfe'tario, -a AG: **prezzo ~** (*da pagare*) fixed o set price; (*da ricevere*) lump sum

'forfora sғ dandruff

'forgia, -ge ['fɔrdʒa] sғ forge

forgi'are [for'dʒare] /**62**/ vт to forge

'forma sғ form; (*aspetto esteriore*) form, shape; (*Dir: procedura*) procedure; (*per calzature*) last; (*stampo da cucina*) mould (BRIT), mold (US) ■ **forme** sғPL (*del corpo*) figure, shape; **le forme** (*convenzioni*) appearances; **errori di ~** stylistic errors; **essere in ~** to be in good shape; **mantenersi in ~** to keep fit; **in ~ ufficiale/privata** officially/privately; **una ~ di formaggio** a (whole) cheese

formag'gino [formad'dʒino] sм processed cheese

for'maggio [for'maddʒo] sм cheese

Italy is a major cheese producer. These may be hard or soft, or from cow's milk, ewe's milk or buffalo milk. There are many regional varieties, the most famous being *parmigiano* (Parmesan) from the Emilia-Romagna region, *mozzarella*, made with either cow's milk or buffalo milk, *pecorino*, the best-known ewe's milk cheese, and *gorgonzola*, with its strong smell and taste.

for'male AG formal

formalità sғ INV formality

formaliz'zare [formalid'dzare] /**72**/ vт to formalize

for'mare /**72**/ vт to form, shape, make; (*numero di telefono*) to dial; (*fig: carattere*) to form, mould (BRIT), mold (US) ■ **formarsi** vPR to form, take shape; **il treno si forma a Milano** the train starts from Milan

for'mato sм format, size

format'tare /**72**/ vт to format

formattazi'one [formattat'tsjone] sғ (*Inform*) formatting

formazi'one [format'tsjone] sғ formation; (*fig: educazione*) training; **~ continua** continuing education; **~ permanente** lifelong learning; **~ professionale** vocational training

for'mica¹, -che sғ ant

'formica²® ['fɔrmika] sғ (*materiale*) Formica®

formi'caio sм anthill

formico'lare /**72**/ vI (*gamba, braccio*) to tingle; (*brulicare: anche fig*): **~ di** to be swarming with; **mi formicola la gamba** I've got pins and needles in my leg, my leg's tingling

formico'lio sм pins and needles pl; swarming

formi'dabile AG powerful, formidable; (*straordinario*) remarkable

for'moso, -a AG shapely

'formula sғ formula; **~ di cortesia** (*nelle lettere*) letter ending

formu'lare /**72**/ vт to formulate; to express

for'nace [for'natʃe] sғ (*per laterizi ecc*) kiln; (*per metalli*) furnace

for'naio, -a sм/ғ baker

for'nello sм (*elettrico, a gas*) ring; (*di pipa*) bowl

for'nire /**55**/ vт: **~ qn di qc, ~ qc a qn** to provide o supply sb with sth, supply sth to sb ■ **fornirsi** vPR: **fornirsi di** (*procurarsi*) to provide o.s. with

for'nito, -a AG: **ben ~** (*negozio*) well-stocked

forni'tore, -'trice AG: **ditta fornitrice di ...** company supplying ... ▶ sм/ғ supplier

forni'tura sғ supply

'forno sм (*di cucina*) oven; (*panetteria*) bakery; (*Tecn: per calce ecc*) kiln; (: *per metalli*) furnace; **fare i forni** (*Med*) to undergo heat treatment; **~ a microonde** microwave oven

'foro sм (*buco*) hole; (*Storia*) forum; (*tribunale*) (law) court

'forse AV perhaps, maybe; (*circa*) about; **essere in ~** to be in doubt

forsen'nato, -a AG mad, crazy, insane

'forte AG strong; (*suono*) loud; (*spesa*) considerable, great; (*passione, dolore*) great, deep ▶ AV strongly; (*velocemente*) fast; (*a voce alta*) loud(ly); (*violentemente*) hard ▶ sм (*edificio*) fort; (*specialità*) forte, strong point; **piatto ~** (*Cuc*) main dish; **avere un ~ mal di testa/raffreddore** to have a bad headache/cold; **essere ~ in qc** to be good at sth; **farsi ~ di qc** to make use of sth; **dare man ~ a qn** to back sb up, support sb; **usare le maniere forti** to use strong-arm tactics

for'tezza [for'tettsa] SF (*morale*) strength; (*luogo fortificato*) fortress

fortifi'care /20/ VT to fortify, strengthen

for'tuito, -a AG fortuitous, chance *cpd*

for'tuna SF (*destino*) fortune, luck; (*buona sorte*) success, fortune; (*eredità, averi*) fortune; **per ~** luckily, fortunately; **di ~** makeshift, improvised; **atterraggio di ~** emergency landing

fortu'nale SM storm

fortunata'mente AV luckily, fortunately

fortu'nato, -a AG lucky, fortunate; (*coronato da successo*) successful

fortu'noso, -a AG (*vita*) eventful; (*avvenimento*) unlucky

fo'runcolo SM (*Med*) boil

forvi'are /19/ VT, VI = **fuorviare**

'forza ['fɔrtsa] SF strength; (*potere*) power; (*Fisica*) force ▸ ESCL come on! ■ **forze** SFPL (*fisiche*) strength *sg*; (*Mil*) forces; **per ~** against one's will; (*naturalmente*) of course; **per ~ di cose** by force of circumstances; **a viva ~** by force; **a ~ di** by dint of; **farsi ~** (*coraggio*) to pluck up one's courage; **bella ~!** (*ironico*) how clever of you (*o* him *etc*)!; **~ lavoro** work force, manpower; **per causa di ~ maggiore** (*Dir*) by reason of an act of God; (*per estensione*) due to circumstances beyond one's control; **la ~ pubblica** the police *pl*; **forze dell'ordine** the forces of law and order; **~ di pace** peacekeeping force; **~ di vendita** (*Comm*) sales force; **~ di volontà** willpower; **le forze armate** the armed forces; **F~ Italia** (*Pol*) moderate right-wing party

for'zare [for'tsare] /72/ VT to force; (*cassaforte, porta*) to force (open); (*voce*) to strain; **~ qn a fare** to force sb to do

for'zato, -a [for'tsato] AG forced ▸ SM (*Dir*) prisoner sentenced to hard labour (BRIT) *o* labor (US)

forzi'ere [for'tsjɛre] SM strongbox; (*di pirati*) treasure chest

for'zista, -i, -e [for'tsista] AG of Forza Italia ▸ SM/F member (*o* supporter) of Forza Italia

for'zuto, -a [for'tsuto] AG big and strong

fos'chia [fos'kia] SF mist, haze

'fosco, -a, -schi, -sche AG dark, gloomy; **dipingere qc a tinte fosche** (*fig*) to paint a gloomy picture of sth

fos'fato SM phosphate

fosfore'scente [fosforeʃ'ʃɛnte] AG phosphorescent; (*lancetta dell'orologio ecc*) luminous

'fosforo SM phosphorous

'fossa SF pit; (*di cimitero*) grave; **~ comune** mass grave; **~ biologica** septic tank

fos'sato SM ditch; (*di fortezza*) moat

fos'setta SF dimple

'fossi *ecc* VB *vedi* **essere**

'fossile AG, SM fossil (*cpd*)

'fosso SM ditch; (*Mil*) trench

'foste *ecc* VB *vedi* **essere**

'foto SF INV photo; **~ ricordo** souvenir photo; **~ tessera** passport(-type) photo

'foto... PREFISSO photo...

foto'camera SF: **~ digitale** digital camera

fotocomposi'tore SM filmsetter

fotocomposizi'one [fotokompozit'tsjone] SF film setting

foto'copia SF photocopy

fotocopi'are /19/ VT to photocopy

fotocopia'trice [fotokopja'tritʃe] SF photocopier

fotocopiste'ria SF photocopy shop

fotofo'nino SM camera phone

foto'genico, -a, -ci, -che [foto'dʒɛniko] AG photogenic

fotogra'fare /72/ VT to photograph

fotogra'fia SF (*procedimento*) photography; (*immagine*) photograph; **fare una ~** to take a photograph; **una ~ a colori/in bianco e nero** a colour/black and white photograph

foto'grafico, -a, -ci, -che AG photographic; **macchina fotografica** camera

fo'tografo, -a SM/F photographer

foto'gramma, -i SM (*Cine*) frame

fotomo'dello, -a SM/F fashion model

fotomon'taggio [fotomon'taddʒo] SM photomontage

fotore'porter SM INV/F INV newspaper (*o* magazine) photographer

fotoro'manzo [fotoro'mandzo] SM romantic picture story

foto'sintesi SF photosynthesis

fotovol'taico, -a, -ci, -che AG photovoltaic; **pannelli fotovoltaici** solar panels

'fottere /1/ VT (!: *avere rapporti sessuali*) to fuck (!), screw (!); (*rubare*) to pinch, swipe; (*fregare*): **mi hanno fottuto** they played a dirty trick on me; **vai a farti ~!** fuck off! (!)

fot'tuto, -a AG (!) bloody, fucking (!)

fou'lard [fu'lar] SM INV scarf

FR SIGLA = Frosinone

fra PREP = **tra**

fracas'sare /72/ VT to shatter, smash ■ **fracassarsi** VPR to shatter, smash; (*veicolo*) to crash

fra'casso SM smash; crash; (*baccano*) din, racket

'fradicio, -a, -ci, -ce ['fraditʃo] AG (*guasto*) rotten; (*molto bagnato*) soaking (wet); **ubriaco ~** blind drunk

'fragile ['fradʒile] AG fragile; (*fig: salute*) delicate; (*nervi, vetro*) brittle

fragilità [fradʒili'ta] SF (vedi ag) fragility; delicacy; brittleness

'**fragola** SF strawberry

fra'gore SM (di cascate, carro armato) roar; (di tuono) rumble

frago'roso, -a AG deafening; **ridere in modo ~** to roar with laughter

fra'grante AG fragrant

frain'tendere /120/ VT to misunderstand

fraintendi'mento SM misunderstanding

frain'teso, -a PP di **fraintendere**

fram'mento SM fragment

fram'misto, -a AG: **~ a** interspersed with

'**frana** SF landslide; (fig: persona): **essere una ~** to be useless, be a walking disaster area

fra'nare /72/ VI to slip, slide down

franca'mente AV frankly

fran'cese [fran'tʃeze] AG French ▶ SMF Frenchman(-woman) ▶ SM (Ling) French; **i Francesi** the French

fran'chezza [fran'kettsa] SF frankness, openness

fran'chigia, -gie [fran'kidʒa] SF (Amm) exemption; (Dir) franchise; (Naut) shore leave; **~ doganale** exemption from customs duty

'**Francia** ['frantʃa] SF: **la ~** France

'**franco, -a, -chi, -che** AG (Comm) free; (sincero) frank, open, sincere ▶ SM (moneta) franc; **farla franca** (fig) to get off scot-free; **~ a bordo** free on board; **~ di dogana** duty-free; **~ a domicilio** delivered free of charge; **~ fabbrica** ex factory, ex works; **prezzo ~ fabbrica** ex-works price; **~ magazzino** ex warehouse; **~ di porto** carriage free; **~ vagone** free on rail; **~ tiratore** sniper (Pol) member of parliament who votes against his own party

franco'bollo SM (postage) stamp

franco-cana'dese AG, SMF French Canadian

Franco'forte SF Frankfurt

fran'gente [fran'dʒɛnte] SM (onda) breaker; (scoglio emergente) reef; (circostanza) situation, circumstance

'**frangia, -ge** ['frandʒa] SF fringe

frangi'flutti [frandʒi'flutti] SM INV breakwater

frangi'vento [frandʒi'vɛnto] SM windbreak

fran'toio SM (Agr) olive press; (Tecn) crusher

frantu'mare /72/ VT, **frantu'marsi** VPR to break into pieces, shatter

fran'tumi SMPL pieces, bits; (schegge) splinters; **andare in ~, mandare in ~** to shatter, smash to pieces o smithereens

frappé SM (Cuc) milk shake

fra'sario SM (gergo) vocabulary, language

'**frasca, -sche** SF (leafy) branch; **saltare di palo in ~** to jump from one subject to another

'**frase** SF (Ling) sentence; (locuzione, espressione, Mus) phrase; **~ fatta** set phrase

fraseolo'gia [frazeolo'dʒia] SF phraseology

'**frassino** SM ash (tree)

frastagli'ato, -a [frastaʎ'ʎato] AG (costa) indented, jagged

frastor'nare /72/ VT (intontire) to daze; (confondere) to bewilder, befuddle

frastor'nato, -a AG dazed; bewildered

frastu'ono SM hubbub, din

'**frate** SM friar, monk

fratel'lanza [fratel'lantsa] SF brotherhood; (associazione) fraternity

fratel'lastro SM stepbrother; (con genitore in comune) half brother

fra'tello SM brother ▪ **fratelli** SMPL brothers; (nel senso di fratelli e sorelle) brothers and sisters

fra'terno, -a AG fraternal, brotherly

fratri'cida, -i, -e [fratri'tʃida] AG fratricidal ▶ SM/F fratricide; **guerra ~** civil war

frat'taglie [frat'taʎʎe] SFPL (Cuc: gen) offal sg; (: di pollo) giblets

frat'tanto AV in the meantime, meanwhile

frat'tempo SM: **nel ~** in the meantime, meanwhile

frat'tura SF fracture; (fig) split, break

frattu'rare /72/ VT to fracture

fraudo'lento, -a AG fraudulent

fraziona'mento [frattsjona'mento] SM division, splitting up

frazio'nare [frattsjo'nare] /72/ VT to divide, split up

frazi'one [frat'tsjone] SF fraction; (anche: frazione di comune) hamlet

'**freccia, -ce** ['frettʃa] SF arrow; **~ di direzione** (Aut) indicator

frec'ciata [fret'tʃata] SF: **lanciare una ~** to make a cutting remark

fred'dare /72/ VT to shoot dead

fred'dezza [fred'dettsa] SF coldness

'**freddo, -a** AG, SM cold; **fa ~** it's cold; **aver ~** to be cold; **soffrire il ~** to feel the cold; **a ~** (fig) deliberately

freddo'loso, -a AG sensitive to the cold

fred'dura SF pun

'**freezer** ['frizer] SM INV fridge-freezer

fre'gare /80/ VT to rub; (col: truffare) to take in, cheat; (: rubare) to swipe, pinch; **fregarsene** (col): **chi se ne frega?** who gives a damn (about it)?

fre'gata SF rub; (col) swindle; (Naut) frigate

frega'tura SF (col: imbroglio) rip-off; (: delusione) let-down

fregherò ecc [frege'rɔ] VB vedi **fregare**

'**fregio** ['fredʒo] SM (Archit) frieze; (ornamento) decoration

'**fremere** /29/ VI: **~ di** to tremble o quiver with; **~ d'impazienza** to be champing at the bit

'fremito SM tremor, quiver

fre'nare /72/ VT (*veicolo*) to slow down; (*cavallo*) to rein in; (*lacrime*) to restrain, hold back ▶ VI to brake ■ **frenarsi** VPR (*fig*) to restrain o.s., control o.s.

fre'nata SF: **fare una ~** to brake

frene'sia SF frenzy

fre'netico, -a, -ci, -che AG frenetic

'freno SM brake; (*morso*) bit; **tenere a ~** (*passioni ecc*) to restrain; **tenere a ~ la lingua** to hold one's tongue; **~ a disco** disc brake; **~ a mano** handbrake

'freon® SM INV (*Chim*) Freon®

frequen'tare /72/ VT (*scuola, corso*) to attend; (*locale, bar*) to go to, frequent; (*persone*) to see (often)

frequen'tato, -a AG (*locale*) busy

fre'quente AG frequent; **di ~** frequently

fre'quenza [fre'kwɛntsa] SF frequency; (*Ins*) attendance

fre'sare /72/ VT (*Tecn*) to mill

fres'chezza [fres'kettsa] SF freshness

'fresco, -a, -schi, -sche AG fresh; (*temperatura*) cool; (*notizia*) recent, fresh ▶ SM: **godere il ~** to enjoy the cool air; **~ di bucato** straight from the wash, newly washed; **stare ~** (*fig*) to be in for it; **mettere al ~** to put in a cool place; (*fig: in prigione*) to put inside *o* in the cooler

fres'cura SF cool

'fresia SF freesia

'fretta SF hurry, haste; **in ~** in a hurry; **in ~ e furia** in a mad rush; **aver ~** to be in a hurry; **far ~ a qn** to hurry sb

frettolosa'mente AV hurriedly, in a rush

fretto'loso, -a AG (*persona*) in a hurry; (*lavoro ecc*) hurried, rushed

fri'abile AG (*terreno*) friable; (*pasta*) crumbly

'friggere ['friddʒere] /56/ VT to fry ▶ VI (*olio ecc*) to sizzle; **vai a farti ~!** (*col*) get lost!

frigidità [fridʒidi'ta] SF frigidity

'frigido, -a ['fridʒido] AG (*Med*) frigid

fri'gnare [frin'ɲare] /15/ VI to whine, snivel

fri'gnone, -a [frin'ɲone] SM/F whiner, sniveller

'frigo, -ghi SM fridge

frigo'bar SM INV minibar

frigo'rifero, -a AG refrigerating ▶ SM refrigerator; **cella frigorifera** cold store

fringu'ello SM chaffinch

'frissi *ecc* VB *vedi* **friggere**

frit'tata SF omelet(te); **fare una ~** (*fig*) to make a mess of things

frit'tella SF (*Cuc*) pancake; (: *ripiena*) fritter

'fritto, -a PP *di* **friggere** ▶ AG fried ▶ SM fried food; **ormai siamo fritti!** (*fig: col*) now we've had it!; **è un argomento ~ e rifritto** that's old hat; **~ misto** mixed fry

frit'tura SF (*cibo*) fried food; **~ di pesce** mixed fried fish

friu'lano, -a AG of (*o* from) Friuli

frivo'lezza [frivo'lettsa] SF frivolity

'frivolo, -a AG frivolous

frizi'one [frit'tsjone] SF friction; (*di pelle*) rub, rub-down; (*Aut*) clutch

friz'zante [frid'dzante] AG (*anche fig*) sparkling

'frizzo ['friddzo] SM witticism

fro'dare /72/ VT to defraud, cheat

'frode SF fraud; **~ fiscale** tax evasion

'frodo SM: **di ~** illegal, contraband; **pescatore di ~, cacciatore di ~** poacher

'frogia, -gie ['frɔdʒa] SF (*di cavallo ecc*) nostril

'frollo, -a AG (*carne*) tender; (: *selvaggina*) high; (*fig: persona*) soft; **pasta frolla** short(crust) pastry

'fronda SF (leafy) branch; (*di partito politico*) internal opposition ■ **fronde** SFPL (*di albero*) foliage *sg*

fron'tale AG frontal; (*scontro*) head-on

'fronte SF (*Anat*) forehead; (*di edificio*) front, façade ▶ SM (*Mil, Pol, Meteor*) front; **a ~, di ~** facing, opposite; **di ~ a** (*posizione*) opposite, facing, in front of; (*a paragone di*) compared with; **far ~ a** (*nemico, problema*) to confront; (*responsabilità*) to face up to; (*spese*) to cope with

fronteggi'are [fronted'dʒare] /62/ VT (*avversari, difficoltà*) to face, stand up to; (*spese*) to cope with

frontes'pizio [frontes'pittsjo] SM (*Archit*) frontispiece; (*di libro*) title page

fronti'era SF border, frontier

fron'tone SM pediment

'fronzolo ['frondzolo] SM frill

'frotta SF crowd; **in ~, a frotte** in their hundreds, in droves

'frottola SF fib; **raccontare un sacco di frottole** to tell a pack of lies

fru'gale AG frugal

fru'gare /80/ VI to rummage ▶ VT to search

frugherò *ecc* [fruge'rɔ] VB *vedi* **frugare**

frui'tore SM user

fruizi'one [fruit'tsjone] SF use

frul'lare /72/ VT (*Cuc*) to whisk ▶ VI (*uccelli*) to flutter; **cosa ti frulla in mente?** what is going on in that mind of yours?

frul'lato SM (*Cuc*) milk shake; (: *con solo frutta*) smoothie

frulla'tore SM electric mixer

frul'lino SM whisk

fru'mento SM wheat **frusci'are** [fruʃ'ʃare] /14/ VI to rustle

fru'scio [fruʃ'ʃio] SM rustle; rustling; (*di acque*) murmur

'frusta SF whip; (*Cuc*) whisk

frus'tare /**72**/ VT to whip

frus'tata SF lash

frus'tino SM riding crop

frus'trare /**72**/ VT to frustrate

frus'trato, -a AG frustrated

frustrazi'one [frustrat'tsjone] SF frustration

'frutta SF fruit; (*portata*) dessert; **~ candita/ secca** candied/dried fruit

frut'tare /**72**/ VI (*investimenti, deposito*) to bear dividends, give a return; **il mio deposito in banca (mi) frutta il 10%** my bank deposits bring (me) in 10%; **quella gara gli fruttò la medaglia d'oro** he won the gold medal in that competition

frut'teto SM orchard

frutticol'tura SF fruit growing

frut'tifero, -a AG (*albero ecc*) fruit-bearing; (*fig: che frutta*) fruitful, profitable; **deposito ~** interest-bearing deposit

frutti'vendolo, -a SM/F greengrocer (BRIT), produce dealer (US)

'frutto SM fruit; (*fig: risultato*) result(s); (*Econ: interesse*) interest; (: *reddito*) income; **è ~ della tua immaginazione** it's a figment of your imagination; **frutti di mare** seafood *sg*; **frutti di bosco** berries

fruttu'oso, -a AG fruitful, profitable

FS ABBR (= *Ferrovie dello Stato*) Italian railways

f.t. ABBR = **fuori testo**

f.to ABBR (= *firmato*) signed

fu VB *vedi* **essere** ▶ AG INV: **il fu Paolo Bianchi** the late Paolo Bianchi

fuci'lare [futʃi'lare] /**72**/ VT to shoot

fuci'lata [futʃi'lata] SF rifle shot

fucilazi'one [futʃilat'tsjone] SF execution (by firing squad)

fu'cile [fu'tʃile] SM rifle, gun; (*da caccia*) shotgun, gun; **~ a canne mozze** sawn-off shotgun

fu'cina [fu'tʃina] SF forge

'fuco, -chi SM drone

'fucsia SF fuchsia

'fuga, -ghe SF escape, flight; (*di gas, liquidi*) leak; (*Mus*) fugue; **mettere qn in ~** to put sb to flight; **~ di cervelli** brain drain

fu'gace [fu'gatʃe] AG fleeting, transient

fu'gare /**80**/ VT (*dubbi, incertezze*) to dispel, drive out

fug'gevole [fud'dʒevole] AG fleeting

fuggi'asco, -a, -schi, -sche [fud'dʒasko] AG, SM/F fugitive

fuggi'fuggi [fuddʒi'fuddʒi] SM scramble, stampede

fug'gire [fud'dʒire] /**31**/ VI to flee, run away; (*fig: passar veloce*) to fly ▶ VT to avoid

fuggi'tivo, -a [fuddʒi'tivo] SM/F fugitive, runaway

'fui VB *vedi* **essere**

'fulcro SM (*Fisica*) fulcrum; (*fig: di teoria, questione*) central o key point

ful'gore SM brilliance, splendour (BRIT), splendor (US)

fu'liggine [fu'liddʒine] SF soot

fulmi'nare /**72**/ VT (*elettricità*) to electrocute; (*con arma da fuoco*) to shoot dead ■ **fulminarsi** VPR (*lampadina*) to go, blow; (*fig: con lo sguardo*) **mi fulminò (con uno sguardo)** he looked daggers at me

'fulmine SM bolt of lightning ■ **fulmini** SMPL lightning *sg*; **~ a ciel sereno** bolt from the blue

ful'mineo, -a AG (*fig: scatto*) rapid; (: *minaccioso*) threatening

'fulvo, -a AG tawny

fumai'olo SM (*di nave*) funnel; (*di fabbrica*) chimney

fu'mante AG (*piatto ecc*) steaming

fu'mare /**72**/ VI to smoke; (*emettere vapore*) to steam ▶ VT to smoke

fu'mario, -a AG: **canna fumaria** flue

fu'mata SF (*segnale*) smoke signal; **farsi una ~** to have a smoke; **~ bianca/nera** (*in Vaticano*) signal that a new pope has/has not been elected

fuma'tore, -'trice SM/F smoker

fu'metto SM comic strip; **giornale a fumetti** comic

'fummo VB *vedi* **essere**

'fumo SM smoke; (*vapore*) steam; (*il fumare tabacco*) smoking ■ **fumi** SMPL (*industriali ecc*) fumes; **vendere ~** to deceive, cheat; **è tutto ~ e niente arrosto** it has no substance to it; **i fumi dell'alcool** (*fig*) the after-effects of drink; **~ passivo** passive smoking

fu'mogeno, -a [fu'mɔdʒeno] AG (*candelotto*) smoke *cpd* ▶ SM smoke bomb; **cortina fumogena** smoke screen

fu'moso, -a AG smoky; (*fig*) muddled

fu'nambolo, -a SM/F tightrope walker

'fune SF rope, cord; (*più grossa*) cable

'funebre AG (*rito*) funeral; (*aspetto*) gloomy, funereal

fune'rale SM funeral

fu'nesto, -a AG (*incidente*) fatal; (*errore, decisione*) fatal, disastrous; (*atmosfera*) gloomy, dismal

'fungere ['fundʒere] /**5**/ VI: **~ da** to act as

'fungo, -ghi SM fungus; (*commestibile*) mushroom; **~ velenoso** toadstool; **crescere come i funghi** (*fig*) to spring up overnight

funico'lare SF funicular railway

funi'via SF cable railway

'funsi ecc VB *vedi* **fungere**

'funto, -a PP *di* **fungere**

funzio'nare [funtsjo'nare] /**72**/ VI to work, function; (*fungere*): **~ da** to act as

funzio'nario [funtsjo'narjo] SM official; **~ statale** civil servant

funzi'one [fun'tsjone] SF function; (carica) post, position; (Rel) service; **in ~** (meccanismo) in operation; **in ~ di** (come) as; **vive in ~ dei figli** he lives for his children; **far ~ di** to act as; **fare la ~ di qn** (farne le veci) to take sb's place

fu'oco, -chi SM fire; (fornello) ring; (Fot, Fisica) focus; **dare ~ a qc** to set fire to sth; **far ~** (sparare) to fire; **prendere ~** to catch fire; **al ~!** fire!; **~ d'artificio** firework; **~ di paglia** flash in the pan; **~ sacro** o **di Sant'Antonio** (Med: col) shingles sg

fuorché [fwor'ke] CONG, PREP except

FU'ORI SIGLA M (= Fronte Unitario Omosessuale Rivoluzionario Italiano) gay liberation movement

fu'ori AV outside; (all'aperto) outdoors, outside; (fuori di casa, Sport) out; (esclamativo) get out! ▶ PREP: **~ (di)** out of, outside ▶ SM outside; **essere in ~** (sporgere) to stick out; **lasciar ~ qc/qn** to leave sth/sb out; **far ~** (col: cioccolatini) to eat up; (: rubare) to nick; **far ~ qn** (col) to kill sb, do sb in; **essere tagliato ~** (da un gruppo, ambiente) to be excluded; **essere ~ di sé** to be beside oneself; **~ luogo** (inopportuno) out of place, uncalled for; **~ mano** out of the way, remote; **~ pasto** between meals; **~ pericolo** out of danger; **~ dai piedi!** get out of the way!; **~ servizio** out of order; **~ stagione** out of season; **illustrazione ~ testo** (Stampa) plate; **~ uso** old-fashioned; obsolete

fuori'bordo SM INV speedboat (with outboard motor); outboard motor

fuori'busta SM INV unofficial payment

fuori'classe SM INV/F INV (undisputed) champion

fuori'corso AG INV (moneta) no longer in circulation; (Ins): **(studente) ~** undergraduate who has not completed a course in due time

fuorigi'oco [fwori'dʒɔko] SM offside

fuori'legge [fwori'leddʒe] SM INV/F INV outlaw

fuoriprog'ramma SM INV (TV, Radio) unscheduled programme; (fig) change of plan o programme

fuori'serie AG INV (auto ecc) custom-built ▶ SF custom-built car

fuoris'trada SM (Aut) cross-country vehicle

fuoru'scito, -a [fworuʃ'ʃito], **fuoriu'scito, -a** [fworiuʃ'ʃito] SM/F exile ▶ SF (di gas) leakage, escape; (di sangue, linfa) seepage

fuorvi'are /60/ VT to mislead; (fig) to lead astray ▶ VI to go astray

furbacchi'one, -a [furbak'kjone] SM/F cunning old devil

fur'bizia [fur'bittsja] SF cleverness; cunning; **una ~** a cunning trick

'furbo, -a AG clever, smart; (peg) cunning ▶ SM/F: **fare il ~** to (try to) be clever o smart; **fatti ~!** show a bit of sense!

fu'rente AG: **~ (contro)** furious (with)

fure'ria SF (Mil) orderly room

fur'retto SM ferret

fur'fante SMF rascal, scoundrel

furgon'cino [furgon'tʃino] SM small van

fur'gone SM van

'furia SF (ira) fury, rage; (fig: impeto) fury, violence; (: fretta) rush; **a ~ di** by dint of; **andare su tutte le furie** to fly into a rage

furi'bondo, -a AG furious

furi'ere SM quartermaster

furi'oso, -a AG furious; (mare, vento) raging

'furono VB vedi **essere**

fu'rore SM fury; (esaltazione) frenzy; **far ~** to be all the rage

furtiva'mente AV furtively

fur'tivo, -a AG furtive

'furto SM theft; **~ con scasso** burglary

'fusa SFPL: **fare le ~** to purr

fu'scello [fuʃ'ʃello] SM twig

fu'seaux SMPL leggings

'fusi ecc VB vedi **fondere**

fu'sibile SM (Elettr) fuse

fusi'one SF (di metalli) fusion, melting; (colata) casting; (Comm) merger; (fig) merging

'fuso, -a PP di **fondere** ▶ SM (Filatura) spindle; **diritto come un ~** as stiff as a ramrod; **~ orario** time zone

fusoli'era SF (Aer) fusillage

fus'tagno [fus'taɲɲo] SM corduroy

fus'tella SF (su scatola di medicinali) tear-off tab

fusti'gare /80/ VT (frustare) to flog; (fig: costumi) to censure, denounce

fus'tino SM (di detersivo) tub

'fusto SM stem; (Anat, di albero) trunk; (recipiente) drum, can; (col) he-man

'futile AG vain, futile

futilità SF INV futility

futu'rismo SM futurism

fu'turo, -a AG, SM future

Gg

G, g [dʒi] SM O F INV (lettera) G, g; **G come Genova** = G for George

g ABBR (= grammo) g

G8 [dʒi'otto] SM (= Gruppo degli Otto) G8

G20 [dʒi'venti] SM (= Gruppo dei Venti) G20

gabar'dine [gabar'din] SM (tessuto) gabardine; (soprabito) gabardine raincoat

gab'bare /72/ VT to take in, dupe ▪ **gabbarsi** VPR: **gabbarsi di qn** to make fun of sb

'gabbia SF cage; (Dir) dock; (da imballaggio) crate; **la ~ degli accusati** (Dir) the dock; **~ dell'ascensore** lift (BRIT) o elevator (US) shaft; **~ toracica** (Anat) rib cage

gabbi'ano SM (sea)gull

gabi'netto SM (Med ecc) consulting room; (Pol) ministry; (di decenza) toilet, lavatory; (Ins: di fisica ecc) laboratory

Ga'bon SM: **il ~** Gabon

ga'elico, -a, -ci, -che AG, SM Gaelic

gaffe [gaf] SF INV blunder, boob (col)

gagli'ardo, -a [gaʎˈʎardo] AG strong, vigorous

gai'ezza [ga'jettsa] SF gaiety, cheerfulness

'gaio, -a AG cheerful

'gala SF (sfarzo) pomp; (festa) gala

ga'lante AG gallant, courteous; (avventura, poesia) amorous

galante'ria SF gallantry

galantu'omo [pl **galantuomini**] SM gentleman

Ga'lapagos SFPL: **le (isole) ~** the Galapagos Islands

ga'lassia SF galaxy

gala'teo SM (good) manners pl, etiquette

gale'otto SM (rematore) galley slave; (carcerato) convict

ga'lera SF (Naut) galley; (prigione) prison

'galla SF: **a ~** afloat; **venire a ~** to surface, come to the surface; (fig: verità) to come out

galleggia'mento [galleddʒaˈmento] SM floating; **linea di ~** (di nave) waterline

galleggi'ante [galled'dʒante] AG floating ▶ SM (natante) barge; (di pescatore, lenza, Tecn) float

galleggi'are [galled'dʒare] /62/ VI to float

galle'ria SF (traforo) tunnel; (Archit, d'arte) gallery; (Teat) circle; (strada coperta con negozi) arcade; **~ del vento** o **aerodinamica** (Aer) wind tunnel

'Galles SM: **il ~** Wales

gal'lese AG Welsh ▶ SMF Welshman(-woman) ▶ SM (Ling) Welsh; **i Gallesi** the Welsh

gal'letta SF cracker; (Naut) ship's biscuit

gal'letto SM young cock, cockerel; (fig) cocky young man; **fare il ~** to play the gallant

'Gallia SF: **la ~** Gaul

gal'lina SF hen; **andare a letto con le galline** to go to bed early

gal'lismo SM machismo

'gallo SM cock; **al canto del ~** at daybreak, at cockcrow; **fare il ~** to play the gallant

gal'lone SM piece of braid; (Mil) stripe; (unità di misura) gallon

galop'pare /72/ VI to gallop

galop'pino SM errand boy; (Pol) canvasser

ga'loppo SM gallop; **al** o **di ~** at a gallop

galvaniz'zare [galvanid'dzare] /72/ VT to galvanize

'gamba SF leg; (asta: di lettera) stem; **in ~** (in buona salute) well; (bravo, sveglio) bright, smart; **prendere qc sotto ~** (fig) to treat sth too lightly; **scappare a gambe levate** to take to one's heels; **gambe!** scatter!

gam'bale SM legging

gambe'retto SM shrimp

'gambero SM (di acqua dolce) crayfish; (di mare) prawn

'Gambia SF: **la ~** the Gambia

gambiz'zare [gambid'dzare] /72/ VT to kneecap

'gambo SM stem; (di frutta) stalk

ga'mella SF mess tin

'gamma SF (Mus) scale; (di colori, fig) range; **~ di prodotti** product range

ga'nascia, -sce [ga'naʃʃa] SF jaw; **ganasce del freno** (Aut) brake shoes

'gancio ['gantʃo] SM hook

'Gange ['gandʒe] SM: **il ~** the Ganges

'gangheri ['gangeri] SMPL: **uscire dai ~** (fig) to fly into a temper

gan'grena SF = **cancrena**

'gara SF competition; (*Sport*) competition; contest; match; (: *corsa*) race; **fare a ~** to compete, vie; **~ d'appalto** (*Comm*) tender

ga'rage [ga'raʒ] SM INV garage

ga'rante SMF guarantor

garan'tire /55/ VT to guarantee; (*debito*) to stand surety for; (*dare per certo*) to assure

garan'tismo SM protection of civil liberties

garan'tista, -i, -e AG concerned with civil liberties

garan'zia [garan'tsia] SF guarantee; (*pegno*) security; **in ~** under guarantee

gar'bare /72/ VI: **non mi garba** I don't like it (*o* him *etc*)

garba'tezza [garba'tettsa] SF courtesy, politeness

gar'bato, -a AG courteous, polite

'garbo SM (*buone maniere*) politeness, courtesy; (*di vestito ecc*) grace, style

gar'buglio [gar'buʎʎo] SM tangle; (*fig*) muddle, mess

gareggi'are [gared'dʒare] /62/ VI to compete

garga'nella SF: **a ~** from the bottle

garga'rismo SM gargle; **fare i gargarismi** to gargle

ga'ritta SF (*di caserma*) sentry box

ga'rofano SM carnation; **chiodo di ~** clove

gar'retto SM hock

gar'rire /55/ VI to chirp

'garrulo, -a AG (*uccello*) chirping; (*persona: loquace*) garrulous, talkative

'garza ['gardza] SF (*per bende*) gauze

gar'zone [gar'dzone] SM (*di negozio*) boy

gas SM INV gas; **a tutto ~** at full speed; **dare ~** (*Aut*) to accelerate; **~ lacrimogeno** tear gas; **~ naturale** natural gas

ga'sare *ecc* /72/ = **gassare** *ecc*

ga'sato, -a SM/F (*col: persona*) freak

gas'dotto SM gas pipeline

ga'solio SM diesel (oil)

ga's(s)are /72/ VT to aerate, carbonate; (*asfissiare*) to gas ■ **gas(s)arsi** VPR (*col*) to get excited

ga's(s)ato, -a AG (*bibita*) aerated, fizzy

gas'soso, -a AG gaseous; gassy ▶ SF fizzy drink

'gastrico, -a, -ci, -che AG gastric

gast'rite SF gastritis

gastroente'rite SF gastroenteritis

gastrono'mia SF gastronomy

gas'tronomo, -a SM/F gourmet, gastronome

G.A.T.T. SIGLA M (= *General Agreement on Tariffs and Trade*) GATT

'gatta SF cat, she-cat; **una ~ da pelare** (*col*) a thankless task; **qui ~ ci cova!** I smell a rat!, there's something fishy going on here!

gatta'buia SF (*col, scherzoso: prigione*) clink

gat'tino SM kitten

'gatto SM cat, tomcat; **~ delle nevi** (*Aut, Sci*) snowcat; **~ a nove code** cat-o'-nine-tails; **~ selvatico** wildcat

gatto'pardo SM: **~ africano** serval; **~ americano** ocelot

gat'tuccio [gat'tuttʃo] SM dogfish

gau'dente SMF pleasure-seeker

'gaudio SM joy, happiness

ga'vetta SF (*Mil*) mess tin; **venire dalla ~** (*Mil, fig*) to rise from the ranks

'gazza ['gaddza] SF magpie

gaz'zarra [gad'dzarra] SF racket, din

gaz'zella [gad'dzɛlla] SF gazelle; (*dei carabinieri*) (high-speed) police car

gaz'zetta [gad'dzetta] SF news sheet; **G~ Ufficiale** *official publication containing details of new laws*

gaz'zoso, -a [gad'dzoso] AG = **gassoso**

Gazz. Uff. ABBR = **Gazzetta Ufficiale**

GB SIGLA (= *Gran Bretagna*) GB

G.C. ABBR = **genio civile**

G.d.F. ABBR = **guardia di finanza**

GE SIGLA = **Genova**

gel [dʒɛl] SM INV gel

ge'lare [dʒe'lare] /72/ VT, VI, VB IMPERS to freeze; **mi ha gelato il sangue** (*fig*) it made my blood run cold

ge'lata [dʒe'lata] SF frost

gela'taio, -a [dʒela'tajo] SM/F ice-cream vendor

gelate'ria [dʒelate'ria] SF ice-cream shop

gela'tina [dʒela'tina] SF gelatine; **~ esplosiva** gelignite; **~ di frutta** fruit jelly

gelati'noso, -a [dʒelati'noso] AG gelatinous, jelly-like

ge'lato, -a [dʒe'lato] AG frozen ▶ SM ice cream

'gelido, -a ['dʒɛlido] AG icy, ice-cold

'gelo ['dʒɛlo] SM (*temperatura*) intense cold; (*brina*) frost; (*fig*) chill

ge'lone [dʒe'lone] SM chilblain

gelo'sia [dʒelo'sia] SF jealousy

ge'loso, -a [dʒe'loso] AG jealous

'gelso ['dʒɛlso] SM mulberry (tree)

gelso'mino [dʒelso'mino] SM jasmine

gemel'laggio [dʒemel'laddʒo] SM twinning

gemel'lare [dʒemel'lare] /72/ AG twin *cpd* ▶ VT (*città*) to twin

ge'mello, -a [dʒe'mɛllo] AG, SM/F twin ■ **gemelli** SMPL (*di camicia*) cufflinks; **Gemelli** Gemini *sg*; **essere dei Gemelli** to be Gemini

ge'mere ['dʒɛmere] /29/ VI to moan, groan; (*cigolare*) to creak; (*gocciolare*) to drip, ooze

'gemito ['dʒɛmito] SM moan, groan

'gemma ['dʒɛmma] SF (*Bot*) bud; (*pietra preziosa*) gem

Gen. ABBR (*Mil*: = *generale*) Gen

gen. ABBR (= *generale, generalmente*) gen

gen'darme [dʒen'darme] SM policeman; (*fig*) martinet

'gene ['dʒɛne] SM gene

genealo'gia, -'gie [dʒenealo'dʒia] SF genealogy

genea'logico, -a, -ci, -che [dʒenea'lɔdʒiko] AG genealogical; **albero ~** family tree

gene'rale [dʒene'rale] AG, SM general; **in ~** (*per sommi capi*) in general terms; (*di solito*) usually, in general; **a ~ richiesta** by popular request

generalità [dʒenerali'ta] SFPL (*dati d'identità*) particulars

generaliz'zare [dʒeneralid'dzare] /72/ VT, VI to generalize

generalizzazi'one [dʒeneraliddzat'tsjone] SF generalization

general'mente [dʒeneral'mente] AV generally

gene'rare [dʒene'rare] /72/ VT (*dar vita*) to give birth to; (*produrre*) to produce; (*causare*) to arouse; (*Tecn*) to produce, generate

genera'tore [dʒenera'tore] SM (*Tecn*) generator

generazi'one [dʒenerat'tsjone] SF generation

'genere ['dʒɛnere] SM kind, type, sort; (*Biol*) genus; (*merce*) article, product; (*Ling*) gender; (*Arte, Letteratura*) genre; **in ~** generally, as a rule; **cose del o di questo ~** such things; **il ~ umano** mankind; **generi alimentari** foodstuffs; **generi di consumo** consumer goods; **generi di prima necessità** basic essentials

ge'nerico, -a, -ci, -che [dʒe'nɛriko] AG generic; (*vago*) vague, imprecise; **medico ~** general practitioner

'genero ['dʒɛnero] SM son-in-law

generosità [dʒenerosi'ta] SF generosity

gene'roso, -a [dʒene'roso] AG generous

'genesi ['dʒɛnezi] SF genesis

ge'netico, -a, -ci, -che [dʒe'nɛtiko] AG genetic ▶ SF genetics *sg*

gen'giva [dʒen'dʒiva] SF (*Anat*) gum

ge'nia [dʒe'nia] SF (*peg*) mob, gang

geni'ale [dʒe'njale] AG (*persona*) of genius; (*idea*) ingenious, brilliant

'genio ['dʒɛnjo] SM genius; (*attitudine, talento*) talent, flair, genius; **andare a ~ a qn** to be to sb's liking, appeal to sb; **~ civile** civil engineers *pl*; **il ~** (*militare*) the Engineers

geni'tale [dʒeni'tale] AG genital ■ **genitali** SMPL genitals

geni'tore [dʒeni'tore] SM parent, father *o* mother ■ **genitori** SMPL parents

genitoriali'tà [dʒenitorjali'ta] SF parenthood

genn. ABBR (= *gennaio*) Jan

gen'naio [dʒen'najo] SM January; *vedi anche* **luglio**

geno'cidio [dʒeno'tʃidjo] SM genocide

ge'noma [dʒe'nɔma] SM genome

'Genova ['dʒɛnova] SF Genoa

geno'vese [dʒeno'vese] AG, SMF Genoese (*pl inv*)

gen'taglia [dʒen'taʎʎa] SF (*peg*) rabble

'gente ['dʒɛnte] SF people *pl*

> *Gente* si traduce **people** con il verbo al plurale. *La gente era simpatica*. **The people were nice.**

gentil'donna [dʒentil'dɔnna] SF lady

gen'tile [dʒen'tile] AG (*persona, atto*) kind; (: *garbato*) courteous, polite; (*nelle lettere*): **G~ Signore** Dear Sir; **G~ Signor Fernando Villa** (*sulla busta*) Mr Fernando Villa

genti'lezza [dʒenti'lettsa] SF kindness; courtesy, politeness; **per ~** (*per favore*) please

gentilu'omo [dʒenti'lwɔmo] (*pl* **gentiluomini**) SM gentleman

genuflessi'one [dʒenufles'sjone] SF genuflection

genu'ino, -a [dʒenu'ino] AG (*prodotto*) natural; (*persona, sentimento*) genuine, sincere

geogra'fia [dʒeogra'fia] SF geography

geo'grafico, -a, -ci, -che [dʒeo'grafiko] AG geographical

ge'ografo, -a [dʒe'ɔgrafo] SM/F geographer

geolocaliz'zare [dʒeolokalid'dzare] VT to geolocate

geolo'gia [dʒeolo'dʒia] SF geology

geo'logico, -a, -ci, -che [dʒeo'lɔdʒiko] AG geological

ge'ometra, -i, -e [dʒe'ɔmetra] SM/F (*professionista*) surveyor

geome'tria [dʒeome'tria] SF geometry

geo'metrico, -a, -ci, -che [dʒeo'mɛtriko] AG geometric(al)

geopo'litico, -a, -ci, -che [dʒeopo'litiko] AG geopolitical

Ge'orgia [dʒe'ɔrdʒa] SF Georgia

geor'giano, -a [dʒeor'dʒano] AG, SM/F Georgian

ge'ranio [dʒe'ranjo] SM geranium

ge'rarca, -chi [dʒe'rarka] SM (*Storia: nel fascismo*) party official

gerar'chia [dʒerar'kia] SF hierarchy

ge'rarchico, -a, -ci, -che [dʒe'rarkiko] AG hierarchical

ge'rente [dʒe'rɛnte] SMF manager (manageress)

ge'renza [dʒe'rɛntsa] SF management

ger'gale [dʒer'gale] AG slang *cpd*

'gergo, -ghi ['dʒɛrgo] SM jargon; slang

geria'tria [dʒerja'tria] SF geriatrics *sg*

geri'atrico, -a, -ci, -che [dʒe'rjatriko] AG geriatric

'gerla [ˈdʒɛrla] SF conical wicker basket

Ger'mania [dʒerˈmanja] SF: **la ~** Germany; **la ~ occidentale/orientale** West/East Germany

'germe [ˈdʒɛrme] SM germ; (fig) seed

germinazi'one [dʒerminatˈtsjone] SF germination

germogli'are [dʒermoʎˈʎare] /**27**/ VI (emettere germogli) to sprout; (germinare) to germinate

ger'moglio [dʒerˈmoʎʎo] SM shoot; (gemma) bud

gero'glifico, -ci [dʒeroˈglifiko] SM hieroglyphic

geron'tologo, -a, -gi, -ghe [dʒeronˈtɔlogo] SM/F specialist in geriatrics

ge'rundio [dʒeˈrundjo] SM gerund

Gerusa'lemme [dʒeruzaˈlɛmme] SF Jerusalem

'gesso [ˈdʒɛsso] SM chalk; (Scultura, Med, Edil) plaster; (statua) plaster figure; (minerale) gypsum

'gesta [ˈdʒɛsta] SFPL (letterario) deeds, feats

ges'tante [dʒesˈtante] SF expectant mother

gestazi'one [dʒestatˈtsjone] SF gestation

gestico'lare [dʒestikoˈlare] /**72**/ VI to gesticulate

gestio'nale [dʒestjoˈnale] AG administrative, management cpd

gesti'one [dʒesˈtjone] SF management; **~ di magazzino** stock control; **~ patrimoniale** investment management

ges'tire [dʒesˈtire] /**55**/ VT to run, manage

'gesto [ˈdʒɛsto] SM gesture

ges'tore [dʒesˈtore] SM manager

Gesù [dʒeˈzu] SM Jesus; **~ bambino** the Christ Child

gesu'ita, -i [dʒezuˈita] SM Jesuit

get'tare [dʒetˈtare] /**72**/ VT to throw; (anche: **gettare via**) to throw away o out; (Scultura) to cast; (Edil) to lay; (acqua) to spout; (grido) to utter ■ **gettarsi** VPR: **gettarsi in** (impresa) to throw o.s. into; (mischia) to hurl o.s. into; (fiume) to flow into; **~ uno sguardo su** to take a quick look at

get'tata [dʒetˈtata] SF (di cemento, gesso, metalli) cast; (diga) jetty

'gettito [ˈdʒettito] SM revenue

'getto [ˈdʒetto] SM (di gas, liquido, Aer) jet; (Bot) shoot; **a ~ continuo** uninterruptedly; **di ~** (fig) straight off, in one go

get'tone [dʒetˈtone] SM token; (per giochi) counter; (: roulette ecc) chip; **~ di presenza** attendance fee; **~ telefonico** telephone token

gettoni'era [dʒettoˈnjɛra] SF telephone-token dispenser

'geyser [ˈɡaizə] SM INV geyser

'Ghana [ˈɡana] SM: **il ~** Ghana

'ghenga, -ghe [ˈɡɛnga] SF (col) gang, crowd

ghe'pardo [ɡeˈpardo] SM cheetah

gher'mire [ɡerˈmire] /**55**/ VT to grasp, clasp, clutch

'ghetta [ˈɡetta] SF (gambale) gaiter

ghettiz'zare [ɡettidˈdzare] /**72**/ VT to segregate

'ghetto [ˈɡetto] SM ghetto

ghiacci'aia [ɡjatˈtʃaja] SF (anche fig) icebox

ghiacci'aio [ɡjatˈtʃajo] SM glacier

ghiacci'are [ɡjatˈtʃare] /**14**/ VT to freeze; (fig): **~ qn** to make sb's blood run cold ▶ VI to freeze, ice over

ghiacci'ato, -a [ɡjatˈtʃato] AG frozen; (bevanda) ice-cold

ghi'accio [ˈɡjattʃo] SM ice

ghiacci'olo [ɡjatˈtʃɔlo] SM icicle; (tipo di gelato) ice lolly (BRIT), popsicle (US)

ghi'aia [ˈɡjaja] SF gravel

ghi'anda [ˈɡjanda] SF (Bot) acorn

ghi'andola [ˈɡjandola] SF gland

ghiando'lare [ɡjandoˈlare] AG glandular

ghigliot'tina [ɡiʎʎotˈtina] SF guillotine

ghi'gnare [ɡiɲˈɲare] /**15**/ VI to sneer

'ghigno [ˈɡiɲɲo] SM (espressione) sneer; (risata) mocking laugh

'ghingheri [ˈɡingeri] SMPL: **in ~** all dolled up; **mettersi in ~** to put on one's Sunday best

ghi'otto, -a [ˈɡjotto] AG greedy; (cibo) delicious, appetizing

ghiot'tone, -a [ɡjotˈtone] SM/F glutton

ghiottone'ria [ɡjottoneˈria] SF greed, gluttony; (cibo) delicacy, titbit (BRIT), tidbit (US)

ghiri'goro [ɡiriˈgoro] SM scribble, squiggle

ghir'landa [ɡirˈlanda] SF garland, wreath

'ghiro [ˈɡiro] SM dormouse

'ghisa [ˈɡiza] SF cast iron

G.I. ABBR = **giudice istruttore**

già [dʒa] AV already; (ex, in precedenza) formerly ▶ ESCL of course!, yes indeed!; **~ che ci sei ...** while you are at it ...

gi'acca, -che [ˈdʒakka] SF jacket; **~ a vento** windcheater (BRIT), windbreaker (US)

giacché [dʒakˈke] CONG since, as

giac'chetta [dʒakˈketta] SF (light) jacket

'giaccio ecc [ˈdʒattʃo] VB vedi **giacere**

giac'cone [dʒakˈkone] SM heavy jacket

gia'cenza [dʒaˈtʃɛntsa] SF: **merce in ~** goods in stock; **capitale in ~** uninvested capital; **giacenze di magazzino** unsold stock

gia'cere [dʒaˈtʃere] /**57**/ VI to lie

giaci'mento [dʒatʃiˈmento] SM deposit

gia'cinto [dʒaˈtʃinto] SM hyacinth

giaci'uto, -a [dʒaˈtʃuto] PP di **giacere**

gi'acqui ecc [ˈdʒakkwi] VB vedi **giacere**

gi'ada [ˈdʒada] SF jade

giaggi'olo [dʒadˈdʒɔlo] SM iris

g

giagu'aro [dʒaˈgwaro] SM jaguar

gial'lastro, -a [dʒalˈlastro] AG yellowish; (*carnagione*) sallow

gi'allo [ˈdʒallo] AG yellow; (*carnagione*) sallow ▶ SM yellow; (*anche: romanzo giallo*) detective novel; (*anche: film giallo*) detective film; ~ **dell'uovo** yolk; **il mar G~** the Yellow Sea

gial'lognolo, -a [dʒalˈloɲɲolo] AG yellowish, dirty yellow

Gia'maica [dʒaˈmaika] SF: **la ~** Jamaica

giamai'cano, -a [dʒamaiˈkano] AG, SM/F Jamaican

giam'mai [dʒamˈmai] AV never

Giap'pone [dʒapˈpone] SM: **il ~** Japan

giappo'nese [dʒappoˈnese] AG, SMF, SM Japanese *inv*

gi'ara [ˈdʒara] SF jar

giardi'naggio [dʒardiˈnaddʒo] SM gardening

giardi'netta [dʒardiˈnetta] SF estate car (BRIT), station wagon (US)

giardini'ere, -a [dʒardiˈnjɛre] SM/F gardener ▶ SF (*misto di sottaceti*) mixed pickles *pl*; (*automobile*) = **giardinetta**

giar'dino [dʒarˈdino] SM garden; ~ **d'infanzia** nursery school; ~ **pubblico** public gardens *pl*, (public) park; ~ **zoologico** zoo

giarretti'era [dʒarretˈtjɛra] SF garter

Gi'ava [ˈdʒava] SF Java

giavel'lotto [dʒavelˈlɔtto] SM javelin

gib'boso, -a [dʒibˈboso] AG (*superficie*) bumpy; (*naso*) crooked

Gibil'terra [dʒibilˈtɛrra] SF Gibraltar

'giga SM INV (*Inform*) gig

giga'byte [dʒigaˈbait] SM INV gigabyte

gi'gante, -'essa [dʒiˈgante] SM/F giant ▶ AG giant, gigantic; (*Comm*) giant-size

gigan'tesco, -a, -schi, -sche [dʒiganˈtesko] AG gigantic

gigantogra'fia [dʒigantograˈfia] SF (*Fot*) blow-up

'giglio [ˈdʒiʎʎo] SM lily

gilè [dʒiˈlɛ] SM INV waistcoat

gin [dʒin] SM INV gin

gin'cana [dʒinˈkana] SF gymkhana

ginecolo'gia [dʒinekoloˈdʒia] SF gynaecology (BRIT), gynecology (US)

gine'cologo, -a, -gi, -ghe [dʒineˈkɔlogo] SM/F gynaecologist (BRIT), gynecologist (US)

gi'nepro [dʒiˈnepro] SM juniper

gi'nestra [dʒiˈnɛstra] SF (*Bot*) broom

Gi'nevra [dʒiˈnevra] SF Geneva; **il Lago di ~** Lake Geneva

gingil'larsi [dʒindʒilˈlarsi] /72/ VPR to fritter away one's time; (*giocare*): ~ **con** to fiddle with

gin'gillo [dʒinˈdʒillo] SM plaything

gin'nasio [dʒinˈnazjo] SM *the 4th and 5th year of secondary school in Italy*

gin'nasta, -i, -e [dʒinˈnasta] SM/F gymnast

gin'nastica [dʒinˈnastika] SF gymnastics *sg*; (*esercizio fisico*) keep-fit exercises *pl*; (*Ins*) physical education

'ginnico, -a, -ci, -che [ˈdʒinniko] AG gymnastic

gi'nocchio [dʒiˈnɔkkjo] (*pl(m)* **ginocchi**, *pl(f)* **ginocchia**) SM knee; **stare in ~** to kneel, be on one's knees; **mettersi in ~** to kneel (down)

ginocchi'oni [dʒinokˈkjoni] AV on one's knees

gio'care [dʒoˈkare] /20/ VT to play; (*scommettere*) to stake, wager, bet; (*ingannare*) to take in ▶ VI to play; (*a roulette ecc*) to gamble; (*fig*) to play a part, be important; (*Tecn: meccanismo*) to be loose; ~ **a** (*gioco, sport*) to play; (*cavalli*) to bet on; ~ **d'astuzia** to be crafty; **giocarsi la carriera** to put one's career at risk; **giocarsi tutto** to risk everything; **a che gioco giochiamo?** what are you playing at?

gioca'tore, -'trice [dʒokaˈtore] SM/F player; gambler

gio'cattolo [dʒoˈkattolo] SM toy

giocherel'lare [dʒokerelˈlare] /72/ VI: ~ **con** (*giocattolo*) to play with; (*distrattamente*) to fiddle with

giocherò *ecc* [dʒokeˈrɔ] VB *vedi* **giocare**

gio'chetto [dʒoˈketto] SM (*gioco*) game; (*tranello*) trick; (*fig*): **è un ~** it's child's play

gi'oco, -chi [ˈdʒɔko] SM game; (*divertimento, Tecn*) play; (*al casinò*) gambling; (*Carte*) hand; (*insieme di pezzi ecc necessari per un gioco*) set; **per ~** for fun; **fare il doppio ~ con** qn to double-cross sb; **prendersi ~ di** qn to pull sb's leg; **stare al ~ di** qn to play along with sb; **è in ~ la mia reputazione** my reputation is at stake; ~ **d'azzardo** game of chance; ~ **per il computer** computer game; ~ **della palla** ball game; ~ **degli scacchi** chess set; **i Giochi Olimpici** the Olympic Games®

gioco'forza [dʒokoˈfɔrtsa] SM: **essere ~** to be inevitable

giocoli'ere [dʒokoˈljɛre] SM juggler

gio'coso, -a [dʒoˈkoso] AG playful, jesting

gio'gaia [dʒoˈgaja] SF (*Geo*) range of mountains

gi'ogo, -ghi [ˈdʒogo] SM yoke

gi'oia [ˈdʒɔja] SF joy, delight; (*pietra preziosa*) jewel, precious stone

gioielle'ria [dʒojelleˈria] SF jeweller's (BRIT) *o* jeweler's (US) craft; (*negozio*) jewel(l)er's (shop)

gioielli'ere, -a [dʒojelˈljɛre] SM/F jeweller (BRIT), jeweler (US)

gioi'ello [dʒoˈjello] SM jewel, piece of jewellery (BRIT) *o* jewelry (US) ■ **gioielli** SMPL (*anelli, collane ecc*) jewellery *sg*; **i miei gioielli** my jewels *o* jewellery; **i gioielli della Corona** the crown jewels

gioi'oso, -a [dʒoˈjoso] AG joyful

Gior'dania [dʒorˈdanja] SF: **la ~** Jordan

Gior'dano [dʒorˈdano] SM: **il ~** the Jordan

gior'dano, -a [dʒor'dano] AG, SM/F Jordanian

giorna'laio, -a [dʒorna'lajo] SM/F newsagent (BRIT), newsdealer (US)

gior'nale [dʒor'nale] SM (news)paper; (diario) journal, diary; (Comm) journal; **~ di bordo** (Naut) ship's log; **~ radio** radio news sg

giorna'letto [dʒorna'letto] SM (children's) comic

giornali'ero, -a [dʒorna'ljero] AG daily; (che varia: umore) changeable ▶ SM/F day labourer (BRIT) o laborer (US)

giorna'lino [dʒorna'lino] SM children's comic

giorna'lismo [dʒorna'lizmo] SM journalism

giorna'lista, -i, -e [dʒorna'lista] SM/F journalist

giorna'listico, -a, -ci, -che [dʒorna'listiko] AG journalistic; **stile ~** journalese

giornal'mente [dʒornal'mente] AV daily

gior'nata [dʒor'nata] SF day; (paga) day's wages, day's pay; **durante la ~ di ieri** yesterday; **fresco di ~** (uovo) freshly laid; **vivere alla ~** to live from day to day; **~ lavorativa** working day

gi'orno ['dʒorno] SM day; (opposto alla notte) day, daytime; (luce del giorno) daylight; **al ~** per day; **di ~** by day; **per ~** day by day; **al ~ d'oggi** nowadays; **tutto il santo ~** all day long; **il G~ dei Morti** All Souls' Day

gi'ostra ['dʒɔstra] SF (per bimbi) merry-go-round; (torneo storico) joust

gios'trare [dʒos'trare] /**72**/ VI (Storia) to joust, tilt ■ **giostrarsi** VPR to manage

giov. ABBR (= giovedì) Thur(s)

giova'mento [dʒova'mento] SM benefit, help

gi'ovane ['dʒovane] AG young; (aspetto) youthful ▶ SM youth, young man ▶ SF girl, young woman; **i giovani** young people; **è ~ del mestiere** he's new to the job

giova'netto, -a [dʒova'netto] SM/F young man(-woman)

giova'nile [dʒova'nile] AG youthful; (scritti) early; (errore) of youth

giova'notto [dʒova'nɔtto] SM young man

gio'vare [dʒo'vare] /**72**/ VI: **~ a** (essere utile) to be useful to; (far bene) to be good for ▶ VB IMPERS (essere bene, utile) to be useful ■ **giovarsi** VPR: **giovarsi di qc** to make use of sth; **a che giova prendersela?** what's the point of getting upset?

Gi'ove ['dʒove] SM (Mitologia) Jove; (Astr) Jupiter

gio'vedì [dʒove'di] SM INV Thursday; **di** o **il ~** on Thursdays; vedi anche **martedì**

gio'venca, -che [dʒo'venka] SF heifer

gioven'tù [dʒoven'tu] SF (periodo) youth; (i giovani) young people pl, youth

giovi'ale [dʒo'vjale] AG jovial, jolly

giovi'nastro [dʒovi'nastro] SM young thug

giovin'cello [dʒovin'tʃello] SM young lad

giovi'nezza [dʒovi'nettsa] SF youth

gip [dʒip] SIGLA M INV (= giudice per le indagini preliminari) judge for preliminary enquiries

gira'dischi [dʒira'diski] SM INV record player

gi'raffa [dʒi'raffa] SF giraffe; (TV, Cine, Radio) boom

gira'mento [dʒira'mento] SM: **~ di testa** fit of dizziness

gira'mondo [dʒira'mondo] SM INV/F INV globe-trotter

gi'randola [dʒi'randola] SF (fuoco d'artificio) Catherine wheel; (giocattolo) toy windmill; (banderuola) weather vane, weathercock

gi'rante [dʒi'rante] SMF (di assegno) endorser

gi'rare [dʒi'rare] /**72**/ VT (far ruotare) to turn; (percorrere, visitare) to go round; (Cine) to shoot; (: film: come regista) to make; (Comm) to endorse ▶ VI to turn; (più veloce) to spin; (andare in giro) to wander, go around ■ **girarsi** VPR to turn; **~ attorno a** to go round; to revolve round; **si girava e rigirava nel letto** he tossed and turned in bed; **far ~ la testa a qn** to make sb dizzy; (fig) to turn sb's head; **gira al largo** keep your distance; **girala come ti pare** (fig) look at it whichever way you like; **gira e rigira ...** after a lot of driving (o walking) about ...; (fig) whichever way you look at it; **cosa ti gira?** (col) what's got into you?; **mi ha fatto ~ le scatole** (col) he drove me crazy

girar'rosto [dʒirar'rɔsto] SM (Cuc) spit

gira'sole [dʒira'sole] SM sunflower

gi'rata [dʒi'rata] SF (passeggiata) stroll; (con veicolo) drive; (Comm) endorsement

gira'tario, -a [dʒira'tarjo] SM/F endorsee

gira'volta [dʒira'vɔlta] SF twirl, turn; (curva) sharp bend; (fig) about-turn

gi'rello [dʒi'rello] SM (di bambino) Babywalker® (BRIT), go-cart (US); (taglio di carne) topside (BRIT), top round (US)

gi'retto [dʒi'retto] SM (passeggiata) walk, stroll; (: in macchina) drive, spin; (: in bicicletta) ride

gi'revole [dʒi'revole] AG revolving, turning

gi'rino [dʒi'rino] SM tadpole

'giro ['dʒiro] SM (circuito, cerchio) circle; (di chiave, manovella) turn; (viaggio) tour, excursion; (passeggiata) stroll, walk; (in macchina) drive; (in bicicletta) ride; (Sport: della pista) lap; (di denaro) circulation; (Carte) hand; (Tecn) revolution; **fare un ~** to go for a walk (o a drive o a ride); **fare il ~ di** (parco, città) to go round; **andare in ~** (a piedi) to go about, walk around; **guardarsi in ~** to look around; **prendere in ~ qn** (fig) to take sb for a ride; **a stretto ~ di posta** by return of post; **nel ~ di un mese** in a month's time; **essere nel ~** (fig) to belong to a circle (of friends); **~ d'affari** (viaggio) business tour; (Comm) turnover; **~ di parole** circumlocution; **~ di prova** (Aut) test drive; **~ turistico** sightseeing tour; **~ vita** waist measurement

g

155

giro'collo [dʒiro'kɔllo] SM: **a ~** crewneck cpd

giro'conto [dʒiro'konto] SM (Econ) credit transfer

gi'rone [dʒi'rone] SM (Sport) series of games; **~ di andata/ritorno** (Calcio) first/second half of the season

gironzo'lare [dʒirondzo'lare] /**72**/ VI to stroll about

giro'tondo [dʒiro'tondo] SM ring-a-ring-o'roses (BRIT), ring-around-the-rosey (US); **in ~** in a circle

girova'gare [dʒirova'gare] /**80**/ VI to wander about

gi'rovago, -a, -ghi, -ghe [dʒi'rɔvago] SM/F (vagabondo) tramp; (venditore) peddler; **una compagnia di girovaghi** (attori) a company of strolling actors

'gita ['dʒita] SF excursion, trip; **fare una ~** to go for a trip, go on an outing

gi'tano, -a [dʒi'tano] SM/F gipsy

gi'tante [dʒi'tante] SMF member of a tour

giù [dʒu] AV down; (dabbasso) downstairs; **in ~** downwards, down; **la mia casa è un po' più in ~** my house is a bit further on; **~ di lì** (pressappoco) thereabouts; **bambini dai 6 anni in ~** children aged 6 and under; **~ per, cadere ~ per le scale** to fall down the stairs; **~ le mani!** hands off!; **essere ~** (fig: di salute) to be run down; (: di spirito) to be depressed; **quel tipo non mi va ~** I can't stand that guy

gi'ubba ['dʒubba] SF jacket

giub'botto [dʒub'bɔtto] SM jerkin; **~ antiproiettile** bulletproof vest; **~ salvagente** life jacket; **~ salvavita** high-visibilty vest

giubi'lare [dʒubi'lare] /**72**/ VI to rejoice

gi'ubilo ['dʒubilo] SM rejoicing

giudi'care [dʒudi'kare] /**20**/ VT to judge; (accusato) to try; (lite) to arbitrate in; **~ qn/qc bello** to consider sb/sth (to be) beautiful

giudi'cato [dʒudi'kato] SM (Dir): **passare in ~** to pass final judgment

gi'udice ['dʒuditʃe] SM judge; **~ collegiale** member of the court; **~ conciliatore** justice of the peace; **~ istruttore** examining (BRIT) o committing (US) magistrate; **~ popolare** member of a jury

giudizi'ale [dʒudit'tsjale] AG judicial

giudizi'ario, -a [dʒudit'tsjarjo] AG legal, judicial

giu'dizio [dʒu'dittsjo] SM judgment; (opinione) opinion; (Dir) judgment, sentence; (: processo) trial; (: verdetto) verdict; **aver ~** to be wise o prudent; **essere in attesa di ~** to be awaiting trial; **citare in ~** to summons; **l'imputato è stato rinviato a ~** the accused has been committed for trial

giudizi'oso, -a [dʒudit'tsjoso] AG prudent, judicious

gi'uggiola ['dʒuddʒola] SF: **andare in brodo di giuggiole** (col) to be over the moon

gi'ugno ['dʒuɲɲo] SM June; vedi anche **luglio**

giu'livo, -a [dʒu'livo] AG merry

giul'lare [dʒul'lare] SM jester

giu'menta [dʒu'menta] SF mare

gi'unco, -chi ['dʒunko] SM (Bot) rush

gi'ungere ['dʒundʒere] /**5**/ VI to arrive ▸ VT (mani ecc) to join; **~ a** to arrive at, reach; **~ nuovo a qn** to come as news to sb; **~ in porto** to reach harbour; (fig) to be brought to a successful outcome

gi'ungla ['dʒungla] SF jungle

gi'unsi ecc ['dʒunsi] VB vedi **giungere**

gi'unto, -a ['dʒunto] PP di **giungere** ▸ SM (Tecn) coupling, joint ▸ SF addition; (organo esecutivo, amministrativo) council, board; **per giunta** into the bargain, in addition; **giunta militare** military junta; vedi anche **Comune; Regione**

giun'tura [dʒun'tura] SF joint

giuo'care [dʒwo'kare] /**20**/ VT, VI = **giocare**

giu'oco ['dʒwɔko] SM = **gioco**

giura'mento [dʒura'mento] SM oath; **~ falso** perjury

giu'rare [dʒu'rare] /**72**/ VT to swear ▸ VI to swear, take an oath; **gliel'ho giurata** I swore I would get even with him

giu'rato, -a [dʒu'rato] AG: **nemico ~** sworn enemy ▸ SM/F juror, juryman(-woman)

giu'ria [dʒu'ria] SF jury

giu'ridico, -a, -ci, -che [dʒu'ridiko] AG legal

giurisdizi'one [dʒurizdit'tsjone] SF jurisdiction

giurispru'denza [dʒurispru'dɛntsa] SF jurisprudence

giu'rista, -i, -e [dʒu'rista] SM/F jurist

giustap'porre [dʒustap'porre] /**77**/ VT to juxtapose

giustapposizi'one [dʒustappozit'tsjone] SF juxtaposition

giustap'posto, -a [dʒustap'posto] PP di **giustapporre**

giustifi'care [dʒustifi'kare] /**20**/ VT to justify ▪ **giustificarsi** VPR: **giustificarsi di** o **per qc** to justify o excuse o.s. for sth

giustifica'tivo, -a [dʒustifika'tivo] AG (Amm): **nota** o **pezza giustificativa** receipt

giustificazi'one [dʒustifikat'tsjone] SF justification; (Ins) (note of) excuse

gius'tizia [dʒus'tittsja] SF justice; **farsi ~ (da sé)** (vendicarsi) to take the law into one's own hands

giustizi'are [dʒustit'tsjare] /**19**/ VT to execute, put to death

giustizi'ere [dʒustit'tsjɛre] SM executioner

gi'usto, -a ['dʒusto] AG (equo) fair, just; (vero) true, correct; (adatto) right, suitable; (preciso) exact, correct ▸ AV (esattamente) exactly, precisely; (per l'appunto, appena) just; **arrivare ~** to arrive just in time; **ho ~ bisogno di te** you're just the person I need

'glabro, -a AG hairless

glaci'ale [gla'tʃale] AG glacial

gla'diolo SM gladiolus

'glandola SF = **ghiandola**

'glassa SF (Cuc) icing

glau'coma SM glaucoma

gli [ʎi] DET MPL (dav V, s impura, gn, pn, ps, x, z) the ► PRON (a lui) to him; (a esso) to it; (in coppia con lo, la, li, le, ne: a lui, a lei, a loro ecc): **gliele do** I'm giving them to him (o her o them); **gliene ho parlato** I spoke to him (o her o them) about it; vedi anche **il**

glice'mia [glitʃe'mia] SF glycaemia

glice'rina [glitʃe'rina] SF glycerine

'glicine ['glitʃine] SM wistaria

gli'ela ecc ['ʎela] vedi **gli**

glo'bale AG overall; (vista) global

globalizza'zione [globalidzat'tsjone] SF globalization

'globo SM globe

'globulo SM (Anat): **~ rosso/bianco** red/white corpuscle

glocalizzazi'one [glokaliddza'tsjone] SF glocalization

'gloria SF glory; **farsi ~ di qc** to pride o.s. on sth, take pride in sth

glori'arsi /72/ VPR: **~ di qc** to pride o.s. on sth, glory o take pride in sth

glorifi'care /20/ VT to glorify

glori'oso, -a AG glorious

glos'sario SM glossary

glu'cosio SM glucose

'gluteo SM gluteus ■ **glutei** SMPL buttocks

GM ABBR = **genio militare**

'gnocchi ['ɲɔkki] SMPL (Cuc) small dumplings made of semolina pasta or potato

'gnomo ['ɲɔmo] SM gnome

'gnorri ['ɲɔrri] SM INV/F INV: **non fare lo ~!** stop acting as if you didn't know anything about it!

GO SIGLA = **Gorizia**

'goal ['goul] SM INV (Sport) goal

'gobba SF (Anat) hump; (protuberanza) bump

'gobbo, -a AG hunchbacked; (ricurvo) round-shouldered ► SM/F hunchback

'Gobi SMPL: **il Deserto dei ~** the Gobi Desert

'goccia, -ce ['gottʃa] SF drop; **~ di rugiada** dewdrop; **somigliarsi come due gocce d'acqua** to be as like as two peas in a pod; **è la ~ che fa traboccare il vaso!** it's the last straw!

'goccio ['gottʃo] SM drop, spot

goccio'lare [gottʃo'lare] /72/ VI, VT to drip

goccio'lio [gottʃo'lio] SM dripping

go'dere /58/ VI: **~ (di)** (compiacersi) to be delighted (at), rejoice (at); **~ di** (trarre vantaggio) to enjoy, to

benefit from ► VT to enjoy; **godersi la vita** to enjoy life; **godersela** to have a good time, enjoy o.s.

godi'mento SM enjoyment

godrò ecc VB vedi **godere**

gof'faggine [gof'faddʒine] SF clumsiness

'goffo, -a AG clumsy, awkward

'gogna ['goɲɲa] SF pillory

gol [gɔl] SM INV (Sport) = **goal**

'gola SF (Anat) throat; (golosità) gluttony, greed; (di camino) flue; (di monte) gorge; **fare ~** (anche fig) to tempt; **ricacciare il pianto o le lacrime in ~** to swallow one's tears

go'letta SF (Naut) schooner

golf SM INV (Sport) golf; (maglia) cardigan

'golfo SM gulf

goli'ardico, -a, -ci, -che AG (canto, vita) student cpd

go'loso, -a AG greedy

'golpe SM INV (Pol) coup

gomi'tata SF: **dare una ~ a qn** to elbow sb; **farsi avanti a (forza o furia di) gomitate** to elbow one's way through; **fare a gomitate per qc** to fight to get sth

'gomito SM elbow; (di strada ecc) sharp bend

go'mitolo SM ball

'gomma SF rubber; (colla) gum; (per cancellare) rubber, eraser; (di veicolo) tyre (BRIT), tire (US); **~ da masticare** chewing gum; **~ a terra** flat tyre

gommapi'uma® SF foam rubber

gom'mino SM rubber tip; (rondella) rubber washer

gom'mista, -i, -e SM/F tyre (BRIT) o tire (US) specialist; (rivenditore) tyre o tire merchant

gom'mone SM rubber dinghy

gom'moso, -a AG rubbery

'gondola SF gondola

gondoli'ere SM gondolier

gonfa'lone SM banner

gonfi'are /19/ VT (pallone) to blow up, inflate; (dilatare, ingrossare) to swell; (fig: notizia) to exaggerate ■ **gonfiarsi** VPR to swell; (fiume) to rise

'gonfio, -a AG swollen; (stomaco) bloated; (palloncino, gomme) inflated, blown up; (con pompa) pumped up; (vela) full; **occhi gonfi di pianto** eyes swollen with tears; **~ di orgoglio** (persona) puffed up (with pride); **avere il portafoglio ~** to have a bulging wallet

gonfi'ore SM swelling

gongo'lare /72/ VI to look pleased with o.s.; **~ di gioia** to be overjoyed

'gonna SF skirt; **~ pantalone** culottes pl

'gonzo ['gondzo] SM simpleton, fool

goo'glare [gu'glare] /72/ VT (Inform) to google

gorgheggi'are [gorged'dʒare] /62/ VI to warble; to trill

g

gor'gheggio [gor'geddʒo] SM (Mus, di uccello) trill

'gorgo, -ghi SM whirlpool

gorgogli'are [gorgoʎ'ʎare] /27/ VI to gurgle

gorgo'glio [gorgoʎ'ʎio] SM gurgling

go'rilla SM INV gorilla; (guardia del corpo) bodyguard

'Gotha SM INV (del cinema, letteratura, industria) leading lights pl

'gotico, -a, -ci, -che AG, SM Gothic

'gotta SF gout

'governance ['gɔvernans] SF INV governance

gover'nante SMF ruler ▶ SF (di bambini) governess; (donna di servizio) housekeeper

gover'nare /72/ VT (stato) to govern, rule; (pilotare, guidare) to steer; (bestiame) to tend, look after

governa'tivo, -a AG (politica, decreto) government cpd, governmental; (stampa) pro-government

governa'tore SM governor

go'verno SM government; **~ ombra** shadow cabinet

'gozzo ['gottso] SM (Zool) crop; (Med) goitre; (fig: col) throat

gozzovigli'are [gottsoviʎ'ʎare] /27/ VI to make merry, carouse

GPA [dʒipi'a] SF (= gestazione per altri) surrogacy

GPL [dʒipi'elle] SIGLA M (= Gas di Petrolio Liquefatto) LPG (= Liquefied Petroleum Gas)

gpm ABBR (= giri per minuto) rpm

GPS [dʒipi'esse] SIGLA M GPS (= Global Positioning System)

GR [dzi'erre] SIGLA = **Grosseto** ▶ SIGLA M (= giornale radio) radio news

gracchi'are [grak'kjare] /19/ VI to caw

graci'dare [gratʃi'dare] /72/ VI to croak

graci'dio, -ii [gratʃi'dio] SM croaking

'gracile ['gratʃile] AG frail, delicate

gra'dasso SM boaster

gradata'mente AV gradually, by degrees

gradazi'one [gradat'tsjone] SF (sfumatura) gradation; **~ alcolica** alcoholic content, strength

gra'devole AG pleasant, agreeable

gradi'mento SM pleasure, satisfaction; **essere di mio (o tuo etc) ~** to be to my (o your etc) liking

gradi'nata SF flight of steps; (in teatro, stadio) tiers pl

gra'dino SM step; (Alpinismo) foothold

gra'dire /55/ VT (accettare con piacere) to accept; (desiderare) to wish, like; **gradisce una tazza di tè?** would you like a cup of tea?

gra'dito, -a AG welcome

'grado SM (Mat, Fisica ecc) degree; (stadio) degree, level; (Mil, sociale) rank; **essere in ~ di fare** to be in a position to do; **di buon ~** willingly; **per gradi** by degrees; **un cugino di primo/secondo**

~ a first/second cousin; subire il terzo ~ (anche fig) to be given the third degree

gradu'ale AG gradual

gradu'are /72/ VT to grade

gradu'ato, -a AG (esercizi) graded; (scala, termometro) graduated ▶ SM (Mil) non-commissioned officer

gradua'toria SF (di concorso) list; (per la promozione) order of seniority

'graffa SF (gancio) clip; (segno grafico) brace

graf'fetta SF paper clip

graffi'are /19/ VT to scratch ▪ **graffiarsi** VPR to get scratched; (con unghie) to scratch o.s.

graffia'tura SF scratch

'graffio SM scratch

graf'fiti SMPL graffiti

gra'fia SF spelling; (scrittura) handwriting

'grafico, -a, -ci, -che AG graphic ▶ SM graph ▶ SM/F (persona) graphic designer ▶ SF graphic arts pl; **~ a torta** pie chart

gra'migna [gra'miɲɲa] SF weed; couch grass

gram'matica, -che SF grammar

grammati'cale AG grammatical

'grammo SM gram(me)

gram'mofono SM gramophone

'gramo, -a AG (vita) wretched

gran AG vedi **grande**

'grana SF (granello, di minerali, corpi spezzati) grain; (col: seccatura) trouble; (: soldi) cash ▶ SM INV cheese similar to Parmesan

gra'naglie [gra'naʎʎe] SFPL corn sg, seed sg

gra'naio SM granary, barn

gra'nata SF (frutto) pomegranate; (pietra preziosa) garnet; (proiettile) grenade

granati'ere SM (Mil) grenadier; (fig) fine figure of a man

Gran Bre'tagna [granbre'taɲɲa] SF: **la ~** Great Britain

gran'cassa SF (Mus) bass drum

'granchio ['grankjo] SM crab; (fig) blunder; **prendere un ~** (fig) to blunder

grandango'lare SM wide-angle lens sg

gran'dangolo SM (Fot) wide-angle lens sg

'grande (qualche volta **gran** + C, **grand'** + V) AG (grosso, largo, vasto) big, large; (alto) tall; (lungo) long; (in sensi astratti) great ▶ SMF (persona adulta) adult, grown-up; (chi ha ingegno e potenza) great man (woman); **mio fratello più ~** my big o older brother; **il gran pubblico** the general public; **di gran classe** (prodotto) high-class; **cosa farai da ~?** what will you be o do when you grow up?; **fare le cose in ~** to do things in style; **fare il ~** (strafare) to act big; **una gran bella donna** a very beautiful woman; **non è una gran cosa** o **un gran che** it's nothing special; **non ne so gran che** I don't know very much about it

grandeggi'are [granded'dʒare] /**62**/ vi (*emergere per grandezza*): **~ su** to tower over; (*darsi arie*) to put on airs

gran'dezza [gran'dettsa] sf (*dimensione*) size; magnitude; (*fig*) greatness; **in ~ naturale** life-size; **manie di ~** delusions of grandeur

grandi'nare /**72**/ vb IMPERS to hail

'grandine sf hail

grandi'oso, -a AG grand, grandiose

gran'duca, -chi sm grand duke

grandu'cato sm grand duchy

grandu'chessa [grandu'kessa] sf grand duchess

gra'nello sm (*di cereali, uva*) seed; (*di frutta*) pip; (*di sabbia, sale ecc*) grain

gra'nita sf kind of water ice

gra'nito sm granite

'grano sm (*in quasi tutti i sensi*) grain; (*frumento*) wheat; (*di rosario, collana*) bead; **~ di pepe** peppercorn

gran'turco sm maize

'granulo sm granule; (*Med*) pellet

'grappa sf rough, strong brandy

'grappolo sm bunch, cluster

'graspo sm bunch (of grapes)

gras'setto sm (*Tip*) bold (type) (BRIT); bold face

'grasso, -a AG fat; (*cibo*) fatty; (*pelle*) greasy; (*terreno*) rich; (*fig: guadagno, annata*) plentiful; (: *volgare*) coarse, lewd ▶ sm (*di persona, animale*) fat; (*sostanza che unge*) grease

gras'soccio, -a, -ci, -ce [gras'sɔttʃo] AG plump

gras'sone, -a sm/f (*col: persona*) dumpling

'grata sf grating

gra'ticcio [gra'tittʃo] sm trellis; (*stuoia*) mat

gra'ticola sf grill

gra'tifica, -che sf bonus; **~ natalizia** Christmas bonus

gratificazi'one [gratifikat'tsjone] sf (*soddisfazione*) satisfaction, reward

grati'nare /**72**/ vt (*Cuc*) to cook au gratin

'gratis AV free, for nothing

grati'tudine sf gratitude

'grato, -a AG grateful; (*gradito*) pleasant, agreeable

gratta'capo sm worry, headache

grattaci'elo [gratta'tʃɛlo] sm skyscraper

gratta e 'sosta sm INV scratch card used to pay for parking

gratta e 'vinci [grattae'vintʃi] sm (*lotteria*) lottery; (*biglietto*) scratchcard

grat'tare /**72**/ vt (*pelle*) to scratch; (*raschiare*) to scrape; (*pane, formaggio, carote*) to grate; (*col: rubare*) to pinch ▶ vi (*stridere*) to grate; (*Aut*) to grind ■ **grattarsi** VPR to scratch o.s.; **grattarsi la pancia** (*fig*) to twiddle one's thumbs

grat'tata sf scratch; **fare una ~** (*Aut: col*) to grind the gears

grat'tugia [grat'tudʒa], **-gie** sf grater

grattugi'are [grattu'dʒare] /**62**/ vt to grate; **pane grattugiato** breadcrumbs *pl*

gratuità sf (*fig*) gratuitousness

gra'tuito, -a AG free; (*fig*) gratuitous

gra'vame sm tax; (*fig*) burden, weight

gra'vare /**72**/ vt to burden ▶ vi: **~ su** to weigh on

'grave AG (*danno, pericolo, peccato ecc*) grave, serious; (*responsabilità*) heavy, grave; (*contegno*) grave, solemn; (*voce, suono*) deep, low-pitched; (*Ling*): **accento ~** grave accent ▶ sm (*Fisica*) (heavy) body; **un malato ~** a person who is seriously ill

grave'mente AV (*ammalato, ferito*) seriously

gravi'danza [gravi'dantsa] sf pregnancy

'gravido, -a AG pregnant

gravità sf seriousness; (*anche Fisica*) gravity

gravi'tare /**72**/ vi (*Fisica*): **~ intorno a** to gravitate round

gra'voso, -a AG heavy, onerous

'grazia ['grattsja] sf grace; (*favore*) favour (BRIT), favor (US); (*Dir*) pardon; **di ~** (*ironico*) if you please; **troppa ~!** (*ironico*) you're too generous!; **quanta ~ di Dio!** what abundance!; **entrare nelle grazie di qn** to win sb's favour; **Ministero di G~ e Giustizia** Ministry of Justice, ≈ Lord Chancellor's Office (BRIT), ≈ Department of Justice (US)

grazi'are [grat'tsjare] /**19**/ vt (*Dir*) to pardon

'grazie ['grattsje] ESCL thank you!; **~ mille!** *o* **tante!** *o* **infinite!** thank you very much!; **~ a** thanks to

grazi'oso, -a [grat'tsjoso] AG charming, delightful; (*gentile*) gracious

'Grecia ['grɛtʃa] sf: **la ~** Greece

'greco, -a, -ci, -che AG, sm/f, sm Greek

gre'gario sm (*Ciclismo*) supporting rider

'gregge ['greddʒe] (*pl*(*f*) **greggi**) sm flock

'greggio, -a, -gi, -ge ['greddʒo] AG raw, unrefined; (*diamante*) rough, uncut; (*tessuto*) unbleached ▶ sm (*anche*: **petrolio greggio**) crude (oil)

grembi'ule sm apron; (*sopravveste*) overall

'grembo sm lap; (*ventre della madre*) womb

gre'mito, -a AG: **~ (di)** packed *o* crowded (with)

'greto sm (exposed) gravel bed of a river

'gretto, -a AG mean, stingy; (*fig*) narrow-minded

'greve AG heavy

'grezzo, -a ['greddzo] AG = **greggio**

gri'dare /**72**/ vi (*per chiamare*) to shout, cry (out); (*strillare*) to scream, yell ▶ vt to shout (out), yell (out); **~ aiuto** to cry *o* shout for help

'grido (*pl*(*m*) **gridi**, *pl*(*f*) **grida**) sm shout, cry; scream, yell; (*di animale*) cry; **di ~** famous; **all'ultimo ~** in the latest style

'grigio ['gridʒo], **-a, -gi, -gie** AG, SM grey (BRIT), gray (US)

'griglia ['griʎʎa] SF (per arrostire) grill; (Elettr) grid; (inferriata) grating; **alla ~** (Cuc) grilled

grigli'ata [griʎ'ʎata] SF (Cuc) grill

gril'letto SM trigger

'grillo SM (Zool) cricket; (fig) whim; **ha dei grilli per la testa** his head is full of nonsense

grimal'dello SM picklock

'grinfia SF: **cadere nelle grinfie di qn** (fig) to fall into sb's clutches

'grinta SF grim expression; (Sport) fighting spirit; **avere molta ~** to be very determined

'grinza ['grintsa] SF crease, wrinkle; (ruga) wrinkle; **il tuo ragionamento non fa una ~** your argument is faultless

grin'zoso, -a [grin'tsoso] AG wrinkled; creased

grip'pare /72/ VI (Tecn) to seize

gris'sino SM bread-stick

groenlan'dese AG Greenland cpd ▶ SMF Greenlander

Groen'landia SF: **la ~** Greenland

'gronda SF eaves pl

gron'daia SF gutter

gron'dante AG dripping

gron'dare /72/ VI to pour; (essere bagnato): **~ di** to be dripping with ▶ VT to drip with

'groppa SF (di animale) back, rump; (col: dell'uomo) back, shoulders pl

'groppo SM tangle; **avere un ~ alla gola** (fig) to have a lump in one's throat

'grossa SF (unità di misura) gross

gros'sezza [gros'settsa] SF size; thickness

gros'sista, -i, -e SM/F (Comm) wholesaler

'grosso, -a AG big, large; (di spessore) thick; (grossolano: anche fig) coarse; (grave, insopportabile) serious, great; (tempo, mare) rough ▶ SM: **il ~ di** the bulk of; **un pezzo ~** (fig) a VIP, a bigwig; **farla grossa** to do something very stupid; **dirle grosse** to tell tall stories (BRIT) o tales (US); **questa è grossa!** that's a good one!; **sbagliarsi di ~** to be completely wrong; **dormire della grossa** to sleep like a log

grossolanità SF coarseness

grosso'lano, -a AG rough, coarse; (fig) coarse, crude; (: errore) stupid

grosso'modo AV roughly

'grotta SF cave; grotto

grot'tesco, -a, -schi, -sche AG grotesque

grovi'era SM o F gruyère (cheese)

gro'viglio [gro'viʎʎo] SM tangle; (fig) muddle

gru SF INV crane

'gruccia, -ce ['gruttʃa] SF (per camminare) crutch; (per abiti) coat-hanger

gru'gnire [gruɲ'ɲire] /55/ VI to grunt

gru'gnito [gruɲ'ɲito] SM grunt

'grugno ['gruɲɲo] SM snout; (col: faccia) mug

'grullo, -a AG silly, stupid

'grumo SM (di sangue) clot; (di farina ecc) lump

gru'moso, -a AG lumpy

'gruppo SM group; **~ sanguigno** blood group

gruvi'era SM o F = **groviera**

'gruzzolo ['gruttsolo] SM (di denaro) hoard

GSM SIGLA M (= Global System for Mobile Communication) GSM

GT ABBR (Aut: = gran turismo) GT

G.U. ABBR = **Gazzetta Ufficiale**

guada'gnare [gwadaɲ'ɲare] /15/ VT (ottenere) to gain; (soldi, stipendio) to earn; (vincere) to win; (raggiungere) to reach; **tanto di guadagnato!** so much the better!

gua'dagno [gwa'daɲɲo] SM earnings pl; (Comm) profit; (vantaggio, utile) advantage, gain; **~ di capitale** capital gains pl; **~ lordo/netto** gross/net earnings pl

gu'ado SM ford; **passare a ~** to ford

gu'ai ESCL: **~ a te** (o lui etc) **!** woe betide you (o him etc) !

gua'ina SF (fodero) sheath; (indumento per donna) girdle

gu'aio SM trouble, mishap; (inconveniente) trouble, snag

gua'ire /55/ VI to whine, yelp

gua'ito SM (di cane) yelp, whine; (il guaire) yelping, whining

gu'ancia, -ce ['gwantʃa] SF cheek

guanci'ale [gwan'tʃale] SM pillow; **dormire fra due guanciali** (fig) to sleep easy, have no worries

gu'anto SM glove; **trattare qn con i guanti** (fig) to handle sb with kid gloves; **gettare/raccogliere il ~** (fig) to throw down/take up the gauntlet

guan'tone SM boxing glove

guarda'boschi [gwarda'bɔski] SM INV forester

guarda'caccia [gwarda'kattʃa] SM INV gamekeeper

guarda'coste SM INV coastguard; (nave) coastguard patrol vessel

guarda'linee SM INV (Sport) linesman

guarda'macchine [gwarda'makkine] SM INV/F INV car-park (BRIT) o parking lot (US) attendant

guar'dare /72/ VT (con lo sguardo: osservare) to look at; (: film, televisione) to watch; (custodire) to look after, take care of ▶ VI to look; (badare): **~ a** to pay attention to; (luoghi: esser orientato): **~ a** to face ■ **guardarsi** VPR to look at o.s.; **~ di** to try to; **guardarsi da** (astenersi) to refrain from; (stare in guardia) to beware of; **guardarsi dal fare** to take care not to do; **guarda di non sbagliare** try not to make a mistake; **ma guarda un po'!** good heavens!; **e guarda caso ...** as if by coincidence ...; **~ qn dall'alto in basso** to look down on sb; **non ~ in faccia a nessuno** (*fig*) to have no regard for anybody; **~ di traverso** to scowl *o* frown at; **~ a vista qn** to keep a close watch on sb

guarda'roba SM INV wardrobe; (*locale*) cloakroom

guardarobi'ere, -a SM/F cloakroom attendant

guardasi'gilli [gwardasi'dʒilli] SM INV ≈ Lord Chancellor (BRIT), ≈ Attorney General (US)

gu'ardia SF (*individuo, corpo*) guard; (*sorveglianza*) watch; **fare la ~ a qc/qn** to guard sth/sb; **stare in ~** (*fig*) to be on one's guard; **il medico di ~** the doctor on call; **il fiume ha raggiunto il livello di ~** the river has reached the high-water mark; **~ carceraria** (prison) warder (BRIT) *o* guard (US); **~ del corpo** bodyguard; **~ di finanza** (*corpo*) customs officer; (*persona*) customs officer; **~ forestale** forest ranger; **~ giurata** security guard; **~ medica** emergency doctor service; **~ municipale** town policeman; **~ notturna** night security guard; **~ di pubblica sicurezza** policeman

> The **Guardia di Finanza** is a military body which reports to the *ministro dell'Economia e delle Finanze* (= Chancellor of the Exchequer). Among its responsibilities are border control, fighting tax evasion, fraud and other financial crime, and combating international drug trafficking.

guardia'caccia [gwardja'kattʃa] SM INV = **guardacaccia**

guardi'ano, -a SM/F (*di carcere*) warder (BRIT), guard (US); (*di villa ecc*) caretaker; (*di museo*) custodian; (*di zoo*) keeper; **~ notturno** night watchman

guar'dina SF cell

guar'dingo, -a, -ghi, -ghe AG wary, cautious

guardi'ola SF porter's lodge; (*Mil*) look-out tower

guarigi'one [gwari'dʒone] SF recovery

gua'rire /55/ VT (*persona, malattia*) to cure; (*ferita*) to heal ▶ VI to recover, be cured; to heal (up)

guarnigi'one [gwarni'dʒone] SF garrison

guar'nire /55/ VT (*ornare: abiti*) to trim; (*Cuc*) to garnish

guarnizi'one [gwarnit'tsjone] SF trimming; garnish; (*Tecn*) gasket

guasta'feste SMF spoilsport

guas'tare /72/ VT to spoil, ruin; (*meccanismo*) to break ■ **guastarsi** VPR (*cibo*) to go bad; (*meccanismo*) to break down; (*tempo*) to change for the worse; (*amici*) to quarrel, fall out

gu'asto, -a AG (*non funzionante*) broken; (: *telefono ecc*) out of order; (*andato a male*) bad, rotten; (: *dente*) decayed, bad; (*fig: corrotto*) depraved ▶ SM breakdown; (*avaria*) failure; **~ al motore** engine failure

Guate'mala SM: **il ~** Guatemala

guatemal'teco, -a, -ci, -che AG, SM/F Guatemalan

gu'ercio, -a, -ci, -ce ['gwertʃo] AG cross-eyed

gu'erra SF war; (*tecnica: atomica, chimica ecc*) warfare; **fare la ~ (a)** to wage war (against); **la ~ fredda** the Cold War; **~ mondiale** world war; **~ preventiva** preventive war; **la prima/seconda ~ mondiale** the First/Second World War

guerrafon'daio SM warmonger

guerreggi'are [gwerred'dʒare] /62/ VI to wage war

guer'resco, -a, -schi, -sche AG (*di guerra*) war *cpd*; (*incline alla guerra*) warlike

guerri'ero, -a AG warlike ▶ SM/F warrior

guer'riglia [gwer'riʎʎa] SF guerrilla warfare

guerrigli'ero, -a [gwerriʎ'ʎɛro] SM/F guerrilla

'gufo SM owl

'guglia ['guʎʎa] SF (*Archit*) spire; (*di roccia*) needle

Gui'ana SF: **la ~ francese** French Guiana

gu'ida SF (*persona*) guide; (*libro*) guide(book); (*comando, direzione*) guidance, direction; (*Aut*) driving; (: *sterzo*) steering; (*tappeto: di tenda, cassetto*) runner; **~ a destra/sinistra** (*Aut*) right-/left-hand drive; **essere alla ~ di** (*governo*) to head; (*spedizione, paese*) to lead; **far da ~ a qn** (*mostrare la strada*) to show sb the way; (*in una città*) to show sb (a)round; **~ telefonica** telephone directory; **~ turistica** tourist guide

gui'dare /72/ VT to guide; (*squadra, rivolta*) to lead; (*auto*) to drive; (*aereo, nave*) to pilot; **sa ~?** can you drive?

guida'tore, -'trice SM/F (*conducente*) driver

Gui'nea SF: **la Repubblica di ~** the Republic of Guinea; **la ~ Equatoriale** Equatorial Guinea

guin'zaglio [gwin'tsaʎʎo] SM leash, lead

gu'isa SF: **a ~ di** like, in the manner of

guiz'zare [gwit'tsare] /72/ VI to dart; to flicker; to leap; **~ via** (*fuggire*) to slip away

gu'izzo ['gwittso] SM (*di animali*) dart; (*di fulmine*) flash

'guru SM INV (*Rel, anche fig*) guru

'guscio ['guʃʃo] SM shell

gus'tare /72/ VT (*cibi*) to taste; (: *assaporare con piacere*) to enjoy, savour (BRIT), savor (US); (*fig*) to enjoy, appreciate ▶ VI: **~ a** to please; **non mi gusta affatto** I don't like it at all

gusta'tivo, -a AG: **papille gustative** taste buds

'gusto SM (*senso*) taste; (*sapore*) taste, flavour (BRIT), flavor (US); (*godimento*) enjoyment; **al ~ di fragola** strawberry-flavoured; **di ~ barocco** in the baroque style; **mangiare di ~** to eat heartily; **prenderci ~: ci ha preso ~** he's acquired a taste for it, he's got to like it

gus'toso, -a AG tasty; (*fig*) agreeable

guttu'rale AG guttural

Gu'yana [gu'jana] SF: **la ~** Guyana

Hh

H, h [ˈakka] SM O F INV (*lettera*) H, h ▶ ABBR (= *ora*) hr; (= *etto, altezza*) h; **H come hotel** ≈ H for Harry (BRIT), H for How (US)

ha¹, 'hai [a, ai] VB *vedi* **avere**

ha² ABBR (= *ettaro*) ha

ha'cker [ˈhaker] SM O F INV hacker

Ha'iti [aˈiti] SF Haiti

haiti'ano, -a [aiˈtjano] AG, SM/F Haitian

hall [hɔːl] SF INV hall, foyer

ham'burger [amˈburger] SM INV (*carne*) hamburger; (*panino*) burger

'handicap [ˈhandikap] SM INV handicap

handicap'pato, -a [andikapˈpato] AG disabled ▶ SM/F person with a disability

'hanno [ˈanno] VB *vedi* **avere**

hard dis'count [ardisˈkaunt] SM INV discount supermarket

hard 'disk [arˈdisk] SM INV hard disk

'hardware [ˈardwer] SM INV hardware

ha'scisc, ha'scisch [aʃˈʃiʃ] SM hashish

'hashtag [ˈaʃteg] SM INV (*su Twitter*) hashtag

hawai'ano, -a [avaˈjano] AG, SM/F Hawaiian

Ha'waii [aˈvai] SFPL: **le ~** Hawaii *sg*

help [ɛlp] SM INV (*Inform*) help

help' desk [ɛlpˈdɛsk] SM INV (*Inform*) help desk

'Helsinki [ˈɛlsinki] SF Helsinki

'herpes [ˈɛrpes] SM (*Med*) herpes *sg*; **~ zoster** shingles *sg*

hg ABBR (= *ettogrammo*) hg

'hi-fi [ˈhaifai] SM INV, AG INV hi-fi

Hima'laia [imaˈlaja] SM: **l'~** the Himalayas *pl*

hl ABBR (= *ettolitro*) hl

ho [ɔ] VB *vedi* **avere**

'hobby [ˈhɔbi] SM INV hobby

'hockey [ˈhɔki] SM hockey; **~ su ghiaccio** ice hockey

'holding [ˈhouldiŋ] SF INV holding company

'home page [ˈhomˈpeidʒ] SF INV home page

Hon'duras [onˈduras] SM Honduras

'Hong Kong [ˈɔkɔg] SF Hong Kong

Hono'lulu [onoˈlulu] SF Honolulu

'hostess [ˈhɔstis] SF INV air hostess (BRIT) o stewardess

'hot dog [ˈhɔtdɔg] SM INV hot dog

ho'tel [oˈtɛl] SM INV hotel

'humour [ˈjumor] SM INV (sense of) humour

'humus SM humus

'husky [ˈaski] SM INV (*cane*) husky

Hz ABBR (= *hertz*) Hz

I i

I, i [i] SM O F INV (*lettera*) I, i; **I come Imola** ≈ I for Isaac (*BRIT*), I for Item (*US*)

i DET MPL the; *vedi anche* **il**

IACP SIGLA M (= *Istituto Autonomo per le Case Popolari*) *public housing association*

i'ato SM hiatus

i'berico, -a, -ci, -che AG Iberian; **la Penisola Iberica** the Iberian Peninsula

iber'nare /72/ VI to hibernate ▸ VT (*Med*) to induce hypothermia in

ibernazi'one [ibernat'tsjone] SF hibernation

ibid. ABBR (= *ibidem*) ib(id)

'ibrido, -a AG, SM hybrid

IC ABBR (= *Intercity*) Intercity

'ICE ['itʃe] SIGLA M (= *Istituto nazionale per il Commercio Estero*) *overseas trade board*

'ICI ['itʃi] SIGLA F (= *Imposta Comunale sugli Immobili*) ≈ Council Tax

i'cona SF (*Rel, Inform, anche fig*) icon

id ABBR (= *idem*) do.

Id'dio SM God

i'dea SF idea; (*opinione*) opinion, view; (*ideale*) ideal; **avere le idee chiare** to know one's mind; **cambiare ~** to change one's mind; **dare l'~ di** to seem, look like; **neanche** o **neppure per ~!** certainly not!, no way!; **~ fissa** obsession

ide'ale AG, SM ideal

idea'lismo SM idealism

idea'lista, -i, -e SM/F idealist

idea'listico, -a, -ci, -che AG idealistic

idealiz'zare [idealid'dzare] /72/ VT to idealize

ide'are /72/ VT (*immaginare*) to think up, conceive; (*progettare*) to plan

idea'tore, -'trice SM/F author

i'dentico, -a, -ci, -che AG identical

identifi'care /20/ VT to identify ▪ **identificarsi** VPR: **identificarsi (con)** to identify o.s. (with)

identificazi'one [identifikat'tsjone] SF identification

identità SF INV identity

ideolo'gia, -'gie [ideolo'dʒia] SF ideology

ideo'logico, -a, -ci, -che [ideo'lɔdʒiko] AG ideological

idil'liaco, -a, -ci, -che AG = **idillico**

i'dillico, -a, -ci, -che AG idyllic

i'dillio SM idyll; **tra di loro è nato un ~** they have fallen in love

idi'oma, -i SM idiom, language

idio'matico, -a, -ci, -che AG idiomatic; **frase idiomatica** idiom

idiosincra'sia SF idiosyncrasy

idi'ota, -i, -e AG idiotic ▸ SM/F idiot

idio'zia [idjot'tsia] SF idiocy; (*atto, discorso*) idiotic thing to do (o say)

ido'latra, -i, -e AG idolatrous ▸ SM/F idolater

idola'trare /72/ VT to worship; (*fig*) to idolize

idola'tria SF idolatry

'idolo SM idol

idonei'tà SF suitability; **esame di ~** qualifying examination

i'doneo, -a AG: **~ a** suitable for, fit for; (*Mil*) fit for; (*qualificato*) qualified for

i'drante SM hydrant

idra'tante AG (*crema*) moisturizing ▸ SM moisturizer

idra'tare /72/ VT (*pelle*) to moisturize

idratazi'one [idratat'tsjone] SF moisturizing

i'draulico, -a, -ci, -che AG hydraulic ▸ SM plumber ▸ SF hydraulics *sg*

'idrico, -a, -ci, -che AG water *cpd*

idrocar'buro SM hydrocarbon

idroe'lettrico, -a, -ci, -che AG hydroelectric

i'drofilo, -a AG: **cotone ~** cotton wool (*BRIT*), absorbent cotton (*US*)

idrofo'bia SF rabies *sg*

i'drofobo, -a AG rabid; (*fig*) furious

i'drogeno [i'drɔdʒeno] SM hydrogen

idroli'pidico, -a, -ci, -che AG hydrolipid

idro'porto SM (*Aer*) seaplane base

idrorepel'lente AG water-repellent

idros'calo SM = **idroporto**

idrovo'lante SM seaplane

i'ella SF bad luck

iel'lato, -a AG plagued by bad luck

i'ena SF hyena

ie'ratico, -a, -ci, -che AG (Rel: scrittura) hieratic; (fig: atteggiamento) solemn

i'eri AV, SM yesterday; **il giornale di ~** yesterday's paper; **~ l'altro** the day before yesterday; **~ sera** yesterday evening

ietta'tore, -'trice SM/F jinx

igi'ene [i'dʒɛne] SF hygiene; **norme d'~** sanitary regulations; **ufficio d'~** public health office; **~ mentale** mental health; **~ pubblica** public health

igi'enico, -a, -ci, -che [i'dʒɛniko] AG hygienic; (salubre) healthy

i'gloo [i'glu] SM INV igloo; (tenda) dome tent

i'gnaro, -a [iɲ'ɲaro] AG: **~ di** unaware of, ignorant of

i'gnifugo, -a, -ghi, -ghe [iɲ'ɲifugo] AG flame-resistant, fireproof

i'gnobile [iɲ'ɲɔbile] AG despicable, vile

igno'minia [iɲɲo'minja] SF ignominy

igno'rante [iɲɲo'rante] AG ignorant

igno'ranza [iɲɲo'rantsa] SF ignorance

igno'rare [iɲɲo'rare] /72/ VT (non sapere, conoscere) to be ignorant o unaware of, not to know; (fingere di non vedere, sentire) to ignore

i'gnoto, -a [iɲ'ɲɔto] AG unknown ▶ SM/F: **figlio di ignoti** child of unknown parentage; **il Milite I~** the Unknown Soldier

---

il

(pl(m) **i**; diventa **lo** (pl **gli**) davanti a s impura, gn, pn, ps, x, z; f **la** (pl **le**)) DET M 1 the; **il libro/lo studente/l'acqua** the book/the student/the water; **gli scolari** the pupils

2 (astrazione): **il coraggio/l'amore/la giovinezza** courage/love/youth

3 (tempo): **il mattino/la sera** in the morning/evening; **il venerdì** (abitualmente) on Fridays; (quel giorno) on (the) Friday; **la settimana prossima** next week

4 (distributivo) a, an; **2 euro il chilo/paio** 2 euros a o per kilo/pair

5 (partitivo) some, any; **hai messo lo zucchero?** have you added sugar?; **hai comprato il latte?** did you buy (some o any) milk?

6 (possesso): **aprire gli occhi** to open one's eyes; **rompersi la gamba** to break one's leg; **avere i capelli neri/il naso rosso** to have dark hair/a red nose; **mettiti le scarpe** put your shoes on

7 (con nomi propri): **il Petrarca** Petrarch; **il Presidente Bush** President Bush; **dov'è la Francesca?** where's Francesca?

8 (con nomi geografici): **il Tevere** the Tiber; **l'Italia** Italy; **il Regno Unito** the United Kingdom; **l'Everest** Everest

---

'ilare AG cheerful

ilarità SF hilarity, mirth

ill. ABBR = **illustrazione**; (= illustrato) ill.

illangui'dire /55/ VI to grow weak o feeble

illazi'one [illat'tsjone] SF inference, deduction

il'lecito, -a [il'letʃito] AG illicit

ille'gale AG illegal

illegalità SF illegality

illeg'gibile [illed'dʒibile] AG illegible

illegittimità [illedʒittimi'ta] SF illegitimacy

ille'gittimo, -a [ille'dʒittimo] AG illegitimate

il'leso, -a AG unhurt, unharmed

illette'rato, -a AG illiterate

illiba'tezza [illiba'tettsa] SF (di donna) virginity

illi'bato, -a AG: **donna illibata** virgin

illimi'tato, -a AG boundless; unlimited

illivi'dire /55/ VI (volto, mani) to turn livid; (cielo) to grow leaden

ill.mo ABBR = **illustrissimo**

il'logico, -a, -ci, -che [il'lɔdʒiko] AG illogical

il'ludere /35/ VT to deceive, delude ■ **illudersi** VPR to deceive o.s., delude o.s.

illumi'nare /72/ VT to light up, illuminate; (fig) to enlighten ■ **illuminarsi** VPR to light up; **~ a giorno** (con riflettori) to floodlight

illumi'nato, -a AG (fig: sovrano, spirito) enlightened

illuminazi'one [illuminat'tsjone] SF lighting; illumination; floodlighting; (fig) flash of inspiration

illumi'nismo SM (Storia): **l'I~** the Enlightenment

il'lusi ecc VB vedi **illudere**

illusi'one SF illusion; **farsi delle illusioni** to delude o.s.; **~ ottica** optical illusion

illusio'nismo SM conjuring

illusio'nista, -i, -e SM/F conjurer

il'luso, -a PP di **illudere**

illu'sorio, -a AG illusory

illus'trare /72/ VT to illustrate

illustra'tivo, -a AG illustrative

illustrazi'one [illustrat'tsjone] SF illustration

il'lustre AG eminent, renowned

illus'trissimo, -a AG (negli indirizzi) very revered

IM SIGLA = **Imperia**

i'mam [i'mam] SM INV imam

imbacuc'care /20/ VT, **imbacuc'carsi** VPR to wrap up

imbaldan'zire [imbaldan'tsire] /55/ VT to give confidence to ■ **imbaldanzirsi** VPR to grow bold

imbal'laggio [imbal'laddʒo] SM packing no pl

imbal'lare /72/ VT to pack; (Aut) to race ■ **imballarsi** VPR (Aut) to race

imbalsa'mare /72/ VT to embalm

imbalsa'mato, -a AG embalmed

imbambo'lato, -a AG (sguardo, espressione) vacant, blank

imban'dire /55/ VT: ~ **un banchetto** to prepare a lavish feast

imban'dito, -a AG: **tavola imbandita** lavishly o sumptuously decked table

imbaraz'zante [imbarat'tsante] AG embarrassing, awkward

imbaraz'zare [imbarat'tsare] /72/ VT (*mettere a disagio*) to embarrass; (*ostacolare: movimenti*) to hamper; (: *stomaco*) to lie heavily on ■ **imbarazzarsi** VPR to become embarrassed

imbaraz'zato, -a [imbarat'tsato] AG embarrassed; **avere lo stomaco** ~ to have an upset stomach

imba'razzo [imba'rattso] SM (*disagio*) embarrassment; (*perplessità*) puzzlement, bewilderment; **essere** o **trovarsi in** ~ to be in an awkward situation o predicament; **mettere in** ~ to embarrass; ~ **di stomaco** indigestion

imbarbari'mento SM (*di civiltà, costumi*) barbarization

imbarca'dero SM landing stage

imbar'care /20/ VT (*passeggeri*) to embark; (*merci*) to load ■ **imbarcarsi** VPR: **imbarcarsi su** to board; **imbarcarsi per l'America** to sail for America; **imbarcarsi in** (*fig: affare*) to embark on

imbarcazi'one [imbarkat'tsjone] SF (small) boat, (small) craft *inv*; ~ **di salvataggio** lifeboat

im'barco, -chi SM embarkation; loading; boarding; (*banchina*) landing stage; **carta d'~** boarding pass (BRIT), boarding card

imbastar'dire /55/ VT to bastardize, debase ■ **imbastardirsi** VPR to degenerate, become debased

imbas'tire /55/ VT (*cucire*) to tack; (*fig: abbozzare*) to sketch, outline

im'battersi /72/ VPR: ~ **in** (*incontrare*) to bump o run into

imbat'tibile AG unbeatable, invincible

imbavagli'are [imbava'ʎʎare] /27/ VT to gag

imbec'care /20/ VT (*uccelli*) to feed; (*fig*) to prompt, put words into sb's mouth

imbec'cata SF (*Teat*) prompt; **dare l'~ a qn** to prompt sb; (*fig*) to give sb their cue

imbe'cille [imbe'tʃille] AG idiotic ▶ SMF idiot; (*Med*) imbecile

imbecillità [imbetʃilli'ta] SF INV (*Med, fig*) imbecility, idiocy; **dire** ~ to talk nonsense

imbellet'tare /72/ VT (*viso*) to make up, put make-up on ■ **imbellettarsi** VPR to make o.s. up, put on one's make-up

imbel'lire /55/ VT to adorn, embellish ▶ VI to grow more beautiful

im'berbe AG beardless; **un giovanotto** ~ a callow youth

imbestia'lire /55/ VT to infuriate ■ **imbestialirsi** VPR to become infuriated, fly into a rage

im'bevere /16/ VT to soak ■ **imbeversi** VPR: **imbeversi di** to soak up, absorb

imbe'vuto, -a AG: ~ **(di)** soaked (in)

imbian'care /20/ VT to whiten; (*muro*) to whitewash ▶ VI to become o turn white

imbianca'tura SF (*di muro: con bianco di calce*) whitewashing; (: *con altre pitture*) painting

imbian'chino [imbjan'kino] SM (house) painter, painter and decorator

imbion'dire /55/ VT (*capelli*) to lighten; (*Cuc: cipolla*) to brown ■ **imbiondirsi** VPR (*capelli*) to lighten, go blonde, go fair; (*messi*) to turn golden, ripen

imbizzar'rirsi [imbiddzar'rirsi] /55/ VPR (*cavallo*) to become frisky

imboc'care /20/ VT (*bambino*) to feed; (*entrare: strada*) to enter, turn into ▶ VI: ~ **in** (*strada*) to lead into; (*fiume*) to flow into

imbocca'tura SF mouth; (*di strada, porto*) entrance; (*Mus, del morso*) mouthpiece

im'bocco, -chi SM entrance

imboni'tore SM (*di spettacolo, circo*) barker

imborghe'sire [imborge'zire] /55/ VI, **imborghe'sirsi** VPR to become bourgeois

imbos'care /20/ VT to hide ■ **imboscarsi** VPR (*Mil*) to evade military service

imbos'cata SF ambush

imbos'cato SMF draft dodger (*US*)

imboschi'mento [imboski'mento] SM afforestation

imbottigli'are [imbotti'ʎʎare] /27/ VT to bottle; (*Naut*) to blockade; (*Mil*) to hem in ■ **imbottigliarsi** VPR to be stuck in a traffic jam

imbot'tire /55/ VT to stuff; (*giacca*) to pad ■ **imbottirsi** VPR (*rimpinzarsi*): **imbottirsi di** to stuff o.s. with

imbot'tito, -a AG stuffed; (*sedia*) upholstered; (*giacca*) padded ▶ SF quilt; **panino** ~ filled roll

imbotti'tura SF stuffing; padding

imbracci'are [imbrat'tʃare] /14/ VT (*fucile*) to shoulder; (*scudo*) to grasp

imbra'nato, -a AG clumsy, awkward ▶ SM/F clumsy person

imbratta'carte SMF (*peg*) scribbler

imbrat'tare /72/ VT to dirty, smear, daub ■ **imbrattarsi** VPR: **imbrattarsi (di)** to dirty o.s. (with)

imbratta'tele SMF (*peg*) dauber

imbrigli'are [imbri'ʎʎare] /27/ VT to bridle

imbroc'care /20/ VT (*fig*) to guess correctly

imbrogli'are [imbro'ʎʎare] /27/ VT to mix up; (*fig: raggirare*) to deceive, cheat; (: *confondere*) to confuse, mix up ■ **imbrogliarsi** VPR to get tangled; (*fig*) to become confused

im'broglio [im'brɔʎʎo] SM (*groviglio*) tangle; (*situazione confusa*) mess; (*truffa*) swindle, trick

165

imbrogli'one, -a [imbroʎ'ʎone] SM/F cheat, swindler

imbronci'ato, -a [imbron'tʃato] AG (*persona*) sulky; (*cielo*) cloudy, threatening

imbru'nire /55/ VI, VB IMPERS to grow dark; **all'~** at dusk

imbrut'tire /55/ VT to make ugly ▶ VI to become ugly

imbu'care /20/ VT to post

imbur'rare /72/ VT to butter

imbuti'forme AG funnel-shaped

im'buto SM funnel

I.M.C.T.C. SIGLA (= *Ispettorato Generale della Motorizzazione Civile e dei Trasporti in Concessione*) ≈ DVLA

i'mene SM hymen

imi'tare /72/ VT to imitate; (*riprodurre*) to copy; (*assomigliare*) to look like

imita'tore, -'trice SM/F (*gen*) imitator; (*Teat*) impersonator, impressionist

imitazi'one [imitat'tsjone] SF imitation

immaco'lato, -a AG spotless; immaculate

immagazzi'nare [immagaddzi'nare] /72/ VT to store

immagi'nabile [immadʒi'nabile] AG imaginable

immagi'nare [immadʒi'nare] /72/ VT to imagine; (*supporre*) to suppose; (*inventare*) to invent; **s'immagini!** don't mention it!, not at all!

immagi'nario, -a [immadʒi'narjo] AG imaginary

immagina'tiva [immadʒina'tiva] SF imagination

immaginazi'one [immadʒinat'tsjone] SF imagination; (*cosa immaginata*) fancy

im'magine [im'madʒine] SF image; (*rappresentazione grafica, mentale*) picture

immagi'noso, -a [immadʒi'noso] AG (*linguaggio, stile*) fantastic

immalinco'nire /55/ VT to sadden, depress ■ **immalinconirsi** VPR to become depressed, become melancholy

imman'cabile AG certain; unfailing

immancabil'mente AV without fail, unfailingly

im'mane AG (*smisurato*) huge; (*spaventoso, inumano*) terrible

imma'nente AG (*Filosofia*) inherent, immanent

immangi'abile [imman'dʒabile] AG inedible

immatrico'lare /72/ VT to register ■ **immatricolarsi** VPR (*Ins*) to matriculate, enrol

immatricolazi'one [immatrikolat'tsjone] SF registration; matriculation; enrolment

immaturità SF immaturity

imma'turo, -a AG (*frutto*) unripe; (*persona*) immature; (*prematuro*) premature

immedesi'marsi /72/ VPR: **~ in** to identify with

immediata'mente AV immediately, at once

immedia'tezza [immedja'tettsa] SF immediacy

immedi'ato, -a AG immediate

immemo'rabile AG immemorial; **da tempo ~** from time immemorial

im'memore AG: **~ di** forgetful of

immensità SF immensity

im'menso, -a AG immense

im'mergere [im'mɛrdʒere] /59/ VT to immerse, plunge ■ **immergersi** VPR to plunge; (*sommergibile*) to dive, submerge; (*dedicarsi a*) **immergersi in** to immerse o.s. in

immeri'tato, -a AG undeserved

immeri'tevole AG undeserving, unworthy

immersi'one SF immersion; (*di sommergibile*) submersion, dive; (*di palombaro*) dive; **linea di ~** (*Naut*) water line

im'merso, -a PP *di* **immergere**

im'messo, -a PP *di* **immettere**

im'mettere /63/ VT: **~ (in)** to introduce (into); **~ dati in un computer** to enter data on a computer

immi'grante AG, SMF immigrant

immi'grare /72/ VI to immigrate

immi'grato, -a SM/F immigrant

immigrazi'one [immigrat'tsjone] SF immigration

immi'nente AG imminent

immi'nenza [immi'nɛntsa] SF imminence

immischi'are [immis'kjare] /19/ VT: **~ qn in** to involve sb in ■ **immischiarsi** VPR: **immischiarsi in** to interfere o meddle in

immiseri'mento SM impoverishment

immise'rire /55/ VT to impoverish

immis'sario SM (*Geo*) affluent, tributary

immissi'one SF (*gen*) introduction; (*di aria, gas*) intake; **~ di dati** (*Inform*) data entry

im'mobile AG motionless, still; **(beni) immobili** real estate *sg*

immobili'are AG (*Dir*) property *cpd*; **patrimonio ~** real estate; **società ~** property company

immobi'lismo SM inertia

immobilità SF immobility

immobiliz'zare [immobilid'dzare] /72/ VT to immobilize; (*Econ*) to lock up

immobi'lizzo [immobi'liddzo] SM: **spese d'~** capital expenditure

immo'destia SF immodesty

immo'desto, -a AG immodest

immo'lare /72/ VT to sacrifice

immondez'zaio [immondet'tsajo] SM rubbish dump

immon'dizia [immon'dittsja] SF dirt, filth;

(*spesso al pl: spazzatura, rifiuti*) rubbish *no pl*, refuse *no pl*

immo'rale AG immoral

immoralità SF immorality

immorta'lare /72/ VT to immortalize

immor'tale AG immortal

immortalità SF immortality

im'mune AG (*esente*) exempt; (*Med, Dir*) immune

immunità SF immunity; **~ diplomatica** diplomatic immunity; **~ parlamentare** parliamentary privilege

immuniz'zare [immunid'dzare] /72/ VT (*Med*) to immunize

immunizzazi'one [immuniddzat'tsjone] SF immunization

immunodefi'cienza [immunodefi'tʃɛntsa] SF: **~ acquisita** acquired immunodeficiency

immuno'logico, -a, -ci, -che [immuno'lɔdʒiko] AG immunological

immu'tabile AG immutable; unchanging

impac'care /20/ VT to pack

impacchet'tare [impakket'tare] /72/ VT to pack up

impacci'are [impat'tʃare] /14/ VT to hinder, hamper

impacci'ato, -a [impat'tʃato] AG awkward, clumsy; (*imbarazzato*) embarrassed

im'paccio [im'pattʃo] SM obstacle; (*imbarazzo*) embarrassment; (*situazione imbarazzante*) awkward situation

im'pacco, -chi SM (*Med*) compress

impadro'nirsi /55/ VPR: **~ di** to seize, take possession of; (*fig: apprendere a fondo*) to master

impa'gabile AG priceless

impagi'nare [impadʒi'nare] /72/ VT (*Tip*) to paginate, page (up)

impaginazi'one [impadʒinat'tsjone] SF pagination

impagli'are [impaʎ'ʎare] /27/ VT to stuff (with straw)

impa'lato, -a AG (*fig*) stiff as a board

impalca'tura SF scaffolding; (*anche fig*) framework

impalli'dire /55/ VI to turn pale; (*fig*) to fade

impalli'nare /72/ VT to riddle with shot

impal'pabile AG impalpable

impa'nare /72/ VT (*Cuc*) to dip (*o* roll) in breadcrumbs, bread (*US*)

impa'nato, -a AG (*Cuc*) coated in breadcrumbs

impanta'narsi /72/ VPR to sink (in the mud); (*fig*) to get bogged down

impape'rarsi /72/ VPR to stumble over a word

impappi'narsi /72/ VPR to stammer, falter

impa'rare /72/ VT to learn; **così impari!** that'll teach you!

impara'ticcio [impara'tittʃo] SM half-baked notions *pl*

impareggi'abile [impared'dʒabile] AG incomparable

imparen'tarsi /72/ VPR: **~ con** (*famiglia*) to marry into

'impari AG INV (*disuguale*) unequal; (*dispari*) odd

impar'tire /55/ VT to bestow, give

imparzi'ale [impar'tsjale] AG impartial, unbiased

imparzialità [impartsjali'ta] SF impartiality

impas'sibile AG impassive

impas'tare /72/ VT (*pasta*) to knead; (*colori*) to mix

im'pasto SM (*l'impastare: di pane*) kneading; (: *di cemento*) mixing; (*pasta*) dough; (*anche fig*) mixture

im'patto SM impact; **~ ambientale** impact on the environment

impau'rire /55/ VT to scare, frighten ▶ VI (*anche:* **impaurirsi**) to become scared *o* frightened

im'pavido, -a AG intrepid, fearless

impazi'ente [impat'tsjɛnte] AG impatient

impazi'enza [impat'tsjɛntsa] SF impatience

impaz'zata [impat'tsata] SF: **all'~** (*precipitosamente*) at breakneck speed; (*colpire*) wildly

impaz'zire [impat'tsire] /55/ VI to go mad; **~ per qn/qc** to be crazy about sb/sth

impec'cabile AG impeccable

impedi'mento SM obstacle, hindrance

impe'dire /55/ VT (*vietare*) **~ a qn di fare** to prevent sb from doing; (*ostruire*) to obstruct; (*impacciare*) to hamper, hinder

impe'gnare [impeɲ'ɲare] /15/ VT (*dare in pegno*) to pawn; (*onore ecc*) to pledge; (*prenotare*) to book, reserve; (*obbligare*) to oblige; (*occupare*) to keep busy; (*Mil: nemico*) to engage ■ **impegnarsi** VPR (*vincolarsi*): **impegnarsi a fare** to undertake to do; (*mettersi risolutamente*): **impegnarsi in qc** to devote o.s. to sth; **impegnarsi con qn** (*accordarsi*) to come to an agreement with sb

impegna'tivo, -a [impeɲɲa'tivo] AG binding; (*lavoro*) demanding, exacting

impe'gnato, -a [impeɲ'ɲato] AG (*occupato*) busy; (*fig: romanzo, autore*) committed, engagé

im'pegno [im'peɲɲo] SM (*obbligo*) obligation; (*promessa*) promise, pledge; (*zelo*) diligence, zeal; (*compito: d'autore*) commitment; **impegni di lavoro** business commitments

impego'larsi /72/ VPR (*fig*): **~ in** to get heavily involved in

impela'garsi /80/ VPR = **impegolarsi**

impel'lente AG pressing, urgent

impene'trabile AG impenetrable

impen'narsi /72/ VPR (*cavallo*) to rear up; (*Aer*) to go into a climb; (*fig*) to bridle

impen'nata SF (*di cavallo*) rearing up; (*di aereo*) climb, nose-up; (*fig: scatto d'ira*) burst of anger; (: *di prezzi ecc*) sudden increase

impen'sabile AG (*inaccettabile*) unthinkable; (*difficile da concepire*) inconceivable

impen'sato, -a AG unforeseen, unexpected

impensie'rirsi /55/ VT to worry ■ **impensierirsi** VPR to worry

impe'rante AG prevailing

impe'rare /72/ VI (*anche fig*) to reign, rule

impera'tivo, -a AG, SM imperative

impera'tore, -'trice SM/F emperor (empress)

impercet'tibile [impertʃet'tibile] AG imperceptible

imperdo'nabile AG unforgivable, unpardonable

imper'fetto, -a AG imperfect ▶ SM (*Ling*) imperfect (tense)

imperfezi'one [imperfet'tsjone] SF imperfection

imperi'ale AG imperial

imperia'lismo SM imperialism

imperia'lista, -i, -e AG imperialist

imperi'oso, -a AG (*persona*) imperious; (*motivo, esigenza*) urgent, pressing

imperi'turo, -a AG everlasting

impe'rizia [impe'rittsja] SF lack of experience

imperma'lirsi /55/ VPR to take offence

imperme'abile AG waterproof ▶ SM raincoat

imperni'are /19/ VT: ~ **qc su** to hinge sth on; (*fig: discorso, relazione ecc*) to base sth on ■ **imperniarsi** VPR (*fig*): **imperniarsi su** to be based on

im'pero SM empire; (*forza, autorità*) rule, control

imperscru'tabile AG inscrutable

imperso'nale AG impersonal

imperso'nare /72/ VT to personify; (*Teat*) to play, act (the part of) ■ **impersonarsi** VPR: **impersonarsi in un ruolo** to get into a part, live a part

imper'territo, -a AG unperturbed, undaunted; impassive

imperti'nente AG impertinent

imperti'nenza [imperti'nɛntsa] SF impertinence

impertur'babile AG imperturbable

imperver'sare /72/ VI to rage

im'pervio, -a AG (*luogo*) inaccessible; (*strada*) impassable

'impeto SM (*moto, forza*) force, impetus; (*assalto*) onslaught; (*fig: impulso*) impulse; (: *slancio*) transport; **con ~** (*parlare*) forcefully, energetically; vehemently

impet'tito, -a AG stiff, erect; **camminare ~** to strut

impetu'oso, -a AG (*vento*) strong, raging; (*persona*) impetuous

impian'tare /72/ VT (*motore*) to install; (*azienda, discussione*) to establish, start

impian'tistica SF plant design and installation

impi'anto SM (*installazione*) installation; (*apparecchiature*) plant; (*sistema*) system; ~ **elettrico** wiring; ~ **di riscaldamento** heating system; ~ **sportivo** sports complex; **impianti di risalita** (*Sci*) ski lifts

impias'trare /72/, **impiastricci'are** [impjastrit'tʃare] VT to smear, dirty

impi'astro SM poultice; (*fig: col: persona*) nuisance

impiccagi'one [impikka'dʒone] SF hanging

impic'care /20/ VT to hang ■ **impiccarsi** VPR to hang o.s.

impicci'are [impit'tʃare] /14/ VT to hinder, hamper ■ **impicciarsi** VPR (*immischiarsi*): **impicciarsi (in)** to meddle (in), interfere (in); **impicciati degli affari tuoi!** mind your own business!

im'piccio [im'pittʃo] SM (*ostacolo*) hindrance; (*seccatura*) trouble, bother; (*affare imbrogliato*) mess; **essere d'~** to be in the way; **cavare o togliere qn dagli impicci** to get sb out of trouble

impicci'one, -a [impit'tʃone] SM/F busybody

impie'gare /80/ VT (*usare*) to use, employ; (*assumere*) to employ, take on; (*spendere: denaro, tempo*) to spend; (*investire*) to invest ■ **impiegarsi** VPR to get a job, obtain employment; **impiego un quarto d'ora per andare a casa** it takes me o I take a quarter of an hour to get home

impiega'tizio, -a [impjega'tittsjo] AG clerical, white-collar *cpd*; **lavoro/ceto ~** clerical o white-collar work/workers *pl*

impie'gato, -a SM/F employee; ~ **statale** state employee

impi'ego, -ghi SM (*uso*) use; (*occupazione*) employment; (*posto di lavoro*) (regular) job, post; (*Econ*) investment; ~ **pubblico** job in the public sector

impieto'sire /55/ VT to move to pity ■ **impietosirsi** VPR to be moved to pity

impie'toso, -a AG pitiless, cruel

impie'trire /55/ VT (*anche fig*) to petrify

impigli'are [impiʎ'ʎare] /27/ VT to catch, entangle ■ **impigliarsi** VPR to get caught up o entangled

impi'grire /55/ VT to make lazy ▶ VI (*anche:* **impigrirsi**) to grow lazy

impingu'are /72/ VT (*maiale ecc*) to fatten; (*fig: tasche, casse dello Stato*) to stuff with money

impiom'bare /72/ VT (*pacco*) to seal (with lead); (*dente*) to fill

impla'cabile AG implacable

implemen'tare /72/ VT to implement

impli'care /20/ VT to imply; (*coinvolgere*) to

involve ■ **implicarsi** VPR: **implicarsi (in)** to become involved (in)

implicazi'one [implikat'tsjone] SF implication

im'plicito, -a [im'plitʃito] AG implicit

implo'rare /72/ VT to implore; (*pietà ecc*) to beg for

implorazi'one [implorat'tsjone] SF plea, entreaty

impolli'nare /72/ VT to pollinate

impollinazi'one [impollinat'tsjone] SF pollination

impolve'rare /72/ VT to cover with dust ■ **impolverarsi** VPR to get dusty

impoma'tare /72/ VT (*pelle*) to put ointment on; (*capelli*) to pomade; (*baffi*) to wax ■ **impomatarsi** VPR (*col*) to get spruced up

imponde'rabile AG imponderable

im'pone *ecc* VB *vedi* **imporre**

impo'nente AG imposing, impressive

im'pongo *ecc* VB *vedi* **imporre**

impo'nibile AG taxable ▸ SM taxable income

impopo'lare AG unpopular

impopolarità SF unpopularity

im'porre /77/ VT to impose; (*costringere*) to force, make; (*far valere*) to impose, enforce ■ **imporsi** VPR (*persona*) to assert o.s.; (*cosa: rendersi necessario*) to become necessary; (*aver successo: moda, attore*) to become popular; **~ a qn di fare** to force sb to do, make sb do

impor'tante AG important

impor'tanza [impor'tantsa] SF importance; **dare ~ a qc** to attach importance to sth; **darsi ~** to give o.s. airs

impor'tare /72/ VT (*introdurre dall'estero*) to import ▸ VI to matter, be important ▸ VB IMPERS (*essere necessario*) to be necessary; (*interessare*) to matter; **non importa!** it doesn't matter!; **non me ne importa!** I don't care!

importa'tore, -'trice AG importing ▸ SM/F importer

importazi'one [importat'tsjone] SF importation; (*merci importate*) imports pl

im'porto SM (total) amount

importu'nare /72/ VT to bother

impor'tuno, -a AG irksome, annoying

im'posi *ecc* VB *vedi* **imporre**

imposizi'one [impozit'tsjone] SF imposition; (*ordine*) order, command; (*onere, imposta*) tax

imposses'sarsi /72/ VPR: **~ di** to seize, take possession of

impos'sibile AG impossible; **fare l'~** to do one's utmost, do all one can

impossibilità SF impossibility; **essere nell'~ di fare qc** to be unable to do sth

impossibili'tato, -a AG: **essere ~ a fare qc** to be unable to do sth

im'posta SF (*di finestra*) shutter; (*tassa*) tax; **~ indiretta sui consumi** excise duty *o* tax; **~ locale sui redditi (ILOR)** tax on unearned income; **~ patrimoniale** property tax; **~ sul reddito** income tax; **~ sul reddito delle persone fisiche** personal income tax; **~ di successione** capital transfer tax (BRIT), inheritance tax (US); **~ sugli utili** tax on profits; **~ sul valore aggiunto** value added tax (US), sales tax (US)

impos'tare /72/ VT (*imbucare*) to post; (*servizio, organizzazione*) to set up; (*lavoro*) to organize, plan; (*resoconto, rapporto*) to plan; (*problema*) to set out, formulate; (*avviare*) to begin, start off; (*Tip: pagina*) to lay out; **~ la voce** (*Mus*) to pitch one's voice

impostazi'one [impostat'tsjone] SF (*di lettera*) posting (BRIT), mailing (US); (*di problema, questione*) formulation, statement; (*di lavoro*) organization, planning; (*di attività*) setting up; (*Mus: di voce*) pitch ■ **impostazioni** SFPL (*di computer*) settings

im'posto, -a PP *di* **imporre**

impos'tore, -a SM/F impostor

impo'tente AG weak, powerless; (*anche Med*) impotent

impo'tenza [impo'tentsa] SF weakness, powerlessness; impotence

impove'rire /55/ VT to impoverish ▸ VI (*anche:* **impoverirsi**) to become poor

imprati'cabile AG (*strada*) impassable; (*campo da gioco*) unplayable

imprati'chire [imprati'kire] /55/ VT to train ■ **impratichirsi** VPR: **impratichirsi in qc** to practise (BRIT) *o* practice (US) sth

impre'care /20/ VI to curse, swear; **~ contro** to hurl abuse at

imprecazi'one [imprekat'tsjone] SF abuse, curse

impreci'sato, -a [impretʃi'zato] AG (*non preciso: quantità, numero*) indeterminate

imprecisi'one [impretʃi'zjone] SF imprecision; inaccuracy

impre'ciso, -a [impre'tʃizo] AG imprecise, vague; (*calcolo*) inaccurate

impre'gnare [impreɲ'ɲare] /15/ VT: **~ (di)** (*imbevere*) to soak *o* impregnate (with); (*riempire: anche fig*) to fill (with)

imprendi'tore, -'trice SM/F (*industriale*) entrepreneur; (*appaltatore*) contractor; **piccolo ~** small businessman(-woman)

imprendito'ria SF enterprise; (*imprenditori*) entrepreneurs pl

imprenditori'ale AG (*ceto, classe*) entrepreneurial

imprepa'rato, -a AG: **~ (a)** (*gen*) unprepared (for); (*lavoratore*) untrained (for); **cogliere qn ~** to catch sb unawares

impreparazi'one [impreparat'tsjone] SF lack of preparation

im'presa SF (*iniziativa*) enterprise; (*azione*) exploit; (*azienda*) firm, concern; **~ familiare** family firm; **~ pubblica** state-owned enterprise

impre'sario SM (*Teat*) manager, impresario; **~ di pompe funebri** funeral director

imprescin'dibile [impreʃʃin'dibile] AG not to be ignored

im'pressi *ecc* VB *vedi* **imprimere**

impressio'nante AG impressive; upsetting

impressio'nare /72/ VT to impress; (*turbare*) to upset; (*Fot*) to expose ▪ **impressionarsi** VPR to be easily upset

impressi'one SF impression; (*fig: sensazione*) sensation, feeling; (*stampa*) printing; **fare ~** (*colpire*) to impress; (*turbare*) to frighten, upset; **fare buona/cattiva ~ a** to make a good/bad impression on

im'presso, -a PP *di* **imprimere**

impres'tare /72/ VT: **~ qc a qn** to lend sth to sb

impreve'dibile AG unforeseeable; (*persona*) unpredictable

imprevi'dente AG lacking in foresight

imprevi'denza [imprevi'dɛntsa] SF lack of foresight

impre'visto, -a AG unexpected, unforeseen ▶ SM unforeseen event; **salvo imprevisti** unless anything unexpected happens

imprezio'sire [imprettsjo'sire] /55/ VT: **~ di** to embellish with

imprigiona'mento [impridʒona'mento] SM imprisonment

imprigio'nare [impridʒo'nare] /72/ VT to imprison

im'primere /50/ VT (*anche fig*) to impress, stamp; (*comunicare: movimento*) to transmit, give

impro'babile AG improbable, unlikely

'improbo, -a AG (*fatica, lavoro*) hard, laborious

improdut'tivo, -a AG (*investimento*) unprofitable; (*terreno*) unfruitful; (*fig: sforzo*) fruitless

im'pronta SF imprint, impression, sign; (*di piede, mano*) print; (*fig*) mark, stamp; **~ di carbonio** carbon footprint; **~ digitale** fingerprint; **rilevamento delle impronte genetiche** genetic fingerprinting

impro'perio SM insult

impropo'nibile AG which cannot be proposed *o* suggested

im'proprio, -a AG improper; **arma impropria** offensive weapon

improro'gabile AG (*termine*) that cannot be extended

improvvisa'mente AV suddenly; unexpectedly

improvvi'sare /72/ VT to improvise ▪ **improvvisarsi** VPR: **improvvisarsi cuoco** to (decide to) act as cook

improvvi'sata SF (pleasant) surprise

improvvisazi'one [improvvizat'tsjone] SF improvisation; **spirito d'~** spirit of invention

improv'viso, -a AG (*imprevisto*) unexpected; (*subitaneo*) sudden; **all'~** unexpectedly; suddenly

impru'dente AG foolish, imprudent; (*osservazione*) unwise, rash

impru'denza [impru'dɛntsa] SF foolishness, imprudence; **è stata un'~** that was a foolish *o* an imprudent thing to do

impu'dente AG impudent

impu'denza [impu'dɛntsa] SF impudence

impudi'cizia [impudi't'ʃittsja] SF immodesty

impu'dico, -a, -chi, -che AG immodest

impu'gnare [impuɲ'ɲare] /15/ VT to grasp, grip; (*Dir*) to contest

impugna'tura [impuɲɲa'tura] SF grip, grasp; (*manico*) handle; (: *di spada*) hilt

impulsività SF impulsiveness

impul'sivo, -a AG impulsive

im'pulso SM impulse; **dare un ~ alle vendite** to boost sales

impune'mente AV with impunity

impunità SF impunity

impun'tarsi /72/ VPR to stop dead, refuse to budge; (*fig*) to be obstinate

impun'tura SF stitching

impurità SF INV impurity

im'puro, -a AG impure

impu'tare /72/ VT (*ascrivere*): **~ qc a** to attribute sth to; (*Dir: accusare*) **~ qn di** to charge sb with, accuse sb of

impu'tato, -a SM/F (*Dir*) accused, defendant

imputazi'one [imputat'tsjone] SF (*Dir*) charge; (*di spese*) allocation

imputri'dire /55/ VI to rot

---

in

(*in + il* = **nel**, *in + lo* = **nello**, *in + l'* = **nell'**, *in + la* = **nella**, *in + i* = **nei**, *in + gli* = **negli**, *in + le* = **nelle**) PREP **1** (*stato in luogo*) in; **vivere in Italia/città** to live in Italy/town; **essere in casa/ufficio** to be at home/the office; **è nel cassetto/in salotto** it's in the drawer/in the sitting room; **se fossi in te** if I were you

2 (*moto a luogo*) to; (: *dentro*) into; **andare in Germania/città** to go to Germany/town; **andare in ufficio** to go to the office; **entrare in macchina/casa** to get into the car/go into the house

3 (*tempo*) in; **nel 1989** in 1989; **in giugno/estate** in June/summer; **l'ha fatto in sei mesi** he did it in six months; **in gioventù, io ...** when I was young, I ...

4 (*modo, maniera*) in; **in silenzio** in silence; **parlare in tedesco** to speak (in) German; **in**

abito da sera in evening dress; **in guerra** at war; **in vacanza** on holiday; **Maria Bianchi in Rossi** Maria Rossi née Bianchi

5 (*mezzo*) by; **viaggiare in autobus/treno** to travel by bus/train

6 (*materia*) made of; **in marmo** made of marble, marble *cpd*; **una collana in oro** a gold necklace

7 (*misura*) in; **siamo in quattro** there are four of us; **in tutto** in all

8 (*fine*): **dare in dono** to give as a gift; **spende tutto in alcool** he spends all his money on drink; **in onore di** in honour of

i'nabile AG: ~ **a** incapable of; (*fisicamente, Mil*) unfit for

inabilità SF: ~ **(a)** unfitness (for)

inabis'sare /**72**/ VT (*nave*) to sink ▪ **inabissarsi** VPR to go down

inabi'tabile AG uninhabitable

inabi'tato, -a AG uninhabited

inacces'sibile [inattʃes'sibile] AG (*luogo*) inaccessible; (*persona*) unapproachable; (*mistero*) unfathomable

inaccet'tabile [inattʃet'tabile] AG unacceptable

inacer'bire [inatʃer'bire] /**55**/ VT to exacerbate ▪ **inacerbirsi** VPR (*persona*) to become embittered

inaci'dire [inatʃi'dire] /**55**/ VT (*persona, carattere*) to embitter ▪ **inacidirsi** VPR (*latte*) to go sour; (*fig: persona, carattere*) to become sour, become embittered

ina'datto, -a AG: ~ **(a)** unsuitable *o* unfit (for)

inadegu'ato, -a AG inadequate

inadempi'ente AG defaulting ▸ SMF defaulter

inadempi'enza [inadem'pjɛntsa] SF: ~ **a un contratto** non-fulfilment of a contract; **dovuto alle inadempienze dei funzionari** due to negligence on the part of the officials

inadempi'mento SM non-fulfilment

inaffer'rabile AG elusive; (*concetto, senso*) difficult to grasp

inaffi'dabile AG unreliable

'INAIL SIGLA M (= *Istituto Nazionale per l'Assicurazione contro gli Infortuni sul Lavoro*) state body providing sickness benefit in the event of accidents at work

ina'lare /**72**/ VT to inhale

inala'tore SM inhaler

inalazi'one [inalat'tsjone] SF inhalation

inalbe'rare /**72**/ VT (*Naut*) to hoist, raise ▪ **inalberarsi** VPR (*fig*) to flare up, fly off the handle

inalte'rabile AG unchangeable; (*colore*) fast, permanent; (*affetto*) constant

inalte'rato, -a AG unchanged

inami'dare /**72**/ VT to starch

inami'dato, -a AG starched

inammis'sibile AG inadmissible

inani'mato, -a AG inanimate; (*senza vita: corpo*) lifeless

inappa'gabile AG insatiable

inappel'labile AG (*decisione*) final, irrevocable; (*Dir*) final, not open to appeal

inappe'tenza [inappe'tɛntsa] SF (*Med*) lack of appetite

inappun'tabile AG irreproachable, flawless

inar'care /**20**/ VT (*schiena*) to arch; (*sopracciglia*) to raise ▪ **inarcarsi** VPR to arch

inaridi'mento SM (*anche fig*) drying up

inari'dire /**55**/ VT to make arid, dry up ▸ VI (*anche:* **inaridirsi**) to dry up, become arid

inarres'tabile AG (*processo*) irreversible; (*emorragia*) that cannot be stemmed; (*corsa del tempo*) relentless

inascol'tato, -a AG unheeded, unheard

inaspettata'mente AV unexpectedly

inaspet'tato, -a AG unexpected

inas'prire /**55**/ VT (*disciplina*) to tighten up, make harsher; (*carattere*) to embitter; (*rapporti*) to make worse ▪ **inasprirsi** VPR to become harsher; to become bitter; to become worse

inattac'cabile AG (*anche fig*) unassailable; (*alibi*) cast-iron

inatten'dibile AG unreliable

inat'teso, -a AG unexpected

inat'tivo, -a AG inactive, idle; (*Chim*) inactive

inattu'abile AG impracticable

inau'dito, -a AG unheard of

inaugu'rale AG inaugural

inaugu'rare /**72**/ VT to inaugurate, open; (*monumento*) to unveil

inaugurazi'one [inaugurat'tsjone] SF inauguration; unveiling

inavve'duto, -a AG careless, inadvertent

inavver'tenza [inavver'tɛntsa] SF carelessness, inadvertence

inavvertita'mente AV inadvertently, unintentionally

inavvici'nabile [inavvitʃi'nabile] AG unapproachable

'Inca AG INV, SM INV/F INV Inca

incagli'are [inkaʎ'ʎare] /**27**/ VI (*Naut: anche:* **incagliarsi**) to run aground

incalco'labile AG incalculable

incal'lito, -a AG calloused; (*fig*) hardened, inveterate; (: *insensibile*) hard

incal'zante [inkal'tsante] AG urgent, insistent; (*crisi*) imminent

incal'zare [inkal'tsare] /**72**/ VT to follow *o* pursue closely; (*fig*) to press ▸ VI (*urgere*) to be pressing; (*essere imminente*) to be imminent

171

incame'rare /72/ VT (Dir) to expropriate

incammi'nare /72/ VT (fig: avviare) to start up ■ **incamminarsi** VPR to set off

incana'lare /72/ VT (anche fig) to channel ■ **incanalarsi** VPR (folla): **incanalarsi verso** to converge on

incancre'nire /55/ VI, **incancre'nirsi** VPR to become gangrenous

incande'scente [inkandeʃ'ʃɛnte] AG incandescent, white-hot

incan'tare /72/ VT to enchant, bewitch ■ **incantarsi** VPR (rimanere intontito) to be spellbound; to be in a daze; (meccanismo: bloccarsi) to jam

incanta'tore, -'trice AG enchanting, bewitching ▶ SM/F enchanter (enchantress)

incan'tesimo SM spell, charm

incan'tevole AG charming, enchanting

in'canto SM spell, charm, enchantment; (asta) auction; **come per ~** as if by magic; **ti sta d'~!** (vestito ecc) it really suits you!; **mettere all'~** to put up for auction

incanu'tire /55/ VI to go white

inca'pace [inka'patʃe] AG incapable

incapacità [inkapatʃi'ta] SF inability; (Dir) incapacity; **~ d'intendere e di volere** diminished responsibility

incapo'nirsi /55/ VPR to be stubborn, be determined

incap'pare /72/ VI: **~ in qc/qn** (anche fig) to run into sth/sb

incappucci'are [inkapput'tʃare] /14/ VT to put a hood on ■ **incappucciarsi** VPR (persona) to put on a hood

incapricci'arsi [inkaprit'tʃarsi] /14/ VPR: **~ di** to take a fancy to o for

incapsu'lare /72/ VT (dente) to crown

incarce'rare [inkartʃe'rare] /72/ VT to imprison

incari'care /20/ VT: **~ qn di fare** to give sb the responsibility of doing ■ **incaricarsi** VPR: **incaricarsi di** to take care o charge of

incari'cato, -a AG: **~ (di)** in charge (of), responsible (for) ▶ SM/F delegate, representative; **docente ~** (di università) lecturer without tenure; **~ d'affari** (Pol) chargé d'affaires

in'carico, -chi SM task, job; (Ins) temporary post

incar'nare /72/ VT to embody ■ **incarnarsi** VPR to be embodied; (Rel) to become incarnate

incarnazi'one [inkarnat'tsjone] SF incarnation; (fig) embodiment

incarta'mento SM dossier, file

incartapeco'rito, -a AG (pelle) wizened, shrivelled (BRIT), shriveled (US)

incar'tare /72/ VT to wrap (in paper)

incasel'lare /72/ VT (posta) to sort; (fig: nozioni) to pigeonhole

incas'sare /72/ VT (merce) to pack (in cases); (gemma: incastonare) to set; (Econ: riscuotere) to collect; (Pugilato: colpi) to take, stand up to

in'casso SM cashing, encashment; (introito) takings pl

incasto'nare /72/ VT to set

incastona'tura SF setting

incas'trare /72/ VT to fit in, insert; (fig: intrappolare) to catch ■ **incastrarsi** VPR (combaciare) to fit together; (restare bloccato) to become stuck

in'castro SM slot, groove; (punto di unione) joint; **gioco a ~** interlocking puzzle

incate'nare /72/ VT to chain up

incatra'mare /72/ VT to tar

incatti'vire /55/ VT to make wicked ■ **incattivirsi** VPR to turn nasty

in'cauto, -a AG imprudent, rash

inca'vare /72/ VT to hollow out

inca'vato, -a AG hollow; (occhi) sunken

in'cavo SM hollow; (solco) groove

incavo'larsi /72/ VPR (col) to lose one's temper, get annoyed

incaz'zarsi [inkat'tsarsi] /72/ VPR (col) to get steamed up

in'cedere [in'tʃedere] /29/ VI (poetico) to advance solemnly ▶ SM solemn gait

incendi'are [intʃen'djare] /19/ VT to set fire to ■ **incendiarsi** VPR to catch fire, burst into flames

incendi'ario, -a [intʃen'djarjo] AG incendiary ▶ SM/F arsonist

in'cendio [in'tʃendjo] SM fire

incene'rire [intʃene'rire] /55/ VT to burn to ashes, incinerate; (cadavere) to cremate ■ **incenerirsi** VPR to be burnt to ashes

inceneri'tore [intʃeneri'tore] SM incinerator

in'censo [in'tʃenso] SM incense

incensu'rato, -a [intʃensu'rato] AG (Dir): **essere ~** to have a clean record

incenti'vare [intʃenti'vare] /72/ VT (produzione, vendite) to boost; (persona) to motivate

incen'tivo [intʃen'tivo] SM incentive

incen'trarsi [intʃen'trarsi] /72/ VPR: **~ su** (fig) to centre (BRIT) o center (US) on

incep'pare [intʃep'pare] /72/ VT to obstruct, hamper ■ **incepparsi** VPR to jam

ince'rata [intʃe'rata] SF (tela) tarpaulin; (impermeabile) oilskins pl

incer'tezza [intʃer'tettsa] SF uncertainty

in'certo, -a [in'tʃerto] AG uncertain; (irresoluto) undecided, hesitating ▶ SM uncertainty; **gli incerti del mestiere** the risks of the job

incespi'care [intʃespi'kare] /20/ VI: **~ (in qc)** to trip (over sth)

inces'sante [intʃes'sante] AG incessant

in'cesto [in'tʃesto] SM incest

incestu'oso, -a [intʃestu'oso] AG incestuous

in'cetta [in'tʃetta] SF buying up; **fare ~ di qc** to buy up sth

inchi'esta [in'kjesta] SF investigation, inquiry

inchi'nare [inki'nare] **/72/** VT to bow ■ **inchinarsi** VPR to bend down; (*per riverenza*) to bow; (: *donna*) to curtsy

in'chino [in'kino] SM bow; curtsy

inchio'dare [inkjo'dare] **/72/** VT to nail (down); **~ la macchina** (*Aut*) to jam on the brakes

inchi'ostro [in'kjɔstro] SM ink; **~ simpatico** invisible ink

inciam'pare [intʃam'pare] **/72/** VI to trip, stumble

inci'ampo [in'tʃampo] SM obstacle; **essere d'~ a qn** (*fig*) to be in sb's way

inciden'tale [intʃiden'tale] AG incidental

incidental'mente [intʃidental'mente] AV (*per caso*) by chance; (*per inciso*) incidentally, by the way

inci'dente [intʃi'dɛnte] SM accident; (*episodio*) incident; **e con questo l'~ è chiuso** and that is the end of the matter; **~ automobilistico** o **d'auto** car accident; **~ diplomatico** diplomatic incident

inci'denza [intʃi'dɛntsa] SF incidence; **avere una forte ~ su qc** to affect sth greatly

in'cidere [in'tʃidere] **/34/** VI: **~ su** to bear upon, affect ▸ VT (*tagliare incavando*) to cut into; (*Arte*) to engrave; to etch; (*canzone*) to record

in'cinta [in'tʃinta] AG F pregnant

incipi'ente [intʃi'pjɛnte] AG incipient

incipri'are [intʃi'prjare] **/19/** VT to powder ■ **incipriarsi** VPR to powder one's face

in'circa [in'tʃirka] AV: **all'~** more or less, very nearly

in'cisi *ecc* [in'tʃizi] VB *vedi* **incidere**

incisi'one [intʃi'zjone] SF cut; (*disegno*) engraving; etching; (*registrazione*) recording; (*Med*) incision

inci'sivo, -a [intʃi'zivo] AG incisive; (*Anat*): (*dente*) **~** incisor

in'ciso, -a [in'tʃizo] PP *di* **incidere** ▸ SM: **per ~** incidentally, by the way

inci'sore [intʃi'zore] SM (*Arte*) engraver

incita'mento [intʃita'mento] SM incitement

inci'tare [intʃi'tare] **/72/** VT to incite

inci'vile [intʃi'vile] AG uncivilized; (*villano*) impolite

incivi'lire [intʃivi'lire] **/55/** VT to civilize

inciviltà [intʃivil'ta] SF (*di popolazione*) barbarism; (*fig: di trattamento*) barbarity; (: *maleducazione*) incivility, rudeness

incl. ABBR (= *incluso*) encl.

incle'mente AG (*giudice, sentenza*) severe, harsh; (*fig: clima*) harsh; (: *tempo*) inclement

incle'menza [inkle'mɛntsa] SF severity; harshness; inclemency

incli'nabile AG (*schienale*) reclinable

incli'nare **/72/** VT to tilt ▸ VI (*fig*): **~ qc/a fare** to incline towards sth/doing; to tend towards sth/to do ■ **inclinarsi** VPR (*barca*) to list; (*aereo*) to bank

incli'nato, -a AG sloping

inclinazi'one [inklinat'tsjone] SF slope; (*fig*) inclination, tendency

in'cline AG: **~ a** inclined to

in'cludere **/3/** VT to include; (*accludere*) to enclose

inclusi'one SF inclusion

inclu'sivo, -a AG: **~ di** inclusive of

in'cluso, -a PP *di* **includere** ▸ AG included; enclosed

incoe'rente AG incoherent; (*contraddittorio*) inconsistent

incoe'renza [inkoe'rɛntsa] SF incoherence; inconsistency

in'cognito, -a [in'kɔɲɲito] AG unknown ▸ SM: **in ~** incognito ▸ SF (*Mat, fig*) unknown quantity

incol'lare **/72/** VT to glue, gum; (*unire con colla*) to stick together; **~ gli occhi addosso a qn** (*fig*) to fix one's eyes on sb

incolla'tura SF (*Ippica*): **vincere/perdere di un'~** to win/lose by a head

incolon'nare **/72/** VT to draw up in columns

inco'lore AG colourless (BRIT), colorless (US)

incol'pare **/72/** VT: **~ qn di** to charge sb with

in'colto, -a AG (*terreno*) uncultivated; (*trascurato: capelli*) neglected; (*persona*) uneducated

in'columE AG safe and sound, unhurt

incolumità SF safety

incom'bente AG (*pericolo*) imminent, impending

incom'benza [inkom'bentsa] SF duty, task

in'combere **/29/** VI (*sovrastare minacciando*): **~ su** to threaten, hang over

incominci'are [inkomin'tʃare] **/14/** VI, VT to begin, start

incomo'dare **/72/** VT to trouble, inconvenience ■ **incomodarsi** VPR to put o.s. out

in'comodo, -a AG uncomfortable; (*inopportuno*) inconvenient ▸ SM inconvenience, bother

incompa'rabile AG incomparable

incompa'tibile AG incompatible

incompatibilità SF incompatibility; **~ di carattere** (mutual) incompatibility

incompe'tente AG incompetent

incompe'tenza [inkompe'tɛntsa] SF incompetence

incompi'uto, -a AG unfinished, incomplete

incom'pleto, -a AG incomplete

incompren'sibile AG incomprehensible

incomprensi'one SF incomprehension

incom'preso, -a AG not understood; misunderstood

inconce'pibile [inkontʃe'pibile] AG inconceivable

inconcili'abile [inkontʃi'ljabile] AG irreconcilable

inconclu'dente AG inconclusive; (*persona*) ineffectual

incondizio'nato, -a [inkondittsjo'nato] AG unconditional

inconfes'sabile AG (*pensiero, peccato*) unmentionable

inconfon'dibile AG unmistakable

inconfu'tabile AG irrefutable

incongru'ente AG inconsistent

incongru'enza [inkongru'εntsa] SF inconsistency

in'congruo, -a AG incongruous

inconsa'pevole AG: ~ **di** unaware of, ignorant of

inconsapevo'lezza [inkonsapevo'lettsa] SF ignorance, lack of awareness

in'conscio, -a, -sci, -sce [in'kɔnʃo] AG unconscious ▶ SM (*Psic*): **l'~** the unconscious

inconsis'tente AG (*patrimonio*) insubstantial; (*dubbio*) unfounded; (*ragionamento, prove*) tenuous, flimsy

inconsis'tenza [inkonsis'tεntsa] SF insubstantial nature; lack of foundation; flimsiness

inconso'labile AG inconsolable

inconsu'eto, -a AG unusual

incon'sulto, -a AG rash

inconte'nibile AG (*rabbia*) uncontrollable; (*entusiasmo*) irrepressible

inconten'tabile AG (*desiderio, avidità*) insatiable; (*persona: capriccioso*) hard to please, very demanding

incontes'tabile AG incontrovertible, indisputable

incontes'tato, -a AG undisputed

inconti'nenza [inkonti'nεntsa] SF incontinence

incon'trare /72/ VT to meet; (*difficoltà*) to meet with ■ **incontrarsi** VPR to meet

incon'trario AV: **all'~** (*sottosopra*) upside down; (*alla rovescia*) back to front; (*all'indietro*) backwards; (*nel senso contrario*) the other way round

incontras'tabile AG incontrovertible, indisputable

incontras'tato, -a AG (*successo, vittoria, verità*) uncontested, undisputed

in'contro AV: ~ **a** (*verso*) towards ▶ SM meeting; (*Sport*) match; meeting; (*fortuito*) encounter; **venire ~ a** (*richieste, esigenze*) to comply with; ~

di calcio football match (BRIT), soccer game (US)

incontrol'labile AG uncontrollable

inconveni'ente SM drawback, snag

incoraggia'mento [inkoraddʒa'mento] SM encouragement; **premio d'~** consolation prize

incoraggi'are [inkorad'dʒare] /62/ VT to encourage

incor'nare /72/ VT to gore

incornici'are [inkorni'tʃare] /14/ VT to frame

incoro'nare /72/ VT to crown

incoronazi'one [inkoronat'tsjone] SF coronation

incorpo'rare /72/ VT to incorporate; (*fig: annettere*) to annex

incorreg'gibile [inkorred'dʒibile] AG incorrigible

in'correre /28/ VI: ~ **in** to meet with, run into

incorrut'tibile AG incorruptible

in'corso, -a PP *di* **incorrere**

incosci'ente [inkoʃ'ʃεnte] AG (*inconscio*) unconscious; (*irresponsabile*) reckless, thoughtless

incosci'enza [inkoʃ'ʃεntsa] SF unconsciousness; recklessness, thoughtlessness

incos'tante AG (*studente, impiegato*) inconsistent; (*carattere*) fickle, inconstant; (*rendimento*) sporadic

incos'tanza [inkos'tantsa] SF inconstancy, fickleness

incostituzio'nale [inkostituttsjo'nale] AG unconstitutional

incre'dibile AG incredible, unbelievable

incredulità SF incredulity

in'credulo, -a AG incredulous, disbelieving

incremen'tare /72/ VT to increase; (*dar sviluppo a*) to promote

incre'mento SM (*sviluppo*) development; (*aumento numerico*) increase, growth

incresci'oso, -a [inkreʃ'ʃoso] AG (*spiacevole*) unpleasant; (*incidente ecc*) regrettable

incres'pare /72/ VT (*capelli*) to curl; (*acque*) to ripple ■ **incresparsi** VPR (*vedi vt*) to curl; to ripple

incrimi'nare /72/ VT (*Dir*) to charge

incriminazi'one [inkriminat'tsjone] SF (*atto d'accusa*) indictment, charge

incri'nare /72/ VT to crack; (*fig: rapporti, amicizia*) to cause to deteriorate ■ **incrinarsi** VPR to crack; to deteriorate

incrina'tura SF crack; (*fig*) rift

incroci'are [inkro'tʃare] /14/ VT to cross; (*incontrare*) to meet ▶ VI (*Naut, Aer*) to cruise ■ **incrociarsi** VPR (*strade*) to cross, intersect; (*persone, veicoli*) to pass each other; ~ **le braccia/le gambe** to fold one's arms/cross one's legs

incrocia'tore [inkrotʃa'tore] SM cruiser

in'crocio [inˈkrotʃo] SM (*anche* Ferr) crossing; (*di strade*) crossroads

incrol'labile AG (*fede*) unshakeable, firm

incros'tare /72/ VT to encrust ▪ **incrostarsi** VPR: **incrostarsi di** to become encrusted with

incrostazi'one [inkrostatˈtsjone] SF encrustation; (*di calcare*) scale; (*nelle tubature*) fur (BRIT), scale

incru'ento, -a AG (*battaglia*) without bloodshed, bloodless

incuba'trice [inkubaˈtritʃe] SF incubator

incubazi'one [inkubatˈtsjone] SF incubation

'incubo SM nightmare

in'cudine SF anvil; **trovarsi** o **essere tra l'~ e il martello** (*fig*) to be between the devil and the deep blue sea

incul'care /20/ VT: **~ qc in** to inculcate sth into, instill sth into

incune'are /72/ VT to wedge

incu'pire /55/ VT (*rendere scuro*) to darken; (*fig: intristire*) to fill with gloom ▶ VI (*vedi vt*) to darken; to become gloomy

incu'rabile AG incurable

incu'rante AG: **~ (di)** heedless (of), careless (of)

in'curia SF negligence

incurio'sire /55/ VT to make curious ▪ **incuriosirsi** VPR to become curious

incursi'one SF raid

incur'vare /72/ VT to bend, curve ▪ **incurvarsi** VPR to bend, curve

in'cusso, -a PP *di* **incutere**

incusto'dito, -a AG unguarded, unattended; **passaggio a livello ~** unmanned level crossing

in'cutere /40/ VT to arouse; **~ timore/rispetto a qn** to strike fear into sb/command sb's respect

'indaco SM indigo

indaffa'rato, -a AG busy

inda'gare /80/ VT to investigate

indaga'tore, -'trice AG (*sguardo, domanda*) searching; (*mente*) inquiring

in'dagine [inˈdadʒine] SF investigation, inquiry; (*ricerca*) research, study; **~ di mercato** market survey

indebita'mente AV (*immeritatamente*) undeservedly; (*erroneamente*) wrongfully

indebi'tare /72/ VT: **~ qn** to get sb into debt ▪ **indebitarsi** VPR to run o get into debt

in'debito, -a AG undeserved; wrongful

indeboli'mento SM weakening; (*debolezza*) weakness

indebo'lire /55/ VT, VI (*anche:* **indebolirsi**) to weaken

inde'cente [indeˈtʃɛnte] AG indecent

inde'cenza [indeˈtʃɛntsa] SF indecency; **è un'~!** (*vergogna*) it's scandalous!, it's a disgrace!

indeci'frabile [indetʃiˈfrabile] AG indecipherable

indecisi'one [indetʃiˈzjone] SF indecisiveness; indecision

inde'ciso, -a [indeˈtʃizo] AG indecisive; (*irresoluto*) undecided

indeco'roso, -a AG (*comportamento*) indecorous, unseemly

inde'fesso, -a AG untiring, indefatigable

indefi'nibile AG indefinable

indefi'nito, -a AG (*anche* Ling) indefinite; (*impreciso, non determinato*) undefined

indefor'mabile AG crushproof

in'degno, -a [inˈdeɲɲo] AG (*atto*) shameful; (*persona*) unworthy

inde'lebile AG indelible

indelica'tezza [indelikaˈtettsa] SF tactlessness

indeli'cato, -a AG (*domanda*) indiscreet, tactless

indemoni'ato, -a AG possessed (by the devil)

in'denne AG unhurt, uninjured

indennità SF INV (*rimborso: di spese*) allowance; (: *di perdita*) compensation, indemnity; **~ di contingenza** cost-of-living allowance; **~ di fine rapporto** severance payment (*on retirement, redundancy or when taking up other employment*); **~ di trasferta** travel expenses *pl*

indenniz'zare [indennidˈdzare] /72/ VT to compensate

inden'nizzo [indenˈniddzo] SM (*somma*) compensation, indemnity

indero'gabile AG binding

indescri'vibile AG indescribable

indeside'rabile AG undesirable

indeside'rato, -a AG unwanted

indetermina'tezza [indeterminaˈtettsa] SF vagueness

indetermina'tivo, -a AG (*Ling*) indefinite

indetermi'nato, -a AG indefinite, indeterminate

in'detto, -a PP *di* **indire**

'India SF: **l'~** India; **le Indie occidentali** the West Indies

indi'ano, -a AG Indian ▶ SM/F (*d'India*) Indian; (*d'America*) Native American, (American) Indian; **l'Oceano I~** the Indian Ocean

indiavo'lato, -a AG possessed (by the devil); (*vivace, violento*) wild

indi'care /20/ VT (*mostrare*) to show, indicate; (: *col dito*) to point to, point out; (*consigliare*) to suggest, recommend

indica'tivo, -a AG indicative ▶ SM (*Ling*) indicative (mood)

indi'cato, -a AG (*consigliato*) advisable; (*adatto*): **~ per** suitable for, appropriate for

indica'tore, -'trice AG indicating ▶ SM (*elenco*) guide; directory; (*Tecn*) gauge; indicator; **cartello ~** sign; **~ della benzina** petrol (BRIT) o gas

(US) gauge, fuel gauge; **~ di velocità** (Aut) speedometer; (Aer) airspeed indicator

indicazi'one [indikat'tsjone] SF indication; (informazione) piece of information; **indicazioni per l'uso** instructions for use

'**indice** ['inditʃe] SM (Anat: dito) index finger, forefinger; (lancetta) needle, pointer; (fig: indizio) sign; (Tecn, Mat, nei libri) index; **~ azionario** share index; **~ di gradimento** (Radio, TV) popularity rating; **~ dei prezzi al consumo** = retail price index

indicherò ecc [indike'rɔ] VB vedi **indicare**

indi'cibile [indi'tʃibile] AG inexpressible

indiciz'zare [inditʃid'dzare] /72/ VT: **~ al costo della vita** to index-link (BRIT), index (US)

indiciz'zato, -a [inditʃid'dzato] AG (polizza, salario ecc) index-linked (BRIT), indexed (US)

indicizzazi'one [inditʃiddzat'tsjone] SF indexing

indietreggi'are [indjetred'dʒare] /62/ VI to draw back, retreat

indi'etro AV back; (guardare) behind, back; (andare, cadere: anche: **all'indietro**) backwards; **rimanere ~** to be left behind; **essere ~** (col lavoro) to be behind; (orologio) to be slow; **rimandare qc ~** to send sth back; **non vado né avanti né ~** (fig) I'm not getting anywhere, I'm getting nowhere

indi'feso, -a AG (città, confine) undefended; (persona) defenceless (BRIT), defenseless (US), helpless

indiffe'rente AG indifferent ▶ SMF: **fare l'~** to pretend to be indifferent, be o act casual; (fingere di non vedere o sentire) to pretend not to notice

indiffe'renza [indiffe'rentsa] SF indifference

in'digeno, -a [in'didʒeno] AG indigenous, native ▶ SM/F native

indi'gente [indi'dʒente] AG poverty-stricken, destitute

indi'genza [indi'dʒentsa] SF extreme poverty

indigesti'one [indidʒes'tjone] SF indigestion

indi'gesto, -a [indi'dʒesto] AG indigestible

indi'gnare [indiɲ'ɲare] /15/ VT to fill with indignation ■ **indignarsi** VPR to be (o get) indignant

indignazi'one [indiɲɲat'tsjone] SF indignation

indimenti'cabile AG unforgettable

'**indio, -a** AG, SM/F (South American) Indian

indipen'dente AG independent

indipendente'mente AV independently; **~ dal fatto che gli piaccia o meno, verrà!** he's coming, whether he likes it or not!

indipen'denza [indipen'dɛntsa] SF independence

in'dire /38/ VT (concorso) to announce; (elezioni) to call

indi'retto, -a AG indirect

indiriz'zare [indirit'tsare] /72/ VT (dirigere) to direct; (mandare) to send; (lettera) to address; **~ la parola a qn** to address sb

indiriz'zario [indirit'tsarjo] SM mailing list

indi'rizzo [indi'rittso] SM address; (direzione) direction; (avvio) trend, course; **~ assoluto** (Inform) absolute address

indisci'plina [indiʃʃi'plina] SF indiscipline

indiscipli'nato, -a [indiʃʃipli'nato] AG undisciplined, unruly

indis'creto, -a AG indiscreet

indiscrezi'one [indiskret'tsjone] SF indiscretion

indiscrimi'nato, -a AG indiscriminate

indis'cusso, -a AG unquestioned

indiscu'tibile AG indisputable, unquestionable

indispen'sabile AG indispensable, essential

indispet'tire /55/ VT to irritate, annoy ▶ VI (anche: **indispettirsi**) to get irritated o annoyed

indispo'nente AG irritating, annoying

indis'porre /77/ VT to antagonize

indisposizi'one [indispozit'tsjone] SF (slight) indisposition

indis'posto, -a PP di **indisporre** ▶ AG indisposed, unwell

indisso'lubile AG indissoluble

indissolubil'mente AV indissolubly

indistinta'mente AV (senza distinzioni) indiscriminately, without exception; (in modo indefinito: vedere, sentire) vaguely, faintly

indis'tinto, -a AG indistinct

indistrut'tibile AG indestructible

in'divia SF endive

individu'ale AG individual

individua'lismo SM individualism

individua'lista, -i, -e SM/F individualist

individualità SF individuality

individual'mente AV individually

individu'are /72/ VT (dar forma distinta a) to characterize; (determinare) to locate; (riconoscere) to single out

indi'viduo SM individual

indivi'sibile AG indivisible; **quei due sono indivisibili** (fig) those two are inseparable

indizi'are [indit'tsjare] /19/ VT: **~ qn di qc** to cast suspicion on sb for sth

indizi'ato, -a [indit'tsjato] AG suspected ▶ SM/F suspect

in'dizio [in'dittsjo] SM (segno) sign, indication; (Polizia) clue; (Dir) piece of evidence

Indo'cina [indo'tʃina] SF: **l'~** Indochina

'**indole** SF nature, character

indo'lente AG indolent

indo'lenza [indo'lɛntsa] SF indolence
indolen'zire [indolen'tsire] /**55**/ VT (gambe, braccia ecc) to make stiff, cause to ache; (: intorpidire) to numb ■ **indolenzirsi** VPR to become stiff; to go numb
indolen'zito, -a [indolen'tsito] AG stiff, aching; (intorpidito) numb
indo'lore AG (anche fig) painless
indo'mani SM: **l'~** the next day, the following day
Indo'nesia SF: **l'~** Indonesia
indonesi'ano, -a AG, SM/F, SM Indonesian
indo'rare /**72**/ VT (rivestire in oro) to gild; (Cuc) to dip in egg yolk; **~ la pillola** (fig) to sugar the pill
indos'sare /**72**/ VT (mettere indosso) to put on; (avere indosso) to have on
indossa'tore, -'trice SM/F model
in'dotto, -a PP di **indurre**
indottri'nare /**72**/ VT to indoctrinate
indovi'nare /**72**/ VT (scoprire) to guess; (immaginare) to imagine, guess; (il futuro) to foretell; **tirare a ~** to make a shot in the dark
indovi'nato, -a AG successful; (scelta) inspired
indovi'nello SM riddle
indo'vino, -a SM/F fortuneteller
indù AG, SMF Hindu
indubbia'mente AV undoubtedly
in'dubbio, -a AG certain, undoubted
in'duco ecc VB vedi **indurre**
indugi'are [indu'dʒare] /**62**/ VI to take one's time, delay
in'dugio [in'dudʒo] SM (ritardo) delay; **senza ~** without delay
indul'gente [indul'dʒɛnte] AG indulgent; (giudice) lenient
indul'genza [indul'dʒɛntsa] SF indulgence; leniency
in'dulgere [in'duldʒere] /**54**/ VI: **~ a** (accondiscendere) to comply with; (abbandonarsi) to indulge in
in'dulto, -a PP di **indulgere** ▶ SM (Dir) pardon
indu'mento SM article of clothing, garment ■ **indumenti** SMPL (vestiti) clothes; **indumenti intimi** underwear sg
induri'mento SM hardening
indu'rire /**55**/ VT to harden ▶ VI (anche: **indurirsi**) to harden, become hard
in'durre /**90**/ VT: **~ qn a fare qc** to induce o persuade sb to do sth; **~ qn in errore** to mislead sb; **~ in tentazione** to lead into temptation
in'dussi ecc VB vedi **indurre**
in'dustria SF industry; **la piccola/grande ~** small/big business
industri'ale AG industrial ▶ SM industrialist
industrializ'zare [industrjalid'dzare] /**72**/ VT to industrialize

industrializzazi'one [industrjaliddzat'tsjone] SF industrialization
industri'arsi /**19**/ VPR to do one's best, try hard
industri'oso, -a AG industrious, hard-working
induzi'one [indut'tsjone] SF induction
inebe'tito, -a AG dazed, stunned
inebri'are /**19**/ VT (anche fig) to intoxicate ■ **inebriarsi** VPR to become intoxicated
inecce'pibile [inettʃe'pibile] AG unexceptionable
i'nedia SF starvation
i'nedito, -a AG unpublished
inef'fabile AG ineffable
effi'cace [ineffi'katʃe] AG ineffective
ineffi'cacia [ineffi'katʃa] SF inefficacy, ineffectiveness
ineffici'ente [ineffi'tʃɛnte] AG inefficient
ineffici'enza [ineffi'tʃɛntsa] SF inefficiency
ineguagli'abile [inegwaʎ'ʎabile] AG incomparable, matchless
ineguagli'anza [inegwaʎ'ʎantsa] SF (sociale) inequality; (di superficie, livello) unevenness
inegu'ale AG unequal; (irregolare) uneven
inelut'tabile AG inescapable
ineluttabilità SF inescapability
inenar'rabile AG unutterable
inequivo'cabile AG unequivocal
ine'rente AG: **~ a** concerning, regarding
i'nerme AG unarmed, defenceless (BRIT), defenseless (US)
inerpi'carsi /**72**/ VPR: **~ (su)** to clamber (up)
i'nerte AG inert; (inattivo) indolent, sluggish
i'nerzia [i'nɛrtsja] SF inertia; indolence, sluggishness
inesat'tezza [inezat'tettsa] SF inaccuracy
ine'satto, -a AG (impreciso) inaccurate, inexact; (erroneo) incorrect; (Amm: non riscosso) uncollected
inesau'ribile AG inexhaustible
inesis'tente AG non-existent
ineso'rabile AG inexorable, relentless
inesorabil'mente AV inexorably
inesperi'enza [inespe'rjɛntsa] SF inexperience
ines'perto, -a AG inexperienced
inespli'cabile AG inexplicable
inesplo'rato, -a AG unexplored
ines'ploso, -a AG unexploded
inespres'sivo, -a AG (viso) expressionless, inexpressive
ines'presso, -a AG unexpressed
inespri'mibile AG inexpressible
inespu'gnabile [inespuɲ'ɲabile] AG (fortezza, torre ecc) impregnable
ineste'tismo SM beauty problem

177

inesti'mabile AG inestimable; (*valore*) incalculable

inestir'pabile AG ineradicable

inestri'cabile AG (*anche fig*) impenetrable

inetti'tudine SF ineptitude

i'netto, -a AG (*incapace*) inept; (*che non ha attitudine*): ~ **(a)** unsuited (to)

ine'vaso, -a AG (*ordine, corrispondenza*) outstanding

inevi'tabile AG inevitable

inevitabil'mente AV inevitably

i'nezia [i'nɛttsja] SF trifle, thing of no importance

infagot'tare /72/ VT to bundle up, wrap up ■ **infagottarsi** VPR to wrap up

infal'libile AG infallible

infallibilità SF infallibility

infa'mante AG (*accusa*) defamatory, slanderous

infa'mare /72/ VT to defame

in'fame AG infamous; (*fig: cosa, compito*) awful, dreadful

in'famia SF infamy

infan'gare /80/ VT (*sporcare*) to cover with mud; (*fig: nome, reputazione*) to sully ■ **infangarsi** VPR to get covered in mud; to be sullied

infan'tile AG child *cpd*; childlike; (*adulto, azione*) childish; **letteratura ~** children's books *pl*

in'fanzia [in'fantsja] SF childhood; (*bambini*) children *pl*; **prima ~** babyhood, infancy

infari'nare /72/ VT to cover with (*o* sprinkle with *o* dip in) flour; ~ **di zucchero** to sprinkle with sugar

infarina'tura SF (*fig*) smattering

in'farto SM (*Med*): ~ **(cardiaco)** coronary

infasti'dire /55/ VT to annoy, irritate ■ **infastidirsi** VPR to get annoyed *o* irritated

infati'cabile AG tireless, untiring

in'fatti CONG as a matter of fact, in fact, actually

infatu'arsi /72/ VPR: ~ **di** *o* **per** to become infatuated with, fall for

infatuazi'one [infatuat'tsjone] SF infatuation

in'fausto, -a AG unpropitious, unfavourable (*BRIT*), unfavorable (*US*)

infecondità SF infertility

infe'condo, -a AG infertile

infe'dele AG unfaithful

infedeltà SF infidelity

infe'lice [infe'litʃe] AG unhappy; (*sfortunato*) unlucky, unfortunate; (*inopportuno*) inopportune, ill-timed; (*mal riuscito: lavoro*) bad, poor

infelicità [infelitʃi'ta] SF unhappiness

infel'trire /55/ VI, **infel'trirsi** VPR (*lana*) to become matted

infe'renza [infe'rɛntsa] SF inference

inferi'ore AG lower; (*per intelligenza, qualità*) inferior ▶ SMF inferior; ~ **a** (*numero, quantità*) less *o* smaller than; (*meno buono*) inferior to; ~ **alla media** below average

inferiorità SF inferiority

infe'rire /55/ VT (*dedurre*) to infer, deduce

inferme'ria SF infirmary; (*di scuola, nave*) sick bay

infermi'ere, -a SM/F nurse

infermità SF INV illness; infirmity; ~ **mentale** mental illness; (*Dir*) insanity

in'fermo, -a AG (*ammalato*) ill; (*debole*) infirm; ~ **di mente** mentally ill

infer'nale AG infernal; (*proposito, complotto*) diabolical; **un tempo ~** (*col*) hellish weather

in'ferno SM hell; **soffrire le pene dell'~** (*fig*) to go through hell

infero'cire [infero'tʃire] /55/ VT to make fierce ▶ VI (*anche:* **inferocirsi**) to become fierce

inferri'ata SF grating

infervo'rare /72/ VT to arouse enthusiasm in ■ **infervorarsi** VPR to get excited, get carried away

infes'tare /72/ VT to infest

infet'tare /72/ VT to infect ■ **infettarsi** VPR to become infected

infet'tivo, -a AG infectious

in'fetto, -a AG infected; (*acque*) polluted, contaminated

infezi'one [infet'tsjone] SF infection

infiac'chire [infjak'kire] /55/ VT to weaken ▶ VI (*anche:* **infiacchirsi**) to grow weak

infiam'mabile AG inflammable

infiam'mare /72/ VT to set alight; (*fig, Med*) to inflame ■ **infiammarsi** VPR to catch fire; (*Med*) to become inflamed; (*fig*) **infiammarsi di** to be fired with

infiammazi'one [infjammat'tsjone] SF (*Med*) inflammation

infias'care /20/ VT to bottle

infici'are [infi'tʃare] /14/ VT (*Dir: atto, dichiarazione*) to challenge

in'fido, -a AG unreliable, treacherous

infie'rire /55/ VI: ~ **su** (*fisicamente*) to attack furiously; (*verbalmente*) to rage at; (*epidemia*) to rage over

in'figgere [in'fiddʒere] /104/ VT: ~ **qc in** to thrust *o* drive sth into

infi'lare /72/ VT (*ago*) to thread; (*mettere: chiave*) to insert; (: *vestito*) to slip *o* put on; (*strada*) to turn into, take ■ **infilarsi** VPR: **infilarsi in** to slip into; (*indossare*) to slip on; ~ **un anello al dito** to slip a ring on one's finger; ~ **l'uscio** to slip in; to slip out; **infilarsi la giacca** to put on one's jacket

infil'trarsi /72/ VPR to penetrate, seep through; (*Mil*) to infiltrate

infil'trato, -a SM/F infiltrator

infiltrazi'one [infiltrat'tsjone] SF infiltration

infil'zare [infil'tsare] /**72**/ VT (*infilare*) to string together; (*trafiggere*) to pierce

'infimo, -a AG lowest; **un albergo di ~ ordine** a third-rate hotel

in'fine AV finally; (*insomma*) in short

infin'gardo, -a AG lazy ▶ SM/F slacker

infinità SF infinity; (*in quantità*): **un'~ di** an infinite number of

infinitesi'male AG infinitesimal

infi'nito, -a AG infinite; (*Ling*) infinitive ▶ SM infinity; (*Ling*) infinitive; **all'~** (*senza fine*) endlessly; (*Ling*) in the infinitive

infinocchi'are [infinok'kjare] /**19**/ VT (*col*) to hoodwink

infiore'scenza [infjoreʃ'ʃɛntsa] SF inflorescence

infir'mare /**72**/ VT (*Dir*) to invalidate

infischi'arsi [infis'kjarsi] /**19**/ VPR: **~ di** not to care about

in'fisso, -a PP *di* **infiggere** ▶ SM fixture; (*di porta, finestra*) frame

infit'tire /**55**/ VT, VI (*anche:* **infittirsi**) to thicken

inflazio'nare [inflattsjo'nare] /**72**/ VT to inflate

inflazi'one [inflat'tsjone] SF inflation

inflazio'nistico, -a, -ci, -che [inflattsjo'nistiko] AG inflationary

infles'sibile AG inflexible; (*ferreo*) unyielding

inflessi'one SF inflexion

in'fliggere [in'fliddʒere] /**104**/ VT to inflict

in'flissi *ecc* VB *vedi* **infliggere**

in'flitto, -a PP *di* **infliggere**

influ'ente AG influential

influ'enza [influ'ɛntsa] SF influence; (*Med*) influenza, flu; **~ aviaria** bird flu; **~ suina** swine flu

influen'zare [influen'tsare] /**72**/ VT to influence, have an influence on

influ'ire /**55**/ VI: **~ su** to influence

in'flusso SM influence

INFN SIGLA M = **Istituto Nazionale di Fisica Nucleare**

info'cato, -a AG = **infuocato**

info'gnarsi [infoɲ'ɲarsi] /**15**/ VPR (*col*) to get into a mess; **~ in un mare di debiti** to be up to one's o the eyes in debt

infol'tire /**55**/ VT, VI to thicken

infon'dato, -a AG unfounded, groundless

in'fondere /**25**/ VT: **~ qc in qn** to instill sth in sb; **~ fiducia in qn** to inspire sb with confidence

infor'care /**20**/ VT to fork (up); (*bicicletta, cavallo*) to get on; (*occhiali*) to put on

infor'male AG informal

infor'mare /**72**/ VT to inform, tell ▪ **informarsi** VPR: **informarsi (di** *o* **su)** to inquire (about);

tenere informato qn to keep sb informed

infor'matico, -a, -ci, -che AG (*settore*) computer *cpd* ▶ SF computer science

informa'tivo, -a AG informative; **a titolo ~** for information only

informatiz'zare [informatid'dzare] /**72**/ VT to computerize

infor'mato, -a AG informed; **tenersi ~** to keep o.s. (well-)informed

informa'tore SM informer

informazi'one [informat'tsjone] SF piece of information ▪ **informazioni** SFPL information *sg*; **chiedere un'~** to ask for (some) information; **~ di garanzia** (*Dir*) = **avviso di garanzia**

i

Informazioni si traduce con **information** che non prende mai la **-s** e si usa con il verbo al singolare.
Queste informazioni sono molto interessanti. **This information is very interesting.**
Per ulteriori informazioni … **For further information …**
Quando si tratta di una singola *informazione* si traduce con **a piece of information**.
Mi hai dato un'informazione preziosa. **You gave me a valuable piece of information.**

in'forme AG shapeless

informico'larsi /**72**/, **informico'lirsi** VPR: **mi si è informicolata una gamba** I've got pins and needles in my leg

infor'nare /**72**/ VT to put in the oven

infor'nata SF (*anche fig*) batch

infortu'narsi /**72**/ VPR to injure o.s., have an accident

infortu'nato, -a AG injured, hurt ▶ SM/F injured person

infor'tunio SM accident; **~ sul lavoro** industrial accident, accident at work

infortu'nistica SF study of (industrial) accidents

infos'sarsi /**72**/ VPR (*terreno*) to sink; (*guance*) to become hollow

infos'sato, -a AG hollow; (*occhi*) deep-set; (: *per malattia*) sunken

infradici'are [infradi'tʃare] /**14**/ VT (*inzuppare*) to soak, drench; (*marcire*) to rot ▪ **infradiciarsi** VPR to get soaked, get drenched; to rot

infra'dito SM INV (*calzatura*) flip flop (BRIT), thong (US)

in'frangere [in'frandʒere] /**37**/ VT to smash; (*fig: legge, patti*) to break ▪ **infrangersi** VPR to smash, break

infran'gibile [infran'dʒibile] AG unbreakable

in'franto, -a PP di **infrangere** ▶ AG broken

infra'rosso, -a AG, SM infrared

infrasettima'nale AG midweek cpd

infrastrut'tura SF infrastructure

infrazi'one [infrat'tsjone] SF: ~ **a** breaking of, violation of

infredda'tura SF slight cold

infreddo'lito, -a AG cold, chilled

infre'quente AG infrequent, rare

infrol'lire /55/ VI, **infrol'lirsi** VPR (selvaggina) to become high

infruttu'oso, -a AG fruitless

infuo'cato, -a AG (metallo) red-hot; (sabbia) burning; (fig: discorso) heated, passionate

infu'ori AV out; **all'~** outwards; **all'~ di** (eccetto) except, with the exception of

infuri'are /19/ VI to rage ▪ **infuriarsi** VPR to fly into a rage

infusi'one SF infusion

in'fuso, -a PP di **infondere** ▶ AG: **scienza infusa** (anche ironico) innate knowledge ▶ SM infusion; **~ di camomilla** camomile tea

Ing. ABBR = **ingegnere**

ingabbi'are /19/ VT to (put in a) cage

ingaggi'are [ingad'dʒare] /62/ VT (assumere con compenso) to take on, hire; (Sport) to sign on; (Mil) to engage

in'gaggio [in'gaddʒo] SM hiring; signing on

ingagliar'dire [ingaʎʎar'dire] /55/ VT to strengthen, invigorate ▶ VI (anche: **ingagliardirsi**) to grow stronger

ingan'nare /72/ VT to deceive; (coniuge) to be unfaithful to; (fisco) to cheat; (eludere) to dodge, elude; (fig: tempo) to while away ▶ VI (apparenza) to be deceptive ▪ **ingannarsi** VPR to be mistaken, be wrong

inganna'tore, -'trice AG deceptive; (persona) deceitful

ingan'nevole AG deceptive

in'ganno SM deceit, deception; (azione) trick; (menzogna, frode) cheat, swindle; (illusione) illusion

ingarbugli'are [ingarbuʎ'ʎare] /27/ VT to tangle; (fig) to confuse, muddle ▪ **ingarbugliarsi** VPR to become confused o muddled

ingarbu'gliato, -a [ingarbuʎ'ʎato] AG tangled; confused, muddled

inge'gnarsi [indʒeɲ'ɲarsi] /15/ VPR to do one's best, try hard; **~ per vivere** to live by one's wits; **basta ~ un po'** you just need a bit of ingenuity

inge'gnere [indʒeɲ'ɲɛre] SM engineer; **~ civile/navale** civil/naval engineer

ingegne'ria [indʒeɲɲe'ria] SF engineering; **~ genetica** genetic engineering

in'gegno [in'dʒeɲɲo] SM (intelligenza) intelligence, brains pl; (capacità creativa) ingenuity; (disposizione) talent

ingegnosità [indʒeɲɲosi'ta] SF ingenuity

inge'gnoso, -a [indʒeɲ'ɲoso] AG ingenious, clever

ingelo'sire [indʒelo'sire] /55/ VT to make jealous ▶ VI (anche: **ingelosirsi**) to become jealous

in'gente [in'dʒɛnte] AG huge, enormous

ingenti'lire [indʒenti'lire] /55/ VT to refine, civilize ▪ **ingentilirsi** VPR to become more refined, become more civilized

ingenuità [indʒenui'ta] SF ingenuousness

in'genuo, -a [in'dʒɛnuo] AG naïve

inge'renza [indʒe'rɛntsa] SF interference

inge'rire [indʒe'rire] /55/ VT to ingest

inges'sare [indʒes'sare] /72/ VT (Med) to put in plaster

ingessa'tura [indʒessa'tura] SF plaster

Inghil'terra [ingil'tɛrra] SF: **l'~** England

inghiot'tire [ingjot'tire] /17/ VT to swallow

in'ghippo [in'gippo] SM trick

ingial'lire [indʒal'lire] /55/ VI to go yellow

ingigan'tire [indʒigan'tire] /55/ VT to enlarge, magnify ▶ VI to become gigantic o enormous

inginocchi'arsi [indʒinok'kjarsi] /19/ VPR to kneel (down)

inginocchia'toio [indʒinokkja'tojo] SM priedieu

ingioiel'lare [indʒojel'lare] /72/ VT to bejewel, adorn with jewels

ingiù [in'dʒu] AV down, downwards

ingi'ungere [in'dʒundʒere] /5/ VT: **~ a qn di fare qc** to enjoin o order sb to do sth

ingi'unto, -a [in'dʒunto] PP di **ingiungere**

ingiunzi'one [indʒun'tsjone] SF injunction, command; **~ di pagamento** final demand

ingi'uria [in'dʒurja] SF insult; (fig: danno) damage

ingiuri'are [indʒu'rjare] /19/ VT to insult, abuse

ingiuri'oso, -a [indʒu'rjoso] AG insulting, abusive

ingiusta'mente [indʒusta'mente] AV unjustly

ingiustifi'cabile [indʒustifi'kabile] AG unjustifiable

ingiustifi'cato, -a [indʒustifi'kato] AG unjustified

ingius'tizia [indʒus'tittsja] SF injustice

ingi'usto, -a [in'dʒusto] AG unjust, unfair

in'glese AG English ▶ SMF Englishman(-woman) ▶ SM (Ling) English; **gli Inglesi** the English; **andarsene o filare all'~** to take French leave

inglori'oso, -a AG inglorious

ingob'bire /55/ VI, **ingob'birsi** VPR to become stooped

ingoi'are /19/ VT to gulp (down); (*fig*) to swallow (up); **ha dovuto ~ il rospo** (*fig*) he had to accept the situation

ingol'fare /72/ VT, **ingol'farsi** VPR (*motore*) to flood

ingolo'sire /55/ VT: **~ qn** to make sb's mouth water; (*fig*) to attract sb ▶ VI (*anche:* **ingolosirsi**): **~ (di)** (*anche fig*) to become greedy (for)

ingom'brante AG cumbersome

ingom'brare /72/ VT (*strada*) to block; (*stanza*) to clutter up

in'gombro, -a AG: **~ di** (*strada*) blocked by; (*stanza*) cluttered up with ▶ SM obstacle; **essere d'~** to be in the way; **per ragioni di ~** for reasons of space

ingor'digia [ingor'didʒa] SF: **~ (di)** greed (for); avidity (for)

in'gordo, -a AG: **~ di** greedy for; (*fig*) greedy o avid for ▶ SM/F glutton

ingor'gare /80/ VT to block ▪ **ingorgarsi** VPR to be blocked up, be choked up

in'gorgo, -ghi SM blockage, obstruction; (*anche:* **ingorgo stradale**) traffic jam

ingoz'zare [ingot'tsare] /72/ VT (*animali*) to fatten; (*fig: persona*) to stuff ▪ **ingozzarsi** VPR: **ingozzarsi (di)** to stuff o.s. (with)

ingra'naggio [ingra'naddʒo] SM (*Tecn*) gear; (*di orologio*) mechanism; **gli ingranaggi della burocrazia** the bureaucratic machinery

ingra'nare /72/ VI to mesh, engage ▶ VT to engage; **~ la marcia** to get into gear

ingrandi'mento SM enlargement; extension; magnification; growth; expansion

ingran'dire /55/ VT (*anche Fot*) to enlarge; (*estendere*) to extend; (*Ottica, fig*) to magnify ▶ VI (*anche:* **ingrandirsi**) to become larger o bigger; (*: aumentare*) to grow, increase; (*: espandersi*) to expand

ingrandi'tore SM (*Fot*) enlarger

ingras'saggio [ingras'saddʒo] SM greasing

ingras'sare /72/ VT to make fat; (*animali*) to fatten; (*Agr: terreno*) to manure; (*lubrificare*) to oil, lubricate ▶ VI (*anche:* **ingrassarsi**) to get fat, put on weight

ingrati'tudine SF ingratitude

in'grato, -a AG ungrateful; (*lavoro*) thankless, unrewarding

ingrazi'are [ingrat'tsjare] /19/ VT: **ingraziarsi qn** to ingratiate o.s. with sb

ingredi'ente SM ingredient

in'gresso SM (*porta*) entrance; (*atrio*) hall; (*l'entrare*) entrance, entry; (*facoltà di entrare*) admission; **"~ libero"** "admission free"; **~ principale** main entrance; **~ di servizio** tradesmen's entrance

ingros'sare /72/ VT to increase; (*folla, livello*) to swell ▶ VI (*anche:* **ingrossarsi**) to increase; to swell

in'grosso AV: **all'~** (*Comm*) wholesale; (*all'incirca*) roughly, about

ingru'gnato, -a [ingruɲ'ɲato] AG grumpy

inguai'arsi /19/ VPR to get into trouble

inguai'nare /72/ VT to sheathe

ingual'cibile [ingwal'tʃibile] AG crease-resistant

ingua'ribile AG incurable

'inguine SM (*Anat*) groin

ingurgi'tare [ingurdʒi'tare] /72/ VT to gulp down

ini'bire /55/ VT to forbid, prohibit; (*Psic*) to inhibit ▪ **inibirsi** VPR to restrain o.s.

ini'bito, -a AG inhibited ▶ SM/F inhibited person

inibi'torio, -a AG (*Psic*) inhibitory, inhibitive; (*provvedimento, misure*) restrictive

inibizi'one [inibit'tsjone] SF prohibition; inhibition

iniet'tare /72/ VT to inject ▪ **iniettarsi** VPR: **iniettarsi di sangue** (*occhi*) to become bloodshot

iniet'tore SM injector

iniezi'one [injet'tsjone] SF injection

inimi'care /20/ VT to alienate, make hostile ▪ **inimicarsi** VPR: **inimicarsi con qn** to fall out with sb; **si è inimicato di un tempo** he has alienated his old friends

inimi'cizia [inimi'tʃittsja] SF animosity

inimi'tabile AG inimitable

inimmagi'nabile [inimmadʒi'nabile] AG unimaginable

ininfiam'mabile AG non-flammable

inintelli'gibile [inintelli'dʒibile] AG unintelligible

ininterrotta'mente AV non-stop, continuously

ininter'rotto, -a AG (*fila*) unbroken; (*rumore*) uninterrupted

iniquità SF INV iniquity; (*atto*) wicked action

i'niquo, -a AG iniquitous

inizi'ale [init'tsjale] AG, SF initial

inizializ'zare [inittsjalid'dzare] /72/ VT (*Inform*) to boot

inizial'mente [inittsjal'mente] AV initially, at first

inizi'are [init'tsjare] /19/ VI, VT to begin, start; **~ qn a** to initiate sb into; (*pittura ecc*) to introduce sb to; **~ a fare qc** to start doing sth

inizia'tiva [inittsja'tiva] SF initiative; **~ privata** private enterprise

inizia'tore, -'trice [inittsja'tore] SM/F initiator

i'nizio [i'nittsjo] SM beginning; **all'~** at the beginning, at the start; **dare ~ a qc** to start sth, get sth going; **essere agli inizi** (*progetto, lavoro ecc*) to be in the initial stages

innaffi'are *ecc* = **annaffiare** *ecc*

innal'zare [innal'tsare] /**72**/ vt (*sollevare, alzare*) to raise; (*rizzare*) to erect ■ **innalzarsi** vpr to rise

innamora'mento sм falling in love

innamo'rare /**72**/ vt to enchant, charm ■ **innamorarsi** vpr: **innamorarsi (di qn)** to fall in love (with sb)

innamo'rato, -a AG: ~ **(di)** (*che nutre amore*) in love (with); ~ **di** (*appassionato*) very fond of ▶ sм/ғ lover; (*anche scherzoso*) sweetheart

in'nanzi [in'nantsi] AV (*stato in luogo*) in front, ahead; (*moto a luogo*) forward, on; (*tempo: prima*) before ▶ PREP (*prima*) before; ~ **a** in front of; **d'ora ~** from now on; **farsi ~** to step forward; ~ **tempo** ahead of time

innanzi'tutto [innantsi'tutto] AV above all; (*per prima cosa*) first of all

in'nato, -a AG innate

innatu'rale AG unnatural

inne'gabile AG undeniable

inneggi'are [inned'dʒare] /**62**/ vi: ~ **a** to sing hymns to; (*fig*) to sing the praises of

innervo'sire /**55**/ vt: ~ **qn** to get on sb's nerves ■ **innervosirsi** vpr to get irritated *o* upset

innes'care /**20**/ vt to prime

in'nesco, -schi sм primer

innes'tare /**72**/ vt (*Bot, Med*) to graft; (*Tecn*) to engage; (*inserire: presa*) to insert

in'nesto sм graft; grafting *no pl*; (*Tecn*) clutch; (*Elettr*) connection

'inno sм hymn; ~ **nazionale** national anthem

inno'cente [inno'tʃɛnte] AG innocent

inno'cenza [inno'tʃɛntsa] sғ innocence

in'nocuo, -a AG innocuous, harmless

innomi'nato, -a AG unnamed

inno'vare /**72**/ vt to change, make innovations in

innova'tivo, -a AG innovative

innovazi'one [innovat'tsjone] sғ innovation

innume'revole AG innumerable

inocu'lare /**72**/ vt (*Med*) to inoculate

ino'doro, -a AG odourless (BRIT), odorless (US)

inoffen'sivo, -a AG harmless

inol'trare /**72**/ vt (*Amm*) to pass on, forward ■ **inoltrarsi** vpr (*addentrarsi*) to advance, go forward

inol'trato, -a AG: **a notte inoltrata** late at night; **a primavera inoltrata** late in the spring

i'noltre AV besides, moreover

i'noltro sм (*Amm*) forwarding

inon'dare /**72**/ vt to flood

inondazi'one [inondat'tsjone] sғ flooding *no pl*; flood

inope'roso, -a AG inactive, idle

inopi'nato, -a AG unexpected

inoppor'tuno, -a AG untimely, ill-timed; (*poco adatto*) inappropriate; (*momento*) inopportune

inoppu'gnabile [inoppuɲ'ɲabile] AG incontrovertible

inor'ganico, -a, -ci, -che AG inorganic

inorgo'glire [inorgoʎ'ʎire] /**55**/ vt to make proud ▶ vi (*anche:* **inorgoglirsi**) to become proud; **inorgoglirsi di qc** to pride o.s. on sth

inorri'dire /**55**/ vt to horrify ▶ vi to be horrified

inospi'tale AG inhospitable

inosser'vante AG: **essere ~ di** to fail to comply with

inosser'vato, -a AG (*non notato*) unobserved; (*non rispettato*) not observed, not kept; **passare ~** to go unobserved, escape notice

inossi'dabile AG stainless

INPS SIGLA м (= *Istituto Nazionale Previdenza Sociale*) social security service

inqua'drare /**72**/ vt (*foto, immagine*) to frame; (*fig*) to situate, set

inquadra'tura sғ (*Cine, Fot: atto*) framing; (: *immagine*) shot; (: *sequenza*) sequence

inqualifi'cabile AG unspeakable

inquie'tante AG disturbing, worrying

inquie'tare /**72**/ vt (*turbare*) to disturb, worry ■ **inquietarsi** vpr to worry, become anxious; (*impazientirsi*) to get upset

inqui'eto, -a AG restless; (*preoccupato*) worried, anxious

inquie'tudine sғ anxiety, worry

inqui'lino, -a sм/ғ tenant

inquina'mento sм pollution

inqui'nante AG polluting ▶ sм pollutant

inqui'nare /**72**/ vt to pollute

inqui'rente AG (*Dir*): **magistrato ~** examining (BRIT) *o* committing (US) magistrate; **commissione ~** commission of inquiry

inqui'sire /**55**/ vt, vi to investigate

inqui'sito, -a AG (*persona*) under investigation

inquisi'tore, -'trice AG (*sguardo*) inquiring

inquisizi'one [inkwizit'tsjone] sғ inquisition

insabbia'mento sм (*fig*) shelving

insabbi'are /**19**/ vt (*fig: pratica*) to shelve ■ **insabbiarsi** vpr (*arenarsi: barca*) to run aground; (*fig: pratica*) to be shelved

insac'care /**20**/ vt (*grano, farina ecc*) to bag, put into sacks; (*carne*) to put into sausage skins

insac'cati sмpʟ (*Cuc*) sausages

insa'lata sғ salad; (*pianta*) lettuce; ~ **mista** mixed salad; ~ **russa** (*Cuc*) Russian salad (*comprised of cold diced cooked vegetables in mayonnaise*)

insalati'era sғ salad bowl

insa'lubre AG unhealthy

insa'nabile AG (*piaga*) which cannot be healed; (*situazione*) irremediable; (*odio*) implacable

insangui'nare /72/ VT to stain with blood

in'sania SF insanity

in'sano, -a AG (*pazzo, folle*) insane

insapo'nare /72/ VT to soap; **insaponarsi le mani** to soap one's hands

insapo'nata SF: **dare un'~ a qc** to give sth a (quick) soaping

insapo'rire /55/ VT to flavour (BRIT), flavor (US); (*con spezie*) to season ▪ **insaporirsi** VPR to acquire flavo(u)r

insa'poro, -a AG tasteless, insipid

insa'puta SF: **all'~ di qn** without sb knowing

insazi'abile [insat'tsjabile] AG insatiable

inscato'lare /72/ VT (*frutta, carne*) to can

insce'nare [inʃe'nare] /72/ VT (*Teat*) to stage, put on; (*fig*) to stage

inscin'dibile [inʃin'dibile] AG (*fattori*) inseparable; (*legame*) indissoluble

insec'chire [insek'kire] /55/ VT (*seccare*) to dry up; (*: piante*) to wither ▶ VI to dry up, become dry; to wither

insedia'mento SM (*Amm: in carica, ufficio*) installation; (*villaggio, colonia*) settlement

insedi'are /19/ VT (*Amm*) to install ▪ **insediarsi** VPR (*Amm*) to take up office; (*colonia, profughi ecc*) to settle; (*Mil*) to take up positions

in'segna [in'seɲɲa] SF sign; (*emblema*) sign, emblem; (*bandiera*) flag, banner ▪ **insegne** SFPL (*decorazioni*) insignia *pl*

insegna'mento [inseɲɲa'mento] SM teaching; **trarre ~ da un'esperienza** to learn from an experience, draw a lesson from an experience; **che ti serva da ~** let this be a lesson to you

inse'gnante [inseɲ'ɲante] AG teaching ▶ SMF teacher; **~ di sostegno** teaching assistant

inse'gnare [inseɲ'ɲare] /15/ VT, VI to teach; **~ a qn qc** to teach sb sth; **~ a qn a fare qc** to teach sb (how) to do sth; **come lei ben m'insegna ...** (*ironico*) as you will doubtless be aware ...

insegui'mento SM pursuit, chase; **darsi all'~ di qn** to give chase to sb

insegu'ire /45/ VT to pursue, chase

insegui'tore, -'trice SM/F pursuer

insel'lare /72/ VT to saddle

inselvati'chire [inselvati'kire] /55/ VT (*persona*) to make unsociable ▶ VI (*anche:* **inselvatichirsi**) to grow wild; (*: persona*) to become unsociable

inseminazi'one [inseminat'tsjone] SF insemination

insena'tura SF inlet, creek

insen'sato, -a AG senseless, stupid

insen'sibile AG (*anche fig*) insensitive

insensibilità SF insensitivity, insensibility

insepa'rabile AG inseparable

inse'polto, -a AG unburied

inseri'mento SM (*gen*) insertion; **problemi di ~** (*di persona*) adjustment problems

inse'rire /55/ VT to insert; (*Elettr*) to connect; (*allegare*) to enclose; (*annuncio*) to put in, place ▪ **inserirsi** VPR (*fig*): **inserirsi in** to become part of; **~ un annuncio sul giornale** to put o place an advertisement in the newspaper

in'serto SM (*pubblicazione*) insert; **~ filmato** (film) clip

inser'vibile AG useless

inservi'ente SMF attendant

inserzi'one [inser'tsjone] SF insertion; (*avviso*) advertisement; **fare un'~ sul giornale** to put an advertisement in the newspaper

inserzio'nista, -i, -e [insertsjo'nista] SM/F advertiser

insetti'cida, -i [insetti'tʃida] SM insecticide

in'setto SM insect

insicu'rezza [insiku'rettsa] SF insecurity

insi'curo, -a AG insecure

in'sidia SF snare, trap; (*pericolo*) hidden danger; **tendere un'~ a qn** to lay o set a trap for sb

insidi'are /19/ VT (*Mil*) to harass; **~ la vita di qn** to make an attempt on sb's life

insidi'oso, -a AG insidious

insi'eme AV together; (*contemporaneamente*) at the same time ▶ PREP: **~ con** together with ▶ SM whole; (*Mat, servizio, assortimento*) set; (*Moda*) ensemble, outfit; **tutti ~** all together; **tutto ~** all together; (*in una volta*) at one go; **nell'~** on the whole; **d'~** (*veduta ecc*) overall

in'signe [in'siɲɲe] AG (*persona*) famous, distinguished, eminent; (*città, monumento*) notable

insignifi'cante [insiɲɲifi'kante] AG insignificant

insi'gnire [insiɲ'ɲire] /55/ VT: **~ qn di** to honour (BRIT) o honor (US) sb with, decorate sb with

insin'cero, -a [insin'tʃero] AG insincere

insinda'cabile AG unquestionable

insinu'ante AG (*osservazione, sguardo*) insinuating; (*maniere*) ingratiating

insinu'are /72/ VT (*fig*) to insinuate, imply; **~ qc in** (*introdurre*) to slip o slide sth into ▪ **insinuarsi** VPR: **insinuarsi in** to seep into; (*fig*) to creep into; to worm one's way into

insinuazi'one [insinuat'tsjone] SF (*fig*) insinuation

in'sipido, -a AG insipid

insis'tente AG insistent; (*pioggia, dolore*) persistent

insistente'mente AV repeatedly

insis'tenza [insis'tɛntsa] SF insistence; persistence

in'sistere /11/ VI: **~ su qc** to insist on sth; **~ in qc/a fare** (*perseverare*) to persist in sth/in doing

insis'tito, -a PP *di* **insistere**

183

'insito, -a AG: ~ **(in)** inherent (in)

insoddis'fatto, -a AG dissatisfied

insoddisfazi'one [insoddisfat'tsjone] SF dissatisfaction

insoffe'rente AG intolerant

insoffe'renza [insoffe'rɛntsa] SF impatience

insolazi'one [insolat'tsjone] SF (Med) sunstroke

inso'lente AG insolent

insolen'tire /55/ VI to grow insolent ▶ VT to insult, be rude to

inso'lenza [inso'lɛntsa] SF insolence

in'solito, -a AG unusual, out of the ordinary

inso'lubile AG insoluble

inso'luto, -a AG (non risolto) unsolved; (non pagato) unpaid, outstanding

insol'vente AG (Dir) insolvent

insol'venza [insol'vɛntsa] SF (Dir) insolvency

insol'vibile AG insolvent

in'somma AV (in breve, in conclusione) in short; (dunque) well ▶ ESCL for heaven's sake!

inson'dabile AG unfathomable

in'sonne AG sleepless

in'sonnia SF insomnia, sleeplessness

insonno'lito, -a AG sleepy, drowsy

insonorizzazi'one [insonoriddzat'tsjone] SF soundproofing

insoppor'tabile AG unbearable

insoppri'mibile AG insuppressible

insor'genza [insor'dʒɛntsa] SF (di malattia) onset

in'sorgere [in'sordʒere] /109/ VI (ribellarsi) to rise up, rebel; (apparire) to come up, arise

insormon'tabile AG (ostacolo) insurmountable, insuperable

in'sorsi ecc VB vedi **insorgere**

in'sorto, -a PP di **insorgere** ▶ SM/F rebel, insurgent

insospet'tabile AG (al di sopra di ogni sospetto) above suspicion; (inatteso) unsuspected

insospet'tire /55/ VT to make suspicious ▶ VI (anche: **insospettirsi**) to become suspicious

insoste'nibile AG (posizione, teoria) untenable; (dolore, situazione) intolerable, unbearable; **le spese di manutenzione sono insostenibili** the maintenance costs are excessive

insostitu'ibile AG (persona) irreplaceable; (aiuto, presenza) invaluable

insoz'zare [insot'tsare] /72/ VT (pavimento) to make dirty; (fig: reputazione, memoria) to tarnish, sully ■ **insozzarsi** VPR to get dirty

inspe'rabile AG: **la guarigione/salvezza era ~** there was no hope of a cure/of rescue; **abbiamo ottenuto risultati insperabili** the results we achieved were far better than we had hoped

inspe'rato, -a AG unhoped-for

inspie'gabile AG inexplicable

inspi'rare /72/ VT to breathe in, inhale

in'stabile AG (carico, indole) unstable; (tempo) unsettled; (equilibrio) unsteady

instabilità SF instability; (di tempo) changeability

instal'lare /72/ VT to install ■ **installarsi** VPR (sistemarsi): **installarsi in** to settle in

installazi'one [installat'tsjone] SF installation

instan'cabile AG untiring, indefatigable

instau'rare /72/ VT to establish, introduce

instaurazi'one [instaurat'tsjone] SF establishment

instil'lare /72/ VT to instil

instra'dare /72/ VT = **istradare**

insù AV up, upwards; **guardare all'~** to look up o upwards; **naso all'~** turned-up nose

insubordinazi'one [insubordinat'tsjone] SF insubordination

insuc'cesso [insut'tʃɛsso] SM failure, flop

insudici'are [insudi'tʃare] /14/ VT to dirty ■ **insudiciarsi** VPR to get dirty

insuffici'ente [insuffi'tʃɛnte] AG insufficient; (compito, allievo) inadequate

insuffici'enza [insuffi'tʃɛntsa] SF insufficiency; inadequacy; (Ins) fail; **~ di prove** (Dir) lack of evidence; **~ renale** renal insufficiency

insu'lare AG insular

insu'lina SF insulin

in'sulso, -a AG (sciocco) inane, silly; (persona) dull, insipid

insul'tare /72/ VT to insult, affront

in'sulto SM insult, affront

insupe'rabile AG (ostacolo, difficoltà) insuperable, insurmountable; (eccellente: qualità, prodotto) unbeatable; (: persona, interpretazione) unequalled

insuper'bire /55/ VT to make proud, make arrogant ■ **insuperbirsi** VPR to become arrogant

insurrezi'one [insurret'tsjone] SF revolt, insurrection

insussis'tente AG non-existent

intac'care /20/ VT (fare tacche) to cut into; (corrodere) to corrode; (fig: cominciare ad usare: risparmi) to break into; (: ledere) to damage

intagli'are [intaʎ'ʎare] /27/ VT to carve

intaglia'tore, -'trice [intaʎʎa'tore] SM/F engraver

in'taglio [in'taʎʎo] SM carving

intan'gibile [intan'dʒibile] AG (bene, patrimonio) untouchable; (fig: diritto) inviolable

in'tanto AV (nel frattempo) meanwhile, in the meantime; (per cominciare) just to begin with; **~ che** cong while

intarsi'are /19/ VT to inlay

in'tarsio SM inlaying *no pl*, marquetry *no pl*; inlay

intasa'mento SM (*ostruzione*) blockage, obstruction; (*Aut: ingorgo*) traffic jam

inta'sare /72/ VT to choke (up), block (up); (*Aut*) to obstruct, block ▪ **intasarsi** VPR to become choked o blocked

intas'care /20/ VT to pocket

in'tatto, -a AG intact; (*puro*) unsullied

intavo'lare /72/ VT to start, enter into

inte'gerrimo, -a [inte'dʒɛrrimo] AG honest, upright

inte'grale AG complete; (*pane, farina*) wholemeal (BRIT), wholewheat (US); **film in versione ~** uncut version of a film; **calcolo ~** (*Mat*) integral calculus; **edizione ~** unabridged edition

inte'grante AG: **parte ~** integral part

inte'grare /72/ VT to complete; (*Mat*) to integrate ▪ **integrarsi** VPR (*persona*) to become integrated

integra'tivo, -a AG (*assegno*) supplementary; (*Ins*): **esame ~** assessment test sat when changing schools

integra'tore SM: **integratori alimentari** nutritional supplements

integrazi'one [integrat'tsjone] SF integration

integrità SF integrity

'integro, -a AG (*intatto, intero*) complete, whole; (*retto*) upright

intelaia'tura SF frame; (*fig*) structure, framework

intel'letto SM intellect

intellettu'ale AG, SMF intellectual

intellettua'loide (*peg*) AG pseudo-intellectual ▶ SMF pseudo-intellectual, would-be intellectual

intelli'gente [intelli'dʒɛnte] AG intelligent

intelli'genza [intelli'dʒɛntsa] SF intelligence

intelli'ghenzia [intelli'gɛntsja] SF intelligentsia

intelli'gibile [intelli'dʒibile] AG intelligible

inteme'rato, -a AG (*persona, vita*) blameless, irreproachable; (*coscienza*) clear; (*fama*) unblemished

intempe'rante AG intemperate, immoderate

intempe'ranza [intempe'rantsa] SF intemperance ▪ **intemperanze** SFPL (*eccessi*) excesses

intem'perie SFPL bad weather *sg*

intempes'tivo, -a AG untimely

inten'dente SM: **~ di Finanza** inland (BRIT) o internal (US) revenue officer

inten'denza [inten'dɛntsa] SF: **~ di Finanza** inland (BRIT) o internal (US) revenue office

in'tendere /120/ VT (*comprendere*) to understand; (*udire*) to hear; (*significare*) to mean; (*avere intenzione*): **~ fare qc** to intend o mean to do sth

intendersi VPR (*conoscere*): **intendersi di** to know a lot about, be a connoisseur of; (*accordarsi*) to get on (well); **intendersi con qn su qc** to come to an agreement with sb about sth; **intendersela con qn** (*avere una relazione amorosa*) to have an affair with sb; **mi ha dato a ~ che ...** he led me to believe that ...; **non vuole ~ ragione** he won't listen to reason; **s'intende!** naturally!, of course!; **intendiamoci** let's get it quite clear; **ci siamo intesi?** is that clear?, is that understood?

intendi'mento SM (*intelligenza*) understanding; (*proposito*) intention

intendi'tore, -'trice SM/F connoisseur, expert; **a buon intenditor poche parole** (*proverbio*) a word is enough to the wise

intene'rire /55/ VT (*fig*) to move (to pity) ▪ **intenerirsi** VPR (*fig*) to be moved

intensifi'care /20/ VT, **intensifi'carsi** VPR to intensify

intensità SF intensity; (*del vento*) force, strength

inten'sivo, -a AG intensive

in'tenso, -a AG (*luce, profumo*) strong; (*colore*) intense, deep

inten'tare /72/ VT (*Dir*): **~ causa contro qn** to start o institute proceedings against sb

inten'tato, -a AG: **non lasciare nulla d'~** to leave no stone unturned, try everything

in'tento, -a AG (*teso, assorto*): **~ (a)** intent (on), absorbed (in) ▶ SM aim, purpose; **fare qc con l'~ di** to do sth with the intention of; **riuscire nell'~** to achieve one's aim

intenzio'nale [intentsjo'nale] AG intentional; (*Dir: omicidio*) premeditated; **fallo ~** (*Sport*) deliberate foul

intenzio'nato, -a [intentsjo'nato] AG: **essere ~ a fare qc** to intend to do sth, have the intention of doing sth; **ben ~** well-meaning, well-intentioned; **mal ~** ill-intentioned

intenzi'one [inten'tsjone] SF intention; (*Dir*) intent; **avere ~ di fare qc** to intend to do sth, have the intention of doing sth

intera'gire [intera'dʒire] /55/ VI to interact

intera'mente AV entirely, completely

interattivi'tà SF interactivity

interat'tivo, -a AG interactive

interazi'one [interat'tsjone] SF interaction

interca'lare /72/ SM pet phrase, stock phrase ▶ VT to insert

interca'pedine SF gap, cavity

inter'cedere [inter'tʃedere] /29/ VI to intercede

intercessi'one [intertʃes'sjone] SF intercession

intercetta'mento [intertʃetta'mento] SM = **intercettazione**

intercet'tare [intertʃet'tare] /72/ VT to intercept

intercettazi'one [intertʃettat'tsjone] SF: ~ **telefonica** telephone tapping

inter'city [inter'siti] SM INV (Ferr) ≈ intercity (train)

intercon'nettere /63/ VT to interconnect

inter'correre /28/ VI (esserci) to exist; (passare: tempo) to elapse

inter'corso, -a PP di **intercorrere**

inter'detto, -a PP di **interdire** ▶ AG forbidden, prohibited; (sconcertato) dumbfounded ▶ SM (Rel) interdict; **rimanere ~** to be taken aback

inter'dire /38/ VT to forbid, prohibit, ban; (Rel) to interdict; (Dir) to deprive of civil rights

interdizi'one [interdit'tsjone] SF prohibition, ban

interessa'mento SM interest; (intervento) intervention, good offices pl

interes'sante AG interesting; **essere in stato ~** to be expecting (a baby)

interes'sare /72/ VT to interest; (concernere) to concern, be of interest to; (far intervenire): ~ **qn a** to draw sb's attention to ▶ VI: ~ **a** to interest, matter to ▪ **interessarsi** VPR (mostrare interesse): **interessarsi a** to take an interest in, be interested in; (occuparsi): **interessarsi di** to take care of; **precipitazioni che interessano le regioni settentrionali** rainfall affecting the north; **si è interessato di farmi avere quei biglietti** he took the trouble to get me those tickets

interes'sato, -a AG (coinvolto) interested, involved; (peg): **essere ~** to act out of pure self-interest ▶ SM/F (coinvolto) person concerned; **a tutti gli interessati** to all those concerned, to all interested parties

inte'resse SM (anche Comm) interest; (tornaconto): **fare qc per ~** to do sth out of self-interest; ~ **maturato** (Econ) accrued interest; ~ **privato in atti di ufficio** (Amm) abuse of public office

interes'senza [interes'sɛntsa] SF (Econ) profit-sharing

inter'faccia, -ce [inter'fattʃa] SF (Inform) interface; ~ **utente** user interface

interfacci'are [interfat'tʃare] /14/ VT (Inform) to interface

interfe'renza [interfe'rɛntsa] SF interference

interfe'rire /55/ VI to interfere

inter'fono SM intercom; (apparecchio) internal phone

interiezi'one [interjet'tsjone] SF exclamation, interjection

'interim SM INV (periodo) interim, interval; (incarico) temporary appointment; **ministro ad ~** acting o interim minister

interi'nale AG: **lavoro ~** temporary work (through an agency); **lavoratore ~** temporary worker

interi'ora SFPL entrails

interi'ore AG inner cpd; **parte ~** inside

interiorità SF inner being

interioriz'zare [interjorid'dzare] /72/ VT to internalize

inter'linea SF (Dattilografia) spacing; (Tip) leading; **doppia ~** double spacing

interlocu'tore, -'trice SM/F speaker

interlocu'torio, -a AG interlocutory

inter'ludio SM (Mus) interlude

intermedi'ario, -a AG, SM/F intermediary

intermediazi'one [intermedjat'tsjone] SF mediation

inter'medio, -a AG intermediate

inter'mezzo [inter'mɛddzo] SM (intervallo) interval; (breve spettacolo) intermezzo

intermi'nabile AG interminable, endless

intermit'tente AG intermittent

intermit'tenza [intermit'tɛntsa] SF: **ad ~** intermittent

interna'mento SM internment; confinement (to a psychiatric hospital)

inter'nare /72/ VT (arrestare) to intern; (Med) to commit (to a psychiatric institution)

inter'nato, -a AG interned; confined (to a psychiatric hospital) ▶ SM/F internee; inmate (of a psychiatric hospital) ▶ SM (collegio) boarding school; (Med) period as a houseman (BRIT) o an intern (US)

inter'nauta SMF internet user

internazio'nale [internattsjo'nale] AG international

'Internet ['internet] SF internet; **in ~** on the internet

inter'nista, -i, -e SM/F specialist in internal medicine

in'terno, -a AG (di dentro) internal, interior, inner; (: mare) inland; (nazionale) domestic; (allievo) boarding ▶ SM inside, interior; (di paese) interior; (fodera) lining; (di appartamento) flat (BRIT) o apartment (US) (number); (Tel) extension ▶ SM/F (Ins) boarder ▪ **interni** SMPL (Cine) interior shots; **commissione interna** (Ins) internal examination board; **"per uso ~"** (Med) "to be taken internally"; **all'~** inside; **Ministero degli Interni** Ministry of the Interior, ≈ Home Office (BRIT), ≈ Department of the Interior (US); **notizie dall'~** (Stampa) home news

in'tero, -a AG (integro, intatto) whole, entire; (completo, totale) complete; (numero) whole; (non ridotto: biglietto) full; (latte) full-cream

interpel'lanza [interpel'lantsa] SF: **presentare un'~** (Pol) to ask a (parliamentary) question; ~ **parlamentare** interpellation

interpel'lare /72/ VT to consult; (Pol) to question

INTER'POL SIGLA F (= International Criminal Police Organization) INTERPOL

inter'porre /77/ VT (*influenza*) to use; (*ostacolo*): ~ **qc a qc** to put sth in the way of sth ■ **interporsi** VPR to intervene; ~ **appello** (*Dir*) to appeal; **interporsi fra** (*mettersi in mezzo*) to come between

inter'posto, -a PP *di* **interporre**

interpre'tare /72/ VT (*spiegare, tradurre*) to interpret; (*Mus, Teat*) to perform; (*personaggio, sonata*) to play; (*canzone*) to sing

interpretari'ato SM interpreting

interpretazi'one [interpretat'tsjone] SF interpretation

in'terprete SMF interpreter; (*Teat*) actor (actress), performer; (*Mus*) performer; **farsi ~ di** to act as a spokesman for

interpunzi'one [interpun'tsjone] SF punctuation; **segni di ~** punctuation marks

inter'rare /72/ VT (*seme, pianta*) to plant; (*tubature ecc*) to lay underground; (*Mil: pezzo d'artiglieria*) to dig in; (*riempire di terra: canale*) to fill in

interregio'nale [interred3o'nale] SM *train that travels between two or more regions of Italy*

> **Interregionali** trains run on a limited number of lines between two or more Italian regions but do not serve stations in major cities.

interro'gare /80/ VT to question; (*Ins*) to test

interroga'tivo, -a AG (*occhi, sguardo*) questioning, inquiring; (*Ling*) interrogative ▶ SM question; (*fig*) mystery

interroga'torio, -a AG interrogatory, questioning ▶ SM (*Dir*) questioning *no pl*

interrogazi'one [interrogat'tsjone] SF questioning *no pl*; (*Ins*) oral test; (*Pol*): ~ **(parlamentare)** question

inter'rompere /97/ VT to interrupt; (*studi, trattative*) to break off, interrupt ■ **interrompersi** VPR to break off, stop

inter'rotto, -a PP *di* **interrompere**

interrut'tore SM switch

interruzi'one [interrut'tsjone] SF (*vedi interrompere*) interruption; break; ~ **di gravidanza** termination of pregnancy

interse'care /20/ VT, **interse'carsi** VPR to intersect

inter'stizio [inter'stittsjo] SM interstice, crack

interur'bano, -a AG inter-city; (*Tel: chiamata, telefono*) long-distance ▶ SF long-distance call

inter'vallo SM interval; (*spazio*) space, gap; ~ **pubblicitario** (*TV*) commercial break

interve'nire /128/ VI (*partecipare*): ~ **a** to take part in; (*intromettersi: anche Pol*) to intervene; (*Med: operare*) to operate

interven'tista, -i, -e AG, SM/F interventionist

inter'vento SM participation; (*intromissione*) intervention; (*Med*) operation; (*breve discorso*) speech; **fare un ~ nel corso di** (*dibattito, programma*) to take part in

interve'nuto, -a PP *di* **intervenire** ▶ SM: **gli intervenuti** those present

inter'vista SF interview

intervis'tare /72/ VT to interview

intervis'tato, -a AG interviewed ▶ SM/F person interviewed, interviewee

intervista'tore, -'trice SM/F interviewer

in'teso, -a PP *di* **intendere** ▶ AG agreed ▶ SF understanding; (*accordo*) agreement, understanding; **resta ~ che ...** it is understood that ...; **non darsi per ~ di qc** to take no notice of sth; **uno sguardo d'intesa** a knowing look

in'tessere /1/ VT to weave together; (*fig: trama, storia*) to weave

intes'tare /72/ VT (*lettera*) to address; (*proprietà*): ~ **a** to register in the name of; ~ **un assegno a qn** to make out a cheque to sb

intesta'tario, -a SM/F holder

intes'tato, -a AG (*proprietà, casa, conto*) in the name of; (*assegno*) made out to; **carta intestata** headed paper

intestazi'one [intestat'tsjone] SF heading; (*su carta da lettere*) letterhead; (*registrazione*) registration

intesti'nale AG intestinal

intes'tino, -a AG (*lotte*) internal, civil ▶ SM (*Anat*) intestine

intiepi'dire /55/ VT (*riscaldare*) to warm (up); (*raffreddare*) to cool (down); (*fig: amicizia ecc*) to cool ■ **intiepidirsi** VPR to warm (up); to cool (down); to cool

Inti'fada SF Intifada

intima'mente AV intimately; **sono ~ convinto che ...** I'm firmly *o* deeply convinced that ...; **i due fatti sono ~ connessi** the two events are closely connected

inti'mare /72/ VT to order, command; ~ **la resa a qn** (*Mil*) to call upon sb to surrender

intimazi'one [intimat'tsjone] SF order, command

intimida'torio, -a AG threatening

intimidazi'one [intimidat'tsjone] SF intimidation

intimi'dire /55/ VT to intimidate ▶ VI (*anche: intimidirsi*) to grow shy

intimità SF intimacy; privacy; (*familiarità*) familiarity

'intimo, -a AG intimate; (*affetti, vita*) private; (*fig: profondo*) inmost ▶ SM (*persona*) intimate *o* close friend; (*dell'animo*) bottom, depths *pl*; **parti intime** (*Anat*) private parts; **rapporti intimi** (*sessuali*) intimate relations

intimo'rire /55/ VT to frighten ■ **intimorirsi** VPR to become frightened

in'tingere [in'tind3ere] /37/ VT to dip

in'tingolo SM sauce; (*pietanza*) stew

in'tinto, -a PP *di* **intingere**

intiriz'zire [intirid'dzire] /**55**/ VT to numb ▸ VI (*anche:* **intirizzirsi**) to go numb

intiriz'zito, -a [intirid'dzito] AG numb (with cold)

intito'lare /**72**/ VT to give a title to; (*dedicare*) to dedicate ■ **intitolarsi** VPR (*libro, film*) to be called

intolle'rabile AG intolerable

intolle'rante AG intolerant

intolle'ranza [intolle'rantsa] SF intolerance

intona'care /**20**/ VT to plaster

in'tonaco (*intonaci o pl* **intonachi**) SM plaster

into'nare /**72**/ VT (*canto*) to start to sing; (*armonizzare*) to match ■ **intonarsi** VPR (*colori*) to go together; **intonarsi a** (*carnagione*) to suit; (*abito*) to go with, match

intonazi'one [intonat'tsjone] SF intonation

inton'tire /**55**/ VT to stun, daze ▸ VI (*anche:* **intontirsi**) to be stunned o dazed

inton'tito, -a AG stunned, dazed; **~ dal sonno** stupid with sleep

in'toppo SM stumbling block, obstacle

intorbi'dire /**55**/ VT (*liquido*) to make turbid; (*mente*) to cloud; **~ le acque** (*fig*) to muddy the waters

in'torno AV around; **~ a** *prep* (*attorno a*) around; (*riguardo, circa*) about

intorpi'dire /**55**/ VT to numb; (*fig*) to make sluggish ▸ VI (*anche:* **intorpidirsi**) to grow numb; (: *fig*) to become sluggish

intossi'care /**20**/ VT to poison

intossicazi'one [intossikat'tsjone] SF poisoning

intradu'cibile [intradu'tʃibile] AG untranslatable

intralci'are [intral'tʃare] /**14**/ VT to hamper, hold up

in'tralcio [in'traltʃo] SM hitch

intrallaz'zare [intrallat'tsare] /**72**/ VI to intrigue, scheme

intral'lazzo [intral'lattso] SM (*Pol*) intrigue, manoeuvre (BRIT), maneuver (US); (*traffico losco*) racket

intramon'tabile AG timeless

intramusco'lare AG intramuscular

'Intranet ['intranet] SF Intranet

intransi'gente [intransi'dʒɛnte] AG intransigent, uncompromising

intransi'genza [intransi'dʒɛntsa] SF intransigence

intransi'tivo, -a AG, SM intransitive

intrappo'lare /**72**/ VT to trap; **rimanere intrappolato** to be trapped; **farsi ~** to get caught

intrapren'dente AG enterprising, go-ahead; (*con le donne*) forward, bold

intrapren'denza [intrapren'dɛntsa] SF audacity, initiative; (*con le donne*) boldness

intra'prendere /**81**/ VT to undertake; (*carriera*) to embark (up)on

intra'preso, -a PP *di* **intraprendere**

intrat'tabile AG intractable

intratte'nere /**121**/ VT (*divertire*) to entertain; (*chiacchierando*) to engage in conversation; (*rapporti*) to have, maintain ■ **intrattenersi** VPR to linger; **intrattenersi su qc** to dwell on sth

intratteni'mento SM entertainment

intrave'dere /**127**/ VT to catch a glimpse of; (*fig*) to foresee

intrecci'are [intret'tʃare] /**14**/ VT (*capelli*) to plait, braid; (*intessere: anche fig*) to weave, interweave, intertwine ■ **intrecciarsi** VPR to intertwine, become interwoven; **~ le mani** to clasp one's hands; **~ una relazione amorosa** (*fig*) to begin an affair

in'treccio [in'trettʃo] SM (*fig: trama*) plot, story

in'trepido, -a AG fearless, intrepid

intri'care /**20**/ VT (*fili*) to tangle; (*fig: faccenda*) to complicate ■ **intricarsi** VPR to become tangled; to become complicated

in'trico, -chi SM (*anche fig*) tangle

intri'gante AG scheming ▸ SMF schemer, intriguer

intri'gare /**80**/ VI to manoeuvre (BRIT), maneuver (US), scheme

in'trigo, -ghi SM plot, intrigue

in'trinseco, -a, -ci, -che AG intrinsic

in'triso, -a AG: **~ (di)** soaked (in)

intris'tire /**55**/ VI (*persona: diventare triste*) to grow sad; (*pianta*) to wilt

intro'dotto, -a PP *di* **introdurre**

intro'durre /**90**/ VT to introduce; (*chiave ecc*): **~ qc in** to insert sth into; (*persona: far entrare*) to show in ■ **introdursi** VPR (*moda, tecniche*) to be introduced; **introdursi in** (*persona: penetrare*) to enter; (: *entrare furtivamente*) to steal o slip into

introduzi'one SF introduction

in'troito SM income, revenue

intro'messo, -a PP *di* **intromettersi**

intro'mettersi /**63**/ VPR to interfere, meddle; (*interporsi*) to intervene

intromissi'one SF interference, meddling; intervention

introspezi'one [introspet'tsjone] SF introspection

intro'vabile AG (*persona, oggetto*) who (o which) cannot be found; (*libro ecc*) unobtainable

intro'verso, -a AG introverted ▸ SM/F introvert

intrufo'larsi /**72**/ VPR: **~ (in)** (*stanza*) to sneak (into), slip (into); (*conversazione*) to butt in (on)

in'truglio [in'truʎʎo] SM concoction

intrusi'one SF intrusion; interference

in'truso, -a SM/F intruder

intu'ire /55/ vt to perceive by intuition; (*rendersi conto*) to realize

in'tuito sm intuition; (*perspicacia*) perspicacity

intuizi'one [intuit'tsjone] sf intuition

inturgi'dire [inturdʒi'dire] /55/ vi, **inturgi'dirsi** vpr to swell

inumanità sf inv inhumanity

inu'mano, -a ag inhuman

inu'mare /72/ vt (*seppellire*) to bury, inter

inumazi'one [inumat'tsjone] sf burial, interment

inumi'dire /55/ vt to dampen, moisten ■ **inumidirsi** vpr to become damp o wet

inurba'mento sm urbanization

inusi'tato, -a ag unusual

i'nutile ag useless; (*superfluo*) pointless, unnecessary; **è stato tutto ~!** it was all in vain!

inutilità sf uselessness; pointlessness

inutiliz'zabile [inutilid'dzabile] ag unusable

inutil'mente av (*senza risultato*) in vain; (*senza utilità, scopo*) unnecessarily, needlessly; **l'ho cercato ~** I looked for him in vain; **ti preoccupi ~** there's nothing for you to worry about, there's no need for you to worry

inva'dente ag (*fig*) interfering, nosey

inva'denza [inva'dɛntsa] sf intrusiveness

in'vadere /52/ vt to invade; (*affollare*) to swarm into, overrun; (*acque*) to flood

invadi'trice [invadi'tritʃe] ag f *vedi* **invasore**

inva'ghirsi [inva'girsi] /55/ vpr: **~ di** to take a fancy to

invali'cabile ag (*montagna*) impassable

invali'dare /72/ vt to invalidate

invalidità sf infirmity; disability; (*Dir*) invalidity

in'valido, -a a ag (*infermo*) infirm, invalid; (*al lavoro*) disabled; (*Dir: nullo*) invalid ▶ sm/f invalid; disabled person; **~ di guerra** disabled ex-serviceman; **~ del lavoro** industrially disabled person

in'valso, -a ag (*diffuso*) established

in'vano av in vain

invari'abile ag invariable

invari'ato, -a ag unchanged

inva'sare /72/ vt (*pianta*) to pot

inva'sato, -a ag possessed (by the devil) ▶ sm/f person possessed by the devil; **urlare come un ~** to shout like a madman

invasi'one sf invasion

in'vaso, -a pp *di* **invadere**

inva'sore, invadi'trice [invadi'tritʃe] ag invading ▶ smf invader

invecchia'mento [invekkja'mento] sm growing old; ageing; **questo whisky ha un ~ di 12 anni** this whisky has been matured for 12 years

invecchi'are [invek'kjare] /19/ vi (*persona*) to grow old; (*vino, popolazione*) to age; (*moda*) to become dated ▶ vt (*far apparire più vecchio*) to make look older; **lo trovo invecchiato** I find he has aged

in'vece [in'vetʃe] av instead; (*al contrario*) on the contrary; **~ di** prep instead of

inve'ire /55/ vi: **~ contro** to rail against

invele'nire /55/ vt to embitter ■ **invelenirsi** vpr to become bitter

inven'duto, -a ag unsold

inven'tare /72/ vt to invent; (*pericoli, pettegolezzi*) to make up, invent

inventari'are /19/ vt to make an inventory of, inventory

inven'tario sm inventory; (*Comm*) stocktaking *no pl*

inven'tivo, -a ag inventive ▶ sf inventiveness

inven'tore, -'trice sm/f inventor

invenzi'one [inven'tsjone] sf invention; (*bugia*) lie, story

invere'condia sf shamelessness, immodesty

inver'nale ag winter *cpd*; (*simile all'inverno*) wintry

in'verno sm winter; **d'~** in (the) winter

invero'simile ag unlikely ▶ sm: **ha dell'~** it's hard to believe, it's incredible

inversi'one sf inversion; reversal; **"divieto d'~"** (*Aut*) "no U-turns"

in'verso, -a ag opposite; (*Mat*) inverse ▶ sm contrary, opposite; **in senso ~** in the opposite direction; **in ordine ~** in reverse order

inverte'brato, -a ag, sm invertebrate

inver'tire /45/ vt to invert, reverse; (*disposizione, posti*) to change; (*ruoli*) to exchange; **~ la marcia** (*Aut*) to do a U-turn; **~ la rotta** (*Naut*) to go about; (*fig*) to do a U-turn

inver'tito, -a sm/f homosexual

investi'gare /80/ vt, vi to investigate

investiga'tivo, -a ag: **squadra investigativa** detective squad

investiga'tore, -'trice sm/f investigator, detective; **~ privato** private investigator

investigazi'one [investigat'tsjone] sf investigation, inquiry

investi'mento sm (*Econ*) investment; (*di veicolo*) crash, collision; (*di pedone*) knocking down

inves'tire /45/ vt (*denaro*) to invest; (*veicolo: pedone*) to knock down; (: *altro veicolo*) to crash into; (*apostrofare*) to assail; (*incaricare*): **~ qn di** to invest sb with ■ **investirsi** vpr (*fig*): **investirsi di una parte** to enter thoroughly into a role

investi'tore, -'trice sm/f driver responsible for an accident

investi'tura sf investiture

invete'rato, -a ag inveterate

invet'tiva SF invective

invi'are /60/ VT to send

invi'ato, -a SM/F envoy; (Stampa) correspondent; **~ speciale** (Pol) special envoy; (di giornale) special correspondent

in'vidia SF envy; **fare ~ a qn** to make sb envious

invidi'abile AG enviable

invidi'are /19/ VT: **~ qn (per qc)** to envy sb (for sth); **~ qc a qn** to envy sb sth; **non aver nulla da ~ a nessuno** to be as good as the next one

invidi'oso, -a AG envious

invin'cibile [invin'tʃibile] AG invincible

in'vio, -'vii SM sending; (insieme di merci) consignment; (tasto) Return (key), Enter (key)

invio'labile AG inviolable

invio'lato, -a AG (diritto, segreto) inviolate; (foresta) virgin cpd; (montagna, vetta) unscaled

invipe'rire /55/ VI, **invipe'rirsi** VPR to become furious, fly into a temper

invipe'rito, -a AG furious

invis'chiare [invis'kjare] /19/ VT (fig): **~ qn in qc** to involve sb in sth, mix sb up in sth ■ **invischiarsi** VPR: **invischiarsi (con qn/in qc)** to get mixed up o involved (with sb/in sth)

invi'sibile AG invisible

in'viso, -a AG: **~ a** unpopular with

invi'tante AG (proposta, odorino) inviting; (sorriso) appealing, attractive

invi'tare /72/ VT to invite; **~ qn a fare** to invite sb to do

invi'tato, -a SM/F guest

in'vito SM invitation; **dietro ~ del sig. Rossi** at Mr Rossi's invitation

invo'care /20/ VT (chiedere: aiuto, pace) to cry out for; (appellarsi: la legge, Dio) to appeal to, invoke

invogli'are [invoʎ'ʎare] /27/ VT: **~ qn a fare** to tempt sb to do, induce sb to do

involon'tario, -a AG (errore) unintentional; (gesto) involuntary

invol'tino SM (Cuc) roulade

in'volto SM (pacco) parcel; (fagotto) bundle

in'volucro SM cover, wrapping

involu'tivo, -a AG: **subire un processo ~** to regress

invo'luto, -a AG involved, intricate

involuzi'one [involut'tsjone] SF (di stile) convolutedness; (regresso): **subire un'~** to regress

invulne'rabile AG invulnerable

inzacche'rare [intsakke'rare] /72/ VT to spatter with mud ■ **inzaccherarsi** VPR to get muddy

inzup'pare [intsup'pare] /72/ VT to soak ■ **inzupparsi** VPR to get soaked; **inzuppò i biscotti nel latte** he dipped the biscuits in the milk

'io PRON I ▶ SM INV: **l'io** the ego, the self; **io stesso(a)** I myself; **sono io** it's me

i'odio SM iodine

i'ogurt SM INV = **yogurt**

i'one SM ion

l'onio SM: **lo ~, il mar ~** the Ionian (Sea)

ionizza'tore [joniddza'tore] SM ioniser

'iosa: **a ~** av in abundance, in great quantity

i'Pad® [ai'pad] SM INV iPad®

i'perbole SF (Letteratura) hyperbole; (Mat) hyperbola

iper'bolico, -a, -ci, -che AG (Letteratura, Mat) hyperbolic(al); (fig: esagerato) exaggerated

ipermer'cato SM hypermarket

ipersen'sibile AG (persona) hypersensitive; (Fot: lastra, pellicola) hypersensitized

ipertecno'logico, -a, -ci, -che [ipertekno'lɔdʒiko] AG hi-tech

ipertensi'one SF high blood pressure, hypertension

iper'testo SM hypertext

ipertestu'ale AG (Inform): **collegamento** o **link ~** hyperlink

i'Phone® [ai'fon] SM INV iPhone®

ip'nosi SF hypnosis

ip'notico, -a, -ci, -che AG hypnotic

ipno'tismo SM hypnotism

ipnotiz'zare [ipnotid'dzare] /72/ VT to hypnotize

ipoaller'genico, -a, -ci, -che [ipoaller'dʒɛniko] AG hypoallergenic

ipocon'dria SF hypochondria

ipocon'driaco, -a, -ci, -che AG, SM/F hypochondriac

ipocri'sia SF hypocrisy

i'pocrita, -i, -e AG hypocritical ▶ SM/F hypocrite

ipo'sodico, -a, -ci, -che AG low sodium cpd

ipo'teca, -che SF mortgage

ipote'care /20/ VT to mortgage

ipote'nusa SF hypotenuse

i'potesi SF INV hypothesis; **facciamo l'~ che ...**, **ammettiamo per ~ che ...** let's suppose o assume that ...; **nella peggiore/migliore delle ~** at worst/best; **nell'~ che venga** should he come, if he comes; **se per ~ io partissi ...** just supposing I were to leave ....

ipo'tetico, -a, -ci, -che AG hypothetical

ipotiz'zare [ipotid'dzare] /72/ VT: **~ che** to form the hypothesis that

'ippico, -a, -ci, -che AG horse cpd ▶ SF horseracing

ippocas'tano SM horse chestnut

ip'podromo SM racecourse

ippo'potamo SM hippopotamus

'ipsilon SM o F INV (lettera) Y, y; (: dell'alfabeto greco) epsilon

IP'SOA SIGLA M (= *Istituto Post-Universitario per lo Studio dell'Organizzazione Aziendale*) *postgraduate institute of business administration*

IR ABBR (*Ferr*: = *Interregionale*) *long distance train which stops frequently*

IRA SIGLA F (= *Irish Republican Army*) IRA

'ira SF anger, wrath

ira'cheno, -a [ira'kɛno] AG, SM/F Iraqi

l'ran SM: **l'~** Iran

irani'ano, -a AG, SM/F Iranian

l'raq SM: **l'~** Iraq

iras'cibile [iraʃ'ʃibile] AG quick-tempered

'IRI SIGLA M (= *Istituto per la Ricostruzione Industriale*) *state-controlled industrial investment office*

'iride SF (*arcobaleno*) rainbow; (*Anat, Bot*) iris

'iris SM INV iris

Ir'landa SF: **l'~** Ireland; **l'~ del Nord** Northern Ireland, Ulster; **la Repubblica d'~** Eire, the Republic of Ireland; **il mar d'~** the Irish Sea

irlan'dese AG Irish ▶ SMF Irishman(-woman); **gli Irlandesi** the Irish

iro'nia SF irony

i'ronico, -a, -ci, -che AG ironic(al)

ironiz'zare [ironid'dzare] /**72**/ VT, VI: **~ su** to be ironical about

i'roso, -a AG (*sguardo, tono*) angry, wrathful; (*persona*) irascible

'IRPEF SIGLA F = **imposta sul reddito delle persone fisiche**

ir'pino, -a AG of (*o* from) Irpinia

irradi'are /**19**/ VT to radiate; (*raggi di luce: illuminare*) to shine on ▶ VI (*diffondersi: anche:* **irradiarsi**) to radiate

irradiazi'one [irradjat'tsjone] SF radiation

irraggiun'gibile [irraddʒun'dʒibile] AG unreachable; (*fig: meta*) unattainable

irragio'nevole [irradʒo'nevole] AG (*privo di ragione*) irrational; (*fig: persona, pretese, prezzo*) unreasonable

irrazio'nale [irrattsjo'nale] AG irrational

irre'ale AG unreal

irrealiz'zabile [irrealid'dzabile] AG (*sogno, desiderio*) unattainable, unrealizable; (*progetto*) unworkable, impracticable

irrealtà SF unreality

irrecupe'rabile AG (*gen*) irretrievable; (*fig: persona*) irredeemable

irrecu'sabile AG (*offerta*) not to be refused; (*prova*) irrefutable

irreden'tista, -i, -e AG, SM/F (*Storia*) Irredentist

irrefre'nabile AG uncontrollable

irrefu'tabile AG irrefutable

irrego'lare AG irregular; (*terreno*) uneven

irregolarità SF INV irregularity; unevenness *no pl*

irremo'vibile AG (*fig*) unshakeable, unyielding

irrepa'rabile AG irreparable; (*fig*) inevitable

irrepe'ribile AG nowhere to be found

irrepren'sibile AG irreproachable

irrequi'eto, -a AG restless

irresis'tibile AG irresistible

irreso'luto, -a AG irresolute

irrespi'rabile AG (*aria*) unbreathable; (*fig: opprimente*) stifling, oppressive; (: *malsano*) unhealthy

irrespon'sabile AG irresponsible

irrestrin'gibile [irrestrin'dʒibile] AG unshrinkable, non-shrink (BRIT)

irre'tire /**55**/ VT to seduce

irrever'sibile AG irreversible

irrevo'cabile AG irrevocable

irricono'scibile [irrikonoʃ'ʃibile] AG unrecognizable

irridu'cibile [irridu'tʃibile] AG irreducible; (*fig*) unshakeable

irrifles'sivo, -a AG thoughtless

irri'gare /**80**/ VT (*annaffiare*) to irrigate; (*fiume ecc*) to flow through

irrigazi'one [irrigat'tsjone] SF irrigation

irrigidi'mento [irridʒidi'mento] SM stiffening; hardening; tightening

irrigi'dire [irridʒi'dire] /**55**/ VT to stiffen; (*disciplina*) to tighten ■ **irrigidirsi** VPR to stiffen; (*posizione, atteggiamento*) to harden

irriguar'doso, -a AG disrespectful

irrile'vante AG (*trascurabile*) insignificant

irrimedi'abile AG: **un errore ~** a mistake which cannot be rectified; **non è ~!** we can do something about it!

irrinunci'abile [irrinun'tʃabile] AG vital; which cannot be abandoned

irripe'tibile AG unrepeatable

irri'solto, -a AG (*problema*) unresolved

irri'sorio, -a AG derisory

irrispet'toso, -a AG disrespectful

irri'tabile AG irritable

irri'tante AG (*atteggiamento*) irritating, annoying; (*Med*) irritant

irri'tare /**72**/ VT (*mettere di malumore*) to irritate, annoy; (*Med*) to irritate ■ **irritarsi** VPR (*stizzirsi*) to become irritated *o* annoyed; (*Med*) to become irritated

irritazi'one [irritat'tsjone] SF irritation; annoyance

irrive'rente AG irreverent

irrobus'tire /**55**/ VT (*persona*) to make stronger, make more robust; (*muscoli*) to strengthen ■ **irrobustirsi** VPR to become stronger

ir'rompere /**97**/ VI: **~ in** to burst into

irro'rare /**72**/ VT to sprinkle; (*Agr*) to spray

ir'rotto, -a PP *di* **irrompere**

191

irru'ente AG (*fig*) impetuous, violent

irru'enza [irru'ɛntsa] SF impetuousness; **con ~** impetuously

ir'ruppi *ecc* VB *vedi* **irrompere**

irruvi'dire /55/ VT to roughen ▶ VI (*anche*: **irruvidirsi**) to become rough

irruzi'one [irrut'tsjone] SF: **fare ~ in** to burst into; (*polizia*) to raid

ir'suto, -a AG (*petto*) hairy; (*barba*) bristly

'irto, -a AG bristly; **~ di** bristling with

Is. ABBR (= *isola*) I

ISBN ABBR (= *International Standard Book Number*) ISBN

is'crissi *ecc* VB *vedi* **iscrivere**

is'critto, -a PP *di* **iscrivere** ▶ SM/F member; **gli iscritti alla gara** the competitors; **per o in ~ in** writing

is'crivere /105/ VT to register, enter; (*persona*): **~ (a)** to register (in), enrol (in) ■ **iscriversi** VPR: **iscriversi (a)** (*club, partito*) to join; (*università*) to register *o* enrol (at); (*esame, concorso*) to register *o* enter (for)

iscrizi'one [iskrit'tsjone] SF (*epigrafe ecc*) inscription; (*a scuola, società ecc*) enrolment, registration; (*registrazione*) registration

'ISEF SIGLA M = **Istituto Superiore di Educazione Fisica**

Is'lam SM: **l'~** Islam

is'lamico, -a, -ci, -che AG Islamic

Is'landa SF: **l'~** Iceland

islan'dese AG Icelandic ▶ SMF Icelander ▶ SM (*Ling*) Icelandic

'isola SF island; **~ pedonale** (*Aut*) pedestrian precinct

isola'mento SM isolation; (*Tecn*) insulation; **essere in cella di ~** to be in solitary confinement; **~ acustico** soundproofing; **~ termico** thermal insulation

iso'lano, -a AG island *cpd* ▶ SM/F islander

iso'lante AG insulating ▶ SM insulator

iso'lare /72/ VT to isolate; (*Tecn*) to insulate; (: *acusticamente*) to soundproof ■ **isolarsi** VPR to isolate o.s.

iso'lato, -a AG isolated; insulated ▶ SM (*edificio*) block

isolazio'nismo [isolattsjo'nismo] SM isolationism

i'sotopo SM isotope

ispessi'mento SM thickening

ispes'sire /55/ VT to thicken ■ **ispessirsi** VPR to get thicker, thicken

ispetto'rato SM inspectorate

ispet'tore, -'trice SM/F inspector; (*Comm*) supervisor; **~ di zona** (*Comm*) area supervisor *o* manager; **~ di reparto** shop walker (BRIT), floor walker (US)

ispezio'nare [ispettsjo'nare] /72/ VT to inspect

ispezi'one [ispet'tsjone] SF inspection

'ispido, -a AG bristly, shaggy

ispi'rare /72/ VT to inspire ■ **ispirarsi** VPR: **ispirarsi a** to draw one's inspiration from; (*conformarsi*) to be based on; **l'idea m'ispira** the idea appeals to me

ispira'tore, -'trice AG inspiring ▶ SM/F inspirer; (*di ribellione*) instigator

ispirazi'one [ispirat'tsjone] SF inspiration; **secondo l'~ del momento** according to the mood of the moment

Isra'ele SM: **l'~** Israel

israeli'ano, -a AG, SM/F Israeli

israe'lita, -i, -e SM/F Jew (Jewess); (*Storia*) Israelite

israe'litico, -a, -ci, -che AG Jewish

is'sare /72/ VT to hoist; **~ l'ancora** to weigh anchor

'Istanbul SF Istanbul

istan'taneo, -a AG instantaneous ▶ SF (*Fot*) snapshot

is'tante SM instant, moment; **all'~, sull'~** instantly, immediately

is'tanza [is'tantsa] SF petition, request; **giudice di prima ~** (*Dir*) judge of the court of first instance; **giudizio di seconda ~** judgment on appeal; **in ultima ~** (*fig*) finally; **~ di divorzio** petition for divorce

'ISTAT SIGLA M = **Istituto Centrale di Statistica**

'ISTEL SIGLA F = **Indagine sull'ascolto delle televisioni in Italia**

is'terico, -a, -ci, -che AG hysterical

isteri'lire /55/ VT (*terreno*) to render infertile; (*fig*: *fantasia*) to dry up ■ **isterilirsi** VPR to become infertile; to dry up

iste'rismo SM hysteria

isti'gare /80/ VT to incite

istigazi'one [istigat'tsjone] SF instigation; **~ a delinquere** (*Dir*) incitement to crime

istin'tivo, -a AG instinctive

is'tinto SM instinct

istitu'ire /55/ VT (*fondare*) to institute, found; (*porre*: *confronto*) to establish; (*intraprendere*: *inchiesta*) to set up

isti'tuto SM institute; (*di università*) department; (*ente, Dir*) institution; **~ di bellezza** beauty salon; **~ di credito** bank, banking institution; **~ di ricerca** research institute; **~ tecnico commerciale** ≈ commercial college; **~ tecnico industriale statale** ≈ technical college

istitu'tore, -'trice SM/F (*fondatore*) founder; (*precettore*) tutor, governess

istituzi'one [istitut'tsjone] SF institution ■ **istituzioni** SFPL (*Dir*) institutes; **lotta alle istituzioni** struggle against the Establishment

'istmo SM (*Geo*) isthmus

isto'gramma, -i SM histogram

istra'dare /72/ VT (*fig*: *persona*): **~ (a/verso)** to direct (to/towards)

istri'ano, -a AG, SM/F Istrian

'istrice ['istritʃe] SM porcupine

istri'one SM (*peg*) ham (actor)

istru'ire /55/ VT (*insegnare*) to teach; (*ammaestrare*) to train; (*informare*) to instruct, inform; (*Dir*) to prepare

istru'ito, -a AG educated

istrut'tivo, -a AG instructive

istrut'tore, -'trice SM/F instructor ▶ AG: **giudice ~** examining (*BRIT*) *o* committing (*US*) magistrate

istrut'toria SF (*Dir*) (preliminary) investigation and hearing; **formalizzare un'~** to proceed to a formal hearing

istruzi'one [istrut'tsjone] SF (*gen*) training; (*Ins, cultura*) education; (*direttiva*) instruction; (*Dir*) = **istruttoria ▪ istruzioni** SFPL (*norme*) instructions; **Ministero della Pubblica I~** Ministry of Education; **istruzioni di spedizione** forwarding instructions; **istruzioni per l'uso** instructions (for use); **~ obbligatoria** (*Ins*) compulsory education

istupi'dire /55/ VT (*colpo*) to stun, daze; (*droga, stanchezza*) to stupefy **▪ istupidirsi** VPR to become stupid

'ISVE SIGLA M (= *Istituto di Studi per lo Sviluppo Economico*) *institute for research into economic development*

I'talia SF: **l'~** Italy

itali'ano, -a AG Italian ▶ SM/F Italian ▶ SM (*Ling*) Italian; **gli Italiani** the Italians

italofo'bia SF anti-Italianism, Italophobia

ITC SIGLA M = **Istituto tecnico commerciale**

'iter SM passage, course; **l'~ burocratico** the bureaucratic process

itine'rante AG wandering, itinerant; **mostra ~** touring exhibition; **spettacolo ~** travelling (*BRIT*) *o* traveling (*US*) show, touring show

itine'rario SM itinerary

'ITIS SIGLA M = **istituto tecnico industriale statale**

itte'rizia [itte'rittsja] SF (*Med*) jaundice

'ittico, -a, -ci, -che AG fish *cpd*; fishing *cpd*

IUD SIGLA M INV (= *intra-uterine device*) IUD

Iugos'lavia SF = **Jugoslavia**

iugos'lavo, -a AG, SM/F = **jugoslavo**

i'uta SF jute

'I.V.A. SIGLA F (= *imposta sul valore aggiunto*) VAT

'ivi AV (*formale, poetico*) therein; (*nelle citazioni*) ibid

Jj

J, j [i'lunga] SM O F INV (*lettera*) J, j; **J come Jersey** ≈ J for Jack (*Brit*), J for Jig (*US*)

jazz [dʒaz] SM jazz

jaz'zista, -i [dʒad'dzista] SM jazz player

jeans [dʒinz] SMPL jeans

Jeep® [dʒip] SF INV jeep

'jersey ['dʒɛrzi] SM INV jersey (cloth)

jihad'ista [dʒiad'ista] SMF jihadist

'jockey ['dʒɔki] SM INV (*Carte*) jack; (*fantino*) jockey

'jogging ['dʒɔgiŋ] SM jogging; **fare ~** to go jogging

'jolly ['dʒɔli] SM INV joker

joys'tick [dʒois'tik] SM INV joystick

jr. ABBR (= *junior*) Jr., jr.

ju'do [dʒu'dɔ] SM judo

Jugos'lavia [jugoz'lavja] SF (*Storia*): **la ~** Yugoslavia; **la ex-Jugoslavia** former Yugoslavia

jugos'lavo, -a AG, SM/F (*Storia*) Yugoslav(ian)

'juke 'box ['dʒuk'bɔks] SM INV jukebox

Kk

K, k ['kappa] SM O F INV (*lettera*) K, k ►ABBR
(= *kilo-, chilo-*) k; (*Inform*) K; **K come Kursaal** ≈ K
for King
kami'kaze [kami'kaddze] SM INV kamikaze
Kam'pala SF Kampala
kara'oke [kara'oke] SM INV karaoke
karatè [kara'tɛ] SM karate
'Kashmir ['kaʃmir] SM: **il ~** Kashmir
ka'yak [ka'jak] SM INV kayak
Ka'zakistan [ka'dzakistan] SM Kazakhstan
ka'zako, -a [ka'dzako] AG, SM/F Kazakh
'Kenia ['kenja] SM: **il ~** Kenya
keni'ano, -a AG, SM/F Kenyan
keni'ota, -i, -e AG, SM/F Kenyan
'Kenya ['kenja] SM: **il ~** Kenya
kero'sene [kero'zɛne] SM = **cherosene**
kg ABBR (= *chilogrammo*) kg
kib'butz [kib'buts] SM INV kibbutz
Kilimangi'aro [kiliman'dʒaro] SM: **il ~** Kilimanjaro
'killer ['killer] SM INV gunman, hired gun

'kilo = **chilo** *ecc*
kilt [kilt] SM INV kilt
ki'mono [ki'mɔno] SM = **chimono**
'Kindle® ['kindœl] SM INV Kindle®
kir'ghiso, -a [kir'gizo] AG, SM/F Kyrgyz
Kir'ghizistan [kir'gidzistan] SM Kyrgyzstan
kitsch [kitʃ] SM kitsch
'kiwi ['kiwi] SM INV kiwi (fruit)
km ABBR (= *chilometro*) km
kmq ABBR (= *chilometro quadrato*) km²
K.'O. [kappa'o] SM INV knockout
ko'ala [ko'ala] SM INV koala (bear)
koso'varo, -a AG, SM/F Kosovan
'Kosovo SM Kosovo
KR SIGLA = **Crotone**
'krapfen ['krapfən] (*Cuc*) SM INV doughnut
Ku'ala Lum'par SF Kuala Lumpur
Ku'wait [ku'vait] SM: **il ~** Kuwait
kW ABBR (= *kilowatt, chilowatt*) kW
kWh ABBR (= *kilowattora*) kW/h

k

L, l ['εlle] SM O F INV (*lettera*) L, l ▶ ABBR (= *lira*) L; **L come Livorno** ≈ L for Lucy (BRIT), L for Love (US)

l ABBR (= *litro*) l

l' DET *vedi* **la; lo**

la DET F (*dav V l'*) the ▶ PRON (*dav V l'*: *oggetto: persona*) her; (: *cosa*) it; (: *forma di cortesia*) you ▶ SM INV (*Mus*) A; (: *solfeggiando la scala*) la; *vedi anche* **il**

là AV there; **di là** (*da quel luogo*) from there; (*in quel luogo*) in there; (*dall'altra parte*) over there; **di là di** beyond; **per di là** that way; **più in là** further on; (*tempo*) later on; **fatti in là** move up; **là dentro/sopra/sotto** in/up *o* on/under there; **là per là** (*sul momento*) there and then; **essere in là con gli anni** to be getting on (in years); **essere più di là che di qua** to be more dead than alive; **va' là!** come off it!; **stavolta è andato troppo in là** this time he's gone too far; *vedi anche* **quello**

'labbro SM (*pl(f)* **labbra**: *Anat*) lip

'labile AG fleeting, ephemeral

labi'rinto SM labyrinth, maze

labora'torio SM (*di ricerca*) laboratory; (*di arti, mestieri*) workshop; **~ linguistico** language laboratory

labori'oso, -a AG (*faticoso*) laborious; (*attivo*) hard-working

labu'rista, -i, -e AG Labour *cpd* (BRIT) ▶ SM/F Labour Party member (BRIT)

'lacca, -che SF lacquer; (*per unghie*) nail varnish (BRIT), nail polish

lac'care /20/ VT (*mobili*) to varnish, lacquer

'laccio ['lattʃo] SM noose; (*legaccio, tirante*) lasso; (*di scarpa*) lace; **~ emostatico** (*Med*) tourniquet

lace'rante [latʃe'rante] AG (*suono*) piercing, shrill

lace'rare [latʃe'rare] /72/ VT to tear to shreds, lacerate ■ **lacerarsi** VPR to tear

lacerazi'one [latʃerat'tsjone] SF (*anche Med*) tear

'lacero, -a ['latʃero] AG (*logoro*) torn, tattered; (*Med*) lacerated; **ferita lacero-contusa** injury with lacerations and bruising

la'conico, -a, -ci, -che AG laconic, brief

'lacrima SF tear; (*goccia*) drop; **in lacrime** in tears

lacri'mare /72/ VI to water

lacri'mevole AG heartrending, pitiful

lacri'mogeno, -a [lakri'mɔdʒeno] AG: **gas ~** tear gas

lacri'moso, -a AG tearful

la'cuna SF (*fig*) gap

la'custre AG lake *cpd*

lad'dove CONG whereas

'ladro, -a SM/F thief; **al ~!** stop thief!

ladro'cinio [ladro'tʃinjo] SM theft, robbery

la'druncolo, -a SM/F petty thief

laggiù [lad'dʒu] AV down there; (*di là*) over there

'lagna ['laɲɲa] SF (*col: persona, cosa*) drag, bore; **fare la ~** to whine, moan

la'gnanza [laɲ'ɲantsa] SF complaint

la'gnarsi [laɲ'ɲarsi] /15/ VPR: **~ (di)** to complain (about)

'lago, -ghi SM lake

'Lagos ['lagos] SF Lagos

'lagrima *ecc* = **lacrima** *ecc*

la'guna SF lagoon

lagu'nare AG lagoon *cpd*

'laico, -a, -ci, -che AG (*apostolato*) lay; (*vita*) secular; (*scuola*) non-denominational ▶ SM/F layman(-woman) ▶ SM lay brother

'laido, -a AG filthy, foul; (*fig: osceno*) obscene, filthy

'lama SF blade ▶ SM INV (*Zool*) llama; (*Rel*) lama

lambic'care /20/ VT to distil; **lambiccarsi il cervello** to rack one's brains

lam'bire /55/ VT (*fig: fiamme*) to lick; (*acqua*) to lap

lam'bretta® SF scooter

la'mella SF (*di metallo ecc*) thin sheet, thin strip; (*di fungo*) gill

lamen'tare /72/ VT to lament ■ **lamentarsi** VPR (*emettere lamenti*) to moan, groan; (*rammaricarsi*) **lamentarsi (di)** to complain (about)

lamen'tela SF complaining *no pl*

lamen'tevole AG (*voce*) complaining, plaintive; (*stato*) lamentable, pitiful

la'mento SM moan, groan; (*per la morte di qn*) lament

lamen'toso, -a AG plaintive

la'metta SF razor blade

lami'era SF sheet metal

'lamina SF (*lastra sottile*) thin sheet (*o* layer *o* plate); **~ d'oro** gold leaf; gold foil

lami'nare /72/ VT to laminate

lami'nato, -a AG laminated; (*tessuto*) lamé ▶ SM laminate

'lampada SF lamp; **~ a petrolio/a gas** oil/gas lamp; **~ a spirito** blowlamp (BRIT), blowtorch; **~ a stelo** standard lamp (BRIT), floor lamp; **~ da tavolo** table lamp

lampa'dario SM chandelier

lampa'dina SF light bulb; **~ tascabile** pocket torch (BRIT), flashlight (US)

lam'pante AG (*fig: evidente*) crystal clear, evident

lam'para SF fishing lamp; (*barca*) boat for fishing by lamplight (*in Mediterranean*)

lampeggi'are [lamped'dʒare] /62/ VI (*luce, fari*) to flash ▶ VB IMPERS: **lampeggia** there's lightning

lampeggia'tore [lampeddʒa'tore] SM (*Aut*) indicator

lampi'one SM street light *o* lamp (BRIT)

'lampo SM (*Meteor*) flash of lightning; (*di luce, fig*) flash ▶ AG INV: **cerniera ~** zip (fastener) (BRIT), zipper (US); **guerra ~** blitzkrieg ▪ **lampi** SMPL (*Meteor*) lightning *no pl*; **passare come un ~** to flash past *o* by

lam'pone SM raspberry

'lana SF wool; **~ d'acciaio** steel wool; **pura ~ vergine** pure new wool; **~ di vetro** glass wool

lan'cetta [lan'tʃetta] SF (*indice*) pointer, needle; (*di orologio*) hand

'lancia, -ce ['lantʃa] SF (*arma*) lance; (: *picca*) spear; (*di pompa antincendio*) nozzle; (*imbarcazione*) launch; **partire ~ in resta** (*fig*) to set off ready for battle; **spezzare una ~ in favore di qn** (*fig*) to come to sb's defence; **~ di salvataggio** lifeboat

lancia'bombe [lantʃa'bombe] SM INV (*Mil*) mortar

lanciafi'amme [lantʃa'fjamme] SM INV flamethrower

lancia'missili [lantʃa'missili] AG INV missile-launching ▶ SM INV missile launcher

lancia'razzi [lantʃa'raddzi] AG INV rocket-launching ▶ SM INV rocket launcher

lanci'are [lan'tʃare] /14/ VT to throw, hurl, fling; (*Sport*) to throw; (*far partire: automobile*) to get up to full speed; (*bombe*) to drop; (*razzo, prodotto, moda*) to launch; (*emettere: grido*) to give out ▪ **lanciarsi** VPR: **lanciarsi contro/su** to throw *o* hurl *o* fling o.s. against/on; **lanciarsi in** (*fig*) to embark on; **~ un cavallo** to give a horse his head; **~ il disco** (*Sport*) to throw the discus; **~ il peso** (*Sport*) to put the shot; **lanciarsi all'inseguimento di qn** to set off in pursuit of sb; **lanciarsi col paracadute** to parachute

lanci'ato, -a [lan'tʃato] AG (*affermato: attore, prodotto*) well-known, famous; (: *veicolo*) speeding along, racing along

lanci'nante [lantʃi'nante] AG (*dolore*) shooting, throbbing; (*grido*) piercing

'lancio ['lantʃo] SM throwing *no pl*; throw; dropping *no pl*; drop; launching *no pl*; launch; **~ del disco** (*Sport*) throwing the discus; **~ del peso** (*Sport*) putting the shot

'landa SF (*Geo*) moor

'languido, -a AG (*fiacco*) languid, weak; (*tenero, malinconico*) languishing

langu'ire /17/ VI to languish; (*conversazione*) to flag

langu'ore SM weakness, languor

lani'ero, -a AG wool *cpd*, woollen (BRIT), woolen (US)

lani'ficio [lani'fitʃo] SM woollen (BRIT) *o* woolen (US) mill

lano'lina SF lanolin(e)

la'noso, -a AG woolly

lan'terna SF lantern; (*faro*) lighthouse

lanter'nino SM: **cercarsele col ~** to be asking for trouble

la'nugine [la'nudʒine] SF down

'Laos SM Laos

lapalissi'ano, -a AG self-evident

La 'Paz [la'pas] SF La Paz

lapi'dare /72/ VT to stone

lapi'dario, -a AG (*fig*) terse

'lapide SF (*di sepolcro*) tombstone; (*commemorativa*) plaque

la'pin [la'pɛ̃] SM INV coney

'lapis SM INV pencil

'lappone AG, SMF, SM Lapp

Lap'ponia SF: **la ~** Lapland

'lapsus SM INV slip

'laptop ['læptɔp] SM INV laptop (computer)

'lardo SM bacon fat, lard

lar'ghezza [lar'gettsa] SF width; breadth; looseness; generosity; **~ di vedute** broad-mindedness

lar'gire [lar'dʒire] /55/ VT to give generously

'largo, -a, -ghi, -ghe AG wide; broad; (*maniche*) wide; (*abito: troppo ampio*) loose; (*fig*) generous ▶ SM width; breadth; (*mare aperto*): **il ~** the open sea ▶ SF: **stare** *o* **tenersi alla larga (da qn/qc)** to keep one's distance (from sb/sth), keep away (from sb/sth); **~ due metri** two metres wide; **~ di spalle** broad-shouldered; **di larghe vedute** broad-minded; **in larga misura** to a great *o* large extent; **su larga scala** on a large scale; **di manica larga** generous, open-handed; **al ~ di Genova** off (the coast of) Genoa; **farsi ~ tra la folla** to push one's way through the crowd

'larice ['laritʃe] SM (*Bot*) larch

la'ringe [la'rindʒe] SF larynx

larin'gite [larin'dʒite] SF laryngitis

laringoi'atra, -i, -e SM/F (*medico*) throat specialist

'larva SF larva; (*fig*) shadow

la'sagne [la'zaɲɲe] SFPL lasagna *sg*

lasciapas'sare [laʃʃapas'sare] SM INV pass, permit

lasci'are [laʃ'ʃare] /**14**/ VT to leave; (*abbandonare*) to leave, abandon, give up; (*cessare di tenere*) to let go of ▶ VB AUS: **~ qn fare qc** to let sb do sth ▶ VI: **~ di fare** (*smettere*) to stop doing ■ **lasciarsi** VPR (*persone*) to part; (*coppia*) to split up; **~ andare** o **correre** o **perdere** to let things go their own way; **~ stare qc/qn** to leave sth/sb alone; **~ qn erede** to make sb one's heir; **~ la presa** to lose one's grip; **~ il segno (su qc)** to leave a mark (on sth); (*fig*) to leave one's mark (on sth); **~ (molto) a desiderare** to leave much to be desired; **ci ha lasciato la vita** it cost him his life; **lasciarsi andare/truffare** to let o.s. go/ be cheated

'lascito ['laʃʃito] SM (*Dir*) legacy

la'scivia [laʃ'ʃivja] SF lust, lasciviousness

la'scivo, -a [laʃ'ʃivo] AG lascivious

'laser ['lazer] AG, SM INV: **(raggio) ~** laser (beam)

lassa'tivo, -a AG, SM laxative

las'sismo SM laxity

'lasso SM: **~ di tempo** interval, lapse of time

lassù AV up there

'lastra SF (*di pietra*) slab; (*di metallo, Fot*) plate; (*di ghiaccio, vetro*) sheet; (*radiografica*) X-ray (plate)

lastri'care /**20**/ VT to pave

lastri'cato SM paving

'lastrico (*pl* **lastrici** o **lastrichi**) SM paving; **essere sul ~** (*fig*) to be penniless; **gettare qn sul ~** (*fig*) to leave sb destitute

las'trone SM (*Alpinismo*) sheer rock face

la'tente AG latent

late'rale AG lateral, side *cpd*; (*uscita, ingresso ecc*) side *cpd* ▶ SM (*Calcio*) half-back

lateral'mente AV sideways

late'rizio [late'rittsjo] SM (*perforated*) brick

latifon'dista, -i, -e SM/F large agricultural landowner

lati'fondo SM large estate

la'tino, -a AG, SM Latin

la'tinoameri'cano, -a AG, SM/F Latin-American

lati'tante AG: **essere ~** to be on the run ▶ SMF fugitive (from justice)

lati'tanza [lati'tantsa] SF: **darsi alla ~** to go into hiding

lati'tudine SF latitude

'lato, -a AG (*fig*) wide, broad; **in senso ~** broadly speaking ▶ SM side; (*fig*) aspect, point of view; **d'altro ~** (*d'altra parte*) on the other hand

la'trare /**72**/ VI to bark

la'trato SM howling

la'trina SF public lavatory

latro'cinio [latro'tʃinjo] SM = **ladrocinio**

'latta SF tin (plate); (*recipiente*) tin, can

lat'taio, -a SM/F (*distributore*) milkman(-woman); (*commerciante*) dairyman(-woman)

lat'tante AG unweaned ▶ SMF breast-fed baby

'latte SM milk; **fratello di ~** foster brother; **avere ancora il ~ alla bocca** (*fig*) to be still wet behind the ears; **tutto ~ e miele** (*fig*) all smiles; **~ detergente** cleansing milk o lotion; **~ intero** full-cream milk; **~ a lunga conservazione** UHT milk, long-life milk; **~ magro** o **scremato** skimmed milk; **~ secco** o **in polvere** dried o powdered milk; **~ solare** suntan lotion

'latteo, -a AG milky; (*dieta, prodotto*) milk *cpd*

latte'ria SF dairy

latti'cini [latti'tʃini] SMPL dairy o milk products

lat'tina SF (*di birra ecc*) can

lat'tuga, -ghe SF lettuce

'laurea SF degree; **~ in ingegneria** engineering degree; **~ in lettere** ≈ arts degree; **~ breve** *university degree awarded at the end of a three-year course*; **avere una ~ in chimica** to have a degree in chemistry o a chemistry degree

The **laurea** (or the *laurea breve* or *triennale*) is awarded to students who successfully complete a three-year course of study. After the *laurea*, students can go on to take a *laurea magistrale*, which lasts another two years and involves writing a longer dissertation than that required for the *laurea breve*.

laure'ando, -a SM/F final-year student

laure'are /**72**/ VT to confer a degree on ■ **laurearsi** VPR to graduate

laure'ato, -a AG, SM/F graduate

'lauro SM laurel

'lauto, -a AG (*pranzo, mancia*) lavish; **lauti guadagni** handsome profits

'lava SF lava

lavabianche'ria [lavabjanke'ria] SF INV washing machine

la'vabo SM washbasin

la'vaggio [la'vaddʒo] SM washing *no pl*; **~ del cervello** brainwashing *no pl*; **~ a secco** dry-cleaning

la'vagna [la'vaɲɲa] SF (*Geo*) slate; (*di scuola*) blackboard; **~ interattiva** interactive whiteboard; **~ luminosa** overhead projector

la'vanda SF (*anche Med*) wash; (*Bot*) lavender; **fare una ~ gastrica a qn** to pump sb's stomach

lavan'daia SF washerwoman

lavande'ria SF (*di ospedale, caserma ecc*) laundry; ~ **automatica** launderette; ~ **a secco** dry-cleaner's

lavan'dino SM (*del bagno*) washbasin

lavapi'atti SF INV (*machine*) dishwasher ▶ SM O F INV (*persona*) dishwasher

la'vare /72/ VT to wash ■ **lavarsi** VPR to wash, have a wash; ~ **a secco** to dry-clean; ~ **i panni sporchi in pubblico** (*fig*) to wash one's dirty linen in public; **lavarsi le mani/i denti** to wash one's hands/clean one's teeth

lava'secco SM O F INV dry-cleaner's

lavasto'viglie [lavasto'viʎʎe] SM O F INV (*macchina*) dishwasher

la'vata SF wash; (*fig*): **dare una ~ di capo a qn** to give sb a good telling-off

lava'tivo, -a SM/F (*buono a nulla*) good-for-nothing, idler

lava'toio SM (*public*) washhouse

lava'trice [lava'tritʃe] SF washing machine

lava'tura SF washing *no pl*; ~ **di piatti** dishwater

la'vello SM (*kitchen*) sink

la'vina SF snowslide

lavo'rante SMF worker

lavo'rare /72/ VI to work; (*fig: bar, studio ecc*) to do good business ▶ VT to work; ~ **a** to work on; ~ **a maglia** to knit; ~ **di fantasia** (*suggestionarsi*) to imagine things; (*fantasticare*) to let one's imagination run free; **lavorarsi qn** (*fig: convincere*) to work on sb

lavora'tivo, -a AG working

lavora'tore, -'trice SM/F worker ▶ AG working

lavorazi'one [lavorat'tsjone] SF (*gen*) working; (*di legno, pietra*) carving; (*di film*) making; (*di prodotto*) manufacture; (*modo di esecuzione*) workmanship

lavo'rio SM intense activity

la'voro SM work; (*occupazione*) job, work *no pl*; (*opera*) piece of work, job; (*Econ*) labour (BRIT), labor (US); **che ~ fa?** what do you do?; **Ministero del L~** Department of Employment (BRIT), Department of Labor (US); **(fare) i lavori di casa** (to do) the housework *sg*; **lavori forzati** hard labour *sg*; **i lavori del parlamento** the parliamentary session *sg*; **lavori pubblici** public works; ~ **interinale** o **in affitto** temporary work

lazi'ale [lat'tsjale] AG of (o from) Lazio

lazza'retto [laddza'retto] SM leper hospital

lazza'rone, -a [laddza'rone] SM/F scoundrel

'lazzo [ˈladdzo] SM jest

LC SIGLA = **Lecco**

LE SIGLA = **Lecce**

le DET FPL the ▶ PRON (*oggetto*) them; (*a lei, a essa*) (to) her; (*forma di cortesia*) (to) you; *vedi anche* **il**

le'ale AG loyal; (*sincero*) sincere; (*onesto*) fair

lea'lista, -i, -e SM/F loyalist

leal'tà SF loyalty; sincerity; fairness

'leasing [ˈliːziŋ] SM leasing; lease

'lebbra SF leprosy

'lecca 'lecca SM INV lollipop

leccapi'edi SMF (*peg*) toady, bootlicker

lec'care /20/ VT to lick; (*gatto, latte ecc*) to lick o lap up; (*fig*) to flatter ■ **leccarsi** VPR (*fig*) to preen o.s.; **leccarsi i baffi** to lick one's lips

lec'cato, -a AG affected ▶ SF lick

leccherò *ecc* [lekke'rɔ] VB *vedi* **leccare**

'leccio [ˈlettʃo] SM holm oak, ilex

leccor'nia SF titbit, delicacy

'lecito, -a [ˈlɛtʃito] AG permitted, allowed; **se mi è ~** if I may; **mi sia ~ far presente che ...** may I point out that ...

'ledere /81/ VT to damage, injure; ~ **gli interessi di qn** to be prejudicial to sb's interests

'lega, -ghe SF (*anche Pol*) league; (*di metalli*) alloy; **metallo di bassa ~** base metal; **gente di bassa ~** common o vulgar people; **L~ Nord** (*Pol*) federalist party

le'gaccio [le'gattʃo] SM string, lace

le'gale AG legal ▶ SMF lawyer; **corso ~ delle monete** official exchange rate; **medicina ~** forensic medicine; **studio ~** lawyer's office

legali'tà SF legality, lawfulness

legaliz'zare [legalid'dzare] /72/ VT to legalize; (*documento*) to authenticate

legalizzazi'one [legaliddzat'tsjone] SF (*vedi vt*) legalization; authentication

le'game SM (*corda, fig: affettivo*) tie, bond; (*nesso logico*) link, connection; ~ **di sangue** o **di parentela** family tie

lega'mento SM (*Anat*) ligament

le'gare /80/ VT (*prigioniero, capelli, cane*) to tie (up); (*libro*) to bind; (*Chim*) to alloy; (*fig: collegare*) to bind, join ▶ VI (*far lega*) to unite; (*fig*) to get on well; **è pazzo da ~** (*col*) he should be locked up

lega'tario, -a SM/F (*Dir*) legatee

le'gato SM (*Rel*) legate; (*Dir*) legacy, bequest

legato'ria SF (*attività*) bookbinding; (*negozio*) bookbinder's

lega'tura SF (*di libro*) binding; (*Mus*) ligature

legazi'one [legat'tsjone] SF legation

le'genda [le'dʒɛnda] SF (*di carta geografica ecc*) = **leggenda**

'legge [ˈleddʒe] SF law; ~ **procedurale** procedural law

leg'genda [led'dʒɛnda] SF (*narrazione*) legend; (*di carta geografica ecc*) key, legend

leggen'dario, -a [leddʒen'darjo] AG legendary

'leggere [ˈlɛddʒere] /61/ VT, VI to read; ~ **il pensiero di qn** to read sb's mind o thoughts

legge'rezza [leddʒe'rettsa] SF lightness; thoughtlessness; fickleness

leg'gero, -a [led'dʒero] AG light; (*agile, snello*)

I

199

nimble, agile, light; (*tè, caffè*) weak; (*fig: non grave, piccolo*) slight; (: *spensierato*) thoughtless; (: *incostante*) fickle; free and easy; **una ragazza leggera** (*fig*) a flighty girl; **alla leggera** thoughtlessly

leggi'adro, -a [led'dʒadro] AG pretty, lovely; (*movimenti*) graceful

leg'gibile [led'dʒibile] AG legible; (*libro*) readable, worth reading

leg'gio, -'gii [led'dʒio] SM lectern; (*Mus*) music stand

legherò *ecc* [lege'rɔ] VB *vedi* **legare**

le'ghismo [le'gismo] SM *political movement with federalist tendencies*

le'ghista, -i, -e [le'gista] AG (*Pol*) of a "lega" (*especially Lega Nord*) ▶ SM/F member (*o* supporter) of a "lega" (*especially Lega Nord*)

legife'rare [ledʒife'rare] /**72**/ VI to legislate

legio'nario [ledʒo'narjo] SM (*romano*) legionary; (*volontario*) legionnaire

legi'one [le'dʒone] SF legion; **~ straniera** foreign legion

legisla'tivo, -a [ledʒizla'tivo] AG legislative

legisla'tore [ledʒizla'tore] SM legislator

legisla'tura [ledʒizla'tura] SF legislature

legislazi'one [ledʒizlat'tsjone] SF legislation

legitti'mare [ledʒitti'mare] /**72**/ VT (*figlio*) to legitimize; (*comportamento ecc*) to justify

legittimità [ledʒittimi'ta] SF legitimacy

le'gittimo, -a [le'dʒittimo] AG legitimate; (*fig: giustificato, lecito*) justified, legitimate; **legittima difesa** (*Dir*) self-defence (BRIT), self-defense (US)

'legna ['leɲɲa] SF firewood

le'gnaia [leɲ'ɲaja] SF woodshed

legnai'olo [leɲɲa'jɔlo] SM woodcutter

le'gname [leɲ'ɲame] SM wood, timber

le'gnata [leɲ'ɲata] SF blow with a stick; **dare a qn un sacco di legnate** to give sb a good hiding

'legno ['leɲɲo] SM wood; (*pezzo di legno*) piece of wood; **di ~** wooden; **~ compensato** plywood

le'gnoso, -a [leɲ'ɲoso] AG (*di legno*) wooden; (*come il legno*) woody; (*carne*) tough

le'gume SM (*Bot*) pulse ▪ **legumi** SMPL (*fagioli, piselli ecc*) pulses

'lei PRON (*soggetto*) she; (*oggetto: per dare rilievo, con preposizione*) her; (*forma di cortesia: anche:* **Lei**) you ▶ SF INV: **la mia ~** my beloved ▶ SM: **dare del ~ a qn** to address sb as "lei"; **~ stessa** she herself; you yourself; **è ~** it's her

> **lei** is the third person singular pronoun. It is used in Italian to address an adult whom you do not know or with whom you are on formal terms.

'lembo SM (*di abito, strada*) edge; (*striscia sottile: di terra*) strip

'lemma, -i SM headword

'lemme 'lemme AV (*very*) very slowly

'lena SF (*fig*) energy, stamina; **di buona ~** (*lavorare, camminare*) at a good pace

Lenin'grado SF Leningrad

le'nire /**55**/ VT to soothe

lenta'mente AV slowly

'lente SF (*Ottica*) lens *sg*; **~ d'ingrandimento** magnifying glass ▪ **lenti** SFPL (*occhiali*) lenses; **lenti a contatto, lenti corneali** contact lenses; **lenti (a contatto) morbide/rigide** soft/hard contact lenses

len'tezza [len'tettsa] SF slowness

len'ticchia [len'tikkja] SF (*Bot*) lentil

len'tiggine [len'tiddʒine] SF freckle

'lento, -a AG slow; (*molle: fune*) slack; (*non stretto: vite, abito*) loose ▶ SM (*ballo*) slow dance

'lenza ['lɛntsa] SF fishing line

lenzu'olo [len'tswɔlo] SM sheet ▪ **lenzuola** SFPL pair of sheets; **~ funebre** shroud

leon'cino [leon'tʃino] SM lion cub

le'one SM lion; **L~** Leo; **essere del L~** to be Leo

leo'pardo SM leopard

lepo'rino, -a AG: **labbro ~** harelip

'lepre SF hare

'lercio, -a, -ci, -ce ['lɛrtʃo] AG filthy

lerci'ume [ler'tʃume] SM filth

'lesbico, -a, -ci, -che AG, SF lesbian

'lesi *ecc* VB *vedi* **ledere**

lesi'nare /**72**/ VT to be stingy with ▶ VI: **~ (su)** to skimp (on), be stingy (with)

lesi'one SF (*Med*) lesion; (*Dir*) injury, damage; (*Edil*) crack

le'sivo, -a AG: **~ (di)** damaging (to), detrimental (to)

'leso, -a PP *di* **ledere** ▶ AG (*offeso*) injured; **parte lesa** (*Dir*) injured party; **lesa maestà** lese-majesty

Le'sotho [le'soto] SM Lesotho

les'sare /**72**/ VT (*Cuc*) to boil

'lessi *ecc* VB *vedi* **leggere**

lessi'cale AG lexical

'lessico, -ci SM vocabulary; (*dizionario*) lexicon

lessicogra'fia SF lexicography

lessi'cografo, -a SM/F lexicographer

'lesso, -a AG boiled ▶ SM boiled meat

'lesto, -a AG quick; (*agile*) nimble; **~ di mano** (*per rubare*) light-fingered; (*per picchiare*) free with one's fists

lesto'fante SM swindler, con man

le'tale AG lethal; fatal

leta'maio SM dunghill

le'tame SM manure, dung

le'targo, -ghi SM lethargy; (*Zool*) hibernation

le'tizia [le'tittsja] SF joy, happiness

'letta SF: **dare una ~ a qc** to glance o look through sth

'lettera SF letter ▪ **lettere** SFPL (*letteratura*) literature *sg*; (*studi umanistici*) arts (subjects); **alla ~** literally; **in lettere** in words, in full; **diventar ~ morta** (*legge*) to become a dead letter; **restar ~ morta** (*consiglio, invito*) to go unheeded; **~ di accompagnamento** accompanying letter; **~ assicurata** registered letter; **~ di cambio** (*Comm*) bill of exchange; **~ di credito** (*Comm*) letter of credit; **~ di intenti** letter of intent; **~ di presentazione** o **raccomandazione** letter of introduction; **~ raccomandata** recorded delivery (*BRIT*) o certified (*US*) letter; **~ di trasporto aereo** (*Comm*) air waybill

lette'rale AG literal

letteral'mente AV literally

lette'rario, -a AG literary

lette'rato, -a AG well-read, scholarly

lettera'tura SF literature

let'tiga, -ghe SF (*portantina*) litter; (*barella*) stretcher

let'tino SM cot (*BRIT*), crib (*US*); (*per il sole*) sun lounger; **~ solare** sunbed

'letto, -a PP *di* **leggere** ▶ SM bed; **andare a ~** to go to bed; **~ a castello** bunk beds *pl*; **~ a una piazza/a due piazze** o **matrimoniale** single/ double bed

'lettone AG, SMF Latvian ▶ SM (*Ling*) Latvian, Lettish

Let'tonia SF: **la ~** Latvia

letto'rato SM (*Ins*) lectorship, assistantship; (*Rel*) lectorate

let'tore, -'trice SM/F reader; (*Ins*) (foreign language) assistant (*BRIT*), (foreign) teaching assistant (*US*) ▶ SM (*Tecn*): **~ di libri digitali** e-reader; **~ ottico (di caratteri)** optical character reader; **~ CD/DVD** CD/DVD player; **~ MP3/ MP4** MP3/MP4 player

let'tura SF reading

leuce'mia [leutʃe'mia] SF leukaemia

'leva SF lever; (*Mil*) conscription; **far ~ su qn** to work on sb; **essere di ~** to be due for call-up; **~ del cambio** (*Aut*) gear lever

le'vante SM east; (*vento*) East wind; **il L~** the Levant

le'vare /72/ VT (*occhi, braccio*) to raise; (*sollevare, togliere: tassa, divieto*) to lift; (: *indumenti*) to take off, remove; (*rimuovere*) to take away; (: *dal di sopra*) to take off; (: *dal di dentro*) to take out ▪ **levarsi** VPR to get up; (*sole*) to rise; **~ le tende** (*fig*) to pack up and leave; **levarsi il pensiero** to put one's mind at rest; **levati di mezzo** o **di lì** o **di torno!** get out of my way!

le'vata SF (*di posta*) collection

leva'taccia, -ce [leva'tattʃa] SF early rise

leva'toio, -a AG: **ponte ~** drawbridge

leva'trice [leva'tritʃe] SF midwife

leva'tura SF intelligence, mental capacity

levi'gare /80/ VT to smooth; (*con carta vetrata*) to sand

levi'gato, -a AG (*superficie*) smooth; (*fig: stile*) polished; (: *viso*) flawless

levità SF lightness

levri'ere SM greyhound

lezi'one [let'tsjone] SF lesson; (*all'università, sgridata*) lecture; **fare ~** to teach; to lecture; **dare una ~ a qn** to teach sb a lesson; **lezioni private** private lessons

lezi'oso, -a [let'tsjoso] AG affected; simpering

'lezzo ['leddzo] SM stench, stink

LI SIGLA = **Livorno**

li PRON PL (*oggetto*) them

lì AV there; **di** o **da lì** from there; **per di lì** that way; **di lì a pochi giorni** a few days later; **lì per lì** there and then; at first; **essere lì (lì) per fare** to be on the point of doing, be about to do; **lì dentro** in there; **lì sotto** under there; **lì sopra** on there; up there; **tutto lì** that's all; *vedi anche* **quello**

libagi'one [liba'dʒone] SF libation

liba'nese AG, SMF Lebanese *inv*

Li'bano SM: **il ~** the Lebanon

'libbra SF (*peso*) pound

li'beccio [li'bettʃo] SM south-west wind

li'bello SM libel

li'bellula SF dragonfly

libe'rale AG, SMF liberal

liberaliz'zare [liberalid'dzare] /72/ VT to liberalize

libe'rare /72/ VT (*rendere libero: prigioniero*) to release; (: *popolo*) to free, liberate; (*sgombrare: passaggio*) to clear; (: *stanza*) to vacate; (*produrre: energia*) to release ▪ **liberarsi** VPR: **liberarsi di qc/qn** to get rid of sth/sb

libera'tore, -'trice AG liberating ▶ SM/F liberator

liberazi'one [liberat'tsjone] SF (*di prigioniero*) release, freeing; (*di popolo*) liberation; rescuing; **che ~!** what a relief!; **la L~** *see note*

The **Liberazione** is a national holiday which falls on 25 April. It commemorates the liberation of Italy in 1945 from German forces and Mussolini's government and marks the end of the war on Italian soil.

li'bercolo SM (*peg*) worthless book

Li'beria SF: **la ~** Liberia

liberi'ano, -a AG, SM/F Liberian

libe'rismo SM (*Econ*) laissez-faire

'libero, -a AG free; (*strada*) clear; (*non occupato: posto ecc*) vacant; free; not taken; empty; (: *Tel*) not engaged; **~ di fare qc** free to do sth; **~ da** free from; **una donna di liberi costumi** a woman of loose morals; **avere via libera** to have a free hand; **dare via libera a qn** to give sb the go-ahead; **via libera!** all clear!; **~ arbitrio** free will; **~ professionista** self-employed professional person; **~ scambio** free trade; **libera uscita** (*Mil*) leave

liberoscam'bismo SM (*Econ*) free trade

libertà SF INV freedom; (*tempo disponibile*) free time ▶ SFPL (*licenza*) liberties; **essere in ~ provvisoria/vigilata** to be released without bail/be on probation; **~ di riunione** right to hold meetings

liber'tario, -a AG libertarian

liber'tino, -a AG, SM/F libertine

'liberty ['liberti] AG INV, SM art nouveau

'Libia SF: **la ~** Libya

'libico, -a, -ci, -che AG, SM/F Libyan

li'bidine SF lust

libidi'noso, -a AG lustful, libidinous

li'bido SF libido

li'braio, -a SM/F bookseller

li'brario, -a AG book *cpd*

li'brarsi /72/ VPR to hover

libre'ria SF (*bottega*) bookshop; (*stanza*) library; (*mobile*) bookcase

---

Do not translate the Italian word **libreria** by (*public*) library.

---

li'bretto SM booklet; (*taccuino*) notebook; (*Mus*) libretto; **~ degli assegni** chequebook (*Brit*), checkbook (*US*); **~ di circolazione** (*Aut*) logbook; **~ di deposito** (bank) deposit book; **~ di risparmio** (savings) bankbook, passbook; **~ universitario** student's report book

'libro SM book; **~ bianco** (*Pol*) white paper; **~ di cassa** cash book; **~ di consultazione** reference book; **~ mastro** ledger; **~ paga** payroll; **~ tascabile** paperback; **~ di testo** textbook; **libri contabili** (account) books; **libri sociali** company records

li'cantropo SM werewolf

lice'ale [litʃe'ale] AG secondary school *cpd* (*Brit*), high school *cpd* (*US*) ▶ SMF secondary school *o* high school pupil

li'cenza [li'tʃɛntsa] SF (*permesso*) permission, leave; (*di pesca, caccia, circolazione*) permit, licence (*Brit*), license (*US*); (*Mil*) leave; (*Ins*) school-leaving certificate; (*libertà*) liberty; licence; (*sfrenatezza*) licentiousness; **andare in ~** (*Mil*) to go on leave; **su ~ di ...** (*Comm*) under licence from ...; **~ di esportazione** export licence; **~ di fabbricazione** manufacturer's licence; **~ poetica** poetic licence

licenzia'mento [litʃentsja'mento] SM dismissal

licenzi'are [litʃen'tsjare] /19/ VT (*impiegato*) to dismiss; (*Comm: per eccesso di personale*) to make redundant; (*Ins*) to award a certificate to ■ **licenziarsi** VPR (*impiegato*) to resign, hand in one's notice; (*Ins*) to obtain one's school-leaving certificate

licenziosità [litʃentsjosi'ta] SF licentiousness

licenzi'oso, -a [litʃen'tsjoso] AG licentious

li'ceo [li'tʃɛo] SM (*Ins*) secondary (*Brit*) *o* high (*US*) school (*for 14- to 19-year-olds*); **~ classico/ scientifico** secondary or high school specializing in classics/scientific subjects

---

After *scuola secondaria di primo grado* (from ages 11–14), Italian children go either to a technical or vocational school or to a **liceo**, which they attend for five years and which prepares them for a university course. There are various types of *liceo*, with curriculums specializing in science, literature, languages, art, etc.

---

li'chene [li'kɛne] SM (*Bot*) lichen

'lido SM beach, shore

'Liechtenstein ['liktənstain] SM: **il ~** Liechtenstein

li'eto, -a AG happy, glad; **"molto ~"** (*nelle presentazioni*) "pleased to meet you"; **a ~ fine** with a happy ending

li'eve AG light; (*di poco conto*) slight; (*sommesso: voce*) faint, soft

lievi'tare /72/ VI (*anche fig*) to rise ▶ VT to leaven

li'evito SM yeast; **~ di birra** brewer's yeast

'ligio, -a, -gi, -gie ['lidʒo] AG faithful, loyal

li'gnaggio [liɲ'naddʒo] SM descent, lineage

'ligure AG Ligurian; **la Riviera L~** the Italian Riviera

Li'kud [li'kud] SM Likud

'lilla, lillà SM INV lilac

'Lima SF Lima

'lima SF file; **~ da unghie** nail file

limacci'oso, -a [limat'tʃoso] AG slimy; muddy

li'mare /72/ VT to file (down); (*fig*) to polish

'limbo SM (*Rel*) limbo

li'metta SF nail file

limi'tare /72/ VT to limit, restrict; (*circoscrivere*) to bound, surround ■ **limitarsi** VPR: **limitarsi nel mangiare** to limit one's eating; **limitarsi a qc/a fare qc** to limit o.s. to sth/to doing sth

limitata'mente AV to a limited extent; **~ alle mie possibilità** in so far as I am able

limi'tato, -a AG limited, restricted

limitazi'one [limitat'tsjone] SF limitation, restriction

'limite SM limit; (*confine*) border, boundary ▶ AG INV: **caso ~** extreme case; **al ~** if the worst comes to the worst (*Brit*), if worst comes to worst (*US*); **~ di velocità** speed limit

---

The *limite di velocità* (speed limit) in Italy is 50 km/h in towns and cities, 90 km/h on secondary roads not in built-up areas, 110 km/h on secondary and major roads, and usually 130 km/h on motorways.

---

li'mitrofo, -a AG neighbouring (BRIT), neighboring (US)

'limo SM mud, slime; (Geo) silt

limo'nata SF lemonade (BRIT), (lemon) soda (US); (spremuta) lemon squash (BRIT), lemonade (US)

li'mone SM (pianta) lemon tree; (frutto) lemon

limpi'dezza [limpi'dettsa] SF clearness; (di discorso) clarity

'limpido, -a AG (acqua) limpid, clear; (cielo) clear; (fig: discorso) clear, lucid

'lince ['lintʃe] SF lynx

linci'aggio [lin'tʃaddʒo] SM lynching

linci'are [lin'tʃare] /14/ VT to lynch

'lindo, -a AG tidy, spick and span; (biancheria) clean

'linea SF (gen) line; (di mezzi pubblici di trasporto: itinerario) route; (: servizio) service; (di prodotto: collezione) collection; (: stile) style; **a grandi linee** in outline; **mantenere la ~** to look after one's figure; **è caduta la ~** (Tel) I (o you etc) have been cut off; **di ~:** **aereo di ~** airliner; **nave di ~** liner; **volo di ~** scheduled flight; **in ~ diretta da** (TV, Radio) coming to you direct from; **~ aerea** airline; **~ continua** solid line; **~ di partenza/d'arrivo** (Sport) starting/finishing line; **~ punteggiata** dotted line; **~ di tiro** line of fire

linea'menti SMPL features; (fig) outlines

line'are AG linear; (fig) coherent, logical

line'etta SF (trattino) dash; (d'unione) hyphen

'linfa SF (Bot) sap; (Anat) lymph; **~ vitale** (fig) lifeblood

lin'gotto SM ingot, bar

'lingua SF (Anat, Cuc) tongue; (idioma) language; **mostrare la ~** to stick out one's tongue; **di ~ italiana** Italian-speaking; **~ madre** mother tongue; **una ~ di terra** a spit of land

lingu'accia [lin'gwattʃa] SF (fig) spiteful gossip

linguacci'uto, -a [lingwat'tʃuto] AG gossipy

lingu'aggio [lin'gwaddʒo] SM language; **~ giuridico** legal language; **~ macchina** (Inform) machine language; **~ di programmazione** (Inform) programming language

lingu'etta SF (di strumento) reed; (di scarpa, Tecn) tongue; (di busta) flap

lingu'ista, -i, -e SM/F linguist

lingu'istico, -a, -ci, -che AG linguistic ▶ SF linguistics sg

lini'mento SM liniment

lin'kare VT to link; **~ qc con** to link sth to

'lino SM (pianta) flax; (tessuto) linen

li'noleum SM INV linoleum, lino

liofiliz'zare [liofilid'dzare] /72/ VT to freeze-dry

liofiliz'zati [liofilid'dzati] SMPL freeze-dried foods

Li'one SF Lyons

liposuzi'one [liposut'tsjone] SF liposuction

'LIPU SIGLA F (= Lega Italiana Protezione Uccelli) society for the protection of birds

liqu'ame SM liquid sewage

lique'fare /41/ VT (render liquido) to liquefy; (fondere) to melt ■ **liquefarsi** VPR to liquefy; to melt

lique'fatto, -a PP di **liquefare**

liqui'dare /72/ VT (società, beni, persona: uccidere) to liquidate; (persona: sbarazzarsene) to get rid of; (conto, problema) to settle; (Comm: merce) to sell off, clear

liquidazi'one [likwidat'tsjone] SF (di società, persona) liquidation; (di conto) settlement; (di problema) settling; (Comm: di merce) clearance sale; (Amm) severance pay (on retirement, redundancy, or when taking up other employment)

liquidità SF liquidity

'liquido, -a AG, SM liquid; **denaro ~** cash, ready money; **~ per freni** brake fluid

liqui'gas® SM INV Calor gas® (BRIT), butane

liqui'rizia [likwi'rittsja] SF liquorice

li'quore SM liqueur

liquo'roso, -a AG: **vino ~** dessert wine

'lira SF (unità monetaria) lira; (Mus) lyre; **~ sterlina** pound sterling

'lirico, -a, -ci, -che AG lyric(al); (Mus) lyric ▶ SF (poesia) lyric poetry; (componimento poetico) lyric; (Mus) opera; **cantante/teatro ~** opera singer/house

li'rismo SM lyricism

Lis'bona SF Lisbon

'lisca, -sche SF (di pesce) fishbone

lisci'are [liʃ'ʃare] /14/ VT to smooth; (fig) to flatter; **lisciarsi i capelli** to straighten one's hair

'liscio, -a, -sci, -sce ['liʃʃo] AG smooth; (capelli) straight; (mobile) plain; (bevanda alcolica) neat; (fig) straightforward, simple ▶ AV: **andare ~** to go smoothly; **passarla liscia** to get away with it

'liso, -a AG worn out, threadbare

'lista SF (striscia) strip; (elenco) list; **~ elettorale** electoral roll; **~ della spesa** shopping list; **~ dei vini** wine list; **~ delle vivande** menu

lis'tare /72/ VT: **~ (di)** to edge (with), border (with)

lis'tato SM (Inform) list, listing

lis'tino SM list; **~ di borsa** the Stock Exchange list; **~ dei cambi** (foreign) exchange rate; **~ dei prezzi** price list

lita'nia SF litany

'lite SF quarrel, argument; (Dir) lawsuit

liti'gare /80/ VI to quarrel; (Dir) to litigate

li'tigio [li'tidʒo] SM quarrel

litigi'oso, -a [liti'dʒoso] AG quarrelsome; (Dir) litigious

litogra'fia SF (sistema) lithography; (stampa) lithograph

lito'grafico, -a, -ci, -che AG lithographic

lito'rale AG coastal, coast *cpd* ▶ SM coast

lito'raneo, -a AG coastal

'litro SM litre (*BRIT*), liter (*US*)

lit'torio, -a AG (*Storia*) lictorial; **fascio ~** fasces *pl*

Litu'ania SF: **la ~** Lithuania

litu'ano, -a AG, SM/F, SM Lithuanian

litur'gia, -'gie [litur'dʒia] SF liturgy

li'uto SM lute

li'vella SF level; **~ a bolla d'aria** spirit level

livel'lare /72/ VT to level, make level ■ **livellarsi** VPR to become level; (*fig*) to level out, balance out

livella'trice [livella'tritʃe] SF steamroller

li'vello SM level; (*fig*) level, standard; **ad alto ~** (*fig*) high-level; **a ~ mondiale** world-wide; **a ~ di confidenza** confidentially; **~ di magazzino** stock level; **~ del mare** sea level; **sul ~ del mare** above sea level; **~ occupazionale** level of employment; **~ retributivo** salary level

'livido, -a AG livid; (*per percosse*) bruised, black and blue; (*cielo*) leaden ▶ SM bruise

li'vore SM malice, spite

Li'vorno SF Livorno, Leghorn

li'vrea SF livery

'lizza ['littsa] SF lists *pl*; **essere in ~ per** (*fig*) to compete for; **scendere in ~** (*anche fig*) to enter the lists

LO SIGLA = **Lodi**

lo DET M (*dav s impura, gn, pn, ps, x, z; dav V* **l'**) the ▶ PRON (*dav V* **l'**: *oggetto: persona*) him; (: *cosa*) it; **lo sapevo** I knew it; **lo so** I know; **sii buono, anche se lui non lo è** be good, even if he isn't; *vedi anche* **il**

lob'bista, -i, -e SM/F lobbyist

'lobby SF INV lobby

'lobo SM lobe; **~ dell'orecchio** ear lobe

lo'cale AG local ▶ SM room; (*luogo pubblico*) premises *pl*; **~ notturno** nightclub

località SF INV locality

localiz'zare [lokalid'dzare] /72/ VT (*circoscrivere*) to confine, localize; (*accertare*) to locate, place

lo'canda SF inn

locandi'ere, -a SM/F innkeeper

locan'dina SF (*Teat*) poster

lo'care /20/ VT (*casa*) to rent out, let; (*macchina*) to hire out (*BRIT*), rent (out)

loca'tario, -a SM/F tenant

loca'tivo, -a AG (*Dir*) rentable

loca'tore, -'trice SM/F landlord (lady)

locazi'one [lokat'tsjone] SF (*da parte del locatario*) renting *no pl*; (*da parte del locatore*) renting out *no pl*, letting *no pl*; (*contratto di*) **~** lease; (*canone di*) **~** rent; **dare in ~** to rent out, let

locomo'tiva SF locomotive

locomo'tore SM electric locomotive

locomot'rice [lokomo'tritʃe] SF = **locomotore**

locomozi'one [lokomot'tsjone] SF locomotion; **mezzi di ~** vehicles, means of transport

'loculo SM burial recess

lo'custa SF locust

locuzi'one [lokut'tsjone] SF phrase, expression

lo'dare /72/ VT to praise

'lode SF praise; (*Ins*): **laurearsi con 110 e ~** to graduate with first-class honours (*BRIT*), ≈ to graduate summa cum laude (*US*)

'loden SM INV (*stoffa*) loden; (*cappotto*) loden overcoat

lo'devole AG praiseworthy

loga'ritmo SM logarithm

log'garsi /72/ VPR (*Inform*) to log in

'loggia, -ge ['lɔddʒa] SF (*Archit*) loggia; (*circolo massonico*) lodge

loggi'one [lod'dʒone] SM (*di teatro*): **il ~** the Gods *sg*

logica'mente [lodʒika'mente] AV naturally, obviously

logicità [lodʒitʃi'ta] SF logicality

'logico, -a, -ci, -che ['lɔdʒiko] AG logical ▶ SF logic

lo'gistica [lo'dʒistika] SF logistics *sg*

'logo SM INV logo

logora'mento SM (*di vestiti ecc*) wear

logo'rante AG exhausting

logo'rare /72/ VT to wear out; (*sciupare*) to waste ■ **logorarsi** VPR to wear out; (*fig*) to wear o.s. out

logo'rio SM wear and tear; (*fig*) strain

'logoro, -a AG (*stoffa*) worn out, threadbare; (*persona*) worn out

'Loira SF: **la ~** the Loire

lom'baggine [lom'baddʒine] SF lumbago

Lombar'dia SF: **la ~** Lombardy

lom'bardo, -a AG, SM/F Lombard

lom'bare AG (*Anat, Med*) lumbar

lom'bata SF (*taglio di carne*) loin

'lombo SM (*Anat*) loin

lom'brico, -chi SM earthworm

londi'nese AG London *cpd* ▶ SMF Londoner

'Londra SF London

lon'ganime AG forbearing

longevità [londʒevi'ta] SF longevity

lon'gevo, -a [lon'dʒevo] AG long-lived

longi'lineo, -a [londʒi'lineo] AG long-limbed

longi'tudine [londʒi'tudine] SF longitude

lontana'mente AV remotely; **non ci pensavo neppure ~** it didn't even occur to me

lonta'nanza [lonta'nantsa] SF distance; absence

lon'tano, -a AG (*distante*) distant, faraway;

(*assente*) absent; (*vago: sospetto*) slight, remote; (*tempo: remoto*) far-off, distant; (*parente*) distant, remote ▶ AV far; **è lontana la casa?** is it far to the house?, is the house far from here?; **è ~ un chilometro** it's a kilometre away *o* a kilometre from here; **più ~** farther; **da** *o* **di ~** from a distance; **~ da** a long way from; **è molto ~ da qui?** is it far from here?; **alla lontana** slightly, vaguely

'lontra SF otter

lo'quace [lo'kwatʃe] AG talkative, loquacious; (*fig: gesto ecc*) eloquent

loquacità [lokwatʃi'ta] SF talkativeness, loquacity

'lordo, -a AG dirty, filthy; (*peso, stipendio*) gross; **~ d'imposta** pre-tax

Lo'rena SF (*Geo*) Lorraine

'loro PRON PL (*oggetto, con preposizione*) them; (*complemento di termine*) to them; (*soggetto*) they; (*forma di cortesia: anche:* **Loro**) you; to you; **il (la) ~**, **i (le) ~** det their; (*forma di cortesia: anche:* **Loro**) your ▶ PRON theirs; (*forma di cortesia: anche:* **Loro**) yours ▶ SM INV: **il ~** their (*o* your) money ▶ SF INV: **la ~** (*opinione*) their (*o* your) view; **i ~** (*famiglia*) their (*o* your) family; (*amici ecc*) their (*o* your) own people; **un ~ amico** a friend of theirs; **è dalla ~** he's on their (*o* your) side; **ne hanno fatto un'altra delle ~** they've (*o* you've) done it again; **~ stessi(e)** they themselves; you yourselves

lo'sanga, -ghe SF diamond, lozenge

Lo'sanna SF Lausanne

'losco, -a, -schi, -sche AG (*fig*) shady, suspicious

'lotta SF struggle, fight; (*Sport*) wrestling; **essere in ~ (con)** to be in conflict (with); **fare la ~ (con)** to wrestle (with); **~ armata** armed struggle; **~ di classe** (*Pol*) class struggle; **~ libera** (*Sport*) all-in wrestling (BRIT), freestyle

lot'tare /**72**/ VI to fight, struggle; to wrestle

lotta'tore, -'trice SM/F wrestler

lotte'ria SF lottery; (*di gara ippica*) sweepstake

lottiz'zare [lottid'dzare] /**72**/ VT to divide into plots; (*fig*) to share out

lottizzazi'one [lottiddzat'tsjone] SF division into plots; (*fig*) share-out

'lotto SM (*gioco*) (state) lottery; (*parte*) lot; (*Edil*) site; **vincere un terno al ~** (*anche fig*) to hit the jackpot

The **Lotto** is an official lottery run by the Italian Finance Ministry. It consists of three draws each week and is very popular.

lozi'one [lot'tsjone] SF lotion

LT SIGLA = **Latina**

LU SIGLA = **Lucca**

lubrifi'cante SM lubricant

lubrifi'care /**20**/ VT to lubricate

lu'cano, -a AG of (*o* from) Lucania

luc'chetto [luk'ketto] SM padlock

lucci'care [luttʃi'kare] /**20**/ VI to sparkle; (*oro*) to glitter; (*stella*) to twinkle; (*occhi*) to glisten

lucci'chio [luttʃi'kio] SM sparkling; glittering; twinkling; glistening

lucci'cone [luttʃi'kone] SM: **avere i lucciconi agli occhi** to have tears in one's eyes

'luccio ['luttʃo] SM (*Zool*) pike

'lucciola ['luttʃola] SF (*Zool*) firefly; glow-worm; (*col: fig: prostituta*) girl (*o* woman) on the game

'luce ['lutʃe] SF light; (*finestra*) window; **alla ~ di** by the light of; **fare qc alla ~ del sole** (*fig*) to do sth in the open; **dare alla ~** (*bambino*) to give birth to; **fare ~ su qc** (*fig*) to shed *o* throw light on sth; **~ del sole/della luna** sun/moonlight

lu'cente [lu'tʃente] AG shining

lucen'tezza [lutʃen'tettsa] SF shine

lu'cerna [lu'tʃerna] SF oil lamp

lucer'nario [lutʃer'narjo] SM skylight

lu'certola [lu'tʃertola] SF lizard

luci'dare [lutʃi'dare] /**72**/ VT to polish; (*ricalcare*) to trace

lucida'trice [lutʃida'tritʃe] SF floor polisher

lucidità [lutʃidi'ta] SF lucidity

'lucido, -a ['lutʃido] AG shining, bright; (*lucidato*) polished; (*fig*) lucid ▶ SM shine, lustre (BRIT), luster (US); (*per scarpe ecc*) polish; (*disegno*) tracing

lu'cignolo [lu'tʃiɲɲolo] SM wick

luc'rare /**72**/ VT to make money out of

lucra'tivo, -a AG lucrative; **a scopo ~** for gain

'lucro SM profit, gain; **a scopo di ~** for gain; **organizzazione senza scopo di ~** non-profit-making (BRIT) *o* non-profit (US) organization

lu'croso, -a AG lucrative, profitable

luculli'ano, -a AG (*pasto*) sumptuous

lu'dibrio SM mockery *no pl*; (*oggetto di scherno*) laughing stock

ludopa'tia SF gambling addiction

'lue SF syphilis

'luglio ['luʎʎo] SM July; **nel mese di ~** in July, in the month of July; **il primo ~** the first of July; **arrivare il 2 ~** to arrive on the 2nd of July; **all'inizio/alla fine di ~** at the beginning/at the end of July; **durante il mese di ~** during July; **a ~ del prossimo anno** in July of next year; **ogni anno a ~** every July; **che fai a ~?** what are you doing in July?; **ha piovuto molto a ~ quest'anno** July was very wet this year

'lugubre AG gloomy

'lui PRON (*soggetto*) he; (*oggetto: per dare rilievo, con preposizione*) him ▶ SM INV: **il mio ~** my beloved; **~ stesso** he himself; **è ~** it's him

lu'maca, -che SF slug; (*chiocciola*) snail

luma'cone SM (large) slug; (*fig*) slowcoach (BRIT), slowpoke (US)

'lume SM light; (*lampada*) lamp; ~ **a olio** oil lamp; **chiedere lumi a qn** (*fig*) to ask sb for advice; **a ~ di naso** (*fig*) by rule of thumb

lumi'cino [lumi'tʃino] SM small *o* faint light; **essere (ridotto) al ~** (*fig*) to be at death's door

lumi'era SF chandelier

lumi'nare SM luminary

lumi'naria SF (*per feste*) illuminations *pl*

lumine'scente [lumineʃ'ʃɛnte] AG luminescent

lu'mino SM small light; **~ da notte** night-light; **~ per i morti** candle for the dead

luminosità SF brightness; (*fig: di sorriso, volto*) radiance

lumi'noso, -a AG (*che emette luce*) luminous; (*cielo, colore, stanza*) bright; (*sorgente*) of light, light *cpd*; (*fig: sorriso*) bright, radiant; **insegna luminosa** neon sign

lun. ABBR (= *lunedì*) Mon.

'luna SF moon; **~ nuova/piena** new/full moon; **avere la ~** to be in a bad mood; **~ di miele** honeymoon

'luna park SM INV amusement park, funfair

lu'nare AG lunar, moon *cpd*

lu'nario SM almanac; **sbarcare il ~** to make ends meet

lu'natico, -a, -ci, -che AG whimsical, temperamental

lunedì SM INV Monday; **di** *o* **il ~** on Mondays; *vedi anche* **martedì**

lun'gaggine [lun'gaddʒine] SF slowness; **lungaggini della burocrazia** red tape

lunga'mente AV (*a lungo*) for a long time; (*estesamente*) at length

lun'garno SM embankment along the Arno

lun'ghezza [lun'gettsa] SF length; **~ d'onda** (*Fisica*) wavelength

'lungi ['lundʒi]: **~ da** *prep* far from

lungimi'rante [lundʒimi'rante] AG far-sighted

'lungo, -a, -ghi, -ghe AG long; (*lento: persona*) slow; (*diluito: caffè, brodo*) weak, watery, thin ▶ SM length ▶ PREP along; **~ 3 metri** 3 metres long; **avere la barba lunga** to be unshaven; **a ~** for a long time; **a ~ andare** in the long run; **di gran lunga** (*molto*) by far; **andare in ~** *o* **per le lunghe** to drag on; **saperla lunga** to know what's what; **in ~ e in largo** far and wide, all over; **~ il corso dei secoli** throughout the centuries; **navigazione di ~ corso** ocean-going navigation

lungofi'ume SM embankment

lungo'lago SM road round a lake

lungo'mare SM promenade

lungome'traggio [lungome'traddʒo] SM (*Cine*) feature film

lungo'tevere SM embankment along the Tiber

lu'notto SM (*Aut*) rear *o* back window; **~ termico** heated rear window

lu'ogo, -ghi SM place; (*posto: di incidente ecc*) scene, site; (*punto, passo di libro*) passage; **in ~ di** instead of; **in primo ~** in the first place; **aver ~** to take place; **dar ~ a** to give rise to; **~ comune** commonplace; **~ del delitto** scene of the crime; **~ geometrico** locus; **~ di nascita** birthplace; (*Amm*) place of birth; **~ di pena** prison, penitentiary; **~ di provenienza** place of origin

luogote'nente SM (*Mil*) lieutenant

lupacchi'otto [lupak'kjɔtto] SM (*Zool*) (wolf) cub

lu'para SF sawn-off shotgun

lu'petto SM (*Zool*) (wolf) cub; (*negli scouts*) cub scout

'lupo, -a SM/F wolf/she-wolf; **cane ~** alsatian (dog) (BRIT), German shepherd (dog); **tempo da lupi** filthy weather

'luppolo SM (*Bot*) hop

'lurido, -a AG filthy

luri'dume SM filth

lu'singa, -ghe SF (*spesso al pl*) flattery *no pl*

lusin'gare /80/ VT to flatter

lusinghi'ero, -a [luzin'gjero] AG flattering, gratifying

lus'sare /72/ VT (*Med*) to dislocate

lussazi'one [lussat'tsjone] SF (*Med*) dislocation

lussembur'ghese [lussembur'gese] AG of (*o* from) Luxembourg ▶ SMF native (*o* inhabitant) of Luxembourg

Lussem'burgo SM (*stato*): **il ~** Luxembourg ▶ SF (*città*) Luxembourg

'lusso SM luxury; **di ~** luxury *cpd*

lussu'oso, -a AG luxurious

lussureggi'are [lussured'dʒare] /62/ VI to be luxuriant

lus'suria SF lust

lussuri'oso, -a AG lascivious, lustful

lus'trare /72/ VT to polish, shine

lustras'carpe SM INV/F INV shoeshine

lus'trino SM sequin

'lustro, -a AG shiny; (*pelliccia*) glossy ▶ SM shine, gloss; (*fig*) prestige, glory; (*quinquennio*) five-year period

lute'rano, -a AG, SM/F Lutheran

'lutto SM mourning; **essere in/portare il ~** to be in/wear mourning

Mm

M, m [ˈɛmme] SM O F INV (*lettera*) M, m; **M come Milano** M for Mary (BRIT), M for Mike (US)

m. ABBR = **mese; metro; miglia; monte**

ma CONG but; **ma insomma!** for goodness sake!; **ma no!** of course not!

ˈmacabro, -a AG gruesome, macabre

maˈcaco, -chi SM (*Zool*) macaque

macché [makˈke] ESCL not at all!, certainly not!

maccheˈroni [makkeˈroni] SMPL macaroni *sg*

ˈmacchia [ˈmakkja] SF stain, spot; (*chiazza di diverso colore*) spot, splash, patch; (*tipo di boscaglia*) scrub; **~ dˈinchiostro** ink stain; **estendersi a ~ dˈolio** (*fig*) to spread rapidly; **darsi/vivere alla ~** (*fig*) to go into/live in hiding

macchiˈare [makˈkjare] /19/ VT (*sporcare*) to stain, mark ■ **macchiarsi** VPR (*persona*) to get o.s. dirty; (*stoffa*) to stain; to get stained o marked; **macchiarsi di un delitto** to be guilty of a crime

macchiˈato, -a [makˈkjato] AG (*pelle, pelo*) spotted; **~ di** stained with; **caffè ~** coffee with a dash of milk

macchiˈetta [makˈkjetta] SF (*disegno*) sketch, caricature; (*Teat*) caricature; (*fig: persona*) character

ˈmacchina [ˈmakkina] SF machine; (*motore, locomotiva*) engine; (*automobile*) car; (*fig: meccanismo*) machinery; **andare in ~** (*Aut*) to go by car; (*Stampa*) to go to press; **salire in ~** to get into the car; **venire in ~** to come by car; **sala macchine** (*Naut*) engine room; **~ da cucire** sewing machine; **~ fotografica** camera; **~ da presa** cine o movie camera; **~ da scrivere** typewriter; **~ utensile** machine tool; **~ a vapore** steam engine

macchinalˈmente [makkinalˈmente] AV mechanically

macchiˈnare [makkiˈnare] /72/ VT to plot

macchiˈnario [makkiˈnarjo] SM machinery

macchinaziˈone [makkinatˈtsjone] SF plot, machination

macchiˈnetta [makkiˈnetta] SF (*col: caffettiera*) percolator; (: *accendino*) lighter

macchiˈnista, -i [makkiˈnista] SM (*di treno*)

engine-driver; (*di nave*) engineer; (*Teat, TV*) stagehand

macchiˈnoso, -a [makkiˈnoso] AG complex, complicated

maˈcedone [maˈtʃɛdone] AG, SMF Macedonian

Maceˈdonia [matʃeˈdɔnja] SF Macedonia

maceˈdonia [matʃeˈdɔnja] SF fruit salad

macelˈlaio, -a [matʃelˈlajo] SM/F butcher

macelˈlare [matʃelˈlare] /72/ VT to slaughter, butcher

macellaziˈone [matʃellatˈtsjone] SF slaughtering, butchering

macelleˈria [matʃelleˈria] SF butcher's (shop)

maˈcello [maˈtʃɛllo] SM (*mattatoio*) slaughterhouse, abattoir (BRIT); (*fig*) slaughter, massacre; (: *disastro*) shambles *sg*

maceˈrare [matʃeˈrare] /72/ VT to macerate; (*Cuc*) to marinate ■ **macerarsi** VPR to waste away; (*fig*) **macerarsi in** to be consumed with

maceraziˈone [matʃeratˈtsjone] SF maceration

maˈcerie [maˈtʃɛrje] SFPL rubble *sg*, debris *sg*

ˈmacero [ˈmatʃero] SM (*operazione*) pulping; (*stabilimento*) pulping mill; **carta da ~** paper for pulping

machiaˈvellico, -a, -ci, -che [makjaˈvɛlliko] AG (*anche fig*) Machiavellian

maˈcigno [maˈtʃiɲɲo] SM (*masso*) rock, boulder

maciˈlento, -a [matʃiˈlɛnto] AG emaciated

ˈmacina [ˈmatʃina] SF (*pietra*) millstone; (*macchina*) grinder

macinacaffè [matʃinakafˈfɛ] SM INV coffee grinder

macinaˈpepe [matʃinaˈpepe] SM INV peppermill

maciˈnare [matʃiˈnare] /72/ VT to grind; (*carne*) to mince (BRIT), grind (US)

maciˈnato, -a [matʃiˈnato] SM meal, flour; (*carne*) minced (BRIT) o ground (US) meat

maciˈnino [matʃiˈnino] SM (*per caffè*) coffee grinder; (*per pepe*) peppermill; (*scherzoso: macchina*) old banger (BRIT), clunker (US)

maciulˈlare [matʃulˈlare] /72/ VT (*canapa, lino*) to brake; (*fig: braccio ecc*) to crush

'macro... PREFISSO macro ...

macrobi'otico, -a AG macrobiotic ▶ SF macrobiotics *sg*

macu'lato, -a AG (*pelo*) spotted

Ma'dama: palazzo ~ *sm* (*Pol*) seat of the Italian Chamber of Senators

made in Italy [meɪdɪ'nɪtəli] SM: **il ~** Italian exports *pl* (*especially fashion goods*)

Ma'dera SF (*Geo*) Madeira ▶ SM INV (*vino*) Madeira

'madido, -a AG: **~ (di)** wet *o* moist (with)

Ma'donna SF (*Rel*) Our Lady

mador'nale AG enormous, huge

'madre SF mother; (*matrice di bolletta*) counterfoil ▶ AG INV mother *cpd*; **ragazza ~** unmarried mother; **scena ~** (*Teat*) principal scene; (*fig*) terrible scene

madre'lingua SF mother tongue, native language

madre'patria SF mother country, native land

madre'perla SF mother-of-pearl

Ma'drid SF Madrid

madri'gale SM madrigal

madri'leno, -a AG of (*o* from) Madrid ▶ SM/F person from Madrid

ma'drina SF godmother

MAECI ABBR = **Ministero degli Affari Esteri e della Cooperazione Internazionale**

maestà SF INV majesty; **Sua M~ la Regina** Her Majesty the Queen

maestosità SF majesty

maes'toso, -a AG majestic

ma'estra SF *vedi* **maestro**

maes'trale SM north-west wind, mistral

maes'tranze [maes'trantse] SFPL workforce *sg*

maes'tria SF mastery, skill

ma'estro, -a SM/F (*Ins: anche:* **maestro di scuola** *o* **elementare**) primary (*Brit*) *o* grade school (*US*) teacher; (*esperto*) expert ▶ SM (*artigiano, fig: guida*) master; (*Mus*) maestro ▶ AG (*principale*) main; (*di grande abilità*) masterly, skilful (*Brit*), skillful (*US*); **un colpo da ~** (*fig*) a masterly move; **muro ~** main wall; **strada maestra** main road; **maestra d'asilo** nursery teacher; **~ di ballo** dancing master; **~ di cerimonie** master of ceremonies; **~ d'orchestra** conductor, director (*US*); **~ di scherma** fencing master; **~ di sci** ski instructor

'mafia SF Mafia

mafi'oso, -a SM/F member of the Mafia

'maga, -ghe SF sorceress

ma'gagna [ma'gaɲɲa] SF defect, flaw, blemish; (*noia, guaio*) problem

ma'gari ESCL (*esprime desiderio*): **~ fosse vero!** if only it were true!; **ti piacerebbe andare in Scozia? — ~!** would you like to go to Scotland?

— I certainly would! ▶ AV (*anche*) even; (*forse*) perhaps

magazzi'naggio [magaddzi'naddʒo] SM: **(spese di) ~** storage charges *pl*, warehousing charges *pl*

magazzini'ere [magaddzi'njere] SM warehouseman

magaz'zino [magad'dzino] SM warehouse; **grande ~** department store; **~ doganale** bonded warehouse

> Do not translate the Italian word **magazzino** by *magazine*.

'maggio ['maddʒo] SM May; *vedi anche* **luglio**

maggio'rana [maddʒo'rana] SF (*Bot*) (sweet) marjoram

maggio'ranza [maddʒo'rantsa] SF majority; **nella ~ dei casi** in most cases

maggio'rare [maddʒo'rare] /**72**/ VT to increase, raise

maggiorazi'one [maddʒorat'tsjone] SF (*Comm*) rise, increase

maggior'domo [maddʒor'dɔmo] SM butler

maggi'ore [mad'dʒore] AG (*comparativo: più grande*) bigger, larger; taller; greater; (*: più vecchio: sorella, fratello*) older, elder; (*: di grado superiore*) senior; (*: più importante: Mil, Mus*) major; (*superlativo*) biggest, largest; tallest; greatest; oldest, eldest ▶ SMF (*di grado*) superior; (*di età*) elder; (*Mil*) major; (*: Aer*) squadron leader; **la maggior parte** the majority; **andare per la ~** (*cantante, attore ecc*) to be very popular, be "in"

maggio'renne [maddʒo'rɛnne] AG of age ▶ SMF person who has come of age

maggiori'tario, -a [maddʒori'tarjo] AG majority *cpd*; (*Pol: anche:* **sistema maggioritario**) first-past-the-post system

maggior'mente [maddʒor'mente] AV much more; (*con senso superlativo*) most

ma'gia [ma'dʒia] SF magic

'magico, -a, -ci, -che ['madʒiko] AG magic; (*fig*) fascinating, charming, magical

'magio ['madʒo] SM (*Rel*): **i re Magi** the Magi, the Three Wise Men

magis'tero [madʒis'tero] SM teaching; (*fig: maestria*) skill; (*Ins*): **Facoltà di M~** ≈ teacher training college

magis'trale [madʒis'trale] AG primary (*Brit*) *o* grade school (*US*) teachers', primary (*Brit*) *o* grade school (*US*) teaching; (*abile*) skilful (*Brit*), skillful (*US*); **istituto ~** secondary school for the training of primary teachers

magis'trato [madʒis'trato] SM magistrate

magistra'tura [madʒistra'tura] SF magistrature; (*magistrati*): **la ~** the Bench

'maglia ['maʎʎa] SF stitch; (*lavoro ai ferri*) knitting *no pl*; (*tessuto, Sport*) jersey; (*maglione*) jersey, sweater; (*di catena*) link; (*di rete*) mesh; **avviare/**

diminuire le maglie to cast on/cast off; **lavorare a ~, fare la ~** to knit; **~ diritta/rovescia** plain/purl

maglie'ria [maʎʎe'ria] SF knitwear; (*negozio*) knitwear shop; **macchina per ~** knitting machine

magli'etta [maʎ'ʎetta] SF (*canottiera*) vest; (*tipo camicia*) T-shirt

magli'ficio [maʎʎi'fitʃo] SM knitwear factory

ma'glina [maʎ'ʎina] SF (*tessuto*) jersey

'maglio ['maʎʎo] SM mallet; (*macchina*) power hammer

magli'one [maʎ'ʎone] SM jumper, sweater

magma SM magma; (*fig*) mass

ma'gnaccia [maɲ'ɲattʃa] SM INV (*peg*) pimp

magnanimità [maɲɲanimi'ta] SF magnanimity

ma'gnanimo, -a [maɲ'ɲanimo] AG magnanimous

ma'gnate [maɲ'ɲate] SM tycoon, magnate

ma'gnesia [maɲ'ɲɛzja] SF (*Chim*) magnesia

ma'gnesio [maɲ'ɲɛzjo] SM (*Chim*) magnesium; **al ~** (*lampada, flash*) magnesium *cpd*

ma'gnete [maɲ'ɲɛte] SM magnet

ma'gnetico, -a, -ci, -che [maɲ'ɲɛtiko] AG magnetic

magne'tismo [maɲɲe'tizmo] SM magnetism

magnetiz'zare [maɲɲetid'dzare] /**72**/ VT (*Fisica*) to magnetize; (*fig*) to mesmerize

magne'tofono [maɲɲe'tɔfono] SM tape recorder

magnifica'mente [maɲɲifika'mente] AV magnificently, extremely well

magnifi'cenza [maɲɲifi'tʃentsa] SF magnificence, splendour (*BRIT*), splendor (*US*)

ma'gnifico, -a, -ci, -che [maɲ'ɲifiko] AG magnificent, splendid; (*ospite*) generous

'magno, -a ['maɲɲo] AG: **aula magna** main hall

ma'gnolia [maɲ'ɲɔlja] SF magnolia

'mago, -ghi SM (*stregone*) magician, wizard; (*illusionista*) magician

ma'grezza [ma'grettsa] SF thinness

'magro, -a AG (very) thin, skinny; (*carne*) lean; (*formaggio*) low-fat; (*fig: scarso, misero*) meagre (*BRIT*), meager (*US*), poor; (: *meschino: scusa*) poor, lame; **mangiare di ~** not to eat meat

'mai AV (*nessuna volta*) never; (*talvolta*) ever; **non ... ~** never; **~ più** never again; **come ~?** why (*o* how) on earth?; **chi/dove/quando ~?** whoever/wherever/whenever?

mai'ale SM (*Zool*) pig; (*carne*) pork

mail ['meil] SF INV = **e-mail**

mai'olica SF majolica

maio'nese SF mayonnaise

Mai'orca SF Majorca

'mais SM maize (*BRIT*), corn (*US*)

mai'uscolo, -a AG (*lettera*) capital; (*fig*) enormous, huge ▶ SF capital letter ▶ SM capital letters *pl*; (*Tip*) upper case; **scrivere tutto (in) ~** to write everything in capitals *o* in capital letters

> In inglese si scrivono in *maiuscolo* anche i mesi, i giorni della settimana, le lingue, gli aggettivi di nazionalità, il pronome personale *io*.

mal AV, SM *vedi* **male**

'mala SF (*gergo*) underworld

malac'corto, -a AG rash, careless

mala'fede SF bad faith

malaf'fare: di ~ ag (*gente*) shady, dishonest; **donna di ~** prostitute

mala'gevole [mala'dʒevole] AG difficult, hard

mala'grazia [mala'grattsja] SF: **con ~** with bad grace, impolitely

mala'lingua (*pl malelingue*) SF gossip (*person*)

mala'mente AV badly; (*sgarbatamente*) rudely

malan'dato, -a AG (*persona: di salute*) in poor health; (: *di condizioni finanziarie*) badly off; (*trascurato*) shabby

ma'lanimo SM ill will, malevolence; **di ~** unwillingly

ma'lanno SM (*disgrazia*) misfortune; (*malattia*) ailment

mala'pena SF: **a ~** hardly, scarcely

ma'laria SF (*Med*) malaria

ma'larico, -a, -ci, -che AG malarial

mala'sorte SF bad luck

mala'ticcio, -a [mala'tittʃo] AG sickly

ma'lato, -a AG ill, sick; (*gamba*) bad; (*pianta*) diseased ▶ SM/F sick person; (*in ospedale*) patient; **darsi ~** (*sul lavoro ecc*) to go sick

> **Ill** e **sick** hanno significati simili, ma si usano in modo leggermente diverso.
> *Non vengo perché sono malata.* **I am not coming because I'm ill.**
> *i malati terminali* **the terminally ill**
> **Ill** non si usa davanti a un nome: *i bambini malati* **sick children**.

malat'tia SF (*infettiva ecc*) illness, disease; (*cattiva salute*) illness, sickness; (*di pianta*) disease; **mettersi in ~** to go on sick leave; **fare una ~ di qc** (*fig: disperarsi*) to get in a state about sth

malaugu'rato, -a AG ill-fated, unlucky

malau'gurio SM bad *o* ill omen; **uccello del ~** bird of ill omen

mala'vita SF underworld

malavi'toso, -a SM/F gangster

mala'voglia [mala'vɔʎʎa]: **di ~** av unwillingly, reluctantly

Ma'lawi [ma'lavi] SM: **il ~** Malawi

Mala'ysia SF Malaysia

malaysi'ano, -a AG, SM/F Malaysian

malcapi'tato, -a AG unlucky, unfortunate
▸ SM/F unfortunate person

mal'concio, -a, -ci, -ce [mal'kontʃo] AG in a sorry state

malcon'tento SM discontent

malcos'tume SM immorality

mal'destro, -a AG (*inabile*) inexpert, inexperienced; (*goffo*) awkward

maldi'cente [maldi'tʃɛnte] AG slanderous

maldi'cenza [maldi'tʃɛntsa] SF malicious gossip

maldis'posto, -a AG: ~ **(verso)** ill-disposed (towards)

Mal'dive SFPL: **le ~** the Maldives

'male AV badly ▸ SM (*ciò che è ingiusto, disonesto*) evil; (*danno, svantaggio*) harm; (*sventura*) misfortune; (*dolore fisico, morale*) pain, ache; **sentirsi ~** to feel ill; **aver mal di cuore/fegato** to have a heart/liver complaint; **aver mal di denti/d'orecchi/di testa** to have toothache/earache/a headache; **aver mal di gola** to have a sore throat; **aver ~ ai piedi** to have sore feet; **far ~** (*dolere*) to hurt; **far ~ alla salute** to be bad for one's health; **far del ~ a qn** to hurt *o* harm sb; **parlar ~ di qn** to speak ill of sb; **restare** *o* **rimanere ~** to be sorry; to be disappointed, to be hurt; **trattar ~ qn** to ill-treat sb; **andare a ~** to go off *o* bad; **come va? — non c'è ~** how are you? — not bad; **di ~ in peggio** from bad to worse; **per ~ che vada** however badly things go; **non avertene a ~, non prendertela a ~** don't take it to heart; **mal comune mezzo gaudio** (*proverbio*) a trouble shared is a trouble halved; **mal d'auto** carsickness; **mal di mare** seasickness

male'detto, -a PP *di* **maledire** ▸ AG cursed, damned; (*fig: col*) damned, blasted

male'dire /38/ VT to curse

maledizi'one [maledit'tsjone] SF curse; **~!** damn it!

maledu'cato, -a AG rude, ill-mannered

maleducazi'one [maledukat'tsjone] SF rudeness

male'fatta SF misdeed

male'ficio [male'fitʃo] SM witchcraft

ma'lefico, -a, -ci, -che AG (*aria, cibo*) harmful, bad; (*influsso, azione*) evil

ma'lese AG, SMF Malay(an) ▸ SM (*Ling*) Malay

Ma'lesia SF Malaya

ma'lessere SM indisposition, slight illness; (*fig*) uneasiness

malevo'lenza [malevo'lɛntsa] SF malevolence

ma'levolo, -a AG malevolent

malfa'mato, -a AG notorious

mal'fatto, -a AG (*persona*) deformed; (*oggetto*) badly made; (*lavoro*) badly done

malfat'tore, -'trice SM/F wrongdoer

mal'fermo, -a AG unsteady, shaky; (*salute*) poor, delicate

malformazi'one [malformat'tsjone] SF malformation

'malga, -ghe SF Alpine hut

malgo'verno SM maladministration

mal'grado PREP in spite of, despite ▸ CONG although; **mio** *o* **tuo** *ecc* ~ against my (*o* your *etc*) will

ma'lia SF spell; (*fig: fascino*) charm

mali'ardo, -a AG (*occhi, sorriso*) bewitching ▸ SF enchantress

maligna'mente [maliɲɲa'mente] AV maliciously

mali'gnare [maliɲ'ɲare] /15/ VI: ~ **su** to malign, speak ill of

malignità [maliɲɲi'ta] SF INV (*qualità*) malice, spite; (*osservazione*) spiteful remark; **con ~** spitefully, maliciously

ma'ligno, -a [ma'liɲɲo] AG (*malvagio*) malicious, malignant; (*Med*) malignant

malinco'nia SF melancholy, gloom

malin'conico, -a, -ci, -che AG melancholy

malincu'ore: a ~ *av* reluctantly, unwillingly

malinfor'mato, -a AG misinformed

malintenzio'nato, -a [malintentsjo'nato] AG ill-intentioned

malin'teso, -a AG misunderstood; (*riguardo, senso del dovere*) mistaken, wrong ▸ SM misunderstanding; **c'è stato un ~** there's been a misunderstanding

ma'lizia [ma'littsja] SF (*malignità*) malice; (*furbizia*) cunning; (*espediente*) trick

malizi'oso, -a [malit'tsjoso] AG malicious; cunning; (*vivace, birichino*) mischievous

malle'abile AG malleable

mal'loppo SM (*col: refurtiva*) loot

malme'nare /72/ VT to beat up; (*fig*) to ill-treat

mal'messo, -a AG shabby

malnu'trito, -a AG undernourished

malnutrizi'one [malnutrit'tsjone] SF malnutrition

'malo, -a AG: **in ~ modo** badly

ma'locchio [ma'lɔkkjo] SM evil eye

ma'lora SF (*col*): **andare in ~** to go to the dogs; **va' in ~!** go to hell!

ma'lore SM (*sudden*) illness

malri'dotto, -a AG (*abiti, scarpe, persona*) in a sorry state; (*casa, macchina*) dilapidated, in a poor state of repair

mal'sano, -a AG unhealthy

malsi'curo, -a AG unsafe

'Malta SF Malta

'malta SF (*Edil*) mortar

mal'tempo SM bad weather

'**malto** SM malt

mal'tolto SM ill-gotten gains pl

maltratta'mento SM ill treatment

maltrat'tare /72/ VT to ill-treat

malu'more SM bad mood; (irritabilità) bad temper; (discordia) ill feeling; **di ~** in a bad mood

'**malva** SF (Bot) mallow ▶ AG, SM INV mauve

mal'vagio, -a, -gi, -gie [mal'vadʒo] AG wicked, evil

malvagità [malvadʒi'ta] SF INV (qualità) wickedness; (azione) wicked deed

malva'sia SF Italian dessert wine

malversazi'one [malversat'tsjone] SF (Dir) embezzlement

malves'tito, -a AG badly dressed, ill-clad

mal'visto, -a AG: **~ (da)** disliked (by), unpopular (with)

malvi'vente SMF criminal

malvolenti'eri AV unwillingly, reluctantly

malvo'lere /131/ VT: **farsi ~ da qn** to make o.s. unpopular with sb ▶ SM: **prendere qn a ~** to take a dislike to sb

'**malware** ['malwer] SM INV (Inform) malware (program)

'**mamma** SF mum(my) (BRIT), mom (US); **~ mia!** my goodness!

mam'mario, -a AG (Anat) mammary

mam'mella SF (Anat) breast; (di vacca, capra ecc) udder

mam'mifero SM mammal

mam'mismo SM excessive attachment to one's mother

'**mammola** SF (Bot) violet

'**manager** ['mænidʒer] SM O F INV manager

manageri'ale [manadʒe'rjale] AG managerial

ma'nata SF (colpo) slap; (quantità) handful

'**manca** SF left (hand); **a destra e a ~** left, right and centre, on all sides

manca'mento SM (di forze) (feeling of) faintness, weakness

man'canza [man'kantsa] SF lack; (carenza) shortage, scarcity; (fallo) fault; (imperfezione) failing, shortcoming; **per ~ di tempo** through lack of time; **in ~ di meglio** for lack of anything better; **sentire la ~ di qc/qn** to miss sth/sb

man'care /20/ VI (essere insufficiente) to be lacking; (venir meno) to fail; (sbagliare) to be wrong, make a mistake; (non esserci) to be missing, not to be there; (essere lontano): **~ (da)** to be away (from) ▶ VT to miss; **~ di** to lack; **~ a** (promessa) to fail to keep; **tu mi manchi** I miss you; **mancò poco che morisse** he very nearly died; **mancano ancora 10 sterline** we're still £10 short; **manca un quarto alle 6** it's a quarter to 6; **non mancherò** I won't forget, I'll make sure I do; **ci**

mancherebbe altro! of course I (o you etc) will!; **~ da casa** to be away from home; **~ di rispetto a** o **verso qn** to be lacking in respect towards sb, be disrespectful towards sb; **~ di parola** not to keep one's word, go back on one's word; **sentirsi ~** to feel faint

man'cato, -a AG (tentativo) unsuccessful; (artista) failed

'**manche** [mãʃ] SF INV (Sport) heat

mancherò ecc [manke'rɔ] VB vedi **mancare**

man'chevole [man'kevole] AG (insufficiente) inadequate, insufficient

manchevo'lezza [mankevo'lettsa] SF (scorrettezza) fault, shortcoming

'**mancia, -ce** ['mantʃa] SF tip; **~ competente** reward

manci'ata [man'tʃata] SF handful

man'cino, -a [man'tʃino] AG (braccio) left; (persona) left-handed; (fig) underhand

'**manco** AV (nemmeno): **~ per sogno** o **per idea!** not on your life!

man'dante SMF (Dir) principal; (istigatore) instigator

manda'rancio [manda'rantʃo] SM clementine

man'dare /72/ VT to send; (far funzionare: macchina) to drive; (emettere) to send out; (: grido) to give, let out; **~ avanti** (persona) to send ahead; (fig: famiglia) to provide for; (: ditta) to look after, run; (: fabbrica) to run, look after; (: pratica) to attend to; **~ a chiamare qn** to send for sb; **~ giù** to send down; (anche fig) to swallow; **~ in onda** (Radio, TV) to broadcast; **~ in rovina** to ruin; **~ via** to send away; (licenziare) to fire

manda'rino SM mandarin (orange); (cinese) mandarin

man'data SF (quantità) lot, batch; (di chiave) turn; **chiudere a doppia ~** to double-lock

manda'tario SM (Dir) representative, agent

man'dato SM (incarico) commission; (Dir: provvedimento) warrant; (di deputato ecc) mandate; (ordine di pagamento) postal o money order; **~ d'arresto, ~ di cattura** warrant for arrest; **~ di comparizione** summons sg; **~ di perquisizione** search warrant

man'dibola SF mandible, jaw

mando'lino SM mandolin(e)

'**mandorla** SF almond

mandor'lato SM nut brittle

'**mandorlo** SM almond tree

'**mandria** SF herd

mandri'ano SM cowherd, herdsman

man'drino SM (Tecn) mandrel

maneg'gevole [maned'dʒevole] AG easy to handle

maneggi'are [maned'dʒare] /62/ VT (creta, cera) to mould (BRIT), mold (US), work, fashion;

(*arnesi, utensili*) to handle; (: *adoperare*) to use; (*fig:
persone, denaro*) to handle, deal with

ma'neggio [ma'neddʒo] SM moulding (BRIT),
molding (US); handling; use; (*intrigo*) plot,
scheme; (*per cavalli*) riding school

ma'nesco, -a, -schi, -sche AG free with one's
fists

ma'nette SFPL handcuffs

manga'nello SM club

manga'nese SM manganese

mange'reccio, -a, -ci, -ce [mandʒe'rettʃo] AG
edible

mangi'abile [man'dʒabile] AG edible, eatable

mangia'dischi [mandʒa'diski] SM INV record
player

mangia'nastri [mandʒa'nastri] SM INV cas-
sette-recorder

mangi'are [man'dʒare] /62/ VT to eat; (*intaccare*)
to eat into o away; (*Carte, Scacchi ecc*) to take ▸ VI
to eat ▸ SM eating; (*cibo*) food; (*cucina*) cooking;
fare da ~ to do the cooking; **mangiarsi le
parole** to mumble; **mangiarsi le unghie** to bite
one's nails

mangia'soldi [mandʒa'sɔldi] AG INV (*col*): **macchinetta ~** one-armed bandit

mangia'toia [mandʒa'toja] SF feeding-trough

man'gime [man'dʒime] SM fodder

mangiucchi'are [mandʒuk'kjare] /19/ VT to
nibble

'mango, -ghi SM mango

ma'nia SF (*Psic*) mania; (*fig*) obsession, craze;
avere la ~ di fare qc to have a habit of doing
sth; **~ di persecuzione** persecution complex o
mania

mania'cale AG (*Psic*) maniacal; (*fanatico*) fanatical

ma'niaco, -a, -ci, -che AG suffering from a
mania; **~ (di)** obsessed (by), crazy (about)

'manica, -che SF sleeve; (*fig: gruppo*) gang,
bunch; (*Geo*): **la M~, il Canale della M~** the
(English) Channel; **senza maniche** sleeveless;
essere in maniche di camicia to be in one's
shirt sleeves; **essere di ~ larga/stretta** to be
easy-going/strict; **~ a vento** (*Aer*) wind sock

manica'retto SM titbit (BRIT), tidbit (US)

mani'chetta [mani'ketta] SF (*Tecn*) hose

mani'chino [mani'kino] SM (*di sarto, vetrina*)
dummy

'manico, -ci SM handle; (*Mus*) neck; **~ di scopa**
broomstick

mani'comio SM psychiatric hospital; (*fig*) madhouse

mani'cotto SM muff; (*Tecn*) coupling; sleeve

mani'cure SM o F INV manicure ▸ SF INV mani-
curist

mani'era SF way, manner; (*stile*) style, manner
■ **maniere** SFPL (*comportamento*) manners; **in ~**

che so that; **in ~ da** so as to; **alla ~ di** in o after
the style of; **in una ~ o nell'altra** one way or
another; **in tutte le maniere** at all costs; **usare
buone maniere con qn** to be polite to sb; **usare
le maniere forti** to use strong-arm tactics

manie'rato, -a AG affected

ma'niero SM manor

manifat'tura SF (*lavorazione*) manufacture;
(*stabilimento*) factory

manifatturi'ero, -a AG manufacturing

manifes'tante SMF demonstrator

manifes'tare /72/ VT to show, display; (*esprimere*) to express; (*rivelare*) to reveal, disclose ▸ VI
to demonstrate ■ **manifestarsi** VPR to show
o.s.; **manifestarsi amico** to prove o.s. (to be) a
friend

manifestazi'one [manifestat'tsjone] SF show,
display, expression; (*sintomo*) sign, symptom;
(*dimostrazione pubblica*) demonstration; (*cerimonia*) event

manifes'tino SM leaflet

mani'festo, -a AG obvious, evident ▸ SM
poster, bill; (*scritto ideologico*) manifesto

ma'niglia [ma'niʎʎa] SF handle; (*sostegno: negli
autobus ecc*) strap

Ma'nila SF Manila

manipo'lare /72/ VT to manipulate; (*alterare:
vino*) to adulterate

manipolazi'one [manipolat'tsjone] SF manipulation; adulteration

ma'nipolo SM (*drappello*) handful

manis'calco, -chi SM blacksmith, farrier (BRIT)

'manna SF (*Rel*) manna

man'naia SF (*del boia*) (executioner's) axe o ax
(US); (*per carni*) cleaver

man'naro, -a AG: **lupo ~** werewolf

'mano, -i SF hand; (*strato: di vernice ecc*) coat; **a ~**
by hand; **cucito a ~** hand-sewn; **fatto a ~**
handmade; **alla ~** (*persona*) easy-going; **fuori ~**
out of the way; **di prima ~** (*notizia*) first-hand;
di seconda ~ second-hand; **man ~** little by
little, gradually; **man ~ che** as; **a piene mani**
(*fig*) generously; **avere le mani bucate** to spend
money like water; **aver le mani in pasta** to be
in the know; **avere qc per le mani** (*progetto,
lavoro*) to have sth in hand; **dare una ~ a qn** to
lend sb a hand; **dare una ~ di vernice a qc** to
give sth a coat of paint; **darsi o stringersi la ~** to
shake hands; **forzare la ~** to go too far; **mettere ~ a qc** to have a hand in sth; **mettere le
mani avanti** (*fig*) to safeguard o.s.; **restare a
mani vuote** to be left empty-handed; **venire
alle mani** to come to blows; **mani in alto!**
hands up!

mano'dopera SF labour (BRIT), labor (US)

mano'messo, -a PP *di* **manomettere**

ma'nometro SM gauge, manometer

mano'mettere /63/ VT (*alterare*) to tamper with; (*aprire indebitamente*) to break open illegally

manomissi'one SF (*di prove ecc*) tampering; (*di lettera*) opening

ma'nopola SF (*dell'armatura*) gauntlet; (*guanto*) mitt; (*di impugnatura*) hand-grip; (*pomello*) knob

manos'critto, -a AG handwritten ▶ SM manuscript

manova'lanza [manova'lantsa] SF unskilled workers *pl*

mano'vale SM labourer (BRIT), laborer (US)

mano'vella SF handle; (*Tecn*) crank

ma'novra SF manoeuvre (BRIT), maneuver (US); (*Ferr*) shunting; **manovre di corridoio** palace intrigues

mano'vrare /72/ VT (*veicolo*) to manoeuvre (BRIT), maneuver (US); (*macchina, congegno*) to operate; (*fig: persona*) to manipulate ▶ VI to manoeuvre

manro'vescio [manro'vɛʃʃo] SM (*with back of hand*) slap

man'sarda SF attic

mansi'one SF task, duty, job

mansu'eto, -a AG (*animale*) tame; (*persona*) gentle, docile

mansue'tudine SF tameness, gentleness, docility

man'tello SM cloak; (*fig: di neve ecc*) blanket, mantle; (*Tecn: involucro*) casing, shell; (*Zool*) coat

mante'nere /121/ VT to maintain; (*adempiere: promesse*) to keep, abide by; (*provvedere a*) to support, maintain ■ **mantenersi** VPR: **mantenersi calmo/giovane** to stay calm/young; **~ i contatti con qn** to keep in touch with sb

manteni'mento SM maintenance

mante'nuto, -a SM/F gigolo/kept woman

'mantice ['mantitʃe] SM bellows *pl*; (*di carrozza, automobile*) hood

'manto SM cloak; **~ stradale** road surface

'Mantova SF Mantua

manto'vano, -a AG of (*o from*) Mantua

manu'ale AG manual ▶ SM (*testo*) manual, handbook

manua'listico, -a, -ci, -che AG textbook *cpd*

manual'mente AV manually, by hand

ma'nubrio SM handle; (*di bicicletta ecc*) handlebars *pl*; (*Sport*) dumbbell

manu'fatto SM manufactured article ■ **manufatti** SMPL manufactured goods

manutenzi'one [manuten'tsjone] SF maintenance, upkeep; (*d'impianti*) maintenance, servicing

'manzo ['mandzo] SM (*Zool*) steer; (*carne*) beef

Mao'metto SM Mohammed

'mappa SF (*Geo*) map

mappa'mondo SM map of the world; (*globo girevole*) globe

ma'rasma, -i SM (*fig*) decay, decline

mara'tona SF marathon

'marca, -che SF mark; (*bollo*) stamp; (*Comm: di prodotti*) brand; (*contrassegno, scontrino*) ticket, check; **prodotti di (gran) ~** high-class products; **~ da bollo** official stamp

mar'care /20/ VT (*munire di contrassegno*) to mark; (*a fuoco*) to brand; (*Sport: gol*) to score; (*: avversario*) to mark; (*accentuare*) to stress; **~ visita** (*Mil*) to report sick

mar'cato, -a AG (*lineamenti, accento ecc*) pronounced

'Marche ['marke] SFPL: **le ~** the Marches (*region of central Italy*)

marcherò *ecc* [marke'rɔ] VB *vedi* **marcare**

mar'chese, -a [mar'keze] SM/F marquis *o* marquess/marchioness

marchi'ano, -a [mar'kjano] AG (*errore*) glaring, gross

marchi'are [mar'kjare] /19/ VT to brand

marchigi'ano, -a [marki'dʒano] AG of (*o from*) the Marches

'marchio ['markjo] SM (*di bestiame, Comm: fig*) brand; **~ depositato** registered trademark; **~ di fabbrica** trademark

'marcia, -ce ['martʃa] SF (*anche Mus, Mil*) march; (*funzionamento*) running; (*il camminare*) walking; (*Aut*) gear; **mettere in ~** to start; **mettersi in ~** to get moving; **far ~ indietro** (*Aut*) to reverse; (*fig*) to back-pedal; **~ forzata** forced march; **~ funebre** funeral march

marciapi'ede [martʃa'pjɛde] SM (*di strada*) pavement (BRIT), sidewalk (US); (*Ferr*) platform

marci'are [mar'tʃare] /14/ VI to march; (*andare: treno, macchina*) to go; (*funzionare*) to run, work

'marcio, -a, -ci, -ce ['martʃo] AG (*frutta, legno*) rotten, bad; (*Med*) festering; (*fig*) corrupt, rotten ▶ SM: **c'è del ~ in questa storia** (*fig*) there's something fishy about this business; **avere torto ~** to be utterly wrong

mar'cire [mar'tʃire] /55/ VI (*andare a male*) to go bad, rot; (*suppurare*) to fester; (*fig*) to rot, waste away

marci'ume [mar'tʃume] SM (*parte guasta: di cibi ecc*) rotten part, bad part; (*: di radice, pianta*) rot; (*fig: corruzione*) rottenness, corruption

'marco, -chi SM (*unità monetaria*) mark

'mare SM sea; **di ~** (*brezza, acqua, uccelli, pesce*) sea *cpd*; **in ~** at sea; **per ~** by sea; **sul ~** (*barca*) on the sea; (*villaggio, località*) by *o* beside the sea; **andare al ~** (*in vacanza ecc*) to go to the seaside; **il mar Caspio** the Caspian Sea; **il mar Morto** the Dead Sea; **il mar Nero** the Black Sea; **il ~ del Nord** the North Sea; **il mar Rosso** the Red Sea; **il mar dei Sargassi** the Sargasso Sea; **i mari del Sud** the South Seas

m

ma'rea SF tide; **alta/bassa ~** high/low tide

mareggi'ata [mared'dʒata] SF heavy sea

ma'remma SF (Geo) maremma, swampy coastal area

marem'mano, -a AG (zona, macchia) swampy; (della Maremma) of (o from) the Maremma

mare'moto SM seaquake

maresci'allo [mareʃ'ʃallo] SM (Mil) marshal; (: sottufficiale) warrant officer

marez'zato, -a [mared'dzato] AG (seta ecc) watered, moiré; (legno) veined; (carta) marbled

marga'rina SF margarine

marghe'rita [marge'rita] SF (ox-eye) daisy, marguerite

margheri'tina [margeri'tina] SF daisy

margi'nale [mardʒi'nale] AG marginal

'margine ['mardʒine] SM margin; (di bosco, via) edge, border; **avere un buon ~ di tempo/denaro** to have plenty of time/money; **~ di guadagno** o **di utile** profit margin; **~ di sicurezza** safety margin

mariju'ana [mæri'wa:nə] SF marijuana

ma'rina SF navy; (costa) coast; (quadro) seascape; **~ mercantile** merchant navy (BRIT) o marine (US); **~ militare** ≈ Royal Navy (BRIT), ≈ Navy (US)

mari'naio SM sailor

mari'nare /72/ VT (Cuc) to marinate; **~ la scuola** to play truant

mari'naro, -a AG (tradizione, popolo) seafaring; (Cuc) with seafood; **alla marinara** (vestito, cappello) sailor cpd; **borgo ~** district where fishing folk live

mari'nata SF marinade

ma'rino, -a AG sea cpd, marine

mario'netta SF puppet

mari'tare /72/ VT to marry ■ **maritarsi** VPR: **maritarsi a** o **con qn** to marry sb, get married to sb

mari'tato, -a AG married

ma'rito SM husband; **prendere ~** to get married; **ragazza (in età) da ~** girl of marriageable age

ma'rittimo, -a AG maritime, sea cpd

mar'maglia [mar'maʎʎa] SF mob, riff-raff

marmel'lata SF jam; (di agrumi) marmalade

mar'mitta SF (recipiente) pot; (Aut) silencer; **~ catalitica** catalytic converter

'marmo SM marble

mar'mocchio [mar'mɔkkjo] SM (col) (little) kid

mar'motta SF (Zool) marmot

maroc'chino, -a [marok'kino] AG, SM/F Moroccan

Ma'rocco SM: **il ~** Morocco

ma'roso SM breaker

'marra SF hoe

Marra'kesh [marra'keʃ] SF Marrakesh

mar'rone AG INV brown ▶ SM (Bot) chestnut

mar'sala SM INV (vino) Marsala (wine)

Mar'siglia [mar'siʎʎa] SF Marseilles

mar'sina SF tails pl, tail coat

mar'supio SM (Zool) pouch, marsupium

mart. ABBR (= martedì) Tue(s)

'Marte SM (Astr, Mitologia) Mars

marte'dì SM INV Tuesday; **di** o **il ~** on Tuesdays; **oggi è ~ 3 aprile** (the date) today is Tuesday 3rd April; **~ stavo male** I wasn't well on Tuesday; **il giornale di ~** Tuesday's newspaper; **~ grasso** Shrove Tuesday

martel'lante AG (fig: dolore) throbbing

martel'lare /72/ VT to hammer ▶ VI (pulsare) to throb; (: cuore) to thump

martel'letto SM (di pianoforte) hammer; (di macchina da scrivere) typebar; (di giudice, nelle vendite all'asta) gavel; (Med) percussion hammer

mar'tello SM hammer; (di uscio) knocker; **suonare a ~** (fig: campane) to sound the tocsin; **~ pneumatico** pneumatic drill

marti'netto SM (Tecn) jack

martin'gala SF (di giacca) half-belt; (di cavallo) martingale

'martire SM/F martyr

mar'tirio SM martyrdom; (fig) agony, torture

martori'are /19/ VT to torment, torture

mar'xismo SM Marxism

mar'xista, -i, -e AG, SM/F Marxist

marza'pane [martsa'pane] SM marzipan

marzi'ale [mar'tsjale] AG martial

'marzo ['martso] SM March; vedi anche **luglio**

marzo'lino, -a [martso'lino] AG March cpd

mascalzo'nata [maskaltso'nata] SF dirty trick

mascal'zone [maskal'tsone] SM rascal, scoundrel

mas'cara SM INV mascara

mascar'pone SM soft cream cheese often used in desserts

ma'scella [maʃ'ʃella] SF (Anat) jaw

'maschera ['maskera] SF mask; (travestimento) disguise; (per un ballo ecc) fancy dress; (Teat, Cine) usher/usherette; (personaggio del teatro) stock character; **in ~** (mascherato) masked; **ballo in ~** fancy-dress ball; **gettare la ~** (fig) to reveal o.s.; **~ antigas/subacquea** gas/diving mask; **~ di bellezza** face pack

masche'rare [maske'rare] /72/ VT to mask; (travestire) to disguise; to dress up; (fig: celare) to hide, conceal; (Mil) to camouflage ■ **mascherarsi** VPR: **mascherarsi da** to disguise o.s. as; to dress up as; (fig) to masquerade as

masche'rina [maske'rina] SF (piccola maschera) mask; (di animale) patch; (di scarpe) toe-cap; (Aut) radiator grill

mas'chile [mas'kile] AG masculine; (sesso, popolazione) male; (abiti) men's; (per ragazzi: scuola) boys'

mas'chilista, -i, -e AG, SM/F (uomo) (male) chauvinist, sexist; (donna) sexist

'maschio, -a ['maskjo] AG (Biol) male; (virile) manly ▶ SM (anche Zool, Tecn) male; (uomo) man; (ragazzo) boy; (figlio) son

masco'lino, -a AG masculine

mas'cotte [mas'kɔt] SF INV mascot

maso'chismo [mazo'kizmo] SM masochism

maso'chista, -i, -e [mazo'kista] AG masochistic ▶ SM/F masochist

'massa SF mass; (di gente) mass, multitude; (Elettr) earth; **una ~ di** (di errori ecc) heaps of, masses of; **in ~** (Comm) in bulk; (tutti insieme) en masse; **adunata in ~** mass meeting; **manifestazione/cultura di ~** mass demonstration/culture; **produrre in ~** to mass-produce; **la ~ (del popolo)** the masses pl

massa'crante AG exhausting, gruelling

massa'crare /72/ VT to massacre, slaughter

mas'sacro SM massacre, slaughter; (fig) mess, disaster

massaggi'are [massad'dʒare] /62/ VT to massage

massaggia'tore, -'trice [massaddʒa'tore] SM/F masseur (masseuse)

mas'saggio [mas'saddʒo] SM massage; **~ cardiaco** cardiac massage

mas'saia SF housewife

masse'ria SF large farm

masse'rizie [masse'rittsje] SFPL (household) furnishings

massicci'ata [massit'tʃata] SF (di strada, ferrovia) ballast

mas'siccio, -a, -ci, -ce [mas'sittʃo] AG (oro, legno) solid; (palazzo) massive; (corporatura) stout ▶ SM (Geo) massif

'massima SF vedi **massimo**

massi'male SM maximum; (Comm) ceiling, limit

'massimo, -a AG, SM maximum ▶ SF (sentenza, regola) maxim; (Meteor) maximum temperature; **in linea di massima** generally speaking; **arrivare entro il tempo ~** to arrive within the time limit; **al ~** at (the) most; **sfruttare qc al ~** to make full use of sth; **arriverò al ~ alle 5** I'll arrive at 5 at the latest; **erano presenti le massime autorità** all the most important dignitaries were there; **il ~ della pena** (Dir) the maximum penalty

mas'sivo, -a AG (intervento) en masse; (emigrazione) mass; (emorragia) massive

'masso SM rock, boulder

mas'sone SM freemason

massone'ria SF freemasonry

mas'sonico, -a, -ci, -che AG masonic

mas'tello SM tub

masteriz'zare [masterid'dzare] /72/ VT (CD, DVD) to burn

masterizza'tore [masteriddza'tore] SM CD burner o writer

masti'care /20/ VT to chew

'mastice ['mastitʃe] SM mastic; (per vetri) putty

mas'tino SM mastiff

masto'dontico, -a, -ci, -che AG gigantic

mastur'barsi /72/ VPR to masturbate

masturbazi'one [masturbat'tsjone] SF masturbation

ma'tassa SF skein

mate'matico, -a, -ci, -che AG mathematical ▶ SM/F mathematician ▶ SF mathematics sg

materas'sino SM mat; **~ gonfiabile** air bed

mate'rasso SM mattress; **~ a molle** spring o interior-sprung mattress

ma'teria SF (Fisica) matter; (Tecn, Comm) material, matter no pl; (disciplina) subject; (argomento) subject matter, material; **in ~ di** (per quanto concerne) on the subject of; **prima di entrare in ~ ...** before discussing the matter in hand ...; **un esperto in ~ (di musica etc)** an expert on the subject (of music etc); **sono ignorante in ~** I know nothing about it; **~ cerebrale** cerebral matter; **~ grassa** fat; **~ grigia** (anche fig) grey matter; **materie plastiche** plastics; **materie prime** raw materials

materi'ale AG material; (fig: grossolano) rough, rude ▶ SM material; (insieme di strumenti ecc) equipment no pl, materials pl; **~ da costruzione** building materials pl

materia'lista, -i, -e AG materialistic ▶ SM/F materialist

materializ'zarsi [materjalid'dzarsi] /72/ VPR to materialize

material'mente AV (fisicamente) materially; (economicamente) financially

mater'nità SF motherhood, maternity; (clinica) maternity hospital; (reparto) maternity ward; **in (congedo di) ~** on maternity leave

ma'terno, -a AG (amore, cura ecc) maternal, motherly; (nonno) maternal; (lingua, terra) mother cpd; vedi anche **scuola**

ma'tita SF pencil; **matite colorate** coloured pencils; **~ per gli occhi** eyeliner (pencil)

ma'trice [ma'tritʃe] SF matrix; (Comm) counterfoil; (fig: origine) background

ma'tricola SF (registro) register; (numero) registration number; (nell'università) freshman, fresher (BRIT col)

ma'trigna [ma'triɲɲa] SF stepmother

matrimoni'ale AG matrimonial, marriage cpd; **camera/letto ~** double room/bed

matri'monio SM marriage, matrimony; (durata) marriage, married life; (cerimonia) wedding

m

ma'trona SF (fig) matronly woman

matta'toio SM abattoir (BRIT), slaughterhouse

mat'tina SF morning; **la** o **alla** o **di ~** in the morning; **di prima ~, la ~ presto** early in the morning; **dalla ~ alla sera** (continuamente) from morning to night; (improvvisamente: cambiare) overnight

matti'nata SF morning; (spettacolo) matinée, afternoon performance; **in ~** in the course of the morning; **nella ~** in the morning; **nella tarda ~** at the end of the morning; **nella tarda ~ di sabato** late on Saturday morning

mattini'ero, -a AG: **essere ~** to be an early riser

mat'tino SM morning; **di buon ~** early in the morning

'matto, -a AG mad, crazy; (fig: falso) false, imitation; (opaco) matt, dull ▶ SM/F madman/woman; **avere una voglia matta di qc** to be dying for sth; **far diventare ~ qn** to drive sb mad o crazy; **una gabbia di matti** (fig) a madhouse

mat'tone SM brick; (fig): **questo libro/film è un ~** this book/film is heavy going

matto'nella SF tile

mattu'tino, -a AG morning cpd

matu'rare /72/ VI (anche: **maturarsi**: frutta, grano) to ripen; (ascesso) to come to a head; (fig: persona, idea, Econ) to mature ▶ VT to ripen, to (make) mature; **~ una decisione** to come to a decision

maturità SF maturity; (di frutta) ripeness, maturity; (Ins) school-leaving examination, ≈ GCE A-levels (BRIT)

> The school-leaving diploma or **maturità** is awarded to students who have passed their final-year examination (also called maturità) at the age of 18 or 19 and is required for entrance to a university.

ma'turo, -a AG mature; (frutto) ripe, mature

ma'tusa SM INV/F INV (scherzoso) old fogey

Mauri'tania SF: **la ~** Mauritania

Mau'rizio SF: (**l'isola di**) **~** Mauritius

mauso'leo SM mausoleum

max. ABBR (= massimo) max

'maxi... PREFISSO maxi...

maxipro'cesso [maksipro'tʃɛsso] SM see note

> A **maxiprocesso** is a criminal trial which is characterized by the large number of co-defendants. These people are usually members of terrorist or criminal organizations. The trials are often lengthy and many witnesses may be called to give evidence.

maxis'chermo [maksis'kermo] SM giant screen

'mazza ['mattsa] SF (bastone) club; (martello) sledge-hammer; (Sport: da golf) club; (: da baseball, cricket) bat

maz'zata [mat'tsata] SF (anche fig) heavy blow

maz'zetta [mat'tsetta] SF (di banconote ecc) bundle; (fig) rake-off

'mazzo ['mattso] SM (di fiori, chiavi ecc) bunch; (di carte da gioco) pack

MC SIGLA = **Macerata**

m.c.d. ABBR (= minimo comune denominatore) lcd

m.c.m. ABBR (= minimo comune multiplo) lcm

ME SIGLA = **Messina**

me PRON me; **me stesso, me stessa** myself; **sei bravo quanto me** you are as clever as I (am) o as me

me'andro SM meander

M.E.C. [mɛk] ABBR M = **Mercato Comune Europeo**

'Mecca SF (anche fig): **La ~** Mecca

meccanica'mente AV mechanically

mec'canico, -a, -ci, -che AG mechanical ▶ SM mechanic ▶ SF mechanics sg; (attività tecnologica) mechanical engineering; (meccanismo) mechanism; **officina meccanica** garage

mecca'nismo SM mechanism

meccaniz'zare [mekkanid'dzare] /72/ VT to mechanize

meccanizzazi'one [mekkaniddzat'tsjone] SF mechanization

meccanogra'fia SF (mechanical) data processing

meccano'grafico, -a, -ci, -che AG: **centro ~** data processing department

mece'nate [metʃe'nate] SM patron

mèche [mɛʃ] SF INV streak; **farsi le ~** to have one's hair streaked

me'daglia [me'daʎʎa] SF medal; **~ d'oro** (oggetto) gold medal; (persona) gold medallist (BRIT) o medalist (US)

medagli'one [medaʎ'ʎone] SM (Archit) medallion; (gioiello) locket

me'desimo, -a AG same; (in persona): **io ~** I myself

'media SF vedi medio

media'mente AV on average

medi'ano, -a AG median; (valore) mean ▶ SM (Calcio) half-back

medi'ante PREP by means of

medi'are /19/ VT (fare da mediatore) to act as mediator in; (Mat) to average

medi'ato, -a AG indirect

media'tore, -'trice SM/F mediator; (Comm) middle man, agent; **fare da ~ fra** to mediate between

mediazi'one [medjat'tsjone] SF mediation; (Comm: azione, compenso) brokerage

medica'mento SM medicine, drug

medi'care /20/ VT to treat; (ferita) to dress

medi'cato, -a AG (garza, shampoo) medicated

medicazi'one [medikat'tsjone] SF treatment, medication dressing; **fare una ~ a qn** to dress sb's wounds

medi'cina [medi'tʃina] SF medicine; **~ legale** forensic medicine

medici'nale [meditʃi'nale] AG medicinal ▶ SM drug, medicine

'medico, -a, -ci, -che AG medical ▶ SM doctor; **~ di bordo** ship's doctor; **~ di famiglia** family doctor; **~ fiscale** doctor who examines patients signed off sick for a lengthy period by their private doctor; **~ generico** general practitioner, GP

medie'vale AG medieval

'medio, -a AG average; (punto, ceto) middle; (altezza, statura) medium ▶ SM (dito) middle finger ▶ SF average; (Mat) mean; (Ins: voto) end-of-term average ■ **medie** SFPL vedi **scuola media**; **licenza media** leaving certificate awarded at the end of 3 years of secondary education; **in media** on average; **al di sopra/sotto della media** above/below average; **viaggiare ad una media di ...** to travel at an average speed of ...; **il M~ Oriente** the Middle East

medi'ocre AG (gen) mediocre; (qualità, stipendio) poor

mediocrità SF mediocrity; poorness

medioe'vale AG = medievale

Medio'evo SM Middle Ages pl

medita'bondo, -a AG thoughtful

medi'tare /72/ VT to ponder over, meditate on; (progettare) to plan, think out ▶ VI to meditate

medi'tato, -a AG (gen) meditated; (parole) carefully-weighed; (vendetta) premeditated; **ben ~** (piano) well worked-out, neat

meditazi'one [meditat'tsjone] SF meditation

mediter'raneo, -a AG Mediterranean; **il (mare) M~** the Mediterranean (Sea)

'medium SM INV/F INV medium

me'dusa SF (Zool) jellyfish

'mega SM INV (Inform) meg

mega'byte SM INV (Inform) megabyte

me'gafono SM megaphone

mega'lomane AG, SMF megalomaniac

me'gera [me'dʒera] SF (peg: donna) shrew

'meglio ['meʎʎo] AV, AG INV better; (con senso superlativo) best ▶ SM (la cosa migliore): **il ~** the best (thing); **faresti ~ ad andartene** you had better leave; **alla ~** as best one can; **andar di bene in ~** to get better and better; **fare del proprio ~** to do one's best; **per il ~** for the best; **aver la ~ su qn** to get the better of sb

'mela SF apple; **~ cotogna** quince

mela'grana SF pomegranate

melan'zana [melan'dzana] SF aubergine (BRIT), eggplant (US)

me'lassa SF molasses sg, treacle

melato'nina SF melatonin

me'lenso, -a AG dull, stupid

me'lissa SF (Bot) balm

mel'lifluo, -a AG (peg) sugary, honeyed

'melma SF mud, mire

'melo SM apple tree

melo'dia SF melody

me'lodico, -a, -ci, -che AG melodic

melodi'oso, -a AG melodious

melo'dramma, -i SM melodrama

me'lone SM (musk) melon

'membra SFPL vedi **membro**

mem'brana SF membrane

'membro SM (pl(m) **membri**: person) member; (pl(f) **membra**: arto) limb

memo'rabile AG memorable

memo'randum SM INV memorandum

'memore AG: **~ di** (ricordando) mindful of; (riconoscente) grateful for

me'moria SF (anche Inform) memory ■ **memorie** SFPL (opera autobiografica) memoirs; **a ~** (imparare, sapere) by heart; **a ~ d'uomo** within living memory; **~ di sola lettura** (Inform) read-only memory; **~ tampone** (Inform) buffer

memori'ale SM (raccolta di memorie) memoirs pl; (Dir) memorial

memoriz'zare [memorid'dzare] /72/ VT (gen) to memorize; (Inform) to store

memorizzazi'one [memoriddzat'tsjone] SF memorization; storage

'mena SF scheme

mena'dito SM: **a ~** av perfectly, thoroughly; **sapere qc a ~** to have sth at one's fingertips

mena'gramo SM INV/F INV jinx, Jonah

me'nare /72/ VT to lead; (picchiare) to hit, beat; (dare: colpi) to deal; **~ la coda** (cane) to wag its tail; **~ qc per le lunghe** to drag sth out; **~ il can per l'aia** (fig) to beat about (BRIT) o around (US) the bush

mendi'cante SMF beggar

mendi'care /20/ VT to beg for ▶ VI to beg

menefre'ghismo [menefre'gizmo] SM (col) couldn't-care-less attitude

me'ninge [me'nindʒe] SF (Med) meninx; **spremersi le meningi** to rack one's brains

menin'gite [menin'dʒite] SF meningitis

me'nisco SM (Anat, Mat, Fisica) meniscus

'meno

AV **1** (in minore misura) less; **dovresti mangiare meno** you should eat less, you shouldn't eat so much; **è sempre meno facile** it's getting less and less easy; **ne voglio di meno** I don't want so much

2 (comparativo): **meno ... di** not as ... as, less ... than; **sono meno alto di te** I'm not as tall as you (are), I'm less tall than you (are);

m

meno ... che not as ... as, less ... than; **meno che mai** less than ever; **è meno intelligente che ricco** he's more rich than intelligent; **meno fumo più mangio** the less I smoke the more I eat; **meno di quanto pensassi** less than I thought

3 (*superlativo*) least; **il meno dotato degli studenti** the least gifted of the students; **è quello che compro meno spesso** it's the one I buy least often

4 (*Mat*) minus; **8 meno 5** 8 minus 5, 8 take away 5; **sono le 8 meno un quarto** it's a quarter to 8; **meno 5 gradi** 5 degrees below zero, minus 5 degrees; **mille euro in meno** a thousand euros less; **ha preso 6 meno** (*a scuola*) he scraped a pass; **cento euro meno le spese** a hundred euros minus *o* less expenses

5 (*fraseologia*): **quanto meno poteva telefonare** he could at least have phoned; **non so se accettare o meno** I don't know whether to accept or not; **non essere da meno di** not to be outdone by; **fare a meno di qc/qn** to do without sth/sb; **non potevo fare a meno di ridere** I couldn't help laughing; **meno male!** thank goodness!; **meno male che sei arrivato** it's a good job that you've come

▶ AG INV (*tempo, denaro*) less; (*errori, persone*) fewer; **ha fatto meno errori di tutti** he made fewer mistakes than anyone, he made the fewest mistakes of all

▶ SM INV **1: il meno** (*il minimo*) the least; **parlare del più e del meno** to talk about this and that; **era il meno che ti potesse succedere** it was the least you could have expected **2** (*Mat*) minus

▶ PREP (*eccetto*) except (for), apart from; **tutti meno lui** everybody apart from *o* except him; **a meno che, a meno di** unless; **a meno che non piova** unless it rains; **non posso, a meno di prendere ferie** I can't, unless I take some leave

vedi anche **più**

meno'mare /72/ VT (*danneggiare*) to maim, disable

meno'mato, -a AG (*persona*) disabled ▶ SM/F disabled person

menomazi'one [menomat'tsjone] SF disablement

meno'pausa SF menopause

'mensa SF (*locale*) canteen; (: *Mil*) mess; (: *nelle università*) refectory

men'sile AG monthly ▶ SM (*periodico*) monthly (magazine); (*stipendio*) monthly salary

mensil'mente AV (*ogni mese*) every month; (*una volta al mese*) monthly

'mensola SF bracket; (*ripiano*) shelf; (*Archit*) corbel

'menta SF mint; (*anche:* **menta piperita**) peppermint; (: *bibita*) peppermint cordial; (: *caramella*) mint, peppermint

men'tale AG mental

mentalità SF INV mentality

mental'mente AV mentally

'mente SF mind; **imparare/sapere qc a ~ to** learn/know sth by heart; **avere in ~ qc** to have sth in mind; **avere in ~ di fare qc** to intend to do sth; **fare venire in ~ qc a qn** to remind sb of sth; **mettersi in ~ di fare qc** to make up one's mind to do sth; **passare di ~ a qn** to slip sb's mind; **tenere a ~ qc** to bear sth in mind; **a ~ fredda** objectively; **lasciami fare ~ locale** let me think

mente'catto, -a AG half-witted ▶ SM/F half-wit, imbecile

men'tire /17/ VI to lie

men'tito, -a AG: **sotto mentite spoglie** under false pretences (BRIT) *o* pretenses (US)

'mento SM chin; **doppio ~** double chin

men'tolo SM menthol

'mentre CONG (*temporale*) while; (*avversativo*) whereas ▶ SM: **in quel ~** at that very moment

menù SM INV (set) menu; **~ turistico** set *o* tourists' menu

menzio'nare [mentsjo'nare] /72/ VT to mention

menzi'one [men'tsjone] SF mention; **fare ~ di** to mention

men'zogna [men'tsɔɲɲa] SF lie

menzo'gnero, -a [mentsoɲ'ɲero] AG false, untrue

mera'viglia [mera'viʎʎa] SF amazement, wonder; (*persona, cosa*) marvel, wonder; **a ~** perfectly, wonderfully

meravigli'are [meraviʎ'ʎare] /27/ VT to amaze, astonish ■ **meravigliarsi** VPR: **meravigliarsi (di)** to marvel (at); (*stupirsi*) to be amazed (at), be astonished (at); **mi meraviglio di te!** I'm surprised at you!; **non c'è da meravigliarsi** it's not surprising

meravigli'oso, -a [meraviʎ'ʎoso] AG wonderful, marvellous (BRIT), marvelous (US)

merc. ABBR (= *mercoledì*) Wed

mer'cante SM merchant; **~ d'arte** art dealer; **~ di cavalli** horse dealer

mercanteggi'are [merkanted'dʒare] /62/ VT (*onore, voto*) to sell ▶ VI to bargain, haggle

mercan'tile AG commercial, mercantile; (*nave, marina*) merchant *cpd* ▶ SM (*nave*) merchantman

mercan'zia [merkan'tsia] SF merchandise, goods *pl*

merca'tino SM (*rionale*) local street market; (*Econ*) unofficial stock market

mer'cato SM market; **~ di** (*economia, prezzo, ricerche*) market *cpd*; **mettere** *o* **lanciare qc sul ~** to launch sth on the market; **a buon ~** cheap; **~**

dei cambi exchange market; **M~ Comune (Europeo)** (European) Common Market; **~ del lavoro** labour market, job market; **~ nero** black market; **~ al rialzo/al ribasso** (*Borsa*) sellers'/buyers' market

'**merce** ['mertʃe] SF goods *pl*, merchandise; **~ deperibile** perishable goods *pl*

mercé [mer'tʃe] SF mercy; **essere alla ~ di qn** to be at sb's mercy

merce'nario, -a [mertʃe'narjo] AG, SM mercenary

merce'ria [mertʃe'ria] SF (*articoli*) haberdashery (*BRIT*), notions *pl* (*US*); (*bottega*) haberdasher's shop (*BRIT*), notions store (*US*)

mercoledì SM INV Wednesday; **di** *o* **il ~** on Wednesdays; **~ delle Ceneri** Ash Wednesday; *vedi anche* **martedì**

mer'curio SM mercury

'**merda** SF (*col*) shit (*!*)

me'renda SF afternoon snack

meren'dina SF snack

meridi'ano, -a AG (*di mezzogiorno*) midday *cpd*, noonday ▶ SM meridian ▶ SF (*orologio*) sundial

meridio'nale AG southern ▶ SMF southerner

meridi'one SM south

me'ringa, -ghe SF (*Cuc*) meringue

meri'tare /72/ VT to deserve, merit ▶ VB IMPERS (*valere la pena*): **merita andare** it's worth going; **non merita neanche parlarne** it's not worth talking about it; **per quel che merita** for what it's worth

meri'tevole AG worthy

'**merito** SM merit; (*valore*) worth; **dare ~ a qn di** to give sb credit for; **finire a pari ~** to finish joint first (*o second etc*); to tie; **in ~ a** as regards, with regard to; **entrare nel ~ di una questione** to go into a matter; **non so niente in ~** I don't know anything about it

meritocra'zia [meritokrat'tsia] SF meritocracy

meri'torio, -a AG praiseworthy

mer'letto SM lace

'**merlo** SM (*Zool*) blackbird; (*Archit*) battlement

mer'luzzo [mer'luttso] SM (*Zool*) cod

'**mescere** ['meʃʃere] /29/ VT to pour (out)

meschinità [meskini'ta] SF wretchedness; meagreness; meanness, narrow-mindedness

mes'chino, -a [mes'kino] AG wretched; (*scarso*) meagre (*BRIT*), meager (*US*), scanty, poor; (*persona: gretta*) mean; (: *limitata*) narrow-minded, petty; **fare una figura meschina** to cut a poor figure

'**mescita** ['meʃʃita] SF wine shop

mesci'uto, -a [meʃ'ʃuto] PP *di* **mescere**

mesco'lanza [mesko'lantsa] SF mixture

mesco'lare /72/ VT to mix; (*vini, colori*) to blend; (*mettere in disordine*) to mix up, muddle up; (*carte*) to shuffle ▪ **mescolarsi** VPR to mix; to blend; to

get mixed up; (*fig*) **mescolarsi in** to get mixed up in, meddle in

'**mese** SM month; **il ~ scorso** last month; **il corrente ~** this month

'**messa** SF (*Rel*) mass; (*il mettere*): **~ a fuoco** focusing; **~ in moto** starting; **~ in piega** (*acconciatura*) set; **~ a punto** (*Tecn*) adjustment; (*Aut*) tuning; (*fig*) clarification; **~ in scena** = **messinscena**

messagge'rie [messaddʒe'rie] SFPL (*ditta: di distribuzione*) distributors; (: *di trasporto*) freight company

messag'gero [messad'dʒero] SM messenger

messag'giare [messa'dzare] /72/ VI (*col*) to message ▶ VT to message; **~ con qn** to message sb; **~ qn su Facebook** to facebook sb ▪ **messaggiarsi** VPR to text; **messaggiamoci** we'll text each other

messag'gino [messad'dʒino] SM (*di telefonino*) text (message)

mes'saggio [mes'saddʒo] SM message; **~ istantaneo** instant message

messag'gistica [messad'dʒistika] SF: **~ immediata** (*Inform*) instant messaging; **programma di ~ immediata** instant messenger

mes'sale SM (*Rel*) missal

'**messe** SF harvest

Mes'sia SM INV (*Rel*): **il ~** the Messiah

messi'cano, -a AG, SM/F Mexican

'**Messico** SM: **il ~** Mexico; **Città del ~** Mexico City

messin'scena [messin'ʃena] SF (*Teat*) production

'**messo, -a** PP *di* **mettere** ▶ SM messenger

mestie'rante SMF (*peg*) money-grubber; (: *scrittore*) hack

mesti'ere SM (*professione*) job; (*artigianale*) craft; (*manuale*) trade; (*fig: abilità nel lavoro*) skill, technique; **di ~** by *o* to trade; **essere del ~** to know the tricks of the trade

mes'tizia [mes'tittsja] SF sadness, melancholy

'**mesto, -a** AG sad, melancholy

'**mestolo** SM (*Cuc*) ladle

mestru'ale AG menstrual

mestruazi'one [mestruat'tsjone] SF menstruation; **avere le mestruazioni** to have one's period

'**meta** SF destination; (*fig*) aim, goal

metà SF INV half; (*punto di mezzo*) middle; **dividere qc** *a o* **per ~** to divide sth in half, halve sth; **fare a ~ (di qc con qn)** to go halves (with sb in sth); **a ~ prezzo** at half price; **a ~ settimana** midweek; **a ~ strada** halfway; **verso la ~ del mese** halfway through the month, towards the middle of the month; **dire le cose a ~** to leave some things unsaid; **fare le cose a ~** to leave things half-done; **la mia dolce ~** (*col, scherzoso*) my better half

metabo'lismo SM metabolism

m

meta'done SM methadone

meta'fisica SF metaphysics *sg*

me'tafora SF metaphor

meta'forico, -a, -ci, -che AG metaphorical

me'tallico, -a, -ci, -che AG (*di metallo*) metal *cpd*; (*splendore, rumore ecc*) metallic

metalliz'zato, -a [metallid'dzato] AG (*verniciatura*) metallic

me'tallo SM metal; **di ~** metal *cpd*

metallur'gia [metallur'dʒia] SF metallurgy

metalmec'canico, -a, -ci, -che AG engineering *cpd* ▶ SM engineering worker

meta'morfosi SF metamorphosis

me'tano SM methane

me'teora SF meteor

meteo'rite SM meteorite

meteorolo'gia [meteorolo'dʒia] SF meteorology

meteoro'logico, -a, -ci, -che [meteoro'lɔdʒiko] AG meteorological, weather *cpd*

meteo'rologo, -a, -ghi, -ghe SM/F meteorologist

me'ticcio, -a, -ci, -ce [me'tittʃo] SM/F halfcaste (!), half-breed (!)

meticolosità SF meticulousness

metico'loso, -a AG meticulous

me'todico, -a, -ci, -che AG methodical

'metodo SM method; (*manuale*) tutor (BRIT), manual; **far qc con/senza ~** to do sth methodically/unmethodically

me'traggio [me'traddʒo] SM (*Sartoria*) length; (*Cine*) footage; **film a lungo ~** feature film; **film a corto ~** short film

metra'tura SF length

'metrico, -a, -ci, -che AG metric; (*Poesia*) metrical ▶ SF metrics *sg*

'metro SM metre (BRIT), meter (US); (*nastro*) tape measure; (*asta*) (metre) rule

metrò SM INV underground (BRIT), subway (US)

metro'notte SM INV night security guard

me'tropoli SF metropolis

metropoli'tano, -a AG metropolitan ▶ SF underground (BRIT), subway (US); **metropolitana leggera** metro (*mainly on the surface*)

metroses'suale AG metrosexual

'mettere /63/ VT to put; (*abito*) to put on; (: *portare*) to wear; (*installare: telefono*) to put in; **~ fame/allegria a qn** (*fig: provocare*) to make sb hungry/happy; (*supporre*): **mettiamo che ...** let's suppose *o* say that ... ▪ **mettersi** VPR (*persona*) to put o.s.; (*oggetto*) to go; (*disporsi: faccenda*) to turn out; **mettersi a** (*cominciare*) to begin to, start to; **mettersi a piangere/ridere** to start crying/laughing, start *o* begin to cry/laugh; **mettersi a sedere** to sit down; **mettersi al lavoro** to set to work; **mettersi a letto** to get

into bed; (*per malattia*) to take to one's bed; **mettersi il cappello** to put on one's hat; **mettersi sotto** to get down to things; **mettersi in società** to set up in business; **si sono messi insieme** (*coppia*) they've started going out together (BRIT) *o* dating (US); **mettersi con qn** (*in società*) to team up with sb; (*in coppia*) to start going out with sb; **metterci: metterci molta cura/molto tempo** to take a lot of care/a lot of time; **mettercela tutta** to do one's best; **ci ho messo 3 ore per venire** it's taken me 3 hours to get here; **~ un annuncio sul giornale** to place an advertisement in the paper; **~ a confronto** to compare; **~ in conto** (*somma ecc*) to put on account; **~ in luce** (*problemi, errori*) to stress, highlight; **~ a tacere qn/qc** to keep sb/sth quiet; **~ su casa** to set up house; **~ su un negozio** to start a shop; **~ su peso** to put on weight; **~ via** to put away

mez'zadro [med'dzadro] SM (*Agr*) sharecropper

mezza'luna [meddza'luna] (*pl* **mezzelune**) SF half-moon; (*dell'islamismo*) crescent; (*coltello*) (semicircular) chopping knife

mezza'nino [meddza'nino] SM mezzanine (floor)

mez'zano, -a [med'dzano] AG (*medio*) average, medium; (*figlio*) middle *cpd* ▶ SM/F (*intermediario*) go-between; (*ruffiano*) pimp

mezza'notte [meddza'nɔtte] SF midnight

'mezzo, -a ['mɛddzo] AG half; **un ~ litro/panino** half a litre/roll ▶ AV half-; **~ morto** half-dead ▶ SM (*metà*) half; (*parte centrale: di strada ecc*) middle; (*per raggiungere un fine*) means *sg*; (*veicolo*) vehicle; (*nell'indicare l'ora*): **le nove e ~** half past nine; **mezzogiorno e ~** half past twelve ▶ SF: **la mezza** half-past twelve (in the afternoon) ▪ **mezzi** SMPL (*possibilità economiche*) means; **di mezza età** middle-aged; **aver una mezza idea di fare qc** to have half a mind to do sth; **è stato un ~ scandalo** it almost caused a scandal; **un soprabito di mezza stagione** a spring (*o* autumn) coat; **a mezza voce** in an undertone; **una volta e ~ più grande** one and a half times bigger; **di ~** middle, in the middle; **andarci di ~** (*patir danno*) to suffer; **esserci di ~** (*ostacolo*) to be in the way; **levarsi** *o* **togliersi di ~** to get out of the way; **mettersi di ~** to interfere; **togliere di ~** (*persona, cosa*) to get rid of; (*col: uccidere*) to bump off; **non c'è una via di ~** there's no middle course; **in ~ a** in the middle of; **nel bel ~ (di)** right in the middle (of); **per** *o* **a ~ di** by means of; **a ~ corriere** by carrier; **mezzi di comunicazione di massa** mass media *pl*; **mezzi pubblici** public transport *sg*; **mezzi di trasporto** means of transport

mezzogi'orno [meddzo'dʒorno] SM midday, noon; (*Geo*) south; **a ~** at 12 (o'clock) *o* midday *o* noon; **il ~ d'Italia** southern Italy

mezz'ora [med'dzora] SF half-hour, half an hour

MI SIGLA = **Milano**

mi PRON (dav lo, la, li, le, ne diventa **me**: oggetto) me; (complemento di termine) (to) me; (riflessivo) myself ▶ SM (Mus) E; (: solfeggiando la scala) mi; **mi aiuti?** will you help me?; **me ne ha parlato** he spoke to me about it, he told me about it; **mi servo da solo** I'll help myself

'**mia** vedi **mio**

miago'lare /72/ VI to miaow, mew

Mib SIGLA M, AG (= indice borsa Milano) Milan Stock Exchange Index

'**mica** SF (Chim) mica ▶ AV (col): **non ... ~** not ... at all; **non sono ~ stanco** I'm not a bit tired; **non sarà ~ partito?** he wouldn't have left, would he?; **~ male** not bad

'**miccia, -ce** ['mittʃa] SF fuse

micidi'ale [mitʃi'djale] AG fatal; (dannosissimo) deadly

'**micio, -a, -ci, -cie** ['mitʃo] SM/F pussy (cat)

microbiolo'gia [mikrobiolo'dʒia] SF microbiology

micro'blog [mikro'blɔg] SM INV microblog

'**microbo** SM microbe

microcir'cuito [mikrotʃir'kuito] SM microcircuit

micro'fibra SF microfibre

micro'film SM INV microfilm

mi'crofono SM microphone

microinfor'matica SF microcomputing

micro'onda SF microwave

microproces'sore [mikroprotʃes'sore] SM microprocessor

micros'copico, -a, -ci, -che AG microscopic

micros'copio SM microscope

micro'solco, -chi SM (solco) microgroove; (disco: a 33 giri) long-playing record, LP; (: a 45 giri) extended-play record, EP

micros'pia SF hidden microphone, bug (col)

mi'dollo (pl(f) **midolla**) SM (Anat) marrow; **~ spinale** spinal cord; **~ osseo** bone marrow

'**mie** vedi **mio**

mi'ele SM honey

mi'etere /29/ VT (Agr) to reap, harvest; (fig: vite) to take, claim

mietitrebbia'trice [mjetitrebbja'tritʃe] SF combine harvester

mieti'trice [mjeti'tritʃe] SF (macchina) harvester

mieti'tura SF (raccolto) harvest; (lavoro) harvesting; (tempo) harvest-time

'**miglia** ['miʎʎa] SFPL di **miglio¹**

migli'aio [miʎ'ʎajo] (pl(f) **migliaia**) SM thousand; **un ~ (di)** about a thousand; **a migliaia** by the thousand, in thousands

'**miglio¹** ['miʎʎo] (pl(f) **miglia**) SM (unità di misura) mile; **~ marino o nautico** nautical mile

'**miglio²** ['miʎʎo] SM (Bot) millet

migliora'mento [miʎʎora'mento] SM improvement

miglio'rare [miʎʎo'rare] /72/ VT, VI to improve

migli'ore [miʎ'ʎore] AG (comparativo) better; (superlativo) best ▶ SM: **il ~** the best (thing) ▶ SMF: **il (la) ~** the best (person); **il miglior vino di questa regione** the best wine in this area; **i migliori auguri** best wishes

miglio'ria [miʎʎo'ria] SF improvement

'**mignolo** ['miɲɲolo] SM (Anat) little finger, pinkie; (: dito del piede) little toe

mi'grare /72/ VI to migrate

migrazi'one [migrat'tsjone] SF migration

'**mila** PL di **mille**

mila'nese AG Milanese ▶ SMF person from Milan; **i milanesi** the Milanese; **cotoletta alla ~** (Cuc) Wiener schnitzel; **risotto alla ~** (Cuc) risotto with saffron

Mi'lano SF Milan

miliar'dario, -a AG, SM/F millionaire

mili'ardo SM thousand million (BRIT), billion (US)

mili'are AG: **pietra ~** milestone

milio'nario, -a AG, SM/F millionaire

mili'one SM million; **un ~ di euro** a million euros

mili'tante AG, SMF militant

mili'tanza [mili'tantsa] SF militancy

mili'tare /72/ VI (Mil) to be a soldier, serve; (fig: in un partito) to be a militant ▶ AG military ▶ SM serviceman; **fare il ~** to do one's military service; **~ di carriera** regular (soldier)

milita'resco, -a, -schi, -sche AG (portamento) military cpd

'**milite** SM soldier

mi'lizia [mi'littsja] SF (corpo armato) militia

milizi'ano [milit'tsjano] SM militiaman

millanta'tore, -'trice SM/F boaster

millante'ria SF (qualità) boastfulness

'**mille** (pl **mila**) NUM a o one thousand; **diecimila** ten thousand; **~ euro** one thousand euros

mille'foglie [mille'fɔʎʎe] SM INV (Cuc) cream o vanilla slice

mil'lennio SM millennium

millepi'edi SM INV centipede

mil'lesimo, -a AG, SM thousandth

milli'grammo SM milligram(me)

mil'lilitro SM millilitre (BRIT), milliliter (US)

mil'limetro SM millimetre (BRIT), millimeter (US)

'**milza** ['miltsa] SF (Anat) spleen

mi'metico, -a, -ci, -che AG (arte) mimetic; **tuta mimetica** (Mil) camouflage

mime'tismo SM camouflage

mimetiz'zare [mimetid'dzare] /72/ VT to camouflage ∎ **mimetizzarsi** VPR to camouflage o.s.

'**mimica** SF (arte) mime

'**mimo** SM (*attore, componimento*) mime

mi'mosa SF mimosa

min. ABBR (= *minuto, minimo*) min

'**mina** SF (*esplosiva*) mine; (*di matita*) lead

mi'naccia, -ce [mi'nattʃa] SF threat; **sotto la ~ di** under threat of

minacci'are [minat'tʃare] /**14**/ VT to threaten; **~ qn di morte** to threaten to kill sb; **~ di fare qc** to threaten to do sth; **minaccia di piovere** it looks like rain

minacci'oso, -a [minat'tʃoso] AG threatening

mi'nare /**72**/ VT (*Mil*) to mine; (*fig*) to undermine

mina'tore SM miner

mina'torio, -a AG threatening

minchi'one, -a [min'kjone] AG (*col*) idiotic ▶ SM/F idiot

mine'rale AG, SM mineral

mineralo'gia [mineralo'dʒia] SF mineralogy

mine'rario, -a AG (*delle miniere*) mining; (*dei minerali*) ore *cpd*

mi'nestra SF soup; **~ in brodo** noodle soup; **~ di verdura** vegetable soup

mines'trone SM thick vegetable and pasta soup

mingher'lino, -a [minger'lino] AG thin, slender

'**mini** AG INV mini ▶ SF INV miniskirt

minia'tura SF miniature

mini'bar SM INV minibar

minielabora'tore SM minicomputer

mini'era SF mine; **~ di carbone** coalmine; (*impresa*) colliery (*BRIT*), coalmine

mini'gonna SF miniskirt

minima'lista, -i, -e AG, SM/F minimalist

minimiz'zare [minimid'dzare] /**72**/ VT to minimize

'**minimo, -a** AG minimum, least, slightest; (*piccolissimo*) very small, slight; (*il più basso*) lowest, minimum ▶ SM minimum; **al ~** at least; **girare al ~** (*Aut*) to idle; **il ~ indispensabile** the bare minimum; **il ~ della pena** the minimum sentence

minis'tero SM (*Pol, Rel*) ministry; (*governo*) government; (*Dir*): **Pubblico M~** State Prosecutor; **M~ delle Finanze** Ministry of Finance, ≈ Treasury

mi'nistro SM (*Pol, Rel*) minister; **M~ delle Finanze** Minister of Finance, ≈ Chancellor of the Exchequer (*BRIT*)

mino'ranza [mino'rantsa] SF minority; **essere in ~** to be in the minority

mino'rato, -a AG disabled ▶ SM/F person with a disability or learning difficulties

minorazi'one [minorat'tsjone] SF handicap

Mi'norca SF Minorca

mi'nore AG (*comparativo*) less; (*più piccolo*) smaller; (*numero*) lower; (*inferiore*) lower, inferior; (*meno importante*) minor; (*più giovane*) younger; (*superlativo*) least; smallest; lowest; least important; youngest ▶ SMF = **minorenne**; **in misura ~** to a lesser extent; **questo è il male ~** this is the lesser evil

mino'renne AG under age ▶ SMF minor, person under age

mino'rile AG juvenile; **carcere ~** young offenders' institution; **delinquenza ~** juvenile delinquency

minori'tario, -a AG minority *cpd*

mi'nuscolo, -a AG (*scrittura, carattere*) small; (*piccolissimo*) tiny ▶ SF small letter ▶ SM small letters *pl*; (*Tip*) lower case; **scrivere tutto (in) ~** to write everything in small letters

mi'nuta SF rough copy, draft

mi'nuto, -a AG tiny, minute; (*pioggia*) fine; (*corporatura*) delicate, fine; (*lavoro*) detailed ▶ SM (*unità di misura*) minute; **al ~** (*Comm*) retail; **avere i minuti contati** to have very little time

mi'nuzia [mi'nuttsja] SF (*cura*) meticulousness; (*particolare*) detail

minuziosa'mente [minuttsjosa'mente] AV meticulously; in minute detail

minuzi'oso, -a [minut'tsjoso] AG (*persona, descrizione*) meticulous; (*esame*) minute

'**mio, 'mia, mi'ei, 'mie** DET: **il ~, la mia** *ecc* my ▶ PRON: **il ~, la mia** *ecc* mine ▶ SM: **ho speso del ~** I spent my own money ▶ SF: **la mia** (*opinione*) my view; **i miei** my family; **un ~ amico** a friend of mine; **per amor ~** for my sake; **è dalla mia** he is on my side; **anch'io ho avuto le mie** (*disavventure*) I've had my problems too; **ne ho fatta una delle mie!** (*sciocchezze*) I've done it again!; **cerco di stare sulle mie** I try to keep myself to myself

'**miope** AG short-sighted

mio'pia SF short-sightedness, myopia; (*fig*) short-sightedness

'**mira** SF (*anche fig*) aim; **avere una buona/cattiva ~** to be a good/bad shot; **prendere la ~** to take aim; **prendere di ~ qn** (*fig*) to pick on sb

mi'rabile AG admirable, wonderful

mi'racolo SM miracle

miraco'loso, -a AG miraculous

mi'raggio [mi'raddʒo] SM mirage

mi'rare /**72**/ VI: **~ a** to aim at

mi'rato, -a AG targeted

mi'riade SF myriad

mi'rino SM (*Tecn*) sight; (*Fot*) viewer, viewfinder

mir'tillo SM bilberry (*BRIT*), blueberry (*US*), whortleberry

'**mirto** SM myrtle

mi'santropo, -a SM/F misanthropist

mi'scela [miʃ'ʃela] SF mixture; (*di caffè*) blend

miscel'lanea [miʃʃel'lanea] SF miscellany

'mischia ['miskja] SF scuffle; (*Rugby*) scrum, scrummage

mischi'are [mis'kjare] /19/ VT, **mischi'arsi** VPR to mix, blend

misco'noscere [misko'noʃʃere] /26/ VT (*qualità, coraggio ecc*) to fail to appreciate

miscre'dente AG (*Rel*) misbelieving; (: *incredulo*) unbelieving ▸ SMF misbeliever; unbeliever

mis'cuglio [mis'kuʎʎo] SM mixture, hotchpotch, jumble

'mise VB *vedi* **mettere**

mise'rabile AG (*infelice*) miserable, wretched; (*povero*) poverty-stricken; (*di scarso valore*) miserable

mi'seria SF extreme poverty; (*infelicità*) misery ■ **miserie** SFPL (*del mondo ecc*) misfortunes, troubles; **costare una ~** to cost next to nothing; **piangere ~** to plead poverty; **ridursi in ~** to be reduced to poverty; **porca ~!** (*col*) (bloody) hell!

miseri'cordia SF mercy, pity

misericordi'oso, -a AG merciful

'misero, -a AG miserable, wretched; (*povero*) poverty-stricken; (*insufficiente*) miserable

mis'fatto SM misdeed, crime

'misi VB *vedi* **mettere**

mi'sogino [mi'zɔdʒino] SM misogynist

'missile SM missile; **~ cruise** *o* **di crociera** cruise missile; **~ terra-aria** surface-to-air missile

missio'nario, -a AG, SM/F missionary

missi'one SF mission

misteri'oso, -a AG mysterious

mis'tero SM mystery; **fare ~ di qc** to make a mystery out of sth; **quanti misteri!** why all the mystery?

'mistico, -a, -ci, -che AG mystic(al) ▸ SM mystic

mistifi'care /20/ VT to fool, bamboozle

'misto, -a AG mixed; (*scuola*) mixed, coeducational ▸ SM mixture; **un tessuto in ~ lino** a linen mix

mis'tura SF mixture

mi'sura SF measure; (*misurazione, dimensione*) measurement; (*taglia*) size; (*provvedimento*) measure, step; (*moderazione*) moderation; (*Mus*) time; (: *divisione*) bar; (*fig: limite*) bounds *pl*, limit; **in ~ di** in accordance with, according to; **nella ~ in cui** inasmuch as, insofar as; **in giusta ~** moderately; **oltre ~** beyond measure; **su ~** made to measure; **in ugual ~** equally, in the same way; **a ~ d'uomo** on a human scale; **passare la ~** to overstep the mark, go too far; **prendere le misure a qn** to take sb's measurements, measure sb; **prendere le misure di qc** to measure sth; **ho preso le mie misure** I've taken the necessary steps; **non ha il senso della ~** he doesn't know when to stop; **~ di lunghezza/capacità** measure of length/capacity; **misure di sicurezza/ prevenzione** safety/precautionary measures

misu'rare /72/ VT (*ambiente, stoffa*) to measure; (*terreno*) to survey; (*abito*) to try on; (*pesare*) to weigh; (*fig: parole ecc*) to weigh up; (: *spese, cibo*) to limit ▸ VI to measure ■ **misurarsi** VPR: **misurarsi con qn** to have a confrontation with sb; (*competere*) to compete with sb

misu'rato, -a AG (*ponderato*) measured; (*prudente*) cautious; (*moderato*) moderate

misurazi'one [mizurat'tsjone] SF measuring; (*di terreni*) surveying

'mite AG mild; (*prezzo*) moderate, reasonable

'mitico, -a, -ci, -che AG mythical

miti'gare /80/ VT to mitigate, lessen; (*lenire*) to soothe, relieve ■ **mitigarsi** VPR (*odio*) to subside; (*tempo*) to become milder

'mitilo SM mussel

'mito SM myth

mitolo'gia, -'gie [mitolo'dʒia] SF mythology

mito'logico, -a, -ci, -che [mito'lɔdʒiko] AG mythological

'mitra SF (*Rel*) mitre (*Brit*), miter (*US*) ▸ SM INV (*arma*) sub-machine gun

mitragli'are [mitraʎ'ʎare] /27/ VT to machine-gun

mitraglia'tore, -'trice [mitraʎʎa'tore] AG: **fucile ~** sub-machine gun ▸ SF machine gun

mitteleuro'peo, -a AG Central European

mit'tente SMF sender

ml ABBR (= *millilitro*) ml

MLD SIGLA M = **Movimento per la Liberazione della Donna**

MM ABBR = **Metropolitana Milanese**

mm ABBR (= *millimetro*) mm

M.M. ABBR = **marina militare**

mms SIGLA M INV (*servizio*) (= *multimedia messaging service*) MMS; (*messaggio*) MMS message

MN SIGLA = **Mantova**

M/N, m/n ABBR (= *motonave*) MV

MO SIGLA = **Modena**

mo SM: **a mo' di** like; **a mo' di esempio** by way of example

M.O. ABBR = **Medio Oriente**

'mobile AG mobile; (*parte di macchina*) moving; (*Dir: bene*) movable, personal ▸ SM (*arredamento*) piece of furniture ■ **mobili** SMPL (*mobilia*) furniture *sg*

Quando si parla in generale di *mobili* si traduce **furniture** che non prende la **–s** e con cui si usa il verbo al singolare.
Tutti i miei mobili sono di seconda mano. **All my furniture is second-hand.**
Quando si vuole specificare un singolo pezzo si usa **a piece of furniture**.
un mobile molto pesante **a very heavy piece of furniture**

---

mo'bilia SF furniture

mobili'are AG (*Dir*) personal, movable

mo'bilio SM = **mobilia**

mobilità SF mobility

mobili'tare /72/ VT to mobilize; ~ **l'opinione pubblica** to rouse public opinion

mobilitazi'one [mobilitat'tsjone] SF mobilization

mocas'sino SM moccasin

mocci'oso, -a [mot'tʃoso] SM/F (*bambino piccolo*) little kid; (*peg*) snotty-nosed kid

'moccolo SM (*di candela*) candle end; (*col: bestemmia*) oath; (: *moccio*) snot; **reggere il ~** to play gooseberry (BRIT), act as chaperon(e)

'moda SF fashion; **alla ~, di ~** fashionable, in fashion

modalità SF INV formality; **seguire attentamente le ~ d'uso** to follow the instructions carefully; **~ giuridiche** legal procedures; **~ di pagamento** method of payment

mo'della SF model

model'lare /72/ VT (*creta*) to model, shape ■ **modellarsi** VPR: **modellarsi su** to model o.s. on

mo'dello SM model; (*stampo*) mould (BRIT), mold (US) ▶ AG INV model *cpd*

'modem SM INV modem

mode'nese AG of (*o* from) Modena

mode'rare /72/ VT to moderate ■ **moderarsi** VPR to restrain o.s.; **~ la velocità** to reduce speed; **~ i termini** to weigh one's words

mode'rato, -a AG moderate

modera'tore, -'trice SM/F moderator

moderazi'one [moderat'tsjone] SF moderation

moderniz'zare [modernid'dzare] /72/ VT to bring up to date, modernize ■ **modernizzarsi** VPR to get up to date

mo'derno, -a AG modern

mo'destia SF modesty; **~ a parte ...** in all modesty ..., though I say it myself ...

mo'desto, -a AG modest

'modico, -a, -ci, -che AG reasonable, moderate

mo'difica, -che SF modification; **subire delle modifiche** to undergo some modifications

modifi'cabile AG modifiable

modifi'care /20/ VT to modify, alter ■ **modificarsi** VPR to alter, change

mo'dista SF milliner

'modo SM way, manner; (*mezzo*) means, way; (*occasione*) opportunity; (*Ling*) mood; (*Mus*) mode ■ **modi** SMPL (*maniere*) manners; **a suo ~, a ~ suo** in his own way; **ad *o* in ogni ~** anyway; **di *o* in ~ che** so that; **in ~ da** so as to; **in tutti i modi** at all costs; (*comunque sia*) anyway; (*in ogni caso*) in any case; **in un certo qual ~** in a way, in some ways; **in qualche ~** somehow or other; **oltre ~**

extremely; **~ di dire** turn of phrase; **per ~ di dire** so to speak; **fare a ~ proprio** to do as one likes; **fare le cose a ~** to do things properly; **una persona a ~** a well-mannered person; **c'è ~ e ~ di farlo** there's a right way and a wrong way of doing it

modu'lare /72/ VT to modulate ▶ AG modular

modulazi'one [modulat'tsjone] SF modulation; **~ di frequenza** frequency modulation

'modulo SM (*modello*) form; (*Archit: lunare, di comando*) module; **~ di domanda** application form; **~ d'iscrizione** enrolment form; **~ di versamento** deposit slip

Moga'discio [moga'diʃʃo] SM Mogadishu

'mogano SM mahogany

'mogio, -a, -gi, -gie ['mɔdʒo] AG down in the dumps, dejected

'moglie ['moʎʎe] SF wife

mo'hair [mɔ'ɛr] SM mohair

mo'ine SFPL cajolery *sg*; (*leziosità*) affectation *sg*; **fare le ~ a qn** to cajole sb

'mola SF millstone; (*utensile abrasivo*) grindstone

mo'lare /72/ VT to grind ▶ AG (*pietra*) mill *cpd* ▶ SM (*dente*) molar

'mole SF mass; (*dimensioni*) size; (*edificio grandioso*) massive structure; **una ~ di lavoro** masses (BRIT) *o* loads of work

mo'lecola SF molecule

moles'tare /72/ VT to bother, annoy

mo'lestia SF annoyance, bother; **recar ~ a qn** to bother sb; **molestie sessuali** sexual harassment *sg*

mo'lesto, -a AG annoying

moli'sano, -a AG of (*o* from) Molise

'molla SF spring ■ **molle** SFPL (*per camino*) tongs; **prendere qn con le molle** to treat sb with kid gloves

mol'lare /72/ VT to release, let go; (*Naut*) to ease; (*fig: ceffone*) to give ▶ VI (*cedere*) to give in; **~ gli ormeggi** (*Naut*) to cast off; **~ la presa** to let go

'molle AG soft; (*muscoli*) flabby; (*fig: debole*) weak, feeble

molleggi'ato, -a [molled'dʒato] AG (*letto*) sprung; (*auto*) with good suspension

mol'leggio [mol'leddʒo] SM (*per veicoli*) suspension; (*elasticità*) springiness; (*Ginnastica*) knee-bends *pl*

mol'letta SF (*per capelli*) hairgrip; (*per panni stesi*) clothes peg (BRIT) *o* pin (US) ■ **mollette** SFPL (*per zucchero*) tongs

mol'lezza [mol'lettsa] SF softness flabbiness weakness, feebleness ■ **mollezze** SFPL: **vivere nelle mollezze** to live in the lap of luxury

mol'lica, -che SF crumb, soft part

mol'liccio, -a, -ci, -ce [mol'littʃo] AG (*terreno, impasto*) soggy; (*frutta*) soft; (*floscio: mano*) limp; (: *muscolo*) flabby

mol'lusco, -schi SM mollusc

'molo SM breakwater; jetty, pier

mol'teplice [mol'teplitʃe] AG (*formato di più elementi*) complex ▪ **molteplici** PL (*svariati: interessi, attività*) numerous, various

molteplicità [molteplitʃi'ta] SF multiplicity

moltipli'care /20/ VT to multiply ▪ **moltiplicarsi** VPR to multiply; (*richieste*) to increase in number

moltiplicazi'one [moltiplikat'tsjone] SF multiplication

molti'tudine SF multitude; **una ~ di** a vast number o a multitude of

---

'molto, -a

DET (*quantità*) a lot of, much; (*numero*) a lot of, many; **molto pane/carbone** a lot of bread/coal; **molta gente** a lot of people, many people; **molti libri** a lot of books, many books; **non ho molto tempo** I haven't got much time; **per molto (tempo)** for a long time; **ci vuole molto (tempo)?** will it take long?; **arriverà fra non molto** he'll arrive soon; **ne hai per molto?** will you be long?

▶ AV **1** a lot, (very) much; **viaggia molto** he travels a lot; **non viaggia molto** he doesn't travel much o a lot

2 (*intensivo: con aggettivi, avverbi*) very; (: *con participio passato*) (very) much; **molto buono** very good; **molto migliore, molto meglio** much o a lot better

▶ PRON much, a lot; **molti, e** (*pl*) many, a lot; **molti pensano che ...** many (people) think that ...; **molte sono rimaste a casa** a lot of them stayed at home; **c'era gente, ma non molta** there were people there, but not many

---

momentanea'mente AV at the moment, at present

momen'taneo, -a AG momentary, fleeting

mo'mento SM moment; **da un ~ all'altro** at any moment; (*all'improvviso*) suddenly; **al ~ di fare** just as I was (o you were o he was *etc*) doing; **a momenti** (*da un momento all'altro*) any time o moment now; (*quasi*) nearly; **per il ~** for the time being; **dal ~ che** ever since; (*dato che*) since; **~ culminante** climax

'monaca, -che SF nun

'Monaco SF Monaco; **~ (di Baviera)** Munich

'monaco, -ci SM monk

mo'narca, -chi SM monarch

monar'chia [monar'kia] SF monarchy

mo'narchico, -a, -ci, -che [mo'narkiko] AG (*stato, autorità*) monarchic; (*partito, fede*) monarchist ▶ SM/F monarchist

monas'tero SM (*di monaci*) monastery; (*di monache*) convent

mo'nastico, -a, -ci, -che AG monastic

'monco, -a, -chi, -che AG maimed; (*fig*) incomplete; **~ d'un braccio** one-armed

mon'cone SM stump

mondanità SF (*frivolezza*) worldliness; **le ~** (*piaceri*) the pleasures of the world

mon'dano, -a AG (*anche fig*) worldly; (*dell'alta società*) society cpd; fashionable

mon'dare /72/ VT (*frutta, patate*) to peel; (*piselli*) to shell; (*pulire*) to clean

mondez'zaio [mondet'tsajo] SM rubbish (BRIT) o garbage (US) dump

mondi'ale AG (*campionato, popolazione*) world cpd; (*influenza*) world-wide; **di fama ~** world famous

'mondo SM world; (*grande quantità*): **un ~ di** lots of, a host of; **il gran** o **bel ~** high society; **per niente al ~, per nessuna cosa al ~** not for all the world; **da che ~ è ~** since time o the world began; **mandare qn all'altro ~** to kill sb; **mettere/venire al ~** to bring/come into the world; **vivere fuori dal ~** to be out of touch with the real world; **(sono) cose dell'altro ~!** it's incredible!; **com'è piccolo il ~!** it's a small world!

mone'gasco, -a, -schi, -sche AG, SM/F Monegasque

monelle'ria SF prank, naughty trick

mo'nello, -a SM/F street urchin; (*ragazzo vivace*) scamp, imp

mo'neta SF coin; (*Econ: valuta*) currency; (*denaro spicciolo*) (small) change; **~ estera** foreign currency; **~ legale** legal tender

mone'tario, -a AG monetary

monetiz'zare [monetid'dzare] VT (*sito web, contenuto*) to monetize

monetizza'zione [monetiddza'tsjone] SF (*di sito web, contenuto*) monetization

mongol'fiera SF hot-air balloon

Mon'golia SF: **la ~** Mongolia

mon'golico, -a, -ci, -che AG Mongolian

'mongolo, -a AG Mongolian ▶ SM/F, SM Mongol, Mongolian

'monito SM warning

'monitor SM INV (*Tecn, TV*) monitor

monito'raggio [monito'radd3o] SM monitoring

monito'rare /72/ VT to monitor

mo'nocolo SM (*lente*) monocle, eyeglass

monoco'lore AG (*Pol*): **governo ~** one-party government

monoga'mia SF monogamy

mo'nogamo, -a AG monogamous ▶ SM monogamist

monogra'fia SF monograph

mono'gramma, -i SM monogram

mono'lingue AG monolingual

monolo'cale SM ≈ studio flat

mo'nologo, -ghi SM monologue

mono'pattino SM scooter

mono'polio SM monopoly; **~ di stato** government monopoly

monopoliz'zare [monopolid'dzare] /**72**/ VT to monopolize

mono'sillabo, -a AG monosyllabic ▶ SM monosyllable

monoto'nia SF monotony

mo'notono, -a AG monotonous

mono'uso AG INV disposable

monovo'lume SF INV (anche: **automobile monovolume**) people carrier, MPV

Mons. ABBR (= Monsignore) Mgr

monsi'gnore [monsiɲ'ɲore] SM (Rel: titolo) Your (o His) Grace

mon'sone SM monsoon

monta'carichi [monta'kariki] SM INV hoist, goods lift

mon'taggio [mon'taddʒo] SM (Tecn) assembly; (Cine) editing

mon'tagna [mon'taɲɲa] SF mountain; (zona montuosa): **la ~** the mountains pl; **andare in ~** to go to the mountains; **aria/strada di ~** mountain air/road; **casa di ~** house in the mountains; **montagne russe** roller coaster sg, big dipper sg (BRIT)

monta'gnoso, -a [montaɲ'ɲoso] AG mountainous

monta'naro, -a AG mountain cpd ▶ SM/F mountain dweller

mon'tano, -a AG mountain cpd; alpine

mon'tante SM (di porta) jamb; (di finestra) upright; (Calcio: palo) post; (Pugilato) upper cut; (Comm) total amount

mon'tare /**72**/ VT to go (o come) up; (cavallo) to ride; (apparecchiatura) to set up, assemble; (Cuc) to whip; (Zool) to cover; (incastonare) to mount, set; (Cine) to edit; (Fot) to mount ▶ VI to go (o come) up; (aumentare di livello, volume) to rise; (a cavallo): **~ bene/male** to ride well/badly ■ **montarsi** VPR to become big-headed; **~ qc** to exaggerate sth; **~ qn o la testa a qn** to turn sb's head; **montarsi la testa** to become big-headed; **~ in bicicletta/macchina/treno** to get on a bicycle/ into a car/on a train; **~ a cavallo** to get on o mount a horse; **~ la guardia** (Mil) to mount guard

monta'tura SF assembling no pl; (di occhiali) frames pl; (di gioiello) mounting, setting; (fig): **~ pubblicitaria** publicity stunt

montavi'vande SM INV dumbwaiter

'monte SM mountain; **a ~** upstream; **andare a ~** (fig) to come to nothing; **mandare a ~ qc** (fig) to upset sth, cause sth to fail; **il M~ Bianco** Mont Blanc; **il M~ Everest** Mount Everest; **~ di pietà** pawnshop; **~ premi** prize

Monteci'torio [montetʃi'torjo] SM: **palazzo ~** (Pol) seat of the Italian Chamber of Deputies

montene'grino, -a AG, SM/F Montenegrin

Monte'negro SM Montenegro

mont'gomery [mənt'gʌməri] SM INV duffel coat

mon'tone SM (Zool) ram; (anche: **giacca di montone**) sheepskin (jacket); **carne di ~** mutton

montuosità SF mountainous nature

montu'oso, -a AG mountainous

monu'mento SM monument

mo'quette [mɔ'kɛt] SF fitted carpet

'mora SF (del rovo) blackberry; (del gelso) mulberry; (Dir) delay; (: somma) arrears pl

mo'rale AG moral ▶ SF (scienza) ethics sg, moral philosophy; (complesso di norme) moral standards pl, morality; (condotta) morals pl; (insegnamento morale) moral ▶ SM morale; **la ~ della favola** the moral of the tale; **essere giù di ~** to be feeling down; **aver il ~ alto/a terra** to be in good/low spirits

mora'lista, -i, -e AG moralistic ▶ SM/F moralist

moralità SF morality; (condotta) morals pl

moraliz'zare [moralid'dzare] /**72**/ VT (costumi, vita pubblica) to set moral standards for

moralizzazi'one [moraliddzat'tsjone] SF setting of moral standards

mora'toria SF (Dir) moratorium

morbi'dezza [morbi'dettsa] SF softness; smoothness; tenderness

'morbido, -a AG soft; (pelle) soft, smooth; (carne) tender

mor'billo SM (Med) measles sg

'morbo SM disease

mor'boso, -a AG (fig) morbid

'morchia ['mɔrkja] SF (residuo grasso) dregs pl; oily deposit

mor'dente SM (fig: di satira, critica) bite; (: di persona) drive

'mordere /**64**/ VT to bite; (addentare) to bite into; (corrodere) to eat into

mordicchi'are [mordik'kjare] /**19**/ VT (gen) to chew at

mo'rente AG dying ▶ SM/F dying man/woman

mor'fina SF morphine

mo'ria SF high mortality

mori'bondo, -a AG dying, moribund

morige'rato, -a [moridʒe'rato] AG of good morals

mo'rire /**65**/ VI to die; (abitudine, civiltà) to die out; **~ di dolore** to die of a broken heart; **~ di fame** to die of hunger; (fig) to be starving; **~ di freddo** to freeze to death; (fig) to be frozen; **~ d'invidia** to be green with envy; **~ di noia/paura** to be bored/scared to death; **~ dalla voglia di fare qc** to be dying to do sth; **fa un caldo da ~** it's terribly hot

mormo'rare /**72**/ VI to murmur; (brontolare) to

grumble; **si mormora che ...** it's rumoured (*BRIT*) *o* rumored (*US*) that ...; **la gente mormora** people are talking

mormo'rio SM murmuring; grumbling

moro, -a AG dark(-haired), dark(-complexioned) ▪ **i Mori** SMPL (*Storia*) the Moors

mo'roso, -a AG in arrears ▸ SM/F (*col: innamorato*) sweetheart

'morsa SF (*Tecn*) vice (*BRIT*), vise (*US*); (*fig: stretta*) grip

mor'setto SM (*Tecn*) clamp; (*Elettr*) terminal

morsi'care /20/ VT to nibble (at), gnaw (at); (*insetto*) to bite

'morso, -a PP *di* **mordere** ▸ SM bite; (*di insetto*) sting; (*parte della briglia*) bit; **dare un ~ a qc/qn** to bite sth/sb; **i morsi della fame** pangs of hunger

morta'della SF (*Cuc*) mortadella (*type of salted pork meat*)

mor'taio SM mortar

mor'tale AG, SM mortal

mortalità SF mortality; (*Statistica*) mortality, death rate

'morte SF death; **in punto di ~** at death's door; **ferito a ~** (*soldato*) mortally wounded; (*in incidente*) fatally injured; **essere annoiato a ~** to be bored to death *o* to tears; **avercela a ~ con qn** to be bitterly resentful of sb; **avere la ~ nel cuore** to have a heavy heart

mortifi'care /20/ VT to mortify

'morto, -a PP *di* **morire** ▸ AG dead ▸ SM/F dead man/woman; **i morti** the dead; **fare il ~** (*nell'acqua*) to float on one's back; **il Mar M~** the Dead Sea; **un ~ di fame** (*fig peg*) a down-and-out; **le campane suonavano a ~** the funeral bells were tolling

mor'torio SM (*anche fig*) funeral

mo'saico, -ci SM mosaic; **l'ultimo tassello del ~** (*fig*) the last piece of the puzzle

'Mosca SF Moscow

'mosca, -sche SF fly; **rimanere** *o* **restare con un pugno di mosche** (*fig*) to be left empty-handed; **non si sentiva volare una ~** (*fig*) you could have heard a pin drop; **~ cieca** blind-man's buff

mos'cato SM muscatel (wine)

mosce'rino [moʃʃe'rino] SM midge, gnat

mos'chea [mos'kɛa] SF mosque

mos'chetto [mos'ketto] SM musket

moschet'tone [mosket'tone] SM (*gancio*) spring clip; (*Alpinismo*) karabiner, snaplink

moschi'cida, -i, -e [moski'tʃida] AG fly *cpd*; **carta ~** flypaper

'moscio, -a, -sci, -sce ['moʃʃo] AG (*fig*) lifeless; **ha la "r" moscia** he can't roll his "r"s

mos'cone SM (*Zool*) bluebottle; (*barca*) pedalo; (: *a remi*) kind of pedalo with oars

mosco'vita, -i, -e AG, SM/F Muscovite

'mossa SF movement; (*nel gioco*) move; **darsi una ~** (*fig*) to give o.s. a shake; **prendere le mosse da qc** to come about as the result of sth

'mossi *ecc* VB *vedi* **muovere**

'mosso, -a PP *di* **muovere** ▸ AG (*mare*) rough; (*capelli*) wavy; (*Fot*) blurred; (*ritmo, prosa*) animated

mos'tarda SF mustard; **~ di Cremona** pickled fruit with mustard

'mosto SM must

'mostra SF exhibition, show; (*ostentazione*) show; **in ~** on show; **far ~ di** (*fingere*) to pretend; **far ~ di sé** to show off; **mettersi in ~** to draw attention to o.s.

mos'trare /72/ VT to show ▸ VI: **~ di fare** to pretend to do ▪ **mostrarsi** VPR to appear; **~ la lingua** to stick out one's tongue

'mostro SM monster

mostru'oso, -a AG monstrous

mo'tel SM INV motel

moti'vare /72/ VT (*causare*) to cause; (*giustificare*) to justify, account for

motivazi'one [motivat'tsjone] SF justification; (*Psic*) motivation

mo'tivo SM (*causa*) reason, cause; (*movente*) motive; (*letterario*) (central) theme; (*disegno*) motif, design, pattern; (*Mus*) motif; **per quale ~?** why?, for what reason?; **per motivi di salute** for health reasons, on health grounds; **motivi personali** personal reasons

'moto SM (*anche Fisica*) motion; (*movimento, gesto*) movement; (*esercizio fisico*) exercise; (*sommossa*) rising, revolt; (*commozione*) feeling, impulse ▸ SF INV (*motocicletta*) motorbike; **fare del ~** to take some exercise; **un ~ d'impazienza** an impatient gesture; **mettere in ~** to set in motion; (*Aut*) to start up; **~ d'acqua** Jet Ski®

moto'carro SM three-wheeler van

motoci'cletta [motot'ʃi'kletta] SF motorcycle

motoci'clismo [motot'ʃi'klizmo] SM motorcycling, motorcycle racing

motoci'clista, -i, -e [motot'ʃi'klista] SM/F motorcyclist

moto'nave SF motor vessel

motopesche'reccio [motopeske'rettʃo] SM motor fishing vessel

mo'tore, -'trice AG motor; (*Tecn*) driving ▸ SM engine, motor ▸ SF (*Tecn*) engine, motor; **albero ~** drive shaft; **forza motrice** driving force; **a ~** motor *cpd*, power-driven; **~ a combustione interna/a reazione** internal combustion/jet engine; **~ di ricerca** (*Inform*) search engine

moto'rino SM moped; **~ di avviamento** (*Aut*) starter

motoriz'zato, -a [motorid'dzato] AG (*truppe*) motorized; (*persona*) having a car *o* transport

motorizzazi'one [motoriddzat'tsjone] SF *(ufficio tecnico e organizzativo)*: **(ufficio della)** ~ road traffic office

motos'cafo SM motorboat

motove'detta SF motor patrol vessel

mo'trice [mo'tritʃe] SF *vedi* **motore**

mot'teggio [mot'teddʒo] SM banter

'motto SM *(battuta scherzosa)* witty remark; *(frase emblematica)* motto, maxim

mountain 'bike ['mauntin 'baik] SF INV mountain bike

'mouse ['maus] SM INV *(Inform)* mouse

mo'vente SM motive

mo'venza [mo'vɛntsa] SF movement

movimen'tare /72/ VT to liven up

movimen'tato, -a AG *(festa, partita)* lively; *(riunione)* animated; *(strada, vita)* busy; *(soggiorno)* eventful

movi'mento SM movement; *(fig)* activity, hustle and bustle; *(Mus)* tempo, movement; **essere sempre in** ~ to be always on the go; **fare un po' di** ~ *(esercizio fisico)* to take some exercise; **c'è molto** ~ **in città** the town is very busy; ~ **di capitali** movement of capital; **M~ per la Liberazione della Donna** Women's Movement

movi'ola SF moviola; **rivedere qc alla** ~ to see an action *(BRIT)* o instant *(US)* replay of sth

Mozam'bico [moddzam'biko] SM: **il** ~ Mozambique

mozi'one [mot'tsjone] SF *(Pol)* motion; ~ **d'ordine** *(Pol)* point of order

mozzafi'ato [mottsa'fjato] AG INV breathtaking

moz'zare [mot'tsare] /72/ VT to cut off; *(coda)* to dock; ~ **il fiato** o **il respiro a qn** *(fig)* to take sb's breath away

mozza'rella [mottsa'rɛlla] SF mozzarella

mozzi'cone [mottsi'kone] SM stub, butt, end; *(anche:* **mozzicone di sigaretta)** cigarette end

'mozzo¹ ['mɔddzo] SM *(Meccanica)* hub

'mozzo² ['mottso] SM *(Naut)* ship's boy; ~ **di stalla** stable boy

mq ABBR *(= metro quadro)* sq.m

MS SIGLA = **Massa Carrara**

Mti ABBR = **monti**

'mucca, -che SF cow; ~ **pazza** BSE; **(morbo della)** ~ **pazza** mad cow disease, BSE; **l'emergenza** ~ **pazza** the mad cow crisis

'mucchio ['mukkjo] SM pile, heap; *(fig)*: **un** ~ **di** lots of, heaps of

mucil'lagine [mutʃil'ladʒine] SF *(Bot)* mucilage *(green slime produced by plants growing in water)*

'muco, -chi SM mucus

mu'cosa SF mucous membrane

'muesli ['mjusli] SM muesli

'muffa SF mould *(BRIT)*, mold *(US)*, mildew; **fare la** ~ to go mouldy *(BRIT)* o moldy *(US)*

mugghi'are [mug'gjare] /19/ VI *(fig: mare, tuono)* to roar; *(: vento)* to howl

mug'gire [mud'dʒire] /55/ VI *(vacca)* to low, moo; *(toro)* to bellow; *(fig)* to roar

mug'gito [mud'dʒito] SM moo; bellow; roar

mu'ghetto [mu'getto] SM lily of the valley

mu'gnaio, -a [muɲ'ɲajo] SM/F miller

mugo'lare /72/ VI *(cane)* to whimper, whine; *(fig: persona)* to moan

mugu'gnare [muguɲ'ɲare] /15/ VI *(col)* to mutter, mumble

mulatti'era SF mule track

mu'latto, -a AG, SM/F mulatto

muli'nare /72/ VI to whirl, spin round (and round)

muli'nello SM *(moto vorticoso)* eddy, whirl; *(di canna da pesca)* reel; *(Naut)* windlass

mu'lino SM mill; ~ **a vento** windmill

'mulo SM mule

'multa SF fine

mul'tare /72/ VT to fine

multico'lore AG multicoloured *(BRIT)*, multicolored *(US)*

multi'etnico, -a, -ci, -che AG multiethnic

multi'forme AG *(paesaggio, attività, interessi)* varied; *(ingegno)* versatile

multimedi'ale AG multimedia *cpd*

multinazio'nale [multinattsjo'nale] AG, SF multinational; **forza** ~ **di pace** multinational peace-keeping force

'multiplo, -a AG, SM multiple

multiraz'ziale [multirat'tsjale] AG multiracial

multi'sala AG INV multiscreen

multiu'tenza [multiu'tɛntsa] SF *(Inform)* time sharing

multivitami'nico, -a, -ci, -che AG: **complesso** ~ multivitamin

'mummia SF mummy

'mungere ['mundʒere] /5/ VT *(anche fig)* to milk

mungi'tura [mundʒi'tura] SF milking

munici'pale [munitʃi'pale] AG *(gen)* municipal; town *cpd*; **palazzo** ~ town hall; **autorità municipali** local authorities *(BRIT)*, local government *sg*

muni'cipio [muni'tʃipjo] SM town council, corporation; *(edificio)* town hall; **sposarsi in** ~ ≈ to get married in a registry office *(BRIT)*, have a civil marriage

munifi'cenza [munifi'tʃɛntsa] SF munificence

mu'nifico, -a, -ci, -che AG munificent, generous

mu'nire /55/ VT: ~ **qc/qn di** to equip sth/sb with; ~ **di firma** *(documento)* to sign

munizi'oni [munit'tsjoni] SFPL *(Mil)* ammunition *sg*

'**munsi** *ecc* VB *vedi* **mungere**

'**munto, -a** PP *di* **mungere**

mu'oio *ecc* VB *vedi* **morire**

mu'overe /66/ VT to move; (*ruota, macchina*) to drive; (*sollevare: questione, obiezione*) to raise, bring up; (: *accusa*) to make, bring forward ■ **muoversi** VPR to move; **~ causa a qn** (*Dir*) to take legal action against sb; **~ a compassione** to move to pity; **~ guerra a** *o* **contro qn** to wage war against sb; **~ mari e monti** to move heaven and earth; **~ al pianto** to move to tears; **~ i primi passi** to take one's first steps; (*fig*) to be starting out; **muoviti!** hurry up!, get a move on!

'**mura** SFPL *vedi* **muro**

mu'raglia [mu'raλλa] SF (high) wall

mu'rale AG wall *cpd*; mural

mu'rare /72/ VT (*persona, porta*) to wall up

mu'rario, -a AG building *cpd*; **arte muraria** masonry

mura'tore SM (*con pietre*) mason; (*con mattoni*) bricklayer

mura'tura SF (*lavoro murario*) masonry; **casa in ~** (*di pietra*) stonebuilt house; (*di mattoni*) brick house

'**muro** SM wall ■ **mura** SFPL (*cinta cittadina*) walls; **a ~** wall *cpd*; (*armadio ecc*) built-in; **mettere al ~** (*fucilare*) to shoot *o* execute (by firing squad); **~ di cinta** surrounding wall; **~ divisorio** dividing wall; **~ del suono** sound barrier

'**musa** SF muse

'**muschio** ['muskjo] SM (*Zool*) musk; (*Bot*) moss

musco'lare AG muscular, muscle *cpd*

muscola'tura SF muscle structure

'**muscolo** SM (*Anat*) muscle

musco'loso, -a AG muscular

mu'seo SM museum

museru'ola SF muzzle

'**musica** SF music; **~ da ballo/camera** dance/chamber music

musi'cale AG musical

musicas'setta SF (pre-recorded) cassette

musi'cista, -i, -e [muzi'tʃista] SM/F musician

musi'comane SMF music lover

'**müsli** ['mysli] SM *vedi* **muesli**

'**muso** SM muzzle; (*di auto, aereo*) nose; **tenere il ~** to sulk

mu'sone, -a SM/F sulky person

'**mussola** SF muslin

mussul'mano, -a AG, SM/F Muslim, Moslem

'**muta** SF (*di animali*) moulting (*BRIT*), molting (*US*); (*di serpenti*) sloughing; (*per immersioni subacquee*) diving suit; (*gruppo di cani*) pack

mu'tabile AG changeable

muta'mento SM change

mu'tande SFPL (*da uomo*) (under)pants

mutan'dine SFPL (*da donna, bambino*) pants (*BRIT*), briefs; **~ di plastica** plastic pants

mu'tare /72/ VT, VI to change, alter

mutazi'one [mutat'tsjone] SF change, alteration; (*Biol*) mutation

mu'tevole AG changeable

muti'lare /72/ VT to mutilate, maim; (*fig*) to mutilate, deface

muti'lato, -a SM/F disabled person (*through loss of limbs*); **~ di guerra** disabled ex-serviceman (*BRIT*) *o* war veteran (*US*)

mutilazi'one [mutilat'tsjone] SF mutilation

mu'tismo SM (*Med*) mutism; (*atteggiamento*) (stubborn) silence

'**muto, -a** AG (*Med*) mute (*peg*); (*emozione, dolore: Cine*) silent; (*Ling*) silent, mute; (*carta geografica*) blank; **~ per lo stupore** *ecc* speechless with amazement *etc*; **ha fatto scena muta** he didn't utter a word

'**mutua** SF (*anche:* **cassa mutua**) health insurance scheme; **medico della ~** ≈ National Health Service doctor (*BRIT*)

mutu'are /72/ VT (*fig*) to borrow

mutu'ato, -a SM/F member of a health insurance scheme

'**mutuo, -a** AG (*reciproco*) mutual ▶ SM (*Econ*) (long-term) loan; **~ ipotecario** mortgage

Nn

N¹, n¹ ['ɛnne] SM O F (*lettera*) N, n; **N come Napoli** ≈ N for Nellie (*BRIT*), N for Nan (*US*)

N² ABBR (= *nord*) N

n² ABBR (= *numero*) no.

NA SIGLA = **Napoli**

na'babbo SM (*anche fig*) nabob

'nacchere ['nakkere] SFPL castanets

Nad SIGLA M = **nucleo anti-droga**

na'dir SM (*Astr*) nadir

'nafta SF naphtha; (*per motori diesel*) diesel oil

nafta'lina SF (*Chim*) naphthalene; (*tarmicida*) mothballs *pl*

'naia SF (*Zool*) cobra; (*Mil*) *slang term for national service*

na'if [na'if] AG INV naïve

'nailon SM = **nylon**

Nai'robi SF Nairobi

'nanna SF (*linguaggio infantile*): **andare a ~** to go to beddy-byes

'nano, -a AG, SM/F dwarf (*peg*)

nanoparti'cella [nanoparti'tʃɛlla] SF nanoparticle

napole'tano, -a AG, SM/F Neapolitan ▶ SF (*macchinetta da caffè*) Neapolitan coffee pot

'Napoli SF Naples

'nappa SF tassel

nar'ciso [nar'tʃizo] SM narcissus

narco'dollari SMPL drug money *sg*

'narcos SM INV (*colombiano*) Colombian drug trafficker

nar'cosi SF general anaesthesia, narcosis

nar'cotico, -ci SM narcotic

narcotraffi'cante SMF drug trafficker

narco'traffico SM drug trade

na'rice [na'ritʃe] SF nostril

nar'rare /72/ VT to tell the story of, recount

narra'tivo, -a AG narrative ▶ SF (*branca*) fiction

narra'tore, -'trice SM/F narrator

narrazi'one [narrat'tsjone] SF narration; (*racconto*) story, tale

N.A.S.A. ['naza] SIGLA F (= *National Aeronautics and Space Administration*) NASA

na'sale AG nasal

na'scente [naʃ'ʃɛnte] AG (*sole, luna*) rising

'nascere ['naʃʃere] /67/ VI (*bambino*) to be born; (*pianta*) to come o spring up; (*fiume*) to rise, have its source; (*sole*) to rise; (*dente*) to come through; (*fig: derivare, conseguire*): **~ da** to arise from, be born out of; **è nata nel 1952** she was born in 1952; **da cosa nasce cosa** one thing leads to another

'nascita ['naʃʃita] SF birth

nasci'turo, -a [naʃʃi'turo] SM/F future child; **come si chiamerà il ~?** what's the baby going to be called?

nas'condere /68/ VT to hide, conceal ■ **nascondersi** VPR to hide

nascon'diglio [naskon'diʎʎo] SM hiding place

nascon'dino SM (*gioco*) hide-and-seek

nas'cosi *ecc* VB *vedi* **nascondere**

nas'costo, -a PP *di* **nascondere** ▶ AG hidden; **di ~** secretly

na'sello SM (*Zool*) hake

'naso SM nose

Nas'sau SF Nassau

'nastro SM ribbon; (*magnetico, isolante: Sport*) tape; **~ adesivo** adhesive tape; **~ trasportatore** conveyor belt

nas'turzio [nas'turtsjo] SM nasturtium

na'tale AG of one's birth ▶ SM (*Rel*): **N~** Christmas; (*giorno della nascita*) birthday ■ **natali** SMPL: **di illustri/umili natali** of noble/humble birth

natalità SF birth rate

nata'lizio, -a [nata'littsjo] AG (*del Natale*) Christmas *cpd*

na'tante SM craft *inv*, boat

'natica, -che SF (*Anat*) buttock

na'tio, -a, -tii, -tie AG native

Natività SF (*Rel*) Nativity

na'tivo, -a AG, SM/F native; **~ digitale** digital native

'nato, -a PP *di* **nascere** ▶ AG: **un attore ~** a born actor; **nata Pieri** née Pieri

'N.A.T.O. SIGLA F NATO (= *North Atlantic Treaty Organization*)

na'tura SF nature; **pagare in ~** to pay in kind; **~ morta** still life

natu'rale AG natural ▶ SM: **al ~** (*alimenti*) served plain; (*ritratto*) life-size; **(ma) è ~!** (*in risposte*) of course!; **a grandezza ~** life-size; **acqua ~** spring water

natura'lezza [natura'lettsa] SF naturalness

natura'lista, -i, -e SM/F naturalist

naturaliz'zare [naturalid'dzare] /**72**/ VT to naturalize

natural'mente AV naturally; (*certamente, sì*) of course

natu'rismo SM naturism, nudism

natu'rista, -i, -e AG, SM/F naturist, nudist

naufra'gare /**80**/ VI (*nave*) to be wrecked; (*persona*) to be shipwrecked; (*fig*) to fall through

nau'fragio [nau'frad3o] SM shipwreck; (*fig*) ruin, failure

'naufrago, -ghi SM castaway, shipwreck victim

'nausea SF nausea; **avere la ~** to feel sick (BRIT) o ill (US); **fino alla ~** ad nauseam

nausea'bondo, -a AG, **nause'ante** AG (*sapore*) disgusting; nauseating, sickening

nause'are /**72**/ VT to nauseate, make (feel) sick (BRIT) o ill (US)

'nautico, -a, -ci, -che AG nautical ▶ SF (art of) navigation; **salone ~** (*mostra*) boat show

na'vale AG naval; **battaglia ~** naval battle; (*gioco*) battleships pl

na'vata SF (*anche:* **navata centrale**) nave; (*anche:* **navata laterale**) aisle

'nave SF ship, vessel; **~ da carico** cargo ship, freighter; **~ cisterna** tanker; **~ da guerra** warship; **~ di linea** liner; **~ passeggeri** passenger ship; **~ portaerei** aircraft carrier; **~ spaziale** spaceship

na'vetta SF shuttle; (*servizio di collegamento*) shuttle (service)

navi'cella [navi't∫ella] SF (*di aerostato*) gondola; **~ spaziale** spaceship

navi'gabile AG navigable

navi'gante SM sailor, seaman

navi'gare /**80**/ VI to sail; **~ in cattive acque** (*fig*) to be in deep water; **~ in Internet** to surf the Net

navi'gato, -a AG (*fig: esperto*) experienced

naviga'tore, -'trice SM: **~ satellitare** satnav, satellite navigator ▶ SM/F (*gen*) navigator; **~ solitario** single-handed sailor

navigazi'one [navigat'tsjone] SF navigation; **dopo una settimana di ~** after a week at sea

na'viglio [na'viλλo] SM fleet, ships pl; (*canale artificiale*) canal; **~ da pesca** fishing fleet

nazio'nale [nattsjo'nale] AG national ▶ SF (*Sport*) national team

naziona'lismo [nattsjona'lizmo] SM nationalism

naziona'lista, -i, -e [nattsjona'lista] AG, SM/F nationalist

nazionalità [nattsjonali'ta] SF INV nationality

nazionaliz'zare [nattsjonalid'dzare] /**72**/ VT to nationalize

nazionalizzazi'one [nattsjonaliddzat'tsjone] SF nationalization

nazi'one [nat'tsjone] SF nation

'naziskin ['nattsiskin] SM INV skinhead (belonging to extreme right-wing group)

na'zismo [nat'tsizmo] SM Nazism

na'zista, -i, -e [nat'tsista] AG, SM/F Nazi

NB ABBR (= *nota bene*) NB

N.d.A. ABBR (= *nota dell'autore*) author's note

N.d.D. ABBR = **nota della direzione**

N.d.E. ABBR (= *nota dell'editore*) publisher's note

N.d.R. ABBR (= *nota della redazione*) editor's note

'ndrangheta [nd'rangeta] SF Calabrian Mafia

N.d.T. ABBR (= *nota del traduttore*) translator's note

---

ne

PRON **1** (*di lui, lei, loro*) of him/her/them; about him/her/them; **ne riconosco la voce** I recognize his (o her) voice

2 (*di questa, quella cosa*) of it; about it; **ne voglio ancora** I want some more (of it o them); **non parliamone più!** let's not talk about it any more!

3 (*da ciò*) from this; **ne deduco che l'avete trovato** I gather you've found it; **ne consegue che ...** it follows therefore that ...

4 (*con valore partitivo*): **hai dei libri? — sì, ne ho** have you any books? — yes, I have (some); **hai del pane? — no, non ne ho** have you any bread? — no, I haven't any; **quanti anni hai? — ne ho 17** how old are you? — I'm 17

▶ AV (*moto da luogo: da lì*) from there; **ne vengo ora** I've just come from there

---

né CONG: **né ... né** neither ... nor; **né l'uno né l'altro lo vuole** neither of them wants it; **né più né meno** no more no less; **non parla né l'italiano né il tedesco** he speaks neither Italian nor German, he doesn't speak either Italian or German; **non piove né nevica** it isn't raining or snowing

N.E. ABBR (= *nordest*) NE

ne'anche [ne'anke] AV, CONG not even; **non ... ~** not even; **~ se volesse potrebbe venire** he couldn't come even if he wanted to; **non l'ho visto — neanch'io** I didn't see him — neither did I o I didn't either; **~ per idea** o **sogno!** not on your life!; **non ci penso ~!** I wouldn't dream of it!; **~ a pagarlo lo farebbe** he wouldn't do it even if you paid him

'nebbia SF fog; (*foschia*) mist

nebbi'oso, -a AG foggy; misty

nebulizza'tore [nebuliddza'tore] SM atomizer

nebu'losa SF nebula

nebulosità SF haziness

nebu'loso, -a AG (*atmosfera, cielo*) hazy; (*fig*) hazy, vague

néces'saire [nese'sɛr] SM INV ~ **da viaggio** overnight case o bag

necessaria'mente [netʃessarja'mente] AV necessarily

neces'sario, -a [netʃes'sarjo] AG necessary ▶ SM: **fare il** ~ to do what is necessary; **lo stretto** ~ the bare essentials pl

necessità [netʃessi'ta] SF INV necessity; (*povertà*) need, poverty; **trovarsi nella** ~ **di fare qc** to be forced o obliged to do sth, have to do sth

necessi'tare [netʃessi'tare] /72/ VT to require ▶ VI (*aver bisogno*): ~ **di** to need

necro'logio [nekro'lɔdʒo] SM obituary notice; (*registro*) register of deaths

ne'fando, -a AG infamous, wicked

ne'fasto, -a AG inauspicious, ill-omened

ne'gare /80/ VT to deny; (*rifiutare*) to deny, refuse; ~ **di aver fatto/che** to deny having done/that

negativa'mente AV negatively; **rispondere** ~ to give a negative response

nega'tivo, -a AG, F, SM negative

negazi'one [negat'tsjone] SF negation

negherò ecc [nege'rɔ] VB vedi **negare**

ne'gletto, -a [ne'glɛtto] AG (*trascurato*) neglected

'negli ['neʎʎi] PREP + DET vedi **in**

négli'gé [negli'ʒe] SM INV negligee

negli'gente [negli'dʒɛnte] AG negligent, careless

negli'genza [negli'dʒɛntsa] SF negligence, carelessness

negozi'abile [negot'tsjabile] AG negotiable

negozi'ante [negot'tsjante] SMF trader, dealer; (*bottegaio*) shopkeeper (BRIT), storekeeper (US)

negozi'are [negot'tsjare] /19/ VT to negotiate ▶ VI: ~ **in** to trade o deal in

negozi'ato [negot'tsjato] SM negotiation

negozia'tore, -'trice [negottsja'tore] SM/F negotiator

ne'gozio [ne'gɔttsjo] SM (*locale*) shop (BRIT), store (US); (*affare*) (piece of) business no pl; (*Dir*): ~ **giuridico** legal transaction; ~ **online** online store o (BRIT) shop; ~ **di vicinato** local shop (BRIT) o store (US)

negri'ere, -a, negri'ero, -a SM/F slave trader; (*fig*) slave driver

'negro, -a (*peg*) AG, SM/F black person

negro'mante SMF necromancer

negroman'zia [negroman'tsia] SF necromancy

nei, nel, nell', 'nella, 'nelle, 'nello PREP + DET vedi **in**

'nembo SM (*Meteor*) nimbus

ne'mico, -a, -ci, -che AG hostile; (*Mil*) enemy cpd ▶ SM/F enemy; **essere** ~ **di** to be strongly averse o opposed to

nem'meno AV, CONG = **neanche**

'nenia SF dirge; (*motivo monotono*) monotonous tune

'neo SM mole; (*fig*) (slight) flaw

'neo... PREFISSO neo...

neofa'scista, -i, -e [neofaʃ'ʃista] SM/F neofascist

neolo'gismo [neolo'dʒizmo] SM neologism

'neon SM (*Chim*) neon

neo'nato, -a AG newborn ▶ SM/F newborn baby

neozelan'dese [neoddzelan'dese] AG New Zealand cpd ▶ SMF New Zealander

Ne'pal SM: **il** ~ Nepal

nepo'tismo SM nepotism

nep'pure AV, CONG = **neanche**

ner'bata SF (*colpo*) blow; (*sferzata*) whiplash

'nerbo SM lash; (*fig*) strength, backbone

nerbo'ruto, -a AG muscular; robust

ne'retto SM (*Tip*) bold type

'nero, -a AG black; (*scuro*) dark ▶ SM/F (*persona*) black man (woman) ▶ SM black; **nella miseria più nera** in utter o abject poverty; **essere di umore** ~, **essere** ~ to be in a filthy mood; **mettere qc** ~ **su bianco** to put sth down in black and white; **vedere tutto** ~ to look on the black side (of things); **il Mar N**~ the Black Sea

nero'fumo SM lampblack

nerva'tura SF (*Anat*) nervous system; (*Bot*) veining; (*Archit, Tecn*) rib

'nervo SM (*Anat*) nerve; (*Bot*) vein; **avere i nervi** to be on edge; **dare sui nervi a qn** to get on sb's nerves; **tenere/avere i nervi saldi** to keep/be calm; **che nervi!** damn (it)!

nervo'sismo SM (*Psic*) nervousness; (*irritazione*) irritability

ner'voso, -a AG nervous; (*irritabile*) irritable ▶ SM (*col*): **far venire il** ~ **a qn** to get on sb's nerves; **farsi prendere dal** ~ to let o.s. get irritated

'nespola SF (*Bot*) medlar; (*fig*) blow, punch

'nespolo SM medlar tree

'nesso SM connection, link

nes'suno, -a

(*det: dav sm* **nessun** + C, V, **nessuno** + *s impura, gn, pn, ps, x, z; dav sf* **nessuna** + C, **nessun'** + V) DET
1 (*non uno*) no
2 (*espressione negativa*) + any; **non c'è nessun libro** there isn't any book, there is no book; **nessun altro** no one else, nobody else; **nessun'altra cosa** nothing else; **in nessun luogo** nowhere
3 (*qualche*) any; **hai nessuna obiezione?** do you have any objections?
▶ PRON 1 (*non uno*) no one, nobody; (*espressione negativa*) any(one); **nessuno è venuto, non è venuto nessuno** nobody came
2 (*cosa: espressione negativa*) none; (: *espressione negativa*) any
3 (*qualcuno*) anyone, anybody; **ha telefonato nessuno?** did anyone phone?

In inglese non c'è la doppia negazione.
Non c'è nessun segreto. **There is no secret/ there isn't any secret.**
Non ho visto nessuno. **I didn't see anyone.**
Non ha telefonato nessuno. **Nobody phoned.**

'netiquette ['nɛtikɛt] SF netiquette
netta'mente AV clearly
net'tare¹ /72/ VT to clean
'nettare² ['nɛttare] SM nectar
net'tezza [net'tettsa] SF cleanness, cleanliness; ~ **urbana** cleansing department (BRIT), department of sanitation (US)
'netto, -a AG (*pulito*) clean; (*chiaro*) clear, clear-cut; (*deciso*) definite; (*Econ*) net; **tagliare qc di ~** to cut sth clean off; **taglio ~ col passato** (*fig*) clean break with the past
nettur'bino SM dustman (BRIT), garbage collector (US)
'neuro... PREFISSO neuro...
neurochirur'gia [neurokirur'dʒia] SF neurosurgery
neurolo'gia [neurolo'dʒia] SF neurology
neuro'logico, -a, -ci, -che [neuro'lɔdʒiko] AG neurological
neu'rologo, -a, -gi, -ghe SM/F neurologist
neu'rosi SF INV = **nevrosi**
neu'trale AG neutral
neutralità SF neutrality
neutraliz'zare [neutralid'dzare] /72/ VT to neutralize
'neutro, -a AG neutral; (*Ling*) neuter ▶ SM (*Ling*) neuter
neu'trone SM neutron
ne'vaio SM snowfield
'neve SF snow; **montare a ~** (*Cuc*) to whip up; ~ **carbonica** dry ice

nevi'care /20/ VB IMPERS to snow
nevi'cata SF snowfall
ne'vischio [ne'viskjo] SM sleet
ne'voso, -a AG snowy; snow-covered
nevral'gia [nevral'dʒia] SF neuralgia
ne'vralgico, -a, -ci, -che [ne'vraldʒiko] AG: **punto ~** (*Med*) nerve centre; (*fig*) crucial point
nevras'tenico, -a, -ci, -che AG (*Med*) neurasthenic; (*fig*) hot-tempered ▶ SM/F neurasthenic; hot-tempered person
ne'vrosi SF INV neurosis
ne'vrotico, -a, -ci, -che AG, SM/F (*anche fig*) neurotic
Nia'gara SM: **le cascate del ~** the Niagara Falls
'nibbio SM (*Zool*) kite
Nica'ragua SM: **il ~** Nicaragua
nicaragu'ense AG, SMF Nicaraguan
'nicchia ['nikkja] SF niche; (*naturale*) cavity, hollow; ~ **di mercato** (*Comm*) niche market
nicchi'are [nik'kjare] /19/ VI to shilly-shally, hesitate
'nichel ['nikel] SM nickel
nichi'lismo [niki'lizmo] SM nihilism
Nico'sia SF Nicosia
nico'tina SF nicotine
nidi'ata SF (*di uccelli: anche fig: di bambini*) brood; (*di altri animali*) litter
nidifi'care /20/ VI to nest
'nido SM nest ▶ AG INV: **asilo ~** day nursery, crèche (*for children aged 0 to 3*); **a ~ d'ape** (*tessuto ecc*) honeycomb *cpd*

ni'ente

PRON 1 (*nessuna cosa*) nothing; **niente può fermarlo** nothing can stop him; **niente di niente** absolutely nothing; **grazie! — di niente!** thank you! — not at all!; **nient'altro** nothing else; **nient'altro che** nothing but, just, only; **niente affatto** not at all, not in the least; **come se niente fosse** as if nothing had happened; **cose da niente** trivial matters; **per niente** (*gratis, invano*) for nothing; **non per niente, ma ...** not for any particular reason, but ...; **poco o niente** next to nothing; **un uomo da niente** a man of no consequence
2 (*qualcosa*): **hai bisogno di niente?** do you need anything?
3: **non ... niente** nothing; (*espressione negativa*) + anything; **non ho visto niente** I saw nothing, I didn't see anything; **non può farci niente** he can't do anything about it; **(non) fa niente** (*non importa*) it doesn't matter; **non ho niente da dire** I have nothing *o* haven't anything to say
▶ AG INV: **niente paura!** never fear!; **e niente scuse!** and I don't want to hear excuses!

▶ SM nothing; **un bel niente** absolutely nothing; **basta un niente per farla piangere** the slightest thing is enough to make her cry; **finire in niente** to come to nothing

▶ AV (*in nessuna misura*): **non … niente** not … at all; **non è (per) niente buono** it isn't good at all; **non ci penso per niente** (*non ne ho nessuna intenzione*) I wouldn't think of it; **niente male!** not bad at all!

nientedi'meno, niente'meno AV actually, even ▶ ESCL really!, I say!

'Niger ['nidʒer] SM: **il ~** Niger; (*fiume*) the Niger

Ni'geria [ni'dʒɛrja] SF: **la ~** Nigeria

nigeri'ano, -a [nidʒe'rjano] AG, SM/F Nigerian

'Nilo SM: **il ~** the Nile

'nimbo SM halo

'ninfa SF nymph

nin'fea SF water lily

nin'fomane SF nymphomaniac

ninna'nanna SF lullaby

'ninnolo SM (*balocco*) plaything; (*gingillo*) knick-knack

ni'pote SMF (*di zii*) nephew (niece); (*di nonni*) grandson (daughter), grandchild

nip'ponico, -a, -ci, -che AG Japanese

niti'dezza [niti'dettsa] SF (*gen*) clearness; (*di stile*) clarity; (*Fot, TV*) sharpness

'nitido, -a AG clear; (*immagine*) sharp; (*specchio*) bright

ni'trato SM nitrate

'nitrico, -a, -ci, -che AG nitric

ni'trire /55/ VI to neigh

ni'trito SM (*di cavallo*) neighing *no pl*; neigh; (*Chim*) nitrite

nitroglice'rina [nitroglitʃe'rina] SF nitroglycerine

'niveo, -a AG snow-white

'Nizza ['nittsa] SF Nice

nn ABBR (= *numeri*) nos

NO SIGLA = **Novara**

no AV (*risposta*) no; **vieni o no?** are you coming or not?; **come no!** of course!, certainly!; **perché no?** why not?; **lo conosciamo? — tu no ma io sì** do we know him? — you don't but I do; **verrai, no?** you'll come, won't you?

N.O. ABBR (= *nordovest*) NW

nobil'donna SF noblewoman

'nobile AG noble ▶ SMF noble, nobleman/woman

nobili'are AG noble

nobili'tare /72/ VT (*anche fig*) to ennoble ■ **nobilitarsi** VPR (*rendersi insigne*) to distinguish o.s.

nobiltà SF nobility; (*di azione ecc*) nobleness

nobilu'omo (*pl* **nobiluomini**) SM nobleman

'nocca, -che SF (*Anat*) knuckle

'noccio *ecc* ['nɔttʃo] VB *vedi* **nuocere**

nocci'ola [not'tʃɔla] SF hazelnut ▶ AG INV (*anche*: **color nocciola**) hazel, light brown

noccio'lina [nottʃo'lina] SF (*anche*: **nocciolina americana**) peanut

'nocciolo[1] ['nɔttʃolo] SM (*di frutto*) stone; (*fig*) heart, core

nocci'olo[2] [nottʃ'ɔlo] SM (*albero*) hazel

'noce ['notʃe] SM (*albero*) walnut tree ▶ SF (*frutto*) walnut; **una ~ di burro** (*Cuc*) a knob of butter (*BRIT*), a dab of butter (*US*); **~ di cocco** coconut; **~ moscata** nutmeg

noce'pesca, -sche [notʃe'pɛska] SF nectarine

no'cevo *ecc* [no'tʃevo] VB *vedi* **nuocere**

noci'uto [no'tʃuto] PP *di* **nuocere**

no'civo, -a [no'tʃivo] AG harmful, noxious

'nocqui *ecc* VB *vedi* **nuocere**

'nodo SM (*di cravatta, legname, Naut*) knot; (*Aut, Ferr*) junction; (*Med, Astr, Bot*) node; (*fig: legame*) bond, tie; (: *punto centrale*) heart, crux; **avere un ~ alla gola** to have a lump in one's throat; **tutti i nodi vengono al pettine** (*proverbio*) your sins will find you out

no'doso, -a AG (*tronco*) gnarled

'nodulo SM (*Anat, Bot*) nodule

no-'global [no-'global] SMF anti-globalization protester ▶ AG (*movimento, manifestante*) anti-globalization

'noi PRON (*soggetto*) we; (*oggetto: per dare rilievo, con preposizione*) us; **~ stessi(e)** we ourselves; (*oggetto*) ourselves; **da ~** (*nel nostro paese*) in our country, where we come from; (*a casa nostra*) at our house

'noia SF boredom; (*disturbo, impaccio*) bother *no pl*, trouble *no pl*; **avere qn/qc a ~** not to like sb/sth; **mi è venuto a ~** I'm tired of it; **dare ~ a** to annoy; **avere delle noie con qn** to have trouble with sb

noi'altri PRON we

noi'oso, -a AG boring; (*fastidioso*) annoying, troublesome

noleggi'are [noled'dʒare] /62/ VT (*prendere a noleggio*) to hire (*BRIT*), rent; (*dare a noleggio*) to hire out (*BRIT*), rent out; (*aereo, nave*) to charter

noleggia'tore, -'trice [noleddʒa'tore] SM/F hirer (*BRIT*), renter; charterer

no'leggio [no'leddʒo] SM hire (*BRIT*), rental; charter

no'lente AG: **volente o ~** whether one likes it or not, willy-nilly

'nolo SM hire (*BRIT*), rental charter; (*per trasporto merci*) freight; **prendere/dare a ~ qc** to hire/hire out sth (*BRIT*), rent/rent out sth

'nomade AG nomadic ▶ SMF nomad

noma'dismo SM nomadism

'nome SM name; (*Ling*) noun; **in o a ~ di** in the name of; **di o per ~** (*chiamato*) called, named;

conoscere qn di ~ to know sb by name; **fare il ~ di qn** to name sb; **faccia pure il mio ~** feel free to mention my name; **~ d'arte** stage name; **~ di battesimo** Christian name; **~ depositato** trade name; **~ di famiglia** surname; **~ da ragazza** maiden name; **~ da sposata** married name; **~ utente** login, username

no'mea SF notoriety

nomencla'tura SF nomenclature

nomenkla'tura SF (*di partito, stato*) nomenklatura

no'mignolo [no'miɲɲolo] SM nickname

'nomina SF appointment

nomi'nale AG nominal; (*Ling*) noun *cpd*

nomi'nare /72/ VT to name; (*eleggere*) to appoint; (*citare*) to mention; **non l'ho mai sentito ~** I've never heard of it (*o him*)

nomi'nation [nomi'neʃʃon] SF INV (*in reality show*) nomination

nomina'tivo, -a AG (*intestato: titolo*) registered; (*: libretto*) personal; (*Ling*) nominative ▶ SM (*Amm: nome*) name; (*Ling*) nominative; **elenco ~** list of names

nomofo'bia SF nomophobia

non AV not ▶ PREFISSO non-; **grazie — ~ c'è di che** thank you — don't mention it; **i ~ credenti** the unbelievers; **~ autosufficiente** (*persona anziana*) needing care; *vedi anche* **affatto**; **appena** *ecc*

nonché [non'ke] CONG (*tanto più, tanto meno*) let alone; (*e inoltre*) as well as

nonconfor'mista, -i, -e AG, SM/F nonconformist

noncu'rante AG: **~ (di)** careless (of), indifferent (to); **con fare ~** with a nonchalant air

noncu'ranza [nonku'rantsa] SF carelessness, indifference; **un'aria di ~** a nonchalant air

nondi'meno CONG (*tuttavia*) however; (*nonostante*) nevertheless

'nonno, -a SM/F grandfather/mother; (*in senso più familiare*) grandma/grandpa ■ **nonni** SMPL grandparents

non'nulla SM INV: **un ~** nothing, a trifle

'nono, -a NUM ninth

nonos'tante PREP in spite of, notwithstanding ▶ CONG although, even though

non plus 'ultra SM INV: **il ~ (di)** the last word (in)

nontiscordardimé SM INV (*Bot*) forget-me-not

nord SM north ▶ AG INV north; (*regione*) northern; **verso ~** north, northwards; **l'America del N~** North America; **il Mare del N~** the North Sea

nor'dest SM north-east

'nordico, -a, -ci, -che AG nordic, northern European

nor'dista, -i, -e AG, SM/F Yankee

nor'dovest SM north-west

Norim'berga SF Nuremberg

'norma SF (*principio*) norm; (*regola*) regulation, rule; (*consuetudine*) custom, rule; **di ~** normally; **a ~ di legge** according to law, as laid down by law; **al di sopra della ~** above average, above the norm; **per sua ~ e regola** for your information; **proporsi una ~ di vita** to set o.s. rules to live by; **norme di sicurezza** safety regulations; **norme per l'uso** instructions for use

nor'male AG normal; standard *cpd*

normalità SF normality

normaliz'zare [normalid'dzare] /72/ VT to normalize, bring back to normal

normal'mente AV normally

Norman'dia SF: **la ~** Normandy

nor'manno, -a AG, SM/F Norman

norma'tivo, -a AG normative ▶ SF regulations *pl*

norve'gese [norve'dʒese] AG, SMF, SM Norwegian

Nor'vegia [nor'vɛdʒa] SF: **la ~** Norway

noso'comio SM hospital

nostal'gia [nostal'dʒia] SF (*di casa, paese*) homesickness; (*del passato*) nostalgia

nos'talgico, -a, -ci, -che [nos'taldʒiko] AG homesick; nostalgic ▶ SM/F (*Pol*) person who hopes for the return of Fascism

nos'trano, -a AG local; national; (*pianta, frutta*) home-produced

'nostro, -a DET: **(il) ~, (la) nostra** our ▶ PRON: **(il) ~, (la) nostra** ours ▶ SM: **il ~** our money; our belongings ▶ SF: **la nostra** (*opinione*) our view; **abbiamo speso del ~** we spent our own money; **i nostri** our family; our own people; **è dei nostri** he's one of us; **è dalla nostra** (*parte*) he's on our side; **anche noi abbiamo avuto le nostre** (*disavventure*) we've had our problems too; **alla nostra!** (*brindisi*) to us!

nos'tromo SM boatswain

'nota SF (*segno*) mark; (*comunicazione scritta: Mus*) note; (*fattura*) bill; (*elenco*) list; **prendere ~ di qc** to note sth, make a note of sth, write sth down; (*fig: fare attenzione*) to note sth, take note of sth; **degno di ~** noteworthy, worthy of note; **note caratteristiche** distinguishing marks *o* features; **note a piè di pagina** footnotes

no'tabile AG notable; (*persona*) important ▶ SM prominent citizen

no'taio SM notary

no'tare /72/ VT (*segnare: errori*) to mark; (*registrare*) to note (down), write down; (*rilevare, osservare*) to note, notice; **farsi ~** to get o.s. noticed

nota'rile AG: **atto ~** legal document (*authorized by a notary*); **studio ~** notary's office

notazi'one [notat'tsjone] SF (*Mus*) notation

235

no'tevole AG (*talento*) notable, remarkable; (*peso*) considerable

no'tifica, -che SF notification

notifi'care /20/ VT (*Dir*): ~ **qc a qn** to notify sb of sth, give sb notice of sth

notificazi'one [notifikat'tsjone] SF notification

no'tizia [no'tittsja] SF (piece of) news *sg*; (*informazione*) piece of information ■ **notizie** SFPL news *sg*; information *sg*

> *Notizie* al plurale si traduce **news**, ma con il verbo al singolare.
> *Le notizie sono scioccanti*. **The news is shocking**.
> Per il singolare si usa **a piece of news** o **(some) news**.
> *una notizia sorprendente* **a surprising piece of news**

---

notizi'ario [notit'tsjarjo] SM (*Radio*, *TV*, *Stampa*) news *sg*

'noto, -a AG (well-)known

notorietà SF fame; notoriety

no'torio, -a AG well-known; (*peg*) notorious

not'tambulo, -a SM/F night-bird (*fig*)

not'tata SF night

'notte SF night; **di ~** at night; (*durante la notte*) in the night, during the night; **questa ~** (*passata*) last night; (*che viene*) tonight; **nella ~ dei tempi** in the mists of time; **come va? — peggio che andar di ~** how are things? — worse than ever; **~ bianca** sleepless night

notte'tempo AV at night; during the night

'nottola SF (*Zool*) noctule

not'turno, -a AG nocturnal; (*servizio, guardiano*) night *cpd* ▶ SF (*Sport*) evening fixture (BRIT) o match

nov. ABBR (= *novembre*) Nov

no'vanta NUM ninety

novan'tenne AG, SMF ninety-year-old

novan'tesimo, -a NUM ninetieth

novan'tina SF: **una ~ (di)** about ninety

'nove NUM nine

novecen'tesco, -a, -schi, -sche [novet-ʃen'tesko] AG twentieth-century

nove'cento [nove'tʃento] NUM nine hundred ▶ SM: **il N~** the twentieth century

no'vella SF (*Letteratura*) short story

novel'lino, -a AG (*pivello*) green, inexperienced

novel'lista, -i, -e SM/F short-story writer

novel'listica SF (*arte*) short-story writing; (*insieme di racconti*) short stories *pl*

no'vello, -a AG (*piante, patate*) new; (*insalata, verdura*) early; (*sposo*) newly-married

no'vembre SM November; *vedi anche* **luglio**

novem'brino, -a AG November *cpd*

nove'mila NUM nine thousand

noven'nale AG (*che dura 9 anni*) nine-year *cpd*; (*ogni 9 anni*) nine-yearly

novi'lunio SM (*Astr*) new moon

novità SF INV novelty; (*innovazione*) innovation; (*cosa originale, insolita*) something new; (*notizia*) (piece of) news *sg*; **le ~ della moda** the latest fashions

novizi'ato [novit'tsjato] SM (*Rel*) novitiate; (*tirocinio*) apprenticeship

no'vizio, -a [no'vittsjo] SM/F (*Rel*) novice; (*tirocinante*) beginner, apprentice

nozi'one [not'tsjone] SF notion, idea ■ **nozioni** SFPL (*rudimenti*) basic knowledge *sg*, rudiments

nozio'nismo [nottsjo'nizmo] SM superficial knowledge

nozio'nistico, -a, -ci, -che [nottsjo'nistiko] AG superficial

'nozze ['nɔttse] SFPL wedding *sg*, marriage *sg*; **~ d'argento/d'oro** silver/golden wedding *sg*

ns . ABBR (*Comm*) = **nostro**

NU SIGLA = **Nuoro**

N.U. SIGLA (= *Nazioni Unite*) UN

'nube SF cloud

nubi'fragio [nubi'fradʒo] SM cloudburst

'nubile AG (*donna*) unmarried, single

'nuca, -che SF nape of the neck

nucle'are AG nuclear ▶ SM: **il ~** nuclear energy

'nucleo SM nucleus; (*gruppo*) team, unit, group; (*Mil, Polizia*) squad; **~ antidroga** anti-drugs squad; **il ~ familiare** the family unit

nu'dismo SM nudism

nu'dista, -i, -e SM/F nudist

nudità SF INV nudity, nakedness; (*di paesaggio*) bareness ▶ SFPL (*parti nude del corpo*) nakedness *sg*

'nudo, -a AG (*persona*) bare, naked, nude; (*membra*) bare, naked; (*montagna*) bare ▶ SM (*Arte*) nude; **a occhio ~** to the naked eye; **a piedi nudi** barefoot; **mettere a ~** (*cuore, verità*) to lay bare; **gli ha detto ~ e crudo che ...** he told him bluntly that ...

'nugolo SM: **un ~ di** a whole host of

'nulla PRON, AV = **niente** ▶ SM: **il ~** nothing; **svanire nel ~** to vanish into thin air; **basta un ~ per farlo arrabbiare** he gets annoyed over the slightest thing

nulla'osta SM INV authorization

nullate'nente AG: **essere ~** to own nothing ▶ SMF person with no property

nullità SF INV nullity; (*persona*) nonentity

'nullo, -a AG useless, worthless; (*Dir*) null (and void); (*Sport*): **incontro ~** draw

nume'rale AG, SM numeral

nume'rare /72/ VT to number

numera'tore SM (*Mat*) numerator; (*macchina*) numbering device

numerazi'one [numerat'tsjone] SF numbering; (*araba, decimale*) notation

nu'merico, -a, -ci, -che AG numerical

'numero SM number; (*romano, arabo*) numeral; (*di spettacolo*) act, turn; **dare i numeri** (*farneticare*) not to be all there; **tanto per fare ~ invitiamo anche lui** why don't we invite him to make up the numbers?; **ha tutti i numeri per riuscire** he's got what it takes to succeed; **che ~ tuo fratello!** your brother is a real character!; **~ civico** house number; **~ chiuso** (*Università*) selective entry system; **~ doppio** (*di rivista*) issue with supplement; **~ di scarpe** shoe size; **~ di telefono** telephone number; **~ verde** (*Tel*) ≈ Freephone®

nume'roso, -a AG numerous, many; (*folla, famiglia*) large

numis'matica SF numismatics *sg*, coin collecting

'nunzio ['nuntsjo] SM (*Rel*) nuncio

nu'occio *ecc* ['nwɔttʃo] VB *vedi* **nuocere**

nu'ocere ['nwɔtʃere] /69/ VI: **~ a** to harm, damage; **il tentar non nuoce** (*proverbio*) there's no harm in trying

nuoci'uto, -a [nwo'tʃuto] PP *di* **nuocere**

nu'ora SF daughter-in-law

nuo'tare /72/ VI to swim; (*galleggiare: oggetti*) to float; **~ a rana/sul dorso** to do the breast stroke/backstroke

nuo'tata SF swim

nuota'tore, -'trice SM/F swimmer

nu'oto SM swimming

nu'ova SF *vedi* **nuovo**

nuova'mente AV again

Nu'ova York SF New York

Nu'ova Ze'landa [-dze'landa] SF: **la ~** New Zealand

nu'ovo, -a AG new ▶ SF (*notizia*) (piece of) news *sg*; **come ~** as good as new; **di ~** again; **fino a ~ ordine** until further notice; **il suo volto non mi è ~** I know his face; **rimettere a ~** (*cosa, macchina*) to do up like new; **anno ~, vita nuova!** it's time to turn over a new leaf!; **~ fiammante** *o* **di zecca** brand-new; **la Nuova Guinea** New Guinea; **la Nuova Inghilterra** New England; **la Nuova Scozia** Nova Scotia

nu'trice [nu'tritʃe] SF wet nurse

nutri'ente AG nutritious, nourishing; (*crema, balsamo*) nourishing

nutri'mento SM food, nourishment

nu'trire /45/ VT to feed; (*fig: sentimenti*) to harbour (*Brit*), harbor (*US*), nurse ■ **nutrirsi** VPR: **nutrirsi di** to feed on, to eat

nutri'tivo, -a AG nutritional; (*alimento*) nutritious

nu'trito, -a AG (*numeroso*) large; (*fitto*) heavy; **ben/mal ~** well/poorly fed

nutrizi'one [nutrit'tsjone] SF nutrition

'nuvolo, -a AG cloudy ▶ SF cloud

nuvolosità SF cloudiness

nuvo'loso, -a AG cloudy

nuzi'ale [nut'tsjale] AG nuptial; wedding *cpd*

'nylon ['nailən] SM nylon

n

Oo

O, o¹ [ɔ] SM O F INV (*lettera*) O, o; **O come Otranto** ≈ O for Oliver (BRIT), O for Oboe (US)

o² CONG (*dav V spesso*): **od** or; **o ... o** either ... or; **o l'uno o l'altro** either (of them); **o meglio** or rather

O. ABBR (= *ovest*) W

'oasi SF INV oasis

obbedi'ente *ecc vedi* **ubbidiente** *ecc*

obbiet'tare *ecc vedi* **obiettare** *ecc*

obbli'gare /80/ VT (*Dir*) to bind; (*costringere*): **~ qn a fare** to force *o* oblige sb to do ■ **obbligarsi** VPR: **obbligarsi a fare** to undertake to do; **obbligarsi per qn** (*Dir*) to stand surety for sb, act as guarantor for sb

obbliga'tissimo, -a AG (*ringraziamento*): **~!** much obliged!

obbli'gato, -a AG (*costretto, grato*) obliged; (*percorso, tappa*) set, fixed; **passaggio ~** (*fig*) essential requirement

obbliga'torio, -a AG compulsory, obligatory

obbligazi'one [obbligat'tsjone] SF obligation; (*Comm*) bond, debenture; **~ dello Stato** government bond; **obbligazioni convertibili** convertible loan stock, convertible debentures

obbligazio'nista, -i, -e [obbligattsjo'nista] SM/F bond-holder

'obbligo, -ghi SM obligation; (*dovere*) duty; **avere l'~ di fare, essere nell'~ di fare** to be obliged to do; **essere d'~** (*discorso, applauso*) to be called for; **avere degli obblighi con** *o* **verso qn** to be under an obligation to sb, be indebted to sb; **le formalità d'~** the necessary formalities

obb.mo ABBR = **obbligatissimo**

ob'brobrio SM disgrace; (*fig*) mess, eyesore

obe'lisco, -schi SM obelisk

obe'rato, -a AG: **~ di** (*lavoro*) overloaded *o* overburdened with; (*debiti*) crippled with

obesità SF obesity

o'beso, -a AG obese

obiet'tare /72/ VT: **~ che** to object that; **~ su qc** to object to sth, raise objections concerning sth

obiettiva'mente AV objectively

obiettività SF objectivity

obiet'tivo, -a AG objective ▶ SM (*Ottica, Fot*) lens *sg*, objective; (*Mil, fig*) objective

obiet'tore SM objector; **~ di coscienza** conscientious objector

obiezi'one [objet'tsjone] SF objection

obi'torio SM morgue

o'bliquo, -a AG oblique; (*inclinato*) slanting; (*fig*) devious, underhand; **sguardo ~** sidelong glance

oblite'rare /72/ VT (*francobollo*) to cancel; (*biglietto*) to stamp

oblitera'trice [oblitera'tritʃe] SF (*anche*: **macchina obliteratrice**) cancelling machine; stamping machine

oblò SM INV porthole

o'blungo, -a, -ghi, -ghe AG oblong

'oboe SM (*Mus*) oboe

'obolo SM (*elemosina*) (small) offering, mite

obsole'scenza [obsoleʃ'ʃentsa] SF (*Econ*) obsolescence

obso'leto, -a AG obsolete

OC ABBR (= *onde corte*) SW

'oca (*pl* **oche**) SF goose

o'caggine [o'kaddʒine] SF silliness, stupidity

occasio'nale AG (*incontro*) chance; (*cliente, guadagni*) casual, occasional

occasi'one SF (*caso favorevole*) opportunity; (*causa, motivo, circostanza*) occasion; (*Comm*) bargain; **all'~** should the need arise; **alla prima ~** at the first, opportunity; **d'~** (*a buon prezzo*) bargain *cpd*; (*usato*) secondhand

occhi'aia [ok'kjaja] SF eye socket ■ **occhiaie** SFPL (*sotto gli occhi*) shadows (under the eyes); **avere le occhiaie** to have shadows under one's eyes

occhi'ali [ok'kjali] SMPL glasses, spectacles; **~ da sole/da vista** sunglasses/(prescription) glasses

occhi'ata [ok'kjata] SF look, glance; **dare un'~ a** to have a look at

occhieggi'are [okkjed'dʒare] /62/ VI (*apparire qua e là*) to peep (out)

occhi'ello [ok'kjello] SM buttonhole; (*asola*) eyelet

'occhio ['ɔkkjo] sm eye; **~!** careful!, watch out!; **a ~ nudo** with the naked eye; **a quattr'occhi** privately, tête-à-tête, in private; **avere ~ to** have a good eye; **chiudere un ~ (su)** (fig) to turn a blind eye (to), shut one's eyes (to); **costare un ~ della testa** to cost a fortune; **dare all'~** o **nell'~ a qn** to catch sb's eye; **fare l'~ a qc** to get used to sth; **tenere d'~ qn** to keep an eye on sb; **vedere di buon/mal ~ qc** to look favourably/unfavourably on sth

occhio'lino [okkjo'lino] sm: **fare l'~ a qn** to wink at sb

occiden'tale [ottʃiden'tale] AG western ▶ smf Westerner

occi'dente [ottʃi'dɛnte] sm west; (Pol): **l'O~** the West; **a ~** in the west

oc'cipite [ot'tʃipite] sm back of the head, occiput (Anat)

oc'cludere /3/ vt to block

occlusi'one sf blockage, obstruction

oc'cluso, -a pp di **occludere**

occor'rente AG necessary ▶ sm all that is necessary

occor'renza [okkor'rɛntsa] sf necessity, need; **all'~** in case of need

oc'correre /28/ vi to be needed, be required ▶ vb impers: **occorre farlo** it must be done; **occorre che tu parta** you must leave, you'll have to leave; **mi occorrono i soldi** I need the money

oc'corso, -a pp di **occorrere**

occulta'mento sm concealment

occul'tare /72/ vt to hide, conceal

oc'culto, -a AG hidden, concealed; (scienze, forze) occult

occu'pante smf (di casa) occupier, occupant; **~ abusivo** squatter

occu'pare /72/ vt to occupy; (manodopera) to employ; (ingombrare) to occupy, take up ■ **occuparsi** vpr to occupy o.s., keep o.s. busy; (impiegarsi) to get a job; **occuparsi di** (interessarsi) to take an interest in; (prendersi cura di) to look after, take care of

occu'pato, -a AG (Mil, Pol) occupied; (persona: affaccendato) busy; (posto, sedia) taken; (toilette, Tel) engaged; **la linea è occupata** the line's engaged

occupazio'nale [okkupattsjo'nale] AG employment cpd, of employment

occupazi'one [okkupat'tsjone] sf occupation; (impiego, lavoro) job; (Econ) employment

Oce'ania [otʃe'anja] sf: **l'~** Oceania

o'ceano [o'tʃɛano] sm ocean

'ocra sf ochre

'OCSE sigla f (= Organizzazione per la Cooperazione e lo Sviluppo Economico) OECD (= Organization for Economic Cooperation and Development)

ocu'lare AG ocular, eye cpd; **testimone ~** eye witness

ocula'tezza [okula'tettsa] sf caution; shrewdness

ocu'lato, -a AG (attento) cautious, prudent; (accorto) shrewd

ocu'lista, -i, -e sm/f eye specialist, oculist

od cong vedi **o**

'ode sf ode

'ode ecc vb vedi **udire**

odi'are /19/ vt to hate, detest

odi'erno, -a AG today's, of today; (attuale) present; **in data odierna** (formale) today

'odio sm hatred; **avere in ~ qc/qn** to hate o detest sth/sb

odi'oso, -a AG hateful, odious; **rendersi ~ (a)** to make o.s. unpopular (with)

'odo ecc vb vedi **udire**

odontoi'atra, -i, -e sm/f dentist, dental surgeon

odontoia'tria sf dentistry

odonto'tecnico, -ci sm dental technician

odo'rare /72/ vt (annusare) to smell; (profumare) to perfume, scent ▶ vi: **~ (di)** to smell (of)

odo'rato sm sense of smell

o'dore sm smell; **gli odori** (Cuc) (aromatic) herbs; **sentire ~ di qc** to smell sth; **morire in ~ di santità** (Rel) to die in the odour (Brit) o odor (US) of sanctity

odo'roso, -a AG sweet-smelling

offendere /36/ vt to offend; (violare) to break, violate; (insultare) to insult; (ferire) to hurt ■ **offendersi** vpr (con senso reciproco) to insult one another; (risentirsi) **offendersi (di)** to take offence (at), be offended (by)

offen'sivo, -a AG, sf offensive

offen'sore sm offender; (Mil) aggressor

offe'rente smf (in aste): **al migliore ~** to the highest bidder

of'ferto, -a pp di **offrire** ▶ sf offer; (donazione: anche Rel) offering; (in gara d'appalto) tender; (in aste) bid; (Econ) supply; **fare un'offerta** to make an offer; (per appalto) to tender; (ad un'asta) to bid; **offerta pubblica d'acquisto** takeover bid; **offerta pubblica di vendita** public offer for sale; **offerta reale** tender; **"offerte d'impiego"** (Stampa) "situations vacant" (Brit), "help wanted" (US); **offerta speciale** special offer

of'feso, -a pp di **offendere** ▶ AG offended; (fisicamente) hurt, injured ▶ sm/f offended party ▶ sf insult, affront; (Mil) attack; (Dir) offence (Brit), offense (US); **essere ~ con qn** to be annoyed with sb; **parte offesa** (Dir) plaintiff

offi'ciare [offi'tʃare] /14/ vi (Rel) to officiate

offi'cina [offi'tʃina] sf workshop

of'frire /70/ vt to offer ■ **offrirsi** vpr (proporsi) to offer (o.s.), volunteer; (occasione) to present

O

itself; (*esporsi*): **offrirsi a** to expose o.s. to; **ti offro da bere** I'll buy you a drink; **"offresi posto di segretaria"** "secretarial vacancy", "vacancy for secretary"; **"segretaria offresi"** "secretary seeks post"

offus'care /2o/ VT to obscure, darken; (*fig: intelletto*) to dim, cloud; (: *fama*) to obscure, overshadow ■ **offuscarsi** VPR to grow dark; to cloud, grow dim; to be obscured

of'talmico, -a, -ci, -che AG ophthalmic

oggettività [oddʒettivi'ta] SF objectivity

ogget'tivo, -a [oddʒet'tivo] AG objective

og'getto [od'dʒɛtto] SM object; (*materia, argomento*) subject (matter); (*in lettere commerciali*): **~ ... re ...**; **essere ~ di** (*critiche, controversia*) to be the subject of; (*odio, pietà ecc*) to be the object of; **essere ~ di scherno** to be a laughing stock; **in ~ a quanto detto** (*in lettere*) as regards the matter mentioned above; **oggetti preziosi** valuables, articles of value; **oggetti smarriti** lost property *sg* (BRIT), lost and found *sg* (US)

'oggi ['ɔddʒi] AV, SM today; **~ stesso** today, this very day; **~ come ~** at present, as things stand; **dall' ~ al domani** from one day to the next; **a tutt'~** up till now, till today; **le spese a tutt'~ sono ...** expenses to date are ...; **~ a otto** a week today

oggigi'orno [oddʒi'dʒorno] AV nowadays

o'giva [o'dʒiva] SF ogive, pointed arch

OGM [ɔdʒi'ɛmme] SIGLA MPL (= *organismi geneticamente modificati*) GMO (= *genetically modified organisms*)

'ogni ['oɲɲi] DET every, each; (*tutti*) all; (*con valore distributivo*) every; **~ uomo è mortale** all men are mortal; **viene ~ due giorni** he comes every two days; **~ cosa** everything; **ad ~ costo** at all costs, at any price; **in ~ luogo** everywhere; **~ tanto** every so often; **~ volta che** every time that

Ognis'santi [oɲɲis'santi] SM All Saints' Day

o'gnuno [oɲ'ɲuno] PRON everyone, everybody

Ognuno/ognuna si traduce con **everyone** o **everybody** con il verbo al singolare e, nel linguaggio corrente, con l'aggettivo possessivo al plurale. Nel linguaggio più formale si usa **his** o **her**.
Ognuno ha la sua idea su questo. **Everyone has their/his/her own view on this**.

'ohi ESCL oh!; (*esprimente dolore*) ow!

ohimè ESCL oh dear!

'OIL SIGLA F (= *Organizzazione Internazionale del Lavoro*) ILO

OL ABBR (= *onde lunghe*) LW

O'landa SF: **l'~** Holland

olan'dese AG Dutch ▶ SM (*Ling*) Dutch ▶ SMF Dutchman/woman; **gli Olandesi** the Dutch

ole'andro SM oleander

ole'ato, -a AG: **carta oleata** greaseproof paper (BRIT), wax paper (US)

oleo'dotto SM oil pipeline

ole'oso, -a AG oily; (*che contiene olio*) oil *cpd*, oil-yielding

o'lezzo [o'leddzo] SM fragrance

ol'fatto SM sense of smell

oli'are /19/ VT to oil

olia'tore SM oil can, oiler

oli'era SF oil cruet

oligar'chia [oligar'kia] SF oligarchy

Olim'piadi SFPL Olympic Games®

o'limpico, -a, -ci, -che AG Olympic®

'olio SM oil; (*Pittura*): **un (quadro a) ~** an oil painting; **sott'~** (*Cuc*) in oil; **oli essenziali** essential oils; **~ di fegato di merluzzo** cod liver oil; **~ d'oliva** olive oil; **~ santo** holy oil; **~ di semi** vegetable oil; **~ solare** suntan oil; **oli essenziali** essential oils

o'liva SF olive

oli'vastro, -a AG olive(-coloured) (BRIT), olive(-colored) (US); (*carnagione*) sallow

oli'veto SM olive grove

o'livo SM olive tree

'olmo SM elm

olo'causto SM holocaust

OLP SIGLA F (= *Organizzazione per la Liberazione della Palestina*) PLO

oltraggi'are [oltrad'dʒare] /62/ VT to offend, insult

ol'traggio [ol'traddʒo] SM outrage; offence (BRIT), offense (US), insult; (*Dir*): **~ a pubblico ufficiale** insulting a public official; (*Dir*): **~ al pudore** indecent behaviour (BRIT) o behavior (US); **~ alla corte** contempt of court

oltraggi'oso, -a [oltrad'dʒoso] AG offensive

ol'tralpe AV beyond the Alps

ol'tranza [ol'trantsa] SF: **a ~** to the last, to the bitter end; **sciopero ad ~** all-out strike

oltran'zismo [oltran'tsizmo] SM (*Pol*) extremism

oltran'zista, -i, -e [oltran'tsista] SM/F (*Pol*) extremist

'oltre AV (*più in là*) further; (*di più: aspettare*) longer, more ▶ PREP (*di là da*) beyond, over, on the other side of; (*più di*) more than, over; (*in aggiunta a*) besides; (*eccetto*): **~ a** except, apart from; **~ a tutto** on top of all that

oltrecor'tina AV behind the Iron Curtain; **paesi d'~** Iron Curtain countries

oltre'manica AV across the Channel

oltre'mare AV overseas

oltre'modo AV extremely, greatly

oltreo'ceano [oltreo'tʃeano] AV overseas ▶ SM: **paesi d'~** overseas countries

oltrepas'sare /72/ VT to go beyond, exceed

oltre'tomba SM INV: **l'~** the hereafter

OM ABBR (= *onde medie*) MW; (*Mil*) = **ospedale militare**

o'maggio [o'maddʒo] SM (*dono*) gift; (*segno di rispetto*) homage, tribute ⬛ **omaggi** SMPL (*complimenti*) respects; **in ~** (*copia, biglietto*) complimentary; **rendere ~ a** to pay homage o tribute to; **presentare i propri omaggi a qn** (*formale*) to pay one's respects to sb

'Oman SM: **l'~** Oman

ombeli'cale AG umbilical

ombe'lico, -chi SM navel

'ombra SF (*zona non assolata, fantasma*) shade; (*sagoma scura*) shadow ▶ AG INV: **bandiera ~** flag of convenience; **governo ~** (*Pol*) shadow cabinet; **sedere all'~** to sit in the shade; **nell'~** (*tramare, agire*) secretly; **restare nell'~** (*fig: persona*) to remain in obscurity; **senza ~ di dubbio** without the shadow of a doubt

ombreggi'are [ombred'dʒare] /62/ VT to shade

om'brello SM umbrella; **~ da sole** parasol, sunshade

ombrel'lone SM beach umbrella

om'bretto SM eyeshadow

om'broso, -a AG shady, shaded; (*cavallo*) nervous, skittish; (*persona*) touchy, easily offended

O.M.C. SIGLA F (= *Organizzazione Mondiale del Commercio*) WTO

ome'lette [ɔmə'lɛt] SF INV omelet(te)

ome'lia SF (*Rel*) homily, sermon

ome'opata SMF hom(o)eopath

omeopa'tia SF hom(o)eopathy

omeo'patico, -a, -ci, -che AG hom(o)eopathic ▶ SM hom(o)eopath

omertà SF conspiracy of silence

o'messo, -a PP di **omettere**

o'mettere /63/ VT to omit, leave out; **~ di fare** to omit o fail to do

omi'cida, -i, -e [omi'tʃida] AG homicidal, murderous ▶ SM/F murderer (murderess)

omi'cidio [omi'tʃidjo] SM murder; **~ colposo** (*Dir*) culpable homicide; **~ premeditato** (*Dir*) murder

o'misi *ecc* VB *vedi* **omettere**

omissi'one SF omission; **reato d'~** criminal negligence; **~ di atti d'ufficio** negligence; **~ di denuncia** failure to report a crime; **~ di soccorso** (*Dir*) failure to stop and give assistance

omogeneiz'zato [omodʒeneid'dzato] SM baby food

omo'geneo, -a [omo'dʒɛneo] AG homogeneous

omogenitoriali'tà [omodʒenitorjali'ta] SF same-sex parenthood

omolo'gare /80/ VT (*Dir*) to approve, recognize; (*ratificare*) to ratify

omologazi'one [omologat'tsjone] SF approval; ratification

o'mologo, -a, -ghi, -ghe AG homologous, corresponding ▶ SM/F opposite number

o'monimo, -a SM/F namesake ▶ SM (*Ling*) homonym

omosessu'ale AG, SMF homosexual

O.M.S. SIGLA F = **Organizzazione Mondiale della Sanità**

On. ABBR (*Pol*) = **onorevole**

'oncia, -ce ['ontʃa] SF ounce

'onda SF wave; **mettere** o **mandare in ~** (*Radio, TV*) to broadcast; **andare in ~** (*Radio, TV*) to go on the air; **onde corte/medie/lunghe** short/medium/long wave sg; **l'~ verde** (*Aut*) synchronized traffic lights pl

on'data SF wave, billow; (*fig*) wave, surge; **a ondate** in waves; **~ di caldo** heatwave; **~ di freddo** cold spell o snap

'onde CONG (*affinché: con il congiuntivo*) so that, in order that; (*: con l'infinito*) so as to, in order to

ondeggi'are [onded'dʒare] /62/ VI (*acqua*) to ripple; (*muoversi sulle onde: barca*) to rock, roll; (*fig: muoversi come le onde, barcollare*) to sway; (*essere incerto*) to waver

on'doso, -a AG (*moto*) of the waves

ondu'lato, -a AG (*capelli*) wavy; (*terreno*) undulating; **cartone ~** corrugated paper; **lamiera ondulata** sheet of corrugated iron

ondula'torio, -a AG undulating; (*Fisica*) undulatory, wave cpd

ondulazi'one [ondulat'tsjone] SF undulation; (*acconciatura*) wave

one'rato, -a AG: **~ di** burdened with, loaded with

'onere SM burden; **~ finanziario** financial charge; **oneri fiscali** taxes

one'roso, -a AG (*fig*) heavy, onerous

onestà SF honesty

onesta'mente AV honestly; fairly, virtuously; (*in verità*) honestly, frankly

o'nesto, -a AG (*probo, retto*) honest; (*giusto*) fair; (*casto*) chaste, virtuous

ONG SIGLA F INV (= *Organizzazione Non Governativa*) NGO

'onice ['ɔnitʃe] SF onyx

o'nirico, -a, -ci, -che AG dreamlike, dream cpd

onnipo'tente AG omnipotent

onnipre'sente AG omnipresent; (*scherzoso*) ubiquitous

onnisci'ente [onniʃ'ʃɛnte] AG omniscient

onniveg'gente [onnived'dʒɛnte] AG all-seeing

ono'mastico, -ci SM name day

onomato'pea SF onomatopoeia

onomato'peico, -a, -ci, -che AG onomatopoeic

241

ono'ranze [ono'rantse] SFPL honours (BRIT), honors (US)

ono'rare /72/ VT to honour (BRIT), honor (US); *(far onore a)* to do credit to ■ **onorarsi** VPR: **onorarsi di qc/di fare qc** to feel hono(u)red by sth/ to do sth

ono'rario, -a AG honorary ▶ SM fee

onora'tissimo, -a AG *(in presentazioni)*: **~!** delighted to meet you!

ono'rato, -a AG *(reputazione, famiglia, carriera)* distinguished; **essere ~ di fare qc** to have the honour to do sth *o* of doing sth; **~ di conoscerla!** (it is) a pleasure to meet you!

o'nore SM honour (BRIT), honor (US); **in ~ di** in hono(u)r of; **fare gli onori di casa** to play host *(o* hostess); **fare ~ a** to honour; *(pranzo)* to do justice to; *(famiglia)* to be a credit to; **farsi ~** to distinguish o.s.; **posto d'~** place of honour; **a onor del vero ...** to tell the truth ...

ono'revole AG honourable (BRIT), honorable (US) ▶ SMF *(Pol)* ≈ Member of Parliament (BRIT), ≈ Congressman/woman (US)

onorifi'cenza [onorifi'tʃɛntsa] SF honour (BRIT), honor (US); decoration

ono'rifico, -a, -ci, -che AG honorary

'onta SF shame, disgrace; **ad ~ di** despite, notwithstanding

on'tano SM *(Bot)* alder

'O.N.U. SIGLA F *(= Organizzazione delle Nazioni Unite)* UN, UNO

'OPA SIGLA F = **offerta pubblica d'acquisto**

o'paco, -a, -chi, -che AG *(vetro)* opaque; *(metallo)* dull, matt

o'pale SM O F opal

'O.P.E.C. SIGLA F *(= Organization of Petroleum Exporting Countries)* OPEC

'opera SF *(gen)* work; *(azione rilevante)* action, deed, work; *(Mus)* work; opus; (: *melodramma)* opera; (: *teatro)* opera house; *(ente)* institution, organization; **per ~ sua** thanks to him; **fare ~ di persuasione presso qn** to try to convince sb; **mettersi/essere all'~** to get down to/be at work; **~ d'arte** work of art; **~ buffa** comic opera; **~ lirica** (grand) opera; **~ pia** religious charity; **opere pubbliche (OO.PP.)** public works; **opere di restauro/di scavo** restoration/excavation work *sg*

ope'raio, -a AG working-class; workers'; *(Zool: ape, formica)* worker *cpd* ▶ SM/F worker; **classe operaia** working class; **~ di fabbrica** factory worker; **~ a giornata** day labourer (BRIT) *o* laborer (US); **~ specializzato** *o* **qualificato** skilled worker; **~ non specializzato** semi-skilled worker

ope'rare /72/ VT to carry out, make; *(Med)* to operate on ▶ VI to operate, work; *(rimedio)* to act, work; *(Med)* to operate ■ **operarsi** VPR to occur, take place; *(Med)* to have an operation; **ope-** rarsi d'appendicite to have one's appendix out; **~ qn d'urgenza** to perform an emergency operation on sb

opera'tivo, -a AG operative, operating; **piano ~** *(Mil)* plan of operations

ope'rato SM *(comportamento)* actions *pl*

opera'tore, -'trice SM/F operator; *(TV, Cine)* cameraman; **aperto solo agli operatori** *(Comm)* open to the trade only; **~ di borsa** dealer on the stock exchange; **~ ecologico** refuse collector; **~ economico** agent, broker; **~ del suono** sound recordist; **~ turistico** tour operator

opera'torio, -a AG *(Med)* operating

operazi'one [operat'tsjone] SF operation

ope'retta SF *(Mus)* operetta, light opera

operosità SF industry

ope'roso, -a AG industrious, hard-working

opi'ficio [opi'fitʃo] SM factory, works *pl*

opi'nabile AG *(discutibile)* debatable, questionable; **è ~** it is a matter of opinion

opini'one SF opinion; **avere il coraggio delle proprie opinioni** to have the courage of one's convictions; **l'~ pubblica** public opinion

opinio'nista, -i, -e SM/F (political) columnist

op là ESCL *(per far saltare)* hup!; *(a bimbo che è caduto)* upsy-daisy!

'oppio SM opium

oppi'omane SMF opium addict

oppo'nente AG opposing ▶ SMF opponent

op'pongo *ecc* VB *vedi* **opporre**

op'porre /77/ VT to oppose ■ **opporsi** VPR: **opporsi (a qc)** to oppose (sth); to object (to sth); **~ resistenza/un rifiuto** to offer resistance/to refuse

opportu'nista, -i, -e SM/F opportunist

opportunità SF INV opportunity; *(convenienza)* opportuneness, timeliness

oppor'tuno, -a AG timely, opportune; *(giusto)* right, appropriate; **a tempo ~** at the right *o* the appropriate time

op'posi *ecc* VB *vedi* **opporre**

opposi'tore, -'trice SM/F opposer, opponent

opposizi'one [oppozit'tsjone] SF opposition; *(Dir)* objection; **essere in netta ~** *(idee, opinioni)* to clash, be in complete opposition; **fare ~ a qn/qc** to oppose sb/sth

op'posto, -a PP *di* **opporre** ▶ AG opposite; *(opinioni)* conflicting ▶ SM opposite, contrary; **all'~** on the contrary

oppressi'one SF oppression

oppres'sivo, -a AG oppressive

op'presso, -a PP *di* **opprimere**

oppres'sore SM oppressor

oppri'mente AG *(caldo, noia)* oppressive; *(persona)* tiresome; *(deprimente)* depressing

op'primere /50/ VT (*premere, gravare*) to weigh down; (*estenuare: caldo*) to suffocate, oppress; (*tiranneggiare: popolo*) to oppress

oppu'gnare [oppuɲˈɲare] /15/ VT (*fig*) to refute

op'pure CONG or (else)

op'tare /72/ VI: ~ **per** (*scegliere*) to opt for, decide upon; (*Borsa*) to take (out) an option on

'optimum SM INV optimum

opu'lento, -a AG (*ricco*) rich, wealthy, affluent; (*arredamento ecc*) opulent

opu'lenza [opuˈlɛntsa] SF (*vedi ag*) richness, wealth, affluence; opulence

o'puscolo SM booklet, pamphlet

OPV SIGLA F = **offerta pubblica di vendita**

opzio'nale [optsjoˈnale] AG optional

opzi'one [opˈtsjone] SF option

OR SIGLA = **Oristano**

'ora SF (*60 minuti*) hour; (*momento*) time ▶ AV (*adesso*) now; (*tra poco*) presently, in a minute; **è uscito proprio ~** (*poco fa*) he's just gone out; **~ ... ~** (*correlativo*) now ... now; **che ~ è?, che ore sono?** what time is it?; **domani a quest'~** this time tomorrow; **non veder l'~ di fare** to long to do, look forward to doing; **fare le ore piccole** to stay up till the early hours (of the morning) *o* the small hours; **è ~ di partire** it's time to go; **di buon' ~** early; **alla buon'~!** at last!; **~ legale** *o* **estiva** summer time (BRIT), daylight saving time (US); **~ di cena** dinner time; **~ locale** local time; **~ di pranzo** lunchtime; **~ di punta** (*Aut*) rush hour; **d'~ in avanti** *o* **poi** from now on; **or ~** just now, a moment ago; **~ come ~** right now, at present; **10 anni or sono** 10 years ago

o'racolo SM oracle

'orafo SM goldsmith

o'rale AG, SM oral

oral'mente AV orally

ora'mai AV = **ormai**

o'rario, -a AG hourly; (*fuso, segnale*) time *cpd*; (*velocità*) per hour ▶ SM timetable, schedule; (*di ufficio, visite ecc*) hours *pl*; time(s); **~ di apertura/chiusura** opening/closing time; **~ di apertura degli sportelli** bank opening hours; **~ elastico** *o* **flessibile** (*Industria*) flexitime; **~ ferroviario** railway timetable; **~ di lavoro/d'ufficio** working/office hours; **in ~** on time

o'rata SF (*Zool*) sea bream

ora'tore, -'trice SM/F speaker; orator

ora'torio, -a AG oratorical ▶ SM (*Rel*) oratory; (*Mus*) oratorio ▶ SF (*arte*) oratory

orazi'one [oratˈtsjone] SF (*Rel*) prayer; (*discorso*) speech, oration

or'bene CONG so, well (then)

'orbita SF (*Astr, Fisica*) orbit; (*Anat*) (eye-)socket

orbi'tare /72/ VI to orbit

'orbo, -a AG blind

'Orcadi SFPL: **le (isole) ~** the Orkney Islands, the Orkneys

or'chestra [orˈkɛstra] SF orchestra

orches'trale [orkesˈtrale] AG orchestral ▶ SMF orchestra player

orches'trare [orkesˈtrare] /72/ VT to orchestrate; (*fig*) to stage-manage

orchi'dea [orkiˈdɛa] SF orchid

'orcio [ˈortʃo] SM jar

'orco, -chi SM ogre

'orda SF horde

or'digno [orˈdiɲɲo] SM: **~ esplosivo** explosive device

ordi'nale AG, SM ordinal

ordina'mento SM order, arrangement; (*regolamento*) regulations *pl*, rules *pl*; **~ scolastico/giuridico** education/legal system

ordi'nanza [ordiˈnantsa] SF (*Dir, Mil*) order; (*Amm: decreto*) decree; (*persona: Mil*) orderly, batman; **d'~** (*Mil*) regulation *cpd*; **ufficiale d'~** orderly; **~ municipale** by(e)-law

ordi'nare /72/ VT (*mettere in ordine*) to arrange, organize; (*Comm*) to order; (*prescrivere: medicina*) to prescribe; (*comandare*): **~ a qn di fare qc** to order *o* command sb to do sth; (*Rel*) to ordain

ordi'nario, -a AG (*comune*) ordinary; everyday; standard; (*grossolano*) coarse, common ▶ SM ordinary; (*Ins: di università*) full professor

ordina'tivo, -a AG regulating, governing ▶ SM (*Comm*) order

ordi'nato, -a AG tidy, orderly

ordinazi'one [ordinatˈtsjone] SF (*Comm*) order; (*Rel*) ordination; **fare un'~ di qc** to put in an order for sth, order sth; **eseguire qc su ~** to make sth to order

'ordine SM order; (*carattere*): **d'~ pratico** of a practical nature; **all'~** (*Comm: assegno*) to order; **di prim'~** first-class; **fino a nuovo ~** until further notice; **essere in ~** (*documenti*) to be in order; (*persona, stanza*) to be tidy; **mettere in ~** to put in order, tidy (up); **richiamare all'~** to call to order; **le forze dell'~** the forces of law and order; **~ d'acquisto** purchase order; **l'~ degli avvocati** ≈ the Bar; **~ del giorno** (*di seduta*) agenda; (*Mil*) order of the day; **l'~ dei medici** ≈ the Medical Association; **~ di pagamento** standing order (BRIT), automatic payment (US); (*Comm*) order for payment; **l'~ pubblico** law and order; **ordini (sacri)** (*Rel*) holy orders

or'dire /55/ VT (*fig*) to plot, scheme

or'dito SM (*di tessuto*) warp

orecchi'abile [orekˈkjabile] AG (*canzone*) catchy

orec'chino [orekˈkino] SM earring

o'recchio [oˈrekkjo] (*pl(f)* **orecchie**) SM (*Anat*) ear; **avere ~** to have a good ear (for music); **venire all'~ di qn** to come to sb's attention; **fare orecchie da mercante (a)** to turn a deaf ear (to)

243

orecchi'oni [orek'kjoni] SMPL (Med) mumps sg

o'refice [o'refitʃe] SM goldsmith; jeweller (BRIT), jeweler (US)

orefice'ria [orefitʃe'ria] SF (arte) goldsmith's art; (negozio) jeweller's (shop) (BRIT), jewelry store (US)

'**orfano, -a** AG orphan(ed) ▶ SM/F orphan; ~ **di padre/madre** fatherless/motherless

orfano'trofio SM orphanage

orga'netto SM barrel organ; (col: armonica a bocca) mouth organ; (: fisarmonica) accordion

or'ganico, -a, -ci, -che AG organic ▶ SM personnel, staff

organi'gramma, -i SM organization chart; (Inform) computer flow chart

orga'nismo SM (Biol) organism; (Anat, Amm) body, organism

orga'nista, -i, -e SM/F organist

organiz'zare [organid'dzare] /72/ VT to organize ■ **organizzarsi** VPR to get organized

organizza'tivo, -a [organiddza'tivo] AG organizational

organizza'tore, -'trice [organiddza'tore] AG organizing ▶ SM/F organizer

organizzazi'one [organiddzat'tsjone] SF (azione) organizing, arranging; (risultato) organization; **O~ Mondiale della Sanità** World Health Organization

'**organo** SM organ; (di congegno) part; (portavoce) spokesman/woman, mouthpiece; **organi di trasmissione** (Tecn) transmission (unit) sg

or'gasmo SM (Fisiol) orgasm; (fig) agitation, anxiety

'**orgia, -ge** ['ɔrdʒa] SF orgy

or'goglio [or'goʎʎo] SM pride

orgogli'oso, -a [orgoʎ'ʎoso] AG proud

orien'tabile AG adjustable

orien'tale AG (paese, regione) eastern; (tappeti, lingua, civiltà) oriental; east

orienta'mento SM positioning; orientation; direction; **senso di ~** sense of direction; **perdere l'~** to lose one's bearings; **~ professionale** careers guidance

orien'tare /72/ VT (situare) to position; (carta, bussola) to orientate; (fig) to direct ■ **orientarsi** VPR to find one's bearings; (fig: tendere) to tend, lean; (indirizzarsi) **orientarsi verso** to take up, go in for

orienta'tivo, -a AG indicative, for guidance; **a scopo ~** for guidance

ori'ente SM east; **l'O~** the East, the Orient; **il Medio/l'Estremo O~** the Middle/Far East; **a ~** in the east

ori'ficio [ori'fitʃo], **ori'fizio** [ori'fittsjo] SM (apertura) opening; (di tubo) mouth; (Anat) orifice

o'rigano SM oregano

origi'nale [oridʒi'nale] AG original; (bizzarro) eccentric ▶ SM original

originalità [oridʒinali'ta] SF originality; eccentricity

origi'nare [oridʒi'nare] /72/ VT to bring about, produce ▶ VI: ~ **da** to arise o spring from

origi'nario, -a [oridʒi'narjo] AG original; **essere ~ di** to be a native of; (provenire da) to originate from; (animale, pianta) to be native to, be indigenous to

o'rigine [o'ridʒine] SF origin; **all'~** originally; **d'~ inglese** of English origin; **avere ~ da** to originate from; **dare ~ a** to give rise to

origli'are [oriʎ'ʎare] /27/ VI: ~ (**a**) to eavesdrop (on)

o'rina SF urine

ori'nale SM chamberpot

ori'nare /72/ VI to urinate ▶ VT to pass

orina'toio SM (public) urinal

ori'undo, -a AG: **essere ~ di Milano** ecc to be of Milanese ecc extraction o origin ▶ SM/F person of foreign extraction o origin

orizzon'tale [oriddzon'tale] AG horizontal

oriz'zonte [orid'dzonte] SM horizon

ORL SIGLA F (Med: = otorinolaringoiatria) ENT

or'lare /72/ VT to hem

orla'tura SF (azione) hemming no pl; (orlo) hem

'**orlo** SM edge, border; (di recipiente) rim, brim; (di vestito ecc) hem; **pieno fino all'~** full to the brim, brimful; **sull'~ della pazzia/della rovina** on the brink o verge of madness/ruin; **~ a giorno** hemstitch

'**orma** SF (di persona) footprint; (di animale) track; (impronta, traccia) mark, trace; **seguire o calcare le orme di qn** to follow in sb's footsteps

or'mai AV by now, by this time; (adesso) now; (quasi) almost, nearly

ormeggi'are [ormed'dʒare] /62/ VT, **ormeggi'arsi** VPR (Naut) to moor

or'meggio [or'meddʒo] SM (atto) mooring no pl; (luogo) moorings pl; **posto d'~** berth

ormo'nale AG hormonal; (disfunzione, cura) hormone cpd; **terapia ~** hormone therapy

or'mone SM hormone

ornamen'tale AG ornamental, decorative

orna'mento SM ornament, decoration

or'nare /72/ VT to adorn, decorate ■ **ornarsi** VPR: **ornarsi (di)** to deck o.s. (out) (with)

or'nato, -a AG ornate

ornitolo'gia [ornitolo'dʒia] SF ornithology

orni'tologo, -a, -gi, -ghe SM/F ornithologist

'**oro** SM gold; **d'~, in ~** gold cpd; **d'~** (colore, occasione) golden; (persona) marvellous (BRIT), marvelous (US); **un affare d'~** a real bargain; **prendere qc per ~ colato** to take sth as gospel (truth); **~ nero** black gold; **~ zecchino** pure gold

orologe'ria [orolodʒe'ria] SF watchmaking *no pl*; watchmaker's (shop), clockmaker's (shop); **bomba a ~** time bomb

orologi'aio [orolo'dʒajo] SM watchmaker; clockmaker

oro'logio [oro'lɔdʒo] SM clock; (*da tasca, da polso*) watch; **~ biologico** biological clock; **~ da polso** wristwatch; **~ al quarzo** quartz watch; **~ a sveglia** alarm clock

o'roscopo SM horoscope

or'rendo, -a AG (*spaventoso*) horrible, awful; (*bruttissimo*) hideous

or'ribile AG horrible

'orrido, -a AG fearful, horrid

orripi'lante AG hair-raising, horrifying

or'rore SM horror; **avere in ~ qn/qc** to loathe *o* detest sb/sth; **mi fanno ~** I loathe *o* detest them

orsacchi'otto [orsak'kjɔtto] SM teddy bear

'orso SM bear; **~ bruno/bianco** brown/polar bear

orsù ESCL come now!

or'taggio [or'taddʒo] SM vegetable

or'tensia SF hydrangea

or'tica, -che SF (stinging) nettle

orti'caria SF nettle rash

orticol'tura SF horticulture

'orto SM vegetable garden, kitchen garden; (*Agr*) market garden (BRIT), truck farm (US); **~ botanico** botanical garden(s)

orto'dosso, -a AG orthodox

ortofrut'ticolo, -a AG fruit and vegetable *cpd*

ortogo'nale AG perpendicular

ortogra'fia SF spelling

orto'lano, -a SM/F (*venditore*) greengrocer (BRIT), produce dealer (US)

ortope'dia SF orthopaedics *sg* (BRIT), orthopedics *sg* (US)

orto'pedico, -a, -ci, -che AG orthopaedic (BRIT), orthopedic (US) ▶ SM orthopaedic specialist (BRIT), orthopedist (US)

orzai'olo [ordza'jɔlo], **orzaiu'olo** [ordza'jwɔlo] SM (*Med*) stye

or'zata [or'dzata] SF barley water

'orzo ['ɔrdzo] SM barley

'OSA SIGLA F (= *Organizzazione degli Stati Americani*) OAS (= *Organization of American States*)

o'sare /72/ VT, VI to dare; **~ fare** to dare (to) do; **come osi?** how dare you?

oscenità [oʃʃeni'ta] SF INV obscenity

o'sceno, -a [oʃ'ʃɛno] AG obscene; (*ripugnante*) ghastly

oscil'lare [oʃʃil'lare] /72/ VI (*pendolo*) to swing; (*dondolare: al vento ecc*) to rock; (*variare*) to fluctuate; (*Tecn*) to oscillate; (*fig*): **~ fra** to waver *o* hesitate between

oscillazi'one [oʃʃillat'tsjone] SF oscillation; (*di prezzi, temperatura*) fluctuation

oscura'mento SM darkening; obscuring; (*in tempo di guerra*) blackout

oscu'rare /72/ VT to darken, obscure; (*fig*) to obscure ▪ **oscurarsi** VPR (*cielo*) to darken, cloud over; (*persona*) **si oscurò in volto** his face clouded over

oscurità SF (*vedi ag*) darkness; obscurity, gloominess

os'curo, -a AG dark; (*fig: incomprensibile*) obscure; (*umile: vita, natali*) humble, lowly, obscure; (*triste: pensiero*) gloomy, sombre ▶ SM: **all'~** in the dark; **tenere qn all'~ di qc** to keep sb in the dark about sth

'Oslo SF Oslo

ospe'dale SM hospital

ospedali'ero, -a AG hospital *cpd*

ospi'tale AG hospitable

ospitalità SF hospitality

ospi'tare /72/ VT to give hospitality to; (*albergo*) to accommodate

'ospite SMF (*persona che ospita*) host/hostess; (*persona ospitata*) guest

os'pizio [os'pittsjo] SM (*per vecchi ecc*) home

'ossa SFPL *vedi* **osso**

os'sario SM (*Mil*) war memorial (*with burial place*)

ossa'tura SF (*Anat*) skeletal structure, frame; (*Tecn: fig*) framework

'osseo, -a AG bony; (*tessuto ecc*) bone *cpd*

osse'quente AG: **~ alla legge** law-abiding

os'sequio SM deference, respect ▪ **ossequi** SMPL (*saluto*) respects, regards; **porgere i propri ossequi a qn** (*formale*) to pay one's respects to sb; **ossequi alla signora!** (give my) regards to your wife!

ossequi'oso, -a AG obsequious

osser'vanza [osser'vantsa] SF observance

osser'vare /72/ VT to observe, watch; (*esaminare*) to examine; (*notare, rilevare*) to notice, observe; (*Dir: la legge*) to observe, respect; (*mantenere: silenzio*) to keep, observe; **far ~ qc a qn** to point sth out to sb

osserva'tore, -'trice AG observant, perceptive ▶ SM/F observer

osserva'torio SM (*Astr*) observatory; (*Mil*) observation post

osservazi'one [osservat'tsjone] SF observation; (*di legge ecc*) observance; (*considerazione critica*) observation, remark; (*rimprovero*) reproof; **in ~** under observation; **fare un'~** to make a remark; to raise an objection; **fare un'~ a qn** to criticize sb

ossessio'nare /72/ VT to obsess, haunt; (*tormentare*) to torment, harass

ossessi'one SF obsession; (*seccatura*) nuisance

osses'sivo, -a AG obsessive, haunting troublesome

os'sesso, -a AG (*spiritato*) possessed

os'sia CONG that is, to be precise

ossi'buchi [ossi'buki] SMPL *di* **ossobuco**

ossi'dare /72/ VT, **ossi'darsi** VPR to oxidize

ossidazi'one [ossidat'tsjone] SF oxidization, oxidation

'ossido SM oxide; ~ **di carbonio** carbon monoxide

ossige'nare [ossidʒe'nare] /72/ VT to oxygenate; (*decolorare*) to bleach; **acqua ossigenata** hydrogen peroxide

os'sigeno [os'sidʒeno] SM oxygen

'osso SM (*pl(f)* **ossa**: *Anat*) bone; **d'~** (*bottone ecc*) of bone, bone *cpd*; **avere le ossa rotte** to be dead *o* dog tired; **bagnato fino all'~** soaked to the skin; **essere ridotto all'~** (*fig: magro*) to be just skin and bone; (: *senza soldi*) to be in dire straits; **rompersi l'~ del collo** to break one's neck; **rimetterci l'~ del collo** (*fig*) to ruin o.s., lose everything; **un ~ duro** (*persona, impresa*) a tough number; **~ di seppia** cuttlebone

osso'buco (*pl* **ossibuchi**) SM (*Cuc*) marrowbone; (*piatto*) *stew made with knuckle of veal in tomato sauce*

os'suto, -a AG bony

ostaco'lare /72/ VT to block, obstruct

os'tacolo SM obstacle; (*Equitazione*) hurdle, jump; **essere di ~ a qn/qc** (*fig*) to stand in the way of sb/sth

os'taggio [os'taddʒo] SM hostage

'oste SM/F innkeeper

osteggi'are [osted'dʒare] /62/ VT to oppose, be opposed to

os'tello SM hostel; ~ **della gioventù** youth hostel

osten'sorio SM (*Rel*) monstrance

osten'tare /72/ VT to make a show of, flaunt

ostentazi'one [ostentat'tsjone] SF ostentation, show

oste'ria SF inn

os'tessa SF *vedi* **oste**

os'tetrico, -a, -ci, -che AG obstetric ▶ SM/F obstetrician ▶ SF midwife

'ostia SF (*Rel*) host; (*per medicinali*) wafer

'ostico, -a, -ci, -che AG (*fig*) harsh; difficult, tough; unpleasant

os'tile AG hostile

ostilità SF hostility ▶ SFPL (*Mil*) hostilities

osti'narsi /72/ VPR to insist, dig one's heels in; ~ **a fare** to persist (obstinately) in doing

osti'nato, -a AG (*caparbio*) obstinate; (*tenace*) persistent, determined

ostinazi'one [ostinat'tsjone] SF obstinacy; persistence

ostra'cismo [ostra'tʃizmo] SM ostracism

'ostrica, -che SF oyster

ostru'ire /55/ VT to obstruct, block

ostruzi'one [ostrut'tsjone] SF obstruction, blockage

ostruzio'nismo [ostruttsjo'nizmo] SM (*Pol*) obstructionism; (*Sport*) obstruction; **fare dell'~ a** (*progetto, legge*) to obstruct; ~ **sindacale** work-to-rule (*BRIT*), slowdown (*US*)

o'tite SF ear infection

oto'rino(laringo'iatra), -i, -e SM/F ear nose and throat specialist

'otre SM (*recipiente*) goatskin

ott. ABBR (= *ottobre*) Oct

ottago'nale AG octagonal

ot'tagono SM octagon

ot'tano SM octane; **numero di ottani** octane rating

ot'tanta NUM eighty

ottan'tenne AG eighty-year-old ▶ SMF octogenarian

ottan'tesimo, -a NUM eightieth

ottan'tina SF: **una ~ (di)** about eighty

ot'tavo, -a NUM eighth ▶ SF octave

ottempe'ranza [ottempe'rantsa] SF: **in ~ a** (*Amm*) in accordance with, in compliance with

ottempe'rare /72/ VI: ~ **a** to comply with, obey

ottene'brare /72/ VT to darken; (*fig*) to cloud

otte'nere /121/ VT to obtain, get; (*risultato*) to achieve, obtain

'ottico, -a, -ci, -che AG (*della vista: nervo*) optic; (*dell'ottica*) optical ▶ SM optician ▶ SF (*scienza*) optics *sg*; (*Fot: lenti, prismi ecc*) optics *pl*

otti'male AG optimal, optimum

ottima'mente AV excellently, very well

otti'mismo SM optimism

otti'mista, -i, -e SM/F optimist

ottimiz'zare [ottimid'dzare] /72/ VT to optimize

ottimizzazi'one [ottimiddzat'tsjone] SF optimization

'ottimo, -a AG excellent, very good

'otto NUM eight

ot'tobre SM October; *vedi anche* **luglio**

otto'brino, -a AG October *cpd*

ottocen'tesco, -a, -schi, -sche [ottotʃen'tesko] AG nineteenth-century

otto'cento [otto'tʃento] NUM eight hundred ▶ SM: **l'O~** the nineteenth century

otto'mila NUM eight thousand

ot'tone SM brass; **gli ottoni** (*Mus*) the brass

ottuage'nario, -a [ottuadʒe'narjo] AG, SM/F octogenarian

ot'tundere /34/ VT (*fig*) to dull

ottu'rare /72/ VT to close (up); (*dente*) to fill ■ **otturarsi** VPR to become *o* get blocked up

ottura'tore SM (*Fot*) shutter; (*nelle armi*) breechblock

otturazi'one [otturat'tsjone] SF closing (up); (*dentaria*) filling

ottusità SF (*vedi ag*) obtuseness; dullness

ot'tuso, -a PP *di* **ottundere** ▸ AG (*Mat: fig*) obtuse; (*suono*) dull

o'vaia SF, **o'vaio** SM (*Anat*) ovary

o'vale AG, SM oval

o'varico, -a AG ovarian

o'vatta SF cotton wool; (*per imbottire*) padding, wadding

ovat'tare /**72**/ VT (*imbottire*) to pad; (*fig: smorzare*) to muffle

ovazi'one [ovat'tsjone] SF ovation

'ovest SM west; **a ~ (di)** west (of); **verso ~** westward(s)

o'vile SM pen, enclosure; **tornare all'~** (*fig*) to return to the fold

o'vino, -a AG sheep *cpd*, ovine

'O.V.N.I. SIGLA M (= *oggetto volante non identificato*) UFO

ovulazi'one [ovulat'tsjone] SF ovulation

'ovulo SM (*Fisiol*) ovum

o'vunque AV = **dovunque**

ov'vero CONG (*ossia*) that is, to be precise; (*oppure*) or (else)

ovvi'are /**19**/ VI: **~ a** to obviate

'ovvio, -a AG obvious

ozi'are [ot'tsjare] /**19**/ VI to laze around, idle

'ozio ['ɔttsjo] SM idleness; (*tempo libero*) leisure; **ore d'~** leisure time; **stare in ~** to be idle

ozi'oso, -a [ot'tsjoso] AG idle

o'zono [od'dzɔno] SM ozone; **lo strato d'~** the ozone layer; **il buco dell'~** the ozone hole

ozonos'fera [oddzonos'fera] SF ozone layer

o

Pp

P¹, p [pi] SM O F INV (*lettera*) P, p; **P come Padova** ≈ P for Peter

P² ABBR (= *peso*) wt; (= *parcheggio*) P; (*Aut*: = *principiante*) L

p. ABBR (= *pagina*) p

P2 ABBR F (= *la (loggia)* P2) the P2 masonic lodge

PA SIGLA = **Palermo**

P.A. ABBR = **Pubblica Amministrazione**

pa'care /20/ VT to calm ■ **pacarsi** VPR (*tempesta, disordini*) to subside

paca'tezza [paka'tettsa] SF quietness, calmness

pa'cato, -a AG quiet, calm

'pacca, -che SF slap

pac'chetto [pak'ketto] SM packet; ~ **applicativo** (*Inform*) applications package; ~ **azionario** (*Finanza*) shareholding; ~ **software** (*Inform*) software package; ~ **turistico** package holiday (BRIT) O tour

pacchi'ano, -a [pak'kjano] AG (*colori*) garish; (*abiti, arredamento*) vulgar, garish

'pacco, -chi SM parcel; (*involto*) bundle; ~ **postale** parcel

paccot'tiglia [pakkot'tiλλa] SF trash, junk

'pace ['patʃe] SF peace; **darsi ~** to resign o.s.; **fare (la) ~ con qn** to make it up with sb

pachis'tano, -a [pakis'tano] AG, SM/F Pakistani

pacifi'care [patʃifi'kare] /20/ VT (*riconciliare*) to reconcile, make peace between; (*mettere in pace*) to pacify

pacificazi'one [patʃifikat'tsjone] SF reconciliation; pacification

pa'cifico, -a, -ci, -che [pa'tʃifiko] AG (*persona*) peaceable; (*vita*) peaceful; (*fig: indiscusso*) indisputable; (: *ovvio*) obvious, clear ► SM: **il P~, l'Oceano P~** the Pacific (Ocean)

paci'fismo [patʃi'fizmo] SM pacifism

paci'fista, -i, -e [patʃi'fista] SM/F pacifist

PACS [paks] SIGLA MPL civil partnerships

pa'dano, -a AG of the Po; **la pianura padana** the Lombardy plain

pa'della SF frying pan; (*per infermi*) bedpan

padigli'one [padiλ'λone] SM pavilion

'Padova SF Padua

pado'vano, -a AG of (o from) Padua

'padre SM father ■ **padri** SMPL (*antenati*) forefathers

Padre'terno SM: **il ~** God the Father

pa'drino SM godfather

padro'nale AG (*scala, entrata*) main, principal; **casa ~** country house

padro'nanza [padro'nantsa] SF command, mastery

padro'nato SM: **il ~** the ruling class

pa'drone, -a SM/F master/mistress; (*proprietario*) owner; (*datore di lavoro*) employer; **essere ~ di sé** to be in control of o.s.; **~/padrona di casa** master/mistress of the house; (*per gli inquilini*) landlord/lady

padroneggi'are [padroned'dʒare] /62/ VT (*fig: sentimenti*) to master, control; (*materia*) to master, know thoroughly ■ **padroneggiarsi** VPR to control o.s.

pae'saggio [pae'zaddʒo] SM landscape

paesag'gista, -i, -e [paezad'dʒista] SM/F (*pittore*) landscape painter

pae'sano, -a AG country *cpd* ► SM/F villager, countryman/woman

pa'ese SM (*nazione*) country, nation; (*terra*) country, land; (*villaggio*) village; **~ di provenienza** country of origin; **i Paesi Bassi** the Netherlands

paf'futo, -a AG chubby, plump

'paga, -ghe SF pay, wages *pl*; **giorno di ~** pay day

pa'gabile AG payable; **~ alla consegna/a vista** payable on delivery/on demand

pa'gaia SF paddle

paga'mento SM payment; **~ anticipato** payment in advance; **~ alla consegna** payment on delivery; **~ all'ordine** cash with order; **la TV a ~** pay TV

pa'gano, -a AG, SM/F pagan

pa'gare /80/ VT to pay; (*acquisto, fig, colpa*) to pay for; (*contraccambiare*) to repay, pay back ► VI to pay; **quanto l'ha pagato?** how much did you pay for it?; **~ con carta di credito** to pay by credit card; **~ in contanti** to pay cash; **~ di persona** (*fig*) to suffer the consequences; **l'ho pagata cara** (*fig*) I paid dearly for it

pa'gella [pa'dʒɛlla] SF (*Ins*) report card

pagel'lino [padʒel'lino] SM (*Ins*) report card

'paggio ['paddʒo] SM page(boy)

paghe'rò [page'rɔ] VB *vedi* **pagare** ▶ SM INV acknowledgement of a debt, IOU; **~ cambiario** promissory note

'pagina ['padʒina] SF page; **Pagine bianche** phone book, telephone directory; **Pagine Gialle**® Yellow Pages®

'paglia ['paʎʎa] SF straw; **avere la coda di ~** (*fig*) to have a guilty conscience; **fuoco di ~** (*fig*) flash in the pan

pagliac'cetto [paʎʎat'tʃetto] SM (*per bambini*) rompers *pl*

pagliac'ciata [paʎʎat'tʃata] SF farce

pagli'accio [paʎ'ʎattʃo] SM clown

pagli'aio [paʎ'ʎajo] SM haystack

paglie'riccio [paʎʎe'rittʃo] SM straw mattress

paglie'rino, -a [paʎʎe'rino] AG: **giallo ~** pale yellow

pagli'etta [paʎ'ʎetta] SF (*cappello per uomo*) (straw) boater; (*per tegami ecc*) steel wool

pagli'uzza [paʎ'ʎuttsa] SF (blade of) straw; (*d'oro ecc*) tiny particle, speck

pa'gnotta [paɲ'ɲɔtta] SF round loaf

'pago, -a, -ghi, -ghe AG: **~ (di)** satisfied (with)

pa'goda SF pagoda

pail'lette [pa'jɛt] SF INV sequin

'paio (*pl(f)* **paia**) SM pair; **un ~ di** (*alcuni*) a couple of; **un ~ di occhiali** a pair of glasses; **è un altro ~ di maniche** (*fig*) that's another kettle of fish

'paio *ecc* VB *vedi* **parere**

pai'olo, paiu'olo SM (copper) pot

'Pakistan SM: **il ~** Pakistan

pakis'tano, -a AG, SM/F = **pachistano**

pal. ABBR = **palude**

'pala SF shovel; (*di remo, ventilatore, elica*) blade; (*di ruota*) paddle

palan'drana SF (*scherzoso: abito lungo e largo*) tent

pa'lata SF shovelful; **fare soldi a palate** to make a mint

pala'tale AG (*Anat, Ling*) palatal

pa'lato SM palate

pa'lazzo [pa'lattso] SM (*reggia*) palace; (*edificio*) building; **~ di giustizia** courthouse; **~ dello sport** sports stadium

pal'chetto [pal'ketto] SM shelf

'palco, -chi SM (*Teat*) box; (*tavolato*) platform, stand; (*ripiano*) layer

palco'scenico, -ci [palkoʃ'ʃɛniko] SM (*Teat*) stage

palermi'tano, -a AG of (*o* from) Palermo ▶ SM/F person from Palermo

Pa'lermo SF Palermo

pale'sare /72/ VT to reveal, disclose ▪ **palesarsi** VPR to reveal *o* show o.s.

pa'lese AG clear, evident

Pales'tina SF: **la ~** Palestine

palesti'nese AG, SM F Palestinian

pa'lestra SF gymnasium; (*esercizio atletico*) exercise, training; (*fig*) training ground, school

'paletot [pal'to] SM INV overcoat

pa'letta SF spade; (*per il focolare*) shovel; (*del capostazione*) signalling disc

pa'letto SM stake, peg; (*spranga*) bolt

palin'sesto SM (*Storia*) palimpsest; (*TV, Radio*) programme (*BRIT*) *o* program (*US*) schedule

'palio SM (*gara*): **il P~** horse race run in Siena; **mettere qc in ~** to offer sth as a prize

---

The **Palio** is a horse race which takes place in a number of Italian towns, the most famous being the *Palio di Siena*. This Tuscan race dates back to the thirteenth century; nowadays it is usually held twice a year, on 2 July and 16 August, in the Piazza del Campo. Ten of the seventeen city districts or *contrade* take part; the winner is the first horse to complete the course, whether or not it still has its rider. The race is preceded by a procession of *contrada* members in period costume.

---

palis'sandro SM rosewood

paliz'zata [palit'tsata] SF palisade

'palla SF ball; (*pallottola*) bullet; **~ di neve** snowball; **~ ovale** rugby ball

pallaca'nestro SF basketball

palla'mano SF handball

pallanu'oto SF water polo

palla'volo SF volleyball

palleggi'are [palled'dʒare] /62/ VI (*Calcio*) to practise (*BRIT*) *o* practice (*US*) with the ball; (*Tennis*) to knock up

pallia'tivo SM palliative; (*fig*) stopgap measure

'pallido, -a AG pale

pal'lina SF (*bilia*) marble

pal'lino SM (*Biliardo*) cue ball; (*Bocce*) jack; (*proiettile*) pellet; (*pois*) dot; **bianco a pallini blu** white with blue dots; **avere il ~ di** (*fig*) to be crazy about

pallon'cino [pallon'tʃino] SM balloon; (*lampioncino*) Chinese lantern

pal'lone SM (*palla*) ball; (*Calcio*) football; (*aerostato*) balloon; **gioco del ~** football

pal'lore SM pallor, paleness

pal'lottola SF pellet; (*proiettile*) bullet

'palma SF (*Anat*) = **palmo**; (*Bot, simbolo*) palm; **~ da datteri** date palm

pal'mato, -a AG (*Zool: piede*) webbed; (*Bot*) palmate

pal'mipede AG web-footed

pal'mizio [pal'mittsjo] SM (*palma*) palm tree; (*ramo*) palm

'palmo SM (*Anat*) palm; **essere alto un ~** (*fig*) to be tiny; **restare con un ~ di naso** (*fig*) to be badly disappointed

'palo SM (*legno appuntito*) stake; (*sostegno*) pole; **fare da** *o* **il ~** (*fig*) to act as look-out; **saltare di ~ in frasca** (*fig*) to jump from one topic to another

palom'baro SM diver

pa'lombo SM (*pesce*) dogfish

pal'pare /72/ VT to feel, finger

'palpebra SF eyelid

palpi'tare /72/ VI (*cuore, polso*) to beat; (*più forte*) to pound, throb; (*fremere*) to quiver

palpitazi'one [palpitat'tsjone] SF palpitation

'palpito SM (*del cuore*) beat; (*fig: d'amore ecc*) throb

paltò SM INV overcoat

pa'lude SF marsh, swamp

palu'doso, -a AG marshy, swampy

pa'lustre AG marsh *cpd*, swamp *cpd*

'pampino SM vine leaf

pana'cea [pana'tʃea] SF panacea

'Panama SF Panama; **il canale di ~** the Panama Canal

pana'mense AG, SMF Panamanian

'panca, -che SF bench

pancarrè SM sliced bread

pan'cetta [pan'tʃetta] SF (*Cuc*) bacon

pan'chetto [pan'ketto] SM stool; footstool

pan'china [pan'kina] SF garden seat; (*di giardino pubblico*) (park) bench

'pancia, -ce ['pantʃa] SF belly, stomach; **mettere** *o* **fare ~** to be getting a paunch; **avere mal di ~** to have stomach ache *o* a sore stomach

panci'era [pan'tʃɛra] SF corset

panci'olle [pan'tʃɔlle] AV: **stare in ~** to lounge about (*BRIT*) *o* around

panci'otto [pan'tʃɔtto] SM waistcoat

pan'ciuto, -a [pan'tʃuto] AG (*persona*) potbellied; (*vaso, bottiglia*) rounded

'pancreas SM INV pancreas

'panda SM INV panda

pande'mia SF pandemic

pande'monio SM pandemonium

pan'doro SM *type of sponge cake eaten at Christmas*

'pane SM bread; (*pagnotta*) loaf (of bread); (*forma*): **un ~ di burro/cera** *ecc* a pat of butter/bar of wax *etc*; **guadagnarsi il ~** to earn one's living; **dire ~ al ~, vino al vino** (*fig*) to call a spade a spade; **rendere pan per focaccia** (*fig*) to give tit for tat; **~ casereccio** homemade bread; **~ a cassetta** sliced bread; **~ integrale** wholemeal bread; **~ di segale** rye bread; **~ di Spagna** sponge cake; **~ tostato** toast

pane'girico [pane'dʒiriko] SM (*fig*) panegyric

panette'ria SF (*forno*) bakery; (*negozio*) baker's (shop), bakery

panetti'ere, -a SM/F baker

panet'tone SM *a kind of spiced brioche with sultanas (eaten at Christmas)*

'panfilo SM yacht

pan'forte SM *Sienese nougat-type delicacy*

pangrat'tato SM breadcrumbs *pl*

'panico, -a, -ci, -che AG, SM panic; **essere in preda al ~** to be panic-stricken; **lasciarsi prendere dal ~** to panic

pani'ere SM basket

panifica'tore, -trice SM/F bread-maker, baker

pani'ficio [pani'fitʃo] SM (*forno*) bakery; (*negozio*) baker's (shop), bakery

pa'nino SM roll; **~ caldo** toasted sandwich; **~ imbottito** filled roll; sandwich

panino'teca, -che SF sandwich bar

'panna SF (*Cuc*) cream; (*Aut*) = **panne**; **~ da cucina** cooking cream; **~ montata** whipped cream

'panne SF INV (*Aut*) breakdown; **essere in ~** to have broken down

pan'nello SM panel; **~ di controllo** control panel; **~ solare** solar panel

'panno SM cloth ■ **panni** SMPL (*abiti*) clothes; **mettiti nei miei panni** (*fig*) put yourself in my shoes

pan'nocchia [pan'nɔkkja] SF (*di mais ecc*) ear

panno'lino SM (*per bambini*) nappy (*BRIT*), diaper (*US*)

panno'lone SM incontinence pad

pano'rama, -i SM panorama

pano'ramico, -a, -ci, -che AG panoramic; **strada panoramica** scenic route

pantacol'lant SMPL leggings

panta'loni SMPL trousers (*BRIT*), pants (*US*), pair *sg* of trousers *o* pants

pan'tano SM bog

pan'tera SF panther

'pantheon ['panteon] SM INV pantheon

pan'tofola SF slipper

panto'mima SF pantomime

pan'zana [pan'tsana] SF fib, tall story

pao'nazzo, -a [pao'nattso] AG purple

'papa, -i SM pope

papà SM INV dad(dy); **figlio di ~** spoilt young man

pa'pale AG papal

pa'pato SM papacy

pa'pavero SM poppy

'papero, -a SM/F (*Zool*) gosling ▶ SF (*fig*) slip of the tongue, blunder

papi'llon [papi'jɔ] SM INV bow tie

pa'piro SM papyrus

'pappa SF baby cereal; **~ reale** royal jelly

pappa'gallo SM parrot; (*fig: uomo*) Romeo, wolf

pappa'gorgia, -ge [pappa'gɔrdʒa] SF double chin

pappar'della SF (*fig*) rigmarole

pap'pare /72/ VT (*col: anche:* **papparsi**) to gobble up

par. ABBR (= *paragrafo*) par

'para SF: **suole di ~** crepe soles

parà ABBR M INV (= *paracadutista*) para

pa'rabola SF (*Mat*) parabola; (*Rel*) parable

para'bolico, -a, -ci, -che AG (*Mat*) parabolic; *vedi anche* **antenna**

para'brezza [para'breddza] SM INV (*Aut*) windscreen (BRIT), windshield (US)

paracadu'tare /72/ VT, **paracadu'tarsi** VPR to parachute

paraca'dute SM INV parachute

paracadu'tismo SM parachuting

paracadu'tista, -i, -e SM/F parachutist; (*Mil*) paratrooper

para'carro SM kerbstone (BRIT), curbstone (US)

paradi'siaco, -a, -ci, -che AG heavenly

para'diso SM paradise; **~ fiscale** tax haven

parados'sale AG paradoxical

para'dosso SM paradox

para'fango, -ghi SM mudguard

paraf'fina SF paraffin, paraffin wax

parafra'sare /72/ VT to paraphrase

pa'rafrasi SF INV paraphrase

para'fulmine SM lightning conductor

pa'raggi [pa'raddʒi] SMPL: **nei ~** in the vicinity, in the neighbourhood (BRIT) o neighborhood (US)

parago'nare /72/ VT: **~ con/a** to compare with/to

para'gone SM comparison; (*esempio analogo*) analogy, parallel; **reggere al ~** to stand comparison

pa'ragrafo SM paragraph

paraguai'ano, -a AG, SM/F Paraguayan

Paragu'ay [para'gwai] SM: **il ~** Paraguay

Paralimp'iadi SMPL Paralympics, Paralympic Games

para'limpico, -a AG Paralympic

pa'ralisi SF INV paralysis

para'litico, -a, -ci, -che AG, SM/F paralytic

paraliz'zare [paralid'dzare] /72/ VT to paralyze

parallela'mente AV in parallel

paralle'lismo SM (*Mat*) parallelism; (*fig: corrispondenza*) similarities *pl*

paral'lelo, -a AG parallel ▶ SM (*Geo*) parallel; (*comparazione*): **fare un ~ tra** to draw a parallel between ▶ SF parallel (line) ■ **parallele** SFPL (*attrezzo ginnico*) parallel bars

para'lume SM lampshade

para'medico, -a, -ci, -che AG paramedical

para'menti SMPL (*Rel*) vestments

pa'rametro SM parameter

paramili'tare AG paramilitary

pa'ranco, -chi SM hoist

para'noia SF paranoia; **andare/mandare in ~** (*col*) to freak/be freaked out

para'noico, -a, -ci, -che AG, SM/F paranoid; (*col: angosciato*) freaked (out)

paranor'male AG paranormal

para'occhi [para'ɔkki] SMPL blinkers (BRIT), blinders (US)

paraolim'piadi SFPL paralympics

para'petto SM parapet

para'piglia [para'piʎʎa] SM commotion

parapsicolo'gia [parapsikolo'dʒia] SF parapsychology

pa'rare /72/ VT (*addobbare*) to adorn, deck; (*proteggere*) to shield, protect; (*scansare: colpo*) to parry; (*Calcio*) to save ▶ VI: **dove vuole andare a ~?** what are you driving at? ■ **pararsi** VPR (*presentarsi*) to appear, present o.s.

parasco'lastico, -a, -ci, -che AG (*attività*) extracurricular

para'sole SM INV parasol, sunshade

paras'sita, -i SM parasite

parassi'tario, -a AG parasitic

parasta'tale AG state-controlled

paras'tato SM *employees in the state-controlled sector*

pa'rata SF (*Sport*) save; (*Mil*) review, parade

pa'rati SMPL hangings *pl*; **carta da ~** wallpaper

para'tia SF (*di nave*) bulkhead

para'urti SM INV (*Aut*) bumper

para'vento SM folding screen; **fare da ~ a qn** (*fig*) to shield sb

par'cella [par'tʃella] SF account, fee (*of lawyer etc*)

parcheggi'are [parked'dʒare] /62/ VT to park

parcheggia'tore, -'trice [parkedddʒa'tore] SM/F parking attendant

par'cheggio [par'kedddʒo] SM parking *no pl*; (*luogo*) car park (BRIT), parking lot (US); (*singolo posto*) parking space; **~ di interscambio** park and ride

par'chimetro [par'kimetro] SM parking meter

'parco¹, -chi SM park; (*spazio per deposito*) depot; (*complesso di veicoli*) fleet

'parco², -a, -chi, -che AG: **~ (in)** (*sobrio*) moderate (in); (*avaro*) sparing (with)

par'cometro SM (*Aut*) (Pay and Display) ticket machine

pa'recchio, -a [pa'rekkjo] DET quite a lot of; (*tempo*) quite a lot of, a long ▶ PRON quite a lot, quite a bit; (*tempo*) quite a while, a long time ▶ AV (*con ag*) quite, rather; (*con vb*) quite a lot, quite a bit ■ **parecchi, e** DET PL, PRON PL quite a lot of, several; quite a lot, several

p

251

pareggi'are [pared'dʒare] /62/ vt to make equal; (*terreno*) to level, make level; (*bilancio, conti*) to balance ▶ vi (*Sport*) to draw

pa'reggio [pa'reddʒo] sm (*Econ*) balance; (*Sport*) draw

paren'tado sm relatives *pl*, relations *pl*

pa'rente smf relative, relation

> Do not translate the Italian word **parente** by *parent*.

paren'tela sf (*vincolo di sangue, fig*) relationship; (*insieme dei parenti*) relations *pl*, relatives *pl*

pa'rentesi sf (*segno grafico*) bracket, parenthesis; (*frase incisa*) parenthesis; (*digressione*) parenthesis, digression; **tra ~** in brackets; (*fig*) incidentally

pa'rere /71/ sm (*opinione*) opinion; (*consiglio*) advice, opinion; **a mio ~** in my opinion ▶ vi to seem, appear ▶ vb impers: **pare che** it seems *o* appears that, they say that; **mi pare che** it seems to me that; **mi pare di sì/no** I think so/ don't think so; **fai come ti pare** do as you like; **che ti pare del mio libro?** what do you think of my book?

pa'rete sf wall

'pargolo, -a sm/f child

'pari ag inv (*uguale*) equal, same; (*in giochi*) equal, drawn, tied; (*Mat*) even ▶ sm inv (*Pol: di Gran Bretagna*) peer ▶ sm o f inv peer, equal; **copiato ~ ~** copied word for word; **siamo ~** (*fig*) we are quits *o* even; **alla ~** on the same level; (*Borsa*) at par; **ragazza alla ~** au pair (girl); **mettersi alla ~ con** to place o.s. on the same level as; **mettersi in ~ con** to catch up with; **andare di ~ passo con qn** to keep pace with sb

parifi'care /20/ vt (*scuola*) to recognize officially

parifi'cato, -a ag: **scuola parificata** officially recognized private school

Pa'rigi [pa'ridʒi] sf Paris

pari'gino, -a [pari'dʒino] ag, sm/f Parisian

pa'riglia [pa'riʎʎa] sf pair; **rendere la ~** to give tit for tat

parità sf parity, equality; (*Sport*) draw, tie

pari'tetico, -a, -ci, -che ag: **commissione paritetica** joint committee; **rapporto ~ equal** relationship

parlamen'tare /72/ ag parliamentary ▶ sm/f ≈ Member of Parliament (*Brit*), ≈ Congressman/woman (*US*) ▶ vi to negotiate, parley

parla'mento sm parliament

> The Italian constitution, which came into force on 1 January 1948, states that the **Parlamento** has legislative power. It is made up of two chambers, the *Camera dei deputati* and the *Senato*. Parliamentary elections are held every 5 years. A motion of no confidence in the government can trigger an early election.

parlan'tina sf (*col*) talkativeness; **avere ~** to have the gift of the gab

par'lare /72/ vi to speak, talk; (*confidare cose segrete*) to talk ▶ vt to speak; **~ (a qn) di** to talk *o* talk (to sb) about; **~ chiaro** to speak one's mind; **~ male di qn/qc** to speak ill of sb/sth; **del più e del meno** to talk of this and that; **ne ho sentito ~** I have heard it mentioned; **non parliamone più** let's just forget about it; **i dati parlano** (*fig*) the facts speak for themselves

> Si usa **talk** quando si tratta di una conversazione mentre **speak** si riferisce al fatto di emettere suoni.
> Si dice quindi **to speak Italian/English**.
> **Speak** si usa anche per fare una domanda in modo educato.
> *Posso parlare con il signor Walton?* **May I speak to Mr Walton?**

par'lata sf (*dialetto*) dialect

parla'tore, -'trice sm/f speaker

parla'torio sm (*di carcere ecc*) visiting room; (*Rel*) parlour (*Brit*), parlor (*US*)

parlot'tare /72/ vi to mutter

parmigi'ano, -a [parmi'dʒano] ag Parma *cpd* of (*o* from) Parma ▶ sm (*grana*) Parmesan (cheese); **alla parmigiana** (*Cuc*) with Parmesan cheese

paro'dia sf parody

parodi'are /19/ vt to parody

pa'rola sf word; (*facoltà*) speech ▪ **parole** sfpl (*chiacchiere*) talk *sg*; **chiedere la ~** to ask permission to speak; **dare la ~ a qn** to call on sb to speak; **dare la propria ~ a qn** to give sb one's word; **mantenere la ~** to keep one's word; **mettere una buona ~ per qn** to put in a good word for sb; **passare dalle parole ai fatti** to get down to business; **prendere la ~** to take the floor; **rimanere senza parole** to be speechless; **rimangiarsi la ~** to go back on one's word; **non ho parole per ringraziarla** I don't know how to thank you; **rivolgere la ~ a qn** to speak to sb; **non è detta l'ultima ~** that's not the end of the matter; **è una persona di ~** he is a man of his word; **in parole povere** in plain English; **~ d'onore** word of honour; **~ d'ordine** (*Mil*) password; **parole incrociate** crossword (puzzle) *sg*

paro'laccia, -ce [paro'lattʃa] sf bad word, swearword

paros'sismo sm paroxysm

par'quet [par'kɛ] sm parquet (flooring)

parrò *ecc* vb *vedi* parere

par'rocchia [par'rɔkkja] sf parish; (*chiesa*) parish church

parrocchi'ano, -a [parrok'kjano] sm/f parishioner

'parroco, -ci sm parish priest

par'rucca, -che sf wig

parrucchi'ere, -a [parruk'kjɛre] SM/F hairdresser ▸ SM barber

parruc'cone SM (*peg*) old fogey

parsi'monia SF frugality, thrift

parsimoni'oso, -a AG frugal, thrifty

'parso, -a PP *di* **parere**

'parte SF part; (*lato*) side; (*quota spettante a ciascuno*) share; (*direzione*) direction; (*Pol*) party; faction; (*Dir*) party; **a ~** *ag* separate ▸ AV separately; **scherzi a ~** joking aside; **a ~ ciò** apart from that; **inviare a ~** (*campioni ecc*) to send under separate cover; **da ~** (*in disparte*) to one side, aside; **mettere/prendere da ~** to put/take aside; **d'altra ~** on the other hand; **da ~ di** (*per conto di*) on behalf of; **da ~ mia** as far as I'm concerned, as for me; **da ~ di madre** on his (*o* her *etc*) mother's side; **essere dalla ~ della ragione** to be in the right; **da ~ a ~** right through; **da qualche ~** somewhere; **da nessuna ~** nowhere; **da questa ~** (*in questa direzione*) this way; **da ogni ~** on all sides, everywhere; (*moto da luogo*) from all sides; **fare ~ di qc** to belong to sth; **prendere ~ a qc** to take part in sth; **prendere le parti di qn** to take sb's side; **mettere qn a ~ di qc** to inform sb of sth; **costituirsi ~ civile contro qn** (*Dir*) to associate in an action with the public prosecutor against sb; **la ~ lesa** (*Dir*) the injured party; **le parti in causa** the parties concerned; **parti sociali** representatives of workers and employers

parteci'pante [partetʃi'pante] SMF: **~ (a)** (*a riunione, dibattito*) participant (in); (*a gara sportiva*) competitor (in); (*a concorso*) entrant (to)

parteci'pare [partetʃi'pare] **/72/** VI: **~ a** to take part in, participate in; (*utili ecc*) to share in; (*spese ecc*) to contribute to; (*dolore, successo di qn*) to share (in) ▸ VT: **~ le nozze (a)** to announce one's wedding (to)

partecipazi'one [partetʃipat'tsjone] SF participation; sharing; (*Econ*) interest; **~ a banda armata** (*Dir*) belonging to an armed gang; **~ di maggioranza/minoranza** controlling/minority interest; **~ agli utili** profit-sharing; **partecipazioni di nozze** wedding announcement card; **ministro delle Partecipazioni statali** minister responsible for companies in which the state has a financial interest

par'tecipe [par'tetʃipe] AG participating; **essere ~ di** to take part in, participate in; (*gioia, dolore*) to share (in); (*consapevole*) to be aware of

parteggi'are [parted'dʒare] **/62/** VI: **~ per** to side with, be on the side of

par'tenza [par'tɛntsa] SF departure; (*Sport*) start; **essere in ~** to be about to leave, be leaving; **passeggeri in ~ per** passengers travelling (BRIT) *o* traveling (US) to; **siamo tornati al punto di ~** (*fig*) we are back where we started; **falsa ~** (*anche fig*) false start

parti'cella [parti'tʃɛlla] SF particle

parti'cipio [parti'tʃipjo] SM participle

partico'lare AG (*specifico*) particular; (*proprio*) personal, private; (*speciale*) special, particular; (*caratteristico*) distinctive, characteristic; (*fuori dal comune*) peculiar ▸ SM detail, particular; **in ~** in particular, particularly; **entrare nei particolari** to go into details

particolareggi'ato, -a [partikolared'dʒato] AG (extremely) detailed

particolarità SF INV (*carattere eccezionale*) peculiarity; (*dettaglio*) particularity, detail; (*caratteristica*) characteristic, feature

partigi'ano, -a [parti'dʒano] AG partisan ▸ SM (*fautore*) supporter, champion; (*Mil*) partisan

par'tire **/45/** VI to go, leave; (*allontanarsi*) to go (*o* drive *etc*) away *o* off; (*petardo, colpo*) to go off; (*fig: avere inizio, Sport*) to start; **sono partita da Roma alle 7** I left Rome at 7; **il volo parte da Ciampino** the flight leaves from Ciampino; **a ~ da** from; **la seconda a ~ da destra** the second from the right; **~ in quarta** to drive off at top speed; (*fig*) to be very enthusiastic

par'tita SF (*Comm*) lot, consignment; (*Econ: registrazione*) entry, item; (*Carte, Sport: gioco*) game; (*: competizione*) match, game; **~ di caccia** hunting party; **numero di ~ IVA** VAT registration number; **~ semplice/doppia** (*Comm*) single-/double-entry book-keeping

par'tito SM (*Pol*) party; (*decisione*) decision, resolution; (*persona da maritare*) match; **per ~ preso** on principle; **mettere la testa a ~** to settle down

partitocra'zia [partitokrat'tsia] SF hijacking of institutions by the party system

parti'tura SF (*Mus*) score

'parto SM (*Med*) labour (BRIT), labor (US), delivery, (child)birth; **sala ~** labo(u)r room; **morire di ~** to die in childbirth

partori'ente SF woman in labour (BRIT) *o* labor (US)

parto'rire **/55/** VT to give birth to; (*fig*) to produce

par'venza [par'vɛntsa] SF semblance

'parvi *ecc* VB *vedi* **parere**

parzi'ale [par'tsjale] AG (*limitato*) partial; (*non obiettivo*) biased, partial

parzialità [partsjali'ta] SF: **~ a favore di** partiality (for), bias (towards); **~ contro** bias (against)

'pascere ['paʃʃere] **/29/** VI to graze ▸ VT (*brucare*) to graze on; (*far pascolare*) to graze, pasture

pasci'uto, -a [paʃ'ʃuto] PP *di* **pascere** ▸ AG: **ben ~** plump

pasco'lare **/72/** VT, VI to graze

'pascolo SM pasture

'Pasqua SF Easter; **isola di ~** Easter Island

pas'quale AG Easter *cpd*

Pasqu'etta SF Easter Monday

pas'sabile AG fairly good, passable

pas'saggio [pas'saddʒo] SM passing *no pl*, passage; (*traversata*) crossing *no pl*, passage; (*luogo, prezzo della traversata, brano di libro ecc*) passage; (*su veicolo altrui*) lift (BRIT), ride; (*Sport*) pass; **di ~** (*persona*) passing through; **~ pedonale/a livello** pedestrian/level (BRIT) *o* grade (US) crossing; **~ di proprietà** transfer of ownership

passamane'ria SF braid, trimming

passamon'tagna [passamon'taɲɲa] SM INV balaclava

pas'sante SMF passer-by ▶ SM loop

passa'porto SM passport

pas'sare /72/ VI (*andare*) to go; (*veicolo, pedone*) to pass (by), go by; (*fare una breve sosta: postino ecc*) to come, call; (: *amico: per fare una visita*) to call *o* drop in; (*sole, aria, luce*) to get through; (*trascorrere: giorni, tempo*) to pass, go by; (*fig: proposta di legge*) to be passed; (: *dolore*) to pass, go away; (*Carte*) to pass ▶ VT (*attraversare*) to cross; (*trasmettere: messaggio*) **~ qc a qn** to pass sth on to sb; (*dare*): **~ qc a qn** to pass sth to sb, give sb sth; (*trascorrere: tempo*) to spend; (*superare: esame*) to pass; (*triturare: verdura*) to strain; (*approvare*) to pass, approve; (*oltrepassare, sorpassare: anche fig*) to go beyond, pass; (*fig: subire*) to go through; **~ da ... a** to pass from ... to; **~ di padre in figlio** to be handed down *o* to pass from father to son; **~ per** (*anche fig*) to go through; **~ per stupido/un genio** to be taken for a fool/a genius; **~ sopra** (*anche fig*) to pass over; **~ attraverso** (*anche fig*) to go through; **~ ad altro** to change the subject; (*in una riunione*) to discuss the next item; **~ in banca/ufficio** to call (in) at the bank/office; **~ alla storia** to pass into history; **~ a un esame** to go up (to the next class) after an exam; **~ inosservato** to go unnoticed; **~ di moda** to go out of fashion; **~ a prendere qc/qn** to call and pick sth/sb up; **le passo il Signor X** (*al telefono*) here is Mr X; I'm putting you through to Mr X; **farsi ~ per** to pass o.s. off as, pretend to be; **lasciar ~ qn/qc** to let sb/sth through; **col ~ degli anni** (*riferito al presente*) as time goes by; (*riferito al passato*) as time passed *o* went by; **il peggio è passato** the worst is over; **30 anni e passa** well over 30 years ago; **~ una mano di vernice su qc** to give sth a coat of paint; **passarsela, come te la passi?** how are you getting on *o* along?

pas'sata SF: **dare una ~ di vernice a qc** to give sth a coat of paint; **dare una ~ al giornale** to have a look at the paper, skim through the paper

passa'tempo SM pastime, hobby

pas'sato, -a AG (*scorso*) last; (*finito: gloria, generazioni*) past; (*usanze*) out of date; (*sfiorito*) faded ▶ SM past; (*Ling*) past (tense); **l'anno ~** last year; **nel corso degli anni passati** over the past years; **nei tempi passati** in the past; **sono le 8 passate** it's past *o* after 8 o'clock; **è acqua passata** (*fig*) it's over and done with; **~ prossimo** (*Ling*) present perfect; **~ remoto** (*Ling*) past historic; **~ di verdura** (*Cuc*) vegetable purée

passa'tutto, passaver'dura SM INV vegetable mill

passeg'gero, -a [passed'dʒɛro] AG passing ▶ SM/F passenger

passeggi'are [passed'dʒare] /62/ VI to go for a walk; (*in veicolo*) to go for a drive

passeggi'ata [passed'dʒata] SF walk; drive; (*luogo*) promenade; **fare una ~** to go for a walk (*o* drive)

passeg'gino [passed'dʒino] SM pushchair (BRIT), stroller (US)

pas'seggio [pas'seddʒo] SM walk, stroll; (*luogo*) promenade; **andare a ~** to go for a walk *o* a stroll

passe'rella SF footbridge; (*di nave, aereo*) gangway; (*pedana*) catwalk

'passero SM sparrow

pas'sibile AG: **~ di** liable to

passio'nale AG (*temperamento*) passionate; **delitto ~** crime of passion

passi'one SF passion

passività SF (*qualità*) passivity, passiveness; (*Comm*) liability

pas'sivo, -a AG passive ▶ SM (*Ling*) passive; (*Econ*) debit; (*complesso dei debiti*) liabilities *pl*

'passo SM step; (*andatura*) pace; (*rumore*) (foot)step; (*orma*) footprint; (*passaggio, fig: brano*) passage; (*valico*) pass; **a ~ d'uomo** at walking pace; (*Aut*) dead slow; **~ (a) ~** step by step; **fare due *o* quattro passi** to go for a walk *o* a stroll; **andare al ~ coi tempi** to keep up with the times; **di questo ~** (*fig*) at this rate; **fare i primi passi** (*anche fig*) to take one's first steps; **fare il gran ~** (*fig*) to take the plunge; **fare un ~ falso** (*fig*) to make the wrong move; **tornare sui propri passi** to retrace one's steps; **"~ carraio"** "vehicle entrance — keep clear"

'password ['pasword] SF INV (*Inform*) password

'pasta SF (*Cuc*) dough; (: *impasto per dolce*) pastry; (: *anche*: **pasta alimentare**) pasta; (*massa molle di materia*) paste; (*fig: indole*) nature ■ **paste** SFPL (*pasticcini*) pastries; **~ in brodo** noodle soup; **~ sfoglia** puff pastry *o* paste (US)

pastasci'utta [pasta'ʃʃutta] SF pasta

pasteggi'are [pasted'dʒare] /62/ VI: **~ a vino/champagne** to have wine/champagne with one's meal

pas'tella SF batter

pas'tello SM pastel

pas'tetta SF (*Cuc*) = **pastella**

pas'ticca, -che SF = **pastiglia**

pasticce'ria [pastittʃe'ria] SF (*pasticcini*) pastries *pl*, cakes *pl*; (*negozio*) cake shop; (*arte*) confectionery

pasticci'are [pastit'tʃare] /**14**/ VT to mess up, make a mess of ▶ VI to make a mess

pasticci'ere, -a [pastit'tʃɛre] SM/F pastrycook; confectioner

pastic'cino [pastit'tʃino] SM petit four

pas'ticcio [pas'tittʃo] SM (Cuc) pie; (lavoro disordinato, imbroglio) mess; **trovarsi nei pasticci** to get into trouble

pasti'ficio [pasti'fitʃo] SM pasta factory

pas'tiglia [pas'tiʎʎa] SF pastille, lozenge

pas'tina SF small pasta shapes used in soup

pasti'naca, -che SF parsnip

'pasto SM meal; **vino da ~** table wine

pas'toia SF (fig): **~ burocratica** red tape

pas'tone SM (per animali) mash; (peg) overcooked stodge

pasto'rale AG pastoral

pas'tore, -a SM/F shepherd; (Rel) pastor, minister; (anche: **cane pastore**) sheepdog; **~ scozzese** (Zool) collie; **~ tedesco** (Zool) Alsatian (dog) (BRIT) German shepherd (dog)

pasto'rizia [pasto'rittsja] SF sheep-rearing, sheep farming

pastoriz'zare [pastorid'dzare] /**72**/ VT to pasteurize

pas'toso, -a AG doughy; pasty; (fig: voce, colore) mellow, soft

pas'trano SM greatcoat

pa'tacca, -che SF (distintivo) medal, decoration; (fig: macchia) grease spot, grease mark; (articolo scadente) bit of rubbish

pa'tata SF potato; **patate fritte** chips (BRIT), French fries

pata'tine SFPL (potato) crisps (BRIT) o chips (US); **~ fritte** chips

pata'trac SM (crollo: anche fig) crash

pâté [pa'te] SM INV pâté; **~ di fegato d'oca** pâté de foie gras

pa'tella SF (Zool) limpet

pa'tema, -i SM anxiety, worry

paten'tato, -a AG (munito di patente) licensed, certified; (fig: scherzoso: qualificato) utter, thorough

pa'tente SF licence (BRIT), license (US); (anche: **patente di guida**) driving licence (BRIT), driver's license (US); **~ a punti** driving licence with penalty points

Do not translate the Italian word **patente** by patent.

paten'tino SM temporary licence (BRIT) o license (US)

paterna'lismo SM paternalism

paterna'lista SM paternalist

paterna'listico, -a, -ci, -che AG paternalistic

paternità SF paternity, fatherhood

pa'terno, -a AG (affetto, consigli) fatherly; (casa, autorità) paternal

pa'tetico, -a, -ci, -che AG pathetic; (commovente) moving, touching

'pathos ['patos] SM pathos

pa'tibolo SM gallows sg, scaffold

pati'mento SM suffering

'patina SF (su rame ecc) patina; (sulla lingua) fur, coating

pa'tire /**55**/ VT, VI to suffer

pa'tito, -a SM/F enthusiast, fan, lover

patolo'gia [patolo'dʒia] SF pathology

pato'logico, -a, -ci, -che [pato'lɔdʒiko] AG pathological

pa'tologo, -a, -gi, -ghe SM/F pathologist

'patria SF homeland; **amor di ~** patriotism

patri'arca, -chi SM patriarch

pa'trigno [pa'triɲɲo] SM stepfather

patrimoni'ale AG (rendita) from property ▶ SF (anche: **imposta patrimoniale**) property tax

patri'monio SM estate, property; (fig) heritage; **mi è costato un ~** (fig) it cost me a fortune, I paid a fortune for it; **~ spirituale/culturale** spiritual/cultural heritage; **~ ereditario** (fig) hereditary characteristics pl; **~ pubblico** public property

'patrio, -a, -ii, -ie AG (di patria) native cpd, of one's country; (Dir): **patria potestà** parental authority; **amor ~** love of one's country

patri'ota, -i, -e SM/F patriot

patri'ottico, -a, -ci, -che AG patriotic

patriot'tismo SM patriotism

patroci'nare [patrotʃi'nare] /**72**/ VT (Dir: difendere) to defend; (sostenere) to sponsor, support

patro'cinio [patro'tʃinjo] SM defence (BRIT), defense (US); support, sponsorship

patro'nato SM patronage; (istituzione benefica) charitable institution o society

pa'trono SM/F (Rel) patron saint; (socio di patronato) patron; (Dir) counsel

'patta SF flap; (dei pantaloni) fly

patteggia'mento [patteddʒa'mento] SM (Dir) plea bargaining

patteggi'are [patted'dʒare] /**62**/ VT, VI to negotiate; (Dir) to plea-bargain

patti'naggio [patti'naddʒo] SM skating; **~ a rotelle/sul ghiaccio** roller-/ice-skating

patti'nare /**72**/ VI to skate; **~ sul ghiaccio** to ice-skate

pattina'tore, -'trice SM/F skater

'pattino¹ SM skate; (di slitta) runner; (Aer) skid; (Tecn) sliding block; **pattini (da ghiaccio)** (ice) skates; **pattini in linea** rollerblades®; **pattini a rotelle** roller skates

pat'tino² SM (barca) kind of pedalo with oars

pat'tista, -i, -e AG (Pol) of Patto per l'Italia

P

▶ SM/F (*Pol*) member (*o* supporter) of Patto per l'Italia

'patto SM (*accordo*) pact, agreement; (*condizione*) term, condition; **a ~ che** on condition that; **a nessun ~** under no circumstances; **venire *o* scendere a patti (con)** to come to an agreement (with); **P~ per l'Italia** (*Pol*) centrist party

pat'tuglia [pat'tuʎʎa] SF (*Mil*) patrol

pattugli'are [pattuʎˈʎare] /27/ VT to patrol

pattu'ire /55/ VT to reach an agreement on

pattumi'era SF (dust)bin (BRIT), ashcan (US)

pa'ura SF fear; **aver ~ di/di fare/che** to be frightened *o* afraid of/of doing/that; **far ~ a** to frighten; **per ~ di/che** for fear of/that; **ho ~ di sì/no** I am afraid so/not

pau'roso, -a AG (*che fa paura*) frightening; (*che ha paura*) fearful, timorous

'pausa SF (*sosta*) break; (*nel parlare: Mus*) pause

paven'tato, -a AG much-feared

pa'vese AG of (*o* from) Pavia

'pavido, -a AG (*letterario*) fearful

pavimen'tare /72/ VT (*stanza*) to floor; (*strada*) to pave

pavimentazi'one [pavimentat'tsjone] SF flooring; paving

pavi'mento SM floor

> Do not translate the Italian word **pavimento** by *pavement*.

pa'vone SM peacock

pavoneggi'arsi [pavoned'dʒarsi] /62/ VPR to strut about, show off

'paywall [ˈpeiwɔl] SM INV paywall

pazien'tare [pattsjen'tare] /72/ VI to be patient

pazi'ente [pat'tsjɛnte] AG, SMF patient

pazi'enza [pat'tsjɛntsa] SF patience; **perdere la ~** to lose (one's) patience

pazza'mente [pattsa'mente] AV madly; **essere ~ innamorato** to be madly in love

paz'zesco, -a, -schi, -sche [pat'tsesko] AG mad, crazy

paz'zia [pat'tsia] SF (*Med*) madness, insanity; (*di azione, decisione*) madness, folly; **è stata una ~!** it was sheer madness!

'pazzo, -a [ˈpattso] AG (*Med*) mad, insane; (*strano*) wild, mad ▶ SM/F madman/woman; **~ di** (*gioia, amore ecc*) mad *o* crazy with; **~ per qc/qn** mad *o* crazy about sth/sb; **essere ~ da legare** to be raving mad *o* a raving lunatic

PC SIGLA = **Piacenza** ▶ SIGLA M INV [piˈtʃi] (= *personal computer*) PC; **PC portatile** laptop

p.c. ABBR = **per condoglianze; per conoscenza**

p.c.c. ABBR (= *per copia conforme*) cc

P.C.I. SIGLA M (= *Partito Comunista Italiano*) former political party

PCUS SIGLA M = **Partito Comunista dell'Unione Sovietica**

PD SIGLA = **Padova**

P.D . ABBR = **partita doppia**

PE SIGLA = **Pescara**

'pecca, -che SF defect, flaw, fault

peccami'noso, -a AG sinful

pec'care /20/ VI to sin; (*fig*) to err

pec'cato SM sin; **è un ~ che** it's a pity that; **che ~!** what a shame *o* pity!; **un ~ di gioventù** (*fig*) a youthful error *o* indiscretion

pecca'tore, -'trice SM/F sinner

peccherò *ecc* [pekke'rɔ] VB *vedi* **peccare**

'pece [ˈpetʃe] SF pitch

pechi'nese [pekiˈnese] AG, SMF Pekin(g)ese *inv* ▶ SM (*anche*: **cane pechinese**) Pekin(g)ese *inv*, Peke

Pe'chino [peˈkino] SF Beijing, Peking

'pecora SF sheep; **~ nera** (*fig*) black sheep

peco'raio SM shepherd

peco'rella SF lamb; **la ~ smarrita** the lost sheep; **cielo a pecorelle** (*fig: nuvole*) mackerel sky

peco'rino SM sheep's milk cheese

pecu'lato SM (*Dir*) embezzlement

peculi'are AG: **~ di** peculiar to

peculiarità SF peculiarity

pecuni'ario, -a AG financial, money *cpd*

pe'daggio [peˈdaddʒo] SM toll

pedago'gia [pedagoˈdʒia] SF pedagogy, educational methods *pl*

peda'gogico, -a, -ci, -che [pedaˈgɔdʒiko] AG pedagogic(al)

peda'gogo, -a, -ghi, -ghe SM/F pedagogue

peda'lare /72/ VI to pedal; (*andare in bicicletta*) to cycle

pe'dale SM pedal

pe'dana SF footboard; (*Sport: nel salto*) springboard; (*: nella scherma*) piste

pe'dante AG pedantic ▶ SMF pedant

pedante'ria SF pedantry

pe'data SF (*impronta*) footprint; (*colpo*) kick; **prendere a pedate qn/qc** to kick sb/sth

pede'rasta, -i SM pederast

pe'destre AG prosaic, pedestrian

pedi'atra, -i, -e SM/F paediatrician (BRIT), pediatrician (US)

pedia'tria SF paediatrics *sg* (BRIT), pediatrics *sg* (US)

pedi'atrico, -a, -ci, -che AG pediatric

pedi'cure SM INV/F INV chiropodist (BRIT), podiatrist (US)

'pedigree [ˈpedigriː] SM INV pedigree

pedi'luvio SM footbath

pe'dina SF (*della dama*) draughtsman (BRIT), draughtsman (US); (*fig*) pawn

pedi'nare /72/ VT to shadow, tail

pe'dofilo, -a AG, SM/F paedophile

pedo'nale AG pedestrian

pe'done, -a SM/F pedestrian ▶ SM (Scacchi) pawn

'peeling ['piling] SM INV (Cosmesi) facial scrub

'peggio ['pɛddʒo] AV, AG INV worse ▶ SM O F: **il o la ~** the worst; **cambiare in ~** to get o become worse; **alla ~** at worst, if the worst comes to the worst; **tirare avanti alla meno ~** to get along as best one can; **avere la ~** to come off worse, get the worst of it

peggiora'mento [peddʒora'mento] SM worsening

peggio'rare [peddʒo'rare] /72/ VT to make worse, worsen ▶ VI to grow worse, worsen

peggiora'tivo, -a [peddʒora'tivo] AG pejorative

peggi'ore [ped'dʒore] AG (comparativo) worse; (superlativo) worst ▶ SMF: **il (la) ~** the worst (person); **nel ~ dei casi** if the worst comes to the worst

'pegno ['peɲɲo] SM (Dir) security, pledge; (nei giochi di società) forfeit; (fig) pledge, token; **dare in ~ qc** to pawn sth; **in ~ d'amicizia** as a token of friendship; **banco dei pegni** pawnshop

pelapa'tate SM INV potato peeler

pe'lare /72/ VT (spennare) to pluck; (spellare) to skin; (sbucciare) to peel; (fig) to make pay through the nose ■ **pelarsi** VPR to go bald

pe'lato, -a AG (sbucciato) peeled; (calvo) bald; **(pomodori) pelati** peeled tomatoes

pel'lame SM skins pl, hides pl

'pelle SF skin; (di animale) skin, hide; (cuoio) leather; **essere ~ ed ossa** to be skin and bone; **avere la ~ d'oca** to have goose pimples o goose flesh; **avere i nervi a fior di ~** to be edgy; **non stare più nella ~ dalla gioia** to be beside o.s. with delight; **lasciarci la ~** to lose one's life; **amici per la ~** firm o close friends

pellegri'naggio [pellegri'naddʒo] SM pilgrimage

pelle'grino, -a SM/F pilgrim

pelle'rossa (pl pellirosse) SM/F (peg) Red Indian (!)

pellette'ria SF (articoli) leather goods pl; (negozio) leather goods shop

pelli'cano SM pelican

pellicce'ria [pellittʃe'ria] SF (negozio) furrier's (shop); (quantità di pellicce) furs pl

pel'liccia, -ce [pel'littʃa] SF (mantello di animale) coat, fur; (indumento) fur coat; **~ ecologica** fake fur

pellicci'aio, -a [pellit'tʃajo] SM/F furrier

pel'licola SF (membrana sottile) film, layer; (Fot, Cine) film

pelli'rossa SMF = **pellerossa**

'pelo SM hair; (pelame) coat, hair; (pelliccia) fur; (di tappeto) pile; (di liquido) surface; **per un ~: per un ~ non ho perduto il treno** I very nearly missed

the train; **c'è mancato un ~ che affogasse** he narrowly escaped drowning; **cercare il ~ nell'uovo** (fig) to pick holes, split hairs; **non aver peli sulla lingua** (fig) to speak one's mind

pe'loso, -a AG hairy

'peltro SM pewter

pe'luche [pə'lyʃ] SM plush; **giocattoli di ~** soft toys

pe'luria SF down

'pelvi SF INV pelvis

pel'vico, -a, -ci, -che AG pelvic

'pena SF (Dir) sentence; (punizione) punishment; (sofferenza) sadness no pl, sorrow; (fatica) trouble no pl, effort; (difficoltà) difficulty; **far ~** to be pitiful; **mi fai ~** I feel sorry for you; **essere o stare in ~ (per qc/qn)** to worry o be anxious (about sth/sb); **prendersi o darsi la ~ di fare** to go to the trouble of doing; **vale la ~ farlo** it's worth doing, it's worth it; **non ne vale la ~** it's not worth the effort, it's not worth it; **~ di morte** death sentence; **~ pecuniaria** fine

pe'nale AG penal ▶ SF (anche: clausola penale) penalty clause; **causa ~** criminal trial; **diritto ~** criminal law; **pagare la ~** to pay the penalty

pena'lista, -i, -e SM/F (avvocato) criminal lawyer

penalità SF INV penalty

penaliz'zare [penalid'dzare] /72/ VT (Sport) to penalize

penalizzazi'one [penaliddzat'tsjone] SF (Sport) penalty

pe'nare /72/ VI (patire) to suffer; (faticare) to struggle

pen'dente AG hanging; leaning ▶ SM (ciondolo) pendant; (orecchino) drop earring

pen'denza [pen'dɛntsa] SF slope, slant; (grado d'inclinazione) gradient; (Econ) outstanding account

'pendere /8/ VI (essere appeso): **~ da** to hang from; (essere inclinato) to lean; (fig: incombere) **~ su** to hang over

pen'dice [pen'ditʃe] SF (di monte) slope

pen'dio, -ii SM slope, slant; (luogo in pendenza) slope

'pendola SF pendulum clock

pendo'lare AG pendulum cpd, pendular ▶ SMF commuter

pendola'rismo SM commuting

pendo'lino SM high-speed train

'pendolo SM (peso) pendulum; (anche: **orologio a pendolo**) pendulum clock

'pene SM penis

pene'trante AG piercing, penetrating

pene'trare /72/ VI to come o get in ▶ VT to penetrate; **~ in** to enter; (proiettile) to penetrate; (acqua, aria) to go o come into

penetrazi'one [penetrat'tsjone] SF penetration

penicil'lina [penitʃil'lina] SF penicillin

peninsu'lare AG peninsular; **l'Italia ~** mainland Italy

pe'nisola SF peninsula

peni'tente SMF penitent

peni'tenza [peni'tɛntsa] SF penitence; (*punizione*) penance

penitenzi'ario [peniten'tsjarjo] SM prison

'**penna** SF (*di uccello*) feather; (*per scrivere*) pen ■ **penne** SFPL (*Cuc*) quills (*type of pasta*); **~ a feltro/stilografica/a sfera** felt-tip/fountain/ballpoint pen

pen'nacchio [pen'nakkjo] SM (*ornamento*) plume; **un ~ di fumo** (*fig*) a plume o spiral of smoke

penna'rello SM felt(-tip) pen

pennel'lare /72/ VI to paint

pennel'lata SF brushstroke

pen'nello SM brush; (*per dipingere*) (paint)brush; **a ~** (*perfettamente*) to perfection, perfectly; **~ per la barba** shaving brush

pen'netta SF (*Inform*) dongle; **~ USB** memory stick

Pen'nini SMPL: **i ~** the Pennines

pen'nino SM nib

pen'none SM (*Naut*) yard; (*stendardo*) banner, standard

pen'nuto SM bird

pe'nombra SF half-light, dim light

pe'noso, -a AG painful, distressing; (*faticoso*) tiring, laborious

pen'sare /72/ VI to think ▶ VT to think; (*inventare, escogitare*) to think out; **~ a** to think of; (*amico, vacanze*) to think of o about; (*problema*) to think about; **~ di fare qc** to think of doing sth; **~ bene/male di qn** to think well/badly of sb, have a good/bad opinion of sb; **penso di sì** I think so; **penso di no** I don't think so; **a pensarci bene ...** on second thoughts (*BRIT*) o thought (*US*) ...; **non voglio nemmeno pensarci** I don't even want to think about it; **ci penso io** I'll see to o take care of it

pen'sata SF (*trovata*) idea, thought

pensa'tore, -'trice SM/F thinker

pensie'rino SM (*dono*) little gift; (*pensiero*): **ci farò un ~** I'll think about it

pensi'ero SM thought; (*modo di pensare, dottrina*) thinking *no pl*; (*preoccupazione*) worry, care, trouble; **darsi ~ per qc** to worry about sth; **stare in ~ per qn** to be worried about sb; **un ~ gentile** (*anche fig: dono ecc*) a kind thought

pensie'roso, -a AG thoughtful

'**pensile** AG hanging ▶ SM (*in cucina*) wall cupboard

pensi'lina SF (*in stazione*) platform roof

pensiona'mento SM retirement; **~ anticipato** early retirement

pensio'nandi SMPL *people about to retire*

pensio'nante SMF (*presso una famiglia*) lodger; (*di albergo*) guest

pensio'nato, -a SM/F pensioner ▶ SM (*istituto*) hostel

pensi'one SF (*al prestatore di lavoro*) pension; (*vitto e alloggio*) board and lodging; (*albergo*) boarding house; **andare in ~** to retire; **mezza ~** half board; **~ completa** full board; **~ d'invalidità** disablement pension; **~ per la vecchiaia** old-age pension

pensio'nistico, -a, -ci, -che AG pension *cpd*

pen'soso, -a AG thoughtful, pensive, lost in thought

pen'tagono SM pentagon; **il P~** the Pentagon

pentag'ramma, -i SM (*Mus*) staff, stave

pentapar'tito SM (*Pol*) five-party coalition government

'**pentathlon** ['pɛntatlon] SM (*Sport*) pentathlon

Pente'coste SF Pentecost, Whit Sunday (*BRIT*)

penti'mento SM repentance, contrition

pen'tirsi /45/ VPR: **~ di** to repent of; (*rammaricarsi*) to regret, be sorry for

penti'tismo SM *confessions from terrorists and members of organized crime rackets*

> The practice of **pentitismo** first emerged in Italy during the 1970s, a period marked by major terrorist activity. After their arrests, some members of terrorist groups would collaborate with the authorities by providing information usually in return for a reduced sentence. In recent years some members of Mafia organizations have become *pentiti*, and special legislation has had to be introduced to provide for the sentencing and protection of these informants.

pen'tito, -a SM/F ≈ supergrass (*BRIT*), *terrorist or criminal who turns police informer*

'**pentola** SF pot; **~ a pressione** pressure cooker

pe'nultimo, -a AG last but one (*BRIT*), next to last, penultimate

pe'nuria SF shortage

penzo'lare [pendzo'lare] /72/ VI to dangle, hang loosely

penzo'loni [pendzo'loni] AV dangling, hanging down; **stare ~** to dangle, hang down

pe'pato, -a AG (*condito con pepe*) peppery, hot; (*fig: pungente*) sharp

'**pepe** SM pepper; **~ macinato/in grani/nero** ground/whole/black pepper

pepero'nata SF *stewed peppers, tomatoes and onions*

peperon'cino [peperon'tʃino] SM chilli pepper

pepe'rone SM: **~ (rosso)** red pepper, capsicum; **~ (verde)** green pepper, capsicum; (*piccante*) chili; **rosso come un ~** as red as a beetroot (*BRIT*), fire-engine red (*US*); **peperoni ripieni** stuffed peppers

pe'pita SF nugget

per

PREP **1** (*moto attraverso luogo*) through; **i ladri sono passati per la finestra** the thieves got in (*o* out) through the window; **l'ho cercato per tutta la casa** I've searched the whole house *o* all over the house for it

2 (*moto a luogo*) for, to; **partire per la Germania/il mare** to leave for Germany/the sea; **il treno per Roma** the Rome train, the train for *o* to Rome; **proseguire per Londra** to go on to London

3 (*stato in luogo*): **seduto/sdraiato per terra** sitting/lying on the ground

4 (*tempo*) for; **per anni/lungo tempo** for years/a long time; **per tutta l'estate** throughout the summer, all summer long; **lo rividi per Natale** I saw him again at Christmas; **lo faccio per lunedì** I'll do it for Monday

5 (*mezzo, maniera*) by; **per lettera/ferrovia/** by letter/rail; **prendere qn per un braccio** to take sb by the arm

6 (*causa, scopo*) for; **assente per malattia** absent because of *o* owing to illness; **ottimo per il mal di gola** excellent for sore throats; **per abitudine** out of habit, from habit

7 (*limitazione*) for; **è troppo difficile per lui** it's too difficult for him; **per quel che mi riguarda** as far as I'm concerned; **per poco che sia** however little it may be; **per questa volta ti perdono** I'll forgive you this time

8 (*prezzo, misura*) for; (*distributivo*) a, per; **venduto per 3 milioni** sold for 3 million; **la strada continua per 3 km** the street goes on for 3 km; **15 euro per persona** 15 euros a *o* per person; **uno per volta** one at a time; **uno per uno** one by one; **giorno per giorno** day by day; **due per parte** two either side; **5 per cento** 5 per cent; **3 per 4 fa 12** 3 times 4 equals 12; **dividere/moltiplicare 12 per 4** to divide/multiply 12 by 4

9 (*in qualità di*) as; (*al posto di*) for; **avere qn per professore** to have sb as a teacher; **ti ho preso per Mario** I mistook you for Mario, I thought you were Mario; **dare per morto qn** to give sb up for dead; **lo prenderanno per pazzo** they'll think he's crazy

10 (*seguito da vb: finale*): **per fare qc** (so as) to do sth, in order to do sth; (: *causale*): **per aver fatto qc** for having done sth; **studia per passare l'esame** he's studying in order to *o* (so as) to pass his exam; **l'hanno punito per aver rubato i soldi** he was punished for having stolen the money; (: *consecutivo*): **è abbastanza grande per andarci da solo** he's big enough to go on his own

'pera SF pear

pe'raltro AV moreover, what's more

per'bacco ESCL my goodness!

per'bene AG INV respectable, decent ▸ AV (*con cura*) properly, well

perbe'nismo SM (so-called) respectability

percentu'ale [pertʃentu'ale] SF percentage; (*commissione*) commission

perce'pire [pertʃe'pire] **/55/** VT (*sentire*) to perceive; (*ricevere*) to receive

percet'tibile [pertʃet'tibile] AG perceptible

percezi'one [pertʃet'tsjone] SF perception

perché [per'ke]

AV why; **perché no?** why not?; **perché non vuoi andarci?** why don't you want to go?; **spiegami perché l'hai fatto** tell me why you did it

▸ CONG **1** (*causale*) because; **non posso uscire perché ho da fare** I can't go out because *o* as I've a lot to do

2 (*finale*) in order that, so that; **te lo do perché tu lo legga** I'm giving it to you so (that) you can read it

3 (*consecutivo*): **è troppo forte perché si possa batterlo** he's too strong to be beaten

▸ SM INV reason; **il perché di** the reason for; **non c'è un vero perché** there's no real reason for it

perciò [per'tʃɔ] CONG so, for this *o* that reason

per'correre /28/ VT (*luogo*) to go all over; (*paese*) to travel up and down, go all over; (*distanza*) to cover

percor'ribile AG (*strada*) which can be followed

per'corso, -a PP di **percorrere** ▸ SM (*tragitto*) journey; (*tratto*) route

per'cosso, -a PP di **percuotere** ▸ SF blow

percu'otere /106/ VT to hit, strike

percussi'one SF percussion; **strumenti a ~** (*Mus*) percussion instruments

per'dente AG losing ▸ SMF loser

'perdere /73/ VT to lose; (*lasciarsi sfuggire*) to miss; (*sprecare: tempo, denaro*) to waste; (*mandare in rovina: persona*) to ruin ▸ VI to lose; (*serbatoio ecc*) to leak ■ **perdersi** VPR (*smarrirsi*) to get lost; (*svanire*) to disappear, vanish; **saper ~** to be a good loser; **lascia ~!** forget it!, never mind!; **non ho niente da ~** (*fig*) I've got nothing to lose; **è un'occasione da non ~** it's a marvellous opportunity; (*affare*) it's a great bargain; **è fatica persa** it's a waste of effort; **~ al gioco** to lose money gambling; **~ di vista qn** (*anche fig*) to lose sight of sb; **perdersi di vista** to lose sight of each other; (*fig*) to lose touch; **perdersi alla vista** to disappear from sight; **perdersi in chiacchiere** to waste time talking

perdifi'ato: a ~ av (*correre*) at breathtaking speed; (*gridare*) at the top of one's voice

perdigi'orno [perdi'dʒorno] SM INV/F INV idler, waster

'perdita SF loss; (*spreco*) waste; (*fuoriuscita*) leak; **siamo in ~** (*Comm*) we are running at a loss; **a ~ d'occhio** as far as the eye can see

perdi'tempo SM INV/F INV waster, idler

perdizi'one [perdit'tsjone] SF (*Rel*) perdition, damnation; **luogo di ~** place of ill repute

perdo'nare /72/ VT to pardon, forgive; (*scusare*) to excuse, pardon; **per farsi ~** in order to be forgiven; **perdona la domanda ...** if you don't mind my asking ...; **vogliate ~ il (mio) ritardo** my apologies for being late; **un male che non perdona** an incurable disease

per'dono SM forgiveness; (*Dir*) pardon; **chiedere ~ a qn (per)** to ask for sb's forgiveness (for); (*scusarsi*) to apologize to sb (for)

perdu'rare /72/ VI to go on, last; (*perseverare*) to persist

perduta'mente AV desperately, passionately

per'duto, -a PP *di* **perdere** ▶ AG (*gen*) lost; **sentirsi** *o* **vedersi ~** (*fig*) to realize the hopelessness of one's position; **una donna perduta** (*fig*) a fallen woman

peregri'nare /72/ VI to wander, roam

pe'renne AG eternal, perpetual, perennial; (*Bot*) perennial

peren'torio, -a AG peremptory; (*definitivo*) final

perfetta'mente AV perfectly; **sai ~ che ...** you know perfectly well that ...

per'fetto, -a AG perfect ▶ SM (*Ling*) perfect (tense)

perfeziona'mento [perfettsjona'mento] SM: **~ (di)** improvement (in), perfection (of); **corso di ~** proficiency course

perfezio'nare [perfettsjo'nare] /72/ VT to improve, perfect ▪ **perfezionarsi** VPR to improve

perfezi'one [perfet'tsjone] SF perfection

perfezio'nismo [perfettsjo'nizmo] SM perfectionism

perfezio'nista, -i, -e [perfettsjo'nista] SM/F perfectionist

per'fidia SF perfidy

'perfido, -a AG perfidious, treacherous

per'fino AV even

perfo'rare /72/ VT to pierce; (*Med*) to perforate, to punch a hole (*o* holes) in; (*banda, schede*) to punch; (*trivellare*) to drill

perfora'tore, -'trice SM/F punch-card operator ▶ SM (*utensile*) punch; (*Inform*): **~ di schede** card punch ▶ SF (*Tecn*) boring *o* drilling machine; (*Inform*) card punch

perforazi'one [perforat'tsjone] SF piercing; perforation; punching; drilling

perga'mena SF parchment

'pergola SF pergola

pergo'lato SM pergola

perico'lante AG precarious

pe'ricolo SM danger; **essere fuori ~** to be out of danger; (*Med*) to be off the danger list; **mettere in ~** to endanger, put in danger

perico'loso, -a AG dangerous

perife'ria SF (*anche fig*) periphery; (*di città*) outskirts *pl*

peri'ferico, -a, -ci, -che AG (*Anat, Inform*) peripheral; (*zona*) outlying

pe'rifrasi SF INV circumlocution

pe'rimetro SM perimeter

peri'odico, -a, -ci, -che AG periodic(al); (*Mat*) recurring ▶ SM periodical

pe'riodo SM period; **~ contabile** accounting period; **~ di prova** trial period

peripe'zie [peripet'tsie] SFPL ups and downs, vicissitudes

'periplo SM circumnavigation

pe'rire /55/ VI to perish, die

peris'copio SM periscope

pe'rito, -a AG expert, skilled ▶ SM/F expert; (*agronomo, navale*) surveyor; **un ~ chimico** a qualified chemist

perito'nite SF peritonitis

pe'rizia [pe'rittsja] SF (*abilità*) ability; (*giudizio tecnico*) expert opinion; expert's report; **~ psichiatrica** psychiatrist's report

peri'zoma, -i [peri'dzoma] SM G-string

'perla SF pearl

per'lina SF bead

perli'nato SM matchboarding

perlo'meno AV (*almeno*) at least

perlopiù AV (*quasi sempre*) in most cases, usually

perlus'trare /72/ VT to patrol

perlustrazi'one [perlustrat'tsjone] SF patrol, reconnaissance; **andare in ~** to go on patrol

perma'loso, -a AG touchy

perma'nente AG permanent ▶ SF permanent wave, perm

perma'nenza [perma'nentsa] SF permanence; (*soggiorno*) stay; **buona ~!** enjoy your stay!

perma'nere /93/ VI to remain

per'mango VB *vedi* **permanere**

per'masi *ecc* VB *vedi* **permanere**

perme'abile AG permeable

perme'are /72/ VT to permeate

per'messo, -a PP *di* **permettere** ▶ SM (*autorizzazione*) permission, leave; (*dato a militare, impiegato*) leave; (*licenza*) licence (BRIT), license (US), permit; (*Mil: foglio*) pass; **~?, è ~?** (*posso entrare?*) may I come in?; (*posso passare?*) excuse me; **~ di lavoro/pesca** work/fishing permit; **~ di soggiorno** residence permit

per'mettere /63/ VT to allow, permit; **~ a qn qc/di fare qc** to allow sb sth/to do sth ▪ **permettersi** VPR: **permettersi qc/di fare qc** (*concedersi*) to allow o.s. sth/to do sth; (*avere la possibilità*) to afford sth/to do sth; **permettete che mi pre-**

senti let me introduce myself, may I introduce myself?; **mi sia permesso di sottolineare che ...** may I take the liberty of pointing out that ...

per'misi *ecc* VB *vedi* **permettere**

permis'sivo, -a AG permissive

'permuta SF (*Dir*) transfer; (*Comm*) trade-in; **accettare qc in ~** to take sth as a trade-in; **valore di ~** (*di macchina ecc*) trade-in value

permu'tare /72/ VT to exchange; (*Mat*) to permute

per'nacchia [per'nakkja] SF (*col*): **fare una ~** to blow a raspberry

per'nice [per'nitʃe] SF partridge

'perno SM pivot

pernotta'mento SM overnight stay

pernot'tare /72/ VI to spend the night, stay overnight

'pero SM pear tree

però CONG (*ma*) but; (*tuttavia*) however, nevertheless

pero'rare /72/ VT (*Dir: fig*): **~ la causa di qn** to plead sb's case

perpendico'lare AG, SF perpendicular

perpen'dicolo SM: **a ~** perpendicularly

perpe'trare /72/ VT to perpetrate

perpetu'are /72/ VT to perpetuate

per'petuo, -a AG perpetual

perplessità SF INV perplexity

per'plesso, -a AG perplexed, puzzled; uncertain

perqui'sire /55/ VT to search

perquisizi'one [perkwizit'tsjone] SF (*police*) search; **mandato di ~** search warrant

'perse *ecc* VB *vedi* **perdere**

persecu'tore, -trice SM/F persecutor

persecuzi'one [persekut'tsjone] SF persecution

persegu'ibile AG (*Dir*): **essere ~ per legge** to be liable to prosecution

persegu'ire /45/ VT to pursue; (*Dir*) to prosecute

persegui'tare /72/ VT to persecute

perseve'rante AG persevering

perseve'ranza [perseve'rantsa] SF perseverance

perseve'rare /72/ VI to persevere

'persi *ecc* VB *vedi* **perdere**

'Persia SF: **la ~** Persia

persi'ano, -a AG, SM/F Persian ▶ SF shutter; **persiana avvolgibile** roller blind

'persico, -a, -ci, -che AG: **il golfo P~** the Persian Gulf; **pesce ~** perch

per'sino AV = **perfino**

persis'tente AG persistent

persis'tenza [persis'tɛntsa] SF persistence

per'sistere /11/ VI to persist; **~ a fare** to persist in doing

persis'tito, -a PP *di* **persistere**

'perso, -a PP *di* **perdere** ▶ AG (*smarrito: anche fig*) lost; (*sprecato*) wasted; **fare qc a tempo ~** to do sth in one's spare time; **~ per ~** I've (*o* we've *etc*) got nothing further to lose

per'sona SF person; (*qualcuno*): **una ~** someone, somebody; (*espressione*) anyone *o* anybody ■ **persone** SFPL people *pl*; **non c'è ~ che ...** there's nobody who ..., there isn't anybody who ...; **in ~, di ~** in person; **per interposta ~** through an intermediary *o* a third party; **~ giuridica** (*Dir*) legal person

perso'naggio [perso'naddʒo] SM (*persona ragguardevole*) personality, figure; (*tipo*) character, individual; (*Letteratura*) character

perso'nale AG personal ▶ SM staff; personnel; (*figura fisica*) build ▶ SF (*mostra*) one-man *o* one-woman exhibition

personalità SF INV personality

personaliz'zare [personalid'dzare] /72/ VT (*arredamento, stile*) to personalize; (*adattare*) to customize

personaliz'zato, -a [personalid'dzato] AG personalized

personal'mente AV personally

personifi'care /20/ VT to personify; (*simboleggiare*) to embody

personificazi'one [personifikat'tsjone] SF (*vedi vb*) personification; embodiment

perspi'cace [perspi'katʃe] AG shrewd, discerning

perspi'cacia [perspi'katʃa] SF perspicacity, shrewdness

persu'adere /88/ VT: **~ qn (di qc/a fare)** to persuade sb (of sth/to do)

persuasi'one SF persuasion

persua'sivo, -a AG persuasive

persu'aso, -a PP *di* **persuadere**

per'tanto CONG (*quindi*) so, therefore

'pertica, -che SF pole

perti'nace [perti'natʃe] AG determined; persistent

perti'nente AG: **~ (a)** relevant (to), pertinent (to)

perti'nenza [perti'nɛntsa] SF (*attinenza*) pertinence, relevance; (*competenza*): **essere di ~ di qn** to be sb's business

per'tosse SF whooping cough

per'tugio [per'tudʒo] SM hole, opening

pertur'bare /72/ VT to disrupt; (*persona*) to disturb, perturb

perturbazi'one [perturbat'tsjone] SF disruption; disturbance; **~ atmosferica** atmospheric disturbance

Perù SM: **il ~** Peru

peru'gino, -a [peru'dʒino] AG of (*o* from), Perugia

P

peruvi'ano, -a AG, SM/F Peruvian

per'vadere /52/ VT to pervade

per'vaso, -a PP di **pervadere**

perve'nire /128/ VI: ~ **a** to reach, arrive at, come to; (*venire in possesso*): **gli pervenne una fortuna** he inherited a fortune; **far ~ qc a** to have sth sent to

perve'nuto, -a PP di **pervenire**

perversi'one SF perversion

perversità SF perversity

per'verso, -a AG perverted; perverse

perver'tire /55/ VT to pervert

perver'tito, -a SM/F pervert

pervi'cace [pervi'kat∫e] AG stubborn, obstinate

pervi'cacia [pervi'kat∫a] SF stubbornness, obstinacy

per'vinca, -che SF periwinkle ▶ SM INV (*colore*) periwinkle (blue)

p.es. ABBR (= *per esempio*) e.g.

'pesa SF weighing *no pl*; weighbridge

pe'sante AG heavy; (*fig: noioso*) dull, boring

pesan'tezza [pesan'tettsa] SF (*anche fig*) heaviness; **avere ~ di stomaco** to feel bloated

pesaper'sone AG INV: **(bilancia) ~ (weighing)** scales *pl*; (*automatica*) weighing machine

pe'sare /72/ VT to weigh ▶ VI (*avere un peso*) to weigh; (*essere pesante*) to be heavy; (*fig*) to carry weight; **~ su** (*fig*) to lie heavy on; to influence; to hang over; **mi pesa sgridarlo** I find it hard to scold him; **tutta la responsabilità pesa su di lui** all the responsibility rests on his shoulders; **è una situazione che mi pesa** it's a difficult situation for me; **il suo parere pesa molto** his opinion counts for a lot; **~ le parole** to weigh one's words

'pesca (*pl* **pesche**) SF (*frutto*) peach; (*il pescare*) fishing; **andare a ~** to go fishing; **~ di beneficenza** (*lotteria*) lucky dip; **~ con la lenza** angling; **~ subacquea** underwater fishing

pes'caggio [pes'kaddʒo] SM (*Naut*) draught (BRIT), draft (US)

pes'care /20/ VT (*pesce*) to fish for; to catch; (*qc nell'acqua*) to fish out; (*fig: trovare*) to get hold of, find; **andare a ~** to go fishing

pesca'tore, -trice SM fisherman ▶ SM/F (*con lenza*) angler

'pesce ['pe∫∫e] SM fish *gen inv*; **Pesci** (*dello zodiaco*) Pisces; **essere dei Pesci** to be Pisces; **non saper che pesci prendere** (*fig*) not to know which way to turn; **~ d'aprile!** April Fool!; **~ martello** hammerhead; **~ rosso** goldfish; **~ spada** swordfish

pesce'cane [pe∫∫e'kane] SM shark

pesche'reccio [peske'rett∫o] SM fishing boat

pesche'ria [peske'ria] SF fishmonger's (shop) (BRIT), fish store (US)

pescherò ecc [peske'rɔ] VB *vedi* **pescare**

peschi'era [pes'kjɛra] SF fishpond

pesci'vendolo, -a [pe∫∫i'vendolo] SM/F fishmonger (BRIT), fish merchant (US)

'pesco, -schi SM peach tree

pes'coso, -a AG teeming with fish

pe'seta SF peseta

'peso SM weight; (*Sport*) shot; **dar ~ a qc** to attach importance to sth; **essere di ~ a qn** (*fig*) to be a burden to sb; **rubare sul ~** to give short weight; **lo portarono via di ~** they carried him away bodily; **avere due pesi e due misure** (*fig*) to have double standards; **~ lordo/netto** gross/net weight; **~ piuma/mosca/gallo/medio/massimo** (*Pugilato*) feather-/fly-/bantam-/middle-/heavyweight

pessi'mismo SM pessimism

pessi'mista, -i, -e AG pessimistic ▶ SM/F pessimist

'pessimo, -a AG very bad, awful; **di pessima qualità** of very poor quality

pes'tare /72/ VT to tread on, trample on; (*sale, pepe*) to grind; (*uva, aglio*) to crush; (*fig: picchiare*): **~ qn** to beat sb up; **~ i piedi** to stamp one's feet; **~ i piedi a qn** (*anche fig*) to tread on sb's toes

'peste SF plague; (*persona*) nuisance, pest

pes'tello SM pestle

pesti'cida, -i [pesti't∫ida] SM pesticide

pes'tifero, -a AG (*anche fig*) pestilential, pestiferous; (*odore*) noxious

pesti'lenza [pesti'lɛntsa] SF pestilence; (*fetore*) stench

'pesto, -a AG: **c'è buio ~** it's pitch dark ▶ SM (*Cuc*) sauce made with basil, garlic, cheese and oil; **occhio ~** black eye

'petalo SM (*Bot*) petal

pe'tardo SM firecracker, banger (BRIT)

petizi'one [petit'tsjone] SF petition; **fare una ~ a** to petition

'peto SM (!) fart (!)

petro'dollaro SM petrodollar

petrol'chimica [petrol'kimika] SF petrochemical industry

petroli'era SF (*nave*) oil tanker

petroli'ere SM (*industriale*) oilman; (*tecnico*) worker in the oil industry

petroli'ero, -a AG oil *cpd*

petro'lifero, -a AG oil *cpd*

pe'trolio SM oil, petroleum; (*per lampada, fornello*) paraffin (BRIT), kerosene (US); **lume a ~** oil *o* paraffin *o* kerosene lamp; **~ grezzo** crude oil

Do not translate the Italian word **petrolio** by *petrol*.

pettego'lare /72/ VI to gossip

pettego'lezzo [pettego'leddzo] SM gossip *no pl*; **fare pettegolezzi** to gossip

pet'tegolo, -a AG gossipy ▶ SM/F gossip

petti'nare /72/ VT to comb (the hair of) ■ **petti-narsi** VPR to comb one's hair

pettina'tura SF (*acconciatura*) hairstyle

'pettine SM comb; (*Zool*) scallop

petti'rosso SM robin

'petto SM chest; (*seno*) breast, bust; (*Cuc: di carne bovina*) brisket; (: *di pollo ecc*) breast; **prendere qn/qc di ~** to face up to sb/sth; **a doppio ~** (*abito*) double-breasted

petto'rale AG pectoral

petto'rina SF (*di grembiule*) bib

petto'ruto, -a AG broad-chested; full-breasted

petu'lante AG insolent

pe'tunia SF petunia

'pezza ['pɛttsa] SF piece of cloth; (*toppa*) patch; (*cencio*) rag, cloth; (*Amm*): **~ d'appoggio** *o* **giustificativa** voucher; **trattare qn come una ~ da piedi** to treat sb like a doormat

pez'zato, -a [pet'tsato] AG piebald

pez'zente [pet'tsɛnte] SMF beggar

'pezzo ['pɛttso] SM (*gen*) piece; (*brandello, frammento*) piece, bit; (*di macchina, arnese ecc*) part; (*Stampa*) article; **aspettare un ~** to wait quite a while *o* some time; **in** *o* **a pezzi** in pieces; **andare a pezzi** to break into pieces; **essere a pezzi** (*oggetto*) to be in pieces *o* bits; (*fig: persona*) to be shattered; **un bel ~ d'uomo** a fine figure of a man; **abito a due pezzi** two-piece suit; **essere tutto d'un ~** (*fig*) to be a man (*o* woman) of integrity; **~ di cronaca** (*Stampa*) report; **~ grosso** (*fig*) bigwig; **~ di ricambio** spare part

PG SIGLA = **Perugia**

P.G. ABBR = **procuratore generale**

pH [pi'akka] SM INV (*Chim*) pH

'phishing ['fiʃin(g)] SM (*Inform*) phishing

PI SIGLA = **Pisa**

P.I. ABBR = **Pubblica Istruzione**

pi'accio *ecc* ['pjattʃo] VB *vedi* **piacere**

pia'cente [pja'tʃɛnte] AG attractive, pleasant

pia'cere [pja'tʃere] /74/ VI to please ▶ SM pleasure; (*favore*) favour (BRIT), favor (US); **una ragazza che piace** (*piacevole*) a likeable girl; (*attraente*) an attractive girl; **mi piace** I like it; **quei ragazzi non mi piacciono** I don't like those boys; **gli piacerebbe andare al cinema** he would like to go to the cinema; **il suo discorso è piaciuto molto** his speech was well received; **"~!"** (*nelle presentazioni*) "pleased to meet you!"; **~ (di conoscerla)** nice to meet you; **con ~** certainly, with pleasure; **per ~** please; **fare un ~ a qn** to do sb a favour; **mi fa ~ per lui** I am pleased for him; **mi farebbe ~ rivederlo** I would like to see him again

pia'cevole [pja'tʃevole] AG pleasant, agreeable

piaci'mento [pjatʃi'mento] SM: **a ~** (*a volontà*) as much as one likes, at will; **lo farà a suo ~** he'll do it when it suits him

piaci'uto, -a [pja'tʃuto] PP *di* **piacere**

pi'acqui *ecc* VB *vedi* **piacere**

pi'aga, -ghe SF (*lesione*) sore; (*ferita: anche fig*) wound; (*fig: flagello*) scourge, curse; (: *persona*) pest, nuisance

piagnis'teo [pjaɲɲis'tɛo] SM whining, whimpering

piagnuco'lare [pjaɲɲuko'lare] /72/ VI to whimper

piagnuco'lio, -ii [pjaɲɲuko'lio] SM whimpering

piagnuco'loso, -a [pjaɲɲuko'loso] AG whiny, whimpering, moaning

pi'alla SF (*arnese*) plane

pial'lare /72/ VT to plane

pialla'trice [pjalla'tritʃe] SF planing machine

pi'ana SF stretch of level ground; (*più esteso*) plain

pianeggi'ante [pjaned'dʒante] AG flat, level

piane'rottolo SM landing

pia'neta SF (*Astr*) planet

pi'angere ['pjandʒere] /75/ VI to cry, weep; (*occhi*) to water ▶ VT to cry, weep; (*lamentare*) to bewail, lament; **~ la morte di qn** to mourn sb's death

pianifi'care /20/ VT to plan

pianificazi'one [pjanifikat'tsjone] SF (*Econ*) planning; **~ aziendale** corporate planning

pia'nista, -i, -e SM/F pianist

pi'ano, -a AG (*piatto*) flat, level; (*Mat*) plane; (*facile*) straightforward, simple; (*chiaro*) clear, plain ▶ AV (*adagio*) slowly; (*a bassa voce*) softly; (*con cautela*) slowly, carefully ▶ SM (*Mat*) plane; (*Geo*) plain; (*livello*) level, plane; (*di edificio*) floor; (*programma*) plan; (*Mus*) piano; **pian ~** very slowly; (*poco a poco*) little by little; **una casa di 3 piani** a 3-storey (BRIT) *o* 3-storied (US) house; **al ~ di sopra/di sotto** on the floor above/below; **all'ultimo ~** on the top floor; **al ~ terra** on the ground floor; **in primo/secondo ~** (*Fot, Cine ecc*) in the foreground/background; **fare un primo ~** (*Fot, Cine*) to take a close-up; **di primo ~** (*fig*) prominent, high-ranking; **un fattore di secondo ~** a secondary *o* minor factor; **passare in secondo ~** to become less important; **mettere tutto sullo stesso ~** to lump everything together, give equal importance to everything; **tutto secondo i piani** all according to plan; **~ di lavoro** (*superficie*) worktop; (*programma*) work plan; **~ regolatore** (*Urbanistica*) town-planning scheme; **~ stradale** road surface

piano'forte SM piano, pianoforte

piano'terra SM INV = **piano terra**

pi'ansi *ecc* VB *vedi* **piangere**

pi'anta SF (*Bot*) plant; (*Anat: anche*: **pianta del piede**) sole (of the foot); (*grafico*) plan; (*cartina topografica*) map; **ufficio a ~ aperta** open-plan office; **in ~ stabile** on the permanent staff; **~ stradale** street map, street plan

piantagi'one [pjanta'dʒone] SF plantation

pianta'grane SM INV/F INV troublemaker

pian'tare /72/ VT to plant; (*conficcare*) to drive o hammer in; (*tenda*) to put up, pitch; (*fig: lasciare*) to leave, desert ▪ **piantarsi** VPR: **piantarsi davanti a qn** to plant o.s. in front of sb; **~ qn in asso** to leave sb in the lurch; **~ grane** (*fig*) to cause trouble; **piantala!** (*col*) cut it out!

pian'tato, -a AG: **ben ~** (*persona*) well-built

pianta'tore SM planter

pianter'reno SM ground floor

pian'tina SF (*di edificio, città*) (small) map; (*Bot*) (small) plant

pi'anto, -a PP *di* **piangere** ▶ SM tears *pl*, crying

pianto'nare /72/ VT to guard, watch over

pian'tone SM (*vigilante*) sentry, guard; (*soldato*) orderly; (*Aut*) steering column

pia'nura SF plain

pi'astra SF plate; (*di pietra*) slab; (*di fornello*) hot-plate; **panino alla ~ =** toasted sandwich; **~ di registrazione** tape deck

pias'trella SF tile

piastrel'lare /72/ VT to tile

pias'trina SF (*Anat*) platelet; (*Mil*) identity disc (BRIT) o tag (US)

piatta'forma SF (*anche fig*) platform; **~ continentale** (*Geo*) continental shelf; **~ girevole** (*Tecn*) turntable; **~ di lancio** (*Mil*) launching pad o platform; **~ rivendicativa** document prepared by the unions in an industry, setting out their claims

piat'tello SM clay pigeon; **tiro al ~** clay-pigeon shooting (BRIT), trapshooting

piat'tino SM (*di tazza*) saucer

pi'atto, -a AG flat; (*fig: scialbo*) dull ▶ SM (*recipiente, vivanda*) dish; (*portata*) course; (*parte piana*) flat (part) ▪ **piatti** SMPL (*Mus*) cymbals; **un ~ di minestra** a plate of soup; **~ fondo** soup dish; **~ forte** main course; **~ del giorno** dish of the day, plat du jour; **~ del giradischi** turntable; **piatti già pronti** (*Cuc*) ready-cooked dishes; **~ piano** dinner plate

pi'azza ['pjattsa] SF square; (*Comm*) market; (*letto, lenzuolo*): **a una ~** single; **a due piazze** double; **far ~ pulita** to make a clean sweep; **mettere in ~** (*fig: rendere pubblico*) to make public; **scendere in ~** (*fig*) to take to the streets, demonstrate; **~ d'armi** (*Mil*) parade ground

piazza'forte [pjattsa'forte] (*pl* **piazzeforti**) SF (*Mil*) stronghold

piaz'zale [pjat'tsale] SM (large) square

piazza'mento [pjattsa'mento] SM (*Sport*) place, placing

piaz'zare [pjat'tsare] /72/ VT to place; (*Comm*) to market, sell ▪ **piazzarsi** VPR (*Sport*) to be placed; **piazzarsi bene** to finish with the leaders o in a good position

piaz'zista, -i [pjat'tsista] SMF (*Comm*) commercial traveller

piaz'zola [pjat'tsɔla] SF (*Aut*) lay-by (BRIT), (roadside) stopping place; (*di tenda*) pitch

'picca, -che SF pike ▪ **picche** SFPL (*Carte*) spades; **rispondere picche a qn** (*fig*) to give sb a flat refusal

pic'cante AG hot, pungent; (*fig*) racy; biting

pic'carsi /20/ VPR: **~ di fare** to pride o.s. on one's ability to do; **~ per qc** to take offence (BRIT) o offense (US) at sth

picchet'taggio [pikket'taddʒo] SM picketing

picchet'tare [pikket'tare] /72/ VT to picket

pic'chetto [pik'ketto] SM (*Mil, di scioperanti*) picket; (*di tenda*) peg

picchi'are [pik'kjare] /19/ VT (*persona: colpire*) to hit, strike; (: *prendere a botte*) to beat (up); (*battere*) to beat; (*sbattere*) to bang ▶ VI (*bussare*) to knock; (: *con forza*) to bang; (*colpire*) to hit, strike; (*sole*) to beat down

picchi'ata [pik'kjata] SF knock; bang; blow; (*percosse*) beating, thrashing; (*Aer*) dive; **scendere in ~** to (nose-)dive

picchiet'tare [pikkjet'tare] /72/ VT (*punteggiare*) to spot, dot; (*colpire*) to tap

'picchio ['pikkjo] SM woodpecker

pic'cino, -a [pit'tʃino] AG tiny, very small

picci'olo [pit'tʃɔlo] SM (*Bot*) stalk

piccio'naia [pittʃo'naja] SF pigeon-loft; (*Teat*): **la ~** the gods *sg* (BRIT), the gallery

picci'one [pit'tʃone] SM pigeon; **pigliare due piccioni con una fava** (*fig*) to kill two birds with one stone

'picco, -chi SM peak; **a ~** vertically; **colare a ~** (*Naut, fig*) to sink

picco'lezza [pikko'lettsa] SF (*dimensione*) smallness; (*fig: grettezza*) meanness, pettiness; (*inezia*) trifle

'piccolo, -a AG small; (*oggetto, mano, di età: bambino*) small, little; (*dav sostantivo: di breve durata: viaggio*) short; (*fig*) mean, petty ▶ SM/F child, little one ▶ SM: **nel mio ~** in my own small way ▪ **piccoli** SMPL (*di animale*) young *pl*; **in ~** in miniature; **la piccola borghesia** the lower middle classes; (*peg*) the petty bourgeoisie

pic'cone SM pick(-axe)

pic'cozza [pik'kɔttsa] SF ice-axe

pic'nic SM INV picnic; **fare un ~** to have a picnic

pidies'sino, -a AG (*Pol*) of P.D.S. ▶ SM/F member (o supporter) of P.D.S.

pi'docchio [pi'dɔkkjo] SM louse

pidocchi'oso, -a [pidok'kjoso] AG (*infestato*) lousy; (*fig: taccagno*) mean, stingy, tight

pidu'ista, -i, -e AG P2 cpd (*masonic lodge*) ▶ SM member of the P2 masonic lodge

piè SM INV: **a ogni ~ sospinto** (*fig*) at every step; **saltare a ~ pari** (*omettere*) to skip; **a ~ di pagina**

at the foot of the page; **note a ~ di pagina** foot-notes

pi'ede SM foot; (*di mobile*) leg; **in piedi** standing; **a piedi** on foot; **a piedi nudi** barefoot; **su due piedi** (*fig*) at once; **mettere qc in piedi** (*azienda ecc*) to set sth up; **prendere ~** (*fig*) to gain ground, catch on; **puntare i piedi** (*fig*) to dig one's heels in; **sentirsi mancare la terra sotto i piedi** to feel lost; **non sta in piedi** (*persona*) he can't stand; (*fig: scusa ecc*) it doesn't hold water; **tenere in piedi** (*persona*) to keep on his (*o* her) feet; (*fig: ditta ecc*) to keep going; **a ~ libero** (*Dir*) on bail; **sul ~ di guerra** (*Mil*) ready for action; **~ di porco** crowbar

piedipi'atti SM INV (*peg: poliziotto*) cop

piedis'tallo, piedes'tallo SM pedestal

pi'ega, -ghe SF (*piegatura, Geo*) fold; (*di gonna*) pleat; (*di pantaloni*) crease; (*grinza*) wrinkle, crease; **prendere una brutta** *o* **cattiva ~** (*fig: persona*) to get into bad ways; (: *situazione*) to take a turn for the worse; **non fa una ~** (*fig: ragionamento*) it's faultless; **non ha fatto una ~** (*fig: persona*) he didn't bat an eye(lid) (*BRIT*) *o* an eye(lash) (*US*)

piega'mento SM folding; bending; **~ sulle gambe** (*Ginnastica*) kneebend

pie'gare /80/ VT to fold; (*braccia, gambe, testa*) to bend ▶ VI to bend ■ **piegarsi** VPR to bend; (*fig*) **piegarsi (a)** to yield (to), submit (to)

piega'tura SF folding *no pl*; bending *no pl*; fold bend

pieghe'rò *ecc* [pjege'rɔ] VB *vedi* **piegare**

pieghet'tare [pjeget'tare] **/72/** VT to pleat

pie'ghevole [pje'gevole] AG pliable, flexible; (*porta*) folding; (*fig*) yielding, docile

Pie'monte SM: **il ~** Piedmont

piemon'tese AG, SMF Piedmontese

pi'ena SF *vedi* **pieno**

pie'nezza [pje'nettsa] SF fullness

pi'eno, -a AG full; (*muro, mattone*) solid ▶ SM (*colmo*) height, peak; (*carico*) full load ▶ SF (*di fiume*) flood, spate; (*gran folla*) crowd, throng; **~ di** full of; **a piene mani** abundantly; **a tempo ~** full-time; **a pieni voti** (*eleggere*) unanimously; **laurearsi a pieni voti** *to graduate with full marks*; **in ~ giorno** in broad daylight; **in ~ inverno** in the depths of winter; **in piena notte** in the middle of the night; **in piena stagione** at the height of the season; **in ~** (*completamente: sbagliare*) completely; (*colpire, centrare*) bang *o* right in the middle; **avere pieni poteri** to have full powers; **nel ~ possesso delle sue facoltà** in full possession of his faculties; **fare il ~ (di benzina)** to fill up (with petrol)

pie'none SM: **c'era il ~ al cinema/al teatro** the cinema/the theatre was packed

'piercing ['pirsing] SM: **farsi il ~ all'ombelico** to have one's navel pierced

pietà SF pity; (*Rel*) piety; **senza ~** (*agire*) ruth-lessly; (*persona*) pitiless, ruthless; **avere ~ di** (*compassione*) to pity, feel sorry for; (*misericordia*) to have pity *o* mercy on; **far ~** to arouse pity; (*peg*) to be terrible

pie'tanza [pje'tantsa] SF dish, course

pie'toso, -a AG (*compassionevole*) pitying, com-passionate; (*che desta pietà*) pitiful

pi'etra SF stone; **mettiamoci una ~ sopra** (*fig*) let bygones be bygones; **~ preziosa** precious stone, gem; **~ dello scandalo** (*fig*) cause of scandal

pie'traia SF (*terreno*) stony ground

pietrifi'care /20/ VT to petrify; (*fig*) to transfix, paralyze

piet'rina SF (*per accendino*) flint

pie'trisco, -schi SM crushed stone, road metal

pi'eve SF parish church

'piffero SM (*Mus*) pipe

pigi'ama [pi'dʒama] SM pyjamas *pl*

'pigia 'pigia ['pidʒa'pidʒa] SM crowd, press

pigi'are [pi'dʒare] **/62/** VT to press

pigia'trice [pidʒa'tritʃe] SF (*macchina*) wine press

pigi'one [pi'dʒone] SF rent

pigli'are [piʎ'ʎare] **/27/** VT to take, grab; (*afferrare*) to catch

'piglio ['piʎʎo] SM look, expression

pig'mento SM pigment

pig'meo, -a SM/F pygmy

'pigna ['piɲɲa] SF pine cone

pignole'ria [piɲɲole'ria] SF fastidiousness, fussiness

pi'gnolo, -a [piɲ'ɲɔlo] AG pernickety

pigno'rare [piɲɲo'rare] **/72/** VT (*Dir*) to distrain

pigo'lare /72/ VI to cheep, chirp

pigo'lio SM cheeping, chirping

pigra'mente AV lazily

pi'grizia [pi'grittsja] SF laziness

'pigro, -a AG lazy; (*fig: ottuso*) slow, dull

PIL SIGLA M (= *prodotto interno lordo*) GDP

'pila SF (*catasta, di ponte*) pile; (*Elettr*) battery; (*col: torcia*) torch (*BRIT*), flashlight; **a ~, a pile** bat-tery-operated

pi'lastro SM pillar

'pile ['pail] SM INV fleece

'pillola SF pill; **prendere la ~** (*contraccettivo*) to be on the pill; **~ del giorno dopo** morning-after pill

pi'lone SM (*di ponte*) pier; (*di linea elettrica*) pylon

pi'lota, -i, -e SM/F pilot; (*Aut*) driver ▶ AG INV pilot *cpd*; **~ automatico** automatic pilot

pilo'taggio [pilo'taddʒo] SM: **cabina di ~** flight deck

pilo'tare /72/ VT to pilot; to drive

piluc'care /20/ VT to nibble at

pi'mento SM pimento, allspice

pim'pante AG lively, full of beans

pinaco'teca, -che SF art gallery
pi'neta SF pinewood
ping-'pong [pɪŋ'pɔŋ] SM table tennis
'pingue AG fat, corpulent
pingu'edine SF corpulence
pingu'ino SM (Zool) penguin
'pinna SF fin; (di cetaceo, per nuotare) flipper
pin'nacolo SM pinnacle
'pino SM pine (tree)
pi'nolo SM pine kernel
'pinta SF pint
'pinza ['pintsa] SF pliers pl; (Med) forceps pl; (Zool) pincer
pin'zette [pin'tsette] SFPL tweezers
'pio, -a, -'pii, -'pie AG pious; (opere, istituzione) charitable, charity cpd
piogge'rella [pjoddʒe'rɛlla] SF drizzle
pi'oggia, -ge ['pjɔddʒa] SF rain; (fig: di regali, fiori) shower; (di insulti) hail; **sotto la ~** in the rain; **~ acida** acid rain
pi'olo SM peg; (di scala) rung
piom'bare /72/ VI to fall heavily; (gettarsi con impeto): **~ su** to fall upon, assail ▶ VT (dente) to fill
piomba'tura SF (di dente) filling
piom'bino SM (sigillo) (lead) seal; (del filo a piombo) plummet; (Pesca) sinker
pi'ombo SM (Chim) lead; (sigillo) (lead) seal; (proiettile) (lead) shot; **a ~** (cadere) straight down; (muro ecc) plumb; **andare con i piedi di ~** (fig) to tread carefully; **senza ~** (benzina) unleaded; **anni di ~** (fig) era of terrorist outrages
pioni'ere, -a SM/F pioneer
pi'oppo SM poplar
pio'vano, -a AG: **acqua piovana** rainwater
pi'overe /76/ VB IMPERS to rain ▶ VI (fig: scendere dall'alto) to rain down; (affluire in gran numero): **~ in** to pour into; **non ci piove sopra** (fig) there's no doubt about it
pioviggi'nare [pjoviddʒi'nare] /72/ VB IMPERS to drizzle
piovosità SF rainfall
pio'voso, -a AG rainy
pi'ovra SF octopus
pi'ovve ecc VB vedi **piovere**
'pipa SF pipe
pipì SF (col): **fare ~** to have a wee (wee)
pipis'trello SM (Zool) bat
pi'ramide SF pyramid
pi'ranha SM INV piranha
pi'rata, -i SM pirate; **~ informatico** hacker; **~ della strada** hit-and-run driver
Pire'nei SMPL: **i ~** the Pyrenees
pi'retro SM pyrethrum
'pirico, -a, -ci, -che AG: **polvere pirica** gunpowder

pi'rite SF pyrite
piro'etta SF pirouette
pi'rofilo, -a AG heat-resistant ▶ SF heat-resistant glass; (tegame) heat-resistant dish
pi'roga, -ghe SF dug-out canoe
pi'romane SMF pyromaniac; arsonist
pi'roscafo SM steamer, steamship
'Pisa SF Pisa
pi'sano, -a AG Pisan
pisci'are [piʃ'ʃare] /14/ VI (col) to piss (!), pee (!)
pi'scina [piʃ'ʃina] SF (swimming) pool
pi'sello SM pea
piso'lino SM nap; **fare un ~** to have a nap
'pista SF (traccia) track, trail; (di stadio) track; (di pattinaggio) rink; (da sci) run; (Aer) runway; (di circo) ring; **~ da ballo** dance floor; **~ ciclabile** cycle lane; **~ di lancio** launch(ing) pad; **~ di rullaggio** (Aer) taxiway; **~ di volo** (Aer) runway
pis'tacchio [pis'takkjo] SM pistachio (tree); pistachio (nut)
pis'tillo SM (Bot) pistil
pis'tola SF pistol, gun; **~ a spruzzo** spray gun; **~ a tamburo** revolver
pis'tone SM piston
pi'tocco, -chi SM skinflint, miser
pito'nato, -a AG python-print
pi'tone SM python
'pittima SF (fig) bore
pit'tore, -'trice SM/F painter
pitto'resco, -a, -schi, -sche AG picturesque
pit'torico, -a, -ci, -che AG of painting, pictorial
pit'tura SF painting; **~ fresca** wet paint
pittu'rare /72/ VT to paint

---

più

AV **1** (in maggiore quantità) more; **più del solito** more than usual; **in più, di più** more; **ne voglio di più** I want some more; **ci sono 3 persone in** o **di più** there are 3 more o extra people; **costa di più** it's more expensive; **una volta di più** once more; **più o meno** more or less; **né più né meno** no more, no less; **per di più** (inoltre) what's more, moreover; **è sempre più difficile** it is getting more and more difficult; **chi più chi meno hanno tutti contribuito** everybody made a contribution of some sort; **più dormo e più dormirei** the more I sleep the more I want to sleep

2 (comparativo) more; (: se monosillabo, spesso) + ... er; **più ... di/che** more ... than; **più intelligente di lui** more intelligent than him; **più furbo di te** smarter than you; **più tardi di ...** later than ...; **lavoro più di te/di Paola** I work harder than you/than Paola; **è più intelligente che ricco** he's more intelligent than rich; **è più fortunato che bravo** he is lucky rather than skilled; **più di quanto pensassi**

more than I thought; **più che altro** mainly; **più che mai** more than ever

3 (*superlativo*) most; (: *se monosillabico, spesso*) + ... est; **il più grande/intelligente** the biggest/most intelligent; **è quello che compro più spesso** that's the one I buy most often; **al più presto** as soon as possible; **al più tardi** at the latest

4 (*negazione*): **non ... più** no more, no longer; **non ho più soldi** I've got no more money, I don't have any more money; **non lavoro più** I'm no longer working, I don't work any more; **non ce n'è più** there isn't any left; **non c'è più nessuno** there's no one left; **non c'è più niente da fare** there's nothing more to be done; **a più non posso** (*gridare*) at the top of one's voice; (*correre*) as fast as one can

5 (*Mat*) plus; **4 più 5 fa 9** 4 plus 5 equals 9; **più 5 gradi** 5 degrees above freezing, plus 5; **6 più** (*a scuola*) just above a pass

▶ PREP plus; **500 più le spese** 500 plus expenses; **siamo in quattro più il nonno** there are four of us plus grandpa

▶ AG INV **1:** **più ... (di)** more ... (than); **più denaro/tempo** more money/time; **più persone di quante ci aspettassimo** more people than we expected

2 (*numerosi, diversi*) several; **l'aspettai per più giorni** I waited for it for several days

▶ SM **1** (*la maggior parte*): **il più è fatto** most of it is done; **il più delle volte** more often than not, generally; **parlare del più e del meno** to talk about this and that

2 (*Mat*) plus (sign)

3: i più the majority

piuccheper'fetto [pjukkeper'fɛtto] SM (*Ling*) pluperfect, past perfect

pi'uma SF feather ■ **piume** SFPL down *sg*; (*piumaggio*) plumage *sg*, feathers

piu'maggio [pju'maddʒo] SM plumage, feathers *pl*

piu'mino SM (eider)down; (*per letto*) eiderdown; (: *tipo danese*) duvet, continental quilt; (*giacca*) quilted jacket (*with goose-feather padding*); (*per cipria*) powder puff; (*per spolverare*) feather duster

piut'tosto AV rather; **~ che** (*anziché*) rather than

'piva SF: **con le pive nel sacco** (*fig*) empty-handed

pi'vello, -a SM/F greenhorn

pixeliz'zare [pikselid'dzare] /**72**/ VT (*Inform*) to pixelate

'pizza ['pittsa] SF (*Cuc*) pizza; (*Cine*) reel

pizze'ria [pittse'ria] SF pizzeria (*place where pizzas are made, sold or eaten*)

pizzi'cagnolo, -a [pittsi'kaɲɲolo] SM/F specialist grocer

pizzi'care [pittsi'kare] /**20**/ VT (*stringere*) to nip, pinch; (*pungere*) to sting; to bite; (*Mus*) to pluck

▶ VI (*prudere*) to itch, be itchy; (*cibo*) to be hot o spicy

pizziche'ria [pittsike'ria] SF delicatessen (shop)

'pizzico, -chi ['pittsiko] SM (*pizzicotto*) pinch, nip; (*piccola quantità*) pinch, dash; (*d'insetto*) sting; bite

pizzi'cotto [pittsi'kɔtto] SM pinch, nip

'pizzo ['pittso] SM (*merletto*) lace; (*barbetta*) goatee beard; (*tangente*) protection money

pla'care /**20**/ VT to placate, soothe ■ **placarsi** VPR to calm down

'placca, -che SF plate; (*con iscrizione*) plaque; (*anche*: **placca dentaria**) (dental) plaque

plac'care /**20**/ VT to plate; **placcato in oro/argento** gold-/silver-plated

pla'centa [pla'tʃɛnta] SF placenta

placidità [platʃidi'ta] SF calm, peacefulness

'placido, -a ['platʃido] AG placid, calm

plafoni'era SF ceiling light

plagi'are [pla'dʒare] /**62**/ VT (*copiare*) to plagiarize; (*Dir: influenzare*) to coerce

'plagio ['pladʒo] SM plagiarism; (*Dir*) duress

plaid [plɛd] SM INV (travelling) rug (BRIT), lap robe (US)

pla'nare /**72**/ VI (*Aer*) to glide

'plancia, -ce ['plantʃa] SF (*Naut*) bridge; (*Aut: cruscotto*) dashboard

'plancton SM INV plankton

plane'tario, -a AG planetary ▶ SM (*locale*) planetarium

planis'fero SM planisphere

plan'tare SM arch support

'plasma SM plasma

plas'mare /**72**/ VT to mould (BRIT), mold (US), shape

'plastico, -a, -ci, -che AG plastic ▶ SM (*rappresentazione*) relief model; (*esplosivo*): **bomba al ~** plastic bomb ▶ SF (*arte*) plastic arts *pl*; (*Med*) plastic surgery; (*sostanza*) plastic; **plastica facciale** face lift; **in materiale ~** plastic

plasti'lina® SF plasticine®

'platano SM plane tree

pla'tea SF (*Teat*) stalls *pl* (BRIT), orchestra (US)

plate'ale AG (*gesto, atteggiamento*) theatrical

plateal'mente AV theatrically

'platino SM platinum

pla'tonico, -a, -ci, -che AG platonic

plau'dire /**45**/ VI: **~ a** to applaud

plau'sibile AG plausible

'plauso SM (*fig*) approval

'playback ['pleibæk] SM: **cantare in ~** to mime

'playboy ['pleibɔi] SM INV playboy

'playmaker ['pleimeiker] SM INV/F INV (*Sport*) playmaker

'play-off ['pleiɔf] SM INV (*Sport*) play-off

ple'baglia [ple'baʎʎa] SF (*peg*) rabble, mob

'plebe SF common people

ple'beo, -a AG plebeian; (*volgare*) coarse, common

plebi'scito [plebiʃˈʃito] SM plebiscite

ple'nario, -a AG plenary

pleni'lunio SM full moon

plenipotenzi'ario, -a [plenipotenˈtsjarjo] AG plenipotentiary

'plenum SM INV plenum

'plettro SM plectrum

'pleura SF (*Anat*) pleura

pleu'rite SF pleurisy

P.L.I. SIGLA M (= *Partito Liberale Italiano*) former political party

'plico, -chi SM (*pacco*) parcel; **in ~ a parte** (*Comm*) under separate cover

plissé [pliˈse] AG INV plissé *cpd* ▶ SM INV (*anche:* **tessuto plissé**) plissé

plisset'tato, -a AG plissé *cpd*

plo'tone SM (*Mil*) platoon; **~ d'esecuzione** firing squad

pug-'in [plaˈgin] AG INV, SM INV (*Inform*) plug-in

'plumbeo, -a AG leaden

plu'rale AG, SM plural

plura'lismo SM pluralism

pluralità SF plurality; (*maggioranza*) majority

plusva'lenza [pluzvaˈlɛntsa] SF capital gain

plusva'lore SM (*Econ*) surplus

plu'tonio SM plutonium

pluvi'ale AG rain *cpd*

pluvi'ometro SM rain gauge

pm ABBR = **peso molecolare**

P.M. ABBR (*Pol*) = **Pubblico Ministero**; (= *Polizia Militare*) MP = *Military Police*)

PMI SIGLA FPL (= *Piccole e Medie Imprese*) SME (= *Small and Medium-sized Enterprises*)

PN SIGLA = **Pordenone**

pneu'matico, -a, -ci, -che AG inflatable; (*Tecn*) pneumatic ▶ SM (*Aut*) tyre (*BRIT*), tire (*US*)

PNL SIGLA M = **prodotto nazionale lordo**

PO SIGLA = **Prato**

Po SM: **il Po** the Po

po' AV, SM *vedi* **poco**

P.O. ABBR = **posta ordinaria**

po'chezza [poˈkettsa] SF insufficiency, shortage; (*fig: meschinità*) meanness, smallness

---

'poco, -a, -chi, -che

AG (*quantità*) little, not much; (*numero*) few, not many; **poco pane/denaro/spazio** little *o* not much bread/money/space; **con poca spesa** without spending much; **a poco prezzo** at a low price, cheap; **poco (tempo) fa** a short time ago; **poche persone/idee** few *o* not many people/ideas; **è un tipo di poche parole** he's a man of few words; **ci**

---

vediamo tra poco (*sottinteso: tempo*) see you soon

▶ AV **1** (*in piccola quantità*) little, not much

2 (*numero limitato*) few, not many; **guadagna poco** he doesn't earn much, he earns little

3 (*con ag, av*) (a) little, not very; **è poco più vecchia di lui** she's a little *o* slightly older than him; **è poco socievole** he's not very sociable; **sta poco bene** he isn't very well

4 (*tempo*): **poco dopo/prima** shortly afterwards/before; **il film dura poco** the film doesn't last very long; **ci vediamo molto poco** we don't see each other very often, we hardly ever see each other

5: **un po'** a little, a bit; **è un po' corto** it's a little *o* a bit short; **arriverà fra un po'** he'll arrive shortly *o* in a little while

6: **a dir poco** to say the least; **a poco a poco** little by little; **per poco non cadevo** I nearly fell; **è una cosa da poco** it's nothing, it's of no importance; **una persona da poco** a worthless person

▶ PRON (a) little; **pochi, poche** pl (*persone*) few (people); (: *cose*) few; **ci vediamo tra poco** see you soon; **pochi lo sanno** not many people know it; **ci vuole tempo ed io ne ho poco** it takes time, and I haven't got much to spare

▶ SM **1** little; **vive del poco che ha** he lives on the little he has

2: **un po'** a little; **un po' di zucchero** a little sugar; **un bel po' di denaro** quite a lot of money; **un po' per ciascuno** a bit each

---

Anche se è possibile tradurre *poco* con **little** (+ nome singolare) e **few** (+ nome plurale) in inglese è più comune una costruzione al negativo: **not much/not many**.
Ho pochi soldi in questo momento. **I don't have much money at the moment.**
Pochi studenti lo sanno. **Not many students know about it.**
Anche con un aggettivo o un verbo, è più comune usare la costruzione al negativo:
un'espressione poco comune **not a very common expression**
Un po' di si traduce **some** quando è seguito da un nome non numerabile.
un po' d'acqua/di pane **some water/bread**

'podcast [ˈpɔdkast] SM podcast

po'dere SM (*Agr*) farm

pode'roso, -a AG powerful

podestà SM INV (*nel fascismo*) podestà, mayor

'podio SM dais, platform; (*Mus*) podium

po'dismo SM (*Sport: marcia*) walking; (: *corsa*) running

po'dista, -i, -e SM/F walker; runner

po'ema, -i SM poem

poe'sia SF (*arte*) poetry; (*componimento*) poem

po'eta, -'essa sm/f poet (poetess)
poe'tare /72/ vi to write poetry
po'etico, -a, -ci, -che ag poetic(al)
poggi'are [pod'dʒare] /62/ vt to lean, rest; (*posare*) to lay, place
poggia'testa [poddʒa'tɛsta] sm inv (*Aut*) headrest
'poggio ['pɔddʒo] sm hillock, knoll
poggi'olo [pod'dʒɔlo] sm balcony
'poi av then; (*alla fine*) finally, at last ▶ sm: **pensare al ~** to think of the future; **e ~** (*inoltre*) and besides; **questa ~ (è bella)!** (*ironico*) that's a good one!; **d'ora in ~** from now on; **da domani in ~** from tomorrow onwards
poi'ana sf buzzard
poiché [poi'ke] cong since, as
pois [pwa] sm inv spot, (polka) dot; **a ~** spotted, polka-dot *cpd*
'poker sm poker
po'lacco, -a, -chi, -che ag Polish ▶ sm/f Pole
po'lare ag polar
polariz'zare [polarid'dzare] /72/ vt (*anche fig*) to polarize
'polca, -che sf polka
po'lemico, -a, -ci, -che ag polemical, controversial ▶ sf controversy; **fare polemiche** to be contentious
polemiz'zare [polemid'dzare] /72/ vi: **~ (su qc)** to argue (about sth)
po'lenta sf (*Cuc*) sort of thick porridge made with maize flour
polen'tone, -a sm/f slowcoach (*Brit*), slowpoke (*US*)
pole'sano, -a ag of (*o* from) Polesine (*area between the Po and the Adige*)
POL'FER abbr f = **Polizia Ferroviaria**
'poli... prefisso poly...
poliambula'torio sm (*Med*) health clinic
poli'clinico, -ci sm general hospital, polyclinic
poli'edro sm polyhedron
poli'estere sm polyester
poliga'mia sf polygamy
polig'lotta, -i, -e ag, sm/f polyglot
po'ligono sm polygon; **~ di tiro** rifle range
Poli'nesia sf: **la ~** Polynesia
polinesi'ano, -a ag, sm/f Polynesian
'polio(mie'lite) sf polio(myelitis)
'polipo sm polyp
polisti'rolo sm polystyrene
poli'tecnico, -ci sm postgraduate technical college
po'litica, -che sf *vedi* **politico**
politica'mente av politically; **~ corretto** politically correct
politi'cante smf (*peg*) petty politician

politiciz'zare [polititʃid'dzare] /72/ vt to politicize
po'litico, -a, -ci, -che ag political ▶ sm/f politician ▶ sf politics *sg*; (*linea di condotta*) policy; **elezioni politiche** parliamentary (*Brit*) *o* congressional (*US*) election(s); **uomo ~** politician; **darsi alla politica** to go into politics; **fare politica** (*militante*) to be a political activist; (*come professione*) to be in politics; **la politica del governo** the government's policies; **politica aziendale** company policy; **politica estera** foreign policy; **politica dei prezzi** prices policy; **politica dei redditi** incomes policy
poliva'lente ag multi-purpose
poli'zia [polit'tsia] sf police; **~ giudiziaria** ≈ Criminal Investigation Department (CID) (*Brit*), Federal Bureau of Investigation (FBI) (*US*); **~ sanitaria/tributaria** health/tax inspectorate; **~ stradale** traffic police; **~ di stato** *see note*

The remit of the **polizia di stato** is to maintain public order, to uphold the law, and to prevent and investigate crime. This is a civilian branch of the police force in which male and female officers perform similar duties. The *polizia di stato* reports to the Minister of the Interior.

In inglese *polizia* si traduce **police** e si usa, in genere, il verbo al plurale.
La polizia ha arrestato venti manifestanti. **The police have arrested twenty demonstrators**.

polizi'esco, -a, -schi, -sche [polit'tsjesko] ag police *cpd*; (*film, romanzo*) detective *cpd*
polizi'otto, -a [polit'tsjɔtto] sm/f policeman; **cane ~** police dog; **donna ~** policewoman; **~ di quartiere** local police officer
po'lizza ['pɔlittsa] sf (*Comm*) bill; **~ di assicurazione** insurance policy; **~ di carico** bill of lading
pol'laio sm henhouse
pollai'olo, -a sm/f poulterer (*Brit*), poultryman
pol'lame sm poultry
pol'lastra sf pullet; (*fig: ragazza*) chick, wench
pol'lastro sm (*Zool*) cockerel
'pollice ['pɔllitʃe] sm thumb; (*unità di*) inch
'polline sm pollen
'pollo sm chicken; **far ridere i polli** (*situazione, persona*) to be utterly ridiculous
polmo'nare ag lung *cpd*, pulmonary
pol'mone sm lung; **~ d'acciaio** (*Med*) iron lung
polmo'nite sf pneumonia; **~ atipica** SARS
'Polo sm (*Pol*) centre-right coalition
'polo sm (*Geo, Fisica*) pole; (*gioco*) polo ▶ sf inv (*maglia*) polo shirt; **il ~ sud/nord** the South/North Pole

Po'lonia SF: **la ~** Poland

'**polpa** SF flesh, pulp; (*carne*) lean meat

pol'paccio [pol'pattʃo] SM (*Anat*) calf

polpas'trello SM fingertip

pol'petta SF (*Cuc*) meatball

polpet'tone SM (*Cuc*) meatloaf

'**polpo** SM octopus

pol'poso, -a AG fleshy

pol'sino SM cuff

'**polso** SM (*Anat*) wrist; (*pulsazione*) pulse; (*fig*: *forza*) drive, vigour (*Brit*), vigor (*US*); **avere ~** (*fig*) to be strong; **un uomo di ~** a man of nerve

pol'tiglia [pol'tiʎʎa] SF (*composto*) mash, mush; (*di fango e neve*) slush

pol'trire /55/ VI to laze about

pol'trona SF armchair; (*Teat*: *posto*) seat in the front stalls (*Brit*) o the orchestra (*US*)

poltron'cina [poltron'tʃina] SF (*Teat*) seat in the back stalls (*Brit*) o the orchestra (*US*)

pol'trone AG lazy, slothful

'**polvere** SF dust; (*sostanza ridotta minutissima*) powder, dust; **caffè in ~** instant coffee; **latte in ~** dried o powdered milk; **sapone in ~** soap powder; **~ d'oro** gold dust; **~ pirica** o **da sparo** gunpowder; **polveri sottili** particulates

polveri'era SF powder magazine

polve'rina SF (*gen, Med*) powder; (*gergo*: *cocaina*) snow

polveriz'zare [polverid'dzare] /72/ VT to pulverize; (*nebulizzare*) to atomize; (*fig*) to crush, pulverize; (*record*) to smash

polve'rone SM thick cloud of dust

polve'roso, -a AG dusty

po'mata SF ointment, cream

po'mello SM knob

pomeridi'ano, -a AG afternoon *cpd*; **nelle ore pomeridiane** in the afternoon

pome'riggio [pome'riddʒo] SM afternoon; **nel primo/tardo ~** in the early/late afternoon

'**pomice** ['pomitʃe] SF pumice

pomici'are [pomi'tʃare] /14/ VI (*col*) to neck

'**pomo** SM (*mela*) apple; (*ornamentale*) knob; (*di sella*) pommel; **~ d'Adamo** (*Anat*) Adam's apple

pomo'doro SM tomato; **pomodori pelati** skinned tomatoes

'**pompa** SF pump; (*sfarzo*) pomp (and ceremony); **~ antincendio** fire hose; **~ di benzina** petrol (*Brit*) o gas (*US*) pump; (*distributore*) filling o gas (*US*) station; **impresa di pompe funebri** funeral parlour *sg* (*Brit*), undertaker's *sg*, mortician's (*US*)

pom'pare /72/ VT to pump; (*trarre*) to pump out; (*gonfiare d'aria*) to pump up

pompei'ano, -a AG of (o from) Pompei

pom'pelmo SM grapefruit

pompi'ere SM fireman

pom'pon [pom'pɔn] SM INV pompom, pompon

pom'poso, -a AG pompous

ponde'rare /72/ VT to ponder over, consider carefully

ponde'roso, -a AG (*anche fig*) weighty

po'nente SM west

'**pongo** VB *vedi* **porre**

'**poni** VB *vedi* **porre**

'**ponte** SM bridge; (*di nave*) deck; (: anche: **ponte di comando**) bridge; (*impalcatura*) scaffold; **vivere sotto i ponti** to be a tramp; **fare il ~** (*fig*) to take the extra day off (*between 2 public holidays*); **governo ~** interim government; **~ aereo** airlift; **~ di barche** (*Mil*) pontoon bridge; **~ di coperta** (*Naut*) upper deck; **~ levatoio** drawbridge; **~ radio** radio link; **~ sospeso** suspension bridge

pon'tefice [pon'tefitʃe] SM (*Rel*) pontiff

ponti'cello [ponti'tʃɛllo] SM (*di occhiali*: *Mus*) bridge

pontifi'care /20/ VI (*anche fig*) to pontificate

pontifi'cato SM pontificate

ponti'ficio, -a, -ci, -cie [ponti'fitʃo] AG papal; **Stato P~** Papal State

pon'tile SM jetty

'**pony** ['pɔni] SM INV pony

pool [pu:l] SM INV (*consorzio*) consortium; (*organismo internazionale*) pool; (*di esperti, ricercatori*) team; (*antimafia, antidroga*) working party

pop [pɔp] AG INV pop *cpd*

'**popcorn** ['pɔpkɔrn] SM INV popcorn

'**popeline** ['pɔpelin] SM poplin

popò SM INV (*sedere*) botty

popo'lano, -a AG popular, of the people ▶ SM/F man/woman of the people

popo'lare /72/ AG popular; (*quartiere, clientela*) working-class; (*Pol*) of P.P.I. ▶ SM/F (*Pol*) member (o supporter) of P.P.I. ▶ VT (*rendere abitato*) to populate ■ **popolarsi** VPR to fill with people, get crowded; **manifestazione ~** mass demonstration; **repubblica ~** people's republic

popolarità SF popularity

popolazi'one [popolat'tsjone] SF population

'**popolo** SM people

popo'loso, -a AG densely populated

po'pone SM melon

'**poppa** SF (*di nave*) stern; (*col*: *mammella*) breast; **a ~** aft, astern

pop'pante SMF unweaned infant; (*fig*) whippersnapper

pop'pare /72/ VT to suck

pop'pata SF (*allattamento*) feed

poppa'toio SM (feeding) bottle

popu'lista, -i, -e AG populist

por'caio SM (*anche fig*) pigsty

por'cata SF (*libro, film ecc*) load of rubbish; **fare una ~ a qn** to play a dirty trick on sb

porcel'lana [portʃel'lana] SF porcelain, china; (*oggetto*) piece of porcelain

porcel'lino, -a [portʃel'lino] SM/F piglet; **~ d'India** guinea pig

porche'ria [porke'ria] SF filth, muck; (*fig: oscenità*) obscenity; (: *azione disonesta*) dirty trick; (: *cosa mal fatta*) rubbish

por'chetta [por'ketta] SF roast sucking pig

por'cile [por'tʃile] SM pigsty

por'cino, -a [por'tʃino] AG of pigs, pork *cpd* ▶ SM (*fungo*) type of edible mushroom

'porco, -ci SM pig; (*carne*) pork

porcos'pino SM porcupine

'porfido SM porphyry

'porgere ['pɔrdʒere] /**115**/ VT to hand, give; (*tendere*) to hold out

'porno AG INV porn, porno

pornogra'fia SF pornography

porno'grafico, -a, -ci, -che AG pornographic

'poro SM pore

po'roso, -a AG porous

'porpora SF purple

'porre /**77**/ VT (*mettere*) to put; (*collocare*) to place; (*posare*) to lay (down), put (down); (*fig: supporre*): **poniamo (il caso) che …** let's suppose that … ■ **porsi** VPR (*mettersi*): **porsi a sedere/in cammino** to sit down/, set off; **~ le basi di** (*fig*) to lay the foundations of, establish; **~ una domanda a qn** to ask sb a question, put a question to sb; **~ la propria fiducia in** to place one's trust in sb; **~ fine** *o* **termine a qc** to put an end *o* a stop to sth; **posto che …** supposing that …, on the assumption that …; **porsi in salvo** to save o.s.

'porro SM (*Bot*) leek; (*Med*) wart

'porsi *ecc* VB *vedi* **porgere; porsi**

'porta SF door; (*Sport*) goal; (*Inform*) port ■ **porte** SFPL (*di città*) gates; **mettere qn alla ~** to throw sb out; **sbattere** *o* **chiudere la ~ in faccia a qn** (*anche fig*) to slam the door in sb's face; **trovare tutte le porte chiuse** (*fig*) to find the way barred; **a porte chiuse** (*Dir*) in camera; **l'inverno è alle porte** (*fig*) winter is upon us; **vendita ~ a ~** door-to-door selling; **~ di servizio** tradesmen's entrance; **~ di sicurezza** emergency exit; **~ stagna** watertight door

portaba'gagli [portaba'gaʎʎi] SM INV (*facchino*) porter; (*Aut, Ferr*) luggage rack

portabandi'era SM INV standard bearer

porta'borse SM INV (*peg*) lackey

portabot'tiglie [portabot'tiʎʎe] SM INV bottle rack

porta-'CD [portatʃi'di] SM INV (*mobile*) CD rack; (*astuccio*) CD holder

porta'cenere [porta'tʃenere] SM INV ashtray

portachi'avi [porta'kjavi] SM INV keyring

porta'cipria [porta'tʃiprja] SM INV powder compact

porta'erei SF INV (*nave*) aircraft carrier ▶ SM INV (*aereo*) aircraft transporter

portafi'nestra (*pl* **portefinestre**) SF French window

porta'foglio [porta'fɔʎʎo] SM (*busta*) wallet; (*cartella*) briefcase; (*Pol, Borsa*) portfolio; **~ titoli** investment portfolio

portafor'tuna SM INV lucky charm; mascot

portagi'oie [porta'dʒɔje], **portagioi'elli** [portadʒo'jelli] SM INV jewellery (BRIT) *o* jewelry (US) box

por'tale SM (*di chiesa, Inform*) portal

porta'lettere SM INV/F INV postman/woman (BRIT), mailman/woman (US)

porta'mento SM carriage, bearing

portamo'nete SM INV purse

por'tante AG (*muro ecc*) supporting, load-bearing

portan'tina SF sedan chair; (*per ammalati*) stretcher

portaog'getti [portaod'dʒetti] AG INV: **vano ~** (*in macchina*) glove compartment

portaom'brelli SM INV umbrella stand

porta'pacchi [porta'pakki] SM INV (*di moto, bicicletta*) luggage rack

porta'penne [porta'penne] SM INV pen holder; (*astuccio*) pencil case

por'tare /**72**/ VT (*sostenere, sorreggere: peso, bambino, pacco*) to carry; (*indossare: abito, occhiali*) to wear; (: *capelli lunghi*) to have; (*avere: nome, titolo*) to have, bear; (*recare*): **~ qc a qn** to take (*o* bring) sth to sb; (*fig: sentimenti*) to bear ■ **portarsi** VPR (*recarsi*) to go; **~ avanti** (*discorso, idea*) to pursue; **~ via** to take away; (*rubare*) to take; **~ i bambini a spasso** to take the children for a walk; **~ fortuna** to bring good luck; **~ qc alla bocca** to lift *o* put sth to one's lips; **porta bene i suoi anni** he's wearing well; **dove porta questa strada?** where does this road lead?, where does this road take you?; **il documento porta la tua firma** the document has *o* bears your signature; **non gli porto rancore** I don't bear him a grudge; **la polizia si è portata sul luogo del disastro** the police went to the scene of the disaster

portarit'ratti SM INV photo(graph) frame

portari'viste SM INV magazine rack

portasa'pone SM INV soap dish

portasiga'rette SM INV cigarette case

portas'pilli SM INV pincushion

por'tata SF (*vivanda*) course; (*Aut*) carrying (*o* loading) capacity; (*di arma*) range; (*volume d'acqua*) (rate of) flow; (*fig: limite*) scope, capability; (: *importanza*) impact, import; **alla ~ di tutti** (*conoscenza*) within everybody's capabilities; (*prezzo*) within everybody's means; **a/fuori ~**

p

(di) within/out of reach (of); **a ~ di mano** within (arm's) reach; **di grande ~** of great importance

por'tatile AG portable

por'tato, -a AG (*incline*): **~ a** inclined *o* apt to

porta'tore, -'trice SM/F (*anche Comm*) bearer; (*Med*) carrier; **pagabile al ~** payable to the bearer; **~ di handicap** person with a disability

portatovagli'olo [portatovaʎ'ʎɔlo] SM napkin ring

portau'ovo SM INV eggcup

porta'voce [porta'votʃe] SM O F INV spokesperson, spokesman(-woman)

por'tello SM (*di portone*) door; (*Naut*) hatch

portel'lone SM (*Naut, Aer*) hold door

por'tento SM wonder, marvel

porten'toso, -a AG wonderful, marvellous (*BRIT*), marvelous (*US*)

porti'cato SM portico

'portico, -ci SM portico; (*riparo*) lean-to

porti'era SF (*Aut*) door

porti'ere, -a SM/F (*portinaio*) concierge, caretaker; (*di hotel*) porter; (*nel calcio*) goalkeeper

porti'naio, -a SM/F concierge, caretaker

portine'ria SF caretaker's lodge

'porto, -a PP *di* **porgere** ▶ SM (*Naut*) harbour (*BRIT*), harbor (*US*), port; (*spesa di trasporto*) carriage ▶ SM INV port (wine); **andare** *o* **giungere in ~** (*fig*) to come to a successful conclusion; **condurre qc in ~** to bring sth to a successful conclusion; **~ d'armi** gun licence (*BRIT*) *o* license (*US*); **~ fluviale** river port; **~ franco** free port; **~ marittimo** seaport; **~ militare** naval base; **~ pagato** carriage paid, post free *o* paid; **~ di scalo** port of call

Porto'gallo SM: **il ~** Portugal

porto'ghese [porto'gese] AG, SMF, SM Portuguese *inv*

por'tone SM main entrance, main door

portori'cano, -a AG, SM/F Puerto Rican

Porto'rico SF Puerto Rico

portu'ale AG harbour *cpd* (*BRIT*), harbor *cpd* (*US*), port *cpd* ▶ SM dock worker

porzi'one [por'tsjone] SF portion, share; (*di cibo*) portion, helping

'posa SF (*Fot*) exposure; (*atteggiamento, di modello*) pose; (*riposo*): **lavorare senza ~** to work without a break; **mettersi in ~** to pose; **teatro di ~** photographic studio

posa'cenere [posa'tʃenere] SM INV ashtray

po'sare /72/ VT to put (down), lay (down) ▶ VI (*ponte, edificio, teoria*): **~ su** to rest on; (*Fot: atteggiarsi*) to pose ▪ **posarsi** VPR (*ape, aereo*) to land; (*uccello*) to alight; (*sguardo*) to settle

po'sata SF piece of cutlery ▪ **posate** SFPL cutlery *sg*

posa'tezza [posa'tettsa] SF (*di persona*) composure; (*di discorso*) balanced nature

po'sato, -a AG steady; (*discorso*) balanced

pos'critto SM postscript

'posi ecc VB *vedi* **porre**

positiva'mente AV positively; (*rispondere*) in the affirmative, affirmatively

posi'tivo, -a AG positive

posizi'one [pozit'tsjone] SF position; **farsi una ~** to make one's way in the world; **prendere ~** (*fig*) to take a stand; **luci di ~** (*Aut*) sidelights

posolo'gia, -'gie [pozolo'dʒia] SF dosage, directions *pl* for use

pos'porre /77/ VT to place after; (*differire*) to postpone, defer

pos'posto, -a PP *di* **posporre**

posse'dere /107/ VT to own, possess; (*qualità, virtù*) to have, possess; (*conoscere a fondo: lingua ecc*) to have a thorough knowledge of; (*ira ecc*) to possess

possedi'mento SM possession

pos'sente AG strong, powerful

posses'sivo, -a AG possessive

pos'sesso SM ownership *no pl*; possession; **essere in ~ di** to be in possession of sth; **prendere ~** to take possession of sth; **entrare in ~** to come into one's inheritance

posses'sore SM owner

pos'sibile AG possible ▶ SM: **fare tutto il ~** to do everything possible; **nei limiti del ~** as far as possible; **al più tardi ~** as late as possible; **vieni prima ~** come as soon as possible

possibi'lista, -i, -e AG: **essere ~** to keep an open mind

possibilità SF INV possibility ▶ SFPL (*mezzi*) means; **aver la ~ di fare** to be in a position to do; to have the opportunity to do; **nei limiti delle nostre ~** in so far as we can

possibil'mente AV if possible

possi'dente SMF landowner

possi'edo ecc VB *vedi* **possedere**

'posso ecc VB *vedi* **potere**

post... PREFISSO post...

'posta SF (*servizio*) post, postal service; (*corrispondenza*) post, mail; (*ufficio postale*) post office; (*nei giochi d'azzardo*) stake; (*Caccia*) hide (*BRIT*), blind (*US*) ▪ **poste** SFPL (*amministrazione*) post office; **fare la ~ a qn** (*fig*) to lie in wait for sb; **la ~ in gioco è troppo alta** (*fig*) there's too much at stake; **a bella ~** (*apposta*) on purpose; **piccola ~** (*su giornale*) letters to the editor, letters page; **~ elettronica** email, electronic mail; **~ in arrivo** inbox; **~ inviata** sent items; **~ in uscita** outbox; **~ ordinaria** ≈ second-class mail; **~ prioritaria** first class (post); **Poste e Telecomunicazioni** *postal and telecommunications service*; **ministro delle Poste e Telecomunicazioni** Postmaster General

In addition to postal services, Italian post offices (ufficio postale) offer various banking and business services. They are usually open only in the morning, Monday to Saturday, but main post offices are open all day.

posta'giro [posta'dʒiro] SM post office cheque (BRIT) o check (US), postal giro (BRIT)

pos'tale AG postal, post office cpd ▸ SM (treno) mail train; (nave) mail boat; (furgone) mail van; **timbro ~** postmark

postazi'one [postat'tsjone] SF (Mil) emplacement

post'bellico, -a, -ci, -che AG postwar

postda'tare /72/ VT to postdate

posteggi'are [posted'dʒare] /62/ VT, VI to park

posteggia'tore, -'trice [posteddʒa'tore] SM/F car-park attendant (BRIT), parking-lot attendant (US)

pos'teggio [pos'teddʒo] SM car park (BRIT), parking lot (US); (di taxi) rank (BRIT), stand (US)

postelegra'fonico, -a, -ci, -che AG postal and telecommunications cpd

'poster SM INV poster

'posteri SMPL posterity sg; **i nostri ~** our descendants

posteri'ore AG (dietro) back; (dopo) later ▸ SM (col: sedere) behind

posteri'ori: a posteri'ori ag inv after the event ▸ AV (dopo sostantivo) looking back

pos'ticcio, -a, -ci, -ce [pos'tittʃo] AG false ▸ SM hairpiece

postici'pare [postitʃi'pare] /72/ VT to defer, postpone

pos'tilla SF marginal note

pos'tino, -a SM/F postman(-woman) (BRIT), mailman(-woman) (US)

'posto, -a PP di **porre** ▸ SM (sito, posizione) place; (impiego) job; (spazio libero) room, space; (di parcheggio) space; (sedile: al teatro, in treno ecc) seat; (Mil) post; **a ~** (in ordine) in place, tidy; (fig) settled; (persona) reliable; **mettere a ~** (riordinare) to tidy (up), put in order; (faccende: sistemare) to straighten out; **prender ~** to take a seat; **al ~ di** in place of; **sul ~** on the spot; **~ di blocco** roadblock; **~ di lavoro** job; **~ di polizia** police station; **~ telefonico pubblico** public telephone; **~ di villeggiatura** holiday (BRIT) o tourist spot; **posti in piedi** (Teat, in autobus) standing room

postopera'torio, -a AG (Med) postoperative

pos'tribolo SM brothel

post'scriptum SM INV postscript

'postumo, -a AG posthumous; (tardivo) belated ▪ **postumi** SMPL (conseguenze) after-effects, consequences

po'tabile AG drinkable; **acqua ~** drinking water

po'tare /72/ VT to prune

po'tassio SM potassium

pota'tura SF pruning

po'tente AG (nazione) strong, powerful; (veleno, farmaco) potent, strong

poten'tino, -a AG of (o from) Potenza

Po'tenza [po'tɛntsa] SF Potenza

po'tenza [po'tɛntsa] SF power; (forza) strength; **all'ennesima ~** to the nth degree; **le Grandi Potenze** the Great Powers; **~ militare** military might o strength

potenzi'ale [poten'tsjale] AG, SM potential

potenzia'mento [potentsja'mento] SM development

potenzi'are [poten'tsjare] /19/ VT to develop

---

po'tere

/78/ SM power; **al potere** (partito ecc) in power; **potere d'acquisto** purchasing power; **potere esecutivo** executive power; **potere giudiziario** legal power; **potere legislativo** legislative power

▸ VB AUS **1** (essere in grado di) can, be able to; **non ha potuto ripararlo** he couldn't o he wasn't able to repair it; **non è potuto venire** he couldn't o he wasn't able to come; **spiacente di non poter aiutare** sorry not to be able to help

2 (avere il permesso) can, may, be allowed to; **posso entrare?** can o may I come in?; **posso chiederti, dove sei stato?** where, may I ask, have you been?

3 (eventualità) may, might, could; **potrebbe essere vero** it might o could be true; **può aver avuto un incidente** he may o might o could have had an accident; **può darsi** perhaps; **può darsi** o **può essere che non venga** he may o might not come

4 (augurio): **potessi almeno parlargli!** if only I could speak to him!

5 (suggerimento): **potresti almeno scusarti!** you could at least apologize!

▸ VT can, be able to; **può molto per noi** he can do a lot for us; **non ne posso più** (per stanchezza) I'm exhausted; (per rabbia) I can't take any more

---

potestà SF (potere) power; (Dir) authority

potrò ecc VB vedi **potere**

pove'raccio, -a, -ci, -ce [pove'rattʃo] SM/F poor devil

'povero, -a AG poor; (disadorno) plain, bare ▸ SM/F poor man/woman; **i poveri** the poor; **~ di** lacking in, having little; **minerale ~ di ferro** ore with a low iron content; **paese ~ di risorse** country short of o lacking in resources

povertà SF poverty; **~ energetica** fuel poverty

pozi'one [pot'tsjone] SF potion

273

p

'**pozza** [ˈpottsa] SF pool

poz'zanghera [potˈtsangera] SF puddle

'**pozzo** [ˈpottso] SM well; (cava: di carbone) pit; (di miniera) shaft; ~ **nero** cesspit; ~ **petrolifero** oil well

pp. ABBR (= pagine) pp

p.p. ABBR (= per procura) pp

PP.TT. ABBR = **Poste e Telecomunicazioni**

PR SIGLA = **Parma** ▶ SIGLA M (Pol) = **Partito Radicale**

P.R. ABBR = **piano regolatore; procuratore della Repubblica**

P.R.A. [pra] SIGLA M (= Pubblico Registro Automobilistico) ≈ DVLA

'**Praga** SF Prague

prag'matico, -a, -ci, -che AG pragmatic

pram'matica SF custom; **essere di** ~ to be customary

pranotera'pia SF pranotherapy

pran'zare [pranˈdzare] /**72**/ VI to dine, have dinner, to lunch, have lunch

'**pranzo** [ˈprandzo] SM dinner; (a mezzogiorno) lunch

'**prassi** SF usual procedure

'**pratica, -che** SF practice; (esperienza) experience; (conoscenza) knowledge, familiarity; (tirocinio) training, practice; (Amm: affare) matter, case; (: incartamento) file, dossier; **in** ~ (praticamente) in practice; **mettere in** ~ to put into practice; **fare le pratiche per** (Amm) to do the paperwork for; ~ **restrittiva** restrictive practice; **pratiche illecite** dishonest practices

prati'cabile AG (progetto) practicable, feasible; (luogo) passable, practicable

pratica'mente AV (in modo pratico) in a practical way, practically; (quasi) practically, almost

prati'cante SMF apprentice, trainee; (Rel) (regular) churchgoer

prati'care /**20**/ VT to practise (BRIT), practice (US); (Sport: tennis ecc) to play; (: nuoto, scherma ecc) to go in for; (eseguire: apertura, buco) to make; ~ **uno sconto** to give a discount

praticità [pratitʃiˈta] SF practicality, practicalness; **per** ~ for practicality's sake

'**pratico, -a, -ci, -che** AG practical; ~ **di** (esperto) experienced o skilled in; (familiare) familiar with; **all'atto** ~ in practice; **è** ~ **del mestiere** he knows his trade; **mi è più** ~ **venire di pomeriggio** it's more convenient for me to come in the afternoon

'**prato** SM meadow; (di giardino) lawn

preal'larme SM warning (signal)

Pre'alpi SFPL: **le** ~ (the) Pre-Alps

preal'pino, -a AG of the Pre-Alps

pre'ambolo SM preamble; **senza tanti preamboli** without beating about (BRIT) o around (US) the bush

preannunci'are [preannunˈtʃare] /**14**/, **preannunzi'are** [preannunˈtsjare] VT to give advance notice of

preavvi'sare /**72**/ VT to give advance notice of

preav'viso SM notice; **telefonata con** ~ personal o person to person call

pre'bellico, -a, -ci, -che AG prewar cpd

precari'ato SM temporary employment

precarietà SF precariousness

pre'cario, -a AG precarious; (Ins) temporary, without tenure

precauzio'nale [prekauttsjoˈnale] AG precautionary

precauzi'one [prekautˈtsjone] SF caution, care; (misura) precaution; **prendere precauzioni** to take precautions

prece'dente [pretʃeˈdɛnte] AG previous ▶ SM precedent; **il discorso/film** ~ the previous o preceding speech/film; **senza precedenti** unprecedented; **precedenti penali** (Dir) criminal record sg

precedente'mente [pretʃedenteˈmente] AV previously

prece'denza [pretʃeˈdɛntsa] SF priority, precedence; (Aut) right of way; **dare** ~ **assoluta a qc** to give sth top priority

pre'cedere [preˈtʃɛdere] /**29**/ VT to precede, go o (come) before

precet'tare [pretʃetˈtare] /**72**/ VT (lavoratori) to order back to work (via an injunction)

precettazi'one [pretʃettatˈtsjone] SF (di lavoratori) order to resume work

pre'cetto [preˈtʃetto] SM precept; (Mil) call-up notice

precet'tore [pretʃetˈtore] SM (private) tutor

precipi'tare [pretʃipiˈtare] /**72**/ VI (cadere) to fall headlong; (fig: situazione) to get out of control ▶ VT (gettare dall'alto in basso) to hurl, fling; (fig: affrettare) to rush ■ **precipitarsi** VPR (gettarsi) to hurl o fling o.s.; (affrettarsi) to rush

precipi'tato, -a [pretʃipiˈtato] AG hasty ▶ SM (Chim) precipitate

precipitazi'one [pretʃipitatˈtsjone] SF (Meteor) precipitation; (fig) haste

precipi'toso, -a [pretʃipiˈtoso] AG (caduta, fuga) headlong; (fig: avventato) rash, reckless; (: affrettato) hasty, rushed

preci'pizio [pretʃiˈpittsjo] SM precipice; **a** ~ (fig: correre) headlong

pre'cipuo, -a [preˈtʃipuo] AG principal, main

precisa'mente [pretʃizaˈmente] AV (gen) precisely; (con esattezza) exactly

preci'sare [pretʃiˈzare] /**72**/ VT to state, specify; (spiegare) to explain (in detail); **vi preciseremo la data in seguito** we'll let you know the exact date later; **tengo a** ~ **che ...** I must point out that ...

precisazi'one [pretʃizatˈtsjone] SF clarification

precisi'one [pretʃiˈzjone] SF precision; accuracy; **strumenti di ~** precision instruments

pre'ciso, -a [preˈtʃizo] AG (esatto) precise; (accurato) accurate, precise; (deciso: idea) precise, definite; (uguale): **2 vestiti precisi** 2 dresses exactly the same; **sono le 9 precise** it's exactly 9 o'clock

pre'cludere /3/ VT to block, obstruct

pre'cluso, -a PP di **precludere**

pre'coce [preˈkɔtʃe] AG early; (bambino) precocious; (vecchiaia) premature

precocità [prekotʃiˈta] SF (di morte) untimeliness; (di bambino) precociousness

precon'cetto, -a [prekonˈtʃetto] AG preconceived ▶ SM preconceived idea, prejudice

pre'correre /28/ VT to anticipate; **~ i tempi** to be ahead of one's time

precorri'tore, -'trice SM/F precursor, forerunner

pre'corso, -a PP di **precorrere**

precur'sore SM forerunner, precursor

'preda SF (bottino) booty; (animale, fig) prey; **essere ~ di** to fall prey to; **essere in ~ a** to be prey to

pre'dare /72/ VT to plunder

preda'tore, -trice SM/F predator

prede'cessore, -a [predetʃesˈsore] SM/F predecessor

pre'della SF platform, dais, altar-step

predesti'nare /72/ VT to predestine

predestinazi'one [predestinatˈtsjone] SF predestination

pre'detto, -a PP di **predire** ▶ AG aforesaid, aforementioned

'predica, -che SF sermon; (fig) lecture, talking-to

predi'care /20/ VT, VI to preach

predica'tivo, -a AG predicative

predi'cato SM (Ling) predicate

predi'letto, -a PP di **prediligere** ▶ AG, SM/F favourite (BRIT), favorite (US)

predilezi'one [prediletˈtsjone] SF fondness, partiality; **avere una ~ per qc/qn** to be partial to sth/fond of sb

predi'ligere [prediˈlidʒere] /117/ VT to prefer, have a preference for

pre'dire /38/ VT to foretell, predict

predis'porre /77/ VT to get ready, prepare; **~ qn a qc** to predispose sb to sth

predisposizi'one [predispozitˈtsjone] SF (Med) predisposition; (attitudine) bent, aptitude; **avere ~ alla musica** to have a bent for music

predis'posto, -a PP di **predisporre**

predizi'one [preditˈtsjone] SF prediction

predomi'nante AG predominant

predomi'nare /72/ VI (prevalere) to predominate; (eccellere) to excel

predo'minio SM predominance; supremacy

preesis'tente AG pre-existent

pree'sistere /11/ VI to pre-exist

preesis'tito, -a PP di **preesistere**

prefabbri'cato, -a AG (Edil) prefabricated

prefazi'one [prefatˈtsjone] SF preface, foreword

prefe'renza [prefeˈrɛntsa] SF preference; **a ~ di** rather than; **di ~** preferably, by preference; **non ho preferenze** I have no preferences either way, I don't mind

preferenzi'ale [preferenˈtsjale] AG preferential; **corsia ~** (Aut) bus and taxi lane

prefe'ribile AG: **~ (a)** preferable (to), better (than); **sarebbe ~ andarsene** it would be better to go

preferibil'mente AV preferably

prefe'rire /55/ VT to prefer, like better; **~ il caffè al tè** to prefer coffee to tea, like coffee better than tea

pre'fetto SM prefect

prefet'tura SF prefecture

pre'figgersi [preˈfiddʒersi] /79/ VPR: **~ uno scopo** to set o.s. a goal

prefigu'rare /72/ VT (simboleggiare) to foreshadow; (prevedere) to foresee

pre'fisso, -a PP di **prefiggersi** ▶ SM (Ling) prefix; (Tel) dialling (BRIT) o dial (US) code

Preg. ABBR = **pregiatissimo**

pre'gare /80/ VI to pray ▶ VT (Rel) to pray to; (implorare) to beg; (chiedere): **~ qn di fare** to ask sb to do; **farsi ~** to need coaxing o persuading

pre'gevole [preˈdʒevole] AG valuable

pregherò ecc [pregeˈrɔ] VB vedi **pregare**

preghi'era [preˈgjɛra] SF (Rel) prayer; (domanda) request

pregi'arsi [preˈdʒarsi] /62/ VPR: **mi pregio di farle sapere che ...** I am pleased to inform you that ...

pregia'tissimo, -a [predʒaˈtissimo] AG (in lettere): **~ Signor G. Agnelli** G. Agnelli Esquire

pregi'ato, -a [preˈdʒato] AG (opera) valuable; (tessuto) fine; (valuta) strong; **vino ~** vintage wine

'pregio [ˈprɛdʒo] SM (stima) esteem, regard; (qualità) (good) quality, merit; (valore) value, worth; **il ~ di questo sistema è ...** the merit of this system is ...; **oggetto di ~** valuable object

pregiudi'care [predʒudiˈkare] /20/ VT to prejudice, harm, be detrimental to

pregiudi'cato, -a [predʒudiˈkato] SM/F (Dir) previous offender

pregiu'dizio [predʒuˈdittsjo] SM (idea errata) prejudice; (danno) harm no pl

preg'nante [prepˈpante] AG (fig) pregnant, meaningful

p

275

'pregno, -a ['preɲɲo] AG (*saturo*): **~ di** full of, saturated with

'prego ESCL (*a chi ringrazia*) don't mention it!; (*invitando qn ad accomodarsi*) please sit down!; (*invitando qn ad andare prima*) after you!

pregus'tare /72/ VT to look forward to

preis'toria SF prehistory

preis'torico, -a, -ci, -che AG prehistoric

pre'lato SM prelate

prela'vaggio [prela'vaddʒo] SM pre-wash

prelazi'one [prelat'tsjone] SF (*Dir*) pre-emption; **avere il diritto di ~ su qc** to have the first option on sth

preleva'mento SM (*Banca*) withdrawal; (*di merce*) picking up, collection

prele'vare /72/ VT (*denaro*) to withdraw; (*campione*) to take; (*merce*) to pick up, collect; (*polizia*) to take, capture

preli'evo SM (*Banca*) withdrawal; (*Med*): **fare un ~ (di)** to take a sample (of); **fare un ~ di sangue** to take a blood sample

prelimi'nare AG preliminary ◼ **preliminari** SMPL preliminary talks; preliminaries

pre'ludere /35/ VI: **~ a** (*preannunciare: crisi, guerra, temporale*) to herald, be a sign of; (*introdurre: dibattito ecc*) to introduce, be a prelude to

pre'ludio SM prelude

pre'luso, -a PP *di* **preludere**

pre-ma'man [prema'mã] SM INV maternity dress

prematrimoni'ale AG premarital

prema'turo, -a AG premature

premedi'tare /72/ VT to premeditate, plan

premeditazi'one [premeditat'tsjone] SF (*Dir*) premeditation; **con ~** AG premeditated ▶ AV with intent

'premere /29/ VT to press ▶ VI: **~ su** to press down on; (*fig*) to put pressure on; **~ a** (*fig: importare*) to matter to; **~ il grilletto** to pull the trigger

pre'messo, -a PP *di* **premettere** ▶ SF introductory statement, introduction; **mancano le premesse per una buona riuscita** we lack the basis for a successful outcome

pre'mettere /63/ VT to put before; (*dire prima*) to start by saying, state first; **premetto che ...** I must say first of all that ...; **premesso che ...** given that ...; **ciò premesso ...** that having been said ...

premi'are /19/ VT to give a prize to; (*fig: merito, onestà*) to reward

premiazi'one [premjat'tsjone] SF prize giving

'premier ['prɛmjer] SM INV premier

premi'nente AG pre-eminent

'premio SM prize; (*ricompensa*) reward; (*Comm*) premium; (*Amm: indennità*) bonus; **in ~ per** as a prize (*o* reward) for; **~ d'ingaggio** (*Sport*) signing-on fee; **~ di produzione** productivity bonus

pre'misi *ecc* VB *vedi* **premettere**

premoni'tore, -'trice AG premonitory

premonizi'one [premonit'tsjone] SF premonition

premu'nirsi /55/ VPR: **~ di** to provide o.s. with; **~ contro** to protect o.s. from, guard o.s. against

pre'mura SF (*fretta*) haste, hurry; (*riguardo*) attention, care ◼ **premure** SFPL (*attenzioni, cure*) care *sg*; **aver ~** to be in a hurry; **far ~ a qn** to hurry sb; **usare ogni ~ nei riguardi di qn, circondare qn di premure** to be very attentive to sb

premu'roso, -a AG thoughtful, considerate

prena'tale AG antenatal

'prendere /81/ VT to take; (*andare a prendere*) to get, fetch; (*ottenere*) to get; (*guadagnare*) to get, earn; (*catturare: ladro, pesce*) to catch; (*: collaboratore, dipendente*) to take on; (*: passeggero*) to pick up; (*chiedere: somma, prezzo*) to charge, ask; (*trattare: persona*) to handle ▶ VI (*colla, cemento*) to set; (*pianta*) to take; (*fuoco: nel camino*) to catch; (*voltare*): **~ a destra** to turn (to the) right ◼ **prendersi** VPR (*azzuffarsi*): **prendersi a pugni** to come to blows; **prende qualcosa?** (*da bere, da mangiare*) would you like something to eat (*o* drink)?; **prendo un caffè** I'll have a coffee; **~ a fare qc** to start doing sth; **~ qn/qc per** (*scambiare*) to take sb/sth for; **~ l'abitudine di** to get into the habit of; **~ fuoco** to catch fire; **~ le generalità di qn** to take down sb's particulars; **~ nota di** to take note of; **~ parte a** to take part in; **prendersi cura di qn/qc** to look after sb/sth; **prendersi un impegno** to take on a commitment; **prendersela** (*adirarsi*) to get annoyed; (*preoccuparsi*) to get upset, worry

prendi'sole SM INV sundress

preno'tare /72/ VT to book, reserve

prenotazi'one [prenotat'tsjone] SF booking, reservation

'prensile AG prehensile

preoccu'pante AG worrying

preoccu'pare /72/ VT to worry; to preoccupy ◼ **preoccuparsi** VPR: **preoccuparsi di qn/qc** to worry about sb/sth; **preoccuparsi per qn** to be anxious for sb

preoccupazi'one [preokkupat'tsjone] SF worry, anxiety

preordi'nato, -a AG preordained

prepa'rare /72/ VT to prepare; (*esame, concorso*) to prepare for ◼ **prepararsi** VPR (*vestirsi*) to get ready; **prepararsi a qc/a fare** to get ready *o* prepare (o.s.) for sth/to do; **~ da mangiare** to prepare a meal

prepa'rativi SMPL preparations

prepa'rato, -a AG (*gen*) prepared; (*pronto*) ready ▶ SM (*prodotto*) preparation

prepara'torio, -a AG preparatory

preparazi'one [preparat'tsjone] SF preparation; **non ha la necessaria ~ per svolgere questo lavoro** he lacks the qualifications necessary for the job

prepensiona'mento SM early retirement

preponde'rante AG predominant

pre'porre /77/ VT to place before; (fig) to prefer

preposizi'one [prepozit'tsjone] SF (Ling) preposition

pre'posto, -a PP di **preporre**

prepo'tente AG (persona) domineering, arrogant; (bisogno, desiderio) overwhelming, pressing ▶ SMF bully

prepo'tenza [prepo'tentsa] SF arrogance; (comportamento) arrogant behaviour (BRIT) o behavior (US)

pre'puzio [pre'puttsjo] SM (Anat) foreskin

preroga'tiva SF prerogative

'presa SF taking no pl; catching no pl; (di città) capture; (induramento: di cemento) setting; (appiglio, Sport) hold; (di acqua, gas) (supply) point; (piccola quantità: di sale ecc) pinch; (Carte) trick; **~ (di corrente)** socket; (al muro) point; **far ~ (colla)** to set; **ha fatto ~ sul pubblico** (fig) it caught the public's imagination; **~ rapida** (cemento) quick-setting; **di forte ~** (fig) with wide appeal; **essere alle prese con qc** (fig) to be struggling with sth; **macchina da ~** (Cine) cine camera (BRIT), movie camera (US); **~ d'aria** air inlet; **~ diretta** (Aut) direct drive; **~ in giro** leg-pull (BRIT), joke; **~ di posizione** stand

pre'sagio [pre'zadʒo] SM omen

presa'gire [preza'dʒire] /55/ VT to foresee

presa'lario SM (Ins) grant

'presbite AG long-sighted

presbiteri'ano, -a AG, SM/F Presbyterian

presbi'terio SM presbytery

pre'scindere [preʃ'ʃindere] /102/ VI: **~ da** to leave out of consideration; **a ~ da** apart from

pre'scisso, -a [preʃ'ʃisso] PP di **prescindere**

presco'lastico, -a, -ci, -che AG pre-school cpd

pres'critto, -a PP di **prescrivere**

pres'crivere /105/ VT to prescribe

prescrizi'one [preskrit'tsjone] SF (Med, Dir) prescription; (norma) rule, regulation; **cadere in ~** (Dir) to become statute-barred

'prese ecc VB vedi **prendere**

presen'tare /72/ VT to present; (Amm: inoltrare) to submit; (far conoscere): **~ qn (a)** to introduce sb (to) ■ **presentarsi** VPR (recarsi, farsi vedere) to present o.s., appear; (farsi conoscere) to introduce o.s.; (occasione) to arise; **~ qc in un'esposizione** to show o display sth at an exhibition; **~ qn in società** to introduce sb into society; **presentarsi come candidato** (Pol) to stand (BRIT) o run (US) as a candidate; **presentarsi bene/male** to have a good/poor appearance; **la situazione si presenta difficile** things aren't looking too good, things look a bit tricky

presentazi'one [prezentat'tsjone] SF presentation; introduction

pre'sente AG present; (questo) this ▶ SM present ▶ SF (lettera): **con la ~ vi comunico …** this is to inform you that … ▶ SMF person present; **i presenti** those present; **aver ~ qc/qn** to remember sth/sb; **essere ~ a una riunione** to be present at o attend a meeting; **tener ~ qn/qc** to keep sb/sth in mind; **esclusi i presenti** present company excepted

presenti'mento SM premonition

pre'senza [pre'zɛntsa] SF presence; (aspetto esteriore) appearance; **in ~ di** in (the) presence of; **di bella ~** of good appearance; **~ di spirito** presence of mind

presenzi'are [prezen'tsjare] /19/ VI: **~ a** to be present at, attend

pre'sepio, pre'sepe SM crib

preser'vare /72/ VT to protect; to save

preserva'tivo SM sheath, condom

'presi ecc VB vedi **prendere**

'preside SMF (Ins) head (teacher) (BRIT), principal (US); (di facoltà universitaria) dean; **~ di facoltà** (Università) dean of faculty

presi'dente SMF (Pol) president; (di assemblea, Comm) chairman(-woman); **il P~ della Camera** (Pol) ≈ the Speaker; **P~ del Consiglio (dei Ministri)** ≈ Prime Minister; **P~ della Repubblica** President of the Republic; see note

> The **Presidente del Consigtlio,** the Italian prime minister, is the leader of the government. He or she submits nominations for ministerial posts to the Presidente della Repubblica, who then appoints them, if approved. The **Presidente del Consiglio** is appointed by the **Presidente della Repubblica**, in consultation with the leaders of the parliamentary parties, former heads of state, the **Presidente della Camera** and the **Presidente del Senato**. The **Presidente della Repubblica** is the head of state. He or she must be an Italian citizen of at least 50 years of age, and is elected for a term of seven years by Parliament and by delegates from each of the Italian regions. He or she has the power to suspend the implementation of legislation and to dissolve one or both chambers of Parliament, and presides over the magistrates' governing body (the Consiglio Superiore della Magistratura).

presiden'tessa SF president; (moglie) president's wife; (di assemblea, Comm) chairwoman

presi'denza [presi'dɛntsa] SF presidency; office of president; chairmanship; **assumere la ~** to become president; to take the chair; **essere alla ~** to be president (o chairman); **candidato alla ~** presidential candidate; candidate for the chairmanship

presidenzi'ale [presidɛn'tsjale] AG presidential

presidi'are /19/ VT to garrison

pre'sidio SM garrison

presi'edere /29/ VT to preside over ▶ VI: ~ **a** to direct, be in charge of

'**preso, -a** PP *di* **prendere**

'**pressa** SF (*Tecn*) press

pres'sante AG (*bisogno, richiesta*) urgent, pressing

pressap'poco AV about, roughly, approximately

pres'sare /72/ VT (*anche fig*) to press; ~ **qn con richieste** to pursue sb with demands

pressi'one SF pressure; **far ~ su qn** to put pressure on sb; **subire forti pressioni** to be under strong pressure; ~ **sanguigna** blood pressure; ~ **atmosferica** atmospheric pressure

'**presso** AV (*vicino*) nearby, close at hand ▶ PREP (*vicino a*) near; (*accanto a*) beside, next to; (*in casa di*): ~ **qn** at sb's home; (*nelle lettere*) care of, c/o; (*alle dipendenza di*): **lavora ~ di noi** he works for o with us ▶ SMPL: **nei pressi di** near, in the vicinity of; **ha avuto grande successo ~ i giovani** it has been a hit with young people

pressoché [presso'ke] AV nearly, almost

pressuriz'zare [pressurid'dzare] /72/ VT to pressurize

prestabi'lire /55/ VT to arrange beforehand, arrange in advance

presta'nome SM INV/F INV (*peg*) figurehead

pres'tante AG good-looking

pres'tanza [pres'tantsa] SF (*robust*) good looks *pl*

pres'tare /72/ VT: ~ **(qc a qn)** to lend (sb sth o sth to sb) ■ **prestarsi** VPR (*offrirsi*): **prestarsi a fare** to offer to do; (*essere adatto*): **prestarsi a** to lend itself to, be suitable for; ~ **aiuto** to lend a hand; ~ **ascolto** o **orecchio** to listen; ~ **attenzione** to pay attention; ~ **fede a qc/qn** to give credence to sth/sb; ~ **giuramento** to take an oath; **la frase si presta a molteplici interpretazioni** the phrase lends itself to numerous interpretations

prestazi'one [prestat'tsjone] SF (*Tecn, Sport*) performance ■ **prestazioni** SFPL (*di persona: servizi*) services

prestigia'tore, -'trice [prestidʒa'tore] SM/F conjurer

pres'tigio [pres'tidʒo] SM (*potere*) prestige; (*illusione*): **gioco di ~** conjuring trick

prestigi'oso, -a [presti'dʒoso] AG prestigious

'**prestito** SM lending *no pl*; loan; **dar in ~** to lend; **prendere in ~** to borrow; ~ **bancario** bank loan; ~ **pubblico** public borrowing

'**presto** AV (*tra poco*) soon; (*in fretta*) quickly; (*di buon'ora*) early; **a ~** see you soon; ~ **o tardi** sooner or later; **fare ~ a fare qc** to hurry up and do sth; (*non costare fatica*) to have no trouble doing sth; **si fa ~ a criticare** it's easy to criticize; **è ancora ~ per decidere** it's still too early o too soon to decide

pre'sumere /12/ VT to presume, assume

presu'mibile AG (*dati, risultati*) likely

pre'sunsi *ecc* VB *vedi* **presumere**

pre'sunto, -a PP *di* **presumere** ▶ AG: **il ~ colpevole** the alleged culprit

presuntu'oso, -a AG presumptuous

presunzi'one [prezun'tsjone] SF presumption

presup'porre /77/ VT to suppose; to presuppose

presup'posto, -a PP *di* **presupporre** ▶ SM (*premessa*) supposition, premise; **partendo dal ~ che ...** assuming that ...; **mancano i presupposti necessari** the necessary conditions are lacking

'**prete** SM priest

preten'dente SMF pretender ▶ SM (*corteggiatore*) suitor

pre'tendere /120/ VT (*esigere*) to demand, require; (*sostenere*): ~ **che** to claim that; **pretende di aver sempre ragione** he thinks he's always right

pretenzi'oso, -a [preten'tsjoso] AG pretentious

preterintenzio'nale [preterintentsjo'nale] AG (*Dir*): **omicidio ~** manslaughter

pre'teso, -a PP *di* **pretendere** ▶ SF (*esigenza*) claim, demand; (*presunzione, sfarzo*) pretentiousness ▶ AV unpretentiously; **avanzare una pretesa** to put forward a claim o demand; **senza pretese** *ag* unpretentious

pre'testo SM pretext, excuse; **con il ~ di** on the pretext of

pretestu'oso, -a AG (*data, motivo*) used as an excuse

pre'tore SM magistrate

pre'tura SF (*Dir: sede*) magistrate's court (BRIT), circuit o superior court (US); (: *magistratura*) magistracy

preva'lente AG prevailing

prevalente'mente AV mainly, for the most part

preva'lenza [preva'lɛntsa] SF predominance

preva'lere /126/ VI to prevail

pre'valso, -a PP *di* **prevalere**

prevari'care /20/ VI (*abusare del potere*) to abuse one's power

prevaricazi'one [prevarikat'tsjone] SF (*abuso di potere*) abuse of power

preve'dere /82/ VT (*indovinare*) to foresee; (*presagire*) to foretell; (*considerare*) to make provision for; **nulla lasciava ~ che ...** there was nothing to suggest o to make one think that ...; **come previsto** as expected; **spese previste** anticipated expenditure; **previsto per martedì** scheduled for Tuesday

prev'edibile AG predictable; **non era assolutamente ~ che ...** no one could have foreseen that ...

prevedibil'mente AV as one would expect

preve'nire /128/ VT (*anticipare: obiezione*) to forestall; (: *domanda*) to anticipate; (*evitare*) to avoid, prevent; (*avvertire*): ~ **qn (di)** to warn sb (of); to inform sb (of)

preventi'vare /72/ vt (*Comm*) to estimate

preven'tivo, -a AG preventive ▶ SM (*Comm*) estimate; **fare un ~** to give an estimate; **bilancio ~** budget; **carcere ~** custody (*pending trial*)

preve'nuto, -a AG (*mal disposto*): ~ **(contro qc/qn)** prejudiced (against sth/sb)

prevenzi'one [preven'tsjone] SF prevention; (*preconcetto*) prejudice

previ'dente AG showing foresight; prudent

previ'denza [previ'dɛntsa] SF foresight; **istituto di ~** provident institution; **~ sociale** social security (*Brit*), welfare (*US*)

pre'vidi *ecc* VB *vedi* **prevedere**

'previo, -a AG (*Comm*): **~ avviso** upon notice; **~ pagamento** upon payment

previsi'one SF forecast, prediction; **previsioni meteorologiche** *o* **del tempo** weather forecast *sg*

pre'visto, -a PP *di* **prevedere** ▶ SM: **piú/meno del ~** more/less than expected; **prima del ~** earlier than expected

prezi'oso, -a [pret'tsjoso] AG precious; (*aiuto, consiglio*) invaluable ▶ SM jewel; valuable

prez'zemolo [pret'tsemolo] SM parsley

'prezzo ['prɛttso] SM price; **a ~ di costo** at cost, at cost price (*Brit*); **tirare sul ~** to bargain, haggle; **il ~ pattuito è di 1000 euro** the agreed price is 1000 euros; **~ d'acquisto/di vendita** purchase/selling price; **~ di fabbrica** factory price; **~ di mercato** market price; **~ scontato** reduced price; **~ unitario** unit price

P.R.I. SIGLA M (= *Partito Repubblicano Italiano*) *former political party*

prigi'one [pri'dʒone] SF prison

prigio'nia [pridʒo'nia] SF imprisonment

prigioni'ero, -a [pridʒo'njɛro] AG captive ▶ SM/F prisoner

'prima SF *vedi* **primo** ▶ AV before; (*in anticipo*) in advance, beforehand; (*per l'addietro*) at one time, formerly; (*più presto*) sooner, earlier; (*in primo luogo*) first ▶ CONG: **~ di fare/che parta** before doing/he leaves; **~ di** *prep* before; **~ o poi** sooner or later; **due giorni ~** two days before *o* earlier; **~ d'ora** before now

pri'mario, -a AG primary; (*principale*) chief, leading, primary ▶ SM/F (*medico*) head physician, chief physician

pri'mate SM (*Rel, Zool*) primate

prima'tista, -i, -e SM/F (*Sport*) record holder

pri'mato SM supremacy; (*Sport*) record

prima'vera SF spring

primave'rile AG spring *cpd*

primeggi'are [primed'dʒare] /62/ VI to excel, be one of the best

primi'tivo, -a AG (*gen*) primitive; (*significato*) original

pri'mizie [pri'mittsje] SFPL early produce *sg*

'primo, -a AG first; (*fig*) initial; basic; prime ▶ SM/F first (one) ▶ SM (*Cuc*) first course; (*in date*): **il ~ luglio** the first of July ▶ SF (*Teat*) first night; (*Cine*) première; (*Aut*) first (gear); **le prime ore del mattino** the early hours of the morning; **di prima mattina** early in the morning; **in prima pagina** (*Stampa*) on the front page; **ai primi freddi** at the first sign of cold weather; **ai primi di maggio** at the beginning of May; **i primi del Novecento** the early twentieth century; **viaggiare in prima** to travel first-class; **per prima cosa** firstly; **in ~ luogo** first of all, in the first place; **di prim'ordine** *o* **prima qualità** first-class, first-rate; **in un ~ tempo** *o* **momento** at first; **prima donna** leading lady; (*di opera lirica*) prima donna

primo'genito, -a [primo'dʒɛnito] AG, SM/F firstborn

pri'mordi SMPL beginnings

primordi'ale AG primordial

'primula SF primrose

princi'pale [printʃi'pale] AG main, principal ▶ SM manager, boss; **sede ~** head office

principal'mente [printʃipal'mente] AV mainly, principally

princi'pato [printʃi'pato] SM principality

'principe ['printʃipe] SM prince; **~ ereditario** crown prince

princi'pesco, -a, -schi, -sche [printʃi'pesko] AG (*anche fig*) princely

princi'pessa [printʃi'pessa] SF princess

principi'ante [printʃi'pjante] SMF beginner

principi'are [printʃi'pjare] /19/ VT, VI to start, begin

prin'cipio [prin'tʃipjo] SM (*inizio*) beginning, start; (*origine*) origin, cause; (*concetto, norma*) principle ▪ **principi** SMPL (*concetti fondamentali*) principles; **al** *o* **in ~** at first; **fin dal ~** right from the start; **per ~** on principle; **una questione di ~** a matter of principle; **~ attivo** active ingredient; **una persona di sani principi morali** a person of sound moral principles

pri'ore SM (*Rel*) prior

pri'ori: a pri'ori *ag inv* prior; a priori ▶ AV at first glance; initially; a priori

priorità SF priority; **avere la ~ (su)** to have priority (over)

priori'tario, -a AG of utmost importance; (*scelta*) first; (*interesse*) overriding; **posta prioritaria** first class (post)

'prisma, -i SM prism

pri'vare /72/ VT: **~ qn di** to deprive sb of ▪ **privarsi** VPR: **privarsi di** to go *o* do without

priva'tiva SF (*Econ*) monopoly

privatiz'zare [privatid'dzare] /72/ VT to privatize

privatizzazi'one [privatiddzat'tsjone] SF privatization

pri'vato, -a AG private ▶ SM/F (*anche:* **privato cittadino**) private citizen; **in ~** in private; **diritto ~** (*Dir*) civil law; **ritirarsi a vita privata** to withdraw from public life; **"non vendiamo a privati"** "wholesale only"

privazi'one [privat'tsjone] SF privation, hardship

privilegi'are [privile'dʒare] /62/ VT to favour (*BRIT*), favor (*US*), to grant a privilege to

privilegi'ato, -a [privile'dʒato] AG (*individuo, classe*) privileged; (*trattamento, Comm: credito*) preferential; **azioni privilegiate** preference shares (*BRIT*), preferred stock (*US*)

privi'legio [privi'lɛdʒo] SM privilege; **avere il ~ di fare** to have the privilege of doing, be privileged to do

'privo, -a AG: **~ di** without, lacking

pro PREP for, on behalf of ▶ SM INV (*utilità*) advantage, benefit; **a che ~?** what's the use?; **il ~ e il contro** the pros and cons

pro'babile AG probable, likely

probabilità SF INV probability; **con molta ~** very probably, in all probability

probabil'mente AV probably

pro'bante AG convincing

pro'blema, -i SM problem

proble'matico, -a, -ci, -che AG problematic; (*incerto*) doubtful ▶ SF problems *pl*

pro'boscide [pro'bɔʃʃide] SF (*di elefante*) trunk

procacci'are [prokat'tʃare] /14/ VT to get, obtain

procaccia'tore [prokattʃa'tore] SM: **~ d'affari** sales executive

pro'cace [pro'katʃe] AG (*donna, aspetto*) provocative

pro'cedere [pro'tʃedere] /29/ VI to proceed; (*comportarsi*) to behave; (*iniziare*): **~ a** to start; **~ contro** (*Dir*) to start legal proceedings against; **~ oltre** to go on ahead; **prima di ~ oltre** before going any further; **gli affari procedono bene** business is going well; **bisogna ~ con cautela** we have to proceed cautiously; **non luogo a ~** (*Dir*) nonsuit

procedi'mento [protʃedi'mento] SM (*modo di condurre*) procedure; (*di avvenimenti*) course; (*Tecn*) process; **~ penale** (*Dir*) criminal proceedings *pl*

proce'dura [protʃe'dura] SF (*Dir*) procedure

proces'sare [protʃes'sare] /72/ VT (*Dir*) to try

processi'one [protʃes'sjone] SF procession

pro'cesso [pro'tʃesso] SM (*Dir*) trial; proceedings *pl*; (*metodo*) process; **essere sotto ~** to be on trial; **mettere sotto ~** (*anche fig*) to put on trial; **~ di fabbricazione** manufacturing process; **~ di pace** peace process

processu'ale [protʃessu'ale] AG (*Dir*): **atti processuali** records of a trial; **spese processuali** legal costs

Proc. Gen. ABBR = **procuratore generale**

pro'cinto [pro'tʃinto] SM: **in ~ di fare** about to do, on the point of doing

pro'clama, -i SM proclamation

procla'mare /72/ VT to proclaim

proclamazi'one [proklamat'tsjone] SF proclamation, declaration

procrasti'nare /72/ VT (*data*) to postpone; (*pagamento*) to defer

procre'are /72/ VT to procreate

pro'cura SF (*Dir*) proxy, power of attorney; (*ufficio*) attorney's office; **per ~** by proxy; **la P~ della Repubblica** the Public Prosecutor's Office

procu'rare /72/ VT: **~ qc a qn** (*fornire*) to get *o* obtain sth for sb; (*causare: noie ecc*) to bring *o* give sb sth

procura'tore, -'trice SM/F (*Dir*) ≈ solicitor; (*: chi ha la procura*) holder of power of attorney; **~ generale** (*in corte d'appello*) public prosecutor; (*in corte di cassazione*) Attorney General; **~ legale** ≈ solicitor (*BRIT*), lawyer; **~ della Repubblica** (*in corte d'assise, tribunale*) public prosecutor

prodi'gare /80/ VT to be lavish with ▪ **prodigarsi** VPR: **prodigarsi per qn** to do all one can for sb

pro'digio [pro'didʒo] SM marvel, wonder; (*persona*) prodigy

prodigi'oso, -a [prodi'dʒoso] AG prodigious; phenomenal

'prodigo, -a, -ghi, -ghe AG lavish, extravagant

pro'dotto, -a PP *di* **produrre** ▶ SM product; **~ di base** primary product; **~ finale** end product; **~ interno lordo** gross domestic product; **~ nazionale lordo** gross national product; **prodotti agricoli** farm produce *sg*; **prodotti di bellezza** cosmetics; **prodotti chimici** chemicals

pro'duco *ecc* VB *vedi* **produrre**

pro'durre /90/ VT to produce

pro'dussi *ecc* VB *vedi* **produrre**

produttività SF productivity

produt'tivo, -a AG productive

produt'tore, -'trice AG producing *cpd* ▶ SM/F producer; **paese ~ di petrolio** oil-producing country

produzi'one [produt'tsjone] SF production; (*rendimento*) output; **~ in serie** mass production

pro'emio SM introduction, preface

Prof. ABBR (= *professore*) Prof

profa'nare /72/ VT to desecrate

pro'fano, -a AG (*mondano*) secular, profane; (*sacrilego*) profane

profe'rire /55/ VT to utter

profes'sare /72/ VT to profess; (*medicina ecc*) to practise (*BRIT*), practice (*US*)

professio'nale AG professional; **scuola ~** training college

professi'one SF profession; **di ~** professional, by profession; **libera ~** profession

professio'nista, -i, -e SM/F professional

profes'sore, -'essa SM/F (*Ins*) teacher; (: *di università*) lecturer; (: *titolare di cattedra*) professor; **~ d'orchestra** member of an orchestra

pro'feta, -i SM prophet

pro'fetico, -a, -ci, -che AG prophetic

profetiz'zare [profetid'dzare] /**72**/ VT to prophesy

profe'zia [profet'tsia] SF prophecy

pro'ficuo, -a AG useful, profitable

profi'lare /**72**/ VT to outline; (*ornare: vestito*) to edge ■ **profilarsi** VPR to stand out, be silhouetted; to loom up

profi'lassi SF (*Med*) preventive treatment, prophylaxis

profi'lattico, -a, -ci, -che AG prophylactic ▶ SM (*anticoncezionale*) sheath, condom

pro'filo SM profile; (*breve descrizione*) sketch, outline; **di ~** in profile

profit'tare /**72**/ VI: **~ di** (*trarre profitto*) to profit by; (*approfittare*) to take advantage of

pro'fitto SM advantage, profit, benefit; (*fig: progresso*) progress; (*Comm*) profit; **ricavare un ~ da** to make a profit from *o* out of; **vendere con ~** to sell at a profit; **conto profitti e perdite** profit and loss account

pro'fondere /**25**/ VT (*lodi*) to lavish; (*denaro*) to squander ■ **profondersi** VPR: **profondersi in** to be profuse in

profondità SF INV depth

pro'fondo, -a AG deep; (*rancore, meditazione*) profound ▶ SM depth(s), bottom; **~ 8 metri** 8 metres deep

pro'forma AG routine *cpd* ▶ SM INV formality ▶ AV: **fare qc ~** to do sth as a formality

'profugo, -a, -ghi, -ghe SM/F refugee

profu'mare /**72**/ VT to perfume ▶ VI to be fragrant ■ **profumarsi** VPR to put on perfume *o* scent

profumata'mente AV: **pagare qc ~** to pay through the nose for sth

profu'mato, -a AG (*fiore, aria*) fragrant; (*fazzoletto, saponetta*) scented; (*pelle*) sweet-smelling; (*persona*) with perfume on

profume'ria SF perfumery; (*negozio*) perfume shop

pro'fumo SM (*prodotto*) perfume, scent; (*fragranza*) scent, fragrance

profusi'one SF profusion; **a ~** in plenty

pro'fuso, -a PP *di* **profondere**

progeni'tore, -'trice [prodʒeni'tore] SM/F ancestor

proget'tare [prodʒet'tare] /**72**/ VT to plan; (*Tecn: edificio*) to plan, design; **~ di fare qc** to plan to do sth

progettazi'one [prodʒettat'tsjone] SF planning; **in corso di ~** at the planning stage

proget'tista, -i, -e [prodʒet'tista] SM/F designer

pro'getto [pro'dʒetto] SM plan; (*idea*) plan, project; **avere in ~ di fare qc** to be planning to do sth; **~ di legge** (*Pol*) bill

'prognosi ['proɲɲozi] SF (*Med*) prognosis; **essere in ~ riservata** to be on the danger list

pro'gramma, -i SM programme (*BRIT*), program (*US*); (*TV, Radio*) programmes *pl*; (*Ins*) syllabus, curriculum; (*Inform*) program; **avere in ~ di fare qc** to be planning to do sth; **~ applicativo** (*Inform*) application program

program'mare /**72**/ VT (*TV, Radio*) to put on; (*Inform*) to program; (*Econ*) to plan

programma'tore, -'trice SM/F (*Inform*) computer programmer (*BRIT*) *o* programer (*US*)

programmazi'one [programmat'tsjone] SF programming (*BRIT*), programing (*US*); planning

progre'dire /**55**/ VI to progress, make progress

progressi'one SF progression

progres'sista, -i, -e AG, SM/F progressive

progressiva'mente AV progressively

progres'sivo, -a AG progressive

pro'gresso SM progress *no pl*; **fare progressi** to make progress

proi'bire /**55**/ VT to forbid, prohibit; **~ a qn di fare qc** (*vietare*) to forbid sb to do sth; (*impedire*) to prevent sb from doing sth

proi'bitivo, -a AG prohibitive

proi'bito, -a AG forbidden; **"è ~ l'accesso"** "no admittance"; **"è ~ fumare"** "no smoking"

proibizi'one [proibit'tsjone] SF prohibition

proibizio'nismo [proibittsjo'nizmo] SM prohibition

proiet'tare /**72**/ VT (*gen, Geom, Cine*) to project; (: *presentare*) to show, screen; (*luce, ombra*) to throw, cast, project

proi'ettile SM projectile, bullet, shell *etc*

proiet'tore SM (*Cine*) projector; (*Aut*) headlamp; (*Mil*) searchlight

proiezi'one [projet'tsjone] SF (*Cine*) projection; showing

'prole SF children *pl*, offspring

proletari'ato SM proletariat

prole'tario, -a AG, SM/F proletarian

prolife'rare /**72**/ VI (*fig*) to proliferate

pro'lifico, -a, -ci, -che AG prolific

pro'lisso, -a AG verbose

'prologo, -ghi SM prologue

pro'lunga, -ghe SF (*di cavo elettrico ecc*) extension

prolunga'mento SM (*gen*) extension; (*di strada*) continuation

prolun'gare /80/ VT (discorso, attesa) to prolong; (linea, termine) to extend

prome'moria SM INV memorandum

pro'messa SF promise; fare/mantenere una ~ to make/keep a promise

pro'messo, -a PP di promettere

promet'tente AG promising

pro'mettere /63/ VT to promise ▶ VI to be o look promising; ~ a qn di fare to promise sb that one will do

promi'nente AG prominent

promi'nenza [promi'nentsa] SF prominence

promiscuità SF promiscuousness

pro'miscuo, -a AG: matrimonio ~ mixed marriage; nome ~ (Ling) common-gender noun

pro'misi ecc VB vedi promettere

promon'torio SM promontory, headland

pro'mosso, -a PP di promuovere

promo'tore, -'trice SM/F promoter, organizer

promozio'nale [promottsjo'nale] AG promotional; "vendita ~" "special offer"

promozi'one [promot'tsjone] SF promotion; ~ delle vendite sales promotion

promul'gare /80/ VT to promulgate

promulgazi'one [promulgat'tsjone] SF promulgation

promu'overe /66/ VT to promote

proni'pote SMF (di nonni) great-grandchild, great-grandson/granddaughter; (di zii) great-nephew/niece ■ pronipoti SMPL (discendenti) descendants

pro'nome SM (Ling) pronoun

pronomi'nale AG pronominal

pronosti'care /20/ VT to foretell, predict

pro'nostico, -ci SM forecast

pron'tezza [pron'tettsa] SF readiness; quickness, promptness; ~ di riflessi quick reflexes; ~ di spirito/mente readiness of wit/mind

'pronto, -a AG ready; (rapido) fast, quick, prompt; ~! (Tel) hello!; essere ~ a fare qc to be ready to do sth; ~ all'ira quick-tempered; a pronta cassa (Comm) cash (BRIT) o collect (US) on delivery; pronta consegna (Comm) prompt delivery; ~ soccorso (trattamento) first aid; (reparto) A&E (BRIT), ER (US)

prontu'ario SM manual, handbook

pro'nuncia [pro'nuntʃa] SF pronunciation

pronunci'are [pronun'tʃare] /14/ VT (parola, sentenza) to pronounce; (dire) to utter; (discorso) to deliver ■ pronunciarsi VPR to declare one's opinion; pronunciarsi a favore di/contro to pronounce o.s. in favour of/against; non mi pronuncio I'm not prepared to comment

pronunci'ato, -a [pronun'tʃato] AG (spiccato) pronounced, marked; (sporgente) prominent

pro'nunzia ecc [pro'nuntsja] = pronuncia ecc

propa'ganda SF propaganda

propagan'dare /72/ VT (idea) to propagandize; (prodotto, invenzione) to push, plug (col)

propa'gare /80/ VT (Fisica, Biol) to propagate; (notizia, idea, malattia) to spread ■ propagarsi VPR to propagate; to spread

propagaz'ione [propagat'tsjone] SF (vedi vb) propagation; spreading

prope'deutico, -a, -ci, -che AG (corso, trattato) introductory

pro'pendere /8/ VI: ~ per to favour (BRIT), favor (US), lean towards

propensi'one SF inclination, propensity; avere ~ a credere che ... to be inclined to think that ...

pro'penso, -a PP di propendere ▶ AG: essere ~ a qc to be in favour (BRIT) o favor (US) of sth; essere ~ a fare qc to be inclined to do sth

propi'nare /72/ VT to administer

pro'pizio, -a [pro'pittsjo] AG favourable (BRIT), favorable (US)

pro'porre /77/ VT (suggerire): ~ qc (a qn) to suggest sth (to sb); (candidato) to put forward; (legge, brindisi) to propose; ~ di fare to suggest o propose doing; proporsi di fare to propose o intend to do; proporsi una meta to set o.s. a goal

proporzio'nale [proportsjo'nale] AG proportional; (sistema) ~ (Pol) proportional representation system

proporzio'nato, -a [proportsjo'nato] AG: ~ a proportionate to, proportional to; ben ~ well-proportioned

proporzi'one [propor'tsjone] SF proportion; in ~ a in proportion to ■ proporzioni SFPL (dimensioni) proportions; di vaste proporzioni huge

pro'posito SM (intenzione) intention, aim; (argomento) subject, matter; a ~ di regarding, with regard to; a questo ~ on this subject; di ~ (apposta) deliberately, on purpose; a ~ by the way; capitare a ~ (cosa, persona) to turn up at the right time

proposizi'one [propozit'tsjone] SF (Ling) clause; (: periodo) sentence

pro'posto, -a PP di proporre ▶ SF proposal; (suggerimento) suggestion; fare una proposta to put forward a proposal; to make a suggestion; proposta di legge (Pol) bill

propria'mente AV (correttamente) properly, correctly; (in modo specifico) specifically; ~ detto in the strict sense of the word

proprietà SF INV (ciò che si possiede) property, estate; (caratteristica) property; (correttezza) correctness; essere di ~ di qn to belong to sb; ~ edilizia (developed) property; ~ privata private property

proprie'tario, -a SM/F owner; (di albergo ecc) proprietor, owner; (per l'inquilino) landlord/lady; ~ terriero landowner

'proprio, -a AG (*possessivo*) own; (: *impersonale*) one's; (*esatto*) exact, correct, proper; (*senso, significato*) literal; (*Ling: nome*) proper; (*particolare*): **~ di** characteristic of, peculiar to ▶ AV (*precisamente*) just, exactly; (*davvero*) really; (*affatto*): **non ... ~** not ... at all ▶ SM (*Comm*): **mettersi in ~** to set up on one's own; **l'ha visto con i (suoi) propri occhi** he saw it with his own eyes

propu'gnare [propuɲ'ɲare] **/15/** VT to support

propulsi'one SF propulsion; **a ~ atomica** atomic-powered

propul'sore SM (*Tecn*) propeller

'prora SF (*Naut*) bow(s), prow

'proroga, -ghe SF extension; postponement

proro'gare **/80/** VT to extend; (*differire*) to postpone, defer

pro'rompere **/97/** VI to burst out

pro'rotto, -a PP *di* **prorompere**

pro'ruppi *ecc* VB *vedi* **prorompere**

'prosa SF prose; (*Teat*): **la stagione della ~** the theatre season; **attore di ~** theatre actor; **compagnia di ~** theatrical company

pro'saico, -a, -ci, -che AG (*fig*) prosaic, mundane

pro'sciogliere [proʃ'ʃɔʎʎere] **/103/** VT to release; (*Dir*) to acquit

prosciogli'mento [proʃʃoʎʎi'mento] SM acquittal

prosci'olto, -a [proʃ'ʃɔlto] PP *di* **prosciogliere**

prosciu'gare [proʃʃu'gare] **/80/** VT (*terreni*) to drain, reclaim ■ **prosciugarsi** VPR to dry up

prosci'utto [proʃ'ʃutto] SM ham; **~ cotto/crudo** cooked/cured ham

pros'critto, -a PP *di* **proscrivere** ▶ SM/F exile; outlaw

pros'crivere **/105/** VT to exile, banish

proscrizi'one [proskrit'tsjone] SF (*esilio*) banishment, exile

prosecuzi'one [prosekut'tsjone] SF continuation

prosegui'mento SM continuation; **buon ~!** all the best!; (*a chi viaggia*) enjoy the rest of your journey!

prosegu'ire **/45/** VT to carry on with, continue ▶ VI to carry on, go on

pro'selito SM (*Rel, Pol*) convert

prospe'rare **/72/** VI to thrive

prosperità SF prosperity

'prospero, -a AG (*fiorente*) flourishing, thriving, prosperous

prospe'roso, -a AG (*robusto*) hale and hearty; (*ragazza*) buxom

prospet'tare **/72/** VT (*esporre*) to point out, show; (*ipotesi*) to advance; (*affare*) to outline ■ **prospettarsi** VPR to look, appear

prospet'tiva SF (*Arte*) perspective; (*veduta*) view; (*fig: previsione, possibilità*) prospect

pros'petto SM (*Disegno*) elevation; (*veduta*) view, prospect; (*facciata*) façade, front; (*tabella*) table; (*sommario*) summary

prospici'ente [prospi'tʃɛnte] AG: **~ qc** facing o overlooking sth

prossima'mente AV soon

prossimità SF nearness, proximity; **in ~ di** near (to), close to; **in ~ delle feste natalizie** as Christmas approaches

'prossimo, -a AG (*che viene subito dopo*) next; (*parente*) close; (*vicino*): **~ a** near (to), close to ▶ SM neighbour (*BRIT*), neighbor (*US*), fellow man; **nei prossimi giorni** in the next few days; **in un ~ futuro** in the near future; **~ venturo (pv)** (*Amm*): **venerdì ~ venturo** next Friday

prostata SF prostate (gland)

prostitu'irsi **/55/** VPR to prostitute o.s.

prosti'tuta SF prostitute

prostituzi'one [prostitut'tsjone] SF prostitution

pros'trare **/72/** VT (*fig*) to exhaust, wear out ■ **prostrarsi** VPR (*fig*) to humble o.s.; **prostrato dal dolore** overcome o prostrate with grief

prostrazi'one [prostrat'tsjone] SF prostration

protago'nista, -i, -e SM/F protagonist

pro'teggere [pro'tɛddʒere] **/83/** VT to protect

proteggi'slip [protɛddʒi'slip] SM INV panty liner

pro'teico, -a, -ci, -che AG protein *cpd*; **altamente ~** high in protein

prote'ina SF protein

pro'tendere **/120/** VT to stretch out

'protesi SF INV (*Med*) prosthesis

pro'teso, -a PP *di* **protendere**

pro'testa SF protest

protes'tante AG, SMF Protestant

protes'tare **/72/** VT, VI to protest ■ **protestarsi** VPR: **protestarsi innocente** *ecc* to protest one's innocence o that one is innocent *etc*

pro'testo SM (*Dir*) protest; **mandare una cambiale in ~** to dishonour (*BRIT*) o dishonor (*US*) a bill

protet'tivo, -a AG protective

pro'tetto, -a PP *di* **proteggere**

protetto'rato SM protectorate

protet'tore, -'trice SM/F protector; (*sostenitore*) patron ▶ AG (*Rel*): **santo ~** patron saint; **società protettrice dei consumatori** consumer protection society

protezi'one [protet'tsjone] SF protection; (*patrocinio*) patronage; **misure di ~** protective measures; **~ civile** civil defence (*BRIT*) o defense (*US*)

protezio'nismo [protettsjo'nizmo] SM protectionism

protocol'lare /72/ VT to register ▶ AG formal; of protocol

proto'collo SM protocol; (*registro*) register of documents ▶ AG INV: **foglio ~** foolscap; **numero di ~** reference number

pro'tone SM proton

pro'totipo SM prototype

pro'trarre /123/ VT (*prolungare*) to prolong ■ **protrarsi** VPR to go on, continue

pro'tratto, -a AG *di* **protrarre**

protube'ranza [protube'rantsa] SF protuberance, bulge

Prov. ABBR (= *provincia*) Prov

'prova SF (*esperimento, cimento*) test, trial; (*tentativo*) attempt, try; (*Mat*) proof *no pl*; (*Dir*) evidence *no pl*, proof *no pl*; (*Ins*) exam, test; (*Teat*) rehearsal; (*di abito*) fitting; **a ~ di** (*in testimonianza di*) as proof of; **a ~ di fuoco** fireproof; **assumere in ~** (*per lavoro*) to employ on a trial basis; **essere in ~** (*persona: per lavoro*) to be on trial; **mettere alla ~** to put to the test; **giro di ~** test *o* trial run; **fino a ~ contraria** until (it's) proved otherwise; **~ a carico/a discarico** (*Dir*) evidence for the prosecution/for the defence; **~ documentale** (*Dir*) documentary evidence; **~ generale** (*Teat*) dress rehearsal; **~ testimoniale** (*Dir*) testimonial evidence

pro'vare /72/ VT (*sperimentare*) to test; (*tentare*) to try, attempt; (*assaggiare*) to try, taste; (*sperimentare in sé*) to experience; (*sentire*) to feel; (*cimentare*) to put to the test; (*dimostrare*) to prove; (*abito*) to try on ■ **provarsi** VPR: **provarsi (a fare)** to try *o* attempt (to do); **~ a fare** to try *o* attempt to do

proveni'enza [prove'njɛntsa] SF origin, source

prove'nire /128/ VI: **~ da** to come from

pro'venti SMPL revenue *sg*

prove'nuto, -a PP *di* **provenire**

Pro'venza [pro'ventsa] SF: **la ~** Provence

proven'zale [proven'tsale] AG Provençal

pro'verbio SM proverb

pro'vetta SF test tube; **bambino in ~** test-tube baby

pro'vetto, -a AG skilled, experienced

pro'vider [pro'vaider] SM INV (*Inform*) service provider

pro'vincia, -ce *o* **-cie** [pro'vintʃa] SF province

provinci'ale [provin'tʃale] AG provincial; **(strada) ~** main road (BRIT), highway (US)

pro'vino SM (*Cine*) screen test; (*campione*) specimen

provo'cante AG (*attraente*) provocative

provo'care /20/ VT (*causare*) to cause, bring about; (*eccitare: riso, pietà*) to arouse; (*irritare, sfidare*) to provoke

provoca'tore, -'trice SM/F agitator ▶ AG: **agente ~** agent provocateur

provoca'torio, -a AG provocative

provocazi'one [provokat'tsjone] SF provocation

provve'dere /82/ VI (*prendere un provvedimento*) to take steps, act; (*disporre*): **~ (a)** to provide (for) ▶ VT: **~ qc a qn** to supply sth to sb ■ **provvedersi** VPR: **provvedersi di** to provide o.s. with

provvedi'mento SM measure; (*di previdenza*) precaution; **~ disciplinare** disciplinary measure

provvedito'rato SM (*Amm*): **~ agli studi** divisional education offices *pl*

provvedi'tore SM (*Amm*): **~ agli studi** divisional director of education

provvi'denza [provvi'dɛntsa] SF: **la ~** providence

provvidenzi'ale [provviden'tsjale] AG providential

provvigi'one [provvi'dʒone] SF (*Comm*) commission; **lavoro/stipendio a ~** job/salary on a commission basis

provvi'sorio, -a AG temporary; (*governo*) temporary, provisional

prov'vista SF (*riserva*) supply, stock; **fare ~ di** to stock up with

prov'visto, -a PP *di* **provvedere** ▶ SF provision, supply

pro'zia [prot'tsia] SF great-aunt

pro'zio, -zii [prot'tsio] SM great-uncle

'prua SF (*Naut*) bow(s), prow

pru'dente AG cautious, prudent; (*assennato*) sensible, wise

pru'denza [pru'dɛntsa] SF prudence, caution; wisdom; **per ~** as a precaution, to be on the safe side

'prudere /29/ VI to itch, be itchy

'prugna ['pruɲɲa] SF plum; **~ secca** prune

prurigi'noso, -a [pruridʒi'noso] AG itchy

pru'rito SM itchiness *no pl*; itch

PS SIGLA = **Pesaro**

P.S. ABBR (= *postscriptum*) PS; (*Comm*) = **partita semplice** ▶ SIGLA F (*Polizia*) = **Pubblica Sicurezza**

P.S.D.I. SIGLA M (= *Partito Socialista Democratico Italiano*) *former political party*

pseu'donimo SM pseudonym

PSI SIGLA M (= *Partito Socialista Italiano*) *former political party*

psica'nalisi SF psychoanalysis

psicana'lista, -i, -e SM/F psychoanalyst

psicanaliz'zare [psikanalid'dzare] /72/ VT to psychoanalyse

'psiche ['psike] SF (*Psic*) psyche

psiche'delico, -a, -ci, -che [psike'dɛliko] AG psychedelic

psichi'atra, -i, -e [psi'kjatra] SM/F psychiatrist

psichia'tria [psikja'tria] SF psychiatry

psichi'atrico, -a, -ci, -che [psi'kjatriko] AG

(*caso*) psychiatric; (*reparto, ospedale*) psychiatric, mental

'psichico, -a, -ci, -che ['psikiko] AG psychological

psico'farmaco, -ci SM (*Med*) drug used in treatment of mental conditions

psicolo'gia [psikolo'dʒia] SF psychology

psico'logico, -a, -ci, -che [psiko'lɔdʒiko] AG psychological

psi'cologo, -a, -gi, -ghe SM/F psychologist

psico'patico, -a, -ci, -che AG psychopathic ▶ SM/F psychopath

psi'cosi SF INV (*Med*) psychosis; (*fig*) obsessive fear

psicoso'matico, -a, -ci, -che AG psychosomatic

PT SIGLA = **Pistoia**

Pt. ABBR (*Geo*: = *punta*) Pt

P.T. ABBR (= *Posta e Telegrafi*) ≈ PO (= *Post Office*); (*Fisco*) = **polizia tributaria**

P.ta ABBR = **porta**

pubbli'care /20/ VT to publish

pubblicazi'one [pubblikat'tsjone] SF publication; **~ periodica** periodical; **pubblicazioni (matrimoniali)** (marriage) banns

pubbli'cista, -i, -e [pubbli'tʃista] SM/F (*Stampa*) freelance journalist

pubblicità [pubblitʃi'ta] SF (*diffusione*) publicity; (*attività*) advertising; (*annunci nei giornali*) advertisements *pl*; **fare ~ a qc** to advertise sth

pubblici'tario, -a [pubblitʃi'tarjo] AG advertising *cpd*; (*trovata, film*) publicity *cpd* ▶ SM/F advertising agent; **annuncio** *o* **avviso ~** advertisement

'pubblico, -a, -ci, -che AG public; (*statale: scuola ecc*) state *cpd* ▶ SM public; (*spettatori*) audience; **in ~** in public; **la pubblica amministrazione** public administration; **un ~ esercizio** a catering (*o* hotel *o* entertainment) business; **~ funzionario** civil servant; **Ministero della Pubblica Istruzione** ≈ Department of Education and Science (*BRIT*), ≈ Department of Health, Education and Welfare (*US*); **P~ Ministero** Public Prosecutor's Office; **la Pubblica Sicurezza** the police

'pube SM (*Anat*) pubis

pubertà SF puberty

'pudico, -a, -ci, -che AG modest

pu'dore SM modesty

puericul'tura SF infant care

pue'rile AG childish

pu'erpera SF woman who has just given birth

pugi'lato [pudʒi'lato] SM boxing

'pugile ['pudʒile] SM boxer

pugli'ese [puʎ'ʎese] AG of (*o* from) Puglia

pugna'lare [puɲɲa'lare] /72/ VT to stab

pu'gnale [puɲ'ɲale] SM dagger

'pugno ['puɲɲo] SM fist; (*colpo*) punch; (*quantità*) fistful; **avere qn in ~** to have sb in the palm of one's hand; **tenere la situazione in ~** to have control of the situation; **scrivere qc di proprio ~** to write sth in one's own hand

'pulce ['pultʃe] SF flea

pul'cino [pul'tʃino] SM chick

pu'ledro, -a SM/F colt/filly

pu'leggia, -ge [pu'leddʒa] SF pulley

pu'lire /55/ VT to clean; (*lucidare*) to polish; **far ~ qc** to have sth cleaned; **~ a secco** to dry-clean

pu'lito, -a AG (*anche fig*) clean; (*ordinato*) neat, tidy ▶ SF quick clean; **avere la coscienza pulita** to have a clear conscience

puli'tura SF cleaning; **~ a secco** dry-cleaning

puli'zia [pulit'tsia] SF (*atto*) cleaning; (*condizione*) cleanness; **fare le pulizie** to do the cleaning, do the housework; **~ etnica** ethnic cleansing

'pullman SM INV coach (*BRIT*), bus

pul'lover SM INV pullover, jumper

pullu'lare /72/ VI to swarm, teem

pul'mino SM minibus

'pulpito SM pulpit

pul'sante SM (push-)button

pul'sare /72/ VI to pulsate, beat

pulsazi'one [pulsat'tsjone] SF beat

pul'viscolo SM fine dust; **~ atmosferico** specks *pl* of dust

'puma SM INV puma

pun'gente [pun'dʒɛnte] AG prickly; stinging; (*anche fig*) biting

'pungere ['pundʒere] /84/ VT to prick; (*insetto, ortica*) to sting; (*freddo*) to bite; **~ qn sul vivo** (*fig*) to cut sb to the quick

pungigli'one [pundʒiʎ'ʎone] SM sting

pungo'lare /72/ VT to goad

pu'nire /55/ VT to punish

puni'tivo, -a AG punitive

punizi'one [punit'tsjone] SF punishment; (*Sport*) penalty

'punsi *ecc* VB *vedi* **pungere**

'punta SF point; (*parte terminale*) tip, end; (*di monte*) peak; (*di costa*) promontory; (*minima parte*) touch, trace; **in ~ di piedi** on tiptoe; **ore di ~** peak hours; **uomo di ~** (*Sport, Pol*) front-rank *o* leading man; **doppie punte** split ends

pun'tare /72/ VT (*piedi a terra, gomiti sul tavolo*) to plant; (*dirigere: pistola*) to point; (*scommettere*): **~ su** to bet on ▶ VI (*mirare*): **~ a** to aim at; (*avviarsi*): **~ su** to head *o* make for; (*fig: contare*): **~ su** to count *o* rely on

puntas'pilli SM INV = **portaspilli**

pun'tata SF (*gita*) short trip; (*scommessa*) bet; (*parte di opera*) instalment (*BRIT*), installment (*US*); **farò una ~ a Parigi** I'll pay a flying visit to Paris; **romanzo a puntate** serial

punteggi'are [punted'dʒare] /62/ VT to punctuate

punteggia'tura [puntedd͡ʒa'tura] SF (Ling) punctuation

pun'teggio [pun'tedd͡ʒo] SM score

puntel'lare /72/ VT to support

pun'tello SM prop, support

punteru'olo SM (Tecn) punch; (per stoffa) bodkin

pun'tiglio [pun'tiʎʎo] SM obstinacy, stubbornness

puntigli'oso, -a [puntiʎ'ʎoso] AG punctilious

pun'tina SF: ~ da disegno drawing pin (BRIT), thumb tack (US) ▪ **puntine** SFPL (Aut) points

pun'tino SM dot; **fare qc a ~** to do sth properly; **arrivare a ~** to arrive just at the right moment; **cotto a ~** cooked to perfection; **mettere i puntini sulle "i"** (fig) to dot the i's and cross the t's

'punto, -a PP di **pungere** ▸ SM point; (segno, macchiolina) dot; (Ling) full stop; (di indirizzo e-mail) dot; (posto) spot; (a scuola) mark; (nel cucire, nella maglia, Med) stitch ▸ AV: **non … ~** not … at all; **due punti** (inv: Ling) colon; **ad un certo ~** at a certain point; **fino ad un certo ~** (fig) to a certain extent; **sul ~ di fare** (just) about to do; **fare il ~** (Naut) to take a bearing; **fare il ~ della situazione** (analisi) to take stock of the situation; (riassunto) to sum up the situation; **alle 6 in ~** at 6 o'clock sharp o on the dot; **essere a buon ~** to have reached a satisfactory stage; **mettere a ~** to adjust; (motore) to tune; (cannocchiale) to focus; (fig) to settle; **venire al ~** to come to the point; **vestito di tutto ~** all dressed up; **di ~ in bianco** point-blank; **~ d'arrivo** arrival point; **~ cardinale** point of the compass, cardinal point; **~ debole** weak point; **~ esclamativo/interrogativo** exclamation/question mark; **~ d'incontro** meeting place, meeting point; **~ morto** standstill; **~ nero** (comedone) blackhead; **~ nevralgico** (anche fig) nerve centre (BRIT) o center (US); **~ di partenza** (anche fig) starting point; **~ di riferimento** landmark; (fig) point of reference; **~ di vendita** retail outlet; **~ e virgola** semicolon; **~ di vista** (fig) point of view; **punti di sospensione** suspension points

puntu'ale AG punctual

puntualità SF punctuality

puntualiz'zare [puntualid'dzare] /72/ VT to make clear

puntual'mente AV (gen) on time; (ironico: al solito) as usual

pun'tura SF (di ago) prick; (di insetto) sting, bite; (Med) puncture; (: iniezione) injection; (dolore) sharp pain

punzecchi'are [puntsek'kjare] /19/ VT to prick; (fig) to tease

punzo'nare [puntso'nare] /72/ VT (Tecn) to stamp

pun'zone [pun'tsone] SM (per metalli) stamp, die

può VB vedi **potere**

puoi VB vedi **potere**

'pupa SF doll

pu'pazzo [pu'pattso] SM puppet

pu'pillo, -a SM/F (Dir) ward; (prediletto) favourite (BRIT), favorite (US), pet ▸ SF (Anat) pupil

purché [pur'ke] CONG provided that, on condition that

'pure CONG (tuttavia) and yet, nevertheless; (anche se) even if ▸ AV (anche) too, also; **pur di** (al fine di) just to; **faccia ~!** go ahead!, please do!

purè SM, **pu'rea** SF (Cuc) purée; (di patate) mashed potatoes pl

pu'rezza [pu'rettsa] SF purity

'purga, -ghe SF purging no pl; purge

pur'gante SM (Med) purgative, purge

pur'gare /80/ VT (Med, Pol) to purge; (pulire) to clean

purga'torio SM purgatory

purifi'care /20/ VT to purify; (metallo) to refine

purificazi'one [purifikat'tsjone] SF purification; refinement

puri'tano, -a AG, SM/F puritan

'puro, -a AG pure; (acqua) clear, limpid; (vino) undiluted; **di razza pura** thoroughbred; **per ~ caso** by sheer chance, purely by chance

puro'sangue SM INV/F INV thoroughbred

pur'troppo AV unfortunately

pus SM pus

pusil'lanime AG cowardly

'pustola SF pimple

puta'caso AV just supposing, suppose

puti'ferio SM rumpus, row

putre'fare /41/ VI to putrefy, rot

putre'fatto, -a PP di **putrefare**

putrefazi'one [putrefat'tsjone] SF putrefaction

'putrido, -a AG putrid, rotten

put'tana SF (col) whore (!)

'putto SM cupid

'puzza ['puttsa] SF = **puzzo**

puz'zare [put'tsare] /72/ VI to stink; **la faccenda puzza (d'imbroglio)** the whole business stinks

'puzzo ['puttso] SM stink, foul smell

'puzzola ['puttsola] SF polecat

puzzo'lente [puttso'lɛnte] AG stinking

PV SIGLA = **Pavia**

pv ABBR = **prossimo venturo**

P.V.C. [pivi'tʃi] SIGLA M (= polyvinyl chloride) PVC

PZ SIGLA = **Potenza**

p.za ABBR = **piazza**

Qq

Q, q¹ [ku] SM O F INV (*lettera*) Q, q; **Q come Quarto** ≈ Q for Queen

q² ABBR (= *quintale*) q

Qa'tar [ka'tar] SM: **il ~** Qatar

q.b. ABBR (= *quanto basta*) as needed; (= *zucchero q.b.*) sugar to taste

Q.G. ABBR = **quartier generale**

Q.I. ABBR = **quoziente d'intelligenza**

qua AV here; **in ~** (*verso questa parte*) this way; **~ dentro/sotto** *ecc* in/under here *etc*; **da un anno in ~** for a year now; **da quando in ~?** since when?; **per di ~** (*passare*) this way; **al di ~ di** (*fiume, strada*) on this side of; **~ dentro/fuori** *ecc* in/out here *ecc*; *vedi anche* **questo**

'quacchero, -a ['kwakkero] SM/F Quaker

qua'derno SM notebook; (*per scuola*) exercise book

qua'drangolo SM quadrangle

qua'drante SM quadrant; (*di orologio*) face

qua'drare /72/ VI (*bilancio*) to balance, tally; (*fig: corrispondere*): **~ (con)** to correspond (with) ▶ VT (*Mat*) to square; **far ~ il bilancio** to balance the books; **non mi quadra** I don't like it

qua'drato, -a AG square; (*fig: equilibrato*) level-headed, sensible; (*peg*) square ▶ SM (*Mat*) square; (*Pugilato*) ring; **5 al ~** 5 squared

quadret'tato, -a AG (*foglio*) squared; (*tessuto*) checked

qua'dretto SM: **a quadretti** (*tessuto*) checked; (*foglio*) squared

quadrien'nale AG (*che dura 4 anni*) four-year *cpd*; (*che avviene ogni 4 anni*) four-yearly

quadri'foglio [kwadri'fɔʎʎo] SM four-leaf clover

quadri'mestre SM (*periodo*) four-month period; (*Ins*) term

'quadro SM (*pittura*) painting, picture; (*quadrato*) square; (*tabella*) table, chart; (*Tecn*) board, panel; (*Teat*) scene; (*fig: scena, spettacolo*) sight; (: *descrizione*) outline, description ▦ **quadri** SMPL (*Pol*) party organizers; (*Comm*) managerial staff; (*Mil*) cadres; (*Carte*) diamonds; **a quadri** (*disegno*) checked; **fare un ~ della situazione** to outline the situation; **~ clinico** (*Med*) case history; **~ di comando** control panel; **quadri intermedi** middle management *sg*

qua'drupede SM quadruped

quadrupli'care /20/ VT to quadruple

'quadruplo, -a AG, SM quadruple

quaggiù [kwad'dʒu] AV down here

'quaglia ['kwaʎʎa] SF quail

'qualche ['kwalke]

DET **1** some, a few; (*in interrogative*) any; **ho comprato qualche libro** I've bought some *o* a few books; **qualche volta** sometimes; **hai qualche sigaretta?** have you any cigarettes? **2** (*uno*): **c'è qualche medico?** is there a doctor?; **in qualche modo** somehow **3** (*un certo, parecchio*) some; **un personaggio di qualche rilievo** a figure of some importance **4**: **qualche cosa = qualcosa**

---

qualche'duno [kwalke'duno] PRON = **qualcuno**

qual'cosa PRON something; (*in espressioni interrogative*) anything; **qualcos'altro** something else; anything else; **~ di nuovo** something new; anything new; **~ da mangiare** something to eat; anything to eat; **c'è ~ che non va?** is there something wrong?

qual'cuno PRON (*persona*) someone, somebody; (: *in espressioni interrogative*) anyone, anybody; (*alcuni*) some; **~ è favorevole a noi** some are on our side; **qualcun altro** someone *o* somebody else; anyone *o* anybody else

---

Someone/somebody e **anyone/anybody** sono seguiti dal verbo al singolare e, nel linguaggio corrente, dal possessivo al plurale.
Qualcuno ha scritto il suo nome sulla porta. **Somebody has written their name on the door.**
Nel linguaggio più formale si specifica **his** o **her**.
Qualcuno ha portato la sua carta di credito? **Has anyone brought his/her credit card?**

'quale

(*spesso troncato in* **qual**) DET **1** (*interrogativo*) what; (: *scegliendo tra due o più cose o persone*) which; **quale uomo/denaro?** what man/money?; which man/money?; **quali sono i tuoi programmi?** what are your plans?; **quale stanza preferisci?** which room do you prefer?

2 (*relativo: come*): **il risultato fu quale ci si aspettava** the result was as expected **3** (*in elenchi*) such as, like; **piante quali l'edera** plants such as *o* like ivy **4** (*esclamativo*) what; **quale disgrazia!** what bad luck!

5: **in un certo qual modo** in a way, in some ways; **per la qual cosa** for which reason

▶ PRON **1** (*interrogativo*) which; **quale dei due scegli?** which of the two do you want?

2 (*relativo*): **il (la) quale** (*persona: soggetto*) who; (: *oggetto, con preposizione*) whom; (*cosa*) which; (*possessivo*) whose; **suo padre, il quale è avvocato, ...** his father, who is a lawyer, ...; **a tutti coloro i quali fossero interessati ...** to whom it may concern ...; **il signore con il quale parlavo** the gentleman to whom I was speaking; **l'albergo al quale ci siamo fermati** the hotel where we stayed *o* which we stayed at; **la signora della quale ammiriamo la bellezza** the lady whose beauty we admire

▶ AV (*in qualità di, come*) as; **quale sindaco di questa città** as mayor of this town

qua'lifica, -che SF qualification; (*titolo*) title
qualifi'care /20/ VT to qualify; (*definire*): **~ qn/qc come** to describe sb/sth as ▪ **qualificarsi** VPR (*Sport*) to qualify; **qualificarsi a un concorso** to pass a competitive exam

qualifica'tivo, -a AG qualifying
qualifi'cato, -a AG (*dotato di qualifica*) qualified; (*esperto, abile*) skilled; **non mi ritengo ~ per questo lavoro** I don't think I'm qualified for this job; **è un medico molto ~** he is a very distinguished doctor

qualificazi'one [kwalifikat'tsjone] SF qualification; **gara di ~** (*Sport*) qualifying event

qualità SF INV quality; **di ottima** *o* **prima ~** top quality; **in ~ di** in one's capacity as; **in ~ di amica** as a friend; **articoli di ogni ~** all sorts of goods; **controllo (di) ~** quality control; **prodotto di ~** quality product

qualita'tivo, -a AG qualitative
qua'lora CONG in case, if

qual'siasi, qua'lunque DET *inv* any; (*quale che sia*) whatever; (*discriminativo*) whichever; (*posposto: mediocre*) poor, indifferent; ordinary; **mettiti un vestito ~** put on any old dress; **~ cosa** anything; **~ cosa accada** whatever happens; **a ~ costo** at any cost, whatever the cost; **l'uomo ~** the man in the street; **~ persona** anyone, anybody

qualunqu'ista, -i, -e SM/F *person indifferent to politics*

'quando CONG, AV when; **~ sarò ricco** when I'm rich; **da ~** (*dacché*) since; (*interrogativo*) **da ~ sei qui?** how long have you been here?; **di ~ in ~** from time to time; **quand'anche** even if

quantifi'care /20/ VT to quantify

quantità SF INV quantity; **una ~ di** (*gran numero*) a great deal of; a lot of; **in grande ~** in large quantities

quantita'tivo, -a AG quantitative ▶ SM (*Comm: di merce*) amount, quantity

'quanto, -a

DET **1** (*interrogativo: quantità*) how much; (: *numero*) how many; **quanto pane/denaro?** how much bread/money?; **quanti libri/ragazzi?** how many books/boys?; **quanto tempo?** how long?; **quanti anni hai?** how old are you?

2 (*esclamativo*): **quante storie!** what a lot of nonsense!; **quanto tempo sprecato!** what a waste of time!

3 (*relativo: quantità*) as much ... as; (: *numero*) as many ... as; **ho quanto denaro mi occorre** I have as much money as I need; **prendi quanti libri vuoi** take as many books as you like

▶ PRON **1** (*interrogativo: quantità*) how much; (: *numero*) how many; (: *tempo*) how long; **quanto mi dai?** how much will you give me?; **quanti me ne hai portati?** how many did you bring me?; **quanto starai via?** how long will you be away (for)?; **da quanto sei qui?** how long have you been here?; **quanti ne abbiamo oggi?** what's the date today?

2 (*relativo: quantità*) as much as; (: *numero*) as many as; **farò quanto posso** I'll do as much as I can; **a quanto dice lui** according to him; **in risposta a quanto esposto nella sua lettera ...** in answer to the points raised in your letter; **possono venire quanti sono stati invitati** all those who have been invited can come

▶ AV **1** (*interrogativo: con ag, av*) how; (: *con vb*) how much; **quanto stanco ti sembrava?** how tired did he seem to you?; **quanto corre la tua moto?** how fast can your motorbike go?; **quanto costa?** how much does it cost?; **quant'è?** how much is it?

2 (*esclamativo: con ag, av*) how; (: *con vb*) how much; **quanto sono felice!** how happy I am!; **sapessi quanto abbiamo camminato!** if you knew how far we've walked!; **studierò quanto posso** I'll study as much as *o* all I can; **quanto prima** as soon as possible; **quanto più ... tanto meno** the more ... the less; **quanto più ... tanto più** the more ... the more **3**: **in quanto** (*in qualità di*) as; (*perché, per il fatto che*) as, since; **in quanto legale della signora** as the lady's lawyer; **non è possibile in**

quanto non possiamo permettercelo it isn't possible, since we can't afford it; **(in) quanto a** (per ciò che riguarda) as for, as regards; **(in) quanto a lui** as far as he's concerned 4: **per quanto** (nonostante, anche se) however; **per quanto si sforzi, non ce la farà** try as he may, he won't manage it; **per quanto sia brava, fa degli errori** however good she may be, she makes mistakes; **per quanto io sappia** as far as I know

quan'tunque CONG although, though
qua'ranta NUM forty
quaran'tena SF quarantine
quaran'tenne AG, SMF forty-year-old
quaran'tennio SM (period of) forty years
quaran'tesimo, -a NUM fortieth
quaran'tina SF: **una ~ (di)** about forty
quaran'totto SM INV forty-eight; **fare un ~** (col) to raise hell
Qua'resima SF: **la ~** Lent
'quarta SF vedi **quarto**
quar'tetto SM quartet(te)
quarti'ere SM district, area; (Mil) quarters pl; **~ generale** headquarters pl; **~ residenziale** residential area o district; **i quartieri alti** the smart districts
'quarto, -a AG fourth ▶ SM fourth; (quarta parte) quarter ▶ SF (Aut) fourth (gear); (Ins: elementare) fourth year of primary school; (: superiore) seventh year of secondary school; **un ~ di vino** a quarter-litre (BRIT) o quarter-liter (US) bottle of wine; **le 6 e un ~** a quarter past (BRIT) o after (US) 6; **~ d'ora** quarter of an hour; **le otto e tre quarti, le nove meno un ~** (a) quarter to (BRIT) o of (US) nine; **passare un brutto ~ d'ora** (fig) to have a bad o nasty time of it; **quarti di finale** (Sport) quarter finals
'quarzo ['kwartso] SM quartz
'quasi AV almost, nearly ▶ CONG (anche: **quasi che**) as if; **(non) ... ~ mai** hardly ever; **~ ~ me ne andrei** I've half a mind to leave
quas'sù AV up here
'quatto, -a AG crouched, squatting; (silenzioso) silent; **~ ~** very quietly; stealthily
quattordi'cenne [kwattordi'tʃɛnne] AG, SMF fourteen-year-old
quat'tordici [kwat'torditʃi] NUM fourteen
quat'trini SMPL money sg, cash sg
'quattro NUM four; **in ~ e quattr'otto** in less than no time; **dirne ~ a qn** to give sb a piece of one's mind; **fare il diavolo a ~** to kick up a rumpus; **fare ~ chiacchiere** to have a chat; **farsi in ~ per qn** to go out of one's way for sb, put o.s. out for sb; **~ per ~** four-by-four
quat'trocchi [kwat'trɔkki] SM INV (fig: col: persona con occhiali) four-eyes; **a ~** av (tra 2 persone) face to face; (privatamente) in private

quattrocen'tesco, -a, -schi, -sche [kwattrotʃen'tesko] AG fifteenth-century
quattro'cento [kwattro'tʃento] NUM four hundred ▶ SM: **il Q~** the fifteenth century
quattro'mila NUM four thousand

'quello, -a

(dav sm **quel** + C, **quell'** + V, **quello** + s impura, gn, pn, ps, x, z; pl **quei** + C, **quegli** + V o s impura, gn, pn, ps, x, z; dav sf **quella** + C, **quell'** + V; pl **quelle**) DET that; pl those; **quella casa** that house; **quegli uomini** those men; **voglio quella camicia (lì o là)** I want that shirt; **quello è mio fratello** that's my brother
▶ PRON 1 (dimostrativo) that one; pl those ones; (ciò) that; **conosci quella?** do you know her?; **prendo quello bianco** I'll take the white one; **chi è quello?** who's that?; **prendiamo quello (lì o là)** let's take that one (there); **in quel di Milano** in the Milan area o region
2 (relativo): **quello(a) che** (persona) the one (who); (cosa) the one (which), the one (that); **quelli(e) che** (persone) those who; (cose) those which; **è lui quello che non voleva venire** he's the one who didn't want to come; **ho fatto quello che potevo** I did what I could; **è quella che ti ho prestato** that's the one I lent you; **è proprio quello che gli ho detto** that's exactly what I told him; **da quello che ho sentito** from what I've heard

'quercia, -ce ['kwɛrtʃa] SF oak (tree); (legno) oak; **la Q~** (Pol) symbol of P.D.S.
que'rela SF (Dir) (legal) action
quere'lare /72/ VT to bring an action against
que'sito SM question, query; problem
'questi PRON (poetico) this person
questio'nario SM questionnaire
questi'one SF problem, question; (controversia) issue; (litigio) quarrel; **in ~** in question; **il caso in ~** the matter at hand; **la persona in ~** the person involved; **non voglio essere chiamato in ~** I don't want to be dragged into the argument; **fuor di ~** out of the question; **è ~ di tempo** it's a matter o question of time

---

'questo, -a

DET 1 (dimostrativo) this; pl these; **questo libro (qui o qua)** this book; **io prendo questo cappotto, tu quello** I'll take this coat, you take that one; **quest'oggi** today; **questa sera** this evening
2 (enfatico): **non fatemi più prendere di queste paure** don't frighten me like that again
▶ PRON (dimostrativo) this (one); pl these (ones); (ciò) this; **prendo questo (qui o qua)** I'll take this one; **preferisci questi o quelli?** do you prefer these (ones) or those (ones)?;

questo intendevo io this is what I meant; **vengono Paolo e Luca: questo da Roma, quello da Palermo** Paolo and Luca are coming: the former from Palermo, the latter from Rome; **questo non dovevi dirlo** you shouldn't have said that; **e con questo?** so what?; **e con questo se n'è andato** and with that he left; **con tutto questo** in spite of this, despite all this; **questo è quanto** that's all

ques'tore SM *public official in charge of the police in the provincial capital, reporting to the prefetto,* ≈ chief constable (BRIT), ≈ police commissioner (US)

'**questua** SF collection (of alms)

ques'tura SF police headquarters *pl*

questu'rino SM (*col: poliziotto*) cop

qui AV here; **da** *o* **di ~** from here; **di ~ in avanti** from now on; **di ~ a poco/una settimana** in a little while/a week's time; **~ dentro/sopra/vicino** in/up/near here; *vedi anche* **questo**

quie'scenza [kwjeʃ'ʃɛntsa] SF (*Amm*): **porre qn in ~** to retire sb

quie'tanza [kwje'tantsa] SF receipt

quie'tare /72/ VT to calm, soothe

qui'ete SF quiet, quietness; calmness; stillness; peace; **turbare la ~ pubblica** (*Dir*) to disturb the peace

qui'eto, -a AG quiet; (*notte*) calm, still; (*mare*) calm; **l'ho fatto per il ~ vivere** I did it for a quiet life

'**quindi** AV then ▶ CONG therefore, so

quindi'cenne [kwindi'tʃɛnne] AG, SMF fifteen-year-old

'**quindici** ['kwinditʃi] NUM fifteen; **~ giorni** a fortnight (BRIT), two weeks

quindi'cina [kwindi'tʃina] SF (*serie*): **una ~ (di)** about fifteen; **fra una ~ di giorni** in a fortnight (BRIT) *o* two weeks

quindici'nale [kwinditʃi'nale] AG fortnightly (BRIT), semimonthly (US) ▶ SM (*rivista*) fortnightly magazine (BRIT), semimonthly (US)

quinquen'nale AG (*che dura 5 anni*) five-year *cpd*; (*che avviene ogni 5 anni*) five-yearly

quin'quennio SM period of five years

'**quinta** SF *vedi* **quinto**

quin'tale SM quintal (*100 kg*)

quin'tetto SM quintet(te)

'**quinto, -a** NUM fifth ▶ SF (*Aut*) fifth (gear); (*Ins: elementare*) fifth year of primary school; (*: superiore*) final year of secondary school; (*Teat*) wing; **un ~ della popolazione** a fifth of the population; **tre quinti** three fifths; **in quinta pagina** on the fifth page, on page five

qui pro quo SM INV misunderstanding

Quiri'nale SM *see note*

The **Quirinale** takes its name from one of the Seven Hills of Rome on which it stands. It is the official residence of the *Presidente della Repubblica*. The term *Quirinale* is also used simply to mean 'the president'.

'**Quito** SF Quito

quiz [kwidz] SM INV (*domanda*) question; (*anche: gioco a quiz*) quiz game

'**quorum** SM quorum

'**quota** SF (*parte*) quota, share; (*Aer*) height, altitude; (*Ippica*) odds *pl*; **prendere/perdere ~** (*Aer*) to gain/lose height *o* altitude; **~ imponibile** taxable income; **~ d'iscrizione** (*Ins*) enrolment fee; (*ad una gara*) entry fee; (*ad un club*) membership fee; **~ di mercato** market share; **quote rosa** (*Pol*) quota for women

quo'tare /72/ VT (*Borsa*) to quote; (*valutare: anche fig*) to value; **è un pittore molto quotato** he is rated highly as a painter

quotazi'one [kwotat'tsjone] SF quotation

quotidiana'mente AV daily, every day

quotidi'ano, -a AG daily; (*banale*) everyday ▶ SM (*giornale*) daily (paper)

quozi'ente [kwot'tsjɛnte] SM (*Mat*) quotient; **~ di crescita zero** zero growth rate; **~ d'intelligenza** intelligence quotient, IQ

Rr

R¹, r [ˈɛrre] SM O F (*lettera*) R, r; **R come Roma** ≈ R for Robert (*BRIT*), R for Roger (*US*)

R² ABBR (*Posta*) = **raccomandato**; (*Ferr*) = **rapido**

RA SIGLA = **Ravenna**

raˈbarbaro SM rhubarb

Raˈbat SF Rabat

rabberciˈare [rabberˈtʃare] /**14**/ VT (*anche fig*) to patch up

ˈrabbia SF (*ira*) anger, rage; (*accanimento, furia*) fury; (*Med: idrofobia*) rabies *sg*

rabˈbino SM rabbi

rabbiˈoso, -a AG angry, furious; (*facile all'ira*) quick-tempered; (*forze, acqua ecc*) furious, raging; (*Med*) rabid, mad

rabboˈnire /**55**/ VT, **rabboˈnirsi** VPR to calm down

rabbriviˈdire /**55**/ VI to shudder, shiver

rabbuiˈarsi /**19**/ VPR to grow dark

rabdoˈmante SMF water diviner

racc. ABBR (*Posta*) = **raccomandato**

raccapezˈzarsi [rakkapetˈtsarsi] /**72**/ VPR: **non ~** to be at a loss

raccapricciˈante [rakkapritˈtʃante] AG horrifying

raccaˈpriccio [rakkaˈprittʃo] SM horror

raccattaˈpalle SM INV (*Sport*) ballboy

raccatˈtare /**72**/ VT to pick up

racˈchetta [rakˈketta] SF (*per tennis*) racket; (*per ping-pong*) bat; **~ da neve** snowshoe; **~ da sci** ski stick

ˈracchio, -a [ˈrakkjo] AG (*col*) ugly

racchiˈudere [rakˈkjudere] /**22**/ VT to contain

racchiˈuso, -a [rakˈkjuso] PP *di* **racchiudere**

racˈcogliere [rakˈkɔʎʎere] /**23**/ VT to collect; (*raccattare*) to pick up; (*frutti, fiori*) to pick, pluck; (*Agr*) to harvest; (*approvazione, voti*) to win; (*profughi*) to take in; (*vele*) to furl; (*capelli*) to put up ■ **raccogliersi** VPR to gather; (*fig*) to gather one's thoughts; to meditate; **non ha raccolto** (*allusione*) he didn't take the hint; (*frecciata*) he took no notice of it; **~ i frutti del proprio lavoro** (*fig*) to reap the benefits of one's work; **~ le idee** (*fig*) to gather one's thoughts

raccogliˈmento [rakkoʎʎiˈmento] SM meditation

raccogliˈtore [rakkoʎʎiˈtore] SM (*cartella*) folder, binder; **~ a fogli mobili** loose-leaf binder

racˈcolta SF *vedi* **raccolto**

racˈcolto, -a PP *di* **raccogliere** ▶ AG (*persona: pensoso*) thoughtful; (*luogo: appartato*) secluded, quiet ▶ SM (*Agr*) crop, harvest ▶ SF collecting *no pl*; collection; (*Agr*) harvesting *no pl*, gathering *no pl*; harvest, crop; (*adunata*) gathering; **fare la raccolta di qc** to collect sth; **chiamare a raccolta** to gather together; **raccolta differenziata** (*dei rifiuti*) separate collection of different kinds of household waste

raccomanˈdabile AG (highly) commendable; **è un tipo poco ~** he is not to be trusted

raccomanˈdare /**72**/ VT to recommend; (*affidare*) to entrust ■ **raccomandarsi** VPR: **raccomandarsi a qn** to commend o.s. to sb; **~ a qn di fare qc** to recommend that sb does sth; **~ a qn di non fare qc** to tell *o* warn sb not to do sth; **~ qn a qn/alle cure di qn** to entrust sb to sb/to sb's care; **mi raccomando!** don't forget!

raccomanˈdato, -a AG (*lettera, pacco*) recorded-delivery (*BRIT*), certified (*US*); (*candidato*) recommended ▶ SM/F: **essere un(a) racdato(a) di ferro** to have friends in high places ▶ SF (*anche:* **lettera raccomandata**) recorded-delivery letter; **raccomandata con ricevuta di ritorno (Rr)** recorded-delivery letter with advice of receipt

raccomandaziˈone [rakkomandatˈtsjone] SF recommendation; **lettera di ~** letter of introduction

raccomoˈdare /**72**/ VT (*riparare*) to repair, mend

racconˈtare /**72**/ VT: **~ (a qn)** (*dire*) to tell (sb); (*narrare*) to relate (to sb), tell (sb) about; **a me non la racconti** don't try and kid me; **cosa mi racconti di nuovo?** what's new?

racˈconto SM telling *no pl*, relating *no pl*; (*fatto raccontato*) story, tale; (*genere letterario*) short story; **racconti per bambini** children's stories

raccorciˈare [rakkorˈtʃare] /**14**/ VT to shorten

raccorˈdare /**72**/ VT to link up, join

racˈcordo SM (*Tecn: giunzione*) connection, joint;

(*Aut: di autostrada*) slip road (BRIT) entrance (*o exit*) ramp (US); ~ **anulare** (*Aut*) ring road (BRIT), beltway (US); ~ **autostradale** slip road (BRIT), entrance (*o exit*) ramp (US); ~ **ferroviario** siding; ~ **stradale** link road

ra'chitico, -a, -ci, -che [ra'kitiko] AG suffering from rickets; (*fig*) scraggy, scrawny

rachi'tismo [raki'tizmo] SM (*Med*) rickets *sg*

racimo'lare [ratʃimo'lare] /72/ VT (*fig*) to scrape together, glean

'rada SF (*natural*) harbour (BRIT) *o* harbor (US)

'radar SM INV radar

raddol'cire [raddol'tʃire] /55/ VT (*persona, carattere*) to soften ∎ **raddolcirsi** VPR (*tempo*) to grow milder; (*persona*) to soften, mellow

raddoppia'mento SM doubling

raddoppi'are /19/ VT, VI to double

rad'doppio SM (*gen*) doubling; (*Biliardo*) double; (*Equitazione*) gallop

raddriz'zare [raddrit'tsare] /72/ VT to straighten; (*fig: correggere*) to put straight, correct

'radere /85/ VT (*barba*) to shave off; (*mento*) to shave; (*fig: rasentare*) to graze; to skim ∎ **radersi** VPR to shave (o.s.); ~ **al suolo** to raze to the ground

radi'ale AG radial

radi'ante AG (*calore, energia*) radiant

radi'are /19/ VT to strike off

radia'tore SM radiator

radiazi'one [radjat'tsjone] SF (*Fisica*) radiation; (*cancellazione*) striking off

'radica SF (*Bot*): ~ **di noce** walnut (wood)

radi'cale AG radical ▶ SM (*Ling*) root; (*Mat*) radical ▶ SMF (*Pol*) radical; **radicali liberi** free radicals

radi'cato, -a AG (*pregiudizio, credenza*) deep-seated, deeply-rooted

ra'dicchio [ra'dikkjo] SM *variety of chicory*

ra'dice [ra'ditʃe] SF root; **segno di** ~ (*Mat*) radical sign; **colpire alla** ~ (*fig*) to strike at the root; **mettere radici** (*idee, odio ecc*) to take root; (*persona*) to put down roots; ~ **quadrata** (*Mat*) square root

'radio SF INV radio ▶ SM (*Chim*) radium; **trasmettere per** ~ to broadcast; **stazione/ponte** ~ radio station/link; ~ **ricevente/trasmittente** receiver/transmitter

radioabbo'nato, -a SM/F radio subscriber

radioama'tore, -'trice SM/F amateur radio operator, ham (*col*)

radioascolta'tore, -'trice SM/F (*radio*) listener

radioattività SF radioactivity

radioat'tivo, -a AG radioactive

radiocoman'dare /72/ VT to operate by remote control

radiocoman'dato, -a AG remote-controlled

radioco'mando SM remote control

radiocomunicazi'one [radjokomunikat'tsjone] SF radio message

radio'cronaca, -che SF radio commentary

radiocro'nista, -i, -e SM/F radio commentator

radiodiffusi'one SF (*radio*) broadcasting

radio'fonico, -a, -ci, -che AG radio *cpd*

radiogra'fare /72/ VT to X-ray

radiogra'fia SF radiography; (*foto*) X-ray photograph

radio'lina SF portable radio, transistor (radio)

radiolo'gia [radjolo'dʒia] SF radiology

radi'ologo, -a, -gi, -ghe SM/F radiologist

radiorice'vente [radjoritʃe'vɛnte] SF (*anche*: **apparecchio radioricevente**) receiver

radi'oso, -a AG radiant

radiostazi'one [radjostat'tsjone] SF radio station

radios'veglia [radjoz'veʎʎa] SF radio alarm

radio'taxi SM INV radio taxi

radio'tecnico, -a, -ci, -che AG radio engineering *cpd* ▶ SM radio engineer

radiotelegra'fista, -i, -e SM/F radiotelegrapher

radiotera'pia SF radiotherapy

radiotrasmit'tente AG (*radio*) broadcasting *cpd* ▶ SF (*radio*) broadcasting station

'rado, -a AG (*capelli*) sparse, thin; (*visite*) infrequent; **di** ~ rarely; **non di** ~ not uncommonly

radu'nare /72/ VT, **radu'narsi** VPR to gather, assemble

radu'nata SF (*Mil*) muster

ra'duno SM gathering, meeting

ra'dura SF clearing

'rafano SM horseradish

raffazzo'nare [raffattso'nare] /72/ VT to patch up

raf'fermo, -a AG stale

'raffica, -che SF (*Meteor*) gust (of wind); ~ **di colpi** (*di fucile*) burst of gunfire

raffigu'rare /72/ VT to represent

raffigurazi'one [raffigurat'tsjone] SF representation, depiction

raffi'nare /72/ VT to refine

raffina'tezza [raffina'tettsa] SF refinement

raffi'nato, -a AG refined

raffinazi'one [raffinat'tsjone] SF (*di sostanza*) refining; ~ **del petrolio** oil refining

raffine'ria SF refinery

raffor'zare [raffor'tsare] /72/ VT to reinforce

rafforza'tivo, -a [raffortsa'tivo] AG (*Ling*) intensifying ▶ SM (*Ling*) intensifier

raffredda'mento SM cooling

raffred'dare /72/ VT to cool; (*fig*) to dampen, have a cooling effect on ■ **raffreddarsi** VPR to grow cold *o* cold; (*prendere un raffreddore*) to catch a cold; (*fig*) to cool (off)

raffred'dato, -a AG (*Med*): **essere ~** to have a cold

raffred'dore SM (*Med*) cold

raffron'tare /72/ VT to compare

raf'fronto SM comparison

'rafia SF (*fibra*) raffia

'rafting ['rafting] SM white-water rafting

raga'nella SF (*Zool*) tree frog

ra'gazzo, -a [ra'gattso] SM/F boy/girl; (*col: fidanzato*) boyfriend/girlfriend ■ **ragazzi** SMPL (*figli*) kids; **nome da ragazza** maiden name; **ragazza madre** unmarried mother; **ragazza squillo** call girl; **ciao ragazzi!** (*gruppo*) hi guys!

ragge'lare [radd3e'lare] /72/ VT, VI, **ragge'larsi** VPR to freeze

raggi'ante [rad'd3ante] AG radiant, shining; **~ di gioia** beaming *o* radiant with joy

raggi'era [rad'd3ɛra] SF (*di ruota*) spokes *pl*; **a ~** with a sunburst pattern

'raggio ['radd3o] SM (*di sole ecc*) ray; (*Mat, distanza*) radius; (*di ruota ecc*) spoke; **nel ~ di 20 km** within a radius of 20 km *o* a 20-km radius; **a largo ~** (*esplorazione, incursione*) wide-ranging; **~ d'azione** range; **~ laser** laser beam; **raggi X** X-rays

raggi'rare [radd3i'rare] /72/ VT to take in, trick

rag'giro [rad'd3iro] SM trick

raggi'ungere [rad'd3und3ere] /5/ VT to reach; (*persona: riprendere*) to catch up (with); (*bersaglio*) to hit; (*fig: meta*) to achieve; **~ il proprio scopo** to reach one's goal, achieve one's aim; **~ un accordo** to come to *o* reach an agreement

raggi'unto, -a [rad'd3unto] PP *di* **raggiungere**

raggomito'larsi /72/ VPR to curl up

raggranel'lare /72/ VT to scrape together

raggrin'zare [raggrin'tsare] /72/ VT, VI (*anche:* **raggrinzarsi**) to wrinkle

raggrin'zire [raggrin'tsire] /55/ VT = **raggrinzare**

raggru'mare /72/ VT, **raggru'marsi** VPR (*sangue, latte*) to clot

raggruppa'mento SM (*azione*) grouping; (*gruppo*) group; (*Mil*) unit

raggrup'pare /72/ VT to group (together)

ragguagli'are [raggwaʎ'ʎare] /27/ VT (*paragonare*) to compare; (*informare*) to inform

raggu'aglio [rag'gwaʎʎo] SM comparison; (*informazione, relazione*) piece of information

ragguar'devole AG (*degno di riguardo*) distinguished, notable; (*notevole: somma*) considerable

'ragia ['rad3a] SF: **acqua ~** turpentine

ragiona'mento [rad3ona'mento] SM reasoning *no pl*; arguing *no pl*; argument

ragio'nare [rad3o'nare] /72/ VI (*usare la ragione*) to reason; (*discorrere*): **~ (di)** to argue (about); **cerca di ~** try and be reasonable

ragi'one [ra'd3one] SF reason; (*dimostrazione, prova*) argument, reason; (*diritto*) right; **aver ~** to be right; **aver ~ di qn** to get the better of sb; **dare ~ a qn** (*persona*) to side with sb; (*fatto*) to prove sb right; **farsi una ~ di qc** to accept sth, come to terms with sth; **in ~ di** at the rate of; to the amount of; according to; **a** *o* **con ~** rightly, justly; **perdere la ~** to become insane; (*fig*) to take leave of one's senses; **a ragion veduta** after due consideration; **per ragioni di famiglia** for family reasons; **~ di scambio** terms of trade; **~ sociale** (*Comm*) corporate name; **ragion di stato** reason of State

ragione'ria [rad3one'ria] SF accountancy; (*ufficio*) accounts department

ragio'nevole [rad3o'nevole] AG reasonable

ragioni'ere, -a [rad3o'njɛre] SM/F accountant

ragli'are [raʎ'ʎare] /27/ VI to bray

ragna'tela [raɲɲa'tela] SF cobweb, spider's web

'ragno ['raɲɲo] SM spider; **non cavare un ~ dal buco** (*fig*) to draw a blank

ragù SM INV (*Cuc*) meat sauce (*for pasta*); stew

RAI ['rai] SIGLA F (= *Radiotelevisione italiana*) Italian Broadcasting Company

rallegra'menti SMPL congratulations

ralle'grare /72/ VT to cheer up ■ **rallegrarsi** VPR to cheer up; (*provare allegrezza*) to rejoice; **rallegrarsi con qn** to congratulate sb

rallenta'mento SM slowing down; slackening

rallen'tare /72/ VT to slow down; (*fig*) to lessen, slacken ▶ VI to slow down; **~ il passo** to slacken one's pace

rallenta'tore SM (*Cine*) slow-motion camera; **al ~** (*anche fig*) in slow motion

raman'zina [raman'dzina] SF lecture, telling-off

ra'mare /72/ VT (*superficie*) to copper, coat with copper; (*Agr: vite*) to spray with copper sulphate

ra'marro SM green lizard

ra'mato, -a AG (*oggetto: rivestito di rame*) copper-coated, coppered; (*capelli, barba*) coppery, copper-coloured (BRIT), copper-colored (US)

'rame SM (*Chim*) copper; **di ~** copper *cpd*; **incisione su ~** copperplate

ramifi'care /20/ VI (*Bot*) to put out branches ■ **ramificarsi** VPR (*diramarsi*) to branch out; (*Med: tumore, vene*) to ramify; **ramificarsi in** (*biforcarsi*) to branch into

ramificazi'one [ramifikat'tsjone] SF ramification

ra'mingo, -a, -ghi, -ghe AG (*poetico*): **andare ~** to go wandering, wander

ra'mino SM (*Carte*) rummy

rammaricarsi – rappresentazione

rammari'carsi /20/ VPR: **~ (di)** (*rincrescersi*) to be sorry (about), regret; (*lamentarsi*) to complain (about)

ram'marico, -chi SM regret

rammen'dare /72/ VT to mend; (*calza*) to darn

ram'mendo SM mending *no pl*; darning *no pl*; mend darn

rammen'tare /72/ VT to remember, recall ■ **rammentarsi** VPR: **rammentarsi (di qc)** to remember (sth); **~ qc a qn** to remind sb of sth

rammol'lire /55/ VT to soften ▶ VI (*anche:* **rammollirsi**) to go soft

rammol'lito, -a AG weak ▶ SM/F weakling

'ramo SM branch; (*di commercio*) field; **non è il mio ~** it's not my field o line

ramo'scello [ramoʃ'ʃello] SM twig

'rampa SF flight (of stairs); **~ di lancio** launching pad

rampi'cante AG (*Bot*) climbing

ram'pino SM (*gancio*) hook; (*Naut*) grapnel

ram'pollo SM (*di acqua*) spring; (*Bot: germoglio*) shoot; (*fig: discendente*) descendant

ram'pone SM harpoon; (*Alpinismo*) crampon

'rana SF frog; **~ pescatrice** angler fish

'rancido, -a ['rantʃido] AG rancid

'rancio ['rantʃo] SM (*Mil*) mess; **ora del ~** mess time

ran'core SM rancour (*BRIT*), rancor (*US*), resentment; **portare ~ a qn, provare ~ per** o **verso qn** to bear sb a grudge

ran'dagio, -a, -gi, -gie o **-ge** [ran'dadʒo] AG (*gatto, cane*) stray

ran'dello SM club, cudgel

'rango, -ghi SM (*grado*) rank; (*condizione sociale*) station, social standing; **persone di ~ inferiore** people of lower standing; **uscire dai ranghi** to fall out; (*fig*) to step out of line

Ran'gun SF Rangoon

rannicchi'arsi [rannik'kjarsi] /19/ VPR to crouch, huddle

rannuvo'larsi /72/ VPR to cloud over, become overcast

ra'nocchio [ra'nɔkkjo] SM (edible) frog

ranto'lare /72/ VI to wheeze

ranto'lio SM (*il respirare affannoso*) wheezing; (*di agonizzante*) death rattle

'rantolo SM wheeze; death rattle

ra'nuncolo SM (*Bot*) buttercup

'rapa SF (*Bot*) turnip

ra'pace [ra'patʃe] AG (*animale*) predatory; (*fig*) rapacious, grasping ▶ SM bird of prey

ra'pare /72/ VT (*capelli*) to crop, cut very short

'rapida SF *vedi* **rapido**

rapida'mente AV quickly, rapidly

rapidità SF speed

'rapido, -a AG fast; (*esame, occhiata*) quick, rapid ▶ SM (*Ferr*) express (train) ▶ SF (*di fiume*) rapid

rapi'mento SM kidnapping; (*fig*) rapture

ra'pina SF robbery; **~ in banca** bank robbery; **~ a mano armata** armed robbery

rapi'nare /72/ VT to rob

rapina'tore, -'trice SM/F robber

ra'pire /55/ VT (*cose*) to steal; (*persone*) to kidnap; (*fig*) to enrapture, delight

ra'pito, -a AG (*persona*) kidnapped; (*fig: in estasi*): **ascoltare ~ qn** to be captivated by sb's words ▶ SM/F kidnapped person

rapi'tore, -'trice SM/F kidnapper

rappacifi'care [rappatʃifi'kare] /20/ VT (*riconciliare*) to reconcile ■ **rappacificarsi** VPR (*uso*) to be reconciled, make it up (*col*)

rappacificazi'one [rappatʃifikat'tsjone] SF reconciliation

rappez'zare [rappet'tsare] /72/ VT to patch

rappor'tare /72/ VT (*confrontare*) to compare; (*riprodurre*) to reproduce

rap'porto SM (*resoconto*) report; (*legame*) relationship; (*Mat, Tecn*) ratio ■ **rapporti** SMPL (*fra persone, paesi*) relations; **in ~ a quanto è successo** with regard to o in relation to what happened; **fare ~ a qn su qc** to report sth to sb; **andare a ~ da qn** to report to sb; **chiamare qn a ~** (*Mil*) to summon sb; **essere in buoni/cattivi rapporti con qn** to be on good/bad terms with sb; **~ d'affari, ~ di lavoro** business relations; **~ di compressione** (*Tecn*) pressure ratio; **~ coniugale** marital relationship; **~ di trasmissione** (*Tecn*) gear; **rapporti sessuali** sexual intercourse *sg*

rap'prendersi /81/ VPR to coagulate, clot; (*latte*) to curdle

rappre'saglia [rappre'saʎʎa] SF reprisal, retaliation

rappresen'tante SMF representative; **~ di commercio** sales representative, sales rep (*col*); **~ sindacale** union delegate o representative

rappresen'tanza [rapprezen'tantsa] SF delegation, deputation; (*Comm: ufficio, sede*) agency; **in ~ di qn** on behalf of sb; **spese di ~** entertainment expenses; **macchina di ~** official car; **avere la ~ di** to be the agent for; **~ esclusiva** sole agency; **avere la ~ esclusiva** to be sole agent

rappresen'tare /72/ VT to represent; (*Teat*) to perform; **farsi ~ dal proprio legale** to be represented by one's lawyer

rappresenta'tivo, -a AG representative ▶ SF (*di partito, sindacale*) representative group; (*Sport: squadra*) representative (team)

rappresentazi'one [rapprezentat'tsjone] SF representation; performing *no pl*; (*spettacolo*) performance; **prima ~ assoluta** world première

rap'preso, -a PP = **rapprendere**

rapso'dia SF rhapsody

'raptus SM INV: ~ **di follia** fit of madness

rara'mente AV seldom, rarely

rare'fare /41/ VT, **rare'farsi** VPR to rarefy

rare'fatto, -a PP *di* **rarefare** ▶ AG rarefied

rarefazi'one [rarefat'tsjone] SF rarefaction

rarità SF INV rarity

'raro, -a AG rare

ra'sare /72/ VT (*barba ecc*) to shave off; (*siepi, erba*) to trim, cut ▪ **rasarsi** VPR to shave (o.s.)

ra'sato, -a AG (*erba*) trimmed, cut; (*tessuto*) smooth; **avere la barba rasata** to be clean-shaven

rasa'tura SF shave

raschia'mento [raskja'mento] SM (*Med*) curettage; ~ **uterino** D and C

raschi'are [ras'kjare] /19/ VT to scrape; (*macchia, fango*) to scrape off ▶ VI to clear one's throat

rasen'tare /72/ VT (*andar rasente*) to keep close to; (*sfiorare*) to skim along (*o* over); (*fig*) to border on

ra'sente PREP: ~ **(a)** close to, very near

'raso, -a PP *di* **radere** ▶ AG (*barba*) shaved; (*capelli*) cropped; (*con misure di capacità*) level; (*pieno: bicchiere*) full to the brim ▶ SM (*tessuto*) satin; ~ **terra** close to the ground; **volare ~ terra** to hedgehop; **un cucchiaio ~** a level spoonful

ra'soio SM razor; ~ **elettrico** electric shaver *o* razor

ras'pare /72/ VT (*levigare*) to rasp; (*grattare*) to scratch

'raspo SM (*di uva*) grape stalk

ras'segna [ras'seɲɲa] SF (*Mil*) inspection, review; (*esame*) inspection; (*resoconto*) review, survey; (*pubblicazione letteraria ecc*) review; (*mostra*) exhibition, show; **passare in ~** (*Mil, fig*) to review

rasse'gnare [rasseɲ'ɲare] /15/ VT: ~ **le dimissioni** to resign, hand in one's resignation ▪ **rassegnarsi** VPR (*accettare*): **rassegnarsi (a qc/a fare)** to resign o.s. (to sth/to doing)

rassegnazi'one [rasseɲɲat'tsjone] SF resignation

rasse're'nare /72/ VT (*persona*) to cheer up ▪ **rasserenarsi** VPR (*tempo*) to clear up

rasset'tare /72/ VT to tidy, put in order; (*aggiustare*) to repair, mend

rassicu'rante AG reassuring

rassicu'rare /72/ VT to reassure ▪ **rassicurarsi** VPR to take heart, recover one's confidence

rassicurazi'one [rassikurat'tsjone] SF reassurance

rasso'dare /72/ VT to harden, stiffen; (*fig*) to strengthen, consolidate ▪ **rassodarsi** VPR to harden, to strengthen

rassomigli'anza [rassomiʎ'ʎantsa] SF resemblance

rassomigli'are [rassomiʎ'ʎare] /27/ VI: ~ **a** to resemble, look like

rastrella'mento SM (*Mil: di polizia*) (thorough) search

rastrel'lare /72/ VT to rake; (*fig: perlustrare*) to comb

rastrelli'era SF rack; (*per piatti*) dish rack

ras'trello SM rake

'rata SF (*quota*) instalment, installment (*US*); **pagare a rate** to pay by instal(l)ments *o* on hire purchase (*BRIT*); **comprare/vendere a rate** to buy/sell on hire purchase (*BRIT*) *o* on the installment plan (*US*)

rate'ale AG: **pagamento ~** payment by instal(l)ments; **vendita ~** hire purchase (*BRIT*), installment plan (*US*)

rate'are /72/ VT to divide into instal(l)ments

rateazi'one [rateat'tsjone] SF division into instal(l)ments

rateiz'zare [rateid'dzare] /72/ VT = **rateare**

'rateo SM (*Comm*) accrual

ra'tifica, -che SF ratification

ratifi'care /20/ VT (*Dir*) to ratify

'ratto SM (*Dir*) abduction; (*Zool*) rat

rattop'pare /72/ VT to patch

rat'toppo SM patching *no pl*; patch

rattrap'pire /55/ VT to make stiff ▪ **rattrappirsi** VPR to be stiff

rattris'tare /72/ VT to sadden ▪ **rattristarsi** VPR to become sad

rau'cedine [rau'tʃedine] SF hoarseness

'rauco, -a, -chi, -che AG hoarse

rava'nello SM radish

raven'nate AG of (*o* from) Ravenna

ravi'oli SMPL ravioli *sg*

ravve'dersi /82/ VPR to mend one's ways

ravvi'are /60/ VT (*capelli*) to tidy; **ravviarsi i capelli** to tidy one's hair

ravvicina'mento [ravvitʃina'mento] SM (*tra persone*) reconciliation; (*Pol: tra paesi ecc*) rapprochement

ravvici'nare [ravvitʃi'nare] /72/ VT (*avvicinare: oggetti*) to bring closer together; (*fig: persone*) to reconcile, bring together; ~ **qc a** to bring sth nearer to ▪ **ravvicinarsi** VPR to be reconciled

ravvi'sare /72/ VT to recognize

ravvi'vare /72/ VT to revive; (*fig*) to brighten up, enliven ▪ **ravvivarsi** VPR to revive; to brighten up

razio'cinio [rattsjo'tʃinjo] SM reasoning *no pl*; reason; (*buon senso*) common sense

razio'nale [rattsjo'nale] AG rational

razionalità [rattsjonali'ta] SF rationality; (*buon senso*) common sense

r

razionaliz'zare [rattsjonalid'dzare] /**72**/ ᴠᴛ (*metodo, lavoro, programma*) to rationalize; (*problema, situazione*) to approach rationally

raziona'mento [rattsjona'mento] sᴍ rationing

razio'nare [rattsjo'nare] /**72**/ ᴠᴛ to ration

razi'one [rat'tsjone] sғ ration; (*porzione*) portion, share

'razza ['rattsa] sғ race; (*Zool*) breed; (*discendenza, stirpe*) stock, race; (*sorta*) sort, kind

raz'zia [rat'tsia] sғ raid, foray

razzi'ale [rat'tsjale] ᴀɢ racial

raz'zismo [rat'tsizmo] sᴍ racism, racialism

raz'zista, -i, -e [rat'tsista] ᴀɢ, sᴍ/ғ racist, racialist

'razzo ['raddzo] sᴍ rocket; **~ di segnalazione** flare; **~ vettore** vector rocket

razzo'lare [rattso'lare] /**72**/ ᴠɪ (*galline*) to scratch about

RC sɪɢʟᴀ = **Reggio Calabria**; (= *partito della Rifondazione Comunista*) *left-wing Italian political party*

RDT sɪɢʟᴀ ғ *vedi* **la Repubblica Democratica Tedesca**

RE sɪɢʟᴀ = **Reggio Emilia**

re sᴍ ɪɴᴠ (*sovrano*) king; (*Mus*) D; (: *solfeggiando la scala*) re; **i Re Magi** the Three Wise Men, the Magi

rea'gente [rea'dʒɛnte] sᴍ reagent

rea'gire [rea'dʒire] /**55**/ ᴠɪ to react

re'ale ᴀɢ real; (*di, da re*) royal ▶ sᴍ: **il ~** reality; **i Reali** the Royal family

rea'lismo sᴍ realism

rea'lista, -i, -e sᴍ/ғ realist; (*Pol*) royalist

rea'listico, -a, -ci, -che ᴀɢ realistic

re'ality [ri'aliti] sᴍ ɪɴᴠ reality show

realiz'zare [realid'dzare] /**72**/ ᴠᴛ (*progetto ecc*) to realize, carry out; (*sogno, desiderio*) to realize, fulfil; (*scopo*) to achieve; (*Comm: titoli ecc*) to realize; (*Calcio ecc*) to score ▪ **realizzarsi** ᴠᴘʀ to be realized

realizzazi'one [realiddzat'tsjone] sғ realization; fulfilment; achievement; **~ scenica** stage production

rea'lizzo [rea'liddzo] sᴍ (*conversione in denaro*) conversion into cash; (*vendita forzata*) clearance sale

real'mente ᴀᴠ really, actually

realtà sғ ɪɴᴠ reality; **in ~** (*in effetti*) in fact; (*a dire il vero*) really; **~ aumentata** augmented reality; **~ virtuale** virtual reality

re'ame sᴍ kingdom, realm; (*fig*) realm

re'ato sᴍ offence (*Brit*), offense (*US*)

reat'tore sᴍ (*Fisica*) reactor; (*Aer: aereo*) jet; (: *motore*) jet engine

reazio'nario, -a [reattsjo'narjo] ᴀɢ, sᴍ/ғ (*Pol*) reactionary

reazi'one [reat'tsjone] sғ reaction; **motore/aereo a ~** jet engine/plane; **forze della ~** reactionary forces; **~ a catena** (*anche fig*) chain reaction

'rebbio sᴍ prong

'rebus sᴍ ɪɴᴠ rebus; (*fig*) puzzle; enigma

recapi'tare /**72**/ ᴠᴛ to deliver

re'capito sᴍ (*indirizzo*) address; (*consegna*) delivery; **~ telefonico** phone number; **ha un ~ telefonico?** do you have a telephone number where you can be reached?; **~ a domicilio** home delivery (service)

re'care /**20**/ ᴠᴛ (*portare*) to bring; (*avere su di sé*) to carry, bear; (*cagionare*) to cause, bring ▪ **recarsi** ᴠᴘʀ to go; **~ danno a qn** to harm sb, cause harm to sb; **recarsi in città/a scuola** to go into town/ to school

re'cedere [re'tʃɛdere] /**29**/ ᴠɪ to withdraw

recensi'one [retʃen'sjone] sғ review

recen'sire [retʃen'sire] /**55**/ ᴠᴛ to review

recen'sore, -a [retʃen'sore] sᴍ/ғ reviewer

re'cente [re'tʃɛnte] ᴀɢ recent; **di ~** recently; **più ~** latest, most recent

recente'mente [retʃɛnte'mente] ᴀᴠ recently

rece'pire [retʃe'pire] /**55**/ ᴠᴛ to understand, take in

recessi'one [retʃes'sjone] sғ (*Econ*) recession

re'cesso [re'tʃɛsso] sᴍ (*azione*) recession, receding; (*Dir*) withdrawal; (*luogo*) recess

recherò *ecc* [reke'rɔ] ᴠʙ *vedi* **recare**

re'cidere [re'tʃidere] /**34**/ ᴠᴛ to cut off, chop off

reci'divo, -a [retʃi'divo] sᴍ/ғ (*Dir*) second (*o* habitual) offender, recidivist ▶ sғ recidivism

recin'tare [retʃin'tare] /**72**/ ᴠᴛ to enclose, fence off

re'cinto [re'tʃinto] sᴍ enclosure; (*ciò che recinge*) fence; surrounding wall

recinzi'one [retʃin'tsjone] sғ (*azione*) enclosure, fencing-off; (*recinto: di legno*) fence; (: *di mattoni*) wall; (*reticolato*) wire fencing; (*a sbarre*) railings pl

recipi'ente [retʃi'pjɛnte] sᴍ container

re'ciproco, -a, -ci, -che [re'tʃiproko] ᴀɢ reciprocal

re'ciso, -a [re'tʃizo] ᴘᴘ *di* **recidere**

'recita ['rɛtʃita] sғ performance

'recital ['rɛtʃital] sᴍ ɪɴᴠ recital

reci'tare [retʃi'tare] /**72**/ ᴠᴛ (*poesia, lezione*) to recite; (*dramma*) to perform; (*ruolo*) to play *o* act (the part of)

recitazi'one [retʃitat'tsjone] sғ recitation; (*di attore*) acting; **scuola di ~** drama school

recla'mare /**72**/ ᴠɪ to complain ▶ ᴠᴛ (*richiedere*) to demand

ré'clame [re'klam] sғ ɪɴᴠ advertising *no pl* advertisement, advert (*Brit*), ad (*col*)

reclamiz'zare [reklamid'dzare] /**72**/ ᴠᴛ to advertise

re'clamo sᴍ complaint; **sporgere ~ a** to complain to, make a complaint to

recli'nabile ᴀɢ (sedile) reclining

recli'nare /**72**/ ᴠᴛ (capo) to bow, lower; (sedile) to tilt

reclusi'one sꜰ (Dir) imprisonment

re'cluso, -a sᴍ/ꜰ prisoner

'recluta sꜰ recruit

recluta'mento sᴍ recruitment

reclu'tare /**72**/ ᴠᴛ to recruit

re'condito, -a ᴀɢ secluded; (fig) secret, hidden

'record ᴀɢ ɪɴᴠ record cpd ▶ sᴍ ɪɴᴠ record; **in tempo ~, a tempo di ~** in record time; **detenere il ~ di** to hold the record for; **~ mondiale** world record

recrimi'nare /**72**/ ᴠɪ: **~ (su qc)** to complain (about sth)

recriminazi'one [rekriminat'tsjone] sꜰ recrimination

recrude'scenza [rekrudeʃ'ʃentsa] sꜰ fresh outbreak

recupe'rare ecc = **ricuperare** ecc

redargu'ire /**55**/ ᴠᴛ to rebuke

re'dassi ecc ᴠʙ vedi **redigere**

re'datto, -a ᴘᴘ di **redigere**

redat'tore, -'trice sᴍ/ꜰ (Stampa) editor; (: di articolo) writer; (di dizionario ecc) compiler; **~ capo** chief editor

redazi'one [redat'tsjone] sꜰ editing; writing; (sede) editorial office(s); (personale) editorial staff; (versione) version

reddi'tizio, -a [reddi'tittsjo] ᴀɢ profitable

'reddito sᴍ income; (dello Stato) revenue; (di un capitale) yield; **~ complessivo** gross income; **~ disponibile** disposable income; **~ fisso** fixed income; **~ imponibile/non imponibile** taxable/non-taxable income; **~ da lavoro** earned income; **~ nazionale** national income; **~ pubblico** public revenue

re'densi ecc ᴠʙ vedi **redimere**

re'dento, -a ᴘᴘ di **redimere**

reden'tore sᴍ: **il R~** the Redeemer

redenzi'one [reden'tsjone] sꜰ redemption

re'digere [re'didʒere] /**47**/ ᴠᴛ to write; (contratto) to draw up

re'dimere /**86**/ ᴠᴛ to deliver; (Rel) to redeem

'redini sꜰᴘʟ reins

redi'vivo, -a ᴀɢ returned to life, reborn

'reduce ['redutʃe] ᴀɢ (gen): **~ da** returning from, back from ▶ sᴍꜰ survivor; (veterano) veteran; **essere ~ da** (esame, colloquio) to have been through; (malattia) to be just over

'refe sᴍ thread

refe'rendum sᴍ ɪɴᴠ referendum

refe'renza [refe'rentsa] sꜰ reference

re'ferto sᴍ medical report

refet'torio sᴍ refectory

refezi'one [refet'tsjone] sꜰ (Ins) school meal

refrat'tario, -a ᴀɢ refractory; (fig): **essere ~ alla matematica** to have no aptitude for mathematics

refrige'rante [refridʒe'rante] ᴀɢ (Tecn) cooling, refrigerating; (bevanda) refreshing ▶ sᴍ (Chim: fluido) coolant; (Tecn: apparecchio) refrigerator

refrige'rare [refridʒe'rare] /**72**/ ᴠᴛ to refrigerate; (rinfrescare) to cool, refresh

refrigerazi'one [refridʒerat'tsjone] sꜰ refrigeration; (Tecn) cooling; **~ ad acqua** (Aut) water-cooling

refri'gerio [refri'dʒerjo] sᴍ: **trovare ~** to find somewhere cool

refur'tiva sꜰ stolen goods pl

Reg. ᴀʙʙʀ (= reggimento) Regt; (Amm) = **regolamento**

rega'lare /**72**/ ᴠᴛ to give (as a present), make a present of

re'gale ᴀɢ regal

re'galo sᴍ gift, present ▶ ᴀɢ ɪɴᴠ: **confezione ~** gift pack; **fare un ~ a qn** to give sb a present; **"articoli da ~"** "gifts"

re'gata sꜰ regatta

reg'gente [red'dʒente] ᴀɢ (proposizione) main; (sovrano) reigning ▶ sᴍꜰ regent; **principe ~** prince regent

reg'genza [red'dʒentsa] sꜰ regency

'reggere ['reddʒere] /**87**/ ᴠᴛ (tenere) to hold; (sostenere) to support, bear, hold up; (portare) to carry, bear; (resistere) to withstand; (dirigere: impresa) to manage, run; (governare) to rule, govern; (Ling) to take, be followed by ▶ ᴠɪ (resistere): **~ a** to stand up to, hold out against; (sopportare): **~ a** to stand; (durare) to last; (fig: teoria ecc) to hold water ■ **reggersi** ᴠᴘʀ (stare ritto) to stand; (fig: dominarsi) to control o.s.; **reggersi sulle gambe o in piedi** to stand up

'reggia, -ge ['reddʒa] sꜰ royal palace

reggi'calze [reddʒi'kaltse] sᴍ ɪɴᴠ suspender belt

reggi'mento [reddʒi'mento] sᴍ (Mil) regiment

reggi'petto [reddʒi'petto], **reggi'seno** [reddʒi'seno] sᴍ bra

re'gia, -'gie [re'dʒia] sꜰ (TV, Cine ecc) direction

re'gime [re'dʒime] sᴍ (Pol) regime; (Dir: aureo, patrimoniale ecc) system; (Med) diet; (Tecn) (engine) speed; **~ di giri** (di motore) revs pl per minute; **~ vegetariano** vegetarian diet

re'gina [re'dʒina] sꜰ queen

'regio, -a, -gi, -gie ['redʒo] ᴀɢ royal

regio'nale [redʒo'nale] ᴀɢ regional ▶ sᴍ local train (stopping frequently)

r

Regionali trains cover only short distances and stop at most stations.

regi'one [re'dʒone] SF (gen) region; (territorio) region, district, area

The **Regione** is the biggest administrative unit in Italy. Each of the 20 *Regioni* consists of a variable number of *Province*, which in turn are subdivided into *Comuni*. Each of the regions has a *capoluogo*, its chief province (for example, Florence is the chief province of the region of Tuscany). Five regions have special status and wider powers: Val d'Aosta, Friuli-Venezia Giulia, Trentino-Alto Adige, Sicily and Sardinia. A *Regione* is run by the *Giunta regionale*, which is appointed by the *Presidente della Regione*. The *Giunta* has legislative powers within the region over the police, public health, schools, town planning and agriculture.

re'gista, -i, -e [re'dʒista] SM/F (TV, *Cine ecc*) director

regis'trare [redʒis'trare] /72/ VT (*Amm*) to register; (*Comm*) to enter; (*notare*) to report, note; (*canzone, conversazione, strumento di misura*) to record; (*mettere a punto*) to adjust, regulate; **~ i bagagli** (*Aer*) to check in one's luggage; **~ i freni** (*Tecn*) to adjust the brakes

registra'tore [redʒistra'tore] SM (*strumento*) recorder, register; (*magnetofono*) tape recorder; **~ di cassa** cash register; **~ a cassette** cassette recorder; **~ di volo** (*Aer*) flight recorder, black box (*col*)

registrazi'one [redʒistrat'tsjone] SF registration; entry; reporting; recording; adjustment; **~ bagagli** (*Aer*) check-in

re'gistro [re'dʒistro] SM register; (*Dir*) registry; (*Comm*): **~ (di cassa)** ledger; **ufficio del ~** registrar's office; **~ di bordo** logbook; **registri contabili** (account) books

re'gnante [reɲ'ɲante] AG reigning, ruling ▶ SMF ruler

re'gnare [reɲ'ɲare] /15/ VI to reign, rule; (*fig*) to reign

'regno ['reɲɲo] SM kingdom; (*periodo*) reign; (*fig*) realm; **il ~ animale/vegetale** the animal/vegetable kingdom; **il R~ Unito** the United Kingdom

'regola SF rule; **a ~ d'arte** duly; perfectly; **essere in ~** (*dipendente*) to be a registered employee; (*fig: essere pulito*) to be clean; **fare le cose in ~** to do things properly; **avere le carte in ~** (*gen*) to have one's papers in order; (*fig: essere adatto*) to be the right person; **per tua (norma e) ~** for your information; **un'eccezione alla ~** an exception to the rule

rego'labile AG adjustable

regolamen'tare /72/ AG (*distanza, velocità*) regulation *cpd*, proper; (*disposizione*) statutory ▶ VT

(*gen*) to control; **entro il tempo ~** within the time allowed, within the prescribed time

regola'mento SM (*complesso di norme*) regulations *pl*; (*di debito*) settlement; **~ di conti** (*fig*) settling of scores

rego'lare /72/ AG regular; (*velocità*) steady; (*superficie*) even; (*passo*) steady, even; (*in regola: documento*) in order ▶ VT to regulate, control; (*apparecchio*) to adjust, regulate; (*questione, conto, debito*) to settle ■ **regolarsi** VPR (*comportarsi*) to behave, act; **regolarsi nel bere/nello spendere** (*moderarsi*) to control one's drinking/spending; **presentare ~ domanda** to apply through the proper channels; **~ i conti** (*fig*) to settle old scores

regolarità SF INV regularity; steadiness; evenness; (*nel pagare*) punctuality

regolariz'zare [regolarid'dzare] /72/ VT (*posizione*) to regularize; (*debito*) to settle

rego'lata SF: **darsi una ~** to pull o.s. together

regola'tezza [regola'tettsa] SF (*ordine*) orderliness; (*moderazione*) moderation

rego'lato, -a AG (*ordinato*) orderly; (*moderato*) moderate

regola'tore SM (*Tecn*) regulator; **~ di frequenza/di volume** frequency/volume control

'regolo SM ruler; **~ calcolatore** slide rule

regre'dire /55/ VI to regress

regressi'one SF regression

re'gresso SM (*fig: declino*) decline

rei'etto, -a SM/F outcast

reincarnazi'one [reinkarnat'tsjone] SF reincarnation

reinte'grare /72/ VT (*produzione*) to restore; (*energie*) to recover; (*dipendente*) to reinstate

reintegrazi'one [reintegrat'tsjone] SF (*di produzione*) restoration; (*di dipendente*) reinstatement

relativa'mente AV relatively

relatività SF relativity

rela'tivo, -a AG relative; (*attinente*) relevant; (*rispettivo*) respective; **~ a** (*che concerne*) relating to, concerning; (*proporzionato*) in proportion to

rela'tore, -'trice SM/F (*gen*) spokesman/woman; (*Ins: di tesi*) supervisor

re'lax [re'laks] SM relaxation

relazi'one [relat'tsjone] SF (*fra cose, persone*) relation(ship); (*resoconto*) report, account ■ **relazioni** SFPL (*conoscenze*) connections; **essere in ~** to be connected; **mettere in ~** (*fatti, elementi*) to make the connection between; **in ~ a quanto detto prima** with regard to what has already been said; **essere in buone relazioni con qn** to be on good terms with sb; **fare una ~** to make a report, give an account; **relazioni pubbliche** public relations

rele'gare /80/ VT to banish; (*fig*) to relegate

religi'one [reli'dʒone] SF religion

Roman Catholicism is the religion (**religione**) of the majority of the Italian population, but all the major religions are recognized and protected.

religi'oso, -a [reli'dʒoso] AG religious ▶ SM/F monk/nun

re'liquia SF relic

re'litto SM wreck; (fig) down-and-out

re'mainder [ri'meindər] SM INV (libro) remainder

're'make [ri:'meik] SM INV (Cine) remake

re'mare /72/ VI to row

remini'scenze [reminiʃ'ʃɛntse] SFPL reminiscences

remissi'one SF remission; (deferenza) submissiveness, compliance; ~ **del debito** remission of debt; ~ **di querela** (Dir) withdrawal of an action

remissività SF submissiveness

remis'sivo, -a AG submissive, compliant

'remo SM oar

'remora SF (poetico: indugio) hesitation

re'moto, -a AG remote

remune'rare ecc = **rimunerare** ecc

'rena SF sand

re'nale AG kidney cpd

'rendere /88/ VT (ridare) to return, give back; (: saluto ecc) to return; (produrre) to yield, bring in; (esprimere, tradurre) to render; (far diventare): ~ **qc possibile** to make sth possible ▶ VI (fruttare: ditta) to be profitable; (: investimento, campo) to yield, be productive; ~ **grazie a qn** to thank sb; ~ **omaggio a qn** to honour sb; ~ **un servizio a qn** to do sb a service; ~ **una testimonianza** to give evidence; ~ **la visita** to pay a return visit; **non so se rendo l'idea** I don't know whether I'm making myself clear; **rendersi utile** to make o.s. useful; **rendersi conto di qc** to realize sth

rendi'conto SM (rapporto) report, account; (Amm, Comm) statement of account

rendi'mento SM (reddito) yield; (di manodopera, Tecn) efficiency; (capacità) output; (di studenti) performance

'rendita SF (di individuo) private o unearned income; (Comm) revenue; ~ **annua** annuity; ~ **vitalizia** life annuity

'rene SM kidney

'reni SFPL back sg

reni'tente AG reluctant, unwilling; ~ **ai consigli di qn** unwilling to follow sb's advice; **essere ~ alla leva** (Mil) to fail to report for military service

'renna SF reindeer inv

'Reno SM: **il ~** the Rhine

'reo, -a SM/F (Dir) offender

re'parto SM department, section; (Mil) detachment; ~ **acquisti** purchasing office

repel'lente AG repulsive; (Chim: insettifugo): **liquido ~** (liquid) repellent

repen'taglio [repen'taʎʎo] SM: **mettere a ~** to jeopardize, risk

repen'tino, -a AG sudden, unexpected

repe'ribile AG available

repe'rire /55/ VT to find, trace

re'perto SM (Archeologia) find; (Med) report; (anche: **reperto giudiziario**) exhibit

reper'torio SM (Teat) repertory; (elenco) index, (alphabetical) list

'replica, -che SF repetition; reply, answer; (obiezione) objection; (Teat, Cine) repeat performance; (copia) replica

repli'care /20/ VT (ripetere) to repeat; (rispondere) to answer, reply

repor'tage [rəpɔr'taʒ] SM INV (Stampa) report

repressi'one SF repression

repres'sivo, -a AG repressive

re'presso, -a PP di **reprimere**

re'primere /50/ VT to suppress, repress

re'pubblica, -che SF republic; **la R~ Democratica Tedesca** the German Democratic Republic; **la R~ Federale Tedesca** the Federal Republic of Germany; **la Prima/la Seconda R~** terms used to refer to Italy before and after the political changes resulting from the 1994 elections; vedi anche **Festa della Repubblica**

repubbli'cano, -a AG, SM/F republican

repu'tare /72/ VT to consider, judge

reputazi'one [reputat'tsjone] SF reputation; **farsi una cattiva ~** to get o.s. a bad name

'requie SF rest; **dare ~ a qn** to give sb some peace; **senza ~** unceasingly

'requiem SM INV (preghiera) requiem, prayer for the dead; (fig: ufficio funebre) requiem

requi'sire /55/ VT to requisition

requi'sito SM requirement; **avere i requisiti necessari per un lavoro** to have the necessary qualifications for a job

requisi'toria SF (Dir) closing speech (for the prosecution)

requisizi'one [rekwizit'tsjone] SF requisition

'resa SF (l'arrendersi) surrender; (restituzione, rendimento) return; ~ **dei conti** rendering of accounts; (fig) day of reckoning

re'scindere [reʃ'ʃindere] **/102/** VT (Dir) to rescind, annul

re'scisso, -a [reʃ'ʃisso] PP di **rescindere**

reset'tare /72/ VT (Inform) to reset

'resi ecc VB vedi **rendere**

resi'dente AG resident

resi'denza [resi'dɛntsa] SF residence

residenzi'ale [residen'tsjale] AG residential

r

residu'ale AG residual

re'siduo, -a AG residual, remaining ▶SM remainder; (*Chim*) residue; **residui industriali** industrial waste *sg*

'resina SF resin

resis'tente AG (*che resiste*): **~ a** resistant to; (*forte*) strong; (*duraturo*) long-lasting, durable; **~ all'acqua** waterproof; **~ al caldo** heat-resistant; **~ al fuoco** fireproof; **~ al gelo** frost-resistant

resis'tenza [resis'tɛntsa] SF (*gen, Elettr*) resistance; (*di persona: fisica*) stamina, endurance; (: *mentale*) endurance, resistance; **opporre ~ (a)** to offer *o* put up resistance (to); (*decisione, scelta*) to show opposition (to); **la R~** *see note*

The Italian **Resistenza** fought against both the Nazis and the Fascists during the Second World War. It was particularly active after the fall of the Fascist government on 25 July 1943, throughout the German occupation and during the period of Mussolini's Republic of Salò in northern Italy. Resistance members spanned the whole political spectrum and played a vital role in the Liberation and in the formation of the new democratic government.

re'sistere /11/ VI to resist; **~ a** (*assalto, tentazioni*) to resist; (*dolore*) to withstand; (*non patir danno*) to be resistant to

resis'tito, -a PP *di* **resistere**

'reso, -a PP *di* **rendere**

reso'conto SM report, account

respin'gente [respin'dʒɛnte] SM (*Ferr*) buffer

res'pingere [res'pindʒere] /114/ VT to drive back, repel; (*rifiutare: pacco, lettera*) to return; (: *invito*) to refuse; (: *proposta*) to reject, turn down; (*Ins: bocciare*) to fail

res'pinto, -a PP *di* **respingere**

respi'rare /72/ VI to breathe; (*fig*) to get one's breath; to breathe again ▶VT to breathe (in), inhale

respira'tore SM respirator

respira'torio, -a AG respiratory

respirazi'one [respirat'tsjone] SF breathing; **~ artificiale** artificial respiration; **~ bocca a bocca** mouth-to-mouth resuscitation, kiss of life (*col*)

res'piro SM breathing *no pl*; (*singolo atto*) breath; (*fig*) respite, rest; **mandare un ~ di sollievo** to give a sigh of relief; **trattenere il ~** to hold one's breath; **lavorare senza ~** to work nonstop; **di ampio ~** (*opera, lavoro*) far-reaching

respon'sabile AG responsible ▶SMF person responsible; (*capo*) person in charge; **~ di** responsible for; (*Dir*) liable for

responsabilità SF INV responsibility; (*legale*) liability; **assumere la ~ di** to take on the responsibility for; **affidare a qn la ~ di** qc to make sb responsible for sth; **~ patrimoniale** debt liability; **~ penale** criminal liability

responsabiliz'zare [responsabilid'dzare] /72/ VT: **~ qn** to make sb feel responsible

res'ponso SM answer; (*Dir*) verdict

'ressa SF crowd, throng

'ressi ecc VB *vedi* **reggere**

res'tare /72/ VI (*rimanere*) to remain, stay; (*avanzare*) to be left, remain; (*diventare*): **~ orfano/cieco** to become *o* be left an orphan/become blind; (*trovarsi*): **~ sorpreso** to be surprised; **~ d'accordo** to agree; **non resta più niente** there's nothing left; **restano pochi giorni** there are only a few days left; **che resti tra di noi** this is just between ourselves; **~ in buoni rapporti** to remain on good terms; **~ senza parole** to be left speechless

restau'rare /72/ VT to restore

restaura'tore, -'trice SM/F restorer

restaurazi'one [restaurat'tsjone] SF (*Pol*) restoration

res'tauro SM (*di edifici ecc*) restoration; **in ~** under repair; **sotto ~** (*dipinto*) being restored; **chiuso per restauri** closed for repairs

res'tio, -a, -'tii, -'tie AG restive; (*persona*): **~ a** reluctant to

restitu'ire /55/ VT to return, give back; (*energie, forze*) to restore

restituzi'one [restitut'tsjone] SF return; (*di soldi*) repayment

'resto SM remainder, rest; (*denaro*) change; (*Mat*) remainder ▪ **resti** SMPL leftovers; (*di città*) remains; **del ~** moreover, besides; **tenga pure il ~** keep the change; **resti mortali** (mortal) remains

res'tringere [res'trindʒere] /117/ VT to reduce; (*vestito*) to take in; (*stoffa*) to shrink; (*fig*) to restrict, limit ▪ **restringersi** VPR (*strada*) to narrow; (*stoffa*) to shrink

restrit'tivo, -a AG restrictive

restrizi'one [restrit'tsjone] SF restriction

resurrezi'one [resurret'tsjone] SF = **risurrezione**

resusci'tare [resuʃʃi'tare] /72/ VT, VI = **risuscitare**

re'tata SF (*Pesca*) haul, catch; **fare una ~ di** (*fig: persone*) to round up

'rete SF net; (*di recinzione*) wire netting; (*Aut, Ferr, di spionaggio ecc*) network; (*fig*) trap, snare; **segnare una ~** (*Calcio*) to score a goal; **~ ferroviaria/stradale/di distribuzione** railway/road/distribution network; **~ del letto** (sprung) bed base; **~ da pesca** fishing net; **~ sociale** social network; **~ (televisiva)** (*sistema*) network; (*canale*) channel; **la R~** the web; **calze a ~** fishnet tights *o* stockings

reti'cente [reti'tʃɛnte] AG reticent

reti'cenza [reti'tʃɛntsa] SF reticence

retico'lato SM grid; (*rete metallica*) wire netting; (*di filo spinato*) barbed wire fence

'retina SF (*Anat*) retina

re'torico, -a, -ci, -che AG rhetorical ▸ SF rhetoric

retribu'ire /55/ VT to pay; (*premiare*) to reward; **un lavoro mal retribuito** a poorly-paid job

retribu'tivo, -a AG pay *cpd*

retribuzi'one [retribut'tsjone] SF payment; reward

re'trivo, -a AG (*fig*) reactionary

'retro SM INV back ▸ AV (*dietro*): **vedi ~** see over(leaf)

retroattività SF retroactivity

retroat'tivo, -a AG (*Dir: legge*) retroactive; (*Amm: salario*) backdated

retrobot'tega, -ghe SF back shop

retro'cedere [retro'tʃɛdere] /29/ VI to withdraw ▸ VT (*Calcio*) to relegate; (*Mil*) to degrade; (*Amm*) to demote

retrocessi'one [retrotʃes'sjone] SF (*di impiegato*) demotion

retro'cesso, -a [retro'tʃɛsso] PP *di* **retrocedere**

retroda'tare /72/ VT (*Amm*) to backdate

re'trogrado, -a AG (*fig*) reactionary, backward-looking

retrogu'ardia SF (*anche fig*) rearguard

retroillumi'nato, -a AG backlit

retro'marcia [retro'martʃa] SF (*Aut*) reverse; (: *dispositivo*) reverse gear

retro'scena [retroʃ'ʃena] SF INV (*Teat*) backstage ▸ SM INV: **i ~** (*fig*) the behind-the-scenes activities

retrospet'tivo, -a AG retrospective ▸ SF (*Arte*) retrospective (exhibition)

retros'tante AG: **~ (a)** at the back (of)

retro'terra SM hinterland

retro'via SF (*Mil*) zone behind the front; **mandare nelle retrovie** to send to the rear

retrovi'sore SM (*Aut*) (rear-view) mirror

'retta SF (*Mat*) straight line; (*di convitto*) charge for bed and board; (*fig: ascolto*): **dar ~ a** to listen to, pay attention to

rettango'lare AG rectangular

ret'tangolo, -a AG right-angled ▸ SM rectangle

ret'tifica, -che SF rectification, correction

rettifi'care /20/ VT (*curva*) to straighten; (*fig*) to rectify, correct

'rettile SM reptile

retti'lineo, -a AG rectilinear

retti'tudine SF rectitude, uprightness

'retto, -a PP *di* **reggere** ▸ AG straight; (*onesto*) honest, upright; (*giusto, esatto*) correct, proper, right; **angolo ~** (*Mat*) right angle

ret'tore SM (*Rel*) rector; (*di università*) ≈ chancellor

re'tweet [ri'twit] SM INV (*su Twitter*) retweet

retwit'tare /72/ VT (*su Twitter*) to retweet

reuma'tismo SM rheumatism

Rev. ABBR (= *Reverendo*) Rev(d)

reve'rendo, -a AG: **il ~ padre Belli** the Reverend Father Belli

reve'rente AG = **riverente**

reve'renza [reve'rɛntsa] SF = **riverenza**

rever'sibile AG reversible

revisio'nare /72/ VT (*conti*) to audit; (*Tecn*) to overhaul, service; (*Dir: processo*) to review; (*componimento*) to revise

revisi'one SF auditing *no pl*; audit; servicing *no pl*; overhaul; review; revision; **~ di bilancio** audit; **~ di bozze** proofreading; **~ contabile interna** internal audit

revi'sore SM: **~ di conti/bozze** auditor/proofreader

re'vival [ri'vaivəl] SM INV revival

'revoca SF revocation

revo'care /20/ VT to revoke

re'volver SM INV revolver

revolve'rata SF revolver shot

'Reykjavik ['reikjavik] SF Reykjavik

RFT SIGLA F *vedi* **la Repubblica Federale Tedesca**

ri'abbia *ecc* VB *vedi* **riavere**

riabili'tare /72/ VT to rehabilitate; (*fig*) to restore to favour (*BRIT*) *o* favor (*US*)

riabilitazi'one [riabilitat'tsjone] SF rehabilitation

riac'cendere [riat'tʃɛndere] /2/ VT (*sigaretta, fuoco, gas*) to light again; (*luce, radio, TV*) to switch on again; (*fig: sentimenti, interesse*) to rekindle, revive ◼ **riaccendersi** VPR (*fuoco*) to catch again; (*luce, radio, TV*) to come back on again; (*fig: sentimenti*) to revive, be rekindled

riac'ceso, -a [riat'tʃeso] PP *di* **riaccendere**

riacqui'stare /72/ VT (*gen*) to buy again; (*ciò che si era venduto*) to buy back; (*fig: buonumore, sangue freddo, libertà*) to regain; **~ la salute** to recover (one's health); **~ le forze** to regain one's strength

Ri'ad SF Riyadh

riaddormen'tare /72/ VT to put to sleep again ◼ **riaddormentarsi** VPR to fall asleep again

riallac'ciare [riallat'tʃare] /14/ VT (*cintura, cavo ecc*) to refasten, tie up *o* fasten again; (*fig: rapporti, amicizia*) to resume, renew ◼ **riallacciarsi** VPR: **riallacciarsi a** (*fig: a discorso, tema*) to resume, take up again

rial'zare [rial'tsare] /72/ VT to raise, lift; (*alzare di più*) to heighten, raise; (*aumentare: prezzi*) to increase, raise ▸ VI (*prezzi*) to rise, increase

rial'zato, -a [rial'tsato] AG: **piano ~** mezzanine, entresol

r

rial'zista, -i [rial'tsista] SM (Borsa) bull

ri'alzo [ri'altso] SM (di prezzi) increase, rise; (sporgenza) rise; **giocare al ~** (Borsa) to bull

rian'dare /6/ VI: **~ (in), ~ (a)** to go back (to), return (to)

riani'mare /72/ VT (Med) to resuscitate; (fig: rallegrare) to cheer up; (: dar coraggio) to give heart to ■ **rianimarsi** VPR to recover consciousness; to cheer up; to take heart

rianimazi'one [rianimat'tsjone] SF (Med) resuscitation; **centro di ~** intensive care unit

ria'perto, -a PP di **riaprire**

riaper'tura SF reopening

riappa'rire /7/ VI to reappear

riap'parso, -a PP di **riapparire**

riap'pendere /8/ VT to rehang; (Tel) to hang up

ria'prire /9/ VT, **ria'prirsi** VPR to reopen, open again

ri'armo SM (Mil) rearmament

ri'arso, -a AG (terreno) arid; (gola) parched; (labbra) dry

riasset'tare /72/ VT (vedi sm) to rearrange; to reorganize

rias'setto SM (di stanza ecc) rearrangement; (ordinamento) reorganization

rias'sumere /12/ VT (riprendere) to resume; (impiegare di nuovo) to re-employ; (sintetizzare) to summarize

rias'sunto, -a PP di **riassumere** ▶ SM summary

riattac'care /20/ VT (attaccare di nuovo): **~ (a)** (manifesto, francobollo) to stick back (on); (bottone) to sew back (on); (quadro, chiavi) to hang back up (on); **~ (il telefono o il ricevitore)** to hang up (the receiver)

riatti'vare /72/ VT to reactivate

ria'vere /13/ VT to have again; (avere indietro) to get back; (riacquistare) to recover ■ **riaversi** VPR to recover; (da svenimento, stordimento) to come round

riba'dire /55/ VT (fig) to confirm

ri'balta SF (sportello) flap; (Teat: proscenio) front of the stage; **luci della ~** footlights pl; (fig) limelight; **tornare alla ~** (personaggio) to make a comeback; (problema) to come up again

ribal'tabile AG (sedile) tip-up

ribal'tare /72/ VT, VI (anche: **ribaltarsi**) to turn over, tip over

ribas'sare /72/ VT to lower, bring down ▶ VI to come down, fall

ribas'sista, -i SM (Borsa) bear

ri'basso SM reduction, fall; **essere in ~** (azioni, prezzi) to be down; (fig: popolarità) to be on the decline; **giocare al ~** (Borsa) to bear

ri'battere /1/ VT (battere di nuovo) to beat again; (con macchina da scrivere) to type again; (palla) to return, hit back; (confutare) to refute; **~ che** to retort that

ribattez'zare [ribatted'dzare] /72/ VT to rename

ribel'larsi /72/ VPR: **~ (a)** to rebel (against)

ri'belle AG (soldati) rebel; (ragazzo) rebellious ▶ SMF rebel

ribelli'one SF rebellion

'ribes SM INV currant; **~ nero** blackcurrant; **~ rosso** redcurrant

ribol'lire /17/ VI (fermentare) to ferment; (fare bolle) to bubble, boil; (fig) to seethe

ri'brezzo [ri'breddzo] SM disgust, loathing; **far ~ a** to disgust

ribut'tante AG disgusting, revolting

ricacci'are [rikat'tʃare] /14/ VT (respingere) to drive back; **~ qn fuori** to throw sb out

rica'dere /18/ VI to fall again; (scendere a terra: fig: nel peccato ecc) to fall back; (vestiti, capelli ecc) to hang (down); (riversarsi: fatiche, colpe): **~ su** to fall on

rica'duta SF (Med) relapse

rical'care /20/ VT (disegni) to trace; (fig) to follow faithfully

ricalci'trare [rikaltʃi'trare] /72/ VI (cavalli, asini, muli) to kick

rica'mare /72/ VT to embroider

ricambi'are /19/ VT to change again; (contraccambiare) to return, repay

ri'cambio SM exchange, return; (Fisiol) metabolism ■ **ricambi** SMPL spare parts; **pezzi di ~** spare parts; **~ della manodopera** labour turnover

ri'camo SM embroidery; **senza ricami** (fig) without frills

ricapitalizza'zione [rikapitaliddza'tsjone] SF bailout

ricapito'lare /72/ VT to recapitulate, sum up

ricapitolazi'one [rikapitolat'tsjone] SF recapitulation, summary

ricari'care /20/ VT (arma, macchina fotografica) to reload; (penna, pipa) to refill; (orologio, giocattolo) to rewind; (Elettr) to recharge

ricat'tare /72/ VT to blackmail

ricatta'tore, -'trice SM/F blackmailer

ri'catto SM blackmail; **fare un ~ a qn** to blackmail sb; **subire un ~** to be blackmailed

rica'vare /72/ VT (estrarre) to draw out, extract; (ottenere) to obtain, gain

rica'vato SM (di vendite) proceeds pl

ri'cavo SM proceeds pl; (Contabilità) revenue

ric'chezza [rik'kettsa] SF wealth; (fig) richness ■ **ricchezze** SFPL (beni) wealth sg, riches; **ricchezze naturali** natural resources

'riccio, -a, -ci, -ce ['rittʃo] AG curly ▶ SM (Zool) hedgehog; (anche: **riccio di mare**) sea urchin

'ricciolo ['rittʃolo] SM curl

ricci'uto, -a [rit'tʃuto] AG curly

'**ricco, -a, -chi, -che** AG rich; (*persona, paese*) rich, wealthy ▶ SM/F rich man/woman; **i ricchi** the rich; **~ di** (*idee, illustrazioni ecc*) full of; (*risorse, fauna ecc*) rich in

ri'cerca, -che [ri'tʃerka] SF search; (*indagine*) investigation, inquiry; (*studio*): **la ~** research; **una ~** a piece of research; **mettersi alla ~ di** to go in search of, look o search o hunt for; **essere alla ~ di** to be searching for, be looking for; **~ di mercato** market research; **~ operativa** operational research

ricer'care [ritʃer'kare] /**20**/ VT (*motivi, cause*) to look for, try to determine; (*successo, piacere*) to pursue; (*onore, gloria*) to seek

ricerca'tezza [ritʃerka'tettsa] SF (*raffinatezza*) refinement; (*peg*) affectation

ricer'cato, -a [ritʃer'kato] AG (*apprezzato*) much sought-after; (*affettato*) studied, affected ▶ SM/F (*Polizia*) wanted man/woman

ricerca'tore, -'trice [ritʃerka'tore] SM/F (*Ins*) researcher

ricetrasmit'tente [ritʃetrazmit'tɛnte] SF two-way radio, transceiver

ri'cetta [ri'tʃetta] SF (*Med*) prescription; (*Cuc*) recipe; (*fig: antidoto*): **~ contro** remedy for

ricet'tacolo [ritʃet'takolo] SM (*peg: luogo malfamato*) den

ricet'tario [ritʃet'tarjo] SM (*Med*) prescription pad; (*Cuc*) recipe book

ricetta'tore, -'trice [ritʃetta'tore] SM/F (*Dir*) receiver (of stolen goods)

ricettazi'one [ritʃettat'tsjone] SF (*Dir*) receiving (stolen goods)

ricet'tivo, -a [ritʃet'tivo] AG receptive

rice'vente [ritʃe'vɛnte] AG (*Radio, TV*) receiving ▶ SMF (*Comm*) receiver

ri'cevere [ri'tʃevere] /**29**/ VT to receive; (*stipendio, lettera*) to get, receive; (*accogliere: ospite*) to welcome; (*vedere: cliente, rappresentante ecc*) to see; **"confermiamo di aver ricevuto tale merce"** (*Comm*) "we acknowledge receipt of these goods"

ricevi'mento [ritʃevi'mento] SM receiving no pl; (*trattenimento*) reception; **al ~ della merce** on receipt of the goods

ricevi'tore [ritʃevi'tore] SM (*Tecn*) receiver; **~ delle imposte** tax collector

ricevito'ria [ritʃevito'ria] SF (*Fisco*): **~ (delle imposte)** Inland Revenue (BRIT) Office, Internal Revenue (US) Office; **~ del lotto** lottery office

rice'vuta [ritʃe'vuta] SF receipt; **accusare ~ di qc** (*Comm*) to acknowledge receipt of sth; **~ fiscale** official receipt (for tax purposes); **~ di ritorno** (*Posta*) advice of receipt; **~ di versamento** receipt of payment

ricezi'one [ritʃet'tsjone] SF (*Radio, TV*) reception

richia'mare [rikja'mare] /**72**/ VT (*chiamare indie-*

tro, ritelefonare) to call back; (*ambasciatore, truppe*) to recall; (*rimproverare*) to reprimand; (*attirare*) to attract, draw ▪ **richiamarsi** VPR: **richiamarsi a** (*riferirsi a*) to refer to; **~ qn all'ordine** to call sb to order; **desidero ~ la vostra attenzione su ...** I would like to draw your attention to ...

richi'amo [ri'kjamo] SM call; recall; reprimand; attraction

richie'dente [rikje'dɛnte] SMF applicant

richi'edere [ri'kjɛdere] /**21**/ VT to ask again for; (*chiedere: per sapere*) to ask; (*: per avere*) to ask for; (*Amm: documenti*) to apply for; (*esigere*) to need, require; (*chiedere indietro*): **~ qc** to ask for sth back; **essere molto richiesto** to be in great demand

richi'esto, -a [ri'kjɛsto] PP di **richiedere** ▶ SF (*domanda*) request; (*Amm*) application, request; (*esigenza*) demand, request; **a richiesta** on request

rici'claggio [ritʃi'kladdʒo] SM (*fig*) laundering; **~ di materiale** recycling; **~ di denaro sporco** money laundering

rici'clare [ritʃi'klare] /**72**/ VT (*vetro, carta, bottiglie*) to recycle; (*fig: personale*) to retrain

'**ricino** [ritʃino] SM: **olio di ~** castor oil

ricogni'tore [rikoɲɲi'tore] SM (*Aer*) reconnaissance aircraft

ricognizi'one [rikoɲɲit'tsjone] SF (*Mil*) reconnaissance; (*Dir*) recognition, acknowledgement

ricolle'gare /**80**/ VT (*collegare nuovamente: gen*) to join again, link again; (*connettere: fatti*): **~ (a, con)** to connect (with) ▪ **ricollegarsi** VPR: **ricollegarsi a** (*fatti: connettersi*) to be connected to; (*persona: riferirsi*) to refer to

ri'colmo, -a AG: **~ (di)** (*bicchiere*) full to the brim (with); (*stanza*) full (of)

ricominci'are [rikomin'tʃare] /**14**/ VT, VI to start again, begin again; **~ a fare qc** to begin doing o to do sth again, start doing o to do sth again

ricom'pensa SF reward

ricompen'sare /**72**/ VT to reward

ricom'porsi /**77**/ VPR to compose o.s., regain one's composure

ricom'posto, -a PP di **ricomporsi**

riconcili'are [rikontʃi'ljare] /**19**/ VT to reconcile ▪ **riconciliarsi** VPR to be reconciled

riconciliazi'one [rikontʃiliat'tsjone] SF reconciliation

ricon'dotto, -a PP di **ricondurre**

ricon'durre /**90**/ VT to bring (o take) back

ricon'ferma SF reconfirmation

riconfer'mare /**72**/ VT to reconfirm

ricongiungi'mento [rikondʒundʒi'mento] SM (*di famiglia, coniugi*) reconciliation; **~ familiare** (*Dir: di immigrati*) family reunification

ricono'scente [rikonoʃ'ʃɛnte] AG grateful

ricono'scenza [rikonoʃ'ʃɛntsa] SF gratitude

r

rico'noscere [riko'noʃʃere] /**26**/ vᴛ to recognize; (Dir: figlio, debito) to acknowledge; (ammettere: errore) to admit, acknowledge; **~ qn colpevole** to find sb guilty

riconosci'mento [rikonoʃʃi'mento] sᴍ recognition; acknowledgement; (identificazione) identification; **come ~ dei servizi resi** in recognition of services rendered; **documento di ~** means of identification; **segno di ~** distinguishing mark; **programma per il ~ vocale** (Inform) voice recognition program

riconosci'uto, -a [rikonoʃ'ʃuto] ᴘᴘ di **riconoscere**

riconquis'tare /**72**/ vᴛ (Mil) to reconquer; (libertà, stima) to win back

rico'perto, -a ᴘᴘ di **ricoprire**

ricopi'are /**19**/ vᴛ to copy

rico'prire /**9**/ vᴛ to re-cover; (coprire) to cover; (occupare: carica) to hold

ricor'dare /**72**/ vᴛ to remember, recall; (richiamare alla memoria): **~ qc a qn** to remind sb of sth ▪ **ricordarsi** vᴘʀ: **ricordarsi (di)** to remember; **ricordarsi di qc/di aver fatto** to remember sth/having done

ri'cordo sᴍ memory; (regalo) keepsake, souvenir; (di viaggio) souvenir ▪ **ricordi** sᴍᴘʟ (memorie) memoirs

ricor'rente ᴀɢ recurrent, recurring

ricor'renza [rikor'rentsa] sᴅ recurrence; (festività) anniversary

ri'correre /**28**/ vɪ (ripetersi) to recur; **~ a** (rivolgersi) to turn to; (Dir) to appeal to; (servirsi di) to have recourse to; **~ in appello** to lodge an appeal

ri'corso, -a ᴘᴘ di **ricorrere** ▸ sᴍ recurrence; (Dir) appeal; **far ~ a** = **ricorrere a**

ricostitu'ente ᴀɢ (Med): **cura ~** tonic treatment, tonic ▸ sᴍ (Med) tonic

ricostitu'ire /**55**/ vᴛ (società) to build up again; (governo, partito) to re-form ▪ **ricostituirsi** vᴘʀ (gruppo ecc) to re-form

ricostru'ire /**55**/ vᴛ (casa) to rebuild; (fatti) to reconstruct

ricostruzi'one [rikostrut'tsjone] sᴅ rebuilding no pl, reconstruction

ri'cotta sᴅ soft white unsalted cheese made from sheep's milk

ricove'rare /**72**/ vᴛ to give shelter to; **~ qn in ospedale** to admit sb to hospital

ricove'rato, -a sᴍ/ꜰ patient

ri'covero sᴍ shelter, refuge; (Mil) shelter; (Med) admission (to hospital); **~ antiaereo** air-raid shelter

ricre'are /**72**/ vᴛ to recreate; (rinvigorire) to restore; (fig: distrarre) to amuse

ricrea'tivo, -a ᴀɢ recreational

ricreazi'one [rikreat'tsjone] sᴅ recreation, entertainment; (Ins) break

ri'credersi /**29**/ vᴘʀ to change one's mind

ricupe'rare /**72**/ vᴛ (rientrare in possesso di) to recover, get back; (tempo perduto) to make up for; (Naut) to salvage; (: naufraghi) to rescue; (delinquente) to rehabilitate; **~ lo svantaggio** (Sport) to close the gap

ri'cupero sᴍ (gen) recovery; (di relitto ecc) salvaging; **capacità di ~** resilience

ricu'sare /**72**/ vᴛ to refuse

ridacchi'are [ridak'kjare] /**19**/ vɪ to snigger

ri'dare /**33**/ vᴛ to return, give back

'ridda sᴅ (di ammiratori ecc) swarm; (di pensieri) jumble

ri'dente ᴀɢ (occhi, volto) smiling; (paesaggio) delightful

'ridere /**89**/ vɪ to laugh; (deridere, beffare): **~ di** to laugh at, make fun of; **non c'è niente da ~, c'è poco da ~** it's not a laughing matter

rides'tare /**72**/ vᴛ (fig: ricordi, passioni) to reawaken

ri'detto, -a ᴘᴘ di **ridire**

ridico'laggine [ridiko'laddʒine] sᴅ (di situazione) absurdity; (cosa detta o fatta) nonsense no pl

ridicoliz'zare [ridikolid'dzare] /**72**/ vᴛ to ridicule

ri'dicolo, -a ᴀɢ ridiculous, absurd ▸ sᴍ: **cadere nel ~** to become ridiculous; **rendersi ~** to make a fool of o.s.

ridimensiona'mento sᴍ reorganization; (di fatto storico) reappraisal

ridimensio'nare /**72**/ vᴛ to reorganize; (fig) to see in the right perspective

ri'dire /**38**/ vᴛ to repeat; (criticare) to find fault with; to object to; **trova sempre qualcosa da ~** he always manages to find fault

ridon'dante ᴀɢ redundant

ri'dosso sᴍ: **a ~ di** (dietro) behind; (contro) against

ri'dotto, -a ᴘᴘ di **ridurre** ▸ ᴀɢ (biglietto) reduced; (formato) small

ri'duco ecc vʙ vedi **ridurre**

ri'durre /**90**/ vᴛ (anche Chim, Mat) to reduce; (prezzo, spese) to cut, reduce; (accorciare: opera letteraria) to abridge; (Radio, TV) to adapt ▪ **ridursi** vᴘʀ (diminuirsi) to be reduced, shrink; **ridursi a** to be reduced to; **ridursi a pelle e ossa** to be reduced to skin and bone

ri'dussi ecc vʙ vedi **ridurre**

ridut'tore sᴍ (Tecn, Chim) reducer; (Elettr) adaptor

riduzi'one [ridut'tsjone] sᴅ reduction; abridgement; adaptation

ri'ebbi ecc vʙ vedi **riavere**

riecheg'giare [rieked'dʒare] /**62**/ vɪ to re-echo

riedu'care /**20**/ vᴛ (persona, arto) to re-educate; (malato) to rehabilitate

rieducazi'one [riedukat'tsjone] sᴅ re-education;

rehabilitation; **centro di ~** rehabilitation centre

rie'leggere [rie'lɛddʒere] /**61**/ vт to re-elect

rie'letto, -a pp di **rieleggere**

riempi'mento sм filling (up)

riem'pire /**91**/ vт to fill (up); (*modulo*) to fill in *o* out ▪ **riempirsi** vpr to fill (up); (*mangiare troppo*) to stuff o.s.; **~ qc di** to fill sth (up) with

riempi'tivo, -a ag filling ▶ sм (*anche fig*) filler

rien'tranza [rien'trantsa] sf recess; indentation

rien'trare /**72**/ vi (*entrare di nuovo*) to go (*o* come) back in; (*tornare*) to return; (*fare una rientranza*) to go in, curve inwards; to be indented; (*riguardare*): **~ in** to be included among, form part of; **~ (a casa)** to get back home; **non rientriamo nelle spese** we are not within our budget

ri'entro sм (*ritorno*) return; (*di astronave*) re-entry; **è iniziato il grande ~** (*estivo*) people are coming back from their (summer) holidays

riepilo'gare /**80**/ vт to summarize ▶ vi to recapitulate

rie'pilogo, -ghi sм recapitulation; **fare un ~ di qc** to summarize sth

rie'same sм re-examination

riesami'nare /**72**/ vт to re-examine

ri'esco *ecc* vв *vedi* **riuscire**

ri'essere /**51**/ vi: **ci risiamo!** (*col*) we're back to this again!

rievo'care /**20**/ vт (*passato*) to recall; (*commemorare: figura, meriti*) to commemorate

rievocazi'one [rievokat'tsjone] sf (*vedi vt*) recalling; commemoration

rifaci'mento [rifatʃi'mento] sм (*di film*) remake; (*di opera letteraria*) rehashing

ri'fare /**53**/ vт to do again; (*ricostruire*) to make again; (*nodo*) to tie again, do up again; (*imitare*) to imitate, copy ▪ **rifarsi** vpr (*risarcirsi*): **rifarsi di** to make up for; (*vendicarsi*): **rifarsi di qc su qn** to get one's own back on sb for sth; (*riferirsi*): **rifarsi a** (*periodo, fenomeno storico*) to go back to; to follow; **~ il letto** to make the bed; **rifarsi una vita** to make a new life for o.s.

ri'fatto, -a pp di **rifare**

riferi'mento sм reference; **in** *o* **con ~ a** with reference to; **far ~ a** to refer to

rife'rire /**55**/ vт (*riportare*) to report; (*ascrivere*): **~ qc a** to attribute sth to ▶ vi to do a report ▪ **riferirsi** vpr: **riferirsi a** to refer to; **riferirò** I'll pass on the message

rifi'lare /**72**/ vт (*tagliare a filo*) to trim; (*col: affibbiare*): **~ qc a qn** to palm sth off on sb

rifi'nire /**55**/ vт to finish off, put the finishing touches to

rifini'tura sf finishing touch ▪ **rifiniture** sfpl (*di mobile, auto*) finish *sg*

rifiu'tare /**72**/ vт to refuse; **~ di fare** to refuse to do

rifi'uto sм refusal ▪ **rifiuti** sмpl (*spazzatura*) rubbish *sg*, refuse *sg*; **rifiuti solidi urbani** solid urban waste *sg*

riflessi'one sf (*Fisica, meditazione*) reflection; (*il pensare*) thought, reflection; (*osservazione*) remark

rifles'sivo, -a ag (*persona*) thoughtful, reflective; (*Ling*) reflexive

ri'flesso, -a pp di **riflettere** ▶ sм (*di luce, allo specchio*) reflection; (*Fisiol*) reflex; (*su capelli*) light; (*fig*) effect; **di** *o* **per ~** indirectly; **avere i riflessi pronti** to have quick reflexes

riflessolo'gia [riflessolo'dʒia] sf: **~ (plantare)** reflexology

ri'flettere /**92**/ vт to reflect ▶ vi to think ▪ **riflettersi** vpr to be reflected; (*ripercuotersi*) **riflettersi su** to have repercussions on; **~ su** to think over

riflet'tore sм reflector; (*proiettore*) floodlight; (*Mil*) searchlight

ri'flusso sм flowing back; (*della marea*) ebb; **un'epoca di ~** an era of nostalgia

rifocil'larsi [rifotʃil'larsi] /**72**/ vpr (*poetico*) to take refreshment

rifondazi'one [rifondat'tsjone] sf (*Pol*): **R~ Comunista** hard left party, originating from former P.C.I.

ri'fondere /**25**/ vт (*rimborsare*) to refund, repay; **~ le spese a qn** to refund sb's expenses; **~ i danni a qn** to compensate sb for damages

ri'forma sf reform; (*Mil*) declaration of unfitness for service; discharge (*on health grounds*); **la R~** (*Rel*) the Reformation

rifor'mare /**72**/ vт to re-form; (*cambiare, innovare*) to reform; (*Mil: recluta*) to declare unfit for service; (*: soldato*) to invalid out, discharge

riforma'tore, -'trice ag reforming ▶ sм/ғ reformer

riforma'torio sм (*Dir*) community home (*Brit*), reformatory (*US*)

rifor'mista, -i, -e ag, sм/ғ reformist

riforni'mento sм supplying, providing; restocking; (*di carburante*) refuelling ▪ **rifornimenti** sмpl (*provviste*) supplies, provisions; **fare ~ di** (*viveri*) to stock up with; (*benzina*) to fill up with; **posto di ~** filling *o* gas (*US*) station

rifor'nire /**55**/ vт (*fornire di nuovo: casa ecc*) to restock; (*provvedere*): **~ di** to supply *o* provide with ▪ **rifornirsi** vpr: **rifornirsi di qc** to stock up on sth

ri'frangere [ri'frandʒere] /**37**/ vт to refract

ri'fratto, -a pp di **rifrangere**

rifrazi'one [rifrat'tsjone] sf refraction

rifug'gire [rifud'dʒire] /**31**/ vi to escape again; (*fig*): **~ da** to shun

rifugi'arsi [rifu'dʒarsi] /**62**/ vpr to take refuge

rifugi'ato, -a [rifu'dʒato] sм/ғ refugee

ri'fugio [ri'fudʒo] SM refuge, shelter; (in montagna) shelter; ~ antiaereo air-raid shelter

ri'fuso, -a PP di rifondere

'riga, -ghe SF line; (striscia) stripe; (di persone, cose) line, row; (regolo) ruler; (scriminatura) parting; mettersi in ~ to line up; a righe (foglio) lined; (vestito) striped; buttare giù due righe (note) to jot down a few notes; mandami due righe appena arrivi drop me a line as soon as you arrive

ri'gagnolo [ri'gaɲɲolo] SM rivulet

ri'gare /80/ VT (foglio) to rule ▶ VI: ~ diritto (fig) to toe the line

rigassifica'tore SM regasification terminal

riga'toni SMPL (Cuc) short, ridged pasta shapes

rigatti'ere SM junk dealer

riga'tura SF (di pagina, quaderno) lining, ruling; (di fucile) rifling

rigene'rare [ridʒene'rare] /72/ VT (gen, Tecn) to regenerate; (forze) to restore; (gomma) to retread ■ rigenerarsi VPR (gen) to regenerate; (ramo, tumore) to regenerate, grow again; gomma rigenerata retread

rigenerazi'one [ridʒenerat'tsjone] SF regeneration

riget'tare [ridʒet'tare] /72/ VT (gettare indietro) to throw back; (fig: respingere) to reject; (vomitare) to bring o throw up

ri'getto [ri'dʒetto] SM (anche Med) rejection

ri'ghello [ri'gɛllo] SM ruler

righerò ecc [rige'rɔ] VB vedi rigare

rigi'dezza [ridʒi'dettsa], rigidità [ridʒidi'ta] SF rigidity, stiffness, severity, rigours pl (BRIT), rigors pl (US); strictness

'rigido, -a ['ridʒido] AG rigid, stiff; (membra ecc: indurite) stiff; (Meteor) harsh, severe; (fig) strict

rigi'rare [ridʒi'rare] /72/ VT to turn ■ rigirarsi VPR to turn round; (nel letto) to turn over; ~ qc tra le mani to turn sth over in one's hands; ~ il discorso to change the subject

'rigo, -ghi SM line; (Mus) staff, stave

rigogli'oso, -a [rigoʎ'ʎoso] AG (pianta) luxuriant; (fig: commercio, sviluppo) thriving

rigonfia'mento SM (Anat) swelling; (su legno, intonaco ecc) bulge

ri'gonfio, -a AG swollen; (grembiule, sporta): ~ di bulging with

ri'gore SM (Meteor) harshness, rigours pl (BRIT), rigors pl (US); (fig) severity, strictness; (anche: calcio di rigore) penalty; di ~ compulsory; "è di ~ l'abito da sera" "evening dress"; area di ~ (Calcio) penalty box (BRIT); a rigor di termini strictly speaking

rigorosità SF strictness; rigour (BRIT), rigor (US)

rigo'roso, -a AG (severo: persona, ordine) strict; (preciso) rigorous

rigover'nare /72/ VT to wash (up)

riguar'dare /72/ VT to look at again; (considerare) to regard, consider; (concernere) to regard, concern ■ riguardarsi VPR (aver cura di sé) to look after o.s.; per quel che mi riguarda as far as I'm concerned; sono affari che non ti riguardano it's none of your business

rigu'ardo SM (attenzione) care; (considerazione) regard, respect; ~ a concerning, with regard to; per ~ a out of respect for; ospite/persona di ~ very important guest/person; non aver riguardi nell'agire/nel parlare to act/speak freely

riguar'doso, -a AG (rispettoso) respectful; (premuroso) considerate, thoughtful

rigurgi'tare [rigurdʒi'tare] /72/ VI (liquido): ~ da to gush out from; (recipiente: traboccare) ~ di to overflow with

ri'gurgito [ri'gurdʒito] SM (Med) regurgitation; (fig: ritorno, risveglio) revival

rilanci'are [rilan'tʃare] /14/ VT (lanciare di nuovo: gen) to throw again; (: moda) to bring back; (: prodotto) to re-launch; ~ un'offerta (asta) to make a higher bid

ri'lancio [ri'lantʃo] SM (Carte: di offerta) raising

rilasci'are [rilaʃ'ʃare] /14/ VT (rimettere in libertà) to release; (Amm: documenti) to issue; (intervista) to give; ~ delle dichiarazioni to make a statement

ri'lascio [ri'laʃʃo] SM release; issue

rilassa'mento SM (gen, Med) relaxation

rilas'sare /72/ VT to relax ■ rilassarsi VPR to relax; (fig: disciplina) to become slack

rilassa'tezza [rilassa'tettsa] SF (fig: di costumi, disciplina) laxity

rilas'sato, -a AG (persona, muscoli) relaxed; (disciplina, costumi) lax

rile'gare /80/ VT (libro) to bind

rilega'tura SF binding

ri'leggere [ri'leddʒere] /61/ VT to reread, read again; (rivedere) to read over

ri'lento: a ~ AV slowly

ri'letto, -a PP di rileggere

rilet'tura SF (vedi vt) rereading; reading over

rileva'mento SM (topografico, statistico) survey; (Naut) bearing

rile'vante AG considerable; important

rile'vanza [rile'vantsa] SF importance

rile'vare /72/ VT (ricavare) to find; (notare) to notice; (mettere in evidenza) to point out; (venire a conoscere: notizia) to learn; (raccogliere: dati) to gather, collect; (Topografia) to survey; (Mil) to relieve; (Comm) to take over

rileva'tore SM: ~ di fumo smoke detector

rilevazi'one [rilevat'tsjone] SF survey

rili'evo SM (Arte, Geo) relief; (fig: rilevanza) importance; (osservazione) point, remark; (Topografia) survey; dar ~ a o mettere in ~ qc (fig) to bring sth out, highlight sth; **di poco/nessun ~** (fig) of little/no importance; **un personaggio di ~** an important person

rilut'tante AG reluctant

rilut'tanza [rilut'tantsa] SF reluctance

'**rima** SF rhyme; (verso) verse; **far ~ con** to rhyme with; **rispondere a qn per le rime** to give sb tit for tat

riman'dare /72/ VT to send again; (restituire, rinviare) to send back, return; **~ qc (a)** (differire) to postpone sth o put sth off (till); **~ qn a** (fare riferimento) to refer sb to; **essere rimandato** (Ins) to have to resit one's exams

ri'mando SM (rinvio) return; (dilazione) postponement; (riferimento) cross-reference

rimaneggi'are [rimaned'dʒare] /62/ VT (testo) to reshape, recast; (Pol) to reshuffle

rima'nente AG remaining ▶ SM rest, remainder; **i rimanenti** (persone) the rest of them, the others

rima'nenza [rima'nɛntsa] SF rest, remainder ■ **rimanenze** SFPL (Comm) unsold stock sg

rima'nere /93/ VI (restare) to remain, stay; (avanzare) to be left, remain; (restare stupito) to be amazed; **rimangono poche settimane a Pasqua** there are only a few weeks left till Easter; **~ vedovo** to be left a widower; **~ confuso/sorpreso** to be confused/surprised; **rimane da vedere se** it remains to be seen whether

rimangi'are [riman'dʒare] /62/ VT to eat again; **rimangiarsi la parola/una promessa** (fig) to go back on one's word/one's promise

ri'mango ecc VB vedi **rimanere**

ri'mare /72/ VT, VI to rhyme

rimargi'nare [rimardʒi'nare] /72/ VT, VI (anche: **rimarginarsi**) to heal

ri'masto, -a PP di **rimanere**

rima'sugli [rima'suʎʎi] SMPL leftovers

rimbal'zare [rimbal'tsare] /72/ VI to bounce back, rebound; (proiettile) to ricochet

rim'balzo [rim'baltso] SM rebound; ricochet

rimbam'bire /55/ VI to be in one's dotage; (rincretinire) to grow foolish

rimbam'bito, -a AG senile, in one's dotage; (col): **un vecchio ~** a doddering old man

rimbec'care /20/ VT (persona) to answer back; (offesa) to return

rimbecil'lire [rimbetʃil'lire] /55/ VI, **rimbecil'lirsi** VPR to become stupid

rimboc'care /20/ VT (orlo) to turn up; (coperta) to tuck in; (maniche, pantaloni) to turn o roll up

rimbom'bare /72/ VI to resound; (artiglieria) to boom; (tuono) to rumble

rim'bombo SM (vedi vi) boom; rumble

rimbor'sare /72/ VT to pay back, repay; **~ qc a qn** to reimburse sb for sth

rim'borso SM repayment; (di spese, biglietto) refund; **~ d'imposta** tax rebate

rimboschi'mento [rimboski'mento] SM reafforestation

rimbos'chire [rimbos'kire] /55/ VT to reafforest

rimbrot'tare /72/ VT to reproach

rim'brotto SM reproach

rimedi'are /19/ VI: **~ a** to remedy ▶ VT (col: procurarsi) to get o scrape together; **~ da vivere** to scrape a living

ri'medio SM (medicina) medicine; (cura, fig) remedy, cure; **porre ~ a qc** to remedy sth; **non c'è ~** there's no way out, there's nothing to be done about it

rimesco'lare /72/ VT to mix well, stir well; (carte) to shuffle; **sentirsi ~ il sangue** (per rabbia) to feel one's blood boil

ri'messa SF (locale: per veicoli) garage; (: per aerei) hangar; (Comm: di merce) consignment; (: di denaro) remittance; (Tennis) return; (Calcio: anche: **rimessa in gioco**) throw-in

ri'messo, -a PP di **rimettere**

rimes'tare /72/ VT (mescolare) to mix well, stir well; (fig: passato) to drag up again

ri'mettere /63/ VT (mettere di nuovo) to put back; (Comm: merci) to deliver; (: denaro) to remit; (vomitare) to bring up; (perdere: anche: **rimetterci**) to lose; (indossare di nuovo): **~ qc** to put sth back on, put sth on again; (restituire) to return, give back; (affidare) to entrust; (decisione) to refer; (condonare) to remit ■ **rimettersi** VPR: **rimettersi a** (affidarsi) to trust; **~ a nuovo** (casa ecc) to do up (BRIT) o over (US); **rimettersi di tasca propria** to be out of pocket; **rimettersi al bello** (tempo) to clear up; **rimettersi in cammino** to set off again; **rimettersi al lavoro** to start working again; **rimettersi in salute** to get better, recover one's health

rimi'nese AG of (o from) Rimini

ri'misi ecc VB vedi **rimettere**

'**rimmel**® SM INV mascara

rimoderna'mento SM modernization

rimoder'nare /72/ VT to modernize

ri'monta SF (Sport: gen) recovery

rimon'tare /72/ VT (meccanismo) to reassemble; (tenda) to put up again ▶ VI (salire di nuovo): **~ in** (macchina, treno) to get back into; (Sport) to close the gap

rimorchi'are [rimor'kjare] /19/ VT to tow; (fig: ragazza) to pick up

rimorchia'tore [rimorkja'tore] SM (Naut) tug(boat)

ri'morchio [ri'mɔrkjo] SM tow; (veicolo) trailer; **andare a ~** to be towed; **prendere a ~** to tow; **cavo da ~** towrope; **autocarro con ~** articulated lorry (BRIT), semi(trailer) (US)

ri'morso SM remorse; **avere il ~ di aver fatto qc** to deeply regret having done sth

ri'mosso, -a PP *di* **rimuovere**

rimos'tranza [rimos'trantsa] SF protest, complaint; **fare le proprie rimostranze a qn** to remonstrate with sb

rimozi'one [rimot'tsjone] SF removal; (*da un impiego*) dismissal; (*Psic*) repression; **"~ forzata"** "illegally parked vehicles will be removed at owner's expense"

rimpas'tare /72/ VT (*Pol: ministero*) to reshuffle

rim'pasto SM (*Pol*) reshuffle; **~ ministeriale** cabinet reshuffle

rimpatri'are /19/ VI to return home ▶ VT to repatriate

rim'patrio SM repatriation

rimpi'angere [rim'pjandʒere] /75/ VT to regret; (*persona*) to miss; **~ di (non) aver fatto qc** to regret (not) having done sth

rimpi'anto, -a PP *di* **rimpiangere** ▶ SM regret

rimpiat'tino SM hide-and-seek

rimpiaz'zare [rimpjat'tsare] /72/ VT to replace

rimpiccio'lire [rimpittʃo'lire] /55/ VT to make smaller ▶ VI (*anche:* **rimpicciolirsi**) to become smaller

rimpin'zare [rimpin'tsare] /72/ VT: **~ di** to cram *o* stuff with ■ **rimpinzarsi** VPR: **rimpinzarsi (di qc)** to stuff o.s. (with sth)

rimprove'rare /72/ VT to rebuke, reprimand

rim'provero SM rebuke, reprimand; **di ~** (*tono, occhiata*) reproachful; (*parole*) of reproach

rimugi'nare [rimudʒi'nare] /72/ VT (*fig*) to turn over in one's mind

rimune'rare /72/ VT (*retribuire*) to remunerate; (*ricompensare: sacrificio ecc*) to reward; **un lavoro ben rimunerato** a well-paid job

rimunera'tivo, -a AG (*lavoro, attività*) remunerative, profitable

rimunerazi'one [rimunerat'tsjone] SF remuneration; (*premio*) reward

rimu'overe /66/ VT to remove; (*destituire*) to dismiss; (*fig: distogliere*) to dissuade

rinascimen'tale [rinaʃʃimen'tale] AG Renaissance *cpd*, of the Renaissance

Rinasci'mento [rinaʃʃi'mento] SM: **il ~** the Renaissance

ri'nascita [ri'naʃʃita] SF rebirth, revival

rincal'zare [rinkal'tsare] /72/ VT (*palo, albero*) to support, prop up; (*lenzuola*) to tuck in

rin'calzo [rin'kaltso] SM support, prop; (*rinforzo*) reinforcement; (*Sport*) reserve (player) ■ **rincalzi** SMPL (*Mil*) reserves

rinca'rare /72/ VT to increase the price of ▶ VI to go up, become more expensive; **~ la dose** (*fig*) to pile it on

rin'caro SM: **~ (di)** (*prezzi, costo della vita*) increase (in); (*prodotto*) increase in the price (of)

rinca'sare /72/ VI to go home

rinchi'udere [rin'kjudere] /22/ VT to shut (*o*

lock) up ■ **rinchiudersi** VPR: **rinchiudersi in** to shut *o.s.* up in; **rinchiudersi in se stesso** to withdraw into o.s.

rinchi'uso, -a [rin'kjuso] PP *di* **rinchiudere**

rincitrul'lirsi [rintʃitrul'lirsi] /55/ VPR to grow foolish

rin'correre /28/ VT to chase, run after

rin'corso, -a PP *di* **rincorrere** ▶ SF short run

rin'crescere [rin'kreʃʃere] /30/ VB IMPERS: **mi rincresce che/di non poter fare** I'm sorry that/I can't do, I regret that/being unable to do

rincresci'mento [rinkreʃʃi'mento] SM regret

rincresci'uto, -a [rinkreʃ'ʃuto] PP *di* **rincrescere**

rincu'lare /72/ VI to draw back; (*arma*) to recoil

rinfacci'are [rinfat'tʃare] /14/ VT (*fig*): **~ qc a qn** to throw sth in sb's face

rinfoco'lare /72/ VT (*fig: odio, passioni*) to rekindle; (*: risentimento, rabbia*) to stir up

rinfor'zare [rinfor'tsare] /72/ VT to reinforce, strengthen ▶ VI (*anche:* **rinforzarsi**) to grow stronger

rin'forzo [rin'fortso] SM: **mettere un ~ a** to strengthen ■ **rinforzi** SMPL (*Mil*) reinforcements; **di ~** (*asse, sbarra*) strengthening; (*esercito*) supporting; (*personale*) extra, additional

rinfran'care /20/ VT to encourage, reassure

rinfres'cante AG (*bibita*) refreshing

rinfres'care /20/ VT (*atmosfera, temperatura*) to cool (down); (*abito, pareti*) to freshen up ▶ VI (*tempo*) to grow cooler ■ **rinfrescarsi** VPR (*ristorarsi*) to refresh o.s.; (*lavarsi*) to freshen up; **~ la memoria a qn** to refresh sb's memory

rin'fresco, -schi SM (*festa*) party ■ **rinfreschi** SMPL (*cibi e bevande*) refreshments

rin'fusa SF: **alla ~** in confusion, higgledy-piggledy

ringhi'are [rin'gjare] /19/ VI to growl, snarl

ringhi'era [rin'gjera] SF railing; (*delle scale*) banister(s)

'ringhio ['ringjo] SM growl, snarl

ringhi'oso, -a [rin'gjoso] AG growling, snarling

ringiova'nire [rindʒova'nire] /55/ VT: **~ qn** (*vestito, acconciatura ecc*) to make sb look younger; (*vacanze ecc*) to rejuvenate sb ▶ VI (*anche:* **ringiovanirsi**) to become (*o* look) younger

ringrazia'mento [ringrattsja'mento] SM thanks *pl*; **lettera/biglietto di ~** thank you letter/card

ringrazi'are [ringrat'tsjare] /19/ VT to thank; **~ qn di qc** to thank sb for sth; **~ qn per aver fatto qc** to thank sb for doing sth

rinne'gare /80/ VT (*fede*) to renounce; (*figlio*) to disown, repudiate

rinne'gato, -a SM/F renegade

rinno'vabile AG (*contratto, energia*) renewable

rinnova'mento SM renewal; (*economico*) revival

rinno'vare /72/ VT to renew; (*ripetere*) to repeat, renew ■ **rinnovarsi** VPR (*fenomeno*) to be repeated, recur

rin'novo SM (*di contratto*) renewal; **"chiuso per ~ (dei) locali"** (*negozio*) "closed for alterations"

rinoce'ronte [rinot∫e'ronte] SM rhinoceros

rino'mato, -a AG renowned, celebrated

rinsal'dare /72/ VT to strengthen

rinsa'vire /55/ VI to come to one's senses

rinsec'chito, -a [rinsek'kito] AG (*vecchio, albero*) thin, gaunt

rinta'narsi /72/ VPR (*animale*) to go into its den; (*persona: nascondersi*) to hide

rintoc'care /20/ VI (*campana*) to toll; (*orologio*) to strike

rin'tocco, -chi SM toll

rintracci'are [rintrat'tʃare] /14/ VT to track down; (*persona scomparsa, documento*) to trace

rintro'nare /72/ VI to boom, roar ▶ VT (*assordare*) to deafen; (*stordire*) to stun

rintuz'zare [rintut'tsare] /72/ VT (*fig: sentimento*) to check, repress; (*: accusa*) to refute

ri'nuncia [ri'nuntʃa] SF renunciation; **~ a** (*carica*) resignation from; (*eredità*) relinquishment of; **~ agli atti del giudizio** (*Dir*) abandonment of a claim

rinunci'are [rinun'tʃare] /14/ VI: **~ a** to give up, renounce; **~ a fare qc** to give up doing sth

rinuncia'tario, -a [rinuntʃa'tarjo] AG defeatist

ri'nunzia ecc [ri'nuntsja] = **rinuncia** ecc

rinveni'mento SM (*ritrovamento*) recovery; (*scoperta*) discovery; (*Metallurgia*) tempering

rinve'nire /128/ VT to find, recover; (*scoprire*) to discover, find out ▶ VI (*riprendere i sensi*) to come round; (*riprendere l'aspetto naturale*) to revive

rinve'nuto, -a PP di **rinvenire**

rinver'dire /55/ VI (*bosco, ramo*) to become green again

rinvi'are /60/ VT (*rimandare indietro*) to send back, return; **~ qc (a)** (*differire*) to postpone sth o put sth off (till); (*seduta*) to adjourn sth (till); **~ qn a** (*fare un rimando*) to refer sb to; **~ a giudizio** (*Dir*) to commit for trial

rinvigo'rire /55/ VT to strengthen

rin'vio, -'vii SM (*rimando*) return; (*differimento*) postponement; (*: di seduta*) adjournment; (*in un testo*) cross-reference; **~ a giudizio** (*Dir*) indictment

riò ecc VB vedi **riavere**

'Rio de Ja'neiro ['rjodedʒa'neiro] SF Rio de Janeiro

rio'nale AG (*mercato, cinema*) local, district cpd

ri'one SM district, quarter

riordina'mento SM (*di ente, azienda*) reorganization

riordi'nare /72/ VT (*rimettere in ordine*) to tidy; (*riorganizzare*) to reorganize

riorganiz'zare [riorganid'dzare] /72/ VT to reorganize

riorganizzazi'one [riorganiddzat'tsjone] SF reorganization

ripa'gare /80/ VT to repay

ripa'rare /72/ VT (*proteggere*) to protect, defend; (*correggere: male, torto*) to make up for; (*: errore*) to put right; (*aggiustare*) to repair ▶ VI (*mettere rimedio*): **~ a** to make up for ■ **ripararsi** VPR (*rifugiarsi*) to take refuge o shelter

ripa'rato, -a AG (*posto*) sheltered

riparazi'one [riparat'tsjone] SF (*di un torto*) reparation; (*di guasto, scarpe*) repairing no pl; repair; (*risarcimento*) compensation; (*Ins*): **esame di ~** resit (BRIT), test retake (US)

ri'paro SM (*protezione*) shelter, protection; (*rimedio*) remedy; **al ~ da** (*sole, vento*) sheltered from; **mettersi al ~** to take shelter; **correre ai ripari** (*fig*) to take remedial action

ripar'tire /45/ VT (*dividere*) to divide up; (*distribuire*) to share out, distribute ▶ VI to set off again; to leave again; (*motore*) to start again

ripartizi'one [ripartit'tsjone] SF division sharing out, distribution; (*Amm: dipartimento*) department

ripas'sare /72/ VI to come (o go) back ▶ VT (*scritto, lezione*) to go over (again)

ri'passo SM (*di lezione*) revision (BRIT), review (US)

ripensa'mento SM second thoughts pl (BRIT), change of mind; **avere un ~** to have second thoughts, change one's mind

ripen'sare /72/ VI to think; (*cambiare idea*) to change one's mind; (*tornare col pensiero*): **~ a** to recall; **a ripensarci ...** on thinking it over ...

riper'correre /28/ VT (*itinerario*) to travel over again; (*strada*) to go along again; (*fig: ricordi, passato*) to go back over

riper'corso, -a PP di **ripercorrere**

riper'cosso, -a PP di **ripercuotersi**

ripercu'otersi /106/ VPR: **~ su** (*fig*) to have repercussions on

ripercussi'one SF (*fig*): **avere una ~ o delle ripercussioni su** to have repercussions on

ripes'care /20/ VT (*pesce*) to catch again; (*persona, cosa*) to fish out; (*fig: ritrovare*) to dig out

ripe'tente SMF student repeating the year, repeater (US)

ri'petere /1/ VT to repeat; (*ripassare*) to go over

ripeti'tore SM (*Radio, TV*) relay

ripetizi'one [ripetit'tsjone] SF repetition; (*di lezione*) revision ■ **ripetizioni** SFPL (*Ins*) private tutoring o coaching sg; **fucile a ~** repeating rifle

ripetuta'mente AV repeatedly, again and again

r

ripi'ano SM (Geo) terrace; (di mobile) shelf

ri'picca SF: **per ~** out of spite

'ripido, -a AG steep

ripiega'mento SM (Mil) retreat

ripie'gare /80/ VT to refold; (piegare più volte) to fold (up) ▶ VI (Mil) to retreat, fall back; (fig: accontentarsi): **~ su** to make do with ■ **ripiegarsi** VPR to bend

ripi'ego, -ghi SM expedient; **una soluzione di ~** a makeshift solution

ripi'eno, -a AG full; (Cuc) stuffed; (: panino) filled ▶ SM (Cuc) stuffing

ri'pone VB vedi **riporre**

ri'pongo ecc VB vedi **riporre**

ri'porre /77/ VT (porre al suo posto) to put back, replace; (mettere via) to put away; (fiducia, speranza): **~ qc in qn** to place o put sth in sb

ripor'tare /72/ VT (portare indietro) to bring (o take) back; (riferire) to report; (citare) to quote; (ricevere) to receive, get; (vittoria) to gain; (successo) to have; (Mat) to carry; (Comm) to carry forward ■ **riportarsi** VPR: **riportarsi a** (anche fig) to go back to; (riferirsi a) to refer to; **~ danni** to suffer damage; **ha riportato gravi ferite** he was seriously injured

ri'porto SM amount carried over; amount carried forward

ripo'sante AG (gen) restful; (musica, colore) soothing

ripo'sare /72/ VT (bicchiere, valigia) to put down; (dare sollievo) to rest ▶ VI to rest ■ **riposarsi** VPR to rest; **qui riposa ...** (su tomba) here lies ...

ripo'sato, -a AG (viso, aspetto) rested; (mente) fresh

ri'posi ecc VB vedi **riporre**

ri'poso SM rest; (Mil): **~!** at ease!; **a ~** (in pensione) retired; **giorno di ~** day off; **"oggi ~"** (Cine, Teat) "no performance today"; (ristorante) "closed today"

ripos'tiglio [ripos'tiʎʎo] SM lumber room (BRIT), storage room (US)

ri'posto, -a PP di **riporre** ▶ AG (fig: senso, significato) hidden

ri'prendere /81/ VT (prigioniero, fortezza) to recapture; (prendere indietro) to take back; (ricominciare: lavoro) to resume; (andare a prendere) to fetch, come back for; (assumere di nuovo: impiegati) to take on again, re-employ; (rimproverare) to tell off; (restringere: abito) to take in; (Cine) to shoot ■ **riprendersi** VPR to recover; (correggersi) to correct o.s.; **~ a fare qc** to start doing sth again; **~ il cammino** to set off again; **~ i sensi** to recover consciousness; **~ sonno** to go back to sleep

ripresen'tare /72/ VT (certificato) to submit again; (domanda) to put forward again; (persona) to introduce again ■ **ripresentarsi** VPR (ritornare: persona) to come back; (: occasione) to arise

again; **ripresentarsi a** (esame) to sit (BRIT) o take (US) again; (concorso) to enter again; **ripresentarsi come candidato** (Pol) to stand (BRIT) o run (US) again (as a candidate)

ri'preso, -a PP di **riprendere** ▶ SF recapture; resumption; (economica, da malattia, emozione) recovery; (Aut) acceleration no pl; (Teat, Cine) rerun; (Cine: presa) shooting no pl; shot; (Sport) second half; (Pugilato) round; **a più riprese** on several occasions, several times; **ripresa cinematografica** shot

ripristi'nare /72/ VT to restore

ri'pristino SM (gen) restoration; (di tradizioni) revival

ripro'dotto, -a PP di **riprodurre**

ripro'durre /90/ VT to reproduce ■ **riprodursi** VPR (Biol) to reproduce; (riformarsi) to form again

riprodut'tivo, -a AG reproductive

riprodut'tore, -'trice AG (organo) reproductive ▶ SM: **~ acustico** pick-up; **~ a cassetta** cassette player

riproduzi'one [riprodut'tsjone] SF reproduction; **~ vietata** all rights reserved

ripro'messo, -a PP di **ripromettersi**

ripro'mettersi /63/ VT (aspettarsi): **~ qc da** to expect sth from; (intendere) **~ di fare qc** to intend to do sth

ripro'porre /77/ VT: **riproporsi di fare qc** to intend to do sth

ripro'posto, -a PP di **riproporre**

ri'prova SF confirmation; **a ~ di** as confirmation of

ripro'vare /72/ VT (provare di nuovo: gen) to try again; (: vestito) to try on again; (: sensazione) to experience again ▶ VI (tentare): **~ (a fare qc)** to try (to do sth) again; **riproverò più tardi** I'll try again later

ripro'vevole AG reprehensible

ripudi'are /19/ VT to repudiate, disown

ri'pudio SM repudiation, disowning

ripu'gnante [ripuɲ'ɲante] AG disgusting, repulsive

ripu'gnanza [ripuɲ'ɲantsa] SF repugnance, disgust

ripu'gnare [ripuɲ'ɲare] /15/ VI: **~ a qn** to repel o disgust sb

ripu'lire /55/ VT to clean up; (ladri) to clean out; (perfezionare) to polish, refine

ripulsi'one SF (Fisica, fig) repulsion

ri'quadro SM square; (Archit) panel

RIS [ris] SIGLA M (= Reparto Investigazioni Scientifiche) ≈ CID, branch of the Carabinieri

ri'sacca, -che SF backwash

ri'saia SF paddy field

risa'lire /98/ VI (ritornare in su) to go back up; **~ a** (ritornare con la mente) to go back to; (datare da) to date back to, go back to

risa'lita SF: **mezzi di ~** (*Sci*) ski lifts

risal'tare /72/ VI (*fig: distinguersi*) to stand out; (*Archit*) to project, jut out

ri'salto SM prominence; (*sporgenza*) projection; **mettere** *o* **porre in ~ qc** to make sth stand out

risana'mento SM (*economico*) improvement; (*bonifica*) reclamation; **~ del bilancio** reorganization of the budget; **~ edilizio** building improvement

risa'nare /72/ VT (*guarire*) to heal, cure; (*palude*) to reclaim; (*economia*) to improve; (*bilancio*) to reorganize

risa'pere /99/ VT: **~ qc** to come to know of sth

risa'puto, -a AG: **è ~ che** ... everyone knows that ..., it's common knowledge that ...

risarci'mento [risart∫i'mento] SM: **~ (di)** compensation (for); **aver diritto al ~ dei danni** to be entitled to damages

risar'cire [risar't∫ire] /55/ VT (*cose*) to pay compensation for; (*persona*): **~ qn di qc** to compensate sb for sth; **~ i danni a qn** to pay sb damages

ri'sata SF laugh

riscalda'mento SM heating; **~ centrale** central heating; **~ globale** global warming

riscal'dare /72/ VT (*scaldare*) to heat; (: *mani, persona*) to warm; (: *minestra*) to reheat ■ **riscaldarsi** VPR to warm up

ris'caldo SM (*col*) (slight) inflammation

riscat'tare /72/ VT (*prigioniero*) to ransom, pay a ransom for; (*Dir*) to redeem ■ **riscattarsi** VPR (*da disonore*) to redeem o.s.

ris'catto SM ransom; redemption

rischia'rare [riskja'rare] /72/ VT (*illuminare*) to light up; (*colore*) to make lighter ■ **rischiararsi** VPR (*tempo*) to clear up; (*cielo*) to clear; (*fig: volto*) to brighten up; **rischiararsi la voce** to clear one's throat

rischi'are [ris'kjare] /19/ VT to risk ▶ VI: **~ di fare qc** to risk *o* run the risk of doing sth

'rischio ['riskjo] SM risk; **a ~** (*zona, situazione*) at risk, vulnerable; **a proprio ~ e pericolo** at one's own risk; **correre il ~ di fare qc** to run the risk of doing sth; **~ del mestiere** occupational hazard

rischi'oso, -a [ris'kjoso] AG risky, dangerous

risciac'quare [ri∫∫ak'kware] /72/ VT to rinse

risci'acquo [ri∫'∫akkwo] SM rinse

riscon'trare /72/ VT (*confrontare: due cose*) to compare; (*esaminare*) to check, verify; (*rilevare*) to find

ris'contro SM comparison check, verification; (*Amm: lettera di risposta*) reply; **mettere a ~** to compare; **in attesa di un vostro cortese ~** we look forward to your reply

risco'perto, -a PP *di* **riscoprire**

risco'prire /9/ VT to rediscover

riscossi'one SF collection

ris'cosso, -a PP *di* **riscuotere** ▶ SF (*riconquista*) recovery, reconquest

riscri'vibile AG (*CD, DVD*) rewritable

riscu'otere /106/ VT (*ritirare una somma dovuta*) to collect; (: *stipendio*) to draw, collect; (: *assegno*) to cash; (*fig: successo ecc*) to win, earn ■ **riscuotersi** VPR: **riscuotersi (da)** to shake o.s. (out of), rouse o.s. (from); **~ un assegno** to cash a cheque

'rise *ecc* VB *vedi* **ridere**

risenti'mento SM resentment

risen'tire /45/ VT to hear again; (*provare*) to feel ▶ VI: **~ di** to feel (*o* show) the effects of ■ **risentirsi** VPR: **risentirsi di** *o* **per** to take offence (BRIT) *o* offense (US) at, resent

risen'tito, -a AG resentful

ri'serbo SM reserve

ri'serva SF reserve; (*di caccia, pesca*) preserve; (*restrizione, di indigeni*) reservation; (*Calcio*) substitute; **fare ~ di** (*cibo*) to get in a supply of; **tenere di ~** to keep in reserve; **con le dovute riserve** with certain reservations; **ha accettato con la ~ di potersi ritirare** he accepted with the proviso that he could pull out

riser'vare /72/ VT (*tenere in serbo*) to keep, put aside; (*prenotare*) to book, reserve ■ **riservarsi** VPR: **riservarsi di fare qc** to intend to do sth; **riservarsi il diritto di fare qc** to reserve the right to do sth

riserva'tezza [riserva'tettsa] SF reserve

riser'vato, -a AG (*prenotato: fig: persona*) reserved; (*confidenziale: lettera, informazione*) confidential

'risi *ecc* VB *vedi* **ridere**

ri'sibile AG laughable

risi'cato, -a AG (*vittoria ecc*) very narrow

risi'edere /29/ VI: **~ a** *o* **in** to reside in

'risma SF (*di carta*) ream; (*fig*) kind, sort

'riso¹, -a PP *di* **ridere** ▶ SM (*pl(f)* **risa**) (*il ridere*): **un ~** a laugh; **il ~** laughter; **uno scoppio di risa** a burst of laughter

'riso² SM (*pianta*) rice

riso'lino SM snigger

risolle'vare /72/ VT (*sollevare di nuovo: testa*) to raise again, lift up again; (*fig: questione*) to raise again, bring up again; (*morale*) to raise ■ **risollevarsi** VPR (*da terra*) to rise again; (*fig: da malattia*) to recover; **~ le sorti di qc** to improve the chances of sth

ri'solsi *ecc* VB *vedi* **risolvere**

ri'solto, -a PP *di* **risolvere**

risolu'tezza [risolu'tettsa] SF determination

risolu'tivo, -a AG (*determinante*) decisive; (*che risolve*) **arrivare ad una formula risolutiva** to come up with a formula to resolve a situation

riso'luto, -a AG determined, resolute

risoluzi'one [risolut'tsjone] SF solving *no pl*; (*Mat*) solution; (*decisione, di schermo, immagine*) resolution; (*Dir: di contratto*) annulment, cancellation

ri'solvere /**94**/ VT (*difficoltà, controversia*) to resolve; (*problema*) to solve; (*decidere*): **~ di fare** to resolve to do ■ **risolversi** VPR (*decidersi*): **risolversi a fare** to make up one's mind to do; (*andare a finire*): **risolversi in** to end up, turn out; **risolversi in nulla** to come to nothing

risol'vibile AG solvable

riso'nanza [riso'nantsa] SF resonance; **aver vasta ~** (*fig: fatto ecc*) to be known far and wide; **~ magnetica** magnetic resonance

riso'nare /**72**/ VT, VI = **risuonare**

ri'sorgere [ri'sɔrdʒere] /**109**/ VI to rise again

risorgimen'tale [risordʒimen'tale] AG of the Risorgimento

risorgi'mento [risordʒi'mento] SM revival; **il R~** (*Storia*) the Risorgimento

> The **Risorgimento**, the period stretching from the early nineteenth century to 1861 and the proclamation of the Kingdom of Italy, saw considerable upheaval and change. Political and personal freedom took on new importance as the events of the French Revolution unfolded. The *Risorgimento* paved the way for the unification of Italy in 1871.

ri'sorsa SF expedient, resort ■ **risorse** SFPL (*naturali, finanziarie ecc*) resources; **persona piena di risorse** resourceful person; **risorse umane** human resources

ri'sorsi *ecc* VB *vedi* **risorgere**

ri'sorto, -a PP *di* **risorgere**

ri'sotto SM (*Cuc*) risotto

risparmi'are /**19**/ VT to save; (*non uccidere*) to spare ▸ VI to save; **~ qc a qn** to spare sb sth; **~ fatica/fiato** to save one's energy/breath; **risparmiati il disturbo** o **la fatica** (*anche ironico*) save yourself the trouble

risparmia'tore, -'trice SM/F saver

ris'parmio SM saving *no pl*; (*denaro*) savings *pl* ■ **risparmi** SMPL (*denaro*) savings

rispecchi'are [rispek'kjare] /**19**/ VT to reflect ■ **rispecchiarsi** VPR to be reflected

rispe'dire /**55**/ VT to send back; **~ qc a qn** to send sth back to sb

rispet'tabile AG respectable; (*considerevole: somma*) sizeable, considerable

rispet'tare /**72**/ VT to respect; (*legge*) to obey, comply with, abide by; (*promessa*) to keep; **farsi ~** to command respect; **~ le distanze** to keep one's distance; **~ i tempi** to keep to schedule; **ogni medico che si rispetti** every self-respecting doctor

rispettiva'mente AV respectively

rispet'tivo, -a AG respective

ris'petto SM respect ■ **rispetti** SMPL (*saluti*)

respects, regards; **~ a** (*in paragone a*) compared to; (*in relazione a*) as regards, as for; **~ (di** o **per)** (*norme, leggi*) observance (of), compliance (with); **portare ~ a qn/qc** to have o feel respect for sb/sth; **mancare di ~ a qn** to be disrespectful to sb; **con ~ parlando** with respect, if you will excuse my saying so; **(porga) i miei rispetti alla signora** (give) my regards to your wife

rispet'toso, -a AG respectful

risplen'dente AG (*giornata, sole*) bright, shining; (*occhi*) sparkling

ris'plendere /**29**/ VI to shine

rispon'dente AG: **~ a** in keeping o conformity with

rispon'denza [rispon'dɛntsa] SF correspondence

ris'pondere /**95**/ VI to answer, reply; (*freni*) to respond; **~ a** (*domanda*) to answer, reply to; (*persona*) to answer; (*invito*) to reply to; (*provocazione, veicolo, apparecchio*) to respond to; (*corrispondere a*) to correspond to; (*speranze, bisogno*) to answer; **~ a qn di qc** (*essere responsabile*) to be answerable to sb for sth

rispo'sarsi /**72**/ VPR to get married again, remarry

ris'posto, -a PP *di* **rispondere** ▸ SF answer, reply; **in risposta a** in reply to; **dare una risposta** to give an answer; **diamo risposta alla vostra lettera del ...** in reply to your letter of ...

'rissa SF brawl

ris'soso, -a AG quarrelsome

rist. ABBR = **ristampa**

ristabi'lire /**55**/ VT to re-establish, restore; (*persona, riposo ecc*) to restore to health ■ **ristabilirsi** VPR to recover

rista'gnare [ristaɲ'ɲare] /**15**/ VI (*acqua*) to become stagnant; (*sangue*) to cease flowing; (*fig: industria*) to stagnate

ris'tagno [ris'taɲɲo] SM stagnation; **c'è un ~ delle vendite** business is slack

ris'tampa SF reprinting *no pl*; reprint

ristam'pare /**72**/ VT to reprint

risto'rante SM restaurant

risto'rare /**72**/ VT (*persona, forze*) to revive, refresh ■ **ristorarsi** VPR (*rifocillarsi*) to have something to eat and drink; (*riposarsi*) to rest, have a rest

ristora'tore, -'trice AG refreshing, reviving ▸ SM/F (*gestore di ristorante*) restaurateur

ris'toro SM (*bevanda, cibo*) refreshment; **posto di ~** (*Ferr*) buffet, snack bar; **servizio di ~** (*Ferr*) refreshments *pl*

ristret'tezza [ristret'tettsa] SF (*strettezza*) narrowness; (*fig: scarsezza*) scarcity, lack; (: *meschinità*) meanness ■ **ristrettezze** SFPL (*povertà*) poverty *sg*

ris'tretto, -a PP *di* **restringere** ▸ AG (*racchiuso*) enclosed, hemmed in; (*angusto*) narrow; (*Cuc*:

brodo) thick; (: *caffè*) extra strong; **~ (a)** (*limitato*) restricted *o* limited (to)

ristruttu'rare /**72**/ vt (*azienda*) to reorganize; (*edificio*) to restore; (*appartamento*) to alter; (*crema, balsamo*) to repair

ristrutturazi'one [ristrutturat'tsjone] sf reorganization; restoration; alteration

risucchi'are [risuk'kjare] /**19**/ vt to suck in

ri'succhio [ri'sukkjo] sm (*di acqua*) undertow, pull; (*di aria*) suction

risul'tare /**72**/ vi (*dimostrarsi*) to prove (to be), turn out (to be); (*riuscire*): **~ vincitore** to emerge as the winner; **~ da** (*provenire*) to result from, be the result of; **mi risulta che ...** I understand that ..., as far as I know ...; **(ne) risulta che ...** it follows that ...; **non mi risulta** not as far as I know

risul'tato sm result

risuo'nare /**72**/ vi (*rimbombare*) to resound

risurrezi'one [risurret'tsjone] sf (*Rel*) resurrection

risusci'tare [risuʃʃi'tare] /**72**/ vt to resuscitate, restore to life; (*fig*) to revive, bring back ▶ vi to rise (from the dead)

risvegli'are [rizveʎ'ʎare] /**27**/ vt (*gen*) to wake up, waken; (*fig: interesse*) to stir up, arouse; (: *curiosità*) to arouse; (: *dall'inerzia ecc*): **~ qn (da)** to rouse sb (from) ▪ **risvegliarsi** vpr to wake up, awaken; (*fig: interesse, curiosità*) to be aroused

ris'veglio [riz'veʎʎo] sm waking up; (*fig*) revival

ris'volto sm (*di giacca*) lapel; (*di pantaloni*) turn-up (Brit), cuff (US); (*di manica*) cuff; (*di tasca*) flap; (*di libro*) inside flap; (*fig*) implication

ritagli'are [rita'ʎʎare] /**27**/ vt (*tagliar via*) to cut out

ri'taglio [ri'taʎʎo] sm (*di giornale*) cutting, clipping; (*di stoffa ecc*) scrap; **nei ritagli di tempo** in one's spare time

ritar'dare /**72**/ vi (*persona, treno*) to be late; (*orologio*) to be slow ▶ vt (*rallentare*) to slow down; (*impedire*) to delay, hold up; (*differire*) to postpone, delay; **~ il pagamento** to defer payment

ritarda'tario, -a sm/f latecomer

ritar'dato, -a ag (*Psic*) retarded

ri'tardo sm delay; (*di persona aspettata*) lateness *no pl*; (*fig: mentale*) learning difficulty; **in ~** late

ri'tegno [ri'teɲɲo] sm restraint

ritem'prare /**72**/ vt (*forze, spirito*) to restore

rite'nere /**121**/ vt (*trattenere*) to hold back; (: *somma*) to deduct; (*giudicare*) to consider, believe

ri'tengo vb *vedi* **ritenere**

ri'tenni *ecc* vb *vedi* **ritenere**

riten'tare /**72**/ vt to try again, make another attempt at

rite'nuta sf (*sul salario*) deduction; **~ d'acconto**

advance deduction of tax; **~ alla fonte** (*Fisco*) taxation at source

riterrò *ecc* vb *vedi* **ritenere**

riti'ene *ecc* vb *vedi* **ritenere**

riti'rare /**72**/ vt to withdraw; (*Pol: richiamare*) to recall; (*andare a prendere: pacco ecc*) to collect, pick up ▪ **ritirarsi** vpr to withdraw; (*da un'attività*) to retire; (*stoffa*) to shrink; (*marea*) to recede; **gli hanno ritirato la patente** they disqualified him from driving (Brit), they took away his licence (Brit) *o* license (US); **ritirarsi a vita privata** to withdraw from public life

riti'rata sf (*Mil*) retreat; (*latrina*) lavatory

riti'rato, -a ag secluded; **fare vita ritirata** to live in seclusion

ri'tiro sm (*di truppe, candidati, soldi*) withdrawal; (*di pacchi*) collection; (*di passaporto*) confiscation; (*da attività*) retirement; (*luogo appartato*) retreat

rit'mato, -a ag rhythmic(al)

'ritmico, -a, -ci, -che ag rhythmic(al)

'ritmo sm rhythm; (*fig*) rate; (: *della vita*) pace, tempo; **al ~ di** at a speed *o* rate of; **ballare al ~ di valzer** to waltz

'rito sm rite; **di ~** usual, customary

ritoc'care /**20**/ vt (*disegno, fotografia*) to touch up; (*testo*) to alter

ri'tocco, -chi sm touching up *no pl*; alteration

ri'torcere [ri'tɔrtʃere] /**106**/ vt (*filato*) to twist; (*fig: accusa, insulto*) to throw back ▪ **ritorcersi** vpr (*tornare a danno di*): **ritorcersi contro** to turn against

ritor'nare /**72**/ vi to return, go (*o* come) back, get back; (*ripresentarsi*) to recur; (*ridiventare*): **~ ricco** to become rich again ▶ vt (*restituire*) to return, give back

ritor'nello sm refrain

ri'torno sm return; **durante il (viaggio di) ~** on the return trip, on the way back; **al ~** (*tornando*) on the way back; **essere di ~** to be back; **far ~** to return; **avere un ~ di fiamma** (*Aut*) to backfire; (*fig: persona*) to be back in love again

ritorsi'one sf (*rappresaglia*) retaliation

ri'torto, -a pp di **ritorcere** ▶ ag (*cotone, corda*) twisted

ri'trarre /**123**/ vt (*trarre indietro, via*) to withdraw; (*distogliere: sguardo*) to turn away; (*rappresentare*) to portray, depict; (*ricavare*) to get, obtain ▪ **ritrarsi** vpr to move back

ritrat'tare /**72**/ vt (*disdire*) to retract, take back; (*trattare nuovamente*) to deal with again

ritrattazi'one [ritrattat'tsjone] sf withdrawal

ritrat'tista, -i, -e sm/f portrait painter

ri'tratto, -a pp di **ritrarre** ▶ sm portrait

ritro'sia sf (*riluttanza*) reluctance, unwillingness; (*timidezza*) shyness

ri'troso, -a ag (*restio*): **~ (a)** reluctant (to); (*schivo*) shy; **andare a ~** to go backwards

r

ritrova'mento SM (di cadavere, oggetto smarrito ecc) finding; (oggetto ritrovato) find

ritro'vare /72/ VT to find; (salute) to regain; (persona) to find; to meet again ■ **ritrovarsi** VPR (essere, capitare) to find o.s.; (raccapezzarsi) to find one's way; (con senso reciproco) to meet (again)

ritro'vato SM discovery

ri'trovo SM meeting place; ~ **notturno** night club

'ritto, -a AG (in piedi) standing, on one's feet; (levato in alto) erect, raised; (: capelli) standing on end; (posto verticalmente) upright

ritu'ale AG, SM ritual

ritwit'tare [ritwit'tare] /72/ VT (su Twitter) to retweet

riuni'one SF (adunanza) meeting; (riconciliazione) reunion; **essere in ~** to be at a meeting

riu'nire /55/ VT (ricongiungere) to join (together); (riconciliare) to reunite, bring together (again) ■ **riunirsi** VPR (adunarsi) to meet; (tornare a stare insieme) to be reunited; **siamo qui riuniti per festeggiare il vostro anniversario** we are gathered here to celebrate your anniversary

riu'scire [riuʃ'ʃire] /125/ VI (uscire di nuovo) to go out again, go back out; (aver esito: fatti, azioni) to go, turn out; (aver successo) to succeed, be successful; (essere, apparire) to be, prove; (raggiungere il fine) to manage, succeed; ~ **a fare qc** to manage o to be able to do sth; **questo mi riesce nuovo** this is new to me

riu'scita [riuʃ'ʃita] SF (esito) result, outcome; (buon esito) success

riutiliz'zare [riutilid'dzare] /72/ VT to use again, re-use

'riva SF (di fiume) bank; (di lago, mare) shore; **in ~ al mare** on the (sea) shore

ri'vale AG rival cpd ▶ SMF rival; **non avere rivali** (anche fig) to be unrivalled

rivaleggi'are [rivaled'dʒare] /62/ VI to compete, vie

rivalità SF rivalry

ri'valsa SF (rivincita) revenge; (risarcimento) compensation; **prendersi una ~ su qn** to take revenge on sb

rivalu'tare /72/ VT (Econ) to revalue

rivalutazi'one [rivalutat'tsjone] SF (Econ) revaluation; (fig) re-evaluation

rivan'gare /80/ VT (ricordi ecc) to dig up (again)

rive'dere /127/ VT to see again; (ripassare) to revise; (verificare) to check

rivedrò ecc VB vedi **rivedere**

rive'lare /72/ VT to reveal; (divulgare) to reveal, disclose; (dare indizio) to reveal, show ■ **rivelarsi** VPR (manifestarsi) to be revealed; **rivelarsi onesto** ecc to prove to be honest etc

rivela'tore, -'trice AG revealing ▶ SM (Tecn) detector; (Fot) developer

rivelazi'one [rivelat'tsjone] SF revelation

ri'vendere /29/ VT (vendere: di nuovo) to resell, sell again; (: al dettaglio) to retail, sell retail

rivendi'care /20/ VT to claim, demand

rivendicazi'one [rivendikat'tsjone] SF claim; **rivendicazioni salariali** wage claims

ri'vendita SF (bottega) retailer's (shop); ~ **di tabacchi** tobacconist's (shop)

rivendi'tore, -'trice SM/F retailer; ~ **autorizzato** (Comm) authorized dealer

riverbe'rare /72/ VT to reflect

ri'verbero SM (di luce, calore) reflection; (di suono) reverberation

rive'rente AG reverent, respectful

rive'renza [rive'rɛntsa] SF reverence; (inchino) bow; curtsey

rive'rire /55/ VT (rispettare) to revere; (salutare) to pay one's respects to

river'sare /72/ VT (anche fig) to pour ■ **riversarsi** VPR (fig: persone) to pour out

rivesti'mento SM covering; coating

rives'tire /45/ VT to dress again; (ricoprire) to cover; (con vernice) to coat; (fig: carica) to hold ■ **rivestirsi** VPR to get dressed again, to change (one's clothes); ~ **di piastrelle** to tile

ri'vidi ecc VB vedi **rivedere**

rivi'era SF coast; **la ~ italiana** the Italian Riviera

ri'vincita [ri'vintʃita] SF (Sport) return match; (fig) revenge; **prendersi la ~ (su qn)** to take o get one's revenge (on sb)

rivis'suto, -a PP di **rivivere**

ri'vista SF review; (periodico) magazine, review; (Teat) revue; variety show

ri'visto, -a PP di **rivedere**

rivitaliz'zante [rivitalid'dzante] AG revitalizing

rivitaliz'zare [rivitalid'dzare] /72/ VT to revitalize

ri'vivere /130/ VI (riacquistare forza) to come alive again; (tornare in uso) to be revived ▶ VT to relive

'rivo SM stream

ri'volgere [ri'vɔldʒere] /96/ VT (attenzione, sguardo) to turn, direct; (parole) to address ■ **rivolgersi** VPR to turn round; **rivolgersi a** (fig: dirigersi per informazioni) to go and see, go and speak to; (: ufficio) to enquire at; ~ **un'accusa/ una critica a qn** to accuse/criticize sb; **rivolgersi all'ufficio competente** to apply to the office concerned

rivolgi'mento [rivoldʒi'mento] SM upheaval

ri'volsi ecc VB vedi **rivolgere**

ri'volta SF revolt, rebellion

rivol'tante AG revolting, disgusting

rivol'tare /72/ VT to turn over; (con l'interno all'esterno) to turn inside out; (disgustare: stomaco) to upset, turn; (: *fig*) to revolt, disgust ■ **rivoltarsi** VPR (*ribellarsi*): **rivoltarsi (a)** to rebel (against)

rivol'tella SF revolver

ri'volto, -a PP *di* **rivolgere**

rivol'toso, -a AG rebellious ▶ SM/F rebel

rivoluzio'nare [rivoluttsjo'nare] /72/ VT to revolutionize

rivoluzio'nario, -a [rivoluttsjo'narjo] AG, SM/F revolutionary

rivoluzi'one [rivolut'tsjone] SF revolution

riz'zare [rit'tsare] /72/ VT to raise, erect ■ **rizzarsi** VPR to stand up; (*capelli*) to stand on end; **rizzarsi in piedi** to stand up, get to one's feet

RN SIGLA = **Rimini**

RNA SIGLA M RNA (= *ribonucleic acid*)

RO SIGLA = **Rovigo**

'**roba** SF stuff, things *pl*; (*possessi, beni*) belongings *pl*, things *pl*, possessions *pl*; **~ da mangiare** things to eat, food; **~ da matti!** it's sheer madness *o* lunacy!

robi'vecchi [robi'vɛkki] SM INV/F INV junk dealer

'**robot** SM INV robot

ro'botica SF robotics *sg*

robus'tezza [robus'tettsa] SF (*di persona, pianta*) robustness, sturdiness; (*di edificio, ponte*) soundness

ro'busto, -a AG robust, sturdy; (*solido: catena*) strong; (: *edificio, ponte*) sound, solid; (: *vino*) full-bodied

'**rocca, -che** SF fortress

rocca'forte SF stronghold

roc'chetto [rok'ketto] SM reel, spool

'**roccia, -ce** ['rɔttʃa] SF rock; **fare ~** (*Sport*) to go rock climbing

roccia'tore, -'trice [rottʃa'tore] SM/F rock climber

rocci'oso, -a [rot'tʃoso] AG rocky; **le Montagne Rocciose** the Rocky Mountains

'**roco, -a, -chi, -che** AG hoarse

ro'daggio [ro'daddʒo] SM running (BRIT) *o* breaking (US) in; **in ~** running *o* breaking in; **periodo di ~** (*fig*) period of adjustment

'**Rodano** SM: **il ~** the Rhone

ro'dare /72/ VT (*Aut, Tecn*) to run (BRIT) *o* break (US) in

ro'deo SM rodeo

rodere /49/ VT to gnaw (at); (*distruggere poco a poco*) to eat into

'**Rodi** SF Rhodes

rodi'tore SM (*Zool*) rodent

rodo'dendro SM rhododendron

'**rogito** ['rɔdʒito] SM (*Dir*) (notary's) deed

'**rogna** ['rɔɲɲa] SF (*Med*) scabies *sg*; (*di animale*) mange; (*fig*) bother, nuisance

ro'gnone [roɲ'ɲone] SM (*Cuc*) kidney

ro'gnoso, -a [roɲ'ɲoso] AG (*persona*) scabby; (*animale*) mangy; (*fig*) troublesome

'**rogo, -ghi** SM (*per cadaveri*) (funeral) pyre; (*supplizio*): **il ~** the stake

rol'lare /72/ VI (*Naut, Aer*) to roll

rol'lino SM = **rullino**

rol'lio SM roll(ing)

'**Roma** SF Rome

roma'gnolo, -a [romaɲ'ɲɔlo] AG of (*o* from) Romagna

roma'nesco, -a, -schi, -sche AG Roman ▶ SM Roman dialect

Roma'nia SF: **la ~** Romania

ro'manico, -a, -ci, -che AG Romanesque

ro'mano, -a AG, SM/F Roman; **fare alla romana** to go Dutch

romantiche'ria [romantike'ria] SF sentimentality

romanti'cismo [romanti'tʃizmo] SM romanticism

ro'mantico, -a, -ci, -che AG romantic

ro'manza [ro'mandza] SF (*Mus, Letteratura*) romance

roman'zare [roman'dzare] /72/ VT to romanticize

roman'zesco, -a, -schi, -sche [roman'dzesko] AG (*stile, personaggi*) fictional; (*fig*) storybook *cpd*

romanzi'ere [roman'dzjɛre] SM novelist

ro'manzo, -a [ro'mandzo] AG (*Ling*) romance *cpd* ▶ SM (*medievale*) romance; (*moderno*) novel; **~ d'amore** love story; **~ d'appendice** serial (story); **~ cavalleresco** tale of chivalry; **~ poliziesco, ~ giallo** detective story; **~ rosa** romantic novel

rom'bare /72/ VI to rumble, thunder, roar

'**rombo** SM rumble, thunder, roar; (*Mat*) rhombus; (*Zool*) turbot; brill

ro'meno, -a AG, SM/F, SM = **rumeno**

'**rompere** /97/ VT to break; (*conversazione, fidanzamento*) to break off ▶ VI to break ■ **rompersi** VPR to break; **mi rompe le scatole** (*col*) he (*o* she) is a pain in the neck; **rompersi un braccio** to break an arm

rompi'capo SM worry, headache; (*indovinello*) puzzle; (*in enigmistica*) brain-teaser

rompi'collo SM daredevil

rompighi'accio [rompi'gjattʃo] SM (*Naut*) icebreaker

rompis'catole SM O F INV (*col*) pest, pain in the neck

'**ronda** SF (*Mil*) rounds *pl*, patrol

ron'della SF (*Tecn*) washer

'**rondine** SF (*Zool*) swallow

ron'done SM (*Zool*) swift

ron'fare /72/ VI (*russare*) to snore

r

315

ron'zare [ron'dzare] /**72**/ VI to buzz, hum

ron'zino [ron'dzino] SM (peg: cavallo) nag

ron'zio, -ii [ron'dzio] SM buzzing, humming; ~ **auricolare** (Med) tinnitus sg

'rosa SF rose; (fig: gruppo): ~ **dei candidati** list of candidates ▶ AG INV, SM pink

ro'saio SM (pianta) rosebush, rose tree; (giardino) rose garden

ro'sario SM (Rel) rosary

ro'sato, -a AG pink, rosy ▶ SM (vino) rosé (wine)

ro'seo, -a AG (anche fig) rosy

ro'seto SM rose garden

ro'setta SF (diamante) rose-cut diamond; (rondella) washer

'rosi VB vedi **rodere**

rosicchi'are [rosik'kjare] /**19**/ VT to gnaw (at); (mangiucchiare) to nibble (at)

rosma'rino SM rosemary

'roso, -a PP di **rodere**

roso'lare /**72**/ VT (Cuc) to brown

roso'lia SF (Med) German measles sg, rubella

ro'sone SM rosette; (vetrata) rose window

'rospo SM (Zool) toad; **mandar giù** o **ingoiare un** o **il ~** (fig) to swallow a bitter pill; **sputa il ~!** out with it!

ros'setto SM (per labbra) lipstick; (per guance) rouge

ros'siccio, -a, -ci, -ce [ros'sittʃo] AG reddish

'rosso, -a AG, SM, SM/F red; **diventare ~ (per la vergogna)** to blush o go red (with o for shame); **il Mar R~** the Red Sea; **~ d'uovo** egg yolk

ros'sore SM flush, blush

rosticce'ria [rostittʃe'ria] SF shop selling roast meat and other cooked food

'rostro SM rostrum; (becco) beak

ro'tabile AG (percorribile): **strada ~** roadway; (Ferr) **materiale ~** rolling stock

ro'taia SF rut, track; (Ferr) rail

ro'tare /**72**/ VT, VI to rotate

rota'tivo, -a AG rotating, rotation cpd

rotazi'one [rotat'tsjone] SF rotation

rote'are /**72**/ VT, VI to whirl; **~ gli occhi** to roll one's eyes

ro'tella SF small wheel; (di mobile) castor

roto'calco, -chi SM (Tip) rotogravure; (rivista) illustrated magazine

roto'lare /**72**/ VT, VI to roll ▪ **rotolarsi** VPR to roll (about)

roto'lio SM rolling

'rotolo SM (di carta, stoffa) roll; (di corda) coil; **andare a rotoli** (fig) to go to rack and ruin; **mandare a rotoli** (fig) to ruin

ro'tondo, -a AG round ▶ SF rotunda

ro'tore SM rotor

'rotta SF (Aer, Naut) course, route; (Mil) rout; **a ~**

di collo at breakneck speed; **essere in ~ con qn** to be on bad terms with sb; **fare ~ su** o **per** o **verso** to head for o towards; **cambiare ~** (anche fig) to change course; **in ~ di collisione** on a collision course; **ufficiale di ~** navigator, navigating officer

rotta'mare /**72**/ VT to scrap old vehicles in return for incentives

rottama'zione [rottamat'tsjone] SF (come incentivo) the scrapping of old vehicles in return for incentives

rot'tame SM fragment, scrap, broken bit ▪ **rottami** SMPL (di nave, aereo ecc) wreckage sg; **rottami di ferro** scrap iron sg

'rotto, -a PP di **rompere** ▶ AG broken; (calzoni) torn, split; (persona: pratico, resistente): ~ **a** accustomed o inured to ▶ SM: **per il ~ della cuffia** by the skin of one's teeth ▪ **rotti** SMPL: **20 euro e rotti** 20-odd euros

rot'tura SF (azione) breaking no pl; break; (di rapporti) breaking off; (Med) fracture, break

rou'lotte [ru'lɔt] SF INV caravan

'router ['ruter] SM INV (Inform) router

ro'vente AG red-hot

'rovere SM oak

ro'vescia [ro'veʃʃa] SF: **alla ~** upside-down; inside-out; **oggi mi va tutto alla ~** everything is going wrong (for me) today

rovesci'are [roveʃ'ʃare] /**14**/ VT (versare in giù) to pour; (: accidentalmente) to spill; (capovolgere) to turn upside down; (gettare a terra) to knock down; (fig: governo) to overthrow; (piegare all'indietro: testa) to throw back ▪ **rovesciarsi** VPR (sedia, macchina) to overturn; (barca) to capsize; (liquido) to spill; (fig: situazione) to be reversed

ro'vescio, -sci [ro'veʃʃo] SM other side, wrong side; (della mano) back; (di moneta) reverse; (pioggia) sudden downpour; (fig) setback; (Maglia: anche: **punto rovescio**) purl (stitch); (Tennis) backhand (stroke); **a ~** (sottosopra) upside-down; (con l'esterno all'interno) inside-out; **capire qc a ~** to misunderstand sth; **~ di fortuna** setback

ro'vina SF ruin ▪ **rovine** SFPL (ruderi) ruins; **andare in ~** (andare a pezzi) to collapse; (fig) to go to rack and ruin; **mandare qc/qn in ~** to ruin sth/sb

rovi'nare /**72**/ VI to collapse, fall down ▶ VT (far cadere giù: casa) to demolish; (danneggiare: fig) to ruin ▪ **rovinarsi** VPR (persona) to ruin o.s.; (oggetto, vestito) to be ruined

rovi'nato, -a AG ruined, damaged; (fig: persona) ruined

rovi'noso, -a AG ruinous

rovis'tare /**72**/ VT (casa) to ransack; (tasche) to rummage in (o through)

'rovo SM (Bot) blackberry o bramble bush

roz'zezza [rod'dzettsa] SF roughness, coarseness

'rozzo, -a ['roddzo] AG rough, coarse

RP SIGLA FPL *vedi* **relazioni pubbliche**

Rr ABBR (*Posta*) = **raccomandata con ricevuta di ritorno**

R.R. ABBR (*Posta*) = **ricevuta di ritorno**

RSVP ABBR (= *répondez s'il vous plaît*) RSVP

'ruba SF: **andare a ~** to sell like hot cakes

rubacu'ori SM INV ladykiller

ru'bare /72/ VT to steal; **~ qc a qn** to steal sth from sb

rubi'condo, -a AG ruddy

rubi'netto SM tap, faucet (*US*)

ru'bino SM ruby

ru'bizzo, -a [ru'bittso] AG lively, sprightly

'rublo SM rouble

ru'brica, -che SF (*di giornale: colonna*) column; (: *pagina*) page; (*quadernetto*) index book; address book; **~ d'indirizzi** address book; **~ telefonica** list of telephone numbers

'rude AG tough, rough

'rudere SM (*rovina*) ruins pl

rudimen'tale AG rudimentary, basic

rudi'menti SMPL rudiments; basic principles; basic knowledge sg

ruffi'ano, -a SM/F pimp; (*fig: leccapiedi*) bootlicker

'ruga, -ghe SF wrinkle

'ruggine ['ruddʒine] SF rust

rug'gire [rud'dʒire] /55/ VI to roar

rug'gito [rud'dʒito] SM roar

rugi'ada [ru'dʒada] SF dew

ru'goso, -a AG wrinkled; (*scabro: superficie ecc*) rough

rul'lare /72/ VI (*tamburo, nave*) to roll; (*aereo*) to taxi

rul'lino SM (*Fot*) (roll of) film, spool

rul'lio, -ii SM (*di tamburi*) roll

'rullo SM (*di tamburi*) roll; (*arnese cilindrico, Tip*) roller; **~ compressore** steam roller; **~ di pellicola** roll of film

rum SM rum

ru'meno, -a AG, SM/F, SM Romanian

rumi'nante SM (*Zool*) ruminant

rumi'nare /72/ VT (*Zool*) to ruminate; (*fig*) to ruminate on *o* over, chew over

ru'more SM: **un ~** a noise, a sound; **il ~** noise; **fare ~** to make a noise; **un ~ di passi** the sound of footsteps; **la notizia ha fatto molto ~** (*fig*) the news aroused great interest

> Do not translate the Italian word **rumore** by *rumour*.

rumoreggi'are [rumored'dʒare] /62/ VI (*tuono ecc*) to rumble; (*fig: folla*) to clamour (BRIT), clamor (US)

rumo'roso, -a AG noisy

ru'olo SM (*Teat, fig*) role, part; (*elenco*) roll, register, list; **di ~** permanent, on the permanent staff; **professore di ~** (*Ins*) ≈ lecturer with tenure; **fuori ~** (*personale, insegnante*) temporary

ru'ota SF wheel; **a ~** (*forma*) circular; **~ anteriore/posteriore** front/back wheel; **andare a ~ libera** to freewheel; **parlare a ~ libera** (*fig*) to speak freely; **~ di scorta** spare wheel

ruo'tare /72/ VT, VI to rotate

'rupe SF cliff, rock

ru'pestre AG rocky

ru'pia SF rupee

'ruppi ecc VB *vedi* **rompere**

ru'rale AG rural, country cpd

ru'scello [ruʃ'ʃello] SM stream

'ruspa SF excavator

rus'pante AG (*pollo*) free-range

rus'sare /72/ VI to snore

'Russia SF: **la ~** Russia

'russo, -a AG, SM/F, SM Russian

'rustico, -a, -ci, -che AG country cpd, rural; (*arredamento*) rustic; (*fig*) rough, unrefined ▸ SM (*fabbricato: per attrezzi*) shed; (: *per abitazione*) farm labourer's (BRIT) *o* farmhand's cottage

'ruta SF (*Bot*) rue

rut'tare /72/ VI to belch

'rutto SM belch

'ruvido, -a AG rough, coarse

ruzzo'lare [ruttso'lare] /72/ VI to tumble down

ruzzo'lone [ruttso'lone] SM tumble, fall

ruzzo'loni [ruttso'loni] AV: **cadere ~** to tumble down; **fare le scale ~** to tumble down the stairs

r

Ss

S', s ['ɛsse] SM O F (*lettera*) S, s; **S come Savona** ≈ S for Sugar

S² ABBR (= *secondo*) sec.

S. ABBR (= *sud*) S; (= *santo*) St

SA SIGLA = **Salerno** ▶ ABBR = **società anonima**

sa VB *vedi* **sapere**

sab. ABBR (= *sabato*) Sat.

'sabato SM Saturday; **di** *o* **il ~** on Saturdays; *vedi anche* **martedì**

'sabbia SF sand; **sabbie mobili** quicksand(s pl)

sabbia'tura SF (*Med*) sand bath; (*Tecn*) sand-blasting; **fare le sabbiature** to take sand baths

sabbi'oso, -a AG sandy

sabo'taggio [sabo'taddʒo] SM sabotage

sabo'tare /**72**/ VT to sabotage

sabota'tore, -'trice SM/F saboteur

'sacca, -che SF bag; (*bisaccia*) haversack; (*insenatura*) inlet; **~ d'aria** air pocket; **~ da viaggio** travelling bag

sacca'rina SF saccharin(e)

sac'cente [sat'tʃɛnte] SMF know-all (BRIT), know-it-all (US)

sacchegg'iare [sakked'dʒare] /**62**/ VT to sack, plunder

sac'cheggio [sak'keddʒo] SM sack(ing)

sac'chetto [sak'ketto] SM (small) bag; (small) sack; **~ di carta/di plastica** paper/plastic bag

'sacco, -chi SM bag; (*per carbone ecc*) sack; (*Anat, Biol*) sac; (*tela*) sacking; (*saccheggio*) sack(ing); (*fig: grande quantità*) **un ~ di** lots of, heaps of; **cogliere** *o* **prendere qn con le mani nel ~** to catch sb red-handed; **vuotare il ~** to confess, spill the beans; **mettere qn nel ~** to cheat sb; **colazione al ~** packed lunch; **~ a pelo** sleeping bag; **~ per i rifiuti** bin bag (BRIT), garbage bag (US)

sacer'dote [satʃer'dɔte] SM priest

sacer'dozio [satʃer'dɔttsjo] SM priesthood

'Sacra Co'rona U'nita SF *the mafia in Puglia*

sacra'mento SM sacrament

sa'crario SM memorial chapel

sacres'tano SM = **sagrestano**

sacres'tia SF = **sagrestia**

sacrifi'care /**20**/ VT to sacrifice ■ **sacrificarsi** VPR to sacrifice o.s.; (*privarsi di qc*) to make sacrifices

sacrifi'cato, -a AG sacrificed; (*non valorizzato*) wasted; **una vita sacrificata** a life of sacrifice

sacri'ficio [sakri'fitʃo] SM sacrifice

sacri'legio [sakri'ledʒo] SM sacrilege

sa'crilego, -a, -ghi, -ghe AG (*Rel*) sacrilegious

'sacro, -a AG sacred

sacro'santo, -a AG sacrosanct

'sadico, -a, -ci, -che AG sadistic ▶ SM/F sadist

sa'dismo SM sadism

sadomaso'chismo [sadomazo'kismo] SM sadomasochism

sa'etta SF arrow; (*fulmine: anche fig*) thunderbolt; flash of lightning

sa'fari SM INV safari

sa'gace [sa'gatʃe] AG shrewd, sagacious

sa'gacia [sa'gatʃa] SF sagacity, shrewdness

sag'gezza [sad'dʒettsa] SF wisdom

sagg'iare [sad'dʒare] /**62**/ VT (*metalli*) to assay; (*fig*) to test

'saggio, -a, -gi, -ge ['saddʒo] AG wise ▶ SM (*persona*) sage; (*operazione sperimentale*) test; (*: dell'oro*) assay; (*fig: prova*) proof; (*campione indicativo*) sample; (*scritto: letterario*) essay; (*: Ins*) written test; **dare ~ di** to give proof of; **in ~** as a sample

sag'gistica [sad'dʒistika] SF ≈ non-fiction

Sagit'tario [sadʒit'tarjo] SM Sagittarius; **essere del ~** to be Sagittarius

'sagoma SF (*profilo*) outline, profile; (*forma*) form, shape; (*Tecn*) template; (*bersaglio*) target; (*fig: persona*) character

'sagra SF festival

A **sagra** is a rural festival held in the open air with folk music, dancing and games, and the chance to sample one or more culinary specialities. They usually take place during the summer months.

---

sa'grato SM churchyard

sagres'tano SM sacristan; sexton

sagres'tia SF sacristy; (*culto protestante*) vestry

Sa'hara [sa'ara] SM: **il (Deserto del)** ~ the Sahara (Desert)

sahari'ana [saa'rjana] SF bush jacket

'sai VB *vedi* **sapere**

'saio SM (*Rel*) habit

'sala SF hall; (*stanza*) room; (*Cine: di proiezione*) cinema; ~ **d'aspetto** waiting room; ~ **da ballo** ballroom; ~ **(dei) comandi** control room; ~ **per concerti** concert hall; ~ **per conferenze** (*Ins*) lecture hall; (*in aziende*) conference room; ~ **corse** betting shop; ~ **giochi** amusement arcade; ~ **da gioco** gaming room; ~ **macchine** (*Naut*) engine room; ~ **operatoria** (*Med*) operating theatre (*BRIT*) *o* room (*US*); ~ **da pranzo** dining room; ~ **per ricevimenti** banqueting hall; ~ **delle udienze** (*Dir*) courtroom

sa'lace [sa'latʃe] AG (*spinto, piccante*) salacious, saucy; (*mordace*) cutting, biting

sala'mandra SF salamander

sa'lame SM salami *no pl*, salami sausage

sala'moia SF (*Cuc*) brine

sa'lare /72/ VT to salt

salari'ale AG wage *cpd*, pay *cpd*; **aumento** ~ wage *o* pay increase (*BRIT*) *o* raise (*US*)

salari'ato, -a SM/F wage-earner

sa'lario SM pay, wages *pl*; ~ **base** basic wage; ~ **minimo garantito** guaranteed minimum wage

salas'sare /72/ VT (*Med*) to bleed

sa'lasso SM (*Med*) bleeding, bloodletting; (*fig: forte spesa*) drain

sala'tino SM cracker, salted biscuit

sa'lato, -a AG (*sapore*) salty; (*Cuc*) salted, salt *cpd*; (*fig: discorso ecc*) biting, sharp; (: *prezzi*) steep, stiff

sal'dare /72/ VT (*congiungere*) to join, bind; (*parti metalliche*) to solder; (: *con saldatura autogena*) to weld; (*conto*) to settle, pay

salda'tore SM (*operaio*) solderer; welder; (*utensile*) soldering iron

salda'trice [salda'tritʃe] SF (*macchina*) welder, welding machine; ~ **ad arco** arc welder

salda'tura SF soldering; welding; (*punto saldato*) soldered joint; weld; ~ **autogena** welding; ~ **dolce** soft soldering

sal'dezza [sal'dettsa] SF firmness, strength

'saldo, -a AG (*resistente, forte*) strong, firm; (*fermo*) firm, steady, stable; (*fig*) firm, steadfast ▶ SM (*svendita*) sale; (*di conto*) settlement; (*Econ*) balance ■ **saldi** SMPL (*Comm*) sales; **pagare a** ~ to pay in full; ~ **attivo** credit; ~ **passivo** deficit; ~ **da riportare** balance carried forward; **essere** ~ **nella propria fede** (*fig*) to stick to one's guns

'sale SM salt; (*fig*) wit ■ **sali** SMPL (*Med: da annusare*) smelling salts; **sotto** ~ salted; **restare di** ~ (*fig*) to be dumbfounded; **ha poco** ~ **in zucca** he doesn't have much sense; ~ **da cucina,** ~

grosso cooking salt; ~ **da tavola,** ~ **fino** table salt; **sali da bagno** bath salts; **sali minerali** mineral salts; **sali e tabacchi** tobacconist's (shop)

sal'gemma [sal'dʒemma] SM rock salt

'salgo *ecc* VB *vedi* **salire**

'salice ['salitʃe] SM willow; ~ **piangente** weeping willow

sali'ente AG (*fig*) salient, main

sali'era SF salt cellar

sa'lino, -a AG saline ▶ SF saltworks *sg*

sa'lire /98/ VI to go (*o come*) up; (*aereo ecc*) to climb, go up; (*passeggero*) to get on; (*sentiero, prezzi, livello*) to go up, rise ▶ VT (*scale, gradini*) to go (*o come*) up; ~ **su** to climb (up); ~ **sul treno/ sull'autobus** to board the train/the bus; ~ **in macchina** to get into the car; ~ **a cavallo** to mount; ~ **al potere** to rise to power; ~ **al trono** to ascend the throne; ~ **alle stelle** (*prezzi*) to rocket

sali'scendi [saliʃ'ʃendi] SM INV latch

sa'lita SF climb, ascent; (*erta*) hill, slope; **in** ~ *ag, av* uphill

sa'liva SF saliva

'salma SF corpse

sal'mastro, -a AG (*acqua*) salt *cpd*; (*sapore*) salty ▶ SM (*sapore*) salty taste; (*odore*) salty smell

salmì SM (*Cuc*) salmi; **lepre in** ~ salmi of hare

'salmo SM psalm

sal'mone SM salmon

salmo'nella SF salmonella

Salo'mone: le isole ~ *sfpl* the Solomon Islands

sa'lone SM (*stanza*) sitting room, lounge; (*in albergo*) lounge; (*di ricevimento*) reception room; (*su nave*) lounge, saloon; (*mostra*) show, exhibition; (*negozio: di parrucchiere*) hairdresser's (salon); ~ **dell'automobile** motor show; ~ **di bellezza** beauty salon

salo'pette [salɔ'pɛt] SF INV dungarees *pl*

salotti'ero, -a AG mundane

sa'lotto SM lounge, sitting room; (*mobilio*) lounge suite

sal'pare /72/ VI (*Naut*) to set sail; (*anche:* **salpare l'ancora**) to weigh anchor

'salsa SF (*Cuc*) sauce; **in tutte le salse** (*fig*) in all kinds of ways; ~ **di pomodoro** tomato sauce

sal'sedine SF (*del mare, vento*) saltiness; (*incrostazione*) (dried) salt

sal'siccia, -ce [sal'sittʃa] SF pork sausage

salsi'era SF sauceboat (*BRIT*), gravy boat

'salso SM saltiness

sal'tare /72/ VI to jump, leap; (*esplodere*) to blow up, explode; (: *valvola*) to blow; (*venir via*) to pop off; (*non aver luogo: corso ecc*) to be cancelled ▶ VT to jump (over), leap (over); (*fig: pranzo, capitolo*) to skip, miss (out); (*Cuc*) to sauté; **far** ~ to blow up; to burst open; (*serratura: forzare*) to break; **far**

S

~ **il banco** (*Gioco*) to break the bank; **farsi ~ le cervella** to blow one's brains out; **ma che ti salta in mente?** what are you thinking of?; ~ **da un argomento all'altro** to jump from one subject to another; ~ **addosso a qn** (*aggredire*) to attack sb; ~ **fuori** to jump out, leap out; (*venire trovato*) to turn up; ~ **fuori con** (*frase, commento*) to come out with; ~ **giù da qc** to jump off sth, jump down from sth

saltel'lare /**72**/ vɪ to skip; to hop

sal'tello sᴍ hop, little jump

saltim'banco, -chi sᴍ acrobat

'**salto** sᴍ jump; (*Sport*) jumping; (*dislivello*) drop; **fare un ~** to jump, leap; **fare un ~ da qn** to pop over to sb's (place); ~ **in alto/lungo** high/long jump; ~ **con l'asta** pole vaulting; ~ **mortale** somersault; **un ~ di qualità** (*miglioramento*) significant improvement

saltu'ario, -a ᴀɢ occasional, irregular

sa'lubre ᴀɢ healthy, salubrious

sa'lume sᴍ (*Cuc*) cured pork ∎ **salumi** sᴍᴘʟ (*insaccati*) cured pork meats

salume'ria sғ delicatessen

salumi'ere, -a sᴍ/ғ ≈ delicatessen owner

salumi'ficio [salumi'fitʃo] sᴍ cured pork meat factory

salu'tare /**72**/ ᴀɢ healthy; (*fig*) salutary, beneficial ▶ vᴛ (*per dire buon giorno, fig*) to greet; (*per dire addio*) to say goodbye to; (*Mil*) to salute; **mi saluti sua moglie** my regards to your wife

sa'lute sғ health; ~**!** (*a chi starnutisce*) bless you!; (*nei brindisi*) cheers!; **bere alla ~ di qn** to drink (to) sb's health; **la ~ pubblica** public welfare; **godere di buona ~** to be healthy, enjoy good health

sa'luto sᴍ (*gesto*) wave; (*parola*) greeting; (*Mil*) salute; **gli ha tolto il ~** he no longer says hello to him; **cari saluti, tanti saluti** best regards; **vogliate gradire i nostri più distinti saluti** yours faithfully; **i miei saluti alla sua signora** my regards to your wife

'**salva** sғ salvo

salvacon'dotto sᴍ (*Mil*) safe-conduct

salvada'naio sᴍ moneybox, piggy bank

salvado'regno, -a [salvado'reɲɲo] ᴀɢ, sᴍ/ғ Salvadorean

salva'gente [salva'dʒɛnte] sᴍ (*Naut*) lifebuoy; (*pl inv: stradale*) traffic island; ~ **a ciambella** lifebelt; ~ **a giubbotto** lifejacket (*Bʀɪт*), life preserver (*US*)

salvaguar'dare /**72**/ vᴛ to safeguard

salvagu'ardia sғ safeguard; **a ~ di** for the safeguard of

sal'vare /**72**/ vᴛ to save; (*trarre da un pericolo*) to rescue; (*proteggere*) to protect ∎ **salvarsi** vᴘʀ to save o.s.; to escape; ~ **la vita a qn** to save sb's life; ~ **le apparenze** to keep up appearances; **si salvi chi può!** every man for himself!

salvas'chermo [salvas'kermo] sᴍ (*Inform*) screen saver

salva'slip® sᴍ ɪɴv panty liner

salva'taggio [salva'taddʒo] sᴍ rescue

salva'tore, -'trice sᴍ/ғ saviour (*Bʀɪт*), savior (*US*)

salvazi'one [salvat'tsjone] sғ (*Rel*) salvation

'**salve** ᴇsᴄʟ (*col*) hi!

sal'vezza [sal'vettsa] sғ salvation; (*sicurezza*) safety

'**salvia** sғ (*Bot*) sage

salvi'etta sғ napkin, serviette; ~ **umidificata** baby wipe

'**salvo, -a** ᴀɢ safe, unhurt, unharmed; (*fuori pericolo*) safe, out of danger ▶ sᴍ: **in ~** safe ▶ ᴘʀᴇᴘ (*eccetto*) except; ~ **che** cong (*a meno che*) unless; (*eccetto che*) except (that); **mettere qc in ~** to put sth in a safe place; **mettersi in ~** to reach safety; **portare qn in ~** to lead sb to safety; ~ **contrordini** barring instructions to the contrary; ~ **errori e omissioni** errors and omissions excepted; ~ **imprevisti** barring accidents

sam'buca sғ (*liquore*) sambuca (*type of anisette*)

sam'buco sᴍ elder (tree)

sa'nare /**72**/ vᴛ to heal, cure; (*economia*) to put right

sana'toria sғ (*Dir*) act of indemnity

sana'torio sᴍ sanatorium (*Bʀɪт*), sanitarium (*US*)

san'cire [san'tʃire] /**55**/ vᴛ to sanction

'**sandalo** sᴍ (*Bot*) sandalwood; (*calzatura*) sandal

sang'ria [san'gria] sғ (*bibita*) sangria

'**sangue** sᴍ blood; **farsi cattivo ~** to fret, get worked up; **all'ultimo ~** (*duello, lotta*) to the death; **non corre buon ~ tra di loro** there's bad blood between them; **buon ~ non mente!** blood will out!; ~ **freddo** (*fig*) sang-froid, calm; **a ~ freddo** in cold blood

sangu'igno, -a [san'gwiɲɲo] ᴀɢ blood cpd; (*colore*) blood-red

sangui'nante ᴀɢ bleeding

sangui'nare /**72**/ vɪ to bleed

sangui'nario, -a ᴀɢ bloodthirsty

sangui'noso, -a ᴀɢ bloody

sangui'suga, -ghe sғ leech

sanità sғ health; (*salubrità*) healthiness; **Ministero della S~** Department of Health; ~ **mentale** sanity; ~ **pubblica** public health

sani'tario, -a ᴀɢ health cpd; (*condizioni*) sanitary ▶ sᴍ (*Amm*) doctor; **Ufficiale S~** Health Officer ∎ **sanitari** (*impianti*) bathroom o sanitary fittings

San Ma'rino sғ: **la Repubblica di ~** the Republic of San Marino

'**sanno** vʙ *vedi* **sapere**

'sano, -a AG healthy; *(denti, costituzione)* healthy, sound; *(integro)* whole, unbroken; *(fig: politica, consigli)* sound; **~ di mente** sane; **di sana pianta** completely, entirely; **~ e salvo** safe and sound

San Sil'vestro SM *(giorno)* New Year's Eve

Santi'ago SF: **~ (del Cile)** Santiago (de Chile)

santifi'care /20/ VT to sanctify; *(feste)* to observe

san'tino SM holy picture

san'tissimo, -a AG: **il S~ Sacramento** the Holy Sacrament; **il Padre S~** *(papa)* the Holy Father

santità SF sanctity; holiness; **Sua/Vostra ~** *(titolo di papa)* His/Your Holiness

'santo, -a AG holy; *(fig)* saintly; *(seguito da nome proprio: dav sm* **san** *+ C,* **sant'** *+ V,* **santo** *+ s impura, gn, pn, ps, x, z; dav sf* **santa** *+ C,* **sant'** *+ V)* saint ▶ SM/F saint; **parole sante!** very true!; **tutto il ~ giorno** the whole blessed day, all day long; **non c'è ~ che tenga!** that's no excuse!; **la Santa Sede** the Holy See

> Every Italian town has its own **santo patrono** (patron saint) in whose honour celebrations are held every year. These are primarily religious, but often contain elements taken from local history or even pagan tradition. Schools are closed and the faithful and tourists can enjoy historical parades and fireworks displays, as well as sampling special local desserts. The main event, however, is the procession: after the priest has said mass, statues and relics of the saint are carried through the streets, which are lit up with special illuminations.

san'tone SM holy man

santu'ario SM sanctuary

sanzio'nare [santsjo'nare] /72/ VT to sanction

sanzi'one [san'tsjone] SF sanction; *(penale, civile)* sanction, penalty; **sanzioni economiche** economic sanctions

sa'pere /99/ VT to know; *(essere capace di)*: **so nuotare** I know how to swim, I can swim ▶ VI: **~ di** *(aver sapore)* to taste of; *(aver odore)* to smell of ▶ SM knowledge; **far ~ qc a qn** to inform sb about sth, let sb know sth; **venire a ~ qc (da qn)** to find out *o* hear about sth (from sb); **non ne vuole più ~ di lei** he doesn't want to have anything more to do with her; **mi sa che non sia vero** I don't think that's true; **non lo so** I don't know; **non so l'inglese** I don't speak English

sapi'ente AG *(dotto)* learned; *(che rivela abilità)* masterly ▶ SMF scholar

sapien'tone, -a SM/F *(peg)* know-all (BRIT), know-it-all (US)

sapi'enza [sa'pjɛntsa] SF wisdom

sa'pone SM soap; **~ da barba** shaving soap; **~ da bucato** washing soap; **~ liquido** liquid soap; **~ in scaglie** soapflakes *pl*

sapo'netta SF cake *o* bar *o* tablet of soap

sa'pore SM taste, flavour (BRIT), flavor (US)

sapo'rito, -a AG tasty; *(fig: arguto)* witty; *(: piccante)* racy

sappi'amo VB *vedi* **sapere**

saprò *ecc* VB *vedi* **sapere**

sapu'tello, -a SM/F know-all (BRIT), know-it-all (US)

sarà *ecc* VB *vedi* **essere**

sara'banda SF *(fig)* uproar

saraci'nesca, -sche [saratʃi'neska] SF *(serranda)* rolling shutter

sar'casmo SM sarcasm *no pl*; sarcastic remark

sar'castico, -a, -ci, -che AG sarcastic

sarchi'are [sar'kjare] /19/ VT *(Agr)* to hoe

sar'cofago *(pl* **sarcofagi** *o* **sarcofaghi***)* SM sarcophagus

Sar'degna [sar'deɲɲa] SF: **la ~** Sardinia

sar'dina SF sardine

'sardo, -a AG, SM/F Sardinian

sar'donico, -a, -ci, -che AG sardonic

sa'rei *ecc* VB *vedi* **essere**

SARS SF (= *severe acute respiratory syndrome*) SARS

'sarta SF *vedi* **sarto**

'sartia SF *(Naut)* stay

'sarto, -a SM/F tailor/dressmaker; **~ d'alta moda** couturier

sarto'ria SF tailor's (shop); dressmaker's (shop); *(casa di moda)* fashion house; *(arte)* couture

sassai'ola SF hail of stones

sas'sata SF blow with a stone; **tirare una ~ contro** *o* **a qc/qn** to throw a stone at sth/sb

'sasso SM stone; *(ciottolo)* pebble; *(masso)* rock; **restare** *o* **rimanere di ~** to be dumbfounded

sassofo'nista, -i, -e SM/F saxophonist

sas'sofono SM saxophone

sas'sone AG, SMF, SM Saxon

sas'soso, -a AG stony; pebbly

'Satana SM Satan

sa'tanico, -a, -ci, -che AG satanic, fiendish

satelli'tare AG satellite *cpd*

sa'tellite SM, AG satellite

'satira SF satire

satireggi'are [satired'dʒare] /62/ VT to satirize ▶ VI *(fare della satira)* to be satirical; *(scrivere satire)* to write satires

sa'tirico, -a, -ci, -che AG satiric(al)

sa'tollo, -a AG full, replete

satu'rare /72/ VT to saturate

saturazi'one [saturat'tsjone] SF saturation

'saturo, -a AG saturated; *(fig)*: **~ di** full of; **~ d'acqua** *(terreno)* waterlogged

SAUB SIGLA F (= *Struttura Amministrativa Unificata di Base*) state welfare system

'sauna SF sauna; **fare la ~** to have o take a sauna

sa'vana SF savannah

'savio, -a AG wise, sensible ▶ SM wise man

Sa'voia SF: **la ~** Savoy

savoi'ardo, -a AG of Savoy, Savoyard ▶ SM (biscotto) sponge finger

sazi'are [sat'tsjare] /**19**/ VT to satisfy, satiate ■ **saziarsi** VPR (riempirsi di cibo): **saziarsi (di)** to eat one's fill (of); (fig): **saziarsi di** to grow tired o weary of

sazietà [sattsje'ta] SF satiety, satiation

'sazio, -a ['sattsjo] AG: **~ (di)** sated (with), full (of); (fig: stufo) fed up (with), sick (of); **sono ~** I'm full (up)

sbada'taggine [zbada'taddʒine] SF (sventatezza) carelessness; (azione) oversight

sba'dato, -a AG careless, inattentive

sbadigli'are [zbadiʎ'ʎare] /**27**/ VI to yawn

sba'diglio [zba'diʎʎo] SM yawn; **fare uno ~** to yawn

'sbafo SM: **a ~** at somebody else's expense

sbagli'are [zbaʎ'ʎare] /**27**/ VT to make a mistake in, get wrong ▶ VI (fare errori) to make a mistake (o mistakes), be mistaken; (ingannarsi) to be wrong; (operare in modo non giusto) to err ■ **sbagliarsi** VPR to make a mistake, be mistaken, be wrong; **~ la mira/strada** to miss one's target/take the wrong road; **scusi, ho sbagliato numero** (Tel) sorry, I've got the wrong number; **non c'è da sbagliarsi** there can be no mistake

sbagli'ato, -a [zbaʎ'ʎato] AG (gen) wrong; (compito) full of mistakes; (conclusione) erroneous

'sbaglio ['zbaʎʎo] SM mistake, error; (morale) error; **fare uno ~** to make a mistake

sbales'trato, -a AG (persona: scombussolato) unsettled

sbal'lare /**72**/ VT (merce) to unpack ▶ VI (nel fare un conto) to overestimate; (Droga: gergo) to get high

sbal'lato, -a AG (calcolo) wrong; (col: ragionamento, persona) screwy

'sballo SM (Droga: gergo) trip

sballot'tare /**72**/ VT to toss (about)

sbalor'dire /**55**/ VT to stun, amaze ▶ VI to be stunned, be amazed

sbalordi'tivo, -a AG amazing; (prezzo) incredible, absurd

sbal'zare [zbal'tsare] /**72**/ VT to throw, hurl; (fig: da una carica) to remove, dismiss ▶ VI (balzare) to bounce; (saltare) to leap, bound

'sbalzo ['zbaltso] SM (spostamento improvviso) jolt, jerk; **a sbalzi** jerkily; (fig) in fits and starts; **uno ~ di temperatura** a sudden change in temperature

sban'care /**20**/ VT (nei giochi) to break the bank at (o of); (fig) to ruin, bankrupt

sbanda'mento SM (Naut) list; (Aut) skid; (fig: di persona) confusion; **ha avuto un periodo di ~** he went off the rails for a bit

sban'dare /**72**/ VI (Naut) to list; (Aut) to skid; (Aer) to bank ■ **sbandarsi** VPR (folla) to disperse; (truppe) to scatter; (fig: famiglia) to break up

sban'data SF (Aut) skid; (Naut) list; **prendere una ~ per qn** (fig) to fall for sb

sban'dato, -a SM/F mixed-up person

sbandie'rare /**72**/ VT (bandiera) to wave; (fig) to parade, show off

'sbando SM: **essere allo ~** to drift

sbarac'care /**20**/ VT (libri, piatti ecc) to clear (up)

sbaragli'are [zbaraʎ'ʎare] /**27**/ VT (Mil) to rout; (in gare sportive ecc) to beat, defeat

sba'raglio [zba'raʎʎo] SM rout; defeat; **gettarsi allo ~** (soldato) to throw o.s. into the fray; (fig) to risk everything

sbaraz'zarsi [zbarat'tsarsi] /**72**/ VPR: **~ di** to get rid of, rid o.s. of

sbaraz'zino, -a [zbarat'tsino] AG impish, cheeky

sbar'bare /**72**/ VT, **sbar'barsi** VPR to shave

sbarba'tello SM novice, greenhorn

sbar'care /**20**/ VT (passeggeri) to disembark; (merci) to unload ▶ VI to disembark

'sbarco SM disembarkation; unloading; (Mil) landing

'sbarra SF bar; (di passaggio a livello) barrier; (Dir): **mettere/presentarsi alla ~** to bring/appear before the court

sbarra'mento SM (stradale) barrier; (diga) dam, barrage; (Mil) barrage; (Pol) cut-off point (level of support below which a political party is excluded from representation in Parliament)

sbar'rare /**72**/ VT (bloccare: strada ecc) to block, bar; (cancellare: assegno) to cross (BRIT); **~ il passo** to bar the way; **~ gli occhi** to open one's eyes wide

sbar'rato, -a AG (porta) barred; (passaggio) blocked, barred; (strada) blocked, obstructed; (occhi) staring; (assegno) crossed (BRIT)

'sbattere /**1**/ VT (porta) to bang, slam; (tappeti, ali, Cuc) to beat; (urtare) to knock, hit ▶ VI (porta, finestra) to bang; (agitarsi: ali, vele ecc) to flap; **~ qn fuori/in galera** to throw sb out/into prison; **me ne sbatto!** (col) I don't give a damn!

sbat'tuto, -a AG (viso, aria) dejected, worn out; (uovo) beaten

sba'vare /**72**/ VI to dribble; (colore) to smear, smudge

sbava'tura SF (di persone) dribbling; (di lumache) slime; (di rossetto, vernice) smear

sbelli'carsi /**20**/ VPR: **~ dalle risa** to split one's sides laughing

'sberla SF slap

sber'leffo SM: **fare uno ~ a qn** to make a face at sb

sbia'dire /55/ vi (anche: **sbiadirsi**) to fade ▶ vt to fade

sbia'dito, -a AG faded; (fig) colourless (BRIT), colorless (US), dull

sbian'care /20/ vt to whiten; (tessuto) to bleach ▶ vi (impallidire) to grow pale o white

sbi'eco, -a, -chi, -che AG (storto) squint, askew; **di ~, guardare qn di ~** (fig) to look askance at sb; **tagliare una stoffa di ~** to cut material on the bias

sbigot'tire /55/ vt to dismay, stun ▶ vi (anche: **sbigottirsi**) to be dismayed

sbilanci'are [zbilan'tʃare] /14/ vt to throw off balance ■ **sbilanciarsi** vpr (perdere l'equilibrio) to overbalance, lose one's balance; (fig: compromettersi) to compromise o.s.

sbi'lenco, -a, -chi, -che AG (persona) crooked, misshapen; (fig: idea, ragionamento) twisted

sbirci'are [zbir'tʃare] /14/ vt to cast sidelong glances at, eye

sbirci'ata [zbir'tʃata] SF: **dare una ~ a qc** to glance at sth, have a look at sth

'sbirro SM (peg) cop

sbizzar'rirsi [zbiddzar'rirsi] /55/ vpr to indulge one's whims

sbloc'care /20/ vt to unblock, free; (freno) to release; (prezzi, affitti) to free from controls ■ **sbloccarsi** vpr (gen) to become unblocked; (passaggio, strada) to clear, become unblocked; **la situazione si è sbloccata** things are moving again

'sblocco, -chi SM (vedi vt) unblocking, freeing; release

sboc'care /20/ vi: **~ in** (fiume) to flow into; (strada) to lead into; (persona) to come (out) into; (fig: concludersi) to end (up) in

sboc'cato, -a AG (persona) foul-mouthed; (linguaggio) foul

sbocci'are [zbot'tʃare] /14/ vi (fiore) to bloom, open (out)

'sbocco, -chi SM (di fiume) mouth; (di strada) end; (di tubazione, Comm) outlet; (uscita: anche fig) way out; **una strada senza ~** a dead end; **siamo in una situazione senza sbocchi** there's no way out of this for us

sbocconcel'lare [zbokkontʃel'lare] /72/ vt: **~ (qc)** to nibble (at sth)

sbollen'tare /72/ vt (Cuc) to parboil

sbol'lire /55/ vi (fig) to cool down, calm down

'sbornia SF (col): **prendersi una ~** to get plastered

sbor'sare /72/ vt (denaro) to pay out

sbot'tare /72/ vi: **~ in una risata/per la collera** to burst out laughing/explode with anger

sbotto'nare /72/ vt to unbutton, undo

sbra'cato, -a AG slovenly

sbracci'arsi [zbrat'tʃarsi] /14/ vpr to wave (one's arms about)

sbracci'ato, -a [zbrat'tʃato] AG (camicia) sleeveless; (persona) bare-armed

sbrai'tare /72/ vi to yell, bawl

sbra'nare /72/ vt to tear to pieces

sbricio'lare [zbritʃo'lare] /72/ vt, **sbricio'larsi** vpr to crumble

sbri'gare /80/ vt to deal with, get through; (cliente) to attend to, deal with ■ **sbrigarsi** vpr to hurry (up)

sbriga'tivo, -a AG (persona, modo) quick, expeditious; (giudizio) hasty

sbrina'mento SM defrosting

sbri'nare /72/ vt to defrost

sbrindel'lato, -a AG tattered, in tatters

sbrodo'lare /72/ vt to stain, dirty

'sbronza ['zbrontsa] SF (col): **prendersi una ~** to get plastered

sbron'zarsi [zbron'tsarsi] /72/ vpr (col) to get plastered

sbruf'fone, -a SM/F boaster, braggart

sbu'care /20/ vi to come out, emerge; (improvvisamente) to pop out (o up)

sbucci'are [zbut'tʃare] /14/ vt (arancia, patata) to peel; (piselli) to shell; **sbucciarsi un ginocchio** to graze one's knee

sbucherò ecc [zbuke'rɔ] VB vedi **sbucare**

sbudel'larsi /72/ vpr: **~ dalle risa** to split one's sides laughing

sbuf'fare /72/ vi (persona, cavallo) to snort; (: ansimare) to puff, pant; (treno) to puff

'sbuffo SM (di aria, fumo, vapore) puff; **maniche a ~** puff(ed) sleeves

sc. ABBR (Teat: = scena) sc.

'scabbia SF (Med) scabies sg

'scabro, -a AG rough, harsh; (fig) concise, terse

sca'broso, -a AG (fig: difficile) difficult, thorny; (: imbarazzante) embarrassing; (: sconcio) indecent

scacchi'era [skak'kjɛra] SF chessboard

scac'chiere [skak'kjɛre] SM (Mil) sector; **S~** (in Gran Bretagna) Exchequer

scaccia'cani [skattʃa'kani] SM O F INV pistol with blanks

scacciapensi'eri [skattʃapen'sjɛri] SM INV (Mus) jew's-harp

scacci'are [skat'tʃare] /14/ vt to chase away o out, drive away o out; **~ qn di casa** to turn sb out of the house

'scacco, -chi SM (pezzo del gioco) chessman; (quadretto di scacchiera) square; (fig) setback, reverse ■ **scacchi** SMPL (gioco) chess sg; **a scacchi** (tessuto) check(ed); **subire uno ~** (fig: sconfitta) to suffer a setback

scacco'matto SM checkmate; **dare ~ a qn** (anche fig) to checkmate sb

'scaddi ecc VB vedi **scadere**

sca'dente AG shoddy, of poor quality

S

sca'denza [ska'dɛntsa] SF (*di cambiale, contratto*) maturity; (*di passaporto*) expiry date; **a breve/lunga** ~ short-/long-term; **data di** ~ expiry date; ~ **a termine** fixed deadline

sca'dere /18/ VI (*contratto ecc*) to expire; (*debito*) to fall due; (*valore, forze, peso*) to decline, go down

sca'fandro SM (*di palombaro*) diving suit; (*di astronauta*) spacesuit

scaffala'tura SF shelving, shelves *pl*

scaf'fale SM shelf; (*mobile*) set of shelves

sca'fista SM (*di immigrati*) people smuggler (*by boat*)

'scafo SM (*Naut, Aer*) hull

scagio'nare [skadʒo'nare] /72/ VT to exonerate, free from blame

'scaglia ['skaʎʎa] SF (*Zool*) scale; (*scheggia*) chip, flake

scagli'are [skaʎ'ʎare] /27/ VT (*lanciare: anche fig*) to hurl, fling ■ **scagliarsi** VPR: **scagliarsi su** *o* **contro** to hurl *o* fling o.s. at; (*fig*) to rail at

scagliona'mento [skaʎʎona'mento] SM (*Mil*) arrangement in echelons

scaglio'nare [skaʎʎo'nare] /72/ VT (*pagamenti*) to space out, spread out; (*Mil*) to echelon

scagli'one [skaʎ'ʎone] SM (*Mil*) echelon; (*Geo*) terrace; **a scaglioni** in groups

sca'gnozzo [skaɲ'ɲɔttso] SM (*peg*) lackey

'Scala SF: **la** ~ *see note*

> Milan's **la Scala** first opened its doors in 1778 with a performance of Salieri's opera, *L'Europa riconosciuta*. Built on the site of the church of Santa Maria della Scala, the theatre suffered serious damage in the bombing campaigns of 1943 but reopened in 1946 with a concert conducted by Toscanini. Enjoying world-wide renown for its opera, *la Scala* also has a famous school of classical dance.

'scala SF (*a gradini ecc*) staircase, stairs *pl*; (*a pioli, di corda*) ladder; (*Mus, Geo, di colori, valori, fig*) scale ■ **scale** SFPL (*scalinata*) stairs; **su larga** *o* **vasta** ~ on a large scale; **su piccola** ~, **su** ~ **ridotta** on a small scale; **su** ~ **nazionale/mondiale** on a national/worldwide scale; **in** ~ **di 1 a 100.000** on a scale of 1 cm to 1 km; **riproduzione in** ~ reproduction to scale; ~ **a chiocciola** spiral staircase; ~ **a libretto** stepladder; ~ **di misure** system of weights and measures; ~ **mobile** escalator; (*Econ*) sliding scale; ~ **mobile (dei salari)** index-linked pay scale; ~ **di sicurezza** (*antincendio*) fire escape

sca'lare /72/ VT (*Alpinismo, muro*) to climb, scale; (*debito*) to scale down, reduce; **questa somma vi viene scalata dal prezzo originale** this sum is deducted from the original price

sca'lata SF scaling *no pl*, climbing *no pl*; (*arrampicata, fig*) climb; **dare la** ~ **a** (*fig*) to make a bid for

scala'tore, -'trice SM/F climber

scalca'gnato, -a [skalkaɲ'ɲato] AG (*logoro*) worn; (*persona*) shabby

scalci'are [skal'tʃare] /14/ VI to kick

scalci'nato, -a [skaltʃi'nato] AG (*fig: peg*) shabby

scalda'bagno [skalda'baɲɲo] SM water heater

scal'dare /72/ VT to heat ■ **scaldarsi** VPR to warm up, heat up; (*al fuoco, al sole*) to warm o.s.; (*fig*) to get excited; ~ **la sedia** (*fig*) to twiddle one's thumbs

scaldavi'vande SM INV dish warmer

scal'dino SM (*per mani*) hand-warmer; (*per piedi*) foot-warmer; (*per letto*) bedwarmer

scal'fire /55/ VT to scratch

scalfit'tura SF scratch

scali'nata SF staircase

sca'lino SM (*anche fig*) step; (*di scala a pioli*) rung

scal'mana SF (hot) flush

scalma'narsi /72/ VPR (*affaticarsi*) to rush about, rush around; (*agitarsi, darsi da fare*) to get all hot and bothered; (*arrabbiarsi*) to get excited, get steamed up

scalma'nato, -a SM/F hothead

'scalo SM (*Naut*) slipway; (*: porto d'approdo*) port of call; (*Aer*) stopover; **fare** ~ **(a)** (*Naut*) to call (at), put in (at); (*Aer*) to land (at), make a stop (at); **volo senza** ~ non-stop flight; ~ **merci** (*Ferr*) goods (*Brit*) *o* freight yard

sca'logna [ska'loɲɲa] SF (*col*) bad luck

scalo'gnato, -a [skaloɲ'ɲato] AG (*col*) unlucky

scalop'pina SF (*Cuc*) escalope

scal'pello SM chisel

scalpi'tare /72/ VI (*cavallo*) to paw the ground; (*persona*) to stamp one's feet

scal'pore SM noise, row; **far** ~ (*notizia*) to cause a sensation *o* a stir

'scaltro, -a AG cunning, shrewd

scal'zare [skal'tsare] /72/ VT (*albero*) to bare the roots of; (*muro, fig: autorità*) to undermine

'scalzo, -a ['skaltso] AG barefoot

scambi'are /19/ VT to exchange; (*confondere*): ~ **qn/qc per** to take *o* mistake sb/sth for; **mi hanno scambiato il cappello** they've given me the wrong hat ■ **scambiarsi** VPR (*auguri, confidenze, visite*) to exchange

scambi'evole AG mutual, reciprocal

'scambio SM exchange; (*Comm*) trade; (*Ferr*) points *pl*; **fare (uno)** ~ to make a swap; **libero** ~ free trade; **scambi con l'estero** foreign trade

scamosci'ato, -a [skamoʃ'ʃato] AG suede

scampa'gnata [skampaɲ'ɲata] SF trip to the country

scampa'nare /72/ VI to peal

scam'pare /72/ VT (*salvare*) to rescue, save; (*evitare: morte, prigione*) to escape ▶ VI: ~ **(a qc)** to survive (sth), escape (sth); **scamparla bella** to have a narrow escape '**scampo** SM (*salvezza*) escape; (*Zool*) prawn; **cercare ~ nella fuga** to seek safety in flight; **non c'è (via di) ~** there's no way out

'**scampolo** SM remnant

scanala'tura SF (*incavo*) channel, groove

scandagli'are [skanda'ʎʎare] /27/ VT (*Naut*) to sound; (*fig*) to sound out; to probe

scanda'listico, -a, -ci, -che AG (*settimanale ecc*) sensational

scandaliz'zare [skandalid'dzare] /72/ VT to shock, scandalize ◼ **scandalizzarsi** VPR to be shocked

'**scandalo** SM scandal; **dare ~** to cause a scandal

scanda'loso, -a AG scandalous, shocking

Scandi'navia SF: **la ~** Scandinavia

scandi'navo, -a AG, SM/F Scandinavian

scan'dire /55/ VT (*versi*) to scan; (*parole*) to articulate, pronounce distinctly; **~ il tempo** (*Mus*) to beat time

scan'nare /72/ VT (*animale*) to butcher, slaughter; (*persona*) to cut o slit the throat of

'**scanner** ['skanner] SM INV scanner

scanneriz'zare [skannerid'dzare] /72/ VT to scan

'**scanno** SM seat, bench

scansafa'tiche [skansafa'tike] SM O F INV idler, loafer

scan'sare /72/ VT (*rimuovere*) to move (aside), shift; (*schivare: schiaffo*) to dodge; (*sfuggire*) to avoid ◼ **scansarsi** VPR to move aside

scan'sia SF shelves *pl*; (*per libri*) bookcase

'**scanso** SM: **a ~ di** in order to avoid, as a precaution against; **a ~ di equivoci** to avoid (any) misunderstanding

scanti'nato SM basement

scanto'nare /72/ VI to turn the corner; (*svignarsela*) to sneak off

scanzo'nato, -a [skantso'nato] AG easy-going

scapacci'one [skapat'tʃone] SM clout, slap

scapes'trato, -a AG dissolute

'**scapito** SM (*perdita*) loss; (*danno*) damage, detriment; **a ~ di** to the detriment of

'**scapola** SF shoulder blade

'**scapolo** SM bachelor

scappa'mento SM (*Aut*) exhaust

scap'pare /72/ VI (*fuggire*) to escape; (*andare via in fretta*) to rush off; **~ di prigione** to escape from prison; **~ di mano** (*oggetto*) to slip out of one's hands; **~ di mente a qn** to slip sb's mind; **lasciarsi ~** (*occasione, affare*) to let go by, miss; (*dettaglio*) to overlook; (*parola*) to let slip; (*prigioniero*) to let escape; **mi scappò detto** I let it slip

scap'pata SF quick visit o call

scappa'tella SF escapade

scappa'toia SF way out

scara'beo SM beetle

scarabocchi'are [skarabok'kjare] /19/ VT to scribble, scrawl

scara'bocchio [skara'bɔkkjo] SM scribble, scrawl

scara'faggio [skara'faddʒo] SM cockroach

scaraman'zia [skaraman'tsia] SF: **per ~** for luck

scara'muccia, -ce [skara'muttʃa] SF skirmish

scaraven'tare /72/ VT to fling, hurl ◼ **scaraventarsi** VPR to fling o.s.

scarce'rare [skartʃe'rare] /72/ VT to release (from prison)

scarcerazi'one [skartʃerat'tsjone] SF release (from prison)

scardi'nare /72/ VT: **~ una porta** to take a door off its hinges

'**scarica, -che** SF (*di più armi*) volley of shots; (*di sassi, pugni*) hail, shower; (*Elettr*) discharge; **~ di mitra** burst of machine-gun fire

scari'care /20/ VT (*merci, camion ecc*) to unload; (*passeggeri*) to set down, put off; (*da Internet*) to download; (*arma*) to unload; (: *sparare, anche Elettr*) to discharge; (*corso d'acqua*) to empty, pour; (*fig: liberare da un peso*) to unburden, relieve ◼ **scaricarsi** VPR (*orologio*) to run o wind down; (*batteria, accumulatore*) to go flat (BRIT) o dead; (*fig: rilassarsi*) to unwind; (: *sfogarsi*) to let off steam; **~ le proprie responsabilità su qn** to offload one's responsibilities onto sb; **~ la colpa addosso a qn** to blame sb; **il fulmine si scaricò su un albero** the lightning struck a tree

scarica'tore SM loader; (*di porto*) docker

'**scarico, -a, -chi, -che** AG unloaded; (*orologio*) run down; (*batteria, accumulatore*) dead, flat (BRIT) ▶ SM (*di merci, materiali*) unloading; (*di immondizie*) dumping, tipping (BRIT); (: *luogo*) rubbish dump; (*Tecn: deflusso*) draining; (: *dispositivo*) drain; (*Aut*) exhaust; **~ del lavandino** waste outlet

scarlat'tina SF scarlet fever

scar'latto, -a AG scarlet

'**scarno, -a** AG thin, bony

'**scarpa** SF shoe; **fare le scarpe a qn** (*fig*) to double-cross sb; **scarpe da ginnastica** gym shoes; **scarpe coi tacchi (alti)** high-heeled shoes; **scarpe col tacco basso** low-heeled shoes; **scarpe senza tacco** flat shoes; **scarpe da tennis** tennis shoes

scar'pata SF escarpment

scarpi'era SF shoe rack

scar'pone SM boot; **scarponi da montagna** climbing boots; **scarponi da sci** ski-boots

scarroz'zare [skarrot'tsare] /72/ VT to drive around

scarseggi'are [skarsed'dʒare] /62/ VI to be scarce; **~ di** to be short of, lack

S

scar'sezza [skar'settsa] SF scarcity, lack

'scarso, -a AG (*insufficiente*) insufficient, meagre (BRIT), meager (US); (*povero: annata*) poor, lean; (*Ins: voto*) poor; **~ di** lacking in; **3 chili scarsi** just under 3 kilos, barely 3 kilos

scartabel'lare /72/ VT to skim through, glance through

scarta'faccio [skarta'fattʃo] SM notebook

scarta'mento SM (*Ferr*) gauge; **~ normale/ridotto** standard/narrow gauge

scar'tare /72/ VT (*pacco*) to unwrap; (*idea*) to reject; (*Mil*) to declare unfit for military service; (*carte da gioco*) to discard; (*Calcio*) to dodge (past) ▶ VI to swerve

'scarto SM (*cosa scartata, anche Comm*) reject; (*di veicolo*) swerve; (*differenza*) gap, difference; **~ salariale** wage differential

scar'toffie SFPL (*peg*) papers *pl*

scas'sare /72/ VT (*col: rompere*) to wreck

scassi'nare /72/ VT to break, force

'scasso SM *vedi* **furto**

scate'nare /72/ VT (*fig*) to incite, stir up ■ **scatenarsi** VPR (*temporale*) to break; (*rivolta*) to break out; (*persona: infuriarsi*) to rage

scate'nato, -a AG wild

'scatola SF box; (*di latta*) tin (BRIT), can; **cibi in ~** tinned (BRIT) *o* canned foods; **una ~ di cioccolatini** a box of chocolates; **comprare qc a ~ chiusa** to buy sth sight unseen; **~ cranica** cranium

scato'lone SM (big) box

scat'tante AG quick off the mark; (*agile*) agile

scat'tare /72/ VT (*fotografia*) to take ▶ VI (*congegno, molla ecc*) to be released; (*balzare*) to spring up; (*Sport*) to put on a spurt; (*fig: per l'ira*) to fly into a rage; (*legge, provvedimento*) to come into effect; **~ in piedi** to spring to one's feet; **far ~** to release

'scatto SM (*dispositivo*) release; (: *di arma da fuoco*) trigger mechanism; (*rumore*) click; (*balzo*) jump, start; (*Sport*) spurt; (*fig: di ira ecc*) fit; (: *di stipendio*) increment; **di ~** suddenly; **serratura a ~** spring lock

scatu'rire /55/ VI to gush, spring

scaval'care /20/ VT (*ostacolo*) to pass (*o* climb) over; (*fig*) to get ahead of, overtake

sca'vare /72/ VT (*terreno*) to dig; (*legno*) to hollow out; (*pozzo, galleria*) to bore; (*città sepolta ecc*) to excavate

scava'trice [skava'tritʃe] SF (*macchina*) excavator

scavezza'collo [skavettsa'kɔllo] SM daredevil

'scavo SM excavating *no pl*; excavation

scazzot'tare [skattsot'tare] /72/ VT (*col*) to beat up, give a thrashing to

'scegliere ['ʃeʎʎere] /100/ VT (*gen*) to choose; (*candidato, prodotto*) to choose, select; **~ di fare** to choose to do

sce'icco, -chi [ʃe'ikko] SM sheik

'scelgo *ecc* ['ʃelgo] VB *vedi* **scegliere**

scelle'rato, -a [ʃelle'rato] AG wicked, evil

scel'lino [ʃel'lino] SM shilling

'scelto, -a ['ʃelto] PP *di* **scegliere** ▶ AG (*gruppo*) carefully selected; (*frutta, verdura*) choice, top quality; (*Mil: specializzato*) crack *cpd*, highly skilled ▶ SF choice; (*selezione*) selection, choice; **frutta o formaggi a scelta** choice of fruit or cheese; **fare una scelta** to make a choice, choose; **non avere scelta** to have no choice *o* option; **di prima scelta** top grade *o* quality

sce'mare [ʃe'mare] /72/ VT, VI to diminish

sce'menza [ʃe'mɛntsa] SF stupidity *no pl*; stupid thing (to do *o* say)

'scemo, -a ['ʃemo] AG stupid, silly

'scempio ['ʃempjo] SM slaughter, massacre; (*fig*) ruin; **far ~ di** (*fig*) to play havoc with, ruin

'scena ['ʃena] SF (*gen*) scene; (*palcoscenico*) stage; **le scene** (*fig: teatro*) the stage; **andare in ~** to be staged *o* put on *o* performed; **mettere in ~** to stage; **uscire di ~** to leave the stage; (*fig*) to leave the scene; **fare una ~** (*fig*) to make a scene; **ha fatto ~ muta** (*fig*) he didn't open his mouth

sce'nario [ʃe'narjo] SM scenery; (*di film*) scenario

sce'nata [ʃe'nata] SF row, scene

'scendere ['ʃendere] /101/ VI to go (*o* come) down; (*strada, sole*) to go down; (*notte*) to fall; (*passeggero: fermarsi*) to get out, alight; (*fig: temperatura, prezzi*) to fall, drop ▶ VT (*scale, pendio*) to go (*o* come) down; **~ dalle scale** to go (*o* come) down the stairs; **~ dal treno** to get off *o* out of the train; **~ dalla macchina** to get out of the car; **~ da cavallo** to dismount, get off one's horse; **~ ad un albergo** to put up *o* stay at a hotel

sceneggi'ato [ʃened'dʒato] SM television drama

sceneggia'tore, -'trice [ʃeneddʒa'tore] SM/F script-writer

sceneggia'tura [ʃeneddʒa'tura] SF (*Teat*) scenario; (*Cine*) screenplay, scenario

'scenico, -a, -ci, -che ['ʃɛniko] AG stage *cpd*

sceno'grafia [ʃenogra'fia] SF (*Teat*) stage design; (*Cine*) set design; (*elementi scenici*) scenery

sce'nografo, -a [ʃe'nɔgrafo] SM/F set designer

sce'riffo [ʃe'riffo] SM sheriff

scervel'larsi [ʃervel'larsi] /72/ VPR: **~ (su qc)** to rack one's brains (over sth)

scervel'lato, -a [ʃervel'lato] AG featherbrained

'sceso, -a ['ʃeso] PP *di* **scendere**

scetti'cismo [ʃetti'tʃizmo] SM scepticism (BRIT), skepticism (US)

'scettico, -a, -ci, -che ['ʃettiko] AG sceptical (BRIT), skeptical (US)

'scettro [ˈʃɛttro] SM sceptre (BRIT), scepter (US)

'scheda [ˈskɛda] SF (index) card; (TV, Radio) (brief) report; **~ audio** (Inform) sound card; **~ bianca/nulla** (Pol) unmarked/spoiled ballot paper; **~ a circuito stampato** printed-circuit board; **~ elettorale** ballot paper; **~ madre** (Inform) motherboard; **~ di memoria** (Inform) memory card; **~ perforata** punch card; **~ ricaricabile** (Tel) top-up card; **~ telefonica** phone card; **~ video** (Inform) video card

sche'dare [skeˈdare] /72/ VT (dati) to file; (libri) to catalogue; (registrare: anche Polizia) to put on one's files

sche'dario [skeˈdarjo] SM file; (mobile) filing cabinet

sche'dato, -a [skeˈdato] AG with a (police) record ▶ SM/F person with a (police) record

sche'dina [skeˈdina] SF ≈ pools coupon (BRIT)

'scheggia, -ge [ˈskeddʒa] SF splinter, sliver; **~ impazzita** (fig) maverick

sche'letrico, -a, -ci, -che [skeˈlɛtriko] AG (anche Anat) skeletal; (fig: essenziale) skeleton cpd

'scheletro [ˈskɛletro] SM skeleton; **avere uno ~ nell'armadio** (fig) to have a skeleton in the cupboard

'schema, -i [ˈskɛma] SM (diagramma) diagram, sketch; (progetto, abbozzo) outline, plan; **ribellarsi agli schemi** to rebel against traditional values; **secondo gli schemi tradizionali** in accordance with traditional values

sche'matico, -a, -ci, -che [skeˈmatiko] AG schematic

schematiz'zare [skematidˈdzare] /72/ VT to schematize

'scherma [ˈskerma] SF fencing

scher'maglia [skerˈmaʎʎa] SF (fig) skirmish

scher'mata [skerˈmata] SF screenshot

scher'mirsi [skerˈmirsi] /55/ VPR to defend o.s.

'schermo [ˈskermo] SM shield, screen; (Cine, TV) screen; **a ~ panoramico** (TV) widescreen

schermogra'fia [skermograˈfia] SF X-rays pl

scher'nire [skerˈnire] /55/ VT to mock, sneer at

'scherno [ˈskerno] SM mockery, derision; **farsi ~ di** to sneer at; **essere oggetto di ~** to be a laughing stock

scher'zare [skerˈtsare] /72/ VI to joke

'scherzo [ˈskertso] SM joke; (tiro) trick; (Mus) scherzo; **è uno ~!** (una cosa facile) it's child's play!, it's easy!; **per ~** in jest; for a joke o a laugh; **fare un brutto ~ a qn** to play a nasty trick on sb; **scherzi a parte** seriously, joking apart

scher'zoso, -a [skerˈtsoso] AG (tono, gesto) playful; (osservazione) facetious; **è un tipo ~** he likes a joke

schiaccia'noci [skjattʃaˈnotʃi] SM INV nutcracker

schiacci'ante [skjatˈtʃante] AG overwhelming

schiacci'are [skjatˈtʃare] /14/ VT (dito) to crush; (noci) to crack; **~ un pisolino** to have a nap ▪ **schiacciarsi** VPR (appiattirsi) to get squashed; (frantumarsi) to get crushed

schiaffeggi'are [skjaffedˈdʒare] /62/ VT to slap

schi'affo [ˈskjaffo] SM slap; **prendere qn a schiaffi** to slap sb's face; **uno ~ morale** a slap in the face, a rebuff

schiamaz'zare [skjamatˈtsare] /72/ VI to squawk, cackle

schia'mazzo [skjaˈmattso] SM (fig: chiasso) din, racket

schian'tare [skjanˈtare] /72/ VT to break, tear apart ▪ **schiantarsi** VPR to break (up), shatter; **schiantarsi al suolo** (aereo) to crash (to the ground)

schi'anto [ˈskjanto] SM (rumore) crash; tearing sound; **è uno ~!** (col) it's (o he's o she's) terrific!; **di ~** all of a sudden

schia'rire [skjaˈrire] /55/ VT to lighten, make lighter ▶ VI (anche: **schiarirsi**) to grow lighter; (tornar sereno) to clear, brighten up; **schiarirsi la voce** to clear one's throat

schia'rita [skjaˈrita] SF (Meteor) bright spell; (fig) improvement, turn for the better

schiat'tare [skjatˈtare] /72/ VI to burst; **~ d'invidia** to be green with envy; **~ di rabbia** to be beside o.s. with rage

schiavitù [skjaviˈtu] SF slavery

schiaviz'zare [skjavidˈdzare] /72/ VT to enslave

schi'avo, -a [ˈskjavo] SM/F slave

schi'ena [ˈskjɛna] SF (Anat) back

schie'nale [skjeˈnale] SM (di sedia) back

schi'era [ˈskjɛra] SF (Mil) rank; (gruppo) group, band; **villette a ~** ≈ terraced houses

schiera'mento [skjeraˈmento] SM (Mil, Sport) formation; (fig) alliance

schie'rare [skjeˈrare] /72/ VT (esercito) to line up, draw up, marshal ▪ **schierarsi** VPR to line up; (fig) **schierarsi con o dalla parte di/contro qn** to side with/oppose sb

schi'etto, -a [ˈskjetto] AG (puro) pure; (fig) frank, straightforward

schi'fare [skiˈfare] /72/ VT to disgust

schi'fezza [skiˈfettsa] SF: **essere una ~** (cibo, bibita ecc) to be disgusting; (film, libro) to be dreadful

schifil'toso, -a [skifilˈtoso] AG fussy, difficult

'schifo [ˈskifo] SM disgust; **fare ~** (essere fatto male, dare pessimi risultati) to be awful; **mi fa ~** it makes me sick, it's disgusting; **quel libro è uno ~** that book's rotten

schi'foso, -a [skiˈfoso] AG disgusting, revolting; (molto scadente) rotten, lousy

schioc'care [skjokˈkare] /20/ VT (frusta) to crack; (dita) to snap; (lingua) to click; **~ le labbra** to smack one's lips

schioppet'tata [skjoppet'tata] SF gunshot

schi'oppo ['skjɔppo] SM rifle, gun

schi'udere ['skjudere] /22/ VT, **schi'udersi** VPR to open

schi'uma ['skjuma] SF foam; (di sapone) lather; (di latte) froth; (fig: feccia) scum

schiu'mare [skju'mare] /72/ VT to skim ▶ VI to foam

schi'uso, -a ['skjuso] PP di **schiudere**

schi'vare [ski'vare] /72/ VT to dodge, avoid

'schivo, -a ['skivo] AG (ritroso) stand-offish, reserved; (timido) shy

schizofre'nia [skiddzofre'nia] SF schizophrenia

schizo'frenico, -a, -ci, -che [skiddzo'freniko] AG schizophrenic

schiz'zare [skit'tsare] /72/ VT (spruzzare) to spurt, squirt; (sporcare) to splash, spatter; (fig: abbozzare) to sketch ▶ VI to spurt, squirt; (saltar fuori) to dart up (o off etc); ~ **via** (animale, persona) to dart away; (macchina, moto) to accelerate away

schizzi'noso, -a [skittsi'noso] AG fussy, finicky

'schizzo ['skittso] SM (di liquido) spurt; splash, spatter; (abbozzo) sketch

sci [ʃi] SM INV (attrezzo) ski; (attività) skiing; ~ **di fondo** cross-country skiing, ski touring (US); ~ **d'acqua** o **nautico** water-skiing

'scia ['ʃia] (pl **scie**) SF (di imbarcazione) wake; (di profumo) trail

scià [ʃa] SM INV shah

sci'abola ['ʃabola] SF sabre (BRIT), saber (US)

scia'callo [ʃa'kallo] SM jackal; (fig: peg: profittatore) shark, profiteer; (: ladro) looter

sciac'quare [ʃak'kware] /72/ VT to rinse

scia'gura [ʃa'gura] SF disaster, calamity; misfortune

sciagu'rato, -a [ʃagu'rato] AG unfortunate; (malvagio) wicked

scialac'quare [ʃalak'kware] /72/ VT to squander

scia'lare [ʃa'lare] /72/ VI to throw one's money around

sci'albo, -a ['ʃalbo] AG pale, dull; (fig) dull, colourless (BRIT), colorless (US)

sci'alle ['ʃalle] SM shawl

sci'alo ['ʃalo] SM squandering, waste

scia'luppa [ʃa'luppa] SF (Naut) sloop; (anche: **scialuppa di salvataggio**) lifeboat

scia'mare [ʃa'mare] /72/ VI to swarm

sci'ame ['ʃame] SM swarm

scian'cato, -a [ʃan'kato] AG lame; (mobile) rickety

sci'are [ʃi'are] /60/ VI to ski; **andare a** ~ to go skiing

sci'arpa ['ʃarpa] SF scarf; (fascia) sash

scia'tore, -'trice [ʃia'tore] SM/F skier

sciat'tezza [ʃat'tettsa] SF slovenliness

sci'atto, -a ['ʃatto] AG (persona: nell'aspetto) slovenly, unkempt; (: nel lavoro) sloppy, careless

'scibile ['ʃibile] SM knowledge

scien'tifico, -a, -ci, -che [ʃen'tifiko] AG scientific; **la (polizia) scientifica** the forensic department

sci'enza ['ʃentsa] SF science; (sapere) knowledge ■ **scienze** SFPL (Ins) science sg; **scienze naturali** natural sciences; **scienze politiche** political science sg

scienzi'ato, -a [ʃen'tsjato] SM/F scientist

'Scilly ['ʃilli]: **le isole** ~ sfpl the Scilly Isles

'scimmia ['ʃimmja] SF monkey

scimmiot'tare [ʃimmjot'tare] /72/ VT to ape, mimic

scimpanzé [ʃimpan'tse] SM INV chimpanzee

scimu'nito, -a [ʃimu'nito] AG silly, idiotic

'scindere ['ʃindere] /102/ VT, **'scindersi** VPR to split (up)

scin'tilla [ʃin'tilla] SF spark

scintil'lare [ʃintil'lare] /72/ VI to spark; (acqua, occhi) to sparkle

scintil'lio [ʃintil'lio] SM sparkling

scioc'care [ʃok'kare] /20/ VT to shock

scioc'chezza [ʃok'kettsa] SF stupidity no pl; stupid o foolish thing; **dire sciocchezze** to talk nonsense

sci'occo, -a, -chi, -che ['ʃɔkko] AG stupid, foolish

sci'ogliere ['ʃɔʎʎere] /103/ VT (nodo) to untie; (capelli) to loosen; (persona, animale) to untie, release; (nell'acqua: zucchero ecc) to dissolve; (fig: mistero) to solve; (porre fine a: contratto) to cancel; (: società, matrimonio) to dissolve; (: riunione) to bring to an end; (fig: persona): ~ **da** to release from; (neve) to melt ■ **sciogliersi** VPR to loosen, come untied; to melt; to dissolve; (assemblea, corteo, duo) to break up; ~ **i muscoli** to limber up; ~ **il ghiaccio** (fig) to break the ice; ~ **le vele** (Naut) to set sail; **sciogliersi dai legami** (fig) to free o.s. from all ties

sciogli'lingua [ʃoʎʎi'lingwa] SM INV tongue-twister

sci'olgo ecc ['ʃɔlgo] VB vedi **sciogliere**

sciol'tezza [ʃol'tettsa] SF agility; suppleness; ease

sci'olto, -a ['ʃɔlto] PP di **sciogliere** ▶ AG loose; (agile) agile, nimble; supple; (disinvolto) free and easy; **essere ~ nei movimenti** to be supple; **versi sciolti** (Poesia) blank verse

sciope'rante [ʃope'rante] SM/F striker

sciope'rare [ʃope'rare] /72/ VI to strike, go on strike

sci'opero ['ʃopero] SM strike; **fare** ~ to strike; **entrare in** ~ to go on o come out on strike; ~ **bianco** work-to-rule (BRIT), slowdown (US); ~

della fame hunger strike; **~ selvaggio** wildcat strike; **~ a singhiozzo** on-off strike; **~ di solidarietà** sympathy strike

sciori'nare [ʃori'nare] /**72**/ vT (ostentare) to show off, display

scio'via [ʃio'via] sF ski lift

sciovi'nismo [ʃovi'nizmo] sm chauvinism

sciovi'nista, -i, -e [ʃovi'nista] sm/F chauvinist

sci'pito, -a [ʃi'pito] AG insipid

scip'pare [ʃip'pare] /**72**/ vT: **~ qn** to snatch sb's bag

scippa'tore [ʃippa'tore] sm bag-snatcher

'scippo ['ʃippo] sm bag-snatching

sci'rocco [ʃi'rɔkko] sm sirocco

sci'roppo [ʃi'rɔppo] sm syrup; **~ per la tosse** cough syrup, cough mixture

'scisma, -i ['ʃizma] sm (Rel) schism

scissi'one [ʃis'sjone] sF (anche fig) split, division; (Fisica) fission

'scisso, -a ['ʃisso] pp di **scindere**

sciu'pare [ʃu'pare] /**72**/ vT (abito, libro, appetito) to spoil, ruin; (tempo, denaro) to waste ■ **sciuparsi** vPR to get spoilt o ruined; (rovinarsi la salute) to ruin one's health

scivo'lare [ʃivo'lare] /**72**/ vi to slide o glide along; (involontariamente) to slip, slide

'scivolo ['ʃivolo] sm slide; (Tecn) chute

scivo'loso, -a [ʃivo'loso] AG slippery

scle'rosi sF sclerosis

scoc'care /**20**/ vT (freccia) to shoot ▶ vi (guizzare) to shoot up; (battere: ora) to strike

scoccherò ecc [skokke'rɔ] vB vedi **scoccare**

scocci'are [skot'tʃare] /**14**/ vT to bother, annoy ■ **scocciarsi** vPR to be bothered o annoyed

scoccia'tore, -'trice [skottʃa'tore] sm/F nuisance, pest (col)

scoccia'tura [skottʃa'tura] sF nuisance, bore

sco'della sF bowl

scodinzo'lare [skodintso'lare] /**72**/ vi to wag its tail

scogli'era [skoʎ'ʎɛra] sF reef; (rupe) cliff

'scoglio ['skoʎʎo] sm (al mare) rock; (fig: ostacolo) difficulty, stumbling block

scogli'oso, -a [skoʎ'ʎoso] AG rocky

scoi'attolo sm squirrel

scola'pasta sm inv colander

scolapi'atti sm inv drainer (for plates)

sco'lare /**72**/ AG: **età ~** school age ▶ vT to drain ▶ vi to drip

scola'resca sF schoolchildren pl, pupils pl

sco'laro, -a sm/F pupil, schoolboy(-girl)

sco'lastico, -a, -ci, -che AG (gen) scholastic; (libro, anno, divisa) school cpd

scol'lare /**72**/ vT (staccare) to unstick ■ **scollarsi** vPR to come unstick

scol'lato, -a AG (vestito) low-cut, low-necked; (donna) wearing a low-cut dress (o blouse ecc)

scolla'tura sF neckline

scolle'gare /**80**/ vT (fili, apparecchi) to disconnect ■ **scollegarsi** vPR (da Internet) to disconnect; (da chat-line) to log off

'scolo sm drainage; (sbocco) drain; (acqua) waste water; **canale di ~** drain; **tubo di ~** drainpipe

scolo'rire /**55**/ vT to fade; to discolour (BRIT), discolor (US) ▶ vi (anche: **scolorirsi**) to fade; to become discoloured; (impallidire) to turn pale

scol'pire /**55**/ vT to carve, sculpt

scombi'nare /**72**/ vT to mess up, upset

scombi'nato, -a AG confused, muddled

scombusso'lare /**72**/ vT to upset

scom'messo, -a pp di **scommettere** ▶ sF bet, wager; **fare una scommessa** to bet

scom'mettere /**63**/ vT, vi to bet

scomo'dare /**72**/ vT to trouble, bother, disturb; (fig: nome famoso) to involve, drag in ■ **scomodarsi** vPR to put o.s. out; **scomodarsi a fare** to go to the bother o trouble of doing

scomodità sF inv (di sedia, letto ecc) discomfort; (di orario, sistemazione ecc) inconvenience

'scomodo, -a AG uncomfortable; (sistemazione, posto) awkward, inconvenient

scompagi'nare [skompadʒi'nare] /**72**/ vT to upset, throw into disorder

scompag'nato, -a [skompaɲ'ɲato] AG (calzini, guanti) odd

scompa'rire /**7**/ vi (sparire) to disappear, vanish; (fig) to be insignificant

scom'parso, -a pp di **scomparire** ▶ sF disappearance; (fig: morte) passing away, death

scomparti'mento sm (Ferr) compartment; (sezione) division

scom'parto sm compartment, division

scom'penso sm imbalance, lack of balance

scompigli'are [skompiʎ'ʎare] /**27**/ vT (cassetto, capelli) to mess up, disarrange; (fig: piani) to upset

scom'piglio [skom'piʎʎo] sm mess, confusion

scom'porre /**77**/ vT (parola, numero) to break up; (Chim) to decompose ■ **scomporsi** vPR (Chim) to decompose; (fig) to get upset, lose one's composure; **senza scomporsi** unperturbed

scom'posto, -a pp di **scomporre** ▶ AG (gesto) unseemly; (capelli) ruffled, dishevelled

sco'munica, -che sF excommunication

scomuni'care /**20**/ vT to excommunicate

sconcer'tante [skontʃer'tante] AG disconcerting

sconcer'tare [skontʃer'tare] /**72**/ vT to disconcert, bewilder

'sconcio, -a, -ci, -ce ['skontʃo] AG (osceno) indecent, obscene ▶ sm (cosa riprovevole, mal fatta) disgrace

sconclusio'nato, -a AG incoherent, illogical

sconfes'sare /72/ VT to renounce, disavow; to repudiate

scon'figgere [skon'fiddʒere] /104/ VT to defeat, overcome

sconfi'nare /72/ VI to cross the border; (in proprietà privata) to trespass; (fig): ~ **da** to stray o digress from

sconfi'nato, -a AG boundless, unlimited

scon'fitto, -a PP di **sconfiggere** ▶ SF defeat

sconfor'tante AG discouraging, disheartening

sconfor'tare /72/ VT to discourage, dishearten ■ **sconfortarsi** VPR to become discouraged, become disheartened, lose heart

scon'forto SM despondency

sconge'lare [skondʒe'lare] /72/ VT to defrost

scongiu'rare [skondʒu'rare] /72/ VT (implorare) to beseech, entreat, implore; (eludere: pericolo) to ward off, avert

scongi'uro [skon'dʒuro] SM (esorcismo) exorcism; **fare gli scongiuri** to touch wood (BRIT), knock on wood (US)

scon'nesso, -a AG (fig: discorso) incoherent, rambling

sconosci'uto, -a [skonoʃ'ʃuto] AG unknown; new, strange ▶ SM/F stranger; unknown person

sconquas'sare /72/ VT to shatter, smash

scon'quasso SM (danno) damage; (fig) confusion

sconside'rato, -a AG thoughtless, rash

sconsigli'are [skonsiʎ'ʎare] /27/ VT: ~ **qc a qn** to advise sb against sth; ~ **qn dal fare qc** to advise sb not to do o against doing sth

sconso'lato, -a AG inconsolable; desolate

scon'tare /72/ VT (Comm: detrarre) to deduct; (: debito) to pay off; (: cambiale) to discount; (pena) to serve; (colpa, errori) to pay for, suffer for

scon'tato, -a AG (previsto) foreseen, taken for granted; (prezzo, merce) discounted, at a discount; **dare per ~ che** to take it for granted that

sconten'tare /72/ VT to displease, dissatisfy

sconten'tezza [skonten'tettsa] SF displeasure, dissatisfaction

scon'tento, -a AG: ~ **(di)** discontented o dissatisfied (with) ▶ SM discontent, dissatisfaction

'sconto SM discount; **fare** o **concedere uno ~** to give a discount; **uno ~ del 10%** a 10% discount

scon'trarsi /72/ VPR (treni ecc) to crash, collide; (venire ad uno scontro: fig) to clash; ~ **con** to crash into, collide with

scon'trino SM ticket; (di cassa) receipt

'scontro SM (Mil, fig) clash, encounter; (di veicoli) crash, collision; ~ **a fuoco** shoot-out

scon'troso, -a AG sullen, surly; (permaloso) touchy

sconveni'ente AG unseemly, improper

sconvol'gente [skonvol'dʒente] AG (notizia, brutta esperienza) upsetting, disturbing; (bellezza) amazing; (passione) overwhelming

scon'volgere [skon'vɔldʒere] /96/ VT to throw into confusion, upset; (turbare) to shake, disturb, upset

scon'volto, -a PP di **sconvolgere** ▶ AG (persona) distraught, very upset

'scooter ['skuter] SM INV scooter

'scopa SF broom; (Carte) Italian card game

sco'pare /72/ VT to sweep; (!) to shag (BRIT) (!)

sco'pata SF (!) shag (BRIT) (!)

scoperchi'are [skoper'kjare] /19/ VT (pentola, vaso) to take the lid off, uncover; (casa) to take the roof off

sco'perto, -a PP di **scoprire** ▶ AG uncovered; (capo) uncovered, bare; (macchina) open; (Mil) exposed, without cover; (conto) overdrawn ▶ SF discovery ▶ SM: **allo ~** (dormire ecc) out in the open; **assegno ~** uncovered cheque; **avere un conto ~** to be overdrawn

'scopo SM aim, purpose; **a che ~?** what for?; **adatto allo ~** fit for its purpose; **allo ~ di fare qc** in order to do sth; **a ~ di lucro** for gain o money; **senza ~** (fare, cercare) pointlessly

scoppi'are /19/ VI (spaccarsi) to burst; (esplodere) to explode; (fig) to break out; ~ **in pianto** o **a piangere** to burst out crying; ~ **dalle risa** o **dal ridere** to split one's sides laughing; ~ **dal caldo** to be boiling; ~ **di salute** to be the picture of health

scoppiet'tare /72/ VI to crackle

'scoppio SM explosion; (di tuono, arma ecc) crash, bang; (fig: di risa, ira) fit; (di pneumatico) bang; (fig: di guerra) outbreak; **a ~ ritardato** delayed-action; **reazione a ~ ritardato** delayed o slow reaction; **uno ~ di risa** a burst of laughter; **uno ~ di collera** an explosion of anger

sco'prire /9/ VT to discover; (liberare da ciò che copre) to uncover; (: monumento) to unveil ■ **scoprirsi** VPR to put on lighter clothes; (fig) to give o.s. away

scopri'tore, -'trice SM/F discoverer

scoraggi'are [skorad'dʒare] /62/ VT to discourage ■ **scoraggiarsi** VPR to become discouraged, lose heart

scor'butico, -a, -ci, -che AG (fig) cantankerous

scorcia'toia [skortʃa'toja] SF short cut

'scorcio ['skortʃo] SM (Arte) foreshortening; (di secolo, periodo) end, close; ~ **panoramico** vista

scor'dare /72/ VT to forget ■ **scordarsi** VPR: **scordarsi di qc/di fare** to forget sth/to do

sco'reggia [sko'reddʒa] (!) SF fart (!)

scoreggi'are [skored'dʒare] /62/ (!) VI to fart (!)

'scorgere ['skɔrdʒere] /59/ VT to make out, distinguish, see

sco'ria SF (*di metalli*) slag; (*vulcanica*) scoria; **scorie radioattive** (*Fisica*) radioactive waste *sg*

'scorno SM ignominy, disgrace

scorpacci'ata [skorpat'tʃata] SF: **fare una ~ (di)**, eat one's fill (of)

scorpi'one SM scorpion; **S~** Scorpio; **essere dello S~** to be Scorpio

'scorporo SM (*Pol*) *transfer of votes aimed at increasing the chances of representation for minority parties*

scorraz'zare [skorrat'tsare] /**72**/ VI to run about

'scorrere /**28**/ VT (*giornale, lettera*) to run *o* skim through ▶ VI (*liquido, fiume*) to run, flow; (*fune*) to run; (*cassetto, porta*) to slide easily; (*tempo*) to pass (by); **far ~ verso il basso/l'alto** (*su schermo tattile*) to swipe down/up

scorre'ria SF raid, incursion

scorret'tezza [skorret'tettsa] SF incorrectness; lack of politeness, rudeness; unfairness; **commettere una ~** (*essere sleale*) to be unfair

scor'retto, -a AG (*sbagliato*) incorrect; (*sgarbato*) impolite; (*sconveniente*) improper; (*sleale*) unfair; (*gioco*) foul

scor'revole AG (*porta*) sliding; (*fig: stile*) fluent, flowing

scorri'banda SF (*Mil*) raid; (*escursione*) trip, excursion

'scorsi *ecc* VB *vedi* **scorgere**

'scorso, -a PP *di* **scorrere** ▶ AG last ▶ SF quick look, glance; **lo ~ mese** last month

scor'soio, -a AG: **nodo ~** noose

'scorta SF (*di personalità, convoglio*) escort; (*provvista*) supply, stock; **sotto la ~ di due agenti** escorted by two policemen; **fare ~ di** to stock up with, get in a supply of; **di ~** (*materiali*) spare; **ruota di ~** spare wheel

scor'tare /**72**/ VT to escort

scor'tese AG discourteous, rude

scorte'sia SF discourtesy, rudeness; (*azione*) discourtesy

scorti'care /**20**/ VT to skin

'scorto, -a PP *di* **scorgere**

'scorza ['skɔrdza] SF (*di albero*) bark; (*di agrumi*) peel, skin

sco'sceso, -a [skoʃ'ʃeso] AG steep

'scosso, -a PP *di* **scuotere** ▶ AG (*turbato*) shaken, upset ▶ SF jerk, jolt, shake; (*Elettr, fig*) shock; **prendere la scossa** to get an electric shock; **scossa di terremoto** earth tremor

scos'sone SM: **dare uno ~ a qn** to give sb a shake; **procedere a scossoni** to jolt *o* jerk along

scos'tante AG (*fig*) off-putting (BRIT), unpleasant

scos'tare /**72**/ VT to move (away), shift ▪ **scostarsi** VPR to move away

scostu'mato, -a AG immoral, dissolute

scotch [skɔtʃ] SM INV (*whisky*) Scotch®; (*nastro adesivo*) Scotch tape®, Sellotape®

scot'tante AG (*fig: urgente*) pressing; (: *delicato*) delicate

scot'tare /**72**/ VT (*ustionare*) to burn; (: *con liquido bollente*) to scald ▶ VI to burn; (*caffè*) to be too hot ▪ **scottarsi** VPR to burn/scald o.s.; (*fig*) to have one's fingers burnt

scotta'tura SF burn; scald

'scotto, -a AG overcooked ▶ SM (*fig*): **pagare lo ~ (di)** to pay the penalty (for)

sco'vare /**72**/ VT to drive out, flush out; (*fig*) to discover

'Scozia ['skɔttsja] SF: **la ~** Scotland

scoz'zese [skot'tsese] AG Scottish ▶ SMF Scot

screan'zato, -a [skrean'tsato] AG ill-mannered ▶ SM/F boor

scredi'tare /**72**/ VT to discredit

'screen saver ['skriin'seɪvər] SM INV (*Inform*) screen saver

scre'mare /**72**/ VT to skim

scre'mato, -a AG skimmed; **parzialmente ~** semi-skimmed

screpo'lare /**72**/ VT, **screpo'larsi** VPR to crack

screpo'lato, -a AG (*labbra*) chapped; (*muro*) cracked

screpola'tura SF cracking *no pl*; crack

screzi'ato, -a [skret'tsjato] AG streaked

'screzio ['skrettsjo] SM disagreement

scribac'chino [skribak'kino] SM (*peg: impiegato*) penpusher; (: *scrittore*) hack

scricchio'lare [skrikkjo'lare] /**72**/ VI to creak, squeak

scricchio'lio [skrikkjo'lio] SM creaking

'scricciolo ['skrittʃolo] SM wren

'scrigno ['skriɲɲo] SM casket

scrimina'tura SF parting

'scrissi *ecc* VB *vedi* **scrivere**

'scritto, -a PP *di* **scrivere** ▶ AG written ▶ SM writing; (*lettera*) letter, note ▶ SF inscription ▪ **scritti** SMPL (*letterari ecc*) work(s), writings; **per *o* in ~** in writing

scrit'toio SM writing desk

scrit'tore, -'trice SM/F writer

scrit'tura SF writing; (*Comm*) entry; (*contratto*) contract; (*Rel*): **la Sacra S~** the Scriptures *pl* ▪ **scritture** SFPL (*Comm*) accounts, books

scrittu'rare /**72**/ VT (*Teat, Cine*) to sign up, engage; (*Comm*) to enter

scriva'nia SF desk

scri'vano SM (*amanuense*) scribe; (*impiegato*) clerk

scri'vente SMF writer

'scrivere /**105**/ VT to write; **come si scrive?** how is it spelt?, how do you write it?; **~ qc a qn** to write sth to sb; **~ qc a macchina** to type sth; **~ a penna/matita** to write in pen/pencil; **~ qc maiuscolo/minuscolo** to write sth in capital/small letters

scroc'care /20/ VT (col) to scrounge, cadge

scroc'cone, -a SM/F scrounger

'scrofa SF (Zool) sow

scrol'lare /72/ VT to shake ■ **scrollarsi** VPR (anche fig) to give o.s. a shake; **~ le spalle/il capo** to shrug one's shoulders/shake one's head; **scrollarsi qc di dosso** (anche fig) to shake sth off

scrol'lata SF shake; **~ di spalle** shrug (of one's shoulders)

scrosci'ante [skroʃ'ʃante] AG (pioggia) pouring; (fig: applausi) thunderous

scrosci'are [skroʃ'ʃare] /14/ VI (pioggia) to pour down, pelt down; (torrente, fig: applausi) to thunder, roar

'scroscio ['skrɔʃʃo] SM pelting; thunder, roar; (di applausi) burst

scros'tare /72/ VT (intonaco) to scrape off, strip ■ **scrostarsi** VPR to peel off, flake off

'scrupolo SM scruple; (meticolosità) care, conscientiousness; **essere senza scrupoli** to be unscrupulous

scrupo'loso, -a AG scrupulous; conscientious

scru'tare /72/ VT to scrutinize; (intenzioni, causa) to examine, scrutinize

scruta'tore, -'trice SM/F (Pol) scrutineer

scruti'nare /72/ VT (voti) to count

scru'tinio SM (votazione) ballot; (insieme delle operazioni) poll; (Ins) meeting for assignment of marks at end of a term or year

scu'cire [sku'tʃire] /31/ VT (orlo ecc) to unpick, undo ■ **scucirsi** VPR to come unstitched

scude'ria SF stable

scu'detto SM (Sport) (championship) shield; (distintivo) badge

scu'discio [sku'diʃʃo] SM (riding) crop, (riding) whip

'scudo SM shield; **farsi ~ di** o **con qc** to shield o.s. with sth; **~ aereo/missilistico** air/missile defence (BRIT) o defense (US); **~ termico** heat shield

sculacci'are [skulat'tʃare] /14/ VT to spank

sculacci'one [skulat'tʃone] SM spanking

scul'tore, -'trice SM/F sculptor

scul'tura SF sculpture

scu'ola SF school; **~ elementare** o **primaria** primary (BRIT) o grade (US) school (for children from 6 to 11 years of age); **~ guida** driving school; **~ materna** o **dell'infanzia** nursery school (for children aged 3 to 6); **~ secondaria di primo grado** first 3 years of secondary school, for children from 11 to 14 years of age; **~ secondaria di secondo grado** secondary school (for those aged 14 to 18); **~ media** secondary (BRIT) o high (US) school; **~ dell'obbligo** compulsory education; **~ privata/pubblica** private/state school; **scuole serali** evening classes, night school sg

Italian children first go to school (scuola) at the age of three. They remain at the *scuola materna* until they are six, when they move on to the *scuola primaria* for another five years. After this come three years of *scuola secondaria di primo grado*. Students who wish to continue their schooling attend the *scuola secondaria di secondo grado*, choosing between several types of institution which specialize in different subject areas.

> Quando la parola *scuola* indica l'istituzione non è mai preceduta dall'articolo determinativo.
> *Ho imparato a suonare il piano a scuola.* **I learned to play piano at school.**
> Si usa l'articolo quando ci si riferisce a uno specifico edificio.
> *Siamo dovuti andare alla scuola per parlare ai professori.* **We had to go to the school to talk to the teachers.**

scu'otere /106/ VT to shake ■ **scuotersi** VPR to jump, be startled; (fig: muoversi) to rouse o.s., stir o.s.; (: turbarsi) to be shaken

'scure SF axe, ax (US)

scu'rire /55/ VT to darken, make darker

'scuro, -a AG dark; (fig: espressione) grim ▶ SM darkness; dark colour (BRIT) o color (US); (imposta) (window) shutter; **verde/rosso** ecc **~** dark green/red etc

scur'rile AG scurrilous

'scusa SF excuse ■ **scuse** SFPL apology sg, apologies; **chiedere ~ a qn (per)** to apologize to sb (for); **chiedo ~** I'm sorry; (disturbando ecc) excuse me; **vi prego di accettare le mie scuse** please accept my apologies

scu'sare /72/ VT to excuse ■ **scusarsi** VPR: **scusarsi (di)** to apologize (for); **(mi) scusi** I'm sorry; (per richiamare l'attenzione) excuse me

> Per attirare l'attenzione di qualcuno come quando si vuole un'informazione e per chiedere permesso tra la folla si usa **excuse me**.
> *Scusi, dov'è la banca?* **Excuse me, where is the bank?**
> *Scusi, scusi! Questa è la mia fermata.* **Excuse me, excuse me! This is my stop.**
> Per chiedere scusa invece si dice **sorry**.
> *Scusi! Non volevo urtarla/offenderla!* **Sorry, I didn't mean to bump into you/to offend you!**

S.C.V. SIGLA = Stato della Città del Vaticano

sdebi'tarsi /72/ VPR: **~ (con qn di** o **per qc)** (anche fig) to repay (sb for sth)

sde'gnare [zdeɲ'ɲare] /15/ VT to scorn, despise ■ **sdegnarsi** VPR (adirarsi) to get angry

sde'gnato, -a [zdeɲ'ɲato] AG indignant, angry

'sdegno ['zdeɲɲo] SM scorn, disdain

sdegnosa'mente [zdeɲɲosa'mente] AV scornfully, disdainfully

sde'gnoso, -a [zdeɲ'ɲoso] AG scornful, disdainful

sdilin'quirsi /55/ VPR (*illanguidirsi*) to become sentimental

sdoga'nare /72/ VT (*Comm*) to clear through customs

sdolci'nato, -a [zdoltʃi'nato] AG mawkish, oversentimental

sdoppia'mento SM (*Chim: di composto*) splitting; (*Psic*): ~ **della personalità** split personality

sdoppi'are /19/ VT (*dividere*) to divide o split in two

sdrai'arsi /19/ VPR to stretch out, lie down

'sdraio SM: **sedia a ~** deck chair

sdrammatiz'zare [zdrammatid'dzare] /72/ VT to play down, minimize

sdruccio'lare [zdruttʃo'lare] /72/ VI to slip, slide

sdruccio'levole [zdruttʃo'levole] AG slippery

sdru'cito, -a [zdru'tʃito] AG (*strappato*) torn; (*logoro*) threadbare

---

se

PRON *vedi* **si**

▸ CONG **1** (*condizionale, ipotetica*) if; **se nevica non vengo** I won't come if it snows; **se fossi in te** if I were you; **sarei rimasto se me l'avessero chiesto** I would have stayed if they'd asked me; **non puoi fare altro se non telefonare** all you can do is phone; **se mai** if, if ever; **siamo noi se mai che le siamo grati** it is we who should be grateful to you; **se no** (*altrimenti*) or (else), otherwise; **se non** (*anzi*) if not; (*tranne*) except; **se non altro** if nothing else, at least; **se solo o solamente** if only

2 (*in frasi dubitative, interrogative indirette*) if, whether; **non so se scrivere o telefonare** I don't know whether o if I should write or phone

sé PRON (*gen*) oneself; (*esso, essa, lui, lei, loro*) itself; himself; herself; themselves; **sé stesso(a)** *pron* oneself; itself; himself; herself; **sé stessi(e)** (*pl*) themselves; **di per sé non è un problema** it's no problem in itself; **parlare tra sé e sé** to talk to oneself; **va da sé che ...** it goes without saying that ..., it's obvious that ..., it stands to reason that ...; **è un caso a sé** o **a sé stante** it's a special case; **un uomo che s'è fatto da sé** a self-made man

S.E. ABBR (= *sud-est*) SE; (= *Sua Eccellenza*) HE

S.E.A.T.O. SIGLA F (= *Southeast Asia Treaty Organization*) SEATO

seb'bene CONG although, though

'sebo SM sebum

sec. ABBR (= *secolo*) c.

SECAM SIGLA M (= *séquentiel couleur à mémoire*) SECAM

'secca SF *vedi* **secco**

secca'mente AV (*rispondere, rifiutare*) sharply, curtly

sec'care /20/ VT to dry; (*prosciugare*) to dry up; (*fig: importunare*) to annoy, bother ▸ VI to dry; to dry up ■ **seccarsi** VPR to dry; to dry up; (*fig*) to grow annoyed; **si è seccato molto** he was very annoyed

sec'cato, -a AG (*fig: infastidito*) bothered, annoyed; (: *stufo*) fed up

secca'tore, -'trice SM/F nuisance, bother

secca'tura SF (*fig*) bother *no pl*, trouble *no pl*

seccherò *ecc* [sekke'rɔ] VB *vedi* **seccare**

'secchia ['sekkja] SF bucket, pail

secchi'ello [sek'kjɛllo] SM (*per bambini*) bucket, pail; ~ **del ghiaccio** ice bucket

'secchio ['sekkjo] SM bucket, pail; ~ **della spazzatura** o **delle immondizie** dustbin (BRIT), garbage can (US)

'secco, -a, -chi, -che AG dry; (*fichi, pesce*) dried; (*foglie, ramo*) withered; (*magro: persona*) thin, skinny; (*fig: risposta, modo di fare*) curt, abrupt; (: *colpo*) clean, sharp ▸ SM (*siccità*) drought ▸ SF (*del mare*) shallows *pl*; **restarci ~** (*morire sul colpo*) to drop dead; **avere la gola secca** to feel dry, be parched; **lavare a ~** to dry-clean; **tirare a ~** (*barca*) to beach; **rimanere a ~** (*fig*) to be left in the lurch

secen'tesco, -a, -schi, -sche [setʃen'tesko] AG = **seicentesco**

se'cernere [se'tʃɛrnere] /29/ VT to secrete

seco'lare AG age-old, centuries-old; (*laico, mondano*) secular

'secolo SM century; (*epoca*) age

se'conda SF *vedi* **secondo**; **la S~ Repubblica** term used to refer to Italy after the political changes resulting from the 1994 elections

secondaria'mente AV secondly

secon'dario, -a AG secondary; **scuola/istruzione secondaria** secondary school/education

secon'dino SM prison officer, warder (BRIT)

se'condo, -a AG second ▸ SM second; (*di pranzo*) main course ▸ SF (*Aut*) second (gear); (*Ferr*) second class ▸ PREP according to; (*nel modo prescritto*) in accordance with; **seconda classe** second-class; **di seconda classe** second-class; **di seconda mano** second-hand; **viaggiare in seconda** to travel second-class; **comandante in seconda** second-in-command; **a seconda di** *prep* according to; in accordance with; ~ **me** in my opinion, to my mind; ~ **la legge/quanto si era deciso** in accordance with the law/the decision taken

secondo'genito, -a [sekondo'dʒenito] SM/F second-born

secrezi'one [sekret'tsjone] SF secretion

S

'**sedano** SM celery

se'dare /**72**/ VT (*dolore*) to soothe; (*rivolta*) to put down, suppress

seda'tivo, -a AG, SM sedative

'**sede** SF (*luogo di residenza*) (place of) residence; (*di ditta: principale*) head office; (: *secondaria*) branch (office); (*di organizzazione*) headquarters *pl*; (*di governo, parlamento*) seat; (*Rel*) see; **in ~ di** (*in occasione di*) during; **in altra ~** on another occasion; **in ~ legislativa** in legislative sitting; **prendere ~** to take up residence; **un'azienda con diverse sedi in città** a firm with several branches in the city; **~ centrale** head office; **~ sociale** registered office

seden'tario, -a AG sedentary

se'dere /**107**/ VI to sit, be seated ▶ SM (*deretano*) bottom ■ **sedersi** VPR to sit down; **posto a ~** seat

'**sedia** SF chair; **~ elettrica** electric chair; **~ a rotelle** wheelchair

sedi'cenne [sedi'tʃɛnne] AG, SMF sixteen-year-old

sedi'cente [sedi'tʃɛnte] AG self-styled

sedi'cesimo, -a [sedi'tʃɛzimo] NUM sixteenth

'**sedici** ['seditʃi] NUM sixteen

se'dile SM seat; (*panchina*) bench

sedimen'tare /**72**/ VI to leave a sediment

sedi'mento SM sediment

sedizi'one [sedit'tsjone] SF revolt, rebellion

sedizi'oso, -a [sedit'tsjoso] AG seditious

se'dotto, -a PP *di* **sedurre**

sedu'cente [sedu'tʃɛnte] AG seductive; (*proposta*) very attractive

se'durre /**90**/ VT to seduce

se'duta SF session, sitting; (*riunione*) meeting; **essere in ~** to be in session, be sitting; **~ stante** (*fig*) immediately; **~ spiritica** seance

sedut'tore, -'trice SM/F seducer/seductress

seduzi'one [sedut'tsjone] SF seduction; (*fascino*) charm, appeal

SEeO ABBR (= *salvo errori e omissioni*) E & OE

'**sega, -ghe** SF saw; **~ circolare** circular saw; **~ a mano** handsaw

'**segale** SF rye

se'gare /**80**/ VT to saw; (*recidere*) to saw off

sega'tura SF (*residuo*) sawdust

'**seggio** ['sɛddʒo] SM seat; **~ elettorale** polling station

seggi'ola ['sɛddʒola] SF chair

seggio'lino [sɛddʒo'lino] SM seat; (*per bambini*) child's chair; **~ di sicurezza** (*Aut*) child safety seat

seggio'lone [sɛddʒo'lone] SM (*per bambini*) highchair

seggio'via [sɛddʒo'via] SF chairlift

seghe'ria [sege'ria] SF sawmill

segherò *ecc* [sege'rɔ] VB *vedi* **segare**

seghet'tato, -a [seget'tato] AG serrated

se'ghetto [se'getto] SM hacksaw

seg'mento SM segment

segna'lare [seɲɲa'lare] /**72**/ VT (*essere segno di*) to indicate, be a sign of; (*avvertire*) to signal; (*menzionare*) to indicate; (: *fatto, risultato, aumento*) to report; (: *errore, dettaglio*) to point out; (: *persona*) to single out; (*Aut*) to signal, indicate ■ **segnalarsi** VPR (*distinguersi*) to distinguish o.s.; **~ qn a qn** (*per lavoro ecc*) to bring sb to sb's attention

segnalazi'one [seɲɲalat'tsjone] SF (*azione*) signalling; (*segnale*) signal; (*annuncio*) report; (*raccomandazione*) recommendation

se'gnale [seɲ'ɲale] SM signal; (*cartello*): **~ stradale** road sign; **~ acustico** acoustic o sound signal; (*di segreteria telefonica*) tone; **~ d'allarme** alarm; (*Ferr*) communication cord; **~ di linea libera** (*Tel*) dialling (BRIT) o dial (US) tone; **~ luminoso** light signal; **~ di occupato** (*Tel*) engaged tone (BRIT), busy signal (US); **~ orario** (*Radio*) time signal

segna'letica [seɲɲa'lɛtika] SF signalling, signposting; **~ stradale** road signs *pl*

segna'libro [seɲɲa'libro] SM (*anche Inform*) bookmark

segna'punti [seɲɲa'punti] SM INV/F INV scorer, scorekeeper

se'gnare [seɲ'ɲare] /**15**/ VT to mark; (*prendere nota*) to note; (*indicare*) to indicate, mark; (*Sport: goal*) to score ■ **segnarsi** VPR (*Rel*) to make the sign of the cross, cross o.s.

'**segno** ['seɲɲo] SM sign; (*impronta, contrassegno*) mark; (*limite*) limit, bounds *pl*; (*bersaglio*) target; **fare ~ di sì/no** to nod (one's head)/shake one's head; **fare ~ a qn di fermarsi** to motion (to) sb to stop; **cogliere** o **colpire nel ~** (*fig*) to hit the mark; **in** o **come ~ d'amicizia** as a mark o token of friendship; **"segni particolari"** (*su documento ecc*) "distinguishing marks"; **~ zodiacale** star sign

segre'gare /**80**/ VT to segregate, isolate

segregazi'one [segregat'tsjone] SF segregation

se'greta SF *vedi* **segreto**

segre'tario, -a SM/F secretary; **~ comunale** town clerk; **~ del partito** party leader; **S~ di Stato** Secretary of State

segrete'ria SF (*di ditta, scuola*) (secretary's) office; (*d'organizzazione internazionale*) secretariat; (*Pol ecc: carica*) office of Secretary; **~ telefonica** answering machine

segre'tezza [segre'tettsa] SF secrecy; **notizie della massima ~** confidential information; **in tutta ~** in secret; (*confidenzialmente*) in confidence

se'greto, -a AG secret ▶ SM secret; secrecy *no pl* ▶ SF dungeon; **in ~** in secret, secretly; **il ~ pro-**

fessionale professional secrecy; **un ~ professionale** a professional secret

segu'ace [se'gwatʃe] SMF follower, disciple

segu'ente AG following, next; **nel modo ~** as follows, in the following way

se'gugio [se'gudʒo] SM hound, hunting dog; (*fig*) private eye, sleuth

segu'ire /45/ VT (*anche su Twitter*) to follow; (*frequentare: corso*) to attend ▶ VI to follow; (*continuare: testo*) to continue; **~ i consigli di qn** to follow o to take sb's advice; **~ gli avvenimenti di attualità** to follow o keep up with current events; **come segue** as follows; **"segue"** "to be continued"

segui'tare /72/ VT to continue, carry on with ▶ VI to continue, carry on

'seguito SM (*scorta*) suite, retinue; (*discepoli*) followers *pl*; (*favore*) following; (*serie*) sequence, series *sg*; (*continuazione*) continuation; (*conseguenza*) result; **di ~** at a stretch, on end; **in ~** later on; **in ~ a, a ~ di** following; (*a causa di*) as a result of, owing to; **essere al ~ di qn** to be among sb's suite, be one of sb's retinue; **non aver ~** (*conseguenze*) to have no repercussions; **facciamo ~ alla lettera del ...** further to o in answer to your letter of ...

'sei VB *vedi* **essere** ▶ NUM six

Sei'celle [sei'tʃelle] SFPL: **le ~** the Seychelles

seicen'tesco, -a, -schi, -sche [seitʃen'tesko] AG seventeenth-century

sei'cento [sei'tʃento] NUM six hundred ▶ SM: **il S~** the seventeenth century

sei'mila NUM six thousand

'selce ['seltʃe] SF flint, flintstone

selci'ato [sel'tʃato] SM cobbled surface

selet'tivo, -a AG selective

selet'tore SM (*Tecn*) selector

selezio'nare [selettsjo'nare] /72/ VT to select

selezi'one [selet'tsjone] SF selection; **fare una ~** to make a selection o choice

'selfie ['selfi] SM INV selfie

'sella SF saddle

sel'lare /72/ VT to saddle

sel'lino SM saddle

seltz SM INV soda (water)

'selva SF (*bosco*) wood; (*foresta*) forest

selvag'gina [selvad'dʒina] SF (*animali*) game

sel'vaggio, -a, -gi, -ge [sel'vaddʒo] AG wild; (*tribù*) savage, uncivilized; (*fig: brutale*) savage, brutal; (: *incontrollato: fenomeno, aumento ecc*) uncontrolled ▶ SM/F savage; **inflazione selvaggia** runaway inflation

sel'vatico, -a, -ci, -che AG wild

S.Em. ABBR (= *Sua Eminenza*) HE

se'maforo SM (*Aut*) traffic lights *pl*

se'mantico, -a AG semantic ▶ SF semantics *sg*

sembi'anza [sem'bjantsa] SF (*poetico: aspetto*) appearance ▪ **sembianze** SFPL (*lineamenti*) features; (*fig: falsa apparenza*) semblance *sg*

sem'brare /72/ VI to seem ▶ VB IMPERS: **sembra che** it seems that; **mi sembra che** it seems to me that; (*penso che*) I think (that); **~ di essere** to seem to be; **non mi sembra vero!** I can't believe it!

'seme SM seed; (*sperma*) semen; (*Carte*) suit

se'mente SF seed

semes'trale AG (*che dura 6 mesi*) six-month *cpd*; (*che avviene ogni 6 mesi*) six-monthly

se'mestre SM half-year, six-month period

'semi... PREFISSO semi ...

semi'cerchio [semi'tʃerkjo] SM semicircle

semicondut'tore SM semiconductor

semidetenzi'one [semideten'tsjone] SF *custodial sentence whereby individual must spend a minimum of 10 hours per day in prison*

semifi'nale SF semifinal

semi'freddo, -a AG (*Cuc*) chilled ▶ SM icecream dessert

semilibertà SF *custodial sentence which allows prisoner to study or work outside prison for part of the day*

'semina SF (*Agr*) sowing

semi'nare /72/ VT to sow

semi'nario SM seminar; (*Rel*) seminary

semi'nato SM: **uscire dal ~** (*fig*) to wander off the point

seminter'rato SM basement; (*appartamento*) basement flat (BRIT) o apartment (US)

semi'ologo, -a, -gi, -ghe SM/F semiologist

semi'otica SF semiotics *sg*

se'mitico, -a, -ci, -che AG semitic

semivu'oto, -a AG half-empty

sem'mai = **se mai**

'semola SF bran; **~ di grano duro** durum wheat

semo'lato AG: **zucchero ~** caster sugar

semo'lino SM semolina

'semplice ['semplitʃe] AG simple; (*di un solo elemento*) single; **è una ~ formalità** it's a mere formality

semplice'mente [semplitʃe'mente] AV simply

sempli'cistico, -a, -ci, -che [semplitʃi'stiko] AG simplistic

semplicità [semplitʃi'ta] SF simplicity

semplifi'care /20/ VT to simplify

semplificazi'one [semplifikat'tsjone] SF simplification; **fare una ~ di** to simplify

'sempre AV always; (*ancora*) still; **posso ~ tentare** I can always o still try; **da ~** always; **per ~** forever; **una volta per ~** once and for all; **~ che** *cong* as long as, provided (that); **~ più** more and more; **~ meno** less and less; **va ~ meglio** things are getting better and better; **è ~ più giovane**

S

she gets younger and younger; **è ~ meglio che niente** it's better than nothing; **è (pur) ~ tuo fratello** he is still your brother (however); **c'è ~ la possibilità che ...** there's still a chance that ..., there's always the possibility that ...

sempre've̱rde AG, SM O F (*Bot*) evergreen

Sen. ABBR (= *senatore*) Sen.

'se̱nape SF (*Cuc*) mustard

se'na̱to SM senate; **il S~** *see note*

> The **Senato** is the upper house of the Italian parliament, with similar functions to the *Camera dei deputati*. Candidates must be at least 40 years of age and electors must be 25 or over. Elections are held every five years. Every former head of state (*Presidente della Repubblica*) becomes a senator for life, as do five distinguished members of the public who are chosen by the *Presidente della Repubblica* for their scientific, social, artistic or literary achievements. The chamber is presided over by the *Presidente del Senato*, who is elected by the senators.

sena'to̱re, -'trice SM/F senator

'Se̱negal SM: **il ~** Senegal

senega'le̱se AG, SMF Senegalese *inv*

se'ne̱se AG of (*o* from) Siena

se'ni̱le AG senile

'Se̱nna SF: **la ~** the Seine

'se̱nno SM judgment, (common) sense; **col ~ di poi** with hindsight

sennò AV = **se no**

'se̱no SM (*Anat: petto, mammella*) breast; (: *grembo: anche fig*) womb; (: *cavità*) sinus; (*Geo*) inlet, creek; (*Mat*) sine; **in ~ al partito/all'organizzazione** within the party/the organization

sen'sa̱le SMF (*Comm*) agent

sensa'te̱zza [sensa'tettsa] SF good sense, good judgment

sen'sa̱to, -a AG sensible

sensazio'na̱le [sensattsjo'nale] AG sensational

sensazi'o̱ne [sensat'tsjone] SF feeling, sensation; **fare ~** to cause a sensation, create a stir; **avere la ~ che** to have a feeling that

sen'si̱bile AG sensitive; (*ai sensi*) perceptible; (*rilevante, notevole*) appreciable, noticeable; **~ a** sensitive to

> Do not translate the Italian word **sensibile** by *sensible*.

sensibili̱tà SF sensitivity

sensibiliz'za̱re [sensibilid'dzare] /72/ VT (*fig*) to make aware, awaken

'se̱nso SM (*Fisiol, istinto*) sense; (*impressione, sensazione*) feeling, sensation; (*significato*) meaning, sense; (*direzione*) direction ■ **sensi** SMPL (*coscienza*) consciousness *sg*; (*sensualità*) senses; **perdere/riprendere i sensi** to lose/regain consciousness; **avere ~ pratico** to be practi-cal; **avere un sesto ~** to have a sixth sense; **fare ~ a** (*ripugnare*) to disgust, repel; **ciò non ha ~** that doesn't make sense; **senza *o* privo di ~** meaningless; **nel ~ che** in the sense that; **nel vero ~ della parola** in the true sense of the word; **nel ~ della lunghezza** lengthwise, lengthways; **nel ~ della larghezza** widthwise; **ho dato disposizioni in quel ~** I've given instructions to that end *o* effect; **~ comune** common sense; **~ del dovere** sense of duty; **in ~ opposto** in the opposite direction; **in ~ orario/antiorario** clockwise/anticlockwise; **~ dell'umorismo** sense of humour; **~ di colpa** sense of guilt; **a ~ unico** one-way; **"~ vietato"** (*Aut*) "no entry"

sensu'a̱le AG sensual; sensuous

sensuali̱tà SF sensuality; sensuousness

sen'te̱nza [sen'tentsa] SF (*Dir*) sentence; (*massima*) maxim

sentenzi'a̱re [senten'tsjare] /19/ VI (*Dir*) to pass judgment

senti'e̱ro SM path

sentimen'ta̱le AG sentimental; (*vita, avventura*) love *cpd*

senti'me̱nto SM feeling

senti'ne̱lla SF sentry

sen'ti̱re /45/ VT (*percepire al tatto, fig*) to feel; (*udire*) to hear; (*ascoltare*) to listen to; (*odore*) to smell; (*avvertire con il gusto, assaggiare*) to taste ▶ VI: **~ di** (*avere sapore*) to taste of; (*avere odore*) to smell of ■ **sentirsi** VPR (*uso reciproco*) to be in touch; **sentirsi bene/male** to feel well/unwell *o* ill; **sentirsi di fare qc** (*essere disposto*) to feel like doing sth; **~ la mancanza di qn** to miss sb; **ho sentito dire che ...** I have heard that ...; **a ~ lui ...** to hear him talk ...; **fatti ~** keep in touch; **intendo ~ il mio legale/il parere di un medico** I'm going to consult my lawyer/a doctor

senti̱ta'me̱nte AV sincerely; **ringraziare ~** to thank sincerely

sen'ti̱to, -a AG (*sincero*) sincere, warm; **per ~ dire** by hearsay

sen'to̱re SM rumour (*BRIT*), rumor (*US*), talk; **aver ~ di qc** to hear about sth

'se̱nza ['sentsa] PREP, CONG without; **~ dir nulla** without saying a word; **~ dire che ...** not to mention the fact that ...; **~ contare che ...** without considering that ...; **fare ~ qc** to do without sth; **~ di me** without me; **~ che io lo sapessi** without me *o* my knowing; **~ amici** friendless; **senz'altro** of course, certainly; **~ dubbio** no doubt; **~ scrupoli** unscrupulous; **i ~ lavoro** the jobless, the unemployed; **i ~ tetto** the homeless

senza'te̱tto [sentsa'tetto] SM INV/F INV homeless person; **i ~** the homeless

sepa'ra̱re /72/ VT to separate; (*dividere*) to divide; (*tenere distinto*) to distinguish ■ **separarsi** VPR (*coniugi*) to separate, part; (*amici*) to part, leave each other; **separarsi da** (*coniuge*) to separate *o* part from; (*amico, socio*) to part company with; (*oggetto*) to part with

separata'mente AV separately

sepa'rato, -a AG (*letti, conto ecc*) separate; (*coniugi*) separated

separazi'one [separat'tsjone] SF separation; **~ dei beni** division of property

sépare [sepa're] SM INV screen

se'polcro SM sepulchre (*BRIT*), sepulcher (*US*)

se'polto, -a PP *di* **seppellire**

sepol'tura SF burial; **dare ~ a qn** to bury sb

seppel'lire /55/ VT to bury

'seppi *ecc* VB *vedi* **sapere**

'seppia SF cuttlefish ▶ AG INV sepia

sep'pure CONG even if

se'quela SF (*di avvenimenti*) series, sequence; (*di offese, ingiurie*) string

se'quenza [se'kwentsa] SF sequence

sequenzi'ale [sekwen'tsjale] AG sequential

seques'trare /72/ VT (*Dir*) to impound; (*rapire*) to kidnap; (*costringere in un luogo*) to keep, confine

se'questro SM (*Dir*) impoundment; **~ di persona** kidnapping

se'quoia SF sequoia

'sera SF evening; **di ~** in the evening; **domani ~** tomorrow evening, tomorrow night; **questa ~** this evening, tonight

se'rale AG evening *cpd*; **scuola ~** evening classes *pl*, night school

se'rata SF evening; (*ricevimento*) party

ser'bare /72/ VT to keep; (*mettere da parte*) to put aside; **~ rancore/odio verso qn** to bear sb a grudge/hate sb

serba'toio SM tank; (*cisterna*) cistern

'Serbia SF: **la ~** Serbia

'serbo, -a AG Serbian ▶ SM/F Serbian, Serb ▶ SM (*Ling*) Serbian; (*il serbare*): **mettere/tenere** *o* **avere in ~ qc** to put/keep sth aside

serbocro'ato, -a AG, SM Serbo-Croat

serena'mente AV serenely, calmly

sere'nata SF (*Mus*) serenade

serenità SF serenity

se'reno, -a AG (*tempo, cielo*) clear; (*fig*) serene, calm ▶ SM (*tempo*) good weather; **un fulmine a ciel ~** (*fig*) a bolt from the blue

serg. ABBR (= *sergente*) Sgt.

ser'gente [ser'dʒente] SM (*Mil*) sergeant

seri'ale AG (*Inform*) serial

seria'mente AV (*con serietà, in modo grave*) seriously; **lavorare ~** to take one's job seriously

'serie SF INV (*successione*) series *inv*; (*gruppo, collezione di chiavi ecc*) set; (*Sport*) division; league; (*Comm*): **modello di/fuori ~** standard/custom-built model; **in ~** in quick succession;

(*Comm*) mass *cpd*; **tutta una ~ di problemi** a whole string *o* series of problems

serietà SF seriousness; reliability

'serio, -a AG serious; (*impiegato*) responsible, reliable; (*ditta, cliente*) reliable, dependable; **sul ~** (*davvero*) really, truly; (*seriamente*) seriously, in earnest; **dico sul ~** I'm serious; **faccio sul ~** I mean it; **prendere qc/qn sul ~** to take sth/sb seriously

seri'oso, -a AG (*persona, modi*): **un po' ~** a bit too serious

ser'mone SM sermon

'serpe SF snake; (*fig: peg*) viper

serpeggi'are [serped'dʒare] **/62/** VI to wind; (*fig*) to spread

ser'pente SM snake; **~ a sonagli** rattlesnake

'serra SF greenhouse; hothouse; (*Geo*) sierra

serra'manico SM: **coltello a ~** jack-knife

ser'randa SF roller shutter

ser'rare /72/ VT to close, shut; (*a chiave*) to lock; (*stringere*) to tighten; (*premere: nemico*) to close in on; **~ i pugni/i denti** to clench one's fists/teeth; **~ le file** to close ranks

ser'rata SF (*Industria*) lockout

ser'rato, -a AG (*veloce*): **a ritmo ~** quickly, fast

serra'tura SF lock

'serva SF *vedi* **servo**

'server ['server] SM INV (*Inform*) server

ser'vigio [ser'vidʒo] SM favour (*BRIT*), favor (*US*), service

ser'vire /45/ VT to serve; (*clienti: al ristorante*) to wait on; (: *al negozio*) to serve, attend to; (*fig: giovare*) to aid, help; (*Carte*) to deal ▶ VI (*Tennis*) to serve; (*essere utile*): **~ a qn** to be of use to sb ■ **servirsi** VPR (*usare*): **servirsi di** to use; (*prendere: cibo*): **servirsi (di)** to help o.s. (to); (*essere cliente abituale*): **servirsi da** to be a regular customer at, go to; **non mi serve più** I don't need it any more; **non serve che lei vada** you don't need to go; **~ qc/a fare** (*utensile ecc*) to be used for sth/for doing; **~ (a qn) da** to serve as (for sb); **serviti pure!** help yourself!

servitù SF servitude; slavery; (*personale di servizio*) servants *pl*, domestic staff

servizi'evole [servit'tsjevole] AG obliging, willing to help

ser'vizio [ser'vittsjo] SM service; (*al ristorante: sul conto*) service (charge); (*Stampa, TV, Radio*) report; (*da tè, caffè ecc*) set, service ■ **servizi** SMPL (*di casa*) kitchen and bathroom; (*Econ*) services; **essere di ~** to be on duty; **fuori ~** (*telefono ecc*) out of order; **~ compreso/escluso** service included/not included; **entrata di ~** service *o* tradesman's (*BRIT*) entrance; **casa con doppi servizi** house with two bathrooms; **~ assistenza clienti** customer service; **~ civile** ≈ community service; **~ in diretta** (*TV, Radio*) live coverage; **~ fotografico** (*Stampa*) photo feature; **~ di posate**

337

set of cutlery; **~ militare** military service; **~ d'ordine** (*Polizia*) police patrol; (*di manifestanti*) team of stewards (*responsible for crowd control*); **servizi segreti** secret service *sg*; **servizi di sicurezza** security forces

'**servo, -a** SM/F servant

servo'freno SM (*Aut*) servo brake

servos'terzo [servos'tɛrtso] SM (*Aut*) power steering

'**sesamo** SM (*Bot*) sesame

ses'santa NUM sixty

sessan'tenne AG, SM/F sixty-year-old

sessan'tesimo, -a NUM sixtieth

sessan'tina SF: **una ~ (di)** about sixty

sessantot'tino, -a SM/F *a person who took part in the events of 1968*

sessi'one SF session

'**sesso** SM sex; **il ~ debole/forte** the weaker/stronger sex

sessu'ale AG sexual, sex *cpd*

sessualità SF sexuality

sessu'ologo, -a, -gi, -ghe SM/F sexologist, sex specialist

ses'tante SM sextant

'**sesto, -a** NUM sixth ▶ SM: **rimettere in ~** (*aggiustare*) to put back in order; (*fig: persona*) to put back on his (*o* her) feet; **rimettersi in ~** (*riprendersi*) to recover, get well; (*riassettarsi*) to tidy o.s. up

'**seta** SF silk

setacci'are [setat'tʃare] /**14**/ VT (*farina ecc*) to sift, sieve; (*fig: zona*) to search, comb

se'taccio [se'tattʃo] SM sieve; **passare al ~** (*fig*) to search, comb

'**sete** SF thirst; **avere ~** to be thirsty; **~ di potere** thirst for power

seti'ficio [seti'fitʃo] SM silk factory

'**setola** SF bristle

sett. ABBR (= *settembre*) Sept.

'**setta** SF sect

set'tanta NUM seventy

settan'tenne AG, SM/F seventy-year-old

settan'tesimo, -a NUM seventieth

settan'tina SF: **una ~ (di)** about seventy

set'tare /**72**/ VT (*Inform*) to set up

'**sette** NUM seven

settecen'tesco, -a, -schi, -sche [settet'ʃen'tesko] AG eighteenth-century

sette'cento [sette'tʃento] NUM seven hundred ▶ SM: **il S~** the eighteenth century

set'tembre SM September; *vedi anche* **luglio**

sette'mila NUM seven thousand

settentrio'nale AG northern ▶ SM/F northerner

settentri'one SM north

'**settico, -a, -ci, -che** AG (*Med*) septic

setti'mana SF week; **la ~ scorsa/prossima** last/next week; **a metà ~** in the middle of the week; **~ bianca** winter-sport holiday

settima'nale AG, SM weekly

'**settimo, -a** NUM seventh

set'tore SM sector; **~ privato/pubblico** private/public sector; **~ terziario** service industries *pl*

Se'ul SF Seoul

severità SF severity

se'vero, -a AG severe

sevizi'are [sevit'tsjare] /**19**/ VT to torture

se'vizie [se'vittsje] SFPL torture *sg*

'**sexting** ['sɛksting] SM sexting

'**sexy** ['sɛksi] AG INV sexy

sez. ABBR = **sezione**

sezio'nare [settsjo'nare] /**72**/ VT to divide into sections; (*Med*) to dissect

sezi'one [set'tsjone] SF section; (*Med*) dissection

sfaccen'dato, -a [sfatt'ʃen'dato] AG idle

sfaccetta'tura [sfatt'ʃetta'tura] SF (*azione*) faceting; (*parte sfaccettata, fig*) facet

sfacchi'nare [sfakki'nare] /**72**/ VI (*col*) to toil, drudge

sfacchi'nata [sfakki'nata] SF (*col*) chore, drudgery *no pl*

sfaccia'taggine [sfatt'ʃa'taddʒine] SF insolence, cheek

sfacci'ato, -a [sfat'tʃato] AG (*maleducato*) cheeky, impudent; (*vistoso*) gaudy

sfa'celo [sfa'tʃɛlo] SM (*fig*) ruin, collapse

sfal'darsi /**72**/ VPR to flake (off)

sfal'sare /**72**/ VT to offset

sfa'mare /**72**/ VT (*nutrire*) to feed; (*cibo*) to fill; (*soddisfare la fame*) **~ qn** to satisfy sb's hunger ▪ **sfamarsi** VPR to satisfy one's hunger, fill o.s. up

sfarfal'lio SM (*Cine, TV*) flickering

'**sfarzo** ['sfartso] SM pomp, splendour (*BRIT*), splendor (*US*)

sfar'zoso, -a [sfar'tsoso] AG splendid, magnificent

sfasa'mento SM (*Elettr*) phase displacement; (*fig*) confusion, bewilderment

sfa'sato, -a AG (*Elettr, motore*) out of phase; (*fig: persona*) confused, bewildered

sfasci'are [sfaʃ'ʃare] /**14**/ VT (*ferita*) to unbandage; (*distruggere: porta*) to smash, shatter ▪ **sfasciarsi** VPR (*rompersi*) to smash, shatter

sfa'tare /**72**/ VT (*leggenda*) to explode

sfati'cato, -a SM/F idler, loafer

'**sfatto, -a** AG (*letto*) unmade; (*orlo ecc*) undone; (*gelato, neve*) melted; (*frutta*) overripe; (*riso, pasta ecc*) overdone, overcooked; (*col: persona, corpo*) flabby

sfavil'lare /72/ vi to spark, send out sparks; (*risplendere*) to sparkle

sfa'vore sm disfavour (BRIT), disfavor (US), disapproval

sfavo'revole AG unfavourable (BRIT), unfavorable (US)

sfega'tato, -a AG fanatical

'sfera SF sphere

'sferico, -a, -ci, -che AG spherical

sfer'rare /72/ VT (*fig: colpo*) to land, deal; (: *attacco*) to launch

sfer'zante [sfer'tsante] AG (*critiche, parole*) stinging

sfer'zare [sfer'tsare] /72/ VT to whip; (*fig*) to lash out at

sfian'care /20/ VT to wear out, exhaust ■ **sfiancarsi** VPR to exhaust o.s., wear o.s. out

sfia'tare /72/ vi to allow air (*o gas etc*) to escape

sfiata'toio SM blowhole; (*Tecn*) vent

sfi'brante AG exhausting, energy-sapping

sfi'brare /72/ VT (*indebolire*) to exhaust, enervate

sfi'brato, -a AG exhausted, worn out

'sfida SF challenge

sfi'dante AG challenging ▶ SMF challenger

sfi'dare /72/ VT to challenge; (*fig*) to defy, brave; **~ qn a fare qc** to challenge sb to do sth; **~ un pericolo** to brave a danger; **sfido che ...** I dare say (that) ...

sfi'ducia [sfi'dutʃa] SF distrust, mistrust; **avere ~ in qn/qc** to distrust sb/sth

sfiduci'ato, -a [sfidu'tʃato] AG lacking confidence

sfi'gato, -a (*col*) AG: **essere ~** (*sfortunato*) to be unlucky ▶ SM/F (*fallito, sfortunato*) loser; (*fuori moda*) dork

sfigu'rare /72/ VT (*persona*) to disfigure; (*quadro, statua*) to deface ▶ vi (*far cattiva figura*) to make a bad impression

sfilacci'are [sfilat'tʃare] /14/ VT, VI, **sfilacciarsi** VPR to fray

sfi'lare /72/ VT (*ago*) to unthread; (*abito, scarpe*) to slip off ▶ vi (*truppe*) to march past, parade; (*atleti*) to parade; (*manifestanti*) to march ■ **sfilarsi** VPR (*perle ecc*) to come unstrung; (*orlo, tessuto*) to fray; (*calza*) to run, ladder

sfi'lata SF (*Mil*) parade; (*di manifestanti*) march; **~ di moda** fashion show

'sfilza ['sfiltsa] SF (*di case*) row; (*di errori*) series *inv*

'sfinge ['sfindʒe] SF sphinx

sfini'mento SM exhaustion

sfi'nito, -a AG exhausted

sfio'rare /72/ VT to brush (against); (*argomento*) to touch upon; **~ la velocità di 150 km/h** to touch 150 km/h

sfio'rire /55/ vi to wither, fade

'sfitto, -a AG vacant, empty

sfo'cato, -a AG (*Fot*) out of focus

sfoci'are [sfo'tʃare] /14/ vi: **~ in** to flow into; (*fig: malcontento*) to develop into

sfode'rato, -a AG (*vestito*) unlined

sfo'gare /80/ VT to vent, pour out ■ **sfogarsi** VPR (*sfogare la propria rabbia*) to give vent to one's anger; (*confidarsi*) **sfogarsi (con)** to pour out one's feelings (to); **non sfogarti su di me!** don't take your bad temper out on me!

sfoggi'are [sfod'dʒare] /62/ VT, vi to show off

'sfoggio ['sfɔddʒo] SM show, display; **fare ~ di** to show off, display

sfogherò *ecc* [sfoge'rɔ] VB *vedi* **sfogare**

'sfoglia ['sfɔʎʎa] SF sheet of pasta dough; **pasta ~** (*Cuc*) puff pastry

sfogli'are [sfoʎ'ʎare] /27/ VT (*libro*) to leaf through

'sfogo, -ghi SM outlet; (*eruzione cutanea*) rash; (*fig*) outburst; **dare ~ a** (*fig*) to give vent to

sfolgo'rante AG (*luce*) blazing; (*fig: vittoria*) brilliant

sfolgo'rare /72/ vi to blaze

sfolla'gente [sfolla'dʒente] SM INV truncheon (BRIT), billy (US)

sfol'lare /72/ VT to empty, clear ▶ vi to disperse; **~ da** (*città*) to evacuate

sfol'lato, -a AG evacuated ▶ SM/F evacuee

sfol'tire /55/ VT, **sfol'tirsi** VPR to thin (out)

sfon'dare /72/ VT (*porta*) to break down; (*scarpe*) to wear a hole in; (*cesto, scatola*) to burst, knock the bottom out of; (*Mil*) to break through ▶ vi (*riuscire*) to make a name for o.s.

sfon'dato, -a AG (*scarpe*) worn out; (*scatola*) burst; (*sedia*) broken, damaged; **essere ricco ~** to be rolling in it

'sfondo SM background

sfo'rare /72/ vi to overrun

sfor'mare /72/ VT to put out of shape, knock out of shape ■ **sformarsi** VPR to lose shape, get out of shape

sfor'mato, -a AG (*che ha perso forma*) shapeless ▶ SM (*Cuc*) *type of soufflé*

sfor'nare /72/ VT (*pane*) to take out of the oven; (*fig*) to churn out

sfor'nito, -a AG: **~ di** lacking in, without; (*negozio*) out of

sfor'tuna SF misfortune, ill luck *no pl*; **avere ~** to be unlucky; **che ~!** how unfortunate!

sfortu'nato, -a AG unlucky; (*impresa, film*) unsuccessful

sfor'zare [sfor'tsare] /72/ VT to force; (*voce, occhi*) to strain ■ **sforzarsi** VPR: **sforzarsi di o a o per fare** to try hard to do

'sforzo ['sfɔrtso] SM effort; (*tensione eccessiva, Tecn*) strain; **fare uno ~** to make an effort; **essere sotto ~** (*motore, macchina, fig: persona*) to be under stress

'sfottere /1/ VT (col) to tease

sfracel'lare [sfratʃel'lare] /72/ VT, **sfracel'larsi** VPR to smash

sfrat'tare /72/ VT to evict

'sfratto SM eviction; **dare lo ~ a qn** to give sb notice to quit

sfrecci'are [sfret'tʃare] /14/ VI to shoot o flash past

sfre'gare /80/ VT (strofinare) to rub; (graffiare) to scratch; **sfregarsi le mani** to rub one's hands; **~ un fiammifero** to strike a match

sfregi'are [sfre'dʒare] /62/ VT to slash, gash; (persona) to disfigure; (quadro) to deface

'sfregio ['sfredʒo] SM gash; scar; (fig) insult

sfre'nato, -a AG (fig) unrestrained, unbridled

sfron'dare /72/ VT (albero) to prune, thin out; (fig: discorso, scritto) to prune (down)

sfronta'tezza [sfronta'tettsa] SF impudence, cheek

sfron'tato, -a AG impudent, cheeky; shameless

sfrutta'mento SM exploitation

sfrut'tare /72/ VT (terreno) to overwork, exhaust; (miniera) to exploit, work; (fig: operai, occasione, potere) to exploit

sfrutta'tore, -'trice SM/F exploiter

sfug'gente [sfud'dʒente] AG (fig: sguardo) elusive; (mento) receding

sfug'gire [sfud'dʒire] /31/ VI to escape; **~ a** (custode) to escape (from); (morte) to escape; **~ a qn** (dettaglio, nome) to escape sb; **~ di mano a qn** to slip out of sb's hand (o hands); **lasciarsi ~ un'occasione** to let an opportunity go by; **~ al controllo** (macchina) to go out of control; (situazione) to be no longer under control

sfug'gita [sfud'dʒita] SF: **di ~** (rapidamente, in fretta) in passing

sfu'mare /72/ VT (colori, contorni) to soften, shade off ▶ VI to shade (off), fade; (fig: svanire) to vanish, disappear; (: speranze) to come to nothing

sfuma'tura SF shading off no pl; (tonalità) shade, tone; (fig) touch, hint

sfuo'cato, -a AG = **sfocato**

sfuri'ata SF (scatto di collera) fit of anger; (rimprovero) sharp rebuke

'sfuso, -a AG (caramelle ecc) loose, unpacked; (vino) unbottled; (birra) draught (BRIT), draft (US)

sg. ABBR = **seguente**

sga'bello SM stool

sgabuz'zino [zgabud'dzino] SM lumber room

sgambet'tare /72/ VI to kick one's legs about

sgam'betto SM: **far lo ~ a qn** to trip sb up; (fig) to oust sb

sganasci'arsi [zganaʃ'ʃarsi] /14/ VPR: **~ dalle risa** to roar with laughter

sganci'are [zgan'tʃare] /14/ VT to unhook; (chiusura) to unfasten, undo; (Ferr) to uncouple; (bombe: da aereo) to release, drop; (fig: col: soldi) to fork out ■ **sganciarsi** VPR to come unhooked; to come unfastened, come undone; to uncouple; **sganciarsi (da)** (fig) to get away (from)

sganghe'rato, -a [zgange'rato] AG (porta) off its hinges; (auto) ramshackle; (riso) wild, boisterous

sgar'bato, -a AG rude, impolite

'sgarbo SM: **fare uno ~ a qn** to be rude to sb

sgargi'ante [zgar'dʒante] AG gaudy, showy

sgar'rare /72/ VI (persona) to step out of line; (orologio: essere avanti) to gain; (: essere indietro) to lose

'sgarro SM inaccuracy

sgattaio'lare /72/ VI to sneak away o off

sge'lare [zdʒe'lare] /72/ VI, VT to thaw

'sghembo, -a ['zgembo] AG (obliquo) slanting; (storto) crooked

sghignaz'zare [zgiɲɲat'tsare] /72/ VI to laugh scornfully

sghignaz'zata [zgiɲɲat'tsata] SF scornful laugh

sgob'bare /72/ VI (col: scolaro) to swot; (: operaio) to slog

sgoccio'lare [zgottʃo'lare] /72/ VT (vuotare) to drain (to the last drop) ▶ VI (acqua) to drip; (recipiente) to drain

'sgoccioli ['zgottʃoli] SMPL: **essere agli ~** (lavoro, provviste ecc) to be nearly finished; (periodo) to be nearly over; **siamo agli ~** we've nearly finished, the end is in sight

sgo'larsi /72/ VPR to talk (o shout o sing) o.s. hoarse

sgombe'rare /72/, **sgom'brare** VT (tavolo, stanza) to clear; (andarsene da: stanza) to vacate; (evacuare: piazza, città) to evacuate ▶ VI to move

'sgombero SM vedi **sgombro**

'sgombro, -a AG: **~ (di)** clear (of), free (from) ▶ SM (Zool) mackerel; (anche: **sgombero**) clearing; vacating; evacuation; (trasloco) removal

sgomen'tare /72/ VT to dismay ■ **sgomentarsi** VPR to be dismayed

sgo'mento, -a AG dismayed ▶ SM dismay, consternation

sgomi'nare /72/ VT (nemico) to rout; (avversario) to defeat; (fig: epidemia) to overcome

sgonfi'are /19/ VT to let down, deflate ■ **sgonfiarsi** VPR to go down

'sgonfio, -a AG (pneumatico, pallone) flat

'sgorbio SM blot; scribble

sgor'gare /80/ VI to gush (out)

sgoz'zare [zgot'tsare] /72/ VT to cut the throat of

sgra'devole AG unpleasant, disagreeable

sgra'dito, -a AG unpleasant, unwelcome

sgraffi'gnare [zgraffiɲ'ɲare] /**15**/ ᴠᴛ (*col*) to pinch, swipe

sgrammati'cato, -a ᴀɢ ungrammatical

sgra'nare /**72**/ ᴠᴛ (*piselli*) to shell; **~ gli occhi** to open one's eyes wide

sgran'chirsi [zgran'kire] /**55**/ ᴠʀ (*anche:* **sgranchirsi**) to stretch; **sgranchirsi le gambe** to stretch one's legs

sgranocchi'are [zgranok'kjare] /**19**/ ᴠᴛ to munch

sgras'sare /**72**/ ᴠᴛ to remove the grease from

'sgravio ꜱᴍ: **~ fiscale** *o* **contributivo** tax relief

sgrazi'ato, -a [zgrat'tsjato] ᴀɢ clumsy, ungainly

sgreto'lare /**72**/ ᴠᴛ to cause to crumble ▪ **sgretolarsi** ᴠᴘʀ to crumble

sgri'dare /**72**/ ᴠᴛ to scold

sgri'data ꜱꜰ scolding

sguai'ato, -a ᴀɢ coarse, vulgar

sguai'nare /**72**/ ᴠᴛ to draw, unsheathe

sgual'cire [zgwal'tʃire] /**55**/ ᴠᴛ to crumple (up), crease

sgual'drina ꜱꜰ (*peg*) slut (!)

sgu'ardo ꜱᴍ (*occhiata*) look, glance; (*espressione*) look (in one's eye); **dare uno ~ a qc** to glance at sth, cast a glance *o* an eye over sth; **alzare** *o* **sollevare lo ~** to raise one's eyes, look up; **cercare qc/qn con lo ~** to look around for sth/sb

'sguattero, -a ꜱᴍ/ꜰ scullery boy(-maid)

sguaz'zare [zgwat'tsare] /**72**/ ᴠɪ (*nell'acqua*) to splash about; (*nella melma*) to wallow; **~ nell'oro** to be rolling in money

sguinzagli'are [zgwintsaʎ'ʎare] /**27**/ ᴠᴛ to let off the leash; (*fig: persona*): **~ qn dietro a qn** to set sb on sb

sgusci'are [zguʃ'ʃare] /**14**/ ᴠᴛ to shell ▶ ᴠɪ (*sfuggire di mano*) to slip; **~ via** to slip *o* slink away

'shaker ['ʃeikər] ꜱᴍ ɪɴᴠ (cocktail) shaker

'shampoo ['ʃampo] ꜱᴍ ɪɴᴠ shampoo

'shiatzu ['tʃiatsu] ꜱᴍ ɪɴᴠ, ᴀɢ ɪɴᴠ shiatsu

shoc'care [ʃok'kare] /**20**/ ᴠᴛ = **shockare**

shock [ʃɔk] ꜱᴍ ɪɴᴠ shock

shoc'kare [ʃok'kare] /**72**/ ᴠᴛ to shock

'shottino [ʃot'tino] ꜱᴍ shot

SI ꜱɪɢʟᴀ = **Siena**

---

si

(*dav lo, la, li, le, ne diventa* **se**) ᴘʀᴏɴ **1** (*riflessivo: maschile*) himself; (*: femminile*) herself; (*: neutro*) itself; (*: impersonale*) oneself; *pl* themselves; **lavarsi** to wash (oneself); **si è tagliato** he has cut himself; **si credono importanti** they think a lot of themselves

2 (*riflessivo: con complemento oggetto*): **lavarsi le mani** to wash one's hands; **sporcarsi i pantaloni** to get one's trousers dirty; **si sta**

lavando i capelli he (*o* she) is washing his (*o* her) hair

3 (*reciproco*) one another, each other; **si amano** they love one another *o* each other

4 (*passivo*): **si ripara facilmente** it is easily repaired; **affittasi camera** room to let

5 (*impersonale*): **si dice che ...** they *o* people say that ...; **si vede che è vecchio** one *o* you can see that it's old; **non si fa credito** we do not give credit; **ci si sbaglia facilmente** it's easy to make a mistake

6 (*noi*) we; **tra poco si parte** we're leaving soon

sì ᴀᴠ yes ▶ ꜱᴍ: **non mi aspettavo un sì** I didn't expect him (*o* her *etc*) to say yes; **per me è sì** I should think so, I expect so; **saranno stati sì e no in 20** there must have been about 20 of them; **uno sì e uno no** every other one; **un giorno sì e uno no** every other day; **dire di sì** to say yes; **spero/penso di sì** I hope/think so; **fece di sì col capo** he nodded (his head); **e sì che ...** and to think that ...

'sia¹ ᴄᴏɴɢ: **~ ... ~**: (*o ... o*) **~ che lavori, ~ che non lavori** whether he works or not; (*tanto ... quanto*) **verranno ~ Luigi ~ suo fratello** both Luigi and his brother will be coming

'sia² *ecc* ᴠʙ *vedi* **essere**

SIAE ꜱɪɢʟᴀ ꜰ = **Società Italiana Autori ed Editori**

Si'am ꜱᴍ: **il ~** Siam

sia'mese ᴀɢ, ꜱᴍꜰ siamese *inv*

si'amo ᴠʙ *vedi* **essere**

Si'beria ꜱꜰ: **la ~** Siberia

siberi'ano, -a ᴀɢ, ꜱᴍ/ꜰ Siberian

sibi'lare /**72**/ ᴠɪ to hiss; (*fischiare*) to whistle

'sibilo ꜱᴍ hiss; whistle

si'cario, -a ꜱᴍ/ꜰ hired killer

sicché [sik'ke] ᴄᴏɴɢ (*perciò*) so (that), therefore; (*e quindi*) (and) so

siccità [sittʃi'ta] ꜱꜰ drought

sic'come ᴄᴏɴɢ since, as

Si'cilia [si'tʃilja] ꜱꜰ: **la ~** Sicily

sicili'ano, -a [sitʃi'ljano] ᴀɢ, ꜱᴍ/ꜰ Sicilian

sico'moro ꜱᴍ sycamore

'siculo, -a ᴀɢ, ꜱᴍ/ꜰ Sicilian

si'cura ꜱꜰ (*di arma, spilla*) safety catch; (*Aut: di portiera*) safety lock

sicura'mente ᴀᴠ certainly

sicu'rezza [siku'rettsa] ꜱꜰ safety; security; confidence; certainty; **di ~** safety *cpd*; **la ~ stradale** road safety; **avere la ~ di qc** to be sure *o* certain of sth; **lo so con ~** I am quite certain; **ha risposto con molta ~** he answered very confidently; **~ informatica** cybersecurity

si'curo, -a ᴀɢ safe; (*ben difeso*) secure; (*fiducioso*) confident; (*certo*) sure, certain; (*notizia, amico*) reliable; (*esperto*) skilled ▶ ᴀᴠ (*anche:* **di sicuro**) certainly ▶ ꜱᴍ: **andare sul ~** to play safe;

essere/mettere al ~ to be safe/put in a safe place; **~ di sé** self-confident, sure of o.s.; **sentirsi ~** to feel safe o secure; **essere ~ di/che** to be sure of/that; **da fonte sicura** from reliable sources

siderur'gia [siderur'dʒia] SF iron and steel industry

side'rurgico, -a, -ci, -che [side'rurdʒiko] AG iron and steel *cpd*

'sidro SM cider

si'edo *ecc* VB *vedi* **sedere**

si'epe SF hedge

si'ero SM (*Med*) serum; **~ antivipera** snake bite serum; **~ del latte** whey

sieronegatività SF INV HIV-negative status

sieronega'tivo, -a AG HIV-negative ▶ SM/F HIV-negative person

sieropositività SF HIV-positive status

sieroposi'tivo, -a AG HIV-positive ▶ SM/F HIV-positive person

si'erra SF (*Geo*) sierra

Si'erra Le'one SF: **la ~** Sierra Leone

si'esta SF siesta, (afternoon) nap

si'ete VB *vedi* **essere**

si'filide SF syphilis

si'fone SM siphon

Sig. ABBR (= *signore*) Mr

siga'retta SF cigarette; **~ elettronica** e-cigarette

'sigaro SM cigar

Sigg. ABBR (= *signori*) Messrs

sigil'lare [sidʒil'lare] /**72**/ VT to seal

si'gillo [si'dʒillo] SM seal

'sigla SF (*iniziali*) initials *pl*; (*abbreviazione*) acronym, abbreviation; **~ automobilistica** abbreviation of province on vehicle number plate; **~ musicale** signature tune

si'glare /**72**/ VT to initial

Sig.na ABBR (= *signorina*) Miss

signifi'care [siɲɲifi'kare] /**20**/ VT to mean; **cosa significa?** what does this mean?

significa'tivo, -a [siɲɲifika'tivo] AG significant

signifi'cato [siɲɲifi'kato] SM meaning

si'gnora [siɲ'ɲora] SF lady; **la ~ X** Mrs X; **buon giorno S~/Signore/Signorina** good morning; (*deferente*) good morning Madam/Sir/Madam; (*quando si conosce il nome*) good morning Mrs/Mr/Miss X; **Gentile S~/Signore/Signorina** (*in una lettera*) Dear Madam/Sir/Madam; **Gentile (o Cara) S~ Rossi** Dear Mrs Rossi; **Gentile S~ Anna Rossi** (*sulle buste*) Mrs Anna Rossi; **il signor Rossi e ~** Mr Rossi and his wife; **signore e signori** ladies and gentlemen; **le presento la mia ~** may I introduce my wife?

Davanti al cognome, per evitare la distinzione tradizionale fra signora e signorina, e quindi indipendentemente dallo stato civile della persona, si usa **Ms**.

si'gnore [siɲ'ɲore] SM gentleman; (*padrone*) lord, master; (*Rel*): **il S~** the Lord; **il signor X** Mr X; **signor Presidente** Mr Chairman; **Gentile (o Caro) Signor Rossi** (*in lettere*) Dear Mr Rossi; **Gentile Signor Paolo Rossi** (*sulle buste*) Mr Paolo Rossi; **i signori Bianchi** (*coniugi*) Mr and Mrs Bianchi; *vedi anche* **signora**

signo'ria [siɲɲo'ria] SF (*Storia*) seignory, signoria; **S~ Vostra** (*Amm*) you

signo'rile [siɲɲo'rile] AG refined

signorilità [siɲɲorili'ta] SF (*raffinatezza*) refinement; (*eleganza*) elegance

signo'rina [siɲɲo'rina] SF young lady; **la ~ X** Miss X; **Gentile (o Cara) S~ Rossi** (*in lettere*) Dear Miss Rossi; **Gentile S~ Anna Rossi** (*sulle buste*) Miss Anna Rossi; *vedi anche* **signora**

signo'rino [siɲɲo'rino] SM young master

Sig.ra ABBR (= *signora*) Mrs

silenzia'tore [silentsja'tore] SM silencer

si'lenzio [si'lɛntsjo] SM silence; **fare ~** to be quiet, stop talking; **far passare qc sotto ~** to keep quiet about sth, hush sth up

silenzi'oso, -a [silen'tsjoso] AG silent, quiet

'silice ['silitʃe] SF silica

si'licio [si'litʃo] SM silicon; **piastrina di ~** silicon chip

sili'cone SM silicone

'sillaba SF syllable

silu'rare /**72**/ VT to torpedo; (*fig: privare del comando*) to oust

si'luro SM torpedo

SIM [sim] SIGLA F INV (*Tel*): **~ card** SIM card

simbi'osi SF (*Biol, fig*) symbiosis

simboleggi'are [simboled'dʒare] /**62**/ VT to symbolize

sim'bolico, -a, -ci, -che AG symbolic(al)

simbo'lismo SM symbolism

'simbolo SM symbol

simi'lare AG similar

'simile AG (*analogo*) similar; (*di questo tipo*): **un uomo ~** such a man, a man like this ▶ SMF (*persona*) fellow man; **libri simili** such books; **~ a** similar to; **non ho mai visto niente di ~** I've never seen anything like that; **è insegnante o qualcosa di ~** he's a teacher or something like that; **vendono vasi e simili** they sell vases and things like that; **i suoi simili** one's fellow men, one's peers

simili'tudine SF (*Ling*) simile

simme'tria SF symmetry

sim'metrico, -a, -ci, -che AG symmetric(al)

simpa'tia SF (*qualità*) pleasantness; (*inclinazione*)

liking; **avere ~ per qn** to like sb, have a liking for sb; **con ~** (*su lettera ecc*) with much affection

sim'patico, -a, -ci, -che AG (*persona*) nice, pleasant, likeable; (*casa, albergo ecc*) nice, pleasant

Do not translate the Italian word **simpatico** by *sympathetic*.

simpatiz'zante [simpatid'dzante] SMF sympathizer

simpatiz'zare [simpatid'dzare] /72/ VI: **~ con** to take a liking to

sim'posio SM symposium

simu'lacro SM (*monumento, statua*) image; (*fig*) semblance

simu'lare /72/ VT to sham, simulate; (*Tecn*) to simulate

simulazi'one [simulat'tsjone] SF shamming; simulation

simul'taneo, -a AG simultaneous

sin. ABBR (= *sinistra*) L

sina'goga, -ghe SF synagogue

sincera'mente [sintʃera'mente] AV (*gen*) sincerely; (*francamente*) honestly, sincerely

since'rarsi [sintʃe'rarsi] /72/ VPR: **~ (di qc)** to make sure (of sth)

sincerità [sintʃeri'ta] SF sincerity

sin'cero, -a [sin'tʃero] AG (*genuino*) sincere; (*onesto*) genuine; heartfelt

'sincope SF syncopation; (*Med*) blackout

sincro'nia SF (*di movimento*) synchronism

sin'cronico, -a, -ci, -che AG synchronic

sincroniz'zare [sinkronid'dzare] /72/ VT to synchronize

sinda'cale AG (trade-)union *cpd*

sindaca'lista, -i, -e SM/F trade unionist

sinda'care /20/ VT (*controllare*) to inspect; (*fig: criticare*) to criticize

sinda'cato SM (*di lavoratori*) (trade) union; (*Amm, Econ, Dir*) syndicate, trust, pool; **~ dei datori di lavoro** employers' association

'sindaco, -ci SM mayor

'sindrome SF (*Med*) syndrome

siner'gia, -gie [siner'dʒia] SF (*anche fig*) synergy

sinfo'nia SF (*Mus*) symphony

sin'fonico, -a, -ci, -che AG symphonic; (*orchestra*) symphony *cpd*

singa'lese AG, SMF Sin(g)halese *inv*

Singa'pore SF Singapore

singhioz'zare [singjot'tsare] /72/ VI to sob; to hiccup

singhi'ozzo [sin'gjottso] SM (*di pianto*) sob; (*Med*) hiccup; **avere il ~** to have the hiccups; **a ~** (*fig*) by fits and starts

'single ['singol] AG INV, SM o F INV single

singo'lare AG (*insolito*) remarkable, singular; (*Ling*) singular ▶ SM (*Ling*) singular; (*Tennis*): **~ maschile/femminile** men's(-women's) singles

singolar'mente AV (*separatamente*) individually, one at a time; (*in modo strano*) strangely, peculiarly, oddly

'singolo, -a AG single, individual ▶ SM (*persona*) individual; (*Tennis*) = **singolare**; **ogni ~ individuo** each individual; **camera singola** single room

sinis'trato, -a AG damaged ▶ SM/F disaster victim; **zona sinistrata** disaster area

si'nistro, -a AG left, left-hand; (*fig*) sinister ▶ SM (*incidente*) accident ▶ SF (*Pol*) left (wing); **a sinistra** on the left; (*direzione*) to the left; **a sinistra di** to the left of; **di sinistra** left-wing; **tenere la sinistra** to keep to the left; **guida a sinistra** left-hand drive

'sino PREP = **fino**

si'nonimo, -a AG synonymous ▶ SM synonym; **~ di** synonymous with

sin'tassi SF syntax

sin'tattico, -a, -ci, -che AG syntactic

'sintesi SF synthesis; (*riassunto*) summary, résumé; **in ~** in brief, in short

sin'tetico, -a, -ci, -che AG synthetic; (*conciso*) brief, concise

sintetiz'zare [sintetid'dzare] /72/ VT to synthesize; (*riassumere*) to summarize

sintetizza'tore [sintetiddza'tore] SM (*Mus*) synthesizer; **~ di voce** voice synthesizer

sinto'matico, -a, -ci, -che AG symptomatic

'sintomo SM symptom

sinto'nia SF (*Radio*) tuning; **essere in ~ con qn** (*fig*) to be on the same wavelength as sb

sintoniz'zare [sintonid'dzare] /72/ VT to tune (in) ▪ **sintonizzarsi** VPR: **sintonizzarsi su** to tune in to

sintonizza'tore [sintoniddza'tore] SM tuner

sinu'oso, -a AG (*strada*) winding

sinu'site SF sinusitis

si'pario SM (*Teat*) curtain

si'rena SF (*apparecchio*) siren; (*nella mitologia, fig*) siren, mermaid; **~ d'allarme** (*per incendio*) fire alarm; (*per furto*) burglar alarm

'Siria SF: **la ~** Syria

siri'ano, -a AG, SM/F Syrian

si'ringa, -ghe SF syringe

'sisma, -i SM earthquake

'SISMI SIGLA M (= *Servizio per l'Informazione e la Sicurezza Militari*) military security service

'sismico, -a, -ci, -che AG seismic; (*zona*) earthquake *cpd*

sis'mografo SM seismograph

sissi'gnore [sissiɲ'ɲore] AV (*a un superiore*) yes, sir; (*enfatico*) yes indeed, of course

343

sis'tema, -i SM system; (*metodo*) method, way; **trovare il ~ per fare qc** to find a way to do sth; **~ decimale/metrico** decimal/metric system; **~ nervoso** nervous system; **~ operativo** (*Inform*) operating system; **~ solare** solar system; **~ di vita** way of life

siste'mare /72/ VT (*mettere a posto*) to tidy, put in order; (*risolvere: questione*) to sort out, settle; (*procurare un lavoro a*) to find a job for; (*dare un alloggio a*) to settle, find accommodation (BRIT) o accommodations (US) for ▪ **sistemarsi** VPR (*problema*) to be settled; (*persona: trovare alloggio*) to find accommodation(s); (: *trovarsi un lavoro*) to get fixed up with a job; **ti sistemo io!** I'll soon sort you out!; **~ qn in un albergo** to fix sb up with a hotel

sistematica'mente AV systematically

siste'matico, -a, -ci, -che AG systematic

sistemazi'one [sistemat'tsjone] SF arrangement, order; settlement; employment; accommodation (BRIT), accommodations (US)

'sito, -a AG (*Amm*) situated ▪ SM (*letterario*) place; **~ Internet** website

sitogra'fia SF webliography, sitography

situ'are /72/ VT to site, situate

situ'ato, -a AG: **~ a/su** situated at/on

situazi'one [situat'tsjone] SF situation; **vista la sua ~ familiare** given your family situation o circumstances; **nella sua ~** in your position o situation; **mi trovo in una ~ critica** I'm in a very difficult situation o position

'skai® SM Leatherette®

ski-lift [ski'lift] SM INV ski tow

ski pass [ski'pas] SM INV ski pass

slacci'are [zlat't∫are] /14/ VT to undo, unfasten

slanci'arsi [zlan't∫arsi] /14/ VPR to dash, fling o.s.

slanci'ato, -a [zlan't∫ato] AG slender

'slancio ['zlant∫o] SM dash, leap; (*fig*) surge; **in uno ~ d'affetto** in a burst o rush of affection; **di ~** impetuously

sla'vato, -a AG faded, washed out; (*fig: viso, occhi*) pale, colourless (BRIT), colorless (US)

sla'vina SF snowslide

'slavo, -a AG Slav(onic), Slavic

sle'ale AG disloyal; (*concorrenza ecc*) unfair

slealtà SF disloyalty; unfairness

sle'gare /80/ VT to untie

slip [zlip] SM INV (*mutandine*) briefs pl; (*da bagno: per uomo*) (swimming) trunks pl; (: *per donna*) bikini bottoms pl

'slitta SF sledge; (*trainata*) sleigh

slitta'mento SM slipping; skidding; postponement; **~ salariale** wage drift

slit'tare /72/ VI to slip, slide; (*Aut*) to skid; (*incontro, conferenza*) to be put off, be postponed

s.l.m. ABBR (= *sul livello del mare*) a.s.l.

slo'gare /80/ VT (*Med*) to dislocate; (: *caviglia, polso*) to sprain

sloga'tura SF dislocation; sprain

sloggi'are [zlod'dʒare] /62/ VT (*inquilino*) to turn out; (*nemico*) to drive out, dislodge ▪ VI to move out

Slo'vacchia [zlo'vakkja] SF Slovakia

slo'vacco, -a, -ci, -che AG, SM/F Slovak, Slovakian; **la Repubblica Slovacca** the Slovak Republic

Slo'venia SF Slovenia

slo'veno, -a AG, SM/F Slovene, Slovenian ▪ SM (*Ling*) Slovene

S.M. ABBR (*Mil*) = **Stato Maggiore**; (= *Sua Maestà*) HM

smac'cato, -a AG (*fig*) excessive

smacchi'are [zmak'kjare] /19/ VT to remove stains from

smacchia'tore [zmakkja'tore] SM stain remover

'smacco, -chi SM humiliating defeat

smagli'ante [zmaʎ'ʎante] AG brilliant, dazzling

smagli'are [zmaʎ'ʎare] /27/ VT, **smagli'arsi** VPR (*calza*) to ladder

smaglia'tura [zmaʎʎa'tura] SF (*su maglia, calza*) ladder (BRIT), run; (*Med: sulla pelle*) stretch mark

sma'grire /55/ VT to make thin ▪ VI to get o grow thin, lose weight

sma'grito, -a AG: **essere ~** to have lost a lot of weight

smalizi'ato, -a [zmalit'tsjato] AG shrewd, cunning

smal'tare /72/ VT to enamel; (*ceramica*) to glaze; (*unghie*) to varnish

smalti'mento SM (*di rifiuti*) disposal

smal'tire /55/ VT (*merce*) to sell off; (*rifiuti*) to dispose of; (*cibo*) to digest; (*peso*) to lose; (*rabbia*) to get over; **~ la sbornia** to sober up

'smalto SM (*anche di denti*) enamel; (*per ceramica*) glaze; **~ per unghie** nail varnish

smance'rie [zmant∫e'rie] SFPL mawkishness sg

'smania SF agitation, restlessness; (*fig*): **~ di** thirst for, craving for; **avere la ~ addosso** to have the fidgets; **avere la ~ di fare** to long o yearn to do

smani'are /19/ VI (*agitarsi*) to be restless o agitated; (*fig*): **~ di fare** to long o yearn to do

smantella'mento SM dismantling

smantel'lare /72/ VT to dismantle

smar'carsi /20/ VPR (*Sport*) to get free of marking

smargi'asso [zmar'dʒasso] SM show-off

smarri'mento SM loss; (*fig*) bewilderment; dismay

smar'rire /55/ VT to lose; (*non riuscire a trovare*) to mislay ▪ **smarrirsi** VPR (*perdersi*) to lose one's way, get lost; (: *oggetto*) to go astray

smar'rito, -a AG (*oggetto*) lost; (*fig: confuso: persona*) bewildered, nonplussed; (: *sguardo*) bewildered; **ufficio oggetti smarriti** lost property office (BRIT), lost and found (US)

'smartphone ['zmartfɔn] SM INV smartphone

smasche'rare [zmaske'rare] /**72**/ VT to unmask

SME ABBR = **Stato Maggiore Esercito** ▸ SIGLA M (= *Sistema Monetario Europeo*) EMS (= *European Monetary System*)

smem'brare /**72**/ VT (*gruppo, partito ecc*) to split ▪ **smembrarsi** VPR to split up

smemo'rato, -a AG forgetful

smen'tire /**55**/ VT (*negare*) to deny; (*testimonianza*) to refute; (*reputazione*) to give the lie to ▪ **smentirsi** VPR to be inconsistent

smen'tita SF denial; refutation

sme'raldo SM, AG INV emerald

smerci'are [zmer'tʃare] /**14**/ VT (*Comm*) to sell; (: *svendere*) to sell off

'smercio ['zmertʃo] SM sale; **avere poco/molto ~** to have poor/good sales

smerigli'ato, -a [zmeriʎ'ʎato] AG: **carta smerigliata** emery paper; **vetro ~** frosted glass

sme'riglio [zme'riʎʎo] SM emery

'smesso, -a PP *di* **smettere** ▸ AG: **abiti smessi** cast-offs

'smettere /**63**/ VT to stop; (*vestiti*) to stop wearing ▸ VI to stop, cease; **~ di fare** to stop doing

smidol'lato, -a AG spineless ▸ SM/F spineless person

smilitarizzazi'one [zmilitariddzat'tsjone] SF demilitarization

'smilzo, -a ['zmiltso] AG thin, lean

sminu'ire /**72**/ VT to diminish, lessen; (*fig*) to belittle; **~ l'importanza di qc** to play sth down

sminuz'zare [zminut'tsare] /**72**/ VT to break into small pieces; to crumble

'smisi *ecc* VB *vedi* **smettere**

smista'mento SM (*di posta*) sorting; (*Ferr*) shunting

smis'tare /**72**/ VT (*pacchi ecc*) to sort; (*Ferr*) to shunt

smisu'rato, -a AG boundless, immeasurable; (*grandissimo*) immense, enormous

smitiz'zare [zmitid'dzare] /**72**/ VT to debunk

smobili'tare /**72**/ VT to demobilize

smobilitazi'one [zmobilitat'tsjone] SF demobilization

smobi'lizzo [zmobi'liddzo] SM (*Comm*) disinvestment

smo'dato, -a AG excessive, unrestrained

smode'rato, -a AG immoderate

smog [zmɔg] SM INV smog

'smoking ['zmoukiŋ] SM INV dinner jacket (BRIT), tuxedo (US)

smon'tare /**72**/ VT (*mobile, macchina ecc*) to take to pieces, dismantle; (*fig: scoraggiare*) to dishearten ▸ VI (*scendere: da cavallo*) to dismount; (: *da treno*) to get off; (*terminare il lavoro*) to stop (work) ▪ **smontarsi** VPR to lose heart; to lose one's enthusiasm

'smorfia SF grimace; (*atteggiamento lezioso*) simpering; **fare smorfie** to make faces; to simper

smorfi'oso, -a AG simpering

'smorto, -a AG (*viso*) pale, wan; (*colore*) dull

smor'zare [zmor'tsare] /**72**/ VT (*suoni*) to deaden; (*colori*) to tone down; (*luce*) to dim; (*sete*) to quench; (*entusiasmo*) to dampen ▪ **smorzarsi** VPR (*suono, luce*) to fade; (*entusiasmo*) to dampen

'smosso, -a PP *di* **smuovere**

smotta'mento SM landslide

sms ['ɛsse'ɛmme'ɛsse] SM INV text (message)

'smunto, -a AG haggard, pinched

smu'overe /**66**/ VT to move, shift; (*fig: commuovere*) to move; (: *dall'inerzia*) to rouse, stir ▪ **smuoversi** VPR to move, shift

smus'sare /**72**/ VT (*angolo*) to round off, smooth; (*lama ecc*) to blunt ▪ **smussarsi** VPR to become blunt

s.n. ABBR = **senza numero**

snatu'rato, -a AG inhuman, heartless

snazionaliz'zare [znattsjonalid'dzare] /**72**/ VT to denationalize

snelli'mento SM (*di traffico*) speeding up; (*di procedura*) streamlining

snel'lire /**55**/ VT (*persona*) to make slim; (*traffico*) to speed up; (*procedura*) to streamline ▪ **snellirsi** VPR (*persona*) to (get) slim; (*traffico*) to speed up

'snello, -a AG (*agile*) agile; (*svelto*) slender, slim

sner'vante AG (*attesa, lavoro*) exasperating

sner'vare /**72**/ VT to enervate, wear out ▪ **snervarsi** VPR to become enervated

sni'dare /**72**/ VT to drive out, flush out

snif'fare [znif'fare] /**72**/ VT (*col: cocaina*) to snort

snob'bare /**72**/ VT to snub

sno'bismo SM snobbery

snoccio'lare [znottʃo'lare] /**72**/ VT (*frutta*) to stone; (*fig: orazioni*) to rattle off; (: *verità*) to blab; (: *col: soldi*) to shell out

sno'dabile AG (*lampada*) adjustable; (*tubo, braccio*) hinged; **rasoio con testina ~** swivel-head razor

sno'dare /**72**/ VT to untie, undo; (*rendere agile, mobile*) to loosen ▪ **snodarsi** VPR to come loose; (*articolarsi*) to bend; (*strada, fiume*) to wind

sno'dato, -a AG (*articolazione, persona*) flexible; (*fune ecc*) undone

'snowboard ['znobord] SM INV (*tavola*) snowboard; (*sport*) snowboarding; **fare ~** to go snowboarding

SO SIGLA = **Sondrio**

S

so VB *vedi* **sapere**

S.O. ABBR (= *sudovest*) SW

so'ave AG (*voce, maniera*) gentle; (*volto*) delicate, sweet; (*musica*) soft, sweet; (*profumo*) delicate

soavità SF gentleness; delicacy; sweetness; softness

sobbal'zare [sobbal'tsare] /**72**/ VI to jolt, jerk; (*trasalire*) to jump, start

sob'balzo [sob'baltso] SM jerk, jolt; jump, start

sobbar'carsi /**20**/ VPR: ~ **a** to take on, undertake

sob'borgo, -ghi SM suburb

sobil'lare /**72**/ VT to stir up, incite

'sobrio, -a AG sober

Soc. ABBR (= *società*) Soc.

socchi'udere [sok'kjudere] /**22**/ VT (*porta*) to leave ajar; (*occhi*) to half-close

socchi'uso, -a [sok'kjuso] PP *di* **socchiudere** ▶ AG (*porta, finestra*) ajar; (*occhi*) half-closed

soc'combere /**29**/ VI to succumb, give way

soc'correre /**28**/ VT to help, assist

soccorri'tore, -'trice SM/F rescuer

soc'corso, -a PP *di* **soccorrere** ▶ SM help, aid, assistance ■ **soccorsi** SMPL relief *sg*, aid *sg*; **prestare ~ a qn** to help o assist sb; **venire in ~ di qn** to help sb, come to sb's aid; **operazioni di ~** rescue operations; **~ stradale** breakdown service

socialdemo'cratico, -a, -ci, -che [sotʃaldemo'kratiko] SM/F Social Democrat

soci'ale [so'tʃale] AG social; (*di associazione*) club *cpd*, association *cpd*

socia'lismo [sotʃa'lizmo] SM socialism

socia'lista, -i, -e [sotʃa'lista] AG, SM/F socialist

socializ'zare [sotʃalid'dzare] /**72**/ VI to socialize

'social 'network ['səuʃl 'nɛtwərk] SM INV social network

società [sotʃe'ta] SF INV society; (*sportiva*) club; (*Comm*) company; **in ~ con qn** in partnership with sb; **mettersi in ~ con qn** to go into business with sb; **l'alta ~** high society; **~ anonima** ≈ limited (BRIT) o incorporated (US) company; **~ per azioni** joint-stock company; **~ di comodo** shell company; **~ fiduciaria** trust company; **~ di mutuo soccorso** friendly society (BRIT), benefit society (US); **~ a responsabilità limitata** *type of limited liability company*

soci'evole [so'tʃevole] AG sociable

socievo'lezza [sotʃevo'lettsa] SF sociableness

'socio ['sɔtʃo] SM (*Dir, Comm*) partner; (*membro di associazione*) member

sociolo'gia [sotʃolo'dʒia] SF sociology

soci'ologo, -a, -gi, -ghe [so'tʃɔlogo] SM/F sociologist

'soda SF (*Chim*) soda; (*acqua gassata*) soda (water)

soda'lizio [soda'littsjo] SM association, society

soddisfa'cente [soddisfa'tʃɛnte] AG satisfactory

soddis'fare /**41**/ VT, VI: ~ **(a)** to satisfy; (*impegno*) to fulfil; (*debito*) to pay off; (*richiesta*) to meet, comply with; (*offesa*) to make amends for

soddis'fatto, -a PP *di* **soddisfare** ▶ AG satisfied, pleased; **essere ~ di** to be satisfied o pleased with

soddisfazi'one [soddisfat'tsjone] SF satisfaction

'sodio SM (*Chim*) sodium

'sodo, -a AG firm, hard; (*uovo*) hard-boiled ▶ SM: **venire al ~** to come to the point ▶ AV (*picchiare, lavorare*) hard; **dormire ~** to sleep soundly

sofà SM INV sofa

soffe'renza [soffe'rɛntsa] SF suffering; (*Comm*): **in ~** unpaid

soffer'to, -a PP *di* **soffrire** ▶ AG (*vittoria*) hard-fought; (*distacco, decisione*) painful

soffi'are /**19**/ VT to blow; (*notizia, segreto*) to whisper ▶ VI to blow; (*sbuffare*) to puff (and blow); **soffiarsi il naso** to blow one's nose; **~ qc/qn a qn** (*fig*) to pinch o steal sth/sb from sb; **~ via qc** to blow sth away

soffi'ata SF (*col*) tip-off; **fare una ~ alla polizia** to tip off the police

'soffice ['sɔffitʃe] AG soft

soffi'etto SM (*Mus, per fuoco*) bellows *pl*; **porta a ~** folding door

'soffio SM (*di vento*) breath; (*di fumo*) puff; (*Med*) murmur

soffi'one SM (*Bot*) dandelion

sof'fitta SF attic

sof'fitto SM ceiling

soffo'cante AG suffocating, stifling

soffo'care /**20**/ VI (*anche*: **soffocarsi**) to suffocate, choke ▶ VT to suffocate, choke; (*fig*) to stifle, suppress

soffocazi'one [soffokat'tsjone] SF suffocation

soffriggere [sof'friddʒere] /**56**/ VT to fry lightly

sof'frire /**70**/ VT to suffer, endure; (*sopportare*) to bear, stand ▶ VI to suffer; to be in pain; **~ (di) qc** (*Med*) to suffer from sth

sof'fritto, -a PP *di* **soffriggere** ▶ SM (*Cuc*) fried mixture of herbs, bacon and onions

sof'fuso, -a AG (*di luce*) suffused

So'fia SF (*Geo*) Sofia

sofisti'care /**20**/ VT (*vino, cibo*) to adulterate

sofisti'cato, -a AG sophisticated; (*vino*) adulterated

sofisticazi'one [sofistikat'tsjone] SF adulteration

'software ['sɔftwɛər] SM: **~ applicativo** applications package

sogget'tivo, -a [soddʒet'tivo] AG subjective

sog'getto, -a [sod'dʒetto] AG: ~ **a** (*sottomesso*) subject to; (*esposto: a variazioni, danni ecc*) subject o liable to ▶ SM subject; ~ **a tassa** taxable; **recitare a** ~ (*Teat*) to improvise

soggezi'one [soddʒet'tsjone] SF subjection; (*timidezza*) awe; **avere ~ di qn** to stand in awe of sb; to be ill at ease in sb's presence

sogghi'gnare [soggiɲ'ɲare] /**15**/ VI to sneer

sog'ghigno [sog'giɲɲo] SM sneer

soggia'cere [soddʒa'tʃere] /**57**/ VI: ~ **a** to be subjected to

soggio'gare [soddʒo'gare] /**80**/ VT to subdue, subjugate

soggior'nare [soddʒor'nare] /**72**/ VI to stay

soggi'orno [sod'dʒorno] SM (*permanenza*) stay; (*stanza*) living room

soggi'ungere [sod'dʒundʒere] /**5**/ VT to add

soggi'unto, -a [sod'dʒunto] PP di **soggiungere**

'soglia ['sɔʎʎa] SF doorstep; (*anche fig*) threshold

'sogliola ['sɔʎʎola] SF (*Zool*) sole

so'gnante [soɲ'ɲante] AG dreamy

so'gnare [soɲ'ɲare] /**15**/ VT, VI to dream; ~ **a occhi aperti** to daydream

sogna'tore, -'trice [soɲɲa'tore] SM/F dreamer

'sogno ['soɲɲo] SM dream

'soia SF (*Bot*) soya

sol SM (*Mus*) G; (: *solfeggiando la scala*) so(h)

so'laio SM (*soffitta*) attic

sola'mente AV only, just

so'lare AG solar, sun *cpd*

sol'care /**20**/ VT (*terreno, fig: mari*) to plough (*Brit*), plow (*US*)

'solco, -chi SM (*scavo, fig: ruga*) furrow; (*incavo*) rut, track; (*di disco*) groove; (*scia*) wake

sol'dato SM soldier; ~ **di leva** conscript; ~ **semplice** private

'soldo SM (*fig*): **non avere un** ~ to be penniless; **non vale un** ~ it's not worth a penny ▪ **soldi** SMPL (*denaro*) money *sg*; **non ho soldi** I haven't got any money

'sole SM sun; (*luce*) sun(light); (*tempo assolato*) sun(shine); **prendere il** ~ to sunbathe; **il S~ che ride** (*Pol*) symbol of the Italian Green party

soleggi'ato, -a [soled'dʒato] AG sunny

so'lenne AG solemn

solennità SF INV solemnity; (*festività*) holiday, feast day

so'lere /**108**/ VT: ~ **fare qc** to be in the habit of doing sth ▶ VB IMPERS: **come suole accadere** as is usually the case, as usually happens; **come si suol dire** as they say

so'lerte AG diligent

so'lerzia [so'lɛrtsja] SF diligence

so'letta SF (*per scarpe*) insole

sol'fato SM sulphate (*Brit*), sulfate (*US*)

sol'forico, -a, -ci, -che AG sulphuric (*Brit*), sulfuric (*US*); **acido** ~ sulphuric o sulfuric acid

sol'furo SM sulphur (*Brit*), sulfur (*US*)

soli'dale AG in agreement; **essere ~ con qn** (*essere d'accordo*) to be in agreement with sb; (*appoggiare*) to be behind sb

solidarietà SF solidarity

solidifi'care /**20**/ VT to solidify ▪ **solidifcarsi** VI to solidify

solidità SF solidity

'solido, -a AG solid; (*forte, robusto*) sturdy, solid; (*fig: ditta*) sound, solid ▶ SM (*Mat*) solid

soli'loquio SM soliloquy

so'lista, -i, -e AG solo ▶ SM/F soloist

solita'mente AV usually, as a rule

soli'tario, -a AG (*senza compagnia*) solitary, lonely; (*solo, isolato*) solitary, lone; (*deserto*) lonely ▶ SM (*gioiello, gioco*) solitaire

'solito, -a AG usual; **essere ~ fare** to be in the habit of doing; **di** ~ usually; **più tardi del** ~ later than usual; **come al** ~ as usual; **siamo alle solite!** (*col*) here we go again!

soli'tudine SF solitude

sollaz'zare [sollat'tsare] /**72**/ VT to entertain ▪ **sollazzarsi** VPR to amuse o.s.

sol'lazzo [sol'lattso] SM amusement

solleci'tare [solletʃi'tare] /**72**/ VT (*lavoro*) to speed up; (*persona*) to urge on; (*chiedere con insistenza*) to press for, request urgently; (*Tecn*) to stress; (*stimolare*): ~ **qn a fare** to urge sb to do

sollecitazi'one [solletʃitat'tsjone] SF entreaty, request; (*fig*) incentive; (*Tecn*) stress; **lettera di** ~ (*Comm*) reminder

sol'lecito, -a [sol'letʃito] AG prompt, quick ▶ SM (*Comm*) reminder; ~ **di pagamento** payment reminder

solleci'tudine [solletʃi'tudine] SF promptness, speed

solleti'care /**20**/ VT to tickle

sol'letico SM tickling; **soffrire il** ~ to be ticklish

solleva'mento SM raising; lifting; (*ribellione*) revolt; ~ **pesi** (*Sport*) weight-lifting

solle'vare /**72**/ VT to lift, raise; (*fig: persona: alleggerire*) ~ **(da)** to relieve (of); (: *dar conforto*) to comfort, relieve; (*questione*) to raise; (*far insorgere*) to stir (to revolt) ▪ **sollevarsi** VPR to rise; (*fig: riprendersi*) to recover; (: *ribellarsi*) to rise up; **sollevarsi da terra** (*persona*) to get up from the ground; (*aereo*) to take off; **sentirsi sollevato** to feel relieved

solli'evo SM relief; (*conforto*) comfort; **con mio grande** ~ to my great relief

'solo, -a AG alone; (*in senso spirituale: isolato*) lonely; (*unico*): **un ~ libro** only one book, a single book; (*con ag numerale*): **veniamo noi tre soli** just o only the three of us are coming ▶ AV (*soltanto*) only, just; ~ **che** cong but; **è il ~ proprietario**

S

he's the sole proprietor; **l'incontrò due sole volte** he only met him twice; **non ~ … ma anche** not only … but also; **fare qc da ~** to do sth (all) by oneself; **vive (da) ~** he lives on his own; **possiamo vederci da soli?** can I see you in private?

sol'stizio [sol'stittsjo] SM solstice

sol'tanto AV only

so'lubile AG (*sostanza*) soluble; **caffè ~** instant coffee

soluzi'one [solut'tsjone] SF solution; **senza ~ di continuità** uninterruptedly

sol'vente AG, SM solvent; **~ per unghie** nail polish remover; **~ per vernici** paint remover

sol'venza [sol'vɛntsa] SF (*Comm*) solvency

'soma SF load, burden; **bestia da ~** beast of burden

So'malia SF: **la ~** Somalia

'somalo, -a AG, SM/F, SM Somali

so'maro SM ass, donkey

so'matico, -a, -ci, -che AG somatic

somigli'anza [somiʎ'ʎantsa] SF resemblance

somigli'are [somiʎ'ʎare] /27/ VI: **~ a** to be like, resemble; (*nell'aspetto fisico*) to look like ▪ **somigliarsi** VPR to be (*o* look) alike

'somma SF (*Mat*) sum; (*di denaro*) sum (of money); (*complesso di varie cose*) whole amount, sum total; **tirare le somme** (*fig*) to sum up; **tirate le somme** (*fig*) all things considered

som'mare /72/ VT to add up; (*aggiungere*) to add; **tutto sommato** all things considered

som'mario, -a AG (*racconto, indagine*) brief; (*giustizia*) summary ▶ SM summary

som'mergere [som'mɛrdʒere] /59/ VT to submerge

sommer'gibile [sommer'dʒibile] SM submarine

som'merso, -a PP *di* **sommergere**

som'messo, -a AG (*voce*) soft, subdued

somminis'trare /72/ VT to give, administer

sommità SF INV summit, top; (*fig*) height

'sommo, -a AG highest; (*rispetto*) highest, greatest; (*poeta, artista*) great, outstanding ▶ SM (*fig*) height; **per sommi capi** in short, in brief

som'mossa SF uprising

sommozza'tore [sommottsa'tore] SM (deep-sea) diver; (*Mil*) frogman

so'naglio [so'naʎʎo] SM (*di mucche ecc*) bell; (*per bambini*) rattle

so'nante AG: **denaro** *o* **moneta ~** (ready) cash

so'nare *ecc* = **suonare** *ecc*

'sonda SF (*Med, Meteor, Aer*) probe; (*Mineralogia*) drill ▶ AG INV: **pallone** *m* **~** weather balloon

son'daggio [son'daddʒo] SM sounding; probe; boring, drilling; (*indagine*) survey; **~ d'opinioni** opinion poll

son'dare /72/ VT (*Naut*) to sound; (*atmosfera, piaga*) to probe; (*Mineralogia*) to bore, drill; (*fig: opinione ecc*) to survey, poll

so'netto SM sonnet

son'nambulo, -a SM/F sleepwalker

sonnecchi'are [sonnek'kjare] /19/ VI to doze, nod

sonnel'lino SM nap

son'nifero SM sleeping drug (*o* pill)

'sonno SM sleep; **aver ~** to be sleepy; **prendere ~** to fall asleep

sonno'lento, -a AG sleepy, drowsy; (*movimenti*) sluggish

sonno'lenza [sonno'lɛntsa] SF sleepiness, drowsiness

'sono VB *vedi* **essere**

sonoriz'zare [sonorid'dzare] /72/ VT (*Ling*) to voice; (*Cine*) to add a sound-track to

so'noro, -a AG (*ambiente*) resonant; (*voce*) sonorous, ringing; (*onde, Cine*) sound *cpd* ▶ SM: **il ~** (*Cine*) the talkies *pl*

sontu'oso, -a AG sumptuous; lavish

so'pire /55/ VT (*fig: dolore, tensione*) to soothe

so'pore SM drowsiness

sopo'rifero, -a AG soporific

sop'palco, -chi SM mezzanine

soppe'rire /55/ VI: **~ a** to provide for; **~ alla mancanza di qc** to make up for the lack of sth

soppe'sare /72/ VT to weigh in one's hand(s), feel the weight of; (*fig*) to weigh up

soppian'tare /72/ VT to supplant

soppi'atto AV: **di ~** secretly; furtively

soppor'tabile AG tolerable, bearable

soppor'tare /72/ VT (*reggere*) to support; (*subire: perdita, spese*) to bear, sustain; (*soffrire: dolore*) to bear, endure; (*cosa, freddo*) to withstand; (*persona, freddo*) to take; (*tollerare*) to put up with, tolerate

sopportazi'one [sopportat'tsjone] SF patience; **avere spirito di ~**, **avere capacità di ~** to be long-suffering

soppressi'one SF abolition; withdrawal; suppression; deletion; elimination, liquidation

sop'presso, -a PP *di* **sopprimere**

sop'primere /50/ VT (*carica, privilegi ecc*) to do away with, abolish; (*servizio*) to withdraw; (*pubblicazione*) to suppress; (*parola, frase*) to delete; (*uccidere*) to eliminate, liquidate

'sopra PREP (*gen*) on; (*al di sopra di, più in alto di*) above; over; (*riguardo a*) on, about ▶ AV on top; (*attaccato, scritto*) on it; (*al di sopra*) above; (*al piano superiore*) upstairs; **donne ~ i 30 anni** women over 30 (years of age); **100 metri ~ il livello del mare** 100 metres above sea level; **5 gradi ~ lo zero** 5 degrees above zero; **abito di ~** I live upstairs; **essere al di ~ di ogni sospetto** to be above suspicion; **per i motivi ~ illustrati** for the above-mentioned reasons, for the reasons shown above; **dormirci ~** (*fig*) to sleep on it; **passar ~ a qc** (*anche fig*) to pass over sth

so'prabito SM overcoat

sopraccen'nato, -a [soprattʃen'nato] AG above-mentioned

soprac'ciglio [soprat'tʃiʎʎo] (*pl(f)* **sopracci-glia**) SM eyebrow

sopracco'perta SF (*di letto*) bedspread; (*di libro*) jacket

soprad'detto, -a AG aforesaid

sopraf'fare /41/ VT to overcome, overwhelm

sopraf'fatto, -a PP *di* **sopraffare**

sopraffazi'one [sopraffat'tsjone] SF over-whelming, overpowering

sopraf'fino, -a AG (*pranzo, vino*) excellent; (*fig*) masterly

sopraggi'ungere [soprad'dʒundʒere] /5/ VI (*giungere all'improvviso*) to arrive (unexpectedly); (*accadere*) to occur (unexpectedly)

sopraggi'unto, -a [soprad'dʒunto] PP *di* **sopraggiungere**

soprallu'ogo, -ghi SM (*di esperti*) inspection; (*di polizia*) on-the-spot investigation

sopram'mobile SM ornament

soprannatu'rale AG supernatural

sopran'nome SM nickname

soprannomi'nare /72/ VT to nickname

sopran'numero AV: **in ~** in excess

so'prano SMF (*persona*) soprano ▶ SM (*voce*) soprano

soprappensi'ero AV lost in thought

soprappiù SM surplus, extra; **in ~** extra, sur-plus; (*per giunta*) besides, in addition

sopras'salto SM: **di ~** with a start, with a jump; suddenly

soprasse'dere /107/ VI: **~ a** to delay, put off

soprat'tassa SF surtax

soprat'tutto AV (*anzitutto*) above all; (*special-mente*) especially

sopravvalu'tare /72/ VT (*persona, capacità*) to overestimate

sopravve'nire /128/ VI to arrive, appear; (*fatto*) to occur

soprav'vento SM: **avere/prendere il ~ su qn** to have/get the upper hand over sb

sopravvis'suto, -a PP *di* **sopravvivere** ▶ SM/F survivor

sopravvi'venza [sopravvi'vɛntsa] SF survival

soprav'vivere /130/ VI to survive; (*continuare a vivere*) **~ (in)** to live on (in); **~ a** (*incidente ecc*) to survive; (*persona*) to outlive

soprele'vata SF (*di strada, ferrovia*) elevated sec-tion

soprinten'dente SMF supervisor; (*statale: di belle arti ecc*) keeper

soprinten'denza [soprinten'dɛntsa] SF super-vision; (*ente*): **~ alle Belle Arti** government depart-ment responsible for monuments and artistic treasures

soprin'tendere /120/ VI: **~ a** to superintend, supervise

soprin'teso, -a PP *di* **soprintendere**

so'pruso SM abuse of power; **subire un ~** to be abused

soq'quadro SM: **mettere a ~** to turn upside-down

sor'betto SM sorbet, water ice (BRIT)

sor'bire /17/ VT to sip; (*fig*) to put up with

'sorcio ['sortʃo] SM mouse

'sordido, -a AG sordid; (*fig: gretto*) stingy

sor'dina SF: **in ~** softly; (*fig*) on the sly

sordità SF deafness

'sordo, -a AG deaf; (*rumore*) muffled; (*dolore*) dull; (*lotta*) silent, hidden; (*odio, rancore*) veiled ▶ SM/F deaf person

sordo'muto, -a AG hearing and speech impaired ▶ SM/F person with a hearing and speech impairment

so'rella SF sister

sorel'lastra SF stepsister; (*con genitore in comune*) half sister

sor'gente [sor'dʒɛnte] SF (*acqua che sgorga*) spring; (*di fiume, Fisica, fig*) source; **acqua di ~** spring water; **~ di calore** source of heat; **~ ter-male** thermal spring

'sorgere ['sordʒere] /109/ VI to rise; (*scaturire*) to spring, rise; (*fig: difficoltà*) to arise ▶ SM: **al ~ del sole** at sunrise

sori'ano, -a AG, SM/F tabby

sormon'tare /72/ VT (*fig*) to overcome, sur-mount

sorni'one, -a AG sly

sorpas'sare /72/ VT (*Aut*) to overtake; (*fig*) to surpass; (*: eccedere*) to exceed, go beyond; **~ in altezza** to be higher than; (*persona*) to be taller than

sorpas'sato, -a AG (*metodo, moda*) outmoded, old-fashioned; (*macchina*) obsolete

sor'passo SM (*Aut*) overtaking

sorpren'dente AG surprising; (*eccezionale, ina-spettato*) astonishing, amazing

sor'prendere /81/ VT (*cogliere: in flagrante ecc*) to catch; (*stupire*) to surprise ▪ **sorprendersi** VPR: **sorprendersi (di)** to be surprised (at)

sor'preso, -a PP *di* **sorprendere** ▶ SF surprise; **fare una sorpresa a qn** to give sb a surprise; **prendere qn di sorpresa** to take sb by surprise *o* unawares

sor'reggere [sor'reddʒere] /87/ VT to support, hold up; (*fig*) to sustain ▪ **sorreggersi** VPR (*tenersi ritto*) to stay upright

sor'retto, -a PP *di* **sorreggere**

sor'ridere /89/ VI to smile

sor'riso, -a PP di **sorridere** ▶ SM smile

sor'sata SF gulp; **bere a sorsate** to gulp

sorseggi'are [sorsed'dʒare] /62/ VT to sip

'sorsi ecc VB vedi **sorgere**

'sorso SM sip; **d'un ~, in un ~ solo** at one gulp

'sorta SF sort, kind; **di ~** whatever, of any kind at all; **ogni ~ di** all sorts of; **di ogni ~** of every kind

'sorte SF (fato) fate, destiny; (evento fortuito) chance; **tirare a ~** to draw lots; **tentare la ~** to try one's luck

sorteggi'are [sorted'dʒare] /62/ VT to draw for

sor'teggio [sor'teddʒo] SM draw

sorti'legio [sorti'lɛdʒo] SM witchcraft no pl; (incantesimo) spell; **fare un ~ a qn** to cast a spell on sb

sor'tire /55/ VT (ottenere) to produce

sor'tita SF (Mil) sortie

'sorto, -a PP di **sorgere**

sorvegli'ante [sorveʎ'ʎante] SMF (di carcere) guard, warder (BRIT); (di fabbrica ecc) supervisor

sorvegli'anza [sorveʎ'ʎantsa] SF watch; supervision; (Polizia, Mil) surveillance

sorvegli'are [sorveʎ'ʎare] /27/ VT (bambino, bagagli, prigioniero) to watch, keep an eye on; (malato) to watch over; (territorio, casa) to watch o keep watch over; (lavori) to supervise

sorvo'lare /72/ VT (territorio) to fly over ▶ VI: **~ su** (fig) to skim over

S.O.S. SIGLA M mayday, SOS

'sosia SM INV double

sos'pendere /8/ VT (appendere) to hang (up); (interrompere, privare di una carica) to suspend; (rimandare) to defer; (appendere) to hang; **~ un quadro al muro/un lampadario al soffitto** to hang a picture on the wall/a chandelier from the ceiling; **~ qn dal suo incarico** to suspend sb from office

sospensi'one SF (anche Chim, Aut) suspension; deferment; **~ condizionale della pena** (Dir) suspended sentence

sos'peso, -a PP di **sospendere** ▶ AG (appeso): **~ a** hanging on (o from); (treno, autobus) cancelled; **in ~** in abeyance; (conto) outstanding; **tenere in ~** (fig) to keep in suspense; **col fiato ~** with bated breath

sospet'tare /72/ VT to suspect ▶ VI: **~ di** to suspect; (diffidare) to be suspicious of

sos'petto, -a AG suspicious ▶ SM suspicion; **destare sospetti** to arouse suspicion

sospet'toso, -a AG suspicious

sos'pingere [sos'pindʒere] /114/ VT to drive, push

sos'pinto, -a PP di **sospingere**

sospi'rare /72/ VI to sigh ▶ VT to long for, yearn for

sos'piro SM sigh; **~ di sollievo** sigh of relief

'sosta SF (fermata) stop, halt; (pausa) pause, break; **senza ~** non-stop, without a break

sostanti'vato, -a AG (Ling): **aggettivo ~** adjective used as a noun

sostan'tivo SM noun, substantive

sos'tanza [sos'tantsa] SF substance ▪ **sostanze** SFPL (ricchezze) wealth sg, possessions; **in ~** in short, to sum up; **la ~ del discorso** the essence of the speech

sostanzi'ale [sostan'tsjale] AG substantial

sostanzi'oso, -a [sostan'tsjoso] AG (cibo) nourishing, substantial

sos'tare /72/ VI (fermarsi) to stop (for a while), stay; (fare una pausa) to take a break

sos'tegno [sos'teɲɲo] SM support; **a ~ di** in support of; **muro di ~** supporting wall

soste'nere /121/ VT to support; (prendere su di sé) to take on, bear; (resistere) to withstand, stand up to; (affermare): **~ che** to maintain that ▪ **sostenersi** VPR to hold o.s. up, support o.s.; (fig) to keep up one's strength; **~ qn** (moralmente) to be a support to sb; (difendere) to stand up for sb, take sb's part; **~ gli esami** to sit exams; **~ il confronto** to bear o stand comparison

soste'nibile AG (tesi) tenable; (spese) bearable; (sviluppo) sustainable

sosteni'tore, -'trice SM/F supporter

sostenta'mento SM maintenance, support; **mezzi di ~** means of support

soste'nuto, -a AG (stile) elevated; (velocità, ritmo) sustained; (prezzo) high ▶ SM/F: **fare il(la) ~(a)** to be standoffish, keep one's distance

sostitu'ire /55/ VT (mettere al posto di): **~ qn/qc a** to substitute sb/sth for; (prendere il posto di) to replace, take the place of

sostitu'tivo, -a AG (Amm: documento, certificato) equivalent

sosti'tuto, -a SM/F substitute; **~ procuratore della Repubblica** (Dir) deputy public prosecutor

sostituzi'one [sostitut'tsjone] SF substitution; **in ~ di** as a substitute for, in place of

sotta'ceti [sotta'tʃeti] SMPL pickles

sot'tana SF (sottoveste) underskirt; (gonna) skirt; (Rel) soutane, cassock

sot'tecchi [sot'tekki] AV: **guardare di ~** to steal a glance at

sotter'fugio [sotter'fudʒo] SM subterfuge

sotter'raneo, -a AG underground ▶ SM cellar

sotter'rare /72/ VT to bury

sottigli'ezza [sottiʎ'ʎettsa] SF thinness; slimness; (fig: acutezza) subtlety; shrewdness ▪ **sottigliezze** SFPL (pedanteria) quibbles

sot'tile AG thin; (figura, caviglia) thin, slim, slender; (fine: polvere, capelli) fine; (fig: leggero) light; (: vista) sharp, keen; (: olfatto) fine, discriminating; (: *mente*) subtle; shrewd ▶ SM: **non andare per il ~** not to mince matters

sottiliz'zare [sottilid'dzare] /**72**/ VI to split hairs

sottin'tendere /**120**/ VT (*intendere qc non espresso*) to understand; (*implicare*) to imply; **lasciare ~ che** to let it be understood that

sottin'teso, -a PP *di* **sottintendere** ▶ SM allusion; **parlare senza sottintesi** to speak plainly

'sotto PREP (*gen*) under; (*più in basso di*) below ▶ AV underneath, beneath; below; (*al piano inferiore*): **(al piano) di ~** downstairs; **~ il monte** at the foot of the mountain; **~ la pioggia/il sole** in the rain/sun(shine); **tutti quelli ~ i 18 anni** all those under 18 (years of age) (BRIT) o under age 18 (US); **~ il livello del mare** below sea level; **~ il chilo** under o less than a kilo; **ha 5 impiegati ~ di sé** he has 5 clerks under him; **siamo ~ Natale/Pasqua** it's nearly Christmas/Easter; **~ un certo punto di vista** in a sense; **~ forma di** in the form of; **~ falso nome** under a false name; **~ terra** underground; **~ voce** in a low voice; **chiuso ~ vuoto** vacuum packed

sotto'banco AV (*di nascosto: vendere, comprare*) under the counter; (: *agire*) in an underhand way

sottobicchi'ere [sottobik'kjɛre] SM mat, coaster

sotto'bosco, -schi SM undergrowth *no pl*

sotto'braccio [sotto'brattʃo] AV by the arm; **prendere qn ~** to take sb by the arm; **camminare ~ a qn** to walk arm in arm with sb

sottochi'ave [sotto'kjave] AV under lock and key

sottoco'perta AV (*Naut*) below deck

sotto'costo AV below cost (price)

sottocu'taneo, -a AG subcutaneous

sottoes'posto, -a AG (*fotografia, pellicola*) underexposed

sotto'fondo SM background; **~ musicale** background music

sotto'gamba AV: **prendere qc ~** not to take sth seriously

sotto'gonna SF underskirt

sottogo'verno SM political patronage

sotto'gruppo SM subgroup; (*di partito*) faction

sottoline'are /**72**/ VT to underline; (*fig*) to emphasize, stress

sot't'olio AV, AG INV in oil

sotto'mano AV (*a portata di mano*) within reach, to hand; (*di nascosto*) secretly

sottoma'rino, -a AG (*flora*) submarine; (*cavo, navigazione*) underwater ▶ SM (*Naut*) submarine

sotto'messo, -a PP *di* **sottomettere** ▶ AG submissive

sotto'mettere /**63**/ VT to subdue, subjugate **~ sottomettersi** VPR to submit

sottomissi'one SF submission

sottopas'saggio [sottopas'saddʒo] SM (*Aut*) underpass; (*pedonale*) subway, underpass

sotto'porre /**77**/ VT (*costringere*) to subject; (*fig: presentare*) to submit **~ sottoporsi** VPR to submit; **sottoporsi a** (*subire*) to undergo

sotto'posto, -a PP *di* **sottoporre**

sottopro'dotto SM by-product

sottoproduzi'one [sottoprodut'tsjone] SF underproduction

sottoproletari'ato SM: **il ~** the underprivileged class

sot'tordine AV: **passare in ~** to become of minor importance

sottos'cala SM INV (*ripostiglio*) cupboard (BRIT) o closet (US) under the stairs; (*stanza*) room under the stairs

sottos'critto, -a PP *di* **sottoscrivere** ▶ SM/F: **io ~, il ~** the undersigned

sottos'crivere /**105**/ VT to sign ▶ VI: **~ a** to subscribe to

sottoscrizi'one [sottoskrit'tsjone] SF signing; subscription

sottosegre'tario SM: **S~ di Stato** undersecretary of state (BRIT), assistant secretary of state (US)

sotto'sopra AV upside-down

sottos'tante AG (*piani*) lower; **nella valle ~** in the valley below

sottos'tare /**116**/ VI: **~ a** (*assoggettarsi a*) to submit to; (: *richieste*) to give in to; (*subire: prova*) to undergo

sottosu'olo SM subsoil

sottosvilup'pato, -a AG underdeveloped

sottosvi'luppo SM underdevelopment

sottote'nente SM (*Mil*) second lieutenant

sotto'terra AV underground

sotto'tetto SM attic

sotto'titolo SM subtitle

sottovalu'tare /**72**/ VT (*persona, prova*) to underestimate, underrate

sotto'vento AV (*Naut*) leeward(s) ▶ AG INV (*lato*) leeward, lee

sotto'veste SF underskirt

sotto'voce [sotto'votʃe] AV in a low voice

sottovu'oto AV: **confezionare ~** to vacuum-pack ▶ AG: **confezione** f **~** vacuum pack

sot'trarre /**123**/ VT (*Mat*) to subtract, take away **~ sottrarsi** VPR: **sottrarsi a** (*sfuggire*) to escape; (*evitare*) to avoid; **~ qn/qc a** (*togliere*) to remove sb/sth from; (*salvare*) to save o rescue sb/sth from; **~ qc a qn** (*rubare*) to steal sth from sb; **sottratte le spese** once expenses have been deducted

sot'tratto, -a PP *di* **sottrarre**

sottrazi'one [sottrat'tsjone] SF (*Mat*) subtraction; (*furto*) removal

S

sottuffici'ale [sottuffi'tʃale] SM (Mil) non-commissioned officer; (Naut) petty officer

soufflé [su'fle] SM INV (Cuc) soufflé

souve'nir [suvə'nir] SM INV souvenir

so'vente AV often

soverchi'are [sover'kjare] /19/ VT to overpower, overwhelm

soverchie'ria [soverkje'ria] SF (prepotenza) abuse (of power)

sovi'etico, -a, -ci, -che AG Soviet ▶ SM/F Soviet citizen

sovrabbon'dante AG overabundant

sovrabbon'danza [sovrabbon'dantsa] SF overabundance; **in ~** in excess

sovraccari'care /20/ VT to overload

sovrac'carico, -a, -chi, -che AG: **~ (di)** overloaded (with) ▶ SM excess load; **~ di lavoro** extra work

sovraesposizi'one [sovraespozit'tsjone] SF (Fot) overexposure

sovraffol'lato, -a AG overcrowded

sovraimmagazzi'nare [sovraimmagaddzi'nare] /72/ VT to overstock

sovranità SF sovereignty; (fig: superiorità) supremacy

sovrannatu'rale AG = **soprannaturale**

so'vrano, -a AG sovereign; (fig: sommo) supreme ▶ SM/F sovereign, monarch

sovrappopolazi'one [sovrappopolat'tsjone] SF overpopulation

sovrap'porre /77/ VT to place on top of, put on top of; (Fot, Geom) to superimpose ■ **sovrapporsi** VPR (fig: aggiungersi) to be added; (Fot) to be superimposed

sovrapposizi'one [sovrapposit'tsjone] SF superimposition

sovrap'posto, -a PP di **sovrapporre**

sovrapproduzi'one [sovrapprodut'tsjone] SF overproduction

sovras'tante AG overhanging; (fig) imminent

sovras'tare /72/ VT (vallata, fiume) to overhang; (fig) to hang over, threaten

sovrastrut'tura SF superstructure

sovrecci'tare [sovrettʃi'tare] /72/ VT to overexcite

sovrimpressi'one SF (Fot, Cine) double exposure; **immagini in ~** superimposed images

sovrinten'dente ecc = **soprintendente** ecc

sovru'mano, -a AG superhuman

sovve'nire /128/ VI (venire in mente): **~ a** to occur to

sovvenzio'nare [sovventsjo'nare] /72/ VT to subsidize

sovvenzi'one [sovven'tsjone] SF subsidy, grant

sovver'sivo, -a AG subversive

sovverti'mento SM subversion, undermining

sovver'tire /45/ VT (Pol: ordine, stato) to subvert, undermine

'sozzo, -a ['sottso] AG filthy, dirty

SP SIGLA = **La Spezia**

S.P. ABBR = **strada provinciale**; vedi **provinciale**

S.p.A. ABBR vedi **società per azioni**

spac'care /20/ VT to split, break; (legna) to chop; (fig) to divide ■ **spaccarsi** VPR to split, break

spacca'tura SF split

spaccherò ecc [spakke'rɔ] VB vedi **spaccare**

spacci'are [spat'tʃare] /14/ VT (vendere) to sell (off); (mettere in circolazione) to circulate; (droga) to peddle, push ■ **spacciarsi** VPR: **spacciarsi per** (farsi credere) to pass o.s. off as, pretend to be

spacci'ato, -a [spat'tʃato] AG (col: malato, fuggiasco): **essere ~** to be done for

spaccia'tore, -'trice [spattʃa'tore] SM/F (di droga) pusher; (di denaro falso) dealer

'spaccio ['spattʃo] SM: **~ (di)** (di merce rubata, droga) trafficking (in); (di denaro falso) passing (of); (vendita) sale; (bottega) shop

'spacco, -chi SM (fenditura) split, crack; (strappo) tear; (di gonna) slit

spac'cone SM boaster, braggart

'spada SF sword

spadroneggi'are [spadroned'dʒare] /62/ VI to swagger

spae'sato, -a AG disorientated, lost

spaghet'tata [spaget'tata] SF spaghetti meal

spa'ghetti [spa'getti] SMPL (Cuc) spaghetti sg

'Spagna ['spaɲɲa] SF: **la ~** Spain

spa'gnolo, -a [spaɲ'ɲɔlo] AG Spanish ▶ SM/F Spaniard ▶ SM (Ling) Spanish; **gli Spagnoli** the Spanish

'spago, -ghi SM string, twine; **dare ~ a qn** (fig) to let sb have his (o her) way

spai'ato, -a AG (calza, guanto) odd

spalan'care /20/ VT, **spalan'carsi** VPR to open wide

spa'lare /72/ VT to shovel

'spalla SF shoulder; (fig: Teat) stooge ■ **spalle** SFPL (dorso) back; **di spalle** from behind; **seduto alle mie spalle** sitting behind me; **prendere/colpire qn alle spalle** to take/hit sb from behind; **mettere qn con le spalle al muro** (fig) to put sb with his (o her) back to the wall; **vivere alle spalle di qn** (fig) to live off sb

spal'lata SF (urto) shove o push with the shoulder; **dare una ~ a qc** to give sth a push o shove with one's shoulder

spalleggi'are [spalled'dʒare] /62/ VT to back up, support

spal'letta SF (parapetto) parapet

spalli'era SF (di sedia ecc) back; (di letto: da capo) head(board); (: da piedi) foot(board); (Ginnastica) wall bars pl

spal'lina SF (*Mil*) epaulette; (*di sottoveste, maglietta*) strap; (*imbottitura*) shoulder pad; **senza spalline** strapless

spal'mare /**72**/ VT to spread

'spalti SMPL (*di stadio*) terraces (BRIT), ≈ bleachers (US)

'spamming ['spammiŋ] SM (*Internet*) spamming

'spandere /**110**/ VT to spread; (*versare*) to pour (out) ■ **spandersi** VPR to spread; **~ lacrime** to shed tears

'spanto, -a PP *di* **spandere**

spa'rare /**72**/ VT to fire ▶ VI (*far fuoco*) to fire; (*tirare*) to shoot; **~ a qn/qc** to shoot sb/sth, fire at sb/sth

spa'rato SM (*di camicia*) dicky

spara'tore, -trice SM/F gunman(-woman)

spara'toria SF exchange of shots

sparecchi'are [sparek'kjare] /**19**/ VT: **~ (la tavola)** to clear the table

spa'reggio [spa'reddʒo] SM (*Sport*) play-off

'spargere ['spardʒere] /**111**/ VT (*sparpagliare*) to scatter; (*versare: vino*) to spill; (*: lacrime, sangue*) to shed; (*diffondere*) to spread; (*emanare*) to give off (*o* out) ■ **spargersi** VPR (*voce, notizia*) to spread; (*persone*) to scatter; **si è sparsa una voce sul suo conto** there is a rumour going round about him

spargi'mento [spardʒi'mento] SM scattering; spilling; shedding; **~ di sangue** bloodshed

spa'rire /**112**/ VI to disappear, vanish; **~ dalla circolazione** (*fig: col*) to lie low, keep a low profile

sparizi'one [spari'tsjone] SF disappearance

spar'lare /**72**/ VI: **~ di** to run down, speak ill of

'sparo SM shot

sparpagli'are [sparpaʎ'ʎare] /**27**/ VT, **sparpagli'arsi** VPR to scatter

'sparso, -a PP *di* **spargere** ▶ AG scattered; (*sciolto*) loose; **in ordine ~** (*Mil*) in open order

sparti'acque SM INV (*Geo*) watershed

sparti'neve SM INV snowplough (BRIT), snowplow (US)

spar'tire /**55**/ VT (*eredità, bottino*) to share out; (*avversari*) to separate

spar'tito SM (*Mus*) score

sparti'traffico SM INV (*Aut*) central reservation (BRIT), median (strip) (US)

spartizi'one [sparti'tsjone] SF division

spa'ruto, -a AG (*viso ecc*) haggard

sparvi'ero SM (*Zool*) sparrowhawk

spasi'mante SM suitor

spasi'mare /**72**/ VI to be in agony; **~ di fare** (*fig*) to yearn to do; **~ per qn** to be madly in love with sb

'spasimo SM pang

'spasmo SM (*Med*) spasm

spas'modico, -a, -ci, -che AG (*angoscioso*) agonizing; (*Med*) spasmodic

spas'sarsela /**72**/ VI to enjoy o.s., have a good time

spassio'nato, -a AG dispassionate, impartial

'spasso SM (*divertimento*) amusement, enjoyment; **andare a ~** to go out for a walk; **essere a ~** (*fig*) to be out of work; **mandare qn a ~** (*fig*) to give sb the sack

spas'soso, -a AG amusing, entertaining

'spastico, -a, -ci, -che AG, SM/F spastic

'spatola SF spatula; (*di muratore*) trowel

spau'racchio [spau'rakkjo] SM scarecrow

spau'rire /**55**/ VT to frighten, terrify

spavalde'ria SF boldness, arrogance

spa'valdo, -a AG arrogant, bold

spaventa'passeri SM INV scarecrow

spaven'tare /**72**/ VT to frighten, scare ■ **spaventarsi** VPR to become frightened, become scared; to get a fright

spa'vento SM fear, fright; **far ~ a qn** to give sb a fright

spaven'toso, -a AG frightening, terrible; (*fig: col*) tremendous, fantastic

spazi'ale [spat'tsjale] AG (*volo, nave, tuta*) space *cpd*; (*Archit, Geom*) spatial

spazia'tura [spattsja'tura] SF (*Tip*) spacing

spazien'tirsi [spattsjen'tirsi] /**55**/ VPR to lose one's patience

'spazio ['spattsjo] SM space; (*posto*) room, space; **fare ~ per qc/qn** to make room for sth/sb; **nello ~ di un'ora** within an hour, in the space of an hour; **dare ~ a** (*fig*) to make room for; **~ aereo** airspace

spazi'oso, -a [spat'tsjoso] AG spacious

spazzaca'mino [spattsaka'mino] SM chimney sweep

spazza'neve [spattsa'neve] SM INV (*spartineve, Sci*) snowplough (BRIT), snowplow (US)

spaz'zare [spat'tsare] /**72**/ VT to sweep; (*foglie ecc*) to sweep up; (*cacciare*) to sweep away

spazza'tura [spattsa'tura] SF sweepings *pl*; (*immondizia*) rubbish

spaz'zino, -a [spat'tsino] SM/F street sweeper

'spazzola ['spattsola] SF brush; **capelli a ~** crew cut *sg*; **~ per abiti** clothesbrush; **~ da capelli** hairbrush

spazzo'lare [spattso'lare] /**72**/ VT to brush

spazzo'lino [spattso'lino] SM (small) brush; **~ da denti** toothbrush

specchi'arsi [spek'kjarsi] /**19**/ VPR to look at o.s. in a mirror; (*riflettersi*) to be mirrored, be reflected

specchi'era [spek'kjera] SF large mirror; (*mobile*) dressing table

specchi'etto [spek'kjetto] SM (*tabella*) table,

S

chart; **~ da borsetta** pocket mirror; **~ retrovisore** (*Aut*) rear-view mirror

'**specchio** ['spɛkkjo] SM mirror; (*tabella*) table, chart; **uno ~ d'acqua** a sheet of water

speci'ale [spe't∫ale] AG special; **in special modo** especially; **inviato ~** (*Radio, TV, Stampa*) special correspondent; **offerta ~** special offer; **poteri/ leggi speciali** (*Pol*) emergency powers/legislation

specia'lista, -i, -e [spet∫a'lista] SM/F specialist

specia'listico, -a, -ci, -che [spet∫a'listiko] AG (*conoscenza, preparazione*) specialized

specialità [spet∫ali'ta] SF INV speciality; (*branca di studio*) special field, speciality

specializ'zare [spet∫alid'dzare] /72/ VT (*industria*) to make more specialized ■ **specializzarsi** VPR: **specializzarsi (in)** to specialize (in)

specializ'zato, -a [spet∫alid'dzato] AG (*manodopera*) skilled; **operaio non ~** semiskilled worker; **essere ~ in** to be a specialist in

specializzazi'one [spet∫aliddzat'tsjone] SF specialization; **prendere la ~ in** to specialize in

special'mente [spet∫al'mente] AV especially, particularly

'**specie** ['spɛt∫e] SF INV (*Biol, Bot, Zool*) species *inv*; (*tipo*) kind, sort ▶ AV especially, particularly; **una ~ di** a kind of; **fare ~ a qn** to surprise sb; **la ~ umana** mankind

spe'cifica, -che [spe't∫ifika] SF specification

specifi'care [spet∫ifi'kare] /20/ VT to specify, state

specificata'mente [spet∫ifikata'mente] AV in detail

spe'cifico, -a, -ci, -che [spe't∫ifiko] AG specific

speck [∫pɛk] SM INV *kind of smoked ham*

specu'lare /72/ VI: **~ su** (*Comm*) to speculate in; (*sfruttare*) to exploit; (*meditare*) to speculate on

specula'tore, -'trice SM/F (*Comm*) speculator

speculazi'one [spekulat'tsjone] SF speculation

spe'dire /55/ VT to send; (*Comm*) to dispatch, forward; **~ per posta** to post (*BRIT*), mail (*US*); **~ per mare** to ship

spedita'mente AV quickly; **camminare ~** to walk at a brisk pace

spe'dito, -a AG (*gen*) quick; **con passo ~** at a brisk pace

spedizi'one [spedit'tsjone] SF sending; (*collo*) consignment; (*scientifica ecc*) expedition; (*Comm*) forwarding; shipping; **fare una ~** to send a consignment; **agenzia di ~** forwarding agency; **spese di ~** postal charges; (*Comm*) forwarding charges

spedizioni'ere [spedittsjo'njɛre] SM forwarding agent, shipping agent

'**spegnere** ['speɲɲere] /113/ VT (*fuoco, sigaretta*) to put out, extinguish; (*apparecchio elettrico*) to

turn *o* switch off; (*gas*) to turn off; (*fig: suoni, passioni*) to stifle; (*debito*) to cancel ■ **spegnersi** VPR to go out; to go off; (*morire*) to pass away; **puoi ~ la luce?** could you switch off the light?

speleolo'gia [speleolo'dʒia] SF (*studio*) speleology; (*pratica*) potholing (*BRIT*), speleology

spele'ologo, -a, -gi, -ghe SM/F speleologist; potholer

spel'lare /72/ VT (*scuoiare*) to skin; (*scorticare*) to graze ■ **spellarsi** VPR to peel

spendacci'one, -a [spendat't∫one] SM/F spendthrift

'**spendere** /8/ VT to spend; **~ una buona parola per qn** (*fig*) to put in a good word for sb

'**spengo** *ecc* VB *vedi* **spegnere**

spen'nare /72/ VT to pluck

'**spensi** *ecc* VB *vedi* **spegnere**

spensiera'tezza [spensjera'tettsa] SF carefreeness, lightheartedness

spensie'rato, -a AG carefree

'**spento, -a** PP *di* **spegnere** ▶ AG (*suono*) muffled; (*colore*) dull; (*sigaretta*) out; (*civiltà, vulcano*) extinct

spe'ranza [spe'rantsa] SF hope; **nella ~ di rivederti** hoping to see *o* in the hope of seeing you again; **pieno di speranze** hopeful; **senza ~** (*situazione*) hopeless; (*amare*) without hope

speran'zoso, -a [speran'tsoso] AG hopeful

spe'rare /72/ VT to hope for ▶ VI: **~ in** to trust in; **~ che/di fare** to hope that/to do; **lo spero, spero di sì** I hope so; **tutto fa ~ per il meglio** everything leads one to hope for the best

sper'duto, -a AG (*isolato*) out-of-the-way; (*persona: smarrita, a disagio*) lost

spergi'uro, -a [sper'dʒuro] SM/F perjurer ▶ SM perjury

sperico'lato, -a AG fearless, daring; (*guidatore*) reckless

sperimen'tale AG experimental; **fare qc in via ~** to try sth out

sperimen'tare /72/ VT to experiment with, test; (*fig*) to test, put to the test

sperimentazi'one [sperimentat'tsjone] SF experimentation

'**sperma, -i** SM (*Biol*) sperm

spermato'zoo, -i [spermatod'dzɔo] SM spermatozoon

spe'rone SM spur

sperpe'rare /72/ VT to squander

'**sperpero** SM (*di denaro*) squandering, waste; (*di cibo, materiali*) waste

'**spesa** SF (*soldi spesi*) expense; (*costo*) cost; (*acquisto*) purchase; (*col: acquisto del cibo quotidiano*) shopping ■ **spese** SFPL expenses; (*Comm*) costs; charges; **ridurre le spese** (*gen*) to cut down; (*Comm*) to reduce expenditure; **fare la ~** to do the shopping; **fare le spese di qc** (*fig*) to pay the price for sth; **a spese di** (*a carico di*) at the expense of; **con la modica ~ di 200 euro** for the modest sum *o* outlay of 200 euros; **~ pubblica** public expenditure; **spese accessorie** incidental expenses; **spese generali** overheads; **spese di gestione** operating expenses; **spese d'impianto** initial outlay; **spese legali** legal costs; **spese di manutenzione, spese di mantenimento** maintenance costs; **spese postali** postage *sg*; **spese di sbarco e sdoganamento** landing charges; **spese di trasporto** handling charge; **spese di viaggio** travelling (BRIT) *o* traveling (US) expenses

spe'sare /72/ VT: **viaggio tutto spesato** all-expenses-paid trip

'speso, -a PP *di* **spendere**

'spesso, -a AG (*fitto*) thick; (*frequente*) frequent ▶ AV often; **spesse volte** frequently, often

spes'sore SM thickness; **ha uno ~ di 20 cm** it is 20 cm thick

Spett. ABBR *vedi* **spettabile**

spet'tabile AG (*in lettere: abbr Spett.*): **~ ditta X** Messrs X and Co; **avvertiamo la ~ clientela ...** we inform our customers ...

spettaco'lare AG spectacular

spet'tacolo SM (*rappresentazione*) performance, show; (*vista, scena*) sight; **dare ~ di sé** to make an exhibition *o* a spectacle of o.s.

spettaco'loso, -a AG spectacular

spet'tanza [spet'tantsa] SF (*competenza*) concern; **non è di mia ~** it's no concern of mine

spet'tare /72/ VI: **~ a** (*decisione*) to be up to; (*stipendio*) to be due to; **spetta a lei decidere** it's up to you to decide

spetta'tore, -'trice SM/F (Cine, Teat) member of the audience; (*di avvenimento*) onlooker, witness

spettego'lare /72/ VI to gossip

spetti'nare /72/ VT: **~ qn** to ruffle sb's hair ▪ **spettinarsi** VPR to get one's hair in a mess

spetti'nato, -a AG dishevelled

spet'trale AG spectral, ghostly

'spettro SM (*fantasma*) spectre (BRIT), specter (US); (*Fisica*) spectrum

'spezie ['spɛttsje] SFPL (Cuc) spices

spez'zare [spet'tsare] /72/ VT (*rompere*) to break; (*fig: interrompere*) to break up ▪ **spezzarsi** VPR to break

spezza'tino [spettsa'tino] SM (Cuc) stew

spez'zato, -a [spet'tsato] AG (*unghia, ramo, braccio*) broken ▶ SM (*abito maschile*) coordinated jacket and trousers (BRIT) *o* pants (US); **fare orario ~** to work a split shift

spezzet'tare [spettset'tare] /72/ VT to break up (*o chop*) into small pieces

spez'zino, -a [spet'tsino] AG (*o from*) La Spezia

spez'zone [spet'tsone] SM (Cine) clip

'spia SF spy; (*confidente della polizia*) informer; (Elettr) indicating light; warning light; (*fessura*) peephole; (*fig: sintomo*) sign, indication; **~ dell'olio** (Aut) oil warning light

spiacci'care [spjattʃi'kare] /20/ VT to squash, crush

spia'cente [spja'tʃɛnte] AG sorry; **essere ~ di qc/di fare qc** to be sorry about sth/for doing sth; **siamo spiacenti di dovervi annunciare che ...** we regret to announce that ...

spia'cevole [spja'tʃevole] AG unpleasant, disagreeable

spi'aggia, -ge ['spjaddʒa] SF beach; **~ libera** public beach

Responsibility for **spiagge** (beaches) in Italy falls to the *comuni* (town councils). On some stretches of the coast the majority of beaches are free of charge, and a number provide some facilities. On others, up to 60% of the beaches are privately run, despite the objections of environmentalists. On these beaches, which often have a restaurant or bar, you can hire beach huts, deckchairs or beach umbrellas, play beach volleyball or take surfing or sailboarding lessons. The busiest beaches even provide swimming pools, thalassotherapy and beauty treatments, Wi-Fi access, and, in the evening, musical entertainment.

spia'nare /72/ VT (*terreno*) to level, make level; (*edificio*) to raze to the ground; (*pasta*) to roll out; (*rendere liscio*) to smooth (out)

spi'ano SM: **a tutto ~** (*lavorare*) non-stop, without a break; (*spendere*) lavishly

spian'tato, -a AG penniless, ruined

spi'are /60/ VT to spy on; (*occasione ecc*) to watch *o* wait for

spi'ata SF tip-off

spiattel'lare /72/ VT (*col: verità, segreto*) to blurt out

spi'azzo ['spjattso] SM open space; (*radura*) clearing

spic'care /20/ VT (*assegno, mandato di cattura*) to issue ▶ VI (*risaltare*) to stand out; **~ il volo** to fly off; (*fig*) to spread one's wings; **~ un balzo** to jump, leap

spic'cato, -a AG (*marcato*) marked, strong; (*notevole*) remarkable

spiccherò *ecc* [spikke'rɔ] VB *vedi* **spiccare**

'spicchio ['spikkjo] SM (*di agrumi*) segment; (*di aglio*) clove; (*parte*) piece, slice

spicci'are [spit'tʃare] /14/ VT (*faccenda, impegno*) to finish off ▪ **spicciarsi** VPR (*fare in fretta*) to hurry up, get a move on

'spiccio, -a, -ci, -ce ['spittʃo] AG (*modi, mezzi*) quick; **andare per le spicce** to be quick off the mark, waste no time

spiccio'lata [spittʃo'lata] AV: **alla ~** in dribs and drabs, a few at a time

'spicciolo, -a ['spittʃolo] AG: **moneta spicciola** (small) change ■ **spiccioli** SMPL (small) change

'spicco, -chi SM: **fare ~** to stand out; **di ~** outstanding, prominent; (*tema*) main, principal

spie'dino SM (*utensile*) skewer; (*cibo*) kebab

spi'edo SM (*Cuc*) spit; **pollo allo ~** spit-roasted chicken

spiega'mento SM (*Mil*): **~ di forze** deployment of forces

spie'gare /80/ VT (*far capire*) to explain; (*tovaglia*) to unfold; (*vele*) to unfurl ■ **spiegarsi** VPR to explain o.s., make o.s. clear; **~ qc a qn** to explain sth to sb; **il problema si spiega** one can understand the problem; **non mi spiego come ...** I can't understand how ...

Quando il verbo **explain** è seguito da un complemento oggetto indiretto bisogna farlo precedere dalla preposizione **to**.
Spiegami come funziona. **Explain to me how it works.**

spiegazi'one [spjegat'tsjone] SF explanation; **avere una ~ con qn** to have it out with sb

spiegaz'zare [spjegat'tsare] /72/ VT to crease, crumple

spiegherò *ecc* [spjege'rɔ] VB *vedi* **spiegare**

spie'tato, -a AG ruthless, pitiless

spiffe'rare /72/ VT (*col*) to blurt out, blab

'spiffero SM draught (*BRIT*), draft (*US*)

'spiga, -ghe SF (*Bot*) ear

spigli'ato, -a [spiʎ'ʎato] AG self-possessed, self-confident

spigo'lare /72/ VT (*anche fig*) to glean

'spigolo SM corner; (*Geom*) edge

spigo'loso, -a AG (*mobile*) angular; (*persona, carattere*) difficult

'spilla SF brooch; (*da cravatta, cappello*) pin; **~ di sicurezza** *o* **da balia** safety pin

spil'lare /72/ VT (*vino, fig*) to tap; **~ denaro/notizie a qn** to tap sb for money/information

'spillo SM pin; (*spilla*) brooch; **tacco a ~** stiletto heel (*BRIT*), spike heel (*US*); **~ di sicurezza** *o* **da balia** safety pin; **~ di sicurezza** (*Mil*) (safety) pin

spilorce'ria [spilortʃe'ria] SF meanness, stinginess

spi'lorcio, -a, -ci, -ce [spi'lortʃo] AG mean, stingy

spilun'gone, -a SM/F beanpole

'spina SF (*Bot*) thorn; (*Zool*) spine, prickle; (*di pesce*) bone; (*Elettr*) plug; (*di botte*) bunghole; **birra alla ~** draught beer; **stare sulle spine** (*fig*) to be on tenterhooks; **~ dorsale** (*Anat*) backbone

spi'nacio [spi'natʃo] SM spinach *no pl*; (*Cuc*): **spinaci** spinach *sg*

spi'nale AG (*Anat*) spinal

spi'nato, -a AG (*fornito di spine*): **filo ~** barbed wire; (*tessuto*) herringbone *cpd*

spi'nello SM (*Droga: gergo*) joint

'spingere ['spindʒere] /114/ VT to push; (*condurre: anche fig*) to drive; (*stimolare*): **~ qn a fare** to urge *o* press sb to do ■ **spingersi** VPR (*inoltrarsi*) to push on, carry on; **spingersi troppo lontano** (*anche fig*) to go too far

'spino SM (*Bot*) thorn bush

spi'noso, -a AG thorny, prickly

'spinsi *ecc* VB *vedi* **spingere**

spinte'rogeno [spinte'rɔdʒeno] SM (*Aut*) coil ignition

'spinto, -a PP *di* **spingere** ▶ SF (*urto*) push; (*Fisica*) thrust; (*fig: stimolo*) incentive, spur; (: *appoggio*) string-pulling *no pl*; **dare una spinta a qn** (*fig*) to pull strings for sb

spinto'nare /72/ VT to shove, push

spin'tone SM push, shove

spio'naggio [spio'naddʒo] SM espionage, spying

spion'cino [spion'tʃino] SM peephole

spi'one, -a SM/F (*spia*) informer; (*ragazzino, collega*) telltale, sneak

spio'nistico, -a, -ci, -che AG (*organizzazione*) spy *cpd*; **rete spionistica** spy ring

spi'overe /76/ VI (*scorrere*) to flow down; (*ricadere*) to hang down, fall

'spira SF coil

spi'raglio [spi'raʎʎo] SM (*fessura*) chink, narrow opening; (*raggio di luce, fig*) glimmer, gleam

spi'rale SF spiral; (*contraccettivo*) coil; **a ~** spiral(-shaped); **~ inflazionistica** inflationary spiral

spi'rare /72/ VI (*vento*) to blow; (*morire*) to expire, pass away

spiri'tato, -a AG possessed; (*fig: persona, espressione*) wild

spiri'tismo SM spiritualism

'spirito SM (*Rel, Chim, disposizione d'animo, di legge ecc, fantasma*) spirit; (*pensieri, intelletto*) mind; (*arguzia*) wit; (*umorismo*) humour, wit; **in buone condizioni di ~** in the right frame of mind; **è una persona di ~** he has a sense of humour (*BRIT*) *o* humor (*US*); **battuta di ~** joke; **~ di classe** class consciousness; **non ha ~ di parte** he never takes sides; **lo S~ Santo** the Holy Spirit *o* Ghost

spirito'saggine [spirito'saddʒine] SF witticism; (*peg*) wisecrack

spiri'toso, -a AG witty

spiritu'ale AG spiritual

splen'dente AG (*giornata*) bright, sunny; (*occhi*) shining; (*pavimento*) shining, gleaming

'splendere /29/ VI to shine

'splendido, -a AG splendid; (*splendente*) shining; (*sfarzoso*) magnificent, splendid

splen'dore SM splendour (BRIT), splendor (US); (*luce intensa*) brilliance, brightness

spodes'tare /**72**/ VT to deprive of power; (*sovrano*) to depose

'spoglia ['spɔʎʎa] SF *vedi* **spoglio**

spogli'are [spoʎ'ʎare] /**27**/ VT (*svestire*) to undress; (*privare, fig: depredare*): **~ qn di qc** to deprive sb of sth; (*togliere ornamenti: anche fig*): **~ qn/qc di** to strip sb/sth of ■ **spogliarsi** VPR to undress, strip; **spogliarsi di** (*ricchezze ecc*) to deprive o.s. of, give up; (*pregiudizi*) to rid o.s. of

spoglia'rello [spoʎʎa'rɛllo] SM striptease

spoglia'toio [spoʎʎa'tojo] SM dressing room; (*di scuola ecc*) cloakroom; (*Sport*) changing room

'spoglio, -a ['spɔʎʎo] AG (*pianta, terreno*) bare; (*privo*): **~ di** stripped of; lacking in, without ▶ SM (*di voti*) counting ▶ SF (*Zool*) skin, hide; (*di rettile*) slough ■ **spoglie** SFPL (*salma*) remains; (*preda*) spoils, booty *sg*

spoile'rare [spɔiler'are] VT to spoil

'spola SF shuttle; (*bobina*) spool; **fare la ~ (fra)** to go to and fro ❍ shuttle (between)

spo'letta SF (*Cucito: bobina*) spool; (*di bomba*) fuse

spol'pare /**72**/ VT to strip the flesh off

spolve'rare /**72**/ VT (*anche Cuc*) to dust; (*con spazzola*) to brush; (*con battipanni*) to beat; (*fig: mangiare*) to polish off ▶ VI to dust

spolve'rino SM (*soprabito*) dust coat

'sponda SF (*di fiume*) bank; (*di mare, lago*) shore; (*bordo*) edge

sponsoriz'zare [sponsorid'dzare] /**72**/ VT to sponsor

sponsorizzazi'one [sponsoriddzat'tsjone] SF sponsorship

spontanea'mente AV (*comportarsi*) naturally; (*agire*) spontaneously; (*reagire*) instinctively, spontaneously

spon'taneo, -a AG spontaneous; (*persona*) unaffected, natural; **di sua spontanea volontà** of his own free will

spopo'lare /**72**/ VT to depopulate ▶ VI (*attirare folla*) to draw the crowds ■ **spopolarsi** VPR to become depopulated

spo'radico, -a, -ci, -che AG sporadic

sporcacci'one, -a [sporkat'tʃone] SM/F (*peg*) pig, filthy person

spor'care /**20**/ VT to dirty, make dirty; (*fig*) to sully, soil ■ **sporcarsi** VPR to get dirty

spor'cizia [spor'tʃittsja] SF (*stato*) dirtiness; (*sudiciume*) dirt, filth; (*cosa sporca*) dirt *no pl*, something dirty; (*fig: cosa oscena*) obscenity

'sporco, -a, -chi, -che AG dirty, filthy; **avere la coscienza sporca** to have a guilty conscience

spor'genza [spor'dʒɛntsa] SF projection

'sporgere ['spɔrdʒere] /**115**/ VT to put out, stretch out ▶ VI (*venire in fuori*) to stick out

■ **sporgersi** VPR to lean out; **~ querela contro qn** (*Dir*) to take legal action against sb

'sporsi *ecc* VB *vedi* **sporgere**

sport SM INV sport

'sporta SF shopping bag

spor'tello SM (*di treno, auto ecc*) door; (*di banca, ufficio*) window, counter; **~ automatico** (*Banca*) cash dispenser, automated telling machine

spor'tivo, -a AG (*gara, giornale*) sports *cpd*; (*persona*) sporty; (*abito*) casual; (*spirito, atteggiamento*) sporting ▶ SM/F sportsman(-woman); **campo ~** playing field; **giacca sportiva** sports (BRIT) ❍ sport (US) jacket

'sporto, -a PP *di* **sporgere**

'sposa SF bride; (*moglie*) wife; **abito** ❍ **vestito da ~** wedding dress

sposa'lizio [spoza'littsjo] SM wedding

spo'sare /**72**/ VT to marry; (*fig: idea, fede*) to espouse ■ **sposarsi** VPR to get married, marry; **sposarsi con qn** to marry sb, get married to sb

spo'sato, -a AG married

'sposo SM (*bride*)groom; (*marito*) husband; **gli sposi** the newlyweds

spos'sante AG exhausting

spossa'tezza [spossa'tettsa] SF exhaustion

spos'sato, -a AG exhausted, weary

sposta'mento SM movement, change of position

spos'tare /**72**/ VT to move, shift; (*cambiare: orario*) to change ■ **spostarsi** VPR to move; **hanno spostato la partenza di qualche giorno** they postponed ❍ put off their departure by a few days

spot [spɔt] ⋅SM INV (*faretto*) spotlight, spot; (*TV*) advert, commercial, ad

'spranga, -ghe SF (*sbarra*) bar; (*catenaccio*) bolt

spran'gare /**80**/ VT to bar; to bolt

spray ['sprai] SM INV (*dispositivo, sostanza*) spray ▶ AG INV (*bombola, confezione*) spray *cpd*

'sprazzo ['sprattso] SM (*di sole ecc*) flash; (*fig: di gioia ecc*) burst

spre'care /**20**/ VT to waste ■ **sprecarsi** VPR (*persona*) to waste one's energy

'spreco, -chi SM waste

spre'gevole [spre'dʒevole] AG contemptible, despicable

'spregio ['sprɛdʒo] SM scorn, disdain

spregiudi'cato, -a [spredʒudi'kato] AG unprejudiced, unbiased; (*peg*) unscrupulous

spre'mere /**62**/ VT to squeeze; **spremersi le meningi** (*fig*) to rack one's brains

spremia'grumi SM INV lemon squeezer

spre'muta SF fresh fruit juice; **~ d'arancia** fresh orange juice

sprez'zante [spret'tsante] AG scornful, contemptuous

'sprezzo ['sprɛttso] SM contempt, scorn, disdain

sprigio'nare [spridʒo'nare] /**72**/ vt to give off, emit ■ **sprigionarsi** vpr to emanate; (*uscire con impeto*) to burst out

spriz'zare [sprit'tsare] /**72**/ vt, vi to spurt; ~ **gioia/salute** to be bursting with joy/health

sprofon'dare /**72**/ vi to sink; (*casa*) to collapse; (*suolo*) to give way, subside ■ **sprofondarsi** vpr: **sprofondarsi in** (*poltrona*) to sink into; (*fig*) to become immersed *o* absorbed in

sproloqui'are /**19**/ vi to ramble on

spro'loquio sm rambling speech

spro'nare /**72**/ vt to spur (on)

'sprone sm (*sperone, fig*) spur

sproporzio'nato, -a [sproportsjo'nato] ag disproportionate, out of all proportion

sproporzi'one [spropor'tsjone] sf disproportion

sproposi'tato, -a ag (*lettera, discorso*) full of mistakes; (*fig: costo*) excessive, enormous

spro'posito sm blunder; **a ~** at the wrong time; (*rispondere, parlare*) irrelevantly

sprovve'duto, -a ag inexperienced, naïve

sprov'visto, -a ag (*mancante*): ~ **di** lacking in, without; **ne siamo sprovvisti** (*negozio*) we are out of it (*o* them); **alla sprovvista** unawares

spruz'zare [sprut'tsare] /**72**/ vt (*a nebulizzazione*) to spray; (*aspergere*) to sprinkle; (*inzaccherare*) to splash

spruzza'tore [spruttsa'tore] sm (*per profumi*) spray, atomizer; (*per biancheria*) sprinkler, spray

'spruzzo ['spruttso] sm spray; splash; **vernicia-tura a ~** spray painting

spudora'tezza [spudora'tettsa] sf shamelessness

spudo'rato, -a ag shameless

'spugna ['spuɲɲa] sf (*Zool*) sponge; (*tessuto*) towelling

spu'gnoso, -a [spuɲ'ɲoso] ag spongy

spulci'are [spul'tʃare] /**14**/ vt (*animali*) to rid of fleas; (*fig: testo, compito*) to examine thoroughly

'spuma sf (*schiuma*) foam; (*bibita*) fizzy drink

spu'mante sm sparkling wine

spumeggi'ante [spumed'dʒante] ag (*vino, fig*) sparkling; (*birra, mare*) foaming

spu'mone sm (*Cuc*) mousse

spun'tare /**72**/ sm : **allo ~ del sole** at sunrise; **allo ~ del giorno** at daybreak ▶ vt (*coltello*) to break the point of; (*capelli*) to trim; (*elenco*) to tick off (BRIT), check off (US) ▶ vi (*uscire: germogli*) to sprout; (*: capelli*) to begin to grow; (*: denti*) to come through; (*apparire*) to appear (suddenly) ■ **spuntarsi** vpr to become blunt, lose its point; **spuntarla** (*fig*) to make it, win through

spun'tino sm snack

'spunto sm (*Teat, Mus*) cue; (*fig*) starting point;

dare lo ~ a (*fig*) to give rise to; **prendere ~ da qc** to take sth as one's starting point

spur'gare /**80**/ vt (*fogna*) to clean, clear ■ **spurgarsi** vpr (*Med*) to expectorate

spu'tare /**72**/ vt to spit out; (*fig*) to belch (out) ▶ vi to spit

'sputo sm spittle *no pl*, spit *no pl*

sputta'nare /**72**/ vt (*col*) to bad-mouth

'spyware ['spaiwer] sm inv (*Inform*) spyware (program)

'squadra sf (*strumento*) (set) square; (*gruppo*) team, squad; (*di operai*) gang, squad; (*Mil*) squad; (*: Aer, Naut*) squadron; (*Sport*) team; **lavoro a squadre** teamwork; ~ **mobile/del buon costume** (*Polizia*) flying/vice squad

squa'drare /**72**/ vt to square, make square; (*osservare*) to look at closely

squa'driglia [skwa'driʎʎa] sf (*Aer*) flight; (*Naut*) squadron

squa'drone sm squadron

squagli'arsi [skwaʎ'ʎarsi] /**27**/ vpr to melt; (*fig*) to sneak off

squa'lifica, -che sf disqualification

squalifi'care /**20**/ vt to disqualify

'squallido, -a ag wretched, bleak

squal'lore sm wretchedness, bleakness

'squalo sm shark

'squama sf scale

squa'mare /**72**/ vt to scale ■ **squamarsi** vpr to flake *o* peel (off)

squarcia'gola [skwartʃa'gola]: **a ~** *av* at the top of one's voice

squarci'are [skwar'tʃare] /**14**/ vt (*muro, corpo*) to rip open; (*tessuto*) to rip; (*fig: tenebre, silenzio*) to split; (*: nuvole*) to pierce

'squarcio ['skwartʃo] sm (*ferita*) gash; (*in lenzuolo, abito*) rip; (*in un muro*) breach; (*in una nave*) hole; (*brano*) passage, excerpt; **uno ~ di sole** a burst of sunlight

squar'tare /**72**/ vt to quarter, cut up; (*cadavere*) to dismember

squattri'nato, -a ag penniless ▶ sm/f pauper

squili'brare /**72**/ vt to unbalance

squili'brato, -a ag (*Psic*) unbalanced ▶ sm/f deranged person

squi'librio sm (*differenza, sbilancio*) imbalance; (*Psic*) derangement

squil'lante ag (*suono*) shrill, sharp; (*voce*) shrill

squil'lare /**72**/ vi (*campanello, telefono*) to ring (out); (*tromba*) to blare

'squillo sm ring, ringing *no pl*; blare ▶ sf inv (*anche:* **ragazza squillo**) call girl

squi'sito, -a ag exquisite; (*cibo*) delicious; (*persona*) delightful

squit'tire /**55**/ vi (*uccello*) to squawk; (*topo*) to squeak

SR SIGLA = Siracusa

sradi'care /20/ VT to uproot; (fig) to eradicate

sragio'nare [zradʒo'nare] /72/ VI to talk nonsense, rave

sregola'tezza [zregola'tettsa] SF (nel mangiare, bere) lack of moderation; (di vita) dissoluteness, dissipation

srego'lato, -a AG (senza ordine: vita) disorderly; (smodato) immoderate; (dissoluto) dissolute

Sri 'Lanka [sri'lanka] SM: **lo ~** Sri Lanka

S.r.l. ABBR vedi **società a responsabilità limitata**

sroto'lare /72/ VT, **sroto'larsi** VPR to unroll

SS SIGLA = Sassari

S.S. ABBR (Rel) = **Sua Santità; Santa Sede; santi, santissimo;** (Aut) = **strada statale;** vedi **statale**

S.S.N. ABBR (= Servizio Sanitario Nazionale) ≈ NHS

sta ecc VB vedi **stare**

'stabbio SM (recinto) pen, fold; (di maiali) pigsty; (letame) manure

'stabile AG stable, steady; (tempo: non variabile) settled; (Teat: compagnia) resident ▶ SM (edificio) building; **teatro ~** civic theatre

stabili'mento SM (edificio) establishment; (fabbrica) plant, factory; **~ balneare** bathing establishment; **~ tessile** textile mill

stabi'lire /55/ VT to establish; (fissare: prezzi, data) to fix; (decidere) to decide ■ **stabilirsi** VPR (prendere dimora) to settle; **resta stabilito che ...** it is agreed that ...

stabilità SF stability

stabiliz'zare [stabilid'dzare] /72/ VT to stabilize

stabilizza'tore [stabiliddza'tore] SM stabilizer; (fig) stabilizing force

stabilizzazi'one [stabiliddzat'tsjone] SF stabilization

stacano'vista, -i, -e SM/F (ironico) eager beaver

stac'care /20/ VT (levare) to detach, remove; (separare: anche fig) to separate, divide; (strappare) to tear off (o out); (scandire: parole) to pronounce clearly; (Sport) to leave behind ■ **staccarsi** VPR (bottone ecc) to come off; (scostarsi) **staccarsi (da)** to move away (from); (fig: separarsi) **staccarsi da** to leave; **non ~ gli occhi da qn** not to take one's eyes off sb; **~ la televisione/il telefono** to disconnect the television/the phone; **~ un assegno** to write a cheque

staccio'nata [stattʃo'nata] SF (gen) fence; (Ippica) hurdle

'stacco, -chi SM (intervallo) gap; (: tra due scene) break; (differenza) difference; (Sport: nel salto) takeoff

sta'dera SF lever scales pl

'stadio SM (Sport) stadium; (periodo, fase) phase, stage

'staffa SF (di sella, Tecn) stirrup; **perdere le staffe** (fig) to fly off the handle

staf'fetta SF (messo) dispatch rider; (Sport) relay race

stagflazi'one [stagflat'tsjone] SF (Econ) stagflation

stagio'nale [stadʒo'nale] AG seasonal ▶ SMF seasonal worker

stagio'nare [stadʒo'nare] /72/ VT (legno) to season; (formaggi, vino) to mature

stagio'nato, -a [stadʒo'nato] AG seasoned; matured; (scherzoso: attempato) getting on in years

stagi'one [sta'dʒone] SF season; **alta/bassa ~** high/low season

sta'gista, -i, -e [sta'dʒista] SM/F trainee, intern (US)

stagli'arsi [staʎ'ʎarsi] /27/ VPR to stand out, be silhouetted

sta'gnante [staɲ'ɲante] AG stagnant

sta'gnare [staɲ'ɲare] /15/ VT (vaso, tegame) to tin-plate; (barca, botte) to make watertight; (sangue) to stop ▶ VI to stagnate

sta'gnino [staɲ'ɲino] SM tinsmith

'stagno, -a ['staɲɲo] AG (a tenuta d'acqua) watertight; (a tenuta d'aria) airtight ▶ SM (acquitrino) pond; (Chim) tin

sta'gnola [staɲ'ɲɔla] SF tinfoil

stalag'mite SF stalagmite

stalat'tite SF stalactite

stali'nismo SM (Pol) Stalinism

'stalla SF (per bovini) cowshed; (per cavalli) stable

stalli'ere SM groom, stableboy

'stallo SM stall, seat; (Scacchi) stalemate; (Aer) stall; **situazione di ~** (fig) stalemate

stal'lone SM stallion

sta'mani, stamat'tina AV this morning

stam'becco, -chi SM ibex

stam'berga, -ghe SF hovel

stami'nale AG: **cellula ~** stem cell; **ricerca sulle cellule staminali** stem-cell research

'stampa SF (Tip, Fot: tecnica) printing; (impressione, copia fotografica) print; (insieme di quotidiani, giornalisti ecc): **la ~** the press; **andare in ~** to go to press; **mandare in ~** to pass for press; **errore di ~** printing error; **prova di ~** print sample; **libertà di ~** freedom of the press; **"stampe"** "printed matter"

stam'pante SF (Inform) printer; **~ seriale/termica** serial/thermal printer

stam'pare /72/ VT to print; (pubblicare) to publish; (coniare) to strike, coin; (imprimere: anche fig) to impress

stampa'tello SM block letters pl

stam'pato, -a AG printed ▶ SM (opuscolo) leaflet; (modulo) form ■ **stampati** SMPL printed matter sg

stam'pella SF crutch

stampigli'are [stampiʎ'ʎare] /**27**/ vт to stamp

stampiglia'tura [stampiʎʎa'tura] sϝ (*atto*) stamping; (*marchio*) stamp

'**stampo** sм mould; (*fig: indole*) type, kind, sort

sta'nare /**72**/ vт to drive out

stan'care /**20**/ vт to tire, make tired; (*annoiare*) to bore; (*infastidire*) to annoy ■ **stancarsi** vpr to get tired, tire o.s. out; **stancarsi (di)** (*stufarsi*) to grow weary (of), grow tired (of)

stan'chezza [stan'kettsa] sϝ tiredness, fatigue

'**stanco, -a, -chi, -che** ag tired; ~ **di** tired of, fed up with

stand [stand] sм inv (*in fiera*) stand

'**standard** ['standərd] sм inv (*livello*) standard

standardiz'zare [standardid'dzare] /**72**/ vт to standardize

stan'dista, -i, -e sм/ϝ (*in una fiera ecc*) person responsible for a stand

'**stanga, -ghe** sм bar; (*di carro*) shaft

stan'gare /**80**/ vт (*fig: cliente*) to overcharge; (: *studente*) to fail

stan'gata sϝ (*colpo: anche fig*) blow; (*cattivo risultato*) poor result; (*Calcio*) shot

stan'ghetta [stan'getta] sϝ (*di occhiali*) leg; (*Mus, di scrittura*) bar

'**stanno** vв *vedi* **stare**

sta'notte av tonight; (*notte passata*) last night

'**stante** prep owing to, because of; **a sé ~** (*appartamento, casa*) independent, separate

stan'tio, -a, -'tii, -'tie ag stale; (*burro*) rancid; (*fig*) old

stan'tuffo sм piston

'**stanza** ['stantsa] sϝ room; (*Poesia*) stanza; **essere di ~ a** (*Mil*) to be stationed in; **~ da bagno** bathroom; **~ da letto** bedroom

stanzia'mento [stantsja'mento] sм allocation

stanzi'are [stan'tsjare] /**19**/ vт to allocate

stan'zino [stan'tsino] sм (*ripostiglio*) storeroom; (*spogliatoio*) changing room (Brit), locker room (US)

stap'pare /**72**/ vт to uncork; (*tappo a corona*) to uncap

star [star] sϝ (*attore, attrice ecc*) star

'**stare** /**116**/ vi (*restare in un luogo*) to stay, remain; (*abitare*) to stay, live; (*essere situato*) to be, be situated; (*anche*: **stare in piedi**) to stand; (*essere, trovarsi*) to be; (*seguito da gerundio*): **sta studiando** he's studying; **se stesse in me** if it were up to me, if it depended on me; **~ per fare qc** to be about to do sth; **starci** (*esserci spazio*): **nel baule non ci sta più niente** there's no more room in the boot; (*accettare*) to accept; **ci stai?** is that okay with you?; **~ a** (*attenersi a*) to follow, stick to; (*seguito dall'infinito*): **~ a sentire** to listen; **staremo a vedere** let's wait and see; **stiamo a discutere** we're talking; (*toccare a*): **sta a te giocare** it's your turn to play; **sta a te decidere** it's

up to you to decide; **~ a qn** (*abiti ecc*) to fit sb; **queste scarpe mi stanno strette** these shoes are tight for me; **il rosso ti sta bene** red suits you; **come sta?** how are you?; **io sto bene/ male** I'm very well/not very well; **~ fermo** to keep o stay still; **~ seduto** to sit, be sitting; **~ zitto** to keep quiet; **stando così le cose** given the situation; **stando a ciò che dice lui** according to him o to his version

'**starlette** ['starlet] sϝ inv starlet

starnaz'zare [starnat'tsare] /**72**/ vi to squawk

starnu'tire /**55**/ vi to sneeze

star'nuto sм sneeze

'**start up** ['startap] sϝ inv start-up

'**startupper** ['startaper] sм o ϝ inv startupper

sta'sera av this evening, tonight

'**stasi** sϝ (*Med, fig*) stasis

sta'tale ag state *cpd*, government *cpd* ▶ sм/ϝ state employee, local authority employee; (*nell'amministrazione*) ≈ civil servant; **bilancio ~** national budget; **strada ~** ≈ trunk (Brit) o main road

stataliz'zare [statalid'dzare] /**72**/ vт to nationalize, put under state control

'**statico, -a, -ci, -che** ag (*Elettr, fig*) static

sta'tista, -i sм statesman

sta'tistico, -a, -ci, -che ag statistical ▶ sϝ statistic; (*scienza*) statistics *sg*; **fare una statistica** to carry out a statistical examination

'**stato, -a** pp *di* **essere**; **stare** ▶ sм (*condizione*) state, condition; (*Pol*) state; (*Dir*) status; **essere in ~ d'accusa** (*Dir*) to be committed for trial; **essere in ~ d'arresto** (*Dir*) to be under arrest; **essere in ~ interessante** to be pregnant; **~ d'assedio/d'emergenza** state of siege/emergency; **~ civile** (*Amm*) marital status; **~ di famiglia** (*Amm*) *certificate giving details of a household and its dependents*; **~ d'animo** mood; **~ maggiore** (*Mil*) general staff; **~ patrimoniale** (*Comm*) statement of assets and liabilities; **gli Stati Uniti (d'America)** the United States (of America)

'**statua** sϝ statue

statuni'tense ag United States *cpd*, of the United States

sta'tura sϝ (*Anat*) height, stature; (*fig*) stature; **essere alto/basso di ~** to be tall/short o small

sta'tuto sм (*Dir*) statute; constitution; **regione a ~ speciale** *Italian region with political autonomy in certain matters*; **~ della società** (*Comm*) articles *pl* of association

sta'volta av this time

staziona'mento [stattsjona'mento] sм (*Aut*) parking; (: *sosta*) waiting; **freno di ~** handbrake

stazio'nare [stattsjo'nare] /**72**/ vi (*veicoli*) to be parked

stazio'nario, -a [stattsjo'narjo] ag stationary; (*fig*) unchanged

stazi'one [stat'tsjone] SF station; (*balneare, invernale ecc*) resort; **~ degli autobus** bus station; **~ balneare** seaside resort; **~ climatica** health resort; **~ ferroviaria** railway (BRIT) *o* railroad (US) station; **~ invernale** winter sports resort; **~ di lavoro** work station; **~ di polizia** police station (*in small town*); **~ di servizio** service *o* petrol (BRIT) *o* filling station; **~ termale** spa; **~ radio base** mobile phone mast (BRIT), cell tower (US)

'stazza ['stattsa] SF tonnage

st. civ. ABBR = **stato civile**

'stecca, -che SF stick; (*di ombrello*) rib; (*di sigaretta*) carton; (*Med*) splint; (*stonatura*): **fare una ~** to sing (*o* play) a wrong note

stec'cato SM fence

stec'chito, -a [stek'kito] AG dried up; (*persona*) skinny; **lasciar ~ qn** (*fig*) to leave sb flabbergasted; **morto ~** stone dead

'stella SF star; **~ alpina** (*Bot*) edelweiss; **~ cadente** *o* **filante** shooting star; **~ di mare** (*Zool*) starfish; **~ di Natale** (*Bot*) poinsettia

stel'lato, -a AG (*cielo, notte*) starry

'stelo SM stem; (*asta*) rod; **lampada a ~** standard lamp (BRIT), floor lamp

'stemma, -i SM coat of arms

'stemmo VB vedi **stare**

stempe'rare /72/ VT (*calce, colore*) to dissolve

stempi'ato, -a AG with a receding hairline

stempia'tura SF receding hairline

sten'dardo SM standard

'stendere /120/ VT (*braccia, gambe*) to stretch (out); (*tovaglia*) to spread (out); (*bucato*) to hang out; (*mettere a giacere*) to lay (down); (*spalmare: colore*) to spread; (*mettere per iscritto*) to draw up ■ **stendersi** VPR (*coricarsi*) to stretch out, lie down; (*estendersi*) to extend, stretch

stendibianche'ria [stendibjanke'ria] SM INV clotheshorse

stendi'toio SM (*locale*) drying room; (*stendibiancheria*) clotheshorse

stenodattilogra'fia SF shorthand typing (BRIT), stenography (US)

stenodatti'lografo, -a SM/F shorthand typist (BRIT), stenographer (US)

stenogra'fare /72/ VT to take down in shorthand

stenogra'fia SF shorthand

ste'nografo, -a SM/F stenographer

sten'tare /72/ VI: **~ a fare** to find it hard to do, have difficulty doing

sten'tato, -a AG (*compito, stile*) laboured (BRIT), labored (US); (*sorriso*) forced

'stento SM (*fatica*) difficulty ■ **stenti** SMPL (*privazioni*) hardship *sg*, privation *sg*; **a ~** *av* with difficulty, barely

'steppa SF steppe

'sterco SM dung

'stereo AG INV stereo ▶ SM INV (*impianto*) stereo

stereofo'nia SF stereophony

stereo('fonico), -a, -ci, -che AG stereophonic

stereoti'pato, -a AG stereotyped

stere'otipo SM stereotype; **pensare per stereotipi** to think in clichés

'sterile AG sterile; (*terra*) barren; (*fig*) futile, fruitless

sterilità SF sterility

steriliz'zare [sterilid'dzare] /72/ VT to sterilize

sterilizzazi'one [steriliddzat'tsjone] SF sterilization

ster'lina SF pound (sterling)

stermi'nare /72/ VT to exterminate, wipe out

stermi'nato, -a AG immense; endless

ster'minio SM extermination, destruction; **campo di ~** death camp

'sterno SM (*Anat*) breastbone

ste'roide SM steroid

ster'paglia [ster'paʎʎa] SF brushwood

'sterpo SM dry twig

ster'rare /72/ VT to excavate

ster'zare [ster'tsare] /72/ VT, VI (*Aut*) to steer

'sterzo ['stertso] SM steering; (*volante*) steering wheel

'steso, -a PP di **stendere**

'stessi ecc VB vedi **stare**

'stesso, -a AG same; (*rafforzativo: in persona, proprio*): **il re ~** the king himself *o* in person ▶ PRON: **lo(la) ~(-a)** the same (one); **quello ~ giorno** that very day; **i suoi stessi avversari lo ammirano** even his enemies admire him; **fa lo ~** it doesn't matter; **parto lo ~** I'm going all the same; **per me è lo ~** it's all the same to me, it doesn't matter to me; *vedi* **io; tu** ecc

ste'sura SF (*azione*) drafting *no pl*, drawing up *no pl*; (*documento*) draft

stetos'copio SM stethoscope

'stetti ecc VB vedi **stare**

'stia¹ SF hutch

'stia² ecc VB vedi **stare**

'stigma, -i SM stigma

'stigmate SFPL (*Rel*) stigmata

sti'lare /72/ VT to draw up, draft

'stile SM style; (*classe*) style, class; (*Sport*): **~ libero** freestyle; **mobili in ~** period furniture; **in grande ~** in great style; **è proprio nel suo ~** (*fig*) it's just like him

sti'lismo SM concern for style

sti'lista, -i, -e SM/F designer

sti'listico, -a, -ci, -che AG stylistic

stiliz'zato, -a [stilid'dzato] AG stylized

stil'lare /72/ VI (*trasudare*) to ooze; (*gocciolare*) to drip

S

stilli'cidio [stilli'tʃidjo] SM (*fig*) continual pestering (*o moaning etc*)

stilo'grafica, -che SF (*anche:* **penna stilografica**) fountain pen

Stim. ABBR = **stimata**

'stima SF (*buona opinione*) respect, esteem; (*Econ, Finanza*) valuation, assessment, estimate; **avere ~ di qn** to have respect for sb; **godere della ~ di qn** to enjoy sb's respect; **fare la ~ di qc** to estimate the value of sth

sti'mare /**72**/ VT (*persona*) to esteem, hold in high regard; (*terreno, casa ecc*) to value; (*stabilire in misura approssimativa*) to estimate, assess; (*ritenere*): **~ che** to consider that; **stimarsi fortunato** to consider o.s. (to be) lucky

Stim.ma ABBR = **stimatissima**

stimo'lante AG stimulating ▶ SM (*Med*) stimulant

stimo'lare /**72**/ VT to stimulate; (*incitare*): **~ qn (a fare)** to spur sb on (to do)

stimolazi'one [stimolat'tsjone] SF stimulation

'stimolo SM (*anche fig*) stimulus

'stinco, -chi SM shin; shinbone

'stingere ['stindʒere] /**37**/ VT, VI (*anche:* **stingersi**) to fade

'stinto, -a PP *di* **stingere**

sti'pare /**72**/ VT to cram, pack ■ **stiparsi** VPR (*accalcarsi*) to crowd, throng

stipendi'are /**19**/ VT (*pagare*) to pay (a salary to)

stipendi'ato, -a AG salaried ▶ SM/F salaried worker

sti'pendio SM salary

'stipite SM (*di porta, finestra*) jamb

stipu'lare /**72**/ VT (*redigere*) to draw up

stipulazi'one [stipulat'tsjone] SF (*di contratto: stesura*) drafting; (*: firma*) signing

stiracchi'are [stirak'kjare] /**19**/ VT (*fig: significato di una parola*) to stretch, force ■ **stiracchiarsi** VPR (*persona*) to stretch

stira'mento SM (*Med*) sprain

sti'rare /**72**/ VT (*abito*) to iron; (*distendere*) to stretch; (*strappare: muscolo*) to strain ■ **stirarsi** VPR (*col*) to stretch (o.s.)

stira'tura SF ironing

'stirpe SF birth, stock; descendants *pl*

stiti'chezza [stiti'kettsa] SF constipation

'stitico, -a, -ci, -che AG constipated

'stiva SF (*di nave*) hold

sti'vale SM boot

stiva'letto SM ankle boot

sti'vare /**72**/ VT to stow, load

'stizza ['stittsa] SF anger, vexation

stiz'zire [stit'tsire] /**55**/ VT to irritate ▶ VI (*anche:* **stizzirsi**) to become irritated, become vexed

stiz'zoso, -a [stit'tsoso] AG (*persona*) quick-tempered, irascible; (*risposta*) angry

stocca'fisso SM stockfish, dried cod

Stoc'carda SF Stuttgart

stoc'cata SF (*colpo*) stab, thrust; (*fig*) gibe, cutting remark

Stoc'colma SF Stockholm

stock [stɔk] SM INV (*Comm*) stock

'stoffa SF material, fabric; (*fig*): **aver la ~ di** to have the makings of; **avere della ~** to have what it takes

stoi'cismo [stoi'tʃizmo] SM stoicism

'stoico, -a, -ci, -che AG stoic(al)

sto'ino SM doormat

'stola SF stole

stol'tezza [stol'tettsa] SF stupidity; (*azione*) foolish action

'stolto, -a AG stupid, foolish

'stomaco, -chi SM stomach; **dare di ~** to vomit, be sick

sto'nare /**72**/ VT to sing (o play) out of tune ▶ VI to be out of tune, sing (o play) out of tune; (*fig*) to be out of place, jar; (*: colori*) to clash

sto'nato, -a AG (*persona*) off-key; (*strumento*) off-key, out of tune

stona'tura SF (*suono*) false note

stop SM INV (*Telegrafia*) stop; (*Aut: cartello*) stop sign; (*: fanalino d'arresto*) brake-light (BRIT), stop-light

'stoppa SF tow

'stoppia SF (*Agr*) stubble

stop'pino SM (*di candela*) wick; (*miccia*) fuse

'storcere ['stɔrtʃere] /**106**/ VT to twist ■ **storcersi** VPR to writhe, twist; **~ il naso** (*fig*) to turn up one's nose; **storcersi la caviglia** to twist one's ankle

stordi'mento SM (*gen*) dizziness; (*da droga*) stupefaction

stor'dire /**55**/ VT (*intontire*) to stun, daze ■ **stordirsi** VPR: **stordirsi col bere** to dull one's senses with drink

stor'dito, -a AG stunned; (*sventato*) scatterbrained, heedless

'storia SF (*scienza, avvenimenti*) history; (*racconto, bugia*) story; (*faccenda, questione*) business *no pl*; (*pretesto*) excuse, pretext ■ **storie** SFPL (*smancerie*) fuss *sg*; **passare alla ~** to go down in history; **non ha fatto storie** he didn't make a fuss

storicità [storitʃi'ta] SF historical authenticity

'storico, -a, -ci, -che AG historic(al) ▶ SM/F historian

storiogra'fia SF historiography

stori'one SM (*Zool*) sturgeon

stor'mire /**55**/ VI to rustle

'stormo SM (*di uccelli*) flock

stor'nare /**72**/ VT (*Comm*) to transfer

stor'nello SM kind of folk song

'storno SM starling

storpi'are /19/ VT to cripple, maim; (*fig: parole*) to mangle; (: *significato*) to twist

storpia'tura SF (*fig: di parola*) twisting, distortion

'**storpio, -a** AG crippled, maimed

'**storsi** *ecc* VB *vedi* **storcere**

'**storto, -a** PP *di* **storcere** ▶ AG (*chiodo*) twisted, bent; (*gamba, quadro*) crooked; (*fig: ragionamento*) false, wrong ▶ SF (*distorsione*) sprain, twist; (*recipiente*) retort ▶ AV: **guardare ~ qn** (*fig*) to look askance at sb; **andar ~** to go wrong

sto'viglie [sto'viʎʎe] SFPL dishes *pl*, crockery *sg*

str. ABBR (*Geo*) = **stretto**

'**strabico, -a, -ci, -che** AG squint-eyed; (*occhi*) squint

strabili'ante AG astonishing, amazing

strabili'are /19/ VI to astonish, amaze

stra'bismo SM squinting

strabuz'zare [strabud'dzare] /72/ VT: **~ gli occhi** to open one's eyes wide

stra'carico, -a, -chi, -che AG overloaded

strac'chino [strak'kino] SM *type of soft cheese*

stracci'are [strat'tʃare] /14/ VT to tear ■ **stracciarsi** VPR to tear

'**straccio, -a, -ci, -ce** ['strattʃo] AG: **carta straccia** waste paper ▶ SM rag; (*per pulire*) cloth, duster ■ **stracci** SMPL (*indumenti*) rags; **si è ridotto a uno ~** he's worn himself out; **non ha uno ~ di lavoro** he's not got a job of any sort

stracci'one, -a [strat'tʃone] SM/F ragamuffin

stracci'vendolo [strattʃi'vendolo] SM ragman

'**stracco, -a, -chi, -che** AG: **~ (morto)** exhausted, dead tired

stra'cotto, -a AG overcooked ▶ SM (*Cuc*) beef stew

'**strada** SF road; (*di città*) street; (*cammino, via, fig*) way; **~ facendo** on the way; **tre ore di ~ (a piedi/in macchina)** three hours' walk/drive; **essere sulla buona ~** (*nella vita*) to be on the right road *o* path; (*con indagine ecc*) to be on the right track; **essere fuori ~** (*fig*) to be on the wrong track; **fare ~ a qn** to show sb the way; **fare** *o* **farsi ~** (*fig: persona*) to get on in life; **portare qn sulla cattiva ~** to lead sb astray; **donna di ~** (*fig: peg*) streetwalker; **ragazzo di ~** (*fig: peg*) street urchin; **~ferrata** railway (BRIT), railroad (US); **~ principale** main road; **~ senza uscita** dead end, cul-de-sac

Italy has a good road network. Main roads **(strade statali)** are indicated by blue signs, while motorways **(autostrade)** have green signs. Italian motorways are numbered A1, A2, A3, etc., and are all toll roads.

stra'dale AG road *cpd*; (*polizia, regolamento*) traffic *cpd*

stra'dario SM street guide

stra'dino SM road worker

strafalci'one [strafal'tʃone] SM blunder, howler

stra'fare /53/ VI to overdo it

stra'fatto, -a PP *di* **strafare**

stra'foro: di ~ *av* (*di nascosto*) on the sly

strafot'tente AG: **è ~** he doesn't give a damn, he couldn't care less

strafot'tenza [strafot'tentsa] SF arrogance

'**strage** ['stradʒe] SF massacre, slaughter

stra'grande AG: **la ~ maggioranza** the overwhelming majority

stralci'are [stral'tʃare] /14/ VT to remove

'**stralcio** ['straltʃo] SM (*Comm*): **vendere in ~** to sell off (at bargain prices) ▶ AG INV: **legge ~** abridged version of an act

stralu'nato, -a AG (*occhi*) rolling; (*persona*) beside o.s., very upset

stramaz'zare [stramat'tsare] /72/ VI to fall heavily

strambe'ria SF eccentricity

'**strambo, -a** AG strange, queer

strampa'lato, -a AG odd, eccentric

strana'mente AV oddly, strangely; **e lui, ~, ha accettato** and surprisingly, he agreed

stra'nezza [stra'nettsa] SF strangeness

strango'lare /72/ VT to strangle ■ **strangolarsi** VPR to choke

strani'ero, -a AG foreign ▶ SM/F foreigner

stra'nito, -a AG dazed

'**strano, -a** AG strange, odd

straordi'nario, -a AG extraordinary; (*treno ecc*) special ▶ SM (*lavoro*) overtime

strapaz'zare [strapat'tsare] /72/ VT to ill-treat ■ **strapazzarsi** VPR to tire o.s. out, overdo things

strapaz'zato, -a [strapat'tsato] AG: **uova strapazzate** scrambled eggs

stra'pazzo [stra'pattso] SM strain, fatigue; **da ~** (*fig*) third-rate

strapi'eno, -a AG full to overflowing

strapi'ombo SM overhanging rock; **a ~** overhanging

strapo'tere SM excessive power

strappa'lacrime AG INV (*col*): **romanzo (***o* **film** *etc*) **~** tear-jerker

strap'pare /72/ VT (*gen*) to tear, rip; (*pagina ecc*) to tear off, tear out; (*sradicare*) to pull up; (*fig*) to wrest sth from sb; (*togliere*): **~ qc a qn** to snatch sth from sb ■ **strapparsi** VPR (*lacerarsi*) to rip, tear; (*rompersi*) to break; **strapparsi un muscolo** to tear a muscle

strap'pato, -a AG torn, ripped

'**strappo** SM (*strattone*) pull, tug; (*lacerazione*) tear, rip; (*fig: col: passaggio*) lift (BRIT), ride (US); **fare uno ~ alla regola** to make an exception to the rule; **~ muscolare** torn muscle

S

strapun'tino SM jump o foldaway seat

strari'pare /72/ VI to overflow

Stras'burgo SF Strasbourg

strasci'care [straʃʃi'kare] /20/ VT to trail; (piedi) to drag; **~ le parole** to drawl

'strascico, -chi ['straʃʃiko] SM (di abito) train; (conseguenza) after-effect

strata'gemma, -i [strata'dʒɛmma] SM stratagem

stra'tega, -ghi SM strategist

strate'gia, -'gie [strate'dʒia] SF strategy

stra'tegico, -a, -ci, -che [stra'tɛdʒiko] AG strategic

'strato SM layer; (rivestimento) coat, coating; (Geo, fig) stratum; (Meteor) stratus; **~ d'ozono** ozone layer

stratos'fera SF stratosphere

strat'tone SM tug, jerk; **dare uno ~ a qc** to tug o jerk sth, give sth a tug o jerk

stravac'cato, -a AG sprawling

strava'gante AG odd, eccentric

strava'ganza [strava'gantsa] SF eccentricity

stra'vecchio, -a [stra'vekkjo] AG very old

strave'dere /127/ VI: **~ per qn** to dote on sb

stra'visto, -a PP di **stravedere**

stra'vizio [stra'vittsjo] SM excess

stra'volgere [stra'vɔldʒere] /96/ VT (volto) to contort; (fig: animo) to trouble deeply; (: verità) to twist, distort

stra'volto, -a PP di **stravolgere** ▶ AG (persona: per stanchezza ecc) in a terrible state; (: per sofferenza) distraught

strazi'ante [strat'tsjante] AG (scena) harrowing; (urlo) bloodcurdling; (dolore) excruciating

strazi'are [strat'tsjare] /19/ VT to torture, torment

'strazio ['strattsjo] SM torture; (fig: cosa fatta male): **essere uno ~** to be appalling; **fare ~ di** (corpo, vittima) to mutilate

'strega, -ghe SF witch

stre'gare /80/ VT to bewitch

stre'gone SM (mago) wizard; (di tribù) witch doctor

stregone'ria SF (pratica) witchcraft; **fare una ~** to cast a spell

'stregua SF: **alla ~ di** by the same standard as

stre'mare /72/ VT to exhaust

'stremo SM: **essere allo ~** to be at the end of one's tether

'strenna SF: **~ natalizia** (regalo) Christmas present; (libro) book published for the Christmas market

'strenuo, -a AG brave, courageous

strepi'tare /72/ VI to yell and shout

'strepito SM (di voci, folla) clamour (BRIT), clamor (US); (di catene) clanking, rattling

strepi'toso, -a AG clamorous, deafening; (fig: successo) resounding

stres'sante AG stressful

stres'sare /72/ VT to put under stress

stres'sato, -a AG under stress

stretch [stretʃ] AG INV stretch

'stretta SF vedi **stretto**

stretta'mente AV tightly; (rigorosamente) strictly

stret'tezza [stret'tettsa] SF narrowness ▪ **strettezze** SFPL (povertà) poverty sg, straitened circumstances

'stretto, -a PP di **stringere** ▶ AG (corridoio, limiti) narrow; (gonna, scarpe, nodo, curva) tight; (intimo: parente, amico) close; (rigoroso: osservanza) strict; (preciso: significato) precise, exact ▶ SM (braccio di mare) strait ▶ SF (di mano) grasp; (finanziaria) squeeze; (fig: dolore, turbamento) pang; **a denti stretti** with clenched teeth; **lo ~ necessario** the bare minimum; **una stretta di mano** a handshake; **una stretta al cuore** a sudden sadness; **essere alle strette** to have one's back to the wall

stret'toia SF bottleneck; (fig) tricky situation

stri'ato, -a AG streaked

stria'tura SF (atto) streaking; (effetto) streaks pl

stric'nina SF strychnine

'strida SFPL screaming sg

stri'dente AG strident

'stridere /89/ VI (porta) to squeak; (animale) to screech, shriek; (colori) to clash

'strido (pl(f) **strida**) SM screech, shriek

stri'dore SM screeching, shrieking

'stridulo, -a AG shrill

'striglia ['striʎʎa] SF currycomb

strigli'are [striʎ'ʎare] /27/ VT (cavallo) to curry

strigli'ata [striʎ'ʎata] SF (di cavallo) currying; (fig): **dare una ~ a qn** to give sb a scolding

stril'lare /72/ VT, VI to scream, shriek

'strillo SM scream, shriek

stril'lone SM newspaper seller

strimin'zito, -a [strimin'tsito] AG (misero) shabby; (molto magro) skinny

strimpel'lare /72/ VT (Mus) to strum

'stringa, -ghe SF lace; (Inform) string

strin'gare /80/ VT (fig: discorso) to condense

strin'gato, -a AG (fig) concise

'stringere ['strindʒere] /117/ VT (avvicinare due cose) to press (together), squeeze (together); (tenere stretto) to hold tight, clasp, clutch; (pugno, mascella, denti) to clench; (labbra) to compress; (avvitare) to tighten; (abito) to take in; (scarpe) to pinch, be tight for; (fig: concludere: patto) to make; (: accelerare: passo) to quicken ▶ VI (essere stretto) to be tight; (tempo: incalzare) to be pressing ▪ **stringersi** VPR (accostarsi): **stringersi a** to press o.s. up against; **~ la mano a qn** to shake sb's hand; **~ gli occhi** to screw up one's eyes; **~ amicizia con qn** to make friends with sb; **stringi stringi** in conclusion; **il tempo stringe** time is short

'strinsi *ecc* VB *vedi* **stringere**

'striscia, -sce ['striʃʃa] SF (*di carta, tessuto ecc*) strip; (*riga*) stripe; **strisce (pedonali)** zebra crossing *sg*; **a strisce** striped

strisci'ante [striʃ'ʃante] AG (*fig: peg*) unctuous; (*Econ: inflazione*) creeping

strisci'are [striʃ'ʃare] /14/ VT (*piedi*) to drag; (*muro, macchina*) to graze ▶ VI to crawl, creep

'striscio ['striʃʃo] SM graze; (*Med*) smear; **colpire di ~** to graze

strisci'one [striʃ'ʃone] SM banner

strito'lare /72/ VT to grind

striz'zare [strit'tsare] /72/ VT (*arancia*) to squeeze; (*panni*) to wring (out); **~ l'occhio** to wink

striz'zata [strit'tsata] SF: **dare una ~ a qc** to give sth a wring; **una ~ d'occhio** a wink

'strofa SF, **'strofe** SF INV strophe

strofi'naccio [strofi'nattʃo] SM duster, cloth; (*per piatti*) dishcloth; (*per pavimenti*) floorcloth

strofi'nare /72/ VT to rub

stron'care /20/ VT to break off; (*fig: ribellione*) to suppress, put down; (: *film, libro*) to tear to pieces

'stronzo ['strontso] SM (*sterco*) turd; (*col: persona*) shit (!)

stropicci'are [stropit'tʃare] /14/ VT to rub

stroz'zare [strot'tsare] /72/ VT (*soffocare*) to choke, strangle ■ **strozzarsi** VPR to choke

strozza'tura [strottsa'tura] SF (*restringimento*) narrowing; (*di strada ecc*) bottleneck

stroz'zino, -a [strot'tsino] SM/F (*usuraio*) usurer; (*fig*) shark

struc'care /20/ VT to remove make-up from ■ **struccarsi** VPR to remove one's make-up

'struggere ['struddʒere] /39/ VT (*fig*) to consume ■ **struggersi** VPR (*fig*): **struggersi di** to be consumed with

struggi'mento [struddʒi'mento] SM (*desiderio*) yearning

strumen'tale AG (*Mus*) instrumental

strumentaliz'zare [strumentalid'dzare] /72/ VT to exploit, use to one's own ends

strumentalizzazi'one [strumentaliddzat'tsjone] SF exploitation

strumentazi'one [strumentat'tsjone] SF (*Mus*) orchestration; (*Tecn*) instrumentation

stru'mento SM (*arnese, fig*) instrument, tool; (*Mus*) instrument; **~ a corda** *o* **ad arco/a fiato** string(ed)/wind instrument

'strussi *ecc* VB *vedi* **struggere**

'strutto SM lard

strut'tura SF structure

struttu'rare /72/ VT to structure

'struzzo ['struttso] SM ostrich; **fare lo ~, fare la politica dello ~** to bury one's head in the sand

stuc'care /20/ VT (*muro*) to plaster; (*vetro*) to putty; (*decorare con stucchi*) to stucco

stucca'tore, -'trice SM/F plasterer; (*artista*) stucco worker

stuc'chevole [stuk'kevole] AG nauseating; (*fig*) tedious, boring

'stucco, -chi SM plaster; (*da vetri*) putty; (*ornamentale*) stucco; **rimanere di ~** (*fig*) to be dumbfounded

stu'dente, -'essa SM/F student; (*scolaro*) pupil, schoolboy(-girl)

studen'tesco, -a, -schi, -sche AG student *cpd*

studi'are /19/ VT to study ■ **studiarsi** VPR (*sforzarsi*): **studiarsi di fare** to try *o* endeavour (BRIT) *o* endeavor (US) to do

studi'ato, -a AG (*modi, sorriso*) affected

'studio SM studying; (*ricerca, saggio, stanza*) study; (*di professionista*) office; (*di artista, Cine, TV, Radio*) studio; (*di medico*) surgery (BRIT), office (US) ■ **studi** SMPL (*Ins*) studies; **alla fine degli studi** at the end of one's course (of studies); **secondo recenti studi, appare che ...** recent research indicates that ...; **la proposta è allo ~** the proposal is under consideration; **~ legale** lawyer's office

studi'oso, -a AG studious, hardworking ▶ SM/F scholar

'stufa SF stove; **~ elettrica** electric fire *o* heater; **~ a legna/carbone** wood-burning/coal stove

stu'fare /72/ VT (*Cuc*) to stew; (*fig: col*) to bore ■ **stufarsi** VPR (*col*): **stufarsi (di)** (*fig*) to get fed up (with)

stu'fato SM (*Cuc*) stew

'stufo, -a AG (*col*): **essere ~ di** to be fed up with, be sick and tired of

stu'oia SF mat

stu'olo SM crowd, host

stupefa'cente [stupefa'tʃente] AG stunning, astounding ▶ SM drug, narcotic

stupe'fare /53/ VT to stun, astound

stupe'fatto, -a PP *di* **stupefare**

stupefazi'one [stupefat'tsjone] SF astonishment

stu'pendo, -a AG marvellous, wonderful

stupi'daggine [stupi'daddʒine] SF stupid thing (to do *o* say)

stupidità SF stupidity

'stupido, -a AG stupid

stu'pire /55/ VT to amaze, stun ▶ VI (*anche:* **stupirsi**): **~ (di)** to be amazed (at), be stunned (by); **non c'è da stupirsi** that's not surprising

stu'pore SM amazement, astonishment

S

stu'prare /**72**/ vt to rape

stupra'tore sm rapist

'stupro sm rape

stu'rare /**72**/ vt (*lavandino*) to clear

stuzzica'denti [stuttsika'dɛnti] sm inv tooth-pick

stuzzi'cante [stuttsi'kante] ag (*gen*) stimulating; (*appetitoso*) appetizing

stuzzi'care [stuttsi'kare] /**20**/ vt (*ferita ecc*) to poke (at), prod (at); (*fig*) to tease; (: *appetito*) to whet; (: *curiosità*) to stimulate; **~ i denti** to pick one's teeth

---

su

(*su + il* = **sul**, *su + lo* = **sullo**, *su + l'* = **sull'**, *su + la* = **sulla**, *su + i* = **sui**, *su + gli* = **sugli**, *su + le* = **sulle**)
PREP **1** (*gen*) on; (*moto*) on(to); (*in cima a*) on (top of); **mettilo sul tavolo** put it on the table; **salire sul treno** to get on the train; **un paesino sul mare** a village by the sea; **è sulla destra** it's on the right; **cento metri sul livello del mare** a hundred metres above sea level; **fecero rotta su Palermo** they set out for Palermo; **sul vestito portava un golf rosso** she was wearing a red sweater over her dress

2 (*argomento*) about, on; **un libro su Cesare** a book on *o* about Caesar

3 (*circa*) about; **costerà sui 3 milioni** it will cost about 3 million; **una ragazza sui 17 anni** a girl of about 17 (years of age)

4: **su misura** made to measure; **su ordinazione** to order; **su richiesta** on request; **3 casi su dieci** 3 cases out of 10

▶ AV **1** (*in alto, verso l'alto*) up; **vieni su** come on up; **guarda su** look up; **andare su e giù** to go up and down; **su le mani!** hands up!; **in su** (*verso l'alto*) up(wards); (*in poi*) onwards; **vieni su da me?** are you going to come up?; **dai 20 anni in su** from the age of 20 onwards

2 (*addosso*) on; **cos'hai su?** what have you got on?

▶ ESCL come on!; **su avanti, muoviti!** come on, hurry up!; **su coraggio!** come on, cheer up!

'sua *vedi* **suo**

sua'dente ag persuasive

sub sm inv/f inv skin-diver

su'bacqueo, -a ag underwater ▶ sm/f skin-diver

subaffit'tare /**72**/ vt to sublet

subaf'fitto sm (*contratto*) sublet

subal'terno, -a ag, sm subordinate; (*Mil*) sub-altern

subappal'tare /**72**/ vt to subcontract

subap'palto sm subcontract

sub'buglio [sub'buʎʎo] sm confusion, turmoil;

essere/mettere in ~ to be in/throw into a turmoil

sub'conscio, -a [sub'kɔnʃo] ag, sm subconscious

subcosci'ente [subkoʃ'ʃɛnte] sm subconscious

'subdolo, -a ag underhand, sneaky

suben'trare /**72**/ vi: **~ a qn in qc** to take over sth from sb; **sono subentrati altri problemi** other problems arose

su'bire /**55**/ vt to suffer, endure

subis'sare /**72**/ vt (*fig*): **~ di** to overwhelm with, load with

subi'taneo, -a ag sudden

'subito AV immediately, at once, straight away

subli'mare /**72**/ vt (*Psic*) to sublimate; (*Chim*) to sublime

su'blime ag sublime

sublo'care /**20**/ vt to sublease

sublocazi'one [sublokat'tsjone] sf sublease

subnor'male ag subnormal ▶ smf person with learning difficulties

subodo'rare /**72**/ vt (*insidia ecc*) to smell, suspect

subordi'nare /**72**/ vt to subordinate

subordi'nato, -a ag subordinate; (*dipendente*): **~ a** dependent on, subject to

subordinazi'one [subordinat'tsjone] sf subordination

su'bordine sm: **in ~** secondarily

sub'prime [sab'praim] ag inv subprime; **mutuo ~** subprime mortgage ▶ sm subprime lending

subur'bano, -a ag suburban

succe'daneo [suttʃe'daneo] sm substitute

suc'cedere [sut'tʃɛdere] /**118**/ vi (*accadere*) to happen; **~ a** (*prendere il posto di*) to succeed; (*venire dopo*) to follow ■ **succedersi** vpr to follow each other; **~ al trono** to succeed to the throne; **sono cose che succedono** these things happen; **cos'è successo?** what happened?

successi'one [suttʃes'sjone] sf succession; **tassa di ~** death duty (*Brit*), inheritance tax (*US*)

successiva'mente [suttʃessiva'mente] AV subsequently

succes'sivo, -a [suttʃes'sivo] ag successive; **il giorno ~** the following day; **in un momento ~** subsequently

suc'cesso, -a [sut'tʃɛsso] PP *di* **succedere** ▶ sm (*esito*) outcome; (*buona riuscita*) success; **di ~** (*libro, personaggio*) successful; **avere ~** (*persona*) to be successful; (*idea*) to be well received

succes'sore [suttʃes'sore] sm successor

succhi'are [suk'kjare] /**19**/ vt to suck (up)

succhi'otto [suk'kjɔtto] sm dummy (*Brit*), pacifier (*US*), comforter (*US*)

suc'cinto, -a [sut't∫into] AG (*discorso*) succinct; (*abito*) brief

'succo, -chi SM juice; (*fig*) essence, gist; **~ di frutta/pomodoro** fruit/tomato juice

suc'coso, -a AG juicy; (*fig*) pithy

'succube SMF victim; **essere ~ di qn** to be dominated by sb

succur'sale SF branch (office)

sud SM south ▶ AG INV south; (*regione*) southern; **verso ~** south, southwards; **l'Italia del S~** Southern Italy; **l'America del S~** South America; **S~ Sudan** South Sudan

Su'dafrica SM: **il ~** South Africa

sudafri'cano, -a AG, SM/F South African

Suda'merica SM: **il ~** South America

sudameri'cano, -a AG, SM/F South American

Su'dan SM: **il ~** (the) Sudan

suda'nese AG, SMF Sudanese *inv*

su'dare /72/ VI to perspire, sweat; **~ freddo** to come out in a cold sweat

su'dato, -a AG (*persona, mani*) sweaty; (*fig: denaro*) hard-earned ▶ SF (*anche fig*) sweat; **una vittoria sudata** a hard-won victory; **ho fatto una bella sudata per finirlo in tempo** it was a real sweat to get it finished in time

sud'detto, -a AG above-mentioned

suddi'tanza [suddi'tantsa] SF subjection; (*cittadinanza*) citizenship

sud'dito, -a SM/F subject

suddi'videre /43/ VT to subdivide

suddivisi'one SF subdivision

suddi'viso, -a PP *di* **suddividere**

su'dest SM south-east; **vento di ~** south-easterly wind; **il ~ asiatico** South-East Asia

sudice'ria [suditʃe'ria] SF (*qualità*) filthiness, dirtiness; (*cosa sporca*) dirty thing

'sudicio, -a, -ci, -ce ['suditʃo] AG dirty, filthy

sudici'ume [sudi'tʃume] SM dirt, filth

su'doku SM INV sudoku

su'dore SM perspiration, sweat

su'dovest SM south-west; **vento di ~** south-westerly wind

'sue *vedi* **suo**

'Suez ['suez] SM: **il Canale di ~** the Suez Canal

suffici'ente [suffi'tʃɛnte] AG enough, sufficient; (*borioso*) self-important; (*Ins*) satisfactory

sufficiente'mente [suffitʃɛnte'mente] AV sufficiently, enough; (*guadagnare, darsi da fare*) enough

suffici'enza [suffi'tʃɛntsa] SF self-importance; (*Ins*) pass mark; **con un'aria di ~** (*fig*) with a condescending air; **a ~** enough; **ne ho avuto a ~!** I've had enough of this!

suf'fisso SM (*Ling*) suffix

suffra'gare /80/ VT to support

suf'fragio [suf'fradʒo] SM (*voto*) vote; **~ universale** universal suffrage

suggel'lare [suddʒel'lare] /72/ VT (*fig*) to seal

sugge'rimento [suddʒeri'mento] SM suggestion; (*consiglio*) piece of advice, advice *no pl*; **dietro suo ~** on his advice

sugge'rire [suddʒe'rire] /55/ VT (*risposta*) to tell; (*consigliare*) to advise; (*proporre*) to suggest; (*Teat*) to prompt; **~ a qn di fare qc** to suggest to sb that he (*o she*) do sth

suggeri'tore, -'trice [suddʒeri'tore] SM/F (*Teat*) prompter

suggestio'nare [suddʒestjo'nare] /72/ VT to influence

suggesti'one [suddʒes'tjone] SF (*Psic*) suggestion; (*istigazione*) instigation

sugges'tivo, -a [suddʒes'tivo] AG (*paesaggio*) evocative; (*teoria*) interesting, attractive

'sughero ['sugero] SM cork

'sugli ['suλλi] PREP + DET *vedi* **su**

'sugo, -ghi SM (*succo*) juice; (*di carne*) gravy; (*condimento*) sauce; (*fig*) gist, essence

su'goso, -a AG (*frutto*) juicy; (*fig: articolo ecc*) pithy

'sui PREP + DET *vedi* **su**

sui'cida, -i, -e [sui'tʃida] AG suicidal ▶ SMF suicide

suici'darsi [suitʃi'darsi] /72/ VPR to commit suicide

sui'cidio [sui'tʃidjo] SM suicide

su'ino, -a AG: **carne suina** pork ▶ SM pig ◼ **suini** SMPL swine *pl*

sul, sull', 'sulla, 'sulle, 'sullo PREP + DET *vedi* **su**

sulfa'midico, -a, -ci, -che AG, SM (*Med*) sulphonamide

sulta'nina SF: **(uva) ~** sultana

sul'tano, -a SM/F sultan (sultana)

Su'matra SF Sumatra

'summit ['summit] SM INV summit

S.U.N.I.A. SIGLA M (= *sindacato unitario nazionale inquilini e assegnatari*) *national association of tenants*

sunnomi'nato, -a AG aforesaid *cpd*

'sunto SM summary

'suo (*f* **sua**, *pl* **sue, suoi**) DET: **il ~, la sua** *ecc* (*di lui*) his; (*di lei*) her; (*di esso*) its; (*con valore indefinito*) one's, his/her; (*forma di cortesia: anche:* **Suo**) your ▶ PRON: **il ~, la sua** *ecc* his; hers; yours ▶ SM: **ha speso del ~** he (*o she etc*) spent his (*o her etc*) own money ▶ SF: **la sua** (*opinione*) his (*o her etc*) view; **i suoi** (*parenti*) his (*o her etc*) family; **un ~ amico** a friend of his (*o hers etc*); **è dalla sua** he's on his (*o her etc*) side; **anche lui ha avuto le sue** (*disavventure*) he's had his problems too; **sta sulle sue** he keeps himself to himself

su'ocero, -a ['swɔtʃero] SM/F father-in-law (mother-in-law); **i suoceri** (*pl*) parents-in-law

su'oi *vedi* **suo**

S

su'ola SF (*di scarpa*) sole

su'olo SM (*terreno*) ground; (*terra*) soil

suo'nare /72/ VT (*Mus*) to play; (*campana*) to ring; (*ore*) to strike; (*clacson, allarme*) to sound ▶ VI to play; (*telefono, campana*) to ring; (*ore*) to strike; (*clacson, fig: parole*) to sound

suo'nato, -a AG (*compiuto*): **ha cinquant'anni suonati** he is well over fifty

suona'tore, -'trice SM/F player; **~ ambulante** street musician

suone'ria SF (*di sveglia*) alarm; (*di telefono*) ring-tone

su'ono SM sound

su'ora SF (*Rel*) nun; **Suor Maria** Sister Maria

'super AG INV: **(benzina) ~** ≈ four-star (petrol) (BRIT), ≈ premium (US)

supera'mento SM (*di ostacolo*) overcoming; (*di montagna*) crossing

supe'rare /72/ VT (*oltrepassare: limite*) to exceed, surpass; (*percorrere*) to cover; (*attraversare: fiume*) to cross; (*sorpassare: veicolo*) to overtake; (*fig: essere più bravo di*) to surpass, outdo; (: *difficoltà*) to overcome; (: *esame*) to get through; **~ qn in altezza/peso** to be taller/heavier than sb; **ha superato la cinquantina** he's over fifty (years of age); **~ i limiti di velocità** to exceed the speed limit; **stavolta ha superato sé stesso** this time he has surpassed himself

supe'rato, -a AG outmoded

supe'rattico, -ci SM penthouse

su'perbia SF pride

su'perbo, -a AG proud; (*fig*) magnificent, superb

supercondut'tore SM superconductor

superena'lotto SM *Italian national lottery*

superfici'ale [superfi'tʃale] AG superficial

superficialità [superfitʃali'ta] SF superficiality

super'ficie, -ci [super'fitʃe] SF surface; **tornare in ~** (*a galla*) to return to the surface; (*fig: problemi ecc*) to resurface; **~ alare** (*Aer*) wing area; **~ velica** (*Naut*) sail area

su'perfluo, -a AG superfluous

superi'ora SF (*Rel: anche:* **madre superiora**) mother superior

superi'ore AG (*piano, arto, classi*) upper; (*più elevato: temperatura, livello*): **~ (a)** higher (than); (*migliore*): **~ (a)** superior (to) ▶ SFPL: **le superiori** (*Ins*) ≈ secondary school (BRIT), ≈ senior high (school) (US); **il corso ~ di un fiume** the upper reaches of a river; **scuola media ~** ≈ senior comprehensive school (BRIT), ≈ senior high (school) (US)

superiorità SF superiority

superla'tivo, -a AG, SM superlative

superla'voro SM overwork

super'market [super'market] SM INV = **supermercato**

supermer'cato SM supermarket

super'nova SF supernova

superpo'tenza [superpo'tentsa] SF (*Pol*) superpower

super'sonico, -a, -ci, -che AG supersonic

su'perstite AG surviving ▶ SMF survivor

superstizi'one [superstit'tsjone] SF superstition

superstizi'oso, -a [superstit'tsjoso] AG superstitious

super'strada SF ≈ expressway

supervisi'one SF supervision

supervi'sore SM supervisor

su'pino, -a AG supine; **accettazione supina** (*fig*) blind acceptance

suppel'lettile SF furnishings *pl*

suppergiù [supper'dʒu] AV more or less, roughly

suppl. ABBR (= *supplemento*) suppl

supplemen'tare AG extra; (*treno*) relief *cpd*; (*entrate*) additional

supple'mento SM supplement

To travel on *Intercity* and *Eurocity* trains, you have to pay a **supplemento**, which you buy when getting your ticket before boarding.

---

sup'plente AG temporary; (*insegnante*) supply *cpd* (BRIT), substitute *cpd* (US) ▶ SMF temporary member of staff; supply (*o* substitute) teacher

sup'lenza [sup'plɛntsa] SF: **fare ~** to do supply (BRIT) *o* substitute (US) teaching

supple'tivo, -a AG (*gen*) supplementary; (*sessione d'esami*) extra

'supplica, -che SF (*preghiera*) plea; (*domanda scritta*) petition, request

suppli'care /20/ VT to implore, beseech

suppli'chevole [suppli'kevole] AG imploring

sup'plire /45/ VI: **~ a** to make up for, compensate for

sup'plizio [sup'plittsjo] SM torture

sup'pongo, sup'poni *ecc* VB *vedi* **supporre**

sup'porre /77/ VT to suppose; **supponiamo che ...** let's *o* just suppose that ...

sup'porto SM (*sostegno*) support

supposizi'one [suppozit'tsjone] SF supposition

sup'posta SF (*Med*) suppository

sup'posto, -a PP *di* **supporre**

suppu'rare /72/ VI to suppurate

suprema'zia [supremat'tsia] SF supremacy

su'premo, -a AG supreme; **Suprema Corte (di Cassazione)** Supreme Court

surclas'sare /72/ VT to outclass

surge'lare [surdʒe'lare] /72/ VT to (deep-)freeze

surge'lato, -a [surdʒe'lato] AG (deep-)frozen ▶ SMPL: **i surgelati** frozen food *sg*

surme'nage [syrmə'naʒ] SM (*fisico*) overwork; (*mentale*) mental strain; (*Sport*) overtraining

sur'plus SM INV (*Econ*) surplus; **~ di manodopera** overmanning

surre'ale AG surrealistic

surriscalda'mento SM (*gen, Tecn*) overheating

surriscal'dare /72/ VT to overheat

surro'gato SM substitute

suscet'tibile [suʃʃet'tibile] AG (*sensibile*) touchy, sensitive; (*soggetto*): **~ di miglioramento** that can be improved, open to improvement

suscettibilità [suʃʃettibili'ta] SF touchiness; **urtare la ~ di qn** to hurt sb's feelings

susci'tare [suʃʃi'tare] /72/ VT to provoke, arouse

su'sina SF plum

su'sino SM plum (tree)

sussegu'ire /45/ VT to follow ■ **susseguirsi** VPR to follow one another

sussidi'ario, -a AG subsidiary; (*treno*) relief *cpd*; (*fermata*) extra

sus'sidio SM subsidy; (*aiuto*) aid; **sussidi didattici/audiovisivi** teaching/audiovisual aids; **~ di disoccupazione** unemployment benefit (*BRIT*) *o* benefits (*US*); **~ per malattia** sickness benefit

sussi'ego SM haughtiness; **con aria di ~** haughtily

sussis'tenza [sussis'tɛntsa] SF subsistence

sus'sistere /11/ VI to exist; (*essere fondato*) to be valid *o* sound

sussul'tare /72/ VI to shudder

sus'sulto SM start

sussur'rare /72/ VT, VI to whisper, murmur; **si sussurra che ...** it's rumoured (*BRIT*) *o* rumored (*US*) that ...

sus'surro SM whisper, murmur

su'tura SF (*Med*) suture

sutu'rare /72/ VT to stitch up, suture

suv'via ESCL come on!

SV SIGLA = **Savona**

S.V. ABBR = **Signoria Vostra**

sva'gare /80/ VT (*divertire*) to amuse; (*distrarre*): **~ qn** to take sb's mind off things ■ **svagarsi** VPR to amuse o.s.; to take one's mind off things

sva'gato, -a AG (*persona*) absent-minded; (*scolaro*) inattentive

'svago, -ghi SM (*riposo*) relaxation; (*ricreazione*) amusement; (*passatempo*) pastime

svali'giare [zvali'dʒare] /62/ VT to rob, burgle (*BRIT*), burglarize (*US*)

svaligia'tore, -'trice [zvalidʒa'tore] SM/F (*di banca*) robber; (*di casa*) burglar

svalu'tare /72/ VT (*Econ*) to devalue; (*fig*) to belittle ■ **svalutarsi** VPR (*Econ*) to be devalued

svalutazi'one [zvalutat'tsjone] SF devaluation

svalvo'lare VI (*col*) to go nuts

svam'pito, -a AG absent-minded ▶ SM/F absent-minded person

sva'nire /55/ VI to disappear, vanish

sva'nito, -a AG (*fig: persona*) absent-minded

svantaggi'ato, -a [zvantad'dʒato] AG at a disadvantage

svan'taggio [zvan'taddʒo] SM disadvantage; (*inconveniente*) drawback, disadvantage; **tornerà a suo ~** it will work against you

svantaggi'oso, -a [zvantad'dʒoso] AG disadvantageous; **è un'offerta svantaggiosa per me** it's not in my interest to accept this offer; **è un prezzo ~** it is not an attractive price

sva'pare VI to vape

svapo'rare /72/ VI to evaporate

svapo'rato, -a AG (*bibita*) flat

svari'ato, -a AG (*vario, diverso*) varied; (*numeroso*) various

'svastica, -che SF swastika

sve'dese AG Swedish ▶ SMF Swede ▶ SM (*Ling*) Swedish

'sveglia ['zveʎʎa] SF waking up; (*orologio*) alarm (clock); **suonare la ~** (*Mil*) to sound the reveille; **~ telefonica** alarm call

svegli'are [zveʎ'ʎare] /27/ VT to wake up; (*fig*) to awaken, arouse ■ **svegliarsi** VPR to wake up; (*fig*) to be revived, reawaken

'sveglio, -a ['zveʎʎo] AG awake; (*fig*) alert, quick-witted

sve'lare /72/ VT to reveal

svel'tezza [zvel'tettsa] SF (*gen*) speed; (*mentale*) quick-wittedness

svel'tire /55/ VT (*gen*) to speed up; (*procedura*) to streamline

'svelto, -a AG (*passo*) quick; (*mente*) quick, alert; (*linea*) slim, slender; **alla svelta** quickly

'svendere /29/ VT to sell off, clear

'svendita SF (*Comm*) (clearance) sale

sve'nevole AG mawkish

'svengo *ecc* VB *vedi* **svenire**

sveni'mento SM fainting fit, faint

sve'nire /128/ VI to faint

sven'tare /72/ VT to foil, thwart

sventa'tezza [zventa'tettsa] SF (*distrazione*) absent-mindedness; (*mancanza di prudenza*) rashness

sven'tato, -a AG (*distratto*) scatterbrained; (*imprudente*) rash

'sventola SF (*colpo*) slap; **orecchie a ~** sticking-out ears

svento'lare /72/ VT, VI to wave, flutter

sven'trare /72/ VT to disembowel

sven'tura SF misfortune

sventu'rato, -a AG unlucky, unfortunate

sve'nuto, -a PP *di* **svenire**

svergo'gnare [zvergoɲ'ɲare] /15/ VT to shame

svergo'gnato, -a [zvergoɲ'ɲato] AG shameless ▶ SM/F shameless person

sver'nare /72/ VI to spend the winter

sverrò *ecc* VB *vedi* **svenire**

sves'tire /45/ VT to undress ▪ **svestirsi** VPR to get undressed

'Svezia ['zvɛttsja] SF: **la ~** Sweden

svez'zare [zvet'tsare] /72/ VT to wean

svi'are /60/ VT to divert; (*fig*) to lead astray ▪ **sviarsi** VPR to go astray

svico'lare /72/ VI to slip down an alley; (*fig*) to sneak off

svi'gnarsela [zviɲ'ɲarsela] /72/ VPR to slip away, sneak off

svili'mento SM debasement

svi'lire /55/ VT to debase

svilup'pare /72/ VT, **svilup'parsi** VPR to develop

sviluppa'tore, -trice SM/F (*Inform*) developer

svi'luppo SM development; (*di industria*) expansion; **in via di ~** in the process of development; **paesi in via di ~** developing countries; **~ sostenibile** sustainable development

svinco'lare /72/ VT to free, release; (*merce*) to clear

'svincolo SM (*Comm*) clearance; (*stradale*) motorway (BRIT) *o* expressway (US) intersection

svisce'rare [zviʃʃe'rare] /72/ VT (*fig: argomento*) to examine in depth

svisce'rato, -a [zviʃʃe'rato] AG (*amore, odio*) passionate

'svista SF oversight

svi'tare /72/ VT to unscrew

'Svizzera ['zvittsera] SF: **la ~** Switzerland

'svizzero, -a ['zvittsero] AG, SM/F Swiss

svoglia'tezza [zvoʎʎa'tettsa] SF listlessness; indolence

svogli'ato, -a [zvoʎ'ʎato] AG listless; (*pigro*) lazy, indolent

svolaz'zare [zvolat'tsare] /72/ VI to flutter

'svolgere ['zvɔldʒere] /96/ VT to unwind; (*srotolare*) to unroll; (*fig: argomento*) to develop; (*: piano, programma*) to carry out ▪ **svolgersi** VPR to unwind; to unroll; (*fig: aver luogo*) to take place; (*: procedere*) to go on; **tutto si è svolto secondo i piani** everything went according to plan

svolgi'mento [zvoldʒi'mento] SM development; carrying out; (*andamento*) course

'svolsi *ecc* VB *vedi* **svolgere**

'svolta SF (*atto*) turning *no pl*; (*curva*) turn, bend; (*fig*) turning-point; **essere ad una ~ nella propria vita** to be at a crossroads in one's life

svol'tare /72/ VI to turn

'svolto, -a PP *di* **svolgere**

svuo'tare /72/ VT to empty (out)

'Swaziland ['swadziland] SM: **lo ~** Swaziland

Tt

T, t [ti] SM O F INV (*lettera*) T, t; **T come Taranto** ≈ T for Tommy

T ABBR = **tabaccheria**

t ABBR = **tara**; **tonnellata**

TA SIGLA = **Taranto**

tabac'caio, -a [tabak'kajo] SM/F tobacconist

tabacche'ria [tabakke'ria] SF tobacconist's (shop)

> **Tabaccherie** sell cigarettes and tobacco and can easily be identified by their sign, a large white "T" on a black background. In many *tabaccherie* you can play the *Lotto* (state lottery) and buy stamps, bus tickets, newspapers and magazines, stationery, gifts, etc.

tabacchi'era [tabak'kjɛra] SF snuffbox

ta'bacco, -chi SM tobacco

ta'bella SF (*tavola*) table; (*elenco*) list; **~ di marcia** schedule; **~ dei prezzi** price list

tabel'lone SM (*per pubblicità*) billboard; (*per informazioni*) notice board (BRIT), bulletin board (US); (*: in stazione*) timetable board

taber'nacolo SM tabernacle

'tablet ['tablet] SM INV (*Inform*) tablet

tabù AG, SM INV taboo

'tabula 'rasa SF tabula rasa; **fare ~** (*fig*) to make a clean sweep

tabu'lare /72/ VT to tabulate

tabu'lato SM (*Inform*) printout

tabula'tore SM tabulator

TAC SIGLA F (*Med*: = *Tomografia Assiale Computerizzata*) CAT

'tacca, -che SF notch, nick; **di mezza ~** (*fig*) mediocre

taccagne'ria [takkaɲɲe'ria] SF meanness, stinginess

tac'cagno, -a [tak'kaɲɲo] AG mean, stingy

tac'cheggio [tak'keddʒo] SM shoplifting

tac'chino [tak'kino] SM turkey

'taccia, -ce ['tattʃa] SF bad reputation

tacci'are [tat'tʃare] /14/ VT: **~ qn di** (*vigliaccheria ecc*) to accuse sb of

'taccio ecc ['tattʃo] VB *vedi* **tacere**

'tacco, -chi SM heel; **tacchi a spillo** stiletto heels

taccu'ino SM notebook

ta'cere [ta'tʃere] /119/ VI to be silent o quiet; (*smettere di parlare*) to fall silent ▶ VT to keep to oneself, say nothing about; **far ~ qn** to make sb be quiet; (*fig*) to silence sb; **mettere a ~ qc** to hush sth up

tachicar'dia [takikar'dia] SF (*Med*) tachycardia

ta'chimetro [ta'kimetro] SM speedometer

'tacito, -a ['tatʃito] AG silent; (*sottinteso*) tacit, unspoken

taci'turno, -a [tatʃi'turno] AG taciturn

taci'uto, -a [ta'tʃuto] PP *di* **tacere**

'tacqui ecc VB *vedi* **tacere**

ta'fano SM horsefly

taffe'ruglio [taffe'ruʎʎo] SM brawl, scuffle

taffettà SM taffeta

tag'gare /80/ VT to tag

'taglia ['taʎʎa] SF (*statura*) height; (*misura*) size; (*riscatto*) ransom; (*ricompensa*) reward; **taglie forti** (*Abbigliamento*) outsize

taglia'boschi [taʎʎa'bɔski] SM INV woodcutter

taglia'carte [taʎʎa'karte] SM INV paperknife

taglia'legna [taʎʎa'leɲɲa] SM INV woodcutter

tagli'ando [taʎ'ʎando] SM coupon

tagli'are [taʎ'ʎare] /27/ VT to cut; (*recidere, interrompere*) to cut off; (*intersecare*) to cut across, intersect; (*carne*) to carve; (*vini*) to blend ▶ VI to cut; (*prendere una scorciatoia*) to take a short-cut ■ **tagliarsi** VPR to cut o.s.; **~ la strada a qn** to cut across in front of sb; **~ corto** (*fig*) to cut short; **~ la corda** (*fig*) to sneak off; **~ i ponti (con)** (*fig*) to break off relations (with); **mi sono tagliato** I've cut myself

taglia'telle [taʎʎa'telle] SFPL tagliatelle *pl*

tagli'ato, -a [taʎ'ʎato] AG: **essere ~ per qc** (*fig*) to be cut out for sth

taglia'trice [taʎʎa'tritʃe] SF (*Tecn*) cutter

taglia'unghie [taʎʎa'ungje] SM INV nail clippers *pl*

taglieggi'are [taʎʎed'dʒare] /62/ VT to exact a tribute from

tagli'ente [taʎ'ʎɛnte] AG sharp

tagli'ere [taʎ'ʎɛre] SM chopping board; (*per il pane*) bread board

'taglio ['taʎʎo] SM (*anche fig*) cut; (*azione*) cutting no pl; (*di carne*) piece; (*parte tagliente*) cutting edge; (*di abito*) cut, style; (*di stoffa*) length; (*di vini*) blending; **di ~** on edge, edgeways; **banconote di piccolo/grosso ~** notes of small/large denomination; **un bel ~ di capelli** a nice haircut o hairstyle; **pizza al ~** pizza by the slice; **~ cesareo** Caesarean section

tagli'ola [taʎ'ʎɔla] SF trap, snare

tagli'one [taʎ'ʎone] SM: **la legge del ~** the concept of an eye for an eye and a tooth for a tooth

tagliuz'zare [taʎʎut'tsare] /72/ VT to cut into small pieces

Ta'hiti [ta'iti] SF Tahiti

tailan'dese AG, SMF, SM Thai

Tai'landia SF: **la ~** Thailand

tai'lleur [ta'jœr] SM INV lady's suit

'talamo SM (*poetico*) marriage bed

'talco SM talcum powder

'tale

DET **1** (*simile, così grande*) such; **un(a) tale ...** such a ...; **non accetto tali discorsi** I won't allow such talk; **è di una tale arroganza** he is so arrogant; **fa una tale confusione!** he makes such a mess!

2 (*persona o cosa indeterminata*) such-and-such; **il giorno tale all'ora tale** on such-and-such a day at such-and-such a time; **la tal persona** that person; **ha telefonato una tale Giovanna** somebody called Giovanna phoned

3 (*nelle similitudini*): **tale ... tale** like ... like; **tale padre tale figlio** like father, like son; **hai il vestito tale quale il mio** your dress is just o exactly like mine

▶ PRON (*indefinito: persona*): **un(a) tale** someone; **quel** (o **quella**) **tale** that person, that man (o woman); **il tal dei tali** what's-his-name

---

tale'bano SM Taliban

ta'lento SM talent

talis'mano SM talisman

talk-'show [tɔlk'ʃo] SM INV talk o chat show

tallo'nare /72/ VT to pursue; **~ il pallone** (*Calcio, Rugby*) to heel the ball

tallon'cino [tallon'tʃino] SM counterfoil (BRIT), stub; **~ del prezzo** (*di medicinali*) tear-off tag

tal'lone SM heel

tal'mente AV so

ta'lora AV = **talvolta**

'talpa SF (*Zool: anche fig*) mole

tal'volta AV sometimes, at times

tambu'rello SM tambourine

tambu'rino SM drummer boy

tam'buro SM drum; **freni a ~** drum brakes; **pistola a ~** revolver; **a ~ battente** (*fig*) immediately, at once

Ta'migi [ta'midʒi] SM: **il ~** the Thames

tampona'mento SM (*Aut*) collision; **~ a catena** pile-up

tampo'nare /72/ VT (*otturare*) to plug; (*urtare: macchina*) to crash o ram into

tam'pone SM (*Med*) wad, pad; (*per timbri*) inkpad; (*respingente*) buffer; **~ assorbente** tampon

'tamtam SM INV (*fig*) grapevine

'tana SF lair, den; (*fig*) den, hideout

'tanfo SM (*di muffa*) musty smell; (*puzza*) stench

'tanga SM INV G-string

tan'gente [tan'dʒɛnte] AG (*Mat*): **~ a** tangential to ▶ SF tangent; (*quota*) share; (*denaro estorto*) rake-off (*col*), cut

tangen'topoli [tandʒɛn'topoli] SF (*Pol, Media*) Bribesville

tangenzi'ale [tandʒen'tsjale] SF (*strada*) bypass

'Tangeri ['tandʒeri] SF Tangiers

tan'gibile [tan'dʒibile] AG tangible

tangibil'mente [tandʒibilmente] AV tangibly

'tango, -ghi SM tango

'tanica, -che SF (*contenitore*) jerry can

tan'nino SM tannin

tan'tino : **un ~** av (*un po'*) a little, a bit; (*alquanto*) rather

---

'tanto, -a

DET **1** (*molto: quantità*) a lot of, much; (*: numero*) a lot of, many; **tanto pane/latte** a lot of bread/milk; **tanto tempo** a lot of time, a long time; **tanti auguri!** all the best!; **tante grazie** many thanks; **tanto persone** a lot of people, many people; **tante volte** many times, often; **ogni tanti chilometri** every so many kilometres

2 (*così tanto: quantità*) so much, such a lot of; (*: numero*) so many, such a lot of; **tanta fatica per niente!** a lot of trouble for nothing!; **ha tanto coraggio che ...** he's got so much courage that ..., he's so brave that ...; **ho aspettato per tanto tempo** I waited so long o for such a long time

3: **tanto ... quanto** (*quantità*) as much ... as; (*numero*) as many ... as; **ho tanta pazienza quanta ne hai tu** I have as much patience as you have o as you; **ha tanti amici quanti nemici** he has as many friends as he has enemies

▶ PRON **1** (*molto*) much, a lot; (*così tanto*) so much, such a lot; (*tanti: pl*) many, a lot; so many; such a lot; **credevo ce ne fosse tanto** I thought there was (such) a lot, I thought there was plenty; **una persona come tante** a person just like any other; **è passato tanto**

(tempo) it's been so long; **è tanto che aspetto** I've been waiting for a long time; **tanto di guadagnato!** so much the better!

2: tanto quanto *(denaro)* as much as; *(cioccolatini)* as many as; **ne ho tanto quanto basta** I have as much as I need; **due volte tanto** twice as much

3 *(indeterminato)* so much; **tanto per l'affitto, tanto per il gas** so much for the rent, so much for the gas; **costa un tanto al metro** it costs so much per metre; **di tanto in tanto, ogni tanto** every so often; **tanto vale che ... I** *(o we etc)* may as well ...; **tanto meglio!** so much the better!; **tanto peggio per lui!** so much the worse for him!; **se tanto mi dà tanto** if that's how things are; **guardare qc con tanto d'occhi** to gaze wide-eyed at sth

▶ AV **1** *(molto)* very; **vengo tanto volentieri** I'd be very glad to come; **non ci vuole tanto a capirlo** it doesn't take much to understand it **2** *(così tanto: con ag, av)* so; *(: con vb)* so much, such a lot; **è tanto bella!** she's so beautiful!; **non urlare tanto (forte)** don't shout so much; **sto tanto meglio adesso** I'm so much better now; **era tanto bella da non credere** she was incredibly beautiful; **tanto ... che** so ... (that); **tanto ... da** so ... as

3: **tanto ... quanto** as ... as; **conosco tanto Carlo quanto suo padre** I know both Carlo and his father; **non è poi tanto complicato quanto sembra** it's not as difficult as it seems; **è tanto bella quanto buona** she is as good as she is beautiful; **tanto più insisti, tanto più non mollerà** the more you insist, the more stubborn he'll be; **quanto più ... tanto meno** the more ... the less; **quanto più lo conosco tanto meno mi piace** the better I know him the less I like him

4 *(solamente)* just; **tanto per cambiare/scherzare** just for a change/a joke; **una volta tanto** for once

5 *(a lungo)* (for) long

▶ CONG after all; **non insistere, tanto è inutile** don't keep on, it's no use; **lascia stare, tanto è troppo tardi** forget it, it's too late

Tanza'nia [tandza'nia] SF: **la ~ Tanzania**

tapi'oca SF tapioca

ta'piro SM *(Zool)* tapir

'tappa SF *(luogo di sosta, fermata)* stop, halt; *(parte di un percorso)* stage, leg; *(Sport)* lap; **a tappe** in stages; **bruciare le tappe** *(fig)* to be a whizz kid

tappa'buchi [tappa'buki] SM INV stopgap; **fare da ~** to act as a stopgap

tap'pare /72/ VT to plug, stop up; *(bottiglia)* to cork ▪ **tapparsi** VPR: **tapparsi in casa** to shut o.s. up at home; **tapparsi la bocca** to shut up; **tapparsi il naso** to hold one's nose; **tapparsi le orecchie** to turn a deaf ear; **tapparsi gli occhi** to turn a blind eye

tappa'rella SF rolling shutter

tappe'tino SM *(per auto)* car mat; **~ antiscivolo** *(da bagno)* non-slip mat; **~ del mouse** mouse mat

tap'peto SM carpet; *(anche: **tappetino**)* rug; *(di tavolo)* cloth; *(Sport)*: **andare al ~** to go down for the count; **mettere sul ~** *(fig)* to bring up for discussion

tappez'zare [tappet'tsare] /72/ VT *(con carta)* to paper; *(rivestire)*: **~ qc (di)** to cover sth (with)

tappezze'ria [tappettse'ria] SF *(arredamento)* soft furnishings pl; *(tessuto)* tapestry; *(carta da parati)* wallpaper, wall covering; *(arte, di automobile)* upholstery; **far da ~** *(fig)* to be a wallflower

tappezzi'ere [tappet'tsjɛre] SM upholsterer

'tappo SM stopper; *(in sughero)* cork; **~ a corona** bottle top; **~ a vite** screw top

TAR SIGLA M = **Tribunale Amministrativo Regionale**

'tara SF *(peso)* tare; *(Med)* hereditary defect; *(difetto)* flaw

taran'tella SF tarantella

ta'rantola SF tarantula

ta'rare /72/ VT *(Comm)* to tare; *(Tecn)* to calibrate

ta'rato, -a AG *(Comm)* tared; *(Med)* with a hereditary defect

tara'tura SF *(Comm)* taring; *(Tecn)* calibration

tarchi'ato, -a [tar'kjato] AG stocky, thickset

tar'dare /72/ VI to be late ▶ VT to delay; **~ a fare** to delay doing

'tardi AV late; **più ~** later (on); **al più ~** at the latest; **far ~** *(verso sera)* late in the day; **far ~** to be late; *(restare alzato)* to stay up late; **è troppo ~** it's too late

tar'divo, -a AG *(primavera)* late; *(rimedio)* belated, tardy; *(fig: bambino)* retarded

'tardo, -a AG *(lento, fig: ottuso)* slow; *(tempo: avanzato)* late

tar'dona SF *(peg)*: **essere una ~** to be mutton dressed as lamb

'targa, -ghe SF plate; *(Aut)* number (BRIT) *o* license (US) plate; *vedi anche* **circolazione**

tar'gare /80/ VT *(Aut)* to register

targ'hetta [tar'getta] SF *(con nome: su porta)* nameplate; *(: su bagaglio)* name tag

ta'riffa SF *(gen)* rate, tariff; *(di trasporti)* fare; *(elenco)* price list; tariff; **la ~ in vigore** the going rate; **~ normale/ridotta** standard/reduced rate; *(su mezzi di trasporto)* full/concessionary fare; **~ salariale** wage rate; **~ unica** flat rate; **tariffe doganali** customs rates *o* tariff; **tariffe postali/telefoniche** postal/telephone charges

tarif'fario, -ii AG: **aumento ~** increase in charges *o* rates ▶ SM tariff, table of charges

'tarlo SM woodworm

'tarma SF moth

tarmi'cida, -i [tarmi'tʃida] AG, SM moth-killer

ta'rocco, -chi SM tarot card ▪ **tarocchi** SMPL *(gioco)* tarot sg

tar'pare /72/ VT (fig): **~ le ali a qn** to clip sb's wings

tartagli'are [tartaʎ'ʎare] /27/ VI to stutter, stammer

'tartaro, -a AG, SM (in tutti i sensi) tartar

tarta'ruga, -ghe SF tortoise; (di mare) turtle; (materiale) tortoiseshell

tartas'sare /72/ VT (col): **~ qn** to give sb the works; **~ qn a un esame** to give sb a grilling at an exam

tar'tina SF canapé

tar'tufo SM (Bot) truffle

'tasca, -sche SF pocket; **da ~** pocket cpd; **fare i conti in ~ a qn** (fig) to meddle in sb's affairs

tas'cabile AG (libro) pocket cpd

tasca'pane SM haversack

tas'chino [tas'kino] SM breast pocket

Tas'mania SF: **la ~** Tasmania

'tassa SF (imposta) tax; (doganale) duty; (per iscrizione: a scuola ecc) fee; **~ di circolazione/di soggiorno** road/tourist tax

tas'sametro SM taximeter

tas'sare /72/ VT to tax; to levy a duty on

tassa'tivo, -a AG peremptory

tassazi'one [tassat'tsjone] SF taxation; **soggetto a ~** taxable

tas'sello SM (di legno, pietra) plug; (assaggio) wedge

tassì SM INV = **taxi**

tas'sista, -i, -e SM/F taxi driver

'tasso SM (di natalità, d'interesse ecc) rate; (Bot) yew; (Zool) badger; **~ di cambio/d'interesse** rate of exchange/interest; **~ di crescita** growth rate

tas'tare /72/ VT to feel; **~ il terreno** (fig) to see how the land lies

tasti'era SF keyboard

tastie'rino SM keypad; **~ numerico** numeric keypad

'tasto SM key; (tatto) touch, feel; **toccare un ~ delicato** (fig) to touch on a delicate subject; **toccare il ~ giusto** (fig) to strike the right note; **~ funzione** (Inform) function key; **~ delle maiuscole** (su macchina da scrivere ecc) shift key

tas'toni AV: **procedere (a) ~** to grope one's way forward

'tata SF (linguaggio infantile) nanny

'tattico, -a, -ci, -che AG tactical ▶ SF tactics pl

'tatto SM (senso) touch; (fig) tact; **duro al ~** hard to the touch; **aver ~** to be tactful, have tact

tatu'aggio [tatu'addʒo] SM tattooing; (disegno) tattoo

tatu'are /72/ VT to tattoo

tauma'turgico, -a, -ci, -che [tauma'turdʒiko] AG (fig) miraculous

TAV [tav] SM O F INV (= treno alta velocità) high-speed train; (sistema) high-speed rail system

ta'verna SF (osteria) tavern

'tavola SF table; (asse) plank, board; (lastra) tablet; (quadro) panel (painting); (illustrazione) plate; **~ calda** snack bar; **~ pieghevole** folding table; **~ rotonda** (fig) round table; **~ a vela** windsurfer

tavo'lata SF company at table

tavo'lato SM boarding; (pavimento) wooden floor

tavo'letta SF tablet, bar; **a ~** (Aut) flat out

tavo'lino SM small table; (scrivania) desk; **~ da tè/gioco** coffee/card table; **mettersi a ~** to get down to work; **decidere qc a ~** (fig) to decide sth on a theoretical level

'tavolo SM table; **~ da disegno** drawing board; **~ da lavoro** desk; (Tecn) workbench; **~ operatorio** (Med) operating table

tavo'lozza [tavo'lɔttsa] SF (Arte) palette

'taxi SM INV taxi

'tazza ['tattsa] SF cup; **~ da caffè/tè** coffee/tea cup; **una ~ di caffè/tè** a cup of coffee/tea

taz'zina [tat'tsina] SF coffee cup

TBC ABBR F (= tubercolosi) TB

TCI SIGLA M = **Touring Club Italiano**

TE SIGLA = **Teramo**

te PRON (soggetto: in forme comparative, oggetto) you

tè SM INV tea; (trattenimento) tea party

tea'trale AG theatrical

te'atro SM theatre; **~ comico** comedy; **~ di posa** film studio

'techno ['tekno] AG INV (musica) techno

'tecnico, -a, -ci, -che AG technical ▶ SM/F technician ▶ SF technique; (tecnologia) technology

tecnolo'gia [teknolo'dʒia] SF technology; **alta ~** high technology, hi-tech; **tecnologie ambientali** clean technology

tecno'logico, -a, -ci, -che [tekno'lɔdʒiko] AG technological

te'desco, -a, -schi, -sche AG, SM/F, SM German; **~ orientale/occidentale** East/West German

tedi'are /19/ VT (infastidire) to bother, annoy; (annoiare) to bore

'tedio SM tedium, boredom

tedi'oso, -a AG tedious, boring

te'game SM (Cuc) pan; **al ~** fried

'teglia ['teʎʎa] SF (Cuc: per dolci) (baking) tin (BRIT), cake pan (US); (: per arrosti) (roasting) tin

'tegola SF tile

Teh'ran SF Tehran

tei'era SF teapot

te'ina SF (Chim) theine

tel. ABBR (= telefono) tel.

'tela SF (tessuto) cloth; (per vele, quadri) canvas; (dipinto) canvas, painting; **di ~** (calzoni) (heavy) cotton *cpd*; (*scarpe, borsa*) canvas *cpd*; **~ cerata** oilcloth; **~ di ragno** spider's web

te'laio SM (*apparecchio*) loom; (*struttura*) frame

Tel A'viv SF Tel Aviv

'tele... PREFISSO tele...

teleabbo'nato SM television licence holder

tele'camera SF television camera; **~ TVCC** CCTV camera

telecoman'dare /72/ VT to operate by remote control

teleco'mando SM remote control; (*dispositivo*) remote-control device

telecomunicazi'oni [telekomunikat'tsjoni] SFPL telecommunications

teleconfe'renza SF teleconferencing

tele'cronaca, -che SF television report

telecro'nista, -i, -e SM/F (television) commentator

tele'ferica, -che SF cableway

tele'film SM INV television film

telefo'nare /72/ VI to telephone, ring; (*fare una chiamata*) to make a phone call ▶ VT to telephone; **~ a qn** to phone o ring o call sb (up)

telefo'nata SF (telephone) call; **~ urbana/interurbana** local/long-distance call; **~ a carico del destinatario** reverse charge (BRIT) o collect (US) call; **~ con preavviso** person-to-person call

telefonica'mente AV by (tele)phone

tele'fonico, -a, -ci, -che AG (tele)phone *cpd*

telefo'nino SM (*cellulare*) mobile phone

telefo'nista, -i, -e SM/F telephonist; (*d'impresa*) switchboard operator

te'lefono SM telephone; **essere al ~** to be on the (tele)phone; **~ a gettoni** ≈ pay phone; **~ azzurro** ≈ Childline; **~ fisso** landline; **~ interno** internal phone; **~ pubblico** public phone, call box (BRIT); **~ rosa** ≈ rape crisis

telegior'nale [teledʒor'nale] SM television news (programme)

telegra'fare /41/ VT, VI to telegraph, cable

telegra'fia SF telegraphy

tele'grafico, -a, -ci, -che AG telegraph *cpd*, telegraphic

telegra'fista, -i, -e SM/F telegraphist, telegraph operator

te'legrafo SM telegraph; (*ufficio*) telegraph office

tele'gramma, -i SM telegram

telela'voro SM teleworking

tele'matica SF data transmission; telematics *sg*

teleno'vela SF soap opera

teleobiet'tivo SM telephoto lens *sg*

Tele'pass® SM INV *automatic payment card for use on Italian motorways*

telepa'tia SF telepathy

tele'quiz [tele'kwits] SM INV (TV) game show

teles'chermo [teles'kɛrmo] SM television screen

teles'copio SM telescope

telescri'vente SF teleprinter (BRIT), teletypewriter (US)

teleselet'tivo, -a AG: **prefisso ~** dialling code (BRIT), dial code (US)

teleselezi'one [teleselet'tsjone] SF direct dialling

telespetta'tore, -'trice SM/F (television) viewer

tele'text SM INV teletext

tele'vendita [tele'vendita] SF teleshopping

tele'video SM *videotext service*

televisi'one SF television

Three state-owned channels, RAI 1, 2 and 3, and a large number of private companies broadcast television programmes in Italy. Some of the latter function at purely local level, while others are regional; some form part of a network, while others remain independent. As a public corporation, RAI comes under the authority of the *Ministero dello sviluppo economico* (Ministry of Economic Development). Both RAI and the private-sector channels compete for advertising revenues. Everyone with a TV set must pay a licence fee (*canone*), which forms part of a household's electricity bill.

televi'sore SM television set

'telex SM INV telex

'telo SM length of cloth

te'lone SM (*per merci ecc*) tarpaulin; (*sipario*) drop curtain

'tema, -i SM theme; (*Ins*) essay, composition

te'matica SF basic themes *pl*

teme'rario, -a AG rash, reckless

te'mere /29/ VT to fear, be afraid of; (*essere sensibile a: freddo, calore*) to be sensitive to ▶ VI to be afraid; (*essere preoccupato*): **~ per** to worry about, fear for; **~ di/che** to be afraid of/that

'tempera SF (*pittura*) tempera; (*dipinto*) painting in tempera

temperama'tite SM INV pencil sharpener

tempera'mento SM temperament

tempe'rante AG moderate

tempe'rare /72/ VT (*aguzzare*) to sharpen; (*fig*) to moderate, control, temper

tempe'rato, -a AG moderate, temperate; (*clima*) temperate

tempera'tura SF temperature; **~ ambiente** room temperature

tempe'rino SM penknife

tem'pesta SF storm; **~ di sabbia/neve** sand/snowstorm

tempes'tare /72/ VT (*percuotere*): **~ qn di colpi** to rain blows on sb; (*bombardare*) **~ qn di domande** to bombard sb with questions; (*ornare*) to stud

t

tempestività SF timeliness

tempes'tivo, -a AG timely

tempes'toso, -a AG stormy

'tempia SF (*Anat*) temple

'tempio SM (*edificio*) temple

tem'pismo SM sense of timing

tem'pistiche [tem'pistike] SFPL (*Comm*) time and motion

'tempo SM (*Meteor*) weather; (*cronologico*) time; (*epoca*) time, times *pl*; (*di film, gioco: parte*) part; (*Mus*) time; (: *battuta*) beat; (*Ling*) tense; **che ~ fa?** what's the weather like?; **un ~ once**; **da ~** for a long time now; **~ fa** some time ago; **poco ~ dopo** not long after; **a ~ e luogo** at the right time and place; **ogni cosa a suo ~** we'll (*o* you'll *etc*) deal with it in due course; **al ~ stesso** *o* **a un ~** at the same time; **per ~** early; **per qualche ~** for a while; **trovare il ~ di fare qc** to find the time to do sth; **aver fatto il proprio ~** to have had its (*o* his *etc*) day; **primo/ secondo ~** (*Teat*) first/second part; (*Sport*) first/ second half; **rispettare i tempi** to keep to the timetable; **stringere i tempi** to speed things up; **con i tempi che corrono** these days; **in questi ultimi tempi** of late; **ai miei tempi** in my day; **~ di cottura** cooking time; **in ~ utile** in due time *o* course; **a ~ pieno** full-time; **~ libero** free time; **tempi di esecuzione** (*Comm*) time scale *sg*; **tempi di lavorazione** (*Comm*) throughput time *sg*; **tempi morti** (*Comm*) downtime *sg*, idle time *sg*

tempo'rale AG temporal ▶ SM (*Meteor*) (thunder)storm

tempora'lesco, -a, -schi, -sche AG stormy

tempo'raneo, -a AG temporary

temporeggi'are [tempored'dʒare] /62/ VI to play for time, temporize

'tempra SF (*Tecn: atto*) tempering, hardening; (: *effetto*) temper; (*fig: costituzione fisica*) constitution; (: *intellettuale*) temperament

tem'prare /72/ VT to temper

te'nace [te'natʃe] AG strong, tough; (*fig*) tenacious

te'nacia [te'natʃa] SF tenacity

te'naglie [te'naʎʎe] SFPL pincers *pl*

'tenda SF (*riparo*) awning; (*di finestra*) curtain; (*per campeggio ecc*) tent

ten'daggio [ten'daddʒo] SM curtaining, curtains *pl*, drapes *pl* (*US*)

ten'denza [ten'dɛntsa] SF tendency; (*orientamento*) trend; **avere ~ a** *o* **per qc** to have a bent for sth; **~ al rialzo/ribasso** (*Borsa*) upward/ downward trend

tendenziosità [tendentsjosi'ta] SF tendentiousness

tendenzi'oso, -a [tenden'tsjoso] AG tendentious, bias(s)ed

'tendere /120/ VT (*allungare al massimo*) to stretch,

draw tight; (*porgere: mano*) to hold out; (*fig: trappola*) to lay, set ▶ VI: **~ a qc/a fare** to tend towards sth/to do; **tutti i nostri sforzi sono tesi a ...** all our efforts are geared towards ...; **~ l'orecchio** to prick up one's ears; **il tempo tende al caldo** the weather is getting hot; **un blu che tende al verde** a greenish blue

ten'dina SF curtain

'tendine SM tendon, sinew

ten'done SM (*da circo*) big top

ten'dopoli SF INV (large) camp

'tenebre SFPL darkness *sg*

tene'broso, -a AG dark, gloomy

te'nente SM lieutenant

te'nere /121/ VT to hold; (*conservare, mantenere*) to keep; (*ritenere, considerare*) to consider; (*occupare: spazio*) to take up, occupy; (*seguire: strada*) to keep to; (*dare: lezione, conferenza*) to give ▶ VI to hold; (*colori*) to be fast; (*dare importanza*): **~ a** to care about; **~ a fare** to want to do, be keen to do ◼ **tenersi** VPR (*stare in una determinata posizione*) to stand; (*stimarsi*) to consider o.s.; (*aggrapparsi*): **tenersi a** to hold on to; (*attenersi*): **tenersi a** to stick to; **~ in gran conto** *o* **considerazione qn** to have a high regard for sb, think highly of sb; **~ una conferenza** to give a lecture; **~ conto di qc** to take sth into consideration; **~ presente qc** to bear sth in mind; **non ci sono scuse che tengano** I'll take no excuses; **tenersi per la mano** (*uso reciproco*) to hold hands; **tenersi in piedi** to stay on one's feet

tene'rezza [tene'rettsa] SF tenderness

'tenero, -a AG tender; (*pietra, cera, colore*) soft; (*fig*) tender, loving ▶ SM: **tra quei due c'è del ~** there's a romance budding between those two

'tengo *ecc* VB *vedi* **tenere**

'tenia SF tapeworm

'tenni *ecc* VB *vedi* **tenere**

'tennis SM tennis; **~ da tavolo** table tennis

ten'nista, -i, -e SM/F tennis player

te'nore SM (*tono*) tone; (*Mus*) tenor; **~ di vita** way of life; (*livello*) standard of living

tensi'one SF tension; **ad alta ~** (*Elettr*) high-voltage *cpd*, high-tension *cpd*

tentaco'lare AG tentacular; (*fig: città*) magnet-like

ten'tacolo SM tentacle

ten'tare /72/ VT (*indurre*) to tempt; (*provare*): **~ qc/ di fare** to attempt *o* try sth/to do; **~ la sorte** to try one's luck

tenta'tivo SM attempt

tentazi'one [tentat'tsjone] SF temptation; **aver la ~ di fare** to be tempted to do

tentenna'mento SM (*fig*) hesitation, wavering; **dopo molti tentennamenti** after much hesitation

tenten'nare /72/ VI to shake, be unsteady; (*fig*)

to hesitate, waver ▸ VT: **~ il capo** to shake one's head

ten'toni AV: **andare a ~** (*anche fig*) to grope one's way

'tenue AG (*sottile*) fine; (*colore*) soft; (*fig*) slender, slight

te'nuta SF (*capacità*) capacity; (*divisa*) uniform; (*abito*) dress; (*Agr*) estate; **a ~ d'aria** airtight; **~ di strada** roadholding power; **in ~ da lavoro** in one's working clothes; **in ~ da sci** in a skiing outfit

teolo'gia [teolo'dʒia] SF theology

teo'logico, -a, -ci, -che [teo'lɔdʒiko] AG theological

te'ologo, -gi SM theologian

teo'rema, -i SM theorem

teo'ria SF theory; **in ~** in theory, theoretically

te'orico, -a, -ci, -che AG theoretic(al) ▸ SM/F theorist, theoretician; **a livello ~, in linea teorica** theoretically

teoriz'zare [teorid'dzare] /**72**/ VT to theorize

'tepido, -a AG = **tiepido**

te'pore SM warmth

'teppa SF mob, hooligans *pl*

tep'paglia [tep'paʎʎa] SF hooligans *pl*

tep'pismo SM hooliganism

tep'pista, -i SM hooligan

tera'peutico, -a, -ci, -che AG therapeutic

tera'pia SF therapy; **~ di gruppo** group therapy; **~ intensiva** intensive care

tera'pista, -i, -e SM/F therapist

tergicris'tallo [terdʒikris'tallo] SM windscreen (BRIT) o windshield (US) wiper

tergiver'sare [terdʒiver'sare] /**72**/ VI to shilly-shally

'tergo SM: **a ~** behind; **vedi a ~** please turn over

'terital® SM INV Terylene®

ter'male AG thermal; **stazione** *sf* **~** spa

'terme SFPL thermal baths

In Italy you can experience the healing properties of its thermal springs, which were already known to the ancient Romans. Today, however, they come with ultramodern facilities. If your doctor prescribes it, you can enjoy, free of charge, the benefits of these establishments, which offer a whole range of thermal treatments for different conditions or complaints, for example, mud baths, swimming, or inhalation treatments. The most famous **terme** are often decorated with expensive works of art and offer a wide choice of restaurants and hotels. These are often very luxurious, are set in spectacular natural surroundings and offer direct access to the treatment facilities themselves.

'termico, -a, -ci, -che AG thermal; **centrale termica** thermal power station

termi'nale AG (*fase, parte*) final; (*Med*) terminal ▸ SM terminal; **tratto ~** (*di fiume*) lower reaches *pl*

termi'nare /**72**/ VT to end; (*lavoro*) to finish ▸ VI to end

terminazi'one [terminat'tsjone] SF (*fine*) end; (*Ling*) ending; **terminazioni nervose** (*Anat*) nerve endings

'termine SM term; (*fine, estremità*) end; (*di territorio*) boundary, limit; **fissare un ~** to set a deadline; **portare a ~ qc** to bring sth to a conclusion; **contratto a ~** (*Comm*) forward contract; **a breve/lungo ~** short-/long-term; **ai termini di legge** by law; **in altri termini** in other words; **parlare senza mezzi termini** to talk frankly, not to mince one's words

terminolo'gia [terminolo'dʒia] SF terminology

'termite SF termite

termoco'perta SF electric blanket

ter'mometro SM thermometer

termonucle'are AG thermonuclear

'termos SM INV = **thermos**

termosi'fone SM radiator; **(riscaldamento a) ~** central heating

ter'mostato SM thermostat

'terna SF set of three; (*lista di tre nomi*) list of three candidates

'terno SM (*al lotto ecc*) (set of) three winning numbers; **vincere un ~ al lotto** (*fig*) to hit the jackpot

'terra SF (*gen, Elettr*) earth; (*sostanza*) soil, earth; (*opposto al mare*) land *no pl*; (*regione, paese*) land; (*argilla*) clay ■ **terre** SFPL (*possedimento*) lands, land *sg*; **a o per ~** (*stato*) on the ground (o floor); (*moto*) to the ground, down; **mettere a ~** (*Elettr*) to earth; **essere a ~** (*fig: depresso*) to be at rock bottom; **via ~** (*viaggiare*) by land, overland; **strada in ~ battuta** dirt track; **~ di nessuno** no man's land; **la T~ Santa** the Holy Land; **~ di Siena** sienna; **~ ~** (*fig: persona, argomento*) prosaic, pedestrian

'terra-'aria AG INV (*Mil*) ground-to-air

terra'cotta SF terracotta; **vasellame di ~** earthenware

terra'ferma SF dry land, terra firma; (*continente*) mainland

ter'raglia [ter'raʎʎa] SF pottery ■ **terraglie** SFPL (*oggetti*) crockery *sg*, earthenware *sg*

Terra'nova SF: **la ~** Newfoundland

terrapi'eno SM embankment, bank

'terra-'terra AG INV (*Mil*) surface-to-surface

ter'razza [ter'rattsa] SF, **ter'razzo** [ter'rattso] SM terrace

terremo'tato, -a AG (*zona*) devastated by an earthquake ▸ SM/F earthquake victim

terre'moto SM earthquake

ter'reno, -a AG (*vita, beni*) earthly ▸ SM (*suolo, fig*) ground; (*Comm*) land *no pl*, plot (of land); site; (*Sport*, *Mil*) field; **perdere ~** (*anche fig*) to lose ground; **un ~ montuoso** a mountainous terrain; **~ alluvionale** (*Geo*) alluvial soil

ter'reo, -a AG (*viso, colorito*) wan

ter'restre AG (*superficie*) of the earth, earth's; (*di terra: battaglia, animale*) land *cpd*; (*Rel*) earthly, worldly

ter'ribile AG terrible, dreadful

ter'riccio [ter'rittʃo] SM soil

terri'ero, -a AG: **proprietà terriera** landed property; **proprietario ~** landowner

terrifi'cante AG terrifying

ter'rina SF (*zuppiera*) tureen

territori'ale AG territorial

terri'torio SM territory

ter'rone, -a SM/F *derogatory term used by Northern Italians to describe Southern Italians*

ter'rore SM terror; **avere il ~ di qc** to be terrified of sth

terro'rismo SM terrorism

terro'rista, -i, -e SM/F terrorist

terroriz'zare [terrorid'dzare] /**72**/ VT to terrorize

'terso, -a AG clear

'terza ['tɛrtsa] SF *vedi* **terzo**

ter'zetto [ter'tsetto] SM (*Mus*) trio, terzetto; (*di persone*) trio

terzi'ario, -a [ter'tsjarjo] AG (*Geo, Econ*) tertiary

ter'zino [ter'tsino] SM (*Calcio*) fullback, back

'terzo, -a ['tɛrtso] AG third ▶ SM (*frazione*) third; (*Dir*) third party ▶ SF (*gen*) third; (*Aut*) third (gear); (*di trasporti*) third class; (*Ins: elementare*) third year at primary school; (*: media*) third year at secondary school; (*: superiore*) sixth year at secondary school ▪ **terzi** SMPL (*altri*) others, other people; **agire per conto di terzi** to act on behalf of a third party; **assicurazione contro terzi** third-party insurance (*BRIT*), liability insurance (*US*); **la terza età** old age; **il ~ mondo** the Third World; **di terz'ordine** third rate; **la terza pagina** (*Stampa*) the Arts page

'tesa SF brim; **a larghe tese** wide-brimmed

'teschio ['tɛskjo] SM skull

'tesi¹ SF INV thesis; **~ di laurea** degree thesis

'tesi² *ecc* VB *vedi* **tendere**

'teso, -a PP *di* **tendere** ▶ AG (*tirato*) taut, tight; (*fig*) tense

tesore'ria SF treasury

tesori'ere SM treasurer

te'soro SM treasure; **il Ministero del T~** the Treasury; **far ~ dei consigli di qn** to take sb's advice to heart

'tessera SF (*documento*) card; (*di abbonato*) season ticket; (*di giornalista*) pass; **ha la ~ del partito** he's a party member; **~ elettorale** ballot paper

tesse'rare /**72**/ VT (*iscrivere*) to give a membership card to

tesse'rato, -a SM/F (*di società sportiva ecc*) (fully paid-up) member; (*Pol*) (card-carrying) member

'tessere /**1**/ VT to weave; **~ le lodi di qn** (*fig*) to sing sb's praises

'tessile AG, SM textile

tessi'tore, -'trice SM/F weaver

tessi'tura SF weaving

tes'suto SM fabric, material; (*Biol*) tissue; (*fig*) web

'test ['tɛst] SM INV test

'testa SF head; (*di cose: estremità, parte anteriore*) head, front; **50 euro a ~** 50 euros apiece *o* a head *o* per person; **a ~ alta** with one's head held high; **a ~ bassa** (*correre*) headlong; (*con aria dimessa*) with head bowed; **di ~** *ag* (*vettura ecc*) front; **dare alla ~** to go to one's head; **fare di ~ propria** to go one's own way; **in ~** (*Sport*) in the lead; **essere in ~ alla classifica** (*corridore*) to be number one; (*squadra*) to be at the top of the league table; (*disco*) to be top of the charts, be number one; **essere alla ~ di qc** (*società*) to be the head of; (*esercito*) to be at the head of; **tenere ~ a qn** (*nemico ecc*) to stand up to sb; **una ~ d'aglio** a bulb of garlic; **~ o croce?** heads or tails?; **avere la ~ dura** to be stubborn; **~ di serie** (*Tennis*) seed, seeded player

'testa-'coda SM INV (*Aut*) spin

testamen'tario, -a AG (*Dir*) testamentary; **le sue disposizioni testamentarie** the provisions of his will

testa'mento SM (*atto*) will, testament; **l'Antico/il Nuovo T~** (*Rel*) the Old/New Testament; **~ biologico** living will

testar'daggine [testar'daddʒine] SF stubbornness, obstinacy

tes'tardo, -a AG stubborn, pig-headed

tes'tare /**72**/ VT to test

tes'tata SF (*parte anteriore*) head; (*intestazione*) heading; **missile a ~ nucleare** missile with a nuclear warhead

'teste SMF witness

tes'ticolo SM testicle

testi'era SF (*del letto*) headboard; (*di cavallo*) headpiece

testi'mone SMF (*Dir*) witness; **fare da ~ alle nozze di qn** to be a witness at sb's wedding; **~ oculare** eye witness

testimoni'anza [testimo'njantsa] SF (*atto*) deposition; (*effetto*) evidence; (*fig: prova*) proof; **accusare qn di falsa ~** to accuse sb of perjury; **rilasciare una ~** to give evidence

testimoni'are /**19**/ VT to testify; (*fig*) to bear witness to, testify to ▶ VI to give evidence, testify; **~ il vero** to tell the truth; **~ il falso** to perjure o.s.

tes'tina SF (*di giradischi, registratore*) head

'testo SM text; **fare ~** (*opera, autore*) to be authoritative; (*fig: dichiarazione*) to carry weight; **questo libro non fa ~** this book is not essential reading

testoste'rone SM testosterone

testu'ale AG textual; **le sue parole testuali** his (*o* her) actual words

tes'tuggine [tes'tuddʒine] SF tortoise; (*di mare*) turtle

'tetano SM (*Med*) tetanus

'tetro, -a AG gloomy

'tetta SF (*col*) boob, tit

tetta'rella SF teat

'tetto SM roof; **abbandonare il ~ coniugale** to desert one's family; **~ a cupola** dome

tet'toia SF roofing; canopy

tet'tuccio [tet'tuttʃo] SM: **~ apribile** (*Aut*) sunroof

'Tevere SM: **il ~** the Tiber

TG [tid'dʒi], **tg** ABBR M (= *telegiornale*) TV news *sg*

'thermos® ['tɛrmos] SM INV vacuum *o* Thermos® flask

'thriller ['θriler], **'thrilling** ['θrilin] SM INV thriller

ti PRON (*dav lo, la, li, le, ne diventa* **te**: *oggetto*) you; (*complemento di termine*) (to) you; (*riflessivo*) yourself; **ti aiuto?** can I give you a hand?; **te lo ha dato?** did he give it to you?; **ti sei lavato?** have you washed?

ti'ara SF (*Rel*) tiara

'Tibet SM: **il ~** Tibet

tibe'tano, -a AG, SM/F Tibetan

'tibia SF tibia, shinbone

tic SM INV tic, (*nervous*) twitch; (*fig*) mannerism

ticchet'tio [tikket'tio] SM (*di macchina da scrivere*) clatter; (*di orologio*) ticking; (*della pioggia*) patter

'ticchio ['tikkjo] SM (*ghiribizzo*) whim; (*tic*) tic, (*nervous*) twitch

'ticket SM INV (*Med*) prescription charge (BRIT)

The **ticket** is the amount you have to pay for some medical services, including emergency treatment, and for getting prescription medicines.

ti'ene *ecc* VB *vedi* **tenere**

ti'epido, -a AG lukewarm, tepid

ti'fare /72/ VI: **~ per** to be a fan of; (*parteggiare*) to side with

'tifo SM (*Med*) typhus; (*fig*): **fare il ~ per** to be a fan of

tifoi'dea SF typhoid

ti'fone SM typhoon

ti'foso, -a SM/F (*Sport ecc*) fan

tight ['tait] SM INV morning suit

tigì [ti'dʒi] SM INV TV news

'tiglio ['tiʎʎo] SM lime (tree), linden (tree)

'tigna ['tiɲɲa] SF (*Med*) ringworm

ti'grato, -a AG striped

'tigre SF tiger

tilt SM: **andare in ~** (*fig*) to go haywire

tim'ballo SM (*strumento*) kettledrum; (*Cuc*) timbale

tim'brare /72/ VT to stamp; (*annullare: francobolli*) to postmark; **~ il cartellino** to clock in

'timbro SM stamp; (*Mus*) timbre, tone

timi'dezza [timi'dettsa] SF shyness, timidity

'timido, -a AG shy; timid

'timo SM thyme

ti'mone SM (*Naut*) rudder

timoni'ere SM helmsman

timo'rato, -a AG conscientious; **~ di Dio** God-fearing

ti'more SM (*paura*) fear; (*rispetto*) awe; **avere ~ di qc/qn** (*paura*) to be afraid of sth/sb

timo'roso, -a AG timid, timorous

'timpano SM (*Anat*) eardrum; (*Mus*): **timpani** kettledrums, timpani

'tinca, -che SF (*Zool*) tench

ti'nello SM small dining room

'tingere ['tindʒere] /37/ VT to dye

'tino SM vat

ti'nozza [ti'nɔttsa] SF tub

'tinsi *ecc* VB *vedi* **tingere**

'tinta SF (*materia colorante*) dye; (*colore*) colour (BRIT), color (US), shade

tinta'rella SF (*col*) (sun)tan

tintin'nare /72/ VI to tinkle

tintin'nio SM tinkling

'tinto, -a PP *di* **tingere**

tinto'ria SF (*officina*) dyeworks *sg*; (*lavasecco*) dry cleaner's (shop)

tin'tura SF (*operazione*) dyeing; (*colorante*) dye; **~ di iodio** tincture of iodine

'tipico, -a, -ci, -che AG typical

'tipo SM type; (*genere*) kind, type; (*col*) chap, fellow; **che ~ di...?** what kind of ...?; **vestiti di tutti i tipi** all kinds of clothes; **sul ~ di questo** of this sort; **sei un bel ~!** you're a fine one!

tipogra'fia SF typography; (*procedimento*) letterpress (printing); (*officina*) printing house

tipo'grafico, -a, -ci, -che AG typographic(al)

ti'pografo SM typographer

tip 'tap [tip'tap] SM (*ballo*) tap dancing

T.I.R. SIGLA M (= *Transports Internationaux Routiers*) International Heavy Goods Vehicle

'tira e 'molla SM INV tug-of-war

ti'raggio [ti'raddʒo] SM (*di camino ecc*) draught (BRIT), draft (US)

Ti'rana SF Tirana

tiranneggi'are [tiranned'dʒare] /62/ VT to tyrannize

tiran'nia SF tyranny

ti'ranno, -a AG tyrannical ▶ SM tyrant

ti'rante SM (Naut, di tenda ecc) guy; (Edil) brace

tirapi'edi SM INV/F INV hanger-on

tira'pugni [tira'puɲɲi] SM INV knuckle-duster

ti'rare /72/ VT (gen) to pull; (chiudere: tenda ecc) to draw, pull; (tracciare, disegnare) to draw, trace; (lanciare: sasso, palla) to throw; (stampare) to print; (pistola, freccia) to fire; (estrarre): ~ **qc da** to take o pull sth out of; to get sth out of; to extract sth from ▶ VI (pipa, camino) to draw; (vento) to blow; (abito) to be tight; (fare fuoco) to fire; (fare del tiro, Calcio) to shoot; ~ **qn da parte** to take o draw sb aside; ~ **un sospiro (di sollievo)** to heave a sigh (of relief); ~ **a indovinare** to take a guess; ~ **sul prezzo** to bargain; ~ **avanti** vi to struggle on, to keep going; vt (famiglia) to provide for; (: ditta) to look after; ~ **fuori** (estrarre) to take out, pull out; ~ **giù** to pull down; (abbassare) to bring down, to lower; (da scaffale ecc) to take down; ~ **su** to pull up; (capelli) to put up; (fig: bambino) to bring up; **tirar dritto** to keep right on going; ~ **via** (togliere) to take off; **tirarsi indietro** to move back; (fig) to back out; **tirarsi su** to pull o.s. up; (fig) to cheer o.s. up; **tirati su!** cheer up!

ti'rato, -a AG (teso) taut; (fig: teso, stanco) drawn

tira'tore, -trice SM/F gunman(-woman); **un buon** ~ a good shot; ~ **scelto** marksman

tira'tura SF (azione) printing; (di libro) (print) run; (di giornale) circulation

tirchie'ria [tirkje'ria] SF meanness, stinginess

'tirchio, -a ['tirkjo] AG mean, stingy

tiri'tera SF drivel, hot air

'tiro SM shooting no pl, firing no pl; (colpo, sparo) shot; (di palla: lancio) throwing no pl; throw; (fig) trick; **essere a** ~ to be in range; **giocare un brutto** ~ o **un** ~ **mancino a qn** to play a dirty trick on s.b.; **cavallo da** ~ draught (BRIT) o draught (US) horse; ~ **a segno** target shooting; (luogo) shooting range; ~ **con l'arco** archery

tiroci'nante [tirotʃi'nante] AG, SMF apprentice cpd; trainee cpd

tiro'cinio [tiro'tʃinjo] SM apprenticeship; (professionale) training

ti'roide SF thyroid (gland)

tiro'lese AG, SMF Tyrolean, Tyrolese inv

Ti'rolo SM: **il** ~ the Tyrol

tir'rennico, -a, -ci, -che AG Tyrrhenian

Tir'reno SM: **il (mar)** ~ the Tyrrhenian Sea

ti'sana SF herb tea

'tisi SF (Med) consumption

'tisico, -a, -ci, -che AG (Med) consumptive; (fig: gracile) frail ▶ SM/F consumptive (person)

ti'tanico, -a, -ci, -che AG gigantic, enormous

ti'tano SM (Mitologia, fig) titan

tito'lare AG appointed; (sovrano) titular ▶ SMF incumbent; (proprietario) owner; (Calcio) regular player

tito'lato, -a AG (persona) titled

'titolo SM title; (di giornale) headline; (diploma) qualification; (Comm) security; (: azione) share; **a che ~?** for what reason?; **a ~ di amicizia** out of friendship; **a ~ di cronaca** for your information; **a ~ di premio** as a prize; ~ **di credito** share; ~ **obbligazionario** bond; ~ **al portatore** bearer bond; ~ **di proprietà** title deed; **titoli di stato** government securities; **titoli di testa** (Cine) credits

titu'bante AG hesitant, irresolute

tivù SF INV (col) telly (BRIT), TV

'tizio, -a ['tittsjo] SM/F fellow, chap

tiz'zone [tit'tsone] SM brand

T.M.G. ABBR (= tempo medio di Greenwich) GMT

TN SIGLA = **Trento**

TNT SIGLA M (= trinitrotoluolo) TNT

TO SIGLA = **Torino**

toast [toust] SM INV toasted sandwich (generally with ham and cheese)

toc'cante AG touching

toc'care /20/ VT to touch; (tastare) to feel; (fig: riguardare) to concern; (commuovere) to touch, move; (pungere) to hurt, wound; (far cenno a: argomento) to touch on, mention ▶ VI (accadere) to happen to; (spettare) to be up to; **tocca a te difenderci** it's up to you to defend us; **a chi tocca?** whose turn is it?; **mi toccò pagare** I had to pay; ~ **il fondo** (in acqua) to touch the bottom; (fig) to touch rock bottom; ~ **con mano** (fig) to find out for o.s.; ~ **qn sul vivo** to cut sb to the quick

tocca'sana SM INV cure-all, panacea

toccherò ecc [tokke'rɔ] VB vedi **toccare**

'tocco, -chi SM touch; (Arte) stroke, touch

toe'letta SF = **toilette**

'toga, -ghe SF toga; (di magistrato, professore) gown

'togliere ['tɔʎʎere] /122/ VT (rimuovere) to take away (o off), remove; (riprendere, non concedere più) to take away, remove; (Mat) to take away, subtract; (liberare) to free; ~ **qc a qn** to take sth (away) from sb; **ciò non toglie che ...** nevertheless ..., be that as it may ...; **togliersi il cappello** to take off one's hat

'Togo SM: **il** ~ Togo

toi'lette [twa'lɛt] SF INV (gabinetto) toilet; (cosmesi) make-up; (abbigliamento) gown, dress; (mobile) dressing table; **fare** ~ to get made up, make o.s. beautiful

'Tokyo SF Tokyo

to'letta SF = **toilette**

'tolgo ecc VB vedi **togliere**

tolle'rante AG tolerant

tolle'ranza [tolle'rantsa] SF tolerance; **casa di** ~ brothel

tolle'rare /72/ ᴠᴛ to tolerate; **non tollero repli-che** I won't stand for objections; **non sono tol-lerati i ritardi** lateness will not be tolerated

To'losa sF Toulouse

'tolsi *ecc* ᴠʙ *vedi* **togliere**

'tolto, -a ᴘᴘ *di* **togliere**

to'maia sF (*di scarpa*) upper

'tomba sF tomb

tom'bale ᴀɢ: **pietra ~** tombstone, gravestone

tom'bino sᴍ manhole cover

'tombola sF (*gioco*) tombola; (*ruzzolone*) tumble

'tomo sᴍ volume

tomogra'fia sF (*Med*) tomography; **~ assiale computerizzata** computerized axial tomography

'tonaca, -che sF (*Rel*) habit

to'nare /72/ ᴠɪ = **tuonare**

'tondo, -a ᴀɢ round

'tonfo sᴍ splash; (*rumore sordo*) thud; (*caduta*): **fare un ~** to take a tumble

'tonico, -a, -ci, -che ᴀɢ tonic ▶ sᴍ tonic; (*cosmetico*) toner

tonifi'cante ᴀɢ invigorating, bracing

tonifi'care /20/ ᴠᴛ (*muscoli, pelle*) to tone up; (*irro-bustire*) to invigorate, brace

ton'nara sF tuna-fishing nets *pl*

ton'nato, -a ᴀɢ (*Cuc*): **salsa tonnata** tuna fish sauce; **vitello ~** veal with tuna fish sauce

tonnel'laggio [tonnel'laddʒo] sᴍ (*Naut*) ton-nage

tonnel'lata sF ton

'tonno sᴍ tuna (fish)

'tono sᴍ (*gen, Mus*) tone; (: *di pezzo*) key; (*di colore*) shade, tone; **rispondere a ~** (*a proposito*) to answer to the point; (*nello stesso modo*) to answer in kind; (*per le rime*) to answer back

ton'silla sF tonsil

tonsil'lite sF tonsillitis

ton'sura sF tonsure

'tonto, -a ᴀɢ dull, stupid ▶ sᴍ/ꜰ blockhead, dunce; **fare il finto ~** to play dumb

top [tɔp] sᴍ ɪɴᴠ (*vertice, camicetta*) top

to'paia sF (*di topo*) mousehole; (*di ratto*) rat's nest; (*fig: casa ecc*) hovel, dump

to'pazio [to'pattsjo] sᴍ topaz

topi'cida, -i [topi'tʃida] sᴍ rat poison

'topless ['tɔplis] sᴍ ɪɴᴠ topless bathing cos-tume

'topo sᴍ mouse; **~ d'albergo** (*fig*) hotel thief; **~ di biblioteca** (*fig*) bookworm

topogra'fia sF topography

topog'rafico, -a, -ci, -che ᴀɢ topographic, topographical

to'ponimo sᴍ place name

'toppa sF (*serratura*) keyhole; (*pezza*) patch

to'race [to'ratʃe] sᴍ chest

'torba sF peat

'torbido, -a ᴀɢ (*liquido*) cloudy; (*fiume*) muddy; (*fig*) dark; troubled ▶ sᴍ: **pescare nel ~** (*fig*) to fish in troubled waters

'torcere ['tɔrtʃere] /106/ ᴠᴛ to twist; (*biancheria*) to wring (out) ◼ **torcersi** ᴠᴘʀ to twist, writhe; **dare del filo da ~ a qn** to make life *o* things difficult for sb

torchi'are [tor'kjare] /19/ ᴠᴛ to press

'torchio ['tɔrkjo] sᴍ press; **mettere qn sotto il ~** (*fig: col: interrogare*) to grill sb; **~ tipografico** printing press

'torcia, -ce ['tɔrtʃa] sF torch; **~ elettrica** torch (*Brit*), flashlight (*US*)

torci'collo [tortʃi'kɔllo] sᴍ stiff neck

'tordo sᴍ thrush

to'rero sᴍ bullfighter, toreador

tori'nese ᴀɢ of (*o* from) Turin ▶ sᴍꜰ person from Turin

To'rino sF Turin

tor'menta sF snowstorm

tormen'tare /72/ ᴠᴛ to torment ◼ **tormentarsi** ᴠᴘʀ to fret, worry o.s.

tor'mento sᴍ torment

torna'conto sᴍ advantage, benefit

tor'nado sᴍ tornado

tor'nante sᴍ hairpin bend (*Brit*) *o* curve (*US*)

tor'nare /72/ ᴠɪ to return, go (*o* come) back; (*ridi-ventare: anche fig*) to become (again); (*riuscire giusto, esatto: conto*) to work out; (*risultare*) to turn out (to be), prove (to be); **~ al punto di partenza** to start again; **~ a casa** to go (*o* come) home; **i conti tornano** the accounts balance; **~ utile** to prove *o* turn out (to be) useful; **torno a casa martedì** I'm going home on Tuesday

torna'sole sᴍ ɪɴᴠ litmus

tor'neo sᴍ tournament

'tornio sᴍ lathe

tor'nire /55/ ᴠᴛ (*Tecn*) to turn (on a lathe); (*fig*) to shape, polish

tor'nito, -a ᴀɢ (*gambe, caviglie*) well-shaped

'toro sᴍ bull; **T~** Taurus; **essere del T~** to be Taurus

tor'pedine sF torpedo

torpedini'era sF torpedo boat

tor'pore sᴍ torpor

'torre sF tower; (*Scacchi*) rook, castle; **~ di con-trollo** (*Aer*) control tower

torrefazi'one [torrefat'tsjone] sF roasting

torreggi'are [torred'dʒare] /62/ ᴠɪ: **~ (su)** to tower (over)

tor'rente sᴍ torrent

torren'tizio, -a [torren'tittsjo] ᴀɢ torrential

torrenzi'ale [torren'tsjale] ᴀɢ torrential

tor'retta sF turret

'torrido, -a ᴀɢ torrid

t

torri'one SM keep

tor'rone SM nougat

'torsi *ecc* VB *vedi* **torcere**

torsi'one SF twisting; (*Tecn*) torsion

'torso SM torso, trunk; (*Arte*) torso; **a ~ nudo** bare-chested

'torsolo SM (*di cavolo ecc*) stump; (*di frutta*) core

'torta SF cake

tortel'lini SMPL (*Cuc*) tortellini

torti'era SF cake tin (BRIT), cake pan (US)

'torto, -a PP *di* **torcere** ▶ AG (*ritorto*) twisted; (*storto*) twisted, crooked ▶ SM (*ingiustizia*) wrong; (*colpa*) fault; **a ~** wrongly; **a ~ o a ragione** rightly or wrongly; **aver ~** to be wrong; **fare un ~ a qn** to wrong sb; **essere/ passare dalla parte del ~** to be/put o.s. in the wrong; **lui non ha tutti i torti** there's something in what he says

'tortora SF turtle dove

tortu'oso, -a AG (*strada*) twisting; (*fig*) tortuous

tor'tura SF torture

tortu'rare /72/ VT to torture

'torvo, -a AG menacing, grim

tosa'erba SM O F INV (lawn)mower

to'sare /72/ VT (*pecora*) to shear; (*cane*) to clip; (*siepe*) to clip, trim

tosa'tura SF (*di pecore*) shearing; (*di cani*) clipping; (*di siepi*) trimming, clipping

Tos'cana SF: **la ~** Tuscany

tos'cano, -a AG, SM/F Tuscan ▶ SM (*anche:* **sigaro toscano**) strong Italian cigar

'tosse SF cough; **ho la ~** I've got a cough

tossicità [tossitʃi'ta] SF toxicity

'tossico, -a, -ci, -che AG toxic; (*Econ*): **titolo ~** toxic asset

tossicodipen'dente SMF drug addict

tossicodipen'denza [tossikodipen'dɛntsa] SF drug addiction

tossi'comane SMF drug addict

tossicoma'nia SF drug addiction

tos'sina SF toxin

tos'sire /55/ VI to cough

tosta'pane SM INV toaster

tos'tare /72/ VT to toast; (*caffè*) to roast

tosta'tura SF (*di pane*) toasting; (*di caffè*) roasting

'tosto, -a AG: **faccia tosta** cheek ▶ AV at once, immediately; **~ che** as soon as

to'tale AG, SM total

totalità SF: **la ~ di** all of, the total amount (*o* number) of; **the whole** (*+ n sg*)

totali'tario, -a AG totalitarian; (*totale*) complete, total; **adesione totalitaria** complete support

totalita'rismo SM (*Pol*) totalitarianism

totaliz'zare [totalid'dzare] /72/ VT to total; (*Sport: punti*) to score

totalizza'tore [totaliddza'tore] SM (*Tecn*) totalizator; (*Ippica*) totalizator, tote (*col*)

to'tip SM gambling pool betting on horse racing

toto'calcio [toto'kaltʃo] SM gambling pool betting on football results, ≈ (football) pools pl (BRIT)

tou'pet [tu'pɛ] SM INV toupee

tour [tur] SM INV (*giro*) tour; (*Ciclismo*) tour de France

tour de 'force ['tur də 'fɔrs] SM INV (*Sport: anche fig*) tour de force

tour'née [tur'ne] SF tour; **essere in ~** to be on tour

to'vaglia [to'vaʎʎa] SF tablecloth

tovagli'olo [tovaʎ'ʎɔlo] SM napkin

'tozzo, -a ['tɔttso] AG squat ▶ SM: **~ di pane** crust of bread

TP SIGLA = **Trapani**

TR SIGLA = **Terni**

Tr ABBR (*Comm*) = **tratta**

tra PREP (*di due persone, cose*) between; (*di più persone, cose*) among(st); (*tempo: entro*) within, in; **prendere qn ~ le braccia** to take sb in one's arms; **litigano ~ (di) loro** they're fighting amongst themselves; **~ 5 giorni** in 5 days' time; **~ breve** *o* **poco** soon; **~ sé e sé** (*parlare ecc*) to oneself; **sia detto ~ noi ...** between you and me ...; **~ una cosa e l'altra** what with one thing and another

---

Tra si traduce con **among** quando ci sono più di due persone.
tra amici **among friends**
Si usa **between** quando ci sono solo due persone o cose o quando si condivide qualcosa in un gruppo.
tra Roma e Milano **between Rome and Milan**
Ci siamo divisi i soldi tra noi quattro. **We split the money between the four of us.**

---

trabal'lante AG shaky

trabal'lare /72/ VI to stagger, totter

tra'biccolo SM (*peg: auto*) old banger (BRIT), jalopy

traboc'care /20/ VI to overflow

traboc'chetto [trabok'ketto] SM (*fig*) trap ▶ AG INV trap cpd; **domanda ~** trick question

traca'gnotto, -a [trakaɲ'ɲɔtto] AG dumpy ▶ SM/F dumpy person

tracan'nare /72/ VT to gulp down

'traccia, -ce ['trattʃa] SF (*segno, striscia*) trail, track; (*orma*) tracks pl; (*residuo, testimonianza*) trace, sign; (*abbozzo*) outline; **essere sulle tracce di qn** to be on sb's trail

tracci'are [trat'tʃare] /14/ VT to trace, mark (out); (*disegnare*) to draw; (*fig: abbozzare*) to outline; **~ un quadro della situazione** to outline the situation

tracci'ato [trat't∫ato] SM (grafico) layout, plan; ~ **di gara** (Sport) race route

tra'chea [tra'kɛa] SF windpipe, trachea

tra'colla SF shoulder strap; **portare qc a** ~ to carry sth over one's shoulder; **borsa a** ~ shoulder bag

tra'collo SM (fig) collapse, ruin; ~ **finanziario** crash; **avere un** ~ (Med) to have a setback; (Comm) to collapse

traco'tante AG overbearing, arrogant

traco'tanza [trako'tantsa] SF arrogance

trad. ABBR = **traduzione**

tradi'mento SM betrayal; (Dir, Mil) treason; **a** ~ by surprise; **alto** ~ high treason

tra'dire /55/ VT to betray; (coniuge) to be unfaithful to; (doveri: mancare) to fail in; (rivelare) to give away, reveal; **ha tradito le attese di tutti** he let everyone down

tradi'tore, -trice SM/F traitor

tradizio'nale [tradittsjo'nale] AG traditional

tradizi'one [tradit'tsjone] SF tradition

tra'dotto, -a PP di **tradurre** ▶ SF (Mil) troop train

tra'durre /90/ VT to translate; (spiegare) to render, convey; (Dir): ~ **qn in carcere/tribunale** to take sb to prison/court; ~ **in cifre** to put into figures; ~ **in atto** (fig) to put into effect

tradut'tore, -'trice SM/F translator

traduzi'one [tradut'tsjone] SF translation; (Dir) transfer

'trae VB vedi **trarre**

tra'ente SMF (Econ) drawer

trafe'lato, -a AG out of breath

traffi'cante SMF dealer; (peg) trafficker

traffi'care /20/ VI (affaccendarsi) to busy o.s.; (commerciare): ~ **(in)** to trade (in), deal (in) ▶ VT (peg) to traffic in

traffi'cato, -a AG (strada, zona) busy

'traffico, -ci SM traffic; (commercio) trade, traffic; ~ **aereo/ferroviario** air/rail traffic; ~ **di armi/droga** arms/drug trafficking; ~ **stradale** traffic

tra'figgere [tra'fiddʒere] **/104/** VT to run through, stab; (fig) to pierce

tra'fila SF procedure

trafi'letto SM (di giornale) short article

tra'fitto, -a PP di **trafiggere**

trafo'rare /72/ VT to bore, drill

tra'foro SM (azione) boring, drilling; (galleria) tunnel

trafu'gare /80/ VT to purloin

tra'gedia [tra'dʒɛdja] SF tragedy

'traggo ecc VB vedi **trarre**

traghet'tare [traget'tare] **/72/** VT to ferry

tra'ghetto [tra'getto] SM crossing; (barca) ferry(boat)

tragicità [tradʒit∫i'ta] SF tragedy

'tragico, -a, -ci, -che ['tradʒiko] AG tragic ▶ SM/F (autore) tragedian; **prendere tutto sul** ~ (fig) to take everything far too seriously

tragi'comico, -a, -ci, -che [tradʒi'kɔmiko] AG tragicomic

tra'gitto [tra'dʒitto] SM (passaggio) crossing; (viaggio) journey

tragu'ardo SM (Sport) finishing line; (fig) goal, aim

'trai ecc VB vedi **trarre**

traiet'toria SF trajectory

trai'nante AG (cavo, fune) towing; (fig: persona, settore) driving

trai'nare /72/ VT to drag, haul; (rimorchiare) to tow

'training ['treinin] SM INV training

'traino SM (carro) wagon; (slitta) sledge; (carico) load

tralasci'are [trala∫'∫are] **/14/** VT (studi) to neglect; (dettagli) to leave out, omit

'tralcio ['tralt∫o] SM (Bot) shoot

tra'liccio [tra'litt∫o] SM (tela) ticking; (struttura) trellis; (Elettr) pylon

tram SM INV tram (BRIT), streetcar (US)

'trama SF (filo) weft, woof; (fig: argomento, maneggio) plot

traman'dare /72/ VT to pass on, hand down

tra'mare /72/ VT (fig) to scheme, plot

tram'busto SM turmoil

trames'tio SM bustle

tramez'zino [tramed'dzino] SM sandwich

tra'mezzo [tra'mɛddzo] SM partition

'tramite PREP through ▶ SM means pl; **agire/fare da** ~ to act as/be a go-between

tramon'tana SF (Meteor) north wind

tramon'tare /72/ VI to set, go down

tra'monto SM setting; (del sole) sunset

tramor'tire /55/ VI to faint ▶ VT to stun

trampo'lino SM (per tuffi) springboard, diving board; (per lo sci) ski-jump

'trampolo SM stilt

tramu'tare /72/ VT: ~ **in** to change into

trance [tra:ns] SF INV (di medium) trance; **cadere in** ~ to fall into a trance

'trancia, -ce ['trant∫a] SF slice; (cesoia) shearing machine

tranci'are [tran't∫are] **/14/** VT (Tecn) to shear

'trancio ['trant∫o] SM slice

tra'nello SM trap; **tendere un** ~ **a qn** to set a trap for sb; **cadere in un** ~ to fall into a trap

trangugi'are [trangu'dʒare] **/62/** VT to gulp down

'tranne PREP except (for), but (for); ~ **che** cong unless; **tutti i giorni** ~ **il venerdì** every day except o with the exception of Friday

tranquil'lante SM (*Med*) tranquillizer

tranquillità SF calm, stillness; quietness; peace of mind

tranquilliz'zare [trankwillid'dzare] /**72**/ VT to reassure

tran'quillo, -a AG calm, quiet; (*bambino, scolaro*) quiet; (*sereno*) with one's mind at rest; **sta' ~** don't worry

transat'lantico, -a, -ci, -che AG transatlantic ▶ SM transatlantic liner; (*Pol*) *corridor used as a meeting place by members of the lower chamber of the Italian Parliament*

tran'satto, -a PP *di* **transigere**

transazi'one [transat'tsjone] SF compromise; (*Dir*) settlement; (*Comm*) transaction, deal

tran'senna SF barrier

tran'setto SM transept

trans'genico, -a, -ci, -che [trans'dʒɛniko] AG genetically modified, GM; **pianta transgenica** GM crop; **cibo ~** GM food

transiberi'ano, -a AG trans-Siberian

tran'sigere [tran'sidʒere] /**47**/ VI (*Dir*) to reach a settlement; (*venire a patti*) to compromise, come to an agreement

tran'sistor SM INV, **transis'tore** SM transistor

transi'tabile AG passable

transi'tare /**72**/ VI to pass

transi'tivo, -a AG transitive

'transito SM transit; **di ~** (*merci*) in transit; (*stazione*) transit cpd; **"divieto di ~"** "no entry"; **"~ interrotto"** "road closed"

transi'torio, -a AG transitory, transient; (*provvisorio*) provisional

transizi'one [transit'tsjone] SF transition

tran 'tran SM routine; **il solito ~** the same old routine

tran'via SF tramway (BRIT), streetcar line (US)

tranvi'ario, -a AG tram cpd (BRIT), streetcar cpd (US); **linea tranviaria** tramline, streetcar line

tranvi'ere SM (*conducente*) tram driver (BRIT), streetcar driver (US); (*bigliettaio*) tram *o* streetcar conductor

trapa'nare /**72**/ VT (*Tecn*) to drill

'trapano SM (*utensile*) drill; (*Med*) trepan

trapas'sare /**72**/ VT to pierce

trapas'sato SM (*Ling*) past perfect

tra'passo SM passage; **~ di proprietà** (*di case*) conveyancing; (*di auto ecc*) legal transfer

trape'lare /**72**/ VI to leak, drip; (*fig*) to leak out

tra'pezio [tra'pɛttsjo] SM (*Mat*) trapezium; (*attrezzo ginnico*) trapeze

trape'zista, -i, -e [trapet'tsista] SM/F trapeze artist

trapian'tare /**72**/ VT to transplant

trapi'anto SM transplanting; (*Med*) transplant; **~ cardiaco** heart transplant

'trappola SF trap

tra'punta SF quilt

'trarre /**123**/ VT to draw, pull; (*portare*) to take; (*prendere, tirare fuori*) to take (out), draw; (*derivare*) to obtain; **~ beneficio** *o* **profitto da qc** to benefit from sth; **~ le conclusioni** to draw one's own conclusions; **~ esempio da qn** to follow sb's example; **~ guadagno** to make a profit; **~ qn d'impaccio** to get sb out of an awkward situation; **~ origine da qc** to have its origins *o* originate in sth; **~ in salvo** to rescue

trasa'lire /**55**/ VI to start, jump

trasan'dato, -a AG shabby

trasbor'dare /**72**/ VT to transfer; (*Naut*) to tran(s)ship ▶ VI (*Naut*) to change ship; (*Aer*) to change plane; (*Ferr*) to change (trains)

trascenden'tale [traʃʃenden'tale] AG transcendental

tra'scendere [traʃ'ʃendere] /**101**/ VT (*Filosofia, Rel*) to transcend; (*fig: superare*) to surpass, go beyond

tra'sceso, -a [traʃ'ʃeso] PP *di* **trascendere**

trasci'nare [traʃʃi'nare] /**72**/ VT to drag ■ **trascinarsi** VPR to drag o.s. along; (*fig*) to drag on

tras'correre /**28**/ VT (*tempo*) to spend, pass ▶ VI to pass

tras'corso, -a PP *di* **trascorrere** ▶ AG past ▶ SM mistake

tras'critto, -a PP *di* **trascrivere**

tras'crivere /**105**/ VT to transcribe

trascrizi'one [traskrit'tsjone] SF transcription

trascu'rare /**72**/ VT to neglect; (*non considerare*) to disregard

trascura'tezza [traskura'tettsa] SF carelessness, negligence

trascu'rato, -a AG (*casa*) neglected; (*persona*) careless, negligent

traseco'lato, -a AG astounded, amazed

trasferi'mento SM transfer; (*trasloco*) removal, move; **~ di chiamata** (*Tel*) call forwarding

trasfe'rire /**55**/ VT to transfer ■ **trasferirsi** VPR to move

tras'ferta SF transfer; (*indennità*) travelling expenses pl; (*Sport*) away game

trasfigu'rare /**72**/ VT to transfigure

trasfor'mare /**72**/ VT to transform, change ■ **trasformarsi** VPR to be transformed; **trasformarsi in qc** to turn into sth

trasforma'tore SM (*Elettr*) transformer

trasformazi'one [trasformat'tsjone] SF transformation

trasfusi'one SF (*Med*) transfusion

trasgre'dire /**55**/ VT to break, infringe; (*ordini*) to disobey, contravene

trasgressi'one SF breaking, infringement; disobeying

trasgres'sivo, -a AG (*personaggio, atteggiamento*) rule-breaking

trasgres'sore, trasgredi'trice [trazgred-i'tritʃe] SM/F (*Dir*) transgressor

tras'lato, -a AG metaphorical, figurative

traslo'care /20/ VT to move, transfer ■ **traslocarsi** VPR to move

tras'loco, -chi SM removal

tras'messo, -a PP *di* **trasmettere**

tras'mettere /63/ VT (*passare*): **~ qc a qn** to pass sth on to sb; (*mandare*) to send; (*Tecn, Tel, Med*) to transmit; (*TV, Radio*) to broadcast

trasmetti'tore SM transmitter

trasmissi'one SF (*gen, Fisica, Tecn*) transmission; (*passaggio*) transmission, passing on; (*TV, Radio*) broadcast

trasmit'tente SF transmitting *o* broadcasting station

traso'gnato, -a [trasoɲ'ɲato] AG dreamy

traspa'rente AG transparent

traspa'renza [traspa'rɛntsa] SF transparency; **guardare qc in ~** to look at sth against the light

traspa'rire /112/ VI to show (through)

tras'parso, -a PP *di* **trasparire**

traspi'rare /72/ VI to perspire; (*fig*) to come to light, leak out

traspirazi'one [traspirat'tsjone] SF perspiration

tras'porre /77/ VT to transpose

traspor'tare /72/ VT to carry, move; (*merce*) to transport, convey; **lasciarsi ~ (da qc)** (*fig*) to let o.s. be carried away (by sth)

tras'porto SM transport; (*fig*) rapture, passion; **con ~** passionately; **compagnia di ~** carriers *pl*; (*per strada*) hauliers *pl* (*BRIT*), haulers *pl* (*US*); **mezzi di ~** means of transport; **nave/aereo da ~** transport ship/aircraft *inv*; **~ (funebre)** funeral procession; **~ marittimo/aereo** sea/air transport; **~ stradale** (road) haulage; **i trasporti pubblici** public transport

tras'posto, -a PP *di* **trasporre**

'trassi *ecc* VB *vedi* **trarre**

trastul'lare /72/ VT to amuse ■ **trastullarsi** VPR to amuse o.s.

tras'tullo SM game

trasu'dare /72/ VI (*filtrare*) to ooze; (*sudare*) to sweat ▶ VT to ooze with

trasver'sale AG (*taglio, sbarra*) cross(-); (*retta*) transverse; running at right angles; **via ~** side street

trasvo'lare /72/ VT to fly over

'tratta SF (*Econ*) draft; **la ~ delle bianche** the white slave trade; **~ documentaria** documentary bill of exchange

tratta'mento SM treatment; (*servizio*) service; **ricevere un buon ~** (*cliente*) to get good service; **~ di bellezza** beauty treatment; **~ di fine rapporto** (*Comm*) severance pay

trat'tare /72/ VT (*gen*) to treat; (*commerciare*) to deal in; (*svolgere: argomento*) to discuss, deal with; (*negoziare*) to negotiate ▶ VI: **~ di** to deal with; **~ con** (*persona*) to deal with; **si tratta di ...** it's about ...; **si tratterebbe solo di poche ore** it would just be a matter of a few hours

tratta'tiva SF negotiation ■ **trattative** SFPL (*tra governi, stati*) talks; **essere in ~ con** to be in negotiation with

trat'tato SM (*testo*) treatise; (*accordo*) treaty; **~ commerciale** trade agreement; **~ di pace** peace treaty

trattazi'one [trattat'tsjone] SF treatment

tratteggi'are [tratted'dʒare] /62/ VT (*disegnare: a tratti*) to sketch, outline; (*: col tratteggio*) to hatch

trat'teggio [trat'teddʒo] SM hatching

tratte'nere /121/ VT (*far rimanere: persona*) to detain; (*intrattenere: ospiti*) to entertain; (*tenere, frenare, reprimere*) to hold back, keep back; (*astenersi dal consegnare*) to hold, keep; (*detrarre: somma*) to deduct ■ **trattenersi** VPR (*astenersi*) to restrain o.s., stop o.s.; (*soffermarsi*) to stay, remain; **sono stato trattenuto in ufficio** I was delayed at the office

tratteni'mento SM entertainment; (*festa*) party

tratte'nuta SF deduction

trat'tino SM dash; (*in parole composte*) hyphen

'tratto, -a PP *di* **trarre** ▶ SM (*di penna, matita*) stroke; (*parte*) part, piece; (*di strada*) stretch; (*di mare, cielo*) expanse; (*di tempo*) period (of time) ■ **tratti** SMPL (*caratteristiche*) features; (*modo di*) ways, manners; **a un ~, d'un ~** suddenly

trat'tore SM tractor

tratto'ria SF (small) restaurant

'trauma, -i SM trauma; **~ cranico** concussion

trau'matico, -a, -ci, -che AG traumatic

traumatiz'zare [traumatid'dzare] /72/ VT (*Med*) to traumatize; (*fig: impressionare*) to shock

tra'vaglio [tra'vaʎʎo] SM (*angoscia*) pain, suffering; (*Med*) pains *pl*; **~ di parto** labour pains

trava'sare /72/ VT to pour; (*vino*) to decant

tra'vaso SM pouring; decanting

trava'tura SF beams *pl*

'trave SF beam

tra'veggole SFPL: **avere le ~** to be seeing things

tra'versa SF (*trave*) crosspiece; (*via*) sidestreet; (*Ferr*) sleeper (*BRIT*), (railroad) tie (*US*); (*Calcio*) crossbar

traver'sare /72/ VT to cross

traver'sata SF crossing; (*Aer*) flight, trip

traver'sie SFPL mishaps, misfortunes

traver'sina SF (*Ferr*) sleeper (*BRIT*), (railroad) tie (*US*)

tra'verso, -a AG oblique; **di ~** *ag* askew ▶ AV sideways; **andare di ~** (*cibo*) to go down the

385

wrong way; **messo di** ~ sideways on; **guardare di** ~ to look askance at; **via traversa** side road; **ottenere qc per vie traverse** (*fig*) to obtain sth in an underhand way

travesti'mento SM disguise

traves'tire /45/ VT to disguise ■ **travestirsi** VPR to disguise o.s.

traves'tito SM transvestite

travi'are /19/ VT (*fig*) to lead astray

travi'sare /72/ VT (*fig*) to distort, misrepresent

travol'gente [travol'dʒɛnte] AG overwhelming

tra'volgere [tra'vɔldʒere] /96/ VT to sweep away, carry away; (*fig*) to overwhelm

tra'volto, -a PP di **travolgere**

trazi'one [trat'tsjone] SF traction; ~ **anteriore/posteriore** (*Aut*) front-wheel/rear-wheel drive

tre NUM three

tre'alberi SM INV (*Naut*) three-master

'trebbia SF (*Agr: operazione*) threshing; (: *stagione*) threshing season

trebbi'are /19/ VT to thresh

trebbia'trice [trebbja'tritʃe] SF threshing machine

trebbia'tura SF threshing

'treccia, -ce ['trettʃa] SF plait, braid; **lavorato a trecce** (*pullover ecc*) cable-knit

trecen'tesco, -a, -schi, -sche [tretʃen'tesko] AG fourteenth-century

tre'cento [tre'tʃento] NUM three hundred ▶ SM: **il T~** the fourteenth century

tredi'cenne [tredi'tʃɛnne] AG, SMF thirteen-year-old

tredi'cesimo, -a [tredi'tʃɛzimo] NUM thirteenth ▶ SF *Christmas bonus of a month's pay*

'tredici ['treditʃi] NUM thirteen ▶ SM INV: **fare ~** (*Totocalcio*) to win the pools (*Brit*)

'tregua SF truce; (*fig*) respite; **senza ~** non-stop, without stopping, uninterruptedly

tre'mante AG trembling, shaking

tre'mare /72/ VI to tremble, shake; ~ **di** (*freddo ecc*) to shiver o tremble with; (*paura, rabbia*) to shake o tremble with

trema'rella SF shivers pl

tre'mendo, -a AG terrible, awful

tremen'tina SF turpentine

tre'mila NUM three thousand

'tremito SM trembling no pl; shaking no pl; shivering no pl

tremo'lare /72/ VI to tremble; (*luce*) to flicker; (*foglie*) to quiver

tremo'lio SM (*vedi vi*) tremble; flicker; quiver

tre'more SM tremor

'treno SM train; (*Aut*): ~ **di gomme** set of tyres (*Brit*) o tires (*US*); ~ **locale/diretto/espresso** local/fast/express train; ~ **merci** goods (*Brit*) o

freight train; ~ **rapido** express (train) (*for which supplement must be paid*); ~ **straordinario** special train; ~ **viaggiatori** passenger train; *see note*

There are several different types of train in Italy. *Intercity* (IC) and *Eurocity* (EC) trains and *espressi* (E) operate on the long-distance main lines and provide a night service. Of the high-speed trains, the *Frecciarossa* and the ultramodern *Italo* trains, which are owned by the private company NTV, run between the major cities. *Frecciargento* trains provide a high- or normal-speed service and *Frecciabianca* trains offer a normal-speed service. *Regionali* (R) are local trains which stop at every small town and village within regional boundaries.

'trenta NUM thirty ▶ SM INV (*Ins*): ~ **e lode** full marks plus distinction o cum laude

tren'tenne AG, SMF thirty-year-old

tren'tennio SM period of thirty years

tren'tesimo, -a NUM thirtieth

tren'tina SF: **una ~ (di)** thirty or so, about thirty

tren'tino, -a AG of (o from) Trento

trepi'dante AG anxious

trepi'dare /72/ VI to be anxious; ~ **per qn** to be anxious about sb

'trepido, -a AG anxious

treppi'ede SM tripod; (*Cuc*) trivet

tre'quarti SM INV three-quarter-length coat

'tresca, -sche SF (*fig*) intrigue; (: *relazione amorosa*) affair

'trespolo SM trestle

trevigi'ano, -a [trevi'dʒano] AG of (o from) Treviso

triango'lare AG triangular

tri'angolo SM triangle

tribo'lare /72/ VI (*patire*) to suffer; (*fare fatica*) to have a lot of trouble

tribolazi'one [tribolat'tsjone] SF suffering, tribulation

tri'bordo SM (*Naut*) starboard

tribù SF INV tribe

tri'buna SF (*podio*) platform; (*in aule ecc*) gallery; (*di stadio*) stand; ~ **della stampa/riservata al pubblico** press/public gallery

tribu'nale SM court; **presentarsi** o **comparire in** ~ to appear in court; ~ **militare** military tribunal; ~ **supremo** supreme court

tribu'tare /72/ VT to bestow; ~ **gli onori dovuti a qn** to pay tribute to sb

tribu'tario, -a AG (*imposta*) fiscal, tax cpd; (*Geo*): **essere ~ di** to be a tributary of

tri'buto SM tax; (*fig*) tribute

tri'checo, -chi [tri'kɛko] SM (*Zool*) walrus

tri'ciclo [tri'tʃiklo] SM tricycle

trico'lore AG three-coloured (*Brit*), three-colored (US) ▶ SM tricolo(u)r; (*bandiera italiana*) Italian flag

tri'dente SM trident

trien'nale AG (*che dura 3 anni*) three-year *cpd*; (*che avviene ogni 3 anni*) three-yearly

tri'ennio SM period of three years

tries'tino, -a AG of (*o from*) Trieste

tri'fase AG (*Elettr*) three-phase

tri'foglio [tri'fɔʎʎo] SM clover

trifo'lato, -a AG (*Cuc*) cooked in oil, garlic and parsley

'triglia ['triʎʎa] SF red mullet

trigonome'tria SF trigonometry

tril'lare /72/ VI (*Mus*) to trill

'trillo SM trill

tri'mestre SM period of three months; (*Ins*) term, quarter (*US*); (*Comm*) quarter

trimo'tore SM (*Aer*) three-engined plane

'trina SF lace

trin'cea [trin'tʃea] SF trench

trince'rare [trintʃe'rare] /72/ VT to entrench

trinci'are [trin'tʃare] /14/ VT to cut up

'Trinidad SM: ~ e Tobago Trinidad and Tobago

Trinità SF (*Rel*) Trinity

'trio (*pl* **trii**) SM trio

trion'fale AG triumphal, triumphant

trion'fante AG triumphant

trion'fare /72/ VI to triumph, win; ~ su to triumph over, overcome

tri'onfo SM triumph

tripli'care /20/ VT to triple

'triplice ['triplitʃe] AG triple; in ~ copia in triplicate

'triplo, -a AG triple; treble ▶ SM: il ~ (di) three times as much (as); la spesa è tripla it costs three times as much

'tripode SM tripod

'Tripoli SF Tripoli

'trippa SF (*Cuc*) tripe

tri'pudio SM triumph, jubilation; (*fig: di colori*) galaxy

tris SM INV (*Carte*): ~ d'assi/di re *ecc* three aces/kings *etc*

'triste AG sad; (*luogo*) dreary, gloomy

tris'tezza [tris'tettsa] SF sadness; gloominess

'tristo, -a AG (*cattivo*) wicked, evil; (*meschino*) sorry, poor

trita'carne SM INV mincer, grinder (*US*)

trita'ghiaccio [trita'gjattʃo] SM INV ice crusher

tri'tare /72/ VT to mince, grind (*US*)

trita'tutto SM INV mincer, grinder (*US*)

'trito, -a AG (*tritato*) minced, ground (*US*); ~ e ritrito (*idee, argomenti, frasi*) trite, hackneyed

'tritolo SM trinitrotoluene

tri'tone SM (*Zool*) newt

'trittico, -ci SM (*Arte*) triptych

tritu'rare /72/ VT to grind

tri'vella SF drill

trivel'lare /72/ VT to drill

trivellazi'one [trivellat'tsjone] SF drilling; torre di ~ derrick

trivi'ale AG vulgar, low

trivialità SF INV (*volgarità*) coarseness, crudeness; (*: osservazione*) coarse *o* crude remark

tro'feo SM trophy

'trogolo SM (*per maiali*) trough

'troia SF (*Zool*) sow; (*fig: peg*) whore(!)

troll [trɔl] SM INV (*anche Internet*) troll

'tromba SF (*Mus*) trumpet; (*Aut*) horn; ~ d'aria whirlwind; ~ delle scale stairwell

trombet'tista, -i, -e SM/F trumpeter, trumpet (player)

trom'bone SM trombone

trom'bosi SF thrombosis

tron'care /20/ VT to cut off; (*spezzare*) to break off

'tronco, -a, -chi, -che AG cut off; broken off; (*Ling*) truncated; (*fig*) cut short ▶ SM (*Bot, Anat*) trunk; (*fig: tratto*) section; (*: pezzo: di lancia*) stump; licenziare qn in ~ (*fig*) to fire sb on the spot

troneggi'are [troned'dʒare] /62/ VI: ~ (su) to tower (over)

'tronfio, -a AG conceited

'trono SM throne

tropi'cale AG tropical

'tropico, -ci SM tropic; ~ del Cancro/Capricorno Tropic of Cancer/Capricorn; i tropici the tropics

---

'troppo, -a

DET (*in eccesso: quantità*) too much; (*: numero*) too many; ho messo troppo zucchero I put too much sugar in; c'era troppa gente there were too many people; fa troppo caldo it's too hot

▶ PRON (*in eccesso: quantità*) too much; (*: numero*) too many; ne hai messo troppo you've put in too much; meglio troppi che pochi better too many than too few

▶ AV (*eccessivamente: con ag, av*) too; (*: con vb*) too much; troppo amaro/tardi too bitter/late; lavora troppo he works too much; costa troppo it costs too much; troppo buono da parte tua! (*anche ironico*) you're too kind!; di troppo too much; too many; qualche tazza di troppo a few cups too many; 5 euro di troppo 5 euros too much; essere di troppo to be in the way

---

'trota SF trout

trot'tare /72/ VI to trot

trotterel'lare /72/ VI to trot along; (*bambino*) to toddle '**trotto** SM trot

'**trottola** SF spinning top

tro'**vare** /72/ VT to find; (*giudicare*): **trovo che** I find o think that ▪ **trovarsi** VPR (*reciproco: incontrarsi*) to meet; (*essere, stare*) to be; (*arrivare, capitare*) to find o.s.; **andare a ~ qn** to go and see sb; **~ qn colpevole** to find sb guilty; **trovo giusto/sbagliato che ...** I think/don't think it's right that ...; **trovarsi bene/male** (*in un luogo, con qn*) to get on well/badly; **trovarsi d'accordo con qn** to be in agreement with sb

tro'**vata** SF good idea; **~ pubblicitaria** advertising gimmick

trova'**tello, -a** SM/F foundling

truc'**care** /20/ VT (*falsare*) to fake; (*attore ecc*) to make up; (*travestire*) to disguise; (*Sport*) to fix; (*Aut*) to soup up ▪ **truccarsi** VPR to make up (one's face)

trucca'**tore, -'trice** SM/F (*Cine, Teat*) make-up artist

'**trucco, -chi** SM trick; (*cosmesi*) make-up; **i trucchi del mestiere** the tricks of the trade

'**truce** ['trutʃe] AG fierce

truci'**dare** [trutʃi'dare] /72/ VT to slaughter

'**truciolo** ['trutʃolo] SM shaving

'**truffa** SF fraud, swindle

truf'**fare** /72/ VT to swindle, cheat

truffa'**tore, -'trice** SM/F swindler, cheat

'**truppa** SF troop

TS SIGLA = **Trieste**

tu PRON you; **tu stesso(a)** you yourself; **dare del tu a qn** to address sb as "tu"; **trovarsi a tu per tu con qn** to find o.s. face to face with sb

'**tua** *vedi* **tuo**

'**tuba** SF (*Mus*) tuba; (*cappello*) top hat

tu'**bare** /72/ VI to coo

tuba'**tura, tubazi'one** [tubat'tsjone] SF piping *no pl*, pipes *pl*

tuberco'**losi** SF tuberculosis

'**tubero** SM (*Bot*) tuber

tu'**betto** SM tube

tu'**bino** SM (*cappello*) bowler (BRIT), derby (US); (*abito da donna*) sheath dress

'**tubo** SM tube; (*per conduttore*) pipe; **~ digerente** (*Anat*) alimentary canal, digestive tract; **~ di scappamento** (*Aut*) exhaust pipe

tubo'**lare** AG tubular ▶ SM tubeless tyre (BRIT) o tire (US)

'**tue** *vedi* **tuo**

tuf'**fare** /72/ VT to plunge; (*intingere*) to dip ▪ **tuffarsi** VPR to plunge, dive

tuffa'**tore, -'trice** SM/F (*Sport*) diver

'**tuffo** SM dive; (*breve bagno*) dip

tu'**gurio** SM hovel

tuli'**pano** SM tulip

'**tulle** SM (*tessuto*) tulle

tume'**fare** /42/ VT to cause to swell ▪ **tumefarsi** VPR to swell

'**tumido, -a** AG swollen

tu'**more** SM (*Med*) tumour (BRIT), tumor (US)

tumulazi'**one** [tumulat'tsjone] SF burial

tu'**multo** SM uproar, commotion; (*sommossa*) riot; (*fig*) turmoil

tumultu'**oso, -a** AG rowdy, unruly; (*fig*) turbulent, stormy

tungs'**teno** SM tungsten

'**tunica, -che** SF tunic

'**Tunisi** SF Tunis

Tuni'**sia** SF: **la ~** Tunisia

tuni'**sino, -a** AG, SM/F Tunisian

'**tunnel** SM INV tunnel

'**tuo** (*f* **tua**, *pl* **tue, tuoi**) DET: **il ~, la tua** *ecc* your ▶ PRON: **il ~, la tua** *ecc* yours ▶ SM: **hai speso del ~?** did you spend your own money? ▶ SF: **la tua** (*opinione*) your view; **i tuoi** (*genitori, famiglia*) your family; **una tua amica** a friend of yours; **è dalla tua** he is on your side; **alla tua!** (*brindisi*) your health!; **ne hai fatta una delle tue!** (*sciocchezze*) you've done it again!

tuo'**nare** /72/ VI to thunder; **tuona** it is thundering, there's some thunder

tu'**ono** SM thunder

tu'**orlo** SM yolk

tu'**racciolo** [tu'rattʃolo] SM cap, top; (*di sughero*) cork

tu'**rare** /72/ VT to stop, plug; (*con sughero*) to cork; **turarsi il naso** to hold one's nose

'**turba** SF (*folla*) crowd, throng; (*: peg*) mob ▪ **turbe** SFPL disorder(s); **soffrire di turbe psichiche** to suffer from a mental disorder

turba'**mento** SM disturbance; (*di animo*) anxiety, agitation

tur'**bante** SM turban

tur'**bare** /72/ VT to disturb, trouble; **~ la quiete pubblica** (*Dir*) to disturb the peace

tur'**bato, -a** AG upset; (*preoccupato, ansioso*) anxious

tur'**bina** SF turbine; **~ eolica** wind turbine

turbi'**nare** /72/ VI to whirl

'**turbine** SM whirlwind; **~ di neve** swirl of snow; **~ di polvere/sabbia** dust/sandstorm

turbi'**noso, -a** AG (*vento, danza ecc*) whirling

turbo'**lento, -a** AG turbulent; (*ragazzo*) boisterous, unruly

turbo'**lenza** [turbo'lentsa] SF turbulence

turboreat'**tore** SM turbojet engine

tur'**chese** [tur'kese] AG, SM, F turquoise

Tur'chia [tur'kia] SF: **la ~** Turkey

tur'**chino, -a** [tur'kino] AG deep blue

'**turco, -a, -chi, -che** AG Turkish ▶ SM/F Turk (Turkish woman) ▶ SM (*Ling*) Turkish; **parlare ~** (*fig*) to talk double Dutch

'turgido, -a ['turdʒido] AG swollen

tu'rismo SM tourism; tourist industry; **~ ses-suale** sex tourism

tu'rista, -i, -e SM/F tourist

tu'ristico, -a, -ci, -che AG tourist *cpd*

tur'nista, -i, -e SM/F shift worker

'turno SM turn; *(di lavoro)* shift; **di ~** *(soldato, medico, custode)* on duty; **a ~** *(rispondere)* in turn; *(lavorare)* in shifts; **fare a ~ a fare qc** to take turns to do sth; **è il suo ~** it's your (*o* his *etc*) turn

'turpe AG filthy, vile

turpi'loquio SM obscene language

'tuta SF (*Dir*: *di minore*) overalls *pl*; *(Sport)* tracksuit; **~ mimetica** *(Mil)* camouflage clothing; **~ spaziale** space-suit; **~ subacquea** wetsuit

tu'tela SF (*Dir*: *di minore*) guardianship; (: *prote-zione*) protection; *(difesa)* defence (BRIT), defense (US); **~ dell'ambiente** environmental protec-tion; **~ del consumatore** consumer protection

tute'lare /72/ VT to protect, defend ▶ AG *(Dir)*: **giudice ~** *judge with responsibility for guardianship cases*

'Tutor® ['tutor] SM INV *(Aut)* speed monitoring system

tu'tore, -'trice SM/F *(Dir)* guardian

tutta'via CONG nevertheless, yet

'tutto, -a

DET **1**(*intero*) all; **tutto il latte** all the milk; **tutta la notte** all night, the whole night; **tutto il libro** the whole book; **tutta una bottiglia** a whole bottle; **in tutto il mondo** all over the world

2 (*pl, collettivo*) all; every; **tutti i libri** all the books; **tutte le notti** every night; **tutti i venerdì** every Friday; **tutti gli uomini** all the men; (*collettivo*) all men; **tutto l'anno** all year long; **tutte le volte che** every time (that); **tutti e due** both *o* each of us (*o* them *o* you); **tutti e cinque** all five of us (*o* them *o* you)

3 (*completamente*): **era tutta sporca** she was all dirty; **tremava tutto** he was trembling all over; **è tutta sua madre** she's just *o* exactly like her mother

4: **a tutt'oggi** so far, up till now; **a tutta velo-cità** at full *o* top speed

▶ PRON **1** (*ogni cosa*) everything, all; (*qualsiasi cosa*) anything; **ha mangiato tutto** he's eaten everything; **dimmi tutto** tell me all about it; **tutto compreso** all included, all-in (BRIT); **tutto considerato** all things consid-ered; **con tutto che** (*malgrado*) although; **del tutto** completely; **100 euro in tutto** 100 euros in all; **in tutto eravamo 50** there were 50 of us in all; **in tutto e per tutto** com-pletely; **il che è tutto dire** and that's saying a lot

2: **tutti, -e** (*ognuno*) all, everybody; **vengono tutti** they are all coming, everybody's coming; **tutti sanno che** everybody knows that; **tutti quanti** all and sundry

▶ AV (*completamente*) entirely, quite; **è tutto il contrario** it's quite *o* exactly the opposite; **tutt'al più**: **saranno stati tutt'al più una cin-quantina** there were about fifty of them at (the very) most; **tutt'al più possiamo pren-dere un treno** if the worst comes to the worst we can take a train; **tutt'altro** on the con-trary; **è tutt'altro che felice** he's anything but happy; **tutt'intorno** all around; **tutt'a un tratto** suddenly

▶ SM: **il tutto** the whole lot, all of it; **il tutto si è svolto senza incidenti** it all went off with-out incident; **il tutto le costerà due milioni** the whole thing will cost you two million

---

Quando *tutti/e* significa ognuno di voi, si tra-duce con **everyone** *o* **everybody**, seguito dal verbo al singolare e, nel linguaggio corrente, con l'aggettivo possessivo al plurale. Nel lin-guaggio più formale si usa **his** *o* **her**.
Avete tutti finito i compiti? **Has everybody fini-shed their/his/her homework?**

tutto'fare AG INV : **domestica ~** general maid; **ragazzo ~** office boy ▶ SM INV/F INV handy-man(-woman)

tut'tora AV still

tutù SM INV tutu, ballet skirt

TV [ti'vu] SF INV (= *televisione*) TV ▶ SIGLA = **Tre-viso**

twit'tare /72/ VT (*su Twitter*) to tweet

twitta'tore, -trice SM/F tweeter

twittos'fera SF Twittersphere, Twitterverse

U u

U, u [u] SM O F INV (*lettera*) U, u; **U come Udine** ≈ U for Uncle; **inversione ad U** U-turn

ub'bia SF (*letterario*) irrational fear

ubbidi'ente AG obedient

ubbidi'enza [ubbi'djɛntsa] SF obedience

ubbi'dire /55/ VI to obey; **~ a** to obey; (*veicolo, macchina*) to respond to

uberiz'zare [uberid'dzare] /72/ VT to Uberize

ubicazi'one [ubikat'tsjone] SF site, location

ubiquità SF: **non ho il dono dell'~** I can't be everywhere at once

ubria'care /20/ VT: **~ qn** to get sb drunk; (*alcool*) to make sb drunk; (*fig*) to make sb's head spin o reel ▪ **ubriacarsi** VPR to get drunk; **ubriacarsi di** (*fig*) to become intoxicated with

ubria'chezza [ubria'kettsa] SF drunkenness

ubri'aco, -a, -chi, -che AG, SM/F drunk

ubria'cone, -a SM/F drunkard

uccellagi'one [uttʃella'dʒone] SF bird catching

uccelli'era [uttʃel'ljɛra] SF aviary

uccel'lino [uttʃel'lino] SM baby bird, chick

uc'cello [ut'tʃello] SM bird

uc'cidere [ut'tʃidere] /34/ VT to kill ▪ **uccidersi** VPR (*suicidarsi*) to kill o.s.; (*perdere la vita*) to be killed

uccisi'one [uttʃi'zjone] SF killing

uc'ciso, -a [ut'tʃizo] PP *di* **uccidere**

ucci'sore [uttʃi'zore] SM killer

U'craina SF Ukraine

u'craino, -a AG, SM/F Ukrainian

UD SIGLA = **Udine**

U.D.C. SIGLA F (*Pol*: = *Unione di Centro*) *centre party*

u'dente SMF: **i non udenti** the hard of hearing

u'dibile AG audible

udi'enza [u'djɛntsa] SF audience; (*Dir*) hearing; **dare ~ (a)** to grant an audience (to); **~ a porte chiuse** hearing in camera

u'dire /124/ VT to hear

udi'tivo, -a AG auditory

u'dito SM (sense of) hearing

udi'tore, -'trice SM/F listener; (*Ins*) unregistered student (*attending lectures*)

udi'torio SM (*persone*) audience

UE SIGLA F (= *Unione Europea*) EU

U.E. ABBR = **uso esterno**

UEFA SIGLA F UEFA (= *Union of European Football Associations*)

UEM SIGLA F (= *Unione economica e monetaria*) EMU

'uffa ESCL tut!

uffici'ale [uffi'tʃale] AG official ▶ SM (*Amm*) official, officer; (*Mil*) officer; **pubblico ~** public official; **~ giudiziario** clerk of the court; **~ di marina** naval officer; **~ sanitario** health inspector; **~ di stato civile** registrar

ufficializ'zare [uffitʃalid'dzare] /72/ VT to make official

uf'ficio [uf'fitʃo] SM (*gen*) office; (*dovere*) duty; (*mansione*) task, function, job; (*agenzia*) agency, bureau; (*Rel*) service; **d'~** AG office *cpd*; official ▶ AV officially; **provvedere d'~** to act officially; **convocare d'~** (*Dir*) to summons; **difensore o avvocato d'~** (*Dir*) court-appointed counsel for the defence; **~ brevetti** patent office; **~ di collocamento** employment office; **~ informazioni** information bureau; **~ oggetti smarriti** lost property office (*Brit*), lost and found (*US*); **~ postale** post office; **~ vendite/del personale** sales/personnel department

uffici'oso, -a [uffi'tʃoso] AG unofficial

'UFO SM INV (= *unidentified flying object*) UFO

'ufo: a ~ AV free, for nothing

U'ganda SF: **l'~** Uganda

'uggia ['uddʒa] SF (*noia*) boredom; (*fastidio*) bore; **avere/prendere qn in ~** to dislike/take a dislike to sb

uggi'oso, -a [ud'dʒoso] AG tiresome; (*tempo*) dull

'ugola SF uvula

uguagli'anza [ugwaʎ'ʎantsa] SF equality

uguagli'are [ugwaʎ'ʎare] /27/ VT to make equal; (*essere uguale*) to equal, be equal to; (*livellare*) to level ▪ **uguagliarsi** VPR: **uguagliarsi a o con qn** (*paragonarsi*) to compare o.s. to sb

ugu'ale AG equal; (*identico*) identical, the same; (*uniforme*) level, even ▶ AV: **costano ~** they cost the same; **sono bravi ~** they're equally good

ugual'mente AV equally; (*lo stesso*) all the same

U.I. ABBR = **uso interno**

UIL SIGLA F (= *Unione Italiana del Lavoro*) trade union federation

'ulcera ['ultʃera] SF ulcer

ulcerazi'one [ultʃerat'tsjone] SF ulceration

u'liva *ecc* = **oliva** *ecc*

U'livo SM (*Pol*) centre-left coalition

ulteri'ore AG further

ultima'mente AV lately, of late

ulti'mare /72/ VT to finish, complete

ulti'matum SM INV ultimatum

ulti'missime SFPL latest news *sg*

'ultimo, -a AG (*finale*) last; (*estremo*) farthest, utmost; (*recente: notizia, moda*) latest; (*fig: sommo, fondamentale*) ultimate ▸ SM/F last (one); **fino all'~** to the last, until the end; **da ~, in ~** in the end; **per ~** (*entrare, arrivare*) last; **abitare all'~ piano** to live on the top floor; **in ultima pagina** (*di giornale*) on the back page; **negli ultimi tempi** recently; **all'~ momento** at the last minute; **... la vostra lettera del 7 aprile ~ scorso** ... your letter of April 7th last; **in ultima analisi** in the final *o* last analysis; **in ~ luogo** finally

ultrà SMF ultra

ultrasi'nistra SF (*Pol*) extreme left

ultrasu'ono SM ultrasound

ultravio'letto, -a AG ultraviolet

ulu'lare /72/ VI to howl

ulu'lato SM howling *no pl*; howl

umana'mente AV (*con umanità*) humanely; (*nei limiti delle capacità umane*) humanly

uma'nesimo SM humanism

umanità SF humanity

umani'tario, -a AG humanitarian

umaniz'zare [umanid'dzare] /72/ VT to humanize

u'mano, -a AG human; (*comprensivo*) humane

umbi'lico SM = **ombelico**

'umbro, -a AG of (*o* from) Umbria

umet'tare /72/ VT to dampen, moisten

umi'diccio, -a, -ci, -ce [umi'dittʃo] AG (*terreno*) damp; (*mano*) moist, clammy

umidifi'care /20/ VT to humidify

umidifica'tore SM humidifier

umidità SF dampness; moistness; humidity

'umido, -a AG damp; (*mano, occhi*) moist; (*clima*) humid ▸ SM dampness, damp; **carne in ~** stew

'umile AG humble

umili'ante AG humiliating

umili'are /19/ VT to humiliate ▪ **umiliarsi** VPR to humble o.s.

umiliazi'one [umiljat'tsjone] SF humiliation

umiltà SF humility, humbleness

u'more SM (*disposizione d'animo*) mood; (*carattere*) temper; **di buon/cattivo ~** in a good/bad mood

umo'rismo SM humour (BRIT), humor (US); **avere il senso dell'~** to have a sense of humour

umo'rista, -i, -e SM/F humorist

umo'ristico, -a, -ci, -che AG humorous, funny

un, un', una *vedi* **uno**

u'nanime AG unanimous

unanimità SF unanimity; **all'~** unanimously

'una 'tantum AG one-off *cpd* ▸ SF (*imposta*) one-off tax

unci'nato, -a [untʃi'nato] AG (*amo*) barbed; (*ferro*) hooked; **croce uncinata** swastika

unci'netto [untʃi'netto] SM crochet hook

un'cino [un'tʃino] SM hook

undi'cenne [undi'tʃenne] AG, SMF eleven-year-old

undi'cesimo, -a [undi'tʃezimo] AG eleventh

'undici ['unditʃi] NUM eleven

U'NESCO SIGLA F (= *United Nations Educational, Scientific and Cultural Organization*) UNESCO

'ungere ['undʒere] /5/ VT to grease, oil; (*Rel*) to anoint; (*fig*) to flatter, butter up ▪ **ungersi** VPR (*sporcarsi*) to get covered in grease; **ungersi con la crema** to put on cream

unghe'rese [unge'rese] AG, SMF, SM Hungarian

Unghe'ria [unge'ria] SF: **l'~** Hungary

'unghia ['ungja] SF (*Anat*) nail; (*di animale*) claw; (*di rapace*) talon; (*di cavallo*) hoof; **pagare sull'~** (*fig*) to pay on the nail

unghi'ata [un'gjata] SF (*graffio*) scratch

ungu'ento SM ointment

unica'mente AV only

U'NICEF ['unitʃef] SIGLA M (= *United Nations International Children's Emergency Fund*) UNICEF

'unico, -a, -ci, -che AG (*solo*) only; (*ineguagliabile*) unique; (*singolo: binario*) single; **è figlio ~** he's an only child; **atto ~** (*Teat*) one-act play; **agente ~** (*Comm*) sole agent

uni'corno SM unicorn

unifi'care /20/ VT to unite, unify; (*sistemi*) to standardize

unificazi'one [unifikat'tsjone] SF uniting; unification; standardization

unifor'mare /72/ VT (*terreno, superficie*) to level ▪ **uniformarsi** VPR: **uniformarsi a** to conform to; **~ qc a** to adjust *o* relate sth to

uni'forme AG uniform; (*superficie*) even ▸ SF (*divisa*) uniform; **alta ~** dress uniform

uniformità SF uniformity; evenness

unilate'rale AG one-sided; (*Dir, Pol*) unilateral

uninomi'nale AG (*Pol: collegio, sistema*) single-candidate *cpd*

uni'one SF union; (*fig: concordia*) unity, harmony; **l'U~** (*Pol*) coalition of centre-left parties; **U~**

u

economica e monetaria economic and monetary union; **U~ Europea** European Union; **ex U~ Sovietica** former Soviet Union

u'nire /55/ VT to unite; (*congiungere*) to join, connect; (*ingredienti, colori*) to combine; (*in matrimonio*) to unite, join together ■ **unirsi** VPR to unite; (*in matrimonio*) to be joined together; **~ qc a** to unite sth with; to join o connect sth with; to combine sth with; **unirsi a** (*gruppo, società*) to join

u'nisono SM: **all'~** in unison

unità SF INV (*unione, concordia*) unity; (*Mat, Mil, Comm, di misura*) unit; **~ centrale (di elaborazione)** (*Inform*) central processing unit; **~ disco** (*Inform*) disk drive; **~ monetaria** monetary unit; **~ di misura** unit of measurement

uni'tario, -a AG unitary; **prezzo ~** price per unit

u'nito, -a AG (*paese*) united; (*amici, famiglia*) close; **in tinta unita** plain, self-coloured (BRIT), self-colored (US)

univer'sale AG universal; general

universalità SF universality

universal'mente AV universally

università SF INV university

universi'tario, -a AG university *cpd* ▶ SM/F (*studente*) university student; (*insegnante*) academic, university lecturer

uni'verso SM universe

u'nivoco, -a, -ci, -che AG unambiguous

'uno, -a

(*dav sm un + C, V,* **uno** *+ s impura, gn, pn, ps, x, z; dav sf* **un'** *+ V,* **una** *+ C*) DET **1** a; (*dav vocale*) an; **un bambino** a child; **una strada** a street; **uno zingaro** a gypsy

2 (*intensivo*): **ho avuto una paura!** I got such a fright!

▶ PRON **1** one; **ce n'è uno qui** there's one here; **prendine uno** take one (of them); **l'uno o l'altro** either (of them); **l'uno e l'altro** both (of them); **aiutarsi l'un l'altro** to help one another o each other; **sono entrati l'uno dopo l'altro** they came in one after the other; **a uno a uno** one by one; **metà per uno** half each

2 (*un tale*) someone, somebody; **ho incontrato uno che ti conosce** I met somebody who knows you

3 (*con valore impersonale*) one, you; **se uno vuole** if one wants, if you want; **cosa fa uno in quella situazione?** what does one do in that situation?

▶ NUM one; **una mela e due pere** one apple and two pears; **uno più uno fa due** one plus one equals two, one and one are two

▶ SF: **è l'una** it's one (o'clock)

'unsi *ecc* VB *vedi* ungere

'unto, -a PP *di* ungere ▶ AG greasy, oily ▶ SM grease

untu'oso, -a AG greasy, oily

unzi'one [un'tsjone] SF: **l'Estrema U~** (*Rel*) Extreme Unction

u'omo (*pl* **uomini**) SM man; **da ~** (*abito, scarpe*) men's, for men; **a memoria d'~** since the world began; **a passo d'~** at walking pace; **~ d'affari** businessman; **~ d'azione** man of action; **~ di fiducia** right-hand man; **~ di mondo** man of the world; **~ di paglia** stooge; **~ politico** politician; **~ rana** frogman; **l'~ della strada** the man in the street

u'opo SM: **all'~** if necessary

u'ovo (*pl(f)* **uova**) SM egg; **cercare il pelo nell'~** (*fig*) to split hairs; **~ affogato** o **in camicia** poached egg; **~ bazzotto/sodo** soft-/hard-boiled egg; **~ alla coque** boiled egg; **~ di Pasqua** Easter egg; **~ al tegame** o **all'occhio di bue** fried egg; **uova strapazzate** scrambled eggs

ura'gano SM hurricane

U'rali SMPL: **gli ~, i Monti ~** the Urals, the Ural Mountains

u'ranio SM uranium; **~ impoverito** depleted uranium

urba'nista, -i, -e SM/F town planner

urba'nistica SF town planning

urbanità SF urbanity

ur'bano, -a AG urban, city *cpd*, town *cpd*; (*Tel: chiamata*) local; (*fig*) urbane

ur'gente [ur'dʒɛnte] AG urgent

ur'genza [ur'dʒɛntsa] SF urgency; **in caso d'~** in (case of) an emergency; **d'~** *ag* emergency; *av* urgently, as a matter of urgency; **non c'è ~** there's no hurry; **questo lavoro va fatto con ~** this work is urgent

'urgere ['urdʒere] /5/ VI to be needed urgently

u'rina *ecc* = orina *ecc*

ur'lare /72/ VI (*persona*) to scream, yell; (*animale, vento*) to howl ▶ VT to scream, yell

'urlo (*pl(m)* **urli**, *pl(f)* **urla**) SM scream, yell; howl

'urna SF urn; (*elettorale*) ballot box; **andare alle urne** to go to the polls

URP [urp] SIGLA M (= *Ufficio Relazioni con il Pubblico*) PR Office

urrà ESCL hurrah!

U.R.S.S. SIGLA F = **Unione delle Repubbliche Socialiste Sovietiche; l'~** the USSR

ur'tare /72/ VT to bump into, knock against, crash into; (*fig: irritare*) to annoy ▶ VI: **~ contro** o **in** to bump into, knock against; (*fig: imbattersi*) to come up against ■ **urtarsi** VPR (*reciproco: scontrarsi*) to collide; (: *fig*) to clash; (*irritarsi*) to get annoyed

'urto SM (*colpo*) knock, bump; (*scontro*) crash, collision; (*fig*) clash; **terapia d'~** (*Med*) shock treatment

uruguai'ano, -a AG, SM/F Uruguayan

Urugu'ay SM: **l'~** Uruguay

u.s. ABBR = **ultimo scorso**

'USA SMPL: **gli ~** the USA

u'sanza [u'zantsa] SF custom; (*moda*) fashion

u'sare /**72**/ VT to use, employ ▶ VI (*essere di moda*) to be fashionable; (*servirsi*): **~ di** to use; (*diritto*) to exercise; (*essere solito*): **~ fare** to be in the habit of doing, be accustomed to doing ▶ VB IMPERS: **qui usa così** it's the custom round here; **~ la massima cura nel fare qc** to exercise great care when doing sth

u'sato, -a AG used; (*consumato*) worn; (*di seconda mano*) used, second-hand ▶ SM second-hand goods *pl*

u'scente [uʃ'ʃɛnte] AG (*Amm*) outgoing

usci'ere [uʃ'ʃɛre] SM usher

'uscio ['uʃʃo] SM door

u'scire [uʃ'ʃire] /**125**/ VI (*gen*) to come out; (*partire, andare a passeggio, a uno spettacolo ecc*) to go out; (*essere sorteggiato: numero*) to come up; **~ da** (*gen*) to leave; (*posto*) to go (*o* come) out of, leave; (*solco, vasca ecc*) to come out of; (*muro*) to stick out of; (*competenza ecc*) to be outside; (*infanzia, adolescenza*) to leave behind; (*famiglia nobile ecc*) to come from; **~ da** *o* **di casa** to go out; (*fig*) to leave home; **~ in automobile** to go out in the car, go for a drive; **~ di strada** (*Aut*) to go off *o* leave the road

u'scita [uʃ'ʃita] SF (*passaggio, varco*) exit, way out; (*per divertimento*) outing; (*Econ: somma*) expenditure; (*Teat*) entrance; (*fig: battuta*) witty remark; **"vietata l'~"** "no exit"; **~ di sicurezza** emergency exit

user'name [juzer'neim] SM INV username

usi'gnolo [uziɲ'ɲɔlo] SM nightingale

'uso SM (*utilizzazione*) use; (*esercizio*) practice (BRIT), practise (US); (*abitudine*) custom; **fare ~ di qc** to use sth; **con l'~** with practice; **a ~ di** for (the use of); **d'~** (*corrente*) in use; **fuori ~** out of use; **essere in ~** to be in common *o* current use; **per ~ esterno** for external use only

ustio'nare /**72**/ VT to burn ▪ **ustionarsi** VPR to burn o.s.

usti'one SF burn

usu'ale AG common, everyday

usufru'ire /**55**/ VI: **~ di** (*giovarsi di*) to take advantage of, make use of

usu'frutto SM (*Dir*) usufruct

u'sura SF usury; (*logoramento*) wear (and tear)

usu'raio, -a SM/F usurer

usur'pare /**72**/ VT to usurp

usurpa'tore, -'trice SM/F usurper

uten'sile SM tool, implement ▶ AG: **macchina ~** machine tool; **utensili da cucina** kitchen utensils

utensile'ria SF (*utensili*) tools *pl*; (*reparto*) tool room

u'tente SMF user; (*di gas ecc*) consumer; (*del telefono*) subscriber; **~ finale** end user

'utero SM uterus, womb; **~ in affitto** host womb

'utile AG useful ▶ SM (*vantaggio*) advantage, benefit; (*Econ: profitto*) profit; **rendersi ~** to be helpful; **in tempo ~ per** in time for; **unire l'~ al dilettevole** to combine business with pleasure; **partecipare agli utili** (*Econ*) to share in the profits

utilità SF usefulness *no pl*; use; (*vantaggio*) benefit; **essere di grande ~** to be very useful

utili'tario, -a AG utilitarian ▶ SF (*Aut*) economy car

utiliz'zare [utilid'dzare] /**72**/ VT to use, make use of, utilize

utilizzazi'one [utiliddzat'tsjone] SF utilization, use

uti'lizzo [uti'liddzo] SM (*Amm*) utilization; (*Banca: di credito*) availment

util'mente AV usefully, profitably

uto'pia SF utopia; **è pura ~** that's sheer utopianism

uto'pistico, -a, -ci, -che AG utopian

UVA ABBR (= *ultravioletto prossimo*) UVA

'uva SF grapes *pl*; **~ passa** raisins *pl*; **~ spina** gooseberry

UVB ABBR (= *ultravioletto lontano*) UVB

V, v [vi, vu] SM O F INV (*lettera*) V, v; **V come Venezia** ≈ V for Victor

V ABBR (= *volt*) V

v. ABBR (= *vedi*) v.; (= *verso*) v.; (= *versetto*) v.

VA SIGLA = **Varese**

va, va' VB *vedi* **andare**

va'cante AG vacant

va'canza [va'kantsa] SF (*l'essere vacante*) vacancy; (*riposo, ferie*) holiday(s pl) (BRIT), vacation (US); (*giorno di permesso*) day off, holiday ■ **vacanze** SFPL (*periodo di ferie*) holidays, vacation *sg*; **essere/andare in** ~ to be/go on holiday *o* vacation; **far** ~ to have a holiday; **vacanze estive** summer holiday(s) *o* vacation; **vacanze natalizie** Christmas holidays *o* vacation

'vacca, -che SF COW

vacci'nare [vattʃi'nare] /**72**/ VT to vaccinate; **farsi** ~ to have a vaccination, get vaccinated

vaccinazi'one [vattʃinat'tsjone] SF vaccination

vac'cino [vat'tʃino] SM (*Med*) vaccine

vacil'lante [vatʃil'lante] AG (*edificio, vecchio*) shaky, unsteady; (*fiamma*) flickering; (*salute, memoria*) shaky, failing

vacil'lare [vatʃil'lare] /**72**/ VI to sway, wobble; (*fiamma, luce*) to flicker; (*fig: memoria, coraggio*) to be failing, falter

'vacuo, -a AG (*fig*) empty, vacuous ▶ SM vacuum

'vado *ecc* VB *vedi* **andare**

vagabon'daggio [vagabon'daddʒo] SM wandering, roaming; (*Dir*) vagrancy

vagabon'dare /**72**/ VI to roam, wander

vaga'bondo, -a SM/F tramp, vagrant; (*fannullone*) idler, loafer

va'gare /**80**/ VI to wander

vagheggi'are [vagedʒ'dʒare] /**62**/ VT to long for, dream of

vaghe'rò *ecc* [vage'rɔ] VB *vedi* **vagare**

va'ghezza [va'gettsa] SF vagueness

va'gina [va'dʒina] SF vagina

va'gire [va'dʒire] /**55**/ VI to whimper

va'gito [va'dʒito] SM cry, wailing

'vaglia ['vaʎʎa] SM INV money order; ~ **cambiario** promissory note; ~ **postale** postal order

vagli'are [vaʎ'ʎare] /**27**/ VT to sift; (*fig*) to weigh up

'vaglio ['vaʎʎo] SM sieve; **passare al** ~ (*fig*) to examine closely

'vago, -a, -ghi, -ghe AG vague

va'gone SM (*Ferr: per passeggeri*) coach, carriage (BRIT), car (US); (: *per merci*) truck, wagon; ~ **letto** sleeper, sleeping car; ~ **ristorante** dining *o* restaurant car

'vai VB *vedi* **andare**

vai'olo SM smallpox

val. ABBR = **valuta**

va'langa, -ghe SF avalanche

va'lente AG able, talented

va'lenza [va'lɛntsa] SF (*fig: significato*) content; (*Chim*) valency

va'lere /**126**/ VI (*avere forza, potenza*) to have influence; (*essere valido*) to be valid; (*avere vigore, autorità*) to hold, apply; (*essere capace: poeta, studente*) to be good, be able ▶ VT (*prezzo, sforzo*) to be worth; (*corrispondere*) to correspond to; (*procurare*): ~ **qc a qn** to earn sb sth ■ **valersi** VPR: **valersi di** to make use of, take advantage of; **far** ~ (*autorità ecc*) to assert; **far** ~ **le proprie ragioni** to make o.s. heard; **farsi** ~ to make o.s. appreciated *o* respected; **vale a dire** that is to say; ~ **la pena** to be worth the effort *o* worth it; **l'uno vale l'altro** the one is as good as the other, they amount to the same thing; **non vale niente** it's worthless; **valersi dei consigli di qn** to take *o* act upon sb's advice

valeri'ana SF (*Bot, Med*) valerian

va'levole AG valid

'valgo *ecc* VB *vedi* **valere**

vali'care /**20**/ VT to cross

'valico, -chi SM (*passo*) pass

validità SF validity

'valido, -a AG valid; (*rimedio*) effective; (*aiuto*) real; (*persona*) worthwhile; **essere di** ~ **aiuto a qn** to be a great help to sb

valige'ria [validʒe'ria] SF (*assortimento*) leather goods pl; (*fabbrica*) leather goods factory; (*negozio*) leather goods shop

vali'getta [vali'dʒetta] SF briefcase; **~ venti-quattrore** overnight bag o case

va'ligia, -gie, -ge [va'lidʒa] SF (suit)case; **fare le valigie** to pack (up); **~ diplomatica** diplomatic bag

val'lata SF valley

'valle SF valley; **a ~** (di fiume) downstream; **scendere a ~** to go downhill

val'letto SM valet

valligi'ano, -a [valli'dʒano] SM/F inhabitant of a valley

va'lore SM (gen, Comm) value; (merito) merit, worth; (coraggio) valour (BRIT), valor (US), courage; (Finanza: titolo) security ◼ **valori** SMPL (oggetti preziosi) valuables; **crescere/diminuire di ~** to go up/down in value, gain/lose in value; **è di gran ~** it's worth a lot, it's very valuable; **privo di ~** worthless; **~ contabile** book value; **~ effettivo** real value; **~ nominale** o **facciale** nominal value; **~ di realizzo** break-up value; **~ di riscatto** surrender value; **valori bollati** (revenue) stamps

valoriz'zare [valorid'dzare] /72/ VT (terreno) to develop; (fig) to make the most of

valo'roso, -a AG courageous

'valso, -a PP di **valere**

va'luta SF currency, money; (Banca): **~ 15 gennaio** interest to run from January 15th; **~ estera** foreign currency

valu'tare /72/ VT (casa, gioiello, fig) to value; (stabilire: peso, entrate, fig) to estimate

valu'tario, -a AG (Finanza: norme) currency cpd

valutazi'one [valutat'tsjone] SF valuation; estimate

'valva SF (Zool, Bot) valve

'valvola SF (Tecn, Anat) valve; (Elettr) fuse; **~ a farfalla del carburatore** (Aut) throttle; **~ di sicurezza** safety valve

'valzer ['valtser] SM INV waltz

vam'pata SF (di fiamma) blaze; (di calore) blast; (: al viso) flush

vam'piro SM vampire

vana'gloria SF boastfulness

van'dalico, -a, -ci, -che AG vandal cpd; **atto ~** act of vandalism

vanda'lismo SM vandalism

'vandalo SM vandal

vaneggia'mento [vaneddʒa'mento] SM raving, delirium

vaneggi'are [vaned'dʒare] /62/ VI to rave

va'nesio, -a AG vain, conceited

'vanga, -ghe SF spade

van'gare /80/ VT to dig

van'gelo [van'dʒɛlo] SM gospel

vanifi'care /20/ VT to nullify

va'niglia [va'niʎʎa] SF vanilla

vanigli'ato, -a [vaniʎ'ʎato] AG: **zucchero ~** (Cuc) vanilla sugar

vanità SF vanity; (di promessa) emptiness; (di sforzo) futility

vani'toso, -a AG vain, conceited

'vanno VB vedi **andare**

'vano, -a AG vain ▶ SM (spazio) space; (apertura) opening; (stanza) room; **il ~ della porta** the doorway; **il ~ portabagagli** (Aut) the boot (BRIT), the trunk (US)

van'taggio [van'taddʒo] SM advantage; **trarre ~ da qc** to benefit from sth; **essere/portarsi in ~** (Sport) to be in/take the lead

vantaggi'oso, -a [vantad'dʒoso] AG advantageous, favourable (BRIT), favorable (US)

van'tare /72/ VT to praise, speak highly of ◼ **vantarsi** VPR: **vantarsi (di/di aver fatto)** to boast o brag (about/about having done)

vante'ria SF boasting

'vanto SM boasting; (merito) virtue, merit; (gloria) pride

'vanvera SF: **a ~** haphazardly; **parlare a ~** to talk nonsense

va'pore SM vapour (BRIT), vapor (US); (anche: **vapore acqueo**) steam; (nave) steamer; **a ~** (turbina ecc) steam cpd; **al ~** (Cuc) steamed

vapo'retto SM steamer

vapori'era SF (Ferr) steam engine

vaporiz'zare [vaporid'dzare] /72/ VT to vaporize

vaporizza'tore [vaporiddza'tore] SM spray

vaporizzazi'one [vaporiddzat'tsjone] SF vaporization

vapo'roso, -a AG (tessuto) filmy; (capelli) soft and full

va'rare /72/ VT (Naut, fig) to launch; (Dir) to pass

var'care /20/ VT to cross

'varco, -chi SM passage; **aprirsi un ~ tra la folla** to push one's way through the crowd

vare'china [vare'kina] SF bleach

vari'abile AG variable; (tempo, umore) changeable, variable ▶ SF (Mat) variable

vari'ante SF (gen) variation, change; (di piano) modification; (Ling) variant; (Sport) alternative route

vari'are /19/ VT, VI to vary; **~ di opinione** to change one's mind

variazi'one [varjat'tsjone] SF variation, change; (Mus) variation; **una ~ di programma** a change of plan

va'rice [va'ritʃe] SF varicose vein

vari'cella [vari'tʃɛlla] SF chickenpox

vari'coso, -a AG varicose

varie'gato, -a AG variegated

varietà SF INV variety ▶ SM INV variety show

'vario, -a AG varied; (parecchi: col sostantivo al pl)

V

395

various; (*mutevole: umore*) changeable ■ **varie**
SFPL: **varie ed eventuali** (*nell'ordine del giorno*)
any other business

vario'pinto, -a AG multicoloured (BRIT), multicolored (US)

'varo SM (*Naut, fig*) launch; (*di leggi*) passing

varrò *ecc* VB *vedi* **valere**

Var'savia SF Warsaw

va'saio SM potter

'vasca, -sche SF basin; (*anche:* **vasca da bagno**)
bathtub, bath

va'scello [vaʃˈʃello] SM (*Naut*) vessel, ship

vas'chetta [vasˈketta] SF (*per gelato*) tub; (*per sviluppare fotografie*) dish

vase'lina SF vaseline

vasel'lame SM (*stoviglie*) crockery; (: *di porcellana*)
china; **~ d'oro/d'argento** gold/silver plate

'vaso SM (*recipiente*) pot; (: *barattolo*) jar; (: *decora-
tivo*) vase; (*Anat*) vessel; **~ da fiori** vase; (*per
piante*) flowerpot

vas'sallo SM vassal

vas'soio SM tray

vastità SF vastness

'vasto, -a AG vast, immense; **di vaste proporzioni** (*incendio*) huge; (*fenomeno, rivolta*) widespread; **su vasta scala** on a vast o huge scale

Vati'cano SM: **il ~** the Vatican; **la Città del ~** the
Vatican City

VB SIGLA = **Vibo Valenza**

VC SIGLA = **Vercelli**

VE SIGLA = **Venezia** ▶ ABBR = **Vostra Eccellenza**

ve PRON, AV *vedi* **vi**

vecchi'aia [vekˈkjaja] SF old age

'vecchio, -a [ˈvɛkkjo] AG old ▶ SM/F old
man(-woman); **i vecchi** the old; **è un mio ~
amico** he's an old friend of mine; **è un uomo ~
stile** o **stampo** he's an old-fashioned man; **è ~
del mestiere** he's an old hand at the job

'vece [ˈvetʃe] SF: **in ~ di** in the place of, for; **fare
le veci di qn** to take sb's place; **firma del padre
o di chi ne fa le veci** signature of the father or
guardian

ve'dere /127/ VT, VI to see ■ **vedersi** VPR to meet,
see one another; **~ di fare qc** to see (to it) that sth
is done, make sure that sth is done; **avere a che
~ con** to have to do with; **far ~ qc a qn** to show sb
sth; **farsi ~** to show o.s.; (*farsi vivo*) to show one's
face; **vedi di non farlo** make sure o see you don't
do it; **farsi ~ da un medico** to go and see a doctor;
modo di ~ outlook, view of things; **vedi pagina 8**
(*rimando*) see page 8; **è da ~ se ...** it remains to be
seen whether ...; **non vedo la ragione di farlo** I
can't see any reason to do it; **si era visto
costretto a ...** he found himself forced to ...;
non (ci) si vede (*è buio ecc*) you can't see a thing; **ci
vediamo domani!** see you tomorrow!; **non lo
posso ~** (*fig*) I can't stand him

ve'detta SF (*sentinella, posto*) look-out; (*Naut*)
patrol boat

ve'dette [vəˈdɛt] SF INV (*attrice*) star

'vedovo, -a SM/F widower (widow); **rimaner ~**
to be widowed

vedrò *ecc* VB *vedi* **vedere**

ve'duta SF view ■ **vedute** SFPL (*fig: opinioni*)
views; **di larghe** o **ampie vedute** broad-
minded; **di vedute limitate** narrow-minded

vee'mente AG (*discorso, azione*) vehement;
(*assalto*) vigorous; (*passione*) overwhelming

vee'menza [veeˈmɛntsa] SF vehemence; **con ~**
vehemently

ve'gano, -a AG, SM/F vegan

vege'tale [vedʒeˈtale] AG, SM vegetable

vege'tare [vedʒeˈtare] /72/ VI (*fig*) to vegetate

vegetari'ano, -a [vedʒetaˈrjano] AG, SM/F vegetarian

vegeta'tivo, -a AG vegetative

vegetazi'one [vedʒetatˈtsjone] SF vegetation

'vegeto, -a [ˈvɛdʒeto] AG (*pianta*) thriving; (*persona*) strong, vigorous

veg'gente [vedˈdʒɛnte] SMF (*indovino*) clairvoyant

'veglia [ˈveʎʎa] SF wakefulness; (*sorveglianza*)
watch; (*trattenimento*) evening gathering; **tra la
~ e il sonno** half awake; **fare la ~ a un malato**
to watch over a sick person; **~ funebre** wake

vegli'ardo, -a [veʎˈʎardo] SM/F venerable old
man/woman

vegli'are [veʎˈʎare] /27/ VI to stay o sit up; (*stare
vigile*) to watch; to keep watch ▶ VT (*malato,
morto*) to watch over, sit up with

vegli'one [veʎˈʎone] SM ball, dance; **~ di Capodanno** New Year's Eve party

ve'icolo SM vehicle; **~ spaziale** spacecraft *inv*

'vela SF (*Naut: tela*) sail; (: *sport*) sailing; **tutto va
a gonfie vele** (*fig*) everything is going perfectly

ve'lare /72/ VT to veil ■ **velarsi** VPR (*occhi, luna*) to
mist over; (*voce*) to become husky; **velarsi il
viso** to cover one's face (with a veil)

ve'lato, -a AG veiled

vela'tura SF (*Naut*) sails *pl*

veleggi'are [veledˈdʒare] /62/ VI to sail; (*Aer*) to
glide

ve'leno SM poison

vele'noso, -a AG poisonous

ve'letta SF (*di cappello*) veil

veli'ero SM sailing ship

ve'lina SF: **carta ~** (*per imballare*) tissue paper; (*per
copie*) flimsy paper; (*copia*) carbon copy

ve'lista, -i, -e SM/F yachtsman(-woman)

ve'livolo SM aircraft

velleità SF INV vain ambition, vain desire

vellei'tario, -a AG unrealistic

'vello SM fleece

vellu'tato, -a AG (*stoffa, pesca, colore*) velvety; (*voce*) mellow

vel'luto SM velvet; **~ a coste** cord

'velo SM veil; (*tessuto*) voile

ve'loce [ve'lotʃe] AG fast, quick ▶ AV fast, quickly

velo'cista, -i, -e [velo'tʃista] SM/F (*Sport*) sprinter

velocità [velotʃi'ta] SF speed; **a forte ~** at high speed; **~ di crociera** cruising speed

ve'lodromo SM velodrome

ven. ABBR (= *venerdì*) Fri.

'vena SF (*gen*) vein; (*filone*) vein, seam; (*fig: ispirazione*) inspiration; (: *umore*) mood; **essere in ~ di qc** to be in the mood for sth

ve'nale AG (*prezzo, valore*) market cpd; (*fig*) venal; mercenary

venalità SF venality

ve'nato, -a AG (*marmo*) veined, streaked; (*legno*) grained

vena'torio, -a AG hunting; **la stagione venatoria** the hunting season

vena'tura SF (*di marmo*) vein, streak; (*di legno*) grain

ven'demmia SF (*raccolta*) grape harvest; (*quantità d'uva*) grape crop, grapes pl; (*vino ottenuto*) vintage

vendemmi'are /19/ VT to harvest ▶ VI to harvest the grapes

'vendere /29/ VT to sell; **~ all'ingrosso/al dettaglio** o **minuto** to sell wholesale/retail; **~ all'asta** to auction, sell by auction; **"vendesi"** "for sale"

ven'detta SF revenge

vendi'care /20/ VT to avenge ▪ **vendicarsi** VPR: **vendicarsi (di)** to avenge o.s. (for); (*per rancore*) to take one's revenge (for); **vendicarsi su qn** to revenge o.s. on sb

vendica'tivo, -a AG vindictive

'vendita SF sale; **la ~** (*attività*) selling; (*smercio*) sales pl; **in ~** on sale; **mettere in ~** to put on sale; **in ~ presso** on sale at; **contratto di ~** sales agreement; **reparto vendite** sales department; **~ all'asta** sale by auction; **~ per telefono** telesales sg; **~ al dettaglio** o **minuto** retail; **~ all'ingrosso** wholesale

vendi'tore, -'trice SM/F seller, vendor; (*gestore di negozio*) trader, dealer

ven'duto, -a AG (*merce*) sold; (*fig: corrotto*) corrupt

ve'nefico, -a, -ci, -che AG poisonous

vene'rabile, vene'rando, -a AG venerable

vene'rare /72/ VT to venerate

venerazi'one [venerat'tsjone] SF veneration

venerdì SM INV Friday; **di** o **il ~** on Fridays; **V~ Santo** Good Friday; *vedi anche* **martedì**

'Venere SMF Venus

ve'nereo, -a AG venereal

'veneto, -a AG of (o from) the Veneto

'veneto-giuli'ano, -a ['vɛnetodʒu'ljano] AG of (o from) Venezia-Giulia

Ve'nezia [ve'nɛttsja] SF Venice

venezi'ano, -a [venet'tsjano] AG, SM/F Venetian

Venezu'ela [venettsu'ela] SM: **il ~** Venezuela

venezue'lano, -a [venettsue'lano] AG, SM/F Venezuelan

'vengo *ecc* VB *vedi* **venire**

veni'ale AG venial

ve'nire /128/ VI to come; (*riuscire: dolce, fotografia*) to turn out; (*come ausiliare: essere*): **viene ammirato da tutti** he is admired by everyone; **~ da** to come from; **quanto viene?** how much does it cost?; **far ~** (*mandare a chiamare*) to send for; (*medico*) to call, send for; **~ a capo di qc** to unravel sth, sort sth out; **~ al dunque** o **nocciolo** o **fatto** to come to the point; **~ fuori** to come out; **~ giù** to come down; **~ meno** (*svenire*) to faint; **~ meno a qc** not to fulfil sth; **~ su** to come up; **~ via** to come away; **~ a sapere qc** to learn sth; **~ a trovare qn** to come and see sb; **negli anni a ~** in the years to come, in future; **è venuto il momento di ...** the time has come to ...

'venni *ecc* VB *vedi* **venire**

ven'taglio [ven'taʎʎo] SM fan

ven'tata SF gust (of wind)

venten'nale AG (*che dura 20 anni*) twenty-year cpd; (*che ricorre ogni 20 anni*) which takes place every twenty years

ven'tenne AG: **una ragazza ~** a twenty-year-old girl, a girl of twenty ▶ SMF twenty-year-old

ven'tennio SM period of twenty years; **il ~ fascista** the Fascist period

ven'tesimo, -a NUM twentieth

'venti NUM twenty

venti'lare /72/ VT (*stanza*) to air, ventilate; (*fig: idea, proposta*) to air

venti'lato, -a AG (*camera, zona*) airy; **poco ~** airless

ventila'tore SM fan; (*su parete, finestra*) ventilator, fan

ventilazi'one [ventilat'tsjone] SF ventilation

ven'tina SF: **una ~ (di)** around twenty, twenty or so

ventiquattr'ore SFPL (*periodo*) twenty-four hours ▶ SF INV (*Sport*) twenty-four-hour race; (*valigetta*) overnight case

venti'sette NUM twenty-seven; **il ~** (*giorno di paga*) (monthly) pay day

ventitré NUM twenty-three ▶ SFPL: **portava il cappello sulle ~** he wore his hat at a jaunty angle

'vento SM wind; **c'è ~** it's windy; **un colpo di ~** a gust of wind; **contro ~** against the wind; **~ contrario** (*Naut*) headwind

V

'**ventola** SF (*Aut, Tecn*) fan

ven'tosa SF (*Zool*) sucker; (*di gomma*) suction pad

ven'toso, -a AG windy

ven'totto NUM twenty-eight

'**ventre** SM stomach

ven'triloquo SM ventriloquist

ven'tuno NUM twenty-one

ven'tura SF: **andare alla ~** to trust to luck; **soldato di ~** mercenary

ven'turo, -a AG next, coming

ve'nuto, -a PP *di* **venire** ▶ SM/F: **il(la) primo(a) ~(a)** the first person who comes along ▶ SF coming, arrival

ver. ABBR = **versamento**

'**vera** SF wedding ring

ve'race [ve'ratʃe] AG (*testimone*) truthful; (*testimonianza*) accurate; (*cibi*) real, genuine

vera'mente AV really

ve'randa SF veranda(h)

ver'bale AG verbal ▶ SM (*di riunione*) minutes *pl*; **accordo ~** verbal agreement; **mettere a ~** to place in the minutes o on record

'**verbo** SM (*Ling*) verb; (*parola*) word; (*Rel*): **il V~** the Word

ver'boso, -a AG verbose, wordy

ver'dastro, -a AG greenish

'**verde** AG, SM green; **~ bottiglia/oliva** (*inv*) bottle/olive green; **benzina ~** lead-free o unleaded petrol; **i Verdi** (*Pol*) the Greens; **essere al ~** (*fig*) to be broke

verdeggi'ante [verded'dʒante] AG green, verdant

verde'rame SM verdigris

ver'detto SM verdict

ver'dura SF vegetables *pl*

vere'condia SF modesty

vere'condo, -a AG modest

'**verga, -ghe** SF rod

ver'gato, -a AG (*foglio*) ruled

vergi'nale [verdʒi'nale] AG virginal

'**vergine** ['verdʒine] SF virgin; **V~** Virgo ▶ AG virgin; (*ragazza*): **essere ~** to be a virgin; **essere della V~** (*dello zodiaco*) to be Virgo; **pura lana ~** pure new wool; **olio ~ d'oliva** unrefined olive oil

verginità [verdʒini'ta] SF virginity

ver'gogna [ver'goɲɲa] SF shame; (*timidezza*) shyness, embarrassment

vergo'gnarsi [vergoɲ'ɲarsi] /15/ VPR: **~ (di)** to be o feel ashamed (of); to be shy (about), be embarrassed (about)

vergo'gnoso, -a [vergoɲ'ɲoso] AG ashamed; (*timido*) shy, embarrassed; (*causa di vergogna: azione*) shameful

veridicità [veriditʃi'ta] SF truthfulness

ve'ridico, -a, -ci, -che AG truthful

ve'rifica, -che SF checking *no pl*; check; **fare una ~ di** (*freni, testimonianza, firma*) to check; **~ contabile** (*Finanza*) audit

verifi'care /20/ VT (*controllare*) to check; (*confermare*) to confirm, bear out; (*Finanza*) to audit

verità SF INV truth; **a dire la ~, per la ~** truth to tell, actually

veriti'ero, -a AG (*che dice la verità*) truthful; (*conforme a verità*) true

'**verme** SM worm

vermi'celli [vermi'tʃelli] SMPL vermicelli *sg*

ver'miglio [ver'miʎʎo] SM vermilion, scarlet

'**vermut** SM INV vermouth

ver'nacolo SM vernacular

ver'nice [ver'nitʃe] SF (*colorazione*) paint; (*trasparente*) varnish; (*pelle*) patent leather; **"~ fresca"** "wet paint"

vernici'are [verni'tʃare] /14/ VT to paint; to varnish

vernicia'tura [vernitʃa'tura] SF painting; varnishing

'**vero, -a** AG (*veridico: fatti, testimonianza*) true; (*autentico*) real ▶ SM (*verità*) truth; (*realtà*) (real) life; **un ~ e proprio delinquente** a real criminal, an out and out criminal; **tant'è ~ che ...** so much so that ...; **a onor del ~, a dire il ~** to tell the truth

Ve'rona SF Verona

vero'nese AG of (o from) Verona

vero'simile AG likely, probable

verrò *ecc* VB *vedi* **venire**

ver'ruca, -che SF wart

versa'mento SM (*pagamento*) payment; (*deposito di denaro*) deposit

ver'sante SM slopes *pl*, side

ver'sare /72/ VT (*fare uscire: vino, farina*) to pour (out); (*spargere: lacrime, sangue*) to shed; (*rovesciare*) to spill; (*Econ*) to pay; (*: depositare*) to deposit, pay in ▶ VI: **~ in gravi difficoltà** to find o.s. with serious problems ■ **versarsi** VPR (*rovesciarsi*) to spill; (*fiume, folla*) **versarsi (in)** to pour (into)

versa'tile AG versatile

versatilità SF versatility

ver'sato, -a AG: **~ in** to be (well-)versed in

ver'setto SM (*Rel*) verse

versi'one SF version; (*traduzione*) translation

'**verso** SM (*di poesia*) verse, line; (*di animale, uccello, venditore ambulante*) cry; (*direzione*) direction; (*modo*) way; (*di foglio di carta*) verso; (*di moneta*) reverse ■ **versi** SMPL (*poesia*) verse *sg* ▶ PREP (*in direzione di*) toward(s); (*nei pressi di*) near, around (about); (*in senso temporale*) about, around; (*nei confronti di*) for; **per un ~ o per l'altro** one way or another; **prendere qn/qc per il ~ giusto** to approach sb/sth the right way; **rifare il ~ a qn** (*imitare*) to mimic sb; **non c'è ~ di persuaderlo** there's no way of persuading him, he can't be persuaded; **~ di me** towards me; **~ l'alto** upwards; **~ il basso** downwards; **~ sera** towards evening

'**vertebra** SF vertebra

verte'brale AG vertebral; **colonna ~** spinal column, spine

verte'brato, -a AG, SM vertebrate

ver'tenza [ver'tɛntsa] SF (*lite*) lawsuit, case; (*sindacale*) dispute

'**vertere** /45/ VI: **~ su** to deal with, be about

verti'cale AG, SF vertical

'**vertice** ['vertitʃe] SM summit, top; (*Mat*) vertex; **conferenza al ~** (*Pol*) summit conference

ver'tigine [ver'tidʒine] SF dizziness *no pl*; dizzy spell; (*Med*) vertigo; **avere le vertigini** to feel dizzy

vertigi'noso, -a [vertidʒi'noso] AG (*altezza*) dizzy; (*fig*) breathtakingly high (*o deep etc*)

'**verza** ['verdza] SF Savoy cabbage

ve'scica, -che [veʃ'ʃika] SF (*Anat*) bladder; (*Med*) blister

vesco'vile AG episcopal

'**vescovo** SM bishop

'**vespa** SF wasp; (*veicolo*): **~®** (motor) scooter

ves'paio SM wasps' nest; **suscitare un ~** (*fig*) to stir up a hornets' nest

vespasi'ano SM urinal

'**vespro** SM (*Rel*) vespers *pl*

ves'sare /72/ VT to oppress

vessazi'one [vessat'tsjone] SF oppression

ves'sillo SM standard; (*bandiera*) flag

ves'taglia [ves'taʎʎa] SF dressing gown, robe (*US*)

'**veste** SF garment; (*rivestimento*) covering; (*qualità, facoltà*) capacity ■ **vesti** SFPL clothes, clothing *sg*; **in ~ ufficiale** (*fig*) in an official capacity; **in ~ di** in the guise of, as; **~ da camera** dressing gown, robe (*US*); **~ editoriale** layout

vesti'ario SM wardrobe, clothes *pl*; **capo di ~** article of clothing, garment

ves'tibolo SM (entrance) hall

ves'tigia [ves'tidʒa] SFPL (*tracce*) vestiges, traces; (*rovine*) ruins, remains

ves'tire /45/ VT (*bambino, malato*) to dress; (*avere indosso*) to have on, wear ■ **vestirsi** VPR to dress, get dressed; **vestirsi da** (*negozio, sarto*) to buy *o* get one's clothes at

ves'tito, -a AG dressed ▶ SM garment; (*da donna*) dress; (*da uomo*) suit ■ **vestiti** SMPL (*indumenti*) clothes; **~ di bianco** dressed in white

Ve'suvio SM: **il ~** Vesuvius

vete'rano, -a AG, SM/F veteran

veteri'nario, -a AG veterinary ▶ SM/F veteri-

nary surgeon (*BRIT*), veterinarian (*US*), vet ▶ SF veterinary medicine

'**veto** SM INV veto; **porre il ~ a qc** to veto sth

ve'traio SM glassmaker; (*per finestre*) glazier

ve'trato, -a AG (*porta, finestra*) glazed; (*che contiene vetro*) glass *cpd* ▶ SF glass door (*o window*); (*di chiesa*) stained glass window; **carta vetrata** sandpaper

vetre'ria SF (*stabilimento*) glassworks *sg*; (*oggetti di vetro*) glassware

ve'trina SF (*di negozio*) (shop) window; (*armadio*) display cabinet

vetri'nista, -i, -e SM/F window dresser

ve'trino SM slide

vetri'olo SM vitriol

'**vetro** SM glass; (*per finestra, porta*) pane (of glass); **~ blindato** bulletproof glass; **~ infrangibile** shatterproof glass; **~ di sicurezza** safety glass; **i vetri di Murano** Murano glassware *sg*

ve'troso, -a AG vitreous

'**vetta** SF peak, summit, top

vet'tore SM (*Mat, Fisica*) vector; (*chi trasporta*) carrier

vetto'vaglie [vetto'vaʎʎe] SFPL supplies

vet'tura SF (*carrozza*) carriage; (*Ferr*) carriage (*BRIT*), car (*US*); (*auto*) car (*BRIT*), automobile (*US*); **~ di piazza** hackney carriage

vettu'rino SM coach driver, coachman

vezzeggi'are [vettsed'dʒare] /62/ VT to fondle, caress

vezzeggia'tivo [vettseddʒa'tivo] SM (*Ling*) term of endearment

'**vezzo** ['vettso] SM habit ■ **vezzi** SMPL (*smancerie*) affected ways; (*leggiadria*) charms

vez'zoso, -a [vet'tsoso] AG (*grazioso*) charming, pretty; (*lezioso*) affected

V.F. ABBR = **vigili del fuoco**

VI SIGLA = **Vicenza**

vi (*dav lo, la, li, le, ne diventa* **ve**) PRON (*oggetto*) you; (*complemento di termine*) (to) you; (*riflessivo*) yourselves; (*reciproco*) each other ▶ AV (*lì*) there; (*qui*) here; (*per questo/quel luogo*) through here/there; **vi è/sono** there is/are

'**via** SF (*gen*) way; (*strada*) street; (*sentiero, pista*) path, track; (*Amm: procedimento*) channels *pl* ▶ PREP (*passando per*) via, by way of ▶ AV away ▶ ESCL go away!; (*suvvia*) come on!; (*Sport*) go! ▶ SM (*Sport*) starting signal; **per ~ di** (*a causa di*) because of, on account of; **in *o* per ~** on the way; **in ~ di guarigione** (*fig*) on the road to recovery; **per ~ aerea** by air; (*lettere*) by airmail; **~ satellite** by satellite; **andare/essere ~** to go/be away; **~ ~** (*pian piano*) gradually; **~ ~ che** (*a mano a mano*) as; **e ~ dicendo, e ~ di questo passo** and so on (and so forth); **dare il ~** (*Sport*) to give the starting signal; **dare il ~ a** (*fig*) to start; **dare il ~ a un progetto** to give the green light to a project; **hanno dato il ~ ai lavori** they've begun o started work; **in ~ amichevole** in a friendly manner; **comporre una disputa in ~ amichevole** (Dir) to settle a dispute out of court; **in ~ eccezionale** as an exception; **in ~ privata** o **confidenziale** (dire ecc) in confidence; **in ~ provvisoria** provisionally; **V~ lattea** (Astr) Milky Way; **~ di mezzo** middle course; **non c'è ~ di scampo** o **d'uscita** there's no way out; **vie di comunicazione** communication routes

viabilità SF (di strada) practicability; (rete stradale) roads pl, road network

via'dotto SM viaduct

viaggi'are [viad'dʒare] /62/ VI to travel; **le merci viaggiano via mare** the goods go by sea

viaggia'tore, -'trice [viaddʒa'tore] AG travelling (Brit), traveling (US) ▶ SM/F traveller (Brit), traveler (US), passenger

vi'aggio [vi'addʒo] SM travel(ling); (tragitto) journey, trip; **buon ~!** have a good trip!; **~ d'affari** business trip; **~ di nozze** honeymoon; **~ organizzato** package tour o holiday

---

Ci si può confondere tra **journey**, **trip** e **travel**. **Journey** indica quel particolare viaggio.
un lungo viaggio in treno **a long train journey**
Trip comprende l'intera esperienza di andare, stare e tornare.
un viaggio fantastico in India **a fantastic trip to India**
un viaggio d'affari **a business trip**
Travel indica il viaggiare in generale, non ha mai l'articolo.
Il viaggiare apre la mente. **Travel broadens the mind.**
diari di viaggio **travel diaries**

---

vi'ale SM avenue

vian'dante SMF vagrant

vi'atico, -ci SM (Rel) viaticum; (fig) encouragement

via'vai SM coming and going, bustle

vi'brare /72/ VI to vibrate; (agitarsi): **~ (di)** to quiver (with)

vibra'tore SM vibrator

vibrazi'one [vibrat'tsjone] SF vibration

vi'cario SM (apostolico ecc) vicar

'vice ['vitʃe] SMF deputy ▶ PREFISSO vice

vice'console [vitʃe'kɔnsole] SM vice-consul

vicediret'tore, -'trice [vitʃediret'tore] SM/F assistant manager (manageress); (di giornale ecc) deputy editor

vi'cenda [vi'tʃenda] SF event ■ **vicende** SFPL (sorte) fortunes; **a ~** in turn; **con alterne vicende** with mixed fortunes

vicen'devole [vitʃen'devole] AG mutual, reciprocal

vicen'tino, -a [vitʃen'tino] AG of (o from) Vicenza

vicepresi'dente [vitʃepresi'dɛnte] SM vice-president, vice-chairman

vice'versa [vitʃe'vɛrsa] AV vice versa; **da Roma a Pisa e ~** from Rome to Pisa and back

vi'chingo, -a, -ghi, -ghe [vi'kingo] AG, SM/F Viking

vici'nanza [vitʃi'nantsa] SF nearness, closeness ■ **vicinanze** SFPL (paraggi) neighbourhood (Brit), neighborhood (US), vicinity

vici'nato [vitʃi'nato] SM neighbourhood (Brit), neighborhood (US); (vicini) neighbo(u)rs pl

vi'cino, -a [vi'tʃino] AG (gen) near; (nello spazio) near, nearby; (accanto) next; (nel tempo) near, close at hand ▶ SM/F neighbour (Brit), neighbor (US) ▶ AV near, close; **da ~** (guardare) close up; (esaminare, seguire) closely; (conoscere) well, intimately; **~ a** prep near (to), close to; (accanto a) beside; **mi sono stati molto vicini** (fig) they were very supportive towards me; **~ di casa** neighbour

vicissi'tudini [vitʃissi'tudini] SFPL trials and tribulations

'vicolo SM alley; **~ cieco** blind alley

'video SM INV (TV: schermo) screen

video'blog SM INV video blog, vlog

video'camera SF camcorder

videocas'setta SF videocassette

videochia'mare [videokja'mare] /72/ VT to video-call

videochia'mata [videokja'mata] SF video call

video'clip [video'klip] SM INV videoclip

videoconfe'renza [videokonfe'renza] SF videoconference

videodipen'dente SMF telly addict ▶ AG: **un pigrone ~** a couch potato

videofo'nino SM video mobile

videogi'oco, -chi [video'dʒɔko] SM video game

videointer'vista SF video interview

videono'leggio [videono'leddʒo] SM video rental

videoproiet'tore SM video projector

videoproie'zione [videoprojet'tsjone] SF video projection

videoregistra'tore [videoredʒistra'tore] SM (apparecchio) video (recorder)

video'teca, -che SF video shop

videote'lefono SM videophone

videotermi'nale SM visual display unit

'vidi ecc VB vedi **vedere**

vidi'mare /72/ VT (Amm) to authenticate

vidimazi'one [vidimat'tsjone] SF (Amm) authentication

Vi'enna SF Vienna

vien'nese AG, SMF Viennese inv

vie'tare /72/ VT to forbid; (Amm) to prohibit;

(*libro*) to ban; **~ a qn di fare** to forbid sb to do; to prohibit sb from doing

vie'tato, -a AG (*vedi vb*) forbidden; prohibited; banned; **"~ fumare/l'ingresso"** "no smoking/admittance"; **~ ai minori di 14/18 anni** prohibited to children under 14/18; **"senso ~"** (*Aut*) "no entry"; **"sosta vietata"** (*Aut*) "no parking"

Viet'nam SM: **il ~** Vietnam

vietna'mita, -i, -e AG, SM/F, SM Vietnamese *inv*

vi'eto, -a AG worthless

vi'gente [vi'dʒɛnte] AG in force

'vigere ['vidʒere] VI (*difettivo: si usa solo alla terza persona*) to be in force; **in casa mia vige l'abitudine di ...** at home we are in the habit of ...

vigi'lante [vidʒi'lante] AG vigilant, watchful

vigi'lanza [vidʒi'lantsa] SF vigilance; (*sorveglianza: di operai, alunni*) supervision; (: *di sospetti, criminali*) surveillance; **~ notturna** night-watchman service

vigi'lare [vidʒi'lare] /**72**/ VT to watch over, keep an eye on; **~ che** to make sure that, see to it that

vigi'lato, -a [vidʒi'lato] SM/F (*Dir*) person under police surveillance

vigila'trice [vidʒila'tritʃe] SF: **~ d'infanzia** nursery-school teacher; **~ scolastica** school health officer

'vigile ['vidʒile] AG watchful ▶ SM (*anche:* **vigile urbano**) policeman (*in towns*); **~ del fuoco** fireman; *see note*

The **vigili urbani** are a municipal police force attached to the *Comune*. They are responsible for enforcing traffic and parking regulations, and regulations relating to the sale of goods and services.

vigi'lessa [vidʒi'lessa] SF (traffic) policewoman

vi'gilia [vi'dʒilja] SF (*giorno antecedente*) eve; **la ~ di Natale** Christmas Eve

vigliacche'ria [viʎʎakke'ria] SF cowardice

vigli'acco, -a, -chi, -che [viʎ'ʎakko] AG cowardly ▶ SM/F coward

'vigna ['viɲɲa] SF, **vi'gneto** [viɲ'ɲeto] SM vineyard

vi'gnetta [viɲ'ɲetta] SF cartoon; (*Aut: anche:* **vignetta autostradale**: *tassa*) car tax (*for motorways*); (: *adesivo*) sticker showing that this tax has been paid

vi'gogna [vi'goɲɲa] SF vicuña

vi'gore SM vigour (*Brit*), vigor (*US*); (*Dir*): **essere/entrare in ~** to be in/come into force; **non è più in ~** it is no longer in force, it no longer applies

vigo'roso, -a AG vigorous

'vile AG (*spregevole*) low, mean, base; (*codardo*) cowardly

vili'pendere /**8**/ VT to despise, scorn

vili'pendio SM contempt, scorn

vili'peso, -a PP *di* **vilipendere**

'villa SF villa

vil'laggio [vil'laddʒo] SM village; **~ turistico** holiday village

villa'nia SF rudeness, lack of manners; **fare (o dire) una ~ a qn** to be rude to sb

vil'lano, -a AG rude, ill-mannered ▶ SM/F boor

villeggi'ante [villed'dʒante] SMF holiday-maker (*Brit*), vacationer (*US*)

villeggi'are [villed'dʒare] /**62**/ VI to holiday, spend one's holidays, vacation (*US*)

villeggia'tura [villeddʒa'tura] SF holiday(s *pl*) (*Brit*), vacation (*US*); **luogo di ~** (holiday) resort

vil'letta SF, **vil'lino** SM small house (with a garden), cottage

vil'loso, -a AG hairy

viltà SF cowardice *no pl*; (*gesto*) cowardly act

Vimi'nale SM *the Ministry of the Interior, located on one of the Seven Hills of Rome, from which it takes its name*

'vimini SMPL wicker; **mobili di ~** wicker furniture *sg*

vi'naio SM wine merchant

'vincere ['vintʃere] /**129**/ VT (*in guerra, al gioco, a una gara*) to defeat, beat; (*premio, guerra, partita*) to win; (*fig*) to overcome, conquer ▶ VI to win; **~ qn in** (*abilità, bellezza*) to surpass sb in

'vincita ['vintʃita] SF win; (*denaro vinto*) winnings *pl*

vinci'tore, -'trice [vintʃi'tore] SM/F winner; (*Mil*) victor

vinco'lante AG binding

vinco'lare /**72**/ VT to bind; (*Comm: denaro*) to tie up

vinco'lato, -a AG: **deposito ~** (*Comm*) fixed deposit

'vincolo SM (*fig*) bond, tie; (*Dir*) obligation

vi'nicolo, -a AG wine *cpd*; **regione vinicola** wine-producing area

vinificazi'one [vinifikat'tsjone] SF wine-making

'vino SM wine; **~ bianco/rosato/rosso** white/rosé/red wine; **~ da pasto** table wine

Italy is one of the world's major wine-producing countries. High-quality wines have the letters D.O.C. (*denominazione d'origine controllata*) on the bottle label.

'vinsi *ecc* VB *vedi* **vincere**

'vinto, -a PP *di* **vincere** ▶ AG: **darla vinta a qn** to let sb have his (*o* her) way; **darsi per ~** to give up, give in

vi'ola SF (*Bot*) violet; (*Mus*) viola ▶ AG, SM INV (*colore*) purple

vio'lare /72/ VT (*chiesa*) to desecrate, violate; (*giuramento, legge*) to violate

violazi'one [violat'tsjone] SF desecration; violation; ~ **di domicilio** (*Dir*) breaking and entering

violen'tare /72/ VT to use violence on; (*donna*) to rape

vio'lento, -a AG violent

vio'lenza [vio'lɛntsa] SF violence; ~ **carnale** rape; ~ **domestica** domestic violence

vio'letto, -a AG, SM (*colore*) violet ▶ SF (*Bot*) violet

violi'nista, -i, -e SM/F violinist

vio'lino SM violin

violoncel'lista, -i, -e [violont∫el'lista] SM/F cellist, cello player

violon'cello [violon't∫ɛllo] SM cello

vi'ottolo SM path, track

VIP [vip] SM INV/F INV (= *Very Important Person*) VIP

'vipera SF viper, adder

vi'raggio [vi'raddʒo] SM (*Naut, Aer*) turn; (*Fot*) toning

vi'rale AG (*Inform*) viral

vi'rare /72/ VI (*Naut, Aer*) to turn; (*Fot*) to tone; ~ **di bordo** to change course; (*Naut*) to tack

vi'rata SF coming about; turning; change of course

'virgola SF (*Ling*) comma; (*Mat*) point

virgo'lette SFPL inverted commas, quotation marks

vi'rile AG (*proprio dell'uomo*) masculine; (*non puerile, da uomo*) manly, virile

virilità SF masculinity; manliness; (*sessuale*) virility

virtù SF INV virtue; **in** o **per ~ di** by virtue of, by

virtu'ale AG virtual

virtu'oso, -a AG virtuous ▶ SM/F (*Mus ecc*) virtuoso

viru'lento, -a AG virulent

'virus SM INV (*anche Inform*) virus

visa'gista, -i, -e [viza'dʒista] SM/F beautician

visce'rale [vi∫∫e'rale] AG (*Med*) visceral; (*fig*) profound, deep-rooted

'viscere ['vi∫∫ere] SM (*Anat*) internal organ ▶ SFPL (*di animale*) entrails *pl*; (*fig*) depths *pl*, bowels *pl*

'vischio ['viskjo] SM (*Bot*) mistletoe; (*pania*) birdlime

vischi'oso, -a [vis'kjoso] AG sticky

viscidità [vi∫∫idi'ta] SF sliminess

'viscido, -a ['vi∫∫ido] AG slimy

vis'conte, -'essa SM/F viscount (viscountess)

viscosità SF viscosity

vis'coso, -a AG viscous

vi'sibile AG visible

visi'bilio SM: **andare in ~** to go into raptures

visibilità SF visibility

visi'era SF (*di elmo*) visor; (*di berretto*) peak

visio'nare /72/ VT (*gen*) to look at, examine; (*Cine*) to screen

visio'nario, -a AG, SM/F visionary

visi'one SF vision; **prendere ~ di qc** to examine sth, look sth over; **prima/seconda ~** (*Cine*) first/second showing

'visita SF visit; (*Med*) visit, call; (: *esame*) examination; **far ~ a qn, andare in ~ da qn** to visit sb, pay sb a visit; **in ~ ufficiale in Italia** on an official visit to Italy; **orario di visite** (*ospedale*) visiting hours; ~ **di controllo** (*Med*) checkup; ~ **medica** medical examination; ~ **a domicilio** house call; ~ **guidata** guided tour; ~ **sanitaria** sanitary inspection

visi'tare /72/ VT to visit; (*Med*) to visit, call on; (: *esaminare*) to examine

visita'tore, -'trice SM/F visitor

vi'sivo, -a AG visual

'viso SM face; **fare buon ~ a cattivo gioco** to make the best of things

vi'sone SM mink

vi'sore SM (*Fot*) viewer

'vispo, -a AG quick, lively

'vissi *ecc* VB *vedi* **vivere**

vis'suto, -a PP *di* **vivere** ▶ AG (*aria, modo di fare*) experienced

'vista SF (*facoltà*) (eye)sight; (*veduta*) view; (*fatto di vedere*): **la ~ di** the sight of; **con ~ sul lago** with a view over the lake; **sparare a ~** to shoot on sight; **pagabile a ~** payable on demand; **in ~** in sight; **avere in ~ qc** to have sth in view; **mettersi in ~** to draw attention to o.s.; (*peg*) to show off; **perdere qn di ~** to lose sight of sb; (*fig*) to lose touch with sb; **far ~ di fare** to pretend to do; **a ~ d'occhio** as far as the eye can see; (*fig*) before one's very eyes

vis'tare /72/ VT to approve; (*Amm: passaporto*) to visa

'visto, -a PP *di* **vedere** ▶ SM visa; ~ **che** *cong* seeing (that); ~ **d'ingresso/di transito** entry/transit visa; ~ **permanente/di soggiorno** permanent/tourist visa

vis'toso, -a AG gaudy, garish; (*ingente*) considerable

visu'ale AG visual

visualiz'zare [vizualid'dzare] /72/ VT to visualize

visualizza'tore [vizualiddza'tore] SM (*Inform*) visual display unit, VDU

visualizzazi'one [vizualiddzat'tsjone] SF (*Inform*) display

'vita SF life; (*Anat*) waist; **essere in ~** to be alive; **pieno di ~** full of life; **a ~** for life; **membro a ~** life member

vi'tale AG vital

vitalità SF vitality

vita'lizio, -a [vita'littsjo] AG life *cpd* ▶ SM life annuity

vita'mina SF vitamin

'vite SF (*Bot*) vine; (*Tecn*) screw; **giro di ~** (*anche fig*) turn of the screw

vi'tello SM (*Zool*) calf; (*carne*) veal; (*pelle*) calfskin

vi'ticcio [vi'tittʃo] SM (*Bot*) tendril

viticol'tore SM wine grower

viticol'tura SF wine growing

'vitreo, -a AG vitreous; (*occhio, sguardo*) glassy

'vittima SF victim

vitti'mismo SM self-pity

'vitto SM food; (*in un albergo ecc*) board; **~ e alloggio** board and lodging

vit'toria SF victory

vittori'ano, -a AG Victorian

vittori'oso, -a AG victorious

vitupe'rare /**72**/ VT to rail at *o* against

vi'uzza [vi'uttsa] SF (*in città*) alley

'viva ESCL: **~ il re!** long live the king!

vivacchi'are [vivak'kjare] /**19**/ VI to scrape a living

vi'vace [vi'vatʃe] AG (*vivo, animato*) lively; (*mente*) lively, sharp; (*colore*) bright

vivacità [vivatʃi'ta] SF liveliness; brightness

vivaciz'zare [vivatʃid'dzare] /**72**/ VT to liven up

vi'vaio SM (*di pesci*) hatchery; (*Agr*) nursery

viva'mente AV (*commuoversi*) deeply, profoundly; (*ringraziare ecc*) sincerely, warmly

vi'vanda SF food; (*piatto*) dish

viva'voce [viva'votʃe] SM INV (*dispositivo*) loudspeaker ▶ AG INV: **telefono ~** speakerphone; **mettere in ~** to switch on the loudspeaker

vi'vente AG living, alive; **i viventi** the living

'vivere /**130**/ VI to live ▶ VT to live; (*passare: brutto momento*) to live through, go through; (*sentire: gioie, pene di qn*) to share ▶ SM life; (*anche:* **modo di vivere**) way of life ■ **viveri** SMPL (*cibo*) food *sg*, provisions; **~ di** to live on

vi'veur [vi'vœr] SM INV pleasure-seeker

'vivido, -a AG (*colore*) vivid, bright

vivifi'care /**20**/ VT to enliven, give life to; (*piante ecc*) to revive

vivisezi'one [viviset'tsjone] SF vivisection

'vivo, -a AG (*vivente*) alive, living; (: *animale*) live; (*fig*) lively; (: *colore*) bright, brilliant ▶ SM: **entrare nel ~ di una questione** to get to the heart of a matter; **i vivi** the living; **esperimenti su animali vivi** experiments on live *o* living animals; **~ e vegeto** hale and hearty; **farsi ~** (*fig*) to show one's face; to keep in touch; **con ~ rammarico** with deep regret; **congratulazioni vivissime** heartiest congratulations; **con i più vivi ringraziamenti** with deepest *o*

warmest thanks; **ritrarre dal ~** to paint from life; **pungere qn nel ~** (*fig*) to cut sb to the quick

vivrò *ecc* VB *vedi* **vivere**

vizi'are [vit'tsjare] /**19**/ VT (*bambino*) to spoil; (*corrompere moralmente*) to corrupt; (*Dir*) to invalidate

vizi'ato, -a [vit'tsjato] AG spoilt; (*aria, acqua*) polluted; (*Dir*) invalid, invalidated

'vizio ['vittsjo] SM (*morale*) vice; (*cattiva abitudine*) bad habit; (*imperfezione*) flaw, defect; (*errore*) fault, mistake; **~ di forma** *o* irregularity; **~ procedurale** procedural error

vizi'oso, -a [vit'tsjoso] AG depraved; (*inesatto*) incorrect; **circolo ~** vicious circle

V.le ABBR = **viale**

vocabo'lario SM (*dizionario*) dictionary; (*lessico*) vocabulary

vo'cabolo SM word

vo'cale AG vocal ▶ SF vowel

vocazi'one [vokat'tsjone] SF vocation; (*fig*) natural bent

'voce ['votʃe] SF voice; (*diceria*) rumour (BRIT), rumor (US); (*di un elenco: in bilancio*) item; (*di dizionario*) entry; **parlare a alta/bassa ~** to speak in a loud/low *o* soft voice; **fare la ~ grossa** to raise one's voice; **dar ~ a qc** to voice sth, give voice to sth; **a gran ~** in a loud voice, loudly; **te lo dico a ~** I'll tell you when I see you; **a una ~** unanimously; **aver ~ in capitolo** (*fig*) to have a say in the matter; **voci di corridoio** rumours

voci'are [vo'tʃare] /**14**/ VI to shout, yell

vocife'rante [votʃife'rante] AG noisy

vo'cio [vo'tʃio] SM shouting

'vodka SF INV vodka

'voga SF (*Naut*) rowing; (*usanza*): **essere in ~** to be in fashion *o* in vogue

vo'gare /**80**/ VI to row

voga'tore, -'trice SM/F oarsman(-woman) ▶ SM rowing machine

vogherò *ecc* [voge'rɔ] VB *vedi* **vogare**

'voglia ['vɔʎʎa] SF desire, wish; (*macchia*) birthmark; **aver ~ di qc/di fare** to feel like sth/like doing; (*più forte*) to want sth/to do; **di buona ~** willingly

'voglio *ecc* ['vɔʎʎo] VB *vedi* **volere**

vogli'oso, -a [voʎ'ʎoso] AG (*sguardo ecc*) longing; (*più forte*) full of desire

'voi PRON you; **~ stessi(e)** you yourselves

voi'altri PRON you

vol. ABBR (= *volume*) vol.

vo'lano SM (*Sport*) shuttlecock; (*Tecn*) flywheel

vo'lant [vo'lã] SM INV frill

vo'lante AG flying ▶ SM (steering) wheel ▶ SF (*Polizia: anche:* **squadra volante**) flying squad

volanti'naggio [volanti'naddʒo] SM leafleting

volanti'nare /72/ VT (*distribuire volantini*) to leaflet, hand out leaflets

volan'tino SM leaflet

vo'lare /72/ VI (*uccello, aereo, fig*) to fly; (*cappello*) to blow away *o* off, fly away *o* off; **~ via** to fly away *o* off

vo'lata SF flight; (*d'uccelli*) flock, flight; (*corsa*) rush; (*Sport*) final sprint; **passare di ~ da qn** to drop in on sb briefly

vo'latile AG (*Chim*) volatile ▶ SM (*Zool*) bird

volatiliz'zarsi [volatilid'dzarsi] /61/ VPR (*Chim*) to volatilize; (*fig*) to vanish, disappear

vo'lente AG: **verrai ~ o nolente** you'll come whether you like it or not

volente'roso, -a AG willing, keen

volenti'eri AV willingly; **"~"** "with pleasure", "I'd be glad to"

---

vo'lere

/131/ SM will, wish(es); **contro il volere di** against the wishes of; **per volere di qn** in obedience to sb's will *o* wishes

▶ VT **1** (*esigere, desiderare*) to want; **volere fare qc** to want to do sth; **volere che qn faccia qc** to want sb to do sth; **vorrei andarmene** I'd like to go; **vorrei che se ne andasse** I'd like him to go; **vorrei questo/fare** I would *o* I'd like this/to do; **volevo parlartene** I meant to talk to you about it; **come vuoi** as you like; **la vogliono al telefono** there's a call for you; **che tu lo voglia o no** whether you like it or not; **vuoi un caffè?** would you like a coffee?; **senza volere** (*inavvertitamente*) without meaning to, unintentionally; **te la sei voluta** you asked for it; **la tradizione vuole che ...** custom requires that ...; **la leggenda vuole che ...** legend has it that ...

2 (*consentire*): **vogliate attendere, per piacere** please wait; **vogliamo andare?** shall we go?; **vuole essere così gentile da ...?** would you be so kind as to ...?; **non ha voluto ricevermi** he wouldn't see me

3: **volerci** (*essere necessario: materiale, attenzione*) to be needed; (: *tempo*) to take; **quanta farina ci vuole per questa torta?** how much flour do you need for this cake?; **ci vuole un'ora per arrivare a Venezia** it takes an hour to get to Venice; **è quel che ci vuole** it's just what is needed

4: **voler bene a qn** (*amore*) to love sb; (*affetto*) to be fond of sb, like sb very much; **voler male a qn** to dislike sb; **volerne a qn** to bear sb a grudge; **voler dire** to mean; **voglio dire ...** I mean ...; **volevo ben dire!** I thought as much!

---

vol'gare AG vulgar

volgarità SF vulgarity

volgariz'zare [volgarid'dzare] /72/ VT to popularize

volgar'mente AV (*in modo volgare*) vulgarly, coarsely; (*del popolo*) commonly, popularly

'volgere ['vɔldʒere] /96/ VT to turn ▶ VI to turn; (*tendere*): **~ a**: **il tempo volge al brutto/al bello** the weather is breaking/is setting fair; **un rosso che volge al viola** a red verging on purple ■ **volgersi** VPR to turn; **~ al peggio** to take a turn for the worse; **~ al termine** to draw to an end

'volgo SM common people

voli'era SF aviary

voli'tivo, -a AG strong-willed

'volli *ecc* VB *vedi* volere

'volo SM flight; **ci sono due ore di ~ da Londra a Milano** it's a two-hour flight between London and Milan; **colpire qc al ~** to hit sth as it flies past; **prendere al ~** (*autobus, treno*) to catch at the last possible moment; (*palla*) to catch as it flies past; (*occasione*) to seize; **capire al ~** to understand straight away; **veduta a ~ d'uccello** bird's-eye view; **~ charter** charter flight; **~ di linea** scheduled flight

volontà SF INV will; **a ~** (*mangiare, bere*) as much as one likes; **buona/cattiva ~** goodwill/lack of goodwill; **le sue ultime ~** (*testamento*) his last will and testament *sg*

volontaria'mente AV voluntarily

volontari'ato SM (*Mil*) voluntary service; (*lavoro*) voluntary work

volon'tario, -a AG voluntary ▶ SM/F (*Mil*) volunteer

'volpe SF fox

vol'pino, -a AG (*pelo, coda*) fox's; (*aspetto, astuzia*) fox-like ▶ SM (*cane*) Pomeranian

vol'pone, -a SM/F (*fig*) old fox

'volsi *ecc* VB *vedi* volgere

volt SM INV (*Elettr*) volt

'volta SF (*momento, circostanza*) time; (*turno, giro*) turn; (*curva*) turn, bend; (*Archit*) vault; (*direzione*): **partire alla ~ di** to set off for; **a mia** (*o* **tua** *etc*) **~** in turn; **una ~** once; **una ~ sola** only once; **c'era una ~** once upon a time there was; **le cose di una ~** the things of the past; **due volte** twice; **tre volte** three times; **una cosa per ~** one thing at a time; **una ~ o l'altra** one of these days; **una ~ per tutte** once and for all; **una ~ tanto** just for once; **lo facciamo un'altra ~** we'll do it another time *o* some other time; **a volte** at times, sometimes; **di ~ in ~** from time to time; **una ~ che** (*temporale*) once; (*causale*) since; **3 volte 4** 3 times 4; **ti ha dato di ~ il cervello?** have you gone out of your mind?

volta'faccia [volta'fattʃa] SM INV (*fig*) volte-face

vol'taggio [vol'taddʒo] SM (*Elettr*) voltage

vol'tare /72/ VT to turn; (*girare: moneta*) to turn over; (*rigirare*) to turn round ▶ VI to turn ■ **voltarsi** VPR to turn; to turn over; to turn round

voltas'tomaco SM nausea; (fig) disgust

volteggi'are [volted'dʒare] /62/ VI (volare) to circle; (in equitazione) to do trick riding; (in ginnastica) to vault

'volto, -a PP di **volgere** ▶ AG (inteso a): **il mio discorso è ~ a spiegare ...** in my speech I intend to explain ... ▶ SM face

vo'lubile AG changeable, fickle

vo'lume SM volume

volumi'noso, -a AG voluminous, bulky

vo'luta SF (gen) spiral; (Archit) volute

voluttà SF sensual pleasure o delight

voluttu'oso, -a AG voluptuous

vomi'tare /72/ VT, VI to vomit

'vomito SM vomiting no pl; vomit; **ho il ~** I feel sick

'vongola SF clam

vo'race [vo'ratʃe] AG voracious, greedy

voracità [voratʃi'ta] SF voracity, voraciousness

vo'ragine [vo'radʒine] SF abyss, chasm

vorrò ecc VB vedi **volere**

'vortice ['vɔrtitʃe] SM whirlwind; whirlpool; (fig) whirl

vorti'coso, -a AG whirling

'vostro, -a DET: **il (la) ~(a)** ecc your ▶ PRON: **il (la) ~(a)** ecc yours ▶ SM: **avete speso del ~?** did you spend your own money? ▶ SF: **la vostra** (opinione) your view; **i vostri** (famiglia) your family; **un ~ amico** a friend of yours; **è dei vostri**, **è dalla vostra** he's on your side; **l'ultima vostra** (Comm: lettera) your most recent letter; **alla vostra!** (brindisi) here's to you!, your health!

vo'tante SMF voter

vo'tare /72/ VI to vote ▶ VT (sottoporre a votazione) to take a vote on; (approvare) to vote for; (Rel): **~ qc a** to dedicate sth to ■ **votarsi** VPR to devote o.s. to

votazi'one [votat'tsjone] SF vote, voting ■ **votazioni** SFPL (Pol) votes; (Ins) marks

'voto SM (Pol) vote; (Ins) mark (BRIT), grade (US); (Rel) vow; (: offerta) votive offering; **aver voti belli/brutti** (Ins) to get good/bad marks o grades; **prendere i voti** to take one's vows; **~ di fiducia** vote of confidence

V.P. ABBR (= vicepresidente) VP

VR SIGLA = **Verona**

v.r. ABBR (= vedi retro) PTO

vs. ABBR (= vostro) yr

v.s. ABBR = **vedi sopra**

VT SIGLA = **Viterbo**

V.U. ABBR = **vigile urbano**

vul'canico, -a, -ci, -che AG volcanic

vulcanizzazi'one [vulkaniddzat'tsjone] SF vulcanization

vul'cano SM volcano

vulne'rabile AG vulnerable

vulnerabilità SF vulnerability

vu'oi, vu'ole VB vedi **volere**

vuo'tare /72/ VT, **vuo'tarsi** VPR to empty

vu'oto, -a AG empty; (fig: privo): **~ di** (senso ecc) devoid of ▶ SM empty space, gap; (spazio in bianco) blank; (Fisica) vacuum; (fig: mancanza) gap, void; **a mani vuote** empty-handed; **assegno a ~** dud cheque (BRIT), bad check (US); **~ d'aria** air pocket; **"~ a perdere"** "no deposit"; **"~ a rendere"** "returnable bottle"

W, w [ˈdɔppjovu] SM O F INV (*lettera*) W, w; **W come Washington** ≈ W for William

W ABBR = **viva, evviva**

'wafer [ˈvafer] SM INV (*Cuc, Elettr*) wafer

wagon-'lit [vagɔ̃ˈli] SM INV (*Ferr*) sleeping car

'water [ˈvater] SM INV toilet

'water 'closet [ˈvaterˈklɔzɪt] SM INV toilet, lavatory

watt [vat] SM INV (*Elettr*) watt

wat'tora [vatˈtora] SM INV (*Elettr*) watt-hour

WC [vuˈtʃi] SM INV WC

web [ueb] SM: **il ~** the web ▶ AG INV: **pagina ~** webpage; **cercare nel ~** to search the web

web'cam [webˈkam] SF INV (*Inform*) webcam

'webinar [ˈwɛbinar] SM INV (*Inform*) webinar

web'mail [wɛbˈmeil] SF webmail; **delle ~** (*Inform*) webmail services

'weekend [ˈwiːkend] SM INV weekend

'western [ˈwɛstern] AG (*Cine*) cowboy *cpd* ▶ SM INV western, cowboy film; **~ all'italiana** spaghetti western

'whisky [ˈwiski] SM INV whisky

Wi-Fi [uaiˈfai] (*Inform*) SM Wi-Fi ▶ AG INV Wi-Fi

'wiki [ˈwiki] SM INV (*Internet*) wiki

'windsurf [ˈwindsəːf] SM INV (*tavola*) windsurfer, sailboard; (*sport*) windsurfing

'würstel [ˈvyrstəl] SM INV frankfurter

Xx

X, x [iks] SM O F INV (*lettera*) X, x; **X come Xeres** ≈ X for Xmas

xenofo'bia [ksenofo'bia] SF xenophobia

xe'nofobo, -a [kse'nɔfobo] AG xenophobic ▶ SM/F xenophobe

'xeres ['ksɛres] SM INV sherry

xero'copia [ksero'kɔpja] SF xerox®, photocopy

xerocopi'are [kseroko'pjare] /**19**/ VT to photocopy

xi'lofono [ksi'lɔfono] SM xylophone

Yy

Y, y [ˈipsilon] SM O F INV (*lettera*) Y, y; **Y come Yacht** ≈ Y for Yellow (*BRIT*), ≈ Y for Yoke (*US*)

yacht [jɔt] SM INV yacht

'yankee [ˈjæŋki] SM O F INV Yank, Yankee

Y.C.I. ABBR = **Yacht Club d'Italia**

'Yemen [ˈjemen] SM: **lo ~** Yemen

yen [jen] SM INV (*moneta*) yen

'yiddish [ˈjidiʃ] AG INV, SM INV Yiddish

'yoga [ˈjɔga] AG INV, SM yoga (*cpd*)

'yogurt [ˈjɔgurt] SM INV yog(h)urt

'youtuber [ˈjutuber] SM O F INV YouTuber

Zz

Z, z [ˈdzɛta] SM O F INV (*lettera*) Z, z; **Z come Zara** ≈ Z for Zebra

zabai'one [dzabaˈjone] SM *dessert made of egg yolks, sugar and marsala*

zaf'fata [tsafˈfata] SF (*tanfo*) stench

zaffe'rano [dzaffeˈrano] SM saffron

zaf'firo [dzafˈfiro] SM sapphire

'zagara [ˈdzagara] SF orange blossom

zai'netto [dzaiˈnetto] SM (small) rucksack

'zaino [ˈdzaino] SM rucksack

Za'ire [dzaˈire] SM: **lo ~** Zaire

'Zambia [ˈdzambja] SM: **lo ~** Zambia

'zampa [ˈtsampa] SF (*di animale: gamba*) leg; (: *piede*) paw; **a quattro zampe** on all fours; **zampe di gallina** (*calligrafia*) scrawl; (*rughe*) crow's feet

zam'pata [tsamˈpata] SF (*di cane, gatto*) blow with a paw

zampet'tare [tsampetˈtare] /**72**/ VI to scamper

zampil'lare [tsampilˈlare] /**72**/ VI to gush, spurt

zam'pillo [tsamˈpillo] SM gush, spurt

zam'pino [tsamˈpino] SM paw; **qui c'è sotto il suo ~** (*fig*) he's had a hand in this

zam'pogna [tsamˈpoɲɲa] SF *instrument similar to bagpipes*

'zanna [ˈtsanna] SF (*di elefante*) tusk; (*di carnivori*) fang

zan'zara [dzanˈdzara] SF mosquito

zanzari'era [dzandzaˈrjɛra] SF mosquito net

'zappa [ˈtsappa] SF hoe

zap'pare [tsapˈpare] /**72**/ VT to hoe

zappa'tore [tsappaˈtore] SM (*Agr*) hoer

zappa'tura [tsappaˈtura] SF (*Agr*) hoeing

'zapping [ˈtsapɪŋ] SM (*TV*) channel-hopping

zar, za'rina [tsar, tsaˈrina] SM/F tsar (tsarina)

'zattera [ˈdzattera] SF raft

za'vorra [dzaˈvɔrra] SF ballast

'zazzera [ˈtsattsera] SF shock of hair

'zebra [ˈdzɛbra] SF zebra ▪ **zebre** SFPL (*Aut*) zebra crossing *sg* (BRIT), crosswalk *sg* (US)

ze'brato, -a [dzeˈbrato] AG with black and white stripes; **strisce zebrate, attraversamento ~** (*Aut*) zebra crossing (BRIT), crosswalk (US)

'zecca, -che [ˈtsekka] SF (*Zool*) tick; (*officina di monete*) mint

zec'chino [tsekˈkino] SM gold coin; **oro ~** pure gold

ze'lante [dzeˈlante] AG zealous

'zelo [ˈdzɛlo] SM zeal

'zenit [ˈdzɛnit] SM zenith

zen'zero [ˈdzendzero] SM ginger

'zeppa [ˈtseppa] SF wedge

'zeppo, -a [ˈtseppo] AG: **~ di** crammed *o* packed with

zer'bino [dzerˈbino] SM doormat

'zero [ˈdzɛro] SM zero, nought; **vincere per tre a ~** (*Sport*) to win three-nil

> Zero si traduce con **zero** quando si vuole essere precisi o in linguaggio scientifico: *30 gradi sotto zero* **30 degrees below zero**. Nell'inglese parlato è comune usare **nought**. *da zero a 100 in otto secondi* **from nought to 100 in eight seconds**. Nei risultati sportivi, specie il calcio, si usa **nil**. *due a zero* **two nil**

'zeta [ˈdzɛta] SM O F zed, (the letter) z

'zia [ˈtsia] SF aunt

zibel'lino [dzibelˈlino] SM sable

zi'gano, -a [tsiˈgano] AG, SM/F gypsy

'zigomo [ˈdzigomo] SM cheekbone

zigri'nare [dzigriˈnare] /**72**/ VT (*gen*) to knurl; (*pellame*) to grain; (*monete*) to mill

zig'zag [dzigˈdzag] SM INV zigzag; **andare a ~** to zigzag

Zim'babwe [tsimˈbabwe] SM: **lo ~** Zimbabwe

zim'bello [dzimˈbɛllo] SM (*oggetto di burle*) laughing-stock

'zinco [ˈdzinko] SM zinc

zinga'resco, -a, -schi, -sche [dzingaˈresko] AG gypsy *cpd*

'zingaro, -a [ˈdzingaro] SM/F gipsy

'zio [ˈtsio] (*pl* **zii**) SM uncle ▪ **zii** SMPL (*zio e zia*) uncle and aunt

zip'pare [dzipˈpare] /**72**/ VT (*Inform: file*) to zip

zi'tella [dzi'tɛlla] SF (*peg*) spinster; old maid

zit'tire [tsit'tire] /**55**/ VT to silence, hush *o* shut up ▶ VI to hiss

'zitto, -a ['tsitto] AG quiet, silent; **sta' ~!** be quiet!

ziz'zania [dzid'dzanja] SF (*Bot*) darnel; (*fig*) discord; **gettare** *o* **seminare ~** to sow discord

'zoccolo ['tsɔkkolo] SM (*calzatura*) clog; (*di cavallo ecc*) hoof; (*Archit*) plinth; (*di parete*) skirting (board); (*di armadio*) base

zodia'cale [dzodia'kale] AG zodiac *cpd*; **segno ~** sign of the zodiac

zo'diaco [dzo'diako] SM zodiac

zolfa'nello [tsolfa'nɛllo] SM (sulphur) match

'zolfo ['tsolfo] SM sulphur (*Brit*), sulfur (*US*)

'zolla ['dzolla] SF clod (of earth)

zol'letta [dzol'letta] SF sugar lump

'zona ['dzɔna] SF zone, area; **~ di depressione** (*Meteor*) trough of low pressure; **~ disco** (*Aut*) ≈ meter zone; **~ industriale** industrial estate; **~ erogena** erogenous zone; **~ pedonale** pedestrian precinct; **~ verde** (*di abitato*) green area

'zonzo ['dzondzo]: **a ~** *av*: **andare a ~** to wander about, stroll about

'zoo ['dzɔo] SM INV zoo

zoolo'gia [dzoolo'dʒia] SF zoology

zoo'logico, -a, -ci, -che [dzoo'lɔdʒiko] AG zoological

zo'ologo, -a, -gi, -ghe [dzo'ɔlogo] SM/F zoologist

zoosa'fari [dzoosa'fari] SM INV safari park

zoo'tecnico, -a, -ci, -che [dzoo'tɛkniko] AG zootechnical; **il patrimonio ~ di un paese** a country's livestock resources

zoppi'care [tsoppi'kare] /**20**/ VI to limp; (*fig: mobile*) to be shaky, rickety

'zoppo, -a ['tsɔppo] AG lame; (*fig: mobile*) shaky, rickety

zoti'cone [dzoti'kone] SM lout

ZTL [dzetati'ɛlle] SIGLA F (= *Zona a Traffico Limitato*) controlled traffic zone

zu'ava [dzu'ava] SF: **pantaloni alla ~** knickerbockers

'zucca, -che ['tsukka] SF (*Bot*) marrow (*Brit*), vegetable marrow (*US*); pumpkin; (*scherzoso*) head

zucche'rare [tsukke'rare] /**72**/ VT to put sugar in

zucche'rato, -a [tsukke'rato] AG sweet, sweetened

zuccheri'era [tsukke'rjɛra] SF sugar bowl

zuccheri'ficio [tsukkeri'fitʃo] SM sugar refinery

zucche'rino, -a [tsukke'rino] AG sugary, sweet

'zucchero ['tsukkero] SM sugar; **~ di canna** cane sugar; **~ caramellato** caramel; **~ filato** candy floss, cotton candy (*US*); **~ a velo** icing sugar (*Brit*), confectioner's sugar (*US*)

zucche'roso, -a [tsukke'roso] AG sugary

zuc'china [tsuk'kina] SF, **zuc'chino** [tsuk'kino] SM courgette (*Brit*), zucchini (*US*)

zuc'cotto [tsuk'kɔtto] SM ice-cream sponge

'zuffa ['tsuffa] SF brawl

zufo'lare [tsufo'lare] /**72**/ VT, VI to whistle

'zufolo ['tsufolo] SM (*Mus*) flageolet

'zuppa ['tsuppa] SF soup; (*fig*) mixture, muddle; **~ inglese** (*Cuc*) dessert made with sponge cake, custard and chocolate, ≈ trifle (*Brit*)

zuppi'era [tsup'pjɛra] SF soup tureen

'zuppo, -a ['tsuppo] AG: **~ (di)** drenched (with), soaked (with)

Zu'rigo [dzu'rigo] SF Zurich

ENGLISH–ITALIAN

INGLESE–ITALIANO

Aa

A, a [eɪ] N (*letter*) A, a *f inv or m inv*; (*Scol: mark*) ≈ 10 (*ottimo*); (*Mus*): **A** la *m*; **A for Andrew**, (*US*) **A for Able** ≈ A come Ancona; **from A to Z** dall'A alla Z; **A road** n (*BRIT Aut*) ≈ strada statale; **A shares** npl (*BRIT Stock Exchange*) azioni *fpl* senza diritto di voto; **A to Z**® *n* stradario

---

a [ə]

(*before vowel or silent h: an*) INDEF ART **1** un *m*, uno *m* (+ s impure, gn, pn, ps, x, z), una *f*, un' *f* + *vowel*; **a book** un libro; **a mirror** uno specchio; **an apple** una mela; **she's a doctor** è medico

2 (*instead of the number "one"*) un(o) *m*, una *f*; **a year ago** un anno fa; **a hundred/thousand pounds** cento/mille sterline

3 (*in expressing ratios, prices etc*) a, per; **3 a day/ week** 3 al giorno/alla settimana; **10 km an hour** 10 km all'ora; **£5 a person** 5 sterline a persona *or* per persona

a. ABBR = **acre**

A2 N ABBR (*BRIT Scol*) seconda parte del diploma di studi superiori chiamato "A level"

AA N ABBR (*BRIT*: = *Automobile Association*) ≈ A.C.I. *m* (= *Automobile Club d'Italia*); (*US*: = *Associate in/of Arts*) titolo di studio; (= *Alcoholics Anonymous*) A.A. *f* (= *Anonima Alcolisti*); (*Mil*) = **anti-aircraft**

AAA N ABBR (= *American Automobile Association*) ≈ A.C.I. *m* (= *Automobile Club d'Italia*); (*BRIT*) = **Amateur Athletics Association**

A & R N ABBR (*Mus*) = **artists and repertoire**; **~ man** talent scout *m inv*

AASCU N ABBR (*US*) = **American Association of State Colleges and Universities**

AAUP N ABBR (= *American Association of University Professors*) associazione dei professori universitari

AB ABBR (*BRIT*) = **able-bodied seaman**; (*CANADA*) = **Alberta**

aback [ə'bæk] ADV: **to be taken ~** essere sbalordito(-a)

abacus ['æbəkəs] (*pl* **abaci** [-saɪ]) N pallottoliere *m*, abaco

abandon [ə'bændən] VT abbandonare ▶ N abbandono; **to ~ ship** abbandonare la nave; **with ~** sfrenatamente, spensieratamente

abandoned [ə'bændənd] ADJ (*child, house etc*) abbandonato(-a); (*unrestrained: manner*) disinvolto(-a)

abase [ə'beɪs] VT: **to ~ o.s. (so far as to do)** umiliarsi *or* abbassarsi (al punto di fare)

abashed [ə'bæʃt] ADJ imbarazzato(-a)

abate [ə'beɪt] VI calmarsi

abatement [ə'beɪtmənt] N (*of pollution, noise*) soppressione *f*, eliminazione *f*; **noise ~ society** associazione *f* per la lotta contro i rumori

abattoir ['æbətwɑː*ʳ*] N (*BRIT*) mattatoio

abbey ['æbɪ] N abbazia, badia

abbot ['æbət] N abate *m*

abbreviate [ə'briːvɪeɪt] VT abbreviare

abbreviation [əbriːvɪ'eɪʃən] N abbreviazione *f*

ABC N ABBR (= *American Broadcasting Company*) rete televisiva americana

abdicate ['æbdɪkeɪt] VT abdicare a ▶ VI abdicare

abdication [æbdɪ'keɪʃən] N abdicazione *f*

abdomen ['æbdəmən] N addome *m*

abdominal [æb'dɔmɪnl] ADJ addominale

abduct [æb'dʌkt] VT rapire

abduction [æb'dʌkʃən] N rapimento

Aberdonian [æbə'dəʊnɪən] ADJ di Aberdeen ▶ N abitante *mf* di Aberdeen, originario(-a) di Aberdeen

aberration [æbə'reɪʃən] N aberrazione *f*

abet [ə'bɛt] VT *see* **aid**

abeyance [ə'beɪəns] N: **in ~** in sospeso

abhor [əb'hɔː*ʳ*] VT aborrire

abhorrent [əb'hɔrənt] ADJ odioso(-a)

abide [ə'baɪd] VT sopportare; **I can't ~ it/him** non lo posso soffrire *or* sopportare ▶ **abide by** VT FUS conformarsi a

abiding [ə'baɪdɪŋ] ADJ (*memory etc*) persistente, duraturo(-a)

ability [ə'bɪlɪtɪ] N abilità *f inv*; **to the best of my ~** con il massimo impegno

abject ['æbdʒɛkt] ADJ (*poverty*) abietto(-a); (*apology*) umiliante; (*coward*) indegno(-a), vile

ablaze [ə'bleɪz] ADJ in fiamme; **~ with light** risplendente di luce

able ['eɪbl] ADJ capace; **to be ~ to do sth** essere capace di fare qc, poter fare qc

able-bodied ['eɪbl'bɒdɪd] ADJ robusto(-a)

able-bodied seaman N (BRIT) marinaio scelto

ably ['eɪblɪ] ADV abilmente

ABM N ABBR (= anti-ballistic missile) ABM m

abnormal [æb'nɔ:məl] ADJ anormale

abnormality [æbnɔ:'mælɪtɪ] N (condition) anormalità; (instance) anomalia

aboard [ə'bɔ:d] ADV a bordo ▶ PREP a bordo di; **~ the train** in or sul treno

abode [ə'bəud] N (old) dimora; (Law) domicilio, dimora; **of no fixed ~** senza fissa dimora

abolish [ə'bɒlɪʃ] VT abolire

abolition [æbəu'lɪʃən] N abolizione f

abominable [ə'bɒmɪnəbl] ADJ abominevole

aborigine [æbə'rɪdʒɪnɪ] N aborigeno(-a)

abort [ə'bɔ:t] VT (Med, fig) abortire; (Comput) interrompere l'esecuzione di

abortion [ə'bɔ:ʃən] N aborto; **to have an ~** avere un aborto, abortire

abortionist [ə'bɔ:ʃənɪst] N abortista mf

abortive [ə'bɔ:tɪv] ADJ abortivo(-a)

abound [ə'baund] VI abbondare; **to ~ in** abbondare di

---

about [ə'baut]

ADV **1** (approximately) circa, quasi; **about a hundred/thousand** un centinaio/migliaio, circa cento/mille; **it takes about 10 hours** ci vogliono circa 10 ore; **at about 2 o'clock** verso le 2; **I've just about finished** ho quasi finito; **it's about here** è qui intorno, è qui vicino
2 (referring to place) qua e là, in giro; **to leave things lying about** lasciare delle cose in giro; **to run about** correre qua e là; **to walk about** camminare; **is Paul about?** (BRIT) hai visto Paul in giro?; **it's the other way about** (BRIT) è il contrario
3: **to be about to do sth** stare per fare qc; **I'm not about to do all that for nothing** non ho intenzione di fare tutto questo per niente
▶ PREP **1** (relating to) su, di; **a book about London** un libro su Londra; **what is it about?** di che si tratta?; (book, film etc) di cosa tratta?; **we talked about it** ne abbiamo parlato; **do something about it!** fai qualcosa!; **what** or **how about doing this?** che ne dici di fare questo?
2 (referring to place): **to walk about the town** camminare per la città; **her clothes were scattered about the room** i suoi vestiti erano sparsi or in giro per tutta la stanza

---

about-face [ə'baut'feɪs], **about-turn** [ə'baut'tə:n] N (Mil) dietro front m inv

above [ə'bʌv] ADV, PREP sopra; **mentioned ~** suddetto; **costing ~ £10** più caro di 10 sterline; **he's not ~ a bit of blackmail** non rifuggirebbe dal ricatto; **~ all** soprattutto

aboveboard [ə'bʌv'bɔ:d] ADJ aperto(-a); onesto(-a)

abrasion [ə'breɪʒən] N abrasione f

abrasive [ə'breɪzɪv] ADJ abrasivo(-a)

abreast [ə'brest] ADV di fianco; **3 ~** per 3 di fronte; **to keep ~ of** tenersi aggiornato su

abroad [ə'brɔ:d] ADV all'estero; **there is a rumour ~ that ...** (fig) si sente dire in giro che ..., circola la voce che ...

abrupt [ə'brʌpt] ADJ (steep) erto(-a); (sudden) improvviso(-a); (gruff, blunt) brusco(-a)

abscess ['æbsɪs] N ascesso

abscond [əb'skɒnd] VI scappare

absence ['æbsəns] N assenza; **in the ~ of** (person) in assenza di; (thing) in mancanza di

absent ['æbsənt] ADJ assente; **to be ~ without leave** (Mil etc) essere assente ingiustificato

absentee [æbsən'ti:] N assente mf

absenteeism [æbsən'ti:ɪzəm] N assenteismo

absent-minded ['æbsənt'maɪndɪd] ADJ distratto(-a)

absent-mindedness ['æbsənt'maɪndɪdnɪs] N distrazione f

absolute ['æbsəlu:t] ADJ assoluto(-a)

absolutely [æbsə'lu:tlɪ] ADV assolutamente

absolve [əb'zɒlv] VT: **to ~ sb (from)** (sin etc) assolvere qn (da); **to ~ sb from** (oath) sciogliere qn da

absorb [əb'sɔ:b] VT assorbire; **to be absorbed in a book** essere immerso(-a) in un libro

absorbent [əb'sɔ:bənt] ADJ assorbente

absorbent cotton [əb'zɔ:bənt-] N (US) cotone m idrofilo

absorbing [əb'sɔ:bɪŋ] ADJ avvincente, molto interessante

absorption [əb'sɔ:pʃən] N assorbimento

abstain [əb'steɪn] VI: **to ~ (from)** astenersi (da)

abstemious [əb'sti:mɪəs] ADJ astemio(-a)

abstention [əb'stenʃən] N astensione f

abstinence ['æbstɪnəns] N astinenza

abstract ADJ ['æbstrækt] astratto(-a) ▶ N (summary) riassunto ▶ VT [æb'strækt] estrarre

absurd [əb'sə:d] ADJ assurdo(-a)

absurdity [əb'sə:dɪtɪ] N assurdità f inv

ABTA ['æbtə] N ABBR = **Association of British Travel Agents**

Abu Dhabi ['æbu:'dɑ:bɪ] N Abu Dhabi f

abundance [ə'bʌndəns] N abbondanza

abundant [ə'bʌndənt] ADJ abbondante

abuse N [ə'bju:s] abuso; (insults) ingiurie fpl

▶ VT [ə'bjuːz] abusare di; **open to ~** che si presta ad abusi

abusive [ə'bjuːsɪv] ADJ ingiurioso(-a)

abysmal [ə'bɪzməl] ADJ spaventoso(-a)

abyss [ə'bɪs] N abisso

AC N ABBR (US) = **athletic club**

a/c ABBR (Banking etc) = **account**; (= account current) c

academic [ækə'dɛmɪk] ADJ accademico(-a); (pej: issue) puramente formale ▶ N universitario(-a)

academic year N anno accademico

academy [ə'kædəmɪ] N (learned body) accademia; (school) scuola privata; **military/naval ~** scuola militare/navale; **~ of music** conservatorio

ACAS ['eɪkæs] N ABBR (BRIT: = Advisory, Conciliation and Arbitration Service) comitato governativo per il miglioramento della contrattazione collettiva

accede [æk'siːd] VI: **to ~ to** (request) accedere a; (throne) ascendere a

accelerate [æk'sɛləreɪt] VT, VI accelerare

acceleration [æksɛlə'reɪʃən] N accelerazione f

accelerator [æk'sɛləreɪtə'] N acceleratore m

accent ['æksɛnt] N accento

accentuate [æk'sɛntjueɪt] VT (syllable) accentuare; (need, difference etc) accentuare, mettere in risalto or in evidenza

accept [ək'sɛpt] VT accettare

acceptable [ək'sɛptəbl] ADJ accettabile

acceptance [ək'sɛptəns] N accettazione f; **to meet with general ~** incontrare il favore or il consenso generale

access ['æksɛs] N accesso ▶ VT (Comput) accedere a; **to have ~ to** avere accesso a; **the burglars gained ~ through a window** i ladri sono riusciti a penetrare da or attraverso una finestra

accessible [æk'sɛsəbl] ADJ accessibile

accession [æk'sɛʃən] N (addition) aggiunta; (to library) accessione f, acquisto; (of king) ascesa or salita al trono

accessory [æk'sɛsərɪ] N accessorio; (Law): **~ to** complice mf di; **toilet accessories** npl (BRIT) articoli mpl da toilette

access road N strada d'accesso; (to motorway) raccordo di entrata

access time N (Comput) tempo di accesso

accident ['æksɪdənt] N incidente m; (chance) caso; **to meet with** or **to have an ~** avere un incidente; **I've had an ~** ho avuto un incidente; **accidents at work** infortuni mpl sul lavoro; **by ~** per caso

accidental [æksɪ'dɛntl] ADJ accidentale

accidentally [æksɪ'dɛntəlɪ] ADV per caso

Accident and Emergency Department N (BRIT) pronto soccorso

accident insurance N assicurazione f contro gli infortuni

accident-prone ['æksɪdənt'prəun] ADJ: **he's very ~** è un vero passaguai

acclaim [ə'kleɪm] VT acclamare ▶ N acclamazione f

acclamation [æklə'meɪʃən] N (approval) acclamazione f; (applause) applauso

acclimatize [ə'klaɪmətaɪz], (US) **acclimate** [ə'klaɪmeɪt] VT: **to become acclimatized** acclimatarsi

accolade ['ækəleɪd] N encomio

accommodate [ə'kɔmədeɪt] VT alloggiare; (oblige, help) favorire; **this car accommodates 4 people comfortably** quest'auto può trasportare comodamente 4 persone

accommodating [ə'kɔmədeɪtɪŋ] ADJ compiacente

accommodation [əkɔmə'deɪʃən] N, (US) **accommodations** [əkɔmə'deɪʃənz] NPL alloggio; **seating ~** (BRIT) posti a sedere; **"~ to let"** (BRIT) "camere in affitto"; **have you any ~?** avete posto?

accompaniment [ə'kʌmpənɪmənt] N accompagnamento

accompanist [ə'kʌmpənɪst] N (Mus) accompagnatore(-trice)

accompany [ə'kʌmpənɪ] VT accompagnare

accomplice [ə'kʌmplɪs] N complice mf

accomplish [ə'kʌmplɪʃ] VT compiere; (achieve) ottenere; (goal) raggiungere

accomplished [ə'kʌmplɪʃt] ADJ (person) esperto(-a)

accomplishment [ə'kʌmplɪʃmənt] N compimento; realizzazione f; (thing achieved) risultato ■ **accomplishments** NPL (skills) doti fpl

accord [ə'kɔːd] N accordo ▶ VT accordare; **of his own ~** di propria iniziativa; **with one ~** all'unanimità, di comune accordo

accordance [ə'kɔːdəns] N: **in ~ with** in conformità con

according [ə'kɔːdɪŋ]: **~ prep** secondo; **it went ~ to plan** è andata secondo il previsto

accordingly [ə'kɔːdɪŋlɪ] ADV in conformità

accordion [ə'kɔːdɪən] N fisarmonica

accost [ə'kɔst] VT avvicinare

account [ə'kaunt] N (Comm) conto; (report) descrizione f ■ **accounts** NPL (Comm) conti mpl; **"~ payee only"** (BRIT) "assegno non trasferibile"; **to keep an ~ of** tenere nota di; **to bring sb to ~ for sth/for having done sth** chiedere a qn di render conto di qc/per aver fatto qc; **by all accounts** a quanto si dice; **of little ~** di poca importanza; **on ~** in acconto; **to buy sth on ~** comprare qc a credito; **on no ~** per nessun motivo; **on ~ of** a causa di; **to take into ~, take ~ of** tener conto di

▶ **account for** VT FUS (explain) spiegare; giustificare; **all the children were accounted for** nessun bambino mancava all'appello

accountability [ə'kauntə'bılıtı] N responsabilità

accountable [ə'kauntəbl] ADJ responsabile; **to be held ~ for sth** dover rispondere di qc; **~ (to)** responsabile (verso)

accountancy [ə'kauntənsı] N ragioneria

accountant [ə'kauntənt] N ragioniere(-a)

accounting [ə'kauntıŋ] N contabilità

accounting period N esercizio finanziario, periodo contabile

account number N numero di conto

account payable N conto passivo

account receivable N conto da esigere

accredited [ə'krɛdıtıd] ADJ accreditato(-a)

accretion [ə'kri:ʃən] N accrescimento

accrue [ə'kru:] VI (mount up) aumentare; **to ~ to** derivare a; **accrued charges** ratei mpl passivi; **accrued interest** interesse m maturato

accumulate [ə'kju:mjuleıt] VT accumulare ▶ VI accumularsi

accumulation [əkju:mju'leıʃən] N accumulazione f

accuracy ['ækjurəsı] N precisione f

accurate ['ækjurıt] ADJ preciso(-a)

accurately ['ækjurıtlı] ADV precisamente

accusation [ækju'zeıʃən] N accusa

accusative [ə'kju:zətıv] N (Ling) accusativo

accuse [ə'kju:z] VT accusare

accused [ə'kju:zd] N accusato(-a)

accuser [ə'kju:zəʳ] N accusatore(-trice)

accustom [ə'kʌstəm] VT abituare; **to ~ o.s. to sth** abituarsi a qc

accustomed [ə'kʌstəmd] ADJ (usual) abituale; **~ to** abituato(-a) a

AC/DC ABBR (= alternating current/direct current) c.a./c.c.

ACE [eıs] N ABBR = **American Council on Education**

ace [eıs] N asso; **within an ~ of** (BRIT) a un pelo da

acerbic [ə'sə:bık] ADJ (also fig) acido(-a)

acetate ['æsıteıt] N acetato

ache [eık] N male m, dolore m ▶ VI (be sore) far male, dolere; **to ~ to do sth** morire dalla voglia di fare qc; **I've got stomach ~** or (US) **a stomach ~** ho mal di stomaco; **my head aches** mi fa male la testa; **I'm aching all over** mi duole dappertutto

achieve [ə'tʃi:v] VT (aim) raggiungere; (victory, success) ottenere; (task) compiere

achievement [ə'tʃi:vmənt] N compimento; successo

Achilles heel [ə'kılı:z-] N tallone m d'Achille

acid ['æsıd] ADJ acido(-a) ▶ N acido

acidity [ə'sıdıtı] N acidità

acid rain N pioggia acida

acid test N (fig) prova del fuoco

acknowledge [ək'nɔlıdʒ] VT (fact) riconoscere; (letter: also: **acknowledge receipt of**) accusare ricevuta di

acknowledgement [ək'nɔlıdʒmənt] N riconoscimento; (of letter) conferma ▪ **acknowledgements** NPL (in book) ringraziamenti mpl

ACLU N ABBR (= American Civil Liberties Union) unione americana per le libertà civili

acme ['ækmı] N culmine m, acme m

acne ['æknı] N acne f

acorn ['eıkɔ:n] N ghianda

acoustic [ə'ku:stık] ADJ acustico(-a); see also **acoustics**

acoustic coupler [-'kʌpləʳ] N (Comput) accoppiatore m acustico

acoustics [ə'ku:stıks] N, NPL acustica

acquaint [ə'kweınt] VT: **to ~ sb with sth** far sapere qc a qn; **to be acquainted with** (person) conoscere

acquaintance [ə'kweıntəns] N conoscenza; (person) conoscente mf; **to make sb's ~** fare la conoscenza di qn

acquiesce [ækwı'ɛs] VI (agree): **to ~ (in)** acconsentire (a)

acquire [ə'kwaıəʳ] VT acquistare

acquired [ə'kwaıəd] ADJ acquisito(-a); **it's an ~ taste** è una cosa che si impara ad apprezzare

acquisition [ækwı'zıʃən] N acquisto

acquisitive [ə'kwızıtıv] ADJ a cui piace accumulare le cose

acquit [ə'kwıt] VT assolvere; **to ~ o.s. well** comportarsi bene

acquittal [ə'kwıtl] N assoluzione f

acre ['eıkəʳ] N acro (= 4047 m2)

acreage ['eıkərıdʒ] N superficie f in acri

acrid ['ækrıd] ADJ (smell) acre, pungente; (fig) pungente

acrimonious [ækrı'məunıəs] ADJ astioso(-a)

acrobat ['ækrəbæt] N acrobata mf

acrobatic [ækrə'bætık] ADJ acrobatico(-a)

acrobatics [ækrə'bætıks] N acrobatica ▶ NPL acrobazie fpl

acronym ['ækrənım] N acronimo

Acropolis [ə'krɔpəlıs] N: **the ~** l'Acropoli f

across [ə'krɔs] PREP (on the other side) dall'altra parte di; (crosswise) attraverso ▶ ADV dall'altra parte; in larghezza; **to walk ~ (the road)** attraversare (la strada); **to run/swim ~** attraversare di corsa/a nuoto; **to take sb ~ the road** far attraversare la strada a qn; **~ from** di fronte a; **the lake is 12 km ~** il lago ha una larghezza di 12 km or è largo 12 km; **to get sth ~ to sb** (fig) far capire qc a qn

acrylic [ə'krılık] ADJ acrilico(-a) ▶ N acrilico

ACT N ABBR (= *American College Test*) *esame di ammissione a college*

act [ækt] N atto; (*in music-hall etc*) numero; (*Law*) decreto ▶ VI agire; (*Theat*) recitare; (*pretend*) fingere ▶ VT (*part*) recitare; **to catch sb in the ~** cogliere qn in flagrante *or* sul fatto; **it's only an ~** è tutta scena, è solo una messinscena; **~ of God** (*Law*) calamità *f* inv naturale; **to ~ Hamlet** (BRIT) recitare la parte di Amleto; **to ~ the fool** (BRIT) fare lo stupido; **to ~ as** agire da; **it acts as a deterrent** serve da deterrente; **acting in my capacity as chairman, I ...** in qualità di presidente, io ...
  ▶ **act on** VT: **to ~ on sth** agire in base a qc
  ▶ **act out** VT (*event*) ricostruire; (*fantasies*) dare forma concreta a
  ▶ **act up** (*col*) VI (*person*) comportarsi male; (*knee, back, injury*) fare male; (*machine*) non funzionare

acting ['æktıŋ] ADJ che fa le funzioni di ▶ N (*of actor*) recitazione *f*; **to do some ~** fare del teatro (*or* del cinema); **he is the ~ manager** fa le veci del direttore

action ['ækʃən] N azione *f*; (*Mil*) combattimento; (*Law*) processo ▶ VT (*Comm: request*) evadere; (*tasks*) portare a termine; **to take ~** agire; **to put a plan into ~** realizzare un piano; **out of ~** fuori combattimento; (*machine etc*) fuori servizio; **killed in ~** (*Mil*) ucciso in combattimento; **to bring an ~ against sb** (*Law*) intentare causa contro qn

action replay N (BRIT TV) replay *m* inv

activate ['æktıveıt] VT (*mechanism*) fare funzionare, attivare; (*Chem, Physics*) rendere attivo(-a)

active ['æktıv] ADJ attivo(-a); **to play an ~ part in** partecipare attivamente a

active duty N (*US Mil*) = **active service**

actively ['æktıvlı] ADV (*participate*) attivamente; (*discourage, dislike*) vivamente

active partner N (*Comm*) socio effettivo

active service N (BRIT Mil): **to be on ~** prestar servizio in zona di operazioni

activist ['æktıvıst] N attivista *mf*

activity [æk'tıvıtı] N attività *f* inv

activity holiday N vacanza attiva (*in bici, a cavallo, in barca, a vela ecc.*)

actor ['æktə'] N attore *m*

actress ['æktrıs] N attrice *f*

actual ['æktjuəl] ADJ reale, vero(-a)

> La parola inglese **actual** non vuol dire *attuale*.

actually ['æktjuəlı] ADV veramente; (*even*) addirittura

> La parola inglese **actually** non vuol dire *attualmente*.

actuary ['æktjuərı] N attuario(-a)

actuate ['æktjueıt] VT attivare

acuity [ə'kju:ıtı] N acutezza

acumen ['ækjumən] N acume *m*; **business ~** fiuto negli affari

acupuncture ['ækjupʌŋktʃə'] N agopuntura

acute [ə'kju:t] ADJ acuto(-a); (*mind, person*) perspicace

AD ADV ABBR (= *Anno Domini*) d. C. ▶ N ABBR (*US Mil*) = **active duty**

ad [æd] N ABBR = **advertisement**

adamant ['ædəmənt] ADJ irremovibile

Adam's apple ['ædəmz-] N pomo di Adamo

adapt [ə'dæpt] VT adattare ▶ VI: **to ~ (to)** adattarsi (a)

adaptability [ədæptə'bılıtı] N adattabilità

adaptable [ə'dæptəbl] ADJ (*device*) adattabile; (*person*) che sa adattarsi

adaptation [ædæp'teıʃən] N adattamento

adapter, adaptor [ə'dæptə'] N (*Elec*) adattatore *m*

ADC N ABBR (*Mil*) = **aide-de-camp**; (*US:* = *Aid to Dependent Children*) *sussidio per figli a carico*

add [æd] VT aggiungere; (*figures*) addizionare ▶ VI: **to ~ to** (*increase*) aumentare ▶ N (*Internet*): **thanks for the ~** grazie per avermi aggiunto (come amico)
  ▶ **add on** VT aggiungere
  ▶ **add up** VT (*figures*) addizionare ▶ VI (*fig*): **it doesn't ~ up** non ha senso; **it doesn't ~ up to much** non è un granché

adder ['ædə'] N vipera

addict ['ædıkt] N tossicomane *mf*; (*fig*) fanatico(-a); **heroin ~** eroinomane *mf*; **drug ~** tossico-dipendente *mf*, tossicomane *mf*

addicted [ə'dıktıd] ADJ: **to be ~ to** (*drink etc*) essere dedito(-a) a; (*fig: football etc*) essere tifoso(-a) di

addiction [ə'dıkʃən] N (*Med*) tossicodipendenza

addictive [ə'dıktıv] ADJ che dà assuefazione

adding machine ['ædıŋ-] N addizionatrice *f*

Addis Ababa ['ædıs'æbəbə] N Addis Abeba *f*

addition [ə'dıʃən] N addizione *f*; (*thing added*) aggiunta; **in ~** inoltre; **in ~ to** oltre

additional [ə'dıʃənl] ADJ supplementare

additive ['ædıtıv] N additivo

address [ə'drɛs] N (*gen, Comput*) indirizzo; (*talk*) discorso ▶ VT indirizzare; (*speak to*) fare un discorso a; (*issue*) affrontare; **my ~ is ...** il mio indirizzo è ...; **form of ~** (*gen*) formula di cortesia; (*in letters*) formula d'indirizzo *or* di intestazione; **to ~ o.s. to sth** indirizzare le proprie energie verso qc; **absolute/relative ~** (*Comput*) indirizzo assoluto/relativo

address book N rubrica

addressee [ædrɛ'si:] N destinatario(-a)

Aden ['eıdən] N: **the Gulf of ~** il golfo di Aden

adenoids ['ædınɔıdz] NPL adenoidi *fpl*

adept ['ædɛpt] ADJ: **~ at** esperto(-a) in

adequate ['ædɪkwɪt] ADJ (description, reward) adeguato(-a); (amount) sufficiente; **to feel ~ to a task** sentirsi all'altezza di un compito

adequately ['ædɪkwɪtlɪ] ADV adeguatamente; sufficientemente

adhere [əd'hɪə'] VI: **to ~ to** aderire a; (fig: rule, decision) seguire

adhesion [əd'hiːʒən] N adesione f

adhesive [əd'hiːzɪv] ADJ adesivo(-a) ▶ N adesivo; **~ tape** (BRIT: for parcels etc) nastro adesivo; (US Med) cerotto adesivo

ad hoc [æd'hɔk] ADJ (decision) ad hoc inv; (committee) apposito(-a)

ad infinitum ['ædɪnfɪ'naɪtəm] ADV all'infinito

adjacent [ə'dʒeɪsənt] ADJ adiacente; **~ to** accanto a

adjective ['ædʒɛktɪv] N aggettivo

adjoin [ə'dʒɔɪn] VT essere contiguo(-a) a or attiguo(-a) a

adjoining [ə'dʒɔɪnɪŋ] ADJ accanto inv, adiacente ▶ PREP accanto a

adjourn [ə'dʒɜːn] VT rimandare, aggiornare; (US: end) sospendere ▶ VI essere aggiornato(-a); (Parliament) sospendere i lavori; (go) spostarsi; **to ~ a meeting till the following week** aggiornare or rinviare un incontro alla settimana seguente; **they adjourned to the pub** (col) si sono trasferiti al pub

adjournment [ə'dʒɜːnmənt] N rinvio, aggiornamento; sospensione f

Adjt ABBR (Mil) = **adjutant**

adjudicate [ə'dʒuːdɪkeɪt] VT (contest) giudicare; (claim) decidere su

adjudication [ədʒuːdɪ'keɪʃən] N decisione f

adjust [ə'dʒʌst] VT aggiustare; (Comm: change) rettificare ▶ VI: **to ~ (to)** adattarsi (a)

adjustable [ə'dʒʌstəbl] ADJ regolabile

adjuster [ə'dʒʌstə'] N see **loss adjuster**

adjustment [ə'dʒʌstmənt] N (Psych) adattamento; (of machine) regolazione f; (of prices, wages) aggiustamento

adjutant ['ædʒətənt] N aiutante m

ad-lib [æd'lɪb] VT, VI improvvisare ▶ N improvvisazione f ▶ ADV: **ad lib** a piacere, a volontà

adman ['ædmæn] N (irreg) (col) pubblicitario

admin [æd'mɪn] N ABBR (col) = **administration**

administer [əd'mɪnɪstə'] VT amministrare; (justice) somministrare

administration [ədmɪnɪs'treɪʃən] N amministrazione f; **the A~** (US) il Governo

administrative [əd'mɪnɪstrətɪv] ADJ amministrativo(-a)

administrator [əd'mɪnɪstreɪtə'] N amministratore(-trice)

admirable ['ædmərəbl] ADJ ammirevole

admiral ['ædmərəl] N ammiraglio

Admiralty ['ædmərəltɪ] N (BRIT: also: **Admiralty Board**) Ministero della Marina

admiration [ædmə'reɪʃən] N ammirazione f

admire [əd'maɪə'] VT ammirare

admirer [əd'maɪərə'] N ammiratore(-trice)

admiring [əd'maɪərɪŋ] ADJ (glance etc) di ammirazione

admissible [əd'mɪsəbl] ADJ ammissibile

admission [əd'mɪʃən] N ammissione f; (to exhibition, nightclub etc) ingresso; (confession) confessione f; **by his own ~** per sua ammissione; **"~ free", "free ~"** "ingresso gratuito"

admit [əd'mɪt] VT ammettere; far entrare; (agree) riconoscere; **"children not admitted"** "vietato l'ingresso ai bambini"; **this ticket admits two** questo biglietto è valido per due persone; **I must ~ that ...** devo ammettere or confessare che ...
▶ **admit of** VT FUS lasciare adito a
▶ **admit to** VT FUS riconoscere

admittance [əd'mɪtəns] N ingresso; **"no ~"** "vietato l'ingresso"

admittedly [əd'mɪtɪdlɪ] ADV bisogna pur riconoscere (che)

admonish [əd'mɔnɪʃ] VT ammonire

ad nauseam [æd'nɔːzɪæm] ADV fino alla nausea, a non finire

ado [ə'duː] N: **without (any) more ~** senza più indugi

adolescence [ædəu'lɛsns] N adolescenza

adolescent [ædəu'lɛsnt] ADJ, N adolescente mf

adopt [ə'dɔpt] VT adottare

adopted [ə'dɔptɪd] ADJ adottivo(-a)

adoption [ə'dɔpʃən] N adozione f

adore [ə'dɔː'] VT adorare

adoring [ə'dɔːrɪŋ] ADJ adorante; **his ~ wife** sua moglie che lo adora

adoringly [ə'dɔːrɪŋlɪ] ADV con adorazione

adorn [ə'dɔːn] VT ornare

adornment [ə'dɔːnmənt] N ornamento

ADP N ABBR = **automatic data processing**

adrenalin [ə'drɛnəlɪn] N adrenalina; **it gets the ~ going** ti dà una carica

Adriatic [eɪdrɪ'ætɪk] N: **the ~ (Sea)** il mare Adriatico, l'Adriatico

adrift [ə'drɪft] ADV alla deriva; **to come ~** (boat) andare alla deriva; (wire, rope etc) essersi staccato(-a) or sciolto(-a)

adroit [ə'drɔɪt] ADJ abile, destro(-a)

ADSL N ABBR (= asymmetric digital subscriber line) ADSL m

ADT ABBR (US: = Atlantic Daylight Time) ora legale di New York

adult ['ædʌlt] N adulto(-a) ▶ ADJ adulto(-a); (work, education) per adulti

adult education N scuola per adulti

adulterate [ə'dʌltəreɪt] VT adulterare

adulterer [ə'dʌltərəʳ] N adultero

adulteress [ə'dʌltərɪs] N adultera

adultery [ə'dʌltərɪ] N adulterio

adulthood ['ædʌlthud] N età adulta

advance [əd'vɑːns] N avanzamento; (money) anticipo ▶ADJ (booking etc) in anticipo ▶VT avanzare; (date, money) anticipare ▶VI avanzare; **in ~** in anticipo; **to make advances to sb** (gen) fare degli approcci a qn; (amorously) fare delle avances a qn; **do I need to book in ~?** occorre che prenoti in anticipo?

advanced [əd'vɑːnst] ADJ avanzato(-a); (Scol: studies) superiore; **~ in years** avanti negli anni

advancement [əd'vɑːnsmənt] N avanzamento

advance notice N preavviso

advantage [əd'vɑːntɪdʒ] N (also Tennis) vantaggio; **to take ~ of** approfittarsi di; **it's to our ~** è nel nostro interesse, torna a nostro vantaggio

advantageous [ædvən'teɪdʒəs] ADJ vantaggioso(-a)

advent ['ædvənt] N avvento; **A~** (Rel) Avvento

Advent calendar N calendario dell'Avvento

adventure [əd'vɛntʃəʳ] N avventura

adventure playground N area attrezzata di giochi per bambini con funi, strutture in legno ecc

adventurous [əd'vɛntʃərəs] ADJ avventuroso(-a)

adverb ['ædvɜːb] N avverbio

adversary ['ædvəsərɪ] N avversario(-a)

adverse ['ædvɜːs] ADJ avverso(-a); **in ~ circumstances** nelle avversità

adversity [əd'vɜːsɪtɪ] N avversità

advert ['ædvɜːt] N ABBR (BRIT) = **advertisement**

advertise ['ædvətaɪz] VI, VT fare pubblicità or réclame (a), fare un'inserzione (per vendere); **to ~ for** (staff) cercare tramite annuncio

advertisement [əd'vɜːtɪsmənt] N (Comm) réclame f inv, pubblicità f inv; (in classified ads) inserzione f

advertiser ['ædvətaɪzəʳ] N azienda che reclamizza un prodotto; (in newspaper) inserzionista mf

advertising ['ædvətaɪzɪŋ] N pubblicità

advertising agency N agenzia pubblicitaria or di pubblicità

advertising campaign N campagna pubblicitaria

advice [əd'vaɪs] N consigli mpl; (notification) avviso; **piece of ~** consiglio; **to ask (sb) for ~** chiedere il consiglio (di qn), chiedere un consiglio (a qn); **legal ~** consulenza legale; **to take legal ~** consultare un avvocato

---

> Unlike advice, **consiglio** is used with an article, and can be made plural.
> some advice **dei consigli**
> He gave me good advice. **Mi ha dato dei buoni consigli**.

advice note N (BRIT) avviso di spedizione

advisable [əd'vaɪzəbl] ADJ consigliabile

advise [əd'vaɪz] VT consigliare; **to ~ sb of sth** informare qn di qc; **to ~ sb against sth/ against doing sth** sconsigliare qc a qn/a qn di fare qc; **you will be well/ill advised to go** fareste bene/male ad andare

advisedly [əd'vaɪzɪdlɪ] ADV (deliberately) deliberatamente

adviser [əd'vaɪzəʳ] N consigliere(-a); (in business) consulente mf, consigliere(-a)

advisory [əd'vaɪzərɪ] ADJ consultivo(-a); **in an ~ capacity** in veste di consulente

advocate N ['ædvəkɪt] (upholder) sostenitore(-trice); (Law) avvocato (difensore) ▶VT ['ædvəkeɪt] propugnare; **to be an ~ of** essere a favore di

advt. ABBR = **advertisement**

AEA N ABBR (BRIT: = Atomic Energy Authority) ente di controllo sulla ricerca e lo sviluppo dell'energia atomica

AEC N ABBR (US: = Atomic Energy Commission) ente di controllo sulla ricerca e lo sviluppo dell'energia atomica

Aegean (Sea) [iː'dʒiːən-] N (mare m) Egeo

aegis ['iːdʒɪs] N: **under the ~ of** sotto gli auspici di

aeon ['iːən] N eternità f inv

aerial ['ɛərɪəl] N antenna ▶ADJ aereo(-a)

aerobatics ['ɛərəu'bætɪks] NPL acrobazia sg aerea; (stunts) acrobazie fpl aeree

aerobics [ɛə'rəubɪks] N aerobica

aerodrome ['ɛərədrəum] N (BRIT) aerodromo

aerodynamic ['ɛərəudaɪ'næmɪk] ADJ aerodinamico(-a)

aeronautics [ɛərə'nɔːtɪks] N aeronautica

aeroplane ['ɛərəpleɪn] N (BRIT) aeroplano

aerosol ['ɛərəsɔl] N (BRIT) aerosol m inv

aerospace industry ['ɛərəuspeɪs-] N industria aerospaziale

aesthetic [ɪs'θɛtɪk] ADJ estetico(-a)

afar [ə'fɑː'] ADV lontano; **from ~** da lontano

AFB N ABBR (US) = **Air Force Base**

AFDC N ABBR (US: = Aid to Families with Dependent Children) ≈ A.F. (= assegni familiari)

affable ['æfəbl] ADJ affabile

affair [ə'fɛəʳ] N affare m; (also: **love affair**) relazione f amorosa ■ **affairs** NPL (business) affari; **the Watergate ~** il caso Watergate

affect [ə'fɛkt] VT toccare; (influence) influire su, incidere su; (feign) fingere

affectation [æfɛk'teɪʃən] N affettazione f

affected [ə'fɛktɪd] ADJ affettato(-a)

affection [əˈfɛkʃən] N affetto

affectionate [əˈfɛkʃənɪt] ADJ affettuoso(-a)

affectionately [əˈfɛkʃənɪtlɪ] ADV affettuosamente

affidavit [æfɪˈdeɪvɪt] N (Law) affidavit m inv

affiliated [əˈfɪlɪeɪtɪd] ADJ affiliato(-a); ~ **company** filiale f

affinity [əˈfɪnɪtɪ] N affinità f inv

affirm [əˈfəːm] VT affermare, asserire

affirmation [æfəˈmeɪʃən] N affermazione f

affirmative [əˈfəːmətɪv] ADJ affermativo(-a) ▶ N: **in the ~** affermativamente

affix [əˈfɪks] VT apporre; attaccare

afflict [əˈflɪkt] VT affliggere

affliction [əˈflɪkʃən] N afflizione f

affluence [ˈæfluəns] N ricchezza

affluent [ˈæfluənt] ADJ ricco(-a); **the ~ society** la società del benessere

afford [əˈfɔːd] VT permettersi; (provide) fornire; **I can't ~ the time** non ho veramente il tempo; **can we ~ a car?** possiamo permetterci un'automobile?

affordability [əfɔːdəˈbɪlɪtɪ] N economicità f inv

affordable [əˈfɔːdəbl] ADJ (che ha un prezzo) abbordabile

affray [əˈfreɪ] N (BRIT Law) rissa

affront [əˈfrʌnt] N affronto

affronted [əˈfrʌntɪd] ADJ insultato(-a)

Afghan [ˈæfɡæn] ADJ, N afgano(-a)

Afghanistan [æfˈɡænɪstɑːn] N Afganistan m

afield [əˈfiːld] ADV: **far ~** lontano

AFL-CIO N ABBR (= American Federation of Labor and Congress of Industrial Organizations) confederazione sindacale

afloat [əˈfləʊt] ADJ, ADV a galla

afoot [əˈfut] ADV: **there is something ~** si sta preparando qualcosa

aforementioned [əˈfɔːmɛnʃənd] ADJ suddetto(-a)

aforesaid [əˈfɔːsɛd] ADJ suddetto(-a), predetto(-a)

afraid [əˈfreɪd] ADJ impaurito(-a); **to be ~ of** aver paura di; **to be ~ of doing** or **to do** aver paura di fare; **to be ~ that** aver paura che; **I am ~ that I'll be late** mi dispiace, ma farò tardi; **I'm ~ so!** ho paura di sì!, temo proprio di sì!; **I'm ~ not** no, mi dispiace, purtroppo no

afresh [əˈfrɛʃ] ADV di nuovo

Africa [ˈæfrɪkə] N Africa

African [ˈæfrɪkən] ADJ, N africano(-a)

African-American ADJ, N afroamericano(-a)

Afrikaans [æfrɪˈkɑːns] N afrikaans m

Afrikaner [æfrɪˈkɑːnəʳ] N africaner m inv

Afro-American [ˈæfrəʊəˈmɛrɪkən] ADJ afroamericano(-a)

Afro-Caribbean [ˈæfrəʊkærɪˈbɪən] ADJ afrocaraibico(-a)

AFT N ABBR (= American Federation of Teachers) sindacato degli insegnanti

aft [ɑːft] ADV a poppa, verso poppa

after [ˈɑːftəʳ] PREP, ADV dopo ▶ CONJ dopo che; ~ **dinner** dopo cena; **the day ~ tomorrow** dopodomani; **what/who are you ~?** che/chi cerca?; **the police are ~ him** è ricercato dalla polizia; ~ **he left/having done** dopo che se ne fu andato/dopo aver fatto; **to name sb ~ sb** dare a qn il nome di qn; **it's twenty ~ eight** (US) sono le otto e venti; **to ask ~ sb** chiedere di qn; ~ **you!** prima lei!, dopo di lei!; ~ **all** dopo tutto

afterbirth [ˈɑːftəbəːθ] N placenta

aftercare [ˈɑːftəkɛəʳ] N (BRIT Med) assistenza medica post-degenza

after-effects [ˈɑːftərɪfɛkts] NPL conseguenze fpl; (of illness) postumi mpl

afterlife [ˈɑːftəlaɪf] N vita dell'al di là

aftermath [ˈɑːftəmæθ] N conseguenze fpl; **in the ~ of** nel periodo dopo

afternoon [ˈɑːftəˈnuːn] N pomeriggio; **good ~!** buon giorno!

L'**afternoon tea** si consuma fra le 16 e le 17 in un caffè, in un *tea shop* o in una delle tante *tea rooms*, talvolta situate all'interno di un grande magazzino. Le più famose si trovano in alcuni hotel di lusso, come il *Ritz* a Londra. Con il tè si mangiano spesso, *scones* con marmellata e *clotted cream*, una crema a base di panna, tramezzini dolcetti e torte.

---

afterparty [ˈɑːftəpɑːtɪ] N after-party m inv

afters [ˈɑːftəz] N (BRIT col: dessert) dessert m inv

after-sales service [ɑːftəˈseɪlz-] N servizio assistenza clienti

after-shave [ˈɑːftəʃeɪv], **after-shave lotion** [ˈɑːftəʃeɪv-] N dopobarba m inv

aftershock [ˈɑːftəʃɔk] N scossa di assestamento

aftersun [ˈɑːftəsʌn] ADJ: ~ **(lotion/cream)** (lozione f/crema) doposole m inv

aftertaste [ˈɑːftəteɪst] N retrogusto

afterthought [ˈɑːftəθɔːt] N: **as an ~** come aggiunta

afterwards [ˈɑːftəwədz], (US) **afterward** ADV dopo

again [əˈɡɛn] ADV di nuovo; **to begin/see ~** ricominciare/rivedere; **he opened it ~** l'ha aperto di nuovo, l'ha riaperto; **not ... ~** non ... più; ~ **and ~** ripetutamente; **now and ~** di tanto in tanto, a volte

against [əˈɡɛnst] PREP contro; ~ **a blue background** su uno sfondo azzurro; **leaning ~ the desk** appoggiato alla scrivania; **(as) ~** (BRIT) in confronto a, contro

age [eɪdʒ] N età *f inv* ▶ VT, VI invecchiare; **what ~ is he?** quanti anni ha?; **he is 20 years of ~** ha 20 anni; **aged 10** di 10 anni; **under ~** minorenne; **to come of ~** diventare maggiorenne; **it's been ages since ...** sono secoli che ...; **the aged** gli anziani

aged ADJ ['eɪdʒd]: **~ 10** di 10 anni ▶ NPL ['eɪdʒɪd]: **the ~** gli anziani

age group N generazione *f*; **the 40 to 50 ~** le persone fra i 40 e i 50 anni

ageing ['eɪdʒɪŋ] ADJ che diventa vecchio(-a); **an ~ film star** una diva stagionata

ageless ['eɪdʒlɪs] ADJ senza età

age limit N limite *m* d'età

agency ['eɪdʒənsɪ] N agenzia; **through** *or* **by the ~ of** grazie a

agenda [ə'dʒɛndə] N ordine *m* del giorno; **on the ~** all'ordine del giorno

> La parola inglese **agenda** non vuol dire *agenda*.

agent ['eɪdʒənt] N agente *m*

aggravate ['ægrəveɪt] VT aggravare, peggiorare; *(annoy)* esasperare

aggravation [ægrə'veɪʃən] N peggioramento; esasperazione *f*

aggregate ['ægrɪgeɪt] N aggregato; **on ~** *(Sport)* con punteggio complessivo

aggression [ə'grɛʃən] N aggressione *f*

aggressive [ə'grɛsɪv] ADJ aggressivo(-a)

aggressiveness [ə'grɛsɪvnɪs] N aggressività

aggressor [ə'grɛsəʳ] N aggressore *m*

aggrieved [ə'griːvd] ADJ addolorato(-a)

aggro ['ægrəu] N *(BRIT col: behaviour)* aggressività *f inv*; *(: hassle)* rottura

aghast [ə'gɑːst] ADJ sbigottito(-a)

agile ['ædʒaɪl] ADJ agile

agility [ə'dʒɪlɪtɪ] N agilità *f inv*

agitate ['ædʒɪteɪt] VT turbare; agitare ▶ VI: **to ~ for** agitarsi per

agitated ['ædʒɪteɪtɪd] ADJ agitato(-a), turbato(-a)

agitator ['ædʒɪteɪtəʳ] N agitatore(-trice)

AGM N ABBR = **annual general meeting**

agnostic [æg'nɒstɪk] ADJ, N agnostico(-a)

ago [ə'gəu] ADV: **2 days ~** 2 giorni fa; **not long ~** poco tempo fa; **as long ~ as 1960** già nel 1960; **how long ~?** quanto tempo fa?

agog [ə'gɒg] ADJ: **(all) ~ (for)** ansioso(-a) (di), impaziente (di)

agonize ['ægənaɪz] VI: **to ~ (over)** angosciarsi (per)

agonizing ['ægənaɪzɪŋ] ADJ straziante

agony ['ægənɪ] N dolore *m* atroce; **I was in ~** avevo dei dolori atroci

agony aunt N *(BRIT col)* chi tiene la rubrica della posta del cuore

agony column N posta del cuore

agree [ə'griː] VT *(price)* pattuire ▶ VI: **to ~ (with)** essere d'accordo (con); *(Ling)* concordare (con); **to ~ to sth/to do sth** accettare qc/di fare qc; **to ~ on sth** accordarsi su qc; **it was agreed that ...** è stato deciso (di comune accordo) che ...; **garlic doesn't ~ with me** l'aglio non mi va

agreeable [ə'griːəbl] ADJ gradevole; *(willing)* disposto(-a); **are you ~ to this?** è d'accordo con questo?

agreed [ə'griːd] ADJ *(time, place)* stabilito(-a); **to be ~** essere d'accordo

agreement [ə'griːmənt] N accordo; **in ~** d'accordo; **by mutual ~** di comune accordo

agricultural [ægrɪ'kʌltʃərəl] ADJ agricolo(-a)

agriculture ['ægrɪkʌltʃəʳ] N agricoltura

aground [ə'graund] ADV: **to run ~** arenarsi

ahead [ə'hɛd] ADV avanti; davanti; **~ of** davanti a; *(fig: schedule etc)* in anticipo su; **~ of time** in anticipo; **go ~!** avanti!; **go right** *or* **straight ~** tiri diritto; **they were (right) ~ of us** erano (proprio) davanti a noi

AI N ABBR = **Amnesty International**; *(Comput)* = **artificial intelligence**

AID N ABBR = **artificial insemination by donor**; *(US: = Agency for International Development)* A.I.D. *f*

aid [eɪd] N aiuto ▶ VT aiutare; **with the ~ of** con l'aiuto di; **in ~ of** a favore di; **to ~ and abet** *(Law)* essere complice di

aide [eɪd] N *(person)* aiutante *mf*

aide-de-camp ['eɪddə'kɒŋ] N *(Mil)* aiutante *m* di campo

AIDS [eɪdz] N ABBR *(= acquired immune (or immuno-) deficiency syndrome)* AIDS *f*

AIH N ABBR = **artificial insemination by husband**

ailing ['eɪlɪŋ] ADJ sofferente; *(fig: economy, industry etc)* in difficoltà

ailment ['eɪlmənt] N indisposizione *f*

aim [eɪm] VT: **to ~ sth at** *(gun)* mirare qc a, puntare qc a; *(camera, remark)* rivolgere qc a; *(missile)* lanciare qc contro; *(blow etc)* tirare qc a ▶ VI *(also: **take aim**)* prendere la mira ▶ N mira; **to ~ at** mirare; **to ~ to do** aver l'intenzione di fare

aimless ['eɪmlɪs] ADJ senza scopo

aimlessly ['eɪmlɪslɪ] ADV senza scopo

ain't [eɪnt] *(col)* = **am not**; **aren't**; **isn't**

air [ɛəʳ] N aria ▶ VT *(room, bed)* arieggiare; *(clothes)* far prendere aria a; *(idea, grievance)* esprimere pubblicamente, manifestare; *(views)* far conoscere ▶ CPD *(currents)* d'aria; *(attack)* aereo(-a); **to throw sth into the ~** lanciare qc in aria; **by ~** *(travel)* in aereo; **to be on the ~** *(Radio, TV: station)* trasmettere; *(: programme)* essere in onda

air bag N airbag *m inv*

air base N base *f* aerea

airbed [ˈɛəbɛd] N (BRIT) materassino

airborne [ˈɛəbɔːn] ADJ (plane) in volo; (troops) aerotrasportato(-a); **as soon as the plane was ~** appena l'aereo ebbe decollato

air cargo N carico trasportato per via aerea

air-conditioned [ˈɛəkənˈdɪʃənd] ADJ con or ad aria condizionata

air conditioning N condizionamento d'aria

air-cooled [ˈɛəkuːld] ADJ raffreddato(-a) ad aria

aircraft [ˈɛəkrɑːft] N pl inv apparecchio

aircraft carrier N portaerei f inv

air cushion N cuscino gonfiabile; (Tech) cuscino d'aria

airfield [ˈɛəfiːld] N campo d'aviazione

Air Force N aviazione f militare

air freight N spedizione f di merci per via aerea; (goods) carico spedito per via aerea

airgun [ˈɛəgʌn] N fucile m ad aria compressa

air hostess N (BRIT) hostess f inv

airily [ˈɛərɪlɪ] ADV con disinvoltura

airing [ˈɛərɪŋ] N: **to give an ~ to** (linen) far prendere aria a; (room) arieggiare; (fig: ideas etc) ventilare

airing cupboard [ˈɛərɪŋ-] N armadio riscaldato per asciugare panni.

air letter N (BRIT) aerogramma m

airlift [ˈɛəlɪft] N ponte m aereo

airline [ˈɛəlaɪn] N linea aerea

airliner [ˈɛəlaɪnəʳ] N aereo di linea

airlock [ˈɛəlɔk] N cassa d'aria

airmail N posta aerea; **by ~** per via or posta aerea

air mattress N materassino gonfiabile

airplane [ˈɛəpleɪn] N (US) aeroplano

air pocket N vuoto d'aria

airport [ˈɛəpɔːt] N aeroporto

air rage N comportamento aggressivo dei passeggeri di un aereo

air raid N incursione f aerea

air rifle N fucile m ad aria compressa

airsick [ˈɛəsɪk] ADJ: **to be ~** soffrire di mal d'aereo

airspace [ˈɛəspeɪs] N spazio aereo

airspeed [ˈɛəspiːd] N velocità f inv di crociera (Aer)

airstrip [ˈɛəstrɪp] N pista d'atterraggio

air terminal N air-terminal m inv

airtight [ˈɛətaɪt] ADJ ermetico(-a)

air time N (Radio) spazio radiofonico; (TV) spazio televisivo

air traffic control N controllo del traffico aereo

air traffic controller N controllore m del traffico aereo

airway [ˈɛəweɪ] N (Aviat) rotte fpl aeree; (Anat) vie fpl respiratorie

airy [ˈɛərɪ] ADJ arioso(-a); (manners) noncurante

aisle [aɪl] N (of church) navata laterale; navata centrale; (of plane) corridoio

aisle seat N (on plane) posto sul corridoio

ajar [əˈdʒɑːʳ] ADJ socchiuso(-a)

AK ABBR (US) = **Alaska**

aka ABBR (= also known as) alias

akin [əˈkɪn] PREP: **~ to** simile a

AL ABBR (US) = **Alabama**

ALA N ABBR = **American Library Association**

à la carte [ɑːlɑːˈkɑːt] ADV alla carta

alacrity [əˈlækrɪtɪ] N: **with ~** con prontezza

alarm [əˈlɑːm] N allarme m ▶ VT allarmare

alarm call N (in hotel etc) sveglia; **could I have an ~ at 7 a.m., please?** vorrei essere svegliato alle 7, per favore

alarm clock N sveglia

alarmed [əˈlɑːmd] ADJ (person) allarmato(-a); (house, car etc) dotato(-a) di allarme

alarming [əˈlɑːmɪŋ] ADJ allarmante, preoccupante

alarmingly [əˈlɑːmɪŋlɪ] ADV in modo allarmante; **~ close** pericolosamente vicino

alarmist [əˈlɑːmɪst] N allarmista mf

alas [əˈlæs] EXCL ohimè!, ahimè!

Alaska [əˈlæskə] N Alasca

Albania [ælˈbeɪnɪə] N Albania

Albanian [ælˈbeɪnɪən] ADJ albanese ▶ N albanese mf; (Ling) albanese m

albatross [ˈælbətrɔs] N albatro, albatros m inv

albeit [ɔːlˈbiːɪt] CONJ sebbene + sub, benché + sub

album [ˈælbəm] N album m inv; (L.P.) 33 giri m inv, L.P. m inv

albumen [ˈælbjumɪn] N albume m

alchemy [ˈælkɪmɪ] N alchimia

alcohol [ˈælkəhɔl] N alcool m

alcohol-free [ˈælkəhɔlˈfriː] ADJ analcolico(-a)

alcoholic [ælkəˈhɔlɪk] ADJ alcolico(-a) ▶ N alcolizzato(-a)

alcoholism [ˈælkəhɔlɪzəm] N alcolismo

alcopop [ˈælkəpɔp] N (BRIT) alcopop m inv

alcove [ˈælkəuv] N alcova

Ald. ABBR = **alderman**

alderman [ˈɔːldəmən] N (irreg) consigliere m comunale

ale [eɪl] N birra

alert [əˈləːt] ADJ vivo(-a); (watchful) vigile ▶ N allarme m ▶ VT: **to ~ sb (to sth)** avvisare qn (di qc), avvertire qn (di qc); **to ~ sb to the dangers of sth** mettere qn in guardia contro qc; **on the ~** all'erta

Aleutian Islands [əˈluːʃən-] NPL isole fpl Aleutine

A level N (BRIT) diploma di studi superiori

Gli **A levels** (*Advanced levels*) sono gli esami alla fine delle scuole secondarie in Inghilterra, Galles ed Irlanda del Nord. La loro preparazione si estende su due anni e anche il primo anno si conclude con degli esami, detti **AS levels** (*Advanced Subsidiary levels*). I voti ottenuti determinano l'ammissione ai corsi di studio superiori.

Alexandria [ælɪgˈzændrɪə] N Alessandria (d'Egitto)

alfresco [ælˈfrɛskəu] ADJ, ADV all'aperto

algebra [ˈældʒɪbrə] N algebra

Algeria [ælˈdʒɪərɪə] N Algeria

Algerian [ælˈdʒɪərɪən] ADJ, N algerino(-a)

Algiers [ælˈdʒɪəz] N Algeri f

algorithm [ˈælgərɪðəm] N algoritmo

alias [ˈeɪlɪəs] ADV alias ▶ N pseudonimo, falso nome m

alibi [ˈælɪbaɪ] N alibi m inv

alien [ˈeɪlɪən] N straniero(-a); (*extraterrestrial*) alieno(-a) ▶ ADJ: ~ **(to)** estraneo(-a) (a)

alienate [ˈeɪlɪəneɪt] VT alienare

alienation [eɪlɪəˈneɪʃən] N alienazione f

alight [əˈlaɪt] ADJ acceso(-a) ▶ VI scendere; (*bird*) posarsi

align [əˈlaɪn] VT allineare

alignment [əˈlaɪnmənt] N allineamento; **out of ~ (with)** non allineato (con)

alike [əˈlaɪk] ADJ simile ▶ ADV allo stesso modo; **to look ~** assomigliarsi; **winter and summer ~** sia d'estate che d'inverno

alimony [ˈælɪmənɪ] N (*payment*) alimenti mpl

alive [əˈlaɪv] ADJ vivo(-a); (*active*) attivo(-a); ~ **with** pieno(-a) di; ~ **to** conscio(-a) di

alkali [ˈælkəlaɪ] N alcali m inv

---

all [ɔːl]

ADJ tutto(-a); **all day** tutto il giorno; **all night** tutta la notte; **all men** tutti gli uomini; **all five girls** tutt'e cinque le ragazze; **all five came** sono venuti tutti e cinque; **all the books** tutti i libri; **all the food** tutto il cibo; **all the time** tutto il tempo; (*always*) sempre; **all his life** tutta la vita; **for all their efforts** nonostante tutti i loro sforzi

▶ PRON **1** tutto(-a); **is that all?** non c'è altro?; (*in shop*) basta così?; **all of them** tutti(-e); **all of it** tutto(-a); **I ate it all, I ate all of it** l'ho mangiato tutto; **all of us went** tutti noi siamo andati; **all of the boys went** tutti i ragazzi sono andati

2 (*in phrases*): **above all** soprattutto; **after all** dopotutto; **at all: not at all** (*in answer to question*) niente affatto; (*in answer to thanks*) prego!, di niente!, s'immagini!; **I'm not at all tired** non sono affatto stanco; **anything at all will do** andrà bene qualsiasi cosa; **all in all** tutto sommato

▶ ADV: **all alone** tutto(-a) solo(-a); **to be/feel all in** (BRIT col) essere/sentirsi sfinito(-a) or distrutto(-a); **all out** adv: **to go all out** mettercela tutta; **it's not as hard as all that** non è poi così difficile; **all the more/the better** tanto più/meglio; **all but** quasi; **the score is two all** il punteggio è di due a due or è due pari

Allah [ˈælə] N Allah m

allay [əˈleɪ] VT (*fears*) dissipare

all clear N (Mil) cessato allarme m inv; (*fig*) okay m

allegation [ælɪˈgeɪʃən] N asserzione f

allege [əˈlɛdʒ] VT asserire; **he is alleged to have said ...** avrebbe detto che ...

alleged [əˈlɛdʒd] ADJ presunto(-a)

allegedly [əˈlɛdʒɪdlɪ] ADV secondo quanto si asserisce

allegiance [əˈliːdʒəns] N fedeltà

allegory [ˈælɪgərɪ] N allegoria

all-embracing [ˈɔːlɪmˈbreɪsɪŋ] ADJ universale

allergic [əˈlɔːdʒɪk] ADJ: ~ **to** allergico(-a) a

allergy [ˈælədʒɪ] N allergia

alleviate [əˈliːvɪeɪt] VT alleviare, sollevare

alley [ˈælɪ] N vicolo; (*in garden*) vialetto

alleyway [ˈælɪweɪ] N vicolo

alliance [əˈlaɪəns] N alleanza

allied [ˈælaɪd] ADJ alleato(-a)

alligator [ˈælɪgeɪtəʳ] N alligatore m

all-important [ˈɔːlɪmˈpɔːtənt] ADJ importantissimo(-a)

all-in [ˈɔːlɪn] ADJ, ADV (BRIT: *charge*) tutto compreso

all-in wrestling N (BRIT) lotta americana

alliteration [əlɪtəˈreɪʃən] N allitterazione f

all-night [ˈɔːlˈnaɪt] ADJ aperto(-a) (or che dura) tutta la notte

allocate [ˈæləkeɪt] VT (*share out*) distribuire; (*duties, sum, time*): **to ~ sth to** assegnare qc a; **to ~ sth for** stanziare qc per

allocation [æləʊˈkeɪʃən] N: ~ **(of money)** stanziamento

allot [əˈlɔt] VT (*share out*) spartire; **to ~ sth to** (*time*) dare qc a; (*duties*) assegnare qc a; **in the allotted time** nel tempo fissato or prestabilito

allotment [əˈlɔtmənt] N (*share*) spartizione f; (*garden*) lotto di terra

all-out [ˈɔːlaut] ADJ (*effort etc*) totale ▶ ADV: **to go all out for** mettercela tutta per

allow [əˈlau] VT (*practice, behaviour*) permettere; (*sum to spend etc*) accordare; (*sum, time estimated*) dare; (*concede*): **to ~ that** ammettere che; **to ~ sb to do** permettere a qn di fare; **he is allowed to do (it)** lo può fare; **smoking is not allowed** è vietato fumare, non è permesso fumare; **we must ~ 3 days for the journey** dobbiamo calcolare 3 giorni per il viaggio

▶ **allow for** VT FUS tener conto di

allowance [əˈlauəns] N (*money received*) assegno; (*for travelling, accommodation*) indennità f inv; (*Tax*) detrazione f di imposta; **to make ~(s) for** tener conto di; (*person*) scusare

alloy [ˈælɔɪ] N lega

all right ADV (*feel, work*) bene; (*as answer*) va bene

all-round [ˈɔːlˈraund] ADJ completo(-a)

all-rounder [ɔːlˈraundəʳ] N (*BRIT*): **to be a good ~** essere bravo(-a) in tutto

allspice [ˈɔːlspaɪs] N pepe m della Giamaica

all-time [ˈɔːlˈtaɪm] ADJ (*record*) assoluto(-a)

allude [əˈluːd] VI: **to ~ to** alludere a

alluring [əˈljuərɪŋ] ADJ seducente

allusion [əˈluːʒən] N allusione f

alluvium [əˈluːvɪəm] N materiale m alluvionale

ally N [ˈælaɪ] alleato ▶ VT [əˈlaɪ]: **to ~ o.s. with** allearsi con

almighty [ɔːlˈmaɪtɪ] ADJ onnipotente; (*row etc*) colossale

almond [ˈɑːmənd] N mandorla

almost [ˈɔːlməust] ADV quasi; **he ~ fell** per poco non è caduto

alms [ɑːmz] N elemosina

aloft [əˈlɔft] ADV in alto; (*Naut*) sull'alberatura

alone [əˈləun] ADJ, ADV solo(-a); **to leave sb ~** lasciare qn in pace; **to leave sth ~** lasciare stare qc; **let ~ ...** figuriamoci poi ..., tanto meno ...

along [əˈlɔŋ] PREP lungo ▶ ADV: **is he coming ~?** viene con noi?; **he was hopping/limping ~** veniva saltellando/zoppicando; **~ with** insieme con; **all ~** (*all the time*) sempre, fin dall'inizio

alongside [əˈlɔŋˈsaɪd] PREP accanto a; lungo ▶ ADV accanto; (*Naut*) sottobordo; **we brought our boat ~** (*of a pier/shore etc*) abbiamo accostato la barca (al molo/alla riva *etc*)

aloof [əˈluːf] ADJ distaccato(-a) ▶ ADV a distanza, in disparte; **to stand ~** tenersi a distanza *or* in disparte

aloofness [əˈluːfnɪs] N distacco, riserbo

aloud [əˈlaud] ADV ad alta voce

alphabet [ˈælfəbɛt] N alfabeto

alphabetical [ælfəˈbɛtɪkəl] ADJ alfabetico(-a); **in ~ order** in ordine alfabetico

alphanumeric [ælfənjuːˈmɛrɪk] ADJ alfanumerico(-a)

alpine [ˈælpaɪn] ADJ alpino(-a); **~ hut** rifugio alpino; **~ pasture** pascolo alpestre; **~ skiing** sci alpino

Alps [ælps] NPL: **the ~** le Alpi

already [ɔːlˈrɛdɪ] ADV già

alright [ˈɔːlˈraɪt] ADV = **all right**

Alsatian [ælˈseɪʃən] N (*BRIT: dog*) pastore m tedesco, (*cane m*) lupo

also [ˈɔːlsəu] ADV anche

altar [ˈɔltəʳ] N altare m

alter [ˈɔltəʳ] VT, VI alterare

alteration [ɔltəˈreɪʃən] N modificazione f, alterazione f; **alterations** (*Sewing, Archit*) modifiche fpl; **timetable subject to ~** orario soggetto a variazioni

altercation [ɔːltəˈkeɪʃən] N alterco, litigio

alternate ADJ [ɔlˈtəːnɪt] alterno(-a); (*US: plan etc*) alternativo(-a) ▶ VI [ˈɔltəːneɪt] alternare; **to ~ (with)** alternarsi (a); **on ~ days** ogni due giorni

alternately [ɔlˈtəːnɪtlɪ] ADV alternatamente

alternating current [ˈɔltəneɪtɪŋ-] N corrente f alternata

alternative [ɔlˈtəːnətɪv] ADJ (*solutions*) alternativo(-a); (*solution*) altro(-a) ▶ N (*choice*) alternativa; (*other possibility*) altra possibilità

alternatively [ɔlˈtəːnətɪvlɪ] ADV altrimenti, come alternativa

alternative medicine N medicina alternativa

alternator [ˈɔltəːneɪtəʳ] N (*Aut*) alternatore m

although [ɔːlˈðəu] CONJ benché + sub, sebbene + sub

altitude [ˈæltɪtjuːd] N altitudine f

alto [ˈæltəu] N contralto

altogether [ɔːltəˈgɛðəʳ] ADV del tutto, completamente; (*on the whole*) tutto considerato; (*in all*) in tutto; **how much is that ~?** quant'è in tutto?

altruism [ˈæltruːɪzəm] N altruismo

altruistic [æltruˈɪstɪk] ADJ altruistico(-a)

aluminium [æljuˈmɪnɪəm], (*US*) **aluminum** [əˈluːmɪnəm] N alluminio

always [ˈɔːlweɪz] ADV sempre

Alzheimer's [ˈæltshaɪməz] N (*also*: **Alzheimer's disease**) morbo di Alzheimer

AM ABBR (= *amplitude modulation*) AM ▶ N ABBR (= *Assembly Member*) deputato gallese

am [æm] VB *see* **be**

a.m. ADV ABBR (= *ante meridiem*) della mattina

AMA N ABBR = **American Medical Association**

amalgam [əˈmælgəm] N amalgama m

amalgamate [əˈmælgəmeɪt] VT amalgamare ▶ VI amalgamarsi

amalgamation [əmælgəˈmeɪʃən] N amalgamazione f; (*Comm*) fusione f

amass [əˈmæs] VT ammassare

amateur [ˈæmətəʳ] N dilettante mf ▶ ADJ (*Sport*) dilettante; **~ dramatics** n filodrammatica

amateurish [ˈæmətərɪʃ] ADJ (*pej*) da dilettante

amaze [əˈmeɪz] VT stupire

amazed ADJ sbalordito(-a); **to be ~ (at)** essere sbalordito(-a) (da)

amazement [əˈmeɪzmənt] N stupore m

amazing [əˈmeɪzɪŋ] ADJ sorprendente, sbalorditivo(-a); (*bargain, offer*) sensazionale

amazingly [əˈmeɪzɪŋlɪ] ADV incredibilmente, sbalorditivamente

Amazon [ˈæməzən] N (*Mythology*) Amazzone *f*; **the ~** il Rio delle Amazzoni ▶ CPD (*basin, jungle*) amazzonico(-a)

Amazonian [æməˈzəʊnɪən] ADJ amazzonico(-a)

ambassador [æmˈbæsədəʳ] N ambasciatore(-trice)

amber [ˈæmbəʳ] N ambra; **at ~** (*BRIT Aut*) giallo

ambidextrous [æmbɪˈdɛkstrəs] ADJ ambidestro(-a)

ambience [ˈæmbɪəns] N ambiente *m*

ambiguity [æmbɪˈgjuɪtɪ] N ambiguità *f inv*

ambiguous [æmˈbɪgjuəs] ADJ ambiguo(-a)

ambition [æmˈbɪʃən] N ambizione *f*; **to achieve one's ~** realizzare le proprie aspirazioni *or* ambizioni

ambitious [æmˈbɪʃəs] ADJ ambizioso(-a)

ambivalent [æmˈbɪvələnt] ADJ ambivalente

amble [ˈæmbl] VI (*also:* **amble along**) camminare tranquillamente

ambulance [ˈæmbjuləns] N ambulanza

ambush [ˈæmbuʃ] N imboscata ▶ VT fare un'imboscata a

ameba [əˈmiːbə] N (*US*) = **amoeba**

ameliorate [əˈmiːlɪəreɪt] VT migliorare

amen [ˈɑːˈmɛn] EXCL così sia, amen

amenable [əˈmiːnəbl] ADJ: **~ to** (*advice etc*) ben disposto(-a) a

amend [əˈmɛnd] VT (*law*) emendare; (*text*) correggere ▶ VI emendarsi; **to make amends** fare ammenda

amendment [əˈmɛndmənt] N emendamento; correzione *f*

amenities [əˈmiːnɪtɪz] NPL attrezzature *fpl* ricreative e culturali

amenity [əˈmiːnɪtɪ] N amenità *f inv*

America [əˈmɛrɪkə] N America

American [əˈmɛrɪkən] ADJ, N americano(-a)

American football N (*BRIT*) football *m* americano

americanize [əˈmɛrɪkənaɪz] VT americanizzare

amethyst [ˈæmɪθɪst] N ametista

Amex [ˈæmɛks] N ABBR = **American Stock Exchange**

amiable [ˈeɪmɪəbl] ADJ amabile, gentile

amicable [ˈæmɪkəbl] ADJ amichevole

amicably [ˈæmɪkəblɪ] ADV: **to part ~** lasciarsi senza rancori

amid [əˈmɪd], **amidst** [əˈmɪdst] PREP fra, tra, in mezzo a

amiss [əˈmɪs] ADJ, ADV: **there's something ~** c'è qualcosa che non va bene; **don't take it ~** non avertene a male

ammo [ˈæməʊ] N ABBR (*col*) = **ammunition**

ammonia [əˈməʊnɪə] N ammoniaca

ammunition [æmjuˈnɪʃən] N munizioni *fpl*; (*fig*) arma

ammunition dump N deposito di munizioni

amnesia [æmˈniːzɪə] N amnesia

amnesty [ˈæmnɪstɪ] N amnistia; **to grant an ~ to** concedere l'amnistia a, amnistiare

Amnesty International N Amnesty International *f*

amoeba, (*US*) **ameba** [əˈmiːbə] N ameba

amok [əˈmɔk] ADV: **to run ~** diventare pazzo(-a) furioso(-a)

among [əˈmʌŋ], **amongst** [əˈmʌŋst] PREP fra, tra, in mezzo a

amoral [eɪˈmɔrəl] ADJ amorale

amorous [ˈæmərəs] ADJ amoroso(-a)

amorphous [əˈmɔːfəs] ADJ amorfo(-a)

amortization [əmɔːtaɪˈzeɪʃən] N (*Comm*) ammortamento

amount [əˈmaunt] N (*sum of money*) somma; ammontare *m*; (*of bill etc*) importo; (*quantity*) quantità *f inv* ▶ VI: **to ~ to** (*total*) ammontare a; (*be same as*) essere come; **this amounts to a refusal** questo equivale a un rifiuto

amp [ˈæmp], **ampère** [ˈæmpɛəʳ] N ampere *m inv*; **a 13 ~ plug** una spina con fusibile da 13 ampere

ampersand [ˈæmpəsænd] N e *f* commerciale

amphetamine [æmˈfɛtəmiːn] N anfetamina

amphibian [æmˈfɪbɪən] N anfibio

amphibious [æmˈfɪbɪəs] ADJ anfibio(-a)

amphitheatre, (*US*) **amphitheater** [ˈæmfɪθɪətəʳ] N anfiteatro

ample [ˈæmpl] ADJ ampio(-a); spazioso(-a); (*enough*): **this is ~** questo è più che sufficiente; **to have ~ time/room** avere assai tempo/posto

amplifier [ˈæmplɪfaɪəʳ] N amplificatore *m*

amplify [ˈæmplɪfaɪ] VT amplificare

amply [ˈæmplɪ] ADV ampiamente

ampoule, (*US*) **ampule** [ˈæmpuːl] N (*Med*) fiala

amputate [ˈæmpjuteɪt] VT amputare

amputee [æmpjuˈtiː] N mutilato(-a), chi ha subito un'amputazione

Amsterdam [æmstəˈdæm] N Amsterdam *f*

amt ABBR = **amount**

Amtrak [ˈæmtræk] N (*US*) *società ferroviaria americana*

amuck [əˈmʌk] ADV = **amok**

amuse [əˈmjuːz] VT divertire; **to ~ o.s. with sth/by doing sth** divertirsi con qc/a fare qc; **to be amused at** essere divertito da; **he was not amused** non l'ha trovato divertente

amusement [əˈmjuːzmənt] N divertimento; **much to my ~** con mio grande spasso

amusement arcade N sala giochi (*solo con macchinette a gettoni*)

amusement park N luna park *m inv*

amusing [əˈmjuːzɪŋ] ADJ divertente

an [æn, ən, n] INDEF ART see **a**

ANA N ABBR = **American Newspaper Association; American Nurses Association**

anachronism [əˈnækrənɪzəm] N anacronismo

anaemia [əˈniːmɪə] N anemia

anaemic [əˈniːmɪk] ADJ anemico(-a)

anaesthetic [ænɪsˈθɛtɪk] ADJ anestetico(-a) ▶ N anestetico; **local/general ~** anestesia locale/totale; **under the ~** sotto anestesia

anaesthetist [æˈniːsθɪtɪst] N anestesista *mf*

anagram [ˈænəɡræm] N anagramma *m*

anal [ˈeɪnl] ADJ anale

analgesic [ænælˈdʒiːsɪk] ADJ analgesico(-a) ▶ N analgesico

analog, analogue [ˈænəlɒɡ] ADJ (*watch, computer*) analogico(-a)

analogous [əˈnæləɡəs] ADJ: **~ to** or **with** analogo(-a) a

analogy [əˈnælədʒɪ] N analogia; **to draw an ~ between** fare un'analogia tra

analyse, (US) **analyze** [ˈænəlaɪz] VT analizzare

analysis [əˈnæləsɪs] (*pl* **analyses** [-siːz]) N analisi *f inv*; **in the last ~** in ultima analisi

analyst [ˈænəlɪst] N (*political analyst etc*) analista *mf*; (US) (psic)analista *mf*

analytic [ænəˈlɪtɪk], **analytical** [ænəˈlɪtɪkl] ADJ analitico(-a)

analyze [ˈænəlaɪz] VT (US) = **analyse**

anarchic [æˈnɑːkɪk] ADJ anarchico(-a)

anarchist [ˈænəkɪst] ADJ, N anarchico(-a)

anarchy [ˈænəkɪ] N anarchia

anathema [əˈnæθɪmə] N: **it is ~ to him** non ne vuol neanche sentir parlare

anatomical [ænəˈtɒmɪkl] ADJ anatomico(-a)

anatomy [əˈnætəmɪ] N anatomia

ANC N ABBR = **African National Congress**

ancestor [ˈænsɪstə] N antenato(-a)

ancestral [ænˈsɛstrəl] ADJ avito(-a)

ancestry [ˈænsɪstrɪ] N antenati *mpl*; ascendenza

anchor [ˈæŋkə] N ancora ▶ VI (*also:* **to drop anchor**) gettare l'ancora ▶ VT ancorare; **to weigh ~** salpare or levare l'ancora

anchorage [ˈæŋkərɪdʒ] N ancoraggio

anchor man N (*irreg*) (TV, Radio) anchorman *m inv*

anchor woman N (*irreg*) (TV, Radio) anchorwoman *f inv*

anchovy [ˈæntʃəvɪ] N acciuga

ancient [ˈeɪnʃənt] ADJ antico(-a); (*person, car*) vecchissimo(-a); **~ monument** monumento storico

ancillary [ænˈsɪlərɪ] ADJ ausiliario(-a)

and [ænd] CONJ e (*often 'ed' before vowel*); **~ so on** e

così via; **try ~ do it** prova a farlo; **try ~ come** cerca di venire; **he talked ~ talked** non la finiva di parlare; **come ~ sit here** vieni a sedere qui; **better ~ better** sempre meglio; **more ~ more** sempre di più

Andes [ˈændiːz] NPL: **the ~** le Ande

Andorra [ænˈdɔːrə] N Andorra

anecdote [ˈænɪkdəut] N aneddoto

anemia *etc* [əˈniːmɪə] (US) = **anaemia** *etc*

anemone [əˈnɛmənɪ] N (*Bot*) anemone *m*; (*sea anemone*) anemone *m* di mare, attinia

anesthetic *etc* [ænɪsˈθɛtɪk] (US) = **anaesthetic** *etc*

anew [əˈnjuː] ADV di nuovo

angel [ˈeɪndʒəl] N angelo

angel dust N sedativo usato a scopo allucinogeno

anger [ˈæŋɡə] N rabbia ▶ VT arrabbiare

angina [ænˈdʒaɪnə] N angina pectoris

angle [ˈæŋɡl] N angolo ▶ VI: **to ~ for** (*fig*) cercare di avere; **from their ~** dal loro punto di vista

angler [ˈæŋɡlə] N pescatore *m* con la lenza

Anglican [ˈæŋɡlɪkən] ADJ, N anglicano(-a)

anglicize [ˈæŋɡlɪsaɪz] VT anglicizzare

angling [ˈæŋɡlɪŋ] N pesca con la lenza

Anglo- [ˈæŋɡləu] PREFIX, N anglo...; **Anglo-Italian** *adj* italobritannico(-a)

Anglo-Saxon [ˈæŋɡləuˈsæksən] ADJ, N anglosassone *mf*

Angola [æŋˈɡəulə] N Angola

Angolan [æŋˈɡəulən] ADJ, N angolano(-a)

angrily [ˈæŋɡrɪlɪ] ADV con rabbia

angry [ˈæŋɡrɪ] ADJ arrabbiato(-a), furioso(-a); (*wound*) infiammato(-a); **to be ~ with sb/at sth** essere in collera con qn/per qc; **to get ~** arrabbiarsi; **to make sb ~** fare arrabbiare qn

anguish [ˈæŋɡwɪʃ] N angoscia

anguished [ˈæŋɡwɪʃt] ADJ angosciato(-a), pieno(-a) d'angoscia

angular [ˈæŋɡjulə] ADJ angolare

animal [ˈænɪməl] ADJ animale ▶ N animale *m*

animal rights NPL diritti *mpl* degli animali

animate VT [ˈænɪmeɪt] animare ▶ ADJ [ˈænɪmɪt] animato(-a)

animated [ˈænɪmeɪtɪd] ADJ animato(-a)

animation [ænɪˈmeɪʃən] N animazione *f*

animosity [ænɪˈmɒsɪtɪ] N animosità

aniseed [ˈænɪsiːd] N semi *mpl* di anice

Ankara [ˈæŋkərə] N Ankara

ankle [ˈæŋkl] N caviglia

ankle socks NPL calzini *mpl*

annex N [ˈænɛks] (BRIT: *also:* **annexe**) edificio annesso ▶ VT [əˈnɛks] annettere

annexation [ænɛkˈseɪʃən] N annessione *f*

annihilate [əˈnaɪəleɪt] VT annientare

annihilation [ənaɪəˈleɪʃən] N annientamento

anniversary [ænɪˈvɜːsərɪ] N anniversario

anniversary dinner N cena commemorativa

annotate [ˈænəuteɪt] VT annotare

announce [əˈnauns] VT annunciare; **he announced that he wasn't going** ha dichiarato che non (ci) sarebbe andato

announcement [əˈnaunsmənt] N annuncio; (*letter, card*) partecipazione *f*; **I'd like to make an ~** ho una comunicazione da fare

announcer [əˈnaunsəʳ] N (*Radio, TV: between programmes*) annunciatore(-trice); (: *in a programme*) presentatore(-trice)

annoy [əˈnɔɪ] VT dare fastidio a; **to be annoyed (at sth/with sb)** essere seccato *or* irritato (per qc/con qn); **don't get annoyed!** non irritarti!

> La parola inglese **annoy** non vuol dire *annoiare*.

annoyance [əˈnɔɪəns] N fastidio; (*cause of annoyance*) noia

annoying [əˈnɔɪɪŋ] ADJ irritante, seccante

annual [ˈænjuəl] ADJ annuale ▶ N (*Bot*) pianta annua; (*book*) annuario

annual general meeting N (BRIT) assemblea generale

annually [ˈænjuəlɪ] ADV annualmente

annual report N relazione *f* annuale

annuity [əˈnjuːɪtɪ] N annualità *f inv*; **life ~** vitalizio

annul [əˈnʌl] VT annullare; (*law*) rescindere

annulment [əˈnʌlmənt] N annullamento; rescissione *f*

annum [ˈænəm] N *see* **per annum**

Annunciation [ənʌnsɪˈeɪʃən] N Annunciazione *f*

anode [ˈænəud] N anodo

anoint [əˈnɔɪnt] VT ungere

anomalous [əˈnɔmələs] ADJ anomalo(-a)

anomaly [əˈnɔməlɪ] N anomalia

anon. [əˈnɔn] ABBR = **anonymous**

anonymity [ænəˈnɪmɪtɪ] N anonimato

anonymous [əˈnɔnɪməs] ADJ anonimo(-a); **to remain ~** mantenere l'anonimato

anorak [ˈænəræk] N giacca a vento

anorexia [ænəˈrɛksɪə] N (*Med: also:* **anorexia nervosa**) anoressia

anorexic [ænəˈrɛksɪk] ADJ, N anoressico(-a)

another [əˈnʌðəʳ] ADJ: **~ book** (*one more*) un altro libro, ancora un libro; (*a different one*) un altro libro ▶ PRON un altro (un'altra), ancora uno(-a); **~ drink?** ancora qualcosa da bere?; **in ~ 5 years** fra altri 5 anni; *see also* **one**

ANSI N ABBR (= *American National Standards Institution*) *Istituto americano di standardizzazione*

answer [ˈɑːnsəʳ] N risposta; soluzione *f* ▶ VI rispondere ▶ VT (*reply to*) rispondere a; (*problem*) risolvere; (*prayer*) esaudire; **in ~ to your letter** in risposta alla sua lettera; **to ~ the phone** rispondere (al telefono); **to ~ the bell** rispondere al campanello; **to ~ the door** aprire la porta

> ▶ **answer back** VI ribattere
> ▶ **answer for** VT FUS essere responsabile di
> ▶ **answer to** VT FUS (*description*) corrispondere a

answerable [ˈɑːnsərəbl] ADJ: **~ (to sb/for sth)** responsabile (verso qn/di qc); **I am ~ to no-one** non devo rispondere a nessuno

answering machine [ˈɑːnsərɪŋ-] N segreteria telefonica

answerphone [ˈɑːnsəfəun] N (*esp* BRIT) segreteria telefonica

ant [ænt] N formica

ANTA N ABBR = **American National Theater and Academy**

antagonism [ænˈtægənɪzəm] N antagonismo

antagonist [ænˈtægənɪst] N antagonista *mf*

antagonistic [æntægəˈnɪstɪk] ADJ antagonistico(-a)

antagonize [ænˈtægənaɪz] VT provocare l'ostilità di

Antarctic [æntˈɑːktɪk] N: **the ~** l'Antartide *f* ▶ ADJ antartico(-a)

Antarctica [æntˈɑːktɪkə] N Antartide *f*

Antarctic Circle N Circolo polare antartico

Antarctic Ocean N Oceano antartico

ante [ˈæntɪ] N (*Cards, fig*): **to up the ~** alzare la posta in palio

ante... [ˈæntɪ] PREFIX anti..., ante..., pre...

anteater [ˈæntiːtəʳ] N formichiere *m*

antecedent [æntɪˈsiːdənt] N antecedente *m*, precedente *m*

antechamber [ˈæntɪtʃeɪmbəʳ] N anticamera

antelope [ˈæntɪləup] N antilope *f*

antenatal [ˈæntɪˈneɪtl] ADJ prenatale

antenatal clinic N assistenza medica preparto

antenna [ænˈtɛnə] (*pl* **antennae** [-niː]) N antenna

anthem [ˈænθəm] N antifona; **national ~** inno nazionale

ant-hill [ˈænthɪl] N formicaio

anthology [ænˈθɔlədʒɪ] N antologia

anthrax [ˈænθræks] N antrace *m*

anthropologist [ænθrəˈpɔlədʒɪst] N antropologo(-a)

anthropology [ænθrəˈpɔlədʒɪ] N antropologia

anti- [ˈæntɪ] PREFIX anti...

anti-aircraft [ˈæntɪˈɛəkrɑːft] ADJ antiaereo(-a)

anti-aircraft defence N difesa antiaerea

antiballistic [ˈæntɪbəˈlɪstɪk] ADJ antibalistico(-a)

antibiotic [ˈæntɪbaɪˈɔtɪk] ADJ antibiotico(-a) ▶ N antibiotico

antibody ['æntɪbɔdɪ] N anticorpo

anticipate [æn'tɪsɪpeɪt] VT prevedere; pregustare; (wishes, request) prevenire; **as anticipated** come previsto; **this is worse than I anticipated** è peggio di quel che immaginavo or pensavo

anticipation [æntɪsɪ'peɪʃən] N anticipazione f; (expectation) aspettative fpl; **thanking you in ~** vi ringrazio in anticipo

anticlimax ['æntɪ'klaɪmæks] N: **it was an ~** fu una completa delusione

anticlockwise ['æntɪ'klɔkwaɪz] ADJ, ADV in senso antiorario

antics ['æntɪks] NPL buffonerie fpl

anticyclone ['æntɪ'saɪkləun] N anticiclone m

antidote ['æntɪdəut] N antidoto

antifreeze ['æntɪfriːz] N anticongelante m

anti-globalization [æntɪgləubəlaɪ'zeɪʃən] ADJ antiglobalizzazione inv ▶ N antiglobalizzazione f

Antigua and Barbuda [æn'tiːgə ænd bɑː'buːdə] N Stato di Antigua e Barbuda

antihistamine [æntɪ'hɪstəmɪn] N antistaminico

Antilles [æn'tɪliːz] NPL: **the ~** le Antille

antipathy [æn'tɪpəθɪ] N antipatia

antiperspirant ['æntɪ'pəːspərənt] ADJ antitraspirante

Antipodean [æntɪpə'diːən] ADJ degli Antipodi

Antipodes [æn'tɪpədiːz] NPL: **the ~** gli Antipodi

antiquarian [æntɪ'kwɛərɪən] ADJ: **~ bookshop** libreria antiquaria ▶ N antiquario(-a)

antiquated ['æntɪkweɪtɪd] ADJ antiquato(-a)

antique [æn'tiːk] N antichità f inv ▶ ADJ antico(-a)

antique dealer N antiquario(-a)

antique shop N negozio d'antichità

antiquity [æn'tɪkwɪtɪ] N antichità f inv

anti-semitic ['æntɪsɪ'mɪtɪk] ADJ antisemitico(-a), antisemita

anti-semitism ['æntɪ'sɛmɪtɪzəm] N antisemitismo

antiseptic [æntɪ'sɛptɪk] ADJ antisettico(-a) ▶ N antisettico

antisocial ['æntɪ'səuʃəl] ADJ asociale; (against society) antisociale

antitank [æntɪ'tæŋk] ADJ anticarro inv

antithesis [æn'tɪθɪsɪs] (pl **antitheses** [-siːz]) N antitesi f inv; (contrast) carattere m antitetico

anti-trust [æntɪ'trʌst] ADJ (Comm): **~ legislation** legislazione f antitrust inv

antiviral [æntɪ'vaɪərəl] ADJ (Med) antivirale

antivirus [æntɪ'vaɪərəs] ADJ (Comput) antivirus inv; **~ program** antivirus m inv

antivirus software N antivirus m inv

antlers ['æntləz] NPL palchi mpl

Antwerp ['æntwəːp] N Anversa

anus ['eɪnəs] N ano

anvil ['ænvɪl] N incudine f

anxiety [æŋ'zaɪətɪ] N ansia; (keenness): **~ to do** smania di fare

anxious ['æŋkʃəs] ADJ ansioso(-a), inquieto(-a); (worrying) angosciante; (keen): **~ to do/that** impaziente di fare/che + sub; **I'm very ~ about you** sono molto preoccupato or in pensiero per te

anxiously ['æŋkʃəslɪ] ADV ansiosamente, con ansia

---

any ['ɛnɪ]

ADJ **1** (in questions etc): **have you any butter?** hai del burro?, hai un po' di burro?; **have you any children?** hai bambini?; **if there are any tickets left** se ci sono ancora (dei) biglietti, se c'è ancora qualche biglietto

2 (with negative): **I haven't any money/books** non ho soldi/libri; **without any difficulty** senza nessuna or alcuna difficoltà

3 (no matter which) qualsiasi, qualunque; **choose any book you like** scegli un libro qualsiasi

4 (in phrases): **in any case** in ogni caso; **any day now** da un giorno all'altro; **at any moment** in qualsiasi momento, da un momento all'altro; **at any rate** ad ogni modo

▶ PRON **1** (in questions, with negative): **have you got any?** ne hai?; **can any of you sing?** qualcuno di voi sa cantare?; **I haven't any (of them)** non ne ho

2 (no matter which one(s)): **take any of those books (you like)** prendi uno qualsiasi di quei libri

▶ ADV **1** (in questions etc): **do you want any more soup/sandwiches?** vuoi ancora un po' di minestra/degli altri panini?; **are you feeling any better?** ti senti meglio?

2 (with negative): **I can't hear him any more** non lo sento più; **don't wait any longer** non aspettare più

---

anybody ['ɛnɪbɔdɪ] PRON qualsiasi persona; (in interrogative sentences) qualcuno; (in negative sentences) nessuno; (no matter who) chiunque; **can you see ~?** vedi qualcuno or nessuno?; **if ~ should phone ...** se telefona qualcuno ...; **I don't see ~** non vedo nessuno; **~ could do it** chiunque potrebbe farlo

anyhow ['ɛnɪhau] ADV in qualsiasi modo; (haphazardly) come capita; (at any rate) ad ogni modo, comunque; (haphazard): **do it ~ you like** fallo come ti pare; **I shall go ~** ci andrò lo stesso or comunque; **she leaves things just ~** lascia tutto come capita

anyone ['ɛnɪwʌn] PRON = **anybody**

anyplace ['ɛnɪpleɪs] ADV (US col) = **anywhere**

anything ['ɛnɪθɪŋ] PRON qualsiasi cosa; (in

interrogative sentences) qualcosa, niente; (with negative) niente; **you can say ~ you like** (no matter what) puoi dire quello che ti pare; **can you see ~?** vedi niente or qualcosa?; **if ~ happens to me …** se mi dovesse succedere qualcosa …; **I can't see ~** non vedo niente; **~ will do** va bene qualsiasi cosa or tutto; **~ else?** (in shop) basta (così)?; **it can cost ~ between £15 and £20** può costare qualcosa come 15 o 20 sterline

anytime [ˈɛnɪtaɪm] ADV in qualunque momento; quando vuole

anyway [ˈɛnɪweɪ] ADV (at any rate) ad ogni modo, comunque; (besides) ad ogni modo

anywhere [ˈɛnɪwɛəʳ] ADV da qualsiasi parte; (in interrogative sentences) da qualche parte; (with negative) da nessuna parte; (no matter where) da qualsiasi or qualunque parte, dovunque; **can you see him ~?** lo vedi da qualche parte?; **I don't see him ~** non lo vedo da nessuna parte; **~ in the world** dovunque nel mondo

Anzac [ˈænzæk] N ABBR (= Australia-New Zealand Army Corps) ANZAC m; (soldier) soldato dell'ANZAC

Anzac Day N vedi nota

L'**Anzac Day** è una festa nazionale in Australia e Nuova Zelanda che cade il 25 aprile quando si commemorano i morti di tutte le guerre. La data ricorda lo sbarco delle truppe ANZAC (Australian and New Zealand Army Corps) a Gallipoli (Turchia) nel 1915, durante la Prima guerra mondiale.

apart [əˈpɑːt] ADV (to one side) a parte; (separately) separatamente; **with one's legs ~** con le gambe divaricate; **10 miles/a long way ~** a 10 miglia di distanza/molto lontani l'uno dall'altro; **they are living ~** sono separati; **to take ~** smontare; **~ from** prep a parte, eccetto

apartheid [əˈpɑːteɪt] N apartheid f

apartment [əˈpɑːtmənt] N (US) appartamento; (room) locale m ∎ **apartments** NPL appartamento ammobiliato

apartment building N (US) stabile m, caseggiato

apathetic [æpəˈθɛtɪk] ADJ apatico(-a)

apathy [ˈæpəθɪ] N apatia

APB N ABBR (US: police expression: = all points bulletin) espressione della polizia che significa "trovate e arrestate il sospetto"

ape [eɪp] N scimmia ▶ VT scimmiottare

Apennines [ˈæpənaɪnz] NPL: **the ~** gli Apennini

aperitif [əˈpɛrɪtiːf] N aperitivo

aperture [ˈæpətʃuəʳ] N apertura

apex [ˈeɪpɛks] N apice m

aphid [ˈæfɪd] N afide f

aphrodisiac [æfrəʊˈdɪzɪæk] ADJ afrodisiaco(-a) ▶ N afrodisiaco

API N ABBR = **American Press Institute**

apiece [əˈpiːs] ADV ciascuno(-a)

aplomb [əˈplɒm] N disinvoltura

apocalypse [əˈpɒkəlɪps] N apocalisse f

apolitical [eɪpəˈlɪtɪkl] ADJ apolitico(-a)

apologetic [əpɒləˈdʒɛtɪk] ADJ (tone, letter) di scusa; **to be very ~ about** scusarsi moltissimo di

apologetically [əpɒləˈdʒɛtɪkəlɪ] ADV per scusarsi

apologize [əˈpɒlədʒaɪz] VI: **to ~ (for sth to sb)** scusarsi (di qc a qn), chiedere scusa (a qn per qc)

apology [əˈpɒlədʒɪ] N scuse fpl; **please accept my apologies** la prego di accettare le mie scuse

apoplectic [æpəˈplɛktɪk] ADJ (Med) apoplettico(-a); **~ with rage** (col) livido(-a) per la rabbia

apoplexy [ˈæpəplɛksɪ] N apoplessia

apostle [əˈpɒsl] N apostolo

apostrophe [əˈpɒstrəfɪ] N (sign) apostrofo

app N ABBR (col: Comput: = application) applicazione f

appal, (US) **appall** [əˈpɔːl] VT atterrire; sconvolgere

Appalachian Mountains [æpəˈleɪʃən-] NPL: **the ~** i Monti Appalachi

appalling [əˈpɔːlɪŋ] ADJ spaventoso(-a); **she's an ~ cook** è un disastro come cuoca

apparatus [æpəˈreɪtəs] N apparato; (in gymnasium) attrezzatura

apparel [əˈpærl] N (US) abbigliamento, confezioni fpl

apparent [əˈpærənt] ADJ evidente

apparently [əˈpærəntlɪ] ADV evidentemente, a quanto pare

apparition [æpəˈrɪʃən] N apparizione f

appeal [əˈpiːl] VI (Law) appellarsi alla legge ▶ N (Law) appello; (request) richiesta; (charm) attrattiva; **to ~ for** chiedere (con insistenza); **to ~ to** (person) appellarsi a; (thing) piacere a; **to ~ to sb for mercy** chiedere pietà a qn; **it doesn't ~ to me** mi dice poco; **right of ~** diritto d'appello

appealing [əˈpiːlɪŋ] ADJ (moving) commovente; (attractive) attraente

appear [əˈpɪəʳ] VI apparire; (Law) comparire; (publication) essere pubblicato(-a); (seem) sembrare; **it would ~ that** sembra che; **to ~ in Hamlet** recitare nell'Amleto; **to ~ on TV** presentarsi in televisione

appearance [əˈpɪərəns] N apparizione f; apparenza; (look, aspect) aspetto; **to put in or make an ~** fare atto di presenza; **by order of ~** (Theat) in ordine di apparizione; **to keep up appearances** salvare le apparenze; **to all appearances** a giudicar dalle apparenze

appease [əˈpiːz] VT calmare, appagare

appeasement [ə'pi:zmənt] N (Pol) appeasement m inv

append [ə'pɛnd] VT (Comput) aggiungere in coda

appendage [ə'pɛndɪdʒ] N aggiunta

appendicitis [əpɛndɪ'saɪtɪs] N appendicite f

appendix [ə'pɛndɪks] (pl **appendices** [-si:z]) N appendice f; **to have one's ~ out** operarsi or farsi operare di appendicite

appetite ['æpɪtaɪt] N appetito; **that walk has given me an ~** la passeggiata mi ha messo appetito

appetizer ['æpɪtaɪzəʳ] N (food) stuzzichino; (drink) aperitivo

appetizing ['æpɪtaɪzɪŋ] ADJ appetitoso(-a)

applaud [ə'plɔ:d] VT, VI applaudire

applause [ə'plɔ:z] N applauso

apple ['æpl] N mela; (also: **apple tree**) melo; **the ~ of one's eye** la pupilla dei propri occhi

apple pie N torta di mele

apple turnover N sfogliatella alle mele

appliance [ə'plaɪəns] N apparecchio; **electrical appliances** elettrodomestici mpl

applicable [ə'plɪkəbl] ADJ applicabile; **to be ~ to** essere valido per; **the law is ~ from January** la legge entrerà in vigore in gennaio

applicant ['æplɪkənt] N candidato(-a); (Admin: for benefit etc) chi ha fatto domanda or richiesta

application [æplɪ'keɪʃən] N applicazione f; (for a job, a grant etc) domanda; (Comput) applicazione f; **on ~** su richiesta

application form N modulo per la domanda

application program N (Comput) programma applicativo

applications package N (Comput) software m inv applicativo

applied [ə'plaɪd] ADJ applicato(-a); **~ arts** arti fpl applicate

apply [ə'plaɪ] VT: **to ~ (to)** (paint, ointment) dare (a); (theory, technique) applicare (a) ▶ VI: **to ~ to** (ask) rivolgersi a; (be suitable for, relevant to) riguardare, riferirsi a; **to ~ (for)** (permit, grant, job) fare domanda (per); **to ~ the brakes** frenare; **to ~ o.s. to** dedicarsi a

appoint [ə'pɔɪnt] VT nominare

appointee [əpɔɪn'ti:] N incaricato(-a)

appointment [ə'pɔɪntmənt] N nomina; (arrangement to meet) appuntamento; **by ~** su or per appuntamento; **to make an ~ with sb** prendere un appuntamento con qn; **I have an ~ (with) ...** ho un appuntamento (con) ...; **"appointments (vacant)"** (Press) "offerte fpl di impiego"

apportion [ə'pɔ:ʃən] VT attribuire

appraisal [ə'preɪzl] N valutazione f

appraise [ə'preɪz] VT (value) valutare, fare una stima di; (situation etc) fare il bilancio di

appreciable [ə'pri:ʃəbl] ADJ apprezzabile

appreciably [ə'pri:ʃəblɪ] ADV notevolmente, sensibilmente

appreciate [ə'pri:ʃɪeɪt] VT (like) apprezzare; (be grateful for) essere riconoscente di; (be aware of) rendersi conto di ▶ VI (Comm) aumentare; **I'd ~ your help** ti sono grato per l'aiuto

appreciation [əpri:ʃɪ'eɪʃən] N apprezzamento; (Finance) aumento del valore

appreciative [ə'pri:ʃɪətɪv] ADJ (person) sensibile; (comment) elogiativo(-a)

apprehend [æprɪ'hɛnd] VT (arrest) arrestare; (understand) comprendere

apprehension [æprɪ'hɛnʃən] N (fear) inquietudine f

apprehensive [æprɪ'hɛnsɪv] ADJ apprensivo(-a)

apprentice [ə'prɛntɪs] N apprendista mf ▶ VT: **to be apprenticed to** lavorare come apprendista presso

apprenticeship [ə'prɛntɪsʃɪp] N apprendistato; **to serve one's ~** fare il proprio apprendistato or tirocinio

appro. ['æprəʊ] ABBR (BRIT Comm: col) = **approval**

approach [ə'prəʊtʃ] VI avvicinarsi ▶ VT (come near) avvicinarsi a; (ask, apply to) rivolgersi a; (subject, passer-by) avvicinare ▶ N approccio; accesso; (to problem) modo di affrontare; **to ~ sb about sth** rivolgersi a qn per qc

approachable [ə'prəʊtʃəbl] ADJ accessibile

approach road N strada d'accesso

approbation [æprə'beɪʃən] N approvazione f, benestare m

appropriate VT [ə'prəʊprɪeɪt] (take) appropriarsi di ▶ ADJ [ə'prəʊprɪɪt] appropriato(-a), adatto(-a); **it would not be ~ for me to comment** non sta a me fare dei commenti

appropriately [ə'prəʊprɪɪtlɪ] ADV in modo appropriato

appropriation [əprəʊprɪ'eɪʃən] N stanziamento

approval [ə'pru:vəl] N approvazione f; **on ~** (Comm) in prova, in esame; **to meet with sb's ~** soddisfare qn, essere di gradimento di qn

approve [ə'pru:v] VT, VI approvare
▶ **approve of** VT FUS approvare

approved school N (BRIT old) riformatorio

approvingly [ə'pru:vɪŋlɪ] ADV in approvazione

approx. ABBR = **approximately**

approximate ADJ [ə'prɒksɪmɪt] approssimativo(-a) ▶ VT [ə'prɒksɪmeɪt] essere un'approssimazione di, avvicinarsi a

approximately [ə'prɒksɪmətlɪ] ADV circa

approximation [ə'prɒksɪ'meɪʃən] N approssimazione f

apricot ['eɪprɪkɒt] N albicocca

April ['eɪprəl] N aprile m; **~ fool!** pesce d'aprile!; see also **July**

April Fools' Day N vedi nota

April Fools' Day è il primo aprile, il giorno degli scherzi. Il nome deriva dal fatto che, se una persona cade nella trappola che gli è stata tesa, fa la figura del *fool*, cioè dello sciocco. Di recente gli scherzi sono diventati sempre più elaborati e persino i giornalisti a volte inventano vicende incredibili per burlarsi dei lettori.

apron ['eɪprən] N grembiule m; (*Aviat*) area di stazionamento

apse [æps] N (*Archit*) abside f

apt [æpt] ADJ (*suitable*) adatto(-a); (*able*) capace; (*likely*): **to be ~ to do** avere tendenza a fare

apt. ABBR = **apartment**

aptitude ['æptɪtjuːd] N abilità f inv

aptitude test N test m inv attitudinale

aptly ['æptlɪ] ADV appropriatamente, in modo adatto

aqualung ['ækwəlʌŋ] N autorespiratore m

aquarium [ə'kwɛərɪəm] N acquario

Aquarius [ə'kwɛərɪəs] N Acquario; **to be ~** essere dell'Acquario

aquatic [ə'kwætɪk] ADJ acquatico(-a)

aqueduct ['ækwɪdʌkt] N acquedotto

AR ABBR (*US*) = **Arkansas**

ARA N ABBR (*BRIT*) = **Associate of the Royal Academy**

Arab ['ærəb] ADJ, N arabo(-a)

Arabia [ə'reɪbɪə] N Arabia

Arabian [ə'reɪbɪən] ADJ arabo(-a)

Arabian Desert N Deserto arabico

Arabian Sea N mare m Arabico

Arabic ['ærəbɪk] ADJ arabico(-a), arabo(-a) ▶ N arabo

Arabic numerals NPL numeri mpl arabi, numerazione f araba

arable ['ærəbl] ADJ arabile

ARAM N ABBR (*BRIT*) = **Associate of the Royal Academy of Music**

arbiter ['ɑːbɪtər] N arbitro

arbitrary ['ɑːbɪtrərɪ] ADJ arbitrario(-a)

arbitrate ['ɑːbɪtreɪt] VI arbitrare

arbitration [ɑːbɪ'treɪʃən] N (*Law*) arbitrato; (*Industry*) arbitraggio

arbitrator ['ɑːbɪtreɪtər] N arbitro

ARC N ABBR (= *American Red Cross*) C.R.I. f (= *Croce Rossa Italiana*)

arc [ɑːk] N arco

arcade [ɑː'keɪd] N portico; (*passage with shops*) galleria

arch [ɑːtʃ] N arco; (*of foot*) arco plantare ▶ VT inarcare ▶ PREFIX: **~(-)** grande (*before n*); per eccellenza

archaeological [ɑːkɪə'lɔdʒɪkəl] ADJ archeologico(-a)

archaeologist [ɑːkɪ'ɔlədʒɪst] N archeologo(-a)

archaeology [ɑːkɪ'ɔlədʒɪ] N archeologia

archaic [ɑː'keɪɪk] ADJ arcaico(-a)

archangel ['ɑːkeɪndʒəl] N arcangelo

archbishop [ɑːtʃ'bɪʃəp] N arcivescovo

arched [ɑːtʃt] ADJ arcuato(-a), ad arco

arch-enemy ['ɑːtʃ'ɛnɪmɪ] N arcinemico(-a)

archeology etc [ɑːkɪ'ɔlədʒɪ] = **archaeology** etc

archer ['ɑːtʃər] N arciere m

archery ['ɑːtʃərɪ] N tiro all'arco

archetypal ['ɑːkɪtaɪpəl] ADJ tipico(-a)

archetype ['ɑːkɪtaɪp] N archetipo

archipelago [ɑːkɪ'pɛlɪgəu] N arcipelago

architect ['ɑːkɪtɛkt] N architetto

architectural [ɑːkɪ'tɛktʃərəl] ADJ architettonico(-a)

architecture ['ɑːkɪtɛktʃər] N architettura

archive ['ɑːkaɪv] N (*also Comput*) archivio ■ **archives** NPL archivi mpl

archive file N (*Comput*) file m inv di archivio

archivist ['ɑːkɪvɪst] N archivista mf

archway ['ɑːtʃweɪ] N arco

ARCM N ABBR (*BRIT*) = **Associate of the Royal College of Music**

Arctic ['ɑːktɪk] ADJ artico(-a) ▶ N: **the ~** l'Artico

Arctic Circle N Circolo polare artico

Arctic Ocean N Oceano artico

ardent ['ɑːdənt] ADJ ardente

ardour, (*US*) **ardor** ['ɑːdər] N ardore m

arduous ['ɑːdjuəs] ADJ arduo(-a)

are [ɑː] VB see **be**

area ['ɛərɪə] N (*Geom*) area; (*zone*) zona; (: *smaller*) settore m; **dining ~** zona pranzo; **the London ~** la zona di Londra

area code N (*US Tel*) prefisso

arena [ə'riːnə] N arena

aren't [ɑːnt] = **are not**

Argentina [ɑːdʒən'tiːnə] N Argentina

Argentinian [ɑːdʒən'tɪnɪən] ADJ, N argentino(-a)

arguable ['ɑːgjuəbl] ADJ discutibile; **it is ~ whether ...** è una cosa discutibile se ... + sub

arguably ['ɑːgjuəblɪ] ADV: **it is ~ ...** si può sostenere che sia ...

argue ['ɑːgjuː] VI (*quarrel*) litigare; (*reason*) ragionare ▶ VT (*debate: case, matter*) dibattere; **to ~ that** sostenere che; **to ~ about sth (with sb)** litigare per or a proposito di qc (con qn)

argument ['ɑːgjumənt] N (*reasons*) argomento; (*quarrel*) lite f; (*debate*) discussione f; **~ for/against** argomento a or in favore di/contro

argumentative [ɑːgju'mɛntətɪv] ADJ litigioso(-a)

aria ['ɑːrɪə] N aria

ARIBA N ABBR (*BRIT*) = **Associate of the Royal Institute of British Architects**

429

arid [ˈærɪd] ADJ arido(-a)

aridity [əˈrɪdɪtɪ] N aridità

Aries [ˈɛərɪz] N Ariete m; **to be ~** essere dell'Ariete

arise [əˈraɪz] (pt **arose** [əˈrəuz], pp **arisen** [əˈrɪzn]) VI alzarsi; (opportunity, problem) presentarsi; **to ~ from** risultare da; **should the need ~** dovesse presentarsi la necessità, in caso di necessità

aristocracy [ærɪsˈtɒkrəsɪ] N aristocrazia

aristocrat [ˈærɪstəkræt] N aristocratico(-a)

aristocratic [ærɪstəˈkrætɪk] ADJ aristocratico(-a)

arithmetic [əˈrɪθmətɪk] N aritmetica

arithmetical [ærɪθˈmetɪkəl] ADJ aritmetico(-a)

ark [ɑːk] N: **Noah's A~** l'arca di Noè

arm [ɑːm] N braccio; (Mil: branch) arma ▶ VT armare; **~ in ~** a braccetto; see also **arms**

armaments [ˈɑːməmənts] NPL (weapons) armamenti mpl

armband [ˈɑːmbænd] N bracciale m

armchair [ˈɑːmtʃɛəʳ] N poltrona

armed [ɑːmd] ADJ armato(-a)

armed forces NPL forze fpl armate

armed robbery N rapina a mano armata

Armenia [ɑːˈmiːnɪə] N Armenia

Armenian [ɑːˈmiːnɪən] ADJ armeno(-a) ▶ N armeno(-a); (Ling) armeno

armful [ˈɑːmful] N bracciata

armistice [ˈɑːmɪstɪs] N armistizio

armour, (US) **armor** [ˈɑːməʳ] N armatura; (also: **armour-plating**) corazza, blindatura; (Mil: tanks) mezzi mpl blindati

armoured car, (US) **armored car** N autoblinda f inv

armoury, (US) **armory** [ˈɑːmərɪ] N arsenale m

armpit [ˈɑːmpɪt] N ascella

armrest [ˈɑːmrest] N bracciolo

arms [ɑːmz] NPL (weapons) armi fpl; (Heraldry) stemma m

arms control N controllo degli armamenti

arms race N corsa agli armamenti

army [ˈɑːmɪ] N esercito

aroma [əˈrəumə] N aroma

aromatherapy [ərəuməˈθɛrəpɪ] N aromaterapia

aromatic [ærəˈmætɪk] ADJ aromatico(-a)

arose [əˈrəuz] PT of **arise**

around [əˈraund] ADV attorno, intorno ▶ PREP intorno a; (fig: about): **~ £5/3 o'clock** circa 5 sterline/le 3; **is he ~?** è in giro?

arousal [əˈrauzəl] N (sexual etc) eccitazione f; (awakening) risveglio

arouse [əˈrauz] VT (sleeper) svegliare; (curiosity, passions) suscitare

arrange [əˈreɪndʒ] VT sistemare; (programme) preparare ▶ VI: **we have arranged for a taxi to pick you up** la faremo venire a prendere da un taxi; **it was arranged that ...** è stato deciso or stabilito che ...; **to ~ to do sth** mettersi d'accordo per fare qc

arrangement [əˈreɪndʒmənt] N sistemazione f; (agreement) accordo ▪ **arrangements** NPL (plans etc) progetti mpl, piani mpl; **by ~** su richiesta; **to come to an ~ (with sb)** venire ad un accordo (con qn), mettersi d'accordo or accordarsi (con qn); **I'll make arrangements for you to be met** darò disposizioni or istruzioni perché ci sia qualcuno ad incontrarla

arrant [ˈærənt] ADJ: **~ nonsense** colossali sciocchezze fpl

array [əˈreɪ] N fila; (Comput) array m inv, insieme mpl; **~ of** fila di

arrears [əˈrɪəz] NPL arretrati mpl; **to be in ~ with one's rent** essere in arretrato con l'affitto

arrest [əˈrest] VT arrestare; (sb's attention) attirare ▶ N arresto; **under ~** in arresto

arresting [əˈrestɪŋ] ADJ (fig) che colpisce

arrival [əˈraɪvəl] N arrivo; (person) arrivato(-a); **a new ~** un nuovo venuto; (baby) un neonato

arrive [əˈraɪv] VI arrivare
▶ **arrive at** VT FUS arrivare a

arrogance [ˈærəgəns] N arroganza

arrogant [ˈærəgənt] ADJ arrogante

arrow [ˈærəu] N freccia

arse [ɑːs] N (BRIT col!) culo (!)

arsenal [ˈɑːsɪnl] N arsenale m

arsenic [ˈɑːsnɪk] N arsenico

arson [ˈɑːsn] N incendio doloso

art [ɑːt] N arte f; (craft) mestiere m; **work of ~** opera d'arte; see also **arts**

art college N scuola di belle arti

artefact, (US) **artifact** [ˈɑːtɪfækt] N manufatto

arterial [ɑːˈtɪərɪəl] ADJ (Anat) arterioso(-a); (road etc) di grande comunicazione; **~ roads** le (grandi or principali) arterie

artery [ˈɑːtərɪ] N arteria

artful [ˈɑːtful] ADJ furbo(-a)

art gallery N galleria d'arte

arthritis [ɑːˈθraɪtɪs] N artrite f

artichoke [ˈɑːtɪtʃəuk] N carciofo; **Jerusalem ~** topinambur m inv

article [ˈɑːtɪkl] N articolo ▪ **articles** NPL (BRIT Law: training) contratto di tirocinio; **articles of clothing** indumenti mpl

articles of association NPL (Comm) statuto sociale

articulate ADJ [ɑːˈtɪkjulɪt] (person) che si esprime forbitamente; (speech) articolato(-a) ▶ VI [ɑːˈtɪkjuleɪt] articolare

articulated lorry N (BRIT) autotreno

artifact [ˈɑːtɪfækt] N (US) = **artefact**

artifice [ˈɑːtɪfɪs] N (cunning) abilità, destrezza; (trick) artificio

artificial [ɑːtɪˈfɪʃəl] ADJ artificiale

artificial insemination [-ɪnsɛmɪˈneɪʃən] N fecondazione f artificiale

artificial intelligence N intelligenza artificiale

artificial respiration N respirazione f artificiale

artillery [ɑːˈtɪlərɪ] N artiglieria

artisan [ˈɑːtɪzæn] N artigiano(-a)

artist [ˈɑːtɪst] N artista mf

artistic [ɑːˈtɪstɪk] ADJ artistico(-a)

artistry [ˈɑːtɪstrɪ] N arte f

artless [ˈɑːtlɪs] ADJ semplice, ingenuo(-a)

arts [ɑːts] NPL (Scol) lettere fpl

art school N scuola d'arte

artwork [ˈɑːtwəːk] N materiale m illustrativo

ARV N ABBR (= American Revised Version) traduzione della Bibbia

AS N ABBR (US Scol: = Associate in or of Science) titolo di studio

---

as [æz]

CONJ **1** (referring to time) mentre; **as the years went by** col passare degli anni; **he came in as I was leaving** arrivò mentre stavo uscendo; **as from tomorrow** da domani

2 (in comparisons): **as big as** grande come; **twice as big as** due volte più grande di; **as much/many as** tanto quanto/tanti quanti; **as soon as possible** prima possibile

3 (since, because) dal momento che, siccome

4 (referring to manner, way) come; **big as it is** grande com'è; **much as I like them, ...** per quanto mi siano simpatici, ...; **do as you wish** fa' come vuoi; **as she said** come ha detto lei

5 (concerning): **as for** or **to that** per quanto riguarda or quanto a quello

6: **as if** or **though** come se; **he looked as if he was ill** sembrava stare male; see also **long**; **such**; **well**

▶ PREP: **he works as a driver** fa l'autista; **as chairman of the company, he ...** come presidente della compagnia, lui ...; **he gave me it as a present** me lo ha regalato

---

There are various ways of translating as ... as when as is used in comparisons.
Peter's as tall as Michael. **Peter è alto come Michael.**
I haven't got as much money as you. **Non ho tanti soldi quanti ne hai tu.**
Her coat cost twice as much as mine. **Il suo cappotto è costato il doppio del mio.**

ASA N ABBR (= American Standards Association) associazione per la normalizzazione; (BRIT: = Advertising Standards Association) ≈ Istituto di Autodisciplina Pubblicitaria

a.s.a.p. ABBR (= as soon as possible) prima possibile

asbestos [æzˈbɛstəs] N asbesto, amianto

ASBO [ˈæzbəu] N ABBR (BRIT: = antisocial behaviour order) provvedimento restrittivo per comportamento antisociale

ascend [əˈsɛnd] VT salire

ascendancy [əˈsɛndənsɪ] N ascendente m

ascendant [əˈsɛndənt] N: **to be in the ~** essere in auge

ascension [əˈsɛnʃən] N: **the A~** (Rel) l'Ascensione f

Ascension Island N isola dell'Ascensione

ascent [əˈsɛnt] N salita

ascertain [æsəˈteɪn] VT accertare

ascetic [əˈsɛtɪk] ADJ ascetico(-a)

asceticism [əˈsɛtɪsɪzəm] N ascetismo

ASCII [ˈæskiː] N ABBR (= American Standard Code for Information Interchange) ASCII m

ascribe [əˈskraɪb] VT: **to ~ sth to** attribuire qc a

ASE N ABBR = **American Stock Exchange**

ASH [æʃ] N ABBR (BRIT: = Action on Smoking and Health) iniziativa contro il fumo

ash [æʃ] N (dust) cenere f; **~ (tree)** frassino

ashamed [əˈʃeɪmd] ADJ vergognoso(-a); **to be ~ of** vergognarsi di; **to be ~ (of o.s.) for having done** vergognarsi di aver fatto

ashen [ˈæʃən] ADJ (pale) livido(-a)

ashore [əˈʃɔːʳ] ADV a terra; **to go ~** sbarcare

ashtray [ˈæʃtreɪ] N portacenere m

Ash Wednesday N Mercoledì m inv delle Ceneri

Asia [ˈeɪʃə] N Asia

Asia Minor N Asia minore

Asian [ˈeɪʃən] ADJ, N asiatico(-a)

Asiatic [eɪsɪˈætɪk] ADJ asiatico(-a)

aside [əˈsaɪd] ADV da parte ▶ N a parte m; **to take sb ~** prendere qn da parte; **~ from** (as well as) oltre a; (except for) a parte

ask [ɑːsk] VT (request) chiedere; (question) domandare; (invite) invitare; **to ~ about sth** informarsi su or di qc; **to ~ sb sth/sb to do sth** chiedere qc a qn/a qn di fare qc; **to ~ sb about sth** chiedere a qn di qc; **to ~ (sb) a question** fare una domanda (a qn); **to ~ sb the time** chiedere l'ora a qn; **to ~ sb out to dinner** invitare qn a mangiare fuori; **you should ~ at the information desk** dovreste rivolgervi all'ufficio informazioni

▶ **ask after** VT FUS chiedere di

▶ **ask for** VT FUS chiedere; **it's just asking for trouble** or **for it** è proprio (come) andarsele a cercare

askance [əˈskɑːns] ADV: **to look ~ at sb** guardare qn di traverso

askew [əˈskjuː] ADV di traverso, storto

asking price [ˈɑːskɪŋ-] N prezzo di partenza

asleep [əˈsliːp] ADJ addormentato(-a); **to be ~** dormire; **to fall ~** addormentarsi

ASLEF [ˈæzlɛf] N ABBR (BRIT: = Associated Society of Locomotive Engineers and Firemen) sindacato dei conducenti dei treni e dei macchinisti

AS level N ABBR (= Advanced Subsidiary level) prima parte del diploma di studi superiori chiamato "A level"

asp [æsp] N cobra m inv egiziano

asparagus [əsˈpærəgəs] N asparagi mpl

asparagus tips NPL punte fpl d'asparagi

ASPCA N ABBR (= American Society for the Prevention of Cruelty to Animals) ≈ E.N.P.A. m (= Ente Nazionale per la Protezione degli Animali)

aspect [ˈæspɛkt] N aspetto

aspersions [əsˈpəːʃənz] NPL: **to cast ~ on** diffamare

asphalt [ˈæsfælt] N asfalto

asphyxiate [æsˈfɪksɪeɪt] VT asfissiare

asphyxiation [æsfɪksɪˈeɪʃən] N asfissia

aspiration [æspəˈreɪʃən] N aspirazione f ▪ **aspirations** NPL aspirazioni fpl

aspire [əsˈpaɪər] VI: **to ~ to** aspirare a

aspirin [ˈæsprɪn] N aspirina

aspiring [əsˈpaɪərɪŋ] ADJ aspirante

ass [æs] N asino; (col) scemo(-a); (US col!) culo (!)

assail [əˈseɪl] VT assalire

assailant [əˈseɪlənt] N assalitore(-trice)

assassin [əˈsæsɪn] N assassino

assassinate [əˈsæsɪneɪt] VT assassinare

assassination [əsæsɪˈneɪʃən] N assassinio

assault [əˈsɔːlt] N (Mil) assalto; (gen: attack) aggressione f; (Law): **~ (and battery)** minacce e vie di fatto fpl ▶ VT assaltare; aggredire; (sexually) violentare

assemble [əˈsɛmbl] VT riunire; (Tech) montare ▶ VI riunirsi

assembly [əˈsɛmblɪ] N (meeting) assemblea; (construction) montaggio

assembly language N (Comput) linguaggio assemblativo

assembly line N catena di montaggio

assent [əˈsɛnt] N assenso, consenso ▶ VI assentire; **to ~ (to sth)** approvare (qc)

assert [əˈsəːt] VT asserire; (insist on) far valere; **to ~ o.s.** farsi valere

assertion [əˈsəːʃən] N asserzione f

assertive [əˈsəːtɪv] ADJ che sa imporsi

assess [əˈsɛs] VT valutare

assessment [əˈsɛsmənt] N valutazione f; (judgment): **~ (of)** giudizio (su)

assessor [əˈsɛsər] N perito; funzionario del fisco

asset [ˈæsɛt] N vantaggio; (person) elemento prezioso ▪ **assets** NPL (Comm: of individual) beni mpl, disponibilità fpl; (: of company) attivo

asset-stripping [ˈæsɛtˈstrɪpɪŋ] N (Comm) acquisto di una società in fallimento con lo scopo di rivenderne le attività

assiduous [əˈsɪdjuəs] ADJ assiduo(-a)

assign [əˈsaɪn] VT: **to ~ (to)** (task) assegnare (a); (resources) riservare (a); (cause, meaning) attribuire (a); **to ~ a date to sth** fissare la data di qc

assignment [əˈsaɪnmənt] N compito

assimilate [əˈsɪmɪleɪt] VT assimilare

assimilation [əsɪmɪˈleɪʃən] N assimilazione f

assist [əˈsɪst] VT assistere, aiutare

assistance [əˈsɪstəns] N assistenza, aiuto

assistant [əˈsɪstənt] N assistente mf; (BRIT: also: **shop assistant**) commesso(-a)

assistant manager N vicedirettore(-trice)

assizes [əˈsaɪzɪz] NPL assise fpl

associate ADJ [əˈsəuʃɪt] associato(-a); (member) aggiunto(-a) ▶ N [əˈsəuʃɪt] collega mf; (in business) socio(-a) ▶ VT [əˈsəuʃɪeɪt] associare ▶ VI [əˈsəuʃɪeɪt]: **to ~ with sb** frequentare qn

associated company [əˈsəusɪˈeɪtɪd-] N società collegata

associate director N amministratore(-trice) aggiunto(-a)

association [əsəusɪˈeɪʃən] N associazione f; **in ~ with** in collaborazione con

association football N (BRIT) (gioco del) calcio

assorted [əˈsɔːtɪd] ADJ assortito(-a); **in ~ sizes** in diverse taglie

assortment [əˈsɔːtmənt] N assortimento

Asst. ABBR = **assistant**

assuage [əˈsweɪdʒ] VT alleviare

assume [əˈsjuːm] VT supporre; (responsibilities etc) assumere; (attitude, name) prendere

assumed name N nome m falso

assumption [əˈsʌmpʃən] N supposizione f, ipotesi f inv; (of power) assunzione f; **on the ~ that ...** partendo dal presupposto che ...

assurance [əˈʃuərəns] N assicurazione f; (self-confidence) fiducia in se stesso; **I can give you no assurances** non posso assicurarle or garantirle niente

assure [əˈʃuər] VT assicurare

assured [əˈʃuəd] ADJ (confident) sicuro(-a); (certain: promotion etc) assicurato(-a)

AST ABBR (US: = Atlantic Standard Time) ora invernale di New York

asterisk [ˈæstərɪsk] N asterisco

astern [əˈstəːn] ADV a poppa

asteroid [ˈæstərɔɪd] N asteroide m

asthma [ˈæsmə] N asma

asthmatic [æsˈmætɪk] ADJ, N asmatico(-a)

astigmatism [əˈstɪgmətɪzəm] N astigmatismo

astir [əˈstəːʳ] ADV in piedi; (excited) in fermento

astonish [əˈstɒnɪʃ] VT stupire

astonished ADJ stupito(-a), sorpreso(-a); **to be ~ (at)** essere stupito(-a) (da)

astonishing [əˈstɒnɪʃɪŋ] ADJ sorprendente, stupefacente; **I find it ~ that ...** mi stupisce che ...

astonishingly [əˈstɒnɪʃɪŋlɪ] ADV straordinariamente, incredibilmente

astonishment [əˈstɒnɪʃmənt] N stupore m; **to my ~** con mia gran meraviglia, con mio grande stupore

astound [əˈstaund] VT sbalordire

astray [əˈstreɪ] ADV: **to go ~** smarrirsi; (fig) traviarsi; **to lead ~** portare sulla cattiva strada; **to go ~ in one's calculations** sbagliare i calcoli

astride [əˈstraɪd] ADV a cavalcioni ▶ PREP a cavalcioni di

astringent [əsˈtrɪndʒənt] ADJ, N astringente m

astrologer [əsˈtrɒlədʒəʳ] N astrologo(-a)

astrology [əsˈtrɒlədʒɪ] N astrologia

astronaut [ˈæstrənɔːt] N astronauta mf

astronomer [əsˈtrɒnəməʳ] N astronomo(-a)

astronomical [æstrəˈnɒmɪkl] ADJ astronomico(-a)

astronomy [əsˈtrɒnəmɪ] N astronomia

astrophysics [ˈæstrəuˈfɪzɪks] N astrofisica

astute [əsˈtjuːt] ADJ astuto(-a)

asunder [əˈsʌndəʳ] ADV: **to tear ~** strappare

ASV N ABBR (= American Standard Version) traduzione della Bibbia

asylum [əˈsaɪləm] N asilo; (lunatic asylum) manicomio; **to seek political ~** chiedere asilo politico

asymmetric [eɪsɪˈmɛtrɪk], **asymmetrical** [eɪsɪˈmɛtrɪkəl] ADJ asimmetrico(-a)

---

at [æt]

PREP **1** (referring to position, direction) a; **at the top** in cima; **at the desk** al banco, alla scrivania; **at home/school** a casa/scuola; **at Paolo's** da Paolo; **at the baker's** dal panettiere; **to look at sth** guardare qc; **to throw sth at sb** lanciare qc a qn

2 (referring to time) a; **at 4 o'clock** alle 4; **at night** di notte; **at Christmas** a Natale; **at times** a volte

3 (referring to rates, speed etc) a; **at £1 a kilo** a 1 sterlina al chilo; **two at a time** due alla volta, due per volta; **at 50 km/h** a 50 km/h; **at full speed** a tutta velocità

4 (referring to manner): **at a stroke** d'un solo colpo; **at peace** in pace

5 (referring to activity): **to be at work** essere al lavoro; **to play at cowboys** giocare ai cowboy; **to be good at sth/doing sth** essere bravo in qc/a fare qc

6 (referring to cause): **shocked/surprised/annoyed at sth** colpito da/sorpreso da/arrabbiato per qc; **I went at his suggestion** ci sono andato dietro suo consiglio

▶ N (Comput: @ symbol) chiocciola

ate [eɪt] PT of **eat**

atheism [ˈeɪθɪɪzəm] N ateismo

atheist [ˈeɪθɪɪst] N ateo(-a)

Athenian [əˈθiːnɪən] ADJ, N ateniese mf

Athens [ˈæθɪnz] N Atene f

athlete [ˈæθliːt] N atleta mf

athletic [æθˈlɛtɪk] ADJ atletico(-a)

athletics [æθˈlɛtɪks] N atletica

Atlantic [ətˈlæntɪk] ADJ atlantico(-a) ▶ N: **the ~ (Ocean)** l'Atlantico, l'Oceano Atlantico

atlas [ˈætləs] N atlante m

Atlas Mountains NPL: **the ~** i Monti dell'Atlante

ATM ABBR (= automated telling machine) (sportello) Bancomat® m inv

atmosphere [ˈætməsfɪəʳ] N atmosfera; (air) aria

atmospheric [ætməsˈfɛrɪk] ADJ atmosferico(-a)

atmospherics [ætməsˈfɛrɪks] NPL (Radio) scariche fpl

atoll [ˈætɒl] N atollo

atom [ˈætəm] N atomo

atom bomb, atomic bomb N bomba atomica

atomic [əˈtɒmɪk] ADJ atomico(-a)

atomizer [ˈætəmaɪzəʳ] N atomizzatore m

atone [əˈtəun] VI: **to ~ for** espiare

atonement [əˈtəunmənt] N espiazione f

ATP N ABBR = **Association of Tennis Professionals**

atrocious [əˈtrəuʃəs] ADJ atroce, pessimo(-a)

atrocity [əˈtrɒsɪtɪ] N atrocità f inv

atrophy [ˈætrəfɪ] N atrofia ▶ VI atrofizzarsi

attach [əˈtætʃ] VT attaccare; (document, letter) allegare; (importance etc) attribuire; (Mil: troops) assegnare; **to be attached to sb/sth** (to like) essere affezionato(-a) a qn/qc; **the attached letter** la lettera acclusa or allegata

attaché [əˈtæʃeɪ] N addetto(-a)

attaché case N valigetta per documenti

attachment [əˈtætʃmənt] N (tool) accessorio; (Comput) allegato; (love): **~ (to)** affetto (per)

attack [əˈtæk] VT attaccare; (person) aggredire; (task etc) iniziare; (problem) affrontare ▶ N attacco; (also: **heart attack**) infarto

attacker [əˈtækəʳ] N aggressore m, assalitore(-trice)

attain [əˈteɪn] VT (also: **attain to**) arrivare a, raggiungere

attainments [ə'teɪmənts] NPL cognizioni *fpl*

attempt [ə'tɛmpt] N tentativo ▶ VT tentare; **attempted murder** (*Law*) tentato omicidio; **to make an ~ on sb's life** attentare alla vita di qn; **he made no ~ to help** non ha (neanche) tentato *or* cercato di aiutare

attend [ə'tɛnd] VT frequentare; (*meeting, talk*) andare a; (*patient*) assistere
▶ **attend to** VT FUS (*needs, affairs etc*) prendersi cura di; (*customer*) occuparsi di

attendance [ə'tɛndəns] N (*being present*) presenza; (*people present*) gente *f* presente

attendant [ə'tɛndənt] N custode *mf*; persona di servizio ▶ ADJ concomitante

attention [ə'tɛnʃən] N attenzione *f*; **attentions** premure *fpl*, attenzioni *fpl*; **~!** (*Mil*) attenti!; **at ~** (*Mil*) sull'attenti; **for the ~ of** (*Admin*) per l'attenzione di; **it has come to my ~ that ...** sono venuto a conoscenza (del fatto) che ...

attentive [ə'tɛntɪv] ADJ attento(-a); (*kind*) premuroso(-a)

attentively [ə'tɛntɪvlɪ] ADV attentamente

attenuate [ə'tɛnjueɪt] VT attenuare ▶ VI attenuarsi

attest [ə'tɛst] VI: **to ~ to** attestare

attic ['ætɪk] N soffitta

attire [ə'taɪər] N abbigliamento

attitude ['ætɪtjuːd] N (*behaviour*) atteggiamento; (*posture*) posa; (*view*): **~ (to)** punto di vista (nei confronti di)

attorney [ə'təːnɪ] N (*US: lawyer*) avvocato(-essa); (*having proxy*) mandatario; **power of ~** procura

Attorney General N (*BRIT*) Procuratore(-trice) Generale; (*US*) Ministro della Giustizia

attract [ə'trækt] VT attirare

attraction [ə'trækʃən] N (*gen pl: pleasant things*) attrattiva; (*Physics, fig: towards sth*) attrazione *f*

attractive [ə'træktɪv] ADJ attraente; (*idea, offer, price*) allettante, interessante

attribute N ['ætrɪbjuːt] attributo ▶ VT [ə'trɪbjuːt]: **to ~ sth to** attribuire qc a

attrition [ə'trɪʃən] N: **war of ~** guerra di logoramento

Atty. Gen. ABBR = **Attorney General**

atypical [eɪ'tɪpɪkl] ADJ atipico(-a)

AU N ABBR (= *African Union*) Unione Africana

aubergine ['əubəʒiːn] N melanzana

auburn ['ɔːbən] ADJ tizianesco(-a)

auction ['ɔːkʃən] N (*also*: **sale by auction**) asta ▶ VT (*also*: **sell by auction**) vendere all'asta; (*also*: **put up for auction**) mettere all'asta

auctioneer [ɔːkʃə'nɪər] N banditore(-trice)

auction room N sala dell'asta

audacious [ɔː'deɪʃəs] ADJ (*bold*) audace; (*impudent*) sfrontato(-a)

audacity [ɔː'dæsɪtɪ] N audacia

audible ['ɔːdɪbl] ADJ udibile

audience ['ɔːdɪəns] N (*people*) pubblico; spettatori *mpl*; ascoltatori *mpl*; (*interview*) udienza

audio-typist ['ɔːdɪəu'taɪpɪst] N dattilografo(-a) che trascrive da nastro

audiovisual [ɔːdɪəu'vɪzjuəl] ADJ audiovisivo(-a); **~ aids** sussidi *mpl* audiovisivi

audit ['ɔːdɪt] N revisione *f*, verifica ▶ VT rivedere, verificare

audition [ɔː'dɪʃən] N (*Theat*) audizione *f*; (*Cine*) provino ▶ VI fare un'audizione (*or* un provino)

auditor ['ɔːdɪtər] N revisore *m*

auditorium [ɔːdɪ'tɔːrɪəm] N sala, auditorio

Aug. ABBR (= *August*) ago., ag.

augment [ɔːg'mɛnt] VT, VI aumentare

augur ['ɔːgər] VT (*be a sign of*) predire ▶ VI: **it augurs well** promette bene

August ['ɔːgəst] N agosto; *see also* **July**

august [ɔː'gʌst] ADJ augusto(-a)

aunt [ɑːnt] N zia

auntie, aunty ['ɑːntɪ] N zietta

au pair ['əu'pɛər] N (*also*: **au pair girl**) (ragazza *f*) alla pari *inv*

aura ['ɔːrə] N aura

auspices ['ɔːspɪsɪz] NPL: **under the ~ of** sotto gli auspici di

auspicious [ɔːs'pɪʃəs] ADJ propizio(-a)

austere [ɔs'tɪər] ADJ austero(-a)

austerity [ɔs'tɛrɪtɪ] N austerità *f inv*

Australasia [ɔstrə'leɪzɪə] N Australasia

Australia [ɔs'treɪlɪə] N Australia

Australian [ɔs'treɪlɪən] ADJ, N australiano(-a)

Austria ['ɔstrɪə] N Austria

Austrian ['ɔstrɪən] ADJ, N austriaco(-a)

AUT N ABBR (*BRIT*: = *Association of University Teachers*) associazione dei docenti universitari

authentic [ɔː'θɛntɪk] ADJ autentico(-a)

authenticate [ɔː'θɛntɪkeɪt] VT autenticare

authenticity [ɔːθɛn'tɪsɪtɪ] N autenticità

author ['ɔːθər] N autore(-trice)

authoritarian [ɔːθɔrɪ'tɛərɪən] ADJ autoritario(-a)

authoritative [ɔː'θɔrɪtətɪv] ADJ (*account etc*) autorevole; (*manner*) autoritario(-a)

authority [ɔː'θɔrɪtɪ] N autorità *f inv*; (*permission*) autorizzazione *f* ■ **the authorities** NPL (*government etc*) le autorità; **to have ~ to do sth** avere l'autorizzazione a fare *or* il diritto di fare qc

authorization [ɔːθəraɪ'zeɪʃən] N autorizzazione *f*

authorize ['ɔːθəraɪz] VT autorizzare

authorized capital N capitale *m* nominale

authorship ['ɔːθəʃɪp] N paternità (*letteraria ecc*)

autistic [ɔː'tɪstɪk] ADJ autistico(-a)

auto ['ɔːtəu] N (*US*) auto *f inv*

autobiography [ɔːtəbaɪˈɔgrəfɪ] N autobiografia

autocratic [ɔːtəˈkrætɪk] ADJ autocratico(-a)

Autocue® [ˈɔːtəukjuː] N (BRIT) gobbo (TV)

autograph [ˈɔːtəgrɑːf] N autografo ▶ VT firmare

autoimmune [ɔːtəʊɪˈmjuːn] ADJ autoimmune

automat [ˈɔːtəmæt] N (US) tavola calda fornita esclusivamente di distributori automatici

automated [ˈɔːtəmeɪtɪd] ADJ automatizzato(-a)

automatic [ɔːtəˈmætɪk] ADJ automatico(-a) ▶ N (gun) arma automatica; (car) automobile f con cambio automatico; (washing machine) lavatrice f automatica

automatically [ɔːtəˈmætɪklɪ] ADV automaticamente

automatic data processing N elaborazione f automatica dei dati

automation [ɔːtəˈmeɪʃən] N automazione f

automaton [ɔːˈtɔmətən] (pl **automata** [-tə]) N automa m

automobile [ˈɔːtəməbiːl] N (US) automobile f

autonomous [ɔːˈtɔnəməs] ADJ autonomo(-a)

autonomy [ɔːˈtɔnəmɪ] N autonomia

autopsy [ˈɔːtɔpsɪ] N autopsia

autumn [ˈɔːtəm] N autunno

auxiliary [ɔːgˈzɪlɪərɪ] ADJ ausiliario(-a) ▶ N ausiliare mf

AV N ABBR (= Authorized Version) traduzione inglese della Bibbia ▶ ABBR = **audiovisual**

Av. ABBR = **avenue**

avail [əˈveɪl] VT: **to ~ o.s. of** servirsi di; approfittarsi di ▶ N: **to no ~** inutilmente

availability [əveɪləˈbɪlɪtɪ] N disponibilità

available [əˈveɪləbl] ADJ disponibile; **every ~ means** tutti i mezzi disponibili; **to make sth ~ to sb** mettere qc a disposizione di qn; **is the manager ~?** è libero il direttore?

avalanche [ˈævəlɑːnʃ] N valanga

avant-garde [ˈævɑ̃ˈgɑːd] ADJ d'avanguardia

avarice [ˈævərɪs] N avarizia

avaricious [ævəˈrɪʃəs] ADJ avaro(-a)

avatar [ˈævətɑːr] N (Comput) avatar m inv

avdp. ABBR (= avoirdupois) sistema ponderale anglosassone basato su libbra, oncia e multipli

Ave. ABBR = **avenue**

avenge [əˈvɛndʒ] VT vendicare

avenue [ˈævənjuː] N viale m; (fig) strada, via

average [ˈævərɪdʒ] N media ▶ ADJ medio(-a) ▶ VT (also: **average out at**) aggirarsi in media su, essere in media di; **on ~** in media; **above/below (the) ~** sopra/sotto la media

averse [əˈvɜːs] ADJ: **to be ~ to sth/doing** essere contrario(-a) a qc/a fare; **I wouldn't be ~ to a drink** non avrei nulla in contrario a bere qualcosa

aversion [əˈvɜːʃən] N avversione f

avert [əˈvɜːt] VT evitare, prevenire; (one's eyes) distogliere

avian flu [ˈeɪvɪən-] N influenza aviaria

aviary [ˈeɪvɪərɪ] N voliera, uccelliera

aviation [eɪvɪˈeɪʃən] N aviazione f

avid [ˈævɪd] ADJ avido(-a); (supporter etc) accanito(-a)

avidly [ˈævɪdlɪ] ADV avidamente

avocado [ævəˈkɑːdəʊ] N (BRIT: also: **avocado pear**) avocado m inv

avoid [əˈvɔɪd] VT evitare

avoidable [əˈvɔɪdəbl] ADJ evitabile

avoidance [əˈvɔɪdəns] N l'evitare m

avowed [əˈvaʊd] ADJ dichiarato(-a)

AVP N ABBR (US) = **assistant vice-president**

AWACS [ˈeɪwæks] N ABBR (= airborne warning and control system) sistema di allarme e controllo in volo

await [əˈweɪt] VT aspettare; **awaiting attention** (Comm: letter) in attesa di risposta; (: order) in attesa di essere evaso; **long awaited** tanto atteso(-a)

awake [əˈweɪk] (pt **awoke** [əˈwəʊk], pp **awoken** [əˈwəʊkən] or **awaked**) VT svegliare ▶ VI svegliarsi ▶ ADJ sveglio(-a); **~ to** consapevole di

awakening [əˈweɪknɪŋ] N risveglio

award [əˈwɔːd] N premio; (Law) decreto; (sum) risarcimento ▶ VT assegnare; (Law: damages) decretare

aware [əˈwɛər] ADJ: **~ of** (conscious) conscio(-a) di; (informed) informato(-a) di; **to become ~ of** accorgersi di; **politically/socially ~** politicamente/socialmente preparato; **I am fully ~ that ...** mi rendo perfettamente conto che ...

awareness [əˈwɛənɪs] N consapevolezza; coscienza; **to develop people's ~ (of)** sensibilizzare la gente (a)

awash [əˈwɔʃ] ADJ: **~ (with)** inondato(-a) (da)

away [əˈweɪ] ADJ, ADV via; lontano(-a); **two kilometres ~** a due chilometri di distanza; **two hours ~ by car** a due ore di distanza in macchina; **the holiday was two weeks ~** mancavano due settimane alle vacanze; **~ from** lontano da; **he's ~ for a week** è andato via per una settimana; **he's ~ in Milan** è (andato) a Milano; **to take ~** vt portare via; **he was working/pedalling** ~ lavorava/pedalava più che poteva; **to fade ~** scomparire

away game N (Sport) partita fuori casa

awe [ɔː] N timore m

awe-inspiring [ˈɔːɪnspaɪərɪŋ], **awesome** [ˈɔːsəm] ADJ imponente

awestruck [ˈɔːstrʌk] ADJ sgomento(-a)

awful [ˈɔːfəl] ADJ terribile; **an ~ lot of** (people, cars, dogs) un numero incredibile di; (jam, flowers) una quantità incredibile di

awfully [ˈɔːflɪ] ADV (very) terribilmente

awhile [ə'waɪl] ADV (per) un po'

awkward ['ɔːkwəd] ADJ (clumsy) goffo(-a); (inconvenient) scomodo(-a); (embarrassing) imbarazzante; (difficult) delicato(-a), difficile

awkwardness ['ɔːkwədnɪs] N goffaggine f; scomodità; imbarazzo; delicatezza, difficoltà

awl ['ɔːl] N punteruolo

awning ['ɔːnɪŋ] N (of tent) veranda; (of shop, hotel etc) tenda

awoke [ə'wəuk] PT of awake

awoken [ə'wəukən] PP of awake

AWOL ['eɪwɔl] ABBR (Mil etc) = absent without leave

awry [ə'raɪ] ADV di traverso ▸ ADJ storto(-a); **to go ~** andare a monte

axe, (US) **ax** [æks] N scure f ▸ VT (project etc) abolire; (jobs) sopprimere; **to have an ~ to grind** (fig)

fare i propri interessi or il proprio tornaconto

axiom ['æksɪəm] N assioma m

axiomatic [æksɪəu'mætɪk] ADJ assiomatico(-a)

axis ['æksɪs] (pl **axes** [-siːz]) N asse m

axle ['æksl] N (also: **axle-tree**) asse m

ay, aye [aɪ] EXCL (yes) sì

AYH N ABBR = **American Youth Hostels**

AZ ABBR (US) = **Arizona**

azalea [ə'zeɪlɪə] N azalea

Azerbaijan [æzəbaɪ'dʒɑːn] N Azerbaigian m

Azerbaijani [æzəbaɪ'dʒɑːnɪ], **Azeri** [ə'zɛərɪ] ADJ, N azerbaigiano(-a), azero(-a)

Azores [ə'zɔːz] NPL: **the ~** le Azzorre

AZT N ABBR (= azidothymidine) AZT m

Aztec ['æztɛk] ADJ, N azteco(-a)

azure ['eɪʒə'] ADJ azzurro(-a)

Bb

B, b [biː] N (*letter*) B, b f *inv or* m *inv*; (*Scol*: *mark*) ≈ 8 (*buono*); (*Mus*): **B** si m; **B for Benjamin**, (*US*) **B for Baker** ≈ B come Bologna; **B road** n (BRIT *Aut*) ≈ strada secondaria

BA N ABBR = **British Academy**; (*Scol*) = **Bachelor of Arts**

b. ABBR = **born**

babble ['bæbl] VI cianciare; mormorare ▶ N ciance fpl mormorio

babe [beɪb] N (*col*): **she's a real ~** è uno schianto di ragazza

baboon [bə'buːn] N babbuino

baby ['beɪbɪ] N bambino(-a)

baby carriage N (*US*) carrozzina

baby grand N (*also*: **baby grand piano**) pianoforte m a mezza coda

babyhood ['beɪbɪhud] N prima infanzia

babyish ['beɪbɪɪʃ] ADJ infantile

baby-minder ['beɪbɪ'maɪndəʳ] N (BRIT) bambinaia (*che tiene i bambini mentre la madre lavora*)

baby-sit ['beɪbɪsɪt] VI fare il (*or* la) babysitter

baby-sitter ['beɪbɪsɪtəʳ] N baby-sitter mf

baby wipe N salvietta umidificata

bachelor ['bætʃələʳ] N scapolo; **B~ of Arts/Science (BA/BSc)** ≈ laureato(-a) in lettere/scienze; **B~ of Arts/Science degree (BA/BSc)** n ≈ laurea in lettere/scienze

---

Il **Bachelor's degree** è il titolo accademico conferito a chi ha completato un corso di laurea di tre o quattro anni. I *Bachelor's degree* più comuni sono il BA (*Bachelor of Arts*), il BSc (*Bachelor of Science*), il BEd (*Bachelor of Education*), e il LLB (*Bachelor of Laws*); *vedi anche* **doctorate**, **Master's degree**.

---

bachelorhood ['bætʃələhud] N celibato

bachelor party N (*US*) festa di addio al celibato

back [bæk] N (*of person, horse*) dorso, schiena; (*as opposed to front*) dietro; (*of hand*) dorso; (*of house, car*) didietro; (*of train*) coda; (*of chair*) schienale m; (*of page*) rovescio; (*of book*) retro; (*Football*) difensore m ▶ VT (*financially*) finanziare; (*candidate: also*: **back up**) appoggiare; (*horse: at races*) puntare su;

(*car*) guidare a marcia indietro ▶ VI indietreggiare; (*car etc*) fare marcia indietro ▶ ADJ (*in compounds*) posteriore, di dietro; arretrato(-a) ▶ ADV (*not forward*) indietro; (*returned*): **he's ~** è tornato; **~ to front** all'incontrario; **to break the ~ of a job** (BRIT) fare il grosso *or* il peggio di un lavoro; **to have one's ~ to the wall** (*fig*) essere *or* trovarsi con le spalle al muro; **when will you be ~?** quando torni?; **he ran ~** tornò indietro di corsa; **throw the ball ~** (*restitution*) ritira la palla; **can I have it ~?** posso riaverlo?; **he called ~** (*again*) ha richiamato; **~ seats/wheels** (*Aut*) sedili mpl/ruote fpl posteriori; **to take a ~ seat** (*fig*) restare in secondo piano; **~ payments/rent** arretrati mpl; **~ garden/room** giardino/stanza sul retro (della casa)

▶ **back down** VI (*fig*) fare marcia indietro

▶ **back on to** VT FUS: **the house backs on to the golf course** il retro della casa dà sul campo da golf

▶ **back out** VI (*of promise*) tirarsi indietro

▶ **back up** VT (*support*) appoggiare, sostenere; (*Comput*) fare una copia di riserva di

backache ['bækeɪk] N mal m di schiena

backbencher ['bæk'bentʃəʳ] N (BRIT) parlamentare che non ha incarichi né al governo né all'opposizione

back benches NPL posti in Parlamento occupati dai backbenchers; *vedi nota*

Nella *House of Commons*, una delle Camere del Parlamento britannico, sono chiamati **back benches** gli scanni dove siedono i *backbenchers*, parlamentari che non hanno incarichi né al governo né all'opposizione. Nelle file davanti ad essi siedono i *frontbenchers*; *vedi anche* **front bench**.

---

backbiting ['bækbaɪtɪŋ] N maldicenza

backbone ['bækbəun] N spina dorsale; **the ~ of the organization** l'anima dell'organizzazione

backchat ['bæktʃæt] N (BRIT *col*) impertinenza

backcloth ['bækklɔθ] N (BRIT) scena di sfondo

backcomb ['bækkəum] VT (BRIT) cotonare

backdate [bæk'deɪt] VT (*letter*) retrodatare; **backdated pay rise** aumento retroattivo

back door N porta sul retro

backdrop ['bækdrɔp] N = **backcloth**

backer ['bækəʳ] N sostenitore(-trice); (Comm) fautore(-trice)

backfire ['bæk'faɪəʳ] VI (Aut) dar ritorni di fiamma; (plans) fallire

backgammon ['bækgæmən] N tavola reale

background ['bækgraund] N sfondo; (of events, Comput) background m inv; (basic knowledge) base f; (experience) esperienza ▶ CPD (noise, music) di fondo; ~ **reading** letture fpl sull'argomento; **family** ~ ambiente m familiare

backhand ['bækhænd] N (Tennis: also: **backhand stroke**) rovescio

backhanded [bæk'hændɪd] ADJ (fig) ambiguo(-a)

backhander ['bækhændəʳ] N (BRIT: bribe) bustarella

backing ['bækɪŋ] N (Comm) finanziamento; (Mus) accompagnamento; (fig) appoggio

backlash ['bæklæʃ] N contraccolpo, ripercussione f

backlog ['bæklɔg] N: ~ **of work** lavoro arretrato

back number N (of magazine etc) numero arretrato

backpack ['bækpæk] N zaino

backpacker ['bækpækəʳ] N chi viaggia con zaino e sacco a pelo

back pay N arretrato di paga

backpedal ['bækpɛdl] VI pedalare all'indietro; (fig) far marcia indietro

backseat driver ['bæksi:t-] N passeggero che dà consigli non richiesti al guidatore

backside [bæk'saɪd] N (col) sedere m

backslash ['bækslæʃ] N backslash m inv, barra obliqua inversa

backslide ['bækslaɪd] VI ricadere

backspace ['bækspeɪs] VI (in typing) battere il tasto di ritorno

backstage [bæk'steɪdʒ] ADV nel retroscena

back street N vicolo

back-street ['bækstri:t] ADJ: ~ **abortionist** praticante mf di aborti clandestini

backstroke ['bækstrəuk] N nuoto sul dorso

backtrack ['bæktræk] VI = **backpedal**

backup ['bækʌp] ADJ (train, plane) supplementare; (Comput) di riserva ▶ N (support) appoggio, sostegno; (Comput: also: **backup file**) file m inv di riserva

backward ['bækwəd] ADJ (movement) indietro inv; (person) tardivo(-a); (country) arretrato(-a); ~ **and forward movement** movimento avanti e indietro

backwards ['bækwədz] ADV indietro; (fall, walk) all'indietro; **to know sth** ~ or (US) ~ **and forwards** (col) sapere qc a menadito

backwater ['bækwɔːtəʳ] N (fig) posto morto

back yard N cortile m sul retro

bacon ['beɪkən] N pancetta

bacteria [bæk'tɪərɪə] NPL batteri mpl

bacteriology [bæktɪərɪ'ɔlədʒɪ] N batteriologia

bad [bæd] ADJ cattivo(-a); (child) cattivello(-a); (meat, food) andato(-a) a male; **his** ~ **leg** la sua gamba malata; **to go** ~ (meat, food) andare a male; **to have a** ~ **time of it** passarsela male; **I feel** ~ **about it** (guilty) mi sento un po' in colpa; ~ **debt** credito difficile da recuperare; ~ **faith** malafede f

baddie, baddy ['bædɪ] N (col: Cine etc) cattivo(-a)

bade [bæd] PT of **bid**

badge [bædʒ] N insegna; (of police officer) stemma m; (stick-on) adesivo

badger ['bædʒəʳ] N tasso ▶ VT tormentare

badly ['bædlɪ] ADV (work, dress etc) male; **things are going** ~ le cose vanno male; ~ **wounded** gravemente ferito; **he needs it** ~ ne ha gran bisogno; ~ **off** adj povero(-a)

bad-mannered [bæd'mænəd] ADJ maleducato(-a), sgarbato(-a)

badminton ['bædmɪntən] N badminton m

bad-tempered [bæd'tɛmpəd] ADJ irritabile; (in bad mood) di malumore

baffle ['bæfl] VT (puzzle) confondere

baffling ['bæflɪŋ] ADJ sconcertante

bag [bæg] N sacco; (handbag etc) borsa; (of hunter) carniere m; bottino ▶ VT (col: take) mettersi in tasca; prendersi; **bags of** (col: lots of) un sacco di; **to pack one's bags** fare le valigie; **bags under the eyes** borse sotto gli occhi

bagful ['bægful] N sacco (pieno)

baggage ['bægɪdʒ] N bagagli mpl

baggage allowance N peso bagaglio consentito

baggage car N (US) bagagliaio

baggage claim, baggage reclaim N ritiro m bagaglio inv

baggy ['bægɪ] ADJ largo(-a), sformato(-a)

Baghdad [bæg'dæd] N Bagdad f

bag lady N (col) stracciona, barbona

bagpipes ['bægpaɪps] NPL cornamusa

bag-snatcher ['bægsnætʃəʳ] N (BRIT) scippatore(-trice)

bag-snatching ['bægsnætʃɪŋ] N (BRIT) scippo

Bahamas [bə'hɑːməz] NPL: **the** ~ le Bahamas

Bahrain [bɑː'reɪn] N Bahrein m

bail [beɪl] N cauzione f ▶ VT (prisoner: also: **grant bail to**) concedere la libertà provvisoria su cauzione a; (Naut: also: **bail out**) aggottare; **on** ~ in libertà provvisoria su cauzione; **to be released on** ~ essere rilasciato(-a) su cauzione
▶ **bail out** VT (prisoner) ottenere la libertà provvisoria su cauzione di; (fig) tirare fuori dai guai
▶ VI see **bale out**

bailiff [ˈbeɪlɪf] N usciere(-a); fattore(-trice)

bailout [ˈbeɪlaut] N ricapitalizzazione f; **government bailouts of large corporations** ricapitalizzazioni di grosse società da parte del governo

bait [beɪt] N esca ▶ VT (hook) innescare; (trap) munire di esca; (fig) tormentare

bake [beɪk] VT cuocere al forno ▶ VI cuocersi al forno

baked beans [-biːnz] NPL fagioli mpl in salsa di pomodoro

baked potato N patata (con la buccia) cotta al forno

baker [ˈbeɪkəʳ] N fornaio(-a), panettiere(-a)

bakery [ˈbeɪkərɪ] N panetteria

baking [ˈbeɪkɪŋ] N cottura (al forno)

baking powder N lievito in polvere

baking tin N stampo, tortiera

baking tray N teglia

balaclava [bælaˈklɑːvə] N (also: **balaclava helmet**) passamontagna m inv

balance [ˈbæləns] N equilibrio; (Comm: sum) bilancio; (remainder) resto; (scales) bilancia ▶ VT tenere in equilibrio; (pros and cons) soppesare; (budget) far quadrare; (account) pareggiare; (compensate) contrappesare; **~ of trade/payments** bilancia commerciale/dei pagamenti; **~ brought forward** saldo riportato; **~ carried forward** saldo da riportare; **to ~ the books** fare il bilancio

balanced [ˈbælənst] ADJ (personality, diet) equilibrato(-a)

balance sheet N bilancio

balcony [ˈbælkənɪ] N balcone m; (in theatre) balconata

bald [bɔːld] ADJ calvo(-a); (tyre) liscio(-a)

baldness [ˈbɔːldnɪs] N calvizie f

bale [beɪl] N balla
▶ **bale out** VT (Naut: water) vuotare; (: boat) aggottare ▶ VI (of a plane) gettarsi col paracadute

Balearic Islands NPL: **the ~** le Baleari fpl

baleful [ˈbeɪlful] ADJ funesto(-a)

balk [bɔːlk] VI: **to ~ (at)** tirarsi indietro (davanti a); (horse) recalcitrare (davanti a)

Balkan [ˈbɔːlkən] ADJ balcanico(-a) ▶ N: **the Balkans** i Balcani

ball [bɔːl] N palla; (football) pallone m; (for golf) pallina; (of wool, string) gomitolo; (dance) ballo; **to play ~ (with sb)** giocare a palla (con qn); (fig) stare al gioco (di qn); **to be on the ~** (fig: competent) essere in gamba; (alert) stare all'erta; **to start the ~ rolling** (fig) fare la prima mossa; **the ~ is in your court** (fig) a lei la prossima mossa; see also **balls**

ballad [ˈbæləd] N ballata

ballast [ˈbæləst] N zavorra

ball bearing N cuscinetto a sfere

ball cock N galleggiante m

ballerina [bæləˈriːnə] N ballerina

ballet [ˈbæleɪ] N balletto

ballet dancer N ballerino(-a) classico(-a)

ballistic [bəˈlɪstɪk] ADJ balistico(-a)

ballistics [bəˈlɪstɪks] N balistica

balloon [bəˈluːn] N pallone m; (in comic strip) fumetto ▶ VI gonfiarsi

balloonist [bəˈluːnɪst] N aeronauta mf

ballot [ˈbælət] N scrutinio

ballot box N urna (per le schede)

ballot paper N scheda

ballpark [ˈbɔːlpɑːk] N (US) stadio di baseball

ballpark figure N (col) cifra approssimativa

ball-point pen [ˈbɔːlpɔɪnt-] N penna a sfera

ballroom [ˈbɔːlrum] N sala da ballo

balls [bɔːlz] NPL (col!) coglioni mpl (!)

balm [bɑːm] N balsamo

balmy [ˈbɑːmɪ] ADJ (breeze, air) balsamico(-a); (BRIT col) = **barmy**

BALPA [ˈbælpə] N ABBR (= British Airline Pilots' Association) sindacato dei piloti

balsa [ˈbɔːlsə], **balsa wood** N (legno di) balsa

balsam [ˈbɔːlsəm] N balsamo

Baltic [ˈbɔːltɪk] ADJ, N: **the ~ (Sea)** il (mar) Baltico

balustrade [bæləsˈtreɪd] N balaustrata

bamboo [bæmˈbuː] N bambù m

bamboozle [bæmˈbuːzl] VT (col) infinocchiare

ban [bæn] N interdizione f ▶ VT interdire; **he was banned from driving** (BRIT) gli hanno ritirato la patente

banal [bəˈnɑːl] ADJ banale

banana [bəˈnɑːnə] N banana

band [bænd] N banda; (at a dance) orchestra; (Mil) fanfara
▶ **band together** VI collegarsi

bandage [ˈbændɪdʒ] N benda, fascia

Band-Aid® [ˈbændeɪd] N (US) cerotto

B & B N ABBR = **bed and breakfast**

bandit [ˈbændɪt] N bandito

bandstand [ˈbændstænd] N palco dell'orchestra

bandwagon [ˈbændwægən] N: **to jump on the ~** (fig) seguire la corrente

bandy [ˈbændɪ] VT (jokes, insults) scambiare
▶ **bandy about** VT far circolare

bandy-legged [ˈbændɪˈlegɪd] ADJ dalle gambe storte

bane [beɪn] N: **it (or he etc) is the ~ of my life** è la mia rovina

bang [bæŋ] N botta; (of door) lo sbattere; (blow) colpo ▶ VT battere (violentemente); (door) sbattere ▶ VI scoppiare; sbattere ▶ ADV (BRIT col): **to be ~ on time** spaccare il secondo; **to ~ at the door** picchiare alla porta; **to ~ into sth** sbattere contro qc; see also **bangs**

banger [ˈbæŋəʳ] N (BRIT col: car: also: **old banger**) macinino; (: sausage) salsiccia; (firework) mortaretto

Bangkok [ˈbæŋkɔk] N Bangkok f

Bangladesh [baːŋgləˈdeʃ] N Bangladesh m

bangle [ˈbæŋgl] N braccialetto

bangs [bæŋz] NPL (US: fringe) frangia, frangetta

banish [ˈbænɪʃ] VT bandire

banister [ˈbænɪstəʳ] N, **banisters** [ˈbænɪstəz] NPL ringhiera

banjo [ˈbændʒəu] (pl **banjoes** or **banjos**) N banjo m inv

bank [bæŋk] N (for money) banca, banco; (of river, lake) riva, sponda; (of earth) banco ▶ VI (Aviat) inclinarsi in virata; (Comm): **they ~ with Pitt's** sono clienti di Pitt's
▶ **bank on** VT FUS contare su

bank account N conto in banca

bank balance N saldo; **a healthy ~** un solido conto in banca

bank card N carta f assegni inv

bank charges NPL (BRIT) spese fpl bancarie

bank draft N assegno circolare or bancario

banker [ˈbæŋkəʳ] N banchiere m; **~'s card** (BRIT) carta f assegni inv; **~'s order** (BRIT) ordine m di banca

bank giro N bancogiro

bank holiday N (BRIT) giorno di festa

Una **bank holiday**, in Gran Bretagna, è una giornata in cui le banche e molti negozi sono chiusi. Generalmente le bank holidays cadono di lunedì e molti ne approfittano per fare una breve vacanza fuori città. Di conseguenza, durante questi fine settimana lunghi (bank holiday weekends) si verifica un notevole aumento del traffico sulle strade, negli aeroporti e nelle stazioni e molte località turistiche registrano il tutto esaurito.

banking [ˈbæŋkɪŋ] N attività bancaria; professione f di banchiere

banking hours NPL orario di sportello

bank loan N prestito bancario

bank manager N direttore(-trice) di banca

banknote [ˈbæŋknəut] N banconota

bank rate N tasso bancario

bankrupt [ˈbæŋkrʌpt] ADJ, N fallito(-a); **to go ~** fallire

bankruptcy [ˈbæŋkrʌptsɪ] N fallimento

bank statement N estratto conto

banned substance N sostanza al bando (nello sport)

banner [ˈbænəʳ] N striscione m

bannister [ˈbænɪstə] N, **bannisters** [ˈbænɪstəz] NPL see **banister**

banns [bænz] NPL pubblicazioni fpl di matrimonio

banquet [ˈbæŋkwɪt] N banchetto

bantam-weight [ˈbæntəmweit] N peso gallo

banter [ˈbæntəʳ] N scherzi mpl bonari

baptism [ˈbæptɪzəm] N battesimo

Baptist [ˈbæptɪst] ADJ, N battista (mf)

baptize [bæpˈtaɪz] VT battezzare

bar [baːʳ] N (rod) barra; (of window etc) sbarra; (of chocolate) tavoletta; (fig) ostacolo; restrizione f; (pub) bar m inv; (counter: in pub) banco; (Mus) battuta ▶ VT (road, window) sbarrare; (person) escludere; (activity) interdire; **~ of soap** saponetta; **the B~** (Law) l'Ordine m degli avvocati; **behind bars** (prisoner) dietro le sbarre; **~ none** senza eccezione

Barbados [baːˈbeidɔs] N Barbados fsg

barbaric [baːˈbærɪk], **barbarous** [ˈbaːbərəs] ADJ barbaro(-a), barbarico(-a)

barbecue [ˈbaːbɪkjuː] N barbecue m inv

barbed wire [ˈbaːbd-] N filo spinato

barber [ˈbaːbəʳ] N barbiere m

barber's (shop), (US) **barber shop** N barbiere m

barbiturate [baːˈbɪtjurit] N barbiturico

Barcelona [baːsɪˈləunə] N Barcellona

bar chart N diagramma m di frequenza

bar code N codice m a barre

bare [bɛəʳ] ADJ nudo(-a) ▶ VT scoprire, denudare; (teeth) mostrare; **the ~ essentials, the ~ necessities** lo stretto necessario

bareback [ˈbɛəbæk] ADV senza sella

barefaced [ˈbɛəfeist] ADJ sfacciato(-a)

barefoot [ˈbɛəfut] ADJ, ADV scalzo(-a)

bareheaded [bɛəˈhɛdɪd] ADJ, ADV a capo scoperto

barely [ˈbɛəlɪ] ADV appena

Barents Sea [ˈbærənts-] N: **the ~** il mar di Barents

bargain [ˈbaːgɪn] N (transaction) contratto; (good buy) affare m ▶ VI (haggle) tirare sul prezzo; (trade) contrattare; **into the ~** per giunta
▶ **bargain for** VT FUS: **to ~ for sth** aspettarsi qc; **he got more than he bargained for** gli è andata peggio di quel che si aspettasse

bargaining [ˈbaːgənɪŋ] N contrattazione f

bargaining position N: **to be in a weak/strong ~** non avere/avere potere contrattuale

barge [baːdʒ] N chiatta
▶ **barge in** VI (walk in) piombare dentro; (interrupt talk) intromettersi a sproposito
▶ **barge into** VT FUS urtare contro

baritone [ˈbærɪtəun] N baritono

barium meal [ˈbɛərɪəm-] N (pasto di) bario

bark [baːk] N (of tree) corteccia; (of dog) abbaio
▶ VI abbaiare

barley [ˈbaːlɪ] N orzo

barley sugar N zucchero d'orzo

barmaid ['bɑ:meɪd] N cameriera al banco

barman ['bɑ:mən] N (*irreg*) barista *m*

barmy ['bɑ:mɪ] ADJ (*BRIT col*) tocco(-a)

barn [bɑ:n] N granaio; (*for animals*) stalla

barnacle ['bɑ:nəkl] N cirripede *m*

barn owl N barbagianni *m inv*

barometer [bə'rɔmɪtə'] N barometro

baron ['bærən] N barone *m*; (*fig*) magnate *m*; **the oil barons** i magnati del petrolio; **the press barons** i baroni della stampa

baroness ['bærənɪs] N baronessa

baronet ['bærənɪt] N baronetto

barrack ['bærək] VT (*BRIT*): **to ~ sb** subissare qn di grida e fischi

barracking ['bærəkɪŋ] N (*BRIT*): **to give sb a ~** subissare qn di grida e fischi

barracks ['bærəks] NPL caserma

barrage ['bærɑ:ʒ] N (*Mil, dam*) sbarramento; (*fig*) fiume *m*; **a ~ of questions** una raffica di *or* un fuoco di fila di domande

barrel ['bærəl] N barile *m*; (*of gun*) canna

barrel organ N organetto a cilindro

barren ['bærən] ADJ sterile; (*soil*) arido(-a)

barrette [bə'rɛt] N (*US*) fermaglio per capelli

barricade [bærɪ'keɪd] N barricata ▶ VT barricare

barrier ['bærɪə'] N barriera; (*BRIT: also:* **crash barrier**) guardrail *m inv*

barrier cream N (*BRIT*) crema protettiva

barring ['bɑ:rɪŋ] PREP salvo

barrister ['bærɪstə'] N (*BRIT*) avvocato(-essa)

Il **barrister** è un membro della più prestigiosa delle due branche della professione legale (l'altra è quella dei *solicitors*); la sua funzione è quella di rappresentare i propri clienti in tutte le corti (*magistrates' court, crown court* e *Court of Appeal*), generalmente seguendo le istruzioni preparate dai *solicitors*.

---

barrow ['bærəʊ] N (*cart*) carriola

barstool ['bɑ:stu:l] N sgabello

Bart. ABBR (*BRIT*) = **baronet**

bartender ['bɑ:tɛndə'] N (*US*) barista *m*

barter ['bɑ:tə'] N baratto ▶ VT: **to ~ sth for** barattare qc con

base [beɪs] N base *f* ▶ ADJ vile ▶ VT: **to ~ sth on** basare qc su; **to ~ at** (*troops*) mettere di stanza a; **coffee-based** a base di caffè; **a Paris-based firm** una ditta con sede centrale a Parigi; **I'm based in London** sono di base *or* ho base a Londra

baseball ['beɪsbɔ:l] N baseball *m*

baseball cap N berretto da baseball

baseboard ['beɪsbɔ:d] N (*US*) zoccolo, battiscopa *m inv*

base camp N campo *m* base *inv*

Basel [bɑ:l] N = **Basle**

baseline ['beɪslaɪn] N (*Tennis*) linea di fondo

basement ['beɪsmənt] N seminterrato; (*of shop*) piano interrato

base rate N tasso di base

bases ['beɪsi:z] NPL *of* **basis**

bash [bæʃ] VT (*col*) picchiare ▶ N: **I'll have a ~ (at it)** (*BRIT col*) ci proverò; **bashed in** *adj* sfondato(-a)
▶ **bash up** VT (*col: car*) sfasciare; (: *BRIT: person*) riempire di *or* prendere a botte

bashful ['bæʃful] ADJ timido(-a)

BASIC ['beɪsɪk] N (*Comput*) BASIC *m*

basic ['beɪsɪk] ADJ (*principles, precautions, rules*) elementare; (*salary*) base *inv* (*after n*)

basically ['beɪsɪklɪ] ADV fondamentalmente, sostanzialmente

basic rate N (*of tax*) aliquota minima

basics NPL: **the ~** l'essenziale *m*

basil ['bæzl] N basilico

basin ['beɪsn] N (*vessel, also Geo*) bacino; (*also:* **washbasin**) lavabo; (*BRIT: for food*) terrina

basis ['beɪsɪs] (*pl* **bases** [-si:z]) N base *f*; **on a part-time ~** part-time; **on a trial ~** in prova; **on the ~ of what you've said** in base alle sue asserzioni

bask [bɑ:sk] VI: **to ~ in the sun** crogiolarsi al sole

basket ['bɑ:skɪt] N cesta; (*smaller*) cestino; (*with handle*) paniere *m*

basketball ['bɑ:skɪtbɔ:l] N pallacanestro *f*

basketball player N cestista *mf*

Basle [bɑ:l] N Basilea

basmati rice [bəz'mætɪ-] N riso basmati

Basque [bæsk] ADJ, N basco(-a)

bass [beɪs] N (*Mus*) basso

bass clef N chiave *f* di basso

bassoon [bə'su:n] N fagotto

bastard ['bɑ:stəd] N bastardo(-a); (!) stronzo (!)

baste [beɪst] VT (*Culin*) ungere con grasso; (*Sewing*) imbastire

bastion ['bæstɪən] N bastione *m*; (*fig*) baluardo

bat [bæt] N pipistrello; (*for baseball etc*) mazza; (*BRIT: for table tennis*) racchetta; **off one's own ~** di propria iniziativa ▶ VT: **he didn't ~ an eyelid** non battè ciglio

batch [bætʃ] N (*of bread*) infornata; (*of papers*) cumulo; (*of applicants, letters*) gruppo; (*of work*) sezione *f*; (*of goods*) partita, lotto

batch processing N (*Comput*) elaborazione *f* a blocchi

bated ['beɪtɪd] ADJ: **with ~ breath** col fiato sospeso

bath [bɑ:θ] (*pl* **baths** [bɑ:ðz]) N bagno; (*bathtub*) vasca da bagno ▶ VT far fare il bagno a; **to have a ~** fare un bagno; *see also* **baths**

bathchair ['bɑ:θtʃɛə'] N (*BRIT*) poltrona a rotelle

bathe [beɪð] vɪ fare il bagno ▶ vᴛ bagnare; (*wound etc*) lavare

bather [ˈbeɪðəʳ] ɴ bagnante *mf*

bathing [ˈbeɪðɪŋ] ɴ bagni *mpl*

bathing cap ɴ cuffia da bagno

bathing costume, (US) **bathing suit** ɴ costume *m* da bagno

bathmat [ˈbɑːθmæt] ɴ tappetino da bagno

bathrobe [ˈbɑːθrəub] ɴ accappatoio

bathroom [ˈbɑːθrum] ɴ stanza da bagno

baths [bɑːðz] ɴᴘʟ bagni *mpl* pubblici

bath towel ɴ asciugamano da bagno

bathtub [ˈbɑːθtʌb] ɴ (vasca da) bagno

batman [ˈbætmən] ɴ (*irreg*) (Bʀɪᴛ *Mil*) attendente *m*

baton [ˈbætən] ɴ bastone *m*; (*Mus*) bacchetta; (*Athletics*) testimone *m*; (*club*) manganello

battalion [bəˈtælɪən] ɴ battaglione *m*

batten [ˈbætən] ɴ (*Carpentry*) assicella, correntino; (*for flooring*) tavola per pavimenti; (*Naut*) serretta; (: *on sail*) stecca
▶ **batten down** vᴛ (*Naut*): **to ~ down the hatches** chiudere i boccaporti

batter [ˈbætəʳ] vᴛ battere ▶ ɴ pastetta

battered [ˈbætəd] ᴀᴅᴊ (*hat*) sformato(-a); (*pan*) ammaccato(-a); **~ wife/baby** consorte *f*/bambino(-a) maltrattato(-a)

battering ram [ˈbætərɪŋ-] ɴ ariete *m*

battery [ˈbætərɪ] ɴ batteria; (*of torch*) pila

battery charger ɴ caricabatterie *m inv*

battery farming ɴ *allevamento in batteria*

battle [ˈbætl] ɴ battaglia ▶ vɪ battagliare, lottare; **to fight a losing ~** (*fig*) battersi per una causa persa; **that's half the ~** (*col*) è già una mezza vittoria

battle dress ɴ uniforme *f* da combattimento

battlefield [ˈbætlfiːld] ɴ campo di battaglia

battlements [ˈbætlmənts] ɴᴘʟ bastioni *mpl*

battleship [ˈbætlʃɪp] ɴ nave *f* da guerra

batty [ˈbætɪ] ᴀᴅᴊ (*col: person*) svitato(-a), strambo(-a); (: *behaviour, idea*) strampalato(-a)

bauble [ˈbɔːbl] ɴ ninnolo

baud [bɔːd] ɴ (*Comput*) baud *m inv*

baulk [bɔːlk] vɪ = **balk**

bauxite [ˈbɔːksaɪt] ɴ bauxite *f*

Bavaria [bəˈveərɪə] ɴ Bavaria

Bavarian [bəˈveərɪən] ᴀᴅᴊ, ɴ bavarese (*mf*)

bawdy [ˈbɔːdɪ] ᴀᴅᴊ piccante

bawl [bɔːl] vɪ urlare

bay [beɪ] ɴ (*of sea*) baia; (Bʀɪᴛ: *for parking*) piazzola di sosta; (: *for loading*) piazzale *m* di (sosta e) carico; **to hold sb at ~** tenere qn a bada

bay leaf ɴ foglia d'alloro

bayonet [ˈbeɪənɪt] ɴ baionetta

bay tree ɴ alloro

bay window ɴ bovindo

bazaar [bəˈzɑːʳ] ɴ bazar *m inv*; vendita di beneficenza

bazooka [bəˈzuːkə] ɴ bazooka *m inv*

BB ɴ ᴀʙʙʀ (Bʀɪᴛ: = *Boys' Brigade*) organizzazione giovanile a fine educativo

BBB ɴ ᴀʙʙʀ (US: = *Better Business Bureau*) organismo per la difesa dei consumatori

BBC ɴ ᴀʙʙʀ (= *British Broadcasting Corporation*) *vedi nota*

La **BBC** è l'azienda statale che fornisce il servizio radiofonico e televisivo in Gran Bretagna. Pur dovendo rispondere al Parlamento del proprio operato, la BBC non è soggetta al controllo dello stato per scelte e programmi, che non contengono inserti pubblicitari perché si autofinanzia con il ricavato dei canoni d'abbonamento. La BBC ha canali televisivi digitali e terrestri, oltre a diverse emittenti radiofoniche nazionali e locali. Fornisce un servizio di informazione internazionale, il BBC World Service, trasmesso in tutto il mondo in inglese e 40 altre lingue.

BC ᴀᴅᴠ ᴀʙʙʀ (= *before Christ*) a.C. ▶ ᴀʙʙʀ (Cᴀɴᴀᴅᴀ) = **British Columbia**

BCG ɴ ᴀʙʙʀ (= *Bacillus Calmette-Guérin*) vaccino antitubercolare

BD ɴ ᴀʙʙʀ (= *Bachelor of Divinity*) titolo di studio

B/D ᴀʙʙʀ = **bank draft**

BDS ɴ ᴀʙʙʀ (= *Bachelor of Dental Surgery*) titolo di studio

---

be [biː]

(*pt* **was, were**, *pp* **been**) ᴀᴜx ᴠʙ **1** (*with present participle: forming continuous tenses*): **what are you doing?** che fai?, che stai facendo?; **they're coming tomorrow** vengono domani; **I've been waiting for her for hours** sono ore che l'aspetto

2 (*with pp: forming passives*) essere; **to be killed** essere *or* venire ucciso(-a); **the box had been opened** la scatola era stata aperta; **the thief was nowhere to be seen** il ladro non si trovava da nessuna parte

3 (*in tag questions*): **it was fun, wasn't it?** è stato divertente, no?; **he's good-looking, isn't he?** è un bell'uomo, vero?; **she's back, is she?** così è tornata, eh?

4 (*+ to + infinitive*): **the house is to be sold** abbiamo (*or* hanno *etc*) intenzione di vendere casa; **you're to be congratulated for all your work** dovremo farvi i complimenti per tutto il vostro lavoro; **am I to understand that …?** devo dedurre che …?; **he's not to open it** non deve aprirlo; **he was to have come yesterday** sarebbe dovuto venire ieri

▶ ᴠʙ + ᴄᴏᴍᴘʟᴇᴍᴇɴᴛ **1** (*gen*) essere; **I'm English** sono inglese; **I'm tired** sono stanco(-a); **I'm hot/cold** ho caldo/freddo; **he's a doctor** è medico; **2 and 2 are 4** 2 più 2 fa 4; **be careful!** sta attento(-a)!; **be good** sii buono(-a); **if I were you ...** se fossi in te ...

2 (of health) stare; **how are you?** come sta?; **he's very ill** sta molto male

3 (of age): **how old are you?** quanti anni hai?; **I'm sixteen (years old)** ho sedici anni

4 (cost) costare; **how much was the meal?** quant'era or quanto costava il pranzo?; **that'll be £5, please** (sono) 5 sterline, per favore

▶ vi **1** (exist, occur etc) essere, esistere; **the best singer that ever was** il migliore cantante mai esistito or di tutti i tempi; **be that as it may** comunque sia, sia come sia; **so be it** sia pure, e sia

2 (referring to place) essere, trovarsi; **I won't be here tomorrow** non ci sarò domani; **Edinburgh is in Scotland** Edimburgo si trova in Scozia

3 (referring to movement): **where have you been?** dove sei stato?; **I've been to China** sono stato in Cina

▶ IMPERS VB **1** (referring to time, distance) essere; **it's 5 o'clock** sono le 5; **it's the 28th of April** è il 28 aprile; **it's 10 km to the village** di qui al paese sono 10 km

2 (referring to the weather) fare; **it's too hot/cold** fa troppo caldo/freddo; **it's windy** c'è vento

3 (emphatic): **it's me** sono io; **it's only me** sono solo io; **it was Maria who paid the bill** è stata Maria che ha pagato il conto

B/E ABBR = **bill of exchange**

beach [biːtʃ] N spiaggia ▶ VT tirare in secco

beach buggy N dune buggy f inv

beachcomber [ˈbiːtʃkəʊməʳ] N vagabondo (che s'aggira sulla spiaggia)

beachwear [ˈbiːtʃwɛəʳ] N articoli mpl da spiaggia

beacon [ˈbiːkən] N (lighthouse) faro; (marker) segnale m; (also: **radio beacon**) radiofaro

bead [biːd] N perlina; (of dew, sweat) goccia ▪ **beads** NPL (necklace) collana

beady [ˈbiːdɪ] ADJ: **~ eyes** occhi mpl piccoli e penetranti

beagle [ˈbiːgl] N cane m da lepre

beak [biːk] N becco

beaker [ˈbiːkəʳ] N coppa

beam [biːm] N trave f; (of light) raggio; (Radio) fascio (d'onde) ▶ VI brillare; (smile): **to ~ at sb** rivolgere un radioso sorriso a qn; **to drive on full** or **main ~** or (US) **high ~** guidare con gli abbaglianti accesi

beaming [ˈbiːmɪŋ] ADJ (sun, smile) raggiante

bean [biːn] N fagiolo; (coffee bean) chicco; **runner ~** fagiolino

beanpole [ˈbiːnpəʊl] N (col) spilungone(-a)

beansprouts [ˈbiːnsprauts] NPL germogli mpl di soia

bear [bɛəʳ] (pt **bore** [bɔːʳ], pp **borne** [bɔːn]) N orso; (Stock Exchange) ribassista mf ▶ VT (gen) portare; (produce) generare; (: fruit) produrre, dare; (: traces, signs) mostrare; (Comm: interest) fruttare; (endure) sopportare ▶ VI: **to ~ right/left** piegare a destra/sinistra; **to ~ the responsibility of** assumersi la responsabilità di; **to ~ comparison with** reggere al paragone con; **I can't ~ him** non lo posso soffrire or sopportare; **to bring pressure to ~ on sb** fare pressione su qn

▶ **bear out** VT (theory, suspicion) confermare, convalidare

▶ **bear up** VI farsi coraggio; **he bore up well under the strain** ha sopportato bene lo stress

▶ **bear with** VT FUS (sb's moods, temper) sopportare (con pazienza); **~ with me a minute** solo un attimo, prego

bearable [ˈbɛərəbl] ADJ sopportabile

beard [bɪəd] N barba

bearded [ˈbɪədɪd] ADJ barbuto(-a)

bearer [ˈbɛərəʳ] N portatore(-trice); (of passport) titolare mf

bearing [ˈbɛərɪŋ] N portamento; (connection) rapporto ▪ **bearings** NPL (also: **ball bearings**) cuscinetti mpl a sfere; **to take a ~** fare un rilevamento; **to find one's bearings** orientarsi

beast [biːst] N bestia

beastly [ˈbiːstlɪ] ADJ meschino(-a); (weather) da cani

beat [biːt] (pt **~**, pp **beaten** [biːtn]) N colpo; (of heart) battito; (Mus) tempo; battuta; (of police officer) giro ▶ VT battere; (eggs, cream) sbattere; **off the beaten track** fuori mano; **to ~ about the bush** menare il cane per l'aia; **to ~ time** battere il tempo; **that beats everything!** (col) questo è il colmo!; **~ it!** (col) fila!, fuori dai piedi!

▶ **beat down** VT (door) abbattere, buttare giù; (price) far abbassare; (seller) far scendere ▶ VI (rain) scrosciare; (sun) picchiare

▶ **beat off** VT respingere

▶ **beat up** VT (col: person) picchiare; (eggs) sbattere

beater [ˈbiːtəʳ] N (for eggs, cream) frullino

beating [ˈbiːtɪŋ] N botte fpl; (defeat) batosta; **to take a ~** prendere una (bella) batosta

beat-up [biːtˈʌp] ADJ (col) scassato(-a)

beautician [bjuːˈtɪʃən] N estetista mf

beautiful [ˈbjuːtɪful] ADJ bello(-a)

beautifully ADV splendidamente

beautify [ˈbjuːtɪfaɪ] VT abbellire

beauty [ˈbjuːtɪ] N bellezza; (concept) bello; **the ~ of it is that ...** il bello è che ...

beauty contest N concorso di bellezza

beauty parlour [-ˈpɑːləʳ], (US) **beauty parlor** N salone m di bellezza

beauty queen N miss f inv, reginetta di bellezza

beauty salon N istituto di bellezza

beauty sleep N: **to get one's ~** farsi un sonno ristoratore

beauty spot N neo; (BRIT Tourism) luogo pittoresco

beaver ['biːvəʳ] N castoro

becalmed [bɪ'kɑːmd] ADJ in bonaccia

became [bɪ'keɪm] PT of **become**

because [bɪ'kɔz] CONJ perché; **~ of** prep a causa di

beck [bɛk] N: **to be at sb's ~ and call** essere a completa disposizione di qn

beckon ['bɛkən] VT (also: **beckon to**) chiamare con un cenno

become [bɪ'kʌm] VT (irreg: like **come**) diventare; **to ~ fat/thin** ingrassarsi/dimagrire; **to ~ angry** arrabbiarsi; **it became known that...** si è venuto a sapere che ...; **what has ~ of him?** che gli è successo?

becoming [bɪ'kʌmɪŋ] ADJ (behaviour) che si conviene; (clothes) grazioso(-a)

BECTU ['bɛktuː] N ABBR (BRIT) = **Broadcasting Entertainment Cinematographic and Theatre Union**

BEd N ABBR (= Bachelor of Education) laurea con abilitazione all'insegnamento

bed [bɛd] N letto; (of flowers) aiuola; (of coal, clay) strato; (of sea, lake) fondo; **to go to ~** andare a letto
▶ **bed down** VI sistemarsi (per dormire)

bed and breakfast N (terms) camera con colazione; (place) ≈ pensione f familiare

bedbug ['bɛdbʌg] N cimice f

bedclothes ['bɛdkləuðz] NPL coperte e lenzuola fpl

bedcover ['bɛdkʌvəʳ] N copriletto

bedding ['bɛdɪŋ] N coperte e lenzuola fpl

bedevil [bɪ'dɛvl] VT (person) tormentare; (plans) ostacolare continuamente

bedfellow ['bɛdfɛləu] N: **they are strange bedfellows** (fig) fanno una coppia ben strana

bedlam ['bɛdləm] N baraonda

bed linen N biancheria da letto

bedpan ['bɛdpæn] N padella

bedpost ['bɛdpəust] N colonnina del letto

bedraggled [bɪ'drægld] ADJ sbrindellato(-a); (wet) fradicio(-a)

bedridden ['bɛdrɪdən] ADJ costretto(-a) a letto

bedrock ['bɛdrɔk] N (Geo) basamento; (fig) fatti mpl di base

bedroom ['bɛdrum] N camera da letto

bed settee N divano m letto inv

bedside ['bɛdsaɪd] N: **at sb's ~** al capezzale di qn

bedside lamp N lampada da comodino

bedside table N comodino

bedsit ['bɛdsɪt], **bedsitter** ['bɛdsɪtəʳ] N (BRIT) monolocale m

bedspread ['bɛdsprɛd] N copriletto

bedtime ['bɛdtaɪm] N: **it's ~** è ora di andare a letto

bee [biː] N ape f; **to have a ~ in one's bonnet (about sth)** avere la fissazione (di qc)

beech [biːtʃ] N faggio

beef [biːf] N manzo; **roast ~** arrosto di manzo
▶ **beef up** VT (col) rinforzare

beefburger ['biːfbəːgəʳ] N hamburger m inv

Beefeater ['biːfiːtəʳ] N guardia della Torre di Londra

beehive ['biːhaɪv] N alveare m

bee-keeping ['biːkiːpɪŋ] N apicoltura

beeline ['biːlaɪn] N: **to make a ~ for** buttarsi a capo fitto verso

been [biːn] PP of **be**

beep [biːp] N (of horn) colpo di clacson; (of phone etc) segnale m (acustico), bip m inv ▶ VI suonare

beeper ['biːpəʳ] N (of doctor etc) cercapersone m inv

beer [bɪəʳ] N birra

beer belly N (col) stomaco da bevitore

beer can N lattina di birra

beer garden N (BRIT) giardino (di pub)

beet [biːt] N (US: also: **red beet**) barbabietola rossa

beetle ['biːtl] N scarafaggio; coleottero

beetroot ['biːtruːt] N (BRIT) barbabietola

befall [bɪ'fɔːl] VI, VT (irreg: like **fall**) accadere (a)

befit [bɪ'fɪt] VT addirsi a

before [bɪ'fɔːʳ] PREP (in time) prima di; (in space) davanti a ▶ CONJ prima che + sub; prima di ▶ ADV prima; **~ going** prima di andare; **~ she goes** prima che vada; **the week ~** la settimana prima; **I've seen it ~** l'ho già visto; **I've never seen it ~** è la prima volta che lo vedo

beforehand [bɪ'fɔːhænd] ADV in anticipo

befriend [bɪ'frɛnd] VT assistere; mostrarsi amico a

befuddled [bɪ'fʌdld] ADJ confuso(-a)

beg [bɛg] VI chiedere l'elemosina ▶ VT (also: **beg for**) chiedere in elemosina; (: favour) chiedere; (: entreat) pregare; **I ~ your pardon** (apologising) mi scusi; (not hearing) scusi?; **this begs the question of ...** questo presuppone che sia già risolto il problema di ...; **to ~ sb to do** pregare qn di fare

began [bɪ'gæn] PT of **begin**

beggar ['bɛgəʳ] N (also: **beggarman, beggarwoman**) mendicante mf

begin [bɪ'gɪn] (pt **began** [bɪ'gæn], pp **begun** [bɪ'gʌn]) VT, VI cominciare; **to ~ doing** or **to do sth** incominciare or iniziare a fare qc; **I can't ~ to thank you** non so proprio come ringraziarla; **to ~ with, I'd like to know ...** tanto per cominciare vorrei sapere ...; **beginning from Monday** a partire da lunedì

beginner [bɪ'gɪnəʳ] N principiante mf

beginning [bɪ'gɪnɪŋ] N inizio, principio; **right from the ~** fin dall'inizio

begrudge [bɪ'grʌdʒ] VT: **to ~ sb sth** dare qc a qn a malincuore; invidiare qn per qc

beguile [bɪ'gaɪl] VT (*enchant*) incantare

beguiling [bɪ'gaɪlɪŋ] ADJ (*charming*) allettante; (*deluding*) ingannevole

begun [bɪ'gʌn] PP *of* **begin**

behalf [bɪ'hɑːf] N: **on ~ of**, (US) **in ~ of** per conto di; a nome di

behave [bɪ'heɪv] VI comportarsi; (*well: also:* **behave o.s.**) comportarsi bene

behaviour, (US) **behavior** [bɪ'heɪvjəʳ] N comportamento, condotta

behead [bɪ'hɛd] VT decapitare

beheld [bɪ'hɛld] PT, PP *of* **behold**

behind [bɪ'haɪnd] PREP dietro; (*followed by pronoun*) dietro di; (*time*) in ritardo con ▶ ADV dietro; in ritardo; (*leave, stay*) indietro ▶ N didietro; **we're ~ them in technology** siamo più indietro *or* più arretrati di loro nella tecnica; **~ the scenes** dietro le quinte; **to be ~ (schedule) with sth** essere indietro con qc; (*payments*) essere in arretrato con qc; **to leave sth ~** dimenticare di prendere qc

behold [bɪ'həuld] VT (*irreg: like* hold) vedere, scorgere

beige [beɪʒ] ADJ beige *inv*

Beijing [beɪ'dʒɪŋ] N Pechino f

being ['biːɪŋ] N essere m; **to come into ~** cominciare ad esistere

Beirut [beɪ'ruːt] N Beirut f

Belarus ['bɛlærus] N Bielorussia

Belarussian [bɛlə'rʌʃən] ADJ bielorusso(-a) ▶ N bielorusso(-a); (*Ling*) bielorusso

belated [bɪ'leɪtɪd] ADJ tardo(-a)

belch [bɛltʃ] VI ruttare ▶ VT (*gen: also:* **belch out:** *smoke etc*) eruttare

beleaguered [bɪ'liːgəd] ADJ (*city*) assediato(-a); (*army*) accerchiato(-a); (*fig*) assillato(-a)

Belfast ['bɛlfɑːst] N Belfast f

belfry ['bɛlfrɪ] N campanile m

Belgian ['bɛldʒən] ADJ, N belga mf

Belgium ['bɛldʒəm] N Belgio m

Belgrade [bɛl'greɪd] N Belgrado f

belie [bɪ'laɪ] VT smentire; (*give false impression of*) nascondere

belief [bɪ'liːf] N (*opinion*) opinione f, convinzione f; (*trust, faith*) fede f; (*acceptance as true*) credenza; **in the ~ that** nella convinzione che; **it's beyond ~** è incredibile

believe [bɪ'liːv] VT, VI credere; **to ~ in** (*God*) credere in; (*ghosts*) credere a; (*method*) avere fiducia in; **I don't ~ in corporal punishment** sono contrario alle punizioni corporali; **he is believed to be abroad** si pensa (che) sia all'estero

believer [bɪ'liːvəʳ] N (*Rel*) credente mf; (*in idea: activity*): **to be a ~ in** credere in

belittle [bɪ'lɪtl] VT sminuire

Belize [bɛ'liːz] N Belize m

bell [bɛl] N campana; (*small, on door, electric*) campanello; **that rings a ~** (*fig*) mi ricorda qualcosa

bell-bottoms ['bɛlbɔtəmz] NPL calzoni mpl a zampa d'elefante

bellboy ['bɛlbɔɪ], (US) **bellhop** ['bɛlhɔp] N ragazzo d'albergo, fattorino d'albergo

belligerent [bɪ'lɪdʒərənt] ADJ (*at war*) belligerante; (*fig*) bellicoso(-a)

bellow ['bɛləu] VI muggire; (*cry*) urlare (a squarciagola) ▶ VT (*orders*) urlare (a squarciagola)

bellows ['bɛləuz] NPL soffietto

bell pepper N (*esp US*) peperone m

bell push N (*BRIT*) pulsante m del campanello

belly ['bɛlɪ] N pancia

bellyache ['bɛlɪeɪk] N mal m di pancia ▶ VI (*col*) mugugnare

bellybutton ['bɛlɪbʌtn] N ombelico

bellyful ['bɛlɪful] N (*col*): **to have had a ~ of** (*fig*) averne piene le tasche (di)

belong [bɪ'lɔŋ] VI: **to ~ to** appartenere a; (*club etc*) essere socio di; **this book belongs here** questo libro va qui

belongings [bɪ'lɔŋɪŋz] NPL cose fpl, roba; **personal ~** effetti mpl personali

Belorussia [bɛləu'rʌʃə] N Bielorussia

Belorussian [bɛləu'rʌʃən] ADJ, N = **Belarussian**

beloved [bɪ'lʌvɪd] ADJ adorato(-a)

below [bɪ'ləu] PREP sotto, al di sotto di ▶ ADV sotto, di sotto; giù; **see ~** vedi sotto *or* oltre; **temperatures ~ normal** temperature al di sotto del normale

belt [bɛlt] N cintura; (*Tech*) cinghia ▶ VT (*thrash*) picchiare ▶ VI (*BRIT col*) filarsela; **industrial ~** zona industriale
▶ **belt out** VT (*song*) cantare a squarciagola
▶ **belt up** VI (*BRIT col*) chiudere la boccaccia

beltway ['bɛltweɪ] N (*US Aut: ring road*) circonvallazione f; (: *motorway*) autostrada

bemoan [bɪ'məun] VT lamentare

bemused [bɪ'mjuːzd] ADJ perplesso(-a), stupito(-a)

bench [bɛntʃ] N panca; (*in workshop, Pol*) banco; **the B~** (*Law*) la Corte

benchmark ['bɛntʃmɑːk] N banco di prova ▶ VT confrontare con

bend [bɛnd] (*pt, pp* **bent** [bɛnt]) VT curvare; (*leg, arm*) piegare ▶ VI curvarsi; piegarsi ▶ N (*in road*) curva; (*in pipe, river*) gomito
▶ **bend down** VI chinarsi
▶ **bend over** VI piegarsi

bends [bɛndz] NPL (*Med*) embolia

beneath [bɪ'niːθ] PREP sotto, al di sotto di; (*unworthy of*) indegno(-a) di ▶ ADV sotto, di sotto

benefactor [ˈbɛnɪfæktəʳ] N benefattore(-trice)

benefactress [ˈbɛnɪfæktrɪs] N benefattrice f

beneficial [bɛnɪˈfɪʃəl] ADJ che fa bene; vantaggioso(-a); **~ to** che giova a

beneficiary [bɛnɪˈfɪʃərɪ] N (Law) beneficiario(-a)

benefit [ˈbɛnɪfɪt] N beneficio, vantaggio; (allowance of money) indennità f inv ▶ VT far bene a ▶ VI: **he'll ~ from it** ne trarrà beneficio or profitto

benefit performance N spettacolo di beneficenza

Benelux [ˈbɛnɪlʌks] N Benelux m

benevolent [bɪˈnɛvələnt] ADJ benevolo(-a)

BEng N ABBR (= Bachelor of Engineering) laurea in ingegneria

benign [bɪˈnaɪn] ADJ (person, smile) benevolo(-a); (Med) benigno(-a)

Benin [bɛˈniːn] N Benin m

bent [bɛnt] PT, PP of **bend** ▶ N inclinazione f ▶ ADJ (wire, pipe) piegato(-a), storto(-a); (col: dishonest) losco(-a); **to be ~ on** essere deciso(-a) a

bequeath [bɪˈkwiːð] VT lasciare in eredità

bequest [bɪˈkwɛst] N lascito

bereaved [bɪˈriːvd] ADJ in lutto ▶ NPL: **the ~** i familiari in lutto

bereavement [bɪˈriːvmənt] N lutto

beret [ˈbɛreɪ] N berretto

Bering Sea [ˈbɛrɪŋ-] N: **the ~** il mar di Bering

berk [bəːk] N (BRIT pej) coglione(-a) (!)

Berlin [bəːˈlɪn] N Berlino f; **East/West ~** Berlino est/ovest

berm [bəːm] N (US Aut) corsia d'emergenza

Bermuda [bəːˈmjuːdə] N le Bermude

Bermuda shorts NPL bermuda mpl

Bern [bəːn] N Berna f

berry [ˈbɛrɪ] N bacca

berserk [bəˈsəːk] ADJ: **to go ~** montare su tutte le furie

berth [bəːθ] N (bed) cuccetta; (for ship) ormeggio ▶ VI (in harbour) entrare in porto; (at anchor) gettare l'ancora; **to give sb a wide ~** (fig) tenersi alla larga da qn

beseech [bɪˈsiːtʃ] (pt, pp besought [bɪˈsɔːt]) VT implorare

beset [bɪˈsɛt] (pt, pp ~) VT assalire ▶ ADJ: **a policy ~ with dangers** una politica irta or piena di pericoli

besetting [bɪˈsɛtɪŋ] ADJ: **his ~ sin** il suo più grande difetto

beside [bɪˈsaɪd] PREP accanto a; (compared with) rispetto a, in confronto a; **to be ~ o.s. (with anger)** essere fuori di sé; **that's ~ the point** non c'entra

besides [bɪˈsaɪdz] ADV inoltre, per di più ▶ PREP oltre a; (except) a parte

besiege [bɪˈsiːdʒ] VT (town) assediare; (fig) tempestare

besotted [bɪˈsɔtɪd] ADJ (BRIT): **~ with** infatuato(-a) di

besought [bɪˈsɔːt] PT, PP of **beseech**

bespectacled [bɪˈspɛktɪkld] ADJ occhialuto(-a)

bespoke [bɪˈspəuk] ADJ (BRIT: garment) su misura; **~ tailor** sarto

best [bɛst] ADJ migliore ▶ ADV meglio; **the ~ thing to do is ...** la cosa migliore da fare or farsi è ...; **the ~ part of** (quantity) la maggior parte di; **at ~** tutt'al più; **to make the ~ of sth** cavare il meglio possibile da qc; **to do one's ~** fare il proprio meglio; **to the ~ of my knowledge** per quel che ne so; **to the ~ of my ability** al massimo delle mie capacità; **he's not exactly patient at the ~ of times** non è mai molto paziente

best-before date N (Comm): **"~: ..."** da consumarsi preferibilmente entro il ...

best man N (irreg) testimone m dello sposo

bestow [bɪˈstəu] VT: **to ~ sth on sb** conferire qc a qn

bestseller [ˈbɛstˈsɛləʳ] N bestseller m inv

bet [bɛt] (pt, pp ~ or betted [ˈbɛtɪd]) N scommessa ▶ VT, VI scommettere; **to ~ sb sth** scommettere qc con qn; **it's a safe ~** (fig) è molto probabile

Bethlehem [ˈbɛθlɪhɛm] N Betlemme f

betray [bɪˈtreɪ] VT tradire

betrayal [bɪˈtreɪəl] N tradimento

better [ˈbɛtəʳ] ADJ migliore ▶ ADV meglio ▶ VT migliorare ▶ N: **to get the ~ of** avere la meglio su; **you had ~ do it** è meglio che lo faccia; **he thought ~ of it** cambiò idea; **to get ~** migliorare; **a change for the ~** un cambiamento in meglio; **that's ~!** così va meglio!; **I had ~ go** dovrei andare; **~ off** adj più ricco(-a); (fig) **you'd be ~ off this way** starebbe meglio così

betting [ˈbɛtɪŋ] N scommesse fpl

betting shop N (BRIT) ufficio dell'allibratore

between [bɪˈtwiːn] PREP tra ▶ ADV in mezzo, nel mezzo; **the road ~ here and London** la strada da qui a Londra; **we only had £5 ~ us** fra tutti e due avevamo solo 5 sterline

bevel [ˈbɛvl] N (also: **bevel(led) edge**) profilo smussato

beverage [ˈbɛvərɪdʒ] N bevanda

bevy [ˈbɛvɪ] N: **a ~ of** una banda di

bewail [bɪˈweɪl] VT lamentare

beware [bɪˈwɛəʳ] VT, VI: **to ~ (of)** stare attento(-a) (a); **"~ of the dog"** "attenti al cane"

bewildered [bɪˈwɪldəd] ADJ sconcertato(-a), confuso(-a)

bewildering [bɪˈwɪldərɪŋ] ADJ sconcertante, sbalorditivo(-a)

bewitching [bɪˈwɪtʃɪŋ] ADJ affascinante

beyond [bɪˈjɔnd] PREP (in space) oltre; (exceeding) al di sopra di ▶ ADV di là; **~ doubt** senza dubbio; **~ repair** irreparabile

b/f ABBR = **brought forward**

BFPO N ABBR (= *British Forces Post Office*) *recapito delle truppe britanniche all'estero*

bhp N ABBR (*Aut*: = *brake horsepower*) c.v. (= *cavallo vapore*)

Bhutan [buː'tɑːn] N Bhutan *m*

bi... [baɪ] PREFIX bi...

biannual [baɪ'ænjʊəl] ADJ semestrale

bias ['baɪəs] N (*prejudice*) pregiudizio; (*preference*) preferenza

biased, biassed ['baɪəst] ADJ parziale; **to be bias(s)ed against** essere prevenuto(-a) contro

biathlon [baɪ'æθlən] N biathlon *m*

bib [bɪb] N bavaglino

Bible ['baɪbl] N Bibbia

bibliography [bɪblɪ'ɔgrəfɪ] N bibliografia

bicarbonate of soda [baɪ'kɑːbənɪt-] N bicarbonato (di sodio)

bicentenary [baɪsɛn'tiːnərɪ], **bicentennial** [baɪsɛn'tɛnɪəl] N bicentenario

biceps ['baɪsɛps] N bicipite *m*

bicker ['bɪkə'] VI bisticciare

bicycle ['baɪsɪkl] N bicicletta

bicycle path, bicycle track N sentiero ciclabile

bicycle pump N pompa della bicicletta

bid [bɪd] N offerta; (*attempt*) tentativo ▶ VI (*pt, pp* ~) fare un'offerta ▶ VT (*pt* **bade** [bæd], *pp* **bidden** ['bɪdn]) fare un'offerta di; **to ~ sb good day** dire buon giorno a qn

bidder ['bɪdə'] N: **the highest ~** il maggior offerente

bidding ['bɪdɪŋ] N offerte *fpl*

bide [baɪd] VT: **to ~ one's time** aspettare il momento giusto

bidet ['biːdeɪ] N bidè *m inv*

bidirectional ['baɪdɪ'rɛkʃənl] ADJ bidirezionale

biennial [baɪ'ɛnɪəl] ADJ biennale ▶ N (*pianta*) biennale *f*

bier [bɪə'] N bara

bifocals [baɪ'fəuklz] NPL occhiali *mpl* bifocali

big [bɪg] ADJ grande; grosso(-a); **my ~ brother** mio fratello maggiore; **to do things in a ~ way** fare le cose in grande

bigamy ['bɪgəmɪ] N bigamia

Big Apple N vedi nota

Tutti sanno che **the Big Apple**, la Grande Mela, è New York, ma sicuramente i soprannomi di altre città americane non sono così conosciuti. Chicago è soprannominata the *Windy City* perché è ventosa, New Orleans si chiama the *Big Easy* per il modo di vivere tranquillo e rilassato dei suoi abitanti e l'industria automobilistica ha fatto sì che Detroit fosse soprannominata *Motown*.

big dipper [-'dɪpə'] N montagne *fpl* russe, otto *m inv* volante

big end N (*Aut*) testa di biella

biggish ['bɪgɪʃ] ADJ *see* **big**; piuttosto grande, piuttosto grosso(-a); **a ~ rent** un affitto piuttosto alto

bigheaded ['bɪg'hɛdɪd] ADJ presuntuoso(-a)

big-hearted ['bɪg'hɑːtɪd] ADJ generoso(-a)

bigot ['bɪgət] N persona gretta

bigoted ['bɪgətɪd] ADJ gretto(-a)

bigotry ['bɪgətrɪ] N grettezza

big toe N alluce *m*

big top N tendone *m* del circo

big wheel N (*at fair*) ruota (panoramica)

bigwig ['bɪgwɪg] N (*col*) pezzo grosso

bike [baɪk] N bici *f inv*

bike lane N pista ciclabile

bikini [bɪ'kiːnɪ] N bikini *m inv*

bilateral [baɪ'lætərl] ADJ bilaterale

bile [baɪl] N bile *f*

bilingual [baɪ'lɪŋgwəl] ADJ bilingue

bilious ['bɪlɪəs] ADJ biliare; (*fig*) bilioso(-a)

bill [bɪl] N (*in hotel, restaurant*) conto; (*Comm*) fattura; (*for gas, electricity*) bolletta, conto; (*Pol*) atto; (*US: banknote*) banconota; (*notice*) avviso; (*of bird*) becco; (*of show*) locandina; (*Theat*): **on the ~** in cartellone ▶ VT mandare il conto a; **may I have the ~ please?** posso avere il conto per piacere?; **"stick** or **post no bills"** "divieto di affissione"; **to fit** or **fill the ~** (*fig*) fare al caso; **~ of exchange** cambiale *f*, tratta; **~ of lading** polizza di carico; **~ of sale** atto di vendita

billboard ['bɪlbɔːd] N tabellone *m*

billet ['bɪlɪt] N alloggio ▶ VT (*troops etc*) alloggiare

billfold ['bɪlfəuld] N (*US*) portafoglio

billiards ['bɪljədz] N biliardo

billion ['bɪljən] N (*BRIT*) bilione *m*; (*US*) miliardo

billow ['bɪləu] N (*of smoke*) nuvola; (*of sail*) rigonfiamento ▶ VI (*smoke*) alzarsi in volute; (*sail*) gonfiarsi

bills payable NPL effetti *mpl* passivi

bills receivable NPL effetti *mpl* attivi

billy goat ['bɪlɪgəut] N caprone *m*, becco

bimbo ['bɪmbəu] N (*pej*) pollastrella, svampitella

bin [bɪn] N (*for coal, rubbish*) bidone *m*; (*for bread*) cassetta; (*BRIT*) pattumiera; (: *also*: **litter bin**) cestino

binary ['baɪnərɪ] ADJ binario(-a)

bind [baɪnd] (*pt, pp* **bound** [baund]) VT legare; (*oblige*) obbligare ▶ N (*col*) scocciatura
▶ **bind over** VT (*Law*) dare la condizionale a
▶ **bind up** VT (*wound*) fasciare, bendare; **to be bound up in** (*work, research etc*) essere completamente assorbito da; **to be bound up with** (*person*) dedicarsi completamente a

binder ['baɪndə'] N (*file*) classificatore *m*

binding ['baɪndɪŋ] N (*of book*) legatura ▶ ADJ (*contract*) vincolante

binge [bɪndʒ] N (col): **to go on a ~** fare baldoria

binge drinker N persona che di norma beve troppo

bingo ['bɪŋgəu] N gioco simile alla tombola

bin liner N sacchetto per l'immondizia

binoculars [bɪ'nɔkjuləz] NPL binocolo

bio ... [baɪə ...] PREFIX bio

biochemistry [baɪəu'kɛmɪstrɪ] N biochimica

biodegradable ['baɪəudɪ'greɪdəbl] ADJ biodegradabile

biodiesel ['baɪəudi:zl] N biodiesel m

biodiversity ['baɪəudaɪ'və:sɪtɪ] N biodiversità f inv

biofuel ['baɪəufjuəl] N biocarburante m

biographer [baɪ'ɔgrəfər] N biografo(-a)

biographic [baɪə'græfɪk], **biographical** [baɪə'græfɪkl] ADJ biografico(-a)

biography [baɪ'ɔgrəfɪ] N biografia

biological [baɪə'lɔdʒɪkl] ADJ biologico(-a)

biological clock N orologio biologico

biologist [baɪ'ɔlədʒɪst] N biologo(-a)

biology [baɪ'ɔlədʒɪ] N biologia

biometric [baɪəu'mɛtrɪk] ADJ biometrico(-a)

biophysics [baɪəu'fɪzɪks] N biofisica

biopic ['baɪəupɪk] N film m inv biografia inv

biopsy ['baɪɔpsɪ] N biopsia

biosecurity [baɪəusɪ'kjuərɪtɪ] N biosicurezza f

biosphere ['baɪəusfɪər] N biosfera

biotechnology [baɪəutɛk'nɔlədʒɪ] N biotecnologia

bioterrorism [baɪəu'tɛrərɪzəm] N bioterrorismo

bipolar [baɪ'pəulər] ADJ bipolare

birch [bə:tʃ] N betulla

bird [bə:d] N uccello; (BRIT pej: girl) bambola

bird flu N influenza aviaria

bird of prey N (uccello) rapace m

bird's-eye view ['bə:dzaɪ-] N veduta a volo d'uccello

bird watcher N ornitologo(-a) dilettante

birdwatching N birdwatching m

Biro® ['baɪrəu] N biro® f inv

birth [bə:θ] N nascita; **to give ~ to** dare alla luce, partorire; (fig) dare inizio a

birth certificate N certificato di nascita

birth control N controllo delle nascite; contraccezione f

birthday ['bə:θdeɪ] N compleanno ▶ CPD di compleanno

birthmark ['bə:θmɑːk] N voglia

birthplace ['bə:θpleɪs] N luogo di nascita

birth rate N indice m di natalità

Biscay ['bɪskeɪ] N: **the Bay of ~** il golfo di Biscaglia

biscuit ['bɪskɪt] N (BRIT) biscotto; (US) panino al latte

bisect [baɪ'sɛkt] VT tagliare in due (parti); (Math) bisecare

bisexual ['baɪ'sɛksjuəl] ADJ, N bisessuale (mf)

bishop ['bɪʃəp] N vescovo; (Chess) alfiere m

bistro ['bi:strəu] N bistrò m inv

bit [bɪt] PT of **bite** ▶ N pezzo; (of tool) punta; (of horse) morso; (Comput) bit m inv; (US: coin) ottavo di dollaro; **a ~ of** un po' di; **a ~ mad/dangerous** un po' matto/pericoloso; **~ by ~** a poco a poco; **to do one's ~** fare la propria parte; **to come to bits** (break) andare a pezzi; **bring all your bits and pieces** porta tutte le tue cose

bitch [bɪtʃ] N (dog) cagna; (!) puttana (!)

bitcoin ['bɪtkɔɪn] N (Comput) bitcoin m inv

bite [baɪt] (pt **bit** [bɪt], pp **bitten** ['bɪtn]) VT, VI mordere; (insect) pungere ▶ N morso; (insect bite) puntura; (mouthful) boccone m; **let's have a ~ to eat** mangiamo un boccone; **to ~ one's nails** mangiarsi le unghie

biting ['baɪtɪŋ] ADJ pungente

bit part N (Theat) particina

bitten ['bɪtn] PP of **bite**

bitter ['bɪtər] ADJ amaro(-a); (wind, criticism) pungente; (icy: weather) gelido(-a) ▶ N (BRIT: beer) birra amara; **to the ~ end** a oltranza

bitterly ['bɪtəlɪ] ADV (disappoint, complain, weep) amaramente; (oppose, criticise) aspramente; (jealous) profondamente; **it's ~ cold** fa un freddo gelido

bitterness ['bɪtənɪs] N amarezza; gusto amaro

bittersweet ['bɪtəswi:t] ADJ agrodolce

bitty ['bɪtɪ] ADJ (BRIT col) frammentario(-a)

bitumen ['bɪtjumɪn] N bitume m

bivouac ['bɪvuæk] N bivacco

bizarre [bɪ'zɑːr] ADJ bizzarro(-a)

BL N ABBR = **Bachelor of Law(s)**; (= Bachelor of Letters) titolo di studio; (US: = Bachelor of Literature) titolo di studio

B/L ABBR = **bill of lading**

blab [blæb] VI parlare troppo ▶ VT (also: **blab out**) spifferare

black [blæk] ADJ nero(-a) ▶ N nero ▶ VT (BRIT Industry) boicottare; **~ coffee** caffè m inv nero; **to give sb a ~ eye** fare un occhio nero a qn; **in the ~** (in credit) in attivo; **there it is in ~ and white** (fig) eccolo nero su bianco; **~ and blue** adj tutto(-a) pesto(-a)
▶ **black out** VI (faint) svenire

black belt N (Sport) cintura nera

blackberry ['blækbərɪ] N mora

blackbird ['blækbə:d] N merlo

blackboard ['blækbɔ:d] N lavagna

black box N (Aviat) scatola nera

Black Country N (BRIT): **the ~** zona carbonifera del centro dell'Inghilterra

blackcurrant [blæk'kʌrənt] N ribes m inv

black economy N (BRIT) economia sommersa

blacken ['blækn] VT annerire

Black Forest N: **the ~** la Foresta Nera

blackhead ['blækhɛd] N punto nero, comedone m

black hole N (Astron) buco nero

black ice N strato trasparente di ghiaccio

blackjack ['blækdʒæk] N (Cards) ventuno; (US: truncheon) manganello

blackleg ['blæklɛg] N (BRIT) crumiro

blacklist ['blæklɪst] N lista nera ▶ VT mettere sulla lista nera

blackmail ['blækmeɪl] N ricatto ▶ VT ricattare

blackmailer ['blækmeɪlə^r] N ricattatore(-trice)

black market N mercato nero

blackout ['blækaut] N oscuramento; (fainting) svenimento; (TV) interruzione f delle trasmissioni

black pepper N pepe m nero

black pudding N sanguinaccio

Black Sea N: **the ~** il mar Nero

black sheep N pecora nera

blacksmith ['blæksmɪθ] N fabbro ferraio

black spot N (Aut) luogo famigerato per gli incidenti

bladder ['blædə^r] N vescica

blade [bleɪd] N lama; (of oar) pala; **~ of grass** filo d'erba

blame [bleɪm] N colpa ▶ VT: **to ~ sb/sth for sth** dare la colpa di qc a qn/qc; **who's to ~?** chi è colpevole?; **I'm not to ~** non è colpa mia

blameless ['bleɪmlɪs] ADJ irreprensibile

blanch [blɑːntʃ] VI (person) sbiancare in viso ▶ VT (Culin) scottare

bland [blænd] ADJ mite; (taste) blando(-a)

blank [blæŋk] ADJ bianco(-a); (look) distratto(-a) ▶ N spazio vuoto; (cartridge) cartuccia a salve; **to draw a ~** (fig) non aver nessun risultato

blank cheque, (US) **blank check** N assegno in bianco; **to give sb a ~ to do** (fig) dare carta bianca a qn per fare

blanket ['blæŋkɪt] N coperta ▶ ADJ (statement, agreement) globale

blanket cover N: **to give ~** (insurance policy) coprire tutti i rischi

blare [blɛə^r] VI strombettare; (radio) suonare a tutto volume

blasé ['blɑːzeɪ] ADJ blasé inv

blasphemous ['blæsfɪməs] ADJ blasfemo(-a)

blasphemy ['blæsfɪmɪ] N bestemmia

blast [blɑːst] N (of wind) raffica; (of air, steam) getto; (bomb blast) esplosione f ▶ VT far saltare ▶ EXCL (BRIT col) mannaggia!; **(at) full ~** a tutta forza
▶ **blast off** VI (Space) essere lanciato(-a)

blast-off ['blɑːstɔf] N (Space) lancio

blatant ['bleɪtənt] ADJ flagrante

blatantly ['bleɪtəntlɪ] ADV: **it's ~ obvious** è lampante

blaze [bleɪz] N (fire) incendio; (glow: of fire, sun etc) bagliore m; (fig) vampata; splendore m ▶ VI (fire) ardere, fiammeggiare; (fig) infiammarsi; (guns) sparare senza sosta; (fig: eyes) ardere ▶ VT: **to ~ a trail** (fig) tracciare una via nuova; **in a ~ of publicity** circondato da grande pubblicità

blazer ['bleɪzə^r] N blazer m inv

bleach [bliːtʃ] N (also: **household bleach**) varechina ▶ VT (material) candeggiare

bleached ['bliːtʃt] ADJ (hair) decolorato(-a)

bleachers ['bliːtʃəz] NPL (US Sport) posti mpl di gradinata

bleak [bliːk] ADJ (prospect, future) tetro(-a); (landscape) desolato(-a); (weather) gelido(-a) e cupo(-a); (smile) pallido(-a)

bleary-eyed ['blɪərɪˈaɪd] ADJ dagli occhi offuscati

bleat [bliːt] VI belare

bled [blɛd] PT, PP of **bleed**

bleed [bliːd] (pt, pp **bled** [blɛd]) VT dissanguare; (brakes, radiator) spurgare ▶ VI sanguinare; **my nose is bleeding** mi viene fuori sangue dal naso

bleep [bliːp] N breve segnale m acustico, bip m inv ▶ VI suonare ▶ VT (doctor) chiamare con il cercapersone

bleeper ['bliːpə^r] N (of doctor etc) cercapersone m inv

blemish ['blɛmɪʃ] N macchia

blend [blɛnd] N miscela ▶ VT mescolare ▶ VI (colours etc: also: **blend in**) armonizzare

blender ['blɛndə^r] N (Culin) frullatore m

bless [blɛs] (pt, pp **blessed** or **blest** [blɛst]) VT benedire; **~ you!** (sneezing) salute!; **to be blessed with** godere di

blessed ['blɛsɪd] ADJ (Rel: holy) benedetto(-a); (happy) beato(-a); **every ~ day** tutti i santi giorni

blessing ['blɛsɪŋ] N benedizione f; fortuna; **to count one's blessings** ringraziare Iddio, ritenersi fortunato; **it was a ~ in disguise** in fondo è stato un bene

blest [blɛst] PT, PP of **bless**

blew [bluː] PT of **blow**

blight [blaɪt] N (of plants) golpe f ▶ VT (hopes etc) deludere; (life) rovinare

blimey ['blaɪmɪ] EXCL (BRIT col) accidenti!

blind [blaɪnd] ADJ cieco(-a) ▶ N (for window) avvolgibile m; (Venetian blind) veneziana ▶ VT accecare; **~ people** i ciechi; **to turn a ~ eye (on** or **to)** chiudere un occhio (su)

blind alley N vicolo cieco

blind corner N (BRIT) svolta cieca

blind date N appuntamento combinato (tra due persone che non si conoscono)

449

blinders ['blaɪndəz] NPL (US) = **blinkers**

blindfold ['blaɪndfəʊld] N benda ▶ ADJ, ADV bendato(-a) ▶ VT bendare gli occhi a

blinding ['blaɪndɪŋ] ADJ (flash, light) accecante; (pain) atroce

blindly ['blaɪndlɪ] ADV ciecamente

blindness ['blaɪndnɪs] N cecità

blind spot N (Aut etc) punto cieco; (fig) punto debole

bling [blɪŋ] N gioielli vistosi

blink [blɪŋk] VI battere gli occhi; (light) lampeggiare ▶ N: **to be on the ~** (col) essere scassato(-a)

blinkers ['blɪŋkəz] NPL (BRIT) paraocchi mpl

blinking ['blɪŋkɪŋ] ADJ (BRIT col): **this ~ ...** questo(-a) maledetto(-a) ...

blip [blɪp] N (on radar etc) segnale m intermittente; (on graph) piccola variazione f; (fig) momentanea battuta d'arresto

bliss [blɪs] N estasi f

blissful ['blɪsfəl] ADJ (event, day) stupendo(-a), meraviglioso(-a); (smile) beato(-a); **in ~ ignorance** nella (più) beata ignoranza

blissfully ['blɪsfəlɪ] ADV (sigh, smile) beatamente; **~ happy** magnificamente felice

blister ['blɪstər] N (on skin) vescica; (on paintwork) bolla ▶ VI (paint) coprirsi di bolle

BLit, BLitt N ABBR (= Bachelor of Literature) titolo di studio

blithe [blaɪð] ADJ gioioso(-a), allegro(-a)

blithely ['blaɪðlɪ] ADV allegramente

blithering ['blɪðərɪŋ] ADJ (col): **this ~ idiot** questa razza d'idiota

blitz [blɪts] N blitz m; **to have a ~ on sth** (fig) prendere d'assalto qc

blizzard ['blɪzəd] N bufera di neve

bloated ['bləʊtɪd] ADJ gonfio(-a)

blob [blɔb] N (drop) goccia; (stain, spot) macchia

bloc [blɔk] N (Pol) blocco

block [blɔk] N (gen, Comput) blocco; (in pipes) ingombro; (toy) cubo; (of buildings) isolato ▶ VT (gen, Comput) bloccare; **the sink is blocked** il lavandino è otturato; **~ of flats** caseggiato; **3 blocks from here** a 3 isolati di distanza da qui; **mental ~** blocco mentale
▶ **block up** VT bloccare; (pipe) ingorgare, intasare

blockade [blɔ'keɪd] N blocco ▶ VT assediare

blockage ['blɔkɪdʒ] N ostacolo

block and tackle N (Tech) paranco

block booking N prenotazione f in blocco

blockbuster ['blɔkbʌstər] N grande successo

block capitals NPL stampatello

blockhead ['blɔkhɛd] N testa di legno

block letters NPL stampatello

block release N (BRIT) periodo pagato concesso al tirocinante per effettuare studi superiori

block vote N (BRIT) voto per delega

blog [blɔg] N blog m inv ▶ VI scrivere blog, bloggare

blogger [blɔgər] N (Comput) blogger mf

blogging ['blɔgɪŋ] N blogging m ▶ ADJ: **~ website** sito di blogging

blogosphere ['blɔgəsfɪər] N blogosfera

blogpost ['blɔgpəʊst] N post m inv su un blog

bloke [bləʊk] N (BRIT col) tizio

blond, blonde [blɔnd] N (man) biondo; (woman) bionda ▶ ADJ biondo(-a)

blood [blʌd] N sangue m; **new ~** (fig) nuova linfa

blood bank N banca del sangue

blood count N conteggio di globuli rossi e bianchi

bloodcurdling ['blʌdkə:dlɪŋ] ADJ raccapricciante, da far gelare il sangue

blood donor N donatore(-trice) di sangue

blood group N gruppo sanguigno

bloodhound ['blʌdhaund] N segugio

bloodless ['blʌdlɪs] ADJ (pale) smorto(-a), esangue; (coup) senza spargimento di sangue

bloodletting ['blʌdlɛtɪŋ] N (Med) salasso; (fig) spargimento di sangue

blood poisoning N setticemia

blood pressure N pressione f sanguigna; **to have high/low ~** avere la pressione alta/bassa

bloodshed ['blʌdʃɛd] N spargimento di sangue

bloodshot ['blʌdʃɔt] ADJ: **~ eyes** occhi iniettati di sangue

bloodstained ['blʌdsteɪnd] ADJ macchiato(-a) di sangue

bloodstream ['blʌdstri:m] N flusso del sangue

blood test N analisi f inv del sangue

bloodthirsty ['blʌdθə:stɪ] ADJ assetato(-a) di sangue

blood transfusion N trasfusione f di sangue

blood type N gruppo sanguigno

blood vessel N vaso sanguigno

bloody ['blʌdɪ] ADJ (fight) sanguinoso(-a); (nose) sanguinante; (BRIT col!): **this ~ ...** questo maledetto ...; **~ awful/good** (col!) veramente terribile/buono; **a ~ awful day** (col!) una giornata di merda (!)

bloody-minded ['blʌdɪ'maɪndɪd] ADJ (BRIT col) indisponente

bloom [blu:m] N fiore m ▶ VI essere in fiore

blooming ['blu:mɪŋ] ADJ (col): **this ~ ...** questo(-a) dannato(-a) ...

blossom ['blɔsəm] N fiore m; (with pl sense) fiori mpl ▶ VI essere in fiore; **to ~ into** (fig) diventare

blot [blɔt] N macchia ▶ VT macchiare; **to be a ~ on the landscape** rovinare il paesaggio; **to ~ one's copy book** (fig) farla grossa
▶ **blot out** VT (memories) cancellare; (view) nascondere; (nation, city) annientare

blotchy [ˈblɒtʃɪ] ADJ (*complexion*) coperto(-a) di macchie

blotter [ˈblɒtəʳ] N tampone *m* (di carta assorbente)

blotting paper [ˈblɒtɪŋ-] N carta assorbente

blotto [ˈblɒtəu] ADJ (*col*) sbronzo(-a)

blouse [blauz] N camicetta

blow [bləu] (*pt* **blew**, *pp* **blown** [bləun]) N colpo ▶ VI soffiare ▶ VT (*fuse*) far saltare; (*wind*) spingere; (*instrument*) suonare; **to come to blows** venire alle mani; **to ~ one's nose** soffiarsi il naso; **to ~ a whistle** fischiare
▶ **blow away** VI volare via ▶ VT portare via
▶ **blow down** VT abbattere
▶ **blow off** VT far volare via; **to ~ off course** far uscire di rotta
▶ **blow out** VI scoppiare
▶ **blow over** VI calmarsi
▶ **blow up** VI saltare in aria ▶ VT far saltare in aria; (*tyre*) gonfiare; (*Phot*) ingrandire

blow-dry [ˈbləudraɪ] N (*hairstyle*) messa in piega a föhn ▶ VT asciugare con il föhn

blowlamp [ˈbləulæmp] N (BRIT) lampada a benzina per saldare

blown [bləun] PP *of* **blow**

blowout [ˈbləuaut] N (*of tyre*) scoppio; (*col: big meal*) abbuffata

blowtorch [ˈbləutɔːtʃ] N lampada a benzina per saldare

blowzy [ˈblauzɪ] ADJ trasandato(-a)

BLS N ABBR (*US*) = **Bureau of Labor Statistics**

blubber [ˈblʌbəʳ] N grasso di balena ▶ VI (*pej*) piangere forte

bludgeon [ˈblʌdʒən] VT prendere a randellate

blue [bluː] ADJ azzurro(-a), celeste; (*darker*) blu *inv*; (*depressed*) giù *inv*; **~ film/joke** film/barzelletta pornografico(a); **(only) once in a ~ moon** a ogni morte di papa; **out of the ~** (*fig*) all'improvviso; *see also* **blues**

blue baby N neonato cianotico

bluebell [ˈbluːbɛl] N giacinto di bosco

blueberry [ˈbluːbərɪ] N mirtillo

bluebottle [ˈbluːbɒtl] N moscone *m*

blue cheese N formaggio tipo gorgonzola

blue-chip [ˈbluːtʃɪp] ADJ: **~ investment** investimento sicuro

blue-collar worker [ˈbluːkɒləʳ-] N operaio(-a)

blue jeans NPL blue-jeans *mpl*

blueprint [ˈbluːprɪnt] N cianografia; (*fig*): **~ (for)** formula (di)

blues [bluːz] NPL: **the ~** (*Mus*) il blues; **to have the ~** (*col: feeling*) essere a terra

bluetit [ˈbluːtɪt] N cinciarella

bluff [blʌf] VI bluffare ▶ N bluff *m inv*; (*promontory*) promontorio scosceso ▶ ADJ (*person*) brusco(-a); **to call sb's ~** mettere alla prova il bluff di qn

blunder [ˈblʌndəʳ] N abbaglio ▶ VI prendere un abbaglio; **to ~ into sb/sth** andare a sbattere contro qn/qc

blunt [blʌnt] ADJ (*edge*) smussato(-a); (*point*) spuntato(-a); (*knife*) che non taglia; (*person*) brusco(-a) ▶ VT smussare; spuntare; **this pencil is ~** questa matita non ha più la punta; **~ instrument** (*Law*) corpo contundente

bluntly [ˈblʌntlɪ] ADV (*speak*) senza mezzi termini

bluntness [ˈblʌntnɪs] N (*of person*) brutale franchezza

blur [bləːʳ] N forma indistinta ▶ VT offuscare

blurb [bləːb] N trafiletto pubblicitario

blurred [bləːd] ADJ (*photo*) mosso(-a); (*TV*) sfuocato(-a)

blurt out [bləːt-] VT lasciarsi sfuggire

blush [blʌʃ] VI arrossire ▶ N rossore *m*

blusher [ˈblʌʃəʳ] N fard *m inv*

bluster [ˈblʌstəʳ] N spaccconate *fpl*; (*threats*) vuote minacce *fpl* ▶ VI fare lo spaccone; minacciare a vuoto

blustering [ˈblʌstərɪŋ] ADJ (*tone etc*) da spaccone

blustery [ˈblʌstərɪ] ADJ (*weather*) burrascoso(-a)

Blvd ABBR = **boulevard**

BM N ABBR = **British Museum**; (*Scol*: = *Bachelor of Medicine*) titolo di studio

BMA N ABBR = **British Medical Association**

BMJ N ABBR = **British Medical Journal**

BMus N ABBR (= *Bachelor of Music*) titolo di studio

BMX N ABBR (= *bicycle motocross*) BMX *f inv*; **~ bike** mountain bike *f inv* per cross

bn ABBR = **billion**

BO N ABBR (*col*: = *body odour*) odori *mpl* sgradevoli (del corpo); = **box office**

boar [bɔːʳ] N cinghiale *m*

board [bɔːd] N tavola; (*on wall*) tabellone *m*; (*for chess etc*) scacchiera; (*committee*) consiglio, comitato; (*in firm*) consiglio d'amministrazione; (*Naut*, *Aviat*): **on ~** a bordo ▶ VT (*ship*) salire a bordo di; (*train*) salire su; **full ~** (BRIT) pensione *f* completa; **half ~** (BRIT) mezza pensione; **~ and lodging** vitto e alloggio; **above ~** (*fig*) regolare; **across the ~** (*fig*) *adv* per tutte le categorie; *adj* generale; **to go by the ~** venir messo(-a) da parte
▶ **board up** VT (*door*) chiudere con assi

boarder [ˈbɔːdəʳ] N pensionante *mf*; (*Scol*) convittore(-trice)

board game N gioco da tavolo

boarding card [ˈbɔːdɪŋ-] N (*Aviat*, *Naut*) carta d'imbarco

boarding house N pensione *f*

boarding party N squadra di ispezione (*del carico di una nave*)

boarding pass N (BRIT) = **boarding card**

boarding school N collegio

board meeting N riunione f di consiglio

board room N sala del consiglio

boardwalk [ˈbɔːdwɔːk] N (US) passeggiata a mare

boast [bəust] VI: **to ~ (about** or **of)** vantarsi (di) ▶ VT vantare ▶ N vanteria; vanto

boastful [ˈbəustful] ADJ vanaglorioso(-a)

boastfulness [ˈbəustfulnɪs] N vanagloria

boat [bəut] N nave f; (small) barca; **to go by ~** andare in barca or in nave; **we're all in the same ~** (fig) siamo tutti nella stessa barca

boater [ˈbəutəʳ] N (hat) paglietta

boating [ˈbəutɪŋ] N canottaggio

boat people N boat people mpl

boatswain [ˈbəusn] N nostromo

bob [bɔb] VI (boat, cork on water: also: **bob up and down**) andare su e giù ▶ N (BRIT col) = **shilling** ▶ **bob up** VI saltare fuori

bobbin [ˈbɔbɪn] N bobina; (of sewing machine) rocchetto

bobby [ˈbɔbɪ] N (BRIT col) ≈ poliziotto

bobby pin [ˈbɔbɪ-] N (US) fermaglio per capelli

bobsleigh [ˈbɔbsleɪ] N bob m inv

bode [bəud] VI: **to ~ well/ill (for)** essere di buon/cattivo auspicio (per)

bodice [ˈbɔdɪs] N corsetto

bodily [ˈbɔdɪlɪ] ADJ (comfort, needs) materiale; (pain) fisico(-a) ▶ ADV (carry) in braccio; (lift) di peso

body [ˈbɔdɪ] N corpo; (of car) carrozzeria; (of plane) fusoliera; (fig: group) gruppo; (: organization) associazione f, organizzazione f; (quantity) quantità f inv; (of speech, document) parte f principale; (also: **body stocking**) body m inv; **in a ~** in massa; **ruling ~** direttivo; **a wine with ~** un vino corposo

body blow N (fig) duro colpo

body-building [ˈbɔdɪˈbɪldɪŋ] N culturismo

bodyguard [ˈbɔdɪgɑːd] N guardia del corpo

body language N linguaggio del corpo

body repairs NPL (Aut) lavori mpl di carrozzeria

body search N perquisizione f personale; **to submit to** or **undergo a ~** essere sottoposto(-a) a perquisizione personale

bodywork [ˈbɔdɪwɜːk] N carrozzeria

boffin [ˈbɔfɪn] N scienziato

bog [bɔg] N palude f ▶ VT: **to get bogged down** (fig) impantanarsi

bogey [ˈbəugɪ] N (worry) spauracchio; (also: **bogey man**) babau m inv

boggle [ˈbɔgl] VI: **the mind boggles** è incredibile

Bogotá [bəugəˈtɑː] N Bogotà f

bogus [ˈbəugəs] ADJ falso(-a); finto(-a)

Bohemia [bəuˈhiːmɪə] N Boemia

Bohemian [bəuˈhiːmɪən] ADJ, N boemo(-a)

boil [bɔɪl] VT, VI bollire ▶ N (Med) foruncolo; **to come to the** or (US) **a ~** raggiungere l'ebollizione; **to bring to the** or (US) **a ~** portare a ebollizione; **boiled egg** uovo alla coque; **boiled potatoes** patate fpl bollite or lesse
▶ **boil down** VI (fig): **to ~ down to** ridursi a
▶ **boil over** VI traboccare (bollendo)

boiler [ˈbɔɪləʳ] N caldaia

boiler suit N (BRIT) tuta

boiling [ˈbɔɪlɪŋ] ADJ bollente; **I'm ~ (hot)** (col) sto morendo di caldo

boiling point N punto di ebollizione

boil-in-the-bag [bɔɪlɪnðəˈbæg] ADJ (rice etc) da bollire nel sacchetto

boisterous [ˈbɔɪstərəs] ADJ chiassoso(-a)

bold [bəuld] ADJ audace; (pej: child) impudente; (outline) chiaro(-a); (colour) deciso(-a)

boldness [ˈbəuldnɪs] N audacia; impudenza

bold type N (Typ) neretto, grassetto

Bolivia [bəˈlɪvɪə] N Bolivia

Bolivian [bəˈlɪvɪən] ADJ, N boliviano(-a)

bollard [ˈbɔləd] N (Naut) bitta; (BRIT Aut) colonnina luminosa

Bollywood [ˈbɔlɪwud] N Bollywood f

bolshy [ˈbɔlʃɪ] ADJ (BRIT col) piantagrane, ribelle; **to be in a ~ mood** essere in vena di piantar grane

bolster [ˈbəulstəʳ] N capezzale m
▶ **bolster up** VT sostenere

bolt [bəult] N chiavistello; (with nut) bullone m
▶ ADV: **~ upright** diritto(-a) come un fuso ▶ VT serrare; (also: **bolt together**) imbullonare; (food) mangiare in fretta ▶ VI scappare via; **a ~ from the blue** (fig) un fulmine a ciel sereno

bomb [bɔm] N bomba ▶ VT bombardare

bombard [bɔmˈbɑːd] VT bombardare

bombardment [bɔmˈbɑːdmənt] N bombardamento

bombastic [bɔmˈbæstɪk] ADJ ampolloso(-a)

bomb disposal N: **~ expert** artificiere m; **~ unit** corpo degli artificieri

bomber [ˈbɔməʳ] N (Aviat) bombardiere m; (terrorist) dinamitardo(-a)

bombing [ˈbɔmɪŋ] N bombardamento

bomb scare N stato di allarme (per sospetta presenza di una bomba)

bombshell [ˈbɔmʃel] N (fig) notizia bomba

bomb site N luogo bombardato

bona fide [ˈbəunəˈfaɪdɪ] ADJ sincero(-a); (offer) onesto(-a)

bonanza [bəˈnænzə] N cuccagna

bond [bɔnd] N legame m; (binding promise, Finance) obbligazione f; (Comm): **in ~** (of goods) in attesa di sdoganamento

bondage [ˈbɔndɪdʒ] N schiavitù f

bonded warehouse [ˈbɔndɪd-] N magazzino doganale

bone [bəun] N osso; (of fish) spina, lisca ▶ VT disossare; togliere le spine a

> The plural of **osso** is feminine when the *bone* is human.
> *He broke every bone in his left hand.* **Si è rotto tutte le ossa della mano sinistra.**

bone china N porcellana fine

bone-dry [ˈbəunˈdraɪ] ADJ asciuttissimo(-a)

bone idle ADJ: **to be ~** essere un(a) fannullone(-a)

bone marrow N midollo osseo

boner [ˈbəunəʳ] N (US) gaffe f inv

bonfire [ˈbɔnfaɪəʳ] N falò m inv

bonk [bɔŋk] VT, VI (col) scopare (!)

bonkers [ˈbɔŋkəz] ADJ (BRIT col) suonato(-a)

Bonn [bɔn] N Bonn f

bonnet [ˈbɔnɪt] N cuffia; (BRIT: of car) cofano

bonny [ˈbɔnɪ] ADJ (esp SCOTTISH) bello(-a), carino(-a)

bonus [ˈbəunəs] N premio; (on wages) gratifica; (fig) sovrappiù m inv

bony [ˈbəunɪ] ADJ (thin: person) ossuto(-a), angoloso(-a); (arm, face, Med: tissue) osseo(-a); (meat) pieno(-a) di ossi; (fish) pieno(-a) di spine

boo [bu:] EXCL ba! ▶ VT fischiare ▶ N fischio

boob [bu:b] N (col: breast) tetta; (: BRIT: mistake) gaffe f inv

booby prize [ˈbu:bɪ-] N premio per il peggior contendente

booby trap [ˈbu:bɪ-] N trabocchetto; (bomb) congegno che esplode al contatto

booby-trapped [ˈbu:bɪtræpt] ADJ: **a ~ car** una macchina con dell'esplosivo a bordo

book [buk] N libro; (of stamps etc) blocchetto ▶ VT (ticket, seat, room) prenotare; (driver) multare; (football player) ammonire ▪ **books** NPL (Comm) conti mpl; **to keep the books** (Comm) tenere la contabilità; **by the ~** secondo le regole; **to throw the ~ at sb** incriminare qn seriamente or con tutte le aggravanti
  ▶ **book in** VI (BRIT: at hotel) prendere una camera
  ▶ **book up** VT riservare, prenotare; **the hotel is booked up** l'albergo è al completo; **all seats are booked up** è tutto esaurito

bookable [ˈbukəbl] ADJ: **seats are ~** si possono prenotare i posti

bookcase [ˈbukkeɪs] N libreria

book ends NPL reggilibri mpl

booking [ˈbukɪŋ] N (BRIT) prenotazione f

booking office N (BRIT: Rail) biglietteria; (: Theat) botteghino

book-keeping [ˈbukˈki:pɪŋ] N contabilità

booklet [ˈbuklɪt] N opuscolo, libriccino

bookmaker [ˈbukmeɪkəʳ] N allibratore m

bookmark [ˈbukmɑ:k] N (also Comput) segnalibro ▶ VT (Comput) mettere un segnalibro a; (internet) aggiungere a "Preferiti"

bookseller [ˈbukseləʳ] N libraio(-a)

bookshelf [ˈbukʃelf] N mensola (per libri) ▪ **bookshelves** NPL (bookcase) libreria

bookshop [ˈbukʃɔp] N libreria

bookstall [ˈbukstɔ:l] N bancarella di libri

bookstore [ˈbukstɔ:ʳ] N = **bookshop**

book token N buono m libri inv

book value N valore m contabile

bookworm [ˈbukwə:m] N (fig) topo di biblioteca

boom [bu:m] N (noise) rimbombo; (busy period) boom m inv ▶ VI rimbombare; andare a gonfie vele

boomerang [ˈbu:məræŋ] N boomerang m inv ▶ VI avere effetto contrario; **to ~ on sb** (fig) ritorcersi contro qn

boom town N città f inv in rapidissima espansione

boon [bu:n] N vantaggio

boorish [ˈbuərɪʃ] ADJ maleducato(-a)

boost [bu:st] N spinta ▶ VT spingere; (increase: sales, production) incentivare; **to give a ~ to** (morale) tirar su; **it gave a ~ to his confidence** è stata per lui un'iniezione di fiducia

booster [ˈbu:stəʳ] N (Elec) amplificatore m; (TV) amplificatore m di segnale; (also: **booster rocket**) razzo vettore; (Med) richiamo

booster seat N (Aut: for children) seggiolino di sicurezza

boot [bu:t] N stivale m; (ankle boot) stivaletto; (for hiking) scarpone m da montagna; (for football etc) scarpa; (BRIT: of car) portabagagli m inv ▶ VT (Comput) inizializzare; **to ~** (in addition) per giunta, in più; **to give sb the ~** (col) mettere qn alla porta

booth [bu:ð] N (at fair) baraccone m; (of cinema, telephone etc) cabina; (also: **voting booth**) cabina (elettorale)

bootleg [ˈbu:tleg] ADJ di contrabbando; **~ record** registrazione f pirata inv

booty [ˈbu:tɪ] N bottino

booze [bu:z] (col) N alcool m ▶ VI trincare

boozer [ˈbu:zəʳ] N (col: person) beone m; (BRIT col: pub) osteria

border [ˈbɔ:dəʳ] N orlo; margine m; (of a country) frontiera; (for flowers) aiuola (laterale) ▶ VT (road) costeggiare; **the B~** la frontiera tra l'Inghilterra e la Scozia; **the Borders** la zona di confine tra l'Inghilterra e la Scozia
  ▶ **border on** VT FUS confinare con

borderline [ˈbɔ:dəlaɪn] N (fig) linea di demarcazione ▶ ADJ: **~ case** caso limite; **on the ~** incerto(-a)

bore [bɔ:ʳ] PT of **bear** ▶ VT (hole) scavare; (person) annoiare ▸ N (*person*) seccatore(-trice); (*of gun*) calibro

bored ADJ annoiato(-a); **to be ~** annoiarsi; **he's ~ to tears** *or* **~ to death** *or* **~ stiff** è annoiato a morte, si annoia da morire

boredom [ˈbɔːdəm] N noia

boring [ˈbɔːrɪŋ] ADJ noioso(-a)

born [bɔːn] ADJ: **to be ~** nascere; **I was ~ in 1960** sono nato nel 1960; **~ blind** cieco dalla nascita; **a ~ comedian** un comico nato

born-again [bɔːnəˈɡɛn] ADJ: **~ Christian** convertito(-a) alla chiesa evangelica

borne [bɔːn] PP *of* **bear**

Borneo [ˈbɔːnɪəu] N Borneo

borough [ˈbʌrə] N comune *m*

borrow [ˈbɔrəu] VT: **to ~ sth (from sb)** prendere in prestito qc (da qn); **may I ~ your car?** può prestarmi la macchina?

borrower [ˈbɔrəuəʳ] N (*gen*) chi prende a prestito; (*Econ*) mutuatario(-a)

borrowing [ˈbɔrəuɪŋ] N prestito

borstal [ˈbɔːstl] N (*BRIT*) riformatorio

Bosnia [ˈbɔznɪə] N Bosnia

Bosnia and Herzegovina [ˈbɔznɪə ænd hɜrtsəˈɡəuviːnə] N Bosnia ed Erzegovina

Bosnian [ˈbɔznɪən] ADJ, N bosniaco(-a)

bosom [ˈbuzəm] N petto; (*fig*) seno

bosom friend N amico(-a) del cuore

boss [bɔs] N capo ▸ VT (*also:* **boss about**, **boss around**) comandare a bacchetta; **stop bossing everyone about!** smettila di dare ordini a tutti!

bossy [ˈbɔsɪ] ADJ prepotente

bosun [ˈbəusn] N nostromo

botanical [bəˈtænɪkl] ADJ botanico(-a)

botanist [ˈbɔtənɪst] N botanico(-a)

botany [ˈbɔtənɪ] N botanica

botch [bɔtʃ] VT fare un pasticcio di

both [bəuθ] ADJ entrambi(-e), tutt'e due ▸ PRON: **~ of them** entrambi(-e) ▸ ADV: **they sell ~ meat and poultry** vendono insieme la carne ed il pollame; **~ of us went**, **we ~ went** ci siamo andati tutt'e due

bother [ˈbɔðəʳ] VT (*worry*) preoccupare; (*annoy*) infastidire ▸ VI (*gen: also:* **bother o.s.**) preoccuparsi ▸ N: **it is a ~ to have to do** è una seccatura dover fare ▸ EXCL uffa!, accidenti!; **it was no ~** non c'era problema; **to ~ doing sth** darsi la pena di fare qc; **I'm sorry to ~ you** mi dispiace disturbarla; **please don't ~** non si scomodi; **it's no ~** non c'è problema

Botswana [bɔtˈswɑːnə] N Botswana *m*

bottle [ˈbɔtl] N bottiglia; (*of perfume, shampoo etc*) flacone *m*; (*baby's*) biberon *m inv* ▸ VT imbottigliare; **~ of wine/milk** bottiglia di vino/latte; **wine/milk ~** bottiglia da vino/del latte
▸ **bottle up** VT contenere

bottle bank N contenitore *m* per la raccolta del vetro

bottle-fed [ˈbɔtlfɛd] ADJ allattato(-a) artificialmente

bottleneck [ˈbɔtlnɛk] N ingorgo

bottle-opener [ˈbɔtləupnəʳ] N apribottiglie *m inv*

bottom [ˈbɔtəm] N fondo; (*of mountain, tree, hill*) piedi *mpl*; (*buttocks*) sedere *m* ▸ ADJ più basso(-a), ultimo(-a); **at the ~ of** in fondo a; **to get to the ~ of sth** andare al fondo di *or* in fondo a qc

bottomless [ˈbɔtəmlɪs] ADJ senza fondo

bottom line N: **the ~ is ...** in ultima analisi ....

botulism [ˈbɔtjulɪzəm] N botulismo

bough [bau] N ramo

bought [bɔːt] PT, PP *of* **buy**

boulder [ˈbəuldəʳ] N masso (tondeggiante)

boulevard [ˈbuːlvɑːd] N viale *m*

bounce [bauns] VI (*ball*) rimbalzare; (*cheque*) essere restituito(-a) ▸ VT far rimbalzare ▸ N (*rebound*) rimbalzo; **to ~ in** entrare di slancio *or* con foga; **he's got plenty of ~** (*fig*) è molto esuberante

bouncer [ˈbaunsəʳ] N (*col*) buttafuori *m inv*

bouncy castle® [ˈbaunsɪ-] N grande castello gonfiabile per giocare

bound [baund] PT, PP *of* **bind** ▸ N (*gen pl*) limite *m*; (*leap*) salto ▸ VI saltare ▸ VT (*leap*) saltare; (*limit*) delimitare ▸ ADJ: **~ by law** obbligato(-a) per legge; **to be ~ to do sth** (*obliged*) essere costretto(-a) a fare qc; **he's ~ to fail** (*likely*) fallirà di certo; **~ for** diretto(-a) a; **out of bounds** il cui accesso è vietato

boundary [ˈbaundrɪ] N confine *m*

boundless [ˈbaundlɪs] ADJ illimitato(-a)

bountiful [ˈbauntɪful] ADJ (*person*) munifico(-a); (*God*) misericordioso(-a); (*supply*) abbondante

bounty [ˈbauntɪ] N (*generosity*) liberalità, munificenza; (*reward*) taglia

bounty hunter N cacciatore(-trice) di taglie

bouquet [ˈbukeɪ] N bouquet *m inv*

bourbon [ˈbuəbən] N (*US: also:* **bourbon whiskey**) bourbon *m inv*

bourgeois [ˈbuəʒwɑː] ADJ, N borghese (*mf*)

bout [baut] N periodo; (*of malaria etc*) attacco; (*Boxing etc*) incontro

boutique [buːˈtiːk] N boutique *f inv*

bow¹ [bəu] N nodo; (*weapon*) arco; (*Mus*) archetto

bow² [bau] N (*with body*) inchino; (*Naut: also:* **bows**) prua ▸ VI inchinarsi; (*yield*): **to ~ to** *or* **before** sottomettersi a; **to ~ to the inevitable** rassegnarsi all'inevitabile

bowels [bauəlz] NPL intestini *mpl*; (*fig*) viscere *fpl*

bowl [bəul] N (*for eating*) scodella; (*for washing*) bacino; (*ball*) boccia; (*of pipe*) fornello; (*US: stadium*) stadio ▸ VI (*Cricket*) servire (la palla); *see also* **bowls**

▶ **bowl over** VT (*fig*) sconcertare

bow-legged ['bəu'lɛgɪd] ADJ dalle gambe storte

bowler ['bəulə'] N giocatore(-trice) di bocce; (*Cricket*) lanciatore(-trice); (*BRIT: also:* **bowler hat**) bombetta

bowling ['bəulɪŋ] N (*game*) gioco delle bocce; bowling *m*

bowling alley N pista da bowling

bowling green N campo di bocce

bowls [bəulz] N gioco delle bocce

bow tie N cravatta a farfalla

box [bɒks] N scatola; (*also:* **cardboard box**) (scatola di) cartone *m*; (*crate: also for money*) cassetta; (*Theat*) palco; (*BRIT Aut*) area d'incrocio ▶ VI fare pugilato ▶ VT mettere in (una) scatola, inscatolare; (*Sport*) combattere contro

boxer ['bɒksə'] N (*person*) pugile *m*; (*dog*) boxer *m inv*

boxer shorts ['bɒksəʃɔːts] NPL boxer; **a pair of ~** un paio di boxer

boxing ['bɒksɪŋ] N (*Sport*) pugilato

Boxing Day N (*BRIT*) ≈ Santo Stefano

Il **Boxing Day** è un giorno di festa e cade in genere il 26 dicembre, data in cui in molti paesi del Commonwealth iniziano i saldi e si svolgono varie manifestazioni sportive, dal calcio al cricket. Prende il nome dall'usanza di donare pacchi regalo natalizi, un tempo chiamati *Christmas boxes*, a fornitori e dipendenti.

boxing gloves NPL guantoni *mpl* da pugile

boxing ring N ring *m inv*

box number N (*for advertisements*) casella

box office N biglietteria

box room N ripostiglio

boy [bɔɪ] N ragazzo; (*small*) bambino; (*son*) figlio; (*servant*) servo

boy band N gruppo pop di soli ragazzi maschi creato per far presa su un pubblico giovane

boycott ['bɔɪkɒt] N boicottaggio ▶ VT boicottare

boyfriend ['bɔɪfrɛnd] N ragazzo

boyish ['bɔɪɪʃ] ADJ di or da ragazzo

bp ABBR = **bishop**

bra [brɑː] N reggipetto, reggiseno

brace [breɪs] N sostegno; (*on teeth*) apparecchio correttore; (*tool*) trapano; (*Typ: also:* **brace bracket**) graffa ▶ VT rinforzare, sostenere; **to ~ o.s.** (*fig*) farsi coraggio; *see also* **braces**

bracelet ['breɪslɪt] N braccialetto

braces ['breɪsɪz] NPL (*BRIT*) bretelle *fpl*

bracing ['breɪsɪŋ] ADJ invigorante

bracken ['brækən] N felce *f*

bracket ['brækɪt] N (*Tech*) mensola; (*group*) gruppo; (*Typ*) parentesi *f inv* ▶ VT mettere fra parentesi; (*fig: also:* **bracket together**) mettere

insieme; **in brackets** tra parentesi; **round/ square brackets** parentesi tonde/quadre; **income ~** fascia di reddito

brackish ['brækɪʃ] ADJ (*water*) salmastro(-a)

brag [bræg] VI vantarsi

braid [breɪd] N (*trimming*) passamano; (*of hair*) treccia

Braille [breɪl] N braille *m*

brain [breɪn] N cervello ▪ **brains** NPL (*intelligence*) cervella *fpl*; **he's got brains** è intelligente

brainchild ['breɪntʃaɪld] N creatura, creazione *f*

braindead ['breɪndɛd] ADJ (*Med*) che ha subito morte cerebrale; (*col*) cerebroleso(-a), deficiente

brainless ['breɪnlɪs] ADJ deficiente, stupido(-a)

brainstorm ['breɪnstɔːm] N (*fig*) attacco di pazzia; (*US*) = **brainwave**

brainwash ['breɪnwɒʃ] VT fare un lavaggio di cervello a

brainwave ['breɪnweɪv] N lampo di genio

brainy ['breɪnɪ] ADJ intelligente

braise [breɪz] VT brasare

brake [breɪk] N (*on vehicle*) freno ▶ VT, VI frenare

brake light N (fanalino dello) stop *m inv*

brake pedal N pedale *m* del freno

bramble ['bræmbl] N rovo; (*fruit*) mora

bran [bræn] N crusca

branch [brɑːntʃ] N ramo; (*Comm*) succursale *f*, filiale *f*
▶ **branch off** VI diramarsi
▶ **branch out** VI: **to ~ out into** intraprendere una nuova attività nel ramo di

branch line N (*Rail*) linea secondaria

branch manager N direttore(-trice) di filiale

brand [brænd] N marca; (*fig*) tipo ▶ VT (*cattle*) marcare (a ferro rovente); (*fig: pej*): **to ~ sb a communist** *etc* definire qn come comunista *etc*

brandish ['brændɪʃ] VT brandire

brand name N marca

brand-new ['brænd'njuː] ADJ nuovo(-a) di zecca

brandy ['brændɪ] N brandy *m inv*

brash [bræʃ] ADJ sfacciato(-a)

Brasilia [brə'zɪljə] N Brasilia

brass [brɑːs] N ottone *m*; **the ~** (*Mus*) gli ottoni

brass band N fanfara

brassière ['bræsɪə'] N reggipetto, reggiseno

brass tacks NPL: **to get down to ~** (*col*) venire al sodo

brat [bræt] N (*pej*) marmocchio, monello(-a)

bravado [brə'vɑːdəu] N spavalderia

brave [breɪv] ADJ coraggioso(-a) ▶ N guerriero *m* pellerossa *inv* ▶ VT affrontare

bravery ['breɪvərɪ] N coraggio

bravo [brɑː'vəu] EXCL bravo!, bene!

brawl [brɔːl] N rissa ▶ vi azzuffarsi

brawn [brɔːn] N muscolo; (*meat*) carne *f* di testa di maiale

brawny [ˈbrɔːnɪ] ADJ muscoloso(-a)

bray [breɪ] N raglio ▶ vi ragliare

brazen [ˈbreɪzn] ADJ svergognato(-a) ▶ vt: **to ~ it out** fare lo sfacciato

brazier [ˈbreɪzɪəʳ] N braciere *m*

Brazil [brəˈzɪl] N Brasile *m*

Brazilian [brəˈzɪljən] ADJ, N brasiliano(-a)

Brazil nut N noce *f* del Brasile

breach [briːtʃ] vt aprire una breccia in ▶ N (*gap*) breccia, varco; (*estrangement*) rottura; (*of duty*) abuso; (*breaking*): **~ of contract** rottura di contratto; **~ of the peace** violazione *f* dell'ordine pubblico; **~ of trust** abuso di fiducia

bread [brɛd] N pane *m*; (*col: money*) grana; **to earn one's daily ~** guadagnarsi il pane; **to know which side one's ~ is buttered on** saper fare i propri interessi; **~ and butter** *n* pane e burro; (*fig*) mezzi *mpl* di sussistenza

breadbin [ˈbrɛdbɪn] N (BRIT) cassetta *f* portapane *inv*

breadboard [ˈbrɛdbɔːd] N tagliere *m* (*per il pane*); (*Comput*) pannello per esperimenti

breadbox [ˈbrɛdbɔks] N (US) cassetta *f* portapane *inv*

breadcrumbs [ˈbrɛdkrʌmz] NPL briciole *fpl*; (*Culin*) pangrattato

breadline [ˈbrɛdlaɪn] N: **to be on the ~** avere appena denaro per vivere

breadth [brɛtθ] N larghezza; (*fig: of knowledge etc*) ampiezza

breadwinner [ˈbrɛdwɪnəʳ] N chi guadagna il pane per tutta la famiglia

break [breɪk] (*pt* **broke** [brəuk], *pp* **broken** [ˈbrəukən]) vt rompere; (*law*) violare; (*promise*) mancare a ▶ vi rompersi; (*storm*) scoppiare; (*weather*) cambiare; (*dawn*) spuntare; (*news*) saltare fuori ▶ N (*gap*) breccia; (*fracture*) rottura; (*rest*) intervallo; (*: short*) pausa; (*chance*) possibilità *f inv*; (*holiday*) vacanza; **to ~ one's leg** *etc* rompersi la gamba *etc*; **to ~ a record** battere un primato; **to ~ the news to sb** comunicare per primo la notizia a qn; **to ~ with sb** (*fig*) rompere con qn; **to ~ even** vi coprire le spese; **to ~ free** *or* **loose** liberarsi; **without a ~** senza una pausa; **to have** *or* **take a ~** (*few minutes*) fare una pausa; (*holiday*) prendere un po' di riposo; **a lucky ~** un colpo di fortuna

▶ **break down** vt (*figures, data*) analizzare; (*door etc*) buttare giù, abbattere; (*resistance*) stroncare ▶ vi crollare; (*Med*) avere un esaurimento (nervoso); (*Aut*) guastarsi

▶ **break in** vt (*horse etc*) domare ▶ vi (*burglar*) fare irruzione

▶ **break into** vt FUS (*house*) fare irruzione in

▶ **break off** vi (*speaker*) interrompersi; (*branch*) troncarsi ▶ vt (*talks, engagement*) rompere

▶ **break open** vt (*door etc*) sfondare

▶ **break out** vi evadere; **to ~ out in spots** coprirsi di macchie

▶ **break through** vi: **the sun broke through** il sole ha fatto capolino tra le nuvole ▶ vt (*defences, barrier*) sfondare, penetrare in; (*crowd*) aprirsi un varco in *or* tra, aprirsi un passaggio in *or* tra

▶ **break up** vi (*partnership*) sciogliersi; (*friends*) separarsi; **the line's** *or* **you're breaking up** la linea è disturbata ▶ vt fare in pezzi, spaccare; (*fight etc*) interrompere, far cessare; (*marriage*) finire

breakable [ˈbreɪkəbl] ADJ fragile ■ **breakables** NPL oggetti *mpl* fragili

breakage [ˈbreɪkɪdʒ] N rottura; **to pay for breakages** pagare i danni

breakaway [ˈbreɪkəweɪ] ADJ (*group etc*) scissionista, dissidente

break-dancing [ˈbreɪkdɑːnsɪŋ] N breakdance *f*

breakdown [ˈbreɪkdaun] N (*Aut*) guasto; (*in communications*) interruzione *f*; (*of marriage*) rottura; (*Med: also:* **nervous breakdown**) esaurimento nervoso; (*of payments, statistics etc*) resoconto

breakdown service N (BRIT) servizio riparazioni

breakdown truck, breakdown van N carro *m* attrezzi *inv*

breakdown van N *see* **breakdown truck**

breaker [ˈbreɪkəʳ] N frangente *m*

breakeven [ˈbreɪkˈiːvn] CPD: **~ chart** diagramma *m* del punto di rottura *or* pareggio; **~ point** punto di rottura *or* pareggio

breakfast [ˈbrɛkfəst] N colazione *f*

breakfast cereal N fiocchi *mpl* d'avena *or* di mais *etc*

break-in [ˈbreɪkɪn] N irruzione *f*

breaking point [ˈbreɪkɪŋ-] N punto di rottura

breakthrough [ˈbreɪkθruː] N (*Mil*) breccia; (*fig*) passo avanti

break-up [ˈbreɪkʌp] N (*of partnership, marriage*) rottura

break-up value N (*Comm*) valore *m* di realizzo

breakwater [ˈbreɪkwɔːtəʳ] N frangiflutti *m inv*

breast [brɛst] N (*of woman*) seno; (*chest, Culin*) petto

breast-feed [ˈbrɛstfiːd] vt, vi (*irreg: like* **feed**) allattare (al seno)

breast pocket N taschino

breast-stroke [ˈbrɛststrəuk] N nuoto a rana

breath [brɛθ] N respiro; **out of ~** senza fiato; **to go out for a ~ of air** andare a prendere una boccata d'aria

Breathalyser® [ˈbrɛθəlaɪzəʳ] N (BRIT) alcoltest *m inv*

breathe [briːð] vt, vi respirare; **I won't ~ a word about it** non fiaterò

▶ **breathe in** VI inspirare ▶ VT respirare
▶ **breathe out** VT, VI espirare

breather ['bri:ðəʳ] N attimo di respiro

breathing ['bri:ðɪŋ] N respiro, respirazione f

breathing space N (fig) attimo di respiro

breathless ['brɛθlɪs] ADJ senza fiato; (with excitement) con il fiato sospeso

breath-taking ['brɛθteɪkɪŋ] ADJ mozzafiato inv

breath test N ≈ prova del palloncino

bred [brɛd] PT, PP of **breed**

-bred [brɛd] SUFFIX: **to be well/ill-bred** essere ben educato(-a)/maleducato(-a)

breed [bri:d] (pt, pp **bred** [brɛd]) VT allevare; (fig: hate, suspicion) generare, provocare ▶ VI riprodursi ▶ N razza; (type, class) varietà f inv

breeder ['bri:dəʳ] N (Physics: also: **breeder reactor**) reattore m autofertilizzante

breeding ['bri:dɪŋ] N riproduzione f; allevamento

breeze [bri:z] N brezza

breeze block N (BRIT) mattone composto di scorie di coke

breezy ['bri:zɪ] ADJ (day) ventilato(-a); (person) allegro(-a)

Breton ['brɛtən] ADJ, N bretone (mf)

brevity ['brɛvɪtɪ] N brevità

brew [bru:] VT (tea) fare un infuso di; (beer) fare; (plot) tramare ▶ VI (tea) essere in infusione; (beer) essere in fermentazione; (storm, fig: trouble etc) prepararsi

brewer ['bru:əʳ] N birraio

brewery ['bru:ərɪ] N fabbrica di birra

briar ['braɪəʳ] N (thorny bush) rovo; (wild rose) rosa selvatica

bribe [braɪb] N bustarella ▶ VT comprare; **to ~ sb to do sth** pagare qn sottobanco perché faccia qc

bribery ['braɪbərɪ] N corruzione f

bric-a-brac ['brɪkəbræk] N bric-a-brac m

brick [brɪk] N mattone m

bricklayer ['brɪkleɪəʳ] N muratore(-trice)

brickwork ['brɪkwə:k] N muratura in mattoni

brickworks ['brɪkwə:ks] N fabbrica di mattoni

bridal ['braɪdl] ADJ nuziale; **~ party** corteo nuziale

bride [braɪd] N sposa

bridegroom ['braɪdgru:m] N sposo

bridesmaid ['braɪdzmeɪd] N damigella d'onore

bridge [brɪdʒ] N ponte m; (Naut) ponte di comando; (of nose) dorso; (Cards, Dentistry) bridge m inv ▶ VT (river) fare un ponte sopra; (fig: gap) colmare

bridging loan ['brɪdʒɪŋ-] N (BRIT) anticipazione f sul mutuo

bridle ['braɪdl] N briglia ▶ VT tenere a freno;

(horse) mettere la briglia a ▶ VI (in anger etc) adombrarsi, adontarsi

bridle path N sentiero (per cavalli)

brief [bri:f] ADJ breve ▶ N (Law) comparsa; (gen) istruzioni fpl ▶ VT (Mil etc) dare istruzioni a; **in ~ ...** in breve ..., a farla breve ...; **to ~ sb (about sth)** mettere qn al corrente (di qc); see also **briefs**

briefcase ['bri:fkeɪs] N cartella

briefing ['bri:fɪŋ] N istruzioni fpl, briefing m inv

briefly ['bri:flɪ] ADV (speak, visit, explain, say) brevemente; (glimpse, glance) di sfuggita

briefness ['bri:fnɪs] N brevità

briefs [bri:fs] NPL mutande fpl

Brig. ABBR = **brigadier**

brigade [brɪ'geɪd] N (Mil) brigata

brigadier [brɪgə'dɪəʳ] N generale m di brigata

bright [braɪt] ADJ luminoso(-a); (person) sveglio(-a); (colour) vivace; **to look on the ~ side** vedere il lato positivo delle cose

brighten ['braɪtn], **brighten up** VT (room) rendere luminoso(-a); rallegrare ▶ VI schiarirsi; (person) rallegrarsi

brightly ['braɪtlɪ] ADV (shine) vivamente, intensamente; (smile) radiosamente; (talk) con animazione

brill [brɪl] EXCL (BRIT col) stupendo!, fantastico!

brilliance ['brɪljəns] N splendore m; (fig: of person) genialità, talento

brilliant ['brɪljənt] ADJ brillante; (sunshine) sfolgorante; (light, smile) radioso(-a); (col) splendido(-a)

brim [brɪm] N orlo

brimful ['brɪm'ful] ADJ pieno(-a) or colmo(-a) fino all'orlo; (fig) pieno(-a)

brine [braɪn] N acqua salmastra; (Culin) salamoia

bring [brɪŋ] (pt, pp **brought** [brɔ:t]) VT portare; **to ~ sth to an end** mettere fine a qc; **I can't ~ myself to sack him** non so risolvermi a licenziarlo

▶ **bring about** VT causare

▶ **bring back** VT riportare

▶ **bring down** VT (lower) far scendere; (shoot down) abbattere; (government) far cadere

▶ **bring forward** VT portare avanti; (in time) anticipare; (Book-keeping) riportare

▶ **bring in** VT (person) fare entrare; (object) portare; (Pol: bill) presentare; (: legislation) introdurre; (Law: verdict) emettere; (produce: income) rendere

▶ **bring off** VT (task, plan) portare a compimento; (deal) concludere

▶ **bring on** VT (illness, attack) causare, provocare; (player, substitute) far scendere in campo

▶ **bring out** VT (meaning) mettere in evidenza; (new product) lanciare; (book) pubblicare, fare uscire

▶ **bring round, bring to** VT (unconscious person) far rinvenire

▶ **bring up** VT allevare; (question) introdurre

brink [brɪŋk] N orlo; **on the ~ of doing sth** sul punto di fare qc; **she was on the ~ of tears** era lì lì per piangere

brisk [brɪsk] ADJ (person, tone) spiccio(-a), sbrigativo(-a); (: abrupt) brusco(-a); (wind) fresco(-a); (trade etc) vivace, attivo(-a); (pace) svelto(-a); **to go for a ~ walk** fare una camminata di buon passo; **business is ~** gli affari vanno bene

bristle ['brɪsl] N setola ▶ VI rizzarsi; **bristling with** irto(-a) di

bristly ['brɪslɪ] ADJ (chin) ispido(-a); (beard, hair) irsuto(-a), setoloso(-a)

Brit [brɪt] N ABBR (col: = British person) britannico(-a)

Britain ['brɪtən] N (also: **Great Britain**) Gran Bretagna

British ['brɪtɪʃ] ADJ britannico(-a) ▪ **the British** NPL i Britannici; **the ~ Isles** npl le Isole Britanniche

British Summer Time N ora legale (in Gran Bretagna)

Briton ['brɪtən] N britannico(-a)

Brittany ['brɪtənɪ] N Bretagna

brittle ['brɪtl] ADJ fragile

Br(o). ABBR (Rel) = **brother**

broach [brəʊtʃ] VT (subject) affrontare

broad [brɔːd] ADJ largo(-a); (distinction) generale; (accent) spiccato(-a) ▶ N (US pej) bellona; **~ hint** allusione f esplicita; **in ~ daylight** in pieno giorno; **the ~ outlines** le grandi linee

broadband ['brɔːdbænd] ADJ (Comput) a banda larga, ADSL ▶ N banda larga, ADSL m inv

broad bean N fava

broadcast ['brɔːdkɑːst] (pt, pp ~) N trasmissione f ▶ VT trasmettere per radio (or per televisione) ▶ VI fare una trasmissione

broadcaster ['brɔːdkɑːstər] N annunciatore(-trice) radiotelevisivo(-a) (or radiofonico(-a))

broadcasting ['brɔːdkɑːstɪŋ] N radiodiffusione f; televisione f

broadcasting station N stazione f trasmittente

broaden ['brɔːdn] VT allargare ▶ VI allargarsi

broadly ['brɔːdlɪ] ADV (fig) in generale

broad-minded ['brɔːd'maɪndɪd] ADJ di mente aperta

broadsheet ['brɔːdʃiːt] N (BRIT) giornale m (si contrappone al tabloid che è di formato più piccolo)

broccoli ['brɔkəlɪ] N (Bot) broccolo; (Culin) broccoli mpl

brochure ['brəʊʃjʊər] N dépliant m inv

brogue [brəʊg] N (shoe) scarpa rozza in cuoio; (accent) accento irlandese

broil [brɔɪl] VT cuocere a fuoco vivo

broiler ['brɔɪlər] N (US: grill) griglia

broke [brəʊk] PT of **break** ▶ ADJ (col) squattrinato(-a); **to go ~** fare fallimento

broken ['brəʊkən] PP of **break** ▶ ADJ (gen) rotto(-a); (stick, promise, vow) spezzato(-a); (marriage) fallito(-a); **a ~ leg** una gamba rotta; **he comes from a ~ home** i suoi sono divisi; **in ~ French/ English** in un francese/inglese stentato

broken-down ['brəʊkən'daʊn] ADJ (car) in panne, rotto(-a); (machine) guasto(-a), fuori uso; (house) abbandonato(-a), in rovina

broken-hearted ['brəʊkən'hɑːtɪd] ADJ: **to be ~** avere il cuore spezzato

broker ['brəʊkər] N agente m

brokerage ['brəʊkərɪdʒ] N (Comm) commissione f di intermediazione

brolly ['brɔlɪ] N (BRIT col) ombrello

bromance ['brəʊmæns] N (col) forte amicizia maschile platonica

bronchitis [brɔŋ'kaɪtɪs] N bronchite f

bronze [brɔnz] N bronzo

bronzed [brɔnzd] ADJ abbronzato(-a)

brooch [brəʊtʃ] N spilla

brood [bruːd] N covata ▶ VI (hen) covare; (person) rimuginare

broody ['bruːdɪ] ADJ (fig) cupo(-a) e taciturno(-a)

brook [bruk] N ruscello

broom [brum] N scopa; (Bot) ginestra

broomstick ['brumstɪk] N manico di scopa

Bros. ABBR (Comm: = brothers) F.lli (= Fratelli)

broth [brɔθ] N brodo

brothel ['brɔθl] N bordello

brother ['brʌðər] N fratello

brotherhood ['brʌðəhud] N fratellanza; confraternità f inv

brother-in-law ['brʌðərɪnlɔː] N cognato

brotherly ['brʌðəlɪ] ADJ fraterno(-a)

brought [brɔːt] PT, PP of **bring**

brought forward ADJ (Comm) riportato(-a)

brow [braʊ] N fronte f; (rare, gen: also: **eyebrow**) sopracciglio; (of hill) cima

browbeat ['braʊbiːt] VT (irreg: like **beat**) intimidire

brown [braʊn] ADJ bruno(-a), marrone; (hair) castano(-a); (tanned) abbronzato(-a) ▶ N (colour) color m bruno or marrone ▶ VT (Culin) rosolare; **to go ~** (person) abbronzarsi; (leaves) ingiallire

brown bread N pane m integrale, pane nero

Brownie ['braʊnɪ] N giovane esploratrice f

brown paper N carta da pacchi or da imballaggio

brown rice N riso greggio

brown sugar N zucchero greggio

browse [braʊz] VI (animal) brucare; (in bookshop etc) curiosare; (Comput) navigare (in Internet)

▶ VT: **to ~ the web** navigare in Internet ▶ N: **to have a ~ (around)** dare un'occhiata (in giro); **to ~ through a book** sfogliare un libro

browser [brauzəʳ] N (*Comput*) browser *m inv*

bruise [bru:z] N ammaccatura; (*on person*) livido ▶ VT ammaccare; (*one's leg etc*) farsi un livido a; (*fig: feelings*) urtare ▶ VI (*fruit*) ammaccarsi

Brum [brʌm], **Brummagem** [ˈbrʌmədʒəm] N (*col*) = **Birmingham**

Brummie [ˈbrʌmɪ] N (*BRIT col*) abitante *mf* di Birmingham, originario(-a) di Birmingham

brunch [brʌntʃ] N *ricca colazione consumata in tarda mattinata*

Brunei [bruːˈnaɪ, ˈbruːnaɪ] N Brunei *m*

brunette [bruːˈnɛt] N bruna

brunt [brʌnt] N: **the ~ of** (*attack, criticism etc*) il peso maggiore di

brush [brʌʃ] N spazzola; (*for painting, shaving*) pennello; (*quarrel*) schermaglia ▶ VT spazzolare; (*also:* **brush past, brush against**) sfiorare; **to have a ~ with sb** (*verbally*) avere uno scontro con qn; (*physically*) venire a diverbio or alle mani con qn; **to have a ~ with the police** avere delle noie con la polizia
▶ **brush aside** VT scostare
▶ **brush up** VT (*knowledge*) rinfrescare

brushed [brʌʃt] ADJ (*Tech: steel, chrome etc*) sabbiato(-a); (*nylon, denim etc*) pettinato(-a)

brush-off [ˈbrʌʃɔf] N: **to give sb the ~** dare il ben servito a qn

brushwood [ˈbrʌʃwud] N macchia

brusque [bruːsk] ADJ (*person, manner*) brusco(-a); (*tone*) secco(-a)

Brussels [ˈbrʌslz] N Bruxelles *f*

Brussels sprout [-spraut] N cavolo di Bruxelles

brutal [ˈbruːtl] ADJ brutale

brutality [bruːˈtælɪtɪ] N brutalità

brutalize [ˈbruːtəlaɪz] VT (*harden*) abbrutire; (*ill-treat*) brutalizzare

brute [bruːt] N bestia; **by ~ force** con la forza, a viva forza

brutish [ˈbruːtɪʃ] ADJ da bruto

BS N ABBR (*US:* = *Bachelor of Science*) *titolo di studio*

bs ABBR = **bill of sale**

BSA N ABBR (*US*) = **Boy Scouts of America**

BSc N ABBR (*Univ*) = **Bachelor of Science**

BSE N ABBR (= *bovine spongiform encephalopathy*) encefalite *f* bovina spongiforme

BSI N ABBR (= *British Standards Institution*) *associazione per la normalizzazione*

BST ABBR (= *British Summer Time*) *ora legale*

btu N ABBR (= *British thermal unit*) Btu *m* (= 1.054.2 *joules*)

bubble [ˈbʌbl] N bolla ▶ VI ribollire; (*sparkle: fig*) essere effervescente

bubble bath N bagno *m* schiuma *inv*

bubble gum N gomma americana

bubble jet printer [ˈbʌbldʒɛt-] N stampante *f* a getto d'inchiostro

bubbly [ˈbʌblɪ] ADJ (*also fig*) frizzante ▶ N (*col: champagne*) spumante *m*

Bucharest [buːkəˈrɛst] N Bucarest *f*

buck [bʌk] N maschio (*di camoscio, caprone, coniglio ecc*); (*US col*) dollaro ▶ VI sgroppare; **to pass the ~ (to sb)** scaricare (su di qn) la propria responsabilità
▶ **buck up** VI (*cheer up*) rianimarsi ▶ VT: **to ~ one's ideas up** mettere la testa a partito

bucket [ˈbʌkɪt] N secchio ▶ VI (*BRIT col*): **the rain is bucketing (down)** piove a catinelle

bucket list N *elenco di cose da fare prima di morire*

Buckingham Palace [ˈbʌkɪŋəm-] N *vedi nota*

> **Buckingham Palace** è la residenza ufficiale a Londra del sovrano britannico. Costruita nel 1703 per il duca di Buckingham, fu acquistata nel 1762 dal re Giorgio III.

buckle [ˈbʌkl] N fibbia ▶ VT allacciare; (*warp*) deformare ▶ VI (*wheel etc*) piegarsi
▶ **buckle down** VI mettersi sotto

bud [bʌd] N gemma; (*of flower*) bocciolo ▶ VI germogliare; (*flower*) sbocciare

Budapest [bjuːdəˈpɛst] N Budapest *f*

Buddha [ˈbudə] N Budda *m*

Buddhism [ˈbudɪzəm] N buddismo

Buddhist [ˈbudɪst] ADJ, N buddista (*mf*)

budding [ˈbʌdɪŋ] ADJ (*flower*) in boccio; (*poet etc*) in erba

buddy [ˈbʌdɪ] N (*US*) compagno

budge [bʌdʒ] VT scostare; (*fig*) smuovere ▶ VI spostarsi; smuoversi

budgerigar [ˈbʌdʒərɪgɑːʳ] N pappagallino

budget [ˈbʌdʒɪt] N bilancio preventivo ▶ VI: **to ~ for sth** fare il bilancio per qc; **I'm on a tight ~** devo contare la lira; **she works out her ~ every month** fa il preventivo delle spese ogni mese

budgie [ˈbʌdʒɪ] N = **budgerigar**

Buenos Aires [ˈbwɛɪnɔsˈaɪrɪz] N Buenos Aires *f*

buff [bʌf] ADJ color camoscio *inv* ▶ N (*col: enthusiast*) appassionato(-a)

buffalo [ˈbʌfələu] (*pl ~ or* **buffaloes**) N bufalo; (*US*) bisonte *m*

buffer [ˈbʌfəʳ] N respingente *m*; (*Comput*) memoria tampone, buffer *m inv* ▶ VI (*Comput*) fare il buffering, trasferire nella memoria tampone

buffering [ˈbʌfərɪŋ] N buffering *m inv*, trasferimento nella memoria tampone

buffer state N stato cuscinetto

buffer zone N zona *f* cuscinetto *inv*

buffet N [ˈbufeɪ] (*food, BRIT: bar*) buffet *m inv* ▶ VT [ˈbʌfɪt] sferzare; urtare

459

buffet car N (*Brit Rail*) ≈ servizio ristoro

buffet lunch N pranzo in piedi

buffoon [bəˈfuːn] N buffone *m*

bug [bʌg] N (*insect*) cimice *f*; (: *gen*) insetto; (*fig*: *germ*) virus *m inv*; (*spy device*) microfono spia; (*Comput*) bug *m inv*, errore *m* nel programma ▶ VT mettere sotto controllo; (*room*) installare microfoni spia in; (*annoy*) scocciare; **I've got the travel ~** (*fig*) mi è presa la mania dei viaggi

bugbear [ˈbʌgbɛəʳ] N spauracchio

bugger [ˈbʌgəʳ] (*col!*) N bastardo (!) ▶ VI: **~ off!** vaffanculo! (!) ▶ VT: **~ (it)!** merda! (!)

buggy [ˈbʌgɪ] N (*baby buggy*) passeggino

bugle [ˈbjuːgl] N tromba

build [bɪld] (*pt, pp* **built** [bɪlt]) N (*of person*) corporatura ▶ VT costruire
▶ **build on** VT FUS (*fig*) prendere il via da
▶ **build up** VT (*establish*: *business*) costruire; (: *reputation*) fare, consolidare; (*increase*: *production*) allargare, incrementare; **don't ~ your hopes up too soon** non sperarci troppo

builder [ˈbɪldəʳ] N costruttore(-trice)

building [ˈbɪldɪŋ] N costruzione *f*; edificio; (*also*: **building trade**) edilizia

building contractor N costruttore(-trice), imprenditore(-trice) (edile)

building industry N industria edilizia

building site N cantiere *m* di costruzione

building society N società immobiliare e finanziaria

Le **building societies** sono società immobiliari e finanziarie che forniscono anche numerosi servizi bancari ai clienti che vi investono i risparmi e, in particolare, concedono mutui per l'acquisto della casa.

building trade N = **building industry**

build-up [ˈbɪldʌp] N (*of gas etc*) accumulo; (*publicity*): **to give sb/sth a good ~** fare buona pubblicità a qn/qc

built [bɪlt] PT, PP *of* **build**; **well-built** robusto(-a)

built-in [ˈbɪltˈɪn] ADJ (*cupboard*) a muro; (*device*) incorporato(-a)

built-up area [ˈbɪltʌp-] N abitato

bulb [bʌlb] N (*Bot*) bulbo; (*Elec*) lampadina

bulbous [ˈbʌlbəs] ADJ bulboso(-a)

Bulgaria [bʌlˈgɛərɪə] N Bulgaria

Bulgarian [bʌlˈgɛərɪən] ADJ bulgaro(-a) ▶ N bulgaro(-a); (*Ling*) bulgaro

bulge [bʌldʒ] N rigonfiamento; (*in birth rate*, *sales*) punta ▶ VI essere protuberante *or* rigonfio(-a); **to be bulging with** essere pieno(-a) *or* zeppo(-a) di

bulimia [bəˈlɪmɪə] N bulimia

bulimic [bjuːˈlɪmɪk] ADJ, N bulimico(-a)

bulk [bʌlk] N massa, volume *m*; **the ~ of** il grosso di; **(to buy) in ~** (comprare) in grande quantità; (*Comm*) (comprare) all'ingrosso

bulk buying N acquisto di merce in grande quantità

bulk carrier N grossa nave *f* da carico

bulkhead [ˈbʌlkhɛd] N paratia

bulky [ˈbʌlkɪ] ADJ grosso(-a); voluminoso(-a)

bull [bul] N toro; (*male elephant, whale*) maschio; (*Stock Exchange*) rialzista *mf*; (*Rel*) bolla (papale)

bulldog [ˈbuldɔg] N bulldog *m inv*

bulldoze [ˈbuldəuz] VT aprire *or* spianare col bulldozer; **I was bulldozed into doing it** (*fig*: *col*) mi ci hanno costretto con la prepotenza

bulldozer [ˈbuldəuzəʳ] N bulldozer *m inv*

bullet [ˈbulɪt] N pallottola

bulletin [ˈbulɪtɪn] N bollettino

bulletin board N (*Comput*) bulletin board *m inv*

bullet point N punto; **bullet points** elenco *sg* puntato

bullet-proof [ˈbulɪtpruːf] ADJ a prova di proiettile; **~ vest** giubbotto antiproiettile

bullfight [ˈbulfaɪt] N corrida

bullfighter [ˈbulfaɪtəʳ] N torero(-a)

bullfighting [ˈbulfaɪtɪŋ] N tauromachia

bullion [ˈbuljən] N oro *or* argento in lingotti

bullock [ˈbulək] N giovenco

bullring [ˈbulrɪŋ] N arena (per corride)

bull's-eye [ˈbulzaɪ] N centro del bersaglio

bullshit [ˈbulʃɪt] (*col!*) EXCL, N stronzate *fpl* (!)
▶ VI raccontare stronzate (!) ▶ VT raccontare stronzate a (!)

bully [ˈbulɪ] N prepotente *m* ▶ VT angariare; (*frighten*) intimidire

bullying [ˈbulɪŋ] N prepotenze *fpl*

bum [bʌm] N (*col*: *backside*) culo(-a); (: *tramp*) vagabondo(-a); (: *US*: *idler*) fannullone(-a)
▶ **bum around** VI (*col*) fare il vagabondo

bumblebee [ˈbʌmblbiː] N (*Zool*) bombo

bumf [bʌmf] N (*col*: *forms etc*) scartoffie *fpl*

bump [bʌmp] N (*blow*) colpo; (*in car*) piccolo tamponamento; (*jolt*) scossa; (*noise*) botto; (*on road etc*) protuberanza; (*on head*) bernoccolo ▶ VT battere; (*car*) urtare, sbattere
▶ **bump along** VI procedere sobbalzando
▶ **bump into** VT FUS scontrarsi con; (*col*: *meet*) imbattersi in, incontrare per caso

bumper [ˈbʌmpəʳ] N (*Brit*) paraurti *m inv* ▶ ADJ: **~ harvest** raccolto eccezionale

bumper cars NPL (*US*) autoscontri *mpl*

bumph [bʌmf] N = **bumf**

bumptious [ˈbʌmpʃəs] ADJ presuntuoso(-a)

bumpy [ˈbʌmpɪ] ADJ (*road*) dissestato(-a); (*journey, flight*) movimentato(-a)

bun [bʌn] N focaccia; (*of hair*) crocchia

bunch [bʌntʃ] N (*of flowers, keys*) mazzo; (*of bananas*) casco; (*of people*) gruppo; **~ of grapes**

grappolo d'uva ■ **bunches** NPL (*in hair*) codine *fpl*

bundle [ˈbʌndl] N fascio ▸ VT (*also:* **bundle up**) legare in un fascio; (*put:*) **to ~ sth/sb into** spingere qc/qn in
▸ **bundle off** VT (*person*) mandare via in gran fretta
▸ **bundle out** VT far uscire (senza tante cerimonie)

bun fight N (BRIT *col*) tè *m inv* (*ricevimento*)

bung [bʌŋ] N tappo ▸ VT (BRIT: *throw: also:* **bung into**) buttare; (*: also:* **bung up:** *pipe, hole*) tappare, otturare; **my nose is bunged up** (*col*) ho il naso otturato

bungalow [ˈbʌŋgələu] N bungalow *m inv*

bungee jumping [ˈbʌndʒiːˈdʒʌmpɪŋ] N *salto nel vuoto da ponti, grattacieli ecc con un cavo fissato alla caviglia*

bungle [ˈbʌŋgl] VT abborracciare

bunion [ˈbʌnjən] N callo (al piede)

bunk [bʌŋk] N cuccetta
▸ **bunk off** VI (BRIT *col*): **to ~ off school** marinare la scuola; **I'll ~ off at 3 this afternoon** oggi me la filo dal lavoro alle 3

bunk beds NPL letti *mpl* a castello

bunker [ˈbʌŋkəʳ] N (*coal store*) ripostiglio per il carbone; (*Mil, Golf*) bunker *m inv*

bunny [ˈbʌnɪ] N (*also:* **bunny rabbit**) coniglietto

bunny girl N coniglietta

bunny hill N (US *Ski*) pista per principianti

bunting [ˈbʌntɪŋ] N pavesi *mpl*, bandierine *fpl*

buoy [bɔɪ] N boa
▸ **buoy up** VT tenere a galla; (*fig*) sostenere

buoyancy [ˈbɔɪənsɪ] N (*of ship*) galleggiabilità

buoyant [ˈbɔɪənt] ADJ galleggiante; (*fig*) vivace; (*Comm: market*) sostenuto(-a); (*: prices, currency*) stabile

burden [ˈbəːdn] N carico, fardello ▸ VT caricare; (*oppress*) opprimere; **to ~ sb with** caricare qn di; **to be a ~ to sb** essere di peso a qn

bureau [ˈbjuərəu] (*pl* **bureaux** [-z]) N (BRIT: *writing desk*) scrivania; (US: *chest of drawers*) cassettone *m*; (*office*) ufficio, agenzia

bureaucracy [bjuəˈrɔkrəsɪ] N burocrazia

bureaucrat [ˈbjuərəkræt] N burocrate *mf*

bureaucratic [bjuərəˈkrætɪk] ADJ burocratico(-a)

bureau de change [-dəˈʃɑ̃ʒ] (*pl* **bureaux de change**) N cambiavalute *m inv*

bureaux [bjuəˈrəuz] NPL *of* **bureau**

burgeon [ˈbəːdʒən] VI svilupparsi rapidamente

burger [ˈbəːgəʳ] N hamburger *m inv*

burglar [ˈbəːgləʳ] N scassinatore(-trice)

burglar alarm N (allarme *m*) antifurto *m inv*

burglarize [ˈbəːgləraɪz] VT (US) svaligiare

burglary [ˈbəːglərɪ] N furto con scasso

burgle [ˈbəːgl] VT svaligiare

Burgundy [ˈbəːgəndɪ] N Borgogna

burial [ˈbɛrɪəl] N sepoltura

burial ground N cimitero

burkha [ˈbəːkə] N burqa *m inv*

Burkina Faso [baːˈkiːnəˈfæsəu] N Burkina Faso *f*

burly [ˈbəːlɪ] ADJ robusto(-a)

Burma [ˈbəːmə] N Birmania; *see* **Myanmar**

Burmese [bəːˈmiːz] ADJ birmano(-a) ▸ N (*pl inv*) birmano(-a); (*Ling*) birmano

burn [bəːn] (*pt, pp* **burned** [bəːnd] *or* **burnt** [bəːnt]) VT, VI bruciare ▸ N bruciatura, scottatura; (*Med*) ustione *f*; **I've burnt myself!** mi sono bruciato!; **the cigarette burnt a hole in her dress** si è fatta un buco nel vestito con la sigaretta
▸ **burn down** VT distruggere col fuoco
▸ **burn out** VT (*writer etc*): **to ~ o.s. out** esaurirsi

burner [ˈbəːnəʳ] N fornello

burning [ˈbəːnɪŋ] ADJ (*building, forest*) in fiamme; (*sand*) che scotta; (*ambition*) bruciante; (*issue, question*) scottante

burnish [ˈbəːnɪʃ] VT brunire

Burns Night N *vedi nota*

Burns Night è la festa celebrata il 25 gennaio per commemorare la nascita del poeta scozzese Robert Burns (1759–1796). Gli scozzesi festeggiano questa data con una cena, *Burns supper*, il cui piatto principale, l'haggis, viene servito al suono di cornamuse, brindando con whisky. Durante la serata si recitano i poemi di Robert Burns, si pronunciano discorsi alla sua memoria e si canta.

burnt [bəːnt] PT, PP *of* **burn**

burnt sugar N (BRIT) caramello

burp [bəːp] (*col*) N rutto ▸ VI ruttare

burrow [ˈbʌrəu] N tana ▸ VT scavare

bursar [ˈbəːsəʳ] N economo(-a); (BRIT: *student*) borsista *mf*

bursary [ˈbəːsərɪ] N (BRIT) borsa di studio

burst [bəːst] (*pt, pp* **~**) VT far scoppiare *or* esplodere ▸ VI esplodere; (*tyre*) scoppiare ▸ N scoppio; (*also:* **burst pipe**) rottura nel tubo, perdita; **~ of energy/laughter** scoppio d'energia/di risa; **a ~ of applause** uno scroscio d'applausi; **a ~ of speed** uno scatto (di velocità); **~ blood vessel** rottura di un vaso sanguigno; **the river has ~ its banks** il fiume ha rotto gli argini *or* ha straripato; **to ~ into flames/tears** scoppiare in fiamme/lacrime; **to be bursting with** essere pronto a scoppiare di; **to ~ out laughing** scoppiare a ridere; **to ~ open** VI aprirsi improvvisamente; (*door*) spalancarsi
▸ **burst into** VT FUS (*room etc*) irrompere in
▸ **burst out of** VT FUS precipitarsi fuori da

Burundi [bəˈrundɪ] N Burundi *m*

461

bury ['bɛrɪ] VT seppellire; **to ~ one's face in one's hands** nascondere la faccia tra le mani; **to ~ one's head in the sand** (fig) fare (la politica del)lo struzzo; **to ~ the hatchet** (fig) seppellire l'ascia di guerra

bus [bʌs] [pl **buses** ['bʌsɪz]) N autobus m inv

bus boy N (US) aiuto inv cameriere(-a)

bus conductor N autista mf (dell'autobus)

bush [bʊʃ] N cespuglio; (scrub land) macchia; **to beat about the ~** menare il cane per l'aia

bushed [bʊʃt] ADJ (col) distrutto(-a)

bushel ['bʊʃl] N staio

bushfire ['bʊʃfaɪə˕] N grande incendio in aperta campagna

bushy ['bʊʃɪ] ADJ (plant, tail, beard) folto(-a); (eyebrows) irsuto(-a)

busily ['bɪzɪlɪ] ADV con impegno, alacremente

business ['bɪznɪs] N (matter) affare m; (trading) affari mpl; (firm) azienda; (job, duty) lavoro; **to be away on ~** essere andato via per affari; **I'm here on ~** sono qui per affari; **to do ~ with sb** fare affari con qn; **he's in the insurance ~** lavora nel campo delle assicurazioni; **it's none of my ~** questo non mi riguarda; **he means ~** non scherza

business address N indirizzo di lavoro or d'ufficio

business card N biglietto da visita della ditta

business class N (Aviat) business class f

businesslike ['bɪznɪslaɪk] ADJ serio(-a); efficiente

businessman ['bɪznɪsmən] N (irreg) uomo d'affari

business trip N viaggio d'affari

businesswoman ['bɪznɪswʊmən] N (irreg) donna d'affari

busker ['bʌskə˕] N (BRIT) suonatore(-trice) ambulante

bus lane N (BRIT) corsia riservata agli autobus

bus pass N tessera dell'autobus

bus shelter N pensilina (alla fermata dell'autobus)

bus station N stazione f delle corriere, autostazione f

bus stop N fermata d'autobus

bust [bʌst] N (Art) busto; (Anat: bosom) seno ▶ ADJ (col: broken) rotto(-a) ▶ VT (col: Police: arrest) pizzicare, beccare; **to go ~** fallire

bustle ['bʌsl] N movimento, attività ▶ VI darsi da fare

bustling ['bʌslɪŋ] ADJ (person) indaffarato(-a); (town) animato(-a)

bust-up ['bʌstʌp] N (BRIT col) lite f

busty ['bʌstɪ] ADJ (col) tettone(-a)

busy ['bɪzɪ] ADJ occupato(-a); (shop, street) molto frequentato(-a) ▶ VT: **to ~ o.s.** darsi da fare; **he's a ~ man** (normally) è un uomo molto occupato; (temporarily) ha molto da fare, è molto occupato

busybody ['bɪzɪbɔdɪ] N ficcanaso mf

busy signal N (US Tel) segnale m di occupato

---

but [bʌt]

CONJ ma; **I'd love to come, but I'm busy** vorrei tanto venire, ma ho da fare

▶ PREP (apart from, except) eccetto, tranne, meno; **nothing but** nient'altro che; **he was nothing but trouble** non dava altro che guai; **no-one but him** solo lui; **no-one but him can do it** nessuno può farlo tranne lui; **the last but one** (BRIT) il (la) penultimo(-a); **but for you/your help** se non fosse per te/per il tuo aiuto; **anything but that** tutto ma non questo; **anything but finished** tutt'altro che finito

▶ ADV (just, only) solo, soltanto; **she's but a child** è solo una bambina; **had I but known** se solo avessi saputo; **I can but try** tentar non nuoce; **all but finished** quasi finito

---

butane ['bju:teɪn] N (also: **butane gas**) butano

butch [bʊtʃ] ADJ (col: woman: pej) mascolino(-a); (: man) macho inv

butcher ['bʊtʃə˕] N macellaio(-a) ▶ VT macellare; **~'s (shop)** macelleria

butler ['bʌtlə˕] N maggiordomo

butt [bʌt] N (cask) grossa botte f; (thick end) estremità f inv più grossa; (of gun) calcio; (of cigarette) mozzicone m; (BRIT fig: target) oggetto ▶ VT cozzare

▶ **butt in** VI (interrupt) interrompere

butter ['bʌtə˕] N burro ▶ VT imburrare

buttercup ['bʌtəkʌp] N ranuncolo

butter dish N burriera

butterfingers ['bʌtəfɪŋgəz] N (col) mani fpl di ricotta

butterfly ['bʌtəflaɪ] N farfalla; (Swimming: also: **butterfly stroke**) (nuoto a) farfalla

buttocks ['bʌtəks] NPL natiche fpl

button ['bʌtn] N bottone m; (US: badge) distintivo ▶ VT (also: **button up**) abbottonare ▶ VI abbottonarsi

buttonhole ['bʌtnhəʊl] N asola, occhiello ▶ VT (person) attaccar bottone a

buttress ['bʌtrɪs] N contrafforte m

buxom ['bʌksəm] ADJ formoso(-a)

buy [baɪ] (pt, pp **bought** [bɔːt]) VT comprare, acquistare ▶ N acquisto; **a good/bad ~** un buon/cattivo acquisto or affare; **to ~ sb sth/sth from sb** comprare qc per qn/qc da qn; **to ~ sb a drink** offrire da bere a qn

▶ **buy back** VT riprendersi, prendersi indietro

▶ **buy in** VT (BRIT: goods) far provvista di

▶ **buy into** VT FUS (BRIT Comm) acquistare delle azioni di

▶ **buy off** VT (col: bribe) comprare

▶ **buy out** VT (business) rilevare

▶**buy up** VT accaparrare

buyer [ˈbaɪəʳ] N compratore(-trice); **~'s market** mercato favorevole ai compratori

buy-out [ˈbaɪaut] N (*Comm*) *acquisto di una società da parte dei suoi dipendenti*

buzz [bʌz] N ronzio; (*col: phone call*) colpo di telefono ▶VI ronzare ▶VT (*call on intercom*) chiamare al citofono; (: *with buzzer*) chiamare col cicalino; (*Aviat: plane, building*) passare rasente; **my head is buzzing** mi gira la testa
▶**buzz off** VI (*BRIT col*) filare, levarsi di torno

buzzard [ˈbʌzəd] N poiana

buzzer [ˈbʌzəʳ] N cicalino

buzz word N (*col*) termine *m* in voga

---

by [baɪ]

PREP **1** (*referring to cause, agent*) da; **killed by lightning** ucciso da un fulmine; **surrounded by a fence** circondato da uno steccato; **a painting by Picasso** un quadro di Picasso
2 (*referring to method, manner, means*): **by bus/car/train** in autobus/macchina/treno, con l'autobus/la macchina/il treno; **to pay by cheque** pagare con (un) assegno; **by moonlight** al chiaro di luna; **by saving hard, he ...** risparmiando molto, lui ...
3 (*via, through*) per; **we came by Dover** siamo venuti via Dover
4 (*close to, past*) accanto a; **the house by the river** la casa sul fiume; **a holiday by the sea** una vacanza al mare; **she sat by his bed** si sedette accanto al suo letto; **she rushed by me** mi è passata accanto correndo; **I go by the post office every day** passo davanti all'ufficio postale ogni giorno
5 (*not later than*) per, entro; **by 4 o'clock** per *or* entro le 4; **by this time tomorrow** domani a quest'ora; **by the time I got here it was too late** quando sono arrivato era ormai troppo tardi
6 (*during*): **by day/night** di giorno/notte
7 (*amount*) a; **by the kilo** a chili; **paid by the hour** pagato all'ora; **to increase by the hour** aumentare di ora in ora; **one by one** uno per uno; **little by little** a poco a poco
8 (*Math: measure*): **to divide/multiply by 3** dividere/moltiplicare per 3; **a room 3 metres by 4** una stanza di 3 metri per 4; **it's broader by a metre** è un metro più largo, è più largo di un metro
9 (*according to*) per; **to play by the rules** attenersi alle regole; **it's all right by me** per me va bene
10: **(all) by oneself** (tutto-(a)) solo-(a); **he did it (all) by himself** lo ha fatto (tutto) da solo
11: **by the way** a proposito; **this wasn't my idea by the way** tra l'altro l'idea non è stata mia
▶ ADV **1** *see* **go**; **pass** *etc*
2: **by and by** (*in past*) poco dopo; (*in future*) fra breve; **by and large** nel complesso

---

bye [ˈbaɪ], **bye-bye** [ˈbaɪˈbaɪ] EXCL ciao!, arrivederci!

bye-law [ˈbaɪlɔ:] N legge *f* locale

by-election [ˈbaɪlɛkʃən] N (*BRIT*) elezione *f* straordinaria

Byelorussia [bjɛləuˈrʌʃə] N Bielorussia, Belorussia

Byelorussian [bjɛləuˈrʌʃən] ADJ, N = **Belarussian**

bygone [ˈbaɪgɔn] ADJ passato(-a) ▶ N: **let bygones be bygones** mettiamoci una pietra sopra

by-law [ˈbaɪlɔ:] N legge *f* locale

bypass [ˈbaɪpɑ:s] N circonvallazione *f*; (*Med*) by-pass *m inv* ▶ VT fare una deviazione intorno a

by-product [ˈbaɪprɔdʌkt] N sottoprodotto; (*fig*) conseguenza secondaria

byre [ˈbaɪəʳ] N (*BRIT*) stalla

bystander [ˈbaɪstændəʳ] N spettatore(-trice)

byte [baɪt] N (*Comput*) byte *m inv*, bicarattere *m*

byway [ˈbaɪweɪ] N strada secondaria

byword [ˈbaɪwə:d] N: **to be a ~ for** essere sinonimo di

by-your-leave [ˈbaɪjɔ:ˈli:v] N: **without so much as a ~** senza nemmeno chiedere il permesso

Cc

C, c [siː] N (letter) C, c f inv or m inv; (Scol: mark) ≈ 6 (sufficiente); (Mus): **C** do m inv; **C for Charlie** ≈ C come Como

C ABBR (= Celsius, centigrade) C

c. ABBR (= century) sec.; (US etc) = **cent**; (= circa) c

CA ABBR = **Central America**; (US) = **California** ▶ N ABBR (BRIT) = **chartered accountant**

ca. ABBR (= circa) ca

c/a ABBR = **credit account; current account**

CAA N ABBR (BRIT) = **Civil Aviation Authority**; (US: = Civil Aeronautics Authority) organismo di controllo e di sviluppo dell'aviazione civile

CAB N ABBR (BRIT: = Citizens' Advice Bureau) organizzazione per la tutela del consumatore

cab [kæb] N taxi m inv; (of train, truck) cabina; (horsedrawn) carrozza

cabaret ['kæbəreɪ] N cabaret m inv

cabbage ['kæbɪdʒ] N cavolo

cabbie, cabby ['kæbɪ] N (col) tassista mf

cab driver N tassista mf

cabin ['kæbɪn] N capanna; (on ship) cabina

cabin crew N equipaggio

cabin cruiser N cabinato

cabinet ['kæbɪnɪt] N (Pol) consiglio dei ministri; (furniture) armadietto; (also: **display cabinet**) vetrinetta; **cocktail ~** mobile m bar inv

cabinet-maker ['kæbɪnɪt'meɪkə'] N stipettaio

cabinet minister N ministro (membro del Consiglio)

cable ['keɪbl] N cavo; fune f; (Tel) cablogramma m ▶ VT telegrafare

cable-car ['keɪblkɑː'] N funivia

cablegram ['keɪblɡræm] N cablogramma m

cable railway N funicolare f

cable television N televisione f via cavo

cache [kæʃ] N nascondiglio; **a ~ of food** etc un deposito segreto di viveri etc

cackle ['kækl] VI schiamazzare

cactus ['kæktəs] (pl **cacti** [-taɪ]) N cactus m inv

CAD N ABBR (= computer-aided design) progettazione f con l'ausilio dell'elaboratore

caddie ['kædɪ] N caddie m inv

cadet [kə'dɛt] N (Mil) cadetto(-a); **police ~** allievo(-a) poliziotto(-a)

cadge [kædʒ] VT (col) scroccare; **to ~ a meal (off sb)** scroccare un pranzo (a qn)

cadre ['kædrɪ] N quadro

Caesarean, (US) **Cesarean** [siː'zɛərɪən] ADJ: **~ (section)** (taglio) cesareo

CAF ABBR (BRIT: = cost and freight) Caf m

café ['kæfeɪ] N caffè m inv

cafeteria [kæfɪ'tɪərɪə] N self-service m inv

caffein, caffeine ['kæfiːn] N caffeina

cage [keɪdʒ] N gabbia ▶ VT mettere in gabbia

cagey ['keɪdʒɪ] ADJ (col) chiuso(-a); guardingo(-a)

cagoule [kə'guːl] N K-way® m inv

cahoots [kə'huːts] N: **to be in ~ (with sb)** essere in combutta (con qn)

CAI N ABBR (= computer-aided instruction) istruzione f assistita dall'elaboratore

Cairo ['kaɪərəu] N il Cairo

cajole [kə'dʒəul] VT allettare

cake [keɪk] N (large) torta; (small) pasticcino; **~ of soap** saponetta; **it's a piece of ~** (col) è una cosa da nulla; **he wants to have his ~ and eat it (too)** (fig) vuole la botte piena e la moglie ubriaca

caked [keɪkt] ADJ: **~ with** incrostato(-a) di

cake shop N pasticceria

calamitous [kə'læmɪtəs] ADJ disastroso(-a)

calamity [kə'læmɪtɪ] N calamità f inv

calcium ['kælsɪəm] N calcio

calculate ['kælkjuleɪt] VT calcolare; (estimate: chances, effect) valutare
▶ **calculate on** VT FUS: **to ~ on sth/on doing sth** contare su qc/di fare qc

calculated ['kælkjuleɪtɪd] ADJ calcolato(-a), intenzionale; **a ~ risk** un rischio calcolato

calculating ['kælkjuleɪtɪŋ] ADJ calcolatore(-trice)

calculation [kælkju'leɪʃən] N calcolo

calculator ['kælkjuleɪtə'] N calcolatrice f

calculus [ˈkælkjuləs] N calcolo; **integral/differential ~** calcolo integrale/differenziale

calendar [ˈkæləndəʳ] N calendario

calendar year N anno civile

calf [kɑːf] (pl **calves** [kɑːvz]) N (of cow) vitello; (of other animals) piccolo; (also: **calfskin**) (pelle f di) vitello; (Anat) polpaccio

caliber [ˈkælɪbəʳ] N (US) = **calibre**

calibrate [ˈkælɪbreɪt] VT (gun etc) calibrare; (scale of measuring instrument) tarare

calibre, (US) **caliber** [ˈkælɪbəʳ] N calibro

calico [ˈkælɪkəu] N tela grezza, cotone m grezzo; (US) cotonina stampata

California [kælɪˈfɔːnɪə] N California

calipers [ˈkælɪpəz] NPL (US) = **callipers**

call [kɔːl] VT (gen, also Tel) chiamare; (announce: flight) annunciare; (: meeting, strike) indire, proclamare ▶ VI chiamare; (visit: also: **call in, call round**) passare ▶ N (shout) grido, urlo; (visit) visita; (summons: for flight etc) chiamata; (fig: lure) richiamo; (also: **telephone call**) telefonata; **to be called** (person, object) chiamarsi; **to be on ~** essere a disposizione; **to make a ~** telefonare, fare una telefonata; **please give me a ~ at 7** per piacere mi chiami alle 7; **to pay a ~ on sb** fare (una) visita a qn; **there's not much ~ for these items** non c'è molta richiesta di questi articoli; **she's called Jane** si chiama Jane; **who is calling?** (Tel) chi parla?; **London calling** (Radio) qui Londra

▶ **call at** VT FUS (ship) fare scalo a; (train) fermarsi a

▶ **call back** VI (return) ritornare; (Tel) ritelefonare, richiamare ▶ VT (Tel) ritelefonare a, richiamare; **can you ~ back later?** può richiamare più tardi?

▶ **call for** VT FUS (demand: action etc) richiedere; (collect: person) passare a prendere; (: goods) ritirare

▶ **call in** VT (doctor, expert, police) chiamare, far venire

▶ **call off** VT (meeting, race) disdire; (deal) cancellare; (dog) richiamare; **the strike was called off** lo sciopero è stato revocato

▶ **call on** VT FUS (visit) passare da; (request): **to ~ on sb to do** chiedere a qn di fare

▶ **call out** VI (in pain) urlare; (to person) chiamare ▶ VT (doctor, police, troops) chiamare

▶ **call up** VT (Mil) richiamare; (Tel) telefonare a

Callanetics® [kæləˈnɛtɪks] NSG tipo di ginnastica basata sulla ripetizione di piccoli movimenti

callbox [ˈkɔːlbɔks] N (BRIT) cabina telefonica

call centre, (US) **call center** N centro informazioni telefoniche

caller [ˈkɔːləʳ] N persona che chiama; visitatore(-trice); **hold the line, ~!** (Tel) rimanga in linea, signore (or signora)!

call girl N ragazza f squillo inv

call-in [ˈkɔːlɪn] N (US) = **phone-in**

calling [ˈkɔːlɪŋ] N vocazione f

calling card N (US) biglietto da visita

callipers, (US) **calipers** [ˈkælɪpəz] NPL (Med) gambale m; (Math) calibro

callous [ˈkæləs] ADJ indurito(-a), insensibile

callousness [ˈkæləsnɪs] N insensibilità

callow [ˈkæləu] ADJ immaturo(-a)

calm [kɑːm] ADJ calmo(-a) ▶ N calma ▶ VT calmare

▶ **calm down** VI calmarsi ▶ VT calmare

calmly [ˈkɑːmlɪ] ADV con calma

calmness [ˈkɑːmnɪs] N calma

Calor gas® [ˈkæləʳ-] N (BRIT) butano

calorie [ˈkælərɪ] N caloria; **low-calorie product** prodotto a basso contenuto di calorie

calve [kɑːv] VI figliare

calves [kɑːvz] NPL of **calf**

CAM N ABBR (= computer-aided manufacturing) fabbricazione f con l'ausilio dell'elaboratore

camber [ˈkæmbəʳ] N (of road) bombatura

Cambodia [kæmˈbəudʒə] N Cambogia

Cambodian [kæmˈbəudɪən] ADJ, N cambogiano(-a)

camcorder [ˈkæmkɔːdəʳ] N videocamera

came [keɪm] PT of **come**

camel [ˈkæməl] N cammello

cameo [ˈkæmɪəu] N cammeo

camera [ˈkæmərə] N macchina fotografica; (Cine, TV) telecamera; (also: **cinecamera, movie camera**) cinepresa; **in ~** a porte chiuse

cameraman [ˈkæmərəmæn] N (irreg) cameraman m inv

camera phone N telefono cellulare con fotocamera integrata

Cameroon, Cameroun [ˈkæmruːn] N Camerun m

camouflage [ˈkæməflɑːʒ] N (feeling) camuffamento; (Mil, Zool) mimetizzazione f ▶ VT (feeling) camuffare; mimetizzare

camp [kæmp] N campeggio; (Mil) campo ▶ VI campeggiare; accamparsi; **to go camping** andare in campeggio ▶ ADJ effeminato(-a)

campaign [kæmˈpeɪn] N (Mil, Pol etc) campagna ▶ VI: **to ~ (for/against)** (also fig) fare una campagna (per/contro)

campaigner [kæmˈpeɪnəʳ] N: **~ for** fautore(-trice) di; **~ against** oppositore(-trice) di

campbed [ˈkæmpˈbɛd] N (BRIT) brandina

camper [ˈkæmpəʳ] N campeggiatore(-trice); (vehicle) camper m inv

campground N (US) campeggio

camping [ˈkæmpɪŋ] N campeggio; **to go ~** andare in campeggio

camp site [ˈkæmpsaɪt], **camping site** N campeggio

campus [ˈkæmpəs] N campus m inv

camshaft [ˈkæmʃɑːft] N albero a camme

can¹ [kæn] N (*of milk*) scatola; (*of oil*) bidone *m*; (*of water*) tanica; (*tin*) scatola ▶ VT mettere in scatola; **a ~ of beer** una lattina di birra; **to carry the ~** (*BRIT col*) prendere la colpa

---

can² [kæn]

(*negative* **cannot** [ˈkænɔt], **can't** [kɑːnt], *pt, conditional* **could** [kud]) AUX VB 1 (*be able to*) potere; **I can't go any further** non posso andare oltre; **you can do it if you try** sei in grado di farlo - basta provarci; **I'll help you all I can** ti aiuterò come potrò; **I can't see you** non ti vedo; **can you hear me?** mi senti?, riesci a sentirmi? 2 (*know how to*) sapere, essere capace di; **I can swim** so nuotare; **can you speak French?** parla francese? 3 (*may*) potere; **could I have a word with you?** posso parlare un momento? 4 (*expressing disbelief, puzzlement etc*): **it can't be true!** non può essere vero!; **what CAN he want?** cosa può mai volere? 5 (*expressing possibility, suggestion etc*): **he could be in the library** può darsi che sia in biblioteca; **they could have forgotten** potrebbero essersene dimenticati; **she could have been delayed** può aver avuto un contrattempo

---

can is not translated with Italian verbs such as **vedere**, **sentire**, **ricordare** and **parlare**.
I can't hear you. **Non ti sento.**
I can't remember. **Non ricordo.**
Can you speak French? **Parli francese?**

Canada [ˈkænədə] N Canada *m*

Canadian [kəˈneɪdɪən] ADJ, N canadese (*mf*)

canal [kəˈnæl] N canale *m*

canary [kəˈnɛərɪ] N canarino

Canary Islands, Canaries [kəˈnɛərɪz] NPL: **the ~** le (isole) Canarie

Canberra [ˈkænbərə] N Camberra

cancel [ˈkænsəl] VT annullare; (*train*) sopprimere; (*cross out*) cancellare
▶ **cancel out** VT (*Math*) semplificare; (*fig*) annullare; **they ~ each other out** (*also fig*) si annullano a vicenda

cancellation [kænsəˈleɪʃən] N annullamento; soppressione *f*; cancellazione *f*; (*Tourism*) prenotazione *f* annullata

cancer [ˈkænsə'] N cancro; **C~** (*sign*) Cancro; **to be C~** essere del Cancro

cancerous [ˈkænsərəs] ADJ canceroso(-a)

cancer patient N malato(-a) di cancro

cancer research N ricerca sul cancro

c&f ABBR (*BRIT: = cost and freight*) Caf *m*

candid [ˈkændɪd] ADJ onesto(-a)

candidacy [ˈkændɪdəsɪ] N candidatura

candidate [ˈkændɪdeɪt] N candidato(-a)

candidature [ˈkændɪdətʃə'] N (*BRIT*) = **candidacy**

candied [ˈkændɪd] ADJ candito(-a); **~ apple** (*US*) mela caramellata

candle [ˈkændl] N candela; (*in church*) cero

candlelight [ˈkændlˈlaɪt] N: **by ~** a lume di candela

candlestick [ˈkændlstɪk] N (*also:* **candle holder**) bugia; (*bigger, ornate*) candeliere *m*

candour, (*US*) **candor** [ˈkændə'] N sincerità

C & W N ABBR = **country and western (music)**

candy [ˈkændɪ] N zucchero candito; (*US*) caramella; caramelle *fpl*

candy bar N (*US*) *lungo biscotto, in genere ricoperto di cioccolata*

candy-floss [ˈkændɪflɔs] N (*BRIT*) zucchero filato

candy store N (*US*) ≈ pasticceria

cane [keɪn] N canna; (*for baskets, chairs etc*) bambù *m*; (*Scol*) verga; (*for walking*) bastone *m* (da passeggio) ▶ VT (*BRIT Scol*) punire a colpi di verga

canine [ˈkænaɪn] ADJ canino(-a)

canister [ˈkænɪstə'] N scatola metallica

cannabis [ˈkænəbɪs] N canapa indiana

canned [ˈkænd] ADJ (*food*) in scatola; (*col: recorded: music*) registrato(-a); (*BRIT col: drunk*) sbronzo(-a); (*US col: worker*) licenziato(-a)

cannibal [ˈkænɪbəl] N cannibale *mf*

cannibalism [ˈkænɪbəlɪzəm] N cannibalismo

cannon [ˈkænən] (*pl ~ or* **cannons**) N (*gun*) cannone *m*

cannonball [ˈkænənbɔːl] N palla di cannone

cannon fodder N carne *f* da macello

cannot [ˈkænɔt] = **can not**

canny [ˈkænɪ] ADJ furbo(-a)

canoe [kəˈnuː] N canoa; (*Sport*) canotto

canoeing [kəˈnuːɪŋ] N (*sport*) canottaggio

canoeist [kəˈnuːɪst] N canottiere *m*

canon [ˈkænən] N (*clergyman*) canonico; (*standard*) canone *m*

canonize [ˈkænənaɪz] VT canonizzare

can opener [-əupnə'] N apriscatole *m inv*

canopy [ˈkænəpɪ] N baldacchino

cant [kænt] N gergo ▶ VT inclinare ▶ VI inclinarsi

can't [kænt] = **can not**

cantankerous [kænˈtæŋkərəs] ADJ stizzoso(-a)

canteen [kænˈtiːn] N mensa; (*BRIT: of cutlery*) portaposate *m inv*

La parola inglese **canteen** non vuol dire *cantina*.

canter [ˈkæntə'] N piccolo galoppo ▶ VI andare al piccolo galoppo

cantilever [ˈkæntɪliːvə'] N trave *f* a sbalzo

canvas [ˈkænvəs] N tela; **under ~** (*camping*) sotto la tenda; (*Naut*) sotto la vela

canvass [ˈkænvəs] VI (*Pol*): **to ~ for** raccogliere voti per ▶ VT (*Comm: district*) fare un'indagine di mercato in; (*: citizens, opinions*) fare un sondaggio di; (*Pol*: *district*) fare un giro elettorale di; (: *person*) fare propaganda elettorale a

canvasser ['kænvəsə^r] N (*Comm*) agente *mf* viaggiatore, piazzista *mf*; (*Pol*) propagandista *mf* (elettorale)

canvassing ['kænvəsɪŋ] N sollecitazione *f*

canyon ['kænjən] N canyon *m inv*

CAP N ABBR (= *Common Agricultural Policy*) PAC *f*

cap [kæp] N (*Football*: *hat*) berretto; (*of pen*) coperchio; (*of bottle*) tappo; (*for swimming*) cuffia; (*BRIT*: *contraceptive*: *also*: **Dutch cap**) diaframma *m* ▶ VT tappare; (*outdo*) superare; (*limit*) fissare un tetto (a); **capped with** ricoperto(-a) di; **and to ~ it all, he ...** (*BRIT*) e per completare l'opera, lui ...

capability [keɪpə'bɪlɪtɪ] N capacità *f inv*, abilità *f inv*

capable ['keɪpəbl] ADJ capace; **~ of** capace di; suscettibile di

capacious [kə'peɪʃəs] ADJ capace

capacity [kə'pæsɪtɪ] N capacità *f inv*; (*of lift etc*) capienza; **in his ~ as** nella sua qualità di; **to work at full ~** lavorare al massimo delle proprie capacità; **this work is beyond my ~** questo lavoro supera le mie possibilità; **filled to ~** pieno zeppo; **in an advisory ~** a titolo consultivo

cape [keɪp] N (*garment*) cappa; (*Geo*) capo

Cape of Good Hope N Capo di Buona Speranza

caper ['keɪpə^r] N (*Culin*: *gen pl*) cappero; (*leap*) saltello; (*escapade*) birichinata; (*prank*) scherzetto

Cape Town N Città del Capo

Cape Verde [keɪp'və:d] N Capo Verde

capita ['kæpɪtə] *see* **per capita**

capital ['kæpɪtl] N (*also*: **capital city**) capitale *f*; (*money*) capitale *m*; (*also*: **capital letter**) (lettera) maiuscola

> Use **la capitale** for a city, e.g. *the capital of Wales* **la capitale del Galles**. Use **il capitale** to refer to money. And use **la maiuscola** to refer to a letter of the alphabet.

capital account N conto capitale

capital allowance N ammortamento fiscale

capital assets NPL capitale *m* fisso

capital expenditure N spese *fpl* in capitale

capital gains tax N imposta sulla plusvalenza

capital goods N beni *mpl* d'investimento, beni *mpl* capitali

capital-intensive ['kæpɪtlɪn'tɛnsɪv] ADJ ad alta intensità di capitale

capitalism ['kæpɪtəlɪzəm] N capitalismo

capitalist ['kæpɪtəlɪst] ADJ, N capitalista (*mf*)

capitalize ['kæpɪtəlaɪz] VT (*provide with capital*) capitalizzare

▶ **capitalize on** VT FUS (*fig*) trarre vantaggio da

capital punishment N pena capitale

capital transfer tax N (*BRIT*) imposta sui trasferimenti di capitali

Capitol ['kæpɪtl] N: **the ~** il Campidoglio; *vedi nota*

> Il **Capitol** è la sede del Congresso degli Stati Uniti, situato sull'omonimo colle, *Capitol Hill*, a Washington. Il termine *Capitol* viene usato per indicare il Congresso stesso.

capitulate [kə'pɪtjuleɪt] VI capitolare

capitulation [kəpɪtju'leɪʃən] N capitolazione *f*

capricious [kə'prɪʃəs] ADJ capriccioso(-a)

Capricorn ['kæprɪkɔ:n] N Capricorno; **to be ~** essere del Capricorno

caps [kæps] ABBR = **capital letters**

capsize [kæp'saɪz] VT capovolgere ▶ VI capovolgersi

capstan ['kæpstən] N argano

capsule ['kæpsju:l] N capsula

Capt. ABBR (= *captain*) Cap.

captain ['kæptɪn] N capitano ▶ VT capitanare

caption ['kæpʃən] N leggenda

captivate ['kæptɪveɪt] VT avvincere

captive ['kæptɪv] ADJ, N prigioniero(-a)

captivity [kæp'tɪvɪtɪ] N prigionia; **in ~** (*animal*) in cattività

captor ['kæptə^r] N (*lawful*) chi ha catturato; (*unlawful*) rapitore(-trice)

capture ['kæptʃə^r] VT catturare, prendere; (*attention*) attirare; (*Comput*) registrare ▶ N cattura; (*data capture*) registrazione *f* o rilevazione *f* di dati

car [kɑ:^r] N macchina, automobile *f*; (*US Rail*) vagone *m*; **by ~** in macchina

Caracas [kə'rækəs] N Caracas *f*

carafe [kə'ræf] N caraffa

carafe wine N (*in restaurant*) ≈ vino sfuso

caramel ['kærəməl] N caramello

carat ['kærət] N carato; **18 ~ gold** oro a 18 carati

caravan ['kærəvæn] N (*BRIT*) roulotte *f inv*; (*of camels*) carovana

caravan site N (*BRIT*) campeggio per roulotte

caraway ['kærəweɪ] N: **~ seed** seme *m* di cumino

carb [kɑ:b] N (*col*) cibo *m* ad alto contenuto di carboidrati

carbohydrate [kɑ:bəu'haɪdreɪt] N carboidrato

carbolic acid [kɑ:'bɔlɪk-] N acido fenico, fenolo

car bomb N ordigno esplosivo collocato in una macchina; **a ~ went off yesterday** ieri è esplosa un'autobomba

carbon ['kɑ:bən] N carbonio

carbonated ['kɑ:bəneɪtəd] ADJ (*drink*) gassato(-a)

carbon copy N copia *f* carbone *inv*

carbon credit N quota *f* di emissione

carbon dioxide [-daɪ'ɔksaɪd] N diossido di carbonio

carbon footprint N impronta di carbonio

carbon monoxide [-mɔ'nɔksaɪd] N monossido di carbonio

carbon-neutral ADJ carbon neutral, *ad emissioni zero CO2*

carbon offset N riduzione *f* delle emissioni di gas serra

carbon paper N carta carbone

carbon ribbon N nastro carbonato

carburettor, (US) **carburetor** [kɑ:bju'retəʳ] N carburatore *m*

carcass ['kɑ:kəs] N carcassa

carcinogenic [kɑ:sɪnə'dʒenɪk] ADJ cancerogeno(-a)

card [kɑ:d] N carta; (*thin cardboard*) cartoncino; (*visiting card etc*) biglietto; (*membership card*) tessera; (*Christmas card etc*) cartolina; **to play cards** giocare a carte

cardamom ['kɑ:dəməm] N cardamomo

cardboard ['kɑ:dbɔ:d] N cartone *m*

cardboard box N (scatola di) cartone *m*

cardboard city N *luogo dove dormono in scatole di cartone emarginati senzatetto*

card-carrying member ['kɑ:d'kærɪŋ-] N tesserato(-a)

card game N gioco di carte

cardiac ['kɑ:dɪæk] ADJ cardiaco(-a)

cardigan ['kɑ:dɪgən] N cardigan *m inv*

cardinal ['kɑ:dɪnl] ADJ, N cardinale (*m*)

card index N schedario

cardphone ['kɑ:dfəun] N telefono a scheda (magnetica)

cardsharp ['kɑ:dʃɑ:p] N baro

card vote N (BRIT) voto (palese) per delega

CARE [kɛəʳ] N ABBR = **Cooperative for American Relief Everywhere**

care [kɛəʳ] N cura, attenzione *f*; (*worry*) preoccupazione *f* ▶ VI: **to ~ about** curarsi di; (*thing, idea*) interessarsi di; **would you ~ to/for ...?** le piacerebbe ...?; **I wouldn't ~ to do it** non lo vorrei fare; **in sb's ~** alle cure di qn; **to take ~** fare attenzione; **to take ~ of** curarsi di; (*details, arrangements, bill, problem*) occuparsi di; **I don't ~** non me ne importa; **I couldn't ~ less** non me ne importa un bel niente; **~ of (c/o)** (*on letter*) presso; **"with ~"** "fragile"; **the child has been taken into ~** il bambino è stato preso in custodia

▶ **care for** VT FUS aver cura di; (*like*) voler bene a

> *care* is often translated by **importare**, which is an impersonal verb. This means that in Italian you say *it matters to me* rather than *I care about it.*
> *Of course I care about him.* **Certo che m'importa di lui.**
> *Who cares?* **Chi se ne importa?**

careen [kə'ri:n] VI (*ship*) sbandare ▶ VT carenare

career [kə'rɪəʳ] N carriera; (*occupation*) professione *f* ▶ VI (*also*: **career along**) andare di (gran) carriera

career girl N donna dedita alla carriera

careers officer N consulente *mf* d'orientamento professionale

carefree ['kɛəfri:] ADJ sgombro(-a) di preoccupazioni

careful ['kɛəful] ADJ attento(-a); (*cautious*) cauto(-a); **(be) ~!** attenzione!; **he's very ~ with his money** bada molto alle spese

carefully ['kɛəfəlɪ] ADV con cura; cautamente

caregiver N (US: *professional*) badante *mf*; (*unpaid*) *persona che si prende cura di un parente malato o anziano*

careless ['kɛəlɪs] ADJ negligente; (*remark*) privo(-a) di tatto; (*heedless*) spensierato(-a)

carelessly ['kɛəlɪslɪ] ADV negligentemente; senza tatto; (*without thinking*) distrattamente

carelessness ['kɛəlɪsnɪs] N negligenza; mancanza di tatto

carer ['kɛərəʳ] N *chi si occupa di un familiare anziano o invalido*

caress [kə'rɛs] N carezza ▶ VT accarezzare

caretaker ['kɛəteɪkəʳ] N custode *m*

caretaker government N (BRIT) governo *m* ponte *inv*

car-ferry ['kɑ:fɛrɪ] N traghetto

cargo ['kɑ:gəu] (*pl* **cargoes**) N carico

cargo boat N cargo

cargo plane N aereo di linea da carico

car hire N (BRIT) autonoleggio

Caribbean [kærɪ'bi:ən] ADJ caraibico(-a); **the ~ (Sea)** il Mar dei Caraibi

caricature ['kærɪkətjuəʳ] N caricatura

caring ['kɛərɪŋ] ADJ (*person*) premuroso(-a); (*society, organization*) umanitario(-a)

carnage ['kɑ:nɪdʒ] N carneficina

carnal ['kɑ:nl] ADJ carnale

carnation [kɑ:'neɪʃən] N garofano

carnival ['kɑ:nɪvəl] N (*public celebration*) carnevale *m*; (US: *funfair*) luna park *m inv*

carnivorous [kɑ:'nɪvərəs] ADJ carnivoro(-a)

carol ['kærəl] N: **(Christmas) ~** canto di Natale

carouse [kə'rauz] VI far baldoria

carousel [kærə'sel] N (US) giostra

carp [kɑ:p] N (*fish*) carpa
▶ **carp at** VT FUS trovare a ridire su

car park N (BRIT) parcheggio

carpenter ['kɑ:pɪntəʳ] N carpentiere *m*

carpentry ['kɑ:pɪntrɪ] N carpenteria

carpet ['kɑ:pɪt] N tappeto; (BRIT: *fitted carpet*) moquette *f inv* ▶ VT coprire con tappeto

carpet bombing N bombardamento a tappeto

carpet slippers NPL pantofole *fpl*

carpet sweeper N scopatappeti *m inv*
car phone N telefonino per auto
car rental N (*US*) autonoleggio
carriage [ˈkærɪdʒ] N vettura; (*of goods*) trasporto; (*of typewriter*) carrello; (*bearing*) portamento; **~ forward** porto assegnato; **~ free** franco di porto; **~ paid** porto pagato
carriage return N (*on typewriter etc*) leva (*or* tasto) del ritorno a capo
carriageway [ˈkærɪdʒweɪ] N (*BRIT: part of road*) carreggiata
carrier [ˈkærɪəʳ] N (*of disease*) portatore(-trice); (*Comm*) impresa di trasporti; (*Naut*) portaerei *f inv*
carrier bag N (*BRIT*) sacchetto
carrier pigeon N colombo viaggiatore
carrion [ˈkærɪən] N carogna
carrot [ˈkærət] N carota
carry [ˈkærɪ] VT (*person*) portare; (*vehicle*) trasportare; (*a motion, bill*) far passare; (*involve: responsibilities etc*) comportare; (*Med*) essere portatore(-trice) di; (*Comm: goods*) tenere; (*: interest*) avere; (*Math: figure*) riportare ▶ VI (*sound*) farsi sentire; **this loan carries 10% interest** questo prestito è sulla base di un interesse del 10%; **to be** *or* **get carried away** (*fig*) farsi trascinare
▶ **carry forward** VT (*Math, Comm*) riportare
▶ **carry on** VI: **to ~ on with sth/doing** continuare qc/a fare ▶ VT mandare avanti
▶ **carry out** VT (*orders*) eseguire; (*investigation*) svolgere; (*accomplish etc: plan*) realizzare; (*perform, implement: idea, threat*) mettere in pratica
carrycot [ˈkærɪkɔt] N (*BRIT*) culla portabile
carry-on [kærɪˈɔn] N (*col: fuss*) casino, confusione *f*; (*: annoying behaviour*): **I've had enough of your ~!** mi hai proprio scocciato!
cart [kɑːt] N carro ▶ VT (*col*) trascinare, scarrozzare
carte blanche [ˈkɑːtˈblɔ̃ʃ] N: **to give sb ~** dare carta bianca a qn
cartel [kɑːˈtɛl] N (*Comm*) cartello
cartilage [ˈkɑːtɪlɪdʒ] N cartilagine *f*
cartographer [kɑːˈtɔgrəfəʳ] N cartografo(-a)
cartography [kɑːˈtɔgrəfɪ] N cartografia
carton [ˈkɑːtən] N (*box*) scatola di cartone; (*of yogurt*) cartone *m*; (*of cigarettes*) stecca
cartoon [kɑːˈtuːn] N (*in newspaper etc*) vignetta; (*comic strip*) fumetto; (*Cine, TV*) cartone *m* animato; (*Art*) cartone
cartoonist [kɑːˈtuːnɪst] N vignettista *mf*; cartonista *mf*
cartridge [ˈkɑːtrɪdʒ] N (*for gun, pen*) cartuccia; (*for camera*) caricatore *m*; (*music tape*) cassetta; (*of record player*) testina
cartwheel [ˈkɑːtwiːl] N: **to turn a ~** (*Sport etc*) fare la ruota
carve [kɑːv] VT (*meat*) trinciare; (*wood, stone*) intagliare

▶ **carve up** VT (*meat*) tagliare; (*fig: country*) suddividere
carving [ˈkɑːvɪŋ] N (*in wood etc*) scultura
carving knife N trinciante *m*
car wash N lavaggio auto
Casablanca [kæsəˈblæŋkə] N Casablanca
cascade [kæsˈkeɪd] N cascata ▶ VI scendere a cascata
case [keɪs] N caso; (*Law*) causa, processo; (*box*) scatola; (*BRIT: also:* **suitcase**) valigia; (*Typ*): **lower/upper ~** (carattere *m*) minuscolo/maiuscolo; **to have a good ~** avere pretese legittime; **there's a strong ~ for reform** ci sono validi argomenti a favore della riforma; **in ~ of** in caso di; **in ~ he** caso mai lui; **in any ~** in ogni caso; **just in ~** in caso di bisogno
case history N (*Med*) cartella clinica
case-sensitive [ˈkeɪsˈsensɪtɪv] ADJ (*Comput*) sensibile alle maiuscole o minuscole
case study N studio di un caso
cash [kæʃ] N (*coins, notes*) soldi *mpl*, denaro ▶ VT incassare; **I haven't got any ~** non ho contanti; **to pay (in) ~** pagare in contanti; **to be short of ~** essere a corto di soldi; **~ with order/ on delivery (COD)** (*Comm*) pagamento all'ordinazione/alla consegna
▶ **cash in** VT (*insurance policy etc*) riscuotere, riconvertire
▶ **cash in on** VT FUS: **to ~ in on sth** sfruttare qc
cash account N conto *m* cassa *inv*
cash-and-carry [ˈkæʃəndˈkærɪ] N cash and carry *m inv*
cashback N (*discount*) sconto; (*at supermarket etc*) *anticipo di contanti ottenuto presso la cassa di un negozio tramite una carta di debito*
cashbook [ˈkæʃbuk] N giornale *m* di cassa
cash box N cassetta per il denaro spicciolo
cash card N (*BRIT*) carta per prelievi automatici
cash desk N (*BRIT*) cassa
cash discount N sconto per contanti
cash dispenser N (*BRIT*) sportello automatico
cashew [kæˈʃuː] N (*also:* **cashew nut**) anacardio
cash flow N cash-flow *m inv*, liquidità *f inv*
cashier [kæˈʃɪəʳ] N cassiere(-a) ▶ VT (*esp Mil*) destituire
cashless [ˈkæʃlɪs] ADJ cashless *inv*, senza contanti
cashmere [ˈkæʃmɪəʳ] N cachemire *m*
cash payment N pagamento in contanti
cash point N sportello bancario automatico, Bancomat® *m inv*
cash price N prezzo per contanti
cash register N registratore *m* di cassa
cash sale N vendita per contanti
casing [ˈkeɪsɪŋ] N rivestimento
casino [kəˈsiːnəu] N casinò *m inv*

C

cask [kɑːsk] N botte f

casket [ˈkɑːskɪt] N cofanetto; (US: *coffin*) bara

Caspian Sea [ˈkæspɪən-] N: **the ~** il mar Caspio

casserole [ˈkæsərəul] N casseruola; **chicken ~** pollo in casseruola

cassette [kæˈsɛt] N cassetta

cassette deck N piastra di registrazione

cassette player N riproduttore *m* a cassette

cassette recorder N registratore *m* a cassette

cast [kɑːst] (*pt, pp* **~**) VT (*throw*) gettare; (*shed*) perdere; spogliarsi di; (*metal*) gettare, fondere; (*Theat*): **to ~ sb as Hamlet** scegliere qn per la parte di Amleto ▶ N (*Theat*) cast *m inv*; (*mould*) forma; (*also: plaster cast*) ingessatura; **to ~ one's vote** votare, dare il voto
▶ **cast aside** VT (*reject*) mettere da parte
▶ **cast off** VI (*Naut*) salpare ▶ VT (*Naut*) disormeggiare; (*Knitting*) diminuire, calare
▶ **cast on** (*Knitting*) VT avviare ▶ VI avviare (le maglie)

castanets [kæstəˈnɛts] NPL castagnette *fpl*

castaway [ˈkɑːstəwəɪ] N naufrago(-a)

caste [kɑːst] N casta

caster sugar [ˈkɑːstə-] N (BRIT) zucchero semolato

casting vote [ˈkɑːstɪŋ-] N (BRIT) voto decisivo

cast iron N ghisa ▶ ADJ: **cast-iron** (*lit*) di ghisa; (*fig: will, alibi*) di ferro, d'acciaio

castle [ˈkɑːsl] N castello; (*fortified*) rocca

castor [ˈkɑːstəʳ] N (*wheel*) rotella

castor oil N olio di ricino

castrate [kæsˈtreɪt] VT castrare

casual [ˈkæʒjul] ADJ (*chance*) casuale, fortuito(-a); (*irregular: work etc*) avventizio(-a); (*unconcerned*) noncurante, indifferente; **~ wear** casual *m*

casual labour N manodopera avventizia

casually [ˈkæʒjulɪ] ADV con disinvoltura; (*by chance*) casualmente

casualty [ˈkæʒjultɪ] N ferito(-a); (*dead*) morto(-a), vittima; (*Med: department*) pronto soccorso; **heavy casualties** grosse perdite *fpl*

casualty ward N (BRIT) pronto soccorso (*reparto*)

cat [kæt] N gatto

catacombs [ˈkætəkuːmz] NPL catacombe *fpl*

catalogue, (US) **catalog** [ˈkætələɔg] N catalogo ▶ VT catalogare

catalyst [ˈkætəlɪst] N catalizzatore *m*

catalytic converter [kætəˈlɪtɪkkənˈvəːtəʳ] N marmitta catalitica, catalizzatore *m*

catapult [ˈkætəpʌlt] N catapulta; fionda

cataract [ˈkætərækt] N (*also Med*) cateratta

catarrh [kəˈtɑːʳ] N catarro

catastrophe [kəˈtæstrəfɪ] N catastrofe *f*

catastrophic [kætəˈstrɔfɪk] ADJ catastrofico(-a)

catcall [ˈkætkɔːl] N (*at meeting etc*) fischio

catch [kætʃ] (*pt, pp* **caught** [kɔːt]) VT prendere; (*train, thief, cold*) acchiappare; (*ball*) afferrare; (*person: by surprise*) sorprendere; (*understand*) comprendere; (*get entangled*) impigliare; (*attention*) attirare; (*comment, whisper*) cogliere; (*person*) raggiungere ▶ VI (*fire*) prendere ▶ N (*fish etc caught*) retata; (*of ball*) presa; (*trick*) inganno; (*Tech*) gancio; (*game*) catch *m inv*; **to ~ fire** prendere fuoco; **to ~ sight of** scorgere
▶ **catch on** VI (*become popular*) affermarsi, far presa; (*understand*): **to ~ on (to sth)** capire (qc)
▶ **catch out** VT (*BRIT fig: with trick question*) cogliere in fallo
▶ **catch up** VI mettersi in pari ▶ VT (*also*: **catch up with**) raggiungere

catching [ˈkætʃɪŋ] ADJ (*Med*) contagioso(-a)

catchment area [ˈkætʃmənt-] N (BRIT Scol) circoscrizione *f* scolare; (*Geo*) bacino pluviale

catch phrase N slogan *m inv*; frase *f* fatta

catch-22 [ˈkætʃtwɛntɪˈtuː] N: **it's a ~ situation** non c'è via d'uscita

catchy [ˈkætʃɪ] ADJ orecchiabile

catechism [ˈkætɪkɪzəm] N catechismo

categoric [kætɪˈgɔrɪk], **categorical** [kætɪˈgɔrɪkl] ADJ categorico(-a)

categorize [ˈkætɪgəraɪz] VT categorizzare

category [ˈkætɪgərɪ] N categoria

cater [ˈkeɪtəʳ] VI: **to ~ for** (*BRIT: needs*) provvedere a; (: *readers, consumers*) incontrare i gusti di; (: *Comm: provide food*) provvedere alla ristorazione di

caterer [ˈkeɪtərəʳ] N fornitore(-trice)

catering [ˈkeɪtərɪŋ] N approvvigionamento

catering trade N settore *m* ristoranti

caterpillar [ˈkætəpɪləʳ] N (*Zool*) bruco ▶ CPD (*vehicle*) cingolato(-a); **~ track** cingolo

cat flap N gattaiola

cathedral [kəˈθiːdrəl] N cattedrale *f*, duomo

cathode [ˈkæθəud] N catodo

cathode ray tube N tubo a raggi catodici

Catholic [ˈkæθəlɪk] ADJ, N (*Rel*) cattolico(-a)

catholic [ˈkæθəlɪk] ADJ (*wide-ranging*) universale; aperto(-a); eclettico(-a)

CAT scanner [kæt-] N (*Med: = computerized axial tomography scanner*) (rilevatore *m* per la) TAC *f inv*

Catseye® [ˈkætsˈaɪ] N (BRIT Aut) catarifrangente *m*

catsup [ˈkætsəp] N (US) ketchup *m inv*

cattle [ˈkætl] NPL bestiame *m*, bestie *fpl*

catty [ˈkætɪ] ADJ maligno(-a), dispettoso(-a)

catwalk [ˈkætwɔːk] N passerella

Caucasian [kɔːˈkeɪzɪən] ADJ, N caucasico(-a)

Caucasus [ˈkɔːkəsəs] N Caucaso

caucus [ˈkɔːkəs] N (US Pol) (riunione *f* del) comitato elettorale; (BRIT Pol: *group*) comitato di dirigenti

caught [kɔːt] PT, PP *of* **catch**

cauliflower [ˈkɔlɪflauəʳ] N cavolfiore m

cause [kɔːz] N causa ▸ VT causare; **there is no ~ for concern** non c'è ragione di preoccuparsi; **to ~ sb to do sth** far fare qc a qn; **to ~ sth to be done** far fare qc

causeway [ˈkɔːzweɪ] N strada rialzata

caustic [ˈkɔːstɪk] ADJ caustico(-a)

caution [ˈkɔːʃən] N prudenza; (warning) avvertimento ▸ VT avvertire; ammonire

cautious [ˈkɔːʃəs] ADJ cauto(-a), prudente

cautiously [ˈkɔːʃəslɪ] ADV prudentemente

cautiousness [ˈkɔːʃəsnɪs] N cautela

cavalier [kævəˈlɪəʳ] N (knight) cavaliere m ▸ ADJ (pej: offhand) brusco(-a)

cavalry [ˈkævəlrɪ] N cavalleria

cave [keɪv] N caverna, grotta ▸ VI: **to go caving** fare speleologia
▸ **cave in** VI (roof etc) crollare

caveman [ˈkeɪvmæn] N (irreg) uomo delle caverne

cavern [ˈkævən] N caverna

caviar, caviare [ˈkævɪɑːʳ] N caviale m

cavity [ˈkævɪtɪ] N cavità f inv

cavity wall insulation N isolamento per pareti a intercapedine

cavort [kəˈvɔːt] VI far capriole

cayenne [keɪˈɛn], **cayenne pepper** [keɪˈɛn-] N pepe m di Caienna

CB N ABBR (Brit: = Companion (of the Order) of the Bath) titolo

CBC N ABBR = **Canadian Broadcasting Corporation**

CBE N ABBR (Brit: = Companion (of the Order) of the British Empire) titolo

CBI N ABBR (= Confederation of British Industry) ≈ CONFINDUSTRIA (= Confederazione Generale dell'Industria Italiana)

CC ABBR (Brit) = **county council**

cc ABBR (= cubic centimetre) cc; (on letter etc) = **carbon copy**

CCA N ABBR (US: = Circuit Court of Appeals) corte f d'appello itinerante

CCTV N ABBR (= closed-circuit television) televisione f a circuito chiuso

CCTV camera N telecamera f TVCC

CCU N ABBR (US: = coronary care unit) unità coronarica

CD N ABBR (= compact disk) CD m inv; (player) lettore m CD inv; (Mil: Brit) = **Civil Defence (Corps)**; (: US) = **Civil Defense** ▸ ABBR (Brit: = Corps Diplomatique) C.D.

CD burner N masterizzatore m (di) CD

CDC N ABBR (US) = **center for disease control**

CD-I® N CD-I m inv, compact disc m inv interattivo

CD player N lettore m CD

Cdr. ABBR (= commander) Com

CD-ROM [ˈsiːˈdiːˈrɔm] N ABBR (= compact disc read-only memory) CD-ROM m inv

CDT ABBR (US: = Central Daylight Time) ora legale del centro; (Brit Scol: = Craft, Design and Technology) educazione tecnica

CDW N ABBR = **collision damage waiver**

CD writer N masterizzatore m

cease [siːs] VT, VI cessare

ceasefire [ˈsiːsfaɪəʳ] N cessate il fuoco m inv

ceaseless [ˈsiːslɪs] ADJ incessante, continuo(-a)

CED N ABBR (US) = **Committee for Economic Development**

cedar [ˈsiːdəʳ] N cedro

cede [siːd] VT cedere

CEEB N ABBR (US: = College Entrance Examination Board) commissione per l'esame di ammissione al college

ceilidh [ˈkeɪlɪ] N festa con musiche e danze popolari scozzesi o irlandesi

ceiling [ˈsiːlɪŋ] N soffitto; (fig: upper limit) tetto, limite m massimo

celebrate [ˈsɛlɪbreɪt] VT, VI celebrare

celebrated [ˈsɛlɪbreɪtɪd] ADJ celebre

celebration [sɛlɪˈbreɪʃən] N celebrazione f

celebrity [sɪˈlɛbrɪtɪ] N celebrità f inv

celeriac [səˈlɛrɪæk] N sedano m rapa inv

celery [ˈsɛlərɪ] N sedano

celestial [sɪˈlɛstɪəl] ADJ celeste

celibacy [ˈsɛlɪbəsɪ] N celibato

cell [sɛl] N cella; (of revolutionaries, Biol) cellula; (Elec) elemento (di batteria)

cellar [ˈsɛləʳ] N sottosuolo; cantina

cellist [ˈtʃɛlɪst] N violoncellista mf

cello [ˈtʃɛləu] N violoncello

cellophane® [ˈsɛləfeɪn] N cellophane® m

cellphone [ˈsɛlfəun] N cellulare m

cell tower N (US Tel) stazione f radio base

cellular [ˈsɛljuləʳ] ADJ cellulare

celluloid [ˈsɛljulɔɪd] N celluloide f

cellulose [ˈsɛljuləus] N cellulosa

Celsius [ˈsɛlsɪəs] ADJ Celsius inv

Celt [kɛlt, sɛlt] N celta mf

Celtic [ˈkɛltɪk, ˈsɛltɪk] ADJ celtico(-a) ▸ N (Ling) celtico

cement [səˈmɛnt] N cemento ▸ VT cementare

cement mixer N betoniera

cemetery [ˈsɛmɪtrɪ] N cimitero

cenotaph [ˈsɛnətɑːf] N cenotafio

censor [ˈsɛnsəʳ] N censore m ▸ VT censurare

censorship [ˈsɛnsəʃɪp] N censura

censure [ˈsɛnʃəʳ] VT censurare

census [ˈsɛnsəs] N censimento

cent [sɛnt] N (of dollar, euro) centesimo; see also **per cent**

centenary [sɛn'ti:nəri], (US) **centennial** [sɛn'tɛnɪəl] N centenario

center ['sɛntəʳ] N, VT (US) = **centre**

centigrade ['sɛntɪɡreɪd] ADJ centigrado(-a)

centilitre, (US) **centiliter** ['sɛntɪli:təʳ] N centilitro

centimetre, (US) **centimeter** ['sɛntɪmɪ:təʳ] N centimetro

centipede ['sɛntɪpi:d] N centopiedi *m inv*

central ['sɛntrəl] ADJ centrale

Central African Republic N Repubblica centrafricana

Central America N America centrale

central heating N riscaldamento centrale

centralize ['sɛntrəlaɪz] VT accentrare

central processing unit N (*Comput*) unità *f* centrale di elaborazione

central reservation N (BRIT Aut) banchina *f* spartitraffico *inv*

centre, (US) **center** ['sɛntəʳ] N centro ▶ VT centrare; (*concentrate*): **to ~ (on)** concentrare (su)

centrefold, (US) **centerfold** ['sɛntəfəʊld] N (*Press*) poster *m* (all'interno di rivista)

centre-forward ['sɛntə'fɔ:wəd] N (*Sport*) centroavanti *m inv*

centre-half ['sɛntə'hɑ:f] N (*Sport*) centromediano

centrepiece, (US) **centerpiece** ['sɛntəpi:s] N centrotavola *m*; (*fig*) punto centrale

centre spread N (BRIT) pubblicità a doppia pagina

centre-stage [sɛntə'steɪdʒ] N: **to take ~** porsi al centro dell'attenzione

centrifugal [sɛn'trɪfjuɡəl] ADJ centrifugo(-a)

centrifuge ['sɛntrɪfju:ʒ] N centrifuga

century ['sɛntjʊrɪ] N secolo; **in the twentieth ~** nel ventesimo secolo

CEO N ABBR = **chief executive officer**

ceramic [sɪ'ræmɪk] ADJ ceramico(-a)

cereal ['si:rɪəl] N cereale *m*

cerebral ['sɛrɪbrəl] ADJ cerebrale

ceremonial [sɛrɪ'məʊnɪəl] N cerimoniale *m*; (*rite*) rito

ceremony ['sɛrɪmənɪ] N cerimonia; **to stand on ~** fare complimenti

cert [sə:t] N (BRIT col): **it's a dead ~** non c'è alcun dubbio

certain ['sə:tən] ADJ certo(-a); **to make ~ of** assicurarsi di; **for ~** per certo, di sicuro

certainly ['sə:tənlɪ] ADV certamente, certo

certainty ['sə:təntɪ] N certezza

certificate [sə'tɪfɪkɪt] N certificato; diploma *m*

certified letter ['sə:tɪfaɪd-] N (US) lettera raccomandata

certified public accountant ['sə:tɪfaɪd-] N (US) ≈ commercialista *mf*

certify ['sə:tɪfaɪ] VT certificare; (*award diploma to*) conferire un diploma a; (*declare insane*) dichiarare pazzo(-a) ▶ VI: **to ~ to** attestare a

cervical ['sə:vɪkl] ADJ: **~ cancer** cancro della cervice, tumore *m* al collo dell'utero; **~ smear** Paptest *m inv*

cervix ['sə:vɪks] N cervice *f*

Cesarean [si:'zɛərɪən] ADJ, N (US) = **Caesarean**

cessation [sə'seɪʃən] N cessazione *f*; arresto

cesspit ['sɛspɪt] N pozzo nero

CET ABBR (= *Central European Time*) fuso orario

Ceylon [sɪ'lɒn] N Ceylon *f*

cf. ABBR (= *compare*) cfr

c/f ABBR (*Comm*) = **carried forward**

CFC N ABBR (= *chlorofluorocarbon*) CFC *m inv*

CG N ABBR (US) = **coastguard**

cg ABBR (= *centigram*) cg

CH N ABBR (BRIT: = *Companion of Honour*) titolo

ch. ABBR (= *chapter*) cap

Chad [tʃæd] N Chad *m*

chafe [tʃeɪf] VT fregare, irritare ▶ VI (*fig*): **to ~ against** scontrarsi con

chaffinch ['tʃæfɪntʃ] N fringuello

chagrin ['ʃæɡrɪn] N disappunto, dispiacere *m*

chain [tʃeɪn] N catena ▶ VT (*also*: **chain up**) incatenare

chain reaction N reazione *f* a catena

chain-smoke ['tʃeɪnsməʊk] VI fumare una sigaretta dopo l'altra

chain store N negozio a catena

chair [tʃɛəʳ] N sedia; (*armchair*) poltrona; (*of university*) cattedra; (*of meeting*) presidenza ▶ VT (*meeting*) presiedere; **the ~** (US: electric chair) la sedia elettrica

chairlift ['tʃɛəlɪft] N seggiovia

chairman ['tʃɛəmən] N (*irreg*) presidente *m*

chairperson ['tʃɛəpə:sn] N presidente(-essa)

chairwoman ['tʃɛəwʊmən] N (*irreg*) presidentessa

chalet ['ʃæleɪ] N chalet *m inv*

chalice ['tʃælɪs] N calice *m*

chalk [tʃɔ:k] N gesso
▶ **chalk up** VT scrivere col gesso; (*fig*: *success*) ottenere; (: *victory*) riportare

chalkboard N (US) lavagna

challenge ['tʃælɪndʒ] N sfida ▶ VT sfidare; (*statement, right*) mettere in dubbio; **to ~ sb to a fight/game** sfidare qn a battersi/ad una partita; **to ~ sb to do** sfidare qn a fare

challenger ['tʃælɪndʒəʳ] N (*Sport*) sfidante *mf*

challenging ['tʃælɪndʒɪŋ] ADJ (*task*) impegnativo(-a); (*remark*) provocatorio(-a); (*look*) di sfida

chamber ['tʃeɪmbəʳ] N camera; **~ of commerce** camera di commercio

chambermaid ['tʃeɪmbəmeɪd] N cameriera

chamber music N musica da camera

chamberpot ['tʃeɪmbəpɔt] N vaso da notte

chameleon [kə'miːliən] N camaleonte *m*

chamois ['ʃæmwɑː] N camoscio

chamois leather ['ʃæmɪ-] N pelle *f* di camoscio

champagne [ʃæm'peɪn] N champagne *m inv*

champers ['ʃæmpəz] NSG (col) sciampagna

champion ['tʃæmpɪən] N campione(-essa); (of cause) difensore *m* ▶ VT difendere, lottare per

championship ['tʃæmpɪənʃɪp] N campionato

chance [tʃɑːns] N caso; (opportunity) occasione *f*; (likelihood) possibilità *f inv* ▶ VT: **to ~ it** rischiare, provarci ▶ ADJ fortuito(-a); **there is little ~ of his coming** è molto improbabile che venga; **to take a ~** rischiare; **by ~** per caso; **it's the ~ of a lifetime** è un'occasione unica; **the chances are that ...** probabilmente ..., è probabile che ... + sub; **to ~ to do sth** (formal: happen) fare per caso qc
▶ **chance (up)on** VT FUS (person) incontrare per caso, imbattersi in; (thing) trovare per caso

chancel ['tʃɑːnsəl] N coro

chancellor ['tʃɑːnsələʳ] N cancelliere *m*; (of university) rettore(-trice) (onorario(-a)); **C~ of the Exchequer** (BRIT) Cancelliere *m* dello Scacchiere

chandelier [ʃændə'lɪəʳ] N lampadario

change [tʃeɪndʒ] VT cambiare; (transform): **to ~ sb into** trasformare qn in ▶ VI cambiare; (change one's clothes) cambiarsi; (be transformed): **to ~ into** trasformarsi in ▶ N cambiamento; (money) resto; **to ~ one's mind** cambiare idea; **to ~ gear** (Aut) cambiare (marcia); **she changed into an old skirt** si è cambiata e ha messo una vecchia gonna; **a ~ of clothes** un cambio (di vestiti); **for a ~** tanto per cambiare; **small ~** spiccioli *mpl*, moneta; **keep the ~** tenga il resto; **can you give me ~ for £1?** mi può cambiare una sterlina?; **sorry, I don't have any ~** mi dispiace, non ho spiccioli
▶ **change over** VI (from sth to sth) passare; (players etc) scambiarsi (di posto o di campo) ▶ VT cambiare

changeable ['tʃeɪndʒəbl] ADJ (weather) variabile; (person) mutevole

change machine N distributore *m* automatico di monete

changeover ['tʃeɪndʒəuvəʳ] N cambiamento, passaggio

changing ['tʃeɪndʒɪŋ] ADJ che cambia; (colours) cangiante

changing room N (BRIT: in shop) camerino; (: Sport) spogliatoio

channel ['tʃænl] N canale *m*; (of river, sea) alveo ▶ VT canalizzare; (fig: interest, energies): **to ~ into** concentrare su, indirizzare verso; **through the usual channels** per le solite vie; **the (English) C~** la Manica; **green/red ~** (Customs) uscita "niente da dichiarare"/"merci da dichiarare"

channel-hopping ['tʃænlhɔpɪŋ] N (TV) zapping *m*

Channel Islands NPL: **the ~** le Isole Normanne

Channel Tunnel N: **the ~** il tunnel sotto la Manica

chant [tʃɑːnt] N canto; salmodia; (of crowd) slogan *m inv* ▶ VT cantare; salmodiare; **the demonstrators chanted their disapproval** i dimostranti lanciavano slogan di protesta

chaos ['keɪɔs] N caos *m*

chaos theory N teoria del caos

chaotic [keɪ'ɔtɪk] ADJ caotico(-a)

chap [tʃæp] N (BRIT col: man) tipo ▶ VT (skin) screpolare; **old ~** vecchio mio

chapel ['tʃæpl] N cappella

chaperone ['ʃæpərəun] N accompagnatore(-trice) ▶ VT accompagnare

chaplain ['tʃæplɪn] N cappellano

chapped [tʃæpt] ADJ (skin, lips) screpolato(-a)

chapter ['tʃæptəʳ] N capitolo

char [tʃɑːʳ] VT (burn) carbonizzare ▶ VI (BRIT: cleaner) lavorare come domestica (a ore) ▶ N (BRIT) = **charlady**

character ['kærɪktəʳ] N (gen, Comput) carattere *m*; (in novel, film) personaggio; (eccentric) originale *m*; **a person of good ~** una persona a modo

character code N (Comput) codice *m* di carattere

characteristic ['kærɪktə'rɪstɪk] ADJ caratteristico(-a) ▶ N caratteristica; **~ of** tipico(-a) di

characterize ['kærɪktəraɪz] VT caratterizzare; (describe): **to ~ (as)** descrivere (come)

charade [ʃə'rɑːd] N sciarada

charcoal ['tʃɑːkəul] N carbone *m* di legna

charge [tʃɑːdʒ] N accusa; (cost) prezzo; (of gun, battery, Mil: attack) carica; (responsibility) responsabilità ▶ VT (gun, battery, Mil: enemy) caricare; (customer) fare pagare a; (sum) fare pagare; (Law): **to ~ sb (with)** accusare qn (di) ▶ VI (gen with: up, along etc) lanciarsi ■ **charges** NPL: **bank charges** commissioni *fpl* bancarie; **labour charges** costi *mpl* del lavoro; **to reverse the charges** (Tel) fare una telefonata a carico del destinatario; **to ~ in/out** precipitarsi dentro/fuori; **to ~ up/down** lanciarsi su/giù per; **is there a ~?** c'è da pagare?; **there's no ~** non c'è niente da pagare; **extra ~** supplemento; **to take ~ of** incaricarsi di; **to be in ~ of** essere responsabile per; **to have ~ of sb** aver cura di qn; **how much do you ~ for this repair?** quanto chiede per la riparazione?; **to ~ an expense (up) to sb** addebitare una spesa a qn; **~ it to my account** lo metta *or* addebiti sul mio conto

charge account N conto

charge card N (of shop) carta *f* clienti *inv*

chargé d'affaires ['ʃɑːʒeɪdæ'fɛəʳ] N incaricato d'affari

473

chargehand ['tʃɑːdʒhænd] N (BRIT) caposquadra mf

charger ['tʃɑːdʒəʳ] N (also: **battery charger**) caricabatterie m inv; (old: warhorse) destriero

chariot ['tʃærɪət] N carro

charismatic [kærɪz'mætɪk] ADJ carismatico(-a)

charitable ['tʃærɪtəbl] ADJ caritatevole

charity ['tʃærɪtɪ] N carità; (organization) opera pia

charity shop N (BRIT) negozi che vendono articoli di seconda mano e devolvono il ricavato in beneficenza

charlady ['tʃɑːleɪdɪ] N (BRIT) domestica a ore

charlatan ['ʃɑːlətən] N ciarlatano

charm [tʃɑːm] N fascino; (on bracelet) ciondolo ▶ VT affascinare, incantare

charm bracelet N braccialetto con ciondoli

charming ['tʃɑːmɪŋ] ADJ affascinante

chart [tʃɑːt] N tabella; grafico; (map) carta nautica; (weather chart) carta del tempo ▶ VT fare una carta nautica di; (sales, progress) tracciare il grafico di; **to be in the charts** (record, pop group) essere in classifica ▪ **charts** NPL (Mus) hit parade f

charter ['tʃɑːtəʳ] VT (plane) noleggiare ▶ N (document) carta; **on ~** a nolo

chartered accountant ['tʃɑːtəd-] N (BRIT) ragioniere(-a) professionista

charter flight N volo m charter inv

charwoman ['tʃɑːwumən] N (irreg) = **charlady**

chase [tʃeɪs] VT inseguire; (also: **chase away**) cacciare ▶ N caccia
▶ **chase down** VT (US) = **chase up**
▶ **chase up** VT (BRIT: person) scovare; (: information) scoprire, raccogliere

chasm ['kæzəm] N abisso

chassis ['ʃæsɪ] N telaio

chastened ['tʃeɪsnd] ADJ abbattuto(-a), provato(-a)

chastening ['tʃeɪsnɪŋ] ADJ che fa riflettere

chastise [tʃæs'taɪz] VT punire, castigare

chastity ['tʃæstɪtɪ] N castità

chat [tʃæt] VI (also: **have a chat**) chiacchierare; (on the internet) chattare ▶ N chiacchierata; (on the internet) chat f inv
▶ **chat up** VT (BRIT col: girl, boy) abbordare

chatline ['tʃætlaɪn] N servizio telefonico che permette a più utenti di conversare insieme

chat room N (Internet) chat f inv

chat show N (BRIT) talk show m inv, conversazione f televisiva

chattel ['tʃætl] N see **goods**

chatter ['tʃætəʳ] VI (person) ciarlare; (bird) cinguettare; (teeth) battere ▶ N ciarle fpl; cinguettio; **her teeth were chattering** batteva i denti

chatterbox ['tʃætəbɔks] N chiacchierone(-a)

chattering classes ['tʃætərɪŋ-] NPL: **the ~** (pej) ≈ gli intellettuali da salotto

chatty ['tʃætɪ] ADJ (style) familiare; (person) chiacchierino(-a)

chauffeur ['ʃəufəʳ] N autista m

chauvinism ['ʃəuvɪnɪzəm] N (also: **male chauvinism**) maschilismo; (nationalism) sciovinismo

chauvinist ['ʃəuvɪnɪst] N (also: **male chauvinist**) maschilista m; (nationalist) sciovinista mf

chauvinistic [ʃəuvɪ'nɪstɪk] ADJ sciovinistico(-a)

chav [tʃæv] N (BRIT pej) giovane della periferia urbana poco colto che indossa abiti sportivi di particolari marche

ChE ABBR = **chemical engineer**

cheap [tʃiːp] ADJ a buon mercato, economico(-a); (reduced: fare, ticket) ridotto(-a); (joke) grossolano(-a); (poor quality) di cattiva qualità ▶ ADV a buon mercato; **cheaper** meno caro; **~ money** denaro a basso tasso di interesse

cheap day return N biglietto ridotto di andata e ritorno valido in giornata

cheapen ['tʃiːpn] VT ribassare; (fig) avvilire

cheaply ['tʃiːplɪ] ADV a buon prezzo, a buon mercato

cheat [tʃiːt] VI imbrogliare; (at school) copiare ▶ VT ingannare; (rob) defraudare ▶ N imbroglione m; copione m; (trick) inganno; **to ~ sb out of sth** defraudare qn di qc
▶ **cheat on** VT FUS (husband, wife) tradire; **he's been cheating on his wife** ha tradito sua moglie

cheating ['tʃiːtɪŋ] N imbrogliare m; copiare m

Chechnya [tʃɪtʃ'njɑː] N Cecenia

check [tʃɛk] VT verificare; (passport, ticket) controllare; (halt) fermare; (restrain) contenere ▶ VI (official etc) informarsi ▶ N verifica; controllo; (curb) freno; (US: bill) conto; (pattern: gen pl) quadretti mpl; (US) = **cheque** ▶ ADJ (pattern, cloth: also: **checked**) a scacchi, a quadretti; **to ~ with sb** chiedere a qn; **to keep a ~ on sb/sth** controllare qn/qc, fare attenzione a qn/qc
▶ **check in** VI (in hotel) registrare; (at airport) presentarsi all'accettazione ▶ VT (luggage) depositare
▶ **check off** VT segnare
▶ **check out** VI (from hotel) saldare il conto ▶ VT (luggage) ritirare; (investigate: story) controllare, verificare; (: person) prendere informazioni su
▶ **check up** VI: **to ~ up (on sth)** investigare (qc); **to ~ up on sb** informarsi sul conto di qn

checkbook ['tʃɛkbuk] N (US) = **chequebook**

checkered ['tʃɛkəd] ADJ (US) = **chequered**

checkers ['tʃɛkəz] N (US) dama

check guarantee card N (US) carta f assegni inv

check-in ['tʃɛkɪn] N (at airport: also: **check-in desk**) check-in m inv, accettazione f (bagagli inv)

checking account ['tʃɛkɪŋ-] N (US) conto corrente

checklist ['tʃɛklɪst] N lista di controllo

checkmate ['tʃɛkmeɪt] N scaccomatto

checkout ['tʃɛkaut] N (in supermarket) cassa

checkpoint ['tʃɛkpɔɪnt] N posto di blocco

checkroom ['tʃɛkrum] N (US) deposito m bagagli inv

checkup ['tʃɛkʌp] N (Med) controllo medico

cheddar ['tʃɛdəʳ] N formaggio duro di latte di mucca di colore bianco o arancione

cheek [tʃiːk] N guancia; (impudence) faccia tosta

cheekbone ['tʃiːkbəun] N zigomo

cheeky ['tʃiːkɪ] ADJ sfacciato(-a)

cheep [tʃiːp] N (of bird) pigolio ▶ VI pigolare

cheer [tʃɪəʳ] VT applaudire; (gladden) rallegrare ▶ VI applaudire ▶ N grido (di incoraggiamento) ■ **cheers** NPL (of approval, encouragement) applausi mpl; evviva mpl; **cheers!** salute!
  ▶ **cheer on** VT (person etc) incitare
  ▶ **cheer up** VI rallegrarsi, farsi animo ▶ VT rallegrare

cheerful ['tʃɪəful] ADJ allegro(-a)

cheerfulness ['tʃɪəfulnɪs] N allegria

cheerio ['tʃɪərɪ'əu] EXCL (BRIT) ciao!

cheerleader ['tʃɪəliːdəʳ] N cheerleader f inv

cheerless ['tʃɪəlɪs] ADJ triste

cheese [tʃiːz] N formaggio

cheeseboard ['tʃiːzbɔːd] N piatto del (or per il) formaggio

cheeseburger ['tʃiːzbəːgəʳ] N cheeseburger m inv

cheesecake ['tʃiːzkeɪk] N specie di torta di ricotta, a volte con frutta

cheetah ['tʃiːtə] N ghepardo

chef [ʃɛf] N capocuoco

chemical ['kɛmɪkl] ADJ chimico(-a) ▶ N prodotto chimico

chemical engineering N ingegneria chimica

chemist ['kɛmɪst] N (BRIT: pharmacist) farmacista mf; (scientist) chimico(-a); **~'s shop** n (BRIT) farmacia

chemistry ['kɛmɪstrɪ] N chimica

chemo [ki:məu] N chemio f inv

chemotherapy [ki:məu'θerəpɪ] N chemioterapia

cheque, (US) **check** [tʃɛk] N assegno; **to pay by ~** pagare per assegno or con un assegno

chequebook, (US) **checkbook** ['tʃɛkbuk] N libretto degli assegni

cheque card N (BRIT) carta f assegni inv

chequered, (US) **checkered** ['tʃɛkəd] ADJ (fig) movimentato(-a)

cherish ['tʃɛrɪʃ] VT aver caro; (hope etc) nutrire

cheroot [ʃə'ruːt] N sigaro spuntato

cherry ['tʃɛrɪ] N ciliegia; (also: **cherry tree**) ciliegio

chess [tʃɛs] N scacchi mpl

chessboard ['tʃɛsbɔːd] N scacchiera

chessman ['tʃɛsmæn] N (irreg) pezzo degli scacchi

chessplayer ['tʃɛspleɪəʳ] N scacchista mf

chest [tʃɛst] N petto; (box) cassa; **to get sth off one's ~** (col) sputare il rospo

chest measurement N giro m torace inv

chestnut ['tʃɛsnʌt] N castagna; (also: **chestnut tree**) castagno ▶ ADJ castano(-a)

chest of drawers N cassettone m

chesty ['tʃɛstɪ] ADJ: **~ cough** tosse f bronchiale

chew [tʃuː] VT masticare

chewing gum ['tʃuːɪŋ-] N chewing gum m

chic [ʃiːk] ADJ elegante

chick [tʃɪk] N pulcino; (US col) pollastrella

chicken ['tʃɪkɪn] N pollo; (col: coward) coniglio
  ▶ **chicken out** VI (col) avere fifa; **to ~ out of sth** tirarsi indietro da qc per fifa or paura

chicken feed N (fig) miseria

chickenpox ['tʃɪkɪnpɔks] N varicella

chick flick N (col) filmetto rosa

chickpea ['tʃɪkpiː] N cece m

chicory ['tʃɪkərɪ] N cicoria

chide [tʃaɪd] VT rimproverare

chief [tʃiːf] N capo ▶ ADJ principale; **C~ of Staff** (Mil) Capo di Stato Maggiore

chief constable N (BRIT) ≈ questore m

chief executive, (US) **chief executive officer** N direttore(-trice) generale

chiefly ['tʃiːflɪ] ADV per lo più, soprattutto

chief operating officer N direttore(-trice) operativo(-a)

chiffon ['ʃɪfɔn] N chiffon m inv

chilblain ['tʃɪlbleɪn] N gelone m

child [tʃaɪld] (pl **children** ['tʃɪldrən]) N bambino(-a)

child abuse N molestie fpl a minori

child abuser [-ə'bjuːzəʳ] N molestatore(-trice) di minori

child benefit N (BRIT) ≈ assegni mpl familiari

childbirth ['tʃaɪldbəːθ] N parto

childcare ['tʃaɪldkɛəʳ] N servizio m di custodia dei bambini

childhood ['tʃaɪldhud] N infanzia

childish ['tʃaɪldɪʃ] ADJ puerile

childless ['tʃaɪldlɪs] ADJ senza figli

childlike ['tʃaɪldlaɪk] ADJ fanciullesco(-a)

child minder [-'maɪndəʳ] N (BRIT) bambinaia

child prodigy N bambino m prodigio inv

children ['tʃɪldrən] NPL of **child**

children's home N istituto per l'infanzia

Chile ['tʃɪlɪ] N Cile m

Chilean ['tʃɪlɪən] ADJ, N cileno(-a)

chill [tʃɪl] N freddo; (*Med*) infreddatura ▶ ADJ freddo(-a), gelido(-a) ▶ VT raffreddare; (*Culin*) mettere in fresco; **"serve chilled"** "servire fresco"
▶ **chill out** VI (*esp US col*) darsi una calmata

chilli, (*US*) **chili** [ˈtʃɪlɪ] N peperoncino

chilling [ˈtʃɪlɪŋ] ADJ agghiacciante; (*wind*) gelido(-a)

chilly [ˈtʃɪlɪ] ADJ freddo(-a), fresco(-a); (*sensitive to cold*) freddoloso(-a); **to feel ~** sentirsi infreddolito(-a)

chime [tʃaɪm] N carillon *m inv* ▶ VI suonare, scampanare

chimney [ˈtʃɪmnɪ] N camino

chimney sweep N spazzacamino

chimpanzee [tʃɪmpænˈziː] N scimpanzé *m inv*

chin [tʃɪn] N mento

China [ˈtʃaɪnə] N Cina

china [ˈtʃaɪnə] N porcellana

Chinese [tʃaɪˈniːz] ADJ cinese ▶ N (*pl inv*) cinese *mf*; (*Ling*) cinese *m*

chink [tʃɪŋk] N (*opening*) fessura; (*noise*) tintinnio

chinwag [ˈtʃɪnwæg] N (*col*): **to have a ~** fare una chiacchierata

chip [tʃɪp] N (*gen pl: Culin*) patatina fritta; (: *US: also:* **potato chip**) patatina; (*of wood, glass, stone*) scheggia; (*in gambling*) fiche *f inv*; (*Comput: microchip*) chip *m inv* ▶ VT (*cup, plate*) scheggiare; **when the chips are down** (*fig*) al momento critico
▶ **chip in** VI (*col: contribute*) contribuire; (: *interrupt*) intromettersi

chip and PIN N sistema *m* chip e PIN; **~ machine** lettore *m* di carte chip e PIN; **~ card** carta chip e PIN

chipboard [ˈtʃɪpbɔːd] N agglomerato

chipmunk [ˈtʃɪpmʌŋk] N tamia *m* striato

chippings [ˈtʃɪpɪŋz] NPL: **loose ~** brecciame *m*

chip shop N (*BRIT*) *vedi nota*

I **chip shops**, anche chiamati *fish-and-chip shops*, sono friggitorie che vendono principalmente filetti di pesce impanati e patatine fritte che un tempo venivano serviti ai clienti avvolti in carta di giornale.

chiropodist [kɪˈrɔpədɪst] N (*BRIT*) pedicure *mf*

chiropody [kɪˈrɔpədɪ] N (*BRIT*) pedicure *f inv*

chirp [tʃəːp] N cinguettio; (*of crickets*) cri cri *m* ▶ VI cinguettare

chirpy [ˈtʃəːpɪ] ADJ (*col*) frizzante

chisel [ˈtʃɪzl] N cesello

chit [tʃɪt] N biglietto

chitchat [ˈtʃɪtʃæt] N (*col*) chiacchiere *fpl*

chivalrous [ˈʃɪvəlrəs] ADJ cavalleresco(-a)

chivalry [ˈʃɪvəlrɪ] N cavalleria; cortesia

chives [tʃaɪvz] NPL erba cipollina

chloride [ˈklɔːraɪd] N cloruro

chlorinate [ˈklɔrɪneɪt] VT clorare

chlorine [ˈklɔːriːn] N cloro

choc-ice [ˈtʃɔkaɪs] N (*BRIT*) gelato ricoperto al cioccolato

chock [tʃɔk] N zeppa

chock-a-block [ˈtʃɔkəˈblɔk], **chockfull** [ˈtʃɔkˈful] ADJ pieno(-a) zeppo(-a)

chocolate [ˈtʃɔklɪt] N (*substance*) cioccolato, cioccolata; (*drink*) cioccolata; (*a sweet*) cioccolatino

choice [tʃɔɪs] N scelta ▶ ADJ scelto(-a); **a wide ~** un'ampia scelta; **I did it by** *or* **from ~** l'ho fatto di mia volontà *or* per mia scelta

choir [ˈkwaɪəʳ] N coro

choirboy [ˈkwaɪəbɔɪ] N corista *m* fanciullo

choke [tʃəuk] VI soffocare ▶ VT soffocare; (*block*) ingombrare ▶ N (*Aut*) valvola dell'aria; **to be choked with** essere intasato(-a)

cholera [ˈkɔlərə] N colera *m*

cholesterol [kəˈlestərɔl] N colesterolo

chook [tʃuk] N (*AUSTRALIA, NEW ZEALAND col*) gallina

choose [tʃuːz] (*pt* **chose** [tʃəuz], *pp* **chosen** [ˈtʃəuzn]) VT scegliere; **to ~ to do** decidere di fare; preferire fare; **to ~ between** scegliere tra; **to ~ from** scegliere da *or* tra

choosy [ˈtʃuːzɪ] ADJ: **(to be) ~** (fare lo) schizzinoso(-a)

chop [tʃɔp] VT (*wood*) spaccare; (*Culin: also:* **chop up**) tritare ▶ N colpo netto; (*Culin*) costoletta; **to get the ~** (*BRIT col: project*) essere bocciato(-a); (: *person: be sacked*) essere licenziato(-a); *see also* **chops**
▶ **chop down** VT (*tree*) abbattere
▶ **chop off** VT tagliare

choppy [ˈtʃɔpɪ] ADJ (*sea*) mosso(-a)

chops [tʃɔps] NPL (*jaws*) mascelle *fpl*

chopsticks [ˈtʃɔpstɪks] NPL bastoncini *mpl* cinesi

choral [ˈkɔːrəl] ADJ corale

chord [kɔːd] N (*Mus*) accordo

chore [tʃɔːʳ] N faccenda; **household chores** faccende *fpl* domestiche

choreographer [kɔrɪˈɔgrəfəʳ] N coreografo(-a)

choreography [kɔrɪˈɔgrəfɪ] N coreografia

chorister [ˈkɔrɪstəʳ] N corista *mf*

chortle [ˈtʃɔːtl] VI ridacchiare

chorus [ˈkɔːrəs] N coro; (*repeated part of song, also fig*) ritornello

chose [tʃəuz] PT *of* **choose**

chosen [ˈtʃəuzn] PP *of* **choose**

chowder [ˈtʃaudəʳ] N zuppa di pesce

Christ [kraɪst] N Cristo

christen [ˈkrɪsn] VT battezzare

christening [ˈkrɪsnɪŋ] N battesimo

Christian ['krɪstɪən] ADJ, N cristiano(-a)
Christianity [krɪstɪ'ænɪtɪ] N cristianesimo
Christian name N nome m di battesimo
Christmas ['krɪsməs] N Natale m; **happy** or **merry ~!** Buon Natale!
Christmas card N cartolina di Natale
Christmas carol N canto natalizio
Christmas Day N il giorno di Natale
Christmas Eve N la vigilia di Natale
Christmas Island N isola di Christmas
Christmas pudding N (esp BRIT) specie di budino con frutta secca, spezie e brandy
Christmas tree N albero di Natale
chrome [krəum] N cromo
chromium ['krəumɪəm] N cromo; (also: **chromium plating**) cromatura
chromosome ['krəuməsəum] N cromosoma m
chronic ['krɒnɪk] ADJ cronico(-a); (fig: liar, smoker) incallito(-a)
chronicle ['krɒnɪkl] N cronaca
chronological [krɒnə'lɒdʒɪkl] ADJ cronologico(-a)
chrysanthemum [krɪ'sænθəməm] N crisantemo
chubby ['tʃʌbɪ] ADJ paffuto(-a)
chuck [tʃʌk] VT (col) buttare, gettare; **to ~ (up** or **in)** (BRIT col: job, person) piantare
▸ **chuck out** VT (col) buttar fuori
chuckle ['tʃʌkl] VI ridere sommessamente
chuffed [tʃʌft] ADJ (col): **to be ~ about sth** essere arcicontento(-a) di qc
chug [tʃʌg] VI (also: **chug along**: train) muoversi sbuffando
chugger ['tʃʌgə'] N (col) dialogatore(-trice) m/f
chum [tʃʌm] N compagno(-a)
chump [tʃʌmp] N (col) idiota mf
chunk [tʃʌŋk] N pezzo; (of bread) tocco
chunky [tʃʌŋkɪ] ADJ (furniture etc) basso(-a) e largo(-a); (person) ben piantato(-a); (knitwear) di lana grossa
Chunnel ['tʃʌnəl] N = **Channel Tunnel**
church [tʃə:tʃ] N chiesa; **the C~ of England** la Chiesa anglicana
churchyard ['tʃə:tʃjɑ:d] N sagrato
churlish ['tʃə:lɪʃ] ADJ rozzo(-a), sgarbato(-a)
churn [tʃə:n] N (for butter) zangola; (also: **milk churn**) bidone m
▸ **churn out** VT sfornare
chute [ʃu:t] N cascata; (also: **rubbish chute**) canale m di scarico; (BRIT: children's slide) scivolo
chutney ['tʃʌtnɪ] N salsa piccante (di frutta, zucchero e spezie)
CIA N ABBR (US: = Central Intelligence Agency) C.I.A. f
CID N ABBR (BRIT: = Criminal Investigation Department) ≈ polizia giudiziaria

cider ['saɪdə'] N sidro
CIF ABBR (= cost, insurance, and freight) C.I.F. m
cigar [sɪ'gɑ:'] N sigaro
cigarette [sɪgə'rɛt] N sigaretta
cigarette case N portasigarette m inv
cigarette end N mozzicone m
cigarette holder N bocchino
cigarette lighter N accendino
C-in-C ABBR = **commander-in-chief**
cinch [sɪntʃ] N (col): **it's a ~** è presto fatto; (sure thing) è una cosa sicura
cinder ['sɪndə'] N cenere f
Cinderella [sɪndə'rɛlə] N Cenerentola
cine-camera ['sɪnɪ'kæmərə] N (BRIT) cinepresa
cine-film ['sɪnɪfɪlm] N (BRIT) pellicola
cinema ['sɪnəmə] N cinema m inv
cine-projector ['sɪnɪprə'dʒɛktə'] N (BRIT) proiettore m
cinnamon ['sɪnəmən] N cannella
cipher ['saɪfə'] N cifra; (fig: faceless employee etc) persona di nessun conto; **in ~** in codice
circa ['sə:kə] PREP circa
circle ['sə:kl] N cerchio; (of friends etc) circolo; (in cinema) galleria ▸ VI girare in circolo ▸ VT (surround) circondare; (move round) girare intorno a
circuit ['sə:kɪt] N circuito
circuit board N (Comput) tavola dei circuiti
circuitous [sə:'kjuɪtəs] ADJ indiretto(-a)
circular ['sə:kjulə'] ADJ circolare ▸ N (letter) circolare f; (as advertisement) volantino pubblicitario
circulate ['sə:kjuleɪt] VI circolare; (person: socially) girare e andare un po' da tutti ▸ VT far circolare
circulating capital ['sə:kjuleɪtɪŋ-] N (Comm) capitale m d'esercizio
circulation [sə:kju'leɪʃən] N circolazione f; (of newspaper) tiratura
circumcise ['sə:kəmsaɪz] VT circoncidere
circumference [sə'kʌmfərəns] N circonferenza
circumflex ['sə:kəmflɛks] N (also: **circumflex accent**) accento circonflesso
circumscribe ['sə:kəmskraɪb] VT circoscrivere; (fig: limit) limitare
circumspect ['sə:kəmspɛkt] ADJ circospetto(-a)
circumstances ['sə:kəmstənsɪz] NPL circostanze fpl; (financial condition) condizioni fpl finanziarie; **in the ~** date le circostanze; **under no ~** per nessun motivo
circumstantial ['sə:kəm'stænʃəl] ADJ (report, statement) circostanziato(-a), dettagliato(-a); **~ evidence** prova indiretta
circumvent [sə:kəm'vɛnt] VT (rule etc) aggirare
circus ['sə:kəs] N circo; (also: **Circus**: in place names) piazza (di forma circolare)

cirrhosis [sɪˈrəʊsɪs] N (also: **cirrhosis of the liver**) cirrosi f inv (epatica)

CIS N ABBR (= Commonwealth of Independent States) CSI f

cissy [ˈsɪsɪ] N = **sissy**

cistern [ˈsɪstən] N cisterna; (in toilet) serbatoio d'acqua

citation [saɪˈteɪʃən] N citazione f

cite [saɪt] VT citare

citizen [ˈsɪtɪzn] N (Pol: of country) cittadino(-a); (: of town) abitante mf; **the citizens of this town** gli abitanti di questa città

Citizens' Advice Bureau N (BRIT) organizzazione di volontari che offre gratuitamente assistenza su questioni legali e finanziarie

citizenship [ˈsɪtɪznʃɪp] N cittadinanza

citric acid [ˈsɪtrɪk] N acido citrico

citrus fruit [ˈsɪtrəs-] N agrume m

city [ˈsɪtɪ] N città f inv; **the C~** la Città di Londra (centro commerciale)

city centre N centro della città

City Hall N (US) ≈ Comune m

City Technology College N (BRIT) istituto tecnico superiore (finanziato dall'industria)

civic [ˈsɪvɪk] ADJ civico(-a)

civic centre N (BRIT) centro civico

civil [ˈsɪvɪl] ADJ civile; (polite) educato(-a), gentile

civil disobedience N disubbidienza civile

civil engineer N ingegnere m civile

civil engineering N ingegneria civile

civilian [sɪˈvɪlɪən] ADJ, N borghese (mf)

civilization [sɪvɪlaɪˈzeɪʃən] N civiltà f inv

civilized [ˈsɪvɪlaɪzd] ADJ civilizzato(-a); (fig) cortese

civil law N codice m civile; (study) diritto civile

civil liberties NPL libertà fpl civili

civil rights NPL diritti mpl civili

civil servant N impiegato(-a) statale

Civil Service N amministrazione f statale

civil war N guerra civile

civvies [ˈsɪvɪz] NPL (col): **in ~** in borghese

CJD N ABBR (= Creutzfeld-Jakob disease) malattia di Creutzfeldt-Jakob

cl ABBR (= centilitre) cl

clad [klæd] ADJ: **~ (in)** vestito(-a) (di)

claim [kleɪm] VT (rights etc) rivendicare; (damages) richiedere; (assert) sostenere, pretendere ▶ VI (for insurance) fare una domanda d'indennizzo ▶ N rivendicazione f; pretesa; richiesta; (right) diritto; **to ~ that/to be** sostenere che/di essere; **(insurance) ~** domanda d'indennizzo; **to put in a ~ for sth** fare una richiesta di qc

claimant [ˈkleɪmənt] N (Admin, Law) richiedente mf

claim form N (gen) modulo di richiesta; (for expenses) modulo di rimborso spese

clairvoyant [klɛəˈvɔɪənt] N chiaroveggente mf

clam [klæm] N vongola
▶ **clam up** VI (col) azzittirsi

clamber [ˈklæmbəʳ] VI arrampicarsi

clammy [ˈklæmɪ] ADJ (weather) caldo(-a) umido(-a); (hands) viscido(-a)

clamour, (US) **clamor** [ˈklæməʳ] N (noise) clamore m; (protest) protesta ▶ VI: **to ~ for sth** chiedere a gran voce qc

clamp [klæmp] N pinza; morsa ▶ VT stringere con una morsa; (Aut: wheel) applicare le ganasce a
▶ **clamp down** VT FUS (fig): **to ~ down (on)** dare un giro di vite (a)

clampdown [ˈklæmpdaun] N stretta, giro di vite; **a ~ on sth/sb** un giro di vite a qc/qn

clan [klæn] N clan m inv

clandestine [klænˈdɛstɪn] ADJ clandestino(-a)

clang [klæŋ] N fragore m, suono metallico

clanger [ˈklæŋəʳ] N: **to drop a ~** (BRIT col) fare una gaffe

clansman [ˈklænzmən] N (irreg) membro di un clan

clap [klæp] VI applaudire ▶ VT: **to ~ one's hands** battere le mani ▶ N: **a ~ of thunder** un tuono

clapping [ˈklæpɪŋ] N applausi mpl

claptrap [ˈklæptræp] N (col) stupidaggini fpl

claret [ˈklærət] N vino di Bordeaux

clarification [klærɪfɪˈkeɪʃən] N (fig) chiarificazione f, chiarimento

clarify [ˈklærɪfaɪ] VT chiarificare, chiarire

clarinet [klærɪˈnɛt] N clarinetto

clarity [ˈklærɪtɪ] N chiarezza

clash [klæʃ] N frastuono; (fig) scontro ▶ VI (Mil, fig: have an argument) scontrarsi; cozzare; (colours) stridere; (dates, events) coincidere

clasp [klɑːsp] N (hold) stretta; (of necklace, bag) fermaglio, fibbia ▶ VT stringere

class [klɑːs] N classe f; (group, category) tipo, categoria ▶ VT classificare

class-conscious [ˈklɑːskɔnʃəs] ADJ che ha coscienza di classe

class consciousness N coscienza di classe

classic [ˈklæsɪk] ADJ classico(-a) ▶ N classico

classical [ˈklæsɪkəl] ADJ classico(-a)

classics [ˈklæsɪks] NPL (Scol) studi mpl umanistici

classification [klæsɪfɪˈkeɪʃən] N classificazione f

classified [ˈklæsɪfaɪd] ADJ (information) segreto(-a), riservato(-a); **~ ads** annunci economici

classify [ˈklæsɪfaɪ] VT classificare

classless society [ˈklɑːslɪs-] N società f inv senza distinzioni di classe

classmate ['klɑːsmeɪt] N compagno(-a) di classe

classroom ['klɑːsrum] N aula

classroom assistant N assistente *mf* in classe dell'insegnante

classy ['klɑːsɪ] ADJ (*col*) chic *inv*, elegante

clatter ['klætər'] N tintinnio; scalpitio ▶ VI tintinnare; scalpitare

clause [klɔːz] N clausola; (*Ling*) proposizione *f*

claustrophobia [klɔːstrə'fəubɪə] N claustrofobia

claustrophobic [klɔːstrə'fəubɪk] ADJ claustrofobico(-a)

claw [klɔː] N tenaglia; (*of bird of prey*) artiglio; (*of lobster*) pinza ▶ VT graffiare; afferrare

clay [kleɪ] N argilla

clean [kliːn] ADJ pulito(-a); (*outline, break, movement etc*) netto(-a) ▶ VT pulire ▶ ADV: **he ~ forgot** si è completamente dimenticato; **to come ~** (*col: admit guilt*) confessare; **to have a ~ driving licence** or **record** (*US*) non aver mai preso contravvenzioni; **to ~ one's teeth** (*BRIT*) lavarsi i denti
  ▶ **clean off** VT togliere
  ▶ **clean out** VT ripulire
  ▶ **clean up** VI far pulizia ▶ VT (*also fig*) ripulire; (*fig: make profit*): **to ~ up on** fare una barca di soldi con

clean-cut ['kliːn'kʌt] ADJ (*man*) curato(-a); (*situation etc*) ben definito(-a)

cleaner ['kliːnər'] N (*person*) uomo (donna) delle pulizie; (*product*) smacchiatore *m*; (*also: **dry cleaner**) tintore(-a)

cleaner's N (*also: **dry cleaner's**) tintoria

cleaning ['kliːnɪŋ] N pulizia

cleaning lady N donna delle pulizie

cleanliness ['klɛnlɪnɪs] N pulizia

cleanly ['kliːnlɪ] ADV in modo netto

cleanse [klɛnz] VT pulire; purificare

cleanser ['klɛnzər'] N detergente *m*; (*cosmetic*) latte *m* detergente

clean-shaven ['kliːn'ʃeɪvn] ADJ sbarbato(-a)

cleansing department ['klɛnzɪŋ-] N (*BRIT*) nettezza urbana

clean sweep N: **to make a ~ (of)** fare piazza pulita (di)

clean technology N tecnologie *fpl* ambientali

clean-up ['kliːnʌp] N pulizia

clear [klɪər'] ADJ chiaro(-a); (*glass etc*) trasparente; (*road, way*) libero(-a); (*profit, majority*) netto(-a); (*conscience*) pulito(-a) ▶ VT sgombrare; liberare; (*table*) sparecchiare; (*site, woodland*) spianare; (*Comm: goods*) liquidare; (*Law: suspect*) discolpare; (*obstacle*) superare; (*cheque*) fare la compensazione di ▶ VI (*weather*) rasserenarsi; (*fog*) andarsene ▶ ADV: **~ of** distante da ▶ N: **to be in the ~** (*out of debt*) essere in attivo; (*out of suspicion*) essere a posto; (*out of danger*) essere fuori

pericolo; **to ~ the table** sparecchiare (la tavola); **to ~ one's throat** schiarirsi la gola; **to ~ a profit** avere un profitto netto; **to make o.s. ~** spiegarsi bene; **to make it ~ to sb that ...** far capire a qn che ...; **I have a ~ day tomorrow** (*BRIT*) non ho impegni domani; **to keep ~ of sb/sth** tenersi lontano da qn/qc, stare alla larga da qn/qc
  ▶ **clear away** VT (*things, clothes, etc*) mettere a posto; **to ~ away the dishes** sparecchiare la tavola
  ▶ **clear off** VI (*col: leave*) svignarsela
  ▶ **clear up** VI schiarirsi ▶ VT mettere in ordine; (*mystery*) risolvere

clearance ['klɪərəns] N (*removal*) sgombro; (*free space*) spazio; (*permission*) autorizzazione *f*, permesso

clearance sale N vendita di liquidazione

clear-cut ['klɪə'kʌt] ADJ ben delineato(-a), distinto(-a)

clearing ['klɪərɪŋ] N radura; (*BRIT Banking*) clearing *m*

clearing bank N (*BRIT*) banca che fa uso della *camera di compensazione*

clearing house N (*Comm*) camera di compensazione

clearly ['klɪəlɪ] ADV chiaramente

clearway ['klɪəweɪ] N (*BRIT*) strada con divieto di sosta

cleavage ['kliːvɪdʒ] N (*of woman*) scollatura

cleaver ['kliːvər'] N mannaia

clef [klɛf] N (*Mus*) chiave *f*

cleft [klɛft] N (*in rock*) crepa, fenditura

clemency ['klɛmənsɪ] N clemenza

clement ['klɛmənt] ADJ (*weather*) mite, clemente

clench [klɛntʃ] VT stringere

clergy ['kləːdʒɪ] N clero

clergyman ['kləːdʒɪmən] N (*irreg*) ecclesiastico

clerical ['klɛrɪkl] ADJ d'impiegato; (*Rel*) clericale

clerk [klɑːk, (*US*) kləːrk] N (*BRIT*) impiegato(-a); (*US: salesman/woman*) commesso(-a); **C~ of the Court** (*Law*) cancelliere *m*

clever ['klɛvər'] ADJ (*mentally*) intelligente; (*deft, skilful*) abile; (*device, arrangement*) ingegnoso(-a)

cleverly ['klɛvəlɪ] ADV abilmente

clew [kluː] N (*US*) = **clue**

cliché ['kliːʃeɪ] N cliché *m inv*

click [klɪk] VI scattare; (*Comput*) cliccare ▶ VT: **to ~ one's tongue** schioccare la lingua; **to ~ one's heels** battere i tacchi

clickable ['klɪkəbl] ADJ cliccabile

client ['klaɪənt] N cliente *mf*

clientele [kliːɑːn'tɛl] N clientela

cliff [klɪf] N scogliera scoscesa, rupe *f*

cliffhanger ['klɪfhæŋər'] N (*TV, fig*) episodio (*or* situazione *etc*) ricco(-a) di suspense

climactic [klaɪ'mæktɪk] ADJ culminante

climate ['klaımıt] N clima *m*

climate change N cambiamenti *mpl* climatici

climax ['klaımæks] N culmine *m*; (*of play etc*) momento più emozionante; (*sexual*) orgasmo

climb [klaım] vı salire; (*clamber*) arrampicarsi; (*plane*) prendere quota ▸ vᴛ salire; (*Climbing*) scalare ▸ N salita; arrampicata; scalata; **to ~ over a wall** scavalcare un muro
▸ **climb down** vı scendere; (ʙʀıᴛ *fig*) far marcia indietro

climbdown ['klaımdaun] N (ʙʀıᴛ) ritirata

climber ['klaımə^r] N (*also*: **rock climber**) rocciatore(-trice); alpinista *mf*

climbing ['klaımıŋ] N (*also*: **rock climbing**) alpinismo

clinch [klıntʃ] vᴛ (*deal*) concludere

clincher ['klıntʃə^r] N (*col*): **that was the ~** quello è stato il fattore decisivo

cling [klıŋ] (*pt*, *pp* **clung** [klʌŋ]) vı: **to ~ (to)** tenersi stretto(-a) (a), aggrapparsi (a); (*clothes*) aderire strettamente (a)

clingfilm® ['klıŋfılm] N pellicola trasparente (*per alimenti*)

clinic ['klınık] N clinica; (*session*) seduta; serie *f* di sedute

clinical ['klınıkəl] ADJ clinico(-a); (*fig*) freddo(-a), distaccato(-a)

clink [klıŋk] vı tintinnare

clip [klıp] N (*for hair*) forcina; (*also*: **paper clip**) graffetta; (TV, *Cine*) sequenza; (ʙʀıᴛ: *also*: **bulldog clip**) fermafogli *m inv*; (*holding hose etc*) anello d'attacco ▸ vᴛ (*also*: **clip together**: *papers*) attaccare insieme; (*hair*, *nails*) tagliare; (*hedge*) tosare

clippers ['klıpəz] NPL macchinetta per capelli; (*also*: **nail clippers**) forbicine *fpl* per le unghie

clipping ['klıpıŋ] N (*from newspaper*) ritaglio

clique [kli:k] N cricca

cloak [kləuk] N mantello ▸ vᴛ avvolgere

cloakroom ['kləukrum] N (*for coats etc*) guardaroba *m inv*; (ʙʀıᴛ: W.C.) gabinetti *mpl*

clock [klɔk] N orologio; (*of taxi*) tassametro; **around the ~** ventiquatt'ore su ventiquattro; **to sleep round the ~** *or* **the ~ round** dormire un giorno intero; **to work against the ~** lavorare in gara col tempo; **30,000 on the ~** (ʙʀıᴛ *Aut*) 30.000 sul contachilometri
▸ **clock in, clock on** vı (ʙʀıᴛ) timbrare il cartellino (all'entrata)
▸ **clock off, clock out** vı (ʙʀıᴛ) timbrare il cartellino (all'uscita)
▸ **clock up** vᴛ (*miles, hours etc*) fare

clockwise ['klɔkwaız] ADV in senso orario

clockwork ['klɔkwə:k] N movimento *or* meccanismo a orologeria ▸ ADJ (*toy, train*) a molla

clog [klɔg] N zoccolo ▸ vᴛ intasare ▸ vı (*also*: **clog up**) intasarsi, bloccarsi

cloister ['klɔıstə^r] N chiostro

clone [kləun] N clone *m* ▸ vᴛ clonare

close¹ [kləus] ADJ vicino(-a); (*writing, texture*) fitto(-a); (*watch*) stretto(-a); (*examination*) attento(-a); (*contest*) combattuto(-a); (*weather*) afoso(-a) ▸ ADV vicino, dappresso; **~ to** prep vicino a; **~ by**, **~ at hand** qui (*or* lì) vicino; **how ~ is Edinburgh to Glasgow?** quanto dista Edimburgo da Glasgow?; **a ~ friend** un amico intimo; **to have a ~ shave** (*fig*) scamparla bella; **at ~ quarters** da vicino

close² [kləuz] vᴛ chiudere; (*bargain, deal*) concludere ▸ vı (*shop etc*) chiudere; (*lid, door etc*) chiudersi; (*end*) finire ▸ N (*end*) fine *f*; **to bring sth to a ~** terminare qc
▸ **close down** vᴛ chiudere (definitivamente) ▸ vı cessare (definitivamente)
▸ **close in** vı (*hunters*) stringersi attorno; (*evening, night, fog*) calare; **to ~ in on sb** accerchiare qn; **the days are closing in** le giornate si accorciano
▸ **close off** vᴛ (*area*) chiudere

closed [kləuzd] ADJ chiuso(-a)

closed-circuit ['kləuzd'sə:kıt] ADJ: **~ television** televisione *f* a circuito chiuso

closed shop N azienda o fabbrica che impiega solo aderenti ai sindacati

close-knit ['kləus'nıt] ADJ (*family, community*) molto unito(-a)

closely ['kləuslı] ADV (*examine, watch*) da vicino; **we are ~ related** siamo parenti stretti; **a ~ guarded secret** un assoluto segreto

close season ['kləuz-] N (*Football*) periodo di vacanza del campionato; (*Hunting*) stagione *f* di chiusura (*di caccia, pesca ecc*)

closet ['klɔzıt] N (*cupboard*) armadio

close-up ['kləusʌp] N primo piano

closing ['kləuzıŋ] ADJ (*stages, remarks*) conclusivo(-a), finale; **~ price** (*Stock Exchange*) prezzo di chiusura

closing time N orario di chiusura

closure ['kləuʒə^r] N chiusura

clot [klɔt] N (*also*: **blood clot**) coagulo; (*col*: *idiot*) scemo(-a) ▸ vı coagularsi

cloth [klɔθ] N (*material*) tessuto, stoffa; (ʙʀıᴛ: *also*: **teacloth**) strofinaccio; (*also*: **tablecloth**) tovaglia

clothe [kləuð] vᴛ vestire

clothes [kləuðz] NPL abiti *mpl*, vestiti *mpl*; **to put one's ~ on** vestirsi; **to take one's ~ off** togliersi i vestiti, svestirsi

clothes brush N spazzola per abiti

clothes line N corda (per stendere il bucato)

clothes peg, (US) **clothes pin** N molletta

clothing ['kləuðıŋ] N = **clothes**

clotted cream ['klɔtıd-] N (ʙʀıᴛ) panna rappresa

cloud [klaud] N nuvola; (*of dust, smoke, gas*) nube *f* ▸ vᴛ (*liquid*) intorbidire; **to ~ the issue** disto-

gliere dal problema; **every ~ has a silver lining**
(*proverb*) non tutto il male vien per nuocere
▶ **cloud over** vi rannuvolarsi; (*fig*) offuscarsi

cloudburst [ˈklaudbəːst] N acquazzone *m*

cloud computing N cloud computing *m inv*

cloud-cuckoo-land [ˈklaudˈkukuːˈlænd] N
(BRIT) mondo dei sogni

cloudy [ˈklaudɪ] ADJ nuvoloso(-a); (*liquid*) torbi-
do(-a)

clout [klaut] N (*blow*) colpo; (*fig*) influenza ▶ VT
dare un colpo a

clove [kləuv] N chiodo di garofano

clove of garlic N spicchio d'aglio

clover [ˈkləuvəʳ] N trifoglio

cloverleaf [ˈkləuvəliːf] N foglia di trifoglio;
(*Aut*) raccordo a quadrifoglio)

clown [klaun] N pagliaccio ▶ VI (*also*: **clown
about**, **clown around**) fare il pagliaccio

cloying [ˈklɔɪɪŋ] ADJ (*taste, smell*) nauseabon-
do(-a)

club [klʌb] N (*society*) club *m inv*, circolo; (*weapon,
Golf*) mazza ▶ VT bastonare ▶ VI: **to ~ together**
associarsi ■ **clubs** NPL (*Cards*) fiori *mpl*

club car N (*US Rail*) carrozza *or* vagone *m* ristorante

club class N (*Aviat*) classe *f* club *inv*

clubhouse [ˈklʌbhaus] N sede *f* del circolo

club soda N (*US*) = **soda**

cluck [klʌk] VI chiocciare

clue [kluː] N indizio; (*in crosswords*) definizione *f*;
I haven't a ~ non ho la minima idea

clued up, (*US*) **clued in** [kluːd-] ADJ (*col*) (ben)
informato(-a)

clump [klʌmp] N (*of flowers, trees*) gruppo; (*of
grass*) ciuffo

clumsy [ˈklʌmzɪ] ADJ (*person*) goffo(-a), malde-
stro(-a); (*object*) malfatto(-a), mal costruito(-a)

clung [klʌŋ] PT, PP *of* **cling**

cluster [ˈklʌstəʳ] N gruppo ▶ VI raggrupparsi

clutch [klʌtʃ] N (*grip, grasp*) presa, stretta; (*Aut*)
frizione *f* ▶ VT afferrare, stringere forte; **to ~ at**
aggrapparsi a

clutter [ˈklʌtəʳ] VT (*also*: **clutter up**) ingombrare ▶ N confusione *f*, disordine *m*

cm ABBR (= *centimetre*) cm

CNAA N ABBR (BRIT: = *Council for National Academic
Awards*) organizzazione che conferisce premi accade-
mici

CND N ABBR (BRIT) = **Campaign for Nuclear Disarmament**

CO N ABBR (= *commanding officer*) Com.; (BRIT)
= **Commonwealth Office** ▶ ABBR (US) = **Colorado**

Co. ABBR = **county**; (= *company*) C., C.ia

c/o ABBR (= *care of*) presso

coach [kəutʃ] N (*bus*) pullman *m inv*; (*horse-
drawn, of train*) carrozza; (*Sport*) allenato-

re(-trice); (*tutor*) chi dà ripetizioni ▶ VT
allenare; dare ripetizioni a

coach station N (BRIT) stazione *f* delle corriere

coach trip N viaggio in pullman

coagulate [kəuˈægjuleɪt] VT coagulare ▶ VI
coagularsi

coal [kəul] N carbone *m*

coalface [ˈkəulfeɪs] N fronte *f*

coalfield [ˈkəulfiːld] N bacino carbonifero

coalition [kəuəˈlɪʃən] N coalizione *f*

coalman [ˈkəulmən] N (*irreg*) negoziante *m* di
carbone

coalmine [ˈkəulmaɪn] N miniera di carbone

coalminer [ˈkəulmaɪnəʳ] N minatore(-trice)

coalmining [ˈkəulmaɪnɪŋ] N estrazione *f* del
carbone

coarse [kɔːs] ADJ (*salt, sand etc*) grosso(-a); (*cloth,
person*) rozzo(-a); (*vulgar: character, laugh*) volgare

coast [kəust] N costa ▶ VI (*with cycle etc*) scendere
a ruota libera

coastal [ˈkəustəl] ADJ costiero(-a)

coaster [ˈkəustəʳ] N (*Naut*) nave *f* da cabotaggio;
(*for glass*) sottobicchiere *m*

coastguard [ˈkəustgɑːd] N guardia costiera

coastline [ˈkəustlaɪn] N linea costiera

coat [kəut] N cappotto; (*of animal*) pelo; (*of paint*)
mano *f* ▶ VT coprire; **~ of arms** *n* stemma *m*

coat hanger N attaccapanni *m inv*

coating [ˈkəutɪŋ] N rivestimento

co-author [ˈkəuˈɔːθəʳ] N coautore(-trice)

coax [kəuks] VT indurre (con moine)

cob [kɔb] N *see* **corn**

cobbled [ˈkɔbld] ADJ: **~ street** strada pavimen-
tata a ciottoli

cobbler [ˈkɔbləʳ] N calzolaio(-a)

cobbles [ˈkɔblz], **cobblestones** [ˈkɔblstəunz]
NPL ciottoli *mpl*

COBOL [ˈkəubɔl] N COBOL *m*

cobra [ˈkəubrə] N cobra *m inv*

cobweb [ˈkɔbwɛb] N ragnatela

cocaine [kəˈkeɪn] N cocaina

cock [kɔk] N (*rooster*) gallo; (*male bird*) maschio
▶ VT (*gun*) armare; **to ~ one's ears** (*fig*) drizzare
le orecchie

cock-a-hoop [kɔkəˈhuːp] ADJ euforico(-a)

cockerel [ˈkɔkərəl] N galletto

cock-eyed [ˈkɔkaɪd] ADJ (*fig*) storto(-a); stram-
palato(-a)

cockle [ˈkɔkl] N cardio

cockney [ˈkɔknɪ] N cockney *mf* (*abitante dei quartieri popolari dell'East End di Londra*)

cockpit [ˈkɔkpɪt] N abitacolo

cockroach [ˈkɔkrəutʃ] N blatta

cocktail [ˈkɔkteɪl] N cocktail *m inv*; **prawn ~**,
(*US*) **shrimp ~** cocktail *m inv* di gamberetti

cocktail cabinet N mobile *m* bar *inv*

cocktail party N cocktail *m inv*

cocktail shaker N shaker *m inv*

cocky ['kɔkɪ] ADJ spavaldo(-a), arrogante

cocoa ['kəukəu] N cacao

coconut ['kəukənʌt] N noce *f* di cocco

cocoon [kə'ku:n] N bozzolo

COD ABBR = **cash on delivery**; (US) = **collect on delivery**

cod [kɔd] N merluzzo

code [kəud] N codice *m* ▶ VT, VI (*Comput*) codificare; **~ of behaviour** regole *fpl* di condotta; **~ of practice** codice professionale

codeine ['kəudi:n] N codeina

codger ['kɔdʒəʳ] N (*BRIT pej*): **an old ~** un simpatico nonnetto

codicil ['kɔdɪsɪl] N codicillo

codify ['kəudɪfaɪ] VT codificare

cod-liver oil ['kɔdlɪvəʳ-] N olio di fegato di merluzzo

co-driver ['kəu'draɪvəʳ] N (*in race*) copilota *m*; (*of lorry*) secondo autista *m*

co-ed ['kəu'ɛd] ADJ ABBR = **coeducational** ▶ N ABBR (US: *female student*) studentessa presso un'università mista; (*BRIT: school*) scuola mista

coeducational ['kəuɛdju'keɪʃənl] ADJ misto(-a)

coerce [kəu'ə:s] VT costringere

coercion [kəu'ə:ʃən] N coercizione *f*

coexistence ['kəuɪg'zɪstəns] N coesistenza

C. of C. N ABBR = **chamber of commerce**

C of E ABBR = **Church of England**

coffee ['kɔfɪ] N caffè *m inv*; **white ~**, (US) **~ with cream** caffellatte *m*

coffee bar N (*BRIT*) caffè *m inv*

coffee bean N grano *or* chicco di caffè

coffee break N pausa per il caffè

coffee cake ['kɔfɪkeɪk] N (US) panino dolce all'uva

coffee cup N tazzina da caffè

coffee maker N bollitore *m* per il caffè

coffeepot ['kɔfɪpɔt] N caffettiera

coffee shop N ≈ caffè *m inv*

coffee table N tavolino

coffin ['kɔfɪn] N bara

C of I ABBR = **Church of Ireland**

C of S ABBR = **Church of Scotland**

cog [kɔg] N dente *m*

cogent ['kəudʒənt] ADJ convincente

cognac ['kɔnjæk] N cognac *m inv*

cognitive ['kɔgnɪtɪv] ADJ cognitivo(-a)

cogwheel ['kɔgwi:l] N ruota dentata

cohabit [kəu'hæbɪt] VI (*formal*): **to ~ (with sb)** coabitare (con qn)

coherent [kəu'hɪərənt] ADJ coerente

cohesion [kəu'hi:ʒən] N coesione *f*

cohesive [kəu'hi:sɪv] ADJ (*fig*) unificante, coesivo(-a)

COI N ABBR (*BRIT*) = **Central Office of Information**

coil [kɔɪl] N rotolo; (*one loop*) anello; (*Aut, Elec*) bobina; (*contraceptive*) spirale *f*; (*of smoke*) filo ▶ VT avvolgere

coin [kɔɪn] N moneta ▶ VT (*word*) coniare

coinage ['kɔɪnɪdʒ] N sistema *m* monetario

coin-box ['kɔɪnbɔks] N (*BRIT*) cabina telefonica

coincide [kəuɪn'saɪd] VI coincidere

coincidence [kəu'ɪnsɪdəns] N combinazione *f*

coin-operated ['kɔɪn'ɔpəreɪtɪd] ADJ (*machine*) (che funziona) a monete

Coke® [kəuk] N (*Coca-Cola*) coca *f inv*

coke [kəuk] N coke *m*

Col. ABBR = **colonel**; (US) = **Colorado**

COLA N ABBR (US: = *cost-of-living adjustment*) ≈ scala mobile

colander ['kɔləndəʳ] N colino

cold [kəuld] ADJ freddo(-a) ▶ N freddo; (*Med*) raffreddore *m*; **it's ~** fa freddo; **to be ~** (*person*) aver freddo; (*object*) essere freddo(-a); **to catch ~** prendere freddo; **to catch a ~** prendere un raffreddore; **in ~ blood** a sangue freddo; **to have ~ feet** avere i piedi freddi; (*fig*) aver la fifa; **to give sb the ~ shoulder** ignorare qn

cold-blooded [kəuld'blʌdɪd] ADJ (*Zool*) a sangue freddo

cold call N chiamata pubblicitaria non richiesta

cold cream N crema emolliente

coldly ['kəuldlɪ] ADV freddamente

cold sore N erpete *m*

cold sweat N: **to be in a ~ (about sth)** sudare freddo (per qc)

cold turkey N (*col*): **to go ~** avere la scimmia (*drogato*)

Cold War N: **the ~** la guerra fredda

coleslaw ['kəulslɔ:] N *insalata di cavolo bianco*

colic ['kɔlɪk] N colica

colicky ['kɔlɪkɪ] ADJ che soffre di coliche

collaborate [kə'læbəreɪt] VI collaborare

collaboration [kəlæbə'reɪʃən] N collaborazione *f*

collaborator [kə'læbəreɪtəʳ] N collaboratore(-trice)

collage [kɔ'lɑ:ʒ] N (*Art*) collage *m inv*

collagen ['kɔlədʒən] N collageno

collapse [kə'læps] VI (*gen*) crollare; (*government*) cadere; (*Med*) avere un collasso; (*plans*) fallire ▶ N crollo; caduta; (*Med*) collasso; fallimento

collapsible [kə'læpsəbl] ADJ pieghevole

collar ['kɔləʳ] N (*of coat, shirt*) colletto; (*for dog*) collare *m*; (*Tech*) anello, fascetta ▶ VT (*col: person, object*) beccare

collarbone ['kɔləbəʊn] N clavicola

collate [kɔ'leɪt] VT collazionare

collateral [kɔ'lætərəl] N garanzia

collation [kɔ'leɪʃən] N collazione *f*

colleague ['kɔliːg] N collega *mf*

collect [kə'lɛkt] VT (*gen*) raccogliere; (*as a hobby*) fare collezione di; (*BRIT: call for*) prendere; (*money owed, pension*) riscuotere; (*donations, subscriptions*) fare una colletta di ▶ VI (*people*) adunarsi, riunirsi; (*rubbish etc*) ammucchiarsi ▶ ADV (*US Tel*): **to call ~** fare una chiamata a carico del destinatario; **to ~ one's thoughts** raccogliere le idee; **~ on delivery** (*US Comm*) pagamento alla consegna

collected [kə'lɛktɪd] ADJ: **~ works** opere *fpl* raccolte

collection [kə'lɛkʃən] N collezione *f*; raccolta; (*for money*) colletta; (*Post*) levata

collective [kə'lɛktɪv] ADJ collettivo(-a) ▶ N collettivo

collective bargaining N trattative *fpl* (sindacali) collettive

collector [kə'lɛktəʳ] N collezionista *mf*; (*of taxes*) esattore(-trice); **~'s item** *or* **piece** pezzo da collezionista

college ['kɔlɪdʒ] N (*Scol*) college *m inv*; (*of technology, agriculture etc*) istituto superiore; (*body*) collegio; **~ of education** ≈ facoltà *f inv* di Magistero

collide [kə'laɪd] VI: **to ~ (with)** scontrarsi (con)

collie ['kɔlɪ] N (*dog*) collie *m inv*

colliery ['kɔlɪərɪ] N (*BRIT*) miniera di carbone

collision [kə'lɪʒən] N collisione *f*, scontro; **to be on a ~ course** (*also fig*) essere in rotta di collisione

collision damage waiver N (*Insurance*) copertura per i danni alla vettura

colloquial [kə'ləʊkwɪəl] ADJ familiare

collusion [kə'luːʒən] N collusione *f*; **in ~ with** in accordo segreto con

Cologne [kə'ləʊn] N Colonia

cologne [kə'ləʊn] N (*also:* **eau de cologne**) acqua di colonia

Colombia [kə'lɔmbɪə] N Colombia

Colombian [kə'lɔmbɪən] ADJ, N colombiano(-a)

colon ['kəʊlən] N (*sign*) due punti *mpl*; (*Med*) colon *m inv*

colonel ['kəːnl] N colonnello

colonial [kə'ləʊnɪəl] ADJ coloniale

colonize ['kɔlənaɪz] VT colonizzare

colony ['kɔlənɪ] N colonia

color *etc* ['kʌləʳ] (*US*) = **colour** *etc*

Colorado beetle [kɔlə'rɑːdəʊ-] N dorifora

colossal [kə'lɔsl] ADJ colossale

colour, (*US*) **color** ['kʌləʳ] N colore *m* ▶ VT colo-

rare; (*tint, dye*) tingere; (*fig: affect*) influenzare ▶ VI (*blush*) arrossire ▶ CPD (*film, photograph, television*) a colori ■ **colours** NPL (*of party, club*) emblemi *mpl*
▶ **colour in** VT colorare

colour bar, (*US*) **color bar** N discriminazione *f* razziale (*in locali ecc*)

colour-blind, (*US*) **color-blind** ['kʌləblaɪnd] ADJ daltonico(-a)

coloured, (*US*) **colored** ['kʌləd] ADJ colorato(-a); (*photo*) a colori; (*!: person*) di colore

colour film, (*US*) **color film** N (*for camera*) pellicola a colori

colourful, (*US*) **colorful** ['kʌləful] ADJ pieno(-a) di colore, a vivaci colori; (*personality*) colorato(-a)

colouring, (*US*) **coloring** ['kʌlərɪŋ] N colorazione *f*; (*substance*) colorante *m*; (*complexion*) colorito

colour scheme, (*US*) **color scheme** N combinazione *f* di colori

colour supplement N (*BRIT Press*) supplemento a colori

colour television, (*US*) **color television** N televisione *f* a colori

colt [kəʊlt] N puledro

column ['kɔləm] N colonna; (*fashion column, sports column etc*) rubrica; **the editorial ~** l'articolo di fondo

columnist ['kɔləmnɪst] N articolista *mf*

coma ['kəʊmə] N coma *m inv*

comb [kəʊm] N pettine *m* ▶ VT (*hair*) pettinare; (*area*) battere a tappeto

combat ['kɔmbæt] N combattimento ▶ VT combattere, lottare contro

combination [kɔmbɪ'neɪʃən] N combinazione *f*

combination lock N serratura a combinazione

combine[1] VT [kəm'baɪn]: **to ~ (with)** combinare (con); (*one quality with another*): **to ~ sth with sth** unire qc a qc ▶ VI unirsi; (*Chem*) combinarsi ▶ N ['kɔmbaɪn] lega; (*Econ*) associazione *f*; **a combined effort** uno sforzo collettivo

combine[2], **combine harvester** N mietitrebbia

combo ['kɔmbəʊ] N (*Jazz etc*) gruppo

combustible [kəm'bʌstɪbl] ADJ combustibile

combustion [kəm'bʌstʃən] N combustione *f*

come [kʌm] (*pt* **came** [keɪm], *pp* ~ [kʌm]) VI venire; (*arrive*) venire, arrivare; **~ with me** vieni con me; **we've just ~ from Paris** siamo appena arrivati da Parigi; **nothing came of it** non è saltato fuori niente; **to ~ into sight** *or* **view** apparire; **to ~ to** (*decision etc*) raggiungere; **I've ~ to like him** ha cominciato a piacermi; **to ~ undone/loose** slacciarsi/allentarsi; **coming!** vengo!; **if it comes to it** nella peggiore delle ipotesi

▶**come about** vi succedere

▶**come across** vt fus trovare per caso ▶ vi: **to ~ across well/badly** fare una buona/cattiva impressione

▶**come along** vi (*pupil, work*) fare progressi; **~ along!** avanti!, andiamo!, forza!

▶**come apart** vi andare in pezzi; (*become detached*) staccarsi

▶**come away** vi venire via; (*become detached*) staccarsi

▶**come back** vi ritornare; (*reply: col*): **can I ~ back to you on that one?** possiamo riparlarne più tardi?

▶**come by** vt fus (*acquire*) ottenere; procurarsi

▶**come down** vi scendere; (*prices*) calare; (*buildings*) essere demolito(-a)

▶**come forward** vi farsi avanti; presentarsi

▶**come from** vt fus venire da; provenire da

▶**come in** vi entrare

▶**come in for** vt fus (*criticism etc*) ricevere

▶**come into** vt fus (*money*) ereditare

▶**come off** vi (*button*) staccarsi; (*stain*) andar via; (*attempt*) riuscire

▶**come on** vi (*lights*) accendersi; (*electricity*) entrare in funzione; (*pupil, undertaking*) fare progressi; **~ on!** avanti!, andiamo!, forza!

▶**come out** vi uscire; (*strike*) entrare in sciopero; (*stain*) andare via

▶**come over** vt fus: **I don't know what's ~ over him!** non so cosa gli sia successo!

▶**come round** vi (*after faint, operation*) riprendere conoscenza, rinvenire

▶**come through** vi (*survive*) sopravvivere, farcela; **the call came through** ci hanno passato la telefonata

▶**come to** vi rinvenire ▶ vt (*add up to: amount*): **how much does it ~ to?** quanto costa?, quanto viene?

▶**come under** vt fus (*heading*) trovarsi sotto; (*influence*) cadere sotto, subire

▶**come up** vi venire su; (*sun*) salire; (*problem*) sorgere; (*event*) essere in arrivo; (*in conversation*) saltar fuori

▶**come up against** vt fus (*resistance, difficulties*) urtare contro

▶**come up to** vt fus arrivare (fino) a; **the film didn't ~ up to our expectations** il film ci ha delusi

▶**come up with** vt fus: **he came up with an idea** venne fuori con un'idea

▶**come upon** vt fus trovare per caso

comeback [ˈkʌmbæk] N (*Theat etc*) ritorno; (*reaction*) reazione *f*; (*response*) risultato, risposta

comedian [kəˈmiːdɪən] N comico

comedienne [kəmiːdɪˈɛn] N attrice *f* comica

comedown [ˈkʌmdaʊn] N rovescio

comedy [ˈkɒmɪdɪ] N commedia

comet [ˈkɒmɪt] N cometa

comeuppance [kʌmˈʌpəns] N: **to get one's ~** ricevere ciò che si merita

comfort [ˈkʌmfət] N comodità *f inv*, benessere *m*; (*relief*) consolazione *f*, conforto ▶ vt consolare, confortare

comfortable [ˈkʌmfətəbl] ADJ comodo(-a); (*financially*) agiato(-a); (*income, majority*) più che sufficiente; **I don't feel very ~ about it** non mi sento molto tranquillo

comfortably [ˈkʌmfətəblɪ] ADV (*sit*) comodamente; (*live*) bene

comforter [ˈkʌmfətəʳ] N (*US*) trapunta

comforts [ˈkʌmfəts] NPL comforts *mpl*, comodità *fpl*

comfort station N (*US*) gabinetti *mpl*

comic [ˈkɒmɪk] ADJ (*also*: **comical**) comico(-a), divertente ▶ N comico; (*BRIT: magazine*) giornaletto

comic book N (*US*) giornalino (a fumetti)

comic strip N fumetto

coming [ˈkʌmɪŋ] N arrivo ▶ ADJ (*next*) prossimo(-a); (*future*) futuro(-a); **in the ~ weeks** nelle prossime settimane

comings and goings NPL, **coming and going** N andirivieni *m inv*

Comintern [ˈkɒmɪntɜːn] N KOMINTERN *m*

comma [ˈkɒmə] N virgola

command [kəˈmɑːnd] N ordine *m*, comando; (*Mil: authority*) comando; (*mastery*) padronanza; (*Comput*) command *m inv*, comando ▶ vt comandare; **to ~ sb to do** ordinare a qn di fare; **to have/take ~ of** avere/prendere il comando di; **to have at one's ~** (*money, resources etc*) avere a propria disposizione

command economy N = **planned economy**

commandeer [kɒmənˈdɪəʳ] vt requisire

commander [kəˈmɑːndəʳ] N capo; (*Mil*) comandante *m*

commander-in-chief [kəˈmɑːndərɪnˈtʃiːf] N (*Mil*) comandante *m* in capo

commanding [kəˈmɑːndɪŋ] ADJ (*appearance*) imponente; (*voice, tone*) autorevole; (*lead, position*) dominante

commanding officer N comandante *m*

commandment [kəˈmɑːndmənt] N (*Rel*) comandamento

command module N (*Space*) modulo di comando

commando [kəˈmɑːndəʊ] N commando *m inv*; membro di un commando

commemorate [kəˈmɛməreɪt] vt commemorare

commemoration [kəmɛməˈreɪʃən] N commemorazione *f*

commemorative [kəˈmɛmərətɪv] ADJ commemorativo(-a)

commence [kəˈmɛns] vt, vi cominciare

commencement N (*US Univ*) cerimonia di consegna dei diplomi

commend [kəˈmɛnd] vt lodare; raccomandare

commendable [kəˈmɛndəbl] ADJ lodevole

commendation [kɔmɛn'deɪʃən] N lode f; rac-comandazione f; (for bravery etc) encomio

commensurate [kə'mɛnʃərɪt] ADJ: ~ **with** proporzionato(-a) a

comment ['kɔmɛnt] N commento ▶ VI: **to ~ (on)** fare commenti (su); **to ~ that** osservare che; **"no ~"** "niente da dire"

commentary ['kɔməntərɪ] N commentario; (Sport) radiocronaca; telecronaca

commentator ['kɔməntɛɪtəʳ] N commentatore(-trice); (Sport) radiocronista mf; telecronista mf

commerce ['kɔmə:s] N commercio

commercial [kə'mə:ʃəl] ADJ commerciale ▶ N (TV, Radio) pubblicità f inv

commercial bank N banca commerciale

commercial break N intervallo pubblicitario

commercial college N ≈ istituto commerciale

commercialism [kə'mə:ʃəlɪzəm] N affarismo

commercial television N televisione f commerciale

commercial traveller N commesso(-a) viaggiatore(-trice)

commercial vehicle N veicolo commerciale

commiserate [kə'mɪzəreɪt] VI: **to ~ with** condolersi con

commission [kə'mɪʃən] N commissione f; (for salesman) commissione, provvigione f ▶ VT (Mil) nominare (al comando); (work of art) commissionare; **I get 10%** ~ ricevo il 10% sulle vendite; **out of ~** (Naut) in disarmo; (machine) fuori uso; **to ~ sb to do sth** incaricare qn di fare qc; **to ~ sth from sb** (painting etc) commissionare qc a qn; ~ **of inquiry** (BRIT) commissione f d'inchiesta

commissionaire [kəmɪʃə'nɛəʳ] N (BRIT: at shop, cinema etc) portiere m in livrea

commissioner [kə'mɪʃənəʳ] N commissionario; (Police) questore m

commit [kə'mɪt] VT (act) commettere; (to sb's care) affidare; **to ~ o.s. (to do)** impegnarsi (a fare); **to ~ suicide** suicidarsi; **to ~ sb for trial** rinviare qn a giudizio

commitment [kə'mɪtmənt] N impegno; promessa

committed [kə'mɪtɪd] ADJ (writer) impegnato(-a); (Christian) convinto(-a)

committee [kə'mɪtɪ] N comitato, commissione f; **to be on a ~** far parte di un comitato or di una commissione

committee meeting N riunione f di comitato or di commissione

commodity [kə'mɔdɪtɪ] N prodotto, articolo; (food) derrata

commodity exchange N borsa f merci inv

common ['kɔmən] ADJ comune; (pej) volgare; (usual) normale ▶ N terreno comune; **in ~** in

comune; **in ~ use** di uso comune; **it's ~ knowledge that** è di dominio pubblico che; **to the ~ good** nell'interesse generale, per il bene comune; see also **Commons**

common cold N: **the ~** il raffreddore

common denominator N denominatore m comune

commoner ['kɔmənəʳ] N cittadino(-a) (non nobile)

common ground N (fig) terreno comune

common land N terreno di uso pubblico

common law N diritto consuetudinario

common-law ['kɔmənlɔ:] ADJ: ~ **wife** convivente f more uxorio

commonly ['kɔmənlɪ] ADV comunemente, usualmente

Common Market N Mercato Comune

commonplace ['kɔmənpleɪs] ADJ banale, ordinario(-a)

common room ['kɔmənrum] N sala di riunione; (Scol) sala dei professori

Commons ['kɔmənz] NPL (BRIT Pol): **the (House of) ~** la Camera dei Comuni

common sense N buon senso

Commonwealth ['kɔmənwɛlθ] N: **the ~** il Commonwealth

Il **Commonwealth** è un'organizzazione che raggruppa 53 stati sovrani indipendenti e alcuni territori annessi che facevano parte dell'Impero britannico. Ancora oggi molti stati del Commonwealth riconoscono simbolicamente il sovrano britannico come capo di stato e i loro rappresentanti si riuniscono per discutere questioni di comune interesse.

commotion [kə'məuʃən] N confusione f, tumulto

communal ['kɔmju:nl] ADJ (life) comunale; (for common use) pubblico(-a)

commune N ['kɔmju:n] (group) comune f ▶ VI [kə'mju:n]: **to ~ with** mettersi in comunione con

communicate [kə'mju:nɪkeɪt] VT comunicare, trasmettere ▶ VI: **to ~ (with)** comunicare (con)

communication [kəmju:nɪ'keɪʃən] N comunicazione f

communication cord N (BRIT) segnale m d'allarme

communications network N rete f delle comunicazioni

communications satellite N satellite m per telecomunicazioni

communicative [kə'mju:nɪkətɪv] ADJ (gen) loquace

communion [kə'mju:nɪən] N (also: **Holy Communion**) comunione f

communiqué [kə'mju:nɪkeɪ] N comunicato

communism ['kɔmjunɪzəm] N comunismo

485

communist [ˈkɔmjunɪst] ADJ, N comunista (mf)

community [kəˈmjuːnɪtɪ] N comunità f inv

community centre, (US) **community center** N circolo ricreativo

community chest N (US) fondo di beneficenza

community health centre N centro socio-sanitario

community home N (BRIT) riformatorio

community service N (BRIT) ≈ lavoro sostitutivo

community spirit N spirito civico

commutation ticket [kɔmjuˈteɪʃən-] N (US) biglietto di abbonamento

commute [kəˈmjuːt] VI fare il pendolare ▸ VT (Law) commutare

commuter [kəˈmjuːtəʳ] N pendolare mf

Comoros [ˈkɔmərəuz, kəˈmɔːrəuz] NPL Unione f delle Comore

compact ADJ [kəmˈpækt] compatto(-a) ▸ N [ˈkɔmpækt] (also: **powder compact**) portacipria m inv

compact disc N compact disc m inv

compact disc player N lettore m CD inv

companion [kəmˈpænjən] N compagno(-a)

companionship [kəmˈpænjənʃɪp] N compagnia

companionway [kəmˈpænjənweɪ] N (Naut) scala

company [ˈkʌmpənɪ] N (also Comm, Mil, Theat) compagnia; **he's good ~** è di buona compagnia; **we have ~** abbiamo ospiti; **to keep sb ~** tenere compagnia a qn; **to part ~ with** separarsi da; **Smith and C~** Smith e soci

company car N macchina (di proprietà) della ditta

company director N amministratore(-trice), consigliere(-a) di amministrazione

company secretary N (BRIT Comm) segretario(-a) generale

comparable [ˈkɔmpərəbl] ADJ simile; **~ to** or **with** paragonabile a

comparative [kəmˈpærətɪv] ADJ (freedom, cost) relativo(-a); (adjective, adverb etc) comparativo(-a); (literature) comparato(-a)

comparatively [kəmˈpærətɪvlɪ] ADV relativamente

compare [kəmˈpεəʳ] VT: **to ~ sth/sb with/to** confrontare qc/qn con/a ▸ VI: **to ~ (with)** reggere il confronto (con); **compared with** or **to** a paragone di, rispetto a; **how do the prices ~?** che differenza di prezzo c'è?

comparison [kəmˈpærɪsn] N confronto; **in ~ with** confronto a

compartment [kəmˈpɑːtmənt] N compartimento; (Rail) scompartimento

compass [ˈkʌmpəs] N bussola; **(a pair of) com-** **passes** (Math) compasso; **within the ~ of** entro i limiti di

compassion [kəmˈpæʃən] N compassione f

compassionate [kəmˈpæʃənɪt] ADJ compassionevole; **on ~ grounds** per motivi personali

compassionate leave N congedo straordinario (per gravi motivi di famiglia)

compatibility [kəmpætɪˈbɪlɪtɪ] N compatibilità

compatible [kəmˈpætɪbl] ADJ compatibile

compel [kəmˈpεl] VT costringere, obbligare

compelling [kəmˈpεlɪŋ] ADJ (fig: argument) irresistibile

compendium [kəmˈpεndɪəm] N compendio

compensate [ˈkɔmpənseɪt] VT risarcire ▸ VI: **to ~ for** compensare

compensation [kɔmpənˈseɪʃən] N compensazione f; (money) risarcimento

compère [ˈkɔmpεəʳ] N presentatore(-trice)

compete [kəmˈpiːt] VI (take part) concorrere; (vie): **to ~ (with)** fare concorrenza (a)

competence [ˈkɔmpɪtəns] N competenza

competent [ˈkɔmpɪtənt] ADJ competente

competing [kəmˈpiːtɪŋ] ADJ (theories, ideas) opposto(-a); (companies) in concorrenza; **three ~ explanations (of)** tre spiegazioni contrastanti tra di loro (di)

competition [kɔmpɪˈtɪʃən] N gara; concorso; (Sport) gara; (Econ) concorrenza; **in ~ with** in concorrenza con

competitive [kəmˈpεtɪtɪv] ADJ (sports) agonistico(-a); (person) che ha spirito di competizione; che ha spirito agonistico; (Econ) concorrenziale

competitive examination N concorso

competitor [kəmˈpεtɪtəʳ] N concorrente mf

compile [kəmˈpaɪl] VT compilare

complacency [kəmˈpleɪsnsɪ] N compiacenza di sé

complacent [kəmˈpleɪsnt] ADJ compiaciuto(-a) di sé

complain [kəmˈpleɪn] VI lagnarsi, lamentarsi; **to ~ (about)** lagnarsi (di); (in shop etc) reclamare (per)

▸ **complain of** VT FUS (Med) accusare

complaint [kəmˈpleɪnt] N lamento; (in shop etc) reclamo; (Med) malattia

complement N [ˈkɔmplɪmənt] complemento; (especially of ship's crew etc) effettivo ▸ VT [ˈkɔmplɪmεnt] (enhance) accompagnarsi bene a

complementary [kɔmplɪˈmεntərɪ] ADJ complementare

complete [kəmˈpliːt] ADJ completo(-a) ▸ VT completare; (form) riempire; **it's a ~ disaster** è un vero disastro

completely [kəmˈpliːtlɪ] ADV completamente

completion [kəm'pli:ʃən] N completamento; **to be nearing ~** essere in fase di completamento; **on ~ of contract** alla firma del contratto

complex ['kɔmplɛks] ADJ complesso(-a) ▶ N (Psych, buildings etc) complesso

complexion [kəm'plɛkʃən] N (of face) carnagione f; (of event etc) aspetto

complexity [kəm'plɛksɪtɪ] N complessità f inv

compliance [kəm'plaɪəns] N acquiescenza; **in ~ with** (orders, wishes etc) in conformità con

compliant [kəm'plaɪənt] ADJ acquiescente, arrendevole

complicate ['kɔmplɪkeɪt] VT complicare

complicated ['kɔmplɪkeɪtɪd] ADJ complicato(-a)

complication [kɔmplɪ'keɪʃən] N complicazione f

compliment N ['kɔmplɪmənt] complimento ▶ VT ['kɔmplɪmɛnt] fare un complimento a ■ **compliments** NPL complimenti mpl; rispetti mpl; **to pay sb a ~** fare un complimento a qn; **to ~ sb (on sth/on doing sth)** congratularsi or complimentarsi con qn (per qc/per aver fatto qc)

complimentary [kɔmplɪ'mɛntərɪ] ADJ complimentoso(-a), elogiativo(-a); (free) in omaggio

complimentary ticket N biglietto d'omaggio

compliments slip N cartoncino della società

comply [kəm'plaɪ] VI: **to ~ with** assentire a; conformarsi a

component [kəm'pəunənt] ADJ, N componente (m)

compose [kəm'pəuz] VT (music, poem etc) comporre; **to ~ o.s.** ricomporsi; **composed of** composto(-a) di

composed [kəm'pəuzd] ADJ calmo(-a)

composer [kəm'pəuzər] N (Mus) compositore(-trice)

composite ['kɔmpəzɪt] ADJ composito(-a); (Math) composto(-a)

composition [kɔmpə'zɪʃən] N composizione f

compost ['kɔmpɔst] N composta, concime m

composure [kəm'pəuzər] N calma

compound N ['kɔmpaund] (Chem, Ling) composto; (enclosure) recinto ▶ ADJ composto(-a) ▶ VT [kəm'paund] (fig: problem, difficulty) peggiorare

compound fracture N frattura esposta

compound interest N interesse m composto

comprehend [kɔmprɪ'hɛnd] VT comprendere, capire

comprehension [kɔmprɪ'hɛnʃən] N comprensione f

comprehensive [kɔmprɪ'hɛnsɪv] ADJ completo(-a) ▶ N (BRIT: also: **comprehensive school**) scuola secondaria aperta a tutti

comprehensive insurance policy N polizza multi-rischio inv

compress VT [kəm'prɛs] comprimere ▶ N ['kɔmprɛs] (Med) compressa

compression [kəm'prɛʃən] N compressione f

comprise [kəm'praɪz] VT (also: **be comprised of**) comprendere

compromise ['kɔmprəmaɪz] N compromesso ▶ VT compromettere ▶ VI venire a un compromesso ▶ CPD (decision, solution) di compromesso

compulsion [kəm'pʌlʃən] N costrizione f; **under ~** sotto pressioni

compulsive [kəm'pʌlsɪv] ADJ (Psych) incontrollabile; (liar, gambler) che non riesce a controllarsi; (viewing, reading) cui non si può fare a meno

compulsory [kəm'pʌlsərɪ] ADJ obbligatorio(-a)

compulsory purchase N espropriazione f

compunction [kəm'pʌŋkʃən] N scrupolo; **to have no ~ about doing sth** non farsi scrupoli a fare qc

computer [kəm'pju:tər] N computer m inv, elaboratore m elettronico

computer game N gioco per computer

computer-generated ADJ realizzato(-a) al computer

computerization [kəmpju:təraɪ'zeɪʃən] N computerizzazione f

computerize [kəm'pju:təraɪz] VT computerizzare

computer language N linguaggio m macchina inv

computer literate ADJ: **to be ~** essere in grado di usare il computer

computer peripheral N unità periferica

computer program N programma m di computer

computer programmer N programmatore(-trice)

computer programming N programmazione f di computer

computer science N informatica

computer scientist N informatico(-a)

computer studies NPL informatica

computing [kəm'pju:tɪŋ] N informatica

comrade ['kɔmrɪd] N compagno(-a)

comradeship ['kɔmrɪdʃɪp] N cameratismo

Comsat® ['kɔmsæt] N ABBR = **communications satellite**

con [kɔn] VT (col) truffare ▶ N truffa; **to ~ sb into doing sth** indurre qn a fare qc con raggiri

concave ['kɔn'keɪv] ADJ concavo(-a)

conceal [kən'si:l] VT nascondere

concede [kən'si:d] VT concedere; (admit) ammettere ▶ VI cedere

conceit [kən'si:t] N presunzione f, vanità

487

conceited [kən'si:tɪd] ADJ presuntuoso(-a), vanitoso(-a)

conceivable [kən'si:vəbl] ADJ concepibile; **it is ~ that ...** può anche darsi che ...

conceivably [kən'si:vəblɪ] ADV: **he may ~ be right** può anche darsi che abbia ragione

conceive [kən'si:v] VT concepire ▶ VI concepire un bambino; **to ~ of sth/of doing sth** immaginare qc/di fare qc

concentrate ['kɔnsəntreɪt] VI concentrarsi ▶ VT concentrare

concentration [kɔnsən'treɪʃən] N concentrazione f

concentration camp N campo di concentramento

concentric [kɔn'sɛntrɪk] ADJ concentrico(-a)

concept ['kɔnsɛpt] N concetto

conception [kən'sɛpʃən] N concezione f; (idea) idea, concetto

concern [kən'sə:n] N affare m; (Comm) azienda, ditta; (anxiety) preoccupazione f ▶ VT riguardare; **to be concerned (about)** preoccuparsi (di); **to be concerned with** occuparsi di; **as far as I am concerned** per quanto mi riguarda; **"to whom it may ~"** "a tutti gli interessati"; **the department concerned** (under discussion) l'ufficio in questione; (relevant) l'ufficio competente

concerning [kən'sə:nɪŋ] PREP riguardo a, circa

concert ['kɔnsət] N concerto; **in ~** di concerto

concerted [kən'sə:tɪd] ADJ concertato(-a)

concert hall N sala da concerti

concertina [kɔnsə'ti:nə] N piccola fisarmonica ▶ VI ridursi come una fisarmonica

concerto [kən'tʃə:təu] N concerto

concession [kən'sɛʃən] N concessione f

concessionaire [kənsɛʃə'nɛəʳ] N concessionario

concessionary [kən'sɛʃənərɪ] ADJ (ticket, fare) a prezzo ridotto

conciliation [kənsɪlɪ'eɪʃən] N conciliazione f

conciliatory [kən'sɪlɪətrɪ] ADJ conciliativo(-a)

concise [kən'saɪs] ADJ conciso(-a)

conclave ['kɔnkleɪv] N riunione f segreta; (Rel) conclave m

conclude [kən'klu:d] VT concludere ▶ VI (speaker) concludere; (events): **to ~ (with)** concludersi (con)

concluding [kən'klu:dɪŋ] ADJ (remarks etc) conclusivo(-a), finale

conclusion [kən'klu:ʒən] N conclusione f; **to come to the ~ that ...** concludere che ..., arrivare alla conclusione che ...

conclusive [kən'klu:sɪv] ADJ conclusivo(-a)

concoct [kən'kɔkt] VT inventare

concoction [kən'kɔkʃən] N (food, drink) miscuglio

concord ['kɔŋkɔ:d] N (harmony) armonia, concordia; (treaty) accordo

concourse ['kɔŋkɔ:s] N (hall) atrio

concrete ['kɔŋkri:t] N calcestruzzo ▶ ADJ concreto(-a); (Constr) di calcestruzzo

concrete mixer N betoniera

concur [kən'kə:ʳ] VI concordare

concurrently [kən'kʌrntlɪ] ADV simultaneamente

concussion [kən'kʌʃən] N (Med) commozione f cerebrale

condemn [kən'dɛm] VT condannare; (building) dichiarare pericoloso(-a)

condemnation [kɔndɛm'neɪʃən] N condanna

condensation [kɔndɛn'seɪʃən] N condensazione f

condense [kən'dɛns] VI condensarsi ▶ VT condensare

condensed milk N latte m condensato

condescend [kɔndɪ'sɛnd] VI condiscendere; **to ~ to do sth** degnarsi di fare qc

condescending [kɔndɪ'sɛndɪŋ] ADJ condiscendente

condition [kən'dɪʃən] N condizione f; (disease) malattia ▶ VT condizionare, regolare; **in good/poor ~** in buone/cattive condizioni; **to have a heart ~** soffrire di (mal di) cuore; **weather conditions** condizioni meteorologiche; **on ~ that** a condizione che + sub, a condizione di

conditional [kən'dɪʃənl] ADJ condizionale; **to be ~ upon** dipendere da

conditioner [kən'dɪʃənəʳ] N (for hair) balsamo; (for fabrics) ammorbidente m

condo ['kɔndəu] N ABBR (US col) = **condominium**

condolences [kən'dəulənsɪz] NPL condoglianze fpl

condom ['kɔndəm] N preservativo

condominium [kɔndə'mɪnɪəm] N (US) condominio

condone [kən'dəun] VT condonare

conducive [kən'dju:sɪv] ADJ: **~ to** favorevole a

conduct N ['kɔndʌkt] condotta ▶ VT [kən'dʌkt] condurre; (manage) dirigere; amministrare; (Mus) dirigere; **to ~ o.s.** comportarsi

conducted tour [kən'dʌktɪd-] N gita accompagnata

conductor [kən'dʌktəʳ] N (of orchestra) direttore(-trice) d'orchestra; (on bus) bigliettaio; (US Rail) controllore(-a); (Elec) conduttore m

conductress [kən'dʌktrɪs] N (on bus) bigliettaia

conduit ['kɔndɪt] N condotto; tubo

cone [kəun] N cono; (Bot) pigna; (traffic cone) birillo

confectioner [kən'fɛkʃənəʳ] N: **~'s (shop)** = pasticceria

confectionery [kən'fɛkʃənərɪ] N dolciumi mpl

confederate [kən'fɛdərɪt] ADJ confederato(-a)
▶ N (pej) complice mf; (US Hist) confederato

confederation [kənfɛdə'reɪʃən] N confederazione f

confer [kən'fəːʳ] VT: **to ~ sth on** conferire qc a
▶ VI conferire; **to ~ (with sb about sth)** consultarsi (con qn su qc)

conference ['kɔnfərns] N congresso; **to be in ~** essere in riunione

conference room N sala f conferenze inv

confess [kən'fɛs] VT confessare, ammettere
▶ VI confessarsi

confession [kən'fɛʃən] N confessione f

confessional [kən'fɛʃənl] N confessionale m

confessor [kən'fɛsəʳ] N confessore m

confetti [kən'fɛtɪ] N coriandoli mpl

confide [kən'faɪd] VI: **to ~ in** confidarsi con

confidence ['kɔnfɪdns] N confidenza; (trust) fiducia; (also: **self-confidence**) sicurezza di sé; **in ~** (speak, write) in confidenza, confidenzialmente; **to tell sb sth in strict ~** dire qc a qn in via strettamente confidenziale; **to have (every) ~ that ...** essere assolutamente certo(-a) che ...; **motion of no ~** mozione f di sfiducia

confidence trick N truffa

confident ['kɔnfɪdənt] ADJ sicuro(-a); (also: **self-confident**) sicuro(-a) di sé

confidential [kɔnfɪ'dɛnʃəl] ADJ riservato(-a), confidenziale; (secretary) particolare

confidentiality ['kɔnfɪdɛnʃɪ'ælɪtɪ] N riservatezza, carattere m confidenziale

configuration [kən'fɪgju'reɪʃən] N (Comput) configurazione f

confine [kən'faɪn] VT limitare; (shut up) rinchiudere; **to ~ o.s. to doing sth** limitarsi a fare qc; see also **confines**

confined [kən'faɪnd] ADJ (space) ristretto(-a)

confinement [kən'faɪnmənt] N prigionia; (Mil) consegna; (Med) parto

confines ['kɔnfaɪnz] NPL confini mpl

confirm [kən'fəːm] VT confermare; (Rel) cresimare

confirmation [kɔnfə'meɪʃən] N conferma; (Rel) cresima

confirmed [kən'fəːmd] ADJ inveterato(-a)

confiscate ['kɔnfɪskeɪt] VT confiscare

confiscation [kɔnfɪs'keɪʃən] N confisca

conflagration [kɔnflə'greɪʃən] N conflagrazione f

conflict N ['kɔnflɪkt] conflitto ▶ VI [kən'flɪkt] essere in conflitto

conflicting [kən'flɪktɪŋ] ADJ contrastante; (reports, evidence, opinions) contraddittorio(-a)

conform [kən'fɔːm] VI: **to ~ (to)** conformarsi (a)

conformist [kən'fɔːmɪst] N conformista mf

confound [kən'faund] VT confondere; (amaze) sconcertare

confounded [kən'faundɪd] ADJ maledetto(-a)

confront [kən'frʌnt] VT confrontare; (enemy, danger) affrontare

confrontation [kɔnfrən'teɪʃən] N scontro

confrontational [kɔnfrən'teɪʃənəl] ADJ polemico(-a), aggressivo(-a)

confuse [kən'fjuːz] VT imbrogliare; (one thing with another) confondere

confused [kən'fjuːzd] ADJ confuso(-a); **to get ~** confondersi

confusing [kən'fjuːzɪŋ] ADJ che fa confondere

confusion [kən'fjuːʒən] N confusione f

congeal [kən'dʒiːl] VI (blood) congelarsi

congenial [kən'dʒiːnɪəl] ADJ (person) simpatico(-a); (place, work, company) piacevole

congenital [kən'dʒɛnɪtl] ADJ congenito(-a)

conger eel ['kɔngər-] N grongo

congested [kən'dʒɛstɪd] ADJ congestionato(-a); (telephone lines) sovraccarico(-a)

congestion [kən'dʒɛstʃən] N congestione f

congestion charge N pedaggio da pagare per poter circolare in automobile nel centro di alcune città, introdotto per la prima volta a Londra nel 2002

conglomerate [kən'glɔmərɪt] N (Comm) conglomerato

conglomeration [kənglɔmə'reɪʃən] N conglomerazione f

Congo ['kɔŋgəu] N Congo

congratulate [kən'grætjuleɪt] VT: **to ~ sb (on)** congratularsi con qn (per or di)

congratulations [kəngrætju'leɪʃənz] NPL auguri mpl; (on success) complimenti mpl; **~ (on)** congratulazioni fpl (per) ▶ EXCL congratulazioni!, rallegramenti!

congregate ['kɔŋgrɪgeɪt] VI congregarsi, riunirsi

congregation [kɔŋgrɪ'geɪʃən] N congregazione f

congress ['kɔŋgrɛs] N congresso; (US Pol): **C~** il Congresso

Il **Congress** è l'assemblea statunitense che si riunisce a Washington nel Capitol per elaborare e discutere le leggi federali. Comprende la House of Representatives (435 membri, eletti nei vari stati in base al numero degli abitanti) e il Senate (100 senatori, due per ogni stato). I membri della House of Representatives hanno un mandato di 2 anni, i senatori di 6 e tutti sono eletti direttamente dal popolo.

congressman ['kɔŋgrɛsmən] N (irreg) (US) membro del Congresso

congresswoman ['kɔŋgrɛswumən] N (irreg) (US) (donna) membro del Congresso

conical ['kɒnɪkl] ADJ conico(-a)

conifer ['kɒnɪfə^r] N conifero

coniferous [kə'nɪfərəs] ADJ (forest) di conifere

conjecture [kən'dʒɛktʃə^r] N congettura ▶ VT, VI congetturare

conjoined twin [kən'dʒɔɪnd-] N fratello (or sorella) siamese

conjugal ['kɒndʒugl] ADJ coniugale

conjugate ['kɒndʒugeɪt] VT coniugare

conjugation [kɒndʒə'geɪʃən] N coniugazione f

conjunction [kən'dʒʌŋkʃən] N congiunzione f; **in ~ with** in accordo con, insieme con

conjunctivitis [kəndʒʌŋktɪ'vaɪtɪs] N congiuntivite f

conjure ['kʌndʒə^r] VI fare giochi di prestigio ▶ **conjure up** VT (ghost, spirit) evocare; (memories) rievocare

conjurer ['kʌndʒərə^r] N prestigiatore(-trice), prestidigitatore(-trice)

conjuring trick ['kʌndʒərɪŋ-] N gioco di prestigio

conker ['kɒŋkə^r] N (BRIT col) castagna (d'ippocastano)

conk out [kɒŋk-] VI (col) andare in panne

conman ['kɒnmæn] N (irreg) truffatore(-trice)

connect [kə'nɛkt] VT connettere, collegare; (Elec) collegare; (fig) associare ▶ VI (train): **to ~ with** essere in coincidenza con; **to be connected with** (associated) aver rapporti con; essere imparentato(-a) con; **I am trying to ~ you** (Tel) sto cercando di darle la linea

connecting flight N volo in coincidenza

connection [kə'nɛkʃən] N relazione f, rapporto; (Elec) connessione f; (Tel) collegamento; (train, plane etc) coincidenza; **in ~ with** con riferimento a, a proposito di; **what is the ~ between them?** in che modo sono legati?; **business connections** rapporti d'affari; **to miss/get one's ~** (train etc) perdere/prendere la coincidenza

connexion [kə'nɛkʃən] N (BRIT) = **connection**

conning tower ['kɒnɪŋ-] N torretta di comando

connive [kə'naɪv] VI: **to ~ at** essere connivente in

connoisseur [kɒnɪ'sə:^r] N conoscitore(-trice)

connotation [kɒnə'teɪʃən] N connotazione f

connubial [kə'nju:bɪəl] ADJ coniugale

conquer ['kɒŋkə^r] VT conquistare; (feelings) vincere

conqueror ['kɒŋkərə^r] N conquistatore(-trice)

conquest ['kɒŋkwɛst] N conquista

cons [kɒnz] NPL see **pro; convenience**

conscience ['kɒnʃəns] N coscienza; **in all ~** onestamente, in coscienza

conscientious [kɒnʃɪ'ɛnʃəs] ADJ coscienzioso(-a)

conscientious objector N obiettore(-trice) di coscienza

conscious ['kɒnʃəs] ADJ consapevole; (Med) cosciente; (deliberate: insult, error) intenzionale, voluto(-a); **to become ~ of sth/that** rendersi conto di qc/che

consciousness ['kɒnʃəsnɪs] N consapevolezza; (Med) coscienza; **to lose/regain ~** perdere/ riprendere coscienza

conscript ['kɒnskrɪpt] N coscritto

conscription [kən'skrɪpʃən] N coscrizione f

consecrate ['kɒnsɪkreɪt] VT consacrare

consecutive [kən'sɛkjutɪv] ADJ consecutivo(-a); **on 3 ~ occasions** 3 volte di fila

consensus [kən'sɛnsəs] N consenso; **the ~ of opinion** l'opinione f unanime or comune

consent [kən'sɛnt] N consenso ▶ VI: **to ~ (to)** acconsentire (a); **age of ~** età legale (per avere rapporti sessuali); **by common ~** di comune accordo

consenting adults [kən'sɛntɪŋ-] NPL adulti mpl consenzienti

consequence ['kɒnsɪkwəns] N conseguenza, risultato; importanza; **in ~** di conseguenza

consequently ['kɒnsɪkwəntlɪ] ADV di conseguenza, dunque

conservation [kɒnsə'veɪʃən] N conservazione f; (also: **nature conservation**) tutela dell'ambiente; **energy ~** risparmio energetico

conservationist [kɒnsə'veɪʃənɪst] N fautore(-trice) della tutela dell'ambiente

conservative [kən'sə:vətɪv] ADJ, N conservatore(-trice); (cautious) cauto(-a); **C~** adj, n (BRIT Pol) conservatore(-trice); **the C~ Party** il partito conservatore

conservatory [kən'sə:vətrɪ] N (greenhouse) serra; (Mus) conservatorio

conserve [kən'sə:v] VT conservare ▶ N conserva

consider [kən'sɪdə^r] VT considerare; (take into account) tener conto di; **to ~ doing sth** considerare la possibilità di fare qc; **all things considered** tutto sommato or considerato; **~ yourself lucky** puoi dirti fortunato

considerable [kən'sɪdərəbl] ADJ considerevole, notevole

considerably [kən'sɪdərəblɪ] ADV notevolmente, decisamente

considerate [kən'sɪdərɪt] ADJ premuroso(-a)

consideration [kənsɪdə'reɪʃən] N considerazione f; (reward) rimunerazione f; **out of ~ for** per riguardo a; **under ~** in esame; **my first ~ is my family** il mio primo pensiero è per la mia famiglia

considered [kən'sɪdəd] ADJ: **it is my ~ opinion that ...** dopo lunga riflessione il mio parere è che ...

considering [kən'sɪdərɪŋ] PREP in considerazione di; ~ **(that)** se si considera (che)

consign [kən'saɪn] VT consegnare; (*send: goods*) spedire

consignee [kɔnsaɪ'niː] N consegnatario(-a), destinatario(-a)

consignment [kən'saɪnmənt] N (*of goods*) consegna; spedizione f

consignment note N (*Comm*) nota di spedizione

consignor [kən'saɪnə^r] N mittente mf

consist [kən'sɪst] VI: **to ~ of** constare di, essere composto(-a) di

consistency [kən'sɪstənsɪ] N consistenza; (*fig*) coerenza

consistent [kən'sɪstənt] ADJ coerente; (*constant*) costante; ~ **with** compatibile con

consolation [kɔnsə'leɪʃən] N consolazione f

console VT [kən'səul] consolare ▶ N ['kɔnsəul] quadro di comando

consolidate [kən'sɔlɪdeɪt] VT consolidare

consols ['kɔnsɔlz] NPL (*Stock Exchange*) titoli mpl del debito consolidato

consommé [kən'sɔmeɪ] N consommé m inv, brodo ristretto

consonant ['kɔnsənənt] N consonante f

consort N ['kɔnsɔːt] consorte mf; **prince ~** principe m consorte ▶ VI [kən'sɔːt] (*often pej*): **to ~ with sb** frequentare qn

consortium [kən'sɔːtɪəm] N consorzio

conspicuous [kən'spɪkjuəs] ADJ cospicuo(-a); **to make o.s. ~** farsi notare

conspiracy [kən'spɪrəsɪ] N congiura, cospirazione f

conspiratorial [kənspɪrə'tɔːrɪəl] ADJ cospiratorio(-a)

conspire [kən'spaɪə^r] VI congiurare, cospirare

constable ['kʌnstəbl] N (*BRIT: also*: **police constable**) ≈ poliziotto(-a), agente mf di polizia; **chief ~** ≈ questore m

constabulary [kən'stæbjulərɪ] N forze fpl dell'ordine

constant ['kɔnstənt] ADJ costante; continuo(-a)

constantly ['kɔnstəntlɪ] ADV costantemente; continuamente

constellation [kɔnstə'leɪʃən] N costellazione f

consternation [kɔnstə'neɪʃən] N costernazione f

constipated ['kɔnstɪpeɪtɪd] ADJ stitico(-a)

constipation [kɔnstɪ'peɪʃən] N stitichezza

constituency [kən'stɪtjuənsɪ] N collegio elettorale; (*people*) elettori mpl (del collegio)

constituency party N sezione f locale (del partito)

constituent [kən'stɪtjuənt] N elettore(-trice); (*part*) elemento componente

constitute ['kɔnstɪtjuːt] VT costituire

constitution [kɔnstɪ'tjuːʃən] N costituzione f

constitutional [kɔnstɪ'tjuːʃənl] ADJ costituzionale

constitutional monarchy N monarchia costituzionale

constrain [kən'streɪn] VT costringere

constrained [kən'streɪnd] ADJ costretto(-a)

constraint [kən'streɪnt] N (*restraint*) limitazione f, costrizione f; (*embarrassment*) imbarazzo, soggezione f

constrict [kən'strɪkt] VT comprimere; opprimere

construct [kən'strʌkt] VT costruire

construction [kən'strʌkʃən] N costruzione f; (*fig: interpretation*) interpretazione f; **under ~** in costruzione

construction industry N edilizia, industria edile

constructive [kən'strʌktɪv] ADJ costruttivo(-a)

construe [kən'struː] VT interpretare

consul ['kɔnsl] N console m

consulate ['kɔnsjulɪt] N consolato

consult [kən'sʌlt] VT: **to ~ sb (about sth)** consultare qn (su *or* riguardo a qc)

consultancy [kən'sʌltənsɪ] N consulenza

consultancy fee N onorario di consulenza

consultant [kən'sʌltənt] N (*Med*) consulente mf medico; (*other specialist*) consulente mf ▶ CPD: ~ **engineer** n ingegnere mf consulente; ~ **paediatrician** n specialista mf in pediatria; **legal/management ~** consulente mf legale/gestionale

consultation [kɔnsəl'teɪʃən] N (*discussion*) consultazione f; (*Med, Law*) consulto; **in ~ with** consultandosi con

consultative [kən'sʌltətɪv] ADJ di consulenza

consulting room [kən'sʌltɪŋ-] N (*BRIT*) ambulatorio

consume [kən'sjuːm] VT consumare

consumer [kən'sjuːmə^r] N consumatore(-trice); (*of electricity, gas etc*) utente mf

consumer credit N credito al consumatore

consumer durables NPL prodotti mpl di consumo durevole

consumer goods NPL beni mpl di consumo

consumerism [kən'sjuːmərɪzəm] N (*consumer protection*) tutela del consumatore; (*Econ*) consumismo

consumer society N società dei consumi

consumer watchdog N comitato di difesa dei consumatori

consummate ['kɔnsʌmeɪt] VT consumare

consumption [kən'sʌmpʃən] N consumo; (*Med*) consunzione f; **not fit for human ~** non commestibile

cont. ABBR (= *continued*) segue

contact [ˈkɒntækt] N contatto; (*person*) conoscenza ▸ VT mettersi in contatto con; **to be in ~ with sb/sth** essere in contatto con qn/qc; **business contacts** contatti *mpl* d'affari

contact lenses NPL lenti *fpl* a contatto

contactless [ˈkɒntæktlɪs] ADJ contactless *inv*

contagious [kənˈteɪdʒəs] ADJ (*also fig*) contagioso(-a)

contain [kənˈteɪn] VT contenere; **to ~ o.s.** contenersi

container [kənˈteɪnəʳ] N recipiente *m*; (*for shipping etc*) container *m inv*

containerize [kənˈteɪnəraɪz] VT mettere in container

container ship N nave *f* container *inv*

contaminate [kənˈtæmɪneɪt] VT contaminare

contamination [kəntæmɪˈneɪʃən] N contaminazione *f*

contemplate [ˈkɒntəmpleɪt] VT contemplare; (*consider*) pensare a (*or* di)

contemplation [kɒntəmˈpleɪʃən] N contemplazione *f*

contemporary [kənˈtɛmpərərɪ] ADJ contemporaneo(-a); (*design*) moderno(-a) ▸ N contemporaneo(-a); (*of the same age*) coetaneo(-a)

contempt [kənˈtɛmpt] N disprezzo; **~ of court** (*Law*) oltraggio alla Corte

contemptible [kənˈtɛmptəbl] ADJ spregevole, vergognoso(-a)

contemptuous [kənˈtɛmptjuəs] ADJ sdegnoso(-a)

contend [kənˈtɛnd] VT: **to ~ that** sostenere che ▸ VI: **to ~ with** lottare contro; **he has a lot to ~ with** ha un sacco di guai

contender [kənˈtɛndəʳ] N contendente *mf*; concorrente *mf*

content¹ [ˈkɒntɛnt] N contenuto ∎ **contents** NPL (*of box, case etc*) contenuto; (*of barrel etc: capacity*) capacità *f inv*; **(table of) contents** indice *m*

content² [kənˈtɛnt] ADJ contento(-a), soddisfatto(-a) ▸ VT contentare, soddisfare; **to be ~ with** essere contento di; **to ~ o.s. with sth/with doing sth** accontentarsi di qc/di fare qc

contented [kənˈtɛntɪd] ADJ contento(-a), soddisfatto(-a)

contentedly [kənˈtɛntɪdlɪ] ADV con soddisfazione

contention [kənˈtɛnʃən] N contesa; (*assertion*) tesi *f inv*; **bone of ~** pomo della discordia

contentious [kənˈtɛnʃəs] ADJ polemico(-a)

contentment [kənˈtɛntmənt] N contentezza

contest N [ˈkɒntɛst] lotta; (*competition*) gara, concorso ▸ VT [kənˈtɛst] contestare; (*Law*) impugnare; (*compete for*) contendersi

contestant [kənˈtɛstənt] N concorrente *mf*; (*in fight*) avversario(-a)

context [ˈkɒntɛkst] N contesto; **in/out of ~** nel/fuori dal contesto

continent [ˈkɒntɪnənt] N continente *m*; **the C~** (BRIT) l'Europa continentale; **on the C~** in Europa

continental [kɒntɪˈnɛntl] ADJ continentale ▸ N (BRIT) abitante *mf* dell'Europa continentale

continental breakfast N colazione *f* all'europea (*senza piatti caldi*)

continental quilt N (BRIT) piumino

contingency [kənˈtɪndʒənsɪ] N eventualità *f inv*

contingency plan N misura d'emergenza

contingent [kənˈtɪndʒənt] N contingenza ▸ ADJ: **to be ~ upon** dipendere da

continual [kənˈtɪnjuəl] ADJ continuo(-a)

continually [kənˈtɪnjuəlɪ] ADV di continuo

continuation [kəntɪnjuˈeɪʃən] N continuazione *f*; (*after interruption*) ripresa; (*of story*) seguito

continue [kənˈtɪnjuː] VI continuare ▸ VT continuare; (*start again*) riprendere; **to be continued** (*story*) continua; **continued on page 10** segue *or* continua a pagina 10

continuing education [kənˈtɪnjuɪŋ-] N corsi *mpl* per adulti

continuity [kɒntɪˈnjuːɪtɪ] N continuità; (*Cine*) (ordine *m* della) sceneggiatura

continuity girl N (*Cine*) segretaria di edizione

continuous [kənˈtɪnjuəs] ADJ continuo(-a), ininterrotto(-a); **~ performance** (*Cine*) spettacolo continuato; **~ stationery** (*Comput*) carta a moduli continui

continuous assessment N (BRIT) valutazione *f* continua

continuously [kənˈtɪnjuəslɪ] ADV (*repeatedly*) continuamente; (*uninterruptedly*) ininterrottamente

contort [kənˈtɔːt] VT contorcere

contortion [kənˈtɔːʃən] N contorcimento; (*of acrobat*) contorsione *f*

contortionist [kənˈtɔːʃənɪst] N contorsionista *mf*

contour [ˈkɒntuəʳ] N contorno, profilo; (*also:* **contour line**) curva di livello

contraband [ˈkɒntrəbænd] N contrabbando ▸ ADJ di contrabbando

contraception [kɒntrəˈsɛpʃən] N contraccezione *f*

contraceptive [kɒntrəˈsɛptɪv] ADJ contraccettivo(-a) ▸ N contraccettivo

contract N [ˈkɒntrækt] contratto ▸ CPD [ˈkɒntrækt] (*price, date*) del contratto; (*work*) a contratto ▸ VI [kənˈtrækt] (*become smaller*) contrarsi; (*Comm*): **to ~ to do sth** fare un contratto per fare qc ▸ VT [kənˈtrækt] (*illness*) contrarre; **to be under ~ to do sth** avere stipulato un contratto per fare qc; **~ of employment** contratto di lavoro

▸ **contract in** VI impegnarsi (con un contratto); (BRIT Admin) scegliere di pagare i contributi per una pensione

▶ **contract out** VI: **to ~ out (of)** ritirarsi (da); (BRIT Admin) (scegliere di) non pagare i contributi per una pensione

contraction [kənˈtrækʃən] N contrazione f

contractor [kənˈtræktəʳ] N imprenditore(-trice)

contractual [kənˈtræktjuəl] ADJ contrattuale

contradict [kɔntrəˈdɪkt] VT contraddire

contradiction [kɔntrəˈdɪkʃən] N contraddizione f; **to be in ~ with** discordare con

contradictory [kɔntrəˈdɪktərɪ] ADJ contraddittorio(-a)

contralto [kənˈtræltəu] N contralto

contraption [kənˈtræpʃən] N (pej) aggeggio

contrary¹ [ˈkɔntrərɪ] ADJ contrario(-a); (unfavourable) avverso(-a), contrario(-a) ▶ N contrario; **on the ~** al contrario; **unless you hear to the ~** salvo contrordine; **~ to what we thought** a differenza di or contrariamente a quanto pensavamo

contrary² [kənˈtrɛərɪ] ADJ (perverse) bisbetico(-a)

contrast N [ˈkɔntrɑːst] contrasto ▶ VT [kənˈtrɑːst] mettere in contrasto; **in ~ to** or **with** a differenza di, contrariamente a

contrasting [kənˈtrɑːstɪŋ] ADJ contrastante, di contrasto

contravene [kɔntrəˈviːn] VT contravvenire

contravention [kɔntrəˈvɛnʃən] N: **~ (of)** contravvenzione f (a), infrazione f (di)

contribute [kənˈtrɪbjuːt] VI contribuire ▶ VT: **to ~ £10/an article to** dare 10 sterline/un articolo a; **to ~ to** contribuire a; (newspaper) scrivere per; (discussion) partecipare a

contribution [kɔntrɪˈbjuːʃən] N contributo

contributor [kənˈtrɪbjutəʳ] N (to newspaper) collaboratore(-trice)

contributory [kənˈtrɪbjutərɪ] ADJ (cause) che contribuisce; **it was a ~ factor in ...** quello ha contribuito a ...

contributory pension scheme N (BRIT) sistema di pensionamento finanziato congiuntamente dai contributi del lavoratore e del datore di lavoro

contrite [ˈkɔntraɪt] ADJ contrito(-a)

contrivance [kənˈtraɪvəns] N congegno; espediente m

contrive [kənˈtraɪv] VT inventare; escogitare ▶ VI: **to ~ to do** fare in modo di fare

control [kənˈtrəul] VT dominare; (firm, operation etc) dirigere; (check) controllare; (disease, fire) arginare, limitare ▶ N controllo ■ **controls** NPL (of vehicle etc) comandi mpl; **to take ~ of** assumere il controllo di; **to be in ~ of** avere il controllo di; essere responsabile di; **to ~ o.s.** controllarsi; **everything is under ~** tutto è sotto controllo; **to go out of ~** (car) non rispondere ai comandi; (situation) sfuggire di

mano; **circumstances beyond our ~** circostanze fpl che non dipendono da noi

control key N (Comput) tasto di controllo

controlled substance [kənˈtrəuld-] N sostanza stupefacente

controller [kənˈtrəuləʳ] N controllore m

controlling interest [kənˈtrəulɪŋ-] N (Comm) maggioranza delle azioni

control panel N (on aircraft, ship, TV etc) quadro dei comandi

control point N punto di controllo

control room N (Naut, Mil) sala di comando; (Radio, TV) sala di regia

control tower N (Aviat) torre f di controllo

control unit N (Comput) unità f inv di controllo

controversial [kɔntrəˈvəːʃl] ADJ controverso(-a), polemico(-a)

controversy [ˈkɔntrəvəːsɪ] N controversia, polemica

conurbation [kɔnəːˈbeɪʃən] N conurbazione f

convalesce [kɔnvəˈlɛs] VI rimettersi in salute

convalescence [kɔnvəˈlɛsns] N convalescenza

convalescent [kɔnvəˈlɛsnt] ADJ, N convalescente (mf)

convector [kənˈvɛktəʳ] N convettore m

convene [kənˈviːn] VT convocare; (meeting) organizzare ▶ VI convenire, adunarsi

convenience [kənˈviːnɪəns] N comodità f inv; **at your ~** a suo comodo; **at your earliest ~** (Comm) appena possibile; **all modern conveniences**, (BRIT) **all mod cons** tutte le comodità moderne

convenience foods NPL cibi mpl precotti

convenient [kənˈviːnɪənt] ADJ comodo(-a); **if it is ~ to you** se per lei va bene, se non la incomoda

conveniently [kənˈviːnɪəntlɪ] ADV (happen) a proposito; (situated) in un posto comodo

convent [ˈkɔnvənt] N convento

convention [kənˈvɛnʃən] N convenzione f; (meeting) convegno

conventional [kənˈvɛnʃənl] ADJ convenzionale

convent school N scuola retta da suore

converge [kənˈvəːdʒ] VI convergere

conversant [kənˈvəːsnt] ADJ: **to be ~ with** essere al corrente di; essere pratico(-a) di

conversation [kɔnvəˈseɪʃən] N conversazione f

conversational [kɔnvəˈseɪʃənl] ADJ non formale; (Comput) conversazionale; **~ Italian** l'italiano parlato

conversationalist [kɔnvəˈseɪʃnəlɪst] N conversatore(-trice)

converse N [ˈkɔnvəːs] contrario, opposto ▶ VI [kənˈvəːs]: **to ~ (with sb about sth)** conversare (con qn su qc)

conversely [kɔnˈvəːslɪ] ADV al contrario, per contro

conversion [kənˈvəːʃən] N conversione f; (BRIT: *of house*) trasformazione f, rimodernamento

conversion table N tavola di equivalenze

convert VT [kənˈvəːt] (*Rel, Comm*) convertire; (*alter*) trasformare ▶ N [ˈkɔnvəːt] convertito(-a)

convertible [kənˈvəːtəbl] N macchina decappottabile

convex [ˈkɔnvɛks] ADJ convesso(-a)

convey [kənˈveɪ] VT trasportare; (*thanks*) comunicare; (*idea*) dare

conveyance [kənˈveɪəns] N (*of goods*) trasporto; (*vehicle*) mezzo di trasporto

conveyancing [kənˈveɪənsɪŋ] N (*Law*) redazione f di transazioni di proprietà

conveyor belt [kənˈveɪəʳ-] N nastro trasportatore

convict VT [kənˈvɪkt] dichiarare colpevole ▶ N [ˈkɔnvɪkt] carcerato(-a)

conviction [kənˈvɪkʃən] N condanna; (*belief*) convinzione f

convince [kənˈvɪns] VT: **to ~ sb (of sth/that)** convincere qn (di qc/che), persuadere qn (di qc/che)

convinced ADJ: **~ of/that** convinto(-a) di/che

convincing [kənˈvɪnsɪŋ] ADJ convincente

convincingly [kənˈvɪnsɪŋlɪ] ADV in modo convincente

convivial [kənˈvɪvɪəl] ADJ allegro(-a)

convoluted [ˈkɔnvəluːtɪd] ADJ (*shape*) attorcigliato(-a), avvolto(-a); (*argument*) involuto(-a)

convoy [ˈkɔnvɔɪ] N convoglio

convulse [kənˈvʌls] VT sconvolgere; **to be convulsed with laughter** contorcersi dalle risa

convulsion [kənˈvʌlʃən] N convulsione f

COO N ABBR = **chief operating officer**

coo [kuː] VI tubare

cook [kuk] VT cucinare, cuocere; (*meal*) preparare ▶ VI cuocere; (*person*) cucinare ▶ N cuoco(-a)
  ▶ **cook up** VT (*col: excuse, story*) improvvisare, inventare

cookbook [ˈkukbuk] N = **cookery book**

cooker [ˈkukəʳ] N fornello, cucina

cookery N cucina

cookery book N (BRIT) libro di cucina

cookie [ˈkukɪ] N (US) biscotto; (*Comput*) cookie m inv

cooking [ˈkukɪŋ] N cucina ▶ CPD (*apples, chocolate*) da cuocere; (*utensils, salt, foil*) da cucina

cookout [ˈkukaut] N (US) pranzo (cucinato) all'aperto

cool [kuːl] ADJ fresco(-a); (*not afraid*) calmo(-a); (*unfriendly*) freddo(-a); (*impertinent*) sfacciato(-a) ▶ VT raffreddare; (*room*) rinfrescare ▶ VI raffreddarsi; (*air*) rinfrescarsi; **it's ~** (*weather*) fa fresco; **to keep sth ~** *or* **in a ~ place** tenere qc in fresco
  ▶ **cool down** VI raffreddarsi; (*fig: person, situation*) calmarsi
  ▶ **cool off** VI (*become calmer*) calmarsi; (*lose enthusiasm*) perdere interesse

coolant [ˈkuːlənt] N (liquido) refrigerante m

cool box, (US) **cooler** [ˈkuːləʳ] N borsa termica

cooling [ˈkuːlɪŋ] ADJ (*breeze*) fresco(-a)

cooling tower N torre f di raffreddamento

coolly [ˈkuːlɪ] ADV (*calmly*) con calma, tranquillamente; (*audaciously*) come se niente fosse; (*unenthusiastically*) freddamente

coolness [ˈkuːlnɪs] N freschezza; sangue m freddo, calma

coop [kuːp] N stia ▶ VT: **to ~ up** (*fig*) rinchiudere

co-op [ˈkəuɔp] N ABBR (= *cooperative (society)*) coop f

cooperate [kəuˈɔpəreɪt] VI cooperare, collaborare

cooperation [kəuɔpəˈreɪʃən] N cooperazione f, collaborazione f

cooperative [kəuˈɔpərətɪv] ADJ cooperativo(-a) ▶ N cooperativa

coopt [kəuˈɔpt] VT: **to ~ sb into sth** cooptare qn per qc

coordinate VT [kəuˈɔːdɪneɪt] coordinare ▶ N [kəuˈɔːdɪnət] (*Math*) coordinata ■ **coordinates** NPL (*clothes*) coordinati mpl

coordination [kəuɔːdɪˈneɪʃən] N coordinazione f

coot [kuːt] N folaga

co-ownership [kəuˈəunəʃɪp] N comproprietà

cop [kɔp] N (*col*) sbirro

co-parent [kəuˈpɛərənt] VT essere cogenitore(-trice) di

co-parenting [kəuˈpɛərəntɪŋ] N co-parenting m inv, cogenitorialità f inv

cope [kəup] VI farcela; **to ~ with** (*problems*) far fronte a

Copenhagen [kəupənˈheɪgən] N Copenhagen f

copier [ˈkɔpɪəʳ] N (*also: photocopier*) (foto)copiatrice f

co-pilot [ˈkəupaɪlət] N secondo pilota m

copious [ˈkəupɪəs] ADJ copioso(-a), abbondante

copper [ˈkɔpəʳ] N rame m; (*col: police officer*) sbirro ■ **coppers** NPL spiccioli mpl

coppice [ˈkɔpɪs], **copse** [kɔps] N bosco ceduo

copulate [ˈkɔpjuleɪt] VI accoppiarsi

copy [ˈkɔpɪ] N copia; (*book etc*) esemplare m; (*material: for printing*) materiale m, testo ▶ VT (*gen, Comput*) copiare; (*imitate*) imitare; **rough/fair ~** brutta/bella (copia); **to make good ~** (*fig*) fare notizia
  ▶ **copy out** VT ricopiare, trascrivere

copycat [ˈkɔpɪkæt] N (*pej*) copione m

copyright [ˈkɔpɪraɪt] N diritto d'autore; **~ reserved** tutti i diritti riservati

copy typist N dattilografo(-a)

copywriter [ˈkɔpɪraɪtəʳ] N redattore(-trice) pubblicitario(-a)

coral [ˈkɔrəl] N corallo

coral reef N barriera corallina

Coral Sea N: **the ~** il mar dei Coralli

cord [kɔːd] N corda; (Elec) filo; (fabric) velluto a coste ■ **cords** NPL (trousers) calzoni mpl (di velluto) a coste

cordial [ˈkɔːdɪəl] ADJ, N cordiale (m)

cordless [ˈkɔːdlɪs] ADJ senza cavo

cordon [ˈkɔːdn] N cordone m
▶ **cordon off** VT fare cordone intorno a

corduroy [ˈkɔːdərɔɪ] N fustagno

CORE [kɔːʳ] N ABBR (US) = **Congress of Racial Equality**

core [kɔːʳ] N (of fruit) torsolo; (Tech) centro; (of earth, nuclear reactor) nucleo; (of organization etc) cuore m; (of problem etc) cuore m, nocciolo ▶ VT estrarre il torsolo da; **rotten to the ~** marcio fino al midollo

Corfu [kɔːˈfuː] N Corfù f

coriander [kɔrɪˈændəʳ] N coriandolo

cork [kɔːk] N sughero; (of bottle) tappo

corkage [ˈkɔːkɪdʒ] N somma da pagare se il cliente porta il proprio vino

corked [kɔːkt], (US) **corky** [ˈkɔːkɪ] ADJ (wine) che sa di tappo

corkscrew [ˈkɔːkskruː] N cavatappi m inv

cormorant [ˈkɔːmərnt] N cormorano

corn [kɔːn] N (Brit: wheat) grano; (US: maize) granturco; (on foot) callo; **~ on the cob** (Culin) pannocchia cotta

cornea [ˈkɔːnɪə] N cornea

corned beef [ˈkɔːnd-] N carne f di manzo in scatola

corner [ˈkɔːnəʳ] N angolo; (Aut) curva; (Football: also: **corner kick**) corner m inv, calcio d'angolo ▶ VT intrappolare; mettere con le spalle al muro; (Comm: market) accaparrare ▶ VI prendere una curva; **to cut corners** (fig) prendere una scorciatoia

corner flag N (Football) bandierina d'angolo

corner kick N (Football) calcio d'angolo

corner shop N (Brit) piccolo negozio di generi alimentari

cornerstone [ˈkɔːnəstəun] N pietra angolare

cornet [ˈkɔːnɪt] N (Mus) cornetta; (Brit: of ice cream) cono

cornflakes [ˈkɔːnfleɪks] NPL fiocchi mpl di granturco

cornflour [ˈkɔːnflauəʳ] N (Brit) farina finissima di granturco

cornice [ˈkɔːnɪs] N cornicione m; cornice f

Cornish [ˈkɔːnɪʃ] ADJ della Cornovaglia

corn oil N olio di mais

cornstarch [ˈkɔːnstɑːtʃ] N (US) = **cornflour**

cornucopia [kɔːnjuˈkəupɪə] N grande abbondanza

Cornwall [ˈkɔːnwəl] N Cornovaglia

corny [ˈkɔːnɪ] ADJ (col) trito(-a)

corollary [kəˈrɔlərɪ] N corollario

coronary [ˈkɔrənərɪ] N: **~ (thrombosis)** trombosi f coronaria

coronation [kɔrəˈneɪʃən] N incoronazione f

coroner [ˈkɔrənəʳ] N magistrato incaricato di indagare la causa di morte in circostanze sospette

coronet [ˈkɔrənɪt] N diadema m

Corp. ABBR = **corporation**

corporal [ˈkɔːprəl] N caporalmaggiore m ▶ ADJ: **~ punishment** pena corporale

corporate [ˈkɔːpərɪt] ADJ comune; (Comm) costituito(-a) (in corporazione)

corporate hospitality N omaggi mpl ai clienti (come biglietti per spettacoli, cene ecc)

corporate identity, corporate image N (of organization) immagine f di marca

corporation [kɔːpəˈreɪʃən] N (of town) consiglio comunale; (Comm) ente m

corporation tax N = imposta societaria

corps [kɔː] (pl ~ [kɔːz]) N corpo; **press ~** ufficio m stampa inv

corpse [kɔːps] N cadavere m

corpuscle [ˈkɔːpʌsl] N corpuscolo

corral [kəˈrɑːl] N recinto

correct [kəˈrɛkt] ADJ (accurate) corretto(-a), esatto(-a); (proper) corretto(-a) ▶ VT correggere; **you are ~** ha ragione

correction [kəˈrɛkʃən] N correzione f

correlate [ˈkɔrɪleɪt] VT mettere in correlazione ▶ VI: **to ~ with** essere in rapporto con

correlation [kɔrɪˈleɪʃən] N correlazione f

correspond [kɔrɪsˈpɔnd] VI corrispondere

correspondence [kɔrɪsˈpɔndəns] N corrispondenza

correspondence course N corso per corrispondenza

correspondent [kɔrɪsˈpɔndənt] N corrispondente mf

corresponding ADJ corrispondente

corridor [ˈkɔrɪdɔːʳ] N corridoio

corroborate [kəˈrɔbəreɪt] VT corroborare, confermare

corrode [kəˈrəud] VT corrodere ▶ VI corrodersi

corrosion [kəˈrəuʒən] N corrosione f

corrosive [kəˈrəuzɪv] ADJ corrosivo(-a)

corrugated [ˈkɔrəgeɪtd] ADJ increspato(-a), ondulato(-a)

corrugated iron N lamiera di ferro ondulata

corrupt [kəˈrʌpt] ADJ corrotto(-a); (Comput) alterato(-a) ▶ VT corrompere; **~ practices** (dishonesty, bribery) pratiche fpl illecite

C

corruption [kəˈrʌpʃən] N corruzione f

corset [ˈkɔːsɪt] N busto

Corsica [ˈkɔːsɪkə] N Corsica

Corsican [ˈkɔːsɪkən] ADJ, N corso(-a)

cortège [kɔːˈteɪʒ] N corteo

cortisone [ˈkɔːtɪzəun] N cortisone m

coruscating [ˈkɒrəskeɪtɪŋ] ADJ scintillante

cosh [kɒʃ] N (BRIT) randello (corto)

cosignatory [kəuˈsɪgnətərɪ] N cofirmatario(-a)

cosiness [ˈkəuzɪnɪs] N intimità

cos lettuce [ˈkɔs-] N lattuga romana

cosmetic [kɒzˈmɛtɪk] N cosmetico ▶ ADJ (prepara-tion) cosmetico(-a); (fig: reforms, measures) appa-rente

cosmetic surgery N chirurgia plastica

cosmic [ˈkɒzmɪk] ADJ cosmico(-a)

cosmonaut [ˈkɒzmənɔːt] N cosmonauta mf

cosmopolitan [kɒzməˈpɒlɪtn] ADJ cosmopolita

cosmos [ˈkɒzmɒs] N cosmo

cosset [ˈkɒsɪt] VT vezzeggiare

cost [kɒst] (pt, pp ~) N costo ▶ VI costare ▶ VT sta-bilire il prezzo di ■ **costs** NPL (Law) spese fpl; **it costs £5/too much** costa 5 sterline/troppo; **it ~ him his life/job** gli costò la vita/il suo lavoro; **how much does it ~?** quanto costa?, quanto viene?; **what will it ~ to have it repaired?** quanto costerà farlo riparare?; **~ of living** costo della vita; **at all costs** a ogni costo

cost accountant N analizzatore(-trice) dei costi

co-star [ˈkəustɑːʳ] N attore/attrice della stessa importanza del protagonista

Costa Rica [ˈkɒstəˈriːkə] N Costa Rica

cost centre N centro di costo

cost control N controllo dei costi

cost-effective [ˈkɒstɪˈfɛktɪv] ADJ (gen) conve-niente, economico(-a); (Comm) redditizio(-a), conveniente

cost-effectiveness [ˈkɒstɪˈfɛktɪvnɪs] N conve-nienza

costing [ˈkɒstɪŋ] N (determinazione f dei) costi mpl

costly [ˈkɒstlɪ] ADJ costoso(-a), caro(-a)

cost-of-living [ˈkɒstəvˈlɪvɪŋ] ADJ: **~ allowance** indennità f inv di contingenza; **~ index** indice m della scala mobile

cost price N (BRIT) prezzo all'ingrosso

costume [ˈkɒstjuːm] N costume m; (lady's suit) tailleur m inv; (BRIT: also: **swimming costume**) costume da bagno

costume jewellery N bigiotteria

cosy, (US) **cozy** [ˈkəuzɪ] ADJ intimo(-a); (room, atmosphere) accogliente; **I'm very ~ here** sto proprio bene qui

cot [kɒt] N (BRIT: child's) lettino; (US: folding bed) brandina

cot death N improvvisa e inspiegabile morte nel sonno di un neonato

Cotswolds [ˈkɒtswəuldz] NPL: **the ~** zona colli-nare del Gloucestershire

cottage [ˈkɒtɪdʒ] N cottage m inv

cottage cheese N fiocchi mpl di latte magro

cottage industry N industria artigianale basata sul lavoro a cottimo

cottage pie N piatto a base di carne macinata in sugo e purè di patate

cotton [ˈkɒtn] N cotone m; **~ dress** etc vestito etc di cotone
▶ **cotton on** VI (col): **to ~ on (to sth)** afferrare (qc)

cotton bud N (BRIT) cotton fioc® m inv

cotton candy N (US) zucchero filato

cotton wool N (BRIT) cotone m idrofilo

couch [kautʃ] N sofà m inv; (in doctor's surgery) let-tino ▶ VT esprimere

couchette [kuːˈʃɛt] N cuccetta

couch potato N (col) pigrone(-a) teledipen-dente

couchsurfing [ˈkautʃsɜːfɪŋ] N couchsurfing m inv

cough [kɒf] VI tossire ▶ N tosse f; **I've got a ~** ho la tosse

cough drop N pasticca per la tosse

cough mixture, cough syrup N sciroppo per la tosse

could [kud] PT of **can²**

couldn't [ˈkudnt] = **could not**

council [ˈkaunsl] N consiglio; **city** or **town ~** consiglio comunale; **C~ of Europe** Consiglio d'Europa

council estate N (BRIT) quartiere m di case popolari

council house N (BRIT) casa popolare

council housing N alloggi mpl popolari

councillor [ˈkaunsləʳ] N consigliere(-a)

council tax N (BRIT) tassa comunale sulla proprietà

counsel [ˈkaunsl] N avvocato; consultazione f
▶ VT: **to ~ sth/sb to do sth** consigliare qc/a qn di fare qc; **~ for the defence/the prosecution** avvocato difensore/di parte civile

counselling, (US) **counseling** N (Psych) assi-stenza psicologica

counsellor, (US) **counselor** [ˈkaunsləʳ] N con-sigliere(-a); (US: lawyer) avvocato(-essa)

count [kaunt] VT, VI contare ▶ N conto; (noble-man) conte m; **to ~ (up) to 10** contare fino a 10; **to ~ the cost of** calcolare il costo di; **not count-ing the children** senza contare i bambini; **10 counting him** 10 compreso lui; **~ yourself lucky** considerati fortunato; **it counts for very little** non conta molto, non ha molta impor-tanza; **to keep ~ of sth** tenere il conto di qc
▶ **count in** VT (col) includere; **~ me in** ci sto anch'io

▶ **count on** vt fus contare su; **to ~ on doing sth** contare di fare qc

▶ **count up** vt addizionare

countdown ['kauntdaun] N conto alla rovescia

countenance ['kauntɪnəns] N volto, aspetto ▶ vt approvare

counter ['kauntər] N banco; (*position: in post office, bank*) sportello; (*in game*) gettone m; (*Tech*) contatore m ▶ vt opporsi a; (*blow*) parare ▶ ADV: **~ to** contro; in opposizione a; **to buy under the ~** (*fig*) comperare sottobanco; **to ~ sth with sth/by doing sth** rispondere a qc con qc/facendo qc

counteract [kauntər'ækt] vt agire in opposizione a; (*poison etc*) annullare gli effetti di

counterattack ['kauntərətæk] N contrattacco ▶ vi contrattaccare

counterbalance ['kauntəbæləns] vt contrappesare

counter-clockwise ['kauntə'klɔkwaɪz] (*US*) ADV in senso antiorario

counter-espionage [kauntər'ɛspɪənɑːʒ] N controspionaggio

counterfeit ['kauntəfɪt] N contraffazione f, falso ▶ vt contraffare, falsificare ▶ ADJ falso(-a)

counterfoil ['kauntəfɔɪl] N matrice f

counterintelligence ['kauntərɪn'tɛlɪdʒəns] N = **counter-espionage**

countermand ['kauntəmɑːnd] vt annullare

countermeasure ['kauntəmɛʒər] N contromisura

counteroffensive ['kauntərə'fɛnsɪv] N controffensiva

counterpane ['kauntəpeɪn] N copriletto m inv

counterpart ['kauntəpɑːt] N (*of document etc*) copia; (*of person*) corrispondente mf

counterproductive ['kauntəprə'dʌktɪv] ADJ controproducente

counterproposal ['kauntəprə'pəuzl] N controproposta

countersign ['kauntəsaɪn] vt controfirmare

countersink ['kauntəsɪŋk] vt (*hole*) svasare

counterterrorism ['kauntə'terərɪzəm] N antiterrorismo

countess ['kauntɪs] N contessa

countless ['kauntlɪs] ADJ innumerevole

countrified ['kʌntrɪfaɪd] ADJ rustico(-a), campagnolo(-a)

country ['kʌntrɪ] N paese m; (*native land*) patria; (*as opposed to town*) campagna; (*region*) regione f; **in the ~** in campagna; **mountainous ~** territorio montagnoso

country and western, country and western music N musica country e western, country m

country dancing N (*BRIT*) danza popolare

country house N villa in campagna

countryman ['kʌntrɪmən] N (*irreg*) (*national*) compatriota m; (*rural*) contadino

countryside ['kʌntrɪsaɪd] N campagna

country-wide ['kʌntrɪ'waɪd] ADJ diffuso(-a) in tutto il paese ▶ ADV in tutto il paese

county ['kauntɪ] N contea

county council N (*BRIT*) consiglio di contea

county town N (*BRIT*) capoluogo

coup [kuː] (*pl* **coups** [kuːz]) N colpo; (*also:* **coup d'état**) colpo di Stato; (*triumph*) bel colpo

coupé [kuː'peɪ] N coupé m inv

couple ['kʌpl] N coppia ▶ vt (*carriages*) agganciare; (*Tech*) accoppiare; (*ideas, names*) associare; **a ~ of** un paio di

couplet ['kʌplɪt] N distico

coupling ['kʌplɪŋ] N (*Rail*) agganciamento

coupon ['kuːpɔn] N (*voucher*) buono; (*Comm*) coupon m inv

courage ['kʌrɪdʒ] N coraggio

courageous [kə'reɪdʒəs] ADJ coraggioso(-a)

courgette [kuə'ʒɛt] N (*BRIT*) zucchina

courier ['kurɪər] N corriere m; (*for tourists*) guida

course [kɔːs] N corso; (*of ship*) rotta; (*for golf*) campo; (*part of meal*) piatto; **first ~** primo piatto; **of ~** adv senz'altro, naturalmente; **(no) of ~ not!** certo che no!, no di certo!; **in the ~ of the next few days** nel corso dei prossimi giorni; **in due ~** a tempo debito; **~ (of action)** modo d'agire; **the best ~ would be to ...** la cosa migliore sarebbe ...; **we have no other ~ but to ...** non possiamo far altro che ...; **~ of lectures** corso di lezioni; **a ~ of treatment** (*Med*) una cura

court [kɔːt] N corte f; (*Tennis*) campo ▶ vt (*woman*) fare la corte a; (*fig: favour, popularity*) cercare di conquistare; (: *death, disaster*) sfiorare, rasentare; **out of ~** (*Law: settle*) in via amichevole; **to take to ~** citare in tribunale; **C~ of Appeal** corte d'appello

courteous ['kɜːtɪəs] ADJ cortese

courtesan [kɔːtɪ'zæn] N cortigiana

courtesy ['kɜːtəsɪ] N cortesia; **by ~ of** per gentile concessione di

courtesy bus, courtesy coach N navetta gratuita (*di hotel, aeroporto*)

courtesy car N vettura sostitutiva

courtesy light N (*Aut*) luce f interna

court-house ['kɔːthaus] N (*US*) palazzo di giustizia

courtier ['kɔːtɪər] N cortigiano(-a)

court martial (*pl* **courts martial**) N corte f marziale

courtroom ['kɔːtrum] N tribunale m

court shoe N scarpa f décolleté inv

courtyard ['kɔːtjɑːd] N cortile m

cousin ['kʌzn] N cugino(-a); **first ~** cugino di primo grado

cove [kəuv] N piccola baia

covenant ['kʌvənənt] N accordo ▶ VT: **to ~ to do sth** impegnarsi (per iscritto) a fare qc

Coventry ['kɔvəntrɪ] N: **to send sb to ~** (fig) dare l'ostracismo a qn

cover ['kʌvə'] VT (gen) coprire; (distance) coprire, percorrere; (book, table) rivestire; (include) comprendere; (Press: report on) fare un servizio su ▶ N (of pan) coperchio; (over furniture) fodera; (of bed) copriletto; (of book) copertina; (shelter) riparo; (Comm, Insurance, of spy) copertura ■ **covers** NPL (on bed) lenzuola e coperte fpl; **to take ~** mettersi al riparo; **under ~** al riparo; **under ~ of darkness** protetto dall'oscurità; **under separate ~** (Comm) a parte, in plico separato; **£10 will ~ everything** 10 sterline saranno sufficienti ▶ **cover up** VT (hide: truth, facts) nascondere; (child, object): **to ~ up (with)** coprire (di) ▶ VI: **to ~ up for sb** (fig) coprire qn

coverage ['kʌvərɪdʒ] N (Press, TV, Radio): **to give full ~ to** fare un ampio servizio su

coveralls ['kʌvərɔːlz] NPL (US) tuta

cover charge N coperto

covering ['kʌvərɪŋ] N copertura

covering letter, (US) **cover letter** N lettera d'accompagnamento

cover note N (Insurance) polizza (di assicurazione) provvisoria

cover price N prezzo di copertina

covert ['kʌvət] ADJ nascosto(-a); (glance) di sottecchi, furtivo(-a)

cover-up ['kʌvərʌp] N occultamento (di informazioni)

covet ['kʌvɪt] VT bramare

cow [kau] N vacca ▶ CPD femmina ▶ VT (person) intimidire; **~ elephant** n elefantessa

coward ['kauəd] N vigliacco(-a)

cowardice ['kauədɪs] N vigliaccheria

cowardly ['kauədlɪ] ADJ vigliacco(-a)

cowboy ['kaubɔɪ] N cow-boy m inv

cower ['kauə'] VI acquattarsi

cowshed ['kauʃed] N stalla

cowslip ['kauslɪp] N (Bot) primula (odorata)

coxswain ['kɔksn] N (also: **cox**) timoniere m

coy [kɔɪ] ADJ falsamente timido(-a)

coyote [kɔɪ'əutɪ] N coyote m inv

cozy ['kəuzɪ] ADJ (US) = **cosy**

CP N ABBR (= Communist Party) P.C. m

cp. ABBR (= compare) cfr.

CPA N ABBR (US) = **certified public accountant**

CPI N ABBR (US: = Consumer Price Index) indice dei prezzi al consumo

Cpl. ABBR = **corporal**

CP/M N ABBR (= Control Program for Microcomputers) CP/M m

c.p.s. ABBR (= characters per second) c.p.s.

CPSA N ABBR (Brit: = Civil and Public Services Association) sindacato dei servizi pubblici

CPU N ABBR = **central processing unit**

cr. ABBR = **credit**; **creditor**

crab [kræb] N granchio

crab apple N mela selvatica

crack [kræk] N (split, slit) fessura, crepa; incrinatura; (noise) schiocco; (: of gun) scoppio; (joke) battuta; (col: attempt): **to have a ~ at sth** tentare qc; (Drugs) crack m inv ▶ VT spaccare; incrinare; (whip) schioccare; (nut) schiacciare; (solve: problem, case) risolvere; (: code) decifrare ▶ CPD (athlete) di prim'ordine; (troops) fuori classe; **to ~ jokes** (col) dire battute, scherzare; **to get cracking** (col) darsi una mossa
▶ **crack down on** VT FUS prendere serie misure contro, porre freno a
▶ **crack up** VI crollare

crackdown ['krækdaun] N repressione f

cracked [krækt] ADJ (col) matto(-a)

cracker ['krækə'] N cracker m inv; (firework) petardo; (Christmas cracker) mortaretto natalizio (con sorpresa); **a ~ of a ...** (Brit col) un(-a) ... formidabile; **he's crackers** (Brit col) è tocco

crackle ['krækl] VI crepitare

crackling ['kræklɪŋ] N crepitio; (on radio, telephone) disturbo; (of pork) cotenna croccante (del maiale)

crackpot ['krækpɔt] N (col) imbecille mf con idee assurde, assurdo(-a)

cradle ['kreɪdl] N culla ▶ VT (child) tenere fra le braccia; (object) reggere tra le braccia

craft [krɑːft] N mestiere m; (cunning) astuzia; (boat) naviglio

craftsman ['krɑːftsmən] N (irreg) artigiano

craftsmanship ['krɑːftsmənʃɪp] N abilità

crafty ['krɑːftɪ] ADJ furbo(-a), astuto(-a)

crag [kræg] N roccia

cram [kræm] VI (for exams) prepararsi (in gran fretta) ▶ VT (fill): **to ~ sth with** riempire qc di; (put): **to ~ sth into** stipare qc in

cramming ['kræmɪŋ] N (fig: pej) sgobbare m

cramp [kræmp] N crampo ▶ VT soffocare, impedire; **I've got ~ in my leg** ho un crampo alla gamba

cramped [kræmpt] ADJ ristretto(-a)

crampon ['kræmpən] N (Climbing) rampone m

cranberry ['krænbərɪ] N mirtillo

crane [kreɪn] N gru f inv ▶ VT, VI: **to ~ forward, to ~ one's neck** allungare il collo

cranium ['kreɪnɪəm] N (pl **crania** ['kreɪnɪə]) N cranio

crank [kræŋk] N manovella; (person) persona stramba

crankshaft ['kræŋkʃɑːft] N albero a gomiti

cranky ['kræŋkɪ] ADJ eccentrico(-a); (bad-tempered): **to be ~** avere i nervi

cranny ['kræni] N *see* **nook**

crap [kræp] N (*col!*) fesserie *fpl*; **to have a ~** cacare (*!*)

crappy ['kræpi] ADJ (*col!*) di merda (*!*)

crash [kræʃ] N fragore *m*; (*of car*) incidente *m*; (*of plane*) caduta; (*of business*) fallimento; (*Stock Exchange*) crollo ▶ VT fracassare ▶ VI (*plane*) fracassarsi; (*car*) avere un incidente; (*two cars*) scontrarsi; (*fig: business etc*) fallire, andare in rovina; **to ~ into** scontrarsi con; **he crashed the car into a wall** andò a sbattere contro un muro con la macchina

crash barrier N (BRIT Aut) guardrail *m inv*

crash course N corso intensivo

crash helmet N casco

crash landing N atterraggio di fortuna

crass [kræs] ADJ crasso(-a)

crate [kreɪt] N cassa

crater ['kreɪtə'] N cratere *m*

cravat, cravate [krə'væt] N fazzoletto da collo

crave [kreɪv] VT, VI: **to ~ (for)** desiderare ardentemente

craving ['kreɪvɪŋ] N: **~ (for)** (*for food, cigarettes etc*) (gran) voglia (di)

crawl [krɔːl] VI strisciare carponi; (*child*) andare a gattoni; (*vehicle*) avanzare lentamente ▶ N (*Swimming*) crawl *m*; **to ~ to sb** (*col: suck up*) arruffianarsi qn

crawler lane ['krɔːlə'-] N (BRIT Aut) corsia riservata al traffico lento

crayfish ['kreɪfiʃ] N INV (*freshwater*) gambero (d'acqua dolce); (*saltwater*) gambero

crayon ['kreɪən] N matita colorata

craze [kreɪz] N mania

crazed [kreɪzd] ADJ (*look, person*) folle, pazzo(-a); (*pottery, glaze*) incrinato(-a)

crazy ['kreɪzi] ADJ matto(-a); (*col: keen*): **to be ~ about sb** essere pazzo di qn; **to be ~ about sth** andare matto per qc; **to go ~** uscir di senno, impazzire

crazy paving N (BRIT) lastricato a mosaico irregolare

creak [kriːk] VI cigolare, scricchiolare

cream [kriːm] N crema; (*fresh*) panna ▶ ADJ (*colour*) color crema *inv*; **whipped ~** panna montata
▶ **cream off** VT (*best talents, part of profits*) portarsi via

cream cake N torta alla panna

cream cheese N formaggio fresco

creamery ['kriːməri] N (*shop*) latteria; (*factory*) caseificio

creamy ['kriːmɪ] ADJ cremoso(-a)

crease [kriːs] N grinza; (*deliberate*) piega ▶ VT sgualcire ▶ VI sgualcirsi

crease-resistant ['kriːsrɪzɪstənt] ADJ ingualcibile

create [kriː'eɪt] VT creare; (*fuss, noise*) fare

creation [kriː'eɪʃən] N creazione *f*

creative [kriː'eɪtɪv] ADJ creativo(-a)

creativity [kriːeɪ'tɪvɪtɪ] N creatività

creator [kriː'eɪtə'] N creatore(-trice)

creature ['kriːtʃə'] N creatura

crèche, creche [krɛʃ] N asilo infantile

credence ['kriːdns] N credenza, fede *f*

credentials [krɪ'dɛnʃlz] NPL (*papers*) credenziali *fpl*; (*letters of reference*) referenze *fpl*

credibility [krɛdɪ'bɪlɪtɪ] N credibilità

credible ['krɛdɪbl] ADJ credibile; (*witness, source*) attendibile

credit ['krɛdɪt] N credito; onore *m*; (*Scol: esp US*) *certificato del compimento di una parte del corso universitario* ▶ VT (*Comm*) accreditare; (*believe: also:* **give credit to**) credere, prestar fede a; **to ~ £5 to sb** accreditare 5 sterline a qn; **to ~ sb with sth** (*fig*) attribuire qc a qn; **on ~** a credito; **to one's ~** a proprio onore; **to take the ~ for** farsi il merito di; **to be in ~** (*person*) essere creditore(-trice); (*bank account*) essere coperto(-a); **he's a ~ to his family** fa onore alla sua famiglia; *see also* **credits**

creditable ['krɛdɪtəbl] ADJ che fa onore, degno(-a) di lode

credit account N conto di credito

credit agency N (BRIT) agenzia di analisi di credito

credit balance N saldo attivo

credit bureau N (US) agenzia di analisi di credito

credit card N carta di credito

credit control N controllo dei crediti

credit crunch N improvvisa stretta di credito

credit facilities NPL agevolazioni *fpl* creditizie

credit limit N limite *m* di credito

credit note N (BRIT) nota di credito

creditor ['krɛdɪtə'] N creditore(-trice)

credit rating N coefficiente *m* di solvibilità, rating *m inv*

credits ['krɛdɪts] NPL (*Cine*) titoli *mpl*

credit transfer N bancogiro, postagiro

creditworthy ['krɛdɪt'wəːðɪ] ADJ autorizzabile al credito

credulity [krɪ'djuːlɪtɪ] N credulità

creed [kriːd] N credo; dottrina

creek [kriːk] N insenatura; (*US*) piccolo fiume *m*

creel [kriːl] N cestino per il pesce; (*also:* **lobster creel**) nassa

creep [kriːp] (*pt, pp* **crept** [krɛpt]) VI avanzare furtivamente (*or* pian piano); (*plant*) arrampicarsi ▶ N (*col*): **he's a ~** (*pej*) è un tipo viscido; **it gives me the creeps** (*col*) mi fa venire la pelle d'oca; **to ~ up on sb** avvicinarsi quatto quatto a qn; (*fig: old age etc*) cogliere qn alla sprovvista

creeper ['kriːpə'] N pianta rampicante

creepers [ˈkriːpəz] NPL (*US: rompers*) tutina

creepy [ˈkriːpɪ] ADJ (*frightening*) che fa accapponare la pelle

creepy-crawly [ˈkriːpɪˈkrɔːlɪ] N (*col*) bestiolina, insetto

cremate [krɪˈmeɪt] VT cremare

cremation [krɪˈmeɪʃən] N cremazione f

crematorium [kreməˈtɔːrɪəm] (*pl* **crematoria** [-ˈtɔːrɪə]) N forno crematorio

creosote [ˈkrɪəsəut] N creosoto

crêpe [kreɪp] N crespo

crêpe bandage (*BRIT*) fascia elastica

crêpe paper N carta crespa

crêpe sole N suola di para

crept [krɛpt] PT, PP *of* **creep**

crescendo [krɪˈʃɛndəu] N crescendo

crescent [ˈkrɛsnt] N (*shape*) mezzaluna; (*street*) strada semicircolare

cress [krɛs] N crescione *m*

crest [krɛst] N cresta; (*of helmet*) pennacchiera; (*of coat of arms*) cimiero

crestfallen [ˈkrɛstfɔːlən] ADJ mortificato(-a)

Crete [ˈkriːt] N Creta

crevasse [krɪˈvæs] N crepaccio

crevice [ˈkrɛvɪs] N fessura, crepa

crew [kruː] N equipaggio; (*Cine*) troupe *f inv*; (*gang*) banda, compagnia

crew-cut [ˈkruːkʌt] N: **to have a ~** avere i capelli a spazzola

crew-neck [ˈkruːnɛk] N girocollo

crib [krɪb] N culla; (*Rel*) presepio ▶ VT (*col*) copiare

cribbage [ˈkrɪbɪdʒ] N *tipo di gioco di carte*

crick [krɪk] N crampo; **~ in the neck** torcicollo

cricket [ˈkrɪkɪt] N (*insect*) grillo; (*game*) cricket *m*

cricketer [ˈkrɪkɪtəʳ] N giocatore(-trice) di cricket

crime [kraɪm] N (*in general*) criminalità; (*instance*) crimine *m*, delitto

crime wave N ondata di criminalità

criminal [ˈkrɪmɪnl] ADJ, N criminale (*mf*); **C~ Investigation Department (CID)** ≈ polizia giudiziaria

crimp [krɪmp] VT arricciare

crimson [ˈkrɪmzn] ADJ color cremisi *inv*

cringe [krɪndʒ] VI acquattarsi; (*fig*) essere servile; (*in embarrassment*) sentirsi sprofondare

crinkle [ˈkrɪŋkl] VT arricciare, increspare

cripple [ˈkrɪpl] N (!) zoppo(-a) ▶ VT azzoppare; (*ship, plane*) avariare; (*production, exports*) rovinare; **crippled with arthritis** sciancato(-a) per l'artrite

crippling [ˈkrɪplɪŋ] ADJ (*taxes, debts*) esorbitante; (*disease*) molto debilitante

crisis [ˈkraɪsɪs] (*pl* **crises** [-siːz]) N crisi *f inv*

crisp [krɪsp] ADJ croccante; (*fig*) frizzante; vivace; deciso(-a)

crisps [krɪsps] NPL (*BRIT*) patatine *fpl* fritte

crispy ADJ croccante

criss-cross [ˈkrɪskrɔs] ADJ incrociato(-a) ▶ VT incrociarsi

criterion [kraɪˈtɪərɪən] (*pl* **criteria** [-ˈtɪərɪə]) N criterio

critic [ˈkrɪtɪk] N critico(-a)

critical [ˈkrɪtɪkl] ADJ critico(-a); **to be ~ of sb/ sth** criticare qn/qc, essere critico verso qn/qc

critically [ˈkrɪtɪklɪ] ADV criticamente; **~ ill** gravemente malato

criticism [ˈkrɪtɪsɪzəm] N critica

criticize [ˈkrɪtɪsaɪz] VT criticare

critique [krɪˈtiːk] N critica, saggio critico

croak [krəuk] VI gracchiare

Croat [ˈkrəuæt] ADJ, N = **Croatian**

Croatia [krəuˈeɪʃə] N Croazia

Croatian [krəuˈeɪʃən] ADJ croato(-a) ▶ N croato(-a); (*Ling*) croato

crochet [ˈkrəuʃeɪ] N lavoro all'uncinetto

crock [krɔk] N coccio; (*col: person: also*: **old crock**) rottame *m*; (*car etc*) caffettiera, rottame *m*

crockery [ˈkrɔkərɪ] N vasellame *m*; (*plates, cups etc*) stoviglie *fpl*

crocodile [ˈkrɔkədaɪl] N coccodrillo

crocus [ˈkrəukəs] N croco

croft [krɔft] N (*BRIT*) piccolo podere *m*

crofter [ˈkrɔftəʳ] N (*BRIT*) affittuario di un piccolo podere

croissant [ˈkrwasɔŋ] N brioche *f inv*, croissant *m inv*

crone [krəun] N strega

crony [ˈkrəunɪ] N (*col*) amicone(-a)

crook [kruk] N (*col*) truffatore *m*; (*of shepherd*) bastone *m*

crooked [ˈkrukɪd] ADJ curvo(-a), storto(-a); (*person, action*) disonesto(-a)

crop [krɔp] N raccolto; (*produce*) coltivazione *f*; (*amount produced*) raccolto; (*riding crop*) frustino; (*of bird*) gozzo, ingluvie *f* ▶ VT (*cut: hair*) tagliare, rapare; (*animals: grass*) brucare
   ▶ **crop up** VI presentarsi

cropper [ˈkrɔpəʳ] N: **to come a ~** (*col*) fare fiasco

crop spraying N spruzzatura di antiparassitari

croquet [ˈkrəukeɪ] N croquet *m*

croquette [krəˈkɛt] N crocchetta

cross [krɔs] N croce *f*; (*Biol*) incrocio ▶ VT (*street etc*) attraversare; (*arms, legs, Biol*) incrociare; (*cheque*) sbarrare; (*thwart: person, plan*) contrastare, ostacolare ▶ VI: **the boat crosses from … to …** la barca fa la traversata da … a …
   ▶ ADJ di cattivo umore; **to ~ o.s.** fare il segno della croce, segnarsi; **we have a crossed line** (*BRIT: on telephone*) c'è un'interferenza; **they've got their lines crossed** (*fig*) si sono fraintesi; **to**

be/get ~ **with sb (about sth)** essere arrabbiato(-a)/arrabbiarsi con qn (per qc)
  ▶ **cross off** VT cancellare (*tirando una riga con la penna*)
  ▶ **cross out** VT cancellare
  ▶ **cross over** VI attraversare

crossbar ['krɔsbɑːʳ] N traversa

crossbow ['krɔsbəu] N balestra

crossbreed ['krɔsbriːd] N incrocio

cross-Channel ferry ['krɔs'tʃænl-] N traghetto che attraversa la Manica

cross-check ['krɔstʃɛk] N controprova ▶ VI fare una controprova

crosscountry [krɔs'kʌntrɪ], **crosscountry race** [krɔs'kʌntrɪ-] N cross-country *m inv*

cross-dressing [krɔs'drɛsɪŋ] N travestitismo

cross-examination ['krɔsɪgzæmɪ'neɪʃən] N (*Law*) controinterrogatorio

cross-examine ['krɔsɪg'zæmɪn] VT (*Law*) sottoporre a controinterrogatorio

cross-eyed ['krɔsaɪd] ADJ strabico(-a)

crossfire ['krɔsfaɪəʳ] N fuoco incrociato

crossing ['krɔsɪŋ] N incrocio; (*sea-passage*) traversata; (*also:* **pedestrian crossing**) passaggio pedonale

crossing guard N (*US*) *dipendente comunale che aiuta i bambini ad attraversare la strada*

crossing point N valico di frontiera

cross-purposes ['krɔs'pɔːpəsɪz] NPL: **to be at ~ with sb** (*misunderstand*) fraintendere qn; **to talk at ~** fraintendersi

cross-question [krɔs'kwɛstʃən] VT (*Law*) = **cross-examine**; (*fig*) sottoporre ad un interrogatorio

cross-reference ['krɔs'rɛfərəns] N rinvio, rimando

crossroads ['krɔsrəudz] N incrocio

cross section N (*Biol*) sezione *f* trasversale; (*in population*) settore *m* rappresentativo

crosswalk ['krɔswɔːk] N (*US*) strisce *fpl* pedonali, passaggio pedonale

crosswind ['krɔswɪnd] N vento di traverso

crosswise ['krɔswaɪz] ADV di traverso

crossword ['krɔswəːd] N cruciverba *m inv*

crotch [krɔtʃ] N (*Anat*) inforcatura; (*of garment*) pattina

crotchet ['krɔtʃɪt] N (*Mus*) semiminima

crotchety ['krɔtʃɪtɪ] ADJ (*person*) burbero(-a)

crouch [krautʃ] VI acquattarsi; rannicchiarsi

croup [kruːp] N (*Med*) croup *m*

crouton ['kruːtɔn] N crostino

crow [krəu] N (*bird*) cornacchia; (*of cock*) canto del gallo ▶ VI (*cock*) cantare; (*fig*) vantarsi; cantar vittoria

crowbar ['krəubɑːʳ] N piede *m* di porco

crowd [kraud] N folla ▶ VT affollare, stipare

▶ VI affollarsi; **crowds of people** un sacco di gente; **to ~ round/in** affollarsi intorno a/in

crowded ['kraudɪd] ADJ affollato(-a); **~ with** stipato(-a) di

crowd scene N (*Cine, Theat*) scena di massa

crowdsource ['kraudsɔːs] VT ricorrere al crowdsourcing per

crowdsourcing ['kraudsɔːsɪŋ] N crowdsourcing *m*

crown [kraun] N corona; (*of head*) calotta cranica; (*of hat*) cocuzzolo; (*of hill*) cima ▶ VT incoronare; (*tooth*) incapsulare; (*fig: career*) coronare; **and to ~ it all …** (*fig*) e per giunta …, e come se non bastasse …; *vedi nota*

In Inghilterra e Galles, una **crown court** è un tribunale, composto da un giudice e una giuria. Ne esistono circa 90 che si occupano dei casi penali più gravi ad esse rinviati dalle *magistrates' courts*.

crowning ['kraunɪŋ] ADJ (*achievement, glory*) supremo(-a)

crown jewels NPL gioielli *mpl* della Corona

crown prince N principe *m* ereditario

crow's-feet ['krəuzfiːt] NPL zampe *fpl* di gallina

crow's-nest ['krəuznɛst] N (*on sailing-ship*) coffa

crucial ['kruːʃl] ADJ cruciale, decisivo(-a); **~ to** essenziale per

crucifix ['kruːsɪfɪks] N crocifisso

crucifixion [kruːsɪ'fɪkʃən] N crocifissione *f*

crucify ['kruːsɪfaɪ] VT crocifiggere, mettere in croce; (*fig*) distruggere, fare a pezzi

crude [kruːd] ADJ (*materials*) greggio(-a); non raffinato(-a); (*fig: basic*) crudo(-a), primitivo(-a); (*: vulgar*) rozzo(-a), grossolano(-a) ▶ N (*also:* **crude oil**) (petrolio) greggio

cruel ['kruəl] ADJ crudele

cruelty ['kruəltɪ] N crudeltà *f inv*

cruet ['kruːɪt] N ampolla

cruise [kruːz] N crociera ▶ VI andare a velocità di crociera; (*taxi*) circolare

cruise missile N missile *m* cruise *inv*

cruiser ['kruːzəʳ] N incrociatore *m*

cruising speed ['kruːzɪŋ-] N velocità *f inv* di crociera

crumb [krʌm] N briciola

crumble ['krʌmbl] VT sbriciolare ▶ VI sbriciolarsi; (*plaster etc*) sgretolarsi; (*land, earth*) franare; (*building, fig*) crollare

crumbly ['krʌmblɪ] ADJ friabile

crummy ['krʌmɪ] ADJ (*col: cheap*) di infima categoria; (*: depressed*) giù *inv*

crumpet ['krʌmpɪt] N *specie di frittella*

crumple ['krʌmpl] VT raggrinzare, spiegazzare

crunch [krʌntʃ] VT sgranocchiare; (*underfoot*)

scricchiolare ▶ N (fig) punto or momento cruciale

crunchy [ˈkrʌntʃɪ] ADJ croccante

crusade [kruːˈseɪd] N crociata ▶ VI (fig): **to ~ for/against** fare una crociata per/contro

crusader [kruːˈseɪdəʳ] N crociato; (fig): **~ (for)** sostenitore(-trice) (di)

crush [krʌʃ] N folla; (love): **to have a ~ on sb** avere una cotta per qn; (drink): **lemon ~** spremuta di limone ▶ VT schiacciare; (crumple) sgualcire; (grind, break up: garlic, ice) tritare; (: grapes) pigiare

crush barrier N (BRIT) transenna

crushing [ˈkrʌʃɪŋ] ADJ schiacciante

crust [krʌst] N crosta

crustacean [krʌsˈteɪʃən] N crostaceo

crusty [ˈkrʌstɪ] ADJ (bread) croccante; (person) brontolone(-a); (remark) brusco(-a)

crutch [krʌtʃ] N (Med) gruccia; (support) sostegno; (also: **crotch**) pattina

crux [krʌks] N nodo

cry [kraɪ] VI piangere; (shout: also: **cry out**) urlare ▶ N urlo, grido; (of animal) verso; **to ~ for help** gridare aiuto; **what are you crying about?** perché piangi?; **she had a good ~** si è fatta un bel pianto; **it's a far ~ from ...** (fig) è tutt'un'altra cosa da ...
  ▶ **cry off** VI ritirarsi
  ▶ **cry out** VI, VT gridare

crying [ˈkraɪɪŋ] ADJ (fig) palese; urgente

crypt [krɪpt] N cripta

cryptic [ˈkrɪptɪk] ADJ ermetico(-a)

crystal [ˈkrɪstl] N cristallo

crystal-clear [ˈkrɪstlˈklɪəʳ] ADJ cristallino(-a); (fig) chiaro(-a) (come il sole)

crystallize [ˈkrɪstəlaɪz] VI cristallizzarsi ▶ VT (fig) concretizzare, concretare; **crystallized fruits** (BRIT) frutta candita

CSA N ABBR (US) = **Confederate States of America**; (BRIT: = Child Support Agency) istituto a difesa dei figli di coppie separate, che si adopera affinché venga rispettato l'obbligo del mantenimento

CSC N ABBR (= Civil Service Commission) commissione per il reclutamento dei funzionari statali

CS gas N (BRIT) tipo di gas lacrimogeno

CST ABBR (US: = Central Standard Time) fuso orario

CT ABBR (US) = **Connecticut**

ct ABBR = **cent; court**

CTC N ABBR (BRIT: = city technology college) istituto tecnico superiore

cu. ABBR = **cubic**

cub [kʌb] N cucciolo; (also: **cub scout**) lupetto

Cuba [ˈkjuːbə] N Cuba

Cuban [ˈkjuːbən] ADJ, N cubano(-a)

cubbyhole [ˈkʌbɪhəul] N angolino

cube [kjuːb] N cubo ▶ VT (Math) elevare al cubo

cube root N radice f cubica

cubic [ˈkjuːbɪk] ADJ cubico(-a); **~ metre** etc metro etc cubo; **~ capacity** (Aut) cilindrata

cubicle [ˈkjuːbɪkl] N scompartimento separato; cabina

cuckoo [ˈkuku:] N cucù m inv

cuckoo clock N orologio a cucù

cucumber [ˈkjuːkʌmbəʳ] N cetriolo

cud [kʌd] N: **to chew the ~** ruminare

cuddle [ˈkʌdl] VT abbracciare, coccolare ▶ VI abbracciarsi

cuddly [ˈkʌdlɪ] ADJ (person) coccolone(-a); (col) paffuto(-a); **~ toy** (animale m di) peluche m inv

cudgel [ˈkʌdʒl] N randello ▶ VT: **to ~ one's brains** scervellarsi, spremere le meningi

cue [kjuː] N stecca; (Theat etc) segnale m

cuff [kʌf] N (BRIT: of shirt, coat etc) polsino; (US: on trousers) risvolto; (blow) schiaffo ▶ VT dare uno schiaffo a; **off the ~** adv improvvisando

cufflink [ˈkʌflɪŋk] N gemello

cu. ft. ABBR = **cubic feet**

cu. in. ABBR = **cubic inches**

cuisine [kwɪˈziːn] N cucina

cul-de-sac [ˈkʌldəsæk] N vicolo cieco

culinary [ˈkʌlɪnərɪ] ADJ culinario(-a)

cull [kʌl] VT (kill selectively: animals) selezionare e abbattere; (ideas etc) scegliere ▶ N (of animals) abbattimento selettivo

culminate [ˈkʌlmɪneɪt] VI: **to ~ in** culminare con

culmination [kʌlmɪˈneɪʃən] N culmine m

culottes [kjuːˈlɔts] NPL gonna f pantalone inv

culpable [ˈkʌlpəbl] ADJ colpevole

culprit [ˈkʌlprɪt] N colpevole mf

cult [kʌlt] N culto

cult figure N idolo

cultivate [ˈkʌltɪveɪt] VT (also fig) coltivare

cultivation [kʌltɪˈveɪʃən] N coltivazione f

cultural [ˈkʌltʃərəl] ADJ culturale

culture [ˈkʌltʃəʳ] N (also fig) cultura

cultured [ˈkʌltʃəd] ADJ colto(-a)

cumbersome [ˈkʌmbəsəm] ADJ ingombrante

cumin [ˈkʌmɪn] N (spice) cumino

cumulative [ˈkjuːmjulətɪv] ADJ cumulativo(-a)

cunning [ˈkʌnɪŋ] N astuzia, furberia ▶ ADJ astuto(-a), furbo(-a); (clever: device, idea) ingegnoso(-a)

cunt [kʌnt] N (col!) figa (!); (insult) stronzo(-a) (!)

cup [kʌp] N tazza; (prize, of bra) coppa; **a ~ of tea** una tazza di tè

cupboard [ˈkʌbəd] N armadio

cup final N (BRIT Football) finale f di coppa

Cupid [ˈkjuːpɪd] N Cupido; **cupid** cupido

cupidity [kjuːˈpɪdɪtɪ] N cupidigia

cupola ['kju:pələ] N cupola

cuppa ['kʌpə] N (*BRIT col*) tazza di tè

cup-tie ['kʌptaɪ] N (*BRIT Football*) partita di coppa

curable ['kjuərəbl] ADJ curabile

curate ['kjuərɪt] N cappellano

curator [kjuə'reɪtəʳ] N direttore(-trice) (*di museo ecc*)

curb [kə:b] VT tenere a freno; (*expenditure*) limitare ▶ N freno; (*US*) bordo del marciapiede

curd cheese [kə:d-] N cagliata

curdle ['kə:dl] VI cagliare

curds [kə:dz] NPL latte *m* cagliato

cure [kjuəʳ] VT guarire; (*Culin*) trattare; affumicare; essiccare ▶ N rimedio; **to be cured of sth** essere guarito(-a) da qc

cure-all ['kjuərɔ:l] N (*also fig*) panacea, toccasana *m inv*

curfew ['kə:fju:] N coprifuoco

curio ['kjuərɪəu] N curiosità *f inv*

curiosity [kjuərɪ'ɒsɪtɪ] N curiosità

curious ['kjuərɪəs] ADJ curioso(-a); **I'm ~ about him** m'incuriosisce

curiously ['kjuərɪəslɪ] ADV con curiosità; (*strangely*) stranamente; **~ enough, ...** per quanto possa sembrare strano, ...

curl [kə:l] N riccio; (*of smoke etc*) anello ▶ VT ondulare; (*tightly*) arricciare ▶ VI arricciarsi ▶ **curl up** VI avvolgersi a spirale; rannicchiarsi

curler ['kə:ləʳ] N bigodino; (*Sport*) giocatore(-trice) di curling

curlew ['kə:lu:] N chiurlo

curling ['kə:lɪŋ] N (*Sport*) curling *m*

curling tongs, (*US*) **curling irons** NPL (*for hair*) arricciacapelli *m inv*

curly ['kə:lɪ] ADJ ricciuto(-a)

currant ['kʌrnt] N (*dried*) uvetta; (*bush, fruit*) ribes *m inv*

currency ['kʌrnsɪ] N moneta; **foreign ~** divisa estera; **to gain ~** (*fig*) acquistare larga diffusione

current ['kʌrnt] ADJ corrente; (*tendency, price, event*) attuale ▶ N corrente *f*; **in ~ use** in uso corrente, d'uso comune; **the ~ issue of a magazine** l'ultimo numero di una rivista; **direct/alternating ~** (*Elec*) corrente continua/alternata

current account N (*BRIT*) conto corrente

current affairs NPL attualità *fpl*

current assets NPL (*Comm*) attivo realizzabile e disponibile

current liabilities NPL (*Comm*) passività *fpl* correnti

currently ['kʌrntlɪ] ADV attualmente

curriculum [kə'rɪkjuləm] (*pl* **curriculums** *or* **curricula** [-lə]) N curriculum *m inv*

curriculum vitae [-'vi:taɪ] N curriculum vitae *m inv*

curry ['kʌrɪ] N curry *m inv* ▶ VT: **to ~ favour with** cercare di attirarsi i favori di; **chicken ~** pollo al curry

curry powder N curry *m*

curse [kə:s] VT maledire ▶ VI bestemmiare ▶ N maledizione *f*; bestemmia

cursor ['kə:səʳ] N (*Comput*) cursore *m*

cursory ['kə:sərɪ] ADJ superficiale

curt [kə:t] ADJ secco(-a)

curtail [kə:'teɪl] VT (*visit etc*) accorciare; (*expenses etc*) ridurre, decurtare

curtain ['kə:tn] N tenda; (*Theat*) sipario; **to draw the curtains** (*together*) chiudere *or* tirare le tende; (*apart*) aprire le tende

curtain call N (*Theat*) chinata alla ribalta

curtsy, curtsey ['kə:tsɪ] N inchino, riverenza ▶ VI fare un inchino *or* una riverenza

curvature ['kə:vətʃəʳ] N curvatura

curve [kə:v] N curva ▶ VT curvare ▶ VI curvarsi; (*road*) fare una curva

curved [kə:vd] ADJ curvo(-a)

cushion ['kuʃən] N cuscino ▶ VT (*shock*) fare da cuscinetto a

cushy ['kuʃɪ] ADJ (*col*): **a ~ job** un lavoro di tutto riposo; **to have a ~ time** spassarsela

custard ['kʌstəd] N (*for pouring*) crema

custard powder N (*BRIT*) crema pasticcera in polvere

custodial sentence [kʌs'təudɪəl-] N condanna a pena detentiva

custodian [kʌs'təudɪən] N custode *mf*; (*of museum etc*) soprintendente *mf*

custody ['kʌstədɪ] N (*of child*) custodia; (*for offenders*) arresto; **to take sb into ~** mettere qn in detenzione preventiva; **in the ~ of** alla custodia di

custom ['kʌstəm] N costume *m*, usanza; (*Law*) consuetudine *f*; (*Comm*) clientela; *see also* **customs**

customary ['kʌstəmərɪ] ADJ consueto(-a); **it is ~ to do** è consuetudine fare

custom-built ['kʌstəm'bɪlt] ADJ *see* **custom-made**

customer ['kʌstəməʳ] N cliente *mf*; **he's an awkward ~** (*col*) è un tipo incontentabile

customer profile N profilo del cliente

customize ['kʌstəmaɪz] VT customizzare

customized ['kʌstəmaɪzd] ADJ personalizzato(-a); (*car*) fuoriserie *inv*

custom-made ['kʌstəm'meɪd] ADJ (*clothes*) fatto(-a) su misura; (*other goods: also:* **custom-built**) fatto(-a) su ordinazione

customs ['kʌstəmz] NPL dogana; **to go through (the) ~** passare la dogana

Customs and Excise N (*BRIT*) Ufficio Dazi e Dogana

customs officer N doganiere m

cut [kʌt] (pt, pp ~) VT tagliare; (shape, make) intagliare; (reduce) ridurre; (col: avoid: class, lecture, appointment) saltare ▶VI tagliare; (intersect) tagliarsi ▶N taglio; (in salary etc) riduzione f; **cold cuts** npl (US) affettati mpl; **power ~** mancanza di corrente elettrica; **to ~ one's finger** tagliarsi un dito; **I've ~ myself** mi sono tagliato; **to get one's hair ~** farsi tagliare i capelli; **to ~ a tooth** mettere un dente; **to ~ sb/ sth short** interrompere qn/qc; **to ~ sb dead** ignorare qn completamente
▶ **cut back** VT (plants) tagliare; (production, expenditure) ridurre
▶ **cut down** VT (tree) abbattere; (consumption, expenses) ridurre; **to ~ sb down to size** (fig) sgonfiare or ridimensionare qn
▶ **cut down on** VT FUS ridurre
▶ **cut in** VI: **to ~ in (on)** (interrupt conversation) intromettersi (in); (Aut) tagliare la strada (a)
▶ **cut off** VT tagliare; (fig) isolare; **we've been ~ off** (Tel) è caduta la linea
▶ **cut out** VT tagliare; eliminare; (picture) ritagliare
▶ **cut up** VT (gen) tagliare a pezzi

cut-and-dried [ˈkʌtənˈdraɪd] ADJ (also: **cut-and-dry**) assodato(-a)

cutaway [ˈkʌtəweɪ] ADJ, N: **~ (drawing)** spaccato

cutback [ˈkʌtbæk] N riduzione f

cute [kjuːt] ADJ carino(-a); (clever) astuto(-a)

cut glass N cristallo

cuticle [ˈkjuːtɪkl] N (on nail) pellicina, cuticola

cutlery [ˈkʌtlərɪ] N posate fpl

cutlet [ˈkʌtlɪt] N costoletta; (nut cutlet) cotoletta vegetariana

cutoff [ˈkʌtɔf] N (also: **cutoff point**) limite m

cutoff switch N interruttore m

cutout [ˈkʌtaut] N (switch) interruttore m; (paper, cardboard figure) ritaglio

cut-price [ˈkʌtˈpraɪs], (US) **cut-rate** [ˈkʌtˈreɪt] ADJ a prezzo ridotto

cutthroat [ˈkʌtθrəut] N assassino ▶ADJ: **~ competition** concorrenza spietata

cutting [ˈkʌtɪŋ] ADJ tagliente; (fig) pungente ▶N (BRIT: Press) ritaglio (di giornale); (: Rail) trincea; (Cine) montaggio; (from plant) talea

cutting edge N (of knife) taglio, filo; **on or at the ~ of sth** all'avanguardia di qc

cutting-edge [kʌtɪŋˈɛdʒ] ADJ d'avanguardia

cuttlefish [ˈkʌtlfɪʃ] N seppia

cut-up [ˈkʌtʌp] ADJ stravolto(-a)

CV N ABBR = **curriculum vitae**

CWO ABBR (US) = **Chief Warrant Officer**

cwt. ABBR = **hundredweight**

cyanide [ˈsaɪənaɪd] N cianuro

cyberattack [ˈsaɪbərətæk] N cyberattacco m

cyberbully [ˈsaɪbəbulɪ] N cyberbullo(-a) m/f

cyberbullying [ˈsaɪbəbulɪŋ] N bullismo informatico

cybercafé [ˈsaɪbəkæfeɪ] N cybercaffè m inv

cybercrime [ˈsaɪbəkraɪm] N delinquenza informatica

cybernetics [saɪbəˈnɛtɪks] N cibernetica

cybersecurity [saɪbəsɪˈkjurɪtɪ] N sicurezza f informatica

cyberspace [ˈsaɪbəspeɪs] N ciberspazio

cyberterrorism [saɪbəˈtɛrərɪzəm] N ciberterrorismo

cyclamen [ˈsɪkləmən] N ciclamino

cycle [ˈsaɪkl] N ciclo; (bicycle) bicicletta ▶VI andare in bicicletta

cycle hire N noleggio m biciclette inv

cycle lane N pista ciclabile

cycle path N pista ciclabile

cycle race N gara or corsa ciclistica

cycle rack N portabiciclette m inv

cycle track N percorso ciclabile; (in velodrome) pista

cycling [ˈsaɪklɪŋ] N ciclismo; **to go on a ~ holiday** (BRIT) fare una vacanza in bicicletta

cyclist [ˈsaɪklɪst] N ciclista mf

cyclone [ˈsaɪkləun] N ciclone m

cygnet [ˈsɪgnɪt] N cigno giovane

cylinder [ˈsɪlɪndər] N cilindro

cylinder capacity N cilindrata

cylinder head N testata

cylinder head gasket N guarnizione f della testata del cilindro

cymbals [ˈsɪmblz] NPL piatti mpl

cynic [ˈsɪnɪk] N cinico(-a)

cynical [ˈsɪnɪkl] ADJ cinico(-a)

cynicism [ˈsɪnɪsɪzəm] N cinismo

cypress [ˈsaɪprɪs] N cipresso

Cypriot [ˈsɪprɪət] ADJ, N cipriota (mf)

Cyprus [ˈsaɪprəs] N Cipro

cyst [sɪst] N cisti f inv

cystitis [sɪˈstaɪtɪs] N cistite f

CZ N ABBR (US: = Canal Zone) zona del Canale di Panama

czar [zɑːr] N zar m inv

Czech [tʃɛk] ADJ ceco(-a) ▶N ceco(-a); (Ling) ceco

Czechia [ˈtʃɛkɪə] N (Czech Republic) Repubblica Ceca

Czechoslovak [tʃɛkəˈsləuvæk] ADJ, N (Hist) = **Czechoslovakian**

Czechoslovakia [tʃɛkəsləˈvækɪə] N (Hist) Cecoslovacchia

Czechoslovakian [tʃɛkəsləˈvækɪən] ADJ, N (Hist) cecoslovacco(-a)

Czech Republic N: **the ~** la Repubblica Ceca

Dd

D, d [di:] N (*letter*) D, d *f inv or m inv*; (*Mus*): **D** re *m*; **D for David**, (*US*) **D for Dog** ≈ D come Domodossola

D ABBR (*US Pol*) = **democrat**

d ABBR (*BRIT old*) = **penny**

d. ABBR = **died**

DA N ABBR (*US*) = **district attorney**

dab [dæb] VT (*eyes, wound*) tamponare; (*paint, cream*) applicare (con leggeri colpetti); **a ~ of paint** un colpetto di vernice

dabble ['dæbl] VI: **to ~ in** occuparsi (da dilettante) di

Dacca ['dækə] N Dacca *f*

dachshund ['dækshund] N bassotto

dad [dæd], **daddy** ['dædɪ] N babbo, papà *m inv*

daddy-long-legs [dædɪ'lɔŋlɛgz] N tipula, zanzarone *m*

daffodil ['dæfədɪl] N trombone *m*, giunchiglia

daft [dɑːft] ADJ sciocco(-a); **to be ~ about sb** perdere la testa per qn; **to be ~ about sth** andare pazzo per qc

dagger ['dægə^r] N pugnale *m*

dahlia ['deɪljə] N dalia

daily ['deɪlɪ] ADJ quotidiano(-a), giornaliero(-a) ▶ N quotidiano; (*BRIT: servant*) donna di servizio ▶ ADV tutti i giorni; **twice ~** due volte al giorno

dainty ['deɪntɪ] ADJ delicato(-a), grazioso(-a)

dairy ['dɛərɪ] N (*shop*) latteria; (*on farm*) caseificio ▶ CPD caseario(-a)

dairy cow N mucca da latte

dairy farm N caseificio

dairy produce N latticini *mpl*

dais ['deɪɪs] N pedana, palco

daisy ['deɪzɪ] N margherita

daisy wheel N (*on printer*) margherita

daisy-wheel printer ['deɪzɪwiːl-] N stampante *f* a margherita

Dakar ['dækə^r] N Dakar *f*

dale [deɪl] N valle *f*

dally ['dælɪ] VI trastullarsi

dalmatian [dæl'meɪʃən] N (*dog*) dalmata *m*

dam [dæm] N diga; (*reservoir*) bacino artificiale ▶ VT sbarrare; costruire dighe su

damage ['dæmɪdʒ] N danno, danni *mpl*; (*fig*) danno ▶ VT danneggiare; (*fig*) recar danno a; **~ to property** danni materiali

damages NPL (*Law*) danni *mpl*; **to pay £5000 in ~** pagare 5000 sterline di indennizzo

damaging ['dæmɪdʒɪŋ] ADJ: **~ (to)** nocivo(-a) (a)

Damascus [də'mɑːskəs] N Damasco *f*

dame [deɪm] N (*title, US col*) donna; (*Theat*) vecchia signora (*ruolo comico di donna recitato da un uomo*)

damn [dæm] VT condannare; (*curse*) maledire ▶ N (*col*): **I don't give a ~** non me ne frega niente ▶ ADJ (*col: also:* **damned**): **this ~ ...** questo maledetto ...; **~ (it)!** accidenti!

damnable ['dæmnəbl] ADJ (*col: behaviour*) vergognoso(-a); (: *weather*) schifoso(-a)

damnation [dæm'neɪʃən] N (*Rel*) dannazione *f* ▶ EXCL (*col*) dannazione!, diavolo!

damning ['dæmɪŋ] ADJ (*evidence*) schiacciante

damp [dæmp] ADJ umido(-a) ▶ N umidità, umido ▶ VT (*also:* **dampen**: *cloth, rag*) inumidire, bagnare; (: *enthusiasm etc*) spegnere

dampcourse ['dæmpkɔːs] N strato *m* isolante antiumido *inv*

damper ['dæmpə^r] N (*Mus*) sordina; (*of fire*) valvola di tiraggio; **to put a ~ on sth** (*fig: atmosphere*) gelare; (*enthusiasm*) far sbollire

dampness ['dæmpnɪs] N umidità, umido

damson ['dæmzən] N susina damaschina

dance [dɑːns] N danza, ballo; (*ball*) ballo ▶ VI ballare; **to ~ about** saltellare

dance floor N pista da ballo

dance hall N dancing *m inv*, sala da ballo

dancer ['dɑːnsə^r] N danzatore(-trice); (*professional*) ballerino(-a)

dancing ['dɑːnsɪŋ] N danza, ballo

D and C N ABBR (*Med:* = *dilation and curettage*) raschiamento

dandelion ['dændɪlaɪən] N dente *m* di leone

dandruff ['dændrəf] N forfora

D & T N ABBR (BRIT Scol) = **design and technology**

dandy ['dændɪ] N dandy *m inv*, elegantone *m* ▸ ADJ (US col) fantastico(-a)

Dane [deɪn] N danese *mf*

danger ['deɪndʒəʳ] N pericolo; **there is a ~ of fire** c'è pericolo di incendio; **in ~** in pericolo; **out of ~** fuori pericolo; **he was in ~ of falling** rischiava di cadere

danger list N (Med): **on the ~** in prognosi riservata

dangerous ['deɪndʒrəs] ADJ pericoloso(-a)

dangerously ['deɪndʒrəslɪ] ADV: **~ ill** in pericolo di vita

danger zone N area di pericolo

dangle ['dæŋgl] VT dondolare; (fig) far balenare ▸ VI pendolare

Danish ['deɪnɪʃ] ADJ danese ▸ N (Ling) danese *m*

Danish pastry N dolce *m* di pasta sfoglia

dank [dæŋk] ADJ freddo(-a) e umido(-a)

Danube ['dænjuːb] N: **the ~** il Danubio

dapper ['dæpəʳ] ADJ lindo(-a)

Dardanelles [dɑːdə'nɛlz] NPL Dardanelli *mpl*

dare [dɛəʳ] VT: **to ~ sb to do** sfidare qn a fare ▸ VI: **to ~ (to) do sth** osare fare qc; **I daren't tell him** (BRIT) non oso dirglielo; **I ~ say** (I suppose) immagino (che); **I ~ say he'll turn up** immagino che spunterà

daredevil ['dɛədɛvl] N scavezzacollo *mf*

Dar-es-Salaam ['dɑːrɛssə'lɑːm] N Dar-es-Salaam *f*

daring ['dɛərɪŋ] ADJ audace, ardito(-a) ▸ N audacia

dark [dɑːk] ADJ (night, room) buio(-a), scuro(-a); (colour, complexion) scuro(-a); (fig) cupo(-a), tetro(-a), nero(-a) ▸ N: **in the ~** al buio; **it is/is getting ~** è/si sta facendo buio; **in the ~ about** (fig) all'oscuro di; **after ~** a notte fatta; **~ chocolate** cioccolata amara

darken ['dɑːkən] VT (room) oscurare; (photo, painting) far scuro(-a); (colour) scurire ▸ VI (sky, room) oscurarsi; imbrunirsi

dark glasses NPL occhiali *mpl* scuri

dark horse N (fig) incognita

darkly ['dɑːklɪ] ADV (gloomily) cupamente, con aria cupa; (in a sinister way) minacciosamente

darkness ['dɑːknɪs] N oscurità, buio

darkroom ['dɑːkruːm] N camera oscura

darling ['dɑːlɪŋ] ADJ caro(-a) ▸ N tesoro

darn [dɑːn] VT rammendare

dart [dɑːt] N freccetta; (Sewing) pince *f inv* ▸ VI: **to ~ towards** (also: **make a dart towards**) precipitarsi verso; **to ~ along** passare come un razzo; **to ~ away/along** sfrecciare via/lungo; see also **darts**

dartboard ['dɑːtbɔːd] N bersaglio (per freccette)

darts [dɑːts] N tiro al bersaglio (con freccette)

dash [dæʃ] N (sign) lineetta; (small quantity: of liquid) goccio, goccino; (: of soda) spruzzo ▸ VT (missile) gettare; (hopes) infrangere ▸ VI: **to ~ towards** (also: **make a dash towards**) precipitarsi verso
▸ **dash away** VI scappare via

dashboard ['dæʃbɔːd] N (Aut) cruscotto

dashing ['dæʃɪŋ] ADJ ardito(-a)

dastardly ['dæstədlɪ] ADJ vile

DAT N ABBR (= digital audio tape) cassetta *f* digitale audio *inv*

data ['deɪtə] NPL dati *mpl*

database ['deɪtəbeɪs] N database *m inv*, base *f* di dati

data capture N registrazione *f* or rilevazione *f* di dati

data processing N elaborazione *f* (elettronica) dei dati

data transmission N trasmissione *f* di dati

date [deɪt] N data; (appointment) appuntamento; (fruit) dattero ▸ VT datare; (person) uscire con; **what's the ~ today?** quanti ne abbiamo oggi?; **~ of birth** data di nascita; **closing ~** scadenza, termine *m*; **to ~** adv (until now) fino a oggi; **out of ~** scaduto(-a); (old-fashioned) passato(-a) di moda; **up to ~** moderno(-a), aggiornato(-a); **to bring up to ~** (correspondence, information) aggiornare; (method) modernizzare; (person) aggiornare, mettere al corrente; **dated the 13th** datato il 13; **thank you for your letter dated 5th July** or (US) **July 5th** la ringrazio per la sua lettera in data 5 luglio

dated ['deɪtɪd] ADJ passato(-a) di moda

dateline ['deɪtlaɪn] N linea del cambiamento di data

date rape N stupro perpetrato da persona conosciuta

date stamp N timbro datario

daub [dɔːb] VT imbrattare

daughter ['dɔːtəʳ] N figlia

daughter-in-law ['dɔːtərɪnlɔː] N nuora

daunt [dɔːnt] VT intimidire

daunting ['dɔːntɪŋ] ADJ non invidiabile

dauntless ['dɔːntlɪs] ADJ intrepido(-a)

dawdle ['dɔːdl] VI bighellonare; **to ~ over one's work** gingillarsi con il lavoro

dawn [dɔːn] N alba ▸ VI (day) spuntare; (fig) venire in mente; **at ~** all'alba; **from ~ to dusk** dall'alba al tramonto; **it dawned on him that ...** gli è venuto in mente che ...

dawn chorus N (BRIT) coro mattutino degli uccelli

day [deɪ] N giorno; (as duration) giornata; (period of time, age) tempo, epoca; **the ~ before** il giorno avanti or prima; **the ~ after, the following ~** il giorno dopo, il giorno seguente; **the ~ before**

yesterday l'altro ieri; **the ~ after tomorrow** dopodomani; **(on) that ~** quel giorno; **(on) the ~ that ...** il giorno che or in cui ...; **to work an 8-hour ~** avere una giornata lavorativa di 8 ore; **by ~** di giorno; **~ by ~** giorno per giorno; **paid by the ~** pagato(-a) a giornata; **these days, in the present ~** di questi tempi, oggigiorno

Use **giorno** to refer to the whole 24-hour period; **giornata** only refers to the time when you are awake.

daybook ['deɪbuk] N (BRIT) brogliaccio

day boy N (Scol) alunno esterno

daybreak ['deɪbreɪk] N spuntar m del giorno

day care centre N scuola materna

daydream ['deɪdriːm] N sogno a occhi aperti ▶ VI sognare a occhi aperti

day girl N (Scol) alunna esterna

daylight ['deɪlaɪt] N luce f del giorno

daylight robbery N: **it's ~!** (BRIT col) è un vero furto!

Daylight Saving Time N (US) ora legale

day release N: **to be on ~** avere un giorno di congedo alla settimana per formazione professionale

day return, day return ticket N (BRIT) biglietto giornaliero di andata e ritorno

day shift N turno di giorno

daytime ['deɪtaɪm] N giorno

day-to-day ['deɪtə'deɪ] ADJ (routine, life, organization) quotidiano(-a); (expenses) giornaliero(-a); **on a ~ basis** a giornata

day trader N (Stock Exchange) day dealer mf, operatore che compra e vende titoli nel corso della stessa giornata

day trip N gita (di un giorno)

day tripper N gitante mf

daze [deɪz] VT (drug) inebetire; (blow) stordire ▶ N: **in a ~** inebetito(-a), stordito(-a)

dazed [deɪzd] ADJ stordito(-a)

dazzle ['dæzl] VT abbagliare

dazzling ['dæzlɪŋ] ADJ (light) abbagliante; (colour) violento(-a); (smile) smagliante

dB ABBR (= decibel) db

DC ABBR (Elec: = direct current) c.c.; (US) = **District of Columbia**

DCC® N ABBR = **digital compact cassette**

DD N ABBR (= Doctor of Divinity) titolo di studio

DD ABBR = **direct debit**

dd. ABBR (Comm) = **delivered**

D-day ['diː'deɪ] N giorno dello sbarco alleato in Normandia

DDS N ABBR (US) = **Doctor of Dental Science**; (= Doctor of Dental Surgery) titoli di studio

DDT N ABBR (= dichlorodiphenyl trichloroethane) D.D.T. m

DE ABBR (US) = **Delaware**

deacon ['diːkən] N diacono

dead [dɛd] ADJ morto(-a); (numb) intirizzito(-a); (telephone) muto(-a); (battery) scarico(-a) ▶ ADV assolutamente, perfettamente ■ **the dead** NPL i morti; **he was shot ~** fu colpito a morte; **~ on time** in perfetto orario; **~ tired** stanco(-a) morto(-a); **to stop ~** fermarsi di colpo; **the line has gone ~** (Tel) è caduta la linea

dead beat ADJ (col) stanco(-a) morto(-a)

deaden ['dɛdn] VT (blow, sound) ammortire; (make numb) intirizzire

dead end N vicolo cieco

dead-end ['dɛdɛnd] ADJ: **a ~ job** un lavoro senza sbocchi

dead heat N (Sport): **to finish in a ~** finire alla pari

dead-letter office [dɛd'lɛtə-] N ufficio della posta in giacenza

deadline ['dɛdlaɪn] N scadenza; **to work to a ~** avere una scadenza

deadlock ['dɛdlɔk] N punto morto

dead loss N (col): **to be a ~** (person, thing) non valere niente

deadly ['dɛdlɪ] ADJ mortale; (weapon, poison) micidiale ▶ ADV: **~ dull** di una noia micidiale

deadpan ['dɛdpæn] ADJ a faccia impassibile

Dead Sea N: **the ~** il mar Morto

deaf [dɛf] ADJ sordo(-a); **to turn a ~ ear to sth** fare orecchi da mercante a qc

deaf-aid ['dɛfeɪd] N apparecchio per la sordità

deaf-and-dumb ['dɛfən'dʌm] (!) ADJ (person) sordomuto(-a); (alphabet) dei sordomuti

deafen ['dɛfn] VT assordare

deafening ['dɛfnɪŋ] ADJ fragoroso(-a), assordante

deaf-mute ['dɛfmjuːt] (!) N sordomuto(-a)

deafness ['dɛfnɪs] N sordità

deal [diːl] (pt, pp **dealt** [dɛlt]) N accordo; (business deal) affare m ▶ VT (blow, cards) dare; **to strike a ~ with sb** fare un affare con qn; **it's a ~!** (col) affare fatto!; **he got a bad/fair ~ from them** l'hanno trattato male/bene; **a good ~ of, a great ~ of** molto(-a)
▶ **deal in** VT FUS (Comm) occuparsi di
▶ **deal with** VT FUS (Comm) fare affari con, trattare con; (handle) occuparsi di; (be about: book etc) trattare di

dealbreaker ['diːlbreɪkəʳ] N motivo m di rottura

dealer ['diːləʳ] N commerciante mf

dealership ['diːləʃɪp] N rivenditore m

dealings ['diːlɪŋz] NPL (Comm) relazioni fpl; (relations) rapporti mpl; (in goods, shares) transazioni fpl

dealt [dɛlt] PT, PP of **deal**

dean [di:n] N (*Rel*) decano; (*Scol*) preside *m* di facoltà (*or* di collegio)

dear [dɪə^r] ADJ caro(-a) ▶ N: **my ~** caro mio/cara mia ▶ EXCL: **~ me!** Dio mio!; **D~ Sir/Madam** (*in letter*) Egregio Signore/Egregia Signora; **D~ Mr/Mrs X** Gentile Signor/Signora X

dearly [ˈdɪəlɪ] ADV (*love*) moltissimo; (*pay*) a caro prezzo

dear money N (*Comm*) denaro ad alto interesse

dearth [də:θ] N scarsità, carestia

death [dɛθ] N morte *f*; (*Admin*) decesso

deathbed [ˈdɛθbɛd] N letto di morte

death certificate N atto di decesso

death duty N (*Brit*) imposta *or* tassa di successione

deathly [ˈdɛθlɪ] ADJ di morte ▶ ADV come un cadavere

death penalty N pena di morte

death rate N indice *m* di mortalità

death row [-rəu] N (*US*): **to be on ~** essere nel braccio della morte

death sentence N condanna a morte

death squad N squadra della morte

deathtrap [ˈdɛθtræp] N trappola mortale

deb [dɛb] N ABBR (*col*) = **debutante**

debacle [deɪˈbɑːkl] N (*defeat*) disfatta; (*collapse*) sfacelo

debar [dɪˈbɑː^r] VT: **to ~ sb from a club** *etc* escludere qn da un club *etc*; **to ~ sb from doing** vietare a qn di fare

debase [dɪˈbeɪs] VT (*currency*) adulterare; (*person*) degradare

debatable [dɪˈbeɪtəbl] ADJ discutibile; **it is ~ whether …** è in dubbio se …

debate [dɪˈbeɪt] N dibattito ▶ VT dibattere; discutere ▶ VI (*consider*): **to ~ whether** riflettere se

debauchery [dɪˈbɔːtʃərɪ] N dissolutezza

debenture [dɪˈbɛntʃə^r] N (*Comm*) obbligazione *f*

debilitate [dɪˈbɪlɪteɪt] VT debilitare

debit [ˈdɛbɪt] N debito ▶ VT: **to ~ a sum to sb** *or* **to sb's account** addebitare una somma a qn

debit balance N saldo debitore

debit card N carta di debito

debit note N nota di addebito

debonair [dɛbəˈnɛə^r] ADJ gioviale e disinvolto(-a)

debrief [diːˈbriːf] VT chiamare a rapporto (a operazione ultimata)

debriefing [diːˈbriːfɪŋ] N rapporto

debris [ˈdɛbriː] N detriti *mpl*

debt [dɛt] N debito; **to be in ~** essere indebitato(-a); **debts of £5000** debiti per 5000 sterline; **bad ~** debito insoluto

debt collector N agente *m* di recupero crediti

debtor [ˈdɛtə^r] N debitore(-trice)

debug [diːˈbʌg] VT (*Comput*) localizzare e rimuovere errori in

debunk [diːˈbʌŋk] VT (*col: theory*) demistificare; (*: claim*) smentire; (*: person, institution*) screditare

debut [ˈdeɪbjuː] N debutto

debutante [ˈdɛbjutɑːnt] N debuttante *f*

Dec. ABBR (= *December*) dic.

decade [ˈdɛkeɪd] N decennio

decadence [ˈdɛkədəns] N decadenza

decadent [ˈdɛkədənt] ADJ decadente

decaf [ˈdiːkæf] N (*col*) decaffeinato

decaffeinated [dɪˈkæfɪneɪtɪd] ADJ decaffeinato(-a)

decamp [dɪˈkæmp] VI (*col*) filarsela, levare le tende

decant [dɪˈkænt] VT (*wine*) travasare

decanter [dɪˈkæntə^r] N caraffa

decarbonize [diːˈkɑːbənaɪz] VT (*Aut*) decarburare

decathlon [dɪˈkæθlən] N decathlon *m*

decay [dɪˈkeɪ] N decadimento; imputridimento; (*fig*) rovina; (*also:* **tooth decay**) carie *f* ▶ VI (*rot*) imputridire; (*fig*) andare in rovina

decease [dɪˈsiːs] N decesso

deceased [dɪˈsiːst] N: **the ~** il(la) defunto(a)

deceit [dɪˈsiːt] N inganno

deceitful [dɪˈsiːtful] ADJ ingannevole, perfido(-a)

deceive [dɪˈsiːv] VT ingannare; **to ~ o.s.** illudersi, ingannarsi

decelerate [diːˈsɛləreɪt] VT, VI rallentare

December [dɪˈsɛmbə^r] N dicembre *m*; *see also* **July**

decency [ˈdiːsənsɪ] N decenza

decent [ˈdiːsənt] ADJ decente; (*respectable*) per bene; (*kind*) gentile; **they were very ~ about it** si sono comportati da signori riguardo a ciò

decently [ˈdiːsəntlɪ] ADV (*respectably*) decentemente, convenientemente; (*kindly*) gentilmente

decentralization [diːsɛntrəlaɪˈzeɪʃən] N decentramento

decentralize [diːˈsɛntrəlaɪz] VT decentrare

deception [dɪˈsɛpʃən] N inganno

deceptive [dɪˈsɛptɪv] ADJ ingannevole

decibel [ˈdɛsɪbɛl] N decibel *m inv*

decide [dɪˈsaɪd] VT (*person*) far prendere una decisione a; (*question, argument*) risolvere, decidere ▶ VI decidere, decidersi; **to ~ to do/that** decidere di fare/che; **to ~ on** decidere per; **to ~ against doing sth** decidere di non fare qc

decided [dɪˈsaɪdɪd] ADJ (*resolute*) deciso(-a); (*clear, definite*) netto(-a), chiaro(-a)

decidedly [dɪˈsaɪdɪdlɪ] ADV indubbiamente; decisamente

deciding [dɪˈsaɪdɪŋ] ADJ decisivo(-a)

deciduous [dɪˈsɪdjuəs] ADJ deciduo(-a)

decimal [ˈdɛsɪməl] ADJ, N decimale (m); **to 3 ~ places** al terzo decimale

decimalize [ˈdɛsɪməlaɪz] VT (BRIT) convertire al sistema metrico decimale

decimal point N ≈ virgola

decimate [ˈdɛsɪmeɪt] VT decimare

decipher [dɪˈsaɪfəʳ] VT decifrare

decision [dɪˈsɪʒən] N decisione f; **to make a ~** prendere una decisione

decisive [dɪˈsaɪsɪv] ADJ (victory, factor) decisivo(-a); (influence) determinante; (manner, person) risoluto(-a), deciso(-a); (reply) deciso(-a), categorico(-a)

deck [dɛk] N (Naut) ponte m; (of cards) mazzo; **top ~** imperiale m; **to go up on ~** salire in coperta; **below ~** sotto coperta; **cassette ~** piastra (di registrazione); **record ~** piatto (giradischi); (of cards) mazzo

deckchair [ˈdɛktʃɛəʳ] N sedia a sdraio

deck hand N marinaio

declaration [dɛkləˈreɪʃən] N dichiarazione f

declare [dɪˈklɛəʳ] VT dichiarare

declassify [diːˈklæsɪfaɪ] VT rendere accessibile al pubblico

decline [dɪˈklaɪn] N (decay) declino; (lessening) ribasso ▶ VT declinare; rifiutare ▶ VI declinare; diminuire; **~ in living standards** abbassamento del tenore di vita; **to ~ to do sth** rifiutar(si) di fare qc

declutch [diːˈklʌtʃ] VI (BRIT) premere la frizione

declutter [diːˈklʌtə] VI fare il decluttering, eliminare il superfluo

decode [diːˈkəud] VT decifrare

decoder [diːˈkəudəʳ] N (Comput, TV) decodificatore m

decompose [diːkəmˈpəuz] VI decomporre

decomposition [diːkɔmpəˈzɪʃən] N decomposizione f

decompression [diːkəmˈprɛʃən] N decompressione f

decompression chamber N camera di decompressione

decongestant [diːkənˈdʒɛstənt] N decongestionante m

decontaminate [diːkənˈtæmɪneɪt] VT decontaminare

decontrol [diːkənˈtrəul] VT (trade) liberalizzare; (prices) togliere il controllo governativo a

decor [ˈdeɪkɔːʳ] N decorazione f

decorate [ˈdɛkəreɪt] VT (adorn, give a medal to) decorare; (paint and paper) tinteggiare e tappezzare

decoration [dɛkəˈreɪʃən] N (medal etc, adornment) decorazione f

decorative [ˈdɛkərətɪv] ADJ decorativo(-a)

decorator [ˈdɛkəreɪtəʳ] N decoratore(-trice)

decorum [dɪˈkɔːrəm] N decoro

decoy [ˈdiːkɔɪ] N zimbello; **they used him as a ~ for the enemy** l'hanno usato come esca per il nemico

decrease N [ˈdiːkriːs] diminuzione f ▶ VT, VI [diːˈkriːs] diminuire; **to be on the ~** essere in diminuzione

decreasing [diːˈkriːsɪŋ] ADJ sempre meno inv

decree [dɪˈkriː] N decreto ▶ VT: **to ~ (that)** decretare (che + sub); **~ absolute** sentenza di divorzio definitiva; **~ nisi** sentenza provvisoria di divorzio

decrepit [dɪˈkrɛpɪt] ADJ decrepito(-a); (building) cadente

decry [dɪˈkraɪ] VT condannare, deplorare

decrypt [diːˈkrɪpt] VT (Comput, Tel) decriptare

dedicate [ˈdɛdɪkeɪt] VT consacrare; (book etc) dedicare

dedicated [ˈdɛdɪkeɪtɪd] ADJ coscienzioso(-a); (Comput) specializzato(-a), dedicato(-a)

dedication [dɛdɪˈkeɪʃən] N (devotion) dedizione f; (in book) dedica

deduce [dɪˈdjuːs] VT dedurre

deduct [dɪˈdʌkt] VT: **to ~ sth (from)** dedurre qc (da); (from wage etc) trattenere qc (da)

deduction [dɪˈdʌkʃən] N (deducting) deduzione f; (from wage etc) trattenuta; (deducing) deduzione f, conclusione f

deed [diːd] N azione f, atto; (Law) atto; **~ of covenant** atto di donazione

deem [diːm] VT (formal) giudicare, ritenere; **to ~ it wise to do** ritenere prudente fare

deep [diːp] ADJ profondo(-a) ▶ ADV: **~ in snow** affondato(-a) nella neve; **spectators stood 20 ~** c'erano 20 file di spettatori; **knee-deep in water** in acqua fino alle ginocchia; **4 metres ~** profondo(a) 4 metri; **he took a ~ breath** fece un respiro profondo; **how ~ is the water?** quanto è profonda l'acqua?

deepen [ˈdiːpn] VT (hole) approfondire ▶ VI approfondirsi; (darkness) farsi più intenso(-a)

deep-freeze [diːpˈfriːz] N congelatore m ▶ VT congelare

deep-fry [diːpˈfraɪ] VT friggere in olio abbondante

deeply [ˈdiːplɪ] ADV profondamente; **to regret sth ~** rammaricarsi sinceramente di qc

deep-rooted [ˈdiːpˈruːtɪd] ADJ (prejudice) profondamente radicato(-a); (affection) profondo(-a); (habit) inveterato(-a)

deep-sea diver [ˈdiːpˈsiː-] N palombaro

deep-sea diving N immersione f in alto mare

deep-sea fishing N pesca d'alto mare

deep-seated [ˈdiːpˈsiːtɪd] ADJ (beliefs) radicato(-a)

deep-set [ˈdiːpsɛt] ADJ (eyes) infossato(-a)

deep-vein thrombosis [ˈdiːpveɪn-] N trombosi *f* inv venosa profonda

deer [dɪəʳ] N (*pl inv*): **the ~** i cervidi (*Zool*); **(red) ~** cervo; **(fallow) ~** daino; **(roe) ~** capriolo

deerskin [ˈdɪəskɪn] N pelle *f* da daino

deerstalker [ˈdɪəstɔːkəʳ] N berretto da cacciatore

deface [dɪˈfeɪs] VT imbrattare

defamation [dɛfəˈmeɪʃən] N diffamazione *f*

defamatory [dɪˈfæmətərɪ] ADJ diffamatorio(-a)

default [dɪˈfɔːlt] VI (*Law*) essere contumace; (*gen*) essere inadempiente ▶ N (*Comput: also:* **default value**) default *m inv*; **by ~** (*Law*) in contumacia; (*Sport*) per abbandono; **to ~ on a debt** non onorare un debito

defaulter [dɪˈfɔːltəʳ] N (*on debt*) inadempiente *mf*

default option N (*Comput*) opzione *f* di default

defeat [dɪˈfiːt] N sconfitta ▶ VT (*team, opponents*) sconfiggere; (*fig: plans, efforts*) frustrare

defeatism [dɪˈfiːtɪzəm] N disfattismo

defeatist [dɪˈfiːtɪst] ADJ, N disfattista (*mf*)

defecate [ˈdɛfəkeɪt] VI defecare

defect N [ˈdiːfɛkt] difetto ▶ VI [dɪˈfɛkt]: **to ~ to the enemy/the West** passare al nemico/all'Ovest; **physical ~** difetto fisico; **mental ~** anomalia mentale

defective [dɪˈfɛktɪv] ADJ difettoso(-a)

defector [dɪˈfɛktəʳ] N rifugiato(-a) politico(-a)

defence, (*US*) **defense** [dɪˈfɛns] N difesa; **in ~ of** in difesa di; **the Ministry of D~**, (*US*) **the Department of Defense** il Ministero della Difesa; **witness for the ~** teste *mf* a difesa

defenceless [dɪˈfɛnslɪs] ADJ senza difesa

defend [dɪˈfɛnd] VT difendere; (*decision, action*) giustificare; (*opinion*) sostenere

defendant [dɪˈfɛndənt] N imputato(-a)

defender [dɪˈfɛndəʳ] N difensore(-a)

defending champion N (*Sport*) campione(-essa) in carica

defending counsel N (*Law*) avvocato difensore

defense [dɪˈfɛns] N (*US*) = **defence**

defensive [dɪˈfɛnsɪv] ADJ difensivo(-a) ▶ N difensiva; **on the ~** sulla difensiva

defer [dɪˈfəːʳ] VT (*postpone*) differire, rinviare ▶ VI (*submit*): **to ~ to sb/sth** rimettersi a qn/qc

deference [ˈdɛfərəns] N deferenza; riguardo; **out of** *or* **in ~ to** per riguardo a

defiance [dɪˈfaɪəns] N sfida; **in ~ of** a dispetto di

defiant [dɪˈfaɪənt] ADJ (*attitude*) di sfida; (*person*) ribelle

defiantly [dɪˈfaɪəntlɪ] ADV con aria di sfida

deficiency [dɪˈfɪʃənsɪ] N deficienza; carenza; (*Comm*) ammanco

deficiency disease N malattia da carenza

deficient [dɪˈfɪʃənt] ADJ deficiente; insufficiente; **to be ~ in** mancare di

deficit [ˈdɛfɪsɪt] N disavanzo, deficit *m inv*

defile VT [dɪˈfaɪl] contaminare ▶ VI sfilare ▶ N [ˈdiːfaɪl] gola, stretta

define [dɪˈfaɪn] VI (*gen, Comput*) definire

definite [ˈdɛfɪnɪt] ADJ (*fixed*) definito(-a), preciso(-a); (*clear, obvious*) ben definito(-a), esatto(-a); (*Ling*) determinativo(-a); **he was ~ about it** ne era sicuro

definitely [ˈdɛfɪnɪtlɪ] ADV indubbiamente

definition [dɛfɪˈnɪʃən] N definizione *f*

definitive [dɪˈfɪnɪtɪv] ADJ definitivo(-a)

deflate [diːˈfleɪt] VT sgonfiare; (*Econ*) deflazionare; (*pompous person*) fare abbassare la cresta a

deflation [diːˈfleɪʃən] N (*Econ*) deflazione *f*

deflationary [diːˈfleɪʃənrɪ] ADJ (*Econ*) deflazionistico(-a)

deflect [dɪˈflɛkt] VT deflettere, deviare

defog [ˈdiːˈfɒg] VT (*US Aut*) sbrinare

defogger [ˈdiːˈfɒgəʳ] N (*US Aut*) sbrinatore *m*

deform [dɪˈfɔːm] VT deformare

deformed [dɪˈfɔːmd] ADJ deforme

deformity [dɪˈfɔːmɪtɪ] N deformità *f inv*

Defra N ABBR (*BRIT*) = **Department for Environment, Food and Rural Affairs**

defraud [dɪˈfrɔːd] VT: **to ~ (of)** defraudare (di)

defray [dɪˈfreɪ] VT: **to ~ sb's expenses** sostenere le spese di qn

defriend [diːˈfrɛnd] VT (*Internet*) cancellare dagli amici

defrost [diːˈfrɒst] VT (*fridge*) disgelare; (*frozen food*) scongelare

deft [dɛft] ADJ svelto(-a), destro(-a)

defunct [dɪˈfʌŋkt] ADJ defunto(-a)

defuse [diːˈfjuːz] VT disinnescare; (*fig*) distendere

defy [dɪˈfaɪ] VT sfidare; (*efforts etc*) resistere a; (*refuse to obey: person*) rifiutare di obbedire a; **it defies description** supera ogni descrizione

degenerate VI [dɪˈdʒɛnəreɪt] degenerare ▶ ADJ [dɪˈdʒɛnərɪt] degenere

degradation [dɛgrəˈdeɪʃən] N degradazione *f*

degrade [dɪˈgreɪd] VT degradare

degrading [dɪˈgreɪdɪŋ] ADJ degradante

degree [dɪˈgriː] N grado; (*Scol*) laurea (universitaria); **10 degrees below freezing** 10 gradi sotto zero; **a (first) ~ in maths** una laurea in matematica; **a considerable ~ of risk** una grossa percentuale di rischio; **by degrees** (*gradually*) gradualmente, a poco a poco; **to some ~, to a certain ~** fino a un certo punto, in certa misura

dehydrated [diːhaɪˈdreɪtɪd] ADJ disidratato(-a); (*milk, eggs*) in polvere

dehydration [diːhaɪˈdreɪʃən] N disidratazione *f*

de-ice [diːˈaɪs] vt (*windscreen*) disgelare

de-icer [ˈdiːaɪsər] n sbrinatore *m*

deign [deɪn] vi: **to ~ to do** degnarsi di fare

deity [ˈdiːɪtɪ] n divinità *f inv*; dio (dea)

déjà vu [deɪʒɑːˈvuː] n déjà vu *m inv*

dejected [dɪˈdʒɛktɪd] ADJ abbattuto(-a), avvilito(-a)

dejection [dɪˈdʒɛkʃən] n abbattimento, avvilimento

Del. ABBR (*US*) = **Delaware**

delay [dɪˈleɪ] vt (*journey, operation*) ritardare, rinviare; (*travellers, trains*) ritardare; (*payment*) differire ▶ vi: **to ~ (in doing sth)** ritardare (a fare qc) ▶ n ritardo; **without ~** senza ritardo; **to be delayed** subire un ritardo; (*person*) essere trattenuto(-a)

delayed-action [dɪˈleɪdˈækʃən] ADJ a azione ritardata

delectable [dɪˈlɛktəbl] ADJ delizioso(-a)

delegate n [ˈdɛlɪgɪt] delegato(-a) ▶ vt [ˈdɛlɪgeɪt] delegare; **to ~ sth to sb/sb to do sth** delegare qc a qn/qn a fare qc

delegation [dɛlɪˈgeɪʃən] n delegazione *f*; (*of work etc*) delega

delete [dɪˈliːt] vt (*gen, Comput*) cancellare

Delhi [ˈdɛlɪ] n Delhi *f*

deli [ˈdɛlɪ] n = **delicatessen**

deliberate ADJ [dɪˈlɪbərɪt] (*intentional*) intenzionale; (*slow*) misurato(-a) ▶ vi [dɪˈlɪbəreɪt] deliberare, riflettere

deliberately [dɪˈlɪbərɪtlɪ] ADV (*on purpose*) deliberatamente

deliberation [dɪlɪbəˈreɪʃən] n (*consideration*) riflessione *f*; (*discussion*) discussione *f*, deliberazione *f*

delicacy [ˈdɛlɪkəsɪ] n delicatezza

delicate [ˈdɛlɪkɪt] ADJ delicato(-a)

delicately [ˈdɛlɪkɪtlɪ] ADV (*gen*) delicatamente; (*act, express*) con delicatezza

delicatessen [dɛlɪkəˈtɛsn] n ≈ salumeria

delicious [dɪˈlɪʃəs] ADJ delizioso(-a), squisito(-a)

delight [dɪˈlaɪt] n delizia, gran piacere *m* ▶ vt dilettare; **it is a ~ to the eyes** è un piacere guardarlo; **to take ~ in** divertirsi a; **to be the ~ of** essere la gioia di

delighted [dɪˈlaɪtɪd] ADJ: **~ (at or with sth)** contentissimo(-a) (di qc), felice (di qc); **to be ~ to do sth/that** essere felice di fare qc/che + *sub*; **I'd be ~** con grande piacere

delightful [dɪˈlaɪtful] ADJ (*person, place, meal*) delizioso(-a); (*smile, manner*) incantevole

delimit [diːˈlɪmɪt] vt delimitare

delineate [dɪˈlɪnɪeɪt] vt delineare

delinquency [dɪˈlɪŋkwənsɪ] n delinquenza

delinquent [dɪˈlɪŋkwənt] ADJ, n delinquente (*mf*)

delirious [dɪˈlɪrɪəs] ADJ (*Med, fig*) delirante, in delirio; **to be ~** delirare; (*fig*) farneticare

delirium [dɪˈlɪrɪəm] n delirio

deliver [dɪˈlɪvər] vt (*mail*) distribuire; (*goods*) consegnare; (*speech*) pronunciare; (*free*) liberare; (*Med*) far partorire; **to ~ a message** fare un'ambasciata; **to ~ the goods** (*fig*) partorire

deliverables [dɪˈlɪvərəbəlz] NPL risultati *or* prodotti finali *mpl*

deliverance [dɪˈlɪvrəns] n liberazione *f*

delivery [dɪˈlɪvərɪ] n distribuzione *f*; consegna; (*of speaker*) dizione *f*; (*Med*) parto; **to take ~ of** prendere in consegna

delivery note n bolla di consegna

delivery van, (*US*) **delivery truck** n furgoncino (per le consegne)

delta [ˈdɛltə] n delta *m*

delude [dɪˈluːd] vt deludere, illudere

deluge [ˈdɛljuːdʒ] n diluvio ▶ vt (*fig*): **to ~ (with)** subissare (di), inondare (di)

delusion [dɪˈluːʒən] n illusione *f*

de luxe [dəˈlʌks] ADJ di lusso

delve [dɛlv] vi: **to ~ into** frugare in; (*subject*) far ricerche in

Dem. ABBR (*US Pol*) = **democrat**

demagogue [ˈdɛməgɔg] n demagogo

demand [dɪˈmɑːnd] vt richiedere; (*rights*) rivendicare ▶ n richiesta; (*Econ*) domanda; (*claim*) rivendicazione *f*; **to ~ sth (from or of sb)** pretendere qc (da qn), esigere qc (da qn); **in ~** ricercato(-a), richiesto(-a); **on ~** a richiesta

demand draft n (*Comm*) tratta a vista

demanding [dɪˈmɑːndɪŋ] ADJ (*boss*) esigente; (*work*) impegnativo(-a)

demarcation [diːmɑːˈkeɪʃən] n demarcazione *f*

demarcation dispute n (*Industry*) controversia settoriale (*or* di categoria)

demean [dɪˈmiːn] vt: **to ~ o.s.** umiliarsi

demeanour, (*US*) **demeanor** [dɪˈmiːnər] n comportamento; contegno

demented [dɪˈmɛntɪd] ADJ demente, impazzito(-a)

demilitarized zone [diːˈmɪlɪtəraɪzd-] n zona smilitarizzata

demise [dɪˈmaɪz] n decesso

demist [diːˈmɪst] vt (*Brit Aut*) sbrinare

demister [diːˈmɪstər] n (*Brit Aut*) sbrinatore *m*

demo [ˈdɛməu] n ABBR (*col*: = *demonstration*) manifestazione *f*

demobilize [diːˈməubɪlaɪz] vt smobilitare

democracy [dɪˈmɔkrəsɪ] n democrazia

democrat [ˈdɛməkræt] n democratico(-a)

democratic [dɛməˈkrætɪk] ADJ democratico(-a); **the D~ Party** (*US*) il partito democratico

demography [dɪˈmɔgrəfɪ] n demografia

demolish [dɪˈmɔlɪʃ] vт demolire

demolition [dɛmǝˈlɪʃǝn] N demolizione f

demon [ˈdiːmǝn] N (also fig) demonio ▸ CPD: **a ~ squash player** un mago dello squash; **a ~ driver** un guidatore folle

demonstrate [ˈdɛmǝnstreɪt] vт dimostrare, provare ▸ vɪ: **to ~ (for/against)** dimostrare (per/contro), manifestare (per/contro)

demonstration [dɛmǝnˈstreɪʃǝn] N dimostrazione f; (Pol) manifestazione f, dimostrazione; **to hold a ~** (Pol) tenere una manifestazione, fare una dimostrazione

demonstrative [dɪˈmɔnstrǝtɪv] ADJ dimostrativo(-a)

demonstrator [ˈdɛmǝnstreɪtǝʳ] N (Pol) dimostrante mf; (Comm: sales person) dimostratore(-trice); (: car, computer etc) modello per dimostrazione

demoralize [dɪˈmɔrǝlaɪz] vт demoralizzare

demote [dɪˈmǝut] vт far retrocedere

demotion [dɪˈmǝuʃǝn] N retrocessione f, degradazione f

demur [dɪˈmǝːʳ] vɪ (formal): **to ~ (at)** sollevare obiezioni (a or su) ▸ N: **without ~** senza obiezioni

demure [dɪˈmjuǝʳ] ADJ contegnoso(-a)

demurrage [dɪˈmʌrɪdʒ] N diritti mpl di immagazzinaggio; spese fpl di controstallia

den [dɛn] N tana, covo; (room) buco

denationalization [ˈdiːnæʃnǝlaɪˈzeɪʃǝn] N denazionalizzazione f

denationalize [diːˈnæʃnǝlaɪz] vт snazionalizzare

denial [dɪˈnaɪǝl] N diniego; rifiuto

denier [ˈdɛnɪǝʳ] N denaro (di filati, calze)

denigrate [ˈdɛnɪgreɪt] vт denigrare

denim [ˈdɛnɪm] N tessuto di cotone ritorto; see also **denims**

denim jacket N giubbotto di jeans

denims [ˈdɛnɪmz] NPL blue jeans mpl

denizen [ˈdɛnɪzǝn] N (inhabitant) abitante mf; (foreigner) straniero(-a) naturalizzato(-a)

Denmark [ˈdɛnmɑːk] N Danimarca

denomination [dɪnɔmɪˈneɪʃǝn] N (of money) valore m; (Rel) confessione f

denominator [dɪˈnɔmɪneɪtǝʳ] N denominatore m

denote [dɪˈnǝut] vт denotare

denounce [dɪˈnauns] vт denunciare

dense [dɛns] ADJ fitto(-a); (smoke) denso(-a); (col: stupid) ottuso(-a), duro(-a)

densely [ˈdɛnslɪ] ADV: **~ wooded** fittamente boscoso(-a); **~ populated** densamente popolato(-a)

density [ˈdɛnsɪtɪ] N densità f inv; **single/double ~ disk** (Comput) disco a singola/doppia densità di registrazione

dent [dɛnt] N ammaccatura ▸ vт (also: **make a dent in**) ammaccare; (: fig) intaccare

dental [ˈdɛntl] ADJ dentale

dental floss [-flɔs] N filo interdentale

dental surgeon N medico(-a) dentista

dental surgery N studio dentistico

dentist [ˈdɛntɪst] N dentista mf; **~'s surgery** (Brit) studio dentistico

dentistry [ˈdɛntɪstrɪ] N odontoiatria

dentures [ˈdɛntʃǝz] NPL dentiera

denunciation [dɪnʌnsɪˈeɪʃǝn] N denuncia

deny [dɪˈnaɪ] vт negare; (refuse) rifiutare; **he denies having said it** nega di averlo detto

deodorant [diːˈǝudǝrǝnt] N deodorante m

dep. ABBR = **departs**; **departure**

depart [dɪˈpɑːt] vɪ partire; **to ~ from** (leave) allontanarsi da, partire da; (fig) deviare da

departed [dɪˈpɑːtɪd] ADJ estinto(-a) ▸ N: **the ~** il caro estinto/la cara estinta

department [dɪˈpɑːtmǝnt] N (Comm) reparto; (Scol) sezione f, dipartimento; (Pol) ministero; **that's not my ~** (also fig) questo non è di mia competenza; **D~ of State** (US) Dipartimento di Stato

departmental [diːpɑːtˈmɛntl] ADJ (dispute) settoriale; (meeting) di sezione; **~ manager** caporeparto mf

department store N grande magazzino

departure [dɪˈpɑːtʃǝʳ] N partenza; (fig): **~ from** deviazione f da; **a new ~** una svolta (decisiva)

departure lounge N sala d'attesa

depend [dɪˈpɛnd] vɪ: **to ~ (up)on** dipendere da; (rely on) contare su; (be dependent on) dipendere (economicamente) da, essere a carico di; **it depends** dipende; **depending on the result ...** a seconda del risultato ...

dependable [dɪˈpɛndǝbl] ADJ fidato(-a); (car etc) affidabile

dependant [dɪˈpɛndǝnt] N persona a carico

dependence [dɪˈpɛndǝns] N dipendenza

dependent [dɪˈpɛndǝnt] ADJ: **to be ~ (on)** (gen) dipendere (da); (child, relative) essere a carico (di) ▸ N = **dependant**

depict [dɪˈpɪkt] vт (in picture) dipingere; (in words) descrivere

depilatory [dɪˈpɪlǝtǝrɪ] N (also: **depilatory cream**) crema depilatoria

depleted [dɪˈpliːtɪd] ADJ diminuito(-a)

deplorable [dɪˈplɔːrǝbl] ADJ deplorevole, lamentevole

deplore [dɪˈplɔːʳ] vт deplorare

deploy [dɪˈplɔɪ] vт dispiegare

depopulate [diːˈpɔpjuleɪt] vт spopolare

depopulation [ˈdiːpɔpjuˈleɪʃǝn] N spopolamento

deport [dɪˈpɔːt] vт deportare; espellere

deportation [di:pɔːˈteɪʃən] N deportazione f

deportation order N foglio di via obbligatorio

deportee [di:pɔːˈtiː] N deportato(-a)

deportment [dɪˈpɔːtmənt] N portamento

depose [dɪˈpəuz] VT deporre

deposit [dɪˈpɔzɪt] N (Comm, Geo) deposito; (of ore, oil) giacimento; (Chem) sedimento; (part payment) acconto; (for hired goods etc) cauzione f ▶ VT depositare; dare in acconto; (luggage etc) mettere or lasciare in deposito; **to put down a ~ of £50** versare una caparra di 50 sterline

deposit account N conto vincolato

depositor [dɪˈpɔzɪtəʳ] N depositante mf

depository [dɪˈpɔzɪtərɪ] N (person) depositario(-a); (place) deposito

depot [ˈdɛpəu] N deposito; (US) stazione f ferroviaria

depraved [dɪˈpreɪvd] ADJ depravato(-a)

depravity [dɪˈprævɪtɪ] N depravazione f

deprecate [ˈdɛprɪkeɪt] VT deprecare

deprecating [ˈdɛprɪkeɪtɪŋ] ADJ (disapproving) di biasimo; (apologetic): **a ~ smile** un sorriso di scusa

depreciate [dɪˈpriːʃɪeɪt] VT svalutare ▶ VI svalutarsi

depreciation [dɪpriːʃɪˈeɪʃən] N svalutazione f

depress [dɪˈprɛs] VT deprimere; (price, wages) abbassare; (press down) premere

depressant [dɪˈprɛsnt] N (Med) sedativo

depressed [dɪˈprɛst] ADJ (person) depresso(-a), abbattuto(-a); (area) depresso(-a); (Comm: market, trade) stagnante, in ribasso; (: industry) in crisi; **to get ~** deprimersi

depressing [dɪˈprɛsɪŋ] ADJ deprimente

depression [dɪˈprɛʃən] N depressione f

deprivation [dɛprɪˈveɪʃən] N privazione f; (state) indigenza; (Psych) carenza affettiva

deprive [dɪˈpraɪv] VT: **to ~ sb of** privare qn di

deprived [dɪˈpraɪvd] ADJ disgraziato(-a)

dept. ABBR = **department**

depth [dɛpθ] N profondità f inv; **at a ~ of 3 metres** a una profondità di 3 metri, a 3 metri di profondità; **in the depths of** nel profondo di; nel cuore di; **in the depths of winter** in pieno inverno; **to study sth in ~** studiare qc in profondità; **to be out of one's ~** (Brit: swimmer) essere dove non si tocca; (fig) non sentirsi all'altezza della situazione

depth charge N carica di profondità

deputation [dɛpjuˈteɪʃən] N deputazione f, delegazione f

deputize [ˈdɛpjutaɪz] VI: **to ~ for** svolgere le funzioni di

deputy [ˈdɛpjutɪ] N (replacement) supplente mf; (second in command) vice mf; (US: also: **deputy sheriff**) vice-sceriffo ▶ CPD: **~ chairman** vice-presidente m; **~ head** (Brit Scol) vicepreside mf; **~ leader** (Brit Pol) sottosegretario

derail [dɪˈreɪl] VT far deragliare; **to be derailed** deragliare

derailment [dɪˈreɪlmənt] N deragliamento

deranged [dɪˈreɪndʒd] ADJ: **to be (mentally) ~** essere pazzo(a)

derby [ˈdəːbɪ] N (US) bombetta

deregulate [diːˈrɛgjuleɪt] VT eliminare la regolamentazione di

deregulation [ˈdiːrɛgjuˈleɪʃən] N eliminazione f della regolamentazione

derelict [ˈdɛrɪlɪkt] ADJ abbandonato(-a)

deride [dɪˈraɪd] VT deridere

derision [dɪˈrɪʒən] N derisione f

derisive [dɪˈraɪsɪv] ADJ di derisione

derisory [dɪˈraɪsərɪ] ADJ (sum) irrisorio(-a)

derivation [dɛrɪˈveɪʃən] N derivazione f

derivative [dɪˈrɪvətɪv] N derivato ▶ ADJ derivato(-a)

derive [dɪˈraɪv] VT: **to ~ sth from** derivare qc da; trarre qc da ▶ VI: **to ~ from** derivare da

dermatitis [dəːməˈtaɪtɪs] N dermatite f

dermatology [dəːməˈtɔlədʒɪ] N dermatologia

derogatory [dɪˈrɔgətərɪ] ADJ denigratorio(-a)

derrick [ˈdɛrɪk] N gru f inv; (for oil) derrick m inv

derv [dəːv] N (Brit) gasolio

desalination [diːsælɪˈneɪʃən] N desalinizzazione f, dissalazione f

descend [dɪˈsɛnd] VT, VI discendere, scendere; **to ~ from** discendere da; **to ~ to** (lying, begging) abbassarsi a; **in descending order of importance** in ordine decrescente d'importanza
▶ **descend on** VT FUS (enemy, angry person) assalire, piombare su; (misfortune) arrivare addosso a; (fig: gloom, silence) scendere su; **visitors descended (up)on us** ci sono arrivate visite tra capo e collo

descendant [dɪˈsɛndənt] N discendente mf

descent [dɪˈsɛnt] N discesa; (origin) discendenza, famiglia

describe [dɪsˈkraɪb] VT descrivere

description [dɪsˈkrɪpʃən] N descrizione f; (sort) genere m, specie f; **of every ~** di ogni genere e specie

descriptive [dɪsˈkrɪptɪv] ADJ descrittivo(-a)

desecrate [ˈdɛsɪkreɪt] VT profanare

desert N [ˈdɛzət] deserto ▶ VT [dɪˈzəːt] lasciare, abbandonare ▶ VI [dɪˈzəːt] (Mil) disertare; see also **deserts**

deserted [dɪˈzəːtɪd] ADJ deserto(-a)

deserter [dɪˈzəːtəʳ] N disertore(-trice)

desertion [dɪˈzəːʃən] N diserzione f

desert island N isola deserta

deserts [dɪˈzəːts] NPL: **to get one's just ~** avere ciò che si merita

deserve [dɪ'zə:v] vт meritare

deservedly [dɪ'zə:vɪdlɪ] ADV meritatamente, giustamente

deserving [dɪ'zə:vɪŋ] ADJ (*person*) meritevole, degno(-a); (*cause*) meritorio(-a)

desiccated ['desɪkeɪtɪd] ADJ essiccato(-a)

design [dɪ'zaɪn] N (*sketch*) disegno; (: *of dress, car*) modello; (*layout, shape*) linea; (*pattern*) fantasia; (*Comm*) disegno tecnico; (*intention*) intenzione *f* ▶ vт disegnare; progettare; **to have designs on** aver mire su; **well-designed** ben concepito; **industrial ~** disegno industriale

design and technology N (BRIT *Scol*) progettazione *f* e tecnologie *fpl*

designate vт ['dezɪgneɪt] designare ▶ ADJ ['dezɪgnɪt] designato(-a)

designation [dezɪg'neɪʃən] N designazione *f*

designer [dɪ'zaɪnəʳ] N (*Tech*) disegnatore(-trice), progettista *mf*; (*of furniture*) designer *mf*; (*fashion designer*) disegnatore(-trice) di moda; (*of theatre sets*) scenografo(-a)

designer baby N bambino progettato geneticamente prima della nascita

desirability [dɪzaɪərə'bɪlɪtɪ] N desiderabilità; vantaggio

desirable [dɪ'zaɪərəbl] ADJ desiderabile; **it is ~ that** è opportuno che + *sub*

desire [dɪ'zaɪəʳ] N desiderio, voglia ▶ vт desiderare, volere; **to ~ sth/to do sth/that** desiderare qc/di fare qc/che + *sub*

desirous [dɪ'zaɪərəs] ADJ: **~ of** desideroso(-a) di

desk [desk] N (*in office*) scrivania; (*for pupil*) banco; (BRIT: *in shop, restaurant*) cassa; (*in hotel*) ricevimento; (*at airport*) accettazione *f*

desk job N lavoro d'ufficio

desktop ['desktɔp] N desktop *m inv*

desktop computer N personal *m inv*, personal computer *m inv*

desktop publishing N desktop publishing *m*

desolate ['desəlɪt] ADJ desolato(-a)

desolation [desə'leɪʃən] N desolazione *f*

despair [dɪs'pɛəʳ] N disperazione *f* ▶ vɪ: **to ~ of** disperare di; **in ~** disperato(-a)

despatch [dɪs'pætʃ] N, vт = **dispatch**

desperate ['despərɪt] ADJ disperato(-a); (*measures*) estremo(-a); (*fugitive*) capace di tutto; **to be ~ for sth/to do** volere disperatamente qc/fare; **we are getting ~** siamo sull'orlo della disperazione

desperately ['despərɪtlɪ] ADV disperatamente; (*very*) terribilmente, estremamente; **~ ill** in pericolo di vita

desperation [despə'reɪʃən] N disperazione *f*; **in ~** per disperazione

despicable [dɪs'pɪkəbl] ADJ disprezzabile

despise [dɪs'paɪz] vт disprezzare, sdegnare

despite [dɪs'paɪt] PREP malgrado, a dispetto di, nonostante

despondent [dɪs'pɔndənt] ADJ abbattuto(-a), scoraggiato(-a)

despot ['despɔt] N despota *m*

dessert [dɪ'zə:t] N dolce *m*; frutta

dessertspoon [dɪ'zə:tspu:n] N cucchiaio da dolci

destabilize [di:'steɪbɪlaɪz] vт privare di stabilità; (*fig*) destabilizzare

destination [destɪ'neɪʃən] N destinazione *f*

destine ['destɪn] vт destinare

destined ['destɪnd] ADJ: **to be ~ to do sth** essere destinato(a) a fare qc; **~ for London** diretto a Londra, con destinazione Londra

destiny ['destɪnɪ] N destino

destitute ['destɪtju:t] ADJ indigente, bisognoso(-a); **~ of** privo(a) di

destroy [dɪs'trɔɪ] vт distruggere

destroyer [dɪs'trɔɪəʳ] N (*Naut*) cacciatorpediniere *m*

destruction [dɪs'trʌkʃən] N distruzione *f*

destructive [dɪs'trʌktɪv] ADJ distruttivo(-a)

desultory ['desəltərɪ] ADJ (*reading*) disordinato(-a); (*conversation*) sconnesso(-a); (*contact*) saltuario(-a), irregolare

detach [dɪ'tætʃ] vт staccare, distaccare

detachable [dɪ'tætʃəbl] ADJ staccabile

detached [dɪ'tætʃt] ADJ (*attitude*) distante

detached house N villa

detachment [dɪ'tætʃmənt] N (*Mil*) distaccamento; (*fig*) distacco

detail ['di:teɪl] N particolare *m*, dettaglio; (*Mil*) piccolo distaccamento ▶ vт dettagliare, particolareggiare; (*Mil*): **to ~ sb (for)** assegnare qn (a); **in ~** nei particolari; **to go into ~(s)** scendere nei particolari

detailed ['di:teɪld] ADJ particolareggiato(-a)

detain [dɪ'teɪn] vт trattenere; (*in captivity*) detenere

detainee [di:teɪ'ni:] N detenuto(-a)

detect [dɪ'tekt] vт scoprire, scorgere; (*Med, Police, Radar etc*) individuare

detection [dɪ'tekʃən] N scoperta; individuazione *f*; **crime ~** indagini *fpl* criminali; **to escape ~** (*criminal*) eludere le ricerche; (*mistake*) passare inosservato(-a)

detective [dɪ'tektɪv] N investigatore(-trice); **private ~** investigatore *m* privato

detective story N giallo

detector [dɪ'tektəʳ] N rivelatore *m*

détente [deɪ'tɑ:nt] N distensione *f*

detention [dɪ'tenʃən] N detenzione *f*; (*Scol*) permanenza forzata per punizione

deter [dɪ'tə:ʳ] vт dissuadere

detergent [dɪ'tə:dʒənt] N detersivo

deteriorate [dɪˈtɪərɪəreɪt] VI deteriorarsi

deterioration [dɪtɪərɪəˈreɪʃən] N deterioramento

determination [dɪtəːmɪˈneɪʃən] N determinazione f

determine [dɪˈtəːmɪn] VT determinare; **to ~ to do sth** decidere di fare qc

determined [dɪˈtəːmɪnd] ADJ (person) risoluto(-a), deciso(-a); **to be ~ to do sth** essere determinato or deciso a fare qc; **a ~ effort** uno sforzo di volontà

deterrence [dɪˈtɛrəns] N deterrenza

deterrent [dɪˈtɛrənt] N deterrente m; **to act as a ~** fungere da deterrente

detest [dɪˈtɛst] VT detestare

detestable [dɪˈtɛstəbl] ADJ detestabile, abominevole

detonate [ˈdɛtəneɪt] VI detonare ▶ VT far detonare

detonator [ˈdɛtəneɪtər] N detonatore m

detour [ˈdiːtuər] N deviazione f

detox [ˈdiːtɒks] N disintossicazione f

detoxification [diːtɒksɪfɪˈkeɪʃən] N disintossicazione f

detoxify [diːˈtɒksɪfaɪ] VT disintossicare ▶ VI disintossicarsi

detract [dɪˈtrækt] VI: **to ~ from** detrarre da

detractor [dɪˈtræktər] N detrattore(-trice)

detriment [ˈdɛtrɪmənt] N: **to the ~ of** a detrimento di; **without ~ to** senza danno a

detrimental [dɛtrɪˈmɛntl] ADJ: **~ to** dannoso(-a) a, nocivo(-a) a

deuce [djuːs] N (Tennis) quaranta pari m inv

devaluation [diːvæljuˈeɪʃən] N svalutazione f

devalue [ˈdiːˈvæljuː] VT svalutare

devastate [ˈdɛvəsteɪt] VT devastare; **he was devastated by the news** la notizia fu per lui un colpo terribile

devastating [ˈdɛvəsteɪtɪŋ] ADJ devastatore(-trice), sconvolgente

devastation [dɛvəˈsteɪʃən] N devastazione f

develop [dɪˈvɛləp] VT sviluppare; (habit) prendere (gradualmente) ▶ VI svilupparsi; (facts, symptoms: appear) manifestarsi, rivelarsi; **to ~ a taste for sth** imparare a gustare qc; **to ~ into** diventare

developer [dɪˈvɛləpər] N (Phot) sviluppatore m; **property ~** costruttore m (edile)

developing country [dɪˈvɛləpɪŋ-] N paese m in via di sviluppo

development [dɪˈvɛləpmənt] N sviluppo

development area N area di sviluppo industriale

deviant [ˈdiːvɪənt] ADJ deviante

deviate [ˈdiːvɪeɪt] VI: **to ~ (from)** deviare (da)

deviation [diːvɪˈeɪʃən] N deviazione f

device [dɪˈvaɪs] N (apparatus) congegno; (explosive device) ordigno esplosivo

devil [ˈdɛvl] N diavolo(-essa); demonio

devilish [ˈdɛvlɪʃ] ADJ diabolico(-a)

devil-may-care [ˈdɛvlmeɪˈkɛər] ADJ impudente

devil's advocate N: **to play ~** fare l'avvocato del diavolo

devious [ˈdiːvɪəs] ADJ (means) indiretto(-a), tortuoso(-a); (person) subdolo(-a)

devise [dɪˈvaɪz] VT escogitare, concepire

devoid [dɪˈvɔɪd] ADJ: **~ of** privo(-a) di

devolution [diːvəˈluːʃən] N (Pol) decentramento

devolve [dɪˈvɒlv] VI: **to ~ (up)on** ricadere su

devote [dɪˈvəut] VT: **to ~ sth to** dedicare qc a

devoted [dɪˈvəutɪd] ADJ devoto(-a); **to be ~ to** essere molto affezionato(-a) a

devotee [dɛvəuˈtiː] N (Rel) adepto(-a); (Mus, Sport) appassionato(-a)

devotion [dɪˈvəuʃən] N devozione f, attaccamento; (Rel) atto di devozione, preghiera

devour [dɪˈvauər] VT divorare

devout [dɪˈvaut] ADJ pio(-a), devoto(-a)

dew [djuː] N rugiada

dexterity [dɛksˈtɛrɪtɪ] N destrezza

dexterous, dextrous [ˈdɛkstrəs] ADJ (skilful) destro(-a), abile; (movement) agile

DfE N ABBR (Brit: = Department for Education) Ministero della pubblica istruzione

dg ABBR (= decigram) dg

diabetes [daɪəˈbiːtiːz] N diabete m

diabetic [daɪəˈbɛtɪk] ADJ diabetico(-a); (chocolate, jam) per diabetici ▶ N diabetico(-a)

diabolical [daɪəˈbɒlɪkl] ADJ diabolico(-a); (col: dreadful) infernale, atroce

diaerisis [daɪˈɛrɪsɪs] N dieresi f inv

diagnose [daɪəgˈnəuz] VT diagnosticare

diagnosis [daɪəgˈnəusɪs] (pl **diagnoses** [-siːz]) N diagnosi f inv

diagonal [daɪˈægənl] ADJ, N diagonale (f)

diagram [ˈdaɪəgræm] N diagramma m

dial [ˈdaɪəl] N quadrante m; (on radio) lancetta; (on telephone) disco combinatore ▶ VT (number) fare; **to ~ a wrong number** sbagliare numero; **can I ~ London direct?** si può chiamare Londra in teleselezione?

dial. ABBR = **dialect**

dialect [ˈdaɪəlɛkt] N dialetto

dialling code [ˈdaɪəlɪŋ-], (US) **area code** N prefisso

dialling tone [ˈdaɪəlɪŋ-], (US) **dial tone** N segnale m di linea libera

dialogue, (US) **dialog** [ˈdaɪəlɒg] N dialogo

dialysis [daɪˈælɪsɪs] N dialisi f

diameter [daɪˈæmɪtəʳ] N diametro

diametrically [daɪəˈmetrɪklɪ] ADV: **~ opposed (to)** diametralmente opposto(-a) (a)

diamond [ˈdaɪəmənd] N diamante m; (shape) rombo ▪ **diamonds** NPL (Cards) quadri mpl

diamond ring N anello di brillanti; (with one diamond) anello con brillante

diaper [ˈdaɪəpəʳ] N (US) pannolino

diaphragm [ˈdaɪəfræm] N diaframma m

diarrhoea, (US) **diarrhea** [daɪəˈriːə] N diarrea

diary [ˈdaɪərɪ] N (daily account) diario; (book) agenda; **to keep a ~** tenere un diario

diatribe [ˈdaɪətraɪb] N diatriba

dice [daɪs] N (pl inv) dado ▸ VT (Culin) tagliare a dadini

dicey [ˈdaɪsɪ] ADJ (col): **it's a bit ~** è un po' un rischio

dichotomy [daɪˈkɒtəmɪ] N dicotomia

dickhead [ˈdɪkhɛd] N (BRIT!) testa m di cazzo (!)

Dictaphone® [ˈdɪktəfəun] N dittafono

dictate VT [dɪkˈteɪt] dettare ▸ VI: **to ~ to** (person) dare ordini a, dettar legge a ▸ N [ˈdɪkteɪt] dettame m; **I won't be dictated to** non ricevo ordini

dictation [dɪkˈteɪʃən] N (to secretary etc) dettatura; (Scol) dettato; **at ~ speed** a velocità di dettatura

dictator [dɪkˈteɪtəʳ] N dittatore(-trice)

dictatorship [dɪkˈteɪtəʃɪp] N dittatura

diction [ˈdɪkʃən] N dizione f

dictionary [ˈdɪkʃənrɪ] N dizionario

did [dɪd] PT of **do**

didactic [daɪˈdæktɪk] ADJ didattico(-a)

didn't [ˈdɪdnt] = **did not**

die [daɪ] N (pl **dies**) conio; matrice f; stampo ▸ VI morire; **to be dying** star morendo; **to be dying for sth/to do sth** morire dalla voglia di qc/di fare qc; **to ~ (of or from)** morire (di)
▸ **die away** VI spegnersi a poco a poco
▸ **die down** VI abbassarsi
▸ **die out** VI estinguersi

diehard [ˈdaɪhɑːd] N reazionario(-a)

diesel [ˈdiːzl] N (vehicle) diesel m inv

diesel engine N motore m diesel inv

diesel fuel, diesel oil N gasolio (per motori diesel)

diet [ˈdaɪət] N alimentazione f; (restricted food) dieta ▸ VI (also: **be on a diet**) stare a dieta; **to live on a ~ of** nutrirsi di

dietician [daɪəˈtɪʃən] N dietologo(-a)

differ [ˈdɪfəʳ] VI: **to ~ from sth** differire da qc; essere diverso(-a) da qc; **to ~ from sb over sth** essere in disaccordo con qn su qc

difference [ˈdɪfrəns] N differenza; (quarrel) screzio; **it makes no ~ to me** per me è lo stesso; **to settle one's differences** risolvere la situazione

different [ˈdɪfrənt] ADJ diverso(-a)

differential [dɪfəˈrɛnʃəl] N (Aut, in wages) differenziale m

differentiate [dɪfəˈrɛnʃɪeɪt] VI differenziarsi; **to ~ between** discriminare fra, fare differenza fra

differently [ˈdɪfrəntlɪ] ADV diversamente

difficult [ˈdɪfɪkəlt] ADJ difficile; **~ to understand** difficile da capire

difficulty [ˈdɪfɪkəltɪ] N difficoltà f inv; **to have difficulties with** (police, landlord etc) avere noie con; **to be in ~** essere or trovarsi in difficoltà

diffidence [ˈdɪfɪdəns] N mancanza di sicurezza

diffident [ˈdɪfɪdənt] ADJ sfiduciato(-a)

diffuse ADJ [dɪˈfjuːs] diffuso(-a) ▸ VT [dɪˈfjuːz] diffondere, emanare

dig [dɪg] (pt, pp **dug** [dʌg]) VT (hole) scavare; (garden) vangare ▸ VI scavare ▸ N (prod) gomitata; (fig) frecciata; (Archaeology) scavo, scavi mpl; **to ~ into** (snow, soil) scavare; **to ~ into one's pockets for sth** frugarsi le tasche cercando qc; **to ~ one's nails into** conficcare le unghie in; see also **digs**
▸ **dig in** VI (col: eat) attaccare a mangiare; (also: **dig o.s. in**: Mil) trincerarsi; (: fig) insediarsi, installarsi ▸ VT (compost) interrare; (knife, claw) affondare; **to ~ in one's heels** (fig) impuntarsi
▸ **dig out** VT (survivors, car from snow) tirar fuori (scavando), estrarre (scavando)
▸ **dig up** VT scavare; (tree etc) sradicare; (information) scavare fuori

digest VT [daɪˈdʒɛst] digerire ▸ N [ˈdaɪdʒɛst] compendio

digestible [dɪˈdʒɛstəbl] ADJ digeribile

digestion [dɪˈdʒɛstʃən] N digestione f

digestive [dɪˈdʒɛstɪv] ADJ digestivo(-a); **~ system** apparato digerente

digit [ˈdɪdʒɪt] N cifra; (finger) dito

digital [ˈdɪdʒɪtəl] ADJ digitale

digital camera N fotocamera digitale

digital compact cassette N piastra digitale per CD

digital radio N radio digitale

digital TV N televisione f digitale

dignified [ˈdɪgnɪfaɪd] ADJ dignitoso(-a)

dignitary [ˈdɪgnɪtərɪ] N dignitario

dignity [ˈdɪgnɪtɪ] N dignità

digress [daɪˈgrɛs] VI: **to ~ from** divagare da

digression [daɪˈgrɛʃən] N digressione f

digs [dɪgz] NPL (BRIT col) camera ammobiliata

dilapidated [dɪˈlæpɪdeɪtɪd] ADJ cadente

dilate [daɪˈleɪt] VT dilatare ▸ VI dilatarsi

dilatory [ˈdɪlətərɪ] ADJ dilatorio(-a)

dilemma [daɪˈlɛmə] N dilemma m; **to be in a ~** essere di fronte a un dilemma

diligent [ˈdɪlɪdʒənt] ADJ diligente

dill [dɪl] N aneto

dilly-dally [ˈdɪlɪdælɪ] VI gingillarsi

dilute [daɪˈluːt] VT diluire; (*with water*) annacquare ▶ ADJ diluito(-a)

dim [dɪm] ADJ (*light, eyesight*) debole; (*memory, outline*) vago(-a); (*room*) in penombra; (*col: stupid*) ottuso(-a), tonto(-a) ▶ VT (*light: also US Aut*) abbassare; **to take a ~ view of sth** non vedere di buon occhio qc

dime [daɪm] N (*US*) = **10 cents**

dimension [dɪˈmɛnʃən] N dimensione f

-dimensional [dɪˈmɛnʃənl] ADJ SUFFIX: **two-dimensional** bi-dimensionale

diminish [dɪˈmɪnɪʃ] VT, VI diminuire

diminished [dɪˈmɪnɪʃt] ADJ: **~ responsibility** (*Law*) incapacità d'intendere e di volere

diminutive [dɪˈmɪnjutɪv] ADJ minuscolo(-a) ▶ N (*Ling*) diminutivo

dimly [ˈdɪmlɪ] ADV debolmente; indistintamente

dimmer [ˈdɪmə^r] N (*also:* **dimmer switch**) dimmer *m inv*, interruttore *m* a reostato ■ **dimmers** NPL (*US Aut*) anabbaglianti mpl; (*parking lights*) luci fpl di posizione

dimple [ˈdɪmpl] N fossetta

dim-witted [ˈdɪmˈwɪtɪd] ADJ (*col*) sciocco(-a), stupido(-a)

din [dɪn] N chiasso, fracasso ▶ VT: **to ~ sth into sb** (*col*) ficcare qc in testa a qn

dine [daɪn] VI pranzare

diner [ˈdaɪnə^r] N (*person: in restaurant*) cliente mf; (*Rail*) carrozza or vagone *m* ristorante; (*US: eating place*) tavola calda

dinghy [ˈdɪŋɡɪ] N gommone *m*; (*also:* **sailing dinghy**) dinghy *m inv*

dingy [ˈdɪndʒɪ] ADJ grigio(-a)

dining area N zona pranzo *inv*

dining car N (*Brit*) vagone *m* ristorante

dining room N sala da pranzo

dining table N tavolo da pranzo

dinkum [ˈdɪŋkʌm] ADJ (*Australia, New Zealand col*) genuino(-a)

dinner [ˈdɪnə^r] N (*lunch*) pranzo; (*evening meal*) cena; (*public*) banchetto; **~'s ready!** a tavola!

dinner jacket N smoking *m inv*

dinner party N cena

dinner service N servizio da tavola

dinner time N ora di pranzo (*or* cena)

dinosaur [ˈdaɪnəsɔː^r] N dinosauro

dint [dɪnt] N: **by ~ of (doing) sth** a forza di (fare) qc

diocese [ˈdaɪəsɪs] N diocesi f inv

dioxide [daɪˈɔksaɪd] N biossido

dip [dɪp] N (*slope*) discesa; (*in sea*) bagno; (*Culin*) salsetta ▶ VT immergere; bagnare; (*Brit Aut: lights*) abbassare ▶ VI (*road*) essere in pendenza; (*bird, plane*) abbassarsi

Dip. ABBR (*Brit*) = **diploma**

diphtheria [dɪfˈθɪərɪə] N difterite f

diphthong [ˈdɪfθɔŋ] N dittongo

diploma [dɪˈpləumə] N diploma *m*

diplomacy [dɪˈpləuməsɪ] N diplomazia

diplomat [ˈdɪpləmæt] N diplomatico

diplomatic [dɪpləˈmætɪk] ADJ diplomatico(-a); **to break off ~ relations** rompere le relazioni diplomatiche

diplomatic corps N corpo diplomatico

diplomatic immunity N immunità f inv diplomatica

dipstick [ˈdɪpstɪk] N (*Aut*) indicatore *m* di livello dell'olio

dipswitch [ˈdɪpswɪtʃ] N (*Brit Aut*) levetta dei fari

dire [daɪə^r] ADJ terribile; estremo(-a)

direct [daɪˈrɛkt] ADJ diretto(-a); (*manner, person*) franco(-a), esplicito(-a) ▶ VT dirigere; (*order*): **to ~ sb to do sth** dare direttive a qn di fare qc ▶ ADV direttamente; **can you ~ me to ...?** mi può indicare la strada per ...?

direct cost N (*Comm*) costo diretto

direct current N (*Elec*) corrente f continua

direct debit N (*Banking*) addebito effettuato per ordine di un cliente di banca

direct dialling N (*Tel*) ≈ teleselezione f

direct hit N (*Mil*) colpo diretto

direction [dɪˈrɛkʃən] N direzione f; (*of play, film, programme*) regia ■ **directions** NPL (*advice*) chiarimenti mpl; (*instructions: to a place*) indicazioni fpl; **directions for use** istruzioni fpl; **to ask for directions** chiedere la strada; **sense of ~** senso dell'orientamento; **in the ~ of** in direzione di

directive [dɪˈrɛktɪv] N direttiva, ordine *m*; **a government ~** una disposizione governativa

direct labour N manodopera diretta

directly [dɪˈrɛktlɪ] ADV (*in straight line*) direttamente; (*at once*) subito

direct mail N pubblicità diretta

direct mailshot N (*Brit*) materiale *m* pubblicitario ad approccio diretto

directness [daɪˈrɛktnɪs] N (*of person, speech*) franchezza

director [dɪˈrɛktə^r] N direttore(-trice), amministratore(-trice); (*Theat, Cine, TV*) regista mf; **D~ of Public Prosecutions** (*Brit*) ≈ Procuratore(-trice) della Repubblica

directory [dɪˈrɛktərɪ] N elenco; (*street directory*) stradario; (*trade directory*) repertorio del commercio; (*Comput*) directory *m inv*

directory enquiries, (*US*) **directory assistance** N (*Tel*) servizio informazioni, informazioni fpl elenco abbonati

dirt [dəːt] N sporcizia; immondizia; (*earth*) terra; **to treat sb like ~** trattare qn come uno straccio

dirt-cheap [ˈdəːtˈtʃiːp] ADJ da due soldi

dirt road N strada non asfaltata

dirty [ˈdəːtɪ] ADJ sporco(-a) ▶ VT sporcare; **~ bomb** bomba convenzionale contenente materiale radioattivo; **~ story** storia oscena; **~ trick** brutto scherzo

disability [dɪsəˈbɪlɪtɪ] N invalidità f inv; (Law) incapacità f inv

disability allowance N pensione f d'invalidità

disable [dɪsˈeɪbl] VT (illness, accident) rendere invalido(-a); (tank, gun) mettere fuori uso

disabled [dɪsˈeɪbld] ADJ invalido(-a); (maimed) mutilato(-a); (mentally) ritardato(-a); (through illness, old age) inabile; **~ people** gli invalidi

disadvantage [dɪsədˈvɑːntɪdʒ] N svantaggio

disadvantaged [dɪsədˈvɑːntɪdʒd] ADJ (person) svantaggiato(-a)

disadvantageous [dɪsædvɑːnˈteɪdʒəs] ADJ svantaggioso(-a)

disaffected [dɪsəˈfɛktɪd] ADJ: **~ (to or towards)** scontento(-a) di, insoddisfatto(-a) di

disaffection [dɪsəˈfɛkʃən] N malcontento, insoddisfazione f

disagree [dɪsəˈɡriː] VI (differ) discordare; (be against, think otherwise): **to ~ (with)** essere in disaccordo (con), dissentire (da); **I ~ with you** non sono d'accordo con lei; **garlic disagrees with me** l'aglio non mi va

disagreeable [dɪsəˈɡriːəbl] ADJ sgradevole; (person) antipatico(-a)

disagreement [dɪsəˈɡriːmənt] N disaccordo; (quarrel) dissapore m; **to have a ~ with sb** litigare con qn

disallow [ˈdɪsəˈlau] VT respingere; (BRIT Football: goal) annullare

disappear [dɪsəˈpɪəʳ] VI scomparire

disappearance [dɪsəˈpɪərəns] N scomparsa

disappoint [dɪsəˈpɔɪnt] VT deludere

disappointed [dɪsəˈpɔɪntɪd] ADJ deluso(-a)

disappointing [dɪsəˈpɔɪntɪŋ] ADJ deludente

disappointment [dɪsəˈpɔɪntmənt] N delusione f

disapproval [dɪsəˈpruːvəl] N disapprovazione f

disapprove [dɪsəˈpruːv] VI: **to ~ of** disapprovare

disapproving [dɪsəˈpruːvɪŋ] ADJ di disapprovazione

disarm [dɪsˈɑːm] VT disarmare

disarmament [dɪsˈɑːməmənt] N disarmo

disarming [dɪsˈɑːmɪŋ] ADJ (smile) disarmante

disarray [dɪsəˈreɪ] N: **in ~** (troops) in rotta; (thoughts) confuso(-a); (clothes) in disordine; **to throw into ~** buttare all'aria

disaster [dɪˈzɑːstəʳ] N disastro

disaster area N zona disastrata

disastrous [dɪˈzɑːstrəs] ADJ disastroso(-a)

disband [dɪsˈbænd] VT sbandare; (Mil) congedare ▶ VI sciogliersi

disbelief [ˈdɪsbəˈliːf] N incredulità; **in ~** incredulo(-a)

disbelieve [ˈdɪsbəˈliːv] VT (person, story) non credere a, mettere in dubbio; **I don't ~ you** vorrei poterle credere

disc [dɪsk] N disco; (Comput) = **disk**

discard [dɪsˈkɑːd] VT (old things) scartare; (fig) abbandonare

disc brake N freno a disco

discern [dɪˈsəːn] VT discernere, distinguere

discernible [dɪˈsəːnəbl] ADJ percepibile

discerning [dɪˈsəːnɪŋ] ADJ perspicace

discharge VT [dɪsˈtʃɑːdʒ] (duties) compiere; (settle: debt) pagare, estinguere; (Elec, waste etc) scaricare; (Med) emettere; (patient) dimettere; (employee) licenziare; (soldier) congedare; (defendant) liberare ▶ N [ˈdɪstʃɑːdʒ] (Elec) scarica; (Med, of gas, chemicals) emissione f; (vaginal discharge) perdite fpl (bianche); (dismissal) licenziamento; congedo; liberazione f; **to ~ one's gun** fare fuoco

discharged bankrupt [dɪsˈtʃɑːdʒd-] N fallito cui il tribunale ha concesso la riabilitazione

disciple [dɪˈsaɪpl] N discepolo

disciplinary [ˈdɪsɪplɪnərɪ] ADJ disciplinare; **to take ~ action against sb** prendere un provvedimento disciplinare contro qn

discipline [ˈdɪsɪplɪn] N disciplina ▶ VT disciplinare; (punish) punire; **to ~ o.s. to do sth** imporsi di fare qc

disc jockey N disc jockey m inv

disclaim [dɪsˈkleɪm] VT negare, smentire

disclaimer [dɪsˈkleɪməʳ] N smentita; **to issue a ~** pubblicare una smentita

disclose [dɪsˈkləuz] VT rivelare, svelare

disclosure [dɪsˈkləuʒəʳ] N rivelazione f

disco [ˈdɪskəu] N ABBR discoteca

discolour, (US) **discolor** [dɪsˈkʌləʳ] VT scolorire; (sth white) ingiallire ▶ VI sbiadire, scolorirsi; (sth white) ingiallire

discolouration, (US) **discoloration** [dɪskʌləˈreɪʃən] N scolorimento

discoloured, (US) **discolored** [dɪsˈkʌləd] ADJ scolorito(-a), ingiallito(-a)

discomfort [dɪsˈkʌmfət] N disagio; (lack of comfort) scomodità f inv

disconcert [dɪskənˈsəːt] VT sconcertare

disconnect [dɪskəˈnɛkt] VT sconnettere, staccare; (Elec, Radio) staccare; (gas, water) chiudere

disconnected [dɪskəˈnɛktɪd] ADJ (speech, thought) sconnesso(-a)

disconsolate [dɪsˈkɒnsəlɪt] ADJ sconsolato(-a)

discontent [dɪskənˈtɛnt] N scontentezza

discontented – disillusionment

discontented [dɪskən'tɛntɪd] ADJ sconten-to(-a)

discontinue [dɪskən'tɪnjuː] VT smettere, cessare; **"discontinued"** (Comm) "fuori produzione"

discord ['dɪskɔːd] N disaccordo; (Mus) disso-nanza

discordant [dɪs'kɔːdənt] ADJ discordante; dis-sonante

discothèque ['dɪskəutɛk] N discoteca

discount N ['dɪskaunt] sconto ▶ VT [dɪs'kaunt] scontare; (report, idea etc) non badare a; **at a ~** con uno sconto; **to give sb a ~ on sth** fare uno sconto a qn su qc; **~ for cash** sconto m cassa inv

discount house N (Finance) casa di sconto, discount house f inv; (Comm: also: **discount store**) discount m inv

discount rate N tasso di sconto

discourage [dɪs'kʌrɪdʒ] VT scoraggiare; (dis-suade, deter) tentare di dissuadere

discouragement [dɪs'kʌrɪdʒmənt] N (dissua-sion) disapprovazione f; (depression) scoraggia-mento; **to act as a ~** to ostacolare

discouraging [dɪs'kʌrɪdʒɪŋ] ADJ scoraggiante

discourteous [dɪs'kəːtɪəs] ADJ scortese

discover [dɪs'kʌvəʳ] VT scoprire

discovery [dɪs'kʌvərɪ] N scoperta

discredit [dɪs'krɛdɪt] VT screditare; mettere in dubbio ▶ N discredito

discreet [dɪ'skriːt] ADJ discreto(-a)

discreetly [dɪ'skriːtlɪ] ADV con discrezione

discrepancy [dɪ'skrɛpənsɪ] N discrepanza

discretion [dɪ'skrɛʃən] N discrezione f; **use your own ~** giudichi lei

discretionary [dɪs'krɛʃənərɪ] ADJ (powers) discrezionale

discriminate [dɪ'skrɪmɪneɪt] VI: **to ~ between** distinguere tra; **to ~ against** discriminare contro

discriminating [dɪs'krɪmɪneɪtɪŋ] ADJ (ear, taste) fine, giudizioso(-a); (person) esigente; (tax, duty) discriminante

discrimination [dɪskrɪmɪ'neɪʃən] N discrimi-nazione f; (judgement) discernimento; **racial/ sexual ~** discriminazione razziale/sessuale

discus ['dɪskəs] N disco

discuss [dɪ'skʌs] VT discutere; (debate) dibattere

discussion [dɪ'skʌʃən] N discussione f; **under ~** in discussione

discussion forum N (Comput) forum m inv di discussione

disdain [dɪs'deɪn] N disdegno

disease [dɪ'ziːz] N malattia

diseased [dɪ'ziːzd] ADJ malato(-a)

disembark [dɪsɪm'bɑːk] VT, VI sbarcare

disembarkation [dɪsɛmbɑː'keɪʃən] N sbarco

disembodied [dɪsɪm'bɔdɪd] ADJ disincarnato(-a)

disembowel [dɪsɪm'bauəl] VT sbudellare, sventrare

disenchanted [dɪsɪn'tʃɑːntɪd] ADJ disincanta-to(-a); **~ (with)** deluso(-a) (da)

disenfranchise [dɪsɪn'fræntʃaɪz] VT privare del diritto di voto; (Comm) revocare una condizione di privilegio commerciale a

disengage [dɪsɪn'geɪdʒ] VT disimpegnare; (Tech) distaccare; (Aut) disinnestare

disentangle [dɪsɪn'tæŋgl] VT sbrogliare

disfavour, (US) **disfavor** [dɪs'feɪvəʳ] N sfavore m; disgrazia

disfigure [dɪs'fɪgəʳ] VT sfigurare

disgorge [dɪs'gɔːdʒ] VT (river) riversare

disgrace [dɪs'greɪs] N vergogna; (disfavour) disgrazia ▶ VT disonorare, far cadere in disgra-zia

disgraceful [dɪs'greɪsful] ADJ scandaloso(-a), vergognoso(-a)

disgruntled [dɪs'grʌntld] ADJ scontento(-a), di cattivo umore

disguise [dɪs'gaɪz] N travestimento ▶ VT trave-stire; (voice) contraffare; (feelings etc) masche-rare; **to ~ o.s. as** travestirsi da; **in ~** travestito(-a); **there's no disguising the fact that ...** non si può nascondere (il fatto) che ...

disgust [dɪs'gʌst] N disgusto, nausea ▶ VT disgustare, far schifo a

disgusted [dɪs'gʌstɪd] ADJ indignato(-a)

disgusting [dɪs'gʌstɪŋ] ADJ disgustoso(-a), ripugnante

dish [dɪʃ] N piatto; **to do or wash the dishes** fare i piatti
▶ **dish out** VT (food) servire; (advice) elargire; (money) tirare fuori; (exam papers) distribuire
▶ **dish up** VT (food) servire; (facts, statistics) pre-sentare

dishcloth ['dɪʃklɔθ] N strofinaccio dei piatti

dishearten [dɪs'hɑːtn] VT scoraggiare

dishevelled, (US) **disheveled** [dɪ'ʃɛvəld] ADJ arruffato(-a), scapigliato(-a)

dishonest [dɪs'ɔnɪst] ADJ disonesto(-a)

dishonesty [dɪs'ɔnɪstɪ] N disonestà

dishonour, (US) **dishonor** [dɪs'ɔnəʳ] N diso-nore m

dishonourable, (US) **dishonorable** [dɪs'ɔnərəbl] ADJ disonorevole

dish soap N (US) detersivo liquido (per stoviglie)

dishtowel ['dɪʃtauəl] N strofinaccio dei piatti

dishwasher ['dɪʃwɔʃəʳ] N lavastoviglie f inv; (person) sguattero(-a)

dishy ['dɪʃɪ] ADJ (BRIT old) figo(-a)

disillusion [dɪsɪ'luːʒən] VT disilludere, disin-gannare ▶ N disillusione f; **to become disillu-sioned (with)** perdere le illusioni (su)

disillusionment [dɪsɪ'luːʒənmənt] N disillu-sione f

519

disincentive [dɪsɪn'sɛntɪv] N: **to act as a ~ (to)** agire da freno (su); **to be a ~ to** scoraggiare

disinclined [dɪsɪn'klaɪnd] ADJ: **to be ~ to do sth** essere poco propenso(-a) a fare qc

disinfect [dɪsɪn'fɛkt] VT disinfettare

disinfectant [dɪsɪn'fɛktənt] N disinfettante *m*

disinflation [dɪsɪn'fleɪʃən] N disinflazione *f*

disinformation [dɪsɪnfə'meɪʃən] N disinformazione *f*

disinherit [dɪsɪn'hɛrɪt] VT diseredare

disintegrate [dɪs'ɪntɪgreɪt] VI disintegrarsi

disinterested [dɪs'ɪntrəstɪd] ADJ disinteressato(-a)

disjointed [dɪs'dʒɔɪntɪd] ADJ sconnesso(-a)

disk [dɪsk] N (Comput) disco; **double-sided ~** disco a doppia faccia

disk drive N disk drive *m inv*

diskette [dɪs'kɛt] N (Comput) dischetto

disk operating system N sistema *m* operativo a disco

dislike [dɪs'laɪk] N antipatia, avversione *f*; (gen pl) cosa che non piace ▶ VT: **he dislikes it** non gli piace; **I ~ the idea** l'idea non mi va; **to take a ~ to sb/sth** prendere in antipatia qn/qc

dislocate ['dɪsləkeɪt] VT (Med) slogare; (fig) disorganizzare; **he dislocated his shoulder** si è lussato una spalla

dislodge [dɪs'lɔdʒ] VT rimuovere, staccare; (enemy) sloggiare

disloyal [dɪs'lɔɪəl] ADJ sleale

dismal ['dɪzml] ADJ triste, cupo(-a)

dismantle [dɪs'mæntl] VT (machine) smantellare, smontare; (fort, warship) disarmare

dismast [dɪs'mɑːst] VT disalberare

dismay [dɪs'meɪ] N costernazione *f* ▶ VT sgomentare; **much to my ~** con mio gran stupore

dismiss [dɪs'mɪs] VT congedare; (employee) licenziare; (idea) scacciare; (Law) respingere ▶ VI (Mil) rompere i ranghi

dismissal [dɪs'mɪsəl] N congedo; licenziamento

dismount [dɪs'maunt] VI scendere ▶ VT (rider) disarcionare

disobedience [dɪsə'biːdɪəns] N disubbidienza

disobedient [dɪsə'biːdɪənt] ADJ disubbidiente

disobey [dɪsə'beɪ] VT disubbidire a; (rule) trasgredire a

disorder [dɪs'ɔːdə'] N disordine *m*; (rioting) tumulto; (Med) disturbo; **civil ~** disordini *mpl* interni

disorderly [dɪs'ɔːdəlɪ] ADJ disordinato(-a), tumultuoso(-a)

disorderly conduct N (Law) comportamento atto a turbare l'ordine pubblico

disorganize [dɪs'ɔːgənaɪz] VT disorganizzare

disorganized [dɪs'ɔːgənaɪzd] ADJ (person, life) disorganizzato(-a); (system, meeting) male organizzato(-a)

disorientated [dɪs'ɔːrɪenteɪtɪd] ADJ disorientato(-a)

disown [dɪs'əun] VT rinnegare, disconoscere

disparaging [dɪs'pærɪdʒɪŋ] ADJ spregiativo(-a), sprezzante; **to be ~ about sb/sth** denigrare qn/qc

disparate ['dɪspərɪt] ADJ disparato(-a)

disparity [dɪs'pærɪtɪ] N disparità *f inv*

dispassionate [dɪs'pæʃənət] ADJ calmo(-a), freddo(-a); imparziale

dispatch [dɪs'pætʃ] VT spedire, inviare; (deal with: business) sbrigare ▶ N spedizione *f*, invio; (Mil, Press) dispaccio

dispatch department N reparto spedizioni

dispatch rider N (Mil) corriere *m*, portaordini *m inv*

dispel [dɪs'pɛl] VT dissipare, scacciare

dispensary [dɪs'pɛnsərɪ] N farmacia; (in chemist's) dispensario

dispense [dɪs'pɛns] VT distribuire, amministrare; (medicine) preparare e dare; **to ~ sb from** dispensare qn da
▶ **dispense with** VT FUS fare a meno di; (make unnecessary) rendere superfluo(-a)

dispenser [dɪs'pɛnsə'] N (container) distributore *m*

dispensing chemist N (BRIT) farmacista *mf*

dispersal [dɪs'pəːsl] N dispersione *f*

disperse [dɪs'pəːs] VT disperdere; (knowledge) disseminare ▶ VI disperdersi

dispirited [dɪs'pɪrɪtɪd] ADJ scoraggiato(-a), abbattuto(-a)

displace [dɪs'pleɪs] VT spostare

displaced person N (Pol) profugo(-a)

displacement [dɪs'pleɪsmənt] N spostamento

display [dɪs'pleɪ] N mostra; esposizione *f*; (of feeling etc) manifestazione *f*; (military display) parata (militare); (computer display) display *m inv*; (pej) ostentazione *f*; (screen) schermo ▶ VT mostrare; (goods) esporre; (pej) ostentare; (results) affiggere; (departure times) indicare; **on ~** (gen) in mostra; (goods) in vetrina

display advertising N pubblicità tabellare

displease [dɪs'pliːz] VT dispiacere a, scontentare; **displeased with** scontento(-a) di

displeasure [dɪs'plɛʒə'] N dispiacere *m*

disposable [dɪs'pəuzəbl] ADJ (pack etc) a perdere; (income) disponibile; **~ nappy** (BRIT) pannolino di carta

disposal [dɪs'pəuzl] N (of rubbish) smaltimento; (of property etc: by selling) vendita; (: by giving away) cessione *f*; **at one's ~** alla sua disposizione; **to put sth at sb's ~** mettere qc a disposizione di qn

dispose [dɪs'pəuz] VT disporre
▶ **dispose of** VT FUS (time, money) disporre di;

(*Comm: sell*) vendere; (*unwanted goods*) sbarazzarsi di; (*problem*) eliminare

disposed [dɪsˈpəʊzd] ADJ: **~ to do** disposto(-a) a fare

disposition [dɪspəˈzɪʃən] N disposizione f; (*temperament*) carattere m

dispossess [ˈdɪspəˈzɛs] VT: **to ~ sb (of)** spossessare qn (di)

disproportion [dɪsprəˈpɔːʃən] N sproporzione f

disproportionate [dɪsprəˈpɔːʃənət] ADJ sproporzionato(-a)

disprove [dɪsˈpruːv] VT confutare

dispute [dɪsˈpjuːt] N disputa; (*also:* **industrial dispute**) controversia (sindacale) ▶ VT contestare; (*matter*) discutere; (*victory*) disputare; **to be in** or **under** (*matter*) essere in discussione; (*territory*) essere oggetto di contesa

disqualification [dɪskwɔlɪfɪˈkeɪʃən] N squalifica; **~ (from driving)** (BRIT) ritiro della patente

disqualify [dɪsˈkwɔlɪfaɪ] VT (*Sport*) squalificare; **to ~ sb from sth/from doing** rendere qn incapace a qc/a fare; squalificare qn da qc/da fare; **to ~ sb from driving** (BRIT) ritirare la patente a qn

disquiet [dɪsˈkwaɪət] N inquietudine f

disquieting [dɪsˈkwaɪətɪŋ] ADJ inquietante, allarmante

disregard [dɪsrɪˈgɑːd] VT non far caso a, non badare a ▶ N (*indifference*): **~ (for)** (*feelings*) insensibilità (a), indifferenza (verso); (*danger*) noncuranza (di); (*money*) disprezzo (di)

disrepair [dɪsrɪˈpɛəʳ] N cattivo stato; **to fall into ~** (*building*) andare in rovina; (*street*) deteriorarsi

disreputable [dɪsˈrɛpjutəbl] ADJ (*person*) di cattiva fama; (*area*) malfamato(-a), poco raccomandabile

disrepute [ˈdɪsrɪˈpjuːt] N disonore m, vergogna; **to bring into ~** rovinare la reputazione di

disrespectful [dɪsrɪˈspɛktful] ADJ che manca di rispetto

disrupt [dɪsˈrʌpt] VT (*meeting, lesson*) disturbare, interrompere; (*public transport*) creare scompiglio in; (*plans*) scombussolare

disruption [dɪsˈrʌpʃən] N disordine m; interruzione f

disruptive [dɪsˈrʌptɪv] ADJ (*influence*) negativo(-a), deleterio(-a); (*strike action*) paralizzante

dissatisfaction [dɪssætɪsˈfækʃən] N scontentezza, insoddisfazione f

dissatisfied [dɪsˈsætɪsfaɪd] ADJ: **~ (with)** scontento(a) or insoddisfatto(a) (di)

dissect [dɪˈsɛkt] VT sezionare; (*fig*) sviscerare

disseminate [dɪˈsɛmɪneɪt] VT disseminare

dissent [dɪˈsɛnt] N dissenso

dissenter [dɪˈsɛntəʳ] N (*Rel, Pol etc*) dissidente mf

dissertation [dɪsəˈteɪʃən] N (*Scol*) tesi f inv, dissertazione f

disservice [dɪsˈsəːvɪs] N: **to do sb a ~** fare un cattivo servizio a qn

dissident [ˈdɪsɪdnt] ADJ dissidente; (*speech, voice*) di dissenso ▶ N dissidente mf

dissimilar [dɪˈsɪmɪləʳ] ADJ: **~ (to)** dissimile or diverso(a) (da)

dissipate [ˈdɪsɪpeɪt] VT dissipare

dissipated [ˈdɪsɪpeɪtɪd] ADJ dissipato(-a)

dissociate [dɪˈsəʊʃɪeɪt] VT dissociare; **to ~ o.s. from** dichiarare di non avere niente a che fare con

dissolute [ˈdɪsəluːt] ADJ dissoluto(-a), licenzioso(-a)

dissolve [dɪˈzɔlv] VT dissolvere, sciogliere; (*Comm, Pol, marriage*) sciogliere ▶ VI dissolversi, sciogliersi; (*fig*) svanire

dissuade [dɪˈsweɪd] VT: **to ~ sb (from)** dissuadere qn (da)

distaff side [ˈdɪstɑːf-] N ramo femminile di una famiglia

distance [ˈdɪstns] N distanza; **in the ~** in lontananza; **what's the ~ to London?** quanto dista Londra?; **it's within walking ~** ci si arriva a piedi; **at a ~ of 2 metres** a 2 metri di distanza

distant [ˈdɪstnt] ADJ lontano(-a), distante; (*manner*) riservato(-a), freddo(-a)

distaste [dɪsˈteɪst] N ripugnanza

distasteful [dɪsˈteɪstful] ADJ ripugnante, sgradevole

Dist. Atty. ABBR (US) = **district attorney**

distemper [dɪsˈtɛmpəʳ] N (*paint*) tempera; (*of dogs*) cimurro

distend [dɪsˈtɛnd] VT dilatare ▶ VI dilatarsi

distended [dɪsˈtɛndɪd] ADJ (*stomach*) dilatato(-a)

distil, (US) **distill** [dɪsˈtɪl] VT distillare

distillery [dɪsˈtɪlərɪ] N distilleria

distinct [dɪsˈtɪŋkt] ADJ distinto(-a); (*preference, progress*) definito(-a); **as ~ from** a differenza di

distinction [dɪsˈtɪŋkʃən] N distinzione f; (*in exam*) lode f; **to draw a ~ between** fare distinzione tra; **a writer of ~** uno scrittore di notevoli qualità

distinctive [dɪsˈtɪŋktɪv] ADJ distintivo(-a)

distinctly [dɪsˈtɪŋktlɪ] ADV distintamente; (*remember*) chiaramente; (*unhappy, better*) decisamente

distinguish [dɪsˈtɪŋgwɪʃ] VT distinguere; discernere ▶ VI: **to ~ (between)** distinguere (tra); **to ~ o.s.** distinguersi

distinguished [dɪsˈtɪŋgwɪʃt] ADJ (*eminent*) eminente; (*career*) brillante; (*refined*) distinto(-a), signorile

distinguishing [dɪsˈtɪŋgwɪʃɪŋ] ADJ (*feature*) distinto(-a), caratteristico(-a)

distort [dɪsˈtɔːt] VT (*also fig*) distorcere; (*account, news*) falsare; (*Tech*) deformare

distortion [dɪsˈtɔːʃən] N (*gen*) distorsione f; (*of*

truth etc) alterazione *f*; (*of facts*) travisamento; (*Tech*) deformazione *f*

distract [dɪsˈtrækt] VT distrarre

distracted [dɪsˈtræktɪd] ADJ distratto(-a)

distraction [dɪsˈtrækʃən] N distrazione *f*; **to drive sb to ~** spingere qn alla pazzia

distraught [dɪsˈtrɔːt] ADJ stravolto(-a)

distress [dɪsˈtrɛs] N angoscia; (*pain*) dolore *m* ▶VT affliggere; **in ~** (*ship etc*) in pericolo, in difficoltà; **distressed area** (*BRIT*) zona sinistrata

distressing [dɪsˈtrɛsɪŋ] ADJ doloroso(-a), penoso(-a)

distress signal N segnale *m* di pericolo

distribute [dɪsˈtrɪbjuːt] VT distribuire

distribution [dɪstrɪˈbjuːʃən] N distribuzione *f*

distribution cost N costo di distribuzione

distributor [dɪsˈtrɪbjutəʳ] N distributore *m*; (*Comm*) concessionario

district [ˈdɪstrɪkt] N (*of country*) regione *f*; (*of town*) quartiere *m*; (*Admin*) distretto

district attorney N (*US*) ≈ sostituto procuratore *m* della Repubblica

district council N *organo di amministrazione regionale*

district nurse N (*BRIT*) infermiera di quartiere

distrust [dɪsˈtrʌst] N diffidenza, sfiducia ▶VT non aver fiducia in

distrustful [dɪsˈtrʌstful] ADJ diffidente

disturb [dɪsˈtəːb] VT disturbare; (*inconvenience*) scomodare; **sorry to ~ you** scusi se la disturbo

disturbance [dɪsˈtəːbəns] N disturbo; (*political etc*) tumulto; (*by drunks etc*) disordini *mpl*; **~ of the peace** disturbo della quiete pubblica; **to cause a ~** provocare disordini

disturbed [dɪsˈtəːbd] ADJ (*worried, upset*) turbato(-a); **to be emotionally ~** avere turbe emotive; **to be mentally ~** essere malato(-a) di mente

disturbing [dɪsˈtəːbɪŋ] ADJ sconvolgente

disuse [dɪsˈjuːs] N: **to fall into ~** cadere in disuso

disused [dɪsˈjuːzd] ADJ abbandonato(-a)

ditch [dɪtʃ] N fossa ▶VT (*col*) piantare in asso

dither [ˈdɪðəʳ] VI vacillare

ditto [ˈdɪtəu] ADV idem

divan [dɪˈvæn] N divano

divan bed N divano letto *inv*

dive [daɪv] N tuffo; (*of submarine*) immersione *f*; (*Aviat*) picchiata; (*pej*) buco ▶VI tuffarsi; immergersi

diver [ˈdaɪvəʳ] N tuffatore(-trice); (*deep-sea diver*) palombaro

diverge [daɪˈvəːdʒ] VI divergere

divergent [daɪˈvəːdʒənt] ADJ divergente

diverse [daɪˈvəːs] ADJ vario(-a)

diversification [daɪvəːsɪfɪˈkeɪʃən] N diversificazione *f*

diversify [daɪˈvəːsɪfaɪ] VT diversificare

diversion [daɪˈvəːʃən] N (*BRIT Aut*) deviazione *f*; (*distraction*) divertimento

diversionary tactics [daɪˈvəːʃənrɪ-] NPL tattica *fsg* diversiva

diversity [daɪˈvəːsɪtɪ] N diversità *f inv*, varietà *f inv*

divert [daɪˈvəːt] VT (*traffic, river*) deviare; (*train, plane*) dirottare; (*amuse*) divertire

divest [daɪˈvɛst] VT: **to ~ sb of** spogliare qn di

divide [dɪˈvaɪd] VT dividere; (*separate*) separare ▶VI dividersi; **to ~ (between** or **among)** dividere (tra), ripartire (tra); **40 divided by 5** 40 diviso 5
▶**divide out** VT: **to ~ out (between** or **among)** (*sweets etc*) distribuire (tra); (*tasks*) distribuire or ripartire (tra)

divided [dɪˈvaɪdɪd] ADJ (*country*) diviso(-a); (*opinions*) discordi

divided highway N (*US*) strada a doppia carreggiata

divided skirt N gonna *f* pantalone *inv*

dividend [ˈdɪvɪdɛnd] N dividendo

dividend cover N rapporto dividendo profitti

dividers [dɪˈvaɪdəz] NPL compasso a punte fisse

divine [dɪˈvaɪn] ADJ divino(-a) ▶VT (*future*) divinare, predire; (*truth*) indovinare; (*water, metal*) individuare tramite radioestesia

diving [ˈdaɪvɪŋ] N tuffo

diving board N trampolino

diving suit N scafandro

divinity [dɪˈvɪnɪtɪ] N divinità *f inv*; teologia

division [dɪˈvɪʒən] N divisione *f*; separazione *f*; (*BRIT Football*) serie *f inv*; **~ of labour** divisione *f* del lavoro

divisive [dɪˈvaɪsɪv] ADJ che è causa di discordia

divorce [dɪˈvɔːs] N divorzio ▶VT divorziare da; (*dissociate*) separare

divorced [dɪˈvɔːst] ADJ divorziato(-a)

divorcee [dɪvɔːˈsiː] N divorziato(-a)

divot [ˈdɪvət] N (*Golf*) zolla di terra (*sollevata accidentalmente*)

divulge [daɪˈvʌldʒ] VT divulgare, rivelare

Diwali [dɪˈwɑːlɪ], **Divali** [dɪˈvɑːlɪ] N Diwali *m inv*

D.I.Y. ADJ, N ABBR (*BRIT*) = **do-it-yourself**

dizziness [ˈdɪzɪnɪs] N vertigini *fpl*

dizzy [ˈdɪzɪ] ADJ (*height*) vertiginoso(-a); **to feel ~** avere il capogiro; **I feel ~** mi gira la testa, ho il capogiro; **to make sb ~** far girare la testa a qn

DJ N ABBR = **disc jockey**

dj N ABBR = **dinner jacket**

Djakarta [dʒəˈkɑːtə] N Giakarta

DJIA N ABBR (*US Stock Exchange*: = *Dow-Jones Industrial Average*) indice *m* Dow-Jones

Djibouti [dʒɪˈbuːtɪ] N Gibuti *m*

dl ABBR (= *decilitre*) dl

DLit, DLitt N ABBR = **Doctor of Literature; Doctor of Letters**

dm ▶ VI ABBR (= *decimetre*) dm

DMus N ABBR = **Doctor of Music**

DMZ N ABBR (= *demilitarized zone*) zona smilitarizzata

DNA N ABBR (= *deoxyribonucleic acid*) DNA *m*

DNA test N test *m inv* del DNA

---

do [du:]

(*pt* **did** [dɪd], *pp* **done** [dʌn]) AUX VB **1** (*in negative constructions*) *non tradotto*; **I don't understand** non capisco

2 (*to form questions*) *non tradotto*; **didn't you know?** non lo sapevi?; **why didn't you come?** perché non sei venuto?

3 (*for emphasis: in polite expressions*): **she does seem rather late** sembra essere piuttosto in ritardo; **I DO wish I could …** magari potessi …; **but I DO like it!** sì che mi piace!; **do sit down** si accomodi la prego, prego si sieda; **do take care!** mi raccomando, stai attento!

4 (*used to avoid repeating vb*): **she swims better than I do** lei nuota meglio di me; **do you agree? — yes, I do/no, I don't** sei d'accordo? — sì/no; **she lives in Glasgow — so do I** lei vive a Glasgow — anch'io; **he asked me to help him and I did** mi ha chiesto di aiutarlo ed io l'ho fatto; **they come here often — do they?** vengono qui spesso — ah sì?, davvero?

5 (*in question tags*): **you like him, don't you?** ti piace, vero?; **I don't know him, do I?** non lo conosco, vero?

▶ VT (*gen: carry out, perform etc*) fare; **what are you doing tonight?** che fai stasera?; **what can I do for you?** (*in shop*) desidera?; **I'll do all I can** farò tutto il possibile; **to do the cooking** cucinare; **to do the washing-up** fare i piatti; **to do one's teeth** lavarsi i denti; **to do one's hair/nails** farsi i capelli/le unghie; **the car was doing 100** la macchina faceva i 100 all'ora; **how do you like your steak done?** come preferisce la bistecca?; **well done** ben cotto(-a)

▶ VI **1** (*act, behave*) fare; **do as I do** faccia come me, faccia come faccio io; **what did he do with the cat?** che ne ha fatto del gatto?

2 (*get on, fare*) andare; **he's doing well/badly at school** va bene/male a scuola; **how do you do?** piacere!

3 (*suit*) andare bene; **this room will do** questa stanza va bene

4 (*be sufficient*) bastare; **will £10 do?** basteranno 10 sterline?; **that'll do** basta così; **that'll do!** (*in annoyance*) ora basta!; **to make do (with)** arrangiarsi (con)

▶ N (*col: party etc*) festa; **it was rather a grand do** è stato un ricevimento piuttosto importante

▶ **do away with** VT FUS (*col: kill*) far fuori; (*abolish*) abolire

▶ **do for** VT FUS (BRIT *col: clean for*) fare i servizi per

▶ **do out of** VT FUS: **to do sb out of sth** fregare qc a qn

▶ **do up** VT (*laces*) allacciare; (*dress, buttons*) abbottonare; (*renovate: room, house*) rimettere a nuovo, rifare; **to do o.s. up** farsi bello(-a)

▶ **do with** VT FUS (*need*) aver bisogno di; **I could do with some help/a drink** un aiuto/un bicchierino non guasterebbe; **it could do with a wash** una lavata non gli farebbe male; (*be connected*): **what has it got to do with you?** e tu che c'entri?; **I won't have anything to do with it** non voglio avere niente a che farci; **it has to do with money** si tratta di soldi

▶ **do without** VI fare senza ▶ VT FUS fare a meno di

do. ABBR = **ditto**

DOA ABBR (= *dead on arrival*) morto(-a) durante il trasporto

d.o.b. ABBR = **date of birth**

doc [dɔk] N (*col*) dottore(-essa)

docile [ˈdəʊsaɪl] ADJ docile

dock [dɔk] N (*Naut*) bacino; (*wharf*) molo; (*Law*) banco degli imputati ▶ VI entrare in bacino; (*Space*) agganciarsi ▶ VT (*pay etc*) decurtare ■ **docks** NPL (*Naut*) dock *m inv*

dock dues NPL diritti *mpl* di banchina

docker [ˈdɔkəʳ] N scaricatore *m*

docket [ˈdɔkɪt] N (*on parcel etc*) etichetta, cartellino

dockyard [ˈdɔkjɑːd] N cantiere *m* navale

doctor [ˈdɔktəʳ] N medico(-a), dottore(-essa); (*PhD etc*) dottore(-essa) ▶ VT (*interfere with: food, drink*) adulterare; (*: text, document*) alterare, manipolare; **~'s office** (*US*) gabinetto medico, ambulatorio

doctorate [ˈdɔktərɪt] N dottorato di ricerca

Il **doctorate** è il riconoscimento accademico più prestigioso in tutti i campi del sapere; viene conferito in seguito alla presentazione di una tesi, frutto di almeno tre anni di ricerca, di fronte ad una commissione di esperti; *vedi anche* **Bachelor's degree**, **Master's degree**.

Doctor of Philosophy, PhD N dottorato di ricerca; (*person*) titolare *mf* di un dottorato di ricerca

doctrine [ˈdɔktrɪn] N dottrina

docudrama [dɔkjuˈdrɑːmə] N (TV) ricostruzione *f* filmata

document N [ˈdɔkjumənt] documento ▶ VT [ˈdɔkjumɛnt] documentare

documentary [dɔkjuˈmɛntərɪ] ADJ documentario(-a); (*evidence*) documentato(-a) ▶ N documentario

documentation [dɔkjumənˈteɪʃən] N documentazione *f*

DOD N ABBR (*US*) = Department of Defense

doddering [ˈdɔdərɪŋ] ADJ traballante

doddery [ˈdɔdərɪ] ADJ malfermo(-a)

doddle [ˈdɔdl] N: **it's a ~** (*col*) è un gioco da ragazzi

Dodecanese Islands [dəudɪkəˈniːz-] NPL Isole *fpl* del Dodecanneso

dodge [dɔdʒ] N trucco; schivata ▶ VT schivare, eludere ▶ VI scansarsi; (*Sport*) fare una schivata; **to ~ out of the way** scansarsi; **to ~ through the traffic** destreggiarsi nel traffico

Dodgems® [ˈdɔdʒəmz] NPL (*BRIT*) autoscontri *mpl*

dodgy [ˈdɔdʒɪ] ADJ (*BRIT col: uncertain*) rischioso(-a); (: *untrustworthy*) sospetto(-a)

DOE N ABBR (*US*) = Department of Energy

doe [dəu] N (*deer*) femmina di daino; (*rabbit*) coniglia

does [dʌz] *see* **do**

doesn't [ˈdʌznt] = **does not**

dog [dɔg] N cane *m* ▶ VT (*follow closely*) pedinare; (*fig: memory etc*) perseguitare; **to go to the dogs** (*person*) ridursi male, lasciarsi andare; (*nation etc*) in malora

dog biscuits NPL biscotti *mpl* per cani

dog collar N collare *m* di cane; (*fig*) collarino

dog-eared [ˈdɔgɪəd] ADJ (*book*) con orecchie

dog food N cibo per cani

dogged [ˈdɔgɪd] ADJ ostinato(-a), tenace

doggy [ˈdɔgɪ] N (*col*) cane *m*, cagnolino

doggy bag N sacchetto per gli avanzi (*da portare a casa*)

dogma [ˈdɔgmə] N dogma *m*

dogmatic [dɔgˈmætɪk] ADJ dogmatico(-a)

do-gooder [duːˈgudəʳ] N (*pej*): **to be a ~** fare il filantropo

dogsbody [ˈdɔgzbɔdɪ] N (*BRIT*) factotum *m inv*

doily [ˈdɔɪlɪ] N centrino di carta sottopiatto

doing [ˈduːɪŋ] N: **this is your ~** è opera tua, sei stato tu

doings [ˈduɪŋz] NPL attività *fpl*

do-it-yourself [ˈduːɪtjɔːˈself] N il far da sé

doldrums [ˈdɔldrəmz] NPL (*fig*): **to be in the ~** essere giù; (*business*) attraversare un momento difficile

dole [dəul] N (*BRIT*) sussidio di disoccupazione; **to be on the ~** vivere del sussidio ▶ **dole out** VT distribuire

doleful [ˈdəulful] ADJ triste, doloroso(-a)

doll [dɔl] N bambola ▶ **doll up** VT: **to ~ o.s. up** farsi bello(a)

dollar [ˈdɔləʳ] N dollaro

dollop [ˈdɔləp] N (*of food*) cucchiaiata

dolly [ˈdɔlɪ] N bambola

dolphin [ˈdɔlfɪn] N delfino

domain [dəˈmeɪn] N dominio; (*fig*) campo, sfera

dome [dəum] N cupola

domestic [dəˈmɛstɪk] ADJ (*duty, happiness, animal*) domestico(-a); (*policy, affairs, flights*) nazionale; (*news*) dall'interno

domestic appliance N elettrodomestico

domesticated [dəˈmɛstɪkeɪtɪd] ADJ addomesticato(-a); (*person*) casalingo(-a)

domesticity [dəumɛsˈtɪsɪtɪ] N vita di famiglia

domestic servant N domestico(-a)

domicile [ˈdɔmɪsaɪl] N domicilio

dominant [ˈdɔmɪnənt] ADJ dominante

dominate [ˈdɔmɪneɪt] VT dominare

domination [dɔmɪˈneɪʃən] N dominazione *f*

domineering [dɔmɪˈnɪərɪŋ] ADJ dispotico(-a), autoritario(-a)

Dominica [dɔmɪˈniːkə, dəˈmɪnɪkə] N Dominica

Dominican Republic [dəˈmɪnɪkən-] N Repubblica Dominicana

dominion [dəˈmɪnɪən] N dominio; sovranità; (*BRIT Pol*) dominion *m inv*

domino [ˈdɔmɪnəu] (*pl* **dominoes**) N domino ■ **dominoes** NPL (*game*) gioco del domino

don [dɔn] N (*BRIT*) docente *mf* universitario(-a) ▶ VT indossare

donate [dəˈneɪt] VT donare

donation [dəˈneɪʃən] N donazione *f*

done [dʌn] PP *of* **do**

dongle [ˈdɔŋgl] N (*Comput*) chiavetta, pennetta

donkey [ˈdɔŋkɪ] N asino

donkey-work [ˈdɔŋkɪwəːk] N (*BRIT col*) lavoro ingrato

donor [ˈdəunəʳ] N donatore(-trice)

donor card N tessera di donatore di organi

don't [dəunt] = **do not**

donut [ˈdəunʌt] N (*US*) = **doughnut**

doodle [ˈduːdl] N scarabocchio ▶ VI scarabocchiare

doom [duːm] N destino; rovina ▶ VT: **to be doomed (to failure)** essere predestinato(-a) (a fallire)

doomsday [ˈduːmzdeɪ] N il giorno del Giudizio

door [dɔːʳ] N porta; (*of vehicle*) sportello, portiera; **from ~ to ~** di porta in porta

doorbell [ˈdɔːbɛl] N campanello

door handle N maniglia

doorknob [ˈdɔːnɔb] N pomello, maniglia

doorman [ˈdɔːmæn] N (*irreg*) (*in hotel*) portiere *m* in livrea; (*in block of flats*) portinaio

doormat [ˈdɔːmæt] N stuoia della porta

doorstep [ˈdɔːstɛp] N gradino della porta

door-to-door [ˈdɔːtəˈdɔːʳ] ADJ: **~ selling** vendita porta a porta

doorway [ˈdɔːweɪ] N porta; **in the ~** nel vano della porta

dope [dəup] N (col: drugs) roba; (: information) dati mpl ▶ VT (horse etc) drogare

dopey ['dəupɪ] ADJ (col) inebetito(-a)

dormant ['dɔ:mənt] ADJ inattivo(-a); (fig) latente

dormer ['dɔ:məʳ] N (also: dormer window) abbaino

dormice ['dɔ:maɪs] NPL of dormouse

dormitory ['dɔ:mɪtrɪ] N dormitorio; (US: hall of residence) casa dello studente

dormouse ['dɔ:maus] (pl dormice [-maɪs]) N ghiro

DOS [dɔs] N ABBR (= disk operating system) DOS m

dosage ['dəusɪdʒ] N (on medicine bottle) posologia

dose [dəus] N dose f; (BRIT: bout) attacco ▶ VT: to ~ sb with sth somministrare qc a qn; a ~ of flu una bella influenza

dosser ['dɔsəʳ] N (BRIT pej) barbone(-a)

doss house ['dɔs-] N (BRIT) asilo notturno

dossier ['dɔsɪeɪ] N dossier m inv

DOT N ABBR (US) = Department of Transportation

dot [dɔt] N punto; macchiolina ▶ VT: dotted with punteggiato(a) di; on the ~ in punto

dotcom [dɔt'kɔm] N azienda che opera in Internet

dot command N (Comput) dot command m inv

dote [dəut]: to ~ on vt fus essere infatuato(a) di

dot-matrix printer [dɔt'meɪtrɪks-] N stampante f a matrice a punti

dotted line ['dɔtɪd-] N linea punteggiata; to sign on the ~ firmare (nell'apposito spazio); (fig) accettare

dotty ['dɔtɪ] ADJ (col) strambo(-a)

double ['dʌbl] ADJ doppio(-a) ▶ ADV (fold) in due, doppio; (twice): to cost ~ sth costare il doppio (di qc) ▶ N sosia m inv; (Cine) controfigura ▶ VT raddoppiare; (fold) piegare doppio or in due ▶ VI raddoppiarsi; spelt with a ~ "l" scritto con due elle or con doppia elle; ~ five two six (5526) (BRIT Tel) cinque cinque due sei; on the ~, (BRIT) at the ~ a passo di corsa; to ~ as (have two uses etc) funzionare or servire anche da; see also doubles
  ▶ **double back** VI (person) tornare sui propri passi
  ▶ **double up** VI (bend over) piegarsi in due; (share room) dividere la stanza

double bass N contrabbasso

double bed N letto matrimoniale

double-breasted ['dʌbl'brɛstɪd] ADJ a doppio petto

double-check ['dʌbl'tʃɛk] VT, VI ricontrollare

double-click VI (Comput) fare doppio click

double-clutch ['dʌbl'klʌtʃ] VI (US) fare la doppietta

double cream N (BRIT) doppia panna

double-cross ['dʌbl'krɔs] VT fare il doppio gioco con

doubledecker ['dʌbl'dɛkəʳ] N autobus m inv a due piani

double declutch VI (BRIT) fare la doppietta

double exposure N (Phot) sovrimpressione f

double glazing N (BRIT) doppi vetri mpl

double-page ['dʌblpeɪdʒ] ADJ: ~ spread pubblicità a doppia pagina

double parking N parcheggio in doppia fila

double room N camera matrimoniale

doubles ['dʌblz] N (Tennis) doppio

double time N tariffa doppia per lavoro straordinario

double whammy [-'wæmɪ] N doppia mazzata (fig)

double yellow lines NPL (BRIT Aut) linea gialla doppia continua che segnala il divieto di sosta

doubly ['dʌblɪ] ADV doppiamente

doubt [daut] N dubbio ▶ VT dubitare di; to ~ that dubitare che + sub; without (a) ~ senza dubbio; beyond ~ fuor di dubbio; I ~ it very much ho i miei dubbi, nutro seri dubbi in proposito

doubtful ['dautful] ADJ dubbioso(-a), incerto(-a); (person) equivoco(-a); to be ~ about sth avere dei dubbi su qc, non essere convinto di qc; I'm a bit ~ non ne sono sicuro

doubtless ['dautlɪs] ADV indubbiamente

dough [dəu] N pasta, impasto; (col: money) grana

doughnut, (US) **donut** ['dəunʌt] N bombolone m

dour [duəʳ] ADJ arcigno(-a)

douse [daus] VT (with water) infradiciare; (flames) spegnere

dove [dʌv] N colombo(-a)

Dover ['dəuvəʳ] N Dover f

dovetail ['dʌvteɪl] N: ~ joint incastro a coda di rondine ▶ VI (fig) combaciare

dowager ['dauədʒəʳ] N vedova titolata

dowdy ['daudɪ] ADJ trasandato(-a), malvestito(-a)

Dow-Jones average ['dau'dʒəunz-] N (US) indice m Dow-Jones

down [daun] N (fluff) piumino; (hill) collina, colle m ▶ ADV giù, di sotto ▶ PREP giù per ▶ VT (col: drink) scolarsi; ~ there laggiù, là in fondo; ~ here quaggiù; I'll be ~ in a minute scendo tra un minuto; the price of meat is ~ il prezzo della carne è sceso; I've got it ~ in my diary ce l'ho sulla mia agenda; to pay £2 ~ dare 2 sterline in acconto or di anticipo; I've been ~ with flu sono stato a letto con l'influenza; England is two goals ~ l'Inghilterra sta perdendo per due goal; to ~ tools (BRIT) incrociare le braccia; ~ with X! abbasso X!

down-and-out [ˈdaunəndaut] N (*tramp*) barbone m

down-at-heel [ˈdaunətˈhiːl] ADJ scalcagnato(-a); (*fig*) trasandato(-a)

downbeat [ˈdaunbiːt] N (*Mus*) tempo in battere ▶ ADJ (*col*) volutamente distaccato(-a)

downcast [ˈdaunkɑːst] ADJ abbattuto(-a)

downer [ˈdaunəʳ] N (*col: drug*) farmaco depressivo; **to be on a ~** (*depressed*) essere giù

downfall [ˈdaunfɔːl] N caduta; rovina

downgrade [ˈdaungreid] VT (*job, hotel*) declassare; (*employee*) degradare

downhearted [daunˈhɑːtid] ADJ scoraggiato(-a)

downhill [ˈdaunˈhil] ADV verso il basso; **to go ~** andare in discesa; (*business*) lasciarsi andare; andare a rotoli ▶ N (*Ski: also:* **downhill race**) discesa libera

Downing Street [ˈdaunɪŋ-] N: **10 ~** *residenza del primo ministro inglese*

Downing Street è la via di Westminster che porta da Whitehall al parco di St James dove, al numero 10, si trova la residenza del primo ministro britannico. Nella stessa via, al numero 11, si trova la residenza del Cancelliere dello Scacchiere. Spesso si usa *Downing Street* per indicare il governo britannico.

download [ˈdaunləud] VT (*Comput*) scaricare ▶ N (*Comput*) file m *inv* da scaricare

downloadable [daunˈləudəbl] ADJ (*Comput*) scaricabile

down-market [ˈdaunˈmɑːkit] ADJ rivolto(-a) ad una fascia di mercato inferiore

down payment N acconto

downplay [ˈdaunplei] VT (*US*) minimizzare

downpour [ˈdaunpɔːʳ] N scroscio di pioggia

downright [ˈdaunrait] ADJ franco(-a); (*refusal*) assoluto(-a)

Downs [daunz] NPL (*BRIT*): **the ~** *colline ricche di gesso nel sud-est dell'Inghilterra*

downsize [ˈdaunsaiz] VT (*workforce*) ridurre

Down's syndrome N sindrome f di Down

downstairs [ˈdaunˈstɛəz] ADV di sotto; al piano inferiore; **to come ~, go ~** scendere giù

downstream [ˈdaunˈstriːm] ADV a valle

downtime [ˈdauntaim] N (*Comm*) tempi mpl morti

down-to-earth [ˈdauntuˈəːθ] ADJ pratico(-a)

downtown [ˈdaunˈtaun] ADV in città ▶ ADJ (*US*): **~ Chicago** il centro di Chicago

downtrodden [ˈdauntrɔdn] ADJ oppresso(-a)

down under ADV (*Australia etc*) agli antipodi

downward [ˈdaunwəd] ADJ in giù, in discesa; **a ~ trend** una diminuzione progressiva ▶ ADV in giù, in discesa

downwards [ˈdaunwədz] ADV in giù, in discesa

dowry [ˈdauri] N dote f

doz. ABBR = **dozen**

doze [dəuz] VI sonnecchiare
▶ **doze off** VI appisolarsi

dozen [ˈdʌzn] N dozzina; **a ~ books** una dozzina di libri; **80p a ~** 80 pence la dozzina; **dozens of times** centinaia *or* migliaia di volte

DPh, DPhil N ABBR (= *Doctor of Philosophy*) ≈ dottorato di ricerca

DPP N ABBR (*BRIT*) = **Director of Public Prosecutions**

DPT N ABBR (*Med*: = *diphtheria, pertussis, tetanus*) vaccino

Dr, Dr. ABBR (= *doctor*) Dr, Dott./Dott.ssa; (*in street names*) = **drive**

dr ABBR (*Comm*) = **debtor**

drab [dræb] ADJ tetro(-a), grigio(-a)

draft [drɑːft] N abbozzo; (*Pol*) bozza; (*Comm*) tratta; (*US Mil*) contingente m; (: *call-up*) leva ▶ VT abbozzare; (*document, report*) stendere (in versione preliminare); *see also* **draught**

drag [dræg] VT trascinare; (*river*) dragare ▶ VI trascinarsi ▶ N (*Aviat, Naut*) resistenza (aerodinamica); (*col: person*) noioso(-a); (: *task*) noia; (*women's clothing*): **in ~** travestito (da donna)
▶ **drag away** VT: **to ~ away (from)** tirare via (da)
▶ **drag on** VI tirar avanti lentamente

dragnet [ˈdrægnet] N giacchio; (*fig*) rastrellamento

dragon [ˈdrægən] N drago

dragonfly [ˈdrægənflai] N libellula

dragoon [drəˈguːn] N (*cavalryman*) dragone m ▶ VT: **to ~ sb into doing sth** (*BRIT*) costringere qn a fare qc

drain [drein] N canale m di scolo; (*for sewage*) fogna; (*on resources*) salasso ▶ VT (*land, marshes*) prosciugare; (*vegetables*) scolare; (*reservoir etc*) vuotare ▶ VI (*water*) defluire; **to feel drained** sentirsi svuotato(-a), sentirsi sfinito(-a)

drainage [ˈdreinidʒ] N prosciugamento; fognatura

draining board [ˈdreiniŋ-], (*US*) **drainboard** [ˈdreinbɔːd] N piano del lavello

drainpipe [ˈdreinpaip] N tubo di scarico

drake [dreik] N maschio dell'anatra

dram [dræm] N bicchierino (di whisky *etc*)

drama [ˈdrɑːmə] N (*art*) dramma m, teatro; (*play*) commedia; (*event*) dramma

dramatic [drəˈmætik] ADJ drammatico(-a)

dramatically [drəˈmætikli] ADV in modo spettacolare

dramatist [ˈdræmətist] N drammaturgo(-a)

dramatize [ˈdræmətaiz] VT (*events etc*) drammatizzare; (*adapt: novel: for TV*) ridurre *or* adattare per la televisione; (: *for cinema*) ridurre *or* adattare per lo schermo

drank [dræŋk] PT of **drink**

drape [dreɪp] VT drappeggiare; see also **drapes**

draper ['dreɪpə'] N (BRIT) negoziante mf di stoffe

drapes [dreɪps] NPL (US: curtains) tende fpl

drastic ['dræstɪk] ADJ drastico(-a)

drastically ['dræstɪklɪ] ADV drasticamente

draught, (US) **draft** [drɑːft] N corrente f d'aria; (Naut) pescaggio; **on ~** (beer) alla spina; see also **draughts**

draught beer N birra alla spina

draughtboard ['drɑːftbɔːd] N scacchiera

draughts [drɑːfts] N (BRIT) (gioco della) dama

draughtsman, (US) **draftsman** ['drɑːftsmən] N (irreg) disegnatore(-trice)

draughtsmanship, (US) **draftsmanship** ['drɑːftsmənʃɪp] N disegno tecnico; (skill) arte f del disegno

draw [drɔː] (pt **drew** [druː], pp **drawn** [drɔːn]) VT tirare; (take out) estrarre; (attract) attirare; (picture) disegnare; (line, circle) tracciare; (money) ritirare; (formulate: conclusion) trarre, ricavare; (: comparison, distinction): **to ~ (between)** fare (tra) ▶ VI (Sport) pareggiare ▶ N (Sport) pareggio; (in lottery) estrazione f; (attraction) attrazione f; **to ~ to a close** avvicinarsi alla conclusione; **to ~ near** vi avvicinarsi
▶ **draw back** VI: **to ~ back (from)** indietreggiare (di fronte a), tirarsi indietro (di fronte a)
▶ **draw in** VI (BRIT: car) accostarsi; (train) entrare in stazione
▶ **draw on** VT (resources) attingere a; (imagination, person) far ricorso a
▶ **draw out** VI (lengthen) allungarsi ▶ VT (money) ritirare
▶ **draw up** VI (stop) arrestarsi, fermarsi ▶ VT (chair) avvicinare; (document) compilare; (plans) formulare

drawback ['drɔːbæk] N svantaggio, inconveniente m

drawbridge ['drɔːbrɪdʒ] N ponte m levatoio

drawee [drɔː'iː] N trattario

drawer [drɔː'] N cassetto; (of cheque) ['drɔːə'] riscuotitore(-trice)

drawing ['drɔːɪŋ] N disegno

drawing board N tavola da disegno

drawing pin N (BRIT) puntina da disegno

drawing room N salotto

drawl [drɔːl] N pronuncia strascicata

drawn [drɔːn] PP of **draw** ▶ ADJ (haggard: with tiredness) tirato(-a); (: with pain) contratto(-a) (dal dolore)

drawstring ['drɔːstrɪŋ] N laccio (per stringere maglie, sacche ecc)

DRC N ABBR (= Democratic Republic of the Congo) Repubblica Democratica del Congo

dread [drɛd] N terrore m ▶ VT tremare all'idea di

dreadful ['drɛdful] ADJ terribile; **I feel ~!** (ill) mi sento uno straccio!; (ashamed) vorrei scomparire (dalla vergogna)!

dream [driːm] (pt, pp **dreamed** [driːmd] or **dreamt** [drɛmt]) N sogno ▶ VT, VI sognare; **to have a ~ about sb/sth** fare un sogno su qn/qc; **sweet dreams!** sogni d'oro!
▶ **dream up** VT (reason, excuse) inventare; (plan, idea) escogitare

dreamer ['driːmə'] N sognatore(-trice)

dreamt [drɛmt] PT, PP of **dream**

dreamy ['driːmɪ] ADJ (look, voice) sognante; (person) distratto(-a), sognatore(-trice)

dreary ['drɪərɪ] ADJ tetro(-a); monotono(-a)

dredge [drɛdʒ] VT dragare
▶ **dredge up** VT tirare alla superficie; (fig: unpleasant facts) rivangare

dredger ['drɛdʒə'] N draga; (BRIT: also: **sugar dredger**) spargizucchero m inv

dregs [drɛgz] NPL feccia

drench [drɛntʃ] VT inzuppare; **drenched to the skin** bagnato(a) fino all'osso, bagnato(a) fradicio(a)

dress [drɛs] N vestito; (no pl: clothing) abbigliamento ▶ VT vestire; (wound) fasciare; (food) condire; preparare; (shop window) allestire ▶ VI vestirsi; **to ~ o.s., to get dressed** vestirsi; **she dresses very well** veste molto bene
▶ **dress up** VI vestirsi a festa; (in fancy dress) vestirsi in costume

dress circle N (BRIT) prima galleria

dress designer N disegnatore(-trice) di moda

dresser ['drɛsə'] N (Theat) assistente mf del camerino; (also: **window dresser**) vetrinista mf; (furniture) credenza; (US) cassettone m

dressing ['drɛsɪŋ] N (Med) benda; (Culin) condimento

dressing gown N (BRIT) vestaglia

dressing room N (Theat) camerino; (Sport) spogliatoio

dressing table N toilette f inv

dressmaker ['drɛsmeɪkə'] N sarta

dressmaking ['drɛsmeɪkɪŋ] N sartoria; confezioni fpl per donna

dress rehearsal N prova generale

dress shirt N camicia da sera

dressy ['drɛsɪ] ADJ (col) elegante

drew [druː] PT of **draw**

dribble ['drɪbl] VI gocciolare; (baby) sbavare; (Football) dribblare ▶ VT (ball) dribblare

dried [draɪd] ADJ (fruit, beans) secco(-a); (eggs, milk) in polvere

drier ['draɪə'] N = **dryer**

drift [drɪft] N (of current etc) direzione f; forza; (of sand, snow) cumulo; turbine m; (general meaning) senso ▶ VI (boat) essere trasportato(-a) dalla corrente; (sand, snow) ammucchiarsi; **to catch**

sb's ~ capire dove qn vuole arrivare; **to let things** ~ lasciare che le cose vadano come vogliono; **to ~ apart** (*friends*) perdersi di vista; (*lovers*) allontanarsi l'uno dall'altro

drifter [ˈdrɪftəʳ] N *persona che fa una vita da zingaro*

driftwood [ˈdrɪftwʊd] N resti mpl della mareggiata

drill [drɪl] N trapano; (*Mil*) esercitazione f ▶ VT trapanare; (*soldiers*) esercitare, addestrare; (*pupils: in grammar*) fare esercitare ▶ VI (*for oil*) fare trivellazioni

drilling [ˈdrɪlɪŋ] N (*for oil*) trivellazione f

drilling rig N (*on land*) torre f di perforazione; (*at sea*) piattaforma (per trivellazioni subacquee)

drily [ˈdraɪlɪ] ADV = **dryly**

drink [drɪŋk] (*pt* **drank** [dræŋk], *pp* **drunk** [drʌŋk]) N bevanda, bibita; (*alcoholic drink*) bicchierino; (*sip*) sorso ▶ VT, VI bere; **to have a ~** bere qualcosa; **a ~ of water** un po' d'acqua; **would you like something to ~?** vuole qualcosa da bere?; **we had drinks before lunch** abbiamo preso l'aperitivo
▶ **drink in** VT (*person: fresh air*) aspirare; (: *story*) ascoltare avidamente; (: *sight*) ammirare, bersi con gli occhi

drinkable [ˈdrɪŋkəbl] ADJ (*not poisonous*) potabile; (*palatable*) bevibile

drink-driving [ˈdrɪŋkˈdraɪvɪŋ] N guida in stato di ebbrezza

drinker [ˈdrɪŋkəʳ] N bevitore(-trice)

drinking [ˈdrɪŋkɪŋ] N (*drunkenness*) il bere, alcoolismo

drinking fountain N fontanella

drinking water N acqua potabile

drip [drɪp] N goccia; (*dripping*) sgocciolio; (*Med*) fleboclisi f inv; (*col: spineless person*) lavativo(-a) ▶ VI gocciolare; (*washing, tap*) sgocciolare; (*wall*) trasudare

drip-dry [ˈdrɪpˈdraɪ] ADJ (*shirt*) che non si stira

drip-feed [ˈdrɪpfiːd] VT alimentare mediante fleboclisi

dripping [ˈdrɪpɪŋ] N (*Culin*) grasso d'arrosto ▶ ADJ: **~ wet** fradicio(a)

drive [draɪv] (*pt* **drove** [drəʊv], *pp* **driven** [ˈdrɪvn]) N passeggiata *or* giro in macchina; (*also*: **driveway**) viale m d'accesso; (*energy*) energia; (*Psych*) impulso; bisogno; (*push*) sforzo eccezionale; (*campaign*) campagna; (*Sport*) drive m inv; (*Tech*) trasmissione f; (*Comput: also*: **disk drive**) disk drive m inv ▶ VT (*vehicle*) guidare; (*nail*) piantare; (*push*) cacciare, spingere; (*Tech: motor*) azionare; far funzionare ▶ VI (*Aut: at controls*) guidare; (: *travel*) andare in macchina; **to go for a ~** andare a fare un giro in macchina; **it's 3 hours' ~ from London** è a 3 ore di macchina da Londra; **left-/right-hand ~** (*Aut*) guida a sinistra/destra; **front-/rear-wheel ~** (*Aut*) trazione f anteriore/posteriore; **to ~ sb to (do) sth** spingere qn a (fare) qc; **to ~ sb mad** far

impazzire qn; **he drives a taxi** fa il tassista; **to ~ at 50 km an hour** guidare *or* andare a 50 km all'ora
▶ **drive at** VT FUS (*fig: intend, mean*) mirare a, voler dire
▶ **drive on** VI proseguire, andare (più) avanti ▶ VT (*incite, encourage*) sospingere, spingere
▶ **drive out** VT (*force out*) cacciare, mandare via

drive-by [ˈdraɪvbaɪ] N (*also*: **drive-by shooting**) sparatoria dalla macchina; **he was killed in a ~ shooting** lo hanno ammazzato sparandogli da una macchina in corsa

drive-in [ˈdraɪvɪn] ADJ, N (*esp US*) drive-in (m inv)

drive-in window N (*US*) sportello di drive-in

drivel [ˈdrɪvl] N (*col: nonsense*) ciance fpl

driven [ˈdrɪvn] PP *of* **drive**

driver [ˈdraɪvəʳ] N conducente mf; (*of taxi*) tassista m; (*chauffeur: of bus*) autista mf; (*Comput*) driver m inv

driver's license N (*US*) patente f di guida

driveway [ˈdraɪvweɪ] N viale m d'accesso

driving [ˈdraɪvɪŋ] ADJ: **~ rain** pioggia sferzante ▶ N guida

driving force N forza trainante

driving instructor N istruttore(-trice) di scuola guida

driving lesson N lezione f di guida

driving licence N (*Brit*) patente f di guida

driving school N scuola f guida inv

driving test N esame m di guida

drizzle [ˈdrɪzl] N pioggerella ▶ VI piovigginare

droll [drəʊl] ADJ buffo(-a)

dromedary [ˈdrɒmədərɪ] N dromedario

drone [drəʊn] N ronzio; (*male bee*) fuco ▶ VI (*bee, aircraft, engine*) ronzare; (*also*: **drone on**: *person*) continuare a parlare (in modo monotono); (: *voice*) continuare a ronzare

drool [druːl] VI sbavare; **to ~ over sb/sth** (*fig*) andare in estasi per qn/qc

droop [druːp] VI abbassarsi; languire; (*flower*) appassire; (*head, shoulders*) chinarsi

drop [drɒp] N (*of water*) goccia; (*lessening*) diminuzione f; (*fall*) caduta; (: *in price*) calo, ribasso; (: *in salary*) riduzione f, taglio; (*also*: **parachute drop**) lancio; (*steep incline*) salto ▶ VT lasciar cadere; (*voice, eyes, price*) abbassare; (*set down from car*) far scendere; (*name from list*) lasciare fuori ▶ VI cascare; (*decrease: wind, temperature, price*) calare, abbassarsi; (: *numbers, attendance*) diminuire; (*voice*) abbassarsi ■ **drops** NPL (*Med*) gocce fpl; **cough drops** pastiglie fpl per la tosse; **a ~ of 10%** un calo del 10%; **to ~ sb a line** mandare due righe a qn; **to ~ anchor** gettare l'ancora
▶ **drop in** VI (*col: visit*): **to ~ in (on)** fare un salto (da), passare (da)
▶ **drop off** VI (*sleep*) addormentarsi ▶ VT: **to ~ sb off** far scendere qn

▶ **drop out** VI (*withdraw*) ritirarsi; (*student etc*) smettere di studiare

droplet [ˈdrɔplɪt] N gocciolina

dropout [ˈdrɔpaʊt] N (*from society/university*) chi ha abbandonato (la società/gli studi)

dropper [ˈdrɔpəʳ] N (*Med*) contagocce *m inv*

droppings [ˈdrɔpɪŋz] NPL sterco

dross [drɔs] N scoria; scarto

drought [draʊt] N siccità *f inv*

drove [drəʊv] PT *of* **drive** ▶ N: **droves of people** una moltitudine di persone

drown [draʊn] VT affogare; (*fig: noise*) soffocare; (*also:* **drown out:** *sound*) coprire ▶ VI affogare

drowse [draʊz] VI sonnecchiare

drowsy [ˈdraʊzɪ] ADJ sonnolento(-a), assonnato(-a)

drudge [drʌdʒ] N (*person*) uomo (donna) di fatica; (*job*) faticaccia

drudgery [ˈdrʌdʒərɪ] N fatica improba; **housework is sheer ~** le faccende domestiche sono alienanti

drug [drʌg] N farmaco; (*narcotic*) droga ▶ VT drogare; **to be on drugs** drogarsi; (*Med*) prendere medicinali; **hard/soft drugs** droghe pesanti/leggere

drug abuser [-əˈbjuːzəʳ] N chi fa uso di droghe

drug addict N tossicomane *mf*

drug dealer N trafficante *mf* di droga

drug driving N guida *f* sotto l'effetto di droghe

druggist [ˈdrʌgɪst] N (*US*) farmacista *mf*

drug peddler N spacciatore(-trice) di droga

drugstore [ˈdrʌgstɔːʳ] N (*US*) *negozio di generi vari e di articoli di farmacia con un bar*

drum [drʌm] N tamburo; (*for oil, petrol*) fusto ▶ VT: **to ~ one's fingers on the table** tamburellare con le dita sulla tavola ▶ VI tamburellare ■ **drums** NPL (*Mus: set of drums*) batteria ▶ **drum up** VT (*enthusiasm, support*) conquistarsi

drummer [ˈdrʌməʳ] N batterista *mf*

drum roll N rullio di tamburi

drumstick [ˈdrʌmstɪk] N (*Mus*) bacchetta; (*chicken leg*) coscia di pollo

drunk [drʌŋk] PP *of* **drink** ▶ ADJ ubriaco(-a), ebbro(-a) ▶ N ubriacone(-a); **to get ~** ubriacarsi, prendere una sbornia

drunkard [ˈdrʌŋkəd] N ubriacone(-a)

drunken [ˈdrʌŋkən] ADJ ubriaco(-a), da ubriaco; **~ driving** guida in stato di ebbrezza

drunkenness [ˈdrʌŋkənnɪs] N ubriachezza; ebbrezza

dry [draɪ] ADJ secco(-a); (*day, clothes, fig: humour*) asciutto(-a); (*uninteresting: lecture, subject*) poco avvincente ▶ VT seccare; (*clothes, hair, hands*) asciugare ▶ VI asciugarsi; **on ~ land** sulla terraferma; **to ~ one's hands/hair/eyes** asciugarsi le mani/i capelli/gli occhi

▶ **dry off** VI asciugarsi ▶ VT asciugare

▶ **dry up** VI seccarsi; (*source of supply*) esaurirsi; (*fig: imagination etc*) inaridirsi; (*fall silent: speaker*) azzittirsi

dry-clean [draɪˈkliːn] VT pulire *or* lavare a secco

dry-cleaner's [draɪˈkliːnəz] N lavasecco *m inv*

dry-cleaning [draɪˈkliːnɪŋ] N pulitura a secco

dry dock N (*Naut*) bacino di carenaggio

dryer [ˈdraɪəʳ] N (*for hair*) föhn *m inv*, asciugacapelli *m inv*; (*for clothes*) asciugabiancheria *m inv*; (*US: spin-dryer*) centrifuga

dry goods NPL (*Comm*) tessuti *mpl* e mercerie *fpl*

dry goods store N (*US*) negozio di stoffe

dry ice N ghiaccio secco

dryly [ˈdraɪlɪ] ADV con fare asciutto

dryness [ˈdraɪnɪs] N secchezza; (*of ground*) aridità

dry rot N fungo del legno

dry run N (*fig*) prova

dry ski slope N pista artificiale

DSc N ABBR (= *Doctor of Science*) *titolo di studio*

DST ABBR = **Daylight Saving Time**

DTP N ABBR (= *desk-top publishing*) desktop publishing *m inv*; (*Med:* = *diphtheria, tetanus, pertussis*) *vaccino*

DT's N ABBR (*col*) = **delirium tremens**

dual [ˈdjuəl] ADJ doppio(-a)

dual carriageway N (*BRIT*) strada a doppia carreggiata

dual-control [ˈdjuəlkənˈtrəʊl] ADJ con doppi comandi

dual nationality N doppia nazionalità

dual-purpose [ˈdjuəlˈpəːpəs] ADJ a doppio uso

dubbed [dʌbd] ADJ (*Cine*) doppiato(-a); (*nicknamed*) soprannominato(-a)

dubious [ˈdjuːbɪəs] ADJ dubbio(-a); (*character, manner*) ambiguo(-a), equivoco(-a); **I'm very ~ about it** ho i miei dubbi in proposito

Dublin [ˈdʌblɪn] N Dublino *f*

Dubliner [ˈdʌblɪnəʳ] N dublinese *mf*

duchess [ˈdʌtʃɪs] N duchessa

duck [dʌk] N anatra ▶ VI abbassare la testa ▶ VT spingere sotto (acqua)

duckling [ˈdʌklɪŋ] N anatroccolo

duct [dʌkt] N condotto; (*Anat*) canale *m*

dud [dʌd] N (*shell*) proiettile *m* che fa cilecca; (*object, tool*): **it's a ~** è inutile, non funziona ▶ ADJ (*cheque*) a vuoto; (*note, coin*) falso(-a)

due [djuː] ADJ dovuto(-a); (*expected*) atteso(-a); (*fitting*) giusto(-a) ▶ N dovuto ▶ ADV: **~ north** diritto verso nord ■ **dues** NPL (*for club, union*) quota; (*in harbour*) diritti *mpl* di porto; **in ~ course** a tempo debito; finalmente; **~ to** dovuto a; a causa di; **the rent's ~ on the 30th** l'affitto scade il 30; **the train is ~ at 8** il treno è atteso per le 8; **she is ~ back tomorrow**

dovrebbe essere di ritorno domani; **I am ~ 6 days' leave** mi spettano 6 giorni di ferie

due date N data di scadenza

duel ['djuəl] N duello

duet [dju:'ɛt] N duetto

duff [dʌf] ADJ (BRIT col) barboso(-a)

duffelbag, duffle bag ['dʌflbæg] N sacca da viaggio di tela

duffelcoat, duffle coat ['dʌflkəut] N montgomery m inv

duffer ['dʌfəʳ] N (col) schiappa

dug [dʌg] PT, PP of **dig**

dugout ['dʌgaut] N (Football) panchina

duke [dju:k] N duca m

dull [dʌl] ADJ (light) debole; (boring) noioso(-a); (slow-witted) ottuso(-a); (sound, pain) sordo(-a); (weather, day) fosco(-a), scuro(-a); (blade) smussato(-a) ▶ VT (pain, grief) attutire; (mind, senses) intorpidire

duly ['dju:lɪ] ADV (on time) a tempo debito; (as expected) debitamente

dumb [dʌm] ADJ (!) muto(-a); (stupid) stupido(-a); **to be struck ~** (fig) ammutolire, restare senza parole

dumbbell ['dʌmbɛl] N (Sport) manubrio, peso

dumbfounded [dʌm'faundɪd] ADJ stupito(-a), stordito(-a)

dummy ['dʌmɪ] N (tailor's model) manichino; (Sport) finto; (Tech, Comm) riproduzione f; (BRIT: for baby) tettarella ▶ ADJ falso(-a), finto(-a)

dummy run N giro di prova

dump [dʌmp] N (also: **rubbish dump**) mucchio di rifiuti; (place) discarica; (Mil) deposito; (Comput) scaricamento, dump m inv ▶ VT (put down) scaricare; mettere giù; (get rid of) buttar via; (Comm: goods) svendere; (Comput) scaricare; **to be (down) in the dumps** (col) essere giù di corda

dumping ['dʌmpɪŋ] N (Econ) dumping m; **"no ~"** "vietato lo scarico"

dumpling ['dʌmplɪŋ] N specie di gnocco

dumpy ['dʌmpɪ] ADJ tracagnotto(-a)

dunce [dʌns] N asino

dune [dju:n] N duna

dung [dʌŋ] N concime m

dungarees [dʌŋgə'ri:z] NPL tuta

dungeon ['dʌndʒən] N prigione f sotterranea

dunk [dʌŋk] VT inzuppare

duo ['dju:əu] N (gen, Mus) duo m inv

duodenal [dju:əu'di:nl] ADJ (ulcer) duodenale

duodenum [dju:əu'di:nəm] N duodeno

dupe [dju:p] VT gabbare, ingannare

duplex ['dju:plɛks] N (US: house) casa con muro divisorio in comune con un'altra; (: also: **duplex apartment**) appartamento su due piani

duplicate N ['dju:plɪkət] doppio; (copy of letter

etc) duplicato ▶ VT ['dju:plɪkeɪt] duplicare; (on machine) ciclostilare ▶ ADJ (copy) conforme, esattamente uguale; **in ~** in duplice copia; **~ key** duplicato (della chiave)

duplicity [dju:'plɪsɪtɪ] N doppiezza, duplicità

durability [djuərə'bɪlɪtɪ] N durevolezza; resistenza

durable ['djuərəbl] ADJ durevole; (clothes, metal) resistente

duration [djuə'reɪʃən] N durata

duress [djuə'rɛs] N: **under ~** sotto costrizione

Durex® ['djuərɛks] N (BRIT) preservativo

during ['djuərɪŋ] PREP durante, nel corso di

dusk [dʌsk] N crepuscolo

dusky ['dʌskɪ] ADJ scuro(-a)

dust [dʌst] N polvere f ▶ VT (furniture) spolverare; (cake etc): **to ~ with** cospargere con ▶ **dust off** VT rispolverare

dustbin ['dʌstbɪn] N (BRIT) pattumiera

duster ['dʌstəʳ] N straccio per la polvere

dust jacket N sopraccoperta

dustman ['dʌstmən] N (irreg) (BRIT) netturbino

dustpan ['dʌstpæn] N pattumiera

dusty ['dʌstɪ] ADJ polveroso(-a)

Dutch [dʌtʃ] ADJ olandese ▶ N (Ling) olandese m ▶ ADV: **to go ~** or **dutch** (col) fare alla romana; **the ~** gli Olandesi

Dutch auction N asta all'olandese

Dutchman ['dʌtʃmən], **Dutchwoman** ['dʌtʃwumən] N (irreg) olandese mf

dutiable ['dju:tɪəbl] ADJ soggetto(-a) a dazio

dutiful ['dju:tɪful] ADJ (child) rispettoso(-a); (husband) premuroso(-a); (employee) coscienzioso(-a)

duty ['dju:tɪ] N dovere m; (tax) dazio, tassa **■ duties** NPL mansioni fpl; **on ~** di servizio; (Med: in hospital) di guardia; **off ~** libero(a), fuori servizio; **to make it one's ~ to do sth** assumersi l'obbligo di fare qc; **to pay ~ on sth** pagare il dazio su qc

duty-free ['dju:tɪ'fri:] ADJ esente da dazio; **~ shop** duty free m inv

duty officer N (Mil etc) ufficiale m di servizio

duvet ['du:veɪ] N (BRIT) piumino, piumone m

DV ABBR (= Deo volente) D.V.

DVD N ABBR (= digital versatile or video disc) DVD m inv

DVD burner N masterizzatore m (di) DVD

DVD player N lettore m DVD

DVD writer N masterizzatore m (di) DVD

DVLA N ABBR (BRIT: = Driver and Vehicle Licensing Agency) ≈ I.M.C.T.C. m (= Ispettorato Generale della Motorizzazione Civile e dei Trasporti in Concessione)

DVM N ABBR (US: = Doctor of Veterinary Medicine) titolo di studio

DVT N ABBR = **deep-vein thrombosis**

dwarf [dwɔːf] N (!) nano(-a) ▸ VT far apparire piccolo

dwell [dwɛl] (*pt, pp* **dwelt** [dwɛlt]) VI dimorare ▸ **dwell on** VT FUS indugiare su

dweller [ˈdwɛləʳ] N abitante *mf*; **city ~** cittadino(-a)

dwelling [ˈdwɛlɪŋ] N dimora

dwelt [dwɛlt] PT, PP *of* **dwell**

dwindle [ˈdwɪndl] VI diminuire, decrescere

dwindling [ˈdwɪndlɪŋ] ADJ (*strength, interest*) che si affievolisce; (*resources, supplies*) in diminuzione

dye [daɪ] N colore *m*; (*chemical*) colorante *m*, tintura ▸ VT tingere; **hair ~** tinta per capelli

dyestuffs [ˈdaɪstʌfs] NPL coloranti *mpl*

dying [ˈdaɪɪŋ] ADJ morente, moribondo(-a)

dyke [daɪk] N diga; (*channel*) canale *m* di scolo; (*causeway*) sentiero rialzato

dynamic [daɪˈnæmɪk] ADJ dinamico(-a)

dynamics [daɪˈnæmɪks] N, NPL dinamica

dynamite [ˈdaɪnəmaɪt] N dinamite *f* ▸ VT far saltare con la dinamite

dynamo [ˈdaɪnəməu] N dinamo *f inv*

dynasty [ˈdɪnəstɪ] N dinastia

dysentery [ˈdɪsntrɪ] N dissenteria

dyslexia [dɪsˈlɛksɪə] N dislessia

dyslexic [dɪsˈlɛksɪk] ADJ dislessico(-a)

dyspepsia [dɪsˈpɛpsɪə] N dispepsia

dyspraxia [dɪsˈpræksɪə] N disprassia *f*

dystrophy [ˈdɪstrəfɪ] N distrofia; **muscular ~** distrofia muscolare

d

Ee

E, e [iː] N (*letter*) E, e *f inv or m inv*; (*Mus*): **E** mi *m*; **E for Edward**, (*US*) **E for Easy** ≈ E come Empoli

E ABBR (= *east*) E ▶ N ABBR (= *Ecstasy*) ecstasy *f inv*

e- [iː] PREFIX e-

ea. ABBR = **each**

each [iːtʃ] ADJ ogni, ciascuno(-a) ▶ PRON ciascuno(-a), ognuno(-a); **~ one** ognuno(a); **~ other** si (*or* ci *etc*); **they hate ~ other** si odiano (l'un l'altro); **you are jealous of ~ other** siete gelosi l'uno dell'altro; **~ day** ogni giorno; **they have 2 books ~** hanno 2 libri ciascuno; **they cost £5 ~** costano 5 sterline l'uno; **~ of us** ciascuno *or* ognuno di noi

> Use a reflexive verb to translate *each other*.
> They love each other. **Si amano**.
> We write to each other. **Ci scriviamo**.

eager ['iːgəʳ] ADJ impaziente; desideroso(-a); ardente; (*keen: pupil*) appassionato(-a), attento(-a); **to be ~ to do sth** non veder l'ora di fare qc; essere desideroso di fare qc; **to be ~ for** essere desideroso di, aver gran voglia di

eagle ['iːgl] N aquila

E & OE ABBR (= *errors and omissions excepted*) S.E.O.

ear [ɪəʳ] N orecchio; (*of corn*) pannocchia; **up to the ears in debt** nei debiti fino al collo

earache ['ɪəreɪk] N mal *m* d'orecchi

eardrum ['ɪədrʌm] N timpano

earful ['ɪəful] N (*col*): **to give sb an ~** fare una ramanzina a qn

earl [əːl] N (*BRIT*) conte *m*

earlier ['əːlɪəʳ] ADJ (*date etc*) anteriore; (*edition etc*) precedente, anteriore ▶ ADV prima; **I can't come any ~** non posso venire prima

early ['əːlɪ] ADV presto, di buon'ora; (*ahead of time*) in anticipo ▶ ADJ primo(-a); anticipato(-a); (*man*) primitivo(-a); (*quick: reply*) veloce; **~ in the morning/afternoon** nelle prime ore del mattino/del pomeriggio; **you're ~!** sei in anticipo!; **at an ~ hour** di buon'ora; **have an ~ night/start** vada a letto/parta presto; **in the ~** *or* **~ in the spring/19th century** all'inizio della primavera/dell'Ottocento; **she's in her ~ forties** ha appena

passato la quarantina; **at your earliest convenience** (*Comm*) non appena possibile

early retirement N prepensionamento

early warning system N sistema *m* di preallarme

earmark ['ɪəmɑːk] VT: **to ~ sth for** destinare qc a

earn [əːn] VT guadagnare; (*rest, reward*) meritare; (*Comm: yield*) maturare; **to ~ one's living** guadagnarsi da vivere; **this earned him much praise, he earned much praise for this** si è attirato grandi lodi per questo

earned income N reddito da lavoro

earnest ['əːnɪst] ADJ serio(-a) ▶ N (*also:* **earnest money**) caparra; **in ~** adv sul serio

earnings ['əːnɪŋz] NPL guadagni *mpl*; (*of company etc*) proventi *mpl*; (*salary*) stipendio

ear, nose and throat specialist N otorinolaringoiatra *mf*

earphones ['ɪəfəunz] NPL cuffia

earplugs ['ɪəplʌgz] NPL tappi *mpl* per le orecchie

earring ['ɪərɪŋ] N orecchino

earshot ['ɪəʃɒt] N: **out of/within ~** fuori portata/a portata d'orecchio

earth [əːθ] N (*gen, also BRIT Elec*) terra; (*of fox etc*) tana ▶ VT (*BRIT Elec*) mettere a terra

earthenware ['əːθənwɛəʳ] N terracotta; stoviglie *fpl* di terracotta ▶ ADJ di terracotta

earthly ['əːθlɪ] ADJ terreno(-a); **~ paradise** paradiso terrestre; **there is no ~ reason to think …** non vi è ragione di pensare …

earthquake ['əːθkweɪk] N terremoto

earth-shattering ['əːθʃætərɪŋ] ADJ stupefacente

earth tremor N scossa sismica

earthworks ['əːθwəːks] NPL lavori *mpl* di sterro

earthworm ['əːθwəːm] N lombrico

earthy ['əːθɪ] ADJ (*fig*) grossolano(-a)

earwax ['ɪəwæks] N cerume *m*

earwig ['ɪəwɪg] N forbicina

ease [iːz] N agio, comodo ▶ VT (*soothe*) calmare; (*loosen*) allentare ▶ VI (*situation*) allentarsi, distendersi; **life of ~** vita comoda; **with ~** senza

difficoltà; **at ~** a proprio agio; (*Mil*) a riposo; **to feel at ~/ill at ~** sentirsi a proprio agio/a disagio; **to ~ sth out/in** tirare fuori/infilare qc con delicatezza; facilitare l'uscita/l'entrata di qc
▶ **ease off, ease up** vi diminuire; (*slow down*) rallentarsi; (*fig*) rilassarsi

easel ['iːzl] N cavalletto

easily ['iːzɪlɪ] ADV facilmente

easiness ['iːzɪnɪs] N facilità, semplicità; (*of manners*) disinvoltura

east [iːst] N est *m* ▶ ADJ dell'est ▶ ADV a oriente; **the E~** l'Oriente *m*; (*Pol*) i Paesi dell'Est

eastbound ['iːstbaund] ADJ (*traffic*) diretto(-a) a est; (*carriageway*) che porta a est

Easter ['iːstə^r] N Pasqua ▶ ADJ (*holidays*) pasquale, di Pasqua

Easter egg N uovo di Pasqua

Easter Island N isola di Pasqua

easterly ['iːstəlɪ] ADJ dall'est, d'oriente

Easter Monday N Pasquetta

eastern ['iːstən] ADJ orientale, d'oriente; (*Pol*) dell'est; **E~ Europe** l'Europa orientale; **the E~ bloc** (*Pol*) i Paesi dell'Est

Easter Sunday N domenica di Pasqua

East Germany N (*Hist*) Germania dell'Est

East Timor ['iːst'iːmɔː] N Timor Est *m*

eastward ['iːstwəd], **eastwards** ['iːstwədz] ADV verso est, verso levante

easy ['iːzɪ] ADJ facile; (*manner*) disinvolto(-a); (*carefree: life*) agiato(-a), tranquillo(-a) ▶ ADV: **to take it** *or* **things ~** prendersela con calma; **I'm ~** (*col*) non ho problemi; **easier said than done** tra il dire e il fare c'è di mezzo il mare; **payment on ~ terms** (*Comm*) facilitazioni fpl di pagamento

easy chair N poltrona

easy-going ['iːzɪ'gəuɪŋ] ADJ accomodante

eat [iːt] (*pt* **ate** [eɪt], *pp* **eaten** ['iːtn]) VT mangiare
▶ **eat away** VT (*sea*) erodere; (*acid*) corrodere
▶ **eat away at, eat into** VT FUS rodere
▶ **eat out** VI mangiare fuori
▶ **eat up** VT (*meal etc*) finire di mangiare; **it eats up electricity** consuma un sacco di corrente

eatable ['iːtəbl] ADJ mangiabile; (*safe to eat*) commestibile

eaten ['iːtn] PP *of* **eat**

eau de Cologne ['əudəkə'ləun] N acqua di colonia

eaves [iːvz] NPL gronda

eavesdrop ['iːvzdrɔp] VI: **to ~ (on a conversation)** origliare (una conversazione)

e-banking ['iːbæŋkɪŋ] N internet *or* home banking *m inv*

ebb [ɛb] N riflusso ▶ VI rifluire; (*fig: also:* **ebb away**) declinare; **~ and flow** flusso e riflusso; **to be at a low ~** (*fig: person, spirits*) avere il morale a terra; (*: business*) andar male

ebb tide N marea discendente

e-bike ['iːbaɪk] N bici(cletta) elettrica (a pedalata assistita), ebike *f inv*

ebony ['ɛbənɪ] N ebano

e-book ['iːbuk] N libro elettronico

ebullient [ɪ'bʌlɪənt] ADJ esuberante

e-business ['iːbɪznɪs] N (*company*) azienda che opera in Internet; (*commerce*) commercio elettronico

EC N ABBR (= *European Community*) CE *f*

e-card ['iːkɑːd] N e-card *f inv*, cartolina virtuale

ECB N ABBR (= *European Central Bank*) BCE *f*

eccentric [ɪk'sɛntrɪk] ADJ, N eccentrico(-a)

ecclesiastic [ɪkliːzɪ'æstɪk] N ecclesiastico ▶ ADJ ecclesiastico(-a)

ecclesiastical [ɪkliːzɪ'æstɪkəl] ADJ ecclesiastico(-a)

ECG N ABBR = **electrocardiogram**

echo ['ɛkəu] (*pl* **echoes**) N eco *m or f* ▶ VT ripetere; fare eco a ▶ VI echeggiare; dare un eco

e-cigarette ['iːsɪɡəret] N sigaretta elettronica

éclair ['eɪkleə^r] N ≈ bignè *m inv*

eclipse [ɪ'klɪps] N eclissi *f inv* ▶ VT eclissare

eco... ['iːkəu] PREFIX eco...

eco-friendly [iːkəu'frɛndlɪ] ADJ ecologico(-a)

ecological [iːkə'lɔdʒɪkəl] ADJ ecologico(-a)

ecologist [ɪ'kɔlədʒɪst] N ecologo(-a)

ecology [ɪ'kɔlədʒɪ] N ecologia

e-commerce [iː'kɔməːs] N commercio elettronico, e-commerce *m inv*

economic [iːkə'nɔmɪk] ADJ economico(-a); (*profitable: price*) vantaggioso(-a); (*: business*) che rende

economical [iːkə'nɔmɪkəl] ADJ economico(-a); (*person*) economo(-a)

economically [iːkə'nɔmɪklɪ] ADV con economia; (*regarding economics*) dal punto di vista economico

economics [iːkə'nɔmɪks] N economia ▶ NPL (*financial aspect*) lato finanziario

economist [ɪ'kɔnəmɪst] N economista *mf*

economize [ɪ'kɔnəmaɪz] VI risparmiare, fare economia

economy [ɪ'kɔnəmɪ] N economia; **economies of scale** (*Comm*) economie fpl di scala

economy class N (*Aviat etc*) classe *f* turistica

economy class syndrome N sindrome *f* della classe economica

economy size N confezione *f* economica

ecosystem ['iːkəusɪstəm] N ecosistema *m*

eco-tourism [iːkəu'tuərɪzəm] N ecoturismo

ecstasy ['ɛkstəsɪ] N estasi *f inv*; **to go into ecstasies over** andare in estasi davanti a; **E~** (*drug*) ecstasy *f inv*

ecstatic [ɛks'tætɪk] ADJ estatico(-a), in estasi

ECT N ABBR = **electroconvulsive therapy**

ECU, ecu [ˈeɪkjuː] N ABBR (= *European Currency Unit*) ECU *f inv*, ecu *f inv*

Ecuador [ˈɛkwədɔːˈ] N Ecuador *m*

ecumenical [iːkjuˈmɛnɪkl] ADJ ecumenico(-a)

eczema [ˈɛksɪmə] N eczema *m*

eddy [ˈɛdɪ] N mulinello

edge [ɛdʒ] N margine *m*; (*of table, plate, cup*) orlo; (*of knife etc*) taglio ▶ VT bordare ▶ VI: **to ~ away from** sgattaiolare da; **to ~ past** passar rasente; **to ~ forward** avanzare a poco a poco; **on ~** (*fig*) = **edgy**; **to have the ~ on** essere in vantaggio su; **to ~ away from** sgattaiolare da

edgeways [ˈɛdʒweɪz] ADV di fianco; **he couldn't get a word in ~** non riuscì a dire una parola

edging [ˈɛdʒɪŋ] N bordo

edgy [ˈɛdʒɪ] ADJ nervoso(-a)

edible [ˈɛdɪbl] ADJ commestibile; (*meal*) mangiabile

edict [ˈiːdɪkt] N editto

edifice [ˈɛdɪfɪs] N edificio

edifying [ˈɛdɪfaɪɪŋ] ADJ edificante

Edinburgh [ˈɛdɪnbərə] N Edimburgo *f*; *vedi nota*

> Il festival di Edimburgo (**Edinburgh Festival**) si svolge ogni anno in agosto per tre settimane ed è uno dei più famosi in Europa per la qualità degli artisti provenienti da tutte le parti del mondo. Il programma include rappresentazioni teatrali, commedie, opera e balletti, tradizionali e d'avanguardia, presentati sia nella sezione ufficiale che in quella denominata "*The Fringe*". Durante il *Festival*, sulla spianata del castello, si svolgono anche spettacoli di musica militare, l'*Edinburgh Military Tattoo*.

edit [ˈɛdɪt] VT curare; (*newspaper, magazine*) dirigere; (*Comput*) correggere e modificare, editare

edition [ɪˈdɪʃən] N edizione *f*

editor [ˈɛdɪtəˈ] N (*in newspaper*) redattore(-trice); redattore(-trice) capo; (*of sb's work*) curatore(-trice); (*film editor*) responsabile *mf* del montaggio

editorial [ɛdɪˈtɔːrɪəl] ADJ redazionale, editoriale ▶ N editoriale *m*; **the ~ staff** la redazione

EDP N ABBR = **electronic data processing**

EDT ABBR (*US*: = *Eastern Daylight Time*) ora legale di New York

educate [ˈɛdjukeɪt] VT istruire; educare

educated ADJ istruito(-a)

educated guess [ˈɛdjukeɪtɪd-] N ipotesi *f* ben fondata

education [ɛdjuˈkeɪʃən] N (*teaching*) insegnamento; (*schooling*) istruzione *f*; (*knowledge, culture*) cultura; (*Scol: subject etc*) pedagogia; **primary** *or* (*US*) **elementary/secondary ~** scuola primaria/secondaria

educational [ɛdjuˈkeɪʃənl] ADJ pedagogico(-a); scolastico(-a); istruttivo(-a); **~ technology** tecnologie *fpl* applicate alla didattica

Edwardian [ɛdˈwɔːdɪən] ADJ edoardiano(-a)

EEG N ABBR = **electroencephalogram**

eel [iːl] N anguilla

EENT N ABBR (*US Med*) = **eye, ear, nose and throat**

EEOC N ABBR (*US*) = **Equal Employment Opportunity Commission**

eerie [ˈɪərɪ] ADJ che fa accapponare la pelle

EET ABBR (= *Eastern European Time*) fuso orario

effect [ɪˈfɛkt] N effetto ▶ VT effettuare; **to take ~** (*law*) entrare in vigore; (*drug*) fare effetto; **to have an ~ on sb/sth** avere *or* produrre un effetto su qn/qc; **to put into ~** (*plan*) attuare; **in ~** effettivamente; **his letter is to the ~ that ...** il contenuto della sua lettera è che ...; *see also* **effects**

effective [ɪˈfɛktɪv] ADJ efficace; (*actual*) effettivo(-a); (*striking: display, outfit*) che fa colpo; **~ date** data d'entrata in vigore; **to become ~** (*law*) entrare in vigore

effectively [ɪˈfɛktɪvlɪ] ADV (*efficiently*) efficacemente; effettivamente; (*strikingly*) ad effetto; (*in reality*) di fatto; (*in effect*) in effetti

effectiveness [ɪˈfɛktɪvnɪs] N efficacia

effects [ɪˈfɛkts] NPL (*Theat*) effetti *mpl* scenici; (*property*) effetti *mpl*

effeminate [ɪˈfɛmɪnɪt] ADJ effeminato(-a)

effervescent [ɛfəˈvɛsnt] ADJ effervescente

efficacy [ˈɛfɪkəsɪ] N efficacia

efficiency [ɪˈfɪʃənsɪ] N efficienza; rendimento effettivo

efficiency apartment N (*US*) miniappartamento

efficient [ɪˈfɪʃənt] ADJ efficiente; (*remedy, product, system*) efficace; (*machine, car*) che ha un buon rendimento

efficiently [ɪˈfɪʃəntlɪ] ADV efficientemente; efficacemente

effigy [ˈɛfɪdʒɪ] N effigie *f*

effluent [ˈɛfluənt] N effluente *m*

effort [ˈɛfət] N sforzo; **to make an ~ to do sth** sforzarsi di fare qc

effortless [ˈɛfətlɪs] ADJ senza sforzo, facile

effrontery [ɪˈfrʌntərɪ] N sfrontatezza

effusive [ɪˈfjuːsɪv] ADJ (*person*) espansivo(-a); (*welcome, letter*) caloroso(-a); (*thanks, apologies*) interminabile

EFL N ABBR (*Scol*) = **English as a foreign language**

EFTA [ˈɛftə] N ABBR (= *European Free Trade Association*) E.F.T.A. *f*

e.g. ADV ABBR (= *exempli gratia*) per esempio, p.es.

egalitarian [ɪgælɪˈtɛərɪən] ADJ egualitario(-a)

egg [ɛg] N uovo; **hard-boiled/soft-boiled ~** uovo sodo/alla coque
▶ **egg on** VT incitare

eggcup [ˈɛgkʌp] N portauovo *m inv*

eggplant [ˈɛɡplɑːnt] N (esp US) melanzana

eggshell [ˈɛɡʃɛl] N guscio d'uovo ▸ADJ (colour) guscio d'uovo inv

egg-timer [ˈɛgtaɪmər] N clessidra (per misurare il tempo di cottura delle uova)

egg white N albume m, bianco d'uovo

egg yolk N tuorlo, rosso (d'uovo)

ego [ˈiːgəu] N ego m inv

egoism [ˈɛgəuɪzəm] N egoismo

egoist [ˈɛgəuɪst] N egoista mf

egotism [ˈɛgəutɪzəm] N egotismo

egotist [ˈɛgəutɪst] N egotista mf

ego trip N: to be on an ~ gasarsi

Egypt [ˈiːdʒɪpt] N Egitto

Egyptian [ɪˈdʒɪpʃən] ADJ, N egiziano(-a)

eiderdown [ˈaɪdədaun] N piumino

eight [eɪt] NUM otto

eighteen [ˈeɪˈtiːn] NUM diciotto

eighteenth [eɪˈtiːnθ] NUM diciottesimo(-a)

eighth [eɪtθ] NUM ottavo(-a)

eightieth [ˈeɪtɪɪθ] NUM ottantesimo(-a)

eighty [eɪtɪ] NUM ottanta

Eire [ˈɛərə] N Repubblica d'Irlanda

EIS N ABBR (= Educational Institute of Scotland) principale sindacato degli insegnanti in Scozia

either [ˈaɪðər] ADJ l'uno(-a) o l'altro(-a); (both, each) ciascuno(-a); on ~ side su ciascun lato ▸PRON: ~ (of them) (o) l'uno(-a) o l'altro(a); I don't like ~ non mi piace né l'uno né l'altro ▸ADV neanche; no, I don't ~ no, neanch'io ▸CONJ: ~ good or bad o buono o cattivo; I haven't seen ~ one or the other non ho visto né l'uno né l'altro

ejaculation [ɪdʒækjuˈleɪʃən] N (Physiol) eiaculazione f

eject [ɪˈdʒɛkt] VT espellere; lanciare ▸VI (pilot) catapultarsi

ejector seat [ɪˈdʒɛktə-] N sedile m eiettabile

eke [iːk] to ~ out VT far durare; aumentare

EKG N ABBR (US) = **electrocardiogram**

el [ɛl] N ABBR (US col) = **elevated railroad**

elaborate ADJ [ɪˈlæbərɪt] elaborato(-a), minuzioso(-a) ▸VT [ɪˈlæbəreɪt] elaborare ▸VI [ɪˈlæbəreɪt] fornire i dettagli

elapse [ɪˈlæps] VI trascorrere, passare

elastic [ɪˈlæstɪk] ADJ elastico(-a) ▸N elastico

elastic band N (BRIT) elastico

elasticity [ɪlæsˈtɪsɪtɪ] N elasticità

elated [ɪˈleɪtɪd] ADJ pieno(-a) di gioia

elation [ɪˈleɪʃən] N gioia

elbow [ˈɛlbəu] N gomito ▸VT: to ~ one's way through the crowd farsi largo tra la folla a gomitate

elbow grease N: to use a bit of ~ usare un po' di olio di gomiti

elbowroom [ˈɛlbəurum] N spazio

elder [ˈɛldər] ADJ maggiore, più vecchio(-a) ▸N (tree) sambuco; one's elders i più anziani

elderly [ˈɛldəlɪ] ADJ anziano(-a); ~ people gli anziani

elder statesman N (irreg) anziano uomo politico in pensione, ma ancora influente; (of company) anziano(-a) consigliere(-a)

eldest [ˈɛldɪst] ADJ, N: the ~ (child) il(la) maggiore (dei bambini)

elect [ɪˈlɛkt] VT eleggere; (choose): to ~ to do decidere di fare ▸ADJ: the president ~ il presidente designato

election [ɪˈlɛkʃən] N elezione f; to hold an ~ indire un'elezione

election campaign N campagna elettorale

electioneering [ɪlɛkʃəˈnɪərɪŋ] N propaganda elettorale

elector [ɪˈlɛktər] N elettore(-trice)

electoral [ɪˈlɛktərəl] ADJ elettorale

electoral college N collegio elettorale

electoral roll N (BRIT) registro elettorale

electoral system N sistema m elettorale

electorate [ɪˈlɛktərɪt] N elettorato

electric [ɪˈlɛktrɪk] ADJ elettrico(-a)

electrical [ɪˈlɛktrɪkəl] ADJ elettrico(-a)

electrical engineer N ingegnere m elettrotecnico

electrical failure N guasto all'impianto elettrico

electric blanket N coperta elettrica

electric chair N sedia elettrica

electric cooker N cucina elettrica

electric current N corrente f elettrica

electric fire N (BRIT) stufa elettrica

electrician [ɪlɛkˈtrɪʃən] N elettricista m

electricity [ɪlɛkˈtrɪsɪtɪ] N elettricità; to switch on/off the ~ attaccare/staccare la corrente

electricity board N (BRIT) ente m regionale per l'energia elettrica

electric light N luce f elettrica

electric shock N scossa (elettrica)

electrify [ɪˈlɛktrɪfaɪ] VT (Rail) elettrificare; (audience) elettrizzare

electro... [ɪˈlɛktrəu] PREFIX elettro...

electrocardiogram [ɪˈlɛktrəˈkɑːdɪəgræm] N elettrocardiogramma m

electroconvulsive therapy [ɪˈlɛktrəkənˈvʌlsɪv-] N elettroshockterapia

electrocute [ɪˈlɛktrəkjuːt] VT fulminare

electrode [ɪˈlɛktrəud] N elettrodo

electroencephalogram [ɪˈlɛktrəuɛnˈsɛfələgræm] N (Med) elettroencefalogramma m

electrolysis [ɪlɛkˈtrɔlɪsɪs] N elettrolisi f

electromagnetic [ɪˈlɛktrəumægˈnɛtɪk] N elettromagnetico(-a)

e

electron [ɪˈlɛktrɔn] N elettrone m

electronic [ɪlɛkˈtrɔnɪk] ADJ elettronico(-a); *see also* **electronics**

electronic data processing N elaborazione f elettronica di dati

electronic mail N posta elettronica

electronics [ɪlɛkˈtrɔnɪks] N elettronica

electron microscope N microscopio elettronico

electroplated [ɪˈlɛktrəuˈpleɪtɪd] ADJ galvanizzato(-a)

electrotherapy [ɪˈlɛktrəuˈθɛrəpɪ] N elettroterapia

elegance [ˈɛlɪgəns] N eleganza

elegant [ˈɛlɪgənt] ADJ elegante

element [ˈɛlɪmənt] N elemento; (*of heater, kettle etc*) resistenza

elementary [ɛlɪˈmɛntərɪ] ADJ elementare

elementary school N (US) scuola elementare

> Negli Stati Uniti e in Canada, i bambini frequentano la **elementary school** per almeno sei anni, a volte anche per otto. Negli Stati Uniti si chiama anche *grade school* o *grammar school*.

elephant [ˈɛlɪfənt] N elefante(-essa)

elevate [ˈɛlɪveɪt] VT elevare

elevated railroad, el N (US) (ferrovia) soprelevata

elevation [ɛlɪˈveɪʃən] N elevazione f; (*height*) altitudine f

elevator [ˈɛlɪveɪtəʳ] N elevatore m; (US: lift) ascensore m

eleven [ɪˈlɛvn] NUM undici

elevenses [ɪˈlɛvnzɪz] NPL (BRIT) caffè m a metà mattina

eleventh [ɪˈlɛvnθ] ADJ undicesimo(-a); **at the ~ hour** (fig) all'ultimo minuto

elf [ɛlf] (pl **elves** [ɛlvz]) N elfo

elicit [ɪˈlɪsɪt] VT: **to ~ (from)** trarre (da), cavare fuori (da); **to ~ sth (from sb)** strappare qc (a qn)

eligible [ˈɛlɪdʒəbl] ADJ eleggibile; (*for membership*) che ha i requisiti; **to be ~ for a pension** essere pensionabile

eliminate [ɪˈlɪmɪneɪt] VT eliminare

elimination [ɪlɪmɪˈneɪʃən] N eliminazione f; **by process of ~** per eliminazione

élite [eɪˈliːt] N élite f inv

elitist [eɪˈliːtɪst] ADJ (pej) elitario(-a)

elixir [ɪˈlɪksəʳ] N elisir m inv

Elizabethan [ɪlɪzəˈbiːθən] N elisabettiano(-a)

ellipse [ɪˈlɪps] N ellisse f

elliptical [ɪˈlɪptɪkl] ADJ ellittico(-a)

elm [ɛlm] N olmo

elocution [ɛləˈkjuːʃən] N elocuzione f

elongated [ˈiːlɔŋgeɪtɪd] ADJ allungato(-a)

elope [ɪˈləup] VI (*lovers*) scappare

elopement [ɪˈləupmənt] N fuga romantica

eloquence [ˈɛləkwəns] N eloquenza

eloquent [ˈɛləkwənt] ADJ eloquente

El Salvador [ɛl ˈsælvədɔː] N El Salvador m

else [ɛls] ADV altro; **something ~** qualcos'altro; **somewhere ~** altrove; **everywhere ~** in qualsiasi altro luogo; **nobody ~** nessun altro; **where ~?** in quale altro luogo?; **little ~** poco altro; **everyone ~** tutti gli altri; **nothing ~** nient'altro; **or ~** (otherwise) altrimenti; **is there anything ~ I can do?** posso fare qualcos'altro?

elsewhere [ɛlsˈwɛəʳ] ADV altrove

ELT N ABBR (Scol) = **English Language Teaching**

elucidate [ɪˈluːsɪdeɪt] VT delucidare

elude [ɪˈluːd] VT eludere

elusive [ɪˈluːsɪv] ADJ elusivo(-a); (*answer*) evasivo(-a); **he is very ~** è proprio inafferrabile *or* irraggiungibile

elves [ɛlvz] NPL of **elf**

emaciated [ɪˈmeɪsɪeɪtɪd] ADJ emaciato(-a)

email [ˈiːmeɪl] N ABBR (= electronic mail) posta elettronica, e-mail m inv ▶ VT mandare un messaggio di posta elettronica *or* un e-mail a; **to ~ sb** comunicare con qn mediante posta elettronica; **~ account** account m inv di posta elettronica

email address N indirizzo di posta elettronica

emanate [ˈɛməneɪt] VI: **to ~ from** emanare da

emancipate [ɪˈmænsɪpeɪt] VT emancipare

emancipation [ɪmænsɪˈpeɪʃən] N emancipazione f

emasculate [ɪˈmæskjuleɪt] VT (fig) rendere impotente

embalm [ɪmˈbɑːm] VT imbalsamare

embankment [ɪmˈbæŋkmənt] N (of road, railway) massicciata; (riverside) argine m; (dyke) diga

embargo [ɪmˈbɑːgəu] (pl **embargoes**) N (Comm, Naut) embargo ▶ VT mettere l'embargo su; **to put an ~ on sth** mettere l'embargo su qc

embark [ɪmˈbɑːk] VI: **to ~ (on)** imbarcarsi (su) ▶ VT imbarcare; **to ~ on** (fig) imbarcarsi in; (journey) intraprendere

embarkation [ɛmbɑːˈkeɪʃən] N imbarco

embarkation card N carta d'imbarco

embarrass [ɪmˈbærəs] VT imbarazzare

embarrassed ADJ imbarazzato(-a); **to be ~** essere imbarazzato(-a)

embarrassing [ɪmˈbærəsɪŋ] ADJ imbarazzante

embarrassment [ɪmˈbærəsmənt] N imbarazzo

embassy [ˈɛmbəsɪ] N ambasciata; **the Italian E~** l'ambasciata d'Italia

embed [ɪmˈbɛd] VT conficcare; incastrare

embellish [ɪmˈbɛlɪʃ] VT abbellire; **to ~ (with)** (fig: story, truth) infiorare (con)

embers [ˈɛmbəz] NPL braci fpl

embezzle [ɪmˈbɛzl] VT appropriarsi indebitamente di

embezzlement [ɪmˈbɛzlmənt] N appropriazione f indebita, malversazione f

embezzler [ɪmˈbɛzləʳ] N malversatore(-trice)

embitter [ɪmˈbɪtəʳ] VT amareggiare; inasprire

emblem [ˈɛmbləm] N emblema m

embodiment [ɪmˈbɔdɪmənt] N personificazione f, incarnazione f

embody [ɪmˈbɔdɪ] VT (features) racchiudere, comprendere; (ideas) dar forma concreta a, esprimere

embolden [ɪmˈbəʊldn] VT incitare

embolism [ˈɛmbəlɪzəm] N embolia

embossed [ɪmˈbɔst] ADJ in rilievo; goffrato(-a); ~ with ... con in rilievo ...

embrace [ɪmˈbreɪs] VT abbracciare; (include) comprendere ▶ VI abbracciarsi ▶ N abbraccio

embroider [ɪmˈbrɔɪdəʳ] VT ricamare; (fig: story) abbellire

embroidery [ɪmˈbrɔɪdərɪ] N ricamo

embroil [ɪmˈbrɔɪl] VT: **to become embroiled (in sth)** restare invischiato(a) (in qc)

embryo [ˈɛmbrɪəʊ] N (also fig) embrione m

emcee [ɛmˈsiː] N ABBR = **master of ceremonies**

emend [ɪˈmɛnd] VT (text) correggere, emendare

emerald [ˈɛmərəld] N smeraldo

emerge [ɪˈmɜːdʒ] VI apparire, emergere; **it emerges that** (BRIT) risulta che

emergence [ɪˈmɜːdʒəns] N apparizione f; (of nation) nascita

emergency [ɪˈmɜːdʒənsɪ] N emergenza; **in an ~** in caso di emergenza; **to declare a state of ~** dichiarare lo stato di emergenza

emergency brake N (US) freno a mano

emergency exit N uscita di sicurezza

emergency landing N atterraggio forzato

emergency lane N (US Aut) corsia d'emergenza

emergency road service N (US) servizio riparazioni

emergency room (US Med) N pronto soccorso

emergency service N servizio di pronto intervento

emergency stop N (BRIT Aut) frenata improvvisa

emergent [ɪˈmɜːdʒənt] ADJ: **~ nation** paese m in via di sviluppo

emery board [ˈɛmərɪ-] N limetta di carta smerigliata

emery paper N carta smerigliata

emetic [ɪˈmɛtɪk] N emetico

emigrant [ˈɛmɪgrənt] N emigrante mf

emigrate [ˈɛmɪgreɪt] VI emigrare

emigration [ɛmɪˈgreɪʃən] N emigrazione f

émigré [ˈɛmɪgreɪ] N emigrato(-a)

eminence [ˈɛmɪnəns] N eminenza

eminent [ˈɛmɪnənt] ADJ eminente

eminently [ˈɛmɪnəntlɪ] ADV assolutamente, perfettamente

emirate [ɛˈmɪərɪt] N emirato

emission [ɪˈmɪʃən] N (of gas, radiation) emissione f

emit [ɪˈmɪt] VT emettere

emoji [ɪˈməʊdʒɪ] N emoji m inv

emolument [ɪˈmɔljumənt] N (often pl: formal) emolumento

emoticon [ɪˈməʊtɪkən] N (Comput) faccina

emotion [ɪˈməʊʃən] N emozione f; (love, jealousy etc) sentimento

emotional [ɪˈməʊʃənl] ADJ (person) emotivo(-a); (scene) commovente; (tone, speech) carico(-a) d'emozione

emotionally [ɪˈməʊʃnəlɪ] ADV (behave, be involved) sentimentalmente; (speak) con emozione; **~ disturbed** con turbe emotive

emotive [ɪˈməʊtɪv] ADJ emotivo(-a); **~ power** capacità di commuovere

empathy [ˈɛmpəθɪ] N immedesimazione f; **to feel ~ with sb** immedesimarsi con i sentimenti di qn

emperor [ˈɛmpərəʳ] N imperatore(-trice)

emphasis [ˈɛmfəsɪs] (pl **emphases** [-siːz]) N enfasi f inv; importanza; **to lay** or **place ~ on sth** (fig) mettere in risalto or in evidenza qc; **the ~ is on sport** si dà molta importanza allo sport

emphasize [ˈɛmfəsaɪz] VT (word, point) sottolineare; (feature) mettere in evidenza

emphatic [ɪmˈfætɪk] ADJ (strong) vigoroso(-a); (unambiguous, clear) netto(-a), categorico(-a)

emphatically [ɪmˈfætɪkəlɪ] ADV vigorosamente; nettamente

emphysema [ɛmfɪˈsiːmə] N (Med) enfisema m

empire [ˈɛmpaɪəʳ] N impero

empirical [ɛmˈpɪrɪkl] ADJ empirico(-a)

employ [ɪmˈplɔɪ] VT (make use of: thing, method, person) impiegare, servirsi di; (give job to) dare lavoro a, impiegare; **he's employed in a bank** lavora in banca

employee [ɪmplɔɪˈiː] N impiegato(-a)

employer [ɪmˈplɔɪəʳ] N principale mf, datore(-trice) di lavoro

employment [ɪmˈplɔɪmənt] N impiego; **to find ~** trovare impiego or lavoro; **without ~** disoccupato(a); **place of ~** posto di lavoro

employment agency N agenzia di collocamento

employment exchange N (BRIT) ufficio m collocamento inv

empower [ɪmˈpaʊəʳ] VT: **to ~ sb to do** concedere autorità a qn di fare

empress [ˈɛmprɪs] N imperatrice f

emptiness [ˈɛmptɪnɪs] N vuoto

empty [ˈɛmptɪ] ADJ vuoto(-a); (street, area) deserto(-a); (threat, promise) vano(-a) ▶ N (bottle) vuoto ▶ VT vuotare ▶ VI vuotarsi; (liquid) scaricarsi; **on an ~ stomach** a stomaco vuoto; **to ~ into** (river) gettarsi in

empty-handed [ɛmptɪˈhændɪd] ADJ a mani vuote

empty-headed [ɛmptɪˈhɛdɪd] ADJ sciocco(-a)

EMT N ABBR (US) = **emergency medical technician**

EMU N ABBR (= European Monetary Union) Unità f monetaria europea; (= economic and monetary union) UEM f

emulate [ˈɛmjuleɪt] VT emulare

emulsion [ɪˈmʌlʃən] N emulsione f; (also: **emulsion paint**) colore m a tempera

enable [ɪˈneɪbl] VT: **to ~ sb to do** permettere a qn di fare

enact [ɪnˈækt] VT (law) emanare; (play, scene) rappresentare

enamel [ɪˈnæməl] N smalto

enamel paint N vernice f a smalto

enamoured [ɪˈnæməd] ADJ: **~ of** innamorato(-a) di

enc. ABBR (on letters etc: = enclosed, enclosure) all., alleg.

encampment [ɪnˈkæmpmənt] N accampamento

encased [ɪnˈkeɪst] ADJ: **~ in** racchiuso(-a) in, rivestito(-a) di

enchant [ɪnˈtʃɑːnt] VT incantare; (magic spell) catturare

enchanting [ɪnˈtʃɑːntɪŋ] ADJ incantevole, affascinante

encircle [ɪnˈsəːkl] VT accerchiare

encl. ABBR (on letters etc: = enclosed, enclosure) all., alleg.

enclose [ɪnˈkləuz] VT (land) circondare, recingere; (letter etc): **to ~ (with)** allegare (con); **please find enclosed** trovi qui accluso

enclosure [ɪnˈkləuʒəʳ] N recinto; (Comm) allegato

encoder [ɪnˈkəudəʳ] N (Comput) codificatore m

encompass [ɪnˈkʌmpəs] VT comprendere

encore [ɔŋˈkɔːʳ] EXCL, N bis (m inv)

encounter [ɪnˈkauntəʳ] N incontro ▶ VT incontrare

encourage [ɪnˈkʌrɪdʒ] VT incoraggiare; (industry, growth etc) favorire; **to ~ sb to do sth** incoraggiare qn a fare qc

encouragement [ɪnˈkʌrɪdʒmənt] N incoraggiamento

encouraging [ɪnˈkʌrɪdʒɪŋ] ADJ incoraggiante

encroach [ɪnˈkrəutʃ] VI: **to ~ (up)on** (rights) usurpare; (time) abusare di; (land) oltrepassare i limiti di

encrusted [ɪnˈkrʌstɪd] ADJ: **~ with** incrostato(-a) di

encrypt [ɪnˈkrɪpt] VT (Comput, Tel) criptare

encumbered [ɪnˈkʌmbəd] ADJ: **to be ~ (with)** essere carico(-a) di

encyclopedia, encyclopaedia [ɛnsaɪkləuˈpiːdɪə] N enciclopedia

end [ɛnd] N fine f; (aim) fine m; (of table) bordo estremo; (of line, rope etc) estremità f inv; (of pointed object) punta; (of town) parte f ▶ VT finire; (also: **bring to an end, put an end to**) mettere fine a ▶ VI finire; **from ~ to ~** da un'estremità all'altra; **to come to an ~** arrivare alla fine, finire; **to be at an ~** essere finito; **in the ~** alla fine; **at the ~ of the street** in fondo alla strada; **at the ~ of the day** (BRIT fig) in fin dei conti; **on ~** (object) ritto(-a); **to stand on ~** (hair) rizzarsi; **for 5 hours on ~** per 5 ore di fila; **for hours on ~** per ore e ore; **to this ~, with this ~ in view** a questo fine; **to ~ (with)** concludere (con)
▶ **end up** VI: **to ~ up in** finire in

> In Italian **la fine** is used when end means the conclusion of something, e.g. the end of the film **la fine del film**. Use **il fine** when end means the aim you want to achieve, e.g. The end justifies the means. **Il fine giustifica i mezzi**.

endanger [ɪnˈdeɪndʒəʳ] VT mettere in pericolo; **an endangered species** una specie in via di estinzione

endear [ɪnˈdɪəʳ] VT: **to ~ o.s. to sb** accattivarsi le simpatie di qn

endearing [ɪnˈdɪərɪŋ] ADJ accattivante

endearment [ɪnˈdɪəmənt] N: **to whisper endearments** sussurrare tenerezze; **term of ~** vezzeggiativo, parola affettuosa

endeavour, (US) **endeavor** [ɪnˈdɛvəʳ] N sforzo, tentativo ▶ VI: **to ~ to do** cercare or sforzarsi di fare

endemic [ɛnˈdɛmɪk] ADJ endemico(-a)

ending [ˈɛndɪŋ] N fine f, conclusione f; (Ling) desinenza

endive [ˈɛndaɪv] N (curly) indivia (riccia); (smooth, flat) indivia belga

endless [ˈɛndlɪs] ADJ senza fine; (patience, resources) infinito(-a); (possibilities) illimitato(-a)

endorse [ɪnˈdɔːs] VT (cheque) girare; (approve) approvare, appoggiare

endorsee [ɪndɔːˈsiː] N giratario(-a)

endorsement [ɪnˈdɔːsmənt] N (approval) approvazione f; (signature) firma; (BRIT: on driving licence) contravvenzione registrata sulla patente

endorser [ɪnˈdɔːsəʳ] N girante mf

endow [ɪnˈdau] VT (prize) istituire; (hospital) fondare; (provide with money) devolvere denaro a; (equip): **to ~ with** fornire di, dotare di

endowment [ɪnˈdaumənt] N istituzione f; fondazione f; (amount) donazione f

endowment mortgage N *mutuo che viene ripagato sotto forma di un'assicurazione a vita*

endowment policy N polizza-vita mista

end product N (*Industry*) prodotto finito; (*fig*) risultato

end result N risultato finale

endurable [ɪn'djuərəbl] ADJ sopportabile

endurance [ɪn'djuərəns] N resistenza; pazienza

endurance test N prova di resistenza

endure [ɪn'djuə'] VT sopportare, resistere a ▶ VI durare

enduring [ɪn'djuərɪŋ] ADJ duraturo(-a)

end user N (*Comput*) consumatore(-trice) effettivo(-a)

enema ['ɛnɪmə] N (*Med*) clistere *m*

enemy ['ɛnəmɪ] ADJ, N nemico(-a); **to make an ~ of sb** inimicarsi qn

energetic [ɛnə'dʒɛtɪk] ADJ energico(-a), attivo(-a)

energy ['ɛnədʒɪ] N energia; **Department of E~** (*US*) Ministero dell'Energia

energy crisis N crisi *f* energetica

energy drink N bevanda energetica

energy-saving ['ɛnədʒɪ'seɪvɪŋ] ADJ (*policy*) del risparmio energetico; (*device*) che risparmia energia

enervating ['ɛnə:veɪtɪŋ] ADJ debilitante

enforce [ɪn'fɔ:s] VT (*Law*) applicare, far osservare

enforced [ɪn'fɔ:st] ADJ forzato(-a)

enfranchise [ɪn'fræntʃaɪz] VT (*give vote to*) concedere il diritto di voto a; (*set free*) affrancare

engage [ɪn'geɪdʒ] VT (*hire*) assumere; (*lawyer*) incaricare; (*attention, interest*) assorbire; (*Mil*) attaccare; (*Tech*): **to ~ gear/the clutch** innestare la marcia/la frizione ▶ VI (*Tech*) ingranare; **to ~ in** impegnarsi in; **he is engaged in research/a survey** si occupa di ricerca/di un'inchiesta; **to ~ sb in conversation** attaccare conversazione con qn

engaged [ɪn'geɪdʒd] ADJ (*BRIT: busy, in use*) occupato(-a); (*betrothed*) fidanzato(-a); **the line's ~** (*BRIT*) la linea è occupata; **to get ~** fidanzarsi

engaged tone N (*BRIT Tel*) segnale *m* di occupato

engagement [ɪn'geɪdʒmənt] N impegno, obbligo; appuntamento; (*to marry*) fidanzamento; (*Mil*) combattimento; **I have a previous ~** ho già un impegno

engagement ring N anello di fidanzamento

engaging [ɪn'geɪdʒɪŋ] ADJ attraente

engender [ɪn'dʒɛndə'] VT produrre, causare

engine ['ɛndʒɪn] N (*Aut*) motore *m*; (*Rail*) locomotiva

engine driver N (*BRIT: of train*) macchinista *m*

engineer [ɛndʒɪ'nɪə'] N ingegnere *m*; (*BRIT: for domestic appliances*) tecnico; (*US Rail*) macchinista *m*; **civil/mechanical ~** ingegnere civile/meccanico

engineering [ɛndʒɪ'nɪərɪŋ] N ingegneria ▶ CPD (*works, factory, worker etc*) metalmeccanico(-a)

engine failure N guasto al motore

engine trouble N panne *f*

England ['ɪŋglənd] N Inghilterra

English ['ɪŋglɪʃ] ADJ inglese ▶ N (*Ling*) inglese *m* ◼ **the English** NPL gli Inglesi; **to be an ~ speaker** essere anglofono(a)

English Channel N: **the ~** il Canale della Manica

Englishman ['ɪŋglɪʃmən] N (*irreg*) inglese *m*

English-speaking ['ɪŋglɪʃspi:kɪŋ] ADJ di lingua inglese

Englishwoman ['ɪŋglɪʃwumən] N (*irreg*) inglese *f*

engrave [ɪn'greɪv] VT incidere

engraving [ɪn'greɪvɪŋ] N incisione *f*

engrossed [ɪn'grəust] ADJ: **~ in** assorbito(a) da, preso(a) da

engulf [ɪn'gʌlf] VT inghiottire

enhance [ɪn'hɑ:ns] VT accrescere; (*position, reputation*) migliorare

enigma [ɪ'nɪgmə] N enigma *m*

enigmatic [ɛnɪg'mætɪk] ADJ enigmatico(-a)

enjoy [ɪn'dʒɔɪ] VT godere; (*have: success, fortune*) avere; (*have benefit of: health*) godere (di); **I ~ dancing** mi piace ballare; **to ~ o.s.** godersela, divertirsi

---

To translate a sentence like *I enjoy it/doing it* into Italian, you have to rephrase it as *It/Doing it is pleasing to me*. If what you enjoy is singular, the verb is singular; if it is plural, the verb is plural.
Did you enjoy the film? **Ti è piaciuto il film?**
I enjoy reading detective stories. **Mi piace leggere i gialli**.

---

enjoyable [ɪn'dʒɔɪəbl] ADJ piacevole

enjoyment [ɪn'dʒɔɪmənt] N piacere *m*, godimento

enlarge [ɪn'lɑ:dʒ] VT ingrandire ▶ VI: **to ~ on** (*subject*) dilungarsi su

enlarged [ɪn'lɑ:dʒd] ADJ (*edition*) ampliato(-a); (*Med: organ, gland*) ingrossato(-a)

enlargement [ɪn'lɑ:dʒmənt] N (*Phot*) ingrandimento

enlighten [ɪn'laɪtn] VT illuminare; dare chiarimenti a

enlightened [ɪn'laɪtnd] ADJ illuminato(-a)

enlightening [ɪn'laɪtnɪŋ] ADJ istruttivo(-a)

enlightenment [ɪn'laɪtnmənt] N progresso culturale; chiarimenti *mpl*; (*Hist*): **the E~** l'Illuminismo

enlist [ɪnˈlɪst] VT arruolare; (*support*) procurare ▸ VI arruolarsi; **enlisted man** (*US Mil*) soldato semplice

enliven [ɪnˈlaɪvn] VT (*people*) rallegrare; (*events*) ravvivare

enmity [ˈɛnmɪtɪ] N inimicizia

ennoble [ɪˈnəubl] VT nobilitare; (*with title*) conferire un titolo nobiliare a

enormity [ɪˈnɔːmɪtɪ] N enormità *f inv*

enormous [ɪˈnɔːməs] ADJ enorme

enormously [ɪˈnɔːməslɪ] ADV enormemente

enough [ɪˈnʌf] ADJ, N: **~ time/books** assai tempo/libri; **have you got ~?** ne ha abbastanza *or* a sufficienza? ▸ ADV: **big ~** abbastanza grande; **he has not worked ~** non ha lavorato abbastanza; **~!** basta!; **it's hot ~ (as it is)!** fa abbastanza caldo così!; **will £5 be ~?** bastano 5 sterline?; **that's ~, thanks** basta così, grazie; **I've had ~!** non ne posso più!; **I've had ~ of him** ne ho abbastanza di lui; **he was kind ~ to lend me the money** è stato così gentile da prestarmi i soldi; **... which, funnily ~** ... che, strano a dirsi

enquire [ɪnˈkwaɪəʳ] VT, VI (*esp* BRIT) = **inquire**

enquiry [ɪnˈkwaɪərɪ] N (*esp* BRIT) = **inquiry**

enrage [ɪnˈreɪdʒ] VT fare arrabbiare

enrich [ɪnˈrɪtʃ] VT arricchire

enrol, (*US*) **enroll** [ɪnˈrəul] VT iscrivere; (*at university*) immatricolare ▸ VI iscriversi

enrolment, (*US*) **enrollment** [ɪnˈrəulmənt] N iscrizione *f*

en route [ɔnˈruːt] ADV: **~ for/from/to** in viaggio per/da/a

ensconced [ɪnˈskɔnst] ADJ: **~ in** ben sistemato(a) in

ensemble [ãːnˈsãːmbl] N (*Mus*) ensemble *m inv*

enshrine [ɪnˈʃraɪn] VT conservare come una reliquia

ensign N (*Naut*) [ˈɛnsən] bandiera; (*Mil*) [ˈɛnsaɪn] portabandiera *m inv*

enslave [ɪnˈsleɪv] VT fare schiavo

ensue [ɪnˈsjuː] VI seguire, risultare

en suite [ɔnˈswiːt] ADJ: **room with ~ bathroom** camera con bagno

ensure [ɪnˈʃuəʳ] VT assicurare; garantire; **to ~ that** assicurarsi che

ENT N ABBR (*Med*: = *ear, nose and throat*) O.R.L.

entail [ɪnˈteɪl] VT comportare

entangle [ɪnˈtæŋgl] VT (*thread etc*) impigliare; **to become entangled in sth** (*fig*) rimanere impegolato in qc

enter [ˈɛntəʳ] VT (*gen*) entrare in; (*club*) associarsi a; (*profession*) intraprendere; (*army*) arruolarsi in; (*competition*) partecipare a; (*sb for a competition*) iscrivere; (*write down*) registrare; (*Comput: data*) introdurre, inserire ▸ VI entrare
▸ **enter for** VT FUS iscriversi a

▸ **enter into** VT FUS (*explanation*) cominciare a dare; (*debate*) partecipare a; (*agreement*) concludere; (*negotiations*) prendere parte a
▸ **enter (up)on** VT FUS cominciare

enteritis [ɛntəˈraɪtɪs] N enterite *f*

enterprise [ˈɛntəpraɪz] N (*undertaking, company*) impresa; (*spirit*) iniziativa; **free ~** liberalismo economico; **private ~** iniziativa privata

enterprising [ˈɛntəpraɪzɪŋ] ADJ intraprendente

entertain [ɛntəˈteɪn] VT divertire; (*invite*) ricevere; (*idea, plan*) nutrire

entertainer [ɛntəˈteɪnəʳ] N comico(-a)

entertaining [ɛntəˈteɪnɪŋ] ADJ divertente ▸ N: **to do a lot of ~** avere molti ospiti

entertainment [ɛntəˈteɪnmənt] N (*amusement*) divertimento; (*show*) spettacolo

entertainment allowance N spese *fpl* di rappresentanza

enthral [ɪnˈθrɔːl] VT affascinare, avvincere

enthralled [ɪnˈθrɔːld] ADJ affascinato(-a)

enthralling [ɪnˈθrɔːlɪŋ] ADJ avvincente

enthuse [ɪnˈθuːz] VI: **to ~ (about *or* over)** entusiasmarsi (per)

enthusiasm [ɪnˈθuːzɪæzəm] N entusiasmo

enthusiast [ɪnˈθuːzɪæst] N entusiasta *mf*; **a jazz *etc* ~** un appassionato di jazz *etc*

enthusiastic [ɪnθuːzɪˈæstɪk] ADJ entusiasta, entusiastico(-a); **to be ~ about sth/sb** essere appassionato di qc/entusiasta di qn

entice [ɪnˈtaɪs] VT allettare, sedurre

enticing [ɪnˈtaɪsɪŋ] ADJ allettante

entire [ɪnˈtaɪəʳ] ADJ intero(-a)

entirely [ɪnˈtaɪəlɪ] ADV completamente, interamente

entirety [ɪnˈtaɪərətɪ] N: **in its ~** nel suo complesso

entitle [ɪnˈtaɪtl] VT (*give right*): **to ~ sb to sth/to do** dare diritto a qn a qc/a fare

entitled [ɪnˈtaɪtld] ADJ (*book*) che si intitola; **to be ~ to sth** avere diritto a qc; **to be ~ to do sth** avere il diritto di fare qc

entity [ˈɛntɪtɪ] N entità *f inv*

entrails [ˈɛntreɪlz] NPL interiora *fpl*

entrance N [ˈɛntrns] entrata, ingresso; (*of person*) entrata ▸ VT [ɪnˈtrɑːns] incantare, rapire; **to gain ~ to** (*university etc*) essere ammesso a

entrance examination N (*to school*) esame *m* di ammissione

entrance fee N tassa d'iscrizione; (*to museum etc*) prezzo d'ingresso

entrance ramp N (*US Aut*) rampa di accesso

entrancing [ɪnˈtrɑːnsɪŋ] ADJ incantevole

entrant [ˈɛntrnt] N partecipante *mf*; concorrente *mf*; (BRIT: *in exam*) candidato(-a)

entreat [ɛn'triːt] VT supplicare

entreaty [ɪn'triːtɪ] N supplica, preghiera

entrée ['ɔntreɪ] N (Culin) prima portata

entrenched [ɛn'trɛntʃt] ADJ radicato(-a)

entrepreneur ['ɔntrəprə'nəː'] N imprenditore(-trice)

entrepreneurial ['ɔntrəprə'nəːrɪəl] ADJ imprenditoriale

entrust [ɪn'trʌst] VT: **to ~ sth to** affidare qc a

entry ['ɛntrɪ] N entrata; (way in) entrata, ingresso; (item: on list) iscrizione f; (in dictionary) voce f; (in diary, ship's log) annotazione f; (in account book, ledger, list) registrazione f; **"no ~"** "vietato l'ingresso"; (Aut) "divieto di accesso"; **single/double ~ book-keeping** partita semplice/doppia

entry form N modulo d'iscrizione

entry phone N (BRIT) citofono

entwine [ɪn'twaɪn] VT intrecciare

E number N sigla di additivo alimentare

enumerate [ɪ'njuːməreɪt] VT enumerare

enunciate [ɪ'nʌnsɪeɪt] VT enunciare; pronunciare

envelop [ɪn'vɛləp] VT avvolgere, avviluppare

envelope ['ɛnvələup] N busta

enviable ['ɛnvɪəbl] ADJ invidiabile

envious ['ɛnvɪəs] ADJ invidioso(-a)

environment [ɪn'vaɪərənmənt] N ambiente m; **Department of the E~** (BRIT) ≈ Ministero dell'Ambiente

environmental [ɪnvaɪərən'mɛntl] ADJ ecologico(-a); ambientale; **~ studies** (in school etc) ecologia

environmentalist [ɪn'vaɪərən'mɛntəlɪst] N studioso(-a) della protezione dell'ambiente

environmentally [ɪnvaɪərən'mɛntəlɪ] ADV: **~ sound/friendly** che rispetta l'ambiente

Environmental Protection Agency N (US) ≈ Ministero dell'Ambiente

envisage [ɪn'vɪzɪdʒ] VT immaginare; prevedere

envision [ɪn'vɪʒən] VT concepire, prevedere

envoy ['ɛnvɔɪ] N inviato(-a)

envy ['ɛnvɪ] N invidia ▶ VT invidiare; **to ~ sb sth** invidiare qn per qc

enzyme ['ɛnzaɪm] N enzima m

EPA N ABBR (US) = **Environmental Protection Agency**

ephemeral [ɪ'fɛmərəl] ADJ effimero(-a)

epic ['ɛpɪk] N poema m epico ▶ ADJ epico(-a)

epicentre, (US) **epicenter** ['ɛpɪsɛntə'] N epicentro

epidemic [ɛpɪ'dɛmɪk] N epidemia

epilepsy ['ɛpɪlɛpsɪ] N epilessia

epileptic [ɛpɪ'lɛptɪk] ADJ, N epilettico(-a)

epileptic fit N attacco epilettico

epilogue ['ɛpɪlɔg] N epilogo

Epiphany [ɪ'pɪfənɪ] N Epifania

episcopal [ɪ'pɪskəpəl] ADJ episcopale

episode ['ɛpɪsəud] N episodio

epistle [ɪ'pɪsl] N epistola

epitaph ['ɛpɪtɑːf] N epitaffio

epithet ['ɛpɪθɛt] N epiteto

epitome [ɪ'pɪtəmɪ] N epitome f; quintessenza

epitomize [ɪ'pɪtəmaɪz] VT (fig) incarnare

epoch ['iːpɔk] N epoca

epoch-making ['iːpɔkmeɪkɪŋ] ADJ che fa epoca

eponymous [ɪ'pɔnɪməs] ADJ dello stesso nome

equable ['ɛkwəbl] ADJ uniforme; (climate) costante; (character) equilibrato(-a)

equal ['iːkwl] ADJ, N pari (mf) ▶ VT uguagliare; **~ to** (task) all'altezza di

equality [iː'kwɔlɪtɪ] N uguaglianza

equalize ['iːkwəlaɪz] VT, VI pareggiare

equalizer ['iːkwəlaɪzə'] N punto del pareggio

equally ['iːkwəlɪ] ADV ugualmente; **they are ~ clever** sono intelligenti allo stesso modo

Equal Opportunities Commission, (US) **Equal Employment Opportunity Commission** N commissione contro discriminazioni sessuali o razziali nel mondo del lavoro

equal sign, equals sign N segno d'uguaglianza

equanimity [ɛkwə'nɪmɪtɪ] N serenità

equate [ɪ'kweɪt] VT: **to ~ sth with** considerare qc uguale a; (compare) paragonare qc con; **to ~ A to B** mettere in equazione A e B

equation [ɪ'kweɪʃən] N (Math) equazione f

equator [ɪ'kweɪtə'] N equatore m

Equatorial Guinea [ɛkwə'tɔːrɪəl-] N Guinea Equatoriale

equestrian [ɪ'kwɛstrɪən] ADJ equestre ▶ N cavaliere (amazzone)

equilibrium [iːkwɪ'lɪbrɪəm] N equilibrio

equinox ['iːkwɪnɔks] N equinozio

equip [ɪ'kwɪp] VT equipaggiare, attrezzare; **to ~ sb/sth with** fornire qn/qc di; **equipped with** (machinery etc) dotato(a) di; **to be well equipped** (office etc) essere ben attrezzato(-a); **he is well equipped for the job** ha i requisiti necessari per quel lavoro

equipment [ɪ'kwɪpmənt] N attrezzatura; (electrical etc) apparecchiatura

equitable ['ɛkwɪtəbl] ADJ equo(-a), giusto(-a)

equities ['ɛkwɪtɪz] NPL (BRIT Comm) azioni fpl ordinarie

equity ['ɛkwɪtɪ] N equità

equity capital N capitale m azionario

equivalent [ɪ'kwɪvələnt] ADJ, N equivalente (m); **to be ~ to** equivalere a

e

equivocal [ɪˈkwɪvəkl] ADJ equivoco(-a); (*open to suspicion*) dubbio(-a)

equivocate [ɪˈkwɪvəkeɪt] VI esprimersi in modo equivoco

equivocation [ɪkwɪvəˈkeɪʃən] N parole *fpl* equivoche

ER ABBR (*BRIT*) = **Elizabeth Regina**; (*US Med*) = **emergency room**

ERA N ABBR (*US Pol*) = **Equal Rights Amendment**

era [ˈɪərə] N era, età *f inv*

eradicate [ɪˈrædɪkeɪt] VT sradicare

erase [ɪˈreɪz] VT cancellare

eraser [ɪˈreɪzəʳ] N gomma

e-reader [ˈiːriːdəʳ] N e-reader *m inv*, lettore *m* di libri digitali

erect [ɪˈrɛkt] ADJ eretto(-a) ▶ VT costruire; (*assemble*) montare; (*monument, tent*) alzare

erection [ɪˈrɛkʃən] N (*also Physiol*) erezione *f*; (*of building*) costruzione *f*; (*of machinery*) montaggio

ergonomics [əːgəˈnɒmɪks] N ergonomia

ERISA N ABBR (*US*: = *Employee Retirement Income Security Act*) *legge relativa al pensionamento statale*

Eritrea [ɛrɪˈtreɪə] N Eritrea

ERM N ABBR (= *Exchange Rate Mechanism*) ERM *m*, meccanismo dei tassi di cambio

ermine [ˈəːmɪn] N ermellino

ERNIE [ˈəːnɪ] N ABBR (*BRIT*: = *Electronic Random Number Indicator Equipment*) *sistema che seleziona i numeri vincenti di buoni del Tesoro*

erode [ɪˈrəud] VT erodere; (*metal*) corrodere

erogenous zone [ɪˈrɒdʒənəs-] N zona erogena

erosion [ɪˈrəuʒən] N erosione *f*

erotic [ɪˈrɒtɪk] ADJ erotico(-a)

eroticism [ɪˈrɒtɪsɪzəm] N erotismo

err [əːʳ] VI errare; (*Rel*) peccare

errand [ˈɛrənd] N commissione *f*; (*also*: **run errands**) fare commissioni; **~ of mercy** atto di carità

errand boy N fattorino

erratic [ɪˈrætɪk] ADJ imprevedibile; (*person, mood*) incostante

erroneous [ɪˈrəunɪəs] ADJ erroneo(-a)

error [ˈɛrəʳ] N errore *m*; **typing/spelling ~** errore di battitura/di ortografia; **in ~** per errore; **errors and omissions excepted** salvo errori ed omissioni

error message N (*Comput*) messaggio di errore

erstwhile [ˈəːstwaɪl] ADV allora, un tempo ▶ ADJ di allora

erudite [ˈɛrjudaɪt] ADJ erudito(-a)

erupt [ɪˈrʌpt] VI erompere; (*volcano*) mettersi (*or* essere) in eruzione; (*war, crisis*) scoppiare

eruption [ɪˈrʌpʃən] N eruzione *f*; (*of anger, violence*) esplosione *f*; scoppio

ESA N ABBR (= *European Space Agency*) ESA *f*

escalate [ˈɛskəleɪt] VI intensificarsi; (*costs*) salire

escalation [ɛskəˈleɪʃən] N escalation *f*; (*of prices*) aumento

escalation clause N clausola di revisione

escalator [ˈɛskəleɪtəʳ] N scala mobile

escapade [ɛskəˈpeɪd] N scappatella; avventura

escape [ɪˈskeɪp] N evasione *f*; fuga; (*of gas etc*) fuga, fuoriuscita ▶ VI fuggire; (*from jail*) evadere, scappare; (*fig*) sfuggire; (*leak*) uscire ▶ VT sfuggire a; **to ~ from** (*place*) fuggire da; (*person*) sfuggire a; **to ~ to** (*another place*) fuggire in; (*freedom, safety*) fuggire verso; **to ~ notice** passare inosservato(a)

escape artist N mago della fuga

escape clause N clausola scappatoia

escapee [ɪskeɪˈpiː] N evaso(-a)

escape hatch N (*in submarine, space rocket*) portello di sicurezza

escape key N (*Comput*) tasto di escape, tasto per cambio di codice

escape route N percorso della fuga

escapism [ɪsˈkeɪpɪzəm] N evasione *f* (dalla realtà)

escapist [ɪsˈkeɪpɪst] ADJ d'evasione ▶ N persona che cerca di evadere dalla realtà

escapologist [ɛskəˈpɔlədʒɪst] N (*BRIT*) = **escape artist**

escarpment [ɪsˈkɑːpmənt] N scarpata

eschew [ɪsˈtʃuː] VT evitare

escort N [ˈɛskɔːt] scorta; (*to dance etc*): **her ~** il suo cavaliere; **his ~** la sua dama ▶ VT [ɪˈskɔːt] scortare; accompagnare

escort agency N agenzia di hostess

e-shopping [ˈiːʃɔpɪŋ] N shopping *m inv* online

Eskimo [ˈɛskɪməu] (*often !*) ADJ eschimese ▶ N eschimese *mf*; (*Ling*) eschimese *m*

ESL N ABBR (*Scol*) = **English as a Second Language**

esophagus [iːˈsɔfəgəs] N (*US*) = **oesophagus**

esoteric [ɛsəuˈtɛrɪk] ADJ esoterico(-a)

ESP N ABBR = **extrasensory perception**; (*Scol*) = **English for Specific Purposes**; = **English for Special Purposes**

esp. ABBR (= *especially*) spec.

especially [ɪˈspɛʃlɪ] ADV specialmente; (*above all*) soprattutto; (*specifically*) espressamente; (*particularly*) particolarmente

espionage [ˈɛspɪənɑːʒ] N spionaggio

esplanade [ɛspləˈneɪd] N lungomare *m*

espouse [ɪˈspauz] VT abbracciare

Esquire [ɪˈskwaɪəʳ] N (*BRIT*): **J. Brown, ~** Signor J. Brown

essay [ˈɛseɪ] N (*Scol*) composizione *f*; (*Literature*) saggio

essence [ˈɛsns] N essenza; **in ~** in sostanza; **speed is of the ~** la velocità è di estrema importanza

essential [ɪˈsɛnʃəl] ADJ essenziale; (basic) fondamentale ▸ N elemento essenziale; **it is ~ that** è essenziale che + sub

essentially [ɪˈsɛnʃəlɪ] ADV essenzialmente

essentials NPL: **the ~** l'essenziale msg

EST ABBR (US: = Eastern Standard Time) fuso orario

est. ABBR = **established**; **estimate(d)**

establish [ɪˈstæblɪʃ] VT stabilire; (business) mettere su; (one's power etc) affermare; (prove: fact, identity, sb's innocence) dimostrare

establishment [ɪsˈtæblɪʃmənt] N stabilimento; (business) azienda; **the E~** la classe dirigente; **the establishment** m; **a teaching ~** un istituto d'istruzione

estate [ɪˈsteɪt] N proprietà f inv; (Law) beni mpl, patrimonio; (BRIT: also: **housing estate**) complesso edilizio

estate agency N (BRIT) agenzia immobiliare

estate agent N (BRIT) agente m immobiliare

estate car N (BRIT) giardiniera

esteem [ɪˈstiːm] N stima ▸ VT considerare; stimare; **I hold him in high ~** gode di tutta la mia stima

esthetic [ɪsˈθɛtɪk] ADJ (US) = **aesthetic**

estimate N [ˈɛstɪmət] stima; (Comm) preventivo ▸ VT [ˈɛstɪmeɪt] stimare, valutare ▸ VI (BRIT Comm): **to ~ for** fare il preventivo per; **to give sb an ~ of** fare a qn una valutazione approssimativa (or un preventivo) di; **at a rough ~** approssimativamente

estimation [ɛstɪˈmeɪʃən] N stima; opinione f; **in my ~** a mio giudizio, a mio avviso

Estonia [ɛˈstəʊnɪə] N Estonia

Estonian [ɛˈstəʊnɪən] ADJ estone inv ▸ N estone mf; (Ling) estone m

estranged [ɪˈstreɪndʒd] ADJ separato(-a)

estrangement [ɪsˈtreɪndʒmənt] N alienazione f

estrogen [ˈiːstrəʊdʒən] N (US) = **oestrogen**

estuary [ˈɛstjʊərɪ] N estuario

ET ABBR (= Eastern Time) fuso orario; (BRIT: = Employment Training) corso di formazione professionale per disoccupati

ETA N ABBR (= estimated time of arrival) ora di arrivo prevista

e-tailer [ˈiːteɪləʳ] N venditore(-trice) in Internet

e-tailing [ˈiːteɪlɪŋ] N commercio in Internet

et al. ABBR (= et alii) ed altri

etc. ABBR (= et cetera) ecc., etc.

etch [ɛtʃ] VT incidere all'acquaforte

etching [ˈɛtʃɪŋ] N acquaforte f

ETD N ABBR (= estimated time of departure) ora di partenza prevista

eternal [ɪˈtəːnl] ADJ eterno(-a)

eternity [ɪˈtəːnɪtɪ] N eternità

ether [ˈiːθəʳ] N etere m

ethereal [ɪˈθɪərɪəl] ADJ etereo(-a)

ethical [ˈɛθɪkl] ADJ etico(-a), morale

ethics [ˈɛθɪks] N etica ▸ NPL morale f

Ethiopia [iːθɪˈəʊpɪə] N Etiopia

Ethiopian [iːθɪˈəʊpɪən] ADJ, N etiope (mf)

ethnic [ˈɛθnɪk] ADJ etnico(-a)

ethnic cleansing [-ˈklɛnzɪŋ] N pulizia etnica

ethnic minority N minoranza etnica

ethnology [ɛθˈnɔlədʒɪ] N etnologia

ethos [ˈiːθɔs] N (of culture, group) norma di vita

e-ticket [ˈiːtɪkɪt] N e-ticket m inv, biglietto elettronico

etiquette [ˈɛtɪkɛt] N etichetta

ETV N ABBR (US) = **Educational Television**

etymology [ɛtɪˈmɔlədʒɪ] N etimologia

EU N ABBR (= European Union) UE f

eucalyptus [juːkəˈlɪptəs] N eucalipto

eulogy [ˈjuːlədʒɪ] N elogio

euphemism [ˈjuːfəmɪzəm] N eufemismo

euphemistic [juːfəˈmɪstɪk] ADJ eufemistico(-a)

euphoria [juːˈfɔːrɪə] N euforia

Eurasia [jʊəˈreɪʃə] N Eurasia

Eurasian [jʊəˈreɪʃən] ADJ, N eurasiano(-a)

Euratom [jʊəˈrætəm] N ABBR (= European Atomic Energy Community) EURATOM f

euro [ˈjʊərəʊ] N (currency) euro m inv

Euro- [ˈjʊərəʊ] PREFIX euro-

Eurocheque [ˈjʊərəʊtʃɛk] N eurochèque m inv

Eurocrat [ˈjʊərəʊkræt] N eurocrate mf

Eurodollar [ˈjʊərəʊdɔləʳ] N eurodollaro

Euroland [ˈjʊərəʊlænd] N Eurolandia

Europe [ˈjʊərəp] N Europa

European [jʊərəˈpiːən] ADJ, N europeo(-a)

European Community N Comunità Europea

European Court of Justice N Corte f di Giustizia della Comunità Europea

European Union N Unione f europea

Europol [ˈjʊərəʊpɔl] N Europol f

Euro-sceptic [ˈjʊərəʊskɛptɪk] N euroscettico(-a)

Eurostar® [ˈjʊərəʊstɑːʳ] N Eurostar® m inv

Eurozone [ˈjʊərəʊzəʊn] N zona euro

euthanasia [juːθəˈneɪzɪə] N eutanasia

evacuate [ɪˈvækjʊeɪt] VT evacuare

evacuation [ɪvækjuˈeɪʃən] N evacuazione f

evacuee [ɪvækjuˈiː] N sfollato(-a)

evade [ɪˈveɪd] VT eludere; (tax) evadere; (duties etc) sottrarsi a; (person) schivare

evaluate [ɪˈvæljueɪt] VT valutare

evangelist [ɪˈvændʒəlɪst] N evangelista m

evangelize [ɪˈvændʒəlaɪz] VT evangelizzare

evaporate [ɪˈvæpəreɪt] VI evaporare ▸ VT far evaporare

evaporated milk N latte *m* concentrato

evaporation [ɪvæpəˈreɪʃən] N evaporazione *f*

evasion [ɪˈveɪʒən] N evasione *f*

evasive [ɪˈveɪsɪv] ADJ evasivo(-a)

eve [iːv] N: **on the ~ of** alla vigilia di

even [ˈiːvn] ADJ regolare; (*number*) pari *inv* ▶ADV anche, perfino; **~ if**, **~ though** anche se; **~ more** ancora di più; **he loves her ~ more** la ama anche di più; **~ faster** ancora più veloce; **~ so** ciò nonostante; **not ~ ...** nemmeno ...; **to break ~** finire in pari *or* alla pari; **to get ~ with sb** dare la pari a qn
▶ **even out** VI pareggiare

even-handed [ˈiːvnˈhændɪd] ADJ imparziale, equo(-a)

evening [ˈiːvnɪŋ] N sera; (*as duration, event*) serata; **in the ~** la sera; **this ~** stasera, questa sera; **tomorrow/yesterday ~** domani/ieri sera

> Use **sera** in expressions of time, e.g. *at 6 in the evening* **alle 6 di sera**. Use **serata** for the kind of evening it is, e.g. *a lovely evening* **una bella serata**, how you spend it, or to emphasize its duration.

evening class N corso serale

evening dress N (*woman's*) abito da sera; **in ~** (*man*) in abito scuro; (*woman*) in abito lungo

evenly [ˈiːvnlɪ] ADV (*distribute, space, spread*) uniformemente; (*divide*) in parti uguali

evensong [ˈiːvnsɔŋ] N ≈ vespro

event [ɪˈvɛnt] N avvenimento; (*Sport*) gara; **in the ~ of** in caso di; **at all events**, (*BRIT*) **in any ~** in ogni caso; **in the ~** in realtà, di fatto; **in the course of events** nel corso degli eventi

eventful [ɪˈvɛntful] ADJ denso(-a) di eventi

eventing [ɪˈvɛntɪŋ] N (*Horseriding*) concorso ippico

eventual [ɪˈvɛntʃuəl] ADJ finale

eventuality [ɪvɛntʃuˈælɪtɪ] N possibilità *f inv*, eventualità *f inv*

eventually [ɪˈvɛntʃuəlɪ] ADV alla fine

> La parola inglese **eventually** non vuol dire *eventualmente*.

ever [ˈɛvəʳ] ADV mai; (*at all times*) sempre; **for ~** per sempre; **the best ~** il migliore che ci sia mai stato; **hardly ~** non ... quasi mai; **have you ~ seen it?** l'ha mai visto?; **have you ~ been there?** c'è mai stato?; **~ so pretty** così bello(a); **thank you ~ so much** grazie mille; **yours ~** (*BRIT: in letters*) sempre tuo; **~ since** *adv* da allora; *conj* sin da quando

Everest [ˈɛvərɪst] N (*also:* **Mount Everest**) Everest *m*

evergreen [ˈɛvəgriːn] N sempreverde *m*

everlasting [ɛvəˈlɑːstɪŋ] ADJ eterno(-a)

every [ˈɛvrɪ] ADJ ogni; **~ day** tutti i giorni, ogni giorno; **~ other/third day** ogni due/tre giorni; **~ other car** una macchina su due; **~ now and then** ogni tanto, di quando in quando; **I have ~ confidence in him** ho piena fiducia in lui

everybody [ˈɛvrɪbɔdɪ] PRON ognuno, tutti *pl*; **~ else** tutti gli altri; **~ knows about it** lo sanno tutti

everyday [ˈɛvrɪdeɪ] ADJ quotidiano(-a); di ogni giorno; (*use, occurrence, experience*) comune; (*expression*) di uso corrente

everyone [ˈɛvrɪwʌn] = **everybody**

everything [ˈɛvrɪθɪŋ] PRON tutto, ogni cosa; **~ is ready** è tutto pronto; **he did ~ possible** ha fatto tutto il possibile

everywhere [ˈɛvrɪwɛəʳ] ADV in ogni luogo, dappertutto; (*wherever*) ovunque; **~ you go you meet ...** ovunque si vada si trova ...

evict [ɪˈvɪkt] VT sfrattare

eviction [ɪˈvɪkʃən] N sfratto

eviction notice N avviso di sfratto

evidence [ˈɛvɪdəns] N (*proof*) prova; (*of witness*) testimonianza; **to show ~ of** (*sign*) dare segni di; **to give ~** deporre; **in ~** (*obvious*) in evidenza; in vista

evident [ˈɛvɪdənt] ADJ evidente

evidently [ˈɛvɪdəntlɪ] ADV evidentemente

evil [ˈiːvl] ADJ cattivo(-a), maligno(-a) ▶N male *m*

evince [ɪˈvɪns] VT manifestare

evocative [ɪˈvɔkətɪv] ADJ evocativo(-a)

evoke [ɪˈvəuk] VT evocare; (*admiration*) suscitare

evolution [iːvəˈluːʃən] N evoluzione *f*

evolve [ɪˈvɔlv] VT elaborare ▶VI svilupparsi, evolversi

ewe [juː] N pecora

ex [ɛks] N (*col*): **my ex** il mio(-a) ex

ex- [ɛks] PREFIX ex; (*out of*): **the price ex-works** il prezzo franco fabbrica

exacerbate [ɪkˈsæsəbeɪt] VT (*pain*) aggravare; (*fig: relations, situation*) esacerbare, esasperare

exact [ɪgˈzækt] ADJ esatto(-a) ▶VT: **to ~ sth (from)** estorcere qc (da); esigere qc (da)

exacting [ɪgˈzæktɪŋ] ADJ esigente; (*work*) faticoso(-a)

exactitude [ɪgˈzæktɪtjuːd] N esattezza, precisione *f*

exactly [ɪgˈzæktlɪ] ADV esattamente; **~!** esatto!

exaggerate [ɪgˈzædʒəreɪt] VT, VI esagerare

exaggeration [ɪgzædʒəˈreɪʃən] N esagerazione *f*

exalt [ɪgˈzɔːlt] VT esaltare; elevare

exalted [ɪgˈzɔːltɪd] ADJ (*rank, person*) elevato(-a); (*elated*) esaltato(-a)

exam [ɪgˈzæm] N ABBR (*Scol*) = **examination**

examination [ɪgzæmɪˈneɪʃən] N (*Scol*) esame *m*; (*Med*) controllo; **to take** *or* **sit an ~** (*BRIT*) sostenere *or* dare un esame; **the matter is under ~** la questione è all'esame

examine [ɪɡ'zæmɪn] VT esaminare; (*Scol: orally, Law: person*) interrogare; (*inspect: machine, premises*) ispezionare; (*: luggage, passport*) controllare; (*Med*) visitare

examiner [ɪɡ'zæmɪnəʳ] N esaminatore(-trice)

example [ɪɡ'zɑːmpl] N esempio; **for ~** ad *or* per esempio; **to set a good/bad ~** dare il buon/cattivo esempio

exasperate [ɪɡ'zɑːspəreɪt] VT esasperare; **exasperated by** (*or* **at** *or* **with**) esasperato da

exasperated [ɪɡ'zɑːspəreɪtɪd] ADJ esasperato(-a)

exasperating [ɪɡ'zɑːspəreɪtɪŋ] ADJ esasperante

exasperation [ɪɡzɑːspə'reɪʃən] N esasperazione *f*

excavate ['ɛkskəveɪt] VT scavare

excavation [ɛkskə'veɪʃən] N escavazione *f*

excavator ['ɛkskəveɪtəʳ] N scavatore(-trice)

exceed [ɪk'siːd] VT superare; (*one's powers, time limit*) oltrepassare

exceedingly [ɪk'siːdɪŋlɪ] ADV eccessivamente

excel [ɪk'sɛl] VI eccellere ▶ VT sorpassare; **to ~ o.s.** (*BRIT*) superare se stesso

excellence ['ɛksələns] N eccellenza

Excellency ['ɛksələnsɪ] N: **His ~** Sua Eccellenza

excellent ['ɛksələnt] ADJ eccellente

except [ɪk'sɛpt] PREP (*also:* **except for, excepting**) salvo, all'infuori di, eccetto ▶ VT escludere; **~ if/when** salvo se/quando; **~ that** salvo che

exception [ɪk'sɛpʃən] N eccezione *f*; **to take ~ to** trovare a ridire su; **with the ~ of** ad eccezione di

exceptional [ɪk'sɛpʃnl] ADJ eccezionale

exceptionally [ɪk'sɛpʃnəlɪ] ADV eccezionalmente

excerpt ['ɛksəːpt] N estratto

excess [ɪk'sɛs] N eccesso; **in ~ of** al di sopra di

excess baggage N bagaglio in eccedenza

excess fare N supplemento

excessive [ɪk'sɛsɪv] ADJ eccessivo(-a)

excess supply N eccesso di offerta

exchange [ɪks'tʃeɪndʒ] N scambio; (*also:* **telephone exchange**) centralino ▶ VT: **to ~ (for)** scambiare (con); **in ~ for** in cambio di; **foreign ~** (*Comm*) cambio

exchange control N controllo sui cambi

exchange market N mercato dei cambi

exchange rate N tasso di cambio

Exchequer [ɪks'tʃɛkəʳ] N: **the ~** (*BRIT*) lo Scacchiere, ≈ il ministero delle Finanze

excisable [ɪk'saɪzəbl] ADJ soggetto(-a) a dazio

excise N ['ɛksaɪz] imposta, dazio ▶ VT [ɛk'saɪz] recidere

excise duties NPL dazi *mpl*

excitable [ɪk'saɪtəbl] ADJ eccitabile

excite [ɪk'saɪt] VT eccitare; **to get excited** eccitarsi

excited ADJ: **to get ~** essere elettrizzato(-a)

excitement [ɪk'saɪtmənt] N eccitazione *f*; agitazione *f*

exciting [ɪk'saɪtɪŋ] ADJ avventuroso(-a); (*film, book*) appassionante

excl. ABBR (= *excluding, exclusive (of)*) escl.

exclaim [ɪk'skleɪm] VI esclamare

exclamation [ɛksklə'meɪʃən] N esclamazione *f*

exclamation mark, (*US*) **exclamation point** N punto esclamativo

exclude [ɪk'skluːd] VT escludere

excluding [ɪk'skluːdɪŋ] PREP: **~ VAT** IVA esclusa

exclusion [ɪk'skluːʒən] N esclusione *f*; **to the ~ of** escludendo

exclusion clause N clausola di esclusione

exclusion zone N area interdetta

exclusive [ɪk'skluːsɪv] ADJ esclusivo(-a); (*club*) selettivo(-a); (*district*) snob *inv* ▶ ADV (*Comm*) non compreso; **~ of VAT** IVA esclusa; **~ of postage** spese postali escluse; **~ of service** servizio escluso; **from 1st to 15th March ~** dal 1° al 15 marzo esclusi; **~ rights** *npl* (*Comm*) diritti *mpl* esclusivi

exclusively [ɪk'skluːsɪvlɪ] ADV esclusivamente

excommunicate [ɛkskə'mjuːnɪkeɪt] VT scomunicare

excrement ['ɛkskrəmənt] N escremento

excruciating [ɪk'skruːʃɪeɪtɪŋ] ADJ straziante, atroce

excursion [ɪk'skəːʃən] N escursione *f*, gita

excursion ticket N biglietto a tariffa escursionistica

excusable [ɪk'skjuːzəbl] ADJ scusabile

excuse N [ɪk'skjuːs] scusa ▶ VT [ɪk'skjuːz] scusare; (*justify*) giustificare; **to make excuses for sb** trovare giustificazioni per qn; **to ~ sb from** (*activity*) dispensare qn da; **~ me!** mi scusi!; **now if you will ~ me, ...** ora, mi scusi ma ...; **to ~ o.s. (for (doing) sth)** giustificarsi (per (aver fatto) qc)

ex-directory ['ɛksdɪ'rɛktərɪ] ADJ (*BRIT*): **to be ~** non essere sull'elenco; **~ (phone) number** numero non compreso nell'elenco telefonico

execrable ['ɛksɪkrəbl] ADJ (*gen*) pessimo(-a); (*manners*) esecrabile

executable [ɛksɪ'kjuːtəbl] ADJ (*Comput*) eseguibile

execute ['ɛksɪkjuːt] VT (*prisoner*) giustiziare; (*plan etc*) eseguire

execution [ɛksɪ'kjuːʃən] N esecuzione *f*

executioner [ɛksɪ'kjuːʃnəʳ] N boia *m inv*

executive [ɪɡ'zɛkjutɪv] N (*Comm*) dirigente *m*;

(Pol) esecutivo ▸ ADJ esecutivo(-a); (secretary) di direzione; (offices, suite) della direzione; (car, plane) dirigenziale; (position, job, duties) direttivo(-a)

executive director N amministratore(-trice)

executor [ɪgˈzɛkjutəˈ] N esecutore(-trice) testamentario(-a)

exemplary [ɪgˈzɛmplərɪ] ADJ esemplare

exemplify [ɪgˈzɛmplɪfaɪ] VT esemplificare

exempt [ɪgˈzɛmpt] ADJ: ~ (from) (person: from tax) esentato(-a) (da); (: from military service etc) esonerato(-a) (da); (goods) esente (da) ▸ VT: to ~ sb from esentare qn da

exemption [ɪgˈzɛmpʃən] N esenzione f

exercise [ˈɛksəsaɪz] N (keep fit) moto; (Scol, Mil etc) esercizio ▸ VT esercitare; (patience) usare; (dog) portar fuori ▸ VI (also: take exercise) fare del movimento or moto

exercise bike N cyclette® f inv

exercise book N quaderno

exert [ɪgˈzəːt] VT esercitare; (strength, force) impiegare; to ~ o.s. sforzarsi

exertion [ɪgˈzəːʃən] N sforzo

ex gratia [ˈɛksˈɡreɪʃə] ADJ: ~ payment gratifica

exhale [ɛksˈheɪl] VT, VI espirare

exhaust [ɪgˈzɔːst] N (also: exhaust fumes) scappamento; (also: exhaust pipe) tubo di scappamento ▸ VT esaurire; to ~ o.s. sfiancarsi

exhausted [ɪgˈzɔːstɪd] ADJ esaurito(-a)

exhausting [ɪgˈzɔːstɪŋ] ADJ estenuante

exhaustion [ɪgˈzɔːstʃən] N esaurimento; **nervous ~** sovraffaticamento mentale

exhaustive [ɪgˈzɔːstɪv] ADJ esauriente

exhibit [ɪgˈzɪbɪt] N (Art) oggetto esposto; (Law) documento or oggetto esibito ▸ VT esporre; (courage, skill) dimostrare

exhibition [ɛksɪˈbɪʃən] N mostra, esposizione f; (of rudeness etc) spettacolo; **to make an ~ of o.s.** dare spettacolo di sé

exhibitionist [ɛksɪˈbɪʃənɪst] N esibizionista mf

exhibitor [ɪgˈzɪbɪtəˈ] N espositore(-trice)

exhilarating [ɪgˈzɪləreɪtɪŋ] ADJ esilarante; stimolante

exhilaration [ɪgzɪləˈreɪʃən] N esaltazione f, ebbrezza

exhort [ɪgˈzɔːt] VT esortare

exile [ˈɛksaɪl] N esilio; (person) esiliato(-a) ▸ VT esiliare; **in ~** in esilio

exist [ɪgˈzɪst] VI esistere

existence [ɪgˈzɪstəns] N esistenza; **to be in ~** esistere

existentialism [ɛgzɪsˈtɛnʃəlɪzəm] N esistenzialismo

existing [ɪgˈzɪstɪŋ] ADJ esistente; (laws, regime) attuale

exit [ˈɛksɪt] N uscita ▸ VI (Comput, Theat) uscire

exit poll N exit poll m inv, sondaggio all'uscita dei seggi

exit ramp N (US Aut) rampa di uscita

exit visa N visto d'uscita

exodus [ˈɛksədəs] N esodo

ex officio [ˈɛksəˈfɪʃɪəu] ADJ, ADV d'ufficio

exonerate [ɪgˈzɔnəreɪt] VT: **to ~ from** discolpare da

exorbitant [ɪgˈzɔːbɪtənt] ADJ (price) esorbitante; (demands) spropositato(-a)

exorcize [ˈɛksɔːsaɪz] VT esorcizzare

exotic [ɪgˈzɔtɪk] ADJ esotico(-a)

expand [ɪkˈspænd] VT (chest, economy etc) sviluppare; (market, operations) espandere; (influence) estendere; (horizons) allargare ▸ VI svilupparsi; (gas) espandersi; (metal) dilatarsi; **to ~ on** (notes, story etc) ampliare

expanse [ɪkˈspæns] N distesa, estensione f

expansion [ɪkˈspænʃən] N (gen) espansione f; (of town, economy) sviluppo; (of metal) dilatazione f

expansionism [ɪkˈspænʃənɪzəm] N espansionismo

expansionist [ɪkˈspænʃənɪst] ADJ espansionistico(-a)

expatriate N [ɛksˈpætrɪət] espatriato(-a) ▸ VT [ɛksˈpætrɪeɪt] espatriare

expect [ɪkˈspɛkt] VT (anticipate) prevedere, aspettarsi, prevedere or aspettarsi che + sub; (count on) contare su; (hope for) sperare; (require) richiedere, esigere; (suppose) supporre; (await, also baby) aspettare ▸ VI: **to be expecting** essere in stato interessante; **to ~ sb to do** aspettarsi che qn faccia; **to ~ to do sth** pensare or contare di fare qc; **as expected** come previsto; **I ~ so** credo di sì

expectancy [ɪkˈspɛktənsɪ] N attesa; **life ~** probabilità fpl di vita

expectant [ɪkˈspɛktənt] ADJ pieno(-a) di aspettative

expectantly [ɪkˈspɛktəntlɪ] ADV (look, listen) con un'aria d'attesa

expectant mother N gestante f

expectation [ɛkspɛkˈteɪʃən] N aspettativa; speranza; **in ~ of** in previsione di; **against** or **contrary to all ~(s)** contro ogni aspettativa; **to come** or **live up to sb's expectations** rispondere alle attese di qn

expedience [ɪkˈspiːdɪəns], **expediency** [ɪkˈspiːdɪənsɪ] N convenienza; **for the sake of ~** per una questione di comodità

expedient [ɪkˈspiːdɪənt] ADJ conveniente; vantaggioso(-a) ▸ N espediente m

expedite [ˈɛkspədaɪt] VT sbrigare; facilitare

expedition [ɛkspəˈdɪʃən] N spedizione f

expeditionary force [ɛkspəˈdɪʃənərɪ-] N corpo di spedizione

expeditious [ɛkspə'dɪʃəs] ADJ sollecito(-a), rapido(-a)

expel [ɪk'spɛl] VT espellere

expend [ɪk'spɛnd] VT spendere; (*use up*) consumare

expendable [ɪk'spɛndəbl] ADJ sacrificabile

expenditure [ɪk'spɛndɪtʃəʳ] N spesa; (*of time, effort*) dispendio

expense [ɪk'spɛns] N spesa; (*high cost*) costo ■ **expenses** NPL (*Comm*) spese *fpl*, indennità *fpl*; **to go to the ~ of** sobbarcarsi la spesa di; **at great ~** con grande impiego di mezzi; **at the ~ of** a spese di

expense account N conto *m* spese *inv*

expensive [ɪk'spɛnsɪv] ADJ caro(-a), costoso(-a); **she has ~ tastes** le piacciono le cose costose

experience [ɪk'spɪərɪəns] N esperienza ▶VT (*pleasure*) provare; (*hardship*) soffrire; **to learn by ~** imparare per esperienza

experienced [ɪk'spɪərɪənst] ADJ esperto(-a)

experiment N [ɪk'spɛrɪmənt] esperimento, esperienza ▶VI [ɪk'spɛrɪmɛnt] fare esperimenti; **to perform** or **carry out an ~** fare un esperimento; **as an ~** a titolo di esperimento; **to ~ with a new vaccine** sperimentare un nuovo vaccino

experimental [ɪkspɛrɪ'mɛntl] ADJ sperimentale; **at the ~ stage** in via di sperimentazione

expert ['ɛkspə:t] ADJ, N esperto(-a); **~ witness** (*Law*) esperto(-a); **~ in** or **at doing sth** esperto nel fare qc; **an ~ on sth** un esperto di qc

expertise [ɛkspə:'ti:z] N competenza

expire [ɪk'spaɪəʳ] VI (*period of time, licence*) scadere

expiry [ɪk'spaɪərɪ] N scadenza

expiry date N (*of medicine, food item*) data di scadenza

explain [ɪk'spleɪn] VT spiegare
▶ **explain away** VT dar ragione di

explanation [ɛksplə'neɪʃən] N spiegazione *f*; **to find an ~ for sth** trovare la spiegazione di qc

explanatory [ɪk'splænətrɪ] ADJ esplicativo(-a)

expletive [ɪk'spli:tɪv] N imprecazione *f*

explicit [ɪk'splɪsɪt] ADJ esplicito(-a); (*definite*) netto(-a)

explode [ɪk'spləud] VI esplodere ▶VT (*fig: theory*) demolire; **to ~ a myth** distruggere un mito

exploit N ['ɛksplɔɪt] impresa ▶VT [ɪk'splɔɪt] sfruttare

exploitation [ɛksplɔɪ'teɪʃən] N sfruttamento

exploration [ɛksplə'reɪʃən] N esplorazione *f*

exploratory [ɪk'splɔrətrɪ] ADJ (*fig: talks*) esplorativo(-a); **~ operation** (*Med*) intervento d'esplorazione

explore [ɪk'splɔ:ʳ] VT esplorare; (*possibilities*) esaminare

explorer [ɪk'splɔ:rəʳ] N esploratore(-trice)

explosion [ɪk'spləuʒən] N esplosione *f*

explosive [ɪk'spləusɪv] ADJ esplosivo(-a) ▶N esplosivo

exponent [ɪk'spəunənt] N esponente *mf*

export VT [ɛk'spɔ:t] esportare ▶N ['ɛkspɔ:t] esportazione *f*; articolo di esportazione ▶CPD d'esportazione

exportation [ɛkspɔ:'teɪʃən] N esportazione *f*

exporter [ɪk'spɔ:təʳ] N esportatore(-trice)

export licence N licenza d'esportazione

expose [ɪk'spəuz] VT esporre; (*unmask*) smascherare; **to ~ o.s.** (*Law*) oltraggiare il pudore

exposed [ɪk'spəuzd] ADJ (*land, house*) esposto(-a); (*Elec: wire*) scoperto(-a); (*pipe, beam*) a vista

exposition [ɛkspə'zɪʃən] N esposizione *f*

exposure [ɪk'spəuʒəʳ] N esposizione *f*; (*Phot*) posa; (*Med*) assideramento; **to die of ~** morire assiderato(-a)

exposure meter N esposimetro

expound [ɪk'spaund] VT esporre; (*theory, text*) spiegare

express [ɪk'sprɛs] ADJ (*definite*) chiaro(-a), espresso(-a); (*Brit: letter etc*) espresso *inv* ▶N (*train*) espresso ▶ADV: **to send sth ~** spedire qc per espresso ▶VT esprimere; **to ~ o.s.** esprimersi

expression [ɪk'sprɛʃən] N espressione *f*

expressionism [ɪk'sprɛʃənɪzəm] N espressionismo

expressive [ɪk'sprɛsɪv] ADJ espressivo(-a)

expressly [ɪk'sprɛslɪ] ADV espressamente

expressway [ɪk'sprɛsweɪ] N (*US: urban motorway*) autostrada che attraversa la città

expropriate [ɛks'prəuprɪeɪt] VT espropriare

expulsion [ɪk'spʌlʃən] N espulsione *f*

exquisite [ɛk'skwɪzɪt] ADJ squisito(-a)

ex-serviceman ['ɛks'sə:vɪsmən] N (*irreg*) ex combattente *m*

ext. ABBR (*Tel*: = *extension*) int. (= *interno*)

extemporize [ɪk'stɛmpəraɪz] VI improvvisare

extend [ɪk'stɛnd] VT (*visit*) protrarre; (*road, deadline*) prolungare; (*building*) ampliare; (*offer*) offrire, porgere; (*Comm: credit*) accordare ▶VI (*land*) estendersi

extension [ɪk'stɛnʃən] N (*of road, term*) prolungamento; (*of contract, deadline*) proroga; (*building*) annesso; (*to wire, table*) prolunga; (*telephone*) interno; (*: in private house*) apparecchio supplementare; **~ 3718** (*Tel*) interno 3718

extension cable, extension lead N (*Elec*) prolunga

extensive [ɪk'stɛnsɪv] ADJ esteso(-a), ampio(-a); (*damage*) su larga scala; (*alterations*) notevole; (*inquiries, coverage, discussion*) esauriente; (*use*) grande

extensively [ɪk'stɛnsɪvlɪ] ADV (*altered, damaged etc*) radicalmente; **he's travelled ~** ha viaggiato molto

extent [ɪk'stɛnt] N estensione *f*; (*of knowledge, activities, power*) portata; (*degree: of damage, loss*) proporzioni *fpl*; **to some ~** fino a un certo punto; **to a certain/large ~** in certa/larga misura; **to what ~?** fino a che punto?; **to such an ~ that ...** a tal punto che ...; **to the ~ of ...** fino al punto di ...

extenuating [ɪk'stɛnjueɪtɪŋ] ADJ: **~ circumstances** attenuanti *fpl*

exterior [ɛk'stɪərɪəʳ] ADJ esteriore, esterno(-a) ▶ N esteriore *m*, esterno; aspetto (esteriore)

exterminate [ɪk'stə:mɪneɪt] VT sterminare

extermination [ɪkstə:mɪ'neɪʃən] N sterminio

external [ɛk'stə:nl] ADJ esterno(-a), esteriore ▶ N: **the externals** le apparenze; **for ~ use only** (*Med*) solo per uso esterno; **~ affairs** (*Pol*) affari *mpl* esteri

externally [ɛk'stə:nəlɪ] ADV esternamente

extinct [ɪk'stɪŋkt] ADJ estinto(-a)

extinction [ɪk'stɪŋkʃən] N estinzione *f*

extinguish [ɪk'stɪŋgwɪʃ] VT estinguere

extinguisher [ɪk'stɪŋgwɪʃəʳ] N estintore *m*

extol, (*US*) **extoll** [ɪk'stəul] VT (*merits, virtues*) magnificare; (*person*) celebrare

extort [ɪk'stɔ:t] VT: **to ~ sth from** estorcere qc (da)

extortion [ɪk'stɔ:ʃən] N estorsione *f*

extortionate [ɪk'stɔ:ʃənɪt] ADJ esorbitante

extra ['ɛkstrə] ADJ extra *inv*, supplementare ▶ ADV (*in addition*) di più ▶ N extra *m inv*; (*surcharge*) supplemento; (*Theat*) comparso; **wine will cost ~** il vino è extra; **~ large sizes** taglie *fpl* forti

extra... ['ɛkstrə] PREFIX extra...

extract VT [ɪk'strækt] estrarre; (*money, promise*) strappare ▶ N ['ɛkstrækt] estratto; (*passage*) brano

extraction [ɪk'strækʃən] N estrazione *f*; (*descent*) origine *f*

extractor fan [ɪk'stræktə-] N aspiratore *m*

extracurricular [ɛkstrəkə'rɪkjuləʳ] ADJ (*Scol*) parascolastico(-a)

extradite ['ɛkstrədaɪt] VT estradare

extradition [ɛkstrə'dɪʃən] N estradizione *f*

extramarital [ɛkstrə'mærɪtl] ADJ extraconiugale

extramural [ɛkstrə'mjuərl] ADJ fuori dell'università

extraneous [ɛk'streɪnɪəs] ADJ: **~ to** estraneo(a) a

extraordinary [ɪk'strɔ:dnrɪ] ADJ straordinario(-a); **the ~ thing is that ...** la cosa strana è che ...

extraordinary general meeting N assemblea straordinaria

extrapolation [ɪkstræpə'leɪʃən] N estrapolazione *f*

extrasensory perception [ɛkstrə'sɛnsərɪ-] N percezione *f* extrasensoriale

extra time N (*Football*) tempo supplementare

extravagance [ɪk'strævəgəns] N (*excessive spending*) sperpero; (*thing bought*) stravaganza

extravagant [ɪk'strævəgənt] ADJ (*in spending: person*) prodigo(-a); (: *tastes*) dispendioso(-a); (*behaviour*) esagerato(-a)

extreme [ɪk'stri:m] ADJ estremo(-a) ▶ N estremo; **extremes of temperature** eccessivi sbalzi *mpl* di temperatura; **the ~ left/right** (*Pol*) l'estrema sinistra/destra

extremely [ɪk'stri:mlɪ] ADV estremamente

extremist [ɪk'stri:mɪst] ADJ, N estremista (*mf*)

extremity [ɪk'strɛmɪtɪ] N estremità *f inv*

extricate ['ɛkstrɪkeɪt] VT: **to ~ sth from** districare qc (da)

extrovert ['ɛkstrəvə:t] N estroverso(-a)

exuberance [ɪg'zu:bərəns] N esuberanza

exuberant [ɪg'zju:bərənt] ADJ esuberante

exude [ɪg'zju:d] VT trasudare; (*fig*) emanare

exult [ɪg'zʌlt] VI esultare, gioire

exultant [ɪg'zʌltənt] ADJ (*person, smile*) esultante; (*shout, expression*) di giubilo

exultation [ɛgzʌl'teɪʃən] N giubilo; **in ~** per la gioia

eye [aɪ] N occhio; (*of needle*) cruna ▶ VT osservare; **to keep an ~ on** tenere d'occhio; **in the public ~** esposto(a) al pubblico; **as far as the ~ can see** a perdita d'occhio; **with an ~ to doing sth** (*BRIT*) con l'idea di far qc; **to have an ~ for sth** avere occhio per qc; **there's more to this than meets the ~** non è così semplice come sembra

eyeball ['aɪbɔ:l] N globo dell'occhio

eyebath ['aɪbɑ:θ] N occhino

eyebrow ['aɪbrau] N sopracciglio

eyebrow pencil N matita per le sopracciglia

eye-catching ['aɪkætʃɪŋ] ADJ che colpisce l'occhio

eye cup N (*US*) = **eyebath**

eyedrops ['aɪdrɒps] NPL gocce *fpl* oculari, collirio

eyeful ['aɪful] N: **to get an ~ (of sth)** (*col*) avere l'occasione di dare una bella sbirciata (a qc)

eyeglass ['aɪglɑ:s] N monocolo

eyelash ['aɪlæʃ] N ciglio

eyelet ['aɪlɪt] N occhiello

eye-level ['aɪlɛvl] ADJ all'altezza degli occhi

eyelid ['aɪlɪd] N palpebra

eyeliner ['aɪlaɪnəʳ] N eye-liner *m inv*

eye-opener ['aɪəupnəʳ] N rivelazione *f*

eyeshadow ['aɪʃædəu] N ombretto

eyesight ['aɪsaɪt] N vista

eyesore ['aɪsɔːr] N pugno nell'occhio

eyestrain ['aɪstreɪn] N: **to get ~** stancarsi gli occhi

eye-tooth ['aɪtuːθ] (pl **eye-teeth** [-tiːθ]) N canino superiore; **to give one's eye-teeth for sth/to do sth** (fig) dare non so che cosa per qc/per fare qc

eyewash ['aɪwɔʃ] N collirio; (fig) sciocchezze fpl

eye witness N testimone mf oculare

eyrie ['ɪərɪ] N nido (d'aquila)

Ff

F, f [ɛf] N (letter) F, f f inv or m inv; (Mus): **F** fa m; **F for Frederick**, (US) **F for Fox** = F come Firenze

F. ABBR (= Fahrenheit) F

FA N ABBR (BRIT) = **Football Association**

FAA N ABBR (US) = **Federal Aviation Administration**

fable [ˈfeɪbl] N favola

fabric [ˈfæbrɪk] N stoffa, tessuto; (Archit) struttura

La parola inglese **fabric** non vuol dire fabbrica.

fabricate [ˈfæbrɪkeɪt] VT fabbricare

fabrication [fæbrɪˈkeɪʃən] N fabbricazione f

fabric ribbon N (for typewriter) dattilonastro di tessuto

fabulous [ˈfæbjuləs] ADJ favoloso(-a); (col: super) favoloso(-a), fantastico(-a)

façade [fəˈsɑːd] N facciata; (fig) apparenza

face [feɪs] N faccia, viso, volto; (expression) faccia; (grimace) smorfia; (of clock) quadrante m; (of building) facciata; (side, surface) faccia; (of mountain, cliff) parete f ▶ VT fronteggiare; (fig) affrontare; **~ down** (person) bocconi; (object) a faccia in giù; **to lose/save ~** perdere/salvare la faccia; **to pull a ~** fare una smorfia; **in the ~ of** (difficulties etc) di fronte a; **on the ~ of it** a prima vista; **~ to ~** faccia a faccia; **to ~ the fact that …** riconoscere or ammettere che …
▶ **face up to** VT FUS affrontare, far fronte a

Facebook® [ˈfeɪsbuk] N Facebook® m

facebook® [ˈfeɪsbuk] VB messaggiare vt su Facebook/facebook

face cloth N (BRIT) guanto di spugna

face cream N crema per il viso

faceless [ˈfeɪslɪs] ADJ anonimo(-a)

face lift N lifting m inv; (of façade etc) ripulita

face pack N (BRIT) maschera di bellezza

face powder N cipria

face-saving [ˈfeɪsseɪvɪŋ] ADJ che salva la faccia

facet [ˈfæsɪt] N faccetta, sfaccettatura; (fig) sfaccettatura

facetious [fəˈsiːʃəs] ADJ faceto(-a)

face-to-face [ˈfeɪstəˈfeɪs] ADV faccia a faccia

face value [ˈfeɪsˈvæljuː] N (of coin) valore m facciale or nominale; **to take sth at ~** (fig) giudicare qc dalle apparenze

facia [ˈfeɪʃɪə] N = **fascia**

facial [ˈfeɪʃəl] ADJ facciale, del viso ▶ N trattamento del viso

facile [ˈfæsaɪl] ADJ facile; superficiale

facilitate [fəˈsɪlɪteɪt] VT facilitare

facility [fəˈsɪlɪtɪ] N facilità ■ **facilities** NPL attrezzature fpl; **credit facilities** facilitazioni fpl di credito

facing [ˈfeɪsɪŋ] N (of wall etc) rivestimento; (Sewing) paramontura

facsimile [fækˈsɪmɪlɪ] N facsimile m inv

facsimile machine N telecopiatrice f

fact [fækt] N fatto; **in ~** in effetti; **to know for a ~ that …** sapere per certo che …; **the ~ (of the matter) is that …** la verità è che …; **the facts of life** (sex) i fatti riguardanti la vita sessuale; (fig) le realtà della vita

fact-finding [ˈfæktfaɪndɪŋ] ADJ: **a ~ tour/mission** un viaggio/una missione d'inchiesta

faction [ˈfækʃən] N fazione f

factional [ˈfækʃənl] ADJ: **~ fighting** scontri mpl tra fazioni

factor [ˈfæktər] N fattore m; (Comm: company) organizzazione specializzata nell'incasso di crediti per conto terzi; (: agent) agente m depositario ▶ VI incassare crediti per conto terzi; **human ~** elemento umano; **safety ~** coefficiente m di sicurezza

factory [ˈfæktərɪ] N fabbrica, stabilimento

La parola inglese **factory** non vuol dire fattoria.

factory farming N (BRIT) allevamento su scala industriale

factory floor N: **the ~** (workers) gli operai; (area) il reparto produzione; **on the ~** nel reparto produzione

factory ship N nave f fattoria inv

factual [ˈfæktjuəl] ADJ che si attiene ai fatti

faculty [ˈfækəltɪ] N facoltà f inv; (US: teaching

staff) corpo insegnante

fad [fæd] N mania; capriccio

fade [feɪd] vɪ sbiadire, sbiadirsi; *(light, sound, hope)* attenuarsi, affievolirsi; *(flower)* appassire
▶ **fade away** vɪ *(sound)* affievolirsi
▶ **fade in** vt *(picture)* aprire in dissolvenza; *(sound)* aumentare gradualmente d'intensità
▶ **fade out** vt *(picture)* chiudere in dissolvenza; *(sound)* diminuire gradualmente d'intensità

faeces, *(US)* **feces** ['fi:si:z] NPL feci *fpl*

fag [fæg] N *(BRIT col: cigarette)* cicca; *(: chore)* sfacchinata; *(US col: homosexual)* frocio

fag end N *(BRIT col)* mozzicone *m*

fagged out ['fægd-] ADJ *(BRIT col)* stanco(-a) morto(-a)

Fahrenheit ['fɑːrənhaɪt] N Fahrenheit *m inv*

fail [feɪl] vt *(exam)* non superare; *(candidate)* bocciare; *(courage, memory)* mancare a ▶ vɪ fallire; *(student)* essere respinto(-a); *(supplies)* mancare; *(eyesight, health, light: also:* **be failing**) venire a mancare; *(: brakes)* non funzionare; **to ~ to do sth** *(neglect)* mancare di fare qc; *(be unable)* non riuscire a fare qc; **without ~** senza fallo; certamente

failing ['feɪlɪŋ] N difetto ▶ PREP in mancanza di; **~ that** se questo non è possibile

failsafe ['feɪlseɪf] ADJ *(device etc)* di sicurezza

failure ['feɪljəʳ] N fallimento; *(person)* fallito(-a); *(mechanical etc)* guasto; *(in exam)* insuccesso, bocciatura; *(of crops)* perdita; **his ~ to come** il fatto che non sia venuto; **it was a complete ~** è stato un vero fiasco

faint [feɪnt] ADJ debole; *(recollection)* vago(-a); *(mark)* indistinto(-a); *(smell, breeze, trace)* leggero(-a) ▶ N *(Med)* svenimento ▶ vɪ svenire; **to feel ~** sentirsi svenire

faintest ['feɪntɪst] ADJ: **I haven't the ~ idea** non ho la più pallida idea

faint-hearted [feɪnt'hɑːtɪd] ADJ pusillanime

faintly ['feɪntlɪ] ADV debolmente; vagamente

faintness ['feɪntnɪs] N debolezza

fair [fɛəʳ] ADJ *(person, decision)* giusto(-a), equo(-a); *(quite large, quite good)* discreto(-a); *(hair etc)* biondo(-a); *(skin, complexion)* chiaro(-a); *(weather)* bello(-a), clemente; *(good enough)* assai buono(-a); *(sizeable)* bello(-a) ▶ ADV: **to play ~** giocare correttamente ▶ N fiera; *(BRIT: funfair)* luna park *m inv*; *(also:* **trade fair**) fiera campionaria; **it's not ~!** non è giusto!; **a ~ amount of** un bel po' di

fair copy N bella copia

fair game N: **to be ~** *(person)* essere bersaglio legittimo

fairground ['fɛəgraund] N luna park *m inv*

fair-haired [fɛə'hɛəd] ADJ *(person)* biondo(-a)

fairly ['fɛəlɪ] ADV equamente; *(quite)* abbastanza

fairness ['fɛənɪs] N equità, giustizia; **in all ~** per essere giusti, a dire il vero

fair play N correttezza

fair trade N commercio equo solidale

fairway ['fɛəweɪ] N *(Golf)* fairway *m inv*

fairy ['fɛərɪ] N fata

fairy godmother N fata buona

fairy lights NPL *(BRIT)* lanternine *fpl* colorate

fairy tale N fiaba

faith [feɪθ] N fede *f*; *(trust)* fiducia; *(sect)* religione *f*, fede *f*; **to have ~ in sb/sth** avere fiducia in qn/qc

faithful ['feɪθful] ADJ fedele

faithfully ['feɪθfəlɪ] ADV fedelmente; **yours ~** *(BRIT: in letters)* distinti saluti

faith healer N guaritore(-trice)

fake [feɪk] N imitazione *f*; *(picture)* falso; *(person)* impostore(-a) ▶ ADJ falso(-a) ▶ vt *(accounts)* falsificare; *(illness)* fingere; *(painting)* contraffare; **his illness is a ~** fa finta di essere malato

falcon ['fɔːlkən] N falco, falcone *m*

Falkland Islands ['fɔːlklənd-] NPL: **the ~** le isole Falkland

fall [fɔːl] *(pt* **fell** [fɛl]*, pp* **fallen** ['fɔːlən]*)* N caduta; *(decrease)* diminuzione *f*, calo; *(in temperature)* abbassamento; *(in price)* ribasso; *(US: autumn)* autunno ▶ vɪ cadere; *(temperature, price)* scendere; **a ~ of earth** uno smottamento; **a ~ of snow** *(BRIT)* una nevicata; **to ~ in love (with sb/sth)** innamorarsi (di qn/qc); **to ~ short of** *(sb's expectations)* non corrispondere a; **to ~ flat** vɪ *(on one's face)* cadere bocconi; *(joke)* fare cilecca; *(plan)* fallire; *see also* **falls**
▶ **fall apart** vɪ cadere a pezzi
▶ **fall back** vɪ indietreggiare; *(Mil)* ritirarsi
▶ **fall back on** vt fus ripiegare su; **to have sth to ~ back on** avere qc di riserva
▶ **fall behind** vɪ rimanere indietro; *(fig: with payments)* essere in arretrato
▶ **fall down** vɪ *(person)* cadere; *(building, hopes)* crollare
▶ **fall for** vt fus *(person)* prendere una cotta per; **to ~ for a trick** *(or* **a story** *etc)* cascarci
▶ **fall in** vɪ crollare; *(Mil)* mettersi in riga
▶ **fall in with** vt fus *(sb's plans etc)* trovarsi d'accordo con
▶ **fall off** vɪ cadere; *(diminish)* diminuire, abbassarsi
▶ **fall out** vɪ *(hair, teeth)* cadere; *(friends etc)* litigare
▶ **fall over** vɪ cadere
▶ **fall through** vɪ *(plan, project)* fallire

fallacy ['fæləsɪ] N errore *m*

fallback ['fɔːlbæk] ADJ: **~ position** posizione *f* di ripiego

fallen ['fɔːlən] PP *of* **fall**

fallible ['fælɪbl] ADJ fallibile

falling ['fɔːlɪŋ] ADJ: **~ market** *(Comm)* mercato in ribasso

falling-off ['fɔːlɪŋ'ɔf] N calo

fallopian tube [fə'ləupɪən-] N *(Anat)* tuba di Falloppio

fallout ['fɔːlaut] N fall-out m

fallout shelter N rifugio antiatomico

fallow ['fæləu] ADJ incolto(-a); a maggese

falls [fɔːlz] NPL (*waterfall*) cascate *fpl*

false [fɔːls] ADJ falso(-a); **under ~ pretences** con l'inganno

false alarm N falso allarme m

falsehood ['fɔːlshud] N menzogna

falsely ['fɔːlslɪ] ADV (*accuse*) a torto

false teeth NPL (BRIT) denti *mpl* finti

falsify ['fɔːlsɪfaɪ] VT falsificare; (*figures*) alterare

falter ['fɔːltər] VI esitare, vacillare

fame [feɪm] N fama, celebrità

familiar [fə'mɪlɪər] ADJ familiare; (*common*) comune; (*close*) intimo(-a); **to be ~ with** (*subject*) conoscere; **to make o.s. ~ with** familiarizzarsi con; **to be on ~ terms with** essere in confidenza con

familiarity [fəmɪlɪ'ærɪtɪ] N familiarità; intimità

familiarize [fə'mɪlɪəraɪz] VT: **to ~ sb with sth** far conoscere qc a qn; **to ~ o.s. with** familiarizzare con

family ['fæmɪlɪ] N famiglia

family allowance N (BRIT) assegni *mpl* familiari

family business N impresa familiare

family credit N (BRIT) ≈ assegni *mpl* familiari

family doctor N medico di famiglia

family life N vita familiare

family man N (*irreg*) padre m di famiglia

family planning N pianificazione f familiare

family planning clinic N consultorio familiare

family tree N albergo genealogico

famine ['fæmɪn] N carestia

famished ['fæmɪʃt] ADJ affamato(-a); **I'm ~!** (*col*) ho una fame da lupo!

famous ['feɪməs] ADJ famoso(-a)

famously ['feɪməslɪ] ADV (*get on*) a meraviglia

fan [fæn] N (*folding*) ventaglio; (*machine*) ventilatore m; (*person*) ammiratore(-trice); (*Sport*) tifoso(-a) ▶ VT far vento a; (*fire, quarrel*) alimentare ▶ **fan out** VI spargersi (a ventaglio)

fanatic [fə'nætɪk] N fanatico(-a)

fanatical [fə'nætɪkl] ADJ fanatico(-a)

fan belt N cinghia del ventilatore

fancied ['fænsɪd] ADJ immaginario(-a)

fanciful ['fænsɪful] ADJ fantasioso(-a); (*object*) di fantasia

fan club N fan club m inv

fancy ['fænsɪ] N immaginazione f, fantasia; (*whim*) capriccio ▶ CPD (di) fantasia inv ▶ ADJ (*hat*) stravagante; (*hotel, food*) speciale ▶ VT (*feel like, want*) aver voglia di; (*imagine*) immaginare,

credere; **to take a ~ to** incapricciarsi di; **it took** or **caught my ~** mi è piaciuto; **when the ~ takes him** quando ne ha voglia; **to ~ that** immaginare che; **he fancies her** gli piace

fancy dress N costume m (per maschera)

fancy-dress ball N ballo in maschera

fancy goods NPL articoli *mpl* di ogni genere

fanfare ['fænfɛər] N fanfara

fanfold paper ['fænfəuld-] N carta a moduli continui

fang [fæŋ] N zanna; (*of snake*) dente m

fan heater N (BRIT) stufa ad aria calda

fanlight ['fænlaɪt] N lunetta

fanny ['fænɪ] N (BRIT col!) figa (!); (US col) culo (!)

fantasize ['fæntəsaɪz] VI fantasticare, sognare

fantastic [fæn'tæstɪk] ADJ fantastico(-a)

fantasy ['fæntəsɪ] N fantasia, immaginazione f; fantasticheria; chimera

fanzine ['fænziːn] N rivista specialistica (*per appassionati*)

FAO N ABBR (= *Food and Agriculture Organization*) FAO f

FAQ ABBR (= *free alongside quay*) franco lungo banchina; (*Comput*: = *frequently asked question(s)*) FAQ

far [fɑːr] ADJ lontano(-a) ▶ ADV lontano; (*much, greatly*) molto; **is it ~ from here?** è molto lontano da qui?; **it's not ~ (from here)** non è lontano (da qui); **how ~?** quanto lontano?; (*referring to activity etc*) fino a dove?; **how ~ is the town centre?** quanto dista il centro da qui?; **~ away, ~ off** lontano, distante; **the ~ side/end** l'altra parte/l'altro capo; **the ~ left/right** (*Pol*) l'estrema sinistra/destra; **~ better** assai migliore; **~ from** lontano da; **by ~** di gran lunga; **as ~ back as the 13th century** già nel duecento; **go as ~ as the farm** vada fino alla fattoria; **as ~ as I know** per quel che so; **as ~ as possible** nei limiti del possibile; **how ~ have you got with your work?** dov'è arrivato con il suo lavoro?

faraway ['fɑːrəweɪ] ADJ lontano(-a); (*voice, look*) assente

farce [fɑːs] N farsa

farcical ['fɑːsɪkəl] ADJ farsesco(-a)

fare [fɛər] N (*on trains, buses*) tariffa; (*in taxi*) prezzo della corsa; (*food*) vitto, cibo ▶ VI passarsela; **half ~** metà tariffa; **full ~** tariffa intera

Far East N: **the ~** l'Estremo Oriente m

farewell [fɛə'wɛl] EXCL, N addio ▶ CPD (*party etc*) d'addio

far-fetched ['fɑː'fɛtʃt] ADJ (*explanation*) stiracchiato(-a), forzato(-a); (*idea, scheme, story*) inverosimile

farm [fɑːm] N fattoria, podere m ▶ VT coltivare ▶ **farm out** VT (*work*) dare in consegna

farmer ['fɑːmər] N coltivatore(-trice), agricoltore(-trice)

farmhand [ˈfɑːmhænd] N bracciante m agricolo

farmhouse [ˈfɑːmhaus] N fattoria

farming [ˈfɑːmɪŋ] N (gen) agricoltura; (of crops) coltivazione f; (of animals) allevamento; **intensive ~** coltura intensiva; **sheep ~** allevamento di pecore

farm labourer N = **farmhand**

farmland [ˈfɑːmlænd] N terreno da coltivare

farm produce N prodotti mpl agricoli

farm worker N = **farmhand**

farmyard [ˈfɑːmjɑːd] N aia

Faroe Islands [ˈfɛərəu-], **Faroes** [ˈfɛərəuz] NPL: **the ~** le isole Faeroer

far-reaching [ˈfɑːˈriːtʃɪŋ] ADJ di vasta portata

far-sighted [ˈfɑːˈsaɪtɪd] ADJ presbite; (fig) lungimirante

fart [fɑːt] (col!) N scoreggia (!) ▶ VI scoreggiare (!)

farther [ˈfɑːðəʳ] ADV più lontano ▶ ADJ più lontano(-a)

farthest [ˈfɑːðɪst] ADV SUPERLATIVE of **far**

FAS ABBR (BRIT: = free alongside ship) franco banchina nave

fascia [ˈfeɪʃɪə] N (Aut) cruscotto; (of mobile phone) cover f inv

fascinate [ˈfæsɪneɪt] VT affascinare

fascinated ADJ affascinato(-a)

fascinating [ˈfæsɪneɪtɪŋ] ADJ affascinante

fascination [fæsɪˈneɪʃən] N fascino

fascism [ˈfæʃɪzəm] N fascismo

fascist [ˈfæʃɪst] ADJ, N fascista (mf)

fashion [ˈfæʃən] N moda; (manner) maniera, modo ▶ VT foggiare, formare; **in ~** alla moda; **out of ~** passato(a) di moda; **after a ~** (finish, manage etc) così così; **in the Greek ~** alla greca

---

Use **la moda** to refer to fashion, e.g. It's no longer in fashion. **Non è più di moda**. Use **il modo** for the way something is done, e.g. She looked at me in a strange way. **Mi ha guardato in modo strano**.

---

fashionable [ˈfæʃənəbl] ADJ alla moda, di moda; (writer) di grido

fashion designer N disegnatore(-trice) di moda

fashionista [fæʃəˈnɪstə] N fashionista mf, maniaco(-a) della moda

fashion show N sfilata di moda

fast [fɑːst] ADJ rapido(-a), svelto(-a), veloce; (clock): **to be ~** andare avanti; (dye, colour) solido(-a) ▶ ADV rapidamente; (stuck, held) saldamente ▶ N digiuno ▶ VI digiunare; **~ asleep** profondamente addormentato; **as ~ as I can** più in fretta possibile; **my watch is 5 minutes ~** il mio orologio va avanti di 5 minuti; **to make a boat ~** (BRIT) ormeggiare una barca

fasten [ˈfɑːsn] VT chiudere, fissare; (coat) abbottonare, allacciare ▶ VI chiudersi, fissarsi; abbottonarsi, allacciarsi
▶ **fasten (up)on** VT FUS (idea) cogliere al volo

fastener [ˈfɑːsnəʳ], **fastening** [ˈfɑːsnɪŋ] N fermaglio, chiusura; (BRIT: zip fastener) chiusura lampo

fast food N fast food m inv

fastidious [fæsˈtɪdɪəs] ADJ esigente, difficile

fast lane N (Aut) ≈ corsia di sorpasso

fat [fæt] ADJ grasso(-a); (book, profit etc) grosso(-a) ▶ N grasso; **to live off the ~ of the land** vivere nel lusso, avere ogni ben di Dio

fatal [ˈfeɪtl] ADJ fatale; mortale; disastroso(-a)

fatalism [ˈfeɪtəlɪzəm] N fatalismo

fatality [fəˈtælɪtɪ] N (road death etc) morto(-a), vittima

fatally [ˈfeɪtəlɪ] ADV a morte

fate [feɪt] N destino; (of person) sorte f; **to meet one's ~** trovare la morte

fated [ˈfeɪtɪd] ADJ (governed by fate) destinato(-a); (person, project etc) destinato(-a) a finire male

fateful [ˈfeɪtful] ADJ fatidico(-a)

fat-free [ˈfætˈfriː] ADJ senza grassi

father [ˈfɑːðəʳ] N padre m

Father Christmas N Babbo Natale

fatherhood [ˈfɑːðəhuːd] N paternità

father-in-law [ˈfɑːðərɪnlɔː] N suocero

fatherland [ˈfɑːðəlænd] N patria

fatherly [ˈfɑːðəlɪ] ADJ paterno(-a)

fathom [ˈfæðəm] N braccio (= 1828 mm) ▶ VT (mystery) penetrare, sondare

fatigue [fəˈtiːg] N stanchezza; (Mil) corvé f; **metal ~** fatica del metallo

fatness [ˈfætnɪs] N grassezza

fatten [ˈfætn] VT, VI ingrassare; **chocolate is fattening** la cioccolata fa ingrassare

fattening [ˈfætnɪŋ] ADJ (food) che fa ingrassare

fatty [ˈfætɪ] ADJ (food) grasso(-a) ▶ N (pej) ciccione(-a)

fatuous [ˈfætjuəs] ADJ fatuo(-a)

faucet [ˈfɔːsɪt] N (US) rubinetto

fault [fɔːlt] N colpa; (Tennis) fallo; (defect) difetto; (Geo) faglia ▶ VT criticare; **it's my ~** è colpa mia; **to find ~ with** trovare da ridire su; **at ~** in fallo; **generous to a ~** eccessivamente generoso

faultless [ˈfɔːltlɪs] ADJ perfetto(-a); senza difetto; impeccabile

faulty [ˈfɔːltɪ] ADJ difettoso(-a)

fauna [ˈfɔːnə] N fauna

faux pas [fəuˈpɑː] N gaffe f inv

favour, (US) **favor** [ˈfeɪvəʳ] N favore m ▶ VT (proposition) favorire, essere favorevole a; (pupil etc) favorire; (team, horse) dare per vincente; **to do sb a ~** fare un favore or una cortesia a qn; **in ~ of** in favore di; **to be in ~ of sth/of doing sth**

essere favorevole a qc/a fare qc; **to find ~ with sb** (*person*) entrare nelle buone grazie di qn; (*suggestion*) avere l'approvazione di qn

favourable, (*US*) **favorable** [ˈfeɪvərəbl] ADJ favorevole

favourably, (*US*) **favorably** [ˈfeɪvərəblɪ] ADV favorevolmente

favourite, (*US*) **favorite** [ˈfeɪvrɪt] ADJ, N favorito(-a)

favouritism, (*US*) **favoritism** [ˈfeɪvrɪtɪzəm] N favoritismo

fawn [fɔːn] N daino ▶ ADJ (*also:* **fawn-coloured**) marrone chiaro *inv* ▶ VI: **to ~ (up)on** adulare servilmente

fax [fæks] N (*document, machine*) facsimile *m inv*, telecopia; (*machine*) telecopiatrice *f* ▶ VT teletrasmettere, spedire via fax

FBI N ABBR (*US*: = *Federal Bureau of Investigation*) FBI *f*

FCC N ABBR (*US*) = **Federal Communications Commission**

FCO N ABBR (*BRIT*: = *Foreign and Commonwealth Office*) ≈ Ufficio affari esteri

FD N ABBR (*US*) = **fire department**

FDA N ABBR (*US*) = **Food and Drug Administration**

FE N ABBR = **further education**

fear [fɪər] N paura, timore *m* ▶ VT aver paura di, temere ▶ VI: **to ~ for** temere per, essere in ansia per; **~ of heights** vertigini *fpl*; **for ~ of** per paura di; **to ~ that** avere paura di (*or* che + *sub*), temere di (*or* che + *sub*)

fearful [ˈfɪəful] ADJ pauroso(-a); (*sight, noise*) terribile, spaventoso(-a); (*frightened*): **to be ~ of** temere

fearfully [ˈfɪəfəlɪ] ADV (*timidly*) timorosamente; (*old: very*) terribilmente, spaventosamente

fearless [ˈfɪəlɪs] ADJ intrepido(-a), senza paura

fearsome [ˈfɪəsəm] ADJ (*opponent*) formidabile, terribile; (*sight*) terrificante

feasibility [fiːzəˈbɪlɪtɪ] N praticabilità

feasibility study N studio delle possibilità di realizzazione

feasible [ˈfiːzəbl] ADJ fattibile, realizzabile

feast [fiːst] N festa, banchetto; (*Rel: also:* **feast day**) festa ▶ VI banchettare; **to ~ on** godersi, gustare

feat [fiːt] N impresa, fatto insigne

feather [ˈfɛðər] N penna ▶ CPD (*mattress, bed, pillow*) di piume ▶ VT: **to ~ one's nest** (*fig*) arricchirsi

feather-weight [ˈfɛðəweɪt] N peso *m* piuma *inv*

feature [ˈfiːtʃər] N caratteristica; (*article*) articolo ▶ VT (*film*) avere come protagonista ▶ VI figurare ■ **features** NPL (*of face*) fisionomia; **a (special) ~ on sth/sb** un servizio speciale su qc/qn; **it featured prominently in ...** ha avuto un posto di prima importanza in ...

feature film N film *m inv* principale

featureless [ˈfiːtʃəlɪs] ADJ anonimo(-a), senza caratteri distinti

Feb. [fɛb] ABBR (= *February*) feb.

February [ˈfɛbruərɪ] N febbraio; *see also* **July**

feces [ˈfiːsiːz] NPL (*US*) = **faeces**

feckless [ˈfɛklɪs] ADJ irresponsabile, incosciente

Fed [fɛd] ABBR (*US*) = **federal; federation**

fed [fɛd] PT, PP *of* **feed**

Fed. [fɛd] N ABBR (*US col*) = **Federal Reserve Board**

federal [ˈfɛdərəl] ADJ federale

Federal Republic of Germany N Repubblica Federale Tedesca

Federal Reserve Board N (*US*) *organo di controllo del sistema bancario statunitense*

Federal Trade Commission N (*US*) *organismo di protezione contro le pratiche commerciali abusive*

federation [fɛdəˈreɪʃən] N federazione *f*

fed up ADJ: **to be ~** essere stufo(-a)

fee [fiː] N pagamento; (*of doctor, lawyer*) onorario; (*for examination*) tassa d'esame; **school fees** tasse *fpl* scolastiche; **entrance ~, membership ~** quota d'iscrizione; **for a small ~** per una somma modesta

feeble [ˈfiːbl] ADJ debole

feeble-minded [fiːblˈmaɪndɪd] ADJ deficiente

feed [fiːd] N (*pt, pp* **fed** [fɛd]) (*of baby*) pappa; (*of animal*) mangime *m*; (*on printer*) meccanismo di alimentazione ▶ VT nutrire; (*baby*) allattare; (*horse etc*) dare da mangiare a; (*fire, machine*) alimentare ▶ VI (*baby, animal*) mangiare; **to ~ material into sth** introdurre materiale in qc; **to ~ data/information into sth** inserire dati/informazioni in qc
  ▶ **feed back** VT (*results*) riferire
  ▶ **feed on** VT FUS nutrirsi di

feedback [ˈfiːdbæk] N feed-back *m*; (*from person*) reazioni *fpl*

feeder [ˈfiːdər] N (*bib*) bavaglino

feeding bottle [ˈfiːdɪŋ-] N (*BRIT*) biberon *m inv*

feel [fiːl] N (*pt, pp* **felt** [fɛlt]) N sensazione *f*; (*sense of touch*) tatto; (*of substance*) consistenza ▶ VT toccare; palpare; tastare; (*cold, pain, anger*) sentire; (*grief*) provare; (*think, believe*): **to ~ that** pensare che; **I ~ that you ought to do it** penso che dovreste farlo; **to ~ hungry/cold** aver fame/freddo; **to ~ lonely/better** sentirsi solo/meglio; **I don't ~ well** non mi sento bene; **to ~ sorry for** dispiacersi per; **it feels soft** è morbido al tatto; **it feels colder out here** sembra più freddo qui fuori; **it feels like velvet** sembra velluto (al tatto); **to ~ like** (*want*) aver voglia di; **to ~ about** *or* **around for** cercare a tastoni; **to ~ about** *or* **around in one's pocket for** frugarsi in tasca per cercare; **I'm still feeling my way** (*fig*) sto ancora tastando il terreno; **to get the ~ of sth** (*fig*) abituarsi a qc

feeler ['fiːlə'] N (of insect) antenna; **to put out feelers** (fig) fare un sondaggio

feelgood ['fiːlgud] ADJ (film, song) allegro(-a) e a lieto fine

feeling ['fiːlɪŋ] N sensazione f; (emotion) sentimento; (impression) senso, impressione f; **to hurt sb's feelings** offendere qn; **what are your feelings about the matter?** che cosa ne pensa?; **my ~ is that ...** ho l'impressione che ...; **I got the ~ that ...** ho avuto l'impressione che ...; **feelings ran high about it** la cosa aveva provocato grande eccitazione

fee-paying school ['fiːpeɪɪŋ-] N scuola privata

feet [fiːt] NPL of **foot**

feign [feɪn] VT fingere, simulare

felicitous [fɪ'lɪsɪtəs] ADJ felice

fell [fɛl] PT of **fall** ▶ VT (tree) abbattere; (person) atterrare ▶ ADJ: **with one ~ blow** con un colpo terribile; **at one ~ swoop** in un colpo solo ▶ N (BRIT: mountain) monte m; (: moorland): **the fells** la brughiera

fellow ['fɛləu] N individuo, tipo; (comrade) compagno; (of learned society) membro cpd; (of university) ≈ docente mf ▶ CPD: **their ~ prisoners/students** i loro compagni di prigione/studio

fellow citizen N concittadino(-a)

fellow countryman N (irreg) compatriota m

fellow feeling N simpatia

fellow men NPL simili mpl

fellowship ['fɛləuʃɪp] N associazione f; compagnia; (Scol) specie di borsa di studio universitaria

fellow traveller N compagno(-a) di viaggio; (Pol) simpatizzante mf

fell-walking ['fɛlwɔːkɪŋ] N (BRIT) passeggiate fpl in montagna

felon ['fɛlən] N (Law) criminale mf

felony ['fɛlənɪ] N (Law) reato, crimine m

felt [fɛlt] PT, PP of **feel** ▶ N feltro

felt-tip pen ['fɛlttɪp-] N pennarello

female ['fiːmeɪl] N (Zool) femmina; (pej: woman) donna, femmina ▶ ADJ (sex, character) femminile; (Biol, Elec) femmina inv; (vote etc) di donne; **male and ~ students** studenti e studentesse

female impersonator N (Theat) attore comico che fa parti da donna

feminine ['fɛmɪnɪn] ADJ, N femminile (m)

femininity [fɛmɪ'nɪnɪtɪ] N femminilità

feminism ['fɛmɪnɪzəm] N femminismo

feminist ['fɛmɪnɪst] N femminista mf

fen [fɛn] N (BRIT): **the Fens** la regione delle Fen

fence [fɛns] N recinto; (Sport) ostacolo; (col: person) ricettatore(-trice) ▶ VT (also: **fence in**) recingere ▶ VI schermire; **to sit on the ~** (fig) rimanere neutrale; (Sport) tirare di scherma

fencing ['fɛnsɪŋ] N (Sport) scherma

fend [fɛnd] VI: **to ~ for o.s.** arrangiarsi

▶ **fend off** VT (attack, attacker) respingere, difendersi da; (blow) parare; (awkward question) eludere

fender ['fɛndə'] N parafuoco; (on boat) parabordo; (US) parafango; paraurti m inv

fennel ['fɛnl] N finocchio

ferment VI [fə'mɛnt] fermentare ▶ N ['fəːmɛnt] (fig) agitazione f, eccitazione f

fermentation [fəːmɛn'teɪʃən] N fermentazione f

fern [fəːn] N felce f

ferocious [fə'rəuʃəs] ADJ feroce

ferocity [fə'rɔsɪtɪ] N ferocità

ferret ['fɛrɪt] N furetto
▶ **ferret about, ferret around** VI frugare
▶ **ferret out** VT (person) scovare, scoprire; (secret, truth) scoprire

ferry ['fɛrɪ] N (small) traghetto; (large: also: **ferry-boat**) nave f traghetto inv ▶ VT traghettare; **to ~ sth/sb across** or **over** traghettare qc/qn da una parte all'altra

ferryman ['fɛrɪmən] N (irreg) traghettatore(-trice)

fertile ['fəːtaɪl] ADJ fertile; (Biol) fecondo(-a); **~ period** periodo di fecondità

fertility [fə'tɪlɪtɪ] N fertilità; fecondità

fertility drug N farmaco fecondativo

fertilize ['fəːtɪlaɪz] VT fertilizzare; fecondare

fertilizer ['fəːtɪlaɪzə'] N fertilizzante m

fervent ['fəːvənt] ADJ ardente, fervente

fervour, (US) **fervor** ['fəːvə'] N fervore m, ardore m

fester ['fɛstə'] VI suppurare

festival ['fɛstɪvəl] N (Rel) festa; (Art, Mus) festival m inv

festive ['fɛstɪv] ADJ di festa; **the ~ season** (BRIT: Christmas) il periodo delle feste

festivities [fɛs'tɪvɪtɪz] NPL festeggiamenti mpl

festoon [fɛ'stuːn] VT: **to ~ with** ornare di; decorare con

fetch [fɛtʃ] VT andare a prendere; (sell for) essere venduto(-a) per; **how much did it ~?** a or per quanto lo ha venduto?
▶ **fetch up** VI (BRIT) andare a finire

fetching ['fɛtʃɪŋ] ADJ attraente

fête [feɪt] N festa

fetid ['fɛtɪd] ADJ fetido(-a)

fetish ['fɛtɪʃ] N feticcio

fetter ['fɛtə'] VT (person) incatenare; (horse) legare; (fig) ostacolare

fetters ['fɛtəz] NPL catene fpl

fettle ['fɛtl] N (BRIT): **in fine ~** in gran forma

fetus ['fiːtəs] N (US) = **foetus**

feud [fjuːd] N contesa, lotta ▶ VI essere in lotta; **a family ~** una lite in famiglia

feudal ['fjuːdl] ADJ feudale

feudalism [ˈfjuːdəlɪzəm] N feudalesimo
fever [ˈfiːvəʳ] N febbre f; **he has a ~** ha la febbre
feverish [ˈfiːvərɪʃ] ADJ (also fig) febbrile; (person) febbricitante
few [fjuː] ADJ pochi(-e) ▶ PRON alcuni(-e); **~ succeed** pochi ci riescono; **they were ~** erano pochi; **a ~ ...** qualche ...; **I know a ~** ne conosco alcuni; **a good ~, quite a ~** parecchi; **in the next ~ days** nei prossimi giorni; **in the past ~ days** negli ultimi giorni, in questi ultimi giorni; **every ~ days/months** ogni due o tre giorni/mesi; **a ~ more days** qualche altro giorno
fewer [ˈfjuːəʳ] ADJ meno inv; meno numerosi(-e) ▶ PRON meno; **they are ~ now** adesso ce ne sono di meno
fewest [ˈfjuːɪst] ADJ il minor numero di
FFA N ABBR = **Future Farmers of America**
FH ABBR (BRIT) = **fire hydrant**
FHA N ABBR (US) = **Federal Housing Administration**
fiancé [fɪˈɑ̃ːŋseɪ] N fidanzato
fiancée [fɪˈɑ̃ːŋseɪ] N fidanzata
fiasco [fɪˈæskəʊ] N fiasco
fib [fɪb] N piccola bugia
fibre, (US) **fiber** [ˈfaɪbəʳ] N fibra
fibreboard, (US) **fiberboard** [ˈfaɪbəbɔːd] N pannello di fibre
fibreglass, (US) **fiberglass** N fibra di vetro
fibrositis [faɪbrəˈsaɪtɪs] N cellulite f
FICA N ABBR (US) = **Federal Insurance Contributions Act**
fickle [ˈfɪkl] ADJ incostante, capriccioso(-a)
fiction [ˈfɪkʃən] N narrativa, romanzi mpl; (sth made up) finzione f
fictional [ˈfɪkʃənl] ADJ immaginario(-a)
fictionalize [ˈfɪkʃənəlaɪz] VT romanzare
fictitious [fɪkˈtɪʃəs] ADJ fittizio(-a)
fiddle [ˈfɪdl] N (Mus) violino; (cheating) imbroglio; truffa ▶ VT (BRIT: accounts) falsificare, falsare; **tax ~** frode f fiscale; **to work a ~** fare un imbroglio
 ▶ **fiddle with** VT FUS gingillarsi con
fiddler [ˈfɪdləʳ] N violinista mf
fiddly [ˈfɪdlɪ] ADJ (task) da certosino; (object) complesso(-a)
fidelity [fɪˈdɛlɪtɪ] N fedeltà; (accuracy) esattezza
fidget [ˈfɪdʒɪt] VI agitarsi
fidgety [ˈfɪdʒɪtɪ] ADJ agitato(-a)
fiduciary [fɪˈduːʃərɪ] N fiduciario
field [fiːld] N (gen, Comput) campo; **to lead the ~** (Sport, Comm) essere in testa, essere al primo posto; **to have a ~ day** (fig) divertirsi, spassarsela
field glasses NPL binocolo (da campagna)
field hospital N ospedale m da campo
field marshal N feldmaresciallo

fieldwork [ˈfiːldwəːk] N ricerche fpl esterne; (Archaeology, Geo) lavoro sul campo
fiend [fiːnd] N demonio
fiendish [ˈfiːndɪʃ] ADJ demoniaco(-a)
fierce [fɪəs] ADJ (look) fiero(-a); (fighting) accanito(-a); (wind) furioso(-a); (heat) intenso(-a); (animal, person, attack) feroce; (enemy) acerrimo(-a)
fiery [ˈfaɪərɪ] ADJ ardente; infocato(-a)
FIFA [ˈfiːfə] N ABBR (= Fédération Internationale de Football Association) F.I.F.A. f
fifteen [fɪfˈtiːn] NUM quindici
fifteenth NUM quindicesimo(-a)
fifth [fɪfθ] NUM quinto(-a)
fiftieth [ˈfɪftɪɪθ] NUM cinquantesimo(-a)
fifty [ˈfɪftɪ] NUM cinquanta
fifty-fifty [ˈfɪftɪˈfɪftɪ] ADJ: **a ~ chance** una possibilità su due ▶ ADV: **to go ~ with sb** fare a metà con qn
fig [fɪg] N fico
fight [faɪt] (pt, pp **fought** [fɔːt]) N zuffa, rissa; (Mil) battaglia, combattimento; (against cancer etc) lotta ▶ VT (person) azzuffarsi con; (enemy, also Mil) combattere; (cancer, alcoholism, emotion) lottare contro, combattere; (election) partecipare a; (Law: case) difendere ▶ VI battersi, combattere; (quarrel): **to ~ (with sb)** litigare (con qn); (fig): **to ~ (for/against)** lottare (per/contro)
 ▶ **fight back** VI difendersi; (Sport, after illness) riprendersi ▶ VT (tears) ricacciare
 ▶ **fight down** VT (anger, anxiety) vincere; (urge) reprimere
 ▶ **fight off** VT (attack, attacker) respingere; (disease, sleep, urge) lottare contro
 ▶ **fight out** VT: **to ~ it out** risolvere la questione a pugni
fighter [ˈfaɪtəʳ] N combattente m; (plane) aeroplano da caccia
fighter-bomber [ˈfaɪtəbɔməʳ] N cacciabombardiere m
fighter pilot N pilota m di caccia
fighting [ˈfaɪtɪŋ] N combattimento; (in streets) scontri mpl
figment [ˈfɪgmənt] N: **a ~ of the imagination** un parto della fantasia
figurative [ˈfɪgjurətɪv] ADJ figurato(-a)
figure [ˈfɪgəʳ] N (Drawing, Geom, person) figura; (number, cipher) cifra; (body, outline) forma ▶ VT (think: esp US) pensare ▶ VI (appear) figurare; (US: make sense) spiegarsi; essere logico(-a) ▶ VT (US: think, calculate) pensare, immaginare; **public ~** personaggio pubblico; **~ of speech** figura retorica
 ▶ **figure on** VT FUS (US) contare su
 ▶ **figure out** VT riuscire a capire; calcolare
figurehead [ˈfɪgəhɛd] N (Naut) polena; (pej) prestanome mf
figure skating N pattinaggio artistico
Fiji [ˈfiːdʒiː] N, **Fiji Islands** NPL le (isole) Figi

filament ['fɪləmənt] N filamento

filch [fɪltʃ] VT (col: steal) grattare

file [faɪl] N (tool) lima; (for nails) limetta; (dossier) incartamento; (in cabinet) scheda; (folder) cartellina; (for loose leaf) raccoglitore m; (row) fila; (Comput) archivio, file m inv ▸ VT (nails, wood) limare; (papers) archiviare; (Law: claim) presentare; passare agli atti ▸ VI: **to ~ in/out** entrare/ uscire in fila; **to ~ past** marciare in fila davanti a; **to ~ a suit against sb** intentare causa contro qn

file name N (Comput) nome m del file

file sharing [-ʃɛərɪŋ] N (Comput) file sharing m, condivisione f di file

filibuster ['fɪlɪbʌstəʳ] (esp US Pol) N (also: **filibusterer**) ostruzionista mf ▸ VI fare ostruzionismo

filing ['faɪlɪŋ] N archiviare m; see also **filings**

filing cabinet ['faɪlɪŋ-] N casellario

filing clerk N archivista mf

filings ['faɪlɪŋz] NPL limatura

Filipino [fɪlɪ'piːnəu] N filippino(-a); (Ling) tagal m

fill [fɪl] VT riempire; (tooth) otturare; (job) coprire; (supply: order, requirements, need) soddisfare ▸ N: **to eat one's ~** mangiare a sazietà; **we've already filled that vacancy** abbiamo già assunto qualcuno per quel posto
▸ **fill in** VT (hole) riempire; (form) compilare; (details, report) completare ▸ VI: **to ~ in for sb** sostituire qn; **to ~ sb in on sth** (col) mettere qn al corrente di qc
▸ **fill out** VT (form, receipt) riempire
▸ **fill up** VT riempire ▸ VI (Aut) fare il pieno; **~ it up, please** (Aut) il pieno, per favore

fillet ['fɪlɪt] N filetto

fillet steak N bistecca di filetto

filling ['fɪlɪŋ] N (Culin) impasto, ripieno; (for tooth) otturazione f

filling station N stazione f di rifornimento

fillip ['fɪlɪp] N incentivo, stimolo

filly ['fɪlɪ] N puledra

film [fɪlm] N (Cine) film m inv; (Phot) pellicola, rullino; (of powder, liquid) sottile strato; (thin layer) velo ▸ VT (scene) filmare ▸ VI girare

film script N copione m

film star N divo(-a) dello schermo

filmstrip ['fɪlmstrɪp] N filmina

film studio N studio cinematografico

Filofax® ['faɪləufæks] N agenda ad anelli

filter ['fɪltəʳ] N filtro ▸ VT filtrare
▸ **filter in, filter through** VI (news) trapelare

filter coffee N caffè m da passare al filtro

filter lane N (BRIT Aut) corsia di svincolo

filter tip N filtro

filth [fɪlθ] N sporcizia; (fig) oscenità

filthy ['fɪlθɪ] ADJ lordo(-a), sozzo(-a); (language) osceno(-a)

fin [fɪn] N (of fish) pinna

final ['faɪnl] ADJ finale, ultimo(-a); definitivo(-a) ▸ N (Sport) finale f ■ **finals** NPL (Scol) esami mpl finali; **~ demand** ingiunzione f di pagamento

finale [fɪ'nɑːlɪ] N finale m

finalist ['faɪnəlɪst] N (Sport) finalista mf

finality [faɪ'nælɪtɪ] N irrevocabilità; **with an air of ~** con risolutezza

finalize ['faɪnəlaɪz] VT mettere a punto

finally ['faɪnəlɪ] ADV (lastly) alla fine; (eventually) finalmente; (once and for all) definitivamente

finance [faɪ'næns] N finanza; (funds) fondi mpl; (capital) capitale m ▸ VT finanziare ■ **finances** NPL (funds) finanze fpl

financial [faɪ'nænʃəl] ADJ finanziario(-a); **~ statement** estratto conto finanziario

financial adviser N consulente mf finanziario(-a)

financially [faɪ'nænʃəlɪ] ADV finanziariamente

financial year N anno finanziario, esercizio finanziario

financier [faɪ'nænsɪəʳ] N finanziatore(-trice)

find [faɪnd] (pt, pp **found** [faund]) VT trovare; (lost object) ritrovare ▸ N trovata, scoperta; **to ~ (some) difficulty in doing sth** trovare delle difficoltà nel fare qc; **to ~ sb guilty** (Law) giudicare qn colpevole
▸ **find out** VT informarsi di; (truth, secret) scoprire; (person) cogliere in fallo ▸ VI: **to ~ out about** informarsi su; (by chance) venire a sapere

findings ['faɪndɪŋz] NPL (Law) sentenza, conclusioni fpl; (of report) conclusioni

fine [faɪn] ADJ bello(-a); ottimo(-a); (thin, subtle) fine ▸ ADV (well) molto bene; (small) finemente ▸ N (Law) multa ▸ VT (Law) multare; **to be ~** (person) stare bene; (weather) far bello; **you're doing ~** te la cavi benissimo; **to cut it ~** (with time, money) farcela per un pelo

fine arts NPL belle arti fpl

finely ['faɪnlɪ] ADV (splendidly) in modo stupendo; (chop) finemente; (adjust) con precisione

fine print N: **the ~** i caratteri minuti

finery ['faɪnərɪ] N abiti mpl eleganti

finesse [fɪ'nɛs] N finezza

fine-tooth comb ['faɪntuː θ-] N: **to go through sth with a ~** (fig) passare qc al setaccio

finger ['fɪŋgəʳ] N dito ▸ VT toccare, tastare; **little/index ~** mignolo/(dito) indice m

fingernail ['fɪŋgəneɪl] N unghia

fingerprint ['fɪŋgəprɪnt] N impronta digitale ▸ VT (person) prendere le impronte digitali di

fingerstall ['fɪŋgəstɔːl] N ditale m

fingertip ['fɪŋgətɪp] N punta del dito; **to have sth at one's fingertips** (fig) avere qc sulla punta delle dita

finicky ['fɪnɪkɪ] ADJ esigente, pignolo(-a); minuziosoa(-a)

557

finish ['fɪnɪʃ] N fine f; (*Sport: place*) traguardo; (*polish etc*) finitura ▶ VT finire; (*use up*) esaurire ▶ VI finire; (*session*) terminare; **to ~ doing sth** finire di fare qc; **to ~ first/second** (*Sport*) arrivare primo/secondo; **she's finished with him** ha chiuso con lui
▶ **finish off** VT compiere; (*kill*) uccidere
▶ **finish up** VI, VT finire

finished ['fɪnɪʃt] ADJ (*product*) finito(-a); (*performance*) perfetto(-a); (*col: tired*) sfinito(-a)

finishing line ['fɪnɪʃɪŋ-] N linea d'arrivo

finishing school N scuola privata di perfezionamento (*per signorine*)

finishing touches NPL ultimi ritocchi *mpl*

finite ['faɪnaɪt] ADJ limitato(-a); (*verb*) finito(-a)

Finland ['fɪnlənd] N Finlandia

Finn [fɪn] N finlandese *mf*

Finnish ['fɪnɪʃ] ADJ finlandese ▶ N (*Ling*) finlandese *m*

fiord [fjɔːd] N fiordo

fir [fəːr] N abete *m*

fire [faɪər] N fuoco; (*destructive*) incendio; (*gas fire, electric fire*) stufa ▶ VT (*discharge*): **to ~ a gun** fare fuoco; (*arrow*) sparare; (*fig*) infiammare; (*dismiss*) licenziare ▶ VI sparare, far fuoco; **~!** al fuoco!; **on ~** in fiamme; **insured against ~** assicurato contro gli incendi; **electric/gas ~** stufa elettrica/a gas; **to set ~ to sth, set sth on ~** dar fuoco a qc, incendiare qc; **to be/come under ~ (from)** essere/finire sotto il fuoco *or* il tiro (di)

fire alarm N allarme *m* d'incendio

firearm ['faɪərɑːm] N arma da fuoco

fire brigade [-brɪˈgeɪd], (*US*) **fire department** N (*Brit*) (corpo dei) pompieri *mpl*

fire chief N (*US*) = **fire master**

fire department N = **fire brigade**

fire door N porta f rompifuoco *inv*

fire drill N esercitazione f antincendio

fire engine N autopompa

fire escape N scala di sicurezza

fire exit N uscita di sicurezza

fire extinguisher [-ɪkˈstɪŋgwɪʃər] N estintore *m*

firefighter ['faɪəfaɪtər] N pompiere *m*

fireguard ['faɪəgɑːd] N (*Brit*) parafuoco

fire hazard N: **that's a ~** comporta rischi in caso d'incendio

fire hydrant N idrante *m*

fire insurance N assicurazione f contro gli incendi

fire master N (*Brit*) comandante *m* dei vigili del fuoco

fireplace ['faɪəpleɪs] N focolare *m*

fireplug ['faɪəplʌg] N (*US*) = **fire hydrant**

fire practice N = **fire drill**

fireproof ['faɪəpruːf] ADJ resistente al fuoco

fire regulations NPL norme *fpl* antincendio

fire screen N parafuoco

fireside ['faɪəsaɪd] N angolo del focolare

fire station N caserma dei pompieri

firetruck N (*US*) = **fire engine**

firewall ['faɪəwɔːl] N (*Internet*) firewall *m inv*

firewood ['faɪəwud] N legna

fireworks NPL fuochi *mpl* d'artificio

firing ['faɪərɪŋ] N (*Mil*) spari *mpl*, tiro

firing line N linea del fuoco; **to be in the ~** (*fig*) essere sotto tiro

firing squad N plotone *m* d'esecuzione

firm [fəːm] ADJ fermo(-a); (*offer, decision*) definitivo(-a) ▶ N ditta, azienda; **to be a ~ believer in sth** credere fermamente in qc

firmly ['fəːmlɪ] ADV fermamente

firmness ['fəːmnɪs] N fermezza

first [fəːst] ADJ primo(-a) ▶ ADV (*before others*) il primo, la prima; (*before other things*) per primo; (*for the first time*) per la prima volta; (*when listing reasons etc*) per prima cosa ▶ N (*person: in race*) primo(-a); (*Brit Scol*) laurea con lode; (*Aut*) prima; **at ~** dapprima, all'inizio; **~ of all** prima di tutto; **in the ~ instance** prima di tutto, in primo luogo; **I'll do it ~ thing tomorrow** lo farò per prima cosa domani; **from the (very) ~** fin dall'inizio, fin dal primo momento; **the ~ of January** il primo (di) gennaio

first aid N pronto soccorso

first-aid kit ['fəːstˈeɪd-] N cassetta pronto soccorso

first-class ['fəːstˈklɑːs] ADJ di prima classe

first-class mail N ≈ espresso

first-hand ['fəːstˈhænd] ADJ di prima mano; diretto(-a)

first lady N (*US*) moglie f del presidente

firstly ['fəːstlɪ] ADV in primo luogo

first name N prenome *m*

first night N (*Theat*) prima

first-rate ['fəːstˈreɪt] ADJ di prima qualità, ottimo(-a)

first-time buyer ['fəːsttaɪm-] N acquirente *mf* di prima casa

First World War N: **the ~** la prima guerra mondiale

fir tree N abete *m*

fiscal ['fɪskəl] ADJ fiscale; **~ year** anno fiscale

fish [fɪʃ] N (*pl inv*) pesce *m* ▶ VT (*river, area*) pescare in ▶ VI pescare; **to go fishing** andare a pesca
▶ **fish out** VT (*from water*) ripescare; (*from box etc*) tirare fuori

fish-and-chip shop [fɪʃənˈtʃɪp-] N ≈ friggitoria; *see* **chip shop**

fishbone ['fɪʃbəun] N lisca, spina

fisherman ['fɪʃəmən] N (*irreg*) pescatore(-trice)

fishery ['fɪʃərɪ] N zona da pesca

fish factory N (*BRIT*) fabbrica per la lavorazione del pesce

fish farm N vivaio

fish fingers NPL (*BRIT*) bastoncini *mpl* di pesce (surgelati)

fish hook N amo

fishing ['fɪʃɪŋ] N pesca

fishing boat N barca da pesca

fishing industry N industria della pesca

fishing line N lenza

fishing net N rete *f* da pesca

fishing rod N canna da pesca

fishing tackle N attrezzatura da pesca

fish market N mercato del pesce

fishmonger ['fɪʃmʌŋgə'] N pescivendolo; **~'s (shop)** pescheria

fish slice N (*BRIT*) posata per servire il pesce

fish sticks NPL (*US*) = **fish fingers**

fishy ['fɪʃɪ] ADJ (*fig: tale, story*) sospetto(-a)

fission ['fɪʃən] N fissione *f*; **atomic/nuclear ~** fissione atomica/nucleare

fissure ['fɪʃə'] N fessura

fist [fɪst] N pugno

fistfight ['fɪstfaɪt] N scazzottata

fit [fɪt] ADJ (*Med, Sport*) in forma; (*proper*) adatto(-a), appropriato(-a); conveniente ▶ VT (*clothes*) stare bene a; (*match: facts etc*) concordare con; (*: description*) corrispondere a; (*adjust*) aggiustare; (*put in, attach*) mettere; installare; (*equip*) fornire, equipaggiare ▶ VI (*clothes*) stare bene; (*parts*) andare bene, adattarsi; (*in space, gap*) entrare ▶ N (*Med*) accesso, attacco; **~ to** in grado di; **~ for** adatto(-a) a; degno(-a) di; **to keep ~** tenersi in forma; **~ for work** (*after illness*) in grado di riprendere il lavoro; **do as you think** *or* **see ~** faccia come meglio crede; **this dress is a tight/good ~** questo vestito è stretto/sta bene; **~ of anger/enthusiasm** accesso d'ira/d'entusiasmo; **to have a ~** (*Med*) avere un attacco di convulsioni; (*col*) andare su tutte le furie; **by fits and starts** a sbalzi

▶ **fit in** VI accordarsi; adattarsi ▶ VT (*object*) far entrare; (*fig: appointment, visitor*) trovare il tempo per; **to ~ in with sb's plans** adattarsi ai progetti di qn

▶ **fit out** VT (*BRIT: also:* **fit up**) equipaggiare

fitful ['fɪtful] ADJ saltuario(-a)

fitment ['fɪtmənt] N componibile *m*

fitness ['fɪtnɪs] N (*Med*) forma fisica; (*of remark*) appropriatezza

fitness instructor N instruttore(-trice) di fitness

fitted ['fɪtɪd] ADJ: **~ carpet** moquette *f* inv; **~ cupboards** armadi *mpl* a muro; **~ kitchen** (*BRIT*) cucina componibile

fitter ['fɪtə'] N aggiustatore(-trice) *or* montatore(-trice) meccanico(-a); (*Dress*) sarto(-a)

fitting ['fɪtɪŋ] ADJ appropriato(-a) ▶ N (*of dress*) prova; (*of piece of equipment*) montaggio, aggiustaggio; *see also* **fittings**

fitting room N (*in shop*) camerino

fittings ['fɪtɪŋz] NPL (*in building*) impianti *mpl*

five [faɪv] NUM cinque

five-day week ['faɪvdeɪ-] N settimana di 5 giorni (lavorativi)

fiver ['faɪvə'] N (*col: BRIT*) biglietto da cinque sterline; (*: US*) biglietto da cinque dollari

fix [fɪks] VT fissare; (*mend*) riparare; (*make ready: meal, drink*) preparare ▶ N: **to be in a ~** essere nei guai; **the fight was a ~** (*col*) l'incontro è stato truccato

▶ **fix up** VT (*arrange: date, meeting*) fissare, stabilire; **to ~ sb up with sth** procurare qc a qn

fixation [fɪk'seɪʃən] N (*Psych, fig*) fissazione *f*, ossessione *f*

fixed [fɪkst] ADJ (*prices etc*) fisso(-a); **there's a ~ charge** c'è una quota fissa; **how are you ~ for money?** (*col*) a soldi come stai?

fixed assets NPL beni *mpl* patrimoniali

fixed penalty, fixed penalty fine N contravvenzione *f* a importo fisso

fixture ['fɪkstʃə'] N impianto (fisso); (*Sport*) incontro (del calendario sportivo)

fizz [fɪz] VI frizzare

fizzle ['fɪzl] VI frizzare; (*also:* **fizzle out**: *enthusiasm, interest*) smorzarsi, svanire; (*: plan*) fallire

fizzy ['fɪzɪ] ADJ frizzante; gassato(-a)

fjord [fjɔːd] N = **fiord**

FL, Fla. ABBR (*US*) = **Florida**

flabbergasted ['flæbəgɑːstɪd] ADJ sbalordito(-a)

flabby ['flæbɪ] ADJ flaccido(-a)

flag [flæg] N bandiera; (*also:* **flagstone**) pietra da lastricare ▶ VI stancarsi; affievolirsi; **~ of convenience** bandiera di convenienza

▶ **flag down** VT fare segno (di fermarsi) a

flagon ['flægən] N bottiglione *m*

flagpole ['flægpəul] N albero

flagrant ['fleɪgrənt] ADJ flagrante

flag stop N (*US: for bus*) fermata facoltativa, fermata a richiesta

flair [fleə'] N (*for business etc*) fiuto; (*for languages etc*) facilità; (*style*) stile *m*

flak [flæk] N (*Mil*) fuoco d'artiglieria; (*col: criticism*) critiche *fpl*

flake [fleɪk] N (*of rust, paint*) scaglia; (*of snow, soap powder*) fiocco ▶ VI (*also:* **flake off**) sfaldarsi

flaky ['fleɪkɪ] ADJ (*paintwork*) scrostato(-a); (*skin*) squamoso(-a); **~ pastry** (*Culin*) pasta sfoglia

flamboyant [flæm'bɔɪənt] ADJ sgargiante

flame [fleɪm] N fiamma; **old ~** (*col*) vecchia fiamma

flamingo [flə'mɪŋgəu] N fenicottero, fiammingo

flammable ['flæməbl] ADJ infiammabile

flan [flæn] N (BRIT) flan m inv

Flanders ['flɑːndəz] N Fiandre fpl

flange [flændʒ] N flangia; (on wheel) suola

flank [flæŋk] N fianco ▶ VT fiancheggiare

flannel ['flænl] N (BRIT: also: **face flannel**) guanto di spugna; (fabric) flanella ■ **flannels** NPL pantaloni mpl di flanella

flannelette [flænə'lɛt] N flanella di cotone

flap [flæp] N (of pocket) patta; (of envelope) lembo; (Aviat) flap m inv ▶ VT (wings) battere ▶ VI (sail, flag) sbattere; (col: also: **be in a flap**) essere in agitazione

flapjack ['flæpdʒæk] N (US: pancake) frittella; (BRIT: biscuit) biscotto di avena

flare [flɛər] N razzo; (in skirt etc) svasatura ■ **flares** (trousers) pantaloni mpl a zampa d'elefante ▶ **flare up** VI andare in fiamme; (fig: person) infiammarsi di rabbia; (: revolt) scoppiare

flared ['flɛəd] ADJ (trousers) svasato(-a)

flash [flæʃ] N vampata; (also: **news flash**) notizia f lampo inv; (Phot) flash m inv; (US: torch) torcia elettrica, lampadina tascabile ▶ VT accendere e spegnere; (send: message) trasmettere; (: look, smile) lanciare; (flaunt) ostentare ▶ VI brillare; (light on ambulance, eyes etc) lampeggiare; **in a ~** in un lampo; **~ of inspiration** lampo di genio; **to ~ one's headlights** lampeggiare; **he flashed by** or **past** ci passò davanti come un lampo

flashback ['flæʃbæk] N flashback m inv

flashbulb ['flæʃbʌlb] N cubo m flash inv

flash card N (Scol) scheda didattica

flashcube ['flæʃkjuːb] N flash m inv

flash drive N (Comput) chiavetta USB

flasher ['flæʃər] N (Aut) lampeggiatore m

flashlight ['flæʃlaɪt] N (torch) lampadina tascabile

flashpoint ['flæʃpɔɪnt] N punto di infiammabilità; (fig) livello critico

flashy ['flæʃɪ] ADJ (pej) vistoso(-a)

flask [flɑːsk] N fiasco; (Chem) beuta; (also: **vacuum flask**) thermos® m inv

flat [flæt] ADJ piatto(-a); (tyre) sgonfio(-a), a terra; (battery) scarico(-a); (beer) svampito(-a); (denial) netto(-a); (Mus) bemolle inv; (: voice) stonato(-a); (: instrument) scordato(-a) ▶ N (BRIT: rooms) appartamento; (Mus) bemolle m; (Aut) pneumatico sgonfio ▶ ADV: **(to work) ~ out** (lavorare) a più non posso; **~ rate of pay** tariffa unica di pagamento

flat-footed ['flæt'futɪd] ADJ: **to be ~** avere i piedi piatti

flatly ['flætlɪ] ADV categoricamente, nettamente

flatmate ['flætmeɪt] N (BRIT): **he's my ~** divide l'appartamento con me

flatness ['flætnɪs] N (of land) assenza di rilievi

flat-pack ['flætpæk] ADJ: **~ furniture** mobili mpl in kit ▶ N: **flat pack** kit m inv

flatscreen ['flætskriːn] ADJ a schermo piatto ▶ N schermo m piatto

flat-screen ['flætskriːn] ADJ a schermo piatto

flatten ['flætn] VT (also: **flatten out**) appiattire; (: house, city) abbattere, radere al suolo

flatter ['flætər] VT lusingare; (show to advantage) donare a

flatterer ['flætərər] N adulatore(-trice)

flattering ['flætərɪŋ] ADJ lusinghiero(-a); (clothes etc) che dona, che abbellisce

flattery ['flætərɪ] N adulazione f

flatulence ['flætjuləns] N flatulenza

flaunt [flɔːnt] VT fare mostra di

flavour, (US) **flavor** ['fleɪvər] N gusto, sapore m ▶ VT insaporire, aggiungere sapore a; **what flavours do you have?** che gusti avete?; **vanilla-flavoured** al gusto di vaniglia

flavouring, (US) **flavoring** ['fleɪvərɪŋ] N essenza (artificiale)

flaw [flɔː] N difetto

flawless ['flɔːlɪs] ADJ senza difetti

flax [flæks] N lino

flaxen ['flæksən] ADJ biondo(-a)

flea [fliː] N pulce f

flea market N mercato delle pulci

fleck [flɛk] N (of mud, paint, colour) macchiolina; (of dust) granello ▶ VT (with blood, mud etc) macchiettare; **brown flecked with white** marrone screziato di bianco

fled [flɛd] PT, PP of **flee**

fledgeling, fledgling ['flɛdʒlɪŋ] N uccellino

flee [fliː] (pt, pp **fled** [flɛd]) VT fuggire da ▶ VI fuggire, scappare

fleece [fliːs] N vello; (garment) pile m inv ▶ VT (col) pelare

fleecy ['fliːsɪ] ADJ (blanket) soffice; (cloud) come ovatta

fleet [fliːt] N flotta; (of lorries etc) convoglio; (of cars) parco

fleeting ['fliːtɪŋ] ADJ fugace, fuggitivo(-a); (visit) volante

Flemish ['flɛmɪʃ] ADJ fiammingo(-a) ▶ N (Ling) fiammingo ■ **the Flemish** NPL i Fiamminghi

flesh [flɛʃ] N carne f; (of fruit) polpa

flesh wound N ferita superficiale

flew [fluː] PT of **fly**

flex [flɛks] N filo (flessibile) ▶ VT flettere; (muscles) contrarre

flexibility [flɛksɪ'bɪlɪtɪ] N flessibilità

flexible ['flɛksəbl] ADJ flessibile

flexitarian [flɛksɪ'tɛərɪən] N, ADJ flexitariano(-a) m/f

flexitime ['flɛksɪtaɪm] N orario flessibile

flick [flɪk] N colpetto; scarto ▶ VT dare un colpetto a; *see also* **flicks**
▶ **flick through** VT FUS sfogliare

flicker ['flɪkər] VI tremolare ▶ N tremolio; **a ~ of light** un breve bagliore

flick knife N (BRIT) coltello a serramanico

flicks [flɪks] NPL: **the ~** (col) il cine

flier ['flaɪər] N aviatore(-trice)

flies [flaɪz] NPL of **fly**

flight [flaɪt] N volo; (*escape*) fuga; (*also*: **flight of steps**) scalinata; **to take ~** darsi alla fuga; **to put to ~** mettere in fuga

flight attendant N (US) steward m, hostess f inv

flight crew N equipaggio

flight deck N (Aviat) cabina di controllo; (Naut) ponte m di comando

flight path N (*of aircraft*) rotta di volo; (*of rocket, projectile*) traiettoria

flight recorder N registratore m di volo

flimsy ['flɪmzɪ] ADJ (*fabric*) leggero(-a); (*building*) poco solido(-a); (*excuse*) debole

flinch [flɪntʃ] VI ritirarsi; **to ~ from** tirarsi indietro di fronte a

fling [flɪŋ] (*pt, pp* **flung** [flʌŋ]) VT lanciare, gettare ▶ N (*love affair*) avventura

flint [flɪnt] N selce f; (*in lighter*) pietrina

flip [flɪp] N colpetto ▶ VT dare un colpetto a; (*switch*) far scattare; (*coin*) lanciare in aria; (US: *pancake*) far saltare (in aria) ▶ VI: **to ~ for sth** (US) fare a testa e croce per qc
▶ **flip through** VT FUS (*book, records*) dare una scorsa a

flip-flops ['flɪpflɒps] NPL (*esp* BRIT: *sandals*) infradito mpl

flippant ['flɪpənt] ADJ senza rispetto, irriverente

flipper ['flɪpər] N pinna

flip side N (*of record*) retro

flirt [flə:t] VI flirtare ▶ N civetta

flirtation [flə:'teɪʃən] N flirt m inv

flit [flɪt] VI svolazzare

float [fləut] N galleggiante m; (*in procession*) carro; (*sum of money*) somma ▶ VI galleggiare; (*bather*) fare il morto; (Comm: *currency*) fluttuare ▶ VT far galleggiare; (*loan, business*) lanciare; **to ~ an idea** ventilare un'idea

floating ['fləutɪŋ] ADJ a galla; **~ vote** voto oscillante; **~ voter** elettore m indeciso

flock [flɒk] N (*of sheep, Rel*) gregge m; (*of people*) folla; (*of birds*) stormo ▶ VI: **to ~ to** accorrere in massa a

floe [fləu] N (*also*: **ice floe**) banchisa

flog [flɒg] VT flagellare

flood [flʌd] N alluvione f; (*of words, tears etc*) dilu-

vio; (*of letters etc*) marea ▶ VT inondare, allagare; (*people*) invadere; (Aut: *carburettor*) ingolfare ▶ VI (*place*) allagarsi; (*people*): **to ~ into** riversarsi in; **in ~** in pieno; **to ~ the market** (Comm) inondare il mercato

flooding ['flʌdɪŋ] N inondazione f

floodlight ['flʌdlaɪt] N riflettore m ▶ VT (*irreg*: *like* **light**) illuminare a giorno

floodlit ['flʌdlɪt] PT, PP of **floodlight** ▶ ADJ illuminato(-a) a giorno

flood tide N alta marea, marea crescente

floodwater ['flʌdwɔ:tər] N acque fpl (*di inondazione*)

floor [flɔ:r] N pavimento; (*storey*) piano; (*of sea, valley*) fondo; (*fig*: *at meeting*): **the ~** il pubblico ▶ VT pavimentare; (*knock down*) atterrare; (*baffle*) confondere; (*silence*) far tacere; **on the ~** sul pavimento, per terra; **ground ~**, (US) **first ~** pianterreno; **first ~**, (US) **second ~** primo piano; **top ~** ultimo piano; **to have the ~** (*speaker*) prendere la parola

floorboard ['flɔ:bɔ:d] N tavellone m di legno

flooring ['flɔ:rɪŋ] N (*floor*) pavimento; (*material*) materiale m per pavimentazioni

floor lamp N (US) lampada a stelo

floor show N spettacolo di varietà

floorwalker ['flɔ:wɔ:kər] N (*esp* US) ispettore(-trice) di reparto

flop [flɒp] N fiasco ▶ VI (*fail*) far fiasco; (*fall*) lasciarsi cadere

floppy ['flɒpɪ] ADJ floscio(-a), molle ▶ N (Comput) = **floppy disk**; **~ hat** cappello floscio

floppy disk N floppy disk m inv

flora ['flɔ:rə] N flora

floral ['flɔ:rl] ADJ floreale

Florence ['flɒrəns] N Firenze f

Florentine ['flɒrəntaɪn] ADJ fiorentino(-a)

florid ['flɒrɪd] ADJ (*complexion*) florido(-a); (*style*) fiorito(-a)

florist ['flɒrɪst] N fioraio(-a)

florist's, florist's shop N fioraio(-a); **at the florist's (shop)** dal fioraio

flotation [fləu'teɪʃən] N (Comm) lancio

flounce [flauns] N balzo
▶ **flounce out** VI uscire stizzito(-a)

flounder ['flaundər] VI annaspare ▶ N (Zool) passera di mare

flour ['flauər] N farina

flourish ['flʌrɪʃ] VI fiorire ▶ VT brandire ▶ N abbellimento; svolazzo; (*of trumpets*) fanfara; (*bold gesture*): **with a ~** con ostentazione

flourishing ['flʌrɪʃɪŋ] ADJ prosperoso(-a), fiorente

flout [flaut] VT (*order*) contravvenire a; (*convention*) sfidare

flow [fləu] N flusso; circolazione f; (*of river, also*

Elec) corrente *f* ▶ vi fluire; (*traffic, blood in veins*) circolare; (*hair*) scendere

flow chart N schema *m* di flusso

flow diagram N organigramma *m*

flower ['flauə^r] N fiore *m* ▶ vi fiorire; **in ~** in fiore

flower bed N aiuola

flowerpot ['flauəpɔt] N vaso da fiori

flowery ['flauəri] ADJ fiorito(-a)

flown [fləun] PP *of* **fly**

fl. oz. ABBR = **fluid ounce**

flu [flu:] N influenza

fluctuate ['flʌktjueit] vi fluttuare, oscillare

fluctuation [flʌktju'eiʃən] N fluttuazione *f*, oscillazione *f*

flue [flu:] N canna fumaria

fluency ['flu:ənsi] N facilità, scioltezza; **his ~ in English** la sua scioltezza nel parlare l'inglese

fluent ['flu:ənt] ADJ (*speech*) facile, sciolto(-a); corrente; **he's a ~ speaker/reader** si esprime/ legge senza difficoltà; **he speaks ~ Italian, he's ~ in Italian** parla l'italiano correntemente

fluently ['flu:əntli] ADV con facilità; correntemente

fluff [flʌf] N lanugine *f*

fluffy ['flʌfi] ADJ lanuginoso(-a); (*toy*) di peluche

fluid ['flu:id] ADJ fluido(-a) ▶ N fluido; (*in diet*) liquido

fluid ounce N (*BRIT*) = 0.028 l; 0.05 pints

fluke [flu:k] N (*col*) colpo di fortuna

flummox ['flʌməks] vt rendere perplesso(-a)

flung [flʌŋ] PT, PP *of* **fling**

flunky ['flʌŋki] N tirapiedi *mf*

fluorescent [fluə'rɛsnt] ADJ fluorescente

fluoride ['fluəraid] N fluoruro

fluorine ['fluəri:n] N fluoro

flurry ['flʌri] N (*of snow*) tempesta; **a ~ of activity/excitement** un'intensa attività/un'improvvisa agitazione

flush [flʌʃ] N rossore *m*; (*fig*) ebbrezza; (*fig: of youth, beauty etc*) rigoglio, pieno vigore ▶ vt ripulire con un getto d'acqua; (*also*: **flush out**: *birds*) far alzare in volo; (: *animals, fig: criminal*) stanare ▶ vi arrossire ▶ ADJ: **~ with** a livello di, pari a; **~ against** aderente a; **hot flushes** (*Med*) vampate *fpl* di calore; **to ~ the toilet** tirare l'acqua

flushed [flʌʃt] ADJ tutto(-a) rosso(-a)

fluster ['flʌstə^r] N agitazione *f*

flustered ['flʌstəd] ADJ sconvolto(-a)

flute [flu:t] N flauto

flutter ['flʌtə^r] N agitazione *f*; (*of wings*) battito ▶ vi (*bird*) battere le ali

flux [flʌks] N: **in a state of ~** in continuo mutamento

fly [flai] (*pt* **flew** [flu:], *pp* **flown** [fləun]) N (*insect*) mosca; (*on trousers: also*: **flies**) patta ▶ vt pilotare; (*passengers, cargo*) trasportare (in aereo); (*distances*) percorrere ▶ vi volare; (*passengers*) andare in aereo; (*escape*) fuggire; (*flag*) sventolare; **to ~ open** spalancarsi all'improvviso; **to ~ off the handle** perdere le staffe, uscire dai gangheri
▶ **fly away** vi volar via
▶ **fly in** vi (*plane*) arrivare; (*person*) arrivare in aereo
▶ **fly off** vi volare via
▶ **fly out** vi (*plane*) partire; (*person*) partire in aereo

fly-drive N: **~ holiday** fly and drive *m inv*

fly-fishing ['flaifiʃiŋ] N pesca con la mosca

flying ['flaiiŋ] N (*activity*) aviazione *f*; (*action*) volo ▶ ADJ: **~ visit** visita volante; **with ~ colours** con risultati brillanti; **he doesn't like ~** non gli piace viaggiare in aereo

flying buttress N arco rampante

flying picket N picchetto (*proveniente da fabbriche non direttamente coinvolte nello sciopero*)

flying saucer N disco volante

flying squad N (*Police*) (squadra) volante *f*

flying start N: **to get off to a ~** partire come un razzo

flyleaf ['flaili:f] N risguardo

flyover ['flaiəuvə^r] N (*BRIT: bridge*) cavalcavia *m inv*

flypast ['flaipɑ:st] N esibizione *f* della pattuglia aerea

flysheet ['flaiʃi:t] N (*for tent*) sopratetto

flyweight ['flaiweit] N (*Sport*) peso *m* mosca *inv*

flywheel ['flaiwi:l] N volano

FM ABBR = **frequency modulation**; (*BRIT Mil*) = **Field Marshal**

FMB N ABBR (*US*) = **Federal Maritime Board**

FMCS N ABBR (*US*: = *Federal Mediation and Conciliation Services*) organismo di conciliazione in caso di conflitti sul lavoro

FO N ABBR (*BRIT*) = **Foreign Office**

foal [fəul] N puledro

foam [fəum] N schiuma; (*also*: **foam rubber**) gommapiuma® ▶ vi schiumare; (*soapy water*) fare la schiuma

foam rubber N gommapiuma®

FOB ABBR (= *free on board*) franco a bordo

fob [fɔb] vt: **to ~ sb off with** appioppare qn con; sbarazzarsi di qn con ▶ N (*also*: **watch fob**: *chain*) catena per orologio; (: *band of cloth*) nastro per orologio

focal ['fəukəl] ADJ focale

focal point N punto focale

focus ['fəukəs] N (*pl* **focuses**) fuoco; (*of interest*) centro ▶ vt (*light rays*) far convergere ▶ vi: **to ~ on** (*with camera*) mettere a fuoco; (*person*) fissare lo sguardo su; **in ~** a fuoco; **out of ~** sfocato(-a)

focus group N (Pol) gruppo di discussione, focus group m inv

fodder ['fɔdə'] N foraggio

FOE N ABBR (= Friends of the Earth) Amici mpl della Terra; (US: = Fraternal Order of Eagles) organizzazione filantropica

foe [fəu] N nemico

foetus, (US) **fetus** ['fi:təs] N feto

fog [fɔg] N nebbia

fogbound ['fɔgbaund] ADJ fermo(-a) a causa della nebbia

foggy ['fɔgɪ] ADJ nebbioso(-a); **it's ~** c'è nebbia

fog lamp, (US) **fog light** N (Aut) faro m antinebbia inv

foible ['fɔɪbl] N debolezza, punto debole

foil [fɔɪl] VT confondere, frustrare ▶ N lamina di metallo; (also: **kitchen foil**) foglio di alluminio; (Fencing) fioretto; **to act as a ~ to** (fig) far risaltare

foist [fɔɪst] VT: **to ~ sth on sb** rifilare qc a qn

fold [fəuld] N (bend, crease) piega; (Agr) ovile m; (fig) gregge m ▶ VT piegare; **to ~ one's arms** incrociare le braccia
▶ **fold up** VI (map etc) piegarsi; (business) crollare
▶ VT (map etc) piegare, ripiegare

folder ['fəuldə'] N (for papers) cartella; cartellina; (binder) raccoglitore m

folding ['fəuldɪŋ] ADJ (chair, bed) pieghevole

foliage ['fəulɪdʒ] N fogliame m

folk [fəuk] NPL gente f ▶ CPD popolare ■ **folks** NPL: **my folks** i miei

folklore ['fəuklɔ:'] N folclore m

folk music N musica folk inv

folk singer N cantante mf folk inv

folksong ['fəuksɔŋ] N canto popolare

follow ['fɔləu] VT seguire ▶ VI (also on Twitter) seguire; (result) conseguire, risultare; **to ~ sb's advice** seguire il consiglio di qn; **I don't quite ~ you** non ti capisco or seguo affatto; **to ~ in sb's footsteps** seguire le orme di qn; **it follows that ...** ne consegue che ...; **he followed suit** lui ha fatto lo stesso
▶ **follow on** VI (continue): **to ~ on from** seguire
▶ **follow out** VT (implement: idea, plan) eseguire, portare a termine
▶ **follow through** VT = **follow out**
▶ **follow up** VT (victory) sfruttare; (letter, offer) fare seguito a; (case) seguire

follower ['fɔləuə'] N seguace mf, discepolo(-a)

following ['fɔləuɪŋ] ADJ seguente, successivo(-a) ▶ N seguito, discepoli mpl

follow-up ['fɔləuʌp] N seguito

folly ['fɔlɪ] N pazzia, follia

fond [fɔnd] ADJ (memory, look) tenero(-a), affettuoso(-a); **to be ~ of** volere bene a; **she's ~ of swimming** le piace nuotare

fondle ['fɔndl] VT accarezzare

fondly ['fɔndlɪ] ADV (lovingly) affettuosamente; (naïvely): **he ~ believed that ...** ha avuto l'ingenuità di credere che ...

fondness ['fɔndnɪs] N affetto; **~ (for sth)** predilezione f (per qc)

font [fɔnt] N (Rel) fonte m (battesimale); (Typ) stile m di carattere

food [fu:d] N cibo

food chain N catena alimentare

food mixer N frullatore m

food poisoning N intossicazione f alimentare

food processor [-'prəusesə] N tritatutto m inv elettrico

food stamp N (US) buono alimentare dato agli indigenti

foodstuffs ['fu:dstʌfs] NPL generi fpl alimentari

fool [fu:l] N sciocco(-a); (Hist: of king) buffone m; (Culin) frullato ▶ VT ingannare ▶ VI (gen): **~ around** fare lo sciocco; **to make a ~ of sb** prendere in giro qn; **to make a ~ of o.s.** coprirsi di ridicolo; **you can't ~ me** non mi inganna
▶ **fool about, fool around** VI (waste time) perdere tempo

foolhardy ['fu:lhɑ:dɪ] ADJ avventato(-a)

foolish ['fu:lɪʃ] ADJ scemo(-a), stupido(-a); imprudente

foolishly ['fu:lɪʃlɪ] ADV stupidamente

foolishness ['fu:lɪʃnɪs] N stupidità

foolproof ['fu:lpru:f] ADJ (plan etc) sicurissimo(-a)

foolscap ['fu:lskæp] N carta protocollo

foot [fut] (pl **feet** [fi:t]) N piede m; (measure) piede (= 304 mm; = 12 inches); (of animal) zampa; (of page, stairs etc) fondo ▶ VT (bill) pagare; **on ~** a piedi; **to put one's ~ down** (Aut) schiacciare l'acceleratore; (say no) imporsi; **to find one's feet** ambientarsi

footage ['futɪdʒ] N (Cine: length) = metraggio; (: material) sequenza

foot and mouth, foot and mouth disease N afta epizootica

football ['fu:tbɔ:l] N pallone m; (sport: BRIT) calcio; (: US) football m americano

footballer ['fu:tbɔ:lə'] N (BRIT) = **football player**

football ground N campo di calcio

football match N (BRIT) partita di calcio

football player N (BRIT: also: **footballer**) calciatore(-trice); (US) giocatore(-trice) di football americano

footbrake ['fu:tbreɪk] N freno a pedale

footbridge ['fu:tbrɪdʒ] N passerella

footfall ['futfɔ:l] N (footstep) (rumore m del) passo m; (Comm) affluenza (di visitatori), footfall m inv

foothills ['fu:thɪlz] NPL contrafforti fpl

foothold ['futhəuld] N punto d'appoggio

footing [ˈfutɪŋ] N (fig) posizione f; **to lose one's ~** mettere un piede in fallo; **on an equal ~** in condizioni di parità

footlights [ˈfutlaɪts] NPL luci fpl della ribalta

footman [ˈfutmən] N (irreg) lacchè m inv

footnote [ˈfutnəut] N nota (a piè di pagina)

footpath [ˈfutpɑːθ] N sentiero; (in street) marciapiede m

footprint [ˈfutprɪnt] N orma, impronta

footrest [ˈfutrɛst] N poggiapiedi m inv

Footsie [ˈfutsɪ], **Footsie index** [ˈfutsɪ-] N (col) = Financial Times Stock Exchange 100 Index

footsie [ˈfutsɪ] N (col): **to play ~ with sb** fare piedino a qn

footsore [ˈfutsɔːʳ] ADJ: **to be ~** avere mal di piedi

footstep [ˈfutstɛp] N passo

footwear [ˈfutwɛəʳ] N calzatura

FOR ABBR (= free on rail) franco vagone

---

for [fɔːʳ]

PREP **1** (indicating destination, intention, purpose) per; **the train for London** il treno per Londra; **he went for the paper** è andato a prendere il giornale; **it's time for lunch** è ora di pranzo; **what's it for?** a che serve?; **what for?** (why) perché?

2 (on behalf of, representing) per; **to work for sb/sth** lavorare per qn/qc; **I'll ask him for you** glielo chiederò a nome tuo; **G for George** ≈ G come George

3 (because of) per, a causa di; **for this reason** per questo motivo

4 (with regard to) per; **it's cold for July** è freddo per luglio; **for everyone who voted yes, 50 voted no** per ogni voto a favore ce n'erano 50 contro

5 (in exchange for) per; **I sold it for £5** l'ho venduto per 5 sterline

6 (in favour of) per, a favore di; **are you for or against us?** sei con noi o contro di noi?; **I'm all for it** sono completamente a favore

7 (referring to distance, time) per; **there are roadworks for 5 km** ci sono lavori in corso per 5 km; **he was away for 2 years** è stato via per 2 anni; **she will be away for a month** starà via un mese; **it hasn't rained for 3 weeks** non piove da 3 settimane; **can you do it for tomorrow?** può farlo per domani?

8 (with infinitive clauses): **it is not for me to decide** non sta a me decidere; **it would be best for you to leave** sarebbe meglio che lei se ne andasse; **there is still time for you to do it** ha ancora tempo per farlo; **for this to be possible …** perché ciò sia possibile …

9 (in spite of) nonostante; **for all his complaints, he's very fond of her** nonostante tutte le sue lamentele, le vuole molto bene

▶ CONJ (since, as: formal) dal momento che, poiché

When the perfect tense is used with for to describe actions or states that started in the past and are still going on, use da with the present tense of the Italian verb.

He's been learning Italian for two years. **Studia italiano da due anni.**

They've been here for ages. **Sono qui da moltissimo tempo.**

---

forage [ˈfɔrɪdʒ] VI foraggiare

forage cap N bustina

foray [ˈfɔreɪ] N incursione f

forbad, forbade [fəˈbæd] PT of **forbid**

forbearing [fɔːˈbɛərɪŋ] ADJ paziente, tollerante

forbid [fəˈbɪd] (pt **forbad(e)** [-ˈbæd], pp **forbidden** [-ˈbɪdn]) VT vietare, interdire; **to ~ sb to do sth** proibire a qn di fare qc

forbidden PT of **forbid** ▶ ADJ (food) proibito(-a); (area, territory) vietato(-a); (word, subject) tabù inv

forbidding [fəˈbɪdɪŋ] ADJ arcigno(-a), d'aspetto minaccioso

force [fɔːs] N forza ▶ VT forzare; (obtain by force: smile, confession) strappare ■ **the Forces** NPL (BRIT) le forze armate; **in ~** (in large numbers) in gran numero; (law) in vigore; **to come into ~** entrare in vigore; **a ~ 5 wind** un vento forza 5; **to join forces** unire le forze; **the sales ~** (Comm) l'effettivo dei rappresentanti; **to ~ sb to do sth** costringere qn a fare qc

▶ **force back** VT (crowd, enemy) respingere; (tears) ingoiare

▶ **force down** VT (food) sforzarsi di mangiare

forced [fɔːst] ADJ forzato(-a)

force-feed [ˈfɔːsfiːd] VT sottoporre ad alimentazione forzata

forceful [ˈfɔːsful] ADJ forte, vigoroso(-a)

forcemeat [ˈfɔːsmiːt] N (BRIT Culin) ripieno

forceps [ˈfɔːsɪps] NPL forcipe m

forcibly [ˈfɔːsəblɪ] ADV con la forza; (vigorously) vigorosamente

ford [fɔːd] N guado ▶ VT guadare

fore [fɔːʳ] N: **to the ~** in prima linea; **to come to the ~** mettersi in evidenza

forearm [ˈfɔːrɑːm] N avambraccio

forebear [ˈfɔːbɛəʳ] N antenato

foreboding [fɔːˈbəudɪŋ] N presagio di male

forecast [ˈfɔːkɑːst] N (irreg: like **cast**) previsione f; (weather forecast) previsioni fpl del tempo ▶ VT (irreg: like **cast**) prevedere

foreclose [fɔːˈkləuz] VT (Law: also: **foreclose on**) sequestrare l'immobile ipotecato di

foreclosure [fɔːˈkləuʒəʳ] N sequestro di immobile ipotecato

forecourt [ˈfɔːkɔːt] N (of garage) corte f esterna

forefathers [ˈfɔːfɑːðəz] NPL antenati mpl, avi mpl

forefinger [ˈfɔːfɪŋgəʳ] N (dito) indice m

forefront [ˈfɔːfrʌnt] N: **in the ~ of** all'avanguardia di

forego [fɔːˈgəu] VT = **forgo**

foregoing [ˈfɔːgəuɪŋ] ADJ precedente

foregone [ˈfɔːgɒn] PP of **forego** ▶ ADJ: **it's a ~ conclusion** è una conclusione scontata

foreground [ˈfɔːgraund] N primo piano ▶ CPD (*Comput*) foreground *inv*, di primo piano

forehand [ˈfɔːhænd] N (*Tennis*) diritto

forehead [ˈfɒrɪd] N fronte f

foreign [ˈfɒrən] ADJ straniero(-a); (*trade*) estero(-a); (*object, matter*) estraneo(-a)

foreign body N corpo estraneo

foreign currency N valuta estera

foreigner [ˈfɒrənəʳ] N straniero(-a)

foreign exchange N cambio di valuta; (*currency*) valuta estera

foreign exchange market N mercato delle valute

foreign exchange rate N cambio

foreign investment N investimento all'estero

foreign minister N ministro degli Affari esteri

Foreign Office N (*BRIT*) Ministero degli Esteri

foreign secretary N (*BRIT*) ministro degli Affari esteri

foreleg [ˈfɔːlɛg] N zampa anteriore

foreman [ˈfɔːmən] N (*irreg*) caposquadra *m*; (*Law: of jury*) portavoce *m* della giuria

foremost [ˈfɔːməust] ADJ principale; più in vista ▶ ADV: **first and ~** innanzitutto

forename [ˈfɔːneɪm] N nome *m* di battesimo

forensic [fəˈrɛnsɪk] ADJ: **~ medicine** medicina legale; **~ expert** esperto della (polizia) scientifica

foreplay [ˈfɔːpleɪ] N preliminari *mpl*

forerunner [ˈfɔːrʌnəʳ] N precursore *m*

foresee [fɔːˈsiː] (*pt* **foresaw** [-ˈsɔː], *pp* **foreseen** [-ˈsiːn]) VT (*irreg: like* **see**) prevedere

foreseeable [fɔːˈsiːəbl] ADJ prevedibile

foreseen [fɔːˈsiːn] PP of **foresee**

foreshadow [fɔːˈʃædəu] VT presagire, far prevedere

foreshorten [fɔːˈʃɔːtn] VT (*figure, scene*) rappresentare in scorcio

foresight [ˈfɔːsaɪt] N previdenza

foreskin [ˈfɔːskɪn] N (*Anat*) prepuzio

forest [ˈfɒrɪst] N foresta

forestall [fɔːˈstɔːl] VT prevenire

forestry [ˈfɒrɪstrɪ] N silvicoltura

foretaste [ˈfɔːteɪst] N pregustazione f

foretell [fɔːˈtɛl] VT (*irreg: like* **tell**) predire

forethought [ˈfɔːθɔːt] N previdenza

foretold [fɔːˈtəuld] PT, PP of **foretell**

forever [fəˈrɛvəʳ] ADV per sempre; (*fig: endlessly*) sempre, di continuo

forewarn [fɔːˈwɔːn] VT avvisare in precedenza

forewent [fɔːˈwɛnt] PT of **forego**

foreword [ˈfɔːwəːd] N prefazione f

forfeit [ˈfɔːfɪt] N ammenda, pena ▶ VT perdere; (*one's happiness, health*) giocarsi

forgave [fəˈgeɪv] PT of **forgive**

forge [fɔːdʒ] N fucina ▶ VT falsificare; (*signature*) contraffare, falsificare; (*wrought iron*) fucinare, foggiare
▶ **forge ahead** VI tirare avanti

forger [ˈfɔːdʒəʳ] N contraffattore *m*

forgery [ˈfɔːdʒərɪ] N falso; (*activity*) contraffazione f

forget [fəˈgɛt] (*pt* **forgot** [-ˈgɒt], *pp* **forgotten** [-ˈgɒtn]) VT, VI dimenticare

forgetful [fəˈgɛtful] ADJ di corta memoria; **~ of** dimentico(a) di

forgetfulness [fəˈgɛtfulnɪs] N smemoratezza; (*oblivion*) oblio

forget-me-not [fəˈgɛtmɪnɒt] N nontiscordardimé *m inv*

forgive [fəˈgɪv] (*pt* **forgave** [-ˈgeɪv], *pp* **forgiven** [-ˈgɪvn]) VT perdonare; **to ~ sb for sth/for doing sth** perdonare qc a qn/a qn di aver fatto qc

forgiveness [fəˈgɪvnɪs] N perdono

forgiving [fəˈgɪvɪŋ] ADJ indulgente

forgo [fɔːˈgəu] (*pt* **forwent** [-ˈwɛnt], *pp* **forgone** [-ˈgɒn]) VT rinunciare a

forgot [fəˈgɒt] PT of **forget**

forgotten [fəˈgɒtn] PP of **forget**

fork [fɔːk] N (*for eating*) forchetta; (*for gardening*) forca; (*of roads, railways*) bivio, biforcazione f ▶ VI (*road*) biforcarsi
▶ **fork out** (*col: pay*) VT sborsare ▶ VI pagare

forked [fɔːkt] ADJ (*lightning*) a zigzag

fork-lift truck [ˈfɔːklɪft-] N carrello elevatore

forlorn [fəˈlɔːn] ADJ (*person*) sconsolato(-a); (*deserted: cottage*) abbandonato(-a); (*desperate: attempt*) disperato(-a); (*: hope*) vano(-a)

form [fɔːm] N forma; (*Scol*) classe f; (*questionnaire*) modulo ▶ VT formare; (*circle, queue etc*) fare; **in the ~ of** a forma di, sotto forma di; **to be in good ~** (*Sport, fig*) essere in forma; **in top ~** in gran forma; **to ~ part of sth** far parte di qc

formal [ˈfɔːməl] ADJ formale; (*gardens*) simmetrico(-a), regolare; (*offer, receipt*) vero(-a) e proprio(-a); (*person*) cerimonioso(-a); (*occasion, dinner*) formale, ufficiale; (*Art, Philosophy*) formale; **~ dress** abito da cerimonia; (*evening dress*) abito da sera

formality [fɔːˈmælɪtɪ] N formalità f inv

formalize [ˈfɔːməlaɪz] VT rendere ufficiale

formally [ˈfɔːməlɪ] ADV ufficialmente; formalmente; cerimoniosamente; **to be ~ invited** ricevere un invito ufficiale

format [ˈfɔːmæt] N formato ▶ VT (*Comput*) formattare

formation [fɔːˈmeɪʃən] N formazione f

formative [ˈfɔːmətɪv] ADJ: **~ years** anni *mpl* formativi

formatting [ˈfɔːmætɪŋ] N (*Comput*) formattazione f

former [ˈfɔːmə‍ʳ] ADJ vecchio(-a) (*before n*), ex *inv* (*before n*); **the ~ president** l'ex presidente; **the ~ ... the latter** quello ... questo; **the ~ Yugoslavia/Soviet Union** l'ex Jugoslavia/Unione Sovietica

formerly [ˈfɔːməlɪ] ADV in passato

form feed N (*on printer*) alimentazione f modulo

formidable [ˈfɔːmɪdəbl] ADJ formidabile

formula [ˈfɔːmjulə] N formula; **F~ One** (*Aut*) formula uno

formulate [ˈfɔːmjuleɪt] VT formulare

fornicate [ˈfɔːnɪkeɪt] VI fornicare

forsake [fəˈseɪk] (*pt* **forsook** [-ˈsuk], *pp* **forsaken** [-ˈseɪkən]) VT abbandonare

fort [fɔːt] N forte *m*; **to hold the ~** (*fig*) prendere le redini (della situazione)

forte [ˈfɔːtɪ] N forte *m*

forth [fɔːθ] ADV in avanti; **to go back and ~** andare avanti e indietro; **and so ~** e così via

forthcoming [fɔːθˈkʌmɪŋ] ADJ (*event*) prossimo(-a); (*help*) disponibile; (*character*) aperto(-a), comunicativo(-a)

forthright [ˈfɔːθraɪt] ADJ franco(-a), schietto(-a)

forthwith [fɔːθˈwɪθ] ADV immediatamente, subito

fortieth [ˈfɔːtɪɪθ] NUM quarantesimo(-a)

fortification [fɔːtɪfɪˈkeɪʃən] N fortificazione f

fortified wine N vino ad alta gradazione alcolica

fortify [ˈfɔːtɪfaɪ] VT (*city*) fortificare; (*person*) armare

fortitude [ˈfɔːtɪtjuːd] N forza d'animo

fortnight [ˈfɔːtnaɪt] N (*BRIT*) quindici giorni *mpl*, due settimane *fpl*; **it's a ~ since ...** sono due settimane da quando ...

fortnightly [ˈfɔːtnaɪtlɪ] ADJ bimensile ▶ ADV ogni quindici giorni

FORTRAN [ˈfɔːtræn] N FORTRAN *m*

fortress [ˈfɔːtrɪs] N fortezza, rocca

fortuitous [fɔːˈtjuːɪtəs] ADJ fortuito(-a)

fortunate [ˈfɔːtʃənɪt] ADJ fortunato(-a); **he is ~ to have ...** ha la fortuna di avere ...; **it is ~ that** è una fortuna che + *sub*

fortunately [ˈfɔːtʃənɪtlɪ] ADV fortunatamente

fortune [ˈfɔːtʃən] N fortuna; **to make a ~** farsi una fortuna

fortune-teller [ˈfɔːtʃəntɛlə‍ʳ] N indovino(-a)

forty [ˈfɔːtɪ] NUM quaranta

forum [ˈfɔːrəm] N foro; (*fig*) luogo di pubblica discussione

forward [ˈfɔːwəd] ADJ (*ahead of schedule*) in anticipo; (*movement, position*) in avanti; (*not shy*) sfacciato(-a); (*Comm: delivery, sales, exchange*) a termine ▶ ADV avanti ▶ N (*Sport*) avanti *m inv* ▶ VT (*letter*) inoltrare; (*parcel, goods*) spedire; (*fig: career, plans*) promuovere, appoggiare; **to move ~** avanzare; **"please ~"** "si prega di inoltrare"; **~ planning** programmazione f in anticipo

forwarding address N *nuovo recapito cui spedire la posta*

forwards [ˈfɔːwədz] ADV avanti

forward slash N barra obliqua

forwent [fɔːˈwɛnt] PT *of* **forgo**

fossick [ˈfɔsɪk] VI (*AUSTRALIA, NEW ZEALAND col*) cercare; **to ~ in a drawer** rovistare in un cassetto

fossil [ˈfɔsl] ADJ, N fossile (*m*); **~ fuel** combustibile m fossile

foster [ˈfɔstə‍ʳ] VT incoraggiare, nutrire; (*child*) avere in affidamento

foster brother N fratello adottivo (*in affidamento temporaneo presso la propria famiglia*)

foster child N (*irreg*) bambino(-a) preso(-a) in affidamento

foster mother N madre f affidataria

foster sister N sorella adottiva (*in affidamento temporaneo presso la propria famiglia*)

fought [fɔːt] PT, PP *of* **fight**

foul [faul] ADJ (*smell, food*) cattivo(-a); (*weather*) brutto(-a), orribile; (*language*) osceno(-a); (*deed*) infame ▶ N (*Football*) fallo ▶ VT sporcare; (*football player*) commettere un fallo su; (*entangle: anchor, propeller*) impigliarsi in

foul play N (*Sport*) gioco scorretto; **~ is not suspected** si è scartata l'ipotesi dell'atto criminale

found [faund] PT, PP *of* **find** ▶ VT (*establish*) fondare

foundation [faunˈdeɪʃən] N (*act*) fondazione f; (*base*) base f; (*also:* **foundation cream**) fondo tinta ◾ **foundations** NPL (*of building*) fondamenta *fpl*; **to lay the foundations** gettare le fondamenta

foundation stone N prima pietra

founder [ˈfaundə‍ʳ] N fondatore(-trice) ▶ VI affondare

founding [ˈfaundɪŋ] ADJ: **~ fathers** (*US*) padri *mpl* fondatori; **~ member** socio fondatore

foundry [ˈfaundrɪ] N fonderia

fount [faunt] N fonte f; (*Typ*) stile *m* di carattere

fountain [ˈfauntɪn] N fontana

fountain pen N penna stilografica

four [fɔː‍ʳ] NUM quattro; **on all fours** a carponi

four-by-four [fɔːbaɪˈfɔː‍ʳ] N quattro per quattro f inv

four-letter word [ˈfɔːlɛtə-] N parolaccia

four-poster [ˈfɔːˈpəustəʳ] N (also: **four-poster bed**) letto a quattro colonne

foursome [ˈfɔːsəm] N partita a quattro; uscita in quattro

fourteen [ˈfɔːtiːn] NUM quattordici

fourteenth NUM quattordicesimo(-a)

fourth [fɔːθ] NUM quarto(-a) ▸ N (Aut: also: **fourth gear**) quarta

four-wheel drive [ˈfɔːwiːl-] N (Aut): **with ~** con quattro ruote motrici

fowl [faul] N pollame m; volatile m

fox [fɔks] N volpe f ▸ VT confondere

fox fur N volpe f, pelliccia di volpe

foxglove [ˈfɔksglʌv] N (Bot) digitale f

fox-hunting [ˈfɔkshʌntɪŋ] N caccia alla volpe

foyer [ˈfɔɪeɪ] N atrio; (Theat) ridotto

FPA N ABBR (BRIT: = Family Planning Association) ≈ A.I.E.D. f (= Associazione Italiana Educazione Demografica)

Fr. ABBR (Rel) = **father; friar**

fr. ABBR (= franc) fr.

fracas [ˈfrækɑː] N rissa, lite f

fracking [ˈfrækɪŋ] N fracking m inv

fraction [ˈfrækʃən] N frazione f

fractionally [ˈfrækʃnəlɪ] ADV un tantino, minimamente

fractious [ˈfrækʃəs] ADJ irritabile

fracture [ˈfræktʃəʳ] N frattura ▸ VT fratturare

fragile [ˈfrædʒaɪl] ADJ fragile

fragment [ˈfrægmənt] N frammento

fragmentary [ˈfrægməntərɪ] ADJ frammentario(-a)

fragrance [ˈfreɪɡrəns] N fragranza, profumo

fragrant [ˈfreɪɡrənt] ADJ fragrante, profumato(-a)

frail [freɪl] ADJ debole, delicato(-a)

frame [freɪm] N (of building) armatura; (of human, animal) ossatura, corpo; (of picture) cornice f; (of door, window) telaio; (of spectacles: also: **frames**) montatura ▸ VT (picture) incorniciare; **to ~ sb** (col) incastrare qn; **~ of mind** stato d'animo

framework [ˈfreɪmwəːk] N struttura

France [frɑːns] N Francia

franchise [ˈfræntʃaɪz] N (Pol) diritto di voto; (Comm) concessione f

franchisee [fræntʃaɪˈziː] N concessionaria

franchiser [ˈfræntʃaɪzəʳ] N concedente m

frank [fræŋk] ADJ franco(-a), aperto(-a) ▸ VT (letter) affrancare

Frankfurt [ˈfræŋkfəːt] N Francoforte f

frankfurter [ˈfræŋkfəːtəʳ] N würstel m inv

franking machine [ˈfræŋkɪŋ-] N macchina affrancatrice

frankly [ˈfræŋklɪ] ADV francamente, sinceramente

frankness [ˈfræŋknɪs] N franchezza

frantic [ˈfræntɪk] ADJ (activity, pace) frenetico(-a); (desperate: need, desire) pazzo(-a), sfrenato(-a); (: search) affannoso(-a); (person) fuori di sé

frantically [ˈfræntɪklɪ] ADV freneticamente; affannosamente

fraternal [frəˈtəːnl] ADJ fraterno(-a)

fraternity [frəˈtəːnɪtɪ] N (club) associazione f; (spirit) fratellanza

fraternize [ˈfrætənaɪz] VI fraternizzare

fraud [frɔːd] N truffa; (Law) frode f; (person) impostore(-a)

fraudulent [ˈfrɔːdjulənt] ADJ fraudolento(-a)

fraught [frɔːt] ADJ (tense) teso(-a); **~ with** pieno(a) di, intriso(a) da

fray [freɪ] N baruffa ▸ VT logorare ▸ VI logorarsi; **to return to the ~** tornare nella mischia; **tempers were getting frayed** cominciavano ad innervosirsi; **her nerves were frayed** aveva i nervi a pezzi

FRB N ABBR (US) = **Federal Reserve Board**

FRCM N ABBR (BRIT) = **Fellow of the Royal College of Music**

FRCO N ABBR (BRIT) = **Fellow of the Royal College of Organists**

FRCP N ABBR (BRIT) = **Fellow of the Royal College of Physicians**

FRCS N ABBR (BRIT) = **Fellow of the Royal College of Surgeons**

freak [friːk] N fenomeno, mostro; (pej: enthusiast) fanatico(-a) ▸ ADJ (storm, conditions) anormale; (victory) inatteso(-a)
▸ **freak out** VI (col) andare fuori di testa

freakish [ˈfriːkɪʃ] ADJ (result, appearance) strano(-a), bizzarro(-a); (weather) anormale

freckle [ˈfrɛkl] N lentiggine f

free [friː] ADJ libero(-a); (gratis) gratuito(-a); (liberal) generoso(-a) ▸ VT (prisoner, jammed person) liberare; (jammed object) districare; **~ (of charge)** gratuitamente; **admission ~** entrata libera; **to give sb a ~ hand** dare carta bianca a qn; **~ and easy** rilassato

freebie [ˈfriːbɪ] N (col): **it's a ~** è in omaggio

freedom [ˈfriːdəm] N libertà

freedom fighter N combattente mf per la libertà

free enterprise N liberalismo economico

Freefone® [ˈfriːfəun] N (BRIT) ≈ numero verde

free-for-all [ˈfriːfərɔːl] N parapiglia m generale

free gift N regalo, omaggio

freehold [ˈfriːhəuld] N proprietà assoluta

free kick N (Sport) calcio libero

freelance [ˈfriːlɑːns] ADJ indipendente; **~ work** collaborazione f esterna

freeloader [ˈfriːləudəʳ] N (pej) scroccone(-a)

freely [ˈfriːlɪ] ADV liberamente; (liberally) liberalmente

f

free-market economy [fri:'mɑːkɪt-] N economia di libero mercato

freemason ['fri:meɪsn] N massone m

freemasonry ['fri:meɪsnrɪ] N massoneria

Freepost® ['fri:pəʊst] N affrancatura a carica del destinatario

free-range ['fri:'reɪndʒ] ADJ (*hen*) ruspante; (*eggs*) di gallina ruspante

free sample N campione m gratuito

free speech N libertà di parola

freestyle ['fri:staɪl] N (*in swimming*) stile m libero

free trade N libero scambio

Freeview® ['fri:vju:] N (BRIT) piattaforma digitale terrestre che trasmette nel Regno Unito gratuitamente un gran numero di canali

freeway ['fri:weɪ] N (US) superstrada

freewheel [fri:'wi:l] VI andare a ruota libera

freewheeling [fri:'wi:lɪŋ] ADJ a ruota libera

free will N libero arbitrio; **of one's own ~** di spontanea volontà

freeze [fri:z] (*pt* **froze** [frəʊz], *pp* **frozen** ['frəʊzn]) VI gelare ▶ VT gelare; (*food*) congelare; (*prices, salaries*) bloccare ▶ N gelo; blocco
▶ **freeze over** VI (*lake, river*) ghiacciarsi; (*windows, windscreen*) coprirsi di ghiaccio
▶ **freeze up** VI gelarsi

freeze-dried ['fri:zdraɪd] ADJ liofilizzato(-a)

freezer ['fri:zə'] N congelatore m

freezing ['fri:zɪŋ] ADJ (*wind, weather*) gelido(-a); **I'm ~** mi sto congelando ▶ N (*also:* **freezing point**) punto di congelamento; **3 degrees below ~** 3 gradi sotto zero

freight [freɪt] N (*goods*) merce f, merci fpl; (*money charged*) spese fpl di trasporto; **~ forward** spese a carico del destinatario; **~ inward** spese di trasporto sulla merce in entrata

freight car N (US) carro m merci inv

freighter ['freɪtə'] N (Naut) nave f da carico

freight forwarder [-'fɔ:wədə'] N spedizioniere m

freight train N (US) treno m merci inv

French [frɛntʃ] ADJ francese ▶ N (Ling) francese m ▪ **the French** NPL i Francesi

French bean N fagiolino

French bread N baguette f inv

French Canadian ADJ, N franco-canadese (mf)

French dressing N (Culin) condimento per insalata

French fried potatoes, (US) **French fries** NPL patate fpl fritte

French Guiana [-gaɪ'ænə] N Guiana francese

French loaf N = filoncino

Frenchman ['frɛntʃmən] N (irreg) francese m

French Riviera N: **the ~** la Costa Azzurra

French stick N baguette f inv

French window N portafinestra

Frenchwoman ['frɛntʃwumən] N (irreg) francese f

frenetic [frə'netɪk] ADJ frenetico(-a)

frenzy ['frɛnzɪ] N frenesia

frequency ['fri:kwənsɪ] N frequenza

frequency modulation N modulazione f di frequenza

frequent ADJ ['fri:kwənt] frequente ▶ VT [frɪ'kwɛnt] frequentare

frequently ['fri:kwəntlɪ] ADV frequentemente, spesso

fresco ['freskəʊ] N affresco

fresh [freʃ] ADJ fresco(-a); (*new*) nuovo(-a); (*cheeky*) sfacciato(-a); **to make a ~ start** cominciare da capo

freshen ['freʃən] VI (*wind, air*) rinfrescare
▶ **freshen up** VI rinfrescarsi

freshener ['freʃnə'] N: **skin ~** tonico rinfrescante; **air ~** deodorante m per ambienti

fresher ['freʃə'] N (BRIT Scol: col) = **freshman**

freshly ['freʃlɪ] ADV di recente, di fresco

freshman ['freʃmən] N (irreg) (Scol) matricola

freshness ['freʃnɪs] N freschezza

freshwater ['freʃwɔ:tə'] ADJ (*fish*) d'acqua dolce

fret [frɛt] VI agitarsi, affliggersi

fretful ['frɛtful] ADJ (*child*) irritabile

Freudian ['frɔɪdɪən] ADJ freudiano(-a); **~ slip** lapsus m inv freudiano

FRG N ABBR = **Federal Republic of Germany**

Fri. ABBR (= *Friday*) ven.

friar ['fraɪə'] N frate m

friction ['frɪkʃən] N frizione f, attrito

friction feed N (*on printer*) trascinamento ad attrito

Friday ['fraɪdɪ] N venerdì m inv; *see also* **Tuesday**

fridge [frɪdʒ] N (BRIT) frigo, frigorifero

fridge-freezer ['frɪdʒ'fri:zə'] N freezer m inv

fried [fraɪd] PT, PP of **fry** ▶ ADJ fritto(-a); **~ egg** uovo fritto

friend [frɛnd] N amico(-a); **to make friends with** fare amicizia con ▶ VT (*Internet*) aggiungere tra gli amici

friendliness ['frɛndlɪnɪs] N amichevolezza

friendly ['frɛndlɪ] ADJ amichevole ▶ N (*also:* **friendly match**) partita amichevole; **to be ~ with** essere amico di; **to be ~ to** essere cordiale con

friendly fire N fuoco amico

friendly society N società f inv di mutuo soccorso

friendship ['frɛndʃɪp] N amicizia

fries [fraɪz] NPL (*esp US*) patate fpl fritte

frieze [fri:z] N fregio

frigate ['frɪgɪt] N (Naut: modern) fregata

fright [fraɪt] N paura, spavento; **to take ~** spaventarsi; **she looks a ~!** guarda com'è conciata!

frighten ['fraɪtn] vt spaventare, far paura a
▶ **frighten away**, **frighten off** vt (birds, children etc) scacciare (facendogli paura)

frightened ['fraɪtnd] ADJ spaventato(-a); **to be ~ (of)** avere paura (di)

frightening ['fraɪtnɪŋ] ADJ spaventoso(-a), pauroso(-a)

frightful ['fraɪtful] ADJ orribile

frightfully ['fraɪtfulɪ] ADV terribilmente; **I'm ~ sorry** mi dispiace moltissimo

frigid ['frɪdʒɪd] ADJ (woman) frigido(-a)

frigidity [frɪ'dʒɪdɪtɪ] N frigidità

frill [frɪl] N balza; **without frills** (fig) senza fronzoli

frilly ['frɪlɪ] ADJ (clothes, lampshade) pieno(-a) di fronzoli

fringe [frɪndʒ] N (BRIT: of hair) frangia; (edge: of forest etc) margine m; (fig): **on the ~** al margine

fringe benefits NPL vantaggi mpl

fringe theatre N teatro d'avanguardia

Frisbee® ['frɪzbɪ] N frisbee® m inv

frisk [frɪsk] vt perquisire

frisky ['frɪskɪ] ADJ vivace, vispo(-a)

fritter ['frɪtə'] N frittella
▶ **fritter away** vt sprecare

frivolity [frɪ'vɒlɪtɪ] N frivolezza

frivolous ['frɪvələs] ADJ frivolo(-a)

frizzy ['frɪzɪ] ADJ crespo(-a)

fro [frəu] ADV: **to and ~** avanti e indietro

frock [frɒk] N vestito

frog [frɒg] N rana; **to have a ~ in one's throat** avere la voce rauca

frogman ['frɒgmən] N (irreg) uomo m rana inv

frogmarch ['frɒgmɑːtʃ] vt (BRIT): **to ~ sb in/out** portar qn dentro/fuori con la forza

frolic ['frɒlɪk] vi sgambettare

---

from [frɒm]

PREP **1** (indicating starting place, origin etc) da; **where do you come from?**, **where are you from?** da dove viene?, di dov'è?; **where has he come from?** da dove arriva?; **from London to Glasgow** da Londra a Glasgow; **a letter from my sister** una lettera da mia sorella; **tell him from me that ...** gli dica da parte mia che ...
2 (indicating time) da; **from one o'clock to** or **until** or **till two** dall'una alle due; **(as) from Friday** a partire da venerdì; **from January (on)** da gennaio, a partire da gennaio
3 (indicating distance) da; **the hotel is 1 km from the beach** l'albergo è a 1 km dalla spiaggia
4 (indicating price, number etc) da; **from a pound** da una sterlina in su; **prices range from £10 to £50** i prezzi vanno dalle 10 alle 50 sterline
5 (indicating difference) da; **he can't tell red from green** non sa distinguere il rosso dal verde

6 (because of, on the basis of): **from what he says** da quanto dice lui; **weak from hunger** debole per la fame

---

The preposition comes at the beginning of the question in Italian.
Where do you come from? **Da dove vieni?**

---

frond [frɒnd] N fronda

front [frʌnt] N (of house, dress) davanti m inv; (of train) testa; (of book) copertina; (promenade: also: **sea front**) lungomare m; (Mil, Pol, Meteor) fronte m; (fig: appearances) fronte f ▶ ADJ primo(-a); anteriore, davanti inv ▶ vi: **to ~ onto sth** dare su qc, guardare verso qc; **in ~ (of)** davanti (a)

frontage ['frʌntɪdʒ] N facciata

frontal ['frʌntl] ADJ frontale

front bench N posti in Parlamento occupati dai frontbenchers

Nel Parlamento britannico, si chiamano **front benches** gli scanni della House of Commons che si trovano alla sinistra e alla destra dello Speaker davanti ai back benches. I front benches sono occupati dai frontbenchers, parlamentari che ricoprono una carica di governo o che fanno parte dello Shadow Cabinet dell'opposizione.

---

frontbencher ['frʌnt'bentʃə'] N (BRIT) parlamentare con carica al governo o all'opposizione

front desk N (US: in hotel) reception f inv; (: at doctor's) accettazione f

front door N porta d'entrata; (of car) sportello anteriore

frontier ['frʌntɪə'] N frontiera

frontispiece ['frʌntɪspiːs] N frontespizio

front page N prima pagina

front room N (BRIT) salotto

front runner N (fig) favorito(-a)

front-wheel drive ['frʌntwiːl-] N trasmissione f anteriore

frost [frɒst] N gelo; (also: **hoarfrost**) brina

frostbite ['frɒstbaɪt] N congelamento

frosted ['frɒstɪd] ADJ (glass) smerigliato(-a); (US: cake) glassato(-a)

frosting ['frɒstɪŋ] N (US: on cake) glassa

frosty ['frɒstɪ] ADJ (window) coperto(-a) di ghiaccio; (weather, look, welcome) gelido(-a)

froth [frɒθ] N spuma; schiuma

frown [fraun] N cipiglio ▶ vi accigliarsi
▶ **frown on** vt FUS (fig) disapprovare

froze [frəuz] PT of **freeze**

frozen ['frəuzn] PP of **freeze** ▶ ADJ (food) congelato(-a); (Comm: assets) bloccato(-a)

FRS N ABBR (BRIT) = **Fellow of the Royal Society**; (US: = Federal Reserve System) sistema bancario degli Stati Uniti

frugal ['fru:gəl] ADJ frugale; *(person)* economo(-a)

fruit [fru:t] N *(pl inv)* frutto; *(collectively)* frutta

fruiterer ['fru:tərə'] N fruttivendolo; **at the ~'s (shop)** dal fruttivendolo

fruit fly N mosca della frutta

fruitful ['fru:tful] ADJ fruttuoso(-a); *(plant)* fruttifero(-a); *(soil)* fertile

fruition [fru:'ɪʃən] N: **to come to ~** realizzarsi

fruit juice N succo di frutta

fruitless ['fru:tlɪs] ADJ *(fig)* vano(-a), inutile

fruit machine N *(BRIT)* macchina *f* mangiasoldi *inv*

fruit salad N macedonia

frump [frʌmp] N: **to feel a ~** sentirsi infagottato(a)

frustrate [frʌs'treɪt] VT frustrare

frustrated [frʌs'treɪtɪd] ADJ frustrato(-a)

frustrating [frʌs'treɪtɪŋ] ADJ *(job)* frustrante; *(day)* disastroso(-a)

frustration [frʌs'treɪʃən] N frustrazione *f*

fry [fraɪ] *(pt, pp* **fried** [-d]*)* VT friggere ▶ NPL: **the small ~** i pesci piccoli

frying pan ['fraɪŋ-] N padella

FT N ABBR *(BRIT: = Financial Times)* giornale finanziario; **the FT index** l'indice FT

ft. ABBR = **foot; feet**

FTC N ABBR *(US)* = **Federal Trade Commission**

FT-SE 100 Index N ABBR = **Financial Times Stock Exchange 100 Index**

fuchsia ['fju:ʃə] N fucsia

fuck [fʌk] VT, VI *(col!)* fottere *(!)*; **~ off!** vaffanculo! *(!)*

fuddled ['fʌdld] ADJ *(muddled)* confuso(-a); *(col: tipsy)* brillo(-a)

fuddy-duddy ['fʌdɪdʌdɪ] N *(pej)* parruccone *m*

fudge [fʌdʒ] N *(Culin)* specie di caramella a base di latte, burro e zucchero ▶ VT *(issue, problem)* evitare

fuel ['fjuəl] N *(for heating)* combustibile *m*; *(for propelling)* carburante *m* ▶ VT *(furnace etc)* alimentare; *(aircraft, ship etc)* rifornire di carburante

fuel oil N nafta

fuel poverty N povertà energetica

fuel pump N *(Aut)* pompa del carburante

fuel tank N deposito *m* nafta *inv*; *(on vehicle)* serbatoio (della benzina)

fug [fʌg] N *(BRIT)* aria viziata

fugitive ['fju:dʒɪtɪv] N fuggitivo(-a), profugo(-a); *(from prison)* evaso(-a)

fulfil, *(US)* **fulfill** [ful'fɪl] VT *(function)* compiere; *(order)* eseguire; *(wish, desire)* soddisfare, appagare

fulfilled [ful'fɪld] ADJ *(person)* realizzato(-a), soddisfatto(-a)

fulfilment, *(US)* **fulfillment** [ful'fɪlmənt] N *(of wishes)* soddisfazione *f*, appagamento

full [ful] ADJ pieno(-a); *(details, skirt)* ampio(-a); *(price)* intero(-a) ▶ ADV: **to know ~ well that** sapere benissimo che; **~ (up)** *(hotel etc)* al completo; **I'm ~ (up)** sono sazio; **a ~ two hours** due ore intere; **at ~ speed** a tutta velocità; **in ~** per intero; **to pay in ~** pagare tutto; **~ name** nome *m* e cognome *m*; **~ employment** piena occupazione; **~ fare** tariffa completa

fullback ['fulbæk] N *(Rugby, Football)* terzino

full-blooded ['ful'blʌdɪd] ADJ *(vigorous: attack)* energico(-a); *(virile: male)* virile

full-cream ['ful'kri:m] ADJ: **~ milk** *(BRIT)* latte *m* intero

full-grown ['ful'grəun] ADJ maturo(-a)

full-length ['ful'leŋθ] ADJ *(portrait)* in piedi; *(film)* a lungometraggio; *(coat, novel)* lungo(-a)

full moon N luna piena

full-scale ['fulskeɪl] ADJ *(plan, model)* in grandezza naturale; *(attack, search, retreat)* su vasta scala

full-sized ['ful'saɪzd] ADJ *(portrait etc)* a grandezza naturale

full stop N punto

full-time ['ful'taɪm] ADJ, ADV *(work)* a tempo pieno ▶ N *(Sport)* fine *f* partita

fully ['fulɪ] ADV interamente, pienamente, completamente; *(at least)*: **~ as big** almeno così grosso

fully-fledged ['fulɪ'fledʒd] ADJ *(bird)* adulto(-a); *(fig: teacher, member etc)* a tutti gli effetti

fulsome ['fulsəm] ADJ *(pej: praise)* esagerato(-a), eccessivo(-a); *(: manner)* insincero

fumble ['fʌmbl] VI brancolare, andare a tentoni ▶ VT *(ball)* lasciarsi sfuggire
▶ **fumble with** VT FUS trafficare con

fume [fju:m] VI essere furioso(-a) ■ **fumes** NPL esalazioni *fpl*, vapori *mpl*

fumigate ['fju:mɪgeɪt] VT suffumicare

fun [fʌn] N divertimento, spasso; **to have ~** divertirsi; **for ~** per scherzo; **it's not much ~** non è molto divertente; **to make ~ of** prendersi gioco di

function ['fʌŋkʃən] N funzione *f*; cerimonia, ricevimento ▶ VI funzionare; **to ~ as** fungere da, funzionare da

functional ['fʌŋkʃənl] ADJ funzionale

function key N *(Comput)* tasto di funzioni

fund [fʌnd] N fondo, cassa; *(source)* fondo; *(store)* riserva ■ **funds** NPL *(money)* fondi *mpl*

fundamental [fʌndə'mɛntl] ADJ fondamentale ■ **fundamentals** NPL basi *fpl*

fundamentalism [fʌndə'mɛntəlɪzəm] N fondamentalismo

fundamentalist [fʌndə'mɛntəlɪst] N fondamentalista *mf*

fundamentally [fʌndə'mɛntəlɪ] ADV essenzialmente, fondamentalmente

funding ['fʌndɪŋ] N finanziamento

fund-raising [ˈfʌndreɪzɪŋ] N raccolta di fondi

funeral [ˈfjuːnərəl] N funerale m

funeral director N impresario di pompe funebri

funeral parlour [-ˈpɑːləʳ] N impresa di pompe funebri

funeral service N ufficio funebre

funereal [fjuːˈnɪərɪəl] ADJ funereo(-a), lugubre

fun fair [ˈfʌnfɛəʳ] N luna park m inv

fungus [ˈfʌŋgəs] (pl **fungi** [-gaɪ]) N fungo; (mould) muffa

funicular [fjuːˈnɪkjuləʳ] ADJ (also: **funicular railway**) funicolare f

funky [ˈfʌŋkɪ] ADJ (music) funky inv; (col: excellent) figo(-a)

funnel [ˈfʌnl] N imbuto; (of ship) ciminiera

funnily [ˈfʌnɪlɪ] ADV in modo divertente; (oddly) stranamente

funny [ˈfʌnɪ] ADJ divertente, buffo(-a); (strange) strano(-a), bizzarro(-a)

funny bone N osso cubitale

fun run N marcia non competitiva

fur [fəːʳ] N pelo; pelliccia; pelle f; (BRIT: in kettle etc) deposito calcare

fur coat N pelliccia

furious [ˈfjuərɪəs] ADJ furioso(-a); (effort) accanito(-a); (argument) violento(-a)

furiously [ˈfjuərɪəslɪ] ADV furiosamente; accanitamente

furl [fəːl] VT (sail) piegare

furlong [ˈfəːlɔŋ] N 201.17 m (termine ippico)

furlough [ˈfəːləu] N (US) congedo, permesso

furnace [ˈfəːnɪs] N fornace f

furnish [ˈfəːnɪʃ] VT ammobiliare; (supply) fornire; **furnished flat** or (US) **apartment** appartamento ammobiliato

furnishings [ˈfəːnɪʃɪŋz] NPL mobili mpl, mobilia

furniture [ˈfəːnɪtʃəʳ] N mobili mpl; **piece of ~** mobile m

furore [fjuəˈrɔːrɪ] N (protests) scalpore m; (enthusiasm) entusiasmo

furrier [ˈfʌrɪəʳ] N pellicciaio(-a)

furrow [ˈfʌrəu] N solco ▶ VT (forehead) segnare di rughe

furry [ˈfəːrɪ] ADJ (animal) peloso(-a); (toy) di peluche

further [ˈfəːðəʳ] ADJ supplementare, altro(-a); nuovo(-a); più lontano(-a) ▶ ADV più lontano; (more) di più; (moreover) inoltre ▶ VT favorire, promuovere; **until ~ notice** fino a nuovo avviso; **how much ~ is it?** quanto manca or dista?; **~ to your letter of ...** (Comm) con riferimento alla vostra lettera del ...; **to ~ one's interests** fare i propri interessi

further education N ≈ corsi mpl di formazione; **college of ~** istituto statale con corsi specializzati (di formazione professionale, aggiornamento professionale ecc)

furthermore [fəːðəˈmɔːʳ] ADV inoltre, per di più

furthermost [ˈfəːðəməust] ADJ più lontano(-a)

furthest [ˈfəːðɪst] ADV SUPERLATIVE of **far**

furtive [ˈfəːtɪv] ADJ furtivo(-a)

fury [ˈfjuərɪ] N furore m

fuse, (US) **fuze** [fjuːz] N fusibile m; (for bomb etc) miccia, spoletta ▶ VT fondere; (Elec): **to ~ the lights** far saltare i fusibili ▶ VI fondersi; **a ~ has blown** è saltato un fusibile

fuse box N cassetta dei fusibili

fuselage [ˈfjuːzəlɑːʒ] N fusoliera

fuse wire N filo (di fusibile)

fusillade [fjuːzɪˈleɪd] N scarica di fucileria; (fig) fuoco di fila, serie f incalzante

fusion [ˈfjuːʒən] N fusione f

fuss [fʌs] N agitazione f, trambusto, confusione f; (complaining) storie fpl ▶ VT (person) infastidire, scocciare ▶ VI agitarsi; **to make a ~** fare delle storie; **to make a ~ of sb** coprire qn di attenzioni

▶ **fuss over** VT FUS (person) circondare di premure

fusspot [ˈfʌspɔt] N (col): **he's such a ~** fa sempre tante storie

fussy [ˈfʌsɪ] ADJ (person) puntiglioso(-a), esigente; che fa le storie; (dress) carico(-a) di fronzoli; (style) elaborato(-a); **I'm not ~** (col) per me è lo stesso

fusty [ˈfʌstɪ] ADJ (pej: archaic) stantio(-a); (: smell) che sa di stantio

futile [ˈfjuːtaɪl] ADJ futile

futility [fjuːˈtɪlɪtɪ] N futilità

futon [ˈfuːtɔn] N futon m inv, letto giapponese

future [ˈfjuːtʃəʳ] ADJ futuro(-a) ▶ N futuro, avvenire m; (Ling) futuro ■ **futures** NPL (Comm) operazioni fpl a termine; **in ~** in futuro; **in the near ~** in un prossimo futuro; **in the immediate ~** nell'immediato futuro

futuristic [fjuːtʃəˈrɪstɪk] ADJ futuristico(-a)

fuze [fjuːz] N, VT, VI (US) = **fuse**

fuzzy [ˈfʌzɪ] ADJ (Phot) indistinto(-a), sfocato(-a); (hair) crespo(-a)

fwd. ABBR = **forward**

FY ABBR = **fiscal year**

FYI ABBR = **for your information**

Gg

G, g [dʒiː] N (letter) G, g f inv or m inv; (Mus): **G** sol m; **G for George** = G come Genova

G N ABBR (BRIT Scol: mark: = good) = buono; (US Cine: = general audience) per tutti

g ABBR (= gram, gravity) g

G7 N ABBR (Pol: = Group of Seven) G7 mpl

G8 N ABBR (Pol: = Group of Eight) G8 m

G20 N ABBR (Pol: = Group of Twenty) G20 m

GA ABBR (US Post) = **Georgia**

gab [gæb] N (col): **to have the gift of the ~** avere parlantina

gabble ['gæbl] VI borbottare; farfugliare

gaberdine [gæbə'diːn] N gabardine m inv

gable ['geɪbl] N frontone m

Gabon [gə'bɔn] N Gabon m

gad about [gæd-] VI (col) svolazzare (qua e là)

gadget ['gædʒɪt] N aggeggio

Gaelic ['geɪlɪk] ADJ gaelico(-a) ▸ N (language) gaelico

gaffe [gæf] N gaffe f inv

gaffer ['gæfəʳ] N (BRIT col) capo

gag [gæg] N bavaglio; (joke) facezia, scherzo ▸ VT (prisoner etc) imbavagliare ▸ VI (choke) soffocare

gaga ['gɑːgɑː] ADJ: **to go ~** rimbambirsi

gage [geɪdʒ] N, VT (US) = **gauge**

gaiety ['geɪɪtɪ] N gaiezza

gaily ['geɪlɪ] ADV allegramente

gain [geɪn] N guadagno, profitto ▸ VT guadagnare ▸ VI (watch) andare avanti; (benefit): **to ~ (from)** trarre beneficio (da); **to ~ in/by** aumentare di/con; **to ~ 3lbs (in weight)** aumentare di 3 libbre; **to ~ ground** guadagnare terreno ▸ **gain (up)on** VT FUS guadagnare terreno su, accorciare le distanze da

gainful ['geɪnful] ADJ profittevole, lucrativo(-a)

gainfully ['geɪnfəlɪ] ADV: **to be ~ employed** avere un lavoro retribuito

gainsay [geɪn'seɪ] VT (irreg: like **say**) contraddire; negare

gait [geɪt] N andatura

gal. ABBR = **gallon**

gala ['gɑːlə] N gala; **swimming ~** manifestazione f di nuoto

Galapagos Islands [gə'læpəgəs-] NPL: **the ~** le isole Galapagos

galaxy ['gæləksɪ] N galassia

gale [geɪl] N vento forte; burrasca; **~ force 10** vento forza 10

gall [gɔːl] N (Anat) bile f; (fig: impudence) fegato, faccia ▸ VT urtare (i nervi a)

gall. ABBR = **gallon**

gallant ['gælənt] ADJ valoroso(-a); (towards ladies) galante, cortese

gallantry ['gæləntrɪ] N valore m militare; galanteria, cortesia

gall bladder ['gɔːl-] N cistifellea

galleon ['gælɪən] N galeone m

gallery ['gælərɪ] N galleria; loggia; (for spectators) tribuna; (in theatre) loggione m, balconata; (also: **art gallery**: state-owned) museo; (: private) galleria

galley ['gælɪ] N (ship's kitchen) cambusa; (ship) galea; (also: **galley proof**) bozza in colonna

Gallic ['gælɪk] ADJ gallico(-a); (French) francese

galling ['gɔːlɪŋ] ADJ irritante

gallon ['gælən] N gallone m (Brit = 4.543 l; 8 pints; US = 3.785 l)

gallop ['gæləp] N galoppo ▸ VI galoppare; **galloping inflation** inflazione f galoppante

gallows ['gæləuz] N forca

gallstone ['gɔːlstəun] N calcolo biliare

Gallup Poll ['gæləp-] N sondaggio a campione

galore [gə'lɔːʳ] ADV a iosa, a profusione

galvanize ['gælvənaɪz] VT galvanizzare; **to ~ sb into action** (fig) galvanizzare qn, spronare qn all'azione

Gambia ['gæmbɪə] N: **the ~** Gambia m

gambit ['gæmbɪt] N (fig): **(opening) ~** prima mossa

gamble ['gæmbl] N azzardo, rischio calcolato ▸ VT, VI giocare; **to ~ on** (fig) giocare su; **to ~ on the Stock Exchange** giocare in Borsa

gambler ['gæmbləʳ] N giocatore(-trice) d'azzardo

gambling [ˈgæmblɪŋ] N gioco d'azzardo

gambol [ˈgæmbəl] VI saltellare

game [geɪm] N gioco; (*event*) partita; (*Tennis*) game *m inv*; (*Hunting, Culin*) selvaggina ▶ ADJ coraggioso(-a); (*ready*): **to be ~ (for sth/to do)** essere pronto(-a) (a qc/a fare) ◼ **games** NPL (*Scol*) attività *fpl* sportive; **big ~** selvaggina grossa

game bird N uccello selvatico

gamekeeper [ˈgeɪmkiːpəʳ] N guardacaccia *m inv*

gamely [ˈgeɪmlɪ] ADV coraggiosamente

gamer [ˈgeɪməʳ] N *chi gioca con i videogame*

game reserve N riserva di caccia

games console [geɪmz-] N console *f inv* dei videogame

gameshow [ˈgeɪmʃəu] N gioco a premi

gamesmanship [ˈgeɪmzmənʃɪp] N abilità

gaming [ˈgeɪmɪŋ] N gioco d'azzardo; (*Comput*) *il giocare con i videogame*

gammon [ˈgæmən] N (*bacon*) quarto di maiale; (*ham*) prosciutto affumicato

gamut [ˈgæmət] N gamma

gang [gæŋ] N banda, squadra ▶ VI: **to ~ up on sb** far combutta contro qn

Ganges [ˈgændʒiːz] N: **the ~** il Gange

gangland [ˈgæŋlænd] ADJ della malavita; **~ killer** sicario

gangling [ˈgæŋglɪŋ] ADJ allampanato(-a)

gangly [ˈgæŋglɪ] ADJ = **gangling**

gangplank [ˈgæŋplæŋk] N passerella

gangrene [ˈgæŋgriːn] N cancrena

gangster [ˈgæŋstəʳ] N gangster *m inv*

gangway [ˈgæŋweɪ] N passerella; (*Brit: of bus*) passaggio

gantry [ˈgæntrɪ] N (*for crane, railway signal*) cavalletto; (*for rocket*) torre *f* di lancio

GAO N ABBR (*US: = General Accounting Office*) ≈ Corte *f* dei Conti

gaol [dʒeɪl] N, VT (*Brit*) = **jail**

gap [gæp] N (*space*) buco; (*in time*) intervallo; (*fig*) lacuna; vuoto; (*difference*): **~ (between)** divario (tra)

gape [geɪp] VI (*person*) restare a bocca aperta; (*shirt, hole*) essere spalancato(-a)

gaping [ˈgeɪpɪŋ] ADJ (*hole*) squarciato(-a)

gap year N (*Scol*) anno di pausa preso prima di iniziare l'università, per lavorare o viaggiare

garage [ˈgærɑːʒ] N garage *m inv*

garage sale N *vendita di oggetti usati nel garage di un privato*

garb [gɑːb] N abiti *mpl*, veste *f*

garbage [ˈgɑːbɪdʒ] N (*US*) immondizie *fpl*, rifiuti *mpl*; (*col*) sciocchezze *fpl*; (*fig: film, book*) porcheria, robaccia; (*: nonsense*) fesserie *fpl*

garbage can N (*US*) bidone *m* della spazzatura

garbage collector N (*US*) spazzino(-a)

garbage disposal unit N tritarifiuti *m inv*

garbage truck N (*US*) camion *m inv* della spazzatura

garbled [ˈgɑːbld] ADJ deformato(-a); ingarbugliato(-a)

garden [ˈgɑːdn] N giardino ▶ VI lavorare nel giardino ◼ **gardens** NPL (*public*) giardini pubblici; (*private*) parco

garden centre N vivaio

garden city N (*Brit*) città *f inv* giardino *inv*

gardener [ˈgɑːdnəʳ] N giardiniere(-a)

gardening [ˈgɑːdnɪŋ] N giardinaggio

gargle [ˈgɑːgl] VI fare gargarismi ▶ N gargarismo

gargoyle [ˈgɑːgɔɪl] N gargouille *f inv*

garish [ˈgɛərɪʃ] ADJ vistoso(-a)

garland [ˈgɑːlənd] N ghirlanda; corona

garlic [ˈgɑːlɪk] N aglio

garment [ˈgɑːmənt] N indumento

garner [ˈgɑːnəʳ] VT ammucchiare, raccogliere

garnish [ˈgɑːnɪʃ] VT (*food*) guarnire

garret [ˈgærɪt] N soffitta

garrison [ˈgærɪsn] N guarnigione *f* ▶ VT guarnire

garrulous [ˈgærjuləs] ADJ ciarliero(-a), loquace

garter [ˈgɑːtəʳ] N giarrettiera; (*US: suspender*) gancio (di reggicalze)

garter belt N (*US*) reggicalze *m inv*

gas [gæs] N gas *m inv*; (*used as anaesthetic*) etere *m*; (*US: gasoline*) benzina ▶ VT asfissiare con il gas; (*Mil*) gasare

gas cooker N (*Brit*) cucina a gas

gas cylinder N bombola del gas

gaseous [ˈgæsɪəs] ADJ gassoso(-a)

gas fire N (*Brit*) radiatore *m* a gas

gas-fired [ˈgæsfaɪəd] ADJ (alimentato(-a)) a gas

gash [gæʃ] N sfregio ▶ VT sfregiare

gasket [ˈgæskɪt] N (*Aut*) guarnizione *f*

gas mask N maschera *f* antigas *inv*

gas meter N contatore *m* del gas

gasoline [ˈgæsəliːn] N (*US*) benzina

gasp [gɑːsp] N respiro affannoso, ansito ▶ VI ansimare, boccheggiare; (*in surprise*) restare senza fiato

▶ **gasp out** VT dire affannosamente

gas pedal N (*esp US*) pedale *m* dell'acceleratore

gas ring N fornello a gas

gas station N (*US*) distributore *m* di benzina

gas stove N cucina a gas

gassy [ˈgæsɪ] ADJ gassoso(-a)

gas tank N (*US Aut*) serbatoio (di benzina)

gas tap N (*on cooker*) manopola del gas; (*on pipe*) rubinetto del gas

gastric ['gæstrɪk] ADJ gastrico(-a)

gastric band N (Med) sistema m di bendaggio gastrico

gastric ulcer N ulcera gastrica

gastroenteritis ['gæstrəʊɛntə'raɪtɪs] N gastro-enterite f

gastronomy [gæs'trɒnəmɪ] N gastronomia

gastropub ['gæstrəʊpʌb] N gastropub m inv

gasworks ['gæswəːks] N, NPL impianto di pro-duzione del gas

gate [geɪt] N cancello; (of castle, town) porta; (at airport) uscita; (at level crossing) barriera

gâteau ['gætəʊ] (pl **gâteaux** [-z]) N torta

gatecrash ['geɪtkræʃ] (BRIT) VT partecipare senza invito a

gatecrasher ['geɪtkræʃəʳ] N intruso(-a), ospite mf non invitato(-a)

gated community ['geɪtɪd-] N quartiere residen-ziale autonomo, recintato e sorvegliato, con accesso limitato

gatehouse ['geɪthaʊs] N casetta del custode (all'entrata di un parco)

gateway ['geɪtweɪ] N porta

gather ['gæðəʳ] VT (flowers, fruit) cogliere; (pick up) raccogliere; (assemble) radunare; racco-gliere; (understand) capire; (Sewing) increspare ▶ VI (assemble) radunarsi; (dust) accumularsi; (clouds) addensarsi; **to ~ speed** acquistare velo-cità; **to ~ (from/that)** comprendere (da/che), dedurre (da/che); **as far as I can ~** da quel che ho potuto capire

gathering ['gæðərɪŋ] N adunanza

gauche [gəʊʃ] ADJ goffo(-a), maldestro(-a)

gaudy ['gɔːdɪ] ADJ vistoso(-a)

gauge [geɪdʒ] N (standard measure) calibro; (Rail) scartamento; (instrument) indicatore m ▶ VT misurare; (fig: sb's capabilities, character) valutare, stimare; **to ~ the right moment** calcolare il momento giusto; **petrol ~**, (US) **gas ~** indica-tore m or spia della benzina

gaunt [gɔːnt] ADJ scarno(-a); (grim, desolate) desolato(-a)

gauntlet ['gɔːntlɪt] N (fig): **to run the ~ through an angry crowd** passare sotto il fuoco di una folla ostile; **to throw down the ~** gettare il guanto

gauze [gɔːz] N garza

gave [geɪv] PT of **give**

gawky ['gɔːkɪ] ADJ goffo(-a), sgraziato(-a)

gawp [gɔːp] VI: **to ~ at** guardare a bocca aperta

gay [geɪ] ADJ (homosexual) omosessuale; (cheerful) gaio(-a), allegro(-a); (colour) vivace, vivo(-a)

gaze [geɪz] N sguardo fisso ▶ VI: **to ~ at** guar-dare fisso

gazelle [gə'zɛl] N gazzella

gazette [gə'zɛt] N (newspaper) gazzetta; (official publication) gazzetta ufficiale

gazetteer [gæzə'tɪəʳ] N (book) dizionario dei nomi geografici; (section of book) indice m dei nomi geografici

gazump [gə'zʌmp] VT (BRIT): **to ~ sb** nella com-pravendita di immobili, venire meno all'impegno preso con un acquirente accettando un'offerta migliore fatta da altri

GB ABBR (= Great Britain) GB

GBH N ABBR (BRIT Law: col) = **grievous bodily harm**

GC N ABBR (BRIT: = George Cross) decorazione al valore

GCE N ABBR (BRIT: = General Certificate of Education) ≈ diploma m di maturità

GCHQ N ABBR (BRIT: = Government Communications Headquarters) centro per l'intercettazione delle teleco-municazioni straniere

GCSE N ABBR (BRIT: = General Certificate of Secondary Education) diploma di istruzione secondaria conse-guito a 16 anni in Inghilterra e Galles

Il **GCSE** (General Certificate of Secondary Education) consiste in una serie di esami che gli studenti fra i 14 e i 16 anni sostengono in Inghilterra, Galles e Irlanda del Nord. Il successo è una condizione essenziale per continuare gli studi e passare gli A levels. Le materie variano, ma alcune come inglese, matematica e scienze, sono obbligato-rie per tutti gli indirizzi.

Gdns. ABBR = **gardens**

GDP N ABBR = **gross domestic product**

GDR N ABBR (Hist) = **German Democratic Republic**

gear [gɪəʳ] N attrezzi mpl, equipaggiamento; (belongings) roba; (Tech) ingranaggio; (Aut) marcia ▶ VT (fig: adapt): **to ~ sth to** adattare qc a; **top** or **high/low/bottom ~** (US) quinta (or sesta)/seconda/prima; **in ~** in marcia; **out of ~** in folle; **our service is geared to meet the needs of the disabled** la nostra organizza-zione risponde espressamente alle esigenze degli handicappati
▶ **gear up** VI: **to ~ up (to do)** prepararsi (a fare)

gear box N scatola del cambio

gear lever, (US) **gear shift** N leva del cambio

GED N ABBR (US Scol) = **general educational development**

geese [giːs] NPL of **goose**

geezer ['giːzəʳ] N (BRIT col) tizio

Geiger counter ['gaɪgə-] N geiger m inv

gel [dʒɛl] N gel m inv

gelatin, gelatine ['dʒɛlətiːn] N gelatina

gelignite ['dʒɛlɪgnaɪt] N nitroglicerina

gem [dʒɛm] N gemma

Gemini ['dʒɛmɪnaɪ] N Gemelli mpl; **to be ~** essere dei Gemelli

gen [dʒɛn] N (BRIT col): **to give sb the ~ on sth** mettere qn al corrente di qc

Gen. ABBR (*Mil*: = *General*) Gen.

gen. ABBR = **general**; (= *generally*) gen.

gender [ˈdʒɛndə^r] N genere *m*

gene [dʒiːn] N (*Biol*) gene *m*

genealogy [dʒiːnɪˈælədʒɪ] N genealogia

general [ˈdʒɛnərl] N generale *m* ▶ ADJ generale; **in ~** in genere; **the ~ public** il grande pubblico

general anaesthetic, (*US*) **general anesthetic** N anestesia totale

general delivery N (*US*) fermo posta *m*

general election N elezioni *fpl* generali

generalization [ˈdʒɛnrəlaɪˈzeɪʃən] N generalizzazione *f*

generalize [ˈdʒɛnrəlaɪz] VI generalizzare

generally [ˈdʒɛnrəlɪ] ADV generalmente

general manager N direttore(-trice) generale

general practitioner N medico generico

general store N emporio

general strike N sciopero generale

generate [ˈdʒɛnəreɪt] VT generare

generation [dʒɛnəˈreɪʃən] N generazione *f*; (*of electricity etc*) produzione *f*

generator [ˈdʒɛnəreɪtə^r] N generatore *m*

generic [dʒɪˈnɛrɪk] ADJ generico(-a)

generosity [dʒɛnəˈrɔsɪtɪ] N generosità

generous [ˈdʒɛnərəs] ADJ generoso(-a); (*copious*) abbondante

genesis [ˈdʒɛnɪsɪs] N genesi *f*

genetic [dʒɪˈnɛtɪk] ADJ genetico(-a); **~ engineering** ingegneria genetica

genetically modified [dʒɪˈnɛtɪklɪˈmɔdɪfaɪd] ADJ geneticamente modificato(-a), transgenico(-a); **~ organism** organismo geneticamente modificato

genetic fingerprinting [-fɪŋɡəprɪntɪŋ] N rilevamento delle impronte genetiche

genetics [dʒɪˈnɛtɪks] N genetica

Geneva [dʒɪˈniːvə] N Ginevra; **Lake ~** il lago di Ginevra

genial [ˈdʒiːnɪəl] ADJ geniale, cordiale

genitals [ˈdʒɛnɪtlz] NPL genitali *mpl*

genitive [ˈdʒɛnɪtɪv] N genitivo

genius [ˈdʒiːnɪəs] N genio

Genoa [ˈdʒɛnəuə] N Genova

genocide [ˈdʒɛnəusaɪd] N genocidio

Genoese [dʒɛnəuˈiːz] ADJ, N (*pl inv*) genovese (*mf*)

genome [ˈgiːnəum] N (*Biol*) genoma *m inv*

gent [dʒɛnt] N ABBR (*BRIT col*) = **gentleman**

genteel [dʒɛnˈtiːl] ADJ raffinato(-a), distinto(-a)

gentle [ˈdʒɛntl] ADJ delicato(-a); (*person*) dolce

gentleman [ˈdʒɛntlmən] N (*irreg*) signore *m*; (*well-bred man*) gentiluomo; **~'s agreement** impegno sulla parola

gentlemanly [ˈdʒɛntlmənlɪ] ADJ da gentiluomo

gentleness [ˈdʒɛntlnɪs] N delicatezza; dolcezza

gently [ˈdʒɛntlɪ] ADV delicatamente

gentry [ˈdʒɛntrɪ] N nobiltà minore

gents [dʒɛnts] N W.C. *m* (per signori)

genuine [ˈdʒɛnjuɪn] ADJ autentico(-a); sincero(-a)

genuinely [ˈdʒɛnjuɪnlɪ] ADV genuinamente

geographer [dʒɪˈɔɡrəfə^r] N geografo(-a)

geographic [dʒɪəˈgræfɪk], **geographical** [dʒɪəˈgræfɪkl] ADJ geografico(-a)

geography [dʒɪˈɔɡrəfɪ] N geografia

geolocate [dʒiːəuˈləuˈkeɪt] VT geolocalizzare

geological [dʒɪəˈlɔdʒɪkl] ADJ geologico(-a)

geologist [dʒɪˈɔlədʒɪst] N geologo(-a)

geology [dʒɪˈɔlədʒɪ] N geologia

geometric [dʒɪəˈmɛtrɪk], **geometrical** [dʒɪəˈmɛtrɪkl] ADJ geometrico(-a)

geometry [dʒɪˈɔmətrɪ] N geometria

Geordie [ˈdʒɔːdɪ] N (*col*) abitante *mf* del Tyneside; originario(-a) del Tyneside

Georgia [ˈdʒɔːdʒə] N Georgia

Georgian [ˈdʒɔːdʒən] ADJ georgiano(-a) ▶ N georgiano(-a); (*Ling*) georgiano

geranium [dʒɪˈreɪnɪəm] N geranio

geriatric [dʒɛrɪˈætrɪk] ADJ geriatrico(-a)

germ [dʒəːm] N (*Med*) microbo; (*Biol, fig*) germe *m*

German [ˈdʒəːmən] ADJ tedesco(-a) ▶ N tedesco(-a); (*Ling*) tedesco

German Democratic Republic N Repubblica Democratica Tedesca

germane [dʒəːˈmeɪn] ADJ (*formal*): **to be ~ to sth** essere attinente a qc

German measles N (*BRIT*) rosolia

Germany [ˈdʒəːmənɪ] N Germania

germination [dʒəːmɪˈneɪʃən] N germinazione *f*

germ warfare N guerra batteriologica

gerrymandering [ˈdʒɛrɪmændərɪŋ] N manipolazione *f* dei distretti elettorali

gestation [dʒɛsˈteɪʃən] N gestazione *f*

gesticulate [dʒɛsˈtɪkjulert] VI gesticolare

gesture [ˈdʒɛstjə^r] N gesto; **as a ~ of friendship** in segno d'amicizia

---

get [gɛt]

(*pt, pp* **got** [gɔt], *US pp* **gotten** [ˈgɔtn]) VI **1** (*become, be*) diventare, farsi; **to get drunk** ubriacarsi; **to get killed** venire *or* rimanere ucciso(-a); **it's getting late** si sta facendo tardi; **to get old** invecchiare; **to get paid** venire pagato(-a); **when do I get paid?** quando mi pagate?; **to get ready** prepararsi; **to get shaved** farsi la barba; **to get tired** stancarsi; **to get washed** lavarsi

g

2 (*go*): **to get to/from** andare a/da; **to get home** arrivare *or* tornare a casa; **how did you get here?** come sei venuto?; **he got across the bridge** ha attraversato il ponte; **he got under the fence** è passato sotto il recinto
3 (*begin*) mettersi a, cominciare a; **to get to know sb** incominciare a conoscere qn; **let's get going** *or* **started** muoviamoci
4 (*modal aux vb*): **you've got to do it** devi farlo
▶ VT **1**: **to get sth done** (*do*) fare qc; (*have done*) far fare qc; **to get sth/sb ready** preparare qc/qn; **to get one's hair cut** tagliarsi *or* farsi tagliare i capelli; **to get sb to do sth** far fare qc a qn
2 (*obtain*: *money, permission, results*) ottenere; (*find*: *job, flat*) trovare; (*fetch*: *person, doctor*) chiamare; **get me Mr Jones, please** (*Tel*) mi passi il signor Jones, per favore; (: *object*) prendere; **to get sth for sb** prendere *or* procurare qc a qn; **can I get you a drink?** le posso offrire da bere?
3 (*receive*: *present, letter, prize*) ricevere; (: *acquire*: *reputation*) farsi; **how much did you get for the painting?** quanto le hanno dato per il quadro?
4 (*catch*) prendere; **to get sb by the arm/throat** afferrare qn per un braccio/alla gola; **get him!** prendetelo!; **he really gets me** (*fig*: *annoy*) mi dà proprio sui nervi
5 (*hit*: *target etc*) colpire
6 (*take, move*) portare; **to get sth to sb** far avere qc a qn; **do you think we'll get it through the door?** pensi che riusciremo a farlo passare per la porta?
7 (*catch, take*: *plane, bus etc*) prendere; **he got the last bus** ha preso l'ultimo autobus; **she got the morning flight to Milan** ha preso il volo per Milano del mattino; **where do we get the ferry to …?** dove si prende il traghetto per …?
8 (*understand*) afferrare; **I've got it!** ci sono arrivato!, ci sono!
9 (*hear*) sentire; **I'm sorry, I didn't get your name** scusi, non ho capito (*or* sentito) come si chiama
10 (*have, possess*): **to have got** avere; **how many have you got?** quanti ne ha?
▶ **get about** VI muoversi; (*news*) diffondersi
▶ **get across** VT: **to get across (to)** (*message, meaning*) comunicare (a) ▶ VI: **to get across to** (*speaker*) comunicare con
▶ **get along** VI (*agree*) andare d'accordo; (*depart*) andarsene; (*manage*) = **get by**
▶ **get at** VT FUS (*attack*) prendersela con; (*reach*) raggiungere, arrivare a; **what are you getting at?** dove vuoi arrivare?
▶ **get away** VI partire, andarsene; (*escape*) scappare
▶ **get away with** VT FUS cavarsela; farla franca; **he'll never get away with it!** non riuscirà a farla franca!
▶ **get back** VI (*return*) ritornare, tornare ▶ VT

riottenere, riavere; **to get back to** (*start again*) ritornare a; (*contact again*) rimettersi in contatto con; **when do we get back?** quando ritorniamo?
▶ **get back at** VT FUS (*col*): **to get back at sb (for sth)** rendere pan per focaccia a qn (per qc)
▶ **get by** VI (*pass*) passare; (*manage*) farcela; **I can get by in Dutch** mi arrangio in olandese
▶ **get down** VI, VT FUS scendere ▶ VT far scendere; (*depress*) buttare giù
▶ **get down to** VT FUS (*work*) mettersi a (fare); **to get down to business** venire al dunque
▶ **get in** VI entrare; (*train*) arrivare; (*arrive home*) ritornare, tornare ▶ VT (*bring in*: *harvest*) raccogliere; (: *coal, shopping, supplies*) fare provvista di; (*insert*) far entrare, infilare
▶ **get into** VT FUS entrare in; **to get into a rage** incavolarsi; **to get into bed** mettersi a letto
▶ **get off** VI (*from train etc*) scendere; (*depart*: *person, car*) andare via; (*escape*) scamparla ▶ VT (*remove*: *clothes, stain*) levare; (*send off*) spedire; (*have as leave*: *days, time*): **we got 2 days off** abbiamo avuto 2 giorni liberi ▶ VT FUS (*train, bus*) scendere da; **to get off to a good start** (*fig*) cominciare bene
▶ **get on** VI: **how did you get on?** com'è andata?; **he got on quite well** ha fatto bene, (gli) è andata bene; **to get on (with sb)** andare d'accordo (con qn); **how are you getting on?** come va la vita? ▶ VT FUS montare in; (*horse*) montare su
▶ **get on to** VT FUS (BRIT *col*: *contact*: *on phone etc*) contattare, rintracciare; (: *deal with*) occuparsi di
▶ **get out** VI uscire; (*of vehicle*) scendere ▶ VT tirar fuori, far uscire; **to get out (of)** (*money from bank etc*) ritirare (da)
▶ **get out of** VT FUS uscire da; (*duty etc*) evitare; **what will you get out of it?** cosa ci guadagni?
▶ **get over** VT FUS (*illness*) riaversi da; (*communicate*: *idea etc*) comunicare, passare; **let's get it over (with)** togliamoci il pensiero
▶ **get round** VT FUS aggirare; (*fig*: *person*) rigirare ▶ VI: **to get round to doing sth** trovare il tempo di fare qc
▶ **get through** VI (*Tel*) avere la linea ▶ VT FUS (*finish*: *work*) sbrigare; (: *book*) finire
▶ **get through to** VT FUS (*Tel*) parlare a
▶ **get together** VI riunirsi ▶ VT raccogliere; (*people*) adunare
▶ **get up** VI (*rise*) alzarsi ▶ VT FUS salire su per
▶ **get up to** VT FUS (*reach*) raggiungere; (*prank etc*) fare

---

When *get* is used with an adjective, the phrase is often translated by a specific verb in Italian.
to get angry **arrabbiarsi**
to get tired **stancarsi**
to get worse **peggiorare**

getaway ['gɛtəweɪ] N fuga

getaway car N macchina per la fuga

get-together ['gɛttəgeðəʳ] N (piccola) riunione f; (party) festicciola

get-up ['gɛtʌp] N (col: outfit) tenuta

get-well card [gɛt'wɛl-] N cartolina di auguri di pronta guarigione

geyser ['giːzəʳ] N scaldabagno; (Geo) geyser m inv

Ghana ['gɑːnə] N Ghana m

Ghanaian [gɑːˈneɪən] ADJ, N ganaense (mf)

ghastly ['gɑːstlɪ] ADJ orribile, orrendo(-a); (pale) spettrale

gherkin ['gəːkɪn] N cetriolino

ghetto ['gɛtəʊ] N ghetto

ghetto blaster [-'blɑːstəʳ] N maxistereo portatile

ghost [gəʊst] N fantasma m, spettro ▶ VT (book) fare lo scrittore ombra per

ghostly ['gəʊstlɪ] ADJ spettrale

ghostwriter ['gəʊstraɪtəʳ] N scrittore(-trice) ombra inv

ghoul [guːl] N vampiro che si nutre di cadaveri

ghoulish ['guːlɪʃ] ADJ (tastes etc) macabro(-a)

GHQ N ABBR (Mil: = general headquarters) ≈ comando di Stato maggiore

GHz ABBR = **gigahertz**

GI N ABBR (US col: = government issue) G.I. m, soldato americano

giant ['dʒaɪənt] N gigante(-essa) ▶ ADJ gigantesco(-a), enorme; **~ (size) packet** confezione f gigante

giant killer N (Sport) piccola squadra che riesce a batterne una importante

gibber ['dʒɪbəʳ] VI (monkey) squittire confusamente; (idiot) farfugliare

gibberish ['dʒɪbərɪʃ] N parole fpl senza senso

gibe [dʒaɪb] N frecciata ▶ VI: **to ~ at** lanciare frecciate a

giblets ['dʒɪblɪts] NPL frattaglie fpl

Gibraltar [dʒɪ'brɔːltəʳ] N Gibilterra

giddiness ['gɪdɪnɪs] N vertigine f

giddy ['gɪdɪ] ADJ (dizzy): **to be ~** aver le vertigini; (height) vertiginoso(-a); **I feel ~** mi gira la testa

gift [gɪft] N regalo; (donation, ability) dono; (Comm: also: **free gift**) omaggio; **to have a ~ for sth** (talent) avere il dono di qc

gifted ['gɪftɪd] ADJ dotato(-a)

gift shop, (US) **gift store** N negozio di souvenir

gift token, gift voucher N buono (acquisto)

gig [gɪg] N (col: of musician) serata

gigabyte [giːgəbaɪt] N gigabyte m inv

gigantic [dʒaɪ'gæntɪk] ADJ gigantesco(-a)

giggle ['gɪgl] VI ridere scioccamente ▶ N risolino (sciocco)

GIGO ['gaɪgəʊ] ABBR (Comput: col: = garbage in, garbage out) qualità di input = qualità di output

gild [gɪld] VT dorare

gill [dʒɪl] N (measure) = 0.25 pints (Brit = 0.148 l; US = 0.118 l)

gills [gɪlz] NPL (of fish) branchie fpl

gilt [gɪlt] N doratura ▶ ADJ dorato(-a)

gilt-edged ['gɪltɛdʒd] ADJ (stocks, securities) della massima sicurezza

gimlet ['gɪmlɪt] N succhiello

gimmick ['gɪmɪk] N trucco; **sales ~** trovata commerciale

gin [dʒɪn] N (liquor) gin m inv

ginger ['dʒɪndʒəʳ] N zenzero
▶ **ginger up** VT scuotere; animare

ginger ale, ginger beer N bibita gassosa allo zenzero

gingerbread ['dʒɪndʒəbrɛd] N pan m di zenzero

ginger group N (BRIT) gruppo di pressione

ginger-haired ['dʒɪndʒə'hɛəd] ADJ rossiccio(-a)

gingerly ['dʒɪndʒəlɪ] ADV cautamente

gingham ['gɪŋəm] N percalle m a righe (or quadretti)

ginseng ['dʒɪnsɛŋ] N ginseng m

gipsy ['dʒɪpsɪ] N zingaro(-a) ▶ ADJ degli zingari

giraffe [dʒɪ'rɑːf] N giraffa

girder ['gəːdəʳ] N trave f

girdle ['gəːdl] N (corset) guaina

girl [gəːl] N ragazza; (young unmarried woman) signorina; (daughter) figlia, figliola; **a little ~** una bambina

girl band N gruppo pop di sole ragazze creato per far presa su un pubblico giovane

girlfriend ['gəːlfrɛnd] N (female friend) amica; (romantic partner) ragazza

girlish ['gəːlɪʃ] ADJ da ragazza

Girl Scout N (US) Giovane Esploratrice f

Giro ['dʒaɪrəʊ] N: **the National ~** (BRIT) ≈ la or il Bancoposta

giro ['dʒaɪrəʊ] N (bank giro) versamento bancario; (post office giro) postagiro

girth [gəːθ] N circonferenza; (of horse) cinghia

gist [dʒɪst] N succo

give [gɪv] (pt **gave** [geɪv], pp **given** ['gɪvn]) N (of fabric) elasticità ▶ VT dare ▶ VI cedere; **to ~ sb sth, ~ sth to sb** dare qc a qn; **I'll ~ you £5 for it** te lo pago 5 sterline; **to ~ a cry/sigh** emettere un grido/sospiro; **to ~ a speech** fare un discorso; **how much did you ~ for it?** quanto (l')hai pagato?; **12 o'clock, ~ or take a few minutes** mezzogiorno, minuto più minuto meno; **to ~ way** VI cedere; (BRIT Aut) dare la precedenza
▶ **give away** VT dare via; (give free) fare dono di; (betray) tradire; (disclose) rivelare; (bride) condurre all'altare
▶ **give back** VT rendere

▶ **give in** VI cedere ▶ VT consegnare

▶ **give off** VT emettere

▶ **give out** VT distribuire; annunciare ▶ VI (*be exhausted: supplies*) esaurirsi, venir meno; (*fail: engine*) fermarsi; (*: strength*) mancare

▶ **give up** VI rinunciare ▶ VT rinunciare a; **to ~ up smoking** smettere di fumare; **to ~ o.s. up** arrendersi

give-and-take [gɪvən'teɪk] N (*col*) elasticità (da ambo le parti), concessioni *fpl* reciproche

giveaway ['gɪvəweɪ] N (*col*): **her expression was a ~** le si leggeva tutto in volto; **the exam was a ~!** l'esame è stato uno scherzo! ▶ CPD: **~ prices** prezzi stracciati

given ['gɪvn] PP of **give** ▶ ADJ (*fixed: time, amount*) dato(-a), determinato(-a) ▶ CONJ: **~ (that) ...** dato che ...; **~ the circumstances ...** date le circostanze ...

glacial ['gleɪsɪəl] ADJ glaciale

glacier ['glæsɪəʳ] N ghiacciaio

glad [glæd] ADJ lieto(-a), contento(-a); **to be ~ about sth/that** essere contento *or* lieto di qc/che+*sub*; **I was ~ of his help** gli sono stato grato del suo aiuto

gladden ['glædn] VT rallegrare, allietare

glade [gleɪd] N radura

gladioli [glædɪ'əʊlaɪ] NPL gladioli *mpl*

gladly ['glædlɪ] ADV volentieri

glamorous ['glæmərəs] ADJ (*gen*) favoloso(-a); (*person*) affascinante, seducente; (*occasion*) brillante, elegante

glamour, (*US*) **glamor** ['glæməʳ] N fascino

glance [glɑːns] N occhiata, sguardo ▶ VI: **to ~ at** dare un'occhiata a

▶ **glance off** VT FUS (*bullet*) rimbalzare su

glancing ['glɑːnsɪŋ] ADJ (*blow*) che colpisce di striscio

gland [glænd] N ghiandola

glandular ['glændjʊləʳ] ADJ: **~ fever** (BRIT) mononucleosi *f*

glare [glɛəʳ] N (*of anger*) sguardo furioso; (*of light*) riverbero, luce *f* abbagliante; (*of publicity*) chiasso ▶ VI abbagliare; **to ~ at** guardare male

glaring ['glɛərɪŋ] ADJ (*mistake*) madornale

glasnost ['glæznɒst] N glasnost *f*

glass [glɑːs] N (*substance*) vetro; (*tumbler*) bicchiere *m*; (*also:* **looking glass**) specchio; *see also* **glasses**

glass-blowing ['glɑːsbləʊɪŋ] N soffiatura del vetro

glass ceiling N (*fig*) barriera invisibile

glasses ['glɑːsɪz] NPL (*spectacles*) occhiali *mpl*

glass fibre N fibra di vetro

glasshouse ['glɑːshaʊs] N serra

glassware ['glɑːswɛəʳ] N vetrame *m*

glassy ['glɑːsɪ] ADJ (*eyes*) vitreo(-a)

Glaswegian [glæs'wiːdʒən] ADJ di Glasgow ▶ N abitante *mf* di Glasgow, originario(-a) di Glasgow

glaze [gleɪz] VT (*door*) fornire di vetri; (*pottery*) smaltare; (*Culin*) glassare ▶ N smalto; glassa

glazed ['gleɪzd] ADJ (*eye*) vitreo(-a); (*tiles, pottery*) smaltato(-a)

glazier ['gleɪzɪəʳ] N vetraio

gleam [gliːm] N barlume *m*; raggio ▶ VI luccicare; **a ~ of hope** un barlume di speranza

gleaming ['gliːmɪŋ] ADJ lucente

glean [gliːn] VT (*information*) racimolare

glee [gliː] N allegrezza, gioia

gleeful ['gliːfʊl] ADJ allegro(-a), gioioso(-a)

glen [glɛn] N valletta

glib [glɪb] ADJ dalla parola facile; facile

glide [glaɪd] VI scivolare; (*Aviat, birds*) planare ▶ N scivolata; planata

glider ['glaɪdəʳ] N (*Aviat*) aliante *m*

gliding ['glaɪdɪŋ] N (*Aviat*) volo a vela

glimmer ['glɪməʳ] VI luccicare ▶ N barlume *m*

glimpse [glɪmps] N impressione *f* fugace ▶ VT vedere di sfuggita; **to catch a ~ of** vedere di sfuggita

glint [glɪnt] N luccichio ▶ VI luccicare

glisten ['glɪsn] VI luccicare

glitter ['glɪtəʳ] VI scintillare ▶ N scintillio

glitz [glɪts] N (*col*) vistosità, chiassosità

gloat [gləʊt] VI: **to ~ (over)** gongolare di piacere (per)

global ['gləʊbl] ADJ globale; (*world-wide*) mondiale

globalization [gləʊbəlaɪ'zeɪʃən] N globalizzazione *f*

global warming N riscaldamento globale

globe [gləʊb] N globo, sfera

globetrotter ['gləʊbtrɒtəʳ] N giramondo *mf*

globule ['glɒbjuːl] N (*Anat*) globulo; (*of water etc*) gocciolina

gloom [gluːm] N oscurità, buio; (*sadness*) tristezza, malinconia

gloomy ['gluːmɪ] ADJ scuro(-a), fosco(-a), triste; **to feel ~** sentirsi giù *or* depresso

glorification [glɔːrɪfɪ'keɪʃən] N glorificazione *f*

glorify ['glɔːrɪfaɪ] VT glorificare; celebrare, esaltare

glorious ['glɔːrɪəs] ADJ glorioso(-a), magnifico(-a)

glory ['glɔːrɪ] N gloria; splendore *m* ▶ VI: **to ~ in** gloriarsi di *or* in

glory hole N (*col*) ripostiglio

gloss [glɒs] N (*shine*) lucentezza; (*also:* **gloss paint**) vernice *f* a olio

▶ **gloss over** VT FUS scivolare su

glossary ['glɒsərɪ] N glossario

glossy ['glɒsɪ] ADJ lucente ▶ N (*also:* **glossy magazine**) rivista di lusso

glove [glʌv] N guanto

glove compartment N (*Aut*) vano portaoggetti

glow [gləu] VI ardere; (*face*) essere luminoso(-a) ▸ N bagliore *m*; (*of face*) colorito acceso

glower ['glauə^r] VI: **to ~ (at sb)** guardare (qn) in cagnesco

glowing ['gləuɪŋ] ADJ (*fire*) ardente; (*complexion*) luminoso(-a); (*fig: report, description etc*) entusiasta

glow-worm ['gləuwə:m] N lucciola

glucose ['glu:kəus] N glucosio

glue [glu:] N colla ▸ VT incollare

glue-sniffing ['glu:snɪfɪŋ] N sniffare *m* (colla)

glum [glʌm] ADJ abbattuto(-a)

glut [glʌt] N eccesso ▸ VT saziare; (*market*) saturare

glute [glu:t] N (*col*) gluteo *m*

glutinous ['glu:tɪnəs] ADJ colloso(-a), appiccicoso(-a)

glutton ['glʌtn] N ghiottone(-a); **a ~ for work** un(-a) patito(-a) del lavoro

gluttonous ['glʌtənəs] ADJ ghiotto(-a), goloso(-a)

gluttony ['glʌtənɪ] N ghiottoneria; (*sin*) gola

glycerin, glycerine ['glɪsəri:n] N glicerina

GM ADJ ABBR (= *genetically modified*) geneticamente modificato(-a)

gm ABBR = **gram**

GMAT N ABBR (*US*: = *Graduate Management Admissions Test*) esame di ammissione all'ultimo biennio di scuola superiore

GMB N ABBR (*BRIT*) = **General, Municipal, and Boilermakers (Union)**

GM crop N cultura GM

GM food N cibo transgenico

GM-free [dʒi:ɛm'fri:] ADJ privo(-a) di OGM

GMO N ABBR (= *genetically modified organism*) OGM *m inv*

GMT ABBR (= *Greenwich Mean Time*) T.M.G.

gnarled [nɑ:ld] ADJ nodoso(-a)

gnash [næʃ] VT: **to ~ one's teeth** digrignare i denti

gnat [næt] N moscerino

gnaw [nɔ:] VT rodere

gnome [nəum] N gnomo

GNP N ABBR = **gross national product**

go [gəu] VI (*pt* **went** [wɛnt], *pp* **gone** [gɔn]) andare; (*depart*) partire, andarsene; (*work*) funzionare; (*time*) passare; (*break etc*) cedere; (*be sold*): **to go for £10** essere venduto per 10 sterline; (*fit, suit*): **to go with** andare bene con; (*become*): **to go pale** diventare pallido(-a); **to go mouldy** ammuffire ▸ N (*pl* **goes**): **to have a go (at)** provare; **to be on the go** essere in moto; **whose go is it?** a chi tocca?; **to go by car/on**

foot andare in macchina/a piedi; **he's going to do** sta per fare; **to go for a walk** andare a fare una passeggiata; **to go dancing/shopping** andare a ballare/fare la spesa; **just then the bell went** proprio allora suonò il campanello; **to go looking for sb/sth** andare in cerca di qn/qc; **to go to sleep** addormentarsi; **to go and see sb, to go to see sb** andare a trovare qn; **how is it going?** come va (la vita)?; **how did it go?** com'è andato?; **to go round the back/by the shop** passare da dietro/davanti al negozio; **my voice has gone** m'è andata via la voce; **the cake is all gone** il dolce è finito tutto; **I'll take whatever is going** (*BRIT*) prendo quello che c'è; **... to go** (*US: food*) ... da portar via; **the money will go towards our holiday** questi soldi li mettiamo per la vacanza

▸ **go about** VI (*also:* **go around**) aggirarsi; (: *rumour*) correre, circolare ▸ VT FUS: **how do I go about this?** qual è la prassi per questo?; **to go about one's business** occuparsi delle proprie faccende

▸ **go after** VT FUS (*pursue*) correr dietro a, rincorrere; (*job, record etc*) mirare a

▸ **go against** VT FUS (*be unfavourable to*) essere contro; (*be contrary to*) andare contro

▸ **go ahead** VI andare avanti; **go ahead!** faccia pure!

▸ **go along** VI andare, avanzare ▸ VT FUS percorrere; **to go along with** (*accompany*) andare con, accompagnare; (*agree with: idea*) sottoscrivere, appoggiare

▸ **go away** VI partire, andarsene

▸ **go back** VI tornare, ritornare; (*go again*) andare di nuovo

▸ **go back on** VT FUS (*promise*) non mantenere

▸ **go by** VI (*years, time*) scorrere ▸ VT FUS attenersi a, seguire (alla lettera); prestar fede a

▸ **go down** VI scendere; (*ship*) affondare; (*sun*) tramontare ▸ VT FUS scendere; **that should go down well with him** dovrebbe incontrare la sua approvazione

▸ **go for** VT FUS (*fetch*) andare a prendere; (*like*) andar matto(-a) per; (*attack*) attaccare; saltare addosso a

▸ **go in** VI entrare

▸ **go in for** VT FUS (*competition*) iscriversi a; (*be interested in*) interessarsi di

▸ **go into** VT FUS entrare in; (*investigate*) indagare, esaminare; (*embark on*) lanciarsi in

▸ **go off** VI partire, andar via; (*food*) guastarsi; (*explode*) esplodere, scoppiare; (*lights etc*) spegnersi; (*event*) passare ▸ VT FUS: **I've gone off chocolate** la cioccolata non mi piace più; **the gun went off** il fucile si scaricò; **the party went off well** la festa è andata *or* è riuscita bene; **to go off to sleep** addormentarsi

▸ **go on** VI continuare; (*happen*) succedere; (*lights*) accendersi ▸ VT FUS (*be guided by: evidence etc*) basarsi su, fondarsi su; **to go on doing** continuare a fare; **what's going on here?** che succede *or* che sta succedendo qui?

▸ **go on at** VT FUS (*nag*) assillare

▸ **go on with** VT FUS continuare, proseguire

▸ **go out** VI uscire; (*fire, light*) spegnersi; (*ebb*:

tide) calare; **to go out with sb** uscire con qn; **they went out for 3 years** (*couple*) sono stati insieme per 3 anni

▶ **go over** VI (*ship*) ribaltarsi ▶ VT FUS (*check*) esaminare; **to go over sth in one's mind** pensare bene a qc

▶ **go past** VI passare ▶ VT FUS passare davanti a

▶ **go round** VI (*circulate: news, rumour*) circolare; (*revolve*) girare; (*suffice*) bastare (per tutti); **to go round (to sb's)** (*visit*) passare (da qn); **to go round (by)** (*make a detour*) passare (per)

▶ **go through** VT FUS (*town etc*) attraversare; (*search through: files, papers*) vagliare attentamente; (*examine: list, book*) leggere da cima a fondo; (*perform*) fare

▶ **go through with** VT FUS (*plan, crime*) mettere in atto, eseguire; **I couldn't go through with it** non sono riuscito ad andare fino in fondo

▶ **go under** VI (*sink: ship*) affondare, colare a picco; (*: person*) andare sotto; (*fig: business, firm*) fallire

▶ **go up** VI salire ▶ VT FUS salire su per; **to go up in flames** andare in fiamme

▶ **go with** VT FUS (*accompany*) accompagnare

▶ **go without** VT FUS fare a meno di

Use the future tense in Italian to say what you're going to do or what's going to happen. *I'm going to do it tomorrow*. **Lo farò domani**. *It's going to be difficult*. **Sarà difficile**.

---

goad [gəud] VT spronare

go-ahead ['gəuəhɛd] ADJ intraprendente ▶ N: **to give sb/sth the ~** dare il via libera a qn/qc

goal [gəul] N (*Sport*) gol m, rete f; (*: place*) porta; (*fig: aim*) fine m, scopo

goal difference N differenza f reti inv

goalie ['gəuli] N (*col*) portiere m

goalkeeper ['gəulki:pə^r] N portiere m

goalpost ['gəulpəust] N palo (della porta)

goat [gəut] N capra

gobble ['gɔbl] VT (*also:* **gobble down, gobble up**) ingoiare

go-between ['gəubɪtwi:n] N intermediario(-a)

Gobi Desert ['gəubɪ-] N: **the ~** il Deserto dei Gobi

goblet ['gɔblɪt] N calice m, coppa

goblin ['gɔblɪn] N folletto

go-cart ['gəukɑ:t] N go-kart m inv ▶ CPD: **~ racing** n kartismo

god [gɔd] N dio; **G~** Dio

god-awful [gɔd'ɔ:fəl] ADJ (*col*) di merda (!)

godchild ['gɔdtʃaɪld] N (*irreg*) figlioccio(-a)

goddamn ['gɔddæm], (US) **goddamned** ['gɔddæmd] (*esp col*) EXCL: **~!** porca miseria! ▶ ADJ fottuto(-a) (!), maledetto(-a) ▶ ADV maledettamente

goddaughter ['gɔddɔ:tə^r] N figlioccia

goddess ['gɔdɪs] N dea

godfather ['gɔdfɑ:ðə^r] N padrino

god-fearing ['gɔdfɪərɪŋ] ADJ timorato(-a) di Dio

god-forsaken ['gɔdfəseɪkən] ADJ desolato(-a), sperduto(-a)

godmother ['gɔdmʌðə^r] N madrina

godparents ['gɔdpɛərənts] NPL: **the ~** il padrino e la madrina

godsend ['gɔdsɛnd] N dono del cielo

godson ['gɔdsʌn] N figlioccio

goes [gəuz] *see* **go**

gofer ['gəufə^r] N (*col*) tuttofare mf, tirapiedi mf

go-getter ['gəugɛtə^r] N arrivista mf

goggle ['gɔgl] VI: **to ~ (at)** stare con gli occhi incollati or appiccicati (a or addosso a)

goggles ['gɔglz] NPL occhiali mpl (di protezione)

going ['gəuɪŋ] N (*conditions*) andare m, stato del terreno ▶ ADJ: **the ~ rate** la tariffa in vigore; **a ~ concern** un'azienda avviata; **it was slow ~** si andava a rilento

going-over [gəuɪŋ'əuvə^r] N (*col*) controllata; (*violent attack*) pestaggio

goings-on ['gəuɪŋz'ɔn] NPL (*col*) fatti mpl strani, cose fpl strane

go-kart ['gəukɑ:t] N = **go-cart**

gold [gəuld] N oro ▶ ADJ d'oro; (*reserves*) aureo(-a)

golden ['gəuldən] ADJ (*made of gold*) d'oro; (*gold in colour*) dorato(-a)

golden age N età d'oro

golden handshake N (BRIT) gratifica di fine servizio

golden rule N regola principale

goldfish ['gəuldfɪʃ] N pesce m dorato or rosso

gold leaf N lamina d'oro

gold medal N (*Sport*) medaglia d'oro

goldmine ['gəuldmaɪn] N (*also fig*) miniera d'oro

gold-plated ['gəuld'pleɪtɪd] ADJ placcato(-a) oro inv

goldsmith ['gəuldsmɪθ] N orefice m, orafo

gold standard N tallone m aureo

golf [gɔlf] N golf m

golf ball N (*for game*) pallina da golf; (*on typewriter*) pallina

golf club N circolo di golf; (*stick*) bastone m or mazza da golf

golf course N campo di golf

golfer ['gɔlfə^r] N giocatore(-trice) di golf

golfing ['gɔlfɪŋ] N il giocare a golf

gondola ['gɔndələ] N gondola

gondolier [gɔndə'lɪə^r] N gondoliere m

gone [gɔn] PP *of* **go** ▶ ADJ partito(-a)

goner ['gɔnə^r] N (*col*): **I thought you were a ~** pensavo che ormai fossi spacciato

gong [gɔŋ] N gong m inv

good [gud] ADJ buono(-a); (*kind*) buono(-a), gentile; (*child*) bravo(-a) ▶N bene *m*; ~! bene!, ottimo!; **to be ~ at** essere bravo(-a) in; **to be ~ for** andare bene per; **it's ~ for you** fa bene; **it's a ~ thing you were there** meno male che c'era; **she is ~ with children/her hands** ci sa fare coi bambini/è abile nei lavori manuali; **to feel ~** sentirsi bene; **it's ~ to see you** che piacere vederla; **to make ~** (*loss, damage*) compensare; **he's up to no ~** ne sta combinando qualcuna; **it's no ~ complaining** brontolare non serve a niente; **for the common ~** nell'interesse generale, per il bene comune; **for ~** (*for ever*) per sempre, definitivamente; **would you be ~ enough to ...?** avrebbe la gentilezza di ...?; **that's very ~ of you** è molto gentile da parte sua; **is this any ~?** (*will it do?*) va bene questo?; (*what's it like?*) com'è?; **a ~ deal (of)** molto(-a), una buona quantità (di); **a ~ many** molti(-e); **~ morning!** buon giorno!; **~ afternoon/evening!** buona sera!; **~ night!** buona notte!; *see also* **goods**

goodbye [gud'baɪ] EXCL arrivederci!; **to say ~ to** (*person*) salutare

good faith N buona fede

good-for-nothing ['gudfənʌθɪŋ] N buono(-a) a nulla, vagabondo(-a)

Good Friday N Venerdì Santo

good-humoured [gud'hju:məd] ADJ (*person*) di buon umore; (*remark, joke*) bonario(-a)

good-looking [gud'lukɪŋ] ADJ bello(-a)

good-natured [gud'neɪtʃəd] ADJ (*person*) affabile; (*discussion*) amichevole, cordiale

goodness ['gudnɪs] N (*of person*) bontà; **for ~ sake!** per amor di Dio!; **~ gracious!** santo cielo!, mamma mia!

goods [gudz] NPL (*Comm etc*) merci *fpl*, articoli *mpl*; **~ and chattels** beni *mpl* e effetti *mpl*

goods train N (*BRIT*) treno *m* merci *inv*

goodwill [gud'wɪl] N amicizia, benevolenza; (*Comm*) avviamento

goody-goody ['gudɪgudɪ] N (*pej*) santarellino(-a)

gooey ['gu:ɪ] ADJ (*col: sticky*) appiccicoso(-a); (*: cake, dessert*) troppo zuccherato(-a)

Google® ['gu:gl] VT, VI cercare su Google®

goose [gu:s] (*pl* **geese** [gi:s]) N oca

gooseberry ['guzbərɪ] N uva spina; **to play ~** (*BRIT*) tenere la candela

goose bumps ['gu:sbʌmpz] NPL, **gooseflesh** ['gu:sfleʃ] N, **goosepimples** ['gu:spɪmplz] NPL pelle *f* d'oca

goose step N (*Mil*) passo dell'oca

GOP N ABBR (*US Pol: col: = Grand Old Party*) partito repubblicano

gopher ['gəufə'] N = **gofer**

gore [gɔ:'] VT incornare ▶N sangue *m* (coagulato)

gorge [gɔ:dʒ] N gola ▶VT: **to ~ o.s. (on)** ingozzarsi (di)

gorgeous ['gɔ:dʒəs] ADJ magnifico(-a)

gorilla [gə'rɪlə] N gorilla *m inv*

gormless ['gɔ:mlɪs] ADJ (*BRIT: col*) tonto(-a); (*: stronger*) deficiente

gorse [gɔ:s] N ginestrone *m*

gory ['gɔ:rɪ] ADJ sanguinoso(-a)

gosh [gɔʃ] EXCL (*col*) perdinci!

go-slow ['gəu'sləu] N (*BRIT*) rallentamento dei lavori (*per agitazione sindacale*)

gospel ['gɔspl] N vangelo

gossamer ['gɔsəmə'] N (*cobweb*) fili *mpl* della Madonna *or* di ragnatela; (*light fabric*) stoffa sottilissima

gossip ['gɔsɪp] N chiacchiere *fpl*; pettegolezzi *mpl*; (*person*) pettegolo(-a) ▶VI chiacchierare; (*maliciously*) pettegolare; **a piece of ~** un pettegolezzo

gossip column N cronaca mondana

got [gɔt] PT, PP *of* **get**

Gothic ['gɔθɪk] ADJ gotico(-a)

gotten ['gɔtn] (*US*) PP *of* **get**

gouge [gaudʒ] VT (*also:* **gouge out:** *hole etc*) scavare; (*: initials*) scolpire; (*: sb's eyes*) cavare

gourd [guəd] N zucca

gourmet ['guəmeɪ] N buongustaio(-a)

gout [gaut] N gotta

govern ['gʌvən] VT governare; (*Ling*) reggere

governess ['gʌvənɪs] N governante *f*

governing ['gʌvənɪŋ] ADJ (*Pol*) al potere, al governo; **~ body** consiglio di amministrazione

government ['gʌvnmənt] N governo; (*BRIT: ministers*) ministero ▶CPD statale; **local ~** amministrazione *f* locale

governmental [gʌvn'mɛntl] ADJ governativo(-a)

government housing N (*US*) alloggi *mpl* popolari

government stock N titoli *mpl* di stato

governor ['gʌvənə'] N (*of state, bank*) governatore(-trice); (*of school, hospital*) amministratore(-trice); (*BRIT: of prison*) direttore(-trice)

Govt ABBR = **government**

gown [gaun] N vestito lungo; (*of teacher, judge: BRIT*) toga

GP N ABBR (*Med*) = **general practitioner**; **who's your GP?** qual è il suo medico di fiducia?

GPMU N ABBR (*BRIT*) = **Graphical, Paper and Media Union**

GPO N ABBR (*BRIT old*) = **General Post Office**; (*US: = Government Printing Office*) ≈ Poligrafici dello Stato

GPS N ABBR (*= global positioning system*) GPS *m*

gr. ABBR (*Comm*) = **gross**

grab [græb] VT afferrare, arraffare; (*property, power*) impadronirsi di ▶ VI: **to ~ at** cercare di afferrare

grace [greɪs] N grazia; (*graciousness*) garbo, cortesia ▶ VT onorare; **5 days' ~** dilazione f di 5 giorni; **to say ~** dire il benedicite; **with a good/bad ~** volentieri/malvolentieri; **his sense of humour is his saving ~** il suo senso dell'umorismo è quello che lo salva

graceful ['greɪsful] ADJ elegante, aggraziato(-a)

gracious ['greɪʃəs] ADJ grazioso(-a), misericordioso(-a) ▶ EXCL: **(good) ~!** madonna (mia)!

gradation [grə'deɪʃən] N gradazione f

grade [greɪd] N (*Comm*) qualità f inv; classe f; categoria; (*in hierarchy*) grado; (*US Scol*: *mark*) voto; classe; (*gradient*) pendenza, gradiente m ▶ VT classificare; ordinare; graduare; **to make the ~** (*fig*) farcela

grade crossing N (*US*) passaggio a livello

grade school N (*US*) scuola elementare *or* primaria

gradient ['greɪdɪənt] N pendenza, inclinazione m

gradual ['grædjuəl] ADJ graduale

gradually ['grædjuəlɪ] ADV man mano, a poco a poco

graduate N ['grædjuɪt] laureato(-a); (*US Scol*) diplomato(-a), licenziato(-a) ▶ VI ['grædjueɪt] laurearsi; diplomarsi

graduated pension ['grædjueɪtɪd-] N *pensione calcolata sugli ultimi stipendi*

graduation [grædju'eɪʃən] N cerimonia del conferimento della laurea; (*US Scol*) consegna dei diplomi

graffiti [grə'fiːtɪ] NPL graffiti *mpl*

graft [grɑːft] N (*Agr, Med*) innesto; (*col*: *bribery*) corruzione f; (*BRIT col*): **hard ~** duro lavoro ▶ VT innestare; **it's hard ~** (*BRIT col*) è un lavoraccio

grain [greɪn] N (*no pl*: *cereals*) cereali *mpl*; (*US*: *corn*) grano; (*of sand*) granello; (*of wood*) venatura; **it goes against the ~** (*fig*) va contro la mia (*or* la sua *etc*) natura

gram [græm] N grammo

grammar ['græmə'] N grammatica

grammar school N (*BRIT*) ≈ liceo; (*US*) ≈ scuola elementare

grammatical [grə'mætɪkl] ADJ grammaticale

gramme [græm] N = **gram**

gramophone ['græməfəun] N (*BRIT*) grammofono

gran [græn] N (*col*: *BRIT*) nonna

granary ['grænərɪ] N granaio

grand [grænd] ADJ grande, magnifico(-a); grandioso(-a) ▶ N (*col*: *thousand*) mille dollari *mpl* (*or* sterline *fpl*)

grandad ['grændæd] N (*col*) = **granddad**

grandchild ['græntʃaɪld] (*pl* **-children** [-tʃɪldrən]) N nipote m

granddad ['grændæd] N (*col*) nonno

granddaughter ['grændɔːtə'] N nipote f

grandeur ['grændjə'] N (*of style, house*) splendore m; (*of occasion, scenery etc*) grandiosità, maestà

grandfather ['grændfɑːðə'] N nonno

grandiose ['grændɪəus] ADJ grandioso(-a); (*pej*) pomposo(-a)

grand jury N (*US*) giuria (*formata da 12 a 23 membri*)

grandma ['grænmɑː] N (*col*) nonna

grandmother ['grænmʌðə'] N nonna

grandpa ['grænpɑː] N (*col*) = **granddad**

grandparent ['grænpɛərənt] N nonno(-a)

grand piano N pianoforte m a coda

Grand Prix ['grɑ̃:'priː] N (*Aut*) Gran Premio, Grand Prix m inv

grandson ['grænsʌn] N nipote m

grandstand ['grændstænd] N (*Sport*) tribuna

grand total N somma complessiva

granite ['grænɪt] N granito

granny ['grænɪ] N (*col*) nonna

grant [grɑːnt] VT accordare; (*a request*) accogliere; (*admit*) ammettere, concedere ▶ N (*Scol*) borsa; (*Admin*) sussidio, sovvenzione f; **to take sth for granted** dare qc per scontato; **to take sb for granted** dare per scontata la presenza di qn

granular ['grænjulə'] ADJ granulare

granulated ['grænjuleɪtɪd] ADJ: **~ sugar** zucchero cristallizzato

granule ['grænjuːl] N granello

grape [greɪp] N chicco d'uva, acino; **a bunch of grapes** un grappolo d'uva

grapefruit ['greɪpfruːt] N pompelmo

grapevine ['greɪpvaɪn] N vite f; **I heard it on the ~** (*fig*) me l'ha detto l'uccellino

graph [grɑːf] N grafico

graphic ['græfɪk] ADJ grafico(-a); (*vivid*) vivido(-a); *see also* **graphics**

graphic designer N grafico(-a)

graphic equalizer N equalizzatore m grafico

graphics ['græfɪks] N (*art, process*) grafica ▶ NPL (*drawings*) illustrazioni *fpl*

graphite ['græfaɪt] N grafite f

graph paper N carta millimetrata

grapple ['græpl] VI: **to ~ with** essere alle prese con

grappling iron ['græplɪŋ-] N (*Naut*) grappino

grasp [grɑːsp] VT afferrare ▶ N (*grip*) presa; (*fig*) potere m; comprensione f; **to have sth within one's ~** avere qc a portata di mano; **to have a good ~ of** (*subject*) avere una buona padronanza di

▶ **grasp at** VT FUS (*rope etc*) afferrarsi a, aggrapparsi a; (*fig*: *opportunity*) non farsi sfuggire, approfittare di

grasping ['grɑːspɪŋ] ADJ avido(-a)

grass [grɑ:s] N erba; (*pasture*) pascolo, prato; (*BRIT col*: *informer*) informatore(-trice); (*ex-terrorist*) pentito(-a)

grasshopper [ˈgrɑ:shɔpəʳ] N cavalletta

grassland [ˈgrɑ:slænd] N prateria

grass roots NPL (*fig*) base *f*

grass snake N natrice *f*

grassy [ˈgrɑ:sɪ] ADJ erboso(-a)

grate [greɪt] N graticola (del focolare) ▶ VI cigolare, stridere ▶ VT (*Culin*) grattugiare

grateful [ˈgreɪtful] ADJ grato(-a), riconoscente

gratefully [ˈgreɪtfulɪ] ADV con gratitudine

grater [ˈgreɪtəʳ] N grattugia

gratification [grætɪfɪˈkeɪʃən] N soddisfazione *f*

gratify [ˈgrætɪfaɪ] VT appagare; (*whim*) soddisfare

gratifying [ˈgrætɪfaɪɪŋ] ADJ gradito(-a), soddisfacente

grating [ˈgreɪtɪŋ] N (*iron bars*) grata ▶ ADJ (*noise*) stridente, stridulo(-a)

gratitude [ˈgrætɪtju:d] N gratitudine *f*

gratuitous [grəˈtju:ɪtəs] ADJ gratuito(-a)

gratuity [grəˈtju:ɪtɪ] N mancia

grave [greɪv] N tomba ▶ ADJ grave, serio(-a)

gravedigger [ˈgreɪvdɪgəʳ] N becchino

gravel [ˈgrævl] N ghiaia

gravely [ˈgreɪvlɪ] ADV gravemente, solennemente; **~ ill** in pericolo di vita

gravestone [ˈgreɪvstəun] N pietra tombale

graveyard [ˈgreɪvjɑ:d] N cimitero

gravitate [ˈgrævɪteɪt] VI gravitare

gravity [ˈgrævɪtɪ] N (*Physics*) gravità; pesantezza; (*seriousness*) gravità, serietà

gravy [ˈgreɪvɪ] N intingolo della carne; salsa

gravy boat N salsiera

gravy train N: **the ~** (*col*) l'albero della cuccagna

gray [greɪ] ADJ (*US*) = **grey**

graze [greɪz] VI pascolare, pascere ▶ VT (*touch lightly*) sfiorare; (*scrape*) escoriare ▶ N (*Med*) escoriazione *f*

grazing [ˈgreɪzɪŋ] N pascolo

grease [gri:s] N (*fat*) grasso; (*lubricant*) lubrificante *m* ▶ VT ingrassare; lubrificare; **to ~ the skids** (*US fig*) spianare la strada

grease gun N ingrassatore *m*

greasepaint [ˈgri:speɪnt] N cerone *m*

greaseproof paper [ˈgri:spru:f-] N (*BRIT*) carta oleata

greasy [ˈgri:sɪ] ADJ grasso(-a), untuoso(-a); (*BRIT*: *road, surface*) scivoloso(-a); (*hands, clothes*) unto(-a)

great [greɪt] ADJ grande; (*pain, heat*) forte, intenso(-a); (*col*) magnifico(-a), meraviglioso(-a); **they're ~ friends** sono grandi amici; **the ~**

thing is that ... il bello è che ...; **it was ~!** è stato fantastico!; **we had a ~ time** ci siamo divertiti un mondo

Great Barrier Reef N: **the ~** la Grande Barriera Corallina

Great Britain N Gran Bretagna

> Sebbene si usino indifferentemente **Great Britain** (Gran Bretagna) e *United Kingdom* (Regno Unito), questi due termini non sono equivalenti. *Great Britain*, che si formò nel 1707 dall'unione dei due regni, Inghilterra e Galles con la Scozia. Con *United Kingdom* si intende l'unione di Gran Bretagna e Irlanda del Nord.

great-grandchild [greɪtˈgrænʧaɪld] (*pl* **-children** [-ʧɪldrən]) N pronipote *mf*

great-grandfather [greɪtˈgrændfɑ:ðəʳ] N bisnonno

great-grandmother [greɪtˈgrænmʌðəʳ] N bisnonna

Great Lakes NPL: **the ~** i Grandi Laghi

greatly [ˈgreɪtlɪ] ADV molto

greatness [ˈgreɪtnɪs] N grandezza

Grecian [ˈgri:ʃən] ADJ greco(-a)

Greece [gri:s] N Grecia

greed [gri:d] N (*also*: **greediness**) avarizia; (: *for food*) golosità, ghiottoneria

greedily [ˈgri:dɪlɪ] ADV avidamente; golosamente

greedy [ˈgri:dɪ] ADJ avido(-a); goloso(-a), ghiotto(-a)

Greek [gri:k] ADJ greco(-a) ▶ N greco(-a); (*Ling*) greco; **ancient/modern ~** greco antico/moderno

green [gri:n] ADJ (*also Pol*) verde; (*inexperienced*) inesperto(-a), ingenuo(-a) ▶ N verde *m*; (*stretch of grass*) prato; (*also*: **village green**) ≈ piazza del paese; (*of golf course*) green *m inv* ■ **greens** NPL (*vegetables*) verdura; **to have ~ fingers** or (*US*) **a ~ thumb** (*fig*) avere il pollice verde; **the G~ Party** (*BRIT Pol*) i Verdi

green belt N (*round town*) cintura di verde

green card N (*BRIT Aut*) carta verde; (*US Admin*) permesso di soggiorno e di lavoro

greenery [ˈgri:nərɪ] N verde *m*

greenfly [ˈgri:nflaɪ] N afide *f*

greengage [ˈgri:ngeɪʤ] N susina Regina Claudia

greengrocer [ˈgri:ngrəusəʳ] N (*BRIT*) fruttivendolo(-a), erbivendolo(-a)

greenhouse [ˈgri:nhaus] N serra

greenhouse effect N: **the ~** l'effetto serra

greenhouse gas N gas *m inv* responsabile dell'effetto serra

greenish [ˈgri:nɪʃ] ADJ verdastro(-a)

Greenland [ˈgri:nlənd] N Groenlandia

Greenlander [ˈgri:nləndəʳ] N groenlandese *mf*

green light N: **to give sb the ~** dare via libera a qn

green pepper N peperone m verde

green salad N insalata verde

green tax N tassa verde

greet [gri:t] VT salutare

greeting ['gri:tɪŋ] N saluto; **Christmas/birthday greetings** auguri mpl di Natale/di compleanno; **Season's greetings** Buone Feste

greetings card N cartolina d'auguri

gregarious [grə'gɛərɪəs] ADJ gregario(-a), socievole

Grenada [grɛ'neɪdə] N Grenada m

grenade [grə'neɪd] N (also: **hand grenade**) granata

grew [gru:] PT of **grow**

grey, (US) **gray** [greɪ] ADJ grigio(-a); **to go ~** diventar grigio

grey-haired ADJ dai capelli grigi

greyhound ['greɪhaund] N levriere m

grey vote N elettori mpl senior

grid [grɪd] N grata; (Elec) rete f; (US Aut) area d'incrocio

griddle ['grɪdl] N piastra

gridiron ['grɪdaɪən] N graticola

gridlock ['grɪdlɔk] N (traffic jam) paralisi f inv del traffico; **gridlocked** adj paralizzato(-a) dal traffico; (talks etc) in fase di stallo

grief [gri:f] N dolore m; **to come to ~** (plan) naufragare; (person) finire male

grievance ['gri:vəns] N doglianza, lagnanza; (cause for complaint) motivo di risentimento

grieve [gri:v] VI affliggersi ▶ VT addolorare; **to ~ for sb** compiangere qn; (dead person) piangere qn

grievous bodily harm ['gri:vəs-] N (Law) aggressione f

grill [grɪl] N (on cooker) griglia; (also: **mixed grill**) grigliata mista ▶ VT (BRIT) cuocere ai ferri; (col: question) interrogare senza sosta; **grilled meat** (BRIT) carne f ai ferri or alla griglia; see **grillroom**

grille [grɪl] N grata; (Aut) griglia

grillroom ['grɪlrum], **grill** ['grɪl] N rosticceria

grim [grɪm] ADJ sinistro(-a), brutto(-a)

grimace [grɪ'meɪs] N smorfia ▶ VI fare smorfie

grime [graɪm] N sudiciume m

grimy ['graɪmɪ] ADJ sudicio(-a)

grin [grɪn] N sorriso smagliante ▶ VI: **to ~ (at)** sorridere (a), fare un gran sorriso (a)

grind [graɪnd] (pt, pp **ground** [graund]) VT macinare; (US: meat) tritare, macinare; (make sharp) arrotare; (polish: gem, lens) molare ▶ VI (car gears) grattare ▶ N (work) sgobbata; **to ~ one's teeth** digrignare i denti; **to ~ to a halt** (vehicle) arrestarsi con uno stridìo di freni; (fig: talks, scheme)

insabbiarsi; (work, production) cessare del tutto; **the daily ~** (col) il tran tran quotidiano

grinder ['graɪndə'] N (machine: for coffee) macinino

grindstone ['graɪndstəun] N: **to keep one's nose to the ~** darci sotto

grip [grɪp] N impugnatura; presa; (holdall) borsa da viaggio ▶ VT (object) afferrare; (attention) catturare; **to come to grips with** affrontare; cercare di risolvere; **to ~ the road** (tyres) far presa sulla strada; (car) tenere bene la strada; **to lose one's ~** perdere or allentare la presa; (fig) perdere la grinta

gripe [graɪp] N (Med) colica; (col: complaint) lagna ▶ VI (col) brontolare

gripping ['grɪpɪŋ] ADJ avvincente

grisly ['grɪzlɪ] ADJ macabro(-a), orrido(-a)

grist [grɪst] N (fig): **it's (all) ~ to the mill** tutto aiuta

gristle ['grɪsl] N cartilagine f

grit [grɪt] N ghiaia; (courage) fegato ▶ VT (road) coprire di sabbia; **to ~ one's teeth** stringere i denti; **I've got a piece of ~ in my eye** ho un bruscolino nell'occhio

grits [grɪts] NPL (US) macinato grosso (di avena etc)

grizzle ['grɪzl] VI (BRIT) piagnucolare

grizzly ['grɪzlɪ] N (also: **grizzly bear**) orso grigio, grizzly m inv

groan [grəun] N gemito ▶ VI gemere

grocer ['grəusə'] N negoziante m di generi alimentari; **~'s (shop)** negozio di alimentari

groceries ['grəusərɪz] NPL provviste fpl

grocery ['grəusərɪ] N (shop) (negozio di) alimentari

grog [grɔg] N grog m inv

groggy ['grɔgɪ] ADJ barcollante

groin [grɔɪn] N inguine m

groom [gru:m] N palafreniere m; (also: **bridegroom**) sposo ▶ VT (horse) strigliare; (fig): **to ~ sb for** avviare qn a; **well-groomed** (person) curato(-a)

groove [gru:v] N scanalatura, solco

grope [grəup] VI andare a tentoni; **to ~ for sth** cercare qc a tastoni

gross [grəus] ADJ grossolano(-a); (Comm) lordo(-a) ▶ N (pl inv: twelve dozen) grossa ▶ VT (Comm) incassare, avere un incasso lordo di

gross domestic product N prodotto interno lordo

grossly ['grəuslɪ] ADV (greatly) molto

gross national product N prodotto nazionale lordo

grotesque [grəu'tɛsk] ADJ grottesco(-a)

grotto ['grɔtəu] N grotta

grotty ['grɔtɪ] ADJ (BRIT col) squallido(-a)

grouch [graʊtʃ] (col) vi brontolare ▶ N (person) brontolone(-a)

ground [graʊnd] PT, PP of **grind** ▶ ADJ (coffee etc) macinato(-a) ▶ N suolo, terra; (land) terreno; (Sport) campo; (reason: gen pl) ragione f; (US: also: **ground wire**) (presa a) terra ▶ VT (plane) tenere a terra; (US Elec) mettere la presa a terra a ▶ vi (ship) arenarsi ▪ **grounds** NPL (of coffee etc) fondi mpl; (gardens etc) terreno, giardini mpl; **on/to the ~** per/a terra; **below ~** sotterra; **common ~** terreno comune; **to gain/lose ~** guadagnare/ perdere terreno; **he covered a lot of ~ in his lecture** ha toccato molti argomenti nel corso della conferenza

ground cloth N (US) = **groundsheet**

ground control N (Aviat, Space) base f di controllo

ground floor N pianterreno

grounding ['graʊndɪŋ] N (in education) basi fpl

groundless ['graʊndlɪs] ADJ infondato(-a)

groundnut ['graʊndnʌt] N arachide f

ground rent N (BRIT) canone m di affitto di un terreno

ground rules NPL regole fpl fondamentali

groundsheet ['graʊndʃiːt] N (BRIT) telone m impermeabile

groundsman ['graʊndzmən] (irreg), (US) **groundskeeper** ['graʊndzkiːpəʳ] N (Sport) custode m (di campo sportivo)

ground staff N personale m di terra

groundswell ['graʊndswɛl] N maremoto; (fig) movimento

ground-to-air ['graʊndtuˈɛəʳ] ADJ terra-aria inv

ground-to-ground ['graʊntəˈgraʊnd] ADJ: **~ missile** missile m terra-terra

groundwork ['graʊndwəːk] N preparazione f

group [gruːp] N gruppo; (Mus: pop group) complesso, gruppo ▶ VT (also: **group together**) raggruppare ▶ VI (also: **group together**) raggrupparsi

groupie ['gruːpɪ] N groupie mf, fan mf inv scatenato(-a)

group therapy N terapia di gruppo

grouse [graʊs] N (pl inv: bird) tetraone m ▶ VI (complain) brontolare

grove [grəʊv] N boschetto

grovel ['grɔvl] VI (fig): **to ~ (before)** strisciare (di fronte a)

grow [grəʊ] (pt **grew** [gruː], pp **grown** [grəʊn]) VI crescere; (increase) aumentare; (develop) svilupparsi; (become): **to ~ rich/weak** arricchirsi/ indebolirsi ▶ VT coltivare, far crescere; **to ~ tired of waiting** stancarsi di aspettare
   ▶ **grow apart** VI (fig) estraniarsi
   ▶ **grow away from** VT FUS (fig) allontanarsi da, staccarsi da
   ▶ **grow on** VT FUS: **that painting is growing on me** quel quadro più lo guardo più mi piace

   ▶ **grow out of** VT FUS (clothes) diventare troppo grande per indossare; (habit) perdere (col tempo); **he'll ~ out of it** gli passerà
   ▶ **grow up** VI farsi grande, crescere

grower ['grəʊəʳ] N coltivatore(-trice)

growing ['grəʊɪŋ] ADJ (fear, amount) crescente; **~ pains** (also fig) problemi mpl di crescita

growl [graʊl] VI ringhiare

grown [grəʊn] PP of **grow** ▶ ADJ adulto(-a), maturo(-a)

grown-up [grəʊnˈʌp] N adulto(-a), grande mf

growth [grəʊθ] N crescita, sviluppo; (what has grown) crescita; (Med) escrescenza, tumore m

growth rate N tasso di crescita

grub [grʌb] N larva; (col: food) roba (da mangiare)

grubby ['grʌbɪ] ADJ sporco(-a)

grudge [grʌdʒ] N rancore m ▶ VT: **to ~ sb sth** dare qc a qn di malavoglia; invidiare qc a qn; **to bear sb a ~ (for)** serbar rancore a qn (per)

grudgingly ['grʌdʒɪŋlɪ] ADV di malavoglia, di malincuore

gruelling, (US) **grueling** ['gruəlɪŋ] ADJ estenuante

gruesome ['gruːsəm] ADJ orribile

gruff [grʌf] ADJ rozzo(-a)

grumble ['grʌmbl] VI brontolare, lagnarsi

grumpy ['grʌmpɪ] ADJ scorbutico(-a)

grunge [grʌndʒ] N (Mus) grunge m inv; (style) moda f grunge inv

grunt [grʌnt] VI grugnire ▶ N grugnito

G-string ['dʒiːstrɪŋ] N (garment) tanga m inv

GT ABBR (Aut: = gran turismo) GT

GU ABBR (US Post) = **Guam**

guarantee [gærənˈtiː] N garanzia ▶ VT garantire; **he can't ~ (that) he'll come** non può garantire che verrà

guarantor [gærənˈtɔːʳ] N garante mf

guard [gɑːd] N guardia; (protection) riparo, protezione f; (Boxing) difesa; (one man) guardia, sentinella; (BRIT Rail) capotreno; (safety device: on machine) schermo protettivo; (also: **fire guard**) parafuoco ▶ VT fare la guardia a; **to ~ (against or from)** proteggere (da), salvaguardare (da); **to be on one's ~** (fig) stare in guardia
   ▶ **guard against** VI: **to ~ against doing sth** guardarsi dal fare qc

guard dog N cane m da guardia

guarded ['gɑːdɪd] ADJ (fig) cauto(-a), guardingo(-a)

guardian ['gɑːdɪən] N custode m; (of minor) tutore(-trice)

guard's van N (BRIT Rail) vagone m di servizio

Guatemala [gwɑːtəˈmɑːlə] N Guatemala m

Guernsey ['gəːnzɪ] N Guernesey f

guerrilla [gəˈrɪlə] N guerrigliero(-a)

guerrilla warfare N guerriglia

guess [gɛs] vɪ indovinare ▶ vᴛ indovinare; (US) credere, pensare ▶ N congettura; **to take** or **have a ~** provare a indovinare; **my ~ is that ...** suppongo che ...; **to keep sb guessing** tenere qn in sospeso or sulla corda; **I ~ you're right** mi sa che hai ragione

guesstimate ['gɛstɪmɪt] N (col) stima approssimativa

guesswork ['gɛswəːk] N: **I got the answer by ~** ho azzeccato la risposta

guest [gɛst] N ospite mf; (in hotel) cliente mf; **be my ~** (col) fai come (se fossi) a casa tua

guest-house ['gɛsthaus] N pensione f

guest room N camera degli ospiti

guff [gʌf] N (col) stupidaggini fpl, assurdità fpl

guffaw [gʌ'fɔː] N risata sonora ▶ vɪ scoppiare di una risata sonora

guidance ['gaɪdəns] N guida, direzione f; **marriage/vocational ~** consulenza matrimoniale/ per l'avviamento professionale

guide [gaɪd] N (person, book etc) guida; (BRIT: also: **girl guide**) giovane esploratrice f ▶ vᴛ guidare; **to be guided by sb/sth** farsi or lasciarsi guidare da qn/qc

guidebook ['gaɪdbuk] N guida

guided missile N missile m telecomandato

guide dog N (BRIT) cane m guida inv

guided tour N visita guidata; **what time does the ~ start?** a che ora comincia la visita guidata?

guidelines ['gaɪdlaɪnz] NPL (fig) indicazioni fpl, linee fpl direttive

guild [gɪld] N arte f, corporazione f; associazione f

guildhall ['gɪldhɔːl] N (BRIT) palazzo municipale

guile [gaɪl] N astuzia

guileless ['gaɪllɪs] ADJ candido(-a)

guillotine ['gɪlətiːn] N ghigliottina

guilt [gɪlt] N colpevolezza

guilty ['gɪltɪ] ADJ colpevole; **to feel ~ (about)** sentirsi in colpa (per); **to plead ~/not ~** dichiararsi colpevole/innocente

Guinea ['gɪnɪ] N: **Republic of ~** Repubblica di Guinea

guinea ['gɪnɪ] N (BRIT) ghinea (= 21 shillings: valuta ora fuori uso)

Guinea-Bissau ['gɪnɪbɪ'sau] N Guinea-Bissau f

guinea pig ['gɪnɪ-] N cavia

guise [gaɪz] N maschera

guitar [gɪ'tɑːʳ] N chitarra

guitarist [gɪ'tɑːrɪst] N chitarrista mf

gulch [gʌltʃ] N (US) burrone m

gulf [gʌlf] N golfo; (abyss) abisso; **the (Persian) G~** il Golfo Persico

Gulf States NPL: **the ~** i paesi del Golfo Persico

Gulf Stream N: **the ~** la corrente del Golfo

gull [gʌl] N gabbiano

gullet ['gʌlɪt] N gola

gullibility [gʌlɪ'bɪlɪtɪ] N semplicioneria

gullible ['gʌlɪbl] ADJ credulo(-a)

gully ['gʌlɪ] N burrone m; gola; canale m

gulp [gʌlp] vɪ deglutire; (from emotion) avere il nodo in gola ▶ vᴛ (also: **gulp down**) tracannare, inghiottire ▶ N (of liquid) sorso; (of food) boccone m; **in** or **at one ~** in un sorso, d'un fiato

gum [gʌm] N (Anat) gengiva; (glue) colla; (sweet) caramella gommosa; (also: **chewing-gum**) chewing-gum m ▶ vᴛ incollare ▶ **gum up** vᴛ: **to ~ up the works** (col) mettere il bastone tra le ruote

gumboil ['gʌmbɔɪl] N ascesso (dentario)

gumboots ['gʌmbuːts] NPL (BRIT) stivali mpl di gomma

gumption ['gʌmpʃən] N buon senso, senso pratico

gun [gʌn] N fucile m; (small) pistola, rivoltella; (rifle) carabina; (shotgun) fucile da caccia; (cannon) cannone m ▶ vᴛ (also: **gun down**) abbattere a colpi di pistola or fucile; **to stick to one's guns** (fig) tener duro

gunboat ['gʌnbəut] N cannoniera

gun dog N cane m da caccia

gunfire ['gʌnfaɪəʳ] N spari mpl

gung-ho ['gʌŋ'həu] ADJ (col) stupidamente entusiasta

gunk [gʌŋk] N porcherie fpl

gunman ['gʌnmən] N (irreg) bandito armato

gunner ['gʌnəʳ] N artigliere m

gunpoint ['gʌnpɔɪnt] N: **at ~** sotto minaccia di fucile

gunpowder ['gʌnpaudəʳ] N polvere f da sparo

gunrunner ['gʌnrʌnəʳ] N contrabbandiere d'armi

gunrunning ['gʌnrʌnɪŋ] N contrabbando d'armi

gunshot ['gʌnʃɔt] N sparo; **within ~** a portata di fucile

gunsmith ['gʌnsmɪθ] N armaiolo

gurgle ['gəːgl] N gorgoglio ▶ vɪ gorgogliare

guru ['guruː] N guru m inv

gush [gʌʃ] N fiotto, getto ▶ vɪ sgorgare; (fig) abbandonarsi ad effusioni

gushing ['gʌʃɪŋ] ADJ che fa smancerie, smorfioso(-a)

gusset ['gʌsɪt] N gherone m; (in tights, pants) rinforzo

gust [gʌst] N (of wind) raffica; (of smoke) buffata

gusto ['gʌstəu] N entusiasmo

gusty ['gʌstɪ] ADJ (wind) a raffiche; (day) tempestoso(-a)

gut [gʌt] N intestino, budello; (Mus etc) minugia

▶ VT (*poultry, fish*) levare le interiora a, sventrare; (*building*) svuotare; (: *fire*) divorare l'interno di ■ **guts** NPL (*col: innards*) budella *fpl*; (: *of animals*) interiora *fpl*; (*courage*) fegato; **to hate sb's guts** odiare qn a morte

gut reaction N reazione *f* istintiva

gutsy ['gʌtsɪ] ADJ (*col: style*) che ha mordente; (*plucky*) coraggioso(-a)

gutted ['gʌtɪd] ADV (*col: upset*) scioccato(-a)

gutter ['gʌtəʳ] N (*of roof*) grondaia; (*in street*) cunetta

gutter press N: **the ~** la stampa scandalistica

guttural ['gʌtərl] ADJ gutturale

guy [gaɪ] N (*also:* **guyrope**) cavo *or* corda di fissaggio; (*col: man*) tipo, elemento; (*figure*) effigie di *Guy Fawkes*

Guyana [gaɪ'ænə] N Guayana *f*

Guy Fawkes Night [-'fɔːks-] N (BRIT) *vedi nota*

La sera del 5 novembre, in occasione della **Guy Fawkes Night**, o *Bonfire Night*, viene commemorato, con falò e fuochi d'artificio, il fallimento della Congiura delle Polveri contro Giacomo I nel 1605. La festa prende il nome dal principale congiurato della cospirazione, Guy Fawkes, la cui effigie viene bruciata durante i festeggiamenti che si svolgono sia in giardini privati che, in modo più ufficiale, in parchi cittadini.

guzzle ['gʌzl] VI gozzovigliare ▶ VT trangugiare

gym [dʒɪm] N (*also:* **gymnasium**) palestra; (*also:* **gymnastics**) ginnastica

gymkhana [dʒɪm'kɑːnə] N gimkana

gymnasium [dʒɪm'neɪzɪəm] N palestra

gymnast ['dʒɪmnæst] N ginnasta *mf*

gymnastics [dʒɪm'næstɪks] N, NPL ginnastica

gym shoes NPL scarpe *fpl* da ginnastica

gym slip N (BRIT) grembiule *m* da scuola (*per ragazze*)

gynaecologist, (US) **gynecologist** [gaɪnɪ'kɔlədʒɪst] N ginecologo(-a)

gynaecology, (US) **gynecology** [gaɪnə'kɔlədʒɪ] N ginecologia

gypsy ['dʒɪpsɪ] N = **gipsy**

gyrate [dʒaɪ'reɪt] VI girare

gyroscope ['dʒaɪərəskəup] N giroscopio

Hh

H, h [eɪtʃ] N (*letter*) H, h *f inv or* m *inv*; **H for Harry**, (*US*) **H for How** ≈ H come Hotel

habeas corpus [ˈheɪbɪəsˈkɔːpəs] N (*Law*) habeas corpus m *inv*

haberdashery [ˈhæbədæʃərɪ] N (*BRIT*) merceria

habit [ˈhæbɪt] N abitudine f; (*costume*) abito; (*Rel*) tonaca; **to get out of/into the ~ of doing sth** perdere/prendere l'abitudine di fare qc

habitable [ˈhæbɪtəbl] ADJ abitabile

habitat [ˈhæbɪtæt] N habitat m *inv*

habitation [hæbɪˈteɪʃən] N abitazione f

habitual [həˈbɪtjuəl] ADJ abituale; (*drinker, liar*) inveterato(-a)

habitually [həˈbɪtjuəlɪ] ADV abitualmente, di solito

hack [hæk] VT tagliare, fare a pezzi ▶ N (*cut*) taglio; (*blow*) colpo; (*old horse*) ronzino; (*pej: writer*) scribacchino(-a)

hacker [ˈhækəʳ] N (*Comput*) pirata m informatico

hackles [ˈhæklz] NPL: **to make sb's ~ rise** (*fig*) rendere qn furioso

hackney cab [ˈhæknɪ-] N carrozza a nolo

hackneyed [ˈhæknɪd] ADJ comune, trito(-a)

hacksaw [ˈhæksɔː] N seghetto (per metallo)

had [hæd] PT, PP *of* **have**

haddock [ˈhædək] (*pl ~ or* **haddocks**) N eglefino

hadn't [ˈhædnt] = **had not**

haematology, (*US*) **hematology** [hiːməˈtɔlədʒɪ] N ematologia

haemoglobin, (*US*) **hemoglobin** [hiːməuˈɡləubɪn] N emoglobina

haemophilia, (*US*) **hemophilia** [hiːməuˈfɪlɪə] N emofilia

haemorrhage, (*US*) **hemorrhage** [ˈhɛmərɪdʒ] N emorragia

haemorrhoids, (*US*) **hemorrhoids** [ˈhɛmərɔɪdz] NPL emorroidi *fpl*

hag [hæg] N (*ugly*) befana; (*nasty*) megera; (*witch*) strega

haggard [ˈhægəd] ADJ smunto(-a)

haggis [ˈhægɪs] N (*SCOTTISH*) insaccato a base di frattaglie di pecora e avena

haggle [ˈhægl] VI mercanteggiare; **to ~ (over)** contrattare (su); (*argue*) discutere (su)

haggling [ˈhæglɪŋ] N contrattazioni *fpl*

Hague [heɪg] N: **The ~** L'Aia

hail [heɪl] N grandine f; (*of criticism etc*) pioggia ▶ VT (*call*) chiamare; (*flag down: taxi*) fermare; (*greet*) salutare ▶ VI grandinare; **to ~ (as)** acclamare (come); **he hails from Scotland** viene dalla Scozia

hailstone [ˈheɪlstəun] N chicco di grandine

hailstorm [ˈheɪlstɔːm] N grandinata

hair [hɛəʳ] N capelli mpl; (*single hair: on head*) capello; (: *on body*) pelo; **to do one's ~** pettinarsi

> The Italian word for *hair* **capelli** is a plural noun spelt with a single 'p'. The Italian word for *hat* is **cappello**, spelt with a double 'p'.

hairband [ˈhɛəbænd] N (*elastic*) fascia per i capelli; (*rigid*) cerchietto

hairbrush [ˈhɛəbrʌʃ] N spazzola per capelli

haircut [ˈhɛəkʌt] N taglio di capelli; **I need a ~** devo tagliarmi i capelli

hairdo [ˈhɛəduː] N acconciatura, pettinatura

hairdresser [ˈhɛədrɛsəʳ] N parrucchiere(-a)

hairdresser's N parrucchiere(-a)

hair-dryer [ˈhɛədraɪəʳ] N asciugacapelli m *inv*

-haired [hɛəd] SUFFIX: **fair/long-haired** dai capelli biondi/lunghi

hair gel N gel m *inv* per capelli

hairgrip [ˈhɛəgrɪp] N forcina

hairline [ˈhɛəlaɪn] N attaccatura dei capelli

hairline fracture N incrinatura

hairnet [ˈhɛənɛt] N retina (per capelli)

hair oil N brillantina

hairpiece [ˈhɛəpiːs] N toupet m *inv*

hairpin [ˈhɛəpɪn] N forcina

hairpin bend, (*US*) **hairpin curve** N tornante m

hair-raising [ˈhɛəreɪzɪŋ] ADJ orripilante

hair remover N crema depilatoria

hair spray N lacca per capelli

hairstyle ['hɛəstaɪl] N pettinatura, acconciatura

hairy ['hɛərɪ] ADJ irsuto(-a); peloso(-a); (col: frightening) spaventoso(-a)

Haiti ['heɪtɪ] N Haiti f

haka ['hɑːkə] N (NEW ZEALAND) danza eseguita dai giocatori di rugby prima di una partita

hake [heɪk] (pl ~ or hakes) N nasello

halal [hə'lɑːl] N: ~ **meat** carne macellata secondo la legge mussulmana

halcyon ['hælsɪən] ADJ sereno(-a)

hale [heɪl] ADJ: ~ **and hearty** che scoppia di salute

half [hɑːf] N (pl **halves** [hɑːvz]) mezzo, metà f inv; (Sport: of match) tempo; (: of ground) metà campo ▶ ADJ mezzo(-a) ▶ ADV a mezzo, a metà; ~ **an hour** mezz'ora; ~ **a dozen** mezza dozzina; ~ **a pound** mezza libbra; **two and a** ~ due e mezzo; **a week and a** ~ una settimana e mezza; ~ **(of)** la metà di; ~ **(of it)** la metà; ~ **the amount of** la metà di; **to cut sth in** ~ tagliare qc in due; ~ **empty/closed** mezzo vuoto/chiuso, semi-vuoto/semichiuso; ~ **asleep** mezzo(-a) addormentato(-a); ~ **past 3** le 3 e mezza; **to go halves (with sb)** fare a metà (con qn)

half-back ['hɑːfbæk] N (Sport) mediano

half-baked [hɑːf'beɪkt] ADJ (col: idea, scheme) mal combinato(-a), che non sta in piedi

half board N (BRIT) mezza pensione

half-breed ['hɑːfbriːd] N (!) = **half-caste**

half-brother ['hɑːfbrʌðəʳ] N fratellastro

half-caste ['hɑːfkɑːst] N (!) meticcio(-a)

half day N mezza giornata

half fare N tariffa a metà prezzo

half-hearted [hɑːf'hɑːtɪd] ADJ tiepido(-a)

half-hour [hɑːf'auəʳ] N mezz'ora

half-mast ['hɑːf'mɑːst] N: **at** ~ (flag) a mezz'asta

halfpenny ['heɪpnɪ] N mezzo penny m inv

half-price ['hɑːf'praɪs] ADJ, ADV (also: **at half-price**) a metà prezzo

half-sister ['hɑːf'sɪstəʳ] N sorellastra

half term N (BRIT Scol) vacanza a or di metà trimestre

half-time [hɑːf'taɪm] N (Sport) intervallo

halfway [hɑːf'weɪ] ADV a metà strada; **to meet sb** ~ (fig) arrivare a un compromesso con qn

halfway house N (hostel) ostello dove possono alloggiare temporaneamente ex detenuti; (fig) via di mezzo

half-wit ['hɑːfwɪt] N (!) idiota mf

half-yearly [hɑːf'jɪəlɪ] ADV semestralmente, ogni sei mesi ▶ ADJ semestrale

halibut ['hælɪbət] N (pl inv) ippoglosso

halitosis [hælɪ'təusɪs] N alitosi f

hall [hɔːl] N sala, salone m; (entrance way) entrata;

(corridor) corridoio; (mansion) grande villa, maniero

hallmark ['hɔːlmɑːk] N marchio di garanzia; (fig) caratteristica

hallo [hə'ləu] EXCL = **hello**

hall of residence N (BRIT) casa dello studente

Halloween ['hæləu'iːn] N vigilia d'Ognissanti

> Secondo la tradizione anglosassone, durante la notte di **Halloween**, il 31 di ottobre, è possibile vedere le streghe e i fantasmi. I bambini, travestiti da fantasmi, streghe, mostri o simili, vanno di porta in porta e raccolgono dolci e piccoli doni, pronunciando la frase ricattatoria: "trick or treat!".

hallucination [həluːsɪ'neɪʃən] N allucinazione f

hallucinogenic [həluːsɪnəu'dʒɛnɪk] ADJ allucinogeno(-a)

hallway ['hɔːlweɪ] N ingresso; corridoio

halo ['heɪləu] N (of saint etc) aureola; (of sun) alone m

halt [hɔːlt] N fermata ▶ VT fermare ▶ VI fermarsi; **to call a** ~ **(to sth)** (fig) mettere or porre fine (a qc)

halter ['hɔːltəʳ] N (for horse) cavezza

halterneck ['hɔːltənɛk] ADJ allacciato(-a) dietro il collo

halve [hɑːv] VT (apple etc) dividere a metà; (expense) ridurre di metà

halves [hɑːvz] NPL of **half**

ham [hæm] N prosciutto; (col) radioamatore(-trice); (: also: **ham actor**) attore(-trice) senza talento

Hamburg ['hæmbəːg] N Amburgo f

hamburger ['hæmbəːgəʳ] N hamburger m inv

ham-fisted ['hæm'fɪstɪd], (US) **ham-handed** ['hæm'hændɪd] ADJ maldestro(-a)

hamlet ['hæmlɪt] N paesetto

hammer ['hæməʳ] N martello ▶ VT martellare; (fig) sconfiggere duramente ▶ VI (at door) picchiare; **to** ~ **a point home to sb** cacciare un'idea in testa a qn; **to** ~ **on** or **at the door** picchiare alla porta
▶ **hammer out** VT (metal) spianare (a martellate); (fig: solution, agreement) mettere a punto

hammock ['hæmək] N amaca

hamper ['hæmpəʳ] VT impedire ▶ N cesta

hamster ['hæmstəʳ] N criceto

hamstring ['hæmstrɪŋ] N (Anat) tendine m del ginocchio

hand [hænd] N mano f; (of clock) lancetta; (handwriting) scrittura; (at cards) mano; (: game) partita; (worker) operaio(-a); (measurement: of horse) ≈ dieci centimetri ▶ VT dare, passare; **to give sb a** ~ dare una mano a qn; **at** ~ a portata di mano; **in** ~ a disposizione; (work) in corso; **we have the matter in** ~ ci stiamo occupando della cosa; **we have the situation in ~** abbiamo la situazione sotto controllo; **to be on ~** (*person*) essere disponibile; (*emergency services*) essere pronto(-a) a intervenire; **to ~** (*information etc*) a portata di mano; **to force sb's ~** forzare la mano a qn; **to have a free ~** avere carta bianca; **to have in one's ~** (*also fig*) avere in mano *or* in pugno; **on the one ~ ..., on the other ~** da un lato ..., dall'altro

▸ **hand down** vt passare giù; (*tradition, heirloom*) tramandare; (*sentence, verdict*) emettere

▸ **hand in** vt consegnare

▸ **hand out** vt (*leaflets*) distribuire; (*advice*) elargire

▸ **hand over** vt passare; cedere

▸ **hand round** vt (Brit: *information, papers*) far passare; (: *distribute: chocolates etc*) far girare; (: *offer around*) offrire

handbag ['hændbæg] N borsetta

hand baggage N bagaglio a mano

handball ['hændbɔ:l] N pallamano f

handbasin ['hændbeɪsn] N lavandino

handbook ['hændbuk] N manuale m

handbrake ['hændbreɪk] N freno a mano

h & c ABBR (Brit) = **hot and cold (water)**

hand cream N crema per le mani

handcuffs ['hændkʌfs] NPL manette fpl

handful ['hændful] N manciata, pugno

hand-held ['hænd'held] ADJ portatile

handicap ['hændɪkæp] N handicap m inv ▸ vt handicappare

handicraft ['hændɪkrɑːft] N lavoro d'artigiano

handiwork ['hændɪwəːk] N lavorazione f a mano; **this looks like his ~** (*pej*) qui c'è il suo zampino

handkerchief ['hæŋkətʃɪf] N fazzoletto

handle ['hændl] N (*of door etc*) maniglia; (*of cup etc*) ansa; (*of knife etc*) impugnatura; (*of saucepan*) manico; (*for winding*) manovella ▸ vt toccare, maneggiare; manovrare; (*deal with*) occuparsi di; (*treat: people*) trattare; **"~ with care"** "fragile"; **to fly off the ~** (*fig*) perdere le staffe, uscire dai gangheri

> Use **il manico** to refer to the handle of a saucepan, tool, etc. Use **la manica** to refer to the sleeve of a piece of clothing.

handlebar ['hændlbɑː'] N, **handlebars** ['hændlbɑːz] NPL manubrio

handling ['hændlɪŋ] N (Aut) maneggevolezza; (*of issue*) modo di affrontare

handling charges NPL commissione f per la prestazione; (*for goods*) spese fpl di trasporto; (Banking) spese fpl bancarie

hand luggage N bagagli mpl a mano

handmade [hænd'meɪd] ADJ fatto(-a) a mano; (*biscuits etc*) fatto(-a) in casa

handout ['hændaut] N (*money, food*) elemosina; (*leaflet*) volantino; (*at lecture*) prospetto; (*press handout*) comunicato stampa

hand-picked [hænd'pɪkt] ADJ (*produce*) scelto(-a), selezionato(-a); (*staff etc*) scelto(-a)

handrail ['hændreɪl] N (*on staircase etc*) corrimano

handset ['hændset] N (Tel) ricevitore m

hands-free ['hændzfri:] N, ADJ (*telephone, microphone*) vivavoce inv

handshake ['hændʃeɪk] N stretta di mano; (Comput) colloquio

handsome ['hænsəm] ADJ bello(-a); (*reward*) generoso(-a); (*profit, fortune*) considerevole

hands-on ['hændz'ɔn] ADJ: **~ experience** esperienza diretta *or* pratica

handstand ['hændstænd] N: **to do a ~** fare la verticale

hand-to-mouth ['hændtə'mauθ] ADJ (*existence*) precario(-a)

handwriting ['hændraɪtɪŋ] N scrittura

handwritten ['hændrɪtn] ADJ scritto(-a) a mano, manoscritto(-a)

handy ['hændɪ] ADJ (*person*) bravo(-a); (*close at hand*) a portata di mano; (*convenient*) comodo(-a); (*useful: machine etc*) pratico(-a), utile; **to come in ~** servire

handyman ['hændɪmæn] N (*irreg*) tuttofare m inv; **tools for the ~** arnesi per il fatelo-da-voi

hang [hæŋ] (*pt, pp* **hung** [hʌŋ]) vt appendere; (*pt, pp* **hanged**: *criminal*) impiccare ▸ vi pendere; (*painting*) essere appeso(-a); (*hair*) scendere; (*drapery*) cadere; **to get the ~ of (doing) sth** (*col*) cominiciare a capire (come si fa) qc

▸ **hang about** vi bighellonare, ciondolare

▸ **hang back** vi (*hesitate*): **to ~ back (from doing)** essere riluttante (a fare)

▸ **hang down** vi ricadere

▸ **hang on** vi (*wait*) aspettare ▸ vt FUS (*depend on: decision etc*) dipendere da; **to ~ on to** (*keep hold of*) aggrapparsi a, attaccarsi a; (*keep*) tenere

▸ **hang out** vt (*washing*) stendere (fuori) ▸ vi penzolare, pendere; (*col: live*) stare

▸ **hang round** vi = **hang around**

▸ **hang together** vi (*argument etc*) stare in piedi

▸ **hang up** vi (Tel) riattaccare ▸ vt appendere; **to ~ up on sb** (Tel) metter giù il ricevitore a qn

hangar ['hæŋə'] N hangar m inv

hangdog ['hæŋdɔg] ADJ (*guilty: look, expression*) da cane bastonato

hanger ['hæŋə'] N gruccia

hanger-on [hæŋər'ɔn] N parassita m

hang-glider ['hæŋglaɪdə'] N deltaplano

hang-gliding ['hæŋglaɪdɪŋ] N volo col deltaplano

hanging ['hæŋɪŋ] N (*execution*) impiccagione f

hangman ['hæŋmən] N (*irreg*) boia m, carnefice m

hangover [ˈhæŋəʊvəʳ] N *(after drinking)* postumi *mpl* di sbornia

hang-up [ˈhæŋʌp] N complesso

hank [hæŋk] N matassa

hanker [ˈhæŋkəʳ] VI: **to ~ after** bramare

hankering [ˈhæŋkərɪŋ] N: **to have a ~ for sth/ to do sth** avere una gran voglia di qc/di fare qc

hankie, hanky [ˈhæŋkɪ] N ABBR = **handker-chief**

haphazard [hæpˈhæzəd] ADJ a casaccio, alla carlona

hapless [ˈhæplɪs] ADJ disgraziato(-a); *(unfortu-nate)* sventurato(-a)

happen [ˈhæpən] VI accadere, succedere; **she happened to be free** per caso era libera; **to ~ to do sth** fare qc per caso; **if anything happened to him** se dovesse succedergli qualcosa; **as it happens** guarda caso; **what's happening?** cosa succede?, cosa sta succedendo?
  ▶ **happen (up)on** VT FUS capitare su

happening [ˈhæpnɪŋ] N avvenimento

happily [ˈhæpɪlɪ] ADV felicemente; fortunata-mente

happiness [ˈhæpɪnɪs] N felicità, contentezza

happy [ˈhæpɪ] ADJ felice, contento(-a); **~ with** *(arrangements etc)* soddisfatto(-a) di; **to be ~ to do** *(willing)* fare volentieri; **yes, I'd be ~ to** (certo,) con piacere, (ben) volentieri; **~ birth-day!** buon compleanno!; **~ Christmas/New Year!** buon Natale/anno!

happy-go-lucky [ˈhæpɪgəʊˈlʌkɪ] ADJ spensie-rato(-a)

happy hour N *orario in cui i pub hanno prezzi ridotti*

harangue [həˈræŋ] VT arringare

harass [ˈhærəs] VT molestare

harassed [ˈhærəst] ADJ assillato(-a)

harassment [ˈhærəsmənt] N molestia

harbour, (US) **harbor** [ˈhɑːbəʳ] N porto ▶ VT *(hope)* nutrire; *(fear)* avere; *(grudge)* covare; *(crimi-nal)* dare rifugio a

harbour dues, (US) **harbor dues** NPL diritti *mpl* portuali

harbour master, (US) **harbor master** N capitano di porto

hard [hɑːd] ADJ duro(-a) ▶ ADV *(work)* sodo; *(think, try)* bene; **to look ~ at** guardare fissamente; esaminare attentamente; **to drink ~** bere forte; **~ luck!** peccato!; **no ~ feelings!** senza rancore!; **to be ~ of hearing** essere duro(-a) d'o-recchio; **to be ~ on sb** essere severo con qn; **to be ~ done by** essere trattato(-a) ingiusta-mente; **I find it ~ to believe that ...** stento or faccio fatica a credere che ...+*sub*

hard-and-fast [ˈhɑːdənˈfɑːst] ADJ ferreo(-a)

hardback [ˈhɑːdbæk] N libro rilegato

hardboard [ˈhɑːdbɔːd] N legno precompresso

hard-boiled egg [ˈhɑːdˈbɔɪld-] N uovo sodo

hard cash N denaro in contanti

hard copy N *(Comput)* hard copy *f inv*, terminale *m* di stampa

hard-core [ˈhɑːdˈkɔːʳ] ADJ *(pornography)* hard-core *inv*; *(supporters)* irriducibile

hard court N *(Tennis)* campo in terra battuta

hard disk N *(Comput)* hard disk *m inv*, disco rigido

hard drive N *(Comput)* hard drive *m inv*

harden [ˈhɑːdn] VT indurire; *(steel)* temprare; *(fig: determination)* rafforzare ▶ VI *(substance)* indurirsi

hardened [ˈhɑːdnd] ADJ *(criminal)* incallito(-a); **to be ~ to sth** essere (diventato) insensibile a qc

hard graft N: **by sheer ~** lavorando da matti

hard-headed [ˈhɑːdˈhɛdɪd] ADJ pratico(-a)

hard-hearted [ˈhɑːdˈhɑːtɪd] ADJ che non si lascia commuovere, dal cuore duro

hard-hitting [ˈhɑːdˈhɪtɪŋ] ADJ molto duro(-a); **a ~ documentary** un documentario *m* verità *inv*

hard labour N lavori *mpl* forzati

hardliner [hɑːdˈlaɪnəʳ] N fautore(-trice) della linea dura

hard-luck story [hɑːdˈlʌk-] N storia lacrimosa *(con un fine ben preciso)*

hardly [ˈhɑːdlɪ] ADV *(scarcely)* appena, a mala pena; **it's ~ the case** non è proprio il caso; **~ anyone/anywhere** quasi nessuno/da nessuna parte; **~ ever** quasi mai; **I can ~ believe it** stento a crederci

hardness [ˈhɑːdnɪs] N durezza

hard-nosed [ˈhɑːdˈnəʊzd] ADJ *(people)* con i piedi per terra

hard-pressed [ˈhɑːdˈprɛst] ADJ in difficoltà

hard sell N *(Comm)* intensa campagna promo-zionale

hardship [ˈhɑːdʃɪp] N avversità *f inv*; priva-zioni *fpl*

hard shoulder N *(Brit Aut)* corsia d'emergenza

hard-up [hɑːdˈʌp] ADJ *(col)* al verde

hardware [ˈhɑːdwɛəʳ] N ferramenta *fpl*; *(Comput)* hardware *m*; *(Mil)* armamenti *mpl*

hardware shop, (US) **hardware store** N (negozio di) ferramenta *fpl*

hard-wearing [hɑːdˈwɛərɪŋ] ADJ resistente, robusto(-a)

hard-won [ˈhɑːdˈwʌn] ADJ sudato(-a)

hard-working [hɑːdˈwəːkɪŋ] ADJ lavorato-re(-trice)

hardy [ˈhɑːdɪ] ADJ robusto(-a); *(plant)* resistente al gelo

hare [hɛəʳ] N lepre *f*

hare-brained [ˈhɛəbreɪnd] ADJ folle; scervella-to(-a)

harelip [ˈhɛəlɪp] N *(Med)* labbro leporino

harem [hɑːˈriːm] N harem *m inv*

591

hark back [hɑːk-] vi: **to ~ to** (former days) rievocare; (earlier occasion) ritornare a or su

harm [hɑːm] N male m; (wrong) danno ▶ vt (person) fare male a; (thing) danneggiare; **to mean no ~** non avere l'intenzione d'offendere; **out of ~'s way** al sicuro; **there's no ~ in trying** tentar non nuoce

harmful ['hɑːmful] ADJ dannoso(-a)

harmless ['hɑːmlɪs] ADJ innocuo(-a); inoffensivo(-a)

harmonic [hɑːˈmɔnɪk] ADJ armonico(-a)

harmonica [hɑːˈmɔnɪkə] N armonica

harmonics [hɑːˈmɔnɪks] NPL armonia

harmonious [hɑːˈməʊnɪəs] ADJ armonioso(-a)

harmonium [hɑːˈməʊnɪəm] N armonium m inv

harmonize ['hɑːmənaɪz] vt, vi armonizzare

harmony ['hɑːmənɪ] N armonia

harness ['hɑːnɪs] N (for horse) bardatura, finimenti mpl; (for child) briglie fpl; (safety harness) imbracatura ▶ vt (horse) bardare; (resources) sfruttare

harp [hɑːp] N arpa ▶ vi: **to ~ on about** insistere tediosamente su

harpist ['hɑːpɪst] N arpista mf

harpoon [hɑːˈpuːn] N arpione m

harpsichord ['hɑːpsɪkɔːd] N clavicembalo

harrow ['hærəʊ] N (Agr) erpice m

harrowing ['hærəʊɪŋ] ADJ straziante

harry ['hærɪ] vt (Mil) saccheggiare; (person) assillare

harsh [hɑːʃ] ADJ (life, winter) duro(-a); (judge, criticism) severo(-a); (sound) rauco(-a); (colour) chiassoso(-a); (light) violento(-a)

harshly ['hɑːʃlɪ] ADV duramente; severamente

harshness ['hɑːʃnɪs] N durezza; severità

harvest ['hɑːvɪst] N raccolto; (of grapes) vendemmia ▶ vt fare il raccolto di, raccogliere; vendemmiare ▶ vi fare il raccolto; vendemmiare

harvester ['hɑːvɪstə'] N (machine) mietitrice f; (also: **combine harvester**) mietitrebbia; (person) mietitore(-trice)

has [hæz] see **have**

has-been ['hæzbiːn] N (col: person): **he's/she's a ~** ha fatto il suo tempo

hash [hæʃ] N (Culin) specie di spezzatino fatto con carne già cotta; (fig: mess) pasticcio ▶ N ABBR (col) = **hashish**

hashish ['hæʃɪʃ] N hascisc m

hashtag ['hæʃtæg] N (on Twitter) hashtag m inv

hasn't ['hæznt] = **has not**

hassle ['hæsl] N (col) sacco di problemi

haste [heɪst] N fretta; precipitazione f

hasten ['heɪsn] vt affrettare ▶ vi: **to ~ (to)** affrettarsi (a); **I ~ to add that ...** mi preme di aggiungere che ...

hastily ['heɪstɪlɪ] ADV in fretta, precipitosamente

hasty ['heɪstɪ] ADJ affrettato(-a), precipitoso(-a)

hat [hæt] N cappello

The Italian word for hat is **cappello**, spelt with a double 'p'. The Italian word for hair **capelli** is a plural noun spelt with a single 'p'.

---

hatbox ['hætbɔks] N cappelliera

hatch [hætʃ] N (Naut: also: **hatchway**) boccaporto; (BRIT: also: **service hatch**) portello di servizio ▶ vi (bird) uscire dal guscio; (egg) schiudersi ▶ vt covare; (fig: scheme, plot) elaborare, mettere a punto

hatchback ['hætʃbæk] N (Aut) tre (or cinque) porte f inv

hatchet ['hætʃɪt] N accetta

hatchet job N (col) attacco spietato; **to do a ~ on sb** fare a pezzi qn

hatchet man N (irreg) (col) tirapiedi m inv, scagnozzo

hate [heɪt] vt odiare, detestare ▶ N odio; **to ~ to do** or **doing** detestare fare; **I ~ to trouble you, but ...** mi dispiace disturbarla, ma ...

hateful ['heɪtful] ADJ odioso(-a), detestabile

hater ['heɪtə'] N: **cop-hater** persona che odia i poliziotti; **woman-hater** misogino(-a)

hatred ['heɪtrɪd] N odio

hat trick N (BRIT Sport, also fig): **to get a ~** segnare tre punti consecutivi (or vincere per tre volte consecutive)

haughty ['hɔːtɪ] ADJ altero(-a), arrogante

haul [hɔːl] vt trascinare, tirare ▶ N (of fish) pescata; (of stolen goods etc) bottino

haulage ['hɔːlɪdʒ] N trasporto; autotrasporto

haulage contractor N (BRIT: firm) impresa di trasporti; (: person) autotrasportatore(-trice)

haulier ['hɔːlɪə'], (US) **hauler** ['hɔːlə'] N autotrasportatore(-trice)

haunch [hɔːntʃ] N anca; **a ~ of venison** una coscia di cervo

haunt [hɔːnt] vt (fear) pervadere; (person) frequentare ▶ N rifugio; **this house is haunted** questa casa è abitata da un fantasma

haunted ['hɔːntɪd] ADJ (castle etc) abitato(-a) dai fantasmi or dagli spiriti; (look) ossessionato(-a), tormentato(-a)

haunting ['hɔːntɪŋ] ADJ (sight, music) ossessionante, che perseguita

Havana [həˈvænə] N l'Avana

---

have [hæv]

(pt, pp **had**) AUX VB **1** (gen) avere; essere; **to have arrived/gone** essere arrivato(-a)/andato(-a); **to have eaten/slept** avere mangiato/dormito; **he has been kind/promoted** è stato gentile/promosso; **having finished** or **when he had finished, he left** dopo aver finito, se n'è andato

2 (in tag questions): **you've done it, haven't you?** l'hai fatto, (non è) vero?; **he hasn't done it, has he?** non l'ha fatto, vero?

3 (in short answers and questions): **you've made a mistake — no I haven't/so I have** ha fatto un errore — ma no, niente affatto/sì, è vero; **we haven't paid — yes we have!** non abbiamo pagato — ma sì che abbiamo pagato!; **I've been there before, have you?** ci sono già stato, e lei?

▶ MODAL AUX VB (be obliged): **to have (got) to do sth** dover fare qc; **I haven't got** or **I don't have to wear glasses** non ho bisogno di portare gli occhiali; **I had better leave** è meglio che io vada

▶ VT **1** (possess, obtain) avere; **he has (got) blue eyes/dark hair** ha gli occhi azzurri/i capelli scuri; **have you got** or **do you have a car?** ha la macchina?; **may I have your address?** potrebbe darmi il suo indirizzo?; **you can have it for £5** te lo do per 5 sterline

2 (+ noun: take, hold etc): **to have breakfast/a swim/a bath** fare colazione/una nuotata/un bagno; **to have a cigarette** fumare una sigaretta; **to have dinner** cenare; **to have a drink** bere qualcosa; **to have lunch** pranzare; **to have a party** dare or fare una festa; **to have an operation** avere or subire un'operazione; **I'll have a coffee** prendo un caffè; **let me have a try** fammi or lasciami provare

3: **to have sth done** far fare qc; **to have one's hair cut** tagliarsi or farsi tagliare i capelli; **he had a suit made** si fece fare un abito; **to have sb do sth** far fare qc a qn; **he had me phone his boss** mi ha fatto telefonare al suo capo

4 (experience, suffer) avere; **to have a cold/flu** avere il raffreddore/l'influenza; **she had her bag stolen** le hanno rubato la borsa

5 (phrases): (col) **you've been had!** ci sei cascato!; **I won't have it!** (accept) non mi sta affatto bene!; see also **haves**

▶ **have in** VT: **to have it in for sb** (col) avercela con qn

▶ **have on** VT (garment) avere addosso; (be busy with) avere da fare; **I don't have any money on me** non ho soldi con me; **have you anything on tomorrow?** (BRIT) ha qualcosa in programma per domani?; **to have sb on** (BRIT col) prendere in giro qn

▶ **have out** VT: **to have it out with sb** (settle a problem etc) mettere le cose in chiaro con qn

haven ['heɪvn] N porto; (fig) rifugio

haven't ['hævnt] = **have not**

haversack ['hævəsæk] N zaino

haves [hævz] NPL (col): **the ~ and the have-nots** gli abbienti e i non abbienti

havoc ['hævək] N gran subbuglio; **to play ~**

with sth scombussolare qc; **to wreak ~ on sth** mettere in subbuglio qc

Hawaii [hə'waɪ:] N le Hawaii

Hawaiian [hə'waɪjən] ADJ hawaiano(-a) ▶ N hawaiano(-a); (Ling) lingua hawaiana

hawk [hɔːk] N falco ▶ VT (goods for sale) vendere per strada

hawker ['hɔːkəʳ] N venditore(-trice) ambulante

hawkish ['hɔːkɪʃ] ADJ violento(-a)

hawthorn ['hɔːθɔːn] N biancospino

hay [heɪ] N fieno

hay fever N febbre f da fieno

haystack ['heɪstæk] N pagliaio

haywire ['heɪwaɪəʳ] ADJ (col): **to go ~** perdere la testa; impazzire

hazard ['hæzəd] N (chance) azzardo, ventura; (risk) pericolo, rischio ▶ VT (one's life) rischiare, mettere a repentaglio; (guess, remark) azzardare; **to be a health/fire ~** essere pericoloso per la salute/in caso d'incendio; **to ~ a guess** tirare a indovinare

hazardous ['hæzədəs] ADJ pericoloso(-a), rischioso(-a)

hazard pay N (US) indennità di rischio

hazard warning lights NPL (Aut) luci fpl di emergenza

haze [heɪz] N foschia

hazel ['heɪzl] N (tree) nocciolo ▶ ADJ (eyes, color) nocciola inv

hazelnut ['heɪzlnʌt] N nocciola

hazy ['heɪzɪ] ADJ fosco(-a); (idea) vago(-a); (photograph) indistinto(-a)

H-bomb ['eɪtʃbɔm] N bomba H

HD ABBR (= high definition) HD, alta definizione

HDTV N ABBR (= high definition television) televisore m HD, TV f inv ad alta definizione

HE ABBR = **high explosive**; (Rel, Diplomacy: = His (or Her) Excellency) S.E.

he [hiː] PRON lui, egli; **it is he who ...** è lui che ...; **here he is** eccolo; **he-bear** etc orso etc maschio

head [hɛd] N testa, capo; (leader) capo; (of school) preside mf; (on tape recorder, computer etc) testina ▶ VT (list) essere in testa a; (group) essere a capo di; **heads (or tails)** testa (o croce), pari (o dispari); **~ first** a capofitto, di testa; **~ over heels in love** pazzamente innamorato(-a); **£10 a** or **per ~** 10 sterline a testa; **to sit at the ~ of the table** sedersi a capotavola; **to have a ~ for business** essere tagliato per gli affari; **to have no ~ for heights** soffrire di vertigini; **to lose/keep one's ~** perdere/non perdere la testa; **to come to a ~** (fig: situation etc) precipitare; **to ~ the ball** (Sport) dare di testa alla palla

▶ **head for** VT FUS dirigersi verso

▶ **head off** VT (threat, danger) sventare

headache ['hɛdeɪk] N mal m di testa; **to have a ~** aver mal di testa

headband ['hɛdbænd] N fascia per i capelli

headboard ['hɛdbɔːd] N testiera (del letto)

head cold N raffreddore *m* di testa

headdress ['hɛddrɛs] N (*of Native American etc*) copricapo; (*of bride*) acconciatura

headed notepaper ['hɛdɪd-] N carta intestata

header ['hɛdəʳ] N (BRIT col: *Football*) colpo di testa; (: *fall*) caduta di testa

head-first ['hɛd'fɜːst] ADV a testa in giù; (*fig*) senza pensare

headhunt ['hɛdhʌnt] VT: **to be headhunted** avere un'offerta di lavoro da un cacciatore di teste

headhunter ['hɛdhʌntəʳ] N cacciatore(-trice) di teste

heading ['hɛdɪŋ] N titolo; intestazione *f*

headlamp ['hɛdlæmp] N (BRIT) = **headlight**

headland ['hɛdlənd] N promontorio

headlight ['hɛdlaɪt] N fanale *m*

headline ['hɛdlaɪn] N titolo

headlong ['hɛdlɔŋ] ADV (*fall*) a capofitto; (*rush*) precipitosamente

headmaster [hɛd'mɑːstəʳ] N preside *m*

headmistress [hɛd'mɪstrɪs] N preside *f*

head office N sede *f* (centrale)

head-on [hɛd'ɔn] ADJ (*collision*) frontale

headphones ['hɛdfəunz] NPL cuffia

headquarters [hɛd'kwɔːtəz] NPL ufficio centrale; (Mil) quartiere *m* generale

head-rest ['hɛdrɛst] N poggiacapo

headroom ['hɛdrum] N (*in car*) altezza dell'abitacolo; (*under bridge*) altezza limite

headscarf ['hɛdskɑːf] N foulard *m inv*

headset ['hɛdsɛt] N = **headphones**

headstone ['hɛdstəun] N (*on grave*) lapide *f*, pietra tombale

headstrong ['hɛdstrɔŋ] ADJ testardo(-a)

headteacher N (*of primary school*) direttore(-trice); (*of secondary school*) preside *mf*

head waiter N capocameriere *m*

headway ['hɛdweɪ] N: **to make ~** fare progressi *or* passi avanti

headwind ['hɛdwɪnd] N controvento

heady ['hɛdɪ] ADJ che dà alla testa; inebriante

heal [hiːl] VT, VI guarire

health [hɛlθ] N salute *f*; **Department of H~** ≈ Ministero della Sanità

health care N assistenza sanitaria

health centre N (BRIT) poliambulatorio

health food N, **health foods** NPL alimenti *mpl* macrobiotici

health hazard N pericolo per la salute

Health Service N: **the ~** (BRIT) ≈ il Servizio Sanitario Statale

healthy ['hɛlθɪ] ADJ (*person*) sano(-a), in buona

salute; (*climate*) salubre; (*food*) salutare; (*appetite, attitude etc*) sano(-a); (*economy*) florido(-a); (*bank balance*) solido(-a)

heap [hiːp] N mucchio ▶ VT (*stones, sand*): **to ~ (up)** ammucchiare; **heaps (of)** (col: *lots*) un sacco (di), un mucchio (di); **to ~ favours/praise/gifts on sb** ricolmare qn di favori/lodi/regali

hear [hɪəʳ] (*pt, pp* **heard** [hɜːd]) VT sentire; (*news*) ascoltare; (*lecture*) assistere a; (*Law: case*) esaminare ▶ VI sentire; **to ~ about** sentire parlare di; (*have news of*) avere notizie di; **did you ~ about the move?** ha sentito del trasloco?; **to ~ from sb** ricevere notizie da qn
▶ **hear out** VT ascoltare senza interrompere

hearing ['hɪərɪŋ] N (*sense*) udito; (*of witnesses*) audizione *f*; (*of a case*) udienza; **to give sb a ~** dare ascolto a qn

hearing aid N apparecchio acustico

hearsay ['hɪəseɪ] N dicerie *fpl*, chiacchiere *fpl*; **by ~** per sentito dire

hearse [hɜːs] N carro funebre

heart [hɑːt] N cuore *m* ■ **hearts** NPL (*Cards*) cuori *mpl*; **at ~** in fondo; **by ~** (*learn, know*) a memoria; **to take ~** farsi coraggio *or* animo; **to lose ~** perdere coraggio, scoraggiarsi; **to have a weak ~** avere il cuore debole; **to set one's ~ on sth/on doing sth** tenere molto a qc/a fare qc; **the ~ of the matter** il nocciolo della questione

heartache ['hɑːteɪk] N pene *fpl*, dolori *mpl*

heart attack N attacco di cuore

heartbeat ['hɑːtbiːt] N battito del cuore

heartbreak ['hɑːtbreɪk] N immenso dolore *m*

heartbreaking ['hɑːtbreɪkɪŋ] ADJ straziante

heartbroken ['hɑːtbrəukən] ADJ affranto(-a); **to be ~** avere il cuore spezzato

heartburn ['hɑːtbɜːn] N bruciore *m* di stomaco

heart disease N malattia di cuore

-hearted ['hɑːtɪd] SUFFIX: **a kind-hearted person** una persona molto gentile

heartening ['hɑːtnɪŋ] ADJ incoraggiante

heart failure N (Med) arresto cardiaco

heartfelt ['hɑːtfɛlt] ADJ sincero(-a)

hearth [hɑːθ] N focolare *m*

heartily ['hɑːtɪlɪ] ADV (*laugh*) di cuore; (*eat*) di buon appetito; (*agree*) in pieno, completamente; **to be ~ sick of** (BRIT) essere veramente stufo di, essere arcistufo di

heartland ['hɑːtlænd] N zona centrale; **Italy's industrial ~** il cuore dell'industria italiana

heartless ['hɑːtlɪs] ADJ senza cuore, insensibile; crudele

heartstrings ['hɑːtstrɪŋz] NPL: **to tug at sb's ~** toccare il cuore a qn, toccare qn nel profondo

heart-throb ['hɑːtθrɔb] N rubacuori *m inv*

heart-to-heart ['hɑːttə'hɑːt] ADJ, ADV a cuore aperto

heart transplant N trapianto del cuore

heartwarming [ˈhɑːtwɔːmɪŋ] ADJ confortante, che scalda il cuore

hearty [ˈhɑːtɪ] ADJ caloroso(-a); robusto(-a), sano(-a); vigoroso(-a)

heat [hiːt] N calore m; (fig) ardore m; fuoco; (Sport: also: **qualifying heat**) prova eliminatoria ▶ VT scaldare; **in** or (BRIT) **on ~** in calore
▶ **heat up** VI (liquids) scaldarsi; (room) riscaldarsi
▶ VT riscaldare

heated [ˈhiːtɪd] ADJ riscaldato(-a); (fig) appassionato(-a); (argument) acceso(-a)

heater [ˈhiːtəʳ] N radiatore m; (stove) stufa

heath [hiːθ] N (BRIT) landa

heathen [ˈhiːðn] ADJ, N pagano(-a)

heather [ˈhɛðəʳ] N erica

heating [ˈhiːtɪŋ] N riscaldamento

heat-resistant [ˈhiːtrɪzɪstənt] ADJ termoresistente

heat-seeking [ˈhiːtsiːkɪŋ] ADJ termoguidato(-a)

heatstroke [ˈhiːtstrəuk] N colpo di sole

heatwave [ˈhiːtweɪv] N ondata di caldo

heave [hiːv] VT sollevare (con forza) ▶ VI sollevarsi ▶ N (push) grande spinta; **to ~ a sigh** emettere or mandare un sospiro
▶ **heave to** (pt, pp **hove**) VI (Naut) mettersi in cappa

heaven [ˈhɛvn] N paradiso, cielo; **~ forbid!** Dio ce ne guardi!; **for ~'s sake!** (pleading) per amor del cielo!, per carità!; (protesting) santo cielo!, in nome del cielo!; **thank ~!** grazie al cielo!

heavenly [ˈhɛvnlɪ] ADJ divino(-a), celeste

heavily [ˈhɛvɪlɪ] ADV pesantemente; (drink, smoke) molto

heavy [ˈhɛvɪ] ADJ pesante; (sea) grosso(-a); (rain) forte; (weather) afoso(-a); (drinker, smoker) gran (before noun); **it's ~ going** è una gran fatica; **~ industry** industria pesante

heavy cream N (US) doppia panna

heavy-duty [ˈhɛvɪˈdjuːtɪ] ADJ molto resistente

heavy goods vehicle N (BRIT) veicolo per trasporti pesanti

heavy-handed [ˈhɛvɪˈhændɪd] ADJ (clumsy, tactless) pesante

heavy metal N (Mus) heavy metal m

heavy-set [ˈhɛvɪˈsɛt] ADJ (esp US) tarchiato(-a)

heavyweight [ˈhɛvɪweɪt] N (Sport) peso massimo

Hebrew [ˈhiːbruː] ADJ ebreo(-a) ▶ N (Ling) ebraico

Hebrides [ˈhɛbrɪdiːz] NPL: **the ~** le Ebridi

heck [hɛk] (col) EXCL: **oh ~!** oh no! ▶ N: **a ~ of a lot of** un gran bel po' di

heckle [ˈhɛkl] VT interpellare e dare noia a (un oratore)

heckler [ˈhɛkləʳ] N agitatore(-trice)

hectare [ˈhɛktɑːʳ] N (BRIT) ettaro

hectic [ˈhɛktɪk] ADJ movimentato(-a); (busy) frenetico(-a)

hector [ˈhɛktəʳ] VT usare le maniere forti con

he'd [hiːd] = **he would**; **he had**

hedge [hɛdʒ] N siepe f ▶ VI essere elusivo(-a); **as a ~ against inflation** per cautelarsi contro l'inflazione; **to ~ one's bets** (fig) coprirsi dai rischi
▶ **hedge in** VT recintare con una siepe

hedgehog [ˈhɛdʒhɔg] N riccio

hedgerow [ˈhɛdʒrəu] N siepe f

hedonism [ˈhiːdənɪzəm] N edonismo

heed [hiːd] VT (also: **take heed of**) badare a, far conto di ▶ N: **to pay (no) ~ to, to take (no) ~ of** (non) ascoltare, (non) tener conto di

heedless [ˈhiːdlɪs] ADJ sbadato(-a)

heel [hiːl] N (Anat) calcagno; (of shoe) tacco ▶ VT (shoe) rifare i tacchi a; **to bring to ~** addomesticare; **to take to one's heels** (col) darsela a gambe, alzare i tacchi

hefty [ˈhɛftɪ] ADJ (person) solido(-a); (parcel) pesante; (piece, price, profit) grosso(-a)

heifer [ˈhɛfəʳ] N giovenca

height [haɪt] N altezza; (high ground) altura; (fig: of glory) apice m; (: of stupidity) colmo; **what ~ are you?** quanto sei alto?; **of average ~** di statura media; **to be afraid of heights** soffrire di vertigini; **it's the ~ of fashion** è l'ultimo grido della moda

heighten [ˈhaɪtn] VT innalzare; (fig) accrescere

heinous [ˈheɪnəs] ADJ nefando(-a), atroce

heir [ɛəʳ] N erede m

heir apparent N erede mf legittimo(-a)

heiress [ˈɛərɛs] N erede f

heirloom [ˈɛəluːm] N mobile m (or gioiello or quadro) di famiglia

heist [haɪst] N (US col) rapina

held [hɛld] PT, PP of **hold**

helicopter [ˈhɛlɪkɔptəʳ] N elicottero

heliport [ˈhɛlɪpɔːt] N eliporto

helium [ˈhiːlɪəm] N elio

hell [hɛl] N inferno; **a ~ of a ...** (col) un(a) maledetto(-a) ...; **oh ~!** (col) porca miseria!, accidenti!

he'll [hiːl] = **he will**; **he shall**

hell-bent [hɛlˈbɛnt] ADJ (col): **to be ~ on doing sth** voler fare qc a tutti i costi

hellish [ˈhɛlɪʃ] ADJ infernale

hello [həˈləu] EXCL buon giorno!; ciao! (to sb one addresses as "tu"); (surprise) ma guarda!

helm [hɛlm] N (Naut) timone m

helmet [ˈhɛlmɪt] N casco

helmsman [ˈhɛlmzmən] N (irreg) timoniere m

help [hɛlp] N aiuto; (charwoman) donna di servi-

zio; (*assistant etc*) impiegato(-a) ▶ VT aiutare; **~!** aiuto!; **with the ~ of** con l'aiuto di; **to be of ~ to sb** essere di aiuto *or* essere utile a qn; **to ~ sb (to) do sth** aiutare qn a far qc; **can you ~ me?** può aiutarmi?; **can I ~ you?** (*in shop*) desidera?; **~ yourself (to bread)** si serva (del pane); **I can't ~ saying** non posso evitare di dire; **he can't ~ it** non ci può far niente
▶ **help out** VI aiutare ▶ VT: **to ~ sb out** aiutare qn

help desk N (*esp Comput*) help desk *m inv*

helper [ˈhɛlpəʳ] N aiutante *mf*, assistente *mf*

helpful [ˈhɛlpful] ADJ di grande aiuto; (*useful*) utile

helping [ˈhɛlpɪŋ] N porzione *f*

helping hand N: **to give sb a ~** dare una mano a qn

helpless [ˈhɛlplɪs] ADJ impotente; debole; (*baby*) indifeso(-a)

helplessly [ˈhɛlplɪslɪ] ADV (*watch*) senza poter fare nulla

helpline [ˈhɛlplaɪn] N ≈ telefono amico; (*Comm*) servizio *m* informazioni *inv* (*a pagamento*)

Helsinki [ˈhɛlsɪŋkɪ] N Helsinki *f*

helter-skelter [ˈhɛltəˈskɛltəʳ] N (*BRIT: in funfair*) scivolo (a spirale)

hem [hɛm] N orlo ▶ VT fare l'orlo a
▶ **hem in** VT cingere; **to feel hemmed in** (*fig*) sentirsi soffocare

he-man [ˈhiːmæn] N (*irreg*) (*col*) fusto

hematology [hiːməˈtɔlədʒɪ] N (*US*) = **haematology**

hemisphere [ˈhɛmɪsfɪəʳ] N emisfero

hemlock [ˈhɛmlɔk] N cicuta

hemoglobin [hiːməˈgləubɪn] N (*US*) = **haemoglobin**

hemophilia [hiːməˈfɪlɪə] N (*US*) = **haemophilia**

hemorrhage [ˈhɛmərɪdʒ] N (*US*) = **haemorrhage**

hemorrhoids [ˈhɛmərɔɪdz] NPL (*US*) = **haemorrhoids**

hemp [hɛmp] N canapa

hen [hɛn] N gallina; (*female bird*) femmina

hence [hɛns] ADV (*therefore*) dunque; **2 years ~** di qui a 2 anni

henceforth [hɛnsˈfɔːθ] ADV d'ora in poi

henchman [ˈhɛntʃmən] N (*irreg*) (*pej*) caudatario

henna [ˈhɛnə] N henna

hen night N (*col*) addio al nubilato

hen party N (*col*) festa di sole donne

henpecked [ˈhɛnpɛkt] ADJ dominato(-a) dalla moglie

hepatitis [hɛpəˈtaɪtɪs] N epatite *f*

her [həːʳ] PRON (*direct*) la, l' + *vowel*; (*indirect*) le; (*stressed, after prep*) lei ▶ ADJ il (la) suo(-a), i (le) suoi (sue); **I see ~** la vedo; **give ~ a book** le dia un libro; **after ~** dopo (di) lei; *see also* **me**; **my**

herald [ˈhɛrəld] N araldo ▶ VT annunciare

heraldic [hɛˈrældɪk] ADJ araldico(-a)

heraldry [ˈhɛrəldrɪ] N araldica

herb [həːb] N erba ▪ **herbs** NPL (*Culin*) erbette *fpl*

herbaceous [həːˈbeɪʃəs] ADJ erbaceo(-a)

herbal [ˈhəːbəl] ADJ di erbe; **~ tea** tisana

herbicide [ˈhəːbɪsaɪd] N erbicida *m*

herd [həːd] N mandria; (*of wild animals, swine*) branco ▶ VT (*drive, gather: animals*) guidare; (*: people*) radunare; **herded together** ammassati (come bestie)

here [hɪəʳ] ADV qui, qua ▶ EXCL ehi!; **~!** (*at roll call*) presente!; **~ is, ~ are** ecco; **~'s my sister** ecco mia sorella; **~ he/she is** eccolo/eccola; **~ she comes** eccola che viene; **come ~!** vieni qui!; **~ and there** qua e là

hereabouts [ˈhɪərəbauts] ADV da queste parti

hereafter [hɪərˈɑːftəʳ] ADV in futuro; dopo questo ▶ N: **the ~** l'al di là *m*

hereby [hɪəˈbaɪ] ADV (*in letter*) con la presente

hereditary [hɪˈrɛdɪtrɪ] ADJ ereditario(-a)

heredity [hɪˈrɛdɪtɪ] N eredità

heresy [ˈhɛrəsɪ] N eresia

heretic [ˈhɛrətɪk] N eretico(-a)

heretical [hɪˈrɛtɪkl] ADJ eretico(-a)

herewith [hɪəˈwɪð] ADV qui accluso

heritage [ˈhɛrɪtɪdʒ] N eredità; (*of country, nation*) retaggio; **our national ~** il nostro patrimonio nazionale

hermetically [həːˈmɛtɪklɪ] ADV ermeticamente; **~ sealed** ermeticamente chiuso

hermit [ˈhəːmɪt] N eremita *m*

hernia [ˈhəːnɪə] N ernia

hero [ˈhɪərəu] N (*pl* **heroes**) N eroe *m*

heroic [hɪˈrəuɪk] ADJ eroico(-a)

heroin [ˈhɛrəuɪn] N eroina (*droga*)

heroin addict N eroinomane *mf*

heroine [ˈhɛrəuɪn] N eroina (*donna*)

heroism [ˈhɛrəuɪzəm] N eroismo

heron [ˈhɛrən] N airone *m*

hero worship N divismo

herring [ˈhɛrɪŋ] N aringa

hers [həːz] PRON il (la) suo(-a), i (le) suoi (sue); **a friend of ~** un suo amico; **this is ~** questo è (il) suo; *see also* **mine**[1]

herself [həːˈsɛlf] PRON (*reflexive*) si; (*emphatic*) lei stessa; (*after prep*) se stessa, sé; *see also* **oneself**

he's [hiːz] = **he is**; **he has**

hesitant [ˈhɛzɪtənt] ADJ esitante, indeciso(-a); **to be ~ about doing sth** esitare a fare qc

hesitate [ˈhɛzɪteɪt] VI: **to ~ (about/to do)** esitare (su/a fare); **don't ~ to ask (me)** non aver timore *or* paura di chiedermelo

hesitation [hɛzɪ'teɪʃən] N esitazione f; **I have no ~ in saying (that)** ... non esito a dire che ...

hessian ['hɛsɪən] N tela di canapa

heterogeneous [hɛtərəu'dʒiːnɪəs] ADJ eterogeneo(-a)

heterosexual [hɛtərəu'sɛksjuəl] ADJ, N eterosessuale (mf)

het up [hɛt'ʌp] ADJ agitato(-a)

hew [hjuː] VT tagliare (con l'accetta)

hex [hɛks] (US) N stregoneria ▶ VT stregare

hexagon ['hɛksəgən] N esagono

hexagonal [hɛk'sægənl] ADJ esagonale

hey [heɪ] EXCL ehi!

heyday ['heɪdeɪ] N: **the ~ of** i bei giorni di, l'età d'oro di

HF N ABBR (= high frequency) AF

HGV N ABBR = **heavy goods vehicle**

HHS N ABBR (US: = Department of Health and Human Services) ministero della sanità e della previdenza sociale

HI ABBR (US) = **Hawaii**

hi [haɪ] EXCL ciao!

hiatus [haɪ'eɪtəs] N vuoto; (Ling) iato

hibernate ['haɪbəneɪt] VI ibernare

hibernation [haɪbə'neɪʃən] N letargo, ibernazione f

hiccough, hiccup ['hɪkʌp] VI singhiozzare ▶ N singhiozzo; **to have (the) hiccoughs** avere il singhiozzo

hick [hɪk] N (US pej) buzzurro(-a)

hid [hɪd] PT of **hide**

hidden ['hɪdn] PP of **hide** ▶ ADJ nascosto(-a); **there are no ~ extras** è veramente tutto compreso nel prezzo; **~ agenda** programma m occulto

hide [haɪd] (pt **hid** [hɪd], pp **hidden** ['hɪdn]) N (skin) pelle f ▶ VT: **to ~ sth (from sb)** nascondere qc (a qn) ▶ VI: **to ~ (from sb)** nascondersi (da qn)

hide-and-seek ['haɪdən'siːk] N rimpiattino

hideaway ['haɪdəweɪ] N nascondiglio

hideous ['hɪdɪəs] ADJ laido(-a); orribile

hide-out ['haɪdaut] N nascondiglio

hiding ['haɪdɪŋ] N (beating) bastonata; **to be in ~** (concealed) tenersi nascosto(-a)

hiding place N nascondiglio

hierarchy ['haɪərɑːkɪ] N gerarchia

hieroglyphic [haɪərə'glɪfɪk] ADJ geroglifico(-a) ▪ **hieroglyphics** NPL geroglifici mpl

hi-fi ['haɪ'faɪ] ADJ, N ABBR (= high fidelity) hi-fi (m) inv

higgledy-piggledy ['hɪgldɪ'pɪgldɪ] ADV alla rinfusa

high [haɪ] ADJ alto(-a); (speed, respect, number) grande; (wind) forte; (voice) acuto(-a); (BRIT: Culin: meat, game) frollato(-a); (: spoilt) andato(-a)

a male; (col: on drugs) fatto(-a); (: on drink) su di giri ▶ ADV alto, in alto ▶ N: **exports have reached a new ~** le esportazioni hanno toccato un nuovo record; **20m ~** alto(-a) 20m; **to pay a ~ price for sth** pagare (molto) caro qc

highball ['haɪbɔːl] N (US: drink) whisky (or brandy) e soda con ghiaccio

highboy ['haɪbɔɪ] N (US) cassettone m

highbrow ['haɪbrau] ADJ, N intellettuale (mf)

highchair ['haɪtʃɛər] N seggiolone m

high-class ['haɪ'klɑːs] ADJ (neighbourhood) elegante; (hotel) di prim'ordine; (person) di gran classe; (food) raffinato(-a)

High Court N alta corte f

> Nel sistema legale inglese e gallese, la **High Court** si occupa di casi più importanti e complessi di diritto civile. In Scozia, invece, la High Court è la corte che si occupa dei reati penali più gravi e corrisponde alla crown court inglese.

higher ['haɪər] ADJ (form of life, study etc) superiore ▶ ADV più in alto, più in su

higher education N istruzione f superiore or universitaria

highfalutin [haɪfə'luːtɪn] ADJ (col) pretenzioso(-a)

high finance N alta finanza

high-flier, high-flyer [haɪ'flaɪər] N (giovane) promessa (fig)

high-flying [haɪ'flaɪɪŋ] ADJ (fig) promettente

high-handed [haɪ'hændɪd] ADJ prepotente

high-heeled [haɪ'hiːld] ADJ a tacchi alti

high heels NPL (heels) tacchi mpl alti; (shoes) scarpe fpl con i tacchi alti

highjack ['haɪdʒæk] VT, N = **hijack**

high jump N (Sport) salto in alto

highlands ['haɪləndz] NPL zona montuosa; **the H~** le Highlands scozzesi

high-level ['haɪlɛvl] ADJ (talks etc, Comput) ad alto livello

highlight ['haɪlaɪt] N (fig: of event) momento culminante ▶ VT mettere in evidenza ▪ **highlights** NPL (in hair) colpi mpl di sole

highlighter ['haɪlaɪtər] N (pen) evidenziatore m

highly ['haɪlɪ] ADV molto; **~ paid** pagato molto bene; **to speak ~ of** parlare molto bene di

highly-strung ['haɪlɪ'strʌŋ] ADJ teso(-a) di nervi, eccitabile

High Mass N messa cantata or solenne

highness ['haɪnɪs] N altezza; **Her H~** Sua Altezza

high-pitched [haɪ'pɪtʃt] ADJ acuto(-a)

high point N: **the ~** il momento più importante

high-powered ['haɪ'pauəd] ADJ (engine) molto potente, ad alta potenza; (fig: person) di prestigio

597

high-pressure ['haɪpreʃə'] ADJ ad alta pressione; (fig) aggressivo(-a)

high-rise ['haɪraɪz] N (also: **high-rise block**, **high-rise building**) palazzone m

high school N (BRIT) scuola secondaria; (US) istituto d'istruzione secondaria

Negli Stati Uniti la **high school** è un istituto di istruzione secondaria dove si impartiscono sia insegnamenti scolastici che di formazione professionale. Si suddivide in *junior high school* (dal settimo al nono anno di corso) e *senior high school* (dal decimo al dodicesimo anno). Nel Regno Unito molte scuole secondarie si chiamano *high school*.

high season N (BRIT) alta stagione

high spirits NPL buonumore m, euforia; **to be in ~** essere euforico(-a)

high street N (BRIT) strada principale

high-tech ADJ (col) high-tech inv

highway ['haɪweɪ] N strada maestra; **the information ~** l'autostrada telematica

Highway Code N (BRIT) codice m della strada

highwayman ['haɪweɪmən] N (irreg) bandito

hijack ['haɪdʒæk] VT dirottare ▶ N dirottamento; (also: **hijacking**) pirateria aerea

hijacker ['haɪdʒækə'] N dirottatore(-trice)

hike [haɪk] VI fare un'escursione a piedi ▶ N escursione f a piedi; (col: in prices etc) aumento ▶ VT (col) aumentare

hiker ['haɪkə'] N escursionista mf

hiking ['haɪkɪŋ] N escursioni fpl a piedi

hilarious [hɪ'lɛərɪəs] ADJ che fa schiantare dal ridere; (behaviour, event) spassosissimo(-a)

hilarity [hɪ'lærɪtɪ] N ilarità

hill [hɪl] N collina, colle m; (fairly high) montagna; (on road) salita

hillbilly ['hɪlbɪlɪ] N (US) montanaro(-a) dal sud degli Stati Uniti; (pej) zotico(-a)

hillock ['hɪlək] N collinetta, poggio

hillside ['hɪlsaɪd] N fianco della collina

hill start N (Aut) partenza in salita

hill walking N escursioni fpl in collina

hilly ['hɪlɪ] ADJ collinoso(-a)

hilt [hɪlt] N (of sword) elsa; **to the ~** (fig: support) fino in fondo

him [hɪm] PRON (direct) lo, l' + vowel; (indirect) gli; (stressed, after prep) lui; **I see ~** lo vedo; **give ~ a book** gli dia un libro; **after ~** dopo (di) lui

Himalayas [hɪmə'leɪəz] NPL: **the ~** l'Himalaia m

himself [hɪm'self] PRON (reflexive) si; (emphatic) lui stesso, sé; (after prep) se stesso, sé; see also **oneself**

hind [haɪnd] ADJ posteriore ▶ N cerva

hinder ['hɪndə'] VT ostacolare; (delay) tardare; (prevent): **to ~ sb from doing** impedire a qn di fare

hindquarters ['haɪndkwɔ:təz] NPL (Zool) posteriore m

hindrance ['hɪndrəns] N ostacolo, impedimento

hindsight ['haɪndsaɪt] N senno di poi; **with (the benefit of) ~** con il senno di poi

Hindu ['hɪndu:] N indù mf inv

Hinduism N (Rel) induismo

hinge [hɪndʒ] N cardine m ▶ VI (fig): **to ~ on** dipendere da

hint [hɪnt] N (suggestion) allusione f; (advice) consiglio; (sign) accenno ▶ VT: **to ~ that** lasciar capire che ▶ VI: **to ~ at** accennare a, alludere a; **to drop a ~** lasciar capire; **give me a ~** (clue) dammi almeno un'idea, dammi un'indicazione

hip [hɪp] N anca, fianco; (Bot) frutto della rosa canina

hip flask N fiaschetta da liquore tascabile

hip hop N hip-hop m inv

hippie ['hɪpɪ] N hippy mf inv

hippo ['hɪpəu] (pl **hippos**) N ippopotamo

hip pocket N tasca posteriore dei calzoni

hippopotamus [hɪpə'pɔtəməs] (pl **hippopotamuses** or **hippopotami** [-'pɔtəmaɪ]) N ippopotamo

hippy ['hɪpɪ] N = **hippie**

hipster ['hɪpstə'] N (humorous: fashionable person) hipster mf inv

hire ['haɪə'] VT (BRIT: car, equipment) noleggiare; (worker) assumere, dare lavoro a ▶ N nolo, noleggio; **for ~** da nolo; (taxi) libero(-a); **on ~** a nolo
▶ **hire out** VT noleggiare, dare a nolo or noleggio, affittare

hire car, hired car N (BRIT) macchina a nolo

hire purchase N (BRIT) acquisto (or vendita) rateale; **to buy sth on ~** comprare qc a rate

his [hɪz] ADJ, PRON il (la) suo (sua), i (le) suoi (sue); **this is ~** questo è (il) suo; see also **my**; **mine¹**

Hispanic [hɪs'pænɪk] ADJ ispanico(-a)

hiss [hɪs] VI fischiare; (cat, snake) sibilare ▶ N fischio; sibilo

histogram ['hɪstəgræm] N istogramma m

historian [hɪ'stɔ:rɪən] N storico(-a)

historic [hɪ'stɔrɪk], **historical** [hɪ'stɔrɪkl] ADJ storico(-a)

history ['hɪstərɪ] N storia; **there's a long ~ of that illness in his family** ci sono molti precedenti (della malattia) nella sua famiglia

histrionics [hɪstrɪ'ɔnɪks] NPL istrionismo

hit [hɪt] (pt, pp **hit**) VT colpire, picchiare; (knock against) battere; (reach: target) raggiungere; (collide with: car) urtare contro; (fig: affect) colpire; (: find: problem) incontrare ▶ N colpo; (success, song) successo; **to ~ the headlines** far titolo; **to**

~ the road (col) mettersi in cammino; **to ~ it off with sb** andare molto d'accordo con qn; **to get a ~/10,000 hits** (Comput) trovare una pagina Web/10.000 pagine Web; **our web page had 10,000 hits last month** lo scorso mese il nostro sito ha avuto 10.000 visitatori

▶ **hit back** vi: **to ~ back at sb** restituire il colpo a qn

▶ **hit out at** vt fus sferrare dei colpi contro; (fig) attaccare

▶ **hit (up)on** vt fus (answer) imbroccare, azzeccare; (solution) trovare (per caso)

hit-and-run driver [ˈhɪtændˈrʌn-] n pirata m della strada

hitch [hɪtʃ] vt (fasten) attaccare; (also: **hitch up**) tirare su ▶ n (difficulty) intoppo, difficoltà f inv; **technical ~** difficoltà tecnica; **to ~ a lift** fare l'autostop

▶ **hitch up** vt (horse, cart) attaccare

hitch-hike [ˈhɪtʃhaɪk] vi fare l'autostop

hitch-hiker [ˈhɪtʃhaɪkəʳ] n autostoppista mf

hitch-hiking n autostop m

hi-tech [ˈhaɪˈtɛk] adj high-tech inv, a tecnologia avanzata

hitherto [ˈhɪðəˈtuː] adv finora

hit list n libro nero

hitman [ˈhɪtmæn] n (irreg) (col) sicario

hit-or-miss [ˈhɪtəˈmɪs] adj casuale; **it's ~ whether ...** è in dubbio se ...; **the service in this hotel is very ~** il servizio dell'albergo lascia a desiderare

hit parade n hit-parade f inv

HIV n abbr (= human immunodeficiency virus) virus m inv di immunodeficienza; **HIV-negative/-positive** adj sieronegativo(-a)/sieropositivo(-a)

hive [haɪv] n alveare m; **the shop was a ~ of activity** (fig) c'era una grande attività nel negozio

▶ **hive off** vt (col) separare

hl abbr (= hectolitre) hl

HM abbr (= His (or Her) Majesty) S.M. (= Sua Maestà)

HMG abbr (Brit) = **Her Majesty's Government; His Majesty's Government**

HMI n abbr (Brit Scol: = His (or Her) Majesty's Inspector) ≈ ispettore(-trice) scolastico(-a)

HMO n abbr (US: = Health Maintenance Organization) organo per la salvaguardia della salute pubblica

HMS abbr (Brit) = **His Majesty's Ship; Her Majesty's Ship**

HNC n abbr (Brit: = Higher National Certificate) diploma di istituto tecnico o professionale

HND n abbr (Brit: = Higher National Diploma) diploma in materie tecniche equivalente a una laurea

hoard [hɔːd] n (of food) provviste fpl; (of money) gruzzolo ▶ vt ammassare

hoarding [ˈhɔːdɪŋ] n (Brit) tabellone m per affissioni

hoarfrost [ˈhɔːfrɔst] n brina

hoarse [hɔːs] adj rauco(-a)

hoax [həʊks] n scherzo; falso allarme

hob [hɔb] n piastra (con fornelli)

hobble [ˈhɔbl] vi zoppicare

hobby [ˈhɔbɪ] n hobby m inv, passatempo

hobby-horse [ˈhɔbɪhɔːs] n cavallo a dondolo; (fig) chiodo fisso

hobnail boots [ˈhɔbneɪl-], **hobnailed boots** [ˈhɔbneɪld-] n scarponi mpl chiodati

hobnob [ˈhɔbnɔb] vi: **to ~ (with)** mescolarsi (con)

hobo [ˈhəʊbəʊ] n (US) vagabondo

hock [hɔk] n (Brit: wine) vino del Reno; (of animal, Culin) garretto; (col): **to be in ~** avere debiti

hockey [ˈhɔkɪ] n hockey m

hockey stick n bastone m da hockey

hocus-pocus [ˈhəʊkəsˈpəʊkəs] n (trickery) trucco; (words: of magician) abracadabra m inv; (: jargon) parolone fpl

hod [hɔd] n (Tech) cassetta per portare i mattoni

hodgepodge [ˈhɔdʒpɔdʒ] n (esp US) = **hotchpotch**

hoe [həʊ] n zappa ▶ vt (ground) zappare

hog [hɔg] n maiale m ▶ vt (fig) arraffare; **to go the whole ~** farlo fino in fondo

Hogmanay [hɔgməˈneɪ] n (Scottish) ≈ San Silvestro

In Scozia la notte di San Silvestro, la vigilia di Capodanno, si chiama **Hogmanay**. I festeggiamenti più famosi e spettacolari si tengono a Edimburgo, con fiaccolate e fuochi d'artificio. Si si riunisce per attendere la mezzanotte e si osserva ancora la tradizione del *first-footing*: la prima persona a entrare in casa nell'anno nuovo porta in regalo qualcosa da bere, di solito whisky, carbone o biscotti come augurio di prosperità.

---

hogwash [ˈhɔgwɔʃ] n (col) stupidaggini fpl

hoist [hɔɪst] n paranco ▶ vt issare

hoity-toity [hɔɪtɪˈtɔɪtɪ] adj (col) altezzoso(-a)

hold [həʊld] (pt, pp **held** [hɛld]) vt tenere; (contain) contenere; (keep back) trattenere; (believe) mantenere; considerare; (possess) avere, possedere; detenere ▶ vi (withstand pressure) tenere; (be valid) essere valido(-a) ▶ n presa; (fig) potere m; (control): **to have a ~ over** avere controllo su; (Naut) stiva; **~ the line!** (Tel) resti in linea!; **to ~ office** (Pol) essere in carica; **to ~ sb responsible for sth** considerare or ritenere qn responsabile di qc; **to ~ one's own** (fig) difendersi bene; **he holds the view that ...** è del parere che ...; **to ~ firm** or **fast** resistere bene, tenere; **to catch** or **get (a) ~ of** afferrare; **to get ~ of** (fig) trovare; **to get ~ of o.s.** trattenersi

▶ **hold back** VT trattenere; (*secret*) tenere celato(-a); **to ~ sb back from doing sth** impedire a qn di fare qc

▶ **hold down** VT (*person*) tenere a terra; (*job*) tenere

▶ **hold forth** VI fare *or* tenere una concione

▶ **hold off** VT tener lontano ▶ VI (*rain*): **if the rain holds off** se continua a non piovere

▶ **hold on** VI tener fermo; (*wait*) aspettare; **~ on!** (*Tel*) resti in linea!

▶ **hold on to** VT FUS tenersi stretto(-a) a; (*keep*) conservare

▶ **hold out** VT offrire ▶ VI (*resist*): **to ~ out (against)** resistere (a)

▶ **hold over** VT (*meeting etc*) rimandare, rinviare

▶ **hold up** VT (*raise*) alzare; (*support*) sostenere; (*delay*) ritardare; (*traffic*) rallentare; (*rob: bank*) assaltare

holdall [ˈhəʊldɔːl] N (*BRIT*) borsone *m*

holder [ˈhəʊldər] N (*container*) contenitore *m*; (*of ticket, title*) possessore (posseditrice); (*of office etc*) incaricato(-a); (*of passport, post*) titolare; (*of record*) detentore(-trice)

holding [ˈhəʊldɪŋ] N (*share*) azioni *fpl*, titoli *mpl*; (*farm*) podere *m*, tenuta

holding company N holding *f inv*

holdup [ˈhəʊldʌp] N (*robbery*) rapina a mano armata; (*delay*) ritardo; (*BRIT: in traffic*) blocco

hole [həʊl] N buco, buca ▶ VT bucare; **~ in the heart** (*Med*) morbo blu; **to pick holes in** (*fig*) trovare da ridire su

▶ **hole up** VI nascondersi, rifugiarsi

holiday [ˈhɔlədɪ] N vacanza; (*from work*) ferie *fpl*; (*day off*) giorno di vacanza; (*public*) giorno festivo; **to be on ~** essere in vacanza; **tomorrow is a ~** domani è festa

holiday camp N (*BRIT: for children*) colonia (di villeggiatura); (: *also:* **holiday centre**) ≈ villaggio (di vacanze)

holiday home N seconda casa (*per le vacanze*)

holiday job N (*BRIT*) ≈ lavoro estivo

holiday-maker [ˈhɔlədeɪkər] N (*BRIT*) villeggiante *mf*

holiday pay N stipendio delle ferie

holiday resort N luogo di villeggiatura

holiday season N stagione *f* delle vacanze

holiness [ˈhəʊlɪnɪs] N santità

holistic [həʊˈlɪstɪk] ADJ olistico(-a)

Holland [ˈhɔlənd] N Olanda

holler [ˈhɔlər] VI (*col*) gridare, urlare

hollow [ˈhɔləʊ] ADJ cavo(-a); (*container, claim*) vuoto(-a); (*laugh*) forzato(-a), falso(-a); (*sound*) cavernoso(-a) ▶ N cavità *f inv*; (*in land*) valletta, depressione *f*

▶ **hollow out** VT scavare

holly [ˈhɔlɪ] N agrifoglio

hollyhock [ˈhɔlɪhɔk] N malvone *m*

Hollywood [ˈhɔlɪwʊd] N Hollywood *f*

holocaust [ˈhɔləkɔːst] N olocausto

hologram [ˈhɔləgræm] N ologramma *m*

hols [hɔlz] NPL: **the ~** le vacanze

holster [ˈhəʊlstər] N fondina (di pistola)

holy [ˈhəʊlɪ] ADJ santo(-a); (*bread*) benedetto(-a), consacrato(-a); (*ground*) consacrato(-a); **the H~ Father** il Santo Padre

Holy Communion N la Santa Comunione

Holy Ghost, Holy Spirit N Spirito Santo

Holy Land N: **the ~** la Terra Santa

holy orders NPL ordini *mpl* (sacri)

homage [ˈhɔmɪdʒ] N omaggio; **to pay ~ to** rendere omaggio a

home [həʊm] N casa; (*country*) patria; (*institution*) casa, ricovero ▶ CPD (*life*) familiare; (*cooking etc*) casalingo(-a); (*Econ, Pol*) nazionale, interno(-a); (*Sport: team*) di casa; (: *match, win*) in casa ▶ ADV a casa; in patria; (*right in: nail etc*) fino in fondo; **at ~ a** casa; (*in situation*) a proprio agio; **to go (or come) ~** tornare a casa (*or* in patria); **it's near my ~** è vicino a casa mia; **make yourself at ~** si metta a suo agio

▶ **home in on** VT FUS (*missiles*) dirigersi (automaticamente) verso

home address N indirizzo di casa

home-brew [həʊmˈbruː] N birra *or* vino fatto(-a) in casa

homecoming [ˈhəʊmkʌmɪŋ] N ritorno

home computer N home computer *m inv*

Home Counties NPL contee *fpl* intorno a Londra

home economics N economia domestica

home ground N (*fig*): **to be on ~** essere sul proprio terreno

home-grown [həʊmˈgrəʊn] ADJ nostrano(-a), di produzione locale

home help N (*BRIT*) *collaboratore familiare per persone bisognose stipendiato dal comune*

homeland [ˈhəʊmlænd] N patria

homeless [ˈhəʊmlɪs] ADJ senza tetto; spatriato(-a) ▪ **the homeless** NPL i senzatetto

home loan N prestito con garanzia immobiliare

homely [ˈhəʊmlɪ] ADJ semplice, alla buona; accogliente

home-made [həʊmˈmeɪd] ADJ casalingo(-a)

home match N partita in casa

Home Office N (*BRIT*) ministero degli Interni

homeopathy *etc* [həʊmɪˈɔpəθɪ] (*US*) = **homoeopathy** *etc*

home owner N proprietario(-a) di casa

home page N (*Comput*) home page *f inv*

home rule N autogoverno

Home Secretary N (*BRIT*) ministro degli Interni

homesick [ˈhəʊmsɪk] ADJ: **to be ~** avere la nostalgia

homestead [ˈhəumstɛd] N fattoria e terreni

home town N città f inv natale

home truth N: **to tell sb a few ~s** dire a qn qualche amara verità

homeward [ˈhəumwəd] ADJ (journey) di ritorno ▶ ADV verso casa

homewards [ˈhəumwədz] ADV verso casa

homework [ˈhəumwəːk] N compiti mpl (per casa)

homicidal [hɔmɪˈsaɪdl] ADJ omicida

homicide [ˈhɔmɪsaɪd] N (US) omicidio

homily [ˈhɔmɪlɪ] N omelia

homing [ˈhəumɪŋ] ADJ (device, missile) autocercante; **~ pigeon** piccione m viaggiatore

homoeopath, (US) **homeopath** [ˈhəumɪəupæθ] N omeopatico(-a)

homoeopathic, (US) **homeopathic** [ˈhəumɪəuˈpæθɪk] ADJ omeopatico(-a)

homoeopathy, (US) **homeopathy** [həumɪˈɔpəθɪ] N omeopatia

homogeneous [hɔməuˈdʒiːnɪəs] ADJ omogeneo(-a)

homogenize [həˈmɔdʒənaɪz] VT omogenizzare

homosexual [hɔməuˈsɛksjuəl] ADJ, N omosessuale (mf)

Hon. ABBR = **honourable; honorary**

Honduras [hɔnˈdjuərəs] N Honduras m

hone [həun] VT (sharpen) affilare; (fig) affinare

honest [ˈɔnɪst] ADJ onesto(-a); sincero(-a); **to be quite ~ with you ...** se devo dirle la verità ...

honestly [ˈɔnɪstlɪ] ADV onestamente; sinceramente

honesty [ˈɔnɪstɪ] N onestà

honey [ˈhʌnɪ] N miele m; (US col) tesoro, amore m

honeycomb [ˈhʌnɪkəum] N favo ▶ VT (fig): **honeycombed with tunnels** etc pieno(-a) di gallerie etc

honeymoon [ˈhʌnɪmuːn] N luna di miele, viaggio di nozze

honeysuckle [ˈhʌnɪsʌkl] N (Bot) caprifoglio

Hong Kong [ˈhɔŋˈkɔŋ] N Hong Kong f

honk [hɔŋk] N (Aut) colpo di clacson ▶ VI suonare il clacson

Honolulu [hɔnəˈluːluː] N Honolulu f

honorary [ˈɔnərərɪ] ADJ onorario(-a); (duty, title) onorifico(-a)

honour, (US) **honor** [ˈɔnəʳ] VT onorare ▶ N onore m; **in ~ of** in onore di

honourable, (US) **honorable** [ˈɔnərəbl] ADJ onorevole

honour-bound, (US) **honor-bound** [ˈɔnəˈbaund] ADJ: **to be ~ to do** dover fare per una questione di onore

honours degree N (Scol) laurea (con corso di studi di 4 o 5 anni)

In Gran Bretagna esistono titoli universitari di diverso livello. Gli studenti che conseguono ottimi risultati e che approfondiscono una o più materie possono ottenere l'**honours degree**. Questo titolo, abbreviato in Hons., può essere aggiunto al nome e titolo ottenuto, per esempio: Peter Jones BA Hons.; vedi anche **ordinary degree**.

honours list N (BRIT) elenco ufficiale dei destinati al conferimento di onorificenze

La **honours list** è un elenco di cittadini britannici e del Commonwealth che si sono distinti in campo imprenditoriale, militare, sportivo ecc, meritando il conferimento di un titolo o di una decorazione da parte del sovrano. Ogni anno vengono redatte dal primo ministro due honours lists, una a Capodanno e una in occasione del compleanno del sovrano.

Hons. [ɔnz] ABBR (Scol) = **honours degree**

hood [hud] N cappuccio; (on cooker) cappa; (BRIT Aut) capote f; (US Aut) cofano; (col) malvivente mf

hooded [ˈhudɪd] ADJ (robber) mascherato(-a)

hoodie [ˈhudɪ] N felpa con cappuccio

hoodlum [ˈhuːdləm] N malvivente mf

hoodwink [ˈhudwɪŋk] VT infinocchiare

hoof [huːf] (pl **hoofs** or **hooves** [huːvz]) N zoccolo

hook [huk] N gancio; (for fishing) amo ▶ VT uncinare; (dress) agganciare; **to be hooked on** (col) essere fanatico di; **hooks and eyes** gancetti; **by ~ or by crook** in un modo o nell'altro ▶ **hook up** VT (Radio, TV etc) allacciare, collegare

hooligan [ˈhuːlɪgən] N giovinastro, teppista m

hooliganism [ˈhuːlɪgənɪzəm] N teppismo

hoop [huːp] N cerchio

hooray [huːˈreɪ] EXCL = **hurrah**

hoot [huːt] VI (Aut) suonare il clacson; (siren) ululare; (owl) gufare ▶ N colpo di clacson; **to ~ with laughter** farsi una gran risata

hooter [ˈhuːtəʳ] N (Aut) clacson m inv; (Naut, at factory) sirena

hoover® [ˈhuːvəʳ] N (BRIT) aspirapolvere m inv ▶ VT pulire con l'aspirapolvere

hooves [huːvz] NPL of **hoof**

hop [hɔp] VI saltellare, saltare; (on one foot) saltare su una gamba ▶ N salto; see also **hops**

hope [həup] VT: **to ~ that/to do** sperare che/di fare ▶ VI sperare ▶ N speranza; **I ~ so/not** spero di sì/no

hopeful [ˈhəupful] ADJ (person) pieno(-a) di speranza; (situation) promettente; **I'm ~ that she'll manage to come** ho buone speranze che venga

hopefully [ˈhəupfulɪ] ADV con speranza; **~ he will recover** speriamo che si riprenda

hopeless [ˈhəʊplɪs] ADJ senza speranza, disperato(-a); (useless) inutile

hopelessly [ˈhəʊplɪslɪ] ADV (live etc) senza speranza; (involved, complicated) spaventosamente; (late) disperatamente, irrimediabilmente; **I'm ~ confused/lost** sono completamente confuso/perso

hopper [ˈhɒpəʳ] N (chute) tramoggia

hops [hɒps] NPL luppoli mpl

horde [hɔːd] N orda

horizon [həˈraɪzn] N orizzonte m

horizontal [hɒrɪˈzɒntl] ADJ orizzontale

hormone [ˈhɔːməʊn] N ormone m

hormone replacement therapy N terapia ormonale (usata in menopausa)

horn [hɔːn] N (Zool, Mus) corno; (Aut) clacson m inv

horned [hɔːnd] ADJ (animal) cornuto(-a)

hornet [ˈhɔːnɪt] N calabrone m

horny [ˈhɔːnɪ] ADJ corneo(-a); (hands) calloso(-a)

horoscope [ˈhɒrəskəʊp] N oroscopo

horrendous [hɒˈrendəs] ADJ orrendo(-a)

horrible [ˈhɒrɪbl] ADJ orribile, tremendo(-a)

horrid [ˈhɒrɪd] ADJ orrido(-a); (person) odioso(-a)

horrific [hɒˈrɪfɪk] ADJ (accident) spaventoso(-a); (film) orripilante

horrify [ˈhɒrɪfaɪ] VT lasciare inorridito(-a)

horrifying [ˈhɒrɪfaɪɪŋ] ADJ terrificante

horror [ˈhɒrəʳ] N orrore m

horror film N film m inv dell'orrore

horror-struck [ˈhɒrəstrʌk], **horror-stricken** [ˈhɒrəstrɪkn] ADJ inorridito(-a)

hors d'œuvre [ɔːˈdəːvrə] N antipasto

horse [hɔːs] N cavallo

horseback [ˈhɔːsbæk]: **on ~** adj, adv a cavallo

horsebox [ˈhɔːsbɒks] N carro or furgone m per il trasporto dei cavalli

horse chestnut N ippocastano

horse-drawn [ˈhɔːsdrɔːn] ADJ tirato(-a) da cavallo

horsefly [ˈhɔːsflaɪ] N tafano, mosca cavallina

horseman [ˈhɔːsmən] N (irreg) cavaliere m

horsemanship [ˈhɔːsmənʃɪp] N equitazione f

horseplay [ˈhɔːspleɪ] N giochi mpl scatenati

horsepower [ˈhɔːspaʊəʳ] N cavallo (vapore), c/v

horse-racing [ˈhɔːsreɪsɪŋ] N ippica

horseradish [ˈhɔːsrædɪʃ] N rafano

horse riding N (BRIT) equitazione f

horseshoe [ˈhɔːsʃuː] N ferro di cavallo

horse show N concorso ippico, gare fpl ippiche

horse-trading [ˈhɔːstreɪdɪŋ] N mercanteggiamento

horse trials NPL = **horse show**

horsewhip [ˈhɔːswɪp] VT frustare

horsewoman [ˈhɔːswʊmən] N (irreg) amazzone f

horsey [ˈhɔːsɪ] ADJ (col: person) che adora i cavalli; (appearance) cavallino(-a), da cavallo

horticulture [ˈhɔːtɪkʌltʃəʳ] N orticoltura

hose [həʊz] N (also: **hosepipe**) tubo; (also: **garden hose**) tubo per annaffiare
  ▶ **hose down** VT lavare con un getto d'acqua

hosepipe [ˈhəʊzpaɪp] N see **hose**

hosiery [ˈhəʊzɪərɪ] N (in shop) (reparto di) calze fpl e calzini mpl

hospice [ˈhɒspɪs] N ricovero, ospizio

hospitable [hɒˈspɪtəbl] ADJ ospitale

hospital [ˈhɒspɪtl] N ospedale m; **in ~**, (US) **in the ~** all'ospedale

hospitality [hɒspɪˈtælɪtɪ] N ospitalità

hospitalize [ˈhɒspɪtəlaɪz] VT ricoverare (in or all'ospedale)

host [həʊst] N ospite m; (TV, Radio) presentatore(-trice); (Rel) ostia; (large number): **a ~ of** una schiera di ▶ VT (TV programme, games) presentare

hostage [ˈhɒstɪdʒ] N ostaggio(-a)

host country N paese m ospite, paese che ospita

hostel [ˈhɒstl] N ostello; (for students, nurses etc) pensionato; (for homeless people) ospizio, ricovero; (also: **youth hostel**) ostello della gioventù

hostelling [ˈhɒstəlɪŋ] N: **to go (youth) ~** passare le vacanze negli ostelli della gioventù

hostess [ˈhəʊstɪs] N ospite f; (BRIT Aviat) hostess f inv; (in nightclub) entraîneuse f inv

hostile [ˈhɒstaɪl] ADJ ostile

hostility [hɒˈstɪlɪtɪ] N ostilità f inv

hot [hɒt] ADJ caldo(-a); (as opposed to only warm) molto caldo(-a); (spicy) piccante; (fig) accanito(-a); ardente; violento(-a), focoso(-a); **to be ~** (person) aver caldo; (thing) essere caldo(-a); (Meteor) far caldo
  ▶ **hot up** (BRIT col) VI (situation) farsi più teso(-a); (party) scaldarsi ▶ VT (pace) affrettare; (engine) truccare

hot-air balloon [hɒtˈɛə-] N mongolfiera

hotbed [ˈhɒtbed] N (fig) focolaio

hotchpotch [ˈhɒtʃpɒtʃ] N (BRIT) pot-pourri m

hot dog N hot dog m inv

hotel [həʊˈtɛl] N albergo

hotelier [həʊˈtɛljeɪ] N albergatore(-trice)

hotel industry N industria alberghiera

hotel room N camera d'albergo

hot flush N (BRIT) scalmana, caldana

hotfoot [ˈhɒtfut] ADV di gran carriera

hothead [ˈhɒthed] N (fig) testa calda

hotheaded [hɒtˈhedɪd] ADJ focoso(-a), eccitabile

hothouse [ˈhɒthaus] N serra

hot line N (Pol) telefono rosso

hotly ['hɔtlɪ] ADV violentemente

hotplate ['hɔtpleɪt] N fornello; piastra riscaldante

hotpot ['hɔtpɔt] N (BRIT Culin) stufato

hot potato N (BRIT col) patata bollente; **to drop sb/sth like a ~** mollare subito qn/qc

hot seat N (fig) posto che scotta

hotspot ['hɔtspɔt] N (Comput: also: **wireless hotspot**) hotspot m inv Wi-Fi

hot spot N (fig) zona calda

hot spring N sorgente f termale

hot-tempered [hɔt'tempəd] ADJ irascibile

hot-water bottle [hɔt'wɔ:tə-] N borsa dell'acqua calda

hot-wire ['hɔtwaɪəʳ] VT (col: car) avviare mettendo in contatto i fili dell'accensione

hound [haund] VT perseguitare ▶ N segugio; **the hounds** la muta

hour ['auəʳ] N ora; **at 30 miles an ~** a 30 miglia all'ora; **lunch ~** intervallo di pranzo; **to pay sb by the ~** pagare qn a ore

hourly ['auəlɪ] ADJ (ad) ogni ora; (rate) orario(-a) ▶ ADV ogni ora; **~ paid** adj pagato(-a) a ore

house N [haus] (pl **houses** ['hauzɪz]) casa; (Pol) camera; (Theat) sala; pubblico; spettacolo ▶ VT [hauz] (person) ospitare, alloggiare; **at (or to) my ~** a casa mia; **the H~ (of Commons/Lords)** (BRIT) la Camera dei Comuni/Lords; **the H~ (of Representatives)** (US) ≈ la Camera dei Deputati; **on the ~** (fig) offerto(-a) dalla casa

Il Parlamento del Regno Unito è costituito dalla **House of Commons**, presieduta dallo *Speaker* e composta da circa 650 deputati (MPs), eletti a suffragio universale diretto e che ricevono uno stipendio. La *House of Commons* si riunisce per circa 175 giorni all'anno. La **House of Lords**, presieduta dal *Lord Chancellor*, è formata dai *lords* il cui titolo è ereditato o conferito a vita dal sovrano. Recenti riforme hanno ridotto le cariche ereditarie che in futuro saranno abolite. Ha poteri più limitati, ma può proporre ed emendare i disegni di legge che provengono dalla *House of Commons*, ad esclusione delle leggi finanziarie.

Negli Stati Uniti, il parlamento, il *Congress*, è costituito dal *Senate* e dalla **House of Representatives**. Quest'ultima comprende 435 membri, il cui numero è in proporzione agli abitanti di ciascuno stato. È eletta ogni due anni a suffragio universale diretto e si riunisce nell'edificio detto *the Capitol*, a Washington

house arrest N arresti mpl domiciliari

houseboat ['hausbəut] N house boat f inv

housebound ['hausbaund] ADJ confinato(-a) in casa

housebreaking ['hausbreɪkɪŋ] N furto con scasso

house-broken ['hausbrəukn] ADJ (US) = **house-trained**

housecoat ['hauskəut] N vestaglia

household ['haushəuld] N famiglia; casa

householder ['haushəuldəʳ] N padrone(-a) di casa; (head of house) capofamiglia mf

household name N nome m che tutti conoscono

househunting ['haushʌntɪŋ] N: **to go ~** mettersi a cercar casa

housekeeper ['hauski:pəʳ] N governante f

housekeeping ['hauski:pɪŋ] N (work) governo della casa; (also: **housekeeping money**) soldi mpl per le spese di casa; (Comput) ausilio

house-owner ['hausəunəʳ] N possessore mf di casa

house plant N pianta da appartamento

house-proud ['hauspraud] ADJ maniaco(-a) della pulizia

house-to-house ['haustə'haus] ADJ (collection) di porta in porta; (search) casa per casa

house-train ['haustreɪn] VT (BRIT: animal) addestrare a non sporcare in casa

house-trained ['haustreɪnd] ADJ (BRIT: animal) che non sporca in casa

house-warming party ['hauswɔ:mɪŋ-] N festa per inaugurare la casa nuova

housewife ['hauswaɪf] N (irreg) massaia, casalinga

house wine N vino della casa

housework ['hauswə:k] N faccende fpl domestiche

housing ['hauzɪŋ] N alloggio ▶ CPD (problem, shortage) degli alloggi

housing association N cooperativa edilizia

housing benefit N (BRIT) contributo abitativo (ad affittuari)

housing conditions NPL condizioni fpl di abitazione

housing development, (BRIT) **housing estate** N zona residenziale con case popolari e/o private

hovel ['hɔvl] N casupola

hover ['hɔvəʳ] VI (bird) librarsi; (helicopter) volare a punto fisso; **to ~ round sb** aggirarsi intorno a qn

hovercraft ['hɔvəkrɑ:ft] N hovercraft m inv

hoverport ['hɔvəpɔ:t] N porto per hovercraft

how [hau] ADV come; **~ are you?** come sta?; **~ do you do?** piacere!, molto lieto!; **~ far is it to ...?** quanto è lontano ...?; **~ long have you been here?** da quanto tempo è qui?; **~ lovely!** che bello!; **~ many?** quanti(-e)?; **~ much?** quanto(-a)?; **~ many people/much milk?** quante persone/quanto latte?; **~ old are you?**

h

quanti anni ha?; **~'s life?** (*col*) come va (la vita)?; **~ about a drink?** che ne diresti di andare a bere qualcosa?; **~ is it that …?** com'è che …? + *sub*

however [hau'ɛvə^r] ADV in qualsiasi modo *or* maniera che; (+ *adjective*) per quanto + sub; (*in questions*) come ▸ CONJ comunque, però

howitzer ['hauɪtsə^r] N (*Mil*) obice *m*

howl [haul] N ululato ▸ VI ululare; (*baby, person*) urlare

howler ['haulə^r] N marronata

howling ['haulɪŋ] ADJ: **a ~ wind** *or* **gale** un vento terribile

HP N ABBR (*BRIT*) = **hire purchase**

hp ABBR (*Aut*) = **horsepower**

HQ N ABBR (= *headquarters*) Q.G.

HR N ABBR (*US*) = **House of Representatives**; (*human resources: department*) ufficio personale; (*: staff*) risorse umane

hr ABBR (= *hour*) h

HRH ABBR (= *His (or Her) Royal Highness*) S.A.R.

hrs ABBR (= *hours*) h

HRT N ABBR = **hormone replacement therapy**

HS ABBR (*US*) = **high school**

HST ABBR (= *Hawaiian Standard Time*) fuso orario

HT ABBR (= *high tension*) A.T.

HTML N ABBR (*Comput*: = *hypertext markup language*) HTML *m inv*

hub [hʌb] N (*of wheel*) mozzo; (*fig*) fulcro

hubbub ['hʌbʌb] N baccano

hubcap ['hʌbkæp] N (*Aut*) coprimozzo

HUD N ABBR (*US*) = **Department of Housing and Urban Development**

huddle ['hʌdl] VI: **to ~ together** rannicchiarsi l'uno contro l'altro

hue [hju:] N tinta; **~ and cry** *n* clamore *m*

huff [hʌf] N: **in a ~** stizzito(-a); **to take the ~** mettere il broncio

huffy ['hʌfɪ] ADJ (*col*) stizzito(-a), indispettito(-a)

hug [hʌg] VT abbracciare; (*shore, kerb*) stringere ▸ N abbraccio, stretta; **to give sb a ~** abbracciare qn

huge [hju:dʒ] ADJ enorme, immenso(-a)

hulk [hʌlk] N carcassa

hulking ['hʌlkɪŋ] ADJ: **~ (great)** grosso(-a) e goffo(-a)

hull [hʌl] N (*of ship*) scafo

hullabaloo [hʌləbə'lu:] N (*col: noise*) fracasso

hullo [hə'ləu] EXCL = **hello**

hum [hʌm] VT (*tune*) canticchiare ▸ VI canticchiare; (*insect, plane, tool*) ronzare ▸ N (*also Elec*) ronzio; (*of traffic, machines*) rumore *m*; (*of voices etc*) mormorio, brusio

human ['hju:mən] ADJ umano(-a) ▸ N (*also:* **human being**) essere *m* umano

humane [hju:'meɪn] ADJ umanitario(-a)

humanism ['hju:mənɪzəm] N umanesimo

humanitarian [hju:mænɪ'tɛərɪən] ADJ umanitario(-a)

humanity [hju:'mænɪtɪ] N umanità; **the humanities** gli studi umanistici

humanly ['hju:mənlɪ] ADV umanamente

humanoid ['hju:mənɔɪd] ADJ che sembra umano(-a) ▸ N umanoide *mf*

human rights NPL diritti *mpl* dell'uomo

humble ['hʌmbl] ADJ umile, modesto(-a) ▸ VT umiliare

humbly ['hʌmblɪ] ADV umilmente, modestamente

humbug ['hʌmbʌg] N inganno; sciocchezze *fpl*; (*BRIT: sweet*) caramella alla menta

humdrum ['hʌmdrʌm] ADJ monotono(-a), tedioso(-a)

humid ['hju:mɪd] ADJ umido(-a)

humidifier [hju:'mɪdɪfaɪə^r] N umidificatore *m*

humidity [hju:'mɪdɪtɪ] N umidità

humiliate [hju:'mɪlɪeɪt] VT umiliare

humiliating ADJ umiliante

humiliation [hju:mɪlɪ'eɪʃən] N umiliazione *f*

humility [hju:'mɪlɪtɪ] N umiltà

hummus ['huməs] N purè di ceci

humorist ['hju:mərɪst] N umorista *mf*

humorous ['hju:mərəs] ADJ umoristico(-a); (*person*) buffo(-a)

humour, (*US*) **humor** ['hju:mə^r] N umore *m* ▸ VT (*person*) assecondare; **sense of ~** senso dell'umorismo; **to be in a good/bad ~** essere di buon/cattivo umore

humourless, (*US*) **humorless** ['hju:məlɪs] ADJ privo(-a) di umorismo

hump [hʌmp] N gobba

humpback ['hʌmpbæk] N schiena d'asino; (*BRIT: also:* **humpback bridge**) ponte *m* a schiena d'asino

humus ['hju:məs] N humus *m*

hunch [hʌntʃ] N gobba; (*premonition*) intuizione *f*; **I have a ~ that** ho la vaga impressione che

hunchback ['hʌntʃbæk] N gobbo(-a)

hunched [hʌntʃt] ADJ incurvato(-a)

hundred ['hʌndrəd] NUM cento; **about a ~ people** un centinaio di persone; **hundreds of people** centinaia *fpl* di persone; **I'm a ~ per cent sure** sono sicuro al cento per cento

hundredth [-ɪdθ] NUM centesimo(-a)

hundredweight ['hʌndrɪdweɪt] N (*BRIT*) = 50.8 *kg*; = 112 *lb*; (*US*) = 45.3 *kg*; = 100 *lb*

hung [hʌŋ] PT, PP *of* **hang**

Hungarian [hʌŋ'gɛərɪən] ADJ ungherese ▸ N ungherese *mf*; (*Ling*) ungherese *m*

Hungary ['hʌŋgərɪ] N Ungheria

hunger ['hʌŋgə^r] N fame f ▶ VI: **to ~ for** desiderare ardentemente

hunger strike N sciopero della fame

hungover [hʌŋ'əuvə^r] ADJ (col): **to be ~** avere i postumi della sbornia

hungrily ['hʌŋgrəlɪ] ADV voracemente; (fig) avidamente

hungry ['hʌŋgrɪ] ADJ affamato(-a); **to be ~** aver fame; **~ for** (fig) assetato di

hung up ADJ (col) complessato(-a)

hunk [hʌŋk] N bel pezzo

hunt [hʌnt] VT (seek) cercare; (Sport) cacciare ▶ VI: **to ~ (for)** andare a caccia (di) ▶ N caccia
▶ **hunt down** VT scovare

hunter ['hʌntə^r] N cacciatore(-trice); (BRIT: horse) cavallo da caccia

hunting ['hʌntɪŋ] N caccia

hurdle ['hə:dl] N (Sport, fig) ostacolo

hurl [hə:l] VT lanciare con violenza

hurling ['hə:lɪŋ] N (Sport) hurling m

hurly-burly ['hə:lɪ'bə:lɪ] N chiasso, baccano

hurrah [hu'rɑ:], **hurray** [hu'reɪ] EXCL urrà!, evviva!

hurricane ['hʌrɪkən] N uragano

hurried ['hʌrɪd] ADJ affrettato(-a); (work) fatto(-a) in fretta

hurriedly ['hʌrɪdlɪ] ADV in fretta

hurry ['hʌrɪ] N fretta ▶ VI (also: **hurry up**) affrettarsi ▶ VT (also: **hurry up**: person) affrettare; (: work) far in fretta; **to be in a ~** aver fretta; **to do sth in a ~** fare qc in fretta; **to ~ in/out** entrare/uscire in fretta; **to ~ back/home** affrettarsi a tornare indietro/a casa
▶ **hurry along** VI camminare in fretta
▶ **hurry away, hurry off** VI andarsene in fretta
▶ **hurry up** VI sbrigarsi

hurt [hə:t] (pt, pp **~**) VT (cause pain to) far male a; (injure, fig) ferire; (business, interests etc) colpire, danneggiare ▶ VI far male ▶ ADJ ferito(-a); **I ~ my arm** mi sono fatto male al braccio; **where does it ~?** dove ti fa male?

hurtful ['hə:tful] ADJ (remark) che ferisce

hurtle ['hə:tl] VT scagliare ▶ VI: **to ~ past/down** passare/scendere a razzo

husband ['hʌzbənd] N marito

hush [hʌʃ] N silenzio, calma ▶ VT zittire; **~!** zitto(-a)!
▶ **hush up** VT (fact) cercare di far passare sotto silenzio

hush-hush ['hʌʃ'hʌʃ] ADJ (col) segretissimo(-a)

husk [hʌsk] N (of wheat) cartoccio; (of rice, maize) buccia

husky ['hʌskɪ] ADJ roco(-a) ▶ N cane m eschimese

hustings ['hʌstɪŋz] NPL (BRIT Pol) comizi mpl elettorali

hustle ['hʌsl] VT spingere, incalzare ▶ N pigia pigia m inv; **~ and bustle** trambusto

hut [hʌt] N rifugio; (shed) ripostiglio

hutch [hʌtʃ] N gabbia

hyacinth ['haɪəsɪnθ] N giacinto

hybrid ['haɪbrɪd] ADJ ibrido(-a) ▶ N ibrido

hydrangea [haɪ'dreɪndʒə] N ortensia

hydrant ['haɪdrənt] N (also: **fire hydrant**) idrante m

hydraulic [haɪ'drɔlɪk] ADJ idraulico(-a)

hydraulics [haɪ'drɔlɪks] N idraulica

hydrochloric [haɪdrə'klɔrɪk] ADJ: **~ acid** acido cloridrico

hydroelectric [haɪdrəuɪ'lɛktrɪk] ADJ idroelettrico(-a)

hydrofoil ['haɪdrəfɔɪl] N aliscafo

hydrogen ['haɪdrədʒən] N idrogeno

hydrogen bomb N bomba all'idrogeno

hydrophobia [haɪdrə'fəubɪə] N idrofobia

hydroplane ['haɪdrəupleɪn] N idrovolante m

hyena [haɪ'i:nə] N iena

hygiene ['haɪdʒi:n] N igiene f

hygienic [haɪ'dʒi:nɪk] ADJ igienico(-a)

hymn [hɪm] N inno; cantica

hype [haɪp] N (col) battage m inv pubblicitario

hyperactive [haɪpər'æktɪv] ADJ iperattivo(-a)

hyperconnectivity ['haɪpəkɔnɛk'tɪvəti] N iperconnettività f inv

hyperlink ['haɪpəlɪŋk] N link m inv ipertestuale

hypermarket ['haɪpəmɑ:kɪt] N (BRIT) ipermercato

hypertension [haɪpə'tɛnʃən] N (Med) ipertensione f

hypertext ['haɪpətɛkst] N (Comput) ipertesto

hyperventilation [haɪpəventɪ'leɪʃən] N iperventilazione f

hyphen ['haɪfn] N trattino

hypnosis [hɪp'nəusɪs] N ipnosi f

hypnotic [hɪp'nɔtɪk] ADJ ipnotico(-a)

hypnotism ['hɪpnətɪzəm] N ipnotismo

hypnotist ['hɪpnətɪst] N ipnotizzatore(-trice)

hypnotize ['hɪpnətaɪz] VT ipnotizzare

hypoallergenic [haɪpəuælə'dʒɛnɪk] ADJ ipoallergico(-a)

hypochondriac [haɪpə'kɔndrɪæk] N ipocondriaco(-a)

hypocrisy [hɪ'pɔkrɪsɪ] N ipocrisia

hypocrite ['hɪpəkrɪt] N ipocrita mf

hypocritical [hɪpə'krɪtɪkl] ADJ ipocrita

hypodermic [haɪpə'də:mɪk] ADJ ipodermico(-a) ▶ N (syringe) siringa ipodermica

hypotenuse [haɪ'pɔtɪnju:z] N ipotenusa

hypothermia [haɪpəu'θə:mɪə] N ipotermia

h

hypothesis [haɪˈpɔθɪsɪs] (pl **hypotheses** [-siːz])
N ipotesi f inv

hypothetical [haɪpəuˈθɛtɪkl] ADJ ipotetico(-a)

hysterectomy [hɪstəˈrɛktəmɪ] N isterectomia

hysteria [hɪˈstɪərɪə] N isteria

hysterical [hɪˈstɛrɪkl] ADJ isterico(-a); **to become ~** avere una crisi isterica

hysterics [hɪˈstɛrɪks] NPL accesso di isteria; (laughter) attacco di riso; **to have ~** avere una crisi isterica

Ii

I, i [aɪ] N (letter) I, i f inv or m inv; **I for Isaac**, (US) **I for Item** ≈ I come Imola

I [aɪ] PRON io ▶ ABBR (= island, isle) Is.

IA ABBR (US) = **Iowa**

IAEA N ABBR = **International Atomic Energy Agency**

ib. ['ɪb] ABBR (= ibidem) ibid

Iberian [aɪ'bɪərɪən] ADJ iberico(-a)

Iberian Peninsula N: **the ~** la Penisola iberica

IBEW N ABBR (US: = International Brotherhood of Electrical Workers) associazione internazionale degli elettrotecnici

ibid. ['ɪbɪd] ABBR (= ibidem) ibid

i/c ABBR (BRIT) = **in charge**

ICBM N ABBR (= intercontinental ballistic missile) ICBM m inv

ICC N ABBR (= International Chamber of Commerce) C.C.I. f

ice [aɪs] N ghiaccio; (on road) gelo ▶ VT (cake) glassare; (drink) mettere in fresco ▶ VI (also: **ice over**) ghiacciare; (also: **ice up**) gelare; **to keep sth on ~** (fig: plan, project) mettere da parte (per il momento), accantonare

Ice Age N era glaciale

ice axe N piccozza da ghiaccio

iceberg ['aɪsbəːg] N iceberg m inv; **tip of the ~** (also fig) punta dell'iceberg

icebox ['aɪsbɔks] N (US) frigorifero; (BRIT) reparto ghiaccio; (insulated box) frigo portatile

icebreaker ['aɪsbreɪkəʳ] N rompighiaccio m inv

ice bucket N secchiello del ghiaccio

ice-cap ['aɪskæp] N calotta polare

ice-cold [aɪs'kəuld] ADJ gelato(-a)

ice cream N gelato

ice-cream soda N (gelato) affogato al seltz

ice cube N cubetto di ghiaccio

iced [aɪst] ADJ (drink) ghiacciato(-a); (coffee, tea) freddo(-a); (cake) glassato(-a)

ice hockey N hockey m su ghiaccio

Iceland ['aɪslənd] N Islanda

Icelander ['aɪsləndəʳ] N islandese mf

Icelandic [aɪs'lændɪk] ADJ islandese ▶ N (Ling) islandese m

ice lolly N (BRIT) ghiacciolo

ice pick N piccone m per ghiaccio

ice rink N pista di pattinaggio

ice-skate ['aɪsskeɪt] N pattino da ghiaccio ▶ VI pattinare sul ghiaccio

ice skating ['aɪsskeɪtɪŋ] N pattinaggio sul ghiaccio

icicle ['aɪsɪkl] N ghiacciolo

icing ['aɪsɪŋ] N (Aviat etc) patina di ghiaccio; (Culin) glassa

icing sugar N (BRIT) zucchero a velo

ICJ N ABBR = **International Court of Justice**

icon ['aɪkɔn] N icona; (Comput) immagine f

ICR N ABBR (US) = **Institute for Cancer Research**

ICRC N ABBR (= International Committee of the Red Cross) CICR m

ICT N ABBR (BRIT Scol: = Information and Communications Technology) informatica

ICU N ABBR = **intensive care unit**

icy ['aɪsɪ] ADJ ghiacciato(-a); (weather, temperature) gelido(-a)

ID ABBR = **identification document**; (US) = **Idaho**

I'd [aɪd] = **I would**; **I had**

Ida. ABBR (US) = **Idaho**

ID card N = **identity card**

IDD N ABBR (BRIT Tel: = International direct dialling) teleselezione f internazionale

idea [aɪ'dɪə] N idea; **good ~!** buon'idea!; **to have an ~ that** ... aver l'impressione che ...; **I haven't the least ~** non ne ho la minima idea

ideal [aɪ'dɪəl] ADJ, N ideale (m)

idealist [aɪ'dɪəlɪst] N idealista mf

ideally [aɪ'dɪəlɪ] ADV perfettamente, assolutamente; **~ the book should have** ... l'ideale sarebbe che il libro avesse ...

identical [aɪ'dɛntɪkl] ADJ identico(-a)

identification [aɪdɛntɪfɪ'keɪʃən] N identificazione f; **means of ~** carta d'identità

identify [aɪ'dɛntɪfaɪ] VT identificare ▶ VI: **to ~ with** identificarsi con

Identikit® [aɪˈdɛntɪkɪt] N: **~ (picture)** identikit *m inv*

identity [aɪˈdɛntɪtɪ] N identità *f inv*

identity card N carta d'identità

identity parade N (BRIT) confronto all'americana

identity theft N furto d'identità

ideological [aɪdɪəˈlɔdʒɪkəl] ADJ ideologico(-a)

ideology [aɪdɪˈɔlədʒɪ] N ideologia

idiocy [ˈɪdɪəsɪ] N idiozia

idiom [ˈɪdɪəm] N idioma *m*; (*phrase*) espressione *f* idiomatica

idiomatic [ɪdɪəˈmætɪk] ADJ idiomatico(-a)

idiosyncrasy [ɪdɪəuˈsɪŋkrəsɪ] N idiosincrasia

idiot [ˈɪdɪət] N idiota *mf*

idiotic [ɪdɪˈɔtɪk] ADJ idiota

idle [ˈaɪdl] ADJ inattivo(-a); (*lazy*) pigro(-a), ozioso(-a); (*unemployed*) disoccupato(-a); (*question, pleasures*) ozioso(-a) ▸ VI (*engine*) girare al minimo; **to lie ~** stare fermo, non funzionare
▸ **idle away** VT (*time*) sprecare, buttar via

idleness [ˈaɪdlnɪs] N ozio; pigrizia

idler [ˈaɪdləʳ] N ozioso(-a), fannullone(-a)

idle time N tempi *mpl* morti

idol [ˈaɪdl] N idolo

idolize [ˈaɪdəlaɪz] VT idoleggiare

idyllic [ɪˈdɪlɪk] ADJ idillico(-a)

i.e. ABBR (= *id est: that is*) cioè

IED [aɪiːˈdiː] N (= *Improvised Explosive Device*) ordigno esplosivo improvvisato; IED *m inv*

if [ɪf] CONJ se ▸ N: **there are a lot of ifs and buts** ci sono molti se e ma; **I'd be pleased if you could do it** sarei molto contento se potesse farlo; **if I were you …** se fossi in te …, io al tuo posto …; **if so** se è così; **if not** se no; **if necessary** se (è) necessario; **if only** se solo *or* soltanto; **if only he were here** se solo fosse qui; **if only to show him my gratitude** se non altro per esprimergli la mia gratitudine

> The Italian word for *if* **se** has the same form as the reflexive pronoun **si** when it is used before **lo**, **la**, **li**, **le**, or **ne**, e.g. *She forgot about it*. **Se ne è dimenticata**.

iffy [ˈɪfɪ] ADJ (*col*) incerto(-a)

igloo [ˈɪgluː] N igloo *m inv*

ignite [ɪgˈnaɪt] VT accendere ▸ VI accendersi

ignition [ɪgˈnɪʃən] N (*Aut*) accensione *f*; **to switch on/off the ~** accendere/spegnere il motore

ignition key N (*Aut*) chiave *f* dell'accensione

ignoble [ɪgˈnəubl] ADJ ignobile

ignominious [ɪgnəˈmɪnɪəs] ADJ vergognoso(-a), ignominioso(-a)

ignoramus [ɪgnəˈreɪməs] N ignorante *mf*

ignorance [ˈɪgnərəns] N ignoranza; **to keep sb in ~ of sth** tenere qn all'oscuro di qc

ignorant [ˈɪgnərənt] ADJ ignorante; **to be ~ of** (*subject*) essere ignorante in; (*events*) essere ignaro(-a) di

ignore [ɪgˈnɔːʳ] VT non tener conto di; (*person, fact*) ignorare

ikon [ˈaɪkɔn] N = **icon**

IL ABBR (US) = **Illinois**

ILA N ABBR (US: = *International Longshoremen's Association*) associazione internazionale degli scaricatori di porto

ill [ɪl] ADJ (*sick*) malato(-a); (*bad*) cattivo(-a) ▸ N male *m*; **to take** *or* **be taken ~** ammalarsi; **to feel ~** star male; **to speak/think ~ of sb** parlar/pensar male di qn

I'll [aɪl] = **I will; I shall**

ill-advised [ɪləd'vaɪzd] ADJ (*decision*) poco giudizioso(-a); (*person*) mal consigliato(-a)

ill-at-ease [ɪlət'iːz] ADJ a disagio

ill-considered [ɪlkən'sɪdəd] ADJ (*plan*) avventato(-a)

ill-disposed [ɪldɪs'pəuzd] ADJ: **to be ~ towards sb/sth** essere maldisposto(-a) verso qn/qc *or* nei riguardi di qn/qc

illegal [ɪˈliːgl] ADJ illegale

illegally [ɪˈliːgəlɪ] ADV illegalmente

illegible [ɪˈlɛdʒɪbl] ADJ illeggibile

illegitimate [ɪlɪˈdʒɪtɪmət] ADJ illegittimo(-a)

ill-fated [ɪlˈfeɪtɪd] ADJ nefasto(-a)

ill-favoured, (US) **ill-favored** [ɪlˈfeɪvəd] ADJ sgraziato(-a), brutto(-a)

ill feeling N rancore *m*

ill-gotten [ˈɪlgɔtn] ADJ: **~ gains** maltolto

ill health N problemi *mpl* di salute

illicit [ɪˈlɪsɪt] ADJ illecito(-a)

ill-informed [ɪlɪnˈfɔːmd] ADJ (*judgement, speech*) pieno(-a) di inesattezze; (*person*) male informato(-a)

illiterate [ɪˈlɪtərət] ADJ analfabeta, illetterato(-a); (*letter*) scorretto(-a)

ill-mannered [ɪlˈmænəd] ADJ maleducato(-a), sgarbato(-a)

illness [ˈɪlnɪs] N malattia

illogical [ɪˈlɔdʒɪkl] ADJ illogico(-a)

ill-suited [ɪlˈsuːtɪd] ADJ (*couple*) mal assortito(-a); **he is ~ to the job** è inadatto a quel lavoro

ill-timed [ɪlˈtaɪmd] ADJ intempestivo(-a), inopportuno(-a)

ill-treat [ɪlˈtriːt] VT maltrattare

ill-treatment [ɪlˈtriːtmənt] N maltrattamenti *mpl*

illuminate [ɪˈluːmɪneɪt] VT illuminare; **illuminated sign** insegna luminosa

illuminating [ɪˈluːmɪneɪtɪŋ] ADJ chiarificatore(-trice)

illumination [ɪluːmɪˈneɪʃən] N illuminazione f
illusion [ɪˈluːʒən] N illusione f; **to be under the ~ that** avere l'impressione che
illusive [ɪˈluːsɪv], **illusory** [ɪˈluːsərɪ] ADJ illusorio(-a)
illustrate [ˈɪləstreɪt] VT illustrare
illustration [ɪləˈstreɪʃən] N illustrazione f
illustrator [ˈɪləstreɪtəʳ] N illustratore(-trice)
illustrious [ɪˈlʌstrɪəs] ADJ illustre
ill will N cattiva volontà
ILO N ABBR (= International Labour Organization)
IM N (= instant messaging) messaggeria istantanea
I'm [aɪm] = **I am**
image [ˈɪmɪdʒ] N immagine f; (public face) immagine (pubblica)
imagery [ˈɪmɪdʒərɪ] N immagini fpl
imaginable [ɪˈmædʒɪnəbl] ADJ immaginabile, che si possa immaginare
imaginary [ɪˈmædʒɪnərɪ] ADJ immaginario(-a)
imagination [ɪmædʒɪˈneɪʃən] N immaginazione f, fantasia
imaginative [ɪˈmædʒɪnətɪv] ADJ immaginoso(-a)
imagine [ɪˈmædʒɪn] VT immaginare
imam [ɪˈmɑːm] N imam m inv
imbalance [ɪmˈbæləns] N squilibrio
imbecile [ˈɪmbəsiːl] N imbecille mf
imbue [ɪmˈbjuː] VT: **to ~ sth with** impregnare qc di
IMF N ABBR = **International Monetary Fund**
imitate [ˈɪmɪteɪt] VT imitare
imitation [ɪmɪˈteɪʃən] N imitazione f
imitator [ˈɪmɪteɪtəʳ] N imitatore(-trice)
immaculate [ɪˈmækjulət] ADJ immacolato(-a); (dress, appearance) impeccabile
immaterial [ɪməˈtɪərɪəl] ADJ immateriale, indifferente; **it is ~ whether** poco importa se or che + sub
immature [ɪməˈtjuəʳ] ADJ immaturo(-a)
immaturity [ɪməˈtjuərɪtɪ] N immaturità, mancanza di maturità
immeasurable [ɪˈmɛʒərəbl] ADJ incommensurabile
immediacy [ɪˈmiːdɪəsɪ] N immediatezza
immediate [ɪˈmiːdɪət] ADJ immediato(-a)
immediately [ɪˈmiːdɪətlɪ] ADV (at once) subito, immediatamente; **~ next to** proprio accanto a
immense [ɪˈmɛns] ADJ immenso(-a); enorme
immensely ADV immensamente
immensity [ɪˈmɛnsɪtɪ] N (of size, difference) enormità; (of problem etc) vastità
immerse [ɪˈməːs] VT immergere
immersion heater [ɪˈməːʃən-] N (BRIT) scaldaacqua m inv a immersione

immigrant [ˈɪmɪgrənt] N immigrante mf; (already established) immigrato(-a)
immigration [ɪmɪˈgreɪʃən] N immigrazione f
immigration authorities NPL ufficio stranieri
immigration laws NPL leggi fpl relative all'immigrazione
imminent [ˈɪmɪnənt] ADJ imminente
immobile [ɪˈməubaɪl] ADJ immobile
immobilize [ɪˈməubɪlaɪz] VT immobilizzare
immobilizer [ɪˈməubɪlaɪzəʳ] N (Aut) immobilizer m inv, dispositivo di bloccaggio del motore
immoderate [ɪˈmɔdərɪt] ADJ (person) smodato(-a), sregolato(-a); (opinion, reaction, demand) eccessivo(-a)
immodest [ɪˈmɔdɪst] ADJ (indecent) indecente, impudico(-a); (boasting) presuntuoso(-a)
immoral [ɪˈmɔrl] ADJ immorale
immorality [ɪmɔˈrælɪtɪ] N immoralità
immortal [ɪˈmɔːtl] ADJ, N immortale (mf)
immortalize [ɪˈmɔːtəlaɪz] VT rendere immortale
immovable [ɪˈmuːvəbl] ADJ (object) non movibile; (person) irremovibile
immune [ɪˈmjuːn] ADJ: **~ (to)** immune (da)
immune system N sistema m immunitario
immunity [ɪˈmjuːnɪtɪ] N (also fig: of diplomat) immunità; **diplomatic ~** immunità diplomatica
immunization [ɪmjunaɪˈzeɪʃən] N immunizzazione f
immunize [ˈɪmjunaɪz] VT immunizzare
imp [ɪmp] N folletto, diavoletto; (child) diavoletto
impact [ˈɪmpækt] N impatto
impair [ɪmˈpɛəʳ] VT danneggiare
impaired [ɪmˈpɛəd] ADJ indebolito(-a)
-impaired [ɪmˈpɛəd] SUFFIX: **visually-impaired** videoleso(-a)
impale [ɪmˈpeɪl] VT impalare
impart [ɪmˈpɑːt] VT (make known) comunicare; (bestow) impartire
impartial [ɪmˈpɑːʃl] ADJ imparziale
impartiality [ɪmpɑːʃɪˈælɪtɪ] N imparzialità
impassable [ɪmˈpɑːsəbl] ADJ insuperabile; (road) impraticabile
impasse [æmˈpɑːs] N impasse f inv
impassioned [ɪmˈpæʃənd] ADJ appassionato(-a)
impassive [ɪmˈpæsɪv] ADJ impassibile
impatience [ɪmˈpeɪʃəns] N impazienza
impatient [ɪmˈpeɪʃənt] ADJ impaziente; **to get** or **grow ~** perdere la pazienza
impeach [ɪmˈpiːtʃ] VT accusare, attaccare; (public official) mettere sotto accusa

impeachment [ɪmˈpiːtʃmənt] N (Law) imputazione f

impeccable [ɪmˈpɛkəbl] ADJ impeccabile

impecunious [ɪmpɪˈkjuːnɪəs] ADJ povero(-a)

impede [ɪmˈpiːd] VT impedire

impediment [ɪmˈpɛdɪmənt] N impedimento; (also: **speech impediment**) difetto di pronuncia

impel [ɪmˈpɛl] VT (force): **to ~ sb (to do sth)** costringere or obbligare qn (a fare qc)

impending [ɪmˈpɛndɪŋ] ADJ imminente

impenetrable [ɪmˈpɛnɪtrəbl] ADJ impenetrabile

imperative [ɪmˈpɛrətɪv] ADJ imperativo(-a); necessario(-a), urgente; (voice) imperioso(-a) ▶ N (Ling) imperativo

imperceptible [ɪmpəˈsɛptɪbl] ADJ impercettibile

imperfect [ɪmˈpəːfɪkt] ADJ imperfetto(-a); (goods etc) difettoso(-a) ▶ N (Ling: also: **imperfect tense**) imperfetto

imperfection [ɪmpəˈfɛkʃən] N imperfezione f; (flaw) difetto

imperial [ɪmˈpɪərɪəl] ADJ imperiale; (measure) legale

imperialism [ɪmˈpɪərɪəlɪzəm] N imperialismo

imperil [ɪmˈpɛrɪl] VT mettere in pericolo

imperious [ɪmˈpɪərɪəs] ADJ imperioso(-a)

impersonal [ɪmˈpəːsənl] ADJ impersonale

impersonate [ɪmˈpəːsəneɪt] VT spacciarsi per, fingersi; (Theat) imitare

impersonation [ɪmpəːsəˈneɪʃən] N (Law) usurpazione f d'identità; (Theat) imitazione f

impersonator [ɪmˈpəːsəneɪtəʳ] N (gen, Theat) imitatore(-trice)

impertinence [ɪmˈpəːtɪnəns] N impertinenza

impertinent [ɪmˈpəːtɪnənt] ADJ impertinente

imperturbable [ɪmpəˈtəːbəbl] ADJ imperturbabile

impervious [ɪmˈpəːvɪəs] ADJ impermeabile; **~ to** (fig) insensibile a; impassibile di fronte a

impetuous [ɪmˈpɛtjuəs] ADJ impetuoso(-a), precipitoso(-a)

impetus [ˈɪmpətəs] N impeto

impinge [ɪmˈpɪndʒ]: **to ~ on** vt fus (person) colpire; (rights) ledere

impish [ˈɪmpɪʃ] ADJ malizioso(-a), birichino(-a)

implacable [ɪmˈplækəbl] ADJ implacabile

implant [ɪmˈplɑːnt] VT (Med) innestare; (fig: idea, principle) inculcare

implausible [ɪmˈplɔːzɪbl] ADJ non plausibile

implement N [ˈɪmplɪmənt] attrezzo; (for cooking) utensile m ▶ VT [ˈɪmplɪmɛnt] effettuare

implicate [ˈɪmplɪkeɪt] VT implicare

implication [ɪmplɪˈkeɪʃən] N implicazione f; **by ~** implicitamente

implicit [ɪmˈplɪsɪt] ADJ implicito(-a); (complete) completo(-a)

implicitly [ɪmˈplɪsɪtlɪ] ADV implicitamente

implore [ɪmˈplɔːʳ] VT implorare

imply [ɪmˈplaɪ] VT insinuare; suggerire

impolite [ɪmpəˈlaɪt] ADJ scortese

imponderable [ɪmˈpɒndərəbl] ADJ imponderabile

import VT [ɪmˈpɔːt] importare ▶ N [ˈɪmpɔːt] (Comm) importazione f; (meaning) significato, senso ▶ CPD (duty, licence etc) d'importazione

importance [ɪmˈpɔːtns] N importanza; **to be of great/little ~** importare molto/poco, essere molto/poco importante

important [ɪmˈpɔːtnt] ADJ importante; **it's not ~** non ha importanza; **it is ~ that** è importante che+sub

importantly [ɪmˈpɔːtəntlɪ] ADV (pej) con (un'aria d')importanza; **but, more ~, ...** ma, quel che più conta or importa, ...

importation [ɪmpɔːˈteɪʃən] N importazione f

imported [ɪmˈpɔːtɪd] ADJ importato(-a)

importer [ɪmˈpɔːtəʳ] N importatore(-trice)

impose [ɪmˈpəuz] VT imporre ▶ VI: **to ~ on sb** sfruttare la bontà di qn

imposing [ɪmˈpəuzɪŋ] ADJ imponente

imposition [ɪmpəˈzɪʃən] N imposizione f; **to be an ~ on** (person) abusare della gentilezza di

impossibility [ɪmpɒsəˈbɪlɪtɪ] N impossibilità

impossible [ɪmˈpɒsɪbl] ADJ impossibile; **it is ~ for me to leave now** mi è impossibile venir via adesso

impostor [ɪmˈpɒstəʳ] N impostore(-a)

impotence [ˈɪmpətns] N impotenza

impotent [ˈɪmpətnt] ADJ impotente

impound [ɪmˈpaund] VT confiscare

impoverished [ɪmˈpɒvərɪʃt] ADJ impoverito(-a)

impracticable [ɪmˈpræktɪkəbl] ADJ impraticabile

impractical [ɪmˈpræktɪkl] ADJ non pratico(-a)

imprecise [ɪmprɪˈsaɪs] ADJ impreciso(-a)

impregnable [ɪmˈprɛgnəbl] ADJ (fortress) inespugnabile; (fig) inoppugnabile; irrefutabile

impregnate [ˈɪmprɛgneɪt] VT impregnare; (fertilize) fecondare

impresario [ɪmprɪˈsɑːrɪəu] N impresario(-a)

impress [ɪmˈprɛs] VT impressionare; (mark) imprimere, stampare; **to ~ sth on sb** far capire qc a qn

impression [ɪmˈprɛʃən] N impressione f; **to be under the ~ that** avere l'impressione che; **to make a good/bad ~ on sb** fare una buona/cattiva impressione a or su qn

impressionable [ɪmˈprɛʃnəbl] ADJ impressionabile

impressionist [ɪmˈprɛʃənɪst] N impressionista *mf*

impressive [ɪmˈprɛsɪv] ADJ notevole

imprint [ˈɪmprɪnt] N (*Publishing*) sigla editoriale

imprinted [ɪmˈprɪntɪd] ADJ: ~ **on** impresso(-a) in

imprison [ɪmˈprɪzn] VT imprigionare

imprisonment [ɪmˈprɪznmənt] N imprigionamento

improbable [ɪmˈprɒbəbl] ADJ improbabile; (*excuse*) inverosimile

impromptu [ɪmˈprɒmptjuː] ADJ improvvisato(-a) ▶ ADV improvvisando, così su due piedi

improper [ɪmˈprɒpəʳ] ADJ scorretto(-a); (*unsuitable*) inadatto(-a), improprio(-a); sconveniente, indecente

impropriety [ɪmprəˈpraɪətɪ] N sconvenienza; (*of expression*) improprietà

improve [ɪmˈpruːv] VT migliorare ▶ VI migliorare; (*pupil etc*) fare progressi
▶ **improve (up)on** VT FUS (*offer*) aumentare

improvement [ɪmˈpruːvmənt] N miglioramento; progresso; **to make improvements to** migliorare, apportare dei miglioramenti a

improvisation [ɪmprəvaɪˈzeɪʃən] N improvvisazione *f*

improvise [ˈɪmprəvaɪz] VT, VI improvvisare

imprudence [ɪmˈpruːdns] N imprudenza

imprudent [ɪmˈpruːdnt] ADJ imprudente

impudence [ˈɪmpjudns] N impudenza

impudent [ˈɪmpjudnt] ADJ impudente, sfacciato(-a)

impugn [ɪmˈpjuːn] VT impugnare

impulse [ˈɪmpʌls] N impulso; **to act on ~** agire d'impulso *or* impulsivamente

impulse buy N acquisto fatto d'impulso

impulsive [ɪmˈpʌlsɪv] ADJ impulsivo(-a)

impunity [ɪmˈpjuːnɪtɪ] N: **with ~** impunemente

impure [ɪmˈpjuəʳ] ADJ impuro(-a)

impurity [ɪmˈpjuərɪtɪ] N impurità *f inv*

IN ABBR (*US*) = **Indiana**

---

in [ɪn]

PREP **1** (*indicating place, position*) in; **in the house/garden** in casa/giardino; **in the box** nella scatola; **in the fridge** nel frigorifero; **I have it in my hand** ce l'ho in mano; **in town/the country** in città/campagna; **in school** a scuola; **in here/there** qui/lì dentro
2 (*with place names: of town, region, country*): **in London** a Londra; **in England** in Inghilterra; **in the United States** negli Stati Uniti; **in Yorkshire** nello Yorkshire
3 (*indicating time: during, in the space of*) in; **in spring/summer** in primavera/estate; **in 1988** nel 1988; **in May** in *or* a maggio; **I'll see you in July** ci vediamo a luglio; **in the afternoon** nel pomeriggio; **at 4 o'clock in the afternoon** alle 4 del pomeriggio; **I did it in 3 hours/days** l'ho fatto in 3 ore/giorni; **I'll see you in 2 weeks** *or* **in 2 weeks' time** ci vediamo tra 2 settimane; **once in a hundred years** una volta ogni cento anni
4 (*indicating manner etc*) a; **in a loud/soft voice** a voce alta/bassa; **in pencil** a matita; **in English/French** in inglese/francese; **in writing** per iscritto; **the boy in the blue shirt** il ragazzo con la camicia blu
5 (*indicating circumstances*): **in the sun** al sole; **in the shade** all'ombra; **in the rain** sotto la pioggia; **a rise in prices** un aumento dei prezzi
6 (*indicating mood, state*): **in tears** in lacrime; **in anger** per la rabbia; **in despair** disperato(-a); **in good condition** in buono stato, in buone condizioni; **to live in luxury** vivere nel lusso
7 (*with ratios, numbers*): **1 in 10** 1 su 10; **20 pence in the pound** 20 pence per sterlina; **they lined up in twos** si misero in fila per due; **in hundreds** a centinaia
8 (*referring to people, works*) in; **the disease is common in children** la malattia è comune nei bambini; **in (the works of) Dickens** in Dickens, nelle opere di Dickens
9 (*indicating profession etc*) in; **to be in teaching** fare l'insegnante, insegnare; **to be in publishing** lavorare nell'editoria
10 (*after superlative*) di; **the best in the class** il migliore della classe
11 (*with present participle*): **in saying this** dicendo questo, nel dire questo
12: **in that** *conj* poiché
▶ ADV: **to be in** (*person: at home, work*) esserci; (*train, ship, plane*) essere arrivato(-a); (*in fashion*) essere di moda; **their party is in** il loro partito è al potere; **to ask sb in** invitare qn ad entrare; **to run/limp etc in** entrare di corsa/zoppicando *etc*
▶ N: **the ins and outs of the problem** tutti gli aspetti del problema

---

in., ins ABBR = **inch; inches**

inability [ɪnəˈbɪlɪtɪ] N inabilità, incapacità; ~ **to pay** impossibilità di pagare

inaccessible [ɪnəkˈsɛsɪbl] ADJ inaccessibile

inaccuracy [ɪnˈækjurəsɪ] N inaccuratezza; inesattezza; imprecisione *f*

inaccurate [ɪnˈækjurət] ADJ inaccurato(-a); (*figures*) inesatto(-a); (*translation*) impreciso(-a)

inaction [ɪnˈækʃən] N inazione *f*

inactivity [ɪnækˈtɪvɪtɪ] N inattività

inadequacy [ɪnˈædɪkwəsɪ] N insufficienza

inadequate [ɪnˈædɪkwət] ADJ insufficiente

inadmissible [ɪnədˈmɪsəbl] ADJ inammissibile

inadvertent [ɪnədˈvəːtənt] ADJ involontario(-a)

inadvertently [ɪnədˈvəːtntlɪ] ADV senza volerlo

inadvisable [ɪnəd'vaɪzəbl] ADJ sconsigliabile

inane [ɪ'neɪn] ADJ vacuo(-a), stupido(-a)

inanimate [ɪn'ænɪmət] ADJ inanimato(-a)

inapplicable [ɪn'æplɪkəbl] ADJ inapplicabile

inappropriate [ɪnə'prəupriət] ADJ non adatto(-a); (word, expression) improprio(-a)

inapt [ɪn'æpt] ADJ maldestro(-a); fuori luogo

inaptitude [ɪn'æptɪtjuːd] N improprietà

inarticulate [ɪnɑː'tɪkjulət] ADJ (person) che si esprime male; (speech) inarticolato(-a)

inasmuch as [ɪnəz'mʌtʃæz] ADV in quanto che; (seeing that) poiché

inattention [ɪnə'tenʃən] N mancanza di attenzione

inattentive [ɪnə'tentɪv] ADJ disattento(-a), distratto(-a); negligente

inaudible [ɪn'ɔːdɪbl] ADJ che non si riesce a sentire

inaugural [ɪ'nɔːgjurəl] ADJ inaugurale

inaugurate [ɪ'nɔːgjureɪt] VT inaugurare; (president, official) insediare

inauguration [ɪnɔːgju'reɪʃən] N inaugurazione f; insediamento in carica

inauspicious [ɪnɔːs'pɪʃəs] ADJ poco propizio(-a)

in-between [ɪnbɪ'twiːn] ADJ fra i (or le) due

inborn [ɪn'bɔːn] ADJ (feeling) innato(-a); (defect) congenito(-a)

inbox ['ɪnbɔks] N (Comput) posta in arrivo; (US: intray) vaschetta della corrispondenza in arrivo

inbred [ɪn'bred] ADJ innato(-a); (family) connaturato(-a)

inbreeding [ɪn'briːdɪŋ] N incrocio ripetuto di animali consanguinei; unioni fpl fra consanguinei

Inc. ABBR (US: = incorporated) S.A.

Inca ['ɪŋkə] ADJ (also: **Incan**) inca inv ▶ N inca mf

incalculable [ɪn'kælkjuləbl] ADJ incalcolabile

incapability [ɪnkeɪpə'bɪlɪtɪ] N incapacità

incapable [ɪn'keɪpəbl] ADJ: **~ (of doing sth)** incapace (di fare qc)

incapacitate [ɪnkə'pæsɪteɪt] VT: **to ~ sb from doing** rendere qn incapace di fare

incapacitated [ɪnkə'pæsɪteɪtɪd] ADJ (Law) inabilitato(-a)

incapacity [ɪnkə'pæsɪtɪ] N incapacità

incarcerate [ɪn'kɑːsəreɪt] VT imprigionare

incarnate ADJ [ɪn'kɑːnɪt] incarnato(-a) ▶ VT ['ɪnkɑːneɪt] incarnare

incarnation [ɪnkɑː'neɪʃən] N incarnazione f

incendiary [ɪn'sendɪərɪ] ADJ incendiario(-a) ▶ N (bomb) bomba incendiaria

incense N ['ɪnsɛns] incenso ▶ VT [ɪn'sɛns] (anger) infuriare

incense burner N incensiere m

incentive [ɪn'sɛntɪv] N incentivo

incentive scheme N piano di incentivazione

inception [ɪn'sepʃən] N inizio, principio

incessant [ɪn'sesnt] ADJ incessante

incessantly [ɪn'sesntlɪ] ADV di continuo, senza sosta

incest ['ɪnsest] N incesto

inch [ɪntʃ] N pollice m (= 25 mm; 12 in a foot); **within an ~ of** a un pelo da; **he wouldn't give an ~** (fig) non ha ceduto di un millimetro
▶ **inch forward** VI avanzare pian piano

inch tape N (BRIT) metro a nastro (da sarto)

incidence ['ɪnsɪdns] N (of crime, disease) incidenza

incident ['ɪnsɪdnt] N incidente m; (in book) episodio

incidental [ɪnsɪ'dentl] ADJ accessorio(-a), d'accompagnamento; (unplanned) incidentale; **~ to** marginale a; **~ expenses** npl spese fpl accessorie

incidentally [ɪnsɪ'dentəlɪ] ADV (by the way) a proposito

incidental music N sottofondo (musicale), musica di sottofondo

incident room N (Police) centrale f delle operazioni (per indagini)

incinerate [ɪn'sɪnəreɪt] VT incenerire

incinerator [ɪn'sɪnəreɪtə'] N inceneritore m

incipient [ɪn'sɪpɪənt] ADJ incipiente

incision [ɪn'sɪʒən] N incisione f

incisive [ɪn'saɪsɪv] ADJ incisivo(-a); tagliante; acuto(-a)

incisor [ɪn'saɪzə'] N incisivo

incite [ɪn'saɪt] VT incitare

incl. ABBR = **including; inclusive (of)**

inclement [ɪn'klemənt] ADJ inclemente

inclination [ɪnklɪ'neɪʃən] N inclinazione f

incline N ['ɪnklaɪn] pendenza, pendio ▶ VT [ɪn'klaɪn] inclinare ▶ VI (surface) essere inclinato(-a); **to ~ to** tendere a; **to be inclined to** tendere a fare; essere propenso(-a) a fare; **to be well inclined towards sb** essere ben disposto(-a) verso qn

include [ɪn'kluːd] VT includere, comprendere; **the tip is/is not included** la mancia è compresa/esclusa

including [ɪn'kluːdɪŋ] PREP compreso(-a), incluso(-a); **~ tip** mancia compresa, compresa la mancia

inclusion [ɪn'kluːʒən] N inclusione f

inclusive [ɪn'kluːsɪv] ADJ incluso(-a), compreso(-a); **£50, ~ of all surcharges** 50 sterline, incluse tutte le soprattasse; **~ of tax** etc tasse etc comprese

inclusive terms NPL (BRIT) prezzo tutto compreso

incognito [ɪnkɔg'niːtəu] ADV in incognito

incoherent [ɪnkəʊˈhɪərənt] ADJ incoerente

income [ˈɪnkʌm] N reddito; **gross/net ~** reddito lordo/netto; **~ and expenditure account** conto entrate ed uscite

income support N (BRIT) sussidio di indigenza or povertà

income tax N imposta sul reddito

income tax inspector N ispettore(-trice) delle imposte dirette

income tax return N dichiarazione f annuale dei redditi

incoming [ˈɪnkʌmɪŋ] ADJ (passengers, flight, mail) in arrivo; (government, tenant) subentrante; **~ tide** marea montante

incommunicado [ɪnkəmjʊnɪˈkɑːdəʊ] ADJ: **to hold sb ~** tenere qn in segregazione

incomparable [ɪnˈkɒmpərəbl] ADJ incomparabile

incompatible [ɪnkəmˈpætɪbl] ADJ incompatibile

incompetence [ɪnˈkɒmpɪtns] N incompetenza, incapacità

incompetent [ɪnˈkɒmpɪtnt] ADJ incompetente, incapace

incomplete [ɪnkəmˈpliːt] ADJ incompleto(-a)

incomprehensible [ɪnkɒmprɪˈhɛnsɪbl] ADJ incomprensibile

inconceivable [ɪnkənˈsiːvəbl] ADJ inimmaginabile

inconclusive [ɪnkənˈkluːsɪv] ADJ improduttivo(-a); (argument) poco convincente

incongruous [ɪnˈkɒŋgrʊəs] ADJ poco appropriato(-a); (remark, act) incongruo(-a)

inconsequential [ɪnkɒnsɪˈkwɛnʃl] ADJ senza importanza

inconsiderable [ɪnkənˈsɪdərəbl] ADJ: **not ~** non trascurabile

inconsiderate [ɪnkənˈsɪdərət] ADJ sconsiderato(-a)

inconsistency [ɪnkənˈsɪstənsɪ] N (of actions etc) incongruenza; (of work) irregolarità; (of statement etc) contraddizione f

inconsistent [ɪnkənˈsɪstnt] ADJ incoerente; poco logico(-a); contraddittorio(-a); **~ with** in contraddizione con

inconsolable [ɪnkənˈsəʊləbl] ADJ inconsolabile

inconspicuous [ɪnkənˈspɪkjuəs] ADJ incospicuo(-a); (colour) poco appariscente; (dress) dimesso(-a); **to make o.s. ~** cercare di passare inosservato(-a)

inconstant [ɪnˈkɒnstnt] ADJ incostante; mutevole

incontinence [ɪnˈkɒntɪnəns] N incontinenza

incontinent [ɪnˈkɒntɪnənt] ADJ incontinente

incontrovertible [ɪnkɒntrəˈvəːtəbl] ADJ incontrovertibile

inconvenience [ɪnkənˈviːnjəns] N inconveniente m; (trouble) disturbo ▶ VT disturbare; **to put sb to great ~** creare degli inconvenienti a qn; **don't ~ yourself** non si disturbi

inconvenient [ɪnkənˈviːnjənt] ADJ scomodo(-a); **that time is very ~ for me** quell'ora mi è molto scomoda, non è un'ora adatta per me

incorporate [ɪnˈkɔːpəreɪt] VT incorporare; (contain) contenere

incorporated [ɪnˈkɔːpəreɪtɪd] ADJ: **~ company** (US) società f inv registrata

incorrect [ɪnkəˈrɛkt] ADJ scorretto(-a); (statement) inesatto(-a)

incorrigible [ɪnˈkɒrɪdʒəbl] ADJ incorreggibile

incorruptible [ɪnkəˈrʌptɪbl] ADJ incorruttibile

increase N [ˈɪnkriːs] aumento ▶ VI [ɪnˈkriːs] aumentare; **to be on the ~** essere in aumento; **an ~ of £5/10%** un aumento di 5 sterline/del 10%

increasing [ɪnˈkriːsɪŋ] ADJ (number) crescente

increasingly [ɪnˈkriːsɪŋlɪ] ADV sempre più

incredible [ɪnˈkrɛdɪbl] ADJ incredibile

incredibly ADV incredibilmente

incredulous [ɪnˈkrɛdjʊləs] ADJ incredulo(-a)

increment [ˈɪnkrɪmənt] N aumento, incremento

incriminate [ɪnˈkrɪmɪneɪt] VT compromettere

incriminating [ɪnˈkrɪmɪneɪtɪŋ] ADJ incriminante

incubate [ˈɪnkjʊbeɪt] VT (eggs) covare ▶ VI (egg) essere in incubazione; (disease) avere un'incubazione

incubation [ɪnkjʊˈbeɪʃən] N incubazione f

incubation period N (periodo di) incubazione f

incubator [ˈɪnkjʊbeɪtəʳ] N incubatrice f

inculcate [ˈɪnkʌlkeɪt] VT: **to ~ sth in sb** inculcare qc a qn, instillare qc a qn

incumbent [ɪnˈkʌmbənt] ADJ: **it is ~ on him to do …** è suo dovere fare … ▶ N titolare mf

incur [ɪnˈkəːʳ] VT (expenses) incorrere; (debt) contrarre; (loss) subire; (anger, risk) esporsi a

incurable [ɪnˈkjʊərəbl] ADJ incurabile

incursion [ɪnˈkəːʃən] N incursione f

indebted [ɪnˈdɛtɪd] ADJ: **to be ~ to sb (for)** essere obbligato(-a) verso qn (per)

indecency [ɪnˈdiːsnsɪ] N indecenza

indecent [ɪnˈdiːsnt] ADJ indecente

indecent assault N (BRIT) aggressione f a scopo di violenza sessuale

indecent exposure N esibizionismo (di organi genitali)

indecipherable [ɪndɪˈsaɪfərəbl] ADJ indecifrabile

indecision [ɪndɪˈsɪʒən] N indecisione f

indecisive [ɪndɪˈsaɪsɪv] ADJ indeciso(-a); (discussion) non decisivo(-a)

indeed [ɪnˈdiːd] ADV infatti; veramente; **yes ~!** certamente!

indefatigable [ɪndɪˈfætɪgəbl] ADJ infaticabile, instancabile

indefensible [ɪndɪˈfɛnsəbl] ADJ (*conduct*) ingiustificabile

indefinable [ɪndɪˈfaɪnəbl] ADJ indefinibile

indefinite [ɪnˈdɛfɪnɪt] ADJ indefinito(-a); (*answer*) vago(-a); (*period, number*) indeterminato(-a)

indefinitely [ɪnˈdɛfɪnɪtlɪ] ADV (*wait*) indefinitamente

indelible [ɪnˈdɛlɪbl] ADJ indelebile

indelicate [ɪnˈdɛlɪkɪt] ADJ (*tactless*) indelicato(-a), privo(-a) di tatto; (*not polite*) sconveniente

indemnify [ɪnˈdɛmnɪfaɪ] VT indennizzare

indemnity [ɪnˈdɛmnɪtɪ] N (*insurance*) assicurazione *f*; (*compensation*) indennità, indennizzo

indent [ɪnˈdɛnt] VT (*Typ: text*) far rientrare dal margine

indentation [ɪndɛnˈteɪʃən] N dentellatura; (*Typ*) rientranza; (*dent*) tacca

indented [ɪnˈdɛntɪd] ADJ (*Typ*) rientrante

indenture [ɪnˈdɛntʃəʳ] N contratto *m* formazione *inv*

independence [ɪndɪˈpɛndns] N indipendenza

Independence Day N (*US*) vedi nota

> Negli Stati Uniti il 4 luglio si festeggia l'**Independence Day**, il giorno dell'adozione, nel 1776, della Dichiarazione di Indipendenza con la quale tredici colonie britanniche dichiaravano la separazione dalla Gran Bretagna e la propria appartenenza agli Stati Uniti d'America.

independent [ɪndɪˈpɛndnt] ADJ indipendente

independently [ɪndɪˈpɛndntlɪ] ADV indipendentemente; separatamente; **~ of** indipendentemente da

independent school N (*Brit*) istituto scolastico indipendente che si autofinanzia

in-depth [ˈɪnˈdɛpθ] ADJ approfondito(-a)

indescribable [ɪndɪˈskraɪbəbl] ADJ indescrivibile

indestructible [ɪndɪˈstrʌktəbl] ADJ indistruttibile

indeterminate [ɪndɪˈtəːmɪnɪt] ADJ indeterminato(-a)

index [ˈɪndɛks] N (*pl* **indexes**) (*in book*) indice *m*; (*in library etc*) catalogo; (*pl* **indices**: *ratio, sign*) indice *m*

index card N scheda

index finger N (dito) indice *m*

index-linked [ˈɪndɛksˈlɪŋkt], (*US*) **indexed** [ˈɪndɛkst] ADJ legato(-a) al costo della vita

India [ˈɪndɪə] N India

Indian [ˈɪndɪən] ADJ, N indiano(-a)

Indian ink N inchiostro di china

Indian Ocean N: **the ~** l'Oceano Indiano

Indian Summer N (*fig*) estate *f* di San Martino

India paper N carta d'India, carta bibbia

India rubber N caucciù *m*

indicate [ˈɪndɪkeɪt] VT indicare ▸ VI (*Brit Aut*): **to ~ left/right** mettere la freccia a sinistra/a destra

indication [ɪndɪˈkeɪʃən] N indicazione *f*, segno

indicative [ɪnˈdɪkətɪv] ADJ: **~ of** indicativo(-a) di ▸ N (*Ling*) indicativo

indicator [ˈɪndɪkeɪtəʳ] N (*sign*) segno; (*Aut*) indicatore *m* di direzione, freccia

indices [ˈɪndɪsiːz] NPL *of* **index**

indict [ɪnˈdaɪt] VT accusare

indictable [ɪnˈdaɪtəbl] ADJ passibile di pena; **~ offence** atto che costituisce reato

indictment [ɪnˈdaɪtmənt] N accusa

indifference [ɪnˈdɪfrəns] N indifferenza

indifferent [ɪnˈdɪfrənt] ADJ indifferente; (*poor*) mediocre

indigenous [ɪnˈdɪdʒɪnəs] ADJ indigeno(-a)

indigestible [ɪndɪˈdʒɛstɪbl] ADJ indigeribile

indigestion [ɪndɪˈdʒɛstʃən] N indigestione *f*

indignant [ɪnˈdɪgnənt] ADJ: **~ (at sth/with sb)** indignato(-a) (per qc/contro qn)

indignation [ɪndɪgˈneɪʃən] N indignazione *f*

indignity [ɪnˈdɪgnɪtɪ] N umiliazione *f*

indigo [ˈɪndɪgəu] ADJ, N indaco (*inv*)

indirect [ɪndɪˈrɛkt] ADJ indiretto(-a)

indirectly [ɪndɪˈrɛktlɪ] ADV indirettamente

indiscreet [ɪndɪˈskriːt] ADJ indiscreto(-a); (*rash*) imprudente

indiscretion [ɪndɪˈskrɛʃən] N indiscrezione *f*; imprudenza

indiscriminate [ɪndɪˈskrɪmɪnət] ADJ (*person*) che non sa discernere; (*admiration*) cieco(-a); (*killings*) indiscriminato(-a)

indispensable [ɪndɪˈspɛnsəbl] ADJ indispensabile

indisposed [ɪndɪˈspəuzd] ADJ (*unwell*) indisposto(-a)

indisposition [ɪndɪspəˈzɪʃən] N (*illness*) indisposizione *f*

indisputable [ɪndɪˈspjuːtəbl] ADJ incontestabile, indiscutibile

indistinct [ɪndɪˈstɪŋkt] ADJ indistinto(-a); (*memory, noise*) vago(-a)

indistinguishable [ɪndɪˈstɪŋgwɪʃəbl] ADJ indistinguibile

individual [ɪndɪˈvɪdjuəl] N individuo ▸ ADJ individuale; (*characteristic*) particolare, originale

individualist [ɪndɪˈvɪdjuəlɪst] N individualista *mf*

individuality [ɪndɪvɪdjuˈælɪtɪ] N individualità

individually [ˌɪndɪ'vɪdjuəlɪ] ADV singolarmente, uno(-a) per uno(-a)

indivisible [ˌɪndɪ'vɪzɪbl] ADJ indivisibile

Indochina ['ɪndəu'tʃaɪnə] N Indocina

indoctrinate [ɪn'dɔktrɪneɪt] VT indottrinare

indoctrination [ɪndɔktrɪ'neɪʃən] N indottrinamento

indolent ['ɪndələnt] ADJ indolente

Indonesia [ˌɪndəu'niːzɪə] N Indonesia

Indonesian [ˌɪndəu'niːzɪən] ADJ, N indonesiano(-a); (Ling) indonesiano

indoor ['ɪndɔːʳ] ADJ da interno; (plant) d'appartamento; (swimming pool) coperto(-a); (sport, games) fatto(-a) al coperto

indoors [ɪn'dɔːz] ADV all'interno; (at home) in casa

indubitable [ɪn'djuːbɪtəbl] ADJ indubitabile

induce [ɪn'djuːs] VT persuadere; (bring about, Med) provocare; **to ~ sb to do sth** persuadere qn a fare qc

inducement [ɪn'djuːsmənt] N incitamento; (incentive) stimolo, incentivo

induct [ɪn'dʌkt] VT insediare; (fig) iniziare

induction [ɪn'dʌkʃən] N (Med: of birth) parto indotto

induction course N (BRIT) corso di avviamento

indulge [ɪn'dʌldʒ] VT (whim) compiacere, soddisfare; (child) viziare ▶ VI: **to ~ in sth** concedersi qc; abbandonarsi a qc

indulgence [ɪn'dʌldʒəns] N lusso (che uno si permette); (leniency) indulgenza

indulgent [ɪn'dʌldʒənt] ADJ indulgente

industrial [ɪn'dʌstrɪəl] ADJ industriale; (injury) sul lavoro; (dispute) di lavoro

industrial action N azione f rivendicativa

industrial estate N (BRIT) zona industriale

industrialist [ɪn'dʌstrɪəlɪst] N industriale m

industrialize [ɪn'dʌstrɪəlaɪz] VT industrializzare

industrial park N (US) zona industriale

industrial relations NPL relazioni fpl industriali

industrial tribunal N (BRIT) ≈ Tribunale m Amministrativo Regionale

industrial unrest N (BRIT) agitazione f (sindacale)

industrious [ɪn'dʌstrɪəs] ADJ industrioso(-a), assiduo(-a)

industry ['ɪndəstrɪ] N industria; (diligence) operosità

inebriated [ɪ'niːbrɪeɪtɪd] ADJ ubriaco(-a)

inedible [ɪn'edɪbl] ADJ immangiabile; non commestibile

ineffective [ɪnɪ'fektɪv] ADJ inefficace

ineffectual [ɪnɪ'fektʃuəl] ADJ inefficace; incompetente

inefficiency [ɪnɪ'fɪʃənsɪ] N inefficienza

inefficient [ɪnɪ'fɪʃənt] ADJ inefficiente

inelegant [ɪn'elɪgənt] ADJ poco elegante

ineligible [ɪn'elɪdʒɪbl] ADJ (candidate) ineleggibile; **to be ~ for sth** non avere il diritto a qc

inept [ɪ'nept] ADJ inetto(-a)

ineptitude [ɪ'neptɪtjuːd] N inettitudine f, stupidità

inequality [ɪnɪ'kwɔlɪtɪ] N ineguaglianza

inequitable [ɪn'ekwɪtəbl] ADJ iniquo(-a)

ineradicable [ɪnɪ'rædɪkəbl] ADJ inestirpabile

inert [ɪ'nɜːt] ADJ inerte

inertia [ɪ'nɜːʃə] N inerzia

inertia-reel seat belt [ɪ'nɜːʃə'riːl-] N cintura di sicurezza con arrotolatore

inescapable [ɪnɪ'skeɪpəbl] ADJ inevitabile

inessential [ɪnɪ'senʃl] ADJ non essenziale

inestimable [ɪn'estɪməbl] ADJ inestimabile, incalcolabile

inevitable [ɪn'evɪtəbl] ADJ inevitabile

inevitably [ɪn'evɪtəblɪ] ADV inevitabilmente; **as ~ happens …** come immancabilmente succede …

inexact [ɪnɪg'zækt] ADJ inesatto(-a)

inexcusable [ɪnɪks'kjuːzəbl] ADJ imperdonabile

inexhaustible [ɪnɪg'zɔːstɪbl] ADJ inesauribile; (person) instancabile

inexorable [ɪn'eksərəbl] ADJ inesorabile

inexpensive [ɪnɪk'spensɪv] ADJ poco costoso(-a)

inexperience [ɪnɪk'spɪərɪəns] N inesperienza

inexperienced [ɪnɪk'spɪərɪənst] ADJ inesperto(-a), senza esperienza; **to be ~ in sth** essere poco pratico di qc

inexplicable [ɪnɪk'splɪkəbl] ADJ inesplicabile

inexpressible [ɪnɪk'spresəbl] ADJ inesprimibile

inextricable [ɪnɪk'strɪkəbl] ADJ inestricabile

infallibility [ɪnfælə'bɪlɪtɪ] N infallibilità

infallible [ɪn'fælɪbl] ADJ infallibile

infamous ['ɪnfəməs] ADJ infame

infamy ['ɪnfəmɪ] N infamia

infancy ['ɪnfənsɪ] N infanzia

infant ['ɪnfənt] N bambino(-a)

infantile ['ɪnfəntaɪl] ADJ infantile

infant mortality N mortalità infantile

infantry ['ɪnfəntrɪ] N fanteria

infantryman ['ɪnfəntrɪmən] N (irreg) fante m

infant school N (BRIT) scuola elementare (per bambini dall'età di 5 a 7 anni)

infatuated [ɪn'fætjueɪtɪd] ADJ: **~ with** infatuato(-a) di; **to become ~ (with sb)** infatuarsi (di qn)

infatuation [ɪnfætju'eɪʃən] N infatuazione f

615

infect [ɪnˈfɛkt] VT infettare; **infected with** (*illness*) affetto(-a) da; **to become infected** (*wound*) infettarsi

infection [ɪnˈfɛkʃən] N infezione f

infectious [ɪnˈfɛkʃəs] ADJ (*disease*) infettivo(-a), contagioso(-a); (*person, laughter, enthusiasm*) contagioso(-a)

infer [ɪnˈfəːʳ] VT: **to ~ (from)** dedurre (da), concludere (da)

inference [ˈɪnfərəns] N deduzione f, conclusione f

inferior [ɪnˈfɪərɪəʳ] ADJ inferiore; (*goods*) di qualità scadente ▸ N inferiore mf; (*in rank*) subalterno(-a); **to feel ~** sentirsi inferiore

inferiority [ɪnfɪərɪˈɔrɪtɪ] N inferiorità

inferiority complex N complesso di inferiorità

infernal [ɪnˈfəːnl] ADJ infernale

inferno [ɪnˈfəːnəu] N inferno

infertile [ɪnˈfəːtaɪl] ADJ sterile

infertility [ɪnfəːˈtɪlɪtɪ] N sterilità

infested [ɪnˈfɛstɪd] ADJ: **~ (with)** infestato(-a) (di)

infidelity [ɪnfɪˈdɛlɪtɪ] N infedeltà

in-fighting [ˈɪnfaɪtɪŋ] N lotte fpl intestine

infiltrate [ˈɪnfɪltreɪt] VT (*troops etc*) far penetrare; (*enemy line etc*) infiltrare ▸ VI infiltrarsi

infinite [ˈɪnfɪnɪt] ADJ infinito(-a); **an ~ amount of time/money** un'illimitata quantità di tempo/denaro

infinitely [ˈɪnfɪnɪtlɪ] ADV infinitamente

infinitesimal [ɪnfɪnɪˈtɛsɪməl] ADJ infinitesimale

infinitive [ɪnˈfɪnɪtɪv] N infinito

infinity [ɪnˈfɪnɪtɪ] N infinità; (*also Math*) infinito

infirm [ɪnˈfəːm] ADJ infermo(-a)

infirmary [ɪnˈfəːmərɪ] N ospedale m; (*in school, factory*) infermeria

infirmity [ɪnˈfəːmɪtɪ] N infermità f inv

inflamed [ɪnˈfleɪmd] ADJ infiammato(-a)

inflammable [ɪnˈflæməbl] ADJ infiammabile

inflammation [ɪnfləˈmeɪʃən] N infiammazione f

inflammatory [ɪnˈflæmətərɪ] ADJ (*speech*) incendiario(-a)

inflatable [ɪnˈfleɪtəbl] ADJ gonfiabile

inflate [ɪnˈfleɪt] VT (*tyre, balloon*) gonfiare; (*fig*) esagerare; gonfiare; **to ~ the currency** far ricorso all'inflazione

inflated [ɪnˈfleɪtɪd] ADJ (*style*) gonfio(-a); (*value*) esagerato(-a)

inflation [ɪnˈfleɪʃən] N (*Econ*) inflazione f

inflationary [ɪnˈfleɪʃənərɪ] ADJ inflazionistico(-a)

inflexible [ɪnˈflɛksɪbl] ADJ inflessibile, rigido(-a)

inflict [ɪnˈflɪkt] VT: **to ~ on** infliggere a

infliction [ɪnˈflɪkʃən] N inflizione f; afflizione f

in-flight [ˈɪnflaɪt] ADJ a bordo

inflow [ˈɪnfləu] N afflusso

influence [ˈɪnfluəns] N influenza ▸ VT influenzare; **under the ~ of** sotto l'influenza di; **under the ~ of alcohol** sotto l'influenza or l'effetto dell'alcool

influential [ɪnfluˈɛnʃl] ADJ influente

influenza [ɪnfluˈɛnzə] N (*Med*) influenza

influx [ˈɪnflʌks] N afflusso

info [ˈɪnfəu] N (*col*) = **information**

inform [ɪnˈfɔːm] VT: **to ~ sb (of)** informare qn (di) ▸ VI: **to ~ on sb** denunciare qn; **to ~ sb about** mettere qn al corrente di

informal [ɪnˈfɔːml] ADJ (*person, manner*) alla buona, semplice; (*visit, discussion*) informale; (*announcement, invitation*) non ufficiale; **"dress ~"** "non è richiesto l'abito scuro"; **~ language** linguaggio colloquiale

informality [ɪnfɔːˈmælɪtɪ] N semplicità, informalità; carattere m non ufficiale

informally [ɪnˈfɔːməlɪ] ADV senza cerimonie; (*invite*) in modo non ufficiale

informant [ɪnˈfɔːmənt] N informatore(-trice)

informatics [ɪnfəˈmætɪks] N informatica

information [ɪnfəˈmeɪʃən] N informazioni fpl; particolari mpl; **to get ~ on** informarsi su; **a piece of ~** un'informazione; **for your ~** a titolo d'informazione, per sua informazione

> The Italian word **informazione** is often used in the plural.
> *For further information contact the number below.*
> **Per ulteriori informazioni contattate il numero sottostante.**

information bureau N ufficio m informazioni inv

information office N ufficio m informazioni inv

information processing N elaborazione f delle informazioni

information retrieval N ricupero delle informazioni

information superhighway N autostrada informatica

information technology N informatica

informative [ɪnˈfɔːmətɪv] ADJ istruttivo(-a)

informed [ɪnˈfɔːmd] ADJ (*observer*) (ben) informato(-a); **an ~ guess** un'ipotesi fondata

informer [ɪnˈfɔːməʳ] N informatore(-trice)

infra dig [ˈɪnfrəˈdɪg] ADJ ABBR (*col*: = *infra dignitatem*) indecoroso(-a)

infra-red [ɪnfrəˈrɛd] ADJ infrarosso(-a)

infrastructure [ˈɪnfrəstrʌktʃəʳ] N infrastruttura

infrequent [ɪnˈfriːkwənt] ADJ infrequente, raro(-a)

infringe [ɪnˈfrɪndʒ] VT infrangere ▶ VI: **to ~ on** calpestare

infringement [ɪnˈfrɪndʒmənt] N: **~ (of)** infrazione f (di)

infuriate [ɪnˈfjuərɪeɪt] VT rendere furioso(-a)

infuriating [ɪnˈfjuərɪeɪtɪŋ] ADJ molto irritante

infuse [ɪnˈfjuːz] VT (with courage, enthusiasm): **to ~ sb with sth** infondere qc a qn, riempire qn di qc

infusion [ɪnˈfjuːʒən] N (tea etc) infuso, infusione f

ingenious [ɪnˈdʒiːnjəs] ADJ ingegnoso(-a)

ingenuity [ɪndʒɪˈnjuːɪtɪ] N ingegnosità

ingenuous [ɪnˈdʒɛnjuəs] ADJ ingenuo(-a)

ingot [ˈɪŋgət] N lingotto

ingrained [ɪnˈgreɪnd] ADJ radicato(-a)

ingratiate [ɪnˈgreɪʃɪeɪt] VT: **to ~ o.s. with sb** ingraziarsi qn

ingratiating [ɪnˈgreɪʃɪeɪtɪŋ] ADJ (smile, speech) suadente, cattivante; (person) compiacente

ingratitude [ɪnˈgrætɪtjuːd] N ingratitudine f

ingredient [ɪnˈgriːdɪənt] N ingrediente m; elemento

ingrowing [ˈɪngrəʊɪŋ], **ingrown** [ˈɪngrəʊn] ADJ: **~ (toe)nail** unghia incarnita

inhabit [ɪnˈhæbɪt] VT abitare

inhabitable [ɪnˈhæbɪtəbl] ADJ abitabile

inhabitant [ɪnˈhæbɪtnt] N abitante mf

inhale [ɪnˈheɪl] VT inalare ▶ VI (in smoking) aspirare

inhaler [ɪnˈheɪləʳ] N inalatore m

inherent [ɪnˈhɪərənt] ADJ: **~ (in or to)** inerente (a)

inherently [ɪnˈhɪərəntlɪ] ADV (easy, difficult) di per sé, di per se stesso(-a); **~ lazy** pigro di natura

inherit [ɪnˈhɛrɪt] VT ereditare

inheritance [ɪnˈhɛrɪtəns] N eredità

inhibit [ɪnˈhɪbɪt] VT (Psych) inibire; **to ~ sb from doing** impedire a qn di fare

inhibited [ɪnˈhɪbɪtɪd] ADJ (person) inibito(-a)

inhibiting [ɪnˈhɪbɪtɪŋ] ADJ che inibisce

inhibition [ɪnhɪˈbɪʃən] N inibizione f

inhospitable [ɪnhɔsˈpɪtəbl] ADJ inospitale

in-house [ˈɪnˈhaus] ADJ effettuato(-a) da personale interno, interno(-a) ▶ ADV (train) all'interno dell'azienda

inhuman [ɪnˈhjuːmən] ADJ inumano(-a), disumano(-a)

inhumane [ɪnhjuːˈmeɪn] ADJ inumano(-a), disumano(-a)

inimitable [ɪˈnɪmɪtəbl] ADJ inimitabile

iniquity [ɪˈnɪkwɪtɪ] N iniquità f inv

initial [ɪˈnɪʃl] ADJ iniziale ▶ N iniziale f ▶ VT

siglare ▪ **initials** NPL (of name) iniziali fpl; (as signature) sigla

initialize [ɪˈnɪʃəlaɪz] VT (Comput) inizializzare

initially [ɪˈnɪʃəlɪ] ADV inizialmente, all'inizio

initiate [ɪˈnɪʃɪeɪt] VT (start) avviare; intraprendere; iniziare; (person) iniziare; **to ~ sb into sth** iniziare qn a qc; **to ~ sb into a secret** mettere qn a parte di un segreto; **to ~ proceedings against sb** (Law) intentare causa a or contro qn

initiation [ɪnɪʃɪˈeɪʃən] N iniziazione f

initiative [ɪˈnɪʃətɪv] N iniziativa; **to take the ~** prendere l'iniziativa

inject [ɪnˈdʒɛkt] VT (liquid) iniettare; (person) fare un'iniezione a; **to ~ sb with sth** fare a qn un'iniezione di qc; (fig: money): **to ~ into** immettere in

injection [ɪnˈdʒɛkʃən] N iniezione f, puntura; **to have an ~** farsi fare un'iniezione or una puntura

injudicious [ɪndʒuˈdɪʃəs] ADJ poco saggio(-a)

injunction [ɪnˈdʒʌŋkʃən] N (Law) ingiunzione f, intimazione f

injure [ˈɪndʒəʳ] VT ferire; (wrong) fare male or torto a; (damage: reputation etc) nuocere a; (feelings) offendere; **to ~ o.s.** farsi male

injured [ˈɪndʒəd] ADJ (person, leg etc) ferito(-a); (tone, feelings) offeso(-a); **~ party** (Law) parte f lesa

injurious [ɪnˈdʒuərɪəs] ADJ: **~ (to)** nocivo(-a) (a), pregiudizievole (per)

injury [ˈɪndʒərɪ] N ferita; (wrong) torto; **to escape without ~** rimanere illeso

injury time N (Sport) tempo di ricupero

injustice [ɪnˈdʒʌstɪs] N ingiustizia; **you do me an ~** mi fa un torto, è ingiusto verso di me

ink [ɪŋk] N inchiostro

ink-jet printer [ˈɪŋkdʒɛt-] N stampante f a getto d'inchiostro

inkling [ˈɪŋklɪŋ] N sentore m, vaga idea

inkpad [ˈɪŋkpæd] N tampone m, cuscinetto per timbri

inky [ˈɪŋkɪ] ADJ macchiato(-a) or sporco(-a) d'inchiostro

inlaid [ˈɪnleɪd] ADJ incrostato(-a); (table etc) intarsiato(-a)

inland ADJ [ˈɪnlənd] interno(-a) ▶ ADV [ɪnˈlænd] all'interno; **~ waterways** canali e fiumi mpl navigabili

Inland Revenue N (BRIT) Fisco

in-laws [ˈɪnlɔːz] NPL suoceri mpl; famiglia del marito (or della moglie)

inlet [ˈɪnlɛt] N (Geo) insenatura, baia

inlet pipe N (Tech) tubo d'immissione

inmate [ˈɪnmeɪt] N (in prison) carcerato(-a); (in psychiatric hospital) ricoverato(-a)

inmost [ˈɪnməust] ADJ più profondo(-a), più intimo(-a)

inn [ɪn] N locanda

innards ['ɪnədz] NPL (col) interiora fpl, budella fpl

innate [ɪ'neɪt] ADJ innato(-a)

inner ['ɪnə'] ADJ interno(-a), interiore

inner city N centro di una zona urbana

innermost ['ɪnəməust] ADJ = **inmost**

inner tube N camera d'aria

inning ['ɪnɪŋ] N (US Baseball) ripresa; **innings** (Cricket) turno di battuta; (BRIT fig) **he has had a good innings** ha avuto molto dalla vita

innocence ['ɪnəsns] N innocenza

innocent ['ɪnəsnt] ADJ innocente

innocuous [ɪ'nɔkjuəs] ADJ innocuo(-a)

innovation [ɪnəu'veɪʃən] N innovazione f

innovative ['ɪnəu'veɪtɪv] ADJ innovativo(-a)

innuendo [ɪnju'ɛndəu] (pl **innuendoes**) N insinuazione f

innumerable [ɪ'njuːmrəbl] ADJ innumerevole

inoculate [ɪ'nɔkjuleɪt] VT: **to ~ sb with sth/ against sth** inoculare qc a qn/qn contro qc

inoculation [ɪnɔkju'leɪʃən] N inoculazione f

inoffensive [ɪnə'fɛnsɪv] ADJ inoffensivo(-a), innocuo(-a)

inopportune [ɪn'ɔpətjuːn] ADJ inopportuno(-a)

inordinate [ɪ'nɔːdɪnɪt] ADJ eccessivo(-a)

inordinately [ɪ'nɔːdɪnətlɪ] ADV smoderatamente

inorganic [ɪnɔː'gænɪk] ADJ inorganico(-a)

in-patient ['ɪnpeɪʃənt] N ricoverato(-a)

input ['ɪnput] N (Elec) energia, potenza; (of machine) alimentazione f; (of computer) input m ▶ VT (Comput) inserire, introdurre

inquest ['ɪnkwɛst] N inchiesta

inquire [ɪn'kwaɪə'] VI informarsi ▶ VT domandare, informarsi di or su; **to ~ about** informarsi di or su, chiedere informazioni su; **to ~ when/where/whether** informarsi di quando/su dove/se
▶ **inquire after** VT FUS (person) chiedere di; (sb's health) informarsi di
▶ **inquire into** VT FUS indagare su, fare delle indagini or ricerche su

inquiring [ɪn'kwaɪərɪŋ] ADJ (mind) inquisitivo(-a)

inquiry [ɪn'kwaɪərɪ] N domanda; (Law) indagine f, investigazione f; **"inquiries"** "informazioni"; **to hold an ~ into sth** fare un'inchiesta su qc

inquiry desk N (BRIT) banco delle informazioni

inquiry office N (BRIT) ufficio m informazioni inv

inquisition [ɪnkwɪ'zɪʃən] N inquisizione f, inchiesta; (Rel): **the I~** l'Inquisizione

inquisitive [ɪn'kwɪzɪtɪv] ADJ curioso(-a)

inroads ['ɪnrəudz] NPL: **to make ~ into** (savings, supplies) intaccare (seriamente)

ins. ABBR = **inches**

insane [ɪn'seɪn] ADJ matto(-a), pazzo(-a); (Med) alienato(-a)

insanitary [ɪn'sænɪtərɪ] ADJ insalubre

insanity [ɪn'sænɪtɪ] N follia; (Med) alienazione f mentale

insatiable [ɪn'seɪʃəbl] ADJ insaziabile

inscribe [ɪn'skraɪb] VT iscrivere; (book etc): **to ~ (to sb)** dedicare (a qn)

inscription [ɪn'skrɪpʃən] N iscrizione f; (in book) dedica

inscrutable [ɪn'skruːtəbl] ADJ imperscrutabile

inseam ['ɪnsiːm] N (US): **~ measurement** lunghezza interna

insect ['ɪnsɛkt] N insetto

insect bite N puntura or morsicatura di insetto

insecticide [ɪn'sɛktɪsaɪd] N insetticida m

insect repellent N insettifugo

insecure [ɪnsɪ'kjuə'] ADJ malsicuro(-a); (person) insicuro(-a)

insecurity [ɪnsɪ'kjuərɪtɪ] N mancanza di sicurezza

insensible [ɪn'sɛnsɪbl] ADJ insensibile; (unconscious) privo(-a) di sensi

insensitive [ɪn'sɛnsɪtɪv] ADJ insensibile

insensitivity [ɪnsɛnsɪ'tɪvɪtɪ] N mancanza di sensibilità

inseparable [ɪn'sɛprəbl] ADJ inseparabile

insert VT [ɪn'səːt] inserire, introdurre ▶ N ['ɪnsəːt] inserto

insertion [ɪn'səːʃən] N inserzione f

in-service ['ɪn'səːvɪs] ADJ (course, training) dopo l'assunzione

inshore ADJ ['ɪnʃɔː'] costiero(-a) ▶ ADV [ɪn'ʃɔː'] presso la riva; verso la riva

inside ['ɪn'saɪd] N interno, parte f interiore; (of road: BRIT) sinistra; (: US, in Europe etc) destra ▶ ADJ interno(-a), interiore ▶ ADV dentro, all'interno ▶ PREP dentro, all'interno di; (of time): **~ 10 minutes** entro 10 minuti ▪ **insides** NPL (col) ventre m; **~ out** adv alla rovescia; **to turn sth ~ out** rivoltare qc; **to know sth ~ out** conoscere qc a fondo; **~ information** informazioni fpl riservate; **~ story** storia segreta

inside forward N (Sport) mezzala, interno

inside lane N (Aut) corsia di marcia

inside leg measurement N (BRIT) lunghezza interna

insider [ɪn'saɪdə'] N uno(-a) che ha le mani in pasta

insider dealing, insider trading N (Stock Exchange) insider trading m inv

insidious [ɪn'sɪdɪəs] ADJ insidioso(-a)

insight ['ɪnsaɪt] N acume m, perspicacia;

(*glimpse, idea*) percezione *f*; **to gain** *or* **get an ~ into sth** potersi render conto di qc

insignia [ɪnˈsɪgnɪə] NPL insegne *fpl*

insignificant [ɪnsɪgˈnɪfɪknt] ADJ insignificante

insincere [ɪnsɪnˈsɪəʳ] ADJ insincero(-a)

insincerity [ɪnsɪnˈsɛrɪtɪ] N falsità, insincerità

insinuate [ɪnˈsɪnjueɪt] VT insinuare

insinuation [ɪnsɪnjuˈeɪʃən] N insinuazione *f*

insipid [ɪnˈsɪpɪd] ADJ insipido(-a), insulso(-a)

insist [ɪnˈsɪst] VI insistere; **to ~ on doing** insistere per fare; **to ~ that** insistere perché + *sub*; (*claim*) sostenere che

insistence [ɪnˈsɪstəns] N insistenza

insistent [ɪnˈsɪstənt] ADJ insistente

insofar [ɪnsəʊˈfɑːʳ] CONJ: **~ as** in quanto

insole [ˈɪnsəʊl] N soletta; (*fixed part of shoe*) tramezza

insolence [ˈɪnsələns] N insolenza

insolent [ˈɪnsələnt] ADJ insolente

insoluble [ɪnˈsɔljubl] ADJ insolubile

insolvency [ɪnˈsɔlvənsɪ] N insolvenza

insolvent [ɪnˈsɔlvənt] ADJ insolvente

insomnia [ɪnˈsɔmnɪə] N insonnia

insomniac [ɪnˈsɔmnɪæk] N chi soffre di insonnia

inspect [ɪnˈspɛkt] VT ispezionare; (BRIT: *ticket*) controllare

inspection [ɪnˈspɛkʃən] N ispezione *f*; controllo

inspector [ɪnˈspɛktəʳ] N ispettore(-trice); (BRIT: *on buses, trains*) controllore(-a)

inspiration [ɪnspəˈreɪʃən] N ispirazione *f*

inspire [ɪnˈspaɪəʳ] VT ispirare

inspired [ɪnˈspaɪəd] ADJ (*writer, book etc*) ispirato(-a); **in an ~ moment** in un momento d'ispirazione

inspiring [ɪnˈspaɪərɪŋ] ADJ stimolante

inst. [ɪnst] ABBR (BRIT *Comm*: = *instant*) c.m. (= *corrente mese*)

instability [ɪnstəˈbɪlɪtɪ] N instabilità

install [ɪnˈstɔːl], (BRIT) **instal** VT installare

installation [ɪnstəˈleɪʃən] N installazione *f*

installer [ɪnˈstɔːləʳ] N (*person*) installatore(-trice) *m/f*; (*Comput*) installer *m inv*

installment, (US) **instalment** [ɪnˈstɔːlmənt] N rata; (*of TV serial etc*) puntata; **in instalments** (*pay*) a rate; (*receive*) una parte per volta; (*publication*) a fascicoli

installment plan N (US) acquisto a rate

instance [ˈɪnstəns] N esempio, caso; **for ~** per *or* ad esempio; **in that ~** in quel caso; **in the first ~** in primo luogo

instant [ˈɪnstənt] N istante *m*, attimo ▶ ADJ immediato(-a); urgente; (*coffee, food*) in polvere; **the 10th ~** il 10 corrente (mese)

instantaneous [ɪnstənˈteɪnɪəs] ADJ istantaneo(-a)

instantly [ˈɪnstəntlɪ] ADV immediatamente, subito

instant message N messaggio istantaneo

instant messaging N messaggeria istantanea

instant replay N (US TV) replay *m inv*

instead [ɪnˈstɛd] ADV invece; **~ of** invece di; **~ of sb** al posto di qn

instep [ˈɪnstɛp] N collo del piede; (*of shoe*) collo della scarpa

instigate [ˈɪnstɪgeɪt] VT (*rebellion, strike, crime*) istigare; (*new ideas etc*) promuovere

instigation [ɪnstɪˈgeɪʃən] N istigazione *f*; **at sb's ~** per *or* in seguito al suggerimento di qn

instil [ɪnˈstɪl] VT: **to ~ (into)** inculcare (in)

instinct [ˈɪnstɪŋkt] N istinto

instinctive [ɪnˈstɪŋktɪv] ADJ istintivo(-a)

instinctively [ɪnˈstɪŋktɪvlɪ] ADV per istinto

institute [ˈɪnstɪtjuːt] N istituto ▶ VT istituire, stabilire; (*inquiry*) avviare; (*proceedings*) iniziare

institution [ɪnstɪˈtjuːʃən] N istituzione *f*; istituto (d'istruzione); istituto (psichiatrico)

institutional [ɪnstɪˈtjuːʃənl] ADJ istituzionale; **~ care** assistenza presso un istituto

instruct [ɪnˈstrʌkt] VT istruire; **to ~ sb in sth** insegnare qc a qn; **to ~ sb to do** dare ordini a qn di fare

instruction [ɪnˈstrʌkʃən] N istruzione *f*; **instructions (for use)** istruzioni per l'uso

instruction book N libretto di istruzioni

instructive [ɪnˈstrʌktɪv] ADJ istruttivo(-a)

instructor [ɪnˈstrʌktəʳ] N istruttore(-trice); (*for skiing*) maestro(-a)

instrument [ˈɪnstrumənt] N strumento

instrumental [ɪnstruˈmɛntl] ADJ (*Mus*) strumentale; **to be ~ in sth/in doing sth** contribuire fattivamente a qc/a fare qc

instrumentalist [ɪnstruˈmɛntəlɪst] N strumentista *mf*

instrument panel N quadro *m* portastrumenti *inv*

insubordinate [ɪnsəˈbɔːdənɪt] ADJ insubordinato(-a)

insubordination [ɪnsəbɔːdəˈneɪʃən] N insubordinazione *f*

insufferable [ɪnˈsʌfrəbl] ADJ insopportabile

insufficient [ɪnsəˈfɪʃənt] ADJ insufficiente

insufficiently [ɪnsəˈfɪʃəntlɪ] ADV in modo insufficiente

insular [ˈɪnsjuləʳ] ADJ insulare; (*person*) di mente ristretta

insulate [ˈɪnsjuleɪt] VT isolare

insulating tape [ˈɪnsjuleɪtɪŋ-] N nastro isolante

insulation [ɪnsjuˈleɪʃən] N isolamento

insulin [ˈɪnsjulɪn] N insulina

insult N ['ɪnsʌlt] insulto, affronto ▸ VT [ɪn'sʌlt] insultare

insulting [ɪn'sʌltɪŋ] ADJ offensivo(-a), ingiurioso(-a)

insuperable [ɪn'sjuːprəbl] ADJ insormontabile, insuperabile

insurance [ɪn'ʃuərəns] N assicurazione f; **fire/ life ~** assicurazione contro gli incendi/sulla vita; **to take out ~ (against)** fare un'assicurazione (contro), assicurarsi (contro)

insurance agent N agente m d'assicurazioni

insurance broker N broker m inv d'assicurazioni

insurance company N società f inv di assicurazioni

insurance policy N polizza d'assicurazione

insurance premium N premio assicurativo

insure [ɪn'ʃuə'] VT assicurare; **to ~ sb** or **sb's life** assicurare qn sulla vita; **to be insured for £5000** essere assicurato per 5000 sterline

insured [ɪn'ʃuəd] N: **the ~** l'assicurato(-a)

insurer [ɪn'ʃuərə'] N assicuratore(-trice)

insurgent [ɪn'sɔːdʒənt] ADJ ribelle ▸ N insorto(-a), rivoltoso(-a)

insurmountable [ɪnsə'mauntəbl] ADJ insormontabile

insurrection [ɪnsə'rekʃən] N insurrezione f

intact [ɪn'tækt] ADJ intatto(-a)

intake ['ɪnteɪk] N (Tech) immissione f; (of food) consumo; (Brit: of pupils etc) afflusso

intangible [ɪn'tændʒɪbl] ADJ intangibile

integral ['ɪntɪgrəl] ADJ integrale; (part) integrante

integrate ['ɪntɪgreɪt] VT integrare ▸ VI integrarsi

integrated circuit N (Comput) circuito integrato

integration [ɪntɪ'greɪʃən] N integrazione f; **racial ~** integrazione razziale

integrity [ɪn'tegrɪtɪ] N integrità

intellect ['ɪntəlekt] N intelletto

intellectual [ɪntə'lektjuəl] ADJ, N intellettuale (mf)

intelligence [ɪn'telɪdʒəns] N intelligenza; (Mil etc) informazioni fpl

intelligence quotient N quoziente m d'intelligenza

Intelligence Service N servizio segreto

intelligence test N test m inv d'intelligenza

intelligent [ɪn'telɪdʒənt] ADJ intelligente

intelligible [ɪn'telɪdʒɪbl] ADJ intelligibile

intemperate [ɪn'tempərət] ADJ immoderato(-a); (drinking too much) intemperante nel bere

intend [ɪn'tend] VT (gift etc): **to ~ sth for** destinare qc a; **to ~ to do** aver l'intenzione di fare

intended [ɪn'tendɪd] ADJ (insult) intenzionale; (effect) voluto(-a); (journey, route) progettato(-a)

intense [ɪn'tens] ADJ intenso(-a); (person) di forti sentimenti

intensely [ɪn'tenslɪ] ADV intensamente; profondamente

intensify [ɪn'tensɪfaɪ] VT intensificare

intensity [ɪn'tensɪtɪ] N intensità

intensive [ɪn'tensɪv] ADJ intensivo(-a)

intensive care N terapia intensiva; **~ unit** reparto terapia intensiva

intent [ɪn'tent] N intenzione f ▸ ADJ: **~ (on)** intento(-a) (a), immerso(-a) (in); **to all intents and purposes** a tutti gli effetti; **to be ~ on doing sth** essere deciso a fare qc

intention [ɪn'tenʃən] N intenzione f

intentional [ɪn'tenʃənl] ADJ intenzionale, deliberato(-a)

intentionally [ɪn'tenʃənəlɪ] ADV apposta

intently [ɪn'tentlɪ] ADV attentamente

inter [ɪn'tɔː'] VT sotterrare

interact [ɪntər'ækt] VI agire reciprocamente, interagire

interaction [ɪntər'ækʃən] N azione f reciproca, interazione f

interactive [ɪntər'æktɪv] ADJ (Comput) interattivo(-a)

intercede [ɪntə'siːd] VI: **to ~ (with sb/on behalf of sb)** intercedere (presso qn/a favore di qn)

intercept [ɪntə'sept] VT intercettare; (person) fermare

interception [ɪntə'sepʃən] N intercettamento

interchange N ['ɪntətʃeɪndʒ] (exchange) scambio; (on motorway) incrocio pluridirezionale ▸ VT [ɪntə'tʃeɪndʒ] scambiare; sostituire l'uno(-a) per l'altro(-a)

interchangeable [ɪntə'tʃeɪndʒəbl] ADJ intercambiabile

intercity [ɪntə'sɪtɪ] ADJ: **~ (train)** ≈ (treno) rapido

intercom ['ɪntəkəm] N interfono

interconnect [ɪntəkə'nekt] VI (rooms) essere in comunicazione

intercontinental ['ɪntəkɔntɪ'nentl] ADJ intercontinentale

intercourse ['ɪntəkɔːs] N rapporti mpl; (sexual intercourse) rapporti sessuali

interdependent [ɪntədɪ'pendənt] ADJ interdipendente

interest ['ɪntrɪst] N interesse m; (Comm: stake, share) interessi mpl ▸ VT interessare; **compound/simple ~** interesse composto/semplice; **business interests** attività fpl commerciali; **British interests in the Middle East** gli interessi (commerciali) britannici nel Medio Oriente

interested ['ɪntrɪstɪd] ADJ interessato(-a); **to be ~ in** interessarsi di

interest-free ['ɪntrɪst'friː] ADJ senza interesse

interesting ['ɪntrɪstɪŋ] ADJ interessante

interest rate N tasso di interesse

interface ['ɪntəfeɪs] N (*Comput*) interfaccia

interfere [ɪntə'fɪər] VI: **to ~ (in)** (*quarrel, other people's business*) immischiarsi (in); **to ~ with** (*object*) toccare; (*plans, duty*) interferire con

interference [ɪntə'fɪərəns] N interferenza

interfering [ɪntə'fɪərɪŋ] ADJ invadente

interim ['ɪntərɪm] ADJ provvisorio(-a) ▸N: **in the ~** nel frattempo; **~ dividend** (*Comm*) acconto di dividendo

interior [ɪn'tɪərɪər] N interno; (*of country*) entroterra ▸ADJ interiore, interno(-a); (*minister*) degli Interni

interior decorator, interior designer N decoratore(-trice) (d'interni)

interior design N architettura d'interni

interjection [ɪntə'dʒɛkʃən] N interiezione *f*

interlock [ɪntə'lɔk] VI ingranarsi ▸VT ingranare

interloper ['ɪntələupər] N intruso(-a)

interlude ['ɪntəluːd] N intervallo; (*Theat*) intermezzo

intermarry [ɪntə'mærɪ] VI imparentarsi per mezzo di matrimonio; sposarsi tra parenti

intermediary [ɪntə'miːdɪərɪ] N intermediario(-a)

intermediate [ɪntə'miːdɪət] ADJ intermedio(-a); (*Scol: course, level*) medio(-a)

interment [ɪn'tɜːmənt] N (*formal*) inumazione *f*

interminable [ɪn'tɜːmɪnəbl] ADJ interminabile

intermission [ɪntə'mɪʃən] N pausa; (*Theat, Cine*) intermissione *f*, intervallo

intermittent [ɪntə'mɪtnt] ADJ intermittente

intermittently [ɪntə'mɪtntlɪ] ADV a intermittenza

intern VT [ɪn'tɜːn] internare ▸N ['ɪntɜːn] (*US*) medico interno

internal [ɪn'tɜːnl] ADJ interno(-a); **~ injuries** lesioni *fpl* interne

internally [ɪn'tɜːnəlɪ] ADV all'interno; **"not to be taken ~"** "per uso esterno"

Internal Revenue, Internal Revenue Service N (*US*) Fisco

international [ɪntə'næʃənl] ADJ internazionale ▸N (*Brit Sport*) incontro internazionale

International Atomic Energy Agency N Agenzia Internazionale per l'Energia Atomica

International Court of Justice N Corte *f* Internazionale di Giustizia

international date line N linea del cambiamento di data

internationally [ɪntə'næʃnəlɪ] ADV a livello internazionale

International Monetary Fund N Fondo monetario internazionale

international relations NPL rapporti *mpl* internazionali

internecine [ɪntə'niːsaɪn] ADJ sanguinoso(-a)

internee [ɪntəː'niː] N internato(-a)

internet ['ɪntənɛt] N: **the ~** Internet *f*

internet café N cybercaffè *m inv*

internet service provider N Provider *m inv*

internet user N utente *mf* Internet

internment [ɪn'tɜːnmənt] N internamento

interplay ['ɪntəpleɪ] N azione e reazione *f*

Interpol ['ɪntəpɔl] N Interpol *f*

interpret [ɪn'tɜːprɪt] VT interpretare ▸VI fare da interprete

interpretation [ɪntəːprɪ'teɪʃən] N interpretazione *f*

interpreter [ɪn'tɜːprɪtər] N interprete *mf*

interpreting [ɪn'tɜːprɪtɪŋ] N (*profession*) interpretariato

interrelated [ɪntərɪ'leɪtɪd] ADJ correlato(-a)

interrogate [ɪn'tɛrəugeɪt] VT interrogare

interrogation [ɪntɛrəu'geɪʃən] N interrogazione *f*; (*of suspect etc*) interrogatorio

interrogative [ɪntə'rɔgətɪv] ADJ interrogativo(-a) ▸N (*Ling*) interrogativo

interrogator [ɪn'tɛrəgeɪtər] N interrogante *mf*

interrupt [ɪntə'rʌpt] VT, VI interrompere

interruption [ɪntə'rʌpʃən] N interruzione *f*

intersect [ɪntə'sɛkt] VT intersecare ▸VI (*roads*) intersecarsi

intersection [ɪntə'sɛkʃən] N intersezione *f*; (*of roads*) incrocio

intersperse [ɪntə'spəːs] VT: **to ~ with** costellare di

interstate ['ɪntəsteɪt] ADJ (*US*) fra stati

intertwine [ɪntə'twaɪn] VT intrecciare ▸VI intrecciarsi

interval ['ɪntəvl] N intervallo; (*Brit Scol*) ricreazione *f*, intervallo; **bright intervals** (*in weather*) schiarite *fpl*; **at intervals** a intervalli

intervene [ɪntə'viːn] VI (*time*) intercorrere; (*event, person*) intervenire

intervention [ɪntə'vɛnʃən] N intervento

interview ['ɪntəvjuː] N (*Radio, TV etc*) intervista; (*for job*) colloquio ▸VT intervistare; avere un colloquio con

interviewee [ɪntəvju'iː] N (*TV*) intervistato(-a); (*for job*) chi si presenta ad un colloquio di lavoro

interviewer ['ɪntəvjuːər] N intervistatore(-trice)

intestate [ɪn'tɛsteɪt] ADJ intestato(-a)

intestinal [ɪn'tɛstɪnl] ADJ intestinale

intestine [ɪn'tɛstɪn] N intestino; **large/small ~** intestino crasso/tenue

intimacy ['ɪntɪməsɪ] N intimità

intimate ADJ ['ɪntɪmət] intimo(-a); (*knowledge*) profondo(-a) ▶ VT ['ɪntɪmeɪt] lasciar capire

intimately ['ɪntɪmɪtlɪ] ADV intimamente

intimation [ɪntɪ'meɪʃən] N annuncio

intimidate [ɪn'tɪmɪdeɪt] VT intimidire, intimorire

intimidating [ɪn'tɪmɪdeɪtɪŋ] ADJ (*sight*) spaventoso(-a); (*appearance, figure*) minaccioso(-a)

intimidation [ɪntɪmɪ'deɪʃən] N intimidazione *f*

into ['ɪntu] PREP dentro, in; **come ~ the house** entra in casa; **he worked late ~ the night** lavorò fino a tarda notte; **~ pieces** a pezzi; **~ Italian** in italiano; **to change pounds ~ dollars** cambiare delle sterline in dollari

intolerable [ɪn'tɔlərəbl] ADJ intollerabile

intolerance [ɪn'tɔlərns] N intolleranza

intolerant [ɪn'tɔlərnt] ADJ: **~ (of)** intollerante (di)

intonation [ɪntəu'neɪʃən] N intonazione *f*

intoxicate [ɪn'tɔksɪkeɪt] VT inebriare

intoxicated [ɪn'tɔksɪkeɪtɪd] ADJ inebriato(-a)

intoxication [ɪntɔksɪ'keɪʃən] N ebbrezza

intractable [ɪn'træktəbl] ADJ intrattabile; (*illness*) difficile da curare; (*problem*) insolubile

intranet ['ɪntrənɛt] N Intranet *f*

intransigence [ɪn'trænsɪdʒəns] N intransigenza

intransigent [ɪn'trænsɪdʒənt] ADJ intransigente

intransitive [ɪn'trænsɪtɪv] ADJ intransitivo(-a)

intra-uterine device [ɪntrə'juːtəraɪn-] N dispositivo intrauterino

intravenous [ɪntrə'viːnəs] ADJ endovenoso(-a)

in-tray ['ɪntreɪ] N raccoglitore *m* per le carte in arrivo

intrepid [ɪn'trɛpɪd] ADJ intrepido(-a)

intricacy ['ɪntrɪkəsɪ] N complessità *f inv*

intricate ['ɪntrɪkət] ADJ intricato(-a), complicato(-a)

intrigue [ɪn'triːg] N intrigo ▶ VT affascinare ▶ VI complottare, tramare

intriguing [ɪn'triːgɪŋ] ADJ affascinante

intrinsic [ɪn'trɪnsɪk] ADJ intrinseco(-a)

introduce [ɪntrə'djuːs] VT introdurre; **to ~ sb (to sb)** presentare qn (a qn); **to ~ sb to** (*pastime, technique*) iniziare qn a; **may I ~ ...?** permette che le presenti ...?

introduction [ɪntrə'dʌkʃən] N introduzione *f*; (*of person*) presentazione *f*; (*to new experience*) iniziazione *f*; **a letter of ~** una lettera di presentazione

introductory [ɪntrə'dʌktərɪ] ADJ introduttivo(-a); **an ~ offer** un'offerta di lancio; **~ remarks** osservazioni *fpl* preliminari

introspection [ɪntrəu'spɛkʃən] N introspezione *f*

introspective [ɪntrəu'spɛktɪv] ADJ introspettivo(-a)

introvert ['ɪntrəuvəːt] ADJ, N introverso(-a)

intrude [ɪn'truːd] VI (*person*) intromettersi; **to ~ on** (*person*) importunare; **~ on** *or* **into** (*conversation*) intromettersi in; **am I intruding?** disturbo?

intruder [ɪn'truːdəʳ] N intruso(-a)

intrusion [ɪn'truːʒən] N intrusione *f*

intrusive [ɪn'truːsɪv] ADJ importuno(-a)

intuition [ɪntjuː'ɪʃən] N intuizione *f*

intuitive [ɪn'tjuːɪtɪv] ADJ intuitivo(-a); dotato(-a) di intuito

inundate ['ɪnʌndeɪt] VT: **to ~ with** inondare di

inure [ɪn'juəʳ] VT: **to ~ (to)** assuefare (a)

invade [ɪn'veɪd] VT invadere

invader [ɪn'veɪdəʳ] N invasore *m*

invalid N ['ɪnvəlɪd] malato(-a); (*with disability*) invalido(-a) ▶ ADJ [ɪn'vælɪd] (*not valid*) invalido(-a), non valido(-a)

invalidate [ɪn'vælɪdeɪt] VT invalidare

invalid chair N (BRIT) sedia a rotelle

invaluable [ɪn'væljuəbl] ADJ prezioso(-a); inestimabile

invariable [ɪn'vɛərɪəbl] ADJ costante, invariabile

invariably [ɪn'vɛərɪəblɪ] ADV invariabilmente; sempre; **she is ~ late** è immancabilmente in ritardo

invasion [ɪn'veɪʒən] N invasione *f*

invective [ɪn'vɛktɪv] N invettiva

inveigle [ɪn'viːgl] VT: **to ~ sb into (doing) sth** circuire qn per (fargli fare) qc

invent [ɪn'vɛnt] VT inventare

invention [ɪn'vɛnʃən] N invenzione *f*

inventive [ɪn'vɛntɪv] ADJ inventivo(-a)

inventiveness [ɪn'vɛntɪvnɪs] N inventiva

inventor [ɪn'vɛntəʳ] N inventore *mf*

inventory ['ɪnvəntrɪ] N inventario

inventory control N (*Comm*) controllo delle giacenze

inverse [ɪn'vəːs] ADJ inverso(-a) ▶ N inverso, contrario; **in ~ proportion (to)** in modo inversamente proporzionale (a)

inversely [ɪn'vəːslɪ] ADV inversamente

invert [ɪn'vəːt] VT invertire; (*object*) rovesciare

invertebrate [ɪn'vəːtɪbrɪt] N invertebrato

inverted commas [ɪn'vəːtɪd-] NPL (BRIT) virgolette *fpl*

invest [ɪn'vɛst] VT investire; (*fig: time, effort*) impiegare; (*endow*): **to ~ sb with sth** investire qn di qc ▶ VI fare investimenti; **to ~ in** investire in, fare (degli) investimenti in; (*acquire*) comprarsi

investigate [ɪn'vɛstɪgeɪt] VT investigare, indagare; (*crime*) fare indagini su

investigation [ɪnvɛstɪ'geɪʃən] N investigazione f; (of crime) indagine f

investigative [ɪn'vɛstɪɡətɪv] ADJ: **~ journalism** giornalismo investigativo

investigator [ɪn'vɛstɪɡeɪtər] N investigatore(-trice); **a private ~** un investigatore privato, un detective

investiture [ɪn'vɛstɪtʃər] N investitura

investment [ɪn'vɛstmənt] N investimento

investment income N reddito da investimenti

investment trust N fondo comune di investimento

investor [ɪn'vɛstər] N investitore(-trice); (shareholder) azionista mf

inveterate [ɪn'vɛtərət] ADJ inveterato(-a)

invidious [ɪn'vɪdɪəs] ADJ odioso(-a); (task) spiacevole

invigilate [ɪn'vɪdʒɪleɪt] VT, VI (BRIT Scol) sorvegliare

invigilator [ɪn'vɪdʒɪleɪtər] N (BRIT) chi sorveglia agli esami

invigorating [ɪn'vɪɡəreɪtɪŋ] ADJ stimolante; vivificante

invincible [ɪn'vɪnsɪbl] ADJ invincibile

inviolate [ɪn'vaɪələt] ADJ inviolato(-a)

invisible [ɪn'vɪzɪbl] ADJ invisibile

invisible assets NPL (BRIT) beni mpl immateriali

invisible ink N inchiostro simpatico

invisible mending N rammendo invisibile

invitation [ɪnvɪ'teɪʃən] N invito; **by ~ only** esclusivamente su or per invito; **at sb's ~** dietro invito di qn

invite [ɪn'vaɪt] VT invitare; (opinions etc) sollecitare; (trouble) provocare; **to ~ sb (to do)** invitare qn (a fare); **to ~ sb to dinner** invitare qn a cena
▶ **invite out** VT invitare fuori
▶ **invite over** VT invitare (a casa)

inviting [ɪn'vaɪtɪŋ] ADJ invitante, attraente

invoice ['ɪnvɔɪs] N fattura ▶VT fatturare; **to ~ sb for goods** inviare a qn la fattura per le or delle merci

invoke [ɪn'vəʊk] VT invocare

involuntary [ɪn'vɔləntrɪ] ADJ involontario(-a)

involve [ɪn'vɔlv] VT (entail) richiedere, comportare; (associate): **to ~ sb (in)** implicare qn (in); coinvolgere qn (in); **to ~ o.s. in sth** (politics etc) impegnarsi in qc

involved [ɪn'vɔlvd] ADJ involuto(-a), complesso(-a); **to feel ~** sentirsi coinvolto(-a); **to be ~ in** essere coinvolto(-a) in; **to become ~ with sb** (socially) legarsi a qn; (emotionally) legarsi sentimentalmente a qn

involvement [ɪn'vɔlvmənt] N implicazione f; coinvolgimento; impegno; partecipazione f

invulnerable [ɪn'vʌlnərəbl] ADJ invulnerabile

inward ['ɪnwəd] ADJ (movement) verso l'interno; (thought, feeling) interiore, intimo(-a) ▶ADV verso l'interno

inwardly ['ɪnwədlɪ] ADV (feel, think etc) nell'intimo, entro di sé

inwards ['ɪnwədz] ADV verso l'interno

I/O ABBR (Comput: = input/output) I/O

IOC N ABBR (= International Olympic Committee) CIO m (= Comitato Internazionale Olimpico)

iodine ['aɪəudiːn] N iodio

IOM ABBR (BRIT) = **Isle of Man**

ion ['aɪən] N ione m

Ionian Sea [aɪ'əunɪən-] N: **the ~** il mare Ionio

ionizer ['aɪənaɪzər] N ionizzatore m

iota [aɪ'əutə] N (fig) briciolo

IOU N ABBR (= I owe you) pagherò m inv

IOW ABBR (BRIT) = **Isle of Wight**

IPA N ABBR (= International Phonetic Alphabet) I.P.A. m

iPad® ['aɪpæd] N iPad® m inv

IP address N (Comput) indirizzo IP

iPhone® ['aɪfəun] N iPhone® m inv

iPlayer® ['aɪpleɪər] N iPlayer® m (trasmissioni televisive e radiofoniche della BBC trasmesse via Internet e disponibili sia in streaming che in download)

iPod® ['aɪpɔd] N iPod® m inv, lettore m MP3

IQ N ABBR (= intelligence quotient) quoziente m d'intelligenza

IRA N ABBR (= Irish Republican Army) I.R.A. f; (US) = **individual retirement account**

Iran [ɪ'rɑːn] N Iran m

Iranian [ɪ'reɪnɪən] ADJ iraniano(-a) ▶N iraniano(-a); (Ling) iranico

Iraq [ɪ'rɑːk] N Iraq m

Iraqi [ɪ'rɑːkɪ] ADJ iracheno(-a) ▶N iracheno(-a)

irascible [ɪ'ræsɪbl] ADJ irascibile

irate [aɪ'reɪt] ADJ irato(-a)

Ireland ['aɪələnd] N Irlanda; **Republic of ~** Repubblica d'Irlanda, Eire f

iris ['aɪrɪs] (pl irises [-ɪz]) N iride f; (Bot) giaggiolo, iride

Irish ['aɪrɪʃ] ADJ irlandese ▶NPL: **the ~** gli Irlandesi

Irishman ['aɪrɪʃmən] N (irreg) irlandese m

Irish Sea N: **the ~** il mar d'Irlanda

Irishwoman ['aɪrɪʃwumən] N (irreg) irlandese f

irk [əːk] VT seccare

irksome ['əːksəm] ADJ seccante

IRN N ABBR (= Independent Radio News) agenzia d'informazioni per la radio

IRO N ABBR (= International Refugee Organization) O.I.R. f (= Organizzazione Internazionale per i Rifugiati)

iron ['aɪən] N ferro; (for clothes) ferro da stiro ▶ADJ di or in ferro ▶VT (clothes) stirare; see also **irons**

▶ **iron out** VT (*crease*) appianare; (*fig*) spianare; far sparire

Iron Curtain N: **the ~** la cortina di ferro

iron foundry N fonderia

ironic [aɪˈrɔnɪk], **ironical** [aɪˈrɔnɪkl] ADJ ironico(-a)

ironically [aɪˈrɔnɪklɪ] ADV ironicamente

ironing [ˈaɪənɪŋ] N (*act*) stirare m; (*clothes*) roba da stirare

ironing board N asse f da stiro

iron lung N (*Med*) polmone m d'acciaio

ironmonger [ˈaɪənmʌŋɡəʳ] N (BRIT) negoziante m in ferramenta; **~'s (shop)** n negozio di ferramenta

iron ore N minerale m di ferro

irons [ˈaɪənz] NPL (*chains*) catene fpl

ironworks [ˈaɪənwəːks] N ferriera

irony [ˈaɪrənɪ] N ironia

irrational [ɪˈræʃənl] ADJ irrazionale; irragionevole; illogico(-a)

irreconcilable [ɪrɛkənˈsaɪləbl] ADJ irreconciliabile; (*opinion*): **~ with** inconciliabile con

irredeemable [ɪrɪˈdiːməbl] ADJ (*Comm*) irredimibile

irrefutable [ɪrɪˈfjuːtəbl] ADJ irrefutabile

irregular [ɪˈrɛɡjuləʳ] ADJ irregolare

irregularity [ɪrɛɡjuˈlærɪtɪ] N irregolarità f inv

irrelevance [ɪˈrɛləvəns] N inappropriatezza

irrelevant [ɪˈrɛləvənt] ADJ non pertinente

irreligious [ɪrɪˈlɪdʒəs] ADJ irreligioso(-a)

irreparable [ɪˈrɛprəbl] ADJ irreparabile

irreplaceable [ɪrɪˈpleɪsəbl] ADJ insostituibile

irrepressible [ɪrɪˈprɛsəbl] ADJ irrefrenabile

irreproachable [ɪrɪˈprəutʃəbl] ADJ irreprensibile

irresistible [ɪrɪˈzɪstɪbl] ADJ irresistibile

irresolute [ɪˈrɛzəluːt] ADJ irresoluto(-a), indeciso(-a)

irrespective [ɪrɪˈspɛktɪv]: **~ of** prep senza riguardo a

irresponsible [ɪrɪˈspɔnsɪbl] ADJ irresponsabile

irretrievable [ɪrɪˈtriːvəbl] ADJ (*object*) irrecuperabile; (*loss, damage*) irreparabile

irreverent [ɪˈrɛvərnt] ADJ irriverente

irrevocable [ɪˈrɛvəkəbl] ADJ irrevocabile

irrigate [ˈɪrɪɡeɪt] VT irrigare

irrigation [ɪrɪˈɡeɪʃən] N irrigazione f

irritable [ˈɪrɪtəbl] ADJ irritabile

irritant [ˈɪrɪtənt] N sostanza irritante

irritate [ˈɪrɪteɪt] VT irritare

irritating ADJ (*person, sound etc*) irritante

irritation [ɪrɪˈteɪʃən] N irritazione f

IRS N ABBR (US) = **Internal Revenue Service**

is [ɪz] VB *see* **be**

ISA [ˈaɪsə] N ABBR (= *individual savings account*) forma di investimento detassata

ISBN N ABBR (= *International Standard Book Number*) ISBN m

ISDN N ABBR (= *Integrated Services Digital Network*) ISDN f

Islam [ˈɪzlɑːm] N Islam m

Islamic [ɪzˈlæmɪk] ADJ islamico(-a)

island [ˈaɪlənd] N isola; (*also*: **traffic island**) salvagente m

islander [ˈaɪləndəʳ] N isolano(-a)

isle [aɪl] N isola

isn't [ˈɪznt] = **is not**

isolate [ˈaɪsəleɪt] VT isolare

isolated [ˈaɪsəleɪtɪd] ADJ isolato(-a)

isolation [aɪsəˈleɪʃən] N isolamento

isolationism [aɪsəˈleɪʃənɪzəm] N isolazionismo

isotope [ˈaɪsəutəup] N isotopo

ISP N ABBR (*Comput*: = *internet service provider*) provider m inv

Israel [ˈɪzreɪl] N Israele m

Israeli [ɪzˈreɪlɪ] ADJ, N israeliano(-a)

issue [ˈɪʃjuː] N questione f, problema m; (*outcome*) esito, risultato; (*of banknotes etc*) emissione f; (*of newspaper etc*) numero; (*offspring*) discendenza ▶ VT (*statement*) rilasciare; (*rations, equipment*) distribuire; (*orders*) dare; (*book*) pubblicare; (*banknotes, cheques, stamps*) emettere ▶ VI: **to ~ (from)** uscire (da), venir fuori (da); **at ~** in gioco, in discussione; **to avoid the ~** evitare la discussione; **to take ~ with sb (over sth)** prendere posizione contro qn (riguardo a qc); **to confuse** or **obscure the ~** confondere le cose; **to make an ~ of sth** fare un problema di qc; **to ~ sth to sb, ~ sb with sth** consegnare qc a qn

Istanbul [ɪstænˈbuːl] N Istanbul f

isthmus [ˈɪsməs] N istmo

IT N ABBR = **information technology**

---

it [ɪt]

PRON **1** (*specific: subject*) esso(-a) (*mostly omitted in Italian*); (: *direct object*) lo (la), l'; (: *indirect object*) gli (le); **where's my book? — it's on the table** dov'è il mio libro? — è sulla tavola; **what is it?** che cos'è?; (*what's the matter?*) cosa c'è?; **where is it?** dov'è?; **I can't find it** non lo (*or* la) trovo; **give it to me** dammelo (*or* dammela); **about/from/of it** ne; **I spoke to him about it** gliene ho parlato; **what did you learn from it?** quale insegnamento ne hai tratto?; **I'm proud of it** ne sono fiero; **in/to/at it** ci; **put the book in it** mettici il libro; **did you go to it?** ci sei andato?; **I wasn't at it** non c'ero; **above/over it** sopra; **below/under it** sotto; **in front of/behind it** lì davanti/dietro

2 (*impers*): **it's raining** piove; **it's Friday tomorrow** domani è venerdì; **it's 6 o'clock** sono le 6; **it's 2 hours on the train** sono *or* ci vogliono 2 ore di treno; **who is it? — it's me** chi è? — sono io

ITA N ABBR (BRIT: = *initial teaching alphabet*) *alfabeto fonetico semplificato per insegnare a leggere*

Italian [ɪˈtæljən] ADJ italiano(-a) ▶N italiano(-a); (*Ling*) italiano; **the Italians** gli italiani

italic [ɪˈtælɪk] ADJ corsivo(-a) ∎ **italics** NPL corsivo

Italy [ˈɪtəlɪ] N Italia

itch [ɪtʃ] N prurito ▶VI (*person*) avere il prurito; (*part of body*) prudere; **to be itching to do** avere una gran voglia di fare

itchy [ˈɪtʃɪ] ADJ che prude; **my back is ~** ho prurito alla schiena

it'd [ˈɪtd] = **it would; it had**

item [ˈaɪtəm] N articolo; (*on agenda*) punto; (*in programme*) numero; (*also*: **news item**) notizia; **items of clothing** capi *mpl* di abbigliamento

itemize [ˈaɪtəmaɪz] VT specificare, dettagliare

itemized bill [ˈaɪtəmaɪzd-] N conto dettagliato

itinerant [ɪˈtɪnərənt] ADJ ambulante

itinerary [aɪˈtɪnərərɪ] N itinerario

it'll [ˈɪtl] = **it will; it shall**

ITN N ABBR (BRIT: = *Independent Television News*) *agenzia d'informazioni per la televisione*

its [ɪts] ADJ, PRON il (la) suo(-a), i (le) suoi (sue)

it's [ɪts] = **it is; it has**

itself [ɪtˈself] PRON (*emphatic*) esso(-a) stesso(-a); (*reflexive*) si

ITV N ABBR (BRIT: = *Independent Television*) *rete televisiva indipendente*

IUD N ABBR = **intra-uterine device**

I've [aɪv] = **I have**

ivory [ˈaɪvərɪ] N avorio

Ivory Coast N Costa d'Avorio

ivory tower N torre f d'avorio

ivy [ˈaɪvɪ] N edera

Ivy League N (*US*) *vedi nota*

Ivy League è il termine usato per indicare le otto università più prestigiose degli Stati Uniti nordorientali (Brown, Columbia, Cornell, Dartmouth College, Harvard, Princeton, University of Pennsylvania e Yale).

J j

J, j [dʒeɪ] N (*letter*) J, j f *inv or* m *inv*; **J for Jack,** (*US*) **J for Jig** ≈ J come Jersey

JA N ABBR = **judge advocate**

J/A ABBR = **joint account**

jab [dʒæb] VT dare colpetti a; **to ~ sth into** affondare *or* piantare qc dentro ▶ VI: **to ~ at** dare colpetti a ▶ N colpo; (*Med: col*) puntura

jabber ['dʒæbəʳ] VT, VI borbottare

jack [dʒæk] N (*Aut*) cricco; (*Bowls*) boccino, pallino; (*Cards*) fante m
▶ **jack in** VT (*col*) mollare
▶ **jack up** VT sollevare sul cricco; (*raise: prices etc*) alzare

jackal ['dʒækl] N sciacallo

jackass ['dʒækæs] N (*also fig*) asino, somaro(-a)

jackdaw ['dʒækdɔ:] N taccola

jacket ['dʒækɪt] N giacca; (*of book*) copertura

jacket potato N patata con la buccia

jack-in-the-box ['dʒækɪnðəbɔks] N scatola a sorpresa (con pupazzo a molla)

jack-knife ['dʒæknaɪf] VI: **the lorry jack-knifed** l'autotreno si è piegato su se stesso

jack-of-all-trades [dʒækəv'ɔ:ltreɪdz] N uno che fa un po' di tutto

jack plug N (*BRIT*) jack plug f *inv*

jackpot ['dʒækpɔt] N primo premio (in denaro)

Jacuzzi® [dʒə'ku:zɪ] N vasca per idromassaggio Jacuzzi®

jade [dʒeɪd] N (*stone*) giada

jaded ['dʒeɪdɪd] ADJ sfinito(-a), spossato(-a)

jagged ['dʒægɪd] ADJ seghettato(-a); (*cliffs etc*) frastagliato(-a)

jaguar ['dʒægjuəʳ] N giaguaro

jail [dʒeɪl] N prigione f ▶ VT mandare in prigione

jailbird ['dʒeɪlbə:d] N avanzo di galera

jailbreak ['dʒeɪlbreɪk] N evasione f

jailer ['dʒeɪləʳ] N custode m del carcere

jail sentence N condanna al carcere

jalopy [dʒə'lɔpɪ] N (*col*) macinino

jam [dʒæm] N marmellata; (*of shoppers etc*) ressa; (*also:* **traffic jam**) ingorgo; (*col*) pasticcio ▶ VT (*passage etc*) ingombrare, ostacolare; (*mecha-*

nism, drawer etc) bloccare; (*Radio*) disturbare con interferenze ▶ VI (*mechanism, sliding part*) incepparsi, bloccarsi; (*gun*) incepparsi; **to get sb out of a ~** tirare qn fuori dai pasticci; **to ~ sth into** forzare qc dentro; infilare qc a forza dentro; **the telephone lines are jammed** le linee sono sovraccariche

Jamaica [dʒə'meɪkə] N Giamaica

Jamaican [dʒə'meɪkən] ADJ, N giamaicano(-a)

jamb [dʒæm] N stipite m

jammed [dʒæmd] ADJ (*door*) bloccato(-a); (*rifle, printer*) inceppato(-a)

jam-packed [dʒæm'pækt] ADJ: **~ (with)** pieno(-a) zeppo(-a) (di), strapieno(-a) (di)

jam session N improvvisazione f jazzistica

Jan. ABBR (= *January*) gen., genn.

jangle ['dʒæŋgl] VI risuonare; (*bracelet*) tintinnare

janitor ['dʒænɪtəʳ] N (*caretaker*) portiere m; (: *Scol*) bidello

January ['dʒænjuərɪ] N gennaio; *see also* **July**

Japan [dʒə'pæn] N Giappone m

Japanese [dʒæpə'ni:z] ADJ giapponese ▶ N (*pl inv*) giapponese mf; (*Ling*) giapponese m

jar [dʒɑ:ʳ] N (*container*) barattolo, vasetto ▶ VI (*sound*) stridere; (*colours etc*) stonare ▶ VT (*shake*) scuotere

jargon ['dʒɑ:gən] N gergo

jarring ['dʒɑ:rɪŋ] ADJ (*sound, colour*) stonato(-a)

Jas. ABBR = **James**

jasmin, jasmine ['dʒæzmɪn] N gelsomino

jaundice ['dʒɔ:ndɪs] N itterizia

jaundiced ['dʒɔ:ndɪst] ADJ (*fig*) invidioso(-a) e critico(-a)

jaunt [dʒɔ:nt] N gita

jaunty ['dʒɔ:ntɪ] ADJ vivace; disinvolto(-a), spigliato(-a)

Java ['dʒɑ:və] N Giava

javelin ['dʒævlɪn] N giavellotto

jaw [dʒɔ:] N mascella ■ **jaws** NPL (*Tech: of vice etc*) morsa

jawbone ['dʒɔ:bəun] N mandibola

jay [dʒeɪ] N ghiandaia

jaywalker [ˈdʒeɪwɔːkər] N pedone(-a) indisciplinato(-a)

jazz [dʒæz] N jazz m
> **jazz up** VT rendere vivace

jazz band N banda f jazz inv

jazzy [ˈdʒæzɪ] ADJ vistoso(-a), chiassoso(-a)

JCB® N scavatrice f

JCS N ABBR (US) = **Joint Chiefs of Staff**

JD N ABBR (US) titolo di studio; (: = Justice Department) ministero della Giustizia

jealous [ˈdʒɛləs] ADJ geloso(-a)

jealously [ˈdʒɛləslɪ] ADV (enviously) con gelosia; (watchfully) gelosamente

jealousy [ˈdʒɛləsɪ] N gelosia

jeans [dʒiːnz] NPL (blue-)jeans mpl

Jeep® [dʒiːp] N jeep m inv

jeer [dʒɪər] VI: **to ~ (at)** fischiare; beffeggiare; see also **jeers**

jeering [ˈdʒɪərɪŋ] ADJ (crowd) che urla e fischia
> N fischi mpl; parole fpl di scherno

jeers [ˈdʒɪəz] NPL fischi mpl

jeggings [ˈdʒɛgɪŋz] NPL jeggins mpl

Jello® [ˈdʒɛləu] N (US) gelatina di frutta

jelly [ˈdʒɛlɪ] N gelatina

jellyfish [ˈdʒɛlɪfɪʃ] N medusa

jeopardize [ˈdʒɛpədaɪz] VT mettere in pericolo

jeopardy [ˈdʒɛpədɪ] N: **in ~** in pericolo

jerk [dʒəːk] N sobbalzo, scossa; sussulto; (pej) povero(-a) scemo(-a) ▶ VT dare una scossa a ▶ VI (vehicles) sobbalzare

jerkin [ˈdʒəːkɪn] N giubbotto

jerky [ˈdʒəːkɪ] ADJ a scatti; a sobbalzi

jerry-built [ˈdʒɛrɪbɪlt] ADJ fatto(-a) di cartapesta

jerry can [ˈdʒɛrɪ-] N tanica

Jersey [ˈdʒəːzɪ] N Jersey m

jersey [ˈdʒəːzɪ] N maglia; (fabric) jersey m

Jerusalem [dʒəˈruːsələm] N Gerusalemme f

jest [dʒɛst] N scherzo; **in ~** per scherzo

jester [ˈdʒɛstər] N (Hist) buffone m

Jesus [ˈdʒiːzəs] N Gesù m; **~ Christ** Gesù Cristo

jet [dʒɛt] N (of gas, liquid) getto; (Aut) spruzzatore m; (Aviat) aviogetto

jet-black [ˈdʒɛtˈblæk] ADJ nero(-a) come l'ebano, corvino(-a)

jet engine N motore m a reazione

jet lag N (problemi mpl dovuti allo) sbalzo dei fusi orari

jetsam [ˈdʒɛtsəm] N relitti mpl di mare

jet-setter [ˈdʒɛtsɛtər] N membro del jet set

jet-ski N acquascooter m inv

jettison [ˈdʒɛtɪsn] VT gettare in mare

jetty [ˈdʒɛtɪ] N molo

Jew [dʒuː] N ebreo

jewel [ˈdʒuːəl] N gioiello

jeweller, (US) **jeweler** [ˈdʒuːələr] N orefice m, gioielliere(-a); **~'s shop** oreficeria, gioielleria

jewellery, (US) **jewelry** [ˈdʒuːəlrɪ] N gioielli mpl; **jewelry store** (US) oreficeria, gioielleria

Jewess [ˈdʒuːɪs] N (pej) ebrea

Jewish [ˈdʒuːɪʃ] ADJ ebreo(-a), ebraico(-a)

JFK N ABBR (US) = **John Fitzgerald Kennedy International Airport**

jib [dʒɪb] N (Naut) fiocco; (of crane) braccio ▶ VI (horse) impennarsi; **to ~ at doing sth** essere restio a fare qc

jibe [dʒaɪb] N beffa

jiffy [ˈdʒɪfɪ] N (col): **in a ~** in un batter d'occhio

jig [dʒɪg] N (dance, tune) giga

jigsaw [ˈdʒɪgsɔː] N (tool) sega da traforo; (also: **jigsaw puzzle**) puzzle m inv

jilbab [ˈdʒɪlbæb] N jilbab m inv

jilt [dʒɪlt] VT piantare in asso

jingle [ˈdʒɪŋgl] N (advert) sigla pubblicitaria ▶ VI tintinnare, scampanellare

jingoism [ˈdʒɪŋgəuɪzəm] N sciovinismo

jinx [dʒɪŋks] N (col) iettatura; (person) iettatore(-trice)

jitters [ˈdʒɪtəz] NPL (col): **to get the ~** aver fifa

jittery [ˈdʒɪtərɪ] ADJ (col) teso(-a), agitato(-a); **to be ~** aver fifa

jiujitsu [dʒuːˈdʒɪtsuː] N jujitsu m

job [dʒɔb] N lavoro; (employment) impiego, posto; **a part-time/full-time ~** un lavoro a mezza giornata/a tempo pieno; **that's not my ~** non è compito mio; **he's only doing his ~** non fa che il suo dovere; **it's a good ~ that ...** meno male che ...; **just the ~!** proprio quello che ci vuole!

jobber [ˈdʒɔbər] N (BRIT Stock Exchange) intermediario tra agenti di cambio

jobbing [ˈdʒɔbɪŋ] ADJ (BRIT: workman) a ore, a giornata

job centre N (BRIT) ufficio di collocamento

job creation scheme N progetto per la creazione di nuovi posti di lavoro

job description N caratteristiche fpl (di un lavoro)

jobless [ˈdʒɔblɪs] ADJ senza lavoro, disoccupato(-a) ▶ NPL: **the ~** i senza lavoro

job lot N partita di articoli disparati

job satisfaction N soddisfazione f nel lavoro

job security N sicurezza del posto di lavoro

job share VI fare un lavoro ripartito ▶ N lavoro ripartito

job specification N caratteristiche fpl (di un lavoro)

Jock [dʒɔk] N (pej) termine colloquiale per chiamare uno scozzese

jockey [ˈdʒɔkɪ] N fantino, jockey m inv ▶ VI: **to ~**

for position manovrare per una posizione di vantaggio

jockey box N (US Aut) vano portaoggetti

jockstrap ['dʒɔkstræp] N conchiglia (per atleti)

jocular ['dʒɔkjulə'] ADJ gioviale; scherzoso(-a)

jog [dʒɔg] VT urtare ▸ VI (Sport) fare footing, fare jogging; **to ~ along** trottare; (fig) andare avanti pian piano; **to ~ sb's memory** rinfrescare la memoria di qn

jogger ['dʒɔgə'] N persona che fa footing or jogging

jogging ['dʒɔgɪŋ] N footing m, jogging m

john [dʒɔn] N (US col): **the ~** il gabinetto

join [dʒɔɪn] VT unire, congiungere; (become member of) iscriversi a; (meet) raggiungere; riunirsi a ▸ VI (roads, rivers) confluire ▸ N giuntura; **to ~ forces (with)** allearsi (con or a); (fig) mettersi insieme (a); **will you ~ us for dinner?** viene a cena con noi?; **I'll ~ you later** vi raggiungo più tardi
▸ **join in** VT FUS unirsi a, prendere parte a, partecipare a ▸ VI partecipare
▸ **join up** VI incontrarsi; (Mil) arruolarsi

joiner ['dʒɔɪnə'] N (BRIT) falegname m

joinery ['dʒɔɪnərɪ] N falegnameria

joint [dʒɔɪnt] N (Tech) giuntura; giunto; (Anat) articolazione f, giuntura; (BRIT Culin) arrosto; (col: place) locale m; (: of cannabis) spinello ▸ ADJ comune; (responsibility) collettivo(-a); (committee) misto(-a)

joint account N (at bank etc) conto comune

jointly ['dʒɔɪntlɪ] ADV in comune, insieme

joint ownership N comproprietà

joint-stock company ['dʒɔɪntstɔk-] N società f inv per azioni

joist [dʒɔɪst] N trave f

joke [dʒəuk] N scherzo; (funny story) barzelletta; (also: **practical joke**) beffa ▸ VI scherzare; **to play a ~ on** fare uno scherzo a

joker ['dʒəukə'] N buffone(-a), burlone(-a); (Cards) matta, jolly m inv

joking ['dʒəukɪŋ] N scherzi mpl

jollity ['dʒɔlɪtɪ] N allegria

jolly ['dʒɔlɪ] ADJ allegro(-a), gioioso(-a) ▸ ADV (BRIT col) veramente, proprio ▸ VT (BRIT): **to ~ sb along** cercare di tenere qn su (di morale); **~ good!** (BRIT) benissimo!

jolt [dʒəult] N scossa, sobbalzo ▸ VT urtare

Jordan ['dʒɔːdən] N (country) Giordania; (river) Giordano

Jordanian [dʒɔːˈdeɪnɪən] ADJ, N giordano(-a)

joss stick ['dʒɔs-] N bastoncino d'incenso

jostle ['dʒɔsl] VT spingere coi gomiti ▸ VI farsi spazio coi gomiti

jot [dʒɔt] N: **not one ~** nemmeno un po'
▸ **jot down** VT annotare in fretta, buttare giù

jotter ['dʒɔtə'] N (BRIT) quaderno; blocco

journal ['dʒəːnl] N (newspaper) giornale m; (periodical) rivista; (diary) diario

journalese [dʒəːnəˈliːz] N (pej) stile m giornalistico

journalism ['dʒəːnəlɪzəm] N giornalismo

journalist ['dʒəːnəlɪst] N giornalista mf

journey ['dʒəːnɪ] N viaggio; (distance covered) tragitto; **how was your ~?** com'è andato il viaggio?; **the ~ takes two hours** il viaggio dura due ore; **a 5-hour ~** un viaggio or un tragitto di 5 ore

jovial ['dʒəuvɪəl] ADJ gioviale, allegro(-a)

jowl [dʒaul] N mandibola; guancia

joy [dʒɔɪ] N gioia

joyful ['dʒɔɪful], **joyous** ['dʒɔɪəs] ADJ gioioso(-a), allegro(-a)

joyride ['dʒɔɪraɪd] N: **to go for a ~** rubare una macchina per farsi un giro

joyrider ['dʒɔɪraɪdə'] N chi ruba una macchina per andare a farsi un giro

joy stick ['dʒɔɪstɪk] N (Aviat) barra di comando; (Comput) joystick m inv

JP N ABBR = **Justice of the Peace**

Jr. ABBR = **junior**

jubilant ['dʒuːbɪlnt] ADJ giubilante; trionfante

jubilation [dʒuːbɪˈleɪʃən] N giubilo

jubilee ['dʒuːbɪliː] N giubileo; **silver ~** venticinquesimo anniversario

judge [dʒʌdʒ] N giudice mf ▸ VT giudicare; (consider) ritenere; (estimate: weight, size etc) calcolare, valutare ▸ VI: **judging** or **to ~ by his expression** a giudicare dalla sua espressione; **as far as I can ~** a mio giudizio; **I judged it necessary to inform him** ho ritenuto necessario informarlo

judge advocate N (Mil) magistrato militare

judgment, judgement ['dʒʌdʒmənt] N giudizio; (punishment) punizione f; **in my judg(e)ment** a mio giudizio; **to pass judg(e)ment (on)** pronunciare un giudizio (su); (fig) dare giudizi affrettati (su)

judicial [dʒuːˈdɪʃl] ADJ giudiziale, giudiziario(-a)

judiciary [dʒuːˈdɪʃɪərɪ] N magistratura

judicious [dʒuːˈdɪʃəs] ADJ giudizioso(-a)

judo ['dʒuːdəu] N judo

jug [dʒʌg] N brocca, bricco

jugged hare [dʒʌgd-] N (BRIT) lepre f in salmì

juggernaut ['dʒʌgənɔːt] N (BRIT: huge truck) bestione m

juggle ['dʒʌgl] VI fare giochi di destrezza

juggler ['dʒʌglə'] N giocoliere(-a)

Jugoslav ['juːgəuˈslɑːv] ADJ, N = **Yugoslav**

jugular ['dʒʌgjulə'] ADJ: **~ (vein)** vena giugulare

juice [dʒuːs] N succo; (of meat) sugo; **we've run out of ~** (col: petrol) siamo rimasti a secco

juicy ['dʒuːsɪ] ADJ succoso(-a)

jukebox [ˈdʒuːkbɔks] N juke-box *m inv*
Jul. ABBR (= *July*) lug., lu.
July [dʒuːˈlaɪ] N luglio; **the first of ~** il primo luglio; **(on) the eleventh of ~** l'undici luglio; **in the month of ~** nel mese di luglio; **at the beginning/end of ~** all'inizio/alla fine di luglio; **in the middle of ~** a metà luglio; **during ~** durante (il mese di) luglio; **in ~ of next year** a luglio dell'anno prossimo; **each *or* every ~** ogni anno a luglio; **~ was wet this year** ha piovuto molto a luglio quest'anno
jumble [ˈdʒʌmbl] N miscuglio ▶ VT (*also:* **jumble up, jumble together**) mischiare, mettere alla rinfusa
jumble sale N (BRIT) ≈ vendita di beneficenza
jumbo [ˈdʒʌmbəu] ADJ: **~ jet** jumbo-jet *m inv*; **~ size** formato gigante
jump [dʒʌmp] VI saltare, balzare; (*start*) sobbalzare; (*increase*) rincarare ▶ VT saltare ▶ N salto, balzo; sobbalzo; (*Showjumping*) salto; (*fence*) ostacolo; **to ~ the queue** (BRIT) passare davanti agli altri (*in una coda*)
  ▶ **jump about** VI fare salti, saltellare
  ▶ **jump at** VT FUS (*fig*) cogliere *or* afferrare al volo; **he jumped at the offer** si affrettò ad accettare l'offerta
  ▶ **jump down** VI saltare giù
  ▶ **jump up** VI saltare in piedi
jumped-up [ˈdʒʌmptʌp] ADJ (BRIT *pej*) presuntuoso(-a)
jumper [ˈdʒʌmpəʳ] N (BRIT: *pullover*) maglione *m*; (US: *pinafore dress*) scamiciato; (*Sport*) saltatore(-trice)
jump leads, (US) **jumper cables** NPL cavi *mpl* per batteria
jump-start [ˈdʒʌmpstɑːt] VT (*car*) far partire spingendo; (*fig*) dare una spinta a, rimettere in moto
jump suit N tuta
jumpy [ˈdʒʌmpɪ] ADJ nervoso(-a), agitato(-a)
Jun. ABBR (= *June*) giu.
Jun., Junr ABBR = **junior**
junction [ˈdʒʌŋkʃən] N (BRIT: *of roads*) incrocio; (*of rails*) nodo ferroviario
juncture [ˈdʒʌŋktʃəʳ] N: **at this ~** in questa congiuntura
June [dʒuːn] N giugno; *see also* **July**
jungle [ˈdʒʌŋgl] N giungla
junior [ˈdʒuːnɪəʳ] ADJ, N: **he's ~ to me (by 2 years)**, **he's my ~ (by 2 years)** è più giovane di me (di 2 anni); **he's ~ to me** (*seniority*) è al di sotto di me, ho più anzianità di lui
junior executive N giovane dirigente *m*
junior high school N (US) scuola media (*da 12 a 15 anni*)
junior minister N (BRIT *Pol*) ministro che non fa parte del Cabinet
junior partner N socio meno anziano

junior school N (BRIT) scuola elementare (*da 8 a 11 anni*)
junior sizes NPL (*Comm*) taglie *fpl* per ragazzi
juniper [ˈdʒuːnɪpəʳ] N: **~ berry** bacca di ginepro
junk [dʒʌŋk] N (*rubbish*) cianfrusaglie *fpl*; (*cheap goods*) robaccia; (*ship*) giunca ▶ VT disfarsi di
junk bond N (*Comm*) titolo *m* spazzatura *inv*
junk dealer N rigattiere *m*
junket [ˈdʒʌŋkɪt] N (*Culin*) giuncata; (BRIT *col*): **to go on a ~** fare bisboccia
junk food N porcherie *fpl*, cibo a scarso valore nutritivo
junkie [ˈdʒʌŋkɪ] N (*col*) drogato(-a)
junk mail N pubblicità *f inv* in cassetta
junk room N (US) ripostiglio
junk shop N chincaglieria
junta [ˈdʒʌntə] N giunta
Jupiter [ˈdʒuːpɪtəʳ] N (*planet*) Giove *m*
jurisdiction [dʒuərɪsˈdɪkʃən] N giurisdizione *f*; **it falls *or* comes within/outside our ~** è/non è di nostra competenza
jurisprudence [dʒuərɪsˈpruːdəns] N giurisprudenza
juror [ˈdʒuərəʳ] N giurato(-a)
jury [ˈdʒuərɪ] N giuria
jury box N banco della giuria
juryman [ˈdʒuərɪmən] N (*irreg*) = **juror**
just [dʒʌst] ADJ giusto(-a) ▶ ADV: **he's ~ done it/left** lo ha appena fatto/è appena partito; **~ as I expected** proprio come me lo aspettavo; **~ right** proprio giusto; **it's ~ 2 o'clock** sono le 2 precise; **she's ~ as clever as you** è in gamba proprio quanto te; **~ as I arrived** proprio mentre arrivavo; **we were ~ going** stavamo uscendo; **I was ~ about to phone** stavo proprio per telefonare; **~ as he was leaving** proprio mentre se ne stava andando; **it was ~ before/enough/here** era poco prima/appena assai/proprio qui; **it's ~ me** sono solo io; **it's ~ a mistake** non è che uno sbaglio; **~ missed/caught** appena perso/preso; **~ listen to this!** senta un po' questo!; **~ ask someone the way** basta che tu chieda la strada a qualcuno; **it's ~ as good** è altrettanto buono; **it's ~ as well you didn't go** meno male che non ci sei andato; **not ~ now** non proprio adesso; **~ a minute!, ~ one moment!** un attimo!
justice [ˈdʒʌstɪs] N giustizia; **Lord Chief J~** (BRIT) presidente *m* della Corte d'Appello; **this photo doesn't do you ~** questa foto non ti fa giustizia
Justice of the Peace N giudice *m* conciliatore
justifiable [dʒʌstɪˈfaɪəbl] ADJ giustificabile
justifiably [dʒʌstɪˈfaɪəblɪ] ADV legittimamente, con ragione
justification [dʒʌstɪfɪˈkeɪʃən] N giustificazione *f*; (*Typ*) giustezza

justify – juxtaposition

justify [ˈdʒʌstɪfaɪ] VT giustificare; (Typ etc) allineare, giustificare; **to be justified in doing sth** avere ragione di fare qc

justly [ˈdʒʌstlɪ] ADV giustamente

justness [ˈdʒʌstnɪs] N giustezza

jut [dʒʌt] VI (also: **jut out**) sporgersi

jute [dʒuːt] N iuta

juvenile [ˈdʒuːvənaɪl] ADJ giovane, giovanile; (court) dei minorenni; (books) per ragazzi ▶ N giovane mf, minorenne mf

juvenile delinquency N delinquenza minorile

juvenile delinquent N delinquente mf minorenne

juxtapose [ˈdʒʌkstəpəuz] VT giustapporre

juxtaposition [dʒʌkstəpəˈzɪʃən] N giustapposizione f

Kk

K, k [keɪ] N (letter) K, k f inv or m inv; **K for King** ≈ K come Kursaal

K N ABBR (= one thousand) mille ▶ ABBR (BRIT: = Knight) titolo; (= kilobyte) K

kaftan [ˈkæftæn] N caffettano

Kalahari Desert [kæləˈhɑːrɪ-] N Deserto di Calahari

kale [keɪl] N cavolo verde

kaleidoscope [kəˈlaɪdəskəup] N caleidoscopio

kamikaze [kæmɪˈkɑːzɪ] ADJ da kamikaze

Kampala [kæmˈpɑːlə] N Kampala f

Kampuchea [kæmpuˈtʃɪə] N Kampuchea f

kangaroo [kæŋɡəˈruː] N canguro

Kans. ABBR (US) = Kansas

kaput [kəˈput] ADJ (col) kaputt inv

karaoke [kɑːrəˈəukɪ] N karaoke m inv

karate [kəˈrɑːtɪ] N karate m

Kashmir [kæʃˈmɪəʳ] N Kashmir m

Kazakhstan [kæzækˈstɑːn] N Kazakistan m

KC N ABBR (BRIT Law: = King's Counsel) avvocato della Corona; see also QC

kebab [kəˈbæb] N spiedino

keel [kiːl] N chiglia; **on an even ~** (fig) in uno stato normale
▶ **keel over** VI (Naut) capovolgersi; (person) crollare

keen [kiːn] ADJ (interest, desire) vivo(-a); (eye, intelligence) acuto(-a); (competition) serrato(-a); (edge) affilato(-a); (eager) entusiasta; **to be ~ to do** or **on doing sth** avere una gran voglia di fare qc; **to be ~ on sth** essere appassionato(-a) di qc; **to be ~ on sb** avere un debole per qn; **I'm not ~ on going** non mi va di andare

keenly [ˈkiːnlɪ] ADV (enthusiastically) con entusiasmo; (acutely) vivamente; in modo penetrante

keenness [ˈkiːnnɪs] N (eagerness) entusiasmo

keep [kiːp] (pt, pp **kept** [kept]) VT tenere; (hold back) trattenere; (feed: one's family etc) mantenere, sostentare; (a promise) mantenere; (chickens, bees, pigs etc) allevare ▶ VI (food) mantenersi; (remain: in a certain state or place) restare ▶ N (of castle) maschio; (food etc): **enough for his ~** abbastanza per vitto e alloggio; **to ~ doing sth** continuare a fare qc; fare qc di continuo; **to ~ sb from doing/sth from happening** impedire a qn di fare/che qc succeda; **to ~ sb busy/a place tidy** tenere qn occupato(-a)/un luogo in ordine; **to ~ sb waiting** far aspettare qn; **to ~ an appointment** andare ad un appuntamento; **to ~ a record** or **note of sth** prendere nota di qc; **to ~ sth to o.s.** tenere qc per sé; **to ~ sth (back) from sb** celare qc a qn; **to ~ time** (clock) andar bene; **~ the change** tenga il resto; see also **keeps**
▶ **keep away** VT: **to ~ sth/sb away from sb** tenere qc/qn lontano da qn ▶ VI: **to ~ away (from)** stare lontano (da)
▶ **keep back** VT (crowds, tears, money) trattenere ▶ VI tenersi indietro
▶ **keep down** VT (control: prices, spending) contenere, ridurre; (retain: food) trattenere, ritenere ▶ VI tenersi giù, stare giù
▶ **keep in** VT (invalid, child) tenere a casa; (Scol) trattenere a scuola ▶ VI (col): **to ~ in with sb** tenersi buono qn
▶ **keep off** VT (dog, person) tenere lontano da ▶ VI stare alla larga; **~ your hands off!** non toccare!, giù le mani!; **"~ off the grass"** "non calpestare l'erba"
▶ **keep on** VI continuare; **to ~ on doing** continuare a fare; **to ~ on (about sth)** continuare a insistere (su qc)
▶ **keep out** VT tener fuori ▶ VI restare fuori; **"~ out"** "vietato l'accesso"
▶ **keep up** VT continuare, mantenere ▶ VI mantenersi; **to ~ up with** tener dietro a, andare di pari passo con; (work etc) farcela a seguire; **to ~ up with sb** (in race etc) mantenersi al passo con qn

keeper [ˈkiːpəʳ] N custode mf, guardiano(-a)

keep-fit [kiːpˈfɪt] N ginnastica

keeping [ˈkiːpɪŋ] N (care) custodia; **in ~ with** in armonia con; in accordo con

keeps [kiːps] N: **for ~** (col) per sempre

keepsake [ˈkiːpseɪk] N ricordo

keg [kɛɡ] N barilotto

Ken. ABBR (US) = Kentucky

kennel [ˈkɛnl] N canile m ▪ **kennels** NPL canile m; **to put a dog in kennels** mettere un cane al canile

Kenya [ˈkɛnjə] N Kenia m

Kenyan [ˈkɛnjən] ADJ, N Keniano(-a), Keniota (mf)

kept [kɛpt] PT, PP of **keep**

kerb [kəːb] N (BRIT) orlo del marciapiede

kerb crawler [-ˈkrɔːləʳ] N (BRIT) chi va in macchina in cerca di una prostituta

kerbside [ˈkəːbsaɪd] N (BRIT) bordo m del marciapiede

kernel [ˈkəːnl] N nocciolo

kerosene [ˈkɛrəsiːn] N cherosene m

ketchup [ˈkɛtʃəp] N ketchup m inv

kettle [ˈkɛtl] N bollitore m

kettle drum N timpano

kettling [ˈkɛtəlɪŋ] N tecnica di contenimento forzato impiegata dalla polizia per accerchiare i manifestanti

key [kiː] N (gen, Mus) chiave f; (of piano, typewriter) tasto; (on map) leg(g)enda ▶ CPD (vital: position, industry etc) chiave inv
▶ **key in** VT (text) digitare

keyboard [ˈkiːbɔːd] N tastiera ▶ VT (text) comporre su tastiera

keyboarder [ˈkiːbɔːdəʳ] N tastierista mf

keyed up [kiːdˈʌp] ADJ: **to be ~** essere agitato(-a)

keyhole [ˈkiːhəul] N buco della serratura

keyhole surgery N chirurgia mininvasiva

keynote [ˈkiːnəut] N (Mus) tonica; (fig) nota dominante

keypad [ˈkiːpæd] N tastierino; tastierino numerico

key ring N portachiavi m inv

keystroke [ˈkiːstrəuk] N battuta (di un tasto)

kg ABBR (= kilogram) Kg

KGB N ABBR KGB m

khaki [ˈkɑːkɪ] ADJ, N cachi (m inv)

kibbutz [kɪˈbuts] N kibbutz m inv

kick [kɪk] VT calciare, dare calci a; (col: habit etc) liberarsi di ▶ VI (horse) tirar calci ▶ N calcio; (of rifle) contraccolpo; (col: thrill): **he does it for kicks** lo fa giusto per il piacere di farlo
▶ **kick around** VI (col) essere in giro
▶ **kick off** VI (Sport) dare il primo calcio

kick-off [ˈkɪkɔf] N (Sport) calcio d'inizio

kick-start [ˈkɪkstɑːt] N (also: **kick-starter**) pedale m d'avviamento

kid [kɪd] N (col: child) ragazzino(-a); (animal, leather) capretto ▶ VI (col) scherzare ▶ VT (col) prendere in giro

kid gloves NPL: **to treat sb with ~** trattare qn coi guanti

kidnap [ˈkɪdnæp] VT rapire, sequestrare

kidnapper [ˈkɪdnæpəʳ] N rapitore(-trice)

kidnapping [ˈkɪdnæpɪŋ] N sequestro (di persona)

kidney [ˈkɪdnɪ] N (Anat) rene m; (Culin) rognone m

kidney bean N fagiolo borlotto

kidney machine N rene m artificiale

Kilimanjaro [kɪlɪmənˈdʒɑːrəu] N: **Mount ~** il monte Kilimangiaro

kill [kɪl] VT uccidere, ammazzare; (fig) sopprimere; sopraffare; ammazzare ▶ N uccisione f; **to ~ time** ammazzare il tempo
▶ **kill off** VT sterminare; (fig) eliminare, soffocare

killer [ˈkɪləʳ] N uccisore m, killer m inv; assassino(-a)

killer instinct N: **to have a/the ~** essere spietato(-a)

killing [ˈkɪlɪŋ] N assassinio; (massacre) strage f; (col): **to make a ~** fare un bel colpo

kill-joy [ˈkɪldʒɔɪ] N guastafeste mf

kiln [kɪln] N forno

kilo [ˈkiːləu] N ABBR (= kilogram) chilo

kilobyte [ˈkɪləbaɪt] N (Comput) kilobyte m inv

kilogram, kilogramme [ˈkɪləugræm] N chilogrammo

kilometre, (US) kilometer [ˈkɪləmiːtəʳ] N chilometro

kilowatt [ˈkɪləuwɔt] N chilowatt m inv

kilt [kɪlt] N gonnellino scozzese

kilter [ˈkɪltəʳ] N: **out of ~** fuori fase

kimono [kɪˈməunəu] N chimono

kin [kɪn] N see **kith**; **next of kin**

kind [kaɪnd] ADJ gentile, buono(-a) ▶ N sorta, specie f; (species) genere m; **what ~ of …?** che tipo di …?; **to be two of a ~** essere molto simili; **would you be ~ enough to …?, would you be so ~ as to …?** sarebbe così gentile da …?; **it's very ~ of you (to do)** è molto gentile da parte sua (di fare); **in ~** (Comm) in natura; (fig) **to repay sb in ~** ripagare qn della stessa moneta

kindergarten [ˈkɪndəgɑːtn] N giardino d'infanzia

kind-hearted [kaɪndˈhɑːtɪd] ADJ di buon cuore

Kindle® [ˈkɪndl] N Kindle® m inv

kindle [ˈkɪndl] VT accendere, infiammare

kindling [ˈkɪndlɪŋ] N frasche fpl, ramoscelli mpl

kindly [ˈkaɪndlɪ] ADJ pieno(-a) di bontà, benevolo(-a) ▶ ADV con bontà, gentilmente; **will you ~ …** vuole … per favore; **he didn't take it ~** se l'è presa a male

kindness [ˈkaɪndnɪs] N bontà, gentilezza

kindred [ˈkɪndrɪd] ADJ imparentato(-a); **~ spirit** spirito affine

kinetic [kɪˈnɛtɪk] ADJ cinetico(-a)

king [kɪŋ] N re m inv

kingdom [ˈkɪŋdəm] N regno, reame m

kingfisher [ˈkɪŋfɪʃəʳ] N martin m inv pescatore

kingpin [ˈkɪŋpɪn] N (Tech, fig) perno

king-size [ˈkɪŋsaɪz], **king-sized** [ˈkɪŋsaɪzd] ADJ super inv; gigante; (cigarette) extra lungo(-a)

king-size bed, king-sized bed N letto king-size

kink [kɪŋk] N (of rope) attorcigliamento; (in hair) ondina; (fig) aberrazione f

kinky [ˈkɪŋkɪ] ADJ (fig) eccentrico(-a); (: col) dai gusti particolari

kinship [ˈkɪnʃɪp] N parentela

kinsman [ˈkɪnzmən] N (irreg) parente m

kinswoman [ˈkɪnzwumən] N (irreg) parente f

kiosk [ˈkiːɔsk] N edicola, chiosco; (BRIT) cabina (telefonica); (also: **newspaper kiosk**) edicola

kipper [ˈkɪpəʳ] N aringa affumicata

Kirghizia [kəːˈɡɪzɪə] N Kirghizistan

Kiribati [kɪrɪˈbætɪ] N Kiribati fpl

kiss [kɪs] N bacio ▸ VT baciare; **to ~ (each other)** baciarsi; **to ~ sb goodbye** congedarsi da qn con un bacio; **~ of life** (BRIT) respirazione f bocca a bocca

kissagram [ˈkɪsəɡræm] N servizio-burla in cui un modello viene incaricato di porgere gli auguri baciando il festeggiato

kit [kɪt] N equipaggiamento, corredo; (set of tools etc) attrezzi mpl; (for assembly) scatola di montaggio; **tool ~** cassetta or borsa degli attrezzi ▸ **kit out** VT (BRIT) attrezzare, equipaggiare

kitbag [ˈkɪtbæg] N zaino; sacco militare

kitchen [ˈkɪtʃɪn] N cucina

kitchen garden N orto

kitchen sink N acquaio

kitchen unit N (BRIT) elemento da cucina

kitchenware [ˈkɪtʃɪnwɛəʳ] N stoviglie fpl; utensili mpl da cucina

kite [kaɪt] N (toy) aquilone m; (Zool) nibbio

kith [kɪθ] N: **~ and kin** amici e parenti mpl

kitten [ˈkɪtn] N gattino(-a), micino(-a)

kitty [ˈkɪtɪ] N (money) fondo comune

kiwi [ˈkiːwiː], **kiwi fruit** N kiwi m inv

KKK N ABBR (US) = Ku Klux Klan

Kleenex® [ˈkliːnɛks] N fazzolettino di carta

kleptomaniac [klɛptəuˈmeɪnɪæk] N cleptomane mf

km ABBR (= kilometre) km

km/h ABBR (= kilometres per hour) km/h

knack [næk] N: **to have a ~ (for doing)** avere una pratica (per fare); **to have the ~ of** avere l'abilità di; **there's a ~ to doing this** c'è un trucco per fare questo

knackered [ˈnækəd] ADJ (col) fuso(-a)

knapsack [ˈnæpsæk] N zaino, sacco da montagna

knave [neɪv] N (Cards) fante m

knead [niːd] VT impastare

knee [niː] N ginocchio

kneecap [ˈniːkæp] N rotula ▸ VT gambizzare

knee-deep [ˈniːˈdiːp] ADJ: **the water was ~** l'acqua ci arrivava alle ginocchia

kneel [niːl] (pt, pp **knelt** [nɛlt]) VI (also: **kneel down**) inginocchiarsi

kneepad [ˈniːpæd] N ginocchiera

knell [nɛl] N rintocco

knelt [nɛlt] PT, PP of **kneel**

knew [njuː] PT of **know**

knickers [ˈnɪkəz] NPL (BRIT) mutandine fpl

knick-knack [ˈnɪknæk] N ninnolo

knife [naɪf] (pl **knives** [naɪvz]) N coltello ▸ VT accoltellare, dare una coltellata a; **~, fork and spoon** coperto

knife edge N: **to be on a ~** (fig) essere appeso(-a) a un filo

knight [naɪt] N cavaliere m; (Chess) cavallo

knighthood [ˈnaɪthud] N cavalleria; (title): **to get a ~** essere fatto cavaliere

knit [nɪt] VT fare a maglia; (fig): **to ~ together** unire ▸ VI lavorare a maglia; (broken bones) saldarsi; **to ~ one's brows** aggrottare le sopracciglia

knitted [ˈnɪtɪd] ADJ lavorato(-a) a maglia

knitting [ˈnɪtɪŋ] N lavoro a maglia

knitting machine N macchina per maglieria

knitting needle N ferro (da calza)

knitting pattern N modello (per maglia)

knitwear [ˈnɪtwɛəʳ] N maglieria

knives [naɪvz] NPL of **knife**

knob [nɔb] N bottone m; manopola; (BRIT): **a ~ of butter** una noce di burro

knobbly [ˈnɔblɪ], (US) **knobby** [ˈnɔbɪ] ADJ (wood, surface) nodoso(-a); (knee) ossuto(-a)

knock [nɔk] VT (strike) colpire; urtare; (fig: col) criticare ▸ VI (engine) battere; (at door etc): **to ~ at/on** bussare a ▸ N bussata; colpo, botta; **he knocked at the door** ha bussato alla porta; **to ~ a nail into sth** conficcare un chiodo in qc
▸ **knock down** VT abbattere; (pedestrian) investire; (price) abbassare
▸ **knock off** VI (col: finish) smettere (di lavorare) ▸ VT (strike off) far cadere; (col: steal) sgraffignare, grattare; **to ~ off £10** fare uno sconto di 10 sterline
▸ **knock out** VT stendere; (Boxing) mettere K.O., mettere fuori combattimento; (defeat) battere
▸ **knock over** VT (object) far cadere; (pedestrian) investire

knockdown [ˈnɔkdaun] ADJ (price) fortemente scontato(-a)

knocker [ˈnɔkəʳ] N (on door) battente m

knocking [ˈnɔkɪŋ] N colpi mpl

knock-kneed [nɔkˈniːd] ADJ che ha le gambe ad x

knockout [ˈnɔkaut] N (Boxing) knock out m inv ▸ CPD a eliminazione

k

knockout competition N (BRIT) gara ad eliminazione

knock-up ['nɔkʌp] N (*Tennis etc*) palleggio; **to have a ~** palleggiare

knot [nɔt] N nodo ▶ VT annodare; **to tie a ~** fare un nodo

knotty ['nɔtɪ] ADJ (*fig*) spinoso(-a)

know [nəu] (*pt* **knew** [nju:], *pp* **known** [nəun]) VT sapere; (*person, author, place*) conoscere ▶ VI sapere; **to ~ that ...** sapere che ...; **to ~ how to do** sapere fare; **to get to ~ sth** venire a sapere qc; **I ~ nothing about it** non ne so niente; **I don't ~ him** non lo conosco; **to ~ right from wrong** distinguere il bene dal male; **as far as I ~ ...** che io sappia ..., per quanto io ne sappia ...; **yes, I ~** sì, lo so; **I don't ~** non lo so; **to ~ about** *or* **of sth/sb** conoscere qc/qn

> Use **sapere** to refer to facts; use **conoscere** to refer to people, places, or subjects you are acquainted with.

know-all ['nəuɔ:l] N (BRIT *pej*) sapientone(-a)

know-how ['nəuhau] N tecnica; pratica

knowing ['nəuɪŋ] ADJ (*look etc*) d'intesa

knowingly ['nəuɪŋlɪ] ADV (*purposely*) consapevolmente; di complicità; (*smile, look*) con aria d'intesa

know-it-all ['nəuɪtɔ:l] N (US) = **know-all**

knowledge ['nɔlɪdʒ] N consapevolezza; (*learning*) conoscenza, sapere *m*; **to have no ~ of** ignorare, non sapere; **not to my ~** che io sappia, no; **to have a working ~ of Italian** avere una conoscenza pratica dell'italiano; **without my ~** a mia insaputa; **it is common ~ that ...** è risaputo che ...; **it has come to my ~ that ...** sono venuto a sapere che ...

knowledgeable ['nɔlɪdʒəbl] ADJ ben informato(-a)

known [nəun] PP *of* **know** ▶ ADJ (*thief, facts*) noto(-a); (*expert*) riconosciuto(-a)

knuckle ['nʌkl] N nocca
▶ **knuckle down** VI (*col*): **to ~ down to some hard work** mettersi sotto a lavorare
▶ **knuckle under** VI (*col*) cedere

knuckleduster ['nʌkldʌstə'] N tirapugni *m inv*

KO ABBR = **knock out** ▶ N K.O. *m inv* ▶ VT mettere K.O.

koala [kəu'ɑːlə] N (*also:* **koala bear**) koala *m inv*

kook [ku:k] N (US *col*) svitato(-a)

Koran [kɔ'rɑːn] N Corano

Korea [kə'riːə] N Corea; **North/South ~** Corea del Nord/Sud

Korean [kə'riːən] ADJ, N coreano(-a)

kosher ['kəuʃə'] ADJ kasher *inv*

Kosovar, Kosovan ['kɔsəvɑː', 'kɔsəvən] ADJ kosovaro(-a)

Kosovo ['kusəvəu] N Kosovo

kowtow ['kau'tau] VI: **to ~ to sb** mostrarsi ossequioso(-a) verso qn

Kremlin ['krɛmlɪn] N: **the ~** il Cremlino

KS ABBR (US) = **Kansas**

Kt ABBR (BRIT: = *Knight*) titolo

Kuala Lumpur ['kwɑːləˈlumpuə'] N Kuala Lumpur *f*

kudos ['kjuːdɔs] N gloria, fama

Kurd [kəːd] N curdo(-a)

Kuwait [ku'weɪt] N Kuwait *m*

Kuwaiti [ku'weɪtɪ] ADJ, N kuwaitiano(-a)

kW ABBR (= *kilowatt*) kw

KY, Ky. ABBR (US) = **Kentucky**

Kyrgyzstan ['kɪəgɪzstɑːn] N Kirghizistan *m*

Ll

L, l [ɛl] N (letter) L, l f inv or m inv; **L for Lucy,** (US) **L for Love** ≈ L come Livorno

L ABBR (= lake) l; (= large) taglia grande; (= left) sin.; (BRIT Aut) = **learner**

l ABBR (= litre) l

LA N ABBR (US) = **Los Angeles** ▶ ABBR (US) = **Louisiana**

La. ABBR (US) = **Louisiana**

lab [læb] N ABBR (= laboratory) laboratorio

Lab. ABBR (CANADA) = **Labrador**

label ['leɪbl] N etichetta, cartellino; (brand: of record) casa ▶ VT etichettare; classificare

labor etc ['leɪbəʳ] (US) = **labour** etc

laboratory [ləˈbɔrətərɪ] N laboratorio

Labor Day N (US) festa del lavoro

> Negli Stati Uniti e in Canada il **Labor Day**, la festa del lavoro, cade il primo lunedì di settembre. Istituito dal Congresso nel 1894, ha perso in gran parte il suo significato politico ed è un normale giorno di vacanza che conclude, con un fine settimana lungo, le ferie estive.

laborious [ləˈbɔːrɪəs] ADJ laborioso(-a)

labor union N (US) sindacato

Labour ['leɪbəʳ] N (BRIT Pol: also: **the Labour Party**) il partito laburista, i laburisti

labour, (US) **labor** ['leɪbəʳ] N (task) lavoro; (workmen) manodopera; (Med) travaglio del parto, doglie fpl ▶ VI: **to ~ (at)** lavorare duro(a); **to be in ~** (Med) avere le doglie; **hard ~** lavori mpl forzati

labour camp, (US) **labor camp** N campo dei lavori forzati

labour cost, (US) **labor cost** N costo del lavoro

labour dispute, (US) **labor dispute** N conflitto tra lavoratori e datori di lavoro

laboured, (US) **labored** ['leɪbəd] ADJ (breathing) affaticato(-a), affannoso(-a); (style) elaborato(-a), pesante

labourer, (US) **laborer** ['leɪbərəʳ] N manovale m; **farm ~** lavoratore m agricolo

labour force, (US) **labor force** N manodopera

labour-intensive, (US) **labor-intensive** [leɪbərɪnˈtɛnsɪv] ADJ che assorbe molta manodopera

labour market, (US) **labor market** N mercato del lavoro

labour pains, (US) **labor pains** NPL doglie fpl

labour relations, (US) **labor relations** NPL relazioni fpl industriali

labour-saving, (US) **labor-saving** ['leɪbəseɪvɪŋ] ADJ che fa risparmiare fatica or lavoro

labour unrest, (US) **labor unrest** N agitazioni fpl degli operai

labyrinth ['læbɪrɪnθ] N labirinto

lace [leɪs] N merletto, pizzo; (of shoe etc) laccio ▶ VT (shoe: also: **lace up**) allacciare; (drink: fortify with spirits) correggere

lacemaking ['leɪsmeɪkɪŋ] N fabbricazione f dei pizzi or dei merletti

laceration [læsəˈreɪʃən] N lacerazione f

lace-up ['leɪsʌp] ADJ (shoes etc) con i lacci, con le stringhe

lack [læk] N mancanza, scarsità ▶ VT mancare di; **through** or **for ~ of** per mancanza di; **to be lacking** mancare; **to be lacking in** mancare di

lackadaisical [lækəˈdeɪzɪkl] ADJ disinteressato(-a), noncurante

lackey ['lækɪ] N (also fig) lacchè m inv

lacklustre, (US) **lackluster** ['læklʌstəʳ] ADJ (surface) opaco(-a); (style) scialbo(-a); (eyes) spento(-a)

laconic [ləˈkɔnɪk] ADJ laconico(-a)

lacquer ['lækəʳ] N lacca; **hair ~** lacca per (i) capelli

lacy ['leɪsɪ] ADJ (like lace) che sembra un pizzo

lad [læd] N ragazzo, giovanotto; (BRIT: in stable etc) mozzo or garzone m di stalla

ladder ['lædəʳ] N scala; (BRIT: in tights) smagliatura ▶ VT smagliare ▶ VI smagliarsi

laden ['leɪdn] ADJ: **~ (with)** carico(-a) or carica(-a) (di); **fully ~** (truck, ship) a pieno carico

ladle ['leɪdl] N mestolo

lady ['leɪdɪ] N signora; dama; **L~ Smith** lady Smith; **the ladies' (toilets)** i gabinetti per signore; **a ~ doctor** una dottoressa

ladybird ['leɪdɪbəːd], (US) **ladybug** ['leɪdɪbʌg] N coccinella

lady-in-waiting ['leɪdɪɪn'weɪtɪŋ] N dama di compagnia

ladykiller ['leɪdɪkɪləʳ] N dongiovanni m inv

ladylike ['leɪdɪlaɪk] ADJ da signora, distinto(-a)

ladyship ['leɪdɪʃɪp] N: **your L~** signora contessa etc

lag [læg] N (of time) lasso, intervallo ▶ VI (also: **lag behind**) trascinarsi ▶ VT (pipes) rivestire di materiale isolante

lager ['lɑːgəʳ] N lager m inv

lager lout N (BRIT pej) giovinastro ubriaco

lagging ['lægɪŋ] N rivestimento di materiale isolante

lagoon [lə'guːn] N laguna

Lagos ['leɪgɔs] N Lagos f

laid [leɪd] PT, PP of **lay**

laid-back [leɪd'bæk] ADJ (col) rilassato(-a), tranquillo(-a)

lain [leɪn] PP of **lie**

lair [lɛəʳ] N covo, tana

laissez-faire [lɛseɪ'fɛəʳ] N liberismo

laity ['leɪətɪ] N laici mpl

lake [leɪk] N lago

Lake District N: **the ~** (BRIT) la regione dei laghi

lamb [læm] N agnello

lamb chop N cotoletta d'agnello

lambskin ['læmskɪn] N (pelle f d')agnello

lambswool ['læmzwul] N lamb's wool m

lame [leɪm] ADJ zoppo(-a); (excuse etc) zoppicante; **~ duck** (fig: person) persona inetta; (firm) azienda traballante

lamely ['leɪmlɪ] ADV (fig) in modo poco convincente

lament [lə'mɛnt] N lamento ▶ VT lamentare, piangere

lamentable ['læməntəbl] ADJ doloroso(-a); deplorevole

laminated ['læmɪneɪtɪd] ADJ laminato(-a)

lamp [læmp] N lampada

lamplight ['læmplaɪt] N: **by ~** a lume della lampada

lampoon [læm'puːn] N satira

lamppost ['læmppəust] N (BRIT) lampione m

lampshade ['læmpʃeɪd] N paralume m

lance [lɑːns] N lancia ▶ VT (Med) incidere

lance corporal N (BRIT) caporale m

lancet ['lɑːnsɪt] N (Med) bisturi m inv

Lancs [læŋks] ABBR (BRIT) = **Lancashire**

land [lænd] N (as opposed to sea) terra (ferma); (country) paese m; (soil) terreno; suolo; (estate) terreni mpl, terre fpl ▶ VI (from ship) sbarcare; (Aviat) atterrare; (fig: fall) cadere ▶ VT (obtain) acchiappare; (passengers) sbarcare; (goods) scaricare; **to go/travel by ~** andare/viaggiare per via di terra; **to own ~** possedere dei terreni, avere delle proprietà (terriere); **to ~ sb with sth** affibbiare qc a qn; **to ~ on one's feet** cadere in piedi; (fig: to be lucky) cascar bene
▶ **land up** VI andare a finire

landed gentry ['lændɪd-] N proprietari mpl terrieri

landfill site ['lændfɪl-] N discarica dove i rifiuti vengono sepolti

landing ['lændɪŋ] N (from ship) sbarco; (Aviat) atterraggio; (of staircase) pianerottolo

landing card N carta di sbarco

landing craft N mezzo da sbarco

landing gear N (Aviat) carrello d'atterraggio

landing stage N pontile m da sbarco

landing strip N pista d'atterraggio

landlady ['lændleɪdɪ] N padrona or proprietaria di casa

landline ['lændlaɪn] N telefono fisso

landlocked ['lændlɔkt] ADJ senza sbocco sul mare

landlord ['lændlɔːd] N padrone m or proprietario di casa; (of pub etc) padrone m

landlubber ['lændlʌbəʳ] N marinaio d'acqua dolce

landmark ['lændmɑːk] N punto di riferimento; (fig) pietra miliare

landowner ['lændəunəʳ] N proprietario(-a) terriero(-a)

landscape ['lænskeɪp] N paesaggio

landscape architect, landscape gardener N paesaggista mf

landscape painting N (Art) paesaggistica

landslide ['lændslaɪd] N (Geo) frana; (fig: Pol) valanga

lane [leɪn] N (in country) viottolo; (in town) stradina; (Aut, in race) corsia; **shipping ~** rotta (marittima); **"get in ~"** "immettersi in corsia"

language ['læŋgwɪdʒ] N lingua; (way one speaks) linguaggio; **bad ~** linguaggio volgare

> Use **lingua** to refer to a language such as Italian or English; use **linguaggio** for a way of communicating, e.g. scientific language **il linguaggio scientifico**.

language laboratory N laboratorio linguistico

language school N scuola di lingue

languid ['læŋgwɪd] ADJ languente, languido(-a)

languish ['læŋgwɪʃ] VI languire

lank [læŋk] ADJ (hair) liscio(-a) e opaco(-a)

lanky ['læŋkɪ] ADJ allampanato(-a)

lanolin, lanoline ['lænəlɪn] N lanolina

lantern ['læntn] N lanterna

Laos [lauz] N Laos m

lap [læp] N (of track) giro; **in** or **on one's ~** in grembo ▶ VT (also: **lap up**) papparsi, leccare ▶ VI (waves) sciabordare
▶ **lap up** VT (fig: compliments, attention) bearsi di

La Paz [læ'pæz] N La Paz f

lapdog ['læpdɔg] N cane m da grembo

lapel [lə'pɛl] N risvolto

Lapland ['læplænd] N Lapponia

Lapp [læp] ADJ lappone ▶ N lappone mf; (Ling) lappone m

lapse [læps] N lapsus m inv; (longer) caduta; (fault) mancanza; (in behaviour) scorrettezza ▶ VI (law, act) cadere; (ticket, passport, membership, contract) scadere; **to ~ into bad habits** pigliare cattive abitudini; **~ of time** spazio di tempo; **a ~ of memory** un vuoto di memoria

laptop ['læptɔp] N (also: **laptop computer**) laptop m inv

larceny ['lɑ:sənɪ] N furto

lard [lɑ:d] N lardo

larder OPAL['lɑ:dəʳ] N dispensa

large [lɑ:dʒ] ADJ grande; (person, animal) grosso(-a) ▶ ADV: **by and ~** generalmente; **at ~** (free) in libertà; (generally) in generale; nell'insieme; **to make larger** ingrandire; **a ~ number of people** molta gente; **on a ~ scale** su vasta scala

largely ['lɑ:dʒlɪ] ADV in gran parte

large-scale ['lɑ:dʒ'skeɪl] ADJ (map, drawing etc) in grande scala; (reforms, business activities) su vasta scala

lark [lɑ:k] N (bird) allodola; (joke) scherzo, gioco
▶ **lark about** VI fare lo(la) stupido(-a)

larrikin ['lærɪkɪn] N (AUSTRALIA, NEW ZEALAND col) furfante mf

larva ['lɑ:və] N (pl **larvae** [-i:]) N larva

laryngitis [lærɪn'dʒaɪtɪs] N laringite f

larynx ['lærɪŋks] N laringe f

lasagne [lə'zænjə] N lasagne fpl

lascivious [lə'sɪvɪəs] ADJ lascivo(-a)

laser ['leɪzəʳ] N laser m inv

laser beam N raggio m laser inv

laser printer N stampante f laser inv

lash [læʃ] N frustata; (also: **eyelash**) ciglio ▶ VT frustare; (tie) legare; **to ~ to/together** legare a /insieme
▶ **lash down** VT assicurare (con corde) ▶ VI (rain) scrosciare
▶ **lash out** VI: **to ~ out (at** or **against sb/sth)** attaccare (qn/qc); **to ~ out (on sth)** (col: spend) spendere un sacco di soldi (per qc)

lashing ['læʃɪŋ] N (beating) frustata, sferzata; **lashings of** (BRIT old) un mucchio di, una montagna di

lass [læs] N ragazza

lasso [læ'su:] N laccio ▶ VT acchiappare con il laccio

last [lɑ:st] ADJ ultimo(-a); (week, month, year) scorso(-a), passato(-a) ▶ ADV per ultimo ▶ VI durare; **~ week** la settimana scorsa; **~ night** ieri sera, la notte scorsa; **at ~** finalmente, alla fine; **~ but one** penultimo(-a); **the ~ time** l'ultima volta; **it lasts (for) 2 hours** dura 2 ore

last-ditch ['lɑ:st'dɪtʃ] ADJ ultimo(-a) e disperato(-a)

lasting ['lɑ:stɪŋ] ADJ durevole

lastly ['lɑ:stlɪ] ADV infine, per finire, per ultimo

last-minute ['lɑ:stmɪnɪt] ADJ fatto(-a) (or preso(-a) etc) all'ultimo momento

latch [lætʃ] N chiavistello; (automatic lock) serratura a scatto
▶ **latch on to** VT FUS (cling to: person) attaccarsi a, appiccicarsi a; (idea) afferrare, capire

latchkey ['lætʃki:] N chiave f di casa

late [leɪt] ADJ (not on time) in ritardo; (far on in day etc) tardi inv; tardo(-a); (recent) recente, ultimo(-a); (former) ex inv; (dead) defunto(-a) ▶ ADV tardi; (behind time, schedule) in ritardo; **to be (10 minutes) ~** essere in ritardo (di 10 minuti); **to work ~** lavorare fino a tardi; **~ in life** in età avanzata; **sorry I'm ~** scusi il ritardo; **the flight is two hours ~** il volo ha due ore di ritardo; **it's too ~** è troppo tardi; **of ~** di recente; **in the ~ afternoon** nel tardo pomeriggio; **in ~ May** verso la fine di maggio; **the ~ Mr X** il defunto Signor X

latecomer ['leɪtkʌməʳ] N ritardatario(-a)

lately ['leɪtlɪ] ADV recentemente

lateness ['leɪtnɪs] N (of person) ritardo; (of event) tardezza, ora tarda

latent ['leɪtnt] ADJ latente; **~ defect** vizio occulto

later ['leɪtəʳ] ADJ (date etc) posteriore; (version etc) successivo(-a) ▶ ADV più tardi; **~ on today** oggi più tardi

lateral ['lætərl] ADJ laterale

latest ['leɪtɪst] ADJ ultimo(-a), più recente; **at the ~** al più tardi; **the ~ news** le ultime notizie

latex ['leɪtɛks] N latice m

lath [læθ] N (pl **laths** [læðz]) assicella

lathe [leɪð] N tornio

lather ['lɑ:ðəʳ] N schiuma di sapone ▶ VT insaponare ▶ VI far schiuma

Latin ['lætɪn] N latino ▶ ADJ latino(-a)

Latin America N America Latina

Latin American ADJ sudamericano(-a)

latitude ['lætɪtju:d] N latitudine f; (fig: freedom) libertà d'azione

latrine [lə'tri:n] N latrina

latter ['lætəʳ] ADJ secondo(-a); più recente ▶ N: **the ~** quest'ultimo, il secondo

latterly ['lætəlɪ] ADV recentemente, negli ultimi tempi

lattice ['lætɪs] N traliccio; graticolato

lattice window N finestra con vetrata a losanghe

Latvia ['lætvɪə] N Lettonia

Latvian ['lætvɪən] ADJ lettone inv ▶ N lettone mf; (Ling) lettone m

laudable ['lɔ:dəbl] ADJ lodevole

laudatory ['lɔ:dətrɪ] ADJ elogiativo(-a)

laugh [lɑ:f] N risata ▶ VI ridere
▶ **laugh at** VT FUS (misfortune etc) ridere di; **I laughed at his joke** la sua barzelletta mi fece ridere
▶ **laugh off** VT prendere alla leggera

laughable ['lɑ:fəbl] ADJ ridicolo(-a)

laughing ['lɑ:fɪŋ] ADJ (face) ridente; **this is no ~ matter** non è una cosa da ridere

laughing gas N gas m esilarante

laughing stock N: **the ~ of** lo zimbello di

laughter ['lɑ:ftə'] N riso; risate fpl

launch [lɔ:ntʃ] N (of rocket, product etc) lancio; (of new ship) varo; (boat) scialuppa; (also: **motor launch**) lancia ▶ VT (rocket, product) lanciare; (ship, plan) varare
▶ **launch into** VT FUS lanciarsi in
▶ **launch out** VI: **to ~ out (into)** lanciarsi (in)

launching ['lɔ:ntʃɪŋ] N lancio; varo

launch pad, launching pad N rampa di lancio

launder ['lɔ:ndə'] VT lavare e stirare

Launderette® [lɔ:n'drɛt], **Laundromat**® (US) ['lɔ:ndrəmæt] N lavanderia (automatica)

laundry ['lɔ:ndrɪ] N lavanderia; (clothes) biancheria; (: dirty) panni mpl da lavare; **to do the ~** fare il bucato

laureate ['lɔ:rɪət] ADJ see **poet laureate**

laurel ['lɔrl] N lauro, alloro; **to rest on one's laurels** riposare or dormire sugli allori

Lausanne [ləu'zæn] N Losanna

lava ['lɑ:və] N lava

lavatory ['lævətərɪ] N gabinetto

lavatory paper N (BRIT) carta igienica

lavender ['lævəndə'] N lavanda

lavish ['lævɪʃ] ADJ copioso(-a), abbondante; sontuoso(-a); (giving freely): **~ with** prodigo(-a) di, largo(-a) in ▶ VT: **to ~ sth on sb/sth** colmare qn/qc di qc

lavishly ['lævɪʃlɪ] ADV (give, spend) generosamente; (furnished) sontuosamente, lussuosamente

law [lɔ:] N legge f; **against the ~** contro la legge; **to study ~** studiare diritto; **to go to ~** (BRIT) ricorrere alle vie legali; **civil/criminal ~** diritto civile/penale

law-abiding ['lɔ:əbaɪdɪŋ] ADJ ubbidiente alla legge

law and order N l'ordine m pubblico

lawbreaker ['lɔ:breɪkə'] N violatore(-trice) della legge

law court N tribunale m, corte f di giustizia

lawful ['lɔ:ful] ADJ legale, lecito(-a)

lawfully ['lɔ:fəlɪ] ADV legalmente

lawless ['lɔ:lɪs] ADJ senza legge; illegale

Law Lords NPL (BRIT) ≈ Corte f Suprema

lawmaker ['lɔ:meɪkə'] N legislatore(-trice)

lawn [lɔ:n] N tappeto erboso

lawnmower ['lɔ:nməuə'] N tosaerba m inv or f inv

lawn tennis N tennis m su prato

law school N facoltà f inv di legge

law student N studente(-essa) di legge

lawsuit ['lɔ:su:t] N processo, causa; **to bring a ~ against** intentare causa a

lawyer ['lɔ:jə'] N (consultant, with company) giurista mf; (for sales, wills etc) ≈ notaio; (partner, in court) ≈ avvocato(-essa)

lax [læks] ADJ (conduct) rilassato(-a); (person: careless) negligente; (: on discipline) permissivo(-a)

laxative ['læksətɪv] N lassativo

laxity ['læksɪtɪ] N rilassatezza; negligenza

lay [leɪ] PT of **lie** ▶ ADJ laico(-a); secolare; (not expert) profano(-a) ▶ VT (pt, pp **laid** [leɪd]) posare, mettere; (eggs) fare; (trap) tendere; (plans) fare, elaborare; **to ~ the table** apparecchiare la tavola; **to ~ the facts/one's proposals before sb** presentare i fatti/delle proposte a qn; **to get laid** (col!) scopare (!), essere scopato(-a) (!)
▶ **lay aside, lay by** VT mettere da parte
▶ **lay down** VT mettere giù; (rules etc) formulare, fissare; **to ~ down the law** (fig) dettar legge; **to ~ down one's life** dare la propria vita
▶ **lay in** VT fare una scorta di
▶ **lay into** VT FUS (col: attack, scold) aggredire
▶ **lay off** VT (workers) licenziare
▶ **lay on** VT (water, gas) installare, mettere; (provide: meal etc) fornire; (paint) applicare
▶ **lay out** VT (design) progettare; (display) presentare; (spend) sborsare
▶ **lay up** VT (provisions) accumulare; (ship) mettere in disarmo; (person) costringere a letto

layabout ['leɪəbaut] N sfaccendato(-a), fannullone(-a)

lay-by ['leɪbaɪ] N (BRIT) piazzola (di sosta)

lay days NPL (Naut) stallie fpl

layer ['leɪə'] N strato

layette [leɪ'ɛt] N corredino (per neonato)

layman ['leɪmən] N (irreg) laico; profano

lay-off ['leɪɔf] N sospensione f, licenziamento

layout ['leɪaut] N lay-out m inv, disposizione f; (Press) impaginazione f

laze [leɪz] VI oziare

laziness ['leɪzɪnɪs] N pigrizia

lazy ['leɪzɪ] ADJ pigro(-a)

lb. ABBR (= pound (weight)) lb.

lbw ABBR (Cricket: = leg before wicket) fallo dovuto al fatto che il giocatore ha la gamba davanti alla porta

LC N ABBR (*US*) = **Library of Congress**

lc ABBR (*Typ*) = **lower case**

L/C ABBR = **letter of credit**

LCD N ABBR = **liquid crystal display**

Ld ABBR (*BRIT*: = *lord*) titolo

LDS N ABBR (*BRIT*: = *Licentiate in Dental Surgery*) specializzazione dopo la laurea; (= *Latter-day Saints*) Chiesa di Gesù Cristo dei Santi dell'Ultimo Giorno

LEA N ABBR (*BRIT*: = *local education authority*) ≈ Provveditorato degli Studi

lead¹ [li:d] (*pt, pp* **led** [lɛd]) N (*front position*) posizione f di testa; (*distance, time ahead*) vantaggio; (*clue*) indizio; (*Elec*) filo (elettrico); (*for dog*) guinzaglio; (*Theat*) parte f principale ▶ VT menare, guidare, condurre; (*induce*) indurre; (*be leader of*) essere a capo di; (*: orchestra*: *BRIT*) essere il primo violino di; (*: US*) dirigere; (*Sport*) essere in testa a ▶ VI condurre; (*Sport*) essere in testa; **in the ~ in** testa; **to ~ the way** fare strada; **to take the ~** (*Sport*) passare in testa; (*fig*) prendere l'iniziativa; **to ~ to** menare a; condurre a; portare a; **to ~ astray** sviare; **to ~ sb to believe that ...** far credere a qn che ...; **to ~ sb to do sth** portare qn a fare qc
  ▶ **lead away** VT condurre via
  ▶ **lead back** VT riportare, ricondurre
  ▶ **lead off** VT portare ▶ VI partire da
  ▶ **lead on** VT (*tease*) tenere sulla corda
  ▶ **lead on to** VT (*induce*) portare a
  ▶ **lead up to** VT FUS portare a; (*fig*) preparare la strada per

lead² [lɛd] N (*metal*) piombo; (*in pencil*) mina

leaded [ˈlɛdɪd] ADJ (*petrol*) con piombo; **~ windows** vetrate *fpl* (artistiche)

leaden [ˈlɛdn] ADJ di piombo

leader [ˈliːdəʳ] N capo; leader *m inv*; (*in newspaper*) articolo di fondo; (*Sport*) chi è in testa; **they are leaders in their field** (*fig*) sono all'avanguardia nel loro campo; **the L~ of the House** (*BRIT*) il capo della maggioranza ministeriale

leadership [ˈliːdəʃɪp] N direzione f; capacità di comando; **under the ~ of ...** sotto la direzione *or* guida di ...; **qualities of ~** qualità *fpl* di un capo

lead-free [ˈlɛdfriː] ADJ senza piombo

leading [ˈliːdɪŋ] ADJ primo(-a), principale; **a ~ question** una domanda tendenziosa; **~ role** ruolo principale

leading lady N (*Theat*) prima attrice

leading light N (*person*) personaggio di primo piano

leading man N (*irreg*) (*Theat*) primo attore

lead pencil [lɛd-] N matita con la mina di grafite

lead poisoning [lɛd-] N saturnismo

lead singer [liːd-] N *cantante alla testa di un gruppo*

lead time [liːd-] N (*Comm*) tempo di consegna

lead weight [lɛd-] N piombino, piombo

leaf [liːf] (*pl* **leaves** [liːvz]) N foglia; (*of table*) ribalta; **to turn over a new ~** (*fig*) cambiar vita; **to take a ~ out of sb's book** (*fig*) prendere esempio da qn
  ▶ **leaf through** VT (*book*) sfogliare

leaflet [ˈliːflɪt] N dépliant *m inv*; (*Pol, Rel*) volantino

leafleting [ˈliːflətɪŋ] N volantinaggio *m*

leafy [ˈliːfɪ] ADJ ricco(-a) di foglie

league [liːg] N lega; (*Football*) campionato; **to be in ~ with** essere in lega con

league table N classifica

leak [liːk] N (*out*) fuga; (*in*) infiltrazione f; (*fig: of information*) fuga di notizie; (*security leak*) fuga d'informazioni ▶ VI (*roof, bucket*) perdere; (*liquid*) uscire; (*shoes*) lasciar passare l'acqua ▶ VT (*liquid*) spandere; (*information*) divulgare
  ▶ **leak out** VI uscire; (*information*) trapelare

leakage [ˈliːkɪdʒ] N (*of water, gas etc*) perdita

leaky [ˈliːkɪ] ADJ (*pipe, bucket, roof*) che perde; (*shoe*) che lascia passare l'acqua; (*boat*) che fa acqua

lean [liːn] (*pt, pp* **leaned** [liːnd] *or* **leant** [lɛnt]) ADJ magro(-a) ▶ N (*of meat*) carne f magra ▶ VT: **to ~ sth on** appoggiare qc su ▶ VI (*slope*) pendere; (*rest*): **to ~ against** appoggiarsi contro; essere appoggiato(-a) a; **to ~ on** appoggiarsi a
  ▶ **lean back** VT sporgersi indietro
  ▶ **lean forward** VI sporgersi in avanti
  ▶ **lean out** VI: **to ~ out (of)** sporgersi (da)
  ▶ **lean over** VI inclinarsi

leaning [ˈliːnɪŋ] N: **~ (towards)** propensione f (per) ▶ ADJ inclinato(-a), pendente; **the L~ Tower of Pisa** la torre (pendente) di Pisa

leant [lɛnt] PT, PP *of* **lean**

lean-to [ˈliːntuː] N (*roof*) tettoia; (*building*) edificio con tetto appoggiato ad altro edificio

leap [liːp] (*pt, pp* **leaped** [liːpt] *or* **leapt** [lɛpt]) N salto, balzo ▶ VI saltare, balzare; **to ~ at an offer** afferrare al volo una proposta
  ▶ **leap up** VI (*person*) alzarsi d'un balzo, balzare su

leapfrog [ˈliːpfrɔg] N gioco della cavallina ▶ VI: **to ~ over sb/sth** saltare (alla cavallina) qn/qc

leapt [lɛpt] PT, PP *of* **leap**

leap year N anno bisestile

learn [lɜːn] (*pt, pp* **learned** [lɜːnd] *or* **learnt** [lɜːnt]) VT, VI imparare; **to ~ (how) to do sth** imparare a fare qc; **to ~ that ...** apprendere che ...; **to ~ about sth** (*Scol*) studiare qc; (*hear*) apprendere qc; **we were sorry to ~ that it was closing down** la notizia della chiusura ci ha fatto dispiacere

learned [ˈlɜːnɪd] ADJ erudito(-a), dotto(-a)

learner [ˈlɜːnəʳ] N principiante *mf*; apprendista *mf*; **he's a ~ (driver)** (*BRIT*) sta imparando a guidare

learning ['lɜ:nɪŋ] N erudizione f, sapienza

learnt [lɜ:nt] PT, PP of **learn**

lease [li:s] N contratto d'affitto ▸ VT affittare; **on ~** in affitto
▸ **lease back** VT effettuare un lease-back da

leaseback ['li:sbæk] N lease-back m inv

leasehold ['li:shəʊld] N (contract) contratto di affitto (a lungo termine con responsabilità simili a quelle di un proprietario) ▸ ADJ in affitto

leash [li:ʃ] N guinzaglio

least [li:st] ADJ: **the ~** (+ noun) il (la) più piccolo(-a), il (la) minimo(-a); (smallest amount of) il (la) meno ▸ ADV (+ verb) meno; **the ~** (+ adjective): **the ~ beautiful girl** la ragazza meno bella; **the ~ expensive** il (la) meno caro(-a); **the ~ possible effort** il minimo sforzo possibile; **I have the ~ money** ho meno denaro di tutti; **at ~** almeno; **not in the ~** affatto, per nulla

leather ['lɛðəʳ] N (soft) pelle f; (hard) cuoio ▸ CPD di or in pelle; di cuoio; **~ goods** pelletteria, pelletterie fpl

leave [li:v] (pt, pp **left** [lɛft]) VT lasciare; (go away from) partire da ▸ VI partire, andarsene; (bus, train) partire ▸ N (time off) congedo m; (Mil, consent) licenza; **to be left** rimanere; **there's some milk left over** c'è rimasto del latte; **to take one's ~ of** congedarsi di; **he's already left for the airport** è già uscito per andare all'aeroporto; **to ~ school** finire la scuola; **~ it to me!** ci penso io!, lascia fare a me!; **on ~** in congedo; **on ~ of absence** in permesso; (public employee) in congedo; (Mil) in licenza
▸ **leave behind** VT (also fig) lasciare; (forget) dimenticare
▸ **leave off** VT non mettere; (BRIT col: stop): **to ~ off doing sth** smetterla or piantarla di fare qc
▸ **leave on** VT lasciare su; (light, fire, cooker) lasciare acceso(-a)
▸ **leave out** VT omettere, tralasciare

leaver [li:vəʳ] N (BRIT: from EU) sostenitore dell'uscita del Regno Unito dall'Unione Europea

leaves [li:vz] NPL of **leaf**

leavetaking ['li:vteɪkɪŋ] N commiato, addio

Lebanese [lɛbə'ni:z] ADJ, N (pl inv) libanese (mf)

Lebanon ['lɛbənən] N Libano

lecherous ['lɛtʃərəs] ADJ lascivo(-a), lubrico(-a)

lectern ['lɛktə:n] N leggìo

lecture ['lɛktʃəʳ] N conferenza; (Scol) lezione f ▸ VI fare conferenze; fare lezioni ▸ VT (scold): **to ~ sb on** or **about sth** rimproverare qn or fare una ramanzina a qn per qc; **to ~ on** fare una conferenza su; **to give a ~ (on)** (BRIT) fare una conferenza (su); fare lezione (su)

La parola inglese **lecture** non vuol dire lettura.

lecture hall N aula magna

lecturer ['lɛktʃərəʳ] N (speaker) conferenziere(-a); (BRIT: at university) professore(-essa), docente mf; **assistant ~** (BRIT) ≈ professo-

re(-essa) associato(-a); **senior ~** (BRIT) ≈ professore(-essa) ordinario(-a)

lecture theatre N = **lecture hall**

LED N ABBR (Elec: = light-emitting diode) diodo a emissione luminosa

led [lɛd] PT, PP of **lead¹**

ledge [lɛdʒ] N (of window) davanzale m; (on wall etc) sporgenza; (of mountain) cornice f, cengia

ledger ['lɛdʒəʳ] N libro maestro, registro

lee [li:] N lato sottovento; **in the ~ of** a ridosso di, al riparo di

leech [li:tʃ] N sanguisuga

leek [li:k] N porro

leer [lɪəʳ] VI: **to ~ at sb** gettare uno sguardo voglioso (or maligno) su qn

leeward ['li:wəd] ADJ sottovento inv ▸ N lato sottovento; **to ~** sottovento

leeway ['li:weɪ] N (fig): **to have some ~** avere una certa libertà di agire

left [lɛft] PT, PP of **leave** ▸ ADJ sinistro(-a) ▸ ADV a sinistra ▸ N sinistra; **on the ~**, **to the ~** a sinistra; **the L~** (Pol) la sinistra

left-click ['lɛftklɪk] VI (Comput): **to ~ on** cliccare con il pulsante sinistro del mouse su

left-hand ADJ: **the ~ side** il lato or fianco sinistro

left-hand drive ['lɛfthænd-] N, ADJ (BRIT) guida a sinistra

left-handed [lɛft'hændɪd] ADJ mancino(-a); **~ scissors** forbici fpl per mancini

left-hand side ['lɛfthænd-] N lato or fianco sinistro

leftie ['lɛftɪ] N: **a ~** (col) uno(-a) di sinistra

leftist ['lɛftɪst] ADJ (Pol) di sinistra

left-luggage [lɛft'lʌgɪdʒ], (BRIT) **left-luggage office** N deposito m bagagli inv

left-luggage locker N armadietto per deposito bagagli

left-overs ['lɛftəʊvəz] NPL avanzi mpl, resti mpl

left wing N (Mil, Sport) ala sinistra; (Pol) sinistra
▸ ADJ: **left-wing** (Pol) di sinistra

left-winger [lɛft'wɪŋəʳ] N (Pol) uno(-a) di sinistra; (Sport) ala sinistra

lefty ['lɛftɪ] N = **leftie**

leg [lɛg] N gamba; (of animal) zampa; (of furniture) piede m; (Culin: of chicken) coscia; (of journey) tappa; **1st/2nd ~** (Sport) partita di andata/ritorno; **~ of lamb** (Culin) cosciotto d'agnello; **to stretch one's legs** sgranchirsi le gambe

legacy ['lɛgəsɪ] N eredità f inv; (fig) retaggio

legal ['li:gl] ADJ legale; **to take ~ action** or **proceedings against sb** intentare un'azione legale contro qn, far causa a qn

legal adviser N consulente mf legale

legal holiday N (US) giorno festivo, festa nazionale

legality [lɪ'gælɪtɪ] N legalità
legalize ['li:gəlaɪz] VT legalizzare
legally ['li:gəlɪ] ADV legalmente; **~ binding** legalmente vincolante
legal tender N moneta legale
legation [lɪ'geɪʃən] N legazione f
legend ['lɛdʒənd] N leggenda
legendary ['lɛdʒəndərɪ] ADJ leggendario(-a)
-legged ['lɛgɪd] SUFFIX: **two-legged** a due gambe (or zampe), bipede
leggings ['lɛgɪŋz] NPL ghette fpl
leggy ['lɛgɪ] ADJ dalle gambe lunghe
legibility [lɛdʒɪ'bɪlɪtɪ] N leggibilità
legible ['lɛdʒəbl] ADJ leggibile
legibly ['lɛdʒəblɪ] ADV in modo leggibile
legion ['li:dʒən] N legione f
legionnaire [li:dʒə'nɛəʳ] N legionario; **~'s disease** morbo del legionario
legislate ['lɛdʒɪsleɪt] VI legiferare
legislation [lɛdʒɪs'leɪʃən] N legislazione f; **a piece of ~** una legge
legislative ['lɛdʒɪslətɪv] ADJ legislativo(-a)
legislator ['lɛdʒɪsleɪtəʳ] N legislatore(-trice)
legislature ['lɛdʒɪslətʃəʳ] N corpo legislativo
legitimacy [lɪ'dʒɪtɪməsɪ] N legittimità
legitimate [lɪ'dʒɪtɪmət] ADJ legittimo(-a)
legitimize [lɪ'dʒɪtɪmaɪz] VT (gen) legalizzare, rendere legale; (child) legittimare
legless ['lɛglɪs] ADJ (BRIT col) sbronzo(-a), fatto(-a)
leg-room ['lɛgru:m] N spazio per le gambe
leisure ['lɛʒəʳ] N agio, tempo libero; ricreazioni fpl; **at ~** con comodo
leisure centre N centro di ricreazione
leisurely ['lɛʒəlɪ] ADJ tranquillo(-a), fatto(-a) con comodo or senza fretta
leisure suit N (BRIT) tuta (da ginnastica)
lemon ['lɛmən] N limone m
lemonade [lɛmə'neɪd] N limonata
lemon cheese, lemon curd N crema di limone (che si spalma sul pane ecc)
lemon juice N succo di limone
lemon squeezer N spremiagrumi m inv
lemon tea N tè m inv al limone
lend [lɛnd] (pt, pp **lent** [lɛnt]) VT: **to ~ sth (to sb)** prestare qc (a qn); **to ~ a hand** dare una mano
lender ['lɛndəʳ] N prestatore(-trice)
lending library ['lɛndɪŋ-] N biblioteca circolante
length [lɛŋθ] N lunghezza; (distance) distanza; (section: of road, pipe etc) pezzo, tratto; **~ of time** periodo (di tempo); **what ~ is it?** quant'è lungo?; **it is 2 metres in ~** è lungo 2 metri; **to fall full ~** cadere lungo disteso; **at ~** (at last) finalmente, alla fine; (lengthily) a lungo; **to go**

to any ~(s) to do sth fare qualsiasi cosa pur di or per fare qc
lengthen ['lɛŋθən] VT allungare, prolungare ▶ VI allungarsi
lengthways ['lɛŋθweɪz] ADV per il lungo
lengthy ['lɛŋθɪ] ADJ molto lungo(-a)
leniency ['li:nɪənsɪ] N indulgenza, clemenza
lenient ['li:nɪənt] ADJ indulgente, clemente
leniently ['li:nɪəntlɪ] ADV con indulgenza
lens [lɛnz] N lente f; (of camera) obiettivo
Lent [lɛnt] N Quaresima
lent [lɛnt] PT, PP of **lend**
lentil ['lɛntl] N lenticchia
Leo ['li:əu] N Leone m; **to be ~** essere del Leone
leopard ['lɛpəd] N leopardo
leotard ['li:ətɑːd] N calzamaglia
leper ['lɛpəʳ] N lebbroso(-a)
leper colony N lebbrosario
leprosy ['lɛprəsɪ] N lebbra
lesbian ['lɛzbɪən] N lesbica ▶ ADJ lesbico(-a)
lesion ['li:ʒən] N (Med) lesione f
Lesotho [lɪ'su:tu] N Lesotho m
less [lɛs] ADJ, PRON, ADV, PREP meno; **~ tax/10% discount** meno tasse/il 10% di sconto; **~ than you/ever** meno di lei/che mai; **~ than half** meno della metà; **~ than £1/a kilo/3 metres** meno di una sterlina/un chilo/3 metri
lessee [lɛ'si:] N affittuario(-a), locatario(-a)
lessen ['lɛsn] VI diminuire, attenuarsi ▶ VT diminuire, ridurre
lesser ['lɛsəʳ] ADJ minore, più piccolo(-a); **to a ~ extent** or **degree** in grado or misura minore
lesson ['lɛsn] N lezione f; **a maths ~** una lezione di matematica; **to give lessons in** dare or impartire lezioni di; **to teach sb a ~** dare una lezione a qn; **it taught him a ~** (fig) gli è servito di lezione
lessor ['lɛsɔːʳ, lɛ'sɔ:ʳ] N locatore(-trice)
lest [lɛst] CONJ per paura di + infinitive, per paura che + sub
let [lɛt] VT (pt, pp ~) lasciare; (BRIT: lease) dare in affitto; **to ~ sb do sth** lasciar fare qc a qn, lasciare che qn faccia qc; **to ~ sb know sth** far sapere qc a qn; **to ~ sb have sth** dare qc a qn; **he ~ me go** mi ha lasciato andare; **~ and ~** sempre meno; **the ~ water boil and ...** fate bollire l'acqua e ...; **~'s go** andiamo; **~ him come** lo lasci venire; **"to ~"** "affittasi"
▶ **let down** VT (lower) abbassare; (dress) allungare; (hair) sciogliere; (disappoint) deludere; (BRIT: tyre) sgonfiare
▶ **let go** VI mollare ▶ VT mollare; (allow to go) lasciare andare
▶ **let in** VT lasciare entrare; (visitor etc) far entrare; **what have you ~ yourself in for?** in che guai or pasticci sei andato a cacciarti?

▶ **let off** VT (*allow to go*) lasciare andare; (*firework etc*) far partire; (*smell etc*) emettere; (*taxi driver, bus driver*) far scendere; **to ~ off steam** (*fig: col*) sfogarsi, scaricarsi

▶ **let on** VI (*col*): **to ~ on that ...** lasciar capire che ...

▶ **let out** VT lasciare uscire; (*dress*) allargare; (*scream*) emettere; (*rent out*) affittare, dare in affitto

▶ **let up** VI diminuire

let-down ['lɛtdaʊn] N (*disappointment*) delusione *f*

lethal ['liːθl] ADJ letale, mortale

lethargic [lɛ'θɑːdʒɪk] ADJ letargico(-a)

lethargy ['lɛθədʒɪ] N letargia

letter ['lɛtə'] N lettera ▪ **letters** NPL (*Literature*) lettere; **small/capital ~** lettera minuscola/maiuscola; **~ of credit** lettera di credito; **documentary ~ of credit** lettera di credito documentata

letter bomb N lettera esplosiva

letterbox ['lɛtəbɒks] N (*BRIT*) buca delle lettere

letterhead ['lɛtəhɛd] N intestazione *f*

lettering ['lɛtərɪŋ] N iscrizione *f*; caratteri *mpl*

letter-opener ['lɛtərəʊpnə'] N tagliacarte *m inv*

letterpress ['lɛtəprɛs] N (*method*) rilievografia

letter quality N (*of printer*) qualità di stampa

letters patent NPL brevetto di invenzione

lettuce ['lɛtɪs] N lattuga, insalata

let-up ['lɛtʌp] N (*col*) interruzione *f*

leukaemia, (*US*) **leukemia** [luː'kiːmɪə] N leucemia

level ['lɛvl] ADJ piatto(-a), piano(-a); orizzontale ▶ N livello; (*also:* **spirit level**) livella (a bolla d'aria) ▶ VT livellare, spianare; (*gun*) puntare; (*accusation*): **to ~ (against)** lanciare (a *or* contro) ▶ VI (*col*): **to ~ with sb** essere franco(-a) con qn; **to be ~ with** essere alla pari di; **a ~ spoonful** (*Culin*) un cucchiaio raso; **to draw ~ with** (*team*) mettersi alla pari di; (*runner, car*) affiancarsi a; **A levels** *npl* (*BRIT*) ≈ esami *mpl* di maturità; **O levels** *npl* (*BRIT formerly*) diploma di istruzione secondaria conseguito a 16 anni in Inghilterra e Galles, ora sostituito dal GCSE; **on the ~** piatto(-a); (*fig*) onesto(-a)

▶ **level off, level out** VI (*prices etc*) stabilizzarsi; (*ground*) diventare pianeggiante; (*aircraft*) volare in quota

level crossing N (*BRIT*) passaggio a livello

level-headed [lɛvl'hɛdɪd] ADJ equilibrato(-a)

levelling, (*US*) **leveling** ['lɛvlɪŋ] ADJ (*process, effect*) di livellamento

level playing field N: **to compete on a ~** (*fig*) competere ad armi pari

lever ['liːvə'] N leva ▶ VT: **to ~ up/out** sollevare/estrarre con una leva

leverage ['liːvərɪdʒ] N: **~ (on** *or* **with)** forza (su); (*fig*) ascendente *m* (su)

levity ['lɛvɪtɪ] N leggerezza, frivolità

levy ['lɛvɪ] N tassa, imposta ▶ VT imporre

lewd [luːd] ADJ osceno(-a), lascivo(-a)

lexicographer [lɛksɪ'kɒɡrəfə'] N lessicografo(-a)

lexicography [lɛksɪ'kɒɡrəfɪ] N lessicografia

LGBT N LGBT *mpl*, persone lesbiche, gay, bisessuali e transessuali

LGV N ABBR (*BRIT*: = *Large Goods Vehicle*) automezzo pesante

LI ABBR (*US*) = **Long Island**

liabilities [laɪə'bɪlətɪz] NPL debiti *mpl*; (*on balance sheet*) passivo

liability [laɪə'bɪlətɪ] N responsabilità *f inv*; (*handicap*) peso

liable ['laɪəbl] ADJ (*subject*): **~ to** soggetto(-a) a; passibile di; (*responsible*): **~ (for)** responsabile (di); (*likely*): **~ to do** propenso(-a) a fare; **to be ~ to a fine** essere passibile di multa

liaise [liː'eɪz] VI: **to ~ (with)** mantenere i contatti (con)

liaison [liː'eɪzɒn] N relazione *f*; (*Mil*) collegamento

liar ['laɪə'] N bugiardo(-a)

libel ['laɪbl] N libello, diffamazione *f* ▶ VT diffamare

libellous, (*US*) **libelous** ['laɪbləs] ADJ diffamatorio(-a)

liberal ['lɪbərl] ADJ liberale; (*generous*): **to be ~ with** distribuire liberalmente ▶ N (*Pol*): **L~** liberale *mf*

Liberal Democrat N liberaldemocratico(-a)

liberality [lɪbə'rælɪtɪ] N (*generosity*) generosità, liberalità

liberalize ['lɪbərəlaɪz] VT liberalizzare

liberal-minded [lɪbərl'maɪndɪd] ADJ tollerante

liberate ['lɪbəreɪt] VT liberare

liberation [lɪbə'reɪʃən] N liberazione *f*

liberation theology N teologia della liberazione

Liberia [laɪ'bɪərɪə] N Liberia

Liberian [laɪ'bɪərɪən] ADJ, N liberiano(-a)

liberty ['lɪbətɪ] N libertà *f inv*; **at ~** (*criminal*) in libertà; **at ~ to do** libero(-a) di fare; **to take the ~ of** prendersi la libertà di, permettersi di

libido [lɪ'biːdəʊ] N libido *f inv*

Libra ['liːbrə] N Bilancia; **to be ~** essere della Bilancia

librarian [laɪ'brɛərɪən] N bibliotecario(-a)

library ['laɪbrərɪ] N biblioteca

library book N libro della biblioteca

libretto [lɪ'brɛtəʊ] N libretto

Libya ['lɪbɪə] N Libia

Libyan ['lɪbɪən] ADJ, N libico(-a)

lice [laɪs] NPL *of* **louse**

licence, (US) **license** [ˈlaɪsns] N autorizzazione f, permesso; (Comm) licenza; (Radio, TV) canone m, abbonamento; (also: **driving licence,** US: **driver's license**) patente f di guida; (excessive freedom) licenza; **import ~** licenza di importazione; **produced under ~** prodotto su licenza

licence number N (Brit Aut) numero di targa

license [ˈlaɪsns] N (US) = **licence** ▶ VT dare una licenza a; (car) pagare la tassa di circolazione or il bollo di

licensed [ˈlaɪsnst] ADJ (for alcohol) che ha la licenza di vendere bibite alcoliche

licensed trade N commercio di bevande alcoliche con licenza speciale

licensee [laɪsənˈsiː] N (Brit: of pub) detentore(-trice) di autorizzazione alla vendita di bevande alcoliche

license plate N (US Aut) targa (automobilistica)

licensing hours (Brit) NPL orario d'apertura (di un pub)

licentious [laɪˈsɛnʃəs] ADJ licenzioso(-a)

lichen [ˈlaɪkən] N lichene m

lick [lɪk] VT leccare; (col: defeat) suonarle a, stracciare ▶ N leccata; **a ~ of paint** una passata di vernice; **to ~ one's lips** (fig) leccarsi i baffi

licorice [ˈlɪkərɪs] N = **liquorice**

lid [lɪd] N coperchio; (eyelid) palpebra; **to take the ~ off sth** (fig) smascherare qc

lido [ˈlaɪdəu] N piscina all'aperto; (part of the beach) lido, stabilimento balneare

lie [laɪ] N bugia, menzogna ▶ VI (pt, pp lied) mentire, dire bugie; (pt lay [leɪ], pp lain [leɪn]) (rest) giacere, star disteso(-a); (in grave) giacere, riposare; (object: be situated) trovarsi, essere; **to tell lies** raccontare or dire bugie; **to ~ low** (fig) latitare

▶ **lie about, lie around** VI (things) essere in giro; (person) bighellonare

▶ **lie back** VI stendersi

▶ **lie down** VI stendersi, sdraiarsi

▶ **lie up** VI (hide) nascondersi

Liechtenstein [ˈlɪktənstaɪn] N Liechtenstein m

lie detector N macchina della verità

lie-down [ˈlaɪdaun] N (Brit): **to have a ~** sdraiarsi, riposarsi

lie-in [ˈlaɪɪn] N (Brit): **to have a ~** rimanere a letto

lieu [luː] N: **in ~ of** invece di, al posto di

Lieut. ABBR (= lieutenant) Ten.

lieutenant [lɛfˈtɛnənt, (US) luːˈtɛnənt] N tenente m

lieutenant-colonel [lɛfˈtɛnəntˈkəːnl, (US) luːˈtɛnəntˈkəːnl] N tenente colonnello

life [laɪf] N (pl **lives** [laɪvz]) vita ▶ CPD di vita; della vita; a vita; **to come to ~** rianimarsi; **country/city ~** vita di campagna/di città; **to be sent to prison for ~** essere condannato

all'ergastolo; **true to ~** fedele alla realtà; **to paint from ~** dipingere dal vero

life annuity N rendita vitalizia

life assurance N (Brit) = **life insurance**

lifebelt [ˈlaɪfbɛlt] N (Brit) salvagente m

lifeblood [ˈlaɪfblʌd] N (fig) linfa vitale

lifeboat [ˈlaɪfbəut] N scialuppa di salvataggio

life expectancy N durata media della vita

lifeguard [ˈlaɪfɡɑːd] N bagnino(-a)

life imprisonment N ergastolo

life insurance N assicurazione f sulla vita

life jacket N giubbotto di salvataggio

lifeless [ˈlaɪflɪs] ADJ senza vita

lifelike [ˈlaɪflaɪk] ADJ che sembra vero(-a); rassomigliante

lifeline [ˈlaɪflaɪn] N cavo di salvataggio

lifelong [ˈlaɪflɔŋ] ADJ per tutta la vita

life preserver [-prɪˈzəːvəʳ] N (US) salvagente m; giubbotto di salvataggio; (Brit) sfollagente m inv

lifer [ˈlaɪfəʳ] N (col) ergastolano(-a)

life-raft [ˈlaɪfrɑːft] N zattera di salvataggio

life-saver [ˈlaɪfseɪvəʳ] N bagnino(-a)

life sentence N (condanna all')ergastolo

life-sized [ˈlaɪfsaɪzd] ADJ a grandezza naturale

life span N (durata della) vita

life style N stile m di vita

life support system N (Med) respiratore m automatico

lifetime [ˈlaɪftaɪm] N: **in his ~** durante la sua vita; **in a ~** nell'arco della vita; in tutta la vita; **the chance of a ~** un'occasione unica

lift [lɪft] VT sollevare; (ban, rule) levare; (steal) prendere, rubare ▶ VI (fog) alzarsi ▶ N (Brit: elevator) ascensore m; **to give sb a ~** (Brit) dare un passaggio a qn

▶ **lift off** VT togliere ▶ VI (rocket) partire; (helicopter) decollare

▶ **lift out** VT tirar fuori; (troops, evacuees etc) far evacuare per mezzo di elicotteri (or aerei)

▶ **lift up** VT sollevare, alzare

lift-off [ˈlɪftɔf] N decollo

ligament [ˈlɪɡəmənt] N legamento

light [laɪt] (pt, pp **lighted** [ˈlaɪtɪd] or **lit** [lɪt]) N luce f, lume m; (daylight) luce, giorno; (lamp) lampada; (Aut: rear light) luce f di posizione; (: headlamp) fanale m; (for cigarette etc): **have you got a ~?** ha da accendere? ▶ VT (candle, cigarette, fire) accendere; (room) illuminare ▶ ADJ (room, colour) chiaro(-a); (not heavy, also fig) leggero(-a) ▶ ADV (travel) con poco bagaglio ■ **lights** NPL (Aut: traffic lights) semaforo; **in the ~ of** alla luce di; **to turn the ~ on/off** accendere/spegnere la luce; **to come to ~** venire alla luce, emergere; **to cast** or **shed** or **throw ~ on** gettare luce su; **to make ~ of sth** (fig) prendere alla leggera qc, non dar peso a qc; **to be lit by** essere illuminato(-a) da

▶ **light up** VI illuminarsi ▶ VT illuminare

light bulb N lampadina

lighten ['laɪtn] VI schiarirsi ▸ VT (*give light to*) illuminare; (*make lighter*) schiarire; (*make less heavy*) alleggerire

lighter ['laɪtəʳ] N (*also:* **cigarette lighter**) accendino (*boat*) chiatta

light-fingered [laɪt'fɪŋgəd] ADJ lesto(-a) di mano

light-headed ['laɪt'hɛdɪd] ADJ stordito(-a)

light-hearted ['laɪt'hɑːtɪd] ADJ gioioso(-a), gaio(-a)

lighthouse ['laɪthaus] N faro

lighting ['laɪtɪŋ] N illuminazione f

lighting-up time ['laɪtɪŋʌp-] N (BRIT) orario per l'accensione delle luci

lightly ['laɪtlɪ] ADV leggermente; **to get off ~** cavarsela a buon mercato

light meter N (Phot) esposimetro

lightness ['laɪtnɪs] N chiarezza; (*in weight*) leggerezza

lightning ['laɪtnɪŋ] N lampo, fulmine *m*; **a flash of ~** un lampo, un fulmine

lightning conductor, (US) **lightning rod** N parafulmine *m*

lightning strike N (BRIT) sciopero *m* lampo *inv*

light pen N penna luminosa

lightship ['laɪtʃɪp] N battello *m* faro *inv*

lightweight ['laɪtweɪt] ADJ (*suit*) leggero(-a) ▸ N (Boxing) peso leggero

light year ['laɪtjɪəʳ] N anno *m* luce *inv*

Ligurian [lɪ'gjuərɪən] ADJ, N ligure (*mf*)

like [laɪk] VT (*person*) volere bene a; (*activity, object, food*): **I ~ swimming/that book/chocolate** mi piace nuotare/quel libro/il cioccolato ▸ PREP come ▸ ADJ simile, uguale ▸ N: **the ~** uno(-a) uguale; **I would ~, I'd ~** mi piacerebbe, vorrei; **would you ~ a coffee?** gradirebbe un caffè?; **if you ~** se vuoi; **to be/look ~ sb/sth** somigliare a qn/qc; **what does it look/taste ~?** che aspetto/gusto ha?; **what does it sound ~?** come fa?; **what's he ~?** che tipo è?, com'è?; **what's the weather ~?** che tempo fa?; **that's just ~ him** è proprio da lui; **something ~ that** qualcosa del genere; **do it ~ this** fallo così; **I feel ~ a drink** avrei voglia di bere qualcosa; **there's nothing ~ ...** non c'è niente di meglio di *or* niente come ...; **it is nothing ~ ...** non è affatto come ...; **his likes and dislikes** i suoi gusti

To translate a sentence like *I like him/it* into Italian, you have to rephrase it as *He/It is pleasing to me*. If what you like is singular, the verb is singular; if it is plural, the verb is plural.
I like Tom. **Tom mi piace.**
I don't like dogs. **Non mi piacciono i cani.**
I like riding. **Mi piace cavalcare.**

likeable ['laɪkəbl] ADJ simpatico(-a)

likelihood ['laɪklɪhud] N probabilità; **in all ~** con ogni probabilità, molto probabilmente

likely ['laɪklɪ] ADJ probabile; plausibile; **he's ~ to leave** probabilmente partirà, è probabile che parta; **not ~!** (*col*) neanche per sogno!

like-minded ['laɪk'maɪndɪd] ADJ che pensa allo stesso modo

liken ['laɪkən] VT: **to ~ sth to** paragonare qc a

likeness ['laɪknɪs] N (*similarity*) somiglianza

likewise ['laɪkwaɪz] ADV similmente, nello stesso modo

liking ['laɪkɪŋ] N: **~ (for)** simpatia (per); debole *m* (per); **to be to sb's ~** piacere a qn; **to take a ~ to sb** prendere qn in simpatia

lilac ['laɪlək] N, ADJ lilla (*m*) inv

Lilo® ['laɪləu] N materassino gonfiabile

lilt [lɪlt] N cadenza

lilting ['lɪltɪŋ] ADJ melodioso(-a)

lily ['lɪlɪ] N giglio; **~ of the valley** mughetto

Lima ['liːmə] N Lima

limb [lɪm] N arto; **to be out on a ~** (*fig*) sentirsi spaesato(-a) *or* tagliato(-a) fuori

limber ['lɪmbəʳ]: **to ~ up** *vi* riscaldarsi i muscoli

limbo ['lɪmbəu] N: **to be in ~** (*fig*) essere lasciato(-a) nel dimenticatoio

lime [laɪm] N (*tree*) tiglio; (*fruit*) limetta; (Geo) calce *f*

lime juice N succo di limetta

limelight ['laɪmlaɪt] N: **in the ~** (*fig*) alla ribalta, in vista

limerick ['lɪmərɪk] N poesiola umoristica di cinque versi

limestone ['laɪmstəun] N pietra calcarea; (Geo) calcare *m*

limit ['lɪmɪt] N limite *m* ▸ VT limitare; **weight/speed ~** limite di peso/di velocità; **within limits** entro certi limiti

limitation [lɪmɪ'teɪʃən] N limitazione f, limite *m*

limited ['lɪmɪtɪd] ADJ limitato(-a), ristretto(-a); **~ edition** edizione f a bassa tiratura; **to be ~ to** limitarsi a

limited company, limited liability company N (BRIT) ≈ società f inv a responsabilità limitata (S.r.l.)

limitless ['lɪmɪtlɪs] ADJ illimitato(-a)

limousine ['lɪməziːn] N limousine f inv

limp [lɪmp] N: **to have a ~** zoppicare ▸ VI zoppicare ▸ ADJ floscio(-a), flaccido(-a)

limpet ['lɪmpɪt] N patella

limpid ['lɪmpɪd] ADJ (*poet*) limpido(-a)

linchpin ['lɪntʃpɪn] N acciarino, bietta; (*fig*) perno

line [laɪn] N (gen, Comm) linea; (*rope*) corda; (*for fishing*) lenza; (*wire*) filo; (*of poem*) verso; (*row, series*) fila, riga; coda; (*on face*) ruga ▸ VT (*trees,*

crowd) fiancheggiare; **to ~ (with)** (*clothes*) foderare (di); (*box*) rivestire *or* foderare (di); **to cut in ~** (*US*) passare avanti; **in his ~ of business** nel suo ramo; **on the right lines** sulla buona strada; **a new ~ in cosmetics** una nuova linea di cosmetici; **hold the ~ please** (*BRIT Tel*) resti in linea per cortesia; **to be in ~ for sth** (*fig*) essere in lista per qc; **in ~ with** d'accordo con, in linea con; **to bring sth into ~ with sth** mettere qc al passo con qc; **to draw the ~ at doing sth** (*fig*) rifiutarsi di fare qc; **to take the ~ that ...** essere del parere che ...
▶ **line up** VI allinearsi, mettersi in fila ▶ VT mettere in fila; (*event, celebration*) preparare; **to have sth lined up** avere qc in programma; **to have sb lined up** avere qn in mente

linear ['lɪnɪə'] ADJ lineare

lined [laɪnd] ADJ (*paper*) a righe, rigato(-a); (*face*) rugoso(-a); (*clothes*) foderato(-a)

line feed N (*Comput*) avanzamento di una interlinea

linen ['lɪnɪn] N biancheria, panni *mpl*; (*cloth*) tela di lino

line printer N stampante *f* parallela

liner ['laɪnə'] N nave *f* di linea; **dustbin ~** sacchetto per la pattumiera

linesman ['laɪnzmən] N (*irreg*) guardalinee *m inv*, segnalinee *m inv*

line-up ['laɪnʌp] N allineamento, fila; (*also:* **police line-up**) confronto all'americana; (*Sport*) formazione *f* di gioco

linger ['lɪŋɡə'] VI attardarsi; indugiare; (*smell, tradition*) persistere

lingerie ['lænʒəriː] N biancheria intima (femminile)

lingering ['lɪŋɡərɪŋ] ADJ lungo(-a), persistente; (*death*) lento(-a)

lingo ['lɪŋɡəu] N (*pl* **lingoes**) (*pej*) gergo

linguist ['lɪŋɡwɪst] N linguista *mf*; poliglotta *mf*

linguistic [lɪŋ'ɡwɪstɪk] ADJ linguistico(-a)

linguistics [lɪŋ'ɡwɪstɪks] N linguistica

lining ['laɪnɪŋ] N fodera; (*Tech*) rivestimento (interno); (*of brake*) guarnizione *f*

link [lɪŋk] N (*of a chain*) anello; (*relationship*) legame *m*; (*connection*) legame *m*, collegamento; (*Comput*) link *m inv*, collegamento ▶ VT collegare, unire, congiungere; (*Comput*) creare un collegamento con; (*associate*): **to ~ with** *or* **to** collegare a ▶ VI (*Comput*): **to ~ to a site** creare un collegamento con un sitio; **rail ~** collegamento ferroviario; *see also* **links**
▶ **link up** VT collegare, unire ▶ VI riunirsi; associarsi

links [lɪŋks] NPL pista *or* terreno da golf

link-up ['lɪŋkʌp] N legame *m*; (*of roads*) nodo; (*of spaceships*) aggancio; (*Radio, TV*) collegamento

linoleum [lɪ'nəuliəm] N linoleum *m inv*

linseed oil ['lɪnsiːd-] N olio di semi di lino

lint [lɪnt] N garza

lintel ['lɪntl] N architrave *f*

lion ['laɪən] N leone *m*

lion cub N leoncino

lioness ['laɪənɪs] N leonessa

lip [lɪp] N labbro; (*of cup etc*) orlo; (*insolence*) sfacciataggine *f*

liposuction ['lɪpəusʌkʃən] N liposuzione *f*

lipread ['lɪpriːd] VI (*irreg: like* **read**) leggere sulle labbra

lip salve [-sælv] N burro di cacao

lip service N: **to pay ~ to sth** essere favorevole a qc solo a parole

lipstick ['lɪpstɪk] N rossetto

liquefy ['lɪkwɪfaɪ] VT liquefare ▶ VI liquefarsi

liqueur [lɪ'kjuə'] N liquore *m*

liquid ['lɪkwɪd] N liquido ▶ ADJ liquido(-a)

liquid assets NPL attività *fpl* liquide, crediti *mpl* liquidi

liquidate ['lɪkwɪdeɪt] VT liquidare

liquidation [lɪkwɪ'deɪʃən] N liquidazione *f*; **to go into ~** andare in liquidazione

liquidator ['lɪkwɪdeɪtə'] N liquidatore *m*

liquid crystal display N visualizzazione *f* a cristalli liquidi

liquidity [lɪ'kwɪdɪtɪ] N (*Comm*) liquidità

liquidize ['lɪkwɪdaɪz] VT (*BRIT Culin*) passare al frullatore

liquidizer ['lɪkwɪdaɪzə'] N (*BRIT Culin*) frullatore *m* (a brocca)

liquor ['lɪkə'] N alcool *m inv*

liquorice ['lɪkərɪs] N liquirizia

liquor store N (*US*) negozio di liquori

Lisbon ['lɪzbən] N Lisbona

lisp [lɪsp] N pronuncia blesa della "s"

lissom ['lɪsəm] ADJ leggiadro(-a)

list [lɪst] N lista, elenco; (*of ship*) sbandamento ▶ VT (*write down*) mettere in lista; fare una lista di; (*enumerate*) elencare; (*Comput*) stampare (un prospetto di) ▶ VI (*ship*) sbandare; **shopping ~** lista *or* nota della spesa

listed building ['lɪstəd-] N (*BRIT Archit*) edificio sotto la protezione delle Belle Arti

listed company N società *f inv* quotata in Borsa

listen ['lɪsn] VI ascoltare; **to ~ to** ascoltare

listener ['lɪsnə'] N ascoltatore(-trice)

listeria [lɪs'tɪərɪə] N listeria

listing ['lɪstɪŋ] N (*Comput*) lista stampata

listless ['lɪstlɪs] ADJ svogliato(-a); apatico(-a)

listlessly ['lɪstlɪslɪ] ADV svogliatamente; apaticamente

list price N prezzo di listino

lit [lɪt] PT, PP *of* **light**

litany ['lɪtənɪ] N litania

liter ['liːtər] N (US) = **litre**

literacy ['lɪtərəsɪ] N il sapere leggere e scrivere

literacy campaign N lotta contro l'analfabetismo

literal ['lɪtərl] ADJ letterale

literally ['lɪtərəlɪ] ADV alla lettera, letteralmente

literary ['lɪtərərɪ] ADJ letterario(-a)

literate ['lɪtərɪt] ADJ che sa leggere e scrivere

literature ['lɪtərɪtʃər] N letteratura; (brochures etc) materiale m

lithe [laɪð] ADJ agile, snello(-a)

lithography [lɪ'θɔgrəfɪ] N litografia

Lithuania [lɪθjuˈeɪnɪə] N Lituania

Lithuanian [lɪθjuˈeɪnɪən] ADJ lituano(-a) ▶N lituano(-a); (Ling) lituano

litigate ['lɪtɪgeɪt] VT muovere causa a ▶VI litigare

litigation [lɪtɪˈgeɪʃən] N causa

litmus ['lɪtməs] N: **~ paper** cartina di tornasole

litre, (US) **liter** ['liːtər] N litro

litter ['lɪtər] N (rubbish) rifiuti mpl; (young animals) figliata ▶VT sparpagliare; lasciare rifiuti in; **littered with** coperto(-a) di

litter bin N (BRIT) cestino per rifiuti

littered ADJ: **~ with** coperto(-a) di

litter lout, (US) **litterbug** ['lɪtəbʌg] N persona che butta per terra le cartacce o i rifiuti

little ['lɪtl] ADJ (small) piccolo(-a); (not much) poco(-a) ▶ADV poco; **a ~** un po' (di); **a ~ milk** un po' di latte; **a ~ bit** un pochino; **with ~ difficulty** senza fatica or difficoltà; **~ by ~** a poco a poco; **as ~ as possible** il meno possibile; **for a ~ while** per un po'; **to make ~ of** dare poca importanza a

little finger N mignolo

little-known ['lɪtl'nəʊn] ADJ poco noto(-a)

liturgy ['lɪtədʒɪ] N liturgia

live¹ [lɪv] VI vivere; (reside) vivere, abitare; **where do you ~?** dove abita?; **to ~ in London** abitare a Londra
  ▶ **live down** VT far dimenticare (alla gente)
  ▶ **live in** VI essere interno(-a); avere vitto e alloggio
  ▶ **live off** VT FUS (land, fish etc) vivere di; (pej: parents etc) vivere alle spalle or a spese di
  ▶ **live on** VT FUS (food) vivere di ▶VI sopravvivere, continuare a vivere; **to ~ on £50 a week** vivere con 50 sterline la settimana
  ▶ **live out** VI (BRIT: students) essere esterno(-a)
  ▶VT: **to ~ out one's days** or **life** trascorrere gli ultimi anni
  ▶ **live together** VI vivere insieme, convivere
  ▶ **live up** VT: **to ~ it up** (col) fare la bella vita
  ▶ **live up to** VT FUS tener fede a, non venir meno a

live² [laɪv] ADJ (animal) vivo(-a); (issue) scottante, d'attualità; (wire) sotto tensione; (broadcast) diretto(-a); (ammunition: not blank) carico(-a); (: unexploded) inesploso(-a); (performance) dal vivo

liveblog ['laɪvblɔg] N liveblog m inv ▶VI fare live blogging

live-in ['lɪvɪn] ADJ (partner) convivente; (servant) che vive in casa; **he has a ~ girlfriend** la sua ragazza vive con lui

livelihood ['laɪvlɪhud] N mezzi mpl di sostentamento

liveliness ['laɪvlɪnəs] N vivacità

lively ['laɪvlɪ] ADJ vivace, vivo(-a)

liven up ['laɪvn-] VT (room etc) ravvivare; (discussion, evening) animare ▶VI ravvivarsi

liver ['lɪvər] N fegato

liverish ['lɪvərɪʃ] ADJ che soffre di mal di fegato; (fig) scontroso(-a)

Liverpudlian [lɪvəˈpʌdlɪən] ADJ di Liverpool ▶N abitante mf di Liverpool; originario(-a) di Liverpool

livery ['lɪvərɪ] N livrea

lives [laɪvz] NPL of **life**

livestock ['laɪvstɔk] N bestiame m

livestream ['laɪvstriːm] N diretta f streaming inv, live streaming m inv ▶VT trasmettere in (diretta) streaming

live wire [laɪv-] N (col: fig): **to be a ~** essere pieno(-a) di vitalità

livid ['lɪvɪd] ADJ livido(-a); (furious) livido(-a) di rabbia, furibondo(-a)

living ['lɪvɪŋ] ADJ vivo(-a), vivente ▶N: **to earn** or **make a ~** guadagnarsi la vita; **cost of ~** costo della vita, carovita m; **within ~ memory** a memoria d'uomo

living conditions NPL condizioni fpl di vita

living expenses NPL spese fpl di mantenimento

living room N soggiorno

living standards NPL tenore m di vita

living wage N salario sufficiente per vivere

living will N testamento biologico

lizard ['lɪzəd] N lucertola

llama ['lɑːmə] N lama m inv

LLB N ABBR (= Bachelor of Laws) ≈ laurea in legge

LLD N ABBR (= Doctor of Laws) titolo di studio

LMT ABBR (US: = Local Mean Time) tempo medio locale

load [ləud] N (weight) peso; (Elec, Tech, thing carried) carico ▶VT (gun, camera) caricare (con); (also: **load up**): **to ~ (with)** (lorry, ship) caricare (di); **a ~ of, loads of** (fig) un sacco di; **to ~ a program** (Comput) caricare un programma

loaded ['ləudɪd] ADJ (dice) falsato(-a); (question, word) capzioso(-a); (col: rich) pieno(-a) di soldi; **~ (with)** (vehicle) carico(-a) (di)

loading bay ['ləudɪŋ-] N piazzola di carico

loaf [ləuf] (pl **loaves** [ləuvz]) N pane m, pagnotta

▶ VI (*also*: **loaf about, loaf around**) bighellonare

loam [ləum] N terra di marna

loan [ləun] N prestito ▶ VT dare in prestito; **on ~** in prestito

loan account N conto dei prestiti

loan capital N capitale *m* di prestito

loan shark N (*pej*) strozzino(-a)

loath [ləuθ] ADJ: **to be ~ to do** essere restio(-a) a fare

loathe [ləuð] VT detestare, aborrire

loathing [ˈləuðɪŋ] N aborrimento, disgusto

loathsome [ˈləuðsəm] ADJ (*gen*) ripugnante; (*person*) detestabile, odioso(-a)

loaves [ləuvz] NPL *of* **loaf**

lob [lɔb] VT (*ball*) lanciare

lobby [ˈlɔbɪ] N atrio, vestibolo; (*Pol: pressure group*) gruppo di pressione ▶ VT fare pressione su

lobbyist [ˈlɔbɪɪst] N appartenente *mf* ad un gruppo di pressione

lobe [ləub] N lobo

lobster [ˈlɔbstə'] N aragosta

lobster pot N nassa per aragoste

local [ˈləukl] ADJ locale ▶ N (*BRIT*: *pub*) ≈ bar *m inv* all'angolo ■ **the locals** NPL la gente della zona

local anaesthetic N anestesia locale

local authority N ente *m* locale

local call N (*Tel*) telefonata urbana

local government N amministrazione *f* locale

locality [ləuˈkælɪtɪ] N località *f inv*; (*position*) posto, luogo

localize [ˈləukəlaɪz] VT localizzare

locally [ˈləukəlɪ] ADV da queste parti; nel vicinato

locate [ləuˈkeɪt] VT (*find*) trovare; (*situate*) collocare; situare

location [ləuˈkeɪʃən] N posizione *f*; **on ~** (*Cine*) all'esterno

loch [lɔx] N lago

lock [lɔk] N (*of door, box*) serratura; (*of canal*) chiusa; (*of hair*) ciocca, riccio ▶ VT (*with key*) chiudere a chiave; (*immobilize*) bloccare ▶ VI (*door etc*) chiudersi; (*wheels*) bloccarsi, inceparsi; **~, stock, and barrel** (*fig*) in blocco; **on full ~** (*BRIT Aut*) a tutto sterzo
▶ **lock away** VT (*valuables*) tenere (rinchiuso(-a)) al sicuro; (*criminal*) metter dentro
▶ **lock in** VT chiudere dentro (a chiave)
▶ **lock out** VT chiudere fuori; **to ~ workers out** fare una serrata
▶ **lock up** VT (*criminal, psychiatric patient*) rinchiudere; (*house*) chiudere (a chiave) ▶ VI chiudere tutto (a chiave)

lockdown [ˈlɔkdaun] N: **to be in** *or* **under ~** (*place*) essere in lockdown; **to be on ~** (*prisoner*) essere confinato(-a) in cella

locker [ˈlɔkə'] N armadietto

locker-room N (*US Sport*) spogliatoio

locket [ˈlɔkɪt] N medaglione *m*

lockjaw [ˈlɔkdʒɔː] N tetano

lockout [ˈlɔkaut] N (*Industry*) serrata

locksmith [ˈlɔksmɪθ] N magnano

lock-up [ˈlɔkʌp] N (*prison*) prigione *f*; (*cell*) guardina; (*also*: **lock-up garage**) box *m inv*

locomotive [ləukəˈməutɪv] N locomotiva

locum [ˈləukəm] N (*Med*) medico sostituto

locust [ˈləukəst] N locusta

lodge [lɔdʒ] N casetta, portineria; (*hunting lodge*) casino di caccia; (*Freemasonry*) loggia ▶ VI (*person*): **to ~ (with)** essere a pensione (presso *or* da); (*bullet etc*) conficcarsi ▶ VT (*appeal etc*) presentare, fare; **to ~ a complaint** presentare un reclamo; **to ~ (itself) in/between** piantarsi dentro/fra

lodger [ˈlɔdʒə'] N affittuario(-a); (*with room and meals*) pensionante *mf*

lodging [ˈlɔdʒɪŋ] N alloggio; *see also* **board**; **lodgings**

lodging house N (*BRIT*) casa con camere in affitto

lodgings [ˈlɔdʒɪŋz] NPL camera d'affitto; camera ammobiliata

loft [lɔft] N solaio, soffitta; (*Agr*) granaio; (*US*) appartamento ricavato da solaio (*or* granaio *etc*)

lofty [ˈlɔftɪ] ADJ alto(-a); (*haughty*) altezzoso(-a); (*sentiments, aims*) nobile

log [lɔg] N (*of wood*) ceppo; (*also*: **logbook**: *Naut, Aviat*) diario di bordo; (*: Aut*) libretto di circolazione ▶ N ABBR = **logarithm** ▶ VT registrare
▶ **log in, log on** VI (*Comput*) aprire una sessione (*con codice di riconoscimento*)
▶ **log off, log out** VI (*Comput*) terminare una sessione

logarithm [ˈlɔgərɪðm] N logaritmo

logbook [ˈlɔgbuk] N (*Naut, Aviat*) diario di bordo; (*Aut*) libretto di circolazione; (*of lorry driver*) registro di viaggio; (*of events, movement of goods etc*) registro

log cabin N capanna di tronchi

log fire N fuoco di legna

logger [ˈlɔgə'] N boscaiolo, taglialegna *m inv*

loggerheads [ˈlɔgəhɛdz] NPL: **at ~ (with)** ai ferri corti (con)

logic [ˈlɔdʒɪk] N logica

logical [ˈlɔdʒɪkəl] ADJ logico(-a)

logically [ˈlɔdʒɪkəlɪ] ADV logicamente

login [ˈlɔgɪn] N (*Comput*) nome *m* utente *inv*

logistics [lɔˈdʒɪstɪks] N logistica

logjam [ˈlɔgdʒæm] N: **to break the ~** superare l'impasse

logo [ˈləugəu] N logo *m inv*

loin [lɔɪn] N (Culin) lombata ▪ **loins** NPL reni fpl

loin cloth N perizoma m

loiter [ˈlɔɪtəʳ] VI attardarsi; **to ~ (about)** indugiare, bighellonare

LOL ABBR (col: = laugh out loud) LOL, grandi risate (nel gergo di Internet)

loll [lɔl] VI (also: **loll about**) essere stravaccato(-a)

lollipop [ˈlɔlɪpɔp] N lecca lecca m inv

lollipop man, lollipop lady N (irreg) (BRIT) vedi nota

> In Gran Bretagna il **lollipop man** e la **lollipop lady** sono persone incaricate di regolare il traffico in prossimità delle scuole e di aiutare i bambini ad attraversare la strada usando una paletta la cui forma ricorda quella di un lecca lecca, in inglese, appunto, lollipop.

lollop [ˈlɔləp] VI (BRIT) camminare (or correre) goffamente

lolly [ˈlɔlɪ] N (col) lecca lecca m inv; (also: **ice lolly**) ghiacciolo; (money) grana

Lombardy [ˈlɔmbədɪ] N Lombardia

London [ˈlʌndən] N Londra

Londoner [ˈlʌndənəʳ] N londinese mf

lone [ləun] ADJ solitario(-a)

loneliness [ˈləunlɪnɪs] N solitudine f, isolamento

lonely [ˈləunlɪ] ADJ solo(-a); solitario(-a); (place) isolato(-a); **to feel ~** sentirsi solo(-a)

lonely hearts ADJ: **~ ads, ~ column** messaggi mpl personali; **~ club** club m inv dei cuori solitari

lone parent N (unmarried: mother) ragazza madre; (: father) ragazzo padre; (divorced: mother) madre divorziata; (: father) padre divorziato; (widowed: mother) madre vedova; (: father) padre vedovo

loner [ˈləunəʳ] N solitario(-a)

lonesome [ˈləunsəm] ADJ solo(-a)

long [lɔŋ] ADJ lungo(-a) ▶ ADV a lungo, per molto tempo ▶ N: **the ~ and the short of it is that ...** (fig) a farla breve ... ▶ VI: **to ~ for sth/to do** desiderare qc/di fare; non veder l'ora di aver qc/di fare; **he had ~ understood that ...** aveva capito da molto tempo che ...; **how ~ is this river/course?** quanto è lungo questo fiume/corso?; **6 metres ~** lungo 6 metri; **6 months ~** che dura 6 mesi, di 6 mesi; **all night ~** tutta la notte; **he no longer comes** non viene più; **~ before** molto tempo prima; **before ~** (+ future) presto, fra poco; (+ past) poco tempo dopo; **~ ago** molto tempo fa; **don't be ~!** faccia presto!; **I shan't be ~** non ne avrò per molto; **at ~ last** finalmente; **in the ~ run** alla fin fine; **so** or **as ~ as** (while) finché; (provided that) sempre che + sub

> Questions with how long and the perfect tense are translated by **da quanto** and an Italian verb in the present tense.
> How long have you been here? **Da quanto sei qui?**
> How long has he been learning Italian? **Da quanto studia l'italiano?**

long-distance [lɔŋˈdɪstəns] ADJ (race) di fondo; (call) interurbano(-a)

long-haired [lɔŋˈhɛəd] ADJ (person) dai capelli lunghi; (animal) dal pelo lungo

longhand [ˈlɔŋhænd] N scrittura normale

long-haul [ˈlɔŋhɔ:l] ADJ (flight) a lunga percorrenza

longing [ˈlɔŋɪŋ] N desiderio, voglia, brama ▶ ADJ di desiderio; pieno(-a) di nostalgia

longingly [ˈlɔŋɪŋlɪ] ADV con desiderio; con nostalgia

longitude [ˈlɔŋgɪtjuːd] N longitudine f

long johns [-dʒɔnz] NPL mutande fpl lunghe

long jump N salto in lungo

long-life [ˈlɔŋlaɪf] ADJ (milk) a lunga conservazione; (batteries) di lunga durata

long-lost [ˈlɔŋlɔst] ADJ perduto(-a) da tempo

long-playing [ˈlɔŋpleɪɪŋ] ADJ: **~ record** (disco) 33 giri m inv

long-range [lɔŋˈreɪndʒ] ADJ a lunga portata; (weather forecast) a lungo termine

longshoreman [ˈlɔŋʃɔːmən] N (irreg) (US) scaricatore m (di porto), portuale m

long-sighted [lɔŋˈsaɪtɪd] ADJ (BRIT) presbite; (fig) lungimirante

long-standing [ˈlɔŋstændɪŋ] ADJ di vecchia data

long-suffering [lɔŋˈsʌfərɪŋ] ADJ estremamente paziente; infinitamente tollerante

long-term [ˈlɔŋtəːm] ADJ a lungo termine

long wave N (Radio) onde fpl lunghe

long-winded [lɔŋˈwɪndɪd] ADJ prolisso(-a), interminabile

loo [luː] N (BRIT col) W.C. m inv, cesso

loofah [ˈluːfə] N luffa

look [luk] VI guardare; (seem) sembrare, parere; (building etc): **to ~ south/onto the sea** dare a sud/sul mare ▶ N sguardo; (appearance) aspetto, aria ▪ **looks** NPL aspetto; (good looks) bellezza; **to ~ like** assomigliare a; **to ~ ahead** guardare avanti; **it looks about 4 metres long** sarà lungo un 4 metri; **it looks all right to me** a me pare che vada bene; **to have a ~ at sth** dare un'occhiata a qc; **to have a ~ for sth** cercare qc ▶ **look after** VT FUS occuparsi di, prendersi cura di; (keep an eye on) guardare, badare a
▶ **look around** VI guardarsi intorno
▶ **look at** VT FUS guardare
▶ **look back** VI: **to ~ back at sth/sb** voltarsi a guardare qc/qn; **to ~ back on** (event, period) ripensare a

▶ **look down on** VT FUS (*fig*) guardare dall'alto, disprezzare

▶ **look for** VT FUS cercare

▶ **look forward to** VT FUS non veder l'ora di; **I'm not looking forward to it** non ne ho nessuna voglia; **looking forward to hearing from you** (*in letter: to a friend*) aspettando tue notizie; (*: more formal*) in attesa di una vostra gentile risposta

▶ **look in** VI: **to ~ in on sb** (*visit*) fare un salto da qn

▶ **look into** VT FUS (*matter, possibility*) esaminare

▶ **look on** VI fare da spettatore

▶ **look out** VI (*beware*): **to ~ out (for)** stare in guardia (per)

▶ **look out for** VT FUS cercare; (*watch out for*): **to ~ out for sb/sth** guardare se arriva qn/qc

▶ **look over** VT (*essay*) dare un'occhiata a, riguardare; (*town, building*) vedere; (*person*) esaminare

▶ **look round** VI (*turn*) girarsi, voltarsi; (*in shops*) dare un'occhiata; **to ~ round for sth** guardarsi intorno cercando qc

▶ **look through** VT FUS (*papers, book*) scorrere; (*telescope*) guardare attraverso

▶ **look to** VT FUS stare attento(-a) a; (*rely on*) contare su

▶ **look up** VI alzare gli occhi; (*improve*) migliorare ▶ VT (*word*) cercare; (*friend*) andare a trovare

▶ **look up to** VT FUS avere rispetto per

lookout [ˈlukaut] N posto d'osservazione; guardia; **to be on the look-out (for)** stare in guardia (per)

look-up table [ˈlukʌp-] N (*Comput*) tabella di consultazione

loom [luːm] N telaio ▶ VI sorgere; (*fig*) incombere

loony [ˈluːnɪ] ADJ, N (*pej*) pazzo(-a)

loop [luːp] N cappio; (*Comput*) anello ▶ VT: **to ~ sth round sth** passare qc intorno a qc

loophole [ˈluːphəul] N via d'uscita; scappatoia

loose [luːs] ADJ (*knot*) sciolto(-a); (*screw*) allentato(-a); (*stone*) cadente; (*clothes*) ampio(-a), largo(-a); (*animal*) in libertà, scappato(-a); (*life, morals*) dissoluto(-a); (*discipline*) allentato(-a); (*thinking*) poco rigoroso(-a), vago(-a) ▶ N: **to be on the ~** essere in libertà ▶ VT (*untie*) sciogliere; (*slacken*) allentare; (*free*) liberare; (*BRIT: arrow*) scoccare; **~ connection** (*Elec*) filo staccato; **to be at a ~ end** *or* (*US*) **at ~ ends** (*fig*) non saper che fare; **to tie up ~ ends** (*fig*) avere ancora qualcosa da sistemare

loose change N spiccioli *mpl*, moneta

loose-fitting [ˈluːsfɪtɪŋ] ADJ ampio(-a)

loose-leaf [ˈluːsliːf] ADJ: **~ binder** *or* **folder** raccoglitore *m*

loose-limbed [luːsˈlɪmd] ADJ snodato(-a), agile

loosely [ˈluːslɪ] ADV senza stringere; approssimativamente

loosely-knit [ˈluːslɪˈnɪt] ADJ non rigidamente strutturato(-a)

loosen [ˈluːsn] VT sciogliere; (*belt etc*) allentare

▶ **loosen up** VI (*before game*) sciogliere i muscoli, scaldarsi; (*col: relax*) rilassarsi

loot [luːt] N bottino ▶ VT saccheggiare

looter [ˈluːtər] N saccheggiatore(-trice)

looting [ˈluːtɪŋ] N saccheggio

lop [lɔp] VT (*also: lop off*) tagliare via, recidere

lop-sided [ˈlɔpˈsaɪdɪd] ADJ non equilibrato(-a), asimmetrico(-a)

lord [lɔːd] N signore *m*; **L~ Smith** lord Smith; **the L~** (*Rel*) il Signore; **good L~!** buon Dio!; **the (House of) Lords** (*BRIT*) la Camera dei Lord

lordly [ˈlɔːdlɪ] ADJ nobile, maestoso(-a); (*arrogant*) altero(-a)

lordship [ˈlɔːdʃɪp] N (*BRIT*): **your L~** Sua Eccellenza

lore [lɔːʳ] N tradizioni *fpl*

lorry [ˈlɔrɪ] N (*BRIT*) camion *m inv*

lorry driver N (*BRIT*) camionista *m*

lose [luːz] (*pt, pp* **lost** [lɔst]) VT perdere; (*pursuers*) distanziare ▶ VI perdere; **to ~ (time)** (*clock*) ritardare; **to ~ no time (in doing sth)** non perdere tempo (a fare qc); **to get lost** (*person*) perdersi, smarrirsi; (*object*) andare perso *or* perduto

▶ **lose out** VI rimetterci

loser [ˈluːzəʳ] N perdente *mf*; **to be a good/bad ~** saper/non saper perdere

loss [lɔs] N perdita; **to cut one's losses** rimetterci il meno possibile; **to make a ~** subire una perdita; **to sell sth at a ~** vendere qc in perdita; **to be at a ~** essere perplesso(-a); **to be at a ~ to explain sth** non saper come fare a spiegare qc

loss adjuster N (*Insurance*) responsabile *mf* della valutazione dei danni

loss leader N (*Comm*) articolo a prezzo ridottissimo per attirare la clientela

lost [lɔst] PT, PP *of* **lose** ▶ ADJ perduto(-a); **~ in thought** immerso *or* perso nei propri pensieri

lost and found N (*BRIT*) oggetti *mpl* smarriti; **lost property office** *or* **department** ufficio oggetti smarriti

lost property N (*US*) = **lost and found**

lot [lɔt] N (*at auctions*) lotto; (*destiny*) destino, sorte *f*; **the ~** tutto(-a) quanto(-a); tutti(-e) quanti(-e); **a ~** molto; **a ~ of** una gran quantità di, un sacco di; **lots of** molto(-a); **to draw lots (for sth)** tirare a sorte (per qc)

lotion [ˈləuʃən] N lozione *f*

lottery [ˈlɔtərɪ] N lotteria

loud [laud] ADJ forte, alto(-a); (*gaudy*) vistoso(-a), sgargiante ▶ ADV (*speak etc*) forte; **out ~** (*read etc*) ad alta voce

loudhailer [laudˈheɪləʳ] N (*BRIT*) portavoce *m inv*

loudly [ˈlaudlɪ] ADV fortemente, ad alta voce

loudspeaker [laudˈspiːkəʳ] N altoparlante *m*

lounge [laundʒ] N salotto, soggiorno; (*of hotel*) salone *m*; (*of airport*) sala d'attesa; (*BRIT: also:*

lounge bar) bar *m inv* con servizio a tavolino ▶ vi oziare; starsene colle mani in mano

lounge bar N bar *m inv* con servizio a tavolino

lounge suit N (BRIT) completo da uomo

louse [laus] (*pl* **lice** [laɪs]) N pidocchio ▶ **louse up** VT (*col*) rovinare

lousy ['lauzɪ] ADJ (*col*: *fig*) orrendo(-a), schifoso(-a); **to feel ~** stare da cani

lout [laut] N zoticone *m*

louvre, (*US*) **louver** ['luːvəʳ] ADJ (*door, window*) con apertura a gelosia

lovable ['lʌvəbl] ADJ simpatico(-a), carino(-a); amabile

love [lʌv] N amore *m* ▶ VT amare; voler bene a; **I ~ you** ti amo; **to ~ to do: I ~ to do** mi piace fare; **I'd ~ to come** mi piacerebbe molto venire; **to be in ~ with** essere innamorato(-a) di; **to fall in ~ with** innamorarsi di; **to make ~** fare l'amore; **~ at first sight** amore a prima vista, colpo di fulmine; **to send one's ~ to sb** mandare i propri saluti a qn; **~ from Anne, ~, Anne** con affetto, Anne; **"15 ~"** (*Tennis*) "15 a zero"

love affair N relazione *f*

love child N (*irreg*) figlio(-a) dell'amore

loved ones [lʌvd-] NPL: **my ~** i miei cari

love-hate relationship ['lʌv'heɪt-] N rapporto amore-odio *inv*

love letter N lettera d'amore

love life N vita sentimentale

lovely ['lʌvlɪ] ADJ bello(-a); (*delicious: smell, meal*) buono(-a); **we had a ~ time** ci siamo divertiti molto

lover ['lʌvəʳ] N amante *mf*; (*person in love*) innamorato(-a); (*amateur*): **a ~ of** un (un') amante di; un (un') appassionato(-a) di

lovesick ['lʌvsɪk] ADJ malato(-a) d'amore

lovesong ['lʌvsɒŋ] N canzone *f* d'amore

loving ['lʌvɪŋ] ADJ affettuoso(-a), amoroso(-a), tenero(-a)

low [ləu] ADJ basso(-a) ▶ ADV in basso ▶ N (*Meteor*) depressione *f* ▶ VI (*cow*) muggire; **to be ~ on** (*supplies etc*) avere scarsità di; **to feel ~** sentirsi giù; **he's very ~** (*ill*) è molto debole; **to reach a new or an all-time ~** toccare il livello più basso *or* il minimo; **to turn (down) ~** vt abbassare

low-alcohol [ləu'ælkəhɒl] ADJ a basso contenuto alcolico

lowbrow ['ləubrau] ADJ (*person*) senza pretese intellettuali

low-calorie ['ləu'kælərɪ] ADJ a basso contenuto calorico

low-carb [ləu'kɑːb] ADJ (*col*) a basso contenuto di carboidrati

low-cut ['ləukʌt] ADJ (*dress*) scollato(-a)

low-down ['ləudaun] ADJ (*mean*) ignobile ▶ N (*col*): **he gave me the ~ on it** mi ha messo al corrente dei fatti

lower ADJ, ADV COMPARATIVE ['ləuəʳ] (*bottom: of 2 things*) più basso(-a); (*less important*) meno importante ▶ VT (*gen*) calare; (*price, eyes, voice*) abbassare, ridurre; (*resistance*) indebolire ▶ VI ['lauəʳ] (*sky*) minacciare; **to ~ (at sb)** (*person*) dare un'occhiataccia (a qn)

lower case N minuscolo

low-fat ['ləu'fæt] ADJ magro(-a)

low-key ['ləu'kiː] ADJ moderato(-a); (*operation*) condotto(-a) con discrezione

lowland ['ləulənd] N bassopiano, pianura

low-level ['ləulɛvl] ADJ a basso livello; (*flying*) a bassa quota

low-loader ['ləuləudəʳ] N camion *m* a pianale basso

lowly ['ləulɪ] ADJ umile, modesto(-a)

low-lying [ləu'laɪŋ] ADJ a basso livello

low-paid [ləu'peɪd] ADJ mal pagato(-a)

low-rise ['ləuraɪz] ADJ di altezza contenuta

low-tech ['ləu'tɛk] ADJ a basso contenuto tecnologico

loyal ['lɔɪəl] ADJ fedele, leale

loyalist ['lɔɪəlɪst] N lealista *mf*

loyalty ['lɔɪəltɪ] N fedeltà *f inv*, lealtà *f inv*

loyalty card N carta che offre sconti a clienti abituali

lozenge ['lɒzɪndʒ] N (*Med*) pastiglia; (*Geom*) losanga

LP N ABBR (= *long-playing record*) LP *m inv*

LPG N ABBR (= *liquefied petroleum gas*) GPL *m* (= *gas di petrolio liquefatto*)

L-plates ['ɛlpleɪts] NPL (BRIT) ≈ contrassegno P principiante

LPN N ABBR (*US*: = *Licensed Practical Nurse*) ≈ infermiera diplomata

LRAM N ABBR (BRIT: = *Licentiate of the Royal Academy of Music*) specializzazione dopo la laurea

LSD N ABBR (= *lysergic acid diethylamide*) L.S.D. *m*; (BRIT: = *pounds, shillings and pence*) sistema monetario in vigore in Gran Bretagna fino al 1971

LSE N ABBR = **London School of Economics**

LT ABBR (*Elec*: = *low tension*) B.T.

Lt. ABBR (= *lieutenant*) Ten.

Ltd ABBR (*Comm*: = *limited*) ≈ S.r.l.

lubricant ['luːbrɪkənt] N lubrificante *m*

lubricate ['luːbrɪkeɪt] VT lubrificare

lucid ['luːsɪd] ADJ lucido(-a)

lucidity [luː'sɪdɪtɪ] N lucidità

luck [lʌk] N fortuna, sorte *f*; **bad ~** sfortuna, mala sorte; **good ~** (buona) fortuna; **to be in ~** essere fortunato(-a); **to be out of ~** essere sfortunato(-a)

luckily ['lʌkɪlɪ] ADV fortunatamente, per fortuna

luckless ['lʌklɪs] ADJ sventurato(-a)

lucky ['lʌkɪ] ADJ fortunato(-a); (number etc) che porta fortuna

lucrative ['lu:krətɪv] ADJ lucrativo(-a), lucroso(-a), profittevole

ludicrous ['lu:dɪkrəs] ADJ ridicolo(-a), assurdo(-a)

ludo ['lu:dəu] N ≈ gioco dell'oca

lug [lʌg] VT trascinare

luggage ['lʌgɪdʒ] N bagagli mpl

luggage rack N portabagagli m inv

luggage van, (US) **luggage car** N (Rail) bagagliaio

lugubrious [lu'gu:brɪəs] ADJ lugubre

lukewarm ['lu:kwɔ:m] ADJ tiepido(-a)

lull [lʌl] N intervallo di calma ▶ VT (child) cullare; (person, fear) acquietare, calmare; **to ~ sb to sleep** cullare qn finché si addormenta

lullaby ['lʌləbaɪ] N ninnananna

lumbago [lʌm'beɪgəu] N lombaggine f

lumber ['lʌmbə^r] N (wood) legname m; (junk) roba vecchia ▶ VT (BRIT col): **to ~ sb with sth/sb** affibbiare or rifilare qc/qn a qn ▶ VI (also: **lumber about**, **lumber along**) muoversi pesantemente

lumberjack ['lʌmbədʒæk] N boscaiolo

lumber room N (BRIT) sgabuzzino

lumber yard N segheria

luminous ['lu:mɪnəs] ADJ luminoso(-a)

lump [lʌmp] N pezzo; (in sauce) grumo; (swelling) gonfiore m; (also: **sugar lump**) zolletta ▶ VT (also: **lump together**) riunire, mettere insieme

lump sum N somma globale

lumpy ['lʌmpɪ] ADJ (sauce) pieno(-a) di grumi; (bed) bitorzoluto(-a)

lunacy ['lu:nəsɪ] N demenza, follia, pazzia

lunar ['lu:nə^r] ADJ lunare

lunatic ['lu:nətɪk] ADJ, N (!) pazzo(-a), matto(-a)

lunatic asylum N (!) manicomio

lunch [lʌntʃ] N pranzo, colazione f; **to invite sb to** or **for ~** invitare qn a pranzo or a colazione

lunch break N intervallo del pranzo

luncheon ['lʌntʃən] N pranzo

luncheon meat N ≈ mortadella

luncheon voucher N buono m pasto inv

lunch hour N = **lunch break**

lunchtime ['lʌntʃtaɪm] N ora di pranzo

lung [lʌŋ] N polmone m

lung cancer N cancro del polmone

lunge [lʌndʒ] VI (also: **lunge forward**) fare un balzo in avanti; **to ~ at sb** balzare su qn

lupin ['lu:pɪn] N lupino

lurch [lə:tʃ] VI vacillare, barcollare ▶ N scatto improvviso; **to leave sb in the ~** piantare in asso qn

lure [luə^r] N richiamo; lusinga ▶ VT attirare (con l'inganno)

lurid ['luərɪd] ADJ sgargiante; (details etc) impressionante

lurk [lə:k] VI stare in agguato

luscious ['lʌʃəs] ADJ succulento(-a); delizioso(-a)

lush [lʌʃ] ADJ lussureggiante

lust [lʌst] N lussuria; cupidigia; desiderio; (fig): **~ for** sete f di
▶ **lust after** VT FUS bramare, desiderare

luster ['lʌstə^r] N (US) = **lustre**

lustful ['lʌstful] ADJ lascivo(-a), voglioso(-a)

lustre, (US) **luster** ['lʌstə^r] N lustro, splendore m

lusty ['lʌstɪ] ADJ vigoroso(-a), robusto(-a)

lute [lu:t] N liuto

Luxembourg ['lʌksəmbə:g] N (state) Lussemburgo m; (city) Lussemburgo f

luxuriant [lʌg'zjuərɪənt] ADJ lussureggiante

luxurious [lʌg'zjuərɪəs] ADJ sontuoso(-a), di lusso

luxury ['lʌkʃərɪ] N lusso ▶ CPD di lusso

LV N ABBR (BRIT) = **luncheon voucher**

LW ABBR (Radio: = long wave) O.L.

Lycra® ['laɪkrə] N lycra® f inv

lying ['laɪŋ] N bugie fpl, menzogne fpl ▶ ADJ (statement, story) falso(-a); (person) bugiardo(-a)

lynch [lɪntʃ] VT linciare

lynx [lɪŋks] N lince f

Lyons ['laɪənz] N Lione f

lyre ['laɪə^r] N lira

lyric ['lɪrɪk] ADJ lirico(-a) ▪ **lyrics** NPL (of song) parole fpl

lyrical ['lɪrɪkl] ADJ lirico(-a)

lyricism ['lɪrɪsɪzəm] N lirismo

Mm

M, m [ɛm] N (*letter*) M, m f *inv* or m *inv*; **M for Mary,** (*US*) **M for Mike** ≈ M come Milano

M N ABBR (*BRIT*) = **motorway** ▶ ABBR (= *medium*) taglia media; **the M8** ≈ l'A8

m ABBR (= *metre*) m = **mile; million**

MA N ABBR (*Scol*) = **Master of Arts**; (*US*) = **military academy** ▶ ABBR (*US*) = **Massachusetts**

ma [mɑː] N (*col*) mamma

mac [mæk] N (*BRIT*) impermeabile *m*

macabre [məˈkɑːbrə] ADJ macabro(-a)

macaroni [mækəˈrəʊnɪ] N maccheroni *mpl*

macaroon [mækəˈruːn] N amaretto (*biscotto*)

mace [meɪs] N mazza; (*spice*) macis *m* or *f*

Macedonia [mæsɪˈdəʊnɪə] N Macedonia

Macedonian [mæsɪˈdəʊnɪən] ADJ macedone ▶ N macedone *mf*; (*Ling*) macedone *m*

machinations [mækɪˈneɪʃənz] NPL macchinazioni *fpl*, intrighi *mpl*

machine [məˈʃiːn] N macchina ▶ VT (*dress etc*) cucire a macchina; (*Tech*) lavorare (a macchina)

machine code N (*Comput*) codice *m* di macchina, codice assoluto

machine gun N mitragliatrice *f*

machine language N (*Comput*) linguaggio *m* macchina *inv*

machine-readable [məˈʃiːnriːdəbl] ADJ (*Comput*) leggibile dalla macchina

machinery [məˈʃiːnərɪ] N macchinario, macchine *fpl*; (*fig*) macchina

machine shop N officina meccanica

machine tool N macchina utensile

machine washable ADJ lavabile in lavatrice

machinist [məˈʃiːnɪst] N macchinista *mf*

macho [ˈmætʃəʊ] ADJ macho *inv*

mackerel [ˈmækrəl] N (*pl inv*) sgombro

mackintosh [ˈmækɪntɔʃ] N (*BRIT*) impermeabile *m*

macro... [ˈmækrəʊ] PREFIX macro...

macroeconomics [ˈmækrəʊiːkəˈnɔmɪks] N macroeconomia

mad [mæd] ADJ matto(-a), pazzo(-a); (*foolish*) sciocco(-a); (*angry*) furioso(-a); **to go ~** impazzire, diventar matto; **~ (at or with sb)** furibondo(-a) (con qn); **to be ~ (keen) about** or **on sth** (*col*) andar matto(-a) per qc

Madagascar [mædəˈgæskəʳ] N Madagascar *m*

madam [ˈmædəm] N signora; **M~ Chairman** Signora Presidentessa

madcap [ˈmædkæp] ADJ (*col*) senza senso, assurdo(-a)

mad cow disease N encefalite f bovina spongiforme

madden [ˈmædn] VT fare infuriare

maddening [ˈmædnɪŋ] ADJ esasperante

made [meɪd] PT, PP *of* **make**

Madeira [məˈdɪərə] N (*Geo*) Madera; (*wine*) madera *m*

made-to-measure [ˈmeɪdtəˈmɛʒəʳ] ADJ (*BRIT*) fatto(-a) su misura

made-up [ˈmeɪdʌp] ADJ (*story*) inventato(-a)

madhouse [ˈmædhaus] N (*also fig*) manicomio

madly [ˈmædlɪ] ADV follemente; (*love*) alla follia

madman [ˈmædmən] N (*irreg*) pazzo, alienato

madness [ˈmædnɪs] N pazzia

Madrid [məˈdrɪd] N Madrid f

Mafia [ˈmæfɪə] N mafia f

mag [mæg] N ABBR (*BRIT col: Press*) = **magazine**

magazine [mægəˈziːn] N (*Press*) rivista; (*Radio, TV*) rubrica; (*Mil: store*) magazzino, deposito; (*of firearm*) caricatore *m*

maggot [ˈmægət] N baco, verme *m*

magic [ˈmædʒɪk] N magia ▶ ADJ magico(-a)

magical [ˈmædʒɪkəl] ADJ magico(-a)

magician [məˈdʒɪʃən] N mago(-a)

magistrate [ˈmædʒɪstreɪt] N magistrato; giudice *mf*

magistrates' court N *see* **crown court**

magnanimous [mæɡˈnænɪməs] ADJ magnanimo(-a)

magnate [ˈmæɡneɪt] N magnate *m*

magnesium [mæɡˈniːzɪəm] N magnesio

magnet [ˈmægnɪt] N magnete m, calamita
magnetic [mægˈnɛtɪk] ADJ magnetico(-a)
magnetic disk N (*Comput*) disco magnetico
magnetic tape N nastro magnetico
magnetism [ˈmægnɪtɪzəm] N magnetismo
magnification [mægnɪfɪˈkeɪʃən] N ingrandimento
magnificence [mægˈnɪfɪsns] N magnificenza
magnificent [mægˈnɪfɪsnt] ADJ magnifico(-a)
magnify [ˈmægnɪfaɪ] VT ingrandire
magnifying glass [ˈmægnɪfaɪŋ-] N lente f d'ingrandimento
magnitude [ˈmægnɪtjuːd] N grandezza; importanza
magnolia [mægˈnəʊlɪə] N magnolia
magpie [ˈmægpaɪ] N gazza
mahogany [məˈhɔgənɪ] N mogano ▸ CPD di or in mogano
maid [meɪd] N domestica; (*in hotel*) cameriera; **old ~** (*pej*) vecchia zitella
maiden [ˈmeɪdn] N fanciulla ▸ ADJ (*aunt etc*) nubile; (*speech, voyage*) inaugurale
maiden name [ˈmeɪdn-] N nome da m nubile or da ragazza
mail [meɪl] N posta ▸ VT spedire (per posta); **by ~** per posta
mailbox [ˈmeɪlbɔks] N (*US*) cassetta delle lettere; (*Comput*) mailbox f inv
mailing list [ˈmeɪlɪŋ-] N elenco d'indirizzi
mailman [ˈmeɪlmæn] N (*irreg*) (*US*) portalettere m inv, postino
mail-order [ˈmeɪlɔːrˈ] N vendita (or acquisto) per corrispondenza ▸ CPD: **~ firm** or **house** ditta di vendita per corrispondenza
mailshot [ˈmeɪlʃɔt] N mailing m inv
mail train N treno postale
mail truck N (*US Aut*) = **mail van**
mail van N (*BRIT: Aut*) furgone m postale; (: *Rail*) vagone m postale
maim [meɪm] VT mutilare
main [meɪn] ADJ principale ▸ N (*pipe*) conduttura principale; **the mains** (*Elec*) la linea principale; **mains operated** adj che funziona a elettricità; **in the ~** nel complesso, nell'insieme
main course N (*Culin*) piatto principale, piatto forte
mainframe [ˈmeɪnfreɪm] N (*also*: **mainframe computer**) mainframe m inv
mainland [ˈmeɪnlənd] N continente m
mainline [ˈmeɪnlaɪn] ADJ (*Rail*) della linea principale ▸ VT (*drugs slang*) bucarsi di ▸ VI (*drugs slang*) bucarsi
main line N (*Rail*) linea principale
mainly [ˈmeɪnlɪ] ADV principalmente, soprattutto

main road N strada principale
mainstay [ˈmeɪnsteɪ] N (*fig*) sostegno principale
mainstream [ˈmeɪnstriːm] N (*fig*) corrente f principale
main street N strada principale
maintain [meɪnˈteɪn] VT mantenere; (*affirm*) sostenere; **to ~ that ...** sostenere che ...
maintenance [ˈmeɪntənəns] N manutenzione f; (*alimony*) alimenti mpl
maintenance contract N contratto di manutenzione
maintenance order N (*Law*) obbligo degli alimenti
maisonette [meɪzəˈnɛt] N (*BRIT*) appartamento a due piani
maize [meɪz] N granturco, mais m
Maj. ABBR (*Mil*) = **major**
majestic [məˈdʒɛstɪk] ADJ maestoso(-a)
majesty [ˈmædʒɪstɪ] N maestà f inv
major [ˈmeɪdʒəʳ] N (*Mil*) maggiore m ▸ ADJ (*greater, Mus*) maggiore; (*in importance*) principale, importante ▸ VI (*US Scol*): **to ~ (in)** specializzarsi (in); **a ~ operation** (*Med*) una grossa operazione
Majorca [məˈjɔːkə] N Maiorca
major general N (*Mil*) generale m di divisione
majority [məˈdʒɔrɪtɪ] N maggioranza ▸ CPD (*verdict*) maggioritario(-a)
majority holding N (*Comm*): **to have a ~** essere maggiore azionista
make [meɪk] (*pt, pp* **made** [meɪd]) VT fare; (*manufacture*) fare, fabbricare; (*cause to be*): **to ~ sb sad** etc rendere qn triste etc; (*force*): **to ~ sb do sth** costringere qn a fare qc, far fare qc a qn; (*equal*): **2 and 2 ~ 4** 2 più 2 fa 4 ▸ N fabbricazione f; (*brand*) marca; **to ~ a fool of sb** far fare a qn la figura dello scemo; **to ~ a profit** realizzare un profitto; **to ~ a loss** subire una perdita; **to ~ it** (*in time etc*) arrivare; (*succeed*) farcela; **what time do you ~ it?** che ora fai?; **to ~ good** vi (*succeed*) aver successo; vt (*deficit*) colmare; (*losses*) compensare; **to ~ do with** arrangiarsi con
▸ **make for** VT FUS (*place*) avviarsi verso
▸ **make off** VI svignarsela
▸ **make out** VT (*write out*) scrivere; (: *cheque*) emettere; (*understand*) capire; (*see*) distinguere; (: *numbers*) decifrare; (*claim, imply*): **to ~ out (that)** voler far credere (che); **to ~ out a case for sth** presentare delle valide ragioni in favore di qc
▸ **make over** VT (*assign*): **to ~ over (to)** passare (a), trasferire (a)
▸ **make up** VT (*constitute*) formare; (*invent*) inventare; (*parcel*) fare ▸ VI conciliarsi; (*with cosmetics*) truccarsi; **to be made up of** essere composto di or formato da
▸ **make up for** VT FUS compensare; ricuperare
make-believe [ˈmeɪkbɪliːv] N: **a world of ~** un

mondo di favole; **it's just ~** è tutta un'invenzione

makeover [ˈmeɪkəʊvəʳ] N cambio di immagine; **to give sb a ~** far cambiare immagine a qn

maker [ˈmeɪkəʳ] N (of programme etc) creatore(-trice); (manufacturer) fabbricante m

makeshift [ˈmeɪkʃɪft] ADJ improvvisato(-a)

make-up [ˈmeɪkʌp] N trucco

make-up bag N borsa del trucco

make-up remover N struccatore m

making [ˈmeɪkɪŋ] N (fig): **in the ~** in formazione; **he has the makings of an actor** ha la stoffa dell'attore

maladjusted [mæləˈdʒʌstɪd] ADJ disadattato(-a)

maladroit [mæləˈdrɔɪt] ADJ maldestro(-a)

malaise [mæˈleɪz] N malessere m

malaria [məˈlɛərɪə] N malaria

Malawi [məˈlɑːwɪ] N Malawi m

Malay [məˈleɪ] ADJ malese ▶ N malese mf; (Ling) malese m

Malaya [məˈleɪə] N Malesia

Malayan [məˈleɪən] ADJ, N = **Malay**

Malaysia [məˈleɪzɪə] N Malaysia

Malaysian [məˈleɪzɪən] ADJ, N malaysiano(-a)

Maldives [ˈmɔːldaɪvz] NPL: **the ~** le (isole) Maldive

male [meɪl] N (Biol, Elec) maschio ▶ ADJ (gen, sex) maschile; (animal, child) maschio(-a); **~ and female students** studenti e studentesse

male chauvinist N maschilista m

male nurse N infermiere m

malevolence [məˈlɛvələns] N malevolenza

malevolent [məˈlɛvələnt] ADJ malevolo(-a)

malfunction [mælˈfʌŋkʃən] N funzione f difettosa

Mali [ˈmɑːlɪ] N Mali m

malice [ˈmælɪs] N malevolenza

malicious [məˈlɪʃəs] ADJ malevolo(-a); (Law) doloso(-a)

malign [məˈlaɪn] VT malignare su; calunniare

malignant [məˈlɪgnənt] ADJ (Med) maligno(-a)

malingerer [məˈlɪŋgərəʳ] N scansafatiche mf

mall [mɔːl] N (also: **shopping mall**) centro commerciale

malleable [ˈmælɪəbl] ADJ malleabile

mallet [ˈmælɪt] N maglio

malnutrition [mælnjuːˈtrɪʃən] N denutrizione f

malpractice [mælˈpræktɪs] N prevaricazione f; negligenza

malt [mɔːlt] N malto ▶ CPD (whisky) di malto

Malta [ˈmɔːltə] N Malta

Maltese [mɔːlˈtiːz] ADJ, N (pl inv) maltese (mf); (Ling) maltese m

maltreat [mælˈtriːt] VT maltrattare

malware [ˈmælwɛəʳ] N (Comput) malware mpl, software mpl maligni

mammal [ˈmæml] N mammifero

mammoth [ˈmæməθ] N mammut m inv ▶ ADJ enorme, gigantesco(-a)

man [mæn] (pl **men**) N uomo; (Chess) pezzo; (Draughts) pedina ▶ VT fornire d'uomini; stare a; essere di servizio a; **an old ~** un vecchio; **~ and wife** marito e moglie

manacles [ˈmænəklz] NPL manette fpl

manage [ˈmænɪdʒ] VI farcela ▶ VT (be in charge of) occuparsi di; (shop, restaurant) gestire; **to ~ without sth/sb** fare a meno di qc/qn; **to ~ to do sth** riuscire a far qc

manageable [ˈmænɪdʒəbl] ADJ maneggevole; (task etc) fattibile

management [ˈmænɪdʒmənt] N amministrazione f, direzione f; gestione f; (persons: of business, firm) dirigenti mpl; (: of hotel, shop, theatre) direzione f; **"under new ~"** "sotto nuova gestione"

management accounting N contabilità di gestione

management buyout N acquisto di una società da parte dei suoi dirigenti

management consultant N consulente mf aziendale

manager [ˈmænɪdʒəʳ] N direttore(-trice); (of shop, restaurant) gerente mf; (of artist, Sport) manager m inv; **sales ~** direttore(-trice) delle vendite

manageress [mænɪdʒəˈrɛs] N direttrice f; gerente f

managerial [mænəˈdʒɪərɪəl] ADJ dirigenziale

managing director [ˈmænɪdʒɪŋ-] N amministratore(-trice) delegato(-a)

Mancunian [mæŋˈkjuːnɪən] ADJ di Manchester ▶ N abitante mf di Manchester; originario(-a) di Manchester

mandarin [ˈmændərɪn] N (person, fruit) mandarino

mandate [ˈmændeɪt] N mandato

mandatory [ˈmændətərɪ] ADJ obbligatorio(-a); ingiuntivo(-a)

mandolin, mandoline [ˈmændəlɪn] N mandolino

mane [meɪn] N criniera

maneuver etc [məˈnuːvəʳ] (US) = **manoeuvre** etc

manful [ˈmænful] ADJ coraggioso(-a), valoroso(-a)

manfully [ˈmænfəlɪ] ADV valorosamente

manganese [mæŋgəˈniːz] N manganese m

mangetout [ˈmɔnʒˈtuː] N pisello dolce, taccola

mangle [ˈmæŋgl] VT straziare; mutilare ▶ N strizzatoio

mango [ˈmæŋgəʊ] (pl **mangoes**) N mango

mangrove [ˈmæŋɡrəuv] N mangrovia

mangy [ˈmeɪndʒɪ] ADJ rognoso(-a)

manhandle [ˈmænhændl] VT (treat roughly) maltmenare; (move by hand: goods) spostare a mano

manhole [ˈmænhəul] N botola stradale

manhood [ˈmænhud] N età virile; virilità

man-hour [ˈmænauəʳ] N ora di lavoro

manhunt [ˈmænhʌnt] N caccia all'uomo

mania [ˈmeɪnɪə] N mania

maniac [ˈmeɪnɪæk] N maniaco(-a)

manic [ˈmænɪk] ADJ (behaviour, activity) maniacale

manic-depressive [ˈmænɪkdɪˈprɛsɪv] ADJ maniaco-depressivo(-a) ▶ N persona affetta da mania depressiva

manicure [ˈmænɪkjuəʳ] N manicure f inv

manicure set N trousse f inv della manicure

manifest [ˈmænɪfɛst] VT manifestare ▶ ADJ manifesto(-a), palese ▶ N (Aviat, Naut) manifesto

manifestation [mænɪfɛsˈteɪʃən] N manifestazione f

manifesto [mænɪˈfɛstəu] N manifesto

manifold [ˈmænɪfəuld] ADJ molteplice ▶ N (Aut etc): **exhaust ~** collettore m di scarico

Manila [məˈnɪlə] N Manila

manila, manilla [məˈnɪlə] ADJ (paper, envelope) manilla inv

manipulate [məˈnɪpjuleɪt] VT (tool) maneggiare; (controls) azionare; (limb, facts) manipolare

manipulation [mənɪpjuˈleɪʃən] N maneggiare m; capacità di azionare; manipolazione f

mankind [mænˈkaɪnd] N umanità, genere m umano

manliness [ˈmænlɪnɪs] N virilità

manly [ˈmænlɪ] ADJ virile; coraggioso(-a)

man-made [ˈmænˈmeɪd] ADJ sintetico(-a); artificiale

manna [ˈmænə] N manna

mannequin [ˈmænɪkɪn] N (dummy) manichino; (fashion model) indossatrice f

manner [ˈmænəʳ] N maniera, modo; (behaviour) modo di fare; (type, sort): **all ~ of things** ogni genere di cosa ▪ **manners** NPL (conduct) maniere fpl; **(good) manners** buona educazione f, buone maniere; **bad manners** maleducazione f

mannerism [ˈmænərɪzəm] N vezzo, tic m inv

mannerly [ˈmænəlɪ] ADJ educato(-a), civile

manoeuvrable, (US) **maneuverable** [məˈnuːvrəbl] ADJ facile da manovrare; (car) maneggevole

manoeuvre, (US) **maneuver** [məˈnuːvəʳ] VT manovrare ▶ VI far manovre ▶ N manovra; **to ~ sb into doing sth** costringere abilmente qn a fare qc

manor [ˈmænəʳ] N (also: **manor house**) maniero

manpower [ˈmænpauəʳ] N manodopera

manservant [ˈmænsəvənt] (pl **menservants** [ˈmɛn-]) N domestico

mansion [ˈmænʃən] N casa signorile

manslaughter [ˈmænslɔːtəʳ] N colposo

mantelpiece [ˈmæntlpiːs] N mensola del caminetto

mantle [ˈmæntl] N mantello

man-to-man [ˈmæntəˈmæn] ADJ, ADV da uomo a uomo

Mantua [ˈmæntjuə] N Mantova

manual [ˈmænjuəl] ADJ, N manuale (m)

manual worker N manovale m

manufacture [mænjuˈfæktʃəʳ] VT fabbricare ▶ N fabbricazione f, manifattura

manufactured goods NPL manufatti mpl

manufacturer [mænjuˈfæktʃərəʳ] N fabbricante m

manufacturing industries [mænjuˈfæktʃərɪŋ-] NPL industrie fpl manifatturiere

manure [məˈnjuəʳ] N concime m

manuscript [ˈmænjuskrɪpt] N manoscritto

many [ˈmɛnɪ] ADJ molti(-e) ▶ PRON molti(-e), un gran numero; **a great ~** moltissimi(-e), un gran numero (di); **~ a ...** molti(-e) ..., più di un(a) ...; **too ~ difficulties** troppe difficoltà; **twice as ~** due volte tanto; **how ~?** quanti(-e)?

Maori [ˈmaurɪ] ADJ, N maori (mf) inv

map [mæp] N carta (geografica); (of city) cartina ▶ VT fare una carta di

▶ **map out** VT tracciare un piano di; (fig: career, holiday, essay) pianificare

maple [ˈmeɪpl] N acero

mar [mɑːʳ] VT sciupare

Mar. ABBR (= March) mar.

marathon [ˈmærəθən] N maratona ▶ ADJ: **a ~ session** una seduta fiume

marathon runner N maratoneta mf

marauder [məˈrɔːdəʳ] N saccheggiatore(-trice); predatore(-trice)

marble [ˈmɑːbl] N marmo; (toy) pallina, bilia ▪ **marbles** N (game) palline, bilie

March [mɑːtʃ] N marzo; see also **July**

march [mɑːtʃ] VI marciare; sfilare ▶ N marcia; (demonstration) dimostrazione f; **to ~ into a room** entrare a passo deciso in una stanza

marcher [ˈmɑːtʃəʳ] N dimostrante mf

marching [ˈmɑːtʃɪŋ] N: **to give sb his ~ orders** (fig) dare il benservito a qn

march-past [ˈmɑːtʃpɑːst] N sfilata

mare [mɛəʳ] N giumenta

marg [mɑːdʒ] N ABBR (col) = **margarine**

margarine [mɑːdʒəˈriːn] N margarina

marge [mɑːdʒ] N ABBR (col) = **margarine**

margin [ˈmɑːdʒɪn] N margine m

marginal [ˈmɑːdʒɪnl] ADJ marginale; ~ **seat** (Pol) seggio elettorale ottenuto con una stretta maggioranza

marginally [ˈmɑːdʒɪnəlɪ] ADV (bigger, better) lievemente, di poco; (different) un po'

marigold [ˈmærɪɡəuld] N calendola

marijuana [mærɪˈwɑːnə] N marijuana

marina [məˈriːnə] N marina

marinade N [mærɪˈneɪd] marinata ▸ VT [ˈmærɪneɪd] = **marinate**

marinate [ˈmærɪneɪt] VT marinare

marine [məˈriːn] ADJ (animal, plant) marino(-a); (forces, engineering) marittimo(-a) ▸ N (BRIT) fante m di marina; (US) marine m inv

marine insurance N assicurazione f marittima

marital [ˈmærɪtl] ADJ maritale, coniugale; ~ **status** stato coniugale

maritime [ˈmærɪtaɪm] ADJ marittimo(-a)

maritime law N diritto marittimo

marjoram [ˈmɑːdʒərəm] N maggiorana

mark [mɑːk] N segno; (stain) macchia; (of skid etc) traccia; (BRIT Scol) voto; (Sport) bersaglio; (Hist: currency) marco; (BRIT Tech): **M~ 2/3** 1a/2a serie f ▸ VT segnare; (stain) macchiare; (indicate) indicare; (BRIT Scol) dare un voto a; correggere; (Sport: player) marcare; **punctuation marks** segni di punteggiatura; **to be quick off the ~ (in doing)** (fig) non perdere tempo (per fare); **up to the ~** (in efficiency) all'altezza; **to ~ time** segnare il passo
  ▸ **mark down** VT (reduce: prices, goods) ribassare, ridurre
  ▸ **mark off** VT (tick off) spuntare, cancellare
  ▸ **mark out** VT delimitare
  ▸ **mark up** VT (price) aumentare

marked [mɑːkt] ADJ spiccato(-a), chiaro(-a)

markedly [ˈmɑːkɪdlɪ] ADV visibilmente, notevolmente

marker [ˈmɑːkər] N (sign) segno; (bookmark) segnalibro

market [ˈmɑːkɪt] N mercato ▸ VT (Comm) mettere in vendita; (promote) lanciare sul mercato; **to play the ~** giocare or speculare in borsa; **to be on the ~** essere (messo) in vendita or in commercio; **open ~** mercato libero

marketable [ˈmɑːkɪtəbl] ADJ commercializzabile

market analysis N analisi f inv di mercato

market day N giorno di mercato

market demand N domanda del mercato

market economy N economia di mercato

market forces NPL forze fpl di mercato

market garden N (BRIT) orto industriale

marketing [ˈmɑːkɪtɪŋ] N marketing m

marketplace [ˈmɑːkɪtpleɪs] N (piazza del) mercato; (world of trade) piazza, mercato

market price N prezzo di mercato

market research N indagine f or ricerca di mercato

market value N valore m di mercato

marking [ˈmɑːkɪŋ] N (on animal) marcatura di colore; (on road) segnaletica orizzontale

marksman [ˈmɑːksmən] N (irreg) tiratore m scelto

marksmanship [ˈmɑːksmənʃɪp] N abilità nel tiro

mark-up [ˈmɑːkʌp] N (Comm: margin) margine di vendita; (: increase) aumento

marmalade [ˈmɑːməleɪd] N marmellata d'arance

maroon [məˈruːn] VT (fig): **to be marooned (in** or **at)** essere abbandonato(-a) (in) ▸ ADJ bordeaux inv

marquee [mɑːˈkiː] N padiglione m

marquess, marquis [ˈmɑːkwɪs] N marchese m

Marrakech, Marrakesh [mærəˈkɛʃ] N Marrakesh f

marriage [ˈmærɪdʒ] N matrimonio

marriage bureau N agenzia matrimoniale

marriage certificate N certificato di matrimonio

marriage guidance, (US) **marriage counseling** N consulenza matrimoniale

marriage of convenience N matrimonio di convenienza

married [ˈmærɪd] ADJ sposato(-a); (life, love) coniugale, matrimoniale

marrow [ˈmærəu] N midollo; (vegetable) zucca

marry [ˈmærɪ] VT sposare, sposarsi con; (father, priest etc) dare in matrimonio ▸ VI (also: **get married**) sposarsi

Mars [mɑːz] N (planet) Marte m

Marseilles [mɑːˈseɪlz] N Marsiglia

marsh [mɑːʃ] N palude f

marshal [ˈmɑːʃl] N maresciallo; (US: fire marshal) capo; (: police marshal) capitano; (for demonstration, meeting) membro del servizio d'ordine ▸ VT (thoughts, support) ordinare; (soldiers) adunare

marshalling yard [ˈmɑːʃlɪŋ-] N scalo smistamento

Marshall Islands [ˈmɑːʃəl-] NPL Isole fpl Marshall

marshmallow [mɑːʃˈmæləu] N (Bot) altea; (sweet) caramella soffice e gommosa

marshy [ˈmɑːʃɪ] ADJ paludoso(-a)

marsupial [mɑːˈsuːpɪəl] ADJ, N marsupiale (m)

martial [ˈmɑːʃl] ADJ marziale

martial arts NPL arti fpl marziali

martial law N legge f marziale

Martian [ˈmɑːʃən] N marziano(-a)

martin [ˈmɑːtɪn] N (also: **house martin**) balestruccio

martyr ['mɑːtə'] N martire *mf* ▶ VT martiriz-
zare

martyrdom ['mɑːtədəm] N martirio

marvel ['mɑːvl] N meraviglia ▶ VI: **to ~ (at)**
meravigliarsi (di)

marvellous, (*US*) **marvelous** ['mɑːvələs] ADJ
meraviglioso(-a)

Marxism ['mɑːksɪzəm] N marxismo

Marxist ['mɑːksɪst] ADJ, N marxista (*mf*)

marzipan ['mɑːzɪpæn] N marzapane *m*

mascara [mæs'kɑːrə] N mascara *m* *inv*

mascot ['mæskət] N mascotte *f* *inv*

masculine ['mæskjulɪn] ADJ maschile; (*woman*)
mascolino(-a) ▶ N genere *m* maschile

masculinity [mæskju'lɪnɪtɪ] N mascolinità

mash [mæʃ] VT (*Culin*) passare, schiacciare

mashed [mæʃt] ADJ: **~ potatoes** purè *m* di patate

mask [mɑːsk] N (*gen*, *Elec*) maschera ▶ VT
mascherare

masochism ['mæsəkɪzəm] N masochismo

masochist ['mæsəkɪst] N masochista *mf*

mason ['meɪsn] N (*also:* **stonemason**) scalpellino; (*also:* **freemason**) massone *m*

masonic [mə'sɔnɪk] ADJ massonico(-a)

masonry ['meɪsnrɪ] N muratura

masquerade [mæskə'reɪd] N ballo in maschera;
(*fig*) mascherata ▶ VI: **to ~ as** farsi passare per

mass [mæs] N moltitudine *f*, massa; (*Physics*)
massa; (*Rel*) messa ▶ CPD di massa ▶ VI ammassarsi; **the masses** (*ordinary people*) le masse;
masses of (*col*) una montagna di; **to go to ~**
andare a *or* alla messa

massacre ['mæsəkə'] N massacro ▶ VT massacrare

massage ['mæsɑːʒ] N massaggio ▶ VT massaggiare

masseur [mæ'səː'] N massaggiatore *m*

masseuse [mæ'səːz] N massaggiatrice *f*

massive ['mæsɪv] ADJ enorme, massiccio(-a)

mass market N mercato di massa

mass media NPL mass media *mpl*

mass meeting N (*of everyone concerned*) riunione
f generale; (*huge*) adunata popolare

mass-produce ['mæsprə'djuːs] VT produrre in
serie

mass production N produzione *f* in serie

mast [mɑːst] N albero; (*Radio*, *TV*) pilone *m* (a
traliccio)

mastectomy [mæs'tɛktəmɪ] N mastectomia

master ['mɑːstə'] N padrone *m*; (*teacher: in primary school*, *Art etc*) maestro; (*: in secondary school*)
professore *m*; (*title for boys*): **M~ X** Signorino X
▶ VT domare; (*learn*) imparare a fondo; (*understand*) conoscere a fondo; **~ of ceremonies** *n*
maestro di cerimonie; **M~'s degree** *n* vedi nota

Il **Master's degree** è il riconoscimento conferito al termine di un corso di specializzazione
dopo aver conseguito un *Bachelor's degree*. Vi
sono diversi tipi di *Master's degrees*; i più comuni
sono il *Master of Arts* (MA) e il *Master of Science*
(MSc) che si ottengono dopo aver seguito un
corso e aver presentato una tesi originale. Per il
Master of Letters (MLitt) e il *Master of Philosophy*
(MPhil) è invece sufficiente presentare la tesi;
vedi anche **doctorate**.

master disk N (*Comput*) disco *m* master *inv*,
disco principale

masterful ['mɑːstəful] ADJ autoritario(-a),
imperioso(-a)

master key N chiave *f* maestra

masterly ['mɑːstəlɪ] ADJ magistrale

mastermind ['mɑːstəmaɪnd] N mente *f* superiore ▶ VT essere il cervello di

Master of Arts/Science N Master *m* *inv* in let-
tere/scienze

masterpiece ['mɑːstəpiːs] N capolavoro

master plan N piano generale

master stroke N colpo maestro

mastery ['mɑːstərɪ] N dominio; padronanza

mastiff ['mæstɪf] N mastino inglese

masturbate ['mæstəbeɪt] VI masturbare

masturbation [mæstə'beɪʃən] N masturba-
zione *f*

mat [mæt] N stuoia; (*also:* **doormat**) stoino, zer-
bino; (*also:* **table mat**) sottopiatto ▶ ADJ = **matt**

match [mætʃ] N fiammifero; (*game*) partita,
incontro; (*fig*) uguale *mf*; matrimonio; partito
▶ VT intonare; (*go well with*) andare benissimo
con; (*equal*) uguagliare; (*correspond to*) corrispondere a; (*pair: also:* **match up**) accoppiare ▶ VI
intonarsi; **to be a good ~** andare bene
▶ **match up** VT intonare

matchbox ['mætʃbɔks] N scatola per fiammiferi

matching ['mætʃɪŋ] ADJ ben assortito(-a)

matchless ['mætʃlɪs] ADJ senza pari

mate [meɪt] N compagno(-a) di lavoro; (*col:
friend*) amico(-a); (*animal*) compagno(-a); (*in merchant navy*) secondo ▶ VI accoppiarsi ▶ VT accoppiare

material [mə'tɪərɪəl] N (*substance*) materiale *m*,
materia; (*cloth*) stoffa ▶ ADJ materiale; (*important*) essenziale ▪ **materials** NPL (*equipment etc*)
materiali *mpl*; occorrente *m*

materialistic [mətɪərɪə'lɪstɪk] ADJ materialisti-
co(-a)

materialize [mə'tɪərɪəlaɪz] VI materializzarsi,
realizzarsi

materially [mə'tɪərɪəlɪ] ADV dal punto di vista
materiale; sostanzialmente

maternal [mə'təːnl] ADJ materno(-a)

maternity [mə'tə:nɪtɪ] N maternità ▸CPD di maternità; (*clothes*) pre-maman *inv*

maternity benefit N sussidio di maternità

maternity hospital N ≈ clinica ostetrica

maternity leave N congedo di maternità

matey ['meɪtɪ] ADJ (BRIT col) amicone(-a)

math [mæθ] N ABBR (US) = **mathematics**

mathematical [mæθə'mætɪkl] ADJ matematico(-a)

mathematician [mæθəmə'tɪʃən] N matematico(-a)

mathematics [mæθə'mætɪks] N matematica

maths [mæθs] N ABBR (BRIT) = **mathematics**

matinée ['mætɪneɪ] N matinée *f inv*

mating ['meɪtɪŋ] N accoppiamento

mating call N chiamata all'accoppiamento

mating season N stagione *f* degli amori

matriarchal [meɪtrɪ'ɑːkl] ADJ matriarcale

matrices ['meɪtrɪsiːz] NPL of **matrix**

matriculation [mətrɪkju'leɪʃən] N immatricolazione *f*

matrimonial [mætrɪ'məunɪəl] ADJ matrimoniale, coniugale

matrimony ['mætrɪmənɪ] N matrimonio

matrix ['meɪtrɪks] (*pl* **matrices** ['meɪtrɪsiːz]) N matrice *f*

matron ['meɪtrən] N (*in hospital*) capoinfermiera; (*in school*) infermiera

matronly ['meɪtrənlɪ] ADJ da matrona

matt [mæt] ADJ opaco(-a)

matted ['mætɪd] ADJ ingarbugliato(-a)

matter ['mætə'] N questione *f*; (*Physics*) materia, sostanza; (*content*) contenuto; (*Med: pus*) pus *m* ▸VI importare ■ **matters** NPL (*affairs*) questioni; **it doesn't ~** non importa; (*I don't mind*) non fa niente; **what's the ~?** che cosa c'è?; **no ~ what** qualsiasi cosa accada; **that's another ~** quello è un altro affare; **as a ~ of course** come cosa naturale; **as a ~ of fact** in verità; **it's a ~ of habit** è una questione di abitudine; **printed ~** stampe *fpl*; **reading ~** (BRIT) qualcosa da leggere

matter-of-fact [mætərəv'fækt] ADJ prosaico(-a)

matting ['mætɪŋ] N stuoia

mattress ['mætrɪs] N materasso

mature [mə'tjuə'] ADJ maturo(-a); (*cheese*) stagionato(-a) ▸VI maturare; stagionare; (*Comm*) scadere

mature student N *studente universitario che ha più di 25 anni*

maturity [mə'tjuərɪtɪ] N maturità

maudlin ['mɔːdlɪn] ADJ lacrimoso(-a)

maul [mɔːl] VT lacerare

Mauritania [mɔrɪ'teɪnɪə] N Mauritania

Mauritius [mə'rɪʃəs] N Maurizio

mausoleum [mɔːsə'lɪəm] N mausoleo

mauve [məuv] ADJ malva *inv*

maverick ['mævərɪk] N (*fig*) chi sta fuori del branco

mawkish ['mɔːkɪʃ] ADJ sdolcinato(-a); insipido(-a)

max. ABBR = **maximum**

maxim ['mæksɪm] N massima

maxima ['mæksɪmə] NPL of **maximum**

maximize ['mæksɪmaɪz] VT (*profits etc*) massimizzare; (*chances*) aumentare al massimo

maximum ['mæksɪməm] (*pl* **maxima** ['mæksɪmə]) ADJ massimo(-a) ▸N massimo

May [meɪ] N maggio; *see also* **July**

may [meɪ] (*conditional* **might** [maɪt]) VI: (*indicating possibility*) **he ~ come** può darsi che venga; (*be allowed to*) **~ I smoke?** posso fumare?; **~ I sit here?** le dispiace se mi siedo qua?; (*wishes*) **~ God bless you!** Dio la benedica!; **he might be there** può darsi che ci sia; **he might come** potrebbe venire, può anche darsi che venga; **I might as well go** potrei anche andarmene; **you might like to try** forse le piacerebbe provare

maybe ['meɪbɪ] ADV forse, può darsi; **~ he'll ...** può darsi che lui ...+*sub*, forse lui ...; **~ not** forse no, può darsi di no

mayday ['meɪdeɪ] N S.O.S. *m inv*, mayday *m inv*

May Day N il primo maggio

mayhem ['meɪhɛm] N cagnara

mayonnaise [meɪə'neɪz] N maionese *f*

mayor [mɛə'] N sindaco

mayoress ['mɛərɛs] N sindaco (*donna*); moglie *f* del sindaco

maypole ['meɪpəul] N *palo ornato di fiori attorno a cui si danza durante la festa di maggio*

maze [meɪz] N labirinto, dedalo

MB ABBR (*Comput*) = **megabyte**; (CANADA) = **Manitoba**

MBA N ABBR (= *Master of Business Administration*) *titolo di studio*

MBE N ABBR (BRIT: = *Member of the Order of the British Empire*) *titolo*

MBO N ABBR = **management buyout**

MC N ABBR = **master of ceremonies**; (US: = *Member of Congress*) *membro del Congresso*

MCAT N ABBR (US: = *Medical College Admissions Test*) *esame di ammissione a studi superiori di medicina*

MD N ABBR (= *Doctor of Medicine*) *titolo di studio*; (*Comm*) = **managing director** ▸ABBR (US) = **Maryland**

MDT ABBR (US: = *Mountain Daylight Time*) *ora legale delle Montagne Rocciose*

ME ABBR (US) = **Maine** ▸N ABBR (*Med*: = *myalgic encephalomyelitis*) *sindrome f da affaticamento cronico*; (US) = **medical examiner**

me [mi:] PRON mi, m' + *vowel or silent "h"*; (*stressed, after prep*) me; **he heard me** mi ha *or* m'ha sentito; **give me a book** dammi (*or* mi dia) un libro; **it's me** sono io; **it's for me** è per me; **with me** con me; **without me** senza di me

meadow ['mɛdəu] N prato

meagre, (*US*) **meager** ['mi:gə^r] ADJ magro(-a)

meal [mi:l] N pasto; (*flour*) farina; **to go out for a ~** mangiare fuori

meals on wheels N (*BRIT*) distribuzione f di pasti caldi a domicilio (*per persone malate o anziane*)

mealtime ['mi:ltaɪm] N l'ora di mangiare

mealy-mouthed ['mi:lɪmauðd] ADJ che parla attraverso eufemismi

mean [mi:n] (*pt, pp* **meant** [mɛnt]) ADJ (*with money*) avaro(-a), gretto(-a); (*unkind*) meschino(-a), maligno(-a); (*US: vicious: animal*) cattivo(-a); (*: person*) perfido(-a); (*shabby*) misero(-a); (*average*) medio(-a) ▶ VT (*signify*) significare, voler dire; (*intend*): **to ~ to do** aver l'intenzione di fare ▶ N mezzo; (*Math*) media; **to be meant for** essere destinato(-a) a; **do you ~ it?** dice sul serio?; **what do you ~?** che cosa vuol dire?; *see also* **means**

meander [mɪ'ændə^r] VI far meandri; (*fig*) divagare

meaning ['mi:nɪŋ] N significato, senso

meaningful ['mi:nɪŋful] ADJ significativo(-a); (*relationship*) valido(-a)

meaningless ['mi:nɪŋlɪs] ADJ senza senso

meanness ['mi:nnɪs] N avarizia; meschinità

means [mi:nz] NPL (*way, money*) mezzi *mpl*; **by ~ of** per mezzo di; (*person*) a mezzo di; **by all ~** ma certo, prego

means test N (*Admin*) accertamento dei redditi (*per una persona che ha chiesto un aiuto finanziario*)

meant [mɛnt] PT, PP *of* **mean**

meantime ['mi:ntaɪm], **meanwhile** ['mi:nwaɪl] ADV (*also:* **in the meantime**) nel frattempo

measles ['mi:zlz] N morbillo

measly ['mi:zlɪ] ADJ (*col*) miserabile

measurable ['mɛʒərəbl] ADJ misurabile

measure ['mɛʒə^r] VT, VI misurare ▶ N misura; (*ruler*) metro; **a litre ~** una misura da un litro; **some ~ of success** un certo successo; **to take measures to do sth** prendere provvedimenti per fare qc
▶ **measure up** VI: **to ~ up (to)** dimostrarsi *or* essere all'altezza (di)

measured ['mɛʒəd] ADJ misurato(-a)

measurement ['mɛʒəmənt] N (*act*) misurazione f; (*measure*) misura; **chest/hip ~** giro petto/fianchi; **to take sb's measurements** prendere le misure di qn

meat [mi:t] N carne f; **cold meats** (*BRIT*) affettati *mpl*; **crab ~** polpa di granchio

meatball ['mi:tbɔ:l] N polpetta di carne

meat pie N *torta salata in pasta frolla con ripieno di carne*

meaty ['mi:tɪ] ADJ che sa di carne; (*fig*) sostanzioso(-a); (*person*) corpulento(-a); (*part of body*) carnoso(-a); **~ meal** pasto a base di carne

Mecca ['mɛkə] N La Mecca; (*fig*): **a ~ (for)** la Mecca (di)

mechanic [mɪ'kænɪk] N meccanico; *see also* **mechanics**

mechanical [mɪ'kænɪkəl] ADJ meccanico(-a)

mechanical engineering N (*science*) ingegneria meccanica; (*industry*) costruzioni *fpl* meccaniche

mechanics [mə'kænɪks] N meccanica ▶ NPL meccanismo

mechanism ['mɛkənɪzəm] N meccanismo

mechanization [mɛkənaɪ'zeɪʃən] N meccanizzazione f

MEd N ABBR (= *Master of Education*) titolo di studio

medal ['mɛdl] N medaglia

medallion [mɪ'dælɪən] N medaglione m

medallist, (*US*) **medalist** ['mɛdəlɪst] N (*Sport*) vincitore(-trice) di medaglia; **to be a gold ~** essere medaglia d'oro

meddle ['mɛdl] VI: **to ~ in** immischiarsi in, mettere le mani in; **to ~ with** toccare

meddlesome ['mɛdlsəm], **meddling** ['mɛdlɪŋ] ADJ (*interfering*) che mette il naso dappertutto; (*touching things*) che tocca tutto

media ['mi:dɪə] NPL (*Press, Radio, TV*) media *mpl*

media circus N carrozzone m dell'informazione

mediaeval [mɛdɪ'i:vl] ADJ = **medieval**

median ['mi:dɪən] N (*US: also:* **median strip**) banchina f spartitraffico *inv*

media research N sondaggio tra gli utenti dei mass media

mediate ['mi:dɪeɪt] VI interporsi; fare da mediatore(-trice)

mediation [mi:dɪ'eɪʃən] N mediazione f

mediator ['mi:dɪeɪtə^r] N mediatore(-trice)

Medicaid ['mɛdɪkeɪd] N (*US*) *assistenza medica ai poveri*

medical ['mɛdɪkl] ADJ medico(-a); **~ (examination)** *n* visita medica

medical certificate N certificato medico

medical examiner N (*US*) medico legale

medicalize ['mɛdɪkəlaɪz] VT medicalizzare

medical student N studente(-essa) di medicina

Medicare ['mɛdɪkɛə^r] N (*US*) *assistenza medica agli anziani*

medicated ['mɛdɪkeɪtɪd] ADJ medicato(-a)

medication [mɛdɪ'keɪʃən] N (*drugs etc*) medicinali *mpl*, farmaci *mpl*

m

medicinal [mɛˈdɪsɪnl] ADJ medicinale

medicine [ˈmɛdsɪn] N medicina

medicine chest N armadietto farmaceutico

medicine man N (irreg) stregone m

medieval [mɛdɪˈiːvl] ADJ medievale

mediocre [miːdɪˈəukəʳ] ADJ mediocre

mediocrity [miːdɪˈɔkrɪtɪ] N mediocrità

meditate [ˈmɛdɪteɪt] VI: **to ~ (on)** meditare (su)

meditation [mɛdɪˈteɪʃən] N meditazione f

Mediterranean [mɛdɪtəˈreɪnɪən] ADJ mediterraneo(-a); **the ~ (Sea)** il (mare) Mediterraneo

medium [ˈmiːdɪəm] ADJ medio(-a) ▶ N (pl **media**: means) mezzo; (pl **mediums**: person) medium m inv; **a happy ~** una giusta via di mezzo; see also **media**

medium-dry [ˈmiːdɪəmˈdraɪ] ADJ demisec inv

medium-sized [ˈmiːdɪəmsaɪzd] ADJ (tin etc) di grandezza media; (clothes) di taglia media

medium wave N (Radio) onde fpl medie

medley [ˈmɛdlɪ] N selezione f

meek [miːk] ADJ dolce, umile

meet [miːt] (pt, pp **met** [mɛt]) VT incontrare; (for the first time) fare la conoscenza di; (go and fetch) andare a prendere; (fig) affrontare; far fronte a; soddisfare; raggiungere ▶ VI incontrarsi; (in session) riunirsi; (join: objects) unirsi ▶ N (BRIT Hunting) raduno (dei partecipanti alla caccia alla volpe); (US Sport) raduno (sportivo); **I'll ~ you at the station** verrò a prenderla alla stazione; **pleased to ~ you!** piacere (di conoscerla)!
  ▸ **meet up** VI: **to ~ up with sb** incontrare qn
  ▸ **meet with** VT FUS incontrare; **he met with an accident** ha avuto un incidente

meeting [ˈmiːtɪŋ] N incontro; (session: of club etc) riunione f; (interview) intervista; (formal) colloquio; (Sport: rally) raduno; **she's in a ~** (Comm) è in riunione; **to call a ~** convocare una riunione

meeting place N luogo d'incontro

megabit [ˈmɛgəbɪt] N megabit m inv

megabyte [ˈmɛgəbaɪt] N (Comput) megabyte m inv

megalomaniac [mɛgələuˈmeɪnɪæk] N megalomane mf

megaphone [ˈmɛgəfəun] N megafono

megapixel [ˈmɛgəpɪksl] N megapixel m inv

megastore [ˈmɛgəstɔːʳ] N megastore m inv

megawatt [ˈmɛgəwɔt] N megawatt m inv

melancholy [ˈmɛlənkəlɪ] N malinconia ▶ ADJ malinconico(-a)

mellow [ˈmɛləu] ADJ (wine, sound) ricco(-a); (person, light) dolce; (colour) caldo(-a); (fruit) maturo(-a) ▶ VI (person) addolcirsi

melodious [mɪˈləudɪəs] ADJ melodioso(-a)

melodrama [ˈmɛləudrɑːmə] N melodramma m

melodramatic [mɛlədrəˈmætɪk] ADJ melodrammatico(-a)

melody [ˈmɛlədɪ] N melodia

melon [ˈmɛlən] N melone m

melt [mɛlt] VI (gen) sciogliersi, struggersi; (metals) fondersi; (fig) intenerirsi ▶ VT sciogliere, struggere; fondere; (person) commuovere; **melted butter** burro fuso
  ▸ **melt away** VI sciogliersi completamente
  ▸ **melt down** VT fondere

meltdown [ˈmɛltdaun] N melt-down m inv

melting point [ˈmɛltɪŋ-] N punto di fusione

melting pot [ˈmɛltɪŋ-] N (fig) crogiolo; **to be in the ~** essere ancora in discussione

member [ˈmɛmbəʳ] N membro; (of club) socio(-a), iscritto(-a); (of political party) iscritto(-a); **~ country/state** n paese m/stato membro

Member of Congress N (US) membro(-a) del Congresso

Member of Parliament N (BRIT) deputato(-a)

Member of the European Parliament N (BRIT) eurodeputato(-a)

Member of the House of Representatives N (US) membro(-a) della Camera dei Rappresentanti

Member of the Scottish Parliament N (BRIT) deputato(-a) del Parlamento scozzese

membership [ˈmɛmbəʃɪp] N iscrizione f; (numero d')iscritti mpl, membri mpl

membership card N tessera (di iscrizione)

membrane [ˈmɛmbreɪn] N membrana

meme [miːm] N meme m inv

memento [məˈmɛntəu] N ricordo, souvenir m inv

memo [ˈmɛməu] N appunto; (Comm etc) comunicazione f di servizio

memoir [ˈmɛmwɑːʳ] N memoria ■ **memoirs** NPL memorie fpl, ricordi mpl

memo pad N blocchetto per appunti

memorable [ˈmɛmərəbl] ADJ memorabile

memorandum [mɛməˈrændəm] (pl **memoranda** [-də]) N appunto; (Comm etc) comunicazione f di servizio; (Diplomacy) memorandum m inv

memorial [mɪˈmɔːrɪəl] N monumento commemorativo ▶ ADJ commemorativo(-a)

Memorial Day N (US) vedi nota

Negli Stati Uniti il **Memorial Day** è una festa nazionale che cade l'ultimo lunedì di maggio quando si commemorano tutti i soldati americani caduti in guerra.

memorize [ˈmɛməraɪz] VT memorizzare

memory [ˈmɛmərɪ] N (gen, Comput) memoria; (recollection) ricordo; **in ~ of** in memoria di; **to have a good/bad ~** aver buona/cattiva memoria; **loss of ~** amnesia

memory card N (*for digital camera*) scheda di memoria

memory stick N (*Comput*) stick *m inv* di memoria

men [mɛn] NPL *of* **man**

menace [ˈmɛnɪs] N minaccia; (*col: nuisance*) peste *f* ▶ VT minacciare; **a public ~** un pericolo pubblico

menacing [ˈmɛnɪsɪŋ] ADJ minaccioso(-a)

menagerie [mɪˈnædʒərɪ] N serraglio

mend [mɛnd] VT aggiustare, riparare; (*darn*) rammendare ▶ N rammendo; **on the ~** in via di guarigione

mending [ˈmɛndɪŋ] N rammendo; (*items to be mended*) roba da rammendare

menial [ˈmiːnɪəl] ADJ da servo, domestico(-a); umile

meningitis [mɛnɪnˈdʒaɪtɪs] N meningite *f*

menopause [ˈmɛnəupɔːz] N menopausa

menservants [ˈmɛnsəvənts] NPL *of* **manservant**

men's room N: **the ~** (*esp US*) la toilette degli uomini

menstruate [ˈmɛnstrueɪt] VI mestruare

menstruation [mɛnstruˈeɪʃən] N mestruazione *f*

menswear [ˈmɛnzwɛər] N abbigliamento maschile

mental [ˈmɛntl] ADJ mentale; **~ illness** malattia mentale

mentality [mɛnˈtælɪtɪ] N mentalità *f inv*

mentally [ˈmɛntlɪ] ADV: **to be ~ ill** essere malato(-a) di mente

menthol [ˈmɛnθɔl] N mentolo

mention [ˈmɛnʃən] N menzione *f* ▶ VT menzionare, far menzione di; **don't ~ it!** non c'è di che!, prego!; **I need hardly ~ that ...** inutile dire che ...; **not to ~, without mentioning** per non parlare di, senza contare

mentor [ˈmɛntɔːr] N mentore *m* ▶ VT fare da mentore (a)

menu [ˈmɛnjuː] N (*set menu, Comput*) menù *m inv*; (*printed*) carta

menu-driven [ˈmɛnjuːdrɪvn] ADJ (*Comput*) guidato(-a) da menù

MEP N ABBR = **Member of the European Parliament**

mercantile [ˈmɜːkəntaɪl] ADJ mercantile; (*law*) commerciale

mercenary [ˈmɜːsɪnərɪ] ADJ venale ▶ N mercenario

merchandise [ˈmɜːtʃəndaɪz] N merci *fpl* ▶ VT commercializzare

merchandiser [ˈmɜːtʃəndaɪzər] N merchandiser *m inv*

merchant [ˈmɜːtʃənt] N (*trader*) mercante *m*, commerciante *m*; (*shopkeeper*) negoziante *m*; **timber/wine ~** negoziante di legno/vino

merchant bank N (BRIT) banca d'affari

merchantman [ˈmɜːtʃəntmən] N (*irreg*) mercantile *m*

merchant navy, (US) **merchant marine** N marina mercantile

merciful [ˈmɜːsɪful] ADJ pietoso(-a), clemente

mercifully [ˈmɜːsɪflɪ] ADV con clemenza; (*fortunately*) per fortuna

merciless [ˈmɜːsɪlɪs] ADJ spietato(-a)

mercurial [mɜːˈkjuərɪəl] ADJ (*unpredictable*) volubile

mercury [ˈmɜːkjurɪ] N mercurio

mercy [ˈmɜːsɪ] N pietà *f*; (*Rel*) misericordia; **to have ~ on sb** aver pietà di qn; **at the ~ of** alla mercè di

mercy killing N eutanasia

mere [mɪər] ADJ semplice; **by a ~ chance** per mero caso

merely [ˈmɪəlɪ] ADV semplicemente

merge [mɜːdʒ] VT unire; (*Comput: files, text*) fondere ▶ VI fondersi, unirsi; (*Comm*) fondersi

merger [ˈmɜːdʒər] N (*Comm*) fusione *f*

meridian [məˈrɪdɪən] N meridiano

meringue [məˈræŋ] N meringa

merit [ˈmɛrɪt] N merito, valore *m* ▶ VT meritare

meritocracy [mɛrɪˈtɔkrəsɪ] N meritocrazia

mermaid [ˈmɜːmeɪd] N sirena

merriment [ˈmɛrɪmənt] N gaiezza, allegria

merry [ˈmɛrɪ] ADJ gaio(-a), allegro(-a); **M~ Christmas!** Buon Natale!

merry-go-round [ˈmɛrɪɡəuraund] N carosello

mesh [mɛʃ] N maglia; rete *f* ▶ VI (*gears*) ingranarsi; **wire ~** rete metallica

mesmerize [ˈmɛzməraɪz] VT ipnotizzare; affascinare

mess [mɛs] N confusione *f*, disordine *m*; (*fig*) pasticcio; (*dirt*) sporcizia; (*Mil*) mensa; **to be (in) a ~** (*house, room*) essere in disordine (*or* molto sporco); (*fig: marriage, life*) essere un caos; **to be/get o.s. in a ~** (*fig*) essere/cacciarsi in un pasticcio

▶ **mess about, mess around** VI (*col*) trastullarsi

▶ **mess about with, mess around with, mess with** VT FUS (*col*) gingillarsi con; (*: plans*) fare un pasticcio di; (*: challenge, confront*) litigare con (*col*); (*: drugs, drinks*) abusare di

▶ **mess up** VT sporcare; fare un pasticcio di; rovinare

message [ˈmɛsɪdʒ] N messaggio ▶ VT messaggiare; **to get the ~** (*fig: col*) capire l'antifona; **she messaged me on Facebook®** mi ha messaggiato su Facebook®

message board N (*Comput*) bacheca elettronica

message switching N (*Comput*) smistamento *m* messaggi *inv*

messenger ['mɛsɪndʒəʳ] N messaggero(-a)

Messiah [mɪ'saɪə] N Messia *m*

Messrs, Messrs. ['mɛsəz] ABBR (*on letters*: = *messieurs*) Spett.

messy ['mɛsɪ] ADJ sporco(-a); disordinato(-a); (*confused: situation etc*) ingarbugliato(-a)

Met [mɛt] N ABBR (*US*) = **Metropolitan Opera**; **the ~ Office** l'Ufficio Meteorologico

met [mɛt] PT, PP *of* **meet** ▶ ADJ ABBR = **meteorological**

metabolism [mɛ'tæbəlɪzəm] N metabolismo

metal ['mɛtl] N metallo ▶ VT massicciare

metallic [mɛ'tælɪk] ADJ metallico(-a)

metallurgy [mɛ'tælədʒɪ] N metallurgia

metalwork ['mɛtlwəːk] N (*craft*) lavorazione *f* del metallo

metamorphosis [mɛtə'mɔːfəsɪs] (*pl* **metamorphoses** [-siːz]) N metamorfosi *f inv*

metaphor ['mɛtəfəʳ] N metafora

metaphysics [mɛtə'fɪzɪks] N metafisica

mete [miːt]: **to ~ out** *vt fus* infliggere

meteor ['miːtɪəʳ] N meteora

meteoric [miːtɪ'ɔrɪk] ADJ (*fig*) fulmineo(-a)

meteorite ['miːtɪəraɪt] N meteorite *m*

meteorological [miːtɪərə'lɔdʒɪkl] ADJ meteorologico(-a)

meteorology [miːtɪə'rɔlədʒɪ] N meteorologia

meter ['miːtəʳ] N (*instrument*) contatore *m*; (*parking meter*) parchimetro; (*US: unit*) = **metre**

methane ['miːθeɪn] N metano

method ['mɛθəd] N metodo; **~ of payment** modo *or* modalità *f inv* di pagamento

methodical [mɪ'θɔdɪkl] ADJ metodico(-a)

Methodist ['mɛθədɪst] ADJ, N metodista (*mf*)

meths [mɛθs] N (*BRIT*) = **methylated spirits**

methylated spirits ['mɛθɪleɪtɪd-] N (*BRIT: also*: **meths**) alcool *m* denaturato

meticulous [mɛ'tɪkjuləs] ADJ meticoloso(-a)

metre, (*US*) **meter** ['miːtəʳ] N metro

metric ['mɛtrɪk] ADJ metrico(-a); **to go ~** adottare il sistema metrico decimale

metrical ['mɛtrɪkl] ADJ metrico(-a)

metrication [mɛtrɪ'keɪʃən] N conversione *f* al sistema metrico

metric system N sistema *m* metrico decimale

metric ton N tonnellata

metro ['mɛtrəu] N metro *m inv*

metronome ['mɛtrənəum] N metronomo

metropolis [mɪ'trɔpəlɪs] N metropoli *f inv*

metropolitan [mɛtrə'pɔlɪtən] ADJ metropolitano(-a)

Metropolitan Police N (*BRIT*): **the ~** la polizia di Londra

mettle ['mɛtl] N coraggio

mew [mjuː] VI (*cat*) miagolare

mews [mjuːz] N (*BRIT*): **~ flat** appartamentino ricavato da una vecchia scuderia

Mexican ['mɛksɪkən] ADJ, N messicano(-a)

Mexico ['mɛksɪkəu] N Messico

Mexico City N Città del Messico

mezzanine ['mɛtsəniːn] N mezzanino

MFA N ABBR (*US*: = *Master of Fine Arts*) titolo di studio

mfr ABBR = **manufacture; manufacturer**

mg ABBR (= *milligram*) mg

Mgr ABBR (= *Monseigneur; Monsignor*) mons.; (*Comm*) = **manager**

MHR N ABBR (*US*) = **Member of the House of Representatives**

MHz ABBR (= *megahertz*) MHz

MI ABBR (*US*) = **Michigan**

MI5 N ABBR (*BRIT*: = *Military Intelligence, section five*) agenzia di controspionaggio

MI6 N ABBR (*BRIT*: = *Military Intelligence, section six*) agenzia di spionaggio

MIA ABBR = **missing in action**

miaow [miːˈau] VI miagolare

mice [maɪs] NPL *of* **mouse**

micro... ['maɪkrəu] PREFIX micro...

microbe ['maɪkrəub] N microbio

microbiology [maɪkrəubaɪ'ɔlədʒɪ] N microbiologia

microblog ['maɪkrəublɔg] N microblog *m inv*

microchip ['maɪkrəutʃɪp] N microcircuito integrato, chip *m inv*

microcomputer [maɪkrəukəm'pjuːtəʳ] N microcomputer *m inv*

microcosm ['maɪkrəukɔzəm] N microcosmo

microeconomics [maɪkrəuiːkə'nɔmɪks] N microeconomia

microfiche ['maɪkrəufiːʃ] N microfiche *f inv*

microfilm ['maɪkrəufɪlm] N microfilm *m inv* ▶ VT microfilmare

microlight ['maɪkrəulaɪt] N aereo *m* biposto *inv*

micrometer [maɪ'krɔmɪtəʳ] N micrometro, palmer *m inv*

Micronesia [maɪkrəuˈniːzɪə] N: **Federated States of ~** Stati *mpl* Federati di Micronesia

microphone ['maɪkrəfəun] N microfono

microprocessor [maɪkrəu'prəusɛsəʳ] N microprocessore *m*

micro-scooter ['maɪkrəuskuːtəʳ] N monopattino

microscope ['maɪkrəskəup] N microscopio; **under the ~** al microscopio

microscopic [maɪkrə'skɔpɪk] ADJ microscopico(-a)

microwavable, microwaveable ['maɪkrəuweɪvəbl] ADJ adatto(-a) al forno a microonde

microwave [ˈmaɪkrəuweɪv] N (*also:* **micro-wave oven**) forno a microonde

mid [mɪd] ADJ: **~ May** metà maggio; **~ afternoon** metà pomeriggio; **in ~ air** a mezz'aria; **he's in his ~ thirties** avrà circa trentacinque anni

midday [mɪdˈdeɪ] N mezzogiorno

middle [ˈmɪdl] N mezzo; centro; (*waist*) vita ▶ ADJ di mezzo; **I'm in the ~ of reading it** sto proprio leggendolo ora; **in the ~ of the night** nel cuore della notte

middle age N mezza età

middle-aged [mɪdlˈeɪdʒd] ADJ di mezza età

Middle Ages NPL: **the ~** il Medioevo

middle class ADJ (*also:* **middle-class**) ≈ bor-ghese ▶ N: **the ~(es)** ≈ la borghesia

Middle East N: **the ~** il Medio Oriente

middleman [ˈmɪdlmæn] N (*irreg*) intermedia-rio; agente *m* rivenditore

middle management N quadri *mpl* inter-medi

middle name N secondo nome *m*

middle-of-the-road [ˈmɪdləvðəˈrəud] ADJ moderato(-a)

middle school N (*US*) scuola media per ragazzi *dagli 11 ai 14 anni*; (*BRIT*) *scuola media per ragazzi dagli 8 o 9 ai 12 o 13 anni*

middleweight [ˈmɪdlweɪt] N (*Boxing*) peso medio

middling [ˈmɪdlɪŋ] ADJ medio(-a)

midge [mɪdʒ] N moscerino

midget [ˈmɪdʒɪt] N (!) nano(-a)

midi system [ˈmɪdɪ-] N (*hi-fi*) compatto

Midlands [ˈmɪdləndz] NPL *contee del centro dell'In-ghilterra*

midnight [ˈmɪdnaɪt] N mezzanotte *f*; **at ~** a mezzanotte

midriff [ˈmɪdrɪf] N diaframma *m*

midst [mɪdst] N: **in the ~ of** in mezzo a

midsummer [mɪdˈsʌmər] N mezza *or* piena estate *f*

midway [mɪdˈweɪ] ADJ, ADV: **~ (between)** a mezza strada (fra); **~ (through)** a metà (di)

midweek [mɪdˈwiːk] ADV, ADJ a metà settimana

midwife [ˈmɪdwaɪf] (*pl* **midwives** [-vz]) N leva-trice *f*

midwifery [ˈmɪdwɪfərɪ] N ostetrica

midwinter [mɪdˈwɪntər] N pieno inverno

miffed [mɪft] ADJ (*col*) seccato(-a), stizzito(-a)

might [maɪt] VB *see* **may** ▶ N potere *m*, forza

mighty [ˈmaɪtɪ] ADJ forte, potente ▶ ADV (*col*) molto

migraine [ˈmiːgreɪn] N emicrania

migrant [ˈmaɪgrənt] N (*bird, animal*) migratore *m*; (*person*) migrante *mf*; nomade *mf* ▶ ADJ (*bird*) migratore(-trice), nomade; (*worker*) emigra-to(-a)

migrate [maɪˈgreɪt] VI (*bird*) migrare; (*person*) emigrare

migration [maɪˈgreɪʃən] N migrazione *f*

mike [maɪk] N ABBR (= *microphone*) microfono

Milan [mɪˈlæn] N Milano *f*

mild [maɪld] ADJ mite; (*person, voice*) dolce; (*fla-vour*) delicato(-a); (*illness*) leggero(-a); (*interest*) blando(-a) ▶ N (*beer*) birra leggera

mildew [ˈmɪldjuː] N muffa

mildly [ˈmaɪldlɪ] ADV mitemente; dolcemente; delicatamente; leggermente; blandamente; **to put it ~** a dire poco

mildness [ˈmaɪldnɪs] N mitezza; dolcezza; deli-catezza; non gravità

mile [maɪl] N miglio; **to do 20 miles per gallon** ≈ usare 14 litri per cento chilometri

mileage [ˈmaɪlɪdʒ] N distanza in miglia, ≈ chi-lometraggio

mileage allowance N rimborso per miglio

mileometer [maɪˈlɒmɪtər] N (*BRIT*) = **milometer**

milestone [ˈmaɪlstəun] N pietra miliare

milieu [ˈmiːljəː] N ambiente *m*

militant [ˈmɪlɪtnt] ADJ, N militante (*mf*)

militarism [ˈmɪlɪtərɪzəm] N militarismo

militaristic [mɪlɪtəˈrɪstɪk] ADJ militaristico(-a)

military [ˈmɪlɪtərɪ] ADJ militare ▶ N: **the ~** i militari, l'esercito

military service N servizio militare

militate [ˈmɪlɪteɪt] VI: **to ~ against** essere d'o-stacolo a

militia [mɪˈlɪʃə] N milizia

milk [mɪlk] N latte *m* ▶ VT (*cow*) mungere; (*fig*) sfruttare

milk chocolate N cioccolato al latte

milk float N (*BRIT*) furgone *m* del lattaio

milking [ˈmɪlkɪŋ] N mungitura

milkman [ˈmɪlkmən] N (*irreg*) lattaio

milk shake N frappé *m inv*

milk tooth N dente *m* di latte

milk truck N (*US*) = **milk float**

milky [ˈmɪlkɪ] ADJ lattiginoso(-a); (*colour*) latte-o(-a)

Milky Way N Via Lattea

mill [mɪl] N mulino; (*small: for coffee, pepper etc*) macinino; (*factory*) fabbrica; (*spinning mill*) fila-tura ▶ VT macinare ▶ VI (*also:* **mill about**) bruli-care

millennium [mɪˈlɛnɪəm] (*pl* **millenniums** *or* **mil-lennia** [-ˈlɛnɪə]) N millennio

millennium bug N baco di fine millennio

miller [ˈmɪlər] N mugnaio

millet [ˈmɪlɪt] N miglio

milli... [ˈmɪlɪ] PREFIX milli...

milligram, milligramme [ˈmɪlɪgræm] N mil-ligrammo

millilitre, (US) **milliliter** [ˈmɪlɪliːtə^r] N millilitro

millimetre, (US) **millimeter** [ˈmɪlɪmiːtə^r] N millimetro

milliner [ˈmɪlɪnə^r] N modista

millinery [ˈmɪlɪnərɪ] N modisteria

million [ˈmɪljən] NUM milione m

millionaire [mɪljəˈnɛə^r] N milionario, ≈ miliardario

millionth NUM milionesimo(-a)

millipede [ˈmɪlɪpiːd] N millepiedi m inv

millstone [ˈmɪlstəun] N macina

millwheel [ˈmɪlwiːl] N ruota di mulino

milometer [maɪˈlɔmɪtə^r] N ≈ contachilometri m inv

mime [maɪm] N mimo ▶ VT, VI mimare

mimic [ˈmɪmɪk] N imitatore(-trice) ▶ VT (comedian) imitare; (animal, person) scimmiottare

mimicry [ˈmɪmɪkrɪ] N imitazioni fpl; (Zool) mimetismo

Min. ABBR (BRIT Pol: = ministry) Min.

min. ABBR = **minute**; (= minimum) min.

minaret [mɪnəˈrɛt] N minareto

mince [mɪns] VT tritare, macinare ▶ VI (in walking) camminare a passettini ▶ N (BRIT Culin) carne f tritata or macinata; **he does not ~ (his) words** parla chiaro e tondo

mincemeat [ˈmɪnsmiːt] N frutta secca tritata per uso in pasticceria

mince pie N specie di torta con frutta secca

mincer [ˈmɪnsə^r] N tritacarne m inv

mincing [ˈmɪnsɪŋ] ADJ lezioso(-a)

mind [maɪnd] N mente f ▶ VT (attend to, look after) badare a, occuparsi di; (be careful) fare attenzione a, stare attento(-a) a; (object to): **I don't ~ the noise** il rumore non mi dà alcun fastidio; **do you ~ if ...?** le dispiace se ...?; **I don't ~** non m'importa; **~ you, ...** sì, però va detto che ...; **never ~** non importa, non fa niente; (don't worry) non preoccuparti; **it is on my ~** mi preoccupa; **to change one's ~** cambiare idea; **to be in two minds about sth** essere incerto su qc; **to my ~** secondo me, a mio parere; **to be out of one's ~** essere uscito(-a) di mente; **to keep sth in ~** non dimenticare qc; **to bear sth in ~** tener presente qc; **to have sb/sth in ~** avere in mente qn/qc; **to have in ~ to do** aver l'intenzione di fare; **it went right out of my ~** mi è completamente passato di mente, me ne sono completamente dimenticato; **to bring** or **call sth to ~** riportare or richiamare qc alla mente; **to make up one's ~** decidersi; **"~ the step"** "attenzione allo scalino"

mind-boggling [ˈmaɪndbɔglɪŋ] ADJ (col) sconcertante

-minded [ˈmaɪndɪd] ADJ: **fair-minded** imparziale; **an industrially-minded nation** una nazione orientata verso l'industria

minder [ˈmaɪndə^r] N (child minder) bambinaia; (bodyguard) guardia del corpo

mindful [ˈmaɪndful] ADJ: **~ of** attento(-a) a; memore di

mindfulness [ˈmaɪndfulnəs] N mindfulness f inv

mindless [ˈmaɪndlɪs] ADJ idiota; (violence, crime) insensato(-a)

mine[1] [maɪn] PRON il (la) mio(-a); (pl) i (le) miei (mie); **this book is ~** questo libro è mio; **yours is red, ~ is green** il tuo è rosso, il mio è verde; **a friend of ~** un mio amico

mine[2] [maɪn] N miniera; (explosive) mina ▶ VT (coal) estrarre; (ship, beach) minare

mine detector N rivelatore m di mine

minefield [ˈmaɪnfiːld] N campo minato

miner [ˈmaɪnə^r] N minatore(-trice)

mineral [ˈmɪnərəl] ADJ minerale ▶ N minerale m ■ **minerals** NPL (BRIT: soft drinks) bevande fpl gasate

mineralogy [mɪnəˈrælədʒɪ] N mineralogia

mineral water N acqua minerale

minesweeper [ˈmaɪnswiːpə^r] N dragamine m inv

mingle [ˈmɪŋgl] VT mescolare, mischiare ▶ VI: **to ~ with** mescolarsi a, mischiarsi con

mingy [ˈmɪndʒɪ] ADJ (col: amount) misero(-a); (: person) spilorcio(-a)

miniature [ˈmɪnətʃə^r] ADJ in miniatura ▶ N miniatura

minibar [ˈmɪnɪbɑː^r] N minibar m inv

minibus [ˈmɪnɪbʌs] N minibus m inv

minicab [ˈmɪnɪkæb] N (BRIT) ≈ taxi m inv

minicomputer [ˈmɪnɪkəmˈpjuːtə^r] N minicomputer m inv

Minidisc® [ˈmɪnɪdɪsk] N minidisc m inv

minim [ˈmɪnɪm] N (Mus) minima

minima [ˈmɪnɪmə] NPL of **minimum**

minimal [ˈmɪnɪml] ADJ minimo(-a)

minimalist [ˈmɪnɪməlɪst] ADJ, N minimalista (mf)

minimize [ˈmɪnɪmaɪz] VT minimizzare

minimum [ˈmɪnɪməm] (pl **minima** [ˈmɪnɪmə]) N minimo ▶ ADJ minimo(-a); **to reduce to a ~** ridurre al minimo; **~ wage** salario minimo garantito

minimum lending rate N (BRIT) ≈ tasso ufficiale di sconto

mining [ˈmaɪnɪŋ] N industria mineraria ▶ ADJ minerario(-a); di minatori

minion [ˈmɪnjən] N (pej) caudatario; favorito(-a)

mini-series [ˈmɪnɪsɪəriːz] N miniserie f inv

miniskirt [ˈmɪnɪskəːt] N minigonna

minister [ˈmɪnɪstə^r] N (BRIT Pol) ministro; (Rel) pastore m ▶ VI: **to ~ to sb** assistere qn; **to ~ to sb's needs** provvedere ai bisogni di qn

ministerial [mɪnɪsˈtɪərɪəl] ADJ (BRIT Pol) ministeriale

ministry ['mɪnɪstrɪ] N (BRIT Pol) ministero; (Rel): **to go into the ~** diventare pastore

mink [mɪŋk] N visone m

mink coat N pelliccia di visone

minnow ['mɪnəu] N pesciolino d'acqua dolce

minor ['maɪnər] ADJ minore, di poca importanza; (Mus) minore ▶ N (Law) minorenne mf

Minorca [mɪ'nɔːkə] N Minorca

minority [maɪ'nɔrɪtɪ] N minoranza; **to be in a ~** essere in minoranza

minster ['mɪnstər] N cattedrale f (annessa a monastero)

minstrel ['mɪnstrəl] N giullare m, menestrello

mint [mɪnt] N (plant) menta; (sweet) pasticca di menta ▶ VT (coins) battere; **the (Royal) M~** (BRIT), **the (US) M~** (US) la Zecca; **in ~ condition** come nuovo(-a) di zecca

mint sauce N salsa di menta

minuet [mɪnju'et] N minuetto

minus ['maɪnəs] N (also: **minus sign**) segno meno ▶ PREP meno

minuscule ['mɪnəskjuːl] ADJ minuscolo(-a)

minute¹ ['mɪnɪt] N minuto; (official record) processo verbale, resoconto sommario ■ **minutes** NPL (of meeting) verbale m, verbali mpl; **it is 5 minutes past 3** sono le 3 e 5 (minuti); **wait a ~!** (aspetta) un momento!; **at the last ~** all'ultimo momento; **up to the ~** ultimissimo; modernissimo

minute² [maɪ'njuːt] ADJ minuscolo(-a); (detail) minuzioso(-a); **in ~ detail** minuziosamente

minute book ['mɪnɪt-] N libro dei verbali

minute hand ['mɪnɪt-] N lancetta dei minuti

minutely [maɪ'njuːtlɪ] ADV (by a small amount) di poco; (in detail) minuziosamente

minutiae [mɪ'njuːʃiː] NPL minuzie fpl

miracle ['mɪrəkl] N miracolo

miraculous [mɪ'rækjuləs] ADJ miracoloso(-a)

mirage ['mɪrɑːʒ] N miraggio

mire ['maɪər] N pantano, melma

mirror ['mɪrər] N specchio; (in car) specchietto ▶ VT rispecchiare, riflettere

mirror image N immagine f speculare

mirth [məːθ] N gaiezza

misadventure [mɪsəd'ventʃər] N disavventura; **death by ~** (BRIT) morte f accidentale

misanthropist [mɪ'zænθrəpɪst] N misantropo(-a)

misapply [mɪsə'plaɪ] VT impiegare male

misapprehension ['mɪsæprɪ'henʃən] N malinteso

misappropriate [mɪsə'prəuprɪeɪt] VT appropriarsi indebitamente di

misappropriation ['mɪsəprəuprɪ'eɪʃən] N appropriazione f indebita

misbehave [mɪsbɪ'heɪv] VI comportarsi male

misbehaviour, (US) **misbehavior** [mɪsbɪ'heɪvjər] N comportamento scorretto

misc. ABBR = **miscellaneous**

miscalculate [mɪs'kælkjuleɪt] VT calcolare male

miscalculation ['mɪskælkju'leɪʃən] N errore m di calcolo

miscarriage ['mɪskærɪdʒ] N (Med) aborto spontaneo; **~ of justice** errore m giudiziario

miscarry [mɪs'kærɪ] VI (Med) abortire; (fail: plans) andare a monte, fallire

miscellaneous [mɪsɪ'leɪnɪəs] ADJ (items) vario(-a); (selection) misto(-a); **~ expenses** spese varie

miscellany [mɪ'selənɪ] N raccolta

mischance [mɪs'tʃɑːns] N: **by (some) ~** per sfortuna

mischief ['mɪstʃɪf] N (naughtiness) birichineria; (harm) male m, danno; (maliciousness) malizia

mischievous ['mɪstʃɪvəs] ADJ (naughty) birichino(-a); (harmful) dannoso(-a)

misconception [mɪskən'sepʃən] N idea sbagliata

misconduct [mɪs'kɔndʌkt] N cattiva condotta; **professional ~** reato professionale

misconstrue [mɪskən'struː] VT interpretare male

miscount [mɪs'kaunt] VT, VI contare male

misdeed [mɪs'diːd] N (old) misfatto

misdemeanour, (US) **misdemeanor** [mɪsdɪ'miːnər] N misfatto; infrazione f

misdirect [mɪsdɪ'rekt] VT mal indirizzare

miser ['maɪzər] N avaro(-a)

miserable ['mɪzərəbl] ADJ infelice; (wretched) miserabile; (weather) deprimente; (offer, failure) misero(-a); **to feel ~** sentirsi avvilito or giù di morale

miserably ['mɪzərəblɪ] ADV (fail, live, pay) miseramente; (smile, answer) tristemente

miserly ['maɪzəlɪ] ADJ avaro(-a)

misery ['mɪzərɪ] N (unhappiness) tristezza; (pain) sofferenza; (wretchedness) miseria

misfire [mɪs'faɪər] VI far cilecca; (car engine) perdere colpi

misfit ['mɪsfɪt] N (person) spostato(-a)

misfortune [mɪs'fɔːtʃən] N sfortuna

misgiving [mɪs'ɡɪvɪŋ] N, **misgivings** [mɪs'ɡɪvɪŋz] NPL dubbi mpl; **to have misgivings about sth** essere diffidente or avere dei dubbi per quanto riguarda qc

misguided [mɪs'ɡaɪdɪd] ADJ sbagliato(-a); poco giudizioso(-a)

mishandle [mɪs'hændl] VT (treat roughly) maltrattare; (mismanage) trattare male

mishap ['mɪshæp] N disgrazia

mishear [mɪs'hɪər] VT, VI (irreg: like **hear**) capire male

665

mishmash [ˈmɪʃmæʃ] N (col) minestrone *m*, guazzabuglio

misinform [mɪsɪnˈfɔːm] VT informare male

misinterpret [mɪsɪnˈtəːprɪt] VT interpretare male

misinterpretation [ˈmɪsɪntəːprɪˈteɪʃən] N errata interpretazione *f*

misjudge [mɪsˈdʒʌdʒ] VT giudicare male

mislay [mɪsˈleɪ] VT (irreg: like **lay**) smarrire

mislead [mɪsˈliːd] VT (irreg: like **lead**[?]) sviare

misleading [mɪsˈliːdɪŋ] ADJ ingannevole

misled [mɪsˈlɛd] PT, PP of **mislead**

mismanage [mɪsˈmænɪdʒ] VT gestire male; trattare male

mismanagement [mɪsˈmænɪdʒmənt] N cattiva amministrazione *f*

misnomer [mɪsˈnəʊməʳ] N termine *m* sbagliato *or* improprio

misogynist [mɪˈsɔdʒɪnɪst] N misogino

misplace [mɪsˈpleɪs] VT smarrire; collocare fuori posto; **to be misplaced** (trust etc) essere malriposto(-a)

misprint [ˈmɪsprɪnt] N errore *m* di stampa

mispronounce [mɪsprəˈnauns] VT pronunziare male

misquote [mɪsˈkwəut] VT citare erroneamente

misread [mɪsˈriːd] VT (irreg: like **read**) leggere male

misrepresent [mɪsrɛprɪˈzɛnt] VT travisare

Miss [mɪs] N Signorina; **Dear ~ Smith** Cara Signorina; (formal) Gentile Signorina

miss [mɪs] VT (fail to get) perdere; (fail to hit) mancare; (appointment, class) mancare a; (escape, avoid) evitare; (notice loss of: money etc) accorgersi di non avere più; (fail to see): **you can't ~ it** non puoi non vederlo; (regret the absence of): **I ~ him/it** sento la sua mancanza, lui/esso mi manca ▶ VI mancare ▶ N (shot) colpo mancato; (fig): **that was a near ~** c'è mancato poco; **the bus just missed the wall** l'autobus per un pelo non è andato a finire contro il muro; **we missed our train** abbiamo perso il treno; **you're missing the point** non capisce
  ▶ **miss out** VT (BRIT) omettere
  ▶ **miss out on** VT FUS (fun, party) perdersi; (chance, bargain) lasciarsi sfuggire

> To translate a sentence like I'm missing my parents into Italian, you have to rephrase it as My parents are missing to me. If what you are missing is singular, the verb is singular; if it is plural, the verb is plural.
> I'm missing my parents. **Mi mancano i miei genitori**.
> I miss you so much. **Mi manchi tanto**.

missal [ˈmɪsl] N messale *m*

misshapen [mɪsˈʃeɪpən] ADJ deforme

missile [ˈmɪsaɪl] N (Aviat) missile *m*; (object thrown) proiettile *m*

missile base N base *f* missilistica

missile launcher N lancia-missili *m inv*

missing [ˈmɪsɪŋ] ADJ perso(-a), smarrito(-a); (removed) mancante; **to go ~** sparire; **~ person** scomparso(-a); (after disaster) disperso(-a); **~ in action** (Mil) disperso(-a); **to be ~** mancare

mission [ˈmɪʃən] N missione *f*; **on a ~ to sb** in missione da qn

missionary [ˈmɪʃənrɪ] N missionario(-a)

misspell [mɪsˈspɛl] VT (irreg: like **spell**) sbagliare l'ortografia di

misspent [mɪsˈspɛnt] ADJ: **his ~ youth** la sua gioventù sciupata

mist [mɪst] N nebbia, foschia ▶ VI (also: **mist over, mist up**) annebbiarsi; (: BRIT: windows) appannarsi

mistake [mɪsˈteɪk] N sbaglio, errore *m* ▶ VT (irreg: like **take**) sbagliarsi di; fraintendere; **to ~ for** prendere per; **by ~** per sbaglio; **to make a ~** (in writing, calculating etc) fare uno sbaglio *or* un errore, sbagliare; **to make a ~ about sb/sth** sbagliarsi sul conto di qn/su qc; **there must be some ~** ci dev'essere un errore

mistaken [mɪsˈteɪkən] PP of **mistake** ▶ ADJ (idea etc) sbagliato(-a); **to be ~** sbagliarsi

mistaken identity N errore *m* di persona

mistakenly [mɪsˈteɪkənlɪ] ADV per errore

mister [ˈmɪstəʳ] N (col) signore *m*; see also **Mr**

mistletoe [ˈmɪsltəu] N vischio

mistook [mɪsˈtuk] PT of **mistake**

mistranslation [mɪstrænsˈleɪʃən] N traduzione *f* errata

mistreat [mɪsˈtriːt] VT maltrattare

mistress [ˈmɪstrɪs] N padrona; (lover) amante *f*; (BRIT Scol) insegnante *f*

mistrust [mɪsˈtrʌst] VT diffidare di ▶ N: **~ (of)** diffidenza (nei confronti di)

mistrustful [mɪsˈtrʌstful] ADJ: **~ (of)** diffidente (nei confronti di)

misty [ˈmɪstɪ] ADJ nebbioso(-a), brumoso(-a)

misty-eyed [ˈmɪstɪˈaɪd] ADJ trasognato(-a)

misunderstand [mɪsʌndəˈstænd] VT, VI (irreg: like **stand**) capire male, fraintendere

misunderstanding [mɪsʌndəˈstændɪŋ] N malinteso, equivoco; **there's been a ~** c'è stato un malinteso

misunderstood [mɪsʌndəˈstud] PT, PP of **misunderstand**

misuse N [mɪsˈjuːs] cattivo uso; (of power) abuso ▶ VT [mɪsˈjuːz] far cattivo uso di; abusare di

MIT N ABBR (US) = **Massachusetts Institute of Technology**

mite [maɪt] N (small quantity) briciolo; (BRIT: small child): **poor ~!** povera creaturina!

miter [ˈmaɪtərˈ] N (US) = **mitre**

mitigate [ˈmɪtɪɡeɪt] VT mitigare; (*suffering*) alleviare; **mitigating circumstances** circostanze *fpl* attenuanti

mitigation [mɪtɪˈɡeɪʃən] N mitigazione *f*; alleviamento

mitre, (US) **miter** [ˈmaɪtərˈ] N mitra; (*Carpentry*) giunto ad angolo retto

mitt [ˈmɪt], **mitten** [ˈmɪtn] N mezzo guanto; manopola

mix [mɪks] VT mescolare ▶ VI mescolarsi; (*people*): **to ~ with** avere a che fare con ▶ N mescolanza; preparato; **to ~ sth with sth** mischiare qc a qc; **to ~ business with pleasure** unire l'utile al dilettevole; **cake ~** preparato per torta
▶ **mix in** VT (*eggs etc*) incorporare
▶ **mix up** VT mescolare; (*confuse*) confondere; **to be mixed up in sth** essere coinvolto in qc

mixed [mɪkst] ADJ misto(-a)

mixed-ability [ˈmɪkstəˈbɪlɪtɪ] ADJ (*class etc*) con alunni di capacità diverse

mixed bag N miscuglio, accozzaglia; **it's a ~** c'è un po' di tutto

mixed blessing N: **it's a ~** ha i suoi lati positivi e negativi

mixed doubles NPL (*Sport*) doppio misto

mixed economy N economia mista

mixed grill N (BRIT) misto alla griglia

mixed marriage N matrimonio misto

mixed salad N insalata mista

mixed-up [mɪkstˈʌp] ADJ (*confused*) confuso(-a)

mixer [ˈmɪksərˈ] N (*for food: electric*) frullatore *m*; (: *hand*) frullino; **he is a good ~** è molto socievole

mixer tap N miscelatore *m*

mixture [ˈmɪkstʃərˈ] N mescolanza; (*blend: of tobacco etc*) miscela; (*Med*) sciroppo

mix-up [ˈmɪksʌp] N confusione *f*

MK ABBR (BRIT Tech) = **mark**

mk ABBR (*Hist: currency*) = **mark**

mkt ABBR = **market**

ml ABBR (= *millilitre(s)*) ml

MLitt N ABBR = **Master of Literature**; (= *Master of Letters*) titolo di studio

MLR N ABBR (BRIT) = **minimum lending rate**

mm ABBR (= *millimetre*) mm

MMS N ABBR (= *multimedia messaging service*) mms *m inv* (*servizio*); **~ message** mms *m inv*

MN ABBR (BRIT) = **merchant navy**; (US) = **Minnesota**

MO N ABBR = **medical officer**; (*US col: = modus operandi*) modo d'agire ▶ ABBR (US) = **Missouri**

m.o. ABBR = **money order**

moan [məʊn] N gemito ▶ VI gemere; (*col: complain*): **to ~ (about)** lamentarsi (di)

moaner [ˈməʊnərˈ] N (*col*) uno(-a) che si lamenta sempre

moaning [ˈməʊnɪŋ] N gemiti *mpl*

moat [məʊt] N fossato

mob [mɔb] N folla; (*disorderly*) calca; (*pej*): **the ~** la plebaglia ▶ VT accalcarsi intorno a

mobbing [ˈmɔbɪŋ] N mobbing *m inv*

mobile [ˈməʊbaɪl] ADJ mobile ▶ N (*phone*) telefonino, cellulare *m*; (*Art*) mobile *m inv*; **applicants must be ~** (BRIT) i candidati devono essere disposti a viaggiare

mobile home N grande roulotte *f inv* (*utilizzata come domicilio*)

mobile phone N telefono portatile, telefonino

mobile shop N (BRIT) negozio ambulante

mobility [məʊˈbɪlɪtɪ] N mobilità; (*of applicant*) disponibilità a viaggiare

mobilize [ˈməʊbɪlaɪz] VT mobilitare ▶ VI mobilitarsi

moccasin [ˈmɔkəsɪn] N mocassino

mock [mɔk] VT deridere, burlarsi di ▶ ADJ falso(-a) ■ **mocks** NPL (BRIT col: Scol) simulazione *f* degli esami

mockery [ˈmɔkərɪ] N derisione *f*; **to make a ~ of** burlarsi di; (*exam*) rendere una farsa

mocking [ˈmɔkɪŋ] ADJ derisorio(-a)

mockingbird [ˈmɔkɪŋbəːd] N mimo (*uccello*)

mock-up [ˈmɔkʌp] N modello dimostrativo; abbozzo

MOD N ABBR (BRIT) = **Ministry of Defence**; *see* **defence**

mod cons [mɔdˈkɔnz] NPL ABBR (BRIT) = **modern conveniences**

mode [məʊd] N modo; (*of transport*) mezzo; (*Comput*) modalità *f inv*

model [ˈmɔdl] N modello; (*person: for fashion*) indossatore(-trice); (: *for artist*) modello(-a) ▶ VT modellare ▶ VI fare l'indossatore (or l'indossatrice) ▶ ADJ (*small-scale: railway etc*) in miniatura; (*child, factory*) modello *inv*; **to ~ clothes** presentare degli abiti; **to ~ sb/sth on** modellare qn/qc su

modem [ˈməʊdɛm] N modem *m inv*

moderate ADJ [ˈmɔdərɪt] moderato(-a) ▶ N (*Pol*) moderato(-a) ▶ VI [ˈmɔdəreɪt] moderarsi, placarsi ▶ VT moderare

moderately [ˈmɔdərɪtlɪ] ADV (*act*) con moderazione; (*expensive, difficult*) non troppo; (*pleased, happy*) abbastanza, discretamente; **~ priced** a prezzo modico

moderation [mɔdəˈreɪʃən] N moderazione *f*, misura; **in ~** in quantità moderata, con moderazione

moderator [ˈmɔdəreɪtərˈ] N moderatore(-trice); (*Rel*) moderatore in importanti riunioni ecclesiastiche

modern [ˈmɔdən] ADJ moderno(-a); **~ conveniences** comodità *fpl* moderne; **~ languages** lingue *fpl* moderne

m

modernization [mɔdənaɪˈzeɪʃən] N rimodernamento, modernizzazione f

modernize [ˈmɔdənaɪz] VT modernizzare

modest [ˈmɔdɪst] ADJ modesto(-a)

modesty [ˈmɔdɪstɪ] N modestia

modicum [ˈmɔdɪkəm] N: **a ~ of** un minimo di

modification [mɔdɪfɪˈkeɪʃən] N modificazione f; **to make modifications** fare or apportare delle modifiche

modify [ˈmɔdɪfaɪ] VT modificare

modish [ˈməudɪʃ] ADJ (literary) à la page inv

Mods [mɔdz] N ABBR (BRIT: = (Honour) Moderations) esame all'università di Oxford

modular [ˈmɔdjuləʳ] ADJ (filing, unit) modulare

modulate [ˈmɔdjuleɪt] VT modulare

modulation [mɔdjuˈleɪʃən] N modulazione f

module [ˈmɔdjuːl] N modulo

Mogadishu [mɔgəˈdɪʃuː] N Mogadiscio f

mogul [ˈməugl] N (fig) magnate m, pezzo grosso; (Ski) cunetta

MOH N ABBR (BRIT: = Medical Officer of Health) ≈ ufficiale m sanitario

mohair [ˈməuhɛəʳ] N mohair m

Mohammed [məuˈhæmɪd] N Maometto

moist [mɔɪst] ADJ umido(-a)

moisten [ˈmɔɪsn] VT inumidire

moisture [ˈmɔɪstʃəʳ] N umidità; (on glass) goccioline fpl di vapore

moisturize [ˈmɔɪstʃəraɪz] VT (skin) idratare

moisturizer [ˈmɔɪstʃəraɪzəʳ] N idratante f

mojo (col) [ˈməudʒəu] N (US) carisma m

molar [ˈməuləʳ] N molare m

molasses [məuˈlæsɪz] N molassa

mold etc [məuld] (US) = **mould** etc

Moldova [mɔlˈdəuvə] N Moldavia

Moldovan [mɔlˈdəuvən] ADJ moldavo(-a)

mole [məul] N (animal, fig) talpa; (spot) neo

molecule [ˈmɔlɪkjuːl] N molecola

molehill [ˈməulhɪl] N cumulo di terra sulla tana di una talpa

molest [məuˈlɛst] VT molestare

mollusc, (US) **mollusk** [ˈmɔləsk] N mollusco

mollycoddle [ˈmɔlɪkɔdl] VT coccolare, vezzeggiare

Molotov cocktail [ˈmɔlətɔf-] N (bottiglia) Molotov f inv

molt [məult] VI (US) = **moult**

molten [ˈməultən] ADJ fuso(-a)

mom [mɔm] N (US) mamma

moment [ˈməumənt] N momento, istante m; importanza; **at that ~** in quel momento; **at the ~** al momento, in questo momento; **for the ~** per il momento, per ora; **in a ~** tra un momento; **"one ~ please"** (Tel) "attenda, prego"

momentarily [ˈməuməntərɪlɪ] ADV per un momento; (US: very soon) da un momento all'altro

momentary [ˈməuməntərɪ] ADJ momentaneo(-a), passeggero(-a)

momentous [məuˈmɛntəs] ADJ di grande importanza

momentum [məuˈmɛntəm] N velocità acquisita, slancio; (Physics) momento; (fig) impeto; **to gather ~** aumentare di velocità; (fig) prendere or guadagnare terreno

mommy [ˈmɔmɪ] N (US) mamma

Mon. ABBR (= Monday) lun.

Monaco [ˈmɔnəkəu] N Monaco f

monarch [ˈmɔnək] N monarca m

monarchist [ˈmɔnəkɪst] N monarchico(-a)

monarchy [ˈmɔnəkɪ] N monarchia

monastery [ˈmɔnəstərɪ] N monastero

monastic [məˈnæstɪk] ADJ monastico(-a)

Monday [ˈmʌndɪ] N lunedì m inv; see also **Tuesday**

Monegasque [mɔnəˈgæsk] ADJ, N monegasco(-a)

monetarist [ˈmʌnɪtərɪst] N monetarista mf

monetary [ˈmʌnɪtərɪ] ADJ monetario(-a)

monetization [mʌnɪtaɪˈzeɪʃən] N monetizzazione f

monetize [ˈmʌnɪtaɪz] VT monetizzare

money [ˈmʌnɪ] N denaro, soldi mpl; **to make ~** (person) fare (i) soldi; (business) rendere; **danger ~** (BRIT) indennità di rischio; **I've got no ~ left** non ho più neanche una lira

money belt N marsupio (per soldi)

moneyed [ˈmʌnɪd] ADJ ricco(-a)

moneylender [ˈmʌnɪlɛndəʳ] N prestatore(-trice) di denaro

moneymaker [ˈmʌnɪmeɪkəʳ] N (BRIT col: business) affare m d'oro

moneymaking [ˈmʌnɪmeɪkɪŋ] ADJ che rende (bene or molto), lucrativo(-a)

money market N mercato monetario

money order N vaglia m inv

money-spinner [ˈmʌnɪspɪnəʳ] N (col) miniera d'oro (fig)

money supply N liquidità monetaria

Mongol [ˈmɔŋgəl] N mongolo(-a); (Ling) mongolo

Mongolia [mɔŋˈgəulɪə] N Mongolia

Mongolian [mɔŋˈgəulɪən] ADJ mongolico(-a) ▶ N mongolo(-a); (Ling) mongolo

mongoose [ˈmɔŋguːs] N mangusta

mongrel [ˈmʌŋgrəl] N (dog) cane m bastardo

monitor [ˈmɔnɪtəʳ] N (BRIT Scol) capoclasse mf; (US Scol) chi sorveglia agli esami; (TV, Comput) monitor m inv ▶ VT controllare; (foreign station) ascoltare le trasmissioni di

monk [mʌŋk] N monaco

monkey [ˈmʌŋkɪ] N scimmia
monkey business N (col) scherzi mpl
monkey nut N (BRIT) nocciolina americana
monkey wrench N chiave f a rullino
mono [ˈmɔnəu] ADJ mono inv; (broadcast) in mono
mono... [ˈmɔnəu] PREFIX mono...
monochrome [ˈmɔnəkrəum] ADJ monocromo(-a)
monocle [ˈmɔnəkl] N monocolo
monogamous [məˈnɔgəməs] ADJ monogamo(-a)
monogamy [məˈnɔgəmɪ] N monogamia
monogram [ˈmɔnəgræm] N monogramma m
monolith [ˈmɔnəlɪθ] N monolito
monologue [ˈmɔnəlɔg] N monologo
monoplane [ˈmɔnəuplern] N monoplano
monopolize [məˈnɔpəlaɪz] VT monopolizzare
monopoly [məˈnɔpəlɪ] N monopolio
monorail [ˈmɔnəureɪl] N monorotaia
monosodium   glutamate [mɔnəˈsəudɪəmˈgluːtəmeɪt] N glutammato di sodio
monosyllabic [mɔnəsɪˈlæbɪk] ADJ monosillabico(-a); (person) che parla a monosillabi
monosyllable [ˈmɔnəsɪləbl] N monosillabo
monotone [ˈmɔnətəun] N pronunzia (or voce f) monotona; **to speak in a ~** parlare con voce monotona
monotonous [məˈnɔtənəs] ADJ monotono(-a)
monotony [məˈnɔtənɪ] N monotonia
monoxide [mɔˈnɔksaɪd] N: **carbon ~** ossido di carbonio
monsoon [mɔnˈsuːn] N monsone m
monster [ˈmɔnstəʳ] N mostro
monstrosity [mɔnˈstrɔsɪtɪ] N mostruosità f inv
monstrous [ˈmɔnstrəs] ADJ mostruoso(-a)
montage [mɔnˈtɑːʒ] N montaggio
Mont Blanc [mɔ̃blɔ̃] N Monte m Bianco
Montenegro [mɔntɪniˈgrəu] N Montenegro
month [mʌnθ] N mese m; **300 dollars a ~** 300 dollari al mese; **every ~** (happen) tutti i mesi; (pay) mensilmente, ogni mese
monthly [ˈmʌnθlɪ] ADJ mensile ▶ ADV al mese; ogni mese ▶ N (magazine) rivista mensile; **twice ~** due volte al mese
monument [ˈmɔnjumənt] N monumento
monumental [mɔnjuˈmɛntl] ADJ monumentale; (fig) colossale
monumental mason N lapidario
moo [muː] VI muggire, mugghiare
mood [muːd] N umore m; **to be in a good/bad ~** essere di buon/cattivo umore; **to be in the ~ for** essere disposto(-a) a, aver voglia di
moody [ˈmuːdɪ] ADJ (variable) capriccioso(-a), lunatico(-a); (sullen) imbronciato(-a)

moon [muːn] N luna
moonbeam [ˈmuːnbiːm] N raggio di luna
moon landing N allunaggio
moonlight [ˈmuːnlaɪt] N chiaro di luna ▶ VI fare del lavoro nero
moonlighting [ˈmuːnlaɪtɪŋ] N lavoro nero
moonlit [ˈmuːnlɪt] ADJ illuminato(-a) dalla luna; **a ~ night** una notte rischiarata dalla luna
moonshot [ˈmuːnʃɔt] N lancio sulla luna
moonstruck [ˈmuːnstrʌk] ADJ lunatico(-a)
moony [ˈmuːnɪ] ADJ (eyes) sognante
Moor [muəʳ] N moro(-a)
moor [muəʳ] N brughiera ▶ VT (ship) ormeggiare ▶ VI ormeggiarsi
moorings [ˈmuərɪŋz] NPL (chains) ormeggi mpl; (place) ormeggio
Moorish [ˈmuərɪʃ] ADJ moresco(-a)
moorland [ˈmuələnd] N brughiera
moose [muːs] N (pl inv) alce m
moot [muːt] VT sollevare ▶ ADJ: **~ point** punto discutibile
mop [mɔp] N lavapavimenti m inv; (also: **mop of hair**) zazzera ▶ VT lavare con lo straccio; (face) asciugare; **to ~ one's brow** asciugarsi la fronte ▶ **mop up** VT asciugare con uno straccio
mope [məup] VI fare il broncio ▶ **mope about, mope around** VI trascinarsi or aggirarsi con aria avvilita
moped [ˈməupɛd] N (BRIT) ciclomotore m
MOR ADJ ABBR (Mus) = **middle-of-the-road; ~ music** musica leggera
moral [ˈmɔrəl] ADJ morale ▶ N morale f ▪ **morals** NPL (principles) moralità
morale [mɔˈrɑːl] N morale m

> In Italian **la morale** is used for the moral of a story, or to mean morals. Use **il morale** for the morale of a person or team.

morality [məˈrælɪtɪ] N moralità
moralize [ˈmɔrəlaɪz] VI: **to ~ (about)** fare il (or la) moralista (riguardo), moraleggiare (riguardo)
morally [ˈmɔrəlɪ] ADV moralmente
moral victory N vittoria morale
morass [məˈræs] N palude f, pantano
moratorium [mɔrəˈtɔːrɪəm] N moratoria
morbid [ˈmɔːbɪd] ADJ morboso(-a)

---

more [mɔːʳ]

ADJ **1** (greater in number etc) più; **more people/ letters than we expected** più persone/lettere di quante ne aspettavamo; **I have more wine/money than you** ho più vino/soldi di te; **I have more wine than beer** ho più vino che birra

2 (additional) altro(-a), ancora; **do you want**

m

(some) more tea? vuole dell'altro tè?, vuole ancora del tè?; **I have no** or **I don't have any more money** non ho più soldi
▸ PRON **1** (*greater amount*) più; **more than 10** più di 10; **it cost more than we expected** è costato più di quanto ci aspettassimo; **and what's more ...** e per di più ...
2 (*further or additional amount*) ancora; **is there any more?** ce n'è ancora?; **there's no more** non ce n'è più; **a little more** ancora un po'; **many/much more** molti(-e)/molto(-a) di più
▸ ADV: **more dangerous/easily (than)** più pericoloso/facilmente (di); **more and more** sempre di più; **more and more difficult** sempre più difficile; **more or less** più o meno; **more than ever** più che mai; **once more** ancora (una volta), un'altra volta; **no more, not any more** non ... più; **I have no more money, I haven't any more money** non ho più soldi

moreover [mɔːˈrəuvəʳ] ADV inoltre, di più
morgue [mɔːg] N obitorio
MORI [ˈmɔːrɪ] N ABBR (BRIT: = *Market & Opinion Research Institute*) *istituto di sondaggio*
moribund [ˈmɔrɪbʌnd] ADJ moribondo(-a)
morning [ˈmɔːnɪŋ] N mattina, mattino; (*duration*) mattinata ▸ CPD del mattino; **in the ~** la mattina; **this ~** stamattina; **7 o'clock in the ~** le 7 di or della mattina

> Use **mattina** or **mattino** in expressions of time, e.g. *at 6 in the morning* **alle 6 di mattina**. Use **mattinata** for the kind of morning it is, e.g. *a cold morning* **una mattinata fredda**, how you spend it, or to emphasize its duration.

morning-after pill [ˈmɔːnɪŋˈɑːftə-] N pillola del giorno dopo
morning sickness N nausee *fpl* mattutine
Moroccan [məˈrɔkən] ADJ, N marocchino(-a)
Morocco [məˈrɔkəu] N Marocco
moron [ˈmɔːrɔn] N (!) deficiente *mf*
moronic [məˈrɔnɪk] ADJ (!) deficiente
morose [məˈrəus] ADJ cupo(-a), tetro(-a)
morphine [ˈmɔːfiːn] N morfina
morris dancing [ˈmɔrɪs-] N (BRIT) antica danza tradizionale inglese
Morse [mɔːs] N (*also*: **Morse code**) alfabeto Morse
morsel [ˈmɔːsl] N boccone *m*
mortal [ˈmɔːtl] ADJ, N mortale (*m*)
mortality [mɔːˈtælɪtɪ] N mortalità
mortality rate N tasso di mortalità
mortar [ˈmɔːtəʳ] N (*Constr*) malta; (*dish*) mortaio
mortgage [ˈmɔːgɪdʒ] N ipoteca; (*loan*) prestito ipotecario ▸ VT ipotecare; **to take out a ~** contrarre un mutuo (*or* un'ipoteca)

mortgage company N (US) società *f inv* immobiliare
mortgagee [mɔːgɪˈdʒiː] N creditore(-trice) ipotecario(-a)
mortgagor [ˈmɔːgɪdʒəʳ] N debitore(-trice) ipotecario(-a)
mortician [mɔːˈtɪʃən] N (US) impresario di pompe funebri
mortified [ˈmɔːtɪfaɪd] ADJ umiliato(-a)
mortise lock [ˈmɔːtɪs-] N serratura incastrata
mortuary [ˈmɔːtjuərɪ] N camera mortuaria; obitorio
mosaic [məuˈzeɪɪk] N mosaico
Moscow [ˈmɔskəu] N Mosca
Moslem [ˈmɔzləm] ADJ, N = **Muslim**
mosque [mɔsk] N moschea
mosquito [mɔsˈkiːtəu] (*pl* **mosquitoes**) N zanzara
mosquito net N zanzariera
moss [mɔs] N muschio
mossy [ˈmɔsɪ] ADJ muscoso(-a)
most [məust] ADJ (*almost all*) la maggior parte di; il più di; (*largest, greatest*): **who has (the) ~ money?** chi ha più soldi di tutti? ▸ PRON la maggior parte ▸ ADV più; (*work, sleep etc*) di più; (*very*) molto, estremamente; **the ~** (*also*: + *adjective*) il (la) più; **~ fish** la maggior parte dei pesci; **~ of** la maggior parte di; **~ of them** quasi tutti; **I saw ~** ho visto più io; **at the (very) ~** al massimo; **to make the ~ of** trarre il massimo vantaggio da; **a ~ interesting book** un libro estremamente interessante
mostly [ˈməustlɪ] ADV per lo più
MOT N ABBR (BRIT): **~ (test)** *revisione obbligatoria degli autoveicoli*
motel [məuˈtɛl] N motel *m inv*
moth [mɔθ] N farfalla notturna; tarma
mothball [ˈmɔθbɔːl] N pallina di naftalina
moth-eaten [ˈmɔθiːtn] ADJ tarmato(-a)
mother [ˈmʌðəʳ] N madre *f* ▸ VT (*care for*) fare da madre a
mother board N (*Comput*) scheda madre
motherhood [ˈmʌðəhud] N maternità
mother-in-law [ˈmʌðərɪnlɔː] N suocera
mother-of-pearl [mʌðərəvˈpəːl] N madreperla
Mother's Day N la festa della mamma
mother's help N bambinaia
mother-to-be [mʌðətəˈbiː] N futura mamma
mother tongue N madrelingua
mothproof [ˈmɔθpruːf] ADJ antitarmico(-a)
motif [məuˈtiːf] N motivo
motion [ˈməuʃən] N movimento, moto; (*gesture*) gesto; (*at meeting*) mozione *f*; (BRIT: *also*: **bowel motion**) evacuazione *f* ▸ VT, VI: **to ~ (to) sb to do** fare cenno a qn di fare; **to be in ~** (*vehicle*) essere

in moto; **to set in ~** avviare; **to go through the motions of doing sth** (fig) fare qc pro forma

motionless ['məʊʃənlɪs] ADJ immobile

motion picture N film m inv

motivate ['məʊtɪveɪt] VT (act, decision) dare origine a, motivare; (person) spingere

motivated ['məʊtɪveɪtɪd] ADJ motivato(-a)

motivation [məʊtɪ'veɪʃən] N motivazione f

motive ['məʊtɪv] N motivo ▶ ADJ motore(-trice); **from the best motives** con le migliori intenzioni

motley ['mɒtlɪ] ADJ eterogeneo(-a), molto vario(-a)

motor ['məʊtə'] N motore m; (BRIT col: vehicle) macchina ▶ ADJ (industry, accident) automobilistico(-a); **~ vehicle** autoveicolo

motorbike ['məʊtəbaɪk] N moto f inv

motorboat ['məʊtəbəʊt] N motoscafo

motorcade ['məʊtəkeɪd] N corteo di macchine

motorcar ['məʊtəkɑː] N (BRIT) automobile f

motorcoach ['məʊtəkəʊtʃ] N (BRIT) pullman m inv

motorcycle ['məʊtəsaɪkl] N motocicletta

motorcyclist ['məʊtəsaɪklɪst] N motociclista mf

motoring ['məʊtərɪŋ] (BRIT) N turismo automobilistico ▶ ADJ (accident) d'auto, automobilistico(-a); (offence) di guida; **~ holiday** vacanza in macchina

motorist ['məʊtərɪst] N automobilista mf

motorize ['məʊtəraɪz] VT motorizzare

motor oil N olio lubrificante

motor racing N (BRIT) corse fpl automobilistiche

motor scooter N motorscooter m inv

motor vehicle N autoveicolo

motorway ['məʊtəweɪ] N (BRIT) autostrada

mottled ['mɒtld] ADJ chiazzato(-a), marezzato(-a)

motto ['mɒtəʊ] (pl **mottoes**) N motto

mould, (US) **mold** [məʊld] N forma, stampo; (mildew) muffa ▶ VT formare; (fig) foggiare

moulder, (US) **molder** ['məʊldə'] VI (decay) ammuffire

moulding, (US) **molding** ['məʊldɪŋ] N (Archit) modanatura

mouldy, (US) **moldy** ['məʊldɪ] ADJ ammuffito(-a); (smell) di muffa

moult, (US) **molt** [məʊlt] VI far la muta

mound [maʊnd] N rialzo, collinetta; (heap) mucchio

mount [maʊnt] N (Geo) monte m, montagna; (horse) cavalcatura; (for jewel etc) montatura ▶ VT montare; (horse) montare a; (exhibition) organizzare; (attack) sferrare, condurre; (picture, stamp) sistemare ▶ VI salire; (get on a horse) montare a cavallo

▶ **mount up** VI (build up) accumularsi

mountain ['maʊntɪn] N montagna ▶ CPD di montagna; **to make a ~ out of a molehill** fare di una mosca un elefante

mountain bike N mountain bike f inv

mountaineer [maʊntɪ'nɪə'] N alpinista mf

mountaineering [maʊntɪ'nɪərɪŋ] N alpinismo; **to go ~** fare dell'alpinismo

mountainous ['maʊntɪnəs] ADJ montagnoso(-a)

mountain range N catena montuosa

mountain rescue team N ≈ squadra di soccorso alpino

mountainside ['maʊntɪnsaɪd] N fianco della montagna

mounted ['maʊntɪd] ADJ a cavallo

mourn [mɔːn] VT piangere, lamentare ▶ VI: **to ~ (for sb)** piangere (la morte di qn)

mourner ['mɔːnə'] N parente mf (or amico(-a)) del defunto

mourning ['mɔːnɪŋ] N lutto ▶ CPD (dress) da lutto; **in ~** in lutto

mouse [maʊs] (pl **mice** [maɪs]) N topo; (Comput) mouse m inv

mouse mat, mouse pad N (Comput) tappetino del mouse

mousetrap ['maʊstræp] N trappola per i topi

moussaka [muː'sɑːkə] N moussaka

mousse [muːs] N mousse f inv

moustache, (US) **mustache** [məs'tɑːʃ] N baffi mpl

mousy ['maʊsɪ] ADJ (person) timido(-a); (hair) né chiaro(-a) né scuro(-a)

mouth [maʊθ] (pl **mouths** [-ðz]) N bocca; (of river) bocca, foce f; (opening) orifizio

mouthful ['maʊθful] N boccata

mouth organ N armonica

mouthpiece ['maʊθpiːs] N (Mus) imboccatura, bocchino; (Tel) microfono; (of breathing apparatus) boccaglio; (person) portavoce mf

mouth-to-mouth ['maʊθtə'maʊθ] ADJ: **~ resuscitation** respirazione f bocca a bocca

mouthwash ['maʊθwɒʃ] N collutorio

mouth-watering ['maʊθwɔːtərɪŋ] ADJ che fa venire l'acquolina in bocca

movable ['muːvəbl] ADJ mobile

move [muːv] N (movement) movimento; (in game) mossa; (: turn to play) turno; (change: of house) trasloco; (: of job) cambiamento ▶ VT muovere; (change position of) spostare; (emotionally) commuovere; (Pol: resolution etc) proporre ▶ VI (gen) muoversi, spostarsi; (traffic) circolare; (also: **move house**) cambiar casa, traslocare; **to ~ towards** andare verso; **to ~ sb to do sth** indurre or spingere qn a fare qc; **to get a ~ on** affrettarsi, sbrigarsi; **to be moved** (emotionally) essere commosso(-a)

▶ **move about, move around** VI (fidget) agitarsi; (travel) viaggiare

m

▶ **move along** vi muoversi avanti

▶ **move away** vi allontanarsi, andarsene

▶ **move back** vi indietreggiare; (*return*) ritornare

▶ **move forward** vi avanzare ▶ vt avanzare, spostare in avanti; (*people*) far avanzare

▶ **move in** vi (*to a house*) entrare (*in una nuova casa*); (*police etc*) intervenire

▶ **move off** vi partire

▶ **move on** vi riprendere la strada ▶ vt (*onlookers*) far circolare

▶ **move out** vi (*of house*) sgombrare

▶ **move over** vi spostarsi

▶ **move up** vi avanzare

movement [ˈmuːvmənt] N (*gen*) movimento; (*gesture*) gesto; (*of stars, water, physical*) moto; **~ (of the bowels)** (*Med*) evacuazione f

mover [ˈmuːvəʳ] N proponente mf

movie [ˈmuːvɪ] N film m inv; **the movies** il cinema

movie camera N cinepresa

moviegoer [ˈmuːvɪɡəʊəʳ] N (*US*) frequentatore(-trice) di cinema

movie theater N (*US*) cinema m inv

moving [ˈmuːvɪŋ] ADJ mobile; (*causing emotion*) commovente; (*instigating*) animatore(-trice)

mow [məʊ] (*pt* **mowed**, *pp* **mowed** or **mown** [məʊn]) vt falciare; (*grass*) tagliare; (*corn*) mietere ▶ **mow down** vt falciare

mower [ˈməʊəʳ] N (*also:* **lawn mower**) tagliaerba m inv

mown [məʊn] PP *of* **mow**

Mozambique [məʊzəmˈbiːk] N Mozambico

MP N ABBR = **Military Police**; (*BRIT*) = **Member of Parliament**; (*CANADA*) = **Mounted Police**

MP3 N MP3 m inv

MP3 player N lettore m MP3 inv

mpg N ABBR = **miles per gallon**

mph N ABBR = **miles per hour**

MPhil N ABBR (= *Master of Philosophy*) titolo di studio

MPS N ABBR (*BRIT*) = **Member of the Pharmaceutical Society**

Mr, (*US*) **Mr.** [ˈmɪstəʳ] N: **Mr X** Signor X, Sig. X

MRC N ABBR (*BRIT*): = *Medical Research Council*) ufficio governativo per la ricerca medica in Gran Bretagna e nel Commonwealth

MRCP N ABBR (*BRIT*) = **Member of the Royal College of Physicians**

MRCS N ABBR (*BRIT*) = **Member of the Royal College of Surgeons**

MRCVS N ABBR (*BRIT*) = **Member of the Royal College of Veterinary Surgeons**

Mrs, (*US*) **Mrs.** [ˈmɪsɪz] N: **~ X** Signora X, Sig.ra X

MS N ABBR (*US*: = *Master of Science*) titolo di studio; (*Med*) = **multiple sclerosis**; (= *manuscript*) ms ▶ ABBR (*US*) = **Mississippi**

Ms, (*US*) **Ms.** [mɪz] N = **Miss**; **Mrs**; **Ms X** ≈ Signora X, ≈ Sig.ra X

In inglese si usa **Ms** al posto di *Mrs* (Signora) o *Miss* (Signorina) per evitare la distinzione tradizionale tra le donne sposate e quelle nubili.

MSA N ABBR (*US*: = *Master of Science in Agriculture*) titolo di studio

MSc N ABBR = **Master of Science**

MSG ABBR = **monosodium glutamate**

MSP N ABBR (*BRIT*) = **Member of the Scottish Parliament**

MST ABBR (*US*: = *Mountain Standard Time*) ora invernale delle Montagne Rocciose

MSW N ABBR (*US*: = *Master of Social Work*) titolo di studio

MT N ABBR = **machine translation** ▶ ABBR (*US*) = **Montana**

Mt ABBR (*Geo*: = *mount*) M

mth ABBR (= *month*) m

MTV N ABBR = **music television**

---

much [mʌtʃ]

ADJ, PRON molto(-a); **he's done so much work** ha lavorato così tanto; **I have as much money as you** ho tanti soldi quanti ne hai tu; **how much is it?** quant'è?; **it's not much** non è tanto; **it costs too much** costa troppo; **as much as you want** quanto vuoi

▶ ADV **1** (*greatly*) molto, tanto; **thank you very much** molte grazie; **I like it very/so much** mi piace moltissimo/così tanto; **much to my amazement** con mio enorme stupore; **he's very much the gentleman** è il vero gentiluomo; **I read as much as I can** leggo quanto posso; **as much as you** tanto quanto te

2 (*by far*) molto; **it's much the biggest company in Europe** è di gran lunga la più grossa società in Europa

3 (*almost*) grossomodo, praticamente; **they're much the same** sono praticamente uguali

---

muck [mʌk] N (*mud*) fango; (*dirt*) sporcizia

▶ **muck about, muck around** vi (*col*) fare lo(la) stupido(-a); (: *waste time*) gingillarsi; (: *tinker*) armeggiare

▶ **muck in** vi (*BRIT col*) mettersi insieme

▶ **muck out** vt (*stable*) pulire

▶ **muck up** vt (*col*: *dirty*) sporcare; (: *spoil*) rovinare

muckraking [ˈmʌkreɪkɪŋ] (*fig*: *col*) N caccia agli scandali ▶ ADJ scandalistico(-a)

mucky [ˈmʌkɪ] ADJ (*dirty*) sporco(-a), lordo(-a)

mucus [ˈmjuːkəs] N muco

mud [mʌd] N fango

muddle [ˈmʌdl] N confusione f, disordine m; pasticcio ▶ vt (*also:* **muddle up**) mettere sottosopra; confondere; **to be in a ~** (*person*) non riuscire a raccapezzarsi; **to get in a ~** (*while explaining etc*) imbrogliarsi

▶ **muddle along** vi andare avanti a casaccio

▶ **muddle through** VI cavarsela alla meno peggio

muddle-headed [mʌdl'hɛdɪd] ADJ (person) confusionario(-a)

muddy ['mʌdɪ] ADJ fangoso(-a)

mud flats NPL distesa fangosa

mudguard ['mʌdgɑːd] N parafango

mudpack ['mʌdpæk] N maschera di fango

mud-slinging ['mʌdslɪŋɪŋ] N (fig) infangamento

muesli ['mjuːzlɪ] N muesli m inv

muff [mʌf] N manicotto ▶ VT (shot, catch etc) mancare, sbagliare; **to ~ it** sbagliare tutto

muffin ['mʌfɪn] N specie di pasticcino soffice da tè

muffle ['mʌfl] VT (sound) smorzare, attutire; (against cold) imbacuccare

muffled ['mʌfld] ADJ smorzato(-a), attutito(-a)

muffler ['mʌflər] N (scarf) sciarpa (pesante); (US: Aut) marmitta; (: on motorbike) silenziatore m

mufti ['mʌftɪ] N: **in ~** in borghese

mug [mʌg] N (cup) tazzone m; (for beer) boccale m; (col: face) muso; (: fool) scemo(-a) ▶ VT (assault) assalire; **it's a ~'s game** (BRIT) è proprio (una cosa) da fessi
▶ **mug up** VT (BRIT col: also: **mug up on**) studiare bene

mugger ['mʌgər] N aggressore m

mugging ['mʌgɪŋ] N aggressione f (a scopo di rapina)

muggins ['mʌgɪnz] N (BRIT col) semplicione(-a), sprovveduto(-a)

muggy ['mʌgɪ] ADJ afoso(-a)

mug shot N (col) foto f inv segnaletica

mulatto [mjuːˈlætəu] (pl **mulattoes**) N (!) mulatto(-a)

mulberry ['mʌlbərɪ] N (fruit) mora (di gelso); (tree) gelso, moro

mule [mjuːl] N mulo

mull [mʌl]: **to ~ over** VT rimuginare

mulled [mʌld] ADJ: **~ wine** vino caldo

multi... ['mʌltɪ] PREFIX multi...

multi-access [mʌltɪ'ækses] ADJ (Comput) ad accesso multiplo

multicoloured, (US) **multicolored** ['mʌltɪkʌləd] ADJ multicolore, variopinto(-a)

multifarious [mʌltɪ'fɛərɪəs] ADJ molteplice, svariato(-a)

multigrain ['mʌltɪgreɪn] ADJ multicereali inv

multilateral [mʌltɪ'lætərəl] ADJ (Pol) multilaterale

multi-level ['mʌltɪlɛvl] ADJ (US) = **multistorey**

multimedia ['mʌltɪ'miːdɪə] ADJ multimedia inv

multimillionaire [mʌltɪmɪljə'nɛər] N multimiliardario(-a)

multinational [mʌltɪ'næʃənl] ADJ, N multinazionale (f)

multiple ['mʌltɪpl] ADJ multiplo(-a); molte-

plice ▶ N multiplo; (BRIT: also: **multiple store**) grande magazzino che fa parte di una catena

multiple choice (test) N esercizi mpl a scelta multipla

multiple crash N serie f inv di incidenti a catena

multiple sclerosis [-sklɪ'rəusɪs] N sclerosi f a placche

multiplex ['mʌltɪplɛks] N (also: **multiplex cinema**) cinema m inv multisale inv

multiplication [mʌltɪplɪ'keɪʃən] N moltiplicazione f

multiplication table N tavola pitagorica

multiplicity [mʌltɪ'plɪsɪtɪ] N molteplicità f inv

multiply ['mʌltɪplaɪ] VT moltiplicare ▶ VI moltiplicarsi

multiracial [mʌltɪ'reɪʃəl] ADJ multirazziale

multistorey ['mʌltɪ'stɔːrɪ] ADJ (BRIT: building, car park) a più piani

multitask ['mʌltɪtɑːsk] VI essere multitasking

multitasking [mʌltɪ'tɑːskɪŋ] N (also Comput) multitasking m inv; **is ~ a skill that can be learned?** il multitasking è un'abilità che si può imparare?

multitude ['mʌltɪtjuːd] N moltitudine f

mum [mʌm] N (BRIT col) mamma ▶ ADJ: **to keep ~** non aprire bocca; **~'s the word!** acqua in bocca!

mumble ['mʌmbl] VT, VI borbottare

mumbo jumbo ['mʌmbəu-] N (col) parole fpl incomprensibili

mummify ['mʌmɪfaɪ] VT mummificare

mummy ['mʌmɪ] N (BRIT: mother) mamma; (embalmed) mummia

mumps [mʌmps] N orecchioni mpl

munch [mʌntʃ] VT, VI sgranocchiare

mundane [mʌn'deɪn] ADJ terra a terra inv

Munich ['mjuːnɪk] N Monaco f (di Baviera)

municipal [mjuː'nɪsɪpl] ADJ municipale

municipality [mjuːnɪsɪ'pælɪtɪ] N municipio

munitions [mjuː'nɪʃənz] NPL munizioni fpl

mural ['mjuərəl] N dipinto murale

murder ['məːdər] N assassinio, omicidio ▶ VT assassinare; **to commit ~** commettere un omicidio

murderer ['məːdərər] N omicida mf, assassino(-a)

murderess ['məːdərɪs] N omicida f, assassina

murderous ['məːdərəs] ADJ micidiale

murk [məːk] N oscurità, buio

murky ['məːkɪ] ADJ tenebroso(-a), buio(-a)

murmur ['məːmər] N mormorio ▶ VT, VI mormorare; **heart ~** (Med) soffio al cuore

MusB, MusBac N ABBR (= Bachelor of Music) titolo di studio

muscle ['mʌsl] N muscolo; (*fig*) forza
 ▸ **muscle in** VI immischiarsi

muscular ['mʌskjulə'] ADJ muscolare; (*person, arm*) muscoloso(-a)

muscular dystrophy N distrofia muscolare

MusD, MusDoc N ABBR (= *Doctor of Music*) titolo di studio

muse [mju:z] VI meditare, sognare ▸ N musa

museum [mju:'zɪəm] N museo

mush [mʌʃ] N pappa

mushroom ['mʌʃrum] N fungo ▸ VI (*fig*) svilupparsi rapidamente

mushy ['mʌʃɪ] ADJ (*food*) spappolato(-a); (*sentimental*) sdolcinato(-a)

music ['mju:zɪk] N musica

musical ['mju:zɪkəl] ADJ musicale; (*person*) portato(-a) per la musica ▸ N (*show*) commedia musicale

musical box N carillon *m inv*

musical chairs N gioco delle sedie (*in cui bisogna sedersi non appena cessa la musica*); (*fig*) scambio delle poltrone

musical instrument N strumento musicale

music box N carillon *m inv*

music centre N impianto *m* stereo *inv* monoblocco *inv*

music hall N teatro di varietà

musician [mju:'zɪʃən] N musicista *mf*

music stand N leggio

musk [mʌsk] N muschio

musket ['mʌskɪt] N moschetto

muskrat ['mʌskræt] N topo muschiato

musk rose N (*Bot*) rosa muschiata

Muslim ['mʌzlɪm] ADJ, N musulmano(-a)

muslin ['mʌzlɪn] N mussola

musquash ['mʌskwɔʃ] N (*fur*) rat musqué *m inv*

mussel ['mʌsl] N cozza

must [mʌst] AUX VB (*obligation*): **I ~ do it** devo farlo; (*probability*): **he ~ be there by now** dovrebbe essere arrivato ormai; **I ~ have made a mistake** devo essermi sbagliato ▸ N: **this programme/trip is a ~** è un programma/viaggio da non perdersi

mustache ['mʌstæʃ] N (*US*) = **moustache**

mustard ['mʌstəd] N senape *f*, mostarda

mustard gas N iprite *f*

muster ['mʌstə'] VT radunare; (*also*: **muster up**: *strength, courage*) fare appello a

mustiness ['mʌstɪnɪs] N odor di muffa *or* di stantio

mustn't ['mʌsnt] = **must not**

musty ['mʌstɪ] ADJ che sa di muffa *or* di rinchiuso

mutant ['mju:tənt] ADJ, N mutante (*m*)

mutate [mju:'teɪt] VI subire una mutazione

mutation [mju:'teɪʃən] N mutazione *f*

mute [mju:t] ADJ muto(-a)

muted ['mju:tɪd] ADJ (*noise*) attutito(-a), smorzato(-a); (*criticism*) attenuato(-a); (*Mus*) in sordina; (: *trumpet*) con sordina

mutilate ['mju:tɪleɪt] VT mutilare

mutilation [mju:tɪ'leɪʃən] N mutilazione *f*

mutinous ['mju:tɪnəs] ADJ (*troops*) ammutinato(-a); (*attitude*) ribelle

mutiny ['mju:tɪnɪ] N ammutinamento ▸ VI ammutinarsi

mutter ['mʌtə'] VT, VI borbottare, brontolare

mutton ['mʌtn] N carne *f* di montone

mutual ['mju:tʃuəl] ADJ mutuo(-a), reciproco(-a)

mutually ['mju:tʃuəlɪ] ADV reciprocamente

Muzak® ['mju:zæk] N (*often pej*) musica di sottofondo

muzzle ['mʌzl] N muso; (*protective device*) museruola; (*of gun*) bocca ▸ VT mettere la museruola a

MV ABBR (= *motor vessel*) M/N, m/n

MVP N ABBR (*US Sport*: = *most valuable player*) titolo ottenuto da sportivo

MW ABBR (*Radio*: = *medium wave*) O.M.; = **megawatt**

my [maɪ] ADJ il (la) mio(-a); (*pl*) i (le) miei (mie); **my house** la mia casa; **my books** i miei libri; **my brother** mio fratello; **I've washed my hair/cut my finger** mi sono lavato i capelli/tagliato

Myanmar ['maɪænmɑ:'] N Myanma

myopic [maɪ'ɔpɪk] ADJ miope

myriad ['mɪrɪəd] N miriade *f*

myself [maɪ'self] PRON (*reflexive*) mi; (*emphatic*) io stesso(-a); (*after prep*) me; *see also* **oneself**

mysterious [mɪs'tɪərɪəs] ADJ misterioso(-a)

mystery ['mɪstərɪ] N mistero

mystery story N racconto del mistero

mystic ['mɪstɪk] ADJ, N mistico(-a)

mystical ['mɪstɪkəl] ADJ mistico(-a)

mystify ['mɪstɪfaɪ] VT mistificare; (*puzzle*) confondere

mystique [mɪs'ti:k] N fascino

myth [mɪθ] N mito

mythical ['mɪθɪkl] ADJ mitico(-a)

mythological [mɪθə'lɔdʒɪkl] ADJ mitologico(-a)

mythology [mɪ'θɔlədʒɪ] N mitologia

Nn

N, n [ɛn] N (*letter*) N, n f *inv or* m *inv*; **N for Nellie**, (*US*) **N for Nan** ≈ N come Napoli

N ABBR (= *north*) N

NA N ABBR (*US:* = *Narcotics Anonymous*) associazione in aiuto dei tossicodipendenti; (*US*) = **National Academy**

n/a ABBR (= *not applicable*) non pertinente

NAACP N ABBR (*US*) = **National Association for the Advancement of Colored People**

NAAFI ['næfɪ] N ABBR (*BRIT:* = *Navy, Army, & Air Force Institutes*) organizzazione che gestisce negozi, mense ecc. per il personale militare

nab [næb] VT (*col*) beccare, acchiappare

NACU N ABBR (*US*) = **National Association of Colleges and Universities**

nadir ['neɪdɪəʳ] N (*Astron*) nadir m; (*fig*) punto più basso

nag [næg] N (*pej: horse*) ronzino; (*person*) brontolone(-a) ▶ VT tormentare ▶ VI brontolare in continuazione

nagging ['nægɪŋ] ADJ (*doubt, pain*) persistente ▶ N brontolii mpl, osservazioni fpl continue

nail [neɪl] N (*human*) unghia; (*metal*) chiodo ▶ VT inchiodare; **to ~ sb down to a date/price** costringere qn a un appuntamento/ad accettare un prezzo; **to pay cash on the ~** (*BRIT*) pagare a tamburo battente

nailbrush ['neɪlbrʌʃ] N spazzolino da *or* per unghie

nailfile ['neɪlfaɪl] N lima da *or* per unghie

nail polish N smalto da *or* per unghie

nail polish remover N acetone m, solvente m

nail scissors NPL forbici fpl da *or* per unghie

nail varnish N (*BRIT*) = **nail polish**

Nairobi [naɪˈrəubɪ] N Nairobi f

naïve [naɪˈiːv] ADJ ingenuo(-a)

naïveté [naːiːvˈteɪ], **naivety** [naɪˈiːvtɪ] N ingenuità f inv

naked ['neɪkɪd] ADJ nudo(-a); **with the ~ eye** a occhio nudo

nakedness ['neɪkɪdnɪs] N nudità

NAM N ABBR (*US*) = **National Association of Manufacturers**

name [neɪm] N nome m; (*reputation*) nome, reputazione f ▶ VT (*baby etc*) chiamare; (*plant, illness*) nominare; (*person, object*) identificare; (*price, date*) fissare; **by ~** di nome; **she knows them all by ~** li conosce tutti per nome; **in the ~ of** in nome di; **what's your ~?** come si chiama?; **my ~ is Peter** mi chiamo Peter; **to take sb's ~ and address** prendere nome e indirizzo di qn; **to make a ~ for o.s.** farsi un nome; **to get (o.s.) a bad ~** farsi una cattiva fama *or* una brutta reputazione; **to call sb names** insultare qn

name dropping N menzionare qualcuno per fare bella figura

nameless ['neɪmlɪs] ADJ senza nome

namely ['neɪmlɪ] ADV cioè

nameplate ['neɪmpleɪt] N (*on door etc*) targa

namesake ['neɪmseɪk] N omonimo

Namibia [naːˈmɪbɪə] N Namibia

nan bread [naːn-] N tipo di pane indiano poco lievitato di forma allungata

nanny ['nænɪ] N bambinaia

nanny goat N capra

nanobot ['nænəubɔt] N nanorobot m inv

nap [næp] N (*sleep*) pisolino; (*of cloth*) peluria ▶ VI: **to be caught napping** essere preso alla sprovvista; **to have a ~** schiacciare un pisolino

napalm ['neɪpaːm] N napalm m

nape [neɪp] N: **~ of the neck** nuca

napkin ['næpkɪn] N tovagliolo; (*BRIT: for baby*) pannolino

Naples ['neɪplz] N Napoli f

Napoleonic [nəpəulɪˈɔnɪk] ADJ napoleonico(-a)

nappy ['næpɪ] N (*BRIT*) pannolino

nappy liner N (*BRIT*) fogliettino igienico

narcissistic [naːsɪˈsɪstɪk] ADJ narcisistico(-a)

narcissus [naːˈsɪsəs] (*pl* narcissi [-saɪ]) N narciso

narcotic [naːˈkɔtɪk] N (*Med*) narcotico ■ **narcotics** NPL (*drugs*) narcotici, stupefacenti mpl

nark [naːk] VT (*BRIT col*) scocciare

narrate [nəˈreɪt] VT raccontare, narrare

narration [nəˈreɪʃən] N narrazione f

narrative [ˈnærətɪv] N narrativa ▶ ADJ narrativo(-a)

narrator [nəˈreɪtəʳ] N narratore(-trice)

narrow [ˈnærəʊ] ADJ stretto(-a); (*resources, means*) limitato(-a), modesto(-a); (*fig*): **to take a ~ view of** avere una visione limitata di ▶ VI restringersi; **to have a ~ escape** farcela per un pelo ▶ **narrow down** VT (*search, investigation, possibilities*) restringere; (*list*) ridurre; **to ~ sth down to** ridurre qc a

narrow gauge ADJ (*Rail*) a scartamento ridotto

narrowly [ˈnærəʊlɪ] ADV per un pelo; (*time*) per poco; **Maria ~ escaped drowning** per un pelo Maria non è affogata; **he ~ missed hitting the cyclist** per poco non ha investito il ciclista

narrow-minded [nærəʊˈmaɪndɪd] ADJ meschino(-a)

NAS N ABBR (*US*) = **National Academy of Sciences**

NASA [ˈnæsə] N ABBR (*US*: = *National Aeronautics and Space Administration*) N.A.S.A. f

nasal [ˈneɪzl] ADJ nasale

Nassau [ˈnæsɔː] N Nassau f

nastily [ˈnɑːstɪlɪ] ADV con cattiveria

nastiness [ˈnɑːstɪnɪs] N (*of person, remark*) cattiveria; (: *spitefulness*) malignità

nasturtium [nəsˈtəːʃəm] N cappuccina, nasturzio (indiano)

nasty [ˈnɑːstɪ] ADJ (*unpleasant: person, remark*) cattivo(-a); (*spiteful*) maligno(-a); (*rude*) villano(-a); (*smell, wound, situation*) brutto(-a); **to turn ~** (*situation*) mettersi male; (*weather*) guastarsi; (*person*) incattivirsi; **it's a ~ business** è una brutta faccenda, è un brutto affare

NASUWT N ABBR (*BRIT*: = *National Association of Schoolmasters and Union of Women Teachers*) sindacato di insegnanti in Inghilterra e Galles

nation [ˈneɪʃən] N nazione f

national [ˈnæʃnl] ADJ nazionale ▶ N cittadino(-a)

national anthem N inno nazionale

National Curriculum N (*BRIT*) ≈ programma m scolastico ministeriale (*in Inghilterra e Galles*)

national debt N debito pubblico

national dress N costume m nazionale

National Guard N (*US*) milizia nazionale (*volontaria, in ogni stato*)

National Health Service N (*BRIT*) ≈ Servizio sanitario nazionale

> Il **National Health Service** (o **NHS**) è il sistema sanitario nazionale britannico che fornisce assistenza medica dal 1948 ed è il più grande al mondo. Finanziato dalla tassazione, si fonda sul principio della gratuità per tutti, indipendentemente dal reddito. Tranne alcune eccezioni (il servizio odontoiatrico effettuato da dentisti convenzionati e i medicinali in Inghilterra Galles

e Irlanda del Nord), tutte le prestazioni, comprese le visite mediche e le cure ospedaliere, sono gratuite. Ognuna delle quattro nazioni del Regno Unito ha un suo sistema gestito in modo indipendente. Spesso oggetto di critiche per le lunghe liste di attesa e l'insufficienza del personale ospedaliero, il servizio è costantemente oggetto di riforme.

National Insurance N (*BRIT*) ≈ Previdenza Sociale

> Nel Regno Unito il **National Insurance** è il sistema di contribuzione obbligatoria versata dai lavoratori e dai datori di lavoro per finanziare il *welfare*. Introdotto nel 1911 come assicurazione contro la malattia e la disoccupazione, nel 1948 è stato considerevolmente ampliato e ora include le pensioni, il congedo per maternità, l'assegno di disoccupazione e quello di invalidità.

nationalism [ˈnæʃnəlɪzəm] N nazionalismo

nationalist [ˈnæʃnəlɪst] ADJ, N nazionalista (*mf*)

nationality [næʃəˈnælɪtɪ] N nazionalità f inv

nationalization [næʃnəlaɪˈzeɪʃən] N nazionalizzazione f

nationalize [ˈnæʃnəlaɪz] VT nazionalizzare

nationally [ˈnæʃnəlɪ] ADV a livello nazionale

national park N parco nazionale

national press N stampa a diffusione nazionale

National Security Council N (*US*) consiglio nazionale di sicurezza

national service N (*Mil*) servizio militare

National Trust N ≈ sovrintendenza ai beni culturali e ambientali

> Fondato nel 1895, il **National Trust** è un'organizzazione che si occupa della tutela e salvaguardia di edifici e monumenti di interesse storico e di siti di interesse ambientale nel Regno Unito.

nationwide [ˈneɪʃənwaɪd] ADJ diffuso(-a) in tutto il paese ▶ ADV in tutto il paese

native [ˈneɪtɪv] N abitante mf del paese; (!: *in colonies*) indigeno(-a) ▶ ADJ indigeno(-a); (*country*) natio(-a); (*ability*) innato(-a); **a ~ of Russia** un nativo della Russia; **a ~ speaker of French** una persona di madrelingua francese; **~ language** madrelingua

Native American N discendente di tribù dell'America settentrionale

Nativity [nəˈtɪvɪtɪ] N (*Rel*): **the ~** la Natività

nativity play N recita sulla Natività

NATO [ˈneɪtəʊ] N ABBR (= *North Atlantic Treaty Organization*) N.A.T.O. f

natter [ˈnætəʳ] (BRIT col) VI chiacchierare ▸ N chiacchierata

natural [ˈnætʃrəl] ADJ naturale; (ability) innato(-a); (manner) semplice; **death from ~ causes** (Law) morte f per cause naturali

natural childbirth N parto indolore

natural gas N gas m metano

natural history N storia naturale

naturalist [ˈnætʃrəlɪst] N naturalista mf

naturalization [nætʃrəlaɪˈzeɪʃən] N naturalizzazione f; acclimatazione f

naturalize [ˈnætʃrəlaɪz] VT: **to be naturalized** (person) naturalizzarsi; **to become naturalized** (animal, plant) acclimatarsi

naturally [ˈnætʃrəlɪ] ADV naturalmente; (by nature: gifted) di natura

naturalness [ˈnætʃrəlnɪs] N naturalezza

natural resources NPL risorse fpl naturali

natural selection N selezione f naturale

natural wastage N (Industry) diminuzione f di manodopera (per pensionamento, decesso ecc)

nature [ˈneɪtʃəʳ] N natura; (character) natura, indole f; **by ~** di natura; **documents of a confidential ~** documenti mpl di natura privata

-natured [ˈneɪtʃəd] SUFFIX: **ill-natured** maldisposto(-a)

nature reserve N (BRIT) parco naturale

nature trail N percorso tracciato in parchi nazionali ecc con scopi educativi

naturist [ˈneɪtʃərɪst] N naturista mf, nudista mf

naught [nɔːt] N = **nought**

naughtiness [ˈnɔːtɪnɪs] N cattiveria

naughty [ˈnɔːtɪ] ADJ (child) birichino(-a), cattivello(-a); (story, film) spinto(-a)

Nauru [nɑːˈuːruː] N Nauru m

nausea [ˈnɔːsɪə] N (Med) nausea; (fig: disgust) schifo

nauseate [ˈnɔːsɪeɪt] VT nauseare; far schifo a

nauseating [ˈnɔːsɪeɪtɪŋ] ADJ nauseante; (fig) disgustoso(-a)

nauseous [ˈnɔːsɪəs] ADJ nauseabondo(-a); (feeling sick): **to be ~** avere la nausea

nautical [ˈnɔːtɪkl] ADJ nautico(-a)

nautical mile N miglio nautico or marino

naval [ˈneɪvl] ADJ navale

naval officer N ufficiale m di marina

nave [neɪv] N navata centrale

navel [ˈneɪvl] N ombelico

navigable [ˈnævɪgəbl] ADJ navigabile

navigate [ˈnævɪgeɪt] VT percorrere navigando ▸ VI navigare; (Aut) fare da navigatore

navigation [nævɪˈgeɪʃən] N navigazione f

navigator [ˈnævɪgeɪtəʳ] N (Naut, Aviat) ufficiale m di rotta; (explorer) navigatore(-trice); (Aut) copilota mf

navvy [ˈnævɪ] N manovale m

navy [ˈneɪvɪ] N marina; **Department of the N~** (US) Ministero della Marina ▸ ADJ blu scuro inv

navy-blue [ˈneɪvɪˈbluː] ADJ blu scuro inv

Nazareth [ˈnæzərɪθ] N Nazareth f

Nazi [ˈnɑːtsɪ] ADJ, N nazista (mf)

NB ABBR (= nota bene) N.B.; (CANADA) = **New Brunswick**

NBA N ABBR (US: = National Basketball Association) ≈ F.I.P. f (= Federazione Italiana Pallacanestro); = **National Boxing Association**

NBC N ABBR (US: = National Broadcasting Company) compagnia nazionale di radiodiffusione

NC ABBR (Comm etc: = no charge) gratis; (US) = **North Carolina**

NCC N ABBR (US) = **National Council of Churches**

NCO N ABBR (US) = **non-commissioned officer**

ND, N. Dak. ABBR (US) = **North Dakota**

NE ABBR (US) = **Nebraska; New England**

NEA N ABBR (US) = **National Education Association**

neap [niːp] N (also: **neaptide**) marea di quadratura

Neapolitan [nɪəˈpɔlɪtən] ADJ, N napoletano(-a)

near [nɪəʳ] ADJ vicino(-a); (relation) prossimo(-a) ▸ ADV vicino ▸ PREP (also: **near to**) vicino a, presso; (: in time) verso ▸ VT avvicinarsi a; **to come ~** avvicinarsi; **~ here/there** qui/lì vicino; **£25,000 or nearest offer** (BRIT) 25.000 sterline trattabili; **in the ~ future** in un prossimo futuro; **the building is nearing completion** il palazzo è quasi terminato or ultimato

nearby [nɪəˈbaɪ] ADJ vicino(-a) ▸ ADV vicino

Near East N: **the ~** il Medio Oriente

nearer [ˈnɪərəʳ] ADJ più vicino(-a) ▸ ADV più vicino

nearly [ˈnɪəlɪ] ADV quasi; **not ~** non ... affatto; **I ~ lost it** per poco non lo perdevo; **she was ~ crying** era lì lì per piangere

near miss N: **that was a ~** c'è mancato poco

nearness [ˈnɪənɪs] N vicinanza

nearside [ˈnɪəsaɪd] N (right-hand drive) lato sinistro; (left-hand drive) lato destro ▸ ADJ sinistro(-a); destro(-a)

near-sighted [nɪəˈsaɪtɪd] ADJ miope

neat [niːt] ADJ (person, room) ordinato(-a); (work) pulito(-a); (solution, plan) ben indovinato(-a), azzeccato(-a); (spirits) liscio(-a)

neatly [ˈniːtlɪ] ADV con ordine; (skilfully) abilmente

neatness [ˈniːtnɪs] N (tidiness) ordine m; (skilfulness) abilità

nebulous [ˈnɛbjuləs] ADJ nebuloso(-a); (fig) vago(-a)

necessarily [ˈnɛsɪsrɪlɪ] ADV necessariamente; **not ~** non è detto, non necessariamente

n

necessary ['nɛsɪsrɪ] ADJ necessario(-a); **if ~ se** necessario

necessitate [nɪ'sɛsɪteɪt] VT rendere necessario(-a)

necessity [nɪ'sɛsɪtɪ] N necessità *f inv*; **in case of ~** in caso di necessità

neck [nɛk] N collo; (*of garment*) colletto ▸ VI (*col*) pomiciare, sbaciucchiarsi; **~ and ~** testa a testa; **to stick one's ~ out** (*col*) rischiare (forte)

necklace ['nɛklɪs] N collana

neckline ['nɛklaɪn] N scollatura

necktie ['nɛktaɪ] N (*esp US*) cravatta

nectar ['nɛktər] N nettare *m*

nectarine ['nɛktərɪn] N nocepesca

née [neɪ] ADJ: **~ Scott** nata Scott

need [niːd] N bisogno ▸ VT aver bisogno di; **do you ~ anything?** ha bisogno di qualcosa?; **I ~ to do it** lo devo fare, bisogna che io lo faccia; **you don't ~ to go** non deve andare, non c'è bisogno che lei vada; **a signature is needed** occorre *or* ci vuole una firma; **to be in ~ of, have ~ of** aver bisogno di; **£10 will meet my immediate needs** 10 sterline mi basteranno per le necessità più urgenti; **in case of ~** in caso di bisogno *or* necessità; **there's no ~ for ...** non c'è bisogno *or* non occorre che ... + *sub*; **there's no ~ to do ...** non occorre fare ...; **the needs of industry** le esigenze dell'industria

needle ['niːdl] N ago; (*on record player*) puntina ▸ VT (*col*) punzecchiare

needlecord ['niːdlkɔːd] N (*BRIT*) velluto a coste sottili

needless ['niːdlɪs] ADJ inutile; **~ to say, ...** inutile dire che ...

needlessly ['niːdlɪslɪ] ADV inutilmente

needlework ['niːdlwəːk] N cucito

needn't ['niːdnt] = **need not**

needy ['niːdɪ] ADJ bisognoso(-a)

negation [nɪ'geɪʃən] N negazione *f*

negative ['nɛgətɪv] N (*Phot*) negativa, negativo; (*Elec*) polo negativo; (*Ling*) negazione *f* ▸ ADJ negativo(-a); **to answer in the ~** rispondere negativamente *or* di no

negative equity N *situazione in cui l'ammontare del mutuo su un immobile supera il suo valore sul mercato*

neglect [nɪ'glɛkt] VT trascurare ▸ N (*of person, duty*) negligenza; (*of child, house etc*) scarsa cura; **state of ~** stato di abbandono; **to ~ to do sth** trascurare *or* tralasciare di fare qc

neglected [nɪ'glɛktɪd] ADJ trascurato(-a)

neglectful [nɪ'glɛktful] ADJ (*gen*) negligente; **to be ~ of sb/sth** trascurare qn/qc

negligee ['nɛglɪʒeɪ] N négligé *m inv*

negligence ['nɛglɪdʒəns] N negligenza

negligent ['nɛglɪdʒənt] ADJ negligente

negligently ['nɛglɪdʒəntlɪ] ADV con negligenza

negligible ['nɛglɪdʒɪbl] ADJ insignificante, trascurabile

negotiable [nɪ'gəuʃrəbl] ADJ negoziabile; (*cheque*) trasferibile; (*road*) transitabile

negotiate [nɪ'gəuʃɪeɪt] VI negoziare ▸ VT (*Comm*) negoziare; (*obstacle*) superare; (*bend in road*) prendere; **to ~ with sb for sth** trattare con qn per ottenere qc

negotiating table [nɪ'gəuʃɪeɪtɪŋ-] N tavolo delle trattative

negotiation [nɪgəuʃɪ'eɪʃən] N trattativa; (*Pol*) negoziato; **to enter into negotiations with sb** entrare in trattative (*or* intavolare i negoziati) con qn

negotiator [nɪ'gəuʃɪeɪtər] N negoziatore(-trice)

Negress ['niːgrɪs] N (!) negra

Negro ['niːgrəu] (*pl* **Negroes**) ADJ, N (!) negro(-a)

neigh [neɪ] VI nitrire

neighbour, (*US*) **neighbor** ['neɪbər] N vicino(-a)

neighbourhood, (*US*) **neighborhood** ['neɪbəhud] N vicinato

neighbourhood watch N (*BRIT: also:* **neighbourhood watch scheme**) *sistema di vigilanza reciproca in un quartiere*

neighbouring, (*US*) **neighboring** ['neɪbərɪŋ] ADJ vicino(-a)

neighbourly, (*US*) **neighborly** ['neɪbəlɪ] ADJ: **he is a ~ person** è un buon vicino

neither ['naɪðər] ADJ, PRON né l'uno(-a) né l'altro(-a), nessuno(-a) dei due ▸ CONJ neanche, nemmeno, neppure ▸ ADV: **~ good nor bad** né buono né cattivo; **I didn't move and ~ did Claude** io non mi mossi e nemmeno Claude; **... ~ did I refuse ...**, ma non ho nemmeno rifiutato ...

neo... ['niːəu] PREFIX neo...

neolithic [niːəu'lɪθɪk] ADJ neolitico(-a)

neologism [nɪ'ɔlədʒɪzəm] N neologismo

neon ['niːɔn] N neon *m*

neon light N luce *f* al neon

neon sign N insegna al neon

Nepal [nɪ'pɔːl] N Nepal *m*

nephew ['nɛvjuː] N nipote *m*

nepotism ['nɛpətɪzəm] N nepotismo

nerd [nəːd] N (*pej*) sfigato(-a), povero(-a) fesso(-a)

nerve [nəːv] N nervo; (*fig*) coraggio; (*impudence*) faccia tosta; **he gets on my nerves** mi dà ai nervi, mi fa venire i nervi; **a fit of nerves** una crisi di nervi; **to lose one's ~** (*self-confidence*) perdere fiducia in se stesso; **I lost my ~** (*courage*) mi è mancato il coraggio

nerve centre N (*Anat*) centro nervoso; (*fig*) cervello, centro vitale

nerve gas N gas *m* nervino

nerve-racking ['nəːvrækɪŋ] ADJ che spezza i nervi

nervous ['nə:vəs] ADJ nervoso(-a); (*anxious*) agitato(-a), in apprensione

nervous breakdown N esaurimento nervoso

nervously ['nə:vəslɪ] ADV nervosamente

nervousness ['nə:vəsnɪs] N nervosismo

nervous wreck N: **to be a ~** (*col*) essere nevrastenico(-a)

nervy ['nə:vɪ] ADJ agitato(-a), nervoso(-a)

nest [nɛst] N nido; **~ of tables** tavolini *mpl* cicogna *inv* ▸ VI fare il nido, nidificare

nest egg N (*fig*) gruzzolo

nestle ['nɛsl] VI accoccolarsi

nestling ['nɛslɪŋ] N uccellino di nido

net [nɛt] N rete *f*; (*fabric*) tulle *m* ▸ ADJ netto(-a) ▸ VT (*person, profit*) ricavare un utile netto di; (*fish etc*) prendere con la rete; (*deal, sale*) dare un utile netto di; **the N~** (*Internet*) Internet *f*; **~ of tax** netto, al netto di tasse; **he earns £30,000 ~ per year** guadagna 30.000 sterline nette all'anno

netball ['nɛtbɔːl] N *specie di pallacanestro*

net curtains NPL tende *fpl* di tulle

Netherlands ['nɛðələndz] NPL: **the ~** i Paesi Bassi

netiquette ['nɛtɪkɛt] N netiquette *f inv*

net profit N utile *m* netto

netsurfer ['nɛtsə:fə'] N navigatore(-trice) in Internet

nett [nɛt] ADJ = **net**

netting ['nɛtɪŋ] N (*for fence etc*) reticolato; (*fabric*) tulle *m*

nettle ['nɛtl] N ortica

network ['nɛtwə:k] N rete *f*

neuralgia [njuə'rældʒə] N nevralgia

neurological [njuərə'lɔdʒɪkl] ADJ neurologico(-a)

neurosis [njuə'rəusɪs] (*pl* **neuroses** [-si:z]) N nevrosi *f inv*

neurotic [njuə'rɔtɪk] ADJ, N nevrotico(-a)

neuter ['nju:tə'] ADJ neutro(-a) ▸ N neutro ▸ VT (*cat etc*) castrare

neutral ['nju:trəl] ADJ neutro(-a); (*person, nation*) neutrale ▸ N (*Aut*): **in ~** in folle

neutrality [nju:'trælɪtɪ] N neutralità

neutralize ['nju:trəlaɪz] VT neutralizzare

neutron bomb ['nju:trɔn-] N bomba al neutrone

never ['nɛvə'] ADV (*non...*) mai; **~ again** mai più; **I'll ~ go there again** non ci vado più; **~ in my life** mai in vita mia; *see also* **mind**

never-ending [nɛvər'ɛndɪŋ] ADJ interminabile

nevertheless [nɛvəðə'lɛs] ADV tuttavia, ciò nonostante, ciò nondimeno

new [nju:] ADJ nuovo(-a); (*brand new*) nuovo(-a) di zecca; **as good as ~** come nuovo

New Age ADJ, N New Age *f inv*

newbie ['nju:bɪ] N (*Comput, Tech*) utilizzatore(-trice) inesperto(-a); (*to a job or group*) nuovo(-a) arrivato(-a); (*to a hobby or experience*) neofita *mf*

newborn ['nju:bɔ:n] ADJ neonato(-a)

newcomer ['nju:kʌmə'] N nuovo(-a) venuto(-a)

new-fangled ['nju:fæŋgld] ADJ (*pej*) stramoderno(-a)

new-found ['nju:faund] ADJ nuovo(-a)

Newfoundland ['nju:fənlənd] N Terranova

New Guinea N Nuova Guinea

newly ['nju:lɪ] ADV di recente

newly-weds ['nju:lɪwɛdz] NPL sposini *mpl*, sposi *mpl* novelli

new moon N luna nuova

newness ['nju:nɪs] N novità

news [nju:z] N notizie *fpl*; (*Radio*) giornale *m* radio; (*TV*) telegiornale *m*; **a piece of ~** una notizia; **good/bad ~** buone/cattive notizie; **financial ~** (*Press*) pagina economica e finanziaria; (*Radio, TV*) notiziario economico

news agency N agenzia di stampa

newsagent ['nju:zeɪdʒənt] N (*BRIT*) giornalaio

news bulletin N (*Radio, TV*) notiziario

newscaster ['nju:zkɑ:stə'] N (*Radio, TV*) annunciatore(-trice)

newsdealer ['nju:zdi:lə'] N (*US*) = **newsagent**

newsflash ['nju:zflæʃ] N notizia *f* lampo *inv*

newsletter ['nju:zlɛtə'] N bollettino (*di ditta, associazione*)

newspaper ['nju:zpeɪpə'] N giornale *m*; **daily ~** quotidiano; **weekly ~** settimanale *m*

newsprint ['nju:zprɪnt] N carta da giornale

newsreader ['nju:zri:də'] N = **newscaster**

newsreel ['nju:zri:l] N cinegiornale *m*

newsroom ['nju:zrum] N (*Press*) redazione *f*; (*Radio, TV*) studio

news stand N edicola

newsworthy ['nju:zwə:ðɪ] ADJ degno(-a) di menzione (*per radio, TV ecc*); **to be ~** fare notizia

newt [nju:t] N tritone *m*

new town N (*BRIT*) *nuovo centro urbano creato con fondi pubblici*

New Year N Anno Nuovo; **Happy ~!** Buon Anno!; **to wish sb a happy ~** augurare Buon Anno a qn

New Year's Day N il Capodanno

New Year's Eve N la vigilia di Capodanno

New York [-'jɔ:k] N New York *f*, Nuova York *f*; (*also:* **New York State**) stato di New York

New Zealand [-'zi:lənd] N Nuova Zelanda ▸ ADJ neozelandese

New Zealander [-'zi:ləndə'] N neozelandese *mf*

next [nɛkst] ADJ prossimo(-a) ▸ ADV accanto; (*in*

n

time) dopo; **~ to** *prep* accanto a; **~ to nothing** quasi niente; **~ please!** (*avanti*) il prossimo!; **~ time** *adv* la prossima volta; **~ week** la settimana prossima; **the ~ week** la settimana dopo *or* seguente; **the week after ~** fra due settimane; **the ~ day** il giorno dopo, l'indomani; **~ year** l'anno prossimo *or* venturo; **"turn to the ~ page"** "vedi pagina seguente"; **who's ~?** a chi tocca?; **when do we meet ~?** quando ci rincontriamo?

next door ADV, ADJ accanto *inv*

next of kin N parente *mf* prossimo(-a)

NF N ABBR (BRIT *Pol*: = *National Front*) *partito di estrema destra* ► ABBR (CANADA) = **Newfoundland**

NFL N ABBR (US) = **National Football League**

NG ABBR (US) = **National Guard**

NGO N ABBR = **non-governmental organization**

NH ABBR (US) = **New Hampshire**

NHL N ABBR (US: = *National Hockey League*) ≈ F.I.H.P. *f* (= *Federazione Italiana Hockey e Pattinaggio*)

NHS N ABBR (BRIT) = **National Health Service**

NI ABBR = **Northern Ireland**; (BRIT) = **National Insurance**

Niagara Falls [naɪˈægərə-] NPL: **the ~** le cascate del Niagara

nib [nɪb] N (*of pen*) pennino

nibble [ˈnɪbl] VT mordicchiare

Nicaragua [nɪkəˈrægjuə] N Nicaragua *m*

Nicaraguan [nɪkəˈrægjuən] ADJ, N nicaraguense (*mf*)

Nice [niːs] N Nizza

nice [naɪs] ADJ (*holiday, trip*) piacevole; (*flat, picture*) bello(-a); (*person*) simpatico(-a), gentile; (*taste, smell, meal*) buono(-a); (*distinction, point*) sottile

nice-looking [ˈnaɪslukɪŋ] ADJ bello(-a)

nicely [ˈnaɪslɪ] ADV bene; **that will do ~** andrà benissimo

niceties [ˈnaɪsɪtɪz] NPL finezze *fpl*

niche [niːʃ] N (*Archit*) nicchia

nick [nɪk] N taglietto; tacca ► VT intaccare; tagliare; (BRIT *col*: *steal*) rubare; (: *arrest*) beccare; **in the ~ of time** appena in tempo; **in good ~** (BRIT *col*) decente, in buono stato; **to ~ o.s.** farsi un taglietto

nickel [ˈnɪkl] N nichel *m*; (US) *moneta da cinque centesimi di dollaro*

nickname [ˈnɪkneɪm] N soprannome *m* ► VT soprannominare

Nicosia [nɪkəˈsiːə] N Nicosia

nicotine [ˈnɪkətiːn] N nicotina

nicotine patch N cerotto antifumo (*a base di nicotina*)

niece [niːs] N nipote *f*

nifty [ˈnɪftɪ] ADJ (*col*: *car, jacket*) chic *inv*; (: *gadget, tool*) ingegnoso(-a)

Niger [ˈnaɪdʒəʳ] N Niger *m*

Nigeria [naɪˈdʒɪərɪə] N Nigeria

Nigerian [naɪˈdʒɪərɪən] ADJ, N nigeriano(-a)

niggardly [ˈnɪɡədlɪ] ADJ (*person*) tirchio(-a), spilorcio(-a); (*allowance, amount*) misero(-a)

niggle [ˈnɪɡl] VT assillare ► VI fare il(la) pignolo(-a)

niggling [ˈnɪɡlɪŋ] ADJ pignolo(-a); (*detail*) insignificante; (*doubt, pain*) persistente

night [naɪt] N notte *f*; (*evening*) sera; **at ~** la notte; la sera; **by ~** di notte; **in the ~, during the ~** durante la notte; **the ~ before last** l'altro ieri notte; l'altro ieri sera

night-bird [ˈnaɪtbəːd] N uccello notturno; (*fig*) nottambulo(-a)

nightcap [ˈnaɪtkæp] N bicchierino prima di andare a letto

night club N locale *m* notturno

nightdress [ˈnaɪtdres] N camicia da notte

nightfall [ˈnaɪtfɔːl] N crepuscolo

nightie [ˈnaɪtɪ] N camicia da notte

nightingale [ˈnaɪtɪŋɡeɪl] N usignolo

night life [ˈnaɪtlaɪf] N vita notturna

nightly [ˈnaɪtlɪ] ADJ di ogni notte *or* sera; (*by night*) notturno(-a) ► ADV ogni notte *or* sera

nightmare [ˈnaɪtmeəʳ] N incubo

night porter N portiere *m* di notte

night safe N cassa continua

night school N scuola serale

nightshade [ˈnaɪtʃeɪd] N: **deadly ~** (*Bot*) belladonna

nightshift [ˈnaɪtʃɪft] N turno di notte

night-time [ˈnaɪttaɪm] N notte *f*

night watchman N (*irreg*) guardiano notturno

nihilism [ˈnaɪɪlɪzəm] N nichilismo

nil [nɪl] N nulla *m*; (BRIT *Sport*) zero

Nile [naɪl] N: **the ~** il Nilo

nimble [ˈnɪmbl] ADJ agile

nine [naɪn] NUM nove

9-11 N 11 settembre

nineteen [naɪnˈtiːn] NUM diciannove

nineteenth [naɪnˈtiːnθ] NUM diciannovesimo(-a)

ninetieth [ˈnaɪntɪɪθ] NUM novantesimo(-a)

ninety [ˈnaɪntɪ] NUM novanta

ninth [naɪnθ] NUM nono(-a)

nip [nɪp] VT pizzicare; (*bite*) mordere ► VI (BRIT *col*): **to ~ out/down/up** fare un salto fuori/giù/di sopra ► N (*pinch*) pizzico; (*drink*) goccio, bicchierino

nipple [ˈnɪpl] N (*Anat*) capezzolo

nippy [ˈnɪpɪ] ADJ (*weather*) pungente; (BRIT: *car, person*) svelto(-a)

nit [nɪt] N (*of louse*) lendine *m*; (*col*: *idiot*) cretino(-a), scemo(-a)

nit-pick [ˈnɪtpɪk] vɪ (col) cercare il pelo nell'uovo

nitrogen [ˈnaɪtrədʒən] N azoto

nitroglycerin, nitroglycerine [naɪtrəʊ-ˈglɪsəriːn] N nitroglicerina

nitty-gritty [ˈnɪtɪˈɡrɪtɪ] N (col): **to get down to the ~** venire al sodo

nitwit [ˈnɪtwɪt] N (col) scemo(-a)

NJ ABBR (US) = **New Jersey**

NLF N ABBR (= National Liberation Front) ≈ F.L.N. m

NLRB N ABBR (US: = National Labor Relations Board) organismo per la tutela dei lavoratori

NM, N. Mex. ABBR (US) = **New Mexico**

---

no [nəʊ]

ADV (opposite of "yes") no; **are you coming? — no (I'm not)** viene? — no (non vengo); **would you like some more? — no thank you** ne vuole ancora un po'? — no, grazie; **I have no more wine** non ho più vino

▶ ADJ (not any) nessuno(-a); **I have no money/time/books** non ho soldi/tempo/libri; **no student would have done it** nessuno studente lo avrebbe fatto; **there is no reason to believe …** non c'è nessuna ragione per credere …; **"no parking"** "divieto di sosta"; **"no smoking"** "vietato fumare"; **"no entry"** "ingresso vietato"; **"no dogs"** "vietato l'accesso ai cani"

▶ N (pl **noes**) no m inv; **I won't take no for an answer** non accetterò un rifiuto

---

no. ABBR (= number) n.

nobble [ˈnɒbl] vt (BRIT col: bribe: person) comprare, corrompere; (: person to speak to, criminal) bloccare, beccare; (: Racing: horse, dog) drogare

Nobel prize [nəʊˈbɛl-] N premio Nobel

nobility [nəʊˈbɪlɪtɪ] N nobiltà

noble [ˈnəʊbl] ADJ, N nobile m

nobleman [ˈnəʊblmən] N (irreg) nobile m, nobiluomo

nobly [ˈnəʊblɪ] ADV (selflessly) generosamente

nobody [ˈnəʊbədɪ] PRON nessuno

no-claims bonus [ˈnəʊkleɪmz-] N bonus malus m inv

nocturnal [nɒkˈtəːnl] ADJ notturno(-a)

nod [nɒd] vɪ accennare col capo, fare un cenno; (in agreement) annuire con un cenno del capo; (sleep) sonnecchiare ▶ vt: **to ~ one's head** fare di sì col capo ▶ N cenno; **they nodded their agreement** accennarono di sì (col capo)
▶ **nod off** vɪ assopirsi

no-fly zone [nəʊˈflaɪ-] N zona di interdizione aerea

noise [nɔɪz] N rumore m; (din, racket) chiasso

noiseless [ˈnɔɪzlɪs] ADJ silenzioso(-a)

noisily [ˈnɔɪzɪlɪ] ADV rumorosamente

noisy [ˈnɔɪzɪ] ADJ (street, car) rumoroso(-a); (person) chiassoso(-a)

nomad [ˈnəʊmæd] N nomade mf

nomadic [nəʊˈmædɪk] ADJ nomade

no man's land N terra di nessuno

nominal [ˈnɒmɪnl] ADJ nominale; (rent) simbolico(-a)

nominate [ˈnɒmɪneɪt] vt (propose) proporre come candidato; (elect) nominare

nomination [nɒmɪˈneɪʃən] N nomina; candidatura

nominee [nɒmɪˈniː] N persona nominata; candidato(-a)

non... [nɒn] PREFIX non...

non-alcoholic [ˈnɒnælkəˈhɒlɪk] ADJ analcolico(-a)

non-breakable [nɒnˈbreɪkəbl] ADJ infrangibile

nonce word [ˈnɒns-] N parola coniata per l'occasione

nonchalant [ˈnɒnʃələnt] ADJ incurante, indifferente

non-commissioned [nɒnkəˈmɪʃnd] ADJ: **~ officer** sottufficiale m

non-committal [nɒnkəˈmɪtl] ADJ evasivo(-a)

nonconformist [nɒnkənˈfɔːmɪst] N anticonformista mf; (BRIT Rel) dissidente mf ▶ ADJ anticonformista

non-contributory [nɒnkənˈtrɪbjutərɪ] ADJ: **~ pension scheme** or (US) **plan** sistema di pensionamento con i contributi interamente a carico del datore di lavoro

non-cooperation [ˈnɒnkəʊɒpəˈreɪʃən] N non cooperazione f, non collaborazione f

nondescript [ˈnɒndɪskrɪpt] ADJ qualunque inv

none [nʌn] PRON (not one thing) niente; (not one person) nessuno(-a); **~ of you** nessuno(-a) di voi; **I have ~** non ne ho nemmeno uno; **I have ~ left** non ne ho più; **~ at all** proprio niente; (not one) nemmeno uno; **he's ~ the worse for it** non ne ha risentito

nonentity [nɒˈnɛntɪtɪ] N persona insignificante

non-essential [nɒnɪˈsɛnʃl] ADJ non essenziale
▶ N: **non-essentials** superfluo, cose fpl superflue

nonetheless [ˈnʌnðəˈlɛs] ADV nondimeno

non-event [nɒnɪˈvɛnt] N delusione f

non-executive [nɒnɪɡˈzɛkjutɪv] ADJ: **~ director** direttore(-trice) senza potere esecutivo

non-existent [nɒnɪɡˈzɪstənt] ADJ inesistente

non-fiction [nɒnˈfɪkʃən] N qualunque pubblicazione non di narrativa

non-flammable [nɒnˈflæməbl] ADJ ininfiammabile

non-intervention [ˈnɒnɪntəˈvɛnʃən] N non intervento

no-no [ˈnəʊnəʊ] N (col): **it's a ~!** (undesirable) è inaccettabile!; (forbidden) non si può fare!

n

non obst. ABBR (*notwithstanding*: = *non obstante*) nonostante

no-nonsense [nəʊˈnɒnsəns] ADJ che va al sodo

non-payment [nɒnˈpeɪmənt] N mancato pagamento

nonplussed [nɒnˈplʌst] ADJ sconcertato(-a)

non-profit-making [nɒnˈprɒfɪtmeɪkɪŋ] ADJ senza scopo di lucro

nonsense [ˈnɒnsəns] N sciocchezze *fpl*; **~!** che sciocchezze!, che assurdità!; **it is ~ to say that ...** è un'assurdità *or* non ha senso dire che ...

nonsensical [nɒnˈsɛnsɪkl] ADJ assurdo(-a), ridicolo(-a)

non-shrink [nɒnˈʃrɪŋk] ADJ (*BRIT*) irrestringibile

non-skid [nɒnˈskɪd] ADJ antisdrucciolo(-a)

non-smoker [ˈnɒnˈsməʊkəʳ] N non fumatore(-trice)

non-smoking ADJ (*person*) che non fuma; (*area, section*) per non fumatori

non-starter [nɒnˈstɑːtəʳ] N: **it's a ~** è fallito in partenza

non-stick [ˈnɒnˈstɪk] ADJ antiaderente, antiadesivo(-a)

non-stop [ˈnɒnˈstɒp] ADJ continuo(-a); (*train, bus*) direttissimo(-a) ▶ ADV senza sosta

non-taxable [nɒnˈtæksəbl] ADJ: **~ income** reddito non imponibile

non-U [nɒnˈjuː] ADJ ABBR (*BRIT col*) = **non-upper class**

non-volatile [nɒnˈvɒlətaɪl] ADJ: **~ memory** (*Comput*) memoria permanente

non-voting [nɒnˈvəʊtɪŋ] ADJ: **~ shares** azioni *fpl* senza diritto di voto

non-white [ˈnɒnˈwaɪt] ADJ di colore ▶ N (!) persona di colore

noodles [ˈnuːdlz] NPL taglierini *mpl*

nook [nʊk] N: **nooks and crannies** angoli *mpl*

noon [nuːn] N mezzogiorno

no one [ˈnəʊwʌn] PRON = **nobody**

noose [nuːs] N nodo scorsoio, cappio; (*hangman's*) cappio

nor [nɔːʳ] CONJ = **neither** ▶ ADV *see* **neither**

norm [nɔːm] N norma

normal [ˈnɔːml] ADJ normale ▶ N: **to return to ~** tornare alla normalità

normality [nɔːˈmælɪtɪ] N normalità

normally [ˈnɔːməlɪ] ADV normalmente

Normandy [ˈnɔːməndɪ] N Normandia

north [nɔːθ] N nord *m*, settentrione *m* ▶ ADJ nord *inv*, del nord, settentrionale ▶ ADV verso nord

North Africa N Africa del Nord

North African ADJ, N nordafricano(-a)

North America N America del Nord

North American ADJ, N nordamericano(-a)

northbound [ˈnɔːθbaʊnd] ADJ (*traffic*) diretto(-a) a nord; (*carriageway*) nord *inv*

north-east [nɔːθˈiːst] N nord-est *m*

northeastern ADJ nordorientale

northerly [ˈnɔːðəlɪ] ADJ (*wind*) del nord; (*direction*) verso nord

northern [ˈnɔːðən] ADJ del nord, settentrionale

Northern Ireland N Irlanda del Nord

L'Irlanda del Nord (**Northern Ireland**) fa parte del Regno Unito ed è formata da sei contee. È stata creata nel 1921 dopo la divisione dell'isola in Irlanda del Nord e Irlanda del Sud che è uno stato indipendente. La popolazione è composta per la maggioranza da unionisti che desiderano restare uniti al Regno Unito, ma è presente anche una consistente minoranza di repubblicani, per la maggior parte cattolici, a favore di un'Irlanda unificata e indipendente. L'Irlanda del Nord è stata per un lungo periodo teatro di conflitti tra le due comunità. Dalla fine degli anni '60 alla fine degli anni '90, l'epoca di violenza conosciuta come *the Troubles*, ha fatto migliaia di vittime. L'accordo stipulato a Belfast nel 1998 che va sotto il nome di *Good Friday Agreement* (l'accordo del Venerdì Santo) ha segnato una tappa importante sulla via della pace, anche se il settarismo e la segregazione religiosa continuano a creare dei problemi.

North Korea N Corea del Nord

North Pole N: **the ~** il Polo Nord

North Sea N: **the ~** il mare del Nord

North Sea oil N petrolio del mare del Nord

northward [ˈnɔːθwəd], **northwards** [ˈnɔːθwədz] ADV verso nord

north-west [nɔːθˈwɛst] N nord-ovest *m*

northwestern ADJ nordoccidentale

Norway [ˈnɔːweɪ] N Norvegia

Norwegian [nɔːˈwiːdʒən] ADJ norvegese ▶ N norvegese *mf*; (*Ling*) norvegese *m*

nos. ABBR (= *numbers*) nn.

nose [nəʊz] N naso; (*of animal*) muso ▶ VI (*also:* **nose one's way**) avanzare cautamente; **to pay through the ~ (for sth)** (*col*) pagare (qc) un occhio della testa
▶ **nose about, nose around** VI aggirarsi

nosebleed [ˈnəʊzbliːd] N emorragia nasale

nose-dive [ˈnəʊzdaɪv] N picchiata

nose drops NPL gocce *fpl* per il naso

nosey [ˈnəʊzɪ] ADJ curioso(-a)

nostalgia [nɒsˈtældʒɪə] N nostalgia

nostalgic [nɒsˈtældʒɪk] ADJ nostalgico(-a)

nostril [ˈnɒstrɪl] N narice *f*; (*of horse*) frogia

nosy [ˈnəʊzɪ] ADJ = **nosey**

not [nɒt] ADV non; **~ at all** niente affatto; (*after thanks*) prego, s'immagini; **you must ~** *or* **mustn't do this** non deve fare questo; **it's too**

late, isn't it *or* **is it ~?** è troppo tardi, vero?; **he is ~** *or* **isn't here** non è qui, non c'è; **I hope ~** spero di no; **~ that I don't like him** non che (lui) non mi piaccia; **~ yet/now** non ancora/ora

notable ['nəutəbl] ADJ notevole

notably ['nəutəblɪ] ADV notevolmente; (*in particular*) in particolare

notary ['nəutərɪ] N (*also:* **notary public**) notaio

notation [nəu'teɪʃən] N notazione *f*

notch [nɒtʃ] N tacca; (*in saw*) dente *m*
  ▶ **notch up** VT (*score, victory*) marcare, segnare

note [nəut] N nota; (*letter, banknote*) biglietto
  ▶ VT prendere nota di; **to take ~ of** prendere nota di; **to take notes** prendere appunti; **to compare notes** (*fig*) scambiarsi le impressioni; **of ~** eminente, importante; **just a quick ~ to let you know ...** ti scrivo solo due righe per informarti ...

notebook ['nəutbuk] N taccuino; (*for shorthand*) bloc-notes *m inv*

note-case ['nəutkeɪs] N (BRIT) portafoglio

noted ['nəutɪd] ADJ celebre

notepad ['nəutpæd] N bloc-notes *m inv*, blocchetto

notepaper ['nəutpeɪpər] N carta da lettere

noteworthy ['nəutwə:ðɪ] ADJ degno(-a) di nota, importante

nothing ['nʌθɪŋ] N nulla *m*, niente *m*; (*zero*) zero; **he does ~** non fa niente; **~ new** niente di nuovo; **for ~** (*free*) per niente; **~ at all** proprio niente

notice ['nəutɪs] N avviso; (*of leaving*) preavviso; (BRIT: *review: of play etc*) critica, recensione *f* ▶ VT notare, accorgersi di; **to take ~ of** fare attenzione a; **to bring sth to sb's ~** far notare qc a qn; **to give sb ~ of sth** avvisare qn di qc; **to hand in one's ~, give ~** (*employee*) licenziarsi; **without ~** senza preavviso; **at short ~** con un breve preavviso; **until further ~** fino a nuovo avviso; **advance ~** preavviso; **to escape** *or* **avoid ~** passare inosservato; **it has come to my ~ that ...** sono venuto a sapere che ...

noticeable ['nəutɪsəbl] ADJ evidente

notice board N (BRIT) tabellone *m* per affissi

notification [nəutɪfɪ'keɪʃən] N annuncio; notifica; denuncia

notify ['nəutɪfaɪ] VT: **to ~ sth to sb** notificare qc a qn; **to ~ sb of sth** avvisare qn di qc; (*police*) denunciare qc a qn

notion ['nəuʃən] N idea; (*concept*) nozione *f*

notions ['nəuʃənz] NPL (US: *haberdashery*) merceria

notoriety [nəutə'raɪətɪ] N notorietà

notorious [nəu'tɔ:rɪəs] ADJ famigerato(-a)

notoriously [nəu'tɔ:rɪəslɪ] ADV notoriamente

notwithstanding [nɒtwɪθ'stændɪŋ] ADV nondimeno ▶ PREP nonostante, malgrado

nougat ['nu:gɑ:] N torrone *m*

nought [nɔ:t] N zero

noun [naun] N nome *m*, sostantivo

nourish ['nʌrɪʃ] VT nutrire

nourishing ['nʌrɪʃɪŋ] ADJ nutriente

nourishment ['nʌrɪʃmənt] N nutrimento

Nov. ABBR (= *November*) nov.

Nova Scotia ['nəuvə'skəuʃə] N Nuova Scozia

novel ['nɒvl] N romanzo ▶ ADJ nuovo(-a)

novelist ['nɒvəlɪst] N romanziere(-a)

novelty ['nɒvəltɪ] N novità *f inv*

November [nəu'vɛmbər] N novembre *m*; *see also* **July**

novice ['nɒvɪs] N principiante *mf*; (*Rel*) novizio(-a)

NOW [nau] N ABBR (US: = *National Organization for Women*) ≈ U.D.I. *f* (= *Unione Donne Italiane*)

now [nau] ADV ora, adesso ▶ CONJ: **~ (that)** adesso che, ora che; **right ~** subito; **by ~** ormai; **just ~** proprio ora; **that's the fashion just ~** è la moda del momento; **I saw her just ~** l'ho vista proprio adesso; **I'll read it just ~** lo leggo subito; **~ and then, ~ and again** ogni tanto; **from ~ on** da ora in poi; **in 3 days from ~** fra 3 giorni; **between ~ and Monday** da qui a lunedì, entro lunedì; **that's all for ~** per ora basta

nowadays ['nauədeɪz] ADV oggidì

nowhere ['nəuwɛər] ADV in nessun luogo, da nessuna parte; **~ else** in nessun altro posto

no-win situation [nəu'wɪn-] N: **to be in a ~** aver perso in partenza

noxious ['nɒkʃəs] ADJ nocivo(-a)

nozzle ['nɒzl] N (*of hose etc*) boccaglio; (*of fire extinguisher*) lancia

NP N ABBR = **notary public**

nr ABBR (BRIT) = **near**

NS ABBR (CANADA) = **Nova Scotia**

NSC N ABBR (US) = **National Security Council**

NSF N ABBR (US) = **National Science Foundation**

NSPCC N ABBR (BRIT) = **National Society for the Prevention of Cruelty to Children**

NSW ABBR (AUSTRALIA) = **New South Wales**

NT N ABBR (= *New Testament*) N.T. ▶ ABBR (CANADA) = **Northwest Territories**

nth [ɛnθ] ADJ: **for the ~ time** (*col*) per l'ennesima volta

nuance ['nju:ɑ:ns] N sfumatura

nubile ['nju:baɪl] ADJ nubile; (*attractive*) giovane e desiderabile

nuclear ['nju:klɪər] ADJ nucleare; (*warfare*) atomico(-a)

nuclear disarmament N disarmo nucleare

nuclear family N famiglia nucleare

nuclear-free zone ['nju:klɪə'fri:-] N zona denuclearizzata

n

nucleus ['nju:klɪəs] (*pl* **nuclei** ['nju:klɪaɪ]) N nucleo

nude [nju:d] ADJ nudo(-a) ▶ N (*Art*) nudo; **in the ~** tutto(-a) nudo(-a)

nudge [nʌdʒ] VT dare una gomitata a

nudist ['nju:dɪst] N nudista *mf*

nudity ['nju:dɪtɪ] N nudità

nugget ['nʌgɪt] N pepita

nuisance ['nju:sns] N: **it's a ~** è una seccatura; **he's a ~** dà fastidio; **what a ~!** che seccatura!

NUJ N ABBR (*BRIT*: = *National Union of Journalists*) sindacato nazionale dei giornalisti

nuke [nju:k] N (*col*) bomba atomica

null [nʌl] ADJ: **~ and void** nullo(-a)

nullify ['nʌlɪfaɪ] VT annullare

NUM N ABBR (*BRIT*: = *National Union of Mineworkers*) sindacato nazionale dei dipendenti delle miniere

numb [nʌm] ADJ intorpidito(-a) ▶ VT intorpidire; **~ with** (*fear, grief*) paralizzato(-a) da, impietrito(-a) da; **~ with cold** intirizzito(-a) (dal freddo)

number ['nʌmbəʳ] N numero ▶ VT numerare; (*include*) contare; **a ~ of** un certo numero di; **to be numbered among** venire annoverato(-a) tra; **telephone ~** numero di telefono; **wrong ~** (*Tel*) numero sbagliato; **the staff numbers 20** gli impiegati sono in 20; **they were 10 in ~** erano in tutto 10

numbered account ['nʌmbəd-] N (*in bank*) conto numerato

number plate N (*BRIT Aut*) targa

Number Ten N (*BRIT*: = *10 Downing Street*) residenza del Primo Ministro del Regno Unito

numbness ['nʌmnɪs] N intorpidimento; (*due to cold*) intirizzimento

numbskull ['nʌmskʌl] N (*pej*) imbecille *mf*, idiota *mf*

numeral ['nju:mərəl] N numero, cifra

numerate ['nju:mərɪt] ADJ (*BRIT*): **to be ~** saper far di conto

numerical [nju:'mɛrɪkl] ADJ numerico(-a)

numerous ['nju:mərəs] ADJ numeroso(-a)

nun [nʌn] N suora, monaca

nunnery ['nʌnərɪ] N convento

nuptial ['nʌpʃəl] ADJ nuziale

nurse [nə:s] N infermiere(-a); (*also*: **nursemaid**) bambinaia ▶ VT (*patient, cold*) curare; (*baby*: *BRIT*) cullare; (: *US*) allattare, dare il latte a; (*hope*) nutrire

nursery ['nə:sərɪ] N (*room*) camera dei bambini; (*institution*) asilo; (*for plants*) vivaio

nursery rhyme N filastrocca

nursery school N scuola materna

nursery slope N (*BRIT Ski*) pista per principianti

nursing ['nə:sɪŋ] N (*profession*) professione *f* di infermiere (*or* di infermiera); (*care*) cura ▶ ADJ (*mother*) che allatta

nursing home N casa di cura

nurture ['nə:tʃəʳ] VT allevare; nutrire

NUS N ABBR (*BRIT*: = *National Union of Students*) sindacato nazionale degli studenti

NUT N ABBR (*BRIT*: = *National Union of Teachers*) sindacato nazionale degli insegnanti

nut [nʌt] N (*of metal*) dado; (*fruit*) noce *f* (*or* nocciola *or* mandorla *etc*) ▶ ADJ (*chocolate etc*) alla nocciola *etc*; **he's nuts** (*col*) è matto

---

In Italian there is no general word for *nut*.
nuts **frutta secca** (fem sing)

---

nutcase ['nʌtkeɪs] N (*col*) mattarello(-a)

nutcrackers ['nʌtkrækəz] NPL schiaccianoci *m inv*

nutmeg ['nʌtmɛg] N noce *f* moscata

nutrient ['nju:trɪənt] ADJ nutriente ▶ N sostanza nutritiva

nutrition [nju:'trɪʃən] N nutrizione *f*

nutritionist [nju:'trɪʃənɪst] N nutrizionista *mf*

nutritious [nju:'trɪʃəs] ADJ nutriente

nutshell ['nʌtʃɛl] N guscio di noce; **in a ~** in poche parole

nutty ['nʌtɪ] ADJ di noce (*or* nocciola *or* mandorla *etc*); (*BRIT col*) tocco(-a), matto(-a)

nuzzle ['nʌzl] VI: **to ~ up to** strofinare il muso contro

NV ABBR (*US*) = **Nevada**

NVQ N ABBR (*BRIT*) = **National Vocational Qualification**

NWT ABBR (*CANADA*) = **Northwest Territories**

NY ABBR (*US*) = **New York**

NYC ABBR (*US*) = **New York City**

nylon ['naɪlɔn] N nailon *m* ▶ ADJ di nailon ■ **nylons** NPL calze *fpl* di nailon

nymph [nɪmf] N ninfa

nymphomaniac [nɪmfəu'meɪnɪæk] ADJ, N ninfomane (*f*)

NYSE ABBR (*US*) = **New York Stock Exchange**

Oo

O, o [əu] N (*letter*) O, o *f inv or m inv*; (*US Scol*: = *outstanding*) ≈ ottimo; (*number*: *Tel etc*) zero; **O for Oliver**, (*US*) **O for Oboe** ≈ O come Otranto

oaf [əuf] N zoticone *m*

oak [əuk] N quercia ▶ CPD di quercia

OAP N ABBR (*BRIT*) = **old-age pensioner**

oar [ɔːʳ] N remo; **to put** *or* **shove one's ~ in** (*fig*: *col*) intromettersi

oarsman [ˈɔːzmən], **oarswoman** [ˈɔːzwumən] N (*irreg*) rematore(-trice)

OAS N ABBR (= *Organization of American States*) O.S.A. *f* (= *Organizzazione degli Stati Americani*)

oasis [əuˈeɪsɪs] (*pl* **oases** [əuˈeɪsiːz]) N oasi *f inv*

oath [əuθ] N giuramento; (*swear word*) bestemmia; **to take the ~** giurare; **on ~** (*BRIT*) *or* **under ~** sotto giuramento

oatmeal [ˈəutmiːl] N farina d'avena

oats [əuts] NPL avena

obdurate [ˈɔbdjurɪt] ADJ testardo(-a); incallito(-a); ostinato(-a), irremovibile

OBE N ABBR (*BRIT*: = *Order of the British Empire*) titolo

obedience [əˈbiːdɪəns] N ubbidienza; **in ~ to** conformemente a

obedient [əˈbiːdɪənt] ADJ ubbidiente; **to be ~ to sb/sth** ubbidire a qn/qc

obelisk [ˈɔbɪlɪsk] N obelisco

obese [əuˈbiːs] ADJ obeso(-a)

obesity [əuˈbiːsɪtɪ] N obesità

obey [əˈbeɪ] VT ubbidire a; (*instructions, regulations*) osservare ▶ VI ubbidire

obituary [əˈbɪtjuərɪ] N necrologia

object N [ˈɔbdʒɪkt] oggetto; (*purpose*) scopo, intento; (*Ling*) complemento oggetto ▶ VI [əbˈdʒɛkt]: **to ~ to** (*attitude*) disapprovare; (*proposal*) protestare contro, sollevare delle obiezioni contro; **I ~!** mi oppongo!; **he objected that ...** obiettò che ...; **do you ~ to my smoking?** la disturba se fumo?; **what's the ~ of doing that?** a che serve farlo?; **expense is no ~** non si bada a spese

objection [əbˈdʒɛkʃən] N obiezione *f*; (*drawback*) inconveniente *m*; **if you have no ~** se non ha obiezioni; **to make** *or* **raise an ~** sollevare un'obiezione

objectionable [əbˈdʒɛkʃənəbl] ADJ antipatico(-a); (*smell*) sgradevole; (*language*) scostumato(-a)

objective [əbˈdʒɛktɪv] N obiettivo ▶ ADJ obiettivo(-a)

objectivity [ɔbdʒɪkˈtɪvɪtɪ] N obiettività

object lesson N: **~ (in)** dimostrazione *f* (di)

objector [əbˈdʒɛktəʳ] N oppositore(-trice)

obligation [ɔblɪˈgeɪʃən] N obbligo, dovere *m*; (*debt*) obbligo (di riconoscenza); **"without ~"** "senza impegno"; **to be under an ~ to sb/to do sth** essere in dovere verso qn/di fare qc

obligatory [əˈblɪgətərɪ] ADJ obbligatorio(-a)

oblige [əˈblaɪdʒ] VT (*do a favour*) fare una cortesia a; (*force*): **to ~ sb to do** costringere qn a fare; **to be obliged to sb for sth** essere grato a qn per qc; **anything to ~!** (*col*) questo e altro!

obliging [əˈblaɪdʒɪŋ] ADJ servizievole, compiacente

oblique [əˈbliːk] ADJ obliquo(-a); (*allusion*) indiretto(-a) ▶ N (*BRIT Typ*): **~ (stroke)** barra

obliterate [əˈblɪtəreɪt] VT cancellare

oblivion [əˈblɪvɪən] N oblio

oblivious [əˈblɪvɪəs] ADJ: **~ of** incurante di; inconscio(-a) di

oblong [ˈɔblɔŋ] ADJ oblungo(-a) ▶ N rettangolo

obnoxious [əbˈnɔkʃəs] ADJ odioso(-a); (*smell*) disgustoso(-a), ripugnante

oboe [ˈəubəu] N oboe *m*

obscene [əbˈsiːn] ADJ osceno(-a)

obscenity [əbˈsɛnɪtɪ] N oscenità *f inv*

obscure [əbˈskjuəʳ] ADJ oscuro(-a) ▶ VT oscurare; (*hide: sun*) nascondere

obscurity [əbˈskjuərɪtɪ] N oscurità; (*obscure point*) punto oscuro; (*lack of fame*) anonimato

obsequious [əbˈsiːkwɪəs] ADJ ossequioso(-a)

observable [əbˈzəːvəbl] ADJ osservabile; (*appreciable*) notevole

observance [əbˈzəːvns] N osservanza; **religious observances** pratiche *fpl* religiose

observant [əbˈzəːvnt] ADJ attento(-a)

observation [ɔbzəˈveɪʃən] N osservazione f; (by police etc) sorveglianza

observation post N (Mil) osservatorio

observatory [əbˈzəːvətrɪ] N osservatorio

observe [əbˈzəːv] VT osservare; (remark) fare osservare

observer [əbˈzəːvəʳ] N osservatore(-trice)

obsess [əbˈsɛs] VT ossessionare; **to be obsessed by** or **with sb/sth** essere ossessionato da qn/qc

obsession [əbˈsɛʃən] N ossessione f

obsessive [əbˈsɛsɪv] ADJ ossessivo(-a)

obsolescence [ɔbsəˈlɛsns] N obsolescenza; **built-in** or **planned ~** (Comm) obsolescenza programmata

obsolescent [ɔbsəˈlɛsnt] ADJ obsolescente

obsolete [ˈɔbsəliːt] ADJ obsoleto(-a); (word) desueto(-a)

obstacle [ˈɔbstəkl] N ostacolo

obstacle race N corsa agli ostacoli

obstetrician [ɔbstəˈtrɪʃən] N ostetrico(-a)

obstetrics [ɔbˈstɛtrɪks] N ostetrica

obstinacy [ˈɔbstɪnəsɪ] N ostinatezza

obstinate [ˈɔbstɪnɪt] ADJ ostinato(-a)

obstreperous [əbˈstrɛpərəs] ADJ turbolento(-a)

obstruct [əbˈstrʌkt] VT (block) ostruire, ostacolare; (halt) fermare; (hinder) impedire

obstruction [əbˈstrʌkʃən] N ostruzione f; ostacolo

obstructive [əbˈstrʌktɪv] ADJ ostruttivo(-a); che crea impedimenti

obtain [əbˈteɪn] VT ottenere ▶ VI essere in uso; **to ~ sth (for o.s.)** procurarsi qc

obtainable [əbˈteɪnəbl] ADJ ottenibile

obtrusive [əbˈtruːsɪv] ADJ (person) importuno(-a); (smell) invadente; (building etc) imponente e invadente

obtuse [əbˈtjuːs] ADJ ottuso(-a)

obverse [ˈɔbvəːs] N opposto, inverso

obviate [ˈɔbvɪeɪt] VT ovviare a, evitare

obvious [ˈɔbvɪəs] ADJ ovvio(-a), evidente

obviously [ˈɔbvɪəslɪ] ADV ovviamente; **~!** certo!; **~ not!** certo che no!; **he was ~ not drunk** si vedeva che non era ubriaco; **he was not ~ drunk** non si vedeva che era ubriaco

OCAS N ABBR = **Organization of Central American States**

occasion [əˈkeɪʒən] N occasione f; (event) avvenimento ▶ VT cagionare; **on that ~** in quell'occasione, quella volta; **to rise to the ~** mostrarsi all'altezza della situazione

occasional [əˈkeɪʒənl] ADJ occasionale; **I smoke an ~ cigarette** ogni tanto fumo una sigaretta

occasionally [əˈkeɪʒənəlɪ] ADV ogni tanto; **very ~** molto raramente

occasional table N tavolino

occult [ɔˈkʌlt] ADJ occulto(-a) ▶ N: **the ~** l'occulto

occupancy [ˈɔkjupənsɪ] N occupazione f

occupant [ˈɔkjupənt] N occupante mf; (of boat, car etc) persona a bordo

occupation [ɔkjuˈpeɪʃən] N occupazione f; (job) mestiere m, professione f; **unfit for ~** (house) inabitabile

occupational [ɔkjuˈpeɪʃənl] ADJ (disease) professionale; (hazard) del mestiere; **~ accident** infortunio sul lavoro

occupational guidance N (BRIT) orientamento professionale

occupational pension scheme N sistema pensionistico programmato dal datore di lavoro

occupational therapy N ergoterapia

occupier [ˈɔkjupaɪəʳ] N occupante mf

occupy [ˈɔkjupaɪ] VT occupare; **to ~ o.s. by doing** occuparsi a fare; **to be occupied with sth/in doing sth** essere preso da qc/occupato a fare qc

occur [əˈkəːʳ] VI accadere; (difficulty, opportunity) capitare; (phenomenon, error) trovarsi; **to ~ to sb** venire in mente a qn

occurrence [əˈkʌrəns] N caso, fatto; presenza

OCD [əusiːˈdiː] N (= obsessive compulsive disorder) DOC m inv

ocean [ˈəuʃən] N oceano; **oceans of** (col) un sacco di

ocean bed N fondale m oceanico

ocean-going [ˈəuʃəngəuɪŋ] ADJ d'alto mare

Oceania [əuʃɪˈɑːnɪə] N Oceania

ocean liner N transatlantico

ochre, (US) **ocher** [ˈəukəʳ] ADJ ocra inv

o'clock [əˈklɔk] ADV: **it is one o'clock** è l'una; **it is 5 o'clock** sono le 5

> Except for one o'clock, use the plural article and a plural verb when telling the time.
> It's six o'clock. **Sono le sei**.
> at four o'clock **alle quattro**

OCR N ABBR = **optical character reader; optical character recognition**

Oct. ABBR (= October) ott.

octagonal [ɔkˈtægənl] ADJ ottagonale

octane [ˈɔkteɪn] N ottano; **high-octane petrol** or (US) **gas** benzina ad alto numero di ottani

octave [ˈɔktɪv] N ottavo

October [ɔkˈtəubəʳ] N ottobre m; see also **July**

octogenarian [ɔktəudʒɪˈnɛərɪən] N ottuagenario(-a)

octopus [ˈɔktəpəs] N polpo, piovra

odd [ɔd] ADJ (strange) strano(-a), bizzarro(-a); (number) dispari inv; (left over) in più; (not of a set) spaiato(-a); **60-odd** 60 e oltre; **at ~ times** di tanto in tanto; **the ~ one out** l'eccezione f

oddball ['ɔdbɔːl] N (col) eccentrico(-a)

oddity ['ɔdɪtɪ] N bizzarria; (person) originale mf

odd-job man [ɔd'dʒɔb-] N (irreg) tuttofare m inv

odd jobs NPL lavori mpl occasionali

oddly ['ɔdlɪ] ADV stranamente

oddments ['ɔdmənts] NPL (BRIT Comm) rimanenze fpl

odds [ɔdz] NPL (in betting) quota; **the ~ are against his coming** c'è poca probabilità che venga; **it makes no ~** non importa; **at ~** in contesa; **to succeed against all the ~** riuscire contro ogni aspettativa; **~ and ends** avanzi mpl

odds-on [ɔdz'ɔn] ADJ (col) probabile; **~ favourite** (Racing) favorito(-a)

ode [əud] N ode f

odious ['əudɪəs] ADJ odioso(-a), ripugnante

odometer [ɔ'dɔmɪtər] N odometro

odour, (US) **odor** ['əudər] N odore m; (unpleasant) cattivo odore

odourless, (US) **odorless** ['əudəlɪs] ADJ inodoro(-a)

OECD N ABBR (= Organization for Economic Cooperation and Development) O.C.S.E. f (= Organizzazione per la Cooperazione e lo Sviluppo Economico)

oesophagus, (US) **esophagus** [iː'sɔfəgəs] N esofago

oestrogen, (US) **estrogen** ['iːstrəudʒən] N estrogeno

---

of [ɔv, əv]

PREP **1** (gen) di; **a boy of 10** un ragazzo di 10 anni; **a friend of ours** un nostro amico; **that was kind of you** è stato molto gentile da parte sua

2 (expressing quantity, amount, dates etc) di; **a kilo of flour** un chilo di farina; **how much of this do you need?** quanto gliene serve?; **there were four of them** (people) erano in quattro; (objects) ce n'erano quattro; **three of us went** tre di noi sono andati; **the 5th of July** il 5 luglio; **a quarter of 4** (US) le 4 meno un quarto

3 (from, out of) di, in; **made of wood** (fatto) di or in legno

---

Ofcom ['ɔfkɔm] N ABBR (BRIT: = Office of Communications) organismo di regolamentazione delle telecomunicazioni

---

off [ɔf]

ADV **1** (distance, time): **it's a long way off** è lontano; **the game is 3 days off** la partita è tra 3 giorni

2 (departure, removal) via; **to go off to Paris** andarsene a Parigi; **I must be off** devo andare via; **to take off one's coat** togliersi il cappotto; **the button came off** il bottone è venuto via or si è staccato; **10% off** con lo sconto del 10%

---

3 (not at work): **to have a day off** avere un giorno libero; **to be off sick** essere assente per malattia

▶ ADJ (engine) spento(-a); (tap) chiuso(-a); (cancelled) sospeso(-a); (BRIT: food) andato(-a) a male; **to be well/badly off** essere/non essere benestante; **the lid was off** non c'era il coperchio; **I'm afraid the chicken is off** (BRIT: not available) purtroppo il pollo è finito; **on the off chance** nel caso; **to have an off day** non essere in forma; **that's a bit off, isn't it?** (fig: col) non è molto carino, vero?

▶ PREP **1** (motion, removal etc) da

2 (distant from) a poca distanza da; **a street off the square** una strada che parte dalla piazza; **5km off the road** a 5km dalla strada; **off the coast** al largo della costa; **a house off the main road** una casa che non è sulla strada principale

3: **to be off meat** non mangiare più la carne

---

offal ['ɔfl] N (Culin) frattaglie fpl

offbeat ['ɔfbiːt] ADJ eccentrico(-a)

off-centre, (US) **off-center** [ɔf'sentər] ADJ storto(-a), fuori centro

off-colour ['ɔf'kʌlər] ADJ (BRIT: ill) malato(-a), indisposto(-a); **to feel ~** sentirsi poco bene

offence, (US) **offense** [ə'fens] N (Law) contravvenzione f; (: more serious) reato; **to give ~ to** offendere; **to take ~ at** offendersi per; **to commit an ~** commettere un reato

offend [ə'fend] VT (person) offendere ▶ VI: **to ~ against** (law, rule) trasgredire

offender [ə'fendər] N delinquente mf; (against regulations) contravventore(-trice)

offending [ə'fendɪŋ] ADJ (often humorous): **the ~ word/object** la parola incriminata/l'oggetto incriminato

offense [ə'fens] N (US) = **offence**

offensive [ə'fensɪv] ADJ offensivo(-a); (smell etc) sgradevole, ripugnante ▶ N (Mil) offensiva

offer ['ɔfər] N offerta, proposta ▶ VT offrire; **"on ~"** (Comm) "in offerta speciale"; **to make an ~ for sth** fare un'offerta per qc; **to ~ sth to sb, ~ sb sth** offrire qc a qn; **to ~ to do sth** offrirsi di fare qc

offering ['ɔfərɪŋ] N offerta

off-grid [ɔf'grɪd] ADJ non allacciato alla rete elettrica (o dell'acqua, del gas, ecc.)

offhand [ɔf'hænd] ADJ disinvolto(-a), noncurante ▶ ADV all'improvviso; **I can't tell you ~** non posso dirglielo su due piedi

office ['ɔfɪs] N (place) ufficio; (position) carica; **doctor's ~** (US) ambulatorio; **to take ~** entrare in carica

office automation N automazione f d'ufficio, burotica

office bearer N (of club etc) membro dell'amministrazione

office block, office building N complesso di uffici

office boy N garzone *m*

office hours NPL orario d'ufficio; (*US Med*) orario di visite

office manager N capoufficio *mf*

officer [ˈɔfɪsəʳ] N (*Mil etc*) ufficiale *m*; (*of organization*) funzionario; (*also*: **police officer**) agente *m* di polizia

office work N lavoro d'ufficio

office worker N impiegato(-a) d'ufficio

official [əˈfɪʃl] ADJ (*authorized*) ufficiale ▶ N ufficiale *m*; (*civil servant*) impiegato(-a) statale; funzionario

officialdom [əˈfɪʃəldəm] N burocrazia

officially [əˈfɪʃəlɪ] ADV ufficialmente

official receiver N curatore(-trice) fallimentare

officiate [əˈfɪʃɪeɪt] VI (*Rel*) ufficiare; **to ~ as Mayor** esplicare le funzioni di sindaco; **to ~ at a marriage** celebrare un matrimonio

officious [əˈfɪʃəs] ADJ invadente

offing [ˈɔfɪŋ] N: **in the ~** (*fig*) in vista

off-key [ɔfˈkiː] ADJ stonato(-a) ▶ ADV fuori tono

off-licence [ˈɔflaɪsns] N (*BRIT*) spaccio di bevande alcoliche

off-limits [ɔfˈlɪmɪts] ADJ in cui vige il divieto d'accesso

off-line ADJ, ADV (*Comput*) off-line *inv*, non in linea; (: *switched off*) spento(-a)

off-load [ˈɔfləud] VT scaricare

off-peak [ˈɔfˈpiːk] ADJ (*ticket etc*) a tariffa ridotta; (*time*) non di punta

off-putting [ˈɔfputɪŋ] ADJ (*BRIT*) sgradevole

off-season [ˈɔfsiːzn] ADJ, ADV fuori stagione

offset [ˈɔfsɛt] VT (*irreg: like* **set**) (*counteract*) controbilanciare, compensare ▶ N (*also*: **offset printing**) offset *m*

offshoot [ˈɔfʃuːt] N (*fig*) diramazione *f*

offshore [ɔfˈʃɔːʳ] ADJ (*breeze*) di terra; (*island*) vicino alla costa; (*fishing*) costiero(-a); **~ oilfield** giacimento petrolifero in mare aperto

offside [ˈɔfˈsaɪd] ADJ (*Sport*) fuori gioco; (*Aut: with right-hand drive*) destro(-a); (: *with left-hand drive*) sinistro(-a) ▶ N destra; sinistra

offspring [ˈɔfsprɪŋ] N prole *f*, discendenza

offstage [ɔfˈsteɪdʒ] ADV dietro le quinte

off-the-cuff [ɔfðəˈkʌf] ADV improvvisando

off-the-job [ˈɔfðəˈdʒɔb] ADJ: **~ training** addestramento fuori sede

off-the-peg [ˈɔfðəˈpɛg], (*US*) **off-the-rack** [ˈɔfðəˈræk] ADV prêt-à-porter

off-the-record [ˈɔfðəˈrɛkɔːd] ADJ ufficioso(-a) ▶ ADV in via ufficiosa

off-white [ˈɔfwaɪt] ADJ bianco sporco *inv*

Ofgem [ˈɔfdʒɛm] N ABBR (*BRIT*: = *Office of Gas and Electricity Markets*) organo indipendente di controllo per la tutela dei consumatori

often [ˈɔfn] ADV spesso; **how ~ do you go?** quanto spesso ci va?; **as ~ as not** quasi sempre

Ofwat [ˈɔfwɔt] N ABBR (*BRIT*: = *Office of Water Services*) in Inghilterra e Galles, organo indipendente di controllo per la tutela dei consumatori

ogle [ˈəugl] VT occhieggiare

ogre [ˈəugəʳ] N orco

OH ABBR (*US*) = **Ohio**

oh [əu] EXCL oh!

OHMS ABBR (*BRIT*) = **On His Majesty's Service; On Her Majesty's Service**

oil [ɔɪl] N olio; (*petroleum*) petrolio; (*for central heating*) nafta ▶ VT (*machine*) lubrificare

oilcan [ˈɔɪlkæn] N oliatore *m* a mano; (*for storing*) latta da olio

oil change N cambio dell'olio

oilfield [ˈɔɪlfiːld] N giacimento petrolifero

oil filter N (*Aut*) filtro dell'olio

oil-fired [ˈɔɪlfaɪəd] ADJ a nafta

oil gauge N indicatore *m* del livello dell'olio

oil industry N industria del petrolio

oil level N livello dell'olio

oil painting N quadro a olio

oil refinery N raffineria di petrolio

oil rig N derrick *m inv*; (*at sea*) piattaforma per trivellazioni subacquee

oilskins [ˈɔɪlskɪnz] NPL indumenti *mpl* di tela cerata

oil slick N chiazza d'olio

oil tanker N (*ship*) petroliera; (*truck*) autocisterna per petrolio

oil well N pozzo petrolifero

oily [ˈɔɪlɪ] ADJ unto(-a), oleoso(-a); (*food*) grasso(-a)

ointment [ˈɔɪntmənt] N unguento

OK ABBR (*US*) = **Oklahoma**

O.K., okay [əuˈkeɪ] EXCL d'accordo! ▶ VT approvare ▶ N: **to give sth one's ~** approvare qc ▶ ADJ non male *inv*; **is it ~?, are you ~?** tutto bene?; **it's ~ with** *or* **by me** per me va bene; **are you ~ for money?** sei a posto coi soldi?

old [əuld] ADJ vecchio(-a); (*ancient*) antico(-a), vecchio(-a); (*person*) vecchio(-a), anziano(-a); **how ~ are you?** quanti anni ha?; **he's 10 years ~** ha 10 anni; **older brother/sister** fratello/sorella maggiore; **any ~ thing will do** va bene qualsiasi cosa

old age N vecchiaia

old-age pension [ˈəuldeɪdʒ-] N (*BRIT*) pensione *f* di vecchiaia

old-age pensioner [ˈəuldeɪdʒ-] N (*BRIT*) pensionato(-a)

old-fashioned [ˈəuldˈfæʃnd] ADJ antiquato(-a), fuori moda; (*person*) all'antica

old maid N (*pej*) zitella

old people's home N ricovero per anziani
old-style [ˈəuldstaɪl] ADJ (di) vecchio stampo *inv*
old-time [ˈəuldtaɪm] ADJ di una volta
old-timer [əuldˈtaɪməʳ] N veterano(-a)
old wives' tale N vecchia superstizione *f*
O levels NPL (BRIT *formerly*) *diploma di istruzione secondaria conseguito a 16 anni in Inghilterra e Galles, ora sostituito dal GCSE*
oligarch [ˈɔlɪɡɑːk] N oligarca *m(f)*
olive [ˈɔlɪv] N (*fruit*) oliva; (*tree*) olivo ▶ ADJ (*also:* **olive-green**) verde oliva *inv*
olive oil N olio d'oliva
Olympic® [əuˈlɪmpɪk] ADJ olimpico(-a); **the ~ Games**®, **the Olympics**® i giochi olimpici, le Olimpiadi
OM N ABBR (BRIT: = *Order of Merit*) titolo
Oman [əuˈmɑːn] N Oman *m*
OMB N ABBR (US: = *Office of Management and Budget*) *servizio di consulenza al Presidente in materia di bilancio*
omelette, (US) **omelet** [ˈɔmlɪt] N omelette *f inv*; **ham/cheese ~** omelette al prosciutto/al formaggio
omen [ˈəumən] N presagio, augurio
OMG ABBR (*col*) *nel linguaggio degli SMS, esprime sorpresa o entusiasmo*
ominous [ˈɔmɪnəs] ADJ minaccioso(-a); (*event*) di malaugurio
omission [əuˈmɪʃən] N omissione *f*
omit [əuˈmɪt] VT omettere; **to ~ to do sth** tralasciare *or* trascurare di fare qc
omnivorous [ɔmˈnɪvərəs] ADJ onnivoro(-a)
ON ABBR (CANADA) = **Ontario**

---
on [ɔn]

PREP **1** (*indicating position*) su; **on the wall** sulla parete; **on the left** a *or* sulla sinistra; **I haven't any money on me** non ho soldi con me
2 (*indicating means, method, condition etc*): **on foot** a piedi; **on the train/plane** in treno/aereo; **on the telephone** al telefono; **on the radio/television** alla radio/televisione; **to be on drugs** drogarsi; **on holiday** in vacanza; **he's on £36,000 a year** guadagna 36.000 sterline all'anno; **this round's on me** questo giro lo offro io
3 (*referring to time*): **on Friday** venerdì; **on Fridays** il *or* di venerdì; **on June 20th** il 20 giugno; **on Friday, June 20th** venerdì, 20 giugno; **a week on Friday** venerdì a otto; **on his arrival** al suo arrivo; **on seeing this** vedendo ciò
4 (*about, concerning*) su, di; **information on train services** informazioni sui collegamenti ferroviari; **a book on Goldoni/physics** un libro su Goldoni/di *or* sulla fisica
▶ ADV **1** (*referring to dress: covering*): **to have one's coat on** avere indosso il cappotto; **to put**

one's coat on mettersi il cappotto; **what's she got on?** cosa indossa?; **she put her boots/gloves/hat on** si mise gli stivali/i guanti/il cappello; **screw the lid on tightly** avvita bene il coperchio
2 (*further, continuously*): **to walk on, go on** *etc* continuare, proseguire; **to read on** continuare a leggere; **on and off** ogni tanto; **from that day on** da quel giorno in poi; **it was well on in the evening** era sera inoltrata
▶ ADJ **1** (*in operation: machine, TV, light*) acceso(-a); (: *tap*) aperto(-a); (: *brake*) inserito(-a); **is the meeting still on?** (*in progress*) la riunione è ancora in corso?; (*not cancelled*) è confermato l'incontro?; **there's a good film on at the cinema** danno un buon film al cinema; **when is the film on?** quando c'è questo film?; **my father's always on at me to get a job** (*col*) mio padre mi tormenta sempre perché trovi un lavoro
2 (*col*): **that's not on!** (*not acceptable*) non si fa così!; (*not possible*) non se ne parla neanche!

When used with dates and days, *on* is generally not translated.
on June twentieth **il venti giugno**
on my birthday **il giorno del mio compleanno**
on Christmas Day **il giorno di Natale**
on Friday **venerdì**

once [wʌns] ADV una volta ▶ CONJ non appena, quando; **~ he had left/it was done** dopo che se n'era andato/fu fatto; **at ~** subito; (*simultaneously*) a un tempo; **all at ~** (tutto) ad un tratto; **~ a week** una volta alla settimana; **~ more** ancora una volta; **I knew him ~** un tempo *or* in passato lo conoscevo; **~ and for all** una volta per sempre; **~ upon a time there was ...** c'era una volta ...
oncoming [ˈɔnkʌmɪŋ] ADJ (*traffic*) che viene in senso opposto

---
one [wʌn]

NUM uno(-a); **one hundred and fifty** centocinquanta; **one day** un giorno; **it's one (o'clock)** è l'una; **to be one up on sb** essere avvantaggiato(-a) rispetto a qn; **to be at one (with sb)** andare d'accordo (con qn)
▶ ADJ **1** (*sole*) unico(-a); **the one book which** l'unico libro che; **the one man who** l'unico che
2 (*same*) stesso(-a); **they came in the one car** sono venuti nella stessa macchina
▶ PRON **1:** **this one** questo(-a); **that one** quello(-a); **which one do you want?** quale vuole?; **I've already got one/a red one** ne ho già uno/uno rosso; **one by one** uno per uno
2: **one another** l'un l'altro; **to look at one another** guardarsi; **to help one another** aiutarsi l'un l'altro *or* a vicenda

3 (*impersonal*) si; **one never knows** non si sa mai; **to cut one's finger** tagliarsi un dito; **to express one's opinion** esprimere la propria opinione; **one needs to eat** bisogna mangiare

one-armed bandit [ˈwʌnɑːmd-] N slot-machine *f inv*

one-day excursion [ˈwʌndeɪ-] N (*US*) biglietto giornaliero di andata e ritorno

one-hundred share index [ˈwʌnhʌndrəd-] N *indice borsistico del Financial Times*

one-man [ˈwʌnˈmæn] ADJ (*business*) diretto(-a) *etc* da un solo uomo

one-man band N *suonatore ambulante con vari strumenti*

one-off [wʌnˈɔf] (*BRIT col*) N fatto eccezionale ▶ ADJ eccezionale

one-parent family [ˈwʌnpɛərənt-] N famiglia monogenitore

one-piece [ˈwʌnpiːs] ADJ (*bathing suit*) intero(-a)

onerous [ˈɔnərəs] ADJ (*task, duty*) gravoso(-a); (*responsibility*) pesante

oneself [wʌnˈsɛlf] PRON (*reflexive*) si; (*after prep*) sé, se stesso(-a); **to do sth (by)** ~ fare qc da sé; **to hurt** ~ farsi male; **to keep sth for** ~ tenere qc per sé; **to talk to** ~ parlare da solo

one-shot [wʌnˈʃɔt] N, ADJ (*US*) = **one-off**

one-sided [wʌnˈsaɪdɪd] ADJ (*decision, view, argument*) unilaterale; (*judgement, account*) parziale; (*game, contest*) impari *inv*

onesie [ˈwʌnzɪ] N onesie *m inv* (*tuta intera*)

one-time [ˈwʌntaɪm] ADJ ex *inv*

one-to-one [ˈwʌntəwʌn] ADJ (*relationship*) univoco(-a)

one-upmanship [wʌnˈʌpmənʃɪp] N: **the art of** ~ l'arte *f* di primeggiare

one-way [ˈwʌnweɪ] ADJ (*street, traffic*) a senso unico

ongoing [ˈɔngəʊɪŋ] ADJ in corso; in attuazione

onion [ˈʌnjən] N cipolla

online, on-line [ˈɔnlaɪn] (*Comput*) ADJ on-line *inv*, online *inv* ▶ ADV: **to go** ~ andare online; **to put the printer** ~ collegare la stampante

online banking N home *or* online banking *m inv*

online purchase N acquisto *m* online

online shopping N acquisti *mpl* online, shopping *m inv* online

onlooker [ˈɔnlʊkər] N spettatore(-trice)

only [ˈəʊnlɪ] ADV solo, soltanto ▶ ADJ solo(-a), unico(-a) ▶ CONJ solo che, ma; **an** ~ **child** un figlio unico; **not** ~ non solo; **I** ~ **took one** ne ho preso soltanto uno, non ne ho preso che uno; **I saw her** ~ **yesterday** l'ho vista appena ieri; **I'd be** ~ **too pleased to help** sarei proprio felice di essere d'aiuto; **I would come,** ~ **I'm very busy** verrei volentieri, solo che sono molto occupato

ono ABBR = **or nearest offer**; *see* **near**

on-screen [ɔnˈskriːn] ADJ sullo schermo *inv*

onset [ˈɔnsɛt] N inizio; (*of winter*) arrivo

onshore [ˈɔnʃɔːr] ADJ (*wind*) di mare

onslaught [ˈɔnslɔːt] N attacco, assalto

on-the-job [ˈɔnðəˈdʒɔb] ADJ: ~ **training** addestramento in sede

onto [ˈɔntu] PREP su, sopra

onus [ˈəʊnəs] N onere *m*, peso; **the** ~ **is upon him to prove it** sta a lui dimostrarlo

onward [ˈɔnwəd], **onwards** [ˈɔnwədz] ADV (*move*) in avanti; **from this time** ~(**s**) d'ora in poi

onyx [ˈɔnɪks] N onice *f*

oops [ups] EXCL ops! (*esprime rincrescimento per un piccolo contrattempo*); **oops-a-daisy!** oplà!

ooze [uːz] VI stillare

opacity [əʊˈpæsɪtɪ] N opacità

opal [ˈəʊpl] N opale *m or f*

opaque [əʊˈpeɪk] ADJ opaco(-a)

OPEC [ˈəʊpɛk] N ABBR (= *Organization of Petroleum-Exporting Countries*) O.P.E.C. *f*

open [ˈəʊpn] ADJ aperto(-a); (*road*) libero(-a); (*meeting*) pubblico(-a); (*admiration*) evidente, franco(-a); (*question*) insoluto(-a); (*enemy*) dichiarato(-a) ▶ VT aprire ▶ VI (*eyes, door, debate*) aprirsi; (*flower*) sbocciare; (*shop, bank, museum*) aprire; (*book etc: commence*) cominciare; **in the** ~ **(air)** all'aperto; **the** ~ **sea** il mare aperto, l'alto mare; ~ **ground** (*among trees*) radura; (*waste ground*) terreno non edificato; **to have an** ~ **mind (on sth)** non avere ancora deciso (su qc); **is it** ~ **to the public?** è aperto al pubblico?; **what time do you** ~? a che ora aprite?
▶ **open on to** VT FUS (*room, door*) dare su
▶ **open out** VT aprire ▶ VI aprirsi
▶ **open up** VT aprire; (*blocked road*) sgombrare
▶ VI aprirsi; (*shop, business*) aprire

open-air [əʊpnˈɛər] ADJ all'aperto

open-and-shut [ˈəʊpnənˈʃʌt] ADJ: ~ **case** caso indubbio

open day N (*BRIT*) giornata di apertura al pubblico

open-ended [əʊpnˈɛndɪd] ADJ (*fig*) aperto(-a), senza limiti

opener [ˈəʊpnər] N (*also:* **can opener, tin opener**) apriscatole *m inv*

open-heart [əʊpnˈhɑːt] ADJ: ~ **surgery** chirurgia a cuore aperto

opening [ˈəʊpnɪŋ] N apertura; (*opportunity*) occasione *f*, opportunità *f inv*; sbocco; (*job*) posto vacante ▶ ADJ (*speech*) di apertura

opening hours NPL orario d'apertura

opening night N (*Theat*) prima

open learning N *sistema educativo secondo il quale lo studente ha maggior controllo e gestione delle modalità di apprendimento*

openly ['əupnlɪ] ADV apertamente

open-minded [əupn'maɪndɪd] ADJ che ha la mente aperta

open-necked ['əupnnɛkt] ADJ col collo slacciato

openness ['əupnnɪs] N (*frankness*) franchezza, sincerità

open-plan ['əupn'plæn] ADJ senza pareti divisorie

open prison N *istituto di pena dove viene data maggiore libertà ai detenuti*

open sandwich N canapè *m inv*

open shop N *fabbrica o ditta dove sono accolti anche operai non iscritti ai sindacati*

Open University N (*BRIT*) *vedi nota*

La **Open University** (*OU*), fondata in Gran Bretagna nel 1969, organizza corsi universitari per corrispondenza o via Internet, disponibili anche in DVD, e corsi estivi.

opera ['ɔpərə] N opera

opera glasses NPL binocolo da teatro

opera house N opera

opera singer N cantante *mf* d'opera *or* lirico(-a)

operate ['ɔpəreɪt] VT (*machine*) azionare, far funzionare; (*system*) usare ▶ VI funzionare; (*drug, person*) agire; **to ~ on sb (for)** (*Med*) operare qn (di)

operatic [ɔpə'rætɪk] ADJ dell'opera, lirico(-a)

operating ['ɔpəreɪtɪŋ] ADJ (*Comm: costs etc*) di gestione; (*Med*) operatorio(-a)

operating room N (*US*) = **operating theatre**

operating system N (*Comput*) sistema *m* operativo

operating theatre N (*Med*) sala operatoria

operation [ɔpə'reɪʃən] N operazione *f*; **to be in ~** (*machine*) essere in azione *or* funzionamento; (*system*) essere in vigore; **to have an ~ (for)** (*Med*) essere operato(-a) (di)

operational [ɔpə'reɪʃənl] ADJ operativo(-a); (*Comm*) di gestione, d'esercizio; (*ready for use or action*) in attività, in funzione; **when the service is fully ~** quando il servizio sarà completamente in funzione

operative ['ɔpərətɪv] ADJ (*measure*) operativo(-a) ▶ N (*in factory*) operaio(-a); **the ~ word** la parola chiave

operator ['ɔpəreɪtə^r] N (*of machine*) operatore(-trice); (*Tel*) centralinista *mf*

operetta [ɔpə'rɛtə] N operetta

ophthalmologist [ɔfθæl'mɔlədʒɪst] N oftalmologo(-a)

opinion [ə'pɪnjən] N opinione *f*, parere *m*; **in my ~** secondo me, a mio avviso; **to seek a second ~** (*Med etc*) consultarsi con un altro medico *etc*

opinionated [ə'pɪnjəneɪtɪd] ADJ dogmatico(-a)

opinion poll N sondaggio di opinioni

opium ['əupɪəm] N oppio

opponent [ə'pəunənt] N avversario(-a)

opportune ['ɔpətjuːn] ADJ opportuno(-a)

opportunist [ɔpə'tjuːnɪst] N opportunista *mf*

opportunity [ɔpə'tjuːnɪtɪ] N opportunità *f inv*, occasione *f*; **to take the ~ to do** *or* **of doing** cogliere l'occasione per fare

oppose [ə'pəuz] VT opporsi a; **opposed to** contrario(-a) a; **as opposed to** in contrasto con

opposing [ə'pəuzɪŋ] ADJ opposto(-a); (*team*) avversario(-a)

opposite ['ɔpəzɪt] ADJ opposto(-a); (*house etc*) di fronte ▶ ADV di fronte, dirimpetto ▶ PREP di fronte a ▶ N opposto, contrario; (*of word*) contrario; **"see ~ page"** "vedere pagina a fronte"

opposite number N controparte *f*, corrispondente *mf*

opposite sex N: **the ~** l'altro sesso

opposition [ɔpə'zɪʃən] N opposizione *f*

oppress [ə'prɛs] VT opprimere

oppression [ə'prɛʃən] N oppressione *f*

oppressive [ə'prɛsɪv] ADJ oppressivo(-a)

opprobrium [ə'prəubrɪəm] N (*formal*) obbrobrio

opt [ɔpt] VI: **to ~ for** optare per; **to ~ to do** scegliere di fare
▶ **opt out** VI: **to ~ out of** ritirarsi da; (*of NHS*) scegliere di non far più parte di; (*of agreement, arrangement*) scegliere di non partecipare a

optical ['ɔptɪkl] ADJ ottico(-a)

optical character reader N lettore *m* ottico

optical character recognition N lettura ottica di caratteri

optical fibre N fibra ottica

optician [ɔp'tɪʃən] N ottico

optics ['ɔptɪks] N ottica

optimism ['ɔptɪmɪzəm] N ottimismo

optimist ['ɔptɪmɪst] N ottimista *mf*

optimistic [ɔptɪ'mɪstɪk] ADJ ottimistico(-a)

optimum ['ɔptɪməm] ADJ ottimale

option ['ɔpʃən] N scelta; (*Scol*) materia facoltativa; (*Comm*) opzione *f*; **to keep one's options open** (*fig*) non impegnarsi; **I have no ~** non ho scelta

optional ['ɔpʃənl] ADJ facoltativo(-a); (*Comm*) a scelta; **~ extra** optional *m inv*

opulence ['ɔpjuləns] N opulenza

opulent ['ɔpjulənt] ADJ opulento(-a)

OR ABBR (*US*) = **Oregon**

or [ɔː^r] CONJ o, oppure; (*with negative*): **he hasn't seen or heard anything** non ha visto né sentito niente; **or else** se no, altrimenti; oppure

oracle ['ɔrəkl] N oracolo

oral ['ɔːrəl] ADJ orale ▶ N esame *m* orale

orange ['ɒrɪndʒ] N (fruit) arancia ▶ADJ arancione

orangeade [ɒrɪndʒ'eɪd] N aranciata

orange juice N succo d'arancia

orange squash N succo d'arancia (da diluire con l'acqua)

oration [ɔː'reɪʃən] N orazione f

orator ['ɒrətə^r] N oratore(-trice)

oratorio [ɒrə'tɔːrɪəu] N oratorio

orb [ɔːb] N orbe m

orbit ['ɔːbɪt] N orbita ▶VT orbitare intorno a; **to be in/go into ~ (round)** essere/entrare in orbita (attorno a)

orbital ['ɔːbɪtl] N (also: **orbital motorway**) raccordo anulare

orchard ['ɔːtʃəd] N frutteto; **apple ~** meleto

orchestra ['ɔːkɪstrə] N orchestra; (US: seating) platea

orchestral [ɔː'kɛstrəl] ADJ orchestrale; (concert) sinfonico(-a)

orchestrate ['ɔːkɪstreɪt] VT (Mus, fig) orchestrare

orchid ['ɔːkɪd] N orchidea

ordain [ɔː'deɪn] VT (Rel) ordinare; (decide) decretare

ordeal [ɔː'diːl] N prova, travaglio

order ['ɔːdə^r] N ordine m; (Comm) ordinazione f ▶VT ordinare; **to ~ sb to do** ordinare a qn di fare; **in ~** in ordine; (document) in regola; **in ~ of size** in ordine di grandezza; **in ~ to do** per fare; **in ~ that** affinché+sub; **a machine in working ~** una macchina che funziona bene; **out of ~** non in ordine; **to be out of ~** (machine, toilets) essere guasto(-a); (telephone) essere fuori servizio; **to place an ~ for sth with sb** ordinare qc a qn; **to the ~ of** (Banking) all'ordine di; **to be under orders to do sth** avere l'ordine di fare qc; **a point of ~** una questione di procedura; **to be on ~** essere stato ordinato; **made to ~** fatto su commissione; **the lower orders** (pej) i ceti inferiori

order book N copiacommissioni m inv

order form N modulo d'ordinazione

orderly ['ɔːdəlɪ] N (Mil) attendente m; (Med) inserviente m ▶ADJ (room) in ordine; (mind) metodico(-a); (person) ordinato(-a), metodico(-a)

order number N numero di ordinazione

ordinal ['ɔːdɪnl] ADJ (number) ordinale

ordinary ['ɔːdnrɪ] ADJ normale, comune; (pej) mediocre ▶N: **out of the ~** diverso dal solito, fuori dell'ordinario

ordinary degree N laurea

ordinary seaman N (irreg) (BRIT) marinaio semplice

ordinary shares NPL azioni fpl ordinarie

ordination [ɔːdɪ'neɪʃən] N ordinazione f

ordnance ['ɔːdnəns] N (Mil: unit) (reparto di) sussistenza

Ordnance Survey map N (BRIT) ≈ carta topografica dell'IGM

ore [ɔː^r] N minerale m grezzo

oregano [ɒrɪ'gɑːnəu] N origano

organ ['ɔːgən] N organo

organic [ɔː'gænɪk] ADJ organico(-a); (food, produce) biologico(-a)

organism ['ɔːgənɪzəm] N organismo

organist ['ɔːgənɪst] N organista mf

organization [ɔːgənaɪ'zeɪʃən] N organizzazione f

organization chart N organigramma m

organize ['ɔːgənaɪz] VT organizzare; **to get organized** organizzarsi

organized ['ɔːgənaɪzd] ADJ organizzato(-a)

organized crime N criminalità organizzata

organized labour N manodopera organizzata

organizer ['ɔːgənaɪzə^r] N organizzatore(-trice)

orgasm ['ɔːgæzəm] N orgasmo

orgy ['ɔːdʒɪ] N orgia

Orient ['ɔːrɪənt] N: **the ~** l'Oriente m

oriental [ɔːrɪ'ɛntl] ADJ, N orientale (mf)

orientate ['ɔːrɪənteɪt] VT orientare

orientation [ɔːrɪɛn'teɪʃən] N orientamento

orifice ['ɒrɪfɪs] N orifizio

origin ['ɒrɪdʒɪn] N origine f; **country of ~** paese m d'origine

original [ə'rɪdʒɪnl] ADJ originale; (earliest) originario(-a) ▶N originale m

originality [ərɪdʒɪ'nælɪtɪ] N originalità

originally [ə'rɪdʒɪnəlɪ] ADV (at first) all'inizio

originate [ə'rɪdʒɪneɪt] VI: **to ~ from** venire da, essere originario(-a) di; (suggestion) provenire da; **to ~ in** nascere in; (custom) avere origine in

originator [ə'rɪdʒɪneɪtə^r] N iniziatore(-trice)

Orkneys ['ɔːknɪz] NPL: **the ~** (also: **the Orkney Islands**) le (isole) Orcadi

ornament ['ɔːnəmənt] N ornamento; (trinket) ninnolo

ornamental [ɔːnə'mɛntl] ADJ ornamentale

ornamentation [ɔːnəmɛn'teɪʃən] N decorazione f, ornamento

ornate [ɔː'neɪt] ADJ molto ornato(-a)

ornithologist [ɔːnɪ'θɒlədʒɪst] N ornitologo(-a)

ornithology [ɔːnɪ'θɒlədʒɪ] N ornitologia

orphan ['ɔːfn] N orfano(-a) ▶VT: **to be orphaned** diventare orfano

orphanage ['ɔːfənɪdʒ] N orfanotrofio

orthodox ['ɔːθədɒks] ADJ ortodosso(-a)

orthopaedic, (US) **orthopedic** [ɔːθə'piːdɪk] ADJ ortopedico(-a)

OS ABBR (BRIT: = Ordnance Survey) ≈ IGM m = **Istituto Geografico Militare**; (Naut) = **ordinary seaman**; (Dress) = **outsize**

O.S. ABBR = **out of stock**

Oscar [ˈɔskəʳ] N Oscar *m inv*

oscillate [ˈɔsɪleɪt] VI oscillare

OSHA N ABBR (*US*: = *Occupational Safety and Health Administration*) amministrazione per la sicurezza e la salute sul lavoro

Oslo [ˈɔzləu] N Oslo *f*

ostensible [ɔsˈtɛnsɪbl] ADJ preteso(-a); apparente

ostensibly [ɔsˈtɛnsɪblɪ] ADV all'apparenza

ostentation [ɔstɛnˈteɪʃən] N ostentazione *f*

ostentatious [ɔstɛnˈteɪʃəs] ADJ pretenzioso(-a); ostentato(-a)

osteopath [ˈɔstɪəpæθ] N specialista *mf* di osteopatia

ostracize [ˈɔstrəsaɪz] VT dare l'ostracismo a

ostrich [ˈɔstrɪtʃ] N struzzo

OT ABBR (= *Old Testament*) V.T.

OTB N ABBR (*US*: = *off-track betting*) puntate effettuate fuori dagli ippodromi

OTE ABBR (= *on-target earnings*) stipendio compreso le commissioni

other [ˈʌðəʳ] ADJ altro(-a) ▶ PRON: **the ~** l'altro(-a); **the others** gli altri; **the ~ day** l'altro giorno; **some ~ people have still to arrive** (alcuni) altri devono ancora arrivare; **some actor or ~** un certo attore; **somebody or ~** qualcuno; **some thing or ~** qualcosa; **somewhere or ~** da qualche parte; **the ~ day** l'altro giorno; **the others** gli altri; **some ~ people have still to arrive** (alcuni) altri devono ancora arrivare; **some actor or ~** un certo attore; **somebody or ~** qualcuno; **some thing or ~** qualcos'altro che; a parte; **the car was none ~ than Roberta's** la macchina era proprio di Roberta

otherwise [ˈʌðəwaɪz] ADV, CONJ altrimenti; **an ~ good piece of work** un lavoro comunque buono

OTT ABBR (*col*) = **over the top**; *see* **top**

otter [ˈɔtəʳ] N lontra

OU N ABBR (*BRIT*) = **Open University**

ouch [autʃ] EXCL ohi!, ahi!

ought [ɔːt] AUX VB: **I ~ to do it** dovrei farlo; **this ~ to have been corrected** questo avrebbe dovuto essere corretto; **he ~ to win** dovrebbe vincere; **you ~ to go and see it** dovreste andare a vederlo, fareste bene ad andarlo a vedere

ounce [auns] N oncia (= *28.35 g; 16 in a pound*)

our [auəʳ] ADJ il nostro(-a); (*pl*) i nostri(-e)

ours [auəz] PRON il nostro(-a); (*pl*) i nostri(-e); *see also* **mine¹**

ourselves [auəˈsɛlvz] PL PRON (*reflexive*) ci; (*after preposition*) noi; (*emphatic*) noi stessi(-e); **we did it (all) by ~** l'abbiamo fatto (tutto) da soli; *see also* **oneself**

oust [aust] VT cacciare, espellere

---

out [aut]

ADV (*gen*) fuori; **out here/there** qui/là fuori; **to speak out loud** parlare forte; **to have a night out** uscire una sera; **to be out and about** *or* (*US*) **around again** essere di nuovo in

---

piedi; **the boat was 10 km out** la barca era a 10 km dalla costa; **the journey out** l'andata; **3 days out from Plymouth** a 3 giorni da Plymouth

▶ ADJ: **to be out** (*gen*) essere fuori; (*unconscious*) aver perso i sensi; (*style, singer*) essere fuori moda; **before the week was out** prima che la settimana fosse finita; **to be out to do sth** avere intenzione di fare qc; **he's out for all he can get** sta cercando di trarne il massimo profitto; **to be out in one's calculations** aver sbagliato i calcoli

▶ PREP: **out of** (*outside, beyond*) fuori di; (*because of*) per; (*origin*) da; (*without*) senza; **out of 10** (*from among*) su 10; **to go out of the house** uscire di casa; **to look out of the window** guardare fuori dalla finestra; **out of pity** per pietà; **out of boredom** per noia; **made out of wood** (fatto) di *or* in legno; **to drink out of a cup** bere da una tazza; **out of petrol** senza benzina; **it's out of stock** (*Comm*) è esaurito

outage [ˈautɪdʒ] N (*esp US: power failure*) interruzione *f or* mancanza di corrente elettrica

out-and-out [ˈautəndaut] ADJ vero(-a) e proprio(-a)

outback [ˈautbæk] N zona isolata; (*in Australia*) interno, entroterra *m*

outbid [autˈbɪd] (*pt, pp ~*) VT fare un'offerta più alta di

outboard [ˈautbɔːd] N: **~ (motor)** (motore *m*) fuoribordo

outbound [ˈautbaund] ADJ: **~ (for or from)** in partenza (per *or* da)

outbox [ˈautbɔks] N (*Comput*) posta in uscita; (*US: out-tray*) vaschetta della corrispondenza in uscita

outbreak [ˈautbreɪk] N scoppio; epidemia

outbuilding [ˈautbɪldɪŋ] N dipendenza

outburst [ˈautbəːst] N scoppio

outcast [ˈautkɑːst] N esule *mf*; (*socially*) paria *m inv*

outclass [autˈklɑːs] VT surclassare

outcome [ˈautkʌm] N esito, risultato

outcrop [ˈautkrɔp] N affioramento

outcry [ˈautkraɪ] N protesta, clamore *m*

outdated [autˈdeɪtɪd] ADJ (*custom, clothes*) fuori moda; (*idea*) sorpassato(-a)

outdistance [autˈdɪstəns] VT distanziare

outdo [autˈduː] VT (*irreg: like* **do**) sorpassare

outdoor [autˈdɔːʳ] ADJ all'aperto

outdoors [autˈdɔːz] ADV fuori; all'aria aperta

outer [ˈautəʳ] ADJ esteriore; **~ suburbs** estrema periferia

outer space N spazio cosmico

outfit [ˈautfɪt] N equipaggiamento; (*clothes*) completo; (: *for sport*) tenuta; (*col: organization*) organizzazione *f*

693

outfitter [ˈautfɪtə^r] N (BRIT): **"(gent's) outfitters"** "confezioni da uomo"

outgoing [ˈautɡəuɪŋ] ADJ (*president, tenant*) uscente; (*means of transport*) in partenza; (*character*) socievole

outgoings [ˈautɡəuɪŋz] NPL (BRIT: *expenses*) spese fpl, uscite fpl

outgrow [autˈɡrəu] VT (*irreg: like* **grow**) (*clothes*) diventare troppo grande per

outhouse [ˈauthaus] N costruzione f annessa

outing [ˈautɪŋ] N gita; escursione f

outlandish [autˈlændɪʃ] ADJ strano(-a)

outlast [autˈlɑːst] VT sopravvivere a

outlaw [ˈautlɔː] N fuorilegge mf ▶ VT (*person*) mettere fuori della legge; (*practice*) bandire

outlay [ˈautleɪ] N spese fpl; (*investment*) sborsa, spesa

outlet [ˈautlɛt] N (*for liquid etc*) sbocco, scarico; (*for emotion*) sfogo; (*for goods*) sbocco, mercato; (*also*: **retail outlet**) punto di vendita; (*US Elec*) presa di corrente

outline [ˈautlaɪn] N contorno, profilo; (*summary*) abbozzo, grandi linee fpl ▶ VT (*fig*) descrivere a grandi linee

outlive [autˈlɪv] VT sopravvivere a

outlook [ˈautluk] N prospettiva, vista

outlying [ˈautlaɪɪŋ] ADJ periferico(-a)

outmanoeuvre, (*US*) **outmaneuver** [autmənuːvə^r] VT (*rival etc*) superare in strategia

outmoded [autˈməudɪd] ADJ passato(-a) di moda; antiquato(-a)

outnumber [autˈnʌmbə^r] VT superare in numero

out-of-court [autəvˈkɔːt] ADJ extragiudiziale ▶ ADV (*settle*) senza ricorrere al tribunale

out-of-date [autəvˈdeɪt] ADJ (*passport, ticket*) scaduto(-a); (*theory, idea*) sorpassato(-a), superato(-a); (*custom*) antiquato(-a); (*clothes*) fuori moda inv

out-of-doors [autəvˈdɔːz] ADV all'aperto

out-of-the-way [ˈautəvðəˈweɪ] ADJ (*remote*) fuori mano; (*unusual*) originale, insolito(-a)

out-of-town [autəvˈtaun] ADJ (*shopping centre etc*) fuori città inv

outpatient [ˈautpeɪʃənt] N paziente mf esterno(-a)

outpost [ˈautpəust] N avamposto

outpouring [ˈautpɔːrɪŋ] N (*fig*) torrente m

output [ˈautput] N produzione f; (*Comput*) output m inv ▶ VT emettere

outrage [ˈautreɪdʒ] N oltraggio; scandalo ▶ VT oltraggiare

outrageous [autˈreɪdʒəs] ADJ oltraggioso(-a); scandaloso(-a)

outrider [ˈautraɪdə^r] N (*on motorcycle*) battistrada m inv

outright ADV [autˈraɪt] completamente; schiettamente; apertamente; sul colpo ▶ ADJ [ˈautraɪt] completo(-a); schietto(-a) e netto(-a)

outrun [autˈrʌn] VT (*irreg: like* **run**) superare (nella corsa)

outset [ˈautsɛt] N inizio

outshine [autˈʃaɪn] VT (*irreg: like* **shine**) (*fig*) eclissare

outside [autˈsaɪd] N esterno, esteriore m ▶ ADJ esterno(-a), esteriore; (*remote, unlikely*): **an ~ chance** una vaga possibilità ▶ ADV fuori, all'esterno ▶ PREP fuori di, all'esterno di; **at the ~** (*fig*) al massimo; **~ left/right** n (*Football*) ala sinistra/destra

outside broadcast N (*Radio, TV*) trasmissione f in esterno

outside lane N (*Aut*) corsia di sorpasso

outside line N (*Tel*) linea esterna

outsider [autˈsaɪdə^r] N (*in race etc*) outsider m inv; (*stranger*) straniero(-a)

outsize [ˈautsaɪz] ADJ enorme; (*clothes*) per taglie forti

outskirts [ˈautskəːts] NPL sobborghi mpl

outsmart [autˈsmɑːt] VT superare in astuzia

outsourcing [ˈautsɔːsɪŋ] N outsourcing m inv, esternalizzazione f

outspoken [autˈspəukən] ADJ molto franco(-a)

outspread [ˈautsprɛd] ADJ (*wings*) aperto(-a), spiegato(-a)

outstanding [autˈstændɪŋ] ADJ eccezionale, di rilievo; (*unfinished*) non completo(-a); non evaso(-a); non regolato(-a); **your account is still ~** deve ancora saldare il conto

outstay [autˈsteɪ] VT: **to ~ one's welcome** diventare un ospite sgradito

outstretched [autˈstrɛtʃt] ADJ (*hand*) teso(-a); (*body*) disteso(-a)

outstrip [autˈstrɪp] VT (*also fig*) superare

out-tray [ˈauttreɪ] N raccoglitore m per le carte da spedire

outvote [autˈvəut] VT: **to ~ sb (by)** avere la maggioranza rispetto a qn; **to ~ sth (by)** respingere qc

outward [ˈautwəd] ADJ (*sign, appearances*) esteriore; (*journey*) d'andata ▶ ADV verso l'esterno

outwardly [ˈautwədlɪ] ADV esteriormente; in apparenza

outwards [ˈautwədz] ADV (*esp* BRIT) = **outward**

outweigh [autˈweɪ] VT avere maggior peso di

outwit [autˈwɪt] VT superare in astuzia

oval [ˈəuvl] ADJ, N ovale (*m*)

Oval Office N (*US*) *vedi nota*

L'**Oval Office** è una grande stanza di forma ovale nella *White House*, la Casa Bianca, dove ha sede l'ufficio del Presidente degli Stati Uniti. Spesso il termine è usato per indicare la stessa presidenza degli Stati Uniti.

ovarian [əu'vɛərɪən] ADJ ovarico(-a)

ovary ['əuvərɪ] N ovaia

ovation [əu'veɪʃən] N ovazione f

oven ['ʌvn] N forno

oven glove N guanto da forno

ovenproof ['ʌvnpruːf] ADJ da forno

oven-ready ['ʌvnrɛdɪ] ADJ pronto(-a) da infornare

ovenware ['ʌvnwɛəʳ] N vasellame m da mettere in forno

over ['əuvəʳ] ADV al di sopra; (excessively) molto, troppo ▶ ADJ (finished) finito(-a), terminato(-a); (too much) troppo; (remaining) che avanza ▶ PREP su; sopra; (above) al di sopra di; (on the other side of) di là di; (more than) più di; (during) durante; ~ **here** qui; ~ **there** là; **all** ~ (everywhere) dappertutto; (finished) tutto(-a) finito(-a); ~ **and** ~ (again) più e più volte; ~ **and above** oltre (a); **to ask** ~ invitare qn (a passare); **now** ~ **to our Rome correspondent** diamo ora la linea al nostro corrispondente da Roma; **the world** ~ in tutto il mondo; **she's not** ~ **intelligent** (BRIT) non è troppo intelligente; **they fell out** ~ **money** litigarono per una questione di denaro

over... ['əuvəʳ] PREFIX: **overabundant** sovrabbondante

overact [əuvər'ækt] VI (Theat) esagerare or strafare la propria parte

overall ADJ ['əuvərɔːl] totale ▶ N ['əuvərɔːl] (BRIT) grembiule m ▶ ADV [əuvər'ɔːl] nell'insieme, complessivamente ■ **overalls** NPL tuta (da lavoro)

overall majority N maggioranza assoluta

overanxious [əuvər'æŋkʃəs] ADJ troppo ansioso(-a)

overawe [əuvər'ɔː] VT intimidire

overbalance [əuvə'bæləns] VI perdere l'equilibrio

overbearing [əuvə'bɛərɪŋ] ADJ imperioso(-a), prepotente

overboard ['əuvəbɔːd] ADV (Naut) fuori bordo, in acqua; **to go** ~ **for sth** (fig) impazzire per qc

overbook [əuvə'buk] VT sovrapprenotare

overcame [əuvə'keɪm] PT of **overcome**

overcapitalize [əuvə'kæpɪtəlaɪz] VT sovraccapitalizzare

overcast ['əuvəkɑːst] ADJ (sky) coperto(-a)

overcharge [əuvə'tʃɑːdʒ] VT: **to** ~ **sb for sth** far pagare troppo caro a qn per qc

overcoat ['əuvəkəut] N soprabito, cappotto

overcome [əuvə'kʌm] VT (irreg: like **come**) superare; sopraffare; ~ **with grief** sopraffatto(-a) dal dolore

overconfident [əuvə'kɔnfɪdənt] ADJ troppo sicuro(-a) (di sé), presuntuoso(-a)

overcrowded [əuvə'kraudɪd] ADJ sovraffollato(-a)

overcrowding [əuvə'kraudɪŋ] N sovraffollamento; (in bus) calca

overdo [əuvə'duː] VT (irreg: like **do**) esagerare; (overcook) cuocere troppo; **to** ~ **it, to** ~ **things** (work too hard) lavorare troppo

overdone [əuvə'dʌn] ADJ troppo cotto(-a)

overdose ['əuvədəus] N dose f eccessiva

overdraft ['əuvədrɑːft] N scoperto (di conto)

overdrawn [əuvə'drɔːn] ADJ (account) scoperto(-a)

overdrive ['əuvədraɪv] N (Aut) overdrive m inv

overdue [əuvə'djuː] ADJ in ritardo; (recognition) tardivo(-a); (bill) insoluto(-a); **that change was long** ~ quel cambiamento ci voleva da tempo

overemphasis [əuvər'ɛmfəsɪs] N: ~ **on sth** importanza eccessiva data a qc

overemphasize [əuvər'ɛmfəsaɪz] VT dare un'importanza eccessiva a

overestimate [əuvər'ɛstɪmeɪt] VT sopravvalutare

overexcited [əuvərɪk'saɪtɪd] ADJ sovraeccitato(-a)

overexertion [əuvərɪg'zəːʃən] N logorio (fisico)

overexpose [əuvərɪk'spəuz] VT (Phot) sovraesporre

overflow VI [əuvə'fləu] traboccare ▶ N ['əuvəfləu] eccesso; (also: **overflow pipe**) troppopieno

overfly [əuvə'flaɪ] VT (irreg: like **fly**) sorvolare

overgenerous [əuvə'dʒənərəs] ADJ troppo generoso(-a)

overgrown [əuvə'grəun] ADJ (garden) ricoperto(-a) di vegetazione; **he's just an** ~ **schoolboy** è proprio un bambinone

overhang [əuvə'hæŋ] VT (irreg: like **hang**) sporgere da ▶ VI sporgere

overhaul VT [əuvə'hɔːl] revisionare ▶ N ['əuvəhɔːl] revisione f

overhead ADV [əuvə'hɛd] di sopra ▶ ADJ ['əuvəhɛd] aereo(-a); (lighting) verticale ▶ N ['əuvəhɛd] (US) = **overheads**

overhead projector N lavagna luminosa

overheads ['əuvəhɛdz] NPL (BRIT) spese fpl generali

overhear [əuvə'hɪəʳ] VT (irreg: like **hear**) sentire (per caso)

overheat [əuvə'hiːt] VI surriscaldarsi

overjoyed [əuvə'dʒɔɪd] ADJ pazzo(-a) di gioia

overkill ['əuvəkɪl] N (fig) strafare m

overland ['əuvəlænd] ADJ, ADV per via di terra

overlap VI [əuvə'læp] sovrapporsi ▶ N ['əuvəlæp] sovrapposizione f

695

overleaf [əuvə'li:f] ADV a tergo

overload [əuvə'ləud] VT sovraccaricare

overlook [əuvə'luk] VT (have view of) dare su; (miss) trascurare; (forgive) passare sopra a

overlord ['əuvələ:d] N capo supremo

overmanning [əuvə'mænɪŋ] N eccedenza di manodopera

overnight ADV [əuvə'naɪt] (happen) durante la notte; (fig) tutto ad un tratto ▶ ADJ ['əuvənaɪt] di notte; fulmineo(-a); **he stayed there ~** ci ha passato la notte; **if you travel ~ ...** se viaggia di notte ...; **he'll be away ~** passerà la notte fuori

overnight bag N borsa da viaggio

overpass ['əuvəpɑːs] N cavalcavia m inv

overpay [əuvə'peɪ] VT (irreg: like **pay**): **to ~ sb by £50** pagare 50 sterline in più a qn

overplay [əuvə'pleɪ] VT dare troppa importanza a; **to ~ one's hand** sopravvalutare la propria posizione

overpower [əuvə'pauə'] VT sopraffare

overpowering [əuvə'pauərɪŋ] ADJ irresistibile; (heat, stench) soffocante

overproduction ['əuvəprə'dʌkʃən] N sovrapproduzione f

overrate [əuvə'reɪt] VT sopravvalutare

overreach [əuvə'riːtʃ] VT: **to ~ o.s.** volere strafare

overreact [əuvəri:'ækt] VI reagire in modo esagerato

override [əuvə'raɪd] VT (irreg: like **ride**) (order, objection) passar sopra a; (decision) annullare

overriding [əuvə'raɪdɪŋ] ADJ preponderante

overrule [əuvə'ru:l] VT (decision) annullare; (claim) respingere

overrun [əuvə'rʌn] VT (irreg: like **run**) (Mil: country etc) invadere; (time limit etc) superare, andare al di là di ▶ VI protrarsi; **the town is ~ with tourists** la città è invasa dai turisti

overseas [əuvə'si:z] ADV oltremare; (abroad) all'estero ▶ ADJ (trade) estero(-a); (visitor) straniero(-a)

oversee [əuvə'si:] VT (irreg: like **see**) sorvegliare

overseer ['əuvəsɪə'] N (in factory) caposquadra m

overshadow [əuvə'ʃædəu] VT far ombra su; (fig) eclissare

overshoot [əuvə'ʃuːt] VT (irreg: like **shoot**) superare

oversight ['əuvəsaɪt] N omissione f, svista; **due to an ~** per una svista

oversimplify [əuvə'sɪmplɪfaɪ] VT rendere troppo semplice

oversleep [əuvə'sli:p] VI (irreg: like **sleep**) dormire troppo a lungo

overspend [əuvə'spɛnd] VI (irreg: like **spend**) spendere troppo; **we have overspent by 5000 dollars** abbiamo speso 5000 dollari di troppo

overspill ['əuvəspɪl] N eccedenza di popolazione

overstaffed [əuvə'stɑːft] ADJ: **to be ~** avere troppo personale

overstate [əuvə'steɪt] VT esagerare

overstatement [əuvə'steɪtmənt] N esagerazione f

overstay [əuvə'steɪ] VT: **to ~ one's welcome** trattenersi troppo a lungo (come ospite)

overstep [əuvə'stɛp] VT: **to ~ the mark** superare ogni limite

overstock [əuvə'stɔk] VT sovrapprovvigionare, sovraimmagazzinare

overstretched [əuvə'strɛtʃt] ADJ sovraccarico(-a); (budget) arrivato(-a) al limite

overstrike N ['əuvəstraɪk] (on printer) sovrapposizione f (di caratteri) ▶ VT [əuvə'straɪk] (irreg: like **strike**) sovrapporre

overt [əu'və:t] ADJ palese

overtake [əuvə'teɪk] VT (irreg: like **take**) sorpassare

overtaking [əuvə'teɪkɪŋ] N (Aut) sorpasso

overtax [əuvə'tæks] VT (Econ) imporre tasse eccessive a, tassare eccessivamente; (fig: strength, patience) mettere alla prova, abusare di; **to ~ o.s.** chiedere troppo alle proprie forze

overthrow [əuvə'θrəu] VT (irreg: like **throw**) (government) rovesciare

overtime ['əuvətaɪm] N (lavoro) straordinario; **to do** or **work ~** fare lo straordinario

overtime ban N rifiuto sindacale a fare gli straordinari

overtone ['əuvətəun] N (also: **overtones**) sfumatura

overtook [əuvə'tuk] PT of **overtake**

overture ['əuvətʃuə'] N (Mus) ouverture f inv; (fig) approccio

overturn [əuvə'tə:n] VT rovesciare ▶ VI rovesciarsi

overview ['əuvəvju:] N visione f d'insieme

overweight [əuvə'weɪt] ADJ (person) troppo grasso(-a); (luggage) troppo pesante

overwhelm [əuvə'wɛlm] VT sopraffare; sommergere; schiacciare

overwhelming [əuvə'wɛlmɪŋ] ADJ (victory, defeat) schiacciante; (heat, desire) intenso(-a); **one's ~ impression is of heat** l'impressione dominante è quella di caldo

overwhelmingly [əuvə'wɛlmɪŋlɪ] ADV in massa

overwork [əuvə'wə:k] VT far lavorare troppo ▶ VI lavorare troppo, strapazzarsi

overwrite [əuvə'raɪt] VT (irreg: like **write**) (Comput) ricoprire

overwrought [əuvə'rɔ:t] ADJ molto agitato(-a)

ovulation [ɔvju'leɪʃən] N ovulazione f

ow [au] EXCL ahi!

owe [əu] VT dovere; **to ~ sb sth, to ~ sth to sb** dovere qc a qn

owing to [ˈəuɪŋtuː] PREP a causa di

owl [aul] N gufo

own [əun] ADJ proprio(-a) ▶ VT possedere ▶ VI (BRIT): **to ~ to sth** ammettere qc; **to ~ to having done sth** ammettere di aver fatto qc; **a room of my ~** la mia propria camera; **to get one's ~ back** vendicarsi; **on one's ~** tutto(-a) solo(-a); **can I have it for my (very) ~?** posso averlo tutto per me?; **to come into one's ~** mostrare le proprie qualità
▶ **own up** VI confessare

own brand N (Comm) etichetta propria

owner [ˈəunəʳ] N proprietario(-a)

owner-occupier [ˈəunərˈɔkjupaɪəʳ] N proprietario/a della casa in cui abita

ownership [ˈəunəʃɪp] N possesso; **it's under new ~** ha un nuovo proprietario

own goal N (also fig) autogol m inv

ox [ɔks] (pl **oxen** [ˈɔksn]) N bue m

Oxbridge [ˈɔksbrɪdʒ] N le università di Oxford e/o Cambridge

La parola **Oxbridge** deriva dalla fusione dei nomi Ox(ford) e (Cam)bridge e fa riferimento a queste due antiche università.

oxen [ˈɔksn] NPL of **ox**

Oxfam [ˈɔksfæm] N ABBR (BRIT: = Oxford Committee for Famine Relief) organizzazione per aiuti al terzo mondo

oxide [ˈɔksaɪd] N ossido

Oxon. [ˈɔksn] ABBR (BRIT: of Oxford) = **Oxoniensis**

oxtail [ˈɔksteɪl] N: **~ soup** minestra di coda di bue

oxyacetylene [ˈɔksɪəˈsɛtɪliːn] ADJ ossiacetilenico(-a); **~ burner, ~ lamp** cannello ossiacetilenico

oxygen [ˈɔksɪdʒən] N ossigeno

oxygen mask N maschera ad ossigeno

oxygen tent N tenda ad ossigeno

oyster [ˈɔɪstəʳ] N ostrica

oz. ABBR = **ounce**

ozone [ˈəuzəun] N ozono

ozone-friendly [ˈəuzəunˈfrɛndlɪ] ADJ che non danneggia lo strato d'ozono

ozone layer N strato d'ozono, fascia d'ozono

o

Pp

P, p [piː] N (letter) P, p f inv or m inv; **P for Peter** = P come Padova

P ABBR = **president; prince**

p [piː] ABBR (= page) p; (BRIT) = **penny; pence**

PA N ABBR = **personal assistant; public address system** ▶ ABBR (US) = **Pennsylvania**

pa [pɑː] N (col) papà m inv, babbo

p.a. ABBR = **per annum**

PAC N ABBR (US) = **political action committee**

pace [peɪs] N passo; (speed) passo; velocità ▶ VI: **to ~ up and down** camminare su e giù; **to keep ~ with** camminare di pari passo a; (events) tenersi al corrente di; **to put sb through his paces** (fig) mettere qn alla prova; **to set the ~** (running) fare l'andatura; (fig) dare il la or il tono

pacemaker ['peɪsmeɪkəʳ] N (Med) pacemaker m inv, stimolatore m cardiaco; (Sport) chi fa l'andatura

Pacific [pə'sɪfɪk] ADJ pacifico(-a) ▶ N: **the ~ (Ocean)** il Pacifico, l'Oceano Pacifico

pacification [pæsɪfɪ'keɪʃən] N pacificazione f

pacifier ['pæsɪfaɪəʳ] N (US: dummy) succhiotto, ciuccio (col)

pacifist ['pæsɪfɪst] N pacifista mf

pacify ['pæsɪfaɪ] VT pacificare; (soothe) calmare

pack [pæk] N (packet) pacco; (Comm) confezione f; (US: of cigarettes) pacchetto; (of goods) balla; (of hounds) muta; (of wolves) branco; (of thieves etc) banda; (of cards) mazzo ▶ VT (goods) impaccare, imballare; (in suitcase etc) mettere; (box) riempire; (cram) stipare, pigiare; (press down) tamponare; turare; (Comput) comprimere, impaccare ▶ VI: **to ~ one's bags** fare la valigia; **to send sb packing** (col) spedire via qn
▶ **pack in** (BRIT col) VI (watch, car) guastarsi ▶ VT mollare, piantare; **~ it in!** piantala!, dacci un taglio!
▶ **pack off** VT (col: person) spedire
▶ **pack up** VI (BRIT col: machine) guastarsi; (person) far fagotto ▶ VT (belongings, clothes) mettere in una valigia; (goods, presents) imballare

package ['pækɪdʒ] N pacco; balla; (also: **package deal**) pacchetto; forfait m inv ▶ VT (goods) confezionare

package holiday N (BRIT) vacanza organizzata

package tour N viaggio organizzato

packaging ['pækɪdʒɪŋ] N confezione f, imballo

packed [pækt] ADJ (crowded) affollato(-a); **~ lunch** (BRIT) pranzo al sacco

packer ['pækəʳ] N (person) imballatore(-trice)

packet ['pækɪt] N pacchetto

packet switching [-swɪtʃɪŋ] N (Comput) commutazione f di pacchetto

pack ice ['pækaɪs] N banchisa

packing ['pækɪŋ] N imballaggio

packing case N cassa da imballaggio

pact [pækt] N patto, accordo; trattato

pad [pæd] N blocco; (for inking) tampone m; (to prevent friction) cuscinetto; (col: flat) appartamentino ▶ VT imbottire ▶ VI: **to ~ about/in** etc camminare/entrare etc a passi felpati

padded ADJ imbottito(-a)

padded cell ['pædɪd-] N cella imbottita

padding ['pædɪŋ] N imbottitura; (fig) riempitivo

paddle ['pædl] N (oar) pagaia; (US: for table tennis) racchetta da ping-pong ▶ VI sguazzare ▶ VT (boat) fare andare a colpi di pagaia

paddle steamer N battello a ruote

paddling pool ['pædlɪŋ-] N (BRIT) piscina per bambini

paddock ['pædək] N prato recintato; (at racecourse) paddock m inv

paddy ['pædɪ] N (also: **paddy field**) risaia

padlock ['pædlɔk] N lucchetto ▶ VT chiudere con il lucchetto

padre ['pɑːdrɪ] N cappellano

Padua ['pædjuə] N Padova

paediatrician, (US) **pediatrician** [piːdɪə'trɪʃən] N pediatra mf

paediatrics, (US) **pediatrics** [piːdɪ'ætrɪks] N pediatria

paedophile, (US) **pedophile** ['piːdəufaɪl] ADJ, N pedofilo(-a)

pagan ['peɪgən] ADJ, N pagano(-a)

page [peɪdʒ] N pagina; (also: **page boy**) fattorino; (: *at wedding*) paggio ▶ VT (*in hotel etc*) (far) chiamare

pageant [ˈpædʒənt] N spettacolo storico; grande cerimonia

pageantry [ˈpædʒəntrɪ] N pompa

page break N interruzione f di pagina

pager [ˈpeɪdʒəʳ] N (*Tel*) cicalino, cercapersone *m inv*

paginate [ˈpædʒɪneɪt] VT impaginare

pagination [pædʒɪˈneɪʃən] N impaginazione f

pagoda [pəˈɡəudə] N pagoda

paid [peɪd] PT, PP *of* **pay** ▶ ADJ (*work, official*) rimunerato(-a); **to put ~ to** (*BRIT*) mettere fine a

paid-up [ˈpeɪdʌp], (*US*) **paid in** [ˈpeɪdɪn] ADJ (*member*) che ha pagato la sua quota; (*share*) interamente pagato(-a); **~ capital** capitale *m* interamente versato

pail [peɪl] N secchio

pain [peɪn] N dolore *m*; **to be in ~** soffrire, aver male; **to have a ~ in** aver male *or* un dolore a; **to take pains to do** mettercela tutta per fare; **on ~ of death** sotto pena di morte

pained [peɪnd] ADJ addolorato(-a), afflitto(-a)

painful [ˈpeɪnful] ADJ doloroso(-a), che fa male; (*difficult*) difficile, penoso(-a)

painfully [ˈpeɪnfəlɪ] ADV (*fig: very*) fin troppo

painkiller [ˈpeɪnkɪləʳ] N antalgico, antidolorifico

painstaking [ˈpeɪnzteɪkɪŋ] ADJ (*person*) sollecito(-a); (*work*) accurato(-a)

paint [peɪnt] N (*for house etc*) tinta, vernice f; (*Art*) colore *m* ▶ VT (*Art: walls*) dipingere; (*door etc*) verniciare; **a tin of ~** un barattolo di tinta *or* vernice; **to ~ the door blue** verniciare la porta di azzurro; **to ~ in oils** dipingere a olio

paintbox [ˈpeɪntbɔks] N scatola di colori

paintbrush [ˈpeɪntbrʌʃ] N pennello

painter [ˈpeɪntəʳ] N (*artist*) pittore(-trice); (*decorator*) imbianchino(-a)

painting [ˈpeɪntɪŋ] N (*activity: of artist*) pittura; (: *of decorator*) imbiancatura; verniciatura; (*picture*) dipinto, quadro

paint-stripper [ˈpeɪntstrɪpəʳ] N prodotto sverniciante

paintwork [ˈpeɪntwəːk] N (*BRIT*) tinta; (: *of car*) vernice f

pair [peəʳ] N (*of shoes, gloves etc*) paio; (*of people*) coppia; duo *m inv*; **a ~ of scissors/trousers** un paio di forbici/pantaloni
▶ **pair off** VI: **to ~ off (with sb)** fare coppia (con qn)

pajamas [pəˈdʒɑːməz] NPL (*US*) pigiama *m*

Pakistan [pɑːkɪˈstɑːn] N Pakistan *m*

Pakistani [pɑːkɪˈstɑːnɪ] ADJ, N pakistano(-a)

PAL [pæl] N ABBR (*TV*: = *phase alternation line*) PAL *m*

pal [pæl] N (*col*) amico(-a), compagno(-a)

palace [ˈpæləs] N palazzo

palatable [ˈpælɪtəbl] ADJ gustoso(-a)

palate [ˈpælɪt] N palato

palatial [pəˈleɪʃəl] ADJ sontuoso(-a), sfarzoso(-a)

palaver [pəˈlɑːvəʳ] N chiacchiere fpl; storie fpl

pale [peɪl] ADJ pallido(-a) ▶ VI impallidire ▶ N: **to be beyond the ~** aver oltrepassato ogni limite; **to grow** *or* **turn ~** (*person*) diventare pallido(-a), impallidire; **to ~ into insignificance (beside)** perdere d'importanza (nei confronti di); **~ blue** azzurro *or* blu pallido *inv*

paleness [ˈpeɪlnɪs] N pallore *m*

Palestine [ˈpælɪstaɪn] N Palestina

Palestinian [pælɪsˈtɪnɪən] ADJ, N palestinese (*mf*)

palette [ˈpælɪt] N tavolozza

paling [ˈpeɪlɪŋ] N (*stake*) palo; (*fence*) palizzata

palisade [pælɪˈseɪd] N palizzata

pall [pɔːl] N (*of smoke*) cappa ▶ VI: **to ~ (on)** diventare noioso(-a) (a)

pallet [ˈpælɪt] N (*for goods*) paletta

pallid [ˈpælɪd] ADJ pallido(-a), smorto(-a)

pallor [ˈpæləʳ] N pallore *m*

pally [ˈpælɪ] ADJ (*col*) amichevole

palm [pɑːm] N (*Anat*) palma, palmo; (*also*: **palm tree**) palma ▶ VT: **to ~ sth off on sb** (*col*) rifilare qc a qn

palmist [ˈpɑːmɪst] N chiromante *mf*

Palm Sunday N Domenica delle Palme

palpable [ˈpælpəbl] ADJ palpabile

palpitation [pælpɪˈteɪʃən] N palpitazione f; **to have palpitations** avere le palpitazioni

paltry [ˈpɔːltrɪ] ADJ derisorio(-a), insignificante

pamper [ˈpæmpəʳ] VT viziare, coccolare

pamphlet [ˈpæmflət] N dépliant *m inv*; (*political etc*) volantino, manifestino

pan [pæn] N (*also*: **saucepan**) casseruola; (*also*: **frying pan**) padella ▶ VI (*Cine*) fare una panoramica; **to ~ for gold** (lavare le sabbie aurifere per) cercare l'oro

panacea [pænəˈsɪə] N panacea

panache [pəˈnæʃ] N stile *m*

Panama [ˈpænəmɑː] N Panama *m*

Panama Canal N canale *m* di Panama

Panamanian [pænəˈmeɪnɪən] ADJ, N panamense (*mf*)

pancake [ˈpænkeɪk] N frittella

Pancake Day N (*BRIT*) martedì *m* grasso

pancake roll N *crêpe ripiena di verdure alla cinese*

pancreas [ˈpæŋkrɪəs] N pancreas *m inv*

panda [ˈpændə] N panda *m inv*

panda car N (*BRIT*) auto f della polizia

pandemic [pænˈdɛmɪk] N pandemia

pandemonium [pændɪˈməunɪəm] N pandemonio

pander [ˈpændəʳ] VI: **to ~ to** lusingare; concedere tutto a

p

p & h ABBR (US: = postage and handling) affrancatura e trasporto

P & L ABBR (= profit and loss) P.P.

p & p ABBR (BRIT: = postage and packing) affrancatura ed imballaggio

pane [peɪn] N vetro

panel ['pænl] N (of wood, cloth etc) pannello; (Radio, TV) giuria

panel game N (BRIT) quiz m inv a squadre

panelling, (US) **paneling** ['pænəlɪŋ] N rivestimento a pannelli

panellist, (US) **panelist** ['pænəlɪst] N partecipante mf (al quiz, alla tavola rotonda etc)

pang [pæŋ] N: **to feel pangs of remorse** essere torturato(-a) dal rimorso; **pangs of hunger** spasimi mpl della fame; **pangs of conscience** morsi mpl di coscienza

panhandler ['pænhændlər] N (US pej) accattone(-a)

panic ['pænɪk] N panico ▶ VI perdere il sangue freddo

panic buying [-baɪɪŋ] N accaparramento (di generi alimentari ecc)

panicky ['pænɪkɪ] ADJ (person) pauroso(-a)

panic-stricken ['pænɪkstrɪkən] ADJ (person) preso(-a) dal panico, in preda al panico; (look) terrorizzato(-a)

panini [pæ'niːnɪ] N panino m

pannier ['pænɪər] N (on animal) bisaccia; (on bicycle) borsa

panorama [pænə'rɑːmə] N panorama m

panoramic [pænə'ræmɪk] ADJ panoramico(-a)

pansy ['pænzɪ] N (Bot) viola del pensiero, pensée f inv; (!) femminuccia

pant [pænt] VI ansare

pantechnicon [pæn'tɛknɪkən] N (BRIT) grosso furgone m per traslochi

panther ['pænθər] N pantera

panties ['pæntɪz] NPL slip m, mutandine fpl

pantihose ['pæntɪhəuz] N (US) collant m inv

panto ['pæntəu] N (BRIT col) see **pantomime**

pantomime ['pæntəmaɪm] N (BRIT: at Christmas) spettacolo natalizio; (tecnica) pantomima

In Gran Bretagna la **pantomime** (abbreviata in panto) è una sorta di libera interpretazione delle favole più conosciute che vengono messe in scena nei teatri durante il periodo natalizio. Gli attori principali sono la dama, pantomime dame, che è un uomo vestito da donna, il protagonista, principal boy, che è una donna travestita da uomo, e il cattivo, villain. È uno spettacolo per tutta la famiglia, che prevede la partecipazione del pubblico.

pantry ['pæntrɪ] N dispensa

pants [pænts] NPL (BRIT) mutande fpl, slip m; (US: trousers) pantaloni mpl

pantsuit ['pæntsuːt] N (US) completo m or tailleur m inv pantalone inv

papacy ['peɪpəsɪ] N papato

papal ['peɪpəl] ADJ papale, pontificio(-a)

paparazzi [pæpə'rætsiː] NPL paparazzi mpl

paper ['peɪpər] N carta; (also: **wallpaper**) carta da parati, tappezzeria; (also: **newspaper**) giornale m; (study, article) saggio; (exam) prova scritta ▶ ADJ di carta ▶ VT tappezzare; **a piece of ~** (odd bit) un pezzo di carta; (sheet) un foglio (di carta); **to put sth down on ~** mettere qc per iscritto; see also **papers**

paper advance N (on printer) avanzamento della carta

paperback ['peɪpəbæk] N tascabile m; edizione f economica ▶ ADJ: **~ edition** edizione f tascabile

paper bag N sacchetto di carta

paperboy ['peɪpəbɔɪ] N (selling) strillone m; (delivering) ragazzo che recapita i giornali

paper clip N graffetta, clip f inv

paper handkerchief N fazzolettino di carta

paper mill N cartiera

paper money N cartamoneta, moneta cartacea

paper profit N utile m teorico

papers ['peɪpəz] NPL (also: **identity papers**) carte fpl, documenti mpl

paper shop N (BRIT) giornalaio (negozio)

paperweight ['peɪpəweɪt] N fermacarte m inv

paperwork ['peɪpəwəːk] N lavoro amministrativo

papier-mâché ['pæpɪeɪ'mæʃeɪ] N cartapesta

paprika ['pæprɪkə] N paprica

Pap test, Pap smear ['pæp-] N (Med) pap-test m inv

Papua New Guinea N Papua Nuova Guinea

par [pɑːr] N parità, pari f; (Golf) norma; **on a ~ with** alla pari con; **at/above/below ~** (Comm) alla/sopra la/sotto la pari; **above/below ~** (gen, Golf) al di sopra/al di sotto della norma; **to feel below** or **under** or **not up to ~** non sentirsi in forma

parable ['pærəbl] N parabola (Rel)

parabola [pə'ræbələ] N parabola (Math)

paracetamol [pærə'siːtəmɔl] N (BRIT) paracetamolo

parachute ['pærəʃuːt] N paracadute m inv ▶ VI scendere col paracadute

parachute jump N lancio col paracadute

parachutist ['pærəʃuːtɪst] N paracadutista mf

parade [pə'reɪd] N parata; (inspection) rivista, rassegna ▶ VT (fig) fare sfoggio di ▶ VI sfilare in parata; **a fashion ~** (BRIT) una sfilata di moda

parade ground N piazza d'armi

paradise [ˈpærədaɪs] N paradiso

paradox [ˈpærədɔks] N paradosso

paradoxical [pærəˈdɔksɪkl] ADJ paradossale

paradoxically [pærəˈdɔksɪklɪ] ADV paradossalmente

paraffin [ˈpærəfɪn] N (BRIT): ~ **(oil)** paraffina; **liquid** ~ olio di paraffina

paraffin heater N (BRIT) stufa al cherosene

paraffin lamp N (BRIT) lampada al cherosene

paragon [ˈpærəgən] N modello di perfezione or di virtù

paragraph [ˈpærəgrɑːf] N paragrafo; **to begin a new** ~ andare a capo

Paraguay [ˈpærəgwaɪ] N Paraguay m

Paraguayan [pærəˈgwaɪən] ADJ, N paraguaiano(-a)

parallel [ˈpærəlɛl] ADJ (also Comput) parallelo(-a); (fig) analogo(-a) ▶ N (line) parallela; (fig, Geo) parallelo; ~ **(with** or **to)** parallelo(-a) (a)

paralyse, (US) **paralyze** [ˈpærəlaɪz] VT paralizzare

paralysed, (US) **paralyzed** [ˈpærəlaɪzd] ADJ paralizzato(-a)

paralysis [pəˈrælɪsɪs] (pl **paralyses** [-siːz]) N paralisi f inv

paralytic [pærəˈlɪtɪk] ADJ paralitico(-a); (BRIT col: drunk) ubriaco(-a) fradicio(-a)

paralyze [ˈpærəlaɪz] VT (US) = **paralyse**

paramedic [pærəˈmɛdɪk] N paramedico

parameter [pəˈræmɪtər] N parametro

paramilitary [pærəˈmɪlɪtərɪ] ADJ paramilitare

paramount [ˈpærəmaunt] ADJ: **of** ~ **importance** di capitale importanza

paranoia [pærəˈnɔɪə] N paranoia

paranoid [ˈpærənɔɪd] ADJ paranoico(-a)

paranormal [pærəˈnɔːml] ADJ paranormale

paraphernalia [pærəfəˈneɪlɪə] N attrezzi mpl, roba

paraphrase [ˈpærəfreɪz] VT parafrasare

paraplegic [pærəˈpliːdʒɪk] N paraplegico(-a)

parapsychology [pærəsaɪˈkɔlədʒɪ] N parapsicologia

parasite [ˈpærəsaɪt] N parassita m

parasol [ˈpærəsɔl] N parasole m inv

paratrooper [ˈpærətruːpər] N paracadutista m (soldato)

parcel [ˈpɑːsl] N pacco, pacchetto ▶ VT (also: **parcel up**) impaccare
  ▶ **parcel out** VT spartire

parcel bomb N (BRIT) pacchetto esplosivo

parcel post N servizio pacchi

parch [pɑːtʃ] VT riardere

parched [ˈpɑːtʃt] ADJ (person) assetato(-a)

parchment [ˈpɑːtʃmənt] N pergamena

pardon [ˈpɑːdn] N perdono; grazia ▶ VT perdonare; (Law) graziare; ~! scusi!; ~ **me!** mi scusi!; **I beg your** ~! scusi!; **(I beg your)** ~?, (US) ~ **me?** prego?

pare [pɛər] VT (BRIT: nails) tagliarsi; (: fruit etc) sbucciare, pelare

parent [ˈpɛərənt] N padre m (or madre f) ■ **parents** NPL genitori mpl

> La parola inglese **parents** non vuol dire parenti.

parentage [ˈpɛərəntɪdʒ] N natali mpl; **of unknown** ~ di genitori sconosciuti

parental [pəˈrɛntl] ADJ dei genitori

parent company N società madre f inv

parenthesis [pəˈrɛnθɪsɪs] (pl **parentheses** [-siːz]) N parentesi f inv; **in parentheses** fra parentesi

parenthood [ˈpɛərənthud] N paternità or maternità

parenting [ˈpɛərəntɪŋ] N mestiere m di genitore

Paris [ˈpærɪs] N Parigi f

parish [ˈpærɪʃ] N parrocchia; (BRIT: civil) ≈ municipio ▶ ADJ parrocchiale

parish council N (BRIT) ≈ consiglio comunale

parishioner [pəˈrɪʃənər] N parrocchiano(-a)

Parisian [pəˈrɪzɪən] ADJ, N parigino(-a)

parity [ˈpærɪtɪ] N parità

park [pɑːk] N parco; (public) giardino pubblico ▶ VT, VI parcheggiare

parka [ˈpɑːkə] N eskimo

park and ride N parcheggio di interscambio

parking [ˈpɑːkɪŋ] N parcheggio; **"no** ~**"** "sosta vietata"

parking lights NPL luci fpl di posizione

parking lot N (US) posteggio, parcheggio

parking meter N parchimetro

parking offence N (BRIT) infrazione f al divieto di sosta

parking place N posto di parcheggio

parking ticket N multa per sosta vietata

parking violation N (US) = **parking offence**

Parkinson's [ˈpɑːkɪnsənz] N (also: **Parkinson's disease**) morbo di Parkinson

parkour [pɑːˈkuər] N parkour m inv

parkway [ˈpɑːkweɪ] N (US) viale m

parlance [ˈpɑːləns] N: **in common/modern** ~ nel gergo or linguaggio comune/moderno

parliament [ˈpɑːləmənt] N parlamento

> Nel Regno Unito il Parlamento, **Parliament**, è formato da due camere: la House of Commons e la House of Lords. Nella House of Commons siedono 650 parlamentari, chiamati MPs, eletti per votazione diretta del popolo nelle rispettive circoscrizioni elettorali, le constituencies. Le sessioni del Parlamento sono presiedute e

moderate dal presidente della Camera, lo *Speaker*. Alla *House of Lords*, i cui poteri sono più limitati, in passato si accedeva per nomina o per carica ereditaria mentre ora le cariche ereditarie sono state ridotte e in futuro verranno abolite.

parliamentary [pɑ:ləˈmɛntərɪ] ADJ parlamentare

parlour, (US) **parlor** [ˈpɑ:ləʳ] N salotto

parlous [ˈpɑ:ləs] ADJ periglioso(-a)

Parmesan [pɑ:mɪˈzæn] N (*also:* **Parmesan cheese**) parmigiano

parochial [pəˈrəukɪəl] ADJ parrocchiale; (*pej*) provinciale

parody [ˈpærədɪ] N parodia

parole [pəˈrəul] N: **on ~** in libertà per buona condotta

paroxysm [ˈpærəksɪzəm] N (*Med*) parossismo; (*of anger, laughter, coughing*) convulso; (*of grief*) attacco

parquet [ˈpɑ:keɪ] N: **~ floor(ing)** parquet *m*

parrot [ˈpærət] N pappagallo

parrot fashion ADV in modo pappagallesco

parry [ˈpærɪ] VT parare

parsimonious [pɑ:sɪˈməunɪəs] ADJ parsimonioso(-a)

parsley [ˈpɑ:slɪ] N prezzemolo

parsnip [ˈpɑ:snɪp] N pastinaca

parson [ˈpɑ:sn] N prete *m*; (*Church of England*) parroco

part [pɑ:t] N parte *f*; (*of machine*) pezzo; (*Theat etc*) parte, ruolo; (*Mus*) voce *f*; parte; (*US: in hair*) scriminatura ▶ ADJ in parte ▶ ADV = **partly** ▶ VT separare ▶ VI (*people*) separarsi; (*roads*) dividersi; **to take ~ in** prendere parte a; **to take sb's ~** parteggiare per qn, prendere le parti di qn; **on his ~** da parte sua; **for my ~** per parte mia; **for the most ~** in generale; nella maggior parte dei casi; **for the better ~ of the day** per la maggior parte della giornata; **to be ~ and parcel of** essere parte integrante di; **to take sth in good/bad ~** prendere bene/male qc; **~ of speech** (*Ling*) parte del discorso
▶ **part with** VT FUS separarsi da; rinunciare a

partake [pɑ:ˈteɪk] VI (*irreg: like* **take**) (*formal*): **to ~ of sth** consumare qc, prendere qc

part exchange N (*Brit*): **in ~** in pagamento parziale

partial [ˈpɑ:ʃl] ADJ parziale; **to be ~ to** avere un debole per

partially [ˈpɑ:ʃəlɪ] ADV in parte, parzialmente

participant [pɑ:ˈtɪsɪpənt] N: **~ (in)** partecipante *mf* (a)

participate [pɑ:ˈtɪsɪpeɪt] VI: **to ~ (in)** prendere parte (a), partecipare (a)

participation [pɑ:tɪsɪˈpeɪʃən] N partecipazione *f*

participle [ˈpɑ:tɪsɪpl] N participio

particle [ˈpɑ:tɪkl] N particella

particular [pəˈtɪkjuləʳ] ADJ particolare; speciale; (*fussy*) difficile; meticoloso(-a) ▪ **particulars** NPL particolari *mpl*, dettagli *mpl*; (*information*) informazioni *fpl*; **in ~** in particolare, particolarmente; **to be very ~ about** essere molto pignolo(-a) su; **I'm not ~** per me va bene tutto

particularly [pəˈtɪkjuləlɪ] ADV particolarmente; in particolare

parting [ˈpɑ:tɪŋ] N separazione *f*; (*Brit: in hair*) scriminatura ▶ ADJ d'addio; **~ shot** (*fig*) battuta finale

partisan [pɑ:tɪˈzæn] N partigiano(-a) ▶ ADJ partigiano(-a); di parte

partition [pɑ:ˈtɪʃən] N (*Pol*) partizione *f*; (*wall*) tramezzo

partly [ˈpɑ:tlɪ] ADV parzialmente; in parte

partner [ˈpɑ:tnəʳ] N (*Comm*) socio(-a); (*wife, husband etc, Sport*) compagno(-a); (*at dance*) cavaliere (dama)

partnership [ˈpɑ:tnəʃɪp] N associazione *f*; (*Comm*) società *f inv*; **to go into ~ (with), form a ~ (with)** mettersi in società (con), associarsi (a)

part payment N acconto

partridge [ˈpɑ:trɪdʒ] N pernice *f*

part-time [ˈpɑ:tˈtaɪm] ADJ, ADV a orario ridotto, part-time (*inv*)

part-timer [ˈpɑ:tˈtaɪməʳ] N (*also:* **part-time worker**) lavoratore(-trice) part-time

party [ˈpɑ:tɪ] N (*Pol*) partito; (*team*) squadra; gruppo; (*Law*) parte *f*; (*celebration*) ricevimento; serata; festa ▶ ADJ (*Pol*) del partito, di partito; **dinner ~** cena; **to give** *or* **throw a ~** dare una festa *or* un party; **to be a ~ to a crime** essere coinvolto in un reato

party line N (*Pol*) linea del partito; (*Tel*) duplex *m inv*

party piece N: **to do one's ~** (*Brit col*) esibirsi nel proprio pezzo forte a una festa, cena ecc

party political broadcast N comunicato radiotelevisivo di propaganda

pass [pɑ:s] VT (*gen*) passare; (*place*) passare davanti a; (*exam*) passare, superare; (*candidate*) promuovere; (*overtake, surpass*) sorpassare, superare; (*approve*) approvare ▶ VI passare; (*Scol*) essere promosso(-a) ▶ N (*permit*) lasciapassare *m inv*; permesso; (*in mountains*) passo, gola; (*Sport*) passaggio; (*Scol: also:* **pass mark**): **to get a ~** prendere la sufficienza; **to ~ for** passare per; **could you ~ the vegetables round?** potrebbe far passare i contorni?; **to ~ sth through a hole** *etc* far passare qc attraverso un buco *etc*; **to make a ~ at sb** (*col*) fare delle proposte *or* delle avances a qn; **things have come to a pretty ~** (*Brit*) ecco a cosa siamo arrivati
▶ **pass away** VI morire
▶ **pass by** VI passare ▶ VT trascurare

▶**pass down** VT (customs, inheritance) tramandare, trasmettere

▶**pass on** VI (die) spegnersi, mancare ▶VT (hand on): **to ~ on (to)** (news, information, object) passare (a); (cold, illness) attaccare (a); (benefits) trasmettere (a); (price rises) riversare (su)

▶**pass out** VI svenire; (BRIT Mil) uscire dall'accademia

▶**pass over** VI (die) spirare ▶VT lasciare da parte

▶**pass up** VT (opportunity) lasciarsi sfuggire, perdere

passable ['pɑːsəbl] ADJ (road) praticabile; (work) accettabile

passage ['pæsɪdʒ] N (gen) passaggio; (also: **passageway**) corridoio; (in book) brano, passo; (by boat) traversata

passenger ['pæsɪndʒər] N passeggero(-a)

passer-by [pɑːsə'baɪ] N passante mf

passing ['pɑːsɪŋ] ADJ (fig) fuggevole; **to mention sth in ~** accennare a qc di sfuggita

passing place N (Aut) piazzola (di sosta)

passion ['pæʃən] N passione f; amore m; **to have a ~ for sth** aver la passione di or per qc

passionate ['pæʃənɪt] ADJ appassionato(-a)

passion fruit N frutto della passione

passion play N rappresentazione f della Passione di Cristo

passive ['pæsɪv] ADJ (also Ling) passivo(-a)

passive smoking N fumo passivo

passkey ['pɑːskiː] N passe-partout m inv

Passover ['pɑːsəuvər] N Pasqua ebraica

passport ['pɑːspɔːt] N passaporto

passport control N controllo m passaporti inv

passport office N ufficio m passaporti inv

password ['pɑːswəːd] N parola d'ordine

past [pɑːst] PREP (further than) oltre, di là di; dopo; (later than) dopo ▶ADV: **to run ~** passare di corsa; **to walk ~** passare ▶ADJ passato(-a); (president etc) ex inv ▶N passato; **quarter/half ~ four** le quattro e un quarto/e mezzo; **ten/ twenty ~ four** le quattro e dieci/venti; **he's ~ forty** ha più di quarant'anni; **it's ~ midnight** è mezzanotte passata; **ten ~ eight** le otto e dieci; **for the ~ few days** da qualche giorno; in questi ultimi giorni; **for the ~ 3 days** negli ultimi 3 giorni; **in the ~** in or nel passato; (Ling) al passato; **I'm ~ caring** non me ne importa più nulla; **to be ~ it** (BRIT col: person) essere finito(-a)

pasta ['pæstə] N pasta

paste [peɪst] N (glue) colla; (Culin) pâté m inv; pasta ▶VT collare; **tomato ~** concentrato di pomodoro

pastel ['pæstl] ADJ pastello inv

pasteurized ['pæstəraɪzd] ADJ pastorizzato(-a)

pastille ['pæstl] N pastiglia

pastime ['pɑːstaɪm] N passatempo

past master N (BRIT): **to be a ~ at** essere molto esperto(-a) in

pastor ['pɑːstər] N pastore m

pastoral ['pɑːstərl] ADJ pastorale

past participle [-'pɑːtɪsɪpl] N (Ling) participio passato

pastry ['peɪstrɪ] N pasta

pasture ['pɑːstʃər] N pascolo

pasty¹ ['pæstɪ] N pasticcio di carne

pasty² ['peɪstɪ] ADJ pastoso(-a); (complexion) pallido(-a), smorto(-a)

pat [pæt] VT accarezzare, dare un colpetto (affettuoso) a ▶N: **a ~ of butter** un panetto di burro; **to give sb/o.s. a ~ on the back** (fig) congratularsi or compiacersi con qn/se stesso; **he knows it (off) ~**, (US) **he has it down ~** lo conosce or sa a menadito

patch [pætʃ] N (of material) toppa; (eye patch) benda; (spot) macchia; (of land) pezzo ▶VT (clothes) rattoppare; **a bad ~** (BRIT) un brutto periodo

▶**patch up** VT rappezzare

patchwork ['pætʃwəːk] N patchwork m inv

patchy ['pætʃɪ] ADJ irregolare

pate [peɪt] N: **a bald ~** una testa pelata

pâté ['pæteɪ] N pâté m inv

patent ['peɪtnt] N brevetto ▶VT brevettare ▶ADJ patente, manifesto(-a)

patent leather N cuoio verniciato

patently ['peɪtntlɪ] ADV palesemente

patent medicine N specialità f inv medicinale

patent office N ufficio brevetti

paternal [pə'təːnl] ADJ paterno(-a)

paternity [pə'təːnɪtɪ] N paternità

paternity leave [pə'təːnɪtɪ-] N congedo di paternità

paternity suit N (Law) causa di riconoscimento della paternità

path [pɑːθ] N sentiero, viottolo; viale m; (fig) via, strada; (of planet, missile) traiettoria

pathetic [pə'θetɪk] ADJ (pitiful) patetico(-a); (very bad) penoso(-a)

pathological [pæθə'lɔdʒɪkl] ADJ patologico(-a)

pathologist [pə'θɔlədʒɪst] N patologo(-a)

pathology [pə'θɔlədʒɪ] N patologia

pathos ['peɪθɔs] N pathos m

pathway ['pɑːθweɪ] N sentiero, viottolo

patience ['peɪʃns] N pazienza; (BRIT Cards) solitario; **to lose one's ~** spazientirsi

patient ['peɪʃnt] N paziente mf; malato(-a) ▶ADJ paziente; **to be ~ with sb** essere paziente or aver pazienza con qn

patiently ['peɪʃntlɪ] ADV pazientemente

patio ['pætɪəu] N terrazza

patriot ['peɪtrɪət] N patriota mf

patriotic [pætrɪˈɔtɪk] ADJ patriottico(-a)

patriotism [ˈpætrɪətɪzəm] N patriottismo

patrol [pəˈtrəʊl] N pattuglia ▶ VT pattugliare; **to be on ~** fare la ronda; essere in ricognizione; essere in perlustrazione

patrol boat N guardacoste m inv

patrol car N autoradio f inv (della polizia)

patrolman [pəˈtrəʊlmən] N (irreg) (US) poliziotto

patron [ˈpeɪtrən] N (in shop) cliente mf; (of charity) benefattore(-trice); **~ of the arts** mecenate mf

patronage [ˈpætrənɪdʒ] N patronato

patronize [ˈpætrənaɪz] VT essere cliente abituale di; (fig) trattare con condiscendenza

patronizing [ˈpætrənaɪzɪŋ] ADJ condiscendente

patron saint N patrono(-a)

patter [ˈpætəʳ] N picchiettio; (sales talk) propaganda di vendita ▶ VI picchiettare

pattern [ˈpætən] N modello; (Sewing etc) modello (di carta), cartamodello; (design) disegno, motivo; (sample) campione m; **behaviour patterns** tipi mpl di comportamento

patterned [ˈpætənd] ADJ a disegni, a motivi; (material) fantasia inv

paucity [ˈpɔːsɪtɪ] N scarsità

paunch [pɔːntʃ] N pancione m

pauper [ˈpɔːpəʳ] N indigente mf; **~'s grave** fossa comune

pause [pɔːz] N pausa ▶ VI fare una pausa, arrestarsi; **to ~ for breath** fermarsi un attimo per riprender fiato

pave [peɪv] VT pavimentare; **to ~ the way for** aprire la via a

pavement [ˈpeɪvmənt] N (BRIT) marciapiede m; (US) pavimentazione f stradale

> La parola inglese **pavement** non vuol dire pavimento.

pavilion [pəˈvɪlɪən] N padiglione m; tendone m; (Sport) edificio annesso ad un campo sportivo

paving [ˈpeɪvɪŋ] N pavimentazione f

paving stone N lastra di pietra

paw [pɔː] N zampa ▶ VT dare una zampata a; (person: pej) palpare

pawn [pɔːn] N pegno; (Chess) pedone m; (fig) pedina ▶ VT dare in pegno

pawnbroker [ˈpɔːnbrəʊkəʳ] N prestatore(-trice) su pegno

pawnshop [ˈpɔːnʃɔp] N monte m di pietà

pay [peɪ] (pt, pp **paid** [peɪd]) N stipendio; paga ▶ VT pagare; (also fig: be profitable to) convenire a ▶ VI pagare; (be profitable) rendere; **to ~ attention (to)** fare attenzione (a); **to ~ sb a visit** far visita a qn; **to ~ one's respects to sb** porgere i propri rispetti a qn; **I paid £5 for it** l'ho pagato 5 sterline; **how much did you ~ for it?** quanto l'ha pagato?; **to ~ one's way** pagare la propria

parte; (company) coprire le spese; **to ~ dividends** (fig) dare buoni frutti

▶ **pay back** VT rimborsare

▶ **pay for** VT FUS pagare

▶ **pay in** VT versare

▶ **pay off** VT (debts) saldare; (creditor) pagare; (mortgage) estinguere; (workers) licenziare ▶ VI (scheme) funzionare; (patience) dare i frutti; **to ~ sth off in instalments** pagare qc a rate

▶ **pay out** VT (money) sborsare, tirar fuori; (rope) far allentare

▶ **pay up** VT saldare

payable [ˈpeɪəbl] ADJ pagabile; **to make a cheque ~ to sb** intestare un assegno a (nome di) qn

pay-as-you-go [ˈpeɪəzjəˈgəʊ] ADJ (mobile phone) con scheda prepagata ·

pay award N aumento salariale

pay day, payday [ˈpeɪdeɪ] N giorno di paga

payday lender N istituto finanziario che effettua il prestito del giorno di paga

payday lending N prestito m del giorno di busta paga

payday loan N prestito m del giorno di busta paga

PAYE N ABBR (BRIT: = pay as you earn) pagamento di imposte tramite ritenute alla fonte

payee [peɪˈiː] N beneficiario(-a)

pay envelope N (US) busta f paga inv

paying [ˈpeɪɪŋ] ADJ: **~ guest** ospite mf pagante, pensionante mf

payload [ˈpeɪləʊd] N carico utile

payment [ˈpeɪmənt] N pagamento; versamento; saldo; **advance ~** (part sum) anticipo, acconto; (total sum) pagamento anticipato; **deferred ~, ~ by instalments** pagamento dilazionato or a rate; **in ~ for, in ~ of** in pagamento di; **on ~ of £5** dietro pagamento di 5 sterline

payout N pagamento; (in competition) premio

pay packet N (BRIT) busta f paga inv

payphone [ˈpeɪfəʊn] N cabina telefonica

payroll [ˈpeɪrəʊl] N ruolo (organico); **to be on a firm's ~** far parte del personale di una ditta

pay slip N (BRIT) foglio m paga inv

pay station N (US) cabina telefonica

pay television N televisione f a pagamento, pay-tv f inv

paywall [ˈpeɪwɔːl] N (Comput) paywall m inv

PBS N ABBR (US: = Public Broadcasting Service) servizio che collabora alla realizzazione di programmi per la rete televisiva nazionale

PBX ABBR (= private branch exchange) sistema telefonico con centralino

PC N ABBR = **personal computer**; (BRIT) = **police constable** ▶ ABBR (BRIT) = **Privy Councillor** ▶ ADJ ABBR = **politically correct**

pc ABBR = **per cent**; (= postcard) C.P.

p/c ABBR = **petty cash**

PCB N ABBR = **printed circuit board**

pcm ABBR = **per calendar month**

PD N ABBR (*US*) = **police department**

pd ABBR = **paid**

PDA N ABBR (= *personal digital assistant*) PDA *m inv*

PDQ ABBR (*col*) = **pretty damn quick**

PDSA N ABBR (*Brit*: = *People's Dispensary for Sick Animals*) assistenza veterinaria gratuita

PDT ABBR (*US*: = *Pacific Daylight Time*) ora legale del Pacifico

PE N ABBR (= *physical education*) ed. fisica ▶ ABBR (*Canada*) = **Prince Edward Island**

pea [piː] N pisello

peace [piːs] N pace *f*; (*calm*) calma, tranquillità; **to be at ~ with sb/sth** essere in pace con qn/qc; **to keep the ~** (*police*) mantenere l'ordine pubblico; (*citizen*) rispettare l'ordine pubblico

peaceable [ˈpiːsəbl] ADJ pacifico(-a)

peaceful [ˈpiːsful] ADJ pacifico(-a), calmo(-a)

peacekeeping [ˈpiːskiːpɪŋ] N mantenimento della pace; **~ force** forza di pace

peace offering N (*fig*) dono in segno di riconciliazione

peach [piːtʃ] N pesca

peacock [ˈpiːkɔk] N pavone *m*

peak [piːk] N (*of mountain*) cima, vetta; (*mountain itself*) picco; (*of cap*) visiera; (*fig*) massimo; (: *of career*) apice *m*

peak-hour [ˈpiːkauər] ADJ (*traffic etc*) delle ore di punta

peak hours NPL ore *fpl* di punta

peak period N periodo di punta

peak rate N tariffa massima

peaky [ˈpiːkɪ] ADJ (*Brit col*) sbattuto(-a)

peal [piːl] N (*of bells*) scampanio, carillon *m inv*; **peals of laughter** scoppi *mpl* di risa

peanut [ˈpiːnʌt] N arachide *f*, nocciolina americana

peanut butter N burro di arachidi

pear [pɛər] N pera

pearl [pəːl] N perla

peasant [ˈpɛznt] N contadino(-a)

peat [piːt] N torba

pebble [ˈpɛbl] N ciottolo

peck [pɛk] VT (*also*: **peck at**) beccare; (: *food*) mangiucchiare ▶ N colpo di becco; (*kiss*) bacetto

pecking order [ˈpɛkɪŋ-] N (*fig*) ordine *m* gerarchico

peckish [ˈpɛkɪʃ] ADJ (*Brit col*): **I feel ~** ho un languorino

peculiar [pɪˈkjuːlɪər] ADJ strano(-a), bizzarro(-a); (*particular: importance, qualities*) particolare; **~ to** tipico(-a) di, caratteristico(-a) di

peculiarity [pɪkjuːlɪˈærɪtɪ] N peculiarità *f inv*; (*oddity*) bizzarria

pecuniary [pɪˈkjuːnɪərɪ] ADJ pecuniario(-a)

pedal [ˈpɛdl] N pedale *m* ▶ VI pedalare

pedal bin N (*Brit*) pattumiera a pedale

pedalo [ˈpɛdələu] N pedalò *m inv*

pedantic [pɪˈdæntɪk] ADJ pedantesco(-a)

peddle [ˈpɛdl] VT (*goods*) andare in giro a vendere; (*drugs*) spacciare; (*gossip*) mettere in giro

peddler [ˈpɛdlər] N venditore(-trice) ambulante

pedestal [ˈpɛdstl] N piedestallo

pedestrian [pɪˈdɛstrɪən] N pedone(-a) ▶ ADJ pedonale; (*fig*) prosaico(-a), pedestre

pedestrian crossing N (*Brit*) passaggio pedonale

pedestrianized ADJ: **a ~ street** una zona pedonalizzata

pedestrian mall N (*US*) zona pedonale

pedestrian precinct, (*US*) **pedestrian zone** N zona pedonale

pediatrics [piːdɪˈætrɪks] N (*US*) = **paediatrics**

pedigree [ˈpɛdɪgriː] N stirpe *f*; (*of animal*) pedigree *m inv*; (*fig*) background *m inv* ▶ CPD (*animal*) di razza

pedlar [ˈpɛdlər] N = **peddler**

pedophile [ˈpɛdəufaɪl] N (*US*) = **paedophile**

pee [piː] VI (*col*) pisciare

peek [piːk] VI guardare furtivamente

peel [piːl] N buccia; (*of orange, lemon*) scorza ▶ VT sbucciare ▶ VI (*paint etc*) staccarsi
▶ **peel back** VT togliere, levare

peeler [piːlər] N: **potato ~** sbucciapatate *m inv*

peelings [ˈpiːlɪŋz] NPL bucce *fpl*

peep [piːp] N (*look*) sguardo furtivo, sbirciata; (*sound*) pigolio ▶ VI guardare furtivamente
▶ **peep out** VI mostrarsi furtivamente

peephole [ˈpiːphəul] N spioncino

peer [pɪər] VI: **to ~ at** scrutare ▶ N (*noble*) pari *m inv*; (*equal*) pari *mf*, uguale *mf*; (*contemporary*) contemporaneo(-a)

peerage [ˈpɪərɪdʒ] N dignità di pari; pari *mpl*

peerless [ˈpɪəlɪs] ADJ impareggiabile, senza pari

peeved [piːvd] ADJ stizzito(-a)

peevish [ˈpiːvɪʃ] ADJ stizzoso(-a)

peg [pɛg] N caviglia; (*tent peg*) picchetto; (*for coat etc*) attaccapanni *m inv*; (*Brit*: *also*: **clothes peg**) molletta ▶ VT (*clothes*) appendere con le mollette; (*Brit*: *groundsheet*) fissare con i picchetti; (*fig*: *prices, wages*) fissare, stabilizzare; **off the ~** confezionato(-a)

pejorative [pɪˈdʒɔrətɪv] ADJ peggiorativo(-a)

Pekin [piːˈkɪn], **Peking** [piːˈkɪn] N Pechino *f*

pekinese, pekingese [piːkɪˈniːz] N pechinese *m*

pelican [ˈpɛlɪkən] N pellicano

pelican crossing N (*Brit Aut*) attraversamento pedonale con semaforo a controllo manuale

pellet [ˈpɛlɪt] N pallottola, pallina

pell-mell [ˈpɛlˈmɛl] ADV disordinatamente, alla rinfusa

pelmet [ˈpɛlmɪt] N mantovana; cassonetto

pelt [pɛlt] VT: **to ~ sb (with)** bombardare qn (con) ▶ VI (rain) piovere a dirotto; (col: run) filare ▶ N pelle f

pelvis [ˈpɛlvɪs] N pelvi f inv, bacino

pen [pɛn] N penna; (for sheep) recinto; (US col: prison) galera; **to put ~ to paper** prendere la penna in mano

penal [ˈpiːnl] ADJ penale

penalize [ˈpiːnəlaɪz] VT punire; (Sport) penalizzare; (fig) svantaggiare

penal servitude [-ˈsəːvɪtjuːd] N lavori mpl forzati

penalty [ˈpɛnltɪ] N penalità f inv; sanzione f penale; (fine) ammenda; (Sport) penalizzazione f; (Football: also: **penalty kick**) calcio di rigore

penalty area N (BRIT Sport) area di rigore

penalty clause N penale f

penalty kick N (Football) calcio di rigore

penalty shoot-out [-ˈʃuːtaut] N (Football) rigori mpl; **to beat a team in a ~** battere una squadra ai rigori

penance [ˈpɛnəns] N penitenza

pence [pɛns] NPL (BRIT) of **penny**

penchant [ˈpɑ̃ːʃɑ̃ːŋ] N debole m

pencil [ˈpɛnsl] N matita ▶ VT (also: **pencil in**) scrivere a matita

pencil case N astuccio per matite

pencil sharpener N temperamatite m inv

pendant [ˈpɛndnt] N pendaglio

pending [ˈpɛndɪŋ] PREP in attesa di ▶ ADJ in sospeso

pendulum [ˈpɛndjuləm] N pendolo

penetrate [ˈpɛnɪtreɪt] VT penetrare

penetrating [ˈpɛnɪtreɪtɪŋ] ADJ penetrante

penetration [pɛnɪˈtreɪʃən] N penetrazione f

penfriend [ˈpɛnfrɛnd] N (BRIT) corrispondente mf

penguin [ˈpɛŋgwɪn] N pinguino

penicillin [pɛnɪˈsɪlɪn] N penicillina

peninsula [pəˈnɪnsjulə] N penisola

penis [ˈpiːnɪs] N pene m

penitence [ˈpɛnɪtns] N penitenza

penitent [ˈpɛnɪtnt] ADJ penitente

penitentiary [pɛnɪˈtɛnʃərɪ] N (US) carcere m

penknife [ˈpɛnnaɪf] N temperino

pen name N pseudonimo

pennant [ˈpɛnənt] N banderuola

penniless [ˈpɛnɪlɪs] ADJ senza un soldo

Pennines [ˈpɛnaɪnz] NPL: **the ~** i Pennini

penny [ˈpɛnɪ] (pl **pennies** [ˈpɛnɪz] or **pence** [pɛns]) N (BRIT) penny m; (US) centesimo

penpal [ˈpɛnpæl] N corrispondente mf

penpusher [ˈpɛnpuʃəʳ] N (pej) scribacchino(-a)

pension [ˈpɛnʃən] N pensione f
▶ **pension off** VT mandare in pensione

pensionable [ˈpɛnʃənəbl] ADJ (person) che ha diritto a una pensione, pensionabile; (age) pensionabile

pensioner [ˈpɛnʃənəʳ] N (BRIT) pensionato(-a)

pension fund N fondo pensioni

pensive [ˈpɛnsɪv] ADJ pensoso(-a)

pentagon [ˈpɛntəgən] N pentagono; **the P~** (US Pol) il Pentagono

Pentecost [ˈpɛntɪkɔst] N Pentecoste f

penthouse [ˈpɛnthaus] N appartamento (di lusso) nell'attico

pent-up [ˈpɛntʌp] ADJ (feelings) represso(-a)

penultimate [pɪˈnʌltɪmət] ADJ penultimo(-a)

penury [ˈpɛnjurɪ] N indigenza

people [ˈpiːpl] NPL gente f; persone fpl; (citizens) popolo ▶ N (nation, race) popolo ▶ VT popolare; **old ~** i vecchi; **young ~** i giovani; **~ at large** il grande pubblico; **a man of the ~** un uomo del popolo; **4/several ~ came** 4/parecchie persone sono venute; **the room was full of ~** la stanza era piena di gente; **~ say that ...** si dice or la gente dice che ...

> Use a singular verb with **gente**.
> The people were nice. **La gente era simpatica**.

pep [pɛp] N (col) dinamismo
▶ **pep up** VT vivacizzare; (food) rendere più gustoso(-a)

pepper [ˈpɛpəʳ] N pepe m; (vegetable) peperone m ▶ VT pepare; (fig): **to ~ with** spruzzare di

peppermint [ˈpɛpəmɪnt] N (plant) menta peperita; (sweet) pasticca di menta

pepperoni [pɛpəˈrəunɪ] N salsiccia piccante

pepperpot [ˈpɛpəpɔt] N pepaiola

pep talk [ˈpɛptɔːk] N (col) discorso di incoraggiamento

per [pəːʳ] PREP per; a; **~ hour** all'ora; **~ kilo** etc il chilo etc; **~ day** al giorno; **~ week** alla settimana; **~ person** a testa, a or per persona; **as ~ your instructions** secondo le vostre istruzioni

per annum ADV all'anno

per capita ADJ, ADV pro capite

perceive [pəˈsiːv] VT percepire; (notice) accorgersi di

per cent ADV per cento; **a 20 ~ discount** uno sconto del 20 per cento

percentage [pəˈsɛntɪdʒ] N percentuale f; **on a ~ basis** a percentuale

percentage point N punto percentuale

perceptible [pəˈsɛptɪbl] ADJ percettibile

perception [pəˈsɛpʃən] N percezione f; sensibilità; perspicacia

perceptive [pə'sɛptɪv] ADJ percettivo(-a); perspicace

perch [pə:tʃ] N (fish) pesce m persico; (for bird) sostegno, ramo ▶ VI appollaiarsi

percolate ['pə:kəleɪt] VT filtrare

percolator ['pə:kəleɪtə'] N caffettiera a pressione; caffettiera elettrica

percussion [pə'kʌʃən] N percussione f; (Mus) strumenti mpl a percussione

peremptory [pə'rɛmptərɪ] ADJ perentorio(-a)

perennial [pə'rɛnɪəl] ADJ perenne ▶ N pianta perenne

perfect ADJ ['pə:fɪkt] perfetto(-a) ▶ N (also: **perfect tense**) perfetto, passato prossimo ▶ VT [pə'fɛkt] perfezionare; mettere a punto; **he's a ~ stranger to me** mi è completamente sconosciuto

perfection [pə'fɛkʃən] N perfezione f

perfectionist [pə'fɛkʃənɪst] N perfezionista mf

perfectly ['pə:fɪktlɪ] ADV perfettamente, alla perfezione; **I'm ~ happy with the situation** sono completamente soddisfatta della situazione; **you know ~ well** sa benissimo

perforate ['pə:fəreɪt] VT perforare

perforated ulcer ['pə:fəreɪtɪd-] N (Med) ulcera perforata

perforation [pə:fə'reɪʃən] N perforazione f; (line of holes) dentellatura

perform [pə'fɔ:m] VT (carry out) eseguire, fare; (symphony etc) suonare; (play, ballet) dare; (opera) fare ▶ VI suonare; recitare

performance [pə'fɔ:məns] N esecuzione f; (at theatre etc) rappresentazione f, spettacolo; (of an artist) interpretazione f; (of player etc) performance f inv; (of car, engine) prestazione f; **the team put up a good ~** la squadra ha giocato una bella partita

performer [pə'fɔ:mə'] N artista mf

performing [pə'fɔ:mɪŋ] ADJ (animal) ammaestrato(-a)

performing arts NPL: **the ~** le arti dello spettacolo

perfume ['pə:fju:m] N profumo ▶ VT profumare

perfunctory [pə'fʌŋktərɪ] ADJ superficiale, per la forma

perhaps [pə'hæps] ADV forse; **~ he'll come** forse verrà, può darsi che venga; **~ so/not** forse sì/no, può darsi di sì/di no

peril ['pɛrɪl] N pericolo

perilous ['pɛrɪləs] ADJ pericoloso(-a)

perilously ['pɛrɪləslɪ] ADV: **they came ~ close to being caught** sono stati a un pelo dall'esser presi

perimeter [pə'rɪmɪtə'] N perimetro

perimeter wall N muro di cinta

period ['pɪərɪəd] N periodo; (Hist) epoca; (Scol) lezione f; (full stop) punto; (US Football) tempo; (Med) mestruazioni fpl ▶ ADJ (costume, furniture) d'epoca; **for a ~ of three weeks** per un periodo di or per la durata di tre settimane; **the holiday ~** (BRIT) il periodo delle vacanze

periodic [pɪərɪ'ɔdɪk] ADJ periodico(-a)

periodical [pɪərɪ'ɔdɪkl] ADJ periodico(-a) ▶ N periodico

periodically [pɪərɪ'ɔdɪklɪ] ADV periodicamente

period pains NPL (BRIT) dolori mpl mestruali

peripatetic [pɛrɪpə'tɛtɪk] ADJ (salesman) ambulante; (BRIT: teacher) peripatetico(-a)

peripheral [pə'rɪfərəl] ADJ periferico(-a) ▶ N (Comput) unità f inv periferica

periphery [pə'rɪfərɪ] N periferia

periscope ['pɛrɪskəup] N periscopio

perish ['pɛrɪʃ] VI perire, morire; (decay) deteriorarsi

perishable ['pɛrɪʃəbl] ADJ deperibile

perishables ['pɛrɪʃəblz] NPL merci fpl deperibili

perishing ['pɛrɪʃɪŋ] ADJ (BRIT col): **it's ~ (cold)** fa un freddo da morire

peritonitis [pɛrɪtə'naɪtɪs] N peritonite f

perjure ['pə:dʒə'] VT: **to ~ o.s.** spergiurare

perjury ['pə:dʒərɪ] N (Law: in court) falso giuramento; (breach of oath) spergiuro

perk [pə:k] N (col) vantaggio
▶ **perk up** VI (cheer up) rianimarsi

perky ['pə:kɪ] ADJ (cheerful) vivace, allegro(-a)

perm [pə:m] N (for hair) permanente f ▶ VT: **to have one's hair permed** farsi fare la permanente

permanence ['pə:mənəns] N permanenza

permanent ['pə:mənənt] ADJ permanente; (job, position) fisso(-a); (dye, ink) indelebile; **~ address** residenza fissa; **I'm not ~ here** non sono fisso qui

permanently ['pə:mənəntlɪ] ADV definitivamente

permeable ['pə:mɪəbl] ADJ permeabile

permeate ['pə:mɪeɪt] VI penetrare ▶ VT permeare

permissible [pə'mɪsɪbl] ADJ permissibile, ammissibile

permission [pə'mɪʃən] N permesso; **to give sb ~ to do sth** dare a qn il permesso di fare qc

permissive [pə'mɪsɪv] ADJ tollerante; **the ~ society** la società permissiva

permit N ['pə:mɪt] permesso; (entrance pass) lasciapassare m inv ▶ VT, VI [pə'mɪt] permettere; **fishing ~** licenza di pesca; **to ~ sb to do** permettere a qn di fare, dare il permesso a qn di fare; **weather permitting** tempo permettendo

permutation [pə:mju'teɪʃən] N permutazione f

pernicious [pə:'nɪʃəs] ADJ pernicioso(-a), nocivo(-a)

pernickety [pəˈnɪkɪtɪ] ADJ (col: person) pignolo(-a); (: task) da certosino

perpendicular [pəːpənˈdɪkjuləʳ] ADJ, N perpendicolare (f)

perpetrate [ˈpəːpɪtreɪt] VT perpetrare, commettere

perpetual [pəˈpɛtjuəl] ADJ perpetuo(-a)

perpetuate [pəˈpɛtjueɪt] VT perpetuare

perpetuity [pəːpɪˈtjuːɪtɪ] N: **in ~** in perpetuo

perplex [pəˈplɛks] VT lasciare perplesso(-a)

perplexing [pəˈplɛksɪŋ] ADJ che lascia perplesso(-a)

perquisites [ˈpəːkwɪzɪts] NPL (also: **perks**) benefici mpl collaterali

persecute [ˈpəːsɪkjuːt] VT perseguitare

persecution [pəːsɪˈkjuːʃən] N persecuzione f

perseverance [pəːsɪˈvɪərəns] N perseveranza

persevere [pəːsɪˈvɪəʳ] VI perseverare

Persia [ˈpəːʃə] N Persia

Persian [ˈpəːʃən] ADJ persiano(-a) ▶ N (Ling) persiano; **the ~ Gulf** n il Golfo Persico

Persian cat N gatto persiano

persist [pəˈsɪst] VI: **to ~ (in doing)** persistere (nel fare); ostinarsi (a fare)

persistence [pəˈsɪstəns] N persistenza; ostinazione f

persistent [pəˈsɪstənt] ADJ persistente; ostinato(-a); (lateness, rain) continuo(-a); **~ offender** (Law) delinquente mf abituale

persnickety [pəˈsnɪkɪtɪ] ADJ (US col) = **pernickety**

person [ˈpəːsn] N persona; **in ~** di or in persona, personalmente; **on** or **about one's ~** (weapon) su di sé; (money) con sé; **a ~ to ~ call** (Tel) una chiamata con preavviso

personable [ˈpəːsnəbl] ADJ di bell'aspetto

personal [ˈpəːsnl] ADJ personale; individuale; **~ belongings, ~ effects** oggetti mpl d'uso personale; **a ~ interview** un incontro privato

personal allowance N (Tax) quota del reddito non imponibile

personal assistant N segretaria personale

personal call N (Tel) chiamata con preavviso

personal column N messaggi mpl personali

personal computer N personal computer m inv

personal details NPL dati mpl personali

personal identification number N (Comput, Banking) codice m segreto, PIN m inv

personality [pəːsəˈnælɪtɪ] N personalità f inv

personally [ˈpəːsnəlɪ] ADV personalmente; **to take sth ~** prendere qc come una critica personale

personal organizer N agenda; (electronic) agenda elettronica

personal property N beni mpl personali

personal stereo N walkman® m inv

personify [pəːˈsɔnɪfaɪ] VT personificare

personnel [pəːsəˈnɛl] N personale m

personnel department N ufficio del personale

personnel manager N direttore(-trice) del personale

perspective [pəˈspɛktɪv] N prospettiva; **to get sth into ~** ridimensionare qc

Perspex® [ˈpəːspɛks] N (BRIT) plexiglas® m

perspicacity [pəːspɪˈkæsɪtɪ] N perspicacia

perspiration [pəːspɪˈreɪʃən] N traspirazione f, sudore m

perspire [pəˈspaɪəʳ] VI traspirare

persuade [pəˈsweɪd] VT: **to ~ sb to do sth** persuadere qn a fare qc; **to ~ sb of sth/that** persuadere qn di qc/che

persuasion [pəˈsweɪʒən] N persuasione f; (creed) convinzione f, credo

persuasive [pəˈsweɪsɪv] ADJ persuasivo(-a)

pert [pəːt] ADJ (bold) sfacciato(-a), impertinente; (hat) spiritoso(-a)

pertaining [pəːˈteɪnɪŋ]: **~ to** prep che riguarda

pertinent [ˈpəːtɪnənt] ADJ pertinente

perturb [pəˈtəːb] VT turbare

perturbing [pəˈtəːbɪŋ] ADJ inquietante

Peru [pəˈruː] N Perù m

perusal [pəˈruːzl] N attenta lettura

Peruvian [pəˈruːvjən] ADJ, N peruviano(-a)

pervade [pəˈveɪd] VT pervadere

pervasive [pəːˈveɪsɪv] ADJ (smell) penetrante; (influence) dilagante; (gloom, feelings) diffuso(-a)

perverse [pəˈvəːs] ADJ perverso(-a)

perversion [pəˈvəːʃən] N pervertimento, perversione f

perversity [pəˈvəːsɪtɪ] N perversità f inv

pervert N [ˈpəːvəːt] pervertito(-a) ▶ VT [pəˈvəːt] pervertire

pessimism [ˈpɛsɪmɪzəm] N pessimismo

pessimist [ˈpɛsɪmɪst] N pessimista mf

pessimistic [pɛsɪˈmɪstɪk] ADJ pessimistico(-a)

pest [pɛst] N animale m (or insetto) pestifero; (fig) peste f

pest control N disinfestazione f

pester [ˈpɛstəʳ] VT tormentare, molestare

pesticide [ˈpɛstɪsaɪd] N pesticida m

pestilence [ˈpɛstɪləns] N pestilenza

pestle [ˈpɛsl] N pestello

pet [pɛt] N animale m domestico; (favourite) favorito(-a) ▶ VT accarezzare ▶ VI (col) fare il petting; **~ lion** etc leone m etc ammaestrato; **teacher's ~** favorito(-a) del maestro

petal [ˈpɛtl] N petalo

peter [ˈpiːtəʳ]: **to ~ out** vi esaurirsi; estinguersi

petite [pəˈtiːt] ADJ piccolo(-a) e aggraziato(-a)

petition [pə'tɪʃən] N petizione f ▶ VI richiedere; **to ~ for divorce** presentare un'istanza di divorzio

pet name N (BRIT) nomignolo

petrified ['pɛtrɪfaɪd] ADJ (fig) morto(-a) di paura

petrify ['pɛtrɪfaɪ] VT pietrificare; (fig) terrorizzare

petrochemical [pɛtrə'kɛmɪkl] ADJ petrolchimico(-a)

petrodollars ['pɛtrəʊdɒləz] NPL petrodollari mpl

petrol ['pɛtrəl] N (BRIT) benzina

> La parola inglese **petrol** non vuol dire petrolio.

petrol bomb N (BRIT) (bottiglia) molotov f inv

petrol can N (BRIT) tanica per benzina

petrol engine N (BRIT) motore m a benzina

petroleum [pə'trəʊlɪəm] N petrolio

petroleum jelly N vaselina

petrolhead (col) ['petrəlhed] N fanatico(-a) dei motori m/f

petrol pump N (BRIT: in car, at garage) pompa di benzina

petrol station N (BRIT) stazione f di rifornimento

petrol tank N (BRIT) serbatoio della benzina

petticoat ['pɛtɪkəʊt] N sottana

pettifogging ['pɛtɪfɒgɪŋ] ADJ cavilloso(-a)

pettiness ['pɛtɪnɪs] N meschinità

petty ['pɛtɪ] ADJ (mean) meschino(-a); (unimportant) insignificante

petty cash N piccola cassa

petty officer N sottufficiale m di marina

petulant ['pɛtjʊlənt] ADJ irritabile

pew [pju:] N panca (di chiesa)

pewter ['pju:tər] N peltro

Pfc ABBR (US Mil) = **private first class**

PG N ABBR (Cine: = parental guidance) consenso dei genitori richiesto

PG 13 ABBR (US Cine: = Parental Guidance 13) vietato ai minori di 13 anni non accompagnati dai genitori

PGA N ABBR (= Professional Golfers Association) associazione dei giocatori di golf professionisti

PH N ABBR (US Mil: = Purple Heart) decorazione per ferite riportate in guerra

phallic ['fælɪk] ADJ fallico(-a)

phantom ['fæntəm] N fantasma m

Pharaoh ['fɛərəʊ] N faraone m

pharmaceutical [fɑːmə'sju:tɪkl] ADJ farmaceutico(-a) ▶ N: **pharmaceuticals** prodotti mpl farmaceutici

pharmacist ['fɑːməsɪst] N farmacista mf

pharmacy ['fɑːməsɪ] N farmacia

phase [feɪz] N fase f, periodo
> **phase in** VT introdurre gradualmente
> **phase out** VT (machinery) eliminare gradualmente; (product) ritirare gradualmente; (job, subsidy) abolire gradualmente

PhD N ABBR = **Doctor of Philosophy**

pheasant ['fɛznt] N fagiano

phenomena [fə'nɒmɪnə] NPL of **phenomenon**

phenomenal [fɪ'nɒmɪnl] ADJ fenomenale

phenomenon [fə'nɒmɪnən] (pl **phenomena** [-nə]) N fenomeno

phew [fju:] EXCL uff!

phial ['faɪəl] N fiala

philanderer [fɪ'lændərər] N donnaiolo

philanthropic [fɪlən'θrɒpɪk] ADJ filantropico(-a)

philanthropist [fɪ'lænθrəpɪst] N filantropo(-a)

philatelist [fɪ'lætəlɪst] N filatelico(-a)

philately [fɪ'lætəlɪ] N filatelia

Philippines ['fɪlɪpi:nz] NPL (also: **Philippine Islands**): **the ~** le Filippine

philosopher [fɪ'lɒsəfər] N filosofo(-a)

philosophical [fɪlə'sɒfɪkl] ADJ filosofico(-a)

philosophy [fɪ'lɒsəfɪ] N filosofia

phlegm [flɛm] N flemma

phlegmatic [flɛg'mætɪk] ADJ flemmatico(-a)

phobia ['fəʊbjə] N fobia

phone [fəʊn] N telefono ▶ VT telefonare a ▶ VI telefonare; **to be on the ~** avere il telefono; (be calling) essere al telefono
> **phone back** VT, VI richiamare
> **phone up** VT telefonare a ▶ VI telefonare

phone book N guida del telefono, elenco telefonico

phone box, (US) **phone booth** N cabina telefonica

phone call N telefonata

phonecard ['fəʊnkɑːd] N scheda telefonica

phone-in ['fəʊnɪn] N (BRIT Radio, TV) trasmissione radiofonica o televisiva con intervento telefonico degli ascoltatori

phone number N numero di telefono

phone tapping [-tæpɪŋ] N intercettazioni fpl telefoniche

phonetics [fə'nɛtɪks] N fonetica

phoney ['fəʊnɪ] ADJ falso(-a), fasullo(-a) ▶ N (person) ciarlatano(-a)

phonograph ['fəʊnəɡrɑːf] N (US) giradischi m inv

phony ['fəʊnɪ] ADJ, N = **phoney**

phosphate ['fɒsfeɪt] N fosfato

phosphorus ['fɒsfərəs] N fosforo

photo ['fəʊtəʊ] N foto f inv

photo... ['fəʊtəʊ] PREFIX foto...

photo album N (new) album m inv per fotografie; (containing photos) album m inv delle fotografie

photobomb (col) ['fəʊtəʊbɒm] VT fare il photobomb(ing) a

photocall ['fəʊtəʊkɔːl] N convocazione di fotoreporter a scopo pubblicitario

photocopier ['fəʊtəʊkɒpɪər] N fotocopiatrice f

p

photocopy [ˈfəutəukɔpɪ] N fotocopia ▶ VT fotocopiare

photoelectric [fəutəʊɪˈlɛktrɪk] ADJ: ~ **cell** cellula fotoelettrica

Photofit® [ˈfəutəufɪt] N photofit m inv

photogenic [fəutəʊˈdʒɛnɪk] ADJ fotogenico(-a)

photograph [ˈfəutəgræf] N fotografia ▶ VT fotografare; **to take a ~ of sb** fare una fotografia a or fotografare qn

photographer [fəˈtɔgrəfəʳ] N fotografo(-a)

photographic [fəutəˈgræfɪk] ADJ fotografico(-a)

photography [fəˈtɔgrəfɪ] N fotografia

photo opportunity N opportunità di scattare delle foto ad un personaggio importante

Photoshop® [ˈfəutəuʃɔp] N Photoshop® m

Photostat® [ˈfəutəustæt] N fotocopia

photosynthesis [fəutəʊˈsɪnθəsɪs] N fotosintesi f

phrase [freɪz] N espressione f; (Ling) locuzione f; (Mus) frase f ▶ VT esprimere; (letter) redigere

phrasebook [ˈfreɪzbuk] N vocabolarietto

physical [ˈfɪzɪkl] ADJ fisico(-a); ~ **examination** visita medica; ~ **education** educazione f fisica; ~ **exercises** ginnastica

physically [ˈfɪzɪklɪ] ADV fisicamente

physician [fɪˈzɪʃən] N medico

physicist [ˈfɪzɪsɪst] N fisico

physics [ˈfɪzɪks] N fisica

physiological [fɪzɪəˈlɔdʒɪkəl] ADJ fisiologico(-a)

physiology [fɪzɪˈɔlədʒɪ] N fisiologia

physiotherapist [fɪzɪəʊˈθɛrəpɪst] N fisioterapista mf

physiotherapy [fɪzɪəʊˈθɛrəpɪ] N fisioterapia

physique [fɪˈziːk] N fisico; costituzione f

pianist [ˈpiːənɪst] N pianista mf

piano [pɪˈænəu] N pianoforte m

piano accordion N (BRIT) fisarmonica (a tastiera)

piccolo [ˈpɪkələu] N ottavino

pick [pɪk] N (tool: also: **pickaxe**) piccone m ▶ VT scegliere; (gather) cogliere; (remove) togliere; (lock) far scattare; (scab, spot) grattarsi ▶ VI: **to ~ and choose** scegliere con cura; **take your ~** scelga; **the ~ of** il fior fiore di; **to ~ one's nose** mettersi le dita nel naso; **to ~ one's teeth** pulirsi i denti con lo stuzzicadenti; **to ~ sb's brains** farsi dare dei suggerimenti da qn; **to ~ pockets** borseggiare; **to ~ a fight/quarrel with sb** attaccar rissa/briga con qn; **to ~ one's way through** attraversare stando ben attento a dove mettere i piedi
▶ **pick off** VT (kill) abbattere
▶ **pick on** VT FUS (person) avercela con
▶ **pick out** VT scegliere; (distinguish) distinguere
▶ **pick up** VI (improve) migliorarsi ▶ VT raccogliere; (Police) prendere; (collect) passare a prendere; (Aut: give lift to) far salire; (person: for sexual encounter) rimorchiare; (learn) imparare; (Radio, TV, Tel) ricevere; **to ~ o.s. up** rialzarsi; **to ~ up where one left off** riprendere dal punto in cui si era fermati; **to ~ up speed** acquistare velocità

pickaxe, (US) **pickax** [ˈpɪkæks] N piccone m

picket [ˈpɪkɪt] N (in strike) scioperante mf che fa parte di un picchetto; picchetto ▶ VT picchettare

picket line N cordone m degli scioperanti

pickings [ˈpɪkɪŋz] NPL (pilferings): **there are good ~ to be had here** qui ci sono buone possibilità di intascare qualcosa sottobanco

pickle [ˈpɪkl] N (as condiment: also: **pickles**) sottaceti mpl; (fig): **in a ~** nei pasticci ▶ VT mettere sottaceto; mettere in salamoia

pick-me-up [ˈpɪkmiːʌp] N (col: drink) goccetto; (: tonic) tonico

pickpocket [ˈpɪkpɔkɪt] N borsaiolo

pickup [ˈpɪkʌp] N (BRIT: on record player) pick-up m inv; (small truck: also: **pickup truck**, **pickup van**) camioncino

picnic [ˈpɪknɪk] N picnic m inv ▶ VI fare un picnic

picnic area N area per il picnic

picnicker [ˈpɪknɪkəʳ] N chi partecipa a un picnic

pictorial [pɪkˈtɔːrɪəl] ADJ illustrato(-a)

picture [ˈpɪktʃəʳ] N quadro; (painting) pittura; (photograph) foto(grafia); (drawing) disegno; (TV) immagine f; (film) film m inv ▶ VT raffigurarsi; **the pictures** (BRIT) il cinema; **to take a ~ of sb/sth** fare una foto a qn/di qc; **we get a good ~ here** (TV) la ricezione qui è buona; **the overall ~** il quadro generale; **to put sb in the ~** mettere qn al corrente

picture book N libro illustrato

picture frame N cornice m inv

picture messaging N picture messaging m, invio di messaggini con immagini

picturesque [pɪktʃəˈrɛsk] ADJ pittoresco(-a)

picture window N finestra panoramica

piddling [ˈpɪdlɪŋ] ADJ (col) insignificante

pidgin English [ˈpɪdʒɪn-] N inglese semplificato misto ad elementi indigeni

pie [paɪ] N torta; (of meat) pasticcio

piebald [ˈpaɪbɔːld] ADJ pezzato(-a)

piece [piːs] N pezzo; (of land) appezzamento; (Draughts etc) pedina; (item): **a ~ of furniture/ advice** un mobile/consiglio ▶ VT: **to ~ together** mettere insieme; **in pieces** (broken) in pezzi; (not yet assembled) smontato(-a); **to take to pieces** smontare; **~ by ~** poco alla volta; **a 10p ~** (BRIT) una moneta da 10 pence; **a six-piece band** un complesso di sei strumentisti; **in one ~** (object) intatto; **to get back all in one ~** (person) tornare a casa incolume or sano e salvo; **to say one's ~** dire la propria

piecemeal [ˈpiːsmiːl] ADV pezzo a pezzo, a spizzico

piece rate N tariffa a cottimo

piecework ['piːswəːk] N (lavoro a) cottimo

pie chart N grafico a torta

Piedmont ['piːdmɒnt] N Piemonte *m*

pier [pɪə'] N molo; *(of bridge etc)* pila

pierce [pɪəs] VT forare; *(with arrow etc)* trafiggere; **to have one's ears pierced** farsi fare i buchi per gli orecchini

pierced ADJ: **I've got ~ ears** ho i buchi per gli orecchini

piercing ['pɪəsɪŋ] ADJ *(cry)* acuto(-a)

piety ['paɪətɪ] N pietà, devozione *f*

piffling ['pɪflɪŋ] ADJ insignificante

pig [pɪg] N maiale *m*, porco

pigeon ['pɪdʒən] N piccione *m*

pigeonhole ['pɪdʒənhəul] N casella ▶ VT classificare

pigeon-toed ['pɪdʒən'təud] ADJ che cammina con i piedi in dentro

piggy bank ['pɪgɪ-] N salvadanaio

pigheaded ['pɪg'hɛdɪd] ADJ caparbio(-a), cocciuto(-a)

piglet ['pɪglɪt] N porcellino

pigment ['pɪgmənt] N pigmento

pigmentation [pɪgmən'teɪʃən] N pigmentazione *f*

pigmy ['pɪgmɪ] N = **pygmy**

pigskin ['pɪgskɪn] N cinghiale *m*

pigsty ['pɪgstaɪ] N porcile *m*

pigtail ['pɪgteɪl] N treccina

pike [paɪk] N *(spear)* picca; *(fish)* luccio

pilchard ['pɪltʃəd] N *specie di sardina*

pile [paɪl] N *(pillar, of books)* pila; *(heap)* mucchio; *(of carpet)* pelo; **to ~ into** *(car)* stiparsi *or* ammucchiarsi in

▶ **pile up** VT ammucchiare ▶ VI ammucchiarsi; **in a ~** ammucchiato

▶ **pile on** VT: **to ~ it on** *(col)* esagerare, drammatizzare

piles [paɪlz] NPL *(Med)* emorroidi *fpl*

pileup ['paɪlʌp] N *(Aut)* tamponamento a catena

pilfer ['pɪlfə'] VT rubacchiare ▶ VI fare dei furtarelli

pilfering ['pɪlfərɪŋ] N rubacchiare *m*

pilgrim ['pɪlgrɪm] N pellegrino(-a)

I **Pilgrim Fathers** (Padri Pellegrini) erano un gruppo di puritani fuggiti dall'Inghilterra nel 1620 per salvarsi dalle persecuzioni religiose. Attraversato l'Atlantico a bordo della *Mayflower*, fondarono New Plymouth in Nuova Inghilterra, oggi Massachusetts. I Padri Pellegrini sono quindi considerati i fondatori degli Stati Uniti e sono commemorati ogni anno, il giorno di *Thanksgiving* che ricorda il successo del loro primo raccolto.

---

pilgrimage ['pɪlgrɪmɪdʒ] N pellegrinaggio

pill [pɪl] N pillola; **to be on the ~** prendere la pillola

pillage ['pɪlɪdʒ] VT saccheggiare

pillar ['pɪlə'] N colonna

pillar box N *(BRIT)* cassetta delle lettere (a colonnina)

pillion ['pɪljən] N *(of motor cycle)* sellino posteriore; **to ride ~** viaggiare dietro

pillory ['pɪlərɪ] N berlina ▶ VT mettere alla berlina

pillow ['pɪləu] N guanciale *m*

pillowcase ['pɪləukeɪs], **pillowslip** ['pɪləuslɪp] N federa

pilot ['paɪlət] N pilota *mf* ▶ CPD *(scheme etc)* pilota *inv* ▶ VT pilotare

pilot boat N pilotina

pilot light N fiamma *f* pilota *inv*

pimento [pɪ'mɛntəu] N peperoncino

pimp [pɪmp] N mezzano

pimple ['pɪmpl] N foruncolo

pimply ['pɪmplɪ] ADJ foruncoloso(-a)

PIN N ABBR (= *personal identification number*) codice *m* segreto, PIN *m inv*

pin [pɪn] N spillo; *(Tech)* perno; *(BRIT: drawing pin)* puntina da disegno; *(: Elec: of plug)* spinotto ▶ VT attaccare con uno spillo; **pins and needles** formicolio; **to ~ sth on sb** *(fig)* addossare la colpa di qc a qn

▶ **pin down** VT *(fig)*: **to ~ sb down** obbligare qn a pronunziarsi; **there's something strange here but I can't quite ~ it down** c'è qualcosa di strano qua ma non riesco a capire cos'è

pinafore ['pɪnəfɔː'] N *(also:* **pinafore dress***)* scamiciato

pinball ['pɪnbɔːl] N flipper *m inv*

pincers ['pɪnsəz] NPL pinzette *fpl*

pinch [pɪntʃ] N pizzicotto, pizzico ▶ VT pizzicare; *(col: steal)* grattare ▶ VI *(shoe)* stringere; **at a ~** in caso di bisogno; **to feel the ~** *(fig)* trovarsi nelle ristrettezze

pinched [pɪntʃt] ADJ *(drawn)* dai lineamenti tirati; *(short)*: **~ for money/space** a corto di soldi/di spazio; **~ with cold** raggrinzito dal freddo

pincushion ['pɪnkuʃən] N puntaspilli *m inv*

pine [paɪn] N *(also:* **pine tree***)* pino ▶ VI: **to ~ for** struggersi dal desiderio di

▶ **pine away** VI languire

pineapple ['paɪnæpl] N ananas *m inv*

pine cone N pigna

pine needles NPL aghi *mpl* di pino

ping [pɪŋ] N *(noise)* tintinnio

Ping-Pong® ['pɪŋpɔŋ] N ping-pong® *m*

pink [pɪŋk] ADJ rosa *inv* ▶ N *(colour)* rosa *m inv*; *(Bot)* garofano

pinking shears [ˈpɪŋkɪŋ-] N forbici *fpl* a zigzag

pin money N (*BRIT*) denaro per le piccole spese

pinnacle [ˈpɪnəkl] N pinnacolo

pinpoint [ˈpɪnpɔɪnt] VT indicare con precisione

pinstripe [ˈpɪnstraɪp] N stoffa gessata; (*also:* **pinstripe suit**) gessato

pint [paɪnt] N pinta (*Brit = 0.57 l; US = 0.47 l*); (*BRIT col: of beer*) ≈ birra grande

pinup [ˈpɪnʌp] N pin-up *mf inv*

pioneer [paɪəˈnɪəʳ] N pioniere(-a) ▶ VT essere un(a) pioniere in

pious [ˈpaɪəs] ADJ pio(-a)

pip [pɪp] N (*seed*) seme *m*; (*BRIT: time signal on radio*) segnale *m* orario

pipe [paɪp] N tubo; (*for smoking*) pipa; (*Mus*) piffero ▶ VT portare per mezzo di tubazione ■ **pipes** NPL (*also:* **bagpipes**) cornamusa (scozzese)

▶ **pipe down** VI (*col*) calmarsi

pipe cleaner N scovolino

piped music [paɪpt-] N musica di sottofondo

pipe dream N vana speranza

pipeline [ˈpaɪplaɪn] N conduttura; (*for oil*) oleodotto; (*for natural gas*) metanodotto; **it is in the ~** (*fig*) è in arrivo

piper [ˈpaɪpəʳ] N piffero; suonatore(-trice) di cornamusa

pipe tobacco N tabacco da pipa

piping [ˈpaɪpɪŋ] ADV: **~ hot** bollente

piquant [ˈpiːkənt] ADJ (*sauce*) piccante; (*conversation*) stimolante

pique [piːk] N picca

piracy [ˈpaɪərəsɪ] N pirateria

pirate [ˈpaɪərət] N pirata *m* ▶ VT (*record, video, book*) riprodurre abusivamente

pirate radio N (*BRIT*) radio pirata *f inv*

pirouette [pɪruˈɛt] N piroetta ▶ VI piroettare

Pisces [ˈpaɪsiːz] N Pesci *mpl*; **to be ~** essere dei Pesci

piss [pɪs] VI (*col!*) pisciare; **~ off!** vaffanculo! (!)

pissed [pɪst] ADJ (*BRIT col: drunk*) ubriaco(-a) fradicio(-a)

pistol [ˈpɪstl] N pistola

piston [ˈpɪstən] N pistone *m*

pit [pɪt] N buca, fossa; (*also:* **coal pit**) miniera; (*also:* **orchestra pit**) orchestra; (*quarry*) cava ▶ VT: **to ~ sb against sb** opporre qn a qn; **to ~ o.s. against** opporsi a ■ **pits** NPL (*Aut*) box *m*

pitapat [ˈpɪtəˈpæt] ADV (*BRIT*): **to go ~** (*heart*) palpitare, battere forte; (*rain*) picchiettare

pitch [pɪtʃ] N (*throw*) lancia; (*Mus*) tono; (*of voice*) altezza; (*fig: degree*) grado, punto; (*also:* **sales pitch**) discorso di vendita, imbonimento; (*BRIT Sport*) campo; (*Naut*) beccheggio; (*tar*) pece *f* ▶ VT (*throw*) lanciare ▶ VI (*fall*) cascare; (*Naut*) beccheggiare; **to ~ a tent** piantare una tenda; **at**

this ~ a questo ritmo

pitch-black [pɪtʃˈblæk] ADJ nero(-a) come la pece

pitched battle [pɪtʃt-] N battaglia campale

pitcher [ˈpɪtʃəʳ] N brocca

pitchfork [ˈpɪtʃfɔːk] N forcone *m*

piteous [ˈpɪtɪəs] ADJ pietoso(-a)

pitfall [ˈpɪtfɔːl] N trappola

pith [pɪθ] N (*of plant*) midollo; (*of orange*) parte *f* interna della scorza; (*fig*) essenza, succo; vigore *m*

pithead [ˈpɪthɛd] N (*BRIT*) imbocco della miniera

pithy [ˈpɪθɪ] ADJ conciso(-a); vigoroso(-a)

pitiable [ˈpɪtɪəbl] ADJ pietoso(-a)

pitiful [ˈpɪtɪful] ADJ (*touching*) pietoso(-a); (*contemptible*) miserabile

pitifully [ˈpɪtɪfəlɪ] ADV pietosamente; **it's ~ obvious** è penosamente chiaro

pitiless [ˈpɪtɪlɪs] ADJ spietato(-a)

pittance [ˈpɪtns] N miseria, magro salario

pitted [ˈpɪtɪd] ADJ: **~ with** (*potholes*) pieno(-a) di; (*chickenpox*) butterato(-a) da

pity [ˈpɪtɪ] N pietà ▶ VT aver pietà di, compatire, commiserare; **to have** *or* **take ~ on sb** aver pietà di qn; **it is a ~ that you can't come** è un peccato che non possa venire; **what a ~!** che peccato!

pitying [ˈpɪtɪɪŋ] ADJ compassionevole

pivot [ˈpɪvət] N perno ▶ VI imperniarsi

pixel [ˈpɪksl] N (*Comput*) pixel *m inv*

pixie [ˈpɪksɪ] N folletto

pizza [ˈpiːtsə] N pizza

placard [ˈplækɑːd] N affisso

placate [pləˈkeɪt] VT placare, calmare

placatory [pləˈkeɪtərɪ] ADJ conciliante

place [pleɪs] N posto, luogo; (*proper position, rank, seat*) posto; (*house*) casa, alloggio; (*home*): **at/to his ~** a casa sua; (*in street names*): **Laurel P~** via dei Lauri ▶ VT (*object*) posare, mettere; (*identify*) riconoscere; individuare; (*goods*) piazzare; **to take ~** aver luogo; succedere; **out of ~** (*not suitable*) inopportuno(-a); **I feel rather out of ~ here** qui mi sento un po' fuori posto; **in the first ~** in primo luogo; **to change places with sb** scambiare il posto con qn; **to put sb in his ~** (*fig*) mettere a posto qn, mettere qn al suo posto; **from ~ to ~** da un posto all'altro; **all over the ~** dappertutto; **he's going places** (*fig: col*) si sta facendo strada; **it is not my ~ to do it** non sta a me farlo; **how are you placed next week?** com'è messo la settimana prossima?; **to ~ an order with sb (for)** (*Comm*) fare un'ordinazione a qn (di); **to be placed** (*in race, exam*) classificarsi

placebo [pləˈsiːbəu] N placebo *m inv*

place mat N sottopiatto; (*in linen etc*) tovaglietta

placement [ˈpleɪsmənt] N collocamento; (*job*) lavoro

place name N toponimo

placenta [pləˈsɛntə] N placenta

placid [ˈplæsɪd] ADJ placido(-a), calmo(-a)

placidity [pləˈsɪdɪtɪ] N placidità

plagiarism [ˈpleɪdʒərɪzəm] N plagio

plagiarist [ˈpleɪdʒərɪst] N plagiario(-a)

plagiarize [ˈpleɪdʒəraɪz] VT plagiare

plague [pleɪg] N peste f ▶ VT tormentare; **to ~ sb with questions** assillare qn di domande

plaice [pleɪs] N (pl inv) pianuzza

plaid [plæd] N plaid m inv

plain [pleɪn] ADJ (clear) chiaro(-a), palese; (simple) semplice; (frank) franco(-a), aperto(-a); (not handsome) bruttino(-a); (without seasoning etc) scondito(-a); naturale; (in one colour) tinta unita inv ▶ ADV francamente, chiaramente ▶ N pianura; **to make sth ~ to sb** far capire chiaramente qc a qn; **in ~ clothes** (police) in borghese

plain chocolate N cioccolato fondente

plainly [ˈpleɪnlɪ] ADV chiaramente; (frankly) francamente

plainness [ˈpleɪnnɪs] N semplicità

plain speaking N: **there has been some ~ between the two leaders** i due leader si sono parlati chiaro

plaintiff [ˈpleɪntɪf] N attore(-trice)

plaintive [ˈpleɪntɪv] ADJ (voice, song) lamentoso(-a); (look) struggente

plait [plæt] N treccia ▶ VT intrecciare; **to ~ one's hair** farsi una treccia (or le trecce)

plan [plæn] N pianta; (scheme) progetto, piano ▶ VT (think in advance) progettare; (prepare) organizzare; (intend) avere in progetto ▶ VI: **to ~ (for)** far piani or progetti (per); **to ~ to do** progettare di fare, avere l'intenzione di fare; **how long do you ~ to stay?** quanto conta di restare?

plane [pleɪn] N (Aviat) aereo; (tree) platano; (tool) pialla; (Art, Math etc) piano ▶ ADJ piano(-a), piatto(-a) ▶ VT (with tool) piallare

planet [ˈplænɪt] N pianeta m

planetarium [plænɪˈtɛərɪəm] N planetario

plank [plæŋk] N tavola, asse f

plankton [ˈplæŋktən] N plancton m

planned economy [plænd-] N economia pianificata

planner [ˈplænəʳ] N pianificatore(-trice); (chart) calendario; **town** or (US) **city ~** urbanista mf

planning [ˈplænɪŋ] N progettazione f; (Pol, Econ) pianificazione f; **family ~** pianificazione delle nascite

planning permission N (BRIT) permesso di costruzione

plant [plɑːnt] N pianta; (machinery) impianto; (factory) fabbrica ▶ VT piantare; (bomb) mettere

plantation [plænˈteɪʃən] N piantagione f

plant pot N (BRIT) vaso (di fiori)

plaque [plæk] N placca

plasma [ˈplæzmə] N plasma m

plasma TV N TV f inv al plasma

plaster [ˈplɑːstəʳ] N intonaco; (also: **plaster of Paris**) gesso; (BRIT: also: **sticking plaster**) cerotto ▶ VT intonacare; ingessare; (col: mud etc) impiastricciare; (cover): **to ~ with** coprire di; **in ~** (BRIT: leg etc) ingessato(-a)

plasterboard [ˈplɑːstəbɔːd] N lastra di cartone ingessato

plaster cast N (Med) ingessatura, gesso; (model, statue) modello in gesso

plastered [ˈplɑːstəd] ADJ (col) ubriaco(-a) fradicio(-a)

plasterer [ˈplɑːstərəʳ] N intonacatore(-trice)

plastic [ˈplæstɪk] N plastica ▶ ADJ (made of plastic) di or in plastica; (flexible) plastico(-a), malleabile; (art) plastico(-a)

plastic bag N sacchetto di plastica

plastic bullet N pallottola di plastica

plastic explosive N esplosivo al plastico

plasticine® [ˈplæstɪsiːn] N plastilina®

plastic surgery N chirurgia plastica

plate [pleɪt] N (dish) piatto; (sheet of metal) lamiera; (Phot) lastra; (Typ) cliché m inv; (in book) tavola; (on door) targa, targhetta; (Aut: number plate) targa; (dental plate) dentiera; (dishes): **gold/silver ~** vasellame m d'oro/d'argento

plateau [ˈplætəʊ] N (pl **plateaus** or **plateaux** [-z]) N altipiano

plateful [ˈpleɪtful] N piatto

plate glass N vetro piano

platen [ˈplætən] N (on typewriter, printer) rullo

plate rack N scolapiatti m inv

platform [ˈplætfɔːm] N (stage, at meeting) palco; (BRIT: on bus) piattaforma; (Rail) marciapiede m; **the train leaves from ~ 7** il treno parte dal binario 7

platform ticket N (BRIT) biglietto d'ingresso ai binari

platinum [ˈplætɪnəm] N platino

platitude [ˈplætɪtjuːd] N luogo comune

platoon [pləˈtuːn] N plotone m

platter [ˈplætəʳ] N piatto

plaudits [ˈplɔːdɪts] NPL plauso

plausible [ˈplɔːzɪbl] ADJ plausibile, credibile; (person) convincente

play [pleɪ] N gioco; (Theat) commedia ▶ VT (game) giocare a; (team, opponent) giocare contro; (instrument, piece of music) suonare; (record, tape) ascoltare; (Theat, Cine: part) interpretare ▶ VI giocare; suonare; recitare; **to ~ safe** giocare sul sicuro; **to bring** or **call into ~** (plan) mettere in azione; (emotions) esprimere; **~ on words** gioco di parole; **to ~ a trick on sb** fare uno scherzo a qn; **they're playing at soldiers** stanno giocando ai soldati; **to ~ for time** (fig) cercare di

guadagnar tempo; **to ~ into sb's hands** (*fig*) fare il gioco di qn
▶ **play about, play around** VI (*person*) divertirsi; **to ~ about** *or* **around with** (*fiddle with*) giocherellare con; (*idea*) accarezzare
▶ **play along** VI: **to ~ along with** (*fig: person*) stare al gioco di; (*plan, idea*) fingere di assecondare ▶ VT (*fig*): **to ~ sb along** tenere qn in sospeso
▶ **play back** VT riascoltare, risentire
▶ **play down** VT minimizzare
▶ **play on** VT FUS (*sb's feelings, credulity*) giocare su; **to ~ on sb's nerves** dare sui nervi a qn
▶ **play up** VI (*cause trouble*) fare i capricci

playact ['pleɪækt] VI fare la commedia
playboy ['pleɪbɔɪ] N playboy *m inv*
played-out ['pleɪd'aut] ADJ spossato(-a)
player ['pleɪə^r] N giocatore(-trice); (*Theat*) attore(-trice); (*Mus*) musicista *mf*
playful ['pleɪful] ADJ giocoso(-a)
playgoer ['pleɪɡəuə^r] N assiduo(-a) frequentatore(-a) di teatri
playground ['pleɪɡraund] N (*in school*) cortile *m* per la ricreazione; (*in park*) parco *m* giochi *inv*
playgroup ['pleɪɡruːp] N giardino d'infanzia
playing card ['pleɪɪŋ-] N carta da gioco
playing field ['pleɪɪŋ-] N campo sportivo
playmaker ['pleɪmeɪkə^r] N (*Sport*) playmaker *m inv*
playmate ['pleɪmeɪt] N compagno(-a) di gioco
play-off ['pleɪɔf] N (*Sport*) bella
playpen ['pleɪpɛn] N box *m inv*
playroom ['pleɪruːm] N stanza dei giochi
playschool N = **playgroup**
plaything ['pleɪθɪŋ] N giocattolo
playtime ['pleɪtaɪm] N (*Scol*) ricreazione *f*
playwright ['pleɪraɪt] N drammaturgo(-a)
plc ABBR (*Brit*: = *public limited company*) società per azioni a responsabilità limitata quotata in borsa
plea [pliː] N (*request*) preghiera, domanda; (*excuse*) scusa; (*Law*) (argomento di) difesa
plea bargaining N (*Law*) patteggiamento
plead [pliːd] VT patrocinare; (*give as excuse*) addurre a pretesto ▶ VI (*Law*) perorare la causa; (*beg*): **to ~ with sb** implorare qn; **to ~ for sth** implorare qc; **to ~ guilty/not guilty** (*defendant*) dichiararsi colpevole/innocente
pleasant ['plɛznt] ADJ piacevole, gradevole
pleasantly ['plɛzntlɪ] ADV piacevolmente
pleasantry ['plɛzntrɪ] N (*joke*) scherzo; (*polite remark*): **to exchange pleasantries** scambiarsi i convenevoli
please [pliːz] VT piacere a ▶ VI (*think fit*): **do as you ~** faccia come le pare; **~!** per piacere!, per favore!; (*acceptance*) **yes, ~** sì, grazie; **my bill, ~** il conto, per piacere; **~ yourself!** come ti (*or* le) pare!; **~ don't cry!** ti prego, non piangere!

pleased [pliːzd] ADJ (*happy*) felice, lieto(-a); **~ (with)** (*satisfied*) contento(-a) (di); **we are ~ to inform you that ...** abbiamo il piacere di informarla che ...; **~ to meet you!** piacere!
pleasing ['pliːzɪŋ] ADJ piacevole, che fa piacere
pleasurable ['plɛʒərəbl] ADJ molto piacevole, molto gradevole
pleasure ['plɛʒə^r] N piacere *m*; **with ~** con piacere, volentieri; **"it's a ~"** "prego"; **is this trip for business or ~?** è un viaggio d'affari o di piacere?
pleasure cruise N crociera
pleat [pliːt] N piega
plebiscite ['plɛbɪsɪt] N plebiscito
plebs [plɛbz] NPL (*pej*) plebe *f*
plectrum ['plɛktrəm] N plettro
pledge [plɛdʒ] N pegno; (*promise*) promessa ▶ VT impegnare; promettere; **to ~ support for sb** impegnarsi a sostenere qn; **to ~ sb to secrecy** far promettere a qn di mantenere il segreto
plenary ['pliːnərɪ] ADJ plenario(-a); **in ~ session** in seduta plenaria
plentiful ['plɛntɪful] ADJ abbondante, copioso(-a)
plenty ['plɛntɪ] N abbondanza; **~ of** tanto(-a), molto(-a); un'abbondanza di; **we've got ~ of time to get there** abbiamo un sacco di tempo per arrivarci
pleurisy ['pluərɪsɪ] N pleurite *f*
Plexiglas® ['plɛksɪɡlɑːs] N (*US*) plexiglas® *m*
pliable ['plaɪəbl] ADJ flessibile; (*person*) malleabile
pliers ['plaɪəz] NPL pinza
plight [plaɪt] N situazione *f* critica
plimsolls ['plɪmsəlz] NPL (*Brit*) scarpe *fpl* da tennis
plinth [plɪnθ] N plinto; piedistallo
PLO N ABBR (= *Palestine Liberation Organization*) O.L.P. *f*
plod [plɔd] VI camminare a stento; (*fig*) sgobbare
plodder ['plɔdə^r] N sgobbone *m*
plodding ['plɔdɪŋ] ADJ lento(-a) e pesante
plonk [plɔŋk] (*col*) N (*Brit: wine*) vino da poco ▶ VT: **to ~ sth down** buttare giù qc bruscamente
plot [plɔt] N congiura, cospirazione *f*; (*of story, play*) trama; (*of land*) lotto ▶ VT (*mark out*) fare la pianta di; rilevare; (: *diagram etc*) tracciare; (*conspire*) congiurare, cospirare ▶ VI congiurare; **a vegetable ~** (*Brit*) un orticello
plotter ['plɔtə^r] N cospiratore(-trice); (*Comput*) plotter *m inv*, tracciatore *m* di curve
plough, (*US*) **plow** [plau] N aratro ▶ VT (*earth*) arare; **to ~ money into** (*company etc*) investire danaro in
▶ **plough back** VT (*Comm*) reinvestire

▶ **plough through** VT FUS (*snow etc*) procedere a fatica in

ploughing, (*US*) **plowing** [ˈplauɪŋ] N aratura

ploughman, (*US*) **plowman** [ˈplaumən] N (*irreg*) aratore *m*; **~'s lunch** (*BRIT*) semplice pasto a base di pane e formaggio

plow etc [plau] (*US*) = **plough** etc

ploy [plɔɪ] N stratagemma *m*

pls ABBR = **please**

pluck [plʌk] VT (*fruit*) cogliere; (*musical instrument*) pizzicare; (*bird*) spennare; (*hairs*) togliere ▶ N coraggio, fegato; **to ~ one's eyebrows** depilarsi le sopracciglia; **to ~ up courage** farsi coraggio

plucky [ˈplʌkɪ] ADJ coraggioso(-a)

plug [plʌg] N tappo; (*Elec*) spina; (*Aut: also:* **spark(ing) plug**) candela ▶ VT (*hole*) tappare; (*col: advertise*) spingere; **to give sb/sth a ~** fare pubblicità a qn/qc
▶ **plug in** (*Elec*) VI inserire la spina ▶ VT attaccare a una presa

plughole [ˈplʌghəul] N (*BRIT*) scarico

plug-in [ˈplʌgɪn] N (*Comput*) plug-in *m inv*

plum [plʌm] N (*fruit*) susina ▶ CPD: **~ job** (*col*) impiego ottimo *or* favoloso

plumage [ˈpluːmɪdʒ] N piume *fpl*, piumaggio

plumb [plʌm] ADJ verticale ▶ N piombo ▶ ADV (*exactly*) esattamente ▶ VT sondare
▶ **plumb in** VT (*washing machine*) collegare all'impianto idraulico

plumber [ˈplʌmə^r] N idraulico

plumbing [ˈplʌmɪŋ] N (*trade*) lavoro di idraulico; (*piping*) tubature *fpl*

plumbline [ˈplʌmlaɪn] N filo a piombo

plume [pluːm] N piuma, penna; (*decorative*) pennacchio

plummet [ˈplʌmɪt] VI: **to ~ (down)** cadere a piombo

plump [plʌmp] ADJ grassoccio(-a) ▶ VT: **to ~ sth (down) on** lasciar cadere qc di peso su
▶ **plump for** VT FUS (*col: choose*) decidersi per
▶ **plump up** VT sprimacciare

plunder [ˈplʌndə^r] N saccheggio ▶ VT saccheggiare

plunge [plʌndʒ] N tuffo; (*fig*) caduta ▶ VT immergere ▶ VI (*dive*) tuffarsi; (*fall*) cadere, precipitare; **to take the ~** (*fig*) saltare il fosso; **to ~ a room into darkness** far piombare una stanza nel buio

plunger [ˈplʌndʒə^r] N (*for blocked sink*) sturalavandini *m inv*

plunging [ˈplʌndʒɪŋ] ADJ (*neckline*) profondo(-a)

pluperfect [pluːˈpəːfɪkt] N piuccheperfetto

plural [ˈpluərl] ADJ, N plurale (*m*)

plus [plʌs] N (*also:* **plus sign**) segno più ▶ PREP più ▶ ADJ (*Math, Elec*) positivo(-a); **ten/twenty ~** più di dieci/venti; **it's a ~** (*fig*) è un vantaggio

plus fours NPL calzoni *mpl* alla zuava

plush [plʌʃ] ADJ lussuoso(-a) ▶ N felpa

plus-one [ˈplʌsˈwʌn] N accompagnatore(-trice)

plutonium [pluːˈtəunɪəm] N plutonio

ply [plaɪ] N (*of wool*) capo; (*of wood*) strato ▶ VT (*tool*) maneggiare; (*a trade*) esercitare ▶ VI (*ship*) fare il servizio; **three ~ (wool)** lana a tre capi; **to ~ sb with drink** dare da bere continuamente a qn

plywood [ˈplaɪwud] N legno compensato

PM N ABBR (*BRIT*) = **prime minister**

p.m. ADV ABBR (= *post meridiem*) del pomeriggio

PMS N ABBR (= *premenstrual syndrome*) sindrome *f* premestruale

PMT N ABBR (= *premenstrual tension*) sindrome *f* premestruale

pneumatic [njuːˈmætɪk] ADJ pneumatico(-a); **~ drill** martello pneumatico

pneumonia [njuːˈməunɪə] N polmonite *f*

PO N ABBR (= *Post Office*) ≈ P.T. (= *Poste e Telegrafi*) ▶ ABBR (*Naut*) = **petty officer**

po ABBR = **postal order**

POA N ABBR (*BRIT: = Prison Officers' Association*) sindacato delle guardie carcerarie

poach [pəutʃ] VT (*cook: egg*) affogare; (: *fish*) cuocere in bianco; (*steal*) cacciare (*or* pescare) di frodo ▶ VI fare il bracconiere

poached [pəutʃt] ADJ (*egg*) affogato(-a)

poacher [ˈpəutʃə^r] N bracconiere *m*

poaching [ˈpəutʃɪŋ] N caccia (*or* pesca) di frodo

PO box N ABBR = **post office box**

pocket [ˈpɔkɪt] N tasca ▶ VT intascare; **to be out of ~** (*BRIT*) rimetterci; **to be £5 in/out of ~** (*BRIT*) trovarsi con 5 sterline in più/in meno; **air ~** vuoto d'aria

pocketbook [ˈpɔkɪtbuk] N (*US: wallet*) portafoglio; (: *handbag*) busta; (*notebook*) taccuino

pocket knife N temperino

pocket money N paghetta, settimana

pockmarked [ˈpɔkmɑːkt] ADJ (*face*) butterato(-a)

pod [pɔd] N guscio ▶ VT sgusciare

podcast [ˈpɔdkɑːst] N podcast *m inv*

podcasting [ˈpɔdkɑːstɪŋ] N podcasting *m inv*

podgy [ˈpɔdʒɪ] ADJ grassoccio(-a)

podiatrist [pɔˈdiːətrɪst] N (*US*) callista *mf*, pedicure *mf*

podiatry [pɔˈdiːətrɪ] N (*US*) mestiere *m* di callista

podium [ˈpəudɪəm] N podio

POE N ABBR = **port of embarkation**; **port of entry**

poem [ˈpəuɪm] N poesia

poet [ˈpəuɪt] N poeta(-essa)

poetic [pəuˈɛtɪk] ADJ poetico(-a)

poet laureate N (*BRIT*) poeta *m* laureato

715

In Gran Bretagna il **poet laureate** è un poeta che riceve un vitalizio dalla casa reale britannica per scrivere delle poesie commemorative in occasione delle festività ufficiali.

poetry [ˈpəʊɪtrɪ] N poesia

poignant [ˈpɔɪnjənt] ADJ struggente

point [pɔɪnt] N (*gen*) punto; (*tip: of needle etc*) punta; (*BRIT Elec: also:* **power point**) presa (di corrente); (*in time*) punto, momento; (*Scol*) voto; (*main idea, important part*) nocciolo; (*also:* **decimal point**): **2 ~ 3 (2.3)** 2 virgola 3 (2,3) ▶ VT (*show*) indicare; (*gun etc*): **to ~ sth at** puntare qc contro ▶ VI: **to ~ at** mostrare a dito; **to ~ to** indicare; (*fig*) dimostrare ∎ **points** NPL (*Aut*) puntine fpl; (*Rail*) scambio; **to make a ~** fare un'osservazione; **to get/miss the ~** capire/non capire; **to come to the ~** venire al fatto; **when it comes to the ~** quando si arriva al dunque; **to be on the ~ of doing sth** essere sul punto di *or* stare (proprio) per fare qc; **to be beside the ~** non entrarci; **to make a ~ of doing sth** non mancare di fare qc; **there's no ~ (in doing)** è inutile (fare); **in ~ of fact** a dire il vero; **that's the whole ~!** precisamente!, sta tutto lì!; **you've got a ~ there!** giusto!, ha ragione!; **the train stops at Carlisle and all points south** il treno ferma a Carlisle e in tutte le stazioni a sud di Carlisle; **good points** vantaggi *mpl*; (*of person*) qualità *fpl*; **~ of departure** (*also fig*) punto di partenza; **~ of order** mozione *f* d'ordine; **~ of sale** (*Comm*) punto di vendita; **~ of view** punto di vista

▶ **point out** VT far notare

point-blank [ˈpɔɪntˈblæŋk] ADV (*also:* **at point-blank range**) a bruciapelo; (*fig*) categoricamente

point duty N (*BRIT*): **to be on ~** dirigere il traffico

pointed [ˈpɔɪntɪd] ADJ (*shape*) aguzzo(-a), appuntito(-a); (*remark*) specifico(-a)

pointedly [ˈpɔɪntɪdlɪ] ADV in maniera inequivocabile

pointer [ˈpɔɪntəʳ] N (*stick*) bacchetta; (*needle*) lancetta; (*clue*) indicazione *f*; (*advice*) consiglio; (*dog*) pointer *m inv*, cane *m* da punta

pointless [ˈpɔɪntlɪs] ADJ inutile, vano(-a)

poise [pɔɪz] N (*balance*) equilibrio; (*of head, body*) portamento; (*calmness*) calma ▶ VT tenere in equilibrio; **to be poised for** (*fig*) essere pronto(-a) a

poison [ˈpɔɪzn] N veleno ▶ VT avvelenare

poisoning [ˈpɔɪznɪŋ] N avvelenamento

poisonous [ˈpɔɪznəs] ADJ velenoso(-a); (*fumes*) venefico(-a), tossico(-a); (*ideas, literature*) pernicioso(-a); (*rumours, individual*) perfido(-a)

poke [pəʊk] VT (*fire*) attizzare; (*jab with finger, stick etc*) punzecchiare; (*put*): **to ~ sth in(to)** spingere qc dentro ▶ N (*jab*) colpetto; (*with elbow*) gomitata; **to ~ one's head out of the window** mettere la testa fuori dalla finestra; **to ~ fun at sb** prendere in giro qn

▶ **poke about, poke around** VI frugare

▶ **poke out** VI (*stick out*) sporgere fuori

poker [ˈpəʊkəʳ] N attizzatoio; (*Cards*) poker *m*

poker-faced [ˈpəʊkəˈfeɪst] ADJ dal viso impassibile

poky [ˈpəʊkɪ] ADJ piccolo(-a) e stretto(-a)

Poland [ˈpəʊlənd] N Polonia

polar [ˈpəʊləʳ] ADJ polare

polar bear N orso bianco

polarize [ˈpəʊləraɪz] VT polarizzare

Pole [pəʊl] N polacco(-a)

pole [pəʊl] N (*of wood*) palo; (*Elec, Geo*) polo

poleaxe, (*US*) **poleax** [ˈpəʊlæks] VT (*fig*) stendere

pole bean N (*US: runner bean*) fagiolino

polecat [ˈpəʊlkæt] N puzzola; (*US*) moffetta

Pol. Econ. [ˈpɒlɪkɒn] N ABBR = **political economy**

polemic [pɔˈlɛmɪk] N polemica

pole star N stella polare

pole vault N salto con l'asta

police [pəˈliːs] N polizia ▶ VT mantenere l'ordine in; (*streets, city, frontier*) presidiare; **a large number of ~ were hurt** molti poliziotti sono rimasti feriti

police car N macchina della polizia

police constable N (*BRIT*) agente *m* di polizia

police department N (*US*) dipartimento di polizia

police force N corpo di polizia, polizia

policeman [pəˈliːsmən] N (*irreg*) poliziotto, agente *m* di polizia

police officer N = **police constable**

police record N: **to have a ~** avere precedenti penali

police state N stato di polizia

police station N posto di polizia

policewoman [pəˈliːswumən] N (*irreg*) donna *f* poliziotto *inv*

policy [ˈpɒlɪsɪ] N politica; (*of newspaper, company*) linea di condotta, prassi *f inv*; (*also:* **insurance policy**) polizza (d'assicurazione); **to take out a ~** (*Insurance*) stipulare una polizza di assicurazione

policy holder N assicurato(-a)

policy-making [ˈpɒlɪsɪmeɪkɪŋ] N messa a punto di programmi

polio [ˈpəʊlɪəʊ] N polio *f*

Polish [ˈpəʊlɪʃ] ADJ polacco(-a) ▶ N (*Ling*) polacco

polish [ˈpɒlɪʃ] N (*for shoes*) lucido; (*for floor*) cera; (*for nails*) smalto; (*shine*) lucentezza, lustro; (*fig: refinement*) raffinatezza ▶ VT lucidare; (*fig: improve*) raffinare

▶ **polish off** VT (*work*) sbrigare; (*food*) mangiarsi

polished [ˈpɒlɪʃt] ADJ (*fig*) raffinato(-a)

polite [pə'laɪt] ADJ cortese; **it's not ~ to do that** non è educato *or* buona educazione fare questo

politely [pə'laɪtlɪ] ADV cortesemente

politeness [pə'laɪtnɪs] N cortesia

politic ['pɔlɪtɪk] ADJ diplomatico(-a)

political [pə'lɪtɪkl] ADJ politico(-a)

political asylum N asilo politico

politically [pə'lɪtɪklɪ] ADV politicamente

politically correct ADJ politicamente corretto(-a)

politician [pɔlɪ'tɪʃən] N politico

politics ['pɔlɪtɪks] N politica ▶ NPL (*views, policies*) idee *fpl* politiche

polka ['pɔlkə] N polca

polka dot N pois *m inv*

poll [pəul] N scrutinio; (*votes cast*) voti *mpl*; (*also:* **opinion poll**) sondaggio (d'opinioni) ▶ VT ottenere; **to go to the polls** (*voters*) andare alle urne; (*government*) indire le elezioni

pollen ['pɔlən] N polline *m*

pollen count N tasso di polline nell'aria

pollination [pɔlɪ'neɪʃən] N impollinazione *f*

polling ['pəulɪŋ] N (*Pol*) votazione *f*, votazioni *fpl*; (*Tel*) interrogazione *f* ciclica

polling booth N (*BRIT*) cabina elettorale

polling day N (*BRIT*) giorno delle elezioni

polling station N (*BRIT*) sezione *f* elettorale

pollster ['pəulstə^r] N chi esegue sondaggi d'opinione

poll tax N (*BRIT*) *imposta locale sulla persona fisica* (*non più in vigore*)

pollutant [pə'lu:tənt] N sostanza inquinante

pollute [pə'lu:t] VT inquinare

pollution [pə'lu:ʃən] N inquinamento

polo ['pəuləu] N polo

polo neck N collo alto; (*also:* **polo neck sweater**) dolcevita ▶ ADJ a collo alto

polo shirt N polo *f inv*

poly ['pɔlɪ] N ABBR (*BRIT*) = **polytechnic**

poly bag N (*BRIT col*) borsa di plastica

polyester [pɔlɪ'ɛstə^r] N poliestere *m*

polygamy [pə'lɪgəmɪ] N poligamia

polygraph ['pɔlɪgrɑːf] N macchina della verità

Polynesia [pɔlɪ'niːzɪə] N Polinesia

Polynesian [pɔlɪ'niːzɪən] ADJ, N polinesiano(-a)

polyp ['pɔlɪp] N (*Med*) polipo

polystyrene [pɔlɪ'staɪriːn] N polistirolo

polytechnic [pɔlɪ'tɛknɪk] N (*BRIT*) *istituto superiore ora inglobato nella struttura universitaria*

polythene ['pɔlɪθiːn] N politene *m*

polythene bag N sacchetto di plastica

polyurethane ['pɔlɪ'juərɪθeɪn] N poliuretano

pomegranate ['pɔmɪgrænɪt] N melagrana

pommel ['pɔml] N pomo ▶ VT = **pummel**

pomp [pɔmp] N pompa, fasto

pompom ['pɔmpɔm] N pompon *m inv*

pompous ['pɔmpəs] ADJ pomposo(-a); (*person*) pieno(-a) di boria

pond [pɔnd] N pozza; stagno; (*in park*) laghetto

ponder ['pɔndə^r] VI riflettere, meditare ▶ VT ponderare, riflettere su

ponderous ['pɔndərəs] ADJ ponderoso(-a), pesante

pong [pɔŋ] (*BRIT col*) N puzzo ▶ VI puzzare

pontiff ['pɔntɪf] N pontefice *m*

pontificate [pɔn'tɪfɪkeɪt] VI (*fig*): **to ~ (about)** pontificare (su)

pontoon [pɔn'tuːn] N pontone *m*; (*BRIT Cards*) ventuno

pony ['pəunɪ] N pony *m inv*

ponytail ['pəunɪteɪl] N coda di cavallo

pony trekking [-trɛkɪŋ] N (*BRIT*) escursione *f* a cavallo

poodle ['puːdl] N barboncino, barbone *m*

pooh-pooh [puː'puː] VT deridere

pool [puːl] N (*of rain*) pozza; (*pond*) stagno; (*artificial*) vasca; (*also:* **swimming pool**) piscina; (*fig: of light*) cerchio; (*sth shared*) fondo comune; (*Comm: consortium*) pool *m inv*; (*US: monopoly trust*) trust *m inv*; (*billiards*) specie di biliardo a buca ▶ VT mettere in comune; **typing ~**, (*US*) **secretary ~** servizio comune di dattilografia; **to do the (football) pools** ≈ fare la schedina, ≈ giocare al totocalcio

poor [puə^r] ADJ povero(-a); (*mediocre*) mediocre, cattivo(-a) ▶ NPL: **the ~** i poveri; **~ in** povero(-a) di

poorly ['puəlɪ] ADV poveramente; (*badly*) male ▶ ADJ indisposto(-a), malato(-a)

pop [pɔp] N (*noise*) schiocco; (*Mus*) musica pop; (*US col: father*) babbo; (*col: drink*) bevanda gasata ▶ VT (*put*) mettere (in fretta) ▶ VI scoppiare; (*cork*) schioccare; **she popped her head out** (*of the window*) sporse fuori la testa
  ▶ **pop in** VI passare
  ▶ **pop out** VI fare un salto fuori
  ▶ **pop up** VI apparire, sorgere

pop concert N concerto *m* pop *inv*

popcorn ['pɔpkɔːn] N pop-corn *m*

pope [pəup] N papa *m*

poplar ['pɔplə^r] N pioppo

poplin ['pɔplɪn] N popeline *f*

popper ['pɔpə^r] N (*BRIT*) bottone *m* a pressione, bottone *m* automatico

poppy ['pɔpɪ] N papavero

poppycock ['pɔpɪkɔk] N (*col*) scempiaggini *fpl*

Popsicle® ['pɔpsɪkl] N (*US: ice lolly*) ghiacciolo

pop star N pop star *f inv*

populace ['pɔpjuləs] N popolo

popular [ˈpɒpjʊləʳ] ADJ popolare; (*fashionable*) in voga; **to be ~ (with)** (*person*) essere benvoluto(-a) *or* ben visto(-a) (da); (*decision*) essere gradito(-a); **a ~ song** una canzone di successo

popularity [pɒpjʊˈlærɪtɪ] N popolarità

popularize [ˈpɒpjʊləraɪz] VT divulgare; (*science*) volgarizzare

populate [ˈpɒpjʊleɪt] VT popolare

population [pɒpjʊˈleɪʃən] N popolazione f

population explosion N forte espansione f demografica

populous [ˈpɒpjʊləs] ADJ popolato(-a)

pop-up ADJ (*Comput: menu, window*) a comparsa

porcelain [ˈpɔːslɪn] N porcellana

porch [pɔːtʃ] N veranda

porcupine [ˈpɔːkjʊpaɪn] N porcospino

pore [pɔːʳ] N poro ▶ VI: **to ~ over** essere immerso(-a) in

pork [pɔːk] N carne f di maiale

pork chop N braciola *or* costoletta di maiale

pork pie N (BRIT Culin) pasticcio di maiale in crosta

porn [pɔːn] (*col*) N pornografia ▶ ADJ porno *inv*

pornographic [pɔːnəˈgræfɪk] ADJ pornografico(-a)

pornography [pɔːˈnɒgrəfɪ] N pornografia

porous [ˈpɔːrəs] ADJ poroso(-a)

porpoise [ˈpɔːpəs] N focena

porridge [ˈpɒrɪdʒ] N porridge *m inv*

port¹ [pɔːt] N porto; (*opening in ship*) portello; (*Naut: left side*) babordo; (*Comput*) porta; **to ~** (*Naut*) a babordo; **~ of call** (porto di) scalo

port² [pɔːt] N (*wine*) porto

portable [ˈpɔːtəbl] ADJ portatile

portal [ˈpɔːtl] N portale *m*

portcullis [pɔːtˈkʌlɪs] N saracinesca

portent [ˈpɔːtɛnt] N presagio

porter [ˈpɔːtəʳ] N (*for luggage*) facchino, portabagagli *m inv*; (*doorkeeper*) portiere(-a), portinaio(-a); (US Rail) addetto ai vagoni letto

portfolio [pɔːtˈfəʊlɪəʊ] N (*case*) cartella; (*Pol: office, Econ*) portafoglio; (*of artist*) raccolta dei propri lavori

porthole [ˈpɔːthəʊl] N oblò *m inv*

portico [ˈpɔːtɪkəʊ] N portico

portion [ˈpɔːʃən] N porzione f

portly [ˈpɔːtlɪ] ADJ corpulento(-a)

portrait [ˈpɔːtreɪt] N ritratto

portray [pɔːˈtreɪ] VT fare il ritratto di; (*character on stage*) rappresentare; (*in writing*) ritrarre

portrayal [pɔːˈtreɪəl] N ritratto; rappresentazione f

Portugal [ˈpɔːtjʊgl] N Portogallo

Portuguese [pɔːtjʊˈgiːz] ADJ portoghese ▶ N (*pl inv*) portoghese mf; (*Ling*) portoghese m

Portuguese man-of-war [-mænəvˈwɔːʳ] N (*jellyfish*) medusa

pose [pəʊz] N posa ▶ VI posare; (*pretend*): **to ~ as** atteggiarsi a, posare a ▶ VT porre; **to strike a ~** mettersi in posa

poser [ˈpəʊzəʳ] N (*question*) domanda difficile; (*person*) = **poseur**

poseur [pəʊˈzəːʳ] N (*pej*) persona affettata

posh [pɒʃ] ADJ (*col*) elegante; (*family*) per bene ▶ ADV (*col*): **to talk ~** parlare in modo snob

position [pəˈzɪʃən] N posizione f; (*job*) posto ▶ VT sistemare, collocare; **to be in a ~ to do sth** essere nella posizione di fare qc

positive [ˈpɒzɪtɪv] ADJ positivo(-a); (*certain*) sicuro(-a), certo(-a); (*definite*) preciso(-a); definitivo(-a)

positively ADV (*affirmatively, enthusiastically*) positivamente; (*decisively*) decisamente; (*really*) assolutamente

posse [ˈpɒsɪ] N (US) drappello

possess [pəˈzɛs] VT possedere; **like one possessed** come un ossesso; **whatever can have possessed you?** cosa ti ha preso?

possession [pəˈzɛʃən] N possesso; (*object*) bene *m*; **to take ~ of sth** impossessarsi *or* impadronirsi di qc ■ **possessions** NPL (*belongings*) beni *mpl*

possessive [pəˈzɛsɪv] ADJ possessivo(-a)

possessiveness [pəˈzɛsɪvnɪs] N possessività

possessor [pəˈzɛsəʳ] N possessore (posseditrice)

possibility [pɒsɪˈbɪlɪtɪ] N possibilità f inv; **he's a ~ for the part** è uno dei candidati per la parte

possible [ˈpɒsɪbl] ADJ possibile; **it is ~ to do it** è possibile farlo; **if ~** se possibile; **as big as ~** il più grande possibile; **as far as ~** nei limiti del possibile

possibly [ˈpɒsɪblɪ] ADV (*perhaps*) forse; **if you ~ can** se le è possibile; **I cannot ~ come** proprio non posso venire

post [pəʊst] N (BRIT: *mail, letters, delivery*) posta; (: *collection*) levata; (*job, situation*) posto; (Mil) postazione f; (*pole*) palo; (*trading post*) stazione f commerciale; (*on blog, social network*) post *m inv*, commento ▶ VT (BRIT: *send by post*) impostare; (Mil) appostare; (*notice*) affiggere; (*to internet: video*) caricare; (: *comment*) mandare; (BRIT): (*appoint*) **to ~ to** assegnare a; **by ~** (BRIT) per posta; **by return of ~** (BRIT) a giro di posta; **to keep sb posted** tenere qn al corrente

> Int Italian **la posta** is used for post or mail. Use **il posto** for a post or job that you have, and use **il post** for a post that you make on the internet.

post... [pəʊst] PREFIX post...; **post-1990** dopo il 1990

postage [ˈpəʊstɪdʒ] N affrancatura

postage stamp N francobollo

postal ['pəustəl] ADJ postale

postal order N vaglia *m inv* postale

postbag ['pəustbæg] N (BRIT) sacco postale, sacco della posta

postbox ['pəustbɔks] N (BRIT) cassetta delle lettere

postcard ['pəustkɑːd] N cartolina

postcode ['pəustkəud] N (BRIT) codice *m* (di avviamento) postale

postdate ['pəust'deɪt] VT (*cheque*) postdatare

poster ['pəustə^r] N manifesto, affisso

poste restante [pəust'rɛstɑ̃ːnt] N (BRIT) fermo posta *m*

posterior [pɔs'tɪərɪə^r] N (col) deretano, didietro

posterity [pɔs'tɛrɪtɪ] N posterità

poster paint N tempera

post exchange N (US Mil) spaccio militare

post-free [pəust'friː] ADJ, ADV (BRIT) franco di porto

postgraduate ['pəust'grædjuət] N laureato/a che continua gli studi

posthumous ['pɔstjuməs] ADJ postumo(-a)

posthumously ['pɔstjuməslɪ] ADV dopo la mia (or sua etc) morte

posting ['pəustɪŋ] N (BRIT) incarico; (on blog, social network) post *m inv*, commento

postman ['pəustmən] N (irreg) postino

postmark ['pəustmɑːk] N bollo or timbro postale

postmaster ['pəustmɑːstə^r] N direttore(-trice) di un ufficio postale

postmistress ['pəustmɪstrɪs] N direttrice *f* di un ufficio postale

post-mortem [pəust'mɔːtəm] N autopsia; (fig) analisi *f inv* a posteriori

postnatal ['pəust'neɪtl] ADJ post-parto inv

post office N (building) ufficio postale; (organization) poste *fpl*; **the Post Office** ≈ le Poste e Telecomunicazioni

post office box N casella postale

post-paid ['pəust'peɪd] ADJ già affrancato(-a)

postpone [pəust'pəun] VT rinviare

postponement [pəust'pəunmənt] N rinvio

postscript ['pəustskrɪpt] N poscritto

postulate ['pɔstjuleɪt] VT postulare

posture ['pɔstʃə^r] N portamento; (pose) posa, atteggiamento ▶ VI posare

postwar ['pəust'wɔː^r] ADJ del dopoguerra

postwoman ['pəustwumən] N (irreg) (BRIT) postina

posy ['pəuzɪ] N mazzetto di fiori

pot [pɔt] N (for cooking) pentola; casseruola; (teapot) teiera; (coffeepot) caffettiera; (for plants, jam) vaso; (piece of pottery) ceramica; (col: mari-

juana) erba ▶ VT (plant) piantare in vaso; **a ~ of tea for two** tè per due; **to go to ~** (col: work, performance) andare in malora; **pots of** (BRIT col) un sacco di

potash ['pɔtæʃ] N potassa

potassium [pə'tæsɪəm] N potassio

potato [pə'teɪtəu] (pl potatoes) N patata

potato crisps, (US) **potato chips** NPL patatine *fpl*

potato flour N fecola di patate

potato peeler N sbucciapatate *m inv*

potbellied ['pɔtbɛlɪd] ADJ (from overeating) panciuto(-a); (from malnutrition) dal ventre gonfio

potency ['pəutnsɪ] N potenza; (of drink) forza

potent ['pəutnt] ADJ potente, forte

potentate ['pəutnteɪt] N potentato

potential [pə'tɛnʃl] ADJ potenziale ▶ N possibilità *fpl*; **to have ~** essere promettente

potentially [pə'tɛnʃəlɪ] ADV potenzialmente

pothole ['pɔthəul] N (in road) buca; (BRIT: underground) caverna

potholer ['pɔthəulə^r] N (BRIT) speleologo(-a)

potholing ['pɔthəulɪŋ] N (BRIT): **to go ~** fare la speleologia

potion ['pəuʃən] N pozione *f*

potluck [pɔt'lʌk] N: **to take ~** tentare la sorte

pot plant N pianta in vaso

potpourri [pəu'puriː] N (dried petals etc) miscuglio di petali essiccati profumati; (fig) pot-pourri *m inv*

pot roast N brasato

potshot ['pɔtʃɔt] N: **to take potshots at** tirare a casaccio contro

potted ['pɔtɪd] ADJ (food) in conserva; (plant) in vaso; (fig: shortened) condensato(-a)

potter ['pɔtə^r] N vasaio(-a) ▶ VI (BRIT): **to ~ around, ~ about** lavoracchiare; **to ~ round the house** sbrigare con calma le faccende di casa; **~'s wheel** tornio (da vasaio)

pottery ['pɔtərɪ] N ceramiche *fpl*; (factory) fabbrica di ceramiche; **a piece of ~** una ceramica

potty ['pɔtɪ] ADJ (BRIT col: mad) tocco(-a) ▶ N (child's) vasino

potty-trained ['pɔtɪtreɪnd] ADJ che ha imparato a farla nel vasino

pouch [pautʃ] N borsa; (Zool) marsupio

pouf, pouffe [puːf] N (stool) pouf *m inv*

poultice ['pəultɪs] N impiastro, cataplasma *m*

poultry ['pəultrɪ] N pollame *m*

poultry farm N azienda avicola

poultry farmer N pollicoltore(-trice)

pounce [pauns] VI: **to ~ (on)** balzare addosso (a), piombare (su) ▶ N balzo

pound [paund] N (weight) libbra (= 453g, 16 ounces); (money) (lira) sterlina (= 100 pence); (for dogs) canile *m* municipale ▶ VT (beat) battere;

p

(*crush*) pestare, polverizzare ▶ vi (*beat*) battere, martellare; **half a ~** mezza libbra; **a five-pound note** una banconota da cinque sterline

pounding ['paundɪŋ] N: **to take a ~** (*fig*) prendere una batosta

pound sterling N sterlina

pour [pɔːʳ] vt versare ▶ vi riversarsi; (*rain*) piovere a dirotto
▶ **pour away, pour off** vt vuotare
▶ **pour in** vi (*people*) entrare in fiotto; **to come pouring in** (*letters*) entrare a fiotti; (*cars, people*) affluire in gran quantità
▶ **pour out** vi (*people*) riversarsi fuori ▶ vt vuotare; versare; (*fig*) sfogare

pouring ['pɔːrɪŋ] ADJ: **~ rain** pioggia torrenziale

pout [paut] vi sporgere le labbra; fare il broncio

poverty ['pɔvətɪ] N povertà, miseria

poverty line N soglia di povertà

poverty-stricken ['pɔvətɪstrɪkən] ADJ molto povero(-a), misero(-a)

poverty trap N (*BRIT*) circolo vizioso della povertà

POW N ABBR = **prisoner of war**

powder ['paudəʳ] N polvere *f* ▶ vt spolverizzare; (*face*) incipriare; **powdered milk** latte *m* in polvere; **to ~ one's nose** incipriarsi il naso; (*euphemism*) andare alla toilette

powder compact N portacipria *m inv*

powder keg N (*fig: area*) polveriera; (: *situation*) situazione *f* esplosiva

powder puff N piumino della cipria

powder room N toilette *f inv* (per signore)

powdery ['paudərɪ] ADJ polveroso(-a)

power ['pauəʳ] N (*strength*) potenza, forza; (*ability, Pol: of party, leader*) potere *m*; (*Math*) potenza; (*Elec*) corrente *f* ▶ vt fornire di energia; azionare; **to be in ~** essere al potere; **to do all in one's ~ to help sb** fare tutto quello che si può per aiutare qn; **the world powers** le grandi potenze; **mental powers** capacità *fpl* mentali

powerboat ['pauəbaut] N (*BRIT*) motobarca, imbarcazione *f* a motore

power cut N (*BRIT*) interruzione *f or* mancanza di corrente

powered ['pauəd] ADJ: **~ by** azionato(-a) da; **nuclear-powered submarine** sottomarino a propulsione atomica

power failure N interruzione *f* della corrente elettrica

powerful ['pauəful] ADJ potente, forte

powerhouse ['pauəhaus] N (*fig: person*) persona molto dinamica; **a ~ of ideas** una miniera di idee

powerless ['pauəlɪs] ADJ impotente, senza potere; **~ to do** impossibilitato(-a) a fare

power line N linea elettrica

power of attorney N procura

power point N (*BRIT*) presa di corrente

power station N centrale *f* elettrica

power steering N (*Aut: also*: **power-assisted steering**) servosterzo

powwow ['pauwau] N riunione *f*

pp ABBR (= *pages*) pp; (*per procurationem*): **pp J. Smith** per il Signor J. Smith

PPE N ABBR (*BRIT Scol*: = *philosophy, politics, and economics*) *corso di laurea*

PPS N ABBR (*BRIT*: = *parliamentary private secretary*) *parlamentare che assiste un ministro*; = **post postscriptum**

PQ ABBR (*CANADA*) = **Province of Quebec**

PR N ABBR = **proportional representation**; **public relations** ▶ ABBR (*US*) = **Puerto Rico**

Pr. ABBR = **prince**

practicability [præktɪkə'bɪlɪtɪ] N praticabilità

practicable ['præktɪkəbl] ADJ (*scheme*) praticabile

practical ['præktɪkl] ADJ pratico(-a)

practicality [præktɪ'kælɪtɪ] N (*of plan*) fattibilità; (*of person*) senso pratico ■ **practicalities** NPL dettagli *mpl* pratici

practical joke N beffa

practically ['præktɪklɪ] ADV (*almost*) quasi, praticamente

practice ['præktɪs] N pratica; (*of profession*) esercizio; (*at football etc*) allenamento; (*business*) gabinetto; clientela ▶ vt, vi (*US*) = **practise; in ~** (*in reality*) in pratica; **out of ~** fuori esercizio; **2 hours' piano ~** 2 ore di esercizio al pianoforte; **it's common ~** è d'uso; **to put sth into ~** mettere qc in pratica; **target ~** pratica di tiro

practice match N partita di allenamento

practise, (*US*) **practice** ['præktɪs] vt (*work at*: *piano, one's backhand etc*) esercitarsi a; (*train for*: *skiing, running etc*) allenarsi a; (*a sport, religion*) praticare; (*method*) usare; (*profession*) esercitare ▶ vi esercitarsi; (*train*) allenarsi; (*lawyer, doctor*) esercitare; **to ~ for a match** allenarsi per una partita

practised, (*US*) **practiced** ADJ (*person*) esperto(-a); (*performance*) da virtuoso(-a); (*liar*) matricolato(-a); **with a ~ eye** con occhio esperto

practising, (*US*) **practicing** ADJ (*Christian etc*) praticante; (*lawyer*) che esercita la professione; (*homosexual*) attivo(-a)

practitioner [præk'tɪʃənəʳ] N professionista *mf*; (*Med*) medico

pragmatic [præg'mætɪk] ADJ pragmatico(-a)

Prague [prɑːg] N Praga

prairie ['prɛərɪ] N prateria

praise [preɪz] N elogio, lode *f* ▶ vt elogiare, lodare

praiseworthy ['preɪzwəːðɪ] ADJ lodevole

pram [præm] N (*BRIT*) carrozzina

prance [prɑːns] vɪ (*horse*) impennarsi

prank [præŋk] N burla

prat [præt] N (*BRIT col*) cretino(-a)

prattle [ˈprætl] vɪ cinguettare

prawn [prɔːn] N gamberetto

prawn cocktail N cocktail *m inv* di gamberetti

pray [preɪ] vɪ pregare

prayer [prɛəʳ] N preghiera

prayer book N libro di preghiere

pre... [priː] PREFIX pre...; **pre-1970** prima del 1970

preach [priːtʃ] vᴛ, vɪ predicare; **to ~ at sb** fare la predica a qn

preacher [ˈpriːtʃəʳ] N predicatore(-trice); (*US: minister*) pastore *m*

preamble [prɪˈæmbl] N preambolo

prearranged [priːəˈreɪndʒd] ADJ organizzato(-a) in anticipo

precarious [prɪˈkɛərɪəs] ADJ precario(-a)

precaution [prɪˈkɔːʃən] N precauzione *f*

precautionary [prɪˈkɔːʃənərɪ] ADJ (*measure*) precauzionale

precede [prɪˈsiːd] vᴛ, vɪ precedere

precedence [ˈprɛsɪdəns] N precedenza; **to take ~ over** avere la precedenza su

precedent [ˈprɛsɪdənt] N precedente *m*; **to establish** *or* **set a ~** creare un precedente

preceding [prɪˈsiːdɪŋ] ADJ precedente

precept [ˈpriːsɛpt] N precetto

precinct [ˈpriːsɪŋkt] N (*round cathedral*) recinto; (*US: district*) circoscrizione *f* ■ **precincts** NPL (*neighbourhood*) dintorni *mpl*, vicinanze *fpl*; **pedestrian ~** zona pedonale; **shopping ~** (*BRIT*) centro commerciale

precious [ˈprɛʃəs] ADJ prezioso(-a) ▶ ADV (*col*): **~ little/few** ben poco/pochi; **your ~ dog** (*ironic*) il suo amatissimo cane

precipice [ˈprɛsɪpɪs] N precipizio

precipitate ADJ [prɪˈsɪpɪtɪt] (*hasty*) precipitoso(-a) ▶ vᴛ [prɪˈsɪpɪteɪt] accelerare

precipitation [prɪsɪpɪˈteɪʃən] N precipitazione *f*

precipitous [prɪˈsɪpɪtəs] ADJ (*steep*) erto(-a), ripido(-a)

précis [ˈpreɪsiː] (*pl* ~ [-z]) N riassunto

precise [prɪˈsaɪs] ADJ preciso(-a)

precisely [prɪˈsaɪslɪ] ADV precisamente; **~!** appunto!

precision [prɪˈsɪʒən] N precisione *f*

preclude [prɪˈkluːd] vᴛ precludere, impedire; **to ~ sb from doing** impedire a qn di fare

precocious [prɪˈkəuʃəs] ADJ precoce

preconceived [priːkənˈsiːvd] ADJ (*idea*) preconcetto(-a)

preconception [priːkənˈsɛpʃən] N preconcetto

precondition [priːkənˈdɪʃən] N condizione *f* necessaria

precursor [priːˈkəːsəʳ] N precursore *m*

predate [priːˈdeɪt] vᴛ (*precede*) precedere

predator [ˈprɛdətəʳ] N predatore(-trice)

predatory [ˈprɛdətərɪ] ADJ predatore(-trice)

predecessor [ˈpriːdɪsɛsəʳ] N predecessore(-a)

predestination [priːdɛstɪˈneɪʃən] N predestinazione *f*

predetermine [priːdɪˈtəːmɪn] vᴛ predeterminare

predicament [prɪˈdɪkəmənt] N situazione *f* difficile

predicate [ˈprɛdɪkɪt] N (*Ling*) predicativo

predict [prɪˈdɪkt] vᴛ predire

predictable [prɪˈdɪktəbl] ADJ prevedibile

predictably [prɪˈdɪktəblɪ] ADV (*behave, react*) in modo prevedibile; **~, she didn't arrive** come era da prevedere, non è arrivata

prediction [prɪˈdɪkʃən] N predizione *f*

predispose [priːdɪsˈpəuz] vᴛ predisporre

predominance [prɪˈdɔmɪnəns] N predominanza

predominant [prɪˈdɔmɪnənt] ADJ predominante

predominantly [prɪˈdɔmɪnəntlɪ] ADV in maggior parte; soprattutto

predominate [prɪˈdɔmɪneɪt] vɪ predominare

pre-eminent [priːˈɛmɪnənt] ADJ preminente

pre-empt [prɪˈɛmpt] vᴛ acquistare per diritto di prelazione; (*fig*) anticipare

pre-emptive [prɪˈɛmptɪv] ADJ: **~ strike** azione *f* preventiva

preen [priːn] vᴛ: **to ~ itself** (*bird*) lisciarsi le penne; **to ~ o.s.** agghindarsi

prefab [ˈpriːfæb] N casa prefabbricata

prefabricated [priːˈfæbrɪkeɪtɪd] ADJ prefabbricato(-a)

preface [ˈprɛfəs] N prefazione *f*

prefect [ˈpriːfɛkt] N (*BRIT: in school*) studente/essa con funzioni disciplinari; (*Admin: in Italy*) prefetto

prefer [prɪˈfəːʳ] vᴛ preferire; (*Law: charges, complaint*) sporgere; (*: action*) intentare; **to ~ coffee to tea** preferire il caffè al tè; **to ~ doing** *or* **to do** preferire fare

preferable [ˈprɛfrəbl] ADJ preferibile

preferably [ˈprɛfrəblɪ] ADV preferibilmente

preference [ˈprɛfrəns] N preferenza; **in ~ to sth** piuttosto che qc

preference shares NPL (*BRIT*) azioni *fpl* privilegiate

preferential [prɛfəˈrɛnʃəl] ADJ preferenziale; **~ treatment** trattamento di favore

preferred stock [prɪˈfəːd-] N (*US*) = **preference shares**

prefix [ˈpriːfɪks] N prefisso

pregnancy [ˈprɛgnənsɪ] N gravidanza
pregnancy test N test *m inv* di gravidanza
pregnant [ˈprɛgnənt] ADJ incinta *adj f*; (*animal*) gravido(-a); (*fig: remark, pause*) significativo(-a); **3 months ~** incinta di 3 mesi
prehistoric [ˈpriːhɪsˈtɔrɪk] ADJ preistorico(-a)
prehistory [priːˈhɪstərɪ] N preistoria
prejudge [priːˈdʒʌdʒ] VT pregiudicare
prejudice [ˈprɛdʒudɪs] N pregiudizio; (*harm*) torto, danno ▶ VT pregiudicare, ledere; (*bias*): **to ~ sb in favour of/against** disporre bene/male qn verso
prejudiced [ˈprɛdʒudɪst] ADJ (*person*) pieno(-a) di pregiudizi; (*view*) prevenuto(-a); **to be ~ against sb/sth** essere prevenuto contro qn/qc; **~ (in favour of)** ben disposto(-a) (verso)
prelate [ˈprɛlət] N prelato
preliminaries [prɪˈlɪmɪnərɪz] NPL preliminari *mpl*
preliminary [prɪˈlɪmɪnərɪ] ADJ preliminare
prelude [ˈprɛljuːd] N preludio
premarital [ˈpriːˈmærɪtl] ADJ prematrimoniale
premature [ˈprɛmətʃuəʳ] ADJ prematuro(-a); (*arrival*) (molto) anticipato(-a); **you are being a little ~** è un po' troppo precipitoso
premeditated [priːˈmɛdɪteɪtɪd] ADJ premeditato(-a)
premeditation [priːmɛdɪˈteɪʃən] N premeditazione *f*
premenstrual syndrome, premenstrual tension [priːˈmɛnstruəl-] N (*Med*) sindrome *f* premestruale
premier [ˈprɛmɪəʳ] ADJ primo(-a) ▶ N (*Pol*) primo ministro
première [ˈprɛmɪɛəʳ] N prima
Premier League [prɛmɪəˈliːg] N (*Brit*) ≈ serie A
premise [ˈprɛmɪs] N premessa
premises [ˈprɛmɪsɪz] NPL locale *m*; **on the ~** sul posto; **business ~** locali commerciali
premium [ˈpriːmɪəm] N premio; **to be at a ~** (*fig: housing etc*) essere ricercatissimo; **to sell at a ~** (*shares*) vendere sopra la pari
premium bond N (*Brit*) obbligazione *f* a premio
premium deal N (*Comm*) offerta speciale
premium gasoline N (*US*) super *f*
premonition [prɛməˈnɪʃən] N premonizione *f*
preoccupation [priːɔkjuˈpeɪʃən] N preoccupazione *f*
preoccupied [priːˈɔkjupaɪd] ADJ preoccupato(-a)
pre-owned [priːˈəund] ADJ di seconda mano
prepackaged [priːˈpækɪdʒd] ADJ già impacchettato(-a)
prepaid [priːˈpeɪd] ADJ pagato(-a) in anticipo; (*envelope*) affrancato(-a)

preparation [prɛpəˈreɪʃən] N preparazione *f*
■ **preparations** NPL (*for trip, war*) preparativi *mpl*; **in ~ for sth** in vista di qc
preparatory [prɪˈpærətərɪ] ADJ preparatorio(-a); **~ to sth/to doing sth** prima di qc/di fare qc
preparatory school N (*Brit*) scuola elementare privata; (*US*) scuola superiore privata
prepare [prɪˈpɛəʳ] VT preparare ▶ VI: **to ~ for** prepararsi a
prepared [prɪˈpɛəd] ADJ: **~ for** preparato(-a) a; **~ to** pronto(-a) a; **to be ~ to help sb** (*willing*) essere disposto *or* pronto ad aiutare qn
preponderance [prɪˈpɔndərns] N preponderanza
preposition [prɛpəˈzɪʃən] N preposizione *f*
prepossessing [priːpəˈzɛsɪŋ] ADJ simpatico(-a), attraente
preposterous [prɪˈpɔstərəs] ADJ assurdo(-a)
prep school [prɛp-] N = **preparatory school**
prerecord [ˈpriːrɪˈkɔːd] VT registrare in anticipo; **prerecorded broadcast** trasmissione *f* registrata; **prerecorded cassette** (musi)cassetta
prerequisite [priːˈrɛkwɪzɪt] N requisito indispensabile
prerogative [prɪˈrɔgətɪv] N prerogativa
presbyterian [prɛzbɪˈtɪərɪən] ADJ, N presbiteriano(-a)
presbytery [ˈprɛzbɪtərɪ] N presbiterio
preschool [ˈpriːˈskuːl] ADJ (*age*) prescolastico(-a); (*child*) in età prescolastica
prescribe [prɪˈskraɪb] VT (*Med*) prescrivere, ordinare; **prescribed books** (*Brit Scol*) testi *mpl* in programma
prescription [prɪˈskrɪpʃən] N prescrizione *f*; (*Med*) ricetta; **to make up** *or* (*US*) **fill a ~** preparare *or* fare una ricetta; **"only available on ~"** "ottenibile solo dietro presentazione di ricetta medica"
prescription charges NPL (*Brit*) ticket *m inv*
prescriptive [prɪˈskrɪptɪv] ADJ normativo(-a)
presence [ˈprɛzns] N presenza; **~ of mind** presenza di spirito
present ADJ [ˈprɛznt] presente; (*wife, residence, job*) attuale ▶ N (*gift*) regalo; (*also:* **present tense**) tempo presente; **the ~** il presente ▶ VT [prɪˈzɛnt] presentare; (*give*): **to ~ sb with sth** offrire qc a qn; **to be ~ at** essere presente a; **those ~** i presenti; **at ~** al momento; **to give sb a ~** fare un regalo a qn; **to make sb a ~ of sth** regalare qc a qn
presentable [prɪˈzɛntəbl] ADJ presentabile
presentation [prɛznˈteɪʃən] N presentazione *f*; (*gift*) regalo, dono; (*ceremony*) consegna ufficiale; **on ~ of the voucher** dietro presentazione del buono

present-day [ˈprɛzntdeɪ] ADJ attuale, d'oggigiorno

presenter [prɪˈzɛntər] N (BRIT Radio, TV) presentatore(-trice)

presently [ˈprɛzntlɪ] ADV (soon) fra poco, presto; (US: now) adesso, ora

present participle N participio presente

preservation [prɛzəˈveɪʃən] N preservazione f, conservazione f

preservative [prɪˈzɜːvətɪv] N conservante m

preserve [prɪˈzɜːv] VT (keep safe) preservare, proteggere; (maintain) conservare; (food) mettere in conserva ▶ N (for game, fish) riserva; (often pl: jam) marmellata; (: fruit) frutta sciroppata

preshrunk [priːˈʃrʌŋk] ADJ irrestringibile

preside [prɪˈzaɪd] VI: **to ~ (over)** presiedere (a)

presidency [ˈprɛzɪdənsɪ] N presidenza; (US: of company) direzione f

president [ˈprɛzɪdənt] N presidente m; (US: of company) direttore(-trice) generale

presidential [prɛzɪˈdɛnʃl] ADJ presidenziale

press [prɛs] N (tool, machine) pressa; (for wine) torchio; (newspapers) stampa; (crowd) folla ▶ VT (push) premere, pigiare; (doorbell) suonare; (squeeze) spremere; (: hand) stringere; (clothes: iron) stirare; (pursue) incalzare; (insist): **to ~ on sb** far accettare qc da qn; (urge, entreat): **to ~ sb to do** or **into doing sth** fare pressione su qn affinché faccia qc ▶ VI premere; accalcare; **to go to ~** (newspaper) andare in macchina; **to be in the ~** (in the newspapers) essere sui giornali; **we are pressed for time** ci manca il tempo; **to ~ for sth** insistere per avere qc; **to ~ sb for an answer** insistere perché qn risponda; **to ~ charges against sb** (Law) sporgere una denuncia contro qn

▶ **press ahead** VI: **to ~ ahead (with)** andare avanti (con)

▶ **press on** VI continuare

press agency N agenzia di stampa

press clipping N ritaglio di giornale

press conference N conferenza f stampa inv

press cutting N = **press clipping**

press-gang [ˈprɛsgæŋ] VT: **to ~ sb into doing sth** costringere qn a viva forza a fare qc

pressing [ˈprɛsɪŋ] ADJ urgente ▶ N stiratura

press officer N addetto(-a) stampa inv

press release N comunicato m stampa inv

press stud N (BRIT) bottone m a pressione

press-up [ˈprɛsʌp] N (BRIT) flessione f sulle braccia

pressure [ˈprɛʃər] N pressione f ▶ VT: **to put ~ on sb (to do)** mettere qn sotto pressione (affinché faccia); **high/low ~** alta/bassa pressione

pressure cooker N pentola a pressione

pressure gauge N manometro

pressure group N gruppo di pressione

pressurize [ˈprɛʃəraɪz] VT pressurizzare; (fig): **to ~ sb (into doing sth)** fare delle pressioni su qn (per costringerlo a fare qc)

pressurized [ˈprɛʃəraɪzd] ADJ pressurizzato(-a)

prestige [prɛsˈtiːʒ] N prestigio

prestigious [prɛsˈtɪdʒəs] ADJ prestigioso(-a)

presumably [prɪˈzjuːməblɪ] ADV presumibilmente; **~ he did it** penso or presumo che l'abbia fatto

presume [prɪˈzjuːm] VT supporre; **to ~ to do** (dare) permettersi di fare

presumption [prɪˈzʌmpʃən] N presunzione f; (boldness) audacia

presumptuous [prɪˈzʌmpʃəs] ADJ presuntuoso(-a)

presuppose [priːsəˈpəuz] VT presupporre

pre-tax [priːˈtæks] ADJ al lordo d'imposta

pretence, (US) **pretense** [prɪˈtɛns] N (claim) pretesa; (pretext) pretesto, scusa; **to make a ~ of doing** far finta di fare; **on** or **under the ~ of doing sth** con il pretesto or la scusa di fare qc; **she is devoid of all ~** non si nasconde dietro false apparenze; **under false pretences** con l'inganno

pretend [prɪˈtɛnd] VT (feign) fingere ▶ VI far finta; (claim): **to ~ to sth** pretendere a qc; **to ~ to do** far finta di fare

pretense [prɪˈtɛns] N (US) = **pretence**

pretension [prɪˈtɛnʃən] N (claim) pretesa; **to have no pretensions to sth/to being sth** non avere la pretesa di avere qc/di essere qc

pretentious [prɪˈtɛnʃəs] ADJ pretenzioso(-a)

preterite [ˈprɛtərɪt] N preterito

pretext [ˈpriːtɛkst] N pretesto; **on** or **under the ~ of doing sth** col pretesto di fare qc

pretty [ˈprɪtɪ] ADJ grazioso(-a), carino(-a) ▶ ADV abbastanza, assai

prevail [prɪˈveɪl] VI (win, be usual) prevalere; (persuade): **to ~ (up)on sb to do** persuadere qn a fare

prevailing [prɪˈveɪlɪŋ] ADJ dominante

prevalent [ˈprɛvələnt] ADJ (belief) predominante; (customs) diffuso(-a); (fashion) corrente; (disease) comune

prevarication [prɪværɪˈkeɪʃən] N tergiversazione f

prevent [prɪˈvɛnt] VT prevenire; **to ~ sb from doing** impedire a qn di fare; **to ~ sth from happening** impedire che qc succeda

preventable [prɪˈvɛntəbl] ADJ evitabile

preventative [prɪˈvɛntətɪv] ADJ preventivo(-a)

prevention [prɪˈvɛnʃən] N prevenzione f

preventive [prɪˈvɛntɪv] ADJ preventivo(-a)

preview [ˈpriːvjuː] N (of film) anteprima

previous [ˈpriːvɪəs] ADJ precedente; anteriore; **I have a ~ engagement** ho già (preso) un impegno; **~ to doing** prima di fare

p

723

previously [ˈpriːvɪəslɪ] ADV prima

prewar [ˈpriːˈwɔːʳ] ADJ anteguerra *inv*

prey [preɪ] N preda ▶ VI: **to ~ on** far preda di; **it was preying on his mind** lo stava ossessionando

price [praɪs] N prezzo; (*Betting: odds*) quotazione f ▶ VT (*goods*) fissare il prezzo di; valutare; **what is the ~ of ...?** quanto costa ...?; **to go up** *or* **rise in ~** salire *or* aumentare di prezzo; **to put a ~ on sth** valutare *or* stimare qc; **he regained his freedom, but at a ~** ha riconquistato la sua libertà, ma a caro prezzo; **what ~ his promises now?** a che valgono ora le sue promesse?; **to be priced out of the market** (*article*) essere così caro da diventare invendibile; (*producer, nation*) non poter sostenere la concorrenza

price control N controllo dei prezzi

price-cutting [ˈpraɪskʌtɪŋ] N riduzione f dei prezzi

priceless [ˈpraɪslɪs] ADJ di valore inestimabile; (*col: amusing*) impagabile, spassosissimo(-a)

price list N listino (dei) prezzi

price range N gamma di prezzi; **it's within my ~** rientra nelle mie possibilità

price tag N cartellino del prezzo

price war N guerra dei prezzi

pricey [ˈpraɪsɪ] ADJ (*col*) caruccio(-a)

prick [prɪk] N puntura ▶ VT pungere; **to ~ up one's ears** drizzare gli orecchi

prickle [ˈprɪkl] N (*of plant*) spina; (*sensation*) pizzicore m

prickly [ˈprɪklɪ] ADJ spinoso(-a); (*fig: person*) permaloso(-a)

prickly heat N sudamina

prickly pear N fico d'India

pride [praɪd] N orgoglio; (*pej*) superbia ▶ VT: **to ~ o.s. on** essere orgoglioso(-a) di; vantarsi di; **to take (a) ~ in** tenere molto a; essere orgoglioso di; **to take a ~ in doing** andare orgoglioso di fare; **to have ~ of place** (*BRIT*) essere al primo posto

priest [priːst] N prete m, sacerdote m

priestess [ˈpriːstɪs] N sacerdotessa

priesthood [ˈpriːsthud] N sacerdozio

prig [prɪg] N: **he's a ~** è compiaciuto di se stesso

prim [prɪm] ADJ pudico(-a); contegnoso(-a)

primacy [ˈpraɪməsɪ] N primato

prima facie [ˈpraɪməˈfeɪʃɪ] ADJ: **to have a ~ case** (*Law*) presentare una causa in apparenza fondata

primal [ˈpraɪməl] ADJ primitivo(-a), originario(-a)

primarily [ˈpraɪmərɪlɪ] ADV principalmente, essenzialmente

primary [ˈpraɪmərɪ] ADJ primario(-a); (*first in importance*) primo(-a) ▶ N (*US: election*) primarie fpl; *vedi nota*

Negli Stati Uniti, attraverso le **primaries** viene fatta una prima scrematura dei candidati dei partiti alle elezioni presidenziali. La scelta definitiva del candidato da presentare alla presidenza si basa sui risultati delle *primaries* e ha luogo durante le *Conventions* dei partiti, che si tengono in luglio e in agosto.

primary colour N colore m fondamentale

primary school N (*BRIT*) scuola elementare

In Gran Bretagna la **primary school** è la scuola elementare, frequentata dai bambini dai 5 agli 11 anni di età. È suddivisa in *infant school* (5-7 anni) e *junior school* (7-11 anni).

primate [(*Rel*) ˈpraɪmɪt, (*Zool*) ˈpraɪmeɪt] N primate m

prime [praɪm] ADJ primario(-a), fondamentale; (*excellent*) di prima qualità ▶ N: **in the ~ of life** nel fiore della vita ▶ VT (*gun*) innescare; (*pump*) adescare; (*wood*) preparare; (*fig*) mettere al corrente

prime minister N primo ministro

primer [ˈpraɪməʳ] N (*book*) testo elementare; (*paint*) vernice f base *inv*

prime time N (*Radio, TV*) fascia di massimo ascolto

primeval [praɪˈmiːvl] ADJ primitivo(-a)

primitive [ˈprɪmɪtɪv] ADJ primitivo(-a)

primrose [ˈprɪmrəuz] N primavera

primus® [ˈpraɪməs], **primus stove**® N (*BRIT*) fornello a petrolio

prince [prɪns] N principe m

prince charming N principe m azzurro

princess [prɪnˈses] N principessa

principal [ˈprɪnsɪpl] ADJ principale ▶ N (*of school, college etc*) preside mf; (*money*) capitale m; (*in play*) protagonista mf

principality [prɪnsɪˈpælɪtɪ] N principato

principally [ˈprɪnsɪplɪ] ADV principalmente

principle [ˈprɪnsɪpl] N principio; **in ~** in linea di principio; **on ~** per principio

print [prɪnt] N (*mark*) impronta; (*letters*) caratteri mpl; (*fabric*) tessuto stampato; (*Art, Phot*) stampa ▶ VT imprimere; (*publish*) stampare, pubblicare; (*write in capitals*) scrivere in stampatello; **out of ~** esaurito(-a)
  ▶ **print out** VT (*Comput*) stampare

printed circuit board [prɪntɪd-] N circuito stampato

printed matter [prɪntɪd-] N stampe fpl

printer [ˈprɪntəʳ] N tipografo(-a); (*machine*) stampante f

printhead [ˈprɪnthɛd] N testa di stampa

printing [ˈprɪntɪŋ] N stampa

printing press N macchina tipografica

print-out [ˈprɪntaut] N tabulato

print wheel N margherita

prior [ˈpraɪə^r] ADJ precedente; (claim etc) più importante ▶N (Rel) priore m; ~ **to doing** prima di fare; **without ~ notice** senza preavviso; **to have a ~ claim to sth** avere un diritto di precedenza su qc

priority [praɪˈɔrɪtɪ] N priorità f inv; precedenza; **to have** or **take ~ over sth** avere la precedenza su qc

priory [ˈpraɪərɪ] N monastero

prise [praɪz] VT: **to ~ open** forzare

prism [ˈprɪzəm] N prisma m

prison [ˈprɪzn] N prigione f ▶CPD (system) carcerario(-a); (conditions, food) nelle or delle prigioni

prison camp N campo di prigionia

prisoner [ˈprɪznə^r] N prigioniero(-a); **to take sb ~** far prigioniero qn; **the ~ at the bar** l'accusato, l'imputato; **~ of war** prigioniero(-a) di guerra

prissy [ˈprɪsɪ] ADJ perbenino inv

pristine [ˈprɪstiːn] ADJ originario(-a); intatto(-a); immacolato(-a)

privacy [ˈprɪvəsɪ] N solitudine f, intimità

private [ˈpraɪvɪt] ADJ privato(-a); personale ▶N soldato semplice; **"~"** (on envelope) "riservata"; (on door) "privato"; **in ~** in privato; **in (his) ~ life** nella vita privata; **he is a very ~ person** è una persona molto riservata; **~ hearing** (Law) udienza a porte chiuse; **to be in ~ practice** essere medico non convenzionato (con la mutua)

private enterprise N iniziativa privata

private eye N investigatore(-trice) privato(-a)

private limited company N (BRIT) società per azioni non quotata in Borsa

privately [ˈpraɪvɪtlɪ] ADV in privato; (within o.s.) dentro di sé

private parts NPL (Anat) parti f pl intime

private property N proprietà privata

private school N scuola privata

privation [praɪˈveɪʃən] N (state) privazione f; (hardship) privazioni f pl, stenti mpl

privatize [ˈpraɪvɪtaɪz] VT privatizzare

privet [ˈprɪvɪt] N ligustro

privilege [ˈprɪvɪlɪdʒ] N privilegio

privileged [ˈprɪvɪlɪdʒd] ADJ privilegiato(-a); **to be ~ to do sth** avere il privilegio or l'onore di fare qc

privy [ˈprɪvɪ] ADJ: **to be ~ to** essere al corrente di

Privy Council N (BRIT) Consiglio della Corona

Il **Privy Council**, un gruppo di consiglieri del re, era il principale organo di governo durante il regno dei Tudor e degli Stuart. Col tempo ha perso la sua importanza e oggi è un organo senza potere effettivo formato da ministri e altre personalità politiche ed ecclesiastiche.

Privy Councillor N (BRIT) Consigliere m della Corona

prize [praɪz] N premio ▶ADJ (example, idiot) perfetto(-a); (bull, novel) premiato(-a) ▶VT apprezzare, pregiare

prize-fighter [ˈpraɪzfaɪtə^r] N pugile m (che si batte per conquistare un premio)

prize giving N premiazione f

prize money N soldi mpl del premio

prizewinner [ˈpraɪzwɪnə^r] N premiato(-a)

prizewinning [ˈpraɪzwɪnɪŋ] ADJ vincente; (novel, essay etc) premiato(-a)

PRO N ABBR = **public relations officer**

pro [prəʊ] N (Sport) professionista mf ▶PREP pro; **the pros and cons** il pro e il contro

pro- [prəʊ] PREFIX (in favour of) filo...; **pro-Soviet** adj filosovietico(-a)

pro-active [prəʊˈæktɪv] ADJ: **to be ~** agire d'iniziativa

probability [prɔbəˈbɪlɪtɪ] N probabilità f inv; **in all ~** con ogni probabilità

probable [ˈprɔbəbl] ADJ probabile; **it is ~/ hardly ~ that ...** è probabile/poco probabile che ... + sub

probably [ˈprɔbəblɪ] ADV probabilmente

probate [ˈprəʊbɪt] N (Law) omologazione f (di un testamento)

probation [prəˈbeɪʃən] N (in employment) periodo di prova; (Law) libertà vigilata; (Rel) probandato; **on ~** (employee) in prova; (Law) in libertà vigilata

probationary [prəʊˈbeɪʃənərɪ] ADJ: **~ period** periodo di prova

probe [prəʊb] N (Med, Space) sonda; (inquiry) indagine f, investigazione f ▶VT sondare, esplorare; indagare

probity [ˈprəʊbɪtɪ] N probità

problem [ˈprɔbləm] N problema m; **to have problems with the car** avere dei problemi con la macchina; **what's the ~?** che cosa c'è?; **I had no ~ in finding her** non mi è stato difficile trovarla; **no ~!** ma certamente!, non c'è problema!

problematic [prɔbləˈmætɪk] ADJ problematico(-a)

problem-solving [ˈprɔbləmsɔlvɪŋ] N risoluzione f di problemi

procedure [prəˈsiːdʒə^r] N (Admin, Law) procedura; (method) metodo, procedimento

proceed [prəˈsiːd] VI (go forward) avanzare, andare avanti; (go about it) procedere; (continue): **to ~ (with)** continuare; **to ~ to** andare a; passare a; **to ~ to do** mettersi a fare; **to ~ against sb** (Law) procedere contro qn; **I am not sure how to ~** non so bene come fare

proceedings [prəˈsiːdɪŋz] NPL misure f pl; (Law) procedimento; (meeting) riunione f; (records) rendiconti mpl; atti mpl

proceeds [ˈprəusiːdz] NPL profitto, incasso

process N [ˈprəusɛs] processo; (*method*) metodo, sistema *m* ▶ VT trattare; (*information*) elaborare ▶ VI [prəˈsɛs] (BRIT *formal: go in procession*) sfilare, procedere in corteo; **we are in the ~ of moving to** ... stiamo per trasferirci a ...

processed cheese [ˈprəusɛst-], (US) **process cheese** N formaggio fuso

processing [ˈprəusɛsɪŋ] N trattamento; elaborazione *f*

procession [prəˈsɛʃən] N processione *f*, corteo; **funeral ~** corteo funebre

pro-choice [prəuˈtʃɔɪs] ADJ per la libertà di scelta di gravidanza

proclaim [prəˈkleɪm] VT proclamare, dichiarare

proclamation [prɔkləˈmeɪʃən] N proclamazione *f*

proclivity [prəˈklɪvɪtɪ] N tendenza, propensione *f*

procrastination [prəukræstɪˈneɪʃən] N procrastinazione *f*

procreation [prəukrɪˈeɪʃən] N procreazione *f*

Procurator Fiscal [ˈprɔkjureɪtə-] N (SCOTTISH) procuratore(-trice)

procure [prəˈkjuəʳ] VT (*for o.s.*) procurarsi; (*for sb*) procurare

procurement [prəˈkjuəmənt] N approvvigionamento

prod [prɔd] VT dare un colpetto a; pungolare ▶ N (*push, jab*) colpetto

prodigal [ˈprɔdɪgl] ADJ prodigo(-a)

prodigious [prəˈdɪdʒəs] ADJ prodigioso(-a)

prodigy [ˈprɔdɪdʒɪ] N prodigio

produce N [ˈprɔdjuːs] (*Agr*) prodotto, prodotti *mpl* ▶ VT [prəˈdjuːs] produrre; (*show*) esibire, mostrare; (*proof of identity*) produrre, fornire; (*cause*) cagionare, causare; (*Theat*) mettere in scena

producer [prəˈdjuːsəʳ] N (*Theat, Cine, Agr*) produttore(-trice)

product [ˈprɔdʌkt] N prodotto

production [prəˈdʌkʃən] N produzione *f*; (*Theat*) messa in scena; **to put into ~** mettere in produzione

production agreement N (US) accordo sui tempi di produzione

production line N catena di lavorazione

production manager N production manager *mf inv*, direttore(-trice) della produzione

productive [prəˈdʌktɪv] ADJ produttivo(-a)

productivity [prɔdʌkˈtɪvɪtɪ] N produttività

productivity agreement N (BRIT) accordo sui tempi di produzione

productivity bonus N premio di produzione

Prof. ABBR (= *professor*) Prof.

profane [prəˈfeɪn] ADJ profano(-a); (*language*) empio(-a)

profess [prəˈfɛs] VT professare; **I do not ~ to be an expert** non pretendo di essere un esperto

professed [prəˈfɛst] ADJ (*self-declared*) dichiarato(-a)

profession [prəˈfɛʃən] N professione *f*; **the professions** le professioni liberali

professional [prəˈfɛʃənl] N (*Sport*) professionista *mf* ▶ ADJ professionale; (*work*) da professionista; **he's a ~ man** è un professionista; **to take ~ advice** consultare un esperto

professionalism [prəˈfɛʃnəlɪzəm] N professionismo

professionally [prəˈfɛʃnəlɪ] ADV professionalmente, in modo professionale; (*Sport: play*) come professionista; **I only know him ~** con lui ho solo rapporti di lavoro

professor [prəˈfɛsəʳ] N professore *m* (*titolare di una cattedra*); (US: *teacher*) professore(-essa)

professorship [prəˈfɛsəʃɪp] N cattedra

proffer [ˈprɔfəʳ] VT (*remark*) profferire; (*apologies*) porgere, presentare; (*one's hand*) porgere

proficiency [prəˈfɪʃənsɪ] N competenza, abilità

proficient [prəˈfɪʃənt] ADJ competente, abile

profile [ˈprəufaɪl] N profilo; **to keep a low ~** (*fig*) cercare di passare inosservato *or* di non farsi notare troppo; **to maintain a high ~** mettersi in mostra

profit [ˈprɔfɪt] N profitto; beneficio ▶ VI: **to ~ (by** *or* **from)** approfittare (di); **~ and loss account** conto perdite e profitti; **to make a ~** realizzare un profitto; **to sell sth at a ~** vendere qc con un utile

profitability [prɔfɪtəˈbɪlɪtɪ] N redditività

profitable [ˈprɔfɪtəbl] ADJ redditizio(-a); (*fig: beneficial*) vantaggioso(-a); (: *meeting, visit*) fruttuoso(-a)

profit centre N centro di profitto

profiteering [prɔfɪˈtɪərɪŋ] N (*pej*) affarismo

profit-making [ˈprɔfɪtmeɪkɪŋ] ADJ a scopo di lucro

profit margin N margine *m* di profitto

profit-sharing [ˈprɔfɪtʃɛərɪŋ] N compartecipazione *f* agli utili

profits tax N (BRIT) imposta sugli utili

profligate [ˈprɔflɪgɪt] ADJ (*dissolute: behaviour*) dissipato(-a); (: *person*) debosciato(-a); (*extravagant*): **he's very ~ with his money** è uno che sperpera i suoi soldi

pro forma [ˈprəuˈfɔːmə] ADJ: **~ invoice** fattura proforma

profound [prəˈfaund] ADJ profondo(-a)

profuse [prəˈfjuːs] ADJ infinito(-a), abbondante

profusely [prəˈfjuːslɪ] ADV con grande effusione

profusion [prəˈfjuːʒən] N profusione *f*, abbondanza

progeny [ˈprɔdʒɪnɪ] N progenie *f*; discendenti *mpl*

programme, (US) **program** [ˈprəʊɡræm] N
programma m ▶ VT programmare

programmer, (US) **programer** [ˈprəʊɡræməʳ]
N programmatore(-trice)

programming, (US) **programing**
[ˈprəʊɡræmɪŋ] N programmazione f

programming language, (US) **programing
language** N linguaggio di programmazione

progress N [ˈprəʊɡrɛs] progresso ▶ VI [prəˈɡrɛs]
(go forward) avanzare, procedere; (in time) procedere; (also: **make progress**) far progressi; **in ~**
in corso

progression [prəˈɡrɛʃən] N progressione f

progressive [prəˈɡrɛsɪv] ADJ progressivo(-a);
(person) progressista

progressively [prəˈɡrɛsɪvlɪ] ADV progressivamente

progress report N (Med) bollettino medico;
(Admin) rendiconto dei lavori

prohibit [prəˈhɪbɪt] VT proibire, vietare; **to ~ sb
from doing sth** vietare or proibire a qn di fare
qc; **"smoking prohibited"** "vietato fumare"

prohibition [prəʊɪˈbɪʃən] N (US) proibizionismo

prohibitive [prəˈhɪbɪtɪv] ADJ (price etc) proibitivo(-a)

project N [ˈprɔdʒɛkt] (plan) piano; (venture) progetto; (Scol) studio, ricerca ▶ VT [prəˈdʒɛkt] proiettare ▶ VI (stick out) sporgere

projectile [prəˈdʒɛktaɪl] N proiettile m

projection [prəˈdʒɛkʃən] N proiezione f; sporgenza

projectionist [prəˈdʒɛkʃənɪst] N (Cine) proiezionista mf

projection room N (Cine) cabina or sala di proiezione

projector [prəˈdʒɛktəʳ] N proiettore m

proletarian [prəʊlɪˈtɛərɪən] ADJ, N proletario(-a)

proletariat [prəʊlɪˈtɛərɪət] N proletariato

pro-life [prəʊˈlaɪf] ADJ per il diritto alla vita

proliferate [prəˈlɪfəreɪt] VI proliferare

proliferation [prəlɪfəˈreɪʃən] N proliferazione f

prolific [prəˈlɪfɪk] ADJ prolifico(-a); (artist etc)
fecondo(-a)

prologue, (US) **prolog** [ˈprəʊlɔɡ] N prologo

prolong [prəˈlɔŋ] VT prolungare

prom [prɔm] N ABBR = **promenade**; **promenade
concert**; (ball) ballo studentesco

In Gran Bretagna i *Proms* (= *promenade concerts*)
sono concerti di musica classica, i più noti dei
quali sono quelli eseguiti nella *Royal Albert Hall* a
Londra. Prendono il nome dal fatto che in origine
il pubblico li ascoltava stando in piedi o passeggiando. In America e ora anche in Gran Bretagna,
con **prom** si intende il ballo studentesco celebrato alla conclusione delle scuole superiori.

promenade [prɔməˈnɑːd] N (by sea) lungomare m

promenade concert N concerto (con posti in
piedi)

promenade deck N (Naut) ponte m di passeggiata

prominence [ˈprɔmɪnəns] N prominenza;
importanza

prominent [ˈprɔmɪnənt] ADJ (standing out) prominente; (important) importante; **he is ~ in the
field of ...** è un'autorità nel campo di ...

prominently [ˈprɔmɪnəntlɪ] ADV (display, set)
ben in vista; **he figured ~ in the case** ha avuto
una parte di primo piano nella faccenda

promiscuity [prɔmɪsˈkjuːɪtɪ] N (sexual) rapporti
mpl multipli

promiscuous [prəˈmɪskjuəs] ADJ (sexually) di
facili costumi

promise [ˈprɔmɪs] N promessa ▶ VT, VI promettere; **to make sb a ~** fare una promessa a qn; **to
~ sb sth, to ~ sth to sb** promettere qc a qn; **a
young man of ~** un giovane promettente; **to ~
(sb) that/to do sth** promettere (a qn) che/di
fare qc

promising [ˈprɔmɪsɪŋ] ADJ promettente

promissory note [ˈprɔmɪsərɪ-] N pagherò m inv

promontory [ˈprɔməntrɪ] N promontorio

promote [prəˈməʊt] VT promuovere; (venture,
event) organizzare; (product) lanciare, reclamizzare; **the team was promoted to the second
division** (BRIT Football) la squadra è stata promossa in serie B

promoter [prəˈməʊtəʳ] N (of sporting event) organizzatore(-trice); (of cause etc) sostenitore(-trice)

promotion [prəˈməʊʃən] N promozione f

prompt [prɔmpt] ADJ rapido(-a), svelto(-a);
puntuale; (reply) sollecito(-a) ▶ ADV (punctually)
in punto ▶ N (Comput) prompt m inv ▶ VT incitare; provocare; (Theat) suggerire a; **at 8 o'clock
~** alle 8 in punto; **to be ~ to do sth** essere sollecito nel fare qc; **to ~ sb to do** spingere qn a fare

prompter [ˈprɔmptəʳ] N (Theat) suggeritore(-trice)

promptly [ˈprɔmptlɪ] ADV prontamente; puntualmente

promptness [ˈprɔmptnɪs] N prontezza; puntualità

prone [prəʊn] ADJ (lying) prono(-a); **~ to** propenso(-a) a, incline a; **to be ~ to illness** essere soggetto(-a) a malattie; **she is ~ to burst into tears
if ...** può facilmente scoppiare in lacrime se ...

prong [prɔŋ] N rebbio, punta

pronoun [ˈprəʊnaʊn] N pronome m

pronounce [prəˈnaʊns] VT pronunciare ▶ VI: **to
~ (up)on** pronunciare su; **they pronounced
him unfit to drive** lo hanno dichiarato inabile
alla guida; **how do you ~ it?** come si pronuncia?

pronounced [prə'naʊnst] ADJ (*marked*) spiccato(-a)

pronouncement [prə'naʊnsmənt] N dichiarazione f

pronunciation [prənʌnsɪ'eɪʃən] N pronuncia

proof [pru:f] N prova; (*of book*) bozza; (*Phot*) provino; **70%** ~ ≈ 40° in volume ▶ VT (*tent, anorak*) impermeabilizzare ▶ ADJ: ~ **against** a prova di

proofreader ['pru:fri:də'] N correttore(-trice) di bozze

prop [prɔp] N sostegno, appoggio ▶ VT (*also:* **prop up**) sostenere, appoggiare; (*lean*): **to** ~ **sth against** appoggiare qc contro *or* a ■ **props** oggetti m inv di scena

Prop. ABBR (*Comm*) = **proprietor**

propaganda [prɔpə'gændə] N propaganda

propagation [prɔpə'geɪʃən] N propagazione f

propel [prə'pɛl] VT spingere (in avanti), muovere

propeller [prə'pɛlə'] N elica

propelling pencil [prə'pɛlɪŋ-] N (*BRIT*) matita a mina

propensity [prə'pɛnsɪtɪ] N tendenza

proper ['prɔpə'] ADJ (*suited, right*) adatto(-a), appropriato(-a); (*seemly*) decente; (*authentic*) vero(-a); (*col: real*) vero(-a) e proprio(-a); **to go through the** ~ **channels** (*Admin*) seguire la regolare procedura

properly ['prɔpəlɪ] ADV decentemente; (*really, thoroughly*) veramente; (*eat, study*) bene; (*behave*) come si deve

proper noun N nome m proprio

property ['prɔpətɪ] N (*things owned*) beni mpl; (*land, building, Chem etc: quality*) proprietà f inv

property developer N (*BRIT*) costruttore(-trice) edile

property owner N proprietario(-a)

property tax N imposta patrimoniale

prophecy ['prɔfɪsɪ] N profezia

prophesy ['prɔfɪsaɪ] VT predire, profetizzare

prophet ['prɔfɪt] N profeta m

prophetic [prə'fɛtɪk] ADJ profetico(-a)

proportion [prə'pɔ:ʃən] N proporzione f; (*share*) parte f ▶ VT proporzionare, commisurare ■ **proportions** NPL (*size*) proporzioni fpl; **to be in/out of** ~ **to** *or* **with sth** essere in proporzione/sproporzionato rispetto a qc; **to see sth in** ~ (*fig*) dare il giusto peso a qc

proportional [prə'pɔ:ʃənl] ADJ proporzionale

proportional representation N rappresentanza proporzionale

proportionate [prə'pɔ:ʃənɪt] ADJ proporzionato(-a)

proposal [prə'pəuzl] N proposta; (*plan*) progetto; (*of marriage*) proposta di matrimonio

propose [prə'pəuz] VT proporre, suggerire ▶ VI

fare una proposta di matrimonio; **to** ~ **to do** proporsi di fare, aver l'intenzione di fare

proposer [prə'pəuzə'] N (*BRIT: of motion*) proponente mf

proposition [prɔpə'zɪʃən] N proposizione f; (*proposal*) proposta; **to make sb a** ~ proporre qualcosa a qn

propound [prə'paund] VT proporre, presentare

proprietary [prə'praɪətərɪ] ADJ: ~ **article** prodotto con marchio depositato; ~ **brand** marchio di fabbrica

proprietor [prə'praɪətə'] N proprietario(-a)

propriety [prə'praɪətɪ] N (*seemliness*) decoro, rispetto delle convenienze sociali

propulsion [prə'pʌlʃən] N propulsione f

pro rata [prəu'rɑ:tə] ADV in proporzione

prosaic [prəu'zeɪk] ADJ prosaico(-a)

Pros. Atty. ABBR (*US*) = **prosecuting attorney**

proscribe [prə'skraɪb] VT proscrivere

prose [prəuz] N prosa; (*Scol: translation*) traduzione f dalla madrelingua

prosecute ['prɔsɪkju:t] VT (*Law*) perseguire

prosecuting attorney ['prɔsɪkju:tɪŋ-] N (*US*) ≈ procuratore(-trice)

prosecution [prɔsɪ'kju:ʃən] N (*Law*) procedimento giudiziario; (*accusing side*) accusa

prosecutor ['prɔsɪkju:tə'] N (*also:* **public prosecutor**) ≈ procuratore(-trice) della Repubblica

prospect N ['prɔspɛkt] prospettiva; (*hope*) speranza ▶ VT [prə'spɛkt] esplorare ▶ VI: **to** ~ **for gold** cercare l'oro; **there is every** ~ **of an early victory** tutto lascia prevedere una rapida vittoria; *see also* **prospects**

prospecting [prə'spɛktɪŋ] N prospezione f

prospective [prə'spɛktɪv] ADJ (*buyer*) potenziale; (*legislation, son-in-law*) futuro(-a)

prospector [prə'spɛktə'] N prospettore(-trice); **gold** ~ cercatore(-trice) d'oro

prospects ['prɔspɛkts] NPL (*for work etc*) prospettive fpl

prospectus [prə'spɛktəs] N prospetto, programma m

prosper ['prɔspə'] VI prosperare

prosperity [prɔ'spɛrɪtɪ] N prosperità

prosperous ['prɔspərəs] ADJ prospero(-a)

prostate ['prɔsteɪt] N (*also:* **prostate gland**) prostata, ghiandola prostatica

prostitute ['prɔstɪtju:t] N prostituta; **male** ~ uomo che si prostituisce

prostitution [prɔstɪ'tju:ʃən] N prostituzione f

prostrate ADJ ['prɔstreɪt] prostrato(-a) ▶ VT [prɔ'streɪt]: **to** ~ **o.s.** (*before sb*) prostrarsi

protagonist [prə'tægənɪst] N protagonista mf

protect [prə'tɛkt] VT proteggere, salvaguardare

protection [prə'tɛkʃən] N protezione f; **to be under sb's** ~ essere sotto la protezione di qn

protectionism [prə'tɛkʃənɪzəm] N protezionismo

protection racket N racket *m inv*

protective [prə'tɛktɪv] ADJ protettivo(-a); ~ **custody** (*Law*) protezione *f*

protector [prə'tɛktə^r] N protettore(-trice)

protégé ['prəʊtiːʒeɪ] N protetto

protégée ['prəʊtiːʒeɪ] N protetta

protein ['prəʊtiːn] N proteina

pro tem [prəʊ'tɛm] ADV ABBR (*for the time being*: = *pro tempore*) pro tempore

protest N ['prəʊtɛst] protesta ▶ VT, VI [prə'tɛst] protestare; **to do sth under ~** fare qc protestando; **to ~ against/about** protestare contro/per

Protestant ['prɒtɪstənt] ADJ, N protestante (*mf*)

protester, protestor [prə'tɛstə^r] N (*in demonstration*) dimostrante *mf*

protest march N marcia di protesta

protocol ['prəʊtəkɒl] N protocollo

prototype ['prəʊtətaɪp] N prototipo

protracted [prə'træktɪd] ADJ tirato(-a) per le lunghe

protractor [prə'træktə^r] N (*Geom*) goniometro

protrude [prə'truːd] VI sporgere

protuberance [prə'tjuːbərəns] N sporgenza

proud [praʊd] ADJ fiero(-a), orgoglioso(-a); (*pej*) superbo(-a); **to be ~ to do sth** essere onorato(-a) di fare qc; **to do sb ~** non far mancare nulla a qn; **to do o.s. ~** trattarsi bene

proudly ['praʊdlɪ] ADV con orgoglio, fieramente

prove [pruːv] VT provare, dimostrare ▶ VI: **to ~ (to be) correct** *etc* risultare vero(-a) *etc*; **to ~ o.s.** mostrare le proprie capacità; **to ~ o.s./itself (to be) useful** *etc* mostrarsi *or* rivelarsi utile *etc*; **he was proved right in the end** alla fine i fatti gli hanno dato ragione

Provence [prɒvɑ̃s] N Provenza

proverb ['prɒvəːb] N proverbio

proverbial [prə'vəːbɪəl] ADJ proverbiale

provide [prə'vaɪd] VT fornire, provvedere; **to ~ sb with sth** fornire *or* provvedere qn di qc; **to be provided with** essere dotato *or* munito di
▶ **provide for** VT FUS provvedere a; (*future event*) prevedere

provided [prə'vaɪdɪd] CONJ: ~ **(that)** purché + *sub*, a condizione che + *sub*

Providence ['prɒvɪdəns] N Provvidenza

providing [prə'vaɪdɪŋ] CONJ purché + *sub*, a condizione che + *sub*

province ['prɒvɪns] N provincia

provincial [prə'vɪnʃəl] ADJ provinciale

provision [prə'vɪʒən] N (*supply*) riserva; (*supplying*) provvista; rifornimento; (*stipulation*) condizione *f* ▪ **provisions** NPL (*food*) provviste *fpl*; **to**

make ~ for (*one's family, future*) pensare a; **there's no ~ for this in the contract** il contratto non lo prevede

provisional [prə'vɪʒənl] ADJ provvisorio(-a) ▶ N: **P~** (*IRISH Pol*) provisional *m inv*

provisional licence N (*BRIT Aut*) ≈ foglio *m* rosa *inv*

provisionally [prə'vɪʒnəlɪ] ADV provvisoriamente; (*appoint*) a titolo provvisorio

proviso [prə'vaɪzəʊ] N condizione *f*; **with the ~ that** a condizione che + *sub*, a patto che + *sub*

Provo ['prɒvəʊ] N ABBR (*pej*) = **Provisional**

provocation [prɒvə'keɪʃən] N provocazione *f*

provocative [prə'vɒkətɪv] ADJ (*aggressive*) provocatorio(-a); (*thought-provoking*) stimolante; (*seductive*) provocante

provoke [prə'vəʊk] VT provocare; incitare; **to ~ sb to sth/to do** *or* **into doing sth** spingere qn a qc/a fare qc

provoking [prə'vəʊkɪŋ] ADJ irritante, esasperante

provost ['prɒvəst] N (*BRIT*: *of university*) rettore(-trice); (*SCOTTISH*) sindaco(-a)

prow [praʊ] N prua

prowess ['praʊɪs] N prodezza; **his ~ as a footballer** le sue capacità di calciatore

prowl [praʊl] VI (*also*: **prowl about, prowl around**) aggirarsi furtivamente ▶ N: **on the ~** in caccia

prowler ['praʊlə^r] N tipo sospetto (*che s'aggira con l'intenzione di rubare, aggredire ecc*)

proximity [prɒk'sɪmɪtɪ] N prossimità

proxy ['prɒksɪ] N procura; **by ~** per procura

PRP N ABBR (= *performance related pay*) retribuzione *f* commensurata al rendimento

prude [pruːd] N puritano(-a)

prudence ['pruːdns] N prudenza

prudent ['pruːdnt] ADJ prudente

prudish ['pruːdɪʃ] ADJ puritano(-a)

prune [pruːn] N prugna secca ▶ VT potare

pry [praɪ] VI: **to ~ into** ficcare il naso in

PS N ABBR (= *postscript*) P.S.

psalm [sɑːm] N salmo

PSAT® N ABBR (*US*) = **Preliminary Scholastic Aptitude Test**

PSBR N ABBR (*BRIT*: = *public sector borrowing requirement*) fabbisogno di prestiti per il settore pubblico

pseud ['sjuːd] N (*BRIT*: *col*) intellettualoide *mf*

pseudo- ['sjuːdəʊ] PREFIX pseudo...

pseudonym ['sjuːdənɪm] N pseudonimo

PSHE N ABBR (*BRIT Scol*: = *personal, social, health and economic education*) formazione di formazione sociale e sanitaria

PST ABBR (*US*: = *Pacific Standard Time*) ora invernale del Pacifico

psyche ['saɪkɪ] N psiche *f*

p

psychedelic [saɪkɪˈdɛlɪk] ADJ psichedelico(-a)

psychiatric [saɪkɪˈætrɪk] ADJ psichiatrico(-a)

psychiatrist [saɪˈkaɪətrɪst] N psichiatra *mf*

psychiatry [saɪˈkaɪətrɪ] N psichiatria

psychic [ˈsaɪkɪk] ADJ (*also*: **psychical**) psichico(-a); (*person*) dotato(-a) di qualità telepatiche

psycho [ˈsaɪkəu] N (*pej*) folle *mf*, psicopatico(-a)

psychoanalyse [saɪkəuˈænəlaɪz] VT psicanalizzare

psychoanalysis [saɪkəuəˈnælɪsɪs] (*pl* **-ses** [-siːz]) N psicanalisi *f inv*

psychoanalyst [saɪkəuˈænəlɪst] N psicanalista *mf*

psychological [saɪkəˈlɔdʒɪkl] ADJ psicologico(-a)

psychologist [saɪˈkɔlədʒɪst] N psicologo(-a)

psychology [saɪˈkɔlədʒɪ] N psicologia

psychopath [ˈsaɪkəupæθ] N psicopatico(-a)

psychosis [saɪˈkəusɪs] (*pl* **psychoses** [-siːz]) N psicosi *f inv*

psychosomatic [saɪkəusəˈmætɪk] ADJ psicosomatico(-a)

psychotherapy [saɪkəuˈθɛrəpɪ] N psicoterapia

psychotic [saɪˈkɔtɪk] ADJ, N psicotico(-a)

PT N ABBR (BRIT: = *physical training*) ed. fisica

pt ABBR = **pint**; (= *point*) pt

Pt. ABBR (*in place names*: = *Point*) Pt.

PTA N ABBR (= *Parent-Teacher Association*) associazione genitori e insegnanti

Pte. ABBR (BRIT Mil) = **private**

PTO ABBR (= *please turn over*) v.r. (= *vedi retro*)

PTV N ABBR (US) = **pay television**; **public television**

pub [pʌb] N ABBR (= *public house*) pub *m inv*

pub crawl N: **to go on a ~** (BRIT col) fare il giro dei pub

puberty [ˈpjuːbətɪ] N pubertà

pubic [ˈpjuːbɪk] ADJ pubico(-a), del pube

public [ˈpʌblɪk] ADJ pubblico(-a) ▶ N pubblico; **in ~** in pubblico; **the general ~** il pubblico; **to make sth ~** render noto *or* di pubblico dominio qc; **to be ~ knowledge** essere di dominio pubblico; **to go ~** (Comm) emettere le azioni sul mercato

public address system N impianto di amplificazione

publican [ˈpʌblɪkən] N (BRIT) gestore(-trice) (*or* proprietario(-a)) di un pub

publication [pʌblɪˈkeɪʃən] N pubblicazione *f*

public company N ≈ società *f inv* per azioni (*costituita tramite pubblica sottoscrizione*)

public convenience N (BRIT) gabinetti *mpl*

public holiday N (BRIT) giorno festivo, festa nazionale

public house N (BRIT) pub *m inv*

publicity [pʌbˈlɪsɪtɪ] N pubblicità

publicize [ˈpʌblɪsaɪz] VT rendere pubblico(-a), pubblicizzare

public limited company N ≈ società per azioni a responsabilità limitata (*quotata in Borsa*)

publicly [ˈpʌblɪklɪ] ADV pubblicamente

public opinion N opinione *f* pubblica

public ownership N proprietà pubblica *or* sociale; **to be taken into ~** essere statalizzato(-a)

public prosecutor N pubblico ministero; **~'s office** ufficio del pubblico ministero

public relations N pubbliche relazioni *fpl*

public relations officer N addetto(-a) alle pubbliche relazioni

public school N (BRIT) scuola privata; (US) scuola statale; *vedi nota*

In Inghilterra le **public schools** sono scuole o collegi privati di istruzione secondaria, spesso di un certo prestigio. In Scozia e negli Stati Uniti, invece, le *public schools* sono scuole pubbliche gratuite amministrate dallo stato.

public sector N settore *m* pubblico

public service vehicle N (BRIT) mezzo pubblico

public-spirited [pʌblɪkˈspɪrɪtɪd] ADJ che ha senso civico

public transport, (US) **public transportation** N mezzi *mpl* pubblici

public utility N servizio pubblico

public works NPL lavori *mpl* pubblici

publish [ˈpʌblɪʃ] VT pubblicare

publisher [ˈpʌblɪʃər] N editore(-trice); (*firm*) casa editrice

publishing [ˈpʌblɪʃɪŋ] N (*industry*) editoria; (*of a book*) pubblicazione *f*

publishing company N casa *or* società *f inv* editrice

pub lunch N: **to go for a ~** andare a mangiare al pub

puce [pjuːs] ADJ color pulce *inv*

puck [pʌk] N (Ice Hockey) disco

pucker [ˈpʌkər] VT corrugare

pudding [ˈpudɪŋ] N budino; (BRIT: *dessert*) dolce *m*; **black ~**, (US) **blood ~** sanguinaccio; **rice ~** budino di riso

puddle [ˈpʌdl] N pozza, pozzanghera

puerile [ˈpjuəraɪl] ADJ puerile

Puerto Rico [ˈpwəːtəuˈriːkəu] N Portorico

puff [pʌf] N sbuffo; (*also*: **powder puff**) piumino ▶ VT (*also*: **puff out**: *sails, cheeks*) gonfiare ▶ VI uscire a sbuffi; (*pant*) ansare; **to ~ out smoke** mandar fuori sbuffi di fumo; **to ~ one's pipe** tirare sboccate di fumo

puffed [pʌft] ADJ (col: out of breath) senza fiato

puffin ['pʌfɪn] N puffino

puff pastry, (US) **puff paste** N pasta sfoglia

puffy ['pʌfɪ] ADJ gonfio(-a)

pugnacious [pʌg'neɪʃəs] ADJ combattivo(-a)

pull [pul] N (tug) strattone m, tirata; (of moon, magnet, the sea etc) attrazione f; (fig) influenza ▶ VT tirare; (muscle) strappare, farsi uno strappo a; (trigger) premere ▶ VI tirare; **to give sth a ~** tirare su qc; **to ~ a face** fare una smorfia; **to ~ to pieces** fare a pezzi; **to ~ one's punches** (Boxing) risparmiare l'avversario; **not to ~ one's punches** (fig) non avere peli sulla lingua; **to ~ one's weight** dare il proprio contributo; **to ~ o.s. together** ricomporsi, riprendersi; **to ~ sb's leg** prendere in giro qn; **to ~ strings (for sb)** muovere qualche pedina (per qn)

▶ **pull about** VT (BRIT: handle roughly: object) strapazzare; (: person) malmenare

▶ **pull apart** VT (break) fare a pezzi

▶ **pull away** VI (move off: vehicle) muoversi, partire; (: boat) staccarsi dal molo, salpare; (draw back: person) indietreggiare

▶ **pull back** VT (lever etc) tirare indietro; (curtains) aprire ▶ VI (from confrontation etc) tirarsi indietro; (Mil: withdraw) ritirarsi

▶ **pull down** VT (house) demolire; (tree) abbattere

▶ **pull in** VI (Aut: at the kerb) accostarsi; (Rail) entrare in stazione

▶ **pull off** VT (clothes) togliere; (deal etc) portare a compimento

▶ **pull out** VI partire; (withdraw) ritirarsi; (Aut: come out of line) spostarsi sulla mezzeria ▶ VT staccare; far uscire; (withdraw) ritirare

▶ **pull over** VI (Aut) accostare

▶ **pull round** VI (unconscious person) rinvenire; (sick person) ristabilirsi

▶ **pull through** VI farcela

▶ **pull up** VI (stop) fermarsi ▶ VT (uproot) sradicare; (stop) fermare; (raise) sollevare

pulley ['pulɪ] N puleggia, carrucola

pull-out ['pulaut] N inserto ▶ CPD staccabile

pullover ['puləʊvə^r] N pullover m inv

pulp [pʌlp] N (of fruit) polpa; (for paper) pasta per carta; (pej: magazines, books) stampa di qualità e di tono scadenti; **to reduce sth to ~** spappolare qc

pulpit ['pulpɪt] N pulpito

pulsate [pʌl'seɪt] VI battere, palpitare

pulse [pʌls] N polso; (Bot) legume m; **to feel or take sb's ~** sentire or tastare il polso a qn

pulses ['pʌlsəz] NPL (Culin) legumi mpl

pulverize ['pʌlvəraɪz] VT polverizzare

puma ['pju:mə] N puma m inv

pumice ['pʌmɪs], **pumice stone** ['pʌmɪs-] N (pietra) pomice f

pummel ['pʌml] VT dare pugni a

pump [pʌmp] N pompa; (shoe) scarpetta ▶ VT pompare; (fig: col) far parlare; **to ~ sb for infor-** **mation** cercare di strappare delle informazioni a qn

▶ **pump up** VT gonfiare

pumpkin ['pʌmpkɪn] N zucca

pun [pʌn] N gioco di parole

punch [pʌntʃ] N (blow) pugno; (fig: force) forza; (tool) punzone m; (drink) ponce m ▶ VT (hit): **to ~ sb/sth** dare un pugno a qn/qc; **to ~ a hole (in)** fare un buco (in)

▶ **punch in** VI (US) timbrare il cartellino (all'entrata)

▶ **punch out** VI (US) timbrare il cortellino (all'uscita)

punch card, punched card ['pʌntʃt-] N scheda perforata

punch-drunk ['pʌntʃdrʌŋk] ADJ (BRIT) stordito(-a)

punch line N (of joke) battuta finale

punch-up ['pʌntʃʌp] N (BRIT col) rissa

punctual ['pʌŋktjuəl] ADJ puntuale

punctuality [pʌŋktju'ælɪtɪ] N puntualità

punctually ['pʌŋktjuəlɪ] ADV puntualmente; **it will start ~ at 6** comincerà alle 6 precise or in punto

punctuate ['pʌŋktjueɪt] VT punteggiare

punctuation [pʌŋktju'eɪʃən] N interpunzione f, punteggiatura

punctuation mark N segno d'interpunzione

puncture ['pʌŋktʃə^r] N foratura ▶ VT forare; **to have a ~** (Aut) forare (una gomma)

pundit ['pʌndɪt] N sapientone(-a)

pungent ['pʌndʒənt] ADJ piccante; (fig) mordace, caustico(-a)

punish ['pʌnɪʃ] VT punire; **to ~ sb for sth/for doing sth** punire qn per qc/per aver fatto qc

punishable ['pʌnɪʃəbl] ADJ punibile

punishing ['pʌnɪʃɪŋ] ADJ (fig: exhausting) sfiancante

punishment ['pʌnɪʃmənt] N punizione f; **to take a lot of ~** (col: boxer) incassare parecchi colpi; (car) essere messo(-a) a dura prova

punk [pʌŋk] N (person: also: **punk rocker**) punk mf; (music: also: **punk rock**) musica punk, punk rock m; (US col: hoodlum) teppista m

punt [pʌnt] N (boat) barchino; (Football) colpo a volo ▶ VI (BRIT: bet) scommettere

punter ['pʌntə^r] N (BRIT: gambler) scommettitore(-trice)

puny ['pju:nɪ] ADJ gracile

pup [pʌp] N cucciolo(-a)

pupil ['pju:pl] N allievo(-a); (Anat) pupilla

puppet ['pʌpɪt] N burattino

puppet government N governo fantoccio

puppy ['pʌpɪ] N cucciolo(-a), cagnolino(-a)

purchase ['pə:tʃɪs] N acquisto, compera; (grip) presa ▶ VT comprare; **to get a ~ on** (grip) trovare un appoggio su

purchase order N ordine m d'acquisto, ordinazione f

purchase price N prezzo d'acquisto

purchaser ['pəːtʃɪsə^r] N compratore(-trice)

purchase tax N (BRIT) tassa d'acquisto

purchasing power ['pəːtʃɪsɪŋ-] N potere m d'acquisto

pure [pjuə^r] ADJ puro(-a); **a ~ wool jumper** un golf di pura lana; **it's laziness ~ and simple** è pura pigrizia

purebred ['pjuəbred] ADJ di razza pura

purée ['pjuərei] N purè m inv

purely ['pjuəlɪ] ADV puramente

purge [pəːdʒ] N (Med) purga; (Pol) epurazione f ▶ VT purgare; (fig) epurare

purification [pjuərɪfɪ'keɪʃən] N purificazione f

purify ['pjuərɪfaɪ] VT purificare

purist ['pjuərɪst] N purista mf

puritan ['pjuərɪtən] ADJ, N puritano(-a)

puritanical [pjuərɪ'tænɪkl] ADJ puritano(-a)

purity ['pjuərɪtɪ] N purezza

purl [pəːl] N punto rovescio ▶ VT lavorare a rovescio

purloin [pəː'lɔɪn] VT rubare

purple ['pəːpl] ADJ di porpora; viola inv

purport [pəː'pɔːt] VI: **to ~ to be/do** pretendere di essere/fare

purpose ['pəːpəs] N intenzione f, scopo; **on ~** apposta, di proposito; **for illustrative purposes** a titolo illustrativo; **for teaching purposes** per l'insegnamento; **for the purposes of this meeting** agli effetti di questa riunione; **to no ~** senza nessun risultato, inutilmente

purpose-built ['pəːpəs'bɪlt] ADJ (BRIT) costruito(-a) allo scopo

purposeful ['pəːpəsful] ADJ deciso(-a), risoluto(-a)

purposely ['pəːpəslɪ] ADV apposta

purr [pəː^r] N fusa fpl ▶ VI fare le fusa

purse [pəːs] N (BRIT) borsellino; (US: handbag) borsetta, borsa ▶ VT contrarre

purser ['pəːsə^r] N (Naut) commissario di bordo

purse snatcher [-'snætʃə^r] N (US) scippatore(-trice)

pursue [pə'sjuː] VT inseguire; essere alla ricerca di; (fig: inquiry, matter) approfondire; (: activity etc) continuare con; (: aim etc) perseguire

pursuer [pə'sjuːə^r] N inseguitore(-trice)

pursuit [pə'sjuːt] N inseguimento; (occupation) occupazione f, attività f inv; (fig) ricerca; (pastime) passatempo; **in (the) ~ of sth** alla ricerca di qc; **scientific pursuits** ricerche fpl scientifiche

purveyor [pə'veɪə^r] N fornitore(-trice)

pus [pʌs] N pus m

push [puʃ] N spinta; (effort) grande sforzo; (drive) energia ▶ VT spingere; (button) premere; (fig) fare pubblicità a; (thrust): **to ~ sth (into)** ficcare qc (in) ▶ VI spingere; premere; **to ~ a door open/shut** aprire/chiudere una porta con una spinta or spingendola; **to be pushed for time/money** essere a corto di tempo/soldi; **she is pushing 50** (col) va per i 50; **to ~ for** (better pay, conditions etc) insistere per ottenere; **"~"** (on door) "spingere"; (on bell) "suonare"; **at a ~** (BRIT col) in caso di necessità

▶ **push aside** VT scostare

▶ **push in** VI introdursi a forza

▶ **push off** VI (col) filare

▶ **push on** VI (continue) continuare

▶ **push over** VT far cadere

▶ **push through** VI farsi largo spingendo ▶ VT (measure) far approvare

▶ **push up** VT (total, prices) far salire

push-bike ['puʃbaɪk] N (BRIT) bicicletta

push-button ['puʃbʌtn] ADJ a pulsante

pushchair ['puʃtʃɛə^r] N (BRIT) passeggino

pusher ['puʃə^r] N (also: **drug pusher**) spacciatore(-trice) (di droga)

pushover ['puʃəuvə^r] N (col): **it's a ~** è un lavoro da bambini

push-up ['puʃʌp] N (US: press-up) flessione f sulle braccia

pushy ['puʃɪ] ADJ (pej) troppo intraprendente

puss [pus], **pussy(-cat)** ['pusɪ-] N micio(-a)

put [put] (pt, pp ~) VT mettere, porre; (say) dire, esprimere; (a question) fare; (estimate) stimare ▶ ADV: **to stay ~** non muoversi; **to ~ sb to bed** mettere qn a letto; **to ~ sb in a good/bad mood** mettere qn di buon/cattivo umore; **to ~ sb to a lot of trouble** scomodare qn; **to ~ a lot of time into sth** dedicare molto tempo a qc; **to ~ money on a horse** scommettere su un cavallo; **how shall I ~ it?** come dire?; **I ~ it to you that ...** (BRIT) io sostengo che ...

▶ **put about** VI (Naut) virare di bordo ▶ VT (rumour) diffondere

▶ **put across** VT (ideas etc) comunicare, far capire

▶ **put aside** VT (lay down: book etc) mettere da una parte, posare; (save) mettere da parte; (in shop) tenere da parte

▶ **put away** VT (clothes, toys etc) mettere via; (return) mettere a posto

▶ **put back** VT (replace) rimettere (a posto); (postpone) rinviare; (delay) ritardare; (set back: watch, clock) mettere indietro; **this will ~ us back 10 years** questo ci farà tornare indietro di 10 anni

▶ **put by** VT (money) mettere da parte

▶ **put down** VT (parcel etc) posare, mettere giù; (pay) versare; (in writing) mettere per iscritto; (suppress: revolt etc) reprimere, sopprimere; (attribute) attribuire

▶ **put forward** VT (ideas) avanzare, proporre; (date) anticipare

▶ **put in** VT (application, complaint) presentare; (time, effort) mettere

▶**put in for** VT FUS (*job*) far domanda per; (*promotion*) far domanda di

▶**put off** VT (*postpone*) rimandare, rinviare; (*discourage*) dissuadere

▶**put on** VT (*clothes, lipstick etc*) mettere; (*light etc*) accendere; (*play etc*) mettere in scena; (*concert, exhibition etc*) allestire, organizzare; (*extra bus, train etc*) mettere in servizio; (*food, meal*) mettere su; (*brake*) mettere; (*assume: accent, manner*) affettare; (*col: tease*) prendere in giro; (*inform, indicate*): **to ~ sb on to sb/sth** indicare qn/qc a qn; **to ~ on weight** ingrassare; **to ~ on airs** darsi delle arie

▶**put out** VT mettere fuori; (*one's hand*) porgere; (*light etc*) spegnere; (*inconvenience: person*) scomodare; (*dislocate: shoulder, knee*) lussarsi; (: *back*) farsi uno strappo a ▶VI (*Naut*): **to ~ out to sea** prendere il largo; **to ~ out from Plymouth** partire da Plymouth

▶**put through** VT (*Tel: caller*) mettere in comunicazione; (: *call*) passare; (*plan*) far approvare; **~ me through to Miss Blair** mi passi la signorina Blair

▶**put together** VT mettere insieme, riunire; (*assemble: furniture*) montare; (: *meal*) improvvisare

▶**put up** VT (*raise*) sollevare, alzare; (: *umbrella*) aprire; (: *tent*) montare; (*pin up*) affiggere; (*hang*) appendere; (*build*) costruire, erigere; (*increase*) aumentare; (*accommodate*) alloggiare; (*incite*): **to ~ sb up to doing sth** istigare qn a fare qc; **to ~ sth up for sale** mettere in vendita qc

▶**put upon** VT FUS: **to be ~ upon** (*imposed on*) farsi mettere sotto i piedi

▶**put up with** VT FUS sopportare

putrid [ˈpjuːtrɪd] ADJ putrido(-a)

putt [pʌt] VT (*ball*) colpire leggermente ▶N colpo leggero

putter [ˈpʌtər] N (*Golf*) putter *m inv* ▶VI (*US*) = **potter**

putting green [ˈpʌtɪŋ-] N green *m inv*; campo da putting

putty [ˈpʌtɪ] N stucco

put-up [ˈpʌtʌp] ADJ: **~ job** montatura

puzzle [ˈpʌzl] N enigma *m*, mistero; (*jigsaw*) puzzle *m inv*; (*also:* **crossword puzzle**) parole *fpl* incrociate, cruciverba *m inv* ▶VT confondere, rendere perplesso(-a) ▶VI scervellarsi; **to ~ over** (*sb's actions*) cercare di capire; (*mystery, problem*) cercare di risolvere

puzzled ADJ perplesso(-a); **to be ~ about sth** domandarsi il perché di qc

puzzling [ˈpʌzlɪŋ] ADJ (*question*) poco chiaro(-a); (*attitude, set of instructions*) incomprensibile

PVC N ABBR (= *polyvinyl chloride*) P.V.C. *m*

Pvt. ABBR (*US Mil*) = **private**

PW N ABBR (*US*) = **prisoner of war**

pw ABBR = **per week**

PX N ABBR (*US Mil*) = **post exchange**

pygmy [ˈpɪgmɪ] N pigmeo(-a)

pyjamas (BRIT), (US) **pajamas** [pəˈdʒɑːməz] NPL pigiama *m*; **a pair of ~** un pigiama

pylon [ˈpaɪlən] N pilone *m*

pyramid [ˈpɪrəmɪd] N piramide *f*

Pyrenean [pɪrəˈniːən] ADJ pirenaico(-a)

Pyrenees [pɪrəˈniːz] NPL: **the ~** i Pirenei

Pyrex® [ˈpaɪrɛks] N Pirex® *m inv* ▶CPD: **~ dish** pirofila

python [ˈpaɪθən] N pitone *m*

p

Qq

Q, q [kju:] N (*letter*) Q, q f inv or m inv; **Q for Queen** = Q come Quarto

Qatar [kæˈtɑːʳ] N Qatar m

QC N ABBR (*BRIT*: = *Queen's Counsel*) avvocato della Corona

QED ABBR (= *quod erat demonstrandum*) qed

QM N ABBR = **quartermaster**

q.t. N ABBR (*col*) = **quiet**; **on the ~** di nascosto

qty ABBR = **quantity**

quack [kwæk] N (*of duck*) qua qua m inv; (*pej*: *doctor*) ciarlatano(-a)

quad [kwɔd] N ABBR = **quadrangle**; **quadruple**; **quadruplet**

quadrangle [ˈkwɔdræŋgl] N (*Math*) quadrilatero; (*courtyard*) cortile m

quadruped [ˈkwɔdrupɛd] N quadrupede m

quadruple [kwɔˈdrupl] ADJ quadruplo(-a) ▶ N quadruplo ▶ VT quadruplicare ▶ VI quadruplicarsi

quadruplet [kwɔˈdruːplɪt] N uno(-a) di quattro gemelli

quagmire [ˈkwægmaɪəʳ] N pantano

quail [kweɪl] N (*Zool*) quaglia ▶ VI (*person*): **to ~ at** or **before** perdersi d'animo davanti a

quaint [kweɪnt] ADJ bizzarro(-a); (*old-fashioned*) antiquato(-a) e pittoresco(-a)

quake [kweɪk] VI tremare ▶ N ABBR = **earthquake**

Quaker [ˈkweɪkəʳ] N quacchero(-a)

qualification [kwɔlɪfɪˈkeɪʃən] N (*degree etc*) qualifica, titolo; (*ability*) competenza, qualificazione f; (*limitation*) riserva, restrizione f; **what are your qualifications?** quali sono le sue qualifiche?

qualified [ˈkwɔlɪfaɪd] ADJ qualificato(-a); (*able*) competente, qualificato(-a); (*limited*) condizionato(-a); **~ for/to do** qualificato(-a) per/per fare; **he's not ~ for the job** non ha i requisiti necessari per questo lavoro; **it was a ~ success** è stato un successo parziale

qualify [ˈkwɔlɪfaɪ] VT abilitare; (*limit*: *statement*) modificare, precisare ▶ VI: **to ~ (as)** qualificarsi (come); **to ~ (for)** acquistare i requisiti

necessari (per); (*Sport*) qualificarsi (per or a); **to ~ as an engineer** diventare un perito tecnico

qualifying [ˈkwɔlɪfaɪŋ] ADJ (*exam*) di ammissione; (*round*) eliminatorio(-a)

qualitative [ˈkwɔlɪtətɪv] ADJ qualitativo(-a)

quality [ˈkwɔlɪtɪ] N qualità f inv ▶ CPD di qualità; **of good ~** di buona qualità; **of poor ~** scadente; **~ of life** qualità della vita

quality control N controllo di qualità

quality papers NPL, **quality press** N: **the ~** (*BRIT*) la stampa d'informazione

qualm [kwɑːm] N dubbio; scrupolo; **to have qualms about sth** avere degli scrupoli per qc

quandary [ˈkwɔndrɪ] N: **in a ~** in un dilemma

quango [ˈkwæŋgəu] N ABBR (*BRIT*: = *quasi-autonomous non-governmental organization*) commissione consultiva di nomina governativa

quantifiable [ˈkwɔntɪfaɪəbl] ADJ quantificabile

quantify [ˈkwɔntɪfaɪ] VT quantificare

quantitative [ˈkwɔntɪtətɪv] ADJ quantitativo(-a)

quantity [ˈkwɔntɪtɪ] N quantità f inv; **in ~** in grande quantità

quantity surveyor N (*BRIT*) geometra m (*specializzato nel calcolare la quantità e il costo del materiale da costruzione*)

quantum leap [ˈkwɔntəm-] N (*fig*) enorme cambiamento

quarantine [ˈkwɔrntiːn] N quarantena

quark [kwɑːk] N quark m inv

quarrel [ˈkwɔrl] N lite f, disputa ▶ VI litigare; **to have a ~ with sb** litigare con qn; **I've no ~ with him** non ho niente contro di lui; **I can't ~ with that** non ho niente da ridire su questo

quarrelsome [ˈkwɔrəlsəm] ADJ litigioso(-a)

quarry [ˈkwɔrɪ] N (*for stone*) cava; (*animal*) preda ▶ VT (*marble etc*) estrarre

quart [kwɔːt] N due pinte fpl, ≈ litro

quarter [ˈkwɔːtəʳ] N quarto; (*of year*) trimestre m; (*district*) quartiere m; (*US, CANADA*: *25 cents*) quarto di dollaro, 25 centesimi ▶ VT dividere in quattro; (*Mil*) alloggiare ▪ **quarters** NPL (*living quarters*) alloggio; (*Mil*) alloggi mpl, quadrato; **to pay by the ~** pagare trimestralmente; **a ~ of an hour** un quarto d'ora; **it's a ~ to 3**, (US) **it's a ~ of 3** sono le 3 meno un quarto, manca un quarto alle 3; **it's a ~ past 3**, (US) **it's a ~ after 3** sono le 3 e un quarto; **from all quarters** da tutte le parti or direzioni; **at close quarters** a distanza ravvicinata

quarterback ['kwɔːtəbæk] N (US Football) quarterback m inv

quarter-deck ['kwɔːtədɛk] N (Naut) cassero

quarter final N quarto di finale

quarterly ['kwɔːtəlɪ] ADJ trimestrale ▶ ADV trimestralmente ▶ N periodico trimestrale

quartermaster ['kwɔːtəmɑːstəʳ] N (Mil) furiere m

quartet, quartette [kwɔː'tɛt] N quartetto

quarto ['kwɔːtəu] ADJ, N in quarto m inv

quartz [kwɔːts] N quarzo ▶ CPD di quarzo; (watch, clock) al quarzo

quash [kwɔʃ] VT (verdict) annullare

quasi- ['kweɪzaɪ] PREFIX quasi + noun; quasi, pressoché + adjective

quaver ['kweɪvəʳ] N (BRIT Mus) croma ▶ VI tremolare

quay [kiː] N (also: **quayside**) banchina

queasy ['kwiːzɪ] ADJ (stomach) delicato(-a); **to feel ~** aver la nausea

Quebec [kwɪ'bɛk] N Quebec m

queen [kwiːn] N (gen) regina; (Cards etc) regina, donna

queen mother N regina madre

Queen's speech N (BRIT) vedi nota

Durante la sessione di apertura del Parlamento britannico il sovrano legge un discorso redatto dal governo, il **Queen's speech** (se si tratta della regina), che contiene le linee generali del nuovo programma politico.

queer [kwɪəʳ] ADJ strano(-a), curioso(-a); (suspicious) dubbio(-a), sospetto(-a); (BRIT: sick): **I feel ~** mi sento poco bene

quell [kwɛl] VT domare

quench [kwɛntʃ] VT (flames) spegnere; **to ~ one's thirst** dissetarsi

querulous ['kwɛruləs] ADJ querulo(-a)

query ['kwɪərɪ] N domanda, questione f; (doubt) dubbio ▶ VT mettere in questione; (disagree with, dispute) contestare

quest [kwɛst] N cerca, ricerca

question ['kwɛstʃən] N domanda, questione f ▶ VT (person) interrogare; (plan, idea) mettere in questione or in dubbio; **to ask sb a ~, put a ~ to sb** fare una domanda a qn; **to bring** or **call sth into ~** mettere in dubbio qc; **the ~ is …** il problema è …; **it's a ~ of doing** si tratta di fare; **there's some ~ of doing** c'è chi suggerisce di fare; **beyond ~** fuori di dubbio; **out of the ~** fuori discussione, impossibile

questionable ['kwɛstʃənəbl] ADJ discutibile

questioner ['kwɛstʃənəʳ] N interrogante mf

questioning ['kwɛstʃənɪŋ] ADJ interrogativo(-a) ▶ N interrogatorio

question mark N punto interrogativo

questionnaire [kwɛstʃə'nɛəʳ] N questionario

queue [kjuː] (BRIT) N coda, fila ▶ VI fare la coda; **to jump the ~** passare davanti agli altri (in una coda)

quibble ['kwɪbl] VI cavillare

quiche [kiːʃ] N torta salata a base di uova, formaggio, prosciutto o altro

quick [kwɪk] ADJ rapido(-a), veloce; (reply) pronto(-a); (mind) pronto(-a), acuto(-a) ▶ ADV rapidamente, presto ▶ N: **cut to the ~** (fig) toccato(-a) sul vivo; **be ~!** fa presto!; **to be ~ to act** agire prontamente; **she was ~ to see that …** ha visto subito che …

quicken ['kwɪkn] VT accelerare, affrettare; (rouse) animare, stimolare ▶ VI accelerare, affrettarsi

quick fix N soluzione f tampone inv

quicklime ['kwɪklaɪm] N calce f viva

quickly ['kwɪklɪ] ADV rapidamente, velocemente; **we must act ~** dobbiamo agire tempestivamente

quickness ['kwɪknɪs] N rapidità; prontezza; acutezza

quicksand ['kwɪksænd] N sabbie fpl mobili

quickstep ['kwɪkstɛp] N tipo di ballo simile al foxtrot

quick-tempered [kwɪk'tɛmpəd] ADJ che si arrabbia facilmente

quick-witted [kwɪk'wɪtɪd] ADJ pronto(-a) d'ingegno

quid [kwɪd] N (pl inv: BRIT col) sterlina

quid pro quo ['kwɪdprəu'kwəu] N contraccambio

quiet ['kwaɪət] ADJ tranquillo(-a), quieto(-a); (reserved) quieto(-a), taciturno(-a); (ceremony) semplice; (not noisy: engine) silenzioso(-a); (not busy: day) calmo(-a), tranquillo(-a); (colour) discreto(-a) ▶ N tranquillità, calma ▶ VT, VI (US) = **quieten**; **keep ~!** sta zitto!; **on the ~** di nascosto; **I'll have a ~ word with him** gli dirò due parole in privato; **business is ~ at this time of year** questa è la stagione morta

quieten ['kwaɪətn] VI (BRIT: also: **quieten down**) calmarsi, chetarsi ▶ VT calmare, chetare

quietly ['kwaɪətlɪ] ADV tranquillamente, calmamente; silenziosamente

quietness ['kwaɪətnɪs] N tranquillità, calma; silenzio

quill [kwɪl] N penna d'oca

quilt [kwɪlt] N trapunta; **continental ~** piumino

quin [kwɪn] N ABBR = **quintuplet**

quince [kwɪns] N (mela) cotogna; (tree) cotogno

quinine [kwɪˈniːn] N chinino

quintet, quintette [kwɪnˈtɛt] N quintetto

quintuplet [kwɪnˈtjuːplɪt] N uno(-a) di cinque gemelli

quip [kwɪp] N battuta di spirito

quire [ˈkwaɪəʳ] N ventesima parte di una risma

quirk [kwəːk] N ghiribizzo; **by some ~ of fate** per un capriccio della sorte

quirky [ˈkwəːkɪ] ADJ stravagante

quit [kwɪt] (*pt, pp* ~ *or* **quitted**) VT mollare; (*premises*) lasciare, partire da ▶ VI (*give up*) mollare; (*resign*) dimettersi; **to ~ doing** smettere di fare; **~ stalling!** (*US col*) non tirarla per le lunghe!; **notice to ~** (BRIT) preavviso (*dato all'inquilino*)

quite [kwaɪt] ADV (*rather*) assai; (*entirely*) completamente, del tutto; **I ~ understand** capisco perfettamente; **~ a few of them** non pochi di loro; **~ (so)!** esatto!; **~ new** proprio nuovo; **that's not ~ right** non è proprio esatto; **she's ~ pretty** è piuttosto carina

Quito [ˈkiːtəu] N Quito *m*

quits [kwɪts] ADJ: **~ (with)** pari (con); **let's call it ~** adesso siamo pari

quiver [ˈkwɪvəʳ] VI tremare, fremere ▶ N (*for arrows*) faretra

quiz [kwɪz] N (*game*) quiz *m inv*; indovinello ▶ VT interrogare

quizzical [ˈkwɪzɪkəl] ADJ enigmatico(-a)

quoits [kwɔɪts] NPL gioco degli anelli

quorum [ˈkwɔːrəm] N quorum *m inv*

quota [ˈkwəutə] N quota

quotation [kwəuˈteɪʃən] N citazione *f*; (*of shares etc*) quotazione *f*; (*estimate*) preventivo

quotation marks NPL virgolette *fpl*

quote [kwəut] N citazione *f* ▶ VT (*sentence*) citare; (*price*) dare, indicare, fissare; (*shares*) quotare ▶ VI: **to ~ from** citare; **to ~ for a job** dare un preventivo per un lavoro ▪ **quotes** NPL (*col*) = **quotation marks**; **in quotes** tra virgolette; **~ ... unquote** (*in dictation*) aprire le virgolette ... chiudere le virgolette

quotient [ˈkwəuʃənt] N quoziente *m*

qv ABBR (= *quod vide*) v

qwerty keyboard [ˈkwəːtɪ-] N tastiera *f* qwerty *inv*

Rr

R, r [ɑːʳ] N (letter) R, r f inv or m inv; **R for Robert,** (US) **R for Roger** ≈ R come Roma

R ABBR (= Réaumur (scale)) R; (= river) F; (= right) D; (US Cine: = restricted) ≈ vietato; (US Pol) = **republican**; (BRIT) = **Rex; Regina**

RA N ABBR (BRIT) = **Royal Academy; Royal Academician** ▶ ABBR = **rear admiral**

RAAF N ABBR = **Royal Australian Air Force**

Rabat [rə'bɑːt] N Rabat f

rabbi ['ræbaɪ] N rabbino

rabbit ['ræbɪt] N coniglio ▶ VI: **to ~ (on)** (BRIT) blaterare

rabbit hole N tana di coniglio

rabbit hutch N conigliera

rabble ['ræbl] N (pej) canaglia, plebaglia

rabid ['ræbɪd] ADJ rabbioso(-a); (fig) fanatico(-a)

rabies ['reɪbiːz] N rabbia

RAC N ABBR (BRIT: = Royal Automobile Club) ≈ A.C.I. m (= Automobile Club d'Italia)

raccoon, racoon [rə'kuːn] N procione m

race [reɪs] N razza; (competition, rush) corsa ▶ VT (person) gareggiare (in corsa) con; (horse) far correre; (engine) imballare ▶ VI correre; (engine) imballarsi; **the human ~** la razza umana; **he raced across the road** ha attraversato la strada di corsa; **to ~ in/out** etc precipitarsi dentro/fuori etc

race car N (US) = **racing car**

race car driver N (US) = **racing driver**

racecourse ['reɪskɔːs] N campo di corse, ippodromo

racehorse ['reɪshɔːs] N cavallo da corsa

race relations NPL rapporti mpl razziali

racetrack ['reɪstræk] N pista

racial ['reɪʃl] ADJ razziale

racial discrimination N discriminazione f razziale

racialism ['reɪʃəlɪzəm] N razzismo

racialist ['reɪʃəlɪst] ADJ, N razzista mf

racing ['reɪsɪŋ] N corsa

racing car N (BRIT) macchina da corsa

racing driver N (BRIT) corridore m automobilista

racism ['reɪsɪzəm] N razzismo

racist ['reɪsɪst] ADJ, N (pej) razzista mf

rack [ræk] N rastrelliera; (also: **luggage rack**) rete f, portabagagli m inv; (also: **roof rack**) portabagagli; (dish rack) scolapiatti m inv ▶ VT torturare, tormentare; **magazine ~** portariviste m inv; **shoe ~** scarpiera; **toast ~** portatoast m inv; **to go to ~ and ruin** (building) andare in rovina; (business) andare in malora or a catafascio; **to ~ one's brains** scervellarsi; **racked by** torturato(-a) da
▶ **rack up** VT accumulare

racket ['rækɪt] N (for tennis) racchetta; (noise) fracasso; baccano; (swindle) imbroglio, truffa; (organized crime) racket m inv

racketeer [rækɪ'tɪəʳ] N (US) trafficante mf

racoon [rə'kuːn] N = **raccoon**

racquet ['rækɪt] N racchetta

racy ['reɪsɪ] ADJ brioso(-a); piccante

RADA ['rɑːdə] N ABBR (BRIT) = **Royal Academy of Dramatic Art**

radar ['reɪdɑːʳ] N radar m ▶ CPD radar inv

radar trap N controllo della velocità con radar

radial ['reɪdɪəl] ADJ (also: **radial-ply**) radiale

radiance ['reɪdɪəns] N splendore m, radiosità

radiant ['reɪdɪənt] ADJ raggiante; (Physics) radiante

radiate ['reɪdɪeɪt] VT (heat) irraggiare, irradiare ▶ VI (lines) irradiarsi

radiation [reɪdɪ'eɪʃən] N irradiamento; (radioactive) radiazione f

radiation sickness N malattia da radiazioni

radiator ['reɪdɪeɪtə] N radiatore m

radiator cap N tappo del radiatore

radiator grill N (Aut) mascherina, calandra

radical ['rædɪkl] ADJ radicale

radii ['reɪdɪaɪ] NPL of **radius**

radio ['reɪdɪəu] N radio f inv ▶ VT (information) trasmettere per radio; (one's position) comunicare via radio; (person) chiamare via radio ▶ VI: **to ~**

r

to sb comunicare via radio con qn; **on the ~** alla radio

radio... [ˈreɪdɪəu] PREFIX radio...

radioactive [ˈreɪdɪəuˈæktɪv] ADJ radioattivo(-a)

radioactivity [ˈreɪdɪəuækˈtɪvɪtɪ] N radioattività

radio announcer N annunciatore(-trice) della radio

radio-controlled [ˈreɪdɪəukənˈtrəʊld] ADJ radiocomandato(-a), radioguidato(-a)

radiographer [reɪdɪˈɔgrəfəʳ] N (tecnico) radiologo(-a)

radiography [reɪdɪˈɔgrəfɪ] N radiografia

radiologist [reɪdɪˈɔlədʒɪst] N (medico) radiologo(-a)

radiology [reɪdɪˈɔlədʒɪ] N radiologia

radio station N stazione f radio inv

radio taxi N radiotaxi m inv

radiotelephone [ˈreɪdɪəuˈtɛlɪfəun] N radiotelefono

radiotherapist [ˈreɪdɪəuˈθɛrəpɪst] N radioterapista mf

radiotherapy [ˈreɪdɪəuˈθɛrəpɪ] N radioterapia

radish [ˈrædɪʃ] N ravanello

radium [ˈreɪdɪəm] N radio

radius [ˈreɪdɪəs] (pl **radii** [-ɪaɪ]) N raggio; (Anat) radio; **within a ~ of 50 miles** in un raggio di 50 miglia

RAF N ABBR (BRIT) = **Royal Air Force**

raffia [ˈræfɪə] N rafia

raffish [ˈræfɪʃ] ADJ dal look trasandato

raffle [ˈræfl] N lotteria ▶ VT (object) mettere in palio

raft [rɑːft] N zattera; (also: **life raft**) zattera di salvataggio

rafter [ˈrɑːftəʳ] N trave f

rag [ræg] N straccio, cencio; (pej: newspaper) giornalaccio, bandiera; (for charity) iniziativa studentesca a scopo benefico ▶ VT (BRIT) prendere in giro ■ **rags** NPL (torn clothes) stracci mpl, brandelli mpl; **in rags** stracciato

rag-and-bone man [ˈrægənˈbəun-] N (irreg) straccivendolo

ragbag [ˈrægbæg] N (fig) guazzabuglio

rag doll N bambola di pezza

rage [reɪdʒ] N (fury) collera, furia ▶ VI (person) andare su tutte le furie; (storm) infuriare; **it's all the ~** fa furore; **to fly into a ~** andare or montare su tutte le furie

ragged [ˈrægɪd] ADJ (edge) irregolare; (cuff) logoro(-a); (appearance) pezzente

raging [ˈreɪdʒɪŋ] ADJ (all senses) furioso(-a); **in a ~ temper** su tutte le furie

rag trade N (col): **the ~** l'abbigliamento

rag week N (BRIT) settimana di festa studentesca

raid [reɪd] N (Mil) incursione f; (criminal) rapina; (by police) irruzione f ▶ VT fare un'incursione in; rapinare; fare irruzione in

raider [ˈreɪdəʳ] N rapinatore(-trice); (plane) aeroplano da incursione

rail [reɪl] N (on stair) ringhiera; (on bridge, balcony) parapetto; (of ship) battagliola; (for train) rotaia ■ **rails** NPL binario, rotaie fpl; **by ~** per ferrovia, in treno

railcard [ˈreɪlkɑːd] N (BRIT) tessera di riduzione ferroviaria

railing [ˈreɪlɪŋ] N, **railings** [ˈreɪlɪŋz] NPL ringhiere fpl

railroad N (US) = **railway**

railway (BRIT) [ˈreɪlweɪ], (US) **railroad** [ˈreɪlrəud] N ferrovia

railway engine N (BRIT) locomotiva

railway line N (BRIT) linea ferroviaria

railwayman [ˈreɪlweɪmən] N (irreg) (BRIT) ferroviere m

railway station N (BRIT) stazione f ferroviaria

rain [reɪn] N pioggia ▶ VI piovere; **in the ~** sotto la pioggia; **it's raining** piove; **it's raining cats and dogs** piove a catinelle

rainbow [ˈreɪnbəu] N arcobaleno

raincoat [ˈreɪnkəut] N impermeabile m

raindrop [ˈreɪndrɔp] N goccia di pioggia

rainfall [ˈreɪnfɔːl] N pioggia; (measurement) piovosità

rainforest [ˈreɪnfɔrɪst] N foresta pluviale or equatoriale

rainproof [ˈreɪnpruːf] ADJ impermeabile

rainstorm [ˈreɪnstɔːm] N pioggia torrenziale

rainwater [ˈreɪnwɔːtəʳ] N acqua piovana

rainy [ˈreɪnɪ] ADJ piovoso(-a)

raise [reɪz] N aumento ▶ VT (lift) alzare; sollevare; (build) erigere; (increase) aumentare; (a protest, doubt, question) sollevare; (cattle, family) allevare; (crop) coltivare; (army, funds) raccogliere; (loan) ottenere; (end: siege, embargo) togliere; **to ~ one's voice** alzare la voce; **to ~ sb's hopes** accendere le speranze di qn; **to ~ one's glass to sb/sth** brindare a qn/qc; **to ~ a laugh/a smile** far ridere/sorridere

raisin [ˈreɪzn] N uva secca

Raj [rɑːdʒ] N: **the ~** l'impero britannico (in India)

rajah [ˈrɑːdʒə] N ragià m inv

rake [reɪk] N (tool) rastrello; (person) libertino ▶ VT (garden) rastrellare; (with machine gun) spazzare ▶ VI: **to ~ through** (fig: search) frugare tra

rake-off [ˈreɪkɔf] N (col) parte f percentuale, fetta

rakish [ˈreɪkɪʃ] ADJ dissoluto(-a); disinvolto(-a)

rally [ˈrælɪ] N (Pol etc) riunione f; (Aut) rally m inv; (Tennis) scambio ▶ VT riunire, radunare ▶ VI raccogliersi, radunarsi; (sick person, Stock Exchange) riprendersi

▶ **rally round** VT FUS raggrupparsi intorno a; venire in aiuto di

rallying point [ˈrælɪŋ-] N (Pol, Mil) punto di riunione, punto di raduno

RAM [ræm] N ABBR (Comput: = random access memory) RAM f

ram [ræm] N montone m, ariete m; (device) ariete ▶ VT conficcare; (crash into) cozzare, sbattere contro; percuotere; speronare

Ramadan [ræməˈdæn] N Ramadan m inv

ramble [ˈræmbl] N escursione f ▶ VI (pej: also: **ramble on**) divagare

rambler [ˈræmbləʳ] N escursionista mf; (Bot) rosa rampicante

rambling [ˈræmblɪŋ] ADJ (speech) sconnesso(-a); (Bot) rampicante; (house) tutto(-a) nicchie e corridoi

rambunctious [ræmˈbʌŋkʃəs] ADJ (US) = **rumbustious**

RAMC N ABBR (BRIT) = **Royal Army Medical Corps**

ramification [ræmɪfɪˈkeɪʃən] N ramificazione f

ramp [ræmp] N rampa; **on/off** ~ (US Aut) raccordo di entrata/uscita

rampage [ræmˈpeɪdʒ] N: **to go on the** ~ scatenarsi in modo violento ▶ VI: **they went rampaging through the town** si sono scatenati in modo violento per la città

rampant [ˈræmpənt] ADJ (disease etc) che infierisce

rampart [ˈræmpɑːt] N bastione m

ram raiding [-reɪdɪŋ] N il rapinare un negozio sfondandone la vetrina con un veicolo rubato

ramshackle [ˈræmʃækl] ADJ (house) cadente; (car etc) sgangherato(-a)

RAN N ABBR = **Royal Australian Navy**

ran [ræn] PT of **run**

ranch [rɑːntʃ] N ranch m inv

rancher [ˈrɑːntʃəʳ] N (owner) proprietario di un ranch; (ranch hand) cowboy m inv

rancid [ˈrænsɪd] ADJ rancido(-a)

rancour, (US) **rancor** [ˈræŋkəʳ] N rancore m

R & B N ABBR = **rhythm and blues**

R & D N ABBR = **research and development**

random [ˈrændəm] ADJ fatto(-a) or detto(-a) per caso; (Comput, Math) casuale ▶ N: **at** ~ a casaccio

random access N (Comput) accesso casuale

R & R N ABBR (= rest and recreation) ricreazione f; (US Mil) permesso per militari

randy [ˈrændɪ] ADJ (col) arrapato(-a); lascivo(-a)

rang [ræŋ] PT of **ring**

range [reɪndʒ] N (of mountains) catena; (of missile, voice) portata; (of products) gamma; (Mil: also: **shooting range**) campo di tiro; (also: **kitchen range**) fornello, cucina economica ▶ VT (place) disporre, allineare; (roam) vagare per ▶ VI: **to** ~

over coprire; **to** ~ **from ... to** andare da ... a; **price** ~ gamma di prezzi; **do you have anything else in this price** ~? ha nient'altro su or di questo prezzo?; **within (firing)** ~ a portata di tiro; **ranged left/right** (text) allineato(-a) a destra/sinistra

ranger [ˈreɪndʒəʳ] N guardia forestale

Rangoon [ræŋˈguːn] N Rangun f

rank [ræŋk] N fila; (status, Mil) grado; (BRIT: also: **taxi rank**) posteggio di taxi ▶ VI: **to** ~ **among** essere tra ▶ ADJ (smell) puzzolente; (hypocrisy, injustice) vero(-a) e proprio(-a); **the ranks** (Mil) la truppa; **the** ~ **and file** (fig) la gran massa; **to close ranks** (Mil, fig) serrare i ranghi; **I** ~ **him sixth** gli do il sesto posto, lo metto al sesto posto

rankle [ˈræŋkl] VI: **to** ~ **(with sb)** bruciare (a qn)

rank outsider N outsider mf

ransack [ˈrænsæk] VT rovistare; (plunder) saccheggiare

ransom [ˈrænsəm] N riscatto; **to hold sb to** ~ (fig) esercitare pressione su qn

rant [rænt] VI vociare

ranting [ˈræntɪŋ] N vociare m

rap [ræp] N (noise) colpetti mpl; (at a door) bussata; (music) rap m inv ▶ VT dare dei colpetti a; bussare a

rape [reɪp] N violenza carnale, stupro; (Bot) ravizzone m ▶ VT violentare

rape oil, rapeseed oil [ˈreɪpsiːd-] N olio di ravizzone

rapid [ˈræpɪd] ADJ rapido(-a)

rapidity [rəˈpɪdɪtɪ] N rapidità

rapidly [ˈræpɪdlɪ] ADV rapidamente

rapids [ˈræpɪdz] NPL (Geo) rapida

rapist [ˈreɪpɪst] N violentatore(-trice)

rapport [ræˈpɔːʳ] N rapporto

rapt [ræpt] ADJ (attention) rapito(-a), profondo(-a); **to be** ~ **in contemplation** essere in estatica contemplazione

rapture [ˈræptʃəʳ] N estasi f inv; **to go into raptures over** andare in solluchero per

rapturous [ˈræptʃərəs] ADJ estatico(-a)

rare [rɛəʳ] ADJ raro(-a); (Culin: steak) al sangue; **it is** ~ **to find that ...** capita di rado or raramente che ... + sub

rarebit [ˈrɛəbɪt] N see **Welsh rarebit**

rarefied [ˈrɛərɪfaɪd] ADJ (air, atmosphere) rarefatto(-a)

rarely [ˈrɛəlɪ] ADV raramente

raring [ˈrɛərɪŋ] ADJ: **to be** ~ **to go** (col) non veder l'ora di cominciare

rarity [ˈrɛərɪtɪ] N rarità f inv

rascal [ˈrɑːskl] N mascalzone m

rash [ræʃ] ADJ imprudente, sconsiderato(-a) ▶ N (Med) eruzione f; (of events etc) scoppio; **to come out in a** ~ avere uno sfogo

r

rasher ['ræʃəʳ] N fetta sottile (di lardo or prosciutto)

rasp [rɑːsp] N (tool) lima ▶ vt (speak: also: **rasp out**) gracchiare

raspberry ['rɑːzbərɪ] N lampone m

raspberry bush N lampone m (pianta)

rasping ['rɑːspɪŋ] ADJ stridulo(-a)

Rastafarian [ræstəˈfɛərɪən] ADJ, N rastafariano(-a)

rat [ræt] N ratto

ratable ['reɪtəbl] ADJ = **rateable**

ratchet ['rætʃɪt] N: **~ wheel** ruota dentata

rate [reɪt] N (proportion) tasso, percentuale f; (speed) velocità f inv; (price) tariffa ▶ vt valutare; stimare; **to ~ sb/sth as** valutare qn/qc come; **to ~ sb/sth among** annoverare qn/qc tra; **to ~ sb/sth highly** stimare molto qn/qc; **at a ~ of 60 kph** alla velocità di 60 km all'ora; **~ of exchange** tasso di cambio; **~ of flow** flusso medio; **~ of growth** tasso di crescita; **~ of return** tasso di rendimento; **pulse ~** frequenza delle pulsazioni; see also **rates**

rateable value ['reɪtəbl-] N (BRIT) valore m imponibile (agli effetti delle imposte comunali)

ratepayer ['reɪtpeɪəʳ] N (BRIT) contribuente mf (che paga le imposte comunali)

rates [reɪts] NPL (BRIT: property tax) imposte fpl comunali; (fees) tariffe fpl

rather ['rɑːðəʳ] ADV piuttosto; (somewhat) abbastanza; (to some extent) un po'; **it's ~ expensive** è piuttosto caro; (too much) è un po' caro; **there's ~ a lot** ce n'è parecchio; **I would** or **I'd ~ go** preferirei andare; **I had ~ go** farei meglio ad andare; **I'd ~ not leave** preferirei non partire; **or ~** (more accurately) anzi, per essere (più) precisi; **I ~ think he won't come** credo proprio che non verrà

ratification [rætɪfɪˈkeɪʃən] N ratificazione f

ratify ['rætɪfaɪ] vt ratificare

rating ['reɪtɪŋ] N classificazione f; (assessment) valutazione f; (score) punteggio di merito; (Naut: category) classe f; (: BRIT: sailor) marinaio semplice

ratings ['reɪtɪŋz] NPL (Radio, TV) indice m di ascolto

ratio ['reɪʃɪəu] N proporzione f; **in the ~ of 2 to 1** in rapporto di 2 a 1

ration ['ræʃən] N razione f ▶ vt razionare ■ **rations** NPL razioni fpl

rational ['ræʃnl] ADJ razionale, ragionevole; (solution, reasoning) logico(-a)

rationale [ræʃəˈnɑːl] N fondamento logico; giustificazione f

rationalization [ræʃnəlaɪˈzeɪʃən] N razionalizzazione f

rationalize ['ræʃnəlaɪz] vt razionalizzare

rationally ['ræʃnəlɪ] ADV razionalmente; logicamente

rationing ['ræʃnɪŋ] N razionamento

ratpack ['rætpæk] N (BRIT pej) stampa scandalistica

rat poison N veleno per topi

rat race N carrierismo, corsa al successo

rattan [ræˈtæn] N malacca

rattle ['rætl] N tintinnio; (louder) rumore m di ferraglia; (object: of baby) sonaglino; (: of sports fan) raganella ▶ vi risuonare, tintinnare; fare un rumore di ferraglia ▶ vt far tintinnare; (col: disconcert) sconcertare

rattlesnake ['rætlsneɪk] N serpente m a sonagli

ratty ['rætɪ] ADJ (col) incavolato(-a)

raucous ['rɔːkəs] ADJ sguaiato(-a)

raucously ['rɔːkəslɪ] ADV sguaiatamente

raunchy ['rɔːntʃɪ] ADJ (col: person) allupato(-a); (: voice, song) libidinoso(-a)

ravage ['rævɪdʒ] vt devastare

ravages ['rævɪdʒɪz] NPL danni mpl

rave [reɪv] vi (in anger) infuriarsi; (with enthusiasm) andare in estasi; (Med) delirare ▶ N (BRIT): **~ (party)** rave m inv ▶ ADJ (scene, culture, music) del fenomeno rave ▶ CPD: **~ review** (col) critica entusiastica

raven ['reɪvən] N corvo

ravenous ['rævənəs] ADJ affamato(-a)

ravine [rəˈviːn] N burrone m

raving ['reɪvɪŋ] ADJ: **~ lunatic** (!) pazzo(-a) furioso(-a)

ravings ['reɪvɪŋz] NPL vaneggiamenti mpl

ravioli [rævɪˈəulɪ] N ravioli mpl

ravish ['rævɪʃ] vt (delight) estasiare

ravishing ['rævɪʃɪŋ] ADJ incantevole

raw [rɔː] ADJ (uncooked) crudo(-a); (not processed) greggio(-a); (sore) vivo(-a); (inexperienced) inesperto(-a); (weather, day) gelido(-a); **to get a ~ deal** (col: bad bargain) prendere un bidone; (: harsh treatment) venire trattato ingiustamente

Rawalpindi [rɔːlˈpɪndɪ] N Rawalpindi f

raw material N materia prima

ray [reɪ] N raggio; **a ~ of hope** un barlume di speranza

rayon ['reɪɔn] N raion m

raze [reɪz] vt radere, distruggere; (also: **raze to the ground**) radere al suolo

razor ['reɪzəʳ] N rasoio

razor blade N lama di rasoio

razzle ['ræzl] N (BRIT col): **to be/go on the ~** darsi alla pazza gioia

razzmatazz ['ræzmətæz] N (col) clamore m

RC ABBR = **Roman Catholic**

RCAF N ABBR = **Royal Canadian Air Force**

RCMP N ABBR = **Royal Canadian Mounted Police**

RCN N ABBR = **Royal Canadian Navy**

RD ABBR (*US Post*) = **rural delivery**

Rd ABBR = **road**

RE N ABBR (*BRIT Mil*: = *Royal Engineers*) ≈ G.M. (= *Genio Militare*); (*BRIT*) = **religious education**

re [riː] PREP con riferimento a

reach [riːtʃ] N portata; (*of river etc*) tratto ▶ VT raggiungere; arrivare a ▶ VI stendersi; (*stretch out hand: also:* **reach down, reach over, reach across**) allungare una mano; **out of/within ~** (*object*) fuori/a portata di mano; **within easy ~** (*of*) (*place*) a breve distanza (di), vicino (a); **to ~ sb by phone** contattare qn per telefono; **can I ~ you at your hotel?** la posso contattare al suo albergo?
  ▶ **reach out** VT (*hand*) allungare ▶ VI: **to ~ out for** stendere la mano per prendere

react [riːˈækt] VI reagire

reaction [riːˈækʃən] N reazione f

reactionary [riːˈækʃənrɪ] ADJ, N reazionario(-a)

reactor [riːˈæktəʳ] N reattore m

read [riːd] (*pt, pp* = [rɛd]) VI leggere ▶ VT leggere; (*understand*) intendere, interpretare; (*study*) studiare; **do you ~ me?** (*Tel*) mi ricevete?; **to take sth as ~** (*fig*) dare qc per scontato
  ▶ **read out** VT leggere ad alta voce
  ▶ **read over** VT rileggere attentamente
  ▶ **read through** VT (*quickly*) dare una scorsa a; (*thoroughly*) leggere da cima a fondo
  ▶ **read up, read up on** VT studiare bene

readable [ˈriːdəbl] ADJ leggibile; che si legge volentieri

reader [ˈriːdəʳ] N lettore(-trice); (*book*) libro di lettura; (*BRIT: at university*) professore con funzioni preminenti di ricerca

readership [ˈriːdəʃɪp] N (*of paper etc*) numero di lettori

readily [ˈrɛdɪlɪ] ADV volentieri; (*easily*) facilmente; (*quickly*) prontamente

readiness [ˈrɛdɪnɪs] N prontezza; **in ~** (*prepared*) pronto(-a)

reading [ˈriːdɪŋ] N lettura; (*understanding*) interpretazione f; (*on instrument*) indicazione f

reading lamp N lampada da studio

reading room N sala di lettura

readjust [riːəˈdʒʌst] VT raggiustare ▶ VI (*person*): **to ~ (to)** riadattarsi (a)

ready [ˈrɛdɪ] ADJ pronto(-a); (*willing*) pronto(-a), disposto(-a); (*quick*) rapido(-a); (*available*) disponibile ▶ N: **at the ~** (*Mil*) pronto a sparare; (*fig*) tutto(-a) pronto(-a) ▶ VT preparare; **~ for use** pronto per l'uso; **to be ~ to do sth** essere pronto a fare qc; **to get ~** vi prepararsi

ready cash N denaro in contanti

ready-cooked [rɛdɪˈkukt] ADJ già cotto(-a)

ready-made [rɛdɪˈmeɪd] ADJ prefabbricato(-a); (*clothes*) confezionato(-a)

ready reckoner [-ˈrɛkənəʳ] N (*BRIT*) prontuario di calcolo

ready-to-wear [rɛdɪtəˈwɛəʳ] ADJ prêt-à-porter *inv*

reagent [riːˈeɪdʒənt] N: **chemical ~** reagente m chimico

real [rɪəl] ADJ reale; vero(-a) ▶ ADV (*US col: very*) veramente, proprio; **in ~ terms** in realtà; **in ~ life** nella realtà

real ale N birra ad effervescenza naturale

real estate N beni *mpl* immobili

realism [ˈrɪəlɪzəm] N (*Art*) realismo

realist [ˈrɪəlɪst] N realista *mf*

realistic [rɪəˈlɪstɪk] ADJ realistico(-a)

reality [riːˈælɪtɪ] N realtà f *inv*; **in ~** in realtà, in effetti

reality TV N reality TV f

realization [rɪəlaɪˈzeɪʃən] N (*awareness*) presa di coscienza; (*of hopes, project etc*) realizzazione f

realize [ˈrɪəlaɪz] VT (*understand*) rendersi conto di; (*a project, Comm: asset*) realizzare; **I ~ that …** mi rendo conto or capisco che …

really [ˈrɪəlɪ] ADV veramente, davvero; **~!** (*indicating annoyance*) oh, insomma!

realm [rɛlm] N reame m, regno

real time N (*Comput*) tempo reale

Realtor® [ˈrɪəltɔːʳ] N (*US*) agente m immobiliare

ream [riːm] N risma; **reams** (*fig: col*) pagine e pagine *fpl*

reap [riːp] VT mietere; (*fig*) raccogliere

reaper [ˈriːpəʳ] N (*machine*) mietitrice f

reappear [riːəˈpɪəʳ] VI ricomparire, riapparire

reappearance [riːəˈpɪərəns] N riapparizione f

reapply [riːəˈplaɪ] VI: **to ~ for** fare un'altra domanda per

reappraisal [riːəˈpreɪzl] N riesame m

rear [rɪəʳ] ADJ di dietro; (*Aut: wheel etc*) posteriore ▶ N didietro, parte f posteriore ▶ VT (*cattle, family*) allevare ▶ VI (*also:* **rear up**: *animal*) impennarsi

rear admiral N contrammiraglio

rear-engined [ˈrɪərˈɛndʒɪnd] ADJ (*Aut*) con motore posteriore

rearguard [ˈrɪəɡɑːd] N retroguardia

rearm [riːˈɑːm] VT, VI riarmare

rearmament [riːˈɑːməmənt] N riarmo

rearrange [riːəˈreɪndʒ] VT riordinare

rear-view mirror [ˈrɪəvjuː-] N (*Aut*) specchio retrovisivo

rear-wheel drive N trazione *fpl* posteriore

reason [ˈriːzn] N ragione f; (*cause, motive*) ragione, motivo ▶ VI: **to ~ with sb** far ragionare qn; **to have ~ to think** avere motivi per pensare; **it stands to ~ that** è ovvio che; **the ~ for/why** la ragione *or* il motivo di/per cui; **with good ~** a ragione; **all the more ~ why you**

r

741

should not sell it ragione di più per non venderlo

reasonable ['ri:znəbl] ADJ ragionevole; (not bad) accettabile

reasonably ['ri:znəblɪ] ADV ragionevolmente; **one can ~ assume that ...** uno può facilmente supporre che ...

reasoned ['ri:znd] ADJ (argument) ponderato(-a)

reasoning ['ri:znɪŋ] N ragionamento

reassemble [ri:ə'sɛmbl] VT riunire; (machine) rimontare

reassert [ri:ə'sə:t] VT riaffermare

reassurance [ri:ə'ʃuərəns] N rassicurazione f

reassure [ri:ə'ʃuə'] VT rassicurare; **to ~ sb of** rassicurare qn di or su

reassuring [ri:ə'ʃuərɪŋ] ADJ rassicurante

reawakening [ri:ə'weɪknɪŋ] N risveglio

rebate ['ri:beɪt] N rimborso; (on tax etc) sgravio

rebel N ['rɛbl] ribelle mf ▶ VI [rɪ'bɛl] ribellarsi

rebellion [rɪ'bɛljən] N ribellione f

rebellious [rɪ'bɛljəs] ADJ ribelle

rebirth [ri:'bə:θ] N rinascita

rebound VI [rɪ'baund] (ball) rimbalzare ▶ N ['ri:baund] rimbalzo

rebrand [ri:'brænd] VT (product, company, organization) fare il rebranding a; **they are rebranding themselves as new technology experts** adesso si stanno presentando come esperti in nuove tecnologie ▶ N ['ri:ˌbrænd] rebranding m inv

rebuff [rɪ'bʌf] N secco rifiuto ▶ VT respingere

rebuild [ri:'bɪld] VT (irreg: like build) ricostruire

rebuke [rɪ'bju:k] N rimprovero ▶ VT rimproverare

rebut [rɪ'bʌt] VT rifiutare

rebuttal [rɪ'bʌtl] N rifiuto

recalcitrant [rɪ'kælsɪtrənt] ADJ recalcitrante

recall VT [rɪ'kɔ:l] (gen, Comput) richiamare; (remember) ricordare, richiamare alla mente ▶ N ['ri:kɔl] richiamo; **beyond ~** irrevocabile

recant [rɪ'kænt] VI ritrattarsi; (Rel) fare abiura

recap ['ri:kæp] N ricapitolazione f ▶ VT ricapitolare ▶ VI riassumere

recapture [ri:'kæptʃə'] VT riprendere; (atmosphere) ricreare

recd. ABBR = **received**

recede [rɪ'si:d] VI allontanarsi; ritirarsi; calare

receding [rɪ'si:dɪŋ] ADJ (forehead, chin) sfuggente; **he's got a ~ hairline** è stempiato

receipt [rɪ'si:t] N (document) ricevuta; (act of receiving) ricevimento; **to acknowledge ~ of** accusare ricevuta di; **we are in ~ of ...** abbiamo ricevuto ...

receipts [rɪ'si:ts] NPL (Comm) introiti mpl

receivable [rɪ'si:vəbl] ADJ (Comm) esigibile; (: owed) dovuto(-a)

receive [rɪ'si:v] VT ricevere; (guest) ricevere, accogliere; **"received with thanks"** (Comm) "per quietanza"

Received Pronunciation N (BRIT) vedi nota

Si chiama **Received Pronunciation** (RP) l'accento dell'inglese parlato in alcune parti del sud-est dell'Inghilterra. In esso si identifica l'inglese standard delle classi colte, privo di inflessioni regionali e adottato tradizionalmente dagli annunciatori della BBC. È anche l'accento standard dell'inglese insegnato come lingua straniera.

receiver [rɪ'si:və'] N (Tel) ricevitore m; (Radio) apparecchio ricevente; (of stolen goods) ricettatore(-trice); (Law, Comm) curatore(-trice) fallimentare

receivership [rɪ'si:vəʃɪp] N curatela; **to go into ~** andare in amministrazione controllata

recent ['ri:snt] ADJ recente; **in ~ years** negli ultimi anni

recently ['ri:sntlɪ] ADV recentemente; **as ~ as ...** soltanto ...; **until ~** fino a poco tempo fa

receptacle [rɪ'sɛptɪkl] N recipiente m

reception [rɪ'sɛpʃən] N (gen) ricevimento; (welcome) accoglienza; (TV etc) ricezione f

reception centre N (BRIT) centro di raccolta

reception desk N (in hotel) reception f inv; (in hospital, at doctor's) accettazione f; (in large building, offices) portineria

receptionist [rɪ'sɛpʃənɪst] N receptionist mf

receptive [rɪ'sɛptɪv] ADJ ricettivo(-a)

recess [rɪ'sɛs] N (in room) alcova; (Pol etc: holiday) vacanze fpl; (US Law: short break) sospensione f; (US Scol) intervallo

recession [rɪ'sɛʃən] N (Econ) recessione f

recessionista [rɪsɛʃə'nɪstə] N recessionista mf

recharge [ri:'tʃɑːdʒ] VT (battery) ricaricare

rechargeable ['ri:'tʃɑːdʒəbl] ADJ ricaricabile

recipe ['rɛsɪpɪ] N ricetta

recipient [rɪ'sɪpɪənt] N beneficiario(-a); (of letter) destinatario(-a)

reciprocal [rɪ'sɪprəkl] ADJ reciproco(-a)

reciprocate [rɪ'sɪprəkeɪt] VT ricambiare, contraccambiare

recital [rɪ'saɪtl] N recital m inv; concerto (di solista)

recite [rɪ'saɪt] VT (poem) recitare

reckless ['rɛkləs] ADJ (driver etc) spericolato(-a); (spender) incosciente; (spending) folle

recklessly ['rɛkləslɪ] ADV in modo spericolato; da incosciente

reckon ['rɛkən] VT (count) calcolare; (consider) considerare, stimare; (think): **I ~ that ...** penso che .. ▶ VI contare, calcolare; **to ~ without sb/ sth** non tener conto di qn/qc; **he is somebody to be reckoned with** è uno da non sottovalutare

▶ **reckon on** VT FUS contare su

reckoning [ˈrɛknɪŋ] N conto; stima; **the day of ~** il giorno del giudizio

reclaim [rɪˈkleɪm] VT (land) bonificare; (demand back) richiedere, reclamare; (materials) recuperare

reclamation [rɛkləˈmeɪʃən] N bonifica

recline [rɪˈklaɪn] VI stare sdraiato(-a)

reclining [rɪˈklaɪnɪŋ] ADJ (seat) ribaltabile

recluse [rɪˈkluːs] N eremita m, recluso(-a)

recognition [rɛkəgˈnɪʃən] N riconoscimento; **to gain ~** essere riconosciuto(-a); **in ~ of** in or come segno di riconoscimento per; **transformed beyond ~** irriconoscibile

recognizable [ˈrɛkəgnaɪzəbl] ADJ: **~ (by)** riconoscibile (a or da)

recognize [ˈrɛkəgnaɪz] VT: **to ~ (by/as)** riconoscere (a or da/come)

recoil [rɪˈkɔɪl] VI (gun) rinculare; (spring) balzare indietro; (person): **to ~ (from)** indietreggiare (davanti a) ▶ N (gun) rinculo

recollect [rɛkəˈlɛkt] VT ricordare

recollection [rɛkəˈlɛkʃən] N ricordo; **to the best of my ~** per quello che mi ricordo

recommend [rɛkəˈmɛnd] VT raccomandare; (advise) consigliare; **she has a lot to ~ her** ha molti elementi a suo favore

recommendation [rɛkəmɛnˈdeɪʃən] N raccomandazione f; consiglio

recommended retail price [rɛkəˈmɛndɪd-] N (BRIT) prezzo raccomandato al dettaglio

recompense [ˈrɛkəmpɛns] VT ricompensare; (compensate) risarcire ▶ N ricompensa; risarcimento

reconcilable [ˈrɛkənsaɪləbl] ADJ conciliabile

reconcile [ˈrɛkənsaɪl] VT (two people) riconciliare; (two facts) conciliare, quadrare; **to ~ o.s. to** rassegnarsi a

reconciliation [rɛkənsɪlɪˈeɪʃən] N riconciliazione f; conciliazione f

recondite [rɪˈkɒndaɪt] ADJ recondito(-a)

recondition [riːkənˈdɪʃən] VT rimettere a nuovo; rifare

reconfigure [riːkənˈfɪɡəʳ] VT riconfigurare

reconnaissance [rɪˈkɒnɪsns] N (Mil) ricognizione f

reconnoitre, (US) **reconnoiter** [rɛkəˈnɔɪtəʳ] (Mil) VT fare una ricognizione di ▶ VI fare una ricognizione

reconsider [riːkənˈsɪdəʳ] VT riconsiderare

reconstitute [riːˈkɒnstɪtjuːt] VT ricostituire

reconstruct [riːkənˈstrʌkt] VT ricostruire

reconstruction [riːkənˈstrʌkʃən] N ricostruzione f

reconvene [riːkənˈviːn] VT riconvocare ▶ VI radunarsi

record N [ˈrɛkɔːd] ricordo, documento; (of meeting etc) nota, verbale m; (register) registro; (file) pratica, dossier m inv; (Comput) record m inv, registrazione f; (also: **police record**) fedina penale sporca; (Mus: disc) disco; (Sport) record m inv, primato ▶ VT [rɪˈkɔːd] (set down) prendere nota di, registrare; (relate) raccontare; (Comput, Mus: song etc) registrare; **off the ~** adj ufficioso(-a); adv ufficiosamente; **public records** archivi mpl; **Italy's excellent ~** i brillanti successi italiani; **in ~ time** a tempo di record; **to keep a ~ of** tener nota di; **to set the ~ straight** mettere le cose in chiaro; **he is on ~ as saying that ...** ha dichiarato pubblicamente che ...

record card N (in file) scheda

recorded delivery letter [rɪˈkɔːdɪd-] N (BRIT Post) lettera raccomandata

recorder [rɪˈkɔːdəʳ] N (Law) avvocato che funge da giudice; (Mus) flauto diritto

record holder N (Sport) primatista mf

recording [rɪˈkɔːdɪŋ] N (Mus) registrazione f

recording studio N studio di registrazione

record library N discoteca

record player N giradischi m inv

recount [rɪˈkaunt] VT raccontare, narrare

re-count N [ˈriːkaunt] (Pol: of votes) nuovo conteggio ▶ VT [riːˈkaunt] ricontare

recoup [rɪˈkuːp] VT ricuperare; **to ~ one's losses** ricuperare le perdite, rifarsi

recourse [rɪˈkɔːs] N: **to have ~ to** ricorrere a

recover [rɪˈkʌvəʳ] VT ricuperare ▶ VI (from illness) rimettersi (in salute), ristabilirsi; **to ~ (from)** (country, person: from shock) riprendersi (da)

re-cover [riːˈkʌvəʳ] VT (chair etc) ricoprire

recovery [rɪˈkʌvərɪ] N ricupero; ristabilimento; ripresa

recreate [riːkrɪˈeɪt] VT ricreare

recreation [rɛkrɪˈeɪʃən] N ricreazione f; svago

recreational [rɛkrɪˈeɪʃənəl] ADJ ricreativo(-a)

recreational drug N droga usata saltuariamente

recreational vehicle N (US) camper m inv

recrimination [rɪkrɪmɪˈneɪʃən] N recriminazione f

recruit [rɪˈkruːt] N recluta; (in company) nuovo(-a) assunto(-a) ▶ VT reclutare

recruiting office [rɪˈkruːtɪŋ-] N ufficio di reclutamento

recruitment [rɪˈkruːtmənt] N reclutamento

rectangle [ˈrɛktæŋɡl] N rettangolo

rectangular [rɛkˈtæŋɡjuləʳ] ADJ rettangolare

rectify [ˈrɛktɪfaɪ] VT (error) rettificare; (omission) riparare

rector [ˈrɛktəʳ] N (Rel) parroco (anglicano); (in Scottish universities) personalità eletta dagli studenti per rappresentarli

r

rectory [ˈrɛktərɪ] N presbiterio

rectum [ˈrɛktəm] N (Anat) retto

recuperate [rɪˈkjuːpəreɪt] VI ristabilirsi

recur [rɪˈkəː] VI riaccadere; (idea, opportunity) riapparire; (symptoms) ripresentarsi

recurrence [rɪˈkʌrəns] N ripresentarsi m inv; riapparizione f

recurrent [rɪˈkʌrənt] ADJ ricorrente, periodico(-a)

recurring [rɪˈkʌrɪŋ] ADJ (Math) periodico(-a)

recyclable [riːˈsaɪkləbl] ADJ riciclabile

recycle [riːˈsaɪkl] VT riciclare

recycled [riːˈsaɪkld] ADJ riciclato(-a); **~ paper** carta f riciclata

recycling [riːˈsaɪklɪŋ] N riciclaggio

red [rɛd] N rosso; (Pol: pej) rosso(-a) ▶ ADJ rosso(-a); **in the ~** (account) scoperto; (business) in deficit

red alert N allarme m rosso

red-blooded [ˈrɛdˈblʌdɪd] ADJ (col) gagliardo(-a)

red-brick university [ˈrɛdbrɪk-] N (BRIT) università di recente formazione

In Gran Bretagna, con **red-brick university** (letteralmente, università di mattoni rossi) si indicano le università istituite tra la fine dell'Ottocento e i primi del Novecento, per contraddistinguerle dalle università più antiche, i cui edifici sono di pietra; vedi anche **Oxbridge**.

red carpet treatment N cerimonia col gran pavese

Red Cross N Croce f Rossa

redcurrant [ˈrɛdkʌrənt] N ribes m inv

redden [ˈrɛdn] VT arrossare ▶ VI arrossire

reddish [ˈrɛdɪʃ] ADJ rossiccio(-a)

redecorate [riːˈdɛkəreɪt] VT tinteggiare (e tappezzare) di nuovo

redeem [rɪˈdiːm] VT (debt) riscattare; (sth in pawn) ritirare; (fig, also Rel) redimere

redeemable [rɪˈdiːməbl] ADJ con diritto di riscatto; redimibile

redeeming [rɪˈdiːmɪŋ] ADJ (feature) che salva

redefine [riːdɪˈfaɪn] VT ridefinire

redemption [rɪˈdɛmpʃən] N (Rel) redenzione f; **past** or **beyond ~** irrecuperabile

redeploy [riːdɪˈplɔɪ] VT (Mil) riorganizzare lo schieramento di; (resources) riorganizzare

redeployment [riːdɪˈplɔɪmənt] N riorganizzazione f

redevelop [riːdɪˈvɛləp] VT ristrutturare

redevelopment [riːdɪˈvɛləpmənt] N ristrutturazione f

red-haired [rɛdˈhɛəd] ADJ dai capelli rossi

red-handed [rɛdˈhændɪd] ADJ: **to be caught ~** essere preso(-a) in flagrante or con le mani nel sacco

redhead [ˈrɛdhɛd] N rosso(-a)

red herring N (fig) falsa pista

red-hot [rɛdˈhɔt] ADJ arroventato(-a)

redirect [riːdaɪˈrɛkt] VT (mail) far seguire

redistribute [riːdɪˈstrɪbjuːt] VT ridistribuire

red-letter day [ˈrɛdlɛtə-] N giorno memorabile

red light N: **to go through a ~** (Aut) passare col rosso

red-light district [rɛdˈlaɪt-] N quartiere m a luci rosse

red meat N carne f rossa

redness [ˈrɛdnɪs] N rossore m; (of hair) rosso

redo [riːˈduː] VT (irreg: like **do**) rifare

redolent [ˈrɛdələnt] ADJ: **~ of** che sa di; (fig) che ricorda

redouble [riːˈdʌbl] VT: **to ~ one's efforts** raddoppiare gli sforzi

redraft [riːˈdrɑːft] VT fare una nuova stesura di

redress [rɪˈdrɛs] N riparazione f ▶ VT riparare; **to ~ the balance** ristabilire l'equilibrio

Red Sea N: **the ~** il mar Rosso

redskin [ˈrɛdskɪn] N (!) pellerossa mf

red tape N (fig) burocrazia

reduce [rɪˈdjuːs] VT ridurre; (lower) ridurre, abbassare; **"~ speed now"** (Aut) "rallentare"; **to ~ sth by/to** ridurre qc di/a; **to ~ sb to silence/despair/tears** ridurre qn al silenzio/alla disperazione/in lacrime

reduced [rɪˈdjuːst] ADJ (decreased) ridotto(-a); **at a ~ price** scontato(-a); **"greatly ~ prices"** "grandi ribassi"

reduction [rɪˈdʌkʃən] N riduzione f; (of price) ribasso; (discount) sconto

redundancy [rɪˈdʌndənsɪ] N (BRIT) licenziamento (per eccesso di personale); **compulsory ~** licenziamento; **voluntary ~** forma di cassa integrazione volontaria

redundancy payment N (BRIT) indennità f inv di licenziamento

redundant [rɪˈdʌndnt] ADJ (BRIT: worker) licenziato(-a); (detail, object) superfluo(-a); **to be made ~** (BRIT) essere licenziato (per eccesso di personale)

reed [riːd] N (Bot) canna; (Mus: of clarinet etc) ancia

re-educate [riːˈɛdjukeɪt] VT rieducare

reedy [ˈriːdɪ] ADJ (voice, instrument) acuto(-a)

reef [riːf] N (at sea) scogliera; **coral ~** barriera corallina

reek [riːk] VI: **to ~ (of)** puzzare (di)

reel [riːl] N bobina, rocchetto; (Tech) aspo; (Fishing) mulinello; (Cine) rotolo; (dance) danza veloce scozzese ▶ VT (Tech) annaspare; (also: **reel up**)

avvolgere ► vi (*sway*) barcollare, vacillare; **my head is reeling** mi gira la testa
► **reel off** vt snocciolare

re-election [riːɪˈlɛkʃən] N rielezione *f*

re-enter [riːˈɛntəʳ] vt rientrare in

re-entry [riːˈɛntrɪ] N rientro

re-export vt [riːɪkˈspɔːt] riesportare ► N [riːˈɛkspɔːt] merce *f* riesportata, riesportazione *f*

ref [rɛf] N ABBR (*col*: = *referee*) arbitro

ref. ABBR (*Comm*: = *with reference to*) sogg

refectory [rɪˈfɛktərɪ] N refettorio

refer [rɪˈfəːʳ] vt: **to ~ sth to** (*dispute, decision*) deferire qc a; **to ~ sb to** (*inquirer, patient*) indirizzare qn a; (*reader: to text*) rimandare qn a; **he referred me to the manager** mi ha detto di rivolgermi al direttore
► **refer to** vt FUS (*allude to*) accennare a; (*apply to*) riferire a; (*consult*) rivolgersi a; **referring to your letter** (*Comm*) in riferimento alla Vostra lettera

referee [rɛfəˈriː] N arbitro; (*Tennis*) giudice *m* di gara; (*Brit: for job application*) referenza ► vt arbitrare

reference [ˈrɛfrəns] N riferimento *m*; (*mention*) menzione *f*, allusione *f*; (*for job application: letter*) referenza; lettera di raccomandazione; (*: person*) referenza; (*in book*) rimando; **with ~ to** riguardo a; (*Comm: in letter*) in *or* con riferimento a; **"please quote this ~"** (*Comm*) "si prega di far riferimento al numero di protocollo"

reference book N libro di consultazione

reference library N biblioteca per la consultazione

reference number N (*Comm*) numero di riferimento

referendum [rɛfəˈrɛndəm] (*pl* **referenda** [-də]) N referendum *m inv*

referral [rɪˈfəːrəl] N deferimento; (*Med*) richiesta (di visita specialistica)

refill vt [riːˈfɪl] riempire di nuovo; (*pen, lighter etc*) ricaricare ► N [ˈriːfɪl] (*for pen etc*) ricambio

refine [rɪˈfaɪn] vt raffinare

refined [rɪˈfaɪnd] ADJ (*person, taste*) raffinato(-a)

refinement [rɪˈfaɪnmənt] N (*of person*) raffinatezza

refinery [rɪˈfaɪnərɪ] N raffineria

refit N [ˈriːfɪt] (*Naut*) raddobbo ► vt [riːˈfɪt] (*ship*) raddobbare

reflate [riːˈfleɪt] vt (*economy*) rilanciare

reflation [riːˈfleɪʃən] N rilancio

reflationary [riːˈfleɪʃənərɪ] ADJ nuovamente inflazionario(-a)

reflect [rɪˈflɛkt] vt (*light, image*) riflettere; (*fig*) rispecchiare ► vi (*think*) riflettere, considerare; **it reflects badly/well on him** si ripercuote su di lui in senso negativo/positivo

► **reflect on** vt FUS (*discredit*) rispecchiarsi su

reflection [rɪˈflɛkʃən] N riflessione *f*; (*image*) riflesso; (*criticism*): **~ on** giudizio su; attacco a; **on ~** pensandoci sopra

reflector [rɪˈflɛktəʳ] N (*also Aut*) catarifrangente *m*

reflex [ˈriːflɛks] ADJ riflesso(-a) ► N riflesso

reflexive [rɪˈflɛksɪv] ADJ (*Ling*) riflessivo(-a)

reform [rɪˈfɔːm] N (*of sinner etc*) correzione *f*; (*of law etc*) riforma ► vt correggere; riformare

reformat [rɪˈfɔːmæt] vt (*Comput*) riformattare

Reformation [rɛfəˈmeɪʃən] N: **the ~** la Riforma

reformatory [rɪˈfɔːmətərɪ] N (*US*) riformatorio

reformed [rɪˈfɔːmd] ADJ cambiato(-a) (per il meglio)

reformer [rɪˈfɔːməʳ] N riformatore(-trice)

refrain [rɪˈfreɪn] vi: **to ~ from doing** trattenersi dal fare ► N ritornello

refresh [rɪˈfrɛʃ] vt rinfrescare; (*food, sleep*) ristorare

refresher course [rɪˈfrɛʃə-] N (*Brit*) corso di aggiornamento

refreshing [rɪˈfrɛʃɪŋ] ADJ (*drink*) rinfrescante; (*sleep*) riposante, ristoratore(-trice); (*change etc*) piacevole; (*idea, point of view*) originale

refreshment [rɪˈfrɛʃmənt] N (*eating, resting etc*) ristoro; **~(s)** rinfreschi *mpl*

refrigeration [rɪfrɪdʒəˈreɪʃən] N refrigerazione *f*

refrigerator [rɪˈfrɪdʒəreɪtəʳ] N frigorifero

refuel [riːˈfjuəl] vt rifornire (di carburante) ► vi far rifornimento (di carburante)

refuge [ˈrɛfjuːdʒ] N rifugio; **to take ~ in** rifugiarsi in

refugee [rɛfjuˈdʒiː] N rifugiato(-a), profugo(-a)

refugee camp N campo (di) profughi

refund N [ˈriːfʌnd] rimborso ► vt [rɪˈfʌnd] rimborsare

refurbish [riːˈfəːbɪʃ] vt rimettere a nuovo

refurnish [riːˈfəːnɪʃ] vt ammobiliare di nuovo

refusal [rɪˈfjuːzəl] N rifiuto; **to have first ~ on sth** avere il diritto d'opzione su qc

refuse¹ [ˈrɛfjuːs] N rifiuti *mpl*

refuse² [rɪˈfjuːz] vt, vi rifiutare; **to ~ to do sth** rifiutare *or* rifiutarsi di fare qc

refuse collection [ˈrɛfjuːs-] N raccolta di rifiuti

refuse disposal [ˈrɛfjuːs-] N sistema *m* di scarico dei rifiuti

refusenik [rɪˈfjuːznɪk] N ebreo a cui il governo sovietico impediva di lasciare il paese

refute [rɪˈfjuːt] vt confutare

regain [rɪˈɡeɪn] vt riguadagnare; riacquistare, ricuperare

regal [ˈriːɡl] ADJ regale

regale [rɪˈɡeɪl] vt: **to ~ sb with sth** intrattenere qn con qc

745

regalia [rɪˈɡeɪlɪə] NPL insegne *fpl* reali

regard [rɪˈɡɑːd] N riguardo, stima ▶ VT considerare, stimare; **to give one's regards to** porgere i suoi saluti a; **(kind) regards** cordiali saluti; **as regards, with ~ to** riguardo a

regarding [rɪˈɡɑːdɪŋ] PREP riguardo a, per quanto riguarda

regardless [rɪˈɡɑːdlɪs] ADV lo stesso; **~ of** a dispetto di, nonostante

regatta [rɪˈɡætə] N regata

regency [ˈriːdʒənsɪ] N reggenza

regenerate [rɪˈdʒɛnəreɪt] VT rigenerare; *(feelings, enthusiasm)* far rinascere ▶ VI rigenerarsi; rinascere

regent [ˈriːdʒənt] N reggente *m*

reggae [ˈrɛɡeɪ] N reggae *m*

régime [reɪˈʒiːm] N regime *m*

regiment N [ˈrɛdʒɪmənt] reggimento ▶ VT [ˈrɛdʒɪmɛnt] irreggimentare

regimental [rɛdʒɪˈmɛntl] ADJ reggimentale

regimentation [rɛdʒɪmɛnˈteɪʃən] N irreggimentazione *f*

region [ˈriːdʒən] N regione *f*; **in the ~ of** *(fig)* all'incirca di

regional [ˈriːdʒənl] ADJ regionale

regional development N sviluppo regionale

register [ˈrɛdʒɪstəʳ] N registro; *(also:* **electoral register**) lista elettorale ▶ VT registrare; *(vehicle)* immatricolare; *(luggage)* spedire assicurato(-a); *(letter)* assicurare; *(instrument)* segnare ▶ VI iscriversi; *(at hotel)* firmare il registro; *(make impression)* entrare in testa; **to ~ a protest** fare un esposto; **to ~ for a course** iscriversi a un corso

registered [ˈrɛdʒɪstəd] ADJ *(design)* depositato(-a); *(Brit: letter)* assicurato(-a); *(student, voter)* iscritto(-a)

registered company N società *f inv* iscritta al registro

registered nurse N *(US)* infermiere(-a) diplomato(-a)

registered office N sede *f* legale

registered trademark N marchio depositato

registrar [ˈrɛdʒɪstrɑːʳ] N ufficiale *m* di stato civile; segretario

registration [rɛdʒɪsˈtreɪʃən] N *(act)* registrazione *f*; iscrizione *f*; *(Aut: also:* **registration number**) numero di targa

registry [ˈrɛdʒɪstrɪ] N ufficio del registro

registry office N *(Brit)* anagrafe *f*; **to get married in a ~** ≈ sposarsi in municipio

regret [rɪˈɡrɛt] N rimpianto, rincrescimento ▶ VT rimpiangere; **I ~ that I/he cannot help** mi rincresce di non poter aiutare/che lui non possa aiutare; **we ~ to inform you that ...** siamo spiacenti di informarla che ...

regretfully [rɪˈɡrɛtfəlɪ] ADV con rincrescimento

regrettable [rɪˈɡrɛtəbl] ADJ deplorevole

regrettably [rɪˈɡrɛtəblɪ] ADV purtroppo, sfortunatamente

regroup [riːˈɡruːp] VT raggruppare ▶ VI raggrupparsi

regt ABBR (= *regiment*) Reg

regular [ˈrɛɡjuləʳ] ADJ regolare; *(usual)* abituale, normale; *(listener, reader)* fedele; *(soldier)* dell'esercito regolare; *(Comm: size)* normale ▶ N *(client etc)* cliente *mf* abituale

regularity [rɛɡjuˈlærɪtɪ] N regolarità *f inv*

regularly [ˈrɛɡjuləlɪ] ADV regolarmente

regulate [ˈrɛɡjuleɪt] VT regolare

regulation [rɛɡjuˈleɪʃən] N *(rule)* regola, regolamento; *(adjustment)* regolazione *f* ▶ CPD *(Mil)* di ordinanza

rehabilitate [riːəˈbɪlɪteɪt] VT *(criminal, drug addict, invalid)* ricuperare, reinserire

rehabilitation [ˈriːəbɪlɪˈteɪʃən] N *(see vb)* ricupero, reinserimento; *(of offender)* riabilitazione *f*; *(of disabled person)* riadattamento

rehash [riːˈhæʃ] VT *(col)* rimaneggiare

rehearsal [rɪˈhəːsəl] N prova; **dress ~** prova generale

rehearse [rɪˈhəːs] VT provare

rehouse [riːˈhauz] VT rialloggiare

reign [reɪn] N regno ▶ VI regnare

reigning [ˈreɪnɪŋ] ADJ *(monarch)* regnante; *(champion)* attuale

reimburse [riːɪmˈbəːs] VT rimborsare

rein [reɪn] N *(for horse)* briglia; **to give sb free ~** *(fig)* lasciare completa libertà a qn

reincarnation [riːɪnkɑːˈneɪʃən] N reincarnazione *f*

reindeer [ˈreɪndɪəʳ] N *pl inv* renna

reinforce [riːɪnˈfɔːs] VT rinforzare

reinforced concrete [riːɪnˈfɔːst-] N cemento armato

reinforcement [riːɪnˈfɔːsmənt] N *(action)* rinforzamento ▪ **reinforcements** NPL *(Mil)* rinforzi *mpl*

reinstate [riːɪnˈsteɪt] VT reintegrare

reinstatement [riːɪnˈsteɪtmənt] N reintegrazione *f*

reissue [riːˈɪʃuː] VT *(book)* ristampare, ripubblicare; *(film)* distribuire di nuovo

reiterate [riːˈɪtəreɪt] VT reiterare, ripetere

reject N [ˈriːdʒɛkt] *(Comm)* scarto ▶ VT [rɪˈdʒɛkt] rifiutare, respingere; *(Comm: goods)* scartare

rejection [rɪˈdʒɛkʃən] N rifiuto

rejoice [rɪˈdʒɔɪs] VI: **to ~ (at** or **over)** provare diletto (in)

rejoinder [rɪˈdʒɔɪndəʳ] N *(retort)* replica

rejuvenate [rɪˈdʒuːvəneɪt] VT ringiovanire

rekindle [riːˈkɪndl] VT riaccendere

relapse [rɪ'læps] N (Med) ricaduta

relate [rɪ'leɪt] VT (tell) raccontare; (connect) collegare ▶ VI: **to ~ to** (refer to) riferirsi a; (get on with) stabilire un rapporto con

related [rɪ'leɪtɪd] ADJ imparentato(-a); collegato(-a), connesso(-a); **~ to** imparentato(-a) con; collegato(-a) or connesso(-a) con

relating [rɪ'leɪtɪŋ]: **~ to** prep che riguarda, rispetto a

relation [rɪ'leɪʃən] N (person) parente mf; (link) rapporto, relazione f ■ **relations** NPL (relatives) parenti mpl; **in ~ to** con riferimento a; **diplomatic/international relations** rapporti diplomatici/internazionali; **to bear a ~ to** corrispondere a

relationship [rɪ'leɪʃənʃɪp] N rapporto; (personal ties) rapporti mpl, relazioni fpl; (also: **family relationship**) legami mpl di parentela; (: affair) relazione f; **they have a good ~** vanno molto d'accordo

relative ['relətɪv] N parente mf ▶ ADJ relativo(-a); (respective) rispettivo(-a)

relatively ['relətɪvlɪ] ADV relativamente; (fairly, rather) abbastanza

relax [rɪ'læks] VI rilasciarsi; (person: unwind) rilassarsi ▶ VT rilasciare; (mind, person) rilassare; **~!** (calm down) calma!

relaxation [ri:læk'seɪʃən] N rilasciamento; rilassamento; (entertainment) ricreazione f, svago

relaxed [rɪ'lækst] ADJ rilasciato(-a); rilassato(-a)

relaxing [rɪ'læksɪŋ] ADJ rilassante

relay ['ri:leɪ] N (Sport) corsa a staffetta ▶ VT (message) trasmettere

release [rɪ'li:s] N (from prison) rilascio; (from obligation) liberazione f; (of gas etc) emissione f; (of film etc) distribuzione f; (record) disco; (device) disinnesto ▶ VT (prisoner) rilasciare; (from obligation, wreckage etc) liberare; (book, film) fare uscire; (news) rendere pubblico(-a); (gas etc) emettere; (Tech: catch, spring etc) disinnestare; (let go) rilasciare; lasciar andare; sciogliere; **to ~ one's grip** mollare la presa; **to ~ the clutch** (Aut) staccare la frizione

relegate ['reləgeɪt] VT relegare; (BRIT Sport): **to be relegated** essere retrocesso(-a)

relent [rɪ'lent] VI cedere

relentless [rɪ'lentlɪs] ADJ implacabile

relevance ['reləvəns] N pertinenza; **~ of sth to sth** rapporto tra qc e qc

relevant ['reləvənt] ADJ pertinente; (chapter) in questione; **~ to** pertinente a

reliability [rɪlaɪə'bɪlɪtɪ] N (of person) serietà; (of machine) affidabilità

reliable [rɪ'laɪəbl] ADJ (person, firm) fidato(-a), che dà affidamento; (method) sicuro(-a); (machine) affidabile

reliably [rɪ'laɪəblɪ] ADV: **to be ~ informed** sapere da fonti sicure

reliance [rɪ'laɪəns] N: **~ (on)** dipendenza (da)

reliant [rɪ'laɪənt] ADJ: **to be ~ on sth/sb** dipendere da qc/qn

relic ['relɪk] N (Rel) reliquia; (of the past) resto

relief [rɪ'li:f] N (from pain, anxiety) sollievo; (help, supplies) soccorsi mpl; (of guard) cambio; (Art, Geo) rilievo; **by way of light ~** come diversivo

relief map N carta in rilievo

relief road N (BRIT) circonvallazione f

relieve [rɪ'li:v] VT (pain, patient) sollevare; (bring help) soccorrere; (take over from: gen) sostituire; (: guard) rilevare; **to ~ sb of sth** (load) alleggerire qn di qc; **to ~ sb of his command** (Mil) esonerare qn dal comando; **to ~ o.s.** (euphemism) fare i propri bisogni

relieved [rɪ'li:vd] ADJ sollevato(-a); **to be ~ that ...** essere sollevato(-a) (dal fatto) che ...; **I'm ~ to hear it** mi hai tolto un peso con questa notizia

religion [rɪ'lɪdʒən] N religione f

religious [rɪ'lɪdʒəs] ADJ religioso(-a)

religious education N religione f

relinquish [rɪ'lɪŋkwɪʃ] VT abbandonare; (plan, habit) rinunziare a

relish ['relɪʃ] N (Culin) condimento; (enjoyment) gran piacere m ▶ VT (food etc) godere; **to ~ doing** adorare fare

relive [ri:'lɪv] VT rivivere

reload [ri:'ləud] VT ricaricare

relocate [ri:ləu'keɪt] VT (business) trasferire ▶ VI trasferirsi; **to ~ in** trasferire la propria sede a

reluctance [rɪ'lʌktəns] N riluttanza

reluctant [rɪ'lʌktənt] ADJ riluttante, mal disposto(-a); **to be ~ to do sth** essere restio a fare qc

reluctantly [rɪ'lʌktəntlɪ] ADV di mala voglia, a malincuore

rely [rɪ'laɪ]: **to ~ on** vt fus contare su; (be dependent) dipendere da

remain [rɪ'meɪn] VI restare, rimanere; **to ~ silent** restare in silenzio; **I ~, yours faithfully** (BRIT: in letters) distinti saluti

remainder [rɪ'meɪndər] N resto; (Comm) rimanenza

remainer [rɪmeɪnər] N (BRIT: in EU) sostenitore della permanenza del Regno Unito nell'Unione Europea

remaining [rɪ'meɪnɪŋ] ADJ che rimane

remains [rɪ'meɪnz] NPL resti mpl

remand [rɪ'mɑ:nd] N: **on ~** in detenzione preventiva ▶ VT: **to ~ in custody** rinviare in carcere; trattenere a disposizione della legge

remand home N (BRIT) riformatorio, casa di correzione

remark [rɪ'mɑ:k] N osservazione f ▶ VT osser-

r

vare, dire; (*notice*) notare ▶ VI: **to ~ on sth** fare dei commenti su qc

remarkable [rɪˈmɑːkəbl] ADJ notevole; eccezionale

remarry [riːˈmærɪ] VI risposarsi

remedial [rɪˈmiːdɪəl] ADJ (*tuition, classes*) di riparazione

remedy [ˈrɛmədɪ] N: **~ (for)** rimedio (per) ▶ VT rimediare a

remember [rɪˈmɛmbəʳ] VT ricordare, ricordarsi di; **I ~ seeing it, I ~ having seen it** (mi) ricordo di averlo visto; **she remembered to do it** si è ricordata di farlo; **~ me to your wife and children!** saluti sua moglie e i bambini da parte mia!

remembrance [rɪˈmɛmbrəns] N memoria; ricordo

Remembrance Day, (BRIT) **Remembrance Sunday** N *vedi nota*

Nel Regno Unito, la domenica più vicina all'undici novembre, data in cui fu firmato l'armistizio con la Germania nel 1918, ricorre il **Remembrance Day** o **Remembrance Sunday**, giorno in cui vengono commemorati i caduti in guerra. A Londra, durante la cerimonia si depongono corone sul cenotafio eretto in Whitehall. In questa occasione molti portano un papavero di carta appuntato al petto in segno di rispetto.

---

remind [rɪˈmaɪnd] VT: **to ~ sb of sth** ricordare qc a qn; **to ~ sb to do** ricordare a qn di fare; **that reminds me!** a proposito!

reminder [rɪˈmaɪndəʳ] N richiamo; (*note etc*) promemoria *m inv*

reminisce [rɛmɪˈnɪs] VI: **to ~ (about)** abbandonarsi ai ricordi (di)

reminiscences [rɛmɪˈnɪsnsɪz] NPL reminiscenze *fpl*, memorie *fpl*

reminiscent [rɛmɪˈnɪsnt] ADJ: **~ of** che fa pensare a, che richiama

remiss [rɪˈmɪs] ADJ negligente; **it was ~ of me** è stata una negligenza da parte mia

remission [rɪˈmɪʃən] N remissione *f*; (*of fee*) esonero

remit [rɪˈmɪt] VT rimettere

remittance [rɪˈmɪtəns] N rimessa

remnant [ˈrɛmnənt] N resto, avanzo ■ **remnants** NPL (*Comm*) scampoli *mpl*; fine *f* serie

remonstrate [ˈrɛmənstreɪt] VI protestare; **to ~ with sb about sth** fare le proprie rimostranze a qn circa qc

remorse [rɪˈmɔːs] N rimorso

remorseful [rɪˈmɔːsful] ADJ pieno(-a) di rimorsi

remorseless [rɪˈmɔːslɪs] ADJ (*fig*) spietato(-a)

remortgage [riːˈmɔːgɪdʒ] VT accendere una seconda ipoteca su

remote [rɪˈməut] ADJ remoto(-a), lontano(-a); (*person*) distaccato(-a); **there is a ~ possibility that ...** c'è una vaga possibilità che ... + *sub*

remote control N telecomando

remote-controlled [rɪˈməutkənˈtrəuld] ADJ telecomandato(-a)

remotely [rɪˈməutlɪ] ADV remotamente; (*slightly*) vagamente

remoteness [rɪˈməutnɪs] N lontananza

remould [ˈriːməuld] N (BRIT: *tyre*) gomma rivestita

removable [rɪˈmuːvəbl] ADJ (*detachable*) staccabile

removal [rɪˈmuːvəl] N (*taking away*) rimozione *f*; soppressione *f*; (BRIT: *from house*) trasloco; (*from office: sacking*) destituzione *f*; (*Med*) ablazione *f*

removal man N (*irreg*) (BRIT) addetto ai traslochi

removal van N (BRIT) furgone *m* per traslochi

remove [rɪˈmuːv] VT togliere, rimuovere; (*employee*) destituire; (*stain*) far sparire; (*doubt, abuse*) sopprimere, eliminare; **first cousin once removed** cugino di secondo grado

remover [rɪˈmuːvəʳ] N (*for paint*) prodotto sverniciante; (*for varnish*) solvente *m*; **make-up ~** struccatore *m*

remunerate [rɪˈmjuːnəreɪt] VT rimunerare

remuneration [rɪmjuːnəˈreɪʃən] N rimunerazione *f*

Renaissance [rəˈneɪsəns] N: **the ~** il Rinascimento

rename [riːˈneɪm] VT ribattezzare

rend [rɛnd] (*pt, pp* **rent** [rɛnt]) VT lacerare

render [ˈrɛndəʳ] VT rendere; (*Culin: fat*) struggere

rendering [ˈrɛndərɪŋ] N (*Mus etc*) interpretazione *f*

rendez-vous [ˈrɔndɪvuː] N appuntamento; (*place*) luogo d'incontro; (*meeting*) incontro ▶ VI ritrovarsi; (*spaceship*) effettuare un rendez-vous

rendition [rɛnˈdɪʃən] N (*Mus*) interpretazione *f*

renegade [ˈrɛnɪgeɪd] N rinnegato(-a)

renew [rɪˈnjuː] VT rinnovare; (*negotiations*) riprendere

renewable [rɪˈnjuːəbl] ADJ riutilizzabile; (*contract*) rinnovabile; **~ energy, renewables** fonti *mpl* di energia rinnovabile

renewal [rɪˈnjuːəl] N rinnovamento; ripresa

renounce [rɪˈnauns] VT rinunziare a; (*disown*) ripudiare

renovate [ˈrɛnəveɪt] VT rinnovare; (*art work*) restaurare

renovation [rɛnəˈveɪʃən] N rinnovamento; restauro

renown [rɪˈnaun] N rinomanza

renowned [rɪˈnaund] ADJ rinomato(-a)

rent [rɛnt] PT, PP of **rend** ▶ N affitto ▶ VT (*take for rent*) prendere in affitto; (*car, TV*) noleggiare, prendere a noleggio; (*also:* **rent out**) dare in affitto; (: *car, TV*) noleggiare, dare a noleggio

rental ['rɛntl] N (*cost: on TV, telephone*) abbonamento; (: *on car*) noleggio

rent boy N (BRIT col) giovane prostituto

renunciation [rɪnʌnsɪ'eɪʃən] N rinnegamento; (*self-denial*) rinunzia

reoffend [ri:ə'fɛnd] VI ricommettere un reato (*dopo aver scontato una pena*)

reopen [ri:'əupən] VT riaprire

reopening [ri:'əupnɪŋ] N riapertura

reorder [ri:'ɔ:dəʳ] VT ordinare di nuovo; (*rearrange*) riorganizzare

reorganize [ri:'ɔ:gənaɪz] VT riorganizzare

Rep ABBR (US Pol) = **representative**; **republican**

rep [rɛp] N ABBR (Comm: = representative) rappresentante *mf*; (Theat: repertory) teatro di repertorio

repair [rɪ'pɛəʳ] N riparazione *f* ▶ VT riparare; **in good/bad ~** in buono/cattivo stato; **under ~** in riparazione

repair kit N kit *m inv* per riparazioni

repair man N (*irreg*) riparatore *m*

repair shop N (Aut etc) officina

repartee [rɛpɑː'tiː] N risposta pronta

repast [rɪ'pɑːst] N (*formal*) pranzo

repatriate [ri:'pætrɪeɪt] VT rimpatriare

repay [ri:'peɪ] VT (*irreg: like* **pay**) (*money, creditor*) rimborsare, ripagare; (*sb's efforts*) ricompensare; (*favour*) ricambiare

repayment [ri:'peɪmənt] N rimborso

repeal [rɪ'piːl] N (*of law*) abrogazione *f*; (*of sentence*) annullamento ▶ VT abrogare; annullare

repeat [rɪ'piːt] N (Radio, TV) replica ▶ VT ripetere; (*pattern*) riprodurre; (*promise, attack, also* Comm: *order*) rinnovare ▶ VI ripetere

repeatedly [rɪ'piːtɪdlɪ] ADV ripetutamente, spesso

repeat order N (Comm): **to place a ~ (for)** rinnovare l'ordinazione (di)

repeat prescription N (BRIT) ricetta ripetibile

repel [rɪ'pɛl] VT respingere

repellent [rɪ'pɛlənt] ADJ repellente ▶ N: **insect ~** prodotto *m* anti-insetti *inv*; **moth ~** antitarmico

repent [rɪ'pɛnt] VI: **to ~ (of)** pentirsi (di)

repentance [rɪ'pɛntəns] N pentimento

repercussion [riːpə'kʌʃən] N (*consequence*) ripercussione *f*

repertoire ['rɛpətwɑːʳ] N repertorio

repertory ['rɛpətərɪ] N (*also:* **repertory theatre**) teatro di repertorio

repertory company N compagnia di repertorio

repetition [rɛpɪ'tɪʃən] N ripetizione *f*; (Comm: *of order etc*) rinnovo

repetitious [rɛpɪ'tɪʃəs] ADJ (*speech*) pieno(-a) di ripetizioni

repetitive [rɪ'pɛtɪtɪv] ADJ (*movement*) che si ripete; (*work*) monotono(-a); (*speech*) pieno(-a) di ripetizioni

replace [rɪ'pleɪs] VT (*put back*) rimettere a posto; (*take the place of*) sostituire; (Tel): **"~ the receiver"** "riattaccare"

replacement [rɪ'pleɪsmənt] N rimessa; sostituzione *f*; (*person*) sostituto(-a)

replacement part N pezzo di ricambio

replay ['riːpleɪ] N (*of match*) partita ripetuta; (*of tape, film*) replay *m inv*

replenish [rɪ'plɛnɪʃ] VT (*glass*) riempire; (*stock etc*) rifornire

replete [rɪ'pliːt] ADJ: **~ (with)** ripieno(-a) (di); (*well-fed*) sazio(-a) (di)

replica ['rɛplɪkə] N replica, copia

reply [rɪ'plaɪ] N risposta ▶ VI rispondere; **in ~** in risposta; **there's no ~** (Tel) non risponde (nessuno)

reply coupon N buono di risposta

report [rɪ'pɔːt] N rapporto; (Press etc) cronaca; (BRIT: *also:* **school report**) pagella; (*of gun*) sparo ▶ VT riportare; (Press etc) fare una cronaca su; (*bring to notice: occurrence*) segnalare; (: *person*) denunciare ▶ VI (*make a report*) fare un rapporto (*or* una cronaca); (*present o.s.*): **to ~ (to sb)** presentarsi (a qn); **to ~ (on)** fare un rapporto (su); **it is reported that** si dice che; **it is reported from Berlin that ...** ci è stato riferito da Berlino che ...

report card N (US, SCOTTISH) pagella

reportedly [rɪ'pɔːtɪdlɪ] ADV stando a quanto si dice; **he ~ told them to ...** avrebbe detto loro di ...; **she is ~ living in Spain** si dice che vive in Spagna

reported speech [rɪ'pɔːtɪd-] N (Ling) discorso indiretto

reporter [rɪ'pɔːtəʳ] N (Press) cronista *mf*, reporter *mf inv*; (Radio) radiocronista *mf*; (TV) telecronista *mf*

repose [rɪ'pəuz] N: **in ~** in riposo

repossess [riːpə'zɛs] VT rientrare in possesso di

repossession order [riːpə'zɛʃən-] N ordine *m* di espropriazione

reprehensible [rɛprɪ'hɛnsɪbl] ADJ riprensibile

represent [rɛprɪ'zɛnt] VT rappresentare

representation [rɛprɪzɛn'teɪʃən] N rappresentazione *f*; (*petition*) rappresentanza ■ **representations** NPL (*protest*) protesta

representative [rɛprɪ'zɛntətɪv] N rappresentativo(-a); (Comm) rappresentante *m* (di commercio); (US Pol) deputato(-a) ▶ ADJ: **~ (of)** rappresentativo(-a) (di)

r

repress [rɪˈprɛs] VT reprimere

repression [rɪˈprɛʃən] N repressione f

repressive [rɪˈprɛsɪv] ADJ repressivo(-a)

reprieve [rɪˈpriːv] N (Law) sospensione f dell'esecuzione della condanna; (fig) dilazione f ▸ VT sospendere l'esecuzione della condanna a; accordare una dilazione a

reprimand [ˈrɛprɪmɑːnd] N rimprovero ▸ VT rimproverare, redarguire

reprint [ˈriːprɪnt] N ristampa ▸ VT ristampare

reprisal [rɪˈpraɪzl] N rappresaglia; **to take reprisals** fare delle rappresaglie

reproach [rɪˈprəʊtʃ] N rimprovero ▸ VT: **to ~ sb with sth** rimproverare qn di qc; **beyond ~** irreprensibile

reproachful [rɪˈprəʊtʃful] ADJ di rimprovero

reproduce [riːprəˈdjuːs] VT riprodurre ▸ VI riprodursi

reproduction [riːprəˈdʌkʃən] N riproduzione f

reproductive [riːprəˈdʌktɪv] ADJ riproduttore(-trice); riproduttivo(-a)

reproof [rɪˈpruːf] N riprovazione f

reprove [rɪˈpruːv] VT (action) disapprovare; (person): **to ~ (for)** biasimare (per)

reproving [rɪˈpruːvɪŋ] ADJ di disapprovazione

reptile [ˈrɛptaɪl] N rettile m

Repub. ABBR (US Pol) = **republican**

republic [rɪˈpʌblɪk] N repubblica

republican [rɪˈpʌblɪkən] ADJ, N repubblicano(-a)

repudiate [rɪˈpjuːdɪeɪt] VT ripudiare

repugnant [rɪˈpʌgnənt] ADJ ripugnante

repulse [rɪˈpʌls] VT respingere

repulsion [rɪˈpʌlʃən] N ripulsione f

repulsive [rɪˈpʌlsɪv] ADJ ripugnante, ripulsivo(-a)

reputable [ˈrɛpjutəbl] ADJ di buona reputazione; (occupation) rispettabile

reputation [rɛpjuˈteɪʃən] N reputazione f; **he has a ~ for being awkward** ha la fama di essere un tipo difficile

repute [rɪˈpjuːt] N reputazione f

reputed [rɪˈpjuːtɪd] ADJ reputato(-a); **to be ~ to be rich/intelligent** etc essere ritenuto(-a) ricco(-a)/intelligente etc

reputedly [rɪˈpjuːtɪdlɪ] ADV secondo quanto si dice

request [rɪˈkwɛst] N domanda; (formal) richiesta ▸ VT: **to ~ (of or from sb)** chiedere (a qn); **at the ~ of** su richiesta di; **"you are requested not to smoke"** "si prega di non fumare"

request stop N (BRIT: for bus) fermata facoltativa or a richiesta

requiem [ˈrɛkwɪəm] N requiem m inv or f inv

require [rɪˈkwaɪər] VT (need: person) aver bisogno di; (: thing, situation) richiedere; (want) volere; esigere; (order) obbligare; **to ~ sb to do sth/sth of sb** esigere che qn faccia qc/qc da qn; **what qualifications are required?** che requisiti ci vogliono?; **required by law** prescritto dalla legge; **if required** in caso di bisogno

required [rɪˈkwaɪəd] ADJ richiesto(-a)

requirement [rɪˈkwaɪəmənt] N (need) esigenza; bisogno; (condition) requisito; **to meet sb's requirements** soddisfare le esigenze di qn

requisite [ˈrɛkwɪzɪt] N cosa necessaria ▸ ADJ necessario(-a); **toilet requisites** articoli mpl da toletta

requisition [rɛkwɪˈzɪʃən] N: **~ (for)** richiesta (di) ▸ VT (Mil) requisire

reroute [riːˈruːt] VT (train etc) deviare

resale [ˈriːseɪl] N rivendita

resale price maintenance N prezzo minimo di vendita imposto

resat [riːˈsæt] PT, PP of **resit**

rescind [rɪˈsɪnd] VT annullare; (law) abrogare; (judgement) rescindere

rescue [ˈrɛskjuː] N salvataggio; (help) soccorso ▸ VT salvare; **to come/go to sb's ~** venire/andare in aiuto a or di qn

rescue party N squadra di salvataggio

rescuer [ˈrɛskjuər] N salvatore(-trice)

research [rɪˈsəːtʃ] N ricerca, ricerche fpl ▸ VT fare ricerche su ▸ VI: **to ~ (into sth)** fare ricerca (su qc); **a piece of ~** un lavoro di ricerca; **~ and development** ricerca e sviluppo

researcher [rɪˈsəːtʃər] N ricercatore(-trice)

research work N ricerche fpl

resell [riːˈsɛl] VT (irreg: like **sell**) rivendere

resemblance [rɪˈzɛmbləns] N somiglianza; **to bear a strong ~ to** somigliare moltissimo a

resemble [rɪˈzɛmbl] VT assomigliare a

resent [rɪˈzɛnt] VT risentirsi di

resentful [rɪˈzɛntful] ADJ pieno(-a) di risentimento

resentment [rɪˈzɛntmənt] N risentimento

reservation [rɛzəˈveɪʃən] N (booking) prenotazione f; (doubt) dubbio; (protected area) riserva; (BRIT Aut: also: **central reservation**) spartitraffico m inv; **to make a ~ (in an hotel/a restaurant/on a plane)** prenotare (una camera/una tavola/un posto); **with reservations** (doubts) con le dovute riserve

reservation desk N (US: in hotel) reception f inv

reserve [rɪˈzəːv] N riserva ▸ VT (seats etc) prenotare ▪ **reserves** NPL (Mil) riserve fpl; **in ~** in serbo

reserve currency N valuta di riserva

reserved [rɪˈzəːvd] ADJ (shy) riservato(-a); (seat) prenotato(-a)

reserve price N (BRIT) prezzo di riserva, prezzo m base inv

reserve team N (BRIT Sport) seconda squadra

reservist [rɪ'zə:vɪst] N (Mil) riservista m

reservoir ['rɛzəvwɑːʳ] N serbatoio; (artificial lake) bacino idrico

reset [riː'sɛt] VT (irreg: like set) (Comput) azzerare

reshape [riː'ʃeɪp] VT (policy) ristrutturare

reshuffle [riː'ʃʌfl] N: **Cabinet ~** (Pol) rimpasto governativo

reside [rɪ'zaɪd] VI risiedere

residence ['rɛzɪdəns] N residenza; **to take up ~** prendere residenza; **in ~** (queen etc) in sede; (doctor) fisso

residence permit N (BRIT) permesso di soggiorno

resident ['rɛzɪdənt] N (gen) residente mf; (in hotel) cliente mf fisso(-a) ▶ ADJ residente; (doctor) fisso(-a)

residential [rɛzɪ'dɛnʃəl] ADJ di residenza; (area) residenziale; (course, college) a tempo pieno con pernottamento

residue ['rɛzɪdjuː] N resto; (Chem, Physics) residuo

resign [rɪ'zaɪn] VT (one's post) dimettersi da ▶ VI: **to ~ (from)** dimettersi (da), dare le dimissioni (da); **to ~ o.s. to** rassegnarsi a

resignation [rɛzɪg'neɪʃən] N dimissioni fpl; rassegnazione f; **to tender one's ~** dare le dimissioni

resilience [rɪ'zɪlɪəns] N (of material) elasticità, resilienza; (of person) capacità di recupero

resilient [rɪ'zɪlɪənt] ADJ elastico(-a); (person) che si riprende facilmente

resin ['rɛzɪn] N resina

resist [rɪ'zɪst] VT resistere a

resistance [rɪ'zɪstəns] N resistenza

resistant [rɪ'zɪstənt] ADJ: **~ (to)** resistente (a)

resit ['riːsɪt] (BRIT) VT (irreg: like sit) (exam) ripresentarsi a; (subject) ridare l'esame di ▶ N: **he's got his French ~ on Friday** deve ridare l'esame di francese venerdì

resolute ['rɛzəluːt] ADJ risoluto(-a)

resolution [rɛzə'luːʃən] N (resolve) fermo proposito, risoluzione f; (determination) risolutezza; (on screen) risoluzione f; **to make a ~** fare un proposito

resolve [rɪ'zɔlv] N risoluzione f ▶ VI (decide): **to ~ to do** decidere di fare ▶ VT (problem) risolvere

resolved [rɪ'zɔlvd] ADJ risoluto(-a)

resonance ['rɛzənəns] N risonanza

resonant ['rɛzənənt] ADJ risonante

resort [rɪ'zɔːt] N (town) stazione f; (place) località f inv; (recourse) ricorso ▶ VI: **to ~ to** far ricorso a; **seaside/winter sports ~** stazione f balneare/di sport invernali; **as a last ~** come ultima risorsa

resound [rɪ'zaund] VI: **to ~ (with)** risonare (di)

resounding [rɪ'zaundɪŋ] ADJ risonante

resource [rɪ'sɔːs] N risorsa ■ **resources** NPL

risorse fpl; **natural resources** risorse naturali; **to leave sb to his (or her) own resources** (fig) lasciare che qn si arrangi (per conto suo)

resourceful [rɪ'sɔːsful] ADJ pieno(-a) di risorse, intraprendente

resourcefulness [rɪ'sɔːsfəlnɪs] N intraprendenza

respect [rɪs'pɛkt] N rispetto; (point, detail): **in some respects** sotto certi aspetti ▶ VT rispettare ■ **respects** NPL ossequi mpl; **to have or show ~ for** aver rispetto per; **out of ~ for** per rispetto or riguardo a; **with ~ to** rispetto a, riguardo a; **in ~ of** quanto a; **in this ~** per questo riguardo; **with (all) due ~ I …** con rispetto parlando, io …

respectability [rɪspɛktə'bɪlɪtɪ] N rispettabilità

respectable [rɪs'pɛktəbl] ADJ rispettabile; (quite big: amount etc) considerevole; (quite good: player, result etc) niente male inv

respectful [rɪs'pɛktful] ADJ rispettoso(-a)

respective [rɪs'pɛktɪv] ADJ rispettivo(-a)

respectively [rɪs'pɛktɪvlɪ] ADV rispettivamente

respiration [rɛspɪ'reɪʃən] N respirazione f

respirator ['rɛspɪreɪtəʳ] N respiratore m

respiratory ['rɛspərətərɪ] ADJ respiratorio(-a)

respite ['rɛspaɪt] N respiro, tregua

resplendent [rɪs'plɛndənt] ADJ risplendente

respond [rɪs'pɔnd] VI rispondere

respondent [rɪs'pɔndənt] N (Law) convenuto(-a)

response [rɪs'pɔns] N risposta; **in ~ to** in risposta a

responsibility [rɪspɔnsɪ'bɪlɪtɪ] N responsabilità f inv; **to take ~ for sth/sb** assumersi or prendersi la responsabilità di qc/per qn

responsible [rɪs'pɔnsɪbl] ADJ (liable): **~ (for)** responsabile (di); (trustworthy) fidato(-a); (job) di (grande) responsabilità; **to be ~ to sb (for sth)** dover rispondere a qn (di qc)

responsibly [rɪs'pɔnsəblɪ] ADV responsabilmente

responsive [rɪs'pɔnsɪv] ADJ che reagisce

rest [rɛst] N riposo; (stop) sosta, pausa; (Mus) pausa; (support) appoggio, sostegno; (remainder) resto, avanzi mpl ▶ VI riposarsi; (remain) rimanere, restare; (be supported): **to ~ on** appoggiarsi su ▶ VT (far) riposare; (lean): **to ~ sth on/against** appoggiare qc su/contro; **to set sb's mind at ~** tranquillizzare qn; **the ~ of them** gli altri; **to ~ one's eyes or gaze on** posare lo sguardo su; **~ assured that …** stia tranquillo che …; **it rests with him to decide** sta a lui decidere

restart [riː'stɑːt] VT (engine) rimettere in marcia; (work) ricominciare

restaurant ['rɛstərɔŋ] N ristorante m

restaurant car N (BRIT) vagone m ristorante

r

rest cure N cura del riposo

restful [ˈrɛstful] ADJ riposante

rest home N casa di riposo

restitution [rɛstɪˈtjuːʃən] N (*act*) restituzione *f*; (*reparation*) riparazione *f*

restive [ˈrɛstɪv] ADJ agitato(-a), impaziente; (*horse*) restio(-a)

restless [ˈrɛstlɪs] ADJ agitato(-a), irrequieto(-a); **to get ~** spazientirsi

restlessly [ˈrɛstlɪslɪ] ADV in preda all'agitazione

restock [riːˈstɔk] VT rifornire

restoration [rɛstəˈreɪʃən] N restauro; restituzione *f*

restorative [rɪˈstɔrətɪv] ADJ corroborante, ristorativo(-a) ▶ N ricostituente *m*

restore [rɪˈstɔːʳ] VT (*building*) restaurare; (*sth stolen*) restituire; (*peace, health*) ristorare

restorer [rɪsˈtɔːrəʳ] N (*Art etc*) restauratore(-trice)

restrain [rɪsˈtreɪn] VT (*feeling*) contenere, frenare; (*person*): **to ~ (from doing)** trattenere (dal fare)

restrained [rɪsˈtreɪnd] ADJ (*style*) contenuto(-a), sobrio(-a); (*manner*) riservato(-a)

restraint [rɪsˈtreɪnt] N (*restriction*) limitazione *f*; (*moderation*) ritegno; (*of style*) contenutezza; **wage ~** restrizioni *fpl* salariali

restrict [rɪsˈtrɪkt] VT restringere, limitare

restricted area [rɪsˈtrɪktɪd-] N (*Aut*) zona a velocità limitata

restriction [rɪsˈtrɪkʃən] N: **~ (on)** restrizione *f* (di), limitazione *f* (di)

restrictive [rɪsˈtrɪktɪv] ADJ restrittivo(-a)

restrictive practices NPL (*Industry*) pratiche restrittive di produzione

rest room N (*US*) toletta

restructure [riːˈstrʌktʃəʳ] VT ristrutturare

result [rɪˈzʌlt] N risultato ▶ VI: **to ~ in** avere per risultato; **as a ~ (of)** in *or* di conseguenza (a), in seguito (a); **to ~ (from)** essere una conseguenza (di), essere causato(-a) (da)

resultant [rɪˈzʌltənt] ADJ risultante, conseguente

resume [rɪˈzjuːm] VT, VI (*work, journey*) riprendere; (*sum up*) riassumere

résumé [ˈreɪzjuːmeɪ] N riassunto; (*US: curriculum vitae*) curriculum vitae *m inv*

resumption [rɪˈzʌmpʃən] N ripresa

resurgence [rɪˈsəːdʒəns] N rinascita

resurrection [rɛzəˈrɛkʃən] N risurrezione *f*

resuscitate [rɪˈsʌsɪteɪt] VT (*Med*) risuscitare

resuscitation [rɪsʌsɪˈteɪʃən] N rianimazione *f*

retail [ˈriːteɪl] N (vendita al) minuto ▶ CPD al minuto ▶ VT vendere al minuto ▶ VI: **to ~ at** essere in vendita al pubblico al prezzo di

retailer [ˈriːteɪləʳ] N commerciante *mf* al minuto, dettagliante *mf*

retail outlet N punto di vendita al dettaglio

retail price N prezzo al minuto

retail price index N indice *m* dei prezzi al consumo

retain [rɪˈteɪn] VT (*keep*) tenere, serbare

retainer [rɪˈteɪnəʳ] N (*servant*) servitore(-trice); (*fee*) onorario

retaliate [rɪˈtælɪeɪt] VI: **to ~ (against)** vendicarsi (di); **to ~ on sb** fare una rappresaglia contro qn

retaliation [rɪtælɪˈeɪʃən] N rappresaglie *fpl*; **in ~ for** per vendicarsi di

retaliatory [rɪˈtælɪətərɪ] ADJ di rappresaglia, di ritorsione

retarded [rɪˈtɑːdɪd] ADJ (*Med*: !) ritardato(-a); (!: *also:* **mentally retarded**) tardo(-a) (di mente)

retch [rɛtʃ] VI aver conati di vomito

retentive [rɪˈtɛntɪv] ADJ ritentivo(-a)

rethink [ˈriːˈθɪŋk] VT ripensare

reticence [ˈrɛtɪsns] N reticenza

reticent [ˈrɛtɪsnt] ADJ reticente

retina [ˈrɛtɪnə] N retina

retinue [ˈrɛtɪnjuː] N seguito, scorta

retire [rɪˈtaɪəʳ] VI (*give up work*) andare in pensione; (*withdraw*) ritirarsi, andarsene; (*go to bed*) andare a letto, ritirarsi

retired [rɪˈtaɪəd] ADJ (*person*) pensionato(-a)

retirement [rɪˈtaɪəmənt] N pensione *f*; (*act*) pensionamento

retirement age N età *f inv* del pensionamento

retiring [rɪˈtaɪərɪŋ] ADJ (*person*) riservato(-a); (*departing: chairman*) uscente

retort [rɪˈtɔːt] N (*reply*) rimbecco; (*container*) storta ▶ VI rimbeccare

retrace [riːˈtreɪs] VT ricostruire; **to ~ one's steps** tornare sui propri passi

retract [rɪˈtrækt] VT (*statement*) ritrattare; (*claws, undercarriage, aerial*) ritrarre, ritirare ▶ VI ritrarsi

retractable [rɪˈtræktəbl] ADJ retrattile

retrain [riːˈtreɪn] VT (*worker*) riaddestrare

retraining [rɪˈtreɪnɪŋ] N riaddestramento

retread VT [riːˈtrɛd] (*Aut: tyre*) rigenerare ▶ N [ˈriːtrɛd] gomma rigenerata

retreat [rɪˈtriːt] N ritirata; (*place*) rifugio ▶ VI battere in ritirata; (*flood*) ritirarsi; **to beat a hasty ~** (*fig*) battersela

retrial [riːˈtraɪəl] N nuovo processo

retribution [rɛtrɪˈbjuːʃən] N castigo

retrieval [rɪˈtriːvəl] N ricupero

retrieve [rɪˈtriːv] VT (*sth lost*) ricuperare, ritrovare; (*situation, honour*) salvare; (*error, loss*) rimediare a; (*Comput*) ricuperare

retriever [rɪˈtriːvəʳ] N cane *m* da riporto

retroactive [rɛtrəʊˈæktɪv] ADJ retroattivo(-a)

retrograde [ˈrɛtrəʊɡreɪd] ADJ retrogrado(-a)

retrospect [ˈrɛtrəspɛkt] N: **in ~** guardando indietro

retrospective [rɛtrəˈspɛktɪv] ADJ retrospettivo(-a); (*law*) retroattivo(-a) ▶ N (*Art*) retrospettiva

return [rɪˈtɜːn] N (*going or coming back*) ritorno; (*of sth stolen etc*) restituzione f; (*Comm: from land, shares*) profitto, reddito; (: *of merchandise*) resa; (*report*) rapporto; (*reward*): **in ~ (for)** in cambio (di) ▶ CPD (*journey, match*) di ritorno; (*BRIT: ticket*) di andata e ritorno ▶ VI tornare, ritornare ▶ VT rendere, restituire; (*bring back*) riportare; (*send back*) mandare indietro; (*put back*) rimettere; (*Pol: candidate*) eleggere ■ **returns** NPL (*Comm*) incassi *mpl*; profitti *mpl*; **by ~ of post** a stretto giro di posta; **many happy returns (of the day)!** cento di questi giorni!

returnable [rɪˈtɜːnəbl] ADJ: **~ bottle** vuoto a rendere

returner [rɪˈtɜːnəʳ] N *donna che ritorna al lavoro dopo la maternità*

returning officer [rɪˈtɜːnɪŋ-] N (*BRIT Pol*) *funzionario addetto all'organizzazione delle elezioni in un distretto*

return key N (*Comput*) tasto di ritorno

return ticket N (*esp BRIT*) biglietto di andata e ritorno

retweet [riːˈtwiːt] VT (*on Twitter*) retwittare

reunion [riːˈjuːnɪən] N riunione f

reunite [riːjuːˈnaɪt] VT riunire

rev [rɛv] N ABBR (*Aut: = revolution*) giro ▶ VT (*also:* **rev up**) imballare ▶ VI (*also:* **rev up**) imballarsi

Rev., Revd. ABBR = **Reverend**

revaluation [riːvæljuˈeɪʃən] N rivalutazione f

revamp [ˈriːˈvæmp] VT rinnovare; (*firm*) riorganizzare

rev counter N contagiri *m inv*

reveal [rɪˈviːl] VT (*make known*) rivelare, svelare; (*display*) rivelare, mostrare

revealing [rɪˈviːlɪŋ] ADJ rivelatore(-trice); (*dress*) scollato(-a)

reveille [rɪˈvælɪ] N (*Mil*) sveglia

revel [ˈrɛvl] VI: **to ~ in sth/in doing** dilettarsi di qc/a fare

revelation [rɛvəˈleɪʃən] N rivelazione f

reveller [ˈrɛvləʳ] N festaiolo(-a)

revelry [ˈrɛvlrɪ] N baldoria

revenge [rɪˈvɛndʒ] N vendetta; (*in game etc*) rivincita ▶ VT vendicare; **to take ~ on** vendicarsi di; **to get one's ~ (for sth)** vendicarsi (di qc)

revengeful [rɪˈvɛndʒful] ADJ vendicatore(-trice); vendicativo(-a)

revenue [ˈrɛvənjuː] N reddito

reverberate [rɪˈvɜːbəreɪt] VI (*sound*) rimbombare; (*light*) riverberarsi

reverberation [rɪvɜːbəˈreɪʃən] N (*of light, sound*) riverberazione f

revere [rɪˈvɪəʳ] VT venerare

reverence [ˈrɛvərəns] N venerazione f, riverenza

Reverend [ˈrɛvərənd] ADJ (*in titles*) reverendo(-a)

reverent [ˈrɛvərənt] ADJ riverente

reverie [ˈrɛvərɪ] N fantasticheria

reversal [rɪˈvɜːsl] N capovolgimento

reverse [rɪˈvɜːs] N contrario, opposto, (*back*) rovescio; (*Aut: also:* **reverse gear**) marcia indietro ▶ ADJ (*order*) inverso(-a); (*direction*) opposto(-a) ▶ VT (*turn*) invertire, rivoltare; (*change*) capovolgere, rovesciare; (*Law: judgement*) cassare; (*car*) fare marcia indietro con ▶ VI (*BRIT Aut, person etc*) fare marcia indietro; **in ~ order** in ordine inverso; **to go into ~** fare marcia indietro

reverse-charge call [rɪˈvɜːstʃɑːdʒ-] N (*BRIT Tel*) telefonata con addebito al ricevente

reverse video N reverse video *m*

reversible [rɪˈvɜːsəbl] ADJ (*garment*) double-face *inv*; (*procedure*) reversibile

reversing lights [rɪˈvɜːsɪŋ-] NPL (*BRIT Aut*) luci *fpl* per la retromarcia

reversion [rɪˈvɜːʃən] N ritorno

revert [rɪˈvɜːt] VI: **to ~ to** tornare a

review [rɪˈvjuː] N rivista; (*of book, film*) recensione f; (*of situation*) esame *m* ▶ VT passare in rivista; fare la recensione di; fare il punto di; **to come under ~** essere preso in esame

reviewer [rɪˈvjuːəʳ] N recensore(-a)

revile [rɪˈvaɪl] VT insultare

revise [rɪˈvaɪz] VT (*manuscript*) rivedere, correggere; (*opinion*) emendare, modificare; (*study: subject, notes*) ripassare; **revised edition** edizione riveduta

revision [rɪˈvɪʒən] N revisione f; ripasso; (*revised version*) versione riveduta e corretta

revitalize [riːˈvaɪtəlaɪz] VT ravvivare

revival [rɪˈvaɪvəl] N ripresa; ristabilimento; (*of faith*) risveglio

revive [rɪˈvaɪv] VT (*person*) rianimare; (*custom*) far rivivere; (*hope, courage, economy*) ravvivare; (*play, fashion*) riesumare ▶ VI (*person*) rianimarsi; (*hope*) ravvivarsi; (*activity*) riprendersi

revoke [rɪˈvəʊk] VT revocare; (*promise, decision*) rinvenire su

revolt [rɪˈvəʊlt] N rivolta, ribellione f ▶ VI rivoltarsi, ribellarsi; **to ~ (against sb/sth)** ribellarsi (a qn/qc) ▶ VT (far) rivoltare

revolting [rɪˈvəʊltɪŋ] ADJ ripugnante

revolution [rɛvəˈluːʃən] N rivoluzione f; (*of wheel etc*) rivoluzione, giro

revolutionary [rɛvəˈluːʃənrɪ] ADJ, N rivoluzionario(-a)

r

revolutionize [rɛvəˈluːʃənaɪz] vt rivoluzionare

revolve [rɪˈvɒlv] vi girare

revolver [rɪˈvɒlvəʳ] n rivoltella

revolving [rɪˈvɒlvɪŋ] adj girevole

revolving door n porta girevole

revue [rɪˈvjuː] n (*Theat*) rivista

revulsion [rɪˈvʌlʃən] n ripugnanza

reward [rɪˈwɔːd] n ricompensa, premio ▶ vt: **to ~ (for)** ricompensare (per)

rewarding [rɪˈwɔːdɪŋ] adj (*fig*) soddisfacente; **financially ~** conveniente dal punto di vista economico

rewind [riːˈwaɪnd] vt (*irreg: like* **wind**²) (*watch*) ricaricare; (*ribbon etc*) riavvolgere

rewire [riːˈwaɪəʳ] vt (*house*) rifare l'impianto elettrico di

reword [riːˈwəːd] vt formulare *or* esprimere con altre parole

rewritable [riːˈraɪtəbl] adj (*CD, DVD*) riscrivibile

rewrite [riːˈraɪt] vt (*irreg: like* **write**) riscrivere

Reykjavik [ˈreɪkjəviːk] n Reykjavik *f*

RGN n abbr (*Brit*: = *Registered General Nurse*) infermiera diplomata (*dopo corso triennale*)

Rh abbr (= *rhesus*) Rh

rhapsody [ˈræpsədɪ] n (*Mus*) rapsodia; (*fig*) elogio stravagante

rhesus negative [ˈriːsəs-] adj (*Med*) Rh-negativo(-a)

rhesus positive adj (*Med*) Rh-positivo(-a)

rhetoric [ˈrɛtərɪk] n retorica

rhetorical [rɪˈtɒrɪkl] adj retorico(-a)

rheumatic [ruːˈmætɪk] adj reumatico(-a)

rheumatism [ˈruːmətɪzəm] n reumatismo

rheumatoid arthritis [ˈruːmətɔɪd-] n artrite *f* reumatoide

Rhine [raɪn] n: **the ~** il Reno

rhinestone [ˈraɪnstəun] n diamante *m* falso

rhinoceros [raɪˈnɔsərəs] n rinoceronte *m*

Rhodes [rəudz] n Rodi *f*

rhododendron [rəudəˈdɛndrn] n rododendro

Rhone [rəun] n: **the ~** il Rodano

rhubarb [ˈruːbɑːb] n rabarbaro

rhyme [raɪm] n rima; (*verse*) poesia ▶ vi: **to ~ (with)** fare rima (con); **without ~ or reason** senza capo né coda

rhythm [ˈrɪðm] n ritmo

rhythmic [ˈrɪðmɪk], **rhythmical** [ˈrɪðmɪkəl] adj ritmico(-a)

rhythmically [ˈrɪðmɪkəlɪ] adv con ritmo

rhythm method n metodo Ogino-Knauss

RI abbr (*US*) = **Rhode Island** ▶ n abbr (*Brit*) = **religious instruction**

rib [rɪb] n (*Anat*) costola ▶ vt (*tease*) punzecchiare

ribald [ˈrɪbəld] adj licenzioso(-a), volgare

ribbed [rɪbd] adj (*knitting*) a coste

ribbon [ˈrɪbən] n nastro; **in ribbons** (*torn*) a brandelli

rice [raɪs] n riso

ricefield [ˈraɪsfiːld] n risaia

rice pudding n budino di riso

rich [rɪtʃ] adj ricco(-a); (*clothes*) sontuoso(-a); **the ~** npl i ricchi ■ **riches** npl ricchezze *fpl*; **to be ~ in sth** essere ricco di qc

richly [ˈrɪtʃlɪ] adv riccamente; (*dressed*) sontuosamente; (*deserved*) pienamente

rickets [ˈrɪkɪts] n rachitismo

rickety [ˈrɪkɪtɪ] adj zoppicante

rickshaw [ˈrɪkʃɔː] n risciò *m inv*

ricochet [ˈrɪkəʃeɪ] n rimbalzo ▶ vi rimbalzare

rid [rɪd] (*pt, pp* **~**) vt: **to ~ sb of** sbarazzare *or* liberare qn di; **to get ~ of** sbarazzarsi di

riddance [ˈrɪdns] n: **good ~!** che liberazione!

ridden [ˈrɪdn] pp *of* **ride**

riddle [ˈrɪdl] n (*puzzle*) indovinello ▶ vt: **to be riddled with** (*holes*) essere crivellato(-a) di; (*doubts*) essere pieno(-a) di

ride [raɪd] (*pt* **rode** [rəud], *pp* **ridden** [ˈrɪdn]) n (*on horse*) cavalcata; (*outing*) passeggiata; (*distance covered*) cavalcata; corsa ▶ vi (*as sport*) cavalcare; (*go somewhere: on horse, bicycle*) andare (a cavallo or in bicicletta *etc*); (*journey: on bicycle, motorcycle, bus*) andare, viaggiare ▶ vt (*a horse*) montare, cavalcare; **to go for a ~** andare a fare una cavalcata; andare a fare un giro; **can you ~ a bike?** sai andare in bicicletta?; **we rode all day/all the way** abbiamo cavalcato tutto il giorno/per tutto il tragitto; **to ~ a horse/bicycle/camel** montare a cavallo/in bicicletta/in groppa a un cammello; **to ~ at anchor** (*Naut*) essere alla fonda; **horse ~** cavalcata; **car ~** passeggiata in macchina; **to take sb for a ~** (*fig*) prendere in giro qn; fregare qn

▶ **ride out** vt: **to ~ out the storm** (*fig*) mantenersi a galla

rider [ˈraɪdəʳ] n cavalcatore(-trice); (*jockey*) fantino; (*on bicycle*) ciclista *mf*; (*on motorcycle*) motociclista *mf*; (*in document*) clausola addizionale, aggiunta

ridge [rɪdʒ] n (*of hill*) cresta; (*of roof*) colmo; (*of mountain*) giogo; (*on object*) riga (in rilievo)

ridicule [ˈrɪdɪkjuːl] n ridicolo; scherno ▶ vt mettere in ridicolo; **to hold sb/sth up to ~** mettere in ridicolo qn/qc

ridiculous [rɪˈdɪkjuləs] adj ridicolo(-a)

riding [ˈraɪdɪŋ] n equitazione *f*

riding school n scuola d'equitazione

rife [raɪf] adj diffuso(-a); **to be ~ with** abbondare di

riffraff [ˈrɪfræf] n canaglia, gentaglia

rifle [ˈraɪfl] n carabina ▶ vt vuotare

▶**rifle through** VT FUS frugare

rifle range N campo di tiro; (*at fair*) tiro a segno

rift [rɪft] N fessura, crepatura; (*fig: disagreement*) incrinatura, disaccordo

rig [rɪg] N (*also:* **oil rig**: *on land*) derrick *m inv*; (: *at sea*) piattaforma di trivellazione ▶VT (*election etc*) truccare

▶**rig out** VT (*BRIT*) attrezzare; (*pej*) abbigliare, agghindare

▶**rig up** VT allestire

rigging [ˈrɪgɪŋ] N (*Naut*) attrezzatura

right [raɪt] ADJ giusto(-a); (*suitable*) appropriato(-a); (*not left*) destro(-a) ▶N giusto; (*title, claim*) diritto; (*not left*) destra ▶ADV (*answer*) correttamente; (*not on the left*) a destra ▶VT raddrizzare; (*fig*) riparare ▶EXCL bene!; **the ~ time** l'ora esatta; **to be ~** (*person*) aver ragione; (*answer*) essere giusto(-a) *or* corretto(-a); **to get sth ~** far giusto qc; **you did the ~ thing** ha fatto bene; **let's get it ~ this time!** cerchiamo di farlo bene stavolta!; **to put a mistake ~** (*BRIT*) correggere un errore; **~ now** proprio adesso; subito; **~ away** subito; **~ before/after** subito prima/dopo; **to go ~ to the end of sth** andare fino in fondo a qc; **~ against the wall** proprio contro il muro; **~ ahead** sempre diritto; proprio davanti; **~ in the middle** proprio nel mezzo; **by rights** di diritto; **on the ~, to the ~** a destra; **to be in the ~** aver ragione, essere nel giusto; **~ and wrong** il bene e il male; **to have a ~ to sth** aver diritto a qc; **film rights** diritti di riproduzione cinematografica

right angle N angolo retto

right-click [ˈraɪtklɪk] VI (*Comput*): **to ~ on** cliccare con il pulsante destro del mouse su

righteous [ˈraɪtʃəs] ADJ retto(-a), virtuoso(-a); (*anger*) giusto(-a), giustificato(-a)

righteousness [ˈraɪtʃəsnɪs] N rettitudine *f*, virtù *f*

rightful [ˈraɪtful] ADJ (*heir*) legittimo(-a)

rightfully [ˈraɪtfəlɪ] ADV legittimamente

right-hand [ˈraɪthænd] ADJ: **~ drive** guida a destra; **the ~ side** il lato destro; **~ man** braccio destro (*fig*)

right-handed [raɪtˈhændɪd] ADJ (*person*) che adopera la mano destra

rightly [ˈraɪtlɪ] ADV bene, correttamente; (*with reason*) a ragione; **if I remember ~** se mi ricordo bene

right-minded [raɪtˈmaɪndɪd] ADJ sensato(-a)

right of way N diritto di passaggio; (*Aut*) precedenza

rights issue [raɪts-] N (*Stock Exchange*) emissione *f* di azioni riservate agli azionisti

right wing N (*Mil, Sport*) ala destra; (*Pol*) destra ▶ADJ: **right-wing** (*Pol*) di destra

right-winger [raɪtˈwɪŋəʳ] N (*Pol*) uno(-a) di destra; (*Sport*) ala destra

rigid [ˈrɪdʒɪd] ADJ rigido(-a); (*principle*) rigoroso(-a)

rigidity [rɪˈdʒɪdɪtɪ] N rigidità

rigidly [ˈrɪdʒɪdlɪ] ADV rigidamente

rigmarole [ˈrɪgmərəul] N tiritera; commedia

rigor [ˈrɪgəʳ] N (*US*) = **rigour**

rigor mortis [ˈrɪgəˈmɔːtɪs] N rigidità cadaverica

rigorous [ˈrɪgərəs] ADJ rigoroso(-a)

rigorously [ˈrɪgərəslɪ] ADV rigorosamente

rigour, (*US*) **rigor** [ˈrɪgəʳ] N rigore *m*

rig-out [ˈrɪgaut] N (*BRIT col*) tenuta

rile [raɪl] VT irritare, seccare

rim [rɪm] N orlo; (*of spectacles*) montatura; (*of wheel*) cerchione *m*

rimless [ˈrɪmlɪs] ADJ (*spectacles*) senza montatura

rimmed [rɪmd] ADJ bordato(-a); cerchiato(-a)

rind [raɪnd] N (*of bacon*) cotenna; (*of lemon etc*) scorza

ring [rɪŋ] (*pt* **rang** [ræŋ], *pp* **rung** [rʌŋ]) N anello; (*also:* **wedding ring**) fede *f*; (*of people, objects*) cerchio; (*of spies*) giro; (*of smoke etc*) spirale *f*; (*arena*) pista, arena; (*for boxing*) ring *m inv*; (*sound of bell*) scampanio; (*telephone call*) colpo di telefono ▶VI (*person, bell, telephone*) suonare; (*also:* **ring out**: *voice, words*) risuonare; (*Tel*) telefonare; (*ears*) fischiare ▶VT (*BRIT Tel: also:* **ring up**) telefonare a; (*bell, doorbell*) suonare; **to give sb a ~** (*BRIT Tel*) dare un colpo di telefono a qn; **that has the ~ of truth about it** questo ha l'aria d'essere vero; **to ~ the bell** suonare il campanello; **the name doesn't ~ a bell (with me)** questo nome non mi dice niente

▶**ring back** VT, VI (*BRIT Tel*) richiamare

▶**ring off** VI (*BRIT Tel*) mettere giù, riattaccare

ring binder N classificatore *m* a anelli

ring-fence [rɪŋˈfɛns] VT isolare

ring finger N anulare *m*

ringing [ˈrɪŋɪŋ] N (*of bell*) scampanio; (: *louder*) scampanellata; (*of telephone*) squillo; (*in ears*) fischio, ronzio

ringing tone N (*BRIT Tel*) segnale *m* di libero

ringleader [ˈrɪŋliːdəʳ] N (*of gang*) capobanda *m*

ringlets [ˈrɪŋlɪts] NPL boccoli *mpl*

ring road N (*BRIT*) raccordo anulare

ringtone N (*Tel*) suoneria

rink [rɪŋk] N (*also:* **ice rink**) pista di pattinaggio; (*for roller-skating*) pista di pattinaggio (a rotelle)

rinse [rɪns] N risciacquatura; (*hair tint*) cachet *m inv* ▶VT sciacquare

Rio [ˈriːəu], **Rio de Janeiro** [ˈriːəudədʒəˈnɪərəu] N Rio de Janeiro *f*

riot [ˈraɪət] N sommossa, tumulto ▶VI tumultuare; **a ~ of colours** un'orgia di colori; **to run ~** creare disordine

rioter [ˈraɪətəʳ] N dimostrante *mf* (*durante dei disordini*)

riot gear N: **in ~** in assetto di guerra

riotous ['raɪətəs] ADJ tumultuoso(-a); che fa crepare dal ridere

riotously ['raɪətəslɪ] ADV: **~ funny** che fa crepare dal ridere

riot police N ≈ la Celere

RIP ABBR (= requiescat or requiescant in pace) R.I.P.

rip [rɪp] N strappo ▶ VT strappare ▶ VI strapparsi
▶ **rip off** VT (col: cheat) fregare
▶ **rip up** VT stracciare

ripcord ['rɪpkɔːd] N cavo di spiegamento

ripe [raɪp] ADJ (fruit, grain) maturo(-a); (cheese) stagionato(-a)

ripen ['raɪpən] VT maturare ▶ VI maturarsi; stagionarsi

ripeness ['raɪpnɪs] N maturità

rip-off ['rɪpɔf] N (col): **it's a ~!** è un furto!

riposte [rɪ'pɔst] N risposta per le rime

ripple ['rɪpl] N increspamento, ondulazione f; mormorio ▶ VI incresparsi ▶ VT increspare

rise [raɪz] (pt **rose** [rəuz], pp **risen** ['rɪzn]) N (slope) salita, pendio; (hill) altura; (increase: in wages: BRIT) aumento; (: in prices, temperature) rialzo, aumento; (fig: to power etc) ascesa ▶ VI alzarsi, levarsi; (prices) aumentare; (waters, river) crescere; (sun, wind, person: from chair, bed) levarsi; (building: also: **rise up**) ergersi; (rebel) insorgere; ribellarsi; (in rank) salire; **to give ~ to** provocare, dare origine a; **to ~ to the occasion** dimostrarsi all'altezza della situazione

risen ['rɪzn] PP of **rise**

rising ['raɪzɪŋ] ADJ (increasing: number) sempre crescente; (: prices) in aumento; (tide) montante; (sun, moon) nascente, che sorge ▶ N (uprising) sommossa

rising damp N infiltrazioni fpl d'umidità

rising star N (also fig) astro nascente

risk [rɪsk] N rischio; pericolo ▶ VT rischiare; **to take** or **run the ~ of doing** correre il rischio di fare; **at ~** in pericolo; **at one's own ~** a proprio rischio e pericolo; **fire/health ~** rischio d'incendio/per la salute; **I'll ~ it** ci proverò lo stesso

risk capital N capitale m di rischio

risky ['rɪskɪ] ADJ rischioso(-a)

risqué ['riːskeɪ] ADJ (joke) spinto(-a)

rissole ['rɪsəul] N crocchetta

rite [raɪt] N rito; **last rites** l'estrema unzione

ritual ['rɪtjuəl] ADJ, N rituale (m)

rival ['raɪvl] N rivale mf; (in business) concorrente mf ▶ ADJ rivale; che fa concorrenza ▶ VT essere in concorrenza con; **to ~ sb/sth in** competere con qn/qc in

rivalry ['raɪvəlrɪ] N rivalità f inv; concorrenza

river ['rɪvəʳ] N fiume m ▶ CPD (port, traffic) fluviale; **up/down~** a monte/valle

riverbank ['rɪvəbæŋk] N argine m

riverbed ['rɪvəbɛd] N alveo (fluviale)

riverside ['rɪvəsaɪd] N sponda del fiume

rivet ['rɪvɪt] N ribattino, rivetto ▶ VT ribadire; (fig) concentrare, fissare

riveting ['rɪvɪtɪŋ] ADJ (fig) avvincente

Riviera [rɪvɪ'ɛərə] N: **the (French) ~** la Costa Azzurra; **the Italian ~** la Riviera

Riyadh [rɪ'jɑːd] N Riad f

RMT N ABBR (= National Union of Rail, Maritime and Transport Workers) sindacato dei Ferrovieri, Marittimi e Trasportatori

RN N ABBR (BRIT) = **Royal Navy**; (US) = **registered nurse**

RNA N ABBR (= ribonucleic acid) R.N.A. m

RNLI N ABBR (BRIT: = Royal National Lifeboat Institution) associazione volontaria che organizza e dispone di scialuppe di salvataggio

RNZAF N ABBR = **Royal New Zealand Air Force**

RNZN N ABBR = **Royal New Zealand Navy**

road [rəud] N strada; (small) cammino; (in town) via ▶ CPD stradale; **main ~** strada principale; **major/minor ~** strada con/senza diritto di precedenza; **it takes 4 hours by ~** sono 4 ore di macchina (or in camion etc); **on the ~ to success** sulla via del successo; "**~ up**" (BRIT) "attenzione: lavori in corso"

road accident N incidente m stradale

roadblock ['rəudblɔk] N blocco stradale

road haulage N autotrasporti mpl

roadhog ['rəudhɔg] N pirata m della strada

road map N carta stradale

road rage N comportamento aggressivo al volante

road safety N sicurezza sulle strade

roadside ['rəudsaɪd] N margine m della strada; **by the ~** a lato della strada

roadsign ['rəudsaɪn] N cartello stradale

roadsweeper ['rəudswiːpəʳ] N (BRIT: person) spazzino(-a)

road tax N (BRIT) tassa di circolazione

road user N utente mf della strada

roadway ['rəudweɪ] N carreggiata

roadworks ['rəudwəːks] NPL lavori mpl stradali

roadworthy ['rəudwəːðɪ] ADJ in buono stato di marcia

roam [rəum] VI errare, vagabondare ▶ VT vagare per

roar [rɔːʳ] N ruggito; (of crowd) tumulto; (of thunder, storm) muggito; (of laughter) scoppio ▶ VI ruggire; tumultuare; muggire; **to ~ with laughter** scoppiare dalle risa

roaring ['rɔːrɪŋ] ADJ: **a ~ fire** un bel fuoco; **to do a ~ trade** fare affari d'oro; **a ~ success** un successo strepitoso

roast [rəust] N arrosto ▶ VT (meat) arrostire; (coffee) tostare, torrefare

roast beef N arrosto di manzo

roasting ['rəʊstɪŋ] N (col): **to give sb a ~** dare una lavata di capo a qn

rob [rɔb] VT (person) rubare; (bank) svaligiare; **to ~ sb of sth** derubare qn di qc; (fig: deprive) privare qn di qc

robber ['rɔbər] N ladro(-a); (armed) rapinatore(-trice)

robbery ['rɔbərɪ] N furto; rapina

robe [rəʊb] N (for ceremony etc) abito; (also: **bathrobe**) accappatoio; (US: also: **lap robe**) coperta ▶ VT vestire

robin ['rɔbɪn] N pettirosso

robot ['rəʊbɔt] N robot m inv

robotics ['rəʊbɔtɪks] N robotica

robust [rəʊ'bʌst] ADJ robusto(-a); (material, economy) solido(-a)

rock [rɔk] N (substance) roccia; (boulder) masso; roccia; (in sea) scoglio; (US: pebble) ciottolo; (BRIT: sweet) zucchero candito ▶ VT (swing gently: cradle) dondolare; (: child) cullare; (shake) scrollare, far tremare ▶ VI dondolarsi; oscillare; **on the rocks** (drink) col ghiaccio; (ship) sugli scogli; (marriage etc) in crisi; **to ~ the boat** (fig) piantare grane

rock and roll N rock and roll m

rock-bottom ['rɔk'bɔtəm] N (fig) stremo; **to reach** or **touch ~** (price) raggiungere il livello più basso; (person) toccare il fondo

rock climber N rocciatore(-trice), scalatore(-trice)

rock climbing N roccia

rockery ['rɔkərɪ] N giardino roccioso

rocket ['rɔkɪt] N razzo; (Mil) razzo, missile m ▶ VI (prices) salire alle stelle

rocket launcher [-lɔ:ntʃər] N lanciarazzi m inv

rock face N parete f della roccia

rock fall N caduta di massi

rocking chair ['rɔkɪŋ-] N sedia a dondolo

rocking horse ['rɔkɪŋ-] N cavallo a dondolo

rocky ['rɔkɪ] ADJ (hill) roccioso(-a); (path) sassoso(-a); (unsteady: table) traballante; (marriage etc) instabile

Rocky Mountains NPL: **the ~** le Montagne Rocciose

rod [rɔd] N (metallic, Tech) asta; (wooden) bacchetta; (also: **fishing rod**) canna da pesca

rode [rəʊd] PT of **ride**

rodent ['rəʊdnt] N roditore m

rodeo ['rəʊdɪəʊ] N rodeo

roe [rəʊ] N (species: also: **roe deer**) capriolo; (of fish: also: **hard roe**) uova fpl di pesce; **soft ~** latte m di pesce

roe deer N (species) capriolo; (female deer: pl inv) capriolo femmina

rogue [rəʊg] N mascalzone m

roguish ['rəʊgɪʃ] ADJ birbantesco(-a)

role [rəʊl] N ruolo

role model N modello (di comportamento)

role-play ['rəʊlpleɪ], **role-playing** ['rəʊlpleɪɪŋ] N il recitare un ruolo, role-playing m inv

roll [rəʊl] N rotolo; (of banknotes) mazzo; (also: **bread roll**) panino; (register) lista; (sound, of drums etc) rullo; (movement, of ship) rullio ▶ VT rotolare; (also: **roll up**: string) aggomitolare; (: sleeves) rimboccare; (cigarettes) arrotolare; (eyes) roteare; (pastry: also: **roll out**) stendere; (lawn, road etc) spianare ▶ VI rotolare; (wheel) girare; (drum) rullare; (vehicle: also: **roll along**) avanzare; (ship) rollare; **cheese ~** panino al formaggio
  ▶ **roll about, roll around** VI rotolare qua e là; (person) rotolarsi
  ▶ **roll by** VI (time) passare
  ▶ **roll in** VI (mail, cash) arrivare a bizzeffe
  ▶ **roll over** VI rivoltarsi
  ▶ **roll up** VI (col: arrive) arrivare ▶ VT (carpet, cloth, map) arrotolare; (sleeves) rimboccare; **to ~ o.s. up into a ball** raggomitolarsi

roll call N appello

rolled gold [rəʊld-] ADJ d'oro laminato

roller ['rəʊlər] N rullo; (wheel) rotella; (for hair) bigodino

rollerblades® ['rəʊləbleɪdz] NPL pattini mpl in linea

roller blind N (BRIT) avvolgibile m

roller coaster [-'kəʊstər] N montagne fpl russe

roller skates NPL pattini mpl a rotelle

roller-skating ['rəʊləskeɪtɪŋ] N pattinaggio a rotelle; **to go ~** andare a pattinare (con i pattini a rotelle)

rollicking ['rɔlɪkɪŋ] ADJ allegro(-a) e chiassoso(-a); **to have a ~ time** divertirsi pazzamente

rolling ['rəʊlɪŋ] ADJ (landscape) ondulato(-a)

rolling mill N fabbrica di laminati

rolling pin N matterello

rolling stock N (Rail) materiale m rotabile

roll-on-roll-off ['rəʊlɔn'rəʊlɔf] ADJ (BRIT: ferry) roll-on roll-off inv

roly-poly ['rəʊlɪ'pəʊlɪ] N (BRIT Culin) rotolo di pasta con ripieno di marmellata

ROM [rɔm] N ABBR (Comput: = read-only memory) ROM f

Roman ['rəʊmən] ADJ, N romano(-a)

Roman Catholic ADJ, N cattolico(-a)

romance [rə'mæns] N storia (or avventura or film m inv) romantico(-a); (charm) poesia; (love affair) idillio

Romanesque [rəʊmə'nɛsk] ADJ romanico(-a)

Romania [rəʊ'meɪnɪə] N Romania

Romanian [rəʊ'meɪnɪən] ADJ romeno(-a) ▶ N romeno(-a); (Ling) romeno

Roman numeral N numero romano

romantic [rə'mæntɪk] ADJ romantico(-a); sentimentale

r

romanticism [rəˈmæntɪsɪzəm] N romanticismo

Romany [ˈrɔmənɪ] ADJ zingaresco(-a) ▶ N (*person*) zingaro(-a); (*Ling*) lingua degli zingari

Rome [rəum] N Roma

romp [rɔmp] N gioco chiassoso ▶ VI (*also*: **romp about**) giocare chiassosamente; **to ~ home** (*horse*) vincere senza difficoltà, stravincere

rompers [ˈrɔmpəz] NPL pagliaccetto

rondo [ˈrɔndəu] N (*Mus*) rondò *m inv*

roof [ru:f] N tetto; (*of tunnel, cave*) volta ▶ VT coprire (con un tetto); **~ of the mouth** palato

roof garden N giardino pensile

roofing [ˈru:fɪŋ] N materiale *m* per copertura

roof rack N (*Aut*) portabagagli *m inv*

rook [ruk] N (*bird*) corvo nero; (*Chess*) torre *f* ▶ VT (*cheat*) truffare, spennare

rookie [ˈrukɪ] N (*col: esp Mil*) pivellino(-a)

room [ru:m] N (*in house*) stanza; (*bedroom, in hotel*) camera; (*in school etc*) sala; (*space*) posto, spazio ■ **rooms** NPL (*lodging*) alloggio; **"rooms to let"**, (*US*) **"rooms for rent"** "si affittano camere"; **is there ~ for this?** c'è spazio per questo?, ci sta anche questo?; **to make ~ for sb** far posto a qn; **there is ~ for improvement** si potrebbe migliorare

rooming house [ˈru:mɪŋ-] N (*US*) casa in cui si *affittano camere o appartamentini ammobiliati*

roommate [ˈru:mmeɪt] N compagno(-a) di stanza

room service N servizio da camera

room temperature N temperatura ambiente

roomy [ˈru:mɪ] ADJ spazioso(-a); (*garment*) ampio(-a)

roost [ru:st] N appollaiato ▶ VI appollaiarsi

rooster [ˈru:stəʳ] N gallo

root [ru:t] N radice *f* ▶ VI (*plant, belief*) attecchire ▶ VT (*plant, belief*) far radicare; **to take ~** (*plant*) attecchire, prendere; (*idea*) far presa; **the ~ of the problem is that ...** il problema deriva dal fatto che ...
  ▶ **root about** VI (*fig*) frugare
  ▶ **root for** VT FUS (*col*) fare il tifo per
  ▶ **root out** VT estirpare

root beer N (*US*) *bibita dolce a base di estratti di erbe e radici*

rope [rəup] N corda, fune *f*; (*Naut*) cavo ▶ VT (*box*) legare; (*climbers*) legare in cordata; **to ~ sb in** (*fig*) coinvolgere qn; **to know the ropes** (*fig*) conoscere i trucchi del mestiere

rope ladder N scala di corda

ropey [ˈrəupɪ] ADJ (*col*) scadente, da quattro soldi; **to feel ~** (*ill*) sentirsi male

rort [rɔ:t] N (*AUSTRALIA, NEW ZEALAND col*) truffa ▶ VT fregare

rosary [ˈrəuzərɪ] N rosario; roseto

rose [rəuz] PT OF **rise** ▶ N rosa; (*also*: **rosebush**) rosaio; (*on watering can*) rosetta ▶ ADJ rosa *inv*

rosé [ˈrəuzeɪ] N vino rosato

rosebed [ˈrəuzbɛd] N roseto

rosebud [ˈrəuzbʌd] N bocciolo di rosa

rosebush [ˈrəuzbuʃ] N rosaio

rosemary [ˈrəuzmərɪ] N rosmarino

rosette [rəuˈzɛt] N coccarda

ROSPA [ˈrɔspə] N ABBR (*BRIT*: = *Royal Society for the Prevention of Accidents*) ≈ E.N.P.I. *m* (= *Ente Nazionale Prevenzione Infortuni*)

roster [ˈrɔstəʳ] N: **duty ~** ruolino di servizio

rostrum [ˈrɔstrəm] N tribuna

rosy [ˈrəuzɪ] ADJ roseo(-a)

rot [rɔt] N (*decay*) putrefazione *f*; (*col: nonsense*) stupidaggini *fpl* ▶ VT, VI imputridire, marcire; **dry/wet ~** funghi parassiti del legno; **to stop the ~** (*BRIT fig*) salvare la situazione

rota [ˈrəutə] N tabella dei turni; **on a ~ basis** a turno

rotary [ˈrəutərɪ] ADJ rotante

rotate [rəuˈteɪt] VT (*revolve*) far girare; (*change round: jobs*) fare a turno; (: *crops*) avvicendare ▶ VI (*revolve*) girare

rotating [rəuˈteɪtɪŋ] ADJ (*movement*) rotante

rotation [rəuˈteɪʃən] N rotazione *f*; **in ~** a turno, in rotazione

rote [rəut] N: **to learn sth by ~** imparare qc a memoria

rotor [ˈrəutəʳ] N rotore *m*

rotten [ˈrɔtn] ADJ (*decayed*) putrido(-a), marcio(-a); (: *teeth*) cariato(-a); (*dishonest*) corrotto(-a); (*col: bad*) brutto(-a); (: *action*) vigliacco(-a); **to feel ~** (*ill*) sentirsi a pezzi

rotting [ˈrɔtɪŋ] ADJ in putrefazione

rotund [rəuˈtʌnd] ADJ grassoccio(-a); tondo(-a)

rouble, (*US*) **ruble** [ˈru:bl] N rublo

rouge [ru:ʒ] N belletto

rough [rʌf] ADJ (*skin, surface*) ruvido(-a); (*terrain, road*) accidentato(-a); (*voice*) rauco(-a); (*person, manner: coarse*) rozzo(-a), aspro(-a); (: *violent*) brutale; (*district*) malfamato(-a); (*weather*) cattivo(-a); (*sea*) mosso(-a); (*plan*) abbozzato(-a); (*guess*) approssimativo(-a) ▶ N (*Golf*) macchia; **~ estimate** approssimazione *f*; **to ~ it** far vita dura; **to play ~** far il gioco pesante; **to sleep ~** (*BRIT*) dormire all'addiaccio; **to feel ~** (*BRIT*) sentirsi male; **to have a ~ time (of it)** passare un periodaccio; **the sea is ~ today** c'è mare grosso oggi
  ▶ **rough out** VT (*draft*) abbozzare

roughage [ˈrʌfɪdʒ] N alimenti *mpl* ricchi di cellulosa

rough-and-ready [ˈrʌfənˈrɛdɪ] ADJ rudimentale

rough-and-tumble [ˈrʌfənˈtʌmbl] N zuffa

roughcast [ˈrʌfkɑ:st] N intonaco grezzo

rough copy, rough draft N brutta copia

roughen ['rʌfn] VT (a surface) rendere ruvido(-a)

rough justice N giustizia sommaria

roughly ['rʌflɪ] ADV (handle) rudemente, brutalmente; (make) grossolanamente; (speak) bruscamente; (approximately) approssimativamente; **~ speaking** grosso modo, ad occhio e croce

roughness ['rʌfnɪs] N asprezza; rozzezza; brutalità

roughshod ['rʌfʃɔd] ADV: **to ride ~ over** (person) mettere sotto i piedi; (objection) passare sopra a

rough work N (at school etc) brutta copia

roulette [ruː'let] N roulette f

Roumania etc [ruː'meɪnɪə] N = **Romania** etc

round [raund] ADJ rotondo(-a) ▶ N tondo, cerchio; (BRIT: of toast) fetta; (duty: of police officer, milkman etc) giro; (: of doctor) visite fpl; (game: of cards, golf, in competition) partita; (Boxing) round m inv; (of talks) serie f inv ▶ VT (corner) girare; (bend) prendere; (cape) doppiare ▶ PREP intorno a ▶ ADV: **right ~, all ~** tutt'attorno; **the long way ~** il giro più lungo; **all the year ~** tutto l'anno; **in ~ figures** in cifra tonda; **it's just ~ the corner** (also fig) è dietro l'angolo; **to ask sb ~** invitare qn (a casa propria); **I'll be ~ at 6 o'clock** ci sarò alle 6; **to go ~** fare il giro; **to go ~ to sb's (house)** andare da qn; **to go ~ an obstacle** aggirare un ostacolo; **go ~ the back** passi da dietro; **to go ~ a house** visitare una casa; **enough to go ~** abbastanza per tutti; **she arrived ~ (about) noon** è arrivata intorno a mezzogiorno; **~ the clock** 24 ore su 24, ininterrottamente; **to go the rounds** (illness) diffondersi; (story) circolare, passare di bocca in bocca; **the daily ~** (fig) la routine quotidiana; **~ of ammunition** cartuccia; **~ of applause** applausi mpl; **~ of drinks** giro di bibite; **~ of sandwiches** (BRIT) sandwich m inv
▶ **round off** VT (speech etc) finire
▶ **round up** VT radunare; (criminals) fare una retata di; (prices) arrotondare

roundabout ['raundəbaut] N (BRIT: Aut) rotatoria; (: at fair) giostra ▶ ADJ (route, means) indiretto(-a)

rounded ['raundɪd] ADJ arrotondato(-a); (style) armonioso(-a)

rounders ['raundəz] NPL (game) gioco simile al baseball

roundly ['raundlɪ] ADV (fig) chiaro e tondo

round robin N (Sport: also: **round robin tournament**) ≈ torneo all'italiana

round-shouldered [raund'ʃəuldəd] ADJ dalle spalle tonde

round trip N (viaggio di) andata e ritorno

roundup ['raundʌp] N raduno; (of criminals) retata; **a ~ of the latest news** un sommario or riepilogo delle ultime notizie

rouse [rauz] VT (wake up) svegliare; (stir up) destare; provocare; risvegliare

rousing ['rauzɪŋ] ADJ (speech, applause) entusiastico(-a)

rout [raut] N (Mil) rotta ▶ VT mettere in rotta

route [ruːt] N itinerario; (of bus) percorso; (of trade, shipping) rotta; **"all routes"** (Aut) "tutte le direzioni"; **the best ~ to London** la strada migliore per andare a Londra; **en ~ for** in viaggio verso; **en ~ from ... to** viaggiando da ... a

route map N (BRIT: for journey) cartina di itinerario; (for trains etc) pianta dei collegamenti

router ['ruːtə'] N (Comput) router m inv

routine [ruː'tiːn] ADJ (work) corrente, abituale; (procedure) solito(-a) ▶ N (pej) routine f, tran tran m; (Theat) numero; (Comput) sottoprogramma m; **daily ~** orario quotidiano; **~ procedure** prassi f

roving ['rəuvɪŋ] ADJ (life) itinerante

roving reporter N reporter mf inv volante

row¹ [rəu] N (line) riga, fila; (Knitting) ferro; (behind one another: of cars, people) fila; (in boat) remata ▶ VI (in boat) remare; (as sport) vogare ▶ VT (boat) manovrare a remi; **in a ~** (fig) di fila

row² [rau] N (noise) baccano, chiasso; (dispute) lite f; (scolding) sgridata ▶ VI (argue) litigare; **to make a ~** far baccano; **to have a ~** litigare

rowboat ['rəubəut] N (US) barca a remi

rowdiness ['raudɪnɪs] N baccano; (fighting) zuffa

rowdy ['raudɪ] ADJ chiassoso(-a), turbolento(-a) ▶ N teppista mf

rowdyism ['raudɪɪzəm] N teppismo

rowing ['rəuɪŋ] N canottaggio

rowing boat N (BRIT) barca a remi

rowlock ['rɔlək] N scalmo

royal ['rɔɪəl] ADJ reale

Royal Academy N (BRIT) vedi nota

L'Accademia Reale d'Arte britannica, *Royal Academy (of Arts)*, è un'istituzione fondata nel 1768 al fine di incoraggiare la pittura, la scultura e l'architettura. Ogni anno organizza una mostra estiva d'arte contemporanea che si tiene nella sua sede, a Burlington House a Piccadilly, Londra.

Royal Air Force N (BRIT) aeronautica militare britannica

royal blue ADJ blu reale inv

royalist ['rɔɪəlɪst] ADJ, N realista mf

Royal Navy N (BRIT) marina militare britannica

royalty ['rɔɪəltɪ] N (royal persons) (membri mpl della) famiglia reale; (payment: to author) diritti mpl d'autore; (: to inventor) diritti di brevetto

RP N ABBR (BRIT: = received pronunciation) pronuncia standard

RPI ABBR (BRIT) = **retail price index**

rpm ABBR (= revolutions per minute) giri/min

RR ABBR (US: = railroad) Ferr

RRP N ABBR (BRIT) = **recommended retail price**

RSA – rumple

RSA N ABBR (*BRIT*) = **Royal Society of Arts; Royal Scottish Academy**

RSI N ABBR (*Med*: = *repetitive strain injury*) lesione al braccio tipica di violinisti e terminalisti

RSPB N ABBR (*BRIT*: = *Royal Society for the Protection of Birds*) ≈ L.I.P.U. *f* (= *Lega Italiana Protezione Uccelli*)

RSPCA N ABBR (*BRIT*: = *Royal Society for the Prevention of Cruelty to Animals*) ≈ E.N.P.A. *m* (= *Ente Nazionale per la Protezione degli Animali*)

RSVP ABBR (= *répondez s'il vous plaît*) R.S.V.P.

RTA N ABBR (= *road traffic accident*) incidente *m* stradale

Rt. Hon. ABBR (*BRIT*: = *Right Honourable*) ≈ On. (= *Onorevole*)

Rt Rev. ABBR (= *Right Reverend*) Rev.

rub [rʌb] N (*with cloth*) fregata, strofinata; (*on person*) frizione *f*, massaggio; **to give sth a ~** strofinare qc; (*sore place*) massaggiare qc ▶ VT fregare, strofinare; frizionare; massaggiare; (*hands: also*: **rub together**) sfregarsi; **to ~ sb up** *or* (*US*) **~ sb the wrong way** lisciare qn contro pelo
  ▶ **rub down** VT (*body*) strofinare, frizionare; (*horse*) strigliare
  ▶ **rub in** VT (*ointment*) far penetrare (massaggiando *or* frizionando)
  ▶ **rub off** VI andare via; **to ~ off on** lasciare una traccia su
  ▶ **rub out** VT cancellare ▶ VI cancellarsi

rubber [ˈrʌbəʳ] N gomma

rubber band N elastico

rubber bullet N pallottola di gomma

rubber gloves NPL guanti *mpl* di gomma

rubber plant N ficus *m inv*

rubber ring N (*for swimming*) ciambella

rubber stamp N timbro di gomma

rubber-stamp [rʌbəˈstæmp] VT (*fig*) approvare senza discussione

rubbery [ˈrʌbəri] ADJ gommoso(-a)

rubbish [ˈrʌbiʃ] N (*from household*) immondizie *fpl*, rifiuti *mpl*; (*fig, pej*) cose *fpl* senza valore; robaccia; (*nonsense*) sciocchezze *fpl* ▶ VT (*col*) sputtanare; **what you've just said is ~** quello che ha appena detto è una sciocchezza

rubbish bin N (*BRIT*) pattumiera

rubbish dump N discarica

rubbishy [ˈrʌbiʃi] ADJ (*BRIT col*) scadente, che non vale niente

rubble [ˈrʌbl] N macerie *fpl*; (*smaller*) pietrisco

ruble [ˈruːbl] N (*US*) = **rouble**

ruby [ˈruːbi] N rubino

RUC N ABBR (*BRIT*: = *Royal Ulster Constabulary*) forza di polizia dell'Irlanda del Nord

rucksack [ˈrʌksæk] N zaino

ructions [ˈrʌkʃənz] NPL putiferio, finimondo

rudder [ˈrʌdəʳ] N timone *m*

ruddy [ˈrʌdi] ADJ (*face*) fresco(-a); (*col: damned*) maledetto(-a)

rude [ruːd] ADJ (*impolite: person*) scortese, rozzo(-a); (*: word, manners*) grossolano(-a), rozzo(-a); (*shocking*) indecente; **to be ~ to sb** essere maleducato con qn

rudely [ˈruːdli] ADV scortesemente; grossolanamente

rudeness [ˈruːdnis] N scortesia; grossolanità

rudiment [ˈruːdimənt] N rudimento

rudimentary [ruːdiˈmɛntəri] ADJ rudimentale

rue [ruː] VT pentirsi amaramente di

rueful [ˈruːful] ADJ mesto(-a), triste

ruff [rʌf] N gorgiera

ruffian [ˈrʌfiən] N briccone *m*, furfante *m*

ruffle [ˈrʌfl] VT (*hair*) scompigliare; (*clothes, water*) increspare; (*fig: person*) turbare

rug [rʌg] N tappeto; (*BRIT: for knees*) coperta

rugby [ˈrʌgbi] N (*also*: **rugby football**) rugby *m*

rugged [ˈrʌgid] ADJ (*landscape*) aspro(-a); (*features, determination*) duro(-a); (*character*) brusco(-a)

rugger [ˈrʌgəʳ] N (*col*) rugby *m*

ruin [ˈruːin] N rovina ▶ VT rovinare; (*spoil: clothes*) sciupare ■ **ruins** NPL (*of building, castle etc*) rovine *fpl*, ruderi *mpl*; **in ruins** in rovina

ruination [ruːiˈneiʃən] N rovina

ruinous [ˈruːinəs] ADJ rovinoso(-a); (*expenditure*) inverosimile

rule [ruːl] N (*gen*) regola; (*regulation*) regolamento, regola; (*government*) governo; (*ruler*) riga; (*dominion etc*): **under British ~** sotto la sovranità britannica ▶ VT (*country*) governare; (*person*) dominare; (*decide*) decidere ▶ VI regnare; decidere; (*Law*) dichiarare; **to ~ against/in favour of/on** (*Law*) pronunciarsi a sfavore di/in favore di/su; **it's against the rules** è contro le regole *or* il regolamento; **by ~ of thumb** a lume di naso; **as a ~** normalmente, di regola
  ▶ **rule out** VT escludere; **murder cannot be ruled out** non si esclude che si tratti di omicidio

ruled [ruːld] ADJ (*paper*) vergato(-a)

ruler [ˈruːləʳ] N (*sovereign*) sovrano(-a); (*leader*) capo (dello Stato); (*for measuring*) regolo, riga

ruling [ˈruːliŋ] ADJ (*party*) al potere; (*class*) dirigente ▶ N (*Law*) decisione *f*

rum [rʌm] N rum *m inv* ▶ ADJ (*BRIT col*) strano(-a)

Rumania *etc* [ruːˈmeiniə] = **Romania** *etc*

rumble [ˈrʌmbl] N rimbombo; brontolio ▶ VI rimbombare; (*stomach, pipe*) brontolare

rumbustious [rʌmˈbʌstʃəs] ADJ (*person*): **to be ~** essere un terremoto

rummage [ˈrʌmidʒ] VI frugare

rumour, (*US*) **rumor** [ˈruːməʳ] N voce *f* ▶ VT: **it is rumoured that** corre voce che

rump [rʌmp] N (*of animal*) groppa

rumple [ˈrʌmpl] VT (*hair*) arruffare, scompigliare; (*clothes*) spiegazzare, sgualcire

rump steak N bistecca di girello

rumpus ['rʌmpəs] N (col) baccano; (quarrel) rissa; **to kick up a ~** fare un putiferio

run [rʌn] (pt **ran** [ræn], pp **~**) N corsa; (outing) gita (in macchina); (distance travelled) percorso, tragitto; (series) serie f inv; (Theat) periodo di rappresentazione; (Ski) pista; (Cricket, Baseball) meta; (in tights, stockings) smagliatura ▶ VT (distance) correre; (operate: business) gestire, dirigere; (: competition, course) organizzare; (: hotel) gestire; (: house) governare; (Comput: program) eseguire; (water, bath) far scorrere; (force through: rope, pipe): **to ~ sth through** far passare qc attraverso; (pass: hand, finger): **to ~ sth over** passare qc su; (Press: feature) presentare ▶ VI correre; (flee) scappare; (pass: road etc) passare; (work: machine, factory) funzionare, andare; (bus, train: operate) far servizio; (: travel) circolare; (continue: play, contract) durare; (slide: drawer, flow: river, bath) scorrere; (colours, washing) stemperarsi; (in election) presentarsi come candidato(-a); (nose) colare; **to go for a ~** andare a correre; (in car) fare un giro (in macchina); **to break into a ~** mettersi a correre; **a ~ of luck** un periodo di fortuna; **to have the ~ of sb's house** essere libero di andare e venire in casa di qn; **there was a ~ on ...** c'era una corsa a ...; **in the long ~** a lungo andare; in fin dei conti; **in the short ~** sulle prime; **on the ~** in fuga; **to make a ~ for it** scappare, tagliare la corda; **to ~ a race** partecipare ad una gara; **I'll ~ you to the station** la porto alla stazione; **to ~ a risk** correre un rischio; **to ~ errands** andare a fare commissioni; **the train runs between Gatwick and Victoria** il treno collega Gatwick alla stazione Victoria; **the bus runs every 20 minutes** c'è un autobus ogni 20 minuti; **it's very cheap to ~** comporta poche spese; **to ~ on petrol** or (US) **gas/on diesel/off batteries** andare a benzina/a diesel/a batterie; **to ~ for the bus** fare una corsa per prendere l'autobus; **to ~ for president** presentarsi come candidato per la presidenza; **their losses ran into millions** le loro perdite hanno raggiunto i milioni; **to be ~ off one's feet** (BRIT) doversi fare in quattro

▶ **run about** VI (children) correre qua e là
▶ **run across** VT FUS (find) trovare per caso
▶ **run after** VT FUS (to catch up) rincorrere; (chase) correre dietro a
▶ **run away** VI fuggire
▶ **run down** VI (clock) scaricarsi ▶ VT (Aut) investire; (criticize) criticare; (BRIT: reduce: production) ridurre gradualmente; (: factory, shop) rallentare l'attività di; **to be ~ down** (battery) essere scarico(-a); (person) essere spossato(-a)
▶ **run in** VT (BRIT: car) rodare, fare il rodaggio di
▶ **run into** VT FUS (meet: person) incontrare per caso; (: trouble) incontrare, trovare; (collide with) andare a sbattere contro; **to ~ into debt** trovarsi nei debiti
▶ **run off** VI fuggire ▶ VT (water) far defluire; (copies) fare

▶ **run out** VI (person) uscire di corsa; (liquid) colare; (lease) scadere; (money) esaurirsi
▶ **run out of** VT FUS rimanere a corto di; **I've ~ out of petrol** or (US) **gas** sono rimasto senza benzina
▶ **run over** VT (Aut) investire, mettere sotto ▶ VT FUS (revise) rivedere
▶ **run through** VT FUS (instructions) dare una scorsa a; (rehearse: play) riprovare, ripetere
▶ **run up** VT (debt) lasciar accumulare; **to ~ up against** (difficulties) incontrare

runaround ['rʌnəraund] N (col): **to give sb the ~** far girare a vuoto qn

runaway ['rʌnəweɪ] ADJ (person) fuggiasco(-a); (horse) in libertà; (truck) fuori controllo; (inflation) galoppante

rundown ['rʌndaun] N (BRIT: of industry etc) riduzione f graduale dell'attività di

rung [rʌŋ] PP of **ring** ▶ N (of ladder) piolo

run-in ['rʌnɪn] N (col) scontro

runner ['rʌnə'] N (in race) corridore m; (: horse) partente mf; (on sledge) pattino; (for drawer etc, carpet) guida

runner bean N (BRIT) fagiolino

runner-up [rʌnər'ʌp] N secondo(-a) arrivato(-a)

running ['rʌnɪŋ] N corsa; direzione f; organizzazione f; funzionamento ▶ ADJ (water) corrente; (commentary) simultaneo(-a); **6 days ~** 6 giorni di seguito; **to be in/out of the ~ for sth** essere/non essere più in lizza per qc

running costs NPL (of business) costi mpl d'esercizio; (of car) spese fpl di mantenimento

running head N (Typ) testata, titolo corrente

running mate N (US Pol) candidato(-a) alla vicepresidenza

runny ['rʌnɪ] ADJ che cola

run-off ['rʌnɔf] N (in contest, election) confronto definitivo; (extra race) spareggio

run-of-the-mill ['rʌnəvðə'mɪl] ADJ solito(-a), banale

runt [rʌnt] N omuncolo; (Zool) animale m più piccolo del normale

run-through ['rʌnθruː] N prova

run-up ['rʌnʌp] N (BRIT): **~ to sth** (election etc) periodo che precede qc

runway ['rʌnweɪ] N (Aviat) pista (di decollo)

rupture ['rʌptʃə'] N (Med) ernia ▶ VT: **to ~ o.s.** farsi venire un'ernia

rural ['ruərl] ADJ rurale

ruse [ruːz] N trucco

rush [rʌʃ] N corsa precipitosa; (of crowd) afflusso; (hurry) furia, fretta; (of emotion) impeto; (Bot) giunco; (sudden demand): **~ for** corsa a; (current) flusso ▶ VT mandare or spedire velocemente; (attack: town etc) prendere d'assalto ▶ VI precipitarsi; **is there any ~ for this?** è urgente?; **we've had a ~ of orders** abbiamo avuto una valanga di ordinazioni; **I'm in a ~ (to do)** ho fretta *or* premura (di fare); **gold ~** corsa all'oro; **to ~ sth off** spedire con urgenza qc; **don't ~ me!** non farmi fretta!

▶ **rush through** VT (*meal*) mangiare in fretta; (*book*) dare una scorsa frettolosa a; (*town*) attraversare in fretta; (*Comm: order*) eseguire d'urgenza ▶ VT FUS (*work*) sbrigare frettolosamente

rush hour N ora di punta

rush job N (*urgent*) lavoro urgente

rush matting N stuoia

rusk [rʌsk] N fetta biscottata

Russia [ˈrʌʃə] N Russia

Russian [ˈrʌʃən] ADJ russo(-a) ▶ N russo(-a); (*Ling*) russo

rust [rʌst] N ruggine *f* ▶ VI arrugginirsi

rustic [ˈrʌstɪk] ADJ rustico(-a) ▶ N (*pej*) cafone(-a)

rustle [ˈrʌsl] VI frusciare ▶ VT (*paper*) far frusciare; (*US: cattle*) rubare

rustproof [ˈrʌstpruːf] ADJ inossidabile

rustproofing [ˈrʌstpruːfɪŋ] N trattamento antiruggine

rusty [ˈrʌstɪ] ADJ arrugginito(-a)

rut [rʌt] N solco; (*Zool*) fregola; **to be in a ~** (*fig*) essersi fossilizzato(-a)

rutabaga [ruːtəˈbeɪɡə] N (*US*) rapa svedese

ruthless [ˈruːθlɪs] ADJ spietato(-a)

ruthlessness [ˈruːθlɪsnɪs] N spietatezza

RV ABBR (= *revised version*) versione riveduta della Bibbia ▶ N ABBR (*US*) = **recreational vehicle**

RVS N ABBR (*BRIT*) = **Royal Voluntary Service**

Rwanda [ruˈændə] N Ruanda

rye [raɪ] N segale *f*

Ss

S, s [ɛs] N (*letter*) S, s f *inv or m inv*; (*US Scol*: = *satisfactory*) ≈ sufficiente; **S for Sugar** ≈ S come Savona

S ABBR (= *saint*) S.; (*on clothes*) = **small**; (= *south*) S

SA ABBR = **South Africa; South America**

Sabbath ['sæbəθ] N (*Jewish*) sabato; (*Christian*) domenica

sabbatical [sə'bætɪkl] ADJ: **~ year** anno sabbatico

sabotage ['sæbətɑːʒ] N sabotaggio ▶ VT sabotare

saccharin, saccharine ['sækərɪn] N saccarina

sachet ['sæʃeɪ] N bustina

sack [sæk] N (*bag*) sacco ▶ VT (*dismiss*) licenziare, mandare a spasso; (*plunder*) saccheggiare; **to get the ~** essere mandato a spasso; **to give sb the ~** licenziare qn, mandare qn a spasso

sackful ['sækful] N: **a ~ of** un sacco di

sacking ['sækɪŋ] N tela di sacco; (*dismissal*) licenziamento

sacrament ['sækrəmənt] N sacramento

sacred ['seɪkrɪd] ADJ sacro(-a)

sacred cow N (*fig: person*) intoccabile *mf*; (: *institution*) caposaldo; (: *idea, belief*) dogma *m*

sacrifice ['sækrɪfaɪs] N sacrificio ▶ VT sacrificare; **to make sacrifices (for sb)** fare (dei) sacrifici (per qn)

sacrilege ['sækrɪlɪdʒ] N sacrilegio

sacrosanct ['sækrəusæŋkt] ADJ sacrosanto(-a)

sad [sæd] ADJ triste; (*deplorable*) deplorevole

sadden ['sædn] VT rattristare

saddle ['sædl] N sella ▶ VT (*horse*) sellare; **to be saddled with sth** (*col*) avere qc sulle spalle

saddlebag ['sædlbæg] N bisaccia; (*on bicycle*) borsa

sadism ['seɪdɪzəm] N sadismo

sadist ['seɪdɪst] N sadico(-a)

sadistic [sə'dɪstɪk] ADJ sadico(-a)

sadly ['sædlɪ] ADV tristemente; (*regrettably*) sfortunatamente; **~ lacking in** penosamente privo di

sadness ['sædnɪs] N tristezza

sadomasochism [seɪdəu'mæsəkɪzəm] N sadomasochismo

sae ABBR (BRIT: = *stamped addressed envelope*) busta affrancata e con indirizzo

safari [sə'fɑːrɪ] N safari *m inv*

safari park N zoosafari *m inv*

safe [seɪf] ADJ sicuro(-a); (*out of danger*) salvo(-a), al sicuro; (*cautious*) prudente ▶ N cassaforte f; **~ from** al sicuro da; **~ and sound** sano(-a) e salvo(-a); **~ journey!** buon viaggio!; **(just) to be on the ~ side** per non correre rischi; **to play ~** giocare sul sicuro; **it is ~ to say that ...** si può affermare con sicurezza che ...

safe bet N: **it's a ~** è una cosa sicura

safe-breaker ['seɪfbreɪkəʳ] N (BRIT) scassinatore(-trice)

safe-conduct [seɪf'kɔndʌkt] N salvacondotto

safe-cracker ['seɪfkrækəʳ] N = **safe-breaker**

safe-deposit ['seɪfdɪpɔzɪt] N (*vault*) caveau *m inv*; (*box*) cassetta di sicurezza

safeguard ['seɪfgɑːd] N salvaguardia ▶ VT salvaguardare

safe haven N zona sicura *or* protetta

safekeeping ['seɪf'kiːpɪŋ] N custodia

safely ['seɪflɪ] ADV sicuramente; prudentemente; **I can ~ say ...** posso tranquillamente asserire ...

safe passage N passaggio sicuro

safe sex N sesso sicuro

safety ['seɪftɪ] N sicurezza; **~ first!** la prudenza innanzitutto!

safety belt N cintura di sicurezza

safety catch N sicura

safety net N rete f di protezione

safety pin N spilla di sicurezza

safety valve N valvola di sicurezza

saffron ['sæfrən] N zafferano

sag [sæg] VI incurvarsi; afflosciarsi

saga ['sɑːgə] N saga; (*fig*) odissea

sage [seɪdʒ] N (*herb*) salvia; (*man*) saggio

Sagittarius [sædʒɪ'tɛərɪəs] N Sagittario; **to be ~** essere del Sagittario

sago [ˈseɪɡəʊ] N sagù m

Sahara [səˈhɑːrə] N: **the ~ Desert** il Deserto del Sahara

Sahel [sæˈhɛl] N Sahel m

said [sɛd] PT, PP of **say**

Saigon [saɪˈɡɔn] N Saigon f

sail [seɪl] N (on boat) vela; (trip): **to go for a ~** fare un giro in barca a vela ▶ VT (boat) condurre, governare ▶ VI (travel: ship) navigare; (: passenger) viaggiare per mare; (set off) salpare; (Sport) fare della vela; **they sailed into Genoa** entrarono nel porto di Genova
▶ **sail through** VT FUS (fig) superare senza difficoltà ▶ VI farcela senza difficoltà

sailboat [ˈseɪlbəʊt] N (US) barca a vela

sailing [ˈseɪlɪŋ] N (sport) vela; **to go ~** fare della vela

sailing boat N barca a vela

sailing ship N veliero

sailor [ˈseɪlər] N marinaio

saint [seɪnt] N santo(-a)

saintly [ˈseɪntlɪ] ADJ da santo(-a); santo(-a)

sake [seɪk] N: **for the ~ of** per, per amore di; **for pity's ~** per pietà; **for the ~ of argument** tanto per fare un esempio; **art for art's ~** l'arte per l'arte

salad [ˈsæləd] N insalata; **tomato ~** insalata di pomodori

salad bowl N insalatiera

salad cream N (BRIT) (tipo di) maionese f

salad dressing N condimento per insalata

salad oil N olio da tavola

salami [səˈlɑːmɪ] N salame m

salaried [ˈsælərɪd] ADJ stipendiato(-a)

salary [ˈsælərɪ] N stipendio

salary scale N scala dei salari

sale [seɪl] N vendita; (at reduced prices) svendita, liquidazione f; (auction) vendita all'asta ▪ **sales** NPL (total amount sold) vendite fpl; **"for ~"** "in vendita"; **on ~** in vendita; **on ~ or return** da vendere o rimandare; **a closing-down** or (US) **liquidation ~** una liquidazione; **~ and lease back** n lease back m inv

saleroom [ˈseɪlrum] N sala delle aste

sales assistant N (BRIT) commesso(-a)

sales clerk N (US) commesso(-a)

sales conference N riunione f marketing e vendite

sales drive N campagna di vendita, sforzo promozionale

sales force N personale m addetto alle vendite

salesman [ˈseɪlzmən] N (irreg) commesso; (representative) rappresentante m

sales manager N direttore(-trice) commerciale

salesmanship [ˈseɪlzmənʃɪp] N arte f del vendere

salesperson N (irreg) (in shop) commesso(-a); (representative) rappresentante mf di commercio

sales rep N rappresentante mf di commercio

sales tax N (US) imposta sulle vendite

saleswoman [ˈseɪlzwʊmən] N (irreg) commessa; (representative) rappresentante f

salient [ˈseɪlɪənt] ADJ saliente

saline [ˈseɪlaɪn] ADJ salino(-a)

saliva [səˈlaɪvə] N saliva

sallow [ˈsæləʊ] ADJ giallastro(-a)

sally forth, sally out [ˈsælɪ-] VI uscire di gran carriera

salmon [ˈsæmən] N (pl inv) salmone m

salmon trout N (pl inv) trota (di mare)

salon [ˈsælɔn] N (hairdressing salon: for men) parrucchiere; (: for women) parrucchiera; (beauty salon) salone m di bellezza

saloon [səˈluːn] N (US) saloon m inv, bar m inv; (BRIT Aut) berlina; (ship's lounge) salone m

salt [sɔːlt] N sale m ▶ VT salare ▶ CPD di sale; (Culin) salato(-a); **an old ~** un lupo di mare
▶ **salt away** VT ammucchiare, mettere via

salt cellar N saliera

salt-free [ˈsɔːltˈfriː] ADJ senza sale

saltwater [ˈsɔːltwɔːtər] ADJ (fish etc) di mare

salty [ˈsɔːltɪ] ADJ salato(-a)

salubrious [səˈluːbrɪəs] ADJ salubre; (fig: district etc) raccomandabile

salutary [ˈsæljutərɪ] ADJ salutare

salute [səˈluːt] N saluto ▶ VT salutare

salvage [ˈsælvɪdʒ] N (saving) salvataggio; (things saved) beni mpl salvati or recuperati ▶ VT salvare, mettere in salvo

salvage vessel N scialuppa di salvataggio

salvation [sælˈveɪʃən] N salvezza

Salvation Army [sælˈveɪʃən-] N Esercito della Salvezza

salver [ˈsælvər] N vassoio

salvo [ˈsælvəʊ] (pl **salvoes**) N salva

Samaritan [səˈmærɪtən] N: **the Samaritans** (organization) ≈ telefono amico

same [seɪm] ADJ stesso(-a), medesimo(-a)
▶ PRON: **the ~** lo (la) stesso(-a), gli (le) stessi(-e); **the ~ book as** lo stesso libro di (or che); **on the ~ day** lo stesso giorno; **at the ~ time** allo stesso tempo; **all** or **just the ~** tuttavia; **to do the ~** fare la stessa cosa; **to do the ~ as sb** fare come qn; **the ~ again** (in bar etc) un altro; **they're one and the ~** (person/thing) sono la stessa persona/cosa; **and the ~ to you!** altrettanto a lei!; **~ here!** anch'io!

same-sex marriage [ˈseɪmsɛks-] N matrimonio tra persone dello stesso sesso

same-sex relationship [ˈseɪmsɛks-] N relazione f gay or omosessuale

Samoa [səˈməʊə] N Samoa fpl

sample ['sɑːmpl] N campione m ▶ VT (food) assaggiare; (wine) degustare; **to take a ~** prelevare un campione; **free ~** campione omaggio inv

sanatorium [sænə'tɔːrɪəm] (pl **sanatoria** [-rɪə]) N sanatorio

sanctify ['sæŋktɪfaɪ] VT santificare

sanctimonious [sæŋktɪ'məʊnɪəs] ADJ bigotto(-a), bacchettone(-a)

sanction ['sæŋkʃən] N sanzione f ▶ VT sancire, sanzionare ■ **sanctions** NPL (Pol) sanzioni fpl; **to impose economic sanctions on** or **against** adottare sanzioni economiche contro

sanctity ['sæŋktɪtɪ] N santità

sanctuary ['sæŋktjʊərɪ] N (holy place) santuario; (refuge) rifugio; (for wildlife) riserva

sand [sænd] N sabbia ▶ VT cospargere di sabbia; (also: **sand down**: wood etc) cartavetrare; see also **sands**

sandal ['sændl] N sandalo

sandbag ['sændbæg] N sacco di sabbia

sandblast ['sændblɑːst] VT sabbiare

sandbox ['sændbɒks] N (US: for children) buca di sabbia

sandcastle ['sændkɑːsl] N castello di sabbia

sand dune N duna di sabbia

sander ['sændər] N levigatrice f

sandpaper ['sændpeɪpər] N carta vetrata

sandpit ['sændpɪt] N (BRIT: for children) buca di sabbia

sands [sændz] NPL spiaggia

sandstone ['sændstəʊn] N arenaria

sandstorm ['sændstɔːm] N tempesta di sabbia

sandwich ['sændwɪtʃ] N tramezzino, panino, sandwich m inv ▶ VT (also: **sandwich in**) infilare; **cheese/ham ~** sandwich al formaggio/prosciutto; **to be sandwiched between** essere incastrato(-a) fra

sandwich board N cartello pubblicitario (portato da un uomo sandwich)

sandwich course N (BRIT) corso di formazione professionale

sandwich man N uomo m sandwich inv

sandy ['sændɪ] ADJ sabbioso(-a); (colour) color sabbia inv, biondo(-a) rossiccio(-a)

sane [seɪn] ADJ (person) sano(-a) di mente; (outlook) sensato(-a)

sang [sæŋ] PT of **sing**

sanguine ['sæŋgwɪn] ADJ ottimista

sanitarium [sænɪ'tɛərɪəm] (pl **sanitaria** [-rɪə]) N (US) = **sanatorium**

sanitary ['sænɪtərɪ] ADJ (system, arrangements) sanitario(-a); (clean) igienico(-a)

sanitary towel ['sænɪtərɪ-], (US) **sanitary napkin** N assorbente m (igienico)

sanitation [sænɪ'teɪʃən] N (in house) impianti mpl sanitari; (in town) fognature fpl

sanitation department N (US) nettezza urbana

sanity ['sænɪtɪ] N sanità mentale; (common sense) buon senso

sank [sæŋk] PT of **sink**

San Marino [sænmə'riːnəʊ] N San Marino f

Santa Claus [sæntə'klɔːz] N Babbo Natale

Santiago [sæntɪ'ɑːgəʊ] N (also: **Santiago de Chile**) Santiago (del Cile) f

sap [sæp] N (of plants) linfa ▶ VT (strength) fiaccare

sapling ['sæplɪŋ] N alberello

sapphire ['sæfaɪər] N zaffiro

sarcasm ['sɑːkæzm] N sarcasmo

sarcastic [sɑː'kæstɪk] ADJ sarcastico(-a); **to be ~** fare del sarcasmo

sarcophagus [sɑː'kɒfəgəs] (pl **sarcophagi** [-gaɪ]) N sarcofago

sardine [sɑː'diːn] N sardina

Sardinia [sɑː'dɪnɪə] N Sardegna

Sardinian [sɑː'dɪnɪən] ADJ, N sardo(-a)

sardonic [sɑː'dɒnɪk] ADJ sardonico(-a)

sari ['sɑːrɪ] N sari m inv

SARS [sɑːz] N ABBR (= severe acute respiratory syndrome) SARS f, polmonite atipica

sartorial [sɑː'tɔːrɪəl] ADJ di sartoria

SAS N ABBR (BRIT Mil: = Special Air Service) reparto dell'esercito britannico specializzato in operazioni clandestine

SASE N ABBR (US: = self-addressed stamped envelope) busta affrancata e con indirizzo

sash [sæʃ] N fascia

sash window N finestra a ghigliottina

SAT N ABBR (US) = **Scholastic Aptitude Test**; vedi nota

Negli Stati Uniti, i liceali che pensano di proseguire gli studi all'università devono passare un test: il *SAT* che è stato introdotto nel 1926 e la sigla ora sta per *Scholastic Assessment Test*. Nel 2005 è stato ribattezzato *SAT Reasoning Test*. Comprende due prove da completare in tre ore: matematica e lettura critica. Per il saggio, che nel 2016 è diventato facoltativo, sono disponibili altri 50 minuti. Esiste anche un altro esame, l'*ACT* (*American College Test*) introdotto nel 1959 che consta di quattro prove: inglese, matematica, lettura, ragionamento scientifico e un tema facoltativo. In Inghilterra invece i *SATs* (*Standard Assessment Tasks*) sono i test con cui gli studenti di 7 e 11 anni sono valutati, tramite parametri standard che permettono un confronto tra alunni e scuole su scala nazionale.

S

sat [sæt] PT, PP of **sit**

Sat. ABBR (= Saturday) sab.

Satan ['seɪtən] N Satana m

satanic [sə'tænɪk] ADJ satanico(-a)

satchel ['sætʃl] N cartella

sated ['seɪtɪd] ADJ soddisfatto(-a); sazio(-a)

satellite ['sætəlaɪt] ADJ, N satellite m

satellite dish N antenna parabolica

satellite television N televisione f via satellite

satiate ['seɪʃɪeɪt] VT saziare

satin ['sætɪn] N raso, satin m inv ▶ ADJ di or in raso, di or in satin; **with a ~ finish** satinato(-a)

satire ['sætaɪəʳ] N satira

satirical [sə'tɪrɪkl] ADJ satirico(-a)

satirist ['sætərɪst] N (writer etc) scrittore(-trice) etc satirico(-a); (cartoonist) caricaturista mf

satirize ['sætɪraɪz] VT satireggiare

satisfaction [sætɪs'fækʃən] N soddisfazione f; **has it been done to your ~?** ne è rimasto soddisfatto?

satisfactory [sætɪs'fæktərɪ] ADJ soddisfacente

satisfied ['sætɪsfaɪd] ADJ (customer) soddisfatto(-a); **to be ~ (with sth)** essere soddisfatto(-a) (di qc)

satisfy ['sætɪsfaɪ] VT soddisfare; (convince) convincere; **to ~ the requirements** rispondere ai requisiti; **to ~ sb (that)** convincere qn (che), persuadere qn (che); **to ~ o.s. of sth** accertarsi di qc

satisfying ['sætɪsfaɪɪŋ] ADJ soddisfacente

satnav ['sætnæv] N ABBR (= satellite navigation) navigatore m satellitare

SATs N ABBR (BRIT: = standard assessment tasks or tests) esame di fine anno sostenuto dagli allievi delle scuole pubbliche inglesi a 7 o 11 anni

satsuma [sæt'su:mə] N agrume di provenienza giapponese

saturate ['sætʃəreɪt] VT: **to ~ (with)** saturare (di)

saturated fat ['sætʃəreɪtɪd-] N grassi mpl saturi

saturation [sætʃə'reɪʃən] N saturazione f

Saturday ['sætədɪ] N sabato; see also **Tuesday**

sauce [sɔːs] N salsa; (containing meat, fish) sugo

saucepan ['sɔːspən] N casseruola

saucer ['sɔːsəʳ] N sottocoppa m, piattino

saucy ['sɔːsɪ] ADJ impertinente

Saudi ['saʊdɪ], **Saudi Arabian** ADJ, N saudita mf

Saudi Arabia N Arabia Saudita

sauna ['sɔːnə] N sauna

saunter ['sɔːntəʳ] VI andare a zonzo, bighellonare

sausage ['sɔsɪdʒ] N salsiccia; (salami etc) salame m

sausage roll N rotolo di pasta sfoglia ripieno di salsiccia

sauté ['səʊteɪ] ADJ (Culin: potatoes) saltato(-a); (: onions) soffritto(-a) ▶ VT far saltare; far soffriggere

sautéed ['səʊteɪd] ADJ saltato(-a)

savage ['sævɪdʒ] ADJ (cruel, fierce) selvaggio(-a), feroce; (primitive) primitivo(-a) ▶ N selvaggio(-a) ▶ VT attaccare selvaggiamente

savagery ['sævɪdʒrɪ] N crudeltà, ferocia

save [seɪv] VT (person, belongings, Comput) salvare; (money) risparmiare, mettere da parte; (time) risparmiare; (food) conservare; (avoid: trouble) evitare; (Sport) parare ▶ VI (also: **save up**) economizzare ▶ N (Sport) parata ▶ PREP salvo, a eccezione di; **it will ~ me an hour** mi farà risparmiare un'ora; **to ~ face** salvare la faccia; **God ~ the Queen!** Dio salvi la Regina!

saving ['seɪvɪŋ] N risparmio ▶ ADJ: **the ~ grace of** l'unica cosa buona di ▪ **savings** NPL risparmi mpl; **to make savings** fare economia

savings account N libretto di risparmio

savings and loan association N (US) ≈ società di credito immobiliare

savings bank N cassa di risparmio

saviour, (US) **savior** ['seɪvjəʳ] N salvatore(-trice)

savour, (US) **savor** ['seɪvəʳ] N sapore m, gusto ▶ VT gustare

savoury, (US) **savory** ['seɪvərɪ] ADJ saporito(-a); (dish: not sweet) salato(-a)

savvy ['sævɪ] N (col) arguzia

saw [sɔː] PT of **see** ▶ N (tool) sega ▶ VT (pt sawed, pp sawed or sawn [sɔːn]) segare; **to ~ sth up** fare a pezzi qc con la sega

sawdust ['sɔːdʌst] N segatura

sawmill ['sɔːmɪl] N segheria

sawn [sɔːn] PP of **saw**

sawn-off ['sɔːnɔf], (US) **sawed-off** ['sɔːdɔf] ADJ: **~ shotgun** fucile m a canne mozze

saxophone ['sæksəfəun] N sassofono

say [seɪ] (pt, pp said [sɛd]) N: **to have one's ~** fare sentire il proprio parere; **to have a** or **some ~** avere voce in capitolo ▶ VT dire; **could you ~ that again?** potrebbe ripeterlo?; **to ~ yes/no** dire di sì/di no; **she said (that) I was to give you this** ha detto di darle questo; **my watch says 3 o'clock** il mio orologio fa le 3; **shall we ~ Tuesday?** facciamo martedì?; **that doesn't ~ much for him** non torna a suo credito; **when all is said and done** a conti fatti; **there is something** or **a lot to be said for it** ha i suoi lati positivi; **that is to ~** cioè, vale a dire; **to ~ nothing of** per non parlare di; **~ that ...** mettiamo or diciamo che ...; **that goes without saying** va da sé

saying ['seɪɪŋ] N proverbio, detto

SBA N ABBR (US: = Small Business Administration) organismo ausiliario per piccole imprese

SC N ABBR (US) = **supreme court** ▶ ABBR (US) = **South Carolina**

s/c ABBR (= self-contained) indipendente

scab [skæb] N crosta; (*pej*) crumiro(-a)

scabby ['skæbɪ] ADJ crostoso(-a)

scaffold ['skæfəʊld] N impalcatura; (*gallows*) patibolo

scaffolding ['skæfəldɪŋ] N impalcatura

scald [skɔːld] N scottatura ▶ VT scottare

scalding ['skɔːldɪŋ] ADJ (*also:* **scalding hot**) bollente

scale [skeɪl] N scala; (*of fish*) squama ▶ VT (*mountain*) scalare; **pay ~** scala dei salari; **~ of charges** tariffa; **on a large ~** su vasta scala; **to draw sth to ~** disegnare qc in scala; **small-scale model** modello in scala ridotta; *see also* **scales**
▶ **scale down** VT ridurre (proporzionalmente)

scaled-down [skeɪld'daun] ADJ su scala ridotta

scale drawing N disegno in scala

scale model N modello in scala

scales [skeɪlz] NPL (*for weighing*) bilancia

scallion ['skæljən] N cipolla; (*US: shallot*) scalogna; (*: leek*) porro

scallop ['skɔləp] N (*Zool*) pettine m; (*Sewing*) smerlo

scalp [skælp] N cuoio capelluto ▶ VT scotennare

scalpel ['skælpl] N bisturi m inv

scalper ['skælpər] N (*US col: of tickets*) bagarino

scam [skæm] N (*col*) truffa

scamp [skæmp] N (*col: child*) peste f

scamper ['skæmpər] VI: **to ~ away, ~ off** darsela a gambe

scampi ['skæmpɪ] NPL scampi mpl

scan [skæn] VT scrutare; (*glance at quickly*) scorrere, dare un'occhiata a; (*poetry*) scandire; (*TV*) analizzare; (*Radar*) esplorare ▶ N (*Med*) ecografia

scandal ['skændl] N scandalo; (*gossip*) pettegolezzi mpl

scandalize ['skændəlaɪz] VT scandalizzare

scandalous ['skændələs] ADJ scandaloso(-a)

Scandinavia [skændɪ'neɪvɪə] N Scandinavia

Scandinavian [skændɪ'neɪvɪən] ADJ, N scandinavo(-a)

scanner ['skænər] N (*Radar, Med*) scanner m inv

scant [skænt] ADJ scarso(-a)

scantily ['skæntɪlɪ] ADV: **~ clad** or **dressed** succintamente vestito(-a)

scanty ['skæntɪ] ADJ insufficiente; (*swimsuit*) ridotto(-a)

scapegoat ['skeɪpɡəut] N capro espiatorio

scar [skɑː^r] N cicatrice f ▶ VT sfregiare

scarce [skɛəs] ADJ scarso(-a); (*copy, edition*) raro(-a); **to make o.s. ~** (*col*) squagliarsela

scarcely ['skɛəslɪ] ADV appena; **~ anybody** quasi nessuno; **I can ~ believe it** faccio fatica a crederci

scarcity ['skɛəsɪtɪ] N scarsità, mancanza

scarcity value N valore m di rarità

scare [skɛə^r] N spavento, paura; panico ▶ VT spaventare, atterrire; **to ~ sb stiff** spaventare a morte qn; **bomb ~** evacuazione f per sospetta presenza di un ordigno esplosivo; **there was a bomb ~ at the bank** hanno evacuato la banca per paura di un attentato dinamitardo
▶ **scare away, scare off** VT mettere in fuga

scarecrow ['skɛəkrəu] N spaventapasseri m inv

scared [skɛəd] ADJ: **to be ~** aver paura

scaremonger ['skɛəmʌŋɡə^r] N allarmista mf

scarf [skɑːf] (*pl* **scarves** [skɑːvz]) N (*long*) sciarpa; (*square*) fazzoletto da testa, foulard m inv

scarlet ['skɑːlɪt] ADJ scarlatto(-a)

scarlet fever N scarlattina

scarper ['skɑːpə^r] VI (*BRIT col*) darsela a gambe

SCART socket ['skɑːt-] N presa f SCART inv

scarves [skɑːvz] NPL *of* **scarf**

scary ['skɛərɪ] ADJ (*col*) che fa paura

scathing ['skeɪðɪŋ] ADJ aspro(-a); **to be ~ about sth** essere molto critico rispetto a qc

scatter ['skætə^r] VT spargere; (*crowd*) disperdere ▶ VI disperdersi

scatterbrained ['skætəbreɪnd] ADJ scervellato(-a), sbadato(-a)

scattered ['skætəd] ADJ sparso(-a), sparpagliato(-a)

scatty ['skætɪ] ADJ (*col*) scervellato(-a), sbadato(-a)

scavenge ['skævɪndʒ] VI (*person*): **to ~ (for)** frugare tra i rifiuti (alla ricerca di); (*hyenas etc*) nutrirsi di carogne

scavenger ['skævəndʒə^r] N spazzino(-a)

scenario [sɪ'nɑːrɪəu] N (*Theat, Cine*) copione m; (*fig*) situazione f

scene [siːn] N (*Theat, fig etc*) scena; (*of crime, accident*) scena, luogo; (*sight, view*) vista, veduta; **behind the scenes** (*also fig*) dietro le quinte; **to appear** or **come on the ~** (*also fig*) entrare in scena; **the political ~ in Italy** il quadro politico in Italia; **to make a ~** (*col: fuss*) fare una scenata

scenery ['siːnərɪ] N (*Theat*) scenario; (*landscape*) panorama m

scenic ['siːnɪk] ADJ scenico(-a); panoramico(-a)

scent [sɛnt] N odore m, profumo; (*sense of smell*) olfatto, odorato; (*fig: track*) pista; **to put** or **throw sb off the ~** (*fig*) far perdere le tracce a qn, sviare qn

sceptic, (*US*) **skeptic** ['skɛptɪk] N scettico(-a)

sceptical, (*US*) **skeptical** ['skɛptɪkl] ADJ scettico(-a)

scepticism, (*US*) **skepticism** ['skɛptɪsɪzm] N scetticismo

sceptre, (*US*) **scepter** ['sɛptə^r] N scettro

schedule ['ʃedjuːl, (*US*) 'skedjuːl] N programma m, piano; (*of trains*) orario; (*of prices etc*) lista, tabella ▶ VT fissare; **as scheduled** come stabi-

S

lito; **on ~** in orario; **to be ahead of/behind ~** essere in anticipo/ritardo sul previsto; **we are working to a very tight ~** il nostro programma di lavoro è molto intenso; **everything went according to ~** tutto è andato secondo i piani *or* secondo il previsto

scheduled flight ['ʃɛdjuːld, (US) 'skɛdjuːld] N (*date, time*) fissato(-a); (*visit, event*) programmato(-a); (*train, bus, stop*) previsto(-a) (sull'orario); **~ volo di linea**

schematic [skɪ'mætɪk] ADJ schematico(-a)

scheme [skiːm] N piano, progetto; (*method*) sistema *m*; (*dishonest plan, plot*) intrigo, trama; (*arrangement*) disposizione *f*, sistemazione *f*; (*pension scheme etc*) programma *m* ▶ VT progettare; (*plot*) ordire ▶ VI fare progetti; (*intrigue*) complottare; **colour ~** combinazione *f* di colori

scheming ['skiːmɪŋ] ADJ intrigante ▶ N intrighi *mpl*, macchinazioni *fpl*

schism ['skɪzəm] N scisma *m*

schizophrenia [skɪtsə'friːnɪə] N schizofrenia

schizophrenic [skɪtsə'frɛnɪk] ADJ, N schizofrenico(-a)

scholar ['skɒlər] N studioso(-a)

scholarly ['skɒləlɪ] ADJ dotto(-a), erudito(-a)

scholarship ['skɒləʃɪp] N erudizione *f*; (*grant*) borsa di studio

school [skuːl] N (*primary, secondary*) scuola; (*in university*) scuola, facoltà *f inv*; (*US: university*) università *f inv* ▶ CPD scolare, scolastico(-a) ▶ VT (*animal*) addestrare

school age N età scolare

schoolbook ['skuːlbuk] N libro scolastico

schoolboy ['skuːlbɔɪ] N scolaro

schoolchild ['skuːltʃaɪld] (*pl* **-children** [-'tʃɪldrən]) N scolaro(-a)

schooldays ['skuːldeɪz] NPL giorni *mpl* di scuola

schoolgirl ['skuːlgɜːl] N scolara

schooling ['skuːlɪŋ] N istruzione *f*

school-leaver ['skuːlliːvər] N (*BRIT*) ≈ neodiplomato(-a)

schoolmaster ['skuːlmɑːstər] N (*primary*) maestro; (*secondary*) insegnante *m*

schoolmistress ['skuːlmɪstrɪs] N (*primary*) maestra; (*secondary*) insegnante *f*

school report N (*BRIT*) pagella

schoolroom ['skuːlruːm] N classe *f*, aula

schoolteacher ['skuːltiːtʃər] N insegnante *mf*, docente *mf*; (*primary*) maestro(-a)

schoolyard ['skuːljɑːd] N (*US*) cortile *m* della scuola

schooner ['skuːnər] N (*ship*) goletta, schooner *m inv*; (*glass*) bicchiere *m* alto da sherry

sciatica [saɪ'ætɪkə] N sciatica

science ['saɪəns] N scienza; **the sciences** le scienze; (*Scol*) le materie scientifiche

science fiction N fantascienza

scientific [saɪən'tɪfɪk] ADJ scientifico(-a)

scientist ['saɪəntɪst] N scienziato(-a)

sci-fi ['saɪfaɪ] N ABBR (*col*) = **science fiction**

Scilly Isles ['sɪlɪ'aɪlz] NPL, **Scillies** ['sɪlɪz] NPL: **the ~** le isole Scilly

scintillating ['sɪntɪleɪtɪŋ] ADJ scintillante; (*wit, conversation, company*) brillante

scissors ['sɪzəz] NPL forbici *fpl*; **a pair of ~** un paio di forbici

sclerosis [sklɪ'rəusɪs] N sclerosi *f*

scoff [skɒf] VT (*BRIT col: eat*) trangugiare, ingozzare ▶ VI: **to ~ (at)** (*mock*) farsi beffe (di)

scold [skəuld] VT rimproverare

scolding ['skəuldɪŋ] N lavata di capo, sgridata

scone [skɒn] N focaccina da tè

scoop [skuːp] N mestolo; (*for ice cream*) cucchiaio dosatore; (*Press*) colpo giornalistico, notizia (in) esclusiva
  ▶ **scoop out** VT scavare
  ▶ **scoop up** VT tirare su, sollevare

scooter ['skuːtər] N (*motorcycle*) motoretta, scooter *m inv*; (*toy*) monopattino

scope [skəup] N (*capacity: of plan, undertaking*) portata; (: *of person*) capacità *fpl*; (*opportunity*) possibilità *fpl*; **to be within the ~ of** rientrare nei limiti di; **it's well within his ~ to ...** è perfettamente in grado di ...; **there is plenty of ~ for improvement** (*BRIT*) ci sono notevoli possibilità di miglioramento

scorch [skɔːtʃ] VT (*clothes*) strinare, bruciacchiare; (*earth, grass*) seccare, bruciare

scorched earth policy [skɔːtʃt-] N tattica della terra bruciata

scorcher ['skɔːtʃər] N (*col: hot day*) giornata torrida

scorching ['skɔːtʃɪŋ] ADJ cocente, scottante

score [skɔːr] N punti *mpl*, punteggio; (*Mus*) partitura, spartito; (*twenty*): **a ~** venti ▶ VT (*goal, point*) segnare, fare; (*success*) ottenere; (*cut: leather, wood, card*) incidere ▶ VI segnare; (*Football*) fare un goal; (*keep score*) segnare i punti; **on that ~** a questo riguardo; **to have an old ~ to settle with sb** (*fig*) avere un vecchio conto da saldare con qn; **scores of people** (*fig*) un sacco di gente; **to ~ 6 out of 10** prendere 6 su 10
  ▶ **score out** VT cancellare con un segno

scoreboard ['skɔːbɔːd] N tabellone *m* segnapunti

scorecard ['skɔːkɑːd] N cartoncino segnapunti

scoreline ['skɔːlaɪn] N (*Sport*) risultato

scorer ['skɔːrər] N marcatore(-trice); (*keeping score*) segnapunti *mf inv*

scorn [skɔːn] N disprezzo ▶ VT disprezzare

scornful ['skɔːnful] ADJ sprezzante

Scorpio ['skɔːpɪəu] N Scorpione *m*; **to be ~** essere dello Scorpione

scorpion [ˈskɔːpɪən] N scorpione *m*

Scot [skɔt] N scozzese *mf*

Scotch [skɔtʃ] N whisky *m inv* scozzese, scotch *m inv*

scotch [skɔtʃ] VT *(rumour etc)* soffocare

Scotch tape® [ˈskɔtʃ-] N scotch® *m*

scot-free [ˈskɔtˈfriː] ADJ impunito(-a); **to get off ~** *(unpunished)* farla franca; *(unhurt)* uscire illeso(-a)

Scotland [ˈskɔtlənd] N Scozia

Scots [skɔts] ADJ scozzese

Scotsman [ˈskɔtsmən] N *(irreg)* scozzese *m*

Scotswoman [ˈskɔtswumən] N *(irreg)* scozzese *f*

Scottish [ˈskɔtɪʃ] ADJ scozzese; **the ~ National Party** il partito nazionalista scozzese; **the ~ Parliament** il Parlamento scozzese

Nel 1997, la Scozia, dopo circa tre secoli di unione politica con l'Inghilterra, ha optato tramite referendum per un parlamento decentralizzato con sede a Edimburgo. Nel 1999 sono stati eletti 129 deputati con potere legislativo in varie materie come l'istruzione, la sanità, la giustizia, la materia fiscale e l'amministrazione locale. Il capo del governo scozzese è il *First Minister*, ma il sovrano britannico rimane il capo di stato.

scoundrel [ˈskaundrl] N farabutto(-a); *(child)* furfantello(-a)

scour [ˈskauəʳ] VT *(clean)* pulire strofinando; raschiare via; ripulire; *(search)* battere, perlustrare

scourer [ˈskauərəʳ] N *(pad)* paglietta; *(powder)* (detersivo) abrasivo

scourge [skəːdʒ] N flagello

scout [skaut] N *(Mil)* esploratore(-trice); *(also:* **boy scout**) giovane esploratore, scout *m inv*
▶ **scout around** VI cercare in giro

scowl [skaul] VI accigliarsi, aggrottare le sopracciglia; **to ~ at** guardare torvo

Scrabble® [ˈskræbl] N Scarabeo®

scrabble [ˈskræbl] VI *(claw)*: **to ~ (at)** graffiare, grattare; **to ~ about** *or* **around for sth** cercare affannosamente qc

scraggy [ˈskrægɪ] ADJ scarno(-a), molto magro(-a)

scram [skræm] VI *(col)* filare via

scramble [ˈskræmbl] N arrampicata ▶ VI inerpicarsi; **to ~ out** *etc* uscire *etc* in fretta; **to ~ for** azzuffarsi per

scrambled eggs [ˈskræmbld-] NPL uova *fpl* strapazzate

scrambling [ˈskræmblɪŋ] N *(Sport)* motocross *m*; **to go ~** *(Sport)* fare il motocross

scrap [skræp] N pezzo, pezzetto; *(fight)* zuffa; *(also:* **scrap iron**) rottami *mpl* di ferro, ferraglia ▶ VT demolire; *(fig)* scartare ▶ VI: **to ~ (with sb)** fare a botte (con qn) ■ **scraps** NPL *(waste)* scarti

mpl; **to sell sth for ~** vendere qc come ferro vecchio

scrapbook [ˈskræpbuk] N album *m inv* di ritagli

scrap dealer N commerciante *m* di ferraglia

scrape [skreip] VT, VI raschiare, grattare ▶ N: **to get into a ~** cacciarsi in un guaio
▶ **scrape through** VI *(succeed)* farcela per un pelo, cavarsela ▶ VT FUS *(exam)* passare per miracolo, passare per il rotto della cuffia

scraper [ˈskreipəʳ] N raschietto

scrap heap N mucchio di rottami; **to throw sth on the ~** *(fig)* mettere qc nel dimenticatoio

scrap merchant N *(BRIT)* commerciante *mf* di ferraglia

scrap metal N ferraglia

scrap paper N cartaccia

scrappy [ˈskræpɪ] ADJ frammentario(-a), sconnesso(-a)

scrap yard N deposito di rottami; *(for cars)* cimitero delle macchine

scratch [skrætʃ] N graffio ▶ CPD: **~ team** squadra raccogliticcia ▶ VT graffiare, rigare; *(Comput)* cancellare ▶ VI grattare; **to start from ~** cominciare *or* partire da zero; **to be up to ~** essere all'altezza

scratch card N *(BRIT)* cartolina *f* gratta e vinci

scratch pad N *(US)* notes *m inv*, blocchetto

scrawl [skrɔːl] N scarabocchio ▶ VI scarabocchiare

scrawny [ˈskrɔːnɪ] ADJ scarno(-a), pelle e ossa *inv*

scream [skriːm] N grido, urlo ▶ VI urlare, gridare; **to ~ at sb (to do sth)** gridare a qn (di fare qc); **it was a ~** *(fig: col)* era da crepar dal ridere; **he's a ~** *(fig: col)* è una sagoma, è uno spasso

scree [skriː] N ghiaione *m*

screech [skriːtʃ] N strido; *(of tyres, brakes)* stridore *m* ▶ VI stridere

screen [skriːn] N schermo; *(fig)* muro, cortina, velo ▶ VT schermare, fare schermo a; *(from the wind etc)* riparare; *(film)* proiettare; *(book)* adattare per lo schermo; *(candidates etc)* passare al vaglio; *(for illness)* sottoporre a controlli medici

screen editing [-ɛdɪtɪŋ] N *(Comput)* correzione *f* e modifica su schermo

screening [ˈskriːnɪŋ] N *(Med)* dépistage *m inv*; *(of film)* proiezione *f*; *(for security)* controlli *mpl* (di sicurezza)

screen memory N *(Comput)* memoria di schermo

screenplay [ˈskriːnpleɪ] N sceneggiatura

screensaver N *(Comput)* screen saver *m inv*

screenshot N *(Comput)* screenshot *m inv*

screen test N provino (cinematografico)

screw [skruː] N vite *f*; *(propeller)* elica ▶ VT avvitare; **to ~ sth to the wall** fissare qc al muro con viti

▶ **screw up** VT (*paper, material*) spiegazzare; (*col: ruin*) mandare a monte; **to ~ up one's face** fare una smorfia; **to ~ up one's eyes** strizzare gli occhi

screwdriver [ˈskruːdraɪvəʳ] N cacciavite m

screwed-up [ˈskruːdˈʌp] ADJ (*col*): **she's totally ~** è nel pallone

screwy [ˈskruːɪ] ADJ (*col*) svitato(-a)

scribble [ˈskrɪbl] N scarabocchio ▶ VT scribacchiare ▶ VI scarabocchiare; **to ~ sth down** scribacchiare qc

scribe [skraɪb] N scriba m

script [skrɪpt] N (*Cine etc*) copione m; (*in exam*) elaborato or compito d'esame; (*writing*) scrittura

scripted [ˈskrɪptɪd] ADJ (*Radio, TV*) preparato(-a)

Scripture [ˈskrɪptʃəʳ] N Sacre Scritture fpl

scriptwriter [ˈskrɪptraɪtəʳ] N soggettista mf

scroll [skrəul] N rotolo di carta ▶ VT (*Comput*) scorrere

scroll bar N (*Comput*) barra di scorrimento

scrotum [ˈskrəutəm] N scroto

scrounge [skraundʒ] VT (*col*): **to ~ sth (off or from sb)** scroccare qc (a qn) ▶ VI: **to ~ on sb** vivere alle spalle di qn

scrounger [ˈskraundʒəʳ] N scroccone(-a)

scrub [skrʌb] N (*clean*) strofinata; (*land*) boscaglia ▶ VT pulire strofinando; (*reject*) annullare

scrubbing brush [ˈskrʌbɪŋ-] N spazzolone m

scruff [skrʌf] N: **by the ~ of the neck** per la collottola

scruffy [ˈskrʌfɪ] ADJ sciatto(-a)

scrum [skrʌm], **scrummage** [ˈskrʌmɪdʒ] N mischia

scruple [ˈskruːpl] N scrupolo; **to have no scruples about doing sth** non avere scrupoli a fare qc

scrupulous [ˈskruːpjuləs] ADJ scrupoloso(-a)

scrupulously [ˈskruːpjuləslɪ] ADV scrupolosamente; **he tries to be ~ fair/honest** cerca di essere più imparziale/onesto che può

scrutinize [ˈskruːtɪnaɪz] VT scrutare, esaminare attentamente

scrutiny [ˈskruːtɪnɪ] N esame m accurato; **under the ~ of sb** sotto la sorveglianza di qn

scuba [ˈskuːbə] N autorespiratore m

scuba diving [ˈskuːbə-] N immersioni fpl subacquee

scuff [skʌf] VT (*shoes*) consumare strascicando

scuffle [ˈskʌfl] N baruffa, tafferuglio

scullery [ˈskʌlərɪ] N retrocucina m or f inv

sculptor [ˈskʌlptəʳ] N scultore(-trice)

sculpture [ˈskʌlptʃəʳ] N scultura

scum [skʌm] N schiuma; (*pej: people*) feccia

scupper [ˈskʌpəʳ] VT autoaffondare; (BRIT fig) far naufragare

scurrilous [ˈskʌrɪləs] ADJ scurrile, volgare

scurry [ˈskʌrɪ] VI sgambare, affrettarsi

scurvy [ˈskəːvɪ] N scorbuto

scuttle [ˈskʌtl] N (*Naut*) portellino; (*also:* **coal scuttle**) secchio del carbone ▶ VT (*ship*) autoaffondare ▶ VI (*scamper*): **to ~ away, ~ off** darsela a gambe, scappare

scythe [saɪð] N falce f

SD, S. Dak. ABBR (*US*) = **South Dakota**

SDLP N ABBR (BRIT Pol) = **Social Democratic and Labour Party**

sea [siː] N mare m ▶ CPD marino(-a), del mare; (*ship, port, route, transport*) marittimo(-a); (*bird, fish*) di mare; **on the ~** (*boat*) in mare; (*town*) di mare; **to go by ~** andare per mare; **by** or **beside the ~** (*holiday*) al mare; (*village*) sul mare; **to look out to ~** guardare il mare; **out to ~** al largo; **(out) at ~** in mare; **heavy** or **rough ~(s)** mare grosso or agitato; **a ~ of faces** (*fig*) una marea di gente; **to be all at ~** (*fig*) non sapere che pesci pigliare

sea bed N fondo marino

sea bird N uccello di mare

seaboard [ˈsiːbɔːd] N costa

sea breeze N brezza di mare

seafarer [ˈsiːfɛərəʳ] N navigante m

seafaring [ˈsiːfɛərɪŋ] ADJ (*community*) marinaro(-a); (*life*) da marinaio

seafood [ˈsiːfuːd] N frutti mpl di mare

sea front N lungomare m

seagoing [ˈsiːgəuɪŋ] ADJ (*ship*) d'alto mare

seagull [ˈsiːgʌl] N gabbiano

seal [siːl] N (*animal*) foca; (*stamp*) sigillo; (*impression*) impronta del sigillo ▶ VT sigillare; (*decide: sb's fate*) segnare; (: *bargain*) concludere; **~ of approval** beneplacito

▶ **seal off** VT (*close*) sigillare; (*forbid entry to*) bloccare l'accesso a

sea level N livello del mare

sealing wax [ˈsiːlɪŋ-] N ceralacca

sea lion N leone m marino

sealskin [ˈsiːlskɪn] N pelle f di foca

seam [siːm] N cucitura; (*of coal*) filone m; **the hall was bursting at the seams** l'aula era piena zeppa

seaman [ˈsiːmən] N (*irreg*) marinaio

seamanship [ˈsiːmənʃɪp] N tecnica di navigazione

seamless [ˈsiːmlɪs] ADJ senza cucitura

seamy [ˈsiːmɪ] ADJ malfamato(-a); squallido(-a)

seance [ˈseɪɔns] N seduta spiritica

seaplane [ˈsiːpleɪn] N idrovolante m

seaport [ˈsiːpɔːt] N porto di mare

search [səːtʃ] N (*for person, thing*) ricerca; (*of drawer, pockets*) esame m accurato; (Law: *at sb's home*) perquisizione f ▶ VT perlustrare, frugare;

(*scan, examine*) esaminare minuziosamente; (*Comput*) ricercare ▶ VI: **to ~ for** ricercare; **in ~ of** alla ricerca di; **"~ and replace"** (*Comput*) "ricercare e sostituire"
▶ **search through** VT FUS frugare

search engine N (*Comput*) motore *m* di ricerca

searcher ['sə:tʃər] N chi cerca

searching ['sə:tʃɪŋ] ADJ minuzioso(-a); penetrante; (*question*) pressante

searchlight ['sə:tʃlaɪt] N proiettore *m*

search party N squadra di soccorso

search warrant N mandato di perquisizione

searing ['sɪərɪŋ] ADJ (*heat*) rovente; (*pain*) acuto(-a)

seashore ['si:ʃɔ:r] N spiaggia; **on the ~** sulla riva del mare

seasick ['si:sɪk] ADJ che soffre il mal di mare; **to be ~** avere il mal di mare

seaside ['si:saɪd] N spiaggia; **to go to the ~** andare al mare

seaside resort N stazione *f* balneare

season ['si:zn] N stagione *f* ▶ VT condire, insaporire; **to be in/out of ~** essere di/fuori stagione; **the busy ~** (*for shops*) il periodo di punta; (*for hotels etc*) l'alta stagione; **the open ~** (*Hunting*) la stagione della caccia

seasonal ['si:zənl] ADJ stagionale

seasoned ['si:znd] ADJ (*wood*) stagionato(-a); (*fig: worker, actor, troops*) con esperienza; **a ~ campaigner** un veterano

seasoning ['si:znɪŋ] N condimento

season ticket N abbonamento

seat [si:t] N sedile *m*; (*in bus, train: place*) posto; (*Parliament*) seggio; (*centre: of government etc, of infection*) sede *f*; (*buttocks*) didietro; (*of trousers*) fondo ▶ VT far sedere; (*have room for*) avere or essere fornito(-a) di posti a sedere per; **are there any seats left?** ci sono posti?; **to take one's ~** prendere posto; **to be seated** essere seduto(-a); **please be seated** accomodatevi per favore

seat belt N cintura di sicurezza

seating ['si:tɪŋ] N posti *mpl* a sedere

seating arrangements NPL sistemazione *f* or disposizione *f* dei posti

seating capacity N posti *mpl* a sedere

SEATO ['si:təu] N ABBR (= *Southeast Asia Treaty Organization*) SEATO *f*

sea water N acqua di mare

seaweed ['si:wi:d] N alghe *fpl*

seaworthy ['si:wə:ðɪ] ADJ atto(-a) alla navigazione

SEC N ABBR (*US*: = *Securities and Exchange Commission*) commissione di controllo sulle operazioni in Borsa

sec. ABBR = **second¹**

secateurs [sɛkə'tə:z] NPL forbici *fpl* per potare

secede [sɪ'si:d] VI: **to ~ (from)** ritirarsi (da)

secluded [sɪ'klu:dɪd] ADJ isolato(-a), appartato(-a)

seclusion [sɪ'klu:ʒən] N isolamento

second¹ ['sɛkənd] NUM secondo(-a) ▶ ADV (*in race etc*) al secondo posto; (*Rail*) in seconda ▶ N (*unit of time*) secondo; (*in series, position*) secondo(-a); (*BRIT Scol: degree*) laurea con punteggio discreto; (*Aut: also:* **second gear**) seconda; (*Comm: imperfect*) scarto ▶ VT (*motion*) appoggiare; **Charles the S~** Carlo Secondo; **just a ~!** un attimo!; **~ floor** (*BRIT*) secondo piano; (*US*) primo piano; **to ask for a ~ opinion** (*Med*) chiedere un altro *or* ulteriore parere; **~ thoughts** ripensamenti *mpl*; **to have ~ thoughts (about doing sth)** avere dei ripensamenti (quanto a fare qc); **on ~ thoughts** (*BRIT*) *or* **thought** (*US*) a ripensarci, ripensandoci bene

second² [sɪ'kɔnd] VT (*employee*) distaccare

secondary ['sɛkəndərɪ] ADJ secondario(-a)

secondary school N scuola secondaria

second-best [sɛkənd'bɛst] N ripiego; **as a ~** in mancanza di meglio

second-class [sɛkənd'klɑ:s] ADJ di seconda classe ▶ ADV: **to travel ~** viaggiare in seconda (classe); **to send sth ~** spedire qc per posta ordinaria; **~ citizen** cittadino di second'ordine

second cousin N cugino(-a) di secondo grado

seconder ['sɛkəndər] N sostenitore(-trice)

second-guess ['sɛkənd'gɛs] VT (*predict*) anticipare; (*after the event*) giudicare col senno di poi

second hand N (*on clock*) lancetta dei secondi

second-hand [sɛkənd'hænd] ADJ di seconda mano, usato(-a) ▶ ADV (*buy*) di seconda mano; **to hear sth ~** venire a sapere qc da terze persone

second-in-command ['sɛkəndɪnkə'mɑ:nd] N (*Mil*) comandante *m* in seconda; (*Admin*) aggiunto

secondly ['sɛkəndlɪ] ADV in secondo luogo

secondment [sɪ'kɔndmənt] N (*BRIT*) distaccamento

second-rate [sɛkənd'reɪt] ADJ scadente

Second World War N: **the ~** la seconda guerra mondiale

secrecy ['si:krəsɪ] N segretezza

secret ['si:krɪt] ADJ segreto(-a) ▶ N segreto; **in ~** in segreto, segretamente; **to keep sth ~ (from sb)** tenere qc segreto (a qn), tenere qc nascosto (a qn); **keep it ~** che rimanga un segreto; **to make no ~ of sth** non far mistero di qc

secret agent N agente *m* segreto

secretarial [sɛkrɪ'tɛərɪəl] ADJ (*work*) da segretario(-a); (*college, course*) di segretariato

secretariat [sɛkrɪ'tɛərɪət] N segretariato

secretary ['sɛkrətrɪ] N segretario(-a); **S~ of State** (*US Pol*) ≈ Ministro degli Esteri; **S~ of**

State (for) (BRIT Pol) ministro (di)

secretary-general ['sɛkrətrɪ'dʒɛnərl] N segretario generale

secrete [sɪ'kri:t] VT (Med, Anat, Biol) secernere; (hide) nascondere

secretion [sɪ'kri:ʃən] N secrezione f

secretive ['si:krətɪv] ADJ riservato(-a)

secretly ['si:krɪtlɪ] ADV in segreto, segretamente

secret police N polizia segreta

secret service N servizi mpl segreti

sect [sɛkt] N setta

sectarian [sɛk'tɛərɪən] ADJ settario(-a)

section ['sɛkʃən] N sezione f; (of document) articolo ▸ VT sezionare, dividere in sezioni; **the business ~** (Press) la pagina economica

sector ['sɛktər] N settore m

secular ['sɛkjulər] ADJ secolare

secure [sɪ'kjuər] ADJ (free from anxiety) sicuro(-a); (firmly fixed) assicurato(-a), ben fermato(-a); (in safe place) al sicuro ▸ VT (fix) fissare, assicurare; (get) ottenere, assicurarsi; (Comm: loan) garantire; **to make sth ~** fissare bene qc; **to ~ sth for sb** procurare qc per or a qn

secured creditor [sɪ'kjuəd-] N creditore(-trice) privilegiato(-a)

security [sɪ'kjuərɪtɪ] N sicurezza; (for loan) garanzia ▪ **securities** NPL (Stock Exchange) titoli mpl; **to increase/tighten ~** aumentare/intensificare la sorveglianza; **~ of tenure** garanzia del posto di lavoro, garanzia di titolo or di godimento

Security Council N: **the ~** il Consiglio di Sicurezza

security forces NPL forze fpl dell'ordine

security guard N guardia giurata

security risk N rischio per la sicurezza

secy. ABBR = **secretary**

sedan [sə'dæn] N (US Aut) berlina

sedate [sɪ'deɪt] ADJ posato(-a); calmo(-a) ▸ VT calmare

sedation [sɪ'deɪʃən] N (Med): **to be under ~** essere sotto l'azione di sedativi

sedative ['sɛdɪtɪv] N sedativo, calmante m

sedentary ['sɛdntrɪ] ADJ sedentario(-a)

sediment ['sɛdɪmənt] N sedimento

sedition [sɪ'dɪʃən] N sedizione f

seduce [sɪ'dju:s] VT sedurre

seduction [sɪ'dʌkʃən] N seduzione f

seductive [sɪ'dʌktɪv] ADJ seducente

see [si:] (pt **saw**, pp **seen**) VT vedere; (accompany): **to ~ sb to the door** accompagnare qn alla porta ▸ VI vedere; (understand) capire ▸ N sede f vescovile; **to ~ that** (ensure) badare che + sub, fare in modo che + sub; **to go and ~ sb** andare a trovare qn; **~ you soon/later/tomorrow!** a presto/più tardi/domani!; **as far as I can ~** da quanto posso vedere; **there was nobody to be seen** non c'era anima viva; **let me ~** (show me) fammi vedere; (let me think) vediamo (un po'); **~ for yourself** vai a vedere con i tuoi occhi; **I don't know what she sees in him** non so che cosa ci trovi in lui

▸ **see about** VT FUS (deal with) occuparsi di

▸ **see off** VT salutare alla partenza

▸ **see out** VT (take to the door) accompagnare alla porta

▸ **see through** VT portare a termine ▸ VT FUS non lasciarsi ingannare da

▸ **see to** VT FUS occuparsi di

seed [si:d] N seme m; (fig) germe m; (Tennis) testa di serie; **to go to ~** fare seme; (fig) scadere

seedless ['si:dlɪs] ADJ senza semi

seedling ['si:dlɪŋ] N piantina di semenzaio

seedy ['si:dɪ] ADJ (shabby: person) sciatto(-a); (: place) cadente

seeing ['si:ɪŋ] CONJ: **~ (that)** visto che

seek [si:k] (pt, pp **sought** [sɔ:t]) VT cercare; **to ~ advice/help from sb** chiedere consiglio/aiuto a qn

▸ **seek out** VT (person) andare a cercare

seem [si:m] VI sembrare, parere; **there seems to be ...** sembra che ci sia ...; **it seems (that) ...** sembra or pare che ... + sub; **what seems to be the trouble?** cosa c'è che non va?

seemingly ['si:mɪŋlɪ] ADV apparentemente

seen [si:n] PP of **see**

seep [si:p] VI filtrare, trapelare

seer [sɪər] N profeta(-essa), veggente mf

seersucker ['sɪəsʌkər] N cotone m indiano

seesaw ['si:sɔ:] N altalena a bilico

seethe [si:ð] VI ribollire; **to ~ with anger** fremere di rabbia

see-through ['si:θru:] ADJ trasparente

segment ['sɛgmənt] N segmento

segregate ['sɛgrɪgeɪt] VT segregare, isolare

segregation [sɛgrɪ'geɪʃən] N segregazione f

Seine [seɪn] N Senna

seismic ['saɪzmɪk] ADJ sismico(-a)

seize [si:z] VT (grasp) afferrare; (take possession of) impadronirsi di; (Law) sequestrare

▸ **seize up** VI (Tech) grippare

▸ **seize (up)on** VT FUS ricorrere a

seizure ['si:ʒər] N (Med) attacco; (Law) confisca, sequestro

seldom ['sɛldəm] ADV raramente

select [sɪ'lɛkt] ADJ scelto(-a); (hotel, restaurant) chic inv; (club) esclusivo(-a) ▸ VT scegliere, selezionare; **a ~ few** pochi eletti mpl

selection [sɪ'lɛkʃən] N selezione f, scelta

selection committee N comitato di selezione

selective [sɪ'lɛktɪv] ADJ selettivo(-a)

selector [sɪˈlɛktəʳ] N (person) selezionatore(-trice); (Tech) selettore m

self [sɛlf] (pl **selves** [sɛlvz]) N: **the ~** l'io m
▶ PREFIX auto...

self-addressed [ˈsɛlfəˈdrɛst] ADJ: **~ envelope** busta col proprio nome e indirizzo

self-adhesive [sɛlfədˈhiːzɪv] ADJ autoadesivo(-a)

self-assertive [sɛlfəˈsəːtɪv] ADJ autoritario(-a)

self-assurance [sɛlfəˈʃuərəns] N sicurezza di sé

self-assured [sɛlfəˈʃuəd] ADJ sicuro(-a) di sé

self-catering [sɛlfˈkeɪtərɪŋ] ADJ (BRIT) in cui ci si cucina da sé; **~ apartment** appartamento (per le vacanze)

self-centred, (US) **self-centered** [sɛlfˈsɛntəd] ADJ egocentrico(-a)

self-cleaning [sɛlfˈkliːnɪŋ] ADJ autopulente

self-confessed [sɛlfkənˈfɛst] ADJ (alcoholic etc) dichiarato(-a)

self-confidence [sɛlfˈkɔnfɪdəns] N sicurezza di sé

self-confident ADJ sicuro(-a) di sé

self-conscious [sɛlfˈkɔnʃəs] ADJ timido(-a)

self-contained [sɛlfkənˈteɪnd] ADJ (BRIT: flat) indipendente

self-control [sɛlfkənˈtrəul] N autocontrollo

self-defeating [sɛlfdɪˈfiːtɪŋ] ADJ futile

self-defence, (US) **self-defense** [sɛlfdɪˈfɛns] N autodifesa; (Law) legittima difesa

self-discipline [sɛlfˈdɪsɪplɪn] N autodisciplina

self-drive ADJ (BRIT: rented car) senza autista

self-employed [sɛlfɪmˈplɔɪd] ADJ che lavora in proprio

self-esteem [sɛlfɪˈstiːm] N amor proprio m

self-evident [sɛlfˈɛvɪdənt] ADJ evidente

self-explanatory [sɛlfɪkˈsplænətərɪ] ADJ ovvio(-a)

self-governing [sɛlfˈgʌvənɪŋ] ADJ autonomo(-a)

self-harm [sɛlfˈhɑːm] N autolesionismo ▶ VI farsi del male intenzionalmente

self-help [ˈsɛlfˈhɛlp] N iniziativa individuale

selfie [ˈsɛlfɪ] N selfie m inv; **~ stick** asta f or bastone m per selfie, selfie stick m inv

self-importance [sɛlfɪmˈpɔːtns] N sufficienza

self-indulgent [sɛlfɪnˈdʌldʒənt] ADJ indulgente verso se stesso(-a)

self-inflicted [sɛlfɪnˈflɪktɪd] ADJ autoinflitto(-a)

self-interest [sɛlfˈɪntrɪst] N interesse m personale

selfish [ˈsɛlfɪʃ] ADJ egoista

selfishly [ˈsɛlfɪʃlɪ] ADV egoisticamente

selfishness [ˈsɛlfɪʃnɪs] N egoismo

selfless [ˈsɛlflɪs] ADJ altruista

selflessly [ˈsɛlflɪslɪ] ADV altruisticamente

selflessness [ˈsɛlflɪsnɪs] N altruismo

self-made man [ˈsɛlfmeɪd-] N (irreg) self-made man m inv, uomo che si è fatto da sé

self-pity [sɛlfˈpɪtɪ] N autocommiserazione f

self-portrait [sɛlfˈpɔːtrɪt] N autoritratto

self-possessed [sɛlfpəˈzɛst] ADJ controllato(-a)

self-preservation [ˈsɛlfprɛzəˈveɪʃən] N istinto di conservazione

self-raising [sɛlfˈreɪzɪŋ], (US) **self-rising** [sɛlfˈraɪzɪŋ] ADJ: **~ flour** miscela di farina e lievito

self-reliant [sɛlfrɪˈlaɪənt] ADJ indipendente

self-respect [sɛlfrɪsˈpɛkt] N rispetto di sé, amor proprio m

self-respecting [sɛlfrɪsˈpɛktɪŋ] ADJ che ha rispetto di sé

self-righteous [sɛlfˈraɪtʃəs] ADJ soddisfatto(-a) di sé

self-rising [sɛlfˈraɪzɪŋ] ADJ (US) = **self-raising**

self-sacrifice [sɛlfˈsækrɪfaɪs] N abnegazione f

self-same [ˈsɛlfseɪm] ADJ stesso(-a)

self-satisfied [sɛlfˈsætɪsfaɪd] ADJ compiaciuto(-a) di sé

self-sealing [sɛlfˈsiːlɪŋ] ADJ autosigillante

self-service [sɛlfˈsəːvɪs] N autoservizio, self-service m

self-styled [sɛlfˈstaɪld] ADJ sedicente

self-sufficient [sɛlfsəˈfɪʃənt] ADJ autosufficiente

self-supporting [sɛlfsəˈpɔːtɪŋ] ADJ economicamente indipendente

self-taught [sɛlfˈtɔːt] ADJ autodidatta

self-test [ˈsɛlftɛst] N (Comput) autoverifica

sell [sɛl] (pt, pp **sold** [səuld]) VT vendere ▶ VI vendersi; **to ~ at** or **for 100 euros** essere in vendita a 100 euro; **to ~ sb an idea** (fig) far accettare un'idea a qn
  ▶ **sell off** VT svendere, liquidare
  ▶ **sell out** VI: **to ~ out (to sb/sth)** (Comm) vendere (tutto) (a qn/qc) ▶ VT esaurire; **the tickets are all sold out** i biglietti sono esauriti
  ▶ **sell up** VI vendere (tutto)

sell-by date [ˈsɛlbaɪ-] N data di scadenza

seller [ˈsɛləʳ] N venditore(-trice); **~'s market** mercato favorevole ai venditori

selling price [ˈsɛlɪŋ-] N prezzo di vendita

Sellotape® [ˈsɛləuteɪp] N (BRIT) nastro adesivo, scotch® m

sellout [ˈsɛlaut] N (betrayal) tradimento; (Theat): **it was a ~** registrò un tutto esaurito

selves [sɛlvz] NPL of **self**

semantic [sɪˈmæntɪk] ADJ semantico(-a)

semantics [sɪˈmæntɪks] N semantica

S

semaphore [ˈsɛməfɔːʳ] N segnali mpl con bandiere; (Rail) semaforo

semblance [ˈsɛmbləns] N parvenza, apparenza

semen [ˈsiːmən] N sperma m

semester [sɪˈmɛstəʳ] N (US) semestre m

semi... [ˈsɛmɪ] PREFIX semi... ▶ N: **semi** = **semidetached (house)**

semi-breve [ˈsɛmɪbriːv] N (BRIT) semibreve f

semicircle [ˈsɛmɪsəːkl] N semicerchio

semicircular [ˈsɛmɪˈsəːkjuləʳ] ADJ semicircolare

semicolon [sɛmɪˈkəulən] N punto e virgola

semiconductor [sɛmɪkənˈdʌktəʳ] N semiconduttore m

semiconscious [sɛmɪˈkɔnʃəs] ADJ parzialmente cosciente

semidetached (house) [sɛmɪdɪˈtætʃt-] N (BRIT) casa gemella

semifinal [sɛmɪˈfaɪnl] N semifinale f

seminar [ˈsɛmɪnɑːʳ] N seminario

seminary [ˈsɛmɪnərɪ] N (Rel: for priests) seminario

semiprecious [sɛmɪˈprɛʃəs] ADJ semiprezioso(-a)

semiquaver [ˈsɛmɪkweɪvəʳ] N (BRIT) semicroma

semiskilled [ˈsɛmɪˈskɪld] ADJ: **~ worker** operaio(-a) non specializzato(-a)

semi-skimmed [ˈsɛmɪˈskɪmd] ADJ (milk) parzialmente scremato(-a)

semitone [ˈsɛmɪtəun] N (Mus) semitono

semolina [sɛməˈliːnə] N semolino

Sen., sen. ABBR = **senator; senior**

senate [ˈsɛnɪt] N senato

> Il **Senate** è la camera alta del Congress, il parlamento degli Stati Uniti. È composto da 100 senatori, 2 per stato, eletti a suffragio universale diretto ogni 6 anni, con un sistema di mandati tale che un terzo dei senatori è rinnovato a rotazione ogni 2 anni.

senator [ˈsɛnɪtəʳ] N senatore(-trice)

send [sɛnd] (pt, pp **sent** [sɛnt]) VT mandare; **to ~ by post** or (US) **mail** spedire per posta; **to ~ sb for sth** mandare qn a prendere qc; **to ~ word that ...** mandare a dire che ...; **she sends (you) her love** ti saluta affettuosamente; **to ~ sb to Coventry** (BRIT) dare l'ostracismo a qn; **to ~ sb to sleep/into fits of laughter** far addormentare/scoppiare dal ridere qn; **to ~ sth flying** far volare via qc
▶ **send away** VT (letter, goods) spedire; (person) mandare via
▶ **send away for** VT FUS richiedere per posta, farsi spedire
▶ **send back** VT rimandare
▶ **send for** VT FUS mandare a chiamare, far venire; (by post) ordinare per posta
▶ **send in** VT (report, application, resignation) presentare

▶ **send off** VT (goods) spedire; (BRIT Sport: player) espellere
▶ **send on** VT (BRIT: letter) inoltrare; (luggage etc: in advance) spedire in anticipo
▶ **send out** VT (invitation) diramare; (emit: light, heat) mandare, emanare; (: signals) emettere
▶ **send round** VT (letter, document etc) far circolare
▶ **send up** VT (person, price) far salire; (BRIT: parody) mettere in ridicolo

sender [ˈsɛndəʳ] N mittente mf

send-off [ˈsɛndɔf] N: **to give sb a good ~** festeggiare la partenza di qn

Senegal [sɛnɪˈgɔːl] N Senegal m

Senegalese [sɛnɪgəˈliːz] ADJ, N senegalese mf

senile [ˈsiːnaɪl] ADJ senile

senility [sɪˈnɪlɪtɪ] N senilità f

senior [ˈsiːnɪəʳ] ADJ (older) più vecchio(-a); (of higher rank) di grado più elevato ▶ N persona più anziana; (in service) persona con maggiore anzianità; **P. Jones ~** P. Jones senior, P. Jones padre

senior citizen N persona anziana

senior high school N (US) ≈ liceo

seniority [siːnɪˈɔrɪtɪ] N anzianità; (in rank) superiorità

sensation [sɛnˈseɪʃən] N sensazione f; **to create a ~** fare scalpore

sensational [sɛnˈseɪʃənl] ADJ sensazionale; (marvellous) eccezionale

sense [sɛns] N senso; (feeling) sensazione f, senso; (meaning) senso, significato; (wisdom) buonsenso ▶ VT sentire, percepire ■ **senses** NPL (sanity) ragione f; **it makes ~** ha senso; **there is no ~ in (doing) that** non ha senso (farlo); **~ of humour** (senso dell')umorismo; **to come to one's senses** (regain consciousness) riprendere i sensi; (become reasonable) tornare in sé; **to take leave of one's senses** perdere il lume or l'uso della ragione

senseless [ˈsɛnslɪs] ADJ sciocco(-a); (unconscious) privo(-a) di sensi

sensibilities [sɛnsɪˈbɪlɪtɪz] NPL sensibilità fsg

sensible [ˈsɛnsɪbl] ADJ sensato(-a), ragionevole

> La parola inglese **sensible** non vuol dire sensibile.

sensitive [ˈsɛnsɪtɪv] ADJ sensibile; (skin, question) delicato(-a); **~ (to)** sensibile (a); **he is very ~ about it** è un tasto che è meglio non toccare con lui

> La parola inglese **sensitive** non vuol dire sensitivo.

sensitivity [sɛnsɪˈtɪvɪtɪ] N sensibilità f inv

sensual [ˈsɛnsjuəl] ADJ sensuale

sensuous [ˈsɛnsjuəs] ADJ sensuale

sent [sɛnt] PT, PP of **send**

sentence [ˈsɛntns] N (Ling) frase f; (Law: judgement) sentenza; (: punishment) condanna ▶ VT: **to**

~ **sb to death/to 5 years** condannare qn a morte/a 5 anni; **to pass ~ on sb** condannare qn

sentiment ['sɛntɪmənt] N sentimento; (*opinion*) opinione *f*

sentimental [sɛntɪ'mɛntl] ADJ sentimentale

sentimentality [sɛntɪmɛn'tælɪtɪ] N sentimentalità, sentimentalismo

sentry ['sɛntrɪ] N sentinella

sentry duty N: **to be on ~** essere di sentinella

Seoul [səul] N Seul *f*

Sep. ABBR (= *September*) sett., set.

separable ['sɛprəbl] ADJ separabile

separate ADJ ['sɛprɪt] separato(-a) ▶ VT ['sɛpəreɪt] separare ▶ VI separarsi; **~ from** separato da; **under ~ cover** (*Comm*) in plico a parte; **to ~ into** dividere in; *see also* **separates**

separately ['sɛprɪtlɪ] ADV separatamente

separates ['sɛprɪts] NPL (*clothes*) coordinati *mpl*

separation [sɛpə'reɪʃən] N separazione *f*

Sept. ABBR (= *September*) sett., set.

September [sɛp'tɛmbəʳ] N settembre *m*; *see also* **July**

septic ['sɛptɪk] ADJ settico(-a); (*wound*) infettato(-a); **to go ~** infettarsi

septicaemia, (*US*) **septicemia** [sɛptɪ'siːmɪə] N setticemia

septic tank N fossa settica

sequel ['siːkwl] N conseguenza; (*of story*) seguito; (*of film*) sequenza

sequence ['siːkwəns] N (*series*) serie *f* inv; (*order*) ordine *m*; **in ~** in ordine, di seguito; **~ of tenses** concordanza dei tempi

sequencing ['siːkwənsɪŋ] N sequenziamento *m*

sequential [sɪ'kwɛnʃəl] ADJ: **~ access** (*Comput*) accesso sequenziale

sequin ['siːkwɪn] N lustrino, paillette *f* inv

Serb [səːb] ADJ, N = **Serbian**

Serbia ['səːbɪə] N Serbia

Serbian ['səːbɪən] ADJ serbo(-a) ▶ N serbo(-a); (*Ling*) serbo

Serbo-Croat ['səːbəu'krəuæt] N (*Ling*) serbocroato

serenade [sɛrə'neɪd] N serenata ▶ VT fare la serenata a

serene [sɪ'riːn] ADJ sereno(-a), calmo(-a)

serenity [sɪ'rɛnɪtɪ] N serenità, tranquillità

sergeant ['saːdʒənt] N sergente *m*; (*Police*) brigadiere *m*

sergeant major N maresciallo

serial ['sɪərɪəl] N (*Press*) romanzo a puntate; (*Radio, TV*) trasmissione *f* a puntate, serial *m* inv ▶ CPD (*Comput*) seriale

serialize ['sɪərɪəlaɪz] VT pubblicare a puntate; trasmettere a puntate

serial killer N serial killer *mf*

serial number N numero di serie

series ['sɪəriːz] N (*pl inv*) serie *f* inv; (*Publishing*) collana

serious ['sɪərɪəs] ADJ serio(-a), grave; **are you ~ (about it)?** parla sul serio?

seriously ['sɪərɪəslɪ] ADV seriamente; **he's ~ rich** (*col: extremely*) ha un casino di soldi; **to take sth/sb ~** prendere qc/qn sul serio

seriousness ['sɪərɪəsnɪs] N serietà, gravità

sermon ['səːmən] N sermone *m*

serrated [sɪ'reɪtɪd] ADJ seghettato(-a)

serum ['sɪərəm] N siero

servant ['səːvənt] N domestico(-a)

serve [səːv] VT (*employer etc*) servire, essere a servizio di; (*purpose*) servire a; (*customer, food, meal*) servire; (*apprenticeship*) fare; (*prison term*) scontare ▶ VI (*also Tennis*) servire; (*soldier etc*) prestare servizio; (*be useful*): **to ~ as/for/to do** servire da/per/per fare ▶ N (*Tennis*) servizio; **are you being served?** la stanno servendo?; **to ~ on a committee/jury** far parte di un comitato/una giuria; **it serves him right** ben gli sta, se l'è meritata; **it serves my purpose** fa al caso mio, serve al mio scopo

▶ **serve out, serve up** VT (*food*) servire

server ['səːvəʳ] N (*Comput*) server *m* inv

service ['səːvɪs] N servizio; (*Aut: maintenance*) assistenza, revisione *f*; (*Rel*) funzione *f* ▶ VT (*car, washing machine*) revisionare ▪ **services** NPL (*BRIT: on motorway*) stazione *f* di servizio; (*Mil*): **the Services** le forze armate; **to be of ~ to sb, to do sb a ~** essere d'aiuto a qn; **to put one's car in for (a) ~** portare la macchina in officina per una revisione; **dinner ~** servizio da tavola; **~ included/not included** servizio compreso/escluso

serviceable ['səːvɪsəbl] ADJ pratico(-a), utile; (*usable, working*) usabile

service area N (*on motorway*) area di servizio

service charge N (*BRIT*) servizio

service industries NPL settore *m* terziario

serviceman ['səːvɪsmən] N (*irreg*) militare *m*

service provider N (*Comput*) provider *m* inv

service station N stazione *f* di servizio

serviette [səːvɪ'ɛt] N (*BRIT*) tovagliolo

servile ['səːvaɪl] ADJ servile

session ['sɛʃən] N (*sitting*) seduta, sessione *f*; (*Scol*) anno scolastico (*or* accademico); **to be in ~** essere in seduta

session musician N musicista *mf* di studio

set [sɛt] (*pt, pp ~*) N serie *f* inv; (*of cutlery etc*) servizio; (*Radio, TV*) apparecchio; (*Tennis*) set *m* inv; (*group of people*) mondo, ambiente *m*; (*Cine*) scenario; (*Theat: stage*) scena *fpl*; (*: scenery*) scenario; (*Math*) insieme *m*; (*Hairdressing*) messa in piega ▶ ADJ (*fixed*) stabilito(-a), determinato(-a);

S

775

(ready) pronto(-a) ▶ VT (place) posare, mettere; (arrange) sistemare; (fix) fissare; (assign: task, homework) dare, assegnare; (adjust) regolare; (decide: rules etc) stabilire, fissare; (Typ) comporre ▶ VI (sun) tramontare; (jam, jelly) rapprendersi; (concrete) fare presa; **to be ~ on doing** essere deciso a fare; **to be all ~ to do sth** essere pronto fare qc; **to be (dead) ~ against** essere completamente contrario a; **~ in one's ways** abitudinario; **a novel ~ in Rome** un romanzo ambientato a Roma; **to ~ to music** mettere in musica; **to ~ on fire** dare fuoco a; **to ~ free** liberare; **to ~ sth going** mettere in moto qc; **to ~ sail** prendere il mare; **a ~ phrase** una frase fatta; **a ~ of false teeth** una dentiera; **a ~ of dining-room furniture** una camera da pranzo
▶ **set about** VT FUS (task) intraprendere, mettersi a; **to ~ about doing sth** mettersi a fare qc
▶ **set aside** VT mettere da parte
▶ **set back** VT (progress) ritardare; **to ~ back (by)** (in time) mettere indietro (di); **a house ~ back from the road** una casa a una certa distanza dalla strada
▶ **set down** VT (bus, train) lasciare
▶ **set in** VI (infection) svilupparsi; (complications) intervenire; **the rain has ~ in for the day** ormai pioverà tutto il giorno
▶ **set off** VI partire ▶ VT (bomb) far scoppiare; (cause to start) mettere in moto; (show up well) dare risalto a
▶ **set out** VI partire; (aim): **to ~ out to do** proporsi di fare ▶ VT (arrange) disporre; (state) esporre, presentare
▶ **set up** VT (organization) fondare, costituire; (record) stabilire; (monument) innalzare

setback ['sɛtbæk] N (hitch) contrattempo, inconveniente m; (in health) ricaduta

set menu N menù m inv fisso

set square N squadra

settee [sɛ'tiː] N divano, sofà m inv

setting ['sɛtɪŋ] N (background) ambiente m; (of controls) posizione f; (of sun) tramonto; (scenery) sfondo; (of jewel) montatura

setting lotion N fissatore m

settle ['sɛtl] VT (argument, matter) appianare; (problem) risolvere; (pay: bill, account) regolare, saldare; (Med: calm) calmare; (colonize: land) colonizzare ▶ VI (bird, dust etc) posarsi; (sediment) depositarsi; (also: **settle down**) sistemarsi, stabilirsi; (: become calmer) calmarsi; **to ~ to sth** applicarsi a qc; **to ~ for sth** accontentarsi di qc; **to ~ on sth** decidersi per qc; **that's settled then** allora è deciso; **to ~ one's stomach** calmare il mal di stomaco
▶ **settle in** VI sistemarsi
▶ **settle up** VI: **to ~ up with sb** regolare i conti con qn

settlement ['sɛtlmənt] N (payment) pagamento, saldo; (agreement) accordo; (colony) colonia; (village etc) villaggio, comunità f inv; **in ~ of our account** (Comm) a saldo del nostro conto

settler ['sɛtləʳ] N colonizzatore(-trice)

setup ['sɛtʌp] N (arrangement) sistemazione f; (situation) situazione f; (Comput) setup m inv, installazione f

seven ['sɛvn] NUM sette

seventeen [sɛvn'tiːn] NUM diciassette

seventeenth [sɛvn'tiːnθ] NUM diciassettesimo(-a)

seventh ['sɛvnθ] NUM settimo(-a)

seventieth ['sɛvntɪɪθ] NUM settantesimo(-a)

seventy ['sɛvntɪ] NUM settanta

sever ['sɛvəʳ] VT recidere, tagliare; (relations) troncare

several ['sɛvərl] ADJ, PRON alcuni(-e), diversi(-e); **~ of us** alcuni di noi; **~ times** diverse volte

severance ['sɛvərəns] N (of relations) rottura

severance pay N indennità di licenziamento

severe [sɪ'vɪəʳ] ADJ severo(-a); (serious) serio(-a), grave; (hard) duro(-a); (plain) semplice, sobrio(-a)

severely [sɪ'vɪəlɪ] ADV (gen) severamente; (wounded, ill) gravemente

severity [sɪ'vɛrɪtɪ] N severità; gravità; (of weather) rigore m

sew [səu] (pt **sewed** [səud], pp **sewn** [səun]) VT, VI cucire
▶ **sew up** VT ricucire; **it is all sewn up** (fig) è tutto apposto

sewage ['suːɪdʒ] N acque fpl di scolo

sewage works N stabilimento per la depurazione dei liquami

sewer ['suːəʳ] N fogna

sewing ['səuɪŋ] N cucitura; cucito

sewing machine N macchina da cucire

sewn [səun] PP of **sew**

sex [sɛks] N sesso; **to have ~ with** avere rapporti sessuali con

sex act N atto sessuale

sex appeal N sex appeal m inv

sex education N educazione f sessuale

sexism ['sɛksɪzəm] N sessismo

sexist ['sɛksɪst] ADJ, N sessista (mf)

sex life N vita sessuale

sex object N oggetto sessuale; **to be treated like a ~** (woman) essere trattata da donna oggetto

sextet [sɛks'tɛt] N sestetto

sexting (col) ['sɛkstɪŋ] N sexting m inv

sexual ['sɛksjuəl] ADJ sessuale; **~ assault** violenza carnale; **~ harassment** molestie fpl sessuali; **~ intercourse** rapporti mpl sessuali

sexuality [sɛksju'ælɪtɪ] N sessualità

sexy ['sɛksɪ] ADJ provocante, sexy inv

Seychelles [seɪ'ʃɛlz] NPL: **the ~** le Seicelle

SF N ABBR = **science fiction**

SG N ABBR (US) = **Surgeon General**

shabbiness [ˈʃæbɪnɪs] N trasandatezza; squallore m; meschinità

shabby [ˈʃæbɪ] ADJ trasandato(-a); (building) squallido(-a), malandato(-a); (behaviour) meschino(-a)

shack [ʃæk] N baracca, capanna

shackles [ˈʃæklz] NPL ferri mpl, catene fpl

shade [ʃeɪd] N ombra; (for lamp) paralume m; (of colour) tonalità f inv; (US: window shade) veneziana; (small quantity): **a ~ (more/too large)** un po' (di più/troppo grande); **a ~ smaller** un tantino più piccolo ▸ VT ombreggiare, fare ombra a ■ **shades** NPL (sunglasses) occhiali mpl da sole; **in the ~** all'ombra

shadow [ˈʃædəu] N ombra ▸ VT (follow) pedinare; **without** or **beyond a ~ of doubt** senz'ombra di dubbio

shadow cabinet N (BRIT Pol) governo m ombra inv

shadowy [ˈʃædəuɪ] ADJ ombreggiato(-a), ombroso(-a); (dim) vago(-a), indistinto(-a)

shady [ˈʃeɪdɪ] ADJ ombroso(-a); (fig: dishonest) losco(-a), equivoco(-a)

shaft [ʃɑːft] N (of arrow, spear) asta; (Aut, Tech) albero; (of mine) pozzo; (of lift) tromba; (of light) raggio; **ventilator ~** condotto di ventilazione

shaggy [ˈʃægɪ] ADJ ispido(-a)

shake [ʃeɪk] (pt **shook** [ʃuk], pp **shaken** [ˈʃeɪkn]) VT scuotere; (bottle, cocktail) agitare ▸ VI tremare ▸ N scossa; **to ~ one's head** (in refusal, dismay) scuotere la testa; **to ~ hands with sb** stringere or dare la mano a qn
▸ **shake off** VT scrollare (via); (fig) sbarazzarsi di
▸ **shake up** VT scuotere

shake-up [ˈʃeɪkʌp] N riorganizzazione f drastica

shakily [ˈʃeɪkɪlɪ] ADV (reply) con voce tremante; (walk) con passo malfermo; (write) con mano tremante

shaky [ˈʃeɪkɪ] ADJ (hand, voice) tremante; (memory) labile; (knowledge) incerto(-a); (building) traballante

shale [ʃeɪl] N roccia scistosa

shall [ʃæl] AUX VB: **I ~ go** andrò; **~ I open the door?** apro io la porta?; **I'll get some, ~ I?** ne prendo un po', va bene?

shallot [ʃəˈlɔt] N (BRIT) scalogna

shallow [ˈʃæləu] ADJ poco profondo(-a); (fig) superficiale

sham [ʃæm] N finzione f, messinscena; (jewellery, furniture) imitazione f ▸ ADJ finto(-a) ▸ VT fingere, simulare

shambles [ˈʃæmblz] N confusione f, baraonda, scompiglio; **the economy is (in) a complete ~** l'economia è nel caos più totale

shambolic [ʃæmˈbɔlɪk] ADJ (col) incasinato(-a)

shame [ʃeɪm] N vergogna ▸ VT far vergognare; **it is a ~ (that/to do)** è un peccato (che + sub/fare); **what a ~!** che peccato!; **to put sb/sth to ~** (fig) far sfigurare qn/qc

shamefaced [ˈʃeɪmfeɪst] ADJ vergognoso(-a)

shameful [ˈʃeɪmful] ADJ vergognoso(-a)

shameless [ˈʃeɪmlɪs] ADJ sfrontato(-a); (immodest) spudorato(-a)

shampoo [ʃæmˈpuː] N shampoo m inv ▸ VT fare lo shampoo a; **~ and set** shampoo e messa in piega

shamrock [ˈʃæmrɔk] N trifoglio (simbolo nazionale dell'Irlanda)

shandy [ˈʃændɪ] N birra con gassosa

shan't [ʃɑːnt] = **shall not**

shanty town [ˈʃæntɪ-] N bidonville f inv

SHAPE [ʃeɪp] N ABBR (= Supreme Headquarters Allied Powers, Europe) supremo quartier generale delle Potenze Alleate in Europa

shape [ʃeɪp] N forma ▸ VT (clay, stone) dar forma a; (fig: ideas, character) formare; (: course of events) determinare, condizionare; (: statement) formulare ▸ VI (also: **shape up**: events) andare, mettersi; (: person) cavarsela; **to take ~** prendere forma; **in the ~ of a heart** a forma di cuore; **to get o.s. into ~** rimettersi in forma; **I can't bear gardening in any ~ or form** detesto il giardinaggio d'ogni genere e specie

-shaped [ʃeɪpt] SUFFIX: **heart-shaped** a forma di cuore

shapeless [ˈʃeɪplɪs] ADJ senza forma, informe

shapely [ˈʃeɪplɪ] ADJ ben proporzionato(-a)

share [ʃɛəʳ] N (thing received, contribution) parte f; (Comm) azione f ▸ VT dividere; (have in common) condividere, avere in comune; **to ~ out (among** or **between)** dividere (tra); **to ~ in** partecipare a

share capital N capitale m azionario

share certificate N certificato azionario

shareholder [ˈʃɛəhəuldəʳ] N azionista mf

share index N listino di Borsa

shark [ʃɑːk] N squalo, pescecane m

sharp [ʃɑːp] ADJ (razor, knife) affilato(-a); (point) acuto(-a), acuminato(-a); (nose, chin) aguzzo(-a); (outline) netto(-a); (curve, bend) stretto(-a), accentuato(-a); (cold, pain) pungente; (voice) stridulo(-a); (person: quick-witted) sveglio(-a); (: unscrupulous) disonesto(-a); (Mus): **C ~** do m inv diesis inv ▸ N (Mus) diesis m inv ▸ ADV: **at 2 o'clock ~** alle due in punto; **turn ~ left** giri tutto a sinistra; **to be ~ with sb** rimproverare qn; **look ~!** sbrigati!

sharpen [ˈʃɑːpən] VT affilare; (pencil) fare la punta a; (fig) acuire

sharpener [ˈʃɑːpnəʳ] N (also: **pencil sharpener**) temperamatite m inv; (also: **knife sharpener**) affilacoltelli m inv

sharp-eyed [ʃɑːpˈaɪd] ADJ dalla vista acuta

777

S

sharpish [ˈʃɑːpɪʃ] ADV (BRIT col: quickly) subito

sharply [ˈʃɑːplɪ] ADV (abruptly) bruscamente; (clearly) nettamente; (harshly) duramente, aspramente

sharp-tempered [ʃɑːpˈtɛmpəd] ADJ irascibile

shatter [ˈʃætəʳ] VT mandare in frantumi, frantumare; (fig: upset) distruggere; (: ruin) rovinare ▶ VI frantumarsi, andare in pezzi

shattered [ˈʃætəd] ADJ (grief-stricken) sconvolto(-a); (exhausted) a pezzi, distrutto(-a)

shatterproof [ˈʃætəpruːf] ADJ infrangibile

shave [ʃeɪv] VT radere, rasare ▶ VI radersi, farsi la barba ▶ N: **to have a ~** farsi la barba

shaven [ˈʃeɪvn] ADJ (head) rasato(-a), tonsurato(-a)

shaver [ˈʃeɪvəʳ] N (also: **electric shaver**) rasoio elettrico

shaving [ˈʃeɪvɪŋ] N (action) rasatura ▪ **shavings** NPL (of wood etc) trucioli mpl

shaving brush N pennello da barba

shaving cream N crema da barba

shaving foam N = **shaving cream**

shaving soap N sapone m da barba

shawl [ʃɔːl] N scialle m

she [ʃiː] PRON ella, lei; **there ~ is** eccola; **she-bear** orsa; **she-cat** gatta; **she-elephant** elefantessa

sheaf [ʃiːf] (pl **sheaves** [ʃiːvz]) N covone m

shear [ʃɪəʳ] (pt **sheared**, pp **sheared** or **shorn** [ʃɔːn]) VT (sheep) tosare ▶ **shear off** VI (break off) spezzarsi

shears [ˈʃɪəz] NPL (for hedge) cesoie fpl

sheath [ʃiːθ] (pl **sheaths** [ʃiːðz]) N fodero, guaina; (contraceptive) preservativo

sheathe [ʃiːð] VT rivestire; (sword) rinfoderare

sheath knife N coltello (con fodero)

sheaves [ʃiːvz] NPL of **sheaf**

shed [ʃɛd] (pt, pp ~) N capannone m ▶ VT (leaves, fur etc) perdere; (tears, blood) versare; (workers) liberarsi di; **to ~ light on** (problem, mystery) far luce su

she'd [ʃiːd] = **she had; she would**

sheen [ʃiːn] N lucentezza

sheep [ʃiːp] N (pl inv) pecora

sheepdog [ˈʃiːpdɔg] N cane m da pastore

sheep farmer N allevatore(-trice) di pecore

sheepish [ˈʃiːpɪʃ] ADJ vergognoso(-a), timido(-a)

sheepskin [ˈʃiːpskɪn] N pelle f di pecora

sheepskin jacket N (giacca di) montone m

sheer [ʃɪəʳ] ADJ (utter) vero(-a) (e proprio(-a)); (steep) a picco, perpendicolare; (transparent) trasparente; (almost transparent) sottile ▶ ADV a picco; **by ~ chance** per puro caso

sheet [ʃiːt] N (on bed) lenzuolo; (of paper) foglio; (of glass) lastra; (of metal) foglio, lamina

sheet feed N (on printer) alimentazione f di fogli

sheet lightning N lampo diffuso

sheet metal N lamiera

sheet music N fogli mpl di musica

sheik, sheikh [ʃeɪk] N sceicco

shelf [ʃɛlf] (pl **shelves** [ʃɛlvz]) N scaffale m, mensola

shelf life N (Comm) durata di conservazione

shell [ʃɛl] N (on beach) conchiglia; (of egg, nut etc) guscio; (explosive) granata; (of building) scheletro, struttura ▶ VT (peas) sgranare; (Mil) bombardare, cannoneggiare
▶ **shell out** VI (col): **to ~ out (for)** sganciare soldi (per)

she'll [ʃiːl] = **she will; she shall**

shellfish [ˈʃɛlfɪʃ] N (pl inv: crab etc) crostaceo; (: scallop etc) mollusco; (pl: as food) crostacei; molluschi

shellsuit [ˈʃɛlsuːt] N tuta di acetato

shelter [ˈʃɛltəʳ] N riparo, rifugio ▶ VT riparare, proteggere; (give lodging to) dare rifugio or asilo a ▶ VI ripararsi, mettersi al riparo; **to take ~ (from)** mettersi al riparo (da)

sheltered [ˈʃɛltəd] ADJ (life) ritirato(-a); (spot) riparato(-a), protetto(-a)

shelve [ʃɛlv] VT (fig) accantonare, rimandare

shelves [ʃɛlvz] NPL of **shelf**

shelving [ˈʃɛlvɪŋ] N scaffalature fpl

shepherd [ˈʃɛpəd] N pastore m ▶ VT (guide) guidare

shepherdess [ˈʃɛpədɪs] N pastora

shepherd's pie N (BRIT) timballo di carne macinata e purè di patate

sherbet [ˈʃəːbət] N (BRIT: powder) polvere effervescente al gusto di frutta; (US: water ice) sorbetto

sheriff [ˈʃɛrɪf] N (US) sceriffo

sherry [ˈʃɛrɪ] N sherry m inv

she's [ʃiːz] = **she is; she has**

Shetland [ˈʃɛtlənd] N (also: **the Shetlands, the Shetland Isles**) le (isole) Shetland

Shetland pony N pony m inv delle Shetland

shield [ʃiːld] N scudo; (trophy) scudetto; (protection) schermo ▶ VT: **to ~ (from)** riparare (da), proteggere (da or contro)

shift [ʃɪft] N (change) cambiamento; (of workers) turno ▶ VT spostare, muovere; (remove) rimuovere ▶ VI spostarsi, muoversi; **~ in demand** (Comm) variazione f della domanda; **the wind has shifted to the south** il vento si è girato e soffia da sud

shift key N (on typewriter) tasto delle maiuscole

shiftless [ˈʃɪftlɪs] ADJ fannullone(-a)

shift work N: **to do ~** fare i turni

shifty [ˈʃɪftɪ] ADJ ambiguo(-a); (eyes) sfuggente

Shiite [ˈʃiːaɪt] ADJ, N sciita mf

shilling [ˈʃɪlɪŋ] N (BRIT) scellino (12 old pence; 20 in a pound)

shilly-shally [ˈʃɪlɪʃælɪ] vi tentennare, esitare

shimmer [ˈʃɪməʳ] vi brillare, luccicare

shimmering [ˈʃɪmərɪŋ] ADJ (gen) luccicante, scintillante; (haze) tremolante; (satin etc) cangiante

shin [ʃɪn] N tibia ▶ VI: **to ~ up/down a tree** arrampicarsi in cima a/scivolare giù da un albero

shindig [ˈʃɪndɪg] N (col) festa chiassosa

shine [ʃaɪn] (pt, pp **shone** [ʃɔn]) N splendore m, lucentezza ▶ VI (ri)splendere, brillare ▶ VT far brillare, far risplendere; (torch): **to ~ sth on** puntare qc verso

shingle [ˈʃɪŋgl] N (on beach) ciottoli mpl; (on roof) assicella di copertura

shingles [ˈʃɪŋglz] N (Med) herpes zoster m

shining [ˈʃaɪnɪŋ] ADJ (surface, hair) lucente; (light) brillante

shiny [ˈʃaɪnɪ] ADJ lucente, lucido(-a)

ship [ʃɪp] N nave f ▶ VT trasportare (via mare); (send) spedire (via mare); (load) imbarcare, caricare; **on board ~** a bordo

shipbuilder [ˈʃɪpbɪldəʳ] N costruttore(-trice) navale

shipbuilding [ˈʃɪpbɪldɪŋ] N costruzione f navale

ship chandler [-ˈtʃɑːndləʳ] N fornitore(-trice) marittimo(-a)

shipment [ˈʃɪpmənt] N carico

shipowner [ˈʃɪpəunəʳ] N armatore(-trice)

shipper [ˈʃɪpəʳ] N spedizioniere m (marittimo)

shipping [ˈʃɪpɪŋ] N (ships) naviglio; (traffic) navigazione f

shipping agent N agente m marittimo

shipping company N compagnia di navigazione

shipping lane N rotta (di navigazione)

shipping line N = **shipping company**

shipshape [ˈʃɪpʃeɪp] ADJ in perfetto ordine

shipwreck [ˈʃɪprɛk] N relitto; (event) naufragio ▶ VT: **to be shipwrecked** naufragare, fare naufragio

shipyard [ˈʃɪpjɑːd] N cantiere m navale

shire [ˈʃaɪəʳ] N (BRIT) contea

shirk [ʃəːk] VT sottrarsi a, evitare

shirt [ʃəːt] N (man's) camicia; (woman's) camicetta, camicia; **in ~ sleeves** in maniche di camicia

shirty [ˈʃəːtɪ] ADJ (BRIT col) incavolato(-a)

shit [ʃɪt] EXCL (col!) merda (!)

shiver [ˈʃɪvəʳ] N brivido ▶ VI rabbrividire, tremare

shoal [ʃəul] N (of fish) banco

shock [ʃɔk] N (impact) urto, colpo; (Elec) scossa; (emotional) colpo, shock m inv; (Med) shock ▶ VT colpire, scioccare; scandalizzare; **to give sb a ~**

far venire un colpo a qn; **to be suffering from ~** essere in stato di shock; **it came as a ~ to hear that ...** è stata una grossa sorpresa sentire che ...

shock absorber N ammortizzatore m

shocker [ˈʃɔkəʳ] N: **it was a real ~** (col) è stata una vera bomba

shocking [ˈʃɔkɪŋ] ADJ scioccante, traumatizzante; (scandalous) scandaloso(-a); (very bad: weather, handwriting) orribile; (: results) disastroso(-a)

shockproof [ˈʃɔkpruːf] ADJ antiurto inv

shock therapy, shock treatment N (Med) shockterapia

shock wave N onda d'urto; (fig: usually pl) impatto msg

shod [ʃɔd] PT, PP of **shoe**

shoddy [ˈʃɔdɪ] ADJ scadente

shoe [ʃuː] (pt, pp **shod** [ʃɔd]) N scarpa; (also: **horseshoe**) ferro di cavallo; (also: **brake shoe**) ganascia (del freno) ▶ VT (horse) ferrare

shoebrush [ˈʃuːbrʌʃ] N spazzola per le scarpe

shoehorn [ˈʃuːhɔːn] N calzante m

shoelace [ˈʃuːleɪs] N stringa

shoemaker [ˈʃuːmeɪkəʳ] N calzolaio(-a)

shoe polish N lucido per scarpe

shoeshop [ˈʃuːʃɔp] N calzoleria

shoestring [ˈʃuːstrɪŋ] N stringa (delle scarpe); **on a ~** (fig: do sth) con quattro soldi

shoetree [ˈʃuːtriː] N forma per scarpe

shone [ʃɔn] PT, PP of **shine**

shonky [ˈʃɔŋkɪ] ADJ (AUSTRALIA, NEW ZEALAND col: untrustworthy) sospetto(-a)

shoo [ʃuː] EXCL sciò!, via! ▶ VT (also: **shoo away, shoo off**) cacciare (via)

shook [ʃuk] PT of **shake**

shoot [ʃuːt] (pt, pp **shot** [ʃɔt]) N (on branch, seedling) germoglio; (shooting party) partita di caccia; (competition) gara di tiro ▶ VT (game: BRIT) cacciare, andare a caccia di; (person) sparare a; (execute) fucilare; (film) girare ▶ VI (Football) sparare, tirare (forte); **to ~ (at)** (with gun) sparare (a), fare fuoco (su); (with bow) tirare (su); **to ~ past sb** passare vicino a qn come un fulmine; **to ~ in/out** entrare/uscire come una freccia
  ▶ **shoot down** VT (plane) abbattere
  ▶ **shoot up** VI (fig) salire alle stelle

shooting [ˈʃuːtɪŋ] N (shots) sparatoria; (murder) uccisione f (a colpi d'arma da fuoco); (Hunting) caccia; (Cine) riprese fpl

shooting range N poligono (di tiro), tirassegno

shooting star N stella cadente

shop [ʃɔp] N negozio; (workshop) officina ▶ VI (also: **go shopping**) fare spese; **repair ~** officina di riparazione; **to talk ~** (fig) parlare di lavoro
  ▶ **shop around** VI fare il giro dei negozi

S

shopaholic [ˈʃɒpəˈhɒlɪk] N (col) maniaco(-a) dello shopping

shop assistant N (BRIT) commesso(-a)

shop floor N (BRIT fig) operai mpl, maestranze fpl

shopkeeper [ˈʃɒpkiːpəʳ] N negoziante mf, bottegaio(-a)

shoplift [ˈʃɒplɪft] VI taccheggiare

shoplifter [ˈʃɒplɪftəʳ] N taccheggiatore(-trice)

shoplifting [ˈʃɒplɪftɪŋ] N taccheggio

shopper [ˈʃɒpəʳ] N compratore(-trice)

shopping [ˈʃɒpɪŋ] N (goods) spesa, acquisti mpl

shopping bag N borsa per la spesa

shopping cart N (US Comput: shopping trolley) carrello

shopping centre, (US) **shopping center** N centro commerciale

shopping mall N centro commerciale

shopping trolley N (BRIT) carrello del supermercato

shop-soiled [ˈʃɒpsɔɪld] ADJ sciupato(-a) a forza di stare in vetrina

shop steward N (BRIT Industry) rappresentante m sindacale

shop window N vetrina

shore [ʃɔːʳ] N (of sea) riva, spiaggia; (of lake) riva ▶ VT: **to ~ (up)** puntellare; **on ~** a riva

shore leave N (Naut) franchigia

shorn [ʃɔːn] PP of **shear**

short [ʃɔːt] ADJ (not long) corto(-a); (soon finished) breve; (person) basso(-a); (curt) brusco(-a), secco(-a); (insufficient) insufficiente ▶ N (also: **short film**) cortometraggio; **it is ~ for** è l'abbreviazione or il diminutivo di; **a ~ time ago** poco tempo fa; **in the ~ term** nell'immediato futuro; **to be ~ of sth** essere a corto di or mancare di qc; **to run ~ of sth** rimanere senza qc; **to be in ~ supply** scarseggiare; **I'm 3 ~** me ne mancano 3; **in ~** in breve; **~ of doing** a meno che non si faccia; **everything ~ of** tutto fuorché; **to cut ~** (speech, visit) accorciare, abbreviare; (person) interrompere; **to fall ~ of** venire meno a; non soddisfare; **to stop ~** fermarsi di colpo; **to stop ~ of** non arrivare fino a; see also **shorts**

shortage [ˈʃɔːtɪdʒ] N scarsezza, carenza

shortbread [ˈʃɔːtbrɛd] N biscotto di pasta frolla

short-change [ʃɔːtˈtʃeɪndʒ] VT: **to ~ sb** imbrogliare qn sul resto

short-circuit [ʃɔːtˈsəːkɪt] N cortocircuito ▶ VT cortocircuitare ▶ VI fare cortocircuito

shortcoming [ˈʃɔːtkʌmɪŋ] N difetto

shortcrust pastry [ˈʃɔːtkrʌst-], **short pastry** N (BRIT) pasta frolla

shortcut [ˈʃɔːtkʌt] N scorciatoia

shorten [ˈʃɔːtn] VT accorciare, ridurre

shortening [ˈʃɔːtnɪŋ] N grasso per pasticceria

shortfall [ˈʃɔːtfɔːl] N deficit m inv

shorthand [ˈʃɔːthænd] N (BRIT) stenografia; **to take sth down in ~** stenografare qc

shorthand notebook N (BRIT) bloc-notes m inv per stenografia

shorthand typist N (BRIT) stenodattilografo(-a)

short list N (BRIT: for job) rosa dei candidati

short-lived [ˈʃɔːtˈlɪvd] ADJ effimero(-a), di breve durata

shortly [ˈʃɔːtlɪ] ADV fra poco

shortness [ˈʃɔːtnɪs] N brevità; insufficienza

shorts [ʃɔːts] NPL (also: **a pair of shorts**) calzoncini mpl

short-sighted [ʃɔːtˈsaɪtɪd] ADJ (BRIT) miope; (fig) poco avveduto(-a)

short-sleeved [ˈʃɔːtsliːvd] ADJ a maniche corte

short-staffed [ʃɔːtˈstɑːft] ADJ a corto di personale

short story N racconto, novella

short-tempered [ʃɔːtˈtɛmpəd] ADJ irascibile

short-term [ˈʃɔːttəːm] ADJ (effect) di or a breve durata; (borrowing) a breve scadenza

short time N (Industry): **to work ~, be on ~** essere or lavorare a orario ridotto

short wave N (Radio) onde fpl corte

shot [ʃɒt] PT, PP of **shoot** ▶ N sparo, colpo; (shotgun pellets) pallottole fpl; (person) tiratore(-trice); (try) prova; (Football) tiro; (injection) iniezione f; (Phot) foto f inv; **like a ~** come un razzo; (very readily) immediatamente; **to fire a ~ at sb/sth** sparare un colpo a qn/qc; **to have a ~ at sth/doing sth** provarci con qc/a fare qc; **a big ~** (col) un pezzo grosso, un papavero; **to get ~ of sb/sth** (col) sbarazzarsi di qn/qc

shotgun [ˈʃɒtɡʌn] N fucile m da caccia

should [ʃud] AUX VB: **I ~ go now** dovrei andare ora; **he ~ be there now** dovrebbe essere arrivato ora; **I ~ go if I were you** se fossi in lei andrei; **I ~ like to** mi piacerebbe; **~ he phone …** se telefonasse …

shoulder [ˈʃəuldəʳ] N spalla; **hard ~** corsia d'emergenza ▶ VT (fig) addossarsi, prendere sulle proprie spalle; **to look over one's ~** guardarsi alle spalle; **to rub shoulders with sb** (fig) essere a contatto con qn; **to give sb the cold ~** (fig) trattare qn con freddezza

shoulder bag N borsa a tracolla

shoulder blade N scapola

shoulder strap N bretella, spallina

shouldn't [ˈʃudnt] = **should not**

shout [ʃaut] N urlo, grido ▶ VT gridare ▶ VI (also: **shout out**) urlare, gridare; **to give sb a ~** chiamare qn gridando
▶ **shout down** VT zittire gridando

shouting [ˈʃautɪŋ] N urli mpl

shouting match N (col) vivace scambio di opinioni

shove [ʃʌv] VT spingere; (col: put): **to ~ sth in** ficcare qc in ▸ N spintone m; **he shoved me out of the way** mi ha spinto da parte
▸ **shove off** VI (Naut) scostarsi

shovel [ˈʃʌvl] N pala ▸ VT spalare

show [ʃəu] (pt **showed**, pp **shown** [ʃəun]) N (of emotion) dimostrazione f, manifestazione f; (semblance) apparenza; (exhibition) mostra, esposizione f; (Theat, Cine) spettacolo; (Comm, Tech) salone m, fiera ▸ VT far vedere, mostrare; (courage etc) dimostrare, dar prova di; (exhibit) esporre ▸ VI vedersi, essere visibile; **to ~ sb to his seat/to the door** accompagnare qn al suo posto/alla porta; **to ~ a profit/loss** (Comm) registrare un utile/una perdita; **it just goes to ~ that ...** il che sta a dimostrare che ...; **to ask for a ~ of hands** chiedere che si voti per alzata di mano; **to be on ~** essere esposto; **it's just for ~** è solo per far scena; **who's running the ~ here?** (col) chi è il padrone qui?
▸ **show in** VT (person) far entrare
▸ **show off** VI (pej) esibirsi, mettersi in mostra ▸ VT (display) mettere in risalto; (pej) mettere in mostra
▸ **show out** VT (person) accompagnare alla porta
▸ **show up** VI (stand out) essere ben visibile; (col: turn up) farsi vedere ▸ VT mettere in risalto; (unmask) smascherare

showbiz [ˈʃəubɪz] N (col) = **show business**

show business N industria dello spettacolo

showcase [ˈʃəukeɪs] N vetrina, bacheca

showdown [ˈʃəudaun] N prova di forza

shower [ˈʃəuəʳ] N doccia; (rain) acquazzone m; (of stones etc) pioggia; (US: party) festa in cui si fanno regali alla persona festeggiata (di fidanzamento ecc) ▸ VI fare la doccia ▸ VT: **to ~ sb with** (gifts, abuse etc) coprire qn di; (missiles) lanciare contro qn una pioggia di; **to have** or **take a ~** fare la doccia

shower cap N cuffia da doccia

shower gel N gel m inv doccia inv

showerproof [ˈʃəuəpruːf] ADJ impermeabile

showery [ˈʃəuərɪ] ADJ (weather) con piogge intermittenti

showground [ˈʃəugraund] N terreno d'esposizione

showing [ˈʃəuɪŋ] N (of film) proiezione f

show jumping N concorso ippico (di salto ad ostacoli)

showman [ˈʃəumən] N (irreg) (at fair, circus) impresario; (fig) attore m

showmanship [ˈʃəumənʃɪp] N abilità d'impresario

shown [ʃəun] PP of **show**

show-off [ˈʃəuɔf] N (col: person) esibizionista mf

showpiece [ˈʃəupiːs] N (of exhibition) pezzo forte; **that hospital is a ~** è un ospedale modello

showroom [ˈʃəurum] N sala d'esposizione

show trial N processo a scopo dimostrativo (spesso ideologico)

showy [ˈʃəuɪ] ADJ vistoso(-a), appariscente

shrank [ʃræŋk] PT of **shrink**

shrapnel [ˈʃræpnl] N shrapnel m

shred [ʃrɛd] N (gen pl) brandello; (fig: of truth, evidence) briciolo ▸ VT fare a brandelli; (Culin) sminuzzare, tagliuzzare; (documents) distruggere, sminuzzare

shredder [ˈʃrɛdəʳ] N (for documents, papers) distruttore m di documenti, sminuzzatrice f

shrew [ʃruː] N (Zool) toporagno; (fig: pej: woman) strega

shrewd [ʃruːd] ADJ astuto(-a), scaltro(-a)

shrewdness [ˈʃruːdnɪs] N astuzia

shriek [ʃriːk] N strillo ▸ VT, VI strillare

shrift [ʃrɪft] N: **to give sb short ~** sbrigare qn

shrill [ʃrɪl] ADJ acuto(-a), stridulo(-a), stridente

shrimp [ʃrɪmp] N gamberetto

shrine [ʃraɪn] N reliquario; (place) santuario

shrink [ʃrɪŋk] (pt **shrank** [ʃræŋk], pp **shrunk** [ʃrʌŋk]) VI restringersi; (fig) ridursi; (also: **shrink away**) ritrarsi ▸ VT (wool) far restringere ▸ N (col, pej) psicanalista mf; **to ~ from doing sth** rifuggire dal fare qc

shrinkage [ˈʃrɪŋkɪdʒ] N restringimento

shrink-wrap [ˈʃrɪŋkræp] VT confezionare con plastica sottile

shrivel [ˈʃrɪvl], **shrivel up** VT raggrinzare, avvizzire ▸ VI raggrinzirsi, avvizzire

shroud [ʃraud] N lenzuolo funebre ▸ VT: **shrouded in mystery** avvolto(-a) nel mistero

Shrove Tuesday [ˈʃrəuv-] N martedì m grasso

shrub [ʃrʌb] N arbusto

shrubbery [ˈʃrʌbərɪ] N arbusti mpl

shrug [ʃrʌg] N scrollata di spalle ▸ VT, VI: **to ~ (one's shoulders)** alzare le spalle, fare spallucce
▸ **shrug off** VT passare sopra a; (cold, illness) sbarazzarsi di

shrunk [ʃrʌŋk] PP of **shrink**

shrunken [ˈʃrʌŋkən] ADJ rattrappito(-a)

shudder [ˈʃʌdəʳ] N brivido ▸ VI rabbrividire

shuffle [ˈʃʌfl] VT (cards) mescolare; **to ~ (one's feet)** strascicare i piedi

shun [ʃʌn] VT sfuggire, evitare

shunt [ʃʌnt] VT (Rail: direct) smistare; (: divert) deviare ▸ VI: **to ~ (to and fro)** fare la spola

shunting yard N fascio di smistamento

shush [ʃuʃ] EXCL zitto(-a)!

shut [ʃʌt] (pt, pp **~**) VT chiudere ▸ VI chiudersi, chiudere
▸ **shut down** VT, VI chiudere definitivamente
▸ **shut off** VT (stop: power) staccare; (: water) chiudere; (: engine) spegnere; (isolate) isolare

S

▶ **shut out** VT (*person, noise, cold*) non far entrare; (*block: view*) impedire, bloccare; (: *memory*) scacciare

▶ **shut up** VI (*col: keep quiet*) stare zitto(-a), fare silenzio ▶ VT (*close*) chiudere; (*silence*) far tacere

shutdown [ˈʃʌtdaʊn] N chiusura

shutter [ˈʃʌtəʳ] N imposta; (*Phot*) otturatore *m*

shuttle [ˈʃʌtl] N spola, navetta; (*space shuttle*) navetta (spaziale); (*also:* **shuttle service**) servizio *m* navetta *inv* ▶ VI (*vehicle, person*) fare la spola ▶ VT (*to and fro: passengers*) portare (avanti e indietro)

shuttlecock [ˈʃʌtlkɔk] N volano

shuttle diplomacy N frequenti mediazioni *fpl* diplomatiche

shy [ʃaɪ] ADJ timido(-a) ▶ VI: **to ~ away from doing sth** (*fig*) rifuggire dal fare qc; **to fight ~ of** tenersi alla larga da; **to be ~ of doing sth** essere restio a fare qc

shyness [ˈʃaɪnɪs] N timidezza

Siam [saɪˈæm] N Siam *m*

Siamese [saɪəˈmiːz] ADJ: **~ cat** gatto siamese; **~ twins** fratelli *mpl* (*or* sorelle *fpl*) siamesi

Siberia [saɪˈbɪərɪə] N Siberia

sibling [ˈsɪblɪŋ] N (*formal*) fratello/sorella

Sicilian [sɪˈsɪlɪən] ADJ, N siciliano(-a)

Sicily [ˈsɪsɪlɪ] N Sicilia

sick [sɪk] ADJ (*ill*) malato(-a); (*humour*) macabro(-a); **to be ~** (*vomiting*) vomitare; **to feel ~** avere la nausea; **to be ~ of** (*fig*) averne abbastanza di; **a ~ person** un malato; **to be (off) ~** essere assente perché malato; **to fall** *or* **take ~** ammalarsi

sickbag [ˈsɪkbæg] N sacchetto (*da usarsi in caso di malessere*)

sick bay N infermeria

sick building syndrome N *malattia causata da mancanza di ventilazione e luce naturale*

sicken [ˈsɪkn] VT nauseare ▶ VI: **to be sickening for sth** (*cold, flu etc*) covare qc

sickening [ˈsɪknɪŋ] ADJ (*fig*) disgustoso(-a), rivoltante

sickle [ˈsɪkl] N falcetto

sick leave N congedo per malattia

sickle-cell anaemia [ˈsɪklsɛl-] N anemia drepanocitica

sickly [ˈsɪklɪ] ADJ malaticcio(-a); (*causing nausea*) nauseante

sickness [ˈsɪknɪs] N malattia; (*vomiting*) vomito

sickness benefit N indennità di malattia

sick pay N sussidio per malattia

sickroom [ˈsɪkruːm] N stanza di malato

side [saɪd] N (*gen*) lato; (*of person, animal*) fianco; (*of lake*) riva; (*face, surface: gen*) faccia; (: *of paper*) facciata; (*fig: aspect*) aspetto, lato; (*team: Sport*) squadra; (: *Pol etc*) parte *f* ▶ CPD (*door, entrance*) laterale ▶ VI: **to ~ with sb** parteggiare per qn, prendere le parti di qn; **by the ~ of** a fianco di;

(*road*) sul ciglio di; **~ by ~** fianco a fianco; **to take sides (with)** schierarsi (con); **the right/wrong ~** il dritto/rovescio; **from ~ to ~** da una parte all'altra; **~ of beef** quarto di bue

sidebar [ˈsaɪdbɑːʳ] N (*on webpage*) barra *f* laterale

sideboard [ˈsaɪdbɔːd] N credenza

sideboards [ˈsaɪdbɔːdz], (*US*) **sideburns** [ˈsaɪdbəːnz] NPL (*whiskers*) basette *fpl*

sidecar [ˈsaɪdkɑːʳ] N sidecar *m inv*

side dish N contorno

side drum N (*Mus*) piccolo tamburo

side effect N (*Med*) effetto collaterale

sidekick [ˈsaɪdkɪk] N (*col*) compagno(-a)

sidelight [ˈsaɪdlaɪt] N (*Aut*) luce *f* di posizione

sideline [ˈsaɪdlaɪn] N (*Sport*) linea laterale; (*fig*) attività secondaria

sidelong [ˈsaɪdlɔŋ] ADJ obliquo(-a); **to give a ~ glance at sth** guardare qc con la coda dell'occhio

side order N contorno (*pietanza*)

side plate N piattino

side road N strada secondaria

sidesaddle [ˈsaɪdsædl] ADV all'amazzone

side show N attrazione *f*

sidestep [ˈsaɪdstɛp] VT (*question*) eludere; (*problem*) scavalcare ▶ VI (*Boxing etc*) spostarsi di lato

side street N traversa

sidetrack [ˈsaɪdtræk] VT (*fig*) distrarre

sidewalk [ˈsaɪdwɔːk] N (*US*) marciapiede *m*

sideways [ˈsaɪdweɪz] ADV (*move*) di lato, di fianco; (*look*) con la coda dell'occhio

siding [ˈsaɪdɪŋ] N (*Rail*) binario di raccordo

sidle [ˈsaɪdl] VI: **to ~ up (to)** avvicinarsi furtivamente (a)

SIDS N (= *sudden infant death syndrome*) = **cot death**

siege [siːdʒ] N assedio; **to lay ~ to** porre l'assedio a

siege economy N economia da stato d'assedio

Sierra Leone [sɪˈɛrəlɪˈəʊn] N Sierra Leone *f*

sieve [sɪv] N setaccio ▶ VT setacciare

sift [sɪft] VT passare al crivello; (*fig*) vagliare ▶ VI: **to ~ through** esaminare minuziosamente

sigh [saɪ] N sospiro ▶ VI sospirare

sight [saɪt] N (*faculty*) vista; (*spectacle*) spettacolo; (*on gun*) mira ▶ VT avvistare; **in ~** in vista; **on ~** a vista; **out of ~** non visibile; **at first ~** a prima vista; **to catch ~ of sth/sb** scorgere qc/qn; **to lose ~ of sb/sth** perdere di vista qn/qc; **to set one's sights on sth/on doing sth** mirare a qc/a fare qc; **at ~** a vista; **I know her by ~** la conosco di vista

sighted [ˈsaɪtɪd] ADJ che ha il dono della vista; **partially ~** parzialmente cieco

sightseeing [ˈsaɪtsiːɪŋ] N giro turistico; **to go ~** visitare una località

sightseer [ˈsaɪtsiːə^r] N turista *mf*

sign [saɪn] N segno; (*with hand etc*) segno, gesto; (*notice*) insegna, cartello; (*road sign*) segnale *m* ▶VT firmare; (*player*) ingaggiare; **as a ~ of** in segno di; **it's a good/bad ~** è buon/brutto segno; **to show signs/no ~ of doing sth** accennare/non accennare a fare qc; **plus/minus ~** segno del più/meno; **to ~ one's name** firmare, apporre la propria firma
▶**sign away** VT (*rights etc*) cedere (con una firma)
▶**sign for** VT FUS (*item*) firmare per l'accettazione di
▶**sign in** VI firmare il registro (all'arrivo)
▶**sign off** VI (*Radio, TV*) chiudere le trasmissioni
▶**sign on** VI (*Mil etc: enlist*) arruolarsi; (*as unemployed*) iscriversi sulla lista (dell'ufficio di collocamento); (*begin work*) prendere servizio; (*enrol*): **to ~ on for a course** iscriversi a un corso ▶VT (*Mil*) arruolare; (*employee*) assumere
▶**sign out** VI firmare il registro (alla partenza)
▶**sign over** VT: **to ~ sth over to sb** cedere qc con scrittura legale a qn
▶**sign up** VT arruolare; (*Mil: recruits*) reclutare; (*player*) ingaggiare ▶VI arruolarsi; (*for course*) iscriversi

signal [ˈsɪgnl] N segnale *m* ▶VT (*person*) fare segno a; (*message*) comunicare per mezzo di segnali ▶VI (*Aut*) segnalare, mettere la freccia; **to ~ to sb (to do sth)** fare segno a qn (di fare qc); **to ~ a left/right turn** (*Aut*) segnalare un cambiamento di direzione a sinistra/destra

signal box N (*Rail*) cabina di manovra

signalman [ˈsɪgnlmən] N (*irreg*) (*Rail*) deviatore *m*

signatory [ˈsɪgnətərɪ] N firmatario(-a)

signature [ˈsɪgnətʃə^r] N firma

signature tune N sigla musicale

signet ring [ˈsɪgnət-] N anello con sigillo

significance [sɪgˈnɪfɪkəns] N (*of remark*) significato; (*of event*) importanza; **that is of no ~** ciò non ha importanza

significant [sɪgˈnɪfɪkənt] ADJ (*improvement, amount*) notevole; (*discovery, event*) importante; (*evidence, smile*) significativo(-a); **it is ~ that ...** è significativo che ...

significantly [sɪgˈnɪfɪkəntlɪ] ADV (*smile*) in modo eloquente; (*improve, increase*) considerevolmente, decisamente

signify [ˈsɪgnɪfaɪ] VT significare

sign language N linguaggio dei muti

signpost [ˈsaɪnpəust] N cartello indicatore

Sikh [siːk] ADJ, N sikh (*mf*) *inv*

silage [ˈsaɪlɪdʒ] N insilato

silence [ˈsaɪlns] N silenzio ▶VT far tacere, ridurre al silenzio

silencer [ˈsaɪlənsə^r] N (*on gun, BRIT Aut*) silenziatore *m*

silent [ˈsaɪlnt] ADJ silenzioso(-a); (*film*) muto(-a); **to keep** *or* **remain ~** tacere, stare zitto(-a)

silently [ˈsaɪlntlɪ] ADV silenziosamente, in silenzio

silent partner N (*Comm*) socio accomandante

silhouette [sɪluːˈɛt] N silhouette *f inv* ▶VT: **to be silhouetted against** stagliarsi contro

silicon [ˈsɪlɪkən] N silicio

silicon chip [ˈsɪlɪkən-] N chip *m inv* (al silicio)

silicone [ˈsɪlɪkəun] N silicone *m*

silk [sɪlk] N seta ▶CPD di seta

silky [ˈsɪlkɪ] ADJ di seta, come la seta

sill [sɪl] N (*windowsill*) davanzale *m*; (*Aut*) predellino

silly [ˈsɪlɪ] ADJ stupido(-a), sciocco(-a); **to do something ~** fare una sciocchezza

silo [ˈsaɪləu] N silo

silt [sɪlt] N limo

silver [ˈsɪlvə^r] N argento; (*money*) monete da 5, 10, 20 o 50 pence; (*also:* **silverware**) argenteria ▶CPD d'argento

silver foil, (BRIT) **silver paper** N carta argentata, (carta) stagnola

silver-plated [sɪlvəˈpleɪtɪd] ADJ argentato(-a)

silversmith [ˈsɪlvəsmɪθ] N argentiere *m*

silverware [ˈsɪlvəwɛə^r] N argenteria, argento

silvery [ˈsɪlvərɪ] ADJ (*colour*) argenteo(-a); (*sound*) argentino(-a)

SIM card [ˈsɪm-] N (*Tel: = Subscriber Identity Module card*) SIM card *f inv*

similar [ˈsɪmɪlə^r] ADJ: **~ (to)** simile (a)

similarity [sɪmɪˈlærɪtɪ] N somiglianza, rassomiglianza

similarly [ˈsɪmɪləlɪ] ADV (*in a similar way*) allo stesso modo; (*as is similar*) così pure

simile [ˈsɪmɪlɪ] N similitudine *f*

simmer [ˈsɪmə^r] VI cuocere a fuoco lento ▶**simmer down** VI (*fig: col*) calmarsi

simper [ˈsɪmpə^r] VI fare lo(la) smorfioso(-a)

simpering [ˈsɪmpərɪŋ] ADJ lezioso(-a), smorfioso(-a)

simple [ˈsɪmpl] ADJ semplice; **the ~ truth** la pura verità

simple interest N (*Math, Comm*) interesse *m* semplice

simple-minded [sɪmplˈmaɪndɪd] ADJ sempliciotto(-a)

simpleton [ˈsɪmpltən] N semplicione(-a), sempliciotto(-a)

simplicity [sɪmˈplɪsɪtɪ] N semplicità

simplification [sɪmplɪfɪˈkeɪʃən] N semplificazione *f*

simplify [ˈsɪmplɪfaɪ] VT semplificare

simply [ˈsɪmplɪ] ADV semplicemente

simulate [ˈsɪmjuleɪt] VT fingere, simulare

simulation [sɪmjuˈleɪʃən] N simulazione f

simultaneous [sɪməlˈteɪnɪəs] ADJ simultane-o(-a)

simultaneously [sɪməlˈteɪnɪəslɪ] ADV simultaneamente, contemporaneamente

sin [sɪn] N peccato ▶ VI peccare

Sinai [ˈsaɪnaɪ] N Sinai m

since [sɪns] ADV da allora ▶ PREP da ▶ CONJ (time) da quando; (because) poiché, dato che; **~ then**, **ever ~** da allora; **~ Monday** da lunedì; **(ever) ~ I arrived** (fin) da quando sono arrivato

> When describing a state or action that started in the past and is still continuing, translate since by **da** and use the present tense of the Italian verb.
> I've been here since the beginning of June. **Sono qua dall'inizio di giugno**.
> We've been waiting for him since three o'clock. **Siamo qui ad aspettarlo dalle tre**.

sincere [sɪnˈsɪər] ADJ sincero(-a)

sincerely [sɪnˈsɪəlɪ] ADV sinceramente; **Yours ~** (at end of letter) distinti saluti

sincerity [sɪnˈsɛrɪtɪ] N sincerità

sine [saɪn] N (Math) seno

sinew [ˈsɪnjuː] N tendine m ■ **sinews** NPL (muscles) muscoli mpl

sinful [ˈsɪnful] ADJ peccaminoso(-a)

sing [sɪŋ] (pt **sang** [sæŋ], pp **sung** [sʌŋ]) VT, VI cantare

Singapore [sɪŋgəˈpɔːr] N Singapore f

singe [sɪndʒ] VT bruciacchiare

singer [ˈsɪŋər] N cantante mf

Singhalese [sɪŋəˈliːz] ADJ = **Sinhalese**

singing [ˈsɪŋɪŋ] N (of person, bird) canto; (of kettle, bullet, in ears) fischio

single [ˈsɪŋgl] ADJ solo(-a), unico(-a); (unmarried: man) celibe; (: woman) nubile; (not double) semplice ▶ N (BRIT: also: **single ticket**) biglietto di (sola) andata; (record) 45 giri m inv; **not a ~ one was left** non ne è rimasto nemmeno uno; **every ~ day** tutti i santi giorni; see also **singles** ▶ **single out** VT scegliere; (distinguish) distinguere

single bed N letto a una piazza

single-breasted [ˈsɪŋglbrɛstɪd] ADJ a un petto

Single European Market N: **the ~** il Mercato Unico

single file N: **in ~** in fila indiana

single-handed [sɪŋglˈhændɪd] ADV senza aiuto, da solo(-a)

single-minded [sɪŋglˈmaɪndɪd] ADJ tenace, risoluto(-a)

single parent N ragazzo padre/ragazza madre; **~ family** famiglia monoparentale

single room N camera singola

singles [ˈsɪŋglz] NPL (Tennis) singolo; (single people) single mf

singles bar N (esp US) bar m inv per single

single-sex school [ˈsɪŋglsɛks-] N (for boys) scuola maschile; (for girls) scuola femminile

singlet [ˈsɪŋglɪt] N canottiera

singly [ˈsɪŋglɪ] ADV separatamente

singsong [ˈsɪŋsɔŋ] ADJ (tone) cantilenante ▶ N (songs): **to have a ~** farsi una cantata

singular [ˈsɪŋgjulər] ADJ (Ling) singolare; (unusual) strano(-a), singolare ▶ N (Ling) singolare m; **in the feminine ~** al femminile singolare

singularly [ˈsɪŋgjuləlɪ] ADV stranamente

Sinhalese [sɪnhəˈliːz] ADJ singalese

sinister [ˈsɪnɪstər] ADJ sinistro(-a)

sink [sɪŋk] (pt **sank** [sæŋk], pp **sunk** [sʌŋk]) N lavandino, acquaio ▶ VT (ship) (fare) affondare, colare a picco; (foundations) scavare; (piles etc): **to ~ sth into** conficcare qc in ▶ VI affondare, andare a fondo; (ground etc) cedere, avvallarsi; **my heart sank** mi sentii venir meno; **he sank into a chair/the mud** sprofondò in una poltrona/nel fango
▶ **sink in** VI penetrare; **it took a long time to ~ in** ci ho (or ha etc) messo molto a capirlo

sinking [ˈsɪŋkɪŋ] ADJ: **that ~ feeling** una stretta allo stomaco

sinking fund N (Comm) fondo d'ammortamento

sink unit N blocco lavello

sinner [ˈsɪnər] N peccatore(-trice)

Sinn Féin [ʃɪnˈfeɪn] N movimento separatista irlandese

sinuous [ˈsɪnjuəs] ADJ sinuoso(-a)

sinus [ˈsaɪnəs] N (Anat) seno

sip [sɪp] N sorso ▶ VT sorseggiare

siphon [ˈsaɪfən] N sifone m ▶ VT (funds) trasferire
▶ **siphon off** VT travasare (con un sifone)

sir [sər] N signore m; **S~ John Smith** Sir John Smith; **yes ~** sì, signore; **Dear S~** (in letter) Egregio signor (followed by name); **Dear Sirs** Spettabile ditta

siren [ˈsaɪərn] N sirena

sirloin [ˈsəːlɔɪn] N controfiletto

sirloin steak N bistecca di controfiletto

sirocco [sɪˈrɔkəu] N scirocco

sisal [ˈsaɪsəl] N sisal f inv

sissy [ˈsɪsɪ] N (!) femminuccia

sister [ˈsɪstər] N sorella; (nun) suora; (BRIT: nurse) infermiera f caposala inv ▶ CPD: **~ organization** organizzazione f affine; **~ ship** nave f gemella

sister-in-law [ˈsɪstərɪnlɔː] N cognata

sit [sɪt] (pt, pp **sat** [sæt]) VI sedere, sedersi; (dress etc) cadere; (assembly) essere in seduta; (for painter) posare ▶ VT (exam) sostenere, dare; **to ~ on a committee** far parte di una commissione

▶ **sit about, sit around** VI star seduto(-a) (senza far nulla)

▶ **sit back** VI (in seat) appoggiarsi allo schienale

▶ **sit down** VI sedersi; **to be sitting down** essere seduto(-a)

▶ **sit in** VI: **to ~ in on a discussion** assistere ad una discussione

▶ **sit on** VT FUS (jury, committee) far parte di

▶ **sit up** VI tirarsi su a sedere; (not go to bed) stare alzato(-a) fino a tardi

sitcom ['sɪtkɔm] N ABBR (TV: = situation comedy) sceneggiato a episodi (comico)

sit-down ['sɪtdaun] ADJ: **~ strike** sciopero bianco (con occupazione della fabbrica); **a ~ meal** un pranzo

site [saɪt] N posto; (also: **building site**) cantiere m; (Comput) sito ▶ VT situare

sit-in ['sɪtɪn] N (demonstration) sit-in m inv

siting ['saɪtɪŋ] N ubicazione f

sitter ['sɪtə^r] N (for painter) modello(-a); (also: **baby sitter**) babysitter mf inv

sitting ['sɪtɪŋ] N (of assembly etc) seduta; (in canteen) turno

sitting member N (Pol) deputato(-a) in carica

sitting room N soggiorno

sitting tenant N (BRIT) attuale affittuario(-a)

situate ['sɪtjueɪt] VT collocare

situated ['sɪtjueɪtɪd] ADJ situato(-a)

situation [sɪtju'eɪʃən] N situazione f; (job) lavoro; (location) posizione f; **"situations vacant/wanted"** (BRIT) "offerte/domande di impiego"

situation comedy N (Theat) commedia di situazione

six [sɪks] NUM sei

six-pack ['sɪkspæk] N confezione f da sei

sixteen [sɪks'tiːn] NUM sedici

sixteenth [sɪks'tiːnθ] NUM sedicesimo(-a)

sixth [sɪksθ] NUM sesto(-a) ▶ N: **the upper/lower ~** (BRIT Scol) l'ultimo/il penultimo anno di scuola superiore

sixth form N (BRIT) ultimo biennio delle scuole superiori

sixth-form college N istituto che offre corsi di preparazione all'esame di maturità per ragazzi dai 16 ai 18 anni

sixtieth ['sɪkstɪθ] NUM sessantesimo(-a) ▶ PRON (in series) sessantesimo(-a); (fraction) sessantesimo

sixty ['sɪkstɪ] NUM sessanta

size [saɪz] N dimensioni fpl; (of clothing) taglia, misura; (of shoes) numero; (glue) colla; **I take ~ 14 in a dress** = porto la 44 di vestiti; **I'd like the small/large ~** (of soap powder etc) vorrei la confezione piccola/grande

▶ **size up** VT giudicare, farsi un'idea di

sizeable ['saɪzəbl] ADJ considerevole

sizzle ['sɪzl] VI sfrigolare

SK ABBR (CANADA) = **Saskatchewan**

skate [skeɪt] N pattino; (fish: pl inv) razza ▶ VI pattinare

▶ **skate over, skate around** VT (problem, issue) prendere alla leggera, prendere sottogamba

skateboard ['skeɪtbɔːd] N skateboard m inv

skateboarding N skateboard m inv

skatepark ['skeɪtpɑːk] N skatepark m inv

skater ['skeɪtə^r] N pattinatore(-trice)

skating ['skeɪtɪŋ] N pattinaggio

skating rink N pista di pattinaggio

skeleton ['skɛlɪtn] N scheletro

skeleton key N passe-partout m inv

skeleton staff N personale m ridotto

skeptic etc ['skɛptɪk] (US) = **sceptic** etc

sketch [skɛtʃ] N (drawing) schizzo, abbozzo; (Theat etc) scenetta comica, sketch m inv ▶ VT abbozzare, schizzare

sketch book N album m inv per schizzi

sketch pad N blocco per schizzi

sketchy ['skɛtʃɪ] ADJ incompleto(-a), lacunoso(-a)

skew [skjuː] N (BRIT): **on the ~** di traverso

skewer ['skjuːə^r] N spiedo

ski [skiː] N sci m inv ▶ VI sciare

ski boot N scarpone m da sci

skid [skɪd] N slittamento; (sideways slip) sbandamento ▶ VI slittare; sbandare; **to go into a ~** slittare; sbandare

skid mark N segno della frenata

skier ['skiːə^r] N sciatore(-trice)

skiing ['skiːɪŋ] N sci m

ski instructor N maestro(-a) di sci

ski jump N (ramp) trampolino; (event) salto con gli sci

skilful, (US) **skillful** ['skɪlful] ADJ abile

skilfully, (US) **skillfully** ['skɪlfəlɪ] ADV abilmente

ski lift N sciovia

skill [skɪl] N abilità f inv, capacità f inv; (technique) tecnica

skilled [skɪld] ADJ esperto(-a); (worker) qualificato(-a), specializzato(-a)

skillet ['skɪlɪt] N padella

skillful ['skɪlful] ADJ (US) = **skilful**

skillfully ['skɪlfəlɪ] ADV (US) = **skilfully**

skim [skɪm] VT (milk) scremare; (soup) schiumare; (glide over) sfiorare ▶ VI: **to ~ through** (fig) scorrere, dare una scorsa a

skimmed milk [skɪmd-], (US) **skim milk** N latte m scremato

skimp [skɪmp] VI: **to ~ on** (work) fare alla carlona; (cloth etc) lesinare su

skimpy ['skɪmpɪ] ADJ misero(-a); striminzito(-a); frugale

S

skin [skɪn] N pelle f; (of fruit, vegetable) buccia; (on pudding, paint) crosta ▶ VT (fruit etc) sbucciare; (animal) scuoiare, spellare; **wet** or **soaked to the ~** bagnato fino al midollo

skin cancer N cancro alla pelle

skin-deep [skɪn'di:p] ADJ superficiale

skin diver N subacqueo(-a)

skin diving N nuoto subacqueo

skinflint ['skɪnflɪnt] N taccagno(-a), tirchio(-a)

skin graft N innesto epidermico

skinhead ['skɪnhed] N skinhead mf inv

skinny ['skɪnɪ] ADJ molto magro(-a), pelle e ossa inv

skin test N prova di reazione cutanea

skintight ['skɪntaɪt] ADJ aderente

skip [skɪp] N saltello, balzo; (BRIT: container) benna ▶ VI saltare; (with rope) saltare la corda ▶ VT (pass over) saltare; **to ~ school** marinare la scuola

ski pants NPL pantaloni mpl da sci

ski pass N ski pass m inv

ski pole N racchetta (da sci)

skipper ['skɪpə'] N (Naut, Sport) capitano

skipping rope ['skɪpɪŋ-], (US) **skip rope** N corda per saltare

ski resort N località f inv sciistica

skirmish ['skə:mɪʃ] N scaramuccia

skirt [skə:t] N gonna, sottana ▶ VT fiancheggiare, costeggiare

skirting board ['skə:tɪŋ-] N (BRIT) zoccolo

ski run N pista (da sci)

ski slope N pista da sci

ski suit N tuta da sci

skit [skɪt] N parodia; scenetta satirica

ski tow N = **ski lift**

skittle ['skɪtl] N birillo ▪ **skittles** N (game) (gioco dei) birilli mpl

skive [skaɪv] VI (BRIT col) fare il(la) lavativo(-a)

skulk [skʌlk] VI muoversi furtivamente

skull [skʌl] N cranio, teschio

skullcap ['skʌlkæp] N (worn by Jews) zucchetto; (worn by Pope) papalina

skunk [skʌŋk] N moffetta

sky [skaɪ] N cielo; **to praise sb to the skies** portare alle stelle qn

sky-blue [skaɪ'blu:] ADJ azzurro(-a), celeste

sky-diving ['skaɪdaɪvɪŋ] N caduta libera, paracadutismo acrobatico

sky-high [skaɪ'haɪ] ADV (throw) molto in alto ▶ ADJ (col) esorbitante; **prices have gone ~** (col) i prezzi sono saliti alle stelle

skylark ['skaɪlɑ:k] N allodola

skylight ['skaɪlaɪt] N lucernario

skyline ['skaɪlaɪn] N (horizon) orizzonte m; (of city) profilo

sky marshal N agente mf a bordo

Skype® [skaɪp] (Internet, Tel) N Skype® m ▶ VT: **to ~ sb** chiamare qn con Skype

skyscraper ['skaɪskreɪpə'] N grattacielo

slab [slæb] N lastra; (of wood) tavola; (of meat, cheese) fetta

slack [slæk] ADJ (loose) allentato(-a); (slow) lento(-a); (careless) negligente; (Comm: market) stagnante; (: demand) scarso(-a); (period) morto(-a) ▶ N (in rope etc) parte f non tesa; **business is ~** l'attività commerciale è scarsa; see also **slacks**

slacken ['slækn], **slacken off** VI rallentare, diminuire ▶ VT allentare; (pressure) diminuire

slacks [slæks] NPL (trousers) pantaloni mpl

slag [slæg] N scorie fpl

slag heap N ammasso di scorie

slain [sleɪn] PP of **slay**

slake [sleɪk] VT (one's thirst) spegnere

slalom ['slɑ:ləm] N slalom m inv

slam [slæm] VT (door) sbattere; (throw) scaraventare; (criticize) stroncare ▶ VI sbattere

slammer ['slæmə'] N: **the ~** (col) la gattabuia

slander ['slɑ:ndə'] N calunnia; (Law) diffamazione f ▶ VT calunniare; diffamare

slanderous ['slɑ:ndrəs] ADJ calunnioso(-a); diffamatorio(-a)

slang [slæŋ] N gergo, slang m

slanging match ['slæŋɪŋ-] N (BRIT col) rissa verbale

slant [slɑ:nt] N pendenza, inclinazione f; (fig) angolazione f, punto di vista

slanted ['slɑ:ntɪd] ADJ tendenzioso(-a)

slanting ['slɑ:ntɪŋ] ADJ in pendenza, inclinato(-a)

slap [slæp] N manata, pacca; (on face) schiaffo ▶ VT dare una manata a; schiaffeggiare ▶ ADV (directly) in pieno; **it fell ~ in the middle** cadde proprio nel mezzo; **~ a coat of paint on it** dagli una mano di vernice

slapdash ['slæpdæʃ] ADJ abborracciato(-a)

slaphead ['slæphed] N (BRIT col) testa pelata (persona)

slapstick ['slæpstɪk] N (comedy) farsa grossolana

slap-up ['slæpʌp] ADJ (BRIT): **a ~ meal** un pranzo (or una cena) coi fiocchi

slash [slæʃ] VT tagliare; (face) sfregiare; (fig: prices) ridurre drasticamente, tagliare

slat [slæt] N (of wood) stecca

slate [sleɪt] N ardesia; (piece) lastra di ardesia ▶ VT (fig: criticize) stroncare, distruggere

slaughter ['slɔ:tə'] N (of animals) macellazione f; (of people) strage f, massacro ▶ VT (animal) macellare; (people) trucidare, massacrare

slaughterhouse ['slɔ:təhaus] N macello, mattatoio

Slav [slɑːv] ADJ, N slavo(-a)

slave [sleɪv] N schiavo(-a) ▶ VI (*also:* **slave away**) lavorare come uno schiavo; **to ~ (away) at sth/at doing sth** ammazzarsi di fatica *or* sgobbare per qc/per fare qc

slave driver N (*col, pej*) schiavista *mf*

slave labour N lavoro degli schiavi; (*fig*): **we're just ~ here** siamo solamente sfruttati qui dentro

slaver ['slævə\`] VI (*dribble*) sbavare

slavery ['sleɪvərɪ] N schiavitù *f*

Slavic ['slævɪk] ADJ slavo(-a)

slavish ['sleɪvɪʃ] ADJ servile; pedissequo(-a)

slavishly ['sleɪvɪʃlɪ] ADV (*copy*) pedissequa-mente

Slavonic [slə'vɒnɪk] ADJ slavo(-a)

slay [sleɪ] (*pt* **slew** [sluː], *pp* **slain** [sleɪn]) VT (*literary*) uccidere

sleazy ['sliːzɪ] ADJ trasandato(-a)

sled [slɛd] (*US*) = **sledge**

sledge [slɛdʒ] N slitta

sledgehammer ['slɛdʒhæmə\`] N martello da fabbro

sleek [sliːk] ADJ (*hair, fur*) lucido(-a), lucente; (*car, boat*) slanciato(-a), affusolato(-a)

sleep [sliːp] (*pt, pp* **slept** [slɛpt]) N sonno ▶ VI dormire ▶ VT: **we can ~ 4** abbiamo 4 posti letto, possiamo alloggiare 4 persone; **to have a good night's ~** farsi una bella dormita; **to go to ~** addormentarsi; **to ~ lightly** avere il sonno leggero; **to put to ~** (*patient*) far addormentare; (*animal: euphemism: kill*) abbattere; **to ~ with sb** (*euphemism: have sex*) andare a letto con qn
▶ **sleep in** VI (*lie late*) alzarsi tardi; (*oversleep*) dormire fino a tardi
▶ **sleep together** VI (*have sex*) andare a letto insieme

sleeper ['sliːpə\`] N (*person*) dormiente *mf*; (BRIT: *Rail: on track*) traversina; (: *train*) treno di vagoni letto

sleepily ['sliːpɪlɪ] ADV con aria assonnata

sleeping ['sliːpɪŋ] ADJ addormentato(-a)

sleeping bag N sacco a pelo

sleeping car N vagone *m* letto *inv*, carrozza *f* letto *inv*

sleeping partner N (BRIT *Comm*) = **silent partner**

sleeping pill N sonnifero

sleeping sickness N malattia del sonno

sleepless ['sliːplɪs] ADJ (*person*) insonne; **a ~ night** una notte in bianco

sleeplessness ['sliːplɪsnɪs] N insonnia

sleepover ['sliːpəuvə\`] N il dormire a casa di amici, usato in riferimento a bambini

sleepwalk ['sliːpwɔːk] VI camminare nel sonno; (*as a habit*) essere sonnambulo(-a)

sleepwalker ['sliːpwɔːkə\`] N sonnambulo(-a)

sleepy ['sliːpɪ] ADJ assonnato(-a), sonnolen-to(-a); (*fig*) addormentato(-a); **to be** *or* **feel ~** avere sonno

sleet [sliːt] N nevischio

sleeve [sliːv] N manica; (*of record*) copertina

> Use **la manica** to refer to a part of a piece of clothing. Use **il manico** to refer to the handle of a saucepan, tool, etc.

sleeveless ['sliːvlɪs] ADJ (*garment*) senza mani-che

sleigh [sleɪ] N slitta

sleight [slaɪt] N: **~ of hand** gioco di destrezza

slender ['slɛndə\`] ADJ snello(-a), sottile; (*not enough*) scarso(-a), esiguo(-a)

slept [slɛpt] PT, PP *of* **sleep**

sleuth [sluːθ] N (*col*) segugio

slew [sluː] VI (BRIT: *also:* **slew round**) girare ▶ PT *of* **slay**

slice [slaɪs] N fetta ▶ VT affettare, tagliare a fette; **sliced bread** pane *m* a cassetta

slick [slɪk] ADJ (*skilful*) brillante; (*insincere*) untuo-so(-a), falso(-a) ▶ N (*also:* **oil slick**) chiazza di petrolio

slid [slɪd] PT, PP *of* **slide**

slide [slaɪd] (*pt, pp* **slid** [slɪd]) N scivolone *m*; (*in playground*) scivolo; (*Phot*) diapositiva; (*microscope slide*) vetrino; (BRIT: *also:* **hair slide**) ferma-glio (per capelli); (*in prices*) caduta ▶ VT far scivolare ▶ VI scivolare; **to let things ~** (*fig*) lasciare andare tutto, trascurare tutto

slide projector N proiettore *m* per diapositive

slide rule N regolo calcolatore

slide show N (*Comput*) diaporama *m*

sliding ['slaɪdɪŋ] ADJ (*door*) scorrevole; **~ roof** (*Aut*) capotte *f inv*

sliding scale N scala mobile

slight [slaɪt] ADJ (*slim*) snello(-a), sottile; (*frail*) delicato(-a), fragile; (*trivial*) insignificante; (*small*) piccolo(-a) ▶ N offesa, affronto ▶ VT (*offend*) offendere, fare un affronto a; **the slightest** il minimo (*or* la minima); **not in the slightest** affatto, neppure per sogno

slightly ['slaɪtlɪ] ADV lievemente, un po'; **~ built** esile

slim [slɪm] ADJ magro(-a), snello(-a) ▶ VI dima-grire; fare *or* seguire una dieta dimagrante

slime [slaɪm] N limo, melma; viscidume *m*

slimming ['slɪmɪŋ] ADJ (*diet, pills*) dimagrante; (*food*) ipocalorico(-a)

slimy ['slaɪmɪ] ADJ (*also fig: person*) viscido(-a); (*covered with mud*) melmoso(-a)

sling [slɪŋ] (*pt, pp* **slung** [slʌŋ]) N (*Med*) fascia al collo; (*for baby*) marsupio ▶ VT lanciare, tirare; **to have one's arm in a ~** avere un braccio al collo

S

slink [slɪŋk] (*pt, pp* **slunk** [slʌŋk]) vi: **to ~ away, ~ off** svignarsela

slinky ['slɪŋkɪ] ADJ (*clothing*) aderente, attillato(-a)

slip [slɪp] N scivolata, scivolone *m*; (*mistake*) errore *m*, sbaglio; (*underskirt*) sottoveste *f*; (*paper*) foglietto; tagliando, scontrino ▶ vT (*slide*) far scivolare ▶ vi (*slide*) scivolare; (*decline*) declinare; **to ~ into/out of** (*move smoothly*) scivolare in/fuori da; **to give sb the ~** sfuggire qn; **a ~ of paper** un foglietto; **a ~ of the tongue** un lapsus linguae; **to ~ sth on/off** infilarsi/togliersi qc; **to let a chance ~ by** lasciarsi scappare un'occasione; **it slipped from her hand** le sfuggì di mano
  ▶ **slip away** vi svignarsela
  ▶ **slip in** vT introdurre casualmente
  ▶ **slip out** vi uscire furtivamente
  ▶ **slip up** vi sbagliarsi

slip-on ['slɪpɔn] ADJ (*gen*) comodo(-a) da mettere; (*shoes*) senza allacciatura

slipped disc ['slɪpt-] N spostamento delle vertebre

slipper ['slɪpər] N pantofola

slippery ['slɪpərɪ] ADJ scivoloso(-a); **it's ~** si scivola

slip road N (*BRIT: to motorway*) rampa di accesso

slipshod ['slɪpʃɔd] ADJ sciatto(-a), trasandato(-a)

slip-up ['slɪpʌp] N granchio (*fig*)

slipway ['slɪpweɪ] N scalo di costruzione

slit [slɪt] (*pt, pp ~*) N fessura, fenditura; (*cut*) taglio; (*tear*) strappo ▶ vT fendere; tagliare; **to ~ sb's throat** tagliare la gola a qn

slither ['slɪðər] vi scivolare, sdrucciolare

sliver ['slɪvər] N (*of glass, wood*) scheggia; (*of cheese, sausage*) fettina

slob [slɔb] N (*pej*) sciattone(-a)

slog [slɔg] (*BRIT*) N faticata ▶ vi lavorare con accanimento, sgobbare

slogan ['sləugən] N motto, slogan *m inv*

slop [slɔp] vi (*also*: **slop over**) traboccare; versarsi ▶ vT spandere; versare ▶ NPL: **slops** acqua sporca; sbobba

slope [sləup] N pendio; (*side of mountain*) versante *m*; (*ski slope*) pista; (*of roof*) pendenza; (*of floor*) inclinazione *f* ▶ vi: **to ~ down** declinare; **to ~ up** essere in salita

sloping ['sləupɪŋ] ADJ inclinato(-a)

sloppy ['slɔpɪ] ADJ (*work*) tirato(-a) via; (*appearance*) sciatto(-a); (*film etc*) sdolcinato(-a)

slosh [slɔʃ] vi (*col*): **to ~ about** *or* **around** (*person*) sguazzare; (*liquid*) guazzare

sloshed [slɔʃt] ADJ (*col: drunk*) sbronzo(-a)

slot [slɔt] N fessura; (*fig: in timetable, Radio, TV*) spazio ▶ vT: **to ~ into** infilare in

sloth [sləuθ] N (*vice*) pigrizia, accidia; (*Zool*) bradipo

slot machine N (*BRIT: vending machine*) distributore *m* automatico; (*for amusement*) slot-machine *f inv*

slot meter N contatore *m* a gettoni

slouch [slautʃ] vi (*when walking*) camminare dinoccolato(-a); **she was slouched in a chair** era sprofondata in una poltrona
  ▶ **slouch about, slouch around** vi (*laze*) oziare

Slovak ['sləuvæk] ADJ slovacco(-a) ▶ N slovacco(-a); (*Ling*) slovacco; **the ~ Republic** la Repubblica Slovacca

Slovakia [sləu'vækɪə] N Slovacchia

Slovakian [sləu'vækɪən] ADJ, N = **Slovak**

Slovene ['sləuviːn] ADJ sloveno(-a) ▶ N sloveno(-a); (*Ling*) sloveno

Slovenia [sləu'viːnɪə] N Slovenia

Slovenian [sləu'viːnɪən] ADJ, N = **Slovene**

slovenly ['slʌvənlɪ] ADJ sciatto(-a), trasandato(-a)

slow [sləu] ADJ lento(-a); (*watch*): **to be ~** essere indietro ▶ ADV lentamente ▶ vT, vi (*also*: **slow down, slow up**) rallentare; **"~"** (*road sign*) "rallentare"; **at a ~ speed** a bassa velocità; **to be ~ to act/decide** essere lento ad agire/a decidere; **my watch is 20 minutes ~** il mio orologio è indietro di 20 minuti; **business is ~** (*Comm*) gli affari procedono a rilento; **to go ~** (*driver*) andare piano; (*in industrial dispute*) fare uno sciopero bianco

slow-acting ['sləu'æktɪŋ] ADJ che agisce lentamente, ad azione lenta

slowly ['sləulɪ] ADV lentamente; **to drive ~** andare piano

slow motion N: **in ~** al rallentatore

slowness ['sləunɪs] N lentezza

sludge [slʌdʒ] N fanghiglia

slug [slʌg] N lumaca; (*bullet*) pallottola

sluggish ['slʌgɪʃ] ADJ lento(-a); (*business, market, sales*) stagnante, fiacco(-a)

sluice [sluːs] N chiusa ▶ vT: **to ~ down** *or* **out** lavare (con abbondante acqua)

slum [slʌm] N catapecchia

slumber ['slʌmbər] N sonno

slump [slʌmp] N crollo, caduta; (*economic*) depressione *f*, crisi *f inv* ▶ vi crollare; **he was slumped over the wheel** era curvo sul volante

slung [slʌŋ] PT, PP *of* **sling**

slunk [slʌŋk] PT, PP *of* **slink**

slur [sləːr] N pronuncia indistinta; (*stigma*) diffamazione *f*, calunnia; (*Mus*) legatura; (*smear*): **~ (on)** macchia (su) ▶ vT pronunciare in modo indistinto; **to cast a ~ on sb** calunniare qn

slurp [sləːp] vT, vi bere rumorosamente ▶ N rumore fatto bevendo

slurred [sləːd] ADJ (*pronunciation*) inarticolato(-a), disarticolato(-a)

slush [slʌʃ] N neve *f* mista a fango

slush fund N fondi *mpl* neri

slushy ['slʌʃɪ] ADJ (*snow*) che si scioglie; (*BRIT fig*) sdolcinato(-a)

slut [slʌt] N donna trasandata, sciattona

sly [slaɪ] ADJ (*smile, remark*) sornione(-a); (*person*) furbo(-a), scaltro(-a); **on the ~** di soppiatto

SM N ABBR (= *sadomasochism*) sadomasochismo

smack [smæk] N (*slap*) pacca; (*on face*) schiaffo ▶ VT schiaffeggiare; (*child*) picchiare ▶ VI: **to ~ of** puzzare di; **to ~ one's lips** fare uno schiocco con le labbra

smacker ['smækə^r] N (*col: kiss*) bacio; (: *BRIT: pound note*) sterlina; (: *US: dollar bill*) dollaro

small [smɔːl] ADJ piccolo(-a); (*in height*) basso(-a); (*letter*) minuscolo(-a) ▶ N: **the ~ of the back** le reni; **to get** *or* **grow smaller** (*stain, town*) rimpicciolire; (*debt, organization, numbers*) ridursi; **to make smaller** (*amount, income*) ridurre; (*garden, object, garment*) rimpicciolire; **in the ~ hours** alle ore piccole; **a ~ shopkeeper** un piccolo negoziante

small ads NPL (*BRIT*) piccoli annunci *mpl*

small arms NPL armi *fpl* portatili *or* leggere

small business N piccola impresa

small change N moneta, spiccioli *mpl*

smallholder ['smɔːlhəʊldə^r] N (*BRIT*) piccolo proprietario

smallholding ['smɔːlhəʊldɪŋ] N (*BRIT*) piccola tenuta

smallish ['smɔːlɪʃ] ADJ piccolino(-a)

small-minded [smɔːl'maɪndɪd] ADJ meschino(-a)

smallpox ['smɔːlpɔks] N vaiolo

small print N caratteri *mpl* piccoli; (*on document*) parte scritta in piccolo

small-scale ['smɔːlskeɪl] ADJ (*map, model*) in scala ridotta; (*business, farming*) modesto(-a)

small talk N chiacchiere *fpl*

small-time ['smɔːltaɪm] ADJ (*col*) da poco; **a ~ thief** un ladro di polli

small-town ['smɔːltaun] ADJ (*pej*) provinciale, di paese

smarmy ['smɑːmɪ] ADJ (*BRIT pej*) untuoso(-a), strisciante

smart [smɑːt] ADJ elegante; (*fashionable*) alla moda; (*clever*) intelligente; (*quick*) sveglio(-a) ▶ VI bruciare; **the ~ set** il bel mondo; **to look ~** essere elegante; **my eyes are smarting** mi bruciano gli occhi

smartcard N smartcard *f inv*, carta intelligente

smarten up ['smɑːtn-] VI farsi bello(-a) ▶ VT (*people*) fare bello(-a); (*things*) abbellire

smartphone N smartphone *m inv*

smartwatch ['smɑːtwɔtʃ] N smartwatch *m inv*

smash [smæʃ] N (*also:* **smash-up**) scontro, collisione *f*; (*sound*) fracasso; (*also:* **smash-hit**) successone *m* ▶ VT frantumare, fracassare;

(*opponent*) annientare, schiacciare; (*hopes*) distruggere; (*Sport: record*) battere ▶ VI frantumarsi, andare in pezzi

▶ **smash up** VT (*car*) sfasciare; (*room*) distruggere

smash-hit [smæʃ'hɪt] N successone *m*

smashing ['smæʃɪŋ] ADJ (*col*) favoloso(-a), formidabile

smattering ['smætərɪŋ] N: **a ~ of** un'infarinatura di

SME N ABBR (= *small and medium-sized enterprise*) PMI *f inv* (= *Piccola e Media Impresa*)

smear [smɪə^r] N macchia; (*Med*) striscio; (*insult*) calunnia ▶ VT ungere; (*make dirty*) sporcare; (*fig*) denigrare, diffamare; **his hands were smeared with oil/ink** aveva le mani sporche di olio/inchiostro

smear campaign N campagna diffamatoria

smear test N (*BRIT Med*) Pap-test *m inv*

smell [smɛl] (*pt, pp* **smelt** [smɛlt], **smelled** [smɛld]) N odore *m*; (*sense*) olfatto, odorato ▶ VT sentire (l')odore di ▶ VI (*pej*) puzzare, avere un cattivo odore; (*food etc*): **to ~ (of)** avere odore (di); **it smells good** ha un buon odore

smelly ['smɛlɪ] ADJ puzzolente

smelt [smɛlt] PT, PP *of* **smell** ▶ VT (*ore*) fondere

smile [smaɪl] N sorriso ▶ VI sorridere

smiling ['smaɪlɪŋ] ADJ sorridente

smirk [sməːk] N sorriso furbo; sorriso compiaciuto

smith [smɪθ] N fabbro

smithy ['smɪðɪ] N fucina

smitten ['smɪtn] ADJ: **~ with** colpito(-a) da

smock [smɔk] N grembiule *m*, camice *m*

smog [smɔg] N smog *m inv*

smoke [sməuk] N fumo ▶ VT, VI fumare; **to have a ~** fumarsi una sigaretta; **do you ~?** fumi?; **to go up in ~** (*house etc*) bruciare, andare distrutto dalle fiamme; (*fig*) andare in fumo

smoke alarm N rivelatore *f* di fumo

smoked [sməukt] ADJ (*bacon, glass*) affumicato(-a)

smokeless fuel ['sməuklɪs-] N carburante *m* che non da fumo

smokeless zone N (*BRIT*) zona dove sono vietati gli scarichi di fumo

smoker ['sməukə^r] N (*person*) fumatore(-trice); (*Rail*) carrozza per fumatori

smoke screen N cortina fumogena *or* di fumo; (*fig*) copertura

smoke shop N (*US*) tabaccheria

smoking ['sməukɪŋ] N fumo; **"no ~"** (*sign*) "vietato fumare"; **he's given up ~** ha smesso di fumare

smoky ['sməukɪ] ADJ fumoso(-a); (*taste, surface*) affumicato(-a)

smolder ['sməuldə^r] VI (*US*) = **smoulder**

smoochy [ˈsmuːtʃɪ] ADJ (col) romantico(-a)

smooth [smuːð] ADJ liscio(-a); (sauce) omogeneo(-a); (flavour, whisky) amabile; (cigarette) leggero(-a); (movement) regolare; (person) mellifluo(-a); (landing, takeoff, flight) senza scosse ▶ VT lisciare, spianare; (also: **smooth out**: difficulties) appianare
  ▶ **smooth over** VT: **to ~ things over** (fig) sistemare le cose

smoothly [ˈsmuːðlɪ] ADV (easily) liscio; **everything went ~** tutto andò liscio

smother [ˈsmʌðəʳ] VT soffocare

smoulder, (US) **smolder** [ˈsməʊldəʳ] VI covare sotto la cenere

SMS N ABBR (= short message service) SMS m (servizio)

SMS message N SMS m inv, messaggino

smudge [smʌdʒ] N macchia; sbavatura ▶ VT imbrattare, sporcare

smug [smʌg] ADJ soddisfatto(-a), compiaciuto(-a)

smuggle [ˈsmʌgl] VT contrabbandare; **to ~ in/out** (goods etc) far entrare/uscire di contrabbando

smuggler [ˈsmʌgləʳ] N contrabbandiere(-a)

smuggling [ˈsmʌglɪŋ] N contrabbando

smut [smʌt] N (grain of soot) granello di fuliggine; (mark) segno nero; (in conversation etc) sconcezze fpl

smutty [ˈsmʌtɪ] ADJ (fig) osceno(-a), indecente

snack [snæk] N spuntino; **to have a ~** fare uno spuntino

snack bar N tavola calda, snack bar m inv

snag [snæg] N intoppo, ostacolo imprevisto

snail [sneɪl] N chiocciola

snake [sneɪk] N serpente m

snap [snæp] N (sound) schianto, colpo secco; (photograph) istantanea; (game) rubamazzo ▶ ADJ improvviso(-a) ▶ VT (far) schioccare; (break) spezzare di netto; (photograph) scattare un'istantanea di ▶ VI spezzarsi con un rumore secco; (fig: person) crollare; **to ~ at sb** rivolgersi a qn con tono brusco; (dog) cercare di mordere qn; **to ~ open/shut** aprirsi/chiudersi di scatto; **to ~ one's fingers at** (fig) infischiarsi di; **a cold ~** (of weather) un'improvvisa ondata di freddo
  ▶ **snap off** VT (break) schiantare
  ▶ **snap up** VT afferrare

snap fastener N bottone m automatico

snappy [ˈsnæpɪ] ADJ rapido(-a); **make it ~!** (col: hurry up) sbrigati!, svelto!

snapshot [ˈsnæpʃɔt] N istantanea

snare [snɛəʳ] N trappola

snarl [snɑːl] VI ringhiare ▶ VT: **to get snarled up** (wool, plans) ingarbugliarsi; (traffic) intasarsi

snatch [snætʃ] N (fig) furto; (BRIT: small amount): **snatches of** frammenti mpl di ▶ VT strappare (con violenza); (steal) rubare ▶ VI: **don't ~!** non

strappare le cose di mano!; **to ~ a sandwich** mangiarsi in fretta un panino; **to ~ some sleep** riuscire a dormire un po'
  ▶ **snatch up** VT raccogliere in fretta

snazzy [ˈsnæzɪ] ADJ (old: clothes) sciccoso(-a)

sneak [sniːk] (US pt, pp **snuck** [snʌk]) VI: **to ~ in/out** entrare/uscire di nascosto ▶ N (col) spione(-a); **to ~ up on sb** avvicinarsi quatto quatto a qn ▶ VT: **to ~ a look at sth** guardare di sottecchi qc

sneakers [ˈsniːkəz] NPL (esp US) scarpe fpl da ginnastica

sneaking [ˈsniːkɪŋ] ADJ: **to have a ~ feeling/suspicion that …** avere la vaga impressione/il vago sospetto che …

sneaky [ˈsniːkɪ] ADJ falso(-a), disonesto(-a)

sneer [snɪəʳ] N ghigno, sogghigno ▶ VI ghignare, sogghignare; **to ~ at sb/sth** farsi beffe di qn/qc

sneeze [sniːz] N starnuto ▶ VI starnutire

snide [snaɪd] ADJ maligno(-a)

sniff [snɪf] N fiutata, annusata ▶ VI fiutare, annusare; tirare su col naso; (in contempt) arricciare il naso ▶ VT fiutare, annusare; (glue, drug) sniffare
  ▶ **sniff at** VT FUS: **it's not to be sniffed at** non è da disprezzare

sniffer dog [ˈsnɪfə-] N cane m poliziotto (per stupefacenti o esplosivi)

snigger [ˈsnɪgəʳ] N riso represso ▶ VI ridacchiare, ridere sotto i baffi

snip [snɪp] N pezzetto; (bargain) (buon) affare m, occasione f ▶ VT tagliare

sniper [ˈsnaɪpəʳ] N (marksman) franco tiratore m, cecchino

snippet [ˈsnɪpɪt] N frammento

snivelling [ˈsnɪvlɪŋ] ADJ piagnucoloso(-a)

snob [snɔb] N snob mf inv

snobbery [ˈsnɔbərɪ] N snobismo

snobbish [ˈsnɔbɪʃ] ADJ snob inv

snog [snɔg] VI (col) pomiciare

snooker [ˈsnuːkəʳ] N tipo di gioco del biliardo

snoop [snuːp] VI: **to ~ on sb** spiare qn; **to ~ about** curiosare

snooper [ˈsnuːpəʳ] N ficcanaso mf

snooty [ˈsnuːtɪ] ADJ borioso(-a), snob inv

snooze [snuːz] N sonnellino, pisolino ▶ VI fare un sonnellino

snore [snɔːʳ] VI russare

snoring [ˈsnɔːrɪŋ] N russare m

snorkel [ˈsnɔːkl] N (of swimmer) respiratore m a tubo

snort [snɔːt] N sbuffo ▶ VI sbuffare ▶ VT (drugs slang) sniffare

snotty [ˈsnɔtɪ] ADJ (col) moccioso(-a)

snout [snaʊt] N muso

snow [snəu] N neve f ▶ VI nevicare ▶ VT: **to be snowed under with work** essere sommerso di lavoro

snowball ['snəubɔːl] N palla di neve ▶ VI (fig) crescere a vista d'occhio

snowboard ['snəubɔːd] N snowboard m inv; **to go snowboarding** fare snowboard

snowbound ['snəubaund] ADJ bloccato(-a) dalla neve

snow-capped ['snəukæpt] ADJ (mountain) con la cima coperta di neve; (peak) coperto(-a) di neve

snowdrift ['snəudrɪft] N cumulo di neve (ammucchiato dal vento)

snowdrop ['snəudrɔp] N bucaneve m inv

snowfall ['snəufɔːl] N nevicata

snowflake ['snəufleɪk] N fiocco di neve

snowman ['snəumæn] N (irreg) pupazzo di neve

snowplough, (US) **snowplow** ['snəuplau] N spazzaneve m inv

snowshoe ['snəuʃuː] N racchetta da neve

snowstorm ['snəustɔːm] N tormenta

snowy ['snəuɪ] ADJ nevoso(-a)

SNP N ABBR (BRIT Pol) = **Scottish National Party**

snub [snʌb] VT snobbare ▶ N offesa, affronto

snub-nosed [snʌb'nəuzd] ADJ dal naso camuso

snuff [snʌf] N tabacco da fiuto ▶ VT (also: **snuff out**: candle) spegnere

snuff movie N (col) film porno dove una persona viene uccisa realmente

snug [snʌg] ADJ comodo(-a); (room, house) accogliente, comodo(-a); **it's a ~ fit** è attillato

snuggle ['snʌgl] VI: **to ~ down in bed** accovacciarsi a letto; **to ~ up to sb** stringersi a qn

snugly ['snʌglɪ] ADV comodamente; **it fits ~** (object in pocket etc) entra giusto giusto; (garment) sta ben attillato

SO ABBR (Banking) = **standing order**

---

so [səu]

ADV **1** (thus, likewise) così; **if so** se è così, quand'è così; **I didn't do it — you did so!** non l'ho fatto io — sì che l'hai fatto!; **so do I, so am I** anch'io; **it's 5 o'clock — so it is!** sono le 5 — davvero!; **I hope so** lo spero; **I think so** penso di sì; **quite so!** esattamente!; **even so** comunque; **so far** finora, fin qui; (in past) fino ad allora

2 (in comparisons etc: to such a degree) così; **so big (that)** così grande (che); **she's not so clever as her brother** lei non è (così) intelligente come suo fratello

3: so much adj tanto(-a); adv tanto; **I've got so much work/money** ho tanto lavoro/tanti soldi; **I love you so much** ti amo tanto; **so many** tanti(-e)

4 (phrases): **10 or so** circa 10; **so long!** (col: goodbye) ciao!, ci vediamo!; **so to speak** per così dire; **so what?** (col) e allora?, e con questo?

▶ CONJ **1** (expressing purpose): **so as to do** in modo or così da fare; **we hurried so as not to be late** ci affrettammo per non fare tardi; **so (that)** affinché + sub, perché + sub

2 (expressing result): **he didn't arrive so I left** non è venuto così me ne sono andata; **so you see, I could have gone** vedi, sarei potuto andare; **so that's the reason!** allora è questo il motivo!, ecco perché!

---

soak [səuk] VT inzuppare; (clothes) mettere a mollo ▶ VI inzupparsi; (clothes) essere a mollo; **to be soaked through** essere fradicio
▶ **soak in** VI penetrare
▶ **soak up** VT assorbire

soaking ['səukɪŋ] ADJ (also: **soaking wet**) fradicio(-a)

so-and-so ['səuənsəu] N (somebody) un(una) tale; **Mr/Mrs ~** signor/signora tal dei tali

soap [səup] N sapone m

soapbox ['səupbɔks] N palco improvvisato (per orazioni pubbliche)

soapflakes ['səupfleɪks] NPL sapone m in scaglie

soap opera N soap opera f inv

soap powder N detersivo

soapsuds ['səupsʌdz] NPL saponata

soapy ['səupɪ] ADJ insaponato(-a)

soar [sɔːr] VI volare in alto; (price, morale, spirits) salire alle stelle; (building) ergersi

sob [sɔb] N singhiozzo ▶ VI singhiozzare

s.o.b. N ABBR (esp US col!: = son of a bitch) figlio di puttana (!)

sober ['səubər] ADJ non ubriaco(-a); (sedate) serio(-a); (moderate) moderato(-a); (colour, style) sobrio(-a)
▶ **sober up** VT far passare la sbornia a ▶ VI farsi passare la sbornia

sobriety [səu'braɪətɪ] N (not being drunk) sobrietà; (seriousness, sedateness) sobrietà, pacatezza

sob story N (col, pej) storia lacrimosa

Soc. ABBR (= society) Soc

so-called ['səu'kɔːld] ADJ cosiddetto(-a)

soccer ['sɔkər] N calcio

soccer pitch N campo di calcio

soccer player N calciatore m

sociable ['səuʃəbl] ADJ socievole

social ['səuʃl] ADJ sociale ▶ N festa, serata

social climber N arrampicatore(-trice) sociale, arrivista mf

social club N club m inv sociale

Social Democrat N socialdemocratico(-a)

social insurance N (US) assicurazione f sociale

socialism ['səuʃəlɪzəm] N socialismo

socialist ['səuʃəlɪst] ADJ, N socialista (mf)

S

socialite [ˈsəuʃəlaɪt] N persona in vista nel bel mondo

socialize [ˈsəuʃəlaɪz] VI frequentare la gente; farsi degli amici; **to ~ with** socializzare con

social life N vita sociale

socially [ˈsəuʃəlɪ] ADV socialmente, in società

social media NPL social media *mpl*

social network N social network *m inv*, rete *f* sociale

social networking N il comunicare tramite social network

social networking site N social network *m inv*

social science N scienze *fpl* sociali

social security N previdenza sociale

social services NPL servizi *mpl* sociali

social welfare N assistenza sociale

social work N servizio sociale

social worker N assistente *mf* sociale

society [səˈsaɪətɪ] N società *f inv*; (*club*) società, associazione *f*; (*also:* **high society**) alta società ▶ CPD (*party, column*) mondano(-a)

socioeconomic [ˈsəusɪəuɪkəˈnɒmɪk] ADJ socio-economico(-a)

sociological [səusɪəˈlɒdʒɪkl] ADJ sociologico(-a)

sociologist [səusɪˈɒlədʒɪst] N sociologo(-a)

sociology [səusɪˈɒlədʒɪ] N sociologia

sock [sɒk] N calzino ▶ VT (*hit*) dare un pugno a; **to pull one's socks up** (*fig*) darsi una regolata

socket [ˈsɒkɪt] N cavità *f inv*; (*of eye*) orbita; (BRIT *Elec*) presa di corrente; (: *for light bulb*) portalampada *m inv*

sod [sɒd] N (*of earth*) zolla erbosa; (BRIT *pej*) bastardo(-a) (!)
▶ **sod off** VI: **~ off!** (BRIT col!) levati dalle palle! (!)

soda [ˈsəudə] N (*Chem*) soda; (*also:* **soda water**) acqua di seltz; (US: *also:* **soda pop**) gassosa

sodden [ˈsɒdn] ADJ fradicio(-a)

sodium [ˈsəudɪəm] N sodio

sodium chloride N cloruro di sodio

sofa [ˈsəufə] N sofà *m inv*

sofa bed N divano *m* letto *inv*

Sofia [ˈsəufɪə] N Sofia

soft [sɒft] ADJ (*not rough*) morbido(-a); (*not hard*) soffice; (*not loud*) sommesso(-a); (*not bright*) tenue; (*kind*) gentile; (: *look, smile*) dolce; (*not strict*) indulgente; (*weak*) debole; (*stupid*) stupido(-a)

soft-boiled [ˈsɒftbɔɪld] ADJ (*egg*) alla coque

soft drink N analcolico

soft drugs NPL droghe *fpl* leggere

soften [ˈsɒfn] VT ammorbidire; addolcire; attenuare ▶ VI ammorbidirsi; addolcirsi; attenuarsi

softener [ˈsɒfnəʳ] N ammorbidente *m*

soft fruit N (BRIT) ≈ frutti *mpl* di bosco

soft furnishings NPL tessuti *mpl* d'arredo

soft-hearted [sɒftˈhɑːtɪd] ADJ sensibile

softly [ˈsɒftlɪ] ADV dolcemente; morbidamente

softness [ˈsɒftnɪs] N dolcezza; morbidezza

soft option N soluzione *f* (più) facile

soft sell N persuasione *f* all'acquisto

soft target N obiettivo civile (*e quindi facile da colpire*)

soft touch N (*col*): **to be a ~** lasciarsi spillare facilmente denaro

soft toy N giocattolo di peluche

software [ˈsɒftwɛəʳ] N (*Comput*) software *m*

software package N pacchetto di software

soft water N acqua non calcarea

soggy [ˈsɒgɪ] ADJ inzuppato(-a)

soil [sɔɪl] N (*earth*) terreno, suolo ▶ VT sporcare; (*fig*) macchiare

soiled [sɔɪld] ADJ sporco(-a), sudicio(-a)

sojourn [ˈsɒdʒəːn] N (*formal*) soggiorno

solace [ˈsɒlɪs] N consolazione *f*

solar [ˈsəuləʳ] ADJ solare

solarium [səˈlɛərɪəm] (*pl* **solaria** [-rɪə]) N solarium *m inv*

solar panel N pannello solare

solar plexus [-ˈplɛksəs] N (*Anat*) plesso solare

solar power N energia solare

solar system N sistema *m* solare

sold [səuld] PT, PP *of* **sell**

solder [ˈsəuldəʳ] VT saldare ▶ N saldatura

soldier [ˈsəuldʒəʳ] N soldato, militare *m* ▶ VI: **to ~ on** perseverare; **toy ~** soldatino

sold out ADJ (*Comm*) esaurito(-a)

sole [səul] N (*of foot*) pianta (del piede); (*of shoe*) suola; (*fish: pl inv*) sogliola ▶ ADJ solo(-a), unico(-a); (*exclusive*) esclusivo(-a)

solely [ˈsəullɪ] ADV solamente, unicamente; **I will hold you ~ responsible** la considererò il solo responsabile

solemn [ˈsɒləm] ADJ solenne; grave; serio(-a)

sole trader N (*Comm*) commerciante *m* in proprio

solicit [səˈlɪsɪt] VT (*request*) richiedere, sollecitare ▶ VI (*prostitute*) adescare i passanti

solicitor [səˈlɪsɪtəʳ] N (BRIT: *for wills etc*) ≈ notaio; (: *in court*) ≈ avvocato

solid [ˈsɒlɪd] ADJ (*not hollow*) pieno(-a); (*strong, sound, reliable, not liquid*) solido(-a); (*meal*) sostanzioso(-a); (*line*) ininterrotto(-a); (*vote*) unanime ▶ N solido; **to be on ~ ground** essere su terraferma; (*fig*) muoversi su terreno sicuro; **we waited 2 ~ hours** abbiamo aspettato due ore buone

solidarity [sɒlɪˈdærɪtɪ] N solidarietà

solid fuel N combustibile *m* solido

solidify [sə'lɪdɪfaɪ] VI solidificarsi ▶ VT solidificare

solidity [sə'lɪdɪtɪ] N solidità

solid-state ['sɔlɪdsteɪt] ADJ (Elec) a transistor

soliloquy [sə'lɪləkwɪ] N soliloquio

solitaire [sɔlɪ'tɛəʳ] N (game, gem) solitario

solitary ['sɔlɪtərɪ] ADJ solitario(-a)

solitary confinement N (Law): **to be in ~** essere in cella d'isolamento

solitude ['sɔlɪtjuːd] N solitudine f

solo ['səʊləʊ] N (Mus) assolo

soloist ['səʊləʊɪst] N solista mf

Solomon Islands ['sɔləmən-] N: **the ~** le isole Salomone

solstice ['sɔlstɪs] N solstizio

soluble ['sɔljʊbl] ADJ solubile

solution [sə'luːʃən] N soluzione f

solve [sɔlv] VT risolvere

solvency ['sɔlvənsɪ] N (Comm) solvenza, solvibilità

solvent ['sɔlvənt] ADJ (Comm) solvibile ▶ N (Chem) solvente m

solvent abuse N abuso di colle e solventi

Somali [sə'mɑːlɪ] ADJ somalo(-a)

Somalia [səʊ'mɑːlɪə] N Somalia

sombre, (US) **somber** ['sɔmbəʳ] ADJ scuro(-a); (mood, person) triste

---

some [sʌm]

ADJ **1** (a certain amount or number of): **some tea/ water/cream** del tè/dell'acqua/della panna; **there's some milk in the fridge** c'è (del) latte nel frigo; **some children/apples** dei bambini/delle mele; **after some time** dopo un po'; **at some length** a lungo

2 (certain: in contrasts) certo(-a); **some people say that ...** alcuni dicono che ..., certa gente dice che ...

3 (unspecified) un(a) certo(-a), qualche; **some woman was asking for you** una tale chiedeva di lei; **some day** un giorno; **some day next week** un giorno della prossima settimana; **in some form or other** in una forma o nell'altra

▶ PRON **1** (a certain number) alcuni(-e), certi(-e); **I've got some** (books etc) ne ho alcuni; **some (of them) have been sold** alcuni sono stati venduti

2 (a certain amount) un po'; **I've got some** (money, milk) ne ho un po'; **I've read some of the book** ho letto parte del libro; **some (of it) was left** ne è rimasto un po'; **could I have some of that cheese?** potrei avere un po' di quel formaggio?

▶ ADV: **some 10 people** circa 10 persone

---

somebody ['sʌmbədɪ] PRON qualcuno; **~ or other** qualcuno

someday ['sʌmdeɪ] ADV uno di questi giorni, un giorno o l'altro

somehow ['sʌmhaʊ] ADV in un modo o nell'altro, in qualche modo; (for some reason) per qualche ragione

someone ['sʌmwʌn] PRON = **somebody**

someplace ['sʌmpleɪs] ADV (US) = **somewhere**

somersault ['sʌməsɔːlt] N capriola; (in air) salto mortale ▶ VI fare una capriola (or un salto mortale); (car) cappottare

something ['sʌmθɪŋ] PRON qualcosa, qualche cosa; **~ nice** qualcosa di bello; **~ to do** qualcosa da fare; **he's ~ like me** mi assomiglia un po'; **it's ~ of a problem** è un bel problema

sometime ['sʌmtaɪm] ADV (in future) una volta o l'altra; (in past): **~ last month** durante il mese scorso; **I'll finish it ~** lo finirò prima o poi

sometimes ['sʌmtaɪmz] ADV qualche volta

somewhat ['sʌmwɔt] ADV piuttosto

somewhere ['sʌmwɛəʳ] ADV in or da qualche parte; **~ else** da qualche altra parte

son [sʌn] N figlio

sonar ['səʊnɑːʳ] N sonar m

sonata [sə'nɑːtə] N sonata

song [sɔŋ] N canzone f

songbook ['sɔŋbʊk] N canzoniere m

songwriter ['sɔŋraɪtəʳ] N compositore(-trice) di canzoni

sonic ['sɔnɪk] ADJ (boom) sonico(-a)

son-in-law ['sʌnɪnlɔː] N genero

sonnet ['sɔnɪt] N sonetto

sonny ['sʌnɪ] N (col) ragazzo mio

soon [suːn] ADV presto, fra poco; (early) presto; **~ afterwards** poco dopo; **very/quite ~** molto/ abbastanza presto; **as ~ as possible** prima possibile; **I'll do it as ~ as I can** lo farò appena posso; **how ~ can you be ready?** fra quanto tempo sarà pronto?; **see you ~!** a presto!

sooner ['suːnəʳ] ADV (time) prima; (preference): **I would ~ do** preferirei fare; **~ or later** prima o poi; **no ~ said than done** detto fatto; **the ~ the better** prima è meglio è; **no ~ had we left than ...** eravamo appena partiti, quando ...

soot [sʊt] N fuliggine f

soothe [suːð] VT calmare

soothing ['suːðɪŋ] ADJ (ointment etc) calmante; (tone, words etc) rassicurante

SOP N ABBR = **standard operating procedure**

sop [sɔp] N: **that's only a ~** è soltanto un contentino

sophisticated [sə'fɪstɪkeɪtɪd] ADJ sofisticato(-a); raffinato(-a); complesso(-a); (film, mind) sottile

sophistication [səfɪstɪ'keɪʃən] N raffinatezza; (of machine) complessità; (of argument etc) sottigliezza

S

sophomore [ˈsɒfəmɔːʳ] N (US) studente(-essa) del secondo anno

soporific [sɒpəˈrɪfɪk] ADJ soporifero(-a)

sopping [ˈsɒpɪŋ] ADJ (also: **sopping wet**) bagnato(-a) fradicio(-a)

soppy [ˈsɒpɪ] ADJ (col) sentimentale

soprano [səˈprɑːnəu] N (voice) soprano m; (singer) soprano mf

sorbet [ˈsɔːbeɪ] N sorbetto

sorcerer [ˈsɔːsərəʳ] N stregone m, mago

sordid [ˈsɔːdɪd] ADJ sordido(-a)

sore [sɔːʳ] ADJ (painful) dolorante; (col: offended) offeso(-a) ▸ N piaga; **my eyes are ~, I have ~ eyes** mi fanno male gli occhi; **~ throat** mal m di gola; **it's a ~ point** (fig) è un punto delicato

sorely [ˈsɔːlɪ] ADV (tempted) fortemente

sorrel [ˈsɒrəl] N acetosa

sorrow [ˈsɒrəu] N dolore m

sorrowful [ˈsɒrəuful] ADJ triste

sorry [ˈsɒrɪ] ADJ spiacente; (condition, excuse) misero(-a), pietoso(-a); (sight, failure) triste; **~!** scusa! (or scusi! or scusate!); **to feel ~ for sb** rincrescersi per qn; **I'm ~ to hear that ...** mi dispiace sentirci che ...; **to be ~ about sth** essere dispiaciuto or spiacente di qc

sort [sɔːt] N specie f, genere m; (make: of coffee, car etc) tipo ▸ VT (also: **sort out**: papers) classificare; ordinare; (: letters etc) smistare; (: problems) risolvere; (Comput) ordinare; **I shall do nothing of the ~!** nemmeno per sogno!; **it's ~ of awkward** (col) è piuttosto difficile

sortie [ˈsɔːtɪ] N sortita

sorting office [ˈsɔːtɪŋ-] N ufficio m smistamento inv

SOS N S.O.S. m inv

so-so [ˈsəusəu] ADV così così

soufflé [ˈsuːfleɪ] N soufflé m inv

sought [sɔːt] PT, PP of **seek**

sought-after [ˈsɔːtɑːftəʳ] ADJ richiesto(-a)

soul [səul] N anima; **the poor ~ had nowhere to sleep** il poveraccio non aveva dove dormire; **I didn't see a ~** non ho visto anima viva

soul-destroying [ˈsəuldɪˈstrɔɪŋ] ADJ demoralizzante

soulful [ˈsəulful] ADJ pieno(-a) di sentimento

soulless [ˈsəullɪs] ADJ senz'anima, inumano(-a)

soul mate N anima gemella

soul-searching [ˈsəulsəːtʃɪŋ] N: **after much ~** dopo un profondo esame di coscienza

sound [saund] ADJ (healthy) sano(-a); (safe, not damaged) solido(-a), in buono stato; (reliable, not superficial) solido(-a); (sensible) giudizioso(-a), di buon senso; (valid: argument, policy, claim) valido(-a) ▸ ADV: **~ asleep** profondamente addormentato ▸ N (noise) suono; rumore m; (Geo) stretto ▸ VT (alarm) suonare; (also: **sound out**: opinions) sondare ▸ VI suonare; (fig: seem) sembrare; **to ~ like** rassomigliare a; **to be of ~ mind** essere sano di mente; **I don't like the ~ of it** (fig: film etc) non mi dice niente (: news) è preoccupante; **it sounds as if ...** ho l'impressione che ...; **it sounds like French** somiglia al francese; **that sounds like them arriving** mi sembra di sentirli arrivare
▸ **sound off** VI (col): **to ~ off (about)** (give one's opinions) fare dei grandi discorsi (su)

sound barrier N muro del suono

soundbite [ˈsaundbaɪt] N frase f incisiva

sound effects NPL effetti mpl sonori

sound engineer N tecnico del suono

sounding [ˈsaundɪŋ] N (Naut etc) scandagliamento

sounding board N (Mus) cassa di risonanza; (fig): **to use sb as a ~ for one's ideas** provare le proprie idee su qn

soundly [ˈsaundlɪ] ADV (sleep) profondamente; (beat) duramente

soundproof [ˈsaundpruːf] VT insonorizzare, isolare acusticamente ▸ ADJ insonorizzato(-a), isolato(-a) acusticamente

sound system N impianto m audio inv

soundtrack [ˈsaundtræk] N (of film) colonna sonora

soup [suːp] N minestra; (clear) brodo; (thick) zuppa; **in the ~** (fig) nei guai

soup course N minestra

soup kitchen N mensa per i poveri

soup plate N piatto fondo

soupspoon [ˈsuːpspuːn] N cucchiaio da minestra

sour [ˈsauəʳ] ADJ aspro(-a); (fruit) acerbo(-a); (milk) acido(-a), fermentato(-a); (fig) arcigno(-a), acido(-a); **to go** or **turn ~** (milk, wine) inacidirsi; (fig: relationship, plans) guastarsi; **it's ~ grapes** (fig) è soltanto invidia

source [sɔːs] N fonte f, sorgente f; (fig) fonte; **I have it from a reliable ~ that ...** ho saputo da fonte sicura che ...

south [sauθ] N sud m, meridione m, mezzogiorno ▸ ADJ del sud, sud inv, meridionale ▸ ADV verso sud; **(to the) ~ of** a sud di; **the S~ of France** il sud della Francia; **to travel ~** viaggiare verso sud

South Africa N Sudafrica m

South African ADJ, N sudafricano(-a)

South America N Sudamerica m, America del sud

South American ADJ, N sudamericano(-a)

southbound [ˈsauθbaund] ADJ (gen) diretto(-a) a sud; (carriageway) sud inv

south-east [sauθˈiːst] N sud-est m

South-East Asia N Asia sudorientale

southeastern [sauθˈiːstən] ADJ sudorientale

southerly [ˈsʌðəlɪ] ADJ del sud

southern [ˈsʌðən] ADJ del sud, meridionale; (wall) esposto(-a) a sud; **the ~ hemisphere** l'emisfero australe

South Korea N Corea f del Sud

South Pole N Polo Sud

South Sea Islands NPL: **the ~** le isole dei Mari del Sud

South Seas NPL: **the ~** i Mari del Sud

South Sudan N Sud Sudan m

South Vietnam N Vietnam m del Sud

southward [ˈsauθwəd], **southwards** [ˈsauθwədz] ADV verso sud

south-west [sauθ'wɛst] N sud-ovest m

southwestern [sauθ'westən] ADJ sudoccidentale

souvenir [su:vəˈnɪər] N ricordo, souvenir m inv

sovereign [ˈsɔvrɪn] ADJ, N sovrano(-a)

sovereignty [ˈsɔvrəntɪ] N sovranità

soviet [ˈsəuvɪət] ADJ sovietico(-a)

Soviet Union N: **the ~** l'Unione f Sovietica

sow¹ [səu] (pt **sowed**, pp **sown** [səun]) VT seminare

sow² [sau] N scrofa

soya [ˈsɔɪə], (US) **soy** [sɔɪ] N: **~ bean** seme m di soia

soy sauce [sɔɪ-] N salsa di soia

sozzled [ˈsɔzld] ADJ (BRIT col) sbronzo(-a)

spa [spɑː] N (resort) stazione f termale; (also: **health spa**) centro di cure estetiche

space [speɪs] N spazio; (room) posto; spazio; (length of time) intervallo ▶ CPD spaziale ▶ VT (also: **space out**) distanziare; **in a confined ~** in un luogo chiuso; **to clear a ~ for sth** fare posto per qc; **in a short ~ of time** in breve tempo; **(with)in the ~ of an hour/three generations** nell'arco di un'ora/di tre generazioni

space bar N (on keyboard) barra spaziatrice

spacecraft [ˈspeɪskrɑːft] N (pl inv) veicolo spaziale

spaceman [ˈspeɪsmæn] N (irreg) astronauta m, cosmonauta m

spaceship [ˈspeɪsʃɪp] N astronave f, navicella spaziale

space shuttle N shuttle m inv

spacesuit [ˈspeɪssuːt] N tuta spaziale

spacewoman [ˈspeɪswumən] N (irreg) astronauta f, cosmonauta f

spacing [ˈspeɪsɪŋ] N spaziatura; **single/double ~** (Typ etc) spaziatura singola/doppia

spacious [ˈspeɪʃəs] ADJ spazioso(-a), ampio(-a)

spade [speɪd] N (tool) vanga; pala; (child's) paletta ▪ **spades** NPL (Cards) picche fpl

spadework [ˈspeɪdwəːk] N (fig) duro lavoro preparatorio

spaghetti [spəˈɡɛtɪ] N spaghetti mpl

Spain [speɪn] N Spagna

spam [spæm] (Comput) N spamming m ▶ VT: **to ~ sb** inviare a qn messaggi pubblicitari non richiesti via email

spamming [ˈspæmɪŋ] N spamming m inv

span [spæn] N (of bird, plane) apertura alare; (of arch) campata; (in time) periodo; durata ▶ VT attraversare; (fig) abbracciare

Spaniard [ˈspænjəd] N spagnolo(-a)

spaniel [ˈspænjəl] N spaniel m inv

Spanish [ˈspænɪʃ] ADJ spagnolo(-a) ▶ N (Ling) spagnolo; **the ~** npl gli Spagnoli; **~ omelette** frittata di cipolle, pomodori e peperoni

spank [spæŋk] VT sculacciare

spanner [ˈspænər] N (BRIT) chiave f inglese

spar [spɑːr] N asta, palo ▶ VI (Boxing) allenarsi

spare [speər] ADJ di riserva, di scorta; (surplus) in più, d'avanzo ▶ N (part) pezzo di ricambio ▶ VT (do without) fare a meno di; (afford to give) concedere; (refrain from hurting, using) risparmiare; **to ~** (surplus) d'avanzo; **there are 2 going ~** (BRIT) ce ne sono 2 in più; **to ~ no expense** non badare a spese; **can you ~ the time?** ha tempo?; **I've a few minutes to ~** ho un attimino di tempo; **there is no time to ~** non c'è tempo da perdere; **can you ~ (me) £10?** puoi prestarmi 10 sterline?

spare part N pezzo di ricambio

spare room N stanza degli ospiti

spare time N tempo libero

spare tyre, (US) **spare tire** N (Aut) gomma di scorta

spare wheel N (Aut) ruota di scorta

sparing [ˈspɛərɪŋ] ADJ (amount) scarso(-a); (use) parsimonioso(-a); **to be ~ with** essere avaro(-a) di

sparingly [ˈspɛərɪŋlɪ] ADV moderatamente

spark [spɑːk] N scintilla

sparkle [ˈspɑːkl] N scintillio, sfavillio ▶ VI scintillare, sfavillare; (bubble) spumeggiare, frizzare

sparkler [ˈspɑːklər] N fuoco d'artificio

sparkling [ˈspɑːklɪŋ] ADJ scintillante, sfavillante; (wine) spumante

spark plug N candela

sparring partner [ˈspɑːrɪŋ-] N sparring partner m inv; (fig) interlocutore abituale in discussioni, dibattiti, tavole rotonde ecc

sparrow [ˈspærəu] N passero

sparse [spɑːs] ADJ sparso(-a), rado(-a)

spartan [ˈspɑːtən] ADJ (fig) spartano(-a)

spasm [ˈspæzəm] N (Med) spasmo; (fig) accesso, attacco

spasmodic [spæzˈmɔdɪk] ADJ spasmodico(-a); (fig) intermittente

spastic [ˈspæstɪk] N (!) spastico(-a)

S

spat [spæt] PT, PP of **spit** ▶ N battibecco

spate [speɪt] N (fig): **a ~ of** un diluvio or fiume m di; **in ~** (river) in piena

spatial ['speɪʃəl] ADJ spaziale

spatter ['spætə'] VT, VI schizzare

spatula ['spætjulə] N spatola

spawn [spɔːn] VT deporre; (pej) produrre ▶ VI deporre le uova ▶ N uova fpl

SPCA N ABBR (US: = Society for the Prevention of Cruelty to Animals) ≈ E.N.P.A. m (= Ente Nazionale per la Protezione degli Animali)

SPCC N ABBR (US) = **Society for the Prevention of Cruelty to Children**

speak [spiːk] (pt **spoke** [spəuk], pp **spoken** ['spəukn]) VT (language) parlare; (truth) dire ▶ VI parlare; **to ~ to sb/of** or **about sth** parlare a qn/di qc; **~ up!** parli più forte!; **to ~ at a conference/in a debate** partecipare ad una conferenza/ad un dibattito; **speaking!** (on telephone) sono io!; **to ~ one's mind** dire quello che si pensa; **he has no money to ~ of** non si può proprio dire che sia ricco
▶ **speak for** VT FUS: **to ~ for sb** parlare a nome di qn; **that picture is already spoken for** (in shop) quel quadro è già stato venduto

speaker ['spiːkə'] N (in public) oratore(-trice); (also: **loudspeaker**) altoparlante m; (Pol): **the S~** il presidente della Camera dei Comuni or (US) dei Rappresentanti; **are you a Welsh ~?** parla gallese?

speaking ['spiːkɪŋ] ADJ parlante; **Italian-speaking people** persone che parlano italiano; **to be on ~ terms** parlarsi

spear [spɪə'] N lancia ▶ VT infilzare

spearhead ['spɪəhɛd] N punta di lancia; (Mil) reparto d'assalto ▶ VT (attack etc) condurre

spearmint ['spɪəmɪnt] N (Bot etc) menta verde

spec [spɛk] N (BRIT col): **on ~** sperando bene; **to buy sth on ~** comprare qc sperando di fare un affare

special ['spɛʃl] ADJ speciale ▶ N (train) treno supplementare; **nothing ~** niente di speciale; **take ~ care** siate particolarmente prudenti

special agent N agente m segreto

special correspondent N inviato speciale

special delivery N (Post): **by ~** per espresso

special effects NPL (Cine) effetti mpl speciali

specialist ['spɛʃəlɪst] N specialista mf; **a heart ~** (Med) un cardiologo

speciality [spɛʃɪ'ælɪtɪ], (esp US) **specialty** ['spɛʃəltɪ] N specialità f inv

specialize ['spɛʃəlaɪz] VI: **to ~ (in)** specializzarsi (in)

specially ['spɛʃəlɪ] ADV specialmente, particolarmente

special needs ADJ: **~ children** bambini mpl con difficoltà di apprendimento

special offer N (Comm) offerta speciale

special school N (BRIT) scuola speciale

specialty ['spɛʃəltɪ] N (esp US) = **speciality**

species ['spiːʃiːz] N (pl inv) specie f inv

specific [spə'sɪfɪk] ADJ specifico(-a); preciso(-a); **to be ~** avere un legame specifico con

specifically [spə'sɪfɪklɪ] ADV (explicitly: state, warn) chiaramente, esplicitamente; (especially: design, intend) appositamente

specification [spɛsɪfɪ'keɪʃən] N specificazione f ▪ **specifications** NPL (of car, machine) dati mpl caratteristici; (for building) dettagli mpl

specify ['spɛsɪfaɪ] VT specificare, precisare; **unless otherwise specified** salvo indicazioni contrarie

specimen ['spɛsɪmən] N esemplare m, modello; (Med) campione m

specimen copy N campione m

specimen signature N firma depositata

speck [spɛk] N puntino, macchiolina; (particle) granello

speckled ['spɛkld] ADJ macchiettato(-a)

specs [spɛks] NPL (col) occhiali mpl

spectacle ['spɛktəkl] N spettacolo; see also **spectacles**

spectacle case N (BRIT) fodero per gli occhiali

spectacles ['spɛktəklz] NPL (BRIT) occhiali mpl

spectacular [spɛk'tækjulə'] ADJ spettacolare ▶ N (Cine etc) film m inv etc spettacolare

spectator [spɛk'teɪtə'] N spettatore(-trice)

spectator sport N sport m inv come spettacolo

spectra ['spɛktrə] NPL of **spectrum**

spectre, (US) **specter** ['spɛktə'] N spettro

spectrum ['spɛktrəm] (pl **spectra** [-rə]) N spettro; (fig) gamma

speculate ['spɛkjuleɪt] VI speculare; (try to guess): **to ~ about** fare ipotesi su

speculation [spɛkju'leɪʃən] N speculazione f; congetture fpl

speculative ['spɛkjulətɪv] ADJ speculativo(-a)

speculator ['spɛkjuleɪtə'] N speculatore(-trice)

sped [spɛd] PT, PP of **speed**

speech [spiːtʃ] N (faculty) parola; (talk, Theat) discorso; (manner of speaking) parlata; (language) linguaggio; (enunciation) elocuzione f

speech day N (BRIT Scol) giorno della premiazione

speech impediment N difetto di pronuncia

speechless ['spiːtʃlɪs] ADJ ammutolito(-a), muto(-a)

speech therapy N cura dei disturbi del linguaggio

speed [spiːd] N (pt, pp **sped** [spɛd]) N velocità f inv; (promptness) prontezza; (Aut: gear) marcia ▶ VI: **to ~ along** procedere velocemente; **the years sped by** gli anni sono volati; (Aut: exceed speed limit) andare a velocità eccessiva; **at ~** (BRIT)

velocemente; **at full** *or* **top ~** a tutta velocità; **at a ~ of 70 km/h** a una velocità di 70 km l'ora; **shorthand/typing speeds** numero di parole al minuto in stenografia/dattilografia; **a five-speed gearbox** un cambio a cinque marce
▶ **speed up** (*pt, pp* **speeded up**) VI, VT accelerare

speedboat ['spiːdbəut] N motoscafo; fuoribordo *m inv*

speed camera N Autovelox *m inv*

speed dating [-deɪtɪŋ] N *sistema di appuntamenti grazie al quale si possono incontrare in pochissimo tempo diverse persone e scegliere eventualmente chi frequentare*

speedily ['spiːdɪlɪ] ADV velocemente; prontamente

speeding ['spiːdɪŋ] N (*Aut*) eccesso di velocità

speed limit N limite *m* di velocità

speedometer [spɪˈdɔmɪtər] N tachimetro

speed trap N (*Aut*) tratto di strada sul quale la polizia controlla la velocità dei veicoli

speedway (racing) ['spiːdweɪ] N (*Sport*) corsa motociclistica su pista

speedy ['spiːdɪ] ADJ veloce, rapido(-a); (*reply*) pronto(-a)

speleologist [spɛlɪˈɔlədʒɪst] N speleologo(-a)

spell [spɛl] (*pt, pp* **spelt** [spɛlt] *or* **spelled** [spɛld]) N (*also:* **magic spell**) incantesimo; (*period of time*) (breve) periodo ▶ VT (*in writing*) scrivere (lettera per lettera); (*aloud*) dire lettera per lettera; (*fig*) significare; **to cast a ~ on sb** fare un incantesimo a qn; **he can't ~** fa errori di ortografia; **how do you ~ your name?** come si scrive il suo nome?; **can you ~ it for me?** me lo può dettare lettera per lettera?
▶ **spell out** VT (*letter by letter*) dettare lettera per lettera; (*explain*): **to ~ sth out for sb** spiegare qc a qn per filo e per segno

spellbound ['spɛlbaund] ADJ incantato(-a), affascinato(-a)

spellchecker ['spɛltʃɛkər] N correttore *m* ortografico

spelling ['spɛlɪŋ] N ortografia

spelt [spɛlt] PT, PP *of* **spell**

spend [spɛnd] (*pt, pp* **spent** [spɛnt]) VT (*money*) spendere; (*time, life*) passare; **to ~ time/money/effort on sth** dedicare tempo/soldi/energie a qc

spending ['spɛndɪŋ] N: **government ~** spesa pubblica

spending money N denaro per le piccole spese

spending power N potere *m* d'acquisto

spendthrift ['spɛndθrɪft] N spendaccione(-a)

spent [spɛnt] PT, PP *of* **spend** ▶ ADJ (*patience*) esaurito(-a); (*cartridge, bullets, match*) usato(-a)

sperm [spəːm] N sperma *m*

sperm bank N banca dello sperma

sperm whale N capodoglio

spew [spjuː] VT vomitare

sphere [sfɪər] N sfera

spherical ['sfɛrɪkl] ADJ sferico(-a)

sphinx [sfɪŋks] N sfinge *f*

spice [spaɪs] N spezia ▶ VT aromatizzare

spick-and-span ['spɪkən'spæn] ADJ impeccabile

spicy ['spaɪsɪ] ADJ piccante

spider ['spaɪdər] N ragno; **~'s web** ragnatela

spiel [spiːl] N (*col*) tiritera

spike [spaɪk] N punta ■ **spikes** NPL (*Sport*) scarpe *fpl* chiodate

spike heel N (*US*) tacco a spillo

spiky ['spaɪkɪ] ADJ (*bush, branch*) spinoso(-a); (*animal*) ricoperto(-a) di aculei

spill [spɪl] (*pt, pp* **spilt** [-t], **spilled** [-d]) VT versare, rovesciare ▶ VI versarsi, rovesciarsi; **to ~ the beans** (*col*) vuotare il sacco
▶ **spill out** VI riversarsi fuori
▶ **spill over** VI: **to ~ over (into)** (*liquid*) versarsi (in); (*crowd*) riversarsi (in)

spillage ['spɪlɪdʒ] N (*event*) fuoriuscita; (*substance*) sostanza fuoriuscita

spin [spɪn] (*pt, pp* **spun** [spʌn]) N (*revolution of wheel*) rotazione *f*; (*Aviat*) avvitamento; (*trip in car*) giretto ▶ VT (*wool etc*) filare; (*wheel*) far girare; (*Brit: clothes*) mettere nella centrifuga ▶ VI girare; **to ~ a yarn** raccontare una storia; **to ~ a coin** (*Brit*) lanciare in aria una moneta
▶ **spin out** VT far durare

spina bifida ['spaɪnə'bɪfɪdə] N spina bifida

spinach ['spɪnɪtʃ] N spinacio; (*as food*) spinaci *mpl*

spinal ['spaɪnl] ADJ spinale

spinal column N colonna vertebrale, spina dorsale

spinal cord N midollo spinale

spindly ['spɪndlɪ] ADJ lungo(-a) e sottile, filiforme

spin doctor N (*col*) *esperto di comunicazioni responsabile dell'immagine di un partito politico*

spin-dry ['spɪn'draɪ] VT asciugare con la centrifuga

spin-dryer [spɪn'draɪər] N (*Brit*) centrifuga

spine [spaɪn] N spina dorsale; (*thorn*) spina

spine-chilling ['spaɪntʃɪlɪŋ] ADJ agghiacciante

spineless ['spaɪnlɪs] ADJ invertebrato(-a), senza spina dorsale; (*fig*) smidollato(-a)

spinner ['spɪnər] N (*of thread*) tessitore(-trice)

spinning ['spɪnɪŋ] N filatura

spinning top N trottola

spinning wheel N filatoio

spin-off ['spɪnɔf] N applicazione *f* secondaria

spinster ['spɪnstər] N nubile *f*; zitella

spiral ['spaɪərl] N spirale *f* ▶ ADJ a spirale ▶ VI

S

(prices) salire vertiginosamente; **the inflationary ~** la spirale dell'inflazione

spiral staircase N scala a chiocciola

spire ['spaɪə^r] N guglia

spirit ['spɪrɪt] N *(soul)* spirito, anima; *(ghost)* spirito, fantasma *m*; *(mood)* stato d'animo, umore *m*; *(courage)* coraggio ▓ **spirits** NPL *(drink)* alcolici *mpl*; **in good spirits** di buon umore; **in low spirits** triste, abbattuto(-a); **community ~, public ~** senso civico

spirited ['spɪrɪtɪd] ADJ vivace, vigoroso(-a); *(horse)* focoso(-a)

spirit level N livella a bolla (d'aria)

spiritual ['spɪrɪtjuəl] ADJ spirituale ▶ N *(Mus)* spiritual *m inv*

spiritualism ['spɪrɪtjuəlɪzəm] N spiritismo

spit [spɪt] *(pt, pp* **spat** [spæt]) N *(for roasting)* spiedo; *(spittle)* sputo; *(saliva)* saliva ▶ VI sputare; *(fire, fat)* scoppiettare

spite [spaɪt] N dispetto ▶ VT contrariare, far dispetto a; **in ~ of** nonostante, malgrado

spiteful ['spaɪtful] ADJ dispettoso(-a); *(tongue, remark)* maligno(-a), velenoso(-a)

spitroast ['spɪt'rəust] VT cuocere allo spiedo

spitting ['spɪtɪŋ] N: **"~ prohibited"** "vietato sputare" ▶ ADJ: **to be the ~ image of sb** essere il ritratto vivente *or* sputato di qn

spittle ['spɪtl] N saliva; sputo

spiv [spɪv] N *(BRIT col, pej)* imbroglione *m*

splash [splæʃ] N spruzzo; *(sound)* tonfo; *(of colour)* schizzo ▶ VT spruzzare ▶ VI *(also:* **splash about***)* sguazzare; **to ~ paint on the floor** schizzare il pavimento di vernice
▶ **splash out** VI *(BRIT col)* fare spese folli

splashdown ['splæʃdaun] N ammaraggio

splay [spleɪ] ADJ: **~ footed** che ha i piedi piatti

spleen [spli:n] N *(Anat)* milza

splendid ['splɛndɪd] ADJ splendido(-a), magnifico(-a)

splendour, *(US)* **splendor** ['splɛndə^r] N splendore *m*

splice [splaɪs] VT *(rope)* impiombare; *(wood)* calettare

splint [splɪnt] N *(Med)* stecca

splinter ['splɪntə^r] N scheggia ▶ VI scheggiarsi

splinter group N gruppo dissidente

split [splɪt] *(pt, pp* **~***)* N spaccatura; *(fig: division, quarrel)* scissione *f* ▶ VT spaccare; *(party)* dividere; *(work, profits)* spartire, ripartire ▶ VI *(divide)* dividersi; **to do the splits** fare la spaccata; **to ~ the difference** dividersi la differenza
▶ **split up** VI *(couple)* separarsi, rompere; *(meeting)* sciogliersi

split-level ['splɪtlɛvl] ADJ *(house)* a piani sfalsati

split peas NPL piselli *mpl* secchi spaccati

split personality N doppia personalità

split second N frazione *f* di secondo

splitting ['splɪtɪŋ] ADJ: **a ~ headache** un mal di testa da impazzire

splutter ['splʌtə^r] VI farfugliare; sputacchiare

spoil [spɔɪl] *(pt, pp* **spoilt** [-t], **spoiled** [-d]) VT *(damage)* rovinare, guastare; *(mar)* sciupare; *(child)* viziare; *(ballot paper)* rendere nullo(-a), invalidare; **to be spoiling for a fight** morire dalla voglia di litigare

spoils [spɔɪlz] NPL bottino

spoilsport ['spɔɪlspɔːt] N guastafeste *mf*

spoilt [spɔɪlt] PT, PP *of* **spoil** ▶ ADJ *(child)* viziato(-a); *(ballot paper)* nullo(-a)

spoke [spəuk] PT *of* **speak** ▶ N raggio

spoken ['spəukn] PP *of* **speak**

spokesman ['spəuksmən] N *(irreg)* portavoce *m inv*

spokesperson ['spəukspə:sn] N portavoce *mf*

spokeswoman ['spəukswumən] N *(irreg)* portavoce *f inv*

sponge [spʌndʒ] N spugna; *(Culin: also:* **sponge cake***)* pan *m* di Spagna ▶ VT spugnare, pulire con una spugna ▶ VI: **to ~ on** *or* **off** scroccare a

sponge bag N *(BRIT)* nécessaire *m inv*

sponge cake N pan *m* di Spagna

sponger ['spʌndʒə^r] N *(pej)* parassita *mf*, scroccone(-a)

spongy ['spʌndʒɪ] ADJ spugnoso(-a)

sponsor ['spɔnsə^r] N *(Radio, TV, Sport etc)* sponsor *m inv*; *(of enterprise, bill, for fund-raising)* promotore(-trice) ▶ VT sponsorizzare; patrocinare; *(Pol: bill)* presentare; **I sponsored him at 50p a mile** *(in fund-raising race)* ho offerto in beneficenza 50 penny per ogni miglio che fa

sponsorship ['spɔnsəʃɪp] N sponsorizzazione *f*; patrocinio

spontaneity [spɔntə'neɪtɪ] N spontaneità

spontaneous [spɔn'teɪnɪəs] ADJ spontaneo(-a)

spoof [spu:f] N presa in giro, parodia

spooky ['spu:kɪ] ADJ *(col)* che fa accapponare la pelle

spool [spu:l] N bobina

spoon [spu:n] N cucchiaio

spoon-feed ['spu:nfi:d] VT nutrire con il cucchiaio; *(fig)* imboccare

spoonful ['spu:nful] N cucchiaiata

sporadic [spə'rædɪk] ADJ sporadico(-a)

sport [spɔːt] N sport *m inv*; *(person)* persona di spirito; *(amusement)* divertimento ▶ VT sfoggiare; **indoor/outdoor sports** sport *mpl* al chiuso/all'aria aperta; **to say sth in ~** dire qc per scherzo

sporting ['spɔːtɪŋ] ADJ sportivo(-a); **to give sb a ~ chance** dare a qn una possibilità (di vincere)

sport jacket N *(US)* = **sports jacket**

sports car N automobile *f* sportiva

sports centre N *(BRIT)* centro sportivo

sports drink N sport drink *m inv*

sports ground N campo sportivo

sports jacket N (*BRIT*) giacca sportiva

sportsman [ˈspɔːtsmən] N (*irreg*) sportivo

sportsmanship [ˈspɔːtsmənʃɪp] N spirito sportivo

sports page N pagina sportiva

sports utility vehicle N SUV *m inv*

sportswear [ˈspɔːtswɛəʳ] N abiti *mpl* sportivi

sportswoman [ˈspɔːtswumən] N (*irreg*) sportiva

sporty [ˈspɔːtɪ] ADJ sportivo(-a)

spot [spɔt] N punto; (*mark*) macchia; (*dot: on pattern*) pallino; (*pimple*) foruncolo; (*place*) posto; (*Radio, TV: also*: **spot advertisement**) spot *m inv*; (*small amount*): **a ~ of** un po' di ▶ VT (*notice*) individuare, distinguere; **on the ~** sul posto; **to do sth on the ~** fare qc immediatamente *or* su due piedi; **to put sb on the ~** mettere qn in difficoltà; **to come out in spots** coprirsi di foruncoli

spot check N controllo senza preavviso

spotless [ˈspɔtlɪs] ADJ immacolato(-a)

spotlight [ˈspɔtlaɪt] N proiettore *m*; (*Aut*) faro ausiliario

spot-on [spɔtˈɔn] ADJ (*BRIT col*) esatto(-a)

spot price N (*Comm*) prezzo del pronto

spotted [ˈspɔtɪd] ADJ macchiato(-a); a puntini, a pallini; **~ with** punteggiato(-a) di

spotty [ˈspɔtɪ] ADJ (*face*) foruncoloso(-a)

spouse [spaus] N sposo(-a)

spout [spaut] N (*of jug*) beccuccio; (*of liquid*) zampillo, getto ▶ VI zampillare

sprain [spreɪn] N storta, distorsione *f* ▶ VT: **to ~ one's ankle** storcersi una caviglia

sprang [spræŋ] PT *of* **spring**

sprawl [sprɔːl] VI sdraiarsi (in modo scomposto); (*place*) estendersi (disordinatamente) ▶ N: **urban ~** sviluppo urbanistico incontrollato; **to send sb sprawling** mandare qn a gambe all'aria

spray [spreɪ] N spruzzo; (*container*) nebulizzatore *m*, spray *m inv*; (*of flowers*) mazzetto ▶ CPD (*deodorant*) spray *inv* ▶ VT spruzzare; (*crops*) irrorare

spread [sprɛd] (*pt, pp ~*) N diffusione *f*; (*distribution*) distribuzione *f*; (*Press, Typ: two pages*) doppia pagina; (*: across columns*) articolo a più colonne; (*Culin*) pasta (da spalmare); (*col: food*) banchetto ▶ VT (*cloth*) stendere, distendere; (*butter etc*) spalmare; (*disease, knowledge*) propagare, diffondere ▶ VI stendersi, distendersi; spalmarsi; propagarsi, diffondersi; **middle-age ~** pancetta; **repayments will be ~ over 18 months** i versamenti saranno scaglionati lungo un periodo di 18 mesi

▶ **spread out** VI (*move apart*) separarsi

spread-eagled [ˈsprɛdiːgld] ADJ: **to be** *or* **lie ~** essere disteso(-a) a gambe e braccia aperte

spreadsheet [ˈsprɛdʃiːt] N (*Comput*) foglio elettronico

spree [spriː] N: **to go on a ~** fare baldoria

sprig [sprɪg] N ramoscello

sprightly [ˈspraɪtlɪ] ADJ vivace

spring [sprɪŋ] (*pt* **sprang** [spræŋ], *pp* **sprung** [sprʌŋ]) N (*leap*) salto, balzo; (*bounciness*) elasticità; (*coiled metal*) molla; (*season*) primavera; (*of water*) sorgente *f* ▶ VI saltare, balzare ▶ VT: **to ~ a leak** (*pipe etc*) cominciare a perdere; **to walk with a ~ in one's step** camminare con passo elastico; **in ~, in the ~** in primavera; **to ~ from** provenire da; **to ~ into action** entrare (rapidamente) in azione; **he sprang the news on me** mi ha sorpreso con quella notizia

▶ **spring up** VI (*problem*) presentarsi

springboard [ˈsprɪŋbɔːd] N trampolino

spring-clean [sprɪŋˈkliːn] N (*also*: **spring-cleaning**) grandi pulizie *fpl* di primavera

spring onion N (*BRIT*) cipollina

spring roll N involtino fritto di verdure o carne tipico della cucina cinese

springtime [ˈsprɪŋtaɪm] N primavera

springy [ˈsprɪŋɪ] ADJ elastico(-a)

sprinkle [ˈsprɪŋkl] VT spruzzare; spargere; **to ~ water etc on**, **~ with water etc** spruzzare dell'acqua *etc* su; **to ~ sugar etc on**, **~ with sugar etc** spolverizzare di zucchero *etc*; **sprinkled with** (*fig*) cosparso(-a) di

sprinkler [ˈsprɪŋkləʳ] N (*for lawn etc*) irrigatore *m*; (*for fire-fighting*) sprinkler *m inv*

sprinkling [ˈsprɪŋklɪŋ] N (*of water*) qualche goccia; (*of salt, sugar*) pizzico

sprint [sprɪnt] N scatto ▶ VI scattare; **the 200-metres ~** i 200 metri piani

sprinter [ˈsprɪntəʳ] N velocista *mf*

sprite [spraɪt] N elfo, folletto

spritzer [ˈsprɪtsəʳ] N spritz *m inv*

sprocket [ˈsprɔkɪt] N (*on printer etc*) dente *m*, rocchetto

sprout [spraut] VI germogliare

sprouts [sprauts] NPL (*also*: **Brussels sprouts**) cavolini *mpl* di Bruxelles

spruce [spruːs] N abete *m* rosso ▶ ADJ lindo(-a); azzimato(-a)

▶ **spruce up** VT (*tidy*) mettere in ordine; (*smarten up: room etc*) abbellire; **to ~ o.s. up** farsi bello(-a)

sprung [sprʌŋ] PP *of* **spring**

spry [spraɪ] ADJ arzillo(-a), sveglio(-a)

SPUC N ABBR (= *Society for the Protection of Unborn Children*) associazione anti-abortista

spun [spʌn] PT, PP *of* **spin**

spur [spəːʳ] N sperone *m*; (*fig*) sprone *m*, incentivo ▶ VT (*also*: **spur on**) spronare; **on the ~ of the moment** lì per lì

S

spurious [ˈspjuərɪəs] ADJ falso(-a)

spurn [spəːn] VT rifiutare con disprezzo, sdegnare

spurt [spəːt] N (of water) getto; (of energy) esplosione f ▶ VI sgorgare; zampillare; **to put in** or **on a ~** (runner) fare uno scatto; (fig: in work etc) affrettarsi, sbrigarsi

sputter [ˈspʌtər] VI = **splutter**

spy [spaɪ] N spia ▶ CPD (film, story) di spionaggio ▶ VI: **to ~ on** spiare ▶ VT (see) scorgere

spycam [ˈspaɪkæm] N spy cam f inv

spying [ˈspaɪɪŋ] N spionaggio

spyware [ˈspaɪwɛər] N (Comput) spyware m

Sq. ABBR (in address) = **square**

sq. ABBR (Math etc) = **square**

squabble [ˈskwɔbl] N battibecco ▶ VI bisticciarsi

squad [skwɔd] N (Mil) plotone m; (Police) squadra; **flying ~** (Police) volante f

squad car N (BRIT Police) automobile f della polizia

squaddie [ˈskwɔdɪ] N (Mil: col) burba

squadron [ˈskwɔdrn] N (Mil) squadrone m; (Aviat, Naut) squadriglia

squalid [ˈskwɔlɪd] ADJ sordido(-a)

squall [skwɔːl] N burrasca

squalor [ˈskwɔlər] N squallore m

squander [ˈskwɔndər] VT dissipare

square [skwɛər] N quadrato; (in town) piazza; (US: block of houses) blocco, isolato; (instrument) squadra ▶ ADJ quadrato(-a); (honest) onesto(-a); (col: ideas, person) di vecchio stampo ▶ VT (arrange) regolare; (Math) elevare al quadrato; (reconcile) conciliare ▶ VI (agree) accordarsi; **a ~ meal** un pasto abbondante; **2 metres ~** di 2 metri per 2; **1 ~ metre** 1 metro quadrato; **we're back to ~ one** (fig) siamo al punto di partenza; **all ~** pari; **to get one's accounts ~** mettere in ordine i propri conti; **I'll ~ it with him** (col) sistemo io le cose con lui; **can you ~ it with your conscience?** (reconcile) puoi conciliarlo con la tua coscienza?
▶ **square up** VI (BRIT: settle) saldare, pagare; **to ~ up with sb** regolare i conti con qn

square bracket N (Typ) parentesi f inv quadra

squarely [ˈskwɛəlɪ] ADV (directly) direttamente; (honestly, fairly) onestamente

square root N radice f quadrata

squash [skwɔʃ] N (vegetable) zucca; (Sport) squash m; **lemon/orange ~** (BRIT) sciroppo di limone/arancia ▶ VT schiacciare

squat [skwɔt] ADJ tarchiato(-a), tozzo(-a) ▶ VI accovacciarsi; (on property) occupare abusivamente

squatter [ˈskwɔtər] N occupante mf abusivo(-a)

squawk [skwɔːk] VI emettere strida rauche

squeak [skwiːk] VI squittire ▶ N (of hinge, wheel

etc) cigolio; (of shoes) scricchiolio; (of mouse etc) squittio

squeaky [ˈskwiːkɪ] ADJ (col) cigolante; **to be ~ clean** (fig) avere un'immagine pulita

squeal [skwiːl] VI strillare

squeamish [ˈskwiːmɪʃ] ADJ schizzinoso(-a); disgustato(-a)

squeeze [skwiːz] N pressione f; (also Econ) stretta; (credit squeeze) stretta creditizia ▶ VT premere; (hand, arm) stringere ▶ VI (also: **squeeze in**) infilarsi; **to ~ past/under sth** passare vicino/sotto a qc con difficoltà; **a ~ of lemon** una spruzzata di limone
▶ **squeeze out** VT spremere

squelch [skwɛltʃ] VI fare ciac; sguazzare

squib [skwɪb] N petardo

squid [skwɪd] N calamaro

squint [skwɪnt] VI essere strabico(-a); (in the sunlight) strizzare gli occhi ▶ N: **he has a ~** è strabico; **to ~ at sth** guardare qc di traverso; (quickly) dare un'occhiata a qc

squire [ˈskwaɪər] N (BRIT) proprietario terriero

squirm [skwəːm] VI contorcersi

squirrel [ˈskwɪrəl] N scoiattolo

squirt [skwəːt] N schizzo ▶ VI schizzare; zampillare ▶ VT spruzzare

Sr ABBR = **senior; sister**

SRC N ABBR (BRIT: = Students' Representative Council) comitato di rappresentanza studenti

Sri Lanka [srɪˈlæŋkə] N Sri Lanka m

SRO ABBR (US: = standing room only) solo posti in piedi

SS ABBR = **steamship**

SSA N ABBR (US: = Social Security Administration) ≈ Previdenza Sociale

SST N ABBR = **supersonic transport**

ST ABBR (US: = Standard Time) ora ufficiale

St ABBR = **saint; street**

stab [stæb] N (with knife etc) pugnalata; (of pain) fitta; (col: try): **to have a ~ at (doing) sth** provare a fare qc ▶ VT pugnalare; **to ~ sb to death** uccidere qn a coltellate

stabbing [ˈstæbɪŋ] N: **there's been a ~** qualcuno è stato pugnalato ▶ ADJ (pain, ache) lancinante

stability [stəˈbɪlɪtɪ] N stabilità

stabilization [steɪbəlaɪˈzeɪʃən] N stabilizzazione f

stabilize [ˈsteɪbəlaɪz] VT stabilizzare ▶ VI stabilizzarsi

stabilizer [ˈsteɪbəlaɪzər] N (Aviat, Naut) stabilizzatore m

stable [ˈsteɪbl] N (for horses) scuderia; (for cattle) stalla ▶ ADJ stabile; **riding stables** maneggio

staccato [stəˈkɑːtəu] ADV in modo staccato ▶ ADJ (Mus) staccato(-a); (sound) scandito(-a)

stack [stæk] N catasta, pila; (col) mucchio, sacco ▶ vт accatastare, ammucchiare; **there's stacks of time to finish it** (BRIT col) abbiamo un sacco di tempo per finirlo

stadium ['steɪdɪəm] N stadio

staff [stɑːf] N (workforce: gen) personale m; (: BRIT Scol) personale insegnante; (: servants) personale di servizio; (Mil) stato maggiore; (stick) bastone m ▶ vт fornire di personale

staffroom ['stɑːfruːm] N sala dei professori

stag [stæg] N cervo; (BRIT Stock Exchange) rialzista mf su nuove emissioni

stage [steɪdʒ] N (platform) palco; (in theatre) palcoscenico; **the ~** il teatro, la scena; (point) fase f, stadio ▶ vт (play) allestire, mettere in scena; (demonstration) organizzare; (fig: perform: recovery etc) effettuare; **in stages** per gradi; a tappe; **in the early/final stages** negli stadi iniziali/finali; **to go through a difficult ~** attraversare un periodo difficile

stagecoach ['steɪdʒkəʊtʃ] N diligenza

stage door N ingresso degli artisti

stage fright N paura del pubblico

stagehand ['steɪdʒhænd] N macchinista m

stage-manage ['steɪdʒmænɪdʒ] vт allestire le scene per; montare

stage manager N direttore(-trice) di scena

stagger ['stægəʳ] vi barcollare ▶ vт (person) sbalordire; (hours, holidays) scaglionare

staggering ['stægərɪŋ] ADJ (amazing) incredibile, sbalorditivo(-a)

staging post ['steɪdʒɪŋ-] N passaggio obbligato

stagnant ['stægnənt] ADJ stagnante

stagnate [stæg'neɪt] vi (also fig) stagnare

stagnation [stæg'neɪʃən] N stagnazione f, ristagno

stag night, stag party N festa di addio al celibato

staid [steɪd] ADJ posato(-a), serio(-a)

stain [steɪn] N macchia; (colouring) colorante m ▶ vт macchiare; (wood) tingere

stained glass [steɪnd-] N vetro colorato

stained glass window ['steɪnd-] N vetrata

stainless ['steɪnlɪs] ADJ (steel) inossidabile

stain remover N smacchiatore m

stair [stɛəʳ] N (step) gradino ▪ **stairs** NPL (flight of stairs) scale fpl, scala

staircase ['stɛəkeɪs], **stairway** ['stɛəweɪ] N scale fpl, scala

stairwell ['stɛəwɛl] N tromba delle scale

stake [steɪk] N palo, piolo; (Comm) interesse m; (Betting) puntata, scommessa ▶ vт (bet) scommettere; (risk) rischiare; (also: **stake out**: area) delimitare con paletti; **to be at ~** essere in gioco; **to have a ~ in sth** avere un interesse in qc; **to ~ a claim (to sth)** rivendicare (qc)

stakeout ['steɪkaʊt] N sorveglianza

stalactite ['stæləktaɪt] N stalattite f

stalagmite ['stæləgmaɪt] N stalagmite f

stale [steɪl] ADJ (bread) raffermo(-a); (food) stantio(-a); (air) viziato(-a); (beer) svaporato(-a); (smell) di chiuso

stalemate ['steɪlmeɪt] N stallo; (fig) punto morto

stalk [stɔːk] N gambo, stelo ▶ vт inseguire ▶ vi camminare impettito(-a)

stall [stɔːl] N (in street, market etc) bancarella; (in stable) box m inv di stalla ▶ vт (Aut) far spegnere; (fig) bloccare ▶ vi (Aut) spegnersi, fermarsi; (fig) temporeggiare ▪ **stalls** NPL (BRIT: in cinema, theatre) platea; **newspaper/flower ~** chiosco del giornalaio/del fioraio

stallholder ['stɔːlhəʊldəʳ] N (BRIT) bancarellista mf

stallion ['stæljən] N stallone m

stalwart ['stɔːlwət] N membro fidato

stamen ['steɪmɛn] N stame m

stamina ['stæmɪnə] N vigore m, resistenza

stammer ['stæməʳ] N balbuzie f ▶ vi balbettare

stamp [stæmp] N (postage stamp) francobollo; (implement) timbro; (mark, also fig) marchio, impronta; (on document) bollo; timbro ▶ vi (also: **stamp one's foot**) battere il piede ▶ vт battere; (letter) affrancare; (mark with a stamp) timbrare; **stamped addressed envelope** busta affrancata per la risposta
▶ **stamp out** vт (fire) estinguere; (crime) eliminare; (opposition) soffocare

stamp album N album m inv per francobolli

stamp collecting N filatelia

stamp duty N (BRIT) bollo

stampede [stæm'piːd] N fuggi fuggi m inv; (of cattle) fuga precipitosa

stamp machine N distributore m automatico di francobolli

stance [stæns] N posizione f

stand [stænd] (pt, pp **stood** [stud]) N (position) posizione f; (Mil) resistenza; (for taxis) posteggio; (structure) supporto, sostegno; (at exhibition) stand m inv; (in shop) banco; (at market) bancarella; (booth) chiosco; (Sport) tribuna; (also: **music stand**) leggio m ▶ vi stare in piedi; (rise) alzarsi in piedi; (be placed) trovarsi ▶ vт (place) mettere, porre; (tolerate, withstand) resistere a, sopportare; **to make a ~** prendere posizione; **to take a ~ on an issue** prendere posizione su un problema; **to ~ for parliament** (BRIT) presentarsi come candidato (per il parlamento); **to ~ guard** or **watch** (Mil) essere di guardia; **it stands to reason** è logico; **as things ~** stando così le cose; **to ~ sb a drink/meal** offrire da bere/un pranzo a qn; **I can't ~ him** non lo sopporto
▶ **stand aside** vi farsi da parte, scostarsi
▶ **stand back** vi prendere le distanze

S

801

▶ **stand by** VI (*be ready*) tenersi pronto(-a)
▶ VT FUS (*opinion*) sostenere
▶ **stand down** VI (*withdraw*) ritirarsi; (*Law*) lasciare il banco dei testimoni
▶ **stand for** VT FUS (*signify*) rappresentare, significare; (*tolerate*) sopportare, tollerare
▶ **stand in for** VT FUS sostituire
▶ **stand out** VI (*be prominent*) spiccare
▶ **stand up** VI (*rise*) alzarsi in piedi
▶ **stand up for** VT FUS difendere
▶ **stand up to** VT FUS tener testa a, resistere a

stand-alone [ˈstændələun] ADJ (*Comput*) stand-alone *inv*

standard [ˈstændəd] N modello, standard *m inv*; (*level*) livello; (*flag*) stendardo ▶ ADJ (*size etc*) normale, standard *inv*; (*practice*) normale; (*model*) di serie ◾ **standards** NPL (*morals*) principi *mpl*, valori *mpl*; **to be** *or* **come up to ~** rispondere ai requisiti; **below** *or* **not up to ~** (*work*) mediocre; **to apply a double ~** usare metri diversi (nel giudicare *or* fare *etc*); **~ of living** livello di vita

standardization [stændədaɪˈzeɪʃən] N standardizzazione *f*

standardize [ˈstændədaɪz] VT normalizzare, standardizzare

standard lamp N (*BRIT*) lampada a stelo

standard time N ora ufficiale

stand-by [ˈstændbaɪ] N riserva, sostituto; **to be on ~** (*gen*) tenersi pronto(-a); (*doctor*) essere di guardia; **a ~ ticket** un biglietto standby; **to fly ~** essere in lista d'attesa per un volo

stand-by generator N generatore *m* d'emergenza

stand-by passenger N (*Aviat*) passeggero(-a) in lista d'attesa

stand-by ticket N (*Aviat*) biglietto senza garanzia

stand-in [ˈstændɪn] N sostituto(-a); (*Cine*) controfigura

standing [ˈstændɪŋ] ADJ diritto(-a), in piedi; (*permanent: rule*) fisso(-a); (: *army*) regolare; (*grievance*) continuo(-a) ▶ N rango, condizione *f*, posizione *f*; (*duration*): **of 6 months' ~** che dura da 6 mesi; **of many years' ~** che esiste da molti anni; **it's a ~ joke** è diventato proverbiale; **he was given a ~ ovation** tutti si alzarono per applaudirlo; **a man of some ~** un uomo di una certa importanza

standing committee N commissione *f* permanente

standing order N (*BRIT: at bank*) ordine *m* di pagamento (permanente) ◾ **standing orders** NPL (*Mil*) regolamento

standing room N posto all'impiedi

stand-off [ˈstændɔf] N (*stalemate*) situazione *f* di stallo

standoffish [stændˈɔfɪʃ] ADJ scostante, freddo(-a)

standpat [ˈstændpæt] ADJ (*US*) irremovibile

standpipe [ˈstændpaɪp] N fontanella

standpoint [ˈstændpɔɪnt] N punto di vista

standstill [ˈstændstɪl] N: **at a ~** fermo(-a); (*fig*) a un punto morto; **to come to a ~** fermarsi; giungere a un punto morto

stank [stæŋk] PT *of* **stink**

stanza [ˈstænzə] N stanza (*poesia*)

staple [ˈsteɪpl] N (*for papers*) graffetta; (*chief product*) prodotto principale ▶ ADJ (*food etc*) di base; (*crop, industry*) principale ▶ VT cucire

stapler [ˈsteɪplə˭] N cucitrice *f*

star [stɑː˭] N stella; (*celebrity*) divo(-a); (*principal actor*) vedette *f inv* ▶ VI: **to ~ (in)** essere il(la) protagonista (di) ▶ VT (*Cine*) essere interpretato(-a) da ◾ **the stars** NPL (*Astrology*) le stelle; **four-star hotel** ≈ albergo di prima categoria

star attraction N numero principale

starboard [ˈstɑːbəd] N dritta; **to ~** a dritta

starch [stɑːtʃ] N amido

starched [ˈstɑːtʃt] ADJ (*collar*) inamidato(-a)

starchy [ˈstɑːtʃɪ] ADJ (*food*) ricco(-a) di amido

stardom [ˈstɑːdəm] N celebrità

stare [stɛə˭] N sguardo fisso ▶ VI: **to ~ at** fissare

starfish [ˈstɑːfɪʃ] N stella di mare

stark [stɑːk] ADJ (*bleak*) desolato(-a); (*simplicity, colour*) austero(-a); (*reality, poverty, truth*) crudo(-a) ▶ ADV: **~ naked** completamente nudo(-a)

starkers [ˈstɑːkəz] ADJ: **to be ~** (*BRIT col*) essere nudo(-a) come un verme

starlet [ˈstɑːlɪt] N (*Cine*) stellina

starlight [ˈstɑːlaɪt] N: **by ~** alla luce delle stelle

starling [ˈstɑːlɪŋ] N storno

starlit [ˈstɑːlɪt] ADJ stellato(-a)

starry [ˈstɑːrɪ] ADJ stellato(-a)

starry-eyed [stɑːrɪˈaɪd] ADJ (*idealistic, gullible*) ingenuo(-a); (*from wonder*) meravigliato(-a)

Stars and Stripes NPL: **the ~** la bandiera a stelle e strisce

star sign N segno zodiacale

star-studded [ˈstɑːstʌdɪd] ADJ: **a ~ cast** un cast di attori famosi

START [stɑːt] N ABBR (= *Strategic Arms Reduction Treaty*) START *m*

start [stɑːt] N inizio; (*of race*) partenza; (*sudden movement*) sobbalzo; (*advantage*) vantaggio ▶ VT cominciare, iniziare; (*found: business, newspaper*) fondare, creare; (*car*) mettere in moto ▶ VI cominciare; (*on journey*) partire, mettersi in viaggio; (*jump*) sobbalzare; **to ~ doing sth** (in) cominciare a fare qc; **at the ~** all'inizio; **for a ~** tanto per cominciare; **to make an early ~** partire di buon'ora; **to ~ (off) with ...** (*firstly*) per prima cosa ...; (*at the beginning*) all'inizio ...; **to ~ a fire** provocare un incendio
▶ **start off** VI cominciare; (*leave*) partire
▶ **start out** VI (*begin*) cominciare; (*set out*) partire

▶ **start over** VI (US) ricominciare
▶ **start up** VI cominciare; (car) avviarsi ▶ VT iniziare; (car) avviare

starter ['stɑːtəʳ] N (Aut) motorino d'avviamento; (Sport: official) starter m inv; (: runner, horse) partente mf; (BRIT Culin) primo piatto

starting handle ['stɑːtɪŋ-] N (BRIT) manovella d'avviamento

starting point ['stɑːtɪŋ-] N punto di partenza

starting price ['stɑːtɪŋ-] N prezzo m base inv

startle ['stɑːtl] VT far trasalire

startling ['stɑːtlɪŋ] ADJ sorprendente, sbalorditivo(-a)

start-up ['stɑːtʌp] N (new business) startup f inv

star turn N (BRIT) attrazione f principale

starvation [stɑːˈveɪʃən] N fame f, inedia; **to die of ~** morire d'inedia

starve [stɑːv] VI morire di fame; soffrire la fame ▶ VT far morire di fame, affamare; **I'm starving** muoio di fame

stash [stæʃ] VT: **to ~ sth away** (col) nascondere qc

state [steɪt] N stato; (pomp): **in ~** in pompa ▶ VT dichiarare, affermare; annunciare; **to be in a ~** essere agitato(-a); **the ~ of the art** il livello di tecnologia (or cultura etc); **~ of emergency** stato di emergenza; **~ of mind** stato d'animo

state control N controllo statale

stated ['steɪtɪd] ADJ fissato(-a), stabilito(-a)

State Department N (US) Dipartimento di Stato, ≈ Ministero degli Esteri

state education N (BRIT) istruzione f pubblica or statale

stateless ['steɪtlɪs] ADJ apolide

stately ['steɪtlɪ] ADJ maestoso(-a), imponente

stately home N residenza nobiliare (d'interesse storico o artistico spesso aperta al pubblico)

statement ['steɪtmənt] N dichiarazione f; (Law) deposizione f; (Finance) rendiconto; **official ~** comunicato ufficiale; **~ of account, bank ~** estratto conto

state-owned ['steɪtˈəund] ADJ statalizzato(-a)

States [steɪts] NPL: **the ~** (USA) gli Stati Uniti

state school N scuola statale

statesman ['steɪtsmən] N (irreg) statista m

statesmanship ['steɪtsmənʃɪp] N abilità politica

static ['stætɪk] N (Radio) scariche fpl ▶ ADJ statico(-a); **~ electricity** elettricità statica

station ['steɪʃən] N stazione f; (rank) rango, condizione f ▶ VT collocare, disporre; **action stations** posti mpl di combattimento; **to be stationed in** (Mil) essere di stanza in

stationary ['steɪʃənrɪ] ADJ fermo(-a), immobile

stationer ['steɪʃənəʳ] N cartolaio(-a); **~'s shop** cartoleria

stationery ['steɪʃənərɪ] N articoli mpl di cancelleria; (writing paper) carta da lettere

station master N (Rail) capostazione m

station wagon N (US) giardinetta

statistic [stəˈtɪstɪk] N statistica; see also **statistics**

statistical [stəˈtɪstɪkəl] ADJ statistico(-a)

statistics [stəˈtɪstɪks] N (science) statistica

statue ['stætjuː] N statua

statuesque [stætjuˈɛsk] ADJ statuario(-a)

statuette [stætjuˈet] N statuetta

stature ['stætʃəʳ] N statura

status ['steɪtəs] N posizione f, condizione f sociale; (prestige) prestigio; (legal, marital) stato

status quo [-ˈkwəu] N: **the ~** lo statu quo

status symbol N simbolo di prestigio

statute ['stætjuːt] N legge f ▪ **statutes** NPL (of club etc) statuto

statute book N codice m

statutory ['stætjutərɪ] ADJ stabilito(-a) dalla legge, statutario(-a); **~ meeting** (Comm) assemblea ordinaria

staunch [stɔːntʃ] ADJ fidato(-a), leale ▶ VT (flow) arrestare; (blood) arrestare il flusso di

stave [steɪv] N (Mus) rigo ▶ VT: **to ~ off** (attack) respingere; (threat) evitare

stay [steɪ] N (period of time) soggiorno, permanenza ▶ VI rimanere; (reside) alloggiare, stare; (spend some time) trattenersi, soggiornare; **~ of execution** (Law) sospensione f dell'esecuzione; **to ~ put** non muoversi; **to ~ with friends** stare presso amici; **to ~ the night** passare la notte
▶ **stay away** VI (from person, building) stare lontano; (from event) non andare
▶ **stay behind** VI restare indietro
▶ **stay in** VI (at home) stare in casa
▶ **stay on** VI restare, rimanere
▶ **stay out** VI (of house) rimanere fuori (di casa); (strikers) continuare lo sciopero
▶ **stay up** VI (at night) rimanere alzato(-a)

staying power ['steɪɪŋ-] N capacità di resistenza

STD N ABBR (BRIT: = subscriber trunk dialling) teleselezione f; (= sexually transmitted disease) malattia venerea

stead [stɛd] N (BRIT): **in sb's ~** al posto di qn; **to stand sb in good ~** essere utile a qn

steadfast ['stɛdfɑːst] ADJ fermo(-a), risoluto(-a)

steadily ['stɛdɪlɪ] ADV (firmly) saldamente; (constantly) continuamente; (fixedly) fisso; (walk) con passo sicuro

steady ['stɛdɪ] ADJ (not wobbling) stabile, solido(-a), fermo(-a); (regular) costante; (boyfriend etc) fisso(-a); (person, character) serio(-a); (calm) calmo(-a), tranquillo(-a) ▶ VT stabilizzare; calmare; **to ~ o.s.** ritrovare l'equilibrio

steak [steɪk] N (meat) bistecca; (fish) trancia

steakhouse ['steɪkhaʊs] N ristorante specializzato in bistecche

steal [stiːl] (pt **stole** [stəʊl], pp **stolen** ['stəʊln]) VT rubare ▶ VI (thieve) rubare; (move) muoversi furtivamente
▶ **steal away, steal off** VI svignarsela, andarsene alla chetichella

stealth [stɛlθ] N: **by** ~ furtivamente

stealthy ['stɛlθɪ] ADJ furtivo(-a)

steam [stiːm] N vapore m ▶ VT trattare con vapore; (Culin) cuocere a vapore ▶ VI fumare; (ship): **to** ~ **along** filare; **to let off** ~ (fig) sfogarsi; **under one's own** ~ (fig) da solo, con i propri mezzi; **to run out of** ~ (fig: person) non farcela più
▶ **steam up** VI (window) appannarsi; **to get steamed up about sth** (fig) andare in bestia per qc

steam engine N macchina a vapore; (Rail) locomotiva a vapore

steamer ['stiːmə'] N piroscafo, vapore m; (Culin) pentola a vapore

steam iron N ferro a vapore

steamroller ['stiːmrəʊlə'] N rullo compressore

steamship ['stiːmʃɪp] N piroscafo, vapore m

steamy ['stiːmɪ] ADJ (room) pieno(-a) di vapore; (window) appannato(-a)

steed [stiːd] N (literary) corsiero, destriero

steel [stiːl] N acciaio ▶ CPD di acciaio

steel band N banda di strumenti a percussione (tipica dei Caribi)

steel industry N industria dell'acciaio

steel mill N acciaieria

steelworks ['stiːlwəːks] N acciaieria

steely ['stiːlɪ] ADJ (determination) inflessibile; (gaze) duro(-a); (eyes) freddo(-a) come l'acciaio

steep [stiːp] ADJ ripido(-a), scosceso(-a); (price) eccessivo(-a) ▶ VT inzuppare; (washing) mettere a mollo

steeple ['stiːpl] N campanile m

steeplechase ['stiːpltʃeɪs] N corsa a ostacoli, steeplechase m inv

steeplejack ['stiːpldʒæk] N chi ripara campanili e ciminiere

steer [stɪə'] N manzo ▶ VT (ship) governare; (car) guidare ▶ VI (Naut: person) governare; (: ship) rispondere al timone; (car) guidarsi; **to** ~ **clear of sb/sth** (fig) tenersi alla larga da qn/qc

steering ['stɪərɪŋ] N (Aut) sterzo

steering column N piantone m dello sterzo

steering committee N comitato direttivo

steering wheel N volante m

stem [stɛm] N (of flower, plant) stelo; (of tree) fusto; (of glass) gambo; (of fruit, leaf) picciolo ▶ VT contenere, arginare
▶ **stem from** VT FUS provenire da, derivare da

stem cell N cellula staminale

stench [stɛntʃ] N puzzo, fetore m

stencil ['stɛnsl] N (of metal, cardboard) stampino, mascherina; (in typing) matrice f

stenographer [stɛ'nɔgrəfə'] N (US) stenografo(-a)

stenography [stɛ'nɔgrəfɪ] N (US) stenografia

step [stɛp] N passo; (stair) gradino, scalino; (action) mossa, azione f ▶ VI: **to** ~ **forward/back** fare un passo avanti/indietro ■ **steps** NPL (BRIT) = **stepladder**; ~ **by** ~ un passo dietro l'altro; (fig) poco a poco; **to be in/out of** ~ **with** (also fig) stare/non stare al passo con
▶ **step down** VI (fig) ritirarsi
▶ **step in** VI fare il proprio ingresso
▶ **step off** VT FUS scendere da
▶ **step over** VT FUS scavalcare
▶ **step up** VT aumentare; intensificare

step aerobics N step m inv

stepbrother ['stɛpbrʌðə'] N fratellastro

stepchild ['stɛptʃaɪld] N (irreg) figliastro(-a)

stepdad ['stɛpdæd] N papà m inv acquisito

stepdaughter ['stɛpdɔːtə'] N figliastra

stepfather ['stɛpfɑːðə'] N patrigno

stepladder ['stɛplædə'] N scala a libretto

stepmother ['stɛpmʌðə'] N matrigna

stepmum ['stɛpmʌm] N mamma acquisita

stepping stone ['stɛpɪŋ-] N pietra di un guado; (fig) trampolino

step Reebok® [-'riːbɔk] N step m inv

stepsister ['stɛpsɪstə'] N sorellastra

stepson ['stɛpsʌn] N figliastro

stereo ['stɛrɪəʊ] N (system) sistema m stereofonico; (record player) stereo m inv ▶ ADJ (also: **stereophonic**) stereofonico(-a); **in** ~ in stereofonia

stereotype ['stɪərɪətaɪp] N stereotipo

sterile ['stɛraɪl] ADJ sterile

sterility [stɛ'rɪlɪtɪ] N sterilità

sterilization [stɛrɪlaɪ'zeɪʃən] N sterilizzazione f

sterilize ['stɛrɪlaɪz] VT sterilizzare

sterling ['stəːlɪŋ] ADJ (gold, silver) di buona lega; (fig) autentico(-a), genuino(-a) ▶ N (Econ) (lira) sterlina; **a pound** ~ una lira sterlina

sterling area N area della sterlina

stern [stəːn] ADJ severo(-a) ▶ N (Naut) poppa

sternum ['stəːnəm] N sterno

steroid ['stɪərɔɪd] N steroide m

stethoscope ['stɛθəskəʊp] N stetoscopio

stevedore ['stiːvɪdɔː'] N scaricatore m di porto

stew [stjuː] N stufato ▶ VT, VI cuocere in umido; **stewed tea** tè lasciato troppo in infusione; **stewed fruit** frutta cotta

steward ['stjuːəd] N (Aviat, Naut, Rail) steward m inv; (in club etc) dispensiere m; (shop steward) rappresentante mf sindacale

stewardess ['stjuːədɛs] N assistente f di volo, hostess f inv

stewardship [ˈstjuədʃɪp] N amministrazione f

stewing steak [ˈstjuːɪŋ-], (US) **stew meat** N carne f (di manzo) per stufato

St. Ex. ABBR = **stock exchange**

stg ABBR = **sterling**

stick [stɪk] (pt, pp **stuck** [stʌk]) N bastone m; (of rhubarb, celery) gambo; (of dynamite) candelotto ▶ VT (glue) attaccare; (thrust): **to ~ sth into** conficcare or piantare or infiggere qc in; (col: put) ficcare; (: tolerate) sopportare ▶ VI attaccarsi; tenere; (remain) restare, rimanere; (get jammed: door, lift) bloccarsi; **to ~ to** (one's word, promise) mantenere; (principles) tener fede a; **to get hold of the wrong end of the ~** (fig) capire male; **it stuck in my mind** mi è rimasto in mente
  ▶ **stick around** VI (col) restare, fermarsi
  ▶ **stick out** VI sporgere, spuntare ▶ VT: **to ~ it out** (col) tener duro
  ▶ **stick up** VI sporgere, spuntare
  ▶ **stick up for** VT FUS difendere

sticker [ˈstɪkəʳ] N cartellino adesivo

sticking plaster [ˈstɪkɪŋ-] cerotto adesivo

sticking point N (fig) punto di stallo, impasse f inv

stick insect N insetto m stecco inv

stickleback [ˈstɪklbæk] N spinarello

stickler [ˈstɪkləʳ] N: **to be a ~ for** essere pignolo(-a) su, tenere molto a

stick-on [ˈstɪkɔn] ADJ (label) adesivo(-a)

stick shift N (US Aut) cambio manuale

stick-up [ˈstɪkʌp] N (col) rapina a mano armata

sticky [ˈstɪkɪ] ADJ attaccaticcio(-a), vischioso(-a); (label) adesivo(-a); (fig: situation) difficile

stiff [stɪf] ADJ rigido(-a), duro(-a); (muscle) legato(-a), indolenzito(-a); (difficult) difficile, arduo(-a); (cold: manner etc) freddo(-a), formale; (strong) forte; (high: price) molto alto(-a) ▶ ADV: **bored ~** annoiato(-a) a morte; **to be** or **feel ~** (person) essere or sentirsi indolenzito; **to have a ~ neck/back** avere il torcicollo/mal di schiena; **to keep a ~ upper lip** (BRIT fig) conservare il sangue freddo

stiffen [ˈstɪfn] VT irrigidire; rinforzare ▶ VI irrigidirsi; indurirsi

stiffness [ˈstɪfnɪs] N rigidità; indolenzimento; difficoltà; freddezza

stifle [ˈstaɪfl] VT soffocare

stifling [ˈstaɪflɪŋ] ADJ (heat) soffocante

stigma [ˈstɪgmə] N (pl **stigmata** [stɪgˈmɑːtə]: Bot, Med; pl **stigmas**: fig) stigma m

stigmata [stɪgˈmɑːtə] NPL (Rel) stigmate fpl

stile [staɪl] N cavalcasiepe m; cavalcasteccato

stiletto [stɪˈlɛtəu] N (BRIT: also: **stiletto heel**) tacco a spillo

still [stɪl] ADJ fermo(-a); (quiet) silenzioso(-a); (orange juice etc) non gassato(-a) ▶ ADV (up to this time, even) ancora; (nonetheless) tuttavia, ciò nonostante ▶ N (Cine) fotogramma m; **keep ~!**

stai fermo!; **he ~ hasn't arrived** non è ancora arrivato

stillborn [ˈstɪlbɔːn] ADJ nato(-a) morto(-a)

still life N natura morta

stilt [stɪlt] N trampolo; (pile) palo

stilted [ˈstɪltɪd] ADJ freddo(-a), formale; artificiale

stimulant [ˈstɪmjulənt] N stimolante m

stimulate [ˈstɪmjuleɪt] VT stimolare

stimulating [ˈstɪmjuleɪtɪŋ] ADJ stimolante

stimulation [stɪmjuˈleɪʃən] N stimolazione f

stimulus [ˈstɪmjuləs] (pl **stimuli** [ˈstɪmjulaɪ]) N stimolo

sting [stɪŋ] (pt, pp **stung** [stʌŋ]) N puntura; (organ) pungiglione m; (col) trucco ▶ VT pungere ▶ VI bruciare; **my eyes are stinging** mi bruciano gli occhi

stingy [ˈstɪndʒɪ] ADJ spilorcio(-a), tirchio(-a)

stink [stɪŋk] (pt **stank** [stæŋk], pp **stunk** [stʌŋk]) N fetore m, puzzo ▶ VI puzzare

stinker [ˈstɪŋkəʳ] N (col) porcheria; (person) fetente mf

stinking [ˈstɪŋkɪŋ] ADJ (col): **a ~ ...** uno schifo di ..., un maledetto(-a) ...; **~ rich** ricco(-a) da far paura

stint [stɪnt] N lavoro, compito ▶ VI: **to ~ on** lesinare su

stipend [ˈstaɪpɛnd] N stipendio, congrua

stipendiary [staɪˈpɛndɪərɪ] ADJ: **~ magistrate** magistrato stipendiato

stipulate [ˈstɪpjuleɪt] VT stipulare

stipulation [stɪpjuˈleɪʃən] N stipulazione f

stir [stəːʳ] N agitazione f, clamore m ▶ VT mescolare; (move) smuovere, agitare; (fig) risvegliare ▶ VI muoversi; **to give sth a ~** mescolare qc; **to cause a ~** fare scalpore
  ▶ **stir up** VT provocare, suscitare

stir-fry [ˈstəːˈfraɪ] VT saltare in padella ▶ N pietanza al salto

stirring [ˈstəːrɪŋ] ADJ eccitante; commovente

stirrup [ˈstɪrəp] N staffa

stitch [stɪtʃ] N (Sewing) punto; (Knitting) maglia; (Med) punto (di sutura); (pain) fitta ▶ VT cucire, attaccare; suturare

St Kitts and Nevis [-kɪts-] N Federazione f di Saint Kitts e Nevis

St Lucia [-ˈluːʃə] N Santa Lucia

stoat [stəut] N ermellino

stock [stɔk] N riserva, provvista; (Comm) giacenza, stock m inv; (Agr) bestiame m; (Culin) brodo; (Finance) titoli mpl, azioni fpl; (Rail: also: **rolling stock**) materiale m rotabile; (descent, origin) stirpe f ▶ ADJ (fig: reply etc) consueto(-a), solito(-a), classico(-a); (greeting) usuale; (Comm: goods, size) standard inv ▶ VT (have in stock) avere, vendere; **well-stocked** ben fornito(-a); **to have sth in ~** avere qc in magazzino; **out of ~** esauri-

S

to(-a); **to take ~** (fig) fare il punto; **stocks and shares** valori mpl di borsa; **government ~** titoli di Stato
▶ **stock up** VI: **to ~ up (with)** fare provvista (di)

stockade [stɔˈkeɪd] N palizzata

stockbroker [ˈstɔkbrəukəʳ] N agente m di cambio

stock control N gestione f magazzino

stock cube N (BRIT Culin) dado

stock exchange N Borsa (valori)

stockholder [ˈstɔkhəuldəʳ] N (Finance) azionista mf

Stockholm [ˈstɔkhəum] N Stoccolma

stocking [ˈstɔkɪŋ] N calza

stock-in-trade [ˈstɔkɪnˈtreɪd] N (fig): **it's his ~** la sua specialità

stockist [ˈstɔkɪst] N (BRIT) fornitore m

stock market N (BRIT) Borsa, mercato finanziario

stock phrase N cliché m inv

stockpile [ˈstɔkpaɪl] N riserva ▶ VT accumulare riserve di

stockroom [ˈstɔkrum] N magazzino

stocktaking [ˈstɔkteɪkɪŋ] N (BRIT Comm) inventario

stocky [ˈstɔkɪ] ADJ tarchiato(-a), tozzo(-a)

stodgy [ˈstɔdʒɪ] ADJ pesante, indigesto(-a)

stoic [ˈstəuɪk] N stoico(-a)

stoical [ˈstəuɪkəl] ADJ stoico(-a)

stoke [stəuk] VT alimentare

stoker [ˈstəukəʳ] N fochista m

stole [stəul] PT of **steal** ▶ N stola

stolen [ˈstəuln] PP of **steal**

stolid [ˈstɔlɪd] ADJ impassibile

stomach [ˈstʌmək] N stomaco; (abdomen) ventre m; (belly) pancia ▶ VT sopportare, digerire

stomach ache N mal m di stomaco

stomach pump N pompa gastrica

stomach ulcer N ulcera allo stomaco

stomp [stɔmp] VI: **to ~ in/out** etc entrare/uscire etc con passo pesante

stone [stəun] N pietra; (pebble) sasso, ciottolo; (in fruit) nocciolo; (Med) calcolo; (BRIT: weight) 6.348 kg., 14 libbre ▶ CPD di pietra ▶ VT lapidare; (fruit) togliere il nocciolo a; **within a ~'s throw of the station** a due passi dalla stazione

Stone Age N: **the ~** l'età della pietra

stone-cold [stəunˈkəuld] ADJ gelido(-a)

stoned [stəund] ADJ (col: drunk) sbronzo(-a); (: on drugs) fuori inv

stone-deaf [stəunˈdɛf] ADJ sordo(-a) come una campana

stonemason [ˈstəunmeɪsn] N scalpellino

stonewall [stəunˈwɔːl] VI fare ostruzionismo ▶ VT ostacolare

stonework [ˈstəunwəːk] N muratura

stonking (col) [ˈstɔŋkɪŋ] (BRIT) ADJ mega inv ▶ ADV super, mega; **a ~ great sum** una mega somma; **a ~ good idea** un'idea super geniale

stony [ˈstəunɪ] ADJ pietroso(-a), sassoso(-a)

stood [stud] PT, PP of **stand**

stooge [stuːdʒ] N (pej) tirapiedi mf

stool [stuːl] N sgabello

stoop [stuːp] VI (also: **have a stoop**) avere una curvatura; (also: **stoop down**: bend) chinarsi, curvarsi; **to ~ to sth/doing sth** abbassarsi a qc/a fare qc

stop [stɔp] N arresto; (stopping place) fermata; (in punctuation) punto ▶ VT arrestare, fermare; (break off) interrompere; (also: **put a stop to**) porre fine a; (: prevent) impedire ▶ VI fermarsi; (rain, noise etc) cessare, finire; **to ~ doing sth** cessare or finire di fare qc; **to ~ sb (from) doing sth** impedire a qn di fare qc; **to ~ dead** fermarsi di colpo; **~ it!** smettila!, basta!
▶ **stop by** VI passare, fare un salto
▶ **stop off** VI sostare brevemente
▶ **stop up** VT (hole) chiudere, turare

stopcock [ˈstɔpkɔk] N rubinetto di arresto

stopgap [ˈstɔpgæp] N (person) tappabuchi mf; (measure) ripiego ▶ CPD (measures, solution) di fortuna

stoplights [ˈstɔplaɪts] NPL (Aut) stop mpl

stopover [ˈstɔpəuvəʳ] N breve sosta; (Aviat) scalo

stoppage [ˈstɔpɪdʒ] N arresto, fermata; (of pay) trattenuta; (strike) interruzione f del lavoro

stopper [ˈstɔpəʳ] N tappo

stop press N ultimissime fpl

stopwatch [ˈstɔpwɔtʃ] N cronometro

storage [ˈstɔːrɪdʒ] N immagazzinamento; (Comput) memoria

storage heater N (BRIT) radiatore m elettrico che accumula calore

store [stɔːʳ] N provvista, riserva; (depot) deposito; (BRIT: department store) grande magazzino; (US: shop) negozio ▶ VT mettere da parte; conservare; (grain, goods) immagazzinare; (Comput) registrare; **to set great/little ~ by sth** dare molta/poca importanza a qc; **in ~** di riserva; in serbo; **who knows what is in ~ for us?** chissà cosa ci riserva il futuro?
▶ **store up** VT mettere in serbo, conservare

storehouse [ˈstɔːhaus] N magazzino, deposito

storekeeper [ˈstɔːkiːpəʳ] N (US) negoziante mf

storeroom [ˈstɔːrum] N dispensa

storey, (US) **story** [ˈstɔːrɪ] N piano

stork [stɔːk] N cicogna

storm [stɔːm] N tempesta; (also: **thunderstorm**) temporale m, burrasca; uragano; (fig) infuriarsi ▶ VT prendere d'assalto

storm cloud N nube f temporalesca

storm door N controporta

stormy ['stɔːmɪ] ADJ tempestoso(-a), burrascoso(-a)

story ['stɔːrɪ] N storia; favola; racconto; (*Press*) articolo; (*US*) = **storey**

storybook ['stɔːrɪbuk] N libro di racconti

storyteller ['stɔːrɪtɛlə^r] N narratore(-trice)

stout [staut] ADJ solido(-a), robusto(-a); (*brave*) coraggioso(-a); (*supporter*) tenace; (*fat*) corpulento(-a), grasso(-a) ▶ N birra scura

stove [stəuv] N (*for cooking*) fornello; (: *small*) fornelletto; (*for heating*) stufa; **gas/electric ~** cucina a gas/elettrica

stow [stəu] VT mettere via

stowaway ['stəuəweɪ] N passeggero(-a) clandestino(-a)

straddle ['strædl] VT stare a cavalcioni di

strafe [strɑːf] VT mitragliare

straggle ['strægl] VI crescere (*or* estendersi) disordinatamente; trascinarsi; rimanere indietro; **straggled along the coast** disseminati(-e) lungo la costa

straggler ['stræglə^r] N sbandato(-a)

straggling ['stræglɪŋ], **straggly** ['stræglɪ] ADJ (*hair*) in disordine

straight [streɪt] ADJ (*continuous, direct*) dritto(-a); (*frank*) onesto(-a), franco(-a); (*plain, uncomplicated*) semplice; (*Theat: part, play*) serio(-a); (*col: heterosexual*) eterosessuale ▶ ADV diritto; (*drink*) liscio ▶ N: **the ~** la linea retta; (*Rail*) il rettilineo; (*Sport*) la dirittura d'arrivo; **to put** *or* **get ~** mettere in ordine, mettere ordine in; **to be (all) ~** (*tidy*) essere a posto, essere sistemato; (*clarified*) essere chiaro; **ten ~ wins** dieci vittorie di fila; **~ away, ~ off** (*at once*) immediatamente; **~ off, ~ out** senza esitare; **I went ~ home** sono andato direttamente a casa

straighten ['streɪtn] VT (*also:* **straighten out**) raddrizzare; **to ~ things out** mettere le cose a posto

straighteners ['streɪtnəz] NPL (*for hair*) piastra f per capelli

straight-faced [streɪt'feɪst] ADJ impassibile, imperturbabile ▶ ADV con il viso serio

straightforward [streɪt'fɔːwəd] ADJ semplice; (*frank*) onesto(-a), franco(-a)

strain [streɪn] N (*Tech*) sollecitazione f; (*physical*) sforzo; (*mental*) tensione f; (*Med*) strappo; distorsione f; (*streak, trace*) tendenza; elemento; (*breed*) razza; (*of virus*) tipo ▶ VT tendere; (*muscle*) stirare; (*ankle*) slogare; (*friendship, marriage*) mettere a dura prova; (*resources*) pesare su; (*filter*) colare, filtrare; (*food*) colare; passare ▶ VI sforzarsi ■ **strains** NPL (*Mus*) note fpl; **she's under a lot of ~** è molto tesa, è sotto pressione

strained [streɪnd] ADJ (*muscle*) stirato(-a); (*laugh etc*) forzato(-a); (*relations*) teso(-a)

strainer ['streɪnə^r] N passino, colino

strait [streɪt] N (*Geo*) stretto ■ **straits** NPL: **to be in dire straits** (*fig*) essere nei guai

straitjacket ['streɪtdʒækɪt] N camicia di forza

strait-laced [streɪt'leɪst] ADJ puritano(-a)

strand [strænd] N (*of thread*) filo

stranded ADJ nei guai; senza mezzi di trasporto

strange [streɪndʒ] ADJ (*not known*) sconosciuto(-a); (*odd*) strano(-a), bizzarro(-a)

strangely ['streɪndʒlɪ] ADV stranamente

stranger ['streɪndʒə^r] N (*unknown*) sconosciuto(-a); (*from another place*) estraneo(-a); **I'm a ~ here** non sono del posto

strangle ['stræŋgl] VT strangolare

stranglehold ['stræŋglhəuld] N (*fig*) stretta (mortale)

strangulation [stræŋgju'leɪʃən] N strangolamento

strap [stræp] N cinghia; (*of slip, dress*) spallina, bretella ▶ VT legare con una cinghia; (*child etc*) punire (con una cinghia)

straphanging ['stræphæŋɪŋ] N viaggiare *m* in piedi (*su mezzi pubblici reggendosi a un sostegno*)

strapless ['stræplɪs] ADJ (*bra, dress*) senza spalline

strapped [stræpt] ADJ: **~ for cash** a corto di soldi; **financially ~** finanziariamente a terra

strapping ['stræpɪŋ] ADJ ben piantato(-a)

Strasbourg ['stræzbəːg] N Strasburgo *f*

strata ['strɑːtə] NPL *of* **stratum**

stratagem ['strætɪdʒəm] N stratagemma *m*

strategic [strə'tiːdʒɪk] ADJ strategico(-a)

strategist ['strætɪdʒɪst] N stratega *m*

strategy ['strætɪdʒɪ] N strategia

stratosphere ['strætəsfɪə^r] N stratosfera

stratum ['strɑːtəm] (*pl* **strata** ['strɑːtə]) N strato

straw [strɔː] N paglia; (*drinking straw*) cannuccia; **that's the last ~!** è la goccia che fa traboccare il vaso!

strawberry ['strɔːbərɪ] N fragola

stray [streɪ] ADJ (*animal*) randagio(-a); (*bullet*) vagante; (*scattered*) sparso(-a) ▶ VI perdersi; allontanarsi, staccarsi (dal gruppo)

streak [striːk] N striscia; (*of hair*) mèche f inv; **a ~ of** una vena di ▶ VT striare, screziare ▶ VI: **to ~ past** passare come un fulmine; **to have streaks in one's hair** avere le mèche nei capelli; **a winning/losing ~** un periodo fortunato/sfortunato

streaker ['striːkə^r] N streaker *mf*

streaky ['striːkɪ] ADJ screziato(-a), striato(-a)

streaky bacon N (*BRIT*) = pancetta

stream [striːm] N ruscello; corrente f; (*of people, etc*) fiume *m*; (*Comput*) flusso ▶ VT (*Scol*) dividere in livelli di rendimento ▶ VI scorrere; **to ~ in/**

out entrare/uscire a fiotti; **against the ~** controcorrente; **on ~** (*new power plant etc*) in funzione, in produzione

streamer ['striːməʳ] N (*of paper*) stella filante

stream feed N (*on photocopier etc*) alimentazione f continua

streamline ['striːmlaɪn] VT dare una linea aerodinamica a; (*fig*) razionalizzare

streamlined ['striːmlaɪnd] ADJ aerodinamico(-a), affusolato(-a); (*fig*) razionalizzato(-a)

street [striːt] N strada, via; **the back streets** le strade secondarie; **to be on the streets** (*homeless*) essere senza tetto; (*as prostitute*) battere il marciapiede

streetcar ['striːtkaːʳ] N (*US*) tram m inv

street cred [-krɛd] N (*col*) credibilità presso i giovani

street lamp N lampione m

street light N lampione m

street lighting N illuminazione f stradale

street map N pianta (di una città)

street market N mercato all'aperto

street plan N pianta (di una città)

streetwise ['striːtwaɪz] ADJ (*col*) esperto(-a) dei bassifondi

strength [strɛŋθ] N forza; (*of girder, knot etc*) resistenza, solidità; (*of chemical solution*) concentrazione f; (*of wine*) gradazione f alcolica; **on the ~ of** sulla base di, in virtù di; **below/at full ~** con gli effettivi ridotti/al completo

strengthen ['strɛŋθən] VT rinforzare; (*muscles*) irrobustire; fortificare; (*economy, currency*) consolidare

strenuous ['strɛnjuəs] ADJ vigoroso(-a), energico(-a); (*tiring*) duro(-a), pesante

stress [strɛs] N (*force, pressure*) pressione f; (*mental strain*) tensione f; (*accent*) accento; (*emphasis*) enfasi f inv ▶VT insistere su, sottolineare; accentare; **to be under ~** essere sotto tensione; **to lay great ~ on sth** dare grande importanza a qc

stressed ADJ (*tense: person*) stressato(-a); (*Ling, Poetry: syllable*) accentato(-a)

stressful ['strɛsful] ADJ (*job*) difficile, stressante

stretch [strɛtʃ] N (*of sand etc*) distesa; (*of time*) periodo ▶VI stirarsi; (*extend*): **to ~ to** or **as far as** estendersi fino a; (*be enough: money, food*): **to ~ (to)** bastare (per) ▶VT tendere, allungare; (*spread*) distendere; (*fig*) spingere (al massimo); **at a ~** ininterrottamente; **to ~ a muscle** tendere un muscolo; **to ~ one's legs** sgranchirsi le gambe

▶**stretch out** VI allungarsi, estendersi ▶VT (*arm etc*) allungare, tendere; (*spread*) distendere; **to ~ out for sth** allungare la mano per prendere qc

stretcher ['strɛtʃəʳ] N barella, lettiga

stretcher-bearer ['strɛtʃəbɛərəʳ] N barelliere m

stretch marks NPL smagliature fpl

strewn [struːn] ADJ: **~ with** cosparso(-a) di

stricken ['strɪkən] ADJ provato(-a), affranto(-a); **~ with** colpito(-a) da

strict [strɪkt] ADJ (*severe*) rigido(-a), severo(-a); (: *order, rule*) rigoroso(-a); (: *supervision*) stretto(-a); (*precise*) preciso(-a), stretto(-a); **in ~ confidence** in assoluta confidenza

strictly ['strɪktlɪ] ADV severamente; rigorosamente; strettamente; **~ confidential** strettamente confidenziale; **~ speaking** a rigor di termini; **~ between ourselves ...** detto fra noi ...

stride [straɪd] (*pt* **strode** [strəud], *pp* **stridden** ['strɪdn]) N passo lungo ▶VI camminare a grandi passi; **to take in one's ~** (*fig: changes etc*) prendere con tranquillità

strident ['straɪdnt] ADJ stridente

strife [straɪf] N conflitto; litigi mpl

strike [straɪk] (*pt, pp* **struck** [strʌk]) N sciopero; (*of oil etc*) scoperta; (*attack*) attacco ▶VT colpire; (*oil etc*) scoprire, trovare; (*produce, make: coin, medal*) coniare; (: *agreement, deal*) concludere; (: *bargain*) fare; (*fig*): **the thought** or **it strikes me that ...** mi viene in mente che ... ▶VI far sciopero, scioperare; (*attack*) attaccare; (*clock*) suonare; **on ~** (*workers*) in sciopero; **to go on** or **come out on ~** mettersi in sciopero; **to ~ a match** accendere un fiammifero; **to ~ a balance** (*fig*) trovare il giusto mezzo

▶**strike back** VI (*Mil*) fare rappresaglie; (*fig*) reagire

▶**strike down** VT (*fig*) atterrare

▶**strike off** VT (*from list*) cancellare; (: *doctor etc*) radiare

▶**strike out** VT depennare

▶**strike up** VT (*Mus*) attaccare; **to ~ up a friendship with** fare amicizia con

strikebreaker ['straɪkbreɪkəʳ] N crumiro(-a)

striker ['straɪkəʳ] N scioperante mf; (*Sport*) attaccante mf

striking ['straɪkɪŋ] ADJ impressionante

Strimmer® ['strɪməʳ] N tagliabordi m inv

string [strɪŋ] (*pt, pp* **strung** [strʌŋ]) N spago; (*row*) fila; sequenza; catena; (*Comput*) stringa, sequenza; (*Mus*) corda ▶VT: **to ~ out** disporre di fianco; **to ~ together** (*words, ideas*) mettere insieme ∎ **the strings** NPL (*Mus*) gli archi; **~ of pearls** filo di perle; **with no strings attached** (*fig*) senza vincoli, senza obblighi; **to pull strings for sb** (*fig*) raccomandare qn

string bean N fagiolino

stringed instrument [strɪŋd-], **string instrument** N (*Mus*) strumento a corda

stringent ['strɪndʒənt] ADJ rigoroso(-a); (*reasons, arguments*) impellente

string quartet N quartetto d'archi

strip [strɪp] N striscia; (*Sport*): **wearing the Celtic ~** con la divisa del Celtic ▶VT spogliare;

(*paint*) togliere; (*also:* **strip down**: *machine*) smontare ▶ vɪ spogliarsi

▶ **strip off** vᴛ (*paint etc*) staccare ▶ vɪ (*person*) spogliarsi

strip cartoon N fumetto

stripe [straɪp] N striscia, riga; (*Mil, Police*) gallone *m*

striped [straɪpt] ADJ a strisce *or* righe

strip light N (BRIT) tubo al neon

stripper [ˈstrɪpəʳ] N spogliarellista *mf*

strip-search [ˈstrɪpsəːtʃ] vᴛ: **to ~ sb** perquisire qn facendolo(-a) spogliare ▶ N perquisizione *f* (*facendo spogliare il perquisito*)

striptease [ˈstrɪptiːz] N spogliarello

strive [straɪv] (*pt* **strove** [strəuv], *pp* **striven** [ˈstrɪvn]) vɪ: **to ~ to do** sforzarsi di fare

strobe [strəub] N (*also:* **strobe light**) luce *f* stroboscopica

strode [strəud] Pᴛ *of* **stride**

stroke [strəuk] N colpo; (*of piston*) corsa; (*Med*) colpo apoplettico; (*Swimming*) bracciata; (: *style*) stile *m*; (*caress*) carezza ▶ vᴛ accarezzare; **at a ~** in un attimo; **on the ~ of 5** alle 5 in punto, allo scoccare delle 5; **a ~ of luck** un colpo di fortuna; **two-stroke engine** motore a due tempi

stroll [strəul] N giretto, passeggiatina ▶ vɪ andare a spasso; **to go for a ~, have** *or* **take a ~** andare a fare un giretto *or* due passi

stroller [ˈstrəuləʳ] N (US) passeggino

strong [strɔŋ] ADJ (*gen*) forte; (*sturdy: table, fabric etc*) robusto(-a); (*concentrated, intense: bleach, acid*) concentrato(-a); (*protest, letter, measures*) energico(-a) ▶ ADV: **to be going ~** (*company*) andare a gonfie vele; (*person*) essere attivo(-a); **they are 50 ~** sono in 50; **~ language** (*swearing*) linguaggio volgare

strong-arm [ˈstrɔŋɑːm] ADJ (*tactics, methods*) energico(-a)

strongbox [ˈstrɔŋbɔks] N cassaforte *f*

stronghold [ˈstrɔŋhəuld] N fortezza; (*also fig*) roccaforte *f*

strongly [ˈstrɔŋlɪ] ADV fortemente, con forza; solidamente; energicamente; **to feel ~ about sth** avere molto a cuore qc

strongman [ˈstrɔŋmæn] N (*irreg*) personaggio di spicco

strongroom [ˈstrɔŋrum] N camera di sicurezza

stroppy [ˈstrɔpɪ] ADJ (BRIT col) scontroso(-a), indisponente

strove [strəuv] Pᴛ *of* **strive**

struck [strʌk] Pᴛ, PP *of* **strike**

structural [ˈstrʌktʃərəl] ADJ strutturale; (*Constr*) di costruzione; di struttura

structurally [ˈstrʌktʃrəlɪ] ADV dal punto di vista della struttura

structure [ˈstrʌktʃəʳ] N struttura; (*building*) costruzione *f*, fabbricato

struggle [ˈstrʌgl] N lotta ▶ vɪ lottare; **to have a ~ to do sth** avere dei problemi per fare qc

strum [strʌm] vᴛ (*guitar*) strimpellare

strung [strʌŋ] Pᴛ, PP *of* **string**

strut [strʌt] N sostegno, supporto ▶ vɪ pavoneggiarsi

strychnine [ˈstrɪkniːn] N stricnina

stub [stʌb] N mozzicone *m*; (*of ticket etc*) matrice *f*, talloncino ▶ vᴛ: **to ~ one's toe (on sth)** urtare *or* sbattere il dito del piede (contro qc)

▶ **stub out a cigarette** spegnere una sigaretta

stubble [ˈstʌbl] N stoppia; (*on chin*) barba ispida

stubborn [ˈstʌbən] ADJ testardo(-a), ostinato(-a)

stubby [ˈstʌbɪ] ADJ tozzo(-a)

stucco [ˈstʌkəu] N stucco

stuck [stʌk] Pᴛ, PP *of* **stick** ▶ ADJ (*jammed*) bloccato(-a); **to get ~** bloccarsi

stuck-up [stʌkˈʌp] ADJ presuntuoso(-a)

stud [stʌd] N bottoncino; borchia; (*also:* **stud earring**) orecchino a pressione; (*of horses*) scuderia, allevamento di cavalli; (*also:* **stud horse**) stallone *m* ▶ vᴛ (*fig*): **studded with** tempestato(-a) di

student [ˈstjuːdənt] N studente(-essa) ▶ CPD studentesco(-a); universitario(-a); degli studenti; **a law/medical ~** uno studente di legge/di medicina

student driver N (US) conducente *mf* principiante

students' union N (BRIT: *association*) circolo universitario; (: *building*) sede *f* del circolo universitario

studied [ˈstʌdɪd] ADJ studiato(-a), calcolato(-a)

studio [ˈstjuːdɪəu] N studio

studio flat, (US) **studio apartment** N monolocale *m*

studious [ˈstjuːdɪəs] ADJ studioso(-a); (*studied*) studiato(-a), voluto(-a)

studiously [ˈstjuːdɪəslɪ] ADV (*carefully*) deliberatamente, di proposito

study [ˈstʌdɪ] N studio ▶ vᴛ studiare; esaminare ▶ vɪ studiare; **to make a ~ of sth** fare uno studio su qc; **to ~ for an exam** prepararsi a un esame

stuff [stʌf] N (*substance*) materiale *m*; (*belongings*) cose *fpl*, roba ▶ vᴛ imbottire; (*animal: for exhibition*) impagliare; (*Culin*) farcire; (*col: push*) ficcare; **my nose is stuffed up** ho il naso chiuso; **get stuffed!** (*col!*) va' a farti fottere! (!); **stuffed toy** giocattolo di peluche

stuffing [ˈstʌfɪŋ] N imbottitura; (*Culin*) ripieno

stuffy [ˈstʌfɪ] ADJ (*room*) mal ventilato(-a), senz'aria; (*ideas*) antiquato(-a)

stumble [ˈstʌmbl] vɪ inciampare; **to ~ across** (*fig*) imbattersi in

stumbling block [ˈstʌmblɪŋ-] N ostacolo, scoglio

S

809

stump [stʌmp] N ceppo; (of limb) moncone m
▶ VT: **to be stumped** essere sconcertato(-a); **to be stumped for an answer** essere incapace di rispondere

stun [stʌn] VT stordire; (amaze) sbalordire

stung [stʌŋ] PT, PP of **sting**

stunk [stʌŋk] PP of **stink**

stunned [stʌnd] ADJ (from blow) stordito(-a); (amazed, shocked) sbalordito(-a)

stunning ['stʌnɪŋ] ADJ (piece of news etc) sbalorditivo(-a); (girl, dress) stupendo(-a), favoloso(-a)

stunt [stʌnt] N bravata; trucco pubblicitario; (Aviat) acrobazia ▶ VT arrestare

stunted ['stʌntɪd] ADJ stentato(-a), rachitico(-a)

stuntman ['stʌntmæn] N (irreg) cascatore m

stupefaction [stju:pɪ'fækʃən] N stupefazione f, stupore m

stupefy ['stju:pɪfaɪ] VT stordire; intontire; (fig) stupire

stupendous [stju:'pɛndəs] ADJ stupendo(-a), meraviglioso(-a)

stupid ['stju:pɪd] ADJ stupido(-a)

stupidity [stju:'pɪdɪtɪ] N stupidità f inv, stupidaggine f

stupidly ['stju:pɪdlɪ] ADV stupidamente

stupor ['stju:pə^r] N torpore m

sturdy ['stə:dɪ] ADJ robusto(-a), vigoroso(-a); solido(-a)

sturgeon ['stə:dʒən] N storione m

stutter ['stʌtə^r] N balbuzie f ▶ VI balbettare

Stuttgart ['ʃtutgart] N Stoccarda

St Vincent and the Grenadines N Saint Vincent e Grenadine fpl

sty [staɪ] N (of pigs) porcile m

stye [staɪ] N (Med) orzaiolo

style [staɪl] N stile m; (distinction) eleganza, classe f; (hair style) pettinatura; (of dress etc) modello, linea; **in the latest ~** all'ultima moda

styli ['staɪlaɪ] NPL of **stylus**

stylish ['staɪlɪʃ] ADJ elegante

stylist ['staɪlɪst] N: **hair ~** parrucchiere(-a)

stylized ['staɪlaɪzd] ADJ stilizzato(-a)

stylus ['staɪləs] (pl **styluses** or **styli** [-laɪ]) N (of record player) puntina

Styrofoam® ['staɪrəfəum] N (US) = **polystyrene** ▶ ADJ (cup) di polistirene

suave [swɑːv] ADJ untuoso(-a)

sub [sʌb] N ABBR = **submarine**; **subscription**

sub... [sʌb] PREFIX sub..., sotto...

subcommittee ['sʌbkəmɪtɪ] N sottocomitato

subconscious [sʌb'kɔnʃəs] ADJ, N subcosciente m

subcontinent [sʌb'kɔntɪnənt] N: **the (Indian) ~** il subcontinente (indiano)

subcontract N [sʌb'kɔntrækt] subappalto ▶ VT [sʌbkən'trækt] subappaltare

subcontractor ['sʌbkən'træktə^r] N subappaltatore(-trice)

subdivide [sʌbdɪ'vaɪd] VT suddividere

subdivision ['sʌbdɪvɪʒən] N suddivisione f

subdue [səb'dju:] VT sottomettere, soggiogare

subdued [səb'dju:d] ADJ pacato(-a); (light) attenuato(-a); (person) poco esuberante

sub-editor ['sʌb'ɛdɪtə^r] N (BRIT) redattore(-a) aggiunto(-a)

subject N ['sʌbdʒɪkt] soggetto; (citizen etc) cittadino(-a); (Scol) materia ▶ VT [səb'dʒɛkt]: **to ~ to** sottomettere a; esporre a; **to be ~ to** (law) essere sottomesso(-a) a; (disease) essere soggetto(-a) a; **~ to confirmation in writing** a condizione di ricevere conferma scritta; **to change the ~** cambiare discorso

subjection [səb'dʒɛkʃən] N sottomissione f, soggezione f

subjective [səb'dʒɛktɪv] ADJ soggettivo(-a)

subject matter N argomento; contenuto

sub judice [sʌb'dʒuːdɪsɪ] ADJ (Law) sub iudice

subjugate ['sʌbdʒugeɪt] VT sottomettere, soggiogare

subjunctive [səb'dʒʌŋktɪv] ADJ congiuntivo(-a) ▶ N congiuntivo

sublet [sʌb'lɛt] VT, VI (irreg) subaffittare

sublime [sə'blaɪm] ADJ sublime

subliminal [sʌb'lɪmɪnl] ADJ subliminale

submachine gun ['sʌbmə'ʃiːn-] N mitra m inv

submarine [sʌbmə'riːn] N sommergibile m

submerge [səb'mə:dʒ] VT sommergere; immergere ▶ VI immergersi

submersion [səb'mə:ʃən] N sommersione f; immersione f

submission [səb'mɪʃən] N sottomissione f; (to committee etc) richiesta, domanda

submissive [səb'mɪsɪv] ADJ remissivo(-a)

submit [səb'mɪt] VT sottomettere; (proposal, claim) presentare ▶ VI sottomettersi

subnormal [sʌb'nɔːməl] ADJ subnormale

subordinate [sə'bɔ:dɪnət] ADJ, N subordinato(-a)

subpoena [səb'pi:nə] N (Law) citazione f, mandato di comparizione ▶ VT (Law) citare in giudizio

subprime ['sʌbpraɪm] ADJ (Finance) subprime inv; **~ mortgage** mutuo subprime

subroutine ['sʌbruːtiːn] N (Comput) sottoprogramma m

subscribe [səb'skraɪb] VI contribuire; **to ~ to** (opinion) approvare, condividere; (fund) sottoscrivere a; (newspaper) abbonarsi a; essere abbonato(-a) a

subscriber [səb'skraɪbə^r] N (to periodical, telephone) abbonato(-a)

subscript ['sʌbskrɪpt] N deponente *m*

subscription [səb'skrɪpʃən] N sottoscrizione *f*; abbonamento; **to take out a ~ to** abbonarsi a

subsequent ['sʌbsɪkwənt] ADJ (*later*) successivo(-a), seguente; conseguente; (*further*) ulteriore; **~ to** in seguito a

subsequently ['sʌbsɪkwəntlɪ] ADV in seguito, successivamente

subservient [səb'sə:vɪənt] ADJ: **~ (to)** remissivo(-a) (a), sottomesso(-a) (a)

subside [səb'saɪd] VI cedere, abbassarsi; (*flood*) decrescere; (*wind*) calmarsi

subsidence [səb'saɪdns] N cedimento, abbassamento

subsidiarity [səbsɪdɪ'ærɪtɪ] N (*Pol*) *principio del decentramento del potere*

subsidiary [səb'sɪdɪərɪ] ADJ sussidiario(-a); accessorio(-a); (*Brit Scol: subject*) complementare ▶ N filiale *f*

subsidize ['sʌbsɪdaɪz] VT sovvenzionare

subsidy ['sʌbsɪdɪ] N sovvenzione *f*

subsist [səb'sɪst] VI: **to ~ on sth** vivere di qc

subsistence [səb'sɪstəns] N esistenza; mezzi *mpl* di sostentamento

subsistence allowance N indennità *f inv* di trasferta

subsistence level N livello minimo di vita

substance ['sʌbstəns] N sostanza; (*fig*) essenza; **to lack ~** (*argument*) essere debole

substance abuse N abuso di sostanze tossiche

substandard [sʌb'stændəd] ADJ (*goods, housing*) di qualità scadente

substantial [səb'stænʃl] ADJ solido(-a); (*amount, progress etc*) notevole; (*meal*) sostanzioso(-a)

substantially [səb'stænʃəlɪ] ADV sostanzialmente; **~ bigger** molto più grande

substantiate [səb'stænʃɪeɪt] VT comprovare

substitute ['sʌbstɪtjuːt] N (*person*) sostituto(-a); (*thing*) succedaneo, surrogato ▶ VT: **to ~ sth/sb for** sostituire qc/qn a

substitute teacher N (*US*) supplente *mf*

substitution [sʌbstɪ'tjuːʃən] N sostituzione *f*

subterfuge ['sʌbtəfjuːdʒ] N sotterfugio

subterranean [sʌbtə'reɪnɪən] ADJ sotterraneo(-a)

subtitle ['sʌbtaɪtl] N (*Cine*) sottotitolo

subtle ['sʌtl] ADJ sottile; (*flavour, perfume*) delicato(-a)

subtlety ['sʌtltɪ] N sottigliezza

subtly ['sʌtlɪ] ADV sottilmente; delicatamente

subtotal [sʌb'təutl] N somma parziale

subtract [səb'trækt] VT sottrarre

subtraction [səb'trækʃən] N sottrazione *f*

suburb ['sʌbə:b] N sobborgo; **the suburbs** la periferia

suburban [sə'bə:bən] ADJ suburbano(-a)

suburbia [sə'bə:bɪə] N periferia, sobborghi *mpl*

subversion [səb'və:ʃən] N sovversione *f*

subversive [səb'və:sɪv] ADJ sovversivo(-a)

subway ['sʌbweɪ] N (*US: underground*) metropolitana; (*Brit: underpass*) sottopassaggio

subzero [sʌb'zɪərəu] ADJ: **~ temperatures** temperature *fpl* sotto zero

succeed [sək'si:d] VI riuscire; avere successo ▶ VT succedere a; **to ~ in doing** riuscire a fare

succeeding [sək'si:dɪŋ] ADJ (*following*) successivo(-a); **~ generations** generazioni *fpl* future

success [sək'sɛs] N successo

successful [sək'sɛsful] ADJ (*venture*) coronato(-a) da successo, riuscito(-a); **to be ~ (in doing)** riuscire (a fare)

successfully [sək'sɛsfəlɪ] ADV con successo

succession [sək'sɛʃən] N successione *f*; **in ~** di seguito

successive [sək'sɛsɪv] ADJ successivo(-a); consecutivo(-a); **on 3 ~ days** per 3 giorni consecutivi *or* di seguito

successor [sək'sɛsə] N successore *m*

succinct [sək'sɪŋkt] ADJ succinto(-a), breve

succulent ['sʌkjulənt] ADJ succulento(-a) ▶ N (*Bot*): **succulents** piante *fpl* grasse

succumb [sə'kʌm] VI soccombere

such [sʌtʃ] ADJ tale; **~ books** tali libri, libri del genere; (*so much*): **~ courage** tanto coraggio; (*of that kind*): **~ a book** un tale libro, un libro del genere ▶ ADV talmente, così; **~ a long trip** un viaggio così lungo; **~ good books** libri così buoni; **~ a lot of** talmente *or* così tanto(-a); **making ~ a noise that** facendo un rumore tale che; **~ a long time ago** tanto tempo fa; **~ as** (*like*) come; **a noise ~ as to** un rumore tale da; **~ books as I have** quei pochi libri che ho; **as ~** come *or* in quanto tale; **I said no ~ thing** non ho detto niente del genere

such-and-such ['sʌtʃənsʌtʃ] ADJ tale (*after noun*)

suchlike ['sʌtʃlaɪk] PRON (*col*): **and ~** e così via

suck [sʌk] VT succhiare; (*baby*) poppare; (*pump, machine*) aspirare

sucker ['sʌkə] N (*Zool, Tech*) ventosa; (*Bot*) pollone *m*; (*col*) gonzo(-a), babbeo(-a)

suckle ['sʌkl] VT allattare

sucrose ['suːkrəuz] N saccarosio

suction ['sʌkʃən] N succhiamento; (*Tech*) aspirazione *f*

suction pump N pompa aspirante

Sudan [suː'dɑːn] N Sudan *m*

Sudanese [suːdə'niːz] ADJ, N sudanese *mf*

sudden ['sʌdn] ADJ improvviso(-a); **all of a ~** improvvisamente, all'improvviso

811

sudden-death [sʌdn'dɛθ] N: ~ **playoff** (*Sport*) spareggio, bella

suddenly ['sʌdnlɪ] ADV bruscamente, improvvisamente, di colpo

sudoku [su'dəuku:] N sudoku *m inv*

suds [sʌdz] NPL schiuma (di sapone)

sue [su:] VT citare in giudizio ▸ VI: **to ~ (for)** intentare causa (per); **to ~ for divorce** intentare causa di divorzio; **to ~ sb for damages** citare qn per danni

suede [sweɪd] N pelle *f* scamosciata ▸ CPD scamosciato(-a)

suet ['suɪt] N grasso di rognone

Suez ['su:ɪz] N: **the ~ Canal** il Canale di Suez

suffer ['sʌfəʳ] VT soffrire, patire; (*bear*) sopportare, tollerare; (*undergo: loss, setback*) subire ▸ VI soffrire; **to ~ from** soffrire di; **to ~ from the effects of alcohol/a fall** risentire degli effetti dell'alcool/di una caduta

sufferance ['sʌfərəns] N: **he was only there on ~** era più che altro sopportato lì

sufferer ['sʌfərəʳ] N (*Med*): ~ **(from)** malato(-a) (di)

suffering ['sʌfərɪŋ] N sofferenza; (*hardship, deprivation*) privazione *f*

suffice [sə'faɪs] VI essere sufficiente, bastare

sufficient [sə'fɪʃənt] ADJ sufficiente; ~ **money** abbastanza soldi

sufficiently [sə'fɪʃəntlɪ] ADV sufficientemente, abbastanza

suffix ['sʌfɪks] N suffisso

suffocate ['sʌfəkeɪt] VI (*have difficulty breathing*) soffocare; (*die through lack of air*) asfissiare

suffocation [sʌfə'keɪʃən] N soffocamento; (*Med*) asfissia

suffrage ['sʌfrɪdʒ] N suffragio

suffuse [sə'fju:z] VT: **to ~ (with)** (*colour*) tingere (di); (*light*) soffondere (di); **her face was suffused with joy** la gioia si dipingeva sul suo volto

sugar ['ʃugəʳ] N zucchero ▸ VT zuccherare

sugar beet N barbabietola da zucchero

sugar bowl N zuccheriera

sugar cane N canna da zucchero

sugar-coated ['ʃugəkəutɪd] ADJ ricoperto(-a) di zucchero

sugar lump N zolletta di zucchero

sugar refinery N raffineria di zucchero

sugary ['ʃugərɪ] ADJ zuccherino(-a), dolce; (*fig*) sdolcinato(-a)

suggest [sə'dʒɛst] VT proporre, suggerire; (*indicate*) indicare; **what do you ~ I do?** cosa mi suggerisce di fare?

suggestion [sə'dʒɛstʃən] N suggerimento, proposta; indicazione *f*

suggestive [sə'dʒɛstɪv] ADJ suggestivo(-a); (*indecent*) spinto(-a), indecente

suicidal [suɪ'saɪdl] ADJ suicida *inv*; (*fig*) fatale, disastroso(-a)

suicide ['suɪsaɪd] N (*person*) suicida *mf*; (*act*) suicidio; **to commit ~** suicidarsi

suicide attempt, suicide bid N tentato suicidio

suicide bomber N kamikaze *mf*, attentatore(-trice) suicida

suicide bombing N attentato suicida

suit [su:t] N (*man's*) vestito; (*woman's*) completo, tailleur *m inv*; (*lawsuit*) causa; (*Cards*) seme *m*, colore *m* ▸ VT andar bene a *or* per; essere adatto(-a) a *or* per; (*adapt*): **to ~ sth to** adattare qc a; **to be suited to sth** (*suitable for*) essere adatto a qc; **well suited** (*couple*) ben assortito(-a); **to bring a ~ against sb** intentare causa a qn; **to follow ~** (*fig*) fare altrettanto

suitable ['su:təbl] ADJ adatto(-a); appropriato(-a); **would tomorrow be ~?** andrebbe bene domani?; **we found somebody ~** abbiamo trovato la persona adatta

suitably ['su:təblɪ] ADV (*dress*) in modo adatto; (*thank*) adeguatamente

suitcase ['su:tkeɪs] N valigia

suite [swi:t] N (*of rooms*) appartamento; (*Mus*) suite *f inv*; (*furniture*): **bedroom/dining room ~** arredo *or* mobilia per la camera da letto/sala da pranzo; **a three-piece ~** un salotto comprendente un divano e due poltrone

suitor ['su:təʳ] N corteggiatore *m*, spasimante *m*

sulfate ['sʌlfeɪt] N (*US*) = **sulphate**

sulfur *etc* ['sʌlfəʳ] (*US*) = **sulphur** *etc*

sulk [sʌlk] VI fare il broncio

sulky ['sʌlkɪ] ADJ imbronciato(-a)

sullen ['sʌlən] ADJ scontroso(-a); cupo(-a)

sulphate, (*US*) **sulfate** ['sʌlfeɪt] N solfato; **copper ~** solfato di rame

sulphur, (*US*) **sulfur** ['sʌlfəʳ] N zolfo

sulphur dioxide N biossido di zolfo

sulphuric, (*US*) **sulfuric** [sʌl'fjuərɪk] ADJ: ~ **acid** acido solforico

sultan ['sʌltən] N sultano

sultana [sʌl'tɑ:nə] N (*fruit*) uva (secca) sultanina

sultry ['sʌltrɪ] ADJ afoso(-a)

sum [sʌm] N somma; (*Scol etc*) addizione *f* ▸ **sum up** VT riassumere; (*evaluate rapidly*) valutare, giudicare ▸ VI riassumere

Sumatra [su'mɑ:trə] N Sumatra

summarize ['sʌməraɪz] VT riassumere, riepilogare

summary ['sʌmərɪ] N riassunto ▸ ADJ (*justice*) sommario(-a)

summer ['sʌməʳ] N estate *f* ▸ CPD d'estate, estivo(-a); **in (the) ~** d'estate

summer camp N (US) colonia (estiva)

summer holidays NPL vacanze fpl estive

summerhouse ['sʌməhaus] N (in garden) padiglione m

summertime ['sʌmətaɪm] N (season) estate f

summer time N (by clock) ora legale (estiva)

summery ['sʌmərɪ] ADJ estivo(-a)

summing-up [sʌmɪŋ'ʌp] N (Law) ricapitolazione f del processo

summit ['sʌmɪt] N cima, sommità; (Pol) vertice m

summit conference N conferenza al vertice

summon ['sʌmən] VT chiamare, convocare; **to ~ a witness** citare un testimone
▶ **summon up** VT raccogliere, fare appello a

summons N ordine m di comparizione ▶ VT citare; **to serve a ~ on sb** notificare una citazione a qn

sumo ['suːməu] N (also: **sumo wrestling**) sumo

sump [sʌmp] N (Aut) coppa dell'olio

sumptuous ['sʌmptjuəs] ADJ sontuoso(-a)

sun [sʌn] N sole m; **in the ~** al sole; **to catch the ~** prendere sole; **they have everything under the ~** hanno tutto ciò che possono desiderare

Sun. ABBR (= Sunday) dom.

sunbathe ['sʌnbeɪð] VI prendere un bagno di sole

sunbeam ['sʌnbiːm] N raggio di sole

sunbed ['sʌnbɛd] N lettino solare

sunblock ['sʌnblɔk] N crema solare a protezione totale

sunburn ['sʌnbəːn] N (tan) abbronzatura; (painful) scottatura

sunburnt ['sʌnbəːnt], **sunburned** ['sʌnbəːnd] ADJ abbronzato(-a); (painfully) scottato(-a) dal sole

sun cream N crema solare

sundae ['sʌndeɪ] N coppa di gelato guarnita

Sunday ['sʌndɪ] N domenica; see also **Tuesday**

Sunday paper N giornale m della domenica

I **Sunday papers**, i giornali che escono di domenica sono un'istituzione in Gran Bretagna e negli Stati Uniti. Sono generalmente corredati da supplementi e riviste di argomento culturale, sportivo e di attualità ed hanno un'alta tiratura.

Sunday school N ≈ scuola di catechismo

sundial ['sʌndaɪəl] N meridiana

sundown ['sʌndaun] N tramonto

sundries ['sʌndrɪz] NPL articoli diversi, cose diverse

sundry ['sʌndrɪ] ADJ vari(-e), diversi(-e); **all and ~** tutti quanti

sunflower ['sʌnflauə^r] N girasole m

sung [sʌŋ] PP of **sing**

sunglasses ['sʌnɡlɑːsɪz] NPL occhiali mpl da sole

sunk [sʌŋk] PP of **sink**

sunken ['sʌŋkən] ADJ sommerso(-a); (eyes, cheeks) infossato(-a); (bath) incassato(-a)

sunlamp ['sʌnlæmp] N lampada a raggi ultravioletti

sunlight ['sʌnlaɪt] N (luce f del) sole m

sunlit ['sʌnlɪt] ADJ assolato(-a), soleggiato(-a)

sun lounger N sedia a sdraio

sunny ['sʌnɪ] ADJ assolato(-a), soleggiato(-a); (fig) allegro(-a), felice; **it is ~** c'è il sole

sunrise ['sʌnraɪz] N levata del sole, alba

sunroof ['sʌnruːf] N (on building) tetto a terrazzo; (Aut) tetto apribile

sunscreen ['sʌnskriːn] N (protective ingredient) filtro solare; (cream) crema solare protettiva

sunset ['sʌnsɛt] N tramonto

sunshade ['sʌnʃeɪd] N parasole m

sunshine ['sʌnʃaɪn] N (luce f del) sole m

sunspot ['sʌnspɔt] N macchia solare

sunstroke ['sʌnstrəuk] N insolazione f, colpo di sole

suntan ['sʌntæn] N abbronzatura

suntan lotion N lozione f solare

suntanned ['sʌntænd] ADJ abbronzato(-a)

suntan oil N olio solare

suntrap ['sʌntræp] N luogo molto assolato, angolo pieno di sole

super ['suːpə^r] ADJ (col) fantastico(-a)

superannuation [suːpərænju'eɪʃən] N contributi mpl pensionistici, pensione f

superb [suː'pəːb] ADJ magnifico(-a)

Super Bowl N (US Sport) Super Bowl m inv

Il **Super Bowl** è la finale del campionato annuale della National Football League (NFL), la lega professionistica del football americano, lo sport più popolare negli Stati Uniti. Dalla sua prima edizione nel 1967, il Super Bowl Sunday è quasi una festa nazionale, celebre per la quantità di cibo, patatine, pizze e birre consumate guardando l'evento in TV. È la trasmissione con più audience negli Stati Uniti, seguita da oltre 100 milioni di spettatori in tutto il mondo.

supercilious [suːpə'sɪlɪəs] ADJ sprezzante, sdegnoso(-a)

superconductor [suːpəkən'dʌktə^r] N superconduttore m

superficial [suːpə'fɪʃəl] ADJ superficiale

superficially [suːpə'fɪʃəlɪ] ADV superficialmente

superfluous [suː'pəːfluəs] ADJ superfluo(-a)

superfood ['suːpəfuːd] N superfood m inv, supercibo m

S

813

superglue [ˈsuːpəgluː] N colla a presa rapida

superhighway [ˈsuːpəharweɪ] N (US) autostrada; **the information ~** l'autostrada telematica

superhuman [suːpəˈhjuːmən] ADJ sovrumano(-a)

superimpose [ˈsuːpərɪmˈpəuz] VT sovrapporre

superintend [suːpərɪnˈtɛnd] VT dirigere, sovraintendere

superintendent [suːpərɪnˈtɛndənt] N direttore(-trice); (Police) ≈ commissario (capo)

superior [suˈpɪərɪəʳ] ADJ superiore; (Comm: goods, quality) di prim'ordine, superiore; (smug: person) che fa il(la)superiore ▶ N superiore mf; **Mother S~** (Rel) Madre f Superiora, Superiora

superiority [supɪərɪˈɔrɪtɪ] N superiorità

superlative [suˈpəːlətɪv] ADJ superlativo(-a), supremo(-a) ▶ N (Ling) superlativo

superman [ˈsuːpəmæn] N (irreg) superuomo

supermarket [ˈsuːpəmɑːkɪt] N supermercato

supermodel [ˈsuːpəmɔdl] N top model mf

supernatural [suːpəˈnætʃərəl] ADJ, N soprannaturale m

supernova [suːpəˈnəuvə] N supernova

superpower [ˈsuːpəpauəʳ] N (Pol) superpotenza

superscript [ˈsuːpəskrɪpt] N esponente m

supersede [suːpəˈsiːd] VT sostituire, soppiantare

supersonic [ˈsuːpəˈsɔnɪk] ADJ supersonico(-a)

superstar [ˈsuːpəstɑːʳ] ADJ, N superstar f inv

superstition [suːpəˈstɪʃən] N superstizione f

superstitious [suːpəˈstɪʃəs] ADJ superstizioso(-a)

superstore [ˈsuːpəstɔːʳ] N (BRIT) grande supermercato

supertanker [ˈsuːpətæŋkəʳ] N superpetroliera

supertax [ˈsuːpətæks] N soprattassa

supervise [ˈsuːpəvaɪz] VT (person etc) sorvegliare; (organization) sovrintendere a

supervision [suːpəˈvɪʒən] N sorveglianza; supervisione f; **under medical ~** sotto controllo medico

supervisor [ˈsuːpəvaɪzəʳ] N sorvegliante mf; soprintendente mf; (in shop) capocommesso(-a); (at university) relatore(-trice)

supervisory [ˈsuːpəvaɪzərɪ] ADJ di sorveglianza

supine [ˈsuːpaɪn] ADJ supino(-a)

supper [ˈsʌpəʳ] N cena; **to have ~** cenare

supplant [səˈplɑːnt] VT soppiantare

supple [ˈsʌpl] ADJ flessibile; agile

supplement N [ˈsʌplɪmənt] supplemento ▶ VT [sʌplɪˈmɛnt] completare, integrare

supplementary [sʌplɪˈmɛntərɪ] ADJ supplementare

supplier [səˈplaɪəʳ] N fornitore m

supply [səˈplaɪ] VT (a need) soddisfare; **to ~ sth (to sb)** (goods) fornire qc (a qn); **to ~ sb (with sth)** (people, organization) fornire a qn (qc); **to ~ sth (with sth)** (system, machine) alimentare qc (con qc) ▶ N riserva, provvista; (supplying) approvvigionamento; (Tech) alimentazione f ■ **supplies** NPL (food) viveri mpl; (Mil) sussistenza; **office supplies** forniture fpl per ufficio; **to be in short ~** scarseggiare, essere scarso(-a); **the electricity/water/gas ~** l'erogazione f di corrente/d'acqua/di gas; **~ and demand** la domanda e l'offerta; **the car comes supplied with a radio** l'auto viene fornita completa di radio

supply teacher N (BRIT) supplente mf

support [səˈpɔːt] N (moral, financial etc) sostegno, appoggio; (Tech) supporto ▶ VT sostenere; (financially) mantenere; (uphold) sostenere, difendere; (Sport: team) fare il tifo per; **they stopped work in ~ (of)** hanno smesso di lavorare per solidarietà (con); **to ~ o.s.** (financially) mantenersi

supporter [səˈpɔːtəʳ] N (Pol etc) sostenitore(-trice), fautore(-trice); (Sport) tifoso(-a)

supporting [səˈpɔːtɪŋ] ADJ (wall) di sostegno

supporting actor N attore m non protagonista

supporting actress N attrice f non protagonista

supporting role N ruolo non protagonista

supportive [səˈpɔːtɪv] ADJ d'appoggio; **I have a ~ wife/family** mia moglie/la mia famiglia mi appoggia

suppose [səˈpəuz] VT, VI supporre; immaginare; **to be supposed to do** essere tenuto(-a) a fare; **always supposing (that) he comes** ammesso e non concesso che venga; **I don't ~ she'll come** non credo che venga; **he's supposed to be an expert** dicono che sia un esperto, passa per un esperto

supposedly [səˈpəuzɪdlɪ] ADV presumibilmente; (seemingly) apparentemente

supposing [səˈpəuzɪŋ] CONJ se, ammesso che + sub

supposition [sʌpəˈzɪʃən] N supposizione f, ipotesi f inv

suppository [səˈpɔzɪtərɪ] N supposta, suppositorio

suppress [səˈprɛs] VT reprimere; sopprimere, tenere segreto(-a); occultare

suppression [səˈprɛʃən] N repressione f; soppressione f

suppressor [səˈprɛsəʳ] N (Elec etc) soppressore m

supremacy [suˈprɛməsɪ] N supremazia

supreme [suˈpriːm] ADJ supremo(-a)

Supreme Court N (US) Corte f suprema; **~ of**

Judicature *corte di giudizio suprema dell'Inghilterra e del Galles*

La Corte suprema (**Supreme Court**) degli Stati Uniti, istituita nel 1789, è la più alta giurisdizione federale. È composta da un *chief justice* (presidente) e da otto *associate justices* (giudici) nominati dal presidente degli Stati Uniti e confermati dal Senato. I giudici sono nominati a vita, ma possono ritirarsi, per motivi di salute o età. Ogni stato ha poi una sua Corte suprema, che è il giudice di ultima istanza nel sistema federale dello stato in questione.

supremo [su'pri:məu] N autorità *f inv* massima

Supt. ABBR (*Police*) = **superintendent**

surcharge ['sə:tʃɑːdʒ] N supplemento; (*extra tax*) soprattassa

sure [ʃuəʳ] ADJ sicuro(-a); (*definite, convinced*) sicuro(-a), certo(-a) ▶ ADV (*col: US*): **that ~ is pretty, that's ~ pretty** è veramente *or* davvero carino; **~!** (*of course*) senz'altro!, certo!; **~ enough** infatti; **to make ~ of** assicurarsi di; **to be ~ of sth** essere sicuro di qc; **to be ~ of o.s.** essere sicuro di sé; **I'm not ~ how/why/when** non so bene come/perché/quando + *sub*

sure-fire ['ʃuəfaɪəʳ] ADJ (*col*) infallibile

sure-footed [ʃuə'futɪd] ADJ dal passo sicuro

surely ['ʃuəlɪ] ADV sicuramente; certamente; **~ you don't mean that!** non parlerà sul serio!

surety ['ʃuərətɪ] N garanzia; **to go** *or* **stand ~ for sb** farsi garante per qn

surf [sə:f] N (*waves*) cavalloni *mpl*; (*foam*) spuma ▶ VT: **to ~ the Net** navigare in Internet

surface ['sə:fɪs] N superficie *f* ▶ VT (*road*) asfaltare ▶ VI risalire alla superficie; (*fig: person, news, feeling*) venire a galla, farsi vivo(-a); **on the ~ it seems that ...** (*fig*) superficialmente sembra che ...

surface area N superficie *f*

surface mail N posta ordinaria

surface-to-surface ['sə:fɪstə'sə:fɪs] ADJ (*Mil*) terra-terra *inv*

surfboard ['sə:fbɔːd] N tavola per surfing

surfeit ['sə:fɪt] N: **a ~ of** un eccesso di; un'indigestione di

surfer ['sə:fəʳ] N (*in sea*) surfista *mf*; (*on the Internet*) navigatore(-trice)

surfing ['sə:fɪŋ] N surfing *m*

surge [sə:dʒ] N (*strong movement*) ondata; (*of feeling*) impeto; (*Elec*) sovracorrente *f* transitoria ▶ VI (*waves*) gonfiarsi; (*people*) riversarsi; (*Elec: power*) aumentare improvvisamente; **to ~ forward** buttarsi avanti

surgeon ['sə:dʒən] N chirurgo

Surgeon General N (*US*) ≈ Ministro della Sanità

surgery ['sə:dʒərɪ] N chirurgia; (*BRIT Med: room*) studio *or* gabinetto medico, ambulatorio; (*: session*) visita ambulatoriale; (*BRIT: of MP*) incontri *mpl* con gli elettori; (*also:* **surgery hours**) orario delle visite *or* di consultazione; **to undergo ~** subire un intervento chirurgico

surgery hours NPL (*BRIT*) orario delle visite *or* di consultazione

surgical ['sə:dʒɪkl] ADJ chirurgico(-a)

surgical spirit N (*BRIT*) alcool *m inv* denaturato

Suriname [suərɪ'næm] N Suriname *m*

surly ['sə:lɪ] ADJ scontroso(-a), burbero(-a)

surmise [sə:'maɪz] VT supporre, congetturare

surmount [sə:'maunt] VT sormontare

surname ['sə:neɪm] N cognome *m*

surpass [sə:'pɑːs] VT superare

surplus ['sə:pləs] N eccedenza; (*Econ*) surplus *m inv* ▶ ADJ eccedente, d'avanzo; **it is ~ to our requirements** eccede i nostri bisogni; **~ stock** merce *f* in sovrappiù

surprise [sə'praɪz] N sorpresa; (*astonishment*) stupore *m* ▶ VT sorprendere; stupire; **to take by ~** (*person*) cogliere di sorpresa; (*Mil: town, fort*) attaccare di sorpresa

surprised [sə'praɪzd] ADJ (*look, smile*) sorpreso(-a); **to be ~** essere sorpreso, sorprendersi

surprising [sə'praɪzɪŋ] ADJ sorprendente, stupefacente

surprisingly [sə'praɪzɪŋlɪ] ADV (*easy, helpful*) sorprendentemente; **(somewhat) ~, he agreed** cosa (alquanto) sorprendente, ha accettato

surrealism [sə'rɪəlɪzəm] N surrealismo

surrealist [sə'rɪəlɪst] ADJ, N surrealista *mf*

surrender [sə'rɛndəʳ] N resa, capitolazione *f* ▶ VI arrendersi ▶ VT (*claim, right*) rinunciare a

surrender value N (*Comm*) valore *m* di riscatto

surreptitious [sʌrəp'tɪʃəs] ADJ furtivo(-a)

surrogate ['sʌrəgɪt] N (*BRIT: substitute*) surrogato ▶ ADJ surrogato(-a)

surrogate mother N madre *f* sostitutiva

surround [sə'raund] VT circondare; (*Mil etc*) accerchiare

surrounding [sə'raundɪŋ] ADJ circostante

surroundings [sə'raundɪŋz] NPL dintorni *mpl*; (*fig*) ambiente *m*

surtax ['sə:tæks] N soprattassa

surveillance [sə:'veɪləns] N sorveglianza, controllo

survey N ['sə:veɪ] (*comprehensive view: of situation, development*) quadro generale; (*study*) indagine *f*, studio; (*in housebuying etc*) perizia; (*of land*) rilevamento, rilievo topografico ▶ VT [sə:'veɪ] osservare; esaminare; (*Surveying: building*) fare una perizia di; (*: land*) fare il rilevamento di

surveying [sə'veɪɪŋ] N (*of land*) agrimensura

surveyor [sə'veɪəʳ] N perito; geometra *m*; (*of land*) agrimensore *m*

815

survival [səˈvaɪvl] N sopravvivenza; (*relic*) reliquia, vestigio

survival course N corso di sopravvivenza

survival kit N equipaggiamento di prima necessità

survive [səˈvaɪv] VI sopravvivere ▶ VT sopravvivere a

survivor [səˈvaɪvəʳ] N superstite *mf*, sopravvissuto(-a)

susceptible [səˈsɛptəbl] ADJ: ~ **(to)** sensibile (a); (*disease*) predisposto(-a) (a)

suspect ADJ [ˈsʌspɛkt] sospetto(-a) ▶ N [ˈsʌspɛkt] persona sospetta ▶ VT [səsˈpɛkt] sospettare; (*think likely*) supporre; (*doubt*) dubitare di

suspected [səsˈpɛktɪd] ADJ presunto(-a); **to have a ~ facture** avere una sospetta frattura

suspend [səsˈpɛnd] VT sospendere

suspended animation [səsˈpɛndɪd-] N: **in a state of ~** in stato comatoso

suspended sentence [səsˈpɛndɪd-] N condanna con la condizionale

suspender belt [səsˈpɛndəʳ-] N (BRIT) reggicalze *m inv*

suspenders [səsˈpɛndəz] NPL (BRIT) giarrettiere *fpl*; (US) bretelle *fpl*

suspense [səsˈpɛns] N apprensione *f*; (*in film etc*) suspense *m*; **to keep sb in ~** tenere qn in sospeso

suspension [səsˈpɛnʃən] N (*gen, Aut*) sospensione *f*; (*of driving licence*) ritiro temporaneo

suspension bridge N ponte *m* sospeso

suspicion [səsˈpɪʃən] N sospetto; **to be under ~** essere sospettato; **arrested on ~ of murder** arrestato come presunto omicida

suspicious [səsˈpɪʃəs] ADJ (*suspecting*) sospettoso(-a); (*causing suspicion*) sospetto(-a); **to be ~ of** *or* **about sb/sth** nutrire sospetti nei riguardi di qn/qc

suss out VT (BRIT col): **I've sussed it/him out** ho capito come stanno le cose/che tipo è

sustain [səsˈteɪn] VT sostenere; sopportare; (*Law: charge*) confermare; (*suffer*) subire

sustainable [səsˈteɪnəbl] ADJ sostenibile

sustained [səˈsteɪnd] ADJ (*effort*) prolungato(-a)

sustenance [ˈsʌstɪnəns] N nutrimento; mezzi *mpl* di sostentamento

suture [ˈsuːtʃəʳ] N sutura

SUV N ABBR (= *sports utility vehicle*) SUV *m inv*

SW ABBR (*Radio*: = *short wave*) O.C.

swab [swɔb] N (*Med*) tampone *m* ▶ VT (*Naut: also*: **swab down**) radazzare

swagger [ˈswægəʳ] VI pavoneggiarsi

swallow [ˈswɔləu] N (*bird*) rondine *f*; (*of food*) boccone *m*; (*of drink*) sorso ▶ VT inghiottire; (*fig: story*) bere
▶ **swallow up** VT inghiottire

swam [swæm] PT *of* **swim**

swamp [swɔmp] N palude *f* ▶ VT sommergere

swampy [ˈswɔmpɪ] ADJ palludoso(-a), pantanoso(-a)

swan [swɔn] N cigno

swank [swæŋk] VI (*col*: *talk boastfully*) fare lo spaccone; (: *show off*) mettersi in mostra

swan song N (*fig*) canto del cigno

swap [swɔp] N scambio ▶ VT: **to ~ (for)** scambiare (con)

SWAPO [ˈswɑːpəu] N ABBR = **South-West Africa People's Organization**

swarm [swɔːm] N sciame *m* ▶ VI formicolare; (*bees*) sciamare; (*people*) brulicare; (*place*): **to be swarming with** brulicare di

swarthy [ˈswɔːðɪ] ADJ di carnagione scura

swashbuckling [ˈswɔʃbʌklɪŋ] ADJ (*role, hero*) spericolato(-a)

swastika [ˈswɔstɪkə] N croce *f* uncinata, svastica

SWAT [swɔt] N ABBR (*US*: = *Special Weapons and Tactics*) reparto speciale di polizia; (= *a SWAT team*) uno squadrone del reparto speciale (di polizia)

swat [swɔt] VT schiacciare ▶ N (BRIT: *also*: **fly swat**) ammazzamosche *m inv*

swathe [sweɪð] N fascio ▶ VT: **to ~ in** (*bandages, blankets*) avvolgere in

swatter [ˈswɔtəʳ] N (*also*: **fly swatter**) ammazzamosche *m inv*

sway [sweɪ] VI (*building*) oscillare; (*tree*) ondeggiare; (*person*) barcollare ▶ VT (*influence*) influenzare, dominare ▶ N (*rule, power*): **~ (over)** influenza (su); **to hold ~ over sb** dominare qn

Swaziland [ˈswɑːzɪlænd] N Swaziland *m*

swear [sweəʳ] (*pt* **swore** [swɔːʳ], *pp* **sworn** [swɔːn]) VI (*witness etc*) giurare; (*curse*) bestemmiare, imprecare ▶ VT: **to ~ an oath** prestare giuramento; **to ~ to sth** giurare qc
▶ **swear in** VT insediare qn facendogli prestare giuramento

swearword [ˈsweəwəːd] N parolaccia

sweat [swɛt] N sudore *m*, traspirazione *f* ▶ VI sudare; **in a ~** in un bagno di sudore

sweatband [ˈswɛtbænd] N (*Sport*) fascia elastica (per assorbire il sudore)

sweater [ˈswɛtəʳ] N maglione *m*

sweatshirt [ˈswɛtʃəːt] N felpa *f*

sweatshop [ˈswɛtʃɔp] N (*pej*) azienda o fabbrica dove i dipendenti sono sfruttati

sweaty [ˈswɛtɪ] ADJ sudato(-a); bagnato(-a) di sudore

Swede [swiːd] N svedese *mf*

swede [swiːd] N (BRIT) rapa svedese

Sweden [ˈswiːdn] N Svezia

Swedish [ˈswiːdɪʃ] ADJ svedese ▶ N (*Ling*) svedese *m*

sweep [swi:p] (*pt, pp* **swept** [swɛpt]) N spazzata; (*curve*) curva; (*expanse*) distesa; (*range*) portata; (*also:* **chimney sweep**) spazzacamino ▶ VT spazzare, scopare; (*fashion, craze*) invadere; (*current*) spazzare ▶ VI camminare maestosamente; precipitarsi, lanciarsi, (e)stendersi; (*hand*) muoversi con gesto ampio; (*wind*) infuriare
▶ **sweep away** VT spazzare via; trascinare via
▶ **sweep past** VI sfrecciare accanto; passare accanto maestosamente
▶ **sweep up** VT, VI spazzare

sweeper ['swi:pə'] N (*person*) spazzino(-a); (*machine*) spazzatrice *f*; (*Football*) libero

sweeping ['swi:pɪŋ] ADJ (*gesture*) ampio(-a); (*changes, reforms*) ampio(-a), radicale; **a ~ statement** un'affermazione generica

sweepstake ['swi:psteɪk] N lotteria (*spesso abbinata alle corse dei cavalli*)

sweet [swi:t] N (*BRIT: pudding*) dolce *m*; (: *candy*) caramella ▶ ADJ dolce; (*fresh*) fresco(-a); (*fig*) piacevole; delicato(-a), grazioso(-a); (*kind*) gentile; (*cute*) carino(-a) ▶ ADV: **to smell/taste ~** avere un odore/sapore dolce; **~ and sour** *adj* agrodolce

sweetbread ['swi:tbrɛd] N animella

sweetcorn ['swi:tkɔ:n] N granturco dolce

sweeten ['swi:tn] VT addolcire; zuccherare

sweetener ['swi:tnə'] N (*Culin*) dolcificante *m*

sweetheart ['swi:thɑ:t] N innamorato(-a)

sweetly ['swi:tlɪ] ADV dolcemente

sweetness ['swi:tnɪs] N sapore *m* dolce; dolcezza

sweet pea N pisello odoroso

sweet potato N patata americana, patata dolce

sweetshop ['swi:tʃɔp] N (*BRIT*) ≈ pasticceria

sweet tooth N: **to have a ~** avere un debole per i dolci

swell [swɛl] (*pt* **swelled**, *pp* **swollen** ['swəulən] or **swelled**) N (*of sea*) mare *m* lungo ▶ ADJ (*US col: excellent*) favoloso(-a) ▶ VT gonfiare, ingrossare; (*numbers, sales etc*) aumentare ▶ VI gonfiarsi, ingrossarsi; (*sound*) crescere; (*Med: also:* **swell up**) gonfiarsi

swelling ['swɛlɪŋ] N (*Med*) tumefazione *f*, gonfiore *m*

sweltering ['swɛltərɪŋ] ADJ soffocante

swept [swɛpt] PT, PP *of* **sweep**

swerve [swə:v] VI deviare; (*driver*) sterzare; (*boxer*) scartare

swift [swɪft] N (*bird*) rondone *m* ▶ ADJ rapido(-a), veloce

swiftly ['swɪftlɪ] ADV rapidamente, velocemente

swiftness ['swɪftnɪs] N rapidità, velocità

swig [swɪg] N (*col: drink*) sorsata

swill [swɪl] N broda ▶ VT (*also:* **swill out, swill down**) risciacquare

swim [swɪm] (*pt* **swam** [swæm], *pp* **swum** [swʌm]) N: **to go for a ~** andare a fare una nuotata ▶ VI nuotare; (*Sport*) fare del nuoto; (*head, room*) girare ▶ VT (*river, channel*) attraversare *or* percorrere a nuoto; (*pool*) nuotare; **to go swimming** andare a nuotare; **to ~ a length** fare una vasca (a nuoto)

swimmer ['swɪmə'] N nuotatore(-trice)

swimming ['swɪmɪŋ] N nuoto

swimming baths NPL (*BRIT*) piscina

swimming cap N cuffia

swimming costume N (*BRIT*) costume *m* da bagno

swimmingly ['swɪmɪŋlɪ] ADV: **to go ~** (*wonderfully*) andare a gonfie vele

swimming pool N piscina

swimming trunks NPL costume *m* da bagno (da uomo)

swimsuit ['swɪmsu:t] N costume *m* da bagno

swindle ['swɪndl] N truffa ▶ VT truffare

swindler ['swɪndlə'] N truffatore(-trice)

swine [swaɪn] N (*pl inv*) maiale *m*, porco; (*pej*) porco (!)

swine flu N influenza suina

swing [swɪŋ] (*pt, pp* **swung** [swʌŋ]) N altalena; (*movement*) oscillazione *f*; (*Mus*) ritmo; (*also:* **swing music**) swing *m* ▶ VT dondolare, far oscillare; (*also:* **swing round**) far girare ▶ VI oscillare, dondolare; (*also:* **swing round**: *object*) roteare; (: *person*) girarsi, voltarsi; **to be in full ~** (*activity*) essere in piena attività; (*party etc*) essere nel pieno; **a ~ to the left** (*Pol*) una svolta a sinistra; **to get into the ~ of things** entrare nel pieno delle cose; **the road swings south** la strada prende la direzione sud

swing bridge N ponte *m* girevole

swing door N (*BRIT*) porta battente

swingeing ['swɪndʒɪŋ] ADJ (*BRIT: defeat*) violento(-a); (: *price increase*) enorme

swinging ['swɪŋɪŋ] ADJ (*step*) cadenzato(-a), ritmico(-a); (*rhythm, music*) trascinante

swinging door N (*US*) porta battente

swipe [swaɪp] N forte colpo; schiaffo ▶ VT (*hit*) colpire con forza; dare uno schiaffo a; (*col: steal*) sgraffignare; (*credit card etc*) far passare (nell'apposita macchinetta)

swipe card N tessera magnetica

swirl [swə:l] N turbine *m*, mulinello ▶ VI turbinare, far mulinello

swish [swɪʃ] ADJ (*old: smart*) all'ultimo grido, alla moda ▶ N (*sound: of whip*) sibilo; (: *of skirts, grass*) fruscio ▶ VI sibilare

Swiss [swɪs] ADJ, N (*pl inv*) svizzero(-a)

Swiss French ADJ svizzero(-a) francese

Swiss German ADJ svizzero(-a) tedesco(-a)

S

switch [swɪtʃ] N (*for light, radio etc*) interruttore *m*; (*change*) cambiamento ▶ VT (*also:* **switch round, switch over**) cambiare; scambiare
▶ **switch off** VT spegnere
▶ **switch on** VT accendere; (*engine, machine*) mettere in moto, avviare; (*Aut: ignition*) inserire; (BRIT: *water supply*) aprire

switchback ['swɪtʃbæk] N (BRIT) montagne *fpl* russe

switchblade ['swɪtʃbleɪd] N (*also:* **switchblade knife**) coltello a scatto

switchboard ['swɪtʃbɔːd] N (*Tel*) centralino

switchboard operator N centralinista *mf*

Switzerland ['swɪtsələnd] N Svizzera

swivel ['swɪvl] VI (*also:* **swivel round**) girare

swollen ['swəulən] PP *of* **swell** ▶ ADJ (*ankle etc*) gonfio(-a)

swoon [swuːn] VI svenire

swoop [swuːp] N (*by police etc*) incursione *f*; (*of bird etc*) picchiata ▶ VI (*also:* **swoop down**) scendere in picchiata, piombare; (*police*) **to ~ (on)** fare un'incursione (in)

swop [swɔp] N, VT = **swap**

sword [sɔːd] N spada

swordfish ['sɔːdfɪʃ] N pesce *m* spada *inv*

swore [swɔːʳ] PT *of* **swear**

sworn [swɔːn] PP *of* **swear** ▶ ADJ giurato(-a)

swot [swɔt] VT sgobbare su ▶ VI sgobbare

swum [swʌm] PP *of* **swim**

swung [swʌŋ] PT, PP *of* **swing**

sycamore ['sɪkəmɔːʳ] N sicomoro

sycophant ['sɪkəfənt] N leccapiedi *mf inv*

sycophantic [sɪkə'fæntɪk] ADJ ossequioso(-a), adulatore(-trice)

Sydney ['sɪdnɪ] N Sydney *f*

syllable ['sɪləbl] N sillaba

syllabus ['sɪləbəs] N programma *m*; **on the ~** in programma d'esame

symbol ['sɪmbl] N simbolo

symbolical [sɪm'bɔlɪkl] ADJ simbolico(-a); **to be ~ of sth** simboleggiare qc

symbolism ['sɪmbəlɪzəm] N simbolismo

symbolize ['sɪmbəlaɪz] VT simbolizzare

symmetrical [sɪ'mɛtrɪkl] ADJ simmetrico(-a)

symmetry ['sɪmɪtrɪ] N simmetria

sympathetic [sɪmpə'θɛtɪk] ADJ (*showing pity*) compassionevole; (*kind*) comprensivo(-a); **~ towards** ben disposto(-a) verso; **to be ~ to a cause** (*well-disposed*) simpatizzare per una causa

sympathetically [sɪmpə'θɛtɪklɪ] ADV in modo compassionevole; con comprensione

sympathize ['sɪmpəθaɪz] VI: **to ~ with sb** compatire qn; partecipare al dolore di qn; (*understand*) capire qn; **to ~ with a cause** simpatizzare per una causa

sympathizer ['sɪmpəθaɪzəʳ] N (*Pol*) simpatizzante *mf*

sympathy ['sɪmpəθɪ] N compassione *f*; **in ~ with** d'accordo con; (*strike*) per solidarietà con; **with our deepest ~** con le nostre più sincere condoglianze

symphonic [sɪm'fɔnɪk] ADJ sinfonico(-a)

symphony ['sɪmfənɪ] N sinfonia

symphony orchestra N orchestra sinfonica

symposium [sɪm'pəuzɪəm] N simposio

symptom ['sɪmptəm] N sintomo; indizio

symptomatic [sɪmptə'mætɪk] ADJ: **~ (of)** sintomatico(-a) (di)

synagogue ['sɪnəgɔg] N sinagoga

sync [sɪŋk] N (*col*): **in/out of ~** in/fuori sincronia; (*fig: people*): **they are in ~** sono in sintonia

synchromesh [sɪŋkrəu'mɛʃ] N cambio sincronizzato

synchronize ['sɪŋkrənaɪz] VT sincronizzare
▶ VI: **to ~ with** essere contemporaneo(-a) a

synchronized swimming ['sɪŋkrənaɪzd-] N nuoto sincronizzato

syncopated ['sɪŋkəpeɪtɪd] ADJ sincopato(-a)

syndicate ['sɪndɪkɪt] N sindacato; (*Press*) agenzia di stampa

syndrome ['sɪndrəum] N sindrome *f*

synonym ['sɪnənɪm] N sinonimo

synonymous [sɪ'nɔnɪməs] ADJ: **~ (with)** sinonimo(-a) (di)

synopsis [sɪ'nɔpsɪs] (*pl* **synopses** [-siːz]) N sommario, sinossi *f inv*

syntax ['sɪntæks] N sintassi *f inv*

synthesis ['sɪnθəsɪs] (*pl* **syntheses** [-siːz]) N sintesi *f inv*

synthesizer ['sɪnθəsaɪzəʳ] N (*Mus*) sintetizzatore *m*

synthetic [sɪn'θɛtɪk] ADJ sintetico(-a) ▶ N prodotto sintetico; (*Textiles*) fibra sintetica

syphilis ['sɪfɪlɪs] N sifilide *f*

syphon ['saɪfən] = **siphon**

Syria ['sɪrɪə] N Siria

Syrian ['sɪrɪən] ADJ, N siriano(-a)

syringe [sɪ'rɪndʒ] N siringa

syrup ['sɪrəp] N sciroppo; (*also:* **golden syrup**) melassa raffinata

syrupy ['sɪrəpɪ] ADJ sciropposo(-a)

system ['sɪstəm] N sistema *m*; (*network*) rete *f*; (*order*) metodo; (*Anat*) apparato; **it was a shock to his ~** è stato uno shock per il suo organismo

systematic [sɪstə'mætɪk] ADJ sistematico(-a); metodico(-a)

system disk N (*Comput*) disco del sistema

systems analyst N analista *mf* di sistemi

Tt

T, t [tiː] N (letter) T, t m inv or f inv; **T for Tommy** ≈ T come Taranto

TA N ABBR (BRIT) = **Territorial Army**

ta [tɑː] EXCL (BRIT col) grazie!

tab [tæb] N ABBR = **tabulator** ▶ N (loop: on coat etc) laccetto; (label) etichetta; **to keep tabs on** (fig) tenere d'occhio

tabby ['tæbɪ] N (also: **tabby cat**) (gatto) soriano, gatto tigrato

tabernacle ['tæbənækl] N tabernacolo

table ['teɪbl] N tavolo, tavola; (Math, Chem etc) tavola; (chart) tabella ▶ VT (BRIT: motion etc) presentare; **to lay** or **set the ~** apparecchiare or preparare la tavola; **to clear the ~** sparecchiare; **league ~** (Football, Rugby) classifica; **~ of contents** indice m

tablecloth ['teɪblklɔθ] N tovaglia

table d'hôte [tɑːblˈdəut] ADJ (meal) a prezzo fisso

table lamp N lampada da tavolo

tablemat ['teɪblmæt] N sottopiatto

table salt N sale m fino or da tavola

tablespoon ['teɪblspuːn] N cucchiaio da tavola; (also: **tablespoonful**: as measurement) cucchiaiata

tablet ['tæblɪt] N (Med) compressa; (: for sucking) pastiglia; (for writing) blocco; (of stone) targa; (Comput) tablet m inv; **~ of soap** (BRIT) saponetta

table tennis N tennis m da tavolo, ping-pong® m

table wine N vino da tavola

tabloid ['tæblɔɪd] N (newspaper) tabloid m inv (giornale illustrato di formato ridotto); **the tabloids, the ~ press** i giornali popolari

taboo [təˈbuː] ADJ, N tabù m inv

tabulate ['tæbjuleɪt] VT (data, figures) tabulare, disporre in tabelle

tabulator ['tæbjuleɪtər] N tabulatore m

tachograph ['tækəgrɑːf] N tachigrafo

tachometer [tæˈkɔmɪtər] N tachimetro

tacit ['tæsɪt] ADJ tacito(-a)

taciturn ['tæsɪtəːn] ADJ taciturno(-a)

tack [tæk] N (nail) bulletta; (stitch) punto d'imbastitura; (Naut) bordo, bordata; (fig) approccio ▶ VT imbullettare; imbastire ▶ VI bordeggiare; **to change ~** virare di bordo; **on the wrong ~** (fig) sulla strada sbagliata; **to ~ sth on to (the end of) sth** (of letter, book) aggiungere qc alla fine di qc

tackle ['tækl] N (equipment) attrezzatura, equipaggiamento; (for lifting) paranco; (Rugby) placcaggio; (Football) contrasto ▶ VT (difficulty) affrontare; (Rugby) placcare; (Football) contrastare

tacky ['tækɪ] ADJ colloso(-a), appiccicaticcio(-a); ancora bagnato(-a); (col: shabby) scadente (pej: tasteless) di cattivo gusto

tact [tækt] N tatto

tactful ['tæktful] ADJ delicato(-a), discreto(-a); **to be ~** avere tatto

tactfully ['tæktfəlɪ] ADV con tatto

tactical ['tæktɪkl] ADJ tattico(-a)

tactical voting N voto tattico

tactician [tækˈtɪʃən] N tattico(-a)

tactics ['tæktɪks] N, NPL tattica

tactless ['tæktlɪs] ADJ che manca di tatto

tactlessly ['tæktlɪslɪ] ADV senza tatto

tadpole ['tædpəul] N girino

taffy ['tæfɪ] N (US) caramella f mou inv

tag [tæg] N etichetta; **price/name ~** etichetta del prezzo/con il nome
▶ **tag along** VI seguire

Tahiti [təˈhiːti] N Tahiti f

tail [teɪl] N coda; (of shirt) falda ▶ VT (follow) seguire, pedinare; **to turn ~** voltare la schiena ◼ **tails** NPL (formal suit) frac m inv; see also **head**
▶ **tail away, tail off** VI (in size, quality etc) diminuire gradatamente

tailback ['teɪlbæk] N (BRIT) ingorgo

tail coat N marsina

tail end N (of train, procession etc) coda; (of meeting etc) fine f

tailgate ['teɪlgeɪt] N (Aut) portellone m posteriore

tail light N (Aut) fanalino di coda

tailor [ˈteɪləʳ] N sarto ▶ VT: **to ~ sth (to)** adattare qc (alle esigenze di); **~'s (shop)** sartoria (da uomo)

tailoring [ˈteɪlərɪŋ] N (cut) taglio

tailor-made [ˈteɪləˈmeɪd] ADJ (also fig) fatto(-a) su misura

tailwind [ˈteɪlwɪnd] N vento di coda

taint [teɪnt] VT (meat, food) far avariare; (fig: reputation) infangare

tainted [ˈteɪntɪd] ADJ (food) guasto(-a); (water, air) infetto(-a); (fig) corrotto(-a)

Taiwan [taɪˈwɑːn] N Taiwan m

Taiwanese [taɪwəˈniːz] ADJ, N taiwanese

Tajikistan [tɑːdʒɪkɪˈstɑːn] N Tagikistan m

take [teɪk] (pt **took** [tuk], pp **taken** [ˈteɪkn]) VT prendere; (gain: prize) ottenere, vincere; (require: effort, courage) occorrere, volerci; (tolerate) accettare, sopportare; (hold: passengers etc) contenere; (accompany) accompagnare; (bring, carry) portare; (conduct: meeting) condurre; (exam) sostenere, presentarsi a; **to ~ a photo/a shower** fare una fotografia/una doccia ▶ VI (dye, fire etc) prendere; (injection) fare effetto; (plant) attecchire ▶ N (Cine) ripresa; **I ~ it that** suppongo che; **to ~ for a walk** (child, dog) portare a fare una passeggiata; **to ~ sb's hand** prendere qn per mano; **to ~ it upon o.s. to do sth** prendersi la responsabilità di fare qc; **to be taken ill** avere un malore; **to be taken with sb/sth** (attracted) essere tutto preso da qn/qc; **it won't ~ long** non ci vorrà molto tempo; **it takes a lot of time/courage** occorre or ci vuole molto tempo/coraggio; **it will ~ at least 5 litres** contiene almeno 5 litri; **~ the first on the left** prenda la prima a sinistra; **to ~ Russian at university** fare russo all'università; **I took him for a doctor** l'ho preso per un dottore
▶ **take after** VT FUS assomigliare a
▶ **take apart** VT smontare
▶ **take away** VT portare via; togliere; **to ~ away (from)** sottrarre (da)
▶ **take back** VT (return) restituire; riportare; (one's words) ritirare
▶ **take down** VT (building) demolire; (dismantle: scaffolding) smontare; (letter etc) scrivere
▶ **take in** VT (lodger) prendere, ospitare; (orphan) accogliere; (stray dog) raccogliere; (Sewing) stringere; (deceive) imbrogliare, abbindolare; (understand) capire; (include) comprendere, includere
▶ **take off** VI (Aviat) decollare; (go away) andarsene ▶ VT (remove) togliere; (imitate) imitare
▶ **take on** VT (work) accettare, intraprendere; (employee) assumere; (opponent) sfidare, affrontare
▶ **take out** VT portare fuori; (remove) togliere; (licence) prendere, ottenere; **to ~ sth out of** (drawer, pocket etc) tirare qc fuori da; estrarre qc da; **don't ~ it out on me!** non prendertela con me!
▶ **take over** VT (business) rilevare ▶ VI: **to ~ over from sb** prendere le consegne or il controllo da qn

▶ **take to** VT FUS (person) prendere in simpatia; (activity) prendere gusto a; (form habit of): **to ~ to doing sth** prendere or cominciare a fare qc
▶ **take up** VT (one's story) riprendere; (dress) accorciare; (absorb: liquids) assorbire; (accept: offer, challenge) accettare; (occupy: time, space) occupare; (engage in: hobby etc) mettersi a; **to ~ up with sb** fare amicizia con qn; **to ~ sb up on sth** accettare qc da qn

takeaway [ˈteɪkəweɪ] (BRIT) ADJ (food) da portar via ▶ N (shop etc) ≈ rosticceria; (food) pasto per asporto

take-home pay [ˈteɪkhəum-] N stipendio netto

taken [ˈteɪkn] PP of **take**

takeoff [ˈteɪkɔf] N (Aviat) decollo

takeout [ˈteɪkaut] ADJ, N (US) = **takeaway**

takeover [ˈteɪkəuvəʳ] N (Comm) assorbimento

takeover bid N offerta di assorbimento

takings [ˈteɪkɪŋz] NPL (Comm) incasso

talc [tælk] N (also: **talcum powder**) talco

tale [teɪl] N racconto, storia; (pej) fandonia; **to tell tales** (fig: to teacher, parent etc) fare la spia

talent [ˈtælənt] N talento

talented [ˈtæləntɪd] ADJ di talento

talent scout N talent scout mf

talisman [ˈtælɪzmən] N talismano

talk [tɔːk] N discorso; (gossip) chiacchiere fpl; (conversation) conversazione f; (interview) discussione f ▶ VI parlare; (chatter) chiacchierare ∎ **talks** NPL (Pol etc) colloqui mpl; **to give a ~** tenere una conferenza; **to ~ about** parlare di; (converse) discorrere or conversare su; **to ~ sb out of/into doing** dissuadere qn da/convincere qn a fare; **to ~ shop** parlare di lavoro or di affari; **talking of films, have you seen ...?** a proposito di film, ha visto ...?
▶ **talk over** VT discutere

talkative [ˈtɔːkətɪv] ADJ loquace, ciarliero(-a)

talking point [ˈtɔːkɪŋ-] N argomento di conversazione

talking-to [ˈtɔːkɪŋtuː] N: **to give sb a good ~** fare una bella paternale a qn

talk show N (TV, Radio) talk show m inv

tall [tɔːl] ADJ alto(-a); **to be 6 feet ~** ≈ essere alto 1 metro e 80; **how ~ are you?** quanto è alto?

tallboy [ˈtɔːlbɔɪ] N (BRIT) cassettone m alto

tallness [ˈtɔːlnɪs] N altezza

tall story N panzana, frottola

tally [ˈtælɪ] N conto, conteggio ▶ VI: **to ~ (with)** corrispondere (a); **to keep a ~ of sth** tener il conto di qc

talon [ˈtælən] N artiglio

tambourine [tæmbəˈriːn] N tamburello

tame [teɪm] ADJ addomesticato(-a); (fig: story, style) insipido(-a), scialbo(-a)

Tamil [ˈtæmɪl] ADJ tamil inv ▶ N tamil mf inv; (Ling) tamil m

tamper ['tæmpə'] VI: **to ~ with** manomettere

tampon ['tæmpɔn] N tampone *m*

tan [tæn] N (*also:* **suntan**) abbronzatura ▶ VT abbronzare ▶ VI abbronzarsi ▶ ADJ (*colour*) marrone rossiccio *inv*; **to get a ~** abbronzarsi

tandem ['tændəm] N tandem *m inv*

tandoori [tæn'duərɪ] ADJ *nella cucina indiana, detto di carni o verdure cucinate allo spiedo in particolari forni*

tang [tæŋ] N odore *m* penetrante; sapore *m* piccante

tangent ['tændʒənt] N (*Math*) tangente *f*; **to go off at a ~** (*fig*) partire per la tangente

tangerine [tændʒə'ri:n] N mandarino

tangible ['tændʒəbl] ADJ tangibile; **~ assets** patrimonio reale

Tangier [tæn'dʒɪə'] N Tangeri *f*

tangle ['tæŋgl] N groviglio ▶ VT aggrovigliare; **to get in(to) a ~** aggrovigliarsi; (*fig*) combinare un pasticcio

tango ['tæŋgəu] N tango

tank [tæŋk] N serbatoio; (*for processing*) vasca; (*for fish*) acquario; (*Mil*) carro armato

tankard ['tæŋkəd] N boccale *m*

tanker ['tæŋkə'] N (*ship*) nave *f* cisterna *inv*; (*for oil*) petroliera; (*truck*) autobotte *f*, autocisterna

tankini [tæn'ki:nɪ] N tankini *m inv*

tanned [tænd] ADJ abbronzato(-a)

tannin ['tænɪn] N tannino

tanning ['tænɪŋ] N (*of leather*) conciatura

tannoy® ['tænɔɪ] N (*BRIT*) altoparlante *m*; **over the ~** per altoparlante

tantalizing ['tæntəlaɪzɪŋ] ADJ allettante

tantamount ['tæntəmaunt] ADJ: **~ to** equivalente a

tantrum ['tæntrəm] N accesso di collera; **to throw a ~** fare le bizze

Tanzania [tænzə'nɪə] N Tanzania

Tanzanian [tænzə'nɪən] ADJ, N tanzaniano(-a)

tap [tæp] N (*on sink etc*) rubinetto; (*gentle blow*) colpetto ▶ VT dare un colpetto a; (*resources*) sfruttare, utilizzare; (*telephone conversation*) intercettare; (*telephone*) mettere sotto controllo; **on ~** (*beer*) alla spina; (*fig: resources*) a disposizione

tap-dancing ['tæpdɑ:nsɪŋ] N tip tap *m*

tape [teɪp] N nastro; (*also:* **magnetic tape**) nastro (magnetico); (*also:* **sticky tape**) nastro adesivo ▶ VT (*record*) registrare (su nastro); (*stick*) attaccare con nastro adesivo; **on ~** (*song etc*) su nastro

tape deck N piastra di registrazione

tape measure N metro a nastro

taper ['teɪpə'] N candelina ▶ VI assottigliarsi

tape-record ['teɪprɪkɔ:d] VT registrare (su nastro)

tape recorder N registratore *m* (a nastro)

tape recording N registrazione *f*

tapered ['teɪpəd], **tapering** ['teɪpərɪŋ] ADJ affusolato(-a)

tapestry ['tæpɪstrɪ] N arazzo; tappezzeria

tape-worm ['teɪpwə:m] N tenia, verme *m* solitario

tapioca [tæpɪ'əukə] N tapioca

tappet ['tæpɪt] N punteria

tar [tɑ:'] N catrame *m*; **low-/middle-tar cigarettes** sigarette a basso/medio contenuto di nicotina

tarantula [tə'ræntjulə] N tarantola

tardy ['tɑ:dɪ] ADJ tardo(-a); tardivo(-a)

target ['tɑ:gɪt] N bersaglio; (*fig: objective*) obiettivo; **to be on ~** (*project*) essere nei tempi (di lavorazione)

target practice N tiro al bersaglio

tariff ['tærɪf] N tariffa

tarmac ['tɑ:mæk] N (*BRIT: on road*) macadam *m* al catrame; (*Aviat*) pista di decollo ▶ VT (*BRIT*) macadamizzare

tarnish ['tɑ:nɪʃ] VT offuscare, annerire; (*fig*) macchiare

tarot ['tærəu] N tarocco

tarpaulin [tɑ:'pɔ:lɪn] N tela incatramata

tarragon ['tærəgən] N dragoncello

tart [tɑ:t] N (*Culin*) crostata; (*BRIT pej: woman*) sgualdrina ▶ ADJ (*flavour*) aspro(-a), agro(-a) ▶ **tart up** VT (*col*): **to ~ o.s. up** farsi bello(-a); (*pej*) agghindarsi

tartan ['tɑ:tn] N tartan *m inv*

tartar ['tɑ:tə'] N (*on teeth*) tartaro

tartar sauce, tartare sauce N salsa tartara

task [tɑ:sk] N compito; **to take to ~** rimproverare

task force N (*Mil, Police*) unità *f inv* operativa

taskmaster ['tɑ:skmɑ:stə'] N: **he's a hard ~** è un vero tiranno

Tasmania [tæz'meɪnɪə] N Tasmania

tassel ['tæsl] N fiocco

taste [teɪst] N gusto; (*flavour*) sapore *m*, gusto; (*sample*) assaggio; (*fig: glimpse, idea*) idea ▶ VT gustare; (*sample*) assaggiare ▶ VI: **to ~ of** or **like** (*fish etc*) sapere di, avere sapore di; **what does it ~ like?** che sapore or gusto ha?; **it tastes like fish** sa di pesce; **in good/bad** di buon/cattivo gusto; **you can ~ the garlic (in it)** ci si sente il sapore dell'aglio; **can I have a ~?** posso assaggiarlo?; **to have a ~ of sth** assaggiare qc; **can I have a ~ of this wine?** posso assaggiare un po' di questo vino?; **to have a ~ for sth** avere un'inclinazione per qc; **to be in bad** or **poor ~** essere di cattivo gusto

taste bud N papilla gustativa

tasteful ['teɪstful] ADJ di buon gusto

tastefully [ˈteɪstfəlɪ] ADV con gusto

tasteless [ˈteɪstlɪs] ADJ (food) insipido(-a); (remark) di cattivo gusto

tasty [ˈteɪstɪ] ADJ saporito(-a), gustoso(-a)

tattered [ˈtætəd] ADJ see **tatters**

tatters [ˈtætəz] NPL: **in ~** (also: **tattered**) a brandelli, sbrindellato(-a)

tattoo [təˈtuː] N tatuaggio; (spectacle) parata militare ▶ VT tatuare

tatty [ˈtætɪ] ADJ (BRIT col) malandato(-a)

taught [tɔːt] PT, PP of **teach**

taunt [tɔːnt] N scherno ▶ VT schernire

Taurus [ˈtɔːrəs] N Toro; **to be ~** essere del Toro

taut [tɔːt] ADJ teso(-a)

tavern [ˈtævən] N (old) taverna

tawdry [ˈtɔːdrɪ] ADJ pacchiano(-a)

tawny [ˈtɔːnɪ] ADJ fulvo(-a)

tax [tæks] N (on goods) imposta; (on services) tassa; (on income) imposte fpl, tasse fpl ▶ VT tassare; (fig: strain: patience etc) mettere alla prova; **free of ~** esentasse inv, esente da imposte; **before/after ~** al lordo/netto delle tasse

taxable [ˈtæksəbl] ADJ imponibile

tax allowance N detrazione f d'imposta

taxation [tækˈseɪʃən] N tassazione f; tasse fpl, imposte fpl; **system of ~** sistema m fiscale

tax avoidance N l'evitare legalmente il pagamento di imposte

tax collector N esattore m delle imposte

tax disc N (BRIT Aut) ≈ bollo

tax evasion N evasione f fiscale

tax exemption N esenzione f fiscale

tax exile N chi ripara all'estero per evadere le imposte

tax-free [tæksˈfriː] ADJ esente da imposte

tax haven N paradiso fiscale

taxi [ˈtæksɪ] N taxi m inv ▶ VI (Aviat) rullare

taxidermist [ˈtæksɪdəːmɪst] N tassidermista mf

taxi driver N tassista mf

tax inspector N (BRIT) ispettore m delle tasse

taxi rank, (US) **taxi stand** N posteggio dei taxi

taxi stand N (US) = **taxi rank**

tax payer N contribuente mf

tax rebate N rimborso fiscale

tax relief N sgravio fiscale

tax return N dichiarazione f dei redditi

tax shelter N paradiso fiscale

tax year N anno fiscale

TB N ABBR (= tuberculosis) TBC f

tbc ABBR (= to be confirmed) da confermarsi

TD N ABBR (US) = **Treasury Department**; (Football) = **touchdown**

tea [tiː] N tè m inv; (BRIT: snack: for children) merenda; **high ~** (BRIT) cena leggera (presa nel tardo pomeriggio)

tea bag N bustina di tè

tea break N (BRIT) intervallo per il tè

teacake [ˈtiːkeɪk] N (BRIT) panino dolce all'uva

teach [tiːtʃ] (pt, pp **taught** [tɔːt]) VT: **to ~ sb sth**, **~ sth to sb** insegnare qc a qn ▶ VI insegnare; **it taught him a lesson** (fig) gli è servito da lezione

teacher [ˈtiːtʃə'] N (gen) insegnante mf; (in secondary school) professore(-essa); (in primary school) maestro(-a); **French ~** insegnante di francese

teacher training college N (for primary schools) ≈ istituto magistrale; (for secondary schools) scuola universitaria per l'abilitazione all'insegnamento nelle medie superiori

teaching [ˈtiːtʃɪŋ] N insegnamento

teaching aids NPL materiali mpl per l'insegnamento

teaching hospital N (BRIT) clinica universitaria

teaching staff N (BRIT) insegnanti mpl, personale m insegnante

tea cloth N (for dishes) strofinaccio; (BRIT: for trolley) tovaglietta da tè

tea cosy N copriteiera m inv

teacup [ˈtiːkʌp] N tazza da tè

teak [tiːk] N teak m

tea leaves NPL foglie fpl di tè

team [tiːm] N squadra; (of animals) tiro
▶ **team up** VI: **to ~ up (with)** mettersi insieme (a)

team games NPL giochi mpl di squadra

teamwork [ˈtiːmwəːk] N lavoro di squadra

tea party N tè m inv (ricevimento)

teapot [ˈtiːpɒt] N teiera

tear¹ [tɪə'] N lacrima; **in tears** in lacrime; **to burst into tears** scoppiare in lacrime

tear² [tɛə'] (pt **tore** [tɔː'], pp **torn** [tɔːn]) N strappo ▶ VT strappare ▶ VI strapparsi; **to ~ to pieces** or **to bits** or **to shreds** (also fig) fare a pezzi or a brandelli
▶ **tear along** VI (rush) correre all'impazzata
▶ **tear apart** VT (also fig) distruggere
▶ **tear away** VT: **to ~ o.s. away (from sth)** (fig) staccarsi (da qc)
▶ **tear down** VT (building, statue) demolire; (poster, flag) tirare giù
▶ **tear off** VT (sheet of paper etc) strappare; (one's clothes) togliersi di dosso
▶ **tear out** VT (sheet of paper, cheque) staccare
▶ **tear up** VT (sheet of paper etc) strappare

tearaway [ˈtɛərəweɪ] N (col) monello(-a)

teardrop [ˈtɪədrɒp] N lacrima

tearful [ˈtɪəful] ADJ piangente, lacrimoso(-a)

tear gas N gas m lacrimogeno

tearoom [ˈtiːruːm] N sala da tè

tease [tiːz] VT canzonare; (unkindly) tormentare

tea set N servizio da tè

teashop [ˈtiːʃɒp] N (BRIT) sala da tè

teaspoon ['tiːspuːn] N cucchiaino da tè; (*also:* **teaspoonful:** *as measurement*) cucchiaino

tea strainer N colino da tè

teat [tiːt] N capezzolo; (*of bottle*) tettarella

teatime ['tiːtaɪm] N ora del tè

tea towel N (BRIT) strofinaccio (per i piatti)

tea urn N bollitore *m* per il tè

tech [tɛk] N ABBR (*col*) = **technical college; technology**

technical ['tɛknɪkl] ADJ tecnico(-a)

technical college N ≈ istituto tecnico

technicality [tɛknɪ'kælɪtɪ] N tecnicità; (*detail*) dettaglio tecnico; **on a legal ~** grazie a un cavillo legale

technically ['tɛknɪklɪ] ADV dal punto di vista tecnico

technician [tɛk'nɪʃən] N tecnico(-a)

technique [tɛk'niːk] N tecnica

techno ['tɛknəʊ] N (*Mus*) techno *f inv*

technocrat ['tɛknəkræt] N tecnocrate *mf*

technological [tɛknə'lɔdʒɪkl] ADJ tecnologico(-a)

technologist [tɛk'nɔlədʒɪst] N tecnologo(-a)

technology [tɛk'nɔlədʒɪ] N tecnologia

teddy ['tɛdɪ], **teddy bear** N orsacchiotto

tedious ['tiːdɪəs] ADJ noioso(-a), tedioso(-a)

tedium ['tiːdɪəm] N noia, tedio

tee [tiː] N (*Golf*) tee *m inv*

teem [tiːm] VI abbondare, brulicare; **to ~ with** brulicare di; **it is teeming (with rain)** piove a dirotto

teen [tiːn] ADJ = **teenage** ▶ N (US) = **teenager**

teenage ['tiːneɪdʒ] ADJ (*fashions etc*) per giovani, per adolescenti

teenager ['tiːneɪdʒəʳ] N adolescente *mf*

teens [tiːnz] NPL: **to be in one's ~** essere adolescente

tee-shirt ['tiːʃəːt] N = **T-shirt**

teeter ['tiːtəʳ] VI barcollare, vacillare

teeth [tiːθ] NPL *of* **tooth**

teethe [tiːð] VI mettere i denti

teething ring ['tiːðɪŋ-] N dentaruolo

teething troubles ['tiːðɪŋ-] NPL (*fig*) difficoltà *fpl* iniziali

teetotal ['tiː'təʊtl] ADJ astemio(-a)

teetotaller, (US) **teetotaler** ['tiː'təʊtləʳ] N astemio(-a)

TEFL ['tɛfl] N ABBR = **Teaching of English as a Foreign Language**

Teflon® ['tɛflɔn] N teflon® *m*

Tehran [tɛə'rɑːn] N Tehran *f*

tel. ABBR (= *telephone*) tel

Tel Aviv ['tɛlə'viːv] N Tel Aviv *f*

telecast ['tɛlɪkɑːst] VT, VI teletrasmettere

telecommunications ['tɛlɪkəmjuːnɪ'keɪʃənz] N telecomunicazioni *fpl*

teleconferencing ['tɛlɪkɔnfərnsɪŋ] N teleconferenza

telegram ['tɛlɪgræm] N telegramma *m*

telegraph ['tɛlɪgrɑːf] N telegrafo

telegraphic [tɛlɪ'græfɪk] ADJ telegrafico(-a)

telegraph pole N palo del telegrafo

telegraph wire N filo del telegrafo

telepathic [tɛlɪ'pæθɪk] ADJ telepatico(-a)

telepathy [tə'lɛpəθɪ] N telepatia

telephone ['tɛlɪfəʊn] N telefono ▶ VT (*person*) telefonare a; (*message*) comunicare per telefono; **to have a ~,** (BRIT) **to be on the ~** (*subscriber*) avere il telefono; **to be on the ~** (*be speaking*) essere al telefono

telephone book N elenco telefonico

telephone box, (US) **telephone booth** N cabina telefonica

telephone call N telefonata

telephone directory N elenco telefonico

telephone exchange N centralino telefonico

telephone number N numero di telefono

telephone operator N centralinista *mf*

telephone tapping N intercettazione *f* telefonica

telephonist [tə'lɛfənɪst] N (BRIT) telefonista *mf*

telephoto lens ['tɛlɪfəʊtəʊ-] N teleobiettivo

teleprinter ['tɛlɪprɪntəʳ] N telescrivente *f*

Teleprompter® ['tɛlɪprɔmptəʳ] N (US) gobbo

telesales ['tɛlɪseɪlz] N vendita per telefono

telescope ['tɛlɪskəʊp] N telescopio ▶ VI chiudersi a telescopio; (*fig: vehicles*) accartocciarsi

telescopic [tɛlɪs'kɔpɪk] ADJ telescopico(-a); (*umbrella*) pieghevole

Teletext® ['tɛlɪtɛkst] N (*system*) teletext *m inv*; (*in Italy*) televideo

telethon ['tɛlɪθɔn] N maratona televisiva

televise ['tɛlɪvaɪz] VT teletrasmettere

television ['tɛlɪvɪʒən] N televisione *f*; **on ~** alla televisione

television licence N (BRIT) abbonamento alla televisione

television programme N programma *m* televisivo

television set N televisore *m*

teleworking ['tɛlɪwəːkɪŋ] N telelavoro

telex ['tɛlɛks] N telex *m inv* ▶ VT trasmettere per telex ▶ VI mandare un telex; **to ~ sb (about sth)** informare qn via telex (di qc)

tell [tɛl] (*pt, pp* **told** [təʊld]) VT dire; (*relate: story*) raccontare; (*distinguish*): **to ~ sth from** distinguere qc da ▶ VI (*talk*): **to ~ (of)** parlare (di); (*have effect*) farsi sentire, avere effetto; **to ~ sb to do** dire a qn di fare; **to ~ sb about sth** dire a qn di

qc; raccontare qc a qn; **to ~ the time** leggere l'ora; **can you ~ me the time?** può dirmi l'ora?; **(I) ~ you what ...** so io che cosa fare ...; **I couldn't ~ them apart** non riuscivo a distinguerli
▸ **tell off** VT rimproverare, sgridare
▸ **tell on** VT FUS (*inform against*) denunciare

teller ['tɛlər] N (*in bank*) cassiere(-a)

telling ['tɛlɪŋ] ADJ (*remark, detail*) rivelatore(-trice)

telltale ['tɛlteɪl] ADJ (*sign*) rivelatore(-trice) ▸ N (*pej*) malalingua, pettegolo(-a)

telly ['tɛlɪ] N ABBR (*BRIT col*: = *television*) tivù *f inv*

temerity [təˈmɛrɪtɪ] N temerarietà

temp [tɛmp] ABBR (*BRIT col*) = **temporary** ▸ N impiegato(-a) interinale ▸ VI lavorare come impiegato(-a) interinale

temper ['tɛmpər] N (*nature*) carattere *m*; (*mood*) umore *m*; (*fit of anger*) collera ▸ VT (*moderate*) temperare, moderare; **to be in a ~** essere in collera; **to keep one's ~** restare calmo; **to lose one's ~** andare in collera

temperament ['tɛmprəmənt] N (*nature*) temperamento

temperamental [tɛmprəˈmɛntl] ADJ capriccioso(-a)

temperance ['tɛmpərns] N moderazione *f*; (*in drinking*) temperanza nel bere

temperate ['tɛmprət] ADJ moderato(-a); (*climate*) temperato(-a)

temperature ['tɛmprətʃər] N temperatura; **to have** *or* **run a ~** avere la febbre

tempered ['tɛmpəd] ADJ (*steel*) temprato(-a)

tempest ['tɛmpɪst] N tempesta

tempestuous [tɛmˈpɛstjuəs] ADJ (*relationship, meeting*) burrascoso(-a)

tempi ['tɛmpiː] NPL of **tempo**

template, (*US*) **templet** ['tɛmplɪt] N sagoma

temple ['tɛmpl] N (*building*) tempio; (*Anat*) tempia

templet ['tɛmplɪt] N (*US*) = **template**

tempo ['tɛmpəu] (*pl* **tempos, tempi** ['tɛmpiː]) N tempo; (*fig: of life etc*) ritmo

temporal ['tɛmpərl] ADJ temporale

temporarily ['tɛmpərərɪlɪ] ADV temporaneamente

temporary ['tɛmpərərɪ] ADJ temporaneo(-a); (*job, worker*) avventizio(-a), temporaneo(-a); **~ secretary** segretaria temporanea; **~ teacher** supplente *mf*

temporize ['tɛmpəraɪz] VI temporeggiare

tempt [tɛmpt] VT tentare; **to ~ sb into doing** indurre qn a fare; **to be tempted to do sth** essere tentato di fare qc

temptation [tɛmpˈteɪʃən] N tentazione *f*

tempting ['tɛmptɪŋ] ADJ allettante, seducente

ten [tɛn] NUM dieci ▸ N dieci; **tens of thousands** decine di migliaia

tenable ['tɛnəbl] ADJ sostenibile

tenacious [təˈneɪʃəs] ADJ tenace

tenacity [təˈnæsɪtɪ] N tenacia

tenancy ['tɛnənsɪ] N affitto; condizione *f* di inquilino

tenant ['tɛnənt] N inquilino(-a)

tend [tɛnd] VT badare a, occuparsi di; (*sick etc*) prendersi cura di ▸ VI: **to ~ to do** tendere a fare; **to ~ to** (*colour*) tendere a

tendency ['tɛndənsɪ] N tendenza

tender ['tɛndər] ADJ tenero(-a); (*sore*) dolorante; (*fig: subject*) delicato(-a) ▸ N (*Comm: offer*) offerta; (*money*): **legal ~** moneta in corso legale ▸ VT offrire; **to put in a ~ (for)** fare un'offerta (per); **to put work out to ~** (*BRIT*) dare lavoro in appalto; **to ~ one's resignation** presentare le proprie dimissioni

tenderize ['tɛndəraɪz] VT (*Culin*) far intenerire

tenderly ['tɛndəlɪ] ADV teneramente

tenderness ['tɛndənɪs] N tenerezza; sensibilità

tendon ['tɛndən] N tendine *m*

tenement ['tɛnəmənt] N casamento

Tenerife [tɛnəˈriːf] N Tenerife *f*

tenet ['tɛnət] N principio

tenner ['tɛnər] N (*BRIT col*) (banconota da) dieci sterline *fpl*

tennis ['tɛnɪs] N tennis *m*

tennis ball N palla da tennis

tennis court N campo da tennis

tennis elbow N (*Med*) gomito del tennista

tennis match N partita di tennis

tennis player N tennista *mf*

tennis racket N racchetta da tennis

tennis shoes NPL scarpe *fpl* da tennis

tenor ['tɛnər] N (*Mus, of speech etc*) tenore *m*

tenpin bowling ['tɛnpɪn-] N (*BRIT*) bowling *m*

tense [tɛns] ADJ teso(-a) ▸ N (*Ling*) tempo ▸ VT (*tighten: muscles*) tendere

tenseness ['tɛnsnɪs] N tensione *f*

tension ['tɛnʃən] N tensione *f*

tent [tɛnt] N tenda

tentacle ['tɛntəkl] N tentacolo

tentative ['tɛntətɪv] ADJ esitante, incerto(-a); (*conclusion*) provvisorio(-a)

tenterhooks ['tɛntəhuks] NPL: **on ~** sulle spine

tenth [tɛnθ] NUM decimo(-a)

tent peg N picchetto da tenda

tent pole N palo da tenda, montante *m*

tenuous ['tɛnjuəs] ADJ tenue

tenure ['tɛnjuər] N (*of property*) possesso; (*of job*) incarico; (*guaranteed employment*): **to have ~** essere di ruolo

tepid ['tɛpɪd] ADJ tiepido(-a)

Ter. ABBR = **terrace**

term [təːm] N (*limit*) termine *m*; (*word*) vocabolo, termine; (*Scol*) trimestre *m*; (*Law*) sessione *f* ▶ vt chiamare, definire ▪ **terms** NPL (*conditions*) condizioni *fpl*; (*Comm*) prezzi *mpl*, tariffe *fpl*; ~ **of imprisonment** periodo di prigionia; **during his ~ of office** durante il suo incarico; **in the short/long ~** a breve/lunga scadenza; **"easy terms"** (*Comm*) "facilitazioni di pagamento"; **to be on good terms with** essere in buoni rapporti con; **to come to terms with** (*person*) arrivare a un accordo con; (*problem*) affrontare

terminal ['təːmɪnl] ADJ finale, terminale; (*disease*) terminale ▶ N (*Elec*, *Comput*) morsetto; (*Aviat, for oil, ore etc*) terminal *m inv*; (*Brit: also:* **coach terminal**) capolinea *m*

terminate ['təːmɪneɪt] VT mettere fine a ▶ VI: **to ~ in** finire in *or* con

termination [təːmɪ'neɪʃən] N fine *f*; (*of contract*) rescissione *f*; ~ **of pregnancy** (*Med*) interruzione *f* della gravidanza

termini ['təːmɪnaɪ] NPL *of* **terminus**

terminology [təːmɪ'nɔlədʒɪ] N terminologia

terminus ['təːmɪnəs] (*pl* **termini** ['təːmɪnaɪ]) N (*for buses*) capolinea *m*; (*for trains*) stazione *f* terminale

termite ['təːmaɪt] N termite *f*

term paper N (*US Univ*) saggio scritto da consegnare a fine trimestre

Terr. ABBR = **terrace**

terrace ['terəs] N terrazza; (*Brit: row of houses*) fila di case a schiera ▪ **the terraces** NPL (*Brit Sport*) le gradinate

terraced ['terɪst] ADJ (*garden*) a terrazze; (*in a row: house, cottage etc*) a schiera

terrain [te'reɪn] N terreno

terrestrial [tɪ'restrɪəl] ADJ (*life*) terrestre; (*Brit: channel*) terrestre

terrible ['terɪbl] ADJ terribile; (*weather*) bruttissimo(-a); (*performance, report*) pessimo(-a)

terribly ['terəblɪ] ADV terribilmente; (*very badly*) malissimo

terrier ['terɪər] N terrier *m inv*

terrific [tə'rɪfɪk] ADJ incredibile, fantastico(-a); (*wonderful*) formidabile, eccezionale

terrified ['terɪfaɪd] ADJ atterrito(-a)

terrify ['terɪfaɪ] VT terrorizzare; **to be terrified** essere atterrito(-a)

terrifying ADJ terrificante

territorial [terɪ'tɔːrɪəl] ADJ territoriale

territorial waters NPL acque *fpl* territoriali

territory ['terɪtərɪ] N territorio

terror ['terər] N terrore *m*

terror attack N attentato terroristico

terrorism ['terərɪzəm] N terrorismo

terrorist ['terərɪst] N terrorista *mf*

terrorize ['terəraɪz] VT terrorizzare

terse [təːs] ADJ (*style*) conciso(-a); (*reply*) laconico(-a)

tertiary ['təːʃərɪ] ADJ (*gen*) terziario(-a); ~ **education** (*Brit*) educazione *f* superiore post-scolastica

Terylene® ['terəliːn] N (*Brit*) terital® *m*, terilene® *m*

TESL ['tesl] N ABBR = **Teaching of English as a Second Language**

test [test] N (*trial, check: of courage etc*) prova; (*: of goods in factory*) controllo, collaudo; (*Med*) esame *m*; (*Chem*) analisi *f inv*; (*exam: of intelligence etc*) test *m inv*; (*: in school*) compito in classe; (*also:* **driving test**) esame *m* di guida ▶ VT provare; controllare, collaudare; esaminare; analizzare; sottoporre ad esame; **to put sth to the ~** mettere qc alla prova; **to ~ sth for sth** analizzare qc alla ricerca di qc; **to ~ sb in history** esaminare qn in storia

testament ['testəmənt] N testamento; **the Old/New T~** il Vecchio/Nuovo testamento

test ban N (*also:* **nuclear test ban**) divieto di esperimenti nucleari

test case N (*Law, fig*) caso che farà testo

testes ['testiːz] NPL testicoli *mpl*

test flight N volo di prova

testicle ['testɪkl] N testicolo

testify ['testɪfaɪ] VI (*Law*) testimoniare, deporre; **to ~ to sth** (*Law*) testimoniare qc; (*gen*) comprovare *or* dimostrare qc; (*be sign of*) essere una prova di qc

testimonial [testɪ'məunɪəl] N (*reference*) benservito; (*gift*) testimonianza di stima

testimony ['testɪmənɪ] N (*Law*) testimonianza, deposizione *f*

testing ['testɪŋ] ADJ (*difficult: time*) duro(-a)

test match N (*Cricket, Rugby*) partita internazionale

testosterone [tes'tɔstərəun] N testosterone *m*

test paper N (*Scol*) interrogazione *f* scritta

test pilot N pilota *m* collaudatore

test tube N provetta

test-tube baby ['testtjuːb-] N bambino(-a) concepito(-a) in provetta

testy ['testɪ] ADJ irritabile

tetanus ['tetənəs] N tetano

tetchy ['tetʃɪ] ADJ irritabile, irascibile

tether ['teðər] VT legare ▶ N: **at the end of one's ~** al limite (della pazienza)

text [tekst] N testo; (*Tel*) sms *m inv*, messaggino ▶ VT: **to ~ sb** (*col*) mandare un sms a ▶ VI messaggiarsi

textbook ['tekstbuk] N libro di testo

textile ['tekstaɪl] N tessile *m* ▪ **textiles** NPL tessuti *mpl*

texting ['tekstɪŋ] N invio di sms

text message N (*Tel*) sms *m inv*, messaggino

text messaging [-'mɛsɪdʒɪŋ] N il mandarsi sms

textual ['tɛkstjuəl] ADJ testuale, del testo

texture ['tɛkstʃəʳ] N tessitura; (*of skin, paper etc*) struttura

TGIF ABBR (*col*) = thank God it's Friday

Thai [taɪ] ADJ tailandese ▶ N tailandese *mf*; (*Ling*) tailandese *m*

Thailand ['taɪlænd] N Tailandia

thalidomide® [θə'lɪdəmaɪd] N talidomide® *m*

Thames [tɛmz] N: **the ~** il Tamigi

than [ðæn, ðən] CONJ (*in comparisons*) che; (*with numerals, pronouns, proper names*) di; **more ~ 10/ Maria/once** più di 10/Maria/una volta; **I have more/less ~ you** ne ho più/meno di te; **you know her better ~ I do** la conosce meglio di me *or* di quanto non la conosca io; **she has more apples ~ pears** ha più mele che pere; **it is better to phone ~ to write** è meglio telefonare che scrivere; **no sooner did he leave ~ the phone rang** non appena uscì il telefono suonò; **she is older ~ you think** è più vecchia di quanto tu (non) pensi

thank [θæŋk] VT ringraziare; **~ you (very much)** grazie (tante); **~ heavens/God!** grazie al cielo/a Dio!; *see also* **thanks**

thankful ['θæŋkful] ADJ: **~ (for)** riconoscente (per); **~ for/that** (*relieved*) sollevato(a) da/dal fatto che

thankfully ['θæŋkfəlɪ] ADV con riconoscenza; con sollievo; **~ there were few victims** grazie al cielo ci sono state poche vittime

thankless ['θæŋklɪs] ADJ ingrato(-a)

thanks [θæŋks] NPL ringraziamenti *mpl*, grazie *fpl* ▶ EXCL grazie!; **~ to** prep grazie a

Thanksgiving (Day) ['θæŋksgɪvɪŋ-] N (*US*) giorno del ringraziamento

Negli Stati Uniti il quarto giovedì di novembre ricorre il **Thanksgiving (Day)**, festa nazionale in ricordo della celebrazione con cui i Padri Pellegrini, i puritani inglesi che fondarono la colonia di Plymouth nel Massachusetts, ringraziarono Dio del buon raccolto del 1621.

---

that [ðæt]

(*pl* **those**) ADJ (*demonstrative*) quel (quell', quello) *m*; quella (quell') *f*; **that man/ woman/book** quell'uomo/quella donna/ quel libro; (*not "this"*) quell'uomo/quella donna/quel libro là; **that one** quello(-a) là

▶ PRON **1** (*demonstrative*) ciò; (: *not "this one"*) quello(-a); **who's that?** chi è?; **what's that?** cos'è quello?; **is that you?** sei tu?; **I prefer this to that** preferisco questo a quello; **that's what he said** questo è ciò che ha detto; **after that** dopo; **what happened after that?** che è successo dopo?; **that is (to say)** cioè; **at** *or* **with that she ...** con ciò lei ...; **do it like that** fallo così

2 (*relative: direct*) che; (: *indirect*) cui; **the book (that) I read** il libro che ho letto; **the box (that) I put it in** la scatola in cui l'ho messo; **the people (that) I spoke to** le persone con cui *or* con le quali ho parlato; **not that I know of** non che io sappia

3 (*relative: of time*) in cui; **the day (that) he came** il giorno in cui è venuto

▶ CONJ che; **he thought that I was ill** pensava che io fossi malato

▶ ADV (*demonstrative*) così; **I can't work that much** non posso lavorare (così) tanto; **that high** così alto; **the wall's about that high and that thick** il muro è alto circa così e spesso circa così

---

thatched [θætʃt] ADJ (*roof*) di paglia; **~ cottage** cottage *m inv* col tetto di paglia

Thatcherism ['θætʃərɪzəm] N thatcherismo

thaw [θɔː] N disgelo ▶ VI (*ice*) sciogliersi; (*food*) scongelarsi ▶ VT (*food*) (fare) scongelare; **it's thawing** (*weather*) sta sgelando

---

the [ðiː, ðə]

DEF ART **1** (*gen*) il (lo, l') *m*; la (l') *f*; i (gli) *mpl*; le *fpl*; **the boy/girl/ink** il ragazzo/la ragazza/l'inchiostro; **the books/pencils** i libri/le matite; **the history of the world** la storia del mondo; **give it to the postman** dallo al postino; **I haven't the time/money** non ho tempo/soldi; **the rich and the poor** i ricchi e i poveri; **1.5 euros to the dollar** 1.5 euro per un dollaro; **paid by the hour** pagato a ore

2 (*in titles*): **Elizabeth the First** Elisabetta prima; **Peter the Great** Pietro il Grande

3 (*in comparisons*): **the more he works, the more he earns** più lavora più guadagna; **the sooner the better** prima è meglio è

---

theatre, (*US*) **theater** ['θɪətəʳ] N teatro; (*also:* **lecture theatre**) aula magna; (*also:* **operating theatre**) sala operatoria

theatre-goer ['θɪətəgəuəʳ] N frequentatore(-trice) di teatri

theatrical [θɪ'ætrɪkl] ADJ teatrale

theft [θɛft] N furto

their [ðɛəʳ] ADJ il (la) loro, *pl* i (le) loro

theirs [ðɛəz] PRON il (la) loro, *pl* i (le) loro; **it is ~** è loro; **a friend of ~** un loro amico; *see also* **my; mine¹**

them [ðɛm, ðəm] PRON (*direct*) li(le); (*indirect*) gli, loro (*after vb*); (*stressed, after prep: people*) loro; (: *people, things*) essi(-e); **I see ~** li vedo; **give ~ the book** dà loro *or* dagli il libro; **give me a few of ~** dammene un po' *or* qualcuno; *see also* **me**

theme [θiːm] N tema *m*

theme park N parco a tema

theme song, theme tune N tema musicale

themselves [ðəm'selvz] PL PRON (reflexive) si; (emphatic) loro stessi(-e); (after prep) se stessi(-e); **between ~** tra (di) loro

then [ðen] ADV (at that time) allora; (next) poi, dopo; (and also) e poi ▶ CONJ (therefore) perciò, dunque, quindi ▶ ADJ: **the ~ president** il presidente di allora; **by ~** allora; **from ~ on** da allora in poi; **until ~** fino ad allora; **and ~ what?** e poi?, e allora?; **what do you want me to do ~?** allora cosa vuole che faccia?

theologian [θɪə'ləudʒən] N teologo(-a)

theological [θɪə'lɔdʒɪkl] ADJ teologico(-a)

theology [θɪ'ɔlədʒɪ] N teologia

theorem ['θɪərəm] N teorema m

theoretical [θɪə'rɛtɪkl] ADJ teorico(-a)

theorize ['θɪəraɪz] VI teorizzare

theory ['θɪərɪ] N teoria; **in ~** in teoria

therapeutic [θɛrə'pju:tɪk], **therapeutical** [θɛrə'pju:tɪkl] ADJ terapeutico(-a)

therapist ['θɛrəpɪst] N terapista mf

therapy ['θɛrəpɪ] N terapia

---

there [ðɛə^r]

ADV **1: there is** c'è; **there are** ci sono; **there are 3 of them** (people) sono in 3; (things) ce ne sono 3; **there is no-one here** non c'è nessuno qui; **there has been an accident** c'è stato un incidente

2 (referring to place) là, lì; **it's there** è là or lì; **up/in/down there** lassù/là dentro/laggiù; **back there** là dietro; **on there** lassù; **over there** là; **through there** di là; **he went there on Friday** ci è andato venerdì; **it takes two hours to go there and back** ci vogliono due ore per andare e tornare; **I want that book there** voglio quel libro là or lì; **there he is!** eccolo!

3: there, there (esp to child) su, su

---

thereabouts ['ðɛərəbauts] ADV (place) nei pressi, da quelle parti; (amount) giù di lì, all'incirca

thereafter [ðɛər'ɑ:ftə^r] ADV da allora in poi

thereby [ðɛə'baɪ] ADV con ciò

therefore ['ðɛəfɔ:^r] ADV perciò, quindi

there's [ðɛəz] = there is; there has

thereupon [ðɛərə'pɔn] ADV (at that point) a quel punto; (formal: on that subject) in merito

thermal ['θə:ml] ADJ (currents, spring) termale; (underwear, printer) termico(-a); (paper) termosensibile

thermodynamics [θə:məudaɪ'næmɪks] N termodinamica

thermometer [θə'mɔmɪtə^r] N termometro

thermonuclear ['θə:məu'nju:klɪə^r] ADJ termonucleare

Thermos® ['θə:məs] N (also: **Thermos flask**) thermos® m inv

thermostat ['θə:məstæt] N termostato

thesaurus [θɪ'sɔ:rəs] N dizionario dei sinonimi

these [ði:z] PL PRON, ADJ questi(-e)

thesis ['θi:sɪs] (pl **theses** ['θi:si:z]) N tesi f inv

they [ðeɪ] PL PRON essi(-e); (people only) loro; **~ say that ...** (it is said that) si dice che ...

they'd [ðeɪd] = they would; they had

they'll [ðeɪl] = they will; they shall

they're [ðɛə^r] = they are

they've [ðeɪv] = they have

thick [θɪk] ADJ spesso(-a); (crowd) compatto(-a); (col: stupid) ottuso(-a), lento(-a) ▶ N: **in the ~ of** nel folto di; **it's 20 cm =** ha uno spessore di 20 cm

thicken ['θɪkən] VI ispessire ▶ VT (sauce etc) ispessire, rendere più denso(-a)

thicket ['θɪkɪt] N boscaglia

thickly ['θɪklɪ] ADV (spread) a strati spessi; (cut) a fette grosse; (populated) densamente

thickness ['θɪknɪs] N spessore m

thickset [θɪk'sɛt] ADJ tarchiato(-a), tozzo(-a)

thickskinned [θɪk'skɪnd] ADJ (fig) insensibile

thief [θi:f] (pl **thieves** [θi:vz]) N ladro(-a)

thieving ['θi:vɪŋ] N furti mpl

thigh [θaɪ] N coscia

thighbone ['θaɪbəun] N femore m

thimble ['θɪmbl] N ditale m

thin [θɪn] ADJ sottile; (person) magro(-a); (soup) poco denso(-a); (hair, crowd) rado(-a); (fog) leggero(-a) ▶ VT sfoltire ▶ VI (fog) diradarsi; (also: **thin out**: crowd) disperdersi; **to ~ (down)** (sauce, paint) diluire; **his hair is thinning** sta perdendo i capelli

thing [θɪŋ] N cosa; (object) oggetto; (contraption) aggeggio; (mania) ▶ **things** NPL (belongings) cose fpl; **to have a ~ about** essere fissato(-a) con ▶ **things** NPL (belongings) cose fpl; **for one ~** tanto per cominciare; **the best ~ would be to** la cosa migliore sarebbe di; **the ~ is ...** il fatto è che ...; **the main ~ is to ...** la cosa più importante è di ...; **first ~ (in the morning)** come or per prima cosa (di mattina); **last ~ (at night)** come or per ultima cosa (di sera); **poor ~** poveretto(-a); **she's got a ~ about mice** è terrorizzata dai topi; **how are things?** come va?

think [θɪŋk] (pt, pp **thought** [θɔ:t]) VI pensare, riflettere ▶ VT pensare, credere; (imagine) immaginare; **to ~ of** pensare a; **what did you ~ of them?** cosa ne ha pensato?; **to ~ about sth/sb** pensare a qc/qn; **I'll ~ about it** ci penserò; **to ~ of doing** pensare di fare; **I ~ so/not** penso or credo di sì/no; **to ~ well of** avere una buona opinione di; **to ~ aloud** pensare ad alta voce; **~ again!** rifletti!, pensaci su!

▶ **think out** VT (plan) elaborare; (solution) trovare

▶ **think over** VT riflettere su; **I'd like to ~ things over** vorrei pensarci su

▶ **think through** VT riflettere a fondo su

t

▶ **think up** VT ideare

thinking [ˈθɪŋkɪŋ] N: **to my (way of)** ~ a mio parere

think tank N gruppo di esperti

thinly [ˈθɪnlɪ] ADV (cut) a fette sottili; (spread) in uno strato sottile

thinness [ˈθɪnnɪs] N sottigliezza; magrezza

third [θəːd] N terzo(-a) ▶ N terzo(-a); (fraction) terzo, terza parte f; (Aut) terza; (BRIT Scol: degree) laurea col minimo dei voti

third-degree burns [ˈθəːdɪˈgriː-] NPL ustioni fpl di terzo grado

thirdly [ˈθəːdlɪ] ADV in terzo luogo

third party insurance N (BRIT) assicurazione f contro terzi

third-rate [θəːdˈreɪt] ADJ di qualità scadente

Third World N: **the** ~ il Terzo Mondo

thirst [θəːst] N sete f

thirsty [ˈθəːstɪ] ADJ (person) assetato(-a), che ha sete; **to be** ~ aver sete

thirteen [θəːˈtiːn] NUM tredici

thirteenth [-ˈtiːnθ] NUM tredicesmo(-a)

thirtieth [ˈθəːtɪɪθ] NUM trentesimo(-a)

thirty [ˈθəːtɪ] NUM trenta

---

this [ðɪs]

(pl **these**) ADJ (demonstrative) questo(-a); **this man/woman/book** quest'uomo/questa donna/questo libro; (not "that") quest'uomo/questa donna/questo libro qui; **this one** questo(-a) qui; **this time** questa volta; **this time last year** l'anno scorso in questo periodo; **this way** (in this direction) da questa parte; (in this fashion) così

▶ PRON (demonstrative) questo(-a); (: not "that one") questo(-a) qui; **who/what is this?** chi è/ che cos'è questo?; **I prefer this to that** preferisco questo a quello; **this is where I live** io abito qui; **this is what he said** questo è ciò che ha detto; **they were talking of this and that** stavano parlando del più e del meno; **this is Mr Brown** (in introductions, photo) questo è il signor Brown; (on telephone) sono il signor Brown

▶ ADV (demonstrative): **this high/long** etc alto/lungo etc così; **it's about this high** è alto circa così; **I didn't know things were this bad** non sapevo andasse così male

---

thistle [ˈθɪsl] N cardo

thong [θɔŋ] N cinghia

thorn [θɔːn] N spina

thorny [ˈθɔːnɪ] ADJ spinoso(-a)

thorough [ˈθʌrə] ADJ (person) preciso(-a), accurato(-a); (search) minuzioso(-a); (knowledge, research) approfondito(-a), profondo(-a); (person) coscienzioso(-a); (cleaning) a fondo

thoroughbred [ˈθʌrəbrɛd] N (horse) purosangue mf

thoroughfare [ˈθʌrəfɛəʳ] N strada transitabile; **"no** ~**"** (BRIT) "divieto di transito"

thoroughgoing [ˈθʌrəgəʊɪŋ] ADJ (analysis) approfondito(-a); (reform) totale

thoroughly [ˈθʌrəlɪ] ADV accuratamente; (search) minuziosamente, in profondità; (wash, study) a fondo; (very) assolutamente; **he** ~ **agreed** fu completamente d'accordo

thoroughness [ˈθʌrənɪs] N precisione f

those [ðəʊz] PL PRON quelli(-e) ▶ PL ADJ quei (quegli) mpl; quelle fpl

though [ðəʊ] CONJ benché, sebbene ▶ ADV comunque, tuttavia; **even** ~ anche se; **it's not so easy,** ~ tuttavia non è così facile

thought [θɔːt] PT, PP of **think** ▶ N pensiero; (opinion) opinione f; (intention) intenzione f; **after much** ~ dopo molti ripensamenti; **I've just had a** ~ mi è appena venuta un'idea; **to give sth some** ~ prendere qc in considerazione, riflettere su qc

thoughtful [ˈθɔːtful] ADJ pensieroso(-a), pensoso(-a); ponderato(-a); (considerate) premuroso(-a)

thoughtfully [ˈθɔːtfəlɪ] ADV (pensively) con aria pensierosa

thoughtless [ˈθɔːtlɪs] ADJ sconsiderato(-a); (behaviour) scortese

thoughtlessly [ˈθɔːtlɪslɪ] ADV sconsideratamente; scortesemente

thought-provoking [ˈθɔːtprəvəʊkɪŋ] ADJ stimolante

thousand [ˈθaʊzənd] NUM mille; **one** ~ mille; **thousands of** migliaia di

thousandth [ˈθaʊzəntθ] NUM millesimo(-a)

thrash [θræʃ] VT picchiare; bastonare; (defeat) battere

▶ **thrash about** VI dibattersi

▶ **thrash out** VT dibattere, sviscerare

thrashing [ˈθræʃɪŋ] N: **to give sb a** ~ picchiare qn di santa ragione

thread [θrɛd] N filo; (of screw) filetto ▶ VT (needle) infilare; **to** ~ **one's way between** infilarsi tra

threadbare [ˈθrɛdbɛəʳ] ADJ consumato(-a), logoro(-a)

threat [θrɛt] N minaccia; **to be under** ~ **of** (closure, extinction) rischiare di; (exposure) essere minacciato(-a) di

threaten [ˈθrɛtn] VI (storm) minacciare ▶ VT: **to** ~ **sb with sth/to do** minacciare qn con qc/di fare

threatening [ˈθrɛtnɪŋ] ADJ minaccioso(-a)

three [θriː] NUM tre

three-dimensional [θriːdaɪˈmɛnʃənl] ADJ tridimensionale; (film) stereoscopico(-a)

three-piece [ˈθriːpiːs] CPD: ~ **suit** n completo

(con gilè); **~ suite** n salotto comprendente un divano e due poltrone

three-ply [θriːˈplaɪ] ADJ (wood) a tre strati; (wool) a tre fili

three-quarters [θriːˈkwɔːtəz] NPL tre quarti mpl; **~ full** pieno per tre quarti

three-wheeler [θriːˈwiːləʳ] N (car) veicolo a tre ruote

thresh [θrɛʃ] VT (Agr) trebbiare

threshing machine [ˈθrɛʃɪŋ-] N trebbiatrice f

threshold [ˈθrɛʃhəuld] N soglia; **to be on the ~ of** (fig) essere sulla soglia di

threshold agreement N (Econ) ≈ scala mobile

threw [θruː] PT of **throw**

thrift [θrɪft] N parsimonia

thrifty [ˈθrɪftɪ] ADJ economico(-a), parsimonioso(-a)

thrill [θrɪl] N brivido ▶ VI eccitarsi, tremare ▶ VT (audience) elettrizzare

thrilled ADJ (with gift etc) elettrizzato(-a); **I was ~ to get your letter** la tua lettera mi ha fatto veramente piacere

thriller [ˈθrɪləʳ] N thriller m inv

thrilling [ˈθrɪlɪŋ] ADJ (book, play etc) pieno(-a) di suspense; (news, discovery) elettrizzante

thrive [θraɪv] (pt **thrived** or **throve** [θrəuv], pp **thrived** or **thriven** [ˈθrɪvn]) VI crescere or svilupparsi bene; (business) prosperare; **he thrives on it** gli fa bene, ne gode

thriving [ˈθraɪvɪŋ] ADJ (industry etc) fiorente

throat [θrəut] N gola; **to have a sore ~** avere (un or il) mal di gola

throb [θrɔb] N (of heart) battito; (of engine) vibrazione f; (of pain) fitta ▶ VI (heart) palpitare; (engine) vibrare; (with pain) pulsare; **my head is throbbing** mi martellano le tempie

throes [θrəuz] NPL: **in the ~ of** alle prese con; in preda a; **in the ~ of death** in agonia

thrombosis [θrɔmˈbəusɪs] (pl **thromboses** [-siːz]) N trombosi f inv

throne [θrəun] N trono

throng [θrɔŋ] N moltitudine f ▶ VT affollare

throttle [ˈθrɔtl] N (Aut) valvola a farfalla; (on motorcycle) (manopola del) gas m inv ▶ VT strangolare

through [θruː] PREP attraverso; (time) per, durante; (by means of) per mezzo di; (owing to) a causa di ▶ ADJ (ticket, train, passage) diretto(-a) ▶ ADV attraverso; **(from) Monday ~ Friday** (US) da lunedì a venerdì; **I am halfway ~ the book** sono a metà libro; **to let sb ~** lasciar passare qn; **to put sb ~ to sb** (Tel) passare qn a qn; **to be ~** (Tel) ottenere la comunicazione; (have finished) avere finito; **"no ~ traffic"** (US) "divieto d'accesso"; **"no ~ road"** (BRIT) "strada senza sbocco"

throughout [θruːˈaut] PREP (place) dappertutto in; (time) per or durante tutto(-a) ▶ ADV dappertutto; sempre

throughput [ˈθruːput] N (of goods, materials) materiale m in lavorazione; (Comput) volume m di dati immessi

throve [θrəuv] PT of **thrive**

throw [θrəu] (pt **threw** [θruː], pp **thrown** [θrəun]) N tiro, getto; (Sport) lancio ▶ VT tirare, gettare; (Sport) lanciare; (rider) disarcionare; (fig) confondere; (pottery) formare al tornio; **to ~ a party** dare una festa; **to ~ open** (doors, windows) spalancare; (house, gardens etc) aprire al pubblico; (competition, race) aprire a tutti
  ▶ **throw about, throw around** VT (litter etc) spargere
  ▶ **throw away** VT gettare or buttare via
  ▶ **throw in** VT (Sport: ball) rimettere in gioco; (include) aggiungere
  ▶ **throw off** VT sbarazzarsi di
  ▶ **throw out** VT buttare fuori; (reject) respingere
  ▶ **throw together** VT (clothes, meal etc) mettere insieme; (essay) buttar giù
  ▶ **throw up** VI vomitare

throwaway [ˈθrəuəweɪ] ADJ da buttare

throwback [ˈθrəubæk] N: **it's a ~ to** (fig) ciò risale a

throw-in [ˈθrəuɪn] N (Sport) rimessa in gioco

thrown [θrəun] PP of **throw**

thru [θruː] PREP, ADJ, ADV (US) = **through**

thrush [θrʌʃ] N (Zool) tordo; (Med: esp in children) mughetto; (: BRIT: in women) candida

thrust [θrʌst] (pt, pp **~**) N (Tech) spinta ▶ VT spingere con forza; (push in) conficcare

thrusting [ˈθrʌstɪŋ] ADJ (troppo) intraprendente

thud [θʌd] N tonfo

thug [θʌg] N delinquente m

thumb [θʌm] N (Anat) pollice m ▶ VT (book) sfogliare; **to ~ a lift** fare l'autostop; **to give sb/sth the thumbs up/down** approvare/disapprovare qn/qc

thumb index N indice m a rubrica

thumbnail [ˈθʌmneɪl] N unghia del pollice

thumbnail sketch N descrizione f breve

thumbtack [ˈθʌmtæk] N (US) puntina da disegno

thump [θʌmp] N colpo forte; (sound) tonfo ▶ VT (person) picchiare; (object) battere su ▶ VI picchiare; battere

thunder [ˈθʌndəʳ] N tuono ▶ VI tuonare; (train etc): **to ~ past** passare con un rombo

thunderbolt [ˈθʌndəbəult] N fulmine m

thunderclap [ˈθʌndəklæp] N rombo di tuono

thunderous [ˈθʌndərəs] ADJ fragoroso(-a)

thunderstorm [ˈθʌndəstɔːm] N temporale m

thunderstruck [ˈθʌndəstrʌk] ADJ (fig) sbigottito(-a)

thundery [ˈθʌndərɪ] ADJ temporalesco(-a)

829

Thur(s). – till

Thur(s). ABBR (= *Thursday*) gio.

Thursday [ˈθɜːzdɪ] N giovedì *m inv*; *see also* **Tuesday**

thus [ðʌs] ADV così

thwart [θwɔːt] VT contrastare

thyme [taɪm] N timo

thyroid [ˈθaɪrɔɪd] N tiroide *f*

tiara [tɪˈɑːrə] N (*woman's*) diadema *m*

Tiber [ˈtaɪbəʳ] N: **the ~** il Tevere

Tibet [tɪˈbɛt] N Tibet *m*

Tibetan [tɪˈbɛtən] ADJ tibetano(-a) ▶ N (*person*) tibetano(-a); (*Ling*) tibetano

tibia [ˈtɪbɪə] N tibia

tic [tɪk] N tic *m inv*

tick [tɪk] N (*sound, of clock*) tic tac *m inv*; (*mark*) segno; spunta; (*Zool*) zecca; (*BRIT col*): **in a ~** in un attimo; (: *credit*): **to buy sth on ~** comprare qc a credito ▶ VI fare tic tac ▶ VT spuntare; **to put a ~ against sth** fare un segno di fianco a qc
  ▶ **tick off** VT spuntare; (*person*) sgridare
  ▶ **tick over** VI (*BRIT: engine*) andare al minimo

ticker tape [ˈtɪkə-] N nastro di telescrivente; (*US: in celebrations*) stelle *fpl* filanti

ticket [ˈtɪkɪt] N biglietto; (*in shop: on goods*) etichetta; (*for library*) scheda; (*US Pol*) lista dei candidati; **to get a (parking) ~** (*Aut*) prendere una multa (per sosta vietata); **a single/return ~ to …** un biglietto di sola andata/di andata e ritorno per…

ticket agency N (*Theat*) agenzia di vendita di biglietti

ticket barrier N (*BRIT Rail*) *cancelletto d'ingresso*

ticket collector N bigliettaio

ticket holder N persona munita di biglietto

ticket inspector N controllore *m*

ticket machine N distributore *m* di biglietti

ticket office N biglietteria

tickle [ˈtɪkl] N solletico ▶ VT fare il solletico a; (*fig*) stuzzicare; piacere a; far ridere ▶ VI: **it tickles** mi (*or* gli *etc*) fa il solletico

ticklish [ˈtɪklɪʃ] ADJ (*person*) che soffre il solletico; (*blanket, cough*) che provoca prurito; (*problem*) delicato(-a)

tidal [ˈtaɪdl] ADJ di marea

tidal wave N onda anomala

tidbit [ˈtɪdbɪt] N (*US*) = **titbit**

tiddlywinks [ˈtɪdlɪwɪŋks] N gioco della pulce

tide [taɪd] N marea; (*fig: of events*) corso ▶ VT: **will £20 ~ you over till Monday?** ti basteranno 20 sterline fino a lunedì?; **high/low ~** alta/bassa marea; **the ~ of public opinion** l'orientamento dell'opinione pubblica

tidily [ˈtaɪdɪlɪ] ADV in modo ordinato; **to arrange ~** sistemare; **to dress ~** vestirsi perbenino

tidiness [ˈtaɪdɪnɪs] N ordine *m*

tidy [ˈtaɪdɪ] ADJ (*room*) ordinato(-a), lindo(-a); (*dress, work*) curato(-a), in ordine; (*person*) ordinato(-a); (*mind*) organizzato(-a) ▶ VT (*also*: **tidy up**) riordinare, mettere in ordine; **to ~ o.s. up** rassettarsi

tie [taɪ] N (*string etc*) legaccio; (*BRIT: also*: **necktie**) cravatta; (*fig: link*) legame *m*; (*Sport: match*) incontro; (: *draw*) pareggio; (*US Rail*) traversina ▶ VT (*parcel*) legare; (*ribbon*) annodare ▶ VI (*Sport*) pareggiare; **"black/white ~"** "smoking/abito di rigore"; **family ties** legami familiari; **to ~ sth in a bow** annodare qc; **to ~ a knot in sth** fare un nodo a qc
  ▶ **tie down** VT legare, assicurare con una corda; (*fig*): **to ~ sb down to** (*price etc*) costringere qn ad accettare
  ▶ **tie in** VI: **to ~ in (with)** (*correspond*) corrispondere (a)
  ▶ **tie on** VT (*BRIT: label etc*) attaccare
  ▶ **tie up** VT (*parcel, dog*) legare; (*boat*) ormeggiare; (*arrangements*) concludere; **to be tied up** (*busy*) essere occupato *or* preso

tie-break [ˈtaɪbreɪk], **tie-breaker** [ˈtaɪbreɪkəʳ] N (*Tennis*) tie-break *m inv*; (*in quiz*) spareggio

tie-on [ˈtaɪɒn] ADJ (*BRIT: label*) volante

tie-pin [ˈtaɪpɪn] N (*BRIT*) fermacravatta *m inv*

tier [tɪəʳ] N fila; (*of cake*) piano, strato

Tierra del Fuego [tɪˈɛrədɛlˈfweɪɡəu] N Terra del Fuoco

tie tack N (*US*) fermacravatta *m inv*

tiff [tɪf] N battibecco

tiger [ˈtaɪɡəʳ] N tigre *f*

tight [taɪt] ADJ (*rope*) teso(-a), tirato(-a); (*money*) poco(-a); (*clothes, budget, programme, bend*) stretto(-a); (*control*) severo(-a), fermo(-a); (*col: drunk*) sbronzo(-a) ▶ ADV (*squeeze*) fortemente; (*shut*) ermeticamente; **to be packed ~** (*suitcase*) essere pieno zeppo; (*people*) essere pigiati; **everybody hold ~!** tenetevi stretti!; *see also* **tights**

tighten [ˈtaɪtn] VT (*rope*) tendere; (*screw*) stringere; (*control*) rinforzare ▶ VI tendersi; stringersi

tight-fisted [taɪtˈfɪstɪd] ADJ avaro(-a)

tight-lipped [ˈtaɪtˈlɪpt] ADJ: **to be ~** essere reticente; (*angry*) tenere le labbra serrate

tightly [ˈtaɪtlɪ] ADV (*grasp*) bene, saldamente

tightrope [ˈtaɪtrəup] N corda (da acrobata)

tightrope walker N funambolo(-a)

tights [taɪts] NPL (*BRIT*) collant *m inv*

tigress [ˈtaɪɡrɪs] N tigre *f* (femmina)

tilde [ˈtɪldə] N tilde *f*

tile [taɪl] N (*on roof*) tegola; (*on floor, wall*) mattonella, piastrella ▶ VT (*floor, bathroom etc*) piastrellare

tiled [taɪld] ADJ rivestito(-a) di tegole; a mattonelle; a piastrelle

till [tɪl] N registratore *m* di cassa ▶ VT (*land*) coltivare ▶ PREP, CONJ = **until**

tiller [ˈtɪləʳ] N (Naut) barra del timone

tilt [tɪlt] VT inclinare, far pendere ▶ VI inclinarsi, pendere ▶ N (slope) pendio; **to wear one's hat at a ~** portare il cappello sulle ventitrè; **(at) full ~** a tutta velocità

timber [ˈtɪmbəʳ] N (material) legname m; (trees) alberi mpl da legname

time [taɪm] N tempo; (epoch: often pl) epoca, tempo; (by clock) ora; (moment) momento; (occasion, also Math) volta; (Mus) tempo ▶ VT (race) cronometrare; (programme) calcolare la durata di; (fix moment for) programmare; (remark etc): **to ~ sth well/badly** scegliere il momento più/meno opportuno per qc; **a long ~** molto tempo; **for the ~ being** per il momento; **4 at a ~** 4 per or alla volta; **from ~ to ~** ogni tanto; **~ after ~, ~ and again** mille volte; **in ~** (soon enough) in tempo; (after some time) col tempo; (Mus) a tempo; **at times** a volte; **to take one's ~** prenderla con calma; **in a week's ~** fra una settimana; **in no ~** in un attimo; **any ~** in qualsiasi momento; **on ~** puntualmente; **to be 30 minutes behind/ahead of ~** avere 30 minuti di ritardo/anticipo; **by the ~ he arrived** quando è arrivato; **5 times 5** 5 volte 5, 5 per 5; **what ~ is it?** che ora è?, che ore sono?; **what ~ do you make it?** che ora fa?; **to have a good ~** divertirsi; **they had a hard ~ of it** è stato duro per loro; **~'s up!** è (l')ora!; **to be behind the times** vivere nel passato; **I've no ~ for it** (fig) non ho tempo da perdere con cose del genere; **he'll do it in his own (good) ~** (without being hurried) lo farà quando avrà (un minuto di) tempo; **he'll do it in** or (US) **on his own ~** (out of working hours) lo farà nel suo tempo libero; **the bomb was timed to explode 5 minutes later** la bomba era stata regolata in modo da esplodere 5 minuti più tardi

time-and-motion study [ˈtaɪmənd'məuʃən-] N analisi f inv dei tempi e dei movimenti

time bomb N bomba a orologeria

time card N cartellino (da timbrare)

time clock N orologio m marcatempo inv

time-consuming [ˈtaɪmkənsjuːmɪŋ] ADJ che richiede molto tempo

time difference N differenza di fuso orario

time frame N tempi mpl

time-honoured, (US) **time-honored** [ˈtaɪmɔnəd] ADJ consacrato(-a) dal tempo

timekeeper [ˈtaɪmkiːpəʳ] N (Sport) cronometrista mf

time lag N intervallo, ritardo; (in travel) differenza di fuso orario

time-lapse (photography) [ˈtaɪmlæps-] N time-lapse m inv

timeless [ˈtaɪmlɪs] ADJ eterno(-a)

time limit N limite m di tempo

timely [ˈtaɪmlɪ] ADJ opportuno(-a)

time off N tempo libero

timer [ˈtaɪməʳ] N (in kitchen) contaminuti m inv; (Tech: time switch) timer m inv, temporizzatore m

time-saving [ˈtaɪmseɪvɪŋ] ADJ che fa risparmiare tempo

time scale N tempi mpl d'esecuzione

time-share [ˈtaɪmʃɛəʳ] ADJ: **~ apartment/villa** appartamento/villa in multiproprietà

time-sharing [ˈtaɪmʃɛərɪŋ] N (Comput) divisione f di tempo

time sheet N = **time card**

time signal N segnale m orario

time switch N interruttore m a tempo

timetable [ˈtaɪmteɪbl] N orario; (programme of events etc) programma m

time zone N fuso orario

timid [ˈtɪmɪd] ADJ timido(-a); (easily scared) pauroso(-a)

timidity [tɪˈmɪdɪtɪ] N timidezza

timing [ˈtaɪmɪŋ] N sincronizzazione f; (fig) scelta del momento opportuno, tempismo; (Sport) cronometraggio

timing device N (on bomb) timer m inv

timpani [ˈtɪmpəni] NPL timpani mpl

tin [tɪn] N stagno; (also: **tin plate**) latta; (BRIT: can) barattolo (di latta), lattina; (container) scatola; (for baking) teglia; **a ~ of paint** un barattolo di tinta or vernice

tin foil N stagnola

tinge [tɪndʒ] N sfumatura ▶ VT: **tinged with** tinto(-a) di

tingle [ˈtɪŋgl] VI (cheeks, skin: from cold) pungere, pizzicare; (: from bad circulation) formicolare

tinker [ˈtɪŋkəʳ] N (pej) stagnino ambulante; (gipsy) zingaro(-a)
▶ **tinker with** VT FUS armeggiare intorno a; cercare di riparare

tinkle [ˈtɪŋkl] VI tintinnare ▶ N (BRIT col): **to give sb a ~** dare un colpo di telefono a qn

tin mine N miniera di stagno

tinned [tɪnd] ADJ (BRIT: food) in scatola

tinnitus [ˈtɪnɪtəs] N (Med) ronzio auricolare

tinny [ˈtɪnɪ] ADJ metallico(-a)

tin-opener [ˈtɪnəupnəʳ] N (BRIT) apriscatole m inv

tinsel [ˈtɪnsl] N decorazioni fpl natalizie (argentate)

tint [tɪnt] N tinta; (for hair) shampoo m inv colorante ▶ VT (hair) fare uno shampoo colorante a

tinted [ˈtɪntɪd] ADJ (hair) tinto(-a); (spectacles, glass) colorato(-a)

tiny [ˈtaɪnɪ] ADJ minuscolo(-a)

tip [tɪp] N (end) punta; (protective: on umbrella etc) puntale m; (gratuity) mancia; (for coal) discarica; (BRIT: for rubbish) immondezzaio; (advice) suggerimento ▶ VT (waiter) dare la mancia a; (tilt)

831

inclinare; (*overturn: also:* **tip over**) capovolgere; (*empty: also:* **tip out**) scaricare; (*predict: winner*) pronosticare; (*: horse*) dare vincente; **he tipped out the contents of the box** ha rovesciato il contenuto della scatola
▶ **tip off** VT fare una soffiata a

tip-off ['tɪpɔf] N (*hint*) soffiata

tipped ['tɪpt] ADJ (BRIT: *cigarette*) col filtro; **steel-tipped** con la punta d'acciaio

Tipp-Ex® ['tɪpɛks] N (BRIT) liquido correttore

tipple ['tɪpl] (BRIT) VI sbevazzare ▶ N: **to have a ~** prendere un bicchierino

tipster ['tɪpstə'] N (*Racing*) chi vende informazioni sulle corse e altre manifestazioni oggetto di scommesse

tipsy ['tɪpsɪ] ADJ (*col*) brillo(-a)

tiptoe ['tɪptəu] N: **on ~** in punta di piedi

tiptop ['tɪptɔp] ADJ: **in ~ condition** in ottime condizioni

tirade [taɪ'reɪd] N filippica

tire ['taɪə'] VT stancare ▶ VI stancarsi ▶ N (US) = **tyre**
▶ **tire out** VT sfinire, spossare

tired ['taɪəd] ADJ stanco(-a); **to be/feel/look ~** essere/sentirsi/sembrare stanco; **to be ~ of** essere stanco *or* stufo di

tiredness ['taɪədnɪs] N stanchezza

tireless ['taɪəlɪs] ADJ instancabile

tire pressure N (US) = **tyre pressure**

tiresome ['taɪəsəm] ADJ noioso(-a)

tiring ['taɪərɪŋ] ADJ faticoso(-a)

tissue ['tɪʃuː] N tessuto; (*paper handkerchief*) fazzoletto di carta

tissue paper N carta velina

tit [tɪt] N (*bird*) cinciallegra; (*col!: breast*) tetta; **to give ~ for tat** rendere pan per focaccia

titanium [tɪ'teɪnɪəm] N titanio

titbit ['tɪtbɪt], (US) **tidbit** ['tɪdbɪt] N (*food*) leccornia; (*news*) notizia, ghiotta

titillate ['tɪtɪleɪt] VT titillare

titivate ['tɪtɪveɪt] VT agghindare

title ['taɪtl] N titolo; (*Law: right*): **~ (to)** diritto (a)

title deed N (*Law*) titolo di proprietà

title page N frontespizio

title role N ruolo *or* parte *f* principale

titter ['tɪtə'] VI ridere scioccamente

tittle-tattle ['tɪtltætl] N chiacchiere *fpl*, pettegolezzi *mpl*

titular ['tɪtjulə'] ADJ (*in name only*) nominale

tizzy ['tɪzɪ] N (*col*): **to be in a ~** essere in agitazione

T-junction ['tiː'dʒʌŋkʃən] N incrocio a T

TM N ABBR (= *transcendental meditation*) M.T. *f*; (*Comm*) = **trademark**

TN ABBR (US) = **Tennessee**

TNT N ABBR (= *trinitrotoluene*) T.N.T. *m*

---

to [tuː, tə]

PREP **1** (*direction*) a; **to go to France/London/school** andare in Francia/a Londra/a scuola; **to go to town** andare in città; **to go to Paul's/the doctor's** andare da Paul/dal dottore; **the road to Edinburgh** la strada per Edimburgo; **to the left/right** a sinistra/destra

2 (*as far as*) (fino) a; **from here to London** da qui a Londra; **to count to 10** contare fino a 10; **from 40 to 50 people** da 40 a 50 persone

3 (*with expressions of time*): **a quarter to 5** le 5 meno un quarto; **it's twenty to 3** sono le 3 meno venti

4 (*for, of*): **the key to the front door** la chiave della porta d'ingresso; **a letter to his wife** una lettera per la moglie

5 (*expressing indirect object*) a; **to give sth to sb** dare qc a qn; **give it to me** dammelo; **to talk to sb** parlare a qn; **it belongs to him** gli appartiene, è suo; **to be a danger to sb/sth** rappresentare un pericolo per qn/qc

6 (*in relation to*) a; **3 goals to 2** 3 goal a 2; **30 miles to the gallon** ≈ 11 chilometri con un litro; **4 apples to the kilo** 4 mele in un chilo

7 (*purpose: result*): **to come to sb's aid** venire in aiuto a qn; **to sentence sb to death** condannare a morte qn; **to my surprise** con mia sorpresa

▶ WITH VB **1** (*simple infinitive*): **to go/eat** etc andare/mangiare etc

2 (*following another vb*): **to want/try/start to do** volere/cercare di/cominciare a fare

3 (*with vb omitted*): **I don't want to** non voglio (farlo); **you ought to** devi (farlo)

4 (*purpose, result*) per; **I did it to help you** l'ho fatto per aiutarti

5 (*equivalent to relative clause*): **I have things to do** ho da fare; **the main thing is to try** la cosa più importante è provare

6 (*after adjective etc*): **ready to go** pronto(-a) a partire; **too old/young to ...** troppo vecchio(-a)/giovane per ...

▶ ADV: **to push the door to** accostare la porta; **to go to and fro** andare e tornare

---

toad [təud] N rospo

toadstool ['təudstuːl] N fungo (velenoso)

toady ['təudɪ] VI adulare

toast [təust] N (*Culin*) pane *m* tostato; (*drink, speech*) brindisi *m inv* ▶ VT (*Culin*) tostare; (*drink to*) brindare a; **a piece** *or* **slice of ~** una fetta di pane tostato

toaster ['təustə'] N tostapane *m inv*

toastmaster ['təustmɑːstə'] N direttore *m* dei brindisi

toast rack N portatoast *m inv*

tobacco [tə'bækəu] N tabacco; **pipe ~** tabacco da pipa

tobacconist [təˈbækənɪst] N tabaccaio(-a); **~'s (shop)** tabaccheria

Tobago [təˈbeɪgəu] N see **Trinidad and Tobago**

toboggan [təˈbɔgən] N toboga m inv; (child's) slitta

today [təˈdeɪ] ADV, N (also fig) oggi m inv; **what day is it ~?** che giorno è oggi?; **what date is it ~?** quanti ne abbiamo oggi?; **~ is the 4th of March** (oggi) è il 4 di marzo; **~'s paper** il giornale di oggi; **a fortnight ~** quindici giorni a oggi

toddler [ˈtɔdlə'] N bambino(-a) che impara a camminare

toddy [ˈtɔdɪ] N grog m inv

to-do [təˈduː] N (fuss) storie fpl

toe [təu] N dito del piede; (of shoe) punta ▶ VT: **to ~ the line** (fig) stare in riga, conformarsi; **big ~** alluce m; **little ~** mignolino

TOEFL [ˈtəufl] N ABBR = **Test(ing) of English as a Foreign Language**

toehold [ˈtəuhəuld] N punto d'appoggio

toenail [ˈtəuneɪl] N unghia del piede

toffee [ˈtɔfɪ] N caramella

toffee apple N (BRIT) mela caramellata

tofu [ˈtəufuː] N tofu m (latte di soia non fermentato)

toga [ˈtəugə] N toga

together [təˈgɛðə'] ADV insieme; (at same time) allo stesso tempo; **~ with** insieme a

togetherness [təˈgɛðənɪs] N solidarietà; intimità

toggle switch [ˈtɔgl-] N (Comput) tasto bistabile

Togo [ˈtəugəu] N Togo

togs [tɔgz] NPL (col: clothes) vestiti mpl

toil [tɔɪl] N travaglio, fatica ▶ VI affannarsi; sgobbare

toilet [ˈtɔɪlət] N (BRIT: lavatory) gabinetto ▶ CPD (soap etc) da toletta; **to go to the ~** andare al gabinetto or al bagno

toilet bag N (BRIT) nécessaire m inv da toilette

toilet bowl N vaso or tazza del gabinetto

toilet paper N carta igienica

toiletries [ˈtɔɪlɪtrɪz] NPL articoli mpl da toletta

toilet roll N rotolo di carta igienica

toilet water N acqua di colonia

to-ing and fro-ing [ˈtuːɪŋənˈfrəuɪŋ] N (BRIT) andirivieni m inv

token [ˈtəukən] N (sign) segno; (voucher) buono ▶ CPD (fee, strike) simbolico(-a); (substitute coin) gettone m; **book/record/gift ~** (BRIT) buono-libro/-disco/-regalo; **by the same ~** (fig) per lo stesso motivo

tokenism [ˈtəukənɪzəm] N (Pol) concessione f pro forma inv

Tokyo [ˈtəukjəu] N Tokyo f

told [təuld] PT, PP of **tell**

tolerable [ˈtɔlərəbl] ADJ (bearable) tollerabile; (fairly good) passabile

tolerably [ˈtɔlərəblɪ] ADV (good, comfortable) abbastanza

tolerance [ˈtɔlərns] N (also Tech) tolleranza

tolerant [ˈtɔlərnt] ADJ: **~ (of)** tollerante (nei confronti di)

tolerate [ˈtɔləreɪt] VT sopportare; (Med, Tech) tollerare

toleration [tɔləˈreɪʃən] N tolleranza

toll [təul] N (tax, charge) pedaggio ▶ VI (bell) suonare; **the accident ~ on the roads** il numero delle vittime della strada

tollbridge [ˈtəulbrɪdʒ] N ponte m a pedaggio

toll call N (US Tel) (telefonata) interurbana

toll-free [ˈtəulˈfriː] (US) ADJ senza addebito, gratuito(-a) ▶ ADV gratuitamente; **~ number** ≈ numero verde

tomato [təˈmɑːtəu] (pl **tomatoes**) N pomodoro

tomato sauce N salsa di pomodoro

tomb [tuːm] N tomba

tombola [tɔmˈbəulə] N tombola

tomboy [ˈtɔmbɔɪ] N maschiaccio

tombstone [ˈtuːmstəun] N pietra tombale

tombstoning (col) [ˈtuːmstəunɪŋ] N (BRIT) tuffi da un'alta scogliera, un ponte, ecc. nell'acqua sottostante

tomcat [ˈtɔmkæt] N gatto

tomorrow [təˈmɔrəu] ADV, N (also fig) domani m inv; **the day after ~** dopodomani; **a week ~** domani a otto; **~ morning** domani mattina

ton [tʌn] N tonnellata (Brit = 1016 kg; 20 cwt; US = 907 kg; metric = 1000 kg); (Naut: also: **register ton**) tonnellata di stazza (= 2.83 cu.m; 100 cu.ft); **tons of** (col) un mucchio or sacco di

tonal [ˈtəunl] ADJ tonale

tone [təun] N tono; (of musical instrument) timbro ▶ VI (also: **tone in**) intonarsi
▶ **tone down** VT (colour, criticism, sound) attenuare
▶ **tone up** VT (muscles) tonificare

tone-deaf [təunˈdɛf] ADJ che non ha orecchio (musicale)

toner [ˈtəunə'] N (for photocopier) colorante m organico, toner m inv

Tonga [ˈtɔŋgə] N isole fpl Tonga

tongs [tɔŋz] NPL tenaglie fpl; (for coal) molle fpl; (for hair) arricciacapelli m inv

tongue [tʌŋ] N lingua; **~ in cheek** (fig: say, speak) ironicamente

tongue-tied [ˈtʌŋtaɪd] ADJ (fig) muto(-a)

tongue-twister [ˈtʌŋtwɪstə'] N scioglilingua m inv

tonic [ˈtɔnɪk] N (Med) ricostituente m; (skin tonic) tonico; (Mus) nota tonica; (also: **tonic water**) acqua tonica

tonight [təˈnaɪt] ADV stanotte; (this evening) stasera ▶ N questa notte; questa sera; **I'll see you ~** ci vediamo stasera

tonnage [ˈtʌnɪdʒ] N (Naut) tonnellaggio, stazza

tonne [tʌn] N (BRIT: metric ton) tonnellata

tonsil [ˈtɒnsl] N tonsilla; **to have one's tonsils out** farsi operare di tonsille

tonsillitis [tɒnsɪˈlaɪtɪs] N tonsillite f; **to have ~** avere la tonsillite

too [tu:] ADV (excessively) troppo; (also) anche; **it's ~ sweet** è troppo dolce; **I went ~** ci sono andato anch'io; **~ much** adv troppo; adj troppo(-a); **~ many** adj troppi(-e); **~ bad!** tanto peggio!; peggio così!

took [tuk] PT of **take**

tool [tu:l] N utensile m, attrezzo; (fig: person) strumento ▶ VT lavorare con un attrezzo

tool box N cassetta f portautensili inv

tool kit N cassetta di attrezzi

toot [tu:t] VI suonare; (with car horn) suonare il clacson

tooth [tu:θ] (pl **teeth** [ti:θ]) N (Anat, Tech) dente m; **to clean one's teeth** lavarsi i denti; **to have a ~ out** or (US) **pulled** farsi togliere un dente; **by the skin of one's teeth** per il rotto della cuffia

toothache [ˈtu:θeɪk] N mal m di denti; **to have ~** avere il mal di denti

toothbrush N spazzolino da denti

tooth fairy N: **the ~** fatina che porta soldini in regalo a un bimbo quando perde un dentino di latte; ≈ topolino

toothpaste [ˈtu:θpeɪst] N dentifricio

toothpick [ˈtu:θpɪk] N stuzzicadenti m inv

tooth powder N dentifricio in polvere

top [tɒp] N (of mountain, page, ladder) cima; (of box, cupboard, table) sopra m inv, parte f superiore; (lid: of box, jar) coperchio; (: of bottle) tappo; (toy) trottola; (Dress: blouse etc) camicia (or maglietta etc); (of pyjamas) giacca ▶ ADJ più alto(-a); (in rank) primo(-a); (best) migliore ▶ VT (exceed) superare; (be first in) essere in testa a; **on ~ of** sopra, in cima a; (in addition to) oltre a; **from ~ to toe** (BRIT) dalla testa ai piedi; **from ~ to bottom** da cima a fondo; **at the ~ of the stairs/page/street** in cima alle scale/alla pagina/alla strada; **the ~ of the milk** (BRIT) la panna; **at ~ speed** a tutta velocità; **at the ~ of one's voice** (fig) a squarciagola; **over the ~** (col: behaviour etc) eccessivo(-a); **to go over the ~** esagerare
▶ **top up**, (US) **top off** VT riempire; (salary) integrare

topaz [ˈtəʊpæz] N topazio

top-class [ˈtɒpˈklɑ:s] ADJ di prim'ordine

topcoat [ˈtɒpkəʊt] N soprabito

topflight [ˈtɒpflaɪt] ADJ di primaria importanza

top floor N ultimo piano

top hat N cilindro

top-heavy [tɒpˈhɛvɪ] ADJ (object) con la parte superiore troppo pesante

topic [ˈtɒpɪk] N argomento

topical [ˈtɒpɪkəl] ADJ d'attualità

topless [ˈtɒplɪs] ADJ (bather etc) col seno scoperto; **~ swimsuit** topless m inv

top-level [ˈtɒplɛvl] ADJ (talks) ad alto livello

topmost [ˈtɒpməʊst] ADJ il(la) più alto(-a)

top-notch [ˈtɒpˈnɒtʃ] ADJ (col: player, performer) di razza; (: school, car) eccellente

topography [təˈpɒgrəfɪ] N topografia

topping [ˈtɒpɪŋ] N (Culin) guarnizione f

topple [ˈtɒpl] VT rovesciare, far cadere ▶ VI cadere; traballare

top-ranking [ˈtɒpˈræŋkɪŋ] ADJ di massimo grado

top-secret [ˈtɒpˈsi:krɪt] ADJ segretissimo(-a)

top-security [ˈtɒpsɪˈkjʊərɪtɪ] ADJ (BRIT) di massima sicurezza

topsy-turvy [ˈtɒpsɪˈtə:vɪ] ADJ, ADV sottosopra inv

top-up [ˈtɒpʌp] N (for mobile phone: also: **top-up card**) ricarica; **would you like a ~?** vuole che le riempia il bicchiere (or la tazza etc)?

top-up loan N (BRIT) prestito integrativo

torch [tɔ:tʃ] N torcia; (BRIT: electric) lampadina tascabile

tore [tɔ:ʳ] PT of **tear²**

torment N [ˈtɔ:mɛnt] tormento ▶ VT [tɔ:ˈmɛnt] tormentare; (fig: annoy) infastidire

torn [tɔ:n] PP of **tear²** ▶ ADJ: **~ between** (fig) combattuto(-a) tra

tornado [tɔ:ˈneɪdəʊ] (pl **tornadoes**) N tornado

torpedo [tɔ:ˈpi:dəʊ] (pl **torpedoes**) N siluro

torpedo boat N motosilurante f

torpor [ˈtɔ:pəʳ] N torpore m

torrent [ˈtɒrnt] N torrente m

torrential [tɒˈrɛnʃl] ADJ torrenziale

torrid [ˈtɒrɪd] ADJ torrido(-a); (fig) denso(-a) di passione

torso [ˈtɔ:səʊ] N torso

tortoise [ˈtɔ:təs] N tartaruga

tortoiseshell [ˈtɔ:təʃɛl] ADJ di tartaruga

tortuous [ˈtɔ:tjʊəs] ADJ tortuoso(-a)

torture [ˈtɔ:tʃəʳ] N tortura ▶ VT torturare

torturer [ˈtɔ:tʃərəʳ] N torturatore(-trice)

Tory [ˈtɔ:rɪ] ADJ, N (BRIT Pol) tory mf, conservatore(-trice)

toss [tɒs] VT gettare, lanciare; (BRIT: pancake) far saltare; (head) scuotere ▶ N (movement, of head etc) movimento brusco; (of coin) lancio; **to win/lose the ~** vincere/perdere a testa o croce; (Sport) vincere/perdere il sorteggio; **to ~ a coin** fare a testa o croce; **to ~ up for sth** fare a testa o croce per qc; **to ~ and turn** (in bed) girarsi e rigirarsi

tot [tɒt] N (BRIT: drink) bicchierino; (child) bimbo(-a)
▶ **tot up** VT (BRIT: figures) sommare

total [ˈtəutl] ADJ totale ▶ N totale *m* ▶ VT (*add up*) sommare; (*amount to*) ammontare a; **in ~** in tutto

totalitarian [təutælɪˈtɛərɪən] ADJ totalitario(-a)

totality [təuˈtælɪtɪ] N totalità

totally [ˈtəutəlɪ] ADV completamente

tote bag [ˈtəut-] N sporta

totem pole [ˈtəutəm-] N totem *m inv*

totter [ˈtɔtəʳ] VI barcollare; (*object, government*) vacillare

touch [tʌtʃ] N tocco; (*sense*) tatto; (*contact*) contatto; (*Football*) fuori gioco *m* ▶ VT toccare; **a ~ of** (*fig*) un tocco di; un pizzico di; **to get in ~ with** mettersi in contatto con; **to lose ~** (*friends*) perdersi di vista; **I'll be in ~** mi farò sentire; **to be out of ~ with events** essere tagliato fuori; **the personal ~** una nota personale; **to put the finishing touches to sth** dare gli ultimi ritocchi a qc
▶ **touch down** VI (*on land*) atterrare
▶ **touch on** VT FUS (*topic*) sfiorare, accennare a
▶ **touch up** VT (*improve*) ritoccare

touch-and-go [ˈtʌtʃənˈgəu] ADJ incerto(-a); **it was ~ with the sick man** il malato era tra la vita e la morte

touchdown [ˈtʌtʃdaun] N atterraggio; (*on sea*) ammaraggio; (*US Football*) meta

touched [tʌtʃt] ADJ commosso(-a); (*col*) tocco(-a), toccato(-a)

touching [ˈtʌtʃɪŋ] ADJ commovente

touchline [ˈtʌtʃlaɪn] N (*Sport*) linea laterale

touch screen N (*Tech*) schermo *m* touch screen *inv*; **touch-screen mobile** telefono *m* touch screen *inv*; **touch-screen technology** tecnologia *f* touch screen *inv*

touch-sensitive [ˈtʌtʃˈsɛnsɪtɪv] ADJ sensibile al tatto

touch-type [ˈtʌtʃtaɪp] VI dattilografare (senza guardare i tasti)

touchy [ˈtʌtʃɪ] ADJ (*person*) suscettibile

tough [tʌf] ADJ duro(-a); (*resistant*) resistente; (*meat*) duro(-a), tiglioso(-a); (*journey*) faticoso(-a), duro(-a); (*person: rough*) violento(-a), brutale ▶ N (*gangster etc*) delinquente *mf*; **~ luck!** che sfortuna!

toughen [ˈtʌfn] VT indurire, rendere più resistente

toughness [ˈtʌfnɪs] N durezza; resistenza

toupee [ˈtuːpeɪ] N parrucchino

tour [tuəʳ] N viaggio; (*also:* **package tour**) viaggio organizzato *or* tutto compreso (*of town, museum*) visita; (*by artist*) tournée *f inv* ▶ VT visitare; **to go on a ~ of** (*region, country*) fare il giro di; (*museum, castle*) visitare; **to go on ~** andare in tournée

tour guide N guida turistica

touring [ˈtuərɪŋ] N turismo

tourism [ˈtuərɪzəm] N turismo

tourist [ˈtuərɪst] N turista *mf* ▶ ADV (*travel*) in classe turistica ▶ CPD turistico(-a); **the ~ trade** il turismo

tourist class N (*Aviat*) classe *f* turistica

tourist office N pro loco *f inv*

tournament [ˈtuənəmənt] N torneo

tourniquet [ˈtuənɪkeɪ] N (*Med*) laccio emostatico, pinza emostatica

tour operator N (*BRIT*) operatore *m* turistico

tousled [ˈtauzld] ADJ (*hair*) arruffato(-a)

tout [taut] VI: **to ~ for** procacciare, raccogliere; cercare clienti per ▶ N (*BRIT: also:* **ticket tout**) bagarino; **to ~ sth (around)** (*BRIT*) cercare di (ri)vendere qc

tow [təu] VT rimorchiare ▶ N rimorchio; **"on ~"**, (*US*) **"in ~"** (*Aut*) "veicolo rimorchiato"; **to give sb a ~** rimorchiare qn

toward [təˈwɔːd], **towards** [təˈwɔːdz] PREP verso; (*of attitude*) nei confronti di; (*of purpose*) per; **~(s) noon/the end of the year** verso mezzogiorno/la fine dell'anno; **to feel friendly ~(s) sb** provare un sentimento d'amicizia per qn

towel [ˈtauəl] N asciugamano; (*also:* **tea towel**) strofinaccio; **to throw in the ~** (*fig*) gettare la spugna

towelling [ˈtauəlɪŋ] N (*fabric*) spugna

towel rail, (*US*) **towel rack** N portasciugamano

tower [ˈtauəʳ] N torre *f* ▶ VI (*building, mountain*) innalzarsi; **to ~ above** or **over sb/sth** sovrastare qn/qc

tower block N (*BRIT*) palazzone *m*

towering [ˈtauərɪŋ] ADJ altissimo(-a), imponente

towline [ˈtəulaɪn] N (cavo da) rimorchio

town [taun] N città *f inv*; **to go to ~** andare in città; (*fig*) mettercela tutta; **in (the) ~** in città; **to be out of ~** essere fuori città

town centre N centro (città)

town clerk N segretario comunale

town council N consiglio comunale

town crier [-ˈkraɪəʳ] N (*BRIT*) banditore(-trice)

town hall N = municipio

townie [ˈtaunɪ] N (*BRIT col*) uno(-a) di città

town plan N pianta della città

town planner N urbanista *mf*

town planning N urbanistica

township [ˈtaunʃɪp] N township *f inv*

townspeople [ˈtaunzpiːpl] NPL cittadinanza, cittadini *mpl*

towpath [ˈtəupɑːθ] N alzaia

towrope [ˈtəurəup] N (cavo da) rimorchio

tow truck N (*US*) carro *m* attrezzi *inv*

toxic [ˈtɔksɪk] ADJ tossico(-a)

t

toxic asset N (*Econ*) titolo tossico

toxic bank N (*Econ*) banca cattiva (*che investe in titoli tossici*)

toxin ['tɔksɪn] N tossina

toy [tɔɪ] N giocattolo
▶ **toy with** VT FUS giocare con; (*idea*) accarezzare, trastullarsi con

toyshop ['tɔɪʃɔp] N negozio di giocattoli

trace [treɪs] N traccia ▶ VT (*draw*) tracciare; (*follow*) seguire; (*locate*) rintracciare; **without ~** (*disappear*) senza lasciare traccia; **there was no ~ of it** non ne restava traccia

traceability [treɪsə'bɪlɪtɪ] N tracciabilità *f inv*

trace element N oligoelemento

trachea [trə'kɪə] N (*Anat*) trachea

tracing paper ['treɪsɪŋ-] N carta da ricalco

track [træk] N (*mark: of person, animal*) traccia; (*Sport: path, gen*) pista; (*of bullet etc*) traiettoria; (*of suspect, animal*) pista, tracce *fpl*; (*Rail*) binario, rotaie *fpl*; (*Comput*) traccia, pista ▶ VT seguire le tracce di; **to keep ~ of** seguire; **to be on the right ~** (*fig*) essere sulla buona strada
▶ **track down** VT (*prey*) scovare; snidare; (*sth lost*) rintracciare

tracker dog ['trækə-] N (*BRIT*) cane *m* poliziotto *inv*

track events NPL (*Sport*) prove *fpl* su pista

tracking station ['trækɪŋ-] N (*Space*) osservatorio spaziale

track meet N (*US*) meeting *m inv* di atletica

track record N: **to have a good ~** (*fig*) avere un buon curriculum

tracksuit ['træksu:t] N tuta sportiva

tract [trækt] N (*Geo*) tratto, estensione *f*; (*pamphlet*) opuscolo, libretto; **respiratory ~** (*Anat*) apparato respiratorio

traction ['trækʃən] N trazione *f*

tractor ['træktə'] N trattore *m*

trade [treɪd] N commercio; (*skill, job*) mestiere *m*; (*industry*) industria, settore *m* ▶ VI commerciare; **to ~ with/in** commerciare con/in ▶ VT: **to ~ sth (for sth)** barattare qc (con qc); **foreign ~** commercio estero
▶ **trade in** VT (*old car etc*) dare come pagamento parziale

trade barrier N barriera commerciale

trade deficit N bilancio commerciale in deficit

Trade Descriptions Act N (*BRIT*) legge *f* a tutela del consumatore

trade discount N sconto sul listino

trade fair N fiera campionaria

trade-in ['treɪdɪn] N: **to take as a ~** accettare in permuta

trade-in price N prezzo di permuta

trademark ['treɪdmɑːk] N marchio di fabbrica

trade mission N missione *f* commerciale

trade name N marca, nome *m* depositato

trade-off ['treɪdɔf] N compromesso, accomodamento

trader ['treɪdə'] N commerciante *mf*

trade secret N segreto di fabbricazione

tradesman ['treɪdzmən] N (*irreg*) fornitore *m*; (*shopkeeper*) negoziante *m*

trade union N sindacato

trade unionist [-'juːnjənɪst] N sindacalista *mf*

trade wind N aliseo

trading ['treɪdɪŋ] N commercio

trading estate N (*BRIT*) zona industriale

trading stamp N bollo premio

tradition [trə'dɪʃən] N tradizione *f* ■ **traditions** NPL tradizioni, usanze *fpl*

traditional [trə'dɪʃənl] ADJ tradizionale

traffic ['træfɪk] N traffico ▶ VI: **to ~ in** (*liquor, drugs*) trafficare in

traffic calming [-'kɑːmɪŋ] N uso di accorgimenti per rallentare il traffico in zone abitate

traffic circle N (*US*) isola rotatoria

traffic island N salvagente *m*, isola *f* spartitraffico *inv*

traffic jam N ingorgo (del traffico)

trafficker ['træfɪkə'] N trafficante *mf*

traffic lights NPL semaforo

traffic offence N (*BRIT*) infrazione *f* al codice stradale

traffic sign N cartello stradale

traffic violation N (*US*) = **traffic offence**

traffic warden N (*BRIT*) addetto(-a) al controllo del traffico e del parcheggio

tragedy ['trædʒədɪ] N tragedia

tragic ['trædʒɪk] ADJ tragico(-a)

trail [treɪl] N (*tracks*) tracce *fpl*, pista; (*path*) sentiero; (*of smoke etc*) scia ▶ VT trascinare, strascicare; (*follow*) seguire ▶ VI essere al traino; (*dress etc*) strusciare; (*plant*) arrampicarsi; strusciare; (*in game*) essere in svantaggio; **to be on sb's ~** essere sulle orme di qn
▶ **trail away, trail off** VI (*sound*) affievolirsi; (*interest, voice*) spegnersi a poco a poco
▶ **trail behind** VI essere al traino

trailer ['treɪlə'] N (*Aut*) rimorchio; (*US*) roulotte *f inv*; (*Cine*) prossimamente *m inv*

trailer truck N (*US*) autoarticolato

train [treɪn] N treno; (*of dress*) coda, strascico; (*BRIT: series*): **~ of events** serie *f* di avvenimenti a catena ▶ VT (*apprentice, doctor etc*) formare; (*sportsman*) allenare; (*dog*) addestrare; (*memory*) esercitare; (*point: gun etc*): **to ~ sth on** puntare qc contro ▶ VI formarsi; allenarsi; (*learn a skill*) fare pratica, fare tirocinio; **to go by ~** andare in or col treno; **one's ~ of thought** il filo dei propri pensieri; **to ~ sb to do sth** preparare qn a fare qc

train attendant N (US) addetto(-a) ai vagoni letto

trained [treɪnd] ADJ qualificato(-a); allenato(-a), addestrato(-a)

trainee [treɪ'niː] N allievo(-a); (in trade) apprendista mf; **he's a ~ teacher** sta facendo tirocinio come insegnante

trainer ['treɪnər] N (Sport) allenatore(-trice); (of dogs etc) addestratore(-trice) ■ **trainers** NPL (shoes) scarpe fpl da ginnastica

training ['treɪnɪŋ] N formazione f; allenamento; addestramento; **in ~** (Sport) in allenamento; (fit) in forma

training college N istituto professionale

training course N corso di formazione professionale

training shoes NPL scarpe fpl da ginnastica

train wreck N (fig) persona distrutta; (: pej) rottame m; **he's a complete ~** è completamente distrutto, è un rottame

traipse [treɪps] VI: **to ~ in/out** etc entrare/uscire etc trascinandosi

trait [treɪt] N tratto

traitor ['treɪtər] N traditore(-trice)

trajectory [trə'dʒɛktərɪ] N traiettoria

tram [træm] N (BRIT: also: **tramcar**) tram m inv

tramline ['træmlaɪn] N linea tranviaria

tramp [træmp] N (pej: person) vagabondo(-a); (: woman) sgualdrina ►VI camminare con passo pesante ►VT (walk through: town, streets) percorrere a piedi

trample ['træmpl] VT: **to ~ (underfoot)** calpestare

trampoline ['træmpəliːn] N trampolino

trance [trɑːns] N trance f inv; (Med) catalessi f inv; **to go into a ~** cadere in trance

tranquil ['træŋkwɪl] ADJ tranquillo(-a)

tranquillity, (US) **tranquility** [træŋ'kwɪlɪtɪ] N tranquillità

tranquillizer, (US) **tranquilizer** ['træŋkwɪlaɪzər] N (Med) tranquillante m

transact [træn'zækt] VT (business) trattare

transaction [træn'zækʃən] N transazione f ■ **transactions** NPL (minutes) atti mpl; **cash ~** operazione f in contanti

transatlantic ['trænzət'læntɪk] ADJ transatlantico(-a)

transcend [træn'sɛnd] VT trascendere; (excel over) superare

transcendental [trænsɛn'dɛntl] ADJ: **~ meditation** meditazione f trascendentale

transcribe [træn'skraɪb] VT trascrivere

transcript ['trænskrɪpt] N trascrizione f

transcription [træn'skrɪpʃən] N trascrizione f

transept ['trænsɛpt] N transetto

transfer N ['trænsfər] (gen, also Sport) trasferimento; (Pol: of power) passaggio; (picture, design) decalcomania; (: stick-on) autoadesivo ►VT [træns'fəːr] trasferire; passare; decalcare; **by bank ~** tramite trasferimento bancario; **to ~ the charges** (BRIT Tel) fare una chiamata a carico del destinatario

transferable [træns'fəːrəbl] ADJ trasferibile; **not ~** non cedibile, personale

transfix [træns'fɪks] VT trafiggere; (fig): **transfixed with fear** paralizzato dalla paura

transform [træns'fɔːm] VT trasformare

transformation [trænsfə'meɪʃən] N trasformazione f

transformer [træns'fɔːmər] N (Elec) trasformatore m

transfusion [træns'fjuːʒən] N trasfusione f

transgress [træns'grɛs] VT (go beyond) infrangere; (violate) trasgredire, infrangere

tranship [træn'ʃɪp] VT trasbordare

transient ['trænzɪənt] ADJ transitorio(-a), fugace

transistor [træn'zɪstər] N (Elec) transistor m inv; (also: **transistor radio**) radio f inv a transistor

transit ['trænzɪt] N: **in ~** in transito

transit camp N campo (di raccolta) profughi

transition [træn'zɪʃən] N passaggio, transizione f

transitional [træn'zɪʃənl] ADJ di transizione

transitive ['trænzɪtɪv] ADJ (Ling) transitivo(-a)

transit lounge N (Aviat) sala di transito

transitory ['trænzɪtərɪ] ADJ transitorio(-a)

translate [trænz'leɪt] VT: **to ~ (from/into)** tradurre (da/in)

translation [trænz'leɪʃən] N traduzione f; (Scol: as opposed to prose) versione f

translator [trænz'leɪtər] N traduttore(-trice)

translucent [trænz'luːsnt] ADJ traslucido(-a)

transmission [trænz'mɪʃən] N trasmissione f

transmit [trænz'mɪt] VT trasmettere

transmitter [trænz'mɪtər] N trasmettitore m

transparency [træns'pɛərnsɪ] N (Phot) diapositiva

transparent [træns'pærnt] ADJ trasparente

transpire [træns'paɪər] VI (happen) succedere; **it finally transpired that …** alla fine si è venuti a sapere che …

transplant VT [træns'plɑːnt] trapiantare ►N ['trænsplɑːnt] (Med) trapianto; **to have a heart ~** subire un trapianto cardiaco

transport N ['trænspɔːt] trasporto ►VT [træns'pɔːt] trasportare; **public ~** mezzi mpl pubblici; **Department for T~** (BRIT) Ministero dei Trasporti

transportation ['trænspɔː'teɪʃən] N (mezzo di) trasporto; (of prisoners) deportazione f; **Department of T~** (US) Ministero dei Trasporti

t

transport café N (BRIT) trattoria per camionisti

transpose [træns'pəuz] VT trasporre

transsexual [trænz'sɛksjuəl] ADJ, N transessuale *mf*

transverse ['trænzvəːs] ADJ trasversale

transvestite [trænz'vɛstaɪt] N travestito(-a)

trap [træp] N (snare, trick) trappola; (carriage) calesse *m* ▶ VT prendere in trappola, intrappolare; (immobilize) bloccare; (jam) chiudere, schiacciare; **to set** or **lay a ~ (for sb)** tendere una trappola (a qn); **to ~ one's finger in the door** chiudersi il dito nella porta; **shut your ~!** (col) chiudi quella boccaccia!

trap door N botola

trapeze [trə'piːz] N trapezio

trapper ['træpəʳ] N cacciatore *m* di animali da pelliccia

trappings ['træpɪŋz] NPL ornamenti *mpl*; indoratura, sfarzo

trash [træʃ] N (col: goods) ciarpame *m*; (: nonsense) sciocchezze *fpl*; (US: rubbish) rifiuti *mpl*, spazzatura

trash can N (US) secchio della spazzatura

trashy ['træʃɪ] ADJ (col) scadente

trauma ['trɔːmə] N trauma *m*

traumatic [trɔː'mætɪk] ADJ (Psych: fig) traumatico(-a), traumatizzante

travel ['trævl] N viaggio; viaggi *mpl* ▶ VI viaggiare; (move) andare, spostarsi ▶ VT (distance) percorrere; **this wine doesn't ~ well** questo vino non resiste agli spostamenti

travel agency N agenzia (di) viaggi

travel agent N agente *m* di viaggio

travel brochure N dépliant *m inv* di viaggi

travel insurance N assicurazione *f* di viaggio

traveller, (US) **traveler** ['trævləʳ] N viaggiatore(-trice); (Comm) commesso(-a) viaggiatore(-trice)

traveller's cheque, (US) **traveler's check** N assegno turistico

travelling, (US) **traveling** ['trævlɪŋ] N viaggi *mpl* ▶ ADJ (circus, exhibition) itinerante ▶ CPD (bag, clock) da viaggio; (expenses) di viaggio

travelling salesman, (US) **traveling salesman** N (irreg) commesso viaggiatore

travelogue ['trævəlɔg] N (book, film) diario or documentario di viaggio; (talk) conferenza sui viaggi

travel-sick ['trævlsɪk] ADJ: **to get ~** (in vehicle) soffrire di mal d'auto; (in aeroplane) soffrire di mal d'aria; (in boat) soffrire di mal di mare

travel sickness N mal *m* d'auto (or di mare or d'aria)

traverse ['trævəs] VT traversare, attraversare

travesty ['trævəstɪ] N parodia

trawler ['trɔːləʳ] N peschereccio (a strascico)

tray [treɪ] N (for carrying) vassoio; (on desk) vaschetta

treacherous ['trɛtʃərəs] ADJ infido(-a); **road conditions today are ~** oggi il fondo stradale è pericoloso

treachery ['trɛtʃərɪ] N tradimento

treacle ['triːkl] N melassa

tread [trɛd] (pt **trod** [trɔd], pp **trodden** ['trɔdn]) N passo; (sound) rumore *m* di passi; (of stairs) pedata; (of tyre) battistrada *m inv* ▶ VI camminare
   ▶ **tread on** VT FUS calpestare

treadle ['trɛdl] N pedale *m*

treas. ABBR = **treasurer**

treason ['triːzn] N tradimento

treasure ['trɛʒəʳ] N tesoro ▶ VT (value) tenere in gran conto, apprezzare molto; (store) custodire gelosamente

treasure hunt N caccia al tesoro

treasurer ['trɛʒərəʳ] N tesoriere(-a)

treasury ['trɛʒərɪ] N tesoreria; (Pol): **the T~** (BRIT), **the T~ Department** (US) ≈ il Ministero del Tesoro

treasury bill N buono del tesoro

treat [triːt] N regalo ▶ VT trattare; (Med) curare; (consider) considerare; **it was a ~** mi (or ci etc) ha fatto veramente piacere; **to ~ sb to sth** offrire qc a qn; **to ~ sth as a joke** considerare qc uno scherzo

treatise ['triːtɪz] N trattato

treatment ['triːtmənt] N trattamento; **to have ~ for sth** (Med) farsi curare qc

treaty ['triːtɪ] N patto, trattato

treble [trɛbl] ADJ triplo(-a), triplice ▶ N (Mus) soprano *mf* ▶ VT triplicare ▶ VI triplicarsi

treble clef N chiave *f* di violino

tree [triː] N albero

tree-lined ['triːlaɪnd] ADJ fiancheggiato(-a) da alberi

treetop ['triːtɔp] N cima di un albero

tree trunk N tronco d'albero

trek [trɛk] N (hike) escursione *f* a piedi; (in car) escursione *f* in macchina; (tiring walk) camminata sfiancante ▶ VI (as holiday) fare dell'escursionismo

trellis ['trɛlɪs] N graticcio, pergola

tremble ['trɛmbl] VI tremare; (machine) vibrare

trembling ['trɛmblɪŋ] N tremito ▶ ADJ tremante

tremendous [trɪ'mɛndəs] ADJ (enormous) enorme; (excellent) meraviglioso(-a), formidabile

tremendously [trɪ'mɛndəslɪ] ADV incredibilmente; **he enjoyed it ~** gli è piaciuto da morire

tremor [trɛməʳ] N tremore *m*, tremito; (also: **earth tremor**) scossa sismica

trench [trɛntʃ] N trincea

trench coat N trench *m inv*

trench warfare N guerra di trincea

trend [trɛnd] N (*tendency*) tendenza; (*of events*) corso; (*fashion*) moda ▶ VI (*on social media*) fare tendenza; **it was trending on Twitter** faceva tendenza su Twitter; **to be on ~** essere trendy *inv*

trendy [ˈtrɛndɪ] ADJ (*idea*) di moda; (*clothes*) all'ultima moda

trepidation [trɛpɪˈdeɪʃən] N trepidazione *f*, agitazione *f*

trespass [ˈtrɛspəs] VI: **to ~ on** entrare abusivamente in; (*fig*) abusare di; **"no trespassing"** "proprietà privata", "vietato l'accesso"

trespasser [ˈtrɛspəsə^r] N trasgressore (trasgreditrice); **"trespassers will be prosecuted"** "i trasgressori saranno puniti secondo i termini di legge"

trestle [ˈtrɛsl] N cavalletto

trestle table N tavola su cavalletti

trial [ˈtraɪəl] N (*Law*) processo; (*test: of machine etc*) collaudo; (*hardship*) prova, difficoltà *f inv*; (*worry*) cruccio ▪ **trials** NPL (*Athletics*) prove *fpl* di qualificazione; **horse trials** concorso ippico; **to be on ~** (*Law*) essere sotto processo; **~ by jury** processo penale con giuria; **to be sent for ~** essere rinviato a giudizio; **to bring sb to ~ (for a crime)** portare qn in giudizio (per un reato); **by ~ and error** a tentoni

trial balance N (*Comm*) bilancio di verifica

trial basis N: **on a ~** in prova

trial period N periodo di prova

trial run N periodo di prova

triangle [ˈtraɪæŋgl] N (*Math, Mus*) triangolo

triangular [traɪˈæŋgjulə^r] ADJ triangolare

triathlon [traɪˈæθlən] N triathlon *m inv*

tribal [ˈtraɪbəl] ADJ tribale

tribe [traɪb] N tribù *f inv*

tribesman [ˈtraɪbzmən] N (*irreg*) membro della tribù

tribulation [trɪbjuˈleɪʃən] N tribolazione *f*

tribunal [traɪˈbjuːnl] N tribunale *m*

tributary [ˈtrɪbjuːtərɪ] N (*river*) tributario, affluente *m*

tribute [ˈtrɪbjuːt] N tributo, omaggio; **to pay ~ to** rendere omaggio a

trice [traɪs] N: **in a ~** in un attimo

trick [trɪk] N trucco; (*clever act*) stratagemma *m*; (*joke*) tiro; (*Cards*) presa ▶ VT imbrogliare, ingannare; **to play a ~ on sb** giocare un tiro a qn; **it's a ~ of the light** è un effetto ottico; **that should do the ~** (*col*) vedrai che funziona; **to ~ sb into doing sth** convincere qn a fare qc con l'inganno; **to ~ sb out of sth** fregare qc a qn

trickery [ˈtrɪkərɪ] N inganno

trickle [ˈtrɪkl] N (*of water etc*) rivolo; gocciolio

▶ VI gocciolare; **to ~ in/out** (*people*) entrare/uscire alla spicciolata

trick question N domanda *f* trabocchetto *inv*

trickster [ˈtrɪkstə^r] N imbroglione(-a)

tricky [ˈtrɪkɪ] ADJ difficile, delicato(-a)

tricycle [ˈtraɪsɪkl] N triciclo

trifle [ˈtraɪfl] N sciocchezza; (*BRIT Culin*) ≈ zuppa inglese ▶ ADV: **a ~ long** un po' lungo ▶ VI: **to ~ with** prendere alla leggera

trifling [ˈtraɪflɪŋ] ADJ insignificante

trigger [ˈtrɪgə^r] N (*of gun*) grilletto
▶ **trigger off** VT dare l'avvio a

trigonometry [trɪgəˈnɔmətrɪ] N trigonometria

trilby [ˈtrɪlbɪ] N (*BRIT: also:* **trilby hat**) cappello floscio di feltro

trill [trɪl] N (*of bird, Mus*) trillo

trilogy [ˈtrɪlədʒɪ] N trilogia

trim [trɪm] ADJ ordinato(-a); (*house, garden*) ben tenuto(-a); (*figure*) snello(-a) ▶ N (*haircut etc*) spuntata, regolata; (*embellishment*) finiture *fpl*; (*on car*) guarnizioni *fpl* ▶ VT spuntare; (*Naut: a sail*) orientare; (*decorate*): **to ~ (with)** decorare (con); **to keep in (good) ~** mantenersi in forma

trimmings [ˈtrɪmɪŋz] NPL decorazioni *fpl*; (*extras: esp Culin*) guarnizione *f*

Trinidad and Tobago [ˈtrɪnɪdæd-] N Trinidad e Tobago *m*

Trinity [ˈtrɪnɪtɪ] N: **the ~** la Trinità

trinket [ˈtrɪŋkɪt] N gingillo; (*piece of jewellery*) ciondolo

trio [ˈtriːəu] N trio

trip [trɪp] N viaggio; (*excursion*) gita, escursione *f*; (*stumble*) passo falso ▶ VI inciampare; (*go lightly*) camminare con passo leggero; **on a ~** in viaggio
▶ **trip up** VI inciampare ▶ VT fare lo sgambetto a

tripartite [traɪˈpɑːtaɪt] ADJ (*agreement*) tripartito(-a); (*talks*) a tre

tripe [traɪp] N (*Culin*) trippa; (*pej: rubbish*) sciocchezze *fpl*, fesserie *fpl*

triple [ˈtrɪpl] ADJ triplo(-a) ▶ ADV: **~ the distance/the speed** tre volte più lontano/più veloce

triple jump N triplo salto

triplets [ˈtrɪplɪts] NPL bambini(-e) trigemini(-e)

triplicate [ˈtrɪplɪkət] N: **in ~** in triplice copia

tripod [ˈtraɪpɔd] N treppiede *m*

Tripoli [ˈtrɪpəlɪ] N Tripoli *f*

tripper [ˈtrɪpə^r] N (*BRIT*) gitante *mf*

tripwire [ˈtrɪpwaɪə^r] N *filo in tensione che fa scattare una trappola, allarme ecc*

trite [traɪt] ADJ (*pej*) banale, trito(-a)

triumph [ˈtraɪʌmf] N trionfo ▶ VI: **to ~ (over)** trionfare (su)

triumphal [traɪˈʌmfl] ADJ trionfale

triumphant [traɪˈʌmfənt] ADJ trionfante

trivia [ˈtrɪvɪə] NPL banalità fpl

trivial [ˈtrɪvɪəl] ADJ insignificante; (matter) futile; (excuse, comment) banale; (amount) irrisorio(-a); (mistake) di poco conto

La parola inglese **trivial** non vuol dire triviale.

triviality [trɪvɪˈælɪtɪ] N frivolezza; (trivial detail) futilità f inv

trivialize [ˈtrɪvɪəlaɪz] VT sminuire

trod [trɒd] PT of **tread**

trodden [ˈtrɒdn] PP of **tread**

troll [trɒl] N (also Internet) troll m inv

trolley [ˈtrɒlɪ] N carrello; (in hospital) lettiga

trolley bus N filobus m inv

trolling [ˈtrəʊlɪŋ] N (Internet) trolling m inv

trollop [ˈtrɒləp] N (pej) prostituta

trombone [trɒmˈbəʊn] N trombone m

troop [truːp] N gruppo; (Mil) squadrone m
■ **troops** NPL (Mil) truppe fpl; **trooping the colour** (BRIT: ceremony) sfilata della bandiera
▶ **troop in** VI entrare a frotte
▶ **troop out** VI uscire a frotte

troop carrier N (plane) aereo per il trasporto (di) truppe; (Naut: also: **troopship**) nave f per il trasporto (di) truppe

trooper [ˈtruːpəʳ] N (Mil) soldato di cavalleria; (US: police officer) poliziotto(-a) (della polizia di stato)

troopship [ˈtruːpʃɪp] N nave f per il trasporto (di) truppe

trophy [ˈtrəʊfɪ] N trofeo

tropic [ˈtrɒpɪk] N tropico; **in the tropics** ai tropici; **T~ of Cancer/Capricorn** tropico del Cancro/Capricorno

tropical [ˈtrɒpɪkəl] ADJ tropicale

trot [trɒt] N trotto ▶ VI trottare; **on the ~** (BRIT fig) di fila, uno(-a) dopo l'altro(-a)
▶ **trot out** VT (excuse, reason) tirar fuori; (names, facts) recitare di fila

trouble [ˈtrʌbl] N difficoltà f inv, problema m; (problems) difficoltà fpl, problemi mpl; (worry) preoccupazione f; (bother, effort) sforzo; (with sth mechanical) noie fpl; (Pol) conflitti mpl, disordine m; (Med): **stomach** etc ~ disturbi mpl gastrici etc ▶ VT disturbare; (worry) preoccupare ▶ VI: **to ~ to do** disturbarsi a fare ■ **troubles** NPL (Pol etc) disordini mpl; **to be in ~** avere dei problemi; (for doing wrong) essere nei guai; **to go to the ~ of doing** darsi la pena di fare; **it's no ~!** di niente!; **what's the ~?** cosa c'è che non va?; **the ~ is ...** c'è che ..., il guaio è che ...; **to have ~ doing sth** avere delle difficoltà a fare qc; **please don't ~ yourself** non si disturbi

troubled [ˈtrʌbld] ADJ (person) preoccupato(-a), inquieto(-a); (epoch, life) agitato(-a), difficile

trouble-free [ˈtrʌblfriː] ADJ senza problemi

troublemaker [ˈtrʌblmeɪkəʳ] N elemento disturbatore, agitatore(-trice); (child) disloco(-a)

troubleshooter [ˈtrʌblʃuːtəʳ] N (in conflict) conciliatore m

troublesome [ˈtrʌblsəm] ADJ fastidioso(-a), seccante

trouble spot N zona calda

troubling [ˈtrʌblɪŋ] ADJ (thought) preoccupante; **these are ~ times** questi sono tempi difficili

trough [trɒf] N (also: **drinking trough**) abbeveratoio; (also: **feeding trough**) trogolo, mangiatoia; (channel) canale m; **~ of low pressure** (Meteor) depressione f

trounce [trauns] VT (col: defeat) sgominare

troupe [truːp] N troupe f inv

trouser press N stirapantaloni m inv

trousers [ˈtrauzəz] NPL pantaloni mpl, calzoni mpl; **short ~** (BRIT) calzoncini mpl

trouser suit N (BRIT) completo m or tailleur m inv pantalone inv

trousseau [ˈtruːsəʊ] N (pl **trousseaux** or **trousseaus** [-z]) N corredo da sposa

trout [traut] N (pl inv) trota

trowel [ˈtrauəl] N cazzuola

truant [ˈtruːənt] N: **to play ~** (BRIT) marinare la scuola

truce [truːs] N tregua

truck [trʌk] N autocarro, camion m inv; (Rail) carro merci aperto; (for luggage) carrello m portabagagli inv

truck driver, (US) **trucker** [ˈtrʌkəʳ] N camionista mf

truck farm N (US) orto industriale

trucking [ˈtrʌkɪŋ] N (esp US) autotrasporto

trucking company N (esp US) impresa di trasporti

truculent [ˈtrʌkjulənt] ADJ aggressivo(-a), brutale

trudge [trʌdʒ] VI trascinarsi pesantemente

true [truː] ADJ vero(-a); (accurate) accurato(-a), esatto(-a); (genuine) reale; (faithful) fedele; (wall, beam) a piombo; (wheel) centrato(-a); **to come ~** avverarsi; **~ to life** verosimile

truffle [ˈtrʌfl] N tartufo

truly [ˈtruːlɪ] ADV veramente; (truthfully) sinceramente; (faithfully) fedelmente; **yours ~** (in letter-writing) distinti saluti

trump [trʌmp] N (Cards) atout m inv; **to turn up trumps** (fig) fare miracoli

trump card N atout m inv; (fig) asso nella manica

trumped-up [trʌmptˈʌp] ADJ inventato(-a)

trumpet [ˈtrʌmpɪt] N tromba

truncated [trʌŋˈkeɪtɪd] ADJ tronco(-a)

truncheon [ˈtrʌntʃən] N sfollagente m inv

trundle [ˈtrʌndl] VT, VI: **to ~ along** rotolare rumorosamente

trunk [trʌŋk] N (of tree, person) tronco; (of elephant) proboscide f; (case) baule m; (US Aut) bagagliaio

trunk call N (BRIT Tel) (telefonata) interurbana

trunk road N (BRIT) strada principale

trunks [trʌŋks] NPL (also: **swimming trunks**) calzoncini mpl da bagno

truss [trʌs] N (Med) cinto erniario ▶ VT: **to ~ (up)** (Culin) legare

trust [trʌst] N fiducia; (Law) amministrazione f fiduciaria; (Comm) trust m inv ▶ VT (have confidence in) fidarsi di; (rely on) contare su; (entrust): **to ~ sth to sb** affidare qc a qn; (hope): **to ~ (that)** sperare (che); **you'll have to take it on ~** deve credermi sulla parola; **in ~** (Law) in amministrazione fiduciaria

trust company N trust m inv

trusted [ˈtrʌstɪd] ADJ fidato(-a)

trustee [trʌsˈtiː] N (Law) amministratore(-trice) fiduciario(-a); (of school etc) amministratore(-trice)

trustful [ˈtrʌstful] ADJ fiducioso(-a)

trust fund N fondo fiduciario

trusting [ˈtrʌstɪŋ] ADJ = **trustful**

trustworthy [ˈtrʌstwəːðɪ] ADJ fidato(-a), degno(-a) di fiducia

trusty [ˈtrʌstɪ] ADJ fidato(-a)

truth [truːθ] (pl **truths** [truːðz]) N verità f inv

truthful [ˈtruːθful] ADJ (person) sincero(-a); (description) veritiero(-a), esatto(-a)

truthfully [ˈtruːθfəlɪ] ADV sinceramente

truthfulness [ˈtruːθfəlnɪs] N veracità

try [traɪ] N prova, tentativo; (Rugby) meta ▶ VT (Law) giudicare; (test: also: **try out**: sth new) provare; (strain: patience, person) mettere alla prova ▶ VI provare; **to have a ~** fare un tentativo; **to ~ to do** provare a fare; (seek) cercare di fare; **to give sth a ~** provare qc; **to ~ one's (very) best** or **one's (very) hardest** mettercela tutta
▶ **try on** VT (clothes) provare, mettere alla prova; **to ~ it on** (fig) cercare di farla
▶ **try out** VT provare, mettere alla prova

trying [ˈtraɪɪŋ] ADJ (day, experience) logorante, pesante; (child) difficile, insopportabile

tsar [zɑːr] N zar m inv

T-shirt [ˈtiːʃəːt] N maglietta

TSO N ABBR (BRIT: = The Stationery Office) ≈ Poligrafici mpl dello Stato

T-square [ˈtiːskwɛər] N riga a T

tsunami [tsuˈnɑːmɪ] N tsunami m inv

TT ADJ ABBR (BRIT col) = **teetotal** ▶ ABBR (US) = **Trust Territory**

tub [tʌb] N tinozza; mastello; (bath) bagno

tuba [ˈtjuːbə] N tuba

tubby [ˈtʌbɪ] ADJ grassoccio(-a)

tube [tjuːb] N tubo; (BRIT: underground) metropolitana, metrò m inv; (for tyre) camera d'aria; (col: television): **the ~** la tele

tubeless [ˈtjuːblɪs] ADJ (tyre) senza camera d'aria

tuber [ˈtjuːbər] N (Bot) tubero

tuberculosis [tjubəːkjuˈləusɪs] N tubercolosi f inv

tube station N (BRIT) stazione f della metropolitana

tubing [ˈtjuːbɪŋ] N tubazione f; **a piece of ~** un tubo

tubular [ˈtjuːbjulər] ADJ tubolare

TUC N ABBR (BRIT: = Trades Union Congress) confederazione f dei sindacati britannici

tuck [tʌk] N (Sewing) piega ▶ VT (put) mettere
▶ **tuck away** VT riporre; (building): **to be tucked away** essere in un luogo isolato
▶ **tuck in** VT mettere dentro; (child) rimboccare ▶ VI (eat) mangiare di buon appetito; abbuffarsi
▶ **tuck up** VT (child) rimboccare

tucker [ˈtʌkər] N (AUSTRALIA, NEW ZEALAND col) cibo

tuck shop N (BRIT) negozio di pasticceria (in una scuola)

Tue(s)., **Tues.** ABBR (= Tuesday) mar.

Tuesday [ˈtjuːzdɪ] N martedì m inv; **(the date) today is ~ 23 March** oggi è martedì 23 marzo; **on ~** martedì; **on Tuesdays** di martedì; **every ~** tutti i martedì; **every other ~** ogni due martedì; **last/next ~** martedì scorso/prossimo; **~ next** martedì prossimo; **the following ~** (in past) il martedì successivo; (in future) il martedì dopo; **a week/fortnight on ~**, **~ week/fortnight** martedì fra una settimana/quindici giorni; **the ~ before last** martedì di due settimane fa; **the ~ after next** non questo martedì ma il prossimo; **~ morning/lunchtime/afternoon/evening** martedì mattina/all'ora di pranzo/pomeriggio/sera; **~ night** martedì sera; (overnight) martedì notte; **~'s newspaper** il giornale di martedì

tuft [tʌft] N ciuffo

tug [tʌg] N (ship) rimorchiatore m ▶ VT tirare con forza

tug-of-love [tʌgəvˈlʌv] N contesa per la custodia dei figli; **~ children** bambini mpl coinvolti nella contesa per la custodia

tug-of-war [tʌgəvˈwɔːr] N tiro alla fune

tuition [tjuːˈɪʃən] N (BRIT: lessons) lezioni fpl; (: private tuition) lezioni fpl private; (US: fees) tasse fpl scolastiche (or universitarie)

tulip [ˈtjuːlɪp] N tulipano

tumble [ˈtʌmbl] N (fall) capitombolo ▶ VI capitombolare, ruzzolare; (somersault) fare capriole ▶ VT far cadere; **to ~ to sth** (col) realizzare qc

tumbledown [ˈtʌmbldaun] N cadente, diroccato(-a)

841

tumble dryer N (BRIT) asciugatrice f

tumbler ['tʌmbləʳ] N bicchiere m senza stelo

tummy ['tʌmɪ] N (col) pancia

tumour, (US) **tumor** ['tjuːməʳ] N tumore m

tumult ['tjuːmʌlt] N tumulto

tumultuous [tjuːˈmʌltjuəs] ADJ tumultuoso(-a)

tuna ['tjuːnə] N (pl inv: also: **tuna fish**) tonno

tune [tjuːn] N (melody) melodia, aria ▶ VT (Mus) accordare; (Radio, TV, Aut) regolare, mettere a punto; **to be in/out of ~** (instrument) essere accordato(-a)/scordato(-a); (singer) essere intonato(-a)/stonato(-a); **to the ~ of** (fig: amount) per la modesta somma di; **in ~ with** (fig) in accordo con
  ▶**tune in** VI (Radio, TV): **to ~ in (to)** sintonizzarsi (su)
  ▶**tune up** VI (musician) accordare lo strumento

tuneful ['tjuːnful] ADJ melodioso(-a)

tuner ['tjuːnəʳ] N (radio set) sintonizzatore m; **piano ~** accordatore(-trice) di pianoforte

tuner amplifier N amplificatore m di sintonia

tungsten ['tʌŋstn] N tungsteno

tunic ['tjuːnɪk] N tunica

tuning ['tjuːnɪŋ] N messa a punto

tuning fork N diapason m inv

Tunis ['tjuːnɪs] N Tunisi f

Tunisia [tjuːˈnɪzɪə] N Tunisia

Tunisian [tjuːˈnɪzɪən] ADJ, N tunisino(-a)

tunnel ['tʌnl] N galleria ▶ VI scavare una galleria

tunnel vision N (Med) riduzione f del campo visivo; (fig) visuale f ristretta

tunny ['tʌnɪ] N tonno

turban ['təːbən] N turbante m

turbid ['təːbɪd] ADJ torbido(-a)

turbine ['təːbaɪn] N turbina

turbo ['təːbəu] N turbo m inv

turbojet ['təːbəu'dʒɛt] N turboreattore m

turboprop ['təːbəu'prɔp] N turboelica m inv

turbot ['təːbət] N (pl inv) rombo gigante

turbulence ['təːbjuləns] N (Aviat) turbolenza

turbulent ['təːbjulənt] ADJ turbolento(-a); (sea) agitato(-a)

tureen [təˈriːn] N zuppiera

turf [təːf] N terreno erboso; (clod) zolla ▶ VT coprire di zolle erbose; **the T~** l'ippodromo
  ▶**turf out** VT (col) buttar fuori

turf accountant N (BRIT) allibratore m

turgid ['təːdʒɪd] ADJ (speech) ampolloso(-a), pomposo(-a)

Turin [tjuəˈrɪn] N Torino f

Turk [təːk] N turco(-a)

Turkey ['təːkɪ] N Turchia

turkey ['təːkɪ] N tacchino

Turkish ['təːkɪʃ] ADJ turco(-a) ▶ N (Ling) turco

Turkish bath N bagno turco

Turkish delight N gelatine ricoperte di zucchero a velo

Turkmenistan [təːkmɛnɪˈstɑːn] N Turkmenistan m

turmeric ['təːmərɪk] N curcuma

turmoil ['təːmɔɪl] N confusione f, tumulto

turn [təːn] N giro; (change) cambiamento; (in road) curva; (tendency: of mind, events) tendenza; (performance) numero; (chance) turno; (Med) crisi f inv, attacco ▶ VT girare, voltare; (milk) far andare a male; (shape: wood, metal) tornire; (change): **to ~ sth into** trasformare qc in ▶ VI girare; (person: look back) girarsi, voltarsi; (reverse direction) girarsi indietro; (change) cambiare; (milk) andare a male; (become) diventare; **to ~ into** trasformarsi in; **a good ~** un buon servizio; **a bad ~** un brutto tiro; **it gave me quite a ~** mi ha fatto prendere un bello spavento; **"no left ~"** (Aut) "divieto di svolta a sinistra"; **it's your ~** tocca a lei; **in ~** a sua volta; a turno; **to take turns (at sth)** fare (qc) a turno; **at the ~ of the year/century** alla fine dell'anno/del secolo; **to take a ~ for the worse** (situation, events) volgere al peggio; (patient, health) peggiorare; **to ~ left/right** girare a sinistra/destra
  ▶**turn about** VI girarsi indietro
  ▶**turn away** VI girarsi (dall'altra parte) ▶ VT (reject: person) mandar via; (: business) rifiutare
  ▶**turn back** VI ritornare, tornare indietro ▶ VT far tornare indietro; (clock) spostare indietro
  ▶**turn down** VT (refuse) rifiutare; (reduce) abbassare; (fold) ripiegare
  ▶**turn in** VI (col: go to bed) andare a letto ▶ VT (fold) voltare in dentro
  ▶**turn off** VI (from road) girare, voltare ▶ VT (light, radio, engine etc) spegnere
  ▶**turn on** VT (light, radio etc) accendere; (engine) avviare
  ▶**turn out** VT (light, gas) chiudere; spegnere; (produce: goods) produrre; (: novel, good pupils) creare ▶ VI (appear, attend: troops, doctor, voters etc) presentarsi; **to ~ out to be ...** rivelarsi ..., risultare ...
  ▶**turn over** VI (person) girarsi; (car etc) capovolgersi ▶ VT girare
  ▶**turn round** VI girare; (person) girarsi
  ▶**turn to** VT FUS: **to ~ to sb** girarsi verso qn; **to ~ to sb for help** rivolgersi a qn per aiuto
  ▶**turn up** VI (person) arrivare, presentarsi; (lost object) saltar fuori ▶ VT (collar, sound, gas etc) alzare

turnabout ['təːnəbaut], **turnaround** ['təːnəraund] N (fig) dietrofront m inv

turncoat ['təːnkəut] N voltagabbana mf

turned-up ['təːndʌp] ADJ (nose) all'insù

turning ['təːnɪŋ] N (in road) curva; (side road) strada laterale; **the first ~ on the right** la prima a destra

turning circle N (BRIT) diametro di sterzata

turning point N (fig) svolta decisiva

turning radius N (US) = **turning circle**

turnip ['tə:nɪp] N rapa

turnout ['tə:naut] N presenza, affluenza

turnover ['tə:nəuvə'] N (Comm: amount of money) giro di affari; (: of goods) smercio; (Culin): **apple** etc ~ sfogliatella alle mele etc; **there is a rapid ~ in staff** c'è un ricambio molto rapido di personale

turnpike ['tə:npaɪk] N (US) autostrada a pedaggio

turnstile ['tə:nstaɪl] N tornella

turntable ['tə:nteɪbl] N (on record player) piatto

turn-up ['tə:nʌp] N (BRIT: on trousers) risvolto

turpentine ['tə:pəntaɪn] N (also: **turps**) acqua ragia

turquoise [tə:kwɔɪz] N (stone) turchese m ▶ ADJ turchese; di turchese

turret ['tʌrɪt] N torretta

turtle ['tə:tl] N testuggine f

turtleneck (sweater) ['tə:tlnɛk-] N maglione m con il collo alto

Tuscan ['tʌskən] ADJ, N toscano(-a)

Tuscany ['tʌskənɪ] N Toscana

tusk [tʌsk] N zanna

tussle ['tʌsl] N baruffa, mischia

tutor ['tju:tə'] N (in college) docente mf (responsabile di un gruppo di studenti); (private teacher) precettore m

tutorial [tju:'tɔ:rɪəl] N (Scol) lezione f con discussione (a un gruppo limitato)

Tuvalu [tu:və'lu:] N Tuvalu fpl

tuxedo [tʌk'si:dəu] N (US) smoking m inv

TV [ti:'vi:] N ABBR (= television) tivù f inv

TV dinner N pasto surgelato pronto in due minuti

twaddle ['twɔdl] N scemenze fpl

twang [twæŋ] N (of instrument) suono vibrante; (of voice) accento nasale ▶ VI vibrare ▶ VT (guitar) pizzicare le corde di

tweak [twi:k] VT (nose) pizzicare; (ear, hair) tirare

tweed [twi:d] N tweed m inv

tweet [twi:t] N (on Twitter) post m inv su Twitter ▶ VT, VI (on Twitter) twittare

tweetable ['twi:təbl] ADJ twittabile

tweezers ['twi:zəz] NPL pinzette fpl

twelfth [twelfθ] NUM dodicesimo(-a)

Twelfth Night N la notte dell'Epifania

twelve [twelv] NUM dodici; **at ~** alle dodici, a mezzogiorno; (midnight) a mezzanotte

twentieth ['twɛntɪɪθ] NUM ventesimo(-a)

twenty ['twɛntɪ] NUM venti; **in ~ fourteen** nel duemilaquattordici

twerking ['twə:kɪŋ] N twerking m inv

twerp [twə:p] N (col) idiota mf

twice [twaɪs] ADV due volte; **~ as much** due volte tanto; **~ a week** due volte alla settimana; **she is ~ your age** ha il doppio dei suoi anni

twiddle ['twɪdl] VT, VI: **to ~ (with) sth** giocherellare con qc; **to ~ one's thumbs** (fig) girarsi i pollici

twig [twɪg] N ramoscello ▶ VT, VI (col) capire

twilight ['twaɪlaɪt] N (evening) crepuscolo; (morning) alba; **in the ~** nella penombra

twill [twɪl] N spigato

twin [twɪn] ADJ, N gemello(-a) ▶ VT: **to ~ one town with another** fare il gemellaggio di una città con un'altra

twin-bedded room ['twɪn'bɛdɪd-] N stanza con letti gemelli

twin beds NPL letti mpl gemelli

twin-carburettor ['twɪnkɑ:bju'rɛtə'] ADJ a doppio carburatore

twine [twaɪn] N spago, cordicella ▶ VI (plant) attorcigliarsi; (road) serpeggiare

twin-engined ['twɪn'ɛndʒɪnd] ADJ a due motori; **~ aircraft** bimotore m

twinge [twɪndʒ] N (of pain) fitta; **a ~ of conscience/regret** un rimorso/rimpianto

twinkle ['twɪŋkl] N scintillio ▶ VI scintillare; (eyes) brillare

twin room N stanza con letti gemelli

twin town N città f inv gemella

twirl [twə:l] N piroetta ▶ VT far roteare ▶ VI roteare

twist [twɪst] N torsione f; (in wire, flex) piega; (in story) colpo di scena; (bend) svolta, piega; (in road) curva ▶ VT attorcigliare; (ankle) slogare; (weave) intrecciare; (roll around) arrotolare; (fig) distorcere ▶ VI attorcigliarsi; arrotolarsi; (road) serpeggiare; **to ~ one's ankle/wrist** (Med) slogarsi la caviglia/il polso

twisted ['twɪstɪd] ADJ (wire, rope) attorcigliato(-a); (ankle, wrist) slogato(-a); (fig: logic, mind) contorto(-a)

twit [twɪt] N (col) cretino(-a)

twitch [twɪtʃ] N tiratina; (nervous) tic m inv ▶ VI contrarsi; avere un tic

Twitter® ['twɪtə'] N Twitter® m

Twitterati (col) [twɪtə'rɑ:tɪ] NPL Twitterati mpl

Twittersphere (col) ['twɪtəfɪə'] N: **the ~** la twittosfera

two [tu:] NUM due; **~ by ~, in twos** a due a due; **to put ~ and ~ together** (fig) fare uno più uno

two-bit [tu:'bɪt] ADJ (esp US col, pej) da quattro soldi

two-door [tu:'dɔ:'] ADJ (Aut) a due porte

two-faced ['tu:'feɪst] ADJ (pej: person) falso(-a)

twofold ['tu:fəuld] ADV: **to increase ~** aumentare del doppio ▶ ADJ (increase) doppio(-a); (reply) in due punti

t

two-piece [ˈtuːˈpiːs] N *(also:* **two-piece suit**) due pezzi *m inv*; *(also:* **two-piece swimsuit**) (costume *m* da bagno a) due pezzi *m inv*

two-seater [ˈtuːˈsiːtər] N *(plane)* biposto; *(car)* macchina a due posti

twosome [ˈtuːsəm] N *(people)* coppia

two-stroke [ˈtuːstrəuk] N *(engine)* due tempi *m inv* ▶ ADJ a due tempi

two-tone [ˈtuːtəun] ADJ *(colour)* bicolore

two-way [ˈtuːweɪ] ADJ *(traffic)* a due sensi; **~ radio** radio *f inv* ricetrasmittente

TX ABBR *(US)* = **Texas**

tycoon [taɪˈkuːn] N: **(business) ~** magnate *m*

type [taɪp] N *(category)* genere *m*; *(model)* modello; *(example)* tipo; *(Typ)* tipo, carattere *m* ▶ VT *(letter etc)* battere (a macchina), dattilografare; **what ~ do you want?** che tipo vuole?; **in bold/italic ~** in grassetto/corsivo

type-cast [ˈtaɪpkɑːst] ADJ *(actor)* a ruolo fisso

typeface [ˈtaɪpfeɪs] N carattere *m* tipografico

typescript [ˈtaɪpskrɪpt] N dattiloscritto

typeset [ˈtaɪpsɛt] VT *(irreg: like* **set***)* comporre

typesetter [ˈtaɪpsɛtər] N compositore *m*

typewriter [ˈtaɪpraɪtər] N macchina da scrivere

typewritten [ˈtaɪprɪtn] ADJ dattiloscritto(-a), battuto(-a) a macchina

typhoid [ˈtaɪfɔɪd] N tifoidea

typhoon [taɪˈfuːn] N tifone *m*

typhus [ˈtaɪfəs] N tifo

typical [ˈtɪpɪkl] ADJ tipico(-a)

typically ADV tipicamente; **~, he arrived late** come al solito è arrivato tardi

typify [ˈtɪpɪfaɪ] VT essere tipico(-a) di

typing [ˈtaɪpɪŋ] N dattilografia

typing error N errore *m* di battitura

typing pool N ufficio *m* dattilografia *inv*

typist [ˈtaɪpɪst] N dattilografo(-a)

typo [ˈtaɪpəu] N ABBR *(col:* = *typographical error)* refuso

typography [taɪˈpɔgrəfɪ] N tipografia

tyranny [ˈtɪrənɪ] N tirannia

tyrant [ˈtaɪərnt] N tiranno

tyre, *(US)* **tire** [ˈtaɪər] N pneumatico, gomma; **I've got a flat ~** ho una gomma a terra

tyre pressure N pressione *f* (delle gomme)

Tyrol [tɪˈrəul] N Tirolo

Tyrolean [tɪrəˈliːən], **Tyrolese** [tɪrəˈliːz] ADJ, N tirolese *mf*

Tyrrhenian Sea [tɪˈriːnɪən-] N: **the ~** il mar Tirreno

Uu

U, u [ju:] N (*letter*) U, u *m inv or f inv*; **U for Uncle** = U come Udine

U N ABBR (*BRIT Cine*: = *universal*) per tutti

UAW N ABBR (*US*: = *United Automobile Workers*) sindacato degli operai automobilistici

U-bend [ˈjuːbɛnd] N (*in pipe*) sifone *m*

ubiquitous [juːˈbɪkwɪtəs] ADJ onnipresente

UCAS [ˈjuːkæs] N ABBR (*BRIT*) = **Universities and Colleges Admissions Service**

UDA N ABBR (*BRIT*: = *Ulster Defence Association*) organizzazione paramilitare protestante

udder [ˈʌdəʳ] N mammella

UDR N ABBR (*BRIT*: = *Ulster Defence Regiment*) reggimento dell'esercito britannico in Irlanda del Nord

UEFA [juːˈeɪfə] N ABBR (= *Union of European Football Associations*) UEFA *f*

UFO [ˈjuːfəu] N ABBR (= *unidentified flying object*) UFO *m inv*

Uganda [juːˈgændə] N Uganda

Ugandan [juːˈgændən] ADJ, N ugandese *mf*

ugh [əːh] EXCL puah!

ugliness [ˈʌglɪnɪs] N bruttezza

ugly [ˈʌglɪ] ADJ brutto(-a)

UHF ABBR = **ultra-high frequency**

UHT ADJ ABBR (= *ultra heat treated*) UHT inv, a lunga conservazione; **~ milk** latte *m* UHT

UK N ABBR = **United Kingdom**

Ukraine [juːˈkreɪn] N Ucraina

Ukrainian [juːˈkreɪnɪən] ADJ ucraino(-a) ▶ N (*person*) ucraino(-a); (*Ling*) ucraino

ulcer [ˈʌlsəʳ] N ulcera; **mouth ~** afta

Ulster [ˈʌlstəʳ] N Ulster *m*

ulterior [ʌlˈtɪərɪəʳ] ADJ ulteriore; **~ motive** secondo fine *m*

ultimata [ʌltɪˈmeɪtə] NPL *of* **ultimatum**

ultimate [ˈʌltɪmɪt] ADJ ultimo(-a), finale; (*authority*) massimo(-a), supremo(-a) ▶ N: **the ~ in luxury** il non plus ultra del lusso

ultimately [ˈʌltɪmɪtlɪ] ADV alla fine; in definitiva, in fin dei conti

ultimatum [ʌltɪˈmeɪtəm] (*pl* **ultimatums** or **ultimata** [-tə]) N ultimatum *m inv*

ultrasonic [ʌltrəˈsɔnɪk] ADJ ultrasonico(-a)

ultrasound [ʌltrəˈsaund] N ultrasuono; (*Med*) ecografia

ultraviolet [ˈʌltrəˈvaɪəlɪt] ADJ ultravioletto(-a)

umbilical [ʌmˈbɪlɪkl] ADJ: **~ cord** cordone *m* ombelicale

umbrage [ˈʌmbrɪdʒ] N: **to take ~** offendersi, impermalirsi

umbrella [ʌmˈbrɛlə] N ombrello; **under the ~ of** (*fig*) sotto l'egida di

umlaut [ˈumlaut] N Umlaut *m inv*

umpire [ˈʌmpaɪəʳ] N arbitro

umpteen [ʌmpˈtiːn] ADJ non so quanti(-e); **for the umpteenth time** per l'ennesima volta

UMW N ABBR (= *United Mineworkers of America*) unione dei minatori d'America

UN N ABBR (= *United Nations*) ONU *f*

unabashed [ʌnəˈbæʃt] ADJ imperturbato(-a)

unabated [ʌnəˈbeɪtɪd] ADJ non diminuito(-a)

unable [ʌnˈeɪbl] ADJ: **to be ~ to** non potere, essere nell'impossibilità di; (*not to know how to*) essere incapace di, non sapere

unabridged [ʌnəˈbrɪdʒd] ADJ integrale

unacceptable [ʌnəkˈsɛptəbl] ADJ (*proposal, behaviour*) inaccettabile; (*price*) impossibile

unaccompanied [ʌnəˈkʌmpənɪd] ADJ (*person*) non accompagnato(-a); (*singing, song*) senza accompagnamento

unaccountably [ʌnəˈkauntəblɪ] ADV inesplicabilmente

unaccounted [ʌnəˈkauntɪd] ADJ: **two passengers are ~ for** due passeggeri mancano all'appello

unaccustomed [ʌnəˈkʌstəmd] ADJ insolito(-a); **to be ~ to sth** non essere abituato(-a) a qc

unacquainted [ʌnəˈkweɪntɪd] ADJ: **to be ~ with** (*facts*) ignorare, non essere al corrente di

unadulterated [ʌnəˈdʌltəreɪtɪd] ADJ (*gen*) puro(-a); (*wine*) non sofisticato(-a)

unaffected [ʌnəˈfɛktɪd] ADJ (*person, behaviour*) naturale, spontaneo(-a); (*emotionally*): **to be ~ by** non essere toccato(-a) da

unafraid [ʌnəˈfreɪd] ADJ: **to be ~** non aver paura

unaided [ʌnˈeɪdɪd] ADV senza aiuto

unanimity [juːnəˈnɪmɪtɪ] N unanimità

unanimous [juːˈnænɪməs] ADJ unanime

unanimously [juːˈnænɪməslɪ] ADV all'unanimità

unanswered [ʌnˈɑːnsəd] ADJ (question, letter) senza risposta; (criticism) non confutato(-a)

unappetizing [ʌnˈæpɪtaɪzɪŋ] ADJ poco appetitoso(-a)

unappreciative [ʌnəˈpriːʃɪətɪv] ADJ che non apprezza

unarmed [ʌnˈɑːmd] ADJ (person) disarmato(-a); (combat) senz'armi

unashamed [ʌnəˈʃeɪmd] ADJ sfacciato(-a), senza vergogna

unassisted [ʌnəˈsɪstɪd] ADJ, ADV senza nessun aiuto

unassuming [ʌnəˈsjuːmɪŋ] ADJ modesto(-a), senza pretese

unattached [ʌnəˈtætʃt] ADJ senza legami, libero(-a)

unattended [ʌnəˈtɛndɪd] ADJ (car, child, luggage) incustodito(-a)

unattractive [ʌnəˈtræktɪv] ADJ privo(-a) di attrattiva, poco attraente

unauthorized [ʌnˈɔːθəraɪzd] ADJ non autorizzato(-a)

unavailable [ʌnəˈveɪləbl] ADJ (article, room, book) non disponibile; (person) impegnato(-a)

unavoidable [ʌnəˈvɔɪdəbl] ADJ inevitabile

unavoidably [ʌnəˈvɔɪdəblɪ] ADV (detained) per cause di forza maggiore

unaware [ʌnəˈwɛəʳ] ADJ: **to be ~ of** non sapere, ignorare

unawares [ʌnəˈwɛəz] ADV di sorpresa, alla sprovvista

unbalanced [ʌnˈbælənst] ADJ squilibrato(-a)

unbearable [ʌnˈbɛərəbl] ADJ insopportabile

unbeatable [ʌnˈbiːtəbl] ADJ imbattibile

unbeaten [ʌnˈbiːtn] ADJ (team, army) imbattuto(-a); (record) insuperato(-a)

unbecoming [ʌnbɪˈkʌmɪŋ] ADJ (unseemly: language, behaviour) sconveniente; (unflattering: garment) che non dona

unbeknown [ʌnbɪˈnəʊn], **unbeknownst** [ʌnbɪˈnəʊnst] ADV: **~(st) to** all'insaputa di

unbelief [ʌnbɪˈliːf] N incredulità

unbelievable [ʌnbɪˈliːvəbl] ADJ incredibile

unbelievingly [ʌnbɪˈliːvɪŋlɪ] ADV con aria incredula

unbend [ʌnˈbɛnd] VI (irreg: like **bend**) distendersi ▶ VT (wire) raddrizzare

unbending [ʌnˈbɛndɪŋ] ADJ (fig) inflessibile, rigido(-a)

unbiased, unbiassed [ʌnˈbaɪəst] ADJ obiettivo(-a), imparziale

unblemished [ʌnˈblɛmɪʃt] ADJ senza macchia

unblock [ʌnˈblɔk] VT (pipe, road) sbloccare

unborn [ʌnˈbɔːn] ADJ non ancora nato(-a)

unbounded [ʌnˈbaʊndɪd] ADJ sconfinato(-a), senza limite

unbreakable [ʌnˈbreɪkəbl] ADJ infrangibile

unbridled [ʌnˈbraɪdld] ADJ sbrigliato(-a)

unbroken [ʌnˈbrəʊkən] ADJ (intact) intero(-a); (continuous) continuo(-a); (record) insuperato(-a)

unbuckle [ʌnˈbʌkl] VT slacciare

unburden [ʌnˈbəːdn] VT: **to ~ o.s.** sfogarsi

unbutton [ʌnˈbʌtn] VT sbottonare

uncalled-for [ʌnˈkɔːldfɔːʳ] ADJ (remark) fuori luogo inv; (action) ingiustificato(-a)

uncanny [ʌnˈkænɪ] ADJ misterioso(-a), strano(-a)

unceasing [ʌnˈsiːsɪŋ] ADJ incessante

unceremonious [ʌnsɛrɪˈməʊnɪəs] ADJ (abrupt, rude) senza tante cerimonie

uncertain [ʌnˈsəːtn] ADJ incerto(-a); dubbio(-a); **it's ~ whether ...** non è sicuro se ...; **in no ~ terms** chiaro e tondo, senza mezzi termini

uncertainty [ʌnˈsəːtntɪ] N incertezza

unchallenged [ʌnˈtʃælɪndʒd] ADJ incontestato(-a); **to go ~** non venire contestato, non trovare opposizione

unchanged [ʌnˈtʃeɪndʒd] ADJ immutato(-a)

uncharitable [ʌnˈtʃærɪtəbl] ADJ duro(-a), severo(-a)

uncharted [ʌnˈtʃɑːtɪd] ADJ inesplorato(-a)

unchecked [ʌnˈtʃɛkt] ADJ incontrollato(-a)

uncivilized [ʌnˈsɪvɪlaɪzd] ADJ (gen) selvaggio(-a); (fig) incivile, barbaro(-a)

uncle [ˈʌŋkl] N zio

unclear [ʌnˈklɪəʳ] ADJ non chiaro(-a); **I'm still ~ about what I'm supposed to do** non ho ancora ben capito cosa dovrei fare

uncoil [ʌnˈkɔɪl] VT srotolare ▶ VI srotolarsi, svolgersi

uncomfortable [ʌnˈkʌmfətəbl] ADJ scomodo(-a); (uneasy) a disagio, agitato(-a); (unpleasant) fastidioso(-a); (situation) sgradevole

uncomfortably [ʌnˈkʌmfətəblɪ] ADV scomodamente; (uneasily: say) con voce inquieta; (: think) con inquietudine

uncommitted [ʌnkəˈmɪtɪd] ADJ (attitude, country) neutrale

uncommon [ʌnˈkɔmən] ADJ raro(-a), insolito(-a), non comune

uncommunicative [ʌnkəˈmjuːnɪkətɪv] ADJ poco comunicativo(-a), chiuso(-a)

uncomplicated [ʌnˈkɔmplɪkeɪtɪd] ADJ semplice, poco complicato(-a)

uncompromising [ʌnˈkɔmprəmaɪzɪŋ] ADJ intransigente, inflessibile

unconcerned [ʌnkən'sə:nd] ADJ (*unworried*) tranquillo(-a); **to be ~ about** non darsi pensiero di, non preoccuparsi di or per

unconditional [ʌn'kən'dɪʃənl] ADJ incondizionato(-a), senza condizioni

uncongenial [ʌnkən'dʒi:nɪəl] ADJ (*work, surroundings*) poco piacevole

unconnected [ʌnkə'nɛktɪd] ADJ (*unrelated*) senza connessione, senza rapporto; **to be ~ with** essere estraneo(-a) a

unconscious [ʌn'kɒnʃəs] ADJ privo(-a) di sensi, svenuto(-a); (*unaware*) inconsapevole, inconscio(-a) ▶ N: **the ~** l'inconscio; **to knock sb ~** far perdere i sensi a qn con un pugno

unconsciously [ʌn'kɒnʃəslɪ] ADV inconsciamente

unconstitutional [ʌnkɒnstɪ'tju:ʃənl] ADJ incostituzionale

uncontested [ʌnkən'tɛstɪd] ADJ (*champion*) incontestato(-a); (*Pol: seat*) non disputato(-a)

uncontrollable [ʌnkən'trəʊləbl] ADJ incontrollabile; indisciplinato(-a)

uncontrolled [ʌnkən'trəʊld] ADJ (*child, dog, emotion*) sfrenato(-a); (*inflation, price rises*) che sfugge al controllo

unconventional [ʌnkən'vɛnʃənl] ADJ poco convenzionale

unconvinced [ʌnkən'vɪnst] ADJ: **to be** or **remain ~** non essere convinto(-a)

unconvincing [ʌnkən'vɪnsɪŋ] ADJ non convincente, poco persuasivo(-a)

uncork [ʌn'kɔ:k] VT stappare

uncorroborated [ʌnkə'rɒbəreɪtɪd] ADJ non convalidato(-a)

uncouth [ʌn'ku:θ] ADJ maleducato(-a), grossolano(-a)

uncover [ʌn'kʌvəʳ] VT scoprire

unctuous ['ʌŋktjʊəs] ADJ untuoso(-a)

undamaged [ʌn'dæmɪdʒd] ADJ (*goods*) in buono stato; (*fig: reputation*) intatto(-a)

undaunted [ʌn'dɔ:ntɪd] ADJ intrepido(-a)

undecided [ʌndɪ'saɪdɪd] ADJ indeciso(-a)

undelivered [ʌndɪ'lɪvəd] ADJ non recapitato(-a); **if ~, return to sender** in caso di mancato recapito rispedire al mittente

undeniable [ʌndɪ'naɪəbl] ADJ innegabile, indiscutibile

under ['ʌndəʳ] PREP sotto; (*less than*) meno di; al disotto di; (*according to*) secondo, in conformità a ▶ ADV (al) disotto; **from ~ sth** da sotto a or dal disotto di qc; **~ there** là sotto; **in ~ 2 hours** in meno di 2 ore; **~ anaesthetic** sotto anestesia; **~ discussion** in discussione; **~ repair** in riparazione; **~ the circumstances** date le circostanze

under … ['ʌndəʳ] PREFIX sotto…, sub…

under-age [ʌndər'eɪdʒ] ADJ minorenne

underarm ['ʌndərɑ:m] N ascella ▶ ADJ ascellare ▶ ADV da sotto in su

undercapitalized [ʌndə'kæpɪtəlaɪzd] ADJ carente di capitali

undercarriage ['ʌndəkærɪdʒ] N (BRIT Aviat) carrello (d'atterraggio)

undercharge [ʌndə'tʃɑ:dʒ] VT far pagare di meno a

underclass ['ʌndəklɑ:s] N sottoproletariato

underclothes ['ʌndəkləʊðz] NPL biancheria (intima)

undercover ['ʌndəkʌvəʳ] ADJ segreto(-a), clandestino(-a)

undercurrent ['ʌndəkʌrənt] N corrente f sottomarina

undercut [ʌndə'kʌt] VT (*irreg: like* **cut**) vendere a prezzo minore di

underdeveloped ['ʌndədɪ'vɛləpt] ADJ sottosviluppato(-a)

underdog ['ʌndədɒg] N oppresso(-a)

underdone [ʌndə'dʌn] ADJ (*Culin*) al sangue; (*pej*) poco cotto(-a)

under-employment [ʌndərɪm'plɔɪmənt] N sottoccupazione f

underestimate [ʌndər'ɛstɪmeɪt] VT sottovalutare

underexposed [ʌndərɪks'pəʊzd] ADJ (*Phot*) sottoesposto(-a)

underfed [ʌndə'fɛd] ADJ denutrito(-a)

underfoot [ʌndə'fut] ADV sotto i piedi

under-funded ['ʌndə'fʌndɪd] ADJ insufficientemente sovvenzionato(-a)

undergo [ʌndə'gəʊ] VT (*irreg: like* **go**) subire; (*treatment*) sottoporsi a; **the car is undergoing repairs** la macchina è in riparazione

undergraduate [ʌndə'grædjuɪt] N studente(-essa) universitario(-a) ▶ CPD: **~ courses** corsi mpl di laurea

underground ['ʌndəgraʊnd] N (BRIT: *railway*) metropolitana; (*Pol*) movimento clandestino ▶ ADJ sotterraneo(-a); (*fig*) clandestino(-a); (*Art, Cine*) underground inv ▶ ADV sottoterra; clandestinamente; **to go ~** (*fig*) darsi alla macchia

undergrowth ['ʌndəgrəʊθ] N sottobosco

underhand [ʌndə'hænd], **underhanded** [ʌndə'hændɪd] ADJ (*fig*) furtivo(-a), subdolo(-a)

underinsured [ʌndərɪn'ʃuəd] ADJ non sufficientemente assicurato(-a)

underlie [ʌndə'laɪ] VT (*irreg: like* **lie**) essere alla base di; **the underlying cause** il motivo di fondo

underline [ʌndə'laɪn] VT sottolineare

underling ['ʌndəlɪŋ] N (*pej*) subalterno(-a), tirapiedi mf

undermanning [ʌndə'mænɪŋ] N carenza di personale

undermentioned [ˌʌndəˈmɛnʃənd] ADJ (riportato(-a)) qui sotto or qui di seguito

undermine [ˌʌndəˈmaɪn] VT minare

underneath [ˌʌndəˈniːθ] ADV sotto, disotto
▶ PREP sotto, al di sotto di

undernourished [ˌʌndəˈnʌrɪʃt] ADJ denutrito(-a)

underpaid [ˌʌndəˈpeɪd] ADJ mal pagato(-a)

underpants [ˈʌndəpænts] NPL (BRIT) mutande fpl, slip m inv

underpass [ˈʌndəpɑːs] N (BRIT) sottopassaggio

underpin [ˌʌndəˈpɪn] VT puntellare; (argument, case) corroborare

underplay [ˌʌndəˈpleɪ] VT minimizzare

underpopulated [ˌʌndəˈpɒpjuleɪtɪd] ADJ scarsamente popolato(-a), sottopopolato(-a)

underprice [ˌʌndəˈpraɪs] VT fissare un prezzo troppo basso a

underprivileged [ˌʌndəˈprɪvɪlɪdʒd] ADJ svantaggiato(-a)

underrate [ˌʌndəˈreɪt] VT sottovalutare

underscore [ˌʌndəˈskɔːʳ] VT sottolineare

underseal [ˈʌndəsiːl] VT rendere stagno(-a) il fondo di

undersecretary [ˌʌndəˈsɛkrətrɪ] N sottosegretario

undersell [ˈʌndəˈsɛl] VT (irreg: like sell) (competitors) vendere a prezzi più bassi di

undershirt [ˈʌndəʃəːt] N (US) maglietta

undershorts [ˈʌndəʃɔːts] NPL (US) mutande fpl, slip m inv

underside [ˈʌndəsaɪd] N disotto

undersigned [ˈʌndəsaɪnd] ADJ, N sottoscritto(-a)

underskirt [ˈʌndəskəːt] N (BRIT) sottoveste f

understaffed [ˌʌndəˈstɑːft] ADJ a corto di personale

understaffing [ˌʌndəˈstɑːfɪŋ] N carenza f del personale

understand [ˌʌndəˈstænd] VT, VI (irreg: like stand) capire, comprendere; **I don't ~** non capisco; **I ~ that ...** sento che ...; credo di capire che ...; **to make o.s. understood** farsi capire

understandable [ˌʌndəˈstændəbl] ADJ comprensibile

understanding [ˌʌndəˈstændɪŋ] ADJ comprensivo(-a) ▶ N comprensione f; (agreement) accordo; **on the ~ that ...** a patto che or a condizione che ...; **to come to an ~ with sb** giungere ad un accordo con qn

understate [ˌʌndəˈsteɪt] VT minimizzare, sminuire

understatement [ˌʌndəˈsteɪtmənt] N: **that's an ~!** a dire poco!

understood [ˌʌndəˈstud] PT, PP of **understand**
▶ ADJ inteso(-a); (implied) sottinteso(-a)

understudy [ˈʌndəstʌdɪ] N sostituto(-a), attore(-trice) supplente

undertake [ˌʌndəˈteɪk] VT (irreg: like take) intraprendere; **to ~ to do sth** impegnarsi a fare qc

undertaker [ˈʌndəteɪkəʳ] N impresario di pompe funebri

undertaking [ˌʌndəˈteɪkɪŋ] N impresa; (promise) promessa

undertone [ˈʌndətəun] N (low voice) tono sommesso; (of criticism etc) vena, sottofondo; **in an ~** sottovoce

undervalue [ˌʌndəˈvæljuː] VT svalutare, sottovalutare

underwater [ˌʌndəˈwɔːtəʳ] ADV sott'acqua
▶ ADJ subacqueo(-a)

underway [ˌʌndəˈweɪ] ADJ: **to be ~** essere in corso

underwear [ˈʌndəwɛəʳ] N biancheria (intima)

underweight [ˌʌndəˈweɪt] ADJ al di sotto del giusto peso; (person) sottopeso inv

underwent [ˌʌndəˈwɛnt] VB see **undergo**

underworld [ˈʌndəwəːld] N (of crime) malavita

underwrite [ˈʌndəraɪt] VT (irreg: like write) (Finance) sottoscrivere; (Insurance) assicurare

underwriter [ˈʌndəraɪtəʳ] N sottoscrittore(-trice); assicuratore(-trice)

undeserving [ˌʌndɪˈzəːvɪŋ] ADJ: **to be ~ of** non meritare, non essere degno di

undesirable [ˌʌndɪˈzaɪərəbl] ADJ indesiderato(-a)

undeveloped [ˌʌndɪˈvɛləpt] ADJ (land, resources) non sfruttato(-a)

undies [ˈʌndɪz] NPL (col) robina, biancheria intima da donna

undiluted [ˌʌndaɪˈluːtɪd] ADJ non diluito(-a)

undiplomatic [ˌʌndɪpləˈmætɪk] ADJ poco diplomatico(-a)

undischarged [ˈʌndɪsˈtʃɑːdʒd] ADJ: **~ bankrupt** fallito non riabilitato

undisciplined [ʌnˈdɪsɪplɪnd] ADJ indisciplinato(-a)

undisguised [ˌʌndɪsˈɡaɪzd] ADJ (dislike, amusement etc) palese

undisputed [ˌʌndɪsˈpjuːtɪd] ADJ indiscusso(-a)

undistinguished [ˌʌndɪsˈtɪŋɡwɪʃt] ADJ mediocre, qualunque

undisturbed [ˌʌndɪsˈtəːbd] ADJ tranquillo(-a); **to leave sth ~** lasciare qc così com'è

undivided [ˌʌndɪˈvaɪdɪd] ADJ: **I want your ~ attention** esigo tutta la sua attenzione

undo [ʌnˈduː] VT (irreg: like do) disfare

undoing [ʌnˈduːɪŋ] N rovina, perdita

undone [ʌnˈdʌn] PP of **undo**; **to come ~** slacciarsi

undoubted [ʌnˈdautɪd] ADJ sicuro(-a), certo(-a)

undoubtedly [ʌnˈdautɪdlɪ] ADV senza alcun dubbio

undress [ʌnˈdrɛs] vi spogliarsi

undrinkable [ʌnˈdrɪŋkəbl] ADJ (*unpalatable*) imbevibile; (*poisonous*) non potabile

undue [ʌnˈdjuː] ADJ eccessivo(-a)

undulating [ˈʌndjuleɪtɪŋ] ADJ ondeggiante, ondulato(-a)

unduly [ʌnˈdjuːlɪ] ADV eccessivamente

undying [ʌnˈdaɪɪŋ] ADJ imperituro(-a)

unearned [ʌnˈəːnd] ADJ (*praise, respect*) immeritato(-a); **~ income** rendita

unearth [ʌnˈəːθ] VT dissotterrare; (*fig*) scoprire

unearthly [ʌnˈəːθlɪ] ADJ soprannaturale; (*hour*) impossibile

uneasy [ʌnˈiːzɪ] ADJ a disagio; (*worried*) preoccupato(-a); (*peace*) precario(-a); **to feel ~ about doing sth** non sentirsela di fare qc

uneconomic [ˈʌniːkəˈnɔmɪk], **uneconomical** [ˈʌniːkəˈnɔmɪkl] ADJ non economico(-a), antieconomico(-a)

uneducated [ʌnˈɛdjukeɪtɪd] ADJ senza istruzione, incolto(-a)

unemployed [ʌnɪmˈplɔɪd] ADJ disoccupato(-a) ► NPL: **the ~** i disoccupati

unemployment [ʌnɪmˈplɔɪmənt] N disoccupazione f

unemployment benefit, (*US*) **unemployment compensation** N sussidio di disoccupazione

unending [ʌnˈɛndɪŋ] ADJ senza fine

unenviable [ʌnˈɛnvɪəbl] ADJ poco invidiabile

unequal [ʌnˈiːkwəl] ADJ (*length, objects*) disuguale; (*amounts*) diverso(-a); (*division of labour*) ineguale

unequalled, (*US*) **unequaled** [ʌnˈiːkwəld] ADJ senza pari, insuperato(-a)

unequivocal [ʌnɪˈkwɪvəkəl] ADJ (*answer*) inequivocabile; (*person*) esplicito(-a), chiaro(-a).

unerring [ʌnˈəːrɪŋ] ADJ infallibile

UNESCO [juːˈnɛskəu] N ABBR (= *United Nations Educational, Scientific and Cultural Organization*) U.N.E.S.C.O f

unethical [ʌnˈɛθɪkəl] ADJ (*methods*) poco ortodosso(-a), non moralmente accettabile; (*doctor's behaviour*) contrario(-a) all'etica professionale

uneven [ʌnˈiːvn] ADJ ineguale; (*ground*) disuguale, accidentato(-a); (*heartbeat*) irregolare

uneventful [ʌnɪˈvɛntful] ADJ senza sorprese, tranquillo(-a)

unexceptional [ʌnɪkˈsɛpʃənl] ADJ che non ha niente d'eccezionale

unexciting [ʌnɪkˈsaɪtɪŋ] ADJ (*news*) poco emozionante; (*film, evening*) poco interessante

unexpected [ʌnɪkˈspɛktɪd] ADJ inatteso(-a), imprevisto(-a)

unexpectedly [ʌnɪkˈspɛktɪdlɪ] ADV inaspettatamente

unexplained [ʌnɪkˈspleɪnd] ADJ inspiegato(-a)

unexploded [ʌnɪkˈspləudɪd] ADJ inesploso(-a)

unfailing [ʌnˈfeɪlɪŋ] ADJ (*supply, energy*) inesauribile; (*remedy*) infallibile

unfair [ʌnˈfɛəʳ] ADJ: **~ (to)** ingiusto(-a) (nei confronti di); **it's ~ that ...** non è giusto che ... +*sub*

unfair dismissal N licenziamento ingiustificato

unfairly [ʌnˈfɛəlɪ] ADV ingiustamente

unfaithful [ʌnˈfeɪθful] ADJ infedele

unfamiliar [ʌnfəˈmɪlɪəʳ] ADJ sconosciuto(-a), strano(-a); **to be ~ with sth** non essere pratico di qc, non avere familiarità con qc

unfashionable [ʌnˈfæʃnəbl] ADJ (*clothes*) fuori moda *inv*; (*district*) non alla moda

unfasten [ʌnˈfɑːsn] VT slacciare; sciogliere

unfathomable [ʌnˈfæðəməbl] ADJ insondabile

unfavourable, (*US*) **unfavorable** [ʌnˈfeɪvərəbl] ADJ sfavorevole

unfavourably, (*US*) **unfavorably** [ʌnˈfeɪvərəblɪ] ADV: **to look ~ upon** vedere di malocchio

unfeeling [ʌnˈfiːlɪŋ] ADJ insensibile, duro(-a)

unfinished [ʌnˈfɪnɪʃt] ADJ incompiuto(-a)

unfit [ʌnˈfɪt] ADJ inadatto(-a); (*ill*) non in forma; (*incompetent*): **~ (for)** incompetente (in); (*work, Mil*) inabile (a); **~ for habitation** inabitabile

unflagging [ʌnˈflægɪŋ] ADJ instancabile

unflappable [ʌnˈflæpəbl] ADJ calmo(-a), composto(-a)

unflattering [ʌnˈflætərɪŋ] ADJ (*dress, hairstyle*) che non dona

unflinching [ʌnˈflɪntʃɪŋ] ADJ che non indietreggia, risoluto(-a)

unfold [ʌnˈfəuld] VT spiegare; (*fig*) rivelare ► VI (*view*) distendersi; (*story*) svelarsi

unfollow [ʌnˈfɔləu] VT (*on social media*) effettuare l'unfollow di

unforeseeable [ˈʌnfɔːˈsiːəbl] ADJ imprevedibile

unforeseen [ʌnfɔːˈsiːn] ADJ imprevisto(-a)

unforgettable [ʌnfəˈgɛtəbl] ADJ indimenticabile

unforgivable [ʌnfəˈgɪvəbl] ADJ imperdonabile

unformatted [ʌnˈfɔːmætɪd] ADJ (*disk, text*) non formattato(-a)

unfortunate [ʌnˈfɔːtʃnɪt] ADJ sfortunato(-a); (*event, remark*) infelice

unfortunately [ʌnˈfɔːtʃnɪtlɪ] ADV sfortunatamente, purtroppo

unfounded [ʌnˈfaundɪd] ADJ infondato(-a)

unfriend [ʌnˈfrɛnd] VT (*Internet*) cancellare dagli amici

unfriendly [ʌnˈfrɛndlɪ] ADJ poco amichevole, freddo(-a)

unfulfilled [ʌnfulˈfɪld] ADJ (*ambition*) non realiz-

u

zato(-a); (*prophecy*) che non si è avverato(-a); (*desire*) insoddisfatto(-a); (*promise*) non mantenuto(-a); (*terms of contract*) non rispettato(-a); (*person*) frustrato(-a)

unfurl [ʌnˈfəːl] VT spiegare

unfurnished [ʌnˈfəːnɪʃt] ADJ non ammobiliato(-a)

ungainly [ʌnˈɡeɪnlɪ] ADJ goffo(-a), impacciato(-a)

ungodly [ʌnˈɡɔdlɪ] ADJ empio(-a); **at an ~ hour** a un'ora impossibile

ungrateful [ʌnˈɡreɪtful] ADJ ingrato(-a)

unguarded [ʌnˈɡɑːdɪd] ADJ: **in an ~ moment** in un momento di distrazione

unhappily [ʌnˈhæpɪlɪ] ADV (*unfortunately*) purtroppo, sfortunatamente

unhappiness [ʌnˈhæpɪnɪs] N infelicità

unhappy [ʌnˈhæpɪ] ADJ infelice; **~ about/with** (*arrangements etc*) insoddisfatto(-a) di

unharmed [ʌnˈhɑːmd] ADJ incolume, sano(-a) e salvo(-a)

UNHCR N ABBR (= *United Nations High Commissioner for Refugees*) Alto Commissariato delle Nazioni Unite per Rifugiati

unhealthy [ʌnˈhɛlθɪ] ADJ (*gen*) malsano(-a); (*person*) malaticcio(-a)

unheard-of [ʌnˈhəːdɔv] ADJ inaudito(-a), senza precedenti

unhelpful [ʌnˈhɛlpful] ADJ poco disponibile

unhesitating [ʌnˈhɛzɪteɪtɪŋ] ADJ (*loyalty*) che non vacilla; (*reply, offer*) pronto(-a), immediato(-a)

unholy [ʌnˈhəʊlɪ] ADJ: **an ~ alliance** un'alleanza nefasta; **he returned at an ~ hour** è tornato ad un'ora indecente

unhook [ʌnˈhuk] VT sganciare; sfibbiare

unhurt [ʌnˈhəːt] ADJ incolume, illeso(-a)

unhygienic [ʌnhaɪˈdʒiːnɪk] ADJ non igienico(-a)

UNICEF [ˈjuːnɪsɛf] N ABBR (= *United Nations International Children's Emergency Fund*) UNICEF m

unicorn [ˈjuːnɪkɔːn] N unicorno

unidentified [ʌnaɪˈdɛntɪfaɪd] ADJ non identificato(-a)

uniform [ˈjuːnɪfɔːm] N uniforme f, divisa ▸ ADJ uniforme

uniformity [juːnɪˈfɔːmɪtɪ] N uniformità

unify [ˈjuːnɪfaɪ] VT unificare

unilateral [juːnɪˈlætərəl] ADJ unilaterale

unimaginable [ʌnɪˈmædʒɪnəbl] ADJ inimmaginabile, inconcepibile

unimaginative [ʌnɪˈmædʒɪnətɪv] ADJ privo(-a) di fantasia, a corto di idee

unimpaired [ʌnɪmˈpɛəd] ADJ intatto(-a), non danneggiato(-a)

unimportant [ʌnɪmˈpɔːtənt] ADJ senza importanza, di scarsa importanza

unimpressed [ʌnɪmˈprɛst] ADJ niente affatto impressionato(-a)

uninhabited [ʌnɪnˈhæbɪtɪd] ADJ disabitato(-a)

uninhibited [ʌnɪnˈhɪbɪtɪd] ADJ senza inibizioni; senza ritegno

uninjured [ʌnˈɪndʒəd] ADJ incolume

uninspiring [ʌnɪnˈspaɪərɪŋ] ADJ banale

uninstall [ʌnɪnˈstɔːl] VT (*Comput*) disinstallare

unintelligent [ʌnɪnˈtɛlɪdʒənt] ADJ poco intelligente

unintentional [ʌnɪnˈtɛnʃənəl] ADJ involontario(-a)

unintentionally [ʌnɪnˈtɛnʃnəlɪ] ADV senza volerlo, involontariamente

uninvited [ʌnɪnˈvaɪtɪd] ADJ non invitato(-a)

uninviting [ʌnɪnˈvaɪtɪŋ] ADJ (*place, food*) non invitante, poco invitante; (*offer*) poco allettante

union [ˈjuːnjən] N unione f; (*also*: **trade union**) sindacato ▸ CPD sindacale, dei sindacati; **the U~** (*US*) gli stati dell'Unione

unionize [ˈjuːnjənaɪz] VT sindacalizzare, organizzare in sindacato

Union Jack N bandiera nazionale britannica

Union of Soviet Socialist Republics N (*Hist*) Unione f delle Repubbliche Socialiste Sovietiche

union shop N stabilimento in cui tutti gli operai sono tenuti ad aderire ad un sindacato

unique [juːˈniːk] ADJ unico(-a)

unisex [ˈjuːnɪsɛks] ADJ unisex inv

UNISON [ˈjuːnɪsn] N (*trade union*) sindacato generale dei funzionari

unison [ˈjuːnɪsn] N: **in ~** all'unisono

unit [ˈjuːnɪt] N unità f inv; (*section: of furniture etc*) elemento; (*team, squad*) reparto, squadra; **production ~** reparto m, produzione inv; **sink ~** blocco m lavello inv

unit cost N costo unitario

unite [juːˈnaɪt] VT unire ▸ VI unirsi

united [juːˈnaɪtɪd] ADJ unito(-a); unificato(-a); (*efforts*) congiunto(-a)

United Arab Emirates NPL Emirati mpl Arabi Uniti

United Kingdom N Regno Unito

United Nations (Organization) N (Organizzazione f delle) Nazioni fpl Unite

United States (of America) N Stati mpl Uniti (d'America)

unit price N prezzo unitario

unit trust N (*BRIT Comm*) fondo d'investimento

unity [ˈjuːnɪtɪ] N unità

Univ. ABBR = **university**

universal [juːnɪˈvəːsl] ADJ universale

universe [ˈjuːnɪvəːs] N universo

university [ju:nɪ'vɜ:sɪtɪ] N università f inv ▶ CPD (*student, professor, education*) universitario(-a); (*year*) accademico(-a)

university degree N laurea

unjust [ʌn'dʒʌst] ADJ ingiusto(-a)

unjustifiable ['ʌndʒʌstɪ'faɪəbl] ADJ ingiustificabile

unjustified [ʌn'dʒʌstɪfaɪd] ADJ ingiustificato(-a); (*Typ*) non allineato(-a)

unkempt [ʌn'kɛmpt] ADJ trasandato(-a); spettinato(-a)

unkind [ʌn'kaɪnd] ADJ poco gentile, scortese

unkindly [ʌn'kaɪndlɪ] ADV (*speak*) in modo sgarbato; (*treat*) male

unknown [ʌn'nəun] ADJ sconosciuto(-a); ~ **to me** ... a mia insaputa ...; ~ **quantity** (*Math: fig*) incognita

unladen [ʌn'leɪdn] ADJ (*ship, weight*) a vuoto

unlawful [ʌn'lɔ:ful] ADJ illecito(-a), illegale

unleaded ['ʌn'lɛdɪd] ADJ senza piombo; ~ **petrol** benzina verde or senza piombo

unleash [ʌn'li:ʃ] VT sguinzagliare; (*fig*) scatenare

unleavened [ʌn'lɛvnd] ADJ non lievitato(-a), azzimo(-a)

unless [ʌn'lɛs] CONJ a meno che (non) + sub; ~ **otherwise stated** salvo indicazione contraria; ~ **I am mistaken** se non mi sbaglio

unlicensed [ʌn'laɪsənst] ADJ (*BRIT*) senza licenza per la vendita di alcolici

unlike [ʌn'laɪk] ADJ diverso(-a) ▶ PREP a differenza di, contrariamente a

unlikelihood [ʌn'laɪklɪhud] N improbabilità

unlikely [ʌn'laɪklɪ] ADJ improbabile; (*explanation*) inverosimile

unlimited [ʌn'lɪmɪtɪd] ADJ illimitato(-a)

unlisted [ʌn'lɪstɪd] ADJ (*US Tel*): **to be ~** non essere sull'elenco; (*Stock Exchange*) non quotato(-a)

unlit [ʌn'lɪt] ADJ (*room*) senza luce; (*road*) non illuminato(-a)

unload [ʌn'ləud] VT scaricare

unlock [ʌn'lɔk] VT aprire

unlucky [ʌn'lʌkɪ] ADJ sfortunato(-a); (*object, number*) che porta sfortuna, di malaugurio; **to be ~** (*person*) essere sfortunato, non avere fortuna

unmanageable [ʌn'mænɪdʒəbl] ADJ (*tool, vehicle*) poco maneggevole; (*situation*) impossibile

unmanned [ʌn'mænd] ADJ (*spacecraft*) senza equipaggio

unmannerly [ʌn'mænəlɪ] ADJ maleducato(-a)

unmarked [ʌn'mɑ:kt] ADJ (*unstained*) pulito(-a), senza macchie; ~ **police car** civetta della polizia

unmarried [ʌn'mærɪd] ADJ non sposato(-a); (*man only*) scapolo, celibe; (*woman only*) nubile

unmarried mother N ragazza f madre inv

unmask [ʌn'mɑ:sk] VT smascherare

unmatched [ʌn'mætʃt] ADJ senza uguali

unmentionable [ʌn'mɛnʃnəbl] ADJ (*vice, topic*) innominabile; (*word*) irripetibile

unmerciful [ʌn'mə:sɪful] ADJ spietato(-a)

unmistakable, unmistakeable [ʌnmɪs'teɪkəbl] ADJ inconfondibile

unmitigated [ʌn'mɪtɪgeɪtɪd] ADJ (*disaster etc*) totale, assoluto(-a)

unnamed [ʌn'neɪmd] ADJ (*nameless*) senza nome; (*anonymous*) anonimo(-a)

unnatural [ʌn'nætʃrəl] ADJ innaturale; contro natura

unnecessary [ʌn'nɛsəsərɪ] ADJ inutile, superfluo(-a)

unnerve [ʌn'nə:v] VT (*accident*) sgomentare; (*hostile attitude*) bloccare; (*long wait, interview*) snervare

unnoticed [ʌn'nəutɪst] ADJ: **to go** or **pass ~** passare inosservato(-a)

UNO ['ju:nəu] N ABBR (= *United Nations Organization*) ONU f

unobservant [ʌnəb'zə:vənt] ADJ: **to be ~** non avere spirito di osservazione

unobtainable [ʌnəb'teɪnəbl] ADJ (*Tel*) non ottenibile

unobtrusive [ʌnəb'tru:sɪv] ADJ discreto(-a)

unoccupied [ʌn'ɔkjupaɪd] ADJ (*house*) vuoto(-a); (*seat, Mil: zone*) libero(-a), non occupato(-a)

unofficial [ʌnə'fɪʃl] ADJ non ufficiale; (*strike*) non dichiarato(-a) dal sindacato

unopened [ʌn'əupənd] ADJ (*letter*) non aperto(-a); (*present*) ancora incartato(-a)

unopposed [ʌnə'pəuzd] ADJ senza incontrare opposizione

unorthodox [ʌn'ɔ:θədɔks] ADJ non ortodosso(-a)

unpack [ʌn'pæk] VI disfare la valigia (*or* le valigie) ▶ VT disfare

unpaid [ʌn'peɪd] ADJ (*holiday*) non pagato(-a); (*work*) non retribuito(-a); (*bill, debt*) da pagare

unpalatable [ʌn'pælətəbl] ADJ (*food*) immangiabile; (*drink*) imbevibile; (*truth*) sgradevole

unparalleled [ʌn'pærəlɛld] ADJ incomparabile, impareggiabile

unpatriotic ['ʌnpætrɪ'ɔtɪk] ADJ (*person*) poco patriottico(-a); (*speech, attitude*) antipatriottico(-a)

unplanned [ʌn'plænd] ADJ (*visit*) imprevisto(-a); (*baby*) non previsto(-a)

unpleasant [ʌn'plɛznt] ADJ spiacevole; (*person, remark*) antipatico(-a); (*day, experience*) brutto(-a)

unplug [ʌn'plʌg] VT staccare

unpolluted [ʌnpə'lu:tɪd] ADJ non inquinato(-a)

u

unpopular [ʌn'pɒpjʊləʳ] ADJ impopolare; **to make o.s. ~ (with)** rendersi antipatico (a); (*politician etc*) alienarsi le simpatie (di)

unprecedented [ʌn'prɛsɪdəntɪd] ADJ senza precedenti

unpredictable [ʌnprɪ'dɪktəbl] ADJ imprevedibile

unprejudiced [ʌn'prɛdʒʊdɪst] ADJ (*not biased*) obiettivo(-a), imparziale; (*having no prejudices*) senza pregiudizi

unprepared [ʌnprɪ'pɛəd] ADJ (*person*) impreparato(-a); (*speech*) improvvisato(-a)

unprepossessing [ʌnpriːpə'zɛsɪŋ] ADJ insulso(-a)

unpretentious [ʌnprɪ'tɛnʃəs] ADJ senza pretese

unprincipled [ʌn'prɪnsɪpld] ADJ senza scrupoli

unproductive [ʌnprə'dʌktɪv] ADJ improduttivo(-a); (*discussion*) sterile

unprofessional ['ʌnprə'fɛʃənl] ADJ: **~ conduct** scorrettezza professionale

unprofitable [ʌn'prɔfɪtəbl] ADJ (*financially*) non redditizio(-a); (*job, deal*) poco lucrativo(-a)

unprotected ['ʌnprə'tɛktɪd] ADJ (*sex*) non protetto(-a)

unprovoked [ʌnprə'vəʊkt] ADJ non provocato(-a)

unpunished [ʌn'pʌnɪʃt] ADJ: **to go ~** restare impunito(-a)

unqualified [ʌn'kwɔlɪfaɪd] ADJ (*worker*) non qualificato(-a); (*in professions*) non abilitato(-a); (*success*) assoluto(-a), senza riserve

unquestionably [ʌn'kwɛstʃənəblɪ] ADV indiscutibilmente

unquestioning [ʌn'kwɛstʃənɪŋ] ADJ (*obedience, acceptance*) cieco(-a)

unravel [ʌn'rævl] VT dipanare, districare

unreal [ʌn'rɪəl] ADJ irreale

unrealistic [ʌnrɪə'lɪstɪk] ADJ (*idea*) illusorio(-a); (*estimate*) non realistico(-a)

unreasonable [ʌn'riːznəbl] ADJ irragionevole; **to make ~ demands on sb** voler troppo da qn

unrecognizable [ʌn'rɛkəgnaɪzəbl] ADJ irriconoscibile

unrecognized [ʌn'rɛkəgnaɪzd] ADJ (*talent, genius*) misconosciuto(-a); (*Pol: regime*) non ufficialmente riconosciuto(-a)

unrecorded [ʌnrɪ'kɔːdɪd] ADJ non documentato(-a), non registrato(-a)

unrefined [ʌnrɪ'faɪnd] ADJ (*sugar, petroleum*) greggio(-a); (*person*) rozzo(-a)

unrehearsed [ʌnrɪ'həːst] ADJ (*Theat etc*) improvvisato(-a); (*spontaneous*) imprevisto(-a)

unrelated [ʌnrɪ'leɪtɪd] ADJ: **~ (to)** senza rapporto (con); (*by family*) non imparentato(-a) (con)

unrelenting [ʌnrɪ'lɛntɪŋ] ADJ implacabile; accanito(-a)

unreliable [ʌnrɪ'laɪəbl] ADJ (*person, machine*) che non dà affidamento; (*news, source of information*) inattendibile

unrelieved [ʌnrɪ'liːvd] ADJ (*monotony*) uniforme

unremitting [ʌnrɪ'mɪtɪŋ] ADJ incessante, infaticabile

unrepeatable [ʌnrɪ'piːtəbl] ADJ (*offer*) unico(-a)

unrepentant [ʌnrɪ'pɛntənt] ADJ impenitente

unrepresentative [ʌnrɛprɪ'zɛntətɪv] ADJ atipico(-a), poco rappresentativo(-a)

unreserved [ʌnrɪ'zəːvd] ADJ (*seat*) non prenotato(-a), non riservato(-a); (*approval, admiration*) senza riserve

unresponsive [ʌnrɪs'pɒnsɪv] ADJ che non reagisce

unrest [ʌn'rɛst] N agitazione f

unrestricted [ʌnrɪ'strɪktɪd] ADJ (*power, time*) illimitato(-a); (*access*) libero(-a)

unrewarded [ʌnrɪ'wɔːdɪd] ADJ non ricompensato(-a)

unripe [ʌn'raɪp] ADJ acerbo(-a)

unrivalled, (*US*) **unrivaled** [ʌn'raɪvəld] ADJ senza pari

unroll [ʌn'rəʊl] VT srotolare

unruffled [ʌn'rʌfld] ADJ (*person*) calmo(-a) e tranquillo(-a), imperturbato(-a); (*hair*) a posto

unruly [ʌn'ruːlɪ] ADJ indisciplinato(-a)

unsafe [ʌn'seɪf] ADJ pericoloso(-a), rischioso(-a); **~ to drink** non potabile; **~ to eat** non commestibile

unsaid [ʌn'sɛd] ADJ: **to leave sth ~** passare qc sotto silenzio

unsaleable, (*US*) **unsalable** [ʌn'seɪləbl] ADJ invendibile

unsatisfactory ['ʌnsætɪs'fæktərɪ] ADJ che lascia a desiderare, insufficiente

unsavoury, (*US*) **unsavory** [ʌn'seɪvərɪ] ADJ (*person*) losco(-a); (*reputation, subject*) disgustoso(-a), ripugnante

unscathed [ʌn'skeɪðd] ADJ incolume

unscientific ['ʌnsaɪən'tɪfɪk] ADJ poco scientifico(-a)

unscrew [ʌn'skruː] VT svitare

unscrupulous [ʌn'skruːpjʊləs] ADJ senza scrupoli

unseat [ʌn'siːt] VT (*rider*) disarcionare; (*fig: an official*) spodestare

unsecured [ʌnsɪ'kjʊəd] ADJ: **~ creditor** creditore *m* chirografario

unseeded [ʌn'siːdɪd] ADJ (*Sport*) che non è una testa di serie

unseemly [ʌn'siːmlɪ] ADJ sconveniente

unseen [ʌn'siːn] ADJ (*person*) inosservato(-a); (*danger*) nascosto(-a)

unselfish [ʌn'sɛlfɪʃ] ADJ (*person*) altruista; (*act*) disinteressato(-a)

unsettled [ʌnˈsɛtld] ADJ (person, future) incerto(-a); indeciso(-a); turbato(-a); (question) non risolto(-a); (weather, market) instabile; **to feel ~** sentirsi disorientato(-a)

unsettling [ʌnˈsɛtlɪŋ] ADJ inquietante

unshakable, unshakeable [ʌnˈʃeɪkəbl] ADJ irremovibile

unshaven [ʌnˈʃeɪvn] ADJ non rasato(-a)

unsightly [ʌnˈsaɪtlɪ] ADJ brutto(-a), sgradevole a vedersi

unskilled [ʌnˈskɪld] ADJ: **~ worker** operaio(-a) specializzato(-a)

unsociable [ʌnˈsəʊʃəbl] ADJ (person) poco socievole; (behaviour) antipatico(-a)

unsocial [ʌnˈsəʊʃəl] ADJ: **~ hours** orario sconveniente

unsold [ʌnˈsəʊld] ADJ invenduto(-a)

unsolicited [ʌnsəˈlɪsɪtɪd] ADJ non richiesto(-a)

unsophisticated [ʌnsəˈfɪstɪkeɪtɪd] ADJ semplice, naturale

unsound [ʌnˈsaʊnd] ADJ (health) debole, cagionevole; (in construction: floor, foundations) debole, malsicuro(-a); (policy, advice) poco sensato(-a); (judgment, investment) poco sicuro(-a)

unspeakable [ʌnˈspiːkəbl] ADJ (bad) abominevole

unspoiled [ˈʌnˈspɔɪld], **unspoilt** [ˈʌnˈspɔɪlt] ADJ (place) non deturpato(-a)

unspoken [ʌnˈspəʊkən] ADJ (words) non detto(-a); (agreement, approval) tacito(-a)

unstable [ʌnˈsteɪbl] ADJ (gen) instabile; (mentally) squilibrato(-a)

unsteady [ʌnˈstɛdɪ] ADJ instabile, malsicuro(-a)

unstinting [ʌnˈstɪntɪŋ] ADJ (support) incondizionato(-a); (generosity) illimitato(-a); (praise) senza riserve

unstuck [ʌnˈstʌk] ADJ: **to come ~** scollarsi; (fig) fare fiasco

unsubscribe [ʌnsʌbˈskraɪb] VI (Comput) disdire l'abbonamento

unsubstantiated [ʌnsəbˈstænʃɪeɪtɪd] ADJ (rumour, accusation) infondato(-a)

unsuccessful [ʌnsəkˈsɛsful] ADJ (writer, proposal) che non ha successo; (marriage, attempt) mal riuscito(-a), fallito(-a); **to be ~** (in attempting sth) non riuscire; non avere successo; (application) non essere considerato(-a)

unsuccessfully [ʌnsəkˈsɛsfəlɪ] ADV senza successo

unsuitable [ʌnˈsuːtəbl] ADJ inadatto(-a); (moment) inopportuno(-a); sconveniente

unsuited [ʌnˈsuːtɪd] ADJ: **to be ~ for** or **to** non essere fatto(-a) per

unsung [ˈʌnˈsʌŋ] ADJ: **an ~ hero** un eroe misconosciuto

unsupported [ʌnsəˈpɔːtɪd] ADJ (claim) senza fondamento; (theory) non dimostrato(-a)

unsure [ʌnˈʃuəʳ] ADJ: **~ (of** or **about)** incerto(-a) (su); **to be ~ of o.s.** essere insicuro(-a)

unsuspecting [ʌnsəˈspɛktɪŋ] ADJ che non sospetta niente

unsweetened [ʌnˈswiːtnd] ADJ senza zucchero

unswerving [ʌnˈswɜːvɪŋ] ADJ fermo(-a)

unsympathetic [ˈʌnsɪmpəˈθɛtɪk] ADJ (attitude) poco incoraggiante; (person) antipatico(-a); **~ (to)** non solidale (verso)

untangle [ʌnˈtæŋgl] VT sbrogliare

untapped [ʌnˈtæpt] ADJ (resources) non sfruttato(-a)

untaxed [ʌnˈtækst] ADJ (goods) esente da imposte; (income) non imponibile

unthinkable [ʌnˈθɪŋkəbl] ADJ impensabile, inconcepibile

unthinkingly [ˈʌnˈθɪŋkɪŋlɪ] ADV senza pensare

untidy [ʌnˈtaɪdɪ] ADJ (room) in disordine; (appearance, work) trascurato(-a); (person, writing) disordinato(-a)

untie [ʌnˈtaɪ] VT (knot, parcel) disfare; (prisoner, dog) slegare

until [ʌnˈtɪl] PREP fino a; (after negative) prima di ▶ CONJ finché, fino a quando; (in past, after negative) prima che + sub, prima di + infinitive; **~ he comes** finché or fino a quando non arriva; **~ now** finora; **~ then** fino ad allora; **from morning ~ night** dalla mattina alla sera

untimely [ʌnˈtaɪmlɪ] ADJ intempestivo(-a), inopportuno(-a); (death) prematuro(-a)

untold [ʌnˈtəʊld] ADJ incalcolabile; indescrivibile

untouched [ʌnˈtʌtʃt] ADJ (not used etc) non toccato(-a), intatto(-a); (safe: person) incolume; (unaffected): **~ by** insensibile a

untoward [ʌntəˈwɔːd] ADJ sfortunato(-a), sconveniente

untrained [ˈʌnˈtreɪnd] ADJ (worker) privo(-a) di formazione professionale; (troops) privo(-a) di addestramento; **to the ~ eye** ad un occhio inesperto

untrammelled [ʌnˈtræmld] ADJ illimitato(-a)

untranslatable [ʌntrænzˈleɪtəbl] ADJ intraducibile

untrue [ʌnˈtruː] ADJ (statement) falso(-a), non vero(-a)

untrustworthy [ʌnˈtrʌstwəːðɪ] ADJ di cui non ci si può fidare

unusable [ʌnˈjuːzəbl] ADJ inservibile, inutilizzabile

unused[1] [ʌnˈjuːzd] ADJ (new) nuovo(-a); (not made use of) non usato(-a), non utilizzato(-a)

unused[2] [ʌnˈjuːst] ADJ: **to be ~ to sth/to doing sth** non essere abituato(-a) a qc/a fare qc

unusual [ʌnˈjuːʒuəl] ADJ insolito(-a), eccezionale raro(-a)

unusually [ʌnˈjuːʒuəlɪ] ADV insolitamente

u

unveil [ʌn'veɪl] VT scoprire; svelare

unwanted [ʌn'wɒntɪd] ADJ (clothing) smesso(-a); (child) non desiderato(-a)

unwarranted [ʌn'wɒrəntɪd] ADJ ingiustificato(-a)

unwary [ʌn'wɛərɪ] ADJ incauto(-a)

unwavering [ʌn'weɪvərɪŋ] ADJ fermo(-a), incrollabile

unwelcome [ʌn'wɛlkəm] ADJ (gen) non gradito(-a); **to feel ~** sentire che la propria presenza non è gradita

unwell [ʌn'wɛl] ADJ indisposto(-a); **to feel ~** non sentirsi bene

unwieldy [ʌn'wiːldɪ] ADJ poco maneggevole

unwilling [ʌn'wɪlɪŋ] ADJ: **to be ~ to do** non voler fare

unwillingly [ʌn'wɪlɪŋlɪ] ADV malvolentieri

unwind [ʌn'waɪnd] VT (irreg: like **wind**²) svolgere, srotolare ▶ VI (relax) rilassarsi

unwise [ʌn'waɪz] ADJ (decision, act) poco saggio(-a)

unwitting [ʌn'wɪtɪŋ] ADJ involontario(-a)

unwittingly [ʌn'wɪtɪŋlɪ] ADV senza volerlo

unworkable [ʌn'wəːkəbl] ADJ (plan etc) inattuabile

unworthy [ʌn'wəːðɪ] ADJ indegno(-a); **to be ~ of sth/to do sth** non essere degno di qc/di fare qc

unwrap [ʌn'ræp] VT disfare; (present) aprire

unwritten [ʌn'rɪtn] ADJ (agreement) tacito(-a)

unzip [ʌn'zɪp] VT aprire (la chiusura lampo di); (Comput) dezippare

---

up [ʌp]

PREP su; **he went up the stairs/the hill** è salito su per le scale/sulla collina; **the cat was up a tree** il gatto era su un albero; **they live further up the street** vivono un po' più su nella stessa strada

▶ ADV **1** (upwards, higher) su, in alto; **up in the sky/the mountains** su nel cielo/in montagna; **up there** lassù; **up above** su in alto; **up with Leeds United!** viva il Leeds United!

2: **to be up** (out of bed) essere alzato(-a); (prices, level) essere salito(-a); (building) essere terminato(-a); (tent) essere piantato(-a); (curtains, shutters, wallpaper) essere su; **"this side up"** "alto"; **to be up (by)** (in price, value) essere salito(-a) or aumentato(-a) (di); **when the year was up** (finished) finito l'anno; **time's up** il tempo è scaduto; **he's well up in** or **on politics** (BRIT) è molto informato di or sulla politica

3: **up to** (as far as) fino a; **up to now** finora

4: **to be up to** (depending on): **it's up to you** sta a lei, dipende da lei; (equal to): **he's not up to it** (job, task etc) non ne è all'altezza; (be doing: col): **what is he up to?** cosa sta combinando?; **what's up?** (col: wrong) che c'è?; **what's up**

with him? che ha?, che gli prende?
▶ N: **ups and downs** alti e bassi mpl
▶ VI (col): **she upped and left** improvvisamente se ne andò

---

up-and-coming ['ʌpənd'kʌmɪŋ] ADJ pieno(-a) di promesse, promettente

upbeat ['ʌpbiːt] N (Mus) tempo in levare; (in economy, prosperity) incremento ▶ ADJ (col) ottimistico(-a)

upbraid [ʌp'breɪd] VT rimproverare

upbringing ['ʌpbrɪŋɪŋ] N educazione f

upcoming ['ʌpkʌmɪŋ] ADJ imminente, prossimo(-a)

upcycle ['ʌpsaɪkl] VT fare l'upcycling di

update [ʌp'deɪt] VT aggiornare

upend [ʌp'ɛnd] VT rovesciare

upfront [ʌp'frʌnt] ADJ (col) franco(-a), aperto(-a) ▶ ADV (pay) subito

upgrade [ʌp'greɪd] VT promuovere; (job) rivalutare; (house) rimodernare; (employee) avanzare di grado; (Comput) fare un upgrade di

upheaval [ʌp'hiːvl] N sconvolgimento; tumulto

uphill [ʌp'hɪl] ADJ in salita; (fig: task) difficile
▶ ADV: **to go ~** andare in salita, salire

uphold [ʌp'həuld] VT (irreg: like **hold**) approvare; sostenere

upholstery [ʌp'həulstərɪ] N tappezzeria

upkeep ['ʌpkiːp] N manutenzione f

upload ['ʌpləud] VT caricare

up-market [ʌp'mɑːkɪt] ADJ (product) che si rivolge ad una fascia di mercato superiore

upon [ə'pɒn] PREP su

upper ['ʌpə'] ADJ superiore ▶ N (of shoe) tomaia; **the ~ class** ≈ l'alta borghesia

upper case N maiuscolo

upper-class [ʌpə'klɑːs] ADJ dell'alta borghesia; (district) signorile; (accent) aristocratico(-a); (attitude) snob inv

uppercut ['ʌpəkʌt] N uppercut m inv, montante m

upper hand N: **to have the ~** avere il coltello dalla parte del manico

Upper House N: **the ~** (in Britain) la Camera Alta, la Camera dei Lords; (in US etc) il Senato

uppermost ['ʌpəməust] ADJ il (la) più alto(-a); predominante; **it was ~ in my mind** è stata la mia prima preoccupazione

Upper Volta [-'vɒltə] N Alto Volta m

upright ['ʌpraɪt] ADJ diritto(-a); verticale; (fig) diritto(-a), onesto(-a) ▶ N montante m

uprising ['ʌpraɪzɪŋ] N insurrezione f, rivolta

uproar ['ʌprɔː'] N tumulto, clamore m

uproarious [ʌp'rɔːrɪəs] ADJ clamoroso(-a); (hilarious) esilarante; **~ laughter** risata sonora

uproot [ʌp'ruːt] VT sradicare

upset N [ˈʌpsɛt] turbamento; (*to plan etc*) contrattempo ▸ VT [ʌpˈsɛt] (*irreg: like* **set**) (*glass etc*) rovesciare; (*plan, stomach*) scombussolare; (*person: offend*) contrariare; (*: grieve*) addolorare; sconvolgere ▸ ADJ [ʌpˈsɛt] contrariato(-a), addolorato(-a); (*stomach*) scombussolato(-a), disturbato(-a); **to have a stomach ~** (BRIT) avere lo stomaco in disordine *or* scombussolato; **to get ~** contrariarsi; addolorarsi

upset price N (US, SCOTTISH) prezzo di riserva

upsetting [ʌpˈsɛtɪŋ] ADJ (*saddening*) sconvolgente; (*offending*) offensivo(-a); (*annoying*) fastidioso(-a)

upshot [ˈʌpʃɔt] N risultato; **the ~ of it all was that …** la conclusione è stata che …

upside down [ˈʌpsaɪd-] ADV sottosopra; **to turn ~** capovolgere; (*fig*) mettere sottosopra

upstage [ˈʌpˈsteɪdʒ] VT: **to ~ sb** rubare la scena a qn

upstairs [ʌpˈstɛəz] ADV, ADJ di sopra, al piano superiore ▸ N piano di sopra

upstart [ˈʌpstɑːt] N parvenu *m inv*

upstream [ʌpˈstriːm] ADV a monte

upsurge [ˈʌpsəːdʒ] N (*of enthusiasm etc*) ondata

uptake [ˈʌpteɪk] N: **he is quick/slow on the ~** è pronto/lento di comprendonio

uptight [ʌpˈtaɪt] ADJ (*col*) teso(-a)

up-to-date [ˈʌptəˈdeɪt] ADJ moderno(-a); aggiornato(-a)

uptown [ˈʌptaun] (US) ADV verso i quartieri residenziali ▸ ADJ dei quartieri residenziali

upturn [ˈʌptəːn] N (*in luck*) svolta favorevole; (*in value of currency*) rialzo

upturned [ˈʌptəːnd] ADJ (*nose*) all'insù

upward [ˈʌpwəd] ADJ ascendente; verso l'alto ▸ ADV = **upwards**

upwardly-mobile [ˈʌpwədlɪˈməubaɪl] N: **to be ~** salire nella scala sociale

upwards [ˈʌpwədz] ADV in su, verso l'alto

Ural Mountains [ˈjuərəl-] NPL: **the ~** (*also:* **the Urals**) gli Urali, i Monti Urali

uranium [juəˈreɪnɪəm] N uranio

Uranus [juəˈreɪnəs] N (*planet*) Urano

urban [ˈəːbən] ADJ urbano(-a)

urbane [əːˈbeɪn] ADJ civile, urbano(-a), educato(-a)

urbanization [əːbənaɪˈzeɪʃən] N urbanizzazione *f*

urchin [ˈəːtʃɪn] N monello; **sea ~** riccio di mare

Urdu [ˈuəduː] N urdu *m inv*

urge [əːdʒ] N impulso; stimolo; forte desiderio ▸ VT (*caution etc*) raccomandare vivamente; **to ~ sb to do** esortare qn a fare, spingere qn a fare; raccomandare a qn di fare
▸ **urge on** VT spronare

urgency [ˈəːdʒənsɪ] N urgenza; (*of tone*) insistenza

urgent [ˈəːdʒənt] ADJ urgente; (*earnest, persistent: plea*) pressante; (*: tone, voice*) insistente, incalzante

urgently [ˈəːdʒəntlɪ] ADV d'urgenza, urgentemente; con insistenza

urinal [ˈjuərɪnl] N (BRIT: *building*) vespasiano; (*: vessel*) orinale *m*, pappagallo

urinate [ˈjuərɪneɪt] VI orinare

urine [ˈjuərɪn] N orina

URL N ABBR (= *uniform resource locator*) URL *m inv*, indirizzo Internet

urn [əːn] N urna; (*also:* **tea urn**) bollitore *m* per il tè

Uruguay [ˈjuərəgwaɪ] N Uruguay *m*

Uruguayan [juərəˈgwaɪən] ADJ, N uruguaiano(-a)

US N ABBR = **United States**

us [ʌs] PRON ci; (*stressed, after prep*) noi; *see also* **me**

USA N ABBR (*Geo*) = **United States of America**; (*Mil*) = **United States Army**

usable [ˈjuːzəbl] ADJ utilizzabile, usabile

USAF N ABBR = **United States Air Force**

usage [ˈjuːzɪdʒ] N uso

USB stick N pennetta *f* USB *inv*

USCG N ABBR = **United States Coast Guard**

USDA N ABBR = **United States Department of Agriculture**

USDAW [ˈʌzdɔː] N ABBR (BRIT: = *Union of Shop, Distributive and Allied Workers*) sindacato dei dipendenti di negozi, reti di distribuzione e simili

USDI N ABBR = **United States Department of the Interior**

use N [juːs] uso; impiego, utilizzazione *f* ▸ VT [juːz] usare, utilizzare, servirsi di; **she used to do it** lo faceva (una volta), era solita farlo; **in ~** in uso; **out of ~** fuori uso; **to be of ~** essere utile, servire; **to make ~ of sth** far uso di qc, utilizzare qc; **ready for ~** pronto per l'uso; **it's no ~** non serve, è inutile; **to have the ~ of** poter usare; **what's this used for?** a che serve?; **to be used to** avere l'abitudine di; **to get used to** abituarsi a, fare l'abitudine a
▸ **use up** VT finire; (*supplies*) dare fondo a; (*leftovers*) consumare

used [juːzd] ADJ (*car, object*) usato(-a)

useful [ˈjuːsful] ADJ utile; **to come in ~** fare comodo, tornare utile

usefulness [ˈjuːsfəlnɪs] N utilità

useless [ˈjuːslɪs] ADJ inutile; (*unusable: object*) inservibile; (*: person*) inetto(-a)

user [ˈjuːzər] N utente *mf*; (*of petrol, gas etc*) consumatore(-trice)

user-friendly [ˈjuːzəˈfrɛndlɪ] ADJ orientato(-a) all'utente; (*computer*) di facile uso

username [ˈjuːzəneɪm] N (*Comput*) nome *m* utente

USES N ABBR = **United States Employment Service**

u

usher [ˈʌʃəʳ] N usciere m; (in cinema) maschera ▶ VT: **to ~ sb in** far entrare qn

usherette [ʌʃəˈrɛt] N (in cinema) maschera

USM N ABBR = **United States Mint; United States Mail**

USN N ABBR = **United States Navy**

USP N ABBR = **unique selling point; unique selling proposition**

USPHS N ABBR = **United States Public Health Service**

USPO N ABBR = **United States Post Office**

USS ABBR = **United States Ship; United States Steamer**

USSR N ABBR (Hist) = **Union of Soviet Socialist Republics**

usu. ABBR = **usually**

usual [ˈjuːʒuəl] ADJ solito(-a); **as ~** come al solito, come d'abitudine

usually [ˈjuːʒuəlɪ] ADV di solito

usurer [ˈjuːʒərəʳ] N usuraio(-a)

usurp [juːˈzəːp] VT usurpare

UT ABBR (US) = **Utah**

ute [juːt] N (AUSTRALIA, NEW ZEALAND) pick-up m inv

utensil [juːˈtɛnsl] N utensile m; **kitchen utensils** utensili da cucina

uterus [ˈjuːtərəs] N utero

utilitarian [juːtɪlɪˈtɛərɪən] ADJ utilitario(-a)

utility [juːˈtɪlɪtɪ] N utilità; (also: **public utility**) servizio pubblico

utility room N locale adibito alla stiratura dei panni ecc

utilization [juːtɪlaɪˈzeɪʃən] N utilizzazione f

utilize [ˈjuːtɪlaɪz] VT utilizzare; sfruttare

utmost [ˈʌtməust] ADJ estremo(-a) ▶ N: **to do one's ~** fare il possibile or di tutto; **of the ~ importance** della massima importanza; **it is of the ~ importance that ...** è estremamente importante che ... + sub

utter [ˈʌtəʳ] ADJ assoluto(-a), totale ▶ VT pronunciare, proferire; emettere

utterance [ˈʌtərəns] N espressione f; parole fpl

utterly [ˈʌtəlɪ] ADV completamente, del tutto

U-turn [ˈjuːtəːn] N inversione f a U; (fig) voltafaccia m inv

Uzbekistan [ʌzbɛkɪˈstɑːn] N Uzbekistan

Vv

V, v [viː] N (*letter*) V, v m *inv or f inv;* **V for Victor** ≈ V come Venezia

V ABBR (= *verse*) v.; (= *vide*) v., vedi; (= *volt*) V.; (= *versus*) contro

VA, Va. ABBR (*US*) = **Virginia**

vac [væk] N ABBR (*BRIT col*) = **vacation**

vacancy ['veɪkənsɪ] N (*job*) posto libero; (*room*) stanza libera; **"no vacancies"** "completo"; **have you any vacancies?** (*office*) avete bisogno di personale?; (*hotel*) avete una stanza?

vacant ['veɪkənt] ADJ (*job, seat etc*) libero(-a); (*expression*) assente

vacant lot N terreno non occupato; (*for sale*) terreno in vendita

vacate [və'keɪt] VT lasciare libero(-a)

vacation [və'keɪʃən] N (*esp US*) vacanze *fpl;* **to take a ~** prendere una vacanza, prendere le ferie; **on ~** in vacanza, in ferie

vacation course N corso estivo

vacationer, vacationist N (*US*) vacanziere(-a)

vaccinate ['væksɪneɪt] VT vaccinare

vaccination [væksɪ'neɪʃən] N vaccinazione *f*

vaccine ['væksiːn] N vaccino

vacuum ['vækjum] N vuoto

vacuum bottle N (*US*) = **vacuum flask**

vacuum cleaner N aspirapolvere *m inv*

vacuum flask N (*BRIT*) thermos® *m inv*

vacuum-packed ['vækjum'pækt] ADJ confezionato(-a) sottovuoto *inv*

vagabond ['vægəbɔnd] N vagabondo(-a)

vagary ['veɪgərɪ] N capriccio

vagina [və'dʒaɪnə] N vagina

vagrancy ['veɪgrənsɪ] N vagabondaggio

vagrant ['veɪgrənt] N vagabondo(-a)

vague [veɪg] ADJ vago(-a); (*blurred: photo, memory*) sfocato(-a); **I haven't the vaguest idea** non ho la minima *or* più pallida idea

vaguely ['veɪglɪ] ADV vagamente

vain [veɪn] ADJ (*useless*) inutile, vano(-a); (*conceited*) vanitoso(-a); **in ~** inutilmente, invano

valance ['væləns] N volant *m inv,* balza

valedictory [vælɪ'dɪktərɪ] ADJ di commiato

valentine ['væləntaɪn] N (*also:* **valentine card**) cartolina *or* biglietto di San Valentino

Valentine's Day ['væləntaɪnzdeɪ] N San Valentino *m*

valet ['vælɪt] N cameriere *m* personale

valet parking N parcheggio effettuato da un dipendente (dell'albergo ecc)

valet service N (*for clothes*) servizio di lavanderia; (*for car*) servizio completo di lavaggio

valiant ['væljənt] ADJ valoroso(-a), coraggioso(-a)

valid ['vælɪd] ADJ valido(-a), valevole; (*excuse*) valido(-a)

validate ['vælɪdeɪt] VT (*contract, document*) convalidare; (*argument, claim*) comprovare

validity [və'lɪdɪtɪ] N validità

valise [və'liːz] N borsa da viaggio

valley ['vælɪ] N valle *f*

valour, (*US*) **valor** ['vælər] N valore *m*

valuable ['væljuəbl] ADJ (*jewel*) di (grande) valore; (*time, help*) prezioso(-a) ■ **valuables** NPL oggetti *mpl* di valore

valuation [vælju'eɪʃən] N valutazione *f,* stima

value ['væljuː] N valore *m* ▶ VT (*fix price*) valutare, dare un prezzo a; (*cherish*) apprezzare, tenere a ■ **values** NPL (*principles*) valori *mpl;* **to be of great ~ to sb** avere molta importanza per qn; **to lose (in) ~** (*currency*) svalutarsi; (*property*) perdere (di) valore; **to gain (in) ~** (*currency*) guadagnare; (*property*) aumentare di valore; **you get good ~ (for money) in that shop** si compra bene in quel negozio

value added tax N (*BRIT*) imposta sul valore aggiunto

valued ['væluːd] ADJ (*appreciated*) stimato(-a), apprezzato(-a)

valuer ['væljuər] N stimatore(-trice)

valve [vælv] N valvola

vampire ['væmpaɪər] N vampiro

van [væn] N (*Aut*) furgone *m;* (*BRIT Rail*) vagone *m*

V and A N ABBR (*BRIT*) = **Victoria and Albert Museum**

vandal ['vændl] N vandalo(-a)

vandalism ['vændəlɪzəm] N vandalismo

vandalize ['vændəlaɪz] VT vandalizzare

vanguard ['væŋɡɑːd] N avanguardia

vanilla [vəˈnɪlə] N vaniglia ▶ CPD (ice cream) alla vaniglia

vanish ['vænɪʃ] VI svanire, scomparire

vanity ['vænɪtɪ] N vanità f inv

vanity case N valigetta per cosmetici

vantage ['vɑːntɪdʒ] N: ~ point posizione f or punto di osservazione; (fig) posizione vantaggiosa

Vanuatu ['vænuːæːtuː] N Vanuatu fpl

vape [veɪp] VT OR VI svapare

vaper ['veɪpər] N svapatore(-trice)

vaping ['veɪpɪŋ] N vaping m, vapo

vaporize ['veɪpəraɪz] VT vaporizzare ▶ VI vaporizzarsi

vapour, (US) **vapor** ['veɪpər] N vapore m

variable ['vɛərɪəbl] ADJ variabile; (mood) mutevole ▶ N fattore m variabile, variabile f

variance ['vɛərɪəns] N: **to be at ~ (with)** essere in disaccordo (con); (facts) essere in contraddizione (con)

variant ['vɛərɪənt] N variante f

variation [vɛərɪˈeɪʃən] N variazione f; (in opinion) cambiamento

varicose ['værɪkəus] ADJ: ~ **veins** varici fpl

varied ['vɛərɪd] ADJ vario(-a), diverso(-a)

variety [vəˈraɪətɪ] N varietà f inv; (quantity) quantità f inv, numero; **a wide ~ of …** una vasta gamma di …; **for a ~ of reasons** per una serie di motivi

variety show N spettacolo di varietà

various ['vɛərɪəs] ADJ vario(-a), diverso(-a); (several) parecchi(-e), molti(-e); **at ~ times** in momenti diversi; (several) diverse volte

varnish ['vɑːnɪʃ] N vernice f; (nail varnish) smalto ▶ VT verniciare; mettere lo smalto su; **to ~ one's nails** mettersi lo smalto sulle unghie

vary ['vɛərɪ] VT, VI variare, mutare; **to ~ (with** or **according to)** variare (con or a seconda di)

varying ['vɛərɪɪŋ] ADJ variabile

vase [vɑːz] N vaso

vasectomy [væˈsɛktəmɪ] N vasectomia

Vaseline® ['væsɪliːn] N vaselina

vast [vɑːst] ADJ vasto(-a); (amount, success) enorme

vastly ['vɑːstlɪ] ADV enormemente

vastness ['vɑːstnɪs] N vastità

VAT [væt] N ABBR (BRIT: = value added tax) I.V.A. f

vat [væt] N tino

Vatican ['vætɪkən] N: **the ~** il Vaticano; ~ **City** Città del Vaticano f inv

vatman ['vætmæn] N (irreg) (BRIT col): **the ~** ≈ l'ispettore m dell'IVA

vault [vɔːlt] N (of roof) volta; (tomb) tomba; (in bank) camera blindata; (jump) salto ▶ VT (also: **vault over**) saltare (d'un balzo)

vaunted ['vɔːntɪd] ADJ: **much-vaunted** tanto celebrato(-a)

VC N ABBR (BRIT: = Victoria Cross) medaglia al coraggio; = **vice-chairman**

VCR N ABBR = **video cassette recorder**

VD N ABBR = **venereal disease**

VDU N ABBR = **visual display unit**

veal [viːl] N vitello

veer [vɪər] VI girare; virare

veg. [vɛdʒ] N ABBR (BRIT col: = vegetable(s)) ≈ contorno

vegan ['viːɡən] N (BRIT) vegetaliano(-a)

vegeburger, veggieburger ['vɛdʒɪbɜːɡər] N hamburger m inv vegetariano

vegetable ['vɛdʒtəbl] N verdura, ortaggio ▶ ADJ vegetale

vegetable garden N orto

vegetarian [vɛdʒɪˈtɛərɪən] ADJ, N vegetariano(-a)

vegetate ['vɛdʒɪteɪt] VI vegetare

vegetation [vɛdʒɪˈteɪʃən] N vegetazione f

vegetative ['vɛdʒɪtətɪv] ADJ (also Bot) vegetativo(-a)

vehemence ['viːɪməns] N veemenza, violenza

vehement ['viːɪmənt] ADJ veemente, violento(-a); profondo(-a)

vehicle ['viːɪkl] N veicolo; (fig) mezzo

vehicular [vɪˈhɪkjulər] ADJ: **"no ~ traffic"** "chiuso al traffico di veicoli"

veil [veɪl] N velo ▶ VT velare; **under a ~ of secrecy** (fig) protetto da una cortina di segretezza

veiled [veɪld] ADJ (also fig) velato(-a)

vein [veɪn] N vena; (on leaf) nervatura; (fig: mood) vena, umore m

Velcro® ['vɛlkrəu] N velcro® m inv

vellum ['vɛləm] N (writing paper) carta patinata

velocity [vɪˈlɔsɪtɪ] N velocità f inv

velour [vəˈluər] N velours m inv

velvet ['vɛlvɪt] N velluto ▶ ADJ di velluto

vending machine ['vɛndɪŋ-] N distributore m automatico

vendor ['vɛndər] N venditore(-trice); **street ~** venditore ambulante

veneer [vəˈnɪər] N impiallacciatura; (fig) vernice f

venerable ['vɛnərəbl] ADJ venerabile

venereal disease [vɪˈnɪərəl-] N malattia venerea

Venetian [vɪˈniːʃən] ADJ, N veneziano(-a)

Venetian blind N (tenda alla) veneziana

Venezuela [vɛnɪˈzweɪlə] N Venezuela m

Venezuelan [vɛnɪˈzweɪlən] ADJ, N venezuelano(-a)

vengeance [ˈvɛndʒəns] N vendetta; **with a ~** (fig) davvero; furiosamente

vengeful [ˈvɛndʒful] ADJ vendicativo(-a)

Venice [ˈvɛnɪs] N Venezia

venison [ˈvɛnɪsn] N carne f di cervo

venom [ˈvɛnəm] N veleno

venomous [ˈvɛnəməs] ADJ velenoso(-a)

vent [vɛnt] N foro, apertura; (in dress, jacket) spacco ▶ VT (fig: one's feelings) sfogare, dare sfogo a

ventilate [ˈvɛntɪleɪt] VT (room) dare aria a, arieggiare

ventilation [vɛntɪˈleɪʃən] N ventilazione f

ventilation shaft N condotto di aerazione

ventilator [ˈvɛntɪleɪtəʳ] N ventilatore m

ventriloquist [vɛnˈtrɪləkwɪst] N ventriloquo(-a)

venture [ˈvɛntʃəʳ] N impresa (rischiosa) ▶ VT rischiare, azzardare ▶ VI arrischiarsi, azzardarsi; **a business ~** un'iniziativa commerciale; **to ~ to do sth** azzardarsi a fare qc

venture capital N capitale m di rischio

venue [ˈvɛnjuː] N luogo di incontro; (Sport) luogo (designato) per l'incontro

Venus [ˈviːnəs] N (planet) Venere m

veracity [vəˈræsɪtɪ] N veridicità

veranda, verandah [vəˈrændə] N veranda

verb [vəːb] N verbo

verbal [ˈvəːbəl] ADJ verbale; (translation) orale

verbally [ˈvəːbəlɪ] ADV a voce

verbatim [vəːˈbeɪtɪm] ADV, ADJ parola per parola

verbose [vəːˈbəus] ADJ verboso(-a)

verdict [ˈvəːdɪkt] N verdetto; (opinion) giudizio, parere m; **~ of guilty/not guilty** verdetto di colpevolezza/non colpevolezza

verge [vəːdʒ] N bordo, orlo; **"soft verges"** (BRIT) "banchina cedevole"; **on the ~ of doing** sul punto di fare
▶ **verge on** VT FUS rasentare

verger [ˈvəːdʒəʳ] N (Rel) sagrestano

verification [vɛrɪfɪˈkeɪʃən] N verifica

verify [ˈvɛrɪfaɪ] VT verificare; (prove the truth of) confermare

veritable [ˈvɛrɪtəbl] ADJ vero(-a)

vermin [ˈvəːmɪn] NPL animali mpl nocivi; (insects) insetti mpl parassiti

vermouth [ˈvəːməθ] N vermut m inv

vernacular [vəˈnækjuləʳ] N vernacolo

versatile [ˈvəːsətaɪl] ADJ (person) versatile; (machine, tool etc) (che si presta) a molti usi

verse [vəːs] N (of poem) verso; (stanza) stanza, strofa; (in bible) versetto; (no pl: poetry) versi mpl; **in ~** in versi

versed [vəːst] ADJ: **(well-)versed in** versato(-a) in

version [ˈvəːʃən] N versione f

versus [ˈvəːsəs] PREP contro

vertebra [ˈvəːtɪbrə] (pl **vertebrae** [-briː]) N vertebra

vertebrate [ˈvəːtɪbrɪt] N vertebrato

vertical [ˈvəːtɪkl] ADJ, N verticale (m)

vertically [ˈvəːtɪklɪ] ADV verticalmente

vertigo [ˈvəːtɪgəu] N vertigine f; **to suffer from ~** soffrire di vertigini

verve [vəːv] N brio; entusiasmo

very [ˈvɛrɪ] ADV molto ▶ ADJ: **the ~ book which** proprio il libro che; **~ much** moltissimo; **~ well** molto bene; **~ little** molto poco; **at the ~ end** proprio alla fine; **the ~ last** proprio l'ultimo; **at the ~ least** almeno; **the ~ thought (of it) alarms me** il solo pensiero mi spaventa, sono spaventato solo al pensiero

vespers [ˈvɛspəz] NPL vespro

vessel [ˈvɛsl] N (Anat) vaso; (Naut) nave f; (container) recipiente m

vest [vɛst] N (BRIT) maglia; (: sleeveless) canottiera; (US: waistcoat) gilè m inv ▶ VT: **to ~ sb with sth, to ~ sth in sb** conferire qc a qn

vested interest [ˈvɛstɪd-] N: **to have a ~ in doing** avere tutto l'interesse a fare ■ **vested interests** NPL (Comm) diritti mpl acquisiti

vestibule [ˈvɛstɪbjuːl] N vestibolo

vestige [ˈvɛstɪdʒ] N vestigio

vestment [ˈvɛstmənt] N (Rel) paramento liturgico

vestry [ˈvɛstrɪ] N sagrestia

Vesuvius [vɪˈsuːvɪəs] N Vesuvio

vet [vɛt] N ABBR (BRIT: = veterinary surgeon) veterinario(-a); (US col) = **veteran** ▶ VT esaminare minuziosamente; (text) rivedere; **to ~ sb for a job** raccogliere delle informazioni dettagliate su qn prima di offrirgli un posto

veteran [ˈvɛtərn] N veterano; (also: **war veteran**) veterano, reduce m ▶ ADJ: **she's a ~ campaigner for …** lotta da sempre per …

veteran car N auto f inv d'epoca (anteriore al 1919)

veterinarian [vɛtrɪˈnɛərɪən] N (US) = **veterinary surgeon**

veterinary [ˈvɛtrɪnərɪ] ADJ veterinario(-a)

veterinary surgeon, (US) **veterinarian** [vɛtrɪˈnɛərɪən] N veterinario(-a)

veto [ˈviːtəu] (pl **vetoes**) N veto ▶ VT opporre il veto a; **to put a ~ on** opporre il veto a

vetting [ˈvɛtɪŋ] N: **positive ~** indagine per accertare l'idoneità di un aspirante a una carica ufficiale

vex [vɛks] VT irritare, contrariare

vexed [vɛkst] ADJ (question) controverso(-a), dibattuto(-a)

VFD N ABBR (US) = **voluntary fire department**

VG ABBR (BRIT Scol etc: = very good) ottimo

VHF ABBR (= very high frequency) VHF

VI ABBR (US) = **Virgin Islands**

via ['vaɪə] PREP (by way of) via; (by means of) tramite

viability [vaɪə'bɪlɪtɪ] N attuabilità

viable ['vaɪəbl] ADJ attuabile; vitale

viaduct ['vaɪədʌkt] N viadotto

vial ['vaɪəl] N fiala

vibes [vaɪbz] NPL (col): **I got good/bad ~** ho trovato simpatica/antipatica l'atmosfera

vibrant ['vaɪbrənt] ADJ (sound) vibrante; (colour) vivace, vivo(-a)

vibraphone ['vaɪbrəfəun] N vibrafono

vibrate [vaɪ'breɪt] VI: **to ~ (with)** vibrare (di); (resound) risonare (di)

vibration [vaɪ'breɪʃən] N vibrazione f

vibrator [vaɪ'breɪtər] N vibratore m

vicar ['vɪkər] N pastore m

vicarage ['vɪkərɪdʒ] N presbiterio

vicarious [vɪ'kɛərɪəs] ADJ sofferto(-a) al posto di un altro; **to get ~ pleasure out of sth** trarre piacere indirettamente da qc

vice [vaɪs] N (evil) vizio; (Tech) morsa

vice- [vaɪs] PREFIX vice ...

vice-chairman [vaɪs'tʃɛəmən] N (irreg) vicepresidente m

vice-chancellor [vaɪs'tʃɑːnsələr] N (BRIT Scol) rettore m (per elezione)

vice-president [vaɪs'prɛzɪdənt] N vicepresidente m

viceroy ['vaɪsrɔɪ] N viceré m inv

vice squad N (squadra del) buon costume f

vice versa ['vaɪsɪ'və:sə] ADV viceversa

vicinity [vɪ'sɪnɪtɪ] N vicinanze fpl

vicious ['vɪʃəs] ADJ (remark) maligno(-a), cattivo(-a); (dog) cattivo(-a); (blow) violento(-a); **a ~ circle** un circolo vizioso

viciousness ['vɪʃəsnɪs] N malignità, cattiveria; ferocia

vicissitudes [vɪ'sɪsɪtjuːdz] NPL vicissitudini fpl

victim ['vɪktɪm] N vittima; **to be the ~ of** essere vittima di

victimization [vɪktɪmaɪ'zeɪʃən] N persecuzione f; rappresaglie fpl

victimize ['vɪktɪmaɪz] VT perseguitare; compiere delle rappresaglie contro

victor ['vɪktər] N vincitore(-trice)

Victorian [vɪk'tɔːrɪən] ADJ vittoriano(-a)

victorious [vɪk'tɔːrɪəs] ADJ vittorioso(-a)

victory ['vɪktərɪ] N vittoria; **to win a ~ over sb** riportare una vittoria su qn

video ['vɪdɪəu] CPD video... ▶ N (video film) video m inv; (also: **video cassette**) videocassetta; (also: **video recorder**) videoregistratore m

video call N videochiamata

videocam ['vɪdɪəukæm] N videocamera

video camera N videocamera

video cassette N videocassetta

video cassette recorder N videoregistratore m

videodisc ['vɪdɪəudɪsk] N disco ottico

video game N videogioco

video nasty N video estremamente violento o porno

videophone ['vɪdɪəufəun] N videotelefono

video recorder N videoregistratore m

video recording N registrazione f su video

video shop N videonoleggio

video tape N videotape m inv

video wall N schermo m multivideo inv

vie [vaɪ] VI: **to ~ with** competere con, rivaleggiare con

Vienna [vɪ'ɛnə] N Vienna

Vietnam, Viet Nam [vjɛt'næm] N Vietnam m

Vietnamese [vjɛtnə'miːz] ADJ vietnamita ▶ N vietnamita mf; (Ling) vietnamita m

view [vjuː] N vista, veduta; (opinion) opinione f ▶ VT (also fig: situation) considerare; (house) visitare; **on ~** (in museum etc) esposto(-a); **to be in** or **within ~ (of sth)** essere in vista (di qc); **in full ~ of sb** sotto gli occhi di qn; **an overall ~ of the situation** una visione globale della situazione; **in my ~** a mio parere, secondo me; **in ~ of the fact that** considerato che, tenuto conto che; **to take** or **hold the ~ that ...** essere dell'opinione che ...; **with a ~ to doing sth** con l'intenzione di fare qc

viewdata ['vjuːdeɪtə] N (BRIT) sistema di televideo

viewer ['vjuːər] N (viewfinder) mirino; (small projector) visore m; (TV) telespettatore(-trice)

viewfinder ['vjuːfaɪndər] N mirino

viewpoint ['vjuːpɔɪnt] N punto di vista; (place) posizione f

vigil ['vɪdʒɪl] N veglia; **to keep ~** vegliare

vigilance ['vɪdʒɪləns] N vigilanza

vigilant ['vɪdʒɪlənt] ADJ vigile

vigilante [vɪdʒɪ'læntɪ] N cittadino che si fa giustizia da solo

vigorous ['vɪgərəs] ADJ vigoroso(-a)

vigour, (US) **vigor** ['vɪgər] N vigore m

vile [vaɪl] ADJ (action) vile; (smell) disgustoso(-a), nauseante; (temper) pessimo(-a)

vilify ['vɪlɪfaɪ] VT diffamare

villa ['vɪlə] N villa

village ['vɪlɪdʒ] N villaggio

villager ['vɪlɪdʒər] N abitante mf di villaggio

villain ['vɪlən] N (scoundrel) canaglia; (BRIT: criminal) criminale m; (in novel etc) cattivo

VIN N ABBR (US) = **vehicle identification number**

vinaigrette [vɪneɪ'grɛt] N vinaigrette f inv

vindicate ['vɪndɪkeɪt] VT comprovare; giustificare

vindication [vɪndɪ'keɪʃən] N: **in ~ of** per giustificare; a discolpa di

vindictive [vɪn'dɪktɪv] ADJ vendicativo(-a)

vine [vaɪn] N vite f; (climbing plant) rampicante m

vinegar ['vɪnɪgər] N aceto

vine grower N viticoltore m

vine-growing ['vaɪngrəʊɪŋ] ADJ viticolo(-a)
▶ N viticoltura

vineyard ['vɪnjɑːd] N vigna, vigneto

vintage ['vɪntɪdʒ] N (year) annata, produzione f; **the 1990 ~** il vino del 1990 ▶ CPD d'annata

vintage car N auto f inv d'epoca

vintage wine N vino d'annata

vinyl ['vaɪnl] N vinile m

viola [vɪ'əʊlə] N viola

violate ['vaɪəleɪt] VT violare

violation [vaɪə'leɪʃən] N violazione f; **in ~ of sth** violando qc

violence ['vaɪələns] N violenza; (Pol etc) incidenti mpl violenti

violent ['vaɪələnt] ADJ violento(-a); **a ~ dislike of sb/sth** una violenta avversione per qn/qc

violently ['vaɪələntlɪ] ADV violentemente; (ill, angry) terribilmente

violet ['vaɪələt] ADJ (colour) viola inv, violetto(-a)
▶ N (plant) violetta; (colour) violetto

violin [vaɪə'lɪn] N violino

violinist [vaɪə'lɪnɪst] N violinista mf

VIP N ABBR (= very important person) V.I.P. mf

viper ['vaɪpər] N vipera

viral ['vaɪərəl] ADJ (Comput) virale ▶ N (Comput: video) video m inv virale; (: image) foto f inv virale; **to go ~** diventare virale

virgin ['vɜːdʒɪn] N vergine f ▶ ADJ vergine inv; **she is a ~** lei è vergine; **the Blessed V~** la Beatissima Vergine

virginity [vɜː'dʒɪnɪtɪ] N verginità

Virgo ['vɜːgəʊ] N (sign) Vergine f; **to be ~** essere della Vergine

virile ['vɪraɪl] ADJ virile

virility [vɪ'rɪlɪtɪ] N virilità

virtual ['vɜːtjʊəl] ADJ effettivo(-a), vero(-a); (Comput, Physics) virtuale; (in effect): **it's a ~ impossibility** è praticamente impossibile; **the ~ leader** il capo all'atto pratico

virtually ['vɜːtjʊəlɪ] ADV (almost) praticamente; **it is ~ impossible** è praticamente impossibile

virtual reality N (Comput) realtà f inv virtuale

virtue ['vɜːtjuː] N virtù f inv; (advantage) pregio, vantaggio; **by ~ of** grazie a

virtuosity [vɜːtjʊ'ɒsɪtɪ] N virtuosismo

virtuoso [vɜːtjʊ'əʊzəʊ] N virtuoso(-a)

virtuous ['vɜːtjʊəs] ADJ virtuoso(-a)

virulent ['vɪrʊlənt] ADJ virulento(-a)

virus ['vaɪərəs] N (also Comput) virus m inv

visa ['viːzə] N visto

vis-à-vis [viːzə'viː] PREP rispetto a, nei riguardi di

viscount ['vaɪkaunt] N visconte m

viscous ['vɪskəs] ADJ viscoso(-a)

vise [vaɪs] N (US Tech) = **vice**

visibility [vɪzɪ'bɪlɪtɪ] N visibilità

visible ['vɪzəbl] ADJ visibile; **~ exports/imports** esportazioni fpl/importazioni fpl visibili

visibly ['vɪzəblɪ] ADV visibilmente

vision ['vɪʒən] N (sight) vista; (foresight, in dream) visione f

visionary ['vɪʒənərɪ] N visionario(-a)

visit ['vɪzɪt] N visita; (stay) soggiorno ▶ VT (person: US: also: **visit with**) andare a trovare; (place) visitare; **to pay a ~ to** (person) fare una visita a; (place) andare a visitare; **on a private/official ~** in visita privata/ufficiale

visiting ['vɪzɪtɪŋ] ADJ (speaker, professor, team) ospite

visiting card N biglietto da visita

visiting hours NPL (in hospital etc) orario delle visite

visitor ['vɪzɪtər] N visitatore(-trice); (guest) ospite mf

visitor centre, (US) **visitor center** N centro informazioni per visitatori di museo, zoo, parco ecc

visitors' book ['vɪzɪtəz-] N libro d'oro; (in hotel) registro

visor ['vaɪzər] N visiera

vista ['vɪstə] N vista, prospettiva

visual ['vɪzjʊəl] ADJ visivo(-a); visuale; ottico(-a)

visual aid N sussidio visivo

visual arts NPL arti fpl figurative

visual display unit N unità f inv di visualizzazione

visualize ['vɪzjʊəlaɪz] VT immaginare, figurarsi; (foresee) prevedere

visually ['vɪzjʊəlɪ] ADV: **~ appealing** piacevole a vedersi; **~ handicapped** (!) con una menomazione della vista

vital ['vaɪtl] ADJ vitale; **of ~ importance (to sb/sth)** di vitale importanza (per qn/qc)

vitality [vaɪ'tælɪtɪ] N vitalità

vitally ['vaɪtəlɪ] ADV estremamente

vital statistics NPL (of population) statistica demografica; (col: woman's) misure fpl

vitamin ['vɪtəmɪn] N vitamina

vitiate ['vɪʃɪeɪt] VT viziare

vitreous ['vɪtrɪəs] ADJ (rock) vetroso(-a); (china, enamel) vetrificato(-a)

vitriolic [vɪtrɪ'ɒlɪk] ADJ (fig) caustico(-a)

V

viva [ˈvaɪvə] N (also: **viva voce**) (esame m) orale

vivacious [vɪˈveɪʃəs] ADJ vivace

vivacity [vɪˈvæsɪtɪ] N vivacità

vivid [ˈvɪvɪd] ADJ vivido(-a)

vividly [ˈvɪvɪdlɪ] ADV (describe) vividamente; (remember) con precisione

vivisection [vɪvɪˈsɛkʃən] N vivisezione f

vixen [ˈvɪksn] N volpe f femmina; (pej: woman) bisbetica

viz ABBR (= videlicet) cioè

VLF ABBR (= very low frequency) bassissima frequenza

vlog [vlɒg] N vlog m inv, video log m inv

vlogger [ˈvlɒgəʳ] N vlogger mf inv, video logger mf inv

vlogging [ˈvlɒgɪŋ] N vlogging m

V-neck [ˈviːnɛk] N maglione m con lo scollo a V

VOA N ABBR (= Voice of America) voce f dell'America (alla radio)

vocabulary [vəʊˈkæbjulərɪ] N vocabolario

vocal [ˈvəʊkl] ADJ (Mus) vocale; (communication) verbale; (noisy) rumoroso(-a)

vocal cords NPL corde fpl vocali

vocalist [ˈvəʊkəlɪst] N cantante mf (in un gruppo)

vocation [vəʊˈkeɪʃən] N vocazione f

vocational [vəʊˈkeɪʃənl] ADJ professionale; **~ guidance** orientamento professionale; **~ training** formazione f professionale

vociferous [vəˈsɪfərəs] ADJ rumoroso(-a)

vodka [ˈvɒdkə] N vodka f inv

vogue [vəʊg] N moda; (popularity) popolarità, voga; **to be in ~**, **be the ~** essere di moda

voice [vɔɪs] N voce f ▶ VT (opinion) esprimere; **in a loud/soft ~** a voce alta/bassa; **to give ~ to** esprimere

voice mail N servizio di segreteria telefonica

voice-over [ˈvɔɪsəʊvəʳ] N voce f fuori campo

void [vɔɪd] N vuoto ▶ ADJ (invalid) nullo(-a); (empty): **~ of** privo(-a) di

voile [vɔɪl] N voile m

vol. ABBR (= volume) vol.

volatile [ˈvɒlətaɪl] ADJ volatile; (fig) volubile

volcanic [vɒlˈkænɪk] ADJ vulcanico(-a)

volcano [vɒlˈkeɪnəʊ] (pl **volcanoes**) N vulcano

volition [vəˈlɪʃən] N: **of one's own ~** di propria volontà

volley [ˈvɒlɪ] N (of gunfire) salva; (of stones etc) raffica, gragnola; (Tennis etc) volata

volleyball [ˈvɒlɪbɔːl] N pallavolo f

volt [vəʊlt] N volt m inv

voltage [ˈvəʊltɪdʒ] N tensione f, voltaggio; **high/low ~** alta/bassa tensione

voluble [ˈvɒljubl] ADJ loquace, ciarliero(-a)

volume [ˈvɒljuːm] N volume m; (of tank) capacità f inv; **~ one/two** (of book) volume primo/

secondo; **his expression spoke volumes** la sua espressione lasciava capire tutto

volume control N (Radio, TV) regolatore m or manopola del volume

volume discount N (Comm) vantaggio sul volume di vendita

voluminous [vəˈluːmɪnəs] ADJ voluminoso(-a); (notes etc) abbondante

voluntarily [ˈvɒləntrɪlɪ] ADV volontariamente; gratuitamente

voluntary [ˈvɒləntərɪ] ADJ volontario(-a); (unpaid) gratuito(-a), non retribuito(-a)

voluntary liquidation N (Comm) liquidazione f volontaria

volunteer [vɒlənˈtɪəʳ] N volontario(-a) ▶ VT offrire volontariamente ▶ VI (Mil) arruolarsi volontario(-a); **to ~ to do** offrire (volontariamente) di fare

voluptuous [vəˈlʌptjuəs] ADJ voluttuoso(-a)

vomit [ˈvɒmɪt] N vomito ▶ VT, VI vomitare

voracious [vəˈreɪʃəs] ADJ (appetite) smisurato(-a); (reader) avido(-a)

vote [vəʊt] N voto, suffragio; (cast) voto; (franchise) diritto di voto ▶ VI votare ▶ VT (gen) votare; (sum of money etc) votare a favore di; (propose): **to ~ that** approvare la proposta che; **to ~ to do sth** votare a favore di fare qc; **he was voted secretary** è stato eletto segretario; **to put sth to the ~**, **to take a ~ on sth** mettere qc ai voti; **~ for/against** voto a favore/contrario; **to pass a ~ of confidence/no confidence** dare il voto di fiducia/sfiducia; **~ of thanks** discorso di ringraziamento

voter [ˈvəʊtəʳ] N elettore(-trice)

voting [ˈvəʊtɪŋ] N scrutinio

voting paper N (BRIT) scheda elettorale

voting right N diritto di voto

vouch [vautʃ]: **to ~ for** vt fus farsi garante di

voucher [ˈvautʃəʳ] N (for meal, petrol) buono; (receipt) ricevuta; **travel ~** voucher m inv, tagliando

vow [vau] N voto, promessa solenne ▶ VI giurare; **to take** or **make a ~ to do sth** fare voto di fare qc ▶ VT: **to ~ to do/that** giurare di fare/che

vowel [ˈvauəl] N vocale f

voyage [ˈvɔɪɪdʒ] N viaggio per mare, traversata

voyeur [vwɑːˈjɜːʳ] N guardone(-a)

VP N ABBR (= vice-president) V.P.

vs ABBR (= versus) contro

VSO N ABBR (BRIT: = Voluntary Service Overseas) servizio volontario in paesi sottosviluppati

VT, Vt. ABBR (US) = **Vermont**

vulgar [ˈvʌlgəʳ] ADJ volgare

vulgarity [vʌlˈgærɪtɪ] N volgarità f inv

vulnerability [vʌlnərəˈbɪlɪtɪ] N vulnerabilità f inv

vulnerable [ˈvʌlnərəbl] ADJ vulnerabile

vulture [ˈvʌltʃəʳ] N avvoltoio

W, w [ˈdʌbljuː] N (*letter*) W, w *m inv or f inv*; **W for William** ≈ W come Washington

W ABBR (= *west*) O; (*Elec*: = *watt*) w

WA ABBR (*US*) = **Washington**

wad [wɔd] N (*of cotton wool, paper*) tampone *m*; (*of banknotes etc*) fascio

wadding [ˈwɔdɪŋ] N imbottitura

waddle [ˈwɔdl] VI camminare come una papera

wade [weɪd] VI: **to ~ through** camminare a stento in; (*fig: book*) leggere con fatica ▶ VT guadare

wafer [ˈweɪfəʳ] N (*Culin*) cialda; (*Rel*) ostia; (*Comput*) wafer *m inv*

wafer-thin [ˈweɪfəˈθɪn] ADJ molto sottile

waffle [ˈwɔfl] N (*Culin*) cialda; (*col*) ciance *fpl*; riempitivo ▶ VI (*col*) cianciare; parlare a vuoto

waffle iron N stampo per cialde

waft [wɔft] VT portare ▶ VI diffondersi

wag [wæg] VT agitare, muovere ▶ VI agitarsi; **the dog wagged its tail** il cane scodinzolò

wage [weɪdʒ] N (*also*: **wages**) salario, paga ▶ VT: **to ~ war** fare la guerra; **a day's wages** un giorno di paga

wage claim N rivendicazione *f* salariale

wage differential N differenza di salario

wage earner N salariato(-a)

wage freeze N blocco dei salari

wage packet N (*BRIT*) busta *f* paga *inv*

wager [ˈweɪdʒəʳ] N scommessa

waggle [ˈwægl] VT dimenare, agitare ▶ VI dimenarsi, agitarsi

wagon, waggon [ˈwægən] N (*horse-drawn*) carro; (*truck*) furgone *m*; (*BRIT Rail*) vagone *m* (merci)

wail [weɪl] N gemito; (*of siren*) urlo ▶ VI gemere; urlare

waist [weɪst] N vita, cintola

waistcoat [ˈweɪskəut] N (*BRIT*) panciotto, gilè *m inv*

waistline [ˈweɪstlaɪn] N (giro di) vita

wait [weɪt] N attesa ▶ VI aspettare, attendere; **to ~ for** aspettare; **~ for me, please** aspettami,

per favore; **to keep sb waiting** far aspettare qn; **~ a moment!** (aspetti) un momento!; **"repairs while you ~"** "riparazioni lampo"; **I can't ~ to ...** (*fig*) non vedo l'ora di ...; **to lie in ~ for** stare in agguato a
▶ **wait behind** VI rimanere (ad aspettare)
▶ **wait on** VT FUS servire
▶ **wait up** VI restare alzato(-a) (ad aspettare); **don't ~ up for me** non rimanere alzato per me

waiter [ˈweɪtəʳ] N cameriere *m*

waiting [ˈweɪtɪŋ] N: **"no ~"** (*BRIT Aut*) "divieto di sosta"

waiting list N lista d'attesa

waiting room N sala d'aspetto *or* d'attesa

waitress [ˈweɪtrɪs] N cameriera

waive [weɪv] VT rinunciare a, abbandonare

waiver [ˈweɪvəʳ] N rinuncia

wake [weɪk] (*pt* **woke** [wəuk] *or* **waked**, *pp* **woken** [ˈwəukn] *or* **waked**) VT (*also*: **wake up**) svegliare ▶ VI (*also*: **wake up**) svegliarsi ▶ N (*for dead person*) veglia funebre; (*Naut*) scia; **to ~ up to sth** (*fig*) rendersi conto di qc; **in the ~ of** sulla scia di; **to follow in sb's ~** (*fig*) seguire le tracce di qn

wakeboard [ˈweɪkbɔːd] N wakeboard *m inv* ▶ VI fare il wakeboard

waken [ˈweɪkn] VT, VI = **wake**

Wales [weɪlz] N Galles *m*

La **National Assembly for Wales** fu istituita nel 1998, dopo che la maggioranza dell'elettorato gallese si era espressa a favore della decentralizzazione nel referendum indetto l'anno precedente. Rispetto al parlamento scozzese ha un potere legislativo più limitato, ma con l'approvazione di una legge nel 2006 si è iniziato un processo di equiparazione fra le due assemblee. Presieduta dal *First Minister*, è composta da 60 deputati, indicati come *AMs* (*Assembly Members*), eletti ogni cinque anni.

walk [wɔːk] N passeggiata; (*short*) giretto; (*gait*) passo, andatura; (*path*) sentiero; (*in park etc*) sentiero, vialetto ▶ VI camminare; (*for pleasure, exercise*) passeggiare ▶ VT (*distance*) fare *or* percorrere

a piedi; (*dog*) accompagnare, portare a passeggiare; **10 minutes' ~ from** 10 minuti di cammino *or* a piedi da; **to go for a ~** andare a fare quattro passi; andare a fare una passeggiata; **from all walks of life** di tutte le condizioni sociali; **to ~ in one's sleep** essere sonnambulo(-a); **I'll ~ you home** ti accompagno a casa
▸ **walk out** VI (*go out*) uscire; (*as protest*) uscire (in segno di protesta); (*audience*) andarsene; (*strike*) scendere in sciopero; **to ~ out on sb** piantare in asso qn

walkabout ['wɔːkəbaut] N: **to go (on a) ~** avere incontri informali col pubblico (*durante una visita ufficiale*)

walker ['wɔːkəʳ] N (*person*) camminatore(-trice)

walkie-talkie ['wɔːkɪ'tɔːkɪ] N walkie-talkie *m inv*

walking ['wɔːkɪŋ] N camminare *m*; **it's within ~ distance** ci si arriva a piedi

walking holiday N vacanza fatta di lunghe camminate

walking shoes NPL scarpe *fpl* da passeggio

walking stick N bastone *m* da passeggio

walk-on ['wɔːkɔn] ADJ (*Theat: part*) da comparsa

walkout ['wɔːkaut] N (*of workers*) sciopero senza preavviso *or* a sorpresa

walkover ['wɔːkəuvəʳ] N (*col*) vittoria facile, gioco da ragazzi

walkway ['wɔːkweɪ] N passaggio pedonale

wall [wɔːl] N muro; (*internal, of tunnel, cave*) parete *f*; **to go to the ~** (*fig: firm etc*) fallire
▸ **wall in** VT (*garden etc*) circondare con un muro

wall cupboard N pensile *m*

walled [wɔːld] ADJ (*city*) fortificato(-a)

wallet ['wɔlɪt] N portafoglio

wallflower ['wɔːlflauəʳ] N violacciocca; **to be a ~** (*fig*) fare da tappezzeria

wall hanging N tappezzeria

wallop ['wɔləp] VT (*col: person*) suonarle a

wallow ['wɔləu] VI sguazzare, rotolarsi; **to ~ in one's grief** crogiolarsi nel proprio dolore

wallpaper ['wɔːlpeɪpəʳ] N carta da parati; (*Comput*) sfondo ▸ VT (*room*) mettere la carta da parati in

wall-to-wall ['wɔːltə'wɔːl] ADJ: **~ carpeting** moquette *f*

walnut ['wɔːlnʌt] N noce *f*; (*tree*) noce *m*

walrus ['wɔːlrəs] (*pl ~ or* **walruses**) N tricheco

waltz [wɔːlts] N valzer *m inv* ▸ VI ballare il valzer

wan [wɔn] ADJ pallido(-a), smorto(-a); triste

wand [wɔnd] N (*also:* **magic wand**) bacchetta (magica)

wander ['wɔndəʳ] VI (*person*) girare senza meta, girovagare; (*thoughts*) vagare; (*river*) serpeggiare
▸ VT girovagare per

wanderer ['wɔndərəʳ] N vagabondo(-a)

wandering ['wɔndrɪŋ] ADJ (*tribe*) nomade; (*min-*

strel, actor) girovago(-a); (*path, river*) tortuoso(-a); (*glance, mind*) distratto(-a)

wane [weɪn] VI (*moon*) calare; (*reputation*) declinare

wangle ['wæŋgl] (BRIT *col*) VT procurare (con l'astuzia) ▸ N astuzia

wanker ['wæŋkəʳ] N (!) segaiolo (!); (*as insult*) coglione (!) *m*

want [wɔnt] VT volere; (*need*) aver bisogno di; (*lack*) mancare di ▸ N (*poverty*) miseria, povertà
■ **wants** NPL (*needs*) bisogni *mpl*; **for ~ of** per mancanza di; **to ~ to do** volere fare; **to ~ sb to do** volere che qn faccia; **you're wanted on the phone** la vogliono al telefono; **"cook wanted"** "cercasi cuoco"

want ads NPL (US) piccoli annunci *mpl*

wanted ADJ (*criminal*) ricercato(-a); **"~"** (*in adverts*) "cercasi"

wanting ['wɔntɪŋ] ADJ: **to be ~ (in)** mancare (di); **to be found ~** non risultare all'altezza

wanton ['wɔntn] ADJ sfrenato(-a); senza motivo

war [wɔːʳ] N guerra; **to go to ~** entrare in guerra; **to make ~ (on)** far guerra (a)

warble ['wɔːbl] N (*of bird*) trillo ▸ VI trillare

war cry N grido di guerra

ward [wɔːd] N (*in hospital: room*) corsia; (: *section*) reparto; (*Pol*) circoscrizione *f*; (*Law: child: also:* **ward of court**) pupillo(-a)
▸ **ward off** VT parare, schivare

warden ['wɔːdn] N (*of institution*) direttore(-trice); (*of park, game reserve*) guardiano(-a); (BRIT: *also:* **traffic warden**) addetto(-a) al controllo del traffico e del parcheggio

warder ['wɔːdəʳ] N (BRIT) guardia carceraria

wardrobe ['wɔːdrəub] N (*cupboard*) guardaroba *m inv*, armadio; (*clothes*) guardaroba; (*Theat*) costumi *mpl*

warehouse ['wɛəhaus] N magazzino

wares [wɛəz] NPL merci *fpl*

warfare ['wɔːfɛəʳ] N guerra

war game N war game *m inv*

warhead ['wɔːhɛd] N (*Mil*) testata, ogiva

warily ['wɛərɪlɪ] ADV cautamente, con prudenza

warlike ['wɔːlaɪk] ADJ guerriero(-a)

warm [wɔːm] ADJ caldo(-a); (*welcome, applause*) caloroso(-a); (*person, greeting*) cordiale; (*heart*) d'oro; (*supporter*) convinto(-a); **it's ~** fa caldo; **I'm ~** ho caldo; **to keep sth ~** tenere qc al caldo; **with my warmest thanks** con i miei più sentiti ringraziamenti
▸ **warm up** VI scaldarsi, riscaldarsi; (*athlete, discussion*) riscaldarsi ▸ VT scaldare, riscaldare; (*engine*) far scaldare

warm-blooded ['wɔːm'blʌdɪd] ADJ a sangue caldo

war memorial N monumento ai caduti

warm-hearted [wɔːmˈhɑːtɪd] ADJ affettuoso(-a)

warmly [ˈwɔːmlɪ] ADV caldamente; (applaud, welcome) calorosamente; vivamente; (dress) con abiti pesanti

warmonger [ˈwɔːmʌŋgəʳ] N guerrafondaio

warmongering [ˈwɔːmʌŋgrɪŋ] N bellicismo

warmth [wɔːmθ] N calore m

warm-up [ˈwɔːmʌp] N (Sport) riscaldamento

warn [wɔːn] VT avvertire, avvisare; **to ~ sb not to do sth** or **against doing sth** avvertire or avvisare qn di non fare qc; **to ~ sb that** avvertire or avvisare qn che

warning [ˈwɔːnɪŋ] N avvertimento; (notice) avviso; (signal) segnalazione f; **without (any) ~** senza preavviso; **gale ~** avviso di burrasca

warning light N spia luminosa

warning triangle N (Aut) triangolo

warp [wɔːp] N (Textiles) ordito ▶ VI deformarsi ▶ VT deformare; (fig) corrompere

warpath [ˈwɔːpɑːθ] N: **to be on the ~** (fig) essere sul sentiero di guerra

warped [wɔːpt] ADJ (wood) curvo(-a); (fig: character, sense of humour etc) contorto(-a)

warrant [ˈwɔrnt] N (voucher) buono; (Law: to arrest) mandato di cattura; (: to search) mandato di perquisizione ▶ VT (justify, merit) giustificare

warrant officer N sottufficiale m

warranty [ˈwɔrəntɪ] N garanzia; **under ~** (Comm) in garanzia

warren [ˈwɔrən] N (of rabbits) tana

warring [ˈwɔːrɪŋ] ADJ (interests etc) opposto(-a), in lotta; (nations) in guerra

warrior [ˈwɔrɪəʳ] N guerriero(-a)

Warsaw [ˈwɔːsɔː] N Varsavia

warship [ˈwɔːʃɪp] N nave f da guerra

wart [wɔːt] N verruca

wartime [ˈwɔːtaɪm] N: **in ~** in tempo di guerra

wary [ˈwɛərɪ] ADJ prudente; **to be ~ about** or **of doing sth** andare cauto nel fare qc

was [wɔz] PT of **be**

wash [wɔʃ] VT lavare; (sweep, carry: sea etc) portare, trascinare ▶ VI lavarsi; (sea): **to ~ over/ against sth** infrangersi su/contro qc ▶ N lavaggio; (of ship) scia; **to give sth a ~** lavare qc, dare una lavata a qc; **to have a ~** lavarsi; **he was washed overboard** fu trascinato in mare (dalle onde)
▶ **wash away** VT (stain) togliere lavando; (river etc) trascinare via
▶ **wash down** VT lavare
▶ **wash off** VI andare via con il lavaggio
▶ **wash up** VI (BRIT) lavare i piatti; (US: have a wash) lavarsi

washable [ˈwɔʃəbl] ADJ lavabile

washbasin [ˈwɔʃbeɪsn], (US) **washbowl** [ˈwɔʃbəul] N lavabo

washcloth [ˈwɔʃklɔθ] N (US) pezzuola (per lavarsi)

washer [ˈwɔʃəʳ] N (Tech) rondella

washing [ˈwɔʃɪŋ] N (BRIT: linen etc) bucato; **dirty ~** biancheria da lavare

washing line N (BRIT) corda del bucato

washing machine N lavatrice f

washing powder N (BRIT) detersivo (in polvere)

Washington [ˈwɔʃɪŋtən] N Washington f

washing-up [wɔʃɪŋˈʌp] N (dishes) piatti mpl sporchi; **to do the ~** lavare i piatti

washing-up liquid N (BRIT) detersivo liquido (per stoviglie)

wash-out [ˈwɔʃaut] N (col) disastro

washroom [ˈwɔʃrum] N gabinetto

wasn't [ˈwɔznt] = **was not**

Wasp, WASP [wɔsp] N ABBR (US: = White Anglo-Saxon Protestant) W.A.S.P. m (protestante bianco anglosassone)

wasp [wɔsp] N vespa

waspish [ˈwɔspɪʃ] ADJ litigioso(-a)

wastage [ˈweɪstɪdʒ] N spreco; (in manufacturing) scarti mpl

waste [weɪst] N spreco; (of time) perdita; (rubbish) rifiuti mpl; (also: **household waste**) immondizie fpl ▶ ADJ (material) di scarto; (food) avanzato(-a); (energy, heat) sprecato(-a); (land, ground: in city) abbandonato(-a); (: in country) incolto(-a) ▶ VT sprecare; (time, opportunity) perdere ▪ **wastes** NPL distesa desolata; **it's a ~ of money** sono soldi sprecati; **to go to ~** andare sprecato; **to lay ~** devastare
▶ **waste away** VI deperire

wastebasket [ˈweɪstbɑːskɪt] N = **wastepaper basket**

waste disposal, waste disposal unit N (BRIT) eliminatore m di rifiuti

wasteful [ˈweɪstful] ADJ sprecone(-a); (process) dispendioso(-a)

waste ground N (BRIT) terreno incolto or abbandonato

wasteland [ˈweɪstlænd] N terra desolata

wastepaper basket [ˈweɪstpeɪpə-] N cestino per la carta straccia

waste pipe N tubo di scarico

waste products NPL (Industry) materiali mpl di scarto

waster [ˈweɪstəʳ] N (pej) buono(-a) a nulla

watch [wɔtʃ] N (wristwatch) orologio (da polso); (act of watching, vigilance) sorveglianza; (guard: Mil, Naut) guardia; (Naut: spell of duty) quarto ▶ VT (look at) osservare; (: match, programme) guardare; (spy on, guard) sorvegliare, tenere d'occhio; (be careful of) fare attenzione a ▶ VI osservare, guardare; (keep guard) fare or montare la guardia; **to keep a close ~ on sb/sth** tener bene

d'occhio qn/qc; **~ how you drive/what you're doing** attento a come guidi/quel che fai
▶ **watch out** vi fare attenzione

watchband ['wɔtʃbænd] N (US) cinturino da orologio

watchdog ['wɔtʃdɔg] N cane m da guardia; (fig) sorvegliante mf

watchful ['wɔtʃful] ADJ attento(-a), vigile

watchmaker ['wɔtʃmeɪkər] N orologiaio(-a)

watchman ['wɔtʃmən] N (irreg) guardiano; (also: **night watchman**) guardiano notturno

watch stem N (US) corona di carica

watch strap N cinturino da orologio

watchword ['wɔtʃwəːd] N parola d'ordine

water ['wɔːtər] N acqua ▶ VT (plant) annaffiare ▶ VI (eyes) lacrimare; **in British waters** nelle acque territoriali britanniche; **I'd like a drink of ~** vorrei un bicchier d'acqua; **to pass ~** orinare; **to make sb's mouth ~** far venire l'acquolina in bocca a qn
▶ **water down** VT (milk) diluire; (fig: story) edulcorare

waterboarding ['wɔːtəbɔːdɪŋ] N water-boarding m inv

water closet N (BRIT) W.C. m inv, gabinetto

watercolour, (US) **watercolor** ['wɔːtəkʌlər] N (picture) acquerello ▪ **watercolours** NPL colori mpl per acquerelli

water-cooled ['wɔːtəkuːld] ADJ raffreddato(-a) ad acqua

watercress ['wɔːtəkrɛs] N crescione m

waterfall ['wɔːtəfɔːl] N cascata

waterfront ['wɔːtəfrʌnt] N (seafront) lungomare m; (at docks) banchina

water heater N scaldabagno

water hole N pozza d'acqua

water ice N (BRIT) sorbetto

watering can ['wɔːtərɪŋ-] N annaffiatoio

water level N livello dell'acqua; (of flood) livello delle acque

water lily N ninfea

waterline ['wɔːtəlaɪn] N (Naut) linea di galleggiamento

waterlogged ['wɔːtəlɔgd] ADJ saturo(-a) d'acqua; imbevuto(-a) d'acqua; (football pitch etc) allagato(-a)

watermark ['wɔːtəmɑːk] N (on paper) filigrana

watermelon ['wɔːtəmɛlən] N anguria, cocomero

water polo N pallanuoto f

waterproof ['wɔːtəpruːf] ADJ impermeabile

water-repellent ['wɔːtərɪpɛlənt] ADJ idrorepellente

watershed ['wɔːtəʃɛd] N (Geo, fig) spartiacque m

water-skiing ['wɔːtəskiːɪŋ] N sci m acquatico

water softener N addolcitore m; (substance) anti-calcare m

water tank N serbatoio d'acqua

watertight ['wɔːtətaɪt] ADJ stagno(-a)

water vapour N vapore m acqueo

waterway ['wɔːtəweɪ] N corso d'acqua navigabile

waterworks ['wɔːtəwəːks] NPL impianto idrico

watery ['wɔːtərɪ] ADJ (colour) slavato(-a); (coffee) acquoso(-a)

watt [wɔt] N watt m inv

wattage ['wɔtɪdʒ] N wattaggio

wattle ['wɔtl] N graticcio

wave [weɪv] N onda; (of hand) gesto, segno; (in hair) ondulazione f; (fig: of enthusiasm, strikes etc) ondata ▶ VI fare un cenno con la mano; (branches, grass) ondeggiare; (flag) sventolare ▶ VT (hand) fare un gesto con; (handkerchief) sventolare; (stick) brandire; (hair) ondulare; **short/medium/long ~** (Radio) onde corte/medie/lunghe; **the new ~** (Cine, Mus) la new wave; **to ~ sb goodbye, to ~ goodbye to sb** fare un cenno d'addio a qn; **he waved us over to his table** ci invitò con un cenno al suo tavolo
▶ **wave aside**, **wave away** VT (person): **to ~ sb aside** fare cenno a qn di spostarsi; (fig: suggestion, objection) respingere, rifiutare; (: doubts) scacciare

waveband ['weɪvbænd] N gamma di lunghezze d'onda

wavelength ['weɪvlɛŋθ] N lunghezza d'onda

waver ['weɪvər] VI esitare; (voice) tremolare

wavy ['weɪvɪ] ADJ ondulato(-a); ondeggiante

wax [wæks] N cera ▶ VT dare la cera a; (car) lucidare ▶ VI (moon) crescere

waxworks ['wækswəːks] NPL cere fpl; museo delle cere

way [weɪ] N via, strada; (path, access) passaggio; (distance) distanza; (direction) parte f, direzione f; (manner) modo, stile m; (habit) abitudine f; (condition) condizione f; **which ~? — this ~** da che parte or in quale direzione? — da questa parte or per di qua; **to crawl one's ~ to ... ** raggiungere ... strisciando; **he lied his ~ out of it** se l'è cavata mentendo; **to lose one's ~** perdere la strada; **on the ~** (en route) per strada; (expected) in arrivo; **you pass it on your ~ home** ci passi davanti andando a casa; **to be on one's ~** essere in cammino or sulla strada; **to be in the ~** bloccare il passaggio; (fig) essere tra i piedi or d'impiccio; **to keep out of sb's ~** evitare qn; **it's a long ~ away** è molto lontano da qui; **the village is rather out of the ~** il villaggio è abbastanza fuori mano; **to go out of one's ~ to do** (fig) mettercela tutta or fare di tutto per fare; **to be under ~** (work, project) essere in corso; **to lose one's ~** perdere la strada; **to make ~ (for sb/sth)** far strada (a qn/qc); (fig) lasciare il posto or far largo (a qn/qc); **to get one's own ~** fare come si vuole; **put it the right ~ up** (BRIT) mettilo in piedi dalla parte giusta; **to be the wrong ~ round** essere al contrario; **he's in a bad ~** è ridotto male; **in a ~** in un certo senso; **in some ways** sotto certi aspetti; **in the ~ of** come; **by ~ of** (through) attraverso; (as a sort of) come; **"~ in"** (BRIT) "entrata", "ingresso"; **"~ out"** (BRIT) "uscita"; **the ~ back** la via del ritorno; **this ~ and that** di qua e di là; **"give ~"** (BRIT Aut). "dare la precedenza"; **no ~!** (col) neanche per idea!; **by the ~ ...** a proposito ...

> Use **il modo** for the way something is done, e.g. *She looked at me in a strange way*. **Mi ha guardato in modo strano**. Use **la moda** to refer to fashion, e.g. *It's no longer in fashion*. **Non è più di moda**.

waybill ['weɪbɪl] N (*Comm*) bolla di accompagnamento

waylay [weɪ'leɪ] VT (*irreg: like* **lay**) tendere un agguato a; attendere al passaggio; (*fig*): **I got waylaid** ho avuto un contrattempo

wayside ['weɪsaɪd] N bordo della strada; **to fall by the ~** (*fig*) perdersi lungo la strada

way station N (*US Rail*) stazione *f* secondaria; (*fig*) tappa

wayward ['weɪwəd] ADJ capriccioso(-a); testardo(-a)

WC ['dʌblju'siː] N ABBR (BRIT: = *water closet*) W.C. *m inv*, gabinetto

WCC N ABBR (= *World Council of Churches*) Consiglio Ecumenico delle Chiese

we [wiː] PL PRON noi; **here we are** eccoci

weak [wiːk] ADJ debole; (*health*) precario(-a); (*beam etc*) fragile; (*tea, coffee*) leggero(-a); **to grow ~(er)** indebolirsi

weaken ['wiːkən] VI indebolirsi ▶ VT indebolire

weak-kneed ['wiːk'niːd] ADJ (*fig*) debole, codardo(-a)

weakling ['wiːklɪŋ] N smidollato(-a); debole *mf*

weakly ['wiːklɪ] ADJ deboluccio(-a), gracile ▶ ADV debolmente

weakness ['wiːknɪs] N debolezza; (*fault*) punto debole, difetto; **to have a ~ for** avere un debole per

wealth [wɛlθ] N (*money, resources*) ricchezza, ricchezze *fpl*; (*of details*) abbondanza, profusione *f*

wealth tax N imposta sul patrimonio

wealthy ['wɛlθɪ] ADJ ricco(-a)

wean [wiːn] VT svezzare

weapon ['wɛpən] N arma; **weapons of mass destruction** armi di distruzione di massa

wear [wɛəʳ] (*pt* **wore** [wɔːʳ], *pp* **worn** [wɔːn]) N (*use*) uso; (*deterioration through use*) logorio, usura; (*clothing*): **sports/baby ~** abbigliamento sportivo/per neonati ▶ VT (*clothes*) portare; (*put on*)

mettersi; (*look, smile, beard etc*) avere; (*damage: through use*) consumare ▶ VI (*last*) durare; (*rub etc through*) consumarsi; **~ and tear** usura, consumo; **town/evening ~** abiti *mpl or* tenuta da città/sera; **to ~ a hole in sth** bucare qc a furia di usarlo

▶ **wear away** VT consumare; erodere ▶ VI consumarsi; essere eroso(-a)

▶ **wear down** VT consumare; (*strength*) esaurire

▶ **wear off** VI sparire lentamente

▶ **wear on** VI passare

▶ **wear out** VT consumare; (*person, strength*) esaurire

wearable ['wɛərəbl] ADJ indossabile

wearily ['wɪərɪlɪ] ADV stancamente

weariness ['wɪərɪnɪs] N stanchezza

wearisome ['wɪərɪsəm] ADJ (*tiring*) estenuante; (*boring*) noioso(-a)

weary ['wɪərɪ] ADJ stanco(-a); (*tiring*) faticoso(-a) ▶ VT stancare ▶ VI: **to ~ of** stancarsi di

weasel ['wiːzl] N (*Zool*) donnola

weather ['wɛðəʳ] N tempo ▶ VT (*wood*) stagionare; (*storm, crisis*) superare; **what's the ~ like?** che tempo fa?; **under the ~** (*fig: ill*) poco bene

weather-beaten ['wɛðəbiːtn] ADJ (*person*) segnato(-a) dalle intemperie; (*building*) logorato(-a) dalle intemperie

weather forecast N previsioni *fpl* del tempo, bollettino meteorologico

weatherman ['wɛðəmæn] N (*irreg*) meteorologo

weatherproof ['wɛðəpruːf] ADJ (*garment*) impermeabile

weather report N bollettino meteorologico

weave [wiːv] (*pt* **wove** [wəʊv], *pp* **woven** ['wəʊvn]) VT (*cloth*) tessere; (*basket*) intrecciare ▶ VI (*pt, pp* **weaved**) (*fig: move in and out*) zigzagare

weaver ['wiːvəʳ] N tessitore(-trice)

weaving ['wiːvɪŋ] N tessitura

web [wɛb] N (*of spider*) ragnatela; (*on foot*) palma; (*fabric, also fig*) tessuto; **the (World Wide) W~** la Rete

web address N indirizzo *m* Internet *inv*

webbed [wɛbd] ADJ (*foot*) palmato(-a)

webbing ['wɛbɪŋ] N (*on chair*) cinghie *fpl*

webcam ['wɛbkæm] N webcam *f inv*

webinar ['wɛbɪnɑːʳ] N (*Comput*) webinar *m inv*

webmail ['wɛbmeɪl] N (*Comput*) webmail *f*

web page N (*Comput*) pagina *f* web *inv*

website ['wɛbsaɪt] N (*Comput*) sito (Internet)

wed [wɛd] (*pt, pp* **wedded** ['wɛdɪd]) VT sposare ▶ VI sposarsi ▶ N: **the newly-weds** gli sposi novelli

Wed. ABBR (= *Wednesday*) mer.

we'd [wiːd] = **we had; we would**

wedded ['wɛdɪd] PT, PP *of* **wed**

wedding ['wɛdɪŋ] N matrimonio; **silver/golden ~** nozze *fpl* d'argento/d'oro

W

wedding anniversary N anniversario di matrimonio

wedding day N giorno delle nozze *or* del matrimonio

wedding dress N abito nuziale

wedding present N regalo di nozze

wedding ring N fede f

wedge [wɛdʒ] N (*of wood etc*) cuneo; (*under door etc*) zeppa; (*of cake*) spicchio, fetta ▶ VT mettere una zeppa sotto (*or* in); (*fix*) fissare con zeppe; (*pack tightly*) incastrare; **to ~ a door open** tenere aperta una porta con una zeppa

wedge-heeled shoes [ˈwɛdʒhiːld-] NPL scarpe *fpl* con tacco a zeppa

wedlock [ˈwɛdlɔk] N vincolo matrimoniale

Wednesday [ˈwɛnzdɪ] N mercoledì *m inv*; *see also* **Tuesday**

wee [wiː] ADJ (*SCOTTISH*) piccolo(-a)

weed [wiːd] N erbaccia ▶ VT diserbare ▶ **weed out** VT fare lo spoglio di

weed-killer [ˈwiːdkɪlər] N diserbante *m*

weedy [ˈwiːdɪ] ADJ (*man*) allampanato

week [wiːk] N settimana; **once/twice a ~** una volta/due volte alla settimana; **in 2 weeks' time** fra 2 settimane, fra 15 giorni; **Tuesday ~, a ~ on Tuesday** martedì a otto; **a ~ today** oggi a otto

weekday [ˈwiːkdeɪ] N giorno feriale; (*Comm*) giornata lavorativa; **on weekdays** durante la settimana

weekend [wiːkˈɛnd] N fine settimana *m inv or f inv*, weekend *m inv*

weekend case N borsa da viaggio

weekly [ˈwiːklɪ] ADV ogni settimana, settimanalmente ▶ ADJ, N settimanale (*m*)

weep [wiːp] (*pt, pp* **wept** [wɛpt]) VI (*person*) piangere; (*Med: wound etc*) essudare

weeping willow [ˈwiːpɪŋ-] N salice *m* piangente

weepy [ˈwiːpɪ] N (*col*) film *m inv* o storia strappalacrime *inv*

weft [wɛft] N (*Textiles*) trama

weigh [weɪ] VT, VI pesare; **to ~ anchor** salpare *or* levare l'ancora; **to ~ the pros and cons** valutare i pro e i contro ▶ **weigh down** VT (*branch*) piegare; (*fig: with worry*) opprimere, caricare ▶ **weigh out** VT (*goods*) pesare ▶ **weigh up** VT valutare

weighbridge [ˈweɪbrɪdʒ] N bascula

weighing machine [ˈweɪɪŋ-] N pesa

weight [weɪt] N peso; **sold by ~** venduto(-a) a peso; **weights and measures** pesi e misure; **to put on/lose ~** ingrassare/dimagrire

weighting [ˈweɪtɪŋ] N: **~ allowance** indennità *f inv* speciale (*per carovita ecc*)

weightlessness [ˈweɪtlɪsnɪs] N mancanza di peso

weightlifter [ˈweɪtlɪftər] N pesista *mf*

weightlifting N sollevamento pesi

weight training N: **to do ~** allenarsi con i pesi

weighty [ˈweɪtɪ] ADJ pesante; (*fig*) importante, grave

weir [wɪər] N diga

weird [wɪəd] ADJ strano(-a), bizzarro(-a); (*eerie*) soprannaturale

weirdo [ˈwɪədəu] N (*col*) tipo(-a) allucinante

welcome [ˈwɛlkəm] ADJ benvenuto(-a) ▶ N accoglienza, benvenuto ▶ VT accogliere cordialmente; (*also*: **bid welcome**) dare il benvenuto a; (*be glad of*) rallegrarsi di; **to be ~** essere il(la) benvenuto(-a); **to make sb ~** accogliere bene qn; **you're ~** (*after thanks*) prego; **you're ~ to try** provi pure

welcoming [ˈwɛlkəmɪŋ] ADJ accogliente

weld [wɛld] N saldatura ▶ VT saldare

welder [ˈwɛldər] N (*person*) saldatore *m*

welding [ˈwɛldɪŋ] N saldatura (autogena)

welfare [ˈwɛlfɛər] N benessere *m*

welfare state N stato sociale

welfare work N assistenza sociale

well [wɛl] N pozzo ▶ ADV bene ▶ ADJ: **to be ~** (*person*) stare bene ▶ EXCL allora!; ma!; ebbene!; **~ done!** bravo(-a)!; **get ~ soon!** guarisci presto!; **to do ~** andare bene; **to do ~ in sth** riuscire in qc; **to be doing ~** stare bene; **to think ~ of sb** avere una buona opinione di qn; **I don't feel ~** non mi sento bene; **as ~** (*in addition*) anche; **X as ~ as Y** sia X che Y; **he did as ~ as he could** ha fatto come meglio poteva; **you might as ~ tell me** potresti anche dirmelo; **it would be as ~ to ask** sarebbe bene chiedere; **~, as I was saying ...** dunque, come stavo dicendo ... ▶ **well up** VI (*tears, emotions*) sgorgare

we'll [wiːl] = **we will; we shall**

well-behaved [ˈwɛlbɪˈheɪvd] ADJ ubbidiente

well-being [ˈwɛlˈbiːɪŋ] N benessere *m*

well-bred [ˈwɛlˈbrɛd] ADJ educato(-a), beneducato(-a)

well-built [ˈwɛlˈbɪlt] ADJ (*person*) ben fatto(-a)

well-chosen [ˈwɛlˈtʃəuzn] ADJ (*remarks, words*) ben scelto(-a), appropriato(-a)

well-developed [ˈwɛldɪˈvɛləpt] ADJ sviluppato(-a)

well-disposed [ˈwɛldɪsˈpəuzd] ADJ: **~ to(wards)** bendisposto(-a) verso

well-dressed [ˈwɛlˈdrɛst] ADJ ben vestito(-a), vestito(-a) bene

well-earned [ˈwɛlˈəːnd] ADJ (*rest*) meritato(-a)

well-groomed [ˈwɛlˈgruːmd] ADJ curato(-a), azzimato(-a)

well-heeled [ˈwɛlˈhiːld] ADJ (*col: wealthy*) agiato(-a), facoltoso(-a)

wellies [ˈwɛlɪz] NPL (*BRIT col*) stivali *mpl* di gomma

well-informed [ˈwɛlɪnˈfɔːmd] ADJ ben informato(-a)

Wellington [ˈwɛlɪŋtən] N Wellington f

wellingtons [ˈwɛlɪŋtənz] NPL (also: **wellington boots**) stivali mpl di gomma

well-kept [ˈwɛlˈkɛpt] ADJ (house, grounds, secret) ben tenuto(-a); (hair, hands) ben curato(-a)

well-known [ˈwɛlˈnəun] ADJ noto(-a), famoso(-a)

well-mannered [ˈwɛlˈmænəd] ADJ ben educato(-a)

well-meaning [ˈwɛlˈmiːnɪŋ] ADJ ben intenzionato(-a)

well-nigh [ˈwɛlˈnaɪ] ADV: ~ **impossible** quasi impossibile

well-off [ˈwɛlˈɔf] ADJ benestante, danaroso(-a)

well-paid [wɛlˈpeɪd] ADJ ben pagato(-a)

well-read [ˈwɛlˈrɛd] ADJ colto(-a)

well-spoken [ˈwɛlˈspəukn] ADJ che parla bene

well-stocked [ˈwɛlˈstɔkt] ADJ (shop, larder) ben fornito(-a)

well-timed [ˈwɛlˈtaɪmd] ADJ opportuno(-a)

well-to-do [ˈwɛltəˈduː] ADJ abbiente, benestante

well-wisher [ˈwɛlwɪʃəʳ] N ammiratore(-trice); **letters from well-wishers** lettere fpl di incoraggiamento

well-woman clinic [ˈwɛlwumən-] N ≈ consultorio (familiare)

Welsh [wɛlʃ] ADJ gallese ▶ N (Ling) gallese m; **the ~** npl i gallesi; **the ~ National Assembly** il Parlamento gallese

Welshman [ˈwɛlʃmən] N (irreg) gallese m

Welsh rarebit N crostino al formaggio

Welshwoman [ˈwɛlʃwumən] N (irreg) gallese f

welter [ˈwɛltəʳ] N massa, mucchio

went [wɛnt] PT of **go**

wept [wɛpt] PT, PP of **weep**

were [wəːʳ] PT of **be**

we're [wɪəʳ] = **we are**

weren't [wəːnt] = **were not**

werewolf [ˈwɪəwulf] (pl **-wolves** [-wulvz]) N licantropo, lupo mannaro (col)

west [wɛst] N ovest m, occidente m, ponente m ▶ ADJ (a) ovest inv, occidentale ▶ ADV verso ovest; **the W~** l'Occidente

westbound [ˈwɛstbaund] ADJ (traffic) diretto(-a) a ovest; (carriageway) ovest inv

West Country N: **the ~** il sud-ovest dell'Inghilterra

westerly [ˈwɛstəlɪ] ADJ (wind) occidentale, da ovest

western [ˈwɛstən] ADJ occidentale, dell'ovest ▶ N (Cine) western m inv

westerner [ˈwɛstənəʳ] N occidentale mf

westernized [ˈwɛstənaɪzd] ADJ occidentalizzato(-a)

West German ADJ, N (formerly) tedesco(-a) occidentale

West Germany N (formerly) Germania Occidentale

West Indian ADJ delle Indie Occidentali ▶ N abitante mf (or originario(-a)) delle Indie Occidentali

West Indies [-ˈɪndɪz] NPL: **the ~** le Indie Occidentali

Westminster [ˈwɛstmɪnstəʳ] N il parlamento (britannico)

westward [ˈwɛstwəd], **westwards** [ˈwɛstwədz] ADV verso ovest

wet [wɛt] ADJ umido(-a), bagnato(-a); (soaked) fradicio(-a); (rainy) piovoso(-a) ▶ N (BRIT Pol) politico moderato ▶ VT: **to ~ one's pants** or **o.s.** farsi la pipì addosso; **to get ~** bagnarsi; **"~ paint"** "vernice fresca"

wet blanket N (fig) guastafeste mf

wetness [ˈwɛtnɪs] N umidità

wet suit N tuta da sub

we've [wiːv] = **we have**

whack [wæk] VT picchiare, battere

whacked [wækt] ADJ (col: tired) sfinito(-a), a pezzi

whale [weɪl] N (Zool) balena

whaler [ˈweɪləʳ] N (ship) baleniera

whaling [ˈweɪlɪŋ] N caccia alla balena

wharf [wɔːf] (pl **wharves** [wɔːvz]) N banchina

---

what [wɔt]

ADJ **1** (in direct/indirect questions) che; quale; **what size is it?** che taglia è?; **what colour is it?** di che colore è?; **what books do you want?** quali or che libri vuole?; **for what reason?** per quale motivo?

2 (in exclamations) che; **what a mess!** che disordine!

▶ PRON **1** (interrogative) che cosa, cosa, che; **what's in there?** cosa c'è lì dentro?; **what is his address?** qual è il suo indirizzo?; **what will it cost?** quanto costerà?; **what are you doing?** che or (che) cosa fai?; **what are you talking about?** di che cosa parli?; **what's happening?** che or (che) cosa succede?; **what is it called?** come si chiama?; **what about me?** e io?; **what about doing ...?** e se facessimo ...?

2 (relative) ciò che, quello che; **I saw what you did** ho visto quello che hai fatto; **I saw what was on the table** ho visto cosa c'era sul tavolo; **what I want is a cup of tea** ciò che voglio adesso è una tazza di tè

3 (indirect use) (che) cosa; **he asked me what she had said** mi ha chiesto che cosa avesse detto; **tell me what you're thinking about** dimmi a cosa stai pensando; **I don't know what to do** non so cosa fare

▶ EXCL (disbelieving) cosa!, come!

W

whatever [wɔt'ɛvə^r] ADJ: ~ **book** qualunque or qualsiasi libro + sub ▶ PRON: **do ~ is necessary/ you want** faccia qualunque or qualsiasi cosa sia necessaria/lei voglia; ~ **happens** qualunque cosa accada; **no reason ~** or **whatsoever** nessuna ragione affatto or al mondo; ~ **it costs** costi quello che costi; **nothing ~** proprio niente

whatsoever [wɔtsəu'ɛvə^r] ADJ, PRON = **whatever**

wheat [wiːt] N grano, frumento

wheatgerm ['wiːtdʒəːm] N germe m di grano

wheatmeal ['wiːtmiːl] N farina integrale di frumento

wheedle ['wiːdl] VT: **to ~ sb into doing sth** convincere qn a fare qc (con lusinghe); **to ~ sth out of sb** ottenere qc da qn (con lusinghe)

wheel [wiːl] N ruota; (Aut: also: **steering wheel**) volante m; (Naut) (ruota del) timone m ▶ VT spingere ▶ VI (birds) roteare; (also: **wheel round**) girare

wheelbarrow ['wiːlbærəu] N carriola

wheelbase ['wiːlbeɪs] N interasse m

wheelchair ['wiːltʃɛə^r] N sedia a rotelle

wheel clamp N (Aut): ~**s** ganasce fpl (per vetture in sosta vietata)

wheeler-dealer ['wiːlə'diːlə^r] N trafficone m, maneggione m

wheelie-bin ['wiːlɪbɪn] N (BRIT) bidone m (della spazzatura) a rotelle

wheeling ['wiːlɪŋ] N (pej): ~ **and dealing** maneggi mpl

wheeze [wiːz] N respiro affannoso ▶ VI ansimare

wheezy ['wiːzɪ] ADJ (person) che respira con affanno; (breath) sibilante

when [wɛn]

ADV quando; **when did it happen?** quando è successo?

▶ CONJ **1** (at, during, after the time that) quando; **she was reading when I came in** quando sono entrato lei leggeva; **that was when I needed you** era allora che avevo bisogno di te

2 (on, at which): **on the day when I met him** il giorno in cui l'ho incontrato; **one day when it was raining** un giorno che pioveva

3 (whereas) quando, mentre; **you said I was wrong when in fact I was right** mi hai detto che avevo torto, quando in realtà avevo ragione

whenever [wɛn'ɛvə^r] ADV quando mai ▶ CONJ quando; (every time that) ogni volta che; **I go ~ I can** ci vado ogni volta che posso

where [wɛə^r] ADV, CONJ dove; **this is ~** è qui che; ~ **are you from?** di dov'è?; ~ **possible** quando è possibile, se possibile

whereabouts ['wɛərəbauts] ADV dove ▶ N: **sb's** ~ luogo dove qn si trova

whereas [wɛər'æz] CONJ mentre

whereby [wɛə'baɪ] ADV (formal) per cui

whereupon [wɛərə'pɔn] ADV al che

wherever [wɛər'ɛvə^r] ADV dove mai ▶ CONJ dovunque + sub; (interrogative) dove mai; **sit ~ you like** si sieda dove vuole

wherewithal ['wɛəwɪðɔːl] N: **the ~ (to do sth)** i mezzi (per fare qc)

whet [wɛt] VT (tool) affilare; (appetite etc) stimolare

whether ['wɛðə^r] CONJ se; **I don't know ~ to accept or not** non so se accettare o no; **it's doubtful ~** è poco probabile che; ~ **you go or not** che lei vada o no

whey [weɪ] N siero

which [wɪtʃ]

ADJ **1** (interrogative: direct, indirect) quale; **which picture do you want?** quale quadro vuole?; **which one?** quale?; **which one of you did it?** chi di voi lo ha fatto?; **tell me which one you want** mi dica quale vuole

2: **in which case** nel qual caso; **by which time** e a quel punto

▶ PRON **1** (interrogative) quale; **which (of these) are yours?** quali di questi sono suoi?; **which of you are coming?** chi di voi viene?

2 (relative) che; (: indirect) cui, il (la) quale; **the apple which you ate/which is on the table** la mela che hai mangiato/che è sul tavolo; **the chair on which you are sitting** la sedia sulla quale or su cui sei seduto; **the book of which we were speaking** il libro del quale stavamo parlando; **he said he knew, which is true** ha detto che lo sapeva, il che è vero; **I don't mind which** non mi importa quale; **after which** dopo di che

whichever [wɪtʃ'ɛvə^r] ADJ: **take ~ book you prefer** prenda qualsiasi libro che preferisce; ~ **book you take** qualsiasi libro prenda; ~ **way you …** in qualunque modo lei … + sub

whiff [wɪf] N odore m; **to catch a ~ of sth** sentire l'odore di qc

while [waɪl] N momento ▶ CONJ mentre; (as long as) finché; (although) sebbene + sub; per quanto + sub; **for a ~** per un po'; **in a ~** tra poco; **all the ~** tutto il tempo; **we'll make it worth your ~** faremo in modo che le valga la pena
▶ **while away** VT (time) far passare

whilst [waɪlst] CONJ = **while**

whim [wɪm] N capriccio

whimper ['wɪmpə^r] N piagnucolio ▶ VI piagnucolare

whimsical ['wɪmzɪkl] ADJ (person) capriccioso(-a); (look) strano(-a)

whine [waɪn] N gemito ▶ VI gemere; uggiolare; piagnucolare

whip [wɪp] N frusta; (for riding) frustino; (Pol: person) capogruppo (che sovrintende alla disciplina dei colleghi di partito) ▶ VT frustare; (Culin: cream, eggs etc) sbattere; (snatch) sollevare (or estrarre) bruscamente
▶ **whip up** VT (cream) montare, sbattere; (col: meal) improvvisare; (: stir up: support, feeling) suscitare, stimolare

whiplash ['wɪplæʃ] N (Med: also: **whiplash injury**) colpo di frusta

whipped cream ['wɪpt-] N panna montata

whipping boy ['wɪpɪŋ-] N (fig) capro espiatorio

whip-round ['wɪpraund] N (BRIT) colletta

whirl [wə:l] N turbine m ▶ VT (far) girare rapidamente; (far) turbinare ▶ VI turbinare; (dancers) volteggiare; (leaves, water, dust) sollevarsi in un vortice

whirlpool ['wə:lpu:l] N mulinello

whirlwind ['wə:lwɪnd] N turbine m

whirr [wə:ʳ] VI ronzare

whisk [wɪsk] N (Culin) frusta; frullino ▶ VT sbattere, frullare; **to ~ sb away** or **off** portar via qn a tutta velocità

whiskers ['wɪskəz] NPL (of animal) baffi mpl; (of man) favoriti mpl

whisky, (IRISH, US) **whiskey** ['wɪskɪ] N whisky m inv

whisper ['wɪspəʳ] N bisbiglio, sussurro; (rumour) voce f ▶ VT, VI bisbigliare, sussurrare; **to ~ sth to sb** bisbigliare qc a qn

whispering ['wɪspərɪŋ] N bisbiglio

whist [wɪst] N (BRIT) whist m

whistle ['wɪsl] N (sound) fischio; (object) fischietto ▶ VI, VT fischiare; **to ~ a tune** fischiettare un motivetto

whistleblower ['wɪslbləuəʳ] N (in company, organization) whistleblower mf inv

whistleblowing ['wɪslbləuɪŋ] N (in company, organization) whistleblowing m inv

whistle-stop ['wɪslstɔp] ADJ: **~ tour** (Pol, fig) rapido giro

Whit [wɪt] N Pentecoste f

white [waɪt] ADJ bianco(-a); (with fear) pallido(-a) ▶ N bianco; (person) bianco(-a); **to turn** or **go ~** (person) sbiancare; (hair) diventare bianco; **the whites** (washing) i capi bianchi; **tennis whites** completo da tennis

whitebait ['waɪtbeɪt] N bianchetti mpl

whiteboard ['waɪtbɔ:d] N lavagna bianca; **interactive ~** lavagna interattiva

white-collar worker ['waɪtkɔlə-] N impiegato(-a)

white elephant N (fig) oggetto (or progetto) costoso ma inutile

white goods NPL (appliances) elettrodomestici mpl; (linens) biancheria per la casa

white-hot [waɪt'hɔt] ADJ (metal) incandescente

White House N: **the ~** la Casa Bianca

white lie N bugia pietosa

whiteness ['waɪtnɪs] N bianchezza

white noise N rumore m bianco

white paper N (Pol) libro bianco

whitewash ['waɪtwɔʃ] N (paint) bianco di calce ▶ VT imbiancare; (fig) coprire

whiting ['waɪtɪŋ] N (pl inv: fish) merlango

Whit Monday N lunedì m inv di Pentecoste

Whitsun ['wɪtsn] N Pentecoste f

whittle ['wɪtl] VT: **to ~ away**, **~ down** ridurre, tagliare

whizz [wɪz] VI: **to ~ past** or **by** passare sfrecciando

whizz kid N (col) prodigio

WHO N ABBR (= World Health Organization) O.M.S. f (= Organizzazione mondiale della sanità)

---

who [hu:]

PRON **1** (interrogative) chi; **who is it?**, **who's there?** chi è?
2 (relative) che; **the man who spoke to me** l'uomo che ha parlato con me; **those who can swim** quelli che sanno nuotare

---

whodunit [hu:'dʌnɪt] N (col) giallo

whoever [hu:'ɛvəʳ] PRON: **~ finds it** chiunque lo trovi; **ask ~ you like** lo chieda a chiunque vuole; **~ she marries** chiunque sposerà, non importa chi sposerà; **~ told you that?** chi mai gliel'ha detto?

whole [həul] ADJ (complete) tutto(-a), completo(-a); (not broken) intero(-a), intatto(-a) ▶ N (all): **the ~ of** tutto(-a) il(la); (not broken) tutto; **the ~ lot (of it)** tutto; **the ~ lot (of them)** tutti; **the ~ of the time** tutto il tempo; **the ~ of the town** tutta la città, la città intera; **on the ~, as a ~** nel complesso, nell'insieme; **~ villages were destroyed** interi paesi furono distrutti

wholefood ['həulfu:d] N, **wholefoods** ['həulfu:dz] NPL cibo integrale

wholehearted [həul'hɑ:tɪd] ADJ sincero(-a)

wholeheartedly [həul'hɑ:tɪdlɪ] ADV sentitamente, di tutto cuore

wholemeal ['həulmi:l] ADJ (BRIT: flour, bread) integrale

whole note N (US) semibreve f

wholesale ['həulseɪl] N commercio or vendita all'ingrosso ▶ ADJ all'ingrosso; (destruction) totale

wholesaler ['həulseɪləʳ] N grossista mf

wholesome ['həulsəm] ADJ sano(-a); (climate) salubre

wholewheat ['həulwi:t] ADJ = **wholemeal**

wholly ['həulɪ] ADV completamente, del tutto

W

whom [huːm]

PRON **1** (*interrogative*) chi; **whom did you see?** chi hai visto?; **to whom did you give it?** a chi lo hai dato?

2 (*relative*) che, *prep* + il (la) quale; **the man whom I saw** l'uomo che ho visto; **the man to whom I spoke** l'uomo al *or* con il quale ho parlato; **those to whom I spoke** le persone alle *or* con le quali ho parlato

whooping cough [ˈhuːpɪŋ-] N pertosse *f*

whoops [wuːps] EXCL: **whoops-a-daisy!** ops!

whoosh [wuʃ] N: **it came out with a ~** (*sauce etc*) è uscito di getto; (*air*) è uscito con un sibilo

whopper [ˈwɔpəʳ] N (*col: lie*) balla; (: *large thing*) cosa enorme

whopping [ˈwɔpɪŋ] ADJ (*col: big*) enorme

whore [hɔːʳ] N (!) puttana (!)

whose [huːz]

ADJ **1** (*possessive: interrogative*) di chi; **whose book is this?**, **whose is this book?** di chi è questo libro?; **whose daughter are you?** di chi sei figlia?; **whose pencil have you taken?** di chi è la matita che hai preso?

2 (*possessive: relative*): **the man whose son you rescued** l'uomo il cui figlio hai salvato *or* a cui hai salvato il figlio; **the girl whose sister you were speaking to** la ragazza alla cui sorella stavi parlando

▶ PRON di chi; **whose is this?** di chi è questo?; **I know whose it is** so di chi è

Who's Who [ˈhuːzˈhuː] N *elenco di personalità*

why [waɪ]

ADV perché; **why not?** perché no?; **why not do it now?** perché non farlo adesso?

▶ CONJ perché; **I wonder why he said that** mi chiedo perché l'abbia detto; **that's not why I'm here** non è questo il motivo per cui sono qui; **the reason why** il motivo per cui

▶ EXCL (*surprise*) ma guarda un po'!; (*remonstrating*) ma (via)!; (*explaining*) ebbene!

whyever [waɪˈɛvəʳ] ADV perché mai

WI N ABBR (BRIT: = *Women's Institute*) circolo femminile ▶ ABBR (*Geo*) = **West Indies**; (*US*) = **Wisconsin**

wick [wɪk] N lucignolo, stoppino

wicked [ˈwɪkɪd] ADJ cattivo(-a), malvagio(-a); (*mischievous*) malizioso(-a); (*terrible: prices, weather*) terribile

wicker [ˈwɪkəʳ] N vimine *m*; (*also:* **wickerwork**) articoli *mpl* di vimini

wicket [ˈwɪkɪt] N (*Cricket*) porta; area tra le due porte

wicket keeper N (*Cricket*) ≈ portiere *m*

wide [waɪd] ADJ largo(-a); (*region, knowledge*) vasto(-a); (*choice*) ampio(-a) ▶ ADV: **to open ~** spalancare; **to shoot ~** tirare a vuoto *or* fuori bersaglio; **it is 3 metres ~** è largo 3 metri

wide-angle lens [ˈwaɪdæŋgl-] N grandangolare *m*

wide-awake [waɪdəˈweɪk] ADJ completamente sveglio(-a)

wide-eyed [waɪdˈaɪd] ADJ con gli occhi spalancati

widely [ˈwaɪdlɪ] ADV (*different*) molto, completamente; (*believed*) generalmente; **~ spaced** molto distanziato; **to be ~ read** (*author*) essere molto letto; (*reader*) essere molto colto

widen [ˈwaɪdn] VT allargare, ampliare

wideness [ˈwaɪdnɪs] N larghezza; vastità; ampiezza

wide open ADJ spalancato(-a)

wide-ranging [waɪdˈreɪndʒɪŋ] ADJ (*survey, report*) vasto(-a); (*interests*) svariato(-a)

widescreen [ˈwaɪdskriːn] ADJ (*television, TV*) a schermo panoramico

widespread [ˈwaɪdsprɛd] ADJ (*belief etc*) molto *or* assai diffuso(-a)

widget [ˈwɪdʒɪt] N (*Comput*) widget *m inv*

widow [ˈwɪdəu] N vedova

widowed [ˈwɪdəud] ADJ (che è rimasto(-a)) vedovo(-a)

widower [ˈwɪdəuəʳ] N vedovo

width [wɪdθ] N larghezza; **it's 7 metres in ~** è largo 7 metri

widthways [ˈwɪdθweɪz] ADV trasversalmente

wield [wiːld] VT (*sword*) maneggiare; (*power*) esercitare

wife [waɪf] (*pl* **wives** [waɪvz]) N moglie *f*

Wi-Fi [ˈwaɪfaɪ] N Wi-Fi *m*

wig [wɪg] N parrucca

wigging [ˈwɪgɪŋ] N (BRIT *col*) lavata di capo

wiggle [ˈwɪgl] VT dimenare, agitare ▶ VI (*loose screw etc*) traballare; (*worm*) torcersi

wiggly [ˈwɪglɪ] ADJ (*line*) ondulato(-a), sinuoso(-a)

wiki [ˈwɪkɪ] N (*Internet*) wiki *m inv*

wild [waɪld] ADJ (*animal, plant*) selvatico(-a); (*countryside, appearance*) selvaggio(-a); (*sea, weather*) tempestoso(-a); (*idea, life*) folle; stravagante; (*applause*) frenetico(-a); (*col: angry*) arrabbiato(-a), furibondo(-a); (*enthusiastic*): **to be ~ about** andar pazzo(-a) per ▶ N: **the ~** la natura ▪ **wilds** NPL regione *f* selvaggia

wild card N (*Comput*) carattere *m* jolly *inv*

wildcat [ˈwaɪldkæt] N gatto(-a) selvatico(-a)

wildcat strike N ≈ sciopero selvaggio

wilderness [ˈwɪldənɪs] N deserto

wildfire [ˈwaɪldfaɪəʳ] N: **to spread like ~** propagarsi rapidamente

wild-goose chase [waɪld'guːs-] N (fig) pista falsa

wildlife ['waɪldlaɪf] N natura

wildly ['waɪldlɪ] ADV selvaggiamente; (applaud) freneticamente; (hit, guess) a casaccio; (happy) follemente

wiles [waɪlz] NPL astuzie fpl

wilful, (US) **willful** ['wɪlful] ADJ (person) testardo(-a); ostinato(-a); (action) intenzionale; (crime) premeditato(-a)

---

will [wɪl]

AUX VB **1** (forming future tense): **I will finish it tomorrow** lo finirò domani; **I will have finished it by tomorrow** lo finirò entro domani; **will you do it? — yes I will/no I won't** lo farai? — sì (lo farò)/no (non lo farò); **the car won't start** la macchina non parte

2 (in conjectures, predictions): **he will** or **he'll be there by now** a quest'ora dovrebbe essere arrivato; **that will be the postman** sarà il postino

3 (in commands, requests, offers): **will you be quiet!** vuoi stare zitto?; **will you sit down?** (politely) prego, si accomodi; (angrily) vuoi metterti seduto?; **will you come?** vieni anche tu?; **will you help me?** mi aiuti?, mi puoi aiutare?; **you won't lose it, will you?** non lo perderai, vero?; **will you have a cup of tea?** vorrebbe una tazza di tè?; **I won't put up with it!** non lo accetterò!

▶ VT (pt, pp **willed**): **to will sb to do** volere che qn faccia; **he willed himself to go on** continuò grazie a un grande sforzo di volontà

▶ N **1** (desire) volontà; **against sb's will** contro la volontà or il volere di qn; **to do sth of one's own free will** fare qc di propria volontà

2 (Law) testamento; **to make a/one's will** fare testamento

---

willful ['wɪlful] ADJ (US) = **wilful**

willing ['wɪlɪŋ] ADJ volonteroso(-a) ▶ N: **to show ~** dare prova di buona volontà; **~ to do** disposto(-a) a fare

willingly ['wɪlɪŋlɪ] ADV volentieri

willingness ['wɪlɪŋnɪs] N buona volontà

will-o'-the-wisp [wɪləðə'wɪsp] N (also fig) fuoco fatuo

willow ['wɪləu] N salice m

willpower ['wɪlpauər] N forza di volontà

willy-nilly ['wɪlɪ'nɪlɪ] ADV volente o nolente

wilt [wɪlt] VI appassire

wily ['waɪlɪ] ADJ furbo(-a)

wimp [wɪmp] N (col) mezza calzetta

win [wɪn] (pt, pp **won** [wʌn]) N (in sports etc) vittoria ▶ VT (battle, prize, money) vincere; (popularity) guadagnare; (contract) aggiudicarsi ▶ VI vincere

▶ **win over**, (BRIT) **win round** VT convincere

wince [wɪns] N trasalimento, sussulto ▶ VI trasalire

winch [wɪntʃ] N verricello, argano

Winchester disk ['wɪntʃɪstə-] N (Comput) disco Winchester

wind[1] [wɪnd] N vento; (Med) flatulenza, ventosità; (breath) respiro, fiato ▶ VT (take breath away) far restare senza fiato; **the ~(s)** (Mus) i fiati; **into** or **against the ~** controvento; **to get ~ of sth** venire a sapere qc; **to break ~** scoreggiare (col)

wind[2] [waɪnd] (pt, pp **wound** [waund]) VT attorcigliare; (wrap) avvolgere; (clock, toy) caricare ▶ VI (road, river) serpeggiare

▶ **wind down** VT (car window) abbassare; (fig: production, business) diminuire

▶ **wind up** VT (clock) caricare; (debate) concludere

windbreak ['wɪndbreɪk] N frangivento

windcheater ['wɪndtʃiːtər], (US) **windbreaker** ['wɪndbreɪkər] N giacca a vento

winder ['waɪndər] N (BRIT: on watch) corona di carica

windfall ['wɪndfɔːl] N (money) guadagno insperato

wind farm [wɪnd-] N centrale f eolica

winding ['waɪndɪŋ] ADJ (road) serpeggiante; (staircase) a chiocciola

wind instrument [wɪnd-] N (Mus) strumento a fiato

windmill ['wɪndmɪl] N mulino a vento

window ['wɪndəu] N (gen, Comput) finestra; (in car, train, plane) finestrino; (in shop etc) vetrina; (also: **window pane**) vetro

window box N cassetta da fiori

window cleaner N (person) pulitore m di finestre

window dressing N allestimento della vetrina

window envelope N busta a finestra

window frame N telaio di finestra

window ledge N davanzale m

window pane N vetro

window seat N posto finestrino

window-shopping ['wɪndəuʃɔpɪŋ] N: **to go ~** andare a vedere le vetrine

windowsill ['wɪndəusɪl] N davanzale m

windpipe ['wɪndpaɪp] N trachea

wind power [wɪnd-] N energia eolica

windscreen ['wɪndskriːn], (US) **windshield** ['wɪndʃiːld] N parabrezza m inv

windscreen washer, (US) **windshield washer** N lavacristallo

windscreen wiper, (US) **windshield wiper** N tergicristallo

windshield ['wɪndʃiːld] N (US) = **windscreen**

W

windsurfing ['wɪndsɔ:fɪŋ] N windsurf *m inv*

windswept ['wɪndswɛpt] ADJ spazzato(-a) dal vento

wind tunnel [wɪnd-] N galleria aerodinamica *or* del vento

wind turbine ['wɪndtə:baɪn] N pala eolica

windy ['wɪndɪ] ADJ ventoso(-a); **it's ~** c'è vento

wine [waɪn] N vino ▶ VT: **to ~ and dine sb** offrire un ottimo pranzo a qn

wine bar N enoteca *(per degustazione)*

wine cellar N cantina

wine glass N bicchiere *m* da vino

wine list N lista dei vini

wine merchant N commerciante *m* di vino

wine tasting N degustazione *f* dei vini

wine waiter N sommelier *m inv*

wing [wɪŋ] N ala; *(Aut)* fiancata ■ **wings** NPL *(Theat)* quinte *fpl*

winger ['wɪŋəʳ] N *(Sport)* ala

wing mirror N *(Brit)* specchietto retrovisore esterno

wing nut N galletto

wingspan ['wɪŋspæn], **wingspread** ['wɪŋsprɛd] N apertura alare, apertura d'ali

wink [wɪŋk] N occhiolino, strizzatina d'occhi ▶ VI ammiccare, fare l'occhiolino; *(light)* baluginare

winkle ['wɪŋkl] N litorina

winner ['wɪnəʳ] N vincitore(-trice)

winning ['wɪnɪŋ] ADJ *(team)* vincente; *(goal)* decisivo(-a); *(charming)* affascinante; *see also* **winnings**

winning post N traguardo

winnings ['wɪnɪŋz] NPL vincite *fpl*

winsome ['wɪnsəm] ADJ accattivante

winter ['wɪntəʳ] N inverno; **in ~** d'inverno, in inverno

winter sports NPL sport *mpl* invernali

wintertime N inverno, stagione *f* invernale

wintry ['wɪntrɪ] ADJ invernale

wipe [waɪp] N pulita, passata ▶ VT pulire (strofinando); *(erase: tape)* cancellare; *(: dishes)* asciugare; **to give sth a ~** dare una pulita *or* una passata a qc; **to ~ one's nose** soffiarsi il naso
▶ **wipe off** VT cancellare; *(stains)* togliere strofinando
▶ **wipe out** VT *(debt)* pagare, liquidare; *(memory)* cancellare; *(destroy)* annientare
▶ **wipe up** VT asciugare

wire ['waɪəʳ] N filo; *(Elec)* filo elettrico; *(Tel)* telegramma *m* ▶ VT *(Elec: house)* fare l'impianto elettrico di; *(: circuit)* installare; *(also: wire up)* collegare, allacciare; *(person)* telegrafare a

wire brush N spazzola metallica

wire cutters [-kʌtəz] NPL tronchese *m or f*

wireless ['waɪəlɪs] N *(Brit old: set)* apparecchio *m)* radio *f inv* ▶ ADJ wireless *inv*, senza fili

wireless technology N tecnologia wireless

wire netting N rete *f* metallica

wire service N *(US)* = **news agency**

wire-tapping ['waɪə'tæpɪŋ] N intercettazione *f* telefonica

wiring ['waɪərɪŋ] N *(Elec)* impianto elettrico

wiry ['waɪərɪ] ADJ magro(-a) e nerboruto(-a)

wisdom ['wɪzdəm] N saggezza; *(of action)* prudenza

wisdom tooth N dente *m* del giudizio

wise [waɪz] ADJ saggio(-a); *(advice, remark)* prudente; giudizioso(-a); **I'm none the wiser** ne so come prima
▶ **wise up** VI *(col)*: **to ~ up to** divenire più consapevole di

...wise [waɪz] SUFFIX: **timewise** per quanto riguarda il tempo, in termini di tempo

wisecrack ['waɪzkræk] N battuta spiritosa

wish [wɪʃ] N *(desire)* desiderio; *(specific desire)* richiesta ▶ VT desiderare, volere; **best wishes** *(on birthday etc)* i migliori auguri; **with best wishes** *(in letter)* cordiali saluti, con i migliori saluti; **give her my best wishes** le faccia i migliori auguri da parte mia; **to ~ sb goodbye** dire arrivederci a qn; **he wished me well** mi augurò di riuscire; **to ~ to do/sb to do** desiderare *or* volere fare/che qn faccia; **to ~ for** desiderare; **to ~ sth on sb** rifilare qc a qn

wishbone ['wɪʃbəun] N forcella

wishful ['wɪʃful] ADJ: **it's ~ thinking** è prendere i desideri per realtà

wishy-washy ['wɪʃɪ'wɔʃɪ] ADJ *(col)* insulso(-a)

wisp [wɪsp] N ciuffo, ciocca; *(of smoke, straw)* filo

wistful ['wɪstful] ADJ malinconico(-a); *(nostalgic)* nostalgico(-a)

wit [wɪt] N *(gen pl)* intelligenza; presenza di spirito; *(wittiness)* spirito, arguzia; *(person)* bello spirito; **to be at one's wits' end** *(fig)* non sapere più cosa fare; **to have** *or* **keep one's wits about one** avere presenza di spirito; **to ~** *adv* cioè

witch [wɪtʃ] N strega

witchcraft ['wɪtʃkrɑ:ft] N stregoneria

witch doctor N stregone *m*

witch-hunt ['wɪtʃhʌnt] N *(fig)* caccia alle streghe

---

with [wɪð, wɪθ]

PREP **1** *(in the company of)* con; **I was with him** ero con lui; **we stayed with friends** siamo stati da amici; **I'll be with you in a minute** vengo subito

2 *(descriptive)* con; **a room with a view** una camera con vista (sul mare *or* sulle montagne *etc)*; **the man with the grey hat/blue eyes** l'uomo con il cappello grigio/gli occhi blu

3 *(indicating manner, means, cause)*: **with tears in**

her eyes con le lacrime agli occhi; **red with anger** rosso(-a) dalla rabbia; **to shake with fear** tremare di paura; **covered with snow** coperto(-a) di neve

4: I'm with you (*I understand*) la seguo; **to be with it** (*col: up-to-date*) essere alla moda; (*: alert*) essere sveglio(-a); **I'm not really with it today** (*col*) oggi sono un po' fuori

withdraw [wɪθˈdrɔː] VT (*irreg: like* **draw**) ritirare; (*money from bank*) ritirare; prelevare ▶ VI ritirarsi; **to ~ into o.s.** chiudersi in se stesso

withdrawal [wɪθˈdrɔːəl] N ritiro; prelievo; (*of army*) ritirata; (*Med*) stato di privazione

withdrawal symptoms NPL (*Med*) crisi f di astinenza

withdrawn [wɪθˈdrɔːn] PP *of* **withdraw** ▶ ADJ (*person*) distaccato(-a)

withdrew [wɪθˈdruː] PT *of* **withdraw**

wither [ˈwɪðəʳ] VI appassire

withered [ˈwɪðəd] ADJ appassito(-a); (*limb*) atrofizzato(-a)

withhold [wɪθˈhəuld] VT (*irreg: like* **hold**) (*money*) trattenere; (*permission*): **to ~ (from)** rifiutare (a); (*information*) nascondere (a)

within [wɪðˈɪn] PREP all'interno di; (*in time, distances*) entro ▶ ADV all'interno, dentro; **~ reach (of)** alla portata (di); **~ sight (of)** in vista (di); **~ a mile of** entro un miglio da; **~ the week** prima della fine della settimana; **~ an hour from now** da qui a un'ora; **to be ~ the law** restare nei limiti della legge

without [wɪðˈaut] PREP senza; **to go** *or* **do ~ sth** fare a meno di qc; **~ anybody knowing** senza che nessuno lo sappia

withstand [wɪθˈstænd] VT (*irreg: like* **stand**) resistere a

witness [ˈwɪtnɪs] N (*person, also Law*) testimone mf ▶ VT (*event*) essere testimone di; (*document*) attestare l'autenticità di ▶ VI: **to ~ to sth/ having seen sth** testimoniare qc/di aver visto qc; **to bear ~ to sth** testimoniare qc; **~ for the prosecution/defence** testimone a carico/ discarico

witness box, (*US*) **witness stand** N banco dei testimoni

witticism [ˈwɪtɪsɪzəm] N spiritosaggine f

witty [ˈwɪtɪ] ADJ spiritoso(-a)

wives [waɪvz] NPL *of* **wife**

wizard [ˈwɪzəd] N mago

wizened [ˈwɪznd] ADJ raggrinzito(-a)

wk ABBR = **week**

Wm. ABBR = **William**

WMD N ABBR (= *weapons of mass destruction*) armi di distruzione di massa

WO N ABBR = **warrant officer**

wobble [ˈwɔbl] VI tremare; (*chair*) traballare

wobbly [ˈwɔblɪ] ADJ (*hand, voice*) tremante; (*table,*

chair) traballante; (*object about to fall*) che oscilla pericolosamente

woe [wəu] N dolore m; disgrazia

woeful [ˈwəuful] ADJ (*sad*) triste; (*deplorable*) deplorevole

wok [wɔk] N wok m inv (*padella concava usata nella cucina cinese*)

woke [wəuk] PT *of* **wake**

woken [ˈwəukn] PP *of* **wake**

wolf [wulf] (*pl* **wolves** [wulvz]) N lupo

woman [ˈwumən] (*pl* **women** [ˈwɪmɪn]) N donna ▶ CPD: **~ doctor** n dottoressa; **~ friend** n amica; **~ teacher** n insegnante f; **women's page** n (*Press*) rubrica femminile

womanize [ˈwumənaɪz] VI essere un donnaiolo

womanly [ˈwumənlɪ] ADJ femminile

womb [wuːm] N (*Anat*) utero

women [ˈwɪmɪn] NPL *of* **woman**

Women's Movement, Women's Liberation Movement N (*also:* **Women's Lib**) Movimento per la Liberazione della Donna

won [wʌn] PT, PP *of* **win**

wonder [ˈwʌndəʳ] N meraviglia ▶ VI: **to ~ whether/why** domandarsi se/perché; **to ~ at** essere sorpreso(-a) di; meravigliarsi di; **to ~ about** domandarsi di; pensare a; **it's no ~ that** c'è poco *or* non c'è da meravigliarsi che + *sub*

wonderful [ˈwʌndəful] ADJ meraviglioso(-a)

wonderfully [ˈwʌndəfəlɪ] ADV (+ *adjective*) meravigliosamente; (+ *verb*) a meraviglia

wonky [ˈwɔŋkɪ] ADJ (*BRIT col*) traballante

wont [wəunt] N: **as is his/her ~** com'è solito/a fare

won't [wəunt] = **will not**

woo [wuː] VT (*woman*) fare la corte a

wood [wud] N legno; (*timber*) legname m; (*forest*) bosco ▶ CPD di bosco, silvestre

wood carving N scultura in legno, intaglio

wooded [ˈwudɪd] ADJ boschivo(-a); boscoso(-a)

wooden [ˈwudn] ADJ di legno; (*fig*) rigido(-a); inespressivo(-a)

woodland [ˈwudlənd] N zona boscosa

woodpecker [ˈwudpɛkəʳ] N picchio

wood pigeon N colombaccio, palomba

woodwind [ˈwudwɪnd] NPL (*Mus*): **the ~** i legni

woodwork [ˈwudwəːk] N parti fpl in legno; (*craft, subject*) falegnameria

woodworm [ˈwudwəːm] N tarlo del legno

woof [wuf] N (*of dog*) bau bau m inv ▶ VI abbaiare; **~, ~!** bau bau!

wool [wul] N lana; **to pull the ~ over sb's eyes** (*fig*) gettare fumo negli occhi a qn

woollen, (*US*) **woolen** [ˈwulən] ADJ di lana; (*industry*) laniero(-a) ▶ N: **woollens** indumenti mpl di lana

W

woolly, (US) **wooly** [ˈwʊlɪ] ADJ di lana; (fig: ideas) confuso(-a)

woozy [ˈwuːzɪ] ADJ (col) stordito(-a)

word [wəːd] N parola; (news) notizie fpl ▶ VT esprimere, formulare; **~ for ~** parola per parola, testualmente; **what's the ~ for "pen" in Italian?** come si dice "pen" in italiano?; **to put sth into words** esprimere qc a parole; **in other words** in altre parole; **to have a ~ with sb** scambiare due parole con qn; **to have words with sb** (quarrel with) avere un diverbio con qn; **to break/keep one's ~** non mantenere/mantenere la propria parola; **I'll take your ~ for it** la crederò sulla parola; **to send ~ of** avvisare di; **to leave ~ (with** or **for sb) that ...** lasciare detto (a qn) che ...

wording [ˈwəːdɪŋ] N formulazione f

word of mouth N passaparola m; **I learned it by** or **through ~** lo so per sentito dire

word-perfect [ˈwəːdˈpəfɪkt] ADJ (speech etc) imparato(-a) a memoria

word processing N word processing m, elaborazione f testi

word processor N word processor m inv

wordwrap [ˈwəːdræp] N (Comput) ritorno carrello automatico

wordy [ˈwəːdɪ] ADJ verboso(-a), prolisso(-a)

wore [wɔːʳ] PT of **wear**

work [wəːk] N lavoro; (Art, Literature) opera ▶ VI lavorare; (mechanism, plan etc) funzionare; (medicine) essere efficace ▶ VT (clay, wood etc) lavorare; (mine etc) sfruttare; (machine) far funzionare; (cause: effect, miracle) fare; **to be at ~ (on sth)** lavorare (a qc); **to set to ~, to start ~** mettersi all'opera; **to go to ~** andare al lavoro; **to be out of ~** essere disoccupato(-a); **to ~ one's way through a book** riuscire a leggersi tutto un libro; **to ~ one's way through college** lavorare per pagarsi gli studi; **how does this ~?** come funziona?; **the TV isn't working** la TV non funziona; **to ~ hard** lavorare sodo; **to ~ loose** allentarsi; see also **works**

▶ **work on** VT FUS lavorare a; (principle) basarsi su; **he's working on the car** sta facendo dei lavori alla macchina

▶ **work out** VI (plans etc) riuscire, andare bene; (Sport) allenarsi ▶ VT (problem) risolvere; (plan) elaborare; **it works out at £100** fa 100 sterline

workable [ˈwəːkəbl] ADJ (solution) realizzabile

workaholic [wəːkəˈhɔlɪk] N stacanovista mf

workbench [ˈwəːkbɛntʃ] N banco (da lavoro)

worked up ADJ: **to get ~** andare su tutte le furie; eccitarsi

worker [ˈwəːkəʳ] N lavoratore(-trice); (esp Agr, Industry) operaio(-a); **office ~** impiegato(-a)

work experience [ˈwəːkɪkspɪərɪəns] N (previous jobs) esperienze fpl lavorative; (student training placement) tirocinio

work force N forza lavoro

work-in [ˈwəːkɪn] N (BRIT) sciopero alla rovescia

working [ˈwəːkɪŋ] ADJ (day) feriale; (tools, conditions) di lavoro; (clothes) da lavoro; (wife) che lavora; (partner) attivo(-a); **in ~ order** funzionante; **~ knowledge** conoscenza pratica

working capital N (Comm) capitale m d'esercizio

working class N classe f operaia or lavoratrice ▶ ADJ: **working-class** operaio(-a)

working man N (irreg) lavoratore m

working party N (BRIT) commissione f

working week N settimana lavorativa

work-in-progress [ˈwəːkɪnˈprəʊgrɛs] N (products) lavoro in corso; (value) valore m del manufatto in lavorazione

workload [ˈwəːkləʊd] N carico di lavoro

workman [ˈwəːkmən] N (irreg) operaio

workmanship [ˈwəːkmənʃɪp] N (of worker) abilità; (of thing) fattura

workmate [ˈwəːkmeɪt] N collega mf

work of art N opera d'arte

workout [ˈwəːkaut] N (Sport) allenamento

work permit N permesso di lavoro

workplace N posto di lavoro

works [wəːks] N (BRIT: factory) fabbrica ▶ NPL (of clock, machine) meccanismo; **road ~** opere fpl stradali

works council N consiglio aziendale

work sheet N (Comput) foglio col programma di lavoro

workshop [ˈwəːkʃɔp] N officina; (practical session) gruppo di lavoro

work station N stazione f di lavoro

work study N studio di organizzazione del lavoro

work surface N piano di lavoro

worktop [ˈwəːktɔp] N piano di lavoro

work-to-rule [ˈwəːktəˈruːl] N (BRIT) sciopero bianco

world [wəːld] N mondo ▶ CPD (tour, champion) del mondo; (record, power, war) mondiale; **all over the ~** in tutto il mondo; **to think the ~ of sb** (fig) pensare un gran bene di qn; **out of this ~** (fig) formidabile; **what in the ~ is he doing?** che cavolo sta facendo?; **to do sb a ~ of good** fare un gran bene a qn; **W~ War One/Two** la prima/seconda guerra mondiale

world champion N campione(-essa) mondiale

World Cup N (Football) Coppa del Mondo

world-famous [wəːldˈfeɪməs] ADJ di fama mondiale

worldly [ˈwəːldlɪ] ADJ di questo mondo

world music N musica etnica

World Series N: **the ~** (US Baseball) la finalissima di baseball

world-wide [ˈwəːldˈwaɪd] ADJ universale

World-Wide Web N World Wide Web *m*

worm [wəːm] N (*also*: **earthworm**) verme *m*

worn [wɔːn] PP *of* **wear** ▶ ADJ usato(-a)

worn-out [ˈwɔːnaut] ADJ (*object*) consumato(-a), logoro(-a); (*person*) sfinito(-a)

worried [ˈwʌrɪd] ADJ preoccupato(-a); **to be ~ about sth** essere preoccupato per qc

worrier [ˈwʌrɪəʳ] N ansioso(-a)

worrisome [ˈwʌrɪsəm] ADJ preoccupante

worry [ˈwʌrɪ] N preoccupazione *f* ▶ VT preoccupare ▶ VI preoccuparsi; **to ~ about** *or* **over sth/ sb** preoccuparsi di qc/per qn

worrying [ˈwʌrɪɪŋ] ADJ preoccupante

worse [wəːs] ADJ peggiore ▶ ADV, N peggio; **a change for the ~** un peggioramento; **to get ~**, **to grow ~** peggiorare; **he is none the ~ for it** non ha avuto brutte conseguenze; **so much the ~ for you!** tanto peggio per te!

worsen [ˈwəːsn] VT, VI peggiorare

worse off ADJ in condizioni (economiche) peggiori; (*fig*): **you'll be ~ this way** così sarà peggio per lei; **he is now ~ than before** ora è in condizioni peggiori di prima

worship [ˈwəːʃɪp] N culto ▶ VT (*God*) adorare, venerare; (*person*) adorare; **Your W~** (BRIT: *to mayor*) signor sindaco; (: *to judge*) signor giudice

worshipper [ˈwəːʃɪpəʳ] N adoratore(-trice); (*in church*) fedele *mf*, devoto(-a)

worst [wəːst] ADJ il (la) peggiore ▶ ADV, N peggio; **at ~** al peggio, per male che vada; **to come off ~** avere la peggio; **if the ~ comes to the ~** nel peggior dei casi

worst-case [ˈwəːstˈkeɪs] ADJ: **the ~ scenario** la peggiore delle ipotesi

worsted [ˈwustɪd] N: **(wool) ~** lana pettinata

worth [wəːθ] N valore *m* ▶ ADJ: **to be ~** valere; **how much is it ~?** quanto vale?; **it's ~ it** ne vale la pena; **it's not ~ the trouble** non ne vale la pena; **50 pence ~ of apples** 50 pence di mele

worthless [ˈwəːθlɪs] ADJ di nessun valore

worthwhile [ˈwəːθˈwaɪl] ADJ (*activity*) utile; (*cause*) lodevole; **a ~ book** un libro che vale la pena leggere

worthy [ˈwəːðɪ] ADJ (*person*) degno(-a); (*motive*) lodevole; **~ of** degno di

---

would [wud]

AUX VB **1** (*conditional tense*): **if you asked him, he would do it** se glielo chiedesse lo farebbe; **if you had asked him, he would have done it** se glielo avesse chiesto lo avrebbe fatto

2 (*in offers, invitations, requests*): **would you like a biscuit?** vorrebbe *or* vuole un biscotto?; **would you ask him to come in?** lo faccia entrare, per cortesia; **would you open the window please?** apra la finestra, per favore

3 (*in indirect speech*): **I said I would do it** ho detto che l'avrei fatto

4 (*emphatic*): **it WOULD have to snow today!** doveva proprio nevicare oggi!

5 (*insistence*): **she wouldn't do it** non ha voluto farlo

6 (*conjecture*): **it would have been midnight** sarà stata mezzanotte; **it would seem so** sembrerebbe proprio di sì

7 (*indicating habit*): **he would go there on Mondays** andava lì ogni lunedì

---

would-be [ˈwudbiː] ADJ (*pej*) sedicente

wouldn't [ˈwudnt] = **would not**

wound¹ [wuːnd] N ferita ▶ VT ferire; **wounded in the leg** ferito(-a) alla gamba

wound² [waund] PT, PP *of* **wind²**

wove [wəuv] PT *of* **weave**

woven [ˈwəuvn] PP *of* **weave**

WP ABBR (BRIT *col*: = *weather permitting*) tempo permettendo ▶ N ABBR = **word processing**; **word processor**

wpm ABBR (= *words per minute*) p.p.m.

wrangle [ˈræŋgl] N litigio ▶ VI litigare

wrap [ræp] N (*stole*) scialle *m*; (*cape*) mantellina ▶ VT (*also*: **wrap up**) avvolgere; (: *parcel*) incartare; **under wraps** segreto

wrapper [ˈræpəʳ] N (*on chocolate*) carta; (BRIT: *of book*) copertina

wrapping [ˈræpɪŋ] N carta

wrapping paper [ˈræpɪŋ-] N carta da pacchi; (*for gift*) carta da regali

wrath [rɔθ] N collera, ira

wreak [riːk] VT (*destruction*) portare, causare; **to ~ vengeance on** vendicarsi su; **to ~ havoc on** portare scompiglio in

wreath [riːθ] (*pl* **wreaths** [riːðz]) N corona

wreck [rɛk] N (*sea disaster*) naufragio; (*ship*) relitto; (*col: person*) rottame *m* ▶ VT demolire; (*ship*) far naufragare; (*fig*) rovinare

wreckage [ˈrɛkɪdʒ] N rottami *mpl*; (*of building*) macerie *fpl*; (*of ship*) relitti *mpl*

wrecker [ˈrɛkəʳ] N (US: *breakdown van*) carro *m* attrezzi *inv*

WREN [rɛn] N ABBR (BRIT) membro del WRNS

wren [rɛn] N (Zool) scricciolo

wrench [rɛntʃ] N (Tech) chiave *f*; (*tug*) torsione *f* brusca; (*fig*) strazio ▶ VT strappare; storcere; **to ~ sth from** strappare qc a *or* da

wrest [rɛst] VT: **to ~ sth from sb** strappare qc a qn

wrestle [ˈrɛsl] VI: **to ~ (with sb)** lottare (con qn); **to ~ with** (*fig*) combattere *or* lottare contro

wrestler [ˈrɛsləʳ] N lottatore(-trice)

wrestling [ˈrɛslɪŋ] N lotta; (*also*: **all-in wrestling**: BRIT) catch *m*, lotta libera

wrestling match N incontro di lotta (*or* lotta libera)

W

wretch [rɛtʃ] N disgraziato(-a), sciagurato(-a); **little ~!** (often humorous) birbante!

wretched [ˈrɛtʃɪd] ADJ disgraziato(-a); (col: weather, holiday) orrendo(-a), orribile; (: child, dog) pestifero(-a)

wriggle [ˈrɪɡl] N contorsione f ▶ VI (also: **wriggle about**) dimenarsi; (: snake, worm) serpeggiare, muoversi serpeggiando

wring [rɪŋ] (pt, pp **wrung** [rʌŋ]) VT torcere; (wet clothes) strizzare; (fig): **to ~ sth out of** strappare qc a

wringer [ˈrɪŋəʳ] N strizzatoio (manuale)

wringing [ˈrɪŋɪŋ] ADJ (also: **wringing wet**) bagnato(-a) fradicio(-a)

wrinkle [ˈrɪŋkl] N (on skin) ruga; (on paper etc) grinza ▶ VT (nose) torcere; (forehead) corrugare; raggrinzire ▶ VI corrugarsi; (skin, paint) raggrinzirsi

wrinkled [ˈrɪŋkld], **wrinkly** [ˈrɪŋklɪ] ADJ (fabric, paper) stropicciato(-a); (surface) corrugato(-a), increspato(-a); (skin) rugoso(-a)

wrist [rɪst] N polso

wristband [ˈrɪstbænd] N (of shirt) polsino; (of watch) cinturino

wrist watch N orologio da polso

writ [rɪt] N ordine m; mandato; **to issue a ~ against sb, serve a ~ on sb** notificare un mandato di comparizione a qn

write [raɪt] (pt **wrote** [rəut], pp **written** [ˈrɪtn]) VT, VI scrivere; **to ~ sb a letter** scrivere una lettera a qn
  ▶ **write away** VI: **to ~ away for** (information) richiedere per posta; (goods) ordinare per posta
  ▶ **write down** VT annotare; (put in writing) mettere per iscritto
  ▶ **write off** VT (debt, plan) cancellare; (depreciate) deprezzare; (smash up: car) distruggere
  ▶ **write out** VT mettere per iscritto; (cheque, receipt) scrivere; (copy) ricopiare
  ▶ **write up** VT redigere

write-off [ˈraɪtɔf] N perdita completa; **the car is a ~** la macchina va bene per il demolitore

write-protect [ˈraɪtprəˈtɛkt] VT (Comput) proteggere contro scrittura

writer [ˈraɪtəʳ] N autore(-trice), scrittore(-trice)

write-up [ˈraɪtʌp] N (review) recensione f

writhe [raɪð] VI contorcersi

writing [ˈraɪtɪŋ] N scrittura; (of author) scritto, opera; **in ~** per iscritto; **in my own ~** scritto di mio pugno

writing case N nécessaire m inv per la corrispondenza

writing desk N scrivania, scrittoio

writing paper N carta da lettere

written [ˈrɪtn] PP of **write**

wrong [rɔŋ] ADJ sbagliato(-a); (not suitable) inadatto(-a); (wicked) cattivo(-a); (unfair) ingiusto(-a) ▶ ADV in modo sbagliato, erroneamente ▶ N (evil) male m; (injustice) torto ▶ VT fare torto a; **to be ~** (answer) essere sbagliato; (in doing, saying) avere torto; **you are ~ to do it** ha torto a farlo; **you are ~ about that, you've got it ~** si sbaglia; **to be in the ~** avere torto; **what's ~?** cosa c'è che non va?; **there's nothing ~** va tutto bene; **what's ~ with the car?** cos'ha la macchina che non va?; **to go ~** (person) sbagliarsi; (plan) fallire, non riuscire; (machine) guastarsi; **it's ~ to steal, stealing is ~** è male rubare

wrongdoer [ˈrɔŋduːəʳ] N malfattore(-trice)

wrong-foot [rɔŋˈfut] VT (Sport, also fig) prendere in contropiede

wrongful [ˈrɔŋful] ADJ illegittimo(-a); ingiusto(-a); **~ dismissal** licenziamento ingiustificato

wrongly [ˈrɔŋlɪ] ADV (incorrectly, by mistake) in modo sbagliato; (accuse, dismiss) a torto; (answer, do, count) erroneamente; (treat) ingiustamente

wrong number N: **you have the ~** (Tel) ha sbagliato numero

wrong side N (of cloth) rovescio

wrote [rəut] PT of **write**

wrought [rɔːt] ADJ: **~ iron** ferro battuto

wrung [rʌŋ] PT, PP of **wring**

wry [raɪ] ADJ storto(-a)

wt. ABBR = **weight**

WV, W.Va. ABBR (US) = **West Virginia**

WWW N ABBR = **World Wide Web**; **the ~** la Rete

WY, Wyo. ABBR (US) = **Wyoming**

WYSIWYG [ˈwɪzɪwɪɡ] ABBR (Comput) = **what you see is what you get**

Xx

X, x [ɛks] N (*letter*) X, x *f inv or m inv*; (*BRIT Cine: old*)
≈ film vietato ai minori di 18 anni; **X for Xmas**
≈ X come Xeres

Xerox® [ˈzɪərɔks] N (*also:* **Xerox machine**) fotocopiatrice *f*; (: *photocopy*) fotocopia ▶ VT fotocopiare

XL ABBR = **extra large**

Xmas [ˈɛksməs] N ABBR = **Christmas**

X-rated [ˈɛksˈreɪtɪd] ADJ (*US: film*) ≈ vietato(-a) ai
minori di 18 anni

X-ray [ˈɛksˈreɪ] N raggio X; (*photograph*) radiografia ▶ VT radiografare; **to have an ~** farsi fare
una radiografia

xylophone [ˈzaɪləfəun] N xilofono

Yy

Y, y [waɪ] N (*letter*) Y, y f *inv or* m *inv*; **Y for Yellow**, (*US*) **Y for Yoke** ≈ Y come Yacht

yacht [jɔt] N panfilo, yacht m *inv*

yachting ['jɔtɪŋ] N yachting m, sport m della vela

yachtsman ['jɔtsmən] N (*irreg*) yachtsman m *inv*

yam [jæm] N igname m; (*sweet potato*) patata dolce

Yank [jæŋk], **Yankee** ['jæŋkɪ] N (*pej*) yankee mf *inv*, nordamericano(-a)

yank [jæŋk] N strattone m ▶ VT tirare, dare uno strattone a

yap [jæp] VI (*dog*) guaire

yard [jɑːd] N (*of house etc*) cortile m; (*US: garden*) giardino; (*measure*) iarda (= *914 mm; 3 feet*); **builder's ~** deposito di materiale da costruzione

yard sale N (*US*) *vendita di oggetti usati nel cortile di una casa privata*

yardstick ['jɑːdstɪk] N (*fig*) misura, criterio

yarn [jɑːn] N filato; (*tale*) lunga storia

yawn [jɔːn] N sbadiglio ▶ VI sbadigliare

yawning ['jɔːnɪŋ] ADJ (*gap*) spalancato(-a)

yd. ABBR = **yard**

yeah [jɛə] ADV (*col*) sì

year [jɪəʳ] N (*gen, Scol*) anno; (*referring to harvest, wine etc*) annata; **every ~** ogni anno, tutti gli anni; **this ~** quest'anno; **~ in, ~ out** anno dopo anno; **she's three years old** ha tre anni; **an eight-year-old child** un(a) bambino(-a) di otto anni; **a** *or* **per ~** all'anno

yearbook ['jɪəbuk] N annuario

yearly ['jɪəlɪ] ADJ annuale ▶ ADV annualmente; **twice-yearly** semestrale

yearn [jəːn] VI: **to ~ for sth/to do** desiderare ardentemente qc/di fare

yearning ['jəːnɪŋ] N desiderio intenso

yeast [jiːst] N lievito

yell [jɛl] N urlo ▶ VI urlare

yellow ['jɛləu] ADJ giallo(-a)

yellow fever N febbre f gialla

yellowish ['jɛləuɪʃ] ADJ giallastro(-a), giallognolo(-a)

Yellow Pages® NPL pagine fpl gialle

Yellow Sea N: **the ~** il mar Giallo

yelp [jɛlp] N guaito, uggiolio ▶ VI guaire, uggiolare

Yemen ['jɛmən] N Yemen m

yen [jɛn] N (*currency*) yen m *inv*; (*craving*): **~ for/to do** gran voglia di/di fare

yeoman ['jəumən] N (*irreg*): **Y~ of the Guard** guardiano della Torre di Londra

yes [jɛs] ADV, N sì (m *inv*); **to say ~ (to)** dire di sì (a)

yesterday ['jɛstədɪ] ADV, N ieri (m *inv*); **~ morning/evening** ieri mattina/sera; **the day before ~** l'altro ieri; **all day ~** ieri per tutta la giornata

yet [jɛt] ADV ancora; già ▶ CONJ ma, tuttavia; **it is not finished ~** non è ancora finito; **the best ~** finora il migliore; **as ~** finora; **~ again** di nuovo; **must you go just ~?** deve andarsene di già?; **a few days ~** ancora qualche giorno

yew [juː] N tasso (*albero*)

Y-fronts® ['waɪfrʌnts] NPL (*BRIT*) slip m *inv* da uomo

YHA N ABBR (*BRIT*: = *Youth Hostels Association*) Y.H.A. f

Yiddish ['jɪdɪʃ] N yiddish m

yield [jiːld] N produzione f, resa; reddito; (*of crops etc*) raccolto ▶ VT produrre, rendere; (*surrender*) cedere ▶ VI cedere; (*US Aut*) dare la precedenza; **a ~ of 5%** un profitto *or* un interesse del 5%

yikes ['jaɪks] EXCL (*col: esp humorous*) oddìo

YMCA N ABBR (= *Young Men's Christian Association*) Y.M.C.A. m

yob ['jɔb], **yobbo** ['jɔbəu] N (*BRIT pej*) bullo

yodel ['jəudl] VI cantare lo jodel *or* alla tirolese

yoga ['jəugə] N yoga m

yoghurt, yogurt ['jəugət] N iogurt m *inv*

yoke [jəuk] N giogo ▶ VT (*also*: **yoke together**: *oxen*) aggiogare

yolk [jəuk] N tuorlo, rosso d'uovo

yonder ['jɔndəʳ] ADV là

yonks [jɔŋks] NPL: **for ~** (*BRIT col*) da una vita

you [ju:]

PRON **1** (*subject*) tu; (*: polite form*) lei; (*: pl*) voi; (*: formal*) loro; **you Italians enjoy your food** a voi italiani piace mangiare bene; **you and I will go** andiamo io e te (*or* lei ed io); **if I was** *or* **were you** se fossi in te (*or* lei *etc*)

2 (*object: direct*) ti; la; vi; loro (*after vb*); (*: indirect*) ti; le; vi; loro (*after vb*); **I know you** ti (*or* la *or* vi) conosco; **I'll see you tomorrow** ci vediamo domani; **I gave it to you** te l'ho dato; gliel'ho dato; ve l'ho dato; l'ho dato loro

3 (*stressed, after prep, in comparisons*) te; lei; voi; loro; **I told YOU to do it** ho detto a TE (*or* a LEI *etc*) di farlo; **she's younger than you** è più giovane di te (*or* lei *etc*)

4 (*impers: one*) si; **fresh air does you good** l'aria fresca fa bene; **you never know** non si sa mai

you'd [ju:d] = **you had**; **you would**

you'll [ju:l] = **you will**; **you shall**

young [jʌŋ] ADJ giovane ▸ NPL (*of animal*) piccoli *mpl*; **the ~** i giovani, la gioventù; **a ~ man** un giovanotto; **a ~ lady** una signorina; **a ~ woman** una giovane donna; **the younger generation** la nuova generazione; **my younger brother** il mio fratello minore

youngish ['jʌŋɪʃ] ADJ abbastanza giovane

youngster ['jʌŋstəʳ] N giovanotto(-a), ragazzo(-a); (*child*) bambino(-a)

your [jɔːʳ] ADJ il (la) tuo(-a); (*pl*) i (le) tuoi (tue); (*polite form*) il (la) suo(-a); (*pl*) i (le) suoi (sue); (*pl*) il (la) vostro(-a); (*pl*) i (le) vostri(-e); (*: formal*) il (la) loro; (*pl*) i (le) loro

you're [juəʳ] = **you are**

yours [jɔːz] PRON il (la) tuo(-a); (*pl*) i (le) tuoi (tue); (*polite form*) il (la) suo(-a); (*pl*) i (le) suoi (sue); (*pl*) il (la) vostro(-a); (*pl*) i (le) vostri(-e); (*: formal*) il (la) loro; (*pl*) i (le) loro; **~ sincerely/ faithfully** (*in letter*) cordiali/distinti saluti; **a friend of ~** un tuo (*or* suo *etc*) amico; **is it ~?** è tuo (*or* suo *etc*)?; *see also* **mine¹**

yourself [jɔːˈsɛlf] PRON (*reflexive*) ti; (*: polite form*) si; (*after prep*) te; sé; (*emphatic*) tu stesso(-a); lei stesso(-a); **you ~ told me** me l'hai detto proprio tu, tu stesso me l'hai detto

yourselves [jɔːˈsɛlvz] PL PRON (*reflexive*) vi; (*: polite form*) si; (*after prep*) voi; loro; (*emphatic*) voi stessi(-e); loro stessi(-e); *see also* **oneself**

youth [ju:θ] N gioventù *f*; (*pl* **youths** [ju:ðz]: *young man*) giovane *m*, ragazzo; **in my ~** da giovane, quando ero giovane

youth club N centro giovanile

youthful ['ju:θful] ADJ giovane; da giovane; giovanile

youthfulness ['ju:θfəlnɪs] N giovinezza

youth hostel N ostello della gioventù

youth movement N movimento giovanile

you've [ju:v] = **you have**

yowl [jaul] N (*of dog, person*) urlo; (*of cat*) miagolio ▸ VI urlare; miagolare

yr ABBR = **year**

YT ABBR (CANADA) = **Yukon Territory**

Yugoslav ['ju:gəuslɑːv] ADJ, N (*formerly*) jugoslavo(-a)

Yugoslavia [ju:gəuˈslɑːvɪə] N (*formerly*) Jugoslavia

Yugoslavian [ju:gəuˈslɑːvɪən] ADJ, N (*formerly*) jugoslavo(-a)

Yule log [ju:l-] N ceppo nel caminetto a Natale

yuppie ['jʌpɪ] ADJ, N (*col*) yuppie *mf inv*

YWCA N ABBR (= *Young Women's Christian Association*) Y.W.C.A. *m*

y

Zz

Z, z [zɛd, (US) ziː] N (letter) Z, z f inv or m inv; **Z for Zebra** ≈ Z come Zara

Zaire [zɑːˈɪəʳ] N Zaire m

Zambia [ˈzæmbɪə] N Zambia m

Zambian [ˈzæmbɪən] ADJ, N zambiano(-a)

zany [ˈzeɪnɪ] ADJ un po' pazzo(-a)

zap [zæp] VT (Comput) cancellare

zeal [ziːl] N zelo; entusiasmo

zealot [ˈzɛlət] N zelota mf

zealous [ˈzɛləs] ADJ zelante; premuroso(-a)

zebra [ˈziːbrə] N zebra

zebra crossing N (BRIT) (passaggio pedonale a) strisce fpl, zebre fpl

zenith [ˈzɛnɪθ] N zenit m inv; (fig) culmine m

zero [ˈzɪərəu] N zero; **5° below ~** 5° sotto zero

zero hour N l'ora zero

zero option N (Pol) opzione f zero

zero-rated [ˈzɪərəuˈreɪtɪd] ADJ (BRIT) ad aliquota zero

zest [zɛst] N gusto; (Culin) buccia

zigzag [ˈzɪgzæg] N zigzag m inv ▶ VI zigzagare

Zimbabwe [zɪmˈbɑːbwɪ] N Zimbabwe m

Zimbabwean [zɪmˈbɑːbwɪən] ADJ dello Zimbabwe

Zimmer® [ˈzɪməʳ] N (also: **Zimmer frame**) deambulatore m

zinc [zɪŋk] N zinco

Zionism [ˈzaɪənɪzəm] N sionismo

Zionist [ˈzaɪənɪst] ADJ sionistico(-a) ▶ N sionista mf

zip [zɪp] N (also: **zip fastener**) chiusura f or cerniera f lampo inv; (energy) energia, forza ▶ VT (Comput) zippare; (also: **zip up**) chiudere con una cerniera lampo

zip code N (US) codice m di avviamento postale

zipper N (US) cerniera f lampo inv

zit [zɪt] N brufolo

zither [ˈzɪðəʳ] N cetra

zodiac [ˈzəudɪæk] N zodiaco

zombie [ˈzɔmbɪ] N (fig): **like a ~** come un morto che cammina

zone [zəun] N (also Mil) zona

zoo [zuː] N zoo m inv

zoological [zuəˈlɔdʒɪkl] ADJ zoologico(-a)

zoologist [zuːˈɔlədʒɪst] N zoologo(-a)

zoology [zuːˈɔlədʒɪ] N zoologia

zoom [zuːm] VI: **to ~ past** sfrecciare; **to ~ in (on sb/sth)** (Phot, Cine) zumare (su qn/qc)

zoom lens N zoom m inv, obiettivo a focale variabile

zucchini [zuːˈkiːnɪ] N (pl inv: US) zucchina

Zulu [ˈzuːluː] ADJ, N zulù (mf) inv

Zumba® [ˈzumbə] N Zumba® f

Zürich [ˈzjuərɪk] N Zurigo f

Grammar
Grammatica

Using the Grammar

The Grammar Guide deals systematically and comprehensively with all the information you will need in order to communicate accurately in Italian. The user-friendly layout explains the grammar point on a left-hand page, leaving the facing page free for illustrative examples. The numbers, → ❶ etc, direct you to the relevant example in every case.

The Grammar Guide also provides invaluable guidance on the danger of translating English structures with identical structures in Italian. Use of Numbers and Pronunciation are important areas covered towards the end of the section. Finally, the index lists the main words and grammatical terms in both English and Italian.

Italic letters in Italian words show where stress does not follow the usual rules.

Abbreviations

fem.	*feminine*
infin.	*infinitive*
masc.	*masculine*
perf.	*perfect*
plur.	plural
sing.	singular
qc	**qualcosa**
qn	**qualcuno**
sb	somebody
sth	something

Contents

Verbs

Simple Tenses: Formation

In English, tenses are either simple, which means they consist of one word, e.g. *(I) work*, or compound, which means they consist of more than one word, e.g. *I have worked, I have been working*. The same is true in Italian.

In Italian the simple tenses are:

Present → ❶
Imperfect → ❷
Future → ❸
Present Conditional → ❹
Past Historic → ❺
Present Subjunctive → ❻
Imperfect Subjunctive → ❼

They are formed by adding endings to a verb stem. The endings show the number and person of the subject of the verb → ❽

The stem and endings of regular verbs are totally predictable. The following sections show all the patterns for regular verbs. For irregular verbs, see page 80 onwards.

Regular Verbs

There are three regular verb patterns (called conjugations), each identifiable by the ending of the infinitive:

First conjugation verbs end in **-are** e.g. **parlare** to speak

Second conjugation verbs end in **-ere** e.g. **credere** to believe

Third conjugation verbs end in **-ire** e.g. **finire** to finish

These three conjugations are treated in order on the following pages.

Examples

1 **parlo**

    I speak
    I am speaking

  parlo?

    do I speak?

2 **parlavo**

    I spoke
    I was speaking
    I used to speak

3 **parlerò**

    I shall/will/'ll speak

4 **parlerei**

    I should/would/'d speak

5 **parlai**

    I spoke

6 **(che) parli**

    that I speak

7 **(che) parlassi**

    that I should speak

8 **parlo**
  parliamo
  parlerei
  parleremmo

    I speak
    we speak
    I'd speak
    we'd speak

Verbs

Simple Tenses: First Conjugation

The stem is formed by taking the **-are** ending off the infinitive. The stem of **parlare** is **parl-** .

Add the following endings to the stem:

		❶ PRESENT	❷ IMPERFECT	❸ FUTURE
	1st person	**-o**	-avo	-erò
sing.	2nd person	**-i**	-avi	-erai
	3rd person	**-a**	-ava	-erà
	1st person	**-iamo**	-avamo	-eremo
plur.	2nd person	**-ate**	-avate	-erete
	3rd person	**-ano**	-avano	-eranno

		❹ PRESENT CONDITIONAL	❺ PAST HISTORIC
	1st person	**-erei**	-ai
sing.	2nd person	**-eresti**	-asti
	3rd person	**-erebbe**	-ò
	1st person	**-eremmo**	-ammo
plur.	2nd person	**-ereste**	-aste
	3rd person	**-erebbero**	-arono

		❻ PRESENT SUBJUNCTIVE	❼ IMPERFECT SUBJUNCTIVE
sing.	1st, 2nd persons	**-i**	-assi
	3rd person	**-i**	-asse
	1st person	**-iamo**	-assimmo
plur.	2nd person	**-iate**	-aste
	3rd person	**-ino**	-assero

Examples

1 PRESENT
parlo
parli
parla
parliamo
parlate
parlano

2 IMPERFECT
parlavo
parlavi
parlava
parlavamo
parlavate
parlavano

3 FUTURE
parlerò
parlerai
parlerà
parleremo
parlerete
parleranno

4 PRESENT CONDITIONAL
parlerei
parleresti
parlerebbe
parleremmo
parlereste
parlerebbero

5 PAST HISTORIC
parlai
parlasti
parlò
parlammo
parlaste
parlarono

6 PRESENT SUBJUNCTIVE
parli
parli
parli
parliamo
parliate
parlino

7 IMPERFECT SUBJUNCTIVE
parlassi
parlassi
parlasse
parlassimo
parlaste
parlassero

Verbs

Simple Tenses: Second Conjugation

The stem is formed by taking the **-ere** ending off the infinitive. The stem of **credere** is **cred-** .

Add the following endings to the stem:

		❶ PRESENT	❷ IMPERFECT	❸ FUTURE
	1st person	-o	-evo	-erò
sing.	2nd person	-i	-evi	-erai
	3rd person	-e	-eva	-erà
	1st person	-iamo	-evamo	-eremo
plur.	2nd person	-ete	-evate	-erete
	3rd person	-ono	-evano	-eranno

		❹ PRESENT CONDITIONAL	❺ PAST HISTORIC
	1st person	-erei	-ei or -etti
sing.	2nd person	-eresti	-esti
	3rd person	-erebbe	-ette
	1st person	-eremmo	-emmo
plur.	2nd person	-ereste	-este
	3rd person	-erebbero	-ettero

		❻ PRESENT SUBJUNCTIVE	❼ IMPERFECT SUBJUNCTIVE
sing.	1st, 2nd persons	-a	-essi
	3rd person	-a	-esse
	1st person	-iamo	-essimo
plur.	2nd person	-iate	-este
	3rd person	-ano	-essero

Examples

❶ PRESENT
credo
credi
crede
crediamo
credete
credono

❷ IMPERFECT
credevo
credevi
credeva
credevamo
credevate
credevano

❸ FUTURE
crederò
crederai
crederà
crederemo
crederete
crederanno

❹ PRESENT CONDITIONAL
crederei
crederesti
crederebbe
crederemmo
credereste
crederebbero

❺ PAST HISTORIC
credei *or* credetti
credesti
credette
credemmo
credeste
credettero

❻ PRESENT SUBJUNCTIVE
creda
creda
creda
crediamo
crediate
credano

❼ IMPERFECT SUBJUNCTIVE
credessi
credessi
credesse
credessimo
credeste
credessero

Verbs

Simple Tenses: Third Conjugation

Generally, the stem is formed by taking the **-ire** ending off the infinitive. The stem for most tenses of **finire** is **fin-**.

However, in the present tense and present subjunctive, **-isc-** is added to the basic stem (except for the 1st and 2nd person plural):

EXCEPTIONS: **servire** to serve, **dormire** to sleep, **soffrire** to suffer, **coprire** to cover, **sentire** to feel, **partire** to leave, **offrire** to offer, **aprire** to offer

The present tenses of **finire** and **dormire** are as follows:

		finire	dormire
	1st person	fin**isc**o	dormo
sing.	2nd person	fin**isc**i	dormi
	3rd person	fin**isc**e	dorme
	1st person	finiamo	dormiamo
plur.	2nd person	finite	dormite
	3rd person	fin**isc**ono	dormono

Both types of verb take the following endings:

		① PRESENT	② IMPERFECT	③ FUTURE
	1st person	-o	-ivo	-irò
sing.	2nd person	-i	-ivi	-irai
	3rd person	-e	-iva	-irà
	1st person	-iamo	-ivamo	-iremo
plur.	2nd person	-ite	-ivate	-irete
	3rd person	-ono	-ivano	-iranno

		④ PRESENT CONDITIONAL	⑤ PAST HISTORIC
	1st person	-irei	-i
sing.	2nd person	-iresti	-isti
	3rd person	-irebbe	-ì
	1st person	-iremmo	-immo
plur.	2nd person	-ireste	-iste
	3rd person	-irebbero	-irono

Examples

		⑥ PRESENT SUBJUNCTIVE	⑦ IMPERFECT SUBJUNCTIVE
sing.	1st, 2nd persons	-a	-issi
	3rd person	-a	-isse
plur.	1st person	-iamo	-issimmo
	2nd person	-iate	-iste
	3rd person	-ano	-issero

① PRESENT
finisc**o**
finisc**i**
finisc**e**
fin**iamo**
fin**ite**
finisc**ono**

② IMPERFECT
fin**ivo**
fin**ivi**
fin**iva**
fin**ivamo**
fin**ivate**
fin**ivano**

③ FUTURE
fin**irò**
fin**irai**
fin**irà**
fin**iremo**
fin**irete**
fin**iranno**

④ PRESENT SUBJUNCTIVE
fin**irei**
fin**iresti**
fin**irebbe**
fin**iremmo**
fin**ireste**
fin**irebbero**

⑤ PAST HISTORIC
fin**ii**
fin**isti**
fin**ì**
fin**immo**
fin**iste**
fin**irono**

⑥ PRESENT SUBJUNCTIVE
finisc**a**
finisc**a**
finisc**a**
fin**iamo**
fin**iate**
fin**iscano**

⑦ IMPERFECT SUBJUNCTIVE
fin**issi**
fin**issi**
fin**isse**
fin**issimo**
fin**iste**
fin**issero**

Verbs

First Conjugation Spelling Irregularities

Before certain endings, the stems of some **-are** verbs may change slightly.

Verbs ending:	**-care**
Change:	**c** becomes **ch** before **e** or **i**
Tenses affected:	Present, Future, Conditional, Present Subjunctive
Model:	**cercare** to look for → ❶

Why the change occurs: **h** is added to keep the **c** sound hard *k*.

Verbs ending:	**-gare**
Change:	**g** becomes **gh** before **e** or **i**
Tenses affected:	Present, Future, Conditional, Present Subjunctive
Model:	**pagare** to pay → ❷

Why the change occurs: **h** is added to keep the **g** sound hard *g*.

Examples

1 INFINITIVE

cercare

PRESENT	FUTURE
cerco	**cercherò**
cerchi	cercherai
cerca	**cercherà**
cerchiamo	cercheremo
cercate	cercherete
cercano	cercheranno

CONDITIONAL	PRESENT SUBJUNCTIVE
cercherei	**cerchi**
cercheresti	cerchi
cercherebbe	cerchi
cercheremmo	cerchiamo
cerchereste	cerchiate
cercherebbero	**cerchino**

2 INFINITIVE

pagare

PRESENT	FUTURE
pago	**pagherò**
paghi	pagherai
paga	**pagherà**
paghiamo	pagheremo
pagate	pagherete
pagano	pagheranno

CONDITIONAL	PRESENT SUBJUNCTIVE
pagherei	**paghi**
pagheresti	paghi
pagherebbe	paghi
pagheremmo	paghiamo
paghereste	paghiate
pagherebbero	paghino

Verbs

First Conjugation Spelling Irregularities *continued*

Verbs ending:	**-ciare**
Change:	**i** is dropped before **e** or **i**
Tenses affected:	Present, Future, Conditional, Present Subjunctive
Model:	**annunciare** to announce → **❶**

Why the change occurs: the **i** of the infinitive is needed to keep **c** soft *tʃ* before **a** (before **e** and **i**, **c** is soft, so the **i** is unnecessary).

Verbs ending:	**-giare**
Change:	**i** is dropped before **e** or **i**
Tenses affected:	Present, Future, Conditional, Present Subjunctive
Model:	**mangiare** to eat → **❷**

Why the change occurs: the **i** of the infinitive is needed to keep **g** soft *dʒ* before **a** (before **e** and **i**, **g** is soft, so the **i** is unnecessary).

Examples

1 INFINITIVE
annunciare

PRESENT	FUTURE
annuncio	**annuncerò**
annunci	**annuncerai**
annuncia	**annuncerà**
annunciamo	**annunceremo**
annunciate	**annuncerete**
annunciano	**annunceranno**

CONDITIONAL	PRESENT SUBJUNCTIVE
annuncerei	**annunci**
annunceresti	**annunci**
annuncerebbe	**annunci**
annunceremmo	**annunciamo**
annuncereste	**annunciate**
annuncerebbero	**annuncino**

2 INFINITIVE
mangiare

PRESENT	FUTURE
mangio	**mangerò**
mangi	**mangerai**
mangia	**mangerà**
mangiamo	**mangeremo**
mangiate	**mangerete**
mangiano	**mangeranno**

CONDITIONAL	PRESENT SUBJUNCTIVE
mangerei	**mangi**
mangeresti	**mangi**
mangerebbe	**mangi**
mangeremmo	**mangiamo**
mangereste	**mangiate**
mangerebbero	**mangino**

Verbs

First Conjugation Spelling Irregularities *continued*

Verbs ending: **-iare**
Change: **i** is not dropped before another **i**, which is what usually happens
Tenses affected: Present, Present Subjunctive
Model: **inviare** to send, **sciare** to ski → ❶

Why the change occurs: The **i** has to be retained in forms where it is the stressed vowel.

Verbs ending: **-gliare**
Change: **i** is dropped before endings beginning with **-i**
Tenses affected: Present, Present subjunctive, Imperfect Subjunctive, Imperative
Model: **consigliare** to advise, **svegliare** to wake up → ❷

Why the change occurs: There is no need to retain the **i**.

Examples

❶ INFINITIVE
inviare
PRESENT
invio
invii
invia
inviamo
inviate
inviano

❷ INFINITIVE
svegliare
PRESENT
sveglio
svegli
sveglia
svegliamo
svegliate
svegliano

Verbs

The Imperative

The imperative is the form of the verb used to give commands or instructions. It can be used politely, as in English 'Please take a seat'. In Italian, the polite imperative is the 3rd person form, either singular or plural. The 1st person plural (we) is used to make suggestions, as in 'Let's go'.

The imperative is formed by adding endings to the stem of the verb. The endings for the 1st and 2nd persons plural are the same as those for the present tense; the others are different. → ❶

	FIRST		SECOND		THIRD
sing. 2nd pers. **-a**	sing. 2nd pers. **-i**	sing. 2nd pers. **-i**
3rd pers. **-i**	3rd pers. **-a**	3rd pers. **-a**
plur. 1st pers. **-iamo**	plur. 1st pers. **-iamo**	plur. 1st pers. **-iamo**
2nd pers. **-ate**	2nd pers. **-ete**	2nd pers. **-ite**
3rd pers. **-ino**	3rd pers. **-ano**	3rd pers. **-ano**

NB Third conjugation verbs which add **isc** to the stem in the present tense also do so in the imperative → ❷

The imperative of irregular verbs is given in the verb tables (pages 80–125).

Position of object and reflexive pronouns with the imperative:
- they follow imperatives in the 2nd person and the **-iamo** form, and are joined on to make one word → ❸
- they precede 3rd person polite imperatives, and are not joined on to them → ❹

Changes to pronouns following the imperative:
- the first letter of the pronoun is doubled when the imperative is one syllable: **mi** becomes **mmi**, **ti** becomes **tti**, **lo** becomes **llo** etc → ❺
- When the pronouns **mi**, **ti**, **ci** and **vi** are followed by another pronoun they become **-me**, **-te**, **-ce** and **-ve**, and **gli** and **le** become **glie-** → ❻

Negative imperatives:
- **non** precedes the imperative to make it negative (except in the 2nd person singular) → ❼
- in 2nd person singular negative commands, **non** is used before the infinitive instead of the imperative. Pronouns may be joined onto the infinitive, or precede it → ❽

Examples

❶ Compare:
Aspetti, Maria?	Are you waiting, Maria?
and: **Aspetta, Maria!**	Wait, Maria!
Prende l'autobus	He gets the bus
and: **Prenda l'autobus, signora!**	Get the bus, madam!

❷
Finisci l'esercizio, Marco!	Finish the exercise, Marco!
Finisca tutto, signore!	Finish it all, sir!
Finiamo tutto	Let's finish it all
Finite i compiti, ragazzi!	Finish your homework, children!
Finiscano tutto signori!	Finish it all, ladies and gentlemen!

❸
Guardami, mamma!	Look at me, mum!
Aspettateli!	Wait for them!
Proviamolo!	Let's try it!

❹
Mi dia un chilo d'uva, per favore	Give me a kilo of grapes, please
Si accomodi!	Take a seat!
La prenda, signore	Take it, sir

❺
Dimmi!	Tell me!
Fallo subito!	Do it immediately!

❻
Mandameli	Send me them
Daglielo	Give it to him
Mandiamogliela!	Let's send it to them!

❼
Non dimentichiamo	Don't let's forget
Non si preoccupi, signore	Don't worry, sir

❽
Non dire bugie, Andrea!	Don't tell lies, Andrea!
Non dimenticare!	Don't forget!
Non toccarlo! *or* **Non lo toccare!**	Don't touch it!
Non glielo dire! *or* **Non dirglielo**	Don't tell him about it!
Non preoccuparti! *or* **Non ti preoccupare**!	Don't worry!

Verbs

Compound Tenses

Continuous tenses

The simple tense of an Italian verb, e.g. **piove**, can have two meanings:
'it rains' or 'it's raining'; the continuous tense, **sta piovendo** is an
alternative way of expressing the English present continuous (it's raining).

The Present Continuous is used less in Italian than in English. It is formed
with the present tense of the verb **stare**, plus the gerund → **1**

The Past Continuous is formed with the imperfect tense of **stare,**
plus the gerund → **2**

For information on how to form the gerund, see page 52.

The Past Continuous is also used less in Italian than in English,
as the imperfect tense can be used to express this meaning.

Examples

1 **Ci sto pensando**   I'm thinking about it
   Stanno arrivando   They're coming
   Cosa stai facendo?   What are you doing?

2 **Stavo studiando**   I was studying
   Stava morendo   He was dying
   Stavano lavorando   They were working

Verbs

Compound Tenses *continued*

Formed with the past participle

These are:

        Perfect → **①**
        Pluperfect → **②**
        Future Perfect → **③**
        Perfect Conditional → **④**
        Past Anterior → **⑤**
        Perfect Subjunctive → **⑥**
        Pluperfect Subjunctive → **⑦**

They consist of the past past participle and an auxiliary verb. Most verbs take the auxiliary **avere**, but some take *essere* (see page 30).

These tenses are formed in the same way for regular and irregular verbs, the only difference being that an irregular verb may have an irregular past participle.

The Past Participle

The past participle of regular verbs is formed as follows:

      First conjugation: replace the **-are** of the infinitive with **-ato** → **⑧**

      Second conjugation: replace the **-ere** of the infinitive with **-uto** → **⑨**

      Third conjugation: replace the **-ire** of the infinitive with **-ito** → **⑩**

Examples

<table>
<tr><td>with avere</td><td>with essere</td></tr>
</table>

① **ho parlato** I spoke, have spoken   **sono andato** I went, have gone

② **avevo parlato** I had spoken   **ero andato** I had gone

③ **avrò parlato** I will have spoken   **sarò andato** I will have gone

④ **avrei parlato** I would have spoken   **sarei andato** I would have gone

⑤ **ebbi parlato** I had spoken   **fui andato** I had gone

⑥ *a*bbia **parlato** I spoke, have spoken   **sia andato** I went, have gone

⑦ **avessi parlato** I had spoken   **fossi andato** I had gone

⑧ **parlare** to speak → **parlato** spoken

⑨ **credere** to believe → **creduto** believed

⑩ **finire** to finish → **finito** finished

Verbs

Compound Tenses *continued*

Verbs taking the auxiliary avere

PERFECT TENSE
The present tense of **avere** plus the past participle → ❶

PLUPERFECT TENSE
The imperfect tense of **avere** plus the past participle → ❷

FUTURE PERFECT
The future tense of **avere** plus the past participle → ❸

PERFECT CONDITIONAL
The conditional of **avere** plus the past participle → ❹

PAST ANTERIOR
The past historic of **avere** plus the past participle → ❺

PERFECT SUBJUNCTIVE
The present subjunctive of **avere** plus the past participle → ❻

PLUPERFECT SUBJUNCTIVE
The imperfect subjunctive of **avere** plus the past participle → ❼

For how to form the past participle of regular verbs, see page 24. The past participle of irregular verbs is given for each verb in the verb tables, pages 80–125.

The past participle agrees in number and gender with a preceding direct object when it is **lo, la, li** or **le**, e.g.

Le matite? Le ho comprate ieri   The pencils? I bought them yesterday

Examples

① PERFECT

ho parlato	abbiamo parlato
hai parlato	avete parlato
ha parlato	hanno parlato

② PLUPERFECT

avevo parlato	avevamo parlato
avevi parlato	avevate parlato
aveva parlato	avevano parlato

③ FUTURE PERFECT

avrò parlato	avremo parlato
avrai parlato	avrete parlato
avrà parlato	avranno parlato

④ PERFECT CONDITIONAL

avrei parlato	avremmo parlato
avresti parlato	avreste parlato
avrebbe parlato	avrebbero parlato

⑤ PAST ANTERIOR

ebbi parlato	avemmo parlato
avesti parlato	aveste parlato
ebbe parlato	ebbero parlato

⑥ PERFECT SUBJUNCTIVE

abbia parlato	abbiamo parlato
abbia parlato	abbiate parlato
abbia parlato	abbiano parlato

⑦ PLUPERFECT SUBJUNCTIVE

avessi parlato	avessimo parlato
avessi parlato	aveste parlato
avesse parlato	avessero parlato

Verbs

Compound Tenses *continued*

Verbs taking the auxiliary *essere*

PERFECT TENSE
The present tense of **essere** plus the past participle → ❶

PLUPERFECT TENSE
The imperfect tense of **essere** plus the past participle → ❷

FUTURE PERFECT
The future tense of **essere** plus the past participle → ❸

PERFECT CONDITIONAL
The conditional of **essere** plus the past participle → ❹

PAST ANTERIOR
The past historic of **essere** plus the past participle → ❺

PERFECT SUBJUNCTIVE
The present subjunctive of **essere** plus the past participle → ❻

PLUPERFECT SUBJUNCTIVE
The imperfect subjunctive of **essere** plus the past participle → ❼

For how to form the past participle of regular verbs, see page 24. The past participle of irregular verbs is given for each verb in the verb tables, pages 80–125.

For agreement of past participles, see page 56.

For a list of verbs and verb types that take the auxiliary **essere**, see page 30.

Examples

1 PERFECT

sono andato(a)	siamo andati(e)
sei andato(a)	siete andati(e)
è andato(a)	sono andati(e)

2 PLUPERFECT

ero andato(a)	eravamo andati(e)
eri andato(a)	eravate andati(e)
era andato(a)	erano andati(e)

3 FUTURE PERFECT

sarò andato(a)	saremo andati(e)
sarai andato(a)	sarete andati(e)
sarà andato(a)	saranno andati(e)

4 PERFECT CONDITIONAL

sarei andato(a)	saremmo andati(e)
saresti andato(a)	sareste andati(e)
sarebbe andato(a)	sarebbero andati(e)

5 PAST ANTERIOR

fui andato(a)	fummo andati(e)
fosti andato(a)	foste andati(e)
fu andato(a)	furono andati(e)

6 PERFECT SUBJUNCTIVE

sia andato(a)	siamo andati(e)
sia andato(a)	siate andati(e)
sia andato(a)	siano andati(e)

7 PLUPERFECT SUBJUNCTIVE

fossi andato(a)	fossimo andati(e)
fossi andato(a)	foste andati(e)
fosse andato(a)	fossero andati(e)

Verbs

Compound Tenses *continued*

The following verbs take the auxiliary *essere*
Reflexive verbs (see page 32) → ❶

Many intransitive verbs (i.e. verbs not taking a direct object), including the following:

andare to go	**partire** to leave
apparire to appear	**restare** to stay
arrivare to arrive → ❷	**rimanere** to stay
bastare to be enough	**ritornare** to return → ❹
cadere to fall	**riuscire** to succeed/manage → ❺
costare to cost → ❸	**salire** to go up/get on
dipendere to depend	**scadere** to expire
divenire to become	**scappare** to get away
diventare to become	**scendere** to go down
durare to last	**scivolare** to slip
entrare to come in	**sparire** to disappear → ❻
esistere to exist	**stare** to be/stay
essere to be	**succedere** to happen
fuggire to escape	**tornare** to come back
intervenire to intervene	**venire** to come
morire to die	**uscire** to go out
nascere to be born	

The following verbs, often used in impersonal constructions:

bisognare	**occorrere**
convenire	**parere** → ❽
dispiacere	**piacere** → ❾
importare	**sembrare**
mancare → ❼	

Verbs that can be used both transitively and intransitively take the auxiliary **essere** when intransitive and **avere** when transitive → ❿

Impersonal verbs which describe the weather are used with both **essere** and **avere** → ⓫

ⓘ Note that the past participle agrees in gender and number with the subject of verbs conjugated with **essere**.

Examples

① **Mi sono fatto male**   I've hurt *or* I hurt myself
   Si è rotta la gamba   She's broken *or* She broke her leg
   Vi siete divertiti?   Did you have *or* Have you had a nice time?
   Si sono addormentati   They've gone *or* They went to sleep

② **È arrivata**   She's arrived *or* She arrived

③ **È costato parecchio**   It cost a lot *or* It has cost a lot

④ **Siamo ritornati**   We've returned *or* We returned

⑤ **Sei riuscito?**   Did you succeed? *or* Have you succeeded?

⑥ **Sono spariti**   They've disappeared

⑦ **Ti sono mancata?**   Did you miss me?

⑧ **Mi è parso strano**   It seemed strange to me

⑨ **Vi è piaciuta la musica?**   Did you like the music?

⑩ **passare**
   Intransitive
   Sono passati molti anni   Many years have passed
   Transitive
   Ho passato l'esame   I've passed the exam

   saltare
   Intransitive
   Il gatto è saltato sul tavolo   The cat jumped on the table
   Transitive
   Ho saltato il pranzo   I skipped lunch

⑪ **Ha piovuto** *or*
   È piovuto molto   It rained a lot
   Ha nevicato! *or*
   È nevicato!   It's snowed!

Verbs

Reflexive Verbs

A reflexive verb is one accompanied by a reflexive pronoun, e.g. **divertirsi** to enjoy oneself; **annoiarsi** to get bored.
The reflexive pronouns are:

	SINGULAR		PLURAL
1st pers.	**mi**	1st pers.	**ci**
2nd pers.	**ti**	2nd pers.	**vi**
3rd pers.	**si**	3rd pers.	**si**

The Italian reflexive pronoun is often not translated in English → **1**

Plural reflexive pronouns can sometimes be translated as 'each other' → **2**

Simple tenses of reflexive verbs are conjugated in exactly the same way as other verbs, except that the reflexive pronoun is always used. Compound tenses are conjugated with the auxiliary **essere**. A sample reflexive verb is conjugated in full on pages 36 and 37.

Position of Reflexive Pronouns

The pronoun generally comes before the verb → **3**

However, in positive 2nd person commands the pronoun is joined onto the end of the imperative → **4**

In the infinitive, the final **e** is dropped and replaced by the reflexive pronoun → **5**

When the infinitive is used with **non** in negative commands, the reflexive pronoun **ti** either comes first, as a separate word, or is joined on at the end → **6**

Two alternatives also exist
- when the infinitive is used after another verb, the pronoun either goes before the main verb or joins onto the infinitive → **7**
- in continuous tenses the pronoun either goes before the main verb or joins onto the gerund → **8**

Examples

① Mi annoio
    I'm getting bored
    Ti fidi di lui?
    Do you trust him?
    Si vergogna
    He's embarrassed
    Non vi preoccupate!
    Don't worry!

② Si odiano
    They hate each other

③ Mi diverto
    I'm enjoying myself
    Ci prepariamo
    We're getting ready
    Si accomodi!
    Take a seat!

④ Svegliati!
    Wake up!
    Divertitevi!
    Enjoy yourselves!

⑤ Compare:

ordinary infinitive	*reflexive infinitive*
lavare to wash	**lavarsi** to get washed, wash oneself
divertire to amuse	**divertirsi** to enjoy oneself

⑥ Non ti bruciare! *or*
    Non bruciarti!
    Don't burn yourself!
    Non ti preoccupare! *or*
    Non preoccuparti!
    Don't worry!

    Mi voglio abbronzare *or*
    Voglio abbronzarmi
    I want to get a tan
    Ti devi alzare *or*
    Devi alzarti
    You must get up
    Vi dovreste preparare *or*
    Dovreste prepararvi
    You ought to get ready

⑦ Ti stai annoiando? *or*
    Stai annoiandoti?
    Are you getting bored?
    Si stanno alzando? *or*
    Stanno alzandosi?
    Are they getting up?

Verbs

Reflexive Verbs *continued*

Past Participle Agreement

The past participle used in compound tenses of reflexive verbs generally agrees with the subject of the verb → **1**

Here are some common reflexive verbs:

accomodarsi to sit down/take a seat
addormentarsi to go to sleep
alzarsi to get up
annoiarsi to get bored/be bored
arrabbiarsi to get angry
cambiarsi to get changed
chiamarsi to be called
chiedersi to wonder
divertirsi to enjoy oneself/have fun
farsi male to hurt oneself
fermarsi to stop
lavarsi to wash/get washed
perdersi to get lost
pettinarsi to comb one's hair
preoccuparsi to worry
prepararsi to get ready
ricordarsi to remember
sbrigarsi to hurry
sedersi to sit
svegliarsi to wake up
vestirsi to dress/get dressed

Examples

❶ Si è lavato le mani   He washed his hands
   Si è lavata le mani   She washed her hands
   I ragazzi si sono lavati le mani   The boys washed their hands
   Le ragazze si sono lavate le mani   The girls washed their hands

Verbs

Reflexive Verbs *continued*

Conjugation of: **divertirsi** to enjoy oneself – SIMPLE TENSES

PRESENT

mi diverto	ci divertiamo
ti diverti	vi divertite
si diverte	si divertono

IMPERFECT

mi divertivo	ci divertivamo
ti divertivi	vi divertivate
si divertiva	si divertivano

FUTURE

mi divertirò	ci divertiremo
ti divertirai	vi divertirete
si divertirà	si divertiranno

CONDITIONAL

mi divertirei	ci divertiremmo
ti divertiresti	vi divertireste
si divertirebbe	si divertirebbero

PAST HISTORIC

mi divertii	ci divertimmo
ti divertisti	vi divertiste
si divertì	si divertirono

PRESENT SUBJUNCTIVE

mi diverta	ci divertiamo
ti diverta	vi divertiate
si diverta	si divertano

IMPERFECT SUBJUNCTIVE

mi divertissi	ci divertissimo
ti divertissi	vi divertiste
si divertisse	si divertissero

Verbs

Conjugation of: **divertirsi** to enjoy oneself – COMPOUND TENSES

PRESENT CONTINUOUS

mi sto divertendo *or*
sto divertendomi
ti stai divertendo *or*
stai divertendoti
si sta divertendo *or*
sta divertendosi

ci stiamo divertendo *or*
stiamo divertendoci
vi state divertendo *or*
state divertendovi
si stanno divertendo *or*
stanno divertendosi

PERFECT

mi sono divertito(a)
ti sei divertito(a)
si è divertito(a)

ci siamo divertiti(e)
vi siete divertiti(e)
si sono divertiti(e)

PLUPERFECT

mi ero divertito(a)
ti eri divertito(a)
si era divertito(a)

ci eravamo divertiti(e)
vi eravate divertiti(e)
si erano divertiti(e)

FUTURE PERFECT

mi sarò divertito(a)
ti sarai divertito(a)
si sarà divertito(a)

ci saremo divertiti(e)
vi sarete divertiti(e)
si saranno divertiti(e)

PERFECT CONDITIONAL

mi sarei divertito(a)
ti saresti divertito(a)
si sarebbe divertito(a)

ci saremmo divertiti(e)
vi sareste divertiti(e)
si sarebbero divertiti(e)

PAST ANTERIOR

mi fui divertito(a)
ti fosti divertito(a)
si fu divertito(a)

ci fummo divertiti(e)
vi foste divertiti(e)
si furono divertiti(e)

PERFECT SUBJUNCTIVE

mi sia divertito(a)
ti sia divertito(a)
si sia divertito(a)

ci siamo divertiti(e)
vi siate divertiti(e)
si siano divertiti(e)

PLUPERFECT SUBJUNCTIVE

mi fossi divertito(a)
ti fossi divertito(a)
si fosse divertito(a)

ci fossimo divertiti(e)
vi foste divertiti(e)
si fossero divertiti(e)

Verbs

The Passive

In the passive, the subject *receives* the action (e.g. I was hit) as opposed to *performing* it (e.g. I hit him). In English the passive is formed with the verb 'to be' and the past participle, and in Italian the passive is formed in exactly the same way, i.e. a tense of **essere** + *past participle*.

The past participle agrees in gender and number with the subject → **1**

A sample verb is conjugated in the passive on pages 40 and 41.

In English it is possible to make the indirect object of an active sentence into the subject of a passive sentence, e.g. Someone gave it to me → I was given it. This is not possible in Italian; instead a 3ʳᵈ person plural can be used → **2**

The passive is used less overall in Italian. The following alternatives are used:
- active constructions → **3**
- the **si passivante** (preceding an active verb with **si**, to make it passive → **4**
- an impersonal construction with **si** → **5**

Examples

1 È stato costretto a ritirarsi dalla gara
He was forced to withdraw from the competition

L'elettricità è stata tagliata ieri
The electricity was cut off yesterday

La partita è stata rinviata
The match has been postponed

Siamo invitati ad una festa a casa loro
We're invited to a party at their house

I ladri sono stati catturati
The thieves have been caught

Le finestre saranno riparate domani
The windows will be repaired tomorrow

2 Mi hanno dato una chiave
I've been given a key

Gli diranno tutto
He'll be told everything

3 Due persone sono morte
Two people were killed

Mi hanno rubato la macchina la settimana scorsa
My car was stolen last week

C'erano delle microspie nella stanza
The room was bugged

Dicono che sia molto ambizioso
He's said to be very ambitious

4 Dove si trovano i vini migliori?
Where are the best wines to be found?

Non si accettano assegni
Cheques are not accepted

Queste parole non si usano più
These words are no longer used

Questo vino si beve a temperatura ambiente
This wine should be drunk at room temperature

5 Non si fa così
That's not how it's done

Si raccomanda la massima discrezione
The utmost discretion is called for

39

Verbs

The Passive *continued*

Conjugation of: **invitare** to invite

PRESENT

sono invitato(a)   siamo invitati(e)
sei invitato(a)   siete invitati(e)
è invitato(a)   sono invitati(e)

IMPERFECT

ero invitato(a)   eravamo invitati(e)
eri invitato(a)   eravate invitati(e)
era invitato(a)   erano invitati(e)

FUTURE

sarò invitato(a)   saremo invitati(e)
sarai invitato(a)   sarete invitati(e)
sarà invitato(a)   saranno invitati(e)

CONDITIONAL

sarei invitato(a)   saremmo invitati(e)
saresti invitato(a)   sareste invitati(e)
sarebbe invitato(a)   sarebbero invitati(e)

PAST HISTORIC

fui invitato(a)   fummo invitati(e)
fosti invitato(a)   foste invitati(e)
fu invitato(a)   furono invitati(e)

PRESENT SUBJUNCTIVE

sia invitato(a)   siamo invitati(e)
sia invitato(a)   siate invitati(e)
sia invitato(a)   siano invitati(e)

IMPERFECT SUBJUNCTIVE

fossi invitato(a)   fossimo invitati(e)
fossi invitato(a)   foste invitati(e)
fosse invitato(a)   fossero invitati(e)

Verbs

The Passive *continued*

Conjugation of: **invitare** to invite

PERFECT
sono stato(a) invitato(a)   siamo stati(e) invitati(e)
sei stato(a) invitato(a)   siete stati(e) invitati(e)
è stato(a) invitato(a)   sono stati(e) invitati(e)

PLUPERFECT
ero stato(a) invitato(a)   eravamo stati(e) invitati(e)
eri stato(a) invitato(a)   eravate stati(e) invitati(e)
era stato(a) invitato(a)   erano stati(e) invitati(e)

FUTURE PERFECT
sarò stato(a) invitato(a)   saremo stati(e) invitati(e)
sarai stato(a) invitato(a)   sarete stati(e) invitati(e)
sarà stato(a) invitato(a)   saranno stati(e) invitati(e)

PERFECT CONDITIONAL
sarei stato(a) invitato(a)   saremmo stati(e) invitati(e)
saresti stato(a) invitato(a)   sareste stati(e) invitati(e)
sarebbe stato(a) invitato(a)   sarebbero stati(e) invitati(e)

PAST ANTERIOR
fui stato(a) invitato(a)   fummo stati(e) invitati(e)
fosti stato(a) invitato(a)   foste stati(e) invitati(e)
fu stato(a) invitato(a)   furono stati(e) invitati(e)

PERFECT SUBJUNCTIVE
sia stato(a) invitato(a)   siamo stati(e) invitati(e)
sia stato(a) invitato(a)   siate stati(e) invitati(e)
sia stato(a) invitato(a)   siano stati(e) invitati(e)

PLUPERFECT SUBJUNCTIVE
fossi stato(a) invitato(a)   fossimo stati(e) invitati(e)
fossi stato(a) invitato(a)   foste stati(e) invitati(e)
fosse stato(a) invitato(a)   fossero stati(e) invitati(e)

Verbs

Impersonal Verbs

Any verb can be made impersonal by the use of **si** → ❶

si is often used to make the following verbs impersonal:

dire	**si dice che** → ❷ it's said that
potere	**si può** → ❸ it's possible to/you can
trattarsi	**si tratta di** → ❹ it's about/it's a matter of

Impersonal verbs are used only in the infinitive, with a gerund and in the third person singular. No pronoun is used in Italian.

e.g. **Ha iniziato a piovere.**   It started to rain.
Sta piovendo?   Is it raining?
Nevicava da due giorni.   It had been snowing for two days.
È facile capire che…   It's easy to see that…

Common impersonal verbs are:

diluviare	**diluvia**	it's pouring
gelare	**gela**	it's freezing
grandinare	**grandina**	it's hailing
nevicare	**nevica**	it's snowing
piovere	**piove**	it's raining
tuonare	**tuona**	it's thundering

Other verbs are often used impersonally:

bastare	**basta**	that's enough
importare	**non importa**	it doesn't matter

Examples

❶ In quel ristorante si mangia bene e si spende poco

In that restaurant the food's good and it doesn't cost much

❷ Si dice che sia una persona strana

It's said that he's a strange person

❸ Si può visitare il castello tutti i giorni dell'anno

You can visit the castle every day of the year

❹ Di cosa si tratta?
Si tratta di poche ore

What's it about?
It's a matter of a few hours

Verbs

Impersonal Verbs *continued*

The following verbs are used in impersonal constructions:

INFINITIVE	CONSTRUCTIONS
bastare	**basta** + *infinitive* → ❶ you just have to
bisognare	**bisogna** + *infinitive* → ❷ you have to
convenire	*indirect pronoun* + **conviene** + *infinitive* → ❸ it's best to
essere	**è** + *noun to do with time/season* → ❹
sono	+ *plural times of the clock* → ❺ it is **è** + *adjective* + *infinitive* → ❻ **è** + *adjective* + **che** → ❼ it is
fare	**fa** + *adjective describing weather* → ❽ it is **fa** + *noun to do with weather, time of day*
occorrere	**occorre** + *infinitive* → ❾ it would be best to
parere	**pare** + **di** + **sì/no** → ❿ it seems so/not **pare** + **che** → ⓫ it seems/apparently
sembrare	**sembra** + **che** → ⓬ it seems

Examples

1 **Basta chiedere a qualcuno** You just have to ask someone

2 **Bisogna prenotare?** Do you have to book?
Bisogna arrivare un'ora prima You have to get there an hour before

3 **Conviene partire presto** It's best to set off early

4 **È tardi.** It's late
Era presto It was early
Era Pasqua It was Easter
È mezzogiorno It's midday

5 **Sono le otto** It's eight o'clock

6 **È stato stupido buttarli via** It was stupid to throw them away
Sarebbe bello andarci It would be nice to go there

7 **È vero che sono stato impaziente** It's true that I've been impatient
È possibile che abbia sbagliato tu Maybe you made a mistake

8 **Fa caldo** It's hot
Fa freddo It's cold
Faceva bel tempo It was good weather *or* The weather was good
Fa sempre brutto tempo The weather's always bad
Si sta facendo buio It's getting dark

9 **Occorre farlo subito** It would be best to do it immediately

10 **Sono contenti? — Pare di sì.** Are they happy? — It seems so.
L'ha creduto? — Pare di no. Did he believe it? — Apparently not.

11 **Pare che sia stato lui** Apparently it was him

12 **Sembra che tu abbia ragione** It seems you're right

45

Verbs

The Infinitive

The infinitive is the form of the verb found in dictionary entries, e.g.
parlare to speak; **finire** to finish. The infinitive sometimes drops its final **-e**.

All regular verbs have infinitives ending in **-are**, **-ere**, or **-ire**.

A few irregular verbs have infinitives ending in **-rre**, e.g.

comporre	to compose	**condurre**	to lead
porre	to put	**produrre**	to produce
proporre	to propose	**ridurre**	to reduce
supporre	to suppose	**tradurre**	to translate

In Italian the infinitive is used in the following ways:
- after adjectives and nouns that are followed by **di** → **①**
- after another verb → **②**
- to give general instructions or orders, e.g. on signs → **③**
- in 2nd person singular negative imperatives → **④**

See page 20 for negative imperatives

- after prepositions → **⑤**

See pages 190-197 for prepositions

- as the subject or object of a sentence → **⑥**

There are three main types of constructions when the infinitive follows another verb:
- no linking preposition → **⑦**
- linking preposition **a** (see also pages 70-78) → **⑧**
- linking preposition **di** (see also pages 70-78) → **⑨**

Examples

1 **Sono contento di vederti**   I'm glad to see you
   Sono sorpreso di vederti qui   I'm surprised to see you here
   Sono stufo di studiare   I'm fed up with studying
   Non c'è bisogno di prenotare   There's no need to book

2 **Non devi mangiare se non vuoi**   You don't have to eat if you don't want to

   Posso entrare?   Can I come in?
   Cosa ti piacerebbe fare?   What would you like to do?

3 **Rallentare**   Slow down
   Spingere   Push

4 **Non fare sciocchezze!**   Don't do anything silly!
   Non toccarlo!   Don't touch it!

5 **È andato via senza dire niente**   He went away without saying anything

6 **Camminare fa bene**   Walking is good for you
   Mi piace cavalcare   I like riding

7 **Devi aspettare**   You must wait

8 **Hanno cominciato a ridere**   They started to laugh

9 **Quando sono entrato hanno smesso di parlare**   When I came in, they stopped talking

Verbs

The Infinitive *continued*

Verbs followed by the infinitive with no linking preposition

dovere, **potere**, **sapere**, **volere** (i.e. modal auxiliary verbs: page 58).

verbs of seeing and hearing, e.g. **vedere** to see; **sentire** to hear → ①

Verbs used impersonally such as **piacere**, **dispiacere**, **occorrere** and **convenire** → ②

fare → ③

lasciare to let, allow → ④

The following common verbs:

bisognare → ⑤	to be necessary
detestare	to hate
desiderare → ⑥	to want
odiare → ⑦	to hate
preferire → ⑧	to prefer

Examples

❶ Ci ha visto arrivare
   He saw us arriving
   Ti ho sentito cantare
   I heard you singing

❷ Mi piace andare in bici
   I like cycling
   Ci dispiace andar via
   We're sorry to be leaving
   Occorre farlo subito
   It should be done immediately
   Ti conviene partire presto
   You'd best set off early

❸ Non mi far ridere!
   Don't make me laugh!

❹ Lascia fare a me
   Let me do it

❺ Bisogna prenotare
   You need to book

**❻ Desiderava migliorare il suo
   inglese**
   He wanted to improve his
   English

**❼ Odio alzarmi presto al
   mattino**
   I hate getting up early in the
   morning

❽ Preferisco non parlarne
   I prefer not to talk about it

Verbs

The Infinitive *continued*

Set expressions

The following are set in Italian with the meaning shown:

> **far entrare** to let in → ❶
> **far sapere** to inform/let someone know → ❷
> **far fare** to have done → ❸
> **farsi fare** to have done → ❹
> **lasciare stare** to leave alone → ❺
> **sentir dire che** to hear that → ❻
> **sentir parlare di** to hear about → ❼
> **voler dire** to mean → ❽

The Perfect Infinitive

The perfect infinitive is formed using the auxiliary verb **avere** or *essere* (as appropriate) with the past participle of the verb → ❾

The perfect infinitive is found:
- after modal verbs → ❿
- after prepositions → ⓫

Examples

1 **Non mi hanno fatto entrare**   They wouldn't let me in

2 **Ti farò sapere prima possibile**   I'll let you know as soon as
                                          possible

3 **Ho fatto riparare la macchina**   I had the car repaired

4 **Mi sono fatta tagliare i capelli**   I had my hair cut

5 **Lascia stare mia sorella!**   Leave my sister alone!

6 **Ho sentito dire che è stato**   I heard he's been sacked
licenziato

7 **Non ho più sentito parlare di loro**   I haven't heard any more about
                                              them

8 **Non so che cosa vuol dire**   I don't know what it means

9 **aver(e) visto**   to have seen
essere partito   to have gone
essersi fatto male   to have hurt oneself

10 **Può aver avuto un incidente**   He may have had an accident
Dev'essere successo ieri   It must have happened yesterday

11 **senza aver dato un esame**   without having done an exam
dopo essere rimasto chiuso   after having been closed

Verbs

The Gerund

Formation

First conjugation:

Replace the **-are** of the infinitive with **-ando** → **①**

Second and Third conjugations:

Replace the **-ere**, or **-ire** of the infinitive with **-endo** → **②**

Exceptions to these rules are:

fare and verbs made by adding a prefix to **fare** → **③**
dire and verbs made by adding a prefix to **dire** → **④**
porre and verbs made by adding a prefix to **porre** → **⑤**
verbs with infinitives ending in **-durre** → **⑥**

The gerund is invariable.*

*A word that is invariable never changes its ending.

Examples

① **parlare** to speak → **parlando** speaking
andare to go → **andando** going
dare to give → **dando** giving

② **credere** to believe → **credendo** believing
essere to be → **essendo** being
dovere to have to → **dovendo** having to
finire to finish → **finendo** finishing
dormire to sleep → **dormendo** sleeping

③ **fare** to do → **facendo** doing
rifare to redo → **rifacendo** redoing

④ **dire** to say → **dicendo** saying
contraddire to contradict → **contraddicendo** contradicting

⑤ **porre** to put → **ponendo** putting
comporre to compose → **componendo** composing
supporre to suppose → **supponendo** supposing

⑥ **condurre** to lead → **conducendo** leading
produrre to produce → **producendo** producing
ridurre to reduce → **riducendo** reducing

Verbs

The Gerund *continued*

Uses

The gerund is used with the present tense of **stare** to make the present continuous tense → ①

The gerund is used with the imperfect tense of **stare** to make the past continuous tense → ②

ⓘ Note that the Italian past participle is sometimes used with the verbs **stare** or **essere** to make a continuous tense, e.g.

***essere* or stare disteso**	to be lying → ③
***essere* or stare seduto**	to be sitting → ③
***essere* or stare appoggiato**	to be leaning → ③

The gerund can used adverbially, to indicate when or why something happens → ④

Pronouns are usually joined onto the end of the gerund → ⑤

When the gerund is part of a continuous tense the pronoun can either come before **stare** or be joined onto the gerund → ⑥

Examples

① **Sto lavorando**
I'm working

Cosa stai facendo?
What are you doing?

② **Il bambino stava piangendo**
The little boy was crying

Stavo lavando i piatti
I was washing the dishes

③ **Era disteso sul divano**
He was lying on the sofa

Stava seduta accanto a me
She was sitting next to me

La scala era appoggiata al muro
The ladder was leaning against the wall

④ **Entrando ho sentito odore di pesce**
When I came in I could smell fish

Ripensandoci, credo che non fosse colpa sua
Thinking back on it, I reckon it wasn't his fault

Vedendolo solo, è venuta a parlargli
Seeing that he was on his own, she came to speak to him

Sentendomi male, sono andato a letto
Because I felt ill, I went to bed

Volendo, potremmo comprarne un altro
If we wanted to, we could buy another

⑤ **Vedendoli è scoppiata in lacrime**
When she saw them, she burst into tears

Mi sono addormentato ascoltandolo
As I listened to him, I fell asleep

Sbagliando si impara
You learn by making mistakes

⑥ **Ti sto parlando** or
Sto parlandoti
I'm talking to you

Si sta vestendo or
Sta vestendosi
He's getting dressed

Me lo stavano mostrando or
Stavano mostrandomelo
They were showing me it

Verbs

Past Participle Agreement

For the formation of the past participle, see page 24.

Note that many Italian verbs have irregular past participles → ❶

Past participles are sometimes like adjectives, and change their endings. For the rules of agreement, see below:

	MASCULINE			FEMININE	
SING.	1st conj	andato	SING.	1st conj	andata
SING.	2nd conj	caduto	SING.	2nd conj	caduta
SING.	3rd conj	uscito	SING.	3rd conj	uscita
PLUR.	1st conj	andati	PLUR.	1st conj	andate
PLUR.	2nd conj	caduti	PLUR.	2nd conj	cadute
PLUR.	3rd conj	usciti	PLUR.	3rd conj	uscite

Rules of Agreement in Compound Tenses

When the auxiliary verb is **avere**:

> The past participle generally remains in the masculine singular form → ❷

EXCEPTION: When the object of the verb is **la** (*feminine*: her/it), **li** (*masculine plural*: them) or **le** (*feminine plural*: them), the participle agrees with **la**, **li** or **le** → ❸

When the auxiliary verb is **essere**:

> The past participle agrees in number and gender with the subject → ❹

For the agreement of the past participle with reflexive verbs, see page 34.

The Past Participle as an adjective

When a past participles is used as an adjective it agrees in the normal way → ❺

Examples

❶ **crescere** to grow   **cresciuto** grown
  dire to say   **detto** said
  fare to do   **fatto** done
  porre to put   **posto** put

❷ **Mio fratello ha comprato una macchina**   My brother has bought a car
  Mia sorella ha comprato una macchina   My sister has bought a car
  I ragazzi hanno comprato dei gelati   The children bought ice creams

❸ **Dov'è Marco? L'hai visto?**   Where's Marco? Have you seen him?
  Dov'è Silvia? L'hai vista?   Where's Silvia? Have you seen her?
  Dove sono i ragazzi? Li hai visti?   Where are the boys? Have you seen them?
  Dove sone le ragazze? Le hai viste?   Where are the girls? Have you seen them?

❹ **È andato a casa**   He's gone home
  È andata a casa   She's gone home
  I ragazzi sono usciti   The boys have gone out
  Le ragazze sono uscite   The girls have gone out
  Si è fatto male?   Has he hurt himself?
  Si è fatta male?   Has she hurt herself?
  Vi siete fatti male, ragazzi?   Have you hurt yourselves, boys?
  Vi siete fatte male, ragazze?   Have you hurt yourselves, girls?

❺ **È chiuso il supermercato?**   Is the supermarket closed?
  È chiusa la banca?   Is the bank closed?
  Sono chiuse le finestre?   Are the windows closed?

Verbs

Modal Auxiliary Verbs

In Italian, the modal auxiliary verbs (**i verbi servili**) are: **dovere, potere, sapere** and **volere**.

They are followed by the infinitive (without a connecting preposition) and have the following meanings:

dovere   to have to, must → **①**
               to be going to, to be supposed to → **②**
               in the present conditional/perfect conditional:
               should/should have, ought/ought to have → **③**

potere   to be able to, can → **④**
               to be allowed to, can, may → **⑤**
               indicating possibility: may/might/could → **⑥**

sapere   to know how to, can → **⑦**

volere   to want/wish to → **⑧**
               with negative won't/wouldn't → **⑨**
               in polite phrases → **⑩**

Compound Tenses of *dovere* and *potere*

dovere and **potere** are conjugated with **avere** if the following verb is conjugated with **avere**, e.g. **dare**, **risolvere** → **⑪**

dovere and **potere** are generally conjugated with *essere* if the following verb is conjugated with *essere*, e.g. **andare**, **partire**, **alzarsi** → **⑫**

EXCEPTION: **avere** is used in compound tenses of **dovere** and **potere** when followed by *essere*, e.g. **Avrebbe dovuto *essere* più freddo** It should have been colder

Examples

① **Devi farlo proprio adesso?** — Do you have to do it right now?
È dovuta partire — She had to leave
Dev'essere caro — It must be expensive

② **Deve scendere qui?** — Are you going to get off here?
Dovevo venire, ma poi non ho avuto tempo — I was going to come, but then I didn't have time
Dovevano arrivare ieri sera — They were supposed to arrive yesterday evening

③ **Dovresti parlargli** — You should speak to him
Avrei dovuto stare più attento — I should have been more careful

④ **Non potrò venire domani** — I won't be able to come tomorrow
Cosa posso dire? — What can I say?

⑤ **Posso entrare?** — May I come in?
Non si può parcheggiare qui — You can't park here

⑥ **Può anche essere vero** — It may/might even be true
Potrebbe piovere — It may/might/could rain

⑦ **Sai guidare?** — Can you drive?
Non so fare gli gnocchi — I don't know how to make gnocchi

⑧ **Vuole rimanere ancora un giorno** — He wants to stay another day

⑨ **Non vuole aiutarci** — She won't help us
Non voleva ascoltarmi — He wouldn't listen to me

⑩ **Vuole bere qualcosa?** — Would you like something to drink?

⑪ **Ho dovuto darglielo** — I had to give it to him
Ho potuto risolvere il problema — I was able to sort out the problem

⑫ **È dovuta partire subito** — She had to leave immediately
Ci siamo dovuti alzare presto — We had to get up early
Lara è potuta venire — Lara was able to come
Non si sono potuti decidere — They couldn't decide
Si sarebbero potuti sbagliare — They could have been mistaken

Verbs

Use of Tenses

The Present

The Italian simple present can be used to translate both the English simple present, e.g. I work, and the English present continuous, e.g. I'm working → ❶

The Italian present continuous tense is also used for continuous actions → ❷

Italian uses the present tense with the preposition **da** to describe an action that *has been continuing for* some time, or *has continued since* some time in the past → ❸

The Italian present is also used
- for the immediate future → ❹
- for offers → ❺
- for arrangements → ❻
- for predictions → ❼
- when asking for suggestions → ❽

The Future

The future is generally used as in English, but note the following:

> the future tense is used after **quando**, if the verb in the main clause is in the future → ❾

The Future Perfect

It is used as in English to mean 'shall/will have done' → ❿

It is also used in time clauses relating to the future, where English uses the perfect → ⓫

Examples

① Dove abitano? — Where do they live?
Dove abitano adesso? — Where are they living now?
Piove molto qui — It rains a lot here
Ora piove — It's raining now

② Cosa stai facendo? *or* **Cosa fai?** — What are you doing?
Sta piovendo *or* **Piove** — It's raining

③ Studio italiano da due anni — I've been learning Italian for two years

Aspettiamo da un'ora — We've been waiting for an hour
Lavora qui da settembre — She's been working here since September

Non lo vedo da un pezzo — I haven't seen him for a while
Vivono qui dal 2006 — They've lived here since 2006

④ Prendo un espresso — I'll have an espresso
È rotto, lo butto via — It's broken; I'm going to throw it away

⑤ Pago io! — I'll pay!
Devo tornare a casa — Ti porto io! — I need to go home — I'll take you!

⑥ Parto alle due — I'm leaving at two
Domani gioco a tennis — I'm playing tennis tomorrow

⑦ Se fai così lo rompi — If you do that, you'll break it
Se piove non viene nessuno — If it rains, nobody will come

⑧ Dove lo metto? — Where shall I put it?
Cosa facciamo? — What shall we do?

⑨ Quando finirò, verrò da te *or* **Quando finisco, vengo da te** — When I finish, I'll come to yours
Lo comprerò quando avrò abbastanza soldi — I'll buy it when I've got enough money
Quando verrà saremo già in vacanza — When he comes, we'll be on holiday

⑩ Avrò finito fra un'ora — I'll have finished in an hour

⑪ Quando l'avrai letto ritornamelo — When you've read it, let me have it back

Partirò quando avrò finito — I'll leave when I've finished

Verbs

Use of Tenses *continued*

The Imperfect

The imperfect describes:
- an action (or state) in the past without definite time limits → ❶
- habitual action(s) in the past (often translated by 'would' or 'used to') → ❷

Italian uses the imperfect tense with the preposition **da** to describe an action that *had been continuing for* some time, or *had continued since* some time in the past → ❸

The Italian imperfect continuous tense is also used for continuous actions → ❹

The Perfect

The Italian perfect tense corresponds to both the English perfect tense and the English simple past → ❺

The Past Historic

The past historic, used mainly in written Italian, and in the south of Italy, corresponds to the English simple past → ❻

The Past Anterior

This tense is used instead of the pluperfect when a verb in another part of the sentence is in the past historic → ❼

The Perfect Conditional

The perfect conditional, not the present conditional, is used in reported speech → ❽

Examples

① **Avevo la febbre**
I had a temperature

Non ne sapeva niente
He didn't know anything about it

Guardavo la tivù
I was watching TV

② **Ti prendevano in giro, vero?**
They used to tease you, didn't they?

Facevamo lunghissime passeggiate
We would go for very long walks

Mi raccontava delle belle storie
She used to tell me lovely stories

③ **Studiavo italiano da due anni**
I had been learning Italian for two years

Aspettavamo da molto tempo
We had been waiting for a long time

Lavorava a Roma dal 2010
She'd been working in Rome since 2010

Non lo vedevo da un pezzo
I hadn't seen him for a while

④ **Cosa stavo dicendo?** *or* **Cosa dicevo?**
What was I saying?

Stava piovendo *or* **Pioveva**
It was raining

⑤ **Non l'ho mai visto**
I've never seen it

Non l'ho visto ieri
I didn't see it yesterday

Sono stata in città
I've been to town

Stamattina sono stata in città
I went to town this morning

⑥ **Dormimmo profondamente e ci svegliammo riposati**
We slept soundly and awoke refreshed

⑦ **Mi addormentai dopo che se ne furono andati**
I went to sleep after they had gone

⑧ **Ha detto che mi avrebbe aiutato**
He said he would help me

Ho detto che avrei pagato la metà
I said I'd pay half

Hanno promesso che sarebbero venuti
They promised they would come

Verbs

The Subjunctive

When to use it

For how to form the subjunctive, see page 8 onwards.

The subjunctive follows the conjunction **che**:

- when used with verbs expressing belief or hope, such as **credere, pensare** and **sperare** → ❶
- when used with verbs and expressions expressing uncertainty → ❷
- when it is used with **volere**. The Italian subjunctive + **che** corresponds to the infinitive construction in English → ❸
- following impersonal verbs → ❹
- after impersonal constructions which express necessity, possibility etc:

è meglio che	it's better (that) → ❺
è possibile che	it's possible (that) → ❻
è facile che	it's likely (that) → ❼
può darsi che	it's possible (that) → ❽
non è che	it's not that → ❾
sembra che	it seems (that) → ❿

Examples

1 **Penso che sia giusto** — I think it's fair
Credo che partano domani — I think they're leaving tomorrow
Spero che Luca arrivi in tempo — I hope Luca arrives in time

2 **Non so se sia la risposta giusta** — I don't know if it's the right answer

Non sono sicura che tu abbia ragione — I'm not sure you're right

3 **Voglio che i miei ragazzi siano felici** — I want my children to be happy
Vuole che la aiuti — She wants me to help her
Non voglio che mi parlino — I don't want them to speak to me

4 **Mi dispiace che non siano qui** — I'm sorry they're not here

5 **È meglio che tu te ne vada** — You'd better leave

6 **È possibile che siano stranieri** — It's possible they're foreigners

7 **È facile che scelgano quelli rossi** — They'll probably choose those red ones

8 **Può darsi che non venga** — It's possible that he won't come

9 **Non è che si debba sempre dire la verità** — You don't always have to tell the truth

10 **Sembra che abbiano vinto** — It seems they've won

Verbs

The Subjunctive *continued*

The subjunctive is used:

- after the following conjunctions:

prima che	before → ❶
affinché	so that → ❷
a meno che	unless → ❸
benché	although → ❹
nel caso che	in case → ❺
nonostante	even though → ❻
perché	so (that) → ❼
per quanto	however → ❽
purché	as long as → ❾
sebbene	even though → ❿

- after superlatives → ⓫
  la più grande che ci sia   the biggest there is

- after:
  chiunque whoever → ⓬
  qualunque + *noun* whatever → ⓭
  per quanto however → ⓮

Note that **che** is not always followed by the subjunctive.

The indicative follows **che** when it is used with positive uses of **sapere** to know, and with other expressions indicating certainty, such as **Sono sicuro** *I'm sure* → ⓯

Examples

1. **Vuoi parlargli prima che parta?** — Do you want to speak to him before he goes?

2. **Ti do venti euro affinché tu possa comprarlo** — I'll give you twenty euros so that you can buy it

3. **Lo prendo io, a meno che lo voglia tu** — I'll take it, unless you want it

4. **Mi aiutò a fare i compiti benché fosse molto stanca** — She helped me do my homework although she was very tired

5. **Vi do il mio numero di telefono nel caso che veniate a Roma** — I'll give you my phone number in case you come to Rome

6. **Vuole alzarsi, nonostante sia ancora malato** — He wants to get up even though he's still ill

7. **Lo metto qui perché tutti possano usarlo** — I'll put it here so everyone can use it

8. **Per quanto mi sforzi non riesco a capire** — I can't understand, however hard I try

9. **Vengo anch'io, purché possa pagare la mia parte** — I'll come too as long as I can pay my share

10. **Mi prestò il denaro sebbene non ne avesse molto** — She lent me the money even though she hadn't got much

11. **È la persona più simpatica che conosca** — He's the nicest person I know

12. **Chiunque sia, digli che non ci sono** — Whoever it is, tell them I'm not here

13. **qualunque cosa accada** — whatever happens

14. **per quanto bello sia** — however nice it may be

15. **So che non è suo** — I know it's not hers
    Sai che ti piace — You know you like it
    Sono sicura che l'ha preso lui — I'm sure he took it
    Sei sicuro che verranno? — Are you sure they're coming?

67

Verbs

The Subjunctive *continued*

The Perfect Subjunctive

The perfect subjunctive follows the conjunction **che**
- when it follows verbs such as **credere**, **pensare** and **sperare** relating to something in the past → ❶
- when it follows an impersonal expression → ❷
- when it follows a superlative → ❸
- when it follows a conjunction ending in **che** → ❹

The Imperfect Subjunctive

The imperfect subjunctive is used:
- following **che**, and other conjunctions, as above → ❺
- with past tenses of **volere** + **che** → ❻
- following **se** in conditional clauses describing hypothetical situations → ❼

The Pluperfect Subjunctive

The pluperfect subjunctive is used:
- after **che**, in the same way as other tenses of the subjunctive → ❽
- after other conjunctions → ❾
- following **se** in conditional clauses describing past hypothetical situations → ❿

Examples

1 **Penso che sia stata una buona idea** I think it was a good idea
Spero che non si sia fatta male I hope she didn't hurt herself
Spero che *abbia* detto la verit*à* I hope you told the truth

2 **È poss*i*bile che *abbiano* cambiato idea** It's possible they've changed their minds
Mi dispiace che *abbia* fatto brutto tempo I'm sorry the weather was bad

3 **la più bella che *abbia* mai visto** the most beautiful one I've ever seen

4 **Sarà qui fra poco, a meno che *abbia* perso l'*a*utobus** He'll be here soon, unless he's missed the bus

5 **Voleva alzarsi nonostante fosse ancora malato** He wanted to get up, even though he was still ill

6 **Voleva che fossimo pronti alle otto** He wanted us to be ready at eight
Vol*e*vano che tutto fosse in *o*rdine They wanted everything to be tidy
Volevo che andasse più veloce I wanted him to go faster
Non volevo che mi parl*a*ssero I didn't want them to speak to me

7 **Se tu ne avessi bisogno, te lo darei** If you needed it, I'd give it to you
Se potessi dormirei fino a tardi If I could, I'd have a lie-in
Se lo sapesse sarebbe molto deluso If he knew, he'd be very disappointed
Se solo avessi più denaro! If only I had more money!

8 **Non pensavo che l'avesse fatto** I didn't think he'd done it
Credevo che fossero partiti I thought they had left
Ero sicuro che avesse perso il treno I was sure he'd missed the train
la più bella che avessi mai visto the most beautiful one I had ever seen

9 **Non ha detto niente nonostante si fosse fatto male** He didn't say anything even though he'd hurt himself

10 **Se l'avessi saputo non l'avrei mai fatto** If I had known, I'd never have done it
Se fosse stato più furbo non avrebbe detto niente If he'd had more sense, he wouldn't have said anything
Se l'avessi visto mi crederesti If you'd seen it, you'd believe me
Se solo mi avessi creduto! If only you'd believed me!

Verbs

Verbs governing *a* and *di*

The following list (pages 70–79) contain common verbal constructions using the prepositions **a** and **di**

Note the following abbreviations:

infin.	*infinitive*
perf. infin.	*perfect infinitive*
qc	**qualcosa**
qn	**qualcuno**
sb	somebody
sth	something

Verbs governing **a** may be followed by the stressed pronouns **me, te, lui, lei, noi, voi** and **loro** → ❶

More often, however, they are preceded by an unstressed indirect pronoun, without **a** → ❷

For stressed and unstressed pronouns, see page 162.

abituare qn a qc/a + *infin.*	to accustom sb to sth/to doing
abituarsi a + *infin.*	to get used to doing → ❸
acconsentire a qc/a + *infin.*	to agree to sth/to do → ❹
accorgersi di qc	to notice sth → ❺
accusare qn di qc/di + *(perf.) infin.*	to accuse sb of sth/of doing, having done → ❻
affrettarsi a + *infin.*	to hurry to do
aiutare qn a + *infin.*	to help sb to do → ❼
andare a + *infin.*	to go to do
approfittare di qc/di + *infin.*	to take advantage of sth/of doing
aspettarsi di + *infin.*	to expect to do → ❽
assistere a qc	to attend sth, be at sth
assomigliare a qn/qc	to look/be like sb/sth → ❾
aver bisogno di qc /di + *infin.*	to need sth/to do sth
aver paura di qc/di + *infin.*	to be afraid of sth/to do/of doing
aver voglia di qc/di + *infin.*	to want sth/to do
avvicinarsi a qn/qc	to approach sb/sth → ❿
badare a qn/qc	to look after sb/sth
cambiarsi di qc	to change sth → ⓫
cercare di + *infin.*	to try to do → ⓬

Examples

❶ Assomigli a lui, non a lei
You look like him, not like her

❷ Gli ho chiesto i soldi
I asked him for the money

❸ Si è abituato a bere di meno
He got used to drinking less

❹ Non hanno acconsentito a venderlo
They haven't agreed to sell it

❺ Non si è accorto del mio errore
He didn't notice my mistake

❻ Mi ha accusato d'aver mentito
He accused me of lying

❼ Aiutatemi a portare queste valigie
Help me to carry these cases

❽ Si aspettava di vederlo?
Was she expecting to see him?

❾ Assomiglia molto a sua madre
She looks very like her mother

❿ Si è avvicinata a me
She came up to me

⓫ Mi sono cambiato d'abito
I changed my clothes

⓬ Ho cercato di capirla
I tried to understand her

Verbs

Verbs governing *a* and *di* continued

cessare di + *infin.*	to stop doing → **❶**
chiedere qc a qn	to ask sb sth/for sth → **❷**
chiedere a qn di + *infin.*	to ask sb to do → **❸**
cominciare a + *infin.*	to begin to do, to start to do → **❹**
comprare qc a qn	to buy sth from sb/for sb → **❺**
consentire qc a qn	to allow sb sth
consentire a qn di + *infin.*	to allow sb to do
consigliare a qn di + *infin.*	to advise sb to do → **❻**
continuare a + *infin.*	to continue to do
convincere qn a + *infin.*	to persuade sb to do → **❼**
dare la colpa a qn di qc	to blame sb for sth
decidere di + *infin.*	to decide to → **❽**
decidersi a + *infin.*	to resolve to do, to make up one's mind to do
diffidare di qn	to distrust sb
dimenticare di + *infin.*	to forget to do → **❾**
dire a qn di + *infin.*	to tell sb to do → **❿**
discutere di qc	to discuss sth
disobbedire a qn	to disobey sb → **⓫**
dispiacere a qn	to displease sb → **⓬**
divertirsi a + *infin.*	to enjoy doing
domandare qc a qn	to ask sb sth/for sth
dubitare di qc	to doubt sth
esitare a + *infin.*	to hesitate to do
evitare di + *infin.*	to avoid doing → **⓭**
far male a qn	to hurt sb
farcela a + *infin.*	to manage to do
fare a meno di qc	to do/go without sth → **⓮**
fare finta di + *infin.*	to pretend to do → **⓯**
fidarsi di qn	to trust sb → **⓰**
fingere di + *infin.*	to pretend to do → **⓱**
finire di + *infin.*	to finish doing → **⓲**
forzare qn a + *infin.*	to force sb to do
giocare a (+ *sports, games*)	to play → **⓳**
giurare di + *infin.*	to swear to do
godere di qc	to enjoy sth → **⓴**

Examples

1. **Ha cessato di piovere?** — Has it stopped raining?

2. **Ho chiesto a Paola che ora fosse** — I asked Paola what time it was

3. **Chiedi a Francesca di farlo** — Ask Francesca to do it

4. **Comincia a nevicare** — It's starting to snow

5. **Cristina ha comprato a Paolo due biglietti** — Cristina bought two tickets for Paolo

6. **Ha consigliato a Paolo di aspettare** — He advised Paolo to wait

7. **Ci ha convinti a restare** — She persuaded us to stay

8. **Cosa avete deciso di fare?** — What have you decided to do?

9. **Non dimenticarti di prendere l'ombrello** — Don't forget to take your umbrella

10. **Dì a Gigi di stare zitto** — Tell Gigi to be quiet

11. **Disobbediscono spesso ai genitori** — They often disobey their parents

12. **A me non dispiace il loro modo di fare** — I quite like their attitude

13. **Evita di parlarle** — He avoids speaking to her

14. **Ho fatto a meno dell'elettricità per diversi giorni** — I did without electricity for several days

15. **Ho fatto finta di non vederlo** — I pretended not to see him

16. **Non mi fido di quella gente** — I don't trust those people

17. **Finge di dormire** — She's pretending to be asleep

18. **Ha finito di leggere questo giornale?** — Have you finished reading this newspaper?

19. **Gioca a tennis** — She plays tennis

20. **Gode di buona salute** — He enjoys good health

Verbs

Verbs governing *a* and *di* continued

imparare a + *infin.*	to learn to do → **❶**
impedire a qn di + *infin.*	to prevent sb from doing → **❷**
impegnarsi a + *infin.*	to undertake to do
incaricarsi di qc/di + *infin.*	to see to sth/undertake to do
incoraggiare qn a + *infin.*	to encourage sb to do → **❸**
iniziare a + *infin.*	to begin to do
insegnare qc a qn	to teach sb sth
insegnare a qn a + *infin.*	to teach sb to do → **❹**
intendersi di qc	to know about sth
interessarsi a qn/qc	to be interested in sb/sth → **❺**
invitare qn a + *infin.*	to invite sb to do → **❻**
lagnarsi di qc	to complain about sth
lamentarsi di qc	to complain about sth
mancare a qn	to be missed by sb → **❼**
mancare di qc	to lack sth
mancare di + *infin.*	to fail to do → **❽**
meritare di + *infin.*	to deserve to do → **❾**
mettersi a + *infin.*	to begin to do
minacciare di + *infin.*	to threaten to do → **❿**
nascondere qc a qn	to hide sth from sb → **⓫**
nuocere a qc	to harm sth, to damage sth → **⓬**
obbligare qn a + *infin.*	to oblige/force sb to do → **⓭**
occuparsi di qn/qc	to look after sb/sth → **⓮**
offrirsi di + *infin.*	to offer to do → **⓯**
omettere di + *infin.*	to fail to do
ordinare a qn di + *infin.*	to order sb to do → **⓰**
partecipare a qc	to take part in sth
pensare a qn/qc	to think about sb/sth → **⓱**
pentirsi di + *(perf.) infin.*	to regret doing, having done → **⓲**
perdonare qc a qn	to forgive sb for sth
perdonare a qn di + *perf. infin.*	to forgive sb for doing → **⓳**
permettere qc a qn	to allow sb sth
permettere a qn di + *infin.*	to allow sb to do → **⓴**

Examples

1. **Sta imparando a leggere** — She's learning to read

2. **Il rumore mi impedisce di lavorare** — The noise is preventing me from working

3. **Incoraggia i figli ad essere indipendenti** — She encourages her children to be independent

4. **Gli sto insegnando a nuotare** — I'm teaching him to swim

5. **Si interessa molto di sport** — She's very interested in sport

6. **Mi ha invitato a cenare da lui** — He invited me for dinner at his house

7. **Manchi molto ai tuoi genitori** — Your parents miss you very much

8. **Non mancherò di dirglielo** — I'll be sure to tell him about it

9. **Meritano di avere la promozione** — They deserve to be promoted

10. **Ha minacciato di dare le dimissioni** — She threatened to resign

11. **Nascondile il regalo!** — Hide the present from her!

12. **Il fumo nuoce alla salute di tutti** — Smoking damages everybody's health

13. **Li ha obbligati a farlo** — He forced them to do it

14. **Mi occupo di mia nipote** — I'm looking after my niece

15. **Marco si è offerto di venire con noi** — Marco has offered to come with us

16. **Ha ordinato loro di sparare** — He ordered them to shoot

17. **Penso spesso a te** — I often think about you

18. **Mi pento di averglielo detto** — I'm sorry I told him

19. **Hai perdonato Carlo di averti mentito?** — Have you forgiven Carlo for lying to you?

20. **Permettetemi di continuare, per favore** — Allow me to go on, please

75

Verbs

Verbs governing *a* and *di* continued

persuadere qn a + *infin.*	to persuade sb to do
piacere a qn	to please sb → ❶
portare via qc a qn	to take sth away from sb
pregare qn a + *infin.*	to beg sb to do
prendere qc a qn	to take sth from sb → ❷
prendersi gioco di qn/qc	to make fun of sb/sth
preparare qn a + *infin.*	to prepare sb to do
prepararsi a + *infin.*	to get ready to do
proibire a qn di + *infin.*	to forbid sb to do → ❸
promettere qc a qn	to promise sb sth
promettere a qn di + *infin.*	to promise sb to do → ❹
proporre di + *infin.*	to suggest doing → ❺
provare a + *infin.*	to try to do
rammaricarsi di + *(perf.) infin.*	to regret doing, having done
resistere a qc	to resist sth → ❻
ricordarsi di qn/qc/di + *(perf.) infin.*	to remember sb/sth/doing, having done → ❼
ridere di qn/qc	to laugh at sb/sth
rifiutarsi di + *infin.*	to refuse to do → ❽
rimpiangere di + *(perf.) infin.*	to regret doing, having done
rimproverare qc a qn	to reproach sb with/for sth → ❾
ringraziare qn di qc/di + *(perf.) infin.*	to thank sb for sth/for doing, having done → ❿
rinunciare a qc/a + *infin.*	to give up sth /give up doing
rischiare di + *infin.*	to risk doing → ⓫
rispondere a qn	to answer sb
riuscire a + *infin.*	to manage to do → ⓬
rivolgersi a qn	to ask sb
rubare qc a qn	to steal sth from sb
scordare di + *infin.*	to forget to do
scordarsi di + *infin.*	to forget to do
scusarsi di qc/di + *(perf.) infin.*	to apologize for sth/for doing, having done → ⓭
servire a qc/a + *infin.*	to be used for sth/for doing → ⓮
servirsi di qc	to use sth → ⓯
sforzarsi di + *infin.*	to make an effort to do
smettere di + *infin.*	to stop doing → ⓰
sognare di + *infin.*	to dream of doing

Examples

① **A lui piace questo genere di film** He likes this kind of film

② **Gli ho preso il cellulare** I took his mobile phone from him

③ **Ho proibito loro di uscire** I've forbidden them to go out

④ **Hanno promesso a Luca di venire** They promised Luca they would come

⑤ **Ho proposto a mio fratello di invitarli** I suggested to my brother that he should invite them

⑥ **Come riesci a resistere alla tentazione?** How do you manage to resist the temptation?

⑦ **Vi ricordate di Luciana?** Do you remember Luciana?
Non si ricorda di averlo perso He doesn't remember losing it

⑧ **Si è rifiutato di cooperare** He has refused to cooperate

⑨ **Rimproverano alla figlia la sua mancanza d'entusiasmo** They reproach their daughter for her lack of enthusiasm

⑩ **Li abbiamo ringraziati della loro gentilezza** We thanked them for their kindness

⑪ **Rischiate di perdere soldi** You risk losing money

⑫ **Siete riusciti a convincermi** You've managed to convince me

⑬ **Mi scuso del ritardo** I'm sorry I'm late

⑭ **Questo pulsante serve a regolare il volume** This button is for adjusting the volume

⑮ **Si è servito di un cacciavite per aprirlo** He used a screwdriver to open it

⑯ **Smettete di fare rumore!** Stop making so much noise!

77

Verbs

Verbs governing *a* and *di* continued

somigliare a qn/qc	to look/be like sb/sth
sopravvivere a qn	to outlive sb → ❶
spicciarsi a + *infin.*	to hurry to do
spingere qn a + *infin.*	to urge sb to do
strappare via qc a qn	to snatch sth from sb → ❷
stufarsi di qn/qc	to be fed up with sb/sth
stupirsi di qc	to be amazed at sth
succedere a qn	to succeed sb
tardare a + *infin.*	to delay doing → ❸
telefonare a qn	to phone sb
tendere a + *infin.*	to tend to do
tenere a + *infin.*	to be keen to do → ❹
tentare di + *infin.*	to try to do → ❺
togliere qc a qn	to take sth away from sb
trattare di qc	to be about sth
ubbidire a qn	to obey sb
vantarsi di qc	to boast about sth
venire a + *infin.*	to come to do
vietare a qn di + *infin.*	to forbid sb to do → ❻
vivere di qc	to live on sth

Verbs followed by a preposition in Engish but not in Italian.

ascoltare qn/qc	to listen to sb/sth → ❼
aspettare qn/qc	to wait for sb/sth → ❽
cercare qn/qc	to look for sb/sth → ❾
chiedere qc	to ask for sth → ❿
guardare qn/qc	to look at sb/sth → ⓫
pagare qn/qc	to pay for sb/sth → ⓬

Examples

1. **È sopravvissuta a suo marito** — She outlived her husband

2. **Il ladro le ha strappato via la borsa** — The thief snatched her bag

3. **Non ha tardato a prendere una decisione** — He didn't take long to make a decision

4. **Ci tiene a farlo da sola** — She's keen to do it by herself

5. **Ho tentato di darlo ad Alessia** — I tried to give it to Alessia

6. **Ha vietato ai bambini di giocare con i fiammiferi** — He's forbidden the children to play with matches

7. **Mi stai ascoltando?** — Are you listening to me?

8. **Aspettami!** — Wait for me!

9. **Sto cercando la chiave** — I'm looking for my key

10. **Ha chiesto qualcosa da mangiare** — He asked for something to eat

11. **Guarda la sua faccia** — Look at his face

12. **Ho già pagato il biglietto** — I've already paid for my ticket

Verb Tables

Introduction

The Verb Tables in the following section contain tables of Italian verbs (some regular and some irregular) in alphabetical order. Each table shows you the following forms: Present, Present Subjunctive, Perfect, Imperfect, Future, Conditional, Past Historic, Pluperfect, Imperative and the Past Participle and Gerund.

In Italian there are regular verbs (their forms follow the regular patterns of **-are**, **-ere** or **-ire** verbs) and irregular verbs (their forms do not follow the normal rules). Examples of regular verbs in these tables are:

parlare (regular **-are** verb)
credere (regular **-ere** verb)
capire (regular **-ire** verb)

Some irregular verbs are irregular in most of their forms, while others may only have a couple of irregular forms.

accorgersi (to realize)

	PRESENT		IMPERFECT
io	mi accorgo	io	mi accorgevo
tu	ti accorgi	tu	ti accorgevi
lui/lei/Lei	si accorge	lui/lei/Lei	si accorgeva
noi	ci accorgiamo	noi	ci accorgevamo
voi	vi accorgete	voi	vi accorgevate
loro	si accorgono	loro	si accorgevano

	FUTURE		CONDITIONAL
io	mi accorgerò	io	mi accorgerei
tu	ti accorgerai	tu	ti accorgeresti
lui/lei/Lei	si accorgerà	lui/lei/Lei	si accorgerebbe
noi	ci accorgeremo	noi	ci accorgeremmo
voi	vi accorgerete	voi	vi accorgereste
loro	si accorgeranno	loro	si accorgerebbero

	PRESENT SUBJUNCTIVE		PAST HISTORIC
io	mi accorga	io	mi accorsi
tu	ti accorga	tu	ti accorgesti
lui/lei/Lei	si accorga	lui/lei/Lei	si accorse
noi	ci accorgiamo	noi	ci accorgemmo
voi	vi accorgiate	voi	vi accorgeste
loro	si accorgano	loro	si accorsero

PAST PARTICIPLE	IMPERATIVE
accorto	accorgiti
	accorgiamoci
	accorgetevi

GERUND	AUXILIARY
accorgendosi	essere

addormentarsi (to go to sleep)

	PRESENT		IMPERFECT
io	mi addormento	io	mi addormentavo
tu	ti addormenti	tu	ti addormentavi
lui/lei/Lei	si addormenta	lui/lei/Lei	si addormentava
noi	ci addormentiamo	noi	ci addormentavamo
voi	vi addormentate	voi	vi addormentavate
loro	si addormentano	loro	si addormentavano

	FUTURE		CONDITIONAL
io	mi addormenterò	io	mi addormenterei
tu	ti addormenterai	tu	ti addormenteresti
lui/lei/Lei	si addormenterà	lui/lei/Lei	si addormenterebbe
noi	ci addormenteremo	noi	ci addormenteremmo
voi	vi addormenterete	voi	vi addormentereste
loro	si addormenteranno	loro	si addormenterebbero

	PRESENT SUBJUNCTIVE		PAST HISTORIC
io	mi addormenti	io	mi addormentai
tu	ti addormenti	tu	ti addormentasti
lui/lei/Lei	si addormenti	lui/lei/Lei	si addormentò
noi	ci addormentiamo	noi	ci addormentammo
voi	vi addormentiate	voi	vi addormentaste
loro	si addormentino	loro	si addormentarono

PAST PARTICIPLE	IMPERATIVE
addormentato	addormentati
	addormentiamoci
	addormentatevi

GERUND	AUXILIARY
addormentandosi	essere

Verb Tables

andare (to go)

	PRESENT		IMPERFECT
io	**vado**	io	**andavo**
tu	**vai**	tu	**andavi**
lui/lei/Lei	**va**	lui/lei/Lei	**andava**
noi	**andiamo**	noi	**andavamo**
voi	**andate**	voi	**andavate**
loro	**vanno**	loro	**andavano**

	FUTURE		CONDITIONAL
io	**andrò**	io	**andrei**
tu	**andrai**	tu	**andresti**
lui/lei/Lei	**andrà**	lui/lei/Lei	**andrebbe**
noi	**andremo**	noi	**andremmo**
voi	**andrete**	voi	**andreste**
loro	**andranno**	loro	**andrebbero**

	PRESENT SUBJUNCTIVE		PAST HISTORIC
io	**vada**	io	**andai**
tu	**vada**	tu	**andasti**
lui/lei/Lei	**vada**	lui/lei/Lei	**andò**
noi	**andiamo**	noi	**andammo**
voi	**andiate**	voi	**andaste**
loro	**vadano**	loro	**andarono**

PAST PARTICIPLE	IMPERATIVE
andato	**vai**
	andiamo
	andate

GERUND	AUXILIARY
andando	*essere*

Verb Tables

aprire (to open)

	PRESENT		IMPERFECT
io	apro	io	aprivo
tu	apri	tu	aprivi
lui/lei/Lei	apre	lui/lei/Lei	apriva
noi	apriamo	noi	aprivamo
voi	aprite	voi	aprivate
loro	aprono	loro	aprivano

	FUTURE		CONDITIONAL
io	aprirò	io	aprirei
tu	aprirai	tu	apriresti
lui/lei/Lei	aprirà	lui/lei/Lei	aprirebbe
noi	apriremo	noi	apriremmo
voi	aprirete	voi	aprireste
loro	apriranno	loro	aprirebbero

	PRESENT SUBJUNCTIVE		PAST HISTORIC
io	apra	io	aprii
tu	apra	tu	apristi
lui/lei/Lei	apra	lui/lei/Lei	aprì
noi	apriamo	noi	aprimmo
voi	apriate	voi	apriste
loro	aprano	loro	aprirono

PAST PARTICIPLE	IMPERATIVE
aperto	apri
	apriamo
	aprite

GERUND	AUXILIARY
aprendo	avere

assumere (to take on, to employ)

	PRESENT		IMPERFECT
io	assumo	io	assumevo
tu	assumi	tu	assumevi
lui/lei/Lei	assume	lui/lei/Lei	assumeva
noi	assumiamo	noi	assumevamo
voi	assumete	voi	assumevate
loro	assumono	loro	assumevano

	FUTURE		CONDITIONAL
io	assumerò	io	assumerei
tu	assumerai	tu	assumeresti
lui/lei/Lei	assumerà	lui/lei/Lei	assumerebbe
noi	assumeremo	noi	assumeremmo
voi	assumerete	voi	assumereste
loro	assumeranno	loro	assumerebbero

	PRESENT SUBJUNCTIVE		PAST HISTORIC
io	assuma	io	assunsi
tu	assuma	tu	assumesti
lui/lei/Lei	assuma	lui/lei/Lei	assunse
noi	assumiamo	noi	assumemmo
voi	assumiate	voi	assumeste
loro	assumano	loro	assunsero

PAST PARTICIPLE
assunto

IMPERATIVE
assumi
assumiamo
assumete

GERUND
assumendo

AUXILIARY
avere

avere (to have)

	PRESENT		IMPERFECT
io	**ho**	io	**avevo**
tu	**hai**	tu	**avevi**
lui/lei/Lei	**ha**	lui/lei/Lei	**aveva**
noi	**abbiamo**	noi	**avevamo**
voi	**avete**	voi	**avevate**
loro	**hanno**	loro	**avevano**

	FUTURE		CONDITIONAL
io	**avrò**	io	**avrei**
tu	**avrai**	tu	**avresti**
lui/lei/Lei	**avrà**	lui/lei/Lei	**avrebbe**
noi	**avremo**	noi	**avremmo**
voi	**avrete**	voi	**avreste**
loro	**avranno**	loro	**avrebbero**

	PRESENT SUBJUNCTIVE		PAST HISTORIC
io	**abbia**	io	**ebbi**
tu	**abbia**	tu	**avesti**
lui/lei/Lei	**abbia**	lui/lei/Lei	**ebbe**
noi	**abbiamo**	noi	**avemmo**
voi	**abbiate**	voi	**aveste**
loro	**abbiano**	loro	**ebbero**

PAST PARTICIPLE	IMPERATIVE
avuto	**abbi**
	abbiamo
	abbiate

GERUND	AUXILIARY
avendo	**avere**

Verb Tables

bere (to drink)

	PRESENT		IMPERFECT
io	**bevo**	io	**bevevo**
tu	**bevi**	tu	**bevevi**
lui/lei/Lei	**beve**	lui/lei/Lei	**beveva**
noi	**beviamo**	noi	**bevevamo**
voi	**bevete**	voi	**bevevate**
loro	**bevono**	loro	**bevevano**

	FUTURE		CONDITIONAL
io	**berrò**	io	**berrei**
tu	**berrai**	tu	**berresti**
lui/lei/Lei	**berrà**	lui/lei/Lei	**berrebbe**
noi	**berremo**	noi	**berremmo**
voi	**berrete**	voi	**berreste**
loro	**berranno**	loro	**berrebbero**

	PRESENT SUBJUNCTIVE		PAST HISTORIC
io	**beva**	io	**bevvi**
tu	**beva**	tu	**bevesti**
lui/lei/Lei	**beva**	lui/lei/Lei	**bevve**
noi	**beviamo**	noi	**bevemmo**
voi	**beviate**	voi	**beveste**
loro	**bevano**	loro	**bevvero**

PAST PARTICIPLE
bevuto

IMPERATIVE
bevi
beviamo
bevete

GERUND
bevendo

AUXILIARY
avere

cadere (to fall)

	PRESENT		IMPERFECT
io	cado	io	cadevo
tu	cadi	tu	cadevi
lui/lei/Lei	cade	lui/lei/Lei	cadeva
noi	cadiamo	noi	cadevamo
voi	cadete	voi	cadevate
loro	cadono	loro	cadevano

	FUTURE		CONDITIONAL
io	cadrò	io	cadrei
tu	cadrai	tu	cadresti
lui/lei/Lei	cadrà	lui/lei/Lei	cadrebbe
noi	cadremo	noi	cadremmo
voi	cadrete	voi	cadreste
loro	cadranno	loro	cadrebbero

	PRESENT SUBJUNCTIVE		PAST HISTORIC
io	cada	io	caddi
tu	cada	tu	cadesti
lui/lei/Lei	cada	lui/lei/Lei	cadde
noi	cadiamo	noi	cademmo
voi	cadiate	voi	cadeste
loro	cadano	loro	caddero

PAST PARTICIPLE	IMPERATIVE
caduto	cadi
	cadiamo
	cadete

GERUND	AUXILIARY
cadendo	essere

Verb Tables

capire (to understand)

	PRESENT		IMPERFECT
io	capisco	io	capivo
tu	capisci	tu	capivi
lui/lei/Lei	capisce	lui/lei/Lei	capiva
noi	capiamo	noi	capivamo
voi	capite	voi	capivate
loro	capiscono	loro	capivano

	FUTURE		CONDITIONAL
io	capirò	io	capirei
tu	capirai	tu	capiresti
lui/lei/Lei	capirà	lui/lei/Lei	capirebbe
noi	capiremo	noi	capiremmo
voi	capirete	voi	capireste
loro	capiranno	loro	capirebbero

	PRESENT SUBJUNCTIVE		PAST HISTORIC
io	capisca	io	capii
tu	capisca	tu	capisti
lui/lei/Lei	capisca	lui/lei/Lei	capì
noi	capiamo	noi	capimmo
voi	capiate	voi	capiste
loro	capiscano	loro	capirono

PAST PARTICIPLE	IMPERATIVE
capito	capisci
	capiamo
	capite

GERUND	AUXILIARY
capendo	avere

cercare (to look for)

	PRESENT		IMPERFECT
io	cerco	io	cercavo
tu	cerchi	tu	cercavi
lui/lei/Lei	cerca	lui/lei/Lei	cercava
noi	cerchiamo	noi	cercavamo
voi	cercate	voi	cercavate
loro	cercano	loro	cercavano

	FUTURE		CONDITIONAL
io	cercherò	io	cercherei
tu	cercherai	tu	cercheresti
lui/lei/Lei	cercherà	lui/lei/Lei	cercherebbe
noi	cercheremo	noi	cercheremmo
voi	cercherete	voi	cerchereste
loro	cercheranno	loro	cercherebbero

	PRESENT SUBJUNCTIVE		PAST HISTORIC
io	cerchi	io	cercai
tu	cerchi	tu	cercasti
lui/lei/Lei	cerchi	lui/lei/Lei	cercò
noi	cerchiamo	noi	cercammo
voi	cerchiate	voi	cercaste
loro	cerchino	loro	cercarono

PAST PARTICIPLE	IMPERATIVE
cercato	cerca
	cerchiamo
	cercate

GERUND	AUXILIARY
cercando	avere

Verb Tables

chiudere (to close)

	PRESENT		IMPERFECT
io	**chiudo**	io	**chiudevo**
tu	**chiudi**	tu	**chiudevi**
lui/lei/Lei	**chiude**	lui/lei/Lei	**chiudeva**
noi	**chiudiamo**	noi	**chiudevamo**
voi	**chiudete**	voi	**chiudevate**
loro	**chiudono**	loro	**chiudevano**

	FUTURE		CONDITIONAL
io	**chiuderò**	io	**chiuderei**
tu	**chiuderai**	tu	**chiuderesti**
lui/lei/Lei	**chiuderà**	lui/lei/Lei	**chiuderebbe**
noi	**chiuderemo**	noi	**chiuderemmo**
voi	**chiuderete**	voi	**chiudereste**
loro	**chiuderanno**	loro	**chiuderebbero**

	PRESENT SUBJUNCTIVE		PAST HISTORIC
io	**chiuda**	io	**chiusi**
tu	**chiuda**	tu	**chiudesti**
lui/lei/Lei	**chiuda**	lui/lei/Lei	**chiuse**
noi	**chiudiamo**	noi	**chiudemmo**
voi	**chiudiate**	voi	**chiudeste**
loro	**chiudano**	loro	**chiusero**

PAST PARTICIPLE	IMPERATIVE
chiuso	**chiudi**
	chiudiamo
	chiudete

GERUND	AUXILIARY
chiudendo	**avere**

Verb Tables

correre (to run)

	PRESENT		IMPERFECT
io	corro	io	correvo
tu	corri	tu	correvi
lui/lei/Lei	corre	lui/lei/Lei	correva
noi	corriamo	noi	correvamo
voi	correte	voi	correvate
loro	corrono	loro	correvano

	FUTURE		CONDITIONAL
io	correrò	io	correrei
tu	correrai	tu	correresti
lui/lei/Lei	correrà	lui/lei/Lei	correrebbe
noi	correremo	noi	correremmo
voi	correrete	voi	correreste
loro	correranno	loro	correrebbero

	PRESENT SUBJUNCTIVE		PAST HISTORIC
io	corra	io	corsi
tu	corra	tu	corresti
lui/lei/Lei	corra	lui/lei/Lei	corse
noi	corriamo	noi	corremmo
voi	corriate	voi	correste
loro	corrano	loro	corsero

PAST PARTICIPLE	IMPERATIVE
corso	corri
	corriamo
	correte

GERUND	AUXILIARY
correndo	avere

Verb Tables

credere (to believe)

	PRESENT		IMPERFECT
io	**credo**	io	**credevo**
tu	**credi**	tu	**credevi**
lui/lei/Lei	**crede**	lui/lei/Lei	**credeva**
noi	**crediamo**	noi	**credevamo**
voi	**credete**	voi	**credevate**
loro	**credono**	loro	**credevano**

	FUTURE		CONDITIONAL
io	**crederò**	io	**crederei**
tu	**crederai**	tu	**crederesti**
lui/lei/Lei	**crederà**	lui/lei/Lei	**crederebbe**
noi	**crederemo**	noi	**crederemmo**
voi	**crederete**	voi	**credereste**
loro	**crederanno**	loro	**crederebbero**

	PRESENT SUBJUNCTIVE		PAST HISTORIC
io	**creda**	io	**credetti** *or* **credei**
tu	**creda**	tu	**credesti**
lui/lei/Lei	**creda**	lui/lei/Lei	**credette**
noi	**crediamo**	noi	**credemmo**
voi	**crediate**	voi	**credeste**
loro	**credano**	loro	**credettero**

PAST PARTICIPLE	IMPERATIVE
creduto	**credi**
	crediamo
	credete

GERUND	AUXILIARY
credendo	**avere**

crescere (to grow)

	PRESENT		IMPERFECT
io	cresco	io	crescevo
tu	cresci	tu	crescevi
lui/lei/Lei	cresce	lui/lei/Lei	cresceva
noi	cresciamo	noi	crescevamo
voi	crescete	voi	crescevate
loro	crescono	loro	crescevano

	FUTURE		CONDITIONAL
io	crescerò	io	crescerei
tu	crescerai	tu	cresceresti
lui/lei/Lei	crescerà	lui/lei/Lei	crescerebbe
noi	cresceremo	noi	cresceremmo
voi	crescerete	voi	crescereste
loro	cresceranno	loro	crescerebbero

	PRESENT SUBJUNCTIVE		PAST HISTORIC
io	cresca	io	crebbi
tu	cresca	tu	crescesti
lui/lei/Lei	cresca	lui/lei/Lei	crebbe
noi	cresciamo	noi	crescemmo
voi	cresciate	voi	cresceste
loro	crescano	loro	crebbero

PAST PARTICIPLE	IMPERATIVE
cresciuto	cresci
	cresciamo
	crescete

GERUND	AUXILIARY
crescendo	essere

Verb Tables

dare (to give)

	PRESENT		IMPERFECT
io	**do**	io	**davo**
tu	**dai**	tu	**davi**
lui/lei/Lei	**dà**	lui/lei/Lei	**dava**
noi	**diamo**	noi	**davamo**
voi	**date**	voi	**davate**
loro	**danno**	loro	**davano**

	FUTURE		CONDITIONAL
io	**darò**	io	**darei**
tu	**darai**	tu	**daresti**
lui/lei/Lei	**darà**	lui/lei/Lei	**darebbe**
noi	**daremo**	noi	**daremmo**
voi	**darete**	voi	**dareste**
loro	**daranno**	loro	**darebbero**

	PRESENT SUBJUNCTIVE		PAST HISTORIC
io	**dia**	io	**diedi** _or_ **dette**
tu	**dia**	tu	**desti**
lui/lei/Lei	**dia**	lui/lei/Lei	**diede** _or_ **dette**
noi	**diamo**	noi	**demmo**
voi	**diate**	voi	**deste**
loro	**diano**	loro	**diedero** _or_ **dettero**

PAST PARTICIPLE	IMPERATIVE
dato	**dai** _or_ **da'**
	diamo
	date

GERUND	AUXILIARY
dando	**avere**

Verb Tables

dire (to say)

	PRESENT		IMPERFECT
io	**dico**	io	**dicevo**
tu	**dici**	tu	**dicevi**
lui/lei/Lei	**dice**	lui/lei/Lei	**diceva**
noi	**diciamo**	noi	**dicevamo**
voi	**dite**	voi	**dicevate**
loro	**dicono**	loro	**dicevano**

	FUTURE		CONDITIONAL
io	**dirò**	io	**direi**
tu	**dirai**	tu	**diresti**
lui/lei/Lei	**dirà**	lui/lei/Lei	**direbbe**
noi	**diremo**	noi	**diremmo**
voi	**direte**	voi	**direste**
loro	**diranno**	loro	**direbbero**

	PRESENT SUBJUNCTIVE		PAST HISTORIC
io	**dica**	io	**dissi**
tu	**dica**	tu	**dicesti**
lui/lei/Lei	**dica**	lui/lei/Lei	**disse**
noi	**diciamo**	noi	**dicemmo**
voi	**diciate**	voi	**diceste**
loro	**dicano**	loro	**dissero**

PAST PARTICIPLE	IMPERATIVE
detto	**di'**
	diciamo
	dite

GERUND	AUXILIARY
dicendo	**avere**

Verb Tables

dirigere (to direct)

	PRESENT		IMPERFECT
io	**dirigo**	io	**dirigevo**
tu	**dirigi**	tu	**dirigevi**
lui/lei/Lei	**dirige**	lui/lei/Lei	**dirigeva**
noi	**dirigiamo**	noi	**dirigevamo**
voi	**dirigete**	voi	**dirigevate**
loro	**dirigono**	loro	**dirigevano**

	FUTURE		CONDITIONAL
io	**dirigerò**	io	**dirigerei**
tu	**dirigerai**	tu	**dirigeresti**
lui/lei/Lei	**dirigerà**	lui/lei/Lei	**dirigerebbe**
noi	**dirigeremo**	noi	**dirigeremmo**
voi	**dirigerete**	voi	**dirigereste**
loro	**dirigeranno**	loro	**dirigerebbero**

	PRESENT SUBJUNCTIVE		PAST HISTORIC
io	**diriga**	io	**diressi**
tu	**diriga**	tu	**dirigesti**
lui/lei/Lei	**diriga**	lui/lei/Lei	**diresse**
noi	**dirigiamo**	noi	**dirigemmo**
voi	**dirigiate**	voi	**dirigeste**
loro	**dirigano**	loro	**diressero**

PAST PARTICIPLE	IMPERATIVE
diretto	**dirigi**
	dirigiamo
	dirigete

GERUND	AUXILIARY
dirigendo	**avere**

dormire (to sleep)

	PRESENT		IMPERFECT
io	dormo	io	dormivo
tu	dormi	tu	dormivi
lui/lei/Lei	dorme	lui/lei/Lei	dormiva
noi	dormiamo	noi	dormivamo
voi	dormite	voi	dormivate
loro	dormono	loro	dormivano

	FUTURE		CONDITIONAL
io	dormirò	io	dormirei
tu	dormirai	tu	dormiresti
lui/lei/Lei	dormirà	lui/lei/Lei	dormirebbe
noi	dormiremo	noi	dormiremmo
voi	dormirete	voi	dormireste
loro	dormiranno	loro	dormirebbero

	PRESENT SUBJUNCTIVE		PAST HISTORIC
io	dorma	io	dormii
tu	dorma	tu	dormisti
lui/lei/Lei	dorma	lui/lei/Lei	dormì
noi	dormiamo	noi	dormimmo
voi	dormiate	voi	dormiste
loro	dormano	loro	dormirono

PAST PARTICIPLE	IMPERATIVE
dormito	dormi
	dormiamo
	dormite

GERUND	AUXILIARY
dormendo	avere

Verb Tables

dovere (to have to)

	PRESENT		IMPERFECT
io	**devo**	io	**dovevo**
tu	**devi**	tu	**dovevi**
lui/lei/Lei	**deve**	lui/lei/Lei	**doveva**
noi	**dobbiamo**	noi	**dovevamo**
voi	**dovete**	voi	**dovevate**
loro	**devono**	loro	**dovevano**

	FUTURE		CONDITIONAL
io	**dovrò**	io	**dovrei**
tu	**dovrai**	tu	**dovresti**
lui/lei/Lei	**dovrà**	lui/lei/Lei	**dovrebbe**
noi	**dovremo**	noi	**dovremmo**
voi	**dovrete**	voi	**dovreste**
loro	**dovranno**	loro	**dovrebbero**

	PRESENT SUBJUNCTIVE		PAST HISTORIC
io	**debba**	io	**dovetti**
tu	**debba**	tu	**dovesti**
lui/lei/Lei	**debba**	lui/lei/Lei	**dovette**
noi	**dobbiamo**	noi	**dovemmo**
voi	**dobbiate**	voi	**doveste**
loro	**debbano**	loro	**dovettero**

PAST PARTICIPLE
dovuto

IMPERATIVE
–

GERUND
dovendo

AUXILIARY
avere

Verb Tables

essere (to be)

	PRESENT		IMPERFECT
io	**sono**	io	**ero**
tu	**sei**	tu	**eri**
lui/lei/Lei	**è**	lui/lei/Lei	**era**
noi	**siamo**	noi	**eravamo**
voi	**siete**	voi	**eravate**
loro	**sono**	loro	**erano**

	FUTURE		CONDITIONAL
io	**sarò**	io	**sarei**
tu	**sarai**	tu	**saresti**
lui/lei/Lei	**sarà**	lui/lei/Lei	**sarebbe**
noi	**saremo**	noi	**saremmo**
voi	**sarete**	voi	**sareste**
loro	**saranno**	loro	**sarebbero**

	PRESENT SUBJUNCTIVE		PAST HISTORIC
io	**sia**	io	**fui**
tu	**sia**	tu	**fosti**
lui/lei/Lei	**sia**	lui/lei/Lei	**fu**
noi	**siamo**	noi	**fummo**
voi	**siate**	voi	**foste**
loro	**siano**	loro	**furono**

PAST PARTICIPLE	IMPERATIVE
stato	**sii**
	siamo
	siate

GERUND	AUXILIARY
essendo	**essere**

fare (to do, to make)

	PRESENT		IMPERFECT
io	*faccio*	io	facevo
tu	fai	tu	facevi
lui/lei/Lei	fa	lui/lei/Lei	faceva
noi	facciamo	noi	facevamo
voi	fate	voi	facevate
loro	fanno	loro	facevano

	FUTURE		CONDITIONAL
io	farò	io	farei
tu	farai	tu	faresti
lui/lei/Lei	farà	lui/lei/Lei	farebbe
noi	faremo	noi	faremmo
voi	farete	voi	fareste
loro	faranno	loro	farebbero

	PRESENT SUBJUNCTIVE		PAST HISTORIC
io	*faccia*	io	feci
tu	*faccia*	tu	facesti
lui/lei/Lei	*faccia*	lui/lei/Lei	fece
noi	facciamo	noi	facemmo
voi	facciate	voi	faceste
loro	*facciano*	loro	*fecero*

PAST PARTICIPLE	IMPERATIVE
fatto	fai *or* fa'
	facciamo
	fate

GERUND	AUXILIARY
facendo	avere

leggere (to read)

	PRESENT		IMPERFECT
io	leggo	io	leggevo
tu	leggi	tu	leggevi
lui/lei/Lei	legge	lui/lei/Lei	leggeva
noi	leggiamo	noi	leggevamo
voi	leggete	voi	leggevate
loro	leggono	loro	leggevano

	FUTURE		CONDITIONAL
io	leggerò	io	leggerei
tu	leggerai	tu	leggeresti
lui/lei/Lei	leggerà	lui/lei/Lei	leggerebbe
noi	leggeremo	noi	leggeremmo
voi	leggerete	voi	leggereste
loro	leggeranno	loro	leggerebbero

	PRESENT SUBJUNCTIVE		PAST HISTORIC
io	legga	io	lessi
tu	legga	tu	leggesti
lui/lei/Lei	legga	lui/lei/Lei	lesse
noi	leggiamo	noi	leggemmo
voi	leggiate	voi	leggeste
loro	leggano	loro	lessero

PAST PARTICIPLE	IMPERATIVE
letto	leggi
	leggiamo
	leggete

GERUND	AUXILIARY
leggendo	avere

Verb Tables

mettere (to put)

	PRESENT		IMPERFECT
io	metto	io	mettevo
tu	metti	tu	mettevi
lui/lei/Lei	mette	lui/lei/Lei	metteva
noi	mettiamo	noi	mettevamo
voi	mettete	voi	mettevate
loro	mettono	loro	mettevano

	FUTURE		CONDITIONAL
io	metterò	io	metterei
tu	metterai	tu	metteresti
lui/lei/Lei	metterà	lui/lei/Lei	metterebbe
noi	metteremo	noi	metteremmo
voi	metterete	voi	mettereste
loro	metteranno	loro	metterebbero

	PRESENT SUBJUNCTIVE		PAST HISTORIC
io	metta	io	misi
tu	metta	tu	mettesti
lui/lei/Lei	metta	lui/lei/Lei	mise
noi	mettiamo	noi	mettemmo
voi	mettiate	voi	metteste
loro	mettano	loro	misero

PAST PARTICIPLE	IMPERATIVE
messo	metti
	mettiamo
	mettete

GERUND	AUXILIARY
mettendo	avere

morire (to die)

	PRESENT		IMPERFECT
io	muoio	io	morivo
tu	muori	tu	morivi
lui/lei/Lei	muore	lui/lei/Lei	moriva
noi	moriamo	noi	morivamo
voi	morite	voi	morivate
loro	muoiono	loro	morivano

	FUTURE		CONDITIONAL
io	morirò	io	morirei
tu	morirai	tu	moriresti
lui/lei/Lei	morirà	lui/lei/Lei	morirebbe
noi	moriremo	noi	moriremmo
voi	morirete	voi	morireste
loro	moriranno	loro	morirebbero

	PRESENT SUBJUNCTIVE		PAST HISTORIC
io	muoia	io	morii
tu	muoia	tu	moristi
lui/lei/Lei	muoia	lui/lei/Lei	morì
noi	moriamo	noi	morimmo
voi	moriate	voi	moriste
loro	muoiano	loro	morirono

PAST PARTICIPLE	IMPERATIVE
morto	muori
	moriamo
	morite

GERUND	AUXILIARY
morendo	essere

muovere (to move)

	PRESENT		IMPERFECT
io	muovo	io	muovevo
tu	muovi	tu	muovevi
lui/lei/Lei	muove	lui/lei/Lei	muoveva
noi	muoviamo	noi	muovevamo
voi	muovete	voi	muovevate
loro	muovono	loro	muovevano

	FUTURE		CONDITIONAL
io	muoverò	io	muoverei
tu	muoverai	tu	muoveresti
lui/lei/Lei	muoverà	lui/lei/Lei	muoverebbe
noi	muoveremo	noi	muoveremmo
voi	muoverete	voi	muovereste
loro	muoveranno	loro	muoverebbero

	PRESENT SUBJUNCTIVE		PAST HISTORIC
io	muova	io	mossi
tu	muova	tu	muovesti
lui/lei/Lei	muova	lui/lei/Lei	mosse
noi	muoviamo	noi	muovemmo
voi	muoviate	voi	muoveste
loro	muovano	loro	mossero

PAST PARTICIPLE	IMPERATIVE
mosso	muovi
	muoviamo
	muovete

GERUND	AUXILIARY
muovendo	avere

nascere (to be born)

	PRESENT		IMPERFECT
io	nasco	io	nascevo
tu	nasci	tu	nascevi
lui/lei/Lei	nasce	lui/lei/Lei	nasceva
noi	nasciamo	noi	nascevamo
voi	nascete	voi	nascevate
loro	nascono	loro	nascevano

	FUTURE		CONDITIONAL
io	nascerò	io	nascerei
tu	nascerai	tu	nasceresti
lui/lei/Lei	nascerà	lui/lei/Lei	nascerebbe
noi	nasceremo	noi	nasceremmo
voi	nascerete	voi	nascereste
loro	nasceranno	loro	nascerebbero

	PRESENT SUBJUNCTIVE		PAST HISTORIC
io	nasca	io	nacqui
tu	nasca	tu	nascesti
lui/lei/Lei	nasca	lui/lei/Lei	nacque
noi	nasciamo	noi	nascemmo
voi	nasciate	voi	nasceste
loro	nascano	loro	nacquero

PAST PARTICIPLE	IMPERATIVE
nato	nasci
	nasciamo
	nascete

GERUND	AUXILIARY
nascendo	essere

Verb Tables

parlare (to speak)

	PRESENT			IMPERFECT
io	**parlo**		io	**parlavo**
tu	**parli**		tu	**parlavi**
lui/lei/Lei	**parla**		lui/lei/Lei	**parlava**
noi	**parliamo**		noi	**parlavamo**
voi	**parlate**		voi	**parlavate**
loro	**parlano**		loro	**parlavano**

	FUTURE			CONDITIONAL
io	**parlerò**		io	**parlerei**
tu	**parlerai**		tu	**parleresti**
lui/lei/Lei	**parlerà**		lui/lei/Lei	**parlerebbe**
noi	**parleremo**		noi	**parleremmo**
voi	**parlerete**		voi	**parlereste**
loro	**parleranno**		loro	**parlerebbero**

	PRESENT SUBJUNCTIVE			PAST HISTORIC
io	**parli**		io	**parlai**
tu	**parli**		tu	**parlasti**
lui/lei/Lei	**parli**		lui/lei/Lei	**parlò**
noi	**parliamo**		noi	**parlammo**
voi	**parliate**		voi	**parlaste**
loro	**parlino**		loro	**parlarono**

PAST PARTICIPLE	IMPERATIVE
parlato	**parla**
	parliamo
	parlate

GERUND	AUXILIARY
parlando	**avere**

piacere (to be pleasing)

	PRESENT		IMPERFECT
io	**piaccio**	io	**piacevo**
tu	**piaci**	tu	**piacevi**
lui/lei/Lei	**piace**	lui/lei/Lei	**piaceva**
noi	**piacciamo**	noi	**piacevamo**
voi	**piacete**	voi	**piacevate**
loro	**piacciono**	loro	**piacevano**

	FUTURE		CONDITIONAL
io	**piacerò**	io	**piacerei**
tu	**piacerai**	tu	**piaceresti**
lui/lei/Lei	**piacerà**	lui/lei/Lei	**piacerebbe**
noi	**piaceremo**	noi	**piaceremmo**
voi	**piacerete**	voi	**piacereste**
loro	**piaceranno**	loro	**piacerebbero**

	PRESENT SUBJUNCTIVE		PAST HISTORIC
io	**piaccia**	io	**piacqui**
tu	**piaccia**	tu	**piacesti**
lui/lei/Lei	**piaccia**	lui/lei/Lei	**piacque**
noi	**piacciamo**	noi	**piacemmo**
voi	**piacciate**	voi	**piaceste**
loro	**piacciano**	loro	**piacquero**

PAST PARTICIPLE	IMPERATIVE
piaciuto	**piaci**
	piacciamo
	piacciate

GERUND	AUXILIARY
piacendo	**essere**

piovere (to rain)

PRESENT	**IMPERFECT**
piove	pioveva

FUTURE	**CONDITIONAL**
pioverà	pioverebbe

PRESENT SUBJUNCTIVE	**PAST HISTORIC**
piova	piovve

PAST PARTICIPLE	**IMPERATIVE**
piovuto	–

GERUND	**AUXILIARY**
piovendo	essere

potere (to be able)

	PRESENT		IMPERFECT
io	**posso**	io	**potevo**
tu	**puoi**	tu	**potevi**
lui/lei/Lei	**può**	lui/lei/Lei	**poteva**
noi	**possiamo**	noi	**potevamo**
voi	**potete**	voi	**potevate**
loro	**possono**	loro	**potevano**

	FUTURE		CONDITIONAL
io	**potrò**	io	**potrei**
tu	**potrai**	tu	**potresti**
lui/lei/Lei	**potrà**	lui/lei/Lei	**potrebbe**
noi	**potremo**	noi	**potremmo**
voi	**potrete**	voi	**potreste**
loro	**potranno**	loro	**potrebbero**

	PRESENT SUBJUNCTIVE		PAST HISTORIC
io	**possa**	io	**potei**
tu	**possa**	tu	**potesti**
lui/lei/Lei	**possa**	lui/lei/Lei	**poté**
noi	**possiamo**	noi	**potemmo**
voi	**possiate**	voi	**poteste**
loro	**possano**	loro	**poterono**

PAST PARTICIPLE	IMPERATIVE
potuto	–

GERUND	AUXILIARY
potendo	**avere**

prendere (to take)

	PRESENT		IMPERFECT
io	prendo	io	prendevo
tu	prendi	tu	prendevi
lui/lei/Lei	prende	lui/lei/Lei	prendeva
noi	prendiamo	noi	prendevamo
voi	prendete	voi	prendevate
loro	prendono	loro	prendevano

	FUTURE		CONDITIONAL
io	prenderò	io	prenderei
tu	prenderai	tu	prenderesti
lui/lei/Lei	prenderà	lui/lei/Lei	prenderebbe
noi	prenderemo	noi	prenderemmo
voi	prenderete	voi	prendereste
loro	prenderanno	loro	prenderebbero

	PRESENT SUBJUNCTIVE		PAST HISTORIC
io	prenda	io	presi
tu	prenda	tu	prendesti
lui/lei/Lei	prenda	lui/lei/Lei	prese
noi	prendiamo	noi	prendemmo
voi	prendiate	voi	prendeste
loro	prendano	loro	presero

PAST PARTICIPLE	IMPERATIVE
preso	prendi
	prendiamo
	prendete

GERUND	AUXILIARY
prendendo	avere

Verb Tables

rompere (to break)

	PRESENT		IMPERFECT
io	rompo	io	rompevo
tu	rompi	tu	rompevi
lui/lei/Lei	rompe	lui/lei/Lei	rompeva
noi	rompiamo	noi	rompevamo
voi	rompete	voi	rompevate
loro	rompono	loro	rompevano

	FUTURE		CONDITIONAL
io	romperò	io	romperei
tu	romperai	tu	romperesti
lui/lei/Lei	romperà	lui/lei/Lei	romperebbe
noi	romperemo	noi	romperemmo
voi	romperete	voi	rompereste
loro	romperanno	loro	romperebbero

	PRESENT SUBJUNCTIVE		PAST HISTORIC
io	rompa	io	ruppi
tu	rompa	tu	rompesti
lui/lei/Lei	rompa	lui/lei/Lei	ruppe
noi	rompiamo	noi	rompemmo
voi	rompiate	voi	rompeste
loro	rompano	loro	ruppero

PAST PARTICIPLE	IMPERATIVE
rotto	rompi
	rompiamo
	rompete

GERUND	AUXILIARY
rompendo	avere

Verb Tables

salire (to go up)

	PRESENT		IMPERFECT
io	**salgo**	io	**salivo**
tu	**sali**	tu	**salivi**
lui/lei/Lei	**sale**	lui/lei/Lei	**saliva**
noi	**saliamo**	noi	**salivamo**
voi	**salite**	voi	**salivate**
loro	**salgono**	loro	**salivano**

	FUTURE		CONDITIONAL
io	**salirò**	io	**salirei**
tu	**salirai**	tu	**saliresti**
lui/lei/Lei	**salirà**	lui/lei/Lei	**salirebbe**
noi	**saliremo**	noi	**saliremmo**
voi	**salirete**	voi	**salireste**
loro	**saliranno**	loro	**salirebbero**

	PRESENT SUBJUNCTIVE		PAST HISTORIC
io	**salga**	io	**salii**
tu	**salga**	tu	**salisti**
lui/lei/Lei	**salga**	lui/lei/Lei	**salì**
noi	**saliamo**	noi	**salimmo**
voi	**saliate**	voi	**saliste**
loro	**salgano**	loro	**salirono**

PAST PARTICIPLE	IMPERATIVE
salito	**sali**
	saliamo
	salite

GERUND	AUXILIARY
salendo	**essere**

Verb Tables

sapere (to know)

	PRESENT		IMPERFECT
io	**so**	io	**sapevo**
tu	**sai**	tu	**sapevi**
lui/lei/Lei	**sa**	lui/lei/Lei	**sapeva**
noi	**sappiamo**	noi	**sapevamo**
voi	**sapete**	voi	**sapevate**
loro	**sanno**	loro	**sapevano**

	FUTURE		CONDITIONAL
io	**saprò**	io	**saprei**
tu	**saprai**	tu	**sapresti**
lui/lei/Lei	**saprà**	lui/lei/Lei	**saprebbe**
noi	**sapremo**	noi	**sapremmo**
voi	**saprete**	voi	**sapreste**
loro	**sapranno**	loro	**saprebbero**

	PRESENT SUBJUNCTIVE		PAST HISTORIC
io	**sappia**	io	**seppi**
tu	**sappia**	tu	**sapesti**
lui/lei/Lei	**sappia**	lui/lei/Lei	**seppe**
noi	**sappiamo**	noi	**sapemmo**
voi	**sappiate**	voi	**sapeste**
loro	**sappiano**	loro	**seppero**

PAST PARTICIPLE	IMPERATIVE
saputo	**sappi**
	sappiamo
	sappiate

GERUND	AUXILIARY
sapendo	**avere**

Verb Tables

scrivere (to write)

	PRESENT		IMPERFECT
io	scrivo	io	scrivevo
tu	scrivi	tu	scrivevi
lui/lei/Lei	scrive	lui/lei/Lei	scriveva
noi	scriviamo	noi	scrivevamo
voi	scrivete	voi	scrivevate
loro	scrivono	loro	scrivevano

	FUTURE		CONDITIONAL
io	scriverò	io	scriverei
tu	scriverai	tu	scriveresti
lui/lei/Lei	scriverà	lui/lei/Lei	scriverebbe
noi	scriveremo	noi	scriveremmo
voi	scriverete	voi	scrivereste
loro	scriveranno	loro	scriverebbero

	PRESENT SUBJUNCTIVE		PAST HISTORIC
io	scriva	io	scrissi
tu	scriva	tu	scrivesti
lui/lei/Lei	scriva	lui/lei/Lei	scrisse
noi	scriviamo	noi	scrivemmo
voi	scriviate	voi	scriveste
loro	scrivano	loro	scrissero

PAST PARTICIPLE
scritto

IMPERATIVE
scrivi
scriviamo
scrivete

GERUND
scrivendo

AUXILIARY
avere

sedere (to sit)

	PRESENT		IMPERFECT
io	**siedo**	io	**sedevo**
tu	**siedi**	tu	**sedevi**
lui/lei/Lei	**siede**	lui/lei/Lei	**sedeva**
noi	**sediamo**	noi	**sedevamo**
voi	**sedete**	voi	**sedevate**
loro	**siedono**	loro	**sedevano**

	FUTURE		CONDITIONAL
io	**siederò**	io	**sederei**
tu	**siederai**	tu	**sederesti**
lui/lei/Lei	**siederà**	lui/lei/Lei	**sederebbe**
noi	**siederemo**	noi	**sederemmo**
voi	**siederete**	voi	**sedereste**
loro	**siederanno**	loro	**sederebbero**

	PRESENT SUBJUNCTIVE		PAST HISTORIC
io	**sieda**	io	**sedetti**
tu	**sieda**	tu	**sedesti**
lui/lei/Lei	**sieda**	lui/lei/Lei	**sedette**
noi	**sediamo**	noi	**sedemmo**
voi	**sediate**	voi	**sedeste**
loro	**siedano**	loro	**sedettero**

PAST PARTICIPLE	IMPERATIVE
seduto	**siedi**
	sediamo
	sedete

GERUND	AUXILIARY
sedendo	*essere*

Verb Tables

stare (to be)

	PRESENT		IMPERFECT
io	**sto**	io	**stavo**
tu	**stai**	tu	**stavi**
lui/lei/Lei	**sta**	lui/lei/Lei	**stava**
noi	**stiamo**	noi	**stavamo**
voi	**state**	voi	**stavate**
loro	**stanno**	loro	**stavano**

	FUTURE		CONDITIONAL
io	**starò**	io	**starei**
tu	**starai**	tu	**staresti**
lui/lei/Lei	**starà**	lui/lei/Lei	**starebbe**
noi	**staremo**	noi	**staremmo**
voi	**starete**	voi	**stareste**
loro	**staranno**	loro	**starebbero**

	PRESENT SUBJUNCTIVE		PAST HISTORIC
io	**stia**	io	**stetti**
tu	**stia**	tu	**stesti**
lui/lei/Lei	**stia**	lui/lei/Lei	**stette**
noi	**stiamo**	noi	**stemmo**
voi	**stiate**	voi	**steste**
loro	**stiano**	loro	**stettero**

PAST PARTICIPLE	IMPERATIVE
stato	**stai**
	stiamo
	state

GERUND	AUXILIARY
stando	*essere*

succedere (to happen)

	PRESENT		IMPERFECT
sing.	**succede**	*sing.*	**succedeva**
plur.	**succedono**	*plur.*	**succedevano**

	FUTURE		CONDITIONAL
sing.	**succederà**	*sing.*	**succederebbe**
plur.	**succederanno**	*plur.*	**succederebbero**

	PRESENT SUBJUNCTIVE		PAST HISTORIC
sing.	**succeda**	*sing.*	**successe**
plur.	**succedano**	*plur.*	**successero**

PAST PARTICIPLE	IMPERATIVE
successo	–

GERUND	AUXILIARY
succedendo	*essere*

Verb Tables

tenere (to hold)

	PRESENT		IMPERFECT
io	tengo	io	tenevo
tu	tieni	tu	tenevi
lui/lei/Lei	tiene	lui/lei/Lei	teneva
noi	teniamo	noi	tenevamo
voi	tenete	voi	tenevate
loro	tengono	loro	tenevano

	FUTURE		CONDITIONAL
io	terrò	io	terrei
tu	terrai	tu	terresti
lui/lei/Lei	terrà	lui/lei/Lei	terrebbe
noi	terremo	noi	terremmo
voi	terrete	voi	terreste
loro	terranno	loro	terrebbero

	PRESENT SUBJUNCTIVE		PAST HISTORIC
io	tenga	io	tenni
tu	tenga	tu	tenesti
lui/lei/Lei	tenga	lui/lei/Lei	tenne
noi	teniamo	noi	tenemmo
voi	teniate	voi	teneste
loro	tengano	loro	tennero

PAST PARTICIPLE	IMPERATIVE
tenuto	tieni
	teniamo
	tenete

GERUND	AUXILIARY
tenendo	avere

uscire (to go out)

	PRESENT		IMPERFECT
io	**esco**	io	**uscivo**
tu	**esci**	tu	**uscivi**
lui/lei/Lei	**esce**	lui/lei/Lei	**usciva**
noi	**usciamo**	noi	**uscivamo**
voi	**uscite**	voi	**uscivate**
loro	**escono**	loro	**uscivano**

	FUTURE		CONDITIONAL
io	**uscirò**	io	**uscirei**
tu	**uscirai**	tu	**usciresti**
lui/lei/Lei	**uscirà**	lui/lei/Lei	**uscirebbe**
noi	**usciremo**	noi	**usciremmo**
voi	**uscirete**	voi	**uscireste**
loro	**usciranno**	loro	**uscirebbero**

	PRESENT SUBJUNCTIVE		PAST HISTORIC
io	**esca**	io	**uscii**
tu	**esca**	tu	**uscisti**
lui/lei/Lei	**esca**	lui/lei/Lei	**uscì**
noi	**usciamo**	noi	**uscimmo**
voi	**usciate**	voi	**usciste**
loro	**escano**	loro	**uscirono**

PAST PARTICIPLE	IMPERATIVE
uscito	**esci**
	usciamo
	uscite

GERUND	AUXILIARY
uscendo	**essere**

vedere (to see)

	PRESENT		IMPERFECT
io	vedo	io	vedevo
tu	vedi	tu	vedevi
lui/lei/Lei	vede	lui/lei/Lei	vedeva
noi	vediamo	noi	vedevamo
voi	vedete	voi	vedevate
loro	vedono	loro	vedevano

	FUTURE		CONDITIONAL
io	vedrò	io	vedrei
tu	vedrai	tu	vedresti
lui/lei/Lei	vedrà	lui/lei/Lei	vedrebbe
noi	vedremo	noi	vedremmo
voi	vedrete	voi	vedreste
loro	vedranno	loro	vedrebbero

	PRESENT SUBJUNCTIVE		PAST HISTORIC
io	veda	io	vidi
tu	veda	tu	vedesti
lui/lei/Lei	veda	lui/lei/Lei	vide
noi	vediamo	noi	vedemmo
voi	vediate	voi	vedeste
loro	vedano	loro	videro

PAST PARTICIPLE	IMPERATIVE
visto	vedi
	vediamo
	vedete

GERUND	AUXILIARY
vedendo	avere

venire (to come)

	PRESENT		IMPERFECT
io	**vengo**	io	**venivo**
tu	**vieni**	tu	**venivi**
lui/lei/Lei	**viene**	lui/lei/Lei	**veniva**
noi	**veniamo**	noi	**venivamo**
voi	**venite**	voi	**venivate**
loro	**vengono**	loro	**venivano**

	FUTURE		CONDITIONAL
io	**verrò**	io	**verrei**
tu	**verrai**	tu	**verresti**
lui/lei/Lei	**verrà**	lui/lei/Lei	**verrebbe**
noi	**verremo**	noi	**verremmo**
voi	**verrete**	voi	**verreste**
loro	**verranno**	loro	**verrebbero**

	PRESENT SUBJUNCTIVE		PAST HISTORIC
io	**venga**	io	**venni**
tu	**venga**	tu	**venisti**
lui/lei/Lei	**venga**	lui/lei/Lei	**venne**
noi	**veniamo**	noi	**venimmo**
voi	**veniate**	voi	**veniste**
loro	**vengano**	loro	**vennero**

PAST PARTICIPLE	IMPERATIVE
venuto	**vieni**
	veniamo
	venite

GERUND	AUXILIARY
venendo	**essere**

Verb Tables

vincere (to defeat)

	PRESENT		IMPERFECT
io	**vinco**	io	**vincevo**
tu	**vinci**	tu	**vincevi**
lui/lei/Lei	**vince**	lui/lei/Lei	**vinceva**
noi	**vinciamo**	noi	**vincevamo**
voi	**vincete**	voi	**vincevate**
loro	**vincono**	loro	**vincevano**

	FUTURE		CONDITIONAL
io	**vincerò**	io	**vincerei**
tu	**vincerai**	tu	**vinceresti**
lui/lei/Lei	**vincerà**	lui/lei/Lei	**vincerebbe**
noi	**vinceremo**	noi	**vinceremmo**
voi	**vincerete**	voi	**vincereste**
loro	**vinceranno**	loro	**vincerebbero**

	PRESENT SUBJUNCTIVE		PAST HISTORIC
io	**vinca**	io	**vinsi**
tu	**vinca**	tu	**vincesti**
lui/lei/Lei	**vinca**	lui/lei/Lei	**vinse**
noi	**vinciamo**	noi	**vincemmo**
voi	**vinciate**	voi	**vinceste**
loro	**vincano**	loro	**vinsero**

PAST PARTICIPLE	IMPERATIVE
vinto	**vinci**
	vinciamo
	vincete

GERUND	AUXILIARY
vincendo	**avere**

vivere (to live)

	PRESENT		IMPERFECT
io	**vivo**	io	**vivevo**
tu	**vivi**	tu	**vivevi**
lui/lei/Lei	**vive**	lui/lei/Lei	**viveva**
noi	**viviamo**	noi	**vivevamo**
voi	**vivete**	voi	**vivevate**
loro	**vivono**	loro	**vivevano**

	FUTURE		CONDITIONAL
io	**vivrò**	io	**vivrei**
tu	**vivrai**	tu	**vivresti**
lui/lei/Lei	**vivrà**	lui/lei/Lei	**vivrebbe**
noi	**vivremo**	noi	**vivremmo**
voi	**vivrete**	voi	**vivreste**
loro	**vivranno**	loro	**vivrebbero**

	PRESENT SUBJUNCTIVE		PAST HISTORIC
io	**viva**	io	**vissi**
tu	**viva**	tu	**vivesti**
lui/lei/Lei	**viva**	lui/lei/Lei	**visse**
noi	**viviamo**	noi	**vivemmo**
voi	**viviate**	voi	**viveste**
loro	**vivano**	loro	**vissero**

PAST PARTICIPLE	IMPERATIVE
vissuto	**vivi**
	viviamo
	vivete

GERUND	AUXILIARY
vivendo	**avere**

Verb Tables

volere (to want)

	PRESENT		IMPERFECT
io	**voglio**	io	**volevo**
tu	**vuoi**	tu	**volevi**
lui/lei/Lei	**vuole**	lui/lei/Lei	**voleva**
noi	**vogliamo**	noi	**volevamo**
voi	**volete**	voi	**volevate**
loro	**vogliono**	loro	**volevano**

	FUTURE		CONDITIONAL
io	**vorrò**	io	**vorrei**
tu	**vorrai**	tu	**vorresti**
lui/lei/Lei	**vorrà**	lui/lei/Lei	**vorrebbe**
noi	**vorremo**	noi	**vorremmo**
voi	**vorrete**	voi	**vorreste**
loro	**vorranno**	loro	**vorrebbero**

	PRESENT SUBJUNCTIVE		PAST HISTORIC
io	**voglia**	io	**volli**
tu	**voglia**	tu	**volesti**
lui/lei/Lei	**voglia**	lui/lei/Lei	**volle**
noi	**vogliamo**	noi	**volemmo**
voi	**vogliate**	voi	**voleste**
loro	**vogliano**	loro	**vollero**

PAST PARTICIPLE	IMPERATIVE
voluto	**–**

GERUND	AUXILIARY
volendo	**avere**

Nouns

The Gender of Nouns

In Italian, all nouns are either masculine or feminine, whether they denote people, animals or things.

The gender of a noun is often indicated by its final letter. Here are some guidelines to help you determine which gender a noun is:

Nearly all nouns ending in **-o** are masculine, e.g.
il treno the train
l'uomo the man
un topo a mouse
un gatto a (tom)cat
un italiano an Italian (man)

EXCEPTIONS:
la mano the hand
una foto a photo
la radio the radio
una moto a motorbike

Very many nouns ending in **-a** are feminine, e.g.
la casa the house
una donna a woman
una gatta a (she) cat
un'italiana an Italian (woman)

There are, however, numerous exceptions, e.g.
il dramma the drama
il papa the pope
il problema the problem

A few nouns ending in **-a** are feminine, but can refer to a man or a woman, e.g.
una guida a guide (male or female)
una persona a person (male or female)
una vittima a victim (male or female)

Nouns ending in **-ista** denoting people can be masculine or feminine, e.g.
un giornalista a (male) journalist
una giornalista a (female) journalist

Nouns

The Gender of Nouns *continued*

> **un pessimista** a (male) pessimist
> **una pessimista** a (female) pessimist

Nearly all words ending in **-à**, **-sione** and **-zione** are feminine, e.g.
> **una difficoltà** a difficulty
> **un'occasione** an opportunity
> **una conversazione** a conversation

Nouns ending in a consonant are nearly always masculine, e.g.
> **un film** a film
> **un computer** a computer
> **un box** a garage

> EXCEPTIONS:
> **una jeep** a jeep
> **una star** a star

Nouns ending in **-e** or **-i** can be masculine or feminine, e.g.
> **un mese** a month
> **la mente** the mind
> **un brindisi** a toast
> **una crisi** a crisis

The names of languages, and all months, are masculine, whether they end in **-o** or **-e**, e.g.
> **il tedesco** German
> **il francese** French
> **lo scorso febbraio** last February
> **il prossimo dicembre** next December

Suffixes that differentiate between male and female are shown on page 128.

Some words have different meanings depending on their gender, e.g.

il fine the objective	**la fine** the end
un posto a place	**la posta** the post (mail)
il manico the handle	**la manica** the sleeve
un modo a way	**la moda** the fashion
un mostro a monster	**una mostra** an exhibition
il capitale capital (money)	**una capitale** a capital city

Nouns

The Formation of Feminines

As in English, male and female are sometimes differentiated by the use of quite different words, e.g.

> **un fratello** a brother
> **una sorella** a sister
> **un toro** a bull
> **una mucca** a cow

More often, however, words in Italian show gender by their ending:

> Many Italian nouns ending in **-o** can be made feminine by changing the ending to **-a** → ❶
>
> Some nouns ending in **-e** also change the ending to **-a** for the feminine → ❷
>
> Some nouns ending in **-a** or **-e** have no change of ending for the feminine → ❸
>
> Nouns ending in **-ese** that describe nationality are the same for masculine and feminine → ❹
>
> Nouns ending in **-ante** are the same for masculine and feminine → ❺
>
> Nouns ending in **-tore** make the the feminine by substituting the ending **-trice** → ❻
>
> Some nouns ending in **-e** have feminine forms ending in **-essa** → ❼

Examples

❶ un cuoco   a (*male*) cook
una cuoca   a (*female*) cook
uno zio   an uncle
una zia   an aunt
una ragazzo   a boy
una ragazza   a girl
un italiano   an Italian (man)
un'italiana   an Italian (woman)

❷ un signore   a gentleman
una signora   a lady
un infermiere   a (*male*) nurse
un'infermiera   a (*female*) nurse
un parrucchiere   a (*male*) hairdresser
una parrucchiera   a (*female*) hairdresser

❸ un collega   a (*male*) colleague
una collega   a (*female*) colleague
il mio dentista   my dentist (*male*)
la mia dentista   my dentist (*female*)
un nipote   a grandson
una nipote   a granddaughter

❹ un irlandese   an Irishman
un'irlandese   an Irishwoman
uno scozzese   a Scotsman
una scozzese   a Scotswoman

❺ un cantante   a (*male*) singer
una cantante   a (*female*) singer
un amante   a (*male*) lover
un'amante   a (*female*) lover
un principiante   a (*male*) beginner
una principiante   a (*female*) beginner

❻ un attore   a (*male*) actor
un'attrice   a (*female*) actor
un pittore   a (*male*) painter
una pittrice   a (*female*) painter

❼ il professore   the (*male*) teacher
la professoressa   the (*female*) teacher
uno studente   a (*male*) student
una studentessa   a (*female*) student

Nouns

The Formation of Plurals

Masculine nouns, whether they end in **-o, -a** or **-e,** nearly always take the ending **-i** in the plural → **❶**

Feminine nouns ending in **-a** take the ending **-e** in the plural → **❷**

Feminine nouns ending in **-e** take the ending **-i** in the plural → **❸**

Nouns that have no change of ending in the plural

Nouns ending in an accented vowel do not change the ending in the plural → **❹**

Nouns ending in **-i** and **-ie** do not change in the plural → **❺**

Words ending with a consonant remain unchanged in the plural → **❻**

Other common words that do not change in the plural are:

il cinema cinema		**i cinema**
la radio radio		**le radio**
la moto motorbike		**le moto**
l'auto car		**le auto**
la foto photo		**le foto**

Examples

❶ **un anno** — one year
due anni — two years
un ragazzo — a boy
i ragazzi — the boys
un ciclista — a (*male*) cyclist
due ciclisti — two cyclists
un problema — a problem
molti problemi — lots of problems
un mese — one month
due mesi — two months
un francese — a Frenchman
due francesi — two Frenchmen

❷ **una settimana** — one week
due settimane — two weeks
una ragazza — one girl
due ragazze — two girls

❸ **un'inglese** — an Englishwoman
due inglesi — two Englishwomen
la vite — the vine
le viti — the vines

❹ **la città** — the city
le città — the cities
la loro università — their university
le loro università — their universities
un caffè — a coffee
due caffè — two coffees
una virtù — a virtue
le sue virtù — her virtues

❺ **un'analisi** — an analysis
delle analisi — analyses
una serie — a series
due serie — two series
una specie — a sort
varie specie — various sorts

❻ **il film** — the film
i film — the films
il manager — the manager
i manager — the managers
il computer — the computer
i computer — the computers
la jeep — the Jeep®
le jeep — the jeeps

Nouns

Irregular Plural Forms

Some masculine nouns become feminine in the plural, and take the ending **-a** → **❶**

The plural of **uomo** man is *uomini.* The plural of **la mano** hand is **le mani.**

Nouns ending in **-ca** and **-ga** add an **h** before the plural ending, to keep the sound of the **c** and **g** hard → **❷**

Some nouns ending in **-co** and **-go** also add an **h** before the plural ending, to keep the sound of the **c** and **g** hard → **❸**

There are numerous exceptions. You can check the plural of such nouns in the dictionary.

> EXCEPTIONS:
> **amico** friend (*plural* **amici**)
> **nemico** enemy (*plural* **nemici**)
> **psicologo** psychologist (*plural* **psicologi**)
> **geologo** geologist (*plural* **geologi**)

The plurals of compound nouns such as **pescespada** (*swordfish*), **capolavoro** (*masterpiece*), or **apriscatole** (*tin opener*) do not always follow the usual rules. You can find them in the dictionary.

Examples

❶ il dito — the finger
  le dita — the fingers
  un uovo — an egg
  le uova — the eggs
  il lenzuolo — the sheet
  le lenzuola — the sheets

❷ amica — (*female*) friend
  amiche — (*female*) friends
  buca — hole
  buche — holes
  riga — line
  righe — lines
  casalinga — housewife
  casalinghe — housewives

❸ gioco — game
  giochi — games
  fuoco — fire
  fuochi — fires
  luogo — place
  luoghi — places
  borgo — district
  borghi — districts

Articles

The Definite Article

il/lo(l'), la(l'), i/gli;le

	MASCULINE		FEMININE
SING.	il	SING.	la
	lo		
	l'		l'
PLUR.	i	PLUR.	le
	gli		

The form of the Italian article depends on the gender and number of the noun it accompanies. It also depends on the letter the noun starts with.

il is used with masculine nouns starting with most consonants, except for **z**, **gn**, **pn**, **ps**, **x**, **y** and impure **s***; **lo** is used with these. **l'** is used before vowels → ❶

i is used with masculine plural nouns starting with most consonants; **gli** is used before vowels and **z**, **gn**, **pn**, **ps**, **x**, **y** and impure **s*** → ❷

la is used before feminine singular nouns beginning with a consonant, and **l'** is used before a vowel → ❸

le is used with all feminine plural nouns → ❹

If the article is separated from the noun by an adjective, the first letter of the adjective determines the choice of article → ❺

For uses of the definite article, see page 138.

*Impure **s** means **s** + another consonant.

Examples

❶ il ragazzo — the boy
il cellulare — the mobile phone
lo zio — the uncle
lo studente — the student
lo pneumatico — the tyre
lo psichiatra — the psychiatrist
lo yogurt — the yoghurt
l'ospedale — the hospital
l'albergo — the hotel

❷ i fratelli — the brothers
i cellulari — the mobile phones
gli studenti — the students
gli zii — the uncles
gli gnocchi — the gnocchi
gli pneumatici — the tyres
gli yogurt — the yoghurts
gli amici — the friends
gli orari — the timetables

❸ la ragazza — the girl
la macchina — the car
l'amica — the (girl) friend
l'arancia — the orange

❹ le ragazze — the girls
le amiche — the (girl) friends

❺ l'amico the friend   **il migliore amico** the best friend
lo studente the student   **il migliore studente** the best student

gli studenti the students   **i migliori studenti** the best students

Articles

The Definite Article *continued*

The prepositions **a, da, di, in, su** and **con** combine with the article to form one word.

a + article → ❶

SING.	a + il = al	a + la = alla
	a + l' = all'	a + l' = all'
	a + lo = allo	
PLUR.	a + i = ai	a + le = alle
	a + gli = agli	

da + article → ❷

SING.	da + il = dal	da + la = dalla
	da + l' = dall'	da + l' = dall'
	da + lo = dallo	
PLUR.	da + i = dai	da + le = dalle
	da + gli = dagli	

di + article → ❸

SING.	di + il = del	di + la = della
	di + l' = dell'	di + l' = dell'
	di + lo = dello	
PLUR.	di + i = dei	di + le = delle
	di + gli = degli	

in + article → ❹

SING.	in + il = nel	in + la = nella
	in + l' = nell'	in + l' = nell'
	in + lo = nello	
PLUR.	in + i = nei	in + le = nelle
	in + gli = negli	

su + article → ❺

SING.	su + il = sul	su + la = sulla
	su + l' = sull'	su + l' = sull'
	su + lo = sullo	
PLUR.	su + i = sui	su + le = sulle
	su + gli = sugli	

con + article → ❻

SING.	con + il = col	
PLUR.	con + i = coi	con + le = colle

Examples

1 **al cinema**   at *or* to the cinema
    allo stadio   at *or* to the stadium
    ai concerti   at *or* to the concerts
    alle partite   at *or* to the matches

2 **dall'albergo**   from the hotel
    dalla stazione   from the station
    dagli aeroporti   from the airports
    della squadra   of the team
    degli studenti   of the students

3 **nel giardino**   in the garden
    nell'appartamento   in the flat

4 **nei dintorni**   in the vicinity

5 **sullo scoglio**   on the rock
    sulla spiaggia   on the beach

6 **col ghiaccio**   with ice
    coi bambini   with children

Articles

The Definite Article *continued*

Uses of the Definite Article

The definite article is used much more in Italian than it is in English.
It generally translates the English definite article, but is also used in many
contexts where English has no article:

with possessive pronouns → **①**

with plurals and uncountable* nouns → **②**

in generalizations → **③**

with the names of regions and countries → **④**
EXCEPTIONS: no article with countries following the Italian
preposition **in** *in/to* → **⑤**

with parts of the body, replacing the English possessive
adjective → **⑥**

'Ownership' of parts of the body, and of clothes, is often indicated by
an indirect object pronoun or a reflexive pronoun → **⑦**

with the time, dates and years → **⑧**

in expressions of quantity/rate/price → **⑨**

with titles, ranks, professions followed by a proper name, and
colloquially, with female names → **⑩**

---

* An uncountable noun is one which cannot be used in the plural or with
an indefinite article, e.g. *milk*.

Examples

1. **la mia casa**   my house
   le sue figlie   her daughters
   i vostri amici   your friends

2. **I bambini soffrono**   Children are suffering
   Mi piacciono gli animali   I like animals
   Le cose vanno meglio   Things are going better
   Il nuoto è il mio sport preferito   Swimming is my favourite sport
   Non mi piace il riso   I don't like rice

3. **Lo zucchero non fa bene**   Sugar isn't good for you
   La povertà è un grande problema   Poverty is a big problem

4. **L'Australia è molto grande**   Australia is very big
   La Calabria è bella   Calabria is beautiful

5. **Vado in Francia a giugno**   I'm going to France in June
   Lavorano in Germania   They work in Germany

6. **Dammi la mano**   Give me your hand
   Attento alla testa!   Mind your head!

7. **Mi fa male il piede**   My foot is hurting
   Soffiati il naso!   Blow your nose!
   Si è tolto il cappotto   He took off his coat
   Mettiti le scarpe   Put your shoes on

8. **all'una**   at one o'clock
   alle due   at two o'clock
   Era l'una   It was one o'clock
   Sono le due   It's two o'clock
   Sono nata il primo maggio 1990   I was born on May 1, 1990
   Verranno nel 2018   They're coming in 2018

9. **Costano 3 euro al chilo**   They cost 3 euros a kilo
   70 km all'ora   70 km an hour
   50.000 dollari al mese   50,000 dollars per month
   due volte alla settimana   twice a week

10. **La signora Rossi è qui**   Mrs. Rossi is here
    Il dottor Gentile   Doctor Gentile
    la regina Elisabetta   Queen Elizabeth
    Ecco la Silvia!   Here's Silvia!

Articles

The Partitive Article

The partitive article has the sense of 'some' or 'any', although the Italian is not always translated in English.

Forms of the partitive

	WITH MASC. NOUN		WITH FEM. NOUN
SING.	del	SING.	della
	dell'		dell'
	dello		
PLUR.	dei	PLUR.	delle
	degli		

Examples

del burro	some butter
dell'*olio*	some oil
della carta	some paper
dei fiammiferi	some matches
delle uova	some eggs
Hanno rotto dei bicchieri	They broke some glasses
Mi ha fatto vedere delle foto	He showed me some photos
Ci vuole del sale	It needs (some) salt
Aggiungi della farina	Add (some) flour

Articles

The Indefinite Article

MASCULINE	FEMININE
un	**una**
uno	**un'**

The form of the indefinite article depends on the gender of the noun it accompanies. It also depends on the letter the noun starts with.

un is used with masculine nouns starting with vowels and most consonants, except for **z**, **gn**, **pn**, **ps**, **x**, **y** and impure **s*** → ❶

uno is used with these → ❷

una is used before feminine nouns beginning with a consonant, and **un'** is used before a vowel → ❸

If the article is separated from the noun by an adjective, the first letter of the adjective determines the choice of article → ❹

The indefinite article is used in Italian largely as it is in English except: → ❺

- with the words **cento** and **mille**
- when translating *a few* or *a lot*
- in exclamations with **che**

The indefinite article is not used when speaking of someone's profession – either the verb *essere* is used, with no article, or **fare** is used with the definite article → ❻

* impure **s** means **s** + another consonant.

Examples

1 **un cellulare** — a mobile phone
un uomo — a man

2 **uno studente** — a student
uno zio — an uncle
uno psichiatra — a psychiatrist

3 **una ragazza** — a girl
una mela — an apple
un'ora — an hour
un'amica — a (girl) friend
un albergo — a hotel

4 **uno splendido albergo** — a magnificent hotel
uno scultore — a sculptor
un bravo scultore — a good sculptor

5 **cento volte** — a hundred times
mille sterline — a thousand pounds
qualche parola — a few words
molti soldi — a lot of money
Che sorpresa! — What a surprise!
Che peccato! — What a pity!

6 **È medico** — He's a doctor
Sono professori — They're teachers
Faccio l'ingegnere — I'm an engineer
Fa l'avvocato — She's a lawyer

Adjectives

The formation of feminines and plurals

Most adjectives agree in number and gender with the noun or pronoun.

The formation of feminines

If the masculine singular form of the adjective ends in **-o**, the feminine ends in **-a** → **❶**

If the adjective ends in **-e**, the ending does not change for the feminine → **❷**

The formation of plurals

If the masculine singular of the adjective ends in **-o**, the ending changes to **-i** for the masculine plural, and to **-e** for the feminine plural → **❸**

If the adjective ends in **-e**, the ending changes to **-i** for both masculine and feminine plural → **❹**

Invariable adjectives

Some adjectives have no change of ending either for the feminine or the plural → **❺**

Examples

1 **un ragazzo alto**   a tall boy
   una ragazza alta   a tall girl
   un film italiano   an Italian film
   una squadra italiana   an Italian team

2 **un libro inglese**   an English book
   una famiglia inglese   an English family
   un treno veloce   a fast train
   una macchina veloce   a fast car

3 **un fiore rosso**   a red flower
   dei fiori rossi   red flowers
   un computer nuovo   a new computer
   dei computer nuovi   new computers
   una strada pericolosa   a dangerous road
   delle strade pericolose   dangerous roads
   una moto nera   a black motorbike
   delle moto nere   black motorbikes

4 **un esercizio difficile**   a difficult exercise
   degli esercizi difficili   difficult exercises
   un sito web interessante   an interesting website
   dei siti web interessanti   interesting websites
   una storia triste   a sad story
   delle storie tristi   sad stories
   una valigia pesante   a heavy case
   delle valigie pesanti   heavy cases

5 **un calzino rosa**   a pink sock
   una maglietta rosa   a pink T-shirt
   un paio di guanti rosa   a pair of pink gloves

   un tappeto blu   a blue rug
   una macchina blu   a blue car
   delle tende blu   blue curtains

   un gruppo rap   a rap group
   la musica rap   rap music
   dei gruppi rap   rap groups

Adjectives

Irregular Adjectives

When **bello** *beautiful* is used in front of a masculine noun, it has different forms depending on which letter follows it.

MASC. SING.	MASC. PLUR.
bel	bei
bell'	begli
bello	begli

EXAMPLES

before most consonants → ❶

before vowels → ❷

before **z**, **gn**, **pn**, **ps**, **x**, **y** and impure **s*** → ❸

When used after a verb, **bello** has the same endings as any other adjective ending in **-o** → ❹

buono *good* becomes **buon** when used before a masculine singular noun, unless the noun starts with **z**, **gn**, **pn**, **ps**, **x**, **y** or impure **s*** → ❺

grande *big, great* is often shortened to **gran** when it comes before a singular noun starting with a consonant → ❻

*Impure **s** means **s** + another consonant.

Examples

1 **bel tempo**
bei nomi
beautiful weather
beautiful names

2 **un bell'**altero
dei begli alberi
a beautiful tree
beautiful trees

3 **un bello strumento**
dei begli strumenti
a beautiful instrument
beautiful instruments

4 **Il tempo era bello**
I fiori sono belli
The weather was beautiful
The flowers are beautiful

5 **Buon viaggio!**
un buon amico
un buono studente
Have a good journey!
a good friend
a good student

6 **la Gran Bretagna**
un gran numero di macchine
Great Britain
a large number of cars

Adjectives

Comparatives and Superlatives

Comparatives are formed using the following constructions:

> **più ... (di)** more ... (than) → ❶
> **meno ... (di)** less ... (than) → ❷
> **(così) .... come** as ... as → ❸
> **(tanto) .... quanto** as ... as → ❹

Superlatives are formed using the following constructions:

> **il/la/i/le più ... (che)** the most ... (that) → ❺
> **il/la/i/le meno ... (che)** the least ... (that) → ❻

After a superlative the preposition **di** is often translated as 'in' → ❼

If a clause follows a superlative, the verb is in the subjunctive → ❽

Adjectives with irregular comparatives/superlatives

Below are the most common adjectives with irregular comparatives and/or superlatives

buono	→	**migliore**	→	**il migliore**
good	→	better	→	the best
cattivo	→	**peggiore**	→	**il peggiore**
bad	→	worse	→	the worst
grande	→	**maggiore**	→	**il maggiore**
big	→	bigger/older	→	the biggest/oldest
piccolo	→	**minore**	→	**il minore**
small	→	smaller/younger	→	the smallest/youngest
alto	→	**superiore**	→	**il superiore**
high	→	higher	→	the highest
basso	→	**inferiore**	→	**l'inferiore**
low	→	lower	→	the lowest

The above words also have regular comparatives/superlatives → ❾

Emphatic adjectives

For added emphasis, the final vowel of an adjective can be replaced with the ending **-issimo**, or **-issima** → ❿

Examples

① **una macchina più grande** a bigger car
Sono più alto di te I'm taller than you

② **un computer meno caro** a less expensive computer
i suoi film meno interessanti his less interesting films
Quello verde è meno caro del nero The green one is less expensive
than the black one

③ **È alta come sua sorella** She's as tall as her sister
La mia borsa non è pesante come My bag's not as heavy as yours
la tua
Non è così lontano come credi It's not as far as you think

④ **Sono stanca quanto te** I'm just as tired as you are
Ha tanto lavoro quanto ne He's got as much work as you
hai tu have
Non ho tanti soldi quanti ne I haven't got as much money
hai tu as you

⑤ **il più alto** the tallest
Queste sono le scarpe più These shoes are the most
comode comfortable

⑥ **il meno interessante** the least interesting
Gianni è il meno ambizioso Gianni is the least ambitious

⑦ **lo stadio più grande d'Italia** the biggest stadium in Italy
il ristorante più caro della città the most expensive restaurant in
the town

⑧ **la persona più pigra che conosca** the laziest person I know
È una delle cose più belle che It's one of the nicest things
ci siano there is

⑨ **Il libro è migliore del film** The book is better than the film
Questo è più buono This one's better
la loro sorella minore their younger sister
il loro fratello più piccolo their younger brother

⑩ **Il tempo era bellissimo** The weather was really beautiful
Anna è sempre elegantissima Anna is always terribly smart
Sono educatissimi They're extremely polite

Adjectives

Demonstrative Adjectives

questo/questa/questi/queste → ❶

	MASCULINE		FEMININE	
SING.	**questo**	SING.	**questa**	this
PLUR.	**questi**	PLUR.	**queste**	these

quello has different forms, depending on the gender of the following noun, and the letter it starts with.

	MASCULINE		FEMININE	
SING.	**quel**	SING.	**quella**	that
	quello		**quell'**	
	quell'			
PLUR.	**quei**	PLUR.	**quelle**	those
	quegli			

quel is used before most consonants, except for **z**, **gn**, **pn**, **ps**, **x**, **y** and impure **s**. **quello** is used before these letters. **quell'** is used before vowels. **quei** is used before most consonants; **quegli** is used before vowels and **z**, **gn**, **pn**, **ps**, **x**, **y** and impure **s***.

quella is used before feminine singular nouns beginning with a consonant, with **quell'** used before a vowel → ❷

*Impure **s** means **s** + another consonant.

Examples

1 **Questa gonna è troppo stretta**   This skirt is too tight
   Questi pantaloni mi piacciono   I like these trousers
   Queste scarpe sono comode   These shoes are comfortable

2 **quel ragazzo**   that boy
   quello zaino   that rucksack
   quello studente   that student
   quell'albero   that tree
   quei cani   those dogs
   quegli uomini   those men
   quegli studenti   those students
   quella ragazza   that girl
   quell'amica   that friend
   quelle macchine   those cars

Adjectives

Interrogative Adjectives

che? what?

che is invariable → **1**

quale/quali? → **2**

	MASCULINE/FEMININE	
SING.	**quale**	what?; which?
PLUR.	**quali**	what?; which?

quanto/quanta/quanti/quante? → **3**

	MASCULINE			FEMININE	
SING.	**quanto**	how much?	SING.	**quanta**	how much?
PLUR.	**quanti**	how many?	PLUR.	**quante**	how many?

Interrogative adjectives are often preceded by prepositions → **4**

Exclamatory Adjectives

che and **quanto** are used with nouns in exclamations → **5**

che is also used with other adjectives → **6**

Examples

❶ **Che giorno è oggi?**   What day is it today?
  Che ore sono?   What time is it?
  Che gusto preferisci?   Which flavour do you like best?
  Che film hai visto?   Which film did you see?
  Che programmi hai?   What plans have you got?

❷ **Quale tipo vuoi?**   What kind do you want?

❸ **Quanto pane hai comprato?**   How much bread did you buy?
  Quanta minestra vuoi?   How much soup do you want?
  Quanti bicchieri ci sono? How many glasses are there?
  Quante uova vuoi?   How many eggs do you want?

❹ **A che ora ti alzi?**   What time do you get up?
  Di che colore è?   What colour is it?
  Per quale squadra tifi?   What team do you support?

❺ **Che peccato!**   What a pity!
  Che disordine!   What a mess!
  Che bella giornata!   What a lovely day!
  Che brutto tempo!   What awful weather!
  Quanto tempo sprecato! What a waste of time!
  Quanta gente!   What a lot of people!
  Quanti soldi!   What a lot of money!
  Quante storie!   What a fuss!

❻ **Che carino!**   Isn't he sweet!
  Che brutti!   They're horrible!

Adjectives

Possessive Adjectives

WITH SING. NOUN		
MASC.	FEM.	
il mio	la mia	my
il tuo	la tua	your
il suo	la sua	his; her; its; your
il nostro	la nostra	our
il vostro	la vostra	your
il loro	la loro	their

WITH PLUR. NOUN		
MASC.	FEM.	
i miei	le mie	my
i tuoi	le tue	your
i suoi	le sue	his; her; its; your
i nostri	le nostre	our
i vostri	le vostre	your
i loro	le loro	their

Possessive adjectives are generally preceded by the article → ❶

Possessive adjectives agree in number and gender with the noun they describe (i.e. the thing which is owned), not with the owner → ❷

il suo/la sua/i suoi/le sue can mean either 'his' or 'her'. To make clear which is meant, **di lui** can be used for 'his', and **di lei** for 'her' → ❸

The article is not used with any possessive adjective except **loro** when referring to singular family members → ❹

EXCEPTIONS: **mamma**, **babbo** and **papà**

Examples

1 **Dove sono le mie chiavi?**   Where are my keys?
   Luca ha perso il suo portafoglio   Luca has lost his wallet
   Ecco i nostri passaporti   Here are our passports
   Qual è la vostra camera?   Which is your room?
   Il tuo amico ti aspetta   Your friend is waiting for you

2 **Anna ha perso il suo cellulare**   Anna has lost her mobile phone
   Le ragazze hanno i loro biglietti   The girls have got their tickets

3 **Le scarpe di lui sono eleganti**   His shoes are smart
   Le scarpe di lei non mi piacciono   I don't like her shoes

4 **con mia madre**   with my mother
   Dov'è tuo padre?   Where's your father?
   lei e suo marito   she and her husband
   È sua moglie   She's his wife
   Non è il loro padre   He's not their father
   Maria e il suo papà   Maria and her dad

Adjectives

Position of Adjectives

Italian adjectives usually follow the noun → **❶**

Adjectives of colour or nationality *always* follow the noun → **❷**

As in English, demonstrative, possessive, numerical and interrogative adjectives precede the noun → **❸**

The adjectives **ogni**, **qualche** and **nessuno** always precede the noun → **❹**

The following common adjectives can precede the noun:

ottimo very good	**pessimo** very bad
bello beautiful	**brutto** bad, ugly
bravo good	**buono** good
prossimo next	**ultimo** last
povero poor	**grande** big, great
nuovo new	**vecchio** old
breve short	**piccolo** small

The meaning of the following adjectives can be affected by their position:

grande	→ (after noun) big	→ (before noun) great →	**❺**
povero	→ (after noun) poor	→ (before noun) unfortunate →	**❻**
vecchio	→ (after noun) old	→ (before noun) long-standing →	**❼**

Adjectives following the noun are linked by **e** → **❽**

Examples

1 **un gesto spont*a*neo**
    a spontaneous gesture
   una partita importante
    an important match

2 **capelli biondi**
    blonde hair
   pantaloni neri
    black trousers
   una parola italiana
    an Italian word

3 **questo cellulare**
    this mobile phone
   la mia mamma
    my mum
   il primo piano
    the first floor
   Quale gusto?
    What flavour?

4 **ogni giorno**
    every day
   qualche volta
    sometimes
   Non c'è nessun bisogno di andarci
    There's no need to go

5 **un uomo grande**
    a big man
   una grande sorpresa
    a great surprise

6 **gente povera**
    poor people
   Povera Anna!
    Poor Anna!

7 **una casa vecchia**
    an old house
   un mio vecchio amico
    an old friend of mine

8 **un libro lungo e noioso**
    a long, boring book
   ragazze antipatiche e maleducate
    nasty, rude girls

Pronouns

Personal Pronouns

		SUBJECT PRONOUNS
		SINGULAR
1st person		**io** I
2nd person		**tu** you
3rd person (*masc.*)		**lui** he
(*fem.*)		**lei** she
(*used as polite 'you'*)		**lei/Lei** you
		PLURAL
1st person		**noi** we
2nd person		**voi** you
3rd person		**loro** they

Italian verbs are frequently used without subject pronouns → **①**

tu/lei
Lei, as well as being the 3rd person singular feminine, is used when addressing someone politely. As a general rule, use **tu** only when addressing a friend, a child, a fellow student, someone you know very well, or when invited to do so. In other cases use **lei,** which is occasionally spelled with a capital when used to mean *you* **②**

loro
Loro is used only to refer to people, not to things → **③**

Loro is occasionally used as a very formal alternative to **voi** → **④**

Examples

❶ Conosci Paolo?   Do you know Paul?
Parlo italiano   I speak Italian
Costa troppo   It costs too much

❷ Tu cara, cosa prendi?   What are you going to have,
                                                              dear?
Lei, signora, cosa prende?   What are you going to have,
                                                              madam?

❸ Loro chi sono?   Who are they?
Cosa sono? — Sono noci.   What are they? — They're
                                                              walnuts.

❹ Loro cosa prendono?   What will you have, ladies and
                                                              gentlemen?

Pronouns

Personal Pronouns *continued*

3rd Person Pronouns

lui, lei and **loro** are the subject pronouns normally used in spoken Italian. In older written Italian you may find **egli** (masc. sing.), **ella** (fem. sing.), **essi** (masc. plur.) and **esse** (fem. plur.).

esso and **essa** are subject pronouns meaning *it*, but they are very rarely used. In Italian there is normally no pronoun corresponding to *it* at the start of a sentence → ❶

Subject pronouns often follow the verb → ❷

Subject pronouns are used:
- to add emphasis, for clarity, or to attract someone's attention → ❸
- after **anche** *too*, **neanche** *neither* and **pure** *as well* → ❹
- when the verb in Italian is understood → ❺

UNSTRESSED DIRECT OBJECT PRONOUNS			
	SINGULAR		PLURAL
1ˢᵗ pers.	**mi** me	1ˢᵗ pers.	**ci** us
2ⁿᵈ pers.	**ti** you	2ⁿᵈ pers.	**vi** you
3ʳᵈ pers. (*masc.*)	**lo (l')** him; it	3ʳᵈ pers. (*masc.*)	**li** them
(*fem.*)	**la (l')** her; it	(*fem.*)	**le** them
(*used as polite 'you'*)	**la/La (l')** you	(*used as polite 'you'*)	**le** you

mi, **ti**, **ci** and **vi** can (but do not have to) become **m'**, **t'**, **c'** and **v'** before a vowel or mute **h** → ❻

lo and **la** change to **l'** before a vowel or mute **h** → ❼

For information on past participle agreement, see page 56.

lo/la /li/le

lo means *him*, or *it*, when the object referred to is masculine → ❽

la means *her*, or *it*, when the object referred to is feminine → ❾

li refers to people, or objects that are masculine → ❿

le refers to females, or objects that are feminine → ⓫

Examples

1 **Fa caldo** — It's hot
 Sono le tre — It's three o'clock
 È tardi — It's late

2 **Pago io** — I'll pay
 Ci pensiamo noi — We'll see to it

3 **Tu cosa dici?** — What do you think?
 No, l'ha fatto lui — No, he did it
 Lei, signore, cosa prende? — And you sir, what will you have?

4 **Prendi un gelato anche tu?** — Are you going to have an ice cream too?
 Non so perché. — Neanch'io — I don't know why. — Neither do I
 È venuto pure lui — He came as well

5 **Chi è il più bravo? — Lui.** — Who's the best? — He is.
 Viene lui, ma lei no — He's coming, but she isn't

6 **Non c'hanno visto** *or* — They didn't see us
 Non ci hanno visto

7 **Non l'ho visto più** — I didn't see him again
 L'ho incontrata ieri — I met her yesterday

8 **Gianni? Non lo vedo mai** — Gianni? I never see him
 Dov'è il mio cellulare? Non lo vedo — Where's my mobile phone? I can't see it

9 **Chiara? Non la vedo mai** — Chiara? I never see her
 La birra? Non la bevo mai. — Beer? I never drink it.

10 **Marco e Sara — li conosci?** — Marco and Sara — do you know them?
 Hai i biglietti? Sì, li ho nel portafoglio — Have you got the tickets? Yes, I've got them in my wallet

11 **Le sue sorelle? Non le conosco** — His sisters? I don't know them
 Hai le chiavi? Sì, le ho in tasca — Have you got the keys? Yes, I've got them in my pocket

Pronouns

Personal Pronouns *continued*

Position of unstressed direct object pronouns

The pronoun generally comes before the verb → ❶

Unstressed direct pronouns come after the verb

- in imperatives, with the pronoun joined onto the verb → ❷

ⓘ If the verb consists of a single syllable, the initial consonant of the pronoun is doubled, except in the case of **gli** → ❸

- in infinitive constructions, when the final **-e** of the infinitive is dropped, and replaced by the pronoun → ❹

Stressed direct object pronouns

	STRESSED DIRECT OBJECT PRONOUNS		
	SINGULAR		PLURAL
1st pers.	**me**	1st pers.	**noi**
2nd pers.	**te**	2nd pers.	**voi**
3rd pers. (*masc.*)	**lui**	3rd pers. (*masc.*)	**loro**
(*fem.*)	**lei**	(*fem.*)	**loro**
(*used as polite 'you'*)	**lei/Lei**	(*used as polite 'you'*)	**loro**

Stressed direct object pronouns are used:
- for emphasis or contrast → ❺
- after prepositions → ❻
- in comparisons → ❼

For further information, see Order of Object Pronouns, page 166.

Reflexive Pronouns

These are dealt with under reflexive verbs, see page 32.

Examples

❶ Ti amo I love you
Lo invito alla festa I'm inviting him to the party
Non lo mangio I'm not going to eat it
La guardava He was looking at her
Vi cercavo I was looking for you
Li conosciamo We know them

❷ Aiutami! Help me!
Lasciala stare Leave her alone

❸ Fallo subito! Do it right away!

❹ Potresti venire a prendermi? Could you come and get me?
Non posso aiutarvi I can't help you
Devo proprio farlo? Do I really have to do it?

❺ Amo solo te I love only you
Invito lui alla festa, ma lei no I'm inviting him to the party but not her
Non guardava me, guardava lei He wasn't looking at me; he was looking at her

❻ Vengo con te I'll come with you
Sono arrivati dopo di noi They arrived after us

❼ Sei più alto di me You're taller than me
Sono più ricchi di lui They're richer than him

Pronouns

Personal Pronouns *continued*

UNSTRESSED INDIRECT OBJECT PRONOUNS			
SINGULAR			PLURAL
1st pers.	**mi**	1st pers.	**ci**
2nd pers.	**ti**	2nd pers.	**vi**
3rd pers. (*masc.*)	**gli**	3rd pers. (*masc.*)	**gli** or **loro**
(*fem.*)	**le**	(*fem.*)	**gli** or **loro**
(*used as polite 'you'*)	**le**	(*used as polite 'you'*)	**loro**

The pronouns in the above table replace the preposition **a** + *noun*, where the noun is a person or an animal → ❶

Indirect object pronouns are used with verbs governing **a** → ❷

Unstressed indirect pronouns are also used with impersonal verbs which govern **a** → ❸

Position of unstressed indirect object pronouns

Unstressed indirect pronouns generally come before the verb → ❹

Unstressed indirect pronouns come after the verb:
- in imperatives, with the pronoun joined onto the verb → ❺

ⓘ If the verb consists of a single syllable, the initial consonant of the pronoun is doubled, except in the case of **gli** → ❻

- in infinitive constructions. The final **-e** of the infinitive is dropped, and replaced by the pronoun → ❼

Examples

1 **Ho detto la verità a Paola**   I told Paola the truth
Le ho detto la verità   I told her the truth
Hai dato del latte al gatto?   Have you given the cat some milk?

Gli hai dato del latte?   Have you given him some milk?
Potresti dare qualche consiglio ai signori?   Could you give the lady and gentleman some advice?
Potresti dar loro *or* **dargli qualche consiglio?**   Could you give them some advice?

2 **telefonare a qn**   to phone sb
Non le ho telefonato   I didn't phone her
promettere qc a qn   to promise sb sth
Mi ha promesso un regalo   He promised me a present
consigliare a qn di fare qc   to advise sb to do sth
Ci ha consigliato di aspettare   He advised us to wait

3 **Le piacciono i gatti**   She likes cats
Non gli importa il prezzo, sono ricchi   They don't care about the price; they're rich
Se gli interessa può venire con me   If he's interested, he can come with me

4 **Mi assomiglia?**   Does she look like me?
Ti piace?   Do you like it?

5 **Rispondigli!**   Answer him!
Mandami un SMS   Send me a text

6 **Dimmi dov'è**   Tell me where it is
Dacci una mano   Give us a hand

7 **Dovresti scriverle**   You ought to write to her
Luigi? Non voglio parlargli   Luigi? I don't want to talk to him

Pronouns

Personal Pronouns *continued*

Stressed Indirect Pronouns

	STRESSED INDIRECT OBJECT PRONOUNS		
	SINGULAR		PLURAL
1st pers.	**a me**	1st pers.	**a noi**
2nd pers.	**a te**	2nd pers.	**a voi**
3rd pers. (*masc.*)	**a lui**	3rd pers. (*masc.*)	**a loro**
(*fem.*)	**a lei**	(*fem.*)	**a loro**
(*used as polite 'you'*)	**a lei/Lei**	(*used as polite 'you'*)	**a loro**

The above forms are used for special emphasis, either before or after the verb → ❶

For further information, see Order of Object Pronouns, below.

Reflexive Pronouns

These are dealt with under reflexive verbs, page 32.

Order of Object Pronouns

If direct and indirect unstressed pronouns occur together, the indirect pronoun always comes first .

mi/ti/ci/vi when followed by a direct object pronoun become **me**, **te**, **ce** and **ve** → ❷

gli and **le** when followed by a direct object pronoun both become **glie-**, and add the pronoun to make one word: **glielo**, **gliela**, **glieli** or **gliele** → ❸

When an indirect pronoun and a direct pronoun follow an imperative, or an infinitive, they join on to it to make one word → ❹

When a stressed indirect object pronoun and an unstressed direct object pronoun occur together the above rules do not apply → ❺

Examples

❶ Ho scritto a lei, a lui no
    I wrote to her, but not to him

A me piace, ma Luca preferisce l'altro
    I like it, but Luca would rather have the other one

❷ Me la dai?
    Will you give me it?

È mia – non te la do
    It's mine, I'm not going to give it to you

Ce l'hanno promesso
    They promised it to us

Ve lo mando domani
    I'll send it to you tomorrow

❸ Glieli hai promessi
    You promised them to her

Gliel'ha spedite
    He sent them to them

Carlo? Glielo dirò domani
    Carlo? I'll tell him tomorrow

❹ Mi piacciono, ma non vuole comprarmeli
    I like them but she won't buy me them

Ecco la lettera di Rita, puoi dargliela?
    Here's Rita's letter. Can you give it to her?

Ecco le chiavi. Dagliele
    Here are the keys. Give them to her.

Non abbiamo i biglietti – può mandarceli?
    We haven't got the tickets – can you send us them?

❺ Mandale a lui, non a me
    Send them to him, not to me

Pronouns

The pronoun *ne*

ne replaces the preposition **di** + *noun* → ❶

There may be no preposition in the English translation of verbal constructions with **di/ne** → ❷

ne also replaces the partitive article (English = some, any) + *noun* → ❸

When used with amounts or numbers, **ne** represents the noun → ❹

Position: **ne** always follows another pronoun and comes before all verbs except imperatives and infinitives → ❺

Pronouns which precede **ne** change their form:
mi/ti/si/ci/vi before **ne** become **me/te/se/ce/ve** → ❻

ne follows the imperative and joins onto to it to make one word → ❼

ne joins onto the infinitive, which drops the final **-e** → ❽

Pronouns which come between the imperative or infinitive and **ne** change their form: **mi**, **ti**, **ci**, **vi** become **me**, **te**, **ce** and **ve**.
gli and **le** become **glie** → ❾

Examples

1 **Sono conscio del pericolo** — I'm aware of the danger
Ne sono conscio — I'm aware of it
Sono sicura del fatto — I'm sure of the fact
Ne sono sicura — I'm sure of it
Ha scritto della guerra sul giornale — She's written about the war in the paper
Ne ha scritto sul giornale — She's written about it in the paper
Parliamo del futuro. — Sì, parliamone. — Let's talk about the future. — Yes, let's talk about it.

2 **accorgersi di qc** — to realize sth
Non se ne accorge — He doesn't realize it
aver bisogno di qc — to need sth
Hai bisogno della chiave? — No, non ne ho più bisogno. — Do you need the key? — No, I don't need it any more.

3 **Perché non prendi delle fragole?** — Why aren't you having any strawberries?
Perché non ne prendi? — Why aren't you having any?
Vuoi del pane? — Would you like some bread?
Ne vuoi? — Would you like some?

4 **Hai due figli? — No, ne ho tre.** — Have you got two children? — No, I've got three.
Hai dello zucchero? — Ne ho un poco. — Have you got any sugar? — I've got a bit.

5 **Ne hai paura?** — Are you afraid of it?

6 **Ti ricordi di quel giorno?** — Do you remember that day?
Te ne ricordi? — Do you remember it?
Non si accorge degli errori — He doesn't notice mistakes
Non se ne accorge — He doesn't notice them

7 **Assaggiane un po'** — Try a bit

8 **Non voglio parlarne** — I don't want to talk about it

9 **Dammene uno per favore** — Give me one of them please
Dagliene due rossi — Give him two red ones
Non posso dartene uno — I can't give you one
Non posso dargliene due rossi — I can't give him two red ones

Pronouns

The pronoun *ci*

ci replaces the preposition **a** + *noun* → **1**

There may be no preposition in the English translation of verbal constructions with **a/ci** → **2**

Position: like **ne**, **ci** comes before the verb, unless it is an imperative, infinitive, or the gerund → **3**

For **ci** as a personal pronoun, see page 164.

Note that **ci** is also an adverb meaning 'there' → **4**

Examples

❶ Credi ai fantasmi?   Do you believe in ghosts?
   Ci credi?   Do you believe in them?
   Non pensa al futuro   She doesn't think about the future

   Non ci pensa   She doesn't think about it

❷ far caso a qc   to notice sth
   Non ci ho fatto caso   I didn't notice it
   avvicinarsi a qc   to approach sth
   Ci si avvicinò   He approached it

❸ Ci penso io   I'll see to it
   BUT
   Pensaci un po'   Think about it a bit
   Non so che farci   I don't know what to do about it
   Ripensandoci mi sono pentito   When I thought it over, I was sorry

❹ Non voglio andarci   I don't want to go there
   Ci sono molti turisti   There are a lot of tourists

Pronouns

Indefinite Pronouns

The following are indefinite pronouns:

alcuni(e) some → ❶

altro(a, i, e) the other one; another one; other people → ❷

chiunque anyone → ❸

ciascuno(a) each → ❹

molto(a, i, e) a lot, lots → ❺

nessuno(a) nobody, anybody; none → ❻

niente nothing → ❼

nulla nothing → ❽

ognuno(a) each → ❾

parecchio, parecchia, parecchi, parecchie quite a lot → ❿

poco, poca, pochi, poche not much, not many → ⓫

qualcosa something, anything → ⓬

qualcuno(a) somebody, anybody, some, any → ⓭

tanto(a, i, e) lots, so much, so many → ⓮

troppo(a, i, e) too much, too many → ⓯

tutti(e) everybody, all → ⓰

tutto everything, all → ⓱

uno(a) somebody → ⓲

Examples

❶	Ci sono posti liberi? — Sì, alcuni.	Are there any empty seats? — Yes, some.	
	Ci sono ancora delle fragole? — Sì, alcune.	Are there any strawberries left? — Yes, some.	
❷	L'altro è meno caro Non m'interessa quello che dicono gli altri Prendine un altro	The other one is cheaper I don't care what other people say Take another one	
❸	Attacca discorso con chiunque	She'll talk to anyone	
❹	Ne avevamo uno per ciascuno Le torte costano due euro ciascuna	We had one each The cakes cost two euros each	
❺	Ne ha molto molti di noi	He's got lots a lot of us	
❻	Non è venuto nessuno Nessuna delle ragazze è venuta	Nobody came None of the girls came	
❼	Cosa c'è? — Niente.	What's wrong? — Nothing.	
❽	Che cos'hai comprato? — Nulla.	What did you buy? — Nothing.	
❾	ognuno di voi	each of you	
❿	C'è ancora del pane? — Sì, parecchio. Avete avuto problemi? — Sì, parecchi.	Is there any bread left? — Yes, quite a lot. Did you have problems? — Yes, a lot.	
⓫	C'è pane? — Poco. Ci sono turisti? — Pochi.	Is there any bread? — Not much. Are there any tourists? — Not many.	
⓬	Ho qualcosa da dirti Ha bisogno di qualcosa?	I've got something to tell you Do you need anything?	
⓭	Ha telefonato qualcuno Conosci qualcuna delle ragazze?	Somebody phoned Do you know any of the girls?	
⓮	Hai mangiato? — Sì, tanto!	Have you eaten? — Yes, lots!	
⓯	Ci sono errori? — Sì, troppi.	Are there any mistakes? — Yes, too many.	
⓰	Vengono tutti Sono arrivate tutte	Everybody is coming They've all arrived	
⓱	Va tutto bene? L'ho finito tutto	Is everything okay? I've finished it all	
⓲	Ho incontrato uno che ti conosce	I met somebody who knows you	

173

Pronouns

Relative Pronouns

che who; whom; which; that
che is an invariable pronoun that can be the subject or object of a relative clause, and can refer to people or things → **1**

The Italian object pronoun cannot be omitted, though it need not be translated in English → **2**

After a preposition use **cui** → **3**

il che which
This is used to refer to a fact or situation that's just been mentioned → **4**

il quale, **la quale**, **i quali**, **le quali** who; whom; which; that
These are more formal relative pronouns, which agree in number and gender with the noun → **5**

il quale, **la quale**, **i quali** and **le quali** are used most often with prepositions.
The prepositions **di**, **da**, **a**, **in** and **su** combine with the articles **il**, **la**, **i** and **le** → **6**

Article + preposition combinations are dealt with on page 136

il cui, **la cui**, **i cui**, **le cui** whose
These agree in number and gender with the thing possessed → **7**

Use **cui** instead of **che** with a preposition → **8**

quello che, **ciò che** what, the thing which

These can be used as the subject or object of a relative clause. Literally they mean 'that which' → **9**

In combination with **di**, **quello** *or* **ciò che** become **quello di cui** *or* **ciò di cui** → **10**

Examples

① **quella signora che ha un piccolo cane nero**
that lady who has a little black dog

una persona che detesto
a person whom I detest

l'uomo che hanno arrestato
the man that they've arrested

la squadra che ha vinto
the team which won

② **la persona che ammiro di più**
the person (whom) I admire most

il dolce che hai fatto
the pudding (that) you made

③ **la ragazza di cui ti ho parlato**
the girl that I told you about

gli amici con cui andiamo in vacanza
the friends we go on holiday with

la persona a cui si riferiva
the person he was referring to

il quartiere in cui abito
the area in which I live

④ **Non pagano nulla, il che non mi sembra giusto**
They don't pay anything, which doesn't seem fair to me

Dice che non è colpa sua, il che è vero
She says it's not her fault, which is true

⑤ **suo padre, il quale è avvocato**
his father, who is a lawyer

le sue sorelle, le quali studiano a Roma
his sisters, who study in Rome

⑥ **l'albergo nel quale ci siamo fermati**
the hotel that we stayed at

la borsa di studio sulla quale contava
the grant he was counting on

gli amici dai quali ho avuto questo regalo
the friends I got this present from

la medicina della quale ho bisogno
the medicine I need

⑦ **una persona il cui nome mi sfugge**
a person whose name escapes me

la persona i cui bagagli sono qui
the person whose bags are here

⑧ **È quello con cui parlavo**
He's the one I was talking to

⑨ **Ho visto quello** *or* **ciò che c'era sul tavolo**
I saw what was on the table

Quello *or* **ciò che mi preoccupa è che...**
The thing which worries me is that...

Quello *or* **ciò che dici non ha senso**
What you say doesn't make sense

Ho fatto quello *or* **ciò che potevo**
I did what I could

⑩ **Non è quello** *or* **ciò di cui si tratta**
That's not what it's about

Non è quello *or* **ciò di cui si stava parlando**
That's not what he was talking about

Pronouns

Interrogative Pronouns

These pronouns are used in direct questions:
- **chi?** who? whom?
- **che?** what?
- **cosa?** what?
- **che cosa?** what?

These pronouns are invariable, and can be the subject or object of the verb → ❶

che cos'è/cos'è? what is it?
This is used to ask for something to be explained or identified → ❷

Prepositions come before the interrogative pronoun, and never at the end of the question → ❸

di chi? whose → ❹

quale? which? which one? what?
quale is the singular form (**qual** before a vowel), and **quali** the plural → ❺

qual è?/quali sono? what is/what are?
These are used to ask about a particular detail, name, number etc → ❻

quanto(a)? How much? → ❼

quanti(e)? How many? → ❽

All the pronouns used in direct questions can be used in indirect questions → ❾

Examples

① **Chi è?**
Who is it?

  Chi cerca?
Who(m) are you looking for?

  Che vuoi?
What do you want?

  Cosa vuole?
What does he want?

  Che cosa vogliono?
What do they want?

② **Che cos'è? — È un regalo.**
What is it? — It's a present.

③ **A chi l'hai dato?**
Who did you give it to?

  Con chi parlavi?
Who were you talking to?

  Di che cosa hai bisogno?
What do you need?

  Cosa ti aspettavi?
What were you expecting?

④ **Di chi è questa borsa?**
Whose is this bag?

  Di chi sono queste chiavi?
Whose are these keys?

⑤ **Conosco sua sorella. — Quale?**
I know his sister. — Which one?

  Ho rotto dei bicchieri. — Quali?
I broke some glasses. — Which ones?

⑥ **Qual è il suo indirizzo?**
What's her address?

  Qual è la capitale della Finlandia?
What's the capital of Finland?

  Quali sono i loro nomi?
What are their names?

⑦ **Farina? Quanta ce ne vuole?**
Flour? How much is needed?

⑧ **Quante di loro passano la sera a leggere?**
How many of them spend the evening reading?

⑨ **Dimmi chi è**
Tell me who it is

  Non so cosa vuol dire
I don't know what it means

  Ho chiesto di chi era
I asked whose it was

  Può dirmi di che cosa si tratta?
Can you tell me what it's about?

Pronouns

Possessive Pronouns

Singular:

MASCULINE/FEMININE	
il mio/la mia	mine
il tuo/la tua	yours
il suo/la sua	his; hers; its; yours
il nostro/la nostra	ours
il vostro/la vostra	yours
il loro/la loro	theirs

Plural:

MASCULINE/FEMININE	
i miei/le mie	mine
i tuoi/le tue	yours
i suoi/le sue	his; hers; its; yours
i nostri/le nostre	ours
i vostri/le vostre	yours
i loro/le loro	theirs

The pronoun agrees in number and gender with the noun it replaces, not with the owner → ❶

di/da/a/su/in + *possessive pronoun*
These prepositions combine with the article → ❷

Examples

❶ **Paolo, questa borsa non è la mia, è la tua**
Paolo, this bag's not mine; it's yours

La nostra casa è piccola, la vostra è grande
Our house is small; yours is big

I miei genitori e i suoi si conoscono
My parents and hers know each other

❷ **La mia macchina è più vecchia della sua**
My car is older than his

Preferisco il nostro giardino al loro
I prefer our garden to theirs

Pronouns

Demonstrative Pronouns

questo/questa/questi/queste
quello/quella/quelli/quelle

	MASCULINE/FEMININE	
SING.	**questo/questa**	this, this one, this man/ this woman
	quello/quella	that, that one, that man/ that woman
PLUR.	**questi/queste**	these, these ones, these men/ these women
	quelli/quelle	those, those ones, those people

The pronoun agrees in number and gender with the noun it replaces → ❶

quello/a used to mean that man/woman is pejorative → ❷

quello(a, i, e) che the one(s) who/which → ❸

quello(a, i, e) di the one(s) belonging to/the one(s) of
This use is often translated by apostrophe s ('s), or s apostrophe (s') → ❹

questo(a, i, e) qui/qua
qui or **qua** can be used with **questo** for emphasis or to distinguish
between two things → ❺

quello(a, i, e) lì/là
lì or **là** can be used with **quello** for emphasis or to distinguish between
two things → ❻

Examples

1 **Questo è mio marito**
This is my husband
Questa è camera mia
This is my bedroom
Questi sono i miei fratelli
These are my brothers
Quali scarpe ti metti? — Queste
Which shoes are you going to wear? — These ones
Qual è la sua borsa? — Quella
Which is your bag? — That one
Quelli quanto costano?
How much do those cost?

2 **Dice sempre bugie quello**
That man is always telling lies
Quelle non sono mai contente
Those women are never happy

3 **È quello che preferisco**
That's the one (that) I prefer
È quella che parla di più
She's the one who talks most
Sono quelli che sono partiti senza pagare
They're the ones who left without paying
Queste scarpe sono quelle che ha ordinato
These shoes are the ones (that) you ordered

4 **Questo giardino è più grande di quello di Giulia**
This garden is bigger than Giulia's
Preferisco la mia macchina a quella di mio marito
I prefer my car to my husband's
Le mie scarpe sono più belle di quelle di Lucia
My shoes are nicer than Lucia's
i miei genitori e quelli delle mie amiche
my parents and those of my friends
le montagne della Svizzera e quelle della Scozia
the mountains of Switzerland and those of Scotland

5 **Non quello, questo qui**
Not that one, this one here
Voglio queste qua
I want these ones here

6 **Questa gonna non ti sta bene, prova quella là**
This skirt doesn't look good on you; try that one
Quali prendi? — Quelli lì
Which ones are you going to have? — Those over there

Adverbs

Formation

Some adverbs are formed by adding **-mente** to an adjective.

-mente is added to the feminine form, (which ends in **-a**) of an adjective ending in **-o** → ❶

-mente is added to the basic form when an adjective ends in **-e** for both masculine and feminine → ❷

Adjectives ending in **-le** and **-re** drop the final **e** → ❸

Irregular Adverbs

ADJECTIVE	ADVERB
buono good	**bene** well → ❹
cattivo bad	**male** badly → ❺
migliore better	**meglio** better → ❻
peggiore worse	**peggio** worse → ❼

Adjectives used as adverbs

Certain adjectives are used adverbially. These include: **giusto**, **vicino**, **diritto**, **certo**, **solo**, **forte**, **molto**, **poco** → ❽

Examples

① MASC./FEM. ADJECTIVE | ADVERB
lento/lenta slow | **lentamente** slowly
fortunato/fortunata lucky | **fortunatamente** luckily

② MASC./FEM. ADJECTIVE | ADVERB
veloce quick, fast | **velocemente** quickly, fast
corrente fluent | **correntemente** fluently

③ **-le/-re** ADJECTIVE | ADVERB
facile easy | **facilmente** easily
particolare particular | **particolarmente** particularly

④ **Parlano bene l'italiano** | They speak Italian well

⑤ **Ho giocato male** | I played badly

⑥ **Sto meglio** | I'm better

⑦ **Mi sento peggio** | I'm feeling worse

⑧ **Ha risposto giusto** | She answered correctly
Abitano vicino | They live nearby
Siamo andati sempre diritto | We kept straight on
Vieni stasera? — Certo! | Are you coming tonight? — Of course!

L'ho incontrata solo due volte | I've only met her twice
Correva forte | He was running fast
Quel quadro mi piace molto | I like that picture a lot
Vengo in ufficio poco spesso | I don't come into the office very often

Adverbs

Position of Adverbs

When the adverb accompanies a verb in a simple tense, it generally follows the verb → ❶

For emphasis the adverb can come at the beginning of the sentence → ❷

When adverbs such as **mai**, **sempre**, **già** and **appena** accompany a verb in a compound tense, they come between the auxilary verb and the past participle → ❸

When the adverb accompanies an adjective or another adverb, it generally precedes the adjective/adverb → ❹

Comparatives of Adverbs

These are formed as follows:
> **più ... (di)** more ... (than) → ❺
> **meno ... (di)** less ... (than) → ❻

sempre più is used with the adjective to mean *more and more* → ❼

Superlatives of Adverbs

più ... and **meno ...** are also used to express the superlative → ❽
più ... di tutti/meno ... di tutti can be used to emphasize the superlative → ❾

Examples

① **Viene sempre** — He always comes
Parli bene l'italiano — You speak Italian well

② **Ora non posso** — I can't do it just now
Prima non lo sapevo — I didn't know that before

③ **Non sono mai stata a Milano** — I've never been to Milan
È sempre venuto con me — He always came with me
L'ho già letto — I've already read it
Se n'è appena andato — He's just left

④ **Fa troppo freddo** — It's too cold
Vai più piano — Go more slowly

⑤ **più spesso** — more often
più lentamente — more slowly
Correva più forte di me — He was running faster than me

⑥ **meno velocemente** — less quickly
Costa meno — It costs less
Vengo meno spesso di lui — I come less often than he does

⑦ **Le cose vanno sempre meglio** — Things are going better and better
Mio nonno sta sempre peggio — My grandfather's getting worse and worse
Cammina sempre più lento — He's walking more and more slowly

⑧ **È Carlo che viene più spesso** — It's Carlo who comes most often
Sono loro che lavorano meno volontieri — They're the ones who work least willingly

⑨ **Cammina più piano di tutti** — She walks the most slowly (of all)
L'ha fatto meno volentieri di tutti — He did it the least willingly

Adverbs

Adverbs with irregular comparatives/superlatives

bene well	→	**meglio** better/best
male badly	→	**peggio** worse/worst
molto a lot	→	**più** more/most
poco not much	→	**meno** less/least

Emphatic Adverbs

For added emphasis the ending **-issimamente** can be used. It replaces the endings **-amente**, **-emente** or **-mente** → ❶

bene and **male** have irregular emphatic forms: **benissimo** and **malissimo** → ❷

Adverbial phrases

di più and **di meno** are used to say what you do most/least → ❸

Examples

① **lentamente** — slowly
lentissimamente — very slowly
velocemente — quickly
velocissimamente — very quickly

② **Hai fatto benissimo** — You did very well

③ **la cosa che temeva di più** — the thing she feared most
quello che mi piace di meno — the one I like least
Sono quelli che guadagnano di meno — They're the ones who earn least

Adverbs

Some common adverbs and their usage

Some common adverbs:

abbastanza quite; enough → ❶

anche too → ❷

ancora still; yet → ❸

appena just; only just → ❹

certo certainly; of course → ❺

così so; like this; like that → ❻

ecco here → ❼

forse perhaps, maybe → ❽

già already → ❾

mai never; ever → ❿

molto very; very much; much → ⓫

piuttosto quite; rather → ⓬

poco not very; not at all → ⓭

presto soon; early → ⓮

quasi nearly → ⓯

spesso often → ⓰

tanto so; so much → ⓱

troppo too; too much → ⓲

Examples

1 **È abbastanza alta**
She's quite tall
Non studia abbastanza
He doesn't study enough

2 **È venuta anche mia sorella**
My sister came too

3 **Sei ancora a letto?**
Are you still in bed?
Silvia non è ancora arrivata
Silvia's not here yet

4 **L'ho appena fatto**
I've just done it
L'indirizzo era appena leggibile
The address was only just legible

5 **Certo che puoi**
Of course you can
Certo che sì
Certainly

6 **È così simpatica!**
She's so nice!
Si apre così
It opens like this
Non si fa così
You don't do it like that

7 **Ecco l'autobus!**
Here's the bus!
Dov'è Carla? — Eccola!
Where's Carla? — Here she is!

8 **Forse hanno ragione**
Maybe they're right

9 **Te l'ho già detto**
I've already told you

10 **Non sono mai stato in America**
I've never been to America
Sei mai stato in America?
Have you ever been to America?

11 **Sono molto stanca**
I'm very tired
Ti piace? — Sì, molto.
Do you like it? — Yes, very much
Ora mi sento molto meglio
I feel much better now

12 **Fa piuttosto caldo oggi**
It's quite warm today
È piuttosto lontano
It's rather a long way

13 **Mi sento poco bene**
I don't feel very well
Mi piacciono poco
I don't like them at all

14 **Arriverà presto**
He'll be here soon
Mi alzo sempre presto
I always get up early

15 **Sono quasi pronta**
I'm nearly ready

16 **Vanno spesso in centro**
They often go into town

17 **Questo libro è tanto noioso**
This book is so boring
Mi manchi tanto
I miss you so much

18 **È troppo caro**
It's too expensive
Parlano troppo
They talk too much

189

Prepositions

On the following pages you will find some of the most frequent uses of prepositions in Italian. Particular attention is paid to cases where usage differs greatly from English. It is often difficult to give an English equivalent for Italian prepositions, since usage varies so much between the two languages.

In the list below, the broad meaning of the preposition is given on the left, with examples of usage following.

Prepositions are given in alphabetical order, except for **a**, **di**, **da** and **in**. These prepositions, shown first, combine with the definite article to make one word.

For combinations of **a**, **di**, **da**, **in**, **su** and **con** with the definite article, see page 136.

a

at	**alla porta** at the door
	a casa at home
	alla prossima fermata at the next stop
	a 50 chilometri all'ora at 50 km an hour
in	**a Londra** in London
	al sole in the sun
	Sta a letto He's in bed
on	**al terzo piano** on the third floor
	alla radio on the radio
to	**Andiamo al cinema?** Shall we go to the cinema?
	Vai a letto? Are you going to bed?
	Sei mai stato a New York?
	Have you ever been to New York?
	dare qc a qn to give sth to sb
	A chi l'hai dato? Who did you give it to?
	promettere qc a qn to promise sth to sb
	il primo/l'ultimo a fare qc the first/last to do sth
from	**comprare qc a qn** to buy sth from sb
	nascondere qc a qn to hide sth from sb

Examples

| | **prendere qc a qn** to take sth from sb |
| | **rubare qc a qn** to steal sth from sb |

| *see you* | **a presto** see you soon |
| | **a domani** see you tomorrow |

manner	**a piedi** on foot
	a mano by hand
	a poco a poco little by little
	all'antica in the old-fashioned way
	alla milanese in the Milanese way

(made) with	**un gelato alla fragola** a strawberry ice cream
	una torta al cioccolato a chocolate cake
	gli spaghetti al pomodoro
	spaghetti with tomato sauce

time: at	**alle due** at two o'clock
	a mezzanotte at midnight
	a Pasqua at Easter

| *with month*: in | **a maggio** in May |

distance	**a tre chilometri da qui** three kilometres from here
	a due ore di distanza in macchina
	two hours away by car

purpose	**Sono uscita a fare due passi** I went out for a little walk
	Sono andati a fare il bagno
	They've gone to have a swim

| *after certain verbs* | See pages 70-79 |

Prepositions

di

of, belonging to	**un amico di famiglia** a friend of the family
	il padre di Marco Marco's father
	la casa dei miei amici my friends' house
	Di chi è? Whose is it?
	il periodo delle vacanze the holiday season
	il professore di francese the French teacher
	il campione del mondo the world champion
(made) by	**un quadro di Picasso** a picture by Picasso
	una commedia di Shakespeare a play by Shakespeare
from	**È di Firenze** He's from Florence
	Di dove sei? Where are you from?
than (*after comparative*)	**È più alto di me** He's taller than me
	È più brava di lui She's better than him
in (*after superlative*)	**il più grande del mondo** the biggest in the world
	il migliore d'Italia the best in Italy
time	**di domenica** on Sundays
	di notte at night
	d'inverno in winter
contents, composition, material, colour	**una bottiglia di vino** a bottle of wine
	un gruppo di turisti a group of tourists
	una maglietta di cotone a cotton T-shirt
	Di che colore è? What colour is it?
manner	**di rado** rarely
	di solito usually
after certain numbers	**un milione di dollari** a million dollars
	un migliaio di persone about a thousand people
	una ventina di macchine about twenty cars

Prepositions

after certain adjectives	**Le arance sono ricche di vitamina C** Oranges are rich in vitamin C **Era pieno di gente** It was full of people
after certain verbs	see pages 70-79

da

from	**a tre chilometri da qui** three kilometres from here **Viene da Roma** He comes from Rome **da cima a fondo** from top to bottom
off, out of	**Isobel è scesa dal treno** Isobel got off the train **È scesa dalla macchina** She got out of the car
at/to the home of	**Sono da Anna** I'm at Anna's (house) **Andiamo da Gabriele?** Shall we go to Gabriele's (house)?
at/to (*shop, workplace*)	**Laura è dal parrucchiere** Laura's at the hairdresser's **È andato dal dentista** He's gone to the dentist's
for	**Vivo qui da un anno** I've been living here for a year (*note tense*)

since	**da allora** since then
	Ti aspetto dalle tre
	  I've been waiting for you since three o'clock
	  (*note tense*)

by (*with passive agent*)	**dipinto da un grande artista** painted by a great artist **Sono stati catturati dalla polizia** They were caught by the police
to (*with infinitive*)	**C'è molto da fare** There's lots to do **È un film da vedere** It's a film that you've got to see
as	**Da bambino avevo paura del buio** As a child I was afraid of the dark

Prepositions

descriptive	**una ragazza dagli occhi azzurri** a girl with blue eyes **un vestito da cento euro** a dress costing a hundred euros
purpose/use	**un nuovo paio di scarpe da corsa** a new pair of running shoes **Non ho il costume da bagno** I haven't got my swimming costume

in

to, in *(place)*	**in centro** in/to the town centre **in Italia** in/to Italy
into	**Su! Sali in macchina** Come on! Get into the car
on, at *(state)*	**in vacanza** on holiday **in pace** at peace
in *(years, seasons, months)*	**nel duemilasei** in two thousand and six **in estate** in summer **in ottobre** in October
in *(time taken)*	**L'ha fatto in sei mesi** He did it in six months
transport	**in treno** by train **in bici** by bike
language	**in italiano** in Italian

con

with	**Con chi sei stata?** Who were you with?
to	**Hai parlato con lui?** Have you spoken to him?
manner	**con calma** without hurrying **con la forza** by force

Prepositions

davanti a

in front of	**Erano seduti davanti a me nell'autobus**
	They were sitting in front of me in the bus
opposite	**la casa davanti alla mia** the house opposite mine

dopo

after	**dopo cena** after dinner
+ *pronoun* (add **di**)	**dopo di loro** after them

fra/tra

in (*time*)	**Torno fra** *or* **tra un'ora** I'll be back in an hour
between	**fra** *or* **tra la cucina ed il soggiorno**
	between the kitchen and the living room
+ *pronoun* (add **di**)	**fra** *or* **tra di noi** between/among us

per

for	**Questo è per te** This is for you
	È troppo difficile per lui It's too difficult for him
	L'ho comprato per trenta centesimi
	I bought it for thirty cents
	Ho guidato per trecento chilometri
	I drove for three hundred kilometres
	una camera per due notti a room for two nights
	Parte per Milano She's leaving for Milan
(going) to	**il volo per Londra** the flight to London
	il treno per Roma the train to Rome
through	**I ladri sono entrati per la finestra**
	The burglars got in through the window
	Siamo passati per Crewe We went through Crewe

Prepositions

by (means of)	**per posta** by post
	per via aerea by airmail
	per posta elettronica by email
	per ferrovia by rail
	per telefono by phone
	per errore by mistake

| (so as) to | **L'ho fatto per aiutarti** I did it to help you |
| | **Si è chinato per prenderlo** He bent down to get it |

out of	**Ci sono andato per abitudine** I went out of habit
	Non l'ho fatto per pigrizia
	I didn't do it out of laziness

distribution	**uno per uno** one by one
	giorno per giorno day by day
	una per volta one at a time
	due per tre two times three

prima di

| before (+*noun*, *pronoun*) | **prima delle sette** before seven |
| | **prima di me** before me |

| + *infin* | **prima di cominciare** before starting |

| until | **Non sarà pronto prima delle otto** |
| | It won't be ready until eight o'clock |

senza

| without | **Esci senza cappotto?** |
| | Are you going out without a coat? |

| + *pronoun* (add **di**) | **senza di te** without you |

| + *infinitive* | **È uscito senza dire niente** |
| | He went out without saying anything |

Prepositions

sopra

over   **le donne sopra i sessant'anni** women over sixty

above   **cento metri sopra il livello del mare**
                              a hundred metres above sea level

on top of   **sopra l'armadio** on top of the cupboard

su*

on   **sul pavimento** on the floor
                           sulla sinistra on the left
                           un libro sugli animali a book on animals

in   **sul giornale** in the paper

out of (*ratio*)   **in tre casi su dieci** in three cases out of ten
                           due giorni su tre two days out of three

approximation   **sui cinquecento euro** around five hundred euros
                           È sulla trentina She's about thirty

* **su** combines with the definite article to make one word

verso

towards (*place*)   **Correva verso l'uscita**
                           He was running towards the exit

about   **Arriverò verso le sette** I'll arrive about seven

Conjunctions

Conjunctions

Some conjunctions introduce a main clause, e.g. **e** (and), **ma** (but), **o** (or).
Others introduce subordinate clauses, e.g. **perché** (because), **mentre**
(while), **quando** (when), **se** (if). Conjunctions also link single words. Most
are used in much the same way as in English, but note the following:

e and
When followed by another 'e', **e** often becomes **ed** → ❶

> Some Italian conjunctions have to be followed by the subjunctive,
> see page 66

> Some conjunctions are split in Italian, like 'both … and', 'either …
> or' in English.
> **o … o** either … or → ❷
> **né … né** neither … nor, either … or → ❸
> **sia … che** both … and → ❹

In Italian, sentences with split conjunctions can have a singular or a plural
verb → ❺

che that
- is followed by the indicative in statements → ❻
- is followed by the subjunctive after verbs expressing uncertainty;
  see page 64

perché because, so that
When **perché** means 'because', it is followed by the indicative → ❼
When it means 'so that', it is followed by the subjunctive → ❽

Note that **perché?** can also be used as an adverb with the meaning 'why?'

se if, whether
When used in conditional clauses, **se** is followed by the subjunctive → ❾
Followed by the infinitive, **se** means 'whether to' → ❿
Followed by the indicative **se** expresses doubt → ⓫

Conjunctions are sometimes used in phrases where a verb is understood
→ ⓬

Examples

1 **È venuto qui ed è rimasto mezzora**
He came here and stayed for half an hour

2 **o oggi o domani**
either today or tomorrow

3 **Non mi hanno chiamato né Claudio né Luca**
Neither Claudio nor Luca has phoned me
Non avevo né guanti né scarponi
I didn't have either gloves or boots

4 **Verranno sia Luigi che suo fratello**
Both Luigi and his brother are coming

5 **Non vengono** or **Non viene né lui né sua moglie**
Neither he nor his wife is coming

6 **Ha detto che farà tardi**
He said that he'll be late

7 **Sono uscita perché faceva bel tempo**
I went out because it was nice weather

8 **Gliel'ho dato perché lo leggesse**
I gave it him so that he could read it

9 **se fosse qui**
if he was here
Se avessi studiato avresti passato l'esame
If you'd studied, you would have passed the exam

10 **Non so se andarci o no**
I don't know whether to go or not

11 **Mi chiedo se avresti accettato**
I wonder if you would have accepted

12 **Ti dispiace? — Ma no!**
Do you mind? — Of course I don't!
Ho fame. — Anch'io!
I'm hungry. — So am I!
Sì, lo so — strano però
Yes, I know — It's odd, though

Sentence structure

Word Order

Word order in Italian is very flexible, but:

- unstressed object pronouns always come before the verb, except when attached to the end of an infinitive or an imperative → ❶
  For details, see page 166

- most adjectives come after the noun → ❷
  For details, see page 156

- Adverbs of frequency accompanying verbs in a simple tense usually follow the verb, and those used with a compound tense follow the auxiliary verb → ❸
  For details, see page 184

Other parts of speech, however, may be positioned to give emphasis or make a contrast:

- the noun which is the object of a verb generally follows the verb, but for emphasis it may come first → ❹

- a question word generally comes first, but for emphasis a noun subject or object can precede it → ❺

- adjectives generally follow the verb **essere**, but may precede it for emphasis → ❻

- unstressed object pronouns generally precede the verb, but stressed pronouns can be used instead, and these follow the verb → ❼
  For details, see page 166

- subject pronouns are not normally used, but, when added for emphasis, they may come before or after the verb → ❽

Examples

❶ Li vedo!　　　　　　　　　I can see them!
Me l'ha dato　　　　　　　　He gave it to me

❷ la squadra italiana　　　　the Italian team
un vino rosso　　　　　　　a red wine

❸ Ci vado spesso　　　　　　I often go there
Non ci sono mai stato　　　I've never been there

❹ *Normal order:*
Non posso soffrire quel cane　I can't stand that dog
Emphatic order:
Quel cane non lo posso soffrire
note object pronoun added before the verb

❺ *Normal order:*
Dov'è Lidia?　　　　　　　　Where's Lidia?
Di chi sono queste scarpe?　Whose are these shoes?
Dove metto questa borsa?　Where shall I put this bag?
Emphatic order:
Lidia, dov'è?
Queste scarpe di chi sono?
Questa borsa dove la metto?
note added object pronoun

❻ *Normal order:*
Sono belli　　　　　　　　　They're lovely
Sei pazza　　　　　　　　　You're mad
Emphatic order:
Belli sono!　　　　　　　　They're lovely!
Pazza sei!　　　　　　　　You're mad!

❼ *Order with unstressed pronoun:*
Me l'ha dato　　　　　　　He gave it to me
Order with stressed pronoun:
L'ha dato a me (non a te)　He gave it to me (not to you)

❽ *Unemphatic:*
Cosa pensi?　　　　　　　What do you think?
Emphatic:
Tu cosa pensi?/Cosa pensi tu?

Sentence structure

Negatives

In Italian, sentences are generally made negative by adding **non** before the verb → ①

di no is used after verbs such as **dire**, **credere**, **pensare** and **sperare** → ②

o no is used to mean 'or not' → ③

noun/pronoun + **no**
no is used when making a distinction between people or things → ④

non is used in combination with other negative words such as **niente** *nothing*, **nessuno** *nobody*, **mai** *never* → ⑤

When **mai** is used with a compound tense, it usually comes between the auxiliary verb and the past participle → ⑥

When **niente** or **nessuno** are the subject of the verb, they can come first or they can follow the verb. If they come first, **non** is not used → ⑦

More than one negative word can follow a negative verb → ⑧

nessuno, nessuna no
These negative adjectives change their endings according to the letter that follows them, like the indefinite article **uno** → ⑨

non ... né ... né neither ... nor/not ... either ... or
A plural verb is required if there are two subjects → ⑩

Examples

❶ Non posso venire — I can't come
Non l'ho visto — I didn't see it
Non è qui — It's not here

❷ Ha detto di no — He said not
Credo di no — I don't think so
Pensa di no — He doesn't think so
Speriamo di no — Let's hope not

❸ Vieni o no? — Are you coming or not?
che ti piaccia o no — whether you like it or not

❹ Invito lui, lei no — I'm going to invite him, but not her
Loro hanno finito, noi no — They've finished, but we haven't
Lei è brava, io no — She's good, but I'm not
Prendo un dolce, il caffè no — I'll have a sweet, but not a coffee

❺ Non ho niente — I haven't got anything/I've got nothing

Non l'ho detto a nessuno — I haven't told anyone/I've told nobody

Non ci vado mai — I never go there

❻ Non l'ho mai vista — I've never seen her
Non ci siamo mai stati — We've never been there

❼ Niente è cambiato — Nothing has changed
BUT
Non è cambiato niente
Nessuno vuole andarci — Nobody wants to go
BUT
Non vuole andarci nessuno

❽ Non fanno mai niente — They never do anything
Non si confida mai con nessuno — He never confides in anyone
Non vendiamo più niente — We no longer sell anything

❾ Nessun tipo di pianta può viverci — No type of plant can live there
Non ho nessuna voglia di farlo — I have no desire to do it
Non hanno fatto nessuno sforzo — They didn't make any effort

❿ Non verranno né Anna né Maria — Neither Anna nor Maria is coming
BUT
Non invito né Anna né Maria — I'm not inviting either Anna or Maria

Sentence structure

Question Forms

In Italian, questions differ from statements in intonation, or the use of a question mark in writing. Unlike in English, the verb forms in questions are no different from those in statements → **①**

Word order

When the subject of the question is a noun, it comes either before or after the verb → **②**

When the object of the question is a noun, it either comes after the verb or comes first. In the latter case an object pronoun agreeing with the noun is added before the verb → **③**

A subject pronoun may also be added at the end of a question, for special emphasis → **④**

When answering a question, either say **sì** or **no**, or **sì** or **no** with a full statement. There is no Italian equivalent for short answers such as Yes I do or No I don't → **⑤**

Question words such as **dove?** *where?*, **chi?** *who?* **cosa?** *what?* generally come first → **⑥**

However, note the following:
- a noun subject can either follow the verb or precede the question word → **⑦**
- a noun object can follow the verb or precede the question word. In this case an object pronoun agreeing with the noun is added before the verb → **⑧**
- prepositions such as **di**, **con** and **a** must precede question words → **⑨**

Examples

① STATEMENT

Basta That's enough
Sono di qui They're from here
L'ha fatto lui He did it
Va bene That's okay

QUESTION

Basta? Is that enough?
Sono di qui? Are they from here?
L'ha fatto lui? Did he do it?
Va bene? Is that okay?

② **Tua sorella è partita?** *or*
  È partita tua sorella?
  La Calabria è bella? *or*
  È bella la Calabria?
  Gli spaghetti sono buoni? *or*
  Sono buoni gli spaghetti?

Has your sister gone?

Is Calabria beautiful?

Is the spaghetti nice?

③ **Vuoi un gelato?** *or*
  Un gelato lo vuoi?
  Vuoi del latte *or*
  Un po' di latte lo vuoi?

Do you want an ice cream?

Do you want some milk?

④ *Contrast*
  Fai il bucato?
  with
  Il bucato lo fai tu?

Are you doing the washing?

Will you do the washing?

⑤ **Piove? Sì** *or* **Sì piove**
  Capisci? No *or* **No, non capisco**

Is it raining? Yes *or* Yes, it's raining
Do you understand? No *or*
  No, I don't

⑥ **Dove vai?**
  Chi parla?

Where are you going?
Who's speaking?

⑦ **Quanto costano queste scarpe?** *or*
  Queste scarpe, quanto costano?
  Chi è quella signora? *or*
  Quella signora, chi è?

How much are these shoes?

Who is that lady?

⑧ **Chi pagherà il conto?** *or*
  Il conto, chi lo pagherà?

Who will pay the bill?

⑨ **Di che colore è?**
  Con chi parlavi?
  A cosa stai pensando?

What colour is it?
Who were you talking to?
What are you thinking about?

Sentence structure

Question Forms *continued*

no?, vero?

no? or **vero?** is used to check that what you've said is correct, like 'isn't it?' or 'haven't you?' in English → ❶

vero? is used to check a negative statement → ❷

Indirect Questions

Word order in Italian indirect questions is no different from that of statements → ❸

Tenses in indirect questions are generally the same as in English, except for the use of the perfect conditional where the present conditional is used in English → ❹

Examples

1 **Hai finito, no?**   You've finished, haven't you?
Questa è la tua macchina, vero?   This is your car, isn't it?

2 **Non sono partiti, vero?**   They haven't gone, have they?
Non fa molto male, vero?   It doesn't hurt much, does it?

3 **Vorrei sapere quanto costa**   I'd like to know how much it
                                        costs
Mi domando cosa pensano   I wonder what they think

4 **Ha detto che non era colpa sua**   He said it wasn't his fault
Ha detto che verrà   He said he'll come
Aveva detto che sarebbe venuto He'd said he'd come

Use of numbers

Cardinal (one, two, *etc*)		Ordinal (first, second, *etc*)	
zero	0		
uno (una, un)	1	primo	1°
due	2	secondo	2°
tre	3	terzo	3°
quattro	4	quarto	4°
cinque	5	quinto	5°
sei	6	sesto	6°
sette	7	settimo	7°
otto	8	ottavo	8°
nove	9	nono	9°
dieci	10	decimo	10°
undici	11	undicesimo	11°
dodici	12	dodicesimo	12°
tredici	13	tredicesimo	13°
quattordici	14	quattordicesimo	14°
quindici	15	quindicesimo	15°
sedici	16	sedicesimo	16°
diciassette	17	diciassettesimo	17°
diciotto	18	diciottesimo	18°
diciannove	19	diciannovesimo	19°
venti	20	ventesimo	20°
ventuno	21	ventunesimo	21°
ventidue	22	ventiduesimo	22°
ventitré	23	ventitreesimo	23°
trenta	30	trentesimo	30°
quaranta	40	quarantesimo	40°
cinquanta	50	cinquantesimo	50°
sessanta	60	sessantesimo	60°
settanta	70	settantesimo	70°
ottanta	80	ottantesimo	80°
novanta	90	novantesimo	90°
novantanove	99	novantanovesimo	99°

Use of numbers

Cardinal		Ordinal	
cento	100	centesimo	100°
centouno	101	centunesimo	101°
(centouna, centoun)			
centodue	102	centoduesimo	102°
centotré	103	centotreesimo	103°
centodieci	110	centodecimo	110°
centoquarantadue	142	centoquarantaduesimo	142°
duecento	200	duecentesimo	200°
duecentouno	201	duecentunesimo	201°
duecentotré	203	duecentotreesimo	203°
trecento	300	trecentesimo	300°
quattrocento	400	quattrocentesimo	400°
cinquecento	500	cinquecentesimo	500°
seicento	600	seicentesimo	600°
settecento	700	settecentesimo	700°
ottocento	800	ottocentesimo	800°
novecento	900	novecentesimo	900°
mille	1000	millesimo	1000°
milleuno	1001	milleunesimo	1001°
milleduecentodue	1202	milleduecentoduesimo	1202°
duemila	2000	duemillesimo	2000°
cinquemilatrecento	5300	cinquemilatrecentesimo	5300°
un milione	1.000.000	milionesimo	1.000.000°
due milioni	2.000.000	duemilionesimo	2.000.000°

Ordinal numbers are adjectives which tell you the order in which the noun occurs (first, third, etc). They end with either **o** or **a**, depending on whether the noun is masculine or feminine:

il 15° piano	the 15th floor	**la 24ª giornata**	the 24th day

Fractions		Other numerical expressions	
un mezzo	a half	**zero virgola cinque (0,5)**	0.5
un terzo	a third	**uno virgola tre (1,3)**	1.3
due terzi	two thirds	**dieci per cento**	10%
un quarto	a quarter	**sei più due**	6 + 2
tre quarti	three quarters	**sei meno due**	6 − 2
un quinto	a fifth	**due volte sei**	2 × 6
un sesto	a sixth	**sei diviso due**	6 ÷ 2

ⓘ Note the use of commas in decimal numbers and full stops with millions.

Use of numbers

Other Uses

Approximate numbers

- ending in **-ina**

una ventina di DVD	about twenty DVDs
Eravamo una trentina	There were about thirty of us
È sulla quarantina	He's about forty
gente sulla cinquantina	people of around fifty

- ending in **-aio**

un centinaio di persone	about a hundred people
centinaia di volte	hundreds of times
un migliaio di casi	about a thousand cases
due migliaia di macchine	about two thousand cars

Measurements

venti metri quadri	20 square metres
venti metri cubi	20 cubic metres
un ponte lungo cento metri	a bridge 100 metres long
essere largo/alto tre metri	to be 3 metres wide/long

Miscellaneous

Abitano al numero dieci	They live at number 10
nel capitolo sei	in chapter 6
Sono a pagina tre	They're on page 3
Abitano al terzo piano	They live on the 3rd floor
Sono arrivata seconda nella gara	I came second in the competition
su una scala da uno a dieci	on a scale of one to ten

Telephone numbers

The digits in a telephone number are spoken individually:

zero zero tre nove zero sei quattro due otto uno sette sei zero due
(0039 0642817602)

tre quattro sette sette zero tre quattro nove zero cinque
(3477034905)

Use of numbers

Calendar

Che data è oggi?/ **Quanti ne abbiamo oggi?**	What's the date today?
È il primo maggio	It's May 1st
È il due maggio	It's May 2nd
È il ventotto febbraio	It's February 28th
Arrivano il diciannove luglio	They're arriving on July 19th

ⓘ Use cardinal numbers except for the first of the month.

Years

È nata nel 1993	She was born in 1993
il dodici febbraio duemilatredici	(on) 12th February 2013

Other expressions

negli anni sessanta	in the sixties
nel ventunesimo secolo	in the twenty-first century
in *or* **a maggio**	in May
lunedì (quindici)	on Monday (the fifteenth)
di lunedì	on Mondays
fra *or* **tra dieci giorni**	in 10 days' time
otto giorni fa	8 days ago

Use of numbers

The time

Che ore sono?	What time is it?
È l'una	It's one o'clock
Sono le due	It's two o'clock

ⓘ Use **sono** for all times except one o'clock, midday and midnight.

00.00	**mezzanotte** midnight, twelve o'clock
00.10	**mezzanotte e dieci** ten past midnight
00.15	**mezzanotte e un quarto, mezzanotte e quindici**
00.30	**mezzanotte e mezza, mezzanotte e trenta**
00.45	**l'una meno un quarto, l'una meno quindici,** **mezzanotte e quarantacinque**
01.00	**l'una di mattina** one a.m., one o'clock in the morning
01.10	**l'una e dieci (di mattina)**
01.15	**l'una e un quarto, l'una e quindici**
01.30	**l'una e mezza, l'una e trenta**
01.45	**l'una e quarantacinque; le due meno un quarto,** **le due meno quindici**
01.50	**l'una e cinquanta, le due meno dieci**
01.59	**l'una e cinquantanove, le due meno un minuto**
12.00	**mezzogiorno, le dodici** noon, twelve o'clock
12.30	**mezzogiorno e mezza, mezzogiorno e trenta,** **le dodici e mezza**
13.00	**l'una (del pomeriggio), le tredici, le ore tredici**
01.30	**l'una e mezza/trenta (del pomeriggio), le tredici e trenta,** **le ore tredici e trenta**
19.00	**le sette (di sera), le diciannove, le ore diciannove**
19.30	**le sette e mezza/trenta, le diciannove e trenta,** **le ore diciannove e trenta**

ⓘ The twenty-four hour clock is widely used in Italy.

alle diciannove *or*	at seven p.m., at seven in the evening
alle ore diciannove	at nineteen hundred hours

Use of numbers

A che ora venite? — Alle sette	What time are you coming? — At seven
L'ufficio è chiuso da mezzogiorno alle due	The office is closed from twelve to two
alle due di notte/del pomeriggio	at two o'clock in the morning/afternoon; at two a.m./p.m.
alle otto di sera	at eight in the evening; at eight p.m.
alle cinque in punto	at five o'clock sharp
verso le nove	at around nine
poco dopo mezzogiorno	shortly after noon
fra le otto e le nove	between eight and nine o'clock
Erano le tre e mezza passate	It was after half past three
Devi esserci entro le nove	You have to be there by nine
Ci vogliono tre ore	It takes three hours
Ci metto una mezz'ora	It takes me half an hour
È rimasta in bagno per un'ora	She was in the bathroom for an hour
Li aspetto da quaranta minuti	I've been waiting for them for forty minutes
Sono partiti qualche minuto fa	They left a few minutes ago
L'ho fatto in venti minuti	I did it in twenty minutes
Il treno arriva fra un quarto d'ora	The train arrives in a quarter of an hour
Per quanto tempo dovremo aspettare?	How long will we have to wait?

Translation problems

Beware of translating word for word. The following are examples of where Italian tends to differ from English:

> English phrasal verbs (i.e. verbs such as 'to look for'; 'to fall down') are often translated by one word in Italian → **1**
>
> English verbs often require a preposition where there is none in Italian, or vice versa → **2**
>
> Different English prepositions may be translated by the one Italian preposition → **3**
>
> A word which is singular in English may be plural in Italian, or vice versa → **4**
>
> There is no Italian equivalent for the apostrophe s and s apostrophe possessive → **5**

See also **at/in/to**, page 220.

The following pages look at some specific problems.

Examples

① **scappare**   to run away
cadere   to fall down
rendere   to give back

② **pagare qc**   to pay for sth
guardare qc/qn   to look at sth/sb
ascoltare qc/qn   to listen to sth/sb
dire a qn   to tell sb
ubbedire a qn   to obey sb
ricordarsi di qc/qn   to remember sth/sb

③ **meravigliarsi di**   to be surprised at
stufo di   fed up with
rubare qc a   to steal sth from
restio a   reluctant to

④ **gli affari**   business
i suoi capelli   his/her hair
Le lasagne sono ...   Lasagne is...
i bagagli   luggage

⑤ **la macchina di mia sorella**   my sister's car
(literally: ... of my sister)

la camera delle ragazze   the girls' bedroom
(literally... of the girls)

Translation problems

-ing

This is translated by the gerund in Italian:

> 'to be ...-ing' is sometimes translated by **stare** + *gerund* when the verb describes something at the moment, but a simple tense is often used. A simple tense must be used when the verb refers to the future. → ❶

The past participle, not the gerund, is used for physical positions such as lying and sitting → ❷

> to see/hear sb ...-ing: use an infinitive or **che** + *verb* → ❸

'-ing' can also be translated by:

- an infinitive: see page 46 → ❹
- a perfect infinitive: see page 50 → ❺
- the gerund, when used abverbially: see page 52 → ❻
- a noun → ❼

to be

'to be' is generally translated by **essere** → ❽

Examples

1 **Che fai** *or* **stai facendo?**
What are you doing?

Che fai domani sera?
What are you doing tomorrow evening?

Partono *or* **Stanno partendo**
They're leaving

Partono alle sette
They're leaving at seven

2 **Erano seduti in prima fila**
They were sitting in the front row

Era sdraiata sulla sabbia
She was lying on the sand

3 **L'ho visto partire**
I saw him leaving

L'ho visto che partiva

L'ho sentita piangere
I heard her crying

L'ho sentita che piangeva

4 **Mi piace cucinare**
I like cooking

invece di rispondere
instead of answering

prima di partire
before leaving

Iniziò a piovere
It started raining

5 **dopo aver perso molti soldi**
after losing a lot of money

6 **Essendo più timida di me, non ha gli ha parlato**
Being shyer than me, she didn't speak to him

7 **Il fumo fa molto male**
Smoking is very bad for you

8 **È tardi**
It's late

Sono loro
It's them

Siamo stanchi
We're tired

Translation problems

stare is used

- with the gerund to make continuous tenses → **❶**
- in forming the perfect and pluperfect tenses of **essere**, which consist of the present/imperfect tense of **essere** + past participle of **stare** → **❷**
- interchangeably with **essere** when talking about locations → **❸**
- when talking about health → **❹**

In various set expressions **avere** is used (with the final **e** dropped):

aver caldo/freddo	to be hot/cold
aver fame/sete	to be hungry/thirsty
aver paura	to be afraid
aver torto/ragione	to be wrong/right

fare is used to talk about the weather → **❺**

avere is used for ages → **❻**

it is, it's

These are never translated by a pronoun in Italian → **❼**

In expressions of time, use **sono**, except for one o'clock, midday and midnight → **❽**

To describe the weather, see above.

When 'it's' is followed by a pronoun, such as 'me', 'her' or 'them', the form of **essere** agrees with the person referred to → **❾**

can, be able

Ability is generally expressed by **potere** → **❿**

If the meaning is 'to know how to', use **sapere** → **⓫**

'can' with verbs of seeing and hearing is not translated in Italian → **⓬**

Examples

① Ci sto pensando I'm thinking about it
Stavano chiacchierando They were chatting

② Non ci sono mai stata I've never been there
Ero stato malato I had been ill

③ La casa sta *or* **è sulla collina** The house is on the hill
Sta *or* **è fuori** It's outside

④ Sto bene, grazie I'm fine, thanks
Sta male He's not well

⑤ Che tempo fa? What's the weather like?
Fa caldo/freddo It's hot/cold
Fa bel/brutto tempo It's nice/bad weather

⑥ Quanti anni hai? How old are you?
Ho quindici anni I'm fifteen

⑦ Dammelo, è mio Give it to me; it's mine
È molto lontano It's a long way

⑧ Sono le nove It's nine o'clock
È l'una meno un quarto It's a quarter to one

⑨ Sono io It's me
È lei It's her
Sono loro It's them

⑩ Puoi venire? Can you come?

⑪ Non so come spiegarlo I can't explain it

⑫ Si vede il mare You can see the sea
Non ti sento I can't hear you

Translation problems

to like

piacere, the Italian verb used to translate 'to like', means 'to be pleasing', so **Mi piace l'Italia** literally means 'Italy is pleasing to me', and **Gli animali piacciono ai bambini** means 'Animals are pleasing to children'.

Remember the following when using **piacere**:
- the thing(s) liked is/are the subject of the Italian verb → ❶
- if the thing liked is singular, the verb is singular (**piace/è piaciuto** etc); if the things liked are plural, the verb is plural (**piacciono/sono piaciuti** etc) → ❷
- **piacere** is used with **a** or an indirect object pronoun → ❸

to

'to' is often translated by **a**: see page 190 → ❹

When telling the time, e.g. ten to six, use **meno** → ❺

When the meaning is 'in order to', use **per** → ❻

When 'to' is part of the infinitive following an adjective such as 'easy', 'difficult', 'impossible', use the Italian infinitive with **da** → ❼

unless the infinitive has an object → ❽

at/in/to

For 'in' or 'to' + a country, use the Italian preposition **in** → ❾

For 'in' or 'to' + a town, use the Italian preposition **a** → ❿

When the meaning is 'to'/'at' + someone's house/place of business, use **da** → ⓫

Examples

1 **Il cane piace a mio figlio**
   I cani piacciono a mio figlio
                       My son likes the dog
                       My son likes dogs

2 **Il concerto è piaciuto a tutti** — Everyone liked the concert
   I cioccolatini piaceranno a tutti — Everyone will like the chocolates

3 **A mia madre piace molto il giardinaggio** — My mother likes gardening very much
   Ti piace questa canzone? — Do you like this song?
   Non gli piacciono i pomodori — He doesn't like tomatoes

4 **Dallo a Patrizia** — Give it to Patrizia

5 **le sei meno un quarto** — a quarter to six
   l'una meno tre minuti — three minutes to one

6 **L'ho fatto per rassicurarti** — I did it to reassure you
   Si è fermato per guardarlo — He stopped to look at it

7 **facile da capire** — easy to understand
   impossibile da dimenticare — impossible to forget

8 **È facile capirlo** — It's easy to understand it
   È impossibile crederci — It's impossible to believe it

9 **Abitano negli Stati Uniti** — They live in the United States
   Andiamo in Germania il quattro maggio — We're going to Germany on May 4
   una città in Cina — a city in China

10 **È andato a Parigi** — He's gone to Paris
   Vive a Bologna — He lives in Bologna

11 **Andiamo da Anna** — Let's go to Anna's (house)
   È dal parucchiere — She's at the hairdresser's

Pronunciation

General Points

Vowels and consonants are always clearly pronounced in Italian, and each syllable of a word is audible, unlike in English, where letters, and sometimes whole syllables, are often not pronounced. Compare, for example:

lettera (both **e**s are equally clear, audible **r**)
letter (2nd **e** indistinct, **r** usually not pronounced)
interessante, (5 syllables)
interesting (3 syllables)

Diphthongs

A diphthong is a glide between two vowel sounds in the same syllable. The vowels in 'say', 'go' and 'might' are diphthongs. Diphthongs are very common in English, but much less so in Italian, where most vowels are a single sound, as they are in English words such as 'top', 'back' and 'set'
The diphthongs found in Italian are vowels preceded by a **y**, or a **w** sound:

ia [ja] - **chiaro**	**ua** [wa] - **sguardo**
ie [je] - **pieno**	**ue** [we] - **guerra**
io [jo] - **pioggia**	**ui** [wi] - **guidare**
iu [ju] - **chiuso**	**uo** [wo] - **fuoco**

Stress

Italian words are generally stressed on the next to the last syllable, (so two-syllable words are stressed on the first syllable, three-syllable words on the second syllable, and so on):

ca sa	set ti **ma** na
ra **gaz** zo	ge ne ral **men** te

For more details, see pages 224–225.

If the stress comes on the last vowel of a word with more than one syllable, the vowel is always written with an accent:
per **ché**
par le **rò**
un i ver si **tà**

For more details, see page 224.

Pronunciation

Pronunciation of Consonants

Most consonants are pronounced as in English, except that they are always clear, and double consonants are audible. Thus, in **sabbia** *sand*, for example, the **b** sound ending the first syllable carries on to start the second syllable: sab-bya.

Note the following:

		PRONOUNCED	EXAMPLES
c *before* **a, o, u**	[k]	like **k** in **kiss**	**c**amera, **c**ome, **c**ubo
c *before* **e** or **i**	[tʃ]	like **ch** in **China**	**c**erto, **c**inese
ch	[k]	like **k** in **kiss**	**ch**iesa
g *before* **a, o, u**	[g]	like **g** in **good**	**g**ara, lar**g**o, **g**usto
g *before* **e** or **i**	[dʒ]	like **g** in **rage**	**g**elato, **g**iro
gh	[g]	like **g** in **good**	la**gh**i, **gh**iaccio
gl *before* **i**	[ʎ]	like **ll** in **million**	me**gl**io, **gl**i
gl *before other vowels*	[gl]	like **gl** in **piglet**	si**gl**a
gn	[ɲ]	like **ny** in **canyon**	**gn**occhi, ra**gn**o
h is not pronounced		like **h** in **honest**	**h**anno
r	[r]	like **r** in **zero**	**r**aro, **r**apido
sc *before* **a, o, u**	[sk]	like **sk** in **skirt**	**sc**ala, **sc**orso, **sc**uro
sc *before* **e** or **i**	[ʃ]	like **sh** in **ship**	**sc**ena, **sc**i
z	[dz]	like **ds** in **lids**	**z**an**z**ara
z	[ts]	like **ts** in **bits**	raga**zz**o

Pronunciation of Vowels

		PRONOUNCED	EXAMPLES
a	[a]	like **a** in **apple**	**a**nimale
e	[ɛ]	like **e** in **set**	sch**e**ma
e	[e]	like **ay** in **day**	st**e**lla
i	[i]	like **ee** in **sheep**	cl**i**ma
i *before a vowel often*	[j]	like **y** in **yoghurt**	L**i**dia, neg**o**zio
o	[o]	like **o** in **pot**	**o**ra
u	[u]	like **oo** in **soot**	p**u**ro
u *before a vowel often*	[w]	like **w** in **win**	us**u**ale

Pronunciation

Stress: Cases where the normal rule does not apply

In cases where the last syllable of a word is stressed, this is shown by an accent. Most of these are:

- nouns ending in **-tà**, many of which have counterparts in English ending in -ty, such as 'reality' and 'university'

re al tà	reality	**u ni ver si tà**	university
fe li ci tà	happiness, felicity	**fe del tà**	fidelity
cu rio si tà	curiosity	**fa col tà**	faculty
bon tà	goodness	**cit tà**	city
cru del tà	cruelty	**e tà**	age
me tà	half		

- 1st and 3rd person singular future verbs , and 3rd person singular past historics:

sa rò	I will be
fi ni rà	it will finish
as pet te rà	she'll wait
par lò	he spoke
an dò	she went

- adverbs and conjunctions such as

perché	why
però	however
così	so

In cases where the stress is on an unexpected syllable other than the last, there is no accent to show this. In this book, such vowels are shown in italics, e.g.

macchina	car
utile	useful
portatile	laptop

Pronunciation

Stress in present tense verb forms

All present tense forms except the 3rd person plural follow the rule, and stress the next to the last syllable, e.g. **par lo** I speak; **considera** he considers

In the 3rd person plural form the stress is not on the next to the last syllable, but matches that of the 1st person singular:

1st person singular		3rd person plural	
par lo	I speak	**par la no**	they speak
con si de ro	I consider	**con si de ra no**	they consider
mi al le no	I'm training	**si al le na no**	they're training

Stress in 2nd conjugation infinitives

Stress is regular for the infinitives of all 1st and 3^{rd,} and many 2nd conjugation verbs, e.g. **parlare** *to speak*, **finire** *to finish*, **vedere** *to see*. However, there are also many 2nd conjugation infinitives which do not stress the 1st **e** of the **-ere** ending, eg:

essere *to be*, **vendere** *to sell*, **permettere** *to allow*, **dividere** *to divide*.

When learning 2nd conjugation verbs, note which syllable of the infinitive is stressed.

Pronunciation

From Sounds to Spelling

Apart from the occasional problem of unexpected stress, the way Italian is spelled is a good guide to how it should be pronounced. See pages 222-223.

It is also easy to know how to spell words, if the following points are remembered:

-care/-gare verbs

Verbs with infinitives ending in **-care**, or **-gare**, for example **cercare** and **pagare**, add an **h** to keep the **c** or **g** hard in front of endings starting with **e** or **i**:

Vowel that follows **c/g**	Present of **cercare**		Present of **pagare**	
o	**cerco**	I look for	**pago**	I pay
i	**cerchi**	you look for	**paghi**	you pay
a	**cerca**	he/she looks for	**paga**	he/she pays
i	**cerchiamo**	we look for	**paghiamo**	we pay
a	**cercate**	you look for	**pagate**	you pay
a	**cercano**	they look for	**pagano**	they pay

Vowel that follows **c/g**	Future of **cercare**		Future of **pagare**	
e	**cercherò**	I'll look for	**pagherò**	I'll pay
e	**cercherai**	you'll look for	**pagherai**	you'll pay
e	**cercherà**	he/she'll, look for	**pagherà**	he/she'll, pay
e	**cercheremo**	we'll look for	**pagheremo**	we'll pay
e	**cercherete**	you'll look for	**pagherete**	you'll pay
e	**cercheranno**	they'll look for	**pagheranno**	they'll pay

-ca/-ga nouns and adjectives

Nouns and adjectives ending in **-ca** and **-ga** always keep the hard sound of the consonant in the plural, so **h** is added before the plural ending **-e**:

Pronunciation

Singular		Plural	
amica	friend	**amiche**	friends
riga	line	**righe**	lines
ricca	rich	**ricche**	rich
lunga	long	**lunghe**	long

-co/-go nouns and adjectives

Some nouns and adjectives ending in **-co** and **-go** keep the hard sound of the consonant in the plural, so **h** is added before the plural ending **-i**, e.g.:

Singular		Plural	
fuoco	fire	**fuochi**	fires
albergo	hotel	**alberghi**	hotels
ricco	rich	**ricchi**	rich
lungo	long	**lunghi**	long

Other nouns and adjectives ending in **-co** and **-go** change the sound of the consonant in the plural from hard [k] or [g] to soft [tʃ] or [dʒ], so no **h** is added, e.g.:

Singular		Plural	
amico	friend	**amici**	friends
astrologo	astrologer	**astrologi**	astrologers
greco	Greek	**greci**	Greek
psicologico	psychological	**psicologici**	psychological

-io nouns

The plural of nouns ending **-io** is spelled **-ii** if the **i** of the **-io** ending is a stressed vowel, e.g. **zio** *uncle*, plural: **zii**, and **invio** *dispatch*, plural: **invii**.

In cases where the **i** of the **-io** is not a stressed vowel, but is pronounced [j], the plural is spelled with a single **i**, e.g. **occhio** *eye*, plural **occhi**; **figlio** *son*, plural: **figli**.

Pronunciation

-cia/-gia nouns

Generally, if the **i** of the **-cia/-gia** ending of a noun is a stressed vowel, the **i** is retained in the plural, e.g. **farmacia** *chemist*, plural: **farmacie**; **bugia** *lie*, plural: **bugie**. If the **i** of the ending serves to keep the **c/g** soft, and is not pronounced as a vowel, there is no **i** in the plural: **faccia** *face*, plural: **facce**; **spiaggia** *beach*, plural: **spiagge**.

Accents

Use an accent when a word is stressed on the final syllable, e.g. **città**, **cercherò**, **università**. See page 222.

Accents are also used on certain one-syllable words to distinguish them from words that are spelled the same (homographs):

da	from	**dà**	he/she gives
e	and	**è**	is
la	the/it	**là**	there
li	them	**lì**	there
ne	of it/them	**né**	neither
se	if	**sé**	himself/herself/itself/ themselves/oneself
si	himself/herself/itself/ themselves/oneself	**sì**	y
te	you	**tè**	tea

The grave accent (**à**, **è**, **ì**, **ò**, **ù**) is used in most words. The acute accent is used to spell conjunctions ending in **che**, such as **benché** *although*, and **perché** *because*. It is also used on **né** and **sé** (except in the phrases **se stesso** and **se stessa** *himself; herself*).

può, **già**, **ciò**, **più** and **giù** are spelled with an accent for no obvious reason.

Alphabet

The Alphabet

A,a [a]	**J,j** [i'lunga]	**S,s** ['ɛsse]
B,b [bi]	**K,k** ['kappa]	**T,t** [ti]
C,c [tʃi]	**L,l** ['ɛlle]	**U,u** [u]
D,d [di]	**M,m** ['ɛmme]	**V,v** [vi, vu]
E,e [e]	**N,n** ['ɛnne]	**W,w** ['dɔppjovu]
F,f ['ɛffe]	**O,o** [ɔ]	**X,x** [iks]
G,g [dʒi]	**P,p** [pi]	**Y,y** ['ipsilon]
H,h ['akka]	**Q,q** [ku]	**Z,z** [dzɛta]
I,i [i]	**R,r** ['ɛrre]	

Capital letters are used as in English except for the following:

adjectives of nationality
e.g. **una città tedesca**   a German town
     una scrittrice italiana   an Italian writer

languages
e.g. **Parla inglese?**   Do you speak English?
     Parlo francese ed italiano I speak French and Italian

days of the week:
  lunedì Monday
  martedì Tuesday
  mercoledì Wednesday
  giovedì Thursday
  venerdì Friday
  sabato Saturday
  domenica Sunday

months of the year:
  gennaio January   **luglio** July
  febbraio February   **agosto** August
  marzo March   **settembre** September
  aprile April   **ottobre** October
  maggio May   **novembre** November
  giugno June   **dicembre** December

Index

The following index lists comprehensively both grammatical terms and key words in English and Italian.

Index

Index

Index

Index

Index